YALE LINGUISTIC SERIES, 8

DICTIONARY OF SPOKEN CHINESE

Yale Univ. Institute of Far Eastern Languages

Compiled by the Staff of
The Institute of Far Eastern Languages
Yale University

New Haven and London | Yale University Press

This work was developed pursuant to a contract
between the United States Office of Education
and Yale University and is published with permission
of the United States Office of Education, Department of Health, Education, and Welfare.

Acknowledgments

This publication is a revision of War Department Technical Manual TM 30–933, Dictionary of Spoken Chinese, published in Washington, D.C., on November 5,1945, by order of the then Chief of Staff, General G.C. Marshall.

The revision was carried out by staff members of the Institute of Far Eastern Languages, Yale University, pursuant to Contract SAE–8983 between Yale University and the United States Office of Education, Department of Health, Education, and Welfare. This contract also provided for preparation of reproduction copy for the present publication. Costs involved in the revision of the text and preparation of the reproduction copy for publication exceeded the provisions of the original contract, and completion of the work was made possible by financial assistance provided by Yale University and the Yale University Press.

Work on the revision was begun in July 1960. The principal investigator from then until the end of August 1962, when the press of other duties made it necessary for him to resign from the work, was Fred Fang-yu Wang. The over-all plan of the revision was his, and virtually all the innovations which this version of the dictionary embodies are due to him.

Kenny K. Huang was associated with the work of revision from its inception, and after it became necessary for Mr. Wang to leave the project, Mr. Huang assumed responsibility for its completion. As the only person associated with the work of revision throughout its entire course, Mr. Huang has put the Institute deeply in his debt. His painstaking care in all stages of the revision and especially his attention to seeing the reproduction copy through the press made it possible to complete the project.

Mrs. Elena R. Speidel worked on the revision from January 1961 through the end of May 1964, and after Mr. Wang left the project she shared with Mr. Huang the responsibility for seeing the work through to its completion. The Institute is deeply in her debt for her help, not the least of which has been the meticulous care she has given the English of the entries.

In addition, the following persons assisted in the work of revision; they are listed below in alphabetical order with an indication of dates during which they assisted in the project:

Dorothy Chang, October 1961–June 1962; Richard Chang, October 1961–June 1962; C. T. Chow, July–October 1960; Mrs. Marjorie K. Darland, October 1963–June, 1964; William Fender, July 1964–June 1965; Joseph Kuo, July–December 1960; Henry T.K. Kuo, October 1961–March 1962; James Lance, March– July 1962; Paul G. Lo, July–December 1960; Michael J. McCaskey, March 1963–June 1965; B. J. Scholl, July 1960–December 1961; C.R. Sheehan, June–December 1961; Winston H. Sun, July 1960–June 1962; Mrs. Doris J.C. Tai, March 1963–June 1964; J. H. Taylor, September 1961–June 1962; Paul K.Y. Tsai, January–May 1961; Maurice H. Tseng, July 1960–December 1961; George Wang, March 1961–April 1962; Ramon L. Woon, July–August 1960, July–August 1961, July–August 1962; Lorraine Yen, October 1961–June 1962; Roger T. Yeu, June 1961–September 1962.

All the above contributed in some way or other to the content of the completed revision. This list does not include a large number of student assistants whose work consisted largely of cutting up dictionary entries, filing cards, and other clerical tasks.

The following served as consultants on the dates indicated: Nicholas C. Bodman, April 28–29, 1961; Hugh M. Stimson, August 21–25, 1961; Fang-kuei Li, April 28–29, 1961; Charles F. Hockett, October 21, 1961; Lien-sheng Yang, April 28–29, and August 21–25, 1961. In addition, Yuan-ren Chao assisted the staff working on the Dictionary by correspondence on several occasions; and Henry C. Fenn, coordinator of the project until his retirement in July 1962, contributed greatly to the organization and direction of the work.

v

Acknowledgments

Typist-secretaries on the project were Mrs. Doris M. Bovee (January 1961–February 1962), Mrs. Antoinette Ferretti (June 1961–September 1964), and Mrs. F. S. Oliver (July 1960–May 1961). The calligraphy in the Chinese-English portion is the work of Chung-tai Shen.

Roy Andrew Miller

New Haven, Connecticut
May 1965

Contents

Introduction

This Dictionary is designed for use by students of colloquial Mandarin on the intermediate level. It is intended to serve as a tool for the development of advanced conversational skills, and a general grammatical reference guide to basic colloquial usage in modern Mandarin.

The lexical items, as well as the usages, are not exhaustive but are the most common in ordinary speech. The Dictionary not only provides adequate lexical material for conversation on all levels but also contains scientific terms, localisms, and other special terminology. In addition, special uses of characters as transliterations, surnames, and names of dynasties are indicated.

There are few cases, of course, in which the meanings of Chinese and English words coincide exactly, but great care has been taken to provide translations, of both lexical items and examples, which are as close as possible to the original and give the same basic shades of meaning. In cases where the meaning of a word or phrase has no exact equivalent in the target language, rough equivalents are given together with literal translations of the source language material.

Yale romanization is used throughout, and both stress and tone sandhi are indicated as they occur. A comparative table for conversion of Yale romanization to that of other major systems appears at the end.

Chinese-English

The Chinese-English section is intended to be used both for the comprehension and for the production of spoken Chinese. For each entry, comprehension is the first step, production the second. When the student hears a native speaker use a word unfamiliar to him, he can look it up with the aid of the supplied romanization. He may find several words having the same sound that the native speaker used, but should be able to find the right word by looking at the basic meanings given and deciding which meaning fits properly into the context of the sentence in which the native speaker used the word. Having decided which word applies, he may go further and study the various ways in which the word may be used grammatically, as shown by the grammar notations and sample phrases and sentences. It is hoped that after such study he will be able to use the word properly himself, not only in the context in which he heard it but in all other possible contexts.

The student can use the Chinese-English section most profitably not as a glossary for immediate conversation but as a tool for developing his own conversational skills over a period of time. He should carry a pocket-size, glossary-type dictionary with him at all times. When he hears a word he does not understand, he should try to elicit information as to its use from the native speaker, and at the same time find its basic meaning in the glossary. When he has found the glossary listing, he should underline or otherwise mark it. At the end of each day, he should make a list of the words he has marked and then look them up, studying their usage carefully. This not only will add to his knowledge of the use of the word and all its possible meanings, but will reinforce his memory of the word.

He can use the Dictionary as an aid in reading materials in the colloquial language, looking up characters he does not know by means of the radical index at the back. It is recommended that he first find the particular meaning and usage employed in his text and then note the word down for future reference. After he has finished reading his material, he can go back to the Dictionary and study the full meanings and uses of the words, again reinforcing his memory of the words he has just seen used in an actual text. This procedure may also be used, of course, when the student works with classroom materials in the colloquial language. In using the Dictionary as an aid in reading, however, he should remember that written colloquial materials, no matter how close to the spoken language they are, are never quite the same as the spoken language itself.

Introduction

Speakers tend to talk in fragments rather than full sentences, and use popular expressions which can never be decoded by use of a standard dictionary. The present Dictionary is intended to fill this information gap, providing colloquialisms that would rarely or never be seen in print, and ignoring various formal expressions that would not be commonly heard in speech. Students will find it useful as an aid to reading, nevertheless, especially since no adequate dictionary specifically designed for the reading of modern Chinese has yet been written for the use of English-speaking people.

This section will be useful not only to those who are learning the spoken language but also to those relatively fluent in Chinese, who will find that it provides valuable information on those words which they have forgotten or are unsure of.

English-Chinese

The English-Chinese section, intended as an aid in speaking Chinese, is for use in conversation in an actual situation. The student should use it to find the basic Chinese equivalent of English words and phrases he wishes to translate. To find the Chinese equivalent of an English phrase, he should look under the key English word in the phrase. For instance, if he wishes to translate the English phrase "for a change", he should turn to "change" and choose a Chinese version of the phrase. The selection of phrases is meant to be representative rather than exhaustive, and in many cases he will have to construct his own. In order to do so, he should look up all the key English words of a phrase, find their Chinese equivalents, and build his phrase. He is advised to select ordinary English key words, rather than unusual ones. For instance, if he wants to translate the concept "house," he should look under "house" rather than trying to find entries for "dwelling" or "domicile."

Alternate segments of Chinese translations are set off by degree signs, as: "The new baby is a girl." — "Syīn shēng de syǎuhár shr̀ °'nyǔde *or* °ge 'syáujye *or* °ge 'gūnyang." This means that any one of the three elements preceded by degree signs may be added to "Syīn shēng de syǎuhár shr̀ . . . ." to form a sentence of the same meaning.

The English-Chinese section is not intended as a full grammatical guide to Chinese usage. A student interested in knowing the full usage of a Chinese phrase should consult the Chinese section for this information.

SOUNDS

1. Symbols Used

In this Dictionary the sounds of Chinese are indicated by the following letters and other symbols:

Representing *consonant sounds*: b, ch, d, dz, f, g, h, j, k, l, m, n, ng, p, r, s, sh, sy, t, ts, w, y, yw.

Representing *vowel sounds*: a, ai, au, e, ee, ei, o, ou, i, u, r, z.

Representing *tones*: accent marks put over a letter, as follows: neutral tone a (no accent mark), first tone ā, second tone á, third tone ǎ, fourth tone à.

Representing *stress* (or *loudness* or *prominence*): a raised tick (') placed before a syllable.

In the interest of economy, some of the letters or groups of letters, or other symbols, are used to represent more than one sound, but only when (1) the sounds are similar and (2) they occur only in mutually exclusive environments, so that the conditions under which a single symbol represents one or another sound can be clearly defined.

2. Consonants at the Beginning of a Syllable

In the following, the first column lists a symbol, the second column lists the conditions under which that symbol represents the sound described in the third column, and the fourth column gives examples. The order is as follows: **f, l, m, n, r, s, w, y, p, t, k, b, d, g, ts, dz, ch, j, sy, sh, h, ng, yw**; this order is used because it puts the most familiar sounds first and groups together those which represent similar difficulties.

Symbol	Conditions	Description	Examples	
f	everywhere	as in English **fun**.	fěn	"powder"
l	everywhere	as in English **low**.	lòu	"to leak"
m	everywhere	as in English **my**.	mài	"to sell"
n	everywhere	as in English **now**.	nàu	"to annoy"
r	everywhere	as in English **run**, but with no rounding of the lips.	rén	"person"

(The main differences between the Chinese **r-** and the general American **r-** are (1) that the lips are never rounded except when the **r** is followed by a vowel requiring rounding, such as **rwǎn** "be soft"; (2) that there is no curling of the tip of the tongue backward. The whole front surface of the tongue is pulled backward and pushed up, still flat, close to the roof of the mouth.)

s	everywhere	as in English **sigh**.	sài	"to compete"
w	everywhere	as in English **way**.	wèi	"because of"
y	everywhere	as in English **yeah**.	yá	"tooth"

(But note that **yw** is treated as a special symbol)

p	everywhere	as in English **pie**, but with a stronger puff of breath.	pài	"to appoint"
t	everywhere	as in English **tie**, but with a stronger puff of breath.	tài	"too, very"
k	everywhere	as in English **kite**, but with a stronger puff of breath.	kāi	"to open"

(The puff of breath or "aspiration" which follows the first consonant of the English words **pie, tie, kite** can be tested by holding a small slip of very light-weight paper before the lips as the words are spoken. The paper will flutter slightly just as the first consonant ends. For the Chinese sounds written with the same letters, the paper should flutter considerably more.)

b	everywhere	as in English **buy**, but without voicing; or as English p in **pie**, but without any puff of breath.	bài	"to worship"
d	everywhere	as in English **die**, but without voicing; or as English t in **tie**, but without any puff of breath.	dài	"to put on"

| g | everywhere | as in English **guy,** but without voicing; or as English **k** in **kite,** but without any puff of breath. | **gài** | "to cover" |

(There are three ways to acquire these sounds: (1) Practice with the slips of paper as suggested above, and try to say the words so that the paper does not flutter at all. (2) Hold your hands over your ears and say the word **buy, die, guy;** you will hear a buzz that begins with the initial consonant and continues throughout. Then try to say the words so that the buzz does not begin until after the initial consonant. (3) Say the words **spy, sty, sky** with the slip of paper, and notice that it does not flutter. Take the initial **s-** away and try to say the p, t, and k in just the same way, without causing the paper to flutter.)

| ts | everywhere | like the **ts-h** of English **it's high** with the initial i left off. | **tsài** | "vegetable" |
| dz | everywhere | like the **ts** of English **it's I** with the initial i left off. | **dzài** | "again" |

(Pretend you are a phonograph record, with the expressions **it's high** and **it's I** recorded on it; put the needle down just past the place where the i of **it's high** or the i of **it's I** is recorded. The difference between **ts** and **dz** is comparable to the difference between p and b, t and d, or k and g as described earlier.)

ch	(1) before **i, y, yu** or **yw**	much as in English **cheat,** but with the tip of the tongue held down behind the lower front teeth.	**chǐ** **chyán** **chyú** **chywán**	"air" "money" "to go" "whole"
	(2) elsewhere	a cross between **true** and **choose**—as though we said **chrue** instead of **true.**	**chá** **chū**	"tea" "exit"
j	(1) before **i, y, yu** or **yw**	like Chinese ch in the same conditions, except with no puff of breath.	**jǐ** **jyàu** **jyù** **jywé**	"remember" "be called" "according to" "absolutely"
	(2) elsewhere	like Chinese ch in the same conditions, except with no puff of breath.	**jū** **já**	"pig" "to fry"

(The most important thing in correctly pronouncing ch and j when not before **i, y, yu,** or **yw** is to draw the tip of the tongue back and up to the roof of the mouth; avoid scrupulously making a sound like the English **ch** in **chase** or **chair,** or **j** in **Jack** or **jump,** which are made with the tongue much farther forward in the mouth. Note the difference between the ch type of sound, which has a puff of breath, and the j type, which does not.)

| sy | everywhere | much as in English **she,** but with the tip of the tongue held down behind the lower front teeth, and without any rounding of the lips. | **syǐ** **syǎu** | "west" "small" |

sh	everywhere	a cross between the **sh** of **shoe** and the **shr** of **shrew**, with the tongue drawn well back and up.	shū shǎu	"book" "few"
h	everywhere	either like the English h in **how**, or with friction at the back of the mouth, as in German **ach**.	hǎu hú	"OK" "lake"

(Most speakers of Chinese vary between these two; either is acceptable, but to use the English h sound constantly may make your pronounciation occasionally unpleasant to Chinese ears.)

ng	everywhere (occurs only when the preceding syllable ends in **ng**.)	like the **ng** of **singer** (not like the **ng** of **finger**.)	bùsyíng nga! "It won't do!"
yw	everywhere	the sound of y as in **yes** and w as in **won't** pronounced at the same time.	ywè ywǎn	"month" "far"

(The tongue is in the position for y, but the lips are rounded as for w. Sometimes the sound starts just slightly before the lips are rounded, but the two are simultaneous.)

3. Semi-Vowel in the Middle of a Syllable

The following semi-vowels occur after a consonant and before a vowel, with or without another consonant following the last vowel. There are three of them, w, y and yw.

w	everywhere	like the English u in **suave** or **quality**.	hwā lwàn hwáng	"flower" "mess" "yellow"
y	(1) before vowel other than e, u.	Like the English y in **Ilya,** and the i in **California**.	lyǎ dyàn	"two" "electricity"
	(2) before e.	(See #5 under vowel e (2))		
	(3) before u.	(See #5 under vowel u (3))		
yw	(1) before vowel other than e.	like the French u in **nuance**.	jywǎn sywǎn chywán	"to roll" "to elect" "fist"
	(2) before e.	(See #5 under vowel e (2))		

4. Consonants at the End of a Syllable

The following consonants occur at the ends of syllables: They are n, ng, r and ngr.

n	(1) except as mentioned under (2).	like the English n in **can**.	wén tán	"smell" "converse"
	(2) when the next syllable begins with y.	the tongue does not quite reach the roof of the mouth, and the preceding vowel is slightly nasalized.	tán yi tán	"converse a bit"

| ng | everywhere | like the English ng in sing or singer (not like the ng in finger). | táng háng húng | "candy, sugar" "trade" "red" |
| r | everywhere | like the English r in bar, fur. | wár fèr | "to play" "portion" |

(In many varieties of English, r's after a vowel are not pronounced. Whatever variety of English you speak, be sure to pronounce the r in Chinese; but don't trill or roll it; make an English r-sound, not a French or German r-sound.)

| ngr | everywhere | the back of the tongue does not reach the roof of the mouth for the ng; the vowel is strongly nasalized; r as described above. | héngr | "horizontal stroke" |

5. Vowels

The vowels are a, ai, au, e, ee, ei, o, ou, i, u, z, and r.

a	(1) except as detailed below.	like the English a in father or ma.	mǎ	"horse"
	(2) between y and n.	like the English a in hand.	yān dyàn	"smoke" "electricity"
	(3) between yw and n.	like the English a in bat, but variable; some speakers make it like (1), some like (2).	ywàn chywán	"court" "altogether"
	(4) between w and ng.	like (1) or like the English o in long.	hwāng	"nervous"
ai	everywhere	like the English ai in aisle.	pài	"to appoint"
au	everywhere	like the English au in umlaut or Faust.	lǎu	"old"
e	(1) except as specified below.	about like the English u in but or huh.	hē chē hěn	"to drink" "cart" "very"

(When final in the syllable, this sound often begins with the back of the tongue drawn back and up toward the roof of the mouth, like the oo in book without the lips rounded; but it then glides from this to the sound described above.)

	(2) after sy, y or yw, final in the syllable.	like the English e in met or eah or yeah.	yě ywè syè	"also" "month" "to thank"
ei	everywhere	like the English ei in reign.	pèi	"to match"
ee	everywhere	the first e is as above, depending on the preceding sound; the second as (1) above.	héer gēer	"small box" "song"
o	everywhere	like the English u in urn.	wǒ	"I"

ou	everywhere	like the English ow in know.	hòu	"behind"
i	(1) final in the syllable.	like the English ee in see.	mǐ	"rice grain"
	(2) not final in the syllable.	like the English i in pin.	mín	"people"

(Consonants before i are often pronounced with a little y-glide after them, as though one said myín instead of mín.)

u	(1) final and not after sy, y.	like the English oo in moon.	wǔ shū	"five" "book"
	(2) followed by a consonant and not after sy, y.	like the English oo in book.	húng	"red"
	(3) after sy, y.	like the English oo in moon and the ee in see pronounced simultaneously.	syù syún yǔ yùn	"to continue" "to look for" "rain" "to ship"

(The tongue is in the ee-position, and the lips are rounded as for oo. This is the same position as described already for the consonant sound yw.)

z	everywhere	like the English oo in look pronounced without rounding the lips; the throat is tense and the back of the tongue is held down tightly.	dż tsż sż	"word" "jab" "four"

(This sound occurs only after the consonants dz, ts, and s. The consonant dz and the vowel z are transcribed as dz when combined.)

r	everywhere	like the middle-western American English ir in shirt, or ur in hurt, fur; something like French je when it stands alone.	r̀ chr̄ jŕ shr̀	"sun" "to eat" "straight" "is"

(This sound occurs only after the consonants r, ch, j, and sh. When the consonant r and the vowel r are combined, only one r is written.)

6. Tones and Stress

A syllable uttered in isolation has one of four basic *tonal contours* or *tones*. In longer expressions, the individual syllables may have one of a number of allotones, all related to that particular one of the four which the same syllable has in isolation. Syllables also may have no definite tonal contour at all. These last are called *toneless* or *neutral tone* syllables, and are written without any tone mark.

The distinctiveness of the tonal contours described below depends on the loudness or prominence of the syllable in question: more distinct when louder, less distinct when softer.

Tone	Symbol	Conditions	Description	Examples	
first	⁻ (ā)	everywhere	high, level, sometimes	gāu	"high"

			cut off sharply at the end.	tsā	"to scrape"
second	´(a)	everywhere	relatively high, rising with increasing loudness; often cut off sharply at the end.	rén báu ná tsúng	"person" "thin" "to take" "from"
third	ˇ(a)	(1) stressed at end of a phrase (before pause).	low in pitch, rising at the end, and gradually less loud.	mǎ kǔ yǒu hǎu	"horse" "bitter" "there is" "OK"
		(2) before another syllable with third tone (ˇ).	mid-low, rising, sometimes not distinguishable from second tone (´).	wǒ yǒu becomes wó yǒu hǎikǒu becomes háikǒu.	"I have" "seaport"

(Sometimes the tone of the second syllable becomes neutral. As dásau "clean up" derived from dǎsǎu.)

		(3) otherwise	low, with no rise.	yǒu rén mǎchē	"there are people" "horse cart"
fourth	`(a)	(1) stressed	falling from high to mid-low or low.	rè hàu	"hot" "number"
		(2) unstressed	falling but often only slightly, and from whatever level is reached by the preceding syllable; if none, from mid-high.	shàngsyàu kànbujyàn	"colonel" "can't see"
neutral	none	everywhere	short, middle pitch.	tāde rénde wǒde hwàide dehwà	"his" "people's" "mine" "bad ones" "in case"

   Stress means the relative degree of loudness or prominence of syllables when they are joined together. In Chinese, stress follows the scheme below:

(` stands for any one of the four tones)

Two-syllable elements

1. `_ `_ means stress is on the second syllable, both tones pronounced.

2. `_ _ means stress is on the first syllable, the second syllable neutral.

3. '_ `_ means stess is on the first syllable, both tones pronounced.

Three-syllable elements

1. `_ `_ `_ means stress is on the last syllable, all tones pronounced.

2. `_ `_ _ means stress is on the second syllable, the last syllable neutral.

3. In other cases, three-syllable elements should be pronounced according to stress marks indicated.

Introduction

In every case, elements of more than three syllables should be pronounced according to stress marks indicated.

7. Changes of Sound

1. **Occasional changes.** Some elements in Chinese vary in pronunciation without any correlated change in meaning. The most frequent case of this is when an element within certain compounds or contexts loses its tone: bùhǎu "not good", with bù "not"; but hǎubuhǎu "is it good?" with bu toneless. Cases of this kind are properly indicated in the body of the Dictionary. Some elements occur in all possible contexts with either of two tones, or even sometimes with any of three tones.

2. **Regular Changes.** The element -r differs from most constituent elements of expressions in Chinese in that it is joined onto the previous syllable as part of that same syllable instead of constituting a syllable in itself. The merging of a syllable with suffixed -r calls for certain systematic changes in the vowels and consonants of the original first syllable; the tone is not affected. The following table shows the changes made:

Syllables ending in:	When adding -r become:	Examples:	
-a	-ar	hwā	: hwār
-an	-ar	hwān	: hwār
-ai	-ar	hwái	: hwár
-au	-aur	hǎu	: hǎur
-ang	-angr	háng	: hángr
-e	-er	gē	: gēr
	-eer	gē	: gēer

(Speakers differ in the latter usage. With the first and second tones transcription using two e's has generally been used; with the third and fourth tones transcription using one e has been generally used.)

-o	-oer	wō	: wōer
	-or	wō	: wōr

(Speakers differ here also; but all the forms are used.)

-en	-er	gēn	: gēr
-ei	-er	swèi	: swèr
-ou	-our	gǒu	: gǒur
-eng	-engr	héng	: héngr
-i	-yer	dí	: dyèr
(yi)	(yer)	(yí	: yèr)
-in	-yer	jīn	: jyēr
(yin)	(yer)	(yīn	: yēr)
-ing	-ingr	bǐng	: bǐngr
-u	-ur	shù	: shùr
-ung	-ungr	húng	: húngr

-z		-er		sż	: sèr
				tsż	: tsèr
		-zer		dż	: dzèr
(r)		(rer)		(r̀	: rèr)
-r		-er		shr̀	: shèr
				chř	: chèr
				jŕ	: jér

GRAMMATICAL NOTATIONS

Key to Symbols

1.	A	adverb		15.	ON	onomatopoeia
2.	AT	attributive		16.	P	particle
3.	AV	auxiliary verb		17.	PN	pronoun
4.	B	boundform		18.	PT	pattern
5.	CV	coverb		19.	PV	post verb
6.	DC	directional complement		20.	PW	placeword
7.	DV	directional verb		21.	q	question word
8.	FV	functive verb		22.	RC	resultative compound
9.	I	interjection		23.	RE	resultative ending
10.	IE	idiomatic expression		24.	SP	specifier
11.	L	localizer		25.	SV	stative verb
12.	M	measure		26.	TW	timeword
13.	N	noun		27.	VO	verb-object compound
14.	NU	number				

Explanation and Comment

A = Adverb

Adverbs are verbal forms which are used to modify verbs or other adverbs. In every case they come before the verb. However, two groups may be distinguished because of more specific function:

A. One group always immediately precedes the verb or another adverb.

這個真好.	Jèige 'jēn hǎu.	This is **really** good.
我們都去吧.	Wǒmen 'dōu chyù ba.	Let's **all** go.
他很累.	Tā hěn 'lèi.	He is **very** tired.
這根繩儿也太長.	Jèigēn shéngr 'yé tài cháng.	This rope is **also** too long.

B. The second group may stand before the subject, as well as immediately before the verb.

我有錢可是他沒有.	Wó yǒu chyán **kěshr** 'tā méiyou.	I have money, **but** he doesn't.
我有錢他可是沒有.	Wó yǒu chyán 'tā **kěshr** meiyou.	I have money; he **however,** doesn't.
他大概不會寫中國字.	Tā **dàgài** 'búhwèi syě Jūnggwo dž.	He **probably** doesn't know how to write Chinese characters.
大概他不會寫中國字.	**Dàgài** tā 'búhwèi syě Jūnggwo dž.	**Probably,** he doesn't know how to write Chinese characters.

Some adverbs may be followed by (一)點儿(yī)dyar which makes them comparative.

你慢(一)點儿走.	Nǐ **'màn (yī)dyar** dzǒu.	Walk **more slowly.**
我要仔細(一)點儿檢查.	Wǒ yàu **'dǐzsyi (yī)dyar** jyǎnchá.	I want to examine it **more carefully.**

<u>AT = Attributive</u>

Attributives constitute a small group of nominal forms which have two functions:

1. They are used before nouns to modify them.

男孩子	**nán**háidz	**male** child or boy
女學生	**nyǔ**sywésheng	**female** student

2. They are followed by the particle 的 **de** to form nouns.

男的	**nán**de	male
女的	**nyǔ**de	female

<u>AV = Auxiliary Verb</u>

Certain verbs in Chinese are referred to as auxiliary verbs simply because they precede other verbs. Two groups may be distinguished:

A. Auxiliaries which function very much as auxiliary verbs in English in that they act as "aids" to the main verb.

這個可以高一點儿.	Jèige **kéyi** 'gāu yidyǎr.	This **could** be higher.
他不能站起來.	Tā bù**néng** 'jànchilai.	He **can** not stand up.

B. Functive auxiliaries which function as the main verb are always followed by another verb or verb-object compound.

我們喜歡吃魚.	Wǒmen **syǐhwan** chr̄ 'yú.	We **like** to eat fish.
他愛睡.	Tā **aì** 'shwèi.	He **likes** to sleep.

Auxiliary verbs have the following characteristics:

1. They may be modified by certain adverbs such as 很 **hěn,** 太 **tài,** 多麼 **dwóma,** etc., or followed by complements indicating degree, such as the particles 極了 **jíle** and 的很 **dehěn.**

他很不愛念書.	Tā **'hěn** búaì nyànshū.	He doesn't like to read **much.**

| 你看他多麽喜歡那張畫儿. | Nǐ kàn tā 'dwóma syǐhwan nèijāng 'hwàr. | See **how much** he likes that picture. |
| 他們都愛説話的很. | Tāmen dōu ài shwōhwà de'hěn. | They all like to talk a lot. |

2. They are used to form choice-type questions rather than the main verb following them. Such questions are answered by repeating either the positive or negative form of the auxiliary verb.

question: 你可以不可以去?	Nǐ 'kéyi bukéyi chyù?	**Can** you or **can't** you go?
answer: 可以. or 不可以.	Kéyi or Bùkéyi.	I **can.** or I **can't.**
question: 他能不能説英文?	Tā 'néng bunéng shwō Yīngwén?	**Can** he or **can't** he speak English?
answer: 能. or 不能.	Néng. or Bùnéng.	He **can.** or He **can't.**

3. They rarely take the negative 沒 **méi** because they are essentially potential rather than active in their meaning and the idea of completion would be inconsistent in such a case.

B = Unclassified Boundform

Unclassified boundforms are elements which cannot be used as free, independent words, but always appear in combination with other elements. As a group they do not follow any set grammatical patterns. These should not be confused with the "classified" boundforms, such as attributives, resultative endings, post verbs, particles, etc., which also never appear except in combination with other elements but which follow definite patterns to warrant giving them separate notations.

The following are typical examples of unclassified boundforms:

長	jǎng	as in	校長	syàujǎng	"principal"
家	jyā	as in	科學家	kēsywéjyā	"scientist"
損	swǔn	as in	損壞	swǔnhwài	"damage"
子	dz	as in	橘子	jyúdz	"orange"
兒	r	as in	花兒	hwār	"flower"

CV = Coverb

A coverb is a verbal expression followed by a noun which together with the noun precedes the main verb and modifies it. Its function is similar to an English preposition.

他坐飛機去.	Tā **dzwò** fēi'jī chyù	He is going **by** plane.
我跟他到紐約去.	Wǒ **gēn** 'tā dàu Nyǒuywe chyù.	I'm going to New York **with** him.
你從那儿來.	Nǐ **tsúng** 'nǎr lái?	Where do you come **from**?

Coverbs have the following characteristics:

1. They may take the particle 着 **je.**

他們順着這條河走的. Tāmen **shwùnje** jèityáu 'hé dzǒude. They went **along** this river.

他們跟着我們去的. Tāmen **gēnje** 'wǒmen chyùde. They went **with** us.

2. The negative 不 **bù** and 沒 **méi** normally stand before the coverb rather than the main verb.

我不替他做事. Wǒ '**bútì** tā dzwòshr. I'm not working on **behalf** of him.

他沒坐車去. Ta '**méidzwò** chē chyù. He did not go **by** car.

DC = Directional Complement

A directional complement is a verbal expression which is combined with directional verbs to form resultative endings and further helps to clarify the direction of motion.

拿上來 náshanglai carry up (**here**)
搬進去 bànjinchyu move in (**there**)

If there is an object, it is inserted between the directional verb and the complement.

開進車房來 kāijin chēfáng lái drive into the garage (**here**)

搬不進屋子去 bānbujin wūdz chyù cannot move it into the room (**there**)

DV = Directional Verb

Directional verbs are essentially verbs, but they are concerned with the direction of motion and therefore have special characteristics which do not apply to regular functive verbs.

Directional verbs have the following characteristics:

1. They may take a direct object which is often a noun indicating a place.

DV				Examples	
上	shàng	(go) up	上樓	shàng lóu	go upstairs
下	syà	(go) down	下山	syà shān	go down the mountain
進	jìn	(go) into	進門	jìn mén	go in the door
出	chū	(go) out of	出國	chū gwó	go out of a country
過	gwò	(go) over	過橋	gwò chyáu	go over a bridge
回	hwéi	(go) back	回家	hwéi jyā	go back home

2. They take the resultative endings 來 **lái** 去 **chyù** to form resultative compounds. (If there is an object, it is inserted between the two parts of the resultative compound.

出來 chūlai come out (**here**)
上去 shàngchyu go up (**there**)
上樓來 shàng lóu lai come upstairs (**here**)

回國去	hwéi gwó. **chyu**	go back to one's country (**there**)

3. They are commonly used as resultative endings.

他衝出銀行就被捕了.	Tā chūng**chu** yínháng jyòu bèi'bǔ le.	He was arrested as he rushed **out** of the bank.
他走進屋子就死了.	Tā dzǒu**jin** wūdz jyòu 'sž le.	He died as he went **into** the room.

4. They may be used after the coverbs 往 **wǎng**, 望 **wàng**, 向 **syàng**, 朝 **cháu**, and 衝 **chùng**.

往回看	**wǎng** hwéi kàn	look back
向出跑	**syàng** chū pǎu	run out
衝進放	**chùng** jin fàng	fire into

5. Some of the directional verbs, when used as resultative endings in potential forms, lose their directional meanings.

我打不過他.	Wǒ dǎbugwò ta.	I can't beat him.
我吃不起這麼貴的飯.	Wǒ chřbu'**chǐ** dzèmma gwèide 'fàn.	I can't afford to eat such expensive food.
我看不出有甚麼好處.	Wǒ kànbu'**chū** yǒu shémma '**hǎuchu**.	I cannot see any advantage.

FV = Functive Verb

A functive verb predicates an action or event (in contrast to a stative verb which expresses a quality or condition).

1. It may stand as a complete predicate.

他吃.	Tā chř.	He **eats**.
我都要.	Wǒ dōu **yàu**.	I **want** them all。

2. It may be followed by an object or other form of complement.

(By a single object)

學生看書.	Sywésheng kàn **shū**.	Students read **books**.

(By both a direct and indirect object)

他們送給我一張畫儿.	Tāmen sùnggei wǒ yìjāng **hwàr**.	They gave **me a picture**.

(By a sentence object)

他說英文容易.	Tā shwō Yīngwen 'yúngyi.	He says **English is easy**.
他說:"你別去."	Tā shwō, "Nǐ 'byé chyù."	He said "Don't go."
我聽他們唱歌儿.	Wǒ tīng **tāmen chàng'gēer**.	I listened to **their singing**.

(By 一 **yi** plus the
repeated verb)

他看一看就走了. | Tā kàn **yikàn** jyòu dzǒu le. | He took **a look** and then went away.

(By Nu-M)

我去過兩次. | Wǒ chyùgwo **'lyǎngtsż**. | I have been there **twice**.

我要兩個. | Wǒ yàu **'lyǎngge**. | I want **two**.

(By a direct object
plus Nu-M)

我打他兩拳. | Wó dǎ **tā** lyǎngchywán. | I hit **him twice with my fist**.

3. It may form compounds with other elements.

(With postverbs)

他站在桌子上. | Tā jàn**dzai** 'jwōdzshang. | He is standing **on the table**.

(With RE to form resulta-
tive compounds)

我吃飽了. | Wǒ chř**'bǎu** le. | I have eaten **enough**.

4. It may be followed by the particle 着 **je** and stand as an adverbial modifier.

馬站着睡覺. | Mǎ '**jànje** shwèijyàu. | The horses sleep **standing up**.

他在那邊兒坐着看報呢. | Tā dzai nèibyar **dzwòje** kàn 'bàu ne. | He is **sitting** over there reading the newspaper.

I = Interjection

The following are examples:

哎呀 | āiyā | (indicates surprise) | oh!
哎 | ái | (indicates doubt) | hmm.
嗨 | hāi | (used to draw some-one's attention) | hey!
咳 | hài | (indicates disgust) | ugh!

IE = Idiomatic Expression

A number of words in Chinese have, in addition to other grammatical functions, an idiomatic usage which cannot be derived from their other meanings. These are treated under IE at the end of an entry. They take the form of responses in specific situations, as a greeting, words of congratulation, or a polite statement.

早 | Dzǎu. | Good morning.
拜壽 | Bàishòu. | Happy Birthday.
怠慢 | Dàimàn. | I have treated you poorly (said to a guest at the end of a party).

In normal conversation these would often be said twice in a row, as "bàishòu, bàishòu" or "dàimàn, dàimàn."

L = Localizer

Localizers are nominal forms used in combination with other elements to indicate position. They are similar in meaning to such English words as inside, outside, on, under, etc. The common localizers are:

裏	lǐ	inside	東	dūng	east
外	wài	outside	南	nán	south
上	shàng	above	西	syī	west
下	syà	below	北	běi	north
前	chyán	ahead	左	dzwǒ	left
後	hòu	behind	右	yòu	right

Localizers have the following characteristics:

1. They may be followed by 邊 byān, 面 myàn, and 頭 tóu to form placewords.

前頭	chyántou	the area in front; the front of.
裡頭	lǐtou	the area inside; the inside of.
上邊	shàngbyan	the area above; the upper part; the top.
外面	wàimyan	the area outside; the outside of.

2. They may be added to nouns to form placewords.

桌子上	jwōdz shang	(on) the top of the table.
屋子裡	wūdzli	(in) the interior of the room.
國外	gwówài	(in) the region outside one's country.
牀下	chwáng syà	(in) the area under the bed.

3. They may be used before nouns to modify them.

前排	chyánpái	front row
後腿	hòutwěi	hind leg

4. They may be used after the coverbs 往 wǎng, 望 wàng, 向 syàng, 朝 cháu, and 衝 chùng.

往右看	wǎng yoù kàn	look to the **right**
望外搬	wàng **wài** bān	move **out**
朝東去	cháu dūng chyù	go toward the **east**

M = Measure

A measure is a nominal element which is the designator of a unit of measurement or classification. English words with a similar function are such words as "flock" in "a flock of sheep" or "pair" in "a pair of shoes." A measure may be preceded by a number, or a specifier, or both, and is usually followed by a noun.*

Measures may be divided into the following categories:

A. Classificatory measures which assign a noun to a group having (theoretically) some common trait. These are listed after all nouns in this Dictionary which take them.†

把	bǎ	yìbá yǐdz	a chair
張	jāng	yìjāng jr̆	a piece of paper
本	běn	lyángběn shū	two books
位	wèi‡	sānwèi syáujye	three young ladies

The general measure 個 ge may also be used before nouns to indicate an "item" of something. However, most nouns usually have a classificatory measure, the use of which is preferred to 個 ge, though this varies greatly from word to word. If a noun in the Dictionary takes only the measure 個 ge, there is no measure listed after it.

B. Quantitative measures which indicate mathematical quantities rather than homogeneous classifications.

| 斗 | dǒu | peck | | 尺 | chǐ | foot |
| 刻 | kè | quarter-hour | | 寸 | tswùn | inch |

C. Numerical measures which are used in expressing higher numbers.

| 十 | shŕ | ten | | 千 | chyān | thousand |
| 百 | bǎi | hundred | | 萬 | wàn | ten-thousand |

D. Temporary measures which are nouns "borrowed" with considerable freedom to function temporarily as measuring-containers needed in a specific situation, as in the following examples:

一壺水	yìhú shwěi	a pot of water
一屋子烟	yìwūdz yān	a "roomful" of smoke
一身泥	yìshēn ní	a "bodyful" of mud
一瓶子酒	yìpíngdz jyǒu	a bottle of liquor

E. General measures of occurrence can be translated as time.

唱三遍	Chàng sānbyàn	sing three times
我打了他兩次.	Wó dǎle tā lyǎngtsz̀.	I hit him two times.
他去了一回上海.	Tā chyùle yìhwéi Shànghai.	He went to Shanghai once.

---

* In some cases the number 一 yi is dropped as in the sentence 我要 (一)個蘋果. Wǒ yàu (yí) ge pínggwo. I want an apple.

† When 子 dz or 兒 r is added to unclassified boundforms (B) nouns are formed and therefore measures also appear after these.

‡ The measure 位 wèi may be used with all nouns indicating respectable people and is therefore not listed after such nouns in this Dictionary.

F. Specific measures of occurrence are always in the following structure.

我打了他兩拳.　　　Wó dǎle tā lyǎngchywán.　　I hit him **twice** (**with my
　　　　　　　　　　　　　　　　　　　　　　　　fist**).

(Such measures not only indicate occurrence but also indicate the instrument with which
the action is performed.)

N = Noun

In Chinese, nouns are distinguished by the fact that they may be preceded by a
specifier or by the combinations SP-M, SP-NU, or NU-M. Chinese nouns are not in-
flected for case or number, hence singular and plural numbers are determined from the
context.

	人	rén	person
	書	shū	book
	桌子	jwōdz	table
	帽子	màudz	hat
(Preceded by SP)	這人	jèirén	this man
(Preceded by SP-M)	這本書	jèibén shū	this book
(Preceded by SP-NU-M)	這三張桌子	jèisānjāng jwōdz	these three tables
(Preceded by NU-M)	一個帽子	yíge màudz	one hat

NU = Number

Numbers are nominal elements which perform the functions of counting, enumerating,
and measuring. In specific function, however, they differ from their English counterparts.
Several basic types of numbers are distinguished according to their function:

1. Single digit numbers not applied to a noun to indicate quantity but given to something as an identifying mark or label, as in telephone numbers or calendar years.

一九六五	yī-jyǒu-lyòu-wǔ	1965
二〇八六	èr-líng-bā-lyòu	2086
三加四是七	sān jyā sż shr chī	3 plus 4 is 7

2. Single or multi-digit numbers used before measures and applied to nouns to
indicate quantity.

一個人	yíge rén	**one** person
三十六個人	sānshŕlyòuge rén	**thirty-six** people

3. Indefinite numbers used before measures and applied to nouns to indicate an
indefinite quantity.

一些個東西	yìsyēge dūngsyi	**several** things
吃幾個花生	chr jǐge hwāshēng	eat **a few** peanuts
十來個	shŕlaige	**less than** ten
四十多個人	sżshrdwōge rén	forty-**odd** people

4. Post-measure numbers or numbers which come after measures.

Introduction

一個半鐘頭	yígebàn jūngtou	one and **a half** hours
一里來路	yìlílái lù	**about** a mile
三塊多錢	sānkwàidwō chyán	**more than** three dollars

5. Question-forming numbers.

| 這有多少(個)人? | Jèr yǒu **dwōshau**(ge) rén? | **How many** people are here? |
| 幾個帽子是你的? | Jǐge màudz shr nǐde? | **How many** hats are yours? |

ON = Onomatopoetic Term

Onomatopoetic terms in Chinese are basically imitations of natural sounds. They must be combined with other elements to function in a sentence. Most often they are combined with particle 的(or 地) **de** or an expression like 一聲 **yisheng** to form adverbial expressions as in the following examples.

| 咕 gū 鴿子一邊兒吃,
一邊兒咕咕的叫. | Gēdz yìbyar chr,
yìbyar **gūgū**de jyàu. | The pigeon is eating and **cooing** at the same time. |
| gūdūng 他咕鼕一聲倒
在地上了. | Tā **gūdūng** yìsheng dǎu dzài dìshang le. | He fell to the ground **with a thud.** |

P = Particle

Particles are not full words but are indicators whose grammatical significance overshadows any meaning content they may possess. They cannot stand alone or be translated independently of the word or words to which they are attached. To a certain extent they take the place of the inflectional endings in European languages.

Two general categories of particles may be distinguished:

1. Interrogative particles indicate a question or suggestion. They are 嗎 ma, 啊 a, 吧 ba, and 呢 ne.

你吃中國飯嗎?	Nǐ chr Jūnggwo fàn **ma?**	Do you eat Chinese food?
你吃中國飯啊?	Nǐ chr Jūnggwo fàn **a?**	So you eat Chinese food?
你吃中國飯吧?	Nǐ chr Jūnggwo fàn **ba?**	You probably eat Chinese food.
你吃中國飯還是吃外國飯呢?	Nǐ chr Jūnggwo fàn háishr chr wàigwo fàn **ne?**	Do you eat Chinese food or foreign food?

2. Aspect particles which indicate certain qualities the speaker wishes to attribute to the action.

了 le (change of status)
他現在好了. Tā syàndzai hǎule. He is well now.

了 le (completed action)
我已經吃了飯了. Wó yǐjing chrle fàn **le.** I have already eaten.

的 de (interest in attendant circumstances rather than the action itself)
他是昨天來的. Tā shr dzwótyan láide. He came yesterday.

呢 ne (continuing action)

他睡覺呢. Tā shwèijyàu **ne**.   He is sleeping.

着 **je**   (accompanying action)

你閉着眼找, Nǐ bì**je** yán jǎu,   You cannot find it with
找不着.   jǎubujáu.   closed eyes.

過 **gwo**   (experiential action)

我沒吃過這 Wǒ méichr̄**gwo** jèiyangr-   I haven't ever eaten
樣儿的菜.   de tsài.   this kind of food.

PN = Pronoun

Pronouns in Chinese are a small group of words used in place of nouns when a noun is already understood.

我	wǒ	I	我們	wǒmen	we
你	nǐ	you	你們	nǐmen	you
他	tā	he, she, it	他們	tāmen	they
誰	shéi	who			

The particle 的 **de** may be added to pronouns to make them possessive.

我的	wǒde	my, mine	我們的	wǒmende	our, ours
你的	nǐde	your, yours	你們的	nǐmende	your, yours

PT = Pattern

When an entry word is used frequently in conjunction with another word or words, and the resulting phrase is difficult to understand by merely translating each word separately, the special "pattern" of words is treated under PT at the end of the entry. Ellipsis marks in the Chinese indicate where other material may be added and correspond as nearly as possible to those in English.

不但 . . . 並且 . . .   búdàn . . . bìngchyě . . .   not only . . . but also . . .

他不但聰明並且 Tā búdàn tsūngming bìngchyě   He is not only clever
好看.   hǎukàn.   but also handsome.

不管 . . . 也 . . .   bùgwǎn . . . yě . . .   no matter . . . still . . .

不管他是誰, 我也 Bùgwǎn tā shr shéi, wó yě   No matter who he
不叫他進來.   bújyàu tā jìnlai.   is, I still won't let him in.

PV = Post verb

A post verb is a verbal element which is added to a limited number of functive verbs and links the action of the functive verb to the following object.

Post verbs have the following characteristics:

1. The object which follows them varies.

    a. The post verbs 在 **dzài** and 到 **dàu** are followed by placewords (PW) or timewords (TW).

他住在旅馆裡.	Tā jùdzai lyúgwǎnli.	He lived **in** a hotel.
我們念到那儿了?	Wǒmen nyàndau nǎr le?	Where did we read **to**?
我們做到六點.	Wǒmen dzwòdau lyòudyǎn.	We work **until** six.

    b. The postverb 給 **gei** is followed by an indirect object while the direct object is optional.

| 我送給他一個表. | Wǒ sùnggei ta yíge byǎu. | I gave him a watch. |
| (表) 我送給他了. | (Byǎu), wǒ sùnggei tā le. | I gave the watch **to** him. |

    c. The postverbs 成 **chéng** and 做 **dzwò** are followed by a nominal expression.

我把他當做我的孩子.	Wó bǎ tā dàng**dzwo** wǒde háidz.	I regard him **as** my own child.
題目可以分成三部.	Tímu kéyi fēng**cheng** sānbù.	The topic may be divided **into** three parts.
這個叫做什麼?	Jèige jyàu**dzwo** shémma?	What's this called?

    2. In cases where there are two objects, direct and indirect, the direct object is transposed to pre-verbal position.

他把帽子放在桌子上.	Tā bǎ **màudz** fàngdzai jwōdzshang. *or*	He put the hat on the table.
帽子, 他放在桌子上.	**Màudz**, tā fàngdzai jwōdz-shang.	
我把箱子改做桌子(用).	Wó bǎ **syāngdz** gǎidzwo jwōdz (yùng). *or*	I use the box as a table.
箱子, 我改做桌子(用).	**Syāngdz**, wó gǎidzwo jwōdz (yùng).	

    3. A particle stands after the object, not immediately after postverbs 在 **dzài**, 給 **gěi**.

| 我把表掉在地上了. | Wó bá byǎu dyàudzai dìshang **le**. | I dropped the watch on the ground. |

PW = Placeword

    Placewords are indicators or names of places. They are basically nouns in that they may function as the subject or object of the verb. However, they are given a separate category because they also function adverbially. (See also under L, 1 and 2.)

這儿	jèr	here
那儿	nèr	there
哪儿	nǎr	where
中國	Jūnggwo	China
上海	Shànghǎi	Shanghai
裏頭	lǐtou	inside
外頭	wàitou	outside

    (Certain nouns which are names of places where people may reside also function as placewords. These are such words as 家 jyā home, 學校 sywésyàu school, 飯廳 fàntīng dining hall, or 火車站 hwǒchējàn railway station.)

Introduction

Sentence examples showing function as a noun:

中國是一個大國.	Jūnggwo shr yíge dàgwó.	**China** is a big country.
裡頭比外頭好.	Lǐtou bǐ wàitou hǎu.	The **inside** is better than the **outside**.
哪儿都沒這儿好.	Nǎr dōu méi jèr hǎu.	**Nowhere** is better than **here**.

Sentence examples showing function adverbially:

你反面儿寫也成.	Ní fǎnmyàr syě yě chéng.	You may also write **on the reverse side**.
花園裡飛着很多蝴蝶.	Hwāywánli fēije hěn dwō húdyé.	There are many butterflies flying **in the garden**.

q = Question Word

The superscript "q" with grammatical notations indicates that the entry is also a question word, i.e., by its presence in a sentence a question is formed. In this function it is similar to the English pronouns "who," "what," "why," etc.

你是誰?	Nǐ shr **shéi**?	**Who** are you?
你要什麼?	Nǐ yàu **shémma**?	**What** do you want?

Words belonging to this category, in addition to their question forming function, have the following characteristics in common:

1. When followed by 都 dōu or 也 yě they become indefinites, translating as "anyone," "anywhere," "anything," etc.

他誰都不喜歡.	Tā **shéi** dou bùsyǐhwan.	He doesn't like **anyone**.
我什麼也不要.	Wǒ **shémma** yě búyàu.	I don't want **anything**.

2. When preceded by 不 bù or 沒 méi they translate as "not so very" or "not much (or many)," and similar phrases.

他沒有多少錢.	Tā méiyou **dwōshau** chyán.	He doesn't have **very much** money.
他不怎麼高興.	Tā **bùdzěmma** gāusyìng.	He is **not very** happy.

3. When repeated in two clauses in a sentence, they translate as "whatever" or "whoever," "however," etc.

你做多少, 我吃多少.	Nǐ dzwò **dwōshau**, wǒ chr **dwōshau**.	I will eat **as much** of it **as** you cook.
誰先到, 誰先吃.	**Shéi** syān dàu, **shéi** syān chr.	**Whoever** arrives first, eats first.

4. They are used to form exclamatory sentences.

他多高啊!	Tā **dwó** gāu a!	**How** tall he is!
這怎麼好啊!	Jè **dzěmma** hǎu a!	**What** on earth can we do?

5. They are used in reduplicated form in subordinate clauses to translate approximately as "the various kind of," "in various ways" and similar indefinite phrases.

我聽説他請什麼什麼人了.	Wǒ tīngshwo tā chǐng **shémma shémma** rén le.	I heard about **the various** people he invited.

他告訴我他到
那儿那儿去了.

Tā gàusung wǒ tā dàu
nár nǎr chyù le.

He told me about **the
various** places he was
going to.

RC = Resultative Compound

Many verbs, both stative and functive, may be compounded with a second verbal
element, a resultative ending (RE), to form what are known as resultative compounds.
A simple compound of this type indicates a result which actually takes place and is known
as an "acual resultative." By indicating between the basic verb and the resultative ending
either 的 de (positive) or 不 bù (negative) a "potential resultative" is formed.

Actual Resultatives

Positive			Negative		
看見	kànjyan	see	沒看見	méikànjyan	didn't see
吃完了	chīwánle	finished eating	沒吃完	méichīwán	didn't finish eating

Potential Resultatives

Positive			Negative		
看的見	kàndejyàn	can see	看不見	kànbujyàn	cannot see
吃的完	chīdewán	can finish eating	吃不完	chībuwán	cannot finish eating

Sentence examples:

他吃完了飯了. Tā chīwánle fàn le. He has finished eating.
恐怕他看不見. Kǔngpa tā kànbujyàn. I'm afraid he cannot see.

The following points should be noted:

1. Potential resultatives cannot be used with the 把 bǎ construction.

Right: 我買不起汽車. Wó mǎibuchǐ chìchē. I can't afford to buy a car.
Wrong: 我把汽車買不起. Wó bǎ chìchē mǎibuchǐ.

2. In the case of certain compounds, the actual resultative form is not used, only
the potential.

吃不起 chībuchǐ cannot afford eating
跑不了 pǎubulyǎu cannot run away
看的起 kàndechǐ can afford to see

3. Actual resultatives prefix the negative 沒 méi; potential resultatives insert the
negative 不 bù (see "negative" examples above).

4. The particles 了 le, 呢 ne and 的 de, but not 着 je, are used with resultative
compounds.

RE = Resultative Ending

Resultative endings are verbal elements which are added to basic verbs and indicate the result of the action.

Typical examples are:

見	jyàn	as in	看見	kànjyan	see or saw
			聽見	tīngjyan	hear or heard
着	jáu	as in	找着	jǎujáu	find or found
			買着	mǎijáu	buy or bought

Stative verbs are also used freely as resultative endings (see 3 under **SV**).

SP = Specifier

A specifier is a nominal expression which points to a definite thing or things. Its closest English equivalents are the definite article and the demonstrative pronoun. A specifier may stand before a measure or noun or the combination NU-M.

這	jèi	這個	jèige	this, this one
		這個人	jèige rén	this man
		這兩本書	jèilyǎngběn shū	these two books
那	nèi	那個	nèige	that, that one
		那兩張畫儿	nèilyǎngjāng hwàr	those two pictures
		那人	nèi rén	that man
哪	něi	哪個	něige	which, which one
		哪位太太	něiwei tàitai	which lady
每	měi	每禮拜五	méilǐbaiwǔ	every Friday
另	lìng	另一個人	lìngyíge rén	another person

SV = Stative Verb

A stative verb is a verbal expression which describes a quality or condition of the subject. It therefore is static in the sense that no action is involved. It normally translates into English as the verb "to be" followed by an adjective.

A stative verb may have the following functions:

1. It may stand as a complete predicate.

   (Unmodified)

這張畫儿好看.	Jèijāng hwàr **hǎukàn.**	This picture **is attractive.**

   (With adverbial modifier)

這張畫儿很好看.	Jèijāng hwàr **hén** hǎukàn.	This picture is **very** attractive.

   (With a particle indicating degree)

這張畫儿好的很.	Jèijāng hwàr hǎu **dehěn.**	This picture is wonderful.

   (With 了 **le** indicating change of status)

我現在不累了.	Wǒ syàndzai búlèile.	I'm not tired now.

2. It may modify a noun.

(Directly before the noun)

他真是一個好人.   Tā jēn shr yíge **hǎu** rén.   He is really a **good** person.

(With the particle 的 de added between it and the noun)

好看的畫儿   **hǎukànde** hwàr   **attractive** picture

3. It may form part of a resultative compound.

(Standing as the basic verb of a resultative compound)

| 快不了 | kwàibulyǎu | cannot be **faster** |
| 貴起來了 | gwèichilaile | has gotten **expensive** |

(Standing as the resultative ending)

洗乾淨	syǐ**gānjing**	wash **clean**
吃飽	chr̄**bǎu**	eat **to the full**
寫清楚	syě**chǐngchu**	write **clearly**

4. It may be used in comparative sentences in the following patterns:

X yǒu Y (nemma) SV

這張桌子有那張桌子 (那麼)貴嗎?   Jèijāng jwōdz **yǒu** nèijāng jwōdz (**nemma**) **gwèi** ma?   Is this table as expensive as that table?

X bǐ Y (hái) SV

這個山比那個山(還) 高.   Jèige shān **bǐ** nèige shān (**hái**) **gāu.**   This mountain is higher than that one.

X gēn Y (yíyàng) SV

這本書跟那本書 (一樣)貴.   Jèibĕn shū **gēn** nèibĕn shu (**yíyàng**) **gwèi.**   This book is as expensive as that one.

5. It may be reduplicated with the particle 的 de to form words which may modify either verbs or nouns.

When single syllable: **X** becomes **XX** 的

好	hǎu	好好的	hǎuhāurde	well, good
快	kwài	快快的	kwàikwārde	quickly, quick
慢	màn	慢慢的	mànmārde	slowly, slow

When polysyllabic: **XY** becomes **XXYY** 的

清楚	chǐngchu	清清楚楚的	chǐngchingchuchūde	clearly, clear
乾淨	gānjing	乾乾淨淨的	gānganjingjǐngde	cleanly, clean
奇怪	chígwài	奇奇怪怪的	chíchigwaigwàide	strangely, strange

6. It may be followed by (一)點儿 (yǐ)dyǎr which makes it comparative.

| 他好 (一)點儿了. | Tā hǎu (yi)dyǎr le. | He is getting better now. |
| 你再弄清楚一點儿. | Nǐ dzài nùng-chǐngchu yidyǎr. | Make it clearer. |

TW = Timeword

Timewords are indicators of time and include such words as the days of the week, the months of the year, the seasons, etc. They are basically nouns, standing as the subject or the object of a verb, but they are distinctive in that they also function adverbially.

明天	míngtyan	tomorrow
今天	jīntyan	today
禮拜五	Lǐbaiwǔ	Friday
明年	míngnyan	next year
九月	Jyǒuywe	September

Sentence examples showing function as a noun:

今天是禮拜二.	Jīntyan shr Lǐbaièr.	Today is Tuesday.
學生都喜歡禮拜六.	Sywésheng dōu syǐhwan Lǐbailyòu.	All students like **Saturday.**
七月是夏天,不是春天.	**Chíywe** shr **syàtyan,** búshr **chwūntyan.**	July is **summer,** not **spring.**

Sentence examples showing function adverbially:

今天我不能去.	Jīntyan wǒ bùnéng chyù.	I can't go **today.**
夏天我們打算到歐洲去.	**Syàtyan** wǒmen dǎswan dàu Oūjou chyù.	We are planning to go to Europe **this summer.**

VO = Verb-Object Compound

Certain verbs in Chinese have such a close relationship with a generalized object that their meanings combine with that of the object to translate into English as a single verb. Such combinations are called verb-object compounds.

VO		Lit. Trans.	Normal Trans.
吃飯	chīfàn	eat food	eat
睡覺	shwèijyàu	sleep sleep	sleep
唱歌儿	chànggēer	sing songs	sing
說話	shwōhwà	speak speech	speak

The following points should be noted:

1. When a specific object is indicated, it replaces the generalized object and is never used together with it.

Right:	我要吃糖.	Wǒ yàu chī táng.	I want to eat some candy.
Wrong:	我要吃飯糖.	Wǒ yàu chīfàn táng.	

2. When the verb and object of a verb-object compound are separated by other elements in a sentence, they function in the same way as any ordinary verb and object.

他吃了三碗飯了.	Tā **chī**le sānwǎn **fàn** le.	He has **eaten** three bowls of **rice.**
我們可以唱幾個中國歌儿.	Wǒmen kéyi **chàng** jǐge Jūnggwo **gēer.**	We can **sing** several Chinese **songs.**

他睡了一個鐘頭 | Tā **shwèi**le yíge jūngtóu- He **slept** for an hour.
的覺. | de **jyàu**.

ABBREVIATIONS AND INDICATORS

Abbreviations

(*anat.*)	in anatomy
(*arith*.)	in arithmetic
(c)	current mainland usage
cf.	compare with
(*chem.*)	in chemistry
(d)	used mostly in dialectal areas other than Peiping
d	name of a dynasty
(fig.)	figurative(ly)
(*geom.*)	in geometry
(h)	honorific
(lit.)	literal(ly)
(lp)	localism of Peiping
(m)	military term
(*math.*)	in mathematics
(*phys*.)	in physics
s	common surname
SF of	simplified form of
t	commonly used in transliteration

Indicators

q	superscript indicating a question word
~	represents the entry word in examples
*	indicates a second pronunciation (see Explanation, E)
=	is identical to
→	look for more information under
↑	see main entry above for information
↓	examples given below
[ ]	indicates simplified form of the character
{ }	indicates variant form of the character (see Explanation, C)
'	precedes syllable to be stressed
/	indicates beginning of a sentence example
( )	used around explanatory material, grammatical notations, a few abbreviations (see Explanation, B)
°	used in Chinese or English sentences as follows : "He isn't °coming here any more. *or* °going to come here again." Indicates that both are acceptable versions

—	used for any material which is not direct translation or is in parentheses (see Explanation, D)
< >	(see Explanation, A)
.	used after translations of entry and example compounds or sentences, as well as the end of complete sentences, abbreviations, etc. (see Explanation, H)
,	used between two or more English words translating an entry (see Explanation, G)
;	separates example compounds and also measures belonging to different catagories (see Explanation, F)
or	(see Explanation, I)

EXPLANATION OF COMPLEX INDICATORS

A   < >

A.1   Enclosing 儿, -子, -头, and following (B) (see Grammatical Notation [hereafter referred to as GN] 4), indicates that the entry, as a boundform, can combine with 儿, 子 or 头 to form a free noun of the same meaning as the boundform entry. As:

桃 táu (B) <-儿, -子> peach.

日 r̀ (B) <-头 > sun.

means that 桃儿 "peach," 桃子 "peach," and 日头 "sun" are free nouns which may be derived from the entry.

A.2   Enclosing -儿, -子, following (N) (see GN 13), (M) (see GN 12), (PW) (see GN 20), (A) (see GN 1), (SV) (see GN 25) or (VO) (see GN 27), indicates that the entry may be prefixed to -儿 or -子 or not, with no change of meaning. As:

票   pyàu (N) <-子, -儿> ticket.

片   pyàn (M) <-儿> slice, thin piece.

西邊   syībyan (PW) <-儿> 1) (in) the west part or area.

到處   dàuchù (A) <-儿> everywhere.

到底   dàudǐ (VO) <-儿> reach the bottom

時髦   shŕmáu (SV) <-儿> be fashionable, stylish.

means that 票, 票子, 票儿 all mean "ticket," 片, 片儿 both mean "slice, thin piece," 西邊 and 西邊儿 both mean "in the west part or area," 到處 and 到處儿 both mean "everywhere," 到底 and 到底儿 both mean "reach the bottom," and 時髦 and 時髦儿 both mean "be fashionable, stylish."

A.3   Enclosing -着, following (CV) (see GN 5) or (A) (see GN 1) indicates that the entry may be prefixed to -着 or not, without change of meaning. As:

順 shwùn (CV) <-着> along.

這麼 dzèmma (A) <着> in this way; then.

means that 順 and 順着 both mean "along," and 這麼 and 這麼着 both mean "in this way; then."

A.4   Enclosing -着, following (FV) (see GN 8) indicates that the verbal entry often appears in its progressive form, i.e. prefixed to -着 rather than standing by itself. As:

站　jàn (FV) <‐着> stand.

means that 站 "stand" is usually seen in the form 站着 "standing."

B　( )

B.1　Enclosing some abbreviations. As: (c), (d), (h), (lp), (m), *(anat.)*, *(chem.)*, (lit.), (fig.) and so on. (see Abbreviations).

B.2　Enclosing grammatical notations. As: (FV), (N), (SV) and so on.

B.3　Enclosing a capital M with character and its pronunciation following the nominal definition of an entry, indicates that the character is a common measure for that entry under the preceding definition. As:

幼兒園 yòuérywán (N) kindergarten (M 所 swǒ).

means that the character 所 is a common measure for 幼兒園 "kindergarten." (note that this Dictionary does not show cases where measures 個 ge, 種 jǔng, 樣 yàng and 位 wèi would be used, since their application is so general, and since students of elementary Chinese would know where to use them without being told.

B.4　Enclosing lit. plus a phrase or a sentence, indicates that the enclosed material is a literal translation of the material it immediately follows. As:

/ He came just when I was sick. (lit. He perversely waited until I was sick to come.)

B.5　Indicates alternative element, or elements, which may be added when convenient, but are usually not necessary. As:

(PT) ~ . . . 也 (or 還) . . .

means that 還 may be used in this pattern in place of 也 .

/他瘦的(跟)個猴儿似的.

means that the word 跟 is optional in this sentence.

B.6　Enclosing an underlined phrase or word, indicates that the enclosed material qualifies what immediately preceded it. As:

go around (move in a circle around something).

be lively (of a party, meeting, etc.).

everybody (used only as a subject or transposed object).

mercury (metal).

B.7　Enclosing prepositions, indicates that the material which follows may either be used nominally or as a prepositional phrase. As:

西方 syīfang (PW) (in) the west.

means that 西方 may start off a sentence translated into English like "In the west, prices are lower." or "The West has a better climate than the East."

星期日 syīngchīr (TW) (on) Sunday.

means that 星期日 can be used both nominally and adverbially in sentences like "This Sunday will be his birthday." and "Let's go next Sunday."

C　{ }

C.1　Enclosing one character, indicates that the character is an alternate form of the standard entry character. As:

預{豫} yù (B) beforehand.

means that 豫 is an alternate form of the standard character 預.

C.2　Enclosing a sequence of characters and symbols, indicates that the characters serve as alternate forms of the standard entry character only in the cases which the symbols indicate. As:

雕 {彫 (FV) (B), 凋 (B) (1), 鵰 (N)} dyāu

means that 雕 may be replaced by 彫 when 雕 functions as functive verb or boundform; that 雕 may be replaced by 凋 when 雕 has the category (1) meaning of the possible boundform meaning; that 雕 may be replaced by 鵰 when 雕 functions as noun.

的 {得 (1) (2), 底 (3) (4), 地 (5) (6)} de (P)

means that standard entry character 的 has only one grammatical function (when pronounced de) and that in meaning categories (1) and (2) it may be replaced by 得 , in meaning categories (3) and (4) it may be replaced by 底, and in meaning categories (5) and (6) it may be replaced by 地 .

D　___　underline

D.0.　Used to indicate words of explanation which would not appear as part of an English translation. As:

戶　hù (M) <u>for households</u>. 三戶人家 three households.

D.1　Beneath a phrase preceding or following the English definition, indicates that the phrase limits the situation in which the entry may be used. As:

化驗 hwàyàn (FV) analyze <u>chemically</u>.

means that the entry is not used in the sense of "analyze a problem," for instance, but is limited to chemical analysis.

啥 shá (N)^q 2) <u>used after negative verbs</u>, anything. (d)

means that the entry 啥 would be translated as "anything" only if it is used after a negative verb.

D.2　Beneath some abbreviations. As <u>i.e.</u>, <u>lit.</u>, and so on.

E　*

E.1　Following an alternative pronunciation, and marking one or more segments of the entry, indicates that the alternative pronunciation may only be used in that/those segment(s). As:

落 lwò, làu* (FV) 1)* fall, drop.　2) be left behind.

means that the word 落 can be pronounced both as lwò and làu when it means "fall, drop." However, it can only be pronounced as lwò when it means "be left behind."

尿 nyàu, swēi* (N)* urine. (FV) urinate.

means that the word 尿 can be pronounced both as nyàu and swēi when used as a noun; but only as nyàu when it is used as a functive verb.

F　;　semicolon

F.1　Separates measure (M) (see GN 8), with different applications, used to measure the same thing. As:

布　bù (N) cotton cloth (M 疋 pǐ; 塊 kwài).

means that the entry "cotton cloth" may be measured in terms of pieces (塊 kwài) or bolts (疋 pǐ).

F.2 Separates independent phrase examples. As:

參 tsān (B) 1) take part in, participate in. 參戰 participate in war; 參政 participate in politics.

G   ,   comma

G.1 Separates related but distinct definitions of an entry. As:

背心 bèisyīn (N) sleeveless jacket, vest.

G.2 Separates alternative pronunciations of the same entry. As:

矛盾 máudwùn, máushwǔn (SV) be contradictory.

G.3 Separates alternative measures of a nominal entry (see GN 12 and B.3) having essentially the same meaning when translated into English. As:

餐巾 tsānjīn (N) cloth napkin (M 條 tyáu, 張 jāng, 塊 kwài).

means that the three measures all have roughly the same meaning, crudely translatable as "piece."

G.4 Appearing after the last one of two or more items in a definition, indicates that the following underlined or parenthetic qualification (see D.1) applies to all the preceding items. As:

料理 lyàuli (FV) straighten out, manage, arrange, matters, a wedding, funeral, meeting, banquet.

means that the underlined limitation applies to all three meanings preceding it.

G.5 If the comma does not appear after the last item, indicates that the following qualification only applies to the last item. As:

來頭 láitou (N) connection, pull (of a person).

means that the underlined and parenthetic limitation only refers to the word "pull."

H   period

H.1 Appearing after the last one of two or more definitions, indicates that the following measure (see GN 12) applies to all the preceding definitions. As:

早飯 dzǎufàn (N) 1) breakfast. 2) lunch (lp). (M 頓 dwùn).

means that 頓 measures both "breakfast" and "lunch."

H.2 If the period does not appear after the last definition, indicates that the following measure only applies to the last definition. As:

梅花 méihwā (N) <兒> 1) club (in cards). 2) plum blossom (M 朵 dwǒ; 枝 jī).

means that 朵 and 枝 measure "plum blossom" only.

I   *or*   (italic or)

I.1 Separates two subordinate, alternative segments of a definition. As:

扛 káng (FV) 1) carry on one's shoulder *or* on the shoulders of two or more men.

In this case, "carry" may apply to either of the two phrases beginning with "on."

CHINESE TO ENGLISH

啊 **a** (P) 1) used as an interrogative. /你到那兒去～? Where are you going? 2) indicating intimacy. 老弟～ my young friend. 3) indicating irritation or impatience. /我懂～! I understand! 4) indicating an exclamation. /這不行～! This won't do! 5) for lively enumeration. 書～,報～,甚麼的... books, and newspapers, and the like. 6) indicating a deliberate pause. /我～,老實説～,可真不想去. To tell the truth, I really don't want to go. 7) calling for confirmation or an echoed statement. /你不來～? You're not coming? 8) indicating a mild command. /你們先吃～. Go ahead and eat. 9) used after the name of a person one is addressing directly. /李先生～,我看你就答應了吧! Mr. Li, I think you might as well agree with this. → 啊 **ā**,啊 **á**,啊 **ǎ**,啊 **à**. *cf.* 哇 **wa**,呀 **ya**,哪 **na**,啦 **la**.

啊 **ā** (I) 1) indicates an affirmative answer. /A: 你去嗎? B: ～,我去. A: Are you going? B: Yes, I am. → 啊 **ā**,啊 **á**,啊 **ǎ**,啊 **à**.

阿 **ā** → 阿 **à**.

啊 **á** (I) 1) What did you say? *or* What do you mean? 2) implying doubt or surprise. /～? 這是你的? Oh? Is this yours? → 啊 **ā**,啊 **ā**,啊 **ǎ**,啊 **à**.

啊 **ǎ** (I) indicating puzzled surprise. /～,他怎麽知道了? That's strange. How does he know about it? → 啊 **ā**,啊 **ā**,啊 **á**,啊 **à**.

啊 **à** (I) indicating satisfaction. /～! 這就對了. Ah! This is right. → 啊 **ā**,啊 **ā**,啊 **á**,啊 **ǎ**.

阿 **à, ā** (B) used before kinship terms of address or last names to indicate affection (d). ～爹 daddy; ～姐 sis, sister. *t*
  阿姨 **àyí, āyí.** (N) 1) aunt (mother's sister). 2) wife's sister. 3) father's concubine. 4) kindergarten teacher, governess (d).

哎 {嗳,哎,唉} **āi, ēi*** (I) 1) used to get closer attention from someone. /～,你看啊. Say! Look! 2) used to express surprise at a coincidence. /～,我正要找你! I was just

about to look for you! 3)* used to answer a call or request. /A: 老張! B: ～,甚麽事? A: Chang! B: Yes, what is it? → 哎 **ái**,哎 **ǎi**,哎 **ài**.

哎呀 **āiyā** = 哎喲 **āiyāu** (I) 1).

哎喲 **āiyāu** (I) 1) indicating surprise or distress. /～! 已經八點了! Oh my! It's already eight! 2) indicating pain or suffering. /～! 痛死我了. Oh, the pain is killing me. /～,真燙. Ouch! It's really hot.

哎唷 **āiyōu** = 哎喲 **āiyāu.**

挨{捱} **āi, ái*** (FV) 1) touch. /這兩根電線～上了. These two wires are touching. 2) be close (physically). /這兩座房子～得很近. These two buildings are very close together. 3) be at. /你～那兒呢? Where are you? 4)* suffer from. ～了一天餓 suffer from hunger for a whole day. 5) receive a scolding. /他～一頓罵. He got a good scolding. 6)* delay, wait. /我～了一年了. I have waited for a year. (CV) <着> 1) near, next to. /～着他坐. Sit next to him. 2) one after another. ～'家檢查 investigate from house to house.
  挨班兒 **āibār** (VO) take turns. /我們説好了～洗碗. We have agreed to take turns washing dishes.
  挨門兒 **āimér** (A) going from door to door.

哎{嗳,唉,唉} **ái** (I) used to introduce an expression of surprise or bewilderment. /～,這怎麽辦呢? Gosh! What can we do? → 哎 **āi**,哎 **ǎi**,哎 **ài**.

呆 **ái** → 呆 **dāi**.

挨 **ái** → 挨 **āi**.

哎{嗳,唉,唉} **ǎi, ěi** (I) used to introduce a difference of opinion. /～,那就不對了. Uh, uh, that couldn't be right. → 哎 **āi**,哎 **ái**,哎 **ài**.

矮 **ǎi** (SV) 1) be short (not tall). /這個人太～. This person is too short. 2) be low in elevation, pitch, rank. /這座樓很～. This building is very low.
  矮子 **ǎidz** (N) 1) dwarf. 2) shorty (nickname).

哎(嗳,喴,唉) ài (I) used as an expression of regret. /～真糟糕! Oh, what a mess! 哎ài, 哎ài, 哎ài.

愛(爱) ài (FV) love. /他很～你. He loves you very much. (N) love. (AV) 1) like to. /他很～吃糖. He likes to eat candy very much. 2) be apt to. /我女兒～傷風. My daughter catches cold very easily. (PT)～...不...as you please. /你～去不去. Go or not as you please.

愛情 àichíng (N) love, affection (between man and woman).

愛國 àigwó (VO) love one's country. /你～不愛? Do you love your country? (SV) be patriotic. /那個人很～. Thai person is very patriotic.

愛國主義 ài'gwójǔ'yì (N) patriotism.

愛護 'àihù (FV) love and protect. ～自己的子女 love and protect one's own children. (N) love and protection.

愛人 àirén (N) 1) lover. 2) husband (c). 3) wife (c).

愛上 àishang (RC) fall in love with. /他～那個小姐了. He fell in love with that girl.

愛惜 àisyí (FV) cherish or treasure a thing in such a manner as to make use of it sparingly, or a person with regard to his ability. /他不知道～東西. He doesn't know what it is to treasure things. /我～他那個人. I cherish him.

礙(碍) ài (FV) hinder, bother. /我們兩人誰也不～誰. We two don't get in each other's way.

礙事 àishr̀ (VO) hinder matters. /我不礙你的事吧. I am not in your way. (SV) be in the way. /這棵樹很～. This tree is really in the way. → 不礙事 búàishr̀.

礙眼 àiyǎn (SV) 1) be unpleasant to look at. 2) be in the way.

安 ān (SV) be at ease. /他心裏很～. His mind is at ease. (FV) install, set up. ～電燈 install electric lights; ～燈泡 put in an electric light bulb. (B) 1) quiet, peaceful. ～靜 be quiet. 2) secure, stable. ～定 be steady (as of a job). s t

安全 ānchywán (SV) be safe. (N) safety. ～第一. Safety first.

安葬 āndzàng (FV) make ceremonial burial arrangements and bury. /他回家去～他父親. He returned home to arrange the funeral of his father.

安靜 ānjìng (SV) be quiet, still. /大家都睡着了,請你們～點兒. Everyone's gone to bed; please be quiet.

安置 ānjr̀ (FV) 1) arrange something. /～一個家不是容易的. It isn't easy to get a family settled (of someone moving his family from one place to another). 2) place someone in a job. /你把他～在那兒哪? Where (or In what section or In what department) did you put him to work?

安排 ānpái (FV) 1) arrange matters. /這個事情不好～. This matter isn't easy to arrange. 2) arrange things physically, putting them in certain places. /他買了很多傢俱,可是不知道怎麼～ He bought a lot of furniture, but he doesn't know how to arrange it for the best effect.

安培 'ānpéi (N) ampere. (M) ampere.

安心 ānsyīn (SV) be free from worry. (A) 1) unworriedly. ～念書 study without worrying. 2) intentionally, purposely. ～害人 harm people intentionally. (VO) have intent. 沒安好心 have bad intentions.

安慰 ānwèi (FV) comfort. /他失業了,你去～～他吧. He lost his job, go and comfort him. (N) source of satisfaction, comfort. (SV) be content. /我心裏覺得很～. I feel very content.

安穩 'ānwěn (SV) be solid, secure, stable. /那個東西放得很～. That thing is securely placed.

鞍 ān (B) <-子> saddle (M 付 fù).

岸 àn (N) shore, bank, coast. 河～ river bank.

按 àn, èn* (FV)* press with the finger or palm. ～門鈴 ring a doorbell. (CV) <着> 1) according to. /我們得～法律辦. We have to do it according to the law. 2) by the week, month, etc. ～月 by the month, monthly.

按照 'ànjàu (CV) according to. /～你所說的,那麼,這個就對了.

According to what you said, then, this is right.

暗 **àn** (SV) be dark, but not totally lacking light. /那個燈很~. That light is very dim. (B) secret, hidden. ~笑 laugh up one's sleeve; ~礁 hidden rocks.

    暗淡 **àndàn** (SV) be dim (of circumstances or of the future). /大局近來很~. The situation is rather dim these days. /他的前途很~. His future is not very bright.

    暗中 **ànjūng** (A) secretly. /他~幫忙. He helps secretly.

    暗扣儿 **ànkòur** (N) hook-and-eye fastener.

    暗室 **ànshr̀** (N) darkroom (M 間 jyān).

案 **àn** (B) 1) <-子> case at law (M件jyàn, 椿 jwāng). 辦~子 handle a case. 2) proposal, bill, in a legislative meeting. 老人醫藥保險 ~ old age medical care bill; 議~ item on an agenda. 3) legal record. 檔~ official file. 4) table. 畫~ drawing table.

骯(骯) **āng** (B) ↓.

    骯髒 **āngdzang** (SV) be filthy.

ao see **au**.

熬 **āu** (FV) boil, stew. 在小火上~ stew over a low fire. → 熬 áu.

熬 **áu** (FV) 1) decoct, extract, by boiling. 拿骨頭~湯 make soup with bones. 2) endure, stand. ~刑 endure torture. → 熬 āu.

    熬夜 **áuyè** (VO) stay up all night. /昨天他們打牌,熬了一夜. They stayed up all last night playing cards.

噢 **àu** (I) indicating comprehension. /~, 我懂了. Oh, now I understand.

吧{罷(P)} **ba** (P) 1) used at the end of a sentence to indicate a suggestion or a mild command. /讓他說~. Let him speak. 2) used at the end of a sentence to indicate some doubt in the speaker's mind. /他們走了~. I suppose they left. 3) used to mark a pause after a suppositional clause. /我去~,太麻煩,不去~,

又不行. If I go, it'll be a lot of trouble; but it won't do not to go either. 4) used to indicate consent. /好~,就這麼辦~! O.K. Let's do it this way. (ON) sound of two objects striking sharply together. /我~的一巴掌打在他的臉上. I hit him in the face with a loud smack.

八{捌} **bā** (**bá** before a syllable with a fourth tone) (NU) eight. (B) eighth. ~號 the eighth (day of month), number eight.

    八月 **báywè** (TW) 1) (in) August. 2) the eighth month of the lunar calendar.

巴 **bā** (FV) stick to a surface. ~在牆上 stick on a wall. (B) 1) hope. ~不得 earnestly hope to do something. 2) added to other elements to form nouns. 尾~ tail. t

    巴答 **bāda** (ON) sound of smacking the lips or puffing on a pipe.

    巴掌 **bājang** (N) palm of the hand.

    巴結 **bājye** (FV) flatter someone with some ulterior motive. /他很會~人. He knows how to flatter people.

疤 **bā** (B) scar.

    疤瘌 **bāla** (N) scar, pockmark (a depression in the surface, or wrinkles, never a ridge or bump; does not include that of smallpox which is 麻子 **mádz**).

拔 **bá** (FV) pull something up or out. ~鎗 pull out a gun; ~牙 extract a tooth.

把 **bǎ** (**baǐ** (lp)*) (M) 1) for things with handles, such as knives, scissors, etc. 一~斧子 an ax. 2) handful. 一~米 a handful of rice. 3) <-儿> bunch of flowers, vegetables, etc. 一~花儿 a bunch of flowers. (FV) 1) hold something with the hands. /他~着不肯放手. He's holding onto it and won't let it go. 2) guard, watch over. ~門 guard a door. (CV)* used to bring the direct object of the sentence before the verb. /我~他的名字忘了. I forgot his name. → 把 **bǎ**.

    把柄 **bábǐng** (N) shortcoming, defect (of a person, particularly when it is the basis of criticism).

/他抓住我的～了． He seized upon my shortcomings.

把持 bǎchr (FV) monopolize, control through use of undue influence. /他為什麼老要～這件事情？ Why does he always monopolize this matter?

把舵 bǎdwò (VO) steer, handle a rudder (boat only). /我們大家輪流～． We take turns at the rudder.

把守 'bǎshǒu (FV) guard. /有兩個兵～城門． There are two soldiers guarding the city gate.

把戲 bǎsyì (N) 1) act of skill. 2) practical joke.

把兄弟 bǎsyūngdì (N) sworn brothers (people who aren't brothers by birth but assume a comparable relationship).

把握 bǎwo (N) confidence. (FV) seize (fig.). ～機會 seize an opportunity.

靶 bǎ (B) <一子> target (for target practice). 打～ practice shooting.

把 bà (B) <一儿> handle of a small object, such as a knife, pot, kettle, cup, broom (not for lifting and carrying a heavy object, nor for opening and closing something). 一把 bà.

爸 bà (B) father.
爸爸 bàba (N) papa, dad.

罷〔罢〕 bà (B) cease, quit. ～教 go on strike (of teachers). 一吧〔罷〕 ba.

罷工 bàgūng (VO) go on strike (of workers only). /他們已經罷了三天工了． They've been on strike for three days now.

罷課 bàkè (VO) go on strike (of students; usually for political reasons).

罷了 bàle (P) used with 不過 bugwò, 無非 wúfēi, 也就是 yě jyòushr, 只是 jřr, that's all, nothing else. /他不過是說說～． He's only talking, that's all. (FV) call something off. /要是他不肯就～． If he's not willing, then call it off.

罷了 bàlyǎu (SV) be all right, O.K. /他的中國話還～． His Chinese is O.K. (P) = 罷了 bàle (P).

罷免 bàmyǎn (FV) remove from office, impeach. /他被人

民給～了． He was removed from office by the will of the people.

罷市 bàshr̀ (VO) go on strike (of merchants, usually in protest against governmental authorities).

霸 bà (N) bully, tyrant, big shot (one who pushes and dominates). /他是這個地方的一個～． He is one of the local big shots. (B) 1) unreasonable. 2) rule by might rather than by right. ～權 tyranny.

霸道 'bàdàu (SV) be unreasonable, ornery. /他這個人很～你跟他說沒用． That guy is very unreasonable; there's no use arguing with him.

霸佔 'bàjàn (FV) seize and control a territory or position or property, exclusively and by might. /他～我們的地方不還． He took over our land and won't give it back.

耙 bà (FV) harrow. ～地 harrow ground. (N) harrow (M 把 bǎ). 一耙 pá.

掰 {擘擘} bāi (FV) break or split something with both hands (lp). ～開 break apart.

白 bái (SV) 1) be white. ～布 white cloth. 2) be light, fair (of complexion). 3) be wrong in writing or reading a character. (N) white, white color. 雪～ snow white. (A) 1) in vain, for nothing. ～來 come in vain. 2) free of charge. ～給 give something free of charge. (B) clear, obvious. 明～ understand, be easy to understand. 2) plain, unaccompanied. ～開水 plain boiled water. s t

白字 báidž (N) character used incorrectly in place of another which represents the same or similar pronunciation (comparable to a misspelled word in English).

白礬 báifán (N) alum.

白話 báihwà (N) colloquial language.

白金 báijīn (N) platinum.

白種人 'báijǔngrén (N) Caucasian.

白濁 báijwó (N) gonorrhea.

白蘭地 báilándì (N) brandy.

白色 báisè (N) white (color).

白事 báishr̀ (N) funeral (M 次 tsẓ). 辦～ make arrangements

for and manage a funeral.

白薯 **báishǔ** (N) sweet potato.

白糖 **báitáng** (N) white sugar.

白菜 **báitsài** (N) Chinese *or* celery cabbage (M棵 **kē**).

白天 **báityan** (TW) (in) the day-time.

把 **bǎi** → 把 **bǎ**.

百 **bǎi, bwò*** (M) hundred. (B)* all, every. ～發～中 hit the mark every time.

百货公司 **bǎi'hwògūng'sz** (N) department store (lit. hundred goods industry) (M家 **jyā**).

百科全書 **bǎi'kēchywán'shū** (N) encyclopedia (M部 **bù**; 套 **tàu**).

柏(栢) **bǎi** (B) cypress, cedar, arbor vitae.

柏樹 **bǎishù** (N) Chinese juniper (M棵 **kē**).

擺(擺) **bǎi** (FV) 1) display. ～架子 put on airs. 2) arrange, set in order. 擺桌子 set a table. 3) swing, wave. 來回～ wave to and fro. 4) place, put. /你把椅子～在桌子邊兒. Put the chair by the table. (N) pendulum.

擺渡 **'bǎidù** (N) ferry (for going across a stream, of a crude and simple sort) (M隻 **jī**).

敗 **bài** (SV) be defeated in a battle or war. /誰～了? Who was defeated?

敗仗 **bàijàng** (N) lost battle (M回 **hwéi**, 次 **tsż**). 打～ fight and lose a battle.

敗類 **bàilèi** (N) black sheep (in a group of people).

拜 **bài** (FV) hold an initiation *or* a ceremony to establish a new relationship between persons. ～乾媽 take someone as one's godmother. (B) 1) worship. ～祖先 worship one's ancestors. 2) kneel before, bow to. ～佛 do homage to *or* worship Buddha. 3) call on. 回～ pay back a visit. 4) congratulate. ～壽 wish someone a happy birthday. *t*

拜訪 **bàifǎng** (FV) make a formal call on somebody. /他去～他的朋友去了. He's gone to pay a call on his friend.

拜年 **bàinyán** (VO) 1) call on someone on New Year's Day. /今年我想寄賀年片兒算了, 不～

了. I'm not going to call on people this New Year's, I'll just send cards. 2) wish someone a happy New Year. /我給您拜個晚年吧! It's a little late, but a happy New Year to you anyway! (IE) Happy New Year!

拜託 **bàitwō** (FV) request, ask, someone to do something. /這件事情我～您辦吧. I'll have to ask you to handle this matter for me. (IE) Thank you (said after a request has been granted).

班 **bān** (M) 1) class of students. 2) squad of soldiers. 3) for scheduled trains, flights, ships, etc. 第一～飛機 flight one. (B) <一儿> 1) turn to do something, shift. 值～ be on duty. 2) <一子> company, troupe. 馬戲～ circus troupe. 3) <一子> house of prostitution. 4) varicolored, mottled. ～白 be partly grey (of hair); ～竹 mottled bamboo. *t*

班長 **bānjǎng** (N) 1) squad leader (m). 2) monitor (in a class).

斑 **bān** (B) varicolored, mottled. ～馬 zebra.

斑點 **bāndyǎn** (N) spot (on a surface), flaw (as in something like jade).

搬 **bān** (FV) lift *or* move something heavy with palms up, not above the head. ～起來 lift up; ～東西 move things from one place to another. /他把箱子～到樓上去了. He moved the trunk upstairs.

搬家 **bānjyā** (VO) change one's residence, move. /一個月我搬了兩回家. I've moved twice in one month.

瘢 **bān** (B) scar, spot (on the skin). 雀～ freckles.

板 **bǎn** (N) 1) printing block, cut. 2) musical instrument for beating time, made of two pieces of wood. (M) main beat in a bar of music. (SV) be stiff, wooden, stern. (B) <一子, 一儿> board, plank, slab, plate, sheet (M塊 **kwài**). 石～ stone slab; 鐵～ sheet *or* plate of iron.

板車 **bǎnchē** (N) two-wheeled wooden cart (M輛 **lyàng**).

板凳儿 **bǎndèngr** (N) stool, bench, without a back (M張 **jāng**).

板擦儿 **bǎntsār** (N) black-board eraser.

版 **bǎn** (N) 1) printing block, cut. 排~ set type. 2) edition. 絕~ be out of print.

半 **bàn** (NU) 1) half. ~塊錢 half a dollar. 2) added to a NU-M indicates a half more than the unit amount specified by the M. 三寸~ three and a half inches. (M) half. 一大~ the majority. (B) half, semi-. ~獨立 semi-independent. (A) partly, half. ~醒 half awake. (PT)~...不... half. ~睡不睡 half asleep.

半輩子 **bànbèidz** (N) half of one's life. /他念了~的書. He spent half of his life studying.

半球 **bànchyóu** (N) hemisphere.

半島 **bàndǎu** (N) peninsula.

半道儿 **bàndàur** (PW) 1) half-way or part way somewhere. /~我們還得加點儿汽油. We'll have to get some more gas halfway. 2) the middle part, the halfway point. /那輛車走到~就壞了. The car broke down at the halfway point.

半瘋儿 **bànfēngr** (SV) be crazy, nuts. /他比你還~. He is even more crazy than you are. (N) half-wit.

半徑 **bànjìng** (N) radius of a circle.

半中腰 **bànjūngyāu** (PW) 1) the middle part, the halfway point, of something long or high. 樓的~ the middle part of a building. /他的學校在那個山的~. His school is halfway up the mountain. 2) halfway along. /他~改了學歷史了. He changed to history halfway through.

半價 **bànjyà** (N) half of a price. /我算你~好了. OK, I'll charge you half-price. /這個錶是~買的. This watch was bought at half-price.

半空中 **bànkūngjūng** (PW) 1) in mid-air. /一個炮仗在~炸了. A firecracker exploded in mid-air. 2) in the sky, in the air. /~有兩架飛機. There are two air-planes in the sky.

半路 **bànlù** (PW) 1) halfway or part way somewhere. /他~離開大家了. He left the group half-way through. 2) the halfway point.

在~上有一個地方我們可以休息. We can take a rest at the halfway point.

半日 **bànr** (N) half a day. /他走了~還沒到. He walked half a day but didn't get there.

半身像 **bànshēnsyàng** (N) 1) bust (statue). 2) half-length por-trait (M張 **jāng**).

半數 **bànshù** (N) half of some stated quantity. /那些人~以上都是學生. More than half of the people are students.

半天 **bàntyān** (A) 1) for a long time. /他~沒說話. He didn't speak for a long time. 2) <-儿> for half a day. /~作事賺錢很少. You earn less money for work-ing half a day. (N) <-儿> half a day.

半夜 **bànyè** (TW) (at) midnight. /那個小孩~哭起來了. The child started crying at midnight. /~很安靜. Midnight is a quiet time.

半圓規 **bànywángwēi** (N) pro-tractor (instrument).

辦[办] **bàn** (FV) 1) manage, carry out. ~公 transact business; ~酒席 prepare a feast; ~貨 buy or import goods. 2) punish. /我非~你不可. I absolutely must punish you.

辦法 **bànfa** (N) method, way of managing something. 有辦法 **yǒubànfa**.

辦公費 **bàngūngfèi** (N) expense allowance in addition to salary for administrative responsibilities (M 筆 **bǐ**).

辦公室 **bàngūngshr** (N) office (place) (M間 **jyān**).

辦理 **bànlǐ** (FV) manage, carry out, usually some temporary plan or project rather than a continuing en-terprise. /我託他替我~這一件事情. I entrusted him with managing that affair for me.

辦事員 **bànshrywán** (N) of-ficial employee (usually higher than a purely clerical worker).

拌 **bàn** (FV) mix solid, powdery, or thick liquid ingredients. /把醬跟麵~在一塊儿. Mix the sauce and the noodles together.

拌嘴 **bàndzwěi** (VO) quarrel, argue (<u>noisily</u>). /你們拌什麼嘴呢? What are you quarreling about?

絆 **bàn** (FV) trip. /差一點～了我一跤. I almost tripped and fell.

伴 **bàn** (B) 1) <ㄦ> companion. 老～ㄦ wife, husband. 2) keep <u>someone</u> company. 陪～ accompany.

伴郎 **bànláng** (N) best man (<u>at a wedding</u>)

伴侶 **bànlyǔ** (N) companion, partner. 終身～ lifetime companions, husband and wife.

幫(幇)(帮) **bāng** (FV) help. /我要～他, 可是～不上. I wanted to help him but I couldn't. (M) <ㄦ> clique, gang, group. (N) clique, gang, group.

幫助 **bāngjù** (FV) help, assist. /他～我找事情. He helped me find a job. (N) help, assistance.

幫忙 **bāngmáng** (VO) help, assist. /我能幫你甚麼忙嗎? Is there anything I can help you with? (N) help, assistance.

幫手 **'bāngshǒu** (N) helper, assistant.

綁 **bǎng** (FV) 1) tie <u>a rope or a string around something</u>, bind. ～起來 tie up. 2) kidnap. /他的兒子叫人～去了. His son was kidnaped.

綁票ㄦ **bǎngpyàur** (VO) kidnap. /有人想綁他的票ㄦ. Somebody is planning to kidnap him.

榜 **bǎng** (N) publicly posted roll of successful examinees.

榜樣 **bǎngyàng** (N) example, model. /別拿他作～. Don't take him as an example.

膀 **bǎng** (B) <子> 1) upper arm from <u>the elbow through the shoulder blade</u> <u>(of a human or an ape)</u>. 2) wing <u>of a chicken or other bird, especially as cut up for eating</u>.

磅 **bàng** (M) pound (<u>in weight</u>). (N) scale that weighs things in terms of the English system. 過～ weigh something.

傍 **bàng** (B) near a certain time.

傍晚 **bàngwǎn** (TW) 1) the early evening. 2) early in the evening. /他～大概就回來了. He will probably be back early in the evening.

棒 **bàng** (SV) be terrific, great, wonderful (lp). (B) <子> club, bat, stick, <u>like a policeman's stick, always</u> <u>of that shape, usually of wood, and</u> <u>often used for striking</u> (M根 **gēn**).

棒球 **bàngchyóu** (N) 1) a baseball. 2) baseball (<u>the game</u>) (M次 **tsz̀**, 場 **chǎng**).

棒子 **bàngdz** (N) 1) (B)↑. 2) corn, maize (M粒 **lì**; 棵 **kē**).

bao see **bau.**

剝 **bāu** → 剝 **bwō.**

包 **bāu** (FV) 1) wrap. 用紙～上 wrap in paper. 2) plate. ～金 plate with gold. 3) include. /一切都～在裏面. Everything is included. 4) do <u>something under contract</u>. ～工 do <u>work under contract</u>. 5) guarantee. ～換 guarantee to exchange <u>merchandise</u>. (N) 1) <ㄦ> package, bundle. 2) bump, swelling. (B) <ㄦ, 子> steamed stuffed dumpling. *s t*

包辦 **bāubàn** (FV) take care of everything involved in some job <u>without help *or* interference</u>. /所有的事他一個人～了. He did the whole job himself.

包飯 **bāufàn** (VO) have meals, board, someplace. /我在那儿包了三年的飯了. I've boarded there for three years. (N) board. 吃～ to board.

包袱 **bāufu** (N) 1) cloth wrapper. 2) cloth bundle. 3) obstacle <u>in thinking</u> (c).

包管 **bāugwǎn** (A) for sure. /這件事我～三天可以做成. I can complete this work in three days for sure. /他～不知道. He doesn't know for sure. (FV) take care of, hold in trust. /我成年以前, 我的財產由我叔叔～. My money is held in trust by my uncle until I come of age.

包裹 **bāugwǒ** (N) parcel, package (M件 **jyàn**). 打～ wrap up a package.

包含 **bāuhán** (FV) include, contain, consist of. /他的話～很多意思. His words contain a great deal of meaning.

包括 **bāukwò** (FV) include. /這

個價錢~稅嗎? Does this price
include the tax?
　　包廂 bāusyāng (N) reserved
box in a theater.
　　包圍 bāuwéi (FV) hem in, surround, blockade. /我們把敵人
~ 了. We surrounded the enemy.
(PT) 受...的... be influenced by.
/他受那些人的~. He is in-
fluenced by those people.

炮(疱) bāu (N) 1) boil, swelling. /他頭
上長了一個~. A boil devel-
oped on his head.　2) protruding
bump. /他頭上石並了一個~.
He hit his head and got a bump on it.

炮(焦,爆) bāu (FV) fry meat over a very hot
fire, with little or no fat and stirring
constantly. →炮 páu, 炮 pàu.

雹 báu (B) <~子> hailstone. 下~子
to hail.

薄 báu (SV) 1) be thin (in dimension).
2) be thin (of soup) (d).　3) be ungenerous. /他待人很~. He is
ungenerous toward people. 4) be
deficient, weak. 人情很~have
poor relations with someone. → 薄
bwó, 薄 bwò.

保 bǎu (B) 1) protect. ~管 keep safely.
2) insure. ~壽險 get (or have) life
insurance. (FV) 1) guarantee.
/我~他一定還錢. I guarantee
he'll pay back the money. 2) go
bail for. /她把他~出來了. She
bailed him out. (N) bond, security,
guarantee.
　　保不住 bǎubujù (A) might,
may. /~我就把這件事情忘
了. I might forget about this matter.
(RC) be unable to keep, hold on to.
/我該的錢太多了,恐怕我的
房子~了. I owe so much money
that I probably won't be able to keep
my house.
　　保持 bǎuchŕ (FV) maintain,
keep unaltered. ~健康 maintain
one's health.
　　保全 bǎuchywán (FV) keep
something intact, preserve. /我們
撒退為的是~實力. We must
retreat in order to preserve our
strength.
　　保管 bǎugwǎn (FV) hold in
trust, take care of (legally). /他父
親的財產都給一個信託公

司~. His father's property was
held by a trust company.
　　保護 bǎuhù (FV) protect.　(N)
protection.
　　保障 'bǎujàng (FV) safeguard.
~ 權利 protect one's rights.　(N)
1) protection.　2) security. /在政
府做事的人有~嗎? Do govern-
ment employees have security?
　　保證 bǎujèng (FV) guarantee.
/我可以~他. I can vouch for
him.　(N) guarantee.
　　保證人 bǎujèngrén (N) guarantor.
　　保重 bǎujùng (FV) be careful
(of one's physical condition). /您
~吧! Take care of yourself!
　　保留 bǎulyóu (FV) 1) hold in
reserve, reserve. /請你給我~
一個座位. Please reserve this
seat for me. 2) preserve. ~中國
固有文化 preserve the traditional
Chinese culture.
　　保姆 bǎumǔ (N) governess,
nurse (for children).
　　保守 bǎushǒu (SV) be conservative.　(FV) keep, maintain. ~祕
'密 keep a secret.
　　保險 bǎusyǎn (VO) insure.
/你的房子保了險嗎? Is your
house insured? (N) insurance.
/對了,我買了一了. Yes, I
bought insurance.　(FV) guarantee.
/我敢~明天不下雨. I can
guarantee it won't rain tomorrow.
　　保險箱 bǎusyǎnsyāng (N) safe
(for valuables).
　　保存 bǎutswún (FV) preserve,
keep something in a safe place.
/這種東西不容易~. This sort
of thing is not easily preserved.

飽 bǎu (SV) be full, satisfied (from
eating). /我~了. I'm full.
　　飽滿 bǎumǎn (SV) 1) be full
(of one's face).　2) be full of zest.
/他的精神很~. He is full of
zest.

寶(寳)(宝) bǎu (B) 1) precious, rare,
valuable. ~石 precious stone; 無
價之~ priceless thing.　2) your
(h). ~眷 your wife and children.
　　寶貝 'bǎubèi (N) small and
very valuable or precious thing.
　　寶貴 bǎugwèi (SV) be valuable,
precious.

堡 **bǎu, pù** (B) 1) walled village, stronghold. 2) -burg, -berg (in names of cities). 漢～ Hamburg.

　　堡壘 **bǎulěi, pùlei** (N) fort, fortress (M座**dzwò**).

抱 **bàu** (FV) 1) hold, carry, in the arms, as a baby. /那個小孩就喜歡人～. That child always wants to be held. 2) embrace, put one's arms around something. /他太太一下飛機他就過去～着她. When his wife got off the plane, he went over and embraced her. 3) adopt a child. /他的女兒是～來的. His daughter is adopted. 4) take, assume, a point of view, attitude. ～樂觀assume an optimistic attitude.

　　抱不平 **bàubupíng** (VO) bear a grudge, feel indignant. /聽完他的故事,我抱了滿腔的不平. After hearing his story, I became very indignant. (SV) be indignant. /我看見這種事情心裏很～. When I see a thing like that I become indignant. (RC) be unable to hold something level.

　　抱歉 **bàuchyàn** (SV) feel sorry. /對那件事我很～. I feel quite sorry about that. (FV) regret that. /我～我太太不能來. I regret that my wife can't come.

　　抱怨 **bàuywan** (FV) 1) complain. /別～. Don't complain. 2) blame. /別～我. Don't blame me.

報[报] **bàu** (FV) 1) report. ～火警 report a fire. 2) announce, declare. ～喪 announce a death. 3) repay, reciprocate. ～恩. repay a kindness. (N) newspaper (M份儿**fèr**, 張**jāng**).

　　報酬 **bàuchou** (FV) compensate, reward. /我怎樣～你呢? How can I repay you? (N) compensation, reward, payment.

　　報仇 **bàuchóu** (VO) get revenge. /他想～的時候快到了. He felt that the time for revenge was at hand.

　　報答 **'bàudá** (FV) repay someone for a favor or kindness. /我得～你對我的恩惠. I must repay you for the kindness you have shown me.

　　報導 **bàudǎu** (FV) report (in writing). /本地的報紙對那件新聞～的不正確. The local newspapers reported that news inaccurately.

　　報到 **bàudàu** (VO) report one's arrival, sign in. /禮拜一我得趕回去～. I have to hurry back on Monday and sign in.

　　報復 **bàufu** (FV) retaliate for an insult or injury. /他這樣待我, 我非～不可. I'll certainly pay him back for treating me like this. (N) revenge.

　　報告 **bàugàu** (FV) report. /無線電每一個鐘頭～一次新聞. The news is reported over the radio once every hour. (N) report.

　　報館 **bàugwǎn** (N) newspaper publishing company (M家**jyā**).

　　報賬 **bàujàng** (VO) charge expenses to an account. /你旅行時候用的錢可以報公賬. You may charge your traveling expenses to the company's account.

　　報紙 **bàujř** (N) 1) newspaper (M張**jāng**, 份儿**fèr**). 2) newsprint (M張**jāng**).

　　報名 **bàumíng** (VO) enroll in a school, for membership in some society, for an examination, etc. /那個學校～的手續怎麼樣? What's the procedure for enrolling at that school?

　　報社 **bàushè** (N) newspaper office (M家**jyā**).

　　報稅 **bàushwèi** (VO) declare taxes or goods for duty. /你有沒有應該～的東西? Have you anything to declare? /我今年還沒有報入息稅呢. I haven't filed my income tax return yet.

　　報喜 **bàusyǐ** (VO) report good tidings, bring good news (especially of the arrival of a child). /你給我報什麼喜來了? What good news have you for me?

　　報攤儿 **bàutār** (N) newsstand.

　　報應 **bàuying** (FV) get paid back for some evil deed. /他老害人現在～了. He always hurts people and now he's getting paid back. (N) retribution, one's due punishment.

暴 **bàu** (SV) be violent, fierce. ～雨 heavy shower. /他脾氣很～. He has a violent temper. (B) 1) expose.～曬 put out in the sun to dry. 2) cruel. ～君 cruel ruler.

暴躁 '**bàudzàu** (SV) be hot-tempered. /他雖然很～,但是對人很好. Even though he's hot-tempered, he's nice to people.

暴露 **bàulù** (FV) expose, bring out into the open. /報紙～了一個販毒機關. The newspaper exposed a narcotics ring. 2) be exposed, uncovered. /口袋破了,偷的書都～出來了. The bag broke and the stolen books were exposed. (SV) be revealing (of clothes).

爆 **bàu** (FV) 1) explode.～炸 explode. 2) burst, pop. /豆子煮的都～了. The beans were boiled until they burst. 3) boil, fry in hot oil for a very short period. →炮{爆} **bāu**.

爆發 **bàufā** (FV) burst or break out suddenly and violently. /火山～了. The volcano erupted. /革命～了. Revolution has suddenly broken out.

刨{鉋} **bàu** (FV) plane, level off. ～木頭 plane wood. (B) <-子> carpenter's plane (M把**bǎ**). →刨 **páu**.

豹 **bàu** (B) <-子> leopard (M隻**jī**).

杯{盃} **bēi** (B) <-子> cup, glass (M隻**jī**). (M) cup, glass. 一～酒 a glass of wine.

背{揹} **bēi** (FV) 1) carry something on one's back. /他～着一個背包. He's carrying a knapsack on his back. 2) be weighed down by debts, etc. ～了很多債 have a lot of debts. →背 **bèi**.

背包 **bēibāu** (N) 1) knapsack. 2) pack carried on the back.

背帶 **bēidài** (N) suspenders (M條**tyáu**).

卑 **bēi** (B) lowly, inferior. 自～感 inferiority complex.

卑鄙 **bēibǐ** (SV) be base, vulgar.

碑 **bēi** (N) monument, gravestone, memorial, memorial tablet, usually with the material used specified. 石～ stone monument.

悲 **bēi** (B) grieved, sad. ～劇 tragedy.

悲觀 **bēigwān** (SV) be pessimistic.

悲哀 **bēiāi** (SV) be grieved, sad.

北 **běi** (L) north. 從～到南 from north to south; 城～ (the area) north of the city; ～極 (at) the north pole.

北邊 **běibyan** (PW) <-ㄦ> (in) the north part or area. /城的～發水了. The north part of the city was flooded. /美國～有很多湖. There are many lakes in the northern part of the United States. 2) north of something. /他家的～是一個學校. There's a school north of his house.

北方 **běifang** (PW) (in) the north. /～比南方冷. The north is colder than the south. /～產小麥. Wheat is grown in the north.

輩 **bèi** (M) <-ㄦ> generation. /他比我大兩～. He is two generations my senior. (B) 1) kind, class. 無名之～ common people. 2) denotes the plural. 我～ we, us.

背 **bèi** (FV) 1) memorize. 2) recite. ～一課書 recite or memorize a lesson. 3) break a promise. ～約 break a promise. 4) turn away. /把臉～過去了. He turned his face away. (SV) 1) be bad (of luck). ～運 bad luck. 2) be bad (of hearing). /我耳朵有點ㄦ～. My hearing is bad. 3) be quiet, deserted. /這條路～. This street is quiet. (N) back (part of the body, excluding the lower part and waist). ～痛 backache. (B) <-ㄦ> back of something. 手～ back of one's hand. →背 **bēi**

背後 **bèihòu** (PW) 1) behind someone's back. /他常～批評人. He often criticizes people behind their backs. 2) the back part, the area behind. /他在門～. He's behind the door.

背着 **bèije** (CV) 1) going contrary to, against, one's conscience, advice. /他～良心做事. He's doing this against his conscience. 2) behind someone's back (lit. or fig.). /他～手站着. He is standing there with his hands behind his back. /他～你說你的壞話. He talks about you behind your back.

背景 **bèijǐng** (N) 1) background (in a picture *or* of a person), milieu (of a story). 2) backing (as of a candidate).

背面兒 **'bèimyàr** (PW) (on) the reverse side *or* back (of anything flat). /～別寫字. Don't write on the reverse side. /這張紙的～髒了. The back of this piece of paper is dirty.

背心 **bèisyīn** (N) sleeveless jacket, vest (M件 **jyàn**).

倍 **bèi** (M) times, -fold. /這個桌子比那個桌子大兩～ (*or* 一～). This table is twice as large as that table. /他的錢是我的錢的三～. He has three times as much money as I do. /五十是五的十～. Fifty is ten times five. (B) double. ～增 be doubled.

被 **bèi** (N) <-子> quilt (M條 **tyáu**, 床 **chwáng**). (CV) by (marking the agent). /我們的買賣～他給毀了. Our business was ruined by him. (B) followed by FV serves to translate the FV in the passive voice. /他～殺了. He was killed.

被單兒 **bèidār** (N) sheet for a bed (M條 **tyáu**, 床 **chwáng**).

被告 **'bèigàu** (N) the accused, defendant.

被窩 **bèiwo** (N) quilt (M條 **tyáu**, 床 **chwáng**).

被窩兒 **bèiwōr** (N) quilt folded into a kind of sleeping bag (used in Chinese homes).

奔 **bēn** (B) run. ～命 flee for one's life. → 奔 **bèn**.

本 **běn** (M) for books, magazines, and other bound things. 兩～字典 two dictionaries. (B) 1) base, root, foundation. 基～ foundation. 2) original, first. ～文 original text. 3) this. ～公司 this company. ～月 this month. 4) <-兒> capital, money invested. 虧～ lose one's capital. 5) <-兒, -子> booklet. 筆記～ notebook. *t*

本錢 **'běnchyán** (N) capital, money invested. /你給的價錢還不夠～呢. The price you offered is less than what I put into it.

本地 **běndì** (AT) native, in-digenous, to a particular area. ～風俗 indigenous *or* local custom; ～出產 native products.

本分 **běnfen** (N) duty, responsibility. /這是我～以內的事情. This is within my responsibility. /他老不守～. He's forever stepping out of line (fig.).

本家 **běnjyā** (N) member of the same clan, person having the same surname.

本來 **běnlái** (A) 1) originally, at first. /他～不去. Originally he wasn't going. 2) it goes without saying, of course. /這件事情～不應當這樣辦吗! Of course, this matter shouldn't be handled this way!

本領 **běnlǐng** (N) ability.

本人 **'běnrén** (N) 1) oneself (follows designation of someone). /我～不能去,我派一個代表. I can't go myself; I'll send a representative. 2) I (in a direct quotation). /今天～有機會跟諸位談談,覺得很高興. I'm very happy to have this opportunity to speak to you today.

奔 **bèn** (FV) go to, be bound for. /你～那兒? Where are you going? → 奔 **bēn**.

笨 **bèn** (SV) 1) be stupid. 2) be clumsy, awkward.

崩(逬) **bēng** (FV) break *or* split open. /這件衣服太小,一穿上就～了. This dress is too small; when I put it on the seams split.

繃(絣綳) **bēng** (FV) stretch something tightly. /弓上的弦～得很緊. The string on the bow is stretched taut.

繃帶 **bēngdài** (N) bandage (M條 **tyáu**, 圈 **jywǎn**).

甭 **béng** (AV) there's no need to (lp). /這個會現在取消了,你～來了. Now that the party's been canceled, there's no need for you to come.

蹦(逬) **bèng** (FV) jump, hop (lp). /那個螞蚱～到那邊兒去了. That grasshopper jumped over there. (B) <-子, -兒> small coin.

逼 **bī** (FV) compel, force. /他昨天～我還他錢. He forced me

to pay back his money yesterday.

荸 **bí** (B) .

　　荸薺 **bíchí** (N) water chestnut.

鼻 **bí** (B) <-子> nose. ～烟儿 snuff.

　　鼻孔 **bíkǔng** (N) nostril.

　　鼻涕 **bítì** (N) mucus from the nose. 擤～ blow one's nose.

比 **bǐ** (FV) 1) compare. /你把這兩個～一～. Compare these two. 2) compete. /我們兩個人～一～, 看誰作的快. Let's race and see who can do it the fastest. 3) point, aim. 拿槍～着 aim a rifle. 4) gesture with the hands. /他說話老愛用手～. When he talks, he has a habit of gesturing with his hands. (CV) than. /他～你高. He's taller than you. (B) 1) proportion, ratio. ～例 ratio. ～例尺 scale (as on a map). 2) example. ～喻 metaphor. 3) Belgium (contracted form of ～利時 **bǐlíshr**). t

　　比不上 **bǐbushàng** (RC) cannot be compared with. /我～你. I can't compare with you.

　　比起來 **bǐchǐlai** (A) comparing two or more things, comparatively. /～, 這個還不如那個. Comparing the two of them, this isn't even as good as that one. /紅的～好一點儿. The red one is comparatively better.

　　比方 **bǐfang** (N) example, instance. (FV) gesture. /他說話的時候用手～. When he talks he gestures with his hands.

　　比較 **'bǐjyǎu** (FV) compare. /把這兩本書～～. Compare these two books. (A) more . . . , . . . er. /這兩個西瓜那個～大一點儿? Which of these two watermelons is larger?

　　比如 **bǐrú** (A) 1) suppose. /～天下雨了, 我們怎麼辦? Suppose it rains, what shall we do? 2) for example, for instance.

　　比賽 **bǐsài** (FV) compete (as in a game). /他們～網球 They are having a tennis match. (N) contest, competition.

筆[笔] **bǐ** (N) pen, pencil, or any writing or drawing instrument (M 隻jī, 管 **gwǎn**, 桿 **gǎn**). (M) 1) stroke of a pen. /這個字有三～. This character has three strokes. 2) for sums of money. 一～錢 a fund. 3) hand (in writing). 一～好字 a good hand.

　　筆桿儿 **bǐgǎr** (N) shaft of a writing instrument.

　　筆記 **bǐjì** (N) 1) memorandum, notation, notes, taken at a lecture or the like. 2) memoirs. (M 本 **běn**, 段 **dwàn**).

　　筆記本儿 **bǐjìběr** (N) notebook.

　　筆筒 **bǐtǔng** (N) pen and pencil holder.

彼 **bǐ** (B) 1) that. ～處 that place. 2) he, she. ～等 they.

　　彼此 **bǐtsz̀** (A) each other. /他們～幫助. They help each other. /如果～明白, 什麼事都好辦. Everything will be easier to manage if there is mutual understanding. (IE) Same to you. / A: 我希望你成功. B: ～～. A: I hope you're successful. B: Same to you.

閉 **bì** (FV) 1) close (mostly applies to the mouth and eyes). ～上眼睛 close one's eyes. 2) stop up, obstruct, hold back. ～氣 hold one's breath.

　　閉幕 **bìmù** (VO) 1) close a curtain (as on a stage). /第三場已經閉了幕了. The curtain has gone down on the third act. 2) be brought to a close, adjourned. /大會～了. The assembly was adjourned.

篦 **bì** (FV) comb hair with a fine-toothed comb in order to clean it. ～頭 comb the hair (lit. comb the head).

　　篦子 **bìdz** (N) fine-toothed comb (M 把 **bǎ**).

壁 **bì** (B) wall. ～爐 fireplace (in a wall).

必 **bì** (B) 1) necessary, must. 何～ Why is it necessary (to) . . . . 2) certainly. ～定 certainly.

　　必得 **'bìděi** (AV) must, have to. /我～去一趟. I must go once.

　　必然 **bìrán** (A) certainly. /他～不知道. He certainly doesn't know.

　　必須 **bìsyū** (SV) be necessary, essential. ～品 necessities. (AV) must. 你～來. You must come.

(N) necessity, need. /沒有這種
～. There's no such need.
　　必要 bìyàu (SV) be necessary,
essential. 不～的東西 things which
are not essential. (N) necessity,
need. /沒有這種～. There's no
such need.

畢[毕] bì (B) finish. 完～ finish.
　　畢業 bìyè (VO) graduate.
/他～一年了. He graduated a
year ago.

避 bì (FV) avoid, evade. ～雨 take
shelter from rain; 逃～ escape; 躲
～ stay away from, hide from.
　　避免 bìmyǎn (FV) avoid, cir-
cumvent, difficulties, trouble.
/他做這個因為要～很多麻
煩. He's doing this in order to
avoid a lot of trouble.

bian *see* byan.

biao *see* byau.

bie *see* bye.

冰{氷} bīng (N) ice (M塊kwài). (FV) chill.
/啤酒～了嗎? Has the beer been
chilled? /石板地～我的腳.
The stone floor made my feet cold.
　　冰雹 bīngbáu (N) hail.
　　冰凌 bīnglíng (N) icicle.

兵 bīng (N) 1) soldier. 2) troops. 3)
pawn (chess). (B) military. ～器
military weapon.
　　兵工廠 bīnggūngchǎng (N)
arsenal (for production, not storage,
of armament).
　　兵艦 bīngjyàn (N) warship (M
艘sǒu, 隻jr̄).
　　兵營 bīngyíng (N) barracks
(M座dzwò).

餅 bǐng (N) (disc-shaped) cake, bread,
biscuit. (M張jāng, 塊kwài).
　　餅乾 bǐnggān (N) cookie,
cracker (M塊kwài).

並{並,幷,并} bìng (A) actually (used
only with 沒méi or 不bù). 他～沒
去. Actually he didn't go. (B) side
by side, together. ～肩 shoulder to
shoulder.
　　並且 'bìngchyě (A) moreover.
/他願意做,～他很合格. He's
willing to do it; moreover, he is well
qualified.

病 bìng (FV) be ill. /他～了. He
was ill. (N) sickness (M場chǎng).
(B) defect. 通～ universal shortcoming.

bo *see* bwo.

捕 bǔ (FV) arrest, apprehend. /他被
～了. He was arrested.

補[补] bǔ (FV) 1) patch, mend. ～衣裳
mend clothes. 2) fill a hole, vacancy. ～牙 fill a tooth. 3) restore,
replenish. ～身體 restore health.
4) make up lost time. ～一小時
的課 make up an hour of class time.
　　補充 bǔchūng (FV) 1) add,
supplement. /我要～兩句話.
I would like to add a few words.
2) recruit people. /我們還得～
兩個人. We have to recruit two
more people. (AT) supplementary.
～讀物 supplementary reading material.

布 bù (N) cotton cloth (M疋pǐ; 塊kwài).
t →佈{布} bù.
　　布鞋 bùsyé (N) cloth shoe (M
隻jr̄, 雙shwāng).

佈{布} bù (B) 1) inform. 公～ make public; ～道 preach. 2) distribute. 散
～ distribute; ～雷 lay mines.
　　佈告 bùgàu (N) bulletin.
　　佈置 bùjr̄ (N) arrangement.
(FV) 1) arrange, decorate. ～屋子
arrange a room. 2) put in order.
/我得把公司的事情～～. I
must get company matters in order.

步 bù (M) 1) step. /你走兩～我
們看看. Let's see you take a
couple of steps. 2) move in a board
game. /下一～該你了. It's
your move next. (B) 1) on foot.
～兵 infantry; ～行 go on foot. 2)
<子> pace, step. 散～ take a
walk.
　　步鎗 bùchyāng (N) rifle (infantry type) (M枝jr̄).
　　步驟 'bùdzòu, 'bùjòu (N) procedure, steps.

部 bù (M) 1) set of books, sometimes
bound in one volume. 2) for vehicles. 一～汽車 an automobile.
(B) 1) portion, part. 上～ upper
portion; 北～ north part. 2) section,
department (of an organization). 編

輯～editorial department; 交通
～Ministry of Communications.

部隊 bùdwèi (N) 1) troops.
2) unit (m).

部分 bùfen (M) portion, part,
section. 一～人 a part of the people.

部長 bùjǎng (N) head of a governmental department.

部門 bùmén (N) section, de-
partment (of an organization).

部下 bùsyà (N) subordinate,
staff in a governmental or military
organization.

簿 bù (B) <～子> notebook, ledger (M
本 běn). 練習～exercise book.

不 bù (bú before a syllable with a fourth
tone) (A) not. /他～是學生.
He isn't a student. (B) 1) be not,
do not, will not (never before 有 yǒu.
See 沒 méi (B) 1.) /我～去 I'm
not going or I won't go. /我～
喜歡吃魚. I don't like fish. 2)
not want to. /你昨天～來,可
是今天來了. You didn't want to
come yesterday, but you came today.
3) no. /你喝茶嗎?～,我喝
咖啡呢. Are you drinking tea? No,
I'm drinking coffee. 4) used as an
infix in resultative compounds, be
unable to do something. /我拿～
住. I can't hold it. (PT) 1) ～
...～... when two expressions
which are opposite in character are
substituted for the ellipsis marks,
(be) neither...nor.... ～長～短
neither long nor short; ～男～女
neither like a man nor a woman. 2)
～..., ～... when verbal expressions are substituted for the ellipsis
marks and the sentence is said with
a pause between the two clauses,
neither do...nor do.... /他～抽
煙,～喝酒. He neither smokes nor
drinks. 3)～...～.... when verbal
expressions are substituted for the
ellipsis marks and heavy stress is
put on the last full tone syllable of
the first clause with no pause after
it, if not...won't..., or doesn't....
unless..../他～吃飯～喝酒.
He doesn't drink unless he's eating.
4)～(是)...就(是).... if not..., then
.... /～(是)下雨,就(是)下雪. If
it isn't raining, then it's snowing.

不礙事 búàishr (IE) That's all
right. / A: 對不起. B: ～. A:

I'm sorry. B: That's all right.

不必 búbì (AV) not be necessary, do not have to. /你～去了.
You don't have to go now.

不大 búda (A) 1) not very. ～好
not very good. 2) not often. /我們
～吃魚. We don't eat fish often.

不但 búdàn (A) not only, generally used in the pattern ～...而且
(or 并且 or 還). /她～聰明而
且好看. She's not only intelligent
but also pretty.

不得不 bùdébu (AV) can't do anything but. / 我～去. There's
nothing I can do but go.

不得了 bùdélyǎu (SV) 1) be
terrific. /他很～. He is really
terrific. or He's really something.
/我餓得～. I'm extremely
hungry. 2) have no way out. /他
現在～了. He's in for it now.
(IE) My gosh! or This is terrible!

不得已 bùdéyǐ (SV) have no
choice. /我～才去的. I had no
choice but to go.

不怎麽 bùdzěmma (A) not very,
not very much. /他的房子～大.
His house isn't very big. /他～想
到法國去. She doesn't want to
go to France very much.

不怎麽樣 bùdzěmmayang (IE)
It doesn't amount to much. or Nothing special. /A:他的英文好不
好? B: ～. A: Is his English any
good? B: It doesn't amount to much.

不足 bùdzú (FV) be less than.
/他～法定年齡. He is
under age. /這儿的學生～二
百人. There are less than two hundred students here.

不敢當 bùgǎndāng (IE) 1) You
flatter me. 2) I'm much obliged.

不過 búgwò (A) 1) only.
/他～是個學生. He is only a
student. 2) but. /～他已經答
應了. But he has already promised.

不好過 bùhǎugwò (SV) not feel
well, feel bad. /我昨晚上沒睡
好,今天～. I didn't sleep well
last night and don't feel well today.

不好意思 bùhǎuyìsz (SV) be
embarrassed, ashamed. /我比
他還～. I'm even more embar-
rassed than he. (AV) be embarrassed to do something. /我～用
他的錢. I'd be embarrassed to
take his money.

不壞 **búhwài** (SV) be pretty good.

不會 **búhwèi** (AV) 1) don't have the habit of doing something (used in a polite refusal). /謝謝你, 我~抽煙. Thank you, I don't smoke.

不及 **bují** (FV) be not as good as. /我做的~你做的. My work is not as good as yours. (CV) not as...as someone or something. /我~你高. I'm not as tall as you. (RE) too late to do something. /你就是躲避, 也躲避~. Even if you wanted to, it's too late to escape.

不拘 **bùjyū** (B) followed by question words, no matter what, who, how, etc. /~誰都得交稅. Everyone has to pay taxes.

不可 **bùkě** (AV) should not. /你~有這樣的態度. You shouldn't have this kind of attitude. (PT)非(得)...~ must. /你非給錢~. You must give money.

不可不 **bùkěbu** (A) must, be obligated to. /你~去. You must go. or You are obligated to go.

不客氣 **bùkèchi** (IE) 1) You're welcome. or Don't mention it. 2) Please don't bother.

不利 **búli** (SV) be disadvantageous.

不論 **búlwùn** (A) when used in the pattern 不論...都..., regardless, no matter. /~誰都可以來. Anybody can come, no matter who he is. (FV) not consider. 一概~not take anything into consideration.

不咧 **bùlye** (P) that's all, nothing else. /他有錢~. He has money, that's all.

不能不 **bùnéngbu** (AV) can't do anything but, must. /你~給他錢. You cannot do anything but give him the money.

不平 **bùpíng** (SV) 1) be unfair. /我們受的待遇很~. The treatment given us was unfair. 2) be indignant. /我對那件事很~. I was indignant about that.

不如 **bùrú** (FV) be not as good as. /我作的~你作的. My work is not as good as yours. (A) it would be better. /~派他去. It would be better to send him. (CV) not as...as someone or some-

thing. /他~你聰明. He is not as clever as you are.

不是 **búshr** (N) fault. /這是你的~. This is your fault. (IE) No. /A: 你明天去啊? B: ~, 我後天去. A: Are you going tomorrow? B: No, the day after tomorrow. (PT) 1)~...就是.... if it is not...then it must be. /~紅的就是綠的. If it isn't red, it must be green. 2) ~...而是.... It isn't that..., (it's that) .... /我~不會作而是不願意作. It isn't that I don't know how to do it; I don't want to do it.

不失 **bùshr** (A) anyhow, still. /雖然舊式一點, 可是~算一件好衣裳. Even though it's a little bit out of style, it's still a good suit.

不時 **bùshŕ** (A) from time to time. /他~來看我. He comes to see me from time to time.

不送 **búsùng** (IE) 1) Don't bother to accompany me further (said by the guest). 2) Excuse me for not accompanying you any further (said by the host; a polite way of saying goodbye).

不想 **bùsyǎng** (A) unexpectedly. /我本來想去看電影, ~客人來了. I wanted to go to the movies, but guests came unexpectedly.

不希罕 **bùsyīhan** (FV) not care about something. /A: 聽說你要加薪了. B: 我才~呢. A: I heard you are going to get a raise. B: It makes no difference to me.

不幸 **búsyìng** (SV) be unfortunate. (A) unfortunately. /昨天我們打牌, 我~輸了. We played cards yesterday. Unfortunately, I lost.

不測 **bútsè** (N) unforeseen event (usually involving death).

不錯 **bútswò** (SV) be pretty good. /他寫的~. He writes pretty well.

不辭 **bùtsź** (FV) not object to, not mind. /我的姪女~辛苦天天來看我. My niece comes to see me every day in spite of all the trouble it causes her.

不要 **búyàu** (AV) don't. /~哭. Don't cry.

不一會兒 **bùyìhwěr** (A) in a

little while, in a few minutes.
/他～就來. He'll be here in a
few minutes.

不依 bùyī (FV) not listen
to someone. /我怎麼説他也
～. No matter what I say he won't
listen.

不用 búyùng (AV) no need to,
need not. /你～給他錢. You
don't have to give him money.

剝 bwō, bāu (FV) peel (off).～橘子
peel an orange;～樹皮 peel off
bark.

剝削 bwōsywē, bāusywē (FV)
exploit, strip of wealth and rights.
/你不能～我的權利. You can't
deprive me of my rights. (N) exploi-
tation.

玻 bwō (B) ↓.

玻璃 bwōli (N) 1) glass (the
substance). (AT) 1) plastic. ～
皮包 plastic purse. 2) nylon. ～
膜子 nylon stocking.

撥 bwō (FV) 1) move or adjust the
position of something with the tip
of a finger or of an object. ～算盤
move the beads on an abacus. 2) adjust or turn a knob, as on a radio or
other machine. ～表 set a watch. 3)
transfer funds, personnel. ～款 appropriate or transfer funds. /我再
～給你兩個打字員. I'll
transfer two more typists over to you.
(M) ＜一ル＞ part of a total number.
/你的錢我分三～ル還. I'll
pay your money back in three
parts. /客人已經來了兩～ル
了. Two groups of guests have already arrived.

菠 bwō, (bwó (lp)) (B) ↓.

菠菜 bwōtsài, bwótsài (N)
spinach (M棵 kē).

播 bwō (B) spread, scatter. 廣～ broadcast (of television and radio).

播種 bwōjǔng (FV) sow seeds.
/春天已經過了, 我們還沒～
呢. Spring is already over, but we
still haven't done the sowing.

伯 bwó (B) 1) father's elder brother.
2) earl, count. ～爵 earl, count. t

伯伯 bwóbwo (N) 1) uncle
(father's elder brother). 2) used to

address a male friend of one's father.

伯父 bwófù (N) =伯伯 bwóbwo.
伯母 bwómǔ (N) aunt (wife of 伯
伯 bwóbwo).

脖 bwó (B) ＜一ル,一子＞ 1) neck. 2)
back of the neck.

博 bwó (SV) be broad (of knowledge).
/他的學問很～. He has a broad
knowledge of things. (B) 1) gamble.
賭～ gamble. 2) of all kinds. ～覽
會 exposition (the show). t

博士 'bwoshr (N) 1) doctoral
degree. 2) holder of a doctoral degree. (B) Dr. (non-medical) 王～
Dr. Wang.

博物館 bwówùgwǎn (N) museum.

薄 bwó (B) thin, slight, poor, mean. ～
酬 small reward; ～酒 thin wine.
→薄 báu, 薄 bwò.

薄情 bwóchíng (SV) be characterized by weakness of sentiment. /男
人多～. Most men are not very ardent in love.

薄弱 bwórwò (SV) be weak,
feeble (of ability, strength). 能力很
～ have very little ability.

駁[駮] bwó (FV) 1) contradict. ～倒 argue
someone down. /你別～我. Don't
contradict me. 2) reject a proposal.
/總統把他的建議～回來了.
The president rejected his suggestion.
(B) transfer. ～運 transport.

簸 bwǒ (FV) winnow, sift. ～米 winnow
rice. (B) to rock (as a boat). ～
動 to rock. →簸 bwò, 簸 pwǒ.

簸 bwò (B) 1) to rock (as a boat). 簸
動 to rock. 2) ↓. →簸 bwǒ, 簸 pwǒ.

簸箕 bwòji (N) dustpan.

薄 bwò (B) ↓. →薄 bwó, 薄 báu.

薄荷 bwòhe (N) peppermint.

百 bwò → 百 bǎi.

鞭 byān (N) firecracker (M掛 gwà) 放
～ set off a firecracker. (B) ＜一子＞
whip. ～打 flog with a whip.

鞭炮 byānpàu (N) string of
firecrackers.

編 byān (FV) 1) edit, compile. ～字
典 compile a dictionary. 2) plait,
weave. ～草繩 braid hemp. 3) fabricate a story. /沒有那麼回事,
都是他瞎～的. That didn't

really happen; he just made it up.
4) organize, reorganize, a military force. /陸軍新～了五個師. The army organized five new divisions.

編輯 byānji (FV) edit, compile. (N) editor. /體育欄由我～. I edit the sports column.

邊(边) byān (M) <-儿> side. /他是我們這～的. He's on our side. (B) <-儿> 1) part, side. 裏～ inside, the inside part; 右～ (on) the right side. 2) edge. 河～ riverside; 海～ seashore.

邊境 byānjìng (N) border area of a country.

邊界 byānjyè (N) border between two countries or states or provinces (the actual line, not the area) (M條tyáu).

扁 byǎn (SV) be flat, thin, shallow. ～舟 shallow boat; 壓～ flatten something by applying pressure.

扁担 byǎndan (N) flat stick used as a carrying pole (M根gēn).

扁豆 byǎndòu (N) string bean (M棵kē).

辯 byàn (FV) argue about something logically. /你沒什麼可跟他～的. You have nothing to argue about with him.

辯護 byànhù (FV) give the case for the defense, defend. /他請一個律師替他～. He asked a lawyer to take his case.

辯證法 byànjèngfǎ (N) dialectics.

辯論 byànlwùn (FV) argue, debate. /我～不過你. I can't out-argue you. (N) debate.

便 byàn (A) then (old-style Mandarin). /他不給你錢你～怎麼樣? If he doesn't give you the money, then what will you do? (B) 1) convenience. /請你得～來一次. Please come when it's convenient. 2) informal. ～條 informal note. 3) relieve oneself by urinating or defecating. 小～ urine, urinate. →便pyán.

便道 byàndàu (N) sidewalk (M條tyáu).

便帽 byànmàu (N) cap (informal hat) (M頂dǐng).

遍(徧) byàn (M) time (one occurrence of something). /他把那本書念了三～. He read that book three times. (A) throughout, everywhere. /我～找找不着. I looked everywhere and couldn't find it. (RE) throughout, everywhere. /這儿的飯舘我都吃～了. I've eaten in every restaurant here.

變(变) byàn (FV) change, transform, alter. /溫度沒～. The temperature hasn't changed.

變成 byànchéng (RC) change into, become. /他喝酒～一個問題了. His drinking has become a problem.

變動 byàndùng (FV) change, alter, fluctuate. /股票市場最近～得很厲害. Recently the stock market has been fluctuating tremendously. (N) change, fluctuation.

變化 byànhwa (N) change, transformation.

變形蟲 byànsyíngchúng (N) amoeba.

標(标) byāu (FV) quote a price. (B) 1) sign, signal. ～記 marking. 2) target, goal. 目～ objective. 3) bid (commercial). 投～ make a bid.

標點 byāudyǎn (N) punctuation.

標語 byāuyǔ (N) slogan.

表(錶)(N) 1) byǎu (N) 1) watch (timepiece). 2) table, chart, form. 3) meter, gauge. 速度～ speedometer. (B) 1) express. 發～ announce; ～明 make clear. 2) indicates second-degree relatives of a different surname. 3) outside, external. ～皮 skin.

表情 byǎuchíng (N) expression, display of emotion.

表哥 byǎugē (N) cousin (older male, on the maternal side or on the paternal aunt's side).

表格 byǎugé (N) form, blank (to be filled out) (M張jāng).

表決 byǎujywé (FV) reach a decision by voting. /這件事我們應當投票～. We must bring this matter to a vote (and reach a decision).

表面 byǎumyàn (N) 1) surface. 2) exterior, outside. 3) appearance.

/他~很客氣. He's outwardly polite.

表嫂 **byáusǎu** (N) cousin's wife (wife of 表哥 **byáugē**).

表示 **byǎushr** (FV) signify, express, make clear. /他~他不願意來. He made it clear that he didn't wish to come.

表現 **byǎusyàn** (FV) express one's reactions or feelings by facial expression or behavior, or verbally. /他心裡很不高興,可是没~出來. He's unhappy, but he doesn't show it. (N) performance. /他没有什麼~. His performance is very poor (of a job).

表同情 **byǎutúngchíng** (VO) show one's sympathy. /他對窮人很~. She has sympathy for the poor. (SV) be sympathetic.

表演 **byǎuyǎn** (FV) give a demonstration, perform before an audience. /那個演員根本不會~. That actor can't act at all.

表揚 **byǎuyáng** (FV) eulogize, praise publicly. /政府~他的功勞. The government praised him for his merit.

憋 **byē** (FV) 1) repress, hold in. /他~着一口氣. He's holding his breath. / 她~了一肚子委曲. She's harboring a lot of grievances. 2) portend, threaten. /今天~了一天的雨. It threatened rain all day.

別 **byé** (FV) 1) pin, fasten something with a pin. 2) carry something in one's belt. /他皮帶上~着一桿鎗. He carries a gun in his belt. (AV) don't (in giving commands, more polite than 不要 **búyàu**). /~聽他的. Don't listen to him. (AT) other. ~處儿 elsewhere. (B) 1) difference. 分~ difference. 2) to part. 告~ bid someone farewell. t SF of 彆 **byè**.

別客氣 **byékèchi** (IE) 1) You're welcome. or Don't mention it. 2) Please don't bother.

別人 **byéren** (N) other people, others.

彆(別) **byè** (B) irritable, testy.

彆扭 **byènyou** (SV) 1) disagreeable. /他人很~. He's a disagreeable character. 2) be difficult,

hard to manage. /這件事辦起來真~. This matter is really hard to deal with. 3) be uncomfortable (as of clothes). 4) be depressed. /這兩天我心裏很~. I've felt depressed the past few days. 5) be disgusting. /他的樣子看着真~. His manners are disgusting. (N) clash of opinion, disagreement. 鬧~ be at odds, in disagreement.

ca *see* **tsa**.

cai *see* **tsai**.

can *see* **tsan**.

cang *see* **tsang**.

cao *see* **tsau**.

ce *see* **tse**.

cen *see* **tsen**.

ceng *see* **tseng**.

叉 **chā** (B) 1) <-子> fork. (M 把 **bǎ**) 刀~ knife and fork, silverware. 2) <-子, -儿> X-mark. 劃~ make an X. → 叉 **chá**, 叉 **chǎ**. SF of 扠 **chā**.

扠(叉) **chā** (FV) pick up something with a fork, spear. ~魚 spear fish. (B) akimbo. ~腰 with arms akimbo.

差 **chā** (N) difference (*arith.*). /三跟五的~是二. The difference between five and three is two. (B) 1) differ. ~別 difference, dissimilarity. 2) error, mistake. ~池 accident. → 差 **chà**, 差 **chāi**.

插 **chā** (FV) insert something into an opening or between two things. ~進去 insert something into something. /把花~在那個瓶子裏. Put the flowers in that vase.

插銷 **chāsyāu** (N) 1) door bolt. 2) electric plug.

插秧 **chāyāng** (VO) transplant young rice plants.

叉 **chá** (FV) block, jam, a passage. /車把路口都~住了. Cars blocked the intersection. /骨頭~了我的嗓子了. A bone got stuck in my throat. → 叉 **chā**, 叉 **chǎ**.

查 **chá** (FV) 1) investigate. ~案子 investigate a case at law. 2) examine,

inspect. ～帳 audit accounts; ～宿
舍 inspect a dormitory. 3) consult
a dictionary, reference book, etc.
～字典 look something up in a
dictionary. t → 查詁.
    查賬 **chájàng** (VO) audit _or_ in-
vestigate accounts. / 今天的賬
查過了, 沒錯儿. Today's accounts
have been audited, and there were no
errors.

茶 **chá** (N) tea. 喝～ drink tea. 沏～
make tea.
    茶杯 **chábēi** (N) teacup.
    茶點 **chádyǎn** (N) refreshments.
(lit. tea and cakes).
    茶房 **cháfang** (N) bellboy,
waiter, boy.
    茶館 **chágwǎn** (N) <-儿> tea-
house.
    茶壺 **cháhú** (N) teapot.
    茶會 **cháhwèi** (N) tea (reception
at which tea is served)
    茶儿 **chájī** (N) side table, tea
table.
    茶碗 **cháwǎn** (N) teacup. (M
隻/只).
    茶葉 **cháyè** (N) tea leaves.

碴 **chá** (FV) cut oneself on a chipped
dish or the like. / 我的手讓玻璃
璃杯～了. I cut my hand on a
glass.
    碴儿 **chár** (N) 1) small sharp
piece of something, chip. 碗～ fragment of chinaware. 2) special point.
/ 他把那個～給忘了. He for-
got that special point. 3) grudge,
hard feelings. 有～ carry a grudge.
4) shortcoming, fault. / 他盡找
我的～. He's always finding fault
with me.

叉 **chà** (B) spread (usually of the legs).
～開 spread apart. → 叉 **chā**, 叉
chá.

差 **chà** (FV) 1) differ (by). / 他比他
哥哥～遠了. He and his older
brother are very different. 2) be
short, lack. ～一毛錢 be short
ten cents. 3) owe. / 我～他五塊
錢. I owe him five dollars. (SV)
be inferior, poor, in quality. / 素
質很～. The quality is very poor.
(CV) lacking, without. / 我～三個
學分就畢業了. I'm lacking
three credits to graduate. / 我們

～你打不了牌. We can't play cards
without you. (PT) ～ . . . (到)
. . . be so much short of an amount.
/ ～五分(到)四點. It's five min-
utes to four. → 差 **chā**, 差 **chāi**.
    差不多 **chàbudwō** (RC) lack
only a little, be almost the same.
/ 他的帽子跟你的～. His hat
is almost the same as yours. (A)
almost, about. / ～三點了. It's
almost three o'clock. (IE) Not bad.
/ A: 他的中文怎麼樣? B: ～.
A: How is his Chinese? B: Not
bad.
    差一點儿 **chàyidyar** (A) al-
most. / 我～掉在河裡. I al-
most fell into the river. / 我～沒
趕上火車. I almost didn't get to
the train on time.
    差一點儿沒 **chàyidyar méi**
(A) almost. / 我～死. I almost
died.

岔 **chà** (FV) 1) diverge, split off.
/ 這條小河是從那條大河裡
頭～出來的. This small river
branches off from that large one.
2) interrupt. / 他們說話被你
給～開了. You interrupted their
conversation. (B) <-子,-儿> accident. / 出～子了. There's been
an accident.
    岔道 **chàdàu** (N) branch road,
side road (M 條 tyáu).

拆 **chāi** (FV) take something apart, dis-
assemble. ～台 take a stage apart,
prevent someone from accomplishing
something (fig.) / 敵兵還沒過河我
們就把橋～了. Before the ene-
my soldiers crossed the river we
took the bridge down.
    拆信 **chāisyìn** (VO) open a
letter.

差 **chāi** (FV) send, commission. / ～
他去買報. Send him to buy a
paper. (B) official matter. ～事
official assignment. → 差 **chā**, 差 **chà**.
    差事 **chāishr** (N) 1) job (way
of making a living) (M 份 fèr). 2)
mission (task of going somewhere to
accomplish something) (M 件 jyàn).
3) assignment of work (M 份 fèr).
/ 他那份儿～可真輕鬆. His
assignment is really a cinch.

柴 **chái** (N) firewood. 打～gather firewood. *s t*
　　柴火 **cháihwo** (N) firewood, fuel.

攙[攙](FV 2)}[攙] **chān** (FV) 1) assist, support, <u>someone by taking him by the arm</u>. /他～着那個病人走. She's helping that sick person walk. 2) mix, blend. 酒裡～水mix water with wine.

纏[纏] **chán** (FV) 1) wrap around (<u>lit. or fig.</u>). /護士用繃帶把他的傷～上了. The nurse wrapped bandages around his wound. /他現在叫那個女人給～上了. That girl has got him wrapped around her little finger now. 2) roll up (<u>as a string</u>). 3) keep bothering <u>someone</u>. /你別～我. Don't keep bothering me.

產[產][产] **chǎn** (FV) produce. ～米produce rice. (B) 1) bear offspring.～科obstetrics; 生～give birth to. 2) product. 土～local products. 3) property, estate. 私～private property.
　　產量 **chǎnlyàng** (N) volume of production.
　　產生 **chǎnshēng** (FV) produce, create. /這樣就～一個新問題. This produces a new problem. /這個會是怎麼～的? How was this committee formed?
　　產業 **'chǎnyè** (N) property (<u>real estate</u>).

鏟[剷] **chǎn** (FV) shovel.～雪shovel snow. (B) <－子> shovel (M把**bǎ**).

長[长] **cháng** (SV) be long (<u>of space or time</u>). /這個桌子三尺～。 This table is three feet long. (B) excelling.～處good point. → 長 **jǎng**.
　　長城 **chángchéng** (PW) (at) the Great Wall.
　　長蟲 **chángchung** (N) snake (M條**tyáu**).
　　長久 **'chángjyǒu** (SV) be long (<u>in time</u>). /這個不是～的辦法. This isn't a long-term proposition.
　　長袍 **chángpáu** (N) long Chinese gown (M件**jyán**).
　　長篇 **chángpyān** (AT) long (<u>of a story, document, editorial, etc.</u>).

～故事long story;～社論long editorial.
　　長途 **'chángtú** (AT) long-distance.～汽車long-distance (<u>intercity</u>) bus;～電話long-distance phone call.

常 **cháng** (A) often. /我～打網球. I often play tennis. (B) 1) constant, regular.～會regular meeting;～青樹evergreen. 2) common, ordinary. 平～ordinary. 3) normal.～態normal appearance *or* situation. *s*
　　常常 **chángcháng** (A) often, repeatedly. /我～到紐約去. I go to New York often.
　　常見 **chángjyàn** (SV) be common (<u>of something frequently met</u>). /這種汽車很～. This kind of car is very common.
　　常識 **chángshř, chángshr̀** (N) common sense.

腸 **cháng** (B) 1) <－子> intestine. 小～small intestine. 2) <－ル, －子> sausage (M根**gēn**). 香～Chinese sausage.

場 **cháng** →場 **chǎng**.

嘗[嘗](FV)}[嘗] **cháng** (FV) taste, sample. /請你～一～. Would you taste this? (B) ever, once. 未～never.
　　嘗試 **chángshř** (FV) have a try, make an attempt. /教他～～他就知道了. Let him get a taste of it; then he'll know.

場[場] **chǎng**, *cháng* (M) 1) spell, period, <u>of something</u>. 一～病a period of illness; 一～雨a spell of rain; 作一～官serve for a period as an official; 哭一～cry for a while; 一～水災a flood; 一～夢a dream; 一～火a fire. 2) game of foot<u>ball, tennis, etc</u>. 一～球a game of ball. 3) scene <u>of a play or opera</u>. 第二～scene two. 4) <u>for movies, plays, operas</u>. 一～戲a play *or* opera; 一～電影a movie. 5) performance, showing, <u>of a play, movie</u>. 第一～七點開始. The first performance begins at seven o'clock. (B) 1) open field. 飛機～airfield, airport. 2) place where many people gather together. 市～market.

22

敞 chǎng (B) 1) open wide. ～開 open up. 2) unobstructed. 寬～ be spacious, roomy.

敞着 chǎngje (FV) keep something wide open. /天冷,別～門. It's cold; don't leave the door open.

廠[廠](厂) chǎng (N) factory, mill. (B) <一子> open space enclosed by a wall. 木～ lumber yard.

廠長 chǎngjǎng (N) factory manager.

唱 chàng (FV) sing. /她～的很好. She sings very well.

唱歌儿 chànggēr (VO) sing (a song).

唱片 chàngpyàn (N) <一儿> phonograph record (M張jang).

唱戲 chàngsyì (VO) play or sing a part in Chinese drama, or in any drama involving singing.

暢 chàng (B) 1) freely. ～流 flow freely. 2) happy, pleasant. ～談 pleasant conversation.

暢快 chàngkwai (SV) be pleased, happy.

chao see chau.

抄 chāu (FV) 1) copy. /～先生寫的. Copy what the teacher writes. 2) seize, confiscate. ～家 confiscate someone's property. /他把我的帽子～走了. He snatched my hat away from me. 3) scald, parboil. /把青菜～～. / Scald the vegetables. 4) go by a shorter route. ～近路 take a short cut.

抄寫 chāusye (FV) copy in writing. /中古時代的修士每天都要～. Medieval monks spent each day copying.

超 chāu (FV) 1) surpass, exceed. ～額 exceed a quota. 2) overtake. ～車 overtake a car. (B) 1) superior in quality. ～等 highest grade. 2) super-. ～音速 supersonic. (B) release, save (spiritual). ～生 release souls from suffering.

超過 chāugwò (RC) exceed. ～重量 exceed a weight limit.

鈔 chāu (B) paper money.

鈔票 chāupyàu (N) banknote (M張jāng).

朝 cháu (FV) 1) face. /他那間屋子～海. His room faces the ocean. 2) visit, pay one's respects to an elder, superior, holy place. ～聖 go on a pilgrimage. (CV) facing, toward. /他臉～牆站着. He's standing facing the wall. (B) 1) reign. 2) dynasty. 明～ Ming dynasty. 3) imperial. ～廷 the imperial court. 4) Korea (contracted form of ～鮮 cháusyān). → 朝 jāu.

潮 cháu (N) tide. /漲～了. The tide is coming in. (SV) be damp, slightly wet. /這天氣很～. The weather is damp.

吵 chǎu (FV) 1) quarrel. /昨天他們～起來了. They had an argument yesterday. 2) disturb someone by making noise. /別～他. Don't disturb him. (SV) be noisy. /這個地方太～. This place is too noisy.

吵嘴 chǎudzwěi (VO) quarrel. /昨天他們倆～了. They quarreled yesterday.

吵架 chǎujyà (VO) quarrel. /你要怎麼樣好好說,別跟我～. Tell me whatever you want to, but don't quarrel with me.

炒 chǎu (FV) fry in oil, stirring constantly. ～雞蛋 scramble eggs. /把肉～兩分鐘. Fry the meat two minutes.

車[车] chē (N) wheeled vehicle (M輛lyàng). 火～ train; 汽～ automobile; 自行～ bicycle. (B) wheeled device. 滑～ pulley; 紡～ spinning wheel; 風～ windmill. → 車 jyū.

車床 chēchwáng (N) lathe.

車房 chēfáng (N) garage (where a car is kept) (M間jyān).

車夫 chēfū (N) 1) chauffeur. 2) driver (of a pedicab or rickshaw).

車站 chējàn (N) terminal, depot, stop, station.

車軸 chējóu (N) axle.

車間 chējyān (N) 1) machine shop. 2) garage (where a car is kept) (d).

車輛 chēlyàng (N) vehicles, vehicular traffic. /路上的～很擁擠. Traffic is really tied up.

車票 chēpyàu (N) train or bus ticket (M張jāng).

車胎 chētāi (N) tire (M 條 tyáu, 付 fù).

車頭 chētóu (N) locomotive (M 輛 lyàng).

扯 chě (FV) 1) tear with the hands. ~碎 tear into pieces. 2) pull at, haul on. /別~我袖子. Don't pull on my sleeve. 3) talk casually, chat. /我們沒談什麼我們閒~呢. We're not talking about anything important; we're just chatting. 4) make up a story. ~謊 tell a lie.

徹(澈)(彻) chè (B) 1) thorough. 透~ be thorough. 2) clear (of water). 清~ be clear. t

徹底 chèdǐ (SV) be thorough. (A) thoroughly. ~解決 solve completely.

撤 chè (FV) remove, take away. ~兵 withdraw troops. /快把碟子碗~走. Clear the dishes away quickly.

捵(抻) chēn (FV) stretch out, pull, something with the hand, adjusting its position or shape. ~麵 pull dough, as in making noodles. /把你的袖子~~就平了. Pull your sleeve down so it's straight.

沉(沈) chén (FV) sink. ~在水裡 sink into the water. (SV) be heavy (in weight). /水比空氣~. Water is heavier than air. (B) to a great degree. ~睡 be in a deep sleep; ~醉 be dead drunk; ~靜 be dead quiet.

沉底 chéndǐ (VO) <-ル> sink to the bottom. /船都~了. The boat sank to the bottom.

沉悶 'chénmèn (SV) 1) be depressed. /那個電影使得我心情很~. That movie made me very depressed. 2) be dull, uninteresting. /這個電影很~. This movie is very dull.

陳(陈) chén (SV) be aged, seasoned (as wine). /這種酒不夠~. This wine hasn't aged long enough. (B) 1) stale. ~舊 old-fashioned. 2) display, exhibit. ~設 arrange. 3) make a statement or plea. ~訴 plead. d s

陳列 chénlyè (FV) display, exhibit (as in a showcase or museum). ~所 museum, place for displays. /窗户裡頭~了很多貨物.

There are a lot of goods displayed in the window.

塵(尘) chén (B) 1) dust, dirt. 2) the world of reality. ~世 mortal life.

塵土 chéntǔ (N) dust, dirt.

趁 chèn (CV) 1) while there's an opportunity, during. /我得~放假找一個新房子. I must look for a new place to live during the vacation. 2) by a certain kind of conveyance. /我~飛機去. I'm going by plane.

趁便 chènbyàn (A) at one's convenience, when it's convenient. /~到我家來一趟. Come to my house at your convenience.

稱(称) chèn (FV) own property, have so much money. /聽說他~兩百多萬. I've heard that he has more than two million. (B) suitable, agreeable. ~心 in accord with one's wishes; ~職 fill requirements for a post. → 稱 chēng, 秤(稱) chèng.

襯(衬) chèn (FV) 1) wear something underneath an outer garment. /你最好在裏頭~一件毛衣. You'd better wear a sweater underneath. 2) put something underneath. /把一張厚紙~在這一張紙底下. Put a thick piece of paper underneath this paper. 3) make something stand out. /框子把這張畫ル~出來了. The frame made the picture stand out.

襯衫 chènshān (N) shirt (M 件 jyàn).

襯衣 chènyī (N) 1) shirt. 2) undershirt. (M 件 jyan).

稱(称) chēng (FV) 1) weigh. /把這隻雞~一~. Weigh this chicken. 2) address someone as. /你~他什麼? How do you address him? 3) call, designate. /他連聲~好. He repeatedly said it was good. (B) term. 尊~ honorific term. → 稱 chèn, 秤(稱) chèng.

稱讚 chēngdzàn (FV) praise, commend. /人人都~他的勇敢. Everyone praised him for his courage.

稱呼 chēnghu (FV) call someone a certain name. /我們應該~他伯父. We ought to call him uncle.

成 chéng (SV) 1) be O.K., satisfactory.

/這樣不～. This way is unsatisfactory. 2) be capable. /他作甚麼都～. He has the ability to do anything. (FV) 1) accomplish, succeed. /他～不了事. He'll never accomplish anything. 2) become. /看他畫的～了什麼了? What's that thing he's painting supposed to be? (PV) change into. 翻翻～英文 translate into English. /水已經結～冰了. The water has frozen. (RE) finished, completed. /他把書寫～了. He has finished writing the book. (CV) used before a measure, by a given quantity. ～打賣 sell by the dozen; ～千～萬 by the tens of thousands. (M) tenth. 三～ three tenths. (B) 1) mature. ～人 adult. 2) established. ～規 established rule. 3) ready-made. ～品 ready-made goods. s

成本 'chéngběn (N) cost of production.

成分 chéngfen (N) element, constituent, ingredient.

成功 chénggūng (VO) succeed. /我看你成不了功. I don't think you'll succeed. (SV) be successful.

成績 chéngjì (N) achievement, record of attainment.

成就 'chéngjyòu (N) accomplishment.

成立 chénglì (FV) 1) establish, set up. ～一個學校 establish a school. 2) stand, hold true. /你的理論不能～. Your theory won't hold true.

成熟 chéngshú (SV) be mature (of a person).

成心 chéngsyīn (A) on purpose, intentionally. /他～跟我搗亂. He made trouble for me on purpose.

成天 chéngtyān (A) 1) all day. 2) every day. ～念書 study every day or study all day.

呈 chéng (FV) submit, present, a document to a superior. /猶辭職書應該～給誰? To whom should I submit my resignation? (B) 1) <-子> petition. 2) appear as. ～白色 produce a white color, come out white.

承 chéng (B) 1) receive from a predecessor. ～繼 inherit. 2) undertake, manage. ～辦 undertake. 3) admit. 招～ confess (of a criminal).

承認 chéngrèn (FV) 1) admit, concede. /他～他偷了那些東西. He admitted that he stole those things. 2) recognize a government. /我們不要立刻～那個革命政府. We shouldn't recognize the revolutionary government immediately.

城 chéng (N) 1) city (M座 dzwò). ～裏 in the city, downtown. 2) city wall (M道 dàu).

城牆 chéngchyáng (N) city wall (M座 dzwò).

城市 chéngshr̀ (N) city in contrast to the country. ～生活 urban life, life in the city.

乘 chéng (FV) multiply. /二～二得四. Two times two equals four. (B) 1) ride on. ～船 take a boat. 2) avail oneself of an opportunity. ～火打劫. rob a place when it's on fire.

盛 chéng (FV) 1) fill a container. ～飯 fill a bowl with rice. 2) hold, contain. /這個盆～不了那麼多東西. This basin can't hold that much. → 盛 shèng.

程 chéng (M) <-子> period, a while. /這一～子我沒做什麼事. I haven't been doing anything for a while. /送他一～. Go with him part of the way. (B) 1) journey. 起～ start on a journey; 前～ career, future. 2) regulation, standard. 章～ rules, by-laws. s

程度 chéngdu (N) level, extent, degree of advancement. 生活～ living standard.

誠 chéng (SV) be sincere. /那個老太太拜佛很～. That old woman is a devout Buddhist. (B) 1) honest. 2) really, indeed. ～然 really, indeed.

誠懇 chéngkěn (SV) be sincere.

誠實 chéngshr̀ (SV) be honest.

懲 chěng (B) punish. ～戒 to discipline.

懲罰 'chěngfá (N) punishment. 受～ be punished. (FV) punish, inflict a penalty, prison sentence, fine on <u>someone</u>. /我不得不～你. I must punish you.

秤{稱}**chèng** (N) steelyard (M 桿**gǎn**). ～錘 weight used with a steelyard.

chǐ *see* **chr.**

七{柒}**chī** (also **chí** before a syllable with a fourth tone) (NU) seven. (B) seventh. ～馬路 7th Avenue.

    七月 **chīywe, chíywe** (TW) 1) (in) July. 2) the seventh month of the lunar calendar.

妻 **chī** (B) wife. 賢～良母 good wife and mother.

    妻子 **chīdz** (N) 1) wife and children. 2) wife (d).

欺 **chī** (B) 1) cheat. ～日萬 cheat, hoodwink. 2) take unfair advantage of. 仗勢～人 use one's power to take unfair advantage of others.

    欺負 **chīfu** (FV) 1) take (unfair) advantage of a <u>weakness</u>. /她～他老實. She took advantage of his good nature. 2) bully <u>someone</u>. /別～你小弟弟. Don't bully your little brother.

    欺騙 **chīpyàn** (FV) deceive, cheat. /你不能再～我了. You can't deceive me any longer. (N) deception.

期 **chī** (M) 1) issue of <u>a magazine</u>. 2) stage in the development of <u>something</u>. /他到了三～肺病. He has reached the third stage of tuberculosis. 3) installment, payment. /我的汽車分三～付欵. My car is to be paid for in three installments. (B) 1) set period, limit of time. ～滿 expire. 2) date. 日～ (fixed) date. 3) expect, hope. ～望 look forward to <u>something</u>.

沏 **chī** (FV) pour <u>hot water over tea leaves, coffee</u>. ～茶 make tea. /請你在壺裏～點兒開水. Please pour some boiling water into the teapot.

漆 **chī** (FV) paint, varnish. /把那個桌子再～一道. Give that table one more coat. (N) paint.

其 **chí** (B) +.

    其實 **chíshŕ** (A) really, in fact. /他說他知道,～他不

知道. He says that he knows, but in fact he doesn't know.

    其他 **chítā** (AT) other, another. ～辦法 another solution. /你還有～的問題嗎? Do you have other questions?

    其次 **chítsž** (A) next, second. /他先唱,～就該你了. He sings first, you're next. (N) the next best. /那本小說最有意思,～是這本. That novel is the most interesting one; this is the next best.

    其餘的 **chíyúde** (N) the rest, the remaining ones.

奇 **chí** (B) 1) strange. 2) rare and wonderful. ～事 wonderful *or* strange affair; ～花 rare flowers. *t*

    奇怪 **chígwài** (SV) 1) be strange, queer. 2) be rare, unusual. /這個屋子大得～. This room is unusually large. (FV) wonder about. /我～他為什麼不來. I wonder why he didn't come.

棋{碁}**chí** (N) chess <u>and similar games</u> (M 盤**pán**). 下～ play chess; ～子兒 chessman.

旗{旂}**chí** (B) 1) <～子> flag, banner. (M 面**myàn**). 國～ national flag; ～語 flag signal. 2) Manchurian. ～人 Manchurian (person); ～袍 Chinese dress (<u>Manchurian style</u>).

齊{斉}**chí** (SV) 1) be even, regular. /他的鬍子剪的很～. His beard has been evenly trimmed. 2) be complete. /客人都～了. The guests are all here. (FV) come up to <u>the level of something</u>. /水都～了腰了. The water comes up to my waist. (B) together. 一～ all together. *d s*

    齊全 **chíchywán** (SV) be complete, not lacking any part. /傢俱都～了. The furniture is complete (all the necessary pieces have been obtained).

騎 **chí** (FV) 1) sit astride <u>something</u>. ～牆 straddle a fence. 2) ride <u>an animal</u> *or* astride something. ～馬 ride a horse *or* horseback; ～自行車 ride a bicycle.

祈 **chí** (B) request. ～求 entreat.

    祈禱 **chídǎu** (FV) pray. /你天天～嗎? Do you pray every day? (N) prayer.

乞 chǐ (B) beg. ~討 beg for, entreat.
乞丐 chǐgài (N) beggar.

企 chǐ (B) 1) stand erect. ~鵝 penguin. 2) anxious, expectant. ~圖 expectation.
　　企業 chǐyè (N) business enterprise.

起 chǐ (DV) go *or* come up, arise. ~床 get out of bed. 2) begin, start off. ~頭儿 start off, in the beginning; ~飛 take off (of a plane). 3) occur. /那件事情~了變化. A change has occurred in that situation. 4) develop, grow. /他臉上~了一個大包. A boil has developed on his face. 5) remove something lodged tightly. ~釘子 remove a nail. (RE) 1) up. /她拿~皮包就走了. She picked up her purse and left. 2) in potential RC only, up to a certain standard. 吃不~ cannot afford to eat something; 看得~ have a high opinion of.
　　起勁儿 chǐjyèr (SV) be enthusiastic.
　　起來 chǐlái (RC) 1) rise, get up. /~! Get up! 2) start. /戰事起不來. There won't be a war. (RE) indicates a change from one position to another or one situation to another. 站~ stand up; 存~ store away. /下起雨來了. It's starting to rain. /那件事我記不~了. I can't remember that thing.
　　起身 chǐshēn (VO) 1) rise, get up. ~很早 get up very early. 2) start on a journey. /你什麼時候起的身? When did you set out?

啟[啓|启]chǐ (B) 1) begin. ~程 start on a journey. 2) announce, state. ~事 announcement, notice.
　　啟發 chǐfā (FV) inspire, stimulate. /聖經~了我. The Bible inspired me.

汽 chì (B) steam, vapor. 水蒸~ steam.
　　汽車 chìchē (N) automobile. (M輛lyàng, 架jyà). 載重~ truck.
　　汽車站 chìchējàn (N) bus station, bus stop.
　　汽船 chìchwán (N) steamship (M隻jīr, 艘sōu).
　　汽鍋 chìgwō (N) steam boiler.

汽水 chìshwěi (N) <一ル> carbonated drink, soda water.
　　汽油 chìyóu (N) gasoline (M加侖 jyālwún).

氣[气]chì (N) 1) air. /球裏沒有~了. There's no air in the ball. 2) breath (M口 kǒu). 3) anger. 生~ be angry. (FV) make someone angry. /別~我. Don't make me angry. (SV) be angry. (B) 1) gas (as opposed to solid or liquid). 氧~ oxygen. 2) weather. ~象臺 observatory. 3) odor. 臭~ bad odor. 4) spirit, attitude. 勇~ courage.
　　氣球 chìchyóu (N) balloon.
　　氣候 chìhou (N) climate.
　　氣象 'chìsyàng (N) meteor.
　　氣味 chìwèi (N) 1) odor. 2) flavor. (M股gǔ).

侵 chīn (B) invade. ~犯 encroach upon.
　　侵略 chīnlywè (FV) commit aggression against, invade. /一九三七年日本~中國. Japan invaded China in 1937. (N) aggression.

親[亲]chīn (FV) kiss, caress. /那個孩子~他母親. The child kissed his mother. (SV) be closely related. /他們的關係很~. They are closely related. (B) 1) married relationship. 說~ arrange a marriage. 2) parent. 雙~ parents. 3) one's own ~眼看見 see with one's own eyes. 4) intimate, close. ~密 be close. (AT) blood (of relation). ~兄弟 blood brothers. → 親 chìng.
　　親愛的 chīnàide (N) beloved.
　　親戚 chīnchi (N) relative, relation.
　　親自 chīndz (A) in person, personally. /總統~回答記者的問題. The president answered the reporters' questions in person.
　　親熱 chīnre (SV) be friendly, very close.
　　親身 'chīnshēn (A) in person, oneself. /你得~去一趟. You should go yourself once.

秦 chín (B) i. s d t
　　秦椒 chínjyāu (chīnjyāu (lp)) (N) pepper (the plant or vegetable, not the granulated form) (M棵kē).

芹 chín (B) celery.
　　芹菜 chíntsài (N) celery (M把

bǎ;棵 kē).

琴 chín (N)　1) Chinese lute *or* guitar.
2) stringed instrument.　*t*

勤 chín (SV)　1) be diligent, industrious.
2) be frequent. /他的床單換得
很~. She changes the bed sheets
frequently. (A) 1) frequently, often. ~洗 wash frequently. 2) industriously. ~學 study industriously.
　勤謹 chínjin (SV) be diligent,
industrious.
　勤快 chínkwai (SV) be diligent,
industrious.
　勤務員 chínwùywán (N) orderly (m).

青 chǐng (SV) 1) be green (of grass,
plants, etc.). ~草 green grass.
2) be blue (of the sky, granite). ~
天 blue sky. 3) be black (of cloth,
hair, a bruise). ~布 black cloth.
4) be young. ~年會 Young Men's
Christian Association. /他年紀
很~. He is very young (lit. His
age is very young). 5) be unripe
(of fruit). /樹上的菓子還很
~呢. The fruit on the tree is
still not ripe.
　青年 chǐngnyán (N) youth
(period of life *or* the person).
　青菜 chǐngtsài (N) green vegetable (M棵 kē).
　青蛙 chǐngwā (N) frog (M隻
jī).

清 chǐng (SV) be clear. ~水 clear
water; 說不~ be unable to express
oneself clearly. /帳還~了. The
account has been cleared. (FV)
clear accounts. (B) incorrupt,
pure. ~官 honest and incorrupt official; ~白 unsullied.　*d*
　清楚 chǐngchu (SV) 1) be
clear, intelligible. /你所說的
很~. What you said is very clear.
2) be in good order. /圖書館的
書目編的很~. The card cata-
logue in the library is well organized.
　清帳 chǐngjàng (VO) clear up
an account, settle an account. /咱
們就算~了. We'll consider this
account settled.
　清靜 chǐngjing (SV) be se-
cluded, quiet.
　清潔 chǐngjyé (SV) be clean.

　清理 chǐnglǐ (FV) 1) clean
up (lit. or fig.). ~房間 clean up a
room; ~債務 clear up debts.
　清明 chǐngmíng (TW) 1) the
Spring Festival in which people worship at the graves. 2) at the time of
the Spring Festival.
　清醒 chǐngsyǐng (SV) 1) be
alert. /他頭腦很~. He has an
alert mind. 2) be sober (after
drinking), conscious. /他還沒有
~. He's still not sober (or conscious).

氫 chǐng (B) hydrogen.
　氫氣 chǐngchì (N) hydrogen.
　氫彈 chǐngdàn (N) hydrogen
bomb (M棵 kē, 枚 méi).

傾 chǐng (B) 1) incline, lean. 左~ lean
to the left (lit. or fig.). 2) collapse.
~倒 fall flat.
　傾向 'chǐngsyàng (FV) lean
toward (lit. or fig.). /這個人很
~共產主義. This man leans
toward Communism. (N) tendency.
/這個國家的人口有減少的
~. The population of this country
has a tendency to decrease.

蜻 chǐng (B) ﹀.
　蜻蜓 chǐngtíng (N) dragonfly
(M隻 jī).

輕 chǐng (SV) 1) be light (in weight).
/木頭比鐵~. Wood is lighter
than iron. 2) be slight (not serious).
/他的病很~. His illness is not
serious. 3) be young. /他年紀
很~. He is very young. (lit. His
age is very young). (A) 1) lightly,
slightly. ~~一推 push slightly.
2) easily, casually, recklessly. ~
信 believe without consideration; ~
舉妄動 make a reckless move. (B)
1) disrespectful. ~薄 to slight. 2)
hydrogen. ~彈 hydrogen bomb.
　輕視 'chǐngshì (FV) 1) underestimate. /我們不能~敵人的
力量. We must not underestimate
the strength of the enemy. 2) look
down on. /他~教育. He looks
down on education.
　輕鬆 chǐngsūng (SV) be carefree, relaxed.

情 chǐng (B) 1) feeling, emotion. ~
感 affection, friendship, feeling; ~

人 lover. 2) circumstances, conditions. 實 ～ the facts of a case. (N) favor, kindness. 說～ ask a favor, ask someone to forgive someone else. /我領你的～. I'm grateful for your kindness.

情感 chínggǎn (N) affection, love.

情況 chíngkwàng (N) conditions, circumstances.

情人 'chíngrén (N) sweetheart.

情形 chíngsying (N) situation, conditions, circumstances.

情緒 chíngsyu (N) morale, mood. /我今天～很不好. I'm in a bad mood today.

情願 chíngywàn (AV) be willing to. /雖然這個任務很難,可是我～去. I am willing to go, even though this mission is very difficult. 2) would rather, prefer to, do one thing rather than another when neither alternative is very satisfactory. /我～在這儿呆着. I prefer to stay here. (PT) ～．．．也不．．． would rather . . . than . . . /我～死也不去. I would rather die than go.

晴 chíng (SV) be clear (of the sky or weather). /現在天～了. The sky is clear now.

晴天 chíngtyān (N) clear day. (VO) be clear (of the sky). /現在晴了天了. Now the sky is clear.

晴雨表 chíngyúbyǎu (N) barometer.

頃 chǐng (M) for land (about 15.13 acres).

請 chǐng (FV) ask, invite. /他～我吃晚飯. He invited me to dinner. 2) apply for. ～入境證 apply for an entry permit. 3) engage the services of someone. /我想～一位中文先生. I would like to engage a Chinese teacher. (AV) please. /～上樓. Please go upstairs. /您先～. After you, please.

請安 chǐngān (VO) give someone one's best regards (of subordinates to a superior or of a young person to an older person). /請你替我給你老太太～. Send my best regards to your mother.

請求 chǐngchyóu (FV) 1) request formally, petition for. /我要～到海外去. I want to ask to go

abroad. (N) request, petition.

請坐 chǐngdzwò (IE) Please sit down.

請假 chǐngjyà (VO) request leave, ask for time off.

請教 chǐngjyàu (FV) ask someone's advice. /我要跟您～一件事. I would like to ask your advice about something. (IE) Excuse me . . . (preceding a request for information). /～,到紐約怎麼走? Excuse me, could you tell me how to get to New York?

請客 chǐngkè (VO) 1) invite guests, have a party. 2) treat someone to a meal, the movies, a party, etc. /誰～? Who's paying? or Who's having a party?

請示 'chǐngshr (FV) ask for instructions. /跟他～. Ask him for instructions.

請帖 chǐngtyē, chǐngtyè (N) written invitation (M 張 jāng, 份ル fèr). 發～ send out invitations.

請問 chǐngwèn (IE) Would you please tell me . . .

慶〔庆〕ching (B) 1) congratulate. 2) celebrate. ～壽 celebrate a birthday; 國～ national celebration.

慶賀 'chìnghè (FV) offer congratulations to someone. /他得博士的時候有很多人給他～. Many people congratulated him when he got his Ph.D.

慶祝 chìngjù (FV) celebrate. /我們今天～雙十節. We are celebrating the Double Tenth today. (N) celebration.

慶祝會 chìngjùhwèi (N) celebration. 開～ hold a party in celebration.

親〔亲〕chìng (B) 1. →親 chīn.

親家 chìngjya (N) father-in-law or mother-in-law of one's child (used also in direct address).

chong see **chung.**

抽 chōu (FV) 1) pull out, draw out. ～籤 draw lots; ～水 pump out water. 2) smoke a cigarette, pipe, etc. /他改～烟斗了. He changed to a pipe. 3) levy. 　levy a tax. 4) whip. /我～了他一頓. I gave him a whipping. 5) shrink. /這塊布洗一次就～了. This piece of cloth shrank after one washing. 6) draft a person (m).

抽屜 chōuti (N) drawer.

仇[讎] chóu (N) hatred, grudge, score to settle. 報~get revenge.

愁 chóu (SV) 1) be worried. 2) be depressed. (FV) worry about. /你 ~甚麼呢? What are you worrying about?

稠 chóu (SV) be thick (of soup, paste, etc.). ~粥 thick congee (a gruel).

稠密 chóumì (SV) be crowded, dense. 人口~ densely populated.

綢[紬] chóu (B) <-子> silk goods.

籌[篝][籌] chóu (FV) raise money, funds. /造那個醫院的錢我們還沒 ~足呢. We still haven't raised enough money to build the hospital. (B) 1) plan. ~ 辦 make plans for. 2) tally. ~碼儿 poker chip.

籌備 chóubèi (FV) plan, prepare for (as some event or project). /我們正~新年晚會呢. We're now planning a New Year's party.

醜[丑] chóu (SV) 1) be ugly. /他長的 很~. He is very ugly. (B) shameful, disgraceful. ~事 shameful affair; 丟~ disgrace oneself.

醜陋 chóulòu (SV) be ugly looking, shabby.

丑 chǒu (N) <-儿> clown. ~角 clown in Chinese opera. (B) the period from 1 to 3 A.M. SF of 醜 chǒu.

臭 chòu (SV) 1) smell bad. /肉~了. The meat smells bad. 2) be disreputable. /他在教育界的名譽 很~. He has a bad reputation in educational circles. 3) be snobbish. /那個人~極了. That person is a snob.

臭蟲 chòuchung (N) bedbug.

吃[喫] chŕ (FV) 1) eat. /我們常~ 中國飯. We often eat Chinese food. 2) drink (d). ~茶 drink tea. 3) take medicine. /頭痛~一點 阿士皮靈就好了. Your headache will go away if you take some aspirin. 4) take (in chess or mahjong). /他把我的馬~了. He took my knight. 5) smoke a cigarette, pipe, etc. (d). 6) absorb. ~油 absorb oil. 7) suffer, endure. ~ 不住 be unable to bear. (B) <-儿> food

(lp). (ON) sound of hissing through the teeth. 口~ stutter; ~~ 的笑 snicker.

吃飯 chŕfàn (VO) eat (a meal or food). /我還沒~呢. I haven't eaten yet. (FV) make a living. /這年頭儿~太難了. It's very hard to make a living nowadays.

吃驚 chŕjīng (VO) be frightened. /他聽見那個消息大吃一驚. He was extremely frightened when he heard the news.

吃疆 chŕjyāng (VO) take a dare. /結果他不吃我的疆呢. He wouldn't take my dare after all.

吃苦 chŕkǔ (VO) suffer or endure hardship. /年青人應該能 ~. Young people should be able to endure suffering.

吃虧 chŕkwēi (SV) be at a disadvantage. /這樣作很~. If you do it this way, you'll be at a disadvantage. (VO) suffer loss. /我吃 了一個大虧. I suffered a big loss. (A) unfortunately. /我~沒 上過大學. Unfortunately I've never been to college.

吃力 chŕlì (SV) be strenuous. /編字典很~. It requires a lot of effort to compile a dictionary.

吃醋 chŕtsù (SV) be jealous (lit. eat vinegar). /別盡跟他女 朋友說話,他最愛~了. Don't talk to his girl friend all the time, he gets very jealous. (VO) be jealous of someone. /他吃我的 醋. He's jealous of me.

池 chŕ (N) <-子> 1) pond, pool. 2) orchestra (part of a theater). s

池塘 chŕtáng (N) pond, pool.

匙 chŕ (B) <-儿, -子> spoon (M把bǎ). 鑰匙 shr̀.

遲[迟] chŕ (SV) be late. /後悔也太 ~了. It's too late to feel sorry. /他 來~了. He came late. (B) 1) slow.~緩 be slow. 2) delay. ~延 to delay.

遲到 chŕdàu (FV) come late. /今天有三個學生~了. Three students came late today.

尺 chŕ (B) ↓. → 尺 chǐ.

尺寸 chŕtswun (N) size, measurement (in feet and inches). /這個 桌子是什麼~? What size is this table?

尺 chǐ (N) ruler (M 根 gēn). (M) Chinese foot (= 0.3581 meters). → 尺 chǐ.

翅 chǐ (B) 1) <-ㄦ> wing. 2) <-子> fin. 魚~ shark's fin.
翅膀 chǐbǎng (N) wing.

出 chū (DV) 1) come *or* go out. /我刚~電影院就下起雨來了. I had just left the movie theater when it started to rain. 2) come up *or* out (of the sun, moon, etc.). /~太陽了. The sun is up. 3) produce. ~煤 produce coal. 4) supply with, donate. ~力 supply labor; ~主意 make a suggestion. 5) issue, send forth. ~命令 issue an order. 6) happen, appear, come up. /~問題了. A problem came up. (RE) 1) out. /他剛衝~銀行,就被捕了. He was caught right after he ran out of the bank. 2) in potential RC, indicates making out what something is. /我想不~什麼好辦法. I can't think of any good solution. (B) used after CV like 往 wàng, 望 wàng, 向 syàng, etc., out. 往~跑 run out of some place. SF of 齣 chū.

出版 chūbǎn (VO) be published. /你的書出了版了嗎? Has your book been published? (FV) publish something. /那家公司~的那本新書? What company published that new book?

出版社 chūbǎnshè (N) publishing company.

出差 chūchāi (VO) go on an official trip. /我這個月出了三次差. I went on three official trips this month.

出差費 chūchāifèi (N) expense allowance while on an official trip (M 筆 bǐ).

出產 chūchǎn (FV) produce goods. /這個工廠一年~多少噸鋼? How many tons of steel does this plant produce each year? (N) production, output.

出場 chūchǎng (VO) come out to perform (in a play, game, party, political rally, etc.). /他一~就把詞ㄦ給忘了. He forgot his lines as soon as he came out on stage. /棒球比賽快開始了,因為運動員都~了. The baseball game will begin soon since all the players have come out.

出岔ㄦ chūchàr (VO) go astray, go amiss. /希望這回別~. I hope nothing goes wrong this time.

出錢 chūchyán (VO) give the money for, pay for. /他~辦了一個醫院. He gave the money for a hospital. /我們看電影是他出的錢. He paid our way to the movies.

出去 chūchyu (RC) go out. /我父親~了. My father went out. (RE) out (there). /我們把他攆~了. We kicked him out.

出發 chūfā (FV) leave, set out. ~點 starting point. /我們明天早晨~. We leave tomorrow morning.

出範圍 chū'fànwei (VO) 1) be outside the scope of, irrelevant to. /你這句話出了我們討論的範圍了. What you said is irrelevant to our discussion. 2) be beyond someone's jurisdiction. /那件事情出了我們警察的範圍了. That matter is beyond the jurisdiction of our police force.

出鋒頭 chūfēngtou (VO) show off. /他在會場裏喜歡~. He likes to show off at meetings. (SV) be in the limelight. /那個人現在很~. That person is very much in the limelight now.

出汗 chūhàn (VO) sweat, perspire. 出一身汗 perspire all over (one's body).

出疹子 chūjěndz (VO) have measles. /他出過疹子嗎? Has he had the measles?

出主意 chūjúyi (VO) produce a scheme, figure out a plan. /他盡出胡~. He's always thinking up crazy schemes.

出口 chūkǒu (FV) export. /那個公司專門~人造絲. That company only exports rayon. (VO) be exported. /那一批貨已經出了口了. Those goods have already been exported.

出來 chūlai (RC) come out. /太陽~了. The sun is out. (RE) 1) out (here). /他把東西從那個屋子裏搬~了. He moved the things out of that room. 2) in potential RC, indicates making out what something is. /他的意思我看不~. I can't understand his idea.

/噢,那個答案我想～了. Ah, now I've got the solution.

出力 **chūlì** (VO) put effort into some enterprise. /為這件事情他出了不少力. He put a lot of effort into that thing.

出馬 **chūmǎ** (FV) do something oneself instead of having someone else do it, usually preceded by 親自 oneself, in person. /你不必親自～. You don't have to do it yourself.

出賣 **chūmài** (FV) 1) sell. /他要把他全部財産都～了. He wants to sell all his property. 2) betray someone who has trusted you. /他總是～朋友. He always betrays his friends.

出毛病 **chūmáubing** (VO) have something go wrong. /他的車出了毛病了. Something went wrong with his car.

出門儿 **chūmér** (VO) 1) go out (the door). /他出了這個門儿就忘了. He forgot as soon as he got out the door. 2) go away from, leave, one's home, village, country. /他一年以前就～了. He left home a year ago.

出名 **chūmíng** (VO) become famous. /現在他的詩已經出了名了. His poems are famous now. (SV) be well known, famous. /這本書很～. This book is very well known.

出面 **chūmyàn** (VO) 1) appear at, attend. /那個酒會總統也～了. Even the President attended the party. 2) offer oneself for some service. /我父親願意～給他們調停. My father is willing to serve as a mediator for them. 3) sponsor. /那個慈善拍賣會是由女皇～的. That charity auction was sponsored by the Queen.

出牌 **chūpái** (VO) play a card or mah-jong piece. /現在該您～了. It's your turn to play a card (or discard).

出入 **chūrù** (N) 1) income and expenditures. /這個月我們家裡的～相抵. Our family income and expenditures balanced this month. 2) difference. /這兩個辦法的～很大. There's a big difference between these two methods. (FV)

go in and out. /他們在教室裡總是隨便～. They always come in and go out of the classroom as they please.

出色 **chūsè** (SV) be outstanding

出身 **chūshēn** (N) origin, background, (of a person). /他的～很低. He comes from a very humble background.

出聲儿 **chūshēngr** (VO) utter a sound. /你別～! Don't utter a sound!

出事儿 **chūshìr** (VO) have something go amiss, have an accident. /出了什麼事儿了? What went wrong? /又有飛機～了. There was another plane accident.

出現 **chūsyàn** (FV) appear, come into view. /水面儿上～了一個潛水艇. A submarine appeared at the surface of the water.

出血 **chūsyě** (VO) bleed (as from the gums, without gushing out of blood).

出席 **chūsyí** (VO) attend a meeting. /今天開會只有一半會員～了. Only one half of the members attended today's meeting.

出庭 **chūtíng** (VO) appear in court (of a lawyer, judge, plaintiff, defendant). /我不願意～給他作證. I don't want to testify for him in court.

出錯儿 **chūtswòr** (VO) make a mistake. /你不能再～了. You can't make any more mistakes.

出外 **chūwài** (VO) travel far from home. /他～很多年了. He has been away from home for many years.

齒句[出] **chū** (M) for plays or operas. 一～戲 a play, an opera.

初 **chū** (SP) used before NU from one to ten, indicates days of a lunar month. ～三 the third day; ～十 the tenth day. (A) for the first time, first. /我～到那儿的時候甚麼都不熟. When I first arrived there, nothing was familiar. (B) beginning, first. 當～ in the beginning; ～選 primary election.

初級 **chūjí** (AT) 1) junior. ～中學 junior high school. 2)

elementary. ～教育 elementary education.

初中 **chūjūng** (N) junior high (school).

除 **chú** (FV) 1) divide (*arith*.). /四被二～得二. *or* 二～四得二. Four divided by two is two. 2) eliminate, remove. ～根 eradicate. (CV) 1) except. /～我没人會做. There's no one who can do it except me. 2) in addition to, besides. /～你還有誰? Who's there besides you? (PT) ～(了)...以外. 1) in addition to, besides. /～(了)你以外，還有兩個人. Besides you, there are still two others. 2) except. /～(了)你以外，没有別人. There's nobody else except you.

除去 **chúchyu** (FV) in addition to, besides. /～開車的還可以坐五個人. Besides the driver, there's enough room for five people.

除掉 **chúdyau** (FV) eliminate, take out. /把這一段～. Eliminate that passage. (CV) in addition to, besides. /～我，還有誰去? Who else is going besides me? 2) except. /～我没有別人去. Nobody's going except me.

除非 **chúfēi** (A) unless, only if. /～你跟我去,否則我不去. I won't go unless you go with me. /～你告訴我,我才知道呢. I'll only know if you tell me.

除夕 **chúsyī** (TW) (on) New Year's Eve.

廚(厨) **chú** (B) 1) kitchen. ～刀 kitchen knife. 2) <子> cook, chef. 3) closet, cupboard. 衣～ clothes closet.

廚房 **chúfáng** (N) kitchen (M 閒 jyān).

鋤(鉏,耡) **chú** (FV) hoe. ～草 hoe weeds. (B) <頭> hoe (M 把 bǎ).

處 **chǔ →** 處 **chù**.

畜 **chù** (B) domestic animal. 家～ domestic animals. → 畜 **syù**.

畜類 **'chùlèi** (N) animal (as contrasted with man, in Buddhist theory).

畜生 **chùsheng** (N) 1) beast (as distinguished from man). 2) domestic animal.

處(處) **chù, chǔ** (FV) get along with someone *or* in some situation. /那個環境可不好～. It isn't easy to get along in that situation. (B) 1) place which functions as a public service, office, board, department. 衛生～ board of public health; 停車～ parking area. 2) point, feature. 好～ good point. 3) deal with, act on. ～置 dispose of. (M) <一儿> 1) for occurrences of fire, robbery, etc. in different places. 三～搶案 three cases of robbery. 2) for activities scheduled in different places. /我還有三～得去送貨. I still have three deliveries to make. 3) for property, real estate. 兩～'買賣 two stores.

處不來 **chùbulai, chǔbulai** (RC) be unable to get along with someone. /我們兩人～. We two don't get along.

處處 **'chùchù** (A) everywhere. /～都是土. There's dust everywhere.

處罰 **chùfá, chǔfá** (FV) punish. /你不要～他了. Don't punish him. (N) punishment.

處置 **chùjr, chǔjr** (FV) deal with, dispose of, a matter, person. /這件事情他～得很好. He dealt with this matter very well.

處理 **chùlǐ, chǔlǐ** (FV) deal with, dispose of, a matter. /我不會～這種事. I can't handle this kind of thing.

處女 **chùnyǔ, chúnyǔ** (N) virgin. 老～ old maid.

處世 **chùshr, chǔshr** (VO) get along in the world, especially with other people. /有經驗了以後才知道怎麼～. It takes experience to know how to get along in the world.

chuai *see* **chwai**.

chuan *see* **chwan**.

chuang *see* **chwang**.

chui *see* **chwei**.

chun *see* **chwun**.

沖 **chūng** (FV) 1) rush against. /大浪把船～到岸上去了. The waves washed the ship ashore. 2) pour something into or over an object. /那些盤子應該再用水～一便.

Those plates must be rinsed again. SF of 衝 chūng, 衝 chùng.

充 chūng (FV) pretend to be. /他老~行家. He is always pretending to be an expert. (B) fill.補 ~ refill. (B) serve as. 冒 ~ act falsely as.

充足 'chūngdzú (SV) be sufficient. /他們的糧食預備的很~. They have sufficient foodstuffs on hand.

充分 chūngfèn (SV) be sufficient, adequate. /他不去的理由很~. His reasons for not going are quite sufficient. (A) 1) sufficiently. /我~瞭解這件事情 I understand this matter sufficiently. 2) as much as possible, to the fullest extent. /請大家~發表意見. Please express your opinions as much as possible.

充滿 chūngmǎn (FV) be filled with remorse, satisfaction, etc. /他的臉上~了高興的樣子. His face was filled with happiness.

衝(沖)chūng (FV) rush toward. / 人都從那個着了火的房子裏~出來了. The people rushed out of the burning building. (B) thoroughfare. 要 ~ key position. →衝 chùng.

衝突 chūngtu (N) clash, conflict. (FV) clash. /他們兩個人~起來了. Those two are in conflict with each other.

重 chúng (A) over again, once again. /你得~做. You must do it all over again. (FV) be repeated by mistake. /這個字~了. This character was repeated by mistake. (RE) again by mistake. 買 ~ 了 buy another one of something by mistake. (B) 1) duplicate.~複 repetitious. 2) great-grand-children. ~ 孫子 great-grand-son. →重 jùng.

崇 chúng (B) 1) to honor.~敬 to respect. 2) lofty. ~ 山 high mountain.

崇拜 chúngbài (FV) worship a person or deity. /他們~他們的領袖. They worship their leader.

蟲(虫)chúng (B) <-ル, -子> insect, worm (M條tyáu).

衝(沖)chùng (SV) 1) be of great momentum or force (as water from a faucet). 2) be strong (as of an odor). 3) be

bold, frank (lp) . (CV) facing, toward. /他 ~ 東站着. He is standing there facing east. →衝 chūng.

衝盹ル chùngdwǒr (VO) nod from sleepiness. /剛才衝了一會ル盹ル,現在精神好多了. I was nodding for a while before but I feel better now.

chuo see chwo.

攑 chwāi (FV) 1) carry something in a pocket, or in one's clothes near the chest. /他把錢都~在口袋裏了. He carried all his money in his pockets. 2) knead.~麵 knead dough.

穿 chwān (FV) 1) pierce, pass through. /用錐子~一個洞. Make a hole with this awl. /我們從這個球場~過去. We'll cross over by way of this ball field. 2) thread. ~珠子 string pearls. 3) wear, put on, main articles of clothing, as a suit, coat, shoes, etc.~褲子 put on trousers. (RE) through (in one side and out the other, lit. or fig.). 鑽~了 bore through. /我們把他的企圖看~了. I saw right through his intentions.

穿上 chwānshang (RC) 1) put on clothing. /我長胖了,舊衣裳都穿不上了. I've gotten so fat that I can't get on any of my old clothes. 2) thread things together. /珠子已經~了. The beads have already been strung together.

船 chwán (N) ship, boat. (M隻jŕ, 條tyáu,艘sǒu).

船長 chwánjǎng (N) captain of a ship.

船主 chwánjǔ (N) master, owner of a ship.

船頭 chwántóu (N) bow, prow, of a ship.

船尾 chwánwěi (N) stern of a ship.

船位 chwánwèi (N) accommodations on a ship.訂~book passage.

傳 chwán (FV) 1) pass on. 一代 ~ 一代 pass down from one generation to another. 2) summon.~審 summon for trial. 3) spread a rumor or disease. /他老是~謠言. He's always spreading rumors. 4) conduct heat or electricity. ~ 熱

radiate heat. 5) propagate, preach.
～福音 preach the gospel. →傳 jwàn.

傳遍 chwánbyàn (RC) be told everywhere, spread far and wide. /這個消息全國都～了。 This news has been spread all over the country.

傳道 chwándàu (VO) preach, proselytize (<u>particularly of missionaries</u>). ～的 missionary, minister. /他在中國傳了三十年道。 He preached in China for thirty years.

傳教 chwánjyàu (VO) spread a faith, do missionary work. ～士 missionary, minister. /我將來要到鄉下去～. I'm going to the country to preach in the future.

傳教士 chwánjyàushr̀ (N) preacher.

傳令兵 chwánlìngbīng (N) messenger (m).

傳染 chwánrǎn (FV) 1) become infected <u>with a disease</u>. /他～上月市病了. He got tuberculosis. 2) spread <u>a disease</u>. /這種病很容易～. Such a disease is easily spread to others.

傳說 chwánshwō (FV) spread a rumor. /有人～他已經死了. According to what people say, he's already dead. (N) 1) rumor. 2) legend. 3) historical tradition.

傳統 chwántǔng (N) tradition.

喘 chwǎn (FV) breathe quickly *or* heavily. /你為什麼這麼～? Why are you breathing so heavily?

喘氣 chwǎnchì (VO) 1) breathe heavily. /上完三層樓,我直～. When I had gone up three flights I was breathing heavily. 2) catch <u>one's breath</u>, relax. /考試今天完了,我可以喘喘氣了. Exams were over today, so now I can relax a little.

串 chwàn (M) <-儿> string, series. 一～珍珠 a string of pearls. (FV) 1) act <u>in a play</u> (<u>as a guest star</u>). 2) go through and around. /他在樹林子裏～了半夜才找着路. He wandered around the woods half the night before he found the road. ～門子 go visiting from door to door (<u>as a pastime</u>). 3) connect, string together. /他把釣的魚

都～在一塊儿了 . He strung the fish he caught together.

串通 chwàntūng (FV) conspire. /佣人跟賊～着把東西都偷了. The servant and the thief worked together in the robbery.

窗{窓,牕} chwāng (B) <-子> 1) window. ～帘 window curtain. 2) shutter (M 扇 shàn, 面 myàn).

窗戶 chwānghu (N) window (M 面 shàn, 扇 myàn). ～簾子 *or* ～簾儿 window curtain.

創 chwāng (B) wound. ～口 wound, cut, sore. →創 chwǎng.

瘡[疮] chwāng (N) sore, skin ulcer. 長了一個～ have an ulcer (<u>external</u>).

床{牀} chwáng (N) bed (M 張 jāng). (B) <-子> workbench. 車～ lathe. (M) <u>for bedding which covers the length of the bed</u>. 兩～氈子 two blankets.

創{剏} chwǎng, chwàng (FV) create, invent. ～學說 create a theory. (B) establish, found. ～辦學校 found a school. →創 chwāng.

創造 chwǎngdzàu, chwàngdzàu (FV) create. ～新天地 create a new world.

創作 chwǎngdzwò, chwàngdzwò (FV) devise, create, <u>ideas, plans</u>. /這個計劃是誰～的? Who devised this plan? (N) creation, invention.

創牌子 chwǎngpáidz, chwàngpáidz (VO) create a market <u>for a new brand of some product</u>. /公司正為這種香煙～呢 The company is trying to create a market for this new brand of cigarettes.

闖 chwǎng (FV) rush into. /你怎麼不敲門就～進來? How come you rushed in without knocking?

撞 chwàng (FV) crash into, bump into. /他被車子～了. He was hit by a car. /他的頭～在門上了. He bumped his head on the door. →撞 jwàng.

創 chwàng →創 chwǎng.

吹 chwēi (FV) 1) blow (<u>as the wind</u>). /風～得很大. The wind is blowing hard. 2) blow on <u>something</u>. /把蠟燭～滅了. <u>Blow out the</u>

candles. 3) play, blow, a wind instrument. ~ 笛 play a Chinese flute. 4) boast. / 他老愛 ~ . He is always boasting. 5) end unhappily. / 他們倆 ~ 了. Those two have broken up.

炊 chwēi (B) to cook. ~ 事 cooking. 炊事員 chwēishr̀wán (N) cook (m).

搥 {捶} chwéi (FV) beat with the fist, pound. ~ 背 pound on the back. / 他用拳頭 ~ 桌子. He pounded the table with his fist.

錘 {鎚 (B) 2), (FV)} chwéi (B) 1) weight on a steelyard. 秤 ~ weight on a steelyard. 2) < -子 > hammer. (FV) hammer, pound. ~ 鐵 hammer iron; ~ 門 pound on a door.

戳 chwō (FV) jab with a long object, like a pencil. / 我在紙上 ~ 了一個洞. I jabbed a hole in the paper. / 他用他的鉛筆 ~ 我. He jabbed me with his pencil. 2) stand something up. / 他們把死屍 ~ 在門後頭了. They stood the corpse up behind the door. (B) < -子 > stamp, seal.

春 chwūn (B) 1) spring. ~ 假 spring vacation. 2) wanton, lewd, lustful. ~ 意 lewd thoughts. 3) joyful, gay. ~ 風滿面 face full of joy. 4) youth. 青 ~ youthful years.
春季 chwūnjì (TW) (in) the spring season.
春節 chwūnjyé (TW) (on) Chinese New Year's Day. 2) (at the time of) the New Year Festival.
春天 chwūntyan (TW) (in) spring.

椿 chwūn (B) Ailanthus or Cedrela (a tree similar to sumac). Cedrela odorata; 臭 ~ Ailanthus.
椿樹 chwūnshù (N) Ailanthus (M 棵 kē).

純 chwún (SV) be pure, unadulterated (of a thing). ~ 科學 pure science; ~ 種 thoroughbred, purebred. / 這個金子不 ~ . This gold isn't pure.
純潔 ' chwúnjyé (SV) be pure, innocent, unsophisticated. / 小孩子的思想非常 ~ . A child's thoughts are very unsophisticated.

純粹 chwúntswèi (SV) 1) be pure, unadulterated. / 他說的是 ~ 的北平話 . He speaks pure Pekingese. 2) be typical. / 他是個 ~ 英國紳士派 He is a typical English gentleman. (A) truly. / 他 ~ 是一個學者 . He is truly a scholar.

掐 chyā (FV) 1) pinch with two fingers. / 他又 ~ 了我一下 . He pinched me again. 2) strangle with one's hands. ~ 死 strangle to death. 3) break off. ~ 花儿 pick flowers. / 電話公司把我的電話 ~ 了. 因為我沒按時交錢 The telephone company disconnected my telephone because I didn't pay on time. (M) < -子 > small bunch (enough for one handful).

卡 chyǎ (FV) get caught (as when an obstruction catches a moving object). / 一根魚刺 ~ 在他嗓子裏了. A fish bone got caught in his throat. (B) 1) guardhouse at a pass. 關 ~ customs barrier. 2) < -子 > clip, fasteners. → 卡 kǎ.

恰 chyà (SV) be exact, appropriate. / 這個字他用的不 ~ . He uses this word inappropriately. (B) just, exactly. ~ 到好處 just right.
恰巧 chyàchyǎu (A) just happened to. / 他送我的 ~ 是我要的 . What he gave me just happened to be what I wanted.
恰好 chyàhǎu (A) 1) just happened to. / 我去看他,他 ~ 出去了. It just happened he was out when I went to see him. 2) fortunately. / 我 ~ 碰見他了. Fortunately I met him. or I just happened to meet him.

千 {仟} chyān (M) thousand. 兩 ~ 人 two thousand people. (B) many. ~ 里 many miles, a long way.
千萬 chywānwàn (M) 1) ten million. 五 ~ fifty million. (A) by all means, be sure to. / 你 ~ 得來 . You should come by all means. / ~ 別忘 . Be sure not to forget. (B) millions, a vast number. 上 ~ 的人 people by the millions.

牽 [牵] chyān (FV) 1) lead or pull along on a rope. ~ 牛 lead an ox. 2) hold onto a person's hand or clothes. ～着手走 walk holding hands. (B) connect, implicate. ～連 involve.

鉛 chyān (N) 1) lead (the metal). 2) pencil lead.
　　鉛筆 chyānbǐ (N) pencil (M 枝 jr̄).

簽(签) chyān (FV) sign (official). ～名 sign one's name; ～條約 sign a treaty. (B) 1) <-子, -ル> lot (M 根 gēn). 抽～ draw lots. 2) label. 書～ book label.

潛(潜) chyān (B) 1) dive, submerge. ～水 dive into water. 2) hide. ～逃 abscond with something.
　　潛水艇 chyānshwéitǐng (N) submarine (M 隻 jī, 艘 sōu).

謙 chyān (B) humble, modest. ～恭 be courteous.
　　謙虛 chyānsyū (SV) be modest, humble.

前 chyán (L) 1) front, ahead. 向～走 go in front, go forward; 門～ (the area) in front of the door; ～排 (in) the front row. 2) ago. 五年～ five years ago. 3) before. 下雨～ before it rains. 4) previous, former, ex-. ～功 previous feat; ～校長 former principal. (SP) 1) past. ～兩天 the past two days. 2) first. ～五名 the first five names.
　　前邊 chyánbyan (PW) <-ル> 1) in front or in the front part of something. /～走的人是我哥哥 The man walking in front of me is my older brother. /房子～有一個花園. There's a garden in front of the house (or in the front part of the house). 2) the area in front or the front part of something. /～比後邊大. The front part is larger than the back part. (or The area in front is larger than the area in back.)
　　前後 chyánhòu (PW) 1) the front and back. /這個樓的～都有樹. There are trees in front and back of this building. 2) in front and back. /我們被敵人攻擊. We were attacked by the enemy from both front and back. (A) from beginning to end. /今天的茶會～來了五十個人. Fifty people

came to the tea today (from the beginning of the tea to the end). (B) around a certain time. 二月～ around February. /他打算月底～來. He plans to come around the end of the month.
　　前進 chyánjìn (FV) go forward, progress. 無法～ be impossible to go forward. (SV) be progressive. /他們說我思想不夠～. They say my ideas are not progressive enough.
　　前門 chyánmén (PW) (at) the front door or gate.
　　前面 chyánmyan = 前邊 chyánbyan.
　　前年 chyánnyan (TW) the year before last.
　　前任 chyánrèn (N) predecessor.
　　前線 chyánsyàn (N) front line, front (m).
　　前提 chyántí (N) 1) factor, issue. /辦學校錢是一個大～. Money is a major factor in operating a school. 2) logical premise.
　　前頭 chyántou = 前邊 chyánbyan.
　　前途 chyántú (N) future. /他的～很光明. His future is very bright.
　　前天 chyántyan (TW) the day before yesterday.
　　前ル(個) chyár(ge) = 前天 chyántyan (lp).

鉗(箝) chyán (B) 1) pinch, clamp. clamp one's mouth shut, gag someone. 2) <-子> pliers, pincers, tongs. 3) <-子> clippers (M 把 bǎ).
　　鉗子 chyándz (N) 1) ↑. 2) earring (M 付 fù) (lp).

錢 chyán (N) 1) money (M 塊 kwài; 毛 máu; 分 fēn; 筆 bǐ). (M) one tenth of a tael. 五～銀子 half a tael of silver. s t
　　錢包 chyánbāu (N) <-ル> money pouch, money bag, wallet.

淺 chyǎn (SV) 1) be shallow. ～水 shallow water. 2) be superficial. 知識很～ superficial knowledge. 3) be short (in duration). 歷史～ short history. 4) be light (in color). ～綠 light green. 5) be simple, easy to comprehend, elementary. /這本書～. This book is elementary.

欠 chyàn (FV) owe someone something. /你~他多少錢? How much money do you owe him? 2) be short, lack. /這盤菜~一點儿鹽. This dish needs some salt. (B) 1) deserve punishment. ~打 deserve a beating. 2) stand on tip-toe. ~腳 stand on tip-toe. (PT) ~...(不到) ... be so much short of an amount. /~二兩(不到)一磅. It's two ounces short of a pound. /~五分(不到)四點. It's five minutes to four.

搶 chyāng (FV) go against, oppose. ~着風行船 sail against the wind. (RE) in opposition, against. 說~ argue. →搶 chyǎng.

槍{鎗}{抢} chyāng (N) spear, lance. 2) rifle, pistol (M枝 jr, 桿 gǎn). 鎗彈 chyāngdàn (N) bullet (of a rifle or other small arm) (M粒 lì, 發 fā, 顆 kē). 鎗子儿 chyāngdzěr (N) bullet (of a rifle or other small arm) (M 顆 kē, 粒 lì).

腔 chyāng (B) 1) <-子> hollow space (as in one's body). 口~ mouth-cavity. 2) <-儿> tune, intonation. 女娘娘~ girlish voice. 3) <-儿> cadenza. 腔調 chyāngdyàu (N) <-儿> 1) tune, melody. 2) unappealing way of talking and acting. /他這種~給人一個很壞的印象. He gives people a very bad impression because of the way he talks and acts.

強{强,疆} chyáng (SV) 1) be strong. /他身體很~. He has a strong body. 2) be superior, better. /你比他~. You are better than he. (B) 1) following a NU-M, a little more than. 三倍~ a little more than three times. 2) strong nation, power. 五~ the five powers. →強 chyǎng, 強 jyàng. 強大 chyángdà (SV) be strong and great. ~的國家 the great powers. 強壯 chyángjwàng (SV) be strong (of one's body).

牆{墙}{墻} chyáng (N) wall (M堵 dǔ, 道 dàu, 面 myàn). 牆壁 chyángbì (N) wall, partition.

強{强,疆} chyǎng (B) force, compel. →強 chyáng, 強 jyàng. 強辯 chyǎngbyàn (FV) argue stubbornly or obstinately. /他已經知道沒理了,可是還要~. He knows he's wrong, but he still argues stubbornly. 強迫 chyǎngpwò (FV) force, compel. /你不能~她跟他結婚. You can't force her to marry him.

搶 chyǎng (FV) 1) rob. /他們正計劃~那個銀行. They're planning to rob that bank. 2) snatch. /猴子從我手裏把花生~走了. The monkey snatched the peanuts out of my hand. 3) fight to get ahead of someone. /報來的時候,他老~. When the newspaper comes, he always fights to get it first. →搶 chyāng. 搶案 chyǎngàn (N) case of robbery (M次 tsž, 處 chù). /這幾天出了很多次~. There have been several robberies the past few days. 搶着 chyǎngje (A) fighting to get ahead. /他老是~給錢. When it comes to paying the bill, he always beats everyone else to it. /他~說話. He's always the first to speak.

敲 chyāu (FV) 1) knock on, tap. ~門 knock on a door. 2) strike a percussion instrument. ~鑼 beat a gong. 3) extort money from, blackmail. 4) gyp someone. /我叫人~了. I was gypped. or I was blackmailed.

瞧 chyáu (FV) 1) look at, see, watch. /你~什麼呢? What are you looking at? 2) visit, see, a person. /我明天~我奶奶去. I'm going to visit my grandmother tomorrow. 3) examine and treat (of a doctor). /大夫還沒~我呢. The doctor hasn't seen me yet. 4) see a doctor. 5) have an opinion, think. /我~你不敢去. I don't think you dare go. 6) read (silently). ~信 read a letter. 7) followed by a question or choice-type question, depend on. /現在就~你了. Now it only depends on you. 8) see what happens (lp). /我們走着~吧! Let's continue on and see.

僑(侨]chyáu (B) reside abroad. 華～overseas Chinese. *t*

僑民 chyáumín (N) citizen living outside his country.

橋(桥]chyáu (N) bridge (M座 dzwò).

巧 chyáu (SV) 1) be skillful, ingenious. /她手很～. She's very skillful (lit. Her hands are very skillful). 2) be lucky, timely, opportune. ～得很come at an opportune time. /真是一件～事! What a coincidence!

巧妙 'chyáumyàu (SV) be ingenious, clever. /他用的方法很～. The method he uses is very clever.

俏 chyàu (SV) be cute, pretty (of women or children). (B) scarce. ～貨 scarce goods.

俏皮 chyàupí (SV) be cute, smart. ～話 witty remark. /那個女孩儿長得很～. That girl is very cute.

切 chyē (FV) 1) cut, slice, carve. ～肉slice meat. 2) be tangent (*geom.*) /這兩圓相～. These two circles are tangent. →切 chyè.

茄 chyé (B) <-子> eggplant.

切 chyè (A) be sure to (usually used in a command). /你～不可買. Be sure not to buy that. /～記. Don't forget. (B) close to. 親～closely related. →切 chyè.

鞦(秋]chyōu (B) ↓.

鞦千 chyōuchyān (N) a swing (M架 jyà).

秋 chyōu (B) autumn. ～收autumn harvest. 2) period of time. 多事之～ eventful period. SF of 鞦chyōu.

秋季 chyōují (TW) (in) the autumn season.

秋天 chyōutyan (TW) (in) autumn.

求 chyóu (FV) 1) beg, implore. ～人 beg someone to do something. 2) seek. ～學 seek an education.

球 chyóu (N) ball.

球員 chyóuywán (N) ballplayer.

曲 chyū (B) 1) bent, crooked. 彎～ crooked, winding. 2) distort. 歪～ distort. →曲 chyǔ.

曲解 chyūjyě (FV) misinterpret what someone means. /你～了書裡的意思. You misinterpreted the book.

屈 chyū (SV) be wronged. /他心裏覺得很～. He feels that he has been unjustly treated. (B) 1) bend. ～指一算 count on one's fingers (by turning them down). 2) submit to someone unwillingly. ～屈 submit with shame. 3) injustice. 受～be wronged. *s*

屈服 chyūfu (FV) submit to, obey unwillingly. /他向他的敵人～. He bowed to the will of his enemies.

區(区]chyū (N) district, region. (B) 1) small. ～～ trifle. 2) distinguish. ～別 distinguish between, distinction.

蛆 chyū (N) maggot (M條tyáu).

趨(趋]chyū (B) ↓.

趨勢 'chyūshr̀ (N) tendency, trend.

曲 chyǔ (N) <-儿,-子> song, piece of music (M隻 jř). 唱～ sing a song; 作～ compose music. →曲 chyū.

曲藝 chyǔyì (N) vaudeville.

取 chyǔ (FV) 1) take out from, fetch. ～行李claim one's luggage. 2) admit, accept, an applicant or candidate. /學校～了二百名學生. The school admitted two hundred students. (B) 1) approve of someone. 以貌～人 approve of someone by his appearance. 2) obtain, take hold of. ～勝win a victory.

取得 chyǔdé (FV) obtain. ～公民權 obtain citizenship.

取消 chyǔsyāu (FV) cancel, get rid of. /我把那個約會～了. I canceled that appointment.

取笑 chyǔsyàu (FV) make fun of, tease. /請你別拿他～了. Please don't make fun of him.

娶 chyǔ (FV) marry (of a man). /你要～她嗎? Are you going to marry her?

去 chyù (DV) 1) go (to). /他要～臺灣了. He's going to Taiwan. 2) used before FV or VO, go in order to do something. /他～吃飯. He went to eat. 3) send something

39

(there). ～信 send a letter.　4) remove, do away with.　～土 remove
dirt. /把這個字～了.　Take
out this word.　(RE) indicates motion
there or away. /他把書買～了.
He bought the book.　(DC) indicates
motion there or away. /那個箱子
叫他們搬出～了.　They moved
the trunk out (there). /把車開進
車房～.　Drive the car into the
garage (there).　(B) 1) depart,
leave.～國 leave one's country.　2)
last.～冬 last winter.　(PT) 1) 到
...～go to a place. /他到那兒
～了? Where did he go?　2) 讓...
～ let someone or something be
(don't pay any attention). /讓他死
～.　Let him die.　3) ～...go in
order to do something. /他們～看
電影～了.　They went to the
movies.　4) 了～了 (preceded by SV),
very. /那個湖深了～了!　That
lake is bottomless! 5)...來...～back
and forth, over and over. 走來走
～ walk back and forth; 聽來聽～
listen over and over.　6)...來...
～ come and take something (there).
/他來拿了三百塊錢～.　He
came and took three hundred dollars
away with him.　7)...～...來.
go and bring something (here). /～
買一點兒肉來.　Go buy some
meat and bring it here.
　　去年 chyùnyan (TW) last year.
　　去世 chyùshř (VO) depart this
world, pass away. /他父親是去
年去的世.　His father passed away
last year.

羣(群)chyún (M) 1) crowd.—～人 a
crowd of people.　2) flock, herd.—
～牛 a herd of cattle.　(B) group.
人～the masses; ～居 live in groups.
　　羣眾 chyúnjùng (N) the people,
the masses.

裙 chyún (B) <-子> skirt (M條tyáu).

窮[窮]chyúng (SV) be poor, destitute.
(A) pointlessly, aimlessly.～忙
be pointlessly busy.　(B) exhaust.
～途 exhaust all possible ways and
means; 無～inexhaustible.
　　窮苦 chyúngkǔ (SV) be very
poor, in dire need.

圈 chywān (N) <-儿,-子> 1) circle,
ring.　2) scope (as of a topic).

/他說的話出了～子了.　What
he said was off the subject.　(M)
<-儿> time around.轉三～儿 turn
around three times.　(FV) 1) encircle, surround. /我們得造一
道牆把這塊地～起來　We have
to build a wall around this piece of
land.　2) draw a circle.～一個圈
儿. draw a circle.　3) mark with
a circle (either to the side of or
around a thing). /先生把這篇文
章～了.　The teacher has marked
this article.　一圈 jywān,圈 jywàn.

全 chywán (SV) be complete. /這套
書京～.　This set of books isn't
complete.　(A) completely. /我～
忘了.　I completely forgot.　(B)
the whole, all.～年 the whole year.
　　全部chywánbù (A) completely.
/過去的事情,我～都忘了.　I
completely forgot everything that
happened.　(N) the whole thing.
/～都壞了.　The whole thing is
spoiled.
　　全都 'chywándōu (A) 1) all,
both. /他們～死了.　They all
died.　2) completely. /那本書～
壞了.　That book is completely
ruined.
　　全體chywántǐ (N) the whole
group (of people).～出席 full at-
tendance.

泉 chywán (N) spring (of water) (M道
dàu).溫～ hot spring.

拳 chywán (B) <-頭> fist.打～ to box.
(M) blow with the fist.打一～ strike
a blow.　(FV) fold or tuck in.～著
身子 crouch. /那個鳥兒有一
隻腳～著呢.　That bird has one
leg tucked under him.

權[权]chywán (N) 1) power, authority.
有大～ have great power.　2)
right.選舉～ right to vote.　(B) 1)
temporary.～宜 best for the time
being.　2) weigh.～衡 consider,
weigh.
　　權柄chywánbǐng (N) moral
right, power, authority.
　　權力 chywánlì (N) right, power,
authority, given by law or tradition.

勸[劝]chywàn (FV) advise, exhort, persuade.～不動be unable to persuade
someone. /他～我多休息幾天
再去工作.　He advised me to get

more rest before going back to work. /牧師～我去教堂. The pastor persuaded me to go to church.

勸過來 **chywàngwolai** (RC) bring someone around to one's way of thinking. /我好不容易才把他～. It wasn't easy to bring him around to my way of thinking.

勸解 **chywànjyě** (FV) make peace. /你給他們兩人～～. Please make peace between those two.

缺 **chywē** (FV) 1) lack, be short of. ～米 be short of rice. 2) be broken, defective. /那個桌子～了一條腿. That table has a broken leg. (N) vacant post, vacancy. 出了一個～ have a vacancy. (SV) 1) be mean (lp). /這個人真～. This man is really mean. 2) be scarce, hard to get (of a commodity). /這種貨現在很～. This kind of merchandise is very hard to get now.

缺點 **chywēdyǎn** (N) shortcoming, defect.

缺乏 **chywēfá** (FV) lack, be short of. ～資本 be short of capital; ～頭腦 lack intelligence. (N) lack, need, deficiency, shortage. (SV) be scarce. /這種原料～極了. This kind of material is extremely scarce.

缺少 **chywēshǎu** (FV) lack, be short of. /做這件事他還～經驗. He still lacks the experience to do this work.

缺席 **chywēsyí** (VO) fail to attend, be absent from a meeting (very formal). /他～了三天. He's been absent for three days.

瘸 **chywé** (SV) be lame. ～子 lame person, cripple. (FV) limp. /他一走一～. He limps when he walks.

確(确) **chywè** (SV) be true, definite. /這個消息很～. This news is quite true. (A) really, definitely. /～有這麼一件事. There really is such a thing.

確定 **chywèdìng** (FV) decide, settle. /日子～了. The date has been settled. (SV) be certain, definite. ～的消息 definite news.

確實 **chywèshŕ** =確 **chywè**.

ci *see* **tsz**.

cong *see* **tsung**.

cou *see* **tsou**.

cu *see* **tsu**.

cuan *see* **tswan**.

cui *see* **tswei**.

cun *see* **tswun**.

cuo *see* **tswo**.

答 **dā** (B) answer. 回～ to answer, an answer. → 答 **dá**.

答碴儿 **dāchár** (VO) 1) cut in, interrupt, when people are talking. /他們說話,我答不上碴儿. When they talk I can't cut in. 2) answer. /他勸了我半天,我沒～. He tried to persuade me at some length, but I didn't say a word.

答應 **dāying** (FV) 1) answer. /我叫你,你為甚麼不～? Why didn't you answer when I called you? 2) agree to. /他～讓我出去. He agreed to let me go out. 3) promise. ～幫忙 promise to help.

搭 **dā** (FV) 1) lay across, overlay. /他在兩個房子當中～了一個梯子. He put a ladder between the roofs of the two buildings. 2) build, set up, a bridge, scaffolding, etc. ～橋 build a bridge. 3) take a boat, train, etc., to someplace. /我～下班飛機到華盛頓去. I'll take the next plane to Washington. 4) lift, carry (of two or more persons). /把床～過去. Move the bed over there. 5) touch, connect. /這兩根電線～上了. These two wires are touching. 6) suspend, hang. /把溼衣服～在繩子上. Hang the wet clothes on the line.

搭夥 **dāhwǒ** (VO) form a partnership, collaborate. /他們倆～做買賣. Those two formed a business partnership.

搭窩 **dāwō** (VO) build a nest (of a bird). /燕子在我家屋頂下才搭了一個窩. A swallow built a nest under the roof of my house.

打 **dá** (M) dozen. → 打 **dǎ**.

答 **dá** (FV) answer, respond to. /這個

問題我～不上來. I can't answer this question. → 答 dā.

答案 dáàn (N) answer, solution, to a problem, mathematical or otherwise (always in writing).

答復 dáfu (FV) answer. /他已經～了我的問題了. He has already answered my question. (N) answer. /你能給我一個～嗎? Can you give me an answer?

答數儿 dáshùr (N) answer, solution, to a mathematical problem.

達(达) dá (B) 1) reach, arrive at. 直～南京 non-stop to Nanking. 2) attain. ～成目的 attain one's objective. 3) prominent. 發～ succeed in life or in business. t

達到 dádàu (RC) reach, attain. ～目的 reach a goal.

打 dǎ (FV) 1) hit, strike, beat. /你別～他. Don't hit him. 2) break something. /我～了一個石宛. I broke a bowl. 3) carry aloft. ～旗子 carry a flag. 4) knit ～手套 knit gloves. 5) fetch, obtain. ～柴 get firewood; ～醬油 buy soya sauce. 6) play a ball game, cards. ～籃球 play basket ball. 7) send a message. ～電報 send a telegram. 8) hunt game. ～鹿 hunt deer. 9) type. 打一封信 type a letter. 10) pack, roll up, wrap. ～鋪蓋 make up a bedroll. 11) unpack, unwrap. /那些禮物不到聖誕節不許～. Those presents are not to be opened before Christmas. 12) go through some involuntary action, as to hiccup, sneeze. ～噴嚏 sneeze. 13) make a mark. ～圖章 stamp something with a chop. 14) inject a drug. ～血清 inject serum. 15) fire a weapon (at). ～飛機 fire at an airplane. 16) fight. /他們老～. They are always fighting. 17) drill a hole into something. ～洞 drill a hole. 18) estimate, determine, a rate, cost. ～傷耗 determine spoilage, breakage. /每月～出三十塊錢來買菜. I estimate spending thirty dollars a month for food. (CV) 1) from. /你～那儿來? Where are you coming from? 2) by way of a route. /～那條路來? Which way did you come? → 打 dá.

打敗 dǎbài (RC) defeat someone in a fight, game, lawsuit, etc. /他們把敵人～了. They defeated the enemy. /那個國家還沒～呢. That country has not been defeated yet.

打扮 dǎban (FV) 1) dress up (includes facial make-up). /她～得很漂亮. She dresses beautifully. 2) disguise. ～成一個商人 disguise oneself as a merchant. (N) the way one dresses or uses make-up. /我喜歡他的～. I like the way she dresses.

打包 dǎbāu (VO) 1) wrap a package. /我把那幾本書打了包寄走了. I wrapped those books up and mailed them. 2) unwrap a package. /他寄來的書我還沒～呢. I haven't unwrapped the package of books he sent me yet.

打氣 dǎchì (VO) 1) pump air into something, such as a tire. /請你給我前面的車胎打一點氣? Would you please put some air in my front tire? 2) encourage. /咱們得給他打一點氣. We should encourage him a little bit.

打鎗 dǎchyāng (VO) fire a rifle or other small arm. /他對着狼打了一鎗. He fired his rifle at the wolf.

打拳 dǎchywán (VO) hit with the fist, box. /我打了他一拳他就倒了. I hit him with my fist and he fell down. (N) boxing (M 場 chǎng).

打倒 dǎdǎu (RC) knock down. /～帝國主義! Down with imperialism!

打賭 dǎdǔ (VO) bet, place a bet. /咱們打一個賭吧. Do you want to bet?

打盹儿 dǎdwěr (VO) doze off, take a nap. /我聽演講的時候老～. I always fall asleep in lectures.

打電話 dǎdyànhwà (VO) make a phone call, call someone up. /他叫我下午給他打一個電話. He asked me to call him this afternoon.

打字 dǎdz (VO) type (words). /你會不會～? Can you type?

打發 dǎfa (FV) dispatch, send, order, a boy, a servant to do something. /我～一個佣人去送信.

I've sent a servant to deliver the letter.

打嗝儿 **dǎgéer** (VO) 1) hiccup. /他一緊張就～. He always hiccups when he's excited. 2) belch, burp. /打幾個嗝儿胃裡就舒服了. If you burp a couple of times, your stomach will feel better.

打官司 **dǎgwānsz** (VO) engage in a lawsuit. //他跟我打了好幾個月的官司了. He and I have been engaged in a lawsuit for several months.

打哈欠 **dǎhāchr** (VO) yawn. /我很睏,打了好多哈欠了. I'm so sleepy; I've been yawning and yawning.

打仗 **dǎjàng** (VO) be at war. /那兩國打了好幾年仗. Those two countries have been at war for several years.

打招呼 **dǎjāuhu** (VO) 1) gesture to someone (as to wave), greet. /我對他～可是他沒看見. I gestured to him but he didn't see me. 2) tell someone about something. /我得去跟他打個招呼. I have to go and tell him something.

打折扣 **dǎjékou** (VO) 1) give a discount. /我給你打個折扣. I'll give you a discount. 2) discount, discredit (as a story). /他說的這件事我們得打個折扣. We must discount the story he told.

打針 **dǎjēn** (VO) 1) get a shot. /我昨天打了一針盤尼西靈,比較好點了. I got a shot of penicillin yesterday and feel better now. 2) give a shot. /大夫給我打了兩針. The doctor gave me two shots.

打擊 **dǎjī** (FV) give someone a blow or shock. ～敵人 give the enemy a blow. (N) blow, shock. 受～ receive a shock.

打主意 **dǎjúyi** (VO) plan. /你打什麼主意呢? What are you planning?

打架 **dǎjyà** (VO) 1) argue violently. /他一開口就跟人～. He never opens his mouth without arguing. 2) come to blows, fight. /我看見你弟弟在跟人～. I saw your little brother fighting with someone.

打攪 **dǎjyǎu** (FV) inconvenience, bother. /別～他. Don't bother him. (IE) I've inconvenienced you (usually said by a visitor when leaving).

打開 **dǎkai** (RC) 1) open a book, can, box, window. /屋裡很悶,把窗戶～吧. It's stuffy in this room. How about opening the window? 2) turn on a television set, radio, etc. ～無線電 turn on a radio.

打來回儿 **dǎláihwér** (VO) make a round trip. /我到北平打個來回. I made a trip to Peiping and back.

打雷 **dǎléi** (VO) thunder. /乾～不下雨. It's only thundering, not raining.

打鈴 **dǎlíng** (VO) ring a small bell. /我聽見～了,去吃飯吧. I heard the bell ring; let's go eat.

打獵 **dǎlyè** (VO) go hunting. /他們在山裏打了三天獵. They went hunting in the mountains for three days.

打門 **dǎmén** (VO) knock on a door. /我打了半天門沒人答應. I knocked on the door for a long time, but nobody answered.

打拍子 **dǎpāidz** (VO) beat time, keep time. /沒人～我們就唱不齊. We can't stay together if nobody keeps time (when singing).

打牌 **dǎpái** (VO) play cards or mah-jong (or any game involving cards or tiles). /他們連打了兩天牌. They've played cards continuously for two days.

打砲 **dǎpàu** (VO) fire a cannon or other large-caliber weapon. /我們的船被敵人打了一砲. The enemy fired their cannons at our ships.

打破 **dǎpwò** (RC) 1) break something tangible. ～一個碗 break a bowl. 2) exceed, break, a record. ～紀錄 break a record. 3) alter, change, a concept, tradition, etc. ～傳統觀念 change a traditional concept.

打票 **dǎpyàu** (VO) buy or obtain a ticket. 打車票 buy a railroad or bus ticket; 打行李票 get a baggage receipt.

打入 **dǎrù** (RC) 1) branch out

into another line of business. /這
家公司也～鋼鐵工業了. This
company has gone into steel too.
2) force one's way into another area.
/他～了教育界了. He has
forced his way into educational circles.

打掃 dǎsau (FV) clean up.
/請你把這間屋子～～. Please
clean up this room. /你為什麼不
把這點儿醬油給～了? Why
don't you use up this bit of soy sauce?

打閃 dǎshǎn (VO) flash (of
lightning). /很遠的地方～哪.
There was a flash of lightning way
off in the distance.

打勝 dǎshèng (RC) win a victory over someone (in a fight, game,
lawsuit, etc.). /斯巴達人～了雅
典人. The Spartans defeated the
Athenians. /誰～了? Who won?

打手勢 dǎshǒushr (VO) make
hand signals, signal. /警察～叫
我停車. The policeman signaled
to me to stop.

打輸 dǎshū (RC) defeat someone in a fight, game, lawsuit. /誰
把羅馬～了? Who defeated the
Romans? /那個官司他～了.
He was defeated in that lawsuit.

打水 dǎshwěi (VO) fetch water.
/請你打一盆水給我洗洗臉.
Please fetch me a pan of water so I
can wash my face.

打算 dǎswan (FV) plan. /你
應該開始～～了. You should
start to make plans. (AV) plan to.
～回家 plan to go home. (N) plan.

打算盤 dǎswànpan (VO) 1)
calculate on an abacus. /你學過
～嗎? Have you learned how to
calculate on an abacus? 2) plan.
/開始做一件事情以前你得
先打打算盤. Before you start
that business you have to make plans
first. /你別打我的算盤. Don't
plan on my doing it.

打嚏噴 dǎtìfen (VO) sneeze.
/我打了三個口嚏噴. I sneezed
three times.

打聽 dǎtīng (FV) make an inquiry, ask about. /我想跟您～
一件事. I would like to ask you
about something.

打魚 dǎyú (VO) catch fish,
fish (as a profession). /今天有一
百隻魚船出海去～. A hun-
dred boats went out to sea today to
fish.

大 dà (SV) 1) be great, large, big (in
size, capacity, extent). /聲音太
～ The noise is too loud. /他的
權力很～. He has a lot of power.
2) be old (in comparing persons'
ages). /他比我～兩歲. He is
two years older than I. 3) be grown
up. /孩子～了. The children
have grown up. (A) greatly, freely.
～笑 laugh heartily; ～吃一頓 eat
a big meal. (B) oldest, first. ～姐
oldest sister. t→大 dài, 不大 búda.

大便 dàbyàn (FV) have a bowel
movement (euphemistic; lit., great
convenience). (N) manure, dung.

大車 dàchē (N) 1) two-wheeled
wooden cart drawn by an animal
(M輛lyàng). 趕～ drive a cart. 2)
principal assistant to the chief engineer (on a ship).

大清早 dàchīngdzǎu (TW) 1)
the very early morning. 2) very
early in the morning.

大前年 dàchyánnyan (TW) three
years ago.

大前天 dàchyántyan (TW) three
days ago.

大膽 dàdǎn (SV) be bold.

大道 dàdàu (N) main road.

大豆 dàdòu (N) soybean.

大多數儿 dàdwōshùr (N) the
great majority, the largest number.

大方 dàfang (SV) 1) be generous. 用錢很～ be generous with
one's money. 2) be poised. /這位
小姐態度很～. This girl is very
poised. 3) be dignified. /他舉止很
～. His manner was very dignified.

大概 dàgài (A) 1) probably.
/他～不來了. He is probably not
coming. 2) approximately. ～五塊
錢 approximately five dollars. 3)
briefly. /我～跟他說了說. I
talked to him briefly. (N) outline,
general picture. /我就能告訴
你一個～. I can only give you the
general picture.

大綱 dàgāng (N) outline
(written).

大後年 dàhòunyan (TW) three
years from now.

大後天 dàhòutyan (TW) three
days from today.

大話 dàhwà (N) big talk, boasting. 說～boast, talk big.

大會 dàhwèi (N) plenary assembly, general meeting, big rally.

大致 dàjr̀ (A) for the most part, in general. /～不差. It's correct for the most part.

大家 dàjyā (N) 1) everybody. /～都笑了. Everybody burst out laughing. 2) old well-known family (usually well-to-do).

大家彩儿 dàjyāhwǒr (N) the whole group (lp). /我們～全去罷. Let's all go together. /我請你們～吧. Let me treat all of you.

大街 dàjyē (N) main street.

大局 dàjyú (N) the general situation. /我們請校長顧全～,別辭職. We asked the principal to consider the general situation and not to resign.

大陸 dàlù (N) 1) continent. 亞洲～ the continent of Asia. 2) mainland. ～上的人民 people on the China mainland.

大量 dàlyàng (A) on a large scale. /這個工廠～出產汽車. This factory produces automobiles on a large scale.

大麥 dàmài (N) barley.

大門 dàmén (N) front door, main gate.

大米 dàmǐ (N) rice (uncooked).

大名 dàmíng (N) your name (h). /您～怎麼稱呼? May I ask your name?

大拇指 dàmújr̀ (N) thumb.

大炮 dàpàu (N) gun, cannon, artillery.

大人 dàren (N) grownup, adult.

大人物 'dàrénwu (N) personage, important person.

大掃除 dasǎuchú (N) general cleaning-up. (FV) clean up everything, clean house. /明天我們宿舍要～. Tomorrow our dormitory is going to clean house.

大聲 'dàshēng (A) <一儿> out loud, loudly. /你～說. Speak loudly. (VO) make one's voice louder. /你能不能大一點聲儿? Can you speak a little louder?

大使 dàshř (N) ambassador.

大師傅 dàshrfu (N) cook, chef (polite term).

大小 dàsyǎu (N) size.

大學 dàsywé (N) 1) college, university. 2) Great Learning (one of the Four Books).

大學生 dàsywéshēng (N) college student.

大體 dàtǐ (N) essence, essential content, structure, of an argument, essay, situation. /這件事情的～已經成功了. The essential part of this proposition has already been put into effect. (A) generally, essentially. /他這個意見～不錯. This idea of his is generally pretty good.

大廳 dàtīng (N) living room, parlor, in a large house (M間 jyān).

大雁 dàyàn (N) wild goose (M隻jī).

大意 dàyi (SV) be careless. /這回考試你可別～. You had better not be careless on this examination. → 大意 dàyì.

大衣 dàyī (N) topcoat, overcoat (M件 jyàn).

大意 dàyì (N) general idea, gist. /我知道這本書的～. I know what the gist of this book is. → 大意 dàyi.

大約 dàywē (A) 1) approximately. /～有十二個人. There are approximately twelve people. 2) probably. /他～不來了. He probably won't come.

呆[獃] dāi, ái* (SV)* be stupid. (B) silly, simple, idiotic. ～笑 silly laugh. → 待[呆] dāi.

呆板 dāibǎn, áibǎn (SV) 1) be monotonous. /他的生活很～. His life is very monotonous. 2) be rigid, wooden. /他這個人很～. He's a wooden individual.

待[呆] dāi (FV) stay. /我們～了一會儿. We stayed for a while. → 待 dāi.

逮 dǎi (dēi or děi (lp)) (FV) catch, seize. /他們～了一個賊. They caught a thief. → 逮 dài.

歹 dǎi (SV) be morally bad, reprehensible, perverse (of people only).

大 dài (B) ↓. → 大 dà.

大夫 dàifu (N) medical doctor.

代 dài (FV) substitute for. ～課 teach in place of someone. (M) generation. (CV) for. /我～你做. I'll do it for you. (B) 1) age, period, time. 古～ ancient times. 2) dynasty. 唐 ～ T'ang Dynasty.

代表 dàibyǎu (FV) represent. /我～我的學校參加市運會. I represented my school at the city athletic meet. (N) representative.

代價 dàijyà (N) sacrifice, cost. /用戰爭的方法來解決戰爭～太大了. The use of war to end war calls for great sacrifices.

代理 dàilǐ (FV) 1) be in charge as a substitute. /我～他的事情. I take care of his affairs. 2) represent a company. 3) deal with, handle, a product. /我們就～農業用品. We only handle agricultural products. (N) agent. (AT) acting. ～總統 acting president.

代數儿 dàishùr (N) algebra.

代替 dàitì (FV) represent. /你最好找他～你. You'd better ask him to represent you. (CV) in place of. /我～你當主席. I acted as chairman in place of you.

待 dài (FV) treat, deal with, people. /他～我好. He treats me well. (B) wait. 等～ wait for. →待 dāi.

待遇 dàiyù (N) 1) treatment. 公平～ fair treatment. 2) pay, salary. /那個公司～不錯. The salary that company pays is good.

帶[带] dài (FV) 1) carry along with, bring, take along. /把書～來. Bring the book here. 2) wear, put on, glasses, gloves, a flower. ～一朵花 wear a flower. 3) lead. ～路 lead the way. 4) have, contain, include. /這個顏色裏～一點儿綠. This color has a little green in it. /他說話～口音. He speaks with an accent. (M) for zones, regions. 這一～地方 this area. (B) 1) <-ル, -子> belt, string, bandage, ribbon. 鞋～ shoe string; 絲～ silk ribbon. 2) zone. 熱～ tropical zone.

帶勁 dàijìn (SV) 1) be powerful, strong. /他那句話很～. That remark of his carried great weight. 2) be interesting. /一邊喝啤酒一邊下棋真～. Drinking

beer and playing chess at the same time is great fun.

逮 dài (B) arrest, seize. →逮 dǎi.

逮捕 dàibǔ (FV) arrest. /警察～他因為他有謀殺的嫌疑. The police arrested him on suspicion of murder.

戴 dài (FV) wear, put on, glasses, gloves, a hat, a flower. /中國女孩子都不～帽子. Chinese girls don't wear hats. (B) honor. 愛～ love and honor. s

耽[躭] dān (B) delay.

耽擱 dānge (FV) 1) delay. /什麼事情把你～了? Why were you delayed? 2) stay. /他在那儿～了兩個鐘頭. He stayed there a couple of hours. (N) 1) stay. /我在那儿沒有幾天～. My stay there will be quite short. 2) delay.

耽誤 dānwu (FV) 1) procrastinate, delay. ～五分鐘 delay for five minutes. 2) let a chance go by, neglect. /他把那個機會給～了. He let that opportunity go by. 3) waste time. ～功夫 waste time.

單[单] dān (AT) 1) unlined (of clothing). ～衣 unlined garment. 2) single. ～人 single person. (A) solely, alone. /～靠父母不行. One cannot depend solely on one's parents. (B) 1) <-ル, -子> list, bill, ticket, receipt (M 張 jāng). 2) <-子> bed sheet. 床～ bed sheet.

單獨 dāndú (A) all alone. /我想～跟你談一談. I want to talk to you all alone.

單數 dānshù (N) <-ル> odd number (1, 3, 5, 7, etc.).

單位 dānwèi (N) unit.

擔[担] dān (FV) 1) carry with a pole on one's shoulder or on several persons' shoulders. ～着兩桶水 carry two buckets of water. 2) shoulder a responsibility. ～責任 shoulder a responsibility. →擔 dàn.

擔保 dānbǎu (FV) guarantee the performance or behavior of someone or something. /這個錶～一年. This watch is guaranteed for a year. /我～他不是一個賊. I guarantee he is not a thief.

擔負 dānfù (FV) bear a responsibility, burden (particularly financial). /那個學生的學費該我～. It's my responsibility to pay that student's tuition. (N) financial burden.

擔任 **dānrèn** (FV) be responsible for. /他不能～這麼多的工作. He can't be responsible for so much work.

擔心 **dānsyīn** (SV) be worried. /我很替你～. I'm very much worried about you. (VO) worry. /你擔什麼心？ What do you have to worry about? *or* Why should you worry?

膽(胆) **dǎn** (N) 1) gall bladder. 2) inside part of a thermos bottle. (B) <-儿,-子> courage. ～大 be brave, courageous.

膽小 **dǎnsyǎu** (SV) be timid.

撢 **dǎn** (FV) brush *or* dust off with a cloth or feather duster. ～土 brush off dirt.

撢子 **dǎndz** (N) duster made of cloth or feathers, with a handle (M把 **bǎ**).

石 **dàn** (M) picul (= 133⅓ lbs.). → 石 **shŕ**.

但 **dàn** (B) 1) but. 2) merely, only.

但凡 **dànfán** (**dànfēn** (lp)) (A) if, if only. /～能去的話，我一定去. If I can possibly go, I will. /～我有一線希望，我也不自殺. I wouldn't have tried to commit suicide if there had been any hope.

但是 **dànshŕ** (A) but. /我本來要去看電影～下雨了. I was going to go to the movies but it's raining now.

擔(扣) **dàn** (B) <-子> lead (on a carrying-pole). (M) picul (= 133⅓ lbs.). →擔 **dàn**.

淡 **dàn** (SV) 1) be weak, insipid. /我抽的煙很～. I smoke very mild cigarettes. /她做的菜老是很～. The food she cooks is always tasteless. 2) be light, pale (of a color). ～綠 light green. 3) be indifferent, unenthusiastic. /他對錢財看得很～. He is very indifferent about money. 4) be slow, poor (of business). /生意很～. Business is slow.

蛋 **dàn** (N) egg.

彈 **dàn** (B) bullet. 炮～ shell, projectile. →彈 **tán**.

當(当) **dāng, dǎng*** (FV) 1) serve as, become (of a profession). ～兵 become a soldier. 2)* think (mistakenly) that. /我～你不知道. I thought you didn't know. (CV) 1) in the presence of someone. /你別～着他罵他太太. You'd better not criticize his wife in front of him. 2) at *or* in the very same. ～天 (on) the same day. (PT) 1) 拿...～...take...as... /你拿我～傻子可不行. Don't take me for a fool. 2) ～...的時候at a time when...t →當 **dàng**.

當場 **dāngchǎng** (A) at that very place, on the spot. /那個賊～叫人逮住了. The thief was caught at the scene of the crime.

當初 **dāngchū** (TW) originally, in the beginning. /～這兒是一個學校. There was a school here originally. /～我不應該跟你結婚. I shouldn't have married you in the beginning.

當前 **dāngchyán** (AT) present, current. ～的問題 present problem.

當地 **dāngdì** (AT) local. ～新聞 local news.

當中 **dāngjūng** (PW) 1) (in) the middle. /湖～有一個島. There's an island in the middle of the lake. 2) (the space) between. /他在兩棵樹的～栓了一個吊床. He strung a hammock between two trees. /從這兒到那兒～沒有汽油站. There's no gas station between here and there.

當局 **dāngjyú** (N) (governing) authority.

當面 **dāngmyàn** (A) face to face. /這件事情你最好跟他～商量商量. You'd better discuss this matter with him face to face.

當儿 **dāngr** (N) space *or* time in between. 空～ empty space between things.

當然 **dāngrán** (A) of course, naturally. /這樣做～最好. Of course this is the best way to do it.

當時 **dāngshŕ** (TW) 1) that time. ～的式樣 the style of that

time. 2) then, at that (very) moment. /他叫汽車碰了,～就死了. He was struck by a car and died immediately. /昨天我把褲子刮石皮了, ～我没注意. I tore my pants yesterday without realizing it then.

當心 dāngsyīn (SV) be careful. /他做文那件事情很～. He does the work very carefully. (FV) be careful of, watch out for. /你～他. Watch out for him. /～有賊進來. Be careful of burglars getting in.

當選 dāngsywǎn (VO) be elected. /他當不了選. He won't be elected. (FV) be elected to an office. /他～主席了. He was elected chairman.

當 dǎng → 當 dāng.

擋 dǎng (FV) block. /這條路都～上了. This road is blocked. /請你別～路. Please don't block the road.

檔[枱] dǎng (B) files, records. ～卷 archives. → 檔 dàng.

檔案 dàngàn (N) file (M件 jyàn). /我把那封信裝在～裏了. I put that letter in the file.

檔案室 dàngànshr̀ (N) room for keeping files (M間 jyàn).

黨[党] dǎng (N) 1) political party. 共產～ Communist Party. 2) gang, group. 三K～ Ku Klux Klan. s

黨派 dǎngpài (N) party, clique, faction.

黨徒 dǎngtú (N) member, "follower," of a party, gang, group (derogatory).

黨員 dǎngywán (N) party or group member.

檔[枱] dàng (B) ↓. → 檔 dǎng.

檔子 dàngdz (M) for events or affairs, usually put down on record. 一～搶案 a case of robbery. /一～事没完,又出了一～. Before one crisis ends another begins.

當[当] dàng (FV) 1) think (mistakenly) that. /我～你走了呢. I thought you had left. 2) pawn. ～衣裳 pawn garments. (N) pledge. 贖～ redeem a pledge. (PT) ～...的時候 at a time when. → 當 dāng.

當真 dàngjēn (A) really (d). /你～要走嗎? Do you really

want to go? (VO) take something or someone seriously. /我是開玩笑呢,你別～. Don't take it seriously, I'm just joking.

dao see dau.

刀 dāu (N) <-子. -ル> 1) knife. 2) one-edged sword. (M把 bǎ). (M) 1) pack of paper containing one hundred sheets. 2) stroke, slash, with a knife. 切兩～ cut something in two strokes.

刀片ル dāupyàr (N) knife or razor blade (M 片ル pyàr).

倒 dǎu (FV) 1) turn something over or around. /那張畫ル掛～了,請你把它～過來. That picture has been hung upside down. Would you please turn it around? 2) change or switch things around. /把這兩把椅子～一下. Change those two chairs around. 3) buy or sell a store, business. /他把鋪子～出去了. He sold the store. 4) fall down or over. /牆～了. The wall fell down. 5) close down, fail (of an organization). /那家銀行～了. That bank went out of business. (RE) 1) down or over. 碰～ knock something down or over. 2) indicates overwhelming, stumping, confuting. /他把我問～了. He stumped me. → 倒 dàu.

倒換 dǎuhwan (FV) exchange, change. /你們兩個人把座位～一下. You two change seats.

倒換班 dǎuhwànbār (VO) change shifts. /巡警～站崗. Policemen stand guard on shifts.

倒霉 dǎuméi (VO) be out of luck. /我真倒了霉了. I am really out of luck. (SV) be unlucky, unfortunate.

倒手 dáushǒu (VO) change hands (lit. or fig.). /你別老用右手做倒倒手就不累了. Don't use your right hand all the time. If you change hands you won't get tired. /那個鋪子倒了三次手了. That store has changed hands three times.

島 dǎu (N) island.

搗[擣] dǎu (FV) 1) beat, pound. ～石卒 pound to pieces.

搗亂 dǎulwàn (VO) create a

disturbance, make trouble. /别跟
我～. Don't make trouble for me.
搞麻煩 dǎumáfan (VO) stir
up trouble, make trouble. /你老
跟他～. You're always stirring
up trouble with him. *or* You're always making trouble for him.

禱 dǎu (B) pray.
禱告 dǎugàu (FV) pray. /你
們吃飯以前～嗎? Do you pray
before each meal?

導[导] dǎu (B) 1) instruct. 指～ instruct,
direct. 2) conduct, lead. ～熱 conduct heat; 嚮～ a guide.
導演 dǎuyǎn (FV) direct a
play, movie. /他～過很多電
影. He has directed a number of
movies. (N) director.

到 dàu (CV) 1) go or come to a place.
/他～香港去了. He went to
Hong Kong. 2) at a time. /～兩點
我就得走了. I'll have to
leave at two o'clock. (FV) arrive,
reach. /他快～了. He'll arrive
soon. (RE) indicates that a result
has been achieved. /我終於找
～他了. I finally found him. /我
去買那本書可是買不～. I
went to buy that book, but I couldn't
get it. (PV) to a place, time, degree. 搬～學校來 move to the
school (here); 冷～零下十度 go
down to 10° below zero. (IE) Here
(as when answering a roll call).
到案 dàuàn (VO) appear in
court (for a serious crime). /那椿
搶案還有一個人沒有～.
There is still one person in that robbery case that hasn't appeared in
court.
到場 dàuchǎng (VO) be present.
/開會的時候他沒～. He didn't
turn up for the meeting.
到期 dàuchī (VO) reach a prearranged date, become due (of a
note or bond). /這本書已經～了,
該還了. This book is already due;
it's got to be returned.
到處 dàuchù (A) <ール> every-
where. /你上哪儿了? 我～找
你. Where were you? I looked
everywhere for you.
到達 dàudá (FV) arrive at a
place. /明天下午我們就～

香港了. We'll arrive in Hong Kong
tomorrow afternoon.
到底 dàudǐ (A) <ール> 1)
finally, after all, anyway. /～他還
是去了. He went after all.
/～她是你母親哪! After all,
she is your mother! 2) in the world,
in heaven's name (used for emphasis
in a question). /～是誰? Who in
the world is it? (VO) <ール> reach
the bottom. /到了底了沒有? Did
it reach the bottom?
到了兒 dàulyǎur (A) finally.
/～我找着他了. I finally found
him.
到任 dàurèn (VO) take office
after appointment or election. /在
他～以前,一切由你負責. Until
he takes office, you are responsible
for everything.
到頭儿 dàutóur (VO) reach
the end. /這條路已經到了頭儿
了. The road has come to an end.
(A) in the end. /他處處討好,～
還是沒人喜歡他. He flattered
everybody, but in the end people
still didn't like him.

倒 dàu (FV) 1) be inverted, turned upside down. /有的畫儿～着掛好
看. Some pictures look better
hanging upside down. 2) pour. ～茶
pour tea. 3) back up a car. /把
車～到這邊儿來. Back the car
up here. (A) 1) and yet, rather,
but (contrary to what you may say or
expect). /你叫別人捐錢,你
自己～不捐. You tell other people
to contribute money, but you don't
yourself. 2) backwards, upside
down. ～數 count backwards. (RE)
upside down. 掛～了 hang something upside down. (PT) ...～...
可是 (or 不過)... all right, but...
/那本書好～是好,可是太貴.
That book is good all right, but it's
too expensive. →倒 dǎu.
倒退 dàutwèi (FV) move backward. /火車～回去了. The
train backed up.

道 dàu (N) <ール> road, way. 鐵～
railroad. (M) 1) for courses in a
meal or for specific dishes. 一～菜
one course. 2) round of drinks. 3)
for levies of taxes, customs, duties.

/我們得上三～稅哪． We have to pay three different taxes. 4) for stages in any procedure. /第一～手續是填表． The first step is to fill out the forms. 5) for doorways leading into one another. /你得過兩～門才能進那間屋子． You have to go through two doors to get to that room. 6) for objects that are long and narrow. 一～牆 a wall; 一～河 a river. 7) coat of paint. 上一～漆 apply a coat of paint. 8) beam of light. 一～金光 a ray of golden light. 9) for commands or orders. 一～命令 an order. 10) time. 洗了三～ washed three times. (B) 1) <-子,-ㄦ> line. 畫一個～ draw a line. 2) Taoism. 老～ Taoist priest. 3) the way, the truth. 4) speak, say. ～賀 congratulate; ～白 speak the lines of an opera. *t*

道歉 **dàuchyàn** (VO) apologize. /我向他～了． I apologized to him.

道德 **dàudé** (N) morality, virtue.

道理 **dàulǐ** (N) 1) logical reason. 2) basis. /他說的話沒有～． There's no basis for what he says. *or* What he says isn't logical. 3) doctrine, teaching. 耶穌的～ the teachings of Jesus.

道路 **dàulù** (N) way, road (M 條 **tyáu**).

道謝 **dàusyè** (VO) extend thanks, express thanks, often when declining something. /請你替我向他～． Please thank him for me.

道喜 **dàusyǐ** (VO) congratulate. /我跟他道了喜了． I congratulated him. (IE) Congratulations!

稻 **dàu** (B) <-子> rice (the plant or unhulled grain) (M 棵 **kē**, 粒 **lì**).

稻草 **dàutsǎu** (N) rice straw (M 根 **gēn**).

的 de{底 (P) 2), 地 (P) 5) 6) 7), 得 (P) 8) 9)}, (RE)　(P) 1) added to N, PN, PW, TW, AT, NU-M, FV, SV, AV, RC, VO, A, or a clause forms nominal expressions and may translate variously as the one (s) that (who, which, etc.), *or* the . . . one(s) or as the noun suffix -er or in the possessive. Note that when added to FV and followed by SV which describe the manner of action of the FV, the SV may translate adverbially. 打獵～ hunter; 開車～ driver. /他買～都是好． The ones he bought are all good. /我喜歡那個紅～． I like that red one. /這報不是今天～． This isn't today's newspaper. /我～比她～漂亮． Mine is prettier than hers. /我要兩個三毛～． I want two of the thirty-cent ones. /她做飯做～比我做～還難吃． Her cooking is even worse than mine. /他學～非常快． He learns very fast. 2) followed by a noun, indicates that what precedes it modifies the noun. This can either "possess" the noun or describe it. 我～書 my book; 今天～報 today's newspaper; 鐵～櫃子 steel cabinet; 容易～問題 easy problem; 他去年買～那輛車 the car he bought last year; 念書～時候 study time, while studying; 停車～地方 (in) a parking lot *or* parking place. 3) used after FV or VO, or between a verb and its object, indicates the action of the verb is completed. 是 **shr** (不是 **bùshr** in negative sentences) often precedes the element in the sentence to be stressed. /我們在飯館吃～飯 We ate in a restaurant. /他是上禮拜六結婚～． He got married last Saturday. /我們是昨天來～． We came YESTERDAY. /他是從樓上跳下去～, 不是掉下去～． He JUMPED from the building, he didn't fall. 4) used as an infix between a verb and an RE to form the affirmative potential RC, able to do something. /你一天走～到嗎? Can you get there in one day? 5) added to certain SV, forms adverbial expressions. 很快～走 walk quickly. /廣義～說西藏話也算中國話． Broadly speaking, the Tibetan language is also considered Chinese. 6) added to A without any change in their meaning or function. /他突然死了． He died suddenly. 7) added to reduplicated SV, NU-M, ON, or certain combinations of opposites, forms adverbial expressions which can also be used as predicates.

/請你們一個一個～來． Please come in one by one. /這個禮拜天

氣忽冷忽熱～. The weather has been hot and cold off and on all week. /你快快儿～吧! Hurry up! /雨落在傘上的的答答～響. The rain makes a pitter-pat sound on the umbrella. 8) added to SV and followed by expressions which describe the degree of the SV, so ...(that). /他近視～連他太太都認不出來了. He's so near-sighted he can't even recognize his wife. /我累～都走不動了. I'm so tired I can't move. 9) added to FV and followed by a clause or descriptive expression, indicates that the clause or descriptive expression is the result of the FV. /我走～鞋都破了. My shoes are worn out from walking. /A: 你嗓子怎麼啞了? B: 唱～. A: Why are you so hoarse? B: From singing. (PV) 1) to a place, time, degree. /他爬～樹頂儿了. He climbed to the top of the tree. 2) followed by TW or PW, at, in, on. /我住～旅館裡了. I stayed in a hotel. (RE) in potential RC only, safe to. In the affirmative form, the infix (see 4) above) is dropped. /這個橋走～走不～? Is it safe to go across this bridge? /這水當然喝～. Of course this water is drinkable. (B) used between NU-M, plus, and. /兩個～兩個是四個. Two and two are four. (PT) 1) X～X, Y～Y some...some... /那些鷄蛋大～大小～小. Some of those eggs are large, some are small. /在地道車裏邊睡覺～睡覺,看報～看報. Some people sleep on the subway, others read newspapers. 2) 有～ (or 沒～) plus FV, there is something to (or there isn't anything to). /他們兩個人在一塊儿老有～說. They always have something to talk about when they're together. /家裏頭沒～吃. There's nothing to eat at home. → 的 dí, 的 dì.

的多 **dedwō** (P) used after SV or expressions with AV, much more. /這件大衣貴～. This coat is much more expensive. /他比我願意去～. He wants to go more than I do.

的很 **dehěn** (P) 1) used after SV, very. /他說的快～. He spoke very fast. 2) used after clauses with AV, very much. /他喜歡說話～. He likes to talk very much.

的哼 **deheng** (P) used after SV or FV implies that the condition or action stated is causing discomfort or irritation. /我累～. I'm tired. /你不悶～嗎? Aren't you bored?

的話 **dehwà** (P) used at the end of conditional clauses, with or without adverbs, such as 若是 **rwòshr**, 要是 **yòushr**, 如果 **rúgwǒ**, etc., if. /(若是 or 要是 or 如果)他來～,怎麼辦呢? If he comes, what will we do? /要是我是你～,我絕對不幹. If I were you, I definitely wouldn't do it.

的慌 **dehwang** = 的哼 **deheng**.

得 **dé** (FV) 1) obtain, get, receive. /我過生日～了很多禮物. I got many gifts for my birthday. /我溜冰～了一個獎章. I won a medal for my skating. 2) be ready, finished, completed. /飯～沒～? Is dinner ready yet? (RE) indicates readiness. /裁縫說你的衣服已經做～了. The tailor said your suit is ready. → 得 děi, 的 得 de.

得當 **dédàng** (SV) be proper, right. /這件事情他處理得不～. He didn't handle the matter right.

得到 **dédàu** (RC) obtain, get, receive. /你從他那儿得不到一個答案. You can't get an answer from him.

得分儿 **défēr** (VO) score (in a game). /昨天打橋牌我得的分儿最多. I scored highest in the bridge game yesterday.

得獎 **déjyǎng** (VO) win a prize, earn a reward, get a medal. /他得了一個獎. He won a prize.

得了 **déle** (P) indicates a suggestion. /咱們去～. Let's go. (IE) 1) OK OK (that's enough)! /～,我跟你道歉,你別再生氣了. OK OK! I'll apologize, but please don't be mad any more. 2) Oh go on! or Don't hand me that! /～吧!我才不信呢! Oh go on! I don't believe it!

得意 déyi (SV) 1) be satisfied, content. /他死了.你這會可該 ～了. You should be content now; he's dead. 2) be proud of something that one has done. /他那篇文章, 他做得很～. He's proud of the article he wrote. 3) be successful, prosperous. /他現在正是很～ 的時候. He is really enjoying a period of success now.

得 děi (AV) 1) have to, must, need to. /我～去一趟. I have to go there once. 2) certainly will be, must be. /你不快走就～晚. If you don't go quickly, you'll certainly be late. →得 dé, 的 de.

撑[拖]dèn (FV) pull on in sudden tugs, yank (lp). /別～我的衣裳. Don't yank my dress.

登 dēng (FV) 1) mount, ascend. ～山 go up a mountain. 2) press down with the foot. ～三輪儿 pedal a pedicab. 3) publish something in a newspaper or magazine. /這種廣 告～三天多少錢? How much would it cost to put this ad in the paper for three days?
　登記 dēngjì (FV) register, check in. /凡是外國人每年都 要～一次. All foreigners have to register once a year.
　登台 dēngtái (VO) be on the stage (of an actor). /他登過好 幾次台. He has been on the stage many times.

燈[灯]dēng (N) lamp, lantern, light (M 盞 jǎn).
　燈罩 dēngjàu (N) ＜-儿＞ lamp-shade.
　燈籠 dēnglung (N) lantern.
　燈泡儿 dēngpàur (N) light bulb.
　燈塔 dēngtǎ (N) lighthouse (M 座 dzwò).

等 děng (FV) wait for. ～火車 wait for a train. (B) 1) equal. ～號 equal sign. 2) and so on. 金銀銅 鐵～gold, silver, copper, iron, and so on. 3) and similar kinds of. 金銀銅鐵～金屬 gold, silver, copper, iron, and similar kinds of metals. (M) class, rank, grade, degree. 頭～first class. (PT) ～ ...再... wait until...then.

/～他到了我們再走. Wait until he comes, then we'll leave.
　等等 'děngděng (B) = 等 děng (B) 2).
　等候 děnghòu (FV) wait, wait for. /我們～他回來再決定吧. We'll wait until he comes back and then decide.
　等級 'děngjí (N) rank in an official hierarchy.
　等於 děngyu (FV) 1) equal (arith.). /三加二～五. Three plus two equals five. 2) be equal to, amount to. /那樣做～自殺. Doing that is like committing suicide.

戥 děng (B) ＜-子＞ small steelyard for weighing gold, jewels, medicine, letters, etc. ～錘 weight on a small steelyard.

凳[櫈]dèng (B) ＜-儿,-子＞ stool, bench (M 張 jāng, 條 tyáu). 板～stool, bench.

瞪 dèng (FV) stare at. /為什麼你老 ～我? Why do you always stare at me?
　瞪眼 dèngyǎn (VO) 1) open one's eyes wide. /他瞪着眼睡 不着覺. He can't sleep with his eyes wide open. 2) be angry with somebody. /你別跟我～. Don't be mad at me. 3) give someone a dirty look. /他瞪了我一眼. He gave me a dirty look. (A) unabashedly, openly. /他～不認賬. He denied it openly.

低 dī (SV) be low in position, rank, pitch, price, tastes. ～地 lowland. /他趣味很～. He has poor taste. (FV) lower one's head or voice. ～ 頭 bow one's head.

滴 dī (FV) drip. ～在地上 drip on the ground. (M) drop of any liquid. 一 ～水 a drop of water. (ON) sound of dripping, ticking, etc. ～答～答 or ～打～打 tick-tock tick-tock, drip-drop drip-drop.

堤 dī→堤 tí.

提 dī (B) ↓.→提 tí.
　提防 dīfang (FV) be on the alert for, be on guard against. /你 應該～他. You must be on the alert for him.

提溜 **dīlou, dīlyou, dīle** (FV) carry something in the hand with the arm hanging down the side of the body. /你～着這個箱子. You carry this suitcase.

的 **dí** (B) 1. →的 de, 的 dì.

的確 **díchywè** (A) surely, certainly, really. /我～不知道. I really don't know.

笛 **dí** (B) 1) <-子> flute. (M管 gwǎn, 根 gēn, 枝 jī). 2) <-ㄦ> whistle.

敵[敌] **dí** (B) 1) opponent. ～兵 enemy troops. 2) oppose. ～擋 resist; 不～ be no match for.

敵人 **díren** (N) enemy.

底 **dǐ** (N) <-ㄦ,-子> bottom. 鞋～ sole of a shoe. (B) 1) <-ㄦ,-子> background, origin, foundation. ～薪 basic salary. 2) <-子,-ㄦ> copy of a manuscript, receipt, etc., for record or reference. ～樣 copy of a pattern. 3) end. 年～ end of a year. →的{底} de.

底稿ㄦ **dǐgǎur** (N) 1) rough draft, general idea, on which a document or talk will be built by amplification. 2) copy of a manuscript, receipt, etc., for record or reference (M張 jāng). /這封信你最好留一個～. You'd better keep a copy of this letter.

底片 **dǐpyàn** (N) negative (photographic) (M張 jāng).

底下 **dǐsya** (PW) 1) underneath, below. 桌子～ underneath the table. 2) next in order. /～怎麼辦? What's next? 3) the lower part. /那個門上頭是黑的,～是紅的. The upper part of that door is black, the lower part red.

底細 **'dǐsyi** (N) background details, the real story. /你知不知道他的～? Do you know the details of his background (implying that something about them has been concealed)?

抵{牴觝} **dǐ** (FV) 1) substitute for, take the place of. /我～你的缺. I'll take your place. 2) be equivalent to. /他的能力～兩個人. He has the ability of two people. 3) compensate for, offset. /我把我的房子～了四千塊錢的債. I used my house to pay off the four thousand-dollar debt. (B) 1) push against something to hold it. ～住門 push against a door. 2) oppose. ～制 boycott.

抵抗 **dǐkàng** (FV) resist, oppose. /敵人～不了就退走了. The enemy was unable to put up resistance and had to retreat. (N) resistance.

抵押 **dǐyā** (FV) give something as security for borrowing money. /你拿什麼東西～? What are you going to give as security? (N) security.

地 **dì** (N) 1) the earth. 2) land, ground, earth. 荒～ uncultivated land. (B) <-子,-ㄦ> 1) background (as of a picture). 藍～ㄦ白花ㄦ white flowers on a blue background. 2) place, locality, territory. 此～ this place. t →的{地} de.

地板 **dìbǎn** (N) wooden floor.

地產 **dìchǎn** (N) property (land).

地球 **dìchyóu** (N) 1) the earth, the globe. 2) bowling ball. 3) bowling (the game).

地帶 **'dìdài** (N) district, region, zone. 危險～ danger zone.

地道車 **dìdàuchē** (N) 1) subway train (M列 lyè). 2) subway car (M輛 lyàng).

地點 **dìdyǎn** (N) place, location of something.

地方 **dìfang** (N) 1) place, locality, region. 2) space. /～不夠大. The space is not large enough. 3) thing (referring back to something already stated or understood). /這些～是他的長處. These things are her good points. (AT) local. ～政府 local government.

地震 **dìjèn** (N) earthquake.

地基 **dìjī** (N) foundation (of a structure) (M座 dzwò).

地址 **dìjř** (N) address (location).

地主 **dìjǔ** (N) landowner, landlord.

地雷 **dìléi** (N) land mine (m).

地理 **dìlǐ** (N) geography. /這儿的～我不熟. I'm not familiar with the layout of this place.

地名 **dìmíng** (N) <-ㄦ> name or designation of a place.

地平線 **dìpíngsyàn** (N) horizon when on land (M條 **tyáu**).

地線 **dìsyàn** (N) ground wire (M條 **tyáu**, 根 **gēn**).

地毯 **dìtǎn** (N) rug, carpet (M塊 **kwài**, 張 **jāng**).

地圖 **dìtú** (N) map (M張 **jāng**).

地位 **dìwèi** (N) 1) position, job. 2) social status.

地窨子 **dìyìndz** (N) basement, cellar.

弟 **dì** (B) 1) younger brother. 二～ second younger brother. 2) younger male cousin

弟弟 **dìdi** (N) younger brother.

弟兄 **dìsyūng** (N) brothers. /你們～幾個? How many brothers do you have?

的 **dì** (B) bull's-eye (on a target). 目～ aim, purpose. →的**de**, 的**dí**.

帝 **dì** (B) supreme ruler, emperor. ～國 empire; 上～ God.

帝國 **dìgwó** (N) empire.

帝國主義 **dìgwójǔyì** (N) imperialism.

第 **dì** (SP) used before numerals, forms ordinal numbers. ～一 first, in the first place; ～三層樓 the third floor.

遞(遞) **dì** (FV) hand over, pass. /我夠不着,請你～給我吧. I can't reach it; please pass it to me. (B) proportionally. ～加 increase proportionally.

dian see **dyan**.

diao see **dyau**.

die see **dye**.

叮 **dīng** (FV) bite (as a mosquito). /公蚊子不～人. The male mosquito doesn't bite. (B) entreat. ～囑 entreat. (ON) ding. ～噹 ding dong.

盯{釘} **dīng** (FV) 1) stare at. /台下的人都～着我,我很緊張. The whole audience was staring at me and I was very nervous. 2) keep an eye out for, keep an eye on. /送信的快來了,你～着點兒. The postman will come soon. Keep an eye out for him.

釘 **dīng, dìng*** (FV) 1)* drive something into a surface (as a nail), nail. /把板子～在牆上. Board up the windows. 2)* sew something on to something. ～釦子 sew a button on. 3) bear, withstand. /我幾天沒睡覺～不住了. I haven't slept for several days; I can't take it any more. 4) take care of, manage. /不要緊有他～着呢. It's O.K.; he's taking care of it. 5) make sure. ～問 ask for confirmation. (B) <～兒,-子> nail, spike (M根 **gēn**). 螺絲～ screw. →釘{釘}**dīng**.

丁 **dīng** (B) 1) male adult. 兵～ soldier. 2) mourn. ～憂 be in mourning for a parent. 3) <～兒> small chunk. 肉～兒 small chunk of meat. 4) T-shaped (derived from the shape of the character). ～字尺 T-square. s t

丁香 **'dīngsyāng** (N) lilac (flower) (M朵兒 **dwǒr**; 棵 **kē**).

頂 **dǐng** (FV) 1) carry something on one's head. /他頭上～着一個籃子. He's carrying a basket on his head. 2) push one's head against something. ～着風走 go against the wind. /羊～牆. The goat rammed the wall. 3) put something against something to hold it. /拿椅子把門給～上. Put a chair against the door. 4) take business away from someone. /新開的舖子把我們給～了. The newly opened shop has taken all our business away. 5) take the place of, substitute for. /你走了誰～你的缺? Who is going to have your position after you leave? 6) assume someone else's name. /他～別人的名字找事. He tried to get a job under an assumed name. 7) talk back, argue back. /我～了他兩句. I talked back to him. 8) be equivalent to. /他的能力～兩個人. He has the ability of two people. (A) most. ～小的那個孩子 the youngest or smallest child. /我～喜歡中國菜. I like Chinese food best. (N) <～兒> top part of something. 房～ roof. (M) for headgear of any kind. 一～帽子 a hat.

釘 **dìng** →釘**dìng**.

定{訂(FV)} **dìng** (FV) 1) settle, make

something definite, decide. /我～的是明天早上走. What I've decided to do is leave tomorrow morning. 2) order something. ～貨 order merchandise. 3) reserve something. ～座 reserve a seat; ～船 book passage. 4) have something delivered regularly. ～雜誌 subscribe to a magazine; ～牛奶 have milk delivered regularly. (B) certain, definite. 一～ for certain, definitely; ～量 a definite amount.

定錢 dìngchyan (N) money on deposit.

定罪 dìngdzwèi (VO) pass sentence in court. /你知道法官定了他什麼罪了嗎? Do you know what sentence the judge has passed on him?

定做 dìngdzwò (FV) order something made, have something made to order. ～的衣服 tailor-made clothing.

定規 dìnggwei (FV) select and decide on a date, person (among several applicants), place, thing. /買那個房子你～了沒有? Did you decide which house you want to buy?

訂 dìng (FV) enter into a contract. ～條約 sign a treaty. (B) check and make a decision. 校～者 editor. → 定{訂} dìng.

訂婚 dìnghwūn (VO) get engaged (to be married). /他們是上個月訂的婚. They got engaged last month.

diu see dyou.

dong see dung.

都{都} dōu (A) 1) both, all. 2) summarizes and adds up the items specified before it. /他天天～念書. He studies every day. /我父母～不在了. My parents are both dead. /我們不～去. We're not all going. 3) used after question words, every, any. /甚麼～好. Everything is fine. or Anything will do. 4) followed by a clause which contains a question word, -ever as in whatever, whenever. /你跟他說甚麼他～聽不見. Whatever you say to him, he won't listen. 5) used before the predicate of a sentence

ending in 了 and/or at the end of such a sentence, already. /他～四歲了. or 他(一)四歲了～. He's already four years old. /我走得腿～痛了. My legs are already sore from walking. (PT) 1) 連...～... even. /連他～不知道. Even he doesn't know it. 2) 就是...～... even if... still. /就是我有錢,我～不買. Even if I had the money, I still wouldn't buy it. → 都 dū.

兜 dōu (FV) carry something in a pocket made by gathering up the edge or edges of a piece of cloth or the like, such as an apron or a handkerchief. /拿你的手絹～着. Use your handkerchief to carry it. (B) 1) <-ル> pocket (in clothing). 2) encircle. ～抄 round up the enemy. 3) <-子> portable chair or carrier (used in traveling over mountains). 4) try to get customers. ～生意 drum up trade.

斗 dǒu (N) peck measure. (M) Chinese peck (316 cubic feet). 一～米 a peck of rice. (B) dipper-shaped object. 煙～ pipe (for smoking); 北～ the Big Dipper. SF of 鬪 dòu.

陡 dǒu (SV) be steep (as a hillside). /這條山路太～了. This mountain road is very steep. (B) suddenly. ～然 unexpectedly.

抖 dǒu (FV) 1) shake something. /你把身上的雪～一～. Shake the snow off yourself. 2) tremble. /他一看見我就～. As soon as he saw me he started to tremble.

抖摟 dǒulou (FV) shake out (as clothes). /你～～那個毯子. Shake out that blanket.

豆 dòu (B) <-ル,-子> bean, pea (M 粒lì,顆kē). 黃～ soybean; 土～ potato.

豆腐 dòufu (N) bean curd (M 塊kwai).

豆角ル dòujyaur (N) string bean.

豆芽ル dòuyár (N) bean sprout (M根gēn).

豆油 dòuyóu (N) oil extracted from beans.

讀 dòu (B) pause in speaking or reading. ～點ル comma. →讀 dú.

鬥〔鬦,鬪,鬭〕〔斗〕 **dòu** (FV) 1) fight.
~拳 to box. 2) purge (political)
(c). /我們得把他~了. We
must purge him. 3) put things together, combine (d). /把這兩個
桌子~起來. Put these two tables
together.
    鬥爭 **dòujēng** (FV) 1) fight,
struggle against. 跟自然~ fight
nature. 2) purge (c). /工人把廠
長給~了. The workers purged
the factory manager.

都 **dū** (B) 1) metropolis. ~會 city.
2) capital. ~城 capital city. t →
都 **dōu**.
    都市 **dūshr̀** (N) city, munici-
pality.

嘟 **dū** (B) ⼂. (ON) toot.
    嘟嚕 **dūlu** (M) bunch, cluster
(particularly of things joined together
at one end but hanging loose at the
other). 一~葡萄 a bunch or cluster
of grapes; 一~鑰匙 a bunch of keys.
    嘟噥 **dūnang** (FV) complain,
mutter, grumble, about something.
/你嘴裏~些什麼哪? What are
you muttering about?

督 **dū** (B) supervise, direct. 監~ supervise, supervisor.
    督促 **dūtsu** (FV) urge. /~他
們念書. Urge them to study.

讀 **dú** (FV) 1) read aloud. /請你把
這封信~給我聽聽. Please
read this letter to me. 2) take a
course, study. /他~政治. He
studies political science. →讀 **dou**.
    讀書 **dúshū** (VO) 1) read a
book. /我讀過那本書. I've read
that book. 2) study. /你在那個
學校~? At what school are you
studying?

毒 **dú** (SV) 1) be poisonous. /這條
蛇很~. This snake is very
poisonous. 2) be fierce, strong
(of sunlight). /今天太陽~極
了. The sun is really strong today.
3) be cruel. ~計 malicious
scheme. (FV) poison. /她丈夫叫
她給~死了. She poisoned her
husband. (N) poison.
    毒氣 **dúchì** (N) poison gas.
    毒藥 **dúyàu** (N) 1) poison.
2) poisonous drug.

獨 **dú** (B) alone. ~子 only son.
    獨唱 **dúchàng** (FV) sing alone.
/她在音樂會裡~了三個歌.
She sang three solos at the concert.
(N) solo (vocal).
    獨奏 **dúdzòu** (FV) play alone
(instrumental). /我給人家伴奏
過,但從來沒有~過. I've
accompanied people, but I've never
played alone. (N) solo. 鋼琴~
piano solo.
    獨立 **dúlì** (FV) gain indepen-
dence, do things independently. /美
國是那年~的? What year did
the United States gain independence?
/他的兒子可以~了. His son
is on his own now. (N) independence.
(AT) independent. ~國 independent
country.
    獨身 **dúshēn** (AT) unmarried.
~男子 bachelor; ~女子 unmarried
woman.
    獨裁 **dútsái** (SV) be autocratic,
dictatorial. ~者 autocrat, dictator.
/他父親很~. His father is very
dictatorial.

堵 **dǔ** (FV) stop up, block, a passageway or conduit. /我鼻子~上了.
My nose is stopped up. (M) for
walls. 一~厚牆 a thick wall.

賭 **dǔ** (FV) bet, gamble. ~場 gambling
house. /我跟你~五塊錢. I'll
bet you five dollars. (N) bet, wager.

肚 **dǔ** (B) <-儿,-子> tripe. →肚 **dù**.

肚 **dǔ** (B) <-子> stomach, belly. ~臍
navel. →肚 **dù**.
    肚儿 **dùr** (N) wide part of a
container, as a vase, barrel. /花
瓶的~很大. The wide part
of the vase is awfully large.

度 **dù** (M) 1) degree (of anything measured in degrees). 四十五~角
forty-five degree angle; 零下十~
ten degrees below zero. 2) time
(occurrence of doing something).
/他一~去過上海. He went to
Shanghai one time. (B) extent,
degree, rate. 溫~ temperature;
高~ altitude. →渡 **dù**.
    度過 **dùgwò** (RC) pass through
a period of time. 安然~難關 get
through a difficult period safely.
    度數 **dùshù** (N) degree. /那
個表上的~是多少? What does

that meter read (lit. How many degrees are on that meter)?

渡[度](B) dù (FV) ferry across. ～河 ferry across a river. (B) spend a period of time. ～假 spend a holiday.

鍍 dù (FV) gild, plate. ～金 plate something with gold.

duan *see* **dwan.**

dui *see* **dwei.**

dun *see* **dwun.**

冬 dūng (M) winter. 三～兩夏 several years (lit. three winters and two summers). (B) winter. ～大衣 winter coat. SF of 鼕 dūng.

　冬瓜 dūnggwa (N) vegetable marrow, winter melon.

　冬季 dūngjì (TW) (in) the winter season.

　冬至 dūngjr̀ (TW) (at the time of) the winter solstice.

　冬天 dūngtyan (TW) (in) winter.

東[东] dūng (L) east. 城～(the area) east of the city; 往～退却 retreat to the east. (B) 1) host. 作～ be a host. 2) owner, proprietor. 房～ landlord.

　東北 dūngběi (L) northeast. (PW) Manchuria.

　東邊 dūngbyan (PW) <-ㄦ> 1) (in) the east part *or* area. /城的～著火了. The east part of the city is on fire. /這個城白人住～,黑人住西邊. Whites live in the east part of the city, Negroes in the west. 2) to the east of. /我的家～是一個醫院. There's a hospital to the east of my house.

　東方 dūngfāng (PW) 1) (in) the east. 從～來 come from the east. 2) the Orient, the East.

　東家 dūngjya (N) 1) employer (of a servant). 2) owner (of a store or the like).

　東南 dūngnán (L) southeast.

　東西 dūngsyi (N) 1) thing (in the sense of an object, article). /那是甚麼～? What's that thing? 2) used when referring to someone who wishes to insult. Note that to say someone isn't a 東西 is worse than saying he is. /你這個～! You're a louse! /他真不是～. He's a despicable person.

鼕[咚][冬] dūng (ON) sound of beating on a drum. /嚇得我心～～的跳. I was so frightened that my heart was pounding.

懂 dǔng (FV) understand, comprehend. /他對這種事～的很多. He knows a lot about this kind of thing.

　懂事 dǔngshr̀ (SV) be sensible. /你怎麼這麼不～啊? How can you be so senseless?

董 dǔng (B) supervise, direct. 校～ trustees of a school. s

　董事 'dǔngshr̀ (N) member of a board of directors or trustees.

　董事會 dǔngshr̀hwèi (N) board of trustees, trustees.

洞 dùng (N) hole. 山～ mountain cave *or* tunnel. /我鞋底破了一個～. I have a hole in the sole of my shoe. /牙醫給我補了兩個～. The dentist filled two cavities for me.

凍[冻] dùng (FV) freeze. ～死 freeze to death. (SV) be cold, freezing. /這兩天真～得慌. It's been freezing the past two days. (B) <-ㄦ, -子> jelly.

動[动] dùng (FV) 1) move. /把他捆上他就不能～了. Tie him up so he won't be able to move. 2) touch, handle, something. /別～我的書. Don't touch my books. 3) utilize. ～腦筋 apply one's mind; ～武 use force. (RE) move physically or mentally. 勸不～ be unable to persuade someone. /風把汽車吹～了. The wind moved the car. (B) start. ～工 start work. (PT) ～不～就 easily, frequently. /那個孩子～不～就哭. That child cries at the drop of a hat.

　動作 dùngdzwò (N) action, movement.

　動感情 dùnggǎnchíng (VO) become aroused. /他這個人演說的時候很容易～. When that fellow makes a speech he lets his emotions run away with him.

　動機 dùngjī (N) motive, intention. /他的話雖說的粗魯,但～是好的. He may speak rudely, but his intentions are good.

　動脈 dùngmài (N) artery (blood vessel) (M條tyáu).

　動人 dùngrén (SV) be moving,

arousing, exciting. /他的演講很
～. His speech was very moving.
/她長的很～. She's very at-
tractive.

動身 dùngshēn (VO) start on a
trip, set out. /他～了沒有? Has
he left yet?

動手 dùngshǒu (VO) 1) start
to do something. /有這麼多房間要
掃,還不～就來不及了. With
so many rooms to clean, if I don't
start soon, there won't be time
to finish. 2) fight, come to blows.
/他們彼此罵了半天,可是沒～.
They cursed each other for a long
time, but they didn't fight. 3) give
someone a helping hand, participate.
/我洗碗他老不～. He never
helps me with the dishes.

動手術 dùngshǒushù (VO) un-
dergo a surgical operation. /我動
過一次大手術. I've had one ma-
jor operation.

動彈 dùngtan (FV) move. /她
被強盜嚇得半天不能～. She
was so frightened by the burglar she
couldn't move for a long time.

動物 dùngwù (N) animal (as
opposed to plants).

動物園 dùngwuywán (N) zoo.

動議 dùngyì (VO) make a
motion, move (in a meeting). (N)
motion. /今天開會沒人～. No-
body made any motions at today's
meeting.

動員 dùngywán (FV) mobilize.
/全國的軍隊都～了. All the
military forces in the country have
been mobilized. (N) mobilization.

duo *see* **dwo.**

端〔耑〕dwān (FV) carry something with
the hand or hands so that it is level,
as a tray. /那個盤子太重,他～
不動. That tray is too heavy for
him to carry. (B) 1) upright. ～
正 upright. 2) end. 兩～ both ends.

端架子 dwānjyàdz (VO) 1)
make an unnatural and dramatic gesture. /他端着架子走. He walks
stiffly. 2) act haughty in turning
down an invitation or refusing a request. /你跟我端什麼架子呢?
Why are you acting so haughty with
me?

端陽節 dwānyángjyé (N) 1)

(on) the fifth day of the fifth lunar
month. 2) the Dragon-boat Festival.

短 dwǎn (SV) be short in extent or duration. /時間很～. Time is very
short. (FV) 1) lack, be short.
/我就～一本書. I'm only short
one book. 2) owe someone money.
/他～我五塊錢. He owes me
five dollars. (B) shortcoming. 護
～ hide one's shortcomings.

短處 dwǎnchu (N) shortcoming,
fault, defect (especially of a person).

短篇 dwǎnpyān (AT) short
(of a story, document, editorial,
etc.). ～故事 short story.

段 dwàn (M) <-ル> 1) section, part,
piece (of things that have length in
space, as a road, or in time, as an
opera). 一～衣料 a piece of material; 一～戲 a part of an opera.
/這一～公路比那一～寬.
This section of highway is wider than
the other section. 2) paragraph. 一
～文章 a paragraph of an essay.
3) for stories. 一～故事 a story.
s

緞 dwàn (B) <-子> satin. ～帶 satin
ribbon.

斷〔断〕dwàn (FV) 1) break into segments (of something long). /他爬
山的時候繩子～了. When he
was mountain climbing, the rope
broke. 2) discontinue doing something, break a habit, a relationship.
/他們兩人已經～交一年了.
It's already been a year since they
broke off their friendship. 3) judge
a law case, sentence someone.
/法官把他～了一個無期徒刑. The
judge sentenced him to life in prison.
(A) definitely, certainly. ～不可
去 definitely cannot go. (RE) indicates breaking. 折～ bend and break,
break off. (B) judge, decide. 了～
settlement of matters.

斷定 'dwàndìng (FV) judge,
decide. /你怎麼能夠～他做的
不對呢? How did you decide that he
hadn't done it right?

堆 dwēi (dzwēi (M) (lp)) (FV) pile,
heap. /他把書都～在地上了.
He piled all the books on the floor.
(M) <-ル> 1) pile, heap. 擺了一
大～ make a big pile. 2) crowd.

一～人 a crowd of people. (B) pile, heap. 煤～pile of coal.

隊(队)dwèi (M) for groups of men, warships, airplanes, etc., usually in formation.一～兵 a squadron of soldiers. (B) 1) team, squadron. 籃球～ basketball team; 軍～army, troops. 2) line of people. 排～ form a line.

隊長 dwèijǎng (N) leader of a team.

隊員 dwèiywán (N) team member.

對(对)dwèi (FV) 1) face something. /他的窗户～着牆. His window faces a wall. 2) treat someone in some way. /你不能這麼～我. You can't treat me like this. 3) check one thing against another. ～鐘 set a clock to the right time. /～一～看看有沒有錯字. Check and see if there are any wrong words. 4) add one liquid to another. ～水 add water to something. 5) suit, agree with. /這種電影～我的口味. I especially like this kind of movie. (SV) be correct, right. /～,你說的很～. Right. What you say is very true. (CV) 1) to a person. /我～他說... I said to him... 2) facing something or someone. /我～着他坐着. I'm sitting facing him. 3) concerning, with regard to. /～這件事我還有意見. I have more to say concerning this matter. /我這樣說是～事,不是～人. My saying this was to direct attention to the business at hand, not the individual. (M) <-儿> pair. 一～花瓶 a pair of vases; 一～夫妻 a couple (husband and wife). (B) 1) opposite. ～手 opponent. 2) mutually. ～罵 curse each other. 3) <-儿,-子> couplet.

對半儿 dwèibàr (A) in half. /那塊蛋糕他們兩個人～分了. They divided the piece of cake in half. /我們兩個人～出錢吧. Let's go halves.

對不起 dwèibuchǐ (RC) be unfair to someone. /這件事情我～他. I was unfair to him in this matter. (IE) Excuse me. or I'm sorry.

對不住 dwèibujù = 對不起 dwèibuchi.

對待 'dwèidài (FV) treat, deal with, people. /他～我們很好. He treated us very well.

對方 dwèifang (N) 1) opponent. 2) the other party (as in a contract).

對付 dwèifu (FV) 1) get along with, make do. /要是你肯～,這個也可以用. If you can make do, it's also possible to use this. 2) deal with, handle, something which constitutes a problem. /這種事情很難～. This kind of thing is difficult to deal with. /我不知道怎麼～他. I don't know how to handle him. (A) making something do. /這個你先～着用吧. Try to make do with this one first.

對過儿 dwèigwòr (PW) (the place) across from or opposite. /～昨天着了火了. The house across from ours caught fire last night. /他住我～. He lives opposite me.

對勁儿 dwèijyèr (SV) 1) get along together, hit it off. /他們倆很～. Those two get along very well together. 2) be well, right (of a person, situation). /我現在有一點儿不～. I'm not feeling up to par right now. /他一看那個情形不～,他就跑了. He saw immediately that the situation was unfavorable, so he left. (VO) suit someone's taste. /這個大概對了你的勁儿了. This probably suits your taste.

對了 dwèile (IE) That's right.

對門儿 dwèimér (PW) the building or house across the street, river, etc., from another one.

對面 dwèimyàn (PW) <-儿> 1) the space (or place or side) opposite something or someone. /他正坐在我的～儿. He sat in the place directly opposite me. 2) facing each other. /他們兩個人～坐着. Those two are sitting facing each other.

對象 dwèisyàng (N) 1) opponent. /這次賽球你們的～是誰? Who's your opponent in this game? 2) partner. 找～ look for a partner, look for a husband or wife. 3) object under consideration or of one's motivations. 愛的～ object of one's love.

對題 dwèití (SV) be to the point (more often used in the negative). /你說的不～. What you said is not to the point.

對于 dwèiyú (CV) concerning, with respect to, for. /～這件事情你覺得怎麼樣? What are your feelings concerning this matter? /多運動運動～你有好處. More exercise would be good for you.

兌 dwèi (FV) exchange money. /請你給我把這些錢～成美金. Would you please change this money into American dollars for me?

兌換 'dwèihwàn (FV) 1) change money (give smaller denominations for larger, or vice versa). /我有一張兩塊錢的票子,你能不能給我～成兩張一塊錢的. I have a two-dollar bill. Could you give me two one-dollar bills for it? 2) exchange foreign currency. /我能在這ル～美國錢嗎? Can I exchange American dollars here? or Can I get American dollars here?

兌現 dwèisyàn (VO) 1) cash a check, bond, etc. 2) fulfill a pledge or a promise. /他說的話,從來沒兌過現 or 沒～過. He never lived up to his promises. /這張支票今天能不能～? Can this check be cashed today?

多 dwō (SV) be a lot, many, much (must be preceded by an adverb when used to modify a noun). /有很～錯ル. There are a lot of mistakes. (FV) followed by a NU-M, have or be a certain amount more or too much. /我們～五個人就好了. If we had five more people, that would be wonderful. /～出兩尺來. There's two feet too much. (A) 1) more. /你應該～吃一點ル. You ought to eat a little more. 2) too much (or many). /我～給了他五塊錢. I gave him five dollars too much. (NU) more than. 三塊～錢 more than three dollars (but less than four); 四百～年 more than four hundred years (but less than five hundred). t → 多 dwó.

多半 dwōbàn (A) <-ル> 1) for the most part. /去年我們～學法文. We studied French for the most part last year. 2) probably, most likely. /明天～下雨. It'll probably rain tomorrow. (N) <-ル> the greater part. /我太太的薪水佔我們收入的～. My wife's salary makes up the greater part of our income.

多咱 dwōdzen (TW)ᑫ when, at what time (lp). /你～可以來? When can you come?

多嘴 dwōdzwèi (VO) talk too much, open one's mouth at the wrong time. /都是你～,要不然那個買賣就成了. If you hadn't opened your mouth at the wrong time, we would have made a deal.

多會ル dwōhwer = 多咱 dwōdzen.

多了 dwōle (P) used after SV or expressions with AV, much more. /這樣好～. This way is much better. /我太太比我會說～. My wife is much more able to talk than I am.

多少 dwōshau (NU)ᑫ 1) how much, how many (when expecting an answer larger than about ten, or when there is no definite expectation). /他喝了～杯酒? How many glasses of wine did he drink? /我知道他有～錢. I know how much money he has. 2) used as the object of a negative verb, (not) many. /他沒有～. He doesn't have much (or many). /他沒請～客人. He didn't invite many people. (PT) 1) ...～,...～ no matter how much, whatever amount. /你要～我給你～. I'll give you whatever amount you want. 2)～...都(or 也) no matter how much, whatever amount. /那個表你給他～錢,他都(or 也)不賣. No matter how much money you give him for that watch, he won't sell it.

多少 dwōshǎu (A) followed by 一點ルyìdyǎr or 錢jǐ plus a measure indicates a little or a few, it doesn't matter exactly how much or how many. /他～會說句中文. He speaks a little Chinese.

多數 'dwōshù (N) <-ル> the majority. 大～ the great majority. /這些人裏～是學生. The majority of these people are students.

多謝 dwōsyè (IE) Many thanks.

多一半 dwōyíbàn = 多半 dwōbàn.

哆 dwō (B)‡.

哆嗦 dwōswo (FV) quiver, shake, shiver. /他手直～. His hands shake all the time. /他冷得直～. He's shivering from the cold.

奪(夺)dwó (FV) 1) take by force. ～棍子 pull on a pole someone else is pulling the other way. /他把我的手錶從我手裏～走了. He snatched my watch out of my hand. 2) compete for, fight over. /兩條狗～一塊骨頭. Two dogs are fighting over a bone.

多 dwó (A)^q 1) used before SV or AV, how (to what extent). /他有～高? How tall is he? /他～高啊! How tall he is! 2) used after 沒有, (not) so very. /他沒～高. He isn't very tall. (PT) 1) 要～..., 有～... as... as one could possibly want. /那個地方要～好有～好. That place is as good a one as you could possibly want. 2) ～...都 (or 也) it doesn't matter how... /給我一根兒繩子, ～長都行. Give me a piece of rope; it doesn't matter how long it is. → 多 dwō.

多麼 dwóma = 多 dwó.

躲(躱)dwó (FV) 1) avoid. ～雨 take cover from the rain. /他～她. He avoids her. 2) hide. /他在地窖子～着呢. He's hiding in the cellar.

躲避 dwóbì (FV) 1) avoid. /這種事情你～不了的. You can't avoid this. 2) hide. /他來了, 我們～～吧! He's coming. Let's hide!

躲藏 dwótsáng (FV) hide. /他們在山洞裏～了一個禮拜. They hid in a mountain cave for a week.

朶(朵)dwó (M) 1) <-ㄦ> for single flowers. 2) for clouds. 3) for dragon flies (lp).

舵 dwò (N) rudder, helm. 掌～ man a tiller.

舵輪 dwòlwún (N) <-ㄦ> steering wheel.

踩(跺)dwò (FV) stamp on something. /把那個蟑螂～死. Stamp on that cockroach.

跺腳 dwòjyǎu (FV) stamp the foot. /他氣的直～. He stamped his foot in anger.

吨(噸)dwūn (M) ton.

蹲 dwūn (FV) 1) squat, crouch. /他們圍着火～着. They squatted around the fire. 2) stay, reside. (d) /他在上海～過. He has stayed in Shanghai before. →蹲 tswún.

撤 dwūn (FV) 1) jolt, bounce up and down. /那個娃娃太小你別～她. Don't bounce the baby up and down, she's too small. /我們～了一下子. We were given a jolt (physical). 2) tap something on an object in order to pack down its contents, as a cigarette. /把香煙～幾下再點. Tap the cigarette a few times before you light it.

頓 dwùn, dwūn* (FV) 1) pause in reading. /念到這兒得～一下. Read up to here and then pause. 2) *pause in writing a stroke of a Chinese character. ～筆 pause in writing a stroke. (M) 1) short time, spell. 挨一～説 be scolded a bit. 2) for meals. ～飯 a meal. (B) 1) prepare. 安～ get ready for. t

燉(炖)dwùn (FV) 1) stew. /鷄要～多少時候? How long should I let the chicken stew? 2) warm, heat, a liquid. ～酒 warm wine.

鈍 dwùn (SV) be dull, dulled, of a knife blade, etc. (B) dull, not clever. 遲～ dull-witted.

顛 dyān (FV) 1) jolt, joggle. /路不平把我的箱子都～開了. The road was so rough that my suitcase was joggled open. 2) try the weight of something by lifting it. /我一～才知道不輕. As soon as I lifted it I knew it wasn't light. (SV) be rough, bumpy. /這輛車很～. This is a bumpy car. (B) 1) top. 山～ mountain summit. 2) beginning. ～末 from beginning to end. 3) invert. ～倒 upside down.

顛顛 dyāndyan (FV) estimate the weight of something, heft, joggle. /你～這封信重嗎? Does this letter feel overweight to you?

典 dyǎn (FV) 1) borrow money on or

lend money in return for <u>land or a house which is taken over by the lender as security</u>. /我~了兩畝地. I've borrowed money on two acres of land. *or* I've lent out money in return for two acres of land. (N) classical allusion. (B) 1) standard, rule.~章 regulations. 2) book <u>to record standards of some kind</u>. 字~ dictionary.

典故 **dyǎngu** (N) 1) classical allusion. /他的文章用了很多~所以我不太懂. He uses a lot of classical allusions in his writing, so I don't understand it very well. 2) historical *or* legendary basis <u>of a custom, saying, literary work</u>. /那齣戲有什麼~? What's the historical legend behind that Chinese opera?

典型 **dyǎnsyíng** (N) model, example.

點[點][点] **dyǎn** (FV) 1) ignite, light. ~火 light a fire. 2) check one by one.~貨 check over goods. 3) order, select, <u>things from a list of items</u>.~菜 order food (<u>in a restaurant</u>). 4) give <u>someone</u> a hint. /我得拿話~他. I'll have to give him a hint. 5) make a dot <u>with a writing instrument</u>.~一個點儿 make a dot. 6) drop <u>small amounts of liquid</u> into <u>something</u>.~眼藥 put eyedrops in one's eyes. 7) touch lightly. 用竹竿~地 touch the ground lightly with a bamboo rod. 8) undulate. ~手 beckon with the hand. (M) 1) <u>with the noun</u>鐘**jung**, o'clock, hour. 三~鐘 three o'clock *or* three hours. 2) point, matter. /這一~我們得注意. We must focus our attention on this matter. (N) <一儿> point, period. 三~六 three point six; 點一個~ put a period. (B) 1) point in space. 中~ the center. 2) time. 誤~ be late. 3) <一儿,一子> drop of liquid. 雨~ raindrop.

點心 **dyǎnsyīn** (N) 1) snack, refreshment. 2) pastries, cookies. 3) breakfast (lp).

點頭 **dyǎntóu** (VO) 1) nod *or* bow <u>in greeting</u>. /我們見面儿的時候連頭都不點. We don't even nod when we meet. 2) nod

assent. /他聽了以後,點了~. After he listened he nodded his head in agreement. 3) say yes, agree. /他已經~了. He's already said yes.

點儿 **dyǎr** (N) † (N), (B) 3). (M) a little bit <u>of anything</u> (<u>with NU</u> **yī** only). /我要一~水. I want a little water. 2) <u>used after SV or A</u>, (a little)... er. /你早~來. Come earlier. /還是他高~. He is still taller. (B) time. 鐘~ hour. → 一點儿 **yīdyǎr**.

店 **dyàn** (N) 1) store, shop (M家**jyā**). 2) inn (<u>old-fashioned</u>) (M家**jyā**). 住~ stay at an inn.

店員 **dyànywán** (N) clerk.

墊[塾] **dyàn** (FV) 1) pad, cushion. /我找不着什麼東西~椅子. I can't find anything to pad the chair. 2) put <u>something under something in order to make it smooth or level</u>. /桌子腿底下~一點儿紙就平了. Put some paper under the leg of the table and then it'll be level. 3) pay out <u>money</u> for <u>someone</u>, <u>expecting reimbursement</u>. /我給你~了五塊錢. I payed the five dollars for you. (B) <一子,一儿> pad, cushion. 椅~子 chair cushion.

惦 **dyàn** (B) feel concerned about. ~念 feel concerned about.

惦記 **dyànji** (FV) feel concerned about. /你別~我. Don't worry about me.

電[电] **dyàn** (N) electricity. (B) telegram. 來~ incoming telegram.

電報 **dyànbàu** (N) telegram (M 封**fēng**). 翻~ code *or* decode a telegram.

電報機 **dyànbàujī** (N) telegraph apparatus.

電報局 **dyànbàujyú** (N) telegraph office, <u>either a place where telegrams can be sent and received, or a business office</u> (M家**jyā**).

電表 **dyànbyǎu** (N) 1) electric current meter. 2) electric clock.

電車 **dyànchē** (N) streetcar, trolley car (M輛**lyàng**).

電車站 **dyànchējàn** (N) streetcar stop.

電氣 **dyànchi** (N) electricity.

電池 **dyànchŕ** (N) electric battery.

電燈 **dyàndēng** (N) electric light (M 盞 **jǎn**).

電燈泡儿 **dyàndēngpàur** electric light bulb.

電動機 **dyàndùngjī** (N) electric motor.

電話 **dyànhwà** (N) telephone. 打~ make a telephone call.

電話局 **dyànhwàjyú** (N) telephone company *or* exchange.

電熨斗 **dyàn'yùndǒu** (N) electric iron (for clothes).

電鈴儿 **dyànlíngr** (N) electric bell. 按~ ring a bell by pressing a button.

電流 **dyànlyóu** (N) electric current.

電碼儿 **dyànmǎr** (N) 1) telegraph *or* radio code. 2) code signal for a single letter or word. 翻~ encode *or* decode.

電門 **dyànmén** (N) 1) electric switch.

電瓶 **dyànpíng** (N) battery (electric). 乾~ dry cell.

電視 **dyànshr̀** (N) 1) television (medium of communication). 2) television set (M 架 **jyà**).

電線 **dyànsyàn** (N) electric wire (M 條 **tyáu**, 根 **gēn**).

電台 **dyàntái** (N) radio station.

電梯 **dyàntī** (N) elevator (electric).

電影 **dyànyǐng** (N) <-儿> movie (M 張 **jāng**; 場 **cháng**).

電影院 **dyànyǐngywàn** (N) movie theatre (M 家 **jyā**).

雕[彫] (FV) (B), 凋 (B), 鵰 (N) } **dyāu** (FV) carve, sculpture. (N) eagle (M 隻 **jr̄**). (B) withered. ~謝 wilt.

雕刻 **dyāukè** (FV) sculpture, carve. ~家 sculptor. (N) carving, sculpture.

叼 **dyāu** (FV) hold between the teeth, as a pipe. /鳥儿~着一個蟲儿. The bird has a worm in his beak.

掉 **dyàu** (FV) 1) fall, drop. /你的帽子~了. Your hat fell off. 2) lose weight. /我~了二十磅. I've lost twenty pounds. 3) exchange, change (d). /這個帽子太大, 能不能~一個? This hat is too big. May I exchange it for another one? 4) turn around. ~頭

turn the head. 5) lose, misplace. (d). /我~了五塊錢. I've lost five dollars. (RE) off, out. /碰~ knock something off; 洗~ wash out.

掉點儿 **dyàudyǎr** (VO) sprinkle (of rain). /又~了. It's sprinkling again.

釣 **dyàu** (FV) catch with hook and line. ~魚 catch fish, go fishing.

釣竿 **dyàugān** (N) <-儿> fishing rod (M 根 **gēn**).

釣鈎 **dyàugōu** (N) <-儿> fish-hook.

調 **dyàu** (FV) transfer someone. ~兵 move troops. /總公司把他~走了. The head office transferred him. (B) <-子, -儿> melody, tune. 小~儿 folk song. →調 **tyáu**.

調查 **dyàuchá** (FV) investigate. /保險公司已經~過了. The insurance company has already made an investigation. (N) investigation, examination.

調動 **dyàudùng** (FV) move around, shift, personnel or things. /最近我們公司裡~了不少人. Our company has shifted a lot of people around lately. (N) shifting, moving around.

吊[弔] **dyàu** (FV) 1) suspend, hang. /把那個燈~起來. Hang up that lantern. 2) line a garment. /我把那件大衣~了一個皮裏子. I put a fur lining in my overcoat. 3) pay respects to the deceased, visit one's grave. /他去~他死去的朋友. He went to visit the grave of his deceased friend. (B) pay a visit of condolence to. ~唁 condole with.

爹 **dyē** (N) papa, daddy.

跌 **dyē, dyé** (FV) 1) stumble, fall down (d). /他~傷了. He fell and injured himself. 2) drop (of a price). /價錢~了. The price has dropped.

迭 **dyé** (B) repeatedly. ~次 again and again. SF of 疊 **dyé**.

碟 **dyé** (B) <-儿, 子 > plate, dish. 飛~ flying saucer.

疊[疊][迭] **dyé** (FV) fold. /把衣服~

起來. Fold up the clothes. (B) duplicate, repeat. 重～ duplicate.

跌 dyé→跌 dyě.

丢 dyōu (FV) 1) lose, misplace. /我的書～了. My book is lost. 2) leave behind. /他把我們～在家裏不管了. He thought nothing of leaving us behind at home. 3) throw (d). /你別把烟頭儿往字紙簍裏～. Don't throw cigarette butts in the wastebasket. (RE) become lost. 走～了 get lost en route.

　　丢掉 dyōudyàu (RC) 1) lose. /我不願意～你這樣儿的一個朋友. I don't want to lose a friend like you. 2) discard, throw away (d). /他把剩菜都～了. She threw out all the leftovers.

　　丢臉 dyōulyǎn (VO) 1) lose face. /我不覺得我丢什麼臉. I don't feel I lost much face. 2) disgrace someone. /我弟弟偷朋友的錢, 真丢我的臉. I was disgraced when my younger brother stole money from a friend. (SV) be humiliating, shameful, disgraceful.

　　丢人 dyōurén = 丢臉 dyōulyǎn.

子 dz (B) 1) commonly used noun and nominalizing suffix. 椅～chair; 刷～brush; 矮～ short person; 戲～actor. 2) added to certain nouns with a diminutive effect. 刀～ knife. → 子 dz.

資 dz (B) 1) fee. 工～wage. 2) capital. ～本 capital. 3) resources. 天然～源 natural resources. 4) talent. 天～ natural talent. 5) aid, assist. ～敵 help the enemy.

　　資格 dzge (N) qualification for anything. /他不夠～. He's not sufficiently qualified.

　　資本主義 dzběnjǔyì (N) capitalism.

　　資産階級 dzchǎnjyējí (N) capitalist class.

滋 dz (FV) spurt out (lp). /水～出來了. Water spurted out. (B) 1) nourishment. ～養 nourish, be nourishing. 2) taste.

　　滋味 dzwei (N) <-儿> 1) taste, flavor. 2) sensation, taste (of experience). /我沒嘗過當兵的～. I've never had a taste of military life.

姿 dz (B) posture, carriage. 風～ graceful posture.

　　姿勢 'dzshr (N) bodily posture, stance, form, (as when playing some athletic game).

子 dz (B) 1) child, son. ～女 sons and daughters. 2) egg, roe. 魚～ fish roe. 3) <-儿> seed. 瓜～儿 melon seed. 4) <-儿> egg (of poultry). 雞～儿 chicken eggs. 5) <-儿> bullet. 鎗～儿 bullet. 6) <-儿> money, wealth (lp). 7) <-儿> copper (penny). 8) added to certain elements to indicate persons. 男～ man; 女～ woman. 9) added as a title to names of ancient philosophers. 孔～ Confucius; 莊～ Chuang-tzu. 10) <-儿> piece for a board game. 棋～ chessman, checker. (M) skein of wool, thread, etc. 一～線 a skein of thread. → 子 dz.

　　子彈 dzdàn (N) bullet, cartridge (M 顆 kē, 粒 lì, 發 fā).

仔 dz (B) ↓. → 崽{仔} dzǎi.

　　仔細 dzsyì (SV) be careful, attentive, meticulous. /他做事很～. He does his work carefully. (A) carefully. /～點儿寫. Write carefully.

紫 dz (SV) be purple. ～花 purple flower. (N) purple, purple color. 深～ deep purple.

字 dz (N) <-儿> 1) word. 2) character (unit symbol of the Chinese writing system). 3) message. /給他留個～. Leave him a message. 4) courtesy name. /他的～是大成. His courtesy name is Ta-ch'eng. 5) contract, lease, deed.

　　字典 dzdyǎn (N) dictionary (M 本 běn).

　　字母 dzmǔ (N) <-儿> 1) alphabet. 2) letter in an alphabet.

　　字體 dztǐ (N) 1) type-face, type-style. 2) style of handwriting.

　　字紙簍 dzjrlǒu (N) <-儿> wastebasket.

自 dz (B) self, oneself. ～信心 self-confidence. (CV) 1) from. ～始至終 from beginning to end. 2) since a time. ～他來那天 since the day he came. (A) naturally, of course. /～有辦法. Of course there's a way.

自大 **dz̀dà** (SV) be conceited.

自動 **dz̀dùng** (AT) automatic. ~步鎗 automatic rifle; ~手錶 self-winding watch. (A) voluntarily. /他~去的. He went voluntarily.

自己 **dz̀jǐ** (N) oneself. /我~拿. Let me get it myself. /他老誇~. He always brags about himself. (B) on the same side (<u>as in a war</u>). ~人 people belonging to the same group. (A) by oneself. /我不~去. I'm not going alone.

自治區 **dz̀jr̀chyū** (N) self-governing district.

自主 **dz̀jǔ** (FV) decide by oneself. /這件事由我~. This matter will be decided by me alone.

自傳 **dz̀jwàn** (N) autobiography.

自覺 **dz̀jywé** (FV) realize, be aware of. /他做錯了事,他還不~. He still isn't aware of the things he did wrong.

自來水 **dz̀láishwěi** (N) <-ㄦ> tap water, running water.

自來水筆 **dz̀láishwéibǐ** (N) fountain pen (M 管 **gwǎn**, 枝 **jr̄**).

自立 **dz̀lì** (FV) be financially independent. /他現在能~了. He's able to be financially independent now.

自滿 **dz̀mǎn** (SV) be self-satisfied.

自然 **dz̀ran** (SV) be natural, normal. /她的頭髮很~. Her hair is very natural looking. (A) 1) of course, naturally. /他~不會來. Of course he won't come. 2) naturally (<u>not by external means</u>). /讓他們的感情~發展吧. Let their affection develop naturally.

自然 **dz̀rán** (N) 1) nature. ~現象 natural phenomenon. 2) natural science (<u>as a subject</u>).

自殺 **dz̀shā** (FV) commit suicide. /昨天瘋人院裏有一個人~了. Yesterday a patient in the mental hospital committed suicide.

自習 **dz̀syí** (FV) study on one's own. /去年他沒有上學,只在家~. Last year he didn't go to school; he studied at home on his own. 2) do homework. /我今天晚上要~. I've got to do homework tonight. (N) study hall (<u>the class</u>).

自行車 **dz̀syíngchē** (N) bicycle. (M 輛 **lyàng**).

自私 **dz̀sz̄** (SV) be selfish.

自從 **dz̀tsúng** (CV) ever since. /~我得病以後,我就不抽煙了. I haven't been smoking ever since I got sick.

自由 **dz̀yóu** (N) liberty, freedom. (SV) be free (<u>unrestricted</u>). /我們現在沒有小孩,所以很~. We don't have any children yet, so we're not tied down. (A) freely, voluntarily. ~參加 join voluntarily.

紮[紮][扎] **dzā** (FV) bind. ~辮子 fasten the end of a pigtail; ~裹腿 put on puttees. (M) <u>for things such as thread, rope, silk, and the like, tied together in a bundle</u>. 一~線 a bundle of thread.

咱 **dzá** → 咱 **dzán**.

砸 **dzá** (FV) 1) smash, break, <u>something fragile, usually by dropping it unintentionally</u>. /他把你的茶壺~了. He broke your teapot. 3) fail. /那件生意~了. That business failed. (RE) <u>indicates the result of the action has failed</u>. /他辦~了. He failed in doing it.

雜[雜][杂] **dzá** (SV) be mixed, miscellaneous. ~貨鋪 general store. /他請的客人很~. The guests he invited were a mixed group. (FV) mix. /我不喜歡跟那些人~在一塊兒. I don't like to mix with those people.

雜貨 **dzáhwò** (N) groceries.

雜技 **dzájì** (N) variety show, vaudeville.

雜誌 **dzájr̀** (N) magazine (M 本 **běn**, 份 **fèn**).

災[災] **dzāi** (N) disaster, calamity, <u>such as flood, famine, pestilence, etc.</u> 水~ a flood.

災荒 **dzāihwang** (N) calamity, disaster, <u>involving crops</u>.

栽 **dzāi** (FV) 1) plant. ~樹 plant a tree. 2) fall, tumble. /他~到水裏去了. He fell into the water. 3) lose face because of failure. /這囘我算~了. I admit that this time I lost face.

載 **dzǎi, dzài*** (FV)* carry, hold (of a vehicle, boat, or other means of transport). /這輛卡車能～多少貨? How much freight will this truck carry? (B)* 1) to record, register. 登～ contain, carry (as a newspaper). 2) year. 一年半～ a year or so.

載重汽車 **dzǎijùngchì'che, dzàijùngchì'chē** (N) truck, lorry (M輛lyàng).

宰 **dzǎi** (FV) slaughter an animal (as a sacrifice or for eating). ～牛 slaughter a cow. (B) rule, govern. 主～ ruler; ～相 prime minister. t

崽{仔} **dzǎi** (B) 1) <-子,-ル> baby animal (also used as a term of abuse). 狗～ puppy. 2) child. 西～ "boy," servant (working for Westerners, a bit insulting).

在 **dzài** (FV) 1) exist, be alive. /糧食問題還～. The problem of food still exists. /他祖父不～了. His grandfather is dead. 2) followed by a place word, be at or in or on. /他不～家. He isn't at home. 3) be a member of a religious faith or a political group. /他～黨. He is a party member. 4) depend on, be up to. /讓不讓他復學,就～學校當局了. Whether or not he'll be readmitted to the school will depend on the school authorities. (CV) 1) at, in. /我～飯館儿吃午飯. I eat lunch at a restaurant. 2) according to. /～我看,這輛車太貴. As I see it, this car is too expensive. (PV) followed by PW or TW, at, in, on. /放～桌子上. Put it on the table. (A) similar to am, is, are, was, were, etc., followed by a verb plus -ing to show continuous action (usually preceded by 正jèng). /他正～吃飯哪. He is eating.

在乎 **dzàihu** (FV) 1) care about, be concerned with. 滿不～ not care a bit. 2) depend on, be up to. /你去不去～你自己. Whether or not you go depends on you yourself.

再 **dzài** (A) 1) again, once more (in the future). /明天～來一次. Come again tomorrow. 2) then.

/你等吃完了～走. Eat and then go. or Don't leave until you finish eating. 3) used before SV, more, -er. /沒有～好的了. There isn't a better one. /～好沒有了. It couldn't be better. (PT) 1) ～...也 followed by a negative expression even though... still (not).... /你～高也沒有樓高. Even if you were taller, you still wouldn't be as tall as a building. 2) ～也... followed by a negative expression (not) any more. /我～也不去了. I won't go there any more.

再見 **dzàijyàn** (IE) Good-bye. or See you again.

再說 **dzàishwō** (A) usually followed by 又yòu or 也yě, furthermore. /太遠,～.又下雨別去了. Don't go, it's too far, and furthermore it's raining.

載 **dzài** → 載dzǎi.

咱{喒,偺} **dzán, dzá** (PN) I (lp). /～沒錢. I don't have any money.

咱們 **dzámen** (PN) you and I, we, indicating specifically that whoever is spoken to is included (lp). /～到那儿去呀? Where are we going?

攢 **dzǎn** (FV) collect, save. /我給他寫的信他都～着呢. He has saved all the letters I wrote him.

贊{賛} **dzàn** (B) approve. →讚{贊} **dzàn**.

贊成 **dzànchéng** (FV) agree with, approve of, someone, someone's conduct, proposal, or opinion. /我～他的意見. I agree with his ideas.

贊助 **dzànjù** (FV) give backing to, support, a person, a plan, a principle. /假如有人～.我們的計劃就可以實行. If we have someone to give us backing, we can carry out our plans.

讚{賛} **dzàn** (B) praise, eulogize.

讚美 **dzànměi** (FV) praise. /大家都～他勇敢. Everybody praised him for his courage.

髒{腌} **dzāng** (SV) be dirty. /我把手弄～了. I got my hands dirty.

藏 **dzàng** (B) 1) store, treasure. '寶

~ treasure. 2) Tibet (contracted form of 西 ~ **syīdzàng**). ~ 香 Tibetan incense. → 藏 **tsáng**.

葬 **dzàng** (FV) bury. /大家出錢把他給~了. We donated money for his burial.

遭 **dzāu** (FV) meet with misfortune. ~官司 be involved in a lawsuit (of the defendant). (M)<-ㄦ> 1) time around something. /用繩子再多捆一~. Wrap the rope around one more time. 2) trip. /我得到城裏去走一~. I have to make a trip to the city.

糟 **dzāu** (N) 1) dregs, sediment. 2) fermented grain mash (used for sauce or seasoning). (FV) season something with fermented grain mash. (SV) 1) be in a bad state, be a mess. /這件事情叫他辦~了. He made a mess of this matter. 2) be weak, about to fall apart. /布~了. This cloth is about to fall apart.
    糟糕 **dzāugāu** (SV) 1) be a mess, awful. 2) be too bad, unfortunate. (IE) What a mess!
    糟蹋 **dzāuta** (FV) 1) waste. /我~了很多時閒什麼也沒作. I wasted a lot of time doing nothing. 2) spoil, ruin. /你把我的前途給~了. You've ruined my future. 3) insult. /別~我了. Don't insult me.

鑿[凿] **dzáu** (FV) 1) hammer, pound. /別~門. Don't pound on the door. 2) chisel. /他在牆上~了一個窗戶. He chiseled out a window in the wall.
    鑿子 **dzáudz** (N) chisel (M把 **bǎ**).

棗[枣] **dzǎu** (B)<-ㄦ,-子> 1) jujube. 2) date. ~泥 date paste.
    棗樹 **dzǎushù** (N) jujube or date tree (M棵 **kē**).

早 **dzǎu** (SV) be early. /我來得~. I came early. /離開車還~呢. It's still quite a while before the train leaves. (A) 1) early. /你~一點ㄦ來. Come a little early. 2) long ago. /我~知道了. I knew it long ago. (IE) Good morning. /張先生~. Good morning, Mr. Chang.

早晨 **dzǎuchen** (TW) (in the) morning. /~比下午好. The morning is better than the afternoon. /我~在這ㄦ,下午不在. I'll be here in the morning, but not in the afternoon.
    早點 **dzǎudyǎn** (N) breakfast (M頓 **dwùn**, 道 **dàu**).
    早飯 **dzǎufan** (N) 1) breakfast. 2) lunch (lp). (M頓 **dwùn**).
    早就 **dzǎujyou** (A) long ago. /他~到了. He arrived long ago.
    早年 **'dzǎunyán** (TW) 1) (in) the early years of one's life. /~就到外國去了. He went abroad early in his life. 2) a long time ago. /這是~的事了. This happened a long time ago.
    早上 **dzǎushang** = 早晨 **dzǎuchen**.
    早餐 **dzǎutsān** (N) breakfast (M頓 **dwùn**).
    早晚 **'dzáuwǎn** (A) sooner or later. /他~會知道的. He'll find out sooner or later.

澡 **dzǎu** (B) bath. 洗~ take a bath.
    澡堂 **dzǎutáng** (N)<-子> public bath (the place).

造 **dzàu** (FV) 1) build, make, manufacture. ~房子 build houses; ~汽車 manufacture cars. 2) fabricate, start, a story, rumor. ~謠 start rumors. (B) 1) party involved in a law suit. 兩~ both parties; 原~ plaintiff.
    造反 **dzàufǎn** (VO) rebel against the government. /稅太重人民~了. Because of the heavy taxation, the people rebelled.
    造孽 **dzàunyè** (VO) do some kind of wrong or evil thing. /他造了不少的孽. He did many evil things. /少~吧. You have done enough evil things. or Don't add to your crimes.

竈[灶] **dzàu** (N) kitchen stove or range. 電~ electric stove or range.
    竈火 **dzàuhwo** (N) kitchen stove.

躁 **dzàu** (SV) be sour (of a person or one's temper), quick-tempered. /他脾氣很~. He's very sour-tempered. /請你不要這麼~好嗎. Please don't be so quick-tempered.

責 **dzé** (B) 1) responsibility, duty.

責~ be responsible. 2) to blame.
~罵 to reprimand.
　　責備 'dzébèi (FV) reprimand,
scold, rebuke. /我父親當面~
我一頓. My father reprimanded
me (to my face). (N) reprimand,
scolding (M 頓dwùn).
　　責任 dzéren (N) responsibility,
duty.

則 dzé (B) 1) principle, standard. 規
~ rules.   2) then. 否 ~ otherwise.
　　則已 dzéyǐ (P) used at the end
of a clause, if a certain thing is done
then everything will be all right.
/你還我錢~,不然我就告你.
Unless you give me the money back,
I'll sue you (lit. If you give me my
money back everything will be o. k.,
otherwise I'll sue you). /他不寫
字~,一寫就錯. He makes mis-
takes whenever he writes (lit. If he
doesn't write, everything is all
right; whenever he writes he makes
mistakes).

這 dzè (B)ᵗ. →這jè.
　　這麼 dzèmma (SP) this, these.
/他是~一個人. He's just this
kind of person. (A) 1) used before
FV, this way, like this. /這個機
器得~用. You must run this
machine this way. 2) used before
SV, to this extent, so. /這個怎
麼~難? How come this is so difficult? 3) <着> in that case, then.
/~我就去吧. In that case, I'll
go. (FV) <着> be like or do something like this. /我看他一生都
只能~了. I think he'll be like
this all of his life. /我們~吧.
Let's do it like this. (B) used after
CV like 往wǎng, 向 syàng, 朝 cháu,
etc., this direction. /往~搬一
搬. Move over this way a little bit.
　　這麼樣 'dzèmmayang (FV)
<-ㄦ> be like or do something like
this. /我們~吧. Let's do it
this way. /他永遠就~了. He'll
be like this forever. (A) 1) this
way, like this. /別~說. Don't
say it this way. 2) as...as this.
/~有錢的人不多. There are not
many people as rich as this.

賊 dzéi (N) thief. (A) extremely, irritatingly. ~冷 be irritatingly cold.
(SV) be smart, sharp. /他的眼
睛真~. He really has sharp eyes.

怎 dzěn (B) how. ~能 how can.
　　怎麼 dzěmma (A)ᑫ 1) how, in
what way. /你知道~開飛機
嗎? Do you know how to fly an airplane? 2) how come, why. /你
~沒來呢? Why didn't you come?
(SP)ᑫ what kind of. /他倒底是
~一個人? What kind of a person
is he anyway? (PT) 1)~...也
(or都)... no matter how...still
.... /~貴我都要買. No mat-
ter how expensive it is, I still want
to buy it.   2)~...,~...
whatever way.... /你~唱,我~
彈. I'll play it any way you sing it.
→不怎麼 budzěmma.
　　怎麼着 dzěmmaje (IE) What?
/~!你不去了? What? You're not
going? (A)ᑫ how (about).... /你
~? How about you? /你看~?
How do you feel about it?
　　怎麼了 dzěmmale (IE) What's
wrong? or What's happened?
怎麼 　　怎麼樣dzěmmayàng (A)ᑫ =
麼 dzěmma (A)ᑫ 1).(SP)ᑫ=怎
麼 dzěmma (SP)ᑫ. (IE) How are
things going? (PT) =怎麼 dzěmma
(PT) 1) 2).→不怎麼樣 budzěm-
mayang.

增 dzēng (B) increase, add to. ~大
enlarge. t
　　增產 dzēngchǎn (VO) increase
production. /我們得努力~.
We should put all our effort into increasing production.
　　增加 dzēngjyā (FV) increase,
add to. ~一半 increase by half.

曾 dzēng (B) great-grandparents or
children through the male line. ~
祖 great-grandfather. s →曾 tséng.

走 dzǒu (FV) 1) leave, depart. /他
已經~了. He had already left.
2) walk. /他~着來的. He
walked here. 3) move, go (of a
boat, vehicle, machine, etc.).
/火車~的慢. The train is
moving slowly. /錶不~了.
This watch isn't running. 4) go by
way of, take a route. /我們~
這條路. We'll take this road.
5) move (in a board game). /該
誰~了? Whose turn is it to move?
6) get together, have contact. /他
們~得很近. They see each
other often. 7) lose flavor, shape,
pitch, etc. /這雙鞋~了樣子

68

了. This pair of shoes has lost its shape.

走廊 dzŏuláng (N) 1) veranda. 2) corridor.

走運 dzŏuyùn (VO) get the breaks, have a lucky streak. /他又得了頭獎了,他這是走什麼運哪? He won first prize again. Why does he get all the breaks? (SV) be lucky. /他這幾年很~. He has been very lucky for several years.

奏 dzòu (FV) play music. /他~了一段月光曲. He played a section of the Moonlight Sonata.

奏樂 dzòuywè (VO) play music. /奏了半小時樂新娘才進來. They played music for half an hour before the bride came in.

揍 dzòu (FV) hit, strike, sock (lp). /~他一頓. Sock him one.

租 dzū (FV) rent. /我把我的船~給他了. I rented my boat to him. (B) <-子> rent. 房~ house rent.

足 dzú (SV) be sufficient, enough. /水塔裏的水很~. There's enough water in the water tank. (A) 1) fully. /我念了~有兩個鐘頭. I studied fully two hours. 2) sufficiently, enough. /吃~喝~ eat and drink enough. (B) 1) foot. ~跡 footprint. 2) complete, full. ~金 solid gold. → 不足 bùdzú.

足球 dzúchyóu (N) <-儿> 1) a football. 2) football (the game) (M場chǎng).

族 dzú (N) 1) race, racial strain. /他們不屬於一個~. They don't belong to the same race. 2) clan. /姓張的是一個大~. The Changs are a big clan.

祖 dzǔ (B) 1) ancestor. ~宗 handed down from one's ancestors. 2) grandparent. ~父母 grandparents. t

祖父 dzǔfù (N) grandfather.

祖國 dzǔgwó (N) the land of one's ancestors, mother country.

祖母 dzǔmǔ (N) grandmother.

組 dzǔ (FV) organize. ~閣 form a cabinet. (M) section, department, group. /這個公司分六~. This company is divided into six depart-

ments. (B) section, department, group. 人事~ personnel department.

組長 dzǔjǎng (N) section chief.

組織 dzǔjr (FV) organize. /我們要~一個歌唱團. We're going to organize a singing group. (N) 1) organization. 2) the Organization (referring to the Communist Party).

阻 dzǔ (B) obstruct, hinder, block. ~力 resistance.

阻礙 dzǔài (FV) prevent someone's progress, serve as a barrier. /那塊石頭在那兒~我們,請你給挪開. That stone (there) is blocking our way; please push it aside.

阻止 'dzǔjr (FV) stop, block, prevent. /要是他一定要來,我們也沒法子~他. If he insists on coming, we have no way of stopping him.

宗 dzūng (M) 1) case, suit (at law). 一~搶案 a case of robbery. 2) batch of goods. /有一~貨要運到了. There's a new batch of goods coming in. (B) 1) ancestor. 祖~ ancestor. 2) school, sect. 禪~ Zen Buddhism. t

宗教 dzūngjyàu (N) religion.

棕(椶) dzūng (B) 1) palm tree. ~繩 rope made of palm tree fiber. 2) dark brown. ~種人 brown race.

棕樹 dzūngshù (N) palm tree (M棵kē).

蹤(踪) dzūng (B) footprint, trace. 失~ disappear without a trace.

蹤跡 dzūngjī (N) clue, trace. /現在,我們找不着他的~. We can't find his trail now.

總(总) dzǔng (FV) add together. /請你把這幾個數~起來. Would you please add up these numbers? (A) 1) always. /他~哭. He always cries. 2) probably. /他~有一千多塊錢. He probably has more than a thousand dollars. 3) surely, certainly. /明天他~回來了吧! He certainly ought to be back tomorrow. 4) anyway, in any event. /人~得死. People will die anyway. (AT) main, chief. ~公司 main office; ~工程師 chief engineer. (B) all, general. ~罷工 general strike.

總共 **dzǔnggùng** (A) altogether. ~ 二十個人 altogether twenty people.

總之 **dzǔngjr** (A) to put it briefly, in short. /~, 他們都不贊成. In short, none of them agree.

總結 **dzǔngjyé** (FV) 1) total up. /我們每天都把帳~一下. We total up accounts every day. 2) summarize. /我沒法~他所說的話. It's impossible for me to summarize what he said. (N) summary.

總理 **dzúnglǐ** (N) prime minister, premier.

總數 **dzǔngshù** (N) <-ル> total, total amount.

總統 **dzúngtǔng** (N) president (of a government). 副~ vice-president.

縱(縱) **dzùng** (A) even though. /你~不能來, 也該給我打個電話. Even though you can't come, you should call me up. (FV) 1) let someone or something go uncontrolled. /他~着他兒子在街上打架. He lets his son fight in the street. /你不能老~着你的性子 You can't be losing your temper all the time. (B) vertical. ~線 vertical line.

縱然 **dzùngrán** (A) even though. /他~有錢, 恐怕也買不起. Even though he's rich, perhaps he can't afford to buy it.

鑽(鉆) **dzwān** (FV) worm into, enter a hole. ~ 山洞 crawl into a cave. → 鑽 **dzwǎn**, 鑽 **dzwàn**.

鑽(鉆) **dzwǎn** (FV) bore a hole through. /他用小刀在牆上~了一個洞. He used a small knife to bore a hole through the wall. → 鑽 **dzwān**, 鑽 **dzwàn**.

鑽(鉆) **dzwàn** (N) <子> drill (M把bǎ). 電~ electric drill. (B) 1) diamond. 水~ false diamond. 2) bore into. ~穿 drill through. → 鑽 **dzwān**, 鑽 **dzwǎn**.

鑽石 **dzwànshŕ** (N) diamond (jewel) (M顆kē, 粒lì).

攢(攢攢) **dzwàn** (FV) grasp, hold fast. /那個小孩~着汽球不撒手. The child held fast to the balloon and wouldn't let it go. (B) clench. ~拳 (頭) clench one's fist.

嘴 **dzwěi** (N) 1) mouth (of a person or animal) (M張jāng). 2) bill (of a bird). (B) 1) <-ル, -子> nozzle, spout. 茶壺~ル spout of a teapot. 2) way of talking. ~直 be outspoken.

嘴巴 **dzwěiba** (N) 1) slap on the cheek (lp). 2) mouth (d).

嘴巴子 **dzwěibàdz** (N) 1) cheek. 2) slap on the cheek (lp).

嘴唇 **dzwěichwún** (N) lip (of the mouth) (M片 pyàn).

最 **dzwèi** (A) 1) used before SV or A, most, -est. ~遠 farthest. 2) used before L or PW, farthest to or nearest a place, in or at the very .... ~前 nearest or farthest to the front, at the very front; ~左邊 farthest to the left, at the very left.

最初 **dzwèichū** (TW) (at or in) the very beginning. /~我以為他是好人. I thought he was a good person in the very beginning.

最後 **dzwèihòu** (N) the end. /他排在隊伍的~. He stood at the end of the line. (TW) 1) in the end. /~, 我們都高興了. In the end we were all happy. 2) lastly, finally. /~, 我要說一說經濟問題. Lastly, I would like to discuss economic problems. 3) last (after all the rest). /~做這個. Do this last. (AT) last. /我把~的一塊錢也花掉了. I've spent my last dollar.

最近 **dzwèijìn** (TW) 1) (in) the near future. /我~不打算去. I don't plan to go in the near future. /我說的是~, 不是十年以後. I'm talking about the near future, not ten years from now. 2) recently. /我~很忙. I've been very busy recently. (AT) 1) closest. ~的鋪子 the closest store. 2) most recent. ~的新聞 the most recent news.

罪 **dzwèi** (N) 1) sin, crime, wrong. 犯~ commit a crime. 2) suffering, suffer.

罪名 **'dzwèimíng** (N) type of crime, class of offense (e.g., first degree murder, second degree murder, etc.). /他犯的是什麼~? What type of crime did he commit?

醉 **dzwèi** (SV) be drunk. /他已經很~了. He's already very drunk. (FV) pickle things in wine. ~螃蟹

pickle crabs in wine, pickled crabs.
(RE) drunk. 灌～ make <u>someone</u>
drunk with wine. (B) infatuated. ～
心 be infatuated with.

作 **dzwō** (B) 1) workshop. 洗衣～
laundry. 2) invite trouble. ～死 invite death (<u>by one's carelessness</u>).
→ 作 dzwó, 作 dzwò.

昨 **dzwó** (B) <-儿> yesterday.
昨儿個 **dzwóerge** (lp) = 昨天
dzwótyan.
   昨天 **dzwótyan** (TW) yesterday. / 我是～來的. I came
yesterday.

作 **dzwó** (B)↓. → 作 dzwō, 作 dzwò.
   作料 **dzwólyàu** (N) seasoning
(<u>in cooking</u>).

捉 **dzwó** (B)↓. → 捉 jwō.
   捉摸 **dzwóma** (FV) think <u>some-
thing</u> over, cogitate about (lp).
/ 你又～什麼哪? What are you
thinking about now?

左 **dzwó** (L) left. ～邊 left side; 山～
left side of the mountain, to the left
of the mountain; ～眼 left eye; 從～
到右 from left to right. (SV) be
leftist. / 他的思想很～. His
way of thinking is very leftist. (RE)
wrong. 想～了 think incorrectly.
(PT) 1) ～ . . . 右 . . . . . . over
and over again. / 他～一次右一次
的跟我説. He talked with me
over and over again. 2)～也 . . .
右也 . . . . . . either way. / ～也
不對右也不對. It's wrong
either way.
   左不是 **dzwóbushr** (A) nothing
but. / 那個地方沒什麼別出産,
～白糖. They produce nothing but
sugar there.
   左邊 **dzwóbyan** (PW) <-儿>
1) on the left side. 2) the left side
<u>or</u> part.
   左傾 **'dzwóchīng** (SV) be radical, leftist. ～份子 leftist elements.
/ 他的思想有一點～. His ideas
are a bit radical (<u>or</u> leftist).
   左近 **dzwójin** (PW) (in) the
vicinity. / 我把～都找到了還
是沒有. I've searched the whole
vicinity and still can't find it. / ～有
沒有電話? Is there a telephone
in the vicinity?
   左右 **dzwóyòu** (N) <u>used after a</u>

noun indicating a place, the vicinity
of. 在學校～ in the vicinity of the
school. (B) <u>used after NU-M</u>,
about, approximately. / 我有一百
塊錢～. I have about a hundred
dollars. / 我們三點鐘～見吧.
Let's meet about three o'clock.

坐 **dzwò** (FV) 1) sit. / 請～. Please
sit down. 2) travel by <u>or</u> on <u>any</u>
conveyance except those which one
straddles. ～火車 ride on a train.
(CV) by a certain kind of conveyance.
/ ～電梯上去好不好? How
about going up by elevator?
   坐蠟 **dzwòlà** (VO) be on the
spot (<u>a bit vulgar; lit</u>. sit on a
candle). / 他叫我坐過一回蠟.
He put me on the spot once.
   坐牢 **dzwòláu** (VO) be in prison.
/ 他坐了三年牢. He's been in
prison for three years.

座 **dzwò** (M) <u>for buildings, mountains</u>,
<u>and other similar immovable ob-
jects</u>. 一～房子 a house; 一～山 a
mountain. (B) <-儿> seat. 訂～
reserve a seat.
   座儿 **dzwòr** (N) holder, base
(<u>as for a vase</u>).
   座位 **'dzwòwèi** (N) seat, place
to sit.

作{做(FV), (PV)} **dzwò** (FV) 1) serve
as, function as, be. ～總統 serve
as president; ～人 be a human being.
2) engage in <u>something</u>, do. ～生意
do business. 3) get together for.
～生日 have a birthday party. 4)
make, produce, <u>something</u>. ～飯
make a meal, cook; ～準備 make
preparations. 5) play the part of
(<u>in a play</u>). / 他在戲裡～的是
父親. He plays the part of the
father in the play. (PV) used with
verbs, such as 當 dàng, 叫 jyàu, 認
rèn, 看 kàn, 裝 jwāng, as. 當～ regard . . . as; 叫～ call (<u>give a name</u>
<u>to</u>). (B) work (<u>as of a writer or an</u>
<u>artist</u>). 傑～ masterpiece. (PT) ～
. . . 的樣子 pretend to be. / 他～生
氣的樣子. He pretends to be
angry. → 作 dzwō, 作 dzwó.
   作對 **dzwòdwèi** (VO) oppose,
be against. / 他跟我～. He's
against me.
   作工 **dzwògūng** (VO) work
(<u>usually only of physical labor</u>).

/他每禮拜就作兩天工. He
only works two days a week.
作活 dzwòhwó (VO) <-ㄦ> do
some kind of physical work, such as
carpentry, bricklaying, farming,
etc. /這兩天沒有什麼活作.
There hasn't been much work to do
the past few days.
作家 dzwòjyā (N) writer, author.
作假 dzwòjyǎ (VO) cheat.
/打牌要誠實,不許~. You
should be honest when playing cards
and not cheat.
作品 dzwòpǐn (N) work of art,
including books, essays, paintings,
sculpture, musical works (M本běn;
章 jāng; 篇 pyān).
作文 dzwòwén (VO) <-ㄦ>
write a composition. /我一個禮拜
作三篇文. I write three compositions each week.
作用 dzwòyung (N) 1) motive,
underlying purpose, function. /他
說那句話有什麼~? What was
his purpose in saying that? 2) effect. 不起~ be ineffective. 3)
action (by some natural force). 化
學~ chemical action; 反應~ reflex
action.

尊 dzwūn (B) 1) high position. ~位
high rank. 2) respect. ~師 respect
one's teacher. 3) your (h). ~夫
人 your wife. (M) 1) for Buddhist
statues. 一~佛像 a Buddhist
statue. 2) for cannons (artillery). 一
~大砲 a cannon.
尊大人 dzwūndàrén (N) your
father (h).
尊敬 dzwūnjìng (FV) revere,
respect. /他很受人~. He is
greatly respected by people.
尊重 dzwūnjùng (FV) respect.
/我~別人的意見. I respect
other people's opinions.

遵 dzwūn (B) obey, comply. ~令 obey
a command.
遵守 'dzwūnshǒu (FV) obey, observe, follow, rules, principles,
etc. /我總是~學校的規則.
I always obey school regulations.

哦 é, óu (I) indicating surprise. /~?
是那麼回事? Oh? Is that so?
→哦 óu.

鵝 é (N) goose (M隻jī).
蛾 é (B) <-子> moth (M隻jī). 蠶~
silkworm moth.
惡[噁] e (B) ↓. →惡 è, 惡 wù.
惡心 ésyin (SV) be nauseated.
/我喝了那杯橘子水很~. I
felt nauseated after I drank that glass
of orange juice. /別再說了,聽着
很~. Don't say anymore; I feel
nauseated when I hear about it.

惡[惡] è (B) 1) evil, wicked. ~勢力
subversive influence; ~鬼 demon.
2) fierce. ~狗 fierce dog. →惡 é,
惡 wù.
惡劣 èlyè (SV) 1) be serious
(as of a situation). /情形很~.
The situation is very serious. 2) be
inferior, poor, bad. /這個料子的
品質很~. This material is of
very poor quality.

餓 è (SV) be hungry, starved.
鱷 è (B) alligator, crocodile.
鱷魚 èyú (N) alligator, crocodile (M條tyau).

哎 ēi →哎 āi.
哎 éi →哎 ǎi.
按 èn →按 àn.
兒 er →兒 r.

而 ér (B) 1) and. 聰明~勇敢 clever
and brave. 2) and yet, while on the
other hand, but. /富~不仁 rich but
unkind.
而且 érchyě (A) 1) but also
(often preceded by a clause beginning
with 不但 búdàn not only). /她不但
難看~笨. She's not only ugly
but also stupid. 2) moreover, and.
/他聰明~用功. He's clever
and works hard.
而已 éryǐ (P) used at the end
of a sentence, that's all (usually
preceded by 不過 bugwò, 就 jyòu,
祇 jr, or 無非 wúfēi). /他不過是
一個學生~. He's just a student,
that's all.

兒(ㄦ) ér (B) 1) child. 孩~ child; 女
~ daughter. 2) <-子> son. t →
兒 r.
兒童 értúng (N) child.

耳 ěr (B) 1) ear. ~鼓 eardrum; 木~

edible tree fungus (<u>lit.</u> tree ear).
2) that which is to the side. ～ 房
side room.

耳朵 **ěrdwo** (N) ear.

耳子 **ěrdz** (N) handle (<u>as on
one side of a pot</u>).

耳環 **ěrhwán** (N) earring (M
隻 jī; 付 fù).

二{弍,貳} **èr** (NU) two. (B) second. ～
哥 second-oldest elder brother.

二月 **èrywe** (TW) 1) (in) February. 2) the second month of the lunar
calendar.

發[发] **fā** (FV) 1) send out, issue. ～信
send a letter; ～ 通知 issue a notice; ～薪 pay a salary; ～傳單 distribute leaflets. 2) break <u>or</u> burst
out. ～笑 burst out laughing. /飛機
撞在樹上當時就～火了. The plane
crashed into the tree and burst into
flame. /他的舊病又～了. He
had a recurrence of his old disease.
3) ferment, leaven. / 米 ～ 了.
The rice has fermented. /我不會
～麵. I don't know how to leaven
dough. 4) expand, swell. /他吃了
魚臉就～起來了. After he ate
the fish his face swelled up. /麵怎
麼還不～呀. I wonder why
the dough hasn't risen yet. 5) shoot,
fire. ～火箭 fire a rocket. 6) express, state. ～問題 ask a question.
7) be known. /他的罪現在～了.
His crime is known now. (M) <u>for
bullets, cartridges, shells.</u> 三～鎗
彈 three bullets. (B) become, turn
(<u>of a qualitative change</u>). ～ 紅 turn red.

發表 **fābyǎu** (FV) 1) announce,
issue <u>a statement.</u> ～聲明 issue a
statement. 2) publish <u>an article,
speech, etc.</u> /你那篇文章～了
嗎? Has that article of yours been
published?

發愁 **fāchóu** (VO) worry. /別
～啦! Don't worry! /你發什麼
愁呢? What are you worried about?
(SV) be worried, concerned. /他很
～因為沒錢上學. He is very
worried because he doesn't have any
money to go to school.

發出 **fāchū** (RC) 1) send out.
～一封信 send a letter. 2) issue.
～一個命令 issue an order. 3)

make <u>a sound.</u> ～一種怪聲 make a
strange sound.

發怵 **fāchù** (VO) become afraid.
/那個人一看見他太太就～.
As soon as he sees his wife he becomes frightened. (SV) be timid,
afraid. /我對那件事情很～.
I am apprehensive about that matter.

發怯 **fāchyè** (VO) be frightened.
/這是我頭一回到這兒來,所以
有點～. This is my first time
here, so I'm a little frightened.

發球 **fāchyóu** (VO) <-ル>
serve (<u>as in tennis</u>). /他很會～.
He has a very good serve.

發達 **fādá** (SV) 1) be well-developed. /他的肌肉很～. His
muscles are well-developed. 2)
be prosperous. /他的買賣很～.
His business is very prosperous.

發抖 **fādǒu** (VO) quiver, shake.
/冷得我直～. I'm so cold I'm
shaking.

發動機 **fādùngjī** (N) motor,
engine (M 架 jyà).

發行 **fāháng** (FV) sell something wholesale. /我們～勝家
縫紉機. We sell Singer sewing
machines wholesale. → 發行 **fāsyíng**.

發火兒 **fāhwǒr** (VO) get angry.
/他昨天發了兩次火兒. He got
angry twice yesterday. (SV) be
angry. /因為他朋友不願意借
給他錢,他很～. He is very angry
because his friend will not lend him
any money.

發展 **fājǎn** (FV) 1) develop.
～工業 develop industry. 2) expand, extend. /他的勢力已經～
到教育界去了. His influence
has already extended to educational
circles. (N) 1) development. 2)
expansion.

發覺 **fājywé** (FV) discover,
realize (<u>in most cases something un-
pleasant</u>). /上個禮拜三我們才
～他是一個賊. We didn't
realize until last Wednesday that he
was a thief.

發明 **fāmíng** (FV) invent.
/印刷術是中國人～的. The
printing process was invented by the
Chinese. (N) invention.

發脾氣 **fāpíchi** (VO) lose one's
temper. /他剛才又跟我發了一
陣脾氣. He just lost his temper
with me again.

發燒 **fashāu** (VO) have a fever, run a temperature. /他在發高燒. He has a very high fever.

發生 **fashēng** (FV) 1) take place, happen. /~了一件事情. Something happened. 2) arise (as a problem). /我看書的時候心裡~了一個問題. While I was reading, a question arose in my mind.

發現 **fāsyàn** (FV) discover. /他~了一個新法子. He discovered a new method. /他~中文不難. He discovered that Chinese is not difficult. (N) discovery.

發行 **fāsyíng** (FV) 1) issue bank notes, bonds, etc. ~鈔票 issue bank notes. 2) publish, distribute, books, magazines, etc. ~雜誌 publish a magazine. → 發行 **fāháng**.

發財 **fātsái** (VO) make a fortune, become rich. /他是賣舊汽車發的財. He made a fortune selling used cars.

發言 **fāyán** (VO) speak at a meeting, in public. /我們前天開會的時候他發了三次言. During the meeting the day before yesterday he spoke three times.

發言人 **fāyánrén** (N) spokesman.

發揚 **fāyáng** (FV) develop, spread. ~革命精神 develop revolutionary spirit; ~中國文化 spread Chinese culture.

發源 **fāywán** (FV) originate (as of a river or a culture). /這條河從那儿~? Where does this river originate.

發源地 **fāywándì** (N) origin, source. /這條河的~在四川. The source of this river is in Szechwan.

乏 **fá** (SV) 1) be tired, worn-out. 2) be weak (of a person as to his ability). 3) be low (of a fire). (B) be in want of, lack. ~味 be insipid.

法 **fá** (B) <-子. -儿> method, way of doing something. → 沒法子 **méifadz**. → 法 **fá**.

法碼 **fámǎ** (N) <-儿> weight used on a balance.

罰{罰} **fá** (FV) 1) punish. /他得受~.
He must be punished. 2) fine. /法官~他五塊錢. The judge fined him five dollars. (N) punishment.

罰金 **fájīn** (N) fine (legal punishment) (M筆 **bǐ**).

罰款 **fákwǎn** (VO) impose a fine (legal punishment). /法官沒罰他的款. The judge didn't fine him. (N) fine. 交~ pay a fine.

法 **fá, fà*** (B) 1) way of, way to. 看~ way of looking at things. 2) technique. 筆~ writing technique. 3) law. 刑~ criminal law. 4) imitate. 效~ imitate. 5)* Buddhist doctrine. 說~ expound the doctrine of Buddha. 6)* supernatural power. 作~ perform black magic. 7)* France. ~國 France. ᵗ→法 **fá**.

法案 **fǎàn** (N) bill (legislative).

法官 **fǎgwān** (N) judge (in court).

法律 **'fǎlyù** (N) law (M條 **tyáu**).

法庭 **fǎtíng** (N) 1) court of law. 2) courtroom.

法院 **fǎywàn** (N) 1) court of law. 最高~ Supreme Court. 2) courthouse.

法 **fà** → 法 **fá**.

帆{帆} **fān** (N) sail.

帆布 **fānbù** (N) sailcloth, canvas.

帆船 **fānchwán** (N) sailboat (M艘 **sōu**).

番羽{繙} (FV) 3)} **fān** (FV) 1) turn over or upside down. /車~了. The car turned over. 2) look through, search. ~箱子 look through a trunk. 3) translate. ~成英文 translate into English; ~'電報 decode a telegram. 4) go up over. /~過山頭就到了. We'll be there after crossing that mountain. 5) break off a relationship. /她跟我~了. She broke up with me. 6) reproduce something. /你們能~這張底片嗎? Can you reproduce this negative? (RE) 1) over, upside down. 推~ push over, overthrow. 2) indicates separation (of people). 吵~ quarrel and break up. (B) reverse. ~供 retract testimony.

番羽個儿 **fāngèer** (VO) turn something over. /把那條魚翻一個個儿再炸一炸. Turn that fish over and fry it some more.

翻身 **fānshēn** (VO) 1) turn over (of a person in a prone position). /他睡覺的時候常常～. He turns over a lot in his sleep. 2) change one's status (go from poverty to economic equality, or from slavery to freedom) (c). /窮人 ～了. The poor people are no longer poor.

翻譯 **fānyì** (FV) translate. /他～過很多書. He has translated many books. (N) translation.

番 **fān** (M) 1) for acts, deeds. 一～好意 a well-meant act; 三～兩次 several times, repeatedly. /他表演了一～. He performed once. (B) foreign, barbarian. ～邦 culturally undeveloped aboriginal tribe.

番茄 **fānchyé** (N) tomato.
番薯 **fānshu** (N) potato.

凡 **fán** (B) 1) every, all. ～事 all matters, everything. 2) ordinary, common. 平～ be common.

凡是 **fánshr** (B) all those who are, all that which is. ～書 all books; ～有錢的人 all those who are rich.

煩 **fán** (SV) 1) be bored, fed up. 2) be worried, disturbed. (FV) bother, trouble, someone. /我想～您點兒事. May I bother you about something? (B) harassing, troublesome. ～瑣 be complicated.

煩悶 **'fánmèn** (SV) be moody, surly. /他女朋友很久沒來信了，所以他很～. He's very moody because his girl hasn't written him for a long time.

煩惱 **fánnǎu** (SV) be vexed. (N) vexation.

繁(繁) **fán** (B) 1) complicated. ～體字 long form of a character. 2) many, numerous. ～多 be numerous.

繁榮 **fánrúng** (SV) be prosperous, flourishing. /市場很～. The market is flourishing. (N) prosperity.

反 **fán** (FV) 1) rebel. /軍隊～了. The troops rebelled. 2) oppose. /他們老跟我～着. They always oppose me. 3) reverse (with wrong side out or up). ～着穿 wear wrong side out. 4) behave boisterously,

make lots of noise (of children). /你們到外邊兒去～怎麼樣? How about going outside and making noise? (B) anti-. ～共 be anticommunist.

反倒 **'fǎndàu** (A) and yet, showing contrast with what has gone before. /我沒打你，你～打了我了. I didn't strike you, and yet you've struck me.

反動 **fǎndùng** (SV) be reactionary.

反對 **fǎndwèi** (FV) oppose, object to. /他很～他兒子娶那個女的. He is very opposed to his son marrying that girl.

反復 **fànfù** (A) repeatedly. /他～的說. He said it repeatedly. (FV) 1) change one's mind. /你現在不能～了. You can't change your mind now. 2) recur, come back (of a disease). /他的病又～了. His (old) disease has come back.

反攻 **fǎngūng** (FV) counterattack. /我們打算下月六號～. We plan to counterattack on the sixth of next month. (N) counterattack.

反正 **fǎnjèng** (A) anyway, anyhow, in any case. /～我不去. Anyway, I'm not going. (FV) return to the side of the government (as of a rebellious army). /叛軍有兩千人～了. Two thousand rebels returned to the side of the government.

反抗 **fǎnkàng** (FV) oppose, be opposed to, resist, an enemy, higher authority, power, etc. ～政府 oppose the government.

反面 **'fǎnmyàn** (PW) <一儿> (on) the reverse or wrong side. /這個料子的～是紅的. The wrong side of this material is red. /你～寫也成. It's O.K. to write on the reverse side too.

反省 **fǎnsyǐng** (FV) examine oneself, take a look at oneself (fig.). /你應當～～. You ought to take a look at yourself.

反映 **fǎnyìng** (FV) 1) reflect. /鏡子把陽光～在牆上. The mirror is reflecting light onto the wall. /他心裡想的事都在臉上～出來了. His face reflected

his feelings. 2) report (c). /向你
上級～. Report to your supe-
rior. (N) 1) reflection (reflected
image). 2) report (c).

反應 'fǎnyìng (N) reaction,
response. /那個針打了以後有
什麼～沒有? Has there been any
reaction to that injection?

犯 fàn (FV) 1) offend, violate. ～校
規 violate school regulations. 2) recur, come back (of a disease). /他
的病又～了. His (old) disease
came back again. 3) do something
bad. ～官僚主義 practice bureau-
cratism. (B) 1) criminal. 戰～
war criminal. 2) invade. 侵～ invade.

犯不上 fànbushàng (RC) not
be worthwhile. /我～用十塊錢
買那本ㄦ書 It isn't worthwhile
for me to spend ten dollars for that
book.

犯規 fànwéi (VO) break a
rule. /那個學生常常～. That
student often breaks rules.

犯人 fànren (N) criminal,
prisoner.

飯 fàn (N) 1) rice (cooked). 2) meal.
(M頓 dwùn). /～好了. The meal
(or the rice) is ready. 3) food. /沒
～吃. There's nothing to eat.

飯車 fànchē (N) dining car (on
a train) (M輛lyàng).

飯店 fàndyàn (N) 1) hotel
(Western-style) (M家jyā, 所swǒ).
2) restaurant (M家jyā).

飯館 fànwǎn (N) <-子,-ㄦ>
restaurant (M家jyā).

飯廳 fàntīng (N) dining room
(M間jyān).

飯菜 fàntsài (N) food (of a meal).

飯碗 fànwǎn (N) 1) rice bowl.
2) job, employment. /他把～丟
了. He lost his job.

範[范]fàn (B) 1) model, pattern. 模～
model, example. 2) sphere, boundary. ～疇 category. t

範圍 'fànwéi (N) scope, sphere.
勢力～ sphere of influence.

范 fàn (B) s SF of 範fàn.

方 fāng (AT) square. ～盒子 square
box; ～糖 cube sugar. (B) 1)
added to L, part, territory. 東～
east part, east side or the east; 前

～ the front (in a battle). 2) <-ㄦ,
-子> prescription (for medicine)
(M張jāng). 藥～ medical prescription; 開～ write out a prescription.
3) squared. ～尺 square foot; ～根
square root. 4) method. 千～百
計 all sorts of devices. s t

方便 fāngbyàn (SV) be con-
venient, handy. (FV) go to the restroom, use the bathroom. /您要不
要～? Do you want to go to the
restroom? or Would you like to use
the bathroom?

方法 fāngfǎ (N) method, way
of doing something.

方針 fāngjēn (N) aim, purpose,
policy. 定～ set up a policy.

方塊ㄦ fāngkwàr (N) 1)
square, rectangle. /他在紙上畫
了很多～. He drew a lot of
squares on the paper. 2) diamond
(in cards).

方面 fāngmyàn (M) 1) side
(as in negotiation, dispute, litigation).
/中日兩～都贊成. Both sides,
China and Japan, agree. 2) phase,
aspect. 從這～看 looking at it from
this aspect.

方式 fāngshr̀ (N) method, form,
way. 生活～ way of living.

方向 fāngsyàng (N) 1) direction.
/往那個～走. Go in that direction.
2) tendency. 新的～ new tendency.

方言 fāngyán (N) dialect.

防 fáng (FV) guard against. ～賊 guard
against thieves.

防備 fángbèi (FV) prepare for,
guard against. ～敵人 guard against
the enemy. (N) precaution.

防毒劑 fángdújì (N) antiseptic.

防護 fánghù (FV) protect, guard
from danger. /政府派了軍隊去
～那個村子. The government
sent troops to protect the village.

防止 fángjř (FV) prevent. ～
傳染病 prevent the spread of contagious diseases.

防守 fángshǒu (FV) defend,
hold. ～陣地 hold a military position.

防線 fángsyàn (N) line of defense (m) (M條tyáu, 道dàu).

防禦 fángyù (FV) prevent,
guard against an enemy. 必須有
武力才能～敵人的侵略. We

must have military strength before we can prevent enemy aggression.

房 **fáng** (N) 1) <-ㄦ, -子> house (M 所 **swǒ**, 座 **dzwò**). 2) room (M 間 **jyān**) (d). (B) branch of a family. 遠 ~ distant branch of a family.

房產 **fángchǎn** (N) property (houses and buildings only) (M 處 **chù**).

房頂 **fángdǐng** (N) <-ㄦ> roof.

房東 **fángdūng** (N) 1) owner of a house. 2) landlord.

房間 **fángjyān** (N) room (M 間 **jyān**) (d).

房樑 **fánglyáng** (N) horizontal beam in the structure of a house (M 根 **gēn**).

房艙 **fángtsāng** (N) cabin (on a ship) (M 間 **jyān**).

房屋 **fángwū** (N) houses, buildings.

妨 **fáng** (B) hinder, interfere with. 不 ~ it does no harm.

妨礙 **fángài** (FV) hinder (prevent someone from doing something), obstruct. /請別~交通！ Please don't block traffic! (N) hindrance, obstruction, difficulty. /這件事情這樣做沒有什麼~吧. You shouldn't have any difficulty doing it this way.

仿(倣, 髣) **fáng** (FV) imitate, copy. /很多女人都~總統夫人的髮型. Many women copy the hair style of the President's wife. (N) copybook (M 本 **běn**). (B) like, resembling. 相 ~ be very much alike.

仿彿 **fángfu** (A) it seems that, seem to be (often with 似的 **shrde** at the end of the sentence). /他~不願意去(似的). It seems that he doesn't want to go.

仿效 **fángsyàu** (FV) imitate, pattern on, model on, a fashion, a standard, etc. /別~我！ Don't imitate me!

紡 **fáng** (FV) spin, reel. ~棉花 spin cotton. (B) silk (material). 小 ~ fine silk.

紡織 **fángjr** (B) spin and weave. ~工業 textile industry.

訪 **fáng** (FV) search for, dig up, news. /這幾天沒~着什麼新聞. I haven't been able to dig up much news the past few days. (B) visit. 拜 ~

call on someone.

訪問 **fàngwèn** (FV) 1) pay a formal *or* official visit to a person or a country. /總統下月要~英國. The President will visit England next month.

放 **fàng** (FV) 1) put, place. /~在這裏. Put it here. /你茶裏~糖嗎？ Do you use sugar in your tea? 2) release, let something or someone go. /他把賊~了. He let the thief go. 3) fire a weapon. ~鎗 fire a gun. 4) lend someone money, collecting interest. /我~了一千塊錢, 每月得三十塊錢利息. I lent out a thousand dollars, and collect thirty dollars interest each month. 5) make larger, wider, etc. ~ 大 enlarge. 6) tend cows, sheep, etc. ~ 牛 tend cows. (B) open. 開 ~ blossom (of a flower), be open to the public.

放棄 **fàngchì** (FV) abandon, give up, renounce, discard. /你別~你自己的權利. Don't renounce your rights.

放假 **fàngjyà** (VO) 1) have a vacation. /你們什麼時候放寒假？ When will you have your winter vacation? 2) grant a holiday *or* vacation. /我的上司答應放我二天假. My boss gave me a two-day vacation.

放浪 '**fànglàng** (SV) be loose, lax (morally), unrestrained. /那個人的行為很 ~. That man's behavior is very unrestrained.

放炮 **fàngpàu** (VO) 1) fire a gun (large-caliber weapon). /昨天敵人才停止~. The enemy stopped firing just yesterday. 2) blow, burst (as a tire) (lp). /我的車胎忽然~了. My tire suddenly blew.

放屁 **fàngpì** (VO) give off gas (from the rectum). (IE) What rot!

放手 **fàngshou** (VO) let something go. /你拿緊了, 我要~了. Hold tight, I'm going to let go. /那種事他已經~不管了. He has given up taking care of that kind of thing. (A) freely. /你可以~去作. Do it whichever way you wish.

放鬆 **fàngsūng** (RC) 1) loosen a belt, etc. /你的溜冰鞋鬆

得太緊了, ～一點儿吧. Your ice-skates are on too tight; loosen them a little. 2) be less strict. /對學生～一點儿. Be less strict with the students.

放心 **fàngsyīn** (SV) be at ease about, not worried. /我很～因為他從前作過這種事. I'm not worried at all because he's done this before. (VO) stop worrying. /我把定錢給他, 他才放一點儿心. He didn't stop worrying until I gave him the deposit. (FV) trust someone. /我不～他. I don't trust him.

放學 **fàngsywé** (VO) 1) get out of school at the end of class or for a vacation. /我們三點鐘～. We get out of school at three. 2) let out (of a school or class). /明天起學校就～了. School lets out tomorrow.

非 **fēi** (A) 1) followed by a verbal expression with or without 不可 **bùkě** or 不行 **busyíng**, absolutely must, insist on. /我～去(不可). I absolutely must go. 2) followed by a negative expression, unless... (not). /～你去辦不了. Unless you go it can't be done. (B) 1) non-, in-, un-, etc. ～會員 non-member. 2) not be. 並～ it is not that. 3) wrong. 是～ right and wrong.

　　非常 **fēicháng** (A) very, unusually, extraordinarily. /那本書～難懂. That book is very hard to understand.

　　非正式 **'fēijèngshr̀** (AT) 1) informal. 2) unofficial.

飛[飠] **fēi** (FV) fly (as a bird). /鳥儿～了. The bird flew away. 2) fly (pilot a plane). /他～戰鬥機. He flies a fighter plane. 3) fly (travel by plane). /明天我～紐約. I'm flying to New York tomorrow. 4) float in the air. /雪花儿在空中～. Snow flakes floated through the air. (A) very fast, rapidly. ～跑 run very fast; ～漲 rise rapidly (of a river or of prices).

　　飛禽 **fēichín** (N) bird (any that can fly) (M 隻 jr̄).

　　飛機 **fēijī** (N) airplane (M 架 jyà).

飛機場 **fēijīchǎng** (N) airport, airfield.

肥 **féi** (SV) 1) be fat (of an animal or meat; also of a person, but derogatory). ～肉 fatty meat. 2) be loose (of clothing). 3) be rich, fertile (of soil, land). (N) fertilizer. 上～ fertilize.

　　肥皂 **féidzàu** (N) soap (M 塊 kwài).

　　肥皂盒儿 **féidzàuhér** (N) soap-box (for a cake of soap).

　　肥料 **féilyàu** (N) fertilizer.

　　肥沃 **féiwò** (SV) be fertile (of soil, land).

匪 **fěi** (SV) be roguish, fast and loose. /他說話的態度很～. His manner of talking is very roguish (too much profanity, obscenity, and talk of improper things, showing lack of moral responsibility). (B) vagabond, bandit, rebel. 土～ bandit.

肺 **fèi** (N) lung.

　　肺病 **fèibìng** (N) pulmonary tuberculosis.

　　肺炎 **fèiyán** (N) pneumonia.

費 **fèi** (FV) 1) expend, consume. ～勞力 expend energy. 2) waste. ～工夫 waste time. (SV) be quickly used up. /孩子穿鞋很～. Children wear out shoes very quickly. (B) fee, expenditure. 學～ tuition; ～用 expenses. s t

　　費心 **fèisyīn** (VO) use mental effort. /他為這件事費了不少的心. He put a lot of thought into this thing. (IE) Thank you.

　　費用 **'fèiyùng** (N) expense (M 筆 bǐ).

廢 **fèi** (FV) abolish, discard. /國王已經～了. The king has been deposed. (B) useless. ～紙 waste paper. 2) crippled. 殘～ be crippled.

　　廢話 **fèihwà** (N) irrelevant talk, hot air, nonsense.

沸 **fèi** (B) boil.

　　沸點 **'fèidyǎn** (N) boiling point.

分 **fēn** (FV) 1) divide. /你把這些東西～一～. Divide these things. /美國～多少州. How many states are there in the United

States? 2) share, be given a share. /你～給他一點兒. Share a little with him. /我～到了五塊錢. I was given a share of five dollars. 3) distinguish, tell. /我～不出這是誰的字. I can't tell whose handwriting this is. (M) 1) tenth of a Chinese inch, tael, acre. 2) cent. 三～錢 three cents. 3) minute (of an hour or of a degree). 差三～一點 three minutes to one o'clock. 4) <－兒> point (as in the scoring of a game or test). /這回考試我得了八十～兒. I got 8 on this examination. 5) 1% rate of interest. 四～利 4% rate of interest. (B) 1) branch of an organization. ～行 branch office of a bank, branch store. 一份{分} fèn.

分辨 fēnbyàn (FV) distinguish between (in thinking or talking). /他不能～是非. He cannot tell right from wrong.

分別 fēnbye (N) difference. /這兩個沒～. There's no difference between these two.

分別 'fēnbyé (FV) tell the difference. /我～不出來. I can't tell the difference.

分別 fēnbyé (A) separately. /你跟他們～談一談. You talk with them separately.

分岔兒 fēnchàr (VO) divide into branches, fork (as a road). /那條路分三個岔兒的地方應該立一個牌子. There ought to be a sign there where the road divides into three branches.

分期 fēnchī (VO) divide into stages. /這個汽車分三期付款. The car will be paid for in three installments. (A) in stages. /我們的工作～完成. Our work will be completed in stages.

分道 fēndàu (VO) <－兒> take different roads (lit. or fig.). /從這兒起我們得～走. From here on we have to take different roads.

分子 fēndz (N) 1) numerator (arith.). 2) molecule.

分毫 fēnháu (N) the slightest thing. /我～都不知道. I don't know the slightest thing about it.

分之 fēnjr (B) used in giving fractions (NU₁分之=NU₂ in English is NU₂ NU₁ -ths). 二～一 one-half; 十～八 eight-tenths; 百～二十 twenty

percent (lit. twenty one-hundredths).

分開 fēnkai (RC) separate. /請你把紅的跟綠的～. Please separate the red ones from the green ones. /他們兩個人～了. Those two are separated. (A) separately. /那兩件事得～看. We should look at the two matters separately.

分配 fēnpèi (FV) distribute, allocate. ～工作 distribute work. (N) distribution, allocation.

分手 fēnshǒu (VO) part, say good-bye. /我們在車站分的手. We said good-bye to each other at the station.

分數 'fēnshù (N) <－兒> 1) grade (on an exam). 2) score (in a game). /大考的～很要緊. The grade on the final exam is very important.

分析 fēnsyi (FV) analyze. /他們在～他犯罪的動機. They are analyzing his motive for the crime. (N) analysis.

吩 fēn (B) command, give instructions to.

吩咐 'fēnfù (FV) leave or give someone instructions. /請您～他別把這些東西拿走. Please leave instructions for him not to take these things away. (N) instructions.

墳[坟] fén (N) grave, tomb (M座dzwò).

墳地 féndì (N) graveyard (M塊kwài,片pyàn).

墳墓 fénmù (N) grave, tomb (M座dzwò).

粉 fěn (N) powder. (SV) be obscene. ～戲 obscene play. (B) 1) pink. ～色 pink (color). 2) flour. 米～ rice flour.

粉筆 fěnbǐ (N) chalk (for writing) (M根gēn).

粉碎 fěnswèi (FV) smash to pieces, ruin. ～敵人的計劃 ruin the enemy's plan. (RE) indicates fragmentation. /他把花瓶摔得～. He smashed the vase to pieces.

粉條兒 fěntyáur (N) vermicelli (made from bean flour).

份{分} (M), (B) 1) 2)}(M) fèn <－兒> 1) copy, issue, of a newspaper or magazine. 2) subscription to a magazine or newspaper. 3) part, portion. /把錢分成三～. Divide this money into three parts. (B) 1) ＜-ㄦ＞ share, portion. 股～ share in a business. 2) responsibility. ～ㄣ within one's responsibility. 3) section, segment. 月～ 牌 calendar.

份子 fèndz (N) 1) gift (for a wedding, birthday, funeral, etc.). 2) share of a group gift.

份子 fèndž (N) element within an organization. 知識～ intelligentsia.

份量 fènlyang (N) weight (lit. or fig.). /那個鑽石有多少～? How much does that diamond weigh? /他說的話很有～. What he says carries a lot of weight.

份ㄦ fèr (N) ⊦ (B) 1). 2) degree, level, extent. /雖然到了 這個～上,他還不明白. He still doesn't understand, even after going to that extent. 3) position. /他的～很大. He has a very high position. 4) leeway, room. 留 一點ㄦ～ leave some room.

糞 fèn (N) stool, manure, excreta (M 堆 dwēi). 馬～ horse manure.

奮[奋] fèn (B) put forth effort, exert oneself. ～勇 display courage.

奮鬬 fèndòu (FV) struggle hard. /為那件事他～了很久. He has struggled a long time for (or over) that.

風[风] fēng (N) 1) wind. 2) news. /別 走了～. Don't let the news leak out. (B) 1) custom. ～土人情 local manners and customs; 家～ family customs. 2) manner, style, taste. ～度 appearance and bearing, deportment. 3) scenery. ～光 scenery and atmosphere. 4) rumor. ～聞 rumor has it that.

風潮 fēngcháu (N) unrest, agitation, ferment of ideas.

風車 fēngchē (N) ＜-ㄦ＞ 1) windmill. 2) winnowing machine.

風琴 fēngchín (N) organ (the instrument).

風箏 fēngjeng (N) kite.

風景 fēngjǐng (N) scenery, view, landscape.

風俗 fēngsu (N) custom, practice, usage.

風箱 fēngsyang (N) bellows.

封 fēng (FV) 1) seal up. /別忘了～那 封信. Don't forget to seal that letter. /傷口～上了. The wound has healed. 2) bestow honors on. ～侯 confer the title of marquis on someone. (M) for letters, telegrams. 一～信 a letter. (B) ＜-ㄦ＞ envelope. 信～ envelope; 紅工～ㄦ small red envelope containing a tip.

封建主義 fēngjyànjǔyì (N) feudalism.

封條 fēngtyáu (N) seal (as on a liquor bottle) (M張jāng).

蜂 fēng (B) bee, wasp, hornet. 蜜～ bee.

蜂蜜 fēngmì (N) honey.

蜂窩 fēngwō (N) beehive, hornet's nest, wasp's nest.

瘋 fēng (SV) 1) be insane, mad. 2) be wild. /那個女孩子有一點ㄦ ～. That girl is a little wild. (B) used in names of certain sicknesses. 羊角～ epilepsy.

瘋了 fēngle (P) used after a verbal expression, indicates an extreme condition and may translate as become extremely something or become crazy with. 他急～. He has become extremely upset or worried. or He has become crazy with worry.

瘋人院 fēngrénywàn (N) insane asylum, mental institution (M 所 swǒ).

豐[丰] fēng (B) abundant, fruitful, luxuriant. ～收 good harvest. t

豐富 fēngfu (SV) be rich in content, full, broad. /對於歷史 他的知識很～. He has a broad knowledge of history.

丰 fēng (B) graceful. ～采 elegance. SF of 豐 fēng.

丰度 'fēngdù (N) deportment, bearing, manner, conduct, appearance.

縫 féng (FV) sew, mend (usually by hand). ～在一塊ㄦ sew things together. →縫 fèng.

縫級機 féngrènjī (N) sewing machine (M架 jya).

縫 fèng (B)＜-ㄦ,-子＞ 1) crack, split. 2) seam. 3) part (in the hair). → 縫 féng.

奉 **fèng** (B) 1) offer, contribute. ～獻 offer with reverence. 2) receive from a superior. ～令 receive an order. 3) respect. ～公守法 be law-abiding. 4) have the honor to. ～告 have the honor to inform. . . .

奉承 **fèngcheng** (FV) compliment, praise (often with an ulterior motive). /我是不會～人的. I don't like to compliment people (with the intention of getting something).

fo *see* **fwo.**

否 **fǒu** (B) 1) not. 是～ is it so or not? 2) deny. ～定 negate, negation.

否則 **fǒudzé** (A) otherwise. /你得作得好, ～我不給錢. You have to do a good job, otherwise I won't pay you.

否決 **fǒujywé** (FV) veto, turn down, a motion, bill, proposal. /他的提議被我們～了. We vetoed his proposal.

否認 **'fǒurèn** (FV) deny. /我們不應當～自己的錯誤. We should not deny our own mistakes.

夫侠 (B) 3) **fū** (B) 1) man. 匹～ common man, one of the masses. 2) husband. 未婚～ fiancé. 3) <-子> laborer. 挑～ bearer, coolie. *t*

夫妻 **fūchī** (N) husband and wife.

夫婦 **fūfù** (N) husband and wife.

夫人 **fūren** (N) wife (of a man of high rank). (B) Mrs., Madam. 蝴蝶～ Madam Butterfly.

扶 **fú** (FV) 1) hold on to someone or something for support. /他～着牆走. He walks by holding on to the wall for support. 2) support something or someone with the hand. /我來～你吧. Let me help you. (B) give support to, back. ～國民學校 give support to the public schools.

扶手 **fúshou** (N) arm (of a chair), railing, bannister, or any similar object which can be used to support oneself with the hand.

服 **fú** (FV) 1) yield to, submit to, make someone submit. /他不～我. He won't yield to me. /他不能～人. He can't make people submit. 2)

serve in an official capacity. ～兵役 serve as a soldier. 3) swallow, take, medicine, poison. ～毒 take poison. 4) be used to. 不～水土 be unaccustomed to the climate. (RE) indicates yielding. /我把他說～了. I convinced him. /鞋穿～了. These shoes are broken in. (B) garment. 衣～ clothes. → 服 fù.

服侍 **fúshr** (FV) wait on, serve. /我老～你, 你從來也沒～過我. I always wait on you; you've never waited on me.

服從 **fútsúng** (SV) obey. ～命令 obey orders.

服務 **fúwù** (SV) serve (do one's duty). /你在軍隊裏～了多久? How long did you serve in the army? (N) service.

服務員 **fúwùywán** (N) person who serves others (c).

俘 **fú** (FV) capture a person, military equipment. /他被～了. He was captured.

俘虜 **fúlwǒ, fúlǔ** (FV) capture a person, military equipment. /他們～了幾個敵兵. They captured several enemy soldiers. (N) prisoner of war.

符 **fú** (N) written charm, incantation (M 道 dàu). (B) 1) agree with. ～合 reconcile; 不～ be inconsistent. 2) mark, symbol. 音～ note (in written music).

符號 **fúhàu** (N) <-ル> symbol.

福 **fú** (N) good luck, good fortune.

福氣 **fúchi** (N) good luck, good fortune.

福利 **fúlì** (N) welfare.

伏 **fú** (FV) 1) submit, surrender. /敵人已經～了. The enemy has surrendered. 2) recline face down. /他～在床上哭. He lay face down on the bed and cried. /他～在桌子上睡着了. He was sleeping slumped over the table. (B) 1) period of ten days between July and August. 歇～ take a summer vacation. 2) hide, ambush. 埋～ ambusher. 3) admit. ～老 admit that one is old.

伏兵 **fúbīng** (N) ambusher, sniper (m).

浮 **fú** (FV) float (on or in a liquid).
/有很多樹葉子~在水上.
There are lots of leaves floating on
the water. (SV) be flighty, giddy,
superficial. (B) 1) excess. ~報
claim more than what is actually
due. 2) unsubstantial. ~利 unsubstantial profit. →浮 **fù**.

斧 **fú** (B) <-子, -頭> hatchet, ax (M
把 **bǎ**).

腐 **fú** (B) decay. ~爛 decay.
腐敗 **fùbài** (SV) be corrupt,
ineffective, inefficient, spoiled,
decadent, old and useless (of people
or institutions).
腐化 **fúhwà** (SV) be corrupt. ~
份子 corrupt element (in an organization).
腐朽 **fúsyǒu** (SV) 1) be de-
cayed, spoiled. 2) be decadent.

府 **fú** (N) mansion. 總統~ presiden-
tial mansion.
府上 **fúshang** (N) 1) your
home (h). /您~在那儿? Where
is your home? or Where are you
from? 2) your family (h). /您~
都好吧? Is all of your family well?

父 **fù** (B) 1) father. ~母 parents. 2)
male relative who is of an older
generation. 伯~ uncle (father's
older brother).
父親 **fùchin** (N) father.

付{副}(M)} **fù** (FV) pay money that is
due. /我汽車的錢已經~清
了. I've paid the bill for the car
in full. (M) set (for small items).
一~棋 a chess set; 一~牌 a deck
of cards; 一~耳環 a pair of earrings. (B) entrust to, commit to.
付表決 **fùbyǎujywé** (VO) put to
a vote (in a meeting which follows
formal parliamentary procedure).
/主席説我們現在把張先生的
提議~. The chairman says
that we will now put Mr. Chang's
motion to a vote.

複{復} **fù** (B) 1) complex. 繁~ be complicated. 2) repeat. 重~ duplicate.
複雜 '**fùdzá** (SV) be complicated.
複寫紙 **fùsyéjr** (N) carbon
paper (M張 **jāng**).

附{坿} **fù** (FV) 1) be attached. /信裏~

了一張支票. A check was en-
closed in the letter. 2) haunt a person. /他叫鬼~下來了. He is
possessed by a ghost. (B) form an
adjunct. ~品 accessories.
附近 **fùjìn** (PW) (in) the vicinity
or neighborhood. /~有郵局嗎?
Is there a post office around here?
附錄 **fùlù** (N) appendix (of a
book).
附議 **fùyì** (FV) second a motion.
/我~他的提議. I second his
motion.

負 **fù** (B) 1) bear, shoulder. 擔~ bear
a burden, a burden. 2) negative. ~
電 negative electricity; ~號 minus
sign. 3) lose, be defeated. 勝~
victory and defeat. 4) show no gratitude. ~義 be ungrateful for kindness.
負擔 **fùdān** (N) burden (usually
financial). (FV) bear a burden,
responsibility. /這種責任我~
不了. I cannot take on this kind of
responsibility.
負責 **fùdzé** (VO) take on or
have a responsibility. /他在學校
負很多責. He has a lot of
responsibilities at school. (SV) be
responsible, reliable. (FV) be
responsible for something. /那件
事由我~. I'm responsible
for that. (AV) be responsible for
doing something. /他~打掃廁
所. He's responsible for cleaning
the bathroom.

服 **fù** (M) dose of medicine, poison. 一
~藥 a dose of medicine. →服 **fú**.

婦{妇} **fù** (B) 1) wife. 夫~ husband and
wife. 2) woman. ~孺 women and
children.
婦道 **fùdàu** (N) womanly virtue, proper moral conduct.
婦女 **fùnyǔ** (N) women, woman-
kind.

復{覆}(FV), (B) 2)}{复} **fù** (FV) reply
to (in writing). /我没~他的
信. I didn't reply to his letter.
(B) 1) return, recover. ~元 recover one's health; 報~ get revenge.
2) again, anew. ~任 resume office.
復活節 **fùhwójyé** (TW) (at)
Easter.
復原 **fùywán** (FV) recover,
get better. /他的病已經~了.

He has recovered from the illness (lit. His illness has recovered).

復員 fùywán (VO) demobilize. /打仗以後軍隊還没有～呢. The troops haven't been demobilized since the war.

富 fù (SV) be rich, wealthy. (B) abundant. ～饒 in great abundance. s t

富農 fùnúng (N) rich peasant or farmer.

富裕 fùyu (SV) be prosperous, well off. (FV) have extra. /我們～一個位子. We have an extra seat.

副 fù (AT) vice-, assistant. ～總統 vice-president (of a government). (B) secondary, accessory. ～產品 by-product. →付{副}fù.

副官 fùgwān (N) adjutant, aide-de-camp.

副業 fùyè (N) sideline, avocation.

浮 fú (FV) swim. /他是從這儿～過去的. He swam across from here. →浮fú.

浮水衣 fúshwéiyī (N) swimming suit (M件jyàn; 套tàu).

賦 fù (N) poetic essay with alliteration, assonance, and other poetic features, but written in prose form (M篇pyān). (B) 1) write in verse. ～詩 write a poem. 2) give, bestow. 天～ natural gifts. 3) taxation. 田～ land tax.

賦閑 fùsyán (VO) be out of a job. /他賦了三年閑了. He hasn't been working for three years.

佛 fwó (N) Buddha. 拜～ worship Buddha.

軋 gā (B) 1) join, connect together (d). ～朋友 form a friendship. 2) settle a matter. ～賬 settle an account. →軋yà

該 gāi (FV) 1) owe money, etc. /他～你多少錢? How much money does he owe you? 2) be one's turn to do something. /～我説了. It's my turn to say something. (AV) ought to, should. /我不～來. I shouldn't have come. /這個孩子～打. This child ought to be spanked. (B) the said, that. ～人員 the said person.

該死 gāisž (IE) What a crime! or Disgusting! or Shameful!

改 gǎi (FV) 1) change, alter. ～期 change a date; ～衣裳 alter clothes. 2) correct. ～錯 correct a mistake. 3) kid someone (lp). /你別～我了. Don't kid me.

改變 gǎibyàn (FV) change, alter. ～計劃 change plans. (N) change.

改造 gǎidzàu (FV) 1) reform (of a person). /他的思想需要～. He needs to reform his thinking. 2) rebuild (as a machine). /這個機器～一下還可以用. If this machine is rebuilt, it can still be used. (N) reform.

改組 gǎidzǔ (FV) reorganize, change the structure or arrangement of. ～政府 reorganize a government. (N) reorganization.

改革 gǎigé (FV) reform or improve a system. /政府把學校制度～了. The government reformed the school system. (N) reform.

改進 gǎijìn (FV) improve, advance. /假如你想～老有辦法～. If you want to improve, there's always a way to improve. (N) improvement, progress.

改良 gǎilyáng (FV) improve, change something for the better. /最近十年汽車没有～什麼. Cars haven't improved much the past ten years. (N) improvement.

改善 gǎishàn (FV) improve, change a situation for the better. /工人的生活～了很多. The life of the laborer has been greatly improved. (N) improvement.

改選 gǎisywǎn (FV) elect new officers in an organization. /我們學校的董事會已經～了. The board of trustees of our school has already elected its new officers. (N) election for new officers.

蓋{盖} gài (FV) 1) cover. ～上茶壺 cover a teapot. 2) put on a cover. ～上茶壺蓋儿 put the cover on a teapot. 3) erect a building. ～一所房子 build a house. 4) put a seal or chop on something. /我把每張畫都～上我的圖章. I put my chop on every picture. (B) <-子,

—ル > 1) cover, lid. 茶壺~ teapot lid. 2) shell on top of a turtle, crab, beetle. 螃蟹~ crab shell. *t*

乾(乾)[干] **gān** (SV) be dry. /衣服~了. The clothes are dry. (A) without anything else, unaccompanied. ~着急 do nothing but worry; ~唱 sing unaccompanied. (RE) indicates finishing up, using up. 用~了 be all used up. (B) 1) <—ル> something dried. 葡萄~ル raisin. 2) nominal (existing in name only). ~媽 godmother; ~姐姐 older sister (daughter of one's godparents and not one's real sister).
　　乾杯 **gānbēi** (IE) Bottoms up! (lit. Dry the cup!)
　　乾飯 **gānfàn** (N) cooked rice (d).
　　乾果 **gāngwǒ** (N) <—ル, —子> nuts and dried fruit.
　　乾淨 **gānjìng** (SV) be clean. /那家洗衣店洗的衣服真~. That laundry really gets your clothes clean. (RE) indicates finishing up, using up. 賣~了 be sold out.
　　乾洗 **gānsyǐ** (FV) dry-clean. /這種料子只能~. This kind of material can only be dry-cleaned.
　　乾脆 **gāntswèi** (SV) be clear-cut, unequivocal. (A) 1) frankly. /我~跟你說吧. I'll be frank with you. 2) the simplest way is to ..../你們兩個人~結婚吧. The simplest way is for you two to get married.

甘 **gān** (B) 1) sweet. ~泉 sweet spring water. 2) be willing to. ~休 be willing to agree. *s t*
　　甘蔗 **gānje** (N) sugar cane.
　　甘心 **gānsyīn** (SV) be pleased, content. /要是他做我們的頭兒我很~. I'll be very content if he's our boss. (AV) be willing to. /我~受苦. I am willing to suffer.

干 **gān** (B) be concerned with. ~涉 interfere with. SF of 幹 **gàn**, 乾 **gān**.

肝 **gān** (N) 1) liver (the organ). 2) <—ル> liver (as food).

桿[杆] **gān** (B) <—子, —ル> pole, staff. →桿 **gǎn**.

敢 **gǎn** (AV) dare, venture to. /你~打他嗎? Do you dare hit him?

敢情 **gǎnching** (A) 1) of course, naturally. /~他會說中國話. Naturally he knows how to speak Chinese. 2) actually, after all (contrary to expectation or upon sudden realization). /我以為他沒來呢, ~他來了. I thought he didn't come, but actually he did.

桿 **gǎn** (M) for rifles, pistols, spears. —~槍 a rifle. (B) <—ル> stem, handle. 筆~ handle of a pen. →桿 **gān**.

趕[赶] **gǎn** (FV) 1) catch a train, plane, person, etc. ~五點鐘的火車 catch the 5 o'clock train. /把他~上. Catch up with him. 2) rush to do *or* make something. /他三天~了五套衣服. He rushed to make five suits in three days. 3) drive *or* chase a person or animal away. /把他~出去. Chase him out. 4) make an animal move. ~牛車 drive an ox-drawn cart. (A) when, by the time. /~他們來我早走了. By the time they come, I'll be long gone. /他來的時候正~我沒錢 He came just when I didn't have any money. (PT) ~...再... wait until...(then)..../~明天再做吧. Let's wait until tomorrow to do it.
　　趕緊 **gǎnjǐn** = 趕快 **gǎnkwài**.
　　趕快 **gǎnkwài** (A) quickly, immediately, without delay. /你~來. Come here quickly. /我們得~走. We must leave immediately.

擀 **gǎn** (FV) roll out dough. ~皮 roll out dough wrappings.

感 **gǎn** (B) 1) feel. 情感 feeling, emotion, passion. 2) grateful. ~佩 appreciation. 3) move, affect, influence. ~化 influence; ~化院 reformatory.
　　感情 **gǎnching** (N) feeling, emotion, passion. /他跟他太太沒有~. He doesn't have any feeling for his wife.
　　感到 **gǎndau** (FV) feel, sense. /我已經~他不痛快了. I have already sensed that he is unhappy.
　　感動 '**gǎndùng** (FV) move,

84

rouse one's emotions. /這本小説把他~得流眼淚了. This novel moved him to tears. (SV) be moved, touched. /我聽了那位老先生的故事以後~極了. I was greatly touched, hearing that old man's story.

感激 gǎnjí (FV) be grateful to. /我對他很~. or 我很~他. I am very grateful to him. (SV) be grateful. /我們大家都~極了. We are all extremely grateful.

感覺 gǎnjywé (FV) 1) feel (have the physical sensation of). /我~不舒服. I don't feel well. 2) feel (be of the opinion). /我~他不對. I don't feel he's right. (N) attitude, opinion, feeling. /你對這件事的~怎樣? What's your feeling about this matter? 2) feeling (sense of touch). /他的右手沒有~了. He doesn't have any feeling in his right hand.

感冒 gǎnmàu (N) cold, influenza. /我有一點~. I have a slight cold. or I have a touch of the flu.

感想 gánsyǎng (N) feeling, impression.

感謝 gǎnsyè (FV) appreciate, be thankful for. /我~他對我的關心. I appreciate his concern for me. (SV) be appreciative, thankful. /因為你常常幫他的忙所以他很~. He's very appreciative of the help you gave him so often.

撒 gǎn (B) olive.
　　撒欖 gánlǎn (N) olive.

幹(幹)(干) gàn (FV) 1) do, manage. /他~不下去了. He can't go on doing it. 2) pick on someone. /你為什麼老跟我~? Why do you always pick on me? 3) get rid of, take care of, someone undesirable (lp). /我們這邊昨天晚上把他給~了. Our gang took care of him last night. (B) 1) main body. 樹~ trunk of a tree; ~線 main line. 2) capable. ~練 be capable and experienced.

幹部 gànbù (N) cadre.
幹活兒 gànhwór (VO) work. /他好幾天沒~了. He hasn't worked for several days.
幹麼 gànmá (A)q why, how come.

/他~不來? Why isn't he coming? /他告訴我他~不去. He gave me various reasons for not going. (VO) do what. /你~呢? What are you doing? /你願意~就~. Whatever you wish to do, do it. (PT) ~都 (or 也)... no matter what someone does.... /你~都叫我生氣. No matter what you do, it makes me angry.

幹甚麼 gǎnshémma = 幹麼 gànmá.

缸 gāng (N) vat, crock (M 口 kǒu).

剛 gāng (A) 1) just a moment ago. /我~到. I just arrived. 2) just about to. /我~要走他就來了. I was just going to leave when he came in. 3) exactly, just. ~好 just right; ~五塊錢 exactly five dollars. 4) only a certain amount, less than expected. ~八點鐘 only eight o'clock. (B) unyielding, hard. ~直 be firm in principle.

剛剛 gānggāng = 剛 gāng (A).
剛才 gāngtsái (TW) just a moment ago, just. /我~給他打了一個電話. I just called him.

鋼 gāng (N) steel.
鋼筆 gāngbǐ (N) pen (writing instrument) (M 枝 jīr, 管 gwǎn, 根 gēn).
鋼筆尖兒 gāngbǐjyār (N) pen point.
鋼琴 gāngchín (N) piano (M 架 jyà).
鋼精 gāngjīng (N) aluminum.
鋼盔 gāngkwēi (N) helmet (of metal) (M 頂 dǐng).
鋼鐵 gāngtyě (N) steel.

肛 gāng (B) large intestine.
肛門 gāngmén (N) anus.

港 gǎng (N) harbor. (B) Hong Kong (contracted form of 香~ syānggang). ~澳 Hong Kong and Macao.

槓(扛) gàng (B) <-子> 1) stout carrying pole. 2) horizontal bar (gymnastic).

gao see gau.

高 gāu (SV) 1) be high, tall. ~樓 tall building. 2) be high in position, pitch, price. /他的聲調很~. He has a very high-pitched voice. 3) be superior. /他的智力很~.

He is a man of superior intelligence.
(B) great-great-grandparent. ~
祖 great-great-grandfather. *s t*

高大 **gāudà** (SV) be big and tall.

高等 **gāuděng** (AT) 1) high-class, high quality (of people, residential districts, stores, etc.). ~香煙 high quality cigarettes. 2) high in position. ~法院 high court.

高爾夫 **gāuěrfū** (N) golf. 打 ~ play golf.

高個兒 **gāugèr** (N) tall person.

高級 **gāují** (AT) senior, advanced. ~中學 senior high school; ~訓練 advanced training.

高中 **gāujūng** (N) senior high (school).

高粱 **gāulyang** (N) common sorghum, kaoliang.

高粱米 **gāulyangmǐ** (N) kaoliang (grain) (M粒lì).

高明 '**gāumíng** (SV) be good, of excellent quality, intelligent (of a person, method, idea, skill). /他說的話很~. What he said was very intelligent. /你這手兒可不怎麼~. What you said wasn't very smart at all.

高射砲 **gāushepàu** (N) anti-aircraft artillery (M門mén).

高興 **gāusying** (SV) be happy, delighted, elated. (AV) be happy to. /我很~去. I'm happy to go. /我不~要他的錢. I'm not happy about taking his money.

糕 **gāu** (N) cake (M塊kwài).

搞 **gāu** (FV) 1) do, make. /你在那兒~什麼呢? What are you doing there? 2) engage in, do work in the field of. ~建設 engage in reconstruction. 3) run, manage. ~報紙 run a newspaper. 4) obtain, acquire, get. ~錢 make money. /你能不能~到一輛汽車? Can you get a car somewhere? 5) purge. /他怕他們~他. He is afraid they will purge him.

鎬 **gāu** (N) <頭> pick (tool) (M把bǎ).

稿 **gāu** (B) <-子,-兒> draft, manuscript, of an article, essay, speech (M篇pyān). 初~ first draft.

告 **gàu** (FV) sue. /我把他~了. I sued him. (B) 1) tell, inform. 廣 ~ advertisement. 2) ask for. ~貸 ask for a loan.

告假 **gàujyà** (VO) ask for time off. /我想告兩天假. I would like to ask for two days off.

告示 **gàushr** (N) notice, sign, bulletin, of an official nature, posted in a public place (M張jāng).

告訴 **gàusù** (N) accusation. ~人 accuser. →告訴 **gàusung**.

告訴 **gàusung, gàusu** (FV) tell, inform. /他們已經結婚了,我忘了~你. They got married. I forgot to tell you. →告訴 **gàusù**.

個[简][个] **ge** (M) 1) for individual persons or things. 三~人 three people; 桌子 two tables; 一~情形 a situation. 2) used between a verb and an object, with or without 一yī, one instance of doing something. /我洗(一)~手就來. I'll come after I wash my hands. 3) used between FV and SV, with or without 一yī, to the point of. 吃~飽 eat until full; 玩~痛快 play until one is satisfied. /他摔了一~鼻青臉腫. He fell and got a black eye. (B) 1) used after FV plus 的de and before SV, really. /他跑的~快 He can really run fast. /他長的~高. He is really getting tall. 2) used before NU-M, approximately, about. 住~兩天 stay for about two days. /他有~萬把塊錢. He has about ten thousand dollars. (PT) 一~..就 if...once, then... /一~不小心你的錢就都沒了. If you're careless once, you'll lose all your money. →個 **ge**.

哥 **gē** (B) 1) older brother. 大~ oldest brother. 2) older male cousin. 表~ older male cousin.

哥哥 **gēge** (N) older brother.

胳 **gē** (B)↓.

胳臂 **gēbei** (N) arm (part of the body) (M隻jī).

胳臂肘兒 **gēbeijǒur** (N) elbow.

胳肢窩 '**gējewō** (N) armpit.

胳棱瓣兒 **gēlengbàr** (N) knee.

疙 **gē** (B)↓.

疙瘩 **gēde** (N) 1) boil, pimple. 2) wart. 3) knot in string or in wood.

割 **gē** (FV) cut off with a knife. ～草 cut grass. /我的手～了一刀. I cut my hand. (B) surrender, give up. ～愛 give up what one treasures.

歌 **gē** (B) <-ㄦ> song. (M 支 jīr). 國～ national anthem.
歌曲 **gēchyǔ** (N) song. 民間～ folk song.
歌譜 **gēpǔ** (N) musical score (M 本 běn, 張 jāng).
歌舞 **gēwǔ** (N) song and dance (M 場 chǎng, 幕 mù).

擱 **gē** (FV) 1) place, put. /～在桌子上. Put it on the table. 2) put something off, delay. /把這件事～下不談. Let's put off talking about this matter. 3) mix in, put into, add to. /我喝咖啡不～糖. I don't put sugar in my coffee.

鴿 **gē** (B) <-子> dove, pigeon (M 隻 jī). 信～ messenger pigeon.

革 **gé** (B) 1) leather. 皮～ leather. 2) change. ～新 change for the better. 3) remove from an organization. ～職 remove from office.
革命 **géming** (VO) carry out a revolution. /沒有武器不能～. We can't carry out the revolution without arms. (N) revolution.

格 **gé** (B) 1) <-ㄦ, -子> ruled line or space (on paper). ～紙 lined or squared paper. 2) standard, category. 及～ be up to standard, pass an examination. 3) <-ㄦ> compartment. /這個書架子有三～ㄦ. This bookcase has three shelves. t
格外 **géwài** (A) 1) exceptionally, especially. /他對我～好. He treated me exceptionally well. 2) in addition, extra. /他～給了我五塊錢. In addition, he gave me five dollars. or He gave me five dollars extra.

隔 **gé, jyé*, jyē†** (FV) 1)* be apart from. /我們～的太遠. We are too far apart from each other. 2)* be separated by. /他家跟我家～着一條河. His house and mine are separated by a river. 3)* divide, partition. /把這間屋子～

開,好不好？ How about partitioning this room? (CV)‡ every other. /他～一天來一次. He comes once every other day. (B) <-子> partition, screen (M 扇 shàn). →隔 jye.
隔壁 **gébì, jyébì** (PW) next door. /他住在～. He lives next door.

合 **gě** (M) one-tenth of a 升 shēng (=0.109 of a liquid quart). →合 hé.

蛤 **gé** (B) clam. ～蜊 clam. →蛤 há.

各 **gè** (B) 1) each, every. ～個 every one. 2) numerous, various. ～國 various countries; ～種 various kinds.

硌 **gè** (FV) press and rub against or dig into one's flesh (as a sharp corner, stone in one's shoe, etc.). /舊床的彈簧～的我很難受. The springs in that old mattress really jabbed into me.

個{简}{个} **gè** (B) individual. ～別 individually. →個 ge.
個子 **gèdz** =個ㄦ **gèr**.
個ㄦ **gèr** (N) size. 大～的鷄蛋 large-sized eggs. /這個人的～真大. This man has a large build.
個人 **gèrén** (N) oneself. /我～沒有什麼意見. I don't have an opinion myself. (AT) individual, personal. /這是我個人的事情. This is my personal affair.
個人主義 **gèrénjǔyì** (N) individualism.
個性 **'gèsyìng** (N) personal nature, personality. /他的～很强. He has a strong personality (it's hard to change his mind— a good or bad comment).

給 **gěi** (FV) 1) give someone something. 2) give someone the chance to do something, let. /～我看～. Let me have a look at it. (CV) 1) for the benefit of. /請你～我們買一點ㄦ東西. Would you please buy a few things for us? 2) used to bring the direct object of the sentence before the verb, similar to the CV 把 **ba**. /他們～那房子拆了. They've torn that house down. 3) by (marking the agent). /太陽～雲彩擋上了. The sun is covered by clouds.

4) indicates that the verb following it is in the passive voice, and has the implication of its being unfortunate that the object has had to undergo the action. /你看,我的帽子都～弄壞了! Look! My hat is ruined! /房子叫風～刮倒了. The house (unfortunately) was blown down by the wind. (PV) to someone. /我把信交～他了. I handed the letter over to him. →給 jǐ.

根 gēn (N) 1) <-ル> root of a plant. 2) square root. (M) <-ル> for relatively long and thin things. 一～草 a blade of grass; 一～棍ル a rod *or* pole; 一～繩子 a rope. (B) origin. ～源 source.

根本 gēnběn (A) 1) used before a negative expression, completely, absolutely. /我～不知道. I absolutely don't know. 2) from the very beginning. /我～就喜歡他. I liked him from the very beginning. (AT) basic, fundamental. ～問題 basic problem.

根基 gēnji (N) foundation (lit. or fig.).

根據 gēnjyu (FV) base something on. /你說這樣的話～什麼? What do you base your statement on? (CV) according to. /～我的看法他錯了. According to my point of view, he is wrong. (N) basis. /他的話沒有～. There is no basis for what he said.

根據地 gēnjyùdì (N) military base (M 處 chù).

跟 gēn (FV) 1) follow (physically). /你為甚麼老～着我? Why are you always following me? 2) be at a place (lp). /他正～家裏呢. He's at home now. 3) be the common-law wife of (lp). /她～王先生了. She's the common-law wife of Mr. Wang. (CV) 1) <着> with (accompanying). /他～我到紐約去. He's going to New York with me. 2) <着> with the help of. /他～王先生學中文. He's studying Chinese with Mr. Wang. 3) and. /我要筆～紙. I would like a pen and some paper. 4) to (with respect to). /他～我很不客氣. He's very rude to me. (B) <-ル>

heel. 高～ル鞋 high heels (shoes). (PT) 1) ～...一樣 the same as, as much as. /這張桌子～那張一樣. This table is the same as that one. /張太太～我太太一樣愛說話. Mrs. Chang likes to talk as much as my wife. 2) ～...似的 be like, resemble. /他走路～他父親似的. He walks the same way his father does. 3) ～...這麼 (or 那麼)...as...as. /這張桌子～那張桌子那麼好. This table is as good as that one. 4) ～...比 as compared to. /這本書～那本書比好多了. This book, compared to that one, is much better.

跟前 gēnchyan (A) in one's family (lp). /您～有幾個小孩ル? How many children do you have in your family? →跟前 gēnchyán.

跟前 gēnchyǎn = 跟前ル gēnchyǎr.

跟前ル gēnchyǎr (PW) the area in front of something or someone. /門的～有一棵樹. There's a tree right in front of the door.

跟着 gēnje (A) right after, immediately after. /他說完了～就坐下了. Right after he spoke he sat down. (CV) † (CV) 1),2).

跟隨 gēnswéi (FV) 1) follow. /大家都～我來. Everybody follow me. 2) be a devoted follower of someone. /他～總統有十年了. He has been a devoted follower of the President for almost ten years.

跟頭 gēntou (N) 1) fall (head first). 栽～ fall head first, fail unexpectedly and lose face as a result. 2) somersault.

哏 gén (SV) be funny, humorous (lp). /那句話很～. That's a very funny remark. /那個小孩很～. That child is very funny.

更 gēng, jīng * (M)* two-hour period (between 7:00 P.M. and 5:00 A.M.) 三～ third period (11:00 P.M. to 1:00 A.M.); 打～的 night watchman. (B) change, alter. ～名 change one's name. → 更 gèng.

耕 gēng, jīng (B) plow. 春～ spring plowing.

更 gèng (A) even more, even...-er. /你比她～好. You're even better than she is. /你不喝酒我～喜歡你了. I'd like you even more if you'd stop drinking. → 更 gēng.

更加 gèngjyā (A) even more, even...-er. /你要那麼便他～恨你了. If you do that, he'll hate you even more.

gong *see* gung.

鈎[鈎] gōu (FV) 1) hook. /那把傘的傘把儿～着我的腿呢. I got my leg hooked on the umbrella handle. /用鈎子～出來. Pull it out with a hook. 2) be in cahoots. /他們兩個人是～着的. Those two fellows are in cahoots. 3) put a check mark by something. /請你把這本書裏的話～一～. Please put a check mark by the important lines in this book. 4) cancel, write off, an account, bill, debt. /把那筆帳～了. Cancel that account. 5) remind one of something. /他一哭～起我的傷心事來了. His weeping reminds me of my own past sad events. (B) <-儿,-子> 1) hook. ～針 crochet needle. 2) stinger (as of a bee).

溝[泃] gōu (N) gutter, ditch (M條 tyáu). (B) connect. ～通文化 mingle cultures.

狗 gǒu (N) dog (M隻 jī, 條 tyáu).

夠[夠,彀] gòu (SV) be sufficient, enough. /他玩～了. He's played enough. (FV) 1) be sufficient *or* enough for. /五百塊錢不～我上大學. Five hundred dollars isn't enough for me to go to college. 2) reach something by stretching. /他～不着. He can't reach it. (A) sufficiently, enough. /～好了. It's good enough. (AV) be enough to. /十塊錢不～買一個電扇. Ten dollars isn't enough to buy an electric fan.

咕 gū (B) mutter, mumble. 唧唧～～ murmur, whisper. (ON) coo. /鴿子一邊吃一邊～～地叫. Pigeons eat and coo at the same time.
咕咚 gūdūng (ON) 1) sound of someone swallowing a liquid. /他～一聲把牛奶嚥下去了. He swallowed the milk with a gulping sound. 2) sound of a heavy thing falling down. /他～一聲倒在地

上了. He fell to the ground with a thud. (FV) bash in. /他們用炮把城門～開了. They used artillery to bash down the city gate.

姑 gū (B) 1) unmarried girl. 2) father's sister. 3) husband's sister. 大～子 sister-in-law (husband's older sister). 4) temporarily. ～且 for the time being. 5) lenient. ～息政策 policy of appeasement.
姑姑 gūgu (N) aunt (father's sister).
姑母 gūmǔ (N) aunt (father's sister).
姑娘 gūnyang (N) 1) young girl. 2) unmarried woman.

箍 gū (FV) wind something around. /這口箱子快破了, 最好～上一條繩子. This box is going to break; we had better wind some rope around it. (N) <-儿> hoop, circlet (M 道 dau).

估 gū (FV) appraise, estimate. ～價 estimate the value *or* price. /請你～一～這張名畫儿值多少錢. Could you estimate how much this famous painting is worth?
估計 'gūjì (FV) estimate. /我～做這個買賣得用一萬塊錢. I estimate that running this business will require ten thousand dollars. (N) estimate.

孤 gū (B) 1) fatherless. 2) solitary. ～單 be alone.
孤兒 gūér (N) orphan. ～院 orphanage.

軲 gū (B)↓.
軲轆 gūlu (FV) roll something along. /把那個桶～過來吧. Please roll that barrel over here. (N) wheel.

骨 gū (B)↓. → 骨 gǔ.
骨朵儿 gūdwor (N) bud (on a plant).

骨 gú → 骨 gǔ.

古 gǔ (SV) be ancient. ～磁 ancient porcelain. t
古代 gǔdài (N) ancient times.
古董 gǔdung (N) 1) antique. (M件 jyàn). 2) obsolete thing (sometimes said sarcastically of a person) (M件 jyàn). /你的汽車已經成

了 ～了. Your car is already obsolete.

古怪 gǔgwài (SV) be mysterious, strange, queer.

古跡 'gǔjī (N) ancient remains, relic (M 處 chù).

古玩 gǔwán (N) antique (M 件 jyàn). ～店 antique store.

骨 gǔ, gú* (B) 1)* bone. 頭～ skull. 2) framework. 鋼～水泥 reinforced concrete. → 骨 gū.

骨頭 gǔtou, gútou (N) 1) bone (M 根 gēn). 2) moral integrity. /～很硬. He is a person of great moral integrity.

股 gǔ (B) 1) thigh. 屁～ buttocks. 2) <-子, -ㄦ> share, portion (in a business). ～息 dividend. 3) section of an organization. 福利～ welfare section. (M) <-ㄦ, -子> 1) for odors, usually bad. 2) puff, blast, column, of smoke, air, steam. 3) strand of hair, rope, string. 4) for relatively sudden surges of strength, energy. 一～勁ㄦ strength, energy, drive. 5) skein of wool, thread. 6) band of soldiers, robbers. 7) <-ㄦ> share of stock.

股東 gǔdūng (N) part owner of an enterprise, stockholder.

股份 gǔfèn (N) share in some sort of investment.

股票 gǔpyàu (N) stock (M 張 jāng, 股 gǔ). /這種～你有多少股? How many shares of this stock do you have?

鼓 gǔ (N) drum (M 面 myàn). (FV) bulge, stick out. /別～着肚子. Don't stick out your stomach. (SV) be convex, bulging. (B) 1) encourage. ～勵 praise and encourage. 2) agitate for. ～吹革命 foment a revolution.

鼓動 gǔdùng (FV) arouse, incite, instigate. /他～工人罷工. He got the workers to go on strike.

鼓掌 gǔjǎng (VO) applaud. /她唱完台下鼓了很久的掌. The audience applauded a long time after she finished singing.

鼓勵 gǔlì (FV) encourage, stimulate. /他從來不～人. He has never encouraged anybody. (N) encouragement.

穀 [谷] gǔ (B) 1) <-子> millet. 2) grain. 五～ the five cereals (rice, millet, corn, wheat, bean).

膨 gǔ (SV) be bulging, protruding, swollen. /他 (吃的) 肚子很～. His stomach is bulging from eating. (FV) bulge, swell, rise. /蛋糕蒸得～起來了. The cake rose as it steamed.

谷 gǔ (B) valley. 山～ ravine. SF of 穀 gǔ.

固 gù (B) 1) solid, firm. 堅～ strong. 2) originally. ～有 original. 3) obstinate. 頑～ stubborn.

固定 gùdìng (SV) be fixed, permanent, continuing. /這件工作是～的, 不是臨時的. This job is permanent, not temporary.

固執 gùjr (SV) be stubborn, obstinate.

固然 gùrán (A) it is true that . . . . /他～不對可是你也不對. He's not right, it's true; but you aren't either.

故 gù (B) 1) old. ～交 old friend. 2) die. 病～ die of disease. 3) cause, reason 無～ without cause. 4) intentionally. ～殺 intentional murder.

故去 gùchyu (FV) pass away (euphemistic). /他父親早就～了. His father passed away a long time ago.

故事 gùshr (N) story.

故意 gùyì (A) on purpose, purposely. /對不起我不是～的. I'm sorry. I didn't do it on purpose. /他～不告訴我. He purposely won't tell me.

顧 [顾] gù (FV) think of, take into consideration. /你別只～自己. Don't just think of yourself. s

顧慮 gùlyù (N) concern, worry. (FV) be concerned about, worry about. /我們應該～他的安全. We have to worry about his safety.

顧問 gùwèn (N) adviser.

雇 [傭] gù (FV) employ, hire. ～車 hire a taxi, rent a car. /我～不着用人. I can't find a servant (to hire).

gua see gwa.

guai see gwai.

guan *see* **gwan**.

guang *see* **gwang**.

guei *see* **gwei**.

gun *see* **gwun**.

工 **gūng** (N) 1) labor, work. 作~ to work (do manual labor). 2) note in the old Chinese musical scale. (M) day's labor for one man. /作這件 事情需要六~. It will take six days' labor to do this job. (B) 1) craftsman. 木~ carpenter. 2) industry. ~界 industrial world.

工廠 **gūngchǎng** (N) factory, mill.

工程 **gūngchéng** (N) project (engineering), construction job (M件 jyàn).

工程師 **gūngchéngshr** (N) engineer.

工錢 **gūngchyan** (N) wage, pay.

工地 **gūngdì** (PW) (in) the construction area.

工資 **gūngdz** (N) wage.

工作 **gūngdzwò** (N) work, job. (FV) work. /你一天~幾小時? How many hours do you work a day?

工夫 **gūngfu** (N) 1) time, leisure. 抽不出~ cannot find time. 2) time and effort devoted to learning something. 下~彈鋼琴 devote time to playing the piano. 3) skill. ~不錯 be quite skilled.

工會 **gūnghwèi** (N) labor union.

工具 **gūngjyù** (N) tool.

工農 **gūngnúng** (N) workers and peasants (c).

工人 **gūngren** (N) laborer, worker.

工頭儿 **gūngtóur** (N) foreman.

工業 **gūngyè** (N) industry.

工業化 **gūngyèhwà** (FV) industrialize. /總統計劃把農業 地區~. The president plans to industrialize the rural areas. (SV) be industrialized.

工友 **gūngyǒu** (N) <-儿> office boy, servant.

弓 **gūng** (N) 1) bow (weapon) (M 張 jāng). 拉~ draw a bow. 2) <-子> bow (as of a violin).

公 **gūng** (AT) male (not of human beings). ~牛 bull. (B) 1) public. ~法 public law. 2) just, equitable. ~平 fair. 3) father-in-law (of the wife only). 4) grandfather. 外~ maternal grandfather. 5) used before measures of length, surface, weight, etc., forms names of the units in the metric system. ~里 kilometer. 6) old man. 老~~ old man. 7) Mr. (usually for an older man). 張 ~ Mr. Chang.

公安局 **gūngānjyú** (N) police headquarters.

公尺 **gūngchř** (M) meter.

公道 **gūngdau** (SV) be impartial, fair, reasonable. /價錢很~. The prices are quite reasonable.

公公 **gūnggung** (N) 1) father-in-law (of the wife only). 2) grandfather (d).

公共 **gūnggùng** (AT) public (not private). ~電話 public telephone.

公共汽車 **gūnggùngchìchē** (N) public bus.

公債 **gūngjài** (N) government bond. 發~ issue government bonds.

公正 **'gūngjèng** (SV) be just, fair, equitable, impartial.

公雞 **gūngjī** (N) cock (M 隻 jr̄).

公斤 **gūngjīn** (M) kilogram.

公開 **gūngkāi** (SV) be public (not private). (FV) make public. /他把這件事情給~了. He made this matter public. (A) openly. /你可以對他~的說. You can talk to him openly.

公款 **gūngkwǎn** (N) fund, funds (M 筆 bǐ).

公里 **gūnglǐ** (M) kilometer.

公立 **gūnglì** (AT) public. /這 個城裏有三個~中學. There are three public high schools in this city.

公曆 **gūnglì** (N) the Western calendar, official international calendar. /元朝是~一二〇六年開 始的. The Yüan Dynasty began in the (Western calendar) year 1206.

公路 **gūnglù** (N) highway (M 條 tyáu).

公民 **gūngmín** (N) 1) citizen. 2) civics (course in school).

公平 **gūngpíng** (SV) be fair, impartial.

公社 **gūngshè** (N) commune.

公使 **gūngshř** (N) minister (diplomatic).

公事 **gūngshr̀** (N) 1) official business. 2) official document.

公事房 **gūngshr̀fáng** (N) office (place for work) (M間 **jyān**).

公司 **gūngsz̄** (N) company, corporation (M'家 **jyā**).

公文 **gūngwén** (N) official document (M件 **jyàn**, 篇 **pyān**, 張 **jāng**).

公務員 **gūngwùywán** (N) civil employee, government employee.

公寓 **gūngyù** (N) apartment, lodging house (M所 **swǒ**, 家 **jyā**).

公園 **gūngywán** (N) public park.

功 **gūng** (B) 1) merit, achievement. 有~ be meritorious. 2) efficacy. ~效 beneficial outcome. 3) time and effort. 下苦~ devote a lot of time and effort.

功夫 **gūngfu** (N) 1) free time, time. /我沒~去. I don't have any time to go. 2) time and effort devoted to learning something. 下~彈鋼琴 devote time and effort to practicing the piano. 3) skill. /我的~都擱下了. I lost all my skill. or I'm completely out of practice.

功課 **gūngkè** (N) 1) school work. 2) course (M門 **mén**).

功課表 **gūngkèbyǎu** (N) schedule of classes (in school) (M張 **jāng**).

功勞 **gūngláu** (N) merit, credit, for something done.

攻 **gūng** (FV) 1) attack. ~城 attack a city. 2) engage in the study of. 專~文學 specialize in literature.

攻擊 **gūngjí** (FV) attack (lit. or fig.). /報紙現在正~市長呢. The papers are now attacking the mayor.

供 **gūng** (FV) 1) supply someone with something. /他們那個工廠的原料都是我們~的. We supply all the raw materials for that factory. 2) give someone financial aid. /我~他念書. I'm paying for his school expenses. →供 **gùng**.

恭 **gūng** (B) 1) respect. ~維 praise, flatter.

恭敬 **'gūngjìng** (FV) respect, show respect to. /我們得~父母. We must respect (our) parents. (SV) be respectful, deferential.

/那個小孩儿對他的先生很~. That small child is very respectful to his teachers.

恭喜 **gūngsyǐ** (FV) congratulate someone. /我還沒給你~呢! I haven't congratulated you yet. (IE) 1) Congratulations! 2) used as a holiday greeting, similar to "Happy New Year!"

鞏[巩] **gǔng** (B) firm, secure.

鞏固 **gǔnggù** (FV) strengthen. /我們得~我們的防線. We must strengthen our defense line. (SV) be firm, secure.

拱 **gǔng** (FV) 1) push something with the shoulders or head. /牛把門~開了. The cow pushed the door open. 2) worm one's way out or into. /他從人群裏~出來了. He wormed his way out of the crowd. (B) 1) an arch. ~門 archway. 2) raise. ~手 raise one's joined hands in salutation; ~肩 shrug. 3) protect. ~衛 guard.

共 **gùng** (B) 1) collectively. 一~ altogether. 2) together. ~用 share. 3) common, general. ~同目標 common goal. 4) communist. 中~ Chinese Communist Party.

共產黨 **gùngchándǎng** (N) Communist Party.

共產主義 **gùngchánjǔyì** (N) communism.

共產主義青年團 **gùngchánjǔ'yìchīngnyán'twán** (N) Communist Youth Corps.

共青團 **gùngchīngtwán** (N) Communist Youth Corps (abbr. of 共產主義青年團 **gùngchánjú'yìchīngnyán'twán**).

共總 **gùngdzǔng** (A) altogether. /這些東西~值一百塊錢. These things are worth one hundred dollars altogether.

共和 **gūnghé** (AT) republican. ~黨 Republican Party.

共同 **gùngtúng** (AT) general, common. ~權利 common rights. (A) jointly, together. ~管理 manage or control something jointly.

貢 **gùng** (B) offer something to a superior. t

貢獻 **gùngsyàn** (N) contribution. (FV) contribute, offer. /我

想～一點意見. I'd like to offer some suggestions.

供 **gùng** (FV) 1) offer in worship. ～佛 offer <u>something</u> to Buddha. 2) give evidence, confess. /他已經～了. He has already confessed. /那個槍匪～出很多同黨. The robber turned in many of his gang. (B) 1) testimony under oath, confession. 畫～ sign a confession. 2) offering. 上～ place an offering (as before Buddha.) → 供 **gūng**.

guo *see* **gwo**.

瓜 **gwā** (N) melon.
瓜子兒 **gwādzěr** (N) melon seeds.

刮 **gwā** (FV) 1) scrape. /他把牆上的漆都～下去了. He scraped all the paint off the wall. 2) shave. ～臉 shave (lit. shave the face). /他一天得～兩次臉. He has to shave twice a day. SF of 颳 **gwā**.
刮臉刀 **gwālyǎndāu** (N) <ｰ儿> razor (M 把 **bǎ**).

颳[刮] **gwā** (FV) blow (of the wind). /土～得滿天飛. Dust was blown into the air.
颳風 **gwāfēng** (VO) be windy. /已經颳了兩天風了. The wind has been blowing for two days.

絓 **gwǎ** (FV) 1) scratch. /那個樹枝把我臉～了一下. My face was scratched by some branches. 2) catch, <u>as something projecting out catches one's clothes, or two cars catch each other's fenders</u>. /我的衣服～在樹枝上了. My clothes caught on the branch of a tree.

掛[罣][挂] **gwà** (FV) hang <u>something</u> up. /你可以把大衣～在門後頭. You may hang your coat behind the door. (M) string <u>of things</u>. 一～珠子 a string of pearls. (B) anxious. ～念 be anxious.
掛號 **gwàhàu** (VO) 1) make an appointment <u>with a doctor</u>, sign in <u>at a hospital</u> (lit. hang up a number). 2) register a letter, etc. /這封信應該～. This letter should be registered.

袿 **gwà** (B) 1) <ｰ子,ｰ儿> man's Chinese gown, jacket (M 件 **jyàn**). 馬～

儿 half-length formal coat (<u>worn over a long gown</u>).

乖 **gwāi** (SV) be good, well-behaved (<u>of children</u>). (B) clever. ～巧 be clever.

拐[枴] (N) **gwǎi** (FV) 1) make a turn. 往左～ turn to the left. 2) take, steal. /他～走了五百塊錢. He stole five hundred dollars. /他～了一個小孩. He kidnapped a child. (N) crutch, cane.
拐子 **gwǎidz** (N) 1) kidnapper. 2) lame person.
拐棍儿 **gwǎigwèr** (N) walking stick, cane (M 根 **gēn**, 隻 **jī**).

踝 **gwǎi** → 踝 **hwái**.

怪 **gwài** (SV) be strange, queer. (FV) blame. /別～他. Don't blame him. (A) rather. /這個東西～好的. This thing is rather good. (B) strange being. 妖～ apparition.
怪物 **gwàiwu** (N) 1) strange being. 2) queer bird, oddball (irrational, erratic person).

官 **gwān** (N) <ｰ儿> official (governmental). (B) 1) governmental, official. ～事 governmental affairs. 2) organ (in the body). 器～ organ.
官價 **gwānjya** (N) official price (fixed by the government or by local authorities, particularly ceiling prices).
官僚主義 **gwānlyáujǔyi** (N) bureaucracy.
官銜 **gwānsyán** (N) official title. /他的～是什麼? What's his official title? *or* What's his position in the government?
官司 **gwānsz** (N) lawsuit. 打～ sue, be involved in a lawsuit.

關[関,関][关] **gwān** (FV) 1) close. /門～了. The door is closed. /～門. Close the door. 2) turn off. ～燈 turn off a light. 3) imprison, confine. /把他～在家裏. Confine him to his house. 4) draw a salary. ～薪水 draw a salary. (N) mountain pass, gate (<u>as in a city wall</u>). 過～ go through a pass. (B) 1) customs. 海～ customs. 2) concerned. ～懷 be concerned about. 3) connect. ～節 a joint. *s*

93

關照 'gwānjàu (FV) 1) speak to, consult with, report to. /你走的時候請你～我一聲。 Would you let me know when you're ready to go? 2) take care of, look after. /我的兒子在那兒做事，請你～。 My son is working there; please look after him (a bit).

關鍵 'gwānjyàn (N) key factor in a situation. /這個問題的～在那儿? What is the crux of the problem?

關稅 gwānshwèi (N) customs duty.

關餉 gwānsyǎng (VO) give out pay. /今天～了。 Today was payday. /軍隊什麼時候～? When do they pay you in the army?

關係 gwānsyi (N) 1) relation, relationship. /他們是甚麼～? What is their relationship? 2) connection, relevance. /這件事情跟我沒有～. This matter has nothing to do with me. 3) influence, consequence. /這件事～很大. The consequences of this matter are very serious. (FV) involve. /這件事～着很多人的生命. This matter involves many lives. → 沒關係 méigwānsyi.

關心 gwānsyīn (FV) be concerned about. /我很～你. I am very concerned about you.

關於 gwānyú (CV) concerning, with respect to. /～這件事情我沒意見. I have no opinion concerning this matter. /這是一個～中國學生的故事. This is a story about a Chinese student.

觀(观)gwān (B) 1) behold, observe. ～摩 observe and imitate. 2) view, concept. 人生～ philosophy of life. → 觀gwàn.

觀察 gwānchá (FV) observe. /我就是來～～. I've only come to observe. (N) observation, opinion.

觀點 gwāndyǎn (N) view, viewpoint.

觀眾 gwānjùng (N) spectator, audience. /～忽然都笑起來了. The whole audience suddenly burst out laughing.

觀念 'gwānnyàn (N) concept, notion, view.

棺 gwān (B) coffin. ～木 coffin.

棺材 gwāntsai (N) coffin (M 口 kou).

管 gwǎn (FV) 1) manage, control, govern, take care of. ～事情 manage affairs; ～孩子 take care of children. /他老想～着我. He always wants to boss me around. 2) include, provide for. ～水電 include water and electricity. 3) guarantee. /不好～換. We guarantee to change it if it isn't any good. 4) be concerned about. /他只～自己不～別人. He's only concerned about himself, not about others. (M) 1) for pens. 一～筆 a pen. 2) for flutes. 一～笛子 a flute. (B) <～子,～儿> tube, pipe (M根gēn). 水～子 water pipe. (PT) 1) ～...叫 call someone something. ～他叫哥哥 call him elder brother. 2) 不～...都 it doesn't matter who, what, whether, etc. /不～誰作都成. It doesn't matter who does it. s

管保 gwǎnbǎu (FV) guarantee. /我～這個東西可以用三年. I guarantee that this can be used for three years. (A) definitely. /他～不知道. He definitely doesn't know.

管賬 gwǎnjàng (VO) keep accounts. /他在那家飯館～. He keeps accounts for that restaurant.

管家 gwǎnjya (N) 1) butler. 2) housekeeper.

管理 gwǎnlǐ (FV) manage, control, take care of. ～工廠 manage a factory. (N) management, control. 商業～ business management.

管事 gwǎnshr̀ (VO) be in charge (of affairs). /這儿誰～? Who is in charge here? (N) manager. /他們的大～走了. Their head-manager has gone. (SV) be effective. /這個藥很～. This medicine is very effective. /這個鎖一點都不～. This lock just doesn't do the trick. /他說的話不～. What he says doesn't count for much.

慣 gwàn (SV) be accustomed to. /我對這件事已經聽的很～了. I've already gotten quite accustomed to hearing about that. (FV) spoil a child. /他老～着他的孩子. He always spoils his children.

貫 gwàn (B) pierce. ～注 pay sharp attention.

　貫徹 'gwànchè (FV) carry through a plan, policy, etc. /他不能～他自己的計劃. He cannot carry through his own plans.

觀 gwàn (N) Taoist temple. →觀 gwān.

罐 gwàn (B) <-子,-ル> jar, can. 茶～ tea canister.

　罐頭 gwàntou (N) canned food (M罐 gwàr). 吃～ eat canned food. 2) can (for canned food). 空～ empty can.

灌 gwàn (FV) 1) pour something. /把剩下的牛奶～到那個瓶裏. Pour the rest of the milk into that bottle. 2) irrigate. ～田 irrigate land. 3) record something on a tape or disc. /請不要把我的話～進去. Please don't record what I say. (B) assemble. ～聚 assemble together; ～木 shrub.

　灌溉 gwàngài (FV) irrigate. ～稻田 irrigate a rice field, flood a rice field (in growing rice).

光 gwāng, gwǎng * (N) light (M道 dàu). (SV) be smooth (of a surface). (FV) 1) make a part of or the whole body bare. /你～着身子會着涼的. You'll catch cold without any clothes on. /他的頭都～了一半了. He's half bald already. 2) be all gone, used up. /我的錢都～了. I don't have any money left. (A)* only do one thing, nothing else. ～吃肉 only eat meat. (RE) indicates using up, finishing up. 吃～ eat up something.

　光棍兒 gwānggwèr (N) bachelor. 打～ be single (of a man).

　光滑 gwānghwá (SV) be smooth (of a surface). /她的皮膚很～. Her skin is very smooth.

　光明 gwāngmíng (SV) be bright (of the future). ～的前途 bright future. (B) pure in mind. 正大～ be upright and pure in mind.

　光榮 gwāngrúng (SV) 1) be honorable, glorious. ～的行為 glorious deed. 2) be proud, honored. /有這麼好一個兒子,他很覺得～. He feels very proud having such a wonderful son. (N) glory,

honor. 為了國家的～ for the glory of the nation.

　光線 gwāngsyàn (N) beam of light (M道 dàu, 條 tyáu).

　光陰 'gwāngyīn (N) time, time available. /～很寶貴. Time is precious.

光 gwǎng → 光 gwāng.

廣[广] gwǎng (SV) be broad, wide, extensive. /他的科學知識很～. He has a broad knowledge of science. (B) Canton (contracted form of ～東 gwǎngdūng).

　廣播 gwǎngbwō (FV) broadcast. /這個節目專為對海外～. This program was made especially for broadcasting overseas. (N) broadcast.

　廣播台 gwǎngbwōtái (N) radio station (M家 jyā).

　廣場 gwǎngchǎng (N) 1) large field (generally for rallies). 2) square (place). 天安門～ Tien An Men Square (in Peking).

　廣大 gwǎngdà (SV) be large, vast, massive. ～的工作階級 the massive labor class.

　廣告 gwǎnggàu (N) advertisement. 登～ put an advertisement in a paper, magazine, etc; 貼～ post a bill.

　廣告牌 gwǎnggàupái (N) billboard.

　廣義 gwǎngyì (AT) broad (in meaning). ～的說法 broad interpretation; ～的說 in a broad sense.

逛 gwàng (FV) visit a place, go sightseeing, browse around. ～公園 go to the park. /我們那天到紐約～～去吧. Let's go sight-seeing in New York sometime.

規 gwēi (B) 1) rule, regulation. ～則 regulation. 2) compasses. 圓～ compasses; 日～ sundial. 3) correct a fault. ～勸 reprimand. 4) fee. 月～ monthly fee.

　規定 gwēidìng (FV) make a regulation. /學校～不許抽煙. The school made a regulation to prohibit smoking. (N) regulation (M條 tyáu).

　規則 'gwēidzé (N) rule, prescribed procedure (M條 tyáu). /咱們用這個機器應該有一定

的～. There have to be definite rules for operating this machinery.
規矩 **gwēijyu** (N) rule, custom. 按～ according to the rules. (SV) be well-behaved (of a person).
規模 **'gwēimwó** (N) scope. /這個組織的～很大. That organization is quite extensive.

閨 **gwēi** (B) lady's chamber. ～房 lady's chamber.
閨女 **gwēinyu** (N) 1) daughter. 2) unmarried young woman.

歸(归) **gwēi** (FV) 1) gather things together. /把書都～在桌上. Put all the books together on the table. 2) be a possession of. /那個島～英國了. That island became a possession of England. (CV) it is one's responsibility to.... /我母親～我哥哥養. It's my brother's responsibility to support my mother. (B) return. ～國 return to one's native country.
歸了包堆 **'gwēilebāu'dzwēi** (A) altogether, in all, a certain amount. /～我花了十五塊錢. I spent fifteen dollars in all.

鬼 **gwěi** (N) ghost, spirit, demon. 鬧～ be haunted. /他心裏有～. He has something weighing on his conscience (lit. There's a ghost in his heart). (SV) be smart, quick-witted. (B) 1) dishonest. ～話 falsehood. 2) addict. 酒～ drunkard.

貴 **gwèi** (SV) be expensive. (B) 1) your (h). ～國 your country. 2) noble. ～婦 noblewoman.
貴族 **gwèidzú** (N) member of the nobility, aristocrat. /他父親從前是一個～. Formerly his father was a member of the nobility.
貴重 **gwèijùng** (SV) be valuable, precious.
貴姓 **gwèisyìng** (IE) What is your name, please?

跪 **gwèi** (FV) kneel. ～下 kneel down. /我的腿都～麻了. My legs are numb from kneeling.

桂 **gwèi** (B) 1) cassia, cinnamon (Cinnamonum cassia). 2) Kwangsi. ～劇 Kwangsi regional drama. s

桂花 **gwèihwā** (N) cassia or cinnamon blossom.

櫃(匱)(柜) **gwèi** (N) <-子> 1) cupboard, cabinet, bureau, wardrobe. 書～ book cabinet; 衣～ clothes closet. 2) counter showcase. 玻璃～ glass showcase. (B) store. 本～ this store, this company.
櫃臺 **gwèitái** (N) counter, desk, in a hotel or store.

鍋 **gwō** (N) pot, pan. 火～ chafing dish. (B) <-ㄦ, -子> bowl of a pipe.

國(国) **gwó** (N) country, nation, state. (M) country, nation, state. /那條河流過好幾～. That river flows through several countries. (B) 1) used with names of countries. 法～ France. 2) national. ～語 national languages.
國旗 **gwóchí** (N) national flag (M 面 **myàn**).
國慶節 **gwóchìngjyé** (TW) (at the time of) the Anniversary of the Nation (c).
國都 **gwódū** (N) capital of a country.
國防 **gwófáng** (N) national defense.
國會 **gwóhwèi** (N) congress, parliament.
國籍 **gwójí** (N) nationality. /你是那國～? What is your nationality?
國際 **gwójì** (AT) international. ～法 international law.
國際主義 **gwójìjǔyì** (N) internationalism.
國家 **gwójyā** (N) country, nation.
國界 **gwójyè** (N) border between countries, national boundary (M 條 **tyáu**). 劃～ draw a boundary line.
國民 **gwómín** (N) citizen of a country, national.
國民黨 **gwómíndǎng** (N) the Chinese Nationalist Party, Kuomintang.
國術 **gwóshù** (N) Chinese rhythmic exercise practiced to give one skill in self-defense.
國王 **gwówáng** (N) king.

果(菓) (B) 1)} **gwǒ** (B) 1) <-子> fruit. 水～ fruit; ～仁 nut. 2) result, outcome. 結 ~ result, outcome.　3) really, actually. 如 ~ supposing that, if.

果子　**gwǒdz** (N) 1)†(B) 1). 2) puffed fritter (lp).

果子醬　**gwǒdzjyàng** (N) jam, preserves.

果木樹　**gwǒmùshù** (N) fruit tree (M棵**kē**).

果然　**gwǒrán** (A) indeed, actually. /他~辭職了. He actually did leave.

果樹　**gwǒshù** (N) fruit tree (M棵**kē**).

果園　**gwǒywán** (N) <-子> orchard.

裹　**gwǒ** (FV) 1) wrap something. ~傷 bandage a wound. /請你用紙把這個~起來. Would you please wrap this? 2) wrap something around an object. /我~了一條毯子. I wrapped a blanket around myself. 3) coerce, compel. /他小的時候就叫土匪~走了. He was forced to join the bandits when he was young. 4) mix a small amount of something with a larger amount. /他們把次等煙草~在好煙草裏. They mix inferior tobacco leaves with good ones.　(B) package. 包~ package.

過(过)　**gwò** (DV) 1) go or come over or through, cross. /火車剛~河橋就塌了. The bridge collapsed just after the train crossed it. 2) pass or go by. /我們已經~了芝加哥了. We've already passed by Chicago. /春天已經~了. Spring is past. /街上~軍隊哪. The troops are going down the street. 3) spend a period of time. ~夜 spend the night at a place or doing something. 4) exceed a certain time or amount. /~三點了嗎? Is it past three o'clock? 5) celebrate, observe, a certain occasion. ~年 celebrate New Year's. 6) make a practice of doing something. ~份子 make a practice of exchanging gifts on special occasions. /我們兩個~玩笑. We are always kidding each other.　(RE) 1) past or by a place. 走~頭了. walk past one's destination. 2) in potential RC, indicates an ability to win in competition. /我打得~他. I

can beat him in a fight.　(P) added to verbs, indicates that an action has been experienced; in a question, is like saying have you ever...; with 沒 **méi** in a statement, is like saying I've never.... /這本書我看~三次了. I've read this book three times. /你吃~中國飯嗎? Have you ever eaten Chinese food? /我沒上~學. I've never been to school. /我沒來~這儿. I've never been here before.　(B) mistake, wrongdoing. 記~ record a demerit; 大~ serious mistake. → 不過 **búgwò**.

過磅　**gwòbàng** (VO) be weighed (of anything exceeding one pound). /行李都~了嗎? Has all the luggage been weighed?

過期　**gwòchī** (VO) pass the due date, become overdue. /這些書都~了. These books are overdue.

過去　**gwòchyu** (FV) pass away (die). /他什麼時候~的? When did he pass away?　(RC) 1) cross over, go over. /我~看他. I'll go over and see him. 2) in negative potential form only, give someone a hard time. /他老跟我過不去. He's always picking on me.　(RE) 1) indicates a change in position from here to there. 拿~ take something over there. 2) indicates a change from a conscious state to an unconscious one. 暈~ pass out, faint. → 過去 **gwòchyù**.

過去　**gwòchyù** (TW) (in) the past. /~我們都這樣做. We've done it this way in the past. /我說的是~不是現在. I'm talking about the past, not the present. → 過去 **gwòchyu**.

過道儿　**gwòdàur** (N) passageway, corridor, aisle (M條**tyáu**).

過繼　'**gwòjì** (FV) adopt a related child. /在中國~比領養孤兒普通. In China adopting a related child is more common than adopting an orphan.

過重　**gwòjùng** (VO) be overweight (of luggage, letters, packages). /這封信~了. This letter is overweight.

過來　**gwòlai** (RC) cross over, come over. /我~看你. I'll come over to see you.　(RE) 1) indicates a change in position from there to here. 搬～move something over here. 2) indicates a change from an undesirable condition to a desirable one. 甦醒～regain consciousness, become sober; 改～correct, reform. /他現在總算明白～了. Finally he understands.

過ㄦ **gwòr** (M) 1) time, occurrence, of doing something thoroughly. /我念了一～. I read it once. 2) time, occurrence, of turning over. /那輛車翻了兩個～. That car turned over twice.

過眼 **gwòyǎn** (VO) look something over. /你桌子上的東西你都～了嗎? Have you looked over all the things on your desk?

過於 **gwòyu** (A) too, over-. /他～小心. He is over-cautious.

滾 **gwǔn** (FV) roll. 在地上～ roll around on the ground; ～雪球 roll a ball of snow. (B) boiling. ～水 boiling water; ～燙 be boiling hot. (IE) Scram! *or* Beat it!

滾出去 **gwǔnchuchyu** (IE) Get out of here!

滾子 **gwǔndz** (N) roller.

棍 **gwùn** (B) 1) <-子,-ㄦ> rod, stick, club (M 條 **tyáu**). 2) villain. 賭～ professional gambler; 訟～ man who promotes litigation, "ambulance-chaser."

哈 **hā** (FV) blow through the mouth. /擦眼鏡以前你先～一點ㄦ氣ㄦ. Blow on your glasses a little before wiping them. (B) ↓. *t* →哈**hǎ**.

哈哈 **hāhā** (ON) ha ha. ～大笑 hearty laughter *or* laugh heartily. (N) <-ㄦ> joke (lp). 打～ crack a joke.

哈喇 **hāla** (SV) be rancid (of oily things only) (lp).

蛤{蝦} **há** (B) ↓. →蛤**gě**.

蛤蟆 **háma** (N) frog.

哈 **hǎ** (B) ↓. *s* →哈**hā**.

哈巴狗ㄦ **hǎbagǒur** (N) Pekinese (dog) (M 條 **tyáu**, 隻 **jr̄**).

嗨 **hāi** (I) used to draw someone's attention. /～! 你過來! Hey! Come here!

孩 **hái** (B) <-子,-ㄦ> child. ～童 children.

還[还] **hái** (A) 1) still going on. /現在怎麼～下雨? How can it still be raining? /我～吃飯呢. I'm still eating. 2) still (as before). /下雨你～去嗎? If it rains, are you still going? 3) still more, more. /～有一個. There's still another *or* There's one more. 4) again. /我明天～來. I'll come again tomorrow. 5) even. /我～給總統寫過信呢. I even wrote the president. 6) rather, fairly. ～好 fairly good. (PT) 1) 比. . . ～ even . . . -er. 比我～好 even better than I. 2) 不但. . . ～ not only. . . but also. /他不但做事,～念書. He's not only working but also studying. →還**hwán**.

還是 **háishr** (A) 1) still (as before). /我～不去. I'm still not going. 2) after all. /～你對. You were right after all. (PT) (～) . . . ～. . . . . . or. . . (in a question). /(～)你去～他去? Are you going or is he?

還有 **háiyou** (A) furthermore, and also. /別讓他知道,～也別讓他太太知道. Don't let him know; and furthermore don't let his wife know.

海 **hǎi** (N) sea. (B) large, vast. ～碗 large bowl. *t*

海港 **hǎigǎng** (N) harbor.

海關 **hǎigwān** (N) 1) customhouse. 2) customs.

海軍 **hǎijyūn** (N) navy. ～基地 naval base.

海口 **hǎikǒu** (N) seaport.

海棠花 **hǎitánghwā** (N) <-ㄦ> cherry-apple *or* crab-apple blossom (M 朵 **dwǒ**).

海灣 **hǎiwān** (N) bay (saltwater).

害 **hài** (FV) 1) harm. /他的舉動～了很多人. His actions harmed many people. 2) murder. /他被人給～了. He was murdered. 3) suffer from. ～病 be sick. (N) 1) seeds of trouble. 2) bad effect. 有利沒有～ have good effects and no bad effects.

害怕 **hàipà** (SV) be afraid, scared, frightened. /我一個人晚上出去很～. I'm afraid to go out alone at night. (VO) be afraid, scared. /他没害過怕. He has never been afraid.

害臊 **hàisàu** (SV) be shy. (VO) feel ashamed. /他從來没害過臊. He has never felt ashamed.

害羞 **hàisyōu** (SV) be shy. (VO) feel ashamed. /你~不~? Don't you feel ashamed?

咳 **hài** (I) indicates discouragement, regret, disgust. /~! 我真是笨蛋! Darn it! I am so stupid! →咳 **ké.**

寒 **hán** (B) 1) cold. ~流 cold current. 2) in poor circumstances. 貧~ be poor.

寒假 **hánjyà** (TW) (during) winter vacation.

寒毛 **hánmau** (N) fine hair on the human body (M根 **gēn**).

寒暑表 **hánshúbyǎu** thermometer.

含 **hán, hén*** (FV) 1)* hold something in the mouth. /你別~着牛奶, 把它嚥了. Don't hold the milk in your mouth; swallow it. 2) contain, embody. /海水裏~很多鹽. Sea water contains a lot of salt. /他的話~着什麼意思? What do his words mean? (B) hold back, restrain, harbor, emotion, feeling. ~恨 harbor hatred; ~淚 hold back tears.

涵 **hán** (B) 1) contain. ~容 contain. 2) lenient. 包~ be tolerant, forgiving.

涵義 **hányì** (N) concealed meaning, implication. /他的話有什麼~? What's the implication behind what he said?

喊 **hǎn** (FV) 1) cry, shout. ~口號 shout slogans. 2) call someone. /你~他來. Call to him to come.

汗 **hàn** (N) sweat, perspiration. 出~ to sweat, perspire.

汗衫 **hànshān** (N) under-shirt, shirt (M件 **jyàn**).

旱 **hàn** (SV) be dry, dried up, from lack of rain. /今年太~了. It's been very dry this year. (B) 1) drought. ~災 drought. 2) dry land (as opposed to flooded land). ~稻 rice grown on dry land.

漢[囝] **hàn** (B) 1) Han race. ~人 Han people. 2) <-子> man. 老~ old man. *d*

和 **hàn** →和 **hé.**

行 **háng** (M) 1) column, line, row. 排成兩~ form two lines. 2) line of business or study. /您在那~做事? What line of business are you in? (FV) be numbered as (among brothers and/or sisters). /你~幾? Which number are you (among your brothers and sisters)? (B) 1) profession. 內~ be professional, a professional; 外~ be amateur, an amateur. 2) firm, business house. 銀~ bank; 電器~ electrical shop. →行 **syíng.**

行市 **hángshr** (N) 1) current price, exchange rate. 2) market. /這種貨没~. There's no market for this line of goods.

航 **háng** (B) navigate. ~線 air *or* shipping route.

航空 **hángkūng** (AT) aeronautical, air. ~工程 aeronautical engineering. (N) aeronautics.

航空母艦 **hángkūngmǔjyàn** (N) aircraft carrier (M艘 **sǒu**, 隻 **jř**, 條 **tyáu**).

航空信 **hángkūngsyìn** (N) air mail letter (M封 **fēng**).

航線 **hángsyàn** (N) shipping route, flight route (M條 **tyáu**).

航行 **hángsyíng** (FV) navigate, fly, sail. /我們在地中海~了一個禮拜. We sailed for one week on the Mediterranean.

hao *see* **hau.**

號[囝] **háu** (B) call out, cry. ~哭 wail. →號 **hàu.**

毫 **háu** (A) before three-syllable negative expressions, (not) at all. /那件事情~不奇怪. That isn't strange at all. (M) one-thousandth of a 寸 **tswùn**, 錢 **chyán**, *or* 畝 **mǔ**. (B) fine hair. ~毛 fine hair on the body.

好 **hǎu** (SV) 1) be good, nice, fine. ~人 nice person. 2) be repaired, fixed. /汽車~了嗎? Is the car fixed? 3) be ready, done. /飯~了. The food (*or* rice) is ready. 4) be friends. /他們兩個人~

了. Those two are friends again. (RE) indicates finishing satisfactorily. /這件事他作不～. He can't do that job well. (A) 1) the better to, in order to. /快點收拾我們～走. Hurry up and pack so we can leave. 2) followed by SV, very, quite. /～久没見. I haven't seen you for a long long time. 3) used in exclamations, what a . . . , how. . . it is. /～漂亮呀! How beautiful it (or she) is! 4) really. ～傷心 really heart-breaking; ～不高興 really unhappy. /我～説了他幾句. I really bawled him out. (Sometimes, depending on the context, 不 bù precedes SV without negating it. /他中了頭彩～不高興. When he won first prize, he was really happy.) (B) 1) be easy to. ～'買 be easy to buy. 2) be good to. ～喝 be good (to drink). 3) with indefinite numbers, quite a number. ～幾個 quite a few; ～些 many. (IE) in answering a suggestion, O.K. or All right. /～. 我們走吧. O.K. Let's go. →好hàu.

好吃 hǎuchī (SV) 1) be good to eat, delicious. 2) be easy to eat.

好處 hǎuchu (N) good point, advantage.

好處 háuchǔ (SV) be easy to get along with.

好歹 háudǎi (N) good and evil. /他不知道～. He doesn't know good from evil. (A) for good or for evil, no matter what. /～你得去一趟. No matter what it's like, you must go there once.

好的 hǎude (IE) O.K. or All right.

好在 hǎudzài (A) fortunately. /～他還不知道. Fortunately he doesn't know it yet.

好漢 hǎuhàn (N) courageous person (male only) (M條tyáu).

好壞 hǎuhwài (N) 1) quality. /這種貨的～很難説. It's very hard to determine the quality of this kind of merchandise. 2) good and evil. /他不知道～. He doesn't know good from evil. (A) for better or for worse, anyway (even though someone doesn't like it). /～他們已經結婚了. For better or

for worse, they got married. /我知道你不喜歡他,可是他結婚你～得去一下. I know you don't like him, but you should go to his wedding anyway.

好傢伙 hǎujyāhwo (IE) My gosh! or My goodness! /～,你吃得真多啊! My gosh, you really eat a lot!

好看 hǎukàn (SV) 1) be good-looking. 2) be easy to read. 3) be interesting.

好説話 hǎushwōhwà (SV) <-ㄦ> be easy to deal with, pleasant to converse with, affable. /我們的經理很～. Our manager is very easy to deal with.

好像 hǎusyàng (FV) seem like, look like (with or without 似的shrde at the end of the sentence). /他～中國人(似的). He looks like a Chinese. (A) it seems that, seem to be (with or without 似的shrde at the end of the sentence). /他～不來了(似的). It seems that he's not coming. /他～很高興. He seems to be very happy.

好聽 hǎutīng (SV) 1) be pleasant to listen to. 2) be easy to hear. 3) be interesting.

好玩ㄦ hǎuwár (SV) 1) be interesting, fun, to do or play. /游泳真～. Swimming is really fun. 2) be easy to play (as an instrument). 3) be cute, amusing. /那個小女孩真～. That little girl is very cute.

好聞 hǎuwén (SV) 1) smell good. 2) be easy to detect by smelling.

好意 hǎuyì (N) good intentions (M番fān). /我勸他離開是一番～. I had good intentions in persuading him to leave. /謝謝您的～. Thank you for your kindness.

好 hàu (AV) 1) like to, enjoy . . . -ing. ～説話 like to talk. /他～看電影. He enjoys going to the movies. 2) be easy to. /他～傷風. He catches cold easily. (B) enjoyment. 嗜～hobby, habit. →好hǎu.

號[号]hàu (M) 1) day. 八月一～ August 1st. 2) number. 第三～ number three. /你的電話幾～? What's your telephone number? (N) 1) bugle.

100

2) courtesy name. /孫逸仙的～
叫中山. Sun Yat-Sen's courtesy
name is Chung-Shan. (B) 1) name.
國 ～ name of a dynasty. 2) <-ㄦ>
mark, sign. 問 ～ question mark.
3) order, command. ～令 an order.
4) business establishment. 商 ～ store.
5) number. ～頭 number. →號 hàu.

號召 hàujàu (FV) urge, en-
courage. /政府～青年從軍.
The government urged the young men
to join the army.

號碼ㄦ hàumǎr (N) number
assigned for identification; e. g., a
telephone number, a motor's serial
number. /他的電話是什麼～?
What is his telephone number?

號ㄦ hàur (M) size which is
standard, as for shoes, clothes, etc.,
or for things which are classified
small, medium, and large. 頭 ～
largest size; 大 ～ large size or king
size; 中～ medium size. /你穿幾
～的鞋? What size shoe do you
wear? /我的襯衫小了一～.
My shirt is a size too small.

耗 hàu (FV) 1) waste. /他～了很多
時間. He wasted a lot of time. 2)
keep a situation deadlocked. /他們
誰也沒提離婚, 一直～了三年.
Neither of them mentioned divorce
and kept things as they were for
three years.

耗子 hàudz (N) mouse, rat
(M 隻ㄐㄧ).

喝 hē (FV) drink. ～茶 drink tea; ～湯
eat soup. →喝 hè.

喝醉 hēdzwèi (RC) get drunk.
/喝酒沒有關係, 但是不要～.
It's all right to drink, but you
shouldn't get drunk.

合[闔] (FV) 1)} hé (FV) 1) close (usually a book or the eyes). ～上書
close a book; ～眼 close one's eyes.
2) put together, combine, pool. /假
如把那些資料～在一起, 這問
題應當可以解決了. If you put
all those materials together, it
should be possible to solve this problem. 3) be in accord with, agree
with. /他的話正～我的意思.
What he says is very much in agreement with my ideas. 4) add up to,

equal to. /那個～五十塊錢.
It adds up to fifty dollars. /一塊美
金～多少中國錢? What is an
American dollar equal to in Chinese
money? (A) together. /那兩家～
住一棟房子. Those two families
live together in one house. →合 gě.

合併 hébìng (FV) merge, unite.
/～這兩個機關可以省錢.
Merging these two organizations
would save money.

合作 hédzwò (FV) co-operate.
/如果他肯～, 這件事就簡單
了. If he is willing to cooperate,
this matter will be simple. (N) cooperation. (SV) be co-operative.

合作社 hédzwòshè (N) co-
operative.

合法 héfǎ (SV) be legal, according to law. 用～的手續 use
legal methods.

合格 hégé (SV) be qualified,
eligible. /做這件事情他很～.
He is very qualified to do this. (VO)
have the qualifications. /他已經
合了格了. He has the qualifications already.

合股 hégǔ (VO) pool capital,
form a partnership. /我們～開一
個鋪子吧. Let's pool our capital and open up a shop.

合乎 héhu (FV) suit, meet,
needs or demands. ～需要 suit one's
needs.

合夥 héhwǒ (VO) be in business
together, work together to make
money. /我從前跟他合過好幾
次夥做買賣. He and I have been
in business together several times
before.

合脾胃 hépíwèi (VO) suit someone's taste. /這個汽車的顏色不
合他的脾胃. The color of this
car doesn't suit his taste.

合適 héshr (SV) 1) be the right
size, fit. /這帽子很～. This
hat is just the right size. 2) be
suitable, fitting. /這種衣服冬天
穿不～. This kind of clothing
isn't suitable for wearing in the winter. 3) be congenial. /他們兩個
人不～. Those two don't get along.

合算 héswàn (SV) 1) be worthwhile. /跑那麼遠看那種電影
很不～. Going that far to see that

kind of movie isn't worthwhile at all. 2) be worth the money. /買這個汽車不~. This car isn't worth buying.

合同 **hétung** (N) contract (M 張 **jāng**). 簽 ~ sign a contract.

何 **hé** (B) 1) what. 如~ in what way, how, how about; ~人 who. 2) why. ~苦 why suffer through doing something. s

何必 **hébì** (A)ᵖ why is it necessary to do something. /你~來這麼早? Why do you need to come so early?

河 **hé** (N) river (M條 **tyáu**, 道 **dàu**).

河壩 **hébà** (N) dam (across a river).

河道 **hédàu** (N) course of a river, river bed (M條 **tyáu**).

河堤 **hédī**, **hétí** (N) river dike (M條 **tyáu**, 道 **dàu**).

河溝儿 **hégōur** (N) brook, stream (M條 **tyáu**).

河口 **hékǒu** (N) mouth of a river.

河流 **hélyóu** (N) river (M 條 **tyáu**, 道 **dàu**).

和(龢) **hé**, **hàn*** (CV) 1)* with (accompanying). /我~你一塊儿去 I'll go with you. 2)* and. /我要筆~紙. I want a pen and some paper. (FV) 1) come to a draw (in chess). /那盤棋我們~了. We reached a stalemate in that game of chess. 2) make peace after a war. /北方跟南方早就~了. The north and the south made peace with each other a long time ago. 3) be friendly. /他們兩個人不~. Those two are not friendly. 4) rehearse with accompaniment. /我已經自己唱過好幾次了,但是還沒有~過琴. I have already sung it many times by myself, but I haven't rehearsed yet with the piano. (N) sum (arith.). /二跟三的~是五. The sum of two and three is five. (B) harmonious. 平~ be good-natured. →和 **hè**, 和 **hwò**, 和 **hwo**.

和氣 **héchì** (SV) be agreeable, friendly, easy to get along with.

和緩 **'héhwǎn** (SV) 1) be calm (of a situation). /最近戰事比較~了. The war situation has been calmer recently. 2) be moderate,

mild (of one's temperament). /他的性情很~. He has a very mild temperament. (FV) calm down. /他們兩人吵起來了,你想法給他們~~. Those two are quarreling; try to calm them down.

和美 **héměi** (SV) be close knit, harmonious, especially of a family group.

和平 **hépíng** (N) peace (as opposed to war). (SV) be good-natured.

和尚 **héshang** (N) monk (Buddhist).

核(覈) (B) 3)} **hé, hú*** (B) 1)*<-儿> pit, stone (of a fruit). 桃~ peach pit. 2) nucleus of a cell or atom. 細胞~ cell nucleus. 3) check up, investigate. ~准 grant after due consideration.

核對 **hédwèi** (FV) check, compare, collate. ~賬目 audit accounts. /請你~~這兩個版本. Would you please compare these two editions?

核桃 **hétau** (N) walnut.

盒 **hé** (B) <-儿, -子 > small box.

荷 **hé** (B) lotus. ~葉 lotus leaf. t

荷花 **héhwā** (N) <-儿 > 1) lotus, water lily (M棵 **kē**). 2) lotus blossom, water lily (M朵 **dwǒ**, 支 **jīr**).

褐 **hé** (B) dark brown. ~色 dark brown (color).

和 **hè** (FV) compose a poem to match another by using similar rhyming words. /我~了他一首詩. I composed a poem to match his. →和 **hé**, 和 **hwò**, 和 **hwo**.

喝 **hè** (B) shout. ~彩 give a cheer, shout applause. →喝 **hē**.

黑 **hēi** (SV) 1) be black. ~頭髮 black hair. 2) be dark (opposite of bright). /天~了. It's dark out. 3) be dark (opposite of fair). /那個人皮膚很~. That man has a dark complexion. (N) black, black color. 漆~ jet black. (B) 1) secret. ~社會 secret society. 2) evil. ~白 good and evil.

黑暗 **hēiàn** (SV) 1) be dark (opposite of bright). ~的夜晚 dark night. 2) be corrupt, decadent.

~社會 decadent society. /政治很~. The government is very corrupt.

黑板 **hēibǎn** (N) blackboard (M塊**kwài**).

黑色 **hēisè** (N) black (color).

黑下 **hēisya** (TW) (at) night. /等到了~再説. Let's wait till night time. /學校~沒有學生. There aren't any students at the school at night.

嘿 **hēi** (I) 1) indicates approval. /~! 真不錯. Hey! That's really not bad! 2) used to get someone's attention. /看這個,~! Hey! Look at this!

含 **hén** → 含 **hán**.

痕 **hén** (B) mark, streak, trace. 傷~ scar from a wound.

痕跡 **'hénjì** (N) trace, mark left by something. /在這兒你還可以看見第二次世界大戰的~. You can still see traces of World War II here.

很(狠) **hěn** (A) 1) before SV, quite, very. ~好 very good, quite good. 2) before AV or occasionally before FV, very much. /我~想請他. I want very much to invite him. /我~愛他. I love him very much. 3) fiercely, strongly. /我把他~打了一頓. I gave him a good beating. →的很 **dehen**.

很心 **hěnsyīn** (SV) be cruel-hearted, cold-blooded. /你別這麼~ Don't be so cruel-hearted. (VO) make a painful decision. /我很下不下心去. I can't make such a painful decision.

恨 **hèn** (FV) hate. /他最~他父親了. He hates his father most. (N) hatred.

哼 **heng** (I) indicates disapproval or suspicion. /~! 誰信你的? Humph! Who believes what you say? → 哼 **hēng**.

哼 **hēng** (FV) 1) hum. /他一邊走一邊~歌欠. He hummed a tune as he walked along. 2) groan, moan. /他~了半天. He moaned for a long time. → 哼 **heng**.

橫 **héng** (SV) be horizontal. ~線 horizontal line. (FV) make something horizontal. /把這個棍子~過

來. Put this pole in a horizontal position. (N) <-ル > horizontal stroke in a Chinese character. →橫 **hèng**.

橫豎 **héngshù** (A) anyway, no matter what the case may be. /我也不説了,~你不懂. I'm not going to say anything more; you wouldn't understand anyway.

橫 **hèng** (SV) be rude. /他説話很~ He speaks very rudely. (B) accidental. ~財 accidental fortune; ~死 die an accidental death. →橫 **héng**.

hong *see* hung.

喉 **hóu** (B) throat. 咽~ throat.

喉嚨 **hóulung** (N) 1) throat. 2) voice (d). /他的~很好聽. He has a very pleasant voice.

猴 **hóu** (B) <-ル,-子 > monkey (M 隻**jr**).

猴筋儿 **hóu'jyēr** (N) rubber band (M根**gēn**) (lp).

后 **hòu** (B) queen, empress. 皇~ queen. SF of 後**hòu**.

後(后) **hòu** (L) 1) back, behind. 向~走 go back, go behind; 門~ (the area) behind the door; ~排 (in) the back row. 2) later. 兩年~ two years later. 3) after. 下雨~ after it rains. 4) succeeding. ~代 succeeding generation; ~母 step-mother. (SP) 1) second, next. ~半年 the second half of the month. 2) last. ~五名 the last five names. (A) later. /他先到,我~到. He got here first; I arrived later.

後半天 **'hòubàntyān** (TW) (in) the afternoon.

後半夜 **'hòubànyè** (TW) very late at night (from midnight to daybreak).

後邊 **hòubyan** (PW) <-ル > 1) in back of *or* in the back part of something. /那個房子~帶一個很大的車房. There's a big garage in back of the house (*or* in the back part of the house). 2) the area behind *or* the back part of something. /~比前邊大. The back part is larger than the front part. (*or* The area in back is larger than the area in front).

後跟 **hòugēn** (N) <-ル > heel. 鞋~ heel of one's foot; 鞋~ heel of a shoe.

後悔 **hòuhwěi** (FV) regret.

/我~考試以前沒有用功. I regret that I didn't study harder before the examination. (SV) be regretful.

後來 **hòulái** (A) and then, after that. /~怎麼樣了? And then what happened? /他們~搬走了. After that, they moved away.

後面 **hòumyan** = 後邊 **hòubyan**.

後年 **hòunyán** (TW) the year after next.

後儿(個) **hòur(ge)** (lp) = 後天 **hòutyan**.

後臺 **hòutái** (PW) backstage. (N) support, backing. /他的~很硬. He has very strong backing.

後頭 **hòutou** = 後邊 **hòubyan**.

後天 **hòutyan** (TW) (on) the day after tomorrow.

厚 **hòu** (SV) 1) be thick (in dimension). ~大衣 heavy overcoat. /這道牆很~,所以聽不見隔壁說話. This wall is so thick I can't hear what my neighbors are saying. 2) be thick (of soup) (d). 3) be generous, liberal. /他待人很~. He's very generous toward people.

候 **hòu** (FV) 1) wait. /我~著你. I'm waiting for you. 2) take care of the bill (in treating people to food, drinks, etc.). /今天的飯賬我~了. I'll take care of the bill for today's meal. (B) 1) give regards to, greet. 問~ ask after. 2) climate. 測~所 weather station. 3) period of time. 火~ time required to cook something.

候補 **hòubǔ** (FV) take over an office. /總統死了由副總統~. The President died and the Vice-president took his place. (AT) alternate, substitute (of a person). ~球員 substitute ball player; ~演員 understudy.

候選 **hòusywàn** (FV) be a candidate, run for an office. /他~總統. He's running for President.

忽 **hū** (B) 1) suddenly. 2) neglect. ~視 neglect. (PT)~...~... suddenly... then... ~熱~冷 suddenly hot, then cold.

忽略 **'hūlywè** (FV) neglect, overlook. /他~了那件事情. He neglected that matter. (SV) be forgetful, careless.

忽然 **hūrán** (A) all of a sudden, suddenly. /~下起大雨來了. All of a sudden it began to pour.

呼 **hū** (B) 1) exhale. ~氣 exhale. 2) call. ~喊 shout. 3) a snore. 打~ to snore. (ON) whish, whiz. /一輛汽車~的一聲就過去了. A car whizzed by.

呼呼 **hūhū** (ON) sound of the wind. /風~~地颳. The wind is howling.

呼吸 **hūsyī** (FV) breathe. /我們到外面去~一點新鮮空氣吧. Let's go out and breathe some fresh air. (N) breathing. /他的~還不正常呐. His breathing is still not normal.

髯[胡] **hú** (B) <-子> 1) mustache. 2) beard. ~鬚 beard.

胡 **hú** (A) blindly, without knowing how, in a bungling way. ~搞 do something blindly; ~說 talk nonsense. (B) 1) northern barbarian (of ancient times) ~服 northern barbarian. s t SF of 髯 **hú**.

胡椒 **hújyāu** (N) peppercorn. ~麵儿 black pepper (powdered).

胡來 **húlái** (FV) do something without knowing how, fool around. /要是你不知道怎麼修理,你可不許~. If you don't know how to repair it, don't fool with it. /跟他一塊儿做事你可不能~. You can't fool around when you work with him.

胡嚕 **húlu** (FV) 1) stroke. /他老~他的光頭. He is always stroking his bald head. 2) brush or sweep off with the hand. /這些東西都從桌子上~下去了. He brushed the things off the table. 3) dabble in many things. /他什麼事都~著. He has a hand in everything.

胡蘿蔔 **húlwóbwo** (N) carrot (M根**gēn**).

胡塗 **hútu** (SV) be muddled, mixed-up.

胡同 **hútung** (B) street (lp). 金魚~ Golden Fish Street.

胡同儿 **hútùngr** (N) small street (M條**tyáu**) (lp).

核 **hú** → 核 **hé**.

湖 **hú** (N) lake.

狐 hú (B) fox.

狐狸 húli (N) fox (M 隻 jī).

蝴 hú (B) ↓. →蝴 hù.

蝴蝶 húdyé (N) butterfly (M 隻 jī).

糊(餬)(B) hú (FV) paper. ∼牆 paper a wall. (SV) be scorched, burned. /飯又∼了. The rice is burned again. (B) 1) paste, glue. 漿∼ paste. 2) thick gruel. 米∼ rice gruel. 3) unclear. 糢∼ be blurred.

糊塗 húdu (SV) be muddled, mixed-up, confused. /你越說我∼. The more you talk the more confused I get.

糊口 húkǒu (VO) make a bare living. /我的收入剛夠∼怎麼能蓄儲呢? My income is just enough to make a bare living. How can I save any money?

糊裏糊塗 'húlihú'dū (SV) be all mixed up. (A) absent-mindedly, without thinking. /我∼給了他一百塊錢. I gave him one hundred dollars without thinking.

弧 hú (N) arc (geom.).

壺 hú (N) kettle, jug. 茶∼ teapot; 暖∼ thermos bottle (M 把 bǎ).

斛 hú (M) unit of capacity equal to five 斗 dǒu (= 54.5 liquid quarts).

葫 hú (B) ↓.

葫蘆 húlu (N) gourd.

護(护) hù (FV) side with (as in an argument). /你老∼着他. You always side with him. (B) protect. ∼兵 guard.

護照 hùjàu (N) passport (M 本 běn).

護士 hùshr (N) nurse (medical).

互 hù (B) each other, mutually. ∼換 interchange, exchange.

互助 hùjù (FV) help each other. /在困難的時候大家應該∼. When there is trouble, everybody should help each other.

互相 hùsyāng (A) each other. /他們兩人老是∼恭維. Those two are always flattering each other.

戶 hù (M) for households. 三∼人家 three households. (B) class, kind (of people). 漁∼ fisherman.

戶口 hùkǒu (N) 1) population. 2) household.

蝴 hù (B) ↓. →蝴 hú.

蝴蝶儿 hùtyěr (N) butterfly (M 隻 jī) (lp).

hua see hwa.

huai see hwai.

huan see hwan.

huang see hwang.

hui see hwei.

hun see hwun.

轟(轟) hūng (FV) 1) drive, chase. ∼走 drive away. 2) bombard. 砲∼ bombard with cannon. (ON) rumbling sound of thunder, an explosion, carts, etc. /∼的一聲鍋爐炸了. The boiler exploded with a bang.

轟炸 hūngjà (FV) bomb from a plane. /敵機∼了我們的首都. The enemy bombed our capital. (N) bombing.

轟炸機 hūngjàjī (N) bomber (M 架 jyà).

烘 hūng (FV) 1) dry or warm something over heat. /我已經把你的濕衣服∼乾了. I've dried your wet clothes over the fire. 2) shade around an object in a painting to make it stand out. /這張花卉用一層淺藍色∼一∼才更好看. If you use light blue to shade around the flowers in this painting, it will be more attractive.

哄 hūng (B) make noise. ∼動 be stirred up, aroused (as a crowd). SF of 鬨 hùng. →哄 hǔng.

紅 húng (FV) turn red. /他∼了臉. His face turned red. (SV) 1) be red. ∼花 red flower. 2) be popular. ∼角 popular actor or actress. (N) red, red color. 血∼ blood red. (B) 1) communist, "red." ∼軍 the Red Army. 2) lucky, fortunate. ∼運 good luck. 3) bonus, dividend. 分∼ get a bonus.

紅利 húngli (N) bonus, dividend (M 份 fèn).

紅人 'húngrén (N) 1) American Indian. 2) <–ル> person favored and coddled by someone in an influential position.

紅十字會 **húngshŕdzhwèi** (N) the Red Cross.

紅糖 **húngtáng** (N) brown sugar.

紅銅 **húngtúng** (N) copper.

洪 **húng** (B) 1) vast, great. ~亮 be strong and clear (of one's voice). 2) torrent. 山~ mountain torrent. *s t*

洪水 **húngshwěi** (N) flood.

虹 **húng, jyàng** (**gàng** (lp)) (N) rainbow.

哄 **hŭng** (FV) 1) deceive. /別~我. Don't deceive me. 2) coax. ~孩子 coax a child. SF of 鬨 **hùng**. →哄 **hūng**.

鬨[鬨] **hùng** (B) din, noise. 起~ create an uproar.

huo *see* **hwo**.

花{化(FV)} **hwā** (FV) spend. ~錢 spend money. (SV) 1) be blurred, dimmed. /我的眼~了. My eyes are blurred. 2) be far-sighted. 3) be fancy, figured (as cloth). (N) 1) fireworks. 2) cotton. (B) 1) <-ㄦ> flower, blossom (M朵 **dwǒ**, 枝 **jŕ**). 雪~ snowflake. 2) <-ㄦ> plant (potted) (M盆 **pén**, 棵 **kē**). ~匠 gardener. 3) variegated, spotted. ~貓 spotted cat. 4) <-ㄦ> design, pattern. ~樣 design, pattern.

花子 **hwādz** (N) beggar.

花費 **'hwāfèi** (FV) spend money, time, effort, energy, etc. /我在這所房子上~了不少錢. I've spent a lot of money on this house. (N) expense (M筆 **bǐ**).

花骨朵 **hwāgūdwo** (N) <-ㄦ> flower bud.

花生 **hwāshēng** (N) peanut.

花生油 **hwāshēngyóu** (N) peanut oil.

花園 **hwāywán** (N) <-ㄦ> flower garden.

嘩 **hwā** (B) ↓.

嘩嘩 **hwāhwā** (ON) sound of rushing water. /學校的馬桶壞了~~老響. The toilet at school is broken and runs all the time.

嘩啦 **hwāla** (ON) 1) sound of rushing water. /水~~的流. Water rushed out. 2) crash. /~一聲牆就倒了. The wall fell with a crash.

滑 **hwá** (SV) 1) be slippery, smooth. /下雨以後地很~. The ground is very slippery after it rains. 2)

be untrustworthy, shifty, slippery. (FV) slide. /他~到山底下去了. He slid to the bottom of the hill.

滑車 **hwáchē** (N) pulley.

滑稽 **hwáji** (SV) be funny, humorous.

滑頭 **hwátóu** (SV) be untrustworthy, shifty, slippery. (N) wily fellow.

划{劃} 2) 3)} **hwá** (FV) 1) row. ~船 row a boat. 2) scrape, scratch. ~火柴 strike a match. 3) cut something with a sharp object. /他用刀~破了手指. She cut her finger with a knife. (B) calculate (usually involves money). ~價ㄦ bargain for a lower price. SF of 劃 **hwá**.

划子 **hwádz** (N) rowboat (M隻 **jŕ**).

劃{畫}{划} **hwà** (FV) draw a line, make a mark. ~兩條平行線 draw two parallel lines. ~界 delimit boundaries. (N) <-ㄦ> line, stroke. /人字是兩~. The character "人" is made up of two strokes. (B) plan. 計~ plan. →划{劃} **hwá**.

化 **hwà** (FV) 1) melt. /冰~了. The ice has melted. 2) change to a gas (from a liquid), evaporate. /水~成汽了. The water has evaporated. 3) ask for donations for religious purposes. /和尚又下山~錢去了. The monk came down from the mountain to ask for alms. (B) 1) -ize, -fy. 工業~ industrialize; 簡單~ simplify. 2) -ide. 氧~鋅 zinc oxide. 3) chemistry. 理~ physics and chemistry. →花{化} **hwà**.

化裝 **hwàjwāng** (FV) disguise. /他~了一個老頭. He disguised himself as an old man. (VO) put on make-up. /她化好裝了,可以上台了. She has finished making up and is ready to go on the stage.

化學 **hwàsywé** (N) chemistry.

化學家 **hwàsywéjyā** (N) chemist.

化學藥品 **'hwàsywéyàupǐn** (N) chemical substance, chemical.

化驗 **'hwàyàn** (FV) analyze chemically. /把溶液拿到實驗室去~一下. Take this solution to the lab and have it analyzed.

話 **hwà** (N) 1) words, talk, speech (M

句 **jyù**). 2) incident, story, matter. /這~有十年了. This incident took place ten years ago. (B) dialect, language. 上海~ Shanghai dialect; 德國~ German.

話劇 **hwàjyù** (N) play.

畫(画) **hwà** (FV) draw, paint. /他~了一幅風景畫. He painted a landscape. (N) 1) <-儿> painting, picture (M 張 **jāng**, 幅 **fú**). 2) painting (the subject). 學~ study painting. → 劃(畫) **hwà**.

畫報 **hwàbàu** (N) illustrated *or* picture magazine (M 本 **běn**, 張 **jāng**).

畫筆 **hwàbǐ** (N) brush (of an artist) (M 管 **gwǎn**, 枝 **jr̄**).

畫家 **hwàjyā** (N) painter, artist.

槐 **hwái** (B) Sophora japonica (tree similar to the ash).

槐樹 **hwáishù** (N) Sophora japonica (M 棵 **kē**).

懷 **hwái** (N) bosom. (FV) 1) carry something next to the bosom. /他~着偷來的銀盤子走了. He left carrying the stolen silver plate under his coat. 2) be pregnant. /那位太太~了八個月了. That woman is eight months pregnant. 3) have in mind. /他不~好意. He has bad intentions. (B) harbor, cherish, thoughts or feelings. ~恨 harbor hatred; ~希望 cherish hopes.

懷疑 **hwáiyí** (FV) have doubts about, suspect. /我~他. I have doubts about him. (SV) be doubtful, suspicious.

踝 **hwái**, **gwǎi** (B) ankle.

踝子骨 **hwáidzgǔ, gwǎidzgǔ** (N) anklebone.

壞(坏) **hwài** (SV) 1) be bad. /天氣很~. The weather's very bad. /我的字寫得很~. My handwriting is awful. 2) be sly. 3) be spoiled (as of food). 4) be out of order, broken down. /車~了. The car has broken down. (FV) ruin, spoil. /他~了我的事. He ruined things for me. → 不壞 **bùhwài**.

壞處 **hwàichu** (N) bad point, bad feature, drawback, shortcoming.

歡(欢) **hwān** (SV) be lively, energetic. /他們唱得很~. They sang exuberantly. /火很~. The fire is

blazing. (B) joyous. ~呼 cheer, shout for joy.

歡實 **hwānshr** (SV) be active, lively (usually referring to a child or a pet). /那個孩子昨天還很~可是今天忽然就病了. That child was (still) very active yesterday, but he suddenly became ill today.

歡喜 **hwānsyi** (FV) like. /他很~你. He likes you very much. (AV) like to, love to. /他~吃糖. He likes to eat candy.

歡迎 **hwányíng** (FV) welcome. /他們都到飛機場~那個電影明星去了. They all went to the airport to welcome that movie star. (N) welcome. (IE) Welcome!

還(还) **hwán** (FV) 1) return, pay back. ~錢 pay back money. 2) return to, go back. ~鄉 return to one's native place. (PV) back to. /我把書寄~他了. I mailed the book back to him. → 還 **hái**.

環(环) **hwán** (B) 1) ring. 耳~ earring. 2) all around. ~球 the earth, all over the world.

環境 **'hwánjìng** (N) 1) environment, circumstances. /在這種~之下你不能說這句話. You can't say this in these circumstances (you'll hurt someone's feelings or get yourself hurt). /他住的地方~很好. He lives in a good environment. 2) financial circumstances. /他上不起學校因為他家的~不好. He can't afford to go to school because his family is poor.

緩 **hwǎn** (FV) 1) go easy. /雖然這個很好吃,可是你還得~着點儿. Even though this tastes awfully good, you'd better go easy. 2) postpone, delay. /你能不能~兩天? Can you postpone it a couple of days? 3) recuperate. /讓我先~一~,一會儿再去. Let me recuperate first; I'll go after a while. (B) slow. ~和 be moderate.

緩過來 **hwǎngwolai** (RC) 1) come to (after fainting or a dizzy spell). /我暈倒了很久才~. I was out a long time before I came to. 2) return slowly to normal, recuperate. /下過雨,花儿都~了. After the rain, the flowers came to life again.

幻 **hwàn** (B) fantasy, illusion. ～影 unreal image, illusion.

  幻燈 **hwàndēng** (N) slide projector.

  幻想 **hwànsyǎng** (N) hallucination, illusion. (FV) imagine, fancy, dream of. /他～有一天會當總統. He dreamed of one day becoming the president.

換 **hwàn** (FV) 1) exchange, interchange. /我跟你～. I'll exchange with you. 2) change, replace by another. ～衣服 change clothes.

患 **hwàn** (B) 1) suffer. ～病 be ill. 2) calamity, misfortune. 後～ future trouble.

  患難 '**hwànnàn** (N) misfortune, calamity in one's life. ～的朋友 friend in need.

慌 **hwāng** (SV) 1) be nervous. /他心裏有一點儿～. He's a little nervous. 2) be in a hurry. /做事別～. When you do something, don't be in a hurry. →的慌 **dehwang**.

荒 **hwāng** (SV) 1) be desolate, wild, uncultivated. /那一條地方很～. That's a desolate area. 2) be neglected, deserted. 他的草地都～了. His lawn is all overgrown. (B) 1) famine. ～年 year of famine; 水～ water shortage. 2) excessive, reckless. ～唐 be exaggerated (of a story), wild (of a person).

  荒廢 **hwāngfèi** (FV) 1) waste. /別～時候了! Don't waste time! 2) neglect one's work. /他把他的功課～很久了. He let his studies go for a long time.

  荒謬 **hwāngnyòu, hwāngmyòu** (SV) be irrational, absurd. /他做這件事很～. It was utterly absurd for him to do this.

蝗 **hwáng** (B) locust. ～災 plague of locusts.

  蝗蟲 **hwángchung** (N) locust. (M 隻扛).

黃[黄] **hwáng** (SV) 1) be yellow. ～葉 yellow leaf. 2) be brown. ～皮鞋 brown leather shoes. (FV) fail, fall through (lp). /那個買賣～了.

That business failed. (N) yellow color, yellow. 杏～ apricot yellow. (B) <-儿> egg yolk. 雙～蛋 double-yolked egg. s

  黃豆 **hwángdòu** (N) soybean.

  黃瓜 **hwánggwa** (N) cucumber (M條tyáu).

  黃銅 **hwángtúng** (N) brass.

  黃油 **hwángyóu** (N) butter.

皇 **hwáng** (B) 1) emperor. ～太后 empress dowager. 2) supreme. 堂～ be marvelous.

  皇帝 **hwángdì** (N) emperor.

  皇宮 **hwánggūng** (N) palace, residence of an emperor (M座dzwò).

  皇后 **hwánghòu** (N) queen, empress.

  皇上 **hwángshang** (N) emperor (h).

謊 **hwǎng** (N) 1) lie, falsehood. 2) overcharge, exhorbitant price (lp). 要～ state a high price <u>with the intention of being bargained down.</u>

  謊話 **hwǎnghwà** (N) lie, falsehood.

晃 **hwǎng** (SV) be glaring, very bright. /那個燈很～. That light is awfully bright. (FV) 1) dazzle, blind. /太陽～我. The sun blinded me. 2) appear momentarily. /他來是來了,可是一～就走了. He was here all right, but he left as soon as he got here. →晃**hwàng**.

  晃眼 **hwángyǎn** (VO) dazzle, blind. /太陽晃我的眼. The sun is blinding me (lit. blinding my eyes). (SV) be dazzling, glaring.

晃 **hwàng** (FV) 1) sway, swing. /樹枝來回～. The branches are swaying back and forth. /他手裏拿着旗子直～. He waved the flag he was holding. 2) wobble, shake. /這個桌子直～. This table wobbles all the time. 3) loiter. /門口有一個人老在那儿～,他是幹什麼的? There's a man forever loitering at the door. What's he up to? →晃**hwǎng**.

  晃悠 **hwàngyou** = 晃**hwàng**.

灰 **hwēi** (N) 1) <-儿> ashes. 燒成～ burn to ashes. 2) dust (d). (AT) grey, dull-colored. ～鼠 grey squirrel. (N) grey, grey color.

~ silver grey. (B) lime. 生石~ quicklime.

灰塵 hwēichén (N) dust, dirt.

灰色 hwēisè (N) grey (color).

灰心 hwēisyīn (SV) be disheartened, disillusioned (lit. with heart turned to ashes). /我現在很~. I've become very disillusioned. (VO) disillusion, discourage. /我的兒子真叫我~. My son has really made me discouraged.

恢 hwēi (B) 1) great. ~宏 be extensive. 2) ↓.

恢復 hwēifu (FV) recover, get back. ~失地 recover lost land. /他身體已經~了. He's recovered his health.

詼 hwēi (B) funny, ridiculous.

詼諧 'hwēisyé (SV) be humorous, lightly joking. /他說話很~. He's very humorous (when he talks).

徽 hwēi (B) 1) insignia. 校~ school emblem. 2) Anhwei (contracted form of 安~ anhwēi). ~調 musical style from Anhwei. 3) Huichou (contracted form of ~州 hwēijōu). ~墨 ink from Huichow.

徽章 hwēijāng (N) 1) button with an inscription, worn to indicate belief or membership. 2) identification badge.

回{囘,回} hwéi (DV) 1) come or go back. /我現在得~學校了. I have to go back to school now. 2) return something. ~手 return a blow. 3) answer a letter, telegram. ~信 answer a letter, an answering letter. (M) 1) time, occurrence. 上~ last time. /我做過三~. I've done it three times. 2) chapter of a novel. /我看完第一~了. I finished reading the first chapter. (RE) back. 送~北平 send back to Peiping. (B) 1) used after CV like 往 wàng, 望 wàng, 向 syàng, etc., back. 往~看 look back. 2) Mohammedan. ~教 Mohammedanism. SF of 迴 hwéi.

回去 hwéichyu (RC) go back. /我回不去了. I can't go back there any more. (RE) back (there). /我得把書送回圖書館去. I have to take this book back to the library.

回答 'hwéidá (FV) reply, answer. /我已經~他的問題了. I have already answered his question. (N) answer.

回家 hwéijyā (VO) come or go (back) home. /雪太大了,我回不了家. It's snowing too hard; I can't go home.

回來 hwéilai (RC) come back. /我今天回不來. I can't come back today. (RE) back (here). /狗自己就跑~了. The dog came back on its own.

回想 hwéisyǎng (FV) recall, think back to. /他喜歡~他的童年時代. He likes to recall his childhood.

回頭 hwéitóu (VO) 1) turn one's head. /我叫她,她連頭都不回. I called to her and she didn't even turn her head. 2) return (as when reaching the end of a road). /他游過去了,可是還沒~呢. He swam across but hasn't come back yet. 3) change one's mind. /等着瞧吧,你會~的. Just wait. You'll change your mind. (A) later, after a while. /~見. See you later. (N) fried dumpling.

回憶 hwéiyì (FV) recall, think back to. /我喜~我小的時候. I like to think back to my childhood days. (N) recollection.

廻{迴,回} hwéi (B) move in circles, curve back and forth. ~旋 revolve; ~廊 winding corridor.

毀 hwěi (FV) destroy, ruin, break down. /誰把這張畫兒~了? Who ruined that picture? (B) slander. ~罵 revile.

毀謗 hwěibàng (FV) attack, vilify, a person, an institution. /那個記者喜歡~人家的名譽. That reporter has a habit of defaming people.

毀滅 hwěimyè (FV) destroy totally. /敵人把城都~了. The enemy totally destroyed the city.

會{会} hwěi (B) ↓. → 會 hwèi, 會 kwài.

會子 hwěidz = 會兒 hwěr.

會兒 hwěr (M) moment. 那~ (at) that moment or time. /我過一~就回來. I'll be back in a moment.

會[会]**hwèi** (AV) 1) can, know how to. /你～說英國話嗎? Can you speak English? 2) be apt to, liable to. /你要是打他,他～生氣的. If you hit him, he's liable to get mad. 3) followed by a descriptive expression, often with 的de added, will. /葉子一定～綠的. The leaves will certainly turn green. (FV) 1) know how to perform something. /我不～那個歌儿. I can't sing that song. 2) pay a bill (for entertaining somebody). /飯錢他～了. He paid the bill for this meal. 3) meet, see. /我明天要去～～他. I'm going to see him tomorrow. (N) 1) meeting, conference. 開～ hold a meeting. 2) association, club, committee. 同學～ alumni association. (RE) indicates mastering some skill. 練～ master by practicing. (B) 1) understand, apprehend. 理～pay attention to. 2) together. ～餐 eat together. → 會 **hwèi**, 會 **kwài**, 不會 **búhwèi**.

    會場 **hwèichǎng** (N) meeting place.

    會戰 **hwèijàn** (VO) join battle. /兩軍在那儿～. The two sides joined battle there.

    會章 **hwèijāng** (N) 1) insignia showing membership in some organization. 2) emblem of an organization. 3) constitution of an organization (M 份儿 fèr). /請你拿一份～來看看. Please get me a copy of the constitution to read.

    會客 **hwèikè** (VO) receive a guest. /他生病了,今天不～. He's sick so he can't have any guests today.

    會客室 **hwèikèshr̄** (N) sitting room, reception room.

    會議 **hwèiyì** (N) conference.

    會意 **hwèiyì** (VO) catch on, understand. /你看他一眼他就～了. Give him the eye; he'll catch on (to what you want him to do).

    會員 **hwèiywán** (N) member of an organization.

滙[滙][汇]**hwèi** (FV) 1) send money. /他每星期～五塊錢給他兒子. He sends five dollars to his son every week. (B) converge. ～集 gather at one place.

滙報 **hwèibàu** (N) report which includes all aspects of a subject, oral or written.

    滙兌 **hwèidwèi** (N) transmission of money or funds from one place to another. /打仗的時候～很困難. In war time the transmission of money from one place to another is difficult.

    滙率 **hwèilyǜ** (N) rate of exchange. /現在中美的～是多少? What's the current rate of exchange for Chinese and American money?

    滙票 **hwèipyàu** (N) draft, money order (M 張 jāng). 開～ write a draft.

賄 **hwèi** (B) bribery.

    賄賂 **hwèiwo, hwèilù** (FV) bribe. /你不能～他. You can't bribe him. (N) bribe. 受～ accept a bribe.

和 **hwo** (B) added to SV which are sensory in nature, comfortably. 暖～ be comfortably warm; 軟～ be nice and soft. → 和 **hé**, 和 **hè**, 和 **hwò**.

嚄 **hwō** (I) indicates surprise. /～! 那麼大! Good Heavens! That big!

豁 **hwō** (FV) 1) be split, torn, opened. /我的領子～了. My collar is torn. /牆～了. There's a break in the wall. 2) sacrifice, give up. /～着幾百塊錢,我也要把這塊草地弄得好看一點. I would rather spend a few hundred dollars and have the lawn look a little better. →豁 **hwò**.

    豁出去 **hwōchuchyu** (RC) go ahead regardless. /我豁出一夜不睡覺去,都得把這間屋子漆好了. I'm going to finish painting this room even if I lose a night's sleep. /我～了,反正我不讓我兒子娶那個女的. I don't care what happens, I won't let my son marry that female.

活 **hwó** (FV) live. /你要想～最好招了. If you want to live, you'd better confess. /他還～着呢. He's still living. (SV) 1) be active, lively. /他的腦筋很～. He has a very quick mind. 2) be loose. /這個釘子～了. This nail is loose. (AT) 1) living, moving. ～

靶 moving target; ～水 running stream. 2) movable. ～字 movable type; ～頁本ㄦ loose-leaf notebook. (N) <-ㄦ> 1) work, workmanship. 2) needle work. (A) alive ～捉 capture someone alive.

活動 hwódung (FV) 1) move about, stretch, loosen up (of a person). /快看,那個死人～了! Look! That corpse is moving! /他站起來～了一下. He got up and stretched. 2) manipulate a person, pull strings. /他想拿錢～我. He tried to bribe me. /他替我～那個事情. He pulled strings to get me that job. (SV) 1) be loose. /我的牙～了. A tooth of mine is loose. 2) be active. /那個政客越來越～了. That politician is becoming more and more active. (N) activity. 課外～ extracurricular activity.

活該 hwógāi (IE) It serves you (or him, etc.) right! /～,誰叫你不聽我的話? It serves you right. You should have listened to me.

活潑 hwópwo (SV) be lively (of a child).

火 hwǒ (N) 1) fire. 生～ make a fire. 2) indigestion. 敗～ cure indigestion. /這孩子心裏有～. This child is suffering from indigestion. (B) weapon. 開～ fire a weapon; ～藥 gunpowder.

火柴 hwǒchái (N) match (for producing fire) (M根gēn). 借～ borrow a match.

火車 hwǒché (N) 1) train (M列lyè). 2) railway car (M輛lyàng).

火車站 hwǒchéjàn (N) train station.

火災 hwǒdzāi (N) fire (as a disaster) (M次tsz̀,場chǎng).

火警 hwójǐng (N) fire (destructive, as a building burning) (M次tsz̀,場chǎng,處chù). 報～ sound a fire alarm or report a fire.

火箭 hwójyàn (N) missile, rocket.

火箭炮 hwójyànpàu (N) bazooka.

火酒 hwójyǒu (N) ethyl alcohol.

火苗 hwǒmyáu (N) <-ㄦ,-子> flame.

火ㄦ hwǒr (SV) be angry. /他又跟我～了. He's mad at me again. (N) 1) anger. 發～ lose one's temper. 2) match (for producing fire). /您有～嗎? Do you have any matches?

火山 hwǒshān (N) volcano (M座dzwò).

夥[伙] hwǒ (FV) collaborate, be partners. /你怎麼跟他們～在一塊ㄦ? How come you collaborated with them? /打牌的時候,他們兩個人～着. They are partners when they play cards. (M) <-ㄦ,-子> group of people. 一～強盜 a band of robbers. (B) partnership. 搭～ form a partnership.

夥伴 hwǒbàn (N) <-ㄦ> partner, working companion, comrade (business or otherwise).

夥計 hwǒjì (N) waiter, clerk, in a store, restaurant.

伙 hwǒ (B) 1) utensil. 傢～ tool. 2) food. 起～ provide food. SF of 夥 hwǒ.

伙食 hwǒshr (N) food, provisions.

豁 hwò (B) 1) forego. ～免 be exempt from tax. 2) open, broad. ～達 be liberal, broad-minded. →豁hwō.

和 hwò (FV) mix. ～麵 make dough. /油跟水不能～在一塊. You can't mix oil and water together. →和hé,和hè,和hwo.

和攏 hwòlung (FV) stir something (often repeated). /你～～那杯咖啡. Stir that cup of coffee.

霍 hwò (B) ⸱ s

霍亂 hwòlwàn (N) cholera.

或 hwò (A) perhaps, maybe. /他們～要提出一些問題. Perhaps they will raise some questions. (PT) ～...～...(都)... either...or... is possible. /～你～我都可以做那件事. Either you or I can do that. /～貴～賤都沒關係. It doesn't matter whether it's expensive or cheap.

或者 hwòjě (A) perhaps, maybe. /～他不願意來. Perhaps he doesn't want to come. (PT) 1) ...～...～... either do one thing or another. /～你去,～他去. Either you go or he goes. 2) ～...～... (都)... either...or... is possible. /～你說,～我說都沒什麼分別.

It doesn't make any difference whether you speak or I speak.

或是 **hwòshr**＝或者 **hwòjě** (PT).
或許 **hwòsyǔ**＝或者 **hwòjě** (A).

獲[獲] **hwò** (B) obtain. ～利 make a profit.
　　獲得 **hwòdé** (FV) obtain, get.
/他因為做那件事～不少經驗.
He got a lot of experience doing that work.

貨 **hwò** (N) item of merchandise, commodity (M件 **jyàn**, 批 **pī**). ～棧 warehouse.　(B) currency. 通～ currency.
　　貨物 **'hwòwù** (N) commodities, merchandise, cargo, in an economics discussion rather than business or retailing talk.

禍 **hwò** (N) calamity, catastrophe.
　　禍根 **hwògēn** (N) root of trouble, source of evil.
　　禍首 **hwòshǒu** (N) ringleader.

婚 **hwūn** (B) marriage. 結～ marry.
　　婚禮 **hwūnlǐ** (N) wedding, wedding ceremony (M次 **tsż**). 舉行～ hold a wedding.
　　婚姻 **hwūnyīn** (N) marriage.
/他們的～很美滿.　Their marriage has been very successful.
　　婚約 **hwūnywē** (N) engagement (to be married). /他們兩個人的 ～已經解除了.　They have already broken off their engagement.

昏 **hwūn** (FV) faint. /她一聽見那個 消息就～了.　She fainted when she heard the news.　(SV) be dizzy.
/我的頭很～.　I feel dizzy.　(B) dark. 黃～ twilight.

混 **hwǔn** (FV) mix.　/你能把油跟酒 ～在一塊兒嗎?　Can you mix oil and wine together? (RE) indicates confusing, mixing up. 弄～ get two people mixed up. →混 **hwùn**.

混 **hwùn** (FV) 1) fool around.　/他～ 了一天.　He fooled around the whole day (without accomplishing anything). 2) mix.　/油跟水不能 ～在一塊兒.　Oil and water don't mix.　(B) confusedly, disorderly. ～ 說　talk foolishly. →混 **hwǔn**.
　　混飯 **hwùnfàn** (VO) 1) engage in a job for the sake of making a living, without having any real interest in it.　/這種工作有什麼意 義? 我只是在那裡混一碗飯.

What of interest could there possibly be in such a job? I'm just working there for the sake of making a living. 2) get by doing something without having the ability. /他一點能力也 沒有, 不過在那兒～而已.　He doesn't have any ability at all, but he manages to get by in his work there.

渣 **jā** (B) <-子, -ㄦ> sediment, refuse. ～滓 refuse. →渣 **já**.
　　渣子 **jādz**＝渣ㄦ **jár**.
　　渣ㄦ **jár** (N) particle, fragment.
麵包～ bread crumbs.

查 **jā** (B) s t → 查 **chá**.

扎 **jā** (FV) 1) jab with any thin pointed thing. /他拿針在紙上～了一 個小洞.　He jabbed a small hole in the paper with a needle. /我手上 ～了一個刺.　I got a splinter in my finger. 2) dive into. /他一 跳就～到河裏去了.　With a leap, he dived from the cliff into the water.　SF of 紮 **dzā**. →扎 **jā**, 扎 **já**.

扎 **já** (B) 1) to camp. 駐～ be stationed (as an army). 2) freezing. ～的哼 be freezing. 3) strain. 掙～ struggle.　(M) bundle. 一～報紙 a bundle of newspapers.　SF of 紮 **dzā**. →扎 **jā**, 扎 **já**.

炸 **já** (FV) deep-fry, fry in a considerable amount of fat. /我晚上～了 一隻雞.　I fried a chicken for supper. →炸 **jà**.

閘 **já** (N) 1) watergate, floodgate. 2) brake on a vehicle (lp). 踩～ step on a brake. 3) gear (as on a vehicle) (lp). 三～ high gear; 換～ shift gears. 4) switch. 搬～ flip a switch.

渣 **jà** (B) t. →渣 **jā**.
　　渣ㄦ **jár** (N) bad spot (as on a piece of fruit).

眨 **jǎ** (FV) blink. /飛機上的燈一 ～一～的.　The lights on the plane are blinking.
　　眨眼 **jǎyǎn** (VO) wink. 一～的 功夫 in the twinkling of an eye.
/那個男孩子老對她～.　That boy is always winking at her.

扎 **jà** (SV) stick out. /他的頭髮～ 著.　His hair is bushy. /那條裙

子~得太厲害了. That skirt sticks out too much. SF of 紮 dzā. 一扎泊, 扎泊.

炸 jà (FV) 1) explode (lit. or fig.). /火藥庫~了. The ammunition dump exploded. /他一聽就~了. He exploded the minute he heard it. 2) bomb. /我們的飛機把那個橋~了. Our planes bombed that bridge. 3) crack (of a glass container as a result of heat or cold). /我的茶杯~了. My teacup has cracked. 一炸泊.

炸彈 jàdàn (N) bomb (M顆kē).

詐 jà (FV) 1) get information from someone by pretending to know the facts already. /你不必拿話~我. You needn't try to wheedle the information out of me. 2) cheat, swindle. /他~了我五塊錢. He cheated me out of five dollars (and absconded with it). (B) 1) pretend. ~死 play dead, feign death. 2) crafty. 奸~ be artful, crafty.

乍 jà (A) for the first time, at first sight. /~看那個東西不錯. At first sight that thing seemed pretty good. (PT)~...~... suddenly ...then.... 天氣~涼~熱,很容易着涼. The weather is suddenly cold, then hot. It's very easy to catch cold.

摘 jāi, jé* (FV) 1) take off a hat, glasses. /你進去的時候,別忘了帽子. Don't forget to take off your hat when you enter. 2) pick flowers, fruit, etc. /蘋果太青還不能~呢. The apples are too green; you can't pick them yet. 3)* extract information from a book, a document, etc. /這句是從那本書上~下來了. This sentence was taken from that book. 4) borrow a small amount of money, as from a friend. /我想跟您~幾個錢用. Could I borrow a couple of dollars from you?

宅 jái (B) <一子> residence, house (M所 swǒ). /這是李~. This is the Li residence (as when answering a telephone call).

窄 jǎi (SV) be narrow. /這條路太~.

This road is too narrow. /他的心眼儿很~. He is narrow-minded.

債 jài (N) 1) debt. 2) loan. (M筆bǐ). 放~ grant a loan; 還~ pay back a loan.

占 jān (B) divine by casting lots, practice soothsaying. ~夢 interpret dreams. SF of 佔jàn.

氈[毡] jān (B) <一子> 1) felt (material). ~帽 felt hat. 2) felt mat (M條 tyáu). 羊毛~ felt mat made of sheep's wool.

粘 jān (FV) paste, glue, stick. /把這兩塊木頭~在一塊儿. Glue these two pieces of wood together. SF of 黏nyán.

盞 jǎn (M) for lamps, electric lights. 一~電燈 an electric light.

展 jǎn (FV) postpone. /把這個會再往後~兩天. Postpone the meeting for two more days. (B) open out, unfold. 發~ develop, development. s

展期 jǎnchī (VO) postpone. 展一期 put off for a set period (e.g., one semester, one quarter, etc.). /那個會~了. That meeting has been postponed.

展開 jǎnkāi (RC) open out, spread out. /請你把那張地圖~. Would you please spread out that map?

展覽 jǎnlǎn (FV) display, exhibit. /他將他的畫送去~. He sent his paintings to be displayed. (N) exhibition.

展覽會 jǎnlǎnhwèi (N) exhibition.

撢 jǎn (FV) sponge, wipe gently. /給我把桌上的墨水~掉. Wipe up the ink on the table for me.

撢布 jǎnbu (N) dustcloth, dustrag (M塊kwài, 條tyáu).

佔[占] jàn (FV) 1) seize, occupy by force. /敵人把那個城~了. The enemy has seized that town. 2) hold, save, a place for someone, as in a theater. /請你給我~一個座儿. Please save a seat for me. 3) make up, constitute, a certain portion. /這個學校女生~多數. Women constitute the majority of the students at this university.

佔領 **jànlǐng** (FV) seize and occupy by military force. /我們沒有足夠的人～那個城. We don't have enough manpower to occupy that city.

佔優勢 **jàn'yōushr̀** (VO) be in an advantageous position. /這次辯論中,大學生比較～. In this debate the university student is in a more advantageous position.

戰战 **jàn** (B) 1) battle, war. 冷～ cold war; ～犯 war criminal. 2) fight in a war. ～死 die in battle. 3) shiver, tremble. 打～ to shiver.

戰敗 **jànbài** (RC) defeat someone in battle or war. /是誰～了? Who was defeated?

戰爭 **jànjēng** (N) war (M 次**tsz̀**, 場**chǎng**).

戰鬥 **jàndòu** (FV) fight (as in a war). /兩國軍隊～很急烈. The armies of both countries fought very hard.

戰艦 **jànjyàn** (N) battleship (M 條 **tyáu**, 隻**jr̄**, 艘**sōu**).

戰局 **jànjyú** (N) military situation, military development.

戰況 **jànkwàng** (N) military situation, military development.

戰利品 **jànlìpǐn** (N) booty.

戰略 **jànlywè** (N) military strategy.

戰勝 **jànshèng** (RC) win a war or battle. /是誰～了? Who won the war?

戰士 **jànshr̀** (N) fighter, warrior.

暫 **jàn** (A) temporarily. /我～借給你. I'll lend it to you temporarily.

暫且 **jànchyě** (A) for a short time, for the time being, temporarily. /～給他. Give it to him for the time being.

暫時 **jànshr̀** (A) for a short time, for the time being, temporarily. /我～來不了. I can't come right away. (AT) temporary. ～辦法 temporary measure or method.

站 **jàn** (FV) stand. /她坐着我～着. She's sitting, I'm standing. /我想～一會兒. I want to stand for a while. /他現在～在門外頭. He is standing outside the door. (N) 1) station (for trains, buses, etc.). 2) distribution center. 補給～supply center. (N) stop (for a public conveyance).

/下一～離這儿有多遠? How far is the next stop from here?

站臺 **jàntái** (N) platform (as at a railway station).

張 **jāng** (FV) open (usually of the hand or mouth). /他一～手,那個蒼蠅又飛了. He opened his hand and the fly got away. (M) for things which have flat, extended surfaces. 一～桌子 a table; 一～床 a bed; 一～紙 a piece of paper. (B) opening of a store or business. 門～ grand opening. s

張開 **jāngkai** (RC) open up (usually of the hand or mouth). /他牙痛得連嘴都張不開了. His tooth hurt so he couldn't even open his mouth.

章 **jāng** (M) chapter (of a book). 第一～ the first chapter. (B) 1) essay. 文～ essay, article, paper. 2) regulation, rule. 會～ regulation of a club or association. 3) chop, stamp. 橡皮～ rubber stamp. 4) insignia. 勳～medal. s t

章程 **jāngcheng** (N) 1) regulation, rule. 2) constitution (of an organization).

長 **jǎng** (FV) 1) grow, develop. /小孩～大了. The children have grown up. /他臉上～了一個疙瘩. He has a pimple on his face. /這個桃儿～蟲儿了. This peach is wormy. /刀子～鏽了. The knife has rusted. /她～得很好看. She's pretty. 2) increase, improve. ～見識 increase one's knowledge. 3) rise (of a price). /價錢又～了. The price went up again. (B) 1) head, chief. 校～ principal or head of a school; 連～ company commander. 2) elder, senior. ～子 eldest son. (PT)比... ～ be so much older than someone. /我比他～兩歲. I am two years older than he. → 長**cháng**.

長進 **'jǎngjìn** (FV) make progress, improve. /他念書～了不少. He has made considerable progress in his studies. (N) progress, improvement.

長勁 **jǎngjìn** (VO) grow strong (of a person). /光吃米飯長不了勁. You can't grow strong on rice only.

掌 **jǎng** (FV) be in charge of, run. ~ 家 run a household. (B) 1) palm (of the hand). 手~ palm of the hand. 2) bottom of the foot. 脚~ sole of the foot; 馬 ~ bottom of a horse's hoof. 3) <-ル> heel or sole (of a shoe). 前 ~ half sole; 後 ~ heel.

掌權 **jǎngchywán** (VO) exercise authority, be in power. /美國現在由那一個政黨 ~? Which party is in power now in the United States?

掌櫃 **jǎnggwèi** (VO) manage a store or shop. /誰給你們 ~? Who manages the store for you?

掌握 **jǎngwò** (FV) 1) seize, control. ~ 軍權 control military power; ~ 機會 seize an opportunity. 2) have a grasp of, master (c). ~ 馬列主義 grasp the essence of Marxism-Leninism. (N) control.

漲 **jǎng** (FV) 1) go up, rise (of a price). /物價又 ~ 了. Prices have gone up again. 2) rise (of a river). The river is rising. → 漲 **jàng**.

漲水 **jǎngshwěi** (VO) rise (of a river). /這條河又漲了三尺水. The river rose three more feet.

帳{賬(N)} **jàng** (N) 1) account (M 筆 **bǐ**). 記 ~ charge to an account. 2) bill, debt (M 筆 **bǐ**). 欠 ~ be in debt. 3) account book (M 本 **běn**). (B) 1) tent. 營 ~ a camp. 2) <-子> bed curtain. ~ 鈎 curtain hook. 3) <-子> mosquito net. (M 條 **tyáu**). 蚊 ~ mosquito net. 4) <-子> wall hanging (M 條 **tyáu**). 喜 ~ "happiness" wall hanging (a wedding gift).

帳單 **jàngdān** (N) <-ル> bill (presented for payment) (M 張 **jàng**).

帳目 **'jàngmù** (N) financial account (M 本 **běn**).

帳篷 **jàngpeng** (N) tent. 搭 ~ put up a tent.

漲 **jàng** (FV) 1) swell, distend. /這個門 ~ 了, 關不上了. This door has swollen so that it won't close. 2) rise (of a river). /一下雨河水就 ~. Whenever it rains, the river rises. → 漲 **jǎng**.

丈 **jàng** (M) ten Chinese feet (= 141 inches). (B) wife's parents. 岳 ~ father-in-law (wife's father). 2)

husband. 姐 ~ brother-in-law (older sister's husband).

丈夫 **jàngfu** (N) husband. (B) man (one having manly excellence). ~ 氣 be manly, manliness. ·

丈母娘 **jàngmǔnyáng** (N) mother-in-law (wife's mother).

丈人 **jàngrén** (N) father-in-law (wife's father).

仗 **jàng** (FV) rely on, depend on. /這件事全 ~ (着) 你了. This matter depends entirely on you. (B) 1) battle. 打 ~ fight a battle or war; 勝 ~ victory. 2) pole or staff held aloft. 儀 ~ emblems, regalia, etc., carried aloft in a procession, review, or parade.

招 **jāu** (FV) 1) recruit people. ~ 生 recruit students. 2) wave, beckon (with the hand). ~ 手 wave the hand, beckon. 3) attract, invite. /他在街上唱歌 ~ 了一群人. His singing on the street attracted a crowd. /他的行動 ~ 警察的疑惑了. His actions aroused the police's suspicion. 4) tease, provoke. /別 ~ 他. Don't tease him. 5) pass a disease on to someone. /這個病 ~ 人. This disease can be passed on to others. 6) confess. /犯人已經 ~ 了. The prisoner has confessed.

招待 **jāudài** (FV) 1) entertain, be hospitable to. /他們 ~ 了我好幾天. They entertained me for several days. 2) take care of, wait on. /我等了半天才有人 ~ 我. I waited a long time before somebody came to wait on me. (N) 1) usher, steward. 2) hospitality, reception, service.

招呼 **jāuhu** (FV) 1) beckon to, wave to. /這個小孩見人就 ~. This child waves to anybody he sees. 2) let someone know. /你 ~ 他一下咱們一塊儿走. Let him know so we can go together. 3) take care of, look after. /你 ~ 小孩儿, 我去拿行李. You look after the children and I'll go get the luggage.

招牌 **jāupái** (N) store sign.

招上 **jāushang** (RC) 1) catch, contract (a disease). /那個小孩 ~ 麻疹了. That child caught the measles. 2) pass a disease on to someone. /他先傷的風，後來把我～了．First he got a cold, then he gave it to me.

招手 **jāushǒu** (VO) 1) beckon with the hand, asking someone to come (Chinese do this with the palm down). /我看不見你的手，所以不知道你向我～呢．I couldn't see your hand, so I didn't know you were beckoning to me. 2) wave hello. /你跟誰～呢? Whom are you waving at?

招搖 **jāuyau** (SV) be ostentatious (of a person). (FV) show off. /他很喜歡各處去～．He likes to show off wherever he goes.

朝 **jāu** (B) 1) morning. ～氣 vigor of youth (lit. morning air). 2) day. —～ someday. →朝**cháu**.

着 **jāu** (B) receive, suffer from, be troubled with. ～風 catch cold. (IE) That's right (d). /～! 就是那麽回事! That's right! That's exactly what it is! →着 **jáu**, 着 **je**, 着 **jwó**.

着急 **jāují** (VO) worry. /你着什麽急呢? What are you worrying about? (SV) be worried.

着涼 **jāulyáng** (VO) catch cold. /上禮拜我着了一點涼，三天才好．Last week I caught cold and I was sick for three days.

着儿 **jāur** (N) clever method, trick. /我得想一個～把他騙出來．We'll think of some trick to get him to come out. (M) step, stroke, move. /那盤棋不到十～我就贏了．I won that game of chess in ten moves.

着 **jáu** (FV) 1) be ignited, lit. /爐子着了沒有? Is the stove lit? 2) fall asleep. /他躺下就～了．He fell asleep as soon as he lay down. 3) touch. /那個氣球已經～了天花板了．The balloon is touching the ceiling. (RE) 1) indicates success in attaining or getting at something. 找～ find; 買～ succeed in buying. 2) indicates touching, connecting. 踫～ run into (lit. or fig.). →着 **jāu**, 着 **je**, 着 **jwó**.

着地 **jáudì** (VO) touch the ground. /那小孩坐在椅子上腳不能～．The child's feet can't touch the ground when he sits in a chair.

着火 **jáuhwǒ** (VO) have a fire,

be on fire. /那個工廠昨天夜裏着了一場大火．There was a very bad fire in that factory last night. /～了! There's a fire! or Fire!

找 **jǎu** (FV) 1) look for. /～個地方休息一會儿．Look for a place to rest for a while. 2) call on, visit. /請你有空的時候來～我．Please look me up when you have time. 3) go and meet. /我約好在公園門口～他．I have arranged to meet him at the gate of the park. 4) give someone change. /我給他一塊錢，他應該～我兩毛五分．I gave him a dollar; he has to give me 25¢ change.

照 **jàu** (FV) 1) shine on. /用燈～一～．Shine the light on it. 2) look at oneself (as in a mirror). /她每天用湖水～她的影子．Everyday she looked at her reflection in the lake. 3) take a picture or an X-ray. /他們給孩子～了一張像片．They took a picture of the child. (CV) 1) according to. /～他說的....According to what he says.... 2) following, toward. /～着那個方向走．Go in that direction. (B) 1) look after. ～看 look after, take care of, something or someone. 2) permit. 護～ passport. 3) photograph. 五彩～ color picture.

照顧 **'jàugù** (FV) 1) look after, take care of, something or someone. /她請我去替她～小孩．She asked me to take care of her children for her. 2) patronize a store. /他常～我們的舖子．He often patronizes our shop.

照管 **'jàugwǎn** (FV) look after, take care of something or someone. /誰～你的孩子呢? Who's taking care of your children?

照鏡子 **jàujìngdz** (VO) look at oneself in a mirror. /她～了半天鏡子．She looks at herself in the mirror half the day.

照例 **jàulì** (VO) follow a previous method, behave according to custom or tradition. /咱們就照去年的舊例吧．Let's follow last year's method. (A) according to custom. /～吧．Do it the traditional way.

照料 'jàulyàu (FV) look after, take care of, something or someone. /他替他父親～家裏的事情. He's taking care of family matters for his father.

照片 jàupyàn (N) photograph (M張jāng).

照像 jàusyàng (VO) 1) take a picture. /我給他們～. I'll take a picture of them. 2) have a picture taken. /我去～去. I'm going (there) to have my picture taken. or I'll go and take a picture.

照相機 jàusyàngjī (N) camera (M架jyà).

照樣 jàuyàng (A) <-ㄦ> in the same manner, the same way as before. /你再～寫一次. Write it again the same way.

着 je (P) 1) added to the main verb, indicates that the action or condition is going on or continuing and is frequently translated in the progressive form as. . . ing. /別站～, 坐下吧! Don't keep standing; sit down. /他連睡覺的時候都拿～書. Even when he's sleeping he has a book in his hand. /畫ㄦ在牆上掛～沒有? Are there pictures hanging on the wall? /我倒底比你大～兩歲呀. After all, I'm two years older than you. 2) added to FV, forms adverbial or coverbial expressions. /他躺～看報. He reads the newspaper lying down. /我是走～來的. I came here on foot. /他們倆背～坐. Those two are sitting with their backs turned to each other. /這種魚炸～好吃. This kind of fish is good fried. /他吃～飯看報. He reads the newspaper while eating. /他聽～無線電看書. He studies while listening to the radio. 3) added to CV without any change in meaning. /他靠(～)賣報吃飯. He makes a living selling newspapers. 4) added to FV which are then repeated, forms adverbial expressions and translates as while doing something. /你學～學～就會了. While you're studying it, you'll learn it. (PT) 1) . . .～. . .呢 indicates that the action or condition is going on or continuing at a particular point in time.

/那個時候他們吃～飯呢. They were eating at that time. /門現在關～呢. The door is closed now. 2) 等. . .～ wait until (lp). /別忙, 等他吃完飯～. Don't be in a rush; wait until he finishes eating. → 着 jāu, 着 jáu, 着 jwó.

着的呢 jedene = 着呢 jene.

着呢 jene (P) used at the end of a sentence which contains SV or AV, very, very much, very well. (lp). /他們兩個人好～. They are very close friends. or Both of them are very, very good. /那個人會說～. That person can speak very well. /那個狗厲害～. That dog is very vicious.

折 jē (FV) turn upside down or over. ～跟頭 turn a somersault. /他把一碗湯～了. He turned over a bowl of soup. 2) cool a liquid by pouring it back and forth between two containers. /你把那碗茶～～. Cool that cup of tea. SF of 摺jé, 摺jé. → 折jé, 折shé.

遮 jē (FV) 1) cover up. /衣服為的是～身體. People wear clothes to cover their bodies. 2) block out, screen off. /他用窗簾～太陽. He uses a window curtain to keep the sun out.

哲 jé (B) wise. ～人 sage. t
哲學 jésywé (N) philosophy.

折 jé (FV) 1) be worth so much on a trade-in, be traded for. /這輛汽車可以～八百元. This car is worth eight hundred dollars on a trade-in. 2) snap, break. /把鉛筆～成兩截. Break this pencil into two pieces. 3) bend. /信封裏有照片, 請你不要～. There are pictures in this letter. Please don't bend it. 4) lose an investment. ～本ㄦ lose capital. 5) be equal to. /一匹馬～十個人做的工. The work of one horse equals that of ten men. 6) turn back. /他們沒到紐約就～回來了. They turned back before they reached New York. (N) discount. 打～ give a discount. (M) tenth of the original price (indicates the amount a customer must pay). 七折 7/10 of the original price (i. e., 30% discount). /這張桌子我算八～賣給你. I'll sell this table to you at 20% off. SF of 摺jé, 摺jé. 一折jé, 折shé.

摘jé→摘jāi.

摺(捌]jé (FV) fold. ～衣服 fold clothes. (B) <-子> 1) book *or* paper in accordion form. 2) passbook, bankbook (M 本běn). →摺jé.

轍jé (N) 1) track left by a wheel (M 條tyáu, 道dàu). 2) end-rhyme in lines of a song. 合～ to rhyme. → 沒轍méijé.

摺[裀](折]jé (B) <-子,-ル> 1) crease. 2) pleat. 百～裙 finely pleated skirt. →摺jé.

這(这]jé, jèi* (SP)* followed by N, NUM, or M with or without 一 yī, this, these. ～三年 these three years; ～ (一)次 this time. /～個是我的. This is mine. /～錶太慢. This watch is too slow. (N)* 1) this (thing). /～是紙. This is paper. 2) this (situation *or* state of affairs). /～不成. This won't do. (A) 1) used before FV, SV, how... (it is), it is so.... /你看他～吃啊！ Look how he eats! /火車～慢吶！ The train is so slow! 2) now, this moment. /我～就起. I'll get up right away. →這dzè.
這邊 jèbyan, jèibyan (PW) <-ル> 1) this direction. /他正往～走呢. He is coming in this direction. 2) here. /這～沒有人. There's nobody here.
這個 jège, jèige (B) sound of hesitation. /他姓～～張. His last name is ... ah ... Chang.
這就 jèjyou (A) immediately. /我～去. I'll go immediately.
這裏 jèlǐ = 這ル jèr.
這麼 jèmma (SP) this, these. /他是～一個人. He's just this kind of person. (A) 1) used before FV, this way, like this. /這個機器得～用. You must run this machine this way. 2) used before SV, to this extent, so. /這個怎麼～難? How come this is so difficult? 3) <-着> in that case, then. /～我就去吧. In that case, I'll go. (FV) <-着> be like *or* do some-

thing like this. /我看他一生都只能～了. I think he'll be like this all of his life. /我們～吧. Let's do it like this. (B) used after CV like 往wǎng, 向syàng, 朝cháu, etc., this direction. /往～搬一搬. Move over this way a little bit.
這麼樣 'jèmmayàng, 'dzèmmayàng = 這樣jèyang.
這ル jèr (PW) here. /他什麼時候可以到～? When can he get here? /～我找不到什麼好飯馆. I can't find any good restaurants here.
這樣 jèyang, jèiyàng (FV) <-ル> be like *or* do something like this. /我們～吧. Let's do it this way. /他永遠就～了. He'll be like this forever. (A) 1) this way, like this. /別～説. Don't say it this way. 2) as ... as this. /～有錢的人不多. There are few people as rich as this.

這 jèi→這jè.

真(眞]jēn (AT) 1) real, genuine. ～鑽石 real diamond. 2) true. ～事 true story. (A) truly, really. ～好 really good. (RE) in potential RC only, indicates clearness in distinguishing. 聽不～ be unable to hear clearly. (B) truth. 認～ take something seriously. t
真格的 jēngéde (A) actually, really (lp). /你～就不去嗎? Are you really not going? (N) something really good, true, substantial. (lp). /咱們吃點ル～. Let's have something substantial to eat. /你得跟我説～. You must be serious with me.
真正 jēnjèng (A) truly, really. /他～要把事情作好. He really wants to do things well. (AT) real, genuine. /這是～的中國飯. This is real Chinese food.
真空 jēnkūng (AT) vacuum, airless. ～吸塵器 vacuum cleaner.
真空管 jēnkūnggwǎn (N) <-ル> vacuum tube, radio tube.
真理 jēnlǐ (N) truth. 尋求～ search for the truth (as of a philosopher).
真是的 'jēnshìde (IE) That's really too bad! *or* Really! (expression of sympathy).

真相 **jēnsyàng** (N) the truth, the real situation, the true picture. 調查 ~ investigate and try to ascertain the true picture (as of a detective).

針(鍼)**jēn** (N) 1) needle, pin (M 相 **gēn**). 2) injection, shot. 打 ~ give or have an injection. (M) stitch. 縫兩 ~ sew a couple of stitches.

針線活 **jēnsyànhwó** (N) needlework, sewing (M 件 **jyàn**).

診 **jěn, jèn** (B) examine (medically). 出 ~ be out on a house call (of a doctor). 診療所 **jěnlyáuswǒ, jěnlyáuswò** (N) 1) clinic. 2) doctor's office.

疹 **jěn** (B) <-子> measles. 麻 ~ measles.

診 **jěn** → 診 **jěn**.

枕 **jěn** (FV) lay one's head on something. /那個孩子把頭~在他母親的胳臂上了. The child laid his head on his mother's arm. (B) <-頭> pillow.

鎮 **jèn** (N) market town, trading center. (FV) 1) chill something (with ice). /請你把茶(拿冰)~上. Would you please chill this tea? 2) settle (of a liquid). /把這杯水~~就清了. Let this glass of water settle a bit and it will clear up. (B) 1) repress, guard. ~驚 allay fears; ~紙 paperweight. 2) calm, composed.

鎮定 **jèndìng** (SV) be calm, composed. (FV) calm down. /我這樣做為的是~人心. I did this in order to calm people down.

鎮靜 **jènjìng** (SV) be calm, composed, cool and collected.

鎮壓 **jènyā** (FV) repress, put down, an uprising. /那個叛亂已經~下去了. That rebellion has been put down.

陣 **jèn** (M) <-子.-ル> short period, spell. 一~雨 a shower (of rain); 一~風 a gust of wind. (B) disposition of troops. 布 ~ place troops in battle array.

陣地 **'jèndì** (N) position in battle array, area or point in battle formation.

陣亡 **jènwáng** (FV) die in battle. /他~了. He died in action.

賑 **jèn** (B) aid the distressed with money, food or goods. ~款 relief funds.

賑災 **jèndzāi** (VO) give relief in time of flood, famine, fire.

正 **jēng** (B) the first month of the year. 新 ~ the first month of the year. → 正 **jèng**, 整(正) **jěng**.

正月 **jēngywè** (TW) 1) the first month of the lunar calendar. 2) (in) January.

蒸 **jēng** (FV) steam something. ~飯 steam rice, steamed rice. (B) evaporate. ~發 evaporate.

蒸汽 **jēngchì** (N) steam.

蒸氣鍋 **jēngchìgwō** (N) boiler, steam generator.

蒸籠 **jēnglúng** (N) steamer (for cooking).

爭 **jēng** (FV) argue about, fight over. /他們~着給錢. They're arguing about who should pay. /我們~那個東西. We're fighting over that thing.

爭辯 **'jēngbyàn** (FV) argue logically about, debate. /他們正在~那個問題. They're arguing about that problem.

爭吵 **jēngchǎu** (FV) quarrel. /那兩夫妻整天~. That couple quarrels all day long.

爭氣 **jēngchì** (VO) prove one has ability. /他說我不行,我得爭這口氣. He says I'm no good, but I'll show him. (SV) be determined, resolute.

爭取 **jēngchyǔ** (FV) struggle for, work hard to attain, something. ~時間 strive to meet a time limit. /我在敵人統治下~生存. I struggled for my life under the rule of the enemy.

爭論 **jēnglwùn** (FV) argue, dispute. /他們~甚麼問題? What are they arguing about?

睜 **jēng** (FV) open the eyes. /你就~一個眼閉一個眼吧. (lit.) Open one eye and close the other. or (fig.) Don't be too critical. or Let it pass.

徵(征) **jēng** (FV) collect, recruit, levy. ~稅 levy taxes. (B) 1) proof,

evidence. ～候 symptoms of disease.
2) seek, ask for. ～問 ask for.

徵兵 **jēngbīng** (VO) draft *or* induct men for military service. /沒有戰事,所以政府不～. There's no war, so the government is not drafting men.

徵求 **jēngchyóu** (FV) look for, seek to get. /我要～他的意見. I want to get his advice. /我想登報～一個秘書. I'm going to advertise for a secretary.

徵聘 **jēngpìn** (FV) advertise for workers, help. /那個中學正在～教員. That high school is advertising for teachers.

征 **jēng** (B) attack, make an expedition against. ～服 compel submission by force. SF of 徵 jēng.

挣 **jēng** (B) ↓. →挣 **jèng**.

挣扎 **jēngjá** (FV) struggle under adverse circumstances. /他為了生活～了很久. He's been struggling to make a living for a long time.

整{正(B) 2)} **jēng** (FV) 1) tinker with. /他把我的鐘～好了. He tinkered with my clock and fixed it. 2) cause trouble, give one a hard time. /我的汽車真把我～了. My car has really given me a lot of trouble. (AT) whole. ～年 the whole year. /我要一個～的. I want a whole one. (A) exactly so much. /我～有三個. I have exactly three. (B) 1) in good order. ～潔 be neat. 2) used before or after NUM, exactly. ～十塊錢 exactly ten dollars; 兩點～ *or* ～兩點 two o'clock sharp.

整齊 **jēngchí** (SV) be neat, orderly. /他把桌子上的東西收拾的～極了. He arranged the things neatly on the table.

整頓 **jēngdwùn** (FV) rearrange, reorganize, reform. /校長說他要把學校的行政～一下. The principal said he would reform the administration of the school.

整個儿 **jēnggèr** (AT) complete, whole. /我要一個～的. I want a whole one. (A) completely, entirely. /他把那件事情～給忘了. He completely forgot about that.

整理 **jēnglǐ** (FV) straighten out, put in order. /請你把桌子上的

東西～一下. Please straighten out the things on the table. /我的報告已經～好了. I've got my report organized now.

整儿 **jēngr** (N) round number. /我給你一個～吧! How about my making it (the price) a round number?

整天 **jēngtyān** (A) all day. /他～睡覺. He sleeps all day long.

正 **jèng** (FV) straighten the position of something. /把你的領帶～一～. Straighten your tie. 2) correct a mistake. /請你給我～～口音. Please correct my pronunciation. (SV) be upright, straight. /請你看張畫～不～? Would you look and see if this picture is straight? (A) 1) just (now). /他～吃着飯呐. He's eating just now. 2) exactly, just. /這雙鞋～合適. This pair of shoes fits just right. /窗戶～對着他的門. The window is right opposite his doorway. (AT) 1) true, exact, correct. ～南 true south; ～面 right *or* correct side of something. 2) chief, main, principal (in contrast to secondary). ～駕駛 pilot (as opposed to the co-pilot). (B) 1) positive, plus. ～電 positive charge. /負三加～四得～一. A minus three and a plus four give plus one. 2) orthodox, regular. ～派 be orthodox. 2) formal. ～式談判 formal discussion. →正 jēng, 整(正)jēng.

正常 **jèngcháng** (SV) be normal. /他的溫度很～. His temperature is quite normal.

正確 **jèngchywè** (SV) be accurate, true. /這個消息很～. The news is quite accurate.

正當 **jèngdang** (SV) be upright, honest. /這個人用～的方法賺錢. He uses honest methods to make money.

正經 **jèngjing** (SV) 1) be serious. /他的態度很～. He is very serious-minded. 2) be proper, respectable. (A) seriously, /你跟我～說. Tell me seriously.

正楷 **jèngkǎi** (N) orthodox style of Chinese writing.

正式 **jèngshr̀** (A) officially, formally. /那件事昨天已經～

發表了. That was announced officially yesterday. (AT) official, formal. ～提案 formal proposal.

正題 **jèngtí** (N) the thing being talked about, main topic.

政 **jèng** (B) 1) political, governmental. ～令 governmental orders; ～權 regime. 2) administration. 校～ school administration; 家～ domestic management.

政黨 **jèngdǎng** (N) political party.

政府 **jèngfǔ** (N) government.

政治 **jèngjr** (N) 1) politics. 2) political science.

政界 '**jèngjyè** (N) political circles, government circles. /他在～很有名. He's quite well known in government circles.

政客 **jèngkè** (N) politician (bad sense).

政體 **jèngtǐ** (N) system of government. 共和～ republican form of government.

政策 **jèngtsè** (N) policy (political, economic, social, etc.).

政委 **jèngwěi** (N) member of a political committee (c).

證(証) **jèng** (FV) prove. ～幾何題 prove a geometry statement *or* theorem. (B) 1) proof. ～人 witness. 2) certificate. 身份～ identification card; 通行～ travel permit.

證婚 **jènghwūn** (VO) perform a wedding ceremony. /是誰給你們證的婚? Who married you two?

證據 **jèngjyu** (N) evidence, proof. /你說那句話有什麼～沒有? Do you have any evidence to back up that statement?

證明 **jèngming** (FV) prove. /你能～他那天沒來嗎? Can you prove that he didn't come that day? (N) 1) certificate, certification (M張**jāng**). 2) proof. /你有什麼～嗎? What proof do you have?

證書 **jèngshū** (N) certificate (M張**jāng**).

掙 **jèng** (FV) 1) earn, take in, as income. /他沒本事～飯吃. He does not have the ability to make a living. 2) struggle to get away. /那個小孩拼命往外～. That

child struggled to get away. → 掙 **jēng**.

激 **jī** (FV) arouse, stimulate, stir up. /那個參議員的演講～起很多辯論. The senator's speech aroused a lot of debate. /別拿話～他. Don't get him aroused. *or* Don't dare him. 2) spray, squirt. /用水～他. Squirt water at him. (B) 1) violently. ～戰 wage violent war. 2) flow fast under pressure (as water). ～流 swift current.

激烈 **jīlyè** (SV) 1) be violent. /他們打得很～. They fought violently. 2) be radical. /他的思想很～. His ideas are very radical.

積(积) **jī** (FV) accumulate, store up. /我～不下什麼錢. I can't save any money. (N) product (*math.*) (B) accumulation. ～蓄 savings; ～雪 accumulated snow.

積極 **jījí** (SV) be enthusiastic. /他做事很～. He's very enthusiastic about his work. (A) eagerly. ～進行 proceed eagerly. (AT) positive (as of one's attitude). ～意義 positive meaning.

機(机) **jī** (B) 1) machine, mechanism. 洗衣～ washing machine. 2) airplane. 轟炸～ bomber; 敵～ enemy plane. 3) opportunity. 乘～ seize an opportunity. 4) secret and important. ～密 be confidential. 5) alert, cunning. ～警 be sharp, quick-witted. 6) <-子> controlling mechanism on a mechanical device. 鎗～ trigger.

機器 **jīchì** (N) machine (M架 **jyà**).

機子 **jīdz** (N) 1) ↑ (B) 6). 2) loom (M架**jyà**).

機器匠 **jīchìjyàng** (N) mechanic.

機關 '**jīgwān** (N) 1) office, agency, bureau, institution (governmental or private). 2) controlling *or* key mechanism on some mechanical device. 3) trick device (mechanical).

機關鎗 **jīgwānchyāng** (N) machine gun (M挺**tǐng**, 架**jyà**).

機會 **jīhwei** (N) opportunity, chance.

機件 **jījyàn** (N) machine part (M件**jyàn**).

機械 **jīyè** (N) mechanical tool, device (M件 **jyàn**). (SV) be mechanical, like a machine. /我的工作很～. My work is very mechanical.

基 **jī** (B) 1) foundation, base. 房～ foundation of a building; 打好根～ build a sound foundation (lit. or fig.). 2) radical (*chem.*). t

基本 **jīběn** (AT) fundamental, basic. ～問題 basic problem.

基礎 **jīchǔ** (N) foundation. /他中文的～打得很好. He has gotten a good foundation in Chinese.

基督 **jīdū** (N) Jesus Christ.

基督徒 **jīdūtú** (N) Christian.

幾[几] **jī** (B) ↓. →幾 **jǐ**.

幾乎 **jīhu** (A) nearly, almost. /我～忘了. I almost forgot.

鷄[雞][鳮] **jī** (N) fowl, chicken (M隻 **jr̄**). ～ rooster; 母～ hen.

鷄蛋 **jīdàn** (N) chicken egg.

鷄蛋青儿 **jīdànchīngr** (N) egg white, albumen.

鷄蛋黄 **jīdànhwáng** (N) <-儿> egg yolk.

鷄子儿 **jīdzěr** (N) chicken egg (lp).

鷄毛撢子 **jīmáudǎndz** (N) feather duster (M把 **bǎ**).

肌 **jī** (B) flesh, muscle. 不隨意～ involuntary muscle.

肌肉 **jīròu** (N) flesh, muscle.

犄 **jī** (B) horn (of an animal).

犄角 **jījyau** (N) horn (of an animal) (M隻 **jr̄**; 對 **dwèi**).

犄角儿 **jījyǎur** (N) corner (as of a table or a room).

犄裏旮旯儿 **'jīligālar** (A) everywhere, from top to bottom, high and low (lp). /我～都找到了. I've hunted high and low.

几 **jī** (B) small table. 茶～ tea table. SF of 幾 **jī**, 幾 **jǐ**.

擊[击] **jī** (B) beat, strike. 攻～ to attack.

擊退 **jītwèi** (RC) beat back, fight off. /我們把敵人的攻勢～了. They fought off the enemy attack.

及 **jí** (RE) in potential RC only, indicates the reaching of a goal in time. 來的～ be able to do something in time;

躲避不～ be unable to escape in time. (B) 1) reach to. 2) together with, and. 以～ and. 一天及 **bùjí**.

及格 **jígé** (VO) pass an exam. /這回考試我及不了格. I can't pass this exam.

即[卽,即] **jí** (B) 1) at once, immediately. ～刻 at once. 2) even. ～或 even if. 3) precisely, namely. 知識～是力量 knowledge is precisely strength.

即使 **jíshř** (A) even if. /～你去我也不去. Even if you go, I still won't go.

急 **jí** (SV) 1) be angry, upset. /他如果知道我們背後取笑他他准～. If he finds out we were making fun of him behind his back, he'll certainly be angry. 2) be hurried. /他走得很～. He left in a hurry. 3) be worried, anxious. /你別～, 他不會出事的. Don't worry. He won't have an accident. 4) be urgent. /這個命令很～. This order is urgent. (A) in a hurry, hurriedly. /你何必這麼～買那輛車呢? Why are you in such a hurry to buy that car. (B) urgency, emergency. ～難 desperate straits.

急躁 **jídzàu** (SV) be irritable, quick-tempered.

急性 **jísyìng** (AT) quick-acting, acute (of a disease). ～盲腸炎 acute appendicitis.

急於 **'jíyú** (AV) be anxious to. /他～做完他的工作. He's anxious to finish his work.

集 **jí** (N) country fair, open-air market. (B) 1) <-子> collection of writings. 詩～ collection of poems. 2) collect, gather. ～會 assemble.

集合 **jíhé** (FV) collect, assemble. ～意見 collect ideas; ～力量 gather effort. /我們九點鐘～, 十點鐘出發. We'll get together at nine and leave at ten.

集中 **jíjūng** (FV) concentrate, consolidate. /敵人把軍隊～在河的兩岸了. The enemy has collected its troops on both sides of the river. /我不能～精神看書. I can't concentrate on reading.

集體主義 **jítǐjǔyi** (N) collectivism.

極[极] **jí** (A) extremely. ～好 extremely good. /他對人的態度～壞.

His attitude toward people is very poor. (B) pole (electric or magnetic). 陰~ negative pole; 北~ North Pole.

極其 **jíchí** (A) extremely. /他~高興. He's extremely happy.

極端 **jídwān** (A) exceedingly, to the greatest degree. /她父親對她的婚事~反對. Her father is very much opposed to her marriage. (SV) be immoderate, extreme. ~主義 extremism. /他的觀點太~了. His point of view is too extreme. (N) extremity. 地球的兩~ the two extremities of the earth.

極點 **jídyān** (N) extreme point. /這孩子真是聰明到~. This child is really extremely bright (lit. is bright to the extreme point).

極了 **jíle** (P) used after SV or expressions with AV, extremely. /他跑得快~. He runs extremely fast. /那個人愛生氣~. That person gets angry very easily.

極力 **jílî** (A) to one's utmost, very hard. /他~為我找工作. He tried very hard to get work for me.

級 **jí** (M) level, class, grade. /他比我高一~. He's one level higher than I. (B) level, class, grade. 階~ rank; 年~ grade *or* class in school.

脊 **jí** (B) spine. ~背 back (part of the body). → 脊 jì.

脊骨 **jígú** (N) spine, backbone (M條 tyáu).

脊梁 **jíliang** (**jínyang** (lp)) (N) back (part of the body).

吉 **jí** (B) lucky, auspicious. ~祥 good fortune. t

吉利 **'jílî** (SV) be lucky, auspicious.

幾(几) **jí** (NU)q (stressed) 1) how many. /你有~輛汽車? How many cars do you have? /你~歲了? How old are you? (Lit. How many years are you?) 2) what *or* which (one) in a sequence of things. /今天是禮拜~? What day is today? (NU) unstressed) 1) several, a few (any amount up to ten). /我去過~次紐約. I've been to New York several times. 2) and a few (in addition to ten or any multiple of ten). /昨天

來了五十~個人. Fifty or more people came yesterday. → 幾 jî.

幾時 **'jíshŕ** (A)q at what time, when, what date. /你~回來? When will you come back?

幾兒 **jyěr** (TW)q what date *or* day of the month (lp). /禮拜一是~? What is the date on Monday? /你~生日? When is your birthday?

幾兒個 **jyěrge** = 幾兒 **jyěr**.

脊 **jî** (N) ridge (M條 tyáu). 山~ mountain ridge. → 脊 jí.

擠(挤) **jî** (SV) be crowded. /街上很~. The street is crowded. (FV) 1) crowd, jostle, press. /人都~到電梯裏去了. People crowded into the elevator. 2) squeeze (out) something. ~牛奶 milk a cow. /別~你臉上的痘瘡. Don't squeeze the pimples on your face.

給 **jî** (B) supply, provide. 配~ to ration. → 給 gěi.

給養 **jîyǎng** (N) supplies, provisions (m).

紀 **jî** → 紀 jì.

季 **jì** (M) 1) season of the year. 四~ the four seasons. 2) term, semester. /我在那個學校念了兩~. I studied at that school two semesters.

季節 **jìjyé** (N) season.

記 **jì** (FV) 1) remember. /我不願意~那件事. I don't want to remember that. 2) record, take down. /你把電話號碼~在那兒啊? Where did you jot down that telephone number? (N) birthmark (M塊 kwài). (B) mark, sign. 標~ mark, marker.

記得 **jìde** (RC) remember. /我還~他. I still remember him. /我得~鎖門. I must remember to lock the door.

記號兒 **jìhaur** (N) sign, mark, notation, as a reminder.

記者 **jìjě** (N) reporter. 新聞~ news reporter.

記錄 **jìlù** (FV) make a written record of, take minutes. /誰~? Who's going to take the minutes? (N) 1) record, minutes. 2) record (as in competitive sports). 打破~ break a record.

記念 **jìnyan** (FV) commemorate, celebrate the memory of. /我們蓋一個樓~陣亡將士. We erected a building to commemorate the war dead. (N) memento. /我送給他一個表留做~. I gave him a watch as a mememto.

記性 **jìsying** (N) memory. /他~很不好. He has a poor memory.

計 **jì** (N) plan, scheme, plot (M條**tyáu**). 定~ devise a plan. (B) 1) calculate, reckon. 估~ estimate. 2) to plan, scheme. ~議 discuss a plan.

計劃 **'jìhwà** (FV) plan, figure out. /我們~~怎麼做吧. Let's figure out what to do. (N) plan, proposal.

計算 **'jìswàn** (FV) 1) compute, figure out. /你~一下得用多少錢? Please figure out how much money it will cost. 2) wheedle things out of <u>someone</u>. /你別老~你的兄弟. Don't try to wheedle things out of your younger brother all the time.

計算機 **jìswànjī** (N) computer, calculator (M架**jyà**).

既{旣,既}**jì** (A) since, now that. /你~不願意知道,我何必告訴你呢. Since you don't want to know, why should I bother to tell you. /你~喜歡,就拿走吧. Since you like it, (then) take it. (B) already. ~有的榮譽 the fame one already has. (PT) ...又...not only...but also... /她~好看,又聰明. She's not only good looking, but also smart.

既然 **jìrán** (A) since, now that, this being the case. /他~不肯借錢給你,你多說也沒用. Since he has refused to lend you the money, further talk will be useless.

技 **jì** (B) skill. 絕~ unsurpassed skill.

技工 **jìgūng** (N) skilled labor.

技師 **jìshr** (N) technical expert.

技術 **jìshū** (N) technique, skill.

技術員 **jìshùywan** (N) technician.

寄 **jì** (FV) mail, send. /這封信你~給誰? To whom are you sending this letter? (B) 1) entrust. ~售 sell on consignment. 2) reside. ~宿 reside temporarily.

紀 **jì**, **jǐ*** (B) 1) record. 大事~ chronicle. 2) year. 年~ age. 3)* regulation, order. 軍~ military discipline. s

紀律 **jìlyù**, **jǐlyù** (N) order, discipline.

紀念 **jìnyàn** (FV) commemorate. ~陣亡將士 commemorate the war dead. (N) memento. /我送他一個表留做~. I gave him a watch as a memento.

紀元前 **jìywánchyán** (TW) before Christ, B. C. ~一九四五年 the year 1945 B.C.

紀元後 **jìywánhòu** (TW) anno Domini, A. D. ~一九六一年. the year 1961 A.D.

繫 **jì** (FV) tie. ~領帶 tie or put on a necktie. /繩子太短什麼都~不上. The rope is too short to tie up anything. →繫**syi**.

繼{繼,鑯}**jì** (B) continue, succeed to. ~位 succeed to the throne; ~母 stepmother.

繼承 **jìchéng** (FV) inherit, fall heir to. /他~了他父親的產業. He inherited his father's property.

繼續 **jìsyù** (A) continously. /他~工作了兩天. He worked continously for two days. (FV) continue to <u>do something</u>. /那個工作太累,我~不下去了. That work is too tiresome; I can't go on doing it.

鮰{鮰鯯,鯯}**jì** (B) sand perch.

鮰鯯魚 **jìyú** (N) sand perch (M條**tyáu**).

忌 **jì** (FV) abstain from, avoid. /你的病~生冷. You (<u>lit.</u> Your illness) should avoid raw and cold foods. /他現在把酒~了. He's not drinking any more now. (B) taboo, socially unacceptable behavior. 犯~ break a taboo, expose one's failings.

忌口 **jìkǒu** (VO) be on a diet. /他現在~,不能吃鹹的. He's on a diet now; he can't eat anything salty.

嫉 **jì** (B) jealous. ~恨 hate <u>someone</u> because of jealousy.

嫉妒 **'jìdù** (SV) be jealous.

(FV) be jealous of. /他很～你.
He's very jealous of you.

jia see **jya**.

jian see **jyan**.

jiang see **jyang**.

jie see **jye**.

津 **jīn** (B) Tientsin (contracted form of
天～ **tyānjīn**). ～浦鐵路Tientsin-
Pukow Railroad.
  津貼 **jīntyē** (N) pension, subsidy, financial aid, given to supplement other resources (M筆 **bǐ**). (FV)
give as financial aid. /我～了他五
百塊錢. I gave him five hundred
dollars.

金 **jīn** (AT) gold, golden, gold-colored.
～錶gold watch; ～鞋 gold-colored
shoes. (B) 1) money. 現～ cash.
2) metal. 五～行 hardware store.
d s
  金子 **jīndz** (N) gold.
  金鋼鑽儿 **jīngāngdzwàr** (N)
diamond (cut as for a ring) (M粒 **lì**;
卡拉 **kāla**).
  金鋼石 **jīngāngshŕ** (N) diamond
(the substance) (M塊 **kwài**, 粒 **lì**).
  金屬 **'jīnshǔ** (N) metal. /銀子
是一種～. Silver is one kind
of metal.

斤(觔) **jīn** (M) catty (= 1⅓ lbs.)

今 **jīn** (B) at present, now. 至～ up to
the present time; 古～ past and
present.
  今後 **jīnhòu** (TW) 1) from now
on. /～我們得努力一點儿.
We must work harder from now on.
2) the days ahead. /～不會比過
去更壞. The days ahead couldn't
be any worse than past ones have
been.
  今年 **jīnnyán** (TW) this year.
  今天 **jīntyān** (TW) today.
  今儿 **jyēr** = 今天 **jīntyān**.
  今儿個 **jyērge** = 今天 **jīntyān**.

筋 **jīn** (N) 1) tendon. 2) vein (as seen
from outside). 3) nerve. 腦～brain.
4) fiber (as in plants). /芹菜太老
有很多～. This celery is too old;
it's very stringy.

禁(經) **jīn** (AV) can bear or stand to be.
/這種料子很～洗. This kind of
material is washable. → 禁 **jìn**.

禁不住 **jīnbujù** (RC) be unable
to hold, bear, withstand. /這根繩
子～五百磅. This rope can't
hold five hundred pounds. /我～
他打. I can't stand his beating me.
  禁用 **jīnyùng** (SV) be durable,
long-lasting. /鋼筆比毛筆～.
A fountain pen is more durable than
a writing brush.

謹 **jǐn** (B) cautious, attentive. ～防 guard
against.
  謹慎 **jǐnshèn** (SV) be careful,
heedful. /他做事很～. He does
his work very carefully.

僅(仅) **jǐn** (A) barely, merely. /這些米.
僅夠一天用. This is barely
enough rice for one day.
  僅僅 **jǐnjǐn** = 僅 **jǐn**.

緊 **jǐn** (SV) 1) be restricting, tight.
/我的鞋太～. My shoes are too
tight. 2) be intense, strong, force-
ful. /雨下得很～. The rain is
really coming down. 3) be strict,
hard. /我父親管得我很～.
My father is very strict with me. 4)
be urgent, critical. /前方戰事
很～. The war situation at the front
is critical. 5) be in financial straits.
/現在我的日子很～. I'm having
a tough time of it financially these
days. (A) 1) directly, closely.
/那兩條路～接着. Those two
roads are directly connected. 2)
continuously. /他～唱沒完. He
sings continuously without stopping.
3) fast. /我們～走, 天黑以前也
許能到. We may get there before
dark if we walk fast. (FV) tighten.
/把你的鞋帶～一～. Tighten
your shoelaces.
  緊張 **jǐnjāng** (SV) 1) be nervous, tense, excited. /你別～.
Don't be excited. 2) be exciting.
/那個電影很～. That movie is
quite exciting.
  緊急 **jǐnjí** (SV) be urgent,
critical, crucial. /事情已經很
～了. The situation is critical
now.

錦 **jǐn** (B) brocade. ～緞 figured satin.
  錦標 **jǐnbyāu** (N) small banner
given as a reward, trophy.

儘(尽) **jǐn** (CV) <～着> 1) taking something first. /你～舊衣服先穿.

Wear the old clothes first. 2) limiting oneself to. /我一天～五塊錢花. I limit myself to five dollars a day. 3) let someone do something first. /我～我弟弟挑. I'll let my younger brother choose first. (B) the utmost. ～底下 at the very bottom; ～夠 absolutely sufficient.

儘管 jìngwǎn (A) 1) even though. /～你多麼聰明,也要用功才考得上大學. Even though you're intelligent, you have to study hard to get into college. 2) freely. /有什麼問題～問. If you have any questions, feel free to ask them.

儘着 jìnje (FV) let someone have his way. /我老～我太太. I always let my wife have her way. (CV) ↑ (CV).

近 jìn (SV) 1) be close, near. 很～的親戚 close relatives. /我住的離鬧區很～. I live very near the downtown area. 2) be alike, close. /這兩個顏色很～. These two colors are very close. (B) recent. ～年 (in) recent years.

近來 jìnlai (A) recently, lately. /～他沒來. He hasn't been coming recently. (AT) recent. ～的新聞 recent news.

近於 jìnyu (A) approaching, close to, almost. /你說的話有點～空想了. What you say is a bit on the unrealistic side. /他的想法～瘋狂了. His way of thinking borders on insanity.

禁 jìn (B) forbid, prohibit. ～地 forbidden ground; 不～ cannot help doing something. →禁 jīn.

禁止 jìnjr (FV) forbid, prohibit. /你們的宗教～結婚嗎? Does your religion forbid marriage?

盡[尽] jìn (A) entirely, totally. /不要～信他的話. Don't believe everything he says. (FV) fulfill. ～責任 fulfill one's duty. (RE) indicates exhausting, finishing. 用～ use up; 走～ go over every road, try everything possible. (B) use up, exhaust. ～可能 exhaust all possibilities.

盡力 jìnlì (AV) try one's best to. /我～給你想辦法. I'll do the best I can to help you. (VO) try one's best. /我已經盡了我的

力了. I've tried my very best.

盡量 jìnlyàng (A) as much as possible. /你～吃好了. You may eat as much as you can.

進[进] jìn (DV) 1) enter, come or go into. ～站 come or go into a station (as a train). /我剛～城,就下起雨來了. I had just gotten to the city when it started to rain. 2) enroll in, enter, a school, club. ～大學 enter a college. 3) receive, take in, money, goods. ～貨 take in merchandise. /你一個月～多少錢? How much money do you make in a month? (RE) in, into. /她抬～醫院,小孩儿就生了. The baby was born as soon as she was carried into the hospital. (B) 1) advance, progress. ～化 evolve, evolution. 2) used after CV like 往 wǎng, 望 wàng, 向 syàng, etc., in. 往～跑 run in or into.

進步 jìnbù (VO) advance, make progress. /他們又進了一步. They have progressed one more step. (N) progress, advancement, improvement. /那個學生沒有什麼～. That student doesn't show any improvement. (SV) be progressive.

進去 jìnchyù (RC) go in. /屋子裏人太多,我進不去. There are too many people in the room; I can't get in. (RE) 1) in (there). 搬～ move in (there). /把他帶進卧房去. Take him into the bedroom. 2) indicates taking in, absorbing (mentally). 聽不～ be unable to absorb (by listening).

進攻 jìngūng (FV) advance and attack a position (in fighting). /我們不能後退,只能～. We cannot retreat, we can only advance.

進展 jìnjǎn (FV) improve, make progress. /他最近～了不少. He has improved a lot recently. (N) progress.

進口 jìnkǒu (VO) bring something into a country (of goods). /現在鴉片是進不了口了. You can't get opium into the country now. (FV) import. /美國～很多糖. The United States imports a lot of sugar.

進款 jìnkwǎn (N) income (M 筆 bǐ).

進 來 **jìnlái** (RC) come in. /你
不 開門, 我怎麼 ～? If you don't
open the door how can I come in?
(RE) in (here). 走 ～ walk in (here).
/把車開進車房來. Drive the
car into the garage (here).

進 深 **jìnshēn** (N) depth (from
front to back of a building). 戲臺的
～ depth of a stage.

進 行 **jìnsyíng** (FV) 1) go
ahead with, progress with. /你們
什麼時候～試驗? When are
you going ahead with the experiment?
/那個工程～的很慢. The con-
struction is progressing very slowly.
2) pull strings to get a job. /告訴
我你怎麼～的這個差事? Tell
me, what strings did you have to
pull to get that job?

進 行 曲 **jìnsyíngchyǔ** (N) march
(the music)(M 支 **jr̄**). 奏 ～ play a
march.

勁 **jìn** (N) 1)<-ㄦ> strength (M 股
gǔ). /他的 ～ 很大. He has
a lot of strength. 2) <-ㄦ> interesting aspects. /那個電影沒
什麼 ～. That movie is dull. 3)
<-ㄦ> interest, enthusiasm (M 股
gǔ). /他對棒球的～很大. He
is very interested in baseball.

勁 ㄦ **jyèr** (N) 1) ↑. 2) manner, attitude, air (M 股 **gǔ**). /他那
股～真京成. His attitude is unacceptable. /那個女孩ㄦ有一股
特別的～. That girl has a
special air about her. (B) 1) added
to FV, SV, how . . . (in exclamations).
/看他那個忙 ～! How busy he
is! /瞧他這個跑 ～. Look at
how he can run! 2) added to FV, the
way someone or something does
something. /他那說～誰也受
不 了. Nobody can stand the way he
talks.
    勁 ㄦ 的 **jyèrde** = 勁 ㄦ **jyèr** (B).

京 **jīng** (B) capital city. ～ 城 capital. *t*

京 劇 **jīngjyù** (N) Chinese opera
(Peiping style) (M 齣 **chū**, 臺 **tái**).

京 戲 **jīngsyì** = 京 劇 **jīngjyù**.

經 **jīng** (N) Buddhist canon (M 本 **běn**, 部
bù). (CV) because of, due to. /～他
一提我就想起來了. Because
of what he said I remembered. (B)
1) sacred book. 聖 ～ the Holy Bible;

可 蘭 ～ the Koran. 2) the Chinese
classics. 書 ～ Book of History. 3)
pass through. ～ 驗 to experience,
be experienced. 4) manage. ～ 管 be
in charge of something. 5) things
running lengthwise. ～ 度 degree of
longitude. 6) constant, regular. ～
常 費 regular expenses; 月 ～ menses.
一 禁 (經) **jìn**.

經 常 **jīngcháng** (A) 1) regularly,
from time to time. /我們 ～ 去看
他. We visit him regularly. 2) all
the time. /他 ～ 有兩個廚子.
He has two cooks on hand all the
time.

經 費 **jīngfèi** (N) operating
funds of an organization (M 筆 **bǐ**, 份
fèn). /政府給我們的 ～ 不夠.
The government didn't give us
enough funds.

經 過 **jīnggwò** (FV) pass by *or*
through. /從這裏到電影院要
～ 郵局. From here to the theater
you have to go by the post office. (N)
circumstances *or* story behind something. /這件事的～怎麼樣?
What about the circumstances surrounding this matter?

經 濟 **jīngjì** (N) economics. 家
庭 ～ home economics. ～ 地 理 economic geography. (SV) be economical. /這樣辦很～. It's very
economical to do it this way.

經 理 **jīnglǐ** (FV) manage, handle. /他一個人～這間店鋪.
He runs this store by himself. (N)
manager (of a hotel, bank, etc.).

經 歷 **'jīnglì** (FV) experience,
go through. /他～過很多危險.
He's been through a lot of danger.
(N) experience. /他的～很淺.
He hasn't had much experience.

經 商 **jīngshāng** (VO) be engaged
in business, commerce, trade. /他
在中國～很多年. He was in
business for a long time in China.

經 售 **jīngshòu** (FV) have for
sale, carry in stock. /他們～那
種貨. They carry that merchandise.

經 驗 **jīngyàn** (FV) experience,
go through. /他們～過各種痛
苦. They have been through all
kinds of suffering. (N) experience.

經 營 **'jīngyíng** (FV) manage *or*
carry on a business. /他在南美

洲～起來一個樹膠工廠. He has taken on the management of a rubber factory in South America.

耕 **jīng** →耕 **gēng**.

精 **jīng** (SV) 1) be skillful. /那個裁縫的手工很～. That tailor does skillful work. 2) be shrewd, smart. /他做生意很～. He is a shrewd businessman. 3) be refined, pure. ～鋼 pure steel. (N) 1) essence, extract. 杏仁ル～ almond extract. 2) sperm. 3) spook *or* spirit which has human form, monster. 妖～ monster. (A) very (lp). ～濕 be soaking wet; ～薄 be very thin. (B) used before FV, thoroughly. ～通 have a thorough knowledge of; ～修鐘錶 do a good job of repairing clocks and watches.

精明 **jīngmíng** (SV) be shrewd.
精神 **jīngshén** (N) spirit, vitality. 合作～ spirit of cooperation. /他的～很好. He's in very good spirits. (SV) be energetic. /我昨天沒睡覺,所以今天不太～. I didn't sleep last night, so I'm sluggish today.

莖 **jīng** (B) stalk, stem (of a plant). 根～ rhizome.

驚(惊] **jīng** (FV) bolt (as a horse). /看見火,我的馬～了. My horse bolted when he saw the fire. (B) 1) fright. 吃～ be frightened, startled, astonished. 2) frighten, startle. ～人 be amazing.

驚動 **jīngdung** (FV) disturb, arouse, a person. /他在睡覺,別～他. He's sleeping, don't disturb him.
驚慌 **jīnghwāng** (SV) be alarmed, excited, frightened. /他們～了一陣. They were given a scare.
驚訝 **jīngyà** (SV) be surprised. /聽見這句話,他很～. He was very surprised to hear that.

井 **jǐng** (N) 1) well (M 口 **kǒu**). 2) mine shaft (M 口 **kǒu**).

警(儆(B) 1)} **jǐng** (B) 1) warn, caution. ～惕 be cautious. 2) an alarm, alert. 火～ fire alarm. 3) police. ～長 police sergeant.

警報 **jǐngbàu** (N) danger signal, alarm. 空襲～ air-raid signal.

警備 **jǐngbèi** (FV) guard, garrison, a place when an emergency threatens. /這個地方都～好了. This district is well guarded.
警察 **jǐngchá** (N) policeman.
警告 **jǐnggàu** (FV) warn, caution. /我想你在沒出事以前先～他一下. I think you'd better warn him before something happens. (N) warning.
警誡 **jǐngjyè** (FV) warn. /～他下次不要再做這件事. Warn him not to do the same thing next time.
警鈴 **jǐnglíng** (N) alarm bell.

景 **jǐng** (M) scene (as in a play). (B) 1) scenery. 風～ scenery, landscape. 2) prospect. 年～ prospect for the year.
景緻 **jǐngjr** (N) beautiful *or* picturesque scenery.
景象 **jǐngsyàng** (N) actual situation, atmosphere, climate of affairs. /～很慘. The situation is pitiful.

淨[净] **jìng** (A) 1) all the time, keep... ing. /他～說謊話. He lies all the time. /你別～裝窮. Don't keep pretending to be so poor. 2) used after PW, everwhere: /屋子裏～是土. There is dirt everywhere in this room. 3) only, merely. /～吃肉不行. It's not good to eat only meat. 4) used before FV like 拿 **ná**, 得 **dé**, 賺 **jwàn**, 剩 **shèn**, etc., translates together with the FV as net, clear, so much money. /他的買賣每月～賺一千元. His business clears a thousand dollars a month. (FV) clean. /～一～桌面. Clean the top of the table. (RE) indicates finishing. /錢都用～了. The money is all used up. (B) 1) clean. 乾～ be clean. 2) net (as opposed to gross). ～得 net profit.

竟 **jìng** (B) 1) end. 究～ in the end, finally. 2) actually, unexpectedly. ～敢 actually dare.
竟然 **jìngrán** (A) unexpectedly, after all. /他～跟他太太離婚了. He unexpectedly divorced his wife.

靜 **jìng** (SV) be quiet, peaceful. /這ル

真～啊.　It's really quiet here.

敬 jìng (FV) give, present, someone with food, refreshment. /這個菜是飯館～的. This dish is on the house. (B) 1) respect, worship. 恭～ be respectful to, respect; ～神 worship God *or* a god. 2) complimentary gift. 喜～ wedding gift (usually money).

　　敬重 'jìngjùng (FV) respect a person. /如果你～別人,別人也會～你. If you respect others, others will respect you.

　　敬禮 jìnglǐ (VO) salute. /衛兵向我敬了一個禮. The guard saluted me. (N) salutation, formal gesture of greeting.

鏡 jìng (B) 1) <-子> mirror (M 面 myàn). 2) lens. 凸透～convex lens.

　　鏡框儿 jìngkwàngr (N) picture frame with glass.

　　鏡頭 jìngtóu (N) 1) lens (of a microscope, camera, telescope). 2) scene in a motion picture.

境 jìng (B) 1) boundary. 邊～ boundary, frontier. 2) situation, circumstances. ～遇 circumstances.

　　境況 'jìngkwàng (N) situation, circumstances. /～慢慢地好轉了. The situation is slowly changing for the better.

競(竞)jìng (B) compete. ～走 foot-race.

　　競爭 jìngjēng (FV) be in competition, compete. /他向來不跟別人～. He never competes with anybody. (N) competition. /商業上的～很厲害. Competition in business is very keen.

　　競選 jìngsywǎn (FV) compete in an election for, run for the office of. /他～總統. He's running for president. (N) election campaign.

jiong *see* jyung.

jiu *see* jyou.

州 jōu (M) 1) administrative region (c). 2) state (of the U.S.). ～長 governor of a state.

周(週)(M) jōu (M) 1) time around something. 繞場三～ walk around a field three times. 2) week. /我的暑假已經過了兩～了. Two

weeks of my summer vacation have already gone by. (B) 1) around. ～遊 make a circuit. 2) complete, entire. ～身 the whole body. *d s*

　　周到 'jōudàu (SV) be thorough, careful, meticulous. /開始造房子之前,我們得很～地計劃. Before we build a house, we must plan very carefully. /他想得很～. He takes everything into consideration.

　　周密 'jōumì (SV) 1) be careful, thoroughgoing. /他計劃很～. He planned it very carefully. 2) be carefully worked out with attention to detail. /這個地方的警衛很～. The defenses of this position have been worked out in great detail.

　　周末 jōumwò (N) weekend. 上～ last weekend; 這個～this weekend.

　　周圍 jōuwéi (PW) (in) the area around something. /那個房子～都有樹. There are trees all around that house. /我每天都在教堂～散步. I take a walk (in the area) around the church every day. (N) circumference, perimeter.

粥 jōu (N) congee (gruel made of rice or millet).

軸 jóu (N) axle, axis (M根gēn). 車～ axle on a car *or* cart. (M) <-儿> for scrolls. (B) scroll. 橫～ horizontal scroll.

妯 jóu (B) ↓.

　　妯娌 jóulǐ (N) sister-in-law (husband's brother's wife).

皺 jòu (SV) be wrinkled (of any surface). (B) wrinkle the brow.

　　皺眉 jòuméi (VO) knit one's brow, frown. /他老～. He is always frowning.

知 jr̄ (B) 1) know. ～恥 have a sense of shame. 2) knowledge. 無～ be ignorant; 求～慾 desire for knowledge. 3) inform. ～會 tell, inform.

　　知道 jr̄dau (FV) know, know of. /我不～怎麼做. I don't know how to do it. /我沒見過他,但我～他. I have never met him, but I know of him.

　　知識 jr̄shr (N) knowledge.

　　知識份子 jr̄shrfèndž (N) intelligentsia.

知心 **jrsyīn** (SV) have mutual understanding, be intimate (lit. know the heart). /他們兩個人是很～的朋友. Those two are very intimate friends.

支{枝}(M) 1) 3)} 支 **jr** (FV) 1) prop up, support. ～窗戶 prop open a window; ～帳蓬 put up a tent. 2) draw *or* pay out money. /我想先～兩千塊錢. I want to take out two thousand dollars in advance. 3) get rid of, put off. ～日子 put off a date. /我跟他借錢他老拿話～我. When I try to borrow money from him, he always talks his way out of it. (M) 1) detachment of soldiers. 2) watt. 六十～光燈泡 60-watt bulb. 3) for long, thin, inflexible objects. 一～香烟 a cigarette; 一～鉛筆 a pencil. 4) for flowers with stems intact. 一～搟花 a lotus flower. 5) branch of a family. /我們這一～人不多. There are not many people in our branch of the family. (B) 1) direct, order. give orders to. 2) branch, division. ～行 branch office.

支持 **jrchr** (FV) support. /我們的黨～他. Our party is supporting him. (N) support. /他得不到國會的～. He cannot get support from Congress.

支票 **jrpyàu** (N) (bank) check (M張 **jāng**). 開～ write a check.

支使 **jrshr** (FV) order people around. /他常常～人. He's always ordering people around.

芝 **jr** (B) 1) fungus. 靈～ fungus with a purplish stalk. 2) fragrant iris. ～草 fragrant iris. 3) ↓.

芝麻 **jrma** (N) sesame (M粒 **li**).

枝 **jr** (B) 1) <-子> branch, limb, of a tree. 樹～子 branch. 2) <-ㄦ> twig. 一支{枝}兒.

織{紙} **jr** (FV) weave. ～布 weave cotton cloth.

汁 **jr** (B) 1) <-ㄦ> juice, sap. 果～ fruit juice; 橘子～ orange juice. 2) <-子> gravy.

隻{只} **jr** (M) for boats, birds, one of certain paired things, some animals. 一～船 a boat; 一～鳥 a bird; 一～鴨子 a duck; 一～手 a hand; 一～鞋 a shoe; 兩～眼睛 two eyes; 一百～牛 one hundred head of cattle. (B) single. ～身 by oneself, alone.

蜘 **jr** (B) ↓.
蜘蛛 **jrju** (N) spider.

指 **jr** (B) ↓. 一指兒.
指甲 **jrjya** (N) fingernail.

之 **jr** (B) ↓.
之中 **jrjūng** (B) 1) among. 我們～ among us. 2) in an enclosed place. 教室～ in a classroom. 3) in, within a period of time. 三年～ within three years.
之間 **jrjyan** (B) 1) between. 中美～ between China and the United States; 第一堂跟第二堂～ between the first and second classes. 2) in, within. 一個月～ within one month.

植 **jr** (B) 1) to plant. ～樹 plant trees. 2) ↓.
植物 **jrwu** (N) plant (M棵 **kē**).

值 **jr** (FV) 1) be worth so much. /那輛車～五百塊錢. That car is worth five hundred dollars. 2) deserve. ～一頓打 deserve a spanking. (SV) be worthwhile. /那趟旅行～不～? Was the trip worthwhile? (B) 1) value. 價～ value. 2) take one's turn on duty. ～日 be on duty for the day.

值班 **jrbān** (VO) take one's turn on duty, be on duty, be on call. /今ㄦ誰～? Who's on duty today? /他這個月裏已經值過兩次班了. He has already been on duty twice this month.

值得 **jrde** (AV) be worth doing something. /那個電影ㄦ很～看. That movie is really worth seeing.

直 **jr** (SV) 1) be straight. ～線 straight line. 2) be honest, straightforward (of a person). 3) be wide open (of the eyes). /他看見那麼多錢, 眼睛都～了. His eyes opened wide when he saw all that money. 4) be stiff. /他站得腿都～了. He stood so long his legs got stiff. (FV) straighten. /把那根彎管子～過來. Straighten out that bent pipe. (A) 1) keep...ing. ～哭 keep crying. 2) directly, straight. ～譯 translate literally. /往西～走就到了. Go straight west and you'll get there. 3) just, exactly. /他～像個小孩. He's just like a child. (N) vertical stroke used in writing Chinese characters. (B) length. ～三尺橫兩尺 be three feet long and two feet wide.

直骨籠通 'jŕgulūng'tūng (SV) be very plain, ordinary, severe, with no frills or fringes, as a dress.

直接 jŕjyē (SV) be direct, immediate. /我們的關係很～. We are directly related. (A) directly, face to face. /我們～交涉. We talked things over face-to-face. *or* We carried on direct negotiations.

姪[侄]jŕ (B) <-子,-ㄦ> brother's child. 內～ nephew (wife's brother's son). 姪女 jŕnyu (N) niece (brother's daughter).

職[職]jŕ (B) 1) duty, responsibility. 盡～ do one's duty to its full extent. 2) office, official position. 調～ to transfer to another position.
職務 'jŕwù (N) duty, responsibility, business, function. /他有～沒有? Has he been assigned any duties?
職業 jŕyè (N) profession, occupation, job.
職員 jŕywán (N) member of a managerial staff in any large institution.

指jŕ→指jŕ.

執[执]jŕ (B) 1) hold, grasp. ～票人 stockholder. 2) manage, direct, control. ～掌 be in charge of.
執照 jŕjau (N) official license *or* certificate (M張 jāng). 駕駛～ driving license.
執行 jŕsyíng (FV) carry out, put into effect (a matter, a law, a proposal). /這條法律已經～了. This law has already gone into effect. (AT) executive. ～委員會 executive committee.

指jŕ, *jŕ (B) *1) <-頭> digit (finger or toe). 大拇～ thumb, big toe. 2) guide, direct. ～示 give instruction to, instruction. (FV) 1) point at (lit. or fig.). 用棍子～一～ point with a stick; 把錯ㄦ～出來 point out mistakes. 2) depend on, count on. /我現在就～你一個人了. I'm counting on you alone now. (CV)

1) relying on. /他～賣糖吃飯. He makes a living by selling candy. 2) referring to, hinting at. /你～什麼說的? What are you hinting at?→指jŕ.

指不定 jŕbuding (A) not be certain about. /她～嫁給誰呢. It's not certain whom she'll marry.

指導 jŕdǎu (FV) serve as advisor to, direct, guide. /我剛來請您～. I've just arrived. Please tell me what to do. (N) guidance, direction.

指點 'jŕdyǎn (FV) point out and explain, show someone how to do something. /你～他怎麼做. You show him how to do it. /請你～～我們. Please show us how.

指責 jŕdzé (FV) point out faults, find fault with someone. /他愛～別人的錯ㄦ. He likes to find fault with others. (N) blame, censure.

指揮 jŕhwēi (FV) direct, command. ～'軍隊 command an army. (N) command, instruction. 2) director, conductor of an orchestra or a band.

指教 jŕjyàu (FV) instruct someone about something. /我初來, 一切請～. I've just come. Would you please tell me what to do? (N) suggestions for improvement. /您有什麼～. Do you have any suggestions? (Very polite, as when asking for criticism of a book one has written.)

指南針 jŕnánjēn (N) compass (for showing direction).

指示 'jŕshr̀ (FV) point out, indicate, suggest. /請你～一個簡便的方法. Would you please suggest a more simple solution? (N) instructions about how to do something. /黨部最近又發給黨員不少的新～. The party has recently issued many new instructions to members.

只[祇]jŕ (A) only, just exclusively. /他～想妳. He is only thinking of you. SF of 隻jŕ.
只得 jŕdé (A) can do nothing but. /現在我～跟他借錢了. I can do nothing but borrow the money from him.

尺 好 **jřhǎu** (A) can do nothing but. /燈都熄了,我們～睡覺. The lights are all out; the only thing we can do is go to sleep.

尺 是 **jřshř** (A) 1) but, however. /這衣服的式樣不錯,～顏色不好. The style of this dress is O.K., but I don't like the color. 2) only (and no other). /昨天我家人都出去了,～我一人在家. Yesterday all of my family was out. Only I was at home.

只要 **jřyàu** (A) if only. /～你有錢就辦得了. You could do it if only you had the money.

只有 **jřyǒu** (A) can only. /我們～坐在這ㄦ等了. We can only sit here and wait.

紙(帋)**jř** (N) paper, stationery (M 張 **jāng**). (M) for documents. 一 ～ 公文 a document.

紙烟 **jřyān** (N) cigarette (M 根 **gēn**; 枝 **jř**; 包 **bāu**; 條 **tyáu**).

止 **jř** (B) 1) stop. ～血 stop bleeding; ～痛 relieve pain. 2) only. 下～兩個 not just two.

制 **jř** (FV) measure. /用尺～一～. Measure it with a ruler. (B) 1) regulate, restrain. 限～ limit. 2) system, institution. 公～ metric system. SF of 製 **jř**.

制度 **jřdù** (N) system of government, education, farming, economic organization, etc.

制子 **jřdz** (N) measure. /拿這根鉛筆當一個～. Use this pencil as a measure.

制服 **jřfú** (N) uniform (M 套 **tàu**). (RC) subdue, control, by persuasion or force. /他已經把那條獅子～了. He has the lion under control.

製(制)**jř** (FV) 1) make, produce, manufacture. ～藥 compound medicine. 2) process. ～革 process hides.

製造 **jřdzàu** (FV) manufacture (lit. or fig.). /這家工廠一年～一萬輛汽車. This factory manufactures ten thousand cars a year. /他這人老是～謠言. He is always starting rumors.

秩 **jř** (B) order, arrangement.

秩序 **jřsyu** (N) order, arrangement. /卡片的～完全亂了. The cards are completely out of order.

志(誌)(B) 2) ⎫ **jř** (B) 1) will, ambition. ～氣 ambition. 2) record. 雜～ magazines; 地方～ topography.

志向 **jřsyang** (N) ambition. /他的～很大. He has great ambition.

志願 **jřywàn** (N) ambition, will. /他的～是做一個好醫生. His ambition is to be a good doctor.

志願軍 **jřywànjyūn** (N) army of volunteers.

志願書 **jřywànshū** (N) signed pledge, signed agreement to participate and share in profits and losses, to obey rules, etc. (M 張 **jāng**).

治 **jř** (FV) heal, treat. ～病 treat an illness. /大夫把病～好了. The doctor cured the patient. (B) manage. ～理 govern.

治安員 **jřānywán** (N) security agent (c).

治療 **jřlyáu** (FV) treat an illness. /他的病～了很久了. He (lit. his illness) has been under treatment for a long time.

至 **jř** (B) before SV most, -est. ～晚 at the latest. (PT) 由(從,自)...～... from one place or time to another. /從上海～南京有多少里? How many miles is it from Shanghai to Nanking?

至多 **jřdwō** (A) at the very most, at most. /那個錶～值二十塊錢. That watch is worth twenty dollars at the very most. /你不給他寫信～她生氣了. If you don't write her, the most she can do is get mad.

至少 **jřshǎu** (A) at the very least, at least. /～得有二十個人才開得了舞會. There must be at least twenty people to have a dance. (B) minimum. ～數量 minimum amount.

至於 **jřyú** (AV) used in questions and negative sentences, go so far as to. /他那ㄦ～偷東西? How could he go so far as to steal? (B) as for, regarding, with regard to. /～那個我沒有意見. I have nothing to say about that.

致 **jř** (B) 1) send, transmit. ～意 send someone regards. 2) cause, bring about. ～死 cause death.

致敬 **jřjìng** (FV) salute, make

a gesture of respect. /他向國旗 ～. He saluted the flag.

Ju *see* **Jyu.**

豬(猪)**jū** (N) hog, pig (M 口 **kǒu**, 頭 **tóu**). 母～ sow; 公～ boar.
    豬 肉 **jūròu** (N) pork.
    豬 油 **jūyóu** (N) lard.

珠 **jū** (B) 1) <-子,-儿> bead (M 顆 **kē**). 眼～ pupil of the eye; 汗～ bead of sweat; 淚～teardrop. 2) <-子> pearl (M 顆 **kē**). ～寳 jewels.

諸 **jū** (B) all, every. ～般 all sorts. s
    諸 位 **jūwèi** (PN) you (in addressing a group). /～明天不要來了. You need not come tomorrow. (IE) Ladies and gentlemen (in speaking to a group of people formally).

竹 **jú** (B) <-子> bamboo (M 顆 **kē**, 根 **gēn**). ～笋儿 strip of bamboo.
    竹 笋 **júswǔn** (N) bamboo shoot (M 棵 **kē**).

主 **jǔ** (FV) indicate (of natural phenomena). /螞蟻打仗～下雨. Fighting ants indicate rain. (N) the (Christian) Lord. (B) 1)<-儿> owner. 地～ landowner. 2) master. ～婦 lady of the house. 3) principal, chief. ～營 leader. 4) favor, advocate. ～和 favor peace. 5) manage. ～治 rule, control. (PT) 以...為～ regard something as most important. /年青人以求學為～. Young people regard studying as most important. /今天的討論以經濟為～. We will make economics the main part of today's discussion.
    主筆 **jǔbǐ** (N) editor-in-chief.
    主持 **jǔchŕ** (FV) have charge of, preside over, a meeting, ceremony, etc. /這儿的事由我～. I'm in charge here. /今天的會議由你～. You'll be presiding over today's meeting.
    主動 **jǔdùng** (FV) initiate, take the initiative. /這件事全是他～的. He initiated this whole affair. (N) initiative, action.
    主顧 **'jǔgù** (N) customer, patron.
    主觀 **jǔgwān** (SV) be subjective.
    主觀主義 **jǔgwānjǔyì** (N) subjectivism.

主管 **'jǔgwǎn** (FV) have charge of, direct, manage. /誰～這件事情? Who's in charge of this matter? (N) manager.
    主婚 **jǔhwūn** (VO) stand up for the bride or groom at a wedding (similar to the function of a witness in a Western-style ceremony, though more important). /我請我叔父給我～. I asked my uncle to stand up for me.
    主張 **jǔjāng** (FV) advocate, propose, favor, a proposal, motion, plan. /我太太～把房子賣了. My wife proposed that we sell our house. (N) 1) proposal, suggestion. 2) conviction.
    主講 **jǔjyǎng** (FV) give the main speech, be the chief speaker at some function. /由那位教授～. That professor will deliver the main speech.
    主角儿 **jǔjyǎur** (N) leading role, principal character, in a play or story.
    主人 **'jǔrén** (N) 1) host. 2) landlord. 女～ landlady, hostess.
    主任 **jǔrèn** (N) chief executive officer, director, chairman.
    主使 **júshŕ** (FV) instigate, incite (bring about some unfortunate occurrence from behind the scenes). /他常～別人去偷東西. He often gets others to steal things. (N) instigation. /他們受誰的～到這儿來搗亂? Who instigated them to come here and cause trouble?
    主席 **jǔsyí** (N) chairman.
    主修 **jǔsyōu** (FV) specialize in, major in a subject in school. /他是～歷史的. He majors in history.
    主要 **jǔyàu** (SV) be essential.
    主義 **jǔyì** (N) doctrine, -ism. 三民～ The Three Principles of the People; 民族～ nationalism.
    主意 **jǔyì** (**júyi** (lp)) (N) idea, plan. /他又改～了. He's changed his plans (*or* mind) again.

煮 **jǔ** (FV) boil. ～飯 boil *or* cook rice, prepare a meal.

囑(嘱)**jǔ** (B) enjoin, order. 遺～ a will (legal).
    囑咐 **jǔfù** (FV) advise, tell someone to do something. /母親～

她的孩子穿上大衣. The mother told her children to put on their overcoats. /他~我下要到紐約去. He told me not to go to New York.

住 jù (FV) 1) live, reside. /我們~在一塊儿. We live together. 2) stop. /雨~了. The rain has stopped. /~嘴! Shut up! (RE) indicates firmness of action. 記~ bear in mind; 拿~ hold onto something securely; 禁不~ be unable to bear pain, hardship, a weight; 站~ stop, halt; 閞~ stump someone.
  住處 jùchu (N) residence.
  住戶 'jùhù (N) group of people living under a single roof or in a single house, family (M 家 jyā). 這條街有五十家~. There are fifty families (or homes) on this street.
  住址 jùjr̄ (N) address (of a person). /你的~在那儿? What's your address?

注{註 (FV), (B) 2)} jù (FV) comment on, annotate. /他把那本書都給~了. He annotated the entire book. (B) 1) pay attention to, fix the mind on something. 貫~ give thorough attention to. 2) <-儿> note, commentary. ~脚 footnote, note. 3) pour into ~射 inject. 4) <-儿> stake, wager. 下~ make a wager.
  注重 jùjùng (FV) emphasize, stress. /你告訴我應該~那一點. Tell me which point I should emphasize.
  注意 jùyì (FV) pay attention to, watch. /請你~那個生人. Please watch that stranger. (IE) Watch out!

著 jù (FV) write, compose. /他~了很多書. He wrote many books. (B) 1) prominent. 顯~ be apparent. 2) composition. 名~ famous literary work. →著{箸} jwó.
  著作 'jùdzwò (N) literary work (as a book, article, paper, etc.) (M 本 běn; 篇 pyān; 章 jāng).
  著者 jùjě (N) writer, author.
  著名 jùmíng (SV) be famous, well-known (of a thing or person). /這張畫很~. This picture is very famous.

祝 jù (FV) wish someone a Happy Birthday, Merry Christmas, etc. /~你聖誕快樂. Merry Christmas to you. (B) 1) celebrate. 慶~ celebrate. 2) congratulate. ~壽 offer birthday congratulations. 3) bless. ~福 invoke a blessing. s
  祝賀 jùhè (FV) offer someone congratulations on a happy occasion. /他過生日你去~嗎? It's his birthday. Are you going to go and congratulate him (or wish him a happy birthday)?

柱 jù (N) cylinder (geom.). (B) <-子> pillar, post (M 根 gēn).

註 jù (FV) annotate, make notes on, previously written material. /我把先生講的都~在書上了. I've made notes in the book of everything the teacher said. (N) annotation, notes. (B) to note. ~銷 make a note of cancellation. →注{註} jù.
  註冊 jùtsè (VO) register in a school, in a governmental organization, as for the draft, etc. (not in a hotel or hospital). /這學期我還沒~呢. I haven't registered yet this semester.

蛀 jù (FV) eat, bore through (of moths, or other insects eating fabrics or wood). /我的皮大衣都叫蟲子給~了. My fur coat has been eaten by moths.

鑄 jù (FV) cast something out of metal. ~鐘 cast a bell; ~錢 coin money. /他們用鐵~了一個模子. They cast a mold out of iron.

駐 jù (FV) station soldiers, diplomats. /城裏~了很多兵. There are many soldiers stationed in the city.
  駐紮 jùjá (FV) station soldiers at a place. /敵人把軍隊~在城外. The enemy has stationed its army outside the city.

助 jù (B) to help. 協~ assist, assistance.
  助手 'jùshǒu (N) assistant (as to a doctor doing an operation, a lawyer at a trial).

juan see jywan.

jue see jywe.

jun see jyun.

終 **jūng** (B) 1) the end. 年～ the end of a year. 2) all, the whole of. ～身 all of one's life. 3) to finish, end. ～場 to end a performance, the end of a performance.

終於 **jūngyú** (A) finally, in the end, after all. /客人～走了. The visitors finally left. /他～當了總統了. He became president after all.

鐘[钟] **jūng** (N) 1) time, as indicated by the clock; must be used after one of the following M: 點 **dyǎn**, 刻 **kè**, 分 **fēn** or 秒 **myǎu**. 兩點半～ two-thirty; 一分～ a minute. 2) large bell (M 座 **dzwò**). 自由～ Liberty Bell. 3) clock (M 座 **dzwò**).

鐘頭 **jūngtóu** (N) hour.

鍾 **jūng** (B) 1) cup. 酒～ winecup. 2) love, cherish. ～愛 love faithfully and ardently. s

鍾情 **jūngchíng** (FV) fall in love with a person. /他們倆一見～. Those two fell in love at first sight.

忠 **jūng** (B) loyal, faithful. ～心 be faithful.

忠告 **jūnggàu** (FV) advise, counsel, someone to do something. /我～你千萬別跟那個女的結婚. I advise you not to marry that girl under any circumstances. (N) advice, counsel.

中 **jūng** (L) 1) middle. 樹林～ (in) the middle of the forest; ～途 midway; ～年 middle-aged, one's middle years. 2) in, within, a period of time. /他在這兩年～沒看過電影. He hasn't been to the movies in two years. (B) 1) in between. ～立 be neutral. 2) China. ～裝 Chinese dress. 3) be suitable, good to. ～聽 be pleasant to listen to. (PT) 正在...～ be in the process of ...ing. /這件案子正在審判～. The case is in the process of being examined. →中 **jùng**.

中秋節 **jūngchyōujyé** (TW) (at the time of) the Mid-Autumn Festival.

中等 **jūngděng** (AT) 1) medium-level, middle-class. ～教育 medium-level education; ～社會 middle-class society. 2) medium-quality. ～貨色 medium-quality goods.

中國 **jūnggwó** (PW) (in) China.

中間 **jūngjyān** (PW) 1) (in) the middle. /樹林子的～有一個紅房子. There is a red house in the middle of the forest. /那個節目～有很多廣告. There are a lot of commercials during that program. 2) (the space) between. /他坐在他父母的～. He sat between his parents. /張家跟王家～隔着一道牆. There is a wall between the Wang house and the Chang house. (AT) middle. ～路線 the middle course (as in politics).

中間兒 **jūngjyār** = 中間 **jūngjyān**.

中心 **jūngsyīn** (N) center, core. 地球的～ center of the earth; 思想的～ core of thought.

中午 **jūngwǔ** (TW) (at) noon. /我們～走. We'll leave at noon. /～是從十一點到一點. Noontime is from 11 A.M. to 1 P.M.

中央 **jūngyāng** (N) the center, middle part. 湖的～ the center of a lake. (AT) 1) central. ～車站 central railroad station. 2) central governmental. ～軍隊 central governmental army.

中用 **jūngyùng** (SV) be useful. /這件雨衣雖然舊了, 下雨天也還～. This raincoat is old, but it's still useful on rainy days.

種[种] **jǔng** (M) kind, sort (used with any noun). /我不喜歡這～香煙. I don't like this kind of cigarette. (N) species. /這是一個新發見的～. This is a newly discovered species. (B) 1) <一子, 一兒> seed (M 粒 **lì**; 顆 **kē**). 雜～ product of cross-breeding. 2) race. 黃～人 people of the yellow race. →種 **jùng**.

種族 **jǔngdzú** (N) race (of people). ～學 ethnology.

種類 **jǔnglèi** (N) kind, variety, category. /酒的～很多. There are many kinds of wines.

腫[肿] **jǔng** (FV) swell up. /他的眼睛～得很厲害. His eye is all swollen up. (RE) indicates swelling. /他的腳走～了. Her feet are swollen from walking.

種 **jùng** (FV) plant, sow, grow. ～菜 plant vegetables; ～田 till the soil, farm. /他～玉米. He grows corn. →種 jùng.

   種地 **jùngdì** (VO) till the soil, farm. /我種了三年地. I've been farming for three years.

   種痘 **jùngdòu** (VO) vaccinate. /你種了痘了嗎? Have you been vaccinated?

重 **jùng** (SV) 1) be heavy (in weight). /這個箱子太～了, 我拿不起來. This suitcase is so heavy I can't lift it. 2) be heavy (in the sense of concentrated, thick). /他的口音很～. He has a heavy accent. /他的工作很重. He has a heavy work load. /這個衣料的顏色有一點兒～. The color of this material is a little bit too dark. / 我喜歡口味～. I like heavily-seasoned dishes. /她的眉毛太～了. Her eyebrows are too thick. 3) be serious, severe (of illness, a wound, a crime). /他的病很～. He is seriously ill. 4) be weighty, important. /他的責任很～. He has weighty responsibilities. (A) severely, hard. /我非～罰他不可. I must punish him severely. (B) 1) give importance to. ～農 lay stress on agriculture; 自～ respect oneself. 2) high (in price). ～價 high price. 3) weight. 體～ weight (of a person). → 重 chúng.

   重量 **'jùnglyàng** (N) weight. /這個東西的～是多少? How much does this thing weigh?

   重視 **'jùngshr̀** (FV) have high regard for a subordinate or a younger person, regard something as important. /他的教授很～他. His professors have high regard for him. /我們對於這本書能否出版很～. Whether or not this book is published is very important to us.

   重要 **jùngyàu** (SV) be important.

   重音 **jùngyīn** (N) stress, accent, emphasis. /這句話的～在那兒? Where should this sentence be stressed?

中 **jùng** (FV) 1) win a prize. /我～了頭彩了. I won first prize. 2)

be hit by something. /他～了一顆鎗彈. He was hit by a bullet. 3) fall into a trap. /我們～了敵人的埋伏了. We fell into an enemy ambush. (RE) indicates hitting a target, reaching a goal. /我沒法射～紅心. I can't hit the bull's-eye. /他沒考～. He didn't pass the exam. →中 jūng.

   中毒 **jùngdú** (VO) be poisoned. /他是吃東西中的毒. He was poisoned by what he ate.

   中風 **jùngfēng** (VO) have an apoplectic stroke. /他中了風, 差一點兒死了. He had an apoplectic stroke and almost died. (N) apoplexy.

眾[众] **jùng** (B) 1) multitude. 公～食堂 public restaurant. 2) all, the whole of. ～生 all living beings.

   眾多 **jùngdwō** (SV) be numerous.

抓 **jwā** (FV) 1) scratch. /貓～了我一下. The cat scratched me. 2) grasp (lit. or fig.). /那個賊～了一把錢跑了. The thief grabbed a handful of money and ran. /他聽課的時候老～不住要點. When he listens to a lecture, he can't grasp the essential points. 3) catch, arrest. ～賊 catch a thief. 4) draft someone. /他們～我做那件事. They drafted me for that work.

   抓鬮兒 **jwājyōur** (VO) draw lots. /既然沒人願意洗碗我們～吧. Since nobody wants to do the dishes, let's draw lots.

拽 **jwāi** (FV) 1) fling, throw. /把球～過來. Throw the ball here. 2) be crippled (of one's arms) (1p). /他的胳臂～了. His arm is crippled. →拽 jwāi.

拽 **jwài** (FV) pull, drag, with the hands (1p). /你～住這個繩子. Hold on to this rope (pulling it). /要不是你把我～住了, 我一定要跟他打起來. If you hadn't pulled me back, I would certainly have started to fight with him. →拽 jwài.

專[专] **jwān** (A) only, exclusively. /我～看這個人寫的書. I only read the books this person has written. (SV) be engrossed in, devoted to, one thing. /他念書很～. He is very engrossed in his studies. (B) special. ～車 special car.

專制 **jwānjr̀** (SV) be despotic, domineering. /那是一個～的國王. He was a despotic king. /他的父親很～. He has a very domineering father.

專家 **jwānjyā** (N) specialist, expert.

專門 **jwānmén** (AT) specialized, technical. ～教育 technical education; ～人才 expert. (A) only, exclusively, especially. /他～跟我搗亂. He only picks on me. /這盤菜是～為你做的. I made this dish especially for you. (N) specialty.

磚(甎) **jwān** (N) brick, tile (M塊**kwài**).
磚頭 **jwāntóu** (N) 1) brickbat (in north China). 2) brick (in south China). (M塊**kwài**).

轉 **jwǎn** (FV) 1) turn. 向右～ turn to the right. 2) transfer, pass on. ～帳 transfer an account; ～車 transfer to another bus *or* train; ～信 forward mail. →轉**jwàn**.
轉變 **jwǎnbyàn** (FV) change (as one's attitude or a situation). /他對事情的看法還沒～過來. He still hasn't changed his way of looking at things. (N) 1) change. /情形有～嗎? Has there been any change in the situation? 2) turning point.
轉機 **jwǎnjī** (N) turn for the better. /這件事有～了. This matter is now taking a turn for the better.
轉彎 **jwǎnwān** (VO) ＜-ル＞ turn a corner. /再向左轉一個彎就到我家了. Turn the corner to the left again and you'll come to my house. 2) change direction. /轉了幾個彎我就迷路了. I changed direction a couple of times and lost my way. (N) turn.
轉運 **jwǎnyùn** (FV) 1) convey goods. /有的日本貨是從香港～到新加坡. Some Japanese goods are shipped from Hong Kong to Singapore. (VO) have a change of luck. /你快～了. You'll have a change of luck soon.

傳(傳) **jwàn** (B) record, chronicle. 自～ autobiography. →傳**chwán**.

傳記 **jwànjì** (N) biography (M本**běn**, 篇**pyān**).

轉 **jwàn** (FV) turn, revolve. /我～不動這螺絲. I can't turn this screw. →轉**jwǎn**.
轉悠ル **jwànwār** (VO) go around, go here and there. /他正騎着馬在場子裏～. He is riding the horse around the field.

賺 **jwàn** (FV) 1) earn, make, money. /他一個月～多少錢? How much money does he earn a month? /我這個買賣不～錢. The business I'm in doesn't bring in the money. (B) ＜-ル＞ profit (lp). ～頭ル a profit.

裝(裝) **jwāng** (FV) 1) pack, load, a vehicle, container. ～車 load a car. 2) pack something into a container. /把書～在箱子裏. Pack these books into that suitcase. 3) carry, hold (of a container). /那輛車～不下八個人. That car won't hold eight people. 4) install. /～電燈 install electric lights. 5) pretend to be, act the role of. ～傻 pretend to be a fool; ～死 feign death. (B) 1) costume, clothing. 西～ Western clothing. 2) adorn, make up. ～扮 dress up, make up (of a person).
裝訂 **jwāngdìng** (FV) bind (as a book). /我想找個地方把這些畫～成冊. I want to find a place where I can get these pictures bound. (N) binding.
裝飾 **'jwāngshr̀** (FV) 1) decorate. /這家商店的櫥窗～得很漂亮. This store window has been beautifully decorated. 2) dress up, make up (of a person). /我太太不會～. My wife doesn't know how to dress well. (N) 1) adornment, clothes, make-up (of a woman) (M件**jyàn**). 2) decoration.

莊(庄) **jwāng** (N) the first player, dealer (in card games). (B) 1) serious, grave. ～重 be serious and respectful. 2) ＜-子＞ village, hamlet. 3) store. 布～ yard goods store. *s*
莊稼 **jwāngjya** (N) 1) standing crop. 2) farming.
莊嚴 **'jwāngyan** (SV) be dignified, serious, formal. /他的態度很～. He has a very dignified manner.

橋[橛]**jwāng** (M) for affairs, matters, business. 一~事情 a matter; 一~買賣 a business transaction. (B) <-子> stake, post. 打~機 pile driver.

撞 **jwàng** (FV) 1) bump into, collide with, hit. ~車 have a car collision. /我倒車的時候~上電線桿了. When I backed up the car, I hit a utility pole. 2) strike something. ~鐘 strike a bell. 3) swindle. /他~了我一百元. He swindled me out of a hundred dollars. → 撞 **chwàng**.

壯[壯]**jwàng** (SV) be big and strong, healthy. (FV) strengthen one's courage or prestige. /他邀請了省長來~聲勢. He invited the governor to increase his own prestige.
壯膽子 **jwàngdǎndz** (VO) strengthen one's courage. /我喝酒壯壯膽子. I drink to give myself courage.

錐 **jwēi** (B) 1) <-子> awl (M把 **bǎ**). 2) <-子,-ㄦ> sharp-pointed object. 氷~ icicle. (FV) bore with an awl, drill. /他把那個紙盒子~了很多洞. He bored a lot of holes in that cardboard box.

追 **jwēi** (FV) 1) chase after, pursue (lit. or fig.). /狗在花園裏~貓. The dog is chasing the cat around the garden. /他們兩個人都~那個女孩子. Both of them are chasing after that girl. 2) search after, investigate. /我看這件事別再~了. I don't think this matter should be looked into any further.
追究 **'jwēijyōu** (FV) look into, investigate. /他們要~他死的原因. They will investigate the cause of his death.

墜 **jwèi** (FV) 1) fall. /船錨已經~到底了. The anchor has sunk to the bottom. 2) attach a weight to something. /你在那個氣球上~一個重東西. You have to attach a weight to the bottom of the balloon. (B) <-子,-ㄦ> pendant ornament. 錶~ watch charm.
墜子 **jwèidz** (N) 1) ↑(B). 2) pendant earring (M隻 **jī**; 付 **fù**). 3)

stringed instrument of Honan. 4) folksong accompanied by 3).
墜着 **jwèije** (FV) dangle. /燈籠下面~一個繐子. There's a tassel dangling from the lantern.
墜胎 **jwèitāi** (VO) have an abortion. /她墜過兩次胎. She has had two abortions. (N) abortion.

桌[棹]**jwō** (M) table of food or of dinner guests. /我請了三~客. I invited enough guests for three tables. (B) <-子,-ㄦ> 1) table. ~布 tablecloth. 2) desk. (M張 **jāng**).

捉 **jwō** (FV) seize, catch, arrest. ~賊 catch a thief. → 捉 **dzwó**.

着[著]**jwó** (B) belong to a place. 土~ a native. → 着 **jāu**, 着 **jáu**, 着 **je**.

鐲 **jwó** (B) <-子> bracelet (M付 **fù**, 隻 **jī**). 手~ handcuffs.

准 **jwǔn** (FV) allow, permit. /這ㄦ不~抽煙. Smoking isn't allowed here. SF of 準 **jwǔn**.
准許 **jwǔnsyǔ** (FV) allow, permit. /我不~你一個人去. I won't permit you to go alone. (N) permission. /他没得我的~就進來了. He came in without my permission.

準[準][准]**jwǔn** (SV) be accurate (of schedules, timepieces, predictions). /不必等他了,我知道他~不會來的. There's no need to wait for him. I definitely know he won't come. (B) 1) quasi. ~會員 quasi-member. 2) standard. 標~ standard.
準ㄦ **jwěr** (N) 1) certainty. /她心裏有~. She really knows what she wants. /現在的天氣真没~. You can't be certain about the weather now. 2) accuracy. /他放鎗一點~都没有. He doesn't have any accuracy in shooting.
準備 **jwǔnbèi** (FV) get ready, prepare. /明天要開會,今天得~~. There's a meeting tomorrow we have to get ready for today. (AV) intend to, plan to. /我~不吃晚飯了. I don't plan to eat supper. (N) preparation.
準確 **'jwǔnchywè** (SV) be accurate, exact, precise. /他的發音很~. His pronunciation is very accurate.

準時 jwŭnshŕ (A) on time, on schedule. /火車是～到的. The train arrived on time. (SV) be punctual.

夾{挾}[夹] jyā (FV) 1) enclose, insert. /他的信裏～了一張照片. There was a picture enclosed in his letter. /我把信～在書裏了. I put the letter in the book. 2) put under one's arm. /他把小孩儿～起來就走. She carried off the child under her arm. 3) pinch, catch, between two things. /我的領帶～在門裏了. My tie got caught in the door. 4) pick up something with chopsticks, pincers, tongs, or the like. /炭太多了,～出幾塊來. There's too much charcoal; take out a few pieces. (B) <-子> 1) folder. 公文～ portfolio. 2) clip. 錢～子 money clip. 3) tongs, pincers (M把bǎ). 錢～子 steel tongs. → 夾 jyā.

加 jyā (FV) add (to), increase. ～薪 raise a salary. /把鍋裏～一點儿水. Add some water to the pot. /請把這幾個數～在一塊儿. Please add up these figures. (CV) plus (math.) /三～二是五. Three plus two is five. (B) used before a SV, make something more . . . or . . .er. ～寬 make something wider; ～快 speed up. t

加倫 jyālwún (M) gallon. /我的車一～可以開三十五里. My car gets thirty-five miles to the gallon.

加入 jyārù (FV) join an organization. /你～工會了嗎? Have you joined the union?

家 jyā (N) home, family. /他～有多少人? How many are there in his family? (M) for business establishments. 一～書店 a book store. (B) 1) specialist. 專～ specialist; 科學～ scientist; 歷史學～ historian. 2) my (precedes certain kinship terms when referring to a senior member of one's family). ～母 my mother.

家產 jyāchǎn (N) family property, family estate (M份fèn).

家當 jyādang (N) <-儿> family property (M份fèn).

家俱 jyājyu (N) furniture (M件jyàn).

家鄉 jyāsyāng (N) 1) ancestral home. 2) home town.

家庭 jyātíng (N) family. ～婦女 housewife.

家務 jyāwù (N) 1) family matter, family affair. 鬧～ have a family feud. 2) housework.

夾{挾}裌(AT){[夹]} jyā (AT) lined (of a garment). /這件衣服是～的. This garment is lined. (B) 1) enclose. ～道儿 lane between two high walls. 2) carry secretly. ～帶 carry something under one's clothes. → 夾 jyā.

夾襖 jyáǎu (N) lined gown, coat (M件jyàn).

假 jyǎ (SV) be unnatural, artificial. /他的態度很～. He has a very artificial manner. (AT) false, artificial, counterfeit. ～牙 false teeth. /這張票子是～的. This bank note is counterfeit. (B) pretend. ～死 feign death. →假 jyà.

假裝 jyǎjwāng (FV) 1) pretend. /我～沒看見他. I pretended not to see him. 2) disguise oneself as. /他～一個警察. He disguised himself as a policeman.

假如 jyǎrú (A) if, supposing that. /～你肯幫忙,這事就簡單了. If you are willing to help, this will be simple.

假意 jyǎyì (A) with false intent. /他～對我說他很喜歡我. He told me with false intent that he liked me very much.

假 jyà (N) 1) vacation, holiday. 春～ spring vacation. 2) leave. 請～ ask for leave. →假 jyà.

假期 jyàchī (N) holiday, holiday season. /我們在～的時候到海邊去. We go to the shore for the holiday (or during the holidays).

架 jyà (FV) 1) support (as with a framework or scaffolding or with the hands and arms). ～起來 prop up. /那個女孩儿～着她的爺爺在花園裏散步. The little girl is helping her grandfather walk around the garden. 2) assemble, put together. ～橋 erect a bridge; ～鎗 stack arms. 3) take forcibly. /警察把這個醉鬼～走了. The drunkard was forcibly taken away by the policemen. /土匪把一個小孩～走了. The bandits kidnapped a

child.　(M)　1) for machines.　— ~
縫紉機 a sewing machine.　2) for
instruments which rest on a tripod
or stand.　— ~ 電影片機 a movie
camera.　3) for airplanes.　— ~ 飛
機 an airplane.　(B)　1) <-子,-ル>
framework, scaffolding, arbor. 葡
萄 ~ grape arbor.　2) <-子,-ル>
rack, stand, shelf. 書 ~ bookcase.
3) a quarrel, fight. 吵 ~ to quarrel.
　　架子 jyàdz (N)　1) † (B) 1) 2)).
2) snobbishness, proud air. 擺 ~
be snobbish.

駕 jyà (FV) drive a vehicle, pilot a
plane or ship, fly. /我不會 ~ 車.
I don't know how to drive (a car).
(B) you (h). 尊 ~ your excellency.
　　駕駛 jyàshř (FV) drive a
vehicle, pilot a plane or ship, fly.
/我不會 ~ 太空船. I don't
know how to pilot a space ship.　(B)
driver, pilot. 副 ~ co-pilot.
　　駕駛員 jyàshřywán (N) driver,
pilot.

價[价] jyà (B) price. 物 ~ price of goods;
原 ~ original price.
　　價錢 jyàchyan (N) price.
　　價格 jyàgé (N) price.
　　價值 jyàjr (N) value. /他的
話沒 ~ . What he says is of no
value. /這件皮大衣的 ~ 很高.
This fur coat is very valuable.

嫁 jyà (FV)　1) marry, get married (of
a girl). /她都三十多了,怎麼還沒
~ 呢? She is already over thirty,
why isn't she married yet? /我不
會 ~ 你的. I won't marry you.
2) give a daughter in marriage to
someone. /他回家去 ~ 女兒去
了. He went home to arrange the
marriage of his daughter.

尖 jyān (SV)　1) be sharp (of a point).
2) be acute, sharp. /他的眼睛很
~ . He has sharp eyes.　3) be high
in pitch, shrill (of a sound or voice).
(B)　1) <-子,-ル> top. 樹 ~ tree-
top; 頂 ~ ル人物 top man.　2)
<-ル> point. 鋼筆 ~ pen point.
　　尖銳 jyānrwèi (SV)　1) be sharp
(of a point).　2) be acute, sharp. ~
的批評 sharp criticism. /階級鬥
爭越來越 ~ 了. The class strug-
gle is getting more and more intense.

3) be high in pitch, shrill (of a sound
or voice).

堅[坚] jyān (SV) be firm, strong (as one's
beliefs). /他的意志很 ~ . He is
strong-willed.
　　堅持 jyānchŕ (FV) hold to an
idea, insist. /我 ~ 你去. I insist that you go.　(SV) be insistent,
persistent.
　　堅強 jyānchyáng (SV) be strong,
firm, persevering.　(FV) strengthen.
/我們應該 ~ 我們的力量. We
must strengthen our power.
　　堅固 jyāngù (SV) be sturdy,
firm. /這是一座很 ~ 的房子.
This is a very sturdy building.　(FV)
fortify, strengthen. /我們用什麼
來 ~ 我們的信仰呢? What can
we employ to strengthen our faith?
　　堅決 jyānjywé (SV) be fixed in
one's opinion or attitude, resolute.
/他的態度很 ~ . He's very fixed
in his attitude.

肩 jyān (B) the shoulder. ~ 章 epaulet.
　　肩膀ル jyānbǎngr (N) shoulder.

監[监] jyān (B)　1) supervise. ~ 察 inspect, examine.　2) prison. 坐 ~ be
in prison.
　　監督 jyāndū (FV) supervise.
/他 ~ 工人造房子. He super-
vises men building houses.　(N)
supervisor.
　　監禁 jyānjìn (FV) imprison.
/把他 ~ 在那ル哪? Where was he
imprisoned? (N) imprisonment. 六個
月的 ~ six months' imprisonment.
　　監獄 jyānyù (N) prison, jail
(M所 swǒ).

奸 jyān (SV)　1) be crafty, villainous,
wicked.　2) be self-seeking, selfish.
(B) traitor. 鋤 ~ expel traitors.
SF of 姦 jyān.
　　奸笑 jyānsyàu (FV) smile
craftily. /他站在旁邊 ~ . He
stood to the side smiling craftily.

姦[奸] jyān (B) adultery, illicit intercourse. 強 ~ to rape.

煎 jyān (FV)　1) fry on a greased surface without mixing or stirring. ~
鷄蛋 fry an egg, fried egg.　2) simmer. ~ 藥 simmer decoctions of
medicine.

閒 jyān (M) for rooms. 四～屋子 four rooms. (B) 1) area, space. 世～ the world. 2) interval. 夜～ nighttime, at night. →閒 jyàn.

艱[艰] jyān (B) difficult, hard, distressing. 艱難 jyānnán (SV) be difficult to take care of, difficult to control, hard to master (of a matter). (N) difficulty, distress.

鹼[碱] jyǎn (N) 1) lye. 2) alkali.

減[减] jyǎn (CV) minus. /三～二得一. Three minus two equals one. (FV) diminish, decrease. /他的體重～了. He lost some weight. 減價 jyǎnjyà (VO) reduce prices, hold a bargain sale. /你能不能減點兒價? Can you reduce the price a little bit? 減少 jyǎnshǎu (FV) diminish, decrease. /今年汽車出產量比以前～了. Car production this year has decreased compared to the past.

剪[翦] jyǎn (FV) clip, cut. ～指甲 cut one's fingernails; ～草 mow grass. (B) 1) <-子> scissors and similar tools (M把bǎ). ～刀 scissors. 2) eliminate, cut out. ～除 get rid of someone.

繭[茧] jyǎn (N) 1) <-子,-儿> cocoon, chrysalis. 2) <-子> callus.

簡 jyǎn (B) 1) simple, brief. ～字 simplified form of Chinese character. 2) letter. 郵～ air letter. s 簡單 jyǎndān (SV) be simple. /這個問題很～. This is a simple problem. /他的思想很～. He's a simple-minded individual. 簡章 jyǎnjāng (N) rule book, bulletin of an institution or organization (M份fèn, 本běn, 張jāng). 簡直 jyǎnjŕ (A) 1) simply, just. /你～不知道. You just don't know. 2) frankly. /～說吧, 我覺得你根本不應該去. Frankly (speaking), I don't think you should have gone there in the first place. 簡捷了當 jyǎn'jyélyǎu'dàng (SV) be direct, frank, to the point.

檢 jyǎn (B) 1) inspect, check, examine. ～察 inspect. 2) restrict. 不～ be indiscreet.

檢查 jyǎnchá (FV) 1) inspect baggage, goods. /海關人員～每一個客人的行李. Customs officials examine everyone's baggage. 2) examine (as a doctor). /請你等一等, 大夫正在～病人呢. Please wait just a moment. The doctor is examining a patient. (N) 1) inspection. 2) physical examination.

檢討 jyǎntǎu (FV) review a matter. /首先我們要～上次開會提出的問題. First we'll review the problems that were brought up at the last meeting.

檢驗 jyǎnyàn (FV) examine something, test (technically). /我想去～一下我的煞車. I want to go and have my brakes tested.

檢閱 jyǎnywè (FV) review troops. /明天市長要～童子軍. Tomorrow the mayor will review the boy scouts.

儉 jyǎn (B) thrifty, frugal. 節～ be thrifty. 儉樸 'jyǎnpǔ (SV) be thrifty in one's ways, given to a simple life. 儉省 'jyǎnshěng (SV) be thrifty. (FV) save, conserve. /你得～你的精力. You must conserve your strength.

間 jyàn (B) 1) put a space between. ～接 indirect, indirectly; ～歇 be intermittent. 2) separate people. 離～ cause someone's separation (as a married couple or friends). →間 jyàn. 間諜 jyàndyé (N) spy.

件 jyàn (M) 1) for affairs, matters of business, matters in general. 一～事情 an affair, a matter; 一～差事 a job. 2) for official documents. 一～公文 an official document. 3) for clothing. 一～大衣 an overcoat. 4) piece of furniture, baggage, pastry. 一～傢俱 a piece of furniture; 一～行李 a piece of baggage; 一～點心 a piece of pastry. (B) single item. 零～ component part.

毽 jyàn (B) Chinese shuttlecock. 毽子 jyàndz (N) Chinese shuttlecock. 踢～ kick a shuttlecock. 毽兒 jyàr = 毽子 jyàndz.

漸 jyàn (B) gradually. 漸漸地 jyànjyànde (A) gradually. /他的病~好了. He (lit. his illness) is gradually getting better.

健 **jyàn** (B) 1) healthy. ~壯 be strong and healthy. 2) be good at. ~談 be a good conversationalist.

　　健康 **jyànkāng** (SV) be healthy. (N) health.

建 **jyàn** (FV) 1) found, establish. /這所大學是一九〇〇年~的. This university was founded in 1900. 2) erect, build. /我們想~一個新宿舍. We plan to build a new dormitory. (B) Fukien (contracted form of 福~**fújyàn**). ~煙 Fukien tobacco.

　　建築 **jyànjù** (FV) build, make, buildings, bridges, roads, etc. /有一條新的公路正在~. There's a new road being built. (N) 1) architecture. 2) building.

　　建築師 **jyànjùshr** (N) architect.

　　建立 **jyànlì** (FV) 1) establish. /他在商業界~了很好的信譽. He has established a good reputation for himself in the business world. /這座醫院是三年前~的. This hospital was established three years ago. 2) build, erect. /最近在城中區~了一座二十層的大樓. A twenty-story building was built recently in the downtown area.

　　建設 **jyànshè** (FV) 1) build up, develop. /中國正以全力~工業. China is putting all of its effort into developing industry. 2) build, construct. /這個城裏~了很多工廠. Many factories have been built in this city. (N) 1) development. 2) reconstruction.

　　建議 **jyànyì** (FV) suggest, propose. /我~你們一個人捐五塊錢. I suggest that each one of you donate five dollars. (N) proposal, suggestion.

見[见] **jyàn** (FV) 1) see (perceive with the eye). /我沒~過這麼多錢. I've never seen this much money before. 2) meet. /我~過他一次. I've met him before. 3) meet with, see. /我去~總統. I'm going to see the president. /經理不~我. The manager won't see me. 4) ex-

pose. ~光 expose something to the light. (RE) indicates perception. 聽~ hear. (B) 1) appear to be, seem. ~好 seem to be better. 2) opinion, view. 偏~ prejudice. →現{見}**syàn**.

　　見方 **jyànfāng** (B) used after NU-M which indicate length, square. 四里~ four miles square (sixteen square miles). /這塊地是五里~. This piece of land is five miles square.

　　見解 **jyànjyě** (N) view or understanding of a problem, judgment, opinion. /他的~很高. His judgment is sound.

　　見面 **jyànmyàn** (VO) meet, see. /我們見過一次面. We've met once.

劍[剑] **jyàn** (N) double-edged sword (M把 **bǎ**).

賤 **jyàn** (SV) 1) be cheap, inexpensive. /這種材料很~. This kind of material is very cheap. 2) be base, lowly, cheap. /她真是~. She is really cheap. 3) be unresponsive to kind or honest treatment. /這個騾子真~,不打它不走. This mule is so unresponsive, if you don't hit him, he won't go. (A) at a low price. ~賣 sell at a low price. (B) 1) poor, low class. 貧~ poor and humble. 2) my (h). ~姓 my name.

箭 **jyàn** (N) arrow (M枝**jr**, 根**gēn**).

艦[舰] **jyàn** (B) warship. ~隊 fleet; ~長 captain of a ship, skipper.

濺 **jyàn** (FV) splash. /車走過去的時候,~了我一身泥. When the car drove by it splashed mud all over me.

薦[荐] **jyàn** (FV) recommend someone. /我給他~了一個花匠. I recommended a gardener to him.

　　薦信 **jyànsyìn** (N) letter of recommendation or introduction (M封 **fēng**).

江 **jyāng** (N) river (large) (M條**tyáu**). (B) Yangtze River (contracted form of 揚子~ **yángdž jyāng**). ~北人 person from north of the Yangtze. s

薑[姜] **jyāng** (N) ginger.

姜 **jyāng** (B) *s* <u>SF of</u> 薑 **jyāng**.

將(將) **jyāng** (A) 1) barely, just, only. ～
夠 just enough. 2) just a moment
ago, just. /他～下火車. He has
just gotten off the train. 3) be about
to, will. /這件事～對他不利.
This will do him some harm. (FV)
check (in chess). /他連～我三
次. He checked me three times in
a row. /～! Check! (CV) <u>used to
bring the direct object of the sentence
before the verb.</u> /我～他的名字
忘了. I forgot his name. (B)
nurture. ～養 nourish and bring up.
→將 **jyàng**.

將就 **jyāngjyou** (FV) 1) make
do with, put up with, <u>something or
someone.</u> /你能不能～他一點?
Can you put up with him? 2) please
<u>someone.</u> /我這麼做為的是～
你. I'm doing it this way just to
please you. 3) compromise. /他不
肯～. He won't compromise.
(A) <-着> making something do.
/這輛車太舊了,你～開吧. This
car is very old, but you can make do
with (driving) it. /請你～着穿這
件舊的吧. Try to get along
with wearing this old one for now.

將軍 **jyāngjyun** (N) general
(m).

將軍 **jyāngjyūn** (VO) 1) check
(in chess). /他將了我兩次軍.
He checked me twice in a row. 2)
put <u>someone</u> on the spot (lp). /他又
將我一軍. He's put me on the
spot again.

將來 **jyānglái** (TW) (in) the
future. /他～就知道了. He'll
find out later. /～不會比現在
更壞. The future couldn't be
worse than now.

將要 **jyāngyàu** (AV) be about to,
will. /他～去歐洲. He is going
to Europe.

漿(漿) **jyāng** (FV) starch. /請不要～全
件襯衫,只～領子. Please
don't starch the whole shirt, only
the collar. (B) thick fluid. 豆～
soybean milk, 糖～ syrup.

僵(殭) **jyāng** (SV) 1) be stiff, rigid (<u>as
a corpse</u>). /那個死屍還沒有
～. The body isn't stiff yet. 2) be
numb. /我坐了三個鐘頭腿都
～了. I sat for three hours and my

legs got numb. 3) be deadlocked,
reach an impasse. /他們兩人鬧
得很～. They reached an impasse
in their argument. *or* They couldn't
resolve their argument. (FV) dare
<u>someone.</u> /只要你一～他,他
就會幹. You dare him and he'll
do it.

僵局 **'jyāngjyú** (N) deadlock,
impasse. /想法打破這個～.
Think of a way to break this deadlock. /他說了一個笑話把～
給打破了. He broke the ice by
telling a joke.

韁(繮) **jyāng** (B) reins.

韁繩 **'jyāngshéng** (N) reins
(M條 **tyáu**). 拉～ pull on the reins.

獎(奖) **jyǎng** (N) prize, reward. 發～ give
a prize. (B) to praise. 誇～ to
praise.

獎章 **jyǎngjāng** (N) medal, emblem, given as a reward, decoration.

獎金 **jyǎngjīn** (N) monetary reward, prize (M筆 **bǐ**).

獎勵 **jyǎnglì** (FV) commend,
praise. /他演講比賽得了第一
名,老師很～他. His teacher
praised him for receiving first prize
in the speech contest. (N) reward,
prize.

獎品 **jyǎngpǐn** (N) prize. 得～
win a prize.

獎學金 **jyǎngsywéjīn** (N)
scholarship, fellowship (M份 **fèn**, 筆
bǐ).

講(讲) **jyǎng** (FV) 1) talk, speak, say.
～價 bargain. /他～的是那國
話? What language is he speaking?
2) explain, lecture. ～數學 lecture
on mathematics. 3) tell. ～故事
tell a story. 4) be conscientious *or*
careful about, make a practice of.
/她很～衛生. She's very care-
ful about hygiene. /他們家的人
都～早睡. Their family makes a
practice of going to bed early.

講和 **jyǎnghé** (VO) make peace,
settle a dispute. /現在我們不能
跟他們～. We cannot make
peace with them now. /他們已經
～了. They've made up.

講話 **jyǎnghwà** (VO) 1) talk,
speak. /別～. Don't talk. /你
講的這是什麼話? What are you
talking about? 2) make a speech,

speak. /總統昨天在國會～. The president made a speech to Congress yesterday.

講究 **jyǎngjyou** (SV) be meticulous, particular. /別這麼～啦. Don't be so particular. (FV) be meticulous *or* particular about, care a great deal about. /他那個人很 ～衣服. He's very meticulous about his clothes.

講理 **jyǎnglǐ** (SV) be rational. (VO) argue logically, appeal to reason. /你没法跟他～. You can't argue logically with him.

講儿 **jyàngr** (N) meaning (lp). /這個字有很多～. This word has a lot of meanings. /你説的 話没～. What you said doesn't make sense.

講堂 **jyǎngtáng** (N) lecture hall, classroom.

講演 **jyǎngyǎn** (VO) give a speech. /他在這儿講過演嗎? Has he ever given a speech here? (FV) talk formally on, speak on, a subject. /你今天～什麼? What are you speaking on today? (N) speech, lecture (M 篇 **pyān**, 次 **tsz̀**).

虹 **jyàng** → 虹 **húng**.

將[将]**jyàng** (N) general in Chinese chess (equal to a king). (B) general, admiral. 少～ major general, rear admiral. →將 **jyāng**.

醬[酱]**jyàng** (FV) pickle, cook, in soy sauce. ～鴨子 cook duck in soy sauce, pickled duck. (N) 1) thick sauce. 2) jam.

醬油 **jyàngyóu** (N) soy sauce.

糨[糨]**jyàng** (SV) be thick (of gruel, paste). /粥太～了. This congee is too thick. (B) <-子> paste (adhesive).

糨糊 **jyànghú** (N) paste (adhesive).

降 **jyàng** (FV) 1) descend, fall, drop. /溫度又～了五度. The temperature has dropped another five degrees. 2) demote. /我把他～了 一級. I demoted him one grade. (B) send down, lower. ～旗 lower a flag. →降 **syáng**.

降落 **jyànglwò** (FV) descend, come down. /飛機開始～了. The plane is beginning to descend.

/飛機已經～在跑道上了. The plane has landed on the runway.

強[强,彊]**jyàng** (SV) be stubborn, hard to convince. →強 **chyáng**, 強 **chyǎng**.

強嘴 **jyàngdzwěi** (VO) talk back to one's senior. /這個孩子 老跟他母親～. This child always talks back to his mother.

膠[胶]**jyāu** (N) 1) glue. 2) sap, gum. (B) 1) rubber. ～胎 rubber tire. 2) plastic. ～碗 plastic bowl. 3) sticky. ～泥 gluey mud.

膠卷儿 **jyāujywǎr** (N) camera film (in roll form) (M 卷 **jywǎn**).

膠水 **jyāushwěi** (N) <-儿> glue, rubber cement.

膠鞋 **jyāusyé** (N) 1) sneaker (shoe). 2) rubber (worn over a shoe). (M 雙 **shwāng**; 隻 **jr̄**).

交 **jyāu** (FV) 1) hand over, deliver, submit, something to someone. ～ 卷儿 turn in a test paper. /這批 貨還没～呢. The merchandise hasn't been delivered yet. 2) make friends with. /他～了很多壞 人. He made friends with a lot of bad people. (B) 1) communication, intercourse. 絶～ terminate a friendship. 2) alternating, interchanging. ～電流 alternating current. 3) reach, join. ～點 point of intersection; ～好運 have good luck.

交情 **jyāuching** (N) friendship.

交代 **jyāudai** (FV) 1) give someone instructions. /那個工頭 ～完就走了. The foreman finished giving instructions and left. 2) be finished, completed. /我們的 工作就算～了. Our work may be regarded as completed. (N) <-儿> explanation, excuse. /他們 兩人没有個～就走了. Those two left without any explanation.

交代 **jyāudài** (FV) 1) turn over work to someone. /把你的工作 ～給他. Turn your work over to him. 2) explain one's actions, make excuses to the public. 對人民～ explain something to the public. (N) transference of work.

交換 **jyāuhwàn** (FV) trade, exchange, barter. ～名片 exchange visiting cards; ～戰俘 exchange prisoners of war.

交際 **jyāujì** (FV) make social contacts, socialize. /他很會~. He's very good at making social contacts. (N) social relations, social contact. (AT) social. ~舞 social dance.

交界 **jyāujyè** (VO) meet, come together, at a border. /那兩國在那條河那ル~. Those two countries come together at that river. (N) border. (PT) 跟...~ border a country, state. /法國跟德國~. France borders Germany.

交朋友 **jyāupéngyou** (VO) make friends with someone. /我在學校沒交什麼朋友. I didn't make any friends at school. /我不願意跟他~. I don't want to make friends with him.

交涉 **jyāushè** (FV) negotiate. /日本派大使到中國去~通商. Japan sent its ambassador to China to negotiate trade agreements. (N) negotiation.

交響樂 **jyāusyǎngywè** (N) symphony (composition) (M 支 jr̄). ~隊 or ~團 symphony orchestra.

交通 **jyāutūng** (N) 1) communications and transportation. ~部長 Ministry of Communications. 2) traffic. ~警察 traffic cop. /請不要阻碍~. Please don't block traffic.

交易 **jyāuyì** (FV) exchange. /我不願意跟他們~. I don't want to trade with them. (N) exchange, trade, transaction. 股票~ exchange of stocks; ~所 stock exchange.

教 **jyāu** (FV) teach. ~英文 teach English. /這個歌是他~我的. That song is one he taught me. →教 **jyàu**.

教給 **jyāugěi** (FV) teach someone something (lp). /他~我怎麼開車. He's teaching me how to drive.

驕 **jyāu** (B) arrogant, proud.

驕傲 **jyāuàu** (SV) be arrogant, conceited.

焦 **jyāu** (SV) be charred, burned. /飯~了! The rice is burned! (B) 1) anxious. ~急 be worried. 2) <-子> coke (fuel). ~炭 coke. s

澆 **jyāu** (FV) 1) water flowers, land.

/草地該~了. The lawn should be watered. 2) pour over. /他~了我一身水. He poured water all over me.

跤 **jyāu** (B) 1) fall, tumble. 摔了一~ take a tumble. 2) wrestling. 摔~ wrestle.

嚼 **jyáu** (FV) 1) chew. /這牛肉太硬. 我~不動. This beef is too tough; I can't chew it. 2) talk, chatter (derogatory). /他整天窮~. He talks his head off all day.

嚼子 **jyáudz** (N) bit (on a bridle).

繳 **jyǎu** (FV) hand in, hand over. ~考卷 hand in an examination paper; ~稅 pay taxes.

角 **jyǎu** (N) 1) <-ル> angle. 直~ right angle. 2) <-ル> corner. ~門 corner door. 3) <-ル> role (as in a play). 主~ leading role. 4) horn. 牛~ oxhorn. (M) ten cents (d). 三~錢 thirty cents. →腳{角} **jywé**.

腳(脚) **jyǎu** (N) 1) foot (M 隻 jr̄). 2) base, foot, of a mountain, wall, and the like. 山~ foot of a mountain. (M) kick. /他踢了那個狗一~. 看看它還活着沒有. He gave the dog a kick to see if it was still alive. →腳 **jywé**.

腳步ル **jyǎubùr** (N) footstep, pace, step. ~聲音 sound of footsteps. /你做事得站穩了~. You must be able to take a firm stand in what you're doing.

腳行 **jyǎuháng** (N) porter at a station, redcap.

腳後跟 **jyǎuhòugen** (N) heel of the foot.

腳掌 **jyǎujǎng** (N) <-子, -ル> sole of the foot.

腳雞眼 **jyǎujīyan** (N) corn (on one's foot).

腳趾頭 **jyǎujřtou** (N) toe.

腳尖ル **jyǎujyār** (N) toe (forepart of the foot, as opposed to the heel). /你踩我~了. You stepped on my toe.

腳色 **jyǎusè** (N) 1) role, part, in a play. 2) figure (person). /在政治上他還是一個重要的~. He is still an important figure in politics.

腳踏車 **jyǎutàchē** (N) bicycle

(M輛**lyàng**). 騎 ~ ride a bicycle.

脚腕 **jyǎuwàn** (N) <-子,-ㄦ> ankle.

脚印ㄦ **jyǎuyèr** (N) footprint.

餃 **jyǎu** (B) <-子> small case of dough filled with chopped meat and vege-tables (usually boiled).

鉸 **jyǎu** (FV) cut (as with scissors) (lp). /把那根繩子~成兩段. Cut that rope into two pieces. (B) hinge. ~釘 pin of a hinge.

狡 **jyǎu** (B) crafty. ~詐 be cunning, de-ceitful.

狡猾 **jyǎuhwá** (SV) be cunning, wily, sly.

較 **jyǎu, jyàu** (B) in comparison. ~好 be better.

較比 '**jyáubǐ, jyàubǐ** (A) more ...,...er. /這塊地氈~好一點. This rug is somewhat bet-ter.

攪 **jyǎu** (FV) 1) stir, mix. /把湯~一~. Stir the soup a bit. 2) dis-turb, disrupt. /他把這個會~了. He disrupted the meeting.

校 **jyàu** (FV) check, collate. ~改 proof-read and correct mistakes. /你打的那篇文章我已經~過了, 沒錯ㄦ. I've checked the re-port you typed and there are no mis-takes. →校**syàu**.

校對 **jyàudwèi** (FV) proofread. /這篇稿件還沒有~過. This article hasn't been proofread.

校正 '**jyàujèng** (FV) make cor-rections in, correct. /請你給我~我的錯ㄦ. Please correct my errors. /他的發音太壞我~不過來. His pronunciation is so bad I can't correct it.

較 **jyàu** →較**jyǎu**.

教 **jyàu** (FV) 1) tell or ask someone to do something. /~他去買東西. Tell him to go and buy the things. 2) let. /他父親不~他看電影. His father won't let him go to the movies. 3) cause, make. /這事ㄦ~我很着急. This makes me worried. (CV) by (marking the agent). /他~人打了. He was beaten up by someone. /蛋糕~

我吃了. I ate up the cake. (N) religion. 信~ believe in a religion. (B) teach. ~練 train someone, a coach. →教**jyāu**.

教科書 **jyàukeshū** (N) textbook (M本-**běn**).

教會 **jyàuhwèi** (N) the Church. /他們兩人情感不好, 但是~不許他們離婚. They don't get along with each other, but the Church won't allow them to get a divorce. 2) denomination.

教授 **jyàushòu** (N) professor. (FV) teach a subject. /他~鋼琴. He teaches piano.

教師 **jyàushr** (N) teacher, in-structor.

教室 **jyàushr** (N) classroom (M間**jyān**).

教訓 **jyàusyùn** (FV) 1) counsel, teach (as a father might a son). 2) admonish, reprimand. /他被法官~了一頓. He was reprimanded by the judge. (N) 1) lesson (as from some experience). /那件事給我一個很大的~. That taught me a very important lesson. 2) admo-nition, lecture (M頓**dwùn**). /為了花錢我受了我父親一頓~. I was given a lecture by my father on spending money.

教學 **jyàusywé** (N) teaching and learning. /現在政府很注意外國語~. The government is very interested in the teaching and learning of foreign languages.

教條 **jyàutyáu** (N) doctrine, dogma.

教條主義 **jyàutyáujǔyì** (N) doctrinairism, dogmatism.

教育 **jyàuyù** (N) education. 受~ receive an education, be educated. (FV) educate, train, develop. /父母應當好好地~他們的子女. Parents should put effort into educating their children.

教員 **jyàuywán** (N) school-teacher.

叫(呌)**jyàu** (FV) 1) call, summon. ~汽車 call a cab. /他~你呢. He's calling you. 2) be called, named. /這個~什麼? What is this called? 3) whistle, blow. /汽笛~了三次. The steam whistle blew three times. 4) shout, yell. /別~.

Don't shout. 5) call (of animals or birds; also translates with more specific words as bark, neigh, moo, bleat, etc., when the animal is named). /那個貓~了一夜. That cat miaowed all night. 6) order, purchase. ~煤 order coal. 7) tell *or* ask someone to do something. /她~我在這兒等她. She asked me to wait here for her. 8) let. /~他走吧！ Let him go! 9) make, cause. /這輛汽車~我生氣. This car makes me angry. (CV) by (marking the agent). /樹~風颳倒了. The tree was blown over by the wind. /他~人打了. He got beaten up by somebody.

叫電話 jyàudyànhwà (VO) make a phone call, phone. /我給他叫了兩次電話. I phoned him twice.

叫花子 jyàuhwādz (N) beggar.

叫喚 jyàuhwan (FV) 1) call (of animals or birds; also translates with more specific words as bark, neigh, moo, bleat, etc. when the animal is named). /那條狗不~. That dog doesn't bark. 2) shout, yell. /別~. Don't shout.

窖 jyàu (N) cellar for storing things. (FV) store something in a cellar. /把白菜~起來. Store the cabbages in the cellar.

覺[覺] jyàu (N) sleep. /我沒打攪你的~嗎? Did I interrupt your sleep?→覺 jywé.

接 jyē (FV) 1) receive guests, mail, a message. ~信 receive a letter. 2) answer a phone. ~電話 answer a phone *or* receive a phone call. 3) connect, join. /電線沒~上呢. The wires aren't connected. 4) catch something thrown through the air. ~球 catch a ball. 5) meet someone, as at a train station. ~朋友 meet a friend. 6) take over. /我~他的事. I'm taking over his work.

接洽 jyēchyà, jyēsyà (FV) negotiate, talk something over, make arrangements. /我要到房產公司去~租房子的事. I'm going to the realty company to make arrangements for renting a place.

接待 'jyēdài (FV) receive,

take care of, guests. /客人來的時候沒有人~他們. When the guests arrived there was no one there to receive them.

接着 jyējáu (RC) receive, meet, successfully. /我去接他可是沒~. I went to meet him, but I missed him. →接着 jyēje.

接着 jyēje (A) 1) continuously. /他~説了兩個多鐘頭. He talked continuously for more than two hours. 2) after that. /她先唱一個歌,~又跳一個舞. She'll sing a song first; after that she'll do a dance. 3) serially. /他~講昨天沒講完的故事. He will continue telling the story he started yesterday. →接着 jyējáu.

接濟 jyējì (FV) supply someone with some urgently required item. /我們~他們糧食. We supply them with provisions. (N) supplies (of vital importance).

接近 jyējìn (SV) be close (of relations between people). /他們的關係很~. They have a very close relationship. (FV) become close to, get mixed up with, someone. /別跟他~. Don't get mixed up with him.

接見 jyējyàn (FV) receive a visitor, an employee, more or less formally. /他沒功夫~你. He's too busy to see you.

接收 jyēshōu (FV) take over something. /我們把他們的房子~過來了. We've taken over their house.

接受 jyēshòu (FV) accept. ~批評 accept criticism; ~禮物 accept a gift.

接線生 jyēsyànshēng (N) telephone operator.

接洽 jyēsyà →接洽 jyēchyà.

接頭 jyētóu (VO) contact someone to make arrangements. /我跟警察局~了. I've contacted the police. (SV) be familiar with. /那件事我不~. I'm not familiar with that matter.

接吻 jyēwèn (VO) kiss. /我看見他們~了. I saw them kiss.

街 jyē (N) street (M條tyáu, 道dàu).

街坊 jyēfang (N) neighbor.

揭 **jyē** (FV) 1) lift off a cover. /二十
分鐘之內別~鍋蓋. Don't take
the cover off the pot for twenty
minutes. 2) take down, tear off.
/把佈告~下來. Take down that
notice. 3) reveal, make known.
/你別~我的缺點. Don't reveal
my shortcomings.

階[阶] **jyē** (M) 1) <-ㄦ> step of a stairway. /這個樓梯有三十多~.
This stairway has more than thirty
steps. 2) rank, class. /他升了
一~. He was raised a rank. (B)
1) steps to a building. 台~ steps to
a building, platform steps. 2) rank,
class. 官~ official rank.

    階級 **jyējí** (N) 1) class (of
society). 工人~ labor class. 2)
rank (m). 少校~ rank of major.

隔 **jyē**→隔 **gé**.

結 **jyē** (FV) bear fruit (lit. only).
/這棵樹今年什麼都沒~.
This tree didn't bear any fruit at all
this year. →結 **jyé**.

    結實 **jyēshr** (SV) 1) be solid,
strong, durable. /這個桌子很
~. This is a very solid table. 2)
be healthy, strong. /這個小孩
ㄦ不太~. This child isn't very
healthy.

    結實 **jyēshŕ** (VO) bear fruit.
/這種樹一年結兩次實. This
kind of tree bears fruit twice a year.

結 **jyé, jyě*** (FV) tie a knot. (N) 1)*
<-子> knot. 2) <-子> bow. 打~
tie a bow or knot. (B) 1) establish
a relationship. ~仇 become enemies.
2) congeal. 凍~ freeze. 3) conclude.
總~ conclusion. 4) certification.
具~ make an affidavit. →結 **jyé**.

    結冰 **jyébīng** (VO) freeze. /湖
水已經結成冰了. The lake is
already frozen.

    結果 **jyégwǒ** (N) outcome, re-
sult. (A) as a result, in the end.
/~他沒來. He didn't show up in
the end.

    結婚 **jyéhwūn** (VO) get married,
be married. /她結過兩次婚了.
She's been married twice.

    結論 **jyélwùn** (N) deduction,
conclusion. /你得了什麼~了?
What conclusion have you reached?

    結束 **jyéshù** (FV) conclude,

close. /我們的工作已經~了.
Our work has been concluded. (N)
last part of one's work or a job. 辦
~ finish up a job.

隔 **jyé**→隔 **gé**.

節[節,節](节) **jyé** (N) 1) festival. 過~ observe a festival. (M) 1) section of
something long. 一~路 a section of
road; 一~火車 a section of train. 2)
for class periods in school. /我今
天只有一~課. I only have one
class today. 3) section of a chapter,
stanza of a poem, verse of the Bible,
etc. 馬可福音第三章第六~
chapter three, verse six of the Book
of Mark. (B) 1) restrain, limit. ~
制 be temperate in. 2) chastity,
purity. 貞~ chastity. 3) <-ㄦ>
joint. 骨~ joint (between bones); 竹
~ joint in bamboo. 4) tempo. ~奏
rhythm.

    節氣 **jyéchì** (N) day marking
one of the 24 Chinese divisions of the
solar year.

    節略 **jyélywè** (N) 1) summary.
2) memorandum (diplomatic) (M 篇
pyān).

    節目 **'jyémù** (N) 1) program
(performance of what is outlined on
paper). ~單 playbill, (printed) program. /今天的~不好. Today's
program isn't any good. 2) number,
event, on a program. 3) planned
activity. /今天晚上你有什麼
~嗎? Do you have anything planned
for this evening?

截 **jyé** (FV) 1) cut in two. /請你把
這個繩子~成兩斷. Please
cut this rope in two. 2) intercept.
/警察把那輛汽車~住了.
The police stopped that car. (M)
<-子, -ㄦ> segment, portion, piece,
of something which has been cut.
/他把那個木頭砍成兩~了.
He's chopped the log into two pieces.

竭 **jyé** (B) exhaust.
    竭力 **jyélì** (AV) try hard to, en-
deavor to. /我一定~幫你的
忙. I'll try hard to help you.

結 **jyě**→結 **jyé**.

姐[姊] **jyě** (B) 1) older sister. 大~
oldest sister. 2) older female cousin.
表~ older female cousin (on the

mother's side).   3) young lady (un-married). 小 ～ Miss (title), young lady.

姐姐 **jyějye** (N) older sister.

姐妹 **jyěmèi** (N) sisters.

解(觧) **jyě** (FV) 1) relieve, get rid of. 渴 relieve thirst. 2) untie, unfasten. ～扣ㄦ unbutton. (CV) from a place (lp). /我～天津來. I've come from Tientsin. (B) 1) explain. ～説 explain. 2) understand. 了～ understand. →解 **jyè**, 解 **syè**.

解除 **jyěchú** (FV) eliminate, remove. ～條約 terminate a treaty. /學校對於留長頭髮的禁令已經～了. The school's restriction on wearing long hair has been eliminated.

解放 **jyěfàng** (FV) liberate, emancipate, free. /林肯為了～黑人而努力. Lincoln devoted his efforts to liberating the slaves. (N) liberation, freedom. /一離家他就得到～了. He got his freedom when he left home.

解放軍 **jyěfàngjwūn** (N) Liberation Army (c).

解決 **jyějywé** (FV) 1) solve a problem. /我不能～我的經濟問題. I can't solve my financial problems. 2) do away with, kill. /我把他～了. I killed him. (N) solution.

解開 **jyěkāi** (RC) 1) unfasten, untie, unbutton. ～大衣 unbutton an overcoat. 2) resolve a question, solve a puzzle. /他把我的謎語～了. He solved my riddle.

解剖 **jyěpōu** (FV) dissect (as a cadaver). /教授～了一個青蛙給我們看. The professor dissected a frog for us.

解手ㄦ **jyěshǒur** (VO) relieve oneself, go to the bathroom (euphemistic). 解小手ㄦ urinate; 解大手ㄦ defecate, have a bowel movement. /我要解個手ㄦ. I have to go to the bathroom.

解釋 **jyěshr̀** (FV) explain. /請你～你遲到的原因. Please explain your reason for coming late. (N) explanation.

解 **jyè** (FV) transfer under guard. /他們把犯人～到另外一個監獄去了. They've transferred the

convict to another prison. →解 **jyě**, 解 **syè**.

介 **jyè** (B) 1) lie between. ～母 medial (in phonetics). 2) regard as important.

介紹 **jyèshàu** (FV) introduce. /你可不可以給我們～一下? Can you introduce us? (N) introduction.

介意 **jyèyì** (FV) 1) take offense at. /別～. Don't take offense. 2) notice. /他的月要帶斷了他沒～, 後來他的褲子就掉下來了. His belt broke and he didn't notice it; after a while his pants fell down. (SV) be offended. /我沒想到他會那麼～. I didn't expect he would be so offended.

借 **jyè** (FV) 1) borrow. /他跟我～了一本書. He borrowed a book from me. 2) lend. /我～了一點錢給他. I lent him some money.

借字ㄦ **jyèdzèr** (N) promissory note, I.O.U. (M 張 **jāng**).

借光 **jyègwāng** (IE) Excuse me. or May I get by. 2) Excuse me .... /～, 請問到支加哥的火車幾點鐘開? Excuse me, could you tell me when the train leaves for Chicago? 3) I am indebted to you.

借約 **jyèywē** (N) promissory note, I.O.U. (M 張 **jāng**).

界 **jyè** (B) 1) boundary. 邊～ border; ～石 boundary stone. 2) scope, sphere, realm. 教育～ educational circles; 科學～ scientific world; 眼～ field of vision.

藉 **jyè** (CV) ＜着＞ by means of, taking advantage of. /他～我的名義跟人捐錢. He used my name to raise money. /我～這個機會看一點ㄦ書. I'm taking this opportunity to read a little.

隔 **jyè** (B) ↓. →隔 **gé**.

隔壁ㄦ **jyèbyěr** (PW) 1) next door (lp). /～有一個煙捲ㄦ店. There's a cigar store next door. 2) the area next to one's house. /他住在～. He lives next door. (N) next-door neighbor. /我的～是一個老太婆. My next-door neighbor is an elderly woman.

戒 **jyè** (FV) abstain from, quit, a habit.

/他把煙已經~了. He has quit smoking. (B) 1) guard against. ~備 take precautions, be on guard. 2) moral rule, precept. 受~ take vows (as a Buddhist priest, nun); 十~ Ten Commandments. 3) <-子> ring (worn on a finger). 鑽~ diamond ring.

戒指 **jyèjr** (N) ring (worn on a finger).

究 **jyōu** (B) investigate. 研~ do research, study, investigate.

究竟 **jyōujìng** (A) 1) finally, after all, anyway. /他~還是去了. He went after all. 2) in the world, in heaven's name (used for emphasis in a question). /他~是誰? Who in the world is he?

揪 **jyōu** (FV) seize with the hand, grasp. /他~着繩子不撒手. He held tightly to the rope and wouldn't let go. /他~着他的領子打他. He seized him by the collar and hit him.

九(玖) **jyǒu** (NU) nine. (B) ninth. ~樓 ninth floor.

九月 **jyǒuywè** (TW) 1) September. 2) the ninth month of the lunar calendar.

酒 **jyǒu** (N) wine, liquor, alcoholic beverage.

酒館 **jyóugwǎn** (N) <-子,-ㄦ> bar (for selling liquor) (M 家 **jyā**).

酒精 **jyóujīng** alcohol (ethyl, grain).

韭(韮) **jyǒu** (B) chives. ~黃 yellow chives.

韭菜 **jyǒutsài** (N) chives (M 棵 **kē**).

久 **jyǒu** (SV) be long (of time). /你來美國多~了? How long have you been in the United States? (A) for a long time. /我們~不見面了. We haven't seen each other for a long time. t

就 **jyòu** (A) 1) then, in that case. /如果你來,我~高興了. If you come, (then) I'll be happy. /當我生氣的時候,我~喝酒. When I'm angry, (then) I drink. 2) then, afterwards. /我們吃了~走. We'll eat, then go. 他每天下了課~回家. He comes home every day right after class. 3) at once,

very soon. /醫生~要來了. The doctor will be here very soon. 4) only, as little as. /我~有一塊錢. I only have one dollar. 5) as much as, as many as. /白皮鞋他~有三十雙. She has as many as thirty pairs of white leather shoes. 6) as early as, from a certain time in the past. /今天我七點鐘~來了. I was here as early as seven o'clock today. 7) only, merely, nothing else but. /他~會說英文. He can only speak English. /我們~等你的決定了. We're merely waiting for your decision. 8) precisely, exactly. /你~是我要找的那個人. You are precisely the person I'm looking for. 9) used to emphasize an example given in contradiction to a previous statement. /A: 誰都知道. B: 我~不知道. A: Everyone knows. B: (On the contrary) I don't know. 10) simply, just. /我不知道為什麼我~不喜歡他. I don't know why, I just don't like him. (FV) go (eat or drink) with. /我没有東西~飯. I don't have anything to go with my rice. (CV) 1) with, along with (as one food is eaten with another). /我喜歡用魚~酒喝. When I drink wine, I like fish with it. 2) taking advantage of. /~他在這儿,我們為什麼不商量商量呢? Why don't we take advantage of his being here and talk things over? (B) 1) go to, approach. ~醫 see a doctor. 2) complete, accomplish. 成~ accomplishment. (PT) 1) 一...~... as soon as ...,(then).... /我一見他,~生氣. As soon as I see him, I get angry. 2) ~...也(or 還)... even if...(still). /你~生氣也没用. Even if you get angry it won't help. 3) 不...~...if not... then...,either...or... /他不打牌~睡覺. If he's not playing cards, he's sleeping. /不是今天~是明天. If it's not today, it's tomorrow.

就地 **jyòudì** (A) right on the spot, right there, at that very place and time. /我把那個問題~解答了. I solved that problem right on the spot.

就着 **jyòuje** (CV) up next to, near to. /你～桌子吃西瓜. Eat your watermelon over the table.

就職 **jyòujŕ** (VO) assume a position or function. /他來這儿就什麼職? What position is he going to assume here?

就是 **jyòushr** (A) namely. /有兩個人去,～我跟你. There are two people going, namely myself and you. (IE) Yes, that's right. /A:這是不是你說那個? B:～. A: Is that what you were talking about? B: Yes, that's it.

就事 **jyòushr** (VO) take up an office, assume a post. /明天我要到紐約去～. Tomorrow I'll go to New York to assume a new post.

就許 '**jyòusyú** (A) maybe, perhaps. /有一天我的兒子～做了美國總統. Perhaps someday my son will be president of the United States.

舅 **jyòu** (B) 1) maternal uncle. 2) <-子> brother-in-law (wife's brother).
舅父 **jyòufù** (N) maternal uncle.
舅母 **jyòumŭ** (N) aunt (wife of a maternal uncle).

舊[旧] **jyòu** (SV) 1) be old. ～賬 an old account. /這車太～了. The car is too old. 2) be old-fashioned. /他的思想太～. His way of thinking is too old-fashioned. (AT) used, secondhand. ～傢俱 secondhand furniture.

救 **jyòu** (FV) 1) rescue, save. /他～了我. He saved me. 2) help someone do something. /他～他的朋友逃出監獄. He helped his friend escape from jail. (B) help. 求～ ask for help.
救護 '**jyòuhù** (FV) take to safety. ～傷兵 bring in the wounded.
救火車 **jyòuhwŏchē** (N) fire engine (M輛 **lyàng**).
救濟 '**jyòují** (FV) extend relief to, relieve the distress of. ～窮人 help the poor (with money or food).
救生船 **jyòushēngchwán** (N) lifeboat (M隻 **jŕ**,條 **tyáu**).
救生帶 **jyòushēngdài** (N) life belt.

鋸 **jyū** (FV) mend chinaware by reinforcing it with metal staples. /這個碗太碎了,不能～了. This bowl is too badly broken; it can't be mended. 一鋸 **jyū**.
鋸子 **jyūdz** (N) staple used in mending broken chinaware.

居 **jyū** (B) 1) restaurant (in names of restaurants). 金門～ Golden Gate Restaurant. 2) reside. 故～ former residence. s
居然 **jyūrán** (A) actually (contrary to expectations), surprisingly. /他～敢反對政府. He is actually daring to oppose the government.

車 **jyū** (N) chariot in Chinese chess (equal to a castle) (M隻 **jŕ**,條 **tyáu**). 一車 **chē**.

拘 **jyū** (FV) confine, arrest. /把他們都～來. Arrest them all. (B) be limited to. ～禮 be formal. 一不拘 **bùjyū**.
拘泥 **jyūnì** (SV) be petty, formalistic, inclined to stick to all the little regulations.
拘束 **jyūshu** (SV) be ill at ease, feel restrained. /別～. Don't be formal. or Make yourself at home. (N) restriction. /我受不了這種～. I can't stand this kind of restriction. (FV) restrict. /我太太老～我. My wife is always putting restrictions on me.

鞠 **jyú** (B) bend in submission.
鞠躬 **jyúgūng** (VO) bow. /他對觀眾鞠了三個躬. He bowed to the audience three times.

橘[桔] **jyú** (B) <-子> orange, tangerine (M只 **jŕ**). 金～ kumquat (lit. golden orange).

菊 **jyú** (B) chrysanthemum.
菊花 **jyúhwā** (N) <-儿> chrysanthemum (M朵 **dwŏ**, 枝 **jŕ**, 棵 **kē**).

局 **jyú** (B) 1) bureau, department, office. 警察～ police station. 2) store, shop. 書～ bookstore. 3) condition, situation. 政～ political situation. 4) party. 飯～ dinner party. (M) game of chess.
局長 **jyújăng** (N) department or bureau head.

局勢 **jyúshr̀** (N) situation, outlook. 戰爭的~ military situation.

舉[擧][举] **jyǔ** (FV) 1) raise, lift, hold up high. ~手 raise one's hand. /他~着國旗在隊伍前面走. He's marching in front of the line holding the national flag. 2) elect, select. /我們~他做代表. We elected him as our representative. 3) give a reason, example, precedent. /你能~出什麼理由來嗎? Can you give any reason for it? (B) 1) behavior. ~止 manner, behavior. 2) begin, initiate. ~辦 initiate. 3) all, the whole. ~世 the whole world.

舉動 **'jyǔdùng** (N) behavior. /他的~很奇怪. His behavior is very strange.

舉行 **jyǔsyíng** (FV) hold a ceremony, meeting, etc. /明天我們要~一次會議. We are holding a meeting tomorrow. /你們幾時~婚禮? When are you going to have your wedding?

俱[具] **jyù** (B) all, entirely. ~都 all, everyone.

俱樂部 **jyùlèbù** (N) club (social).

具 **jyù** (M) 1) for dead bodies. 一~死屍 a corpse. 2) for machines. 一~縫紉機 a sewing machine. (B) 1) utensil, tool. 農~ farm tools; 家~ furniture. 2) draw up, write out. ~文 prepare a document; ~名 sign one's name.

具體 **jyùtǐ** (SV) be concrete (not abstract). ~的建議 concrete suggestion.

拒 **jyù** (B) resist, refuse. ~捕 resist arrest.

拒絕 **jyùjywé** (FV) reject, refuse. /政府把他的請求~了. The government rejected his petition. /他~答覆. He refused to answer.

鋸 **jyù** (N) <-子> saw (M把**bǎ**). (FV) saw. /請你把這個木板~成兩段. Please saw this board in two. →鋸**jyū**.

颶 **jyù** (B) hurricane, typhoon.

颶風 **jyùfēng** (N) hurricane, typhoon.

距 **jyù** (CV) from a place. /他的家~我家不遠. His house isn't far from mine. (B) distance.

距離 **jyùlí** (N) distance between two points. /這兩個村子的~是十吅哩. These two villages are ten miles apart. (CV) from a place. /那個鋪子~我家只有兩條街. That store is only two blocks from my house.

劇[剧] **jyù** (B) 1) severe, intense. ~毒 powerful poison. 2) play, drama. ~場 a theatre.

劇烈 **'jyùlyè** (SV) be violent, rough, intense. /這件運動很~. This kind of sport is very rough. /戰事這兩天不太~. The fighting hasn't been so intense the past couple of days.

據[据] **jyù** (CV) according to. /~他說,.... According to what he says, ... /~我看,他就是想往上爬. As I see it, he's just trying to get ahead. (B) 1) take possession. 佔~ occupy by force. 2) evidence, proof. 收~ a receipt. 3) basis. 根~ be based on, basis.

據說 **jyùshwō** (A) it is said that, hear someone say that. /~他已經來了. I heard he's already come.

聚 **jyù** (FV) gather, assemble. /咱們~在一塊儿. Let's all go together.

聚會 **jyùhwei**, **jyùhwèi*** (FV) gather together for a meeting, party, etc. /我們~~吧. Let's get together. (N)* get-together, gathering (M次**tsz̀**).

句 **jyù** (M) sentence. /他的演講我一~也不懂. I didn't understand a single part of his speech. (B) <-子> sentence. ~法 syntax.

君 **jyūn** (B) 1) used after surnames, Mr. 張~ Mr. Chang. 2) chief, sovereign. ~主 monarch.

君子 **'jyūndž** (N) man of virtue and good character, gentleman.

均 **jyūn** (SV) be equal, even. /錢分的很~. The money was divided equally. (FV) make portions equal. /我的飯太多了,我們~一~吧. I have too much rice. How

about taking some? (B) equally.
allot equally.

軍 **jyūn** (N) army corps consisting of two or more army divisions.　(B) 1) military. ~犬 military dog.　2) troops. 美~ U. S. troops.

軍器庫 **jyūnchìkù** (N) arsenal, armory (for storage) (M座**dzwò**).

軍隊 **jyūndwèi** (N) troops, armed forces (M支**jř**).

軍官 **jyūngwān** (N) military officer.

軍長 **jyūnjǎng** (N) army corps commander.

軍艦 **jyūnjyàn** (N) warship, naval vessel (M艘**sōu**, 隻**jř**).

軍事 **jyūnshř** (AT) military. ~訓練 military training.

軍需品 **jyūnsyūpǐn** (N) military equipment, supplies.

軍樂隊 **jyūn ywèdwèi** (N) military band (musical).

窘 **jyǔng** (SV) 1) be poor, hard up. /他近來(近日)很~. Recently he's been hard up financially.　2) be embarrassing. /這個情形很~. This situation is very embarrassing.　3) be embarrassed. /那件事情叫我真~. That incident really made me embarrassed.

捐 **jywān** (FV) donate, contribute. /您打算~多少? How much are you planning to donate? (N) temporary *or* special tax. 房~ special tax on houses.

圈 **jywān** (FV) confine, imprison, fence in. /把他~起來. Lock him up. →圈 **chywān**, 圈 **jywàn**.

捲[卷] **jywǎn** (FV) roll up. /你先把袖子~起來再洗碗吧. Roll up your sleeves before you do the dishes. (SV) be curly. /那個狗的毛是~的. That dog's hair is curly. (M)<-儿> roll, reel. 一~電影儿 a reel of movie film.

捲子 **jywǎndz** (N) steamed roll.

捲儿 **jywǎr** (N) 1) roll. 膠~ roll film; 烟~cigarette. 2) curler. /她帶着一腦袋~就到電影院去了. She went to the movies with her hair in curlers. (B) roll, bun (bread). 花~ fancy-shaped steamed roll. (M) ↑(M).

卷 **jywàn** (M) fascicle of a book. 第一~ fascicle one.　(B) 1)<-子,-儿> examination paper. 交~ hand in an examination paper.　2) scroll. 長~ long scroll.　3) document, record. ~宗 archives. SF of 卷**jywǎn**.

圈 **jywàn** (N) pen, fold. 猪~ pen for pigs. →圈 **chywān**, 圈 **jywān**.

撅 **jywē** (FV) 1) break something long by grasping at the ends and applying bending pressure. /他把那根尺~成兩段了. He broke that ruler in two.　2) stick out and up (as the tail of an animal). /猴子~着尾巴. The monkey has his tail stuck up in the air.　3) refuse someone bluntly. /我叫他給~了. He turned me down flat.　4) embarrass people. /你為什麽老當着人~我? Why do you always embarrass me in front of others?

撅嘴 **jywēdzwěi** (VO) purse the lips, pout. /她撅着嘴不理我. She's pouting and won't talk to me.

脚[角] **jywé** (B)<-儿> role (as in a play). 配~ supporting role. →脚 **jyǎu**.

決[决] **jywé** (AV) used before a negative, be determined to. /我~不投降. I am determined not to give in.　(B) 1) decide. ~意 decide; 判~ sentence someone.　2) execute a person. 鎗~ execute by shooting.　3) burst. ~口 breach a dyke.

決定 **jywédìng** (FV) decide. /你怎麽~? What did you decide? (AV) decide to. /我已經~去了. I've decided to go. (N) decision.

決斷 **jywédwàn** (N) ability to make quick and definite decisions. (SV) be decisive.

決賽 **jywésài** (FV) hold *or* participate in the final competition of a series, run the final heat of a race. /今天我們~. Today we hold the final competition. (N) final competition, final heat.

決心 **jywésyīn** (N) determination. (AV) make up one's mind to, decide to. /我~念書了. I've made up my mind to study.

決議 **jywéyì** (N) resolution of an assembly. (FV) decide by a majority, vote. /我們已經在開會時~了去草山旅行. At the meeting we decided to take a trip to Grass Mountain.

掘 **jywé** (FV) dig. ～井 dig a well.

絕 **jywé** (A) 1) extremely. ～早 extremely early. 2) absolutely, definitely. /他～没有太太. He definitely doesn't have a wife. (SV) be unique, peculiar. /他的畫兒真～. His paintings are really unique. (B) 1) cut short, break off. ～交 break off a friendship. 2) extinct. 殺～exterminate. 3) unsurpassed, extraordinary. ～才 extraordinary talent.

絕版 **jywébǎn** (VO) go *or* be out of print (of a book). /這本書已經～了. This book is out of print.

絕對 **jywédwèi** (A) absolutely, definitely. /他～會失敗的. He will definitely fail. (AT) absolute. ～溫度 absolute temperature.

絕交 **jywéjyāu** (VO) break off relations. /那兩國～了. Those two countries have broken off relations. /我跟他～了. I've broken off with him.

絕裂 **jywélyè** (FV) break off relations or negotiations. /我跟他～了. I've broken off with him. /日內瓦談判又要～了. The Geneva talks are about to be broken off again.

覺[觉] **jywé** (B) 1) feel, sense. 感～feel, sense, feeling. 2) sense, sensitivity. 視～sense of sight. →覺 **jyàu**.

覺出來 **jywéchulai** (RC) figure out, sense. /他的意思你還没～嗎. Have you figured out what he meant yet?

覺得 **jywéde** (FV) 1) feel (physically). /我～很冷. I feel cold. 2) be of the opinion that, feel that. /我～他應當去. I feel that he should go.

覺着 **jywéje** (FV) feel (physically). /我～有點兒冷. I feel a bit cold.

覺悟 **jywéwù** (FV) become enlightened, converted, reformed. /他原來不信我們的主義,現在～了. He didn't used to believe what we do, but he's become enlightened.

爵[爵] **jywé** (B) nobility. 公～ duke.

爵位 '**jywéwèi** (N) title of nobility. /他有什麼～? What title does he have?

口客 **kā** (ON) crack (as when wood breaks). /～的一聲桌子的腿斷了. The leg of the table broke with a cracking sound. *t*

口客口赤 **kāchr** (FV) scrape with a sharp tool (as in removing encrusted dirt or paint). /我們可以拿刀子把那層漆～下來. We can scrape off that layer of paint with a knife. (ON) 1) crunch (as when chewing something brittle or crisp). /你別～～地嚼那塊糖. Don't crunch on that piece of candy like that. 2) sound of scraping. /他用刀～～～地刮玻璃上的油漆. He's scraping the paint off the window with a knife (making a scraping sound).

咖 **kā** (B) ‡. *t*

咖啡 **kāfēi** (N) coffee (M 杯 bēi; 壺 hú).

卡 **kǎ** (B) truck. 十輪～ ten-wheel truck. *t* → 卡 chyǎ.

卡車 **kǎchē** (N) truck (M 輛 lyàng, 部 bù).

卡片 **kǎpyàn** (N) <-ㄦ> card (any kind except a playing card) (M 張 jāng).

開[开] **kāi** (FV) 1) open, unlock. ～門 open a door; ～鎖 unlock a lock. 2) operate a car, airplane, ship, etc. ～汽車 drive a car. 3) leave (of a train, bus, ship, etc.). /火車快～了. The train is about to leave. 4) begin, start, open. ～學 start school, start (of school); ～球 start off a ball game. /他～了一個飯館. He has opened a restaurant. 5) turn on a light, radio, machine, etc. ～電門 turn on a switch. 6) operate, conduct, manage (as a store, etc.). ～舖子 operate a store. 7) make a list, write down. /你有什麼問題,請～出來好了. Whatever questions you have, please make a list of them. 8) expel, fire (as an employee). /我們公司今天～了兩個人. Our company fired two men today. 9) serve food, people. /你把晚飯～在花園

裡好了. Would you please serve supper out in the garden? 10) perform surgery on, operate on, a part of the body; ～盲腸 operate on the appendix. 11) dig ore, a well. ～井 dig a well. 12) pay money, a wage. ～工錢 pay a salary. 13) bloom (as a flower). /玫瑰花只在夏天～. Roses bloom only in the summertime. 14) be boiling, boiled. /水～了. The water is boiling. /水還沒有～. This water hasn't been boiled yet. *or* The water hasn't boiled yet. (RE) 1) indicates separation. 離～ leave; 打～ open up. (M) carat (of gold). 十四～金 14-carat gold. (B) division of standard-sized printing paper. 八～ octavo.

開拔 **kāibá** (FV) move (of troops). /新兵～到前線去了. Fresh troops have moved to the front.

開場 **kāichǎng** (VO) begin (of a play, movie, etc.). /戲是八點鐘～. The play began at eight o'clock.

開車執照 **kāichē'jŕjàu** (N) driver's license (M張 jāng).

開除 **kāichú** (FV) expel, kick out, a student, discharge a soldier (dishonorably or without special honor). ～黨籍 expel from a political party. /這個學生功課太壞,學校把他給～了. This student was expelled from school because of his poor grades.

開刀 **kāidāu** (VO) 1) operate (as a surgeon). /大夫馬上要給他的病人～了. The doctor is about to operate on a patient. 2) have an operation. /病人一定得～嗎? Does the patient definitely have to have an operation?

開動 **kāidùng** (RC) start a machine. /這輛破車修了好幾天還是開不動. This jalopy has been worked on for several days but it still won't start.

開放 **kāifàng** (FV) 1) open *or* release something to the public. /白宮每禮拜五～. The White House is open to the public every Friday. 2) bloom (as a flower). /我家園子裏的梅花都～了. The plum blossoms in our garden

are all in bloom.

開關 **kāigwān** (N) electric switch.

開會 **kāihwèi** (VO) 1) hold a meeting. /我們明天要開一個會. We're going to have a meeting tomorrow. 2) attend a meeting. /他～去了. He has gone to the meeting. 3) start a meeting. /會幾點鐘開? *or* 幾點鐘～? When does the meeting start?

開展 **kāijǎn** (FV) expand, develop. /我們正計劃～遠東的市場. We are planning to expand our markets in the Far East. (N) expansion, development.

開支 **kāijŕ** (N) expenditure, expense (M份 fèn, 筆 bǐ). (FV) 1) spend money. /我們學校今年～了多少錢? How much did our school spend this year? 2) pay for. /我的收入還不夠～房錢和飯錢. My income doesn't even pay for my room and board.

開礦 **kāikwàng** (VO) work a mine. /這個礦已經開了二十年了. This mine has already been worked for twenty years.

開幕 **kāimù** (VO) 1) rise, be up (of the curtain on a stage). /現在已經～了. The curtain is already up. 2) have a grand opening. /我們的珠寶店明天～. Our jewelry store has its grand opening tomorrow. 3) begin, open (of a conference). /國民代表大會下禮拜～. The National Assembly begins next week.

開審 **kāishěn** (FV) open a court inquiry. /那件殺人案昨天已經～了. That murder case opened in court yesterday.

開始 **kāishŕ** (FV) start, begin. /電影儿已經～了. The movie has already started. (N) start, beginning. /今天是本學期的～. Today is the beginning of the semester.

開水 **kāishwěi** (N) 1) boiling water. 2) boiled water. 涼～ cold boiled water.

開消 **kāisyau** (N) expenditure, expense (M份 fèn, 筆 bǐ). /我賺的錢不夠我的～. The money I make doesn't cover my expenses. (FV) 1) fire someone. /我把那個偷東西的用人～了. I fired that

thieving servant. 2) pay for. /我父親給我的錢只夠~房租.
The money my father gives me is only enough to pay for my rent.

開心 **kāisyīn** (VO) 1) feel happy. /他中了頭獎, 你開什麼心? He's the one that got first prize. Why are you so happy? 2) make fun of someone. /他拿那個新來的學生開了好一陣心. He has amused himself several times at the expense of that new student. (SV) be happy. /他馬上要結婚了, 所以~的很. He's very happy because he's going to get married soon.

開庭 **kāitíng** (VO) open a court session, be in session. /最高法院已經開了兩天的庭了. The Supreme Court has been in session for two days.

開頭 **kāitóu** (VO) <ール> start, make a start. /這場打架是誰開的頭? Who started this fight? (TW) (from) the beginning. /我~就不喜歡他. I never liked him from the beginning. /我從~就注意了. I was aware of it from the beginning. (N) beginning (as of a book). /那本書的~是我寫的. I wrote the beginning of that book.

開玩笑 **kāiwánsyàu** (VO) crack a joke, joke, kid. /他開了一個玩笑. He cracked a joke. /我不過是跟你開個玩笑, 別着急. Don't get excited, I was only kidding you.

開演 **kāiyǎn** (FV) begin (of a play, movie, etc.). /戲已經~了. The play has already begun.

開夜車 **kāiyèchē** (VO) work very hard studying late at night, cram all night (lit. drive the night train). /考試的時候, 那個學生開了兩三次的夜車. During examinations, that student crammed for two or three nights.

刊 **kān** (B) 1) issue, edition. 月~ monthly edition. 2) engrave, cut. ~字 engrave letters. 3) publish, print. 停~ stop publishing.

刊物 **kānwu** (N) periodical (M期**chī**,份**fèn**).

看 **kān** (FV) 1) look after, take care of. ~孩子 take care of a child. 2) watch, keep an eye on. ~門 guard

a gate. /~着點兒這個箱子, 別叫人拿走了. Keep an eye on this suitcase; don't let anyone make off with it. → 看**kàn**.

看護 **kānhù** (N) nurse (for sick people, not babies). (FV) take care of, nurse. /他病了, 沒有人~他. There's no one to take care of him when he's sick.

看守所 **kānshóuswǒ** (N) jail, prison (for detention before trial, not for imprisonment as punishment).

砍 **kǎn** (FV) 1) chop with a sharp instrument, cut down. /把那棵樹~倒. Chop that tree down. 2) throw something at something or someone. /他用石頭把狗~傷了. He threw a stone at the dog and wounded it.

坎 **kǎn** (B) 1) <ー子,ール> pit, hole. 2) threshold. 門~ threshold. t

坎肩兒 **kǎnjyār** (N) sleeveless upper garment, vest (M件**jyàn**).

坎兒 **kǎr** (N) 1) argot of thieves, tradesmen, etc. 2) ↑B (1).

看 **kàn** (FV) 1) look at, see, watch. ~打球 watch a ball game. /你~什麼呢? What are you looking at? 2) visit, see, a person. /我明天來~你. I'll come to see you tomorrow. 3) examine and treat, see (as a doctor). /大夫還沒給我~呢. The doctor hasn't seen me yet. 4) see a doctor. /你應該去~大夫. You ought to go and see a doctor. 5) be of the opinion, think that. /我~你不應該去. I don't think you should go. 6) read (silently).~報 read a newspaper. 7) depend on. /我們去不去就~你了. Whether we go or not depends on you. 8) see what happens. /你試試~. You try and see. 9) try to avoid. /快一點, ~晚了! Hurry up! Let's not be late! → 看**kān**.

看病 **kànbìng** (VO) 1) see a doctor. /明天我想去~去. I think I'll go and see a doctor tomorrow. 2) examine and treat, see (as a doctor). /張大夫, 您每天都~嗎? Dr. Chang, do you see patients every day?

看遍 **kànbyàn** (RC) 1) look everywhere, search thoroughly (in

/actual form only). /樓上我都~
了. I looked everywhere upstairs.
2) see all of something. /今天的
報紙我都~了. I've seen all of
today's newspapers.

看法 **kànfa** (N) way of looking
at something.

看見 **kànjyàn** (RC) see (with
the eyes). /我從這儿看不見
他. I can't see him from here.

糠康(SV)} **kāng** (N) chaff, bran, husk.
(SV) be dry and pulpy.

康 **kāng** (B) 1) peaceful. ~樂 be happy
and peaceful. 2) Sikang (contracted
form of 西~ **syīkāng**). s t → 糠(康)
kāng.

康健 **kāngjyàn** (SV) be healthy,
in good health.

扛 **káng** (FV) 1) carry on one's shoulder
or on the shoulders of two or more
men. /一個人~那麼大一個
箱子很累. One person carrying
such a big trunk will become exhausted. 2) shoulder, take on, a
responsibility. /我一個~不了
那麼多責任. I can't take on so
many responsibilities.

炕 **kàng** (N) brick platform for sleeping
which can be heated in winter, usually found in northern China (M 座
dzwò). (FV) dry, warm, something
over a fire. /把你的濕衣服
~-~. Dry your wet clothes over
the fire.

抗 **kàng** (B) resist, oppose. ~戰 fight
the enemy; ~命 disobey.

抗告 **kànggàu** (FV) contest a
court decision, appeal a court decision. /他不服法庭的判斷要
~. He didn't go along with the
court's decision, and is going to appeal.

kao see kau.

烤 **kǎu** (FV) 1) bake, roast. /蛋糕已
經~好了. The cake is baked.
2) broil, toast. /請你把這塊
麵包~-~. Would you please toast
this piece of bread? 3) dry, warm,
something over a fire. ~手 warm
one's hands; ~衣服 dry clothes.

考 **kǎu** (FV) 1) test someone. /我~
~你. Let me test you. 2) take
or have an exam. /我們明天~.

We have an exam. 3)
examine, investigate. /請你~一
~這個古錢是那年的. Please
examine this old coin and tell me
what year it is. (N) examination.
大~ final examination. t

考查 **kǎuchá** (FV) investigate.
~地下 survey the lay of the land;
~金鑛 prospect for gold. /他們
到歐洲去~各國的經濟狀況.
They went to Europe to investigate
the economic situation of each
country (there).

考古 **káugǔ** (FV) do archaeological work or research in archaeology.
/他現在正在埃及~呢. He is
doing archaeological work in Egypt
right now.

考卷 **kǎujywàn** (N) <-ㄦ> examination paper (M 張 **jāng,** 份 **fèn**).

考慮 **kǎulyu** (FV) consider,
think over. /讓我~~. Let me
think it over a bit. (N) consideration.

考試 **kǎushr̀** (VO) 1) take or
have an exam. /我昨天考了兩
堂試. I had two exams yesterday.
2) give an exam. /我明天給他
們~. I'm giving them an exam
tomorrow. (N) examination.

靠 **kàu** (FV) 1) lean on. /你別往樹
上~. Don't lean against the tree.
2) depend on, be dependent on.
/他~他兒子. He depends on
his son. 3) be located near or by.
/那個房子~着海邊. That
house is (located) near the beach.
(CV) <着> 1) relying on, depending on. /我~教書吃飯. I
rely on teaching for a living. 2)
leaning on or against. /他~牆
睡着了. He fell asleep leaning
against the wall. 3) along, next to.
/別~河邊騎脚踏車太危險.
Don't ride your bicycle along the
river; it's too dangerous. 4) veering
in a direction. /你~左邊走.
Veer to the left.

靠岸 **kàuàn** (VO) dock. /船已
經靠了岸了. The ship has
docked.

科 **kē** (B) 1) subject for study. ~目
list of subjects for study. 2) curriculum. 文~ liberal arts course. 3)
department. 人事~ personnel
department; 外~ surgery. 4) family

(biol.). 貓 ~ cat family.　t

科長 **kējǎng** (N) head of a department (governmental).

科學 **kēsywé** (N) science. (SV) be scientific. /他們的方法很 ~ . Their methods are very scientific.

磕 **kē** (FV) strike (against), knock. /他把頭~在桌上了. He struck his head on the table. /把煙斗~一~. Knock the ashes out of the pipe. → 磕 **kè**.

磕膝蓋 **kēsyigài** (N) <-ㄦ> front part of the knee, kneecap.

磕頭 **kētóu** (VO) kowtow. /那個老太太給一個佛像磕了好幾個頭. The old woman kowtowed several times to the statue of Buddha. (IE) Many thanks.

瞌 **kē** (B) sleepy.

瞌睡 **kēshwèi** (FV) doze. /他上課的時候老~. He is always dozing off in class. (N) drowsiness. /我~又來了. I'm getting drowsy again.

棵 **kē** (M) for trees, plants. 一~樹 a tree; 一~稻子 a rice plant.

棵儿 **kēr** (N) size of a plant. 大~的白菜 large-sized cabbage.

顆 **kē** (M) 1) for seeds, grain. 一~瓜子 a melon seed; 一~麥子 a grain of wheat. 2) for bullets. 一~子彈 a bullet. 3) for stars. 一~星星 a star. 4) for jewels. 一~紅寶石 a ruby.

咳 **ké** (FV) cough, cough up. /他~了一夜. He coughed all night. → 咳 **hài**.

咳嗽 **késou** (FV) cough. /他~了半夜. He coughed half the night. (N) cough.

殼(壳] **ké** (B) <-ㄦ> husk, shell. 蛋~ eggshell.

可 **kě** (A) 1) however, but. /他叫別人去,他~不去. He told other people to go, but he didn't go himself. 2) indeed, certainly. /你買這個就花五十塊錢,那~便宜. You only paid fifty dollars for this? That's certainly cheap. 3) when stressed, finally, at last. /他~來了. (**Tā 'kě lái le.**) He finally came. (CV) <着> within the

confines of, according to the size or capacity of. /他~屋子的大小織了一張地毯. He made a rug to fit this room. /你就~着這五十塊錢花吧. Don't spend any more than this five dollars. (AV) may, might, can. /這句話裏這個字~不~用? Can I use this word in this sentence? (B) 1) followed by FV, forms SV with a meaning similar to the English -able, -ible. ~佩 be admirable; ~耻 be shameful. 2) total, whole. ~村子的人 people of the whole village. 3) fit, suit. ~口 taste good to someone. (PT) 沒有什麼~...的 there isn't anything to .... /沒有什麼~說的. There isn't anything to talk about. → 不~ **bùkě**.

可愛 **kěài** (SV) be lovable. /他是一個很~的人. He's a lovable sort of person.

可不是 **kěbushr** (IE) That's right. or That's very true. /A:你們這件工作一個月完不了吧. B:~. A: You'll never be able to finish this work in a month. B: That's very true. (PT) ~...嗎 it really is ..., really did do something (as someone said.) /~他嗎! It really is he! /他~昨天死的嗎! He really did die yesterday!

可靠 **kěkàu** (SV) be reliable, dependable.

可憐 **kělyán** (FV) pity, feel sorry for. /我很~他. I really feel sorry for him. (SV) be pitiful, wretched, miserable. /他又窮又病真~. He's both poor and sick. It's really pitiful. /他太太抛下他以後,他很~. He was miserable after his wife left him.

可慮 **kělyu** (SV) be productive of worry, worrisome (of a situation or matter).

可能 **kěnéng** (SV) be possible. (N) possibility. (AV) may, might. /他~沒有錢. He may not have any money.

可能性 **kěnéngsying** (N) chance, possibility.

可怕 **kěpà** (SV) 1) be frightening. /那個電影很~. That was a very frightening movie. 2) be formidable, terrible. /看那個小

孩儿真～. It's terrible taking care of that child. /他是一個最～的競選對手. He is the most formidable of campaign opponents.

可身 **kèshēn** (VO) <-ㄦ> fit well (of clothes). /這件上衣正可他的身. This jacket really fits him well. (SV) <-ㄦ> be a good fit, fit well.

可是 **kěshr̀** (A) but, however. /我想去看電影,～没錢. I want to go to the movies, but I don't have any money. (PT) 雖然..., ～... even though . . . , . . . /雖然他有錢,～他不肯捐. Even though he's wealthy, he won't contribute.

可笑 **kěsyàu** (SV) be funny, humorous. 2) be ridiculous.

可惜 **kěsyī** (SV) be a shame, regrettable. /他没當選,真～. It was a shame he wasn't elected. (A) too bad, what a pity. /～你不能來. What a pity you can't come!

可惡 **kěwù** (SV) be detestable, hateful.

可以 **'kéyĭ, kéyi** (AV) may, can. /你～走了. You may go. (SV) 1) be terrific. /這個人真～. This fellow's really terrific. 2) be all right, OK. /他的中國話説得很～. He speaks Chinese pretty well.

渴 **kě** (SV) be thirsty. /我有一點～. I'm a little thirsty.

磕 **kè** (FV) crack something between one's teeth (lp). ～瓜子ㄦ crack melon seeds. →磕kè.

克 **kè** (M) gram. (B) conquer, overcome. ～復 recapture a fallen city. t

克服 **kèfú** (FV) overcome. /我們必須把這些困難～. We will have to overcome these difficulties.

客 **kè** (N) guest, visitor. (M) for orders of food (as in a restaurant). 一～炒麵 an order of fried noodles. (B) traveler.～棧 inn;～商 traveling merchant.

客氣 **kèchi** (SV) be polite, courteous. /他老是很～. He's always very polite.→不～ **búkèchi**, 别～ **byékèchi**.

客觀 **kègwān** (SV) be objective.

/他的態度很～. He has a very objective outlook. (AT) external. ～環境 external situation.

客廳 **kètīng** (N) living room (M間 **jyān**).

課 **kè** (N) 1) course (in school) (M門 **mén**). 2) class (in school) (M堂 **táng**). /我今天還有兩堂～. I still have two classes today. (M) lesson in a textbook. /這本書裡有十～. There are ten lessons in this book. (B) section (of an organization). 人事～ personnel section.

課本 **kèběn** (N) <-子,-ㄦ> textbook (M本 **běn**).

刻 **kè** (M) quarter of an hour. 一～鐘 a quarter of an hour; 三點一～ quarter after three. (FV) engrave, carve. ～圖章 engrave a chop or seal. (SV) 1) be mean and stingy. /對我别這麽～. Don't be so mean and stingy. 2) be sarcastic. /對我嘴别這麽～. Don't be sarcastic with me.

刻薄 **kèbwo** (SV) 1) be mean, sarcastic. /這個人很～. He's mean (he likes to say and do things that make people unhappy, to find fault). 2) be stingy, niggardly. /他待他的職員很～. He's very stingy with his employees.

肯 **kěn** (AV) be willing to, agree to. /你～幫我的忙嗎? Are you willing to help me? t

啃 **kěn** (FV) gnaw. /我的小狗在桌子底下～骨頭. My dog is under the table gnawing on a bone.

坑 **kēng** (N) <-子,-ㄦ> shallow hole, pit, in a flat, level surface. (FV) cheat, rook, someone (lp). /有人～他. Somebody rooked him.

kong see kung.

摳 **kōu** (SV) be stingy, tight. /他雖然有錢,可是他太太可～了. Even though he's rich, his wife is very stingy. (FV) 1) dig with the fingernail. ～鼻子 pick one's nose. /你别～牆上的紙. Don't dig the wallpaper with your fingernail. 2) carve. /他用一塊木頭～成一個獅子. He carved a lion out of a piece of wood.

摳門ㄦ **kōumér** (SV) be stingy (lp).

口 **kǒu** (M) 1) <-子,-ル> for members of a family. /他們家有四～人. There are four persons in his family. 2) bite (as of a mosquito, insect, dog). /那條狗咬了我一～. That dog took a bite out of me. 3) mouthful. 一～飯 a mouthful of food. 4) for certain objects that have a mouth-like opening. 一～鐘 a bell. 5) for languages one speaks fluently (used only with 一yī). /他說一～中國話. He speaks fluent Chinese. 6) for pigs. 一～猪 a pig. (B) 1) the mouth. ～腔 cavity of the mouth. 2) verbal, oral. ～信 verbal message. 3) entrance, opening. 港～ seaport; 門～ entrance. 4) pass in the Great Wall. ～外 Mongolia (lit. outside the Great Wall.)

口氣 **kǒuchì** (N) implication or tone of words. /看這封信的～好像他很不高興. It seems from the tone of this letter that he's very unhappy. /聽他說話的～, 你知道他心裏是什麼意思. You can tell how he feels from the way he talks.

口琴 **kǒuchín** (N) harmonica (M 隻把).

口輕 **kǒuchīng** (SV) not have much salt, be bland. /這個菜太～了. This dish is too bland (or doesn't have enough salt). /把這條魚做的～一點. Please use less salt in preparing this fish.

口袋 **kǒudài** (N) <-ル> 1) pocket. 2) bag, sack.

口子 **kǒudz** (N) tear, cut, hole, rip, wound, opening, in cloth, skin, the bank of a river, etc. (M) ˈ(M) 1).

口供 **kǒugung** (N) confession, deposition (of a crime). 招～ confess.

口號 **kǒuhàu** (N) (verbal) slogan. 喊～ shout slogans.

口重 **kǒujùng** (SV) have lots of salt, be salty. /我喜歡吃～的菜. I like salty food.

口ル **kǒur** = 口子 kǒudz.

口頭 **ˈkǒutóu** (A) orally, by word of mouth. ～交代 pass on or transmit by word of mouth. /我不給他請帖了, 我就～通知他算了. I won't send him an invitation, I'll just ask him in person. (AT) verbal, oral. ～請求 verbal request.

口味 **ˈkǒuwèi** (N) 1) taste (of food). /中國菜的～很好. Chinese food has a wonderful taste. 2) preference, taste. /這個菜不合他的～. This food doesn't suit his taste.

口勿 **kǒuwěn** (N) manner of speaking, tone of voice. /我聽他的～有一點儿奇怪. I noticed that his manner of speaking was a bit strange.

口音 **ˈkǒuyīn** (N) accent. 廣東～ Cantonese accent. /他說話帶一點儿南方～. He speaks with a bit of a southern accent.

扣(釦) (FV) 1) 2), (B)} **kòu** (FV) 1) button, buckle. /你的襯衫沒～好. Your shirt is unbuttoned. 2) fasten something which has a latch. /把大門～上. Latch the gate. 3) place cups, bowls, etc., upside down. /他把碗都～在桌子上了. He placed all the bowls upside down on the table. 4) cover something with an inverted cup, bowl, etc. /請你用碗把那塊蛋糕～上. Please cover that piece of cake with a bowl. 5) detain, arrest, hold, people or things. /警察把他～起來了. The police arrested him. 6) withhold, deduct, money. /我的老板從我薪水裡～了五塊錢. My boss deducted five dollars from my salary. 7) talk someone into doing something. /你別拿話～我. Don't try to talk me into it. (B) <-子,-ル> button, buckle. ～眼ル buttonhole. (M) tenth of the original price (indicates the amount a customer must pay). 七～ 7/10 of the original price (which is the amount to be paid for an item).

扣襻ル **kòupàr** (N) button loop (made of fabric).

扣ル **kòur** (N) ˈ1) (B). 2) knot. 打～ tie a knot.

哭 **kū** (FV) cry (about). /小孩儿又～了. The baby's crying again. /他～什麼呢? What is he crying about?

窟 **ˈkū** (B) hole, cave.

窟窿 **kūlung** (N) hole, cavity, cave. /賊在牆角儿挖了一個～. The thief dug a hole through the base of the wall.

苦 **kǔ** (SV) 1) be bitter to the taste. ～瓜 bitter melon. 2) be hard, difficult, miserable (of life or an experience). /他的環境很～. His situation is very difficult. (A) intensely, hard.～戰 fight hard. (B) 1) bitterly. ～笑 laugh bitterly. 2) <-子> bitterness, suffering. 吃～ suffer.

苦處 **'kǔchù** (N) hardship, suffering.

苦悶 **kǔmèn** (SV) be lonely, depressed. (N) boredom, depression.

褲(袴) **kù** (B) <-子> trousers, pants (M 條 **tyáu**). ～帶 (trousers) belt.

褲叉儿 **kùchǎr** (N) shorts, undershorts (M 條 **tyáu**).

kua *see* kwa.

kuai *see* kwai.

kuan *see* kwan.

kuang *see* kwang.

kui *see* kwei.

kun *see* kwun.

空 **kūng** (FV) 1) vacate. /房子～出來了. The house has been vacated. 2) leave a space empty, skip a line. /～一行再寫. Skip a line and then write. (AT) 1) empty, vacant, hollow. ～瓶子 empty bottle. /這棵樹是～的. This tree is hollow. 2) meaningless. ～話 meaningless words. (A) in vain. ～想 wish for in vain. (B) space, sky. 太～ outer space. →'空 **kùng**.

空氣 **kūngchì** (N) 1) air, atmosphere. /這儿的～很新鮮. The air here is very fresh. 2) atmosphere (pervading influence). /那天會場的～很緊張. That day the atmosphere of the meeting was very tense.

空前的 **kūngchyánde** (B) unprecedented. ～事件 unprecedented event.

空鐘 **kūngjung** (N) whistling top (toy).

空軍 **kūngjywūn** (N) 1) air force. 2) airman, air force officer.

空曠 **kūngkwàng** (SV) be open, sparsely populated, not crowded.

/紐約市雖然很擁擠,但是長島區就～得多了. New York City is very crowded, but Long Island is more sparsely populated.

空襲 **kūngsyí** (N) air raid (M 次 **tsż**). (FV) raid (by air). ～敵人的後方 raid behind enemy lines.

恐 **kǔng** (B) afraid, fearful. ～嚇 terrify.

恐慌 **kǔnghwāng** (SV) be in a panic. /他們～極了. They are in a great panic. (N) panic, crisis. 經濟～ financial crisis.

恐怕 **kǔngpà** (FV) be afraid that. /我～他不來. I'm afraid he won't come. (A) probably. /～要下雨. It's probably going to rain.

孔 **kǔng** (B) 1) small hole, opening. 鼻～ nostril. 2) Confucius (contracted form of 孔子 **kúngdž**). ～廟 Confucian temple. *s t*

孔子 **'kúngdž** (N) Confucius.

空 **kùng** (FV) 1) empty, vacate. /把這個瓶子～一～. Empty out this bottle. /這幢房子月底一定～出來. This house will be vacated for sure at the end of the month. 2) leave a space empty, skip a line. /把這個格儿～出來,別往裏寫字. Leave this square blank; don't write anything. 3) turn *or* hang something upside down. /把他往下～着. Turn him over. /那個練空中飛人的在空中～着. That trapeze artist is hanging upside down in mid-air. (SV) be only partially occupied, not crowded. /那個停車場很～. The parking lot isn't crowded at all. →空 **kūng**.

空場 **kùngchǎng** (N) <-儿> open space, vacant lot, square.

空子 **kùngdz** (N) empty space. 留一個～ leave a space.

空儿 **kùngr** (N) 1) empty space. /桌子跟桌子之間得留一點儿～. You must leave a little space between tables. 2) spare time. /你有～就來看我. When you have time, come and visit me.

控 **kùng** (B) 1) accuse. ～訴 sue. 2) control.

161

控告 **kùnggàu** (FV) accuse in court, sue someone. /他太太～他重婚. His wife accused him of bigamy.

控制 **kùngjr̀** (FV) control. /我～不了我的脾氣. I can't control my temper. (N) control.

kuo *see* **kwo**.

誇[夸] **kwā** (FV) praise, commend. /他老～他的兒子. He's always praising his son. (B) brag, boast. ～大 boast, exaggerate.

誇獎 **kwājyang** (FV) praise, flatter, a subordinate, younger person, one's student. /老師～他文章寫得好. The teacher praised him for writing such a good composition. (N) praise.

挎 **kwà** (FV) 1) carry in the crook of one's arm. /這個籃子壞了,我沒法儿～. The basket is broken; I can't carry it. 2) carry by a strap over the shoulder. /明天演習不用～鎗. You don't need to carry your rifles in tomorrow's drill. 3) hook arms. /我常看見他們～着胳臂. I often see them arm in arm.

筷 **kwài** (B) <-子> chopstick (M 根 **gēn**, 枝 **jr̄**; 雙 **shwāng**).

快 **kwài** (SV) 1) be fast, rapid, quick. ～車 express train. /他的腦子很～. He has a quick mind. 2) be sharp (of an edge). /這把刀不很～. This knife isn't sharp. (A) 1) quickly, fast. /～點走. Move more quickly. /你～上學吧! Hurry up and get to school! 2) soon. /他～五十歲了. He'll be fifty soon. /汽油～要完了. We'll run out of gas soon. (B) happy. 痛～ be content.

快板儿 **kwàibǎr** (N) fast-tempo singing in Chinese opera.

快活 **kwàihwo** (SV) be happy, in high spirits. (N) joy, happiness.

快樂 **kwàilè** (SV) be happy. (N) happiness. /他把他的～建築在別人的痛苦上. He built his happiness on other peoples' suffering.

快慢 **kwàimàn** (N) speed. /那個電門管～. That switch controls the speed.

會[会] **kwài** (B) ↓.→會 **hwèi**, 會 **hwěi**.

會計 **kwàijì** (N) 1) accounting. 2) accountant, bookkeeper.

塊[块] **kwài** (M) 1) <-儿> piece, hunk, of something. 一～麵包 a piece of bread; 一～石頭 a rock; 一～肉 a piece or hunk of meat; 一～布 a piece of cloth; 一～地 a piece of land; 一～手巾 a towel; 一～油 a spot of grease. 一～胰子 a cake of soap. 2) dollar. 五～五 five dollars and fifty cents.

塊儿 **kwàr** (N) size of objects which take 塊 **kwài** as a measure (see (M) 1) above). /他買的磚～很大. The size of bricks he bought was huge. (M) ↑ (M) 1). (B) 1) lump, hunk. 石頭～ a stone. 2) place. 那～ where; 這～ this place.

寬 **kwān** (SV) be wide, broad. /馬路很～. The streets are wide. 2) be lenient. /對他～一點儿. Be more lenient with him. (FV) 1) take off a jacket, overcoat, etc. /～～衣裳吧. Please take off your coat. 2) extend a time limit. /限期能不能再～幾天? Can the deadline be extended a few more days? (B) wide. 三尺長兩尺～ three feet long, and two feet wide.

寬大 **kwāndà** (SV) 1) be spacious. 2) be loose-fitting. 3) be lenient.

寬厚 **kwānhòu** (SV) be generous, kind.

寬容 **kwānrúng** (SV) be tolerant, big about things. (FV) tolerate someone despite his offenses. /我們不能～這種學生. We cannot tolerate this kind of student.

款 **kwǎn** (N) <-子> money, funds (M 筆 **bǐ**). (M) article in a treaty, contract, regulation, etc. 第三～ article three. (B) 1) <-儿> inscription. 題～ write an inscription. 2) entertain, treat well. ～待 entertain a guest.

筐 **kwāng** (M) basket. 一～橘子 a basket of oranges. (B) <-子,-儿> basket (differs from 籃子 **lándz** in that it is purely utilitarian, usually larger and without a handle). 土～ dirt basket.

狂 **kwáng** (SV) 1) be violent, furious. ～風 high wind. 2) be proud, conceited (of a person). (A) violently, madly. ～笑 laugh hysterically. /大風～吹了一夜. The wind blew violently all night. (B) mad, crazy. 發～ go crazy.

礦(鑛)[矿] **kwàng** (N) 1) mine. 煤～coal mine. 2) ore.
礦物 **kwàngwu** (N) mineral.

況[况] **kwàng** (B) 1) in addition, moreover. 何～ moreover, how much more can you expect of .... 2) situation, state. 近～ recent situation.
況且 **kwàngchyě** (A) moreover, what's more. /我不喜歡那個樣子,～顏色也太深. I don't like the style; what's more, the color is too dark.

框 **kwàng** (B) <－子,－ル> frame, casement, framework.門～ door frame; 窗戶～ window casement; 鏡～picture frame.

曠 **kwàng** (B) 1) open, broad. ～野 desert, wilderness; ～場 open area. 2) neglect. ～課 skip class.

虧(亏)[亏] **kwēi** (FV) 1) lack, be short of. /你還～多少錢? How much money do you still lack? 2) owe. /你還～他幾個月的房錢? How many months' rent do you still owe him? 3) disappoint, let someone down. /我絕不會～你的. I definitely won't let you down. (A) 1) fortunately, happily. /～你告訴我. Fortunately you told me. 2) that's something, that's great (sarcastic). /～你是美國人,連華盛頓是誰都不知道. That's something. You're an American and you don't even know who George Washington was. (B) deficiency, loss, suffer loss.
虧空 **kwēikung** (FV) 1) be so much in debt. /他～了六百塊錢. He's six hundred dollars in debt. 2) embezzle. /他～了很多公款. He embezzled a considerable amount of public funds. (N) 1) debt. 2) embezzlement.

擴 **kwò** (B) enlarge, expand. ～展 expand.

擴充 **kwòchūng** (FV) enlarge, expand, grow (as a business). /那個大學～成十個學院了. That university has grown so that it now has ten colleges.

擴大 **kwòdà** (FV) extend, enlarge, spread. /戰事已經～到邊境了. The war has spread to the border. /他的買賣～了很多. His business has expanded a lot.

擴張 **kwòjāng** (FV) extend, enlarge, spread. /他老想～他的勢力. He's always thinking of ways to extend his influence. /戰事～到邊境了. The war has spread to the border.

闊(濶)[阔] **kwò** (SV) be rich, wealthy. /不知道為什麼他忽然間～起來了. Nobody knows why he became so rich all of a sudden. (B) broad, wide. ～葉樹 broad-leaf tree.

細(捆)[捆] **kwǔn** (FV) tie, bind, things together with rope or string. /把他～上. Tie him up. (M) <－子,－ル> bundle. 一～破布 a bundle of rags.

囷 **kwùn** (FV) 1) trap, maroon. /我們～在那個島上了. We were marooned on that island. 2) besiege. /首都已經被敵人～了三個月了. The capital has been besieged by the enemy for three months. (B) distress. ～境 hardship. SF of 圍困 **kwùn**.
困難 **kwùnnàn** (N) difficulty. (SV) be difficult.

睏[囷] **kwùn** (SV) be sleepy. /我還不～呢. I'm still not sleepy.

啦 **la** (P) fusion of 了 le and 啊 a. /他早就來～! Why, he's been here a long time! →啦 **lā**.

啦 **lā** (B) ↓. →啦 **la**.
啦啦隊 **lālādwèi** (N) cheering section.

垃 **lā** (B) ↓.
垃圾 **lājī, lāsyī** (N) rubbish, garbage.

拉 **lā** (FV) 1) pull, drag. ～抽屜 open a drawer; ～手 shake hands. /這匹

馬會～車. This horse can pull a cart. 2) play a stringed instrument (with a bow). ～提琴 play a violin. 3) defecate. ～屎 defecate. (B) added to FV, indicates a brushing motion. 扒～ brush something out of the way *or* off of something. *t*

拉倒 **lādǎu** (RC) pull down. /他們用三匹馬把這棵大樹～了. They used three horses to pull down this huge tree. (IE) Forget about it. /我好意勸你不要和他來往，你不聽，就～. I tried to convince you not to have any contact with him, but you wouldn't listen. So forget about it.

拉賬 **lājàng** (VO) run into debt (lp). /他拉了很多賬. He's run up a lot of debts.

拉鍊儿 **lālyàr** (N) zipper (M 條 **tyáu**).

剌 **lá** (FV) 1) cut, slash. /他把他的手～了好幾個口子. He cut his hand in several places. 2) cross out. /把他的名字給～了. Cross his name out.

邋 **lá** (B) slovenly. ～雜 be disorderly, garbled (as one's thinking or speech). →邋**là**.

邋遢 **láta** (SV) be careless, sloppy, messy.

喇 **lá** (B) ↓.

喇叭 **lăba** (N) 1) trumpet, bugle. 2) loudspeaker.

喇嘛 **lǎma** (N) lama.

邋(落) **là** (FV) 1) leave something behind *or* out unintentionally. /他～了一個字. He left out a word. /什麼都買了，就是把胰子～了. I bought everything but soap. 2) outdistance. /他～了我一哩多地. He outdistanced me by more than a mile. →邋**lá**.

蠟(蜡) **là** (N) 1) wax. 2) candle (M 枝 **jī**, 根 **gēn**). 點～ light a candle.

臘(腊) **là** (B) 1) preserved, dried (of meat). ～腸 sausage. 2) twelfth month of the lunar calendar. ～八儿 eighth day of the twelfth month.

臘月 **làywè** (N) the twelfth month of the lunar calendar.

辣 **là** (SV) 1) be heavily seasoned, hot, peppery. 2) be cruel, harsh. /這

個手段很～. This measure is very harsh. (FV) burn (as one's mouth from heavily seasoned food). /辣椒～了我的舌頭了. The pepper burned my tongue.

辣椒 **làjyāu** (N) pepper (vegetable) (M 棵 **kē**).

來(来) **lái** (DV) 1) come (to). /請你～學校談談. Please come to the school and talk it over. /客～了. The guests have come. 2) used before FV or VO, come in order to do something. /他們～這儿念書. They come here to study. 3) bring something (here). /再～碗飯. Bring another bowl of rice. 4) have, take. /你～一點儿. Have some. 5) do. /我自己～吧. Let me do it. (RE) 1) indicates motion here. /他把錢拿～了. He brought the money (here). /他們把車開到這儿～了. They drove the car here. 2) used in potential RC only, indicates accomplishment in mastering something. 吃的～ can eat something (but don't like it); 說不～ can't say *or* tell *or* speak, can't get along with someone. (DC) indicates motion here. /把報紙帶上樓～. Bring the newspaper upstairs (here). (NU) about, around. 二十～個 about twenty; 兩丈～高 around twenty feet high; 三年～的 about three years. (B) 1) after a time expression in NU-M form, during the past…. 一年～ during the past year. 2) next. ～年 next year. 3) used after a clause and before a verb, in order to, to. /他把他的房子燒了～騙保險費. He burnt down his house in order to collect the insurance. 4) used after NU, in the first, second, etc., place. /一～我不喜歡它，二～我也沒錢. In the first place, I don't like it; in the second place, I don't have the money. (PT) 1) 到…～ come to a place. /他什麼時候到這儿～? When is he coming here? 2) ～…～ come in order to do something. /他們(～)看我們～了. They came to see us. 3) 去…～ go and bring something here. /我去拿點儿錢～. I'll go and bring back some money. 4) ～…

去 come and take something away. /他~拿了幾本書去. He came and took some books away. 5) ... ~ ... 去 back and forth, over and over. 走~走去 walk back and forth. /這封信,我看~看去還是不懂. I've read this letter over and over again, but still don't understand it.

來不及 **láibují** (RC) be too late to do something. /已經~坐六點鐘的火車了. It's too late to take the six o'clock train.

來得及 **láideji** (RC) have enough time to do something. /現在還~哪. There's still enough time.

來回 **láihwéi** (A) 1) back and forth. /我每天~跑好幾趟學校. I have to go back and forth to so many classes every day. 2) over and over. /他拿着情書~念. He read the love letter over and over. (N) <一ル> round trip. 打~ make a round trip.

來回來去的 **láihweiláichyùde** (A) 1) over and over. /那件事他老~說. He talks about that over and over again. 2) back and forth. /我~跑了好幾趟. I ran back and forth many times.

來着 **láije** (P) used at the end of affirmative sentences only, indicates that an action or state was going on in the past, but this is no longer the case. /我進來的時候,他在這ル站着~. When I came in, he was standing here (but he isn't any longer). /你説什麼~? What were you saying?

來來去去的 **'láiláichyùchyùde** (FV) walk back and forth *or* all around. 這辦公室老有人~,所以很難工作. There are always people walking around this office, so it's very difficult to work. (A) back and forth, all around. /小孩在院子裏~跑. The child is running around in the yard.

來歷 **láilì** (N) background, past history, of a person.

來頭 **láitou** (N) 1) connections, pull (of a person). /他~大的很. He has a lot of pull. 2) important family background.

來往 **láiwǎng** (N) contact. /我跟他没有~. I don't have any con-

tact with him. *or* He and I have nothing to do with each other. (FV) 1) commute. /他天天在新港跟紐約之間~. He commutes between New York and New Haven every day. 2) have social contact with someone. /你們~嗎? Do you have social contact with each other?

來源 **'láiywán** (N) source, place of origin. 稅收的~ source of revenue.

攔(挡) **lán** (FV) 1) stop, hold back. /他們兩個人打架你為什麼不~着點ル? Why don't you stop those two people from fighting so much? /別~着我,我一定得走. Don't stop me; I must go. 2) enclose something. /草地用木欄杆~起來了. The lawn has been enclosed by a wooden fence. 3) separate, cut off. /那兩棟房子中間~着一道牆. Those two houses are separated by a wall.

藍 **lán** (SV) be blue (in color). ~天 blue sky. (N) blue, blue color. 天~ sky blue.

藍圖 **lántú** (N) blueprint (M 張 **jāng**).

籃 **lán** (B) <一子, 一ル> basket (usually with a handle curved over the top). 花~ flower basket. 2) basket (a goal in basketball). 投~ shoot for a basket.

籃球 **lánchyóu** (N) 1) basketball (the game) (M 場 **chǎng**). 2) a basketball.

欄(栏) **lán** (M) column, section, of a newspaper. /那個新聞佔了兩~. That news takes up two columns. (B) 1) column, section (in a newspaper). 社會~ society section; 廣告~ classified ad section. 2) railing. 牛~ pen for cows.

欄杆 **'lángān** (N) <一ル> 1) low fence around something. 2) railing. (M 排 **pái**).

懶(嬾) **lǎn** (SV) be lazy. ~骨頭 lazybones.

懶的 **lǎnde** (AV) not feel like doing something. /我~跟他説話. I don't feel like talking with him.

懶惰 **lǎndwò** (SV) be lazy.

攬 **lǎn** (FV) 1) seize, monopolize. ~

權 seize power. 2) obtain, get, a contract. /他～了好幾筆生意. He obtained a lot of business contracts.

爛[烂]làn (SV) 1) be rotten (as fruit), infected (as a wound). /蘋果都～了. The apples are all rotten. /他手破的地方～了. The cut on his hand is infected. 2) be tender (from cooking). /肉才煮了一小時就～了. I only boiled the meat for an hour and it's tender. 3) be soggy. /玉米花都～了,因為我剛才把一杯水打翻在上面. The popcorn's all soggy because I spilled a glass of water on it. (RE) indicates breaking (d). 打～ smash to pieces. (B) glistening. 燦～ be brilliant (as sunlight).

狼 láng (N) wolf (M條tyáu, 隻jř).

廊[廊] láng (B) <-子> 1) corridor. corridor. 2) veranda, porch. (M 閒jyān, 條tyáu).

浪 làng (N) 1) <頭> wave (in water). 2) vibration, wave. 音～ sound wave. (SV) be sluttish (lp). (B) reckless. ～遊 roam from place to place.
　　浪費 'làngfèi (FV) waste time, money, energy. /他喝酒～了很多錢. He wasted lots of money drinking. /別～時間了. Don't waste time. (SV) be extravagant. /那位小姐太～了. That girl is too extravagant. (N) waste. /你這樣花錢是一種～. Spending money as you do is a waste.
　　浪漫 'làngmàn (SV) 1) be carefree, unconventional, Bohemian. 2) be flirtatious. 3) be romantic.

lao see lau.

撈[捞]lāu (FV) 1) drag for, fish for. /他們把那個屍首～上來了. They fished up that dead body. /你在水裡～什麼? What are you fishing for in the water? 2) get, make, money improperly. /他一分錢也沒～着. He didn't make a single penny.

勞[劳]láu (B) 1) tired. ～累 be tired. 2) to trouble. ～心 be troublesome. 3) toil, labor. ～作 task. s ǐ → 勞 lǎu.
　　勞步 láubù (IE) Thanks for coming to see us (said to guests as they leave).
　　勞動 láudùng (N) manual labor. (FV) cause someone trouble. /我不願意～你替我做飯. I don't want to cause you the trouble of cooking for me.
　　勞動節 láudùngjyé (N) Labor Day, May Day.
　　勞工 láugūng (N) workers, labor.
　　勞駕 láujyà (IE) 1) Excuse me. or Would you please . . . . /～,請問黃石公園還有多遠. Excuse me. Could you tell me how much farther it is to Yellowstone Park? /～您把我的大衣給我. Would you please get my coat? 2) I'm much obliged. or Thank you.

老 lǎu (SV) 1) be old, elderly. ～樹 old tree. /他的父親很～了. His father is very old. 2) be old (not new). ～朋友 old friend. /我買了一架～打字機. I bought an old typewriter. 3) be tough (of food). /這個牛肉太～. This beef is tough. 4) be well cooked, well done. /我喜歡吃～一點儿的牛排. I like steak quite well done. (A) 1) for a long time. /我～沒見他. I haven't seen him for a long time. 2) always . . . ing, . . . all the time. /他～跟我借錢. He is always borrowing money from me. 3) very. ～早 very early. (B) 1) dark (of a color). ～綠 dark green. 2) experienced. ～練 be an old hand at something. 3) used before the surname of a male servant. 4) used before the surname of a good friend or acquaintance. 5) used before NU in designating sons, daughters, brothers, or sisters. ～二 second son or daughter, second brother or sister. 6) Laotzu (contracted form of ～子 láudž). 孔～ Confucius and Laotzu.
　　老百姓 láubǎisyìng (N) 1) the people, common man. /這個政府有～做後盾. This government has the wholehearted support of the people. 2) civilian (as opposed to a military person).
　　老板 láubǎn (N) 1) owner of a store. 2) boss. (B) used after surnames of actors or actresses (h).
　　老大爺 lǎudàye (N) 1) old

gentleman. 2) Sir (direct address to an elderly man) (h).

老虎 làuhu (N) tiger (M 隻 jr̄).

老媽子 lǎumādz (N) maid, married female servant.

老年人 'lǎunyánrén (N) old man *or* woman.

老婆 làupwo (N) wife (not very polite).

老人 lǎurén (N) 1) elderly person. 2) mother and father (elderly). 3) former employee. 4) old hand (long-employed person).

老手 láushǒu (N) old hand at something. /他是廚房的～. He's an old hand at cooking.

老實 làushr (SV) 1) be honest. 2) be well-behaved. /你～點儿吧! You'd better behave! (A) honestly. /我跟你～說,我没錢. To tell you quite honestly, I don't have the money.

老師 làushr̄ (N) teacher, tutor (h).

老鼠 láushu (N) rat (M 隻 jr̄).

老鄉 làusyāng (N) 1) fellow townsman. 2) direct address used by a man to a stranger when asking for directions.

老太婆 lǎutàipwó (N) old woman.

老太太 láutàitai (N) 1) old woman. 2) mother (lp) (h).

老頭子 làutóudz = 老頭儿 lǎutóur.

老頭儿 làutóur (N) 1) old man. 2) the Old Man (referring to one's elderly husband or father) (lp).

老天爺 làutyānyé (N) god (in general parlance). /哎呀,我的～! Oh my god!

老鷹 làuyǐng (N) hawk, eagle, falcon (M 隻 jr̄).

老玉米 lǎuyùmi (N) corn, maize.

落 làu → 落 lwò.

勞[劳] làu (B) encourage, reward. ～軍 raise the morale of troops (by means of rewards, or entertainment). → 勞 láu.

烙 làu (FV) 1) iron clothes. /我有一大堆衣服要～. I have a huge pile of clothes to iron. 2) grill, cook, on a flat surface with a little grease, as pancakes. 3) burn. /強

盜拿炭火～他的手. The bandit burned his hand with a hot coal.

烙餅 làubǐng (N) thin, salty pancake. (VO) grill *or* make pancakes. /我們烙了十個人的餅. We made pancakes for ten people.

烙鐵 làutye (N) flatiron, iron (M 把 bǎ).

了 le (P) 1) indicates the completion of an action in the past or a stated time in the future. /他昨天死～. He died yesterday. /他買～票就進去～. He bought a ticket and went in. /他明天就走～. He'll leave tomorrow. 2) indicates that an action has started and is going on, or will start. /他畫～,可是還没畫完呢. He has started painting, but hasn't finished yet. /他們明天就蓋房子～,大概一年才能蓋好. They will start building tomorrow; it will probably take them a year to finish. 3) indicates a change to a new situation or condition. /孩子都大～. The children are all grown up. /他又想去～. He thinks he'll go now. /她是張太太～. She's Mrs. Chang now. /我的女孩儿今天兩歲～. My daughter is two years old today. 4) indicates an exclamation. /不得了～! Oh my gosh! /都三點～! It's already three o'clock! 5) indicates a conditional phrase. /明天暖～,也到不了六十度. Even if it's mild tomorrow, it'll never get up to sixty degrees. /這個東西丟～,你可得賠. If you lose this, you'll have to pay for it. 6) used after items which are enumerated. /像桌子～,椅子～,床～,他們都有. Tables, chairs, beds—they have them all. (PT) 不...～ not any more, no longer. /我不買～. I won't buy any more. *or* I no longer want to buy it. 7) used as a sentence completer at the end of a sentence in which 了 le appears after the main verb. /他吃～飯～. He has eaten. /他坐～三天車～. He has been riding for three days. → 了 lyǎu.

褚 lē (B) ↓.

褚襤 lēde, lēte (SV) be sloppy, untidy. /你看他穿的那個～勁

儿的. Look at the sloppy way he dresses.

樂[乐]lè (SV) be happy, pleased. (FV) laugh (lp). /那個笑話他還沒說完大家都～了. Everybody laughed before he had finished telling the joke. s → 樂ywè.

樂子 lèdz = 樂儿lèr.

樂觀lègwān (SV) be optimistic. /對那件事你～一點吧. Try to be a bit more optimistic about that.

樂儿 lèr (N) 1) fun. /我們出來是找～來了, 不是找麻煩來了. We're out to have some fun, not to find trouble. 2) disturbance, ruckus. /他喝醉了去上課, ～一定不小. He's on his way to class drunk; there's sure to be a ruckus.

雷 léi (N) thunder. (B) mine (explosive). 魚～torpedo; 地～land mine. s

累 léi (B) burdensome, bothersome. → 累léi, 累lèi.

累贅 léijwèi (N) burden. (SV) be burdensome, troublesome. (FV) be a burden to. /你放心我絕對不會～你的. Don't worry, I won't be a burden to you.

累 léi (B) accumulate, pile up. ～年～月 month after month and year after year. → 累léi, 累lèi.

累 lèi (SV) be tired. (FV) trouble, bother. /今天我又要～您了. I have to bother you again today. (B) 1) implicate, involve. 連～get someone involved, involvement. 2) hardship, tiredness. 受～endure hardship. → 累léi, 累lèi.

類[类]lèi (M) category, class, kind. /這一～樹不結果. This category of trees doesn't bear fruit. /這～小說我都不愛看. I don't enjoy reading this kind of novel. (B) category, class, kind. 人～human beings, mankind; 分～classify. 2) similar. 相～be similar.

類似 lèisz (SV) be similar. (FV) be similar to. /我工作的性質～你的. My work is similar to yours.

棱[稜]léng (B) <-子, -儿> corner, angular part of an object. 三～體 prism. t

冷 lěng (SV) 1) be cold (in temperature). /今天晚上要～. It'll be cold tonight. 2) be unfriendly, cold, indifferent. /你何必對他那麼～哪? Why are you so cold to him? 3) be rarely used or seen. ～字 rarely used character. (B) 1) lonely. ～巷 deserted lane. 2) sudden, unexpected. ～不防 suddenly, unexpectedly.

冷清 lěngching (SV) 1) be lonely. /他一個人住着很～. He's very lonely living all by himself. 2) be quiet. /這地方很～. It's very quiet here.

冷淡 'lěngdàn (SV) 1) be unfriendly, cold, indifferent. /他對我很～. He's very cold to me. 2) be slow (of business). /今天生意很～. Business is very slow today.

冷靜 'lěngjìng (SV) 1) be quiet. /這個地方很～. This place is very quiet. 2) be unemotional, calm. /請你～一點儿. Please calm down.

愣 lèng (SV) be blunt. /他很～. He has a very blunt manner. (FV) stare absent-mindedly. /一聽那個消息, 他～在那儿了. When he heard the news, he just stood there staring. (A) 1) without proof or basis. /他～說張家夫婦離婚了. He said without proof that the Changs were getting a divorce. 2) contrary to expectations. /他～會沒死. He was able to stay alive, contrary to expectations. 3) ignoring social customs, regulations, one's lack of ability. /公路上只許開六十哩, 他～開八十哩. He drives eighty miles an hour, ignoring the sixty-mile speed limit.

釐[厘]lí(M) 1) one thousandth of a foot, dollar, tael. 2) .1% rate of interest. 月利四～monthly interest rate of 0.4%.

犂[犁]lí (FV) plough. ～田 plough the fields. (N) <-頭> plough (M把bǎ).

梨[棃]lí (N) pear. s

離[离]lí (CV) from (in giving distances).

/學校～我家很遠. The school is a long way from home. (B) leave, be away from. ～家 leave home; ～不了 be unable to stay away from something (as liquor).

離奇 'líchí (SV) be strange, mysterious. /他的行為很～. His behavior is very strange.

離婚 líhwūn (VO) be divorced. /她已經離過三次婚了. She has been divorced three times.

離間 líjyàn (FV) cause a rift between, drive a wedge between, two friends, etc. /不要讓他～我們. Don't let him cause a rift between us.

離開 líkāi (RC) leave a place or person. /船已經～碼頭了. The ship has already left the pier. /那個小孩離不開他的母親. The child can't be separated from his mother.

離了 líle (CV) without. /我～你做不了事. I can't work without you.

籬[篱]lí (B) bamboo partition. 竹～ bamboo partition.

籬笆 líba (N) wooden fence (M 道 dàu).

哩 lǐ (M) mile.

李 lǐ (B) <-子> plum (M顆 kē). 桃～ peach and plum. s

李花 líhwā (N) <-ㄦ> plum blossom (M 朵 dwǒ, 枝 jr̄).

里 lǐ (M) Chinese mile (=⅓ of a mile). (B) lane, square (in place names). 平安～ Peace Lane. SF of 裏 lǐ.

理 lǐ (FV) 1) set in order, straighten up or out. /請你把房間～一～. Would you please straighten up this room? /牀還沒～好呢. The bed hasn't been made yet. 2) speak to, say hello to, someone. /他瞪着我,可是沒～我. He stared at me but didn't speak. 3) pay attention to. /別～那條狗. Don't pay any attention to that dog. (N) rational argument, logical reason. /你要是有～你就說吧! If you have any arguments, speak up. (B) natural science. ～工 science and engineering.

理髮 lǐfǎ, lǐfà (VO) 1) get a haircut. /我～去. I'm going to get a haircut. 2) give a haircut.

/我每月給他～一次. I give him a haircut once a month.

理髮館 lǐfàgwǎn (N) barber shop.

理髮員 lǐfàywán (N) barber (c).

理會 lǐhwèi (FV) pay attention to, take note of. /我沒～那件事情. I didn't pay any attention to that.

理智 'lǐjr̀ (SV) be rational. (N) reason, reasonableness /碰到嚴重事情的時候,他的～老控制不住感情. When confronted with a serious matter, his reason always gives way to emotion.

理科 lǐkē (N) science (as a field of study) (M門 mén).

理論 lǐlwùn (N) theory. (FV) dispute, argue. /我得跟他～. I have to argue this out with him.

理想 lǐsyǎng (SV) be ideal. /他找到一個～的伴侶. He found an ideal companion. (N) ideal.

理學士 lǐsywéshr̀ (N) bachelor of science. /他有一個～學位. He has a bachelor of science degree.

理由 lǐyóu (N) reason, cause. /你的～不充足. Your reasons aren't sufficient.

禮[礼]lǐ (N) 1) gift (M份 fèn). 送～ give someone a gift. (B) 1) courtesy, manners. 敬～ salute. 2) ceremony, rite. 婚～ wedding ceremony.

禮拜 lǐbài (N) 1) act of worshiping. 作～ worship, go to church. 2) week. 上～ last week; 這～ this week; 下～ next week. (TW) (on) Sunday. /明天又是～了. Tomorrow is Sunday again. /如果他明天不來,～一定會來的. If he doesn't come tomorrow, he will certainly come on Sunday. (B) weekday. ～一 Monday; ～六 Saturday.

禮服 lǐfú (N) formal or ceremonial attire (M 套 tàu, 件 jyàn).

禮節 'lǐjyé (N) etiquette, courtesy. /中國有許多～跟外國不同. Much of Chinese etiquette is different from that of other countries.

禮帽 lǐmàu (N) top hat (M 頂 dǐng).

禮貌 'lǐmàu (SV) be courteous. (N) politeness, manners.

禮堂 lǐtáng (N) auditorium (M 座 dzwò).

禮物 **lǐwu** (N) gift (M份 **fèn**, 件 **jyàn**).

鯉 **lǐ** (B) carp.

鯉魚 **lǐyú** (N) carp (M條 **tyáu**).

裡[裏][裡] **lǐ** (L) 1) inside. 向～走 go inside; 城～in the city; ～屋 inner room. 2) in, within, a period of time. 夜～at night. /五年～他作了很多事. He got a lot done in five years.

裡邊 **lǐbyan** (PW) <-ル> 1) inside. /～有很多人. There are a lot of people inside. 2) the inside of something. /這所房子～還沒有完工. The inside of this house isn't finished yet. 3) inner surface of something. /這個箱子～是紅的. The inner surface of this box is red.

裡子 **lǐdz** = 裡ル **lyěr** (N) 1).

裡面 **lǐmyan** = 裡邊 **lǐbyan**.

裡頭 **lǐtou** = 裡邊 **lǐbyan**.

裡ル **lyěr** (N) 1) lining (as of a coat). 2) wrong side of cloth that has a right and a wrong side. /這塊布的～沒花，面ル上有花. The wrong side of this cloth has no design on it; the right side does.

立 **lì** (FV) 1) stand. /他在那ル～了半天了. He has stood there for quite a while. 2) set or stand something up, erect. ～一座碑 erect a monument. /把傘～在門後頭. Stand the umbrella behind the door. 3) establish, found. /他們在那ル～了一個學校. They founded a school there. (B) immediately. ～日 on the same day. t

立場 **lìchǎng** (N) standpoint, point of view.

立方 **lìfāng** (N) cube (math.). ～尺 cubic foot; ～根 cube root. /二的～是八. The cube of two is eight.

立刻 **lìkè** (A) immediately, at once. /他看見警察～就跑了. He scrammed as soon as he saw the cop.

立時 **lìshŕ** (A) immediately, at once. /他～就走了. He left immediately.

粒 **lì** (M) <-ル> grain. 一～沙 a grain of sand.

粒ル **lyèr** (B) grain. 米～grain of rice; 麥～grain of wheat. (M) t.

力 **lì** (N) strength, power. 人～man-power; 水～water power. (B) vigorously. ～求進步 strive vigorously to make progress.

力氣 **lìchi** (N) strength, energy (physical). /他的～跟牛一樣大. He has the strength of an ox.

力量 **lìlyang** (N) strength, force, power. /那個黨沒什麼～. That party doesn't have much power.

栗 **lì** (B) <-子> chestnut. 板～chestnut (edible).

例 **lì** (N) <-子> example. (B) customary. ～規 regulation.

例如 **lìrú** (A) such as, for example. /有很多歐洲國家我都沒去過,～英國和法國. There are a number of European countries I haven't been to, such as England and France.

利 **lì** (N) 1) interest on money. 複～compound interest. 2) profit. 淨～net profit. 3) advantage. /他來對你有什麼～? What advantage will you get out of his coming here? (B) 1) sharp (of a blade or a point). ～器 sharp tool. 2) sharp, cutting (of speech). ～嘴 sharp tongue. 3) beneficial. ～於 be beneficial to. s t 不利 **búlì**.

利錢 **lìchyan** (N) interest on an investment. 出 (or給or付)～pay interest.

利害 **lìhai** (N) advantages and disadvantages, consequences. /他不知道～. He doesn't realize what the consequences will be.

利落 **lìlou** (SV) 1) be neat, proficient. /他做事很～. He's very proficient in his work. 2) be clear, distinct. /他說話很～. He speaks very distinctly.

利益 **lìyì** (N) advantage, benefit. /我這麼做是為了你的～. I did this for your own benefit.

利用 **lìyùng** (FV) 1) take advantage of. /你別～他的弱點. Don't take advantage of his weaknesses. 2) make use of. /想法把那些錢都～了. Try to make use of that money.

曆(曆)[历] **lì** (B) calendar. 陰～ lunar calendar.

歷(歷)[历] **lì** (B) pass through. ～來 hitherto, so far. →曆(曆) **lì**.
   歷史 **lìshř** (N) history.

痢 **lì** (B) dysentery, diarrhea. 白～ diarrhea.
   痢疾 **lìji** (N) dysentery.

厲[厉] **lì** (B) severe, harsh. 嚴～ be severe, stern; ～聲 harsh voice. *s*
   厲害 **lìhai** (SV) 1) be fierce, terrible (as a wild animal, or as one's temper). 2) be stern, strict, harsh. /我們老師很～. Our teacher is very strict. 3) be severe, intense (as sickness, or as heat or cold).

lia *see* **lya.**

lian *see* **lyan.**

liang *see* **lyang.**

liao *see* **lyau.**

lie *see* **lye.**

臨[临] **lín** (FV) 1) be (located) near a place. /他的房子～海. His house is near the ocean. 2) copy a painting or calligraphy. /他～那張畫～的很像. He copied that picture very accurately. (B) just before. ～走 just before leaving.
   臨時 **línshř** (A) temporarily. /我們～就用這個辦法吧. Let's use this method temporarily. (TW) (at) the time when something is due or is to happen. /你現在不預備,～怎麼辦呢? If you don't prepare now, what will you do when the time comes? /到了～,我們可以逃到墨西哥去. When the time comes, we can escape to Mexico. (AT) temporary. ～辦法 temporary solution.

淋 **lín, lwun*** (FV) 1) put liquid on something. /～點汽油在火上就燒得更猛了. The fire will burn faster if you pour gasoline on it. /草地太乾了,～一點兒水吧. The lawn is so dry. Why don't you water it? 2)* drench. /他的衣裳被雨～了. His clothes were drenched by the rain. → 淋 **lín.**

鄰[邻] **lín** (B) neighbor. ～國 neighboring country.

鄰居 **línjyu** (N) neighbor.

魚鱗 **lín** (N) scales of a fish (M 片 **pyàn**).

吝 **lín** (B) stingy. ～惜 be unwilling to sacrifice.
   吝嗇 **'línsè** (SV) be stingy, tight. /他～的連洋火都不給人. He's so stingy he won't even give anyone a match.

淋 **lín** (FV) strain, filter. /水裡有很多砂子,得用布～一～. This water has sand in it; you'd better filter it through a cloth. →淋 **lín.**

論 **lín** →論 **lwùn.**

零 **líng** (N) zero. ～下 below zero. (AT) fragmentary, single. ～錢 change (money). /我能不能買～張的信紙? Is it possible to buy single sheets of letter paper? (A) bit by bit, a little at a time. /他的日用錢他太太～給. His wife gives him daily spending money a little at a time. (B) 1) used between a series of NU-M$_2$ and. 一百～三個 one hundred and three; 兩塊～九分 two dollars and nine cents. 2) solitary. ～丁 lonely.
   零度 **língdù** (N) zero degrees. ～以上三十度 thirty degrees above zero.
   零件 **língjyàn** (N) <－ㄦ> 1) part (as to a machine). /這個機器上少了一個～. This motor has a part missing. 2) spare part, accessory. /這個價錢不包括～. This price doesn't include accessories.
   零售 **língshòu** (FV) sell by the piece. /這套家具不能～. We can't sell this set of furniture by the piece. (AT) retail. ～店 retail store.
   零食 **língshř** (N) things to nibble on, snack. /他喜歡吃～. He likes to nibble.

鈴 **líng** (N) <－ㄦ> small bell.
   鈴鐺 **língdang** (N) bell.

伶[伶] (B) 1)] **líng** (B) 1) clever, sprightly. ～便 be supple, limber. 2) actor (in Chinese opera). 女～ actress. 3) lonely. 孤苦～仃 be sad and lonely.
   伶俐 **línglì** (SV) be clever, smart, quick.

靈[灵]**líng** (SV) 1) be effective (of medicine). 2) be in good working order, work. /這個打字機不~了. This typewriter doesn't work well anymore. 3) be alert, keen. /這個孩子~極了. This is a very alert child. /他耳朵很~. His hearing is very good. 4) be satisfactory. /他辦事簡直的不~. His work is simply not satisfactory. (N) coffin (containing the deceased) (M口 kǒu). (B) soul, spirit. 魂~ soul.

靈便 **língbyan** (SV) be supple, limber, flexible. /他經過一次撞車,現在腿不大~. He was in a car accident, so his legs aren't very limber anymore.

靈分 **língfen** (SV) be skillful (lp).

靈活 **línghwó** (SV) 1) be supple, limber. /他雖然六十歲了,但是動作還很~. Even though he's sixty years old, he's still very limber. 2) be alert (as of a person's mind).

靈魂 **línghwún** (N) soul.

領 **líng** (FV) 1) lead, guide, show the way (physically). /誰~你們進來的? Who showed you in? 2) receive something issued or distributed. ~薪水 get paid. 3) adopt a child. /他去年~了一個小女孩. He adopted a little girl last year. 4) take care of children. /因為我找不着人替我~孩子,所以不能去. I can't go because I couldn't find anyone to take care of my children for me. (M) 1) for large mats. 一~蓆 a large mat. 2) ream of paper. 三~報紙 three reams of newsprint. (B) 1)<-子, -ル> collar (M條tyáu). 口ル neck of a dress. 2) have sovereignty over. ~海 territorial waters. 3) receive.~會 comprehend. 4)important element. 要~ important part.

領帶 **língdài** (N) necktie (M 條 tyáu, 根 gēn).

領導 **língdǎu** (FV) guide, direct. /沒人~我們. Nobody directs us. (N) guidance, leadership.

領教 **língjyàu** (FV) consult with someone. /關於這件事情我跟他~遍好幾次. I've consulted with him about this matter

several times. /我有點儿事跟您~~. I have something I'd like to ask you about.

領袖 **língsyòu** (N) leader.

領頭ル **língtóur** (VO) start something, set a pattern. /一個人~,大家也都跟着做了. One person started it, and everybody followed suit.

令 **líng** (M) ream of paper. 一~報紙 ream of newsprint. SF of 伶 líng. → 令 líng.

令 **líng** (FV) make, cause. /你這樣做事不是~人看不起你嗎? If you do things like this, won't you cause people to look down on you? (B) 1) your (precedes certain kinship terms when referring to a member of a friend's family) (h). ~兄 your older brother. 2) an order, command. 訓~ order or instructions from a high official. 3) season. 夏~ summer season. SF of 伶 líng. → 令 líng.

另 **ling** (A) 1) in addition to, besides. /你買一打,我就~送你半打. If you buy a dozen, you get a half dozen free in addition. 2) in place of. /我的房子燒了,我得~找房子. My house burned down, so I have to find another place to live. (SP) different, other (only before the NU yī). ~一件事 another matter.

另外 **lingwài** (A) 1) in addition to, besides. /我雖然有一個,可是我還想~買一個. Even though I already have one, I want to buy another one besides. 2) in place of. /我的車房塌了,我~蓋了一個. My garage collapsed, so I built another one in place of it. (SP) different, other. /~兩個人我不認識. I don't know the other two people. (B) different, other. ~的 extra one; ~那三個人 those other three people.

lîu see lyou.

long see lung.

嘍[娄]**lou** (P) fusion of 了 le and 嘔ou. /他們現在可都走~! But they are all leaving now! → 嘍lóu.

摟 **lōu** (FV) 1) gather up, rake up. /他把他贏的籌碼都~走了.

He raked up all the poker chips he had won. 2) take for oneself, rake in. /他在那椿政府生意上～了很多錢. He raked in a lot of money on that government deal. 3) pull a trigger. ～槍機 pull a trigger. 4) hold up, hike up (as a skirt). /別在客人面前把裙子～起來. Don't hike up your skirt in front of the guests. →摟 lǒu.

嘍[嘍] lóu (B) ↓. →嘍 lou.
　嘍囉 lóulwo (N) follower, subordinate (in a gang of bandits).

樓[楼] lóu (N) building (of two or more stories) (M 座 dzwò; 層 tséng). 上～ go upstairs; 下～ go downstairs. (B) floor, story. 二～ second floor. s
　樓房 'lóufáng (N) building of two or more stories (M 座 dzwò).
　樓梯 lóutí (N) stairs, stairway (M 層 tséng, 段 dwàn, 階 jyē). 一層～ a flight of stairs.

簍 lǒu (B) <-子, -ㄦ> deep basket. 竹～ bamboo basket.

摟[搂] lǒu (FV) embrace, hug. /他們把那小孩找回來以後, 他的母親～着他哭了. When they brought the child back, her mother cried and hugged her. →摟 lóu.

漏 lòu (FV) 1) leak. /那個鍋～了. That pot is leaking. 2) let information leak out. /你千萬不能把這個消息～出去. You absolutely must not let this news leak out. 3) leave out by mistake. /那個合同～了一段. There's a paragraph missing from that contract. (RE) 1) indicates disclosure of some secret. 她丈夫把她的年齡說～了. Her husband revealed her age. 2) indicates omission by mistake. /他抄～了三個字. When he made the copy, he left out three words by mistake. (B) <-子> funnel. ～斗 a funnel.

露 lòu →露 lù.

lü see lyu.

爐[鑪][炉] lú (B) <-子> stove, furnace. 電～ electric stove.

路 lù (N) road, route (M 條 tyáu). 公～ highway. (M) kind, sort. 這～貨 this kind of merchandise. (B) <-子>

method, way (M 條 tyáu). 生～ way to continue living. s
　路程 'lùchéng (N) journey, trip.
　路費 lùfei (N) traveling expenses.
　路過 lùgwò (FV) go past or through. /我～那個鋪子. I'll be going past that store. /我到美國來的時候從日本～. I went through Japan on my way to the United States.
　路線 lùsyàn (N) route, line (as of a railroad) (M 條 tyáu).

轆[櫨] lù (B) wheel, pulley.
　車鹿轆 lùlu (N) 1) windlass, winch. 2) pulley. 3) water wheel.

鹿 lù (N) deer (M 隻 jĭ). s

露 lù, lòu* (FV)* reveal, expose to view. /你的襯裙～出來了. Your slip is showing. (B) 1) dew. ～珠ㄦ dewdrop. 2) juice 果子～ fruit juice.
　露水 lùshwěi (N) dew.
　露天 lùtyān (AT) open air. ～電影 open-air movie. (A) outdoors, in the open air. /你着涼的時候不應該～睡覺. You shouldn't sleep outdoors when you have a cold.
　露營 lùyíng (VO) camp out. /我們在山裡頭露了三天營. We camped out in the mountains for three days.

陸[陆] lù (B) land. 大～ continent, mainland. s →六[陸] lyòu.
　陸軍 lùjyūn (N) army.

聾 lúng (SV) be deaf.
　聾子 lúngdz (N) deaf person.

隆 lúng (FV) start, light, a fire or stove. /我～不着這個火. I can't get this fire started. (B) abundant. 興～ be prosperous. t
　隆重 'lúngjùng (SV) 1) be formal (of a celebration, meeting, ceremony). 2) be impressive. /他們的結婚典禮很～. Their wedding was very impressive.
　隆隆 lúnglúng (ON) rumble, boom. /我聽見雷～地響. I heard thunder rumbling.

龍[龙] lúng (N) dragon (條 tyáu). (B) imperial. ～袍 imperial robe.
　龍頭 lúngtou (N) spigot, tap, faucet. 水～ water faucet.

籠 **lúng** (B)　1) <-子,-ㄦ> cage. 鳥～ birdcage.　2) steamer (for cooking). ～屜 steamer composed of several tiers.　3) envelop. ～罩 envelop. (M) for amounts of steamed food which can be contained by one layer of a steamer composed of several tiers. 一一～饅頭 a layer of steamed bread.
　　籠頭 **lúngtou** (N) bridle.

攏 **lǔng** (FV)　1) tie loosely together, gather together. /把所有的書都～在一塊. Gather all the books together.　2) comb. /叫我給你～一～你的頭髮. Let me comb your hair.
　　攏子 **lǔngdz** (N) comb (M把**bǎ**).
　　攏總 **lǔngdzǔng** (A) altogether. /買這麼多東西,～才花了五塊錢. It will cost five dollars altogether to buy this many things.

luan *see* lwan.

lüe *see* lywe.

lun *see* lwun.

luo *see* lwo.

亂[乱] **lwàn** (SV)　1) be disorderly, tangled. /線～了. The thread is tangled. /這間屋子很～. This room is a mess.　2) be confused, mixed up. /我心裡很～. I'm all mixed up.　3) be confusing. /這本書很～. This book is very confusing.　(A) aimlessly, disorderly. /他在牆上～寫. He scribbled on the wall. /他把衣服往箱子～放. He stuffed the clothes into a suitcase. (B) <-子> disorder, trouble. 叛～ rebellion.
　　亂七八糟 **lwànchibādzāu** (SV) 1) be helter-skelter, all in confusion. /他的屋子～. His room was all in confusion.　2) be indiscreet. /你這麼～可不行. It won't do for you to be so indiscreet.

囉[罗] **lwō** (B) ↓. →叫羅 **lwó**.
　　囉嗦 **lwōswo** (SV) 1) be talkative.　2) be bothersome.　3) be fussy. 4) be poky, dilatory, slow.　(FV) bother. /我要睡了,別～我. I want to sleep; don't bother me.

騾 **lwó** (B) <-子> mule (M頭**tóu**, 匹 **pǐ**). ～馬 mules and horses.

羅[罗] **lwó**(N)　1) silk gauze.　2) fine sifter for flour, sugar, etc.　(M) gross.　(FV) sift. ～麵 sift flour. (B)　1) netting. ～網 net for catching things.　2) arrange. ～列 set out in order. *s t*
　　羅盤 **lwópán** (N) compass (for determining direction) (M面**myàn**).

蘿 **lwó** (B) creeping plant, vine. 藤～ wistaria.
　　蘿葍 **lwóbwo** (N) Chinese white radish and similar edible roots.

鑼 **lwó** (N) gong (M面**myàn**).

螺 **lwó** (B)　1) snail. 田～ fresh-water snail; 響～ conch (animal or shell).　2) spiral. ～旋槳 propeller.
　　螺絲 **lwósz** (N) screw, bolt (M顆 **kē**).
　　螺絲釘 **lwószdīng** (N) <-ㄦ> screw, bolt (M顆 **kē**).

囉[罗] **lwó** (B) *see* 嘍 ～**lōulwó**. →囉 **lwó**.

駱 **lwò** (B) ↓. *s*
　　駱駝 **lwòtwo** (N) camel (M匹 **pǐ**).

落 **lwò, làu*** (FV)　1)* fall, drop. /花瓣～了一地. Flower petals fell all over the ground. /股票(的價錢)又～了. The price of stocks has dropped again.　2)* descend, come down (as a plane). /飛機～下來了. The plane landed.　3)* set (of the sun, moon). /現在八點鐘太陽才～呢. Now the sun doesn't set until eight o'clock.　4) recede (of the tide, a flood). /潮水又～了. The tide is out again. 5) be left (behind). /他們把我～的很遠. They left me far behind.　6)* be left with something not very valuable or desirable. /我唸了那麼多年書就～了一張文憑. After all those years I studied, all I have to show for it is a diploma. (B) settled *or* defined area. 村～ village.
　　落成 **lwòchéng** (FV) be completed (of construction). /金門大橋是那年～的? What year was the Golden Gate Bridge completed?
　　落後 **lwòhòu** (SV) be backward, behind the times. /他的思想很～. His thoughts are behind the times.　(FV) be behind, left behind (fig.). /他們的空軍比我們～

174

五年. Their air force is five years behind ours. (N) backwardness. 工業的~ industrial backwardness.

落花生 lwòhwāshēng (N) peanut.

落伍 lwòwǔ (FV) be behind, left behind (fig.). /我們的海軍比他們~了很多. Our navy is far behind theirs. (SV) be out of date. /他的思想很~. His way of thinking is very out of date.

摞 lwò (FV) pile up, stack. /把這些書~在一塊兒. Stack these books together. (M) <-ㄦ> pile, stack. 一~書 a pile of books.

淋 lwún →淋lín.

輪 lwún (M) cycle of twelve zodiacal years. (B) 1) <-子,-ㄦ> wheel. 三~車 pedicab. 2) steamship. 郵~ passenger steamship; ~渡 steam ferry. 3) rotate, revolve. ~班 take turns in doing something; 頭~電影 first-run movie.
輪船 lwúnchwán (N) steamship (M隻jr).
輪到 lwúndau (FV) be one's turn. /這回~我了. This time it's my turn.
輪流 lwúnlyóu (FV) take turns. /我們大家~,好不好? How about our taking turns? (A) taking turns, in rotation. /我們~到醫院去看他. We'll take turns going to the hospital to see him.

論 lwún (B) ㅓ. →論lwùn.
論語 lwúnyǔ (N) the Confucian Analects.

論 lwùn, lín* (CV)* by a certain unit of measure. /蘋果~磅賣. Apples are sold by the pound. /這個公司~鐘頭給錢. This company pays by the hour. (B) 1) theory, -ism. 唯物~ materialism. 2) discuss. ~文 dissertation, thesis, essay. (PT)以...而~ as far as ... is concerned, as for .... /以我而~,我就不買它. As for me, I wouldn't buy it. →論lwún, 不論 búlwùn, 無論 wúlwùn.

倆 lyǎ (N) two of something (a fusion of the NU 兩lyǎng and M個ge). /你給我~. Give me two. (AT) couple, several, some. ~錢兒 some money.

(B) two people. 哥兒倆 two brothers. 一个倆 lyǎng.

鐮[鐮] lyán (B) scythe, sickle.
鐮刀 lyándāu (N) scythe, sickle (M把bǎ).

連 lyán (FV) join, connect. /把這兩條電線~起來. Connect these two electric wires. (A) <-着> continously, in succession. /他~說了三個鐘頭. He spoke continously for three hours. (CV) including. /~你一共十個人. There are ten people, including you. (N) company, battery (m). (PT) 1) ~...帶.... (both)...and..../~房錢帶飯錢一共多少? How much will rent and food be altogether? 2)~...也(or都or還)...even..../~他都會說中文. Even he can speak Chinese.
連長 lyánjǎng (N) company commander.
連忙 lyánmáng (A) hastily, in a hurry. /他看見老虎來了,~往樹上爬. When he saw the tiger coming, he climbed the tree in a hurry.
連矇帶虎的 lyán'mēngdài'hǔde (A) under false pretenses, by guile. /他~就把她帶走了. He enticed her away under false pretenses.

簾[帘][帘] lyán (B) <-子,-ㄦ> 1) hanging screen. 竹~ bamboo screen. 2) curtain, drape. 窗~ window curtain.

聯[联] lyán (B) 1) unite, join, associate. ~盟 ally. 2) <-ㄦ> couplet. 對~ pair of matching scrolls forming a couplet.
聯合 lyánhé (FV) join together, unite. /大家應該~起來. Everybody should unite. (AT) united, allied, joint. ~公報 joint communiqué.
聯合國 lyánhégwó (N) the United Nations.
聯襟 lyánjīn (N) brother-in-law (wife's sister's husband).
聯絡 lyánlwo (FV) start or keep up personal relations. ~友情 start or keep up a friendship. /多多~ Let's get in touch more often. (N) contact (between people). 失掉~ lose contact.

斂 lyǎn→斂lyàn.

臉 lyǎn (N) 1)<-ㄦ> face (lit. or fig.).
丟～ lose face. /他天天不洗
～. He never washes his face. 2)
front part of something, facade.門
～ facade of a building.
　　臉蛋ㄦ lyǎndàr (N) cheek.
　　臉盆 lyǎnpén (N) wash basin.
　　臉色 lyǎnsè (N) 1) facial expression. 看人的～ speak while
watching another's facial expressions.
2) color (of the face). /他的～不
好. His color isn't very good.

練(練]lyàn (FV) 1) drill, train.～兵
drill soldiers. 2) practice。～琴
practice the piano. /我已經～了
三年了,可是還不會做飯. I've
been practicing for three years, but
I still don't know how to cook. (B)
skilled.～達 be versed in, experienced.
　　練習 lyànsyí (FV) practice.～
說中國話 practice speaking
Chinese. (N) exercise (in a book).
作法文～ do an exercise in
French.
　　練習本 lyànsyíběn (N) <-ㄦ>
exercise book.

戀(恋]lyàn (B) 1) feel attached to.～家
feel attached to one's home. 2)
love, be fond of.～酒 be fond of
wine; 失～ be disappointed in love.
　　戀愛 lyànài (N) love affair.
(FV) be in love. /他們兩個人
在～呢. They are falling in love.

斂 lyàn, lyǎn (FV) collect, gather.～
錢 hoard money.

鍊(鏈]lyàn (B) <-子,-ㄦ> chain (M條
tyáu,根gēn). 表～ watch chain.
→煉(錬]lyàn.

煉(錬(FV) 1)](煉]lyàn (FV) 1) refine,
purify.～銀子 refine silver. 2)
boil down.～豬油 boil down fat to
get lard.

量 lyáng (FV) measure. /～一～這
塊布看看有多長. Measure this
piece of cloth and see how long it is.
(B) weigh, consider carefully. 推～
guess. →量 lyàng.
　　量杯 lyángbēi (N) measuring
cup.

涼 lyáng (SV) be cool, cold. /天氣忽
然～了. The weather has suddenly
gotten cold.

涼快 lyángkwai (SV) be pleasantly cool. (FV) cool off, get cool.
/我們到樹底下～～去. Let's
go cool off under the trees.
　　涼臺 lyángtái (N) porch, veranda, balcony (outside a house in
the open air).

糧(粮]lyáng (B) 1) grain.～商 grain
merchant. 2) provisions, food.兵
～ soldier's rations.
　　糧食 lyángshr (N) provisions,
food.

良 lyáng (B) good, virtuous.～民 good
citizen.
　　良心 'lyángsyīn (N) conscience.

梁(樑(N)} lyáng (N) horizontal beam
(of a building). (B) 1) bridge. 石～
stone bridge. 2)<-子,-ㄦ> handle
on the top of a teapot, bucket, etc.
桶～ㄦ handle of a bucket. 3)
ridge. 山～ mountain ridge. d s

倆 lyàng (B) clever. 伎～ cleverness.
→倆 lyǎ.

兩(两]lyàng (NU) 1) two (used before
most M rather than 二 èr).～塊錢
two dollars. 2) a few, a couple.
/我過～天再來. I'll come again
in a couple of days. (M) tael. 一～
金子 a tael of gold. (B) both sides.
～利 be profitable to both sides.
　　兩口子 lyángkǒudz (N) hus-
band and wife.

亮 lyàng (SV) 1) be bright. /那個電
燈照得很～. That electric
light is very bright. 2) be light (of
the sky). /天還～着呢. It's
still light (in the evening). 3) be enlightened. /你這一說,我心裡
頭～了. I was enlightened by what
you said. (FV) reveal, show someone something.～刀 pull out a knife.
/你真有本事就～幾手ㄦ. If
you are really good at this, show us.
　　亮ㄦ lyàngr (N) light. /拿一
個～來. Bring a light.

輛 lyàng (M) for vehicles
車 a bicycle; 兩～火車 two railroad cars.

諒 lyàng (FV) suppose, guess. /～他
不敢去. I guess he doesn't dare
go. (B) 1) forgive.原～ pardon,
excuse. 2) sympathize. 骨豐～ make
allowances for.

諒解 '**lyàngjyě** (FV) forgive. /他還不～我. He still won't forgive me. (N) 1) forgiveness. /雖然過了這麼多年,我還得不到我太太的～. Even though so many years have gone by, I still can't obtain my wife's forgiveness. 2) understanding. /英國做那件事得到俄國的～. England is doing that with the understanding of Russia.

晾 **lyàng** (FV) 1) hang up to dry. /她把衣裳～在那兒呢? Where did she hang up the clothes? 2) let something cool. /把那個湯～一～. Let the soup cool off a bit.

量 **lyàng** (N) 1) quantity. /這是一個～的問題. This is a problem of quantity. 2) magnanimity, tolerance. /他的～很大. He has a great deal of tolerance. (B) 1) volume, capacity 酒～ capacity for drinking wine. 2) weigh, estimate. ～力 estimate one's own ability or strength. → 量 **lyáng**.

聊 **lyáu** (FV) chat, gab. /你們在～什麼? What are you folks gabbing about?

了{暸(B)} **lyáu** (FV) finish, conclude. /我昨天替朋友～了一件事. I finished up something for a friend of mine yesterday. (RE) in potential RC only, indicates finishing, concluding successfully. 吃的～can finish (eating); 看不～can't finish (reading). (B) clear. 明～understand clearly. → 了 **le**.

了不起 **lyáubuchǐ** (SV) be unusual, extraordinary. /我看他也沒有什麼～. I don't see anything extraordinary about him.

了不得 **lyáubude** (SV) 1) be extreme in manner or action. /他急的～. He's extremely worried. 2) be wonderful, terrific. /他真～. He's really terrific.

了解 **lyáujyě** (FV) comprehend, understand. /我完全～你. I understand you perfectly. (N) understanding, comprehension. /我對物理學的～很差. My understanding of physics is very limited.

暸[?]**lyàu** (B) look off into the distance. ～望台 lookout tower. → 了{暸} **lyàu**.

料 **lyàu** (FV) suppose, guess. /我～他不能來. I guess he can't come. (AT) imitation, glass (of jewels, jewelry). /這個鐲子是～的. This bracelet is glass. (N) <一ㄦ> oaf, clod, schlemiel. /憑他那塊～也想當教授. Even an oaf like him thinks he can be a professor. (B) 1) raw material. 木～ lumber. 2) fodder. 草～ fodder. 3) opium. ～膏 opium (in paste form).

料子 **lyàudz** (N) material (for clothing) (M塊**kwài**).

料理 **lyàulǐ** (FV) straighten out, manage, arrange, matters, a wedding, funeral, meeting, banquet. ～喪事 make arrangements for a funeral. /那件事情由誰～? Who's going to take care of that matter?

咧 **lyē** (B) ㆍ→咧**lyē**, 不咧**bùlye**. 咧咧 **lyēlye** (FV) cry, wail. /那個小孩兒老～. That child is always crying.

咧 **lyě** (B) grimace. ～嘴 draw back the corners of the mouth →咧**lyě**.

裂 **lyè** (FV) crack, split. /那個牆～了一道縫兒. That wall has cracked. (RE) indicates cracking, splitting. /盒子掉在地下摔～了. That box fell on the ground and cracked open.

列 **lyè** (FV) list, arrange in order. /請你把他們的名字～在一張紙上. Please list all of their names on a piece of paper. (M) for trains. ～火車 a train. (B) 1) series, row. ～車 train. 2) all, each one. ～位 all of you. t

烈 **lyè** (B) 1) intense, ardent. ～火 fierce fire; 熱～ be ardent. 2) martyred. 壯～ be valiant.

烈士 '**lyèshr** (N) martyred patriot.

溜 **lyōu** (FV) 1) glide, slide down, coast. /車從山上～下來了. The car coasted down the hill. 2) sneak away. /他沒給錢就～了. He sneaked away without paying. 3) watch, keep an eye on. /你～着他一點,留神他偷東西. Keep an eye on him and see that he doesn't steal anything. 4) sauté in oil, adding cornstarch. ～魚片 sauté

slices of fish, sautéed fish slices.
(B) smooth, glossy. 順 ～ be smooth
and straight. →溜 lyòu.

遛 lyōu (B) walk, stroll. →溜{遛} lyòu.
遛達 lyōuda (FV) go for a
walk. /你上那儿～? Where did
you go for a walk?

留 lyóu (FV) 1) stay. /他在紐約～
了兩天. He stayed in New York
for two days. 2) ask someone to
stay. /我要～他吃飯. I want
to ask him to stay for dinner. 3)
accept, take. /我們的鄰居想把
五個小貓都給我們, 可是我
們就～了一個. Our neighbor
wanted to give us all of their five
kittens, but we only took one. 4) reserve, save. ～座 save a seat. /給
我～一點儿飯. Save some food
for me. 5) leave behind. ～條儿
leave a note.
留神 lyóushén = 留心 lyóusyīn.
留聲機 lyóushēngjī (N) record
player.
留聲片 lyóushēngpyàn (N)
phonograph record.
留心 lyóusyīn (SV) be careful.
/他開車的時候非常～. He is
very careful when he's driving. (A)
carefully, closely. /請你～看
門. Please watch the door closely.
(VO) take care, be careful. /請你
～點儿. Take care or please
be careful. (FV) pay attention to,
watch closely. /他很～股票的
行市. He watches the stock market very closely.

流 lyóu (FV) flow (of liquids). /這條
河向北～. This river flows in a
northerly direction. (M) class (of
people). 第一～作家 a first-class
writer. (B) 1) stray, random. ～
彈 stray bullet. 2) prevalent. ～
弊 prevalent defect. 3) current. 急
～ swift current.
流動 lyóudùng (FV) 1) flow,
circulate. /你可以聽見水在管
子裡～. You can hear the water
flowing through the pipe. 2) move in
air or a liquid. /冰在河裡～很
快. The ice is moving down the
river very fast. (N) mobility. 人口
的～ population mobility.
流露 lyóulù (FV) show, reveal,
one's feelings. /她不容易～感

情. She doesn't show her emotions
easily.
流行 lyóusyíng (SV) be prevalent, popular. /這個歌很～.
This song is very popular. (FV)
become prevalent, spread. /現在
～一種很奇怪的病. There's
a very strange disease spreading
around just now.

硫 lyóu (B) sulphur. ～酸 sulphuric
acid.
硫磺 lyóuhwáng (N) sulphur.

瘤 lyóu (B) <-子> tumor. 毒～cancer.

柳 lyŏu (B) willow tree. 垂～weeping
willow. s t
柳樹 lyŏushù (N) willow tree
(M棵kē).

溜{遛(FV)} lyòu (FV) 1) walk an animal. ～狗 walk a dog. 2) go for a
walk. /我想出去～一～. I
think I'll go out for a walk. (M)
<-儿> line, column, row. 一～松
樹 a row of pines. (N) current (of
a stream). →溜 lyōu.
溜儿 lyòur (N) current trend.
隨～ follow the trend. (M) 1) ↑.
2) area. 這一～ this area.

六{陸} lyòu (NU) six. (B) sixth. ～樓
sixth floor.
六月 'lyòuywè (TW) 1) (in)
June. 2) the sixth month of the lunar
calendar.

馬盧 lyú (N) <-子,-儿> donkey (M頭tóu,
隻jī, 條tyáu, 匹pǐ).

鋁 lyŭ (N) aluminum.

屢{屢} lyŭ (B) repeatedly. ～戰～敗
repeatedly fight and be defeated.
屢次 lyŭtsz (A) repeatedly,
time and again. /我～告訴你你
老是不聽. I've told you time and
again, but you never listen.

旅 lyŭ (N) brigade (m). (B) 1) travel.
～客 traveler. 2) troops. 勁～ strong
military force.
旅館 lyŭgwǎn (N) hotel, inn.
旅長 lyŭjǎng (N) commander of
a brigade.
旅社 lyŭshè (N) hotel, inn.
旅行 lyŭsyíng (FV) take a trip,
travel. /今年夏天我們要去歐
洲～. This summer we're going
to take a trip to Europe. (N) traveling.

縷 **lyǔ** (M) 1) curl of smoke (as from a chimney). 一~烟 a curl of smoke. 2) strand of thread. 一~絲 a strand of silk; 一~線 a strand of thread. (FV) tidy up, straighten out (lp). /我把箱子都~好了. I've straightened out everything in the suitcase. (B) in detail. ~述 state in detail.

履 **lyǔ** (B) carry out. ~約 carry out a contract.
　　履歷 **lyǔlì** (N) record of attainments and qualifications (M張 **jāng**).

綠 **lyù** (SV) be green. (N) green, green color. 草~ grass green.
　　綠豆 **lyùdòu** (N) green lentils.

略 **lywè** (FV) omit. /我把那段給~去了. I omitted that paragraph. (B) 1) simple, rough. 簡~ be simple. 2) outline, sketch. 大~ in outline, roughly. 3) plan, strategy. 戰~ military strategy. *t*

嗎 **ma** (P) 1) used at the end of a sentence on a higher pitch than the beginning of the sentence, indicates that the sentence is a question. /這個是你的~? Is this yours? 2) used to mark a pause after a suppositional clause or a noun. /下雨~, 我就不去了. If it rains, I won't go. /我~, 還是不去好. As for me, I'd better not go. → 嗎 **ma**.

麼 **ma** (P) 1) used at the end of a sentence on a higher pitch than the beginning of the sentence, indicates that the sentence is a question. /你好~? How are you? 2) used at the end of a sentence on a lower pitch than the beginning of the sentence indicates that what precedes it is an obvious fact. /這個是我的~, 當然我可以拿走. This is mine; of course I can take it. 3) used to mark a pause after a suppositional clause or a noun. /戲不好, 觀眾~, 還不少. The show isn't any good; as for the audience it's still pretty large. /你要去~, 我也去. If you go, I'll go. (B) added to 多 **dwó**, 甚 **shén**, 那 **nà**, 這 **jè**, 怎 **dzěn**. 甚~ what; 那~ thus, then, hence.

媽 **mā** (N) ma, mamma (B) 1) woman servant, nurse. 老~子 married woman servant; 奶~ wet nurse. 2) used after surnames of married women servants in polite direct address.
　　媽媽 **māma** (N) 1) mamma. 2) used in direct address to an elderly woman.

螞 **mā** (B) ↑. →螞 **mǎ**, 螞 **mà**.
　　螞蜋 **mālang** (N) dragonfly (M隻 **jī**) (lp).

摩 **mā** (B) ↑. *t* →摩 **mwó**.
　　摩挲 **māsa** (FV) smooth out with the hand something that is wrinkled. /把枕頭套~平了再把枕頭裝進去. Smooth out the pillowcase before you put it on the pillow.

麻{麻(N), 麻(SV), (B)} **má** (N) hemp. ~布 linen. (SV) be numb. /坐的太久了, 我的腿都~了. I sat there so long my legs became numb. (B) <-子> pockmark. ~皮 pockmarked person.
　　麻痺 **mábì** (N) paralysis. 小兒~ poliomyelitis.
　　麻雀 **máchyè** (N) 1) house sparrow (M隻 **jī**). 2) mahjong (M場 **chǎng**). 搖~ play mahjong.
　　麻袋 **mádài** (N) burlap bag.
　　麻子 **mádz** (N) 1) ↑. 2) pockmarked person.
　　麻煩 **máfan** (SV) be troublesome, annoying. (FV) cause someone trouble, bother, disturb. /你別~我. Don't bother me. (N) trouble.
　　麻繩 **máshéng** (N) <-ㄦ> rope (made of hemp) (M根 **gēn**, 條 **tyáu**).
　　麻藥 **máyàu** (N) anaesthetic.

螞 **mǎ** (B) ↑. →螞 **mā**, 螞 **mà**.
　　螞蜂 **mǎfēng** (N) wasp (M隻 **jī**).
　　螞蟥 **mǎhwáng** (N) leech (M條 **tyáu**).
　　螞蟻 **mǎyǐ** (N) ant (M隻 **jī**).

嗎 **mǎ** (B) ↑. *t* →嗎 **ma**.
　　嗎啡 **mǎfēi** (N) morphine.

碼 **mǎ** (FV) pile up neatly on top of one another. /把這些磚都~起來. Pile up those bricks. (M) yard. 兩~料子 two yards of material. (B) counter, marker. 籌~ poker chip; 砝~ weight (metal piece on a scale).
　　碼子 **mǎdz** (N) 1) number,

figure. 2) liquid assets. 3) bridge (as on a violin). 4) poker chip.

石馬頭 **mǎtou** (N) 1) wharf, pier, dock. 2) territory, area, in which one performs or practices, as an entertainer or doctor.

馬[马]**mǎ** (N) 1) horse (M 匹 **pǐ**). 2) horse (in chess, comparable to a knight). *t s*

馬車 **mǎchē** (N) carriage.
馬達 **mǎdá** (N) motor.
馬子 **mǎdz** (N) commode (for a chamber pot).
馬虎 **mǎhu** (SV) be casual, easygoing, careless. /他做事很 ～. He's very casual about his work.
馬克思主義 **mǎkèszjǔyì** (N) Marxism.
馬克思列寧主義 **mǎkè'szlyè'níngjǔyì** (N) Marxism-Leninism.
馬力 **mǎlì** (N) horsepower (M 匹 **pǐ**).
馬鈴薯 **mǎlíngshǔ** (N) potato.
馬路 **mǎlù** (N) avenue (M 條 **tyáu**).
馬趴 **mǎpā** (N) fall (on one's face) (lp). /他蹲了一個 ～. He fell flat on his face.
馬上 **mǎshàng** (A) immediately, at once. /我 ～ 來. I'll come immediately.

螞 **mà** (B) ↓. →螞**mā**, 螞**mǎ**.
螞蚱 **màja** (N) grasshopper.

罵[骂]**mà** (FV) 1) call someone names, curse. /你憑什麼 ～ 我? Why are you calling me names? 2) scold. /他父親 ～ 了他一頓. His father gave him a good scolding. 3) run down, tear apart, criticize. /他時常～市政府. He often runs down the city government.
罵街 **màjyē** (VO) cuss, swear. /他一急了就 ～. He swears when he gets mad.

埋 **mái** (FV) bury. /他把兇器 ～ 了. He buried the murder weapon. (B) lie in wait. ～ 伏 an ambush, to ambush. →埋**mán**.
埋葬 **máidzàng** (FV) bury a person. /他們把羅斯福總統 ～ 在海德公園. President Roosevelt was buried in Hyde Park. /我們將要～你們. We will bury you.

埋没 **'máimwò** (FV) suppress one's real ability, waste talent. /你做那樁事不是把你的才幹都 ～ 了嗎? Aren't you wasting your talent doing that kind of work?
埋怨 **máiywàn** (FV) hold someone responsible, blame. /她結不了婚,她老 ～ 她母親. She always blames her mother for her not being able to get married.

買[买]**mǎi** (FV) 1) buy. /這本書很值得 ～. This book is really worth buying. 2) buy off someone. /他把那個警察 ～ 了. He bought off that cop.
買賣 **mǎimai** (N) 1) business, trade. 作 ～ be in business, do business. 2) business establishment (M 家 **jyā**).

賣[卖]**mài** (FV) 1) sell. /這個東西 ～ 多少錢? What does this thing sell for? 2) sell out, betray. /他把我們都 ～ 了. He betrayed all of us. 3) show off. /你那兩下子不必 ～ 了. Don't show off those abilities of yours.
賣力氣 **màilìchi** (VO) expend effort, work hard. /你做事得多賣點儿力氣. You have to work a little harder. (SV) be industrious.
賣命 **màimìng** (VO) work like a slave. /你為什麼給他 ～ 呢? Why should you work like a slave for him? (SV) be very hard-working.
賣藝 **màiyì** (VO) make a living by entertaining people on the street, particularly by acrobatics, magic tricks, and the like. /在戲院子裡唱戲跟在街口 ～ 不一樣. Performing in a theater is not the same as performing on a street corner.

脈[脉,脈]**mài, mwò** (N) pulse. /他的 ～ 跳的正常嗎? Is his pulse normal? (B) vein, vessel. 動 ～ artery; 靜～vein; 山～mountain range.

麥[麦]**mài** (B) <-子> wheat. (M 粒lì, 棵kē). 大 ～ barley. *s t*

饅 **mán** (B) ↓.
饅頭 **mántou** (N) Chinese steamed bread.

埋 **mán** (B) ↓. →埋**mái**.
埋怨 **mánywàn** (FV) hold some-

one responsible, blame. /你別～我. Don't blame me.

満 **măn** (SV) 1) be full. /油缸～了. The gas tank is full. (FV) expire, terminate. /我們的合同明天就要～了. Our contract will expire tomorrow. (A) 1) used before negative SV, completely. /他對這事～不關心. He is completely unconcerned about it. 2) really, actually. /我～想去看她,可是沒有時間. I really want to visit her, but I don't have any time. 3) quite, very (d). /那個女孩～漂亮. That girl is quite pretty. (B) 1) a whole ... full. ～臉土 a face full of dirt. 2) satisfied. 不～ be dissatisfied. 3) Manchu. ～族 Manchurian (person).

満足 **măndzú** (FV) satisfy. /我們不能～他的要求. We cannot satisfy his demands. (SV) be satisfied. /他給你這麼多錢,你還不～嗎? He gave you all that money and you still aren't satisfied?

満意 **mănyî** (FV) be satisfied with. /我不～他. I'm not satisfied with him. (SV) be contented, satisfied. /我現在已經很～了. I'm very satisfied now.

慢 **màn** (SV) be slow. /他做事很～. He is slow in doing things. /那個鐘～了. That clock is slow. (A) slowly. /你～點兒開. Drive more slowly. (B) impolite. 怠～ treat rudely.

慢走 **'màndzou** (IE) Watch your step! or Be careful! or Don't let anything happen to you! (said to someone who has been visiting you and is leaving).

漫 **màn** (FV) 1) overflow (of a liquid). /油箱太満了,汽油已經～出來了. The tank got too full and the gasoline overflowed. 2) rise, come up to (of a liquid). /水已經～到二層樓了. The water has risen to the second floor. 3) flood. /山洪把莊稼都～了. The water rushing down the mountain flooded the crops. (B) unrestricted, boundless. ～篤 criticize unreasonably.

忙 **máng** (FV) 1) be busy with some-thing. /我～這件事情呢. I'm busy with this matter now. 2) be in a hurry. /時間還早你～什麼? It's still early; what are you in such a hurry about? (SV) be busy. /這幾天你～不～? Are you busy these days? (A) hastily. /客人來了,他～去穿衣服. When the guests came, he hastily put on his clothes.

盲 **máng** (B) blind. 色～ be color-blind, color-blind person.

盲月腸 **mángcháng** (N) appendix (in the body).

mao *see* **mau**.

貓[猫]**māu** (N) cat (M 隻jī).

矛 **máu** (N) lance, spear (M桿gǎn, 根gēn).

矛盾 **máudwùn, máushǔn** (SV) be contradictory. (N) contradiction, clash.

毛 **máu** (N) 1) hair (on the body) (M根gēn). 2) feather (M根gēn). 3) fur (M塊kwài). 4) wool. 5) mold, mildew. 長～了 become mildewed. (M) ten cents. 一～港幣 ten cents Hong Kong currency; 三～錢 thirty cents. (SV) 1) be coarse, rough, scratched (from being rubbed). /我的眼鏡都～了. My glasses are scratched. 2) be nervous, flustered. /他聽說明天考試就～了. He got flustered when he heard there was an exam tomorrow. 3) be worth less than before (of currency). /現在美金～了. The American dollar is now worth less than it was. (B) 1) small, young. ～孩子 child, kid. 2) gross. ～重 gross weight.

毛筆 **máubǐ** (N) brush (for painting or writing) (M桿gǎn,枝jī, 根gēn).

毛病 **máubing** (N) 1) bad habit. 2) defect. 3) trouble. 4) slight illness.

毛巾 **máujīn** (N) towel (M塊kwài,張jāng).

毛腰 **máuyāu** (VO) bend at the waist, stoop over. /你毛着腰幹什麼呢? What are you stooping over for? (SV) be stooped, bent with age.

毛衣 **máuyī** (N) (wool) sweater (M件jyàn).

茅 **máu** (B) thatch, reeds. ～屋 thatched house, hut.

    茅房 **máufáng** (N) outhouse, toilet.

錨 **máu** (N) anchor. 起～ weigh anchor; 下～ drop anchor.

冒 **máu** (FV) give off smoke, gas, fluids, etc. /水壺在～汽,水是不是開了? The kettle is giving off steam; isn't the water boiling? /那個變戲法儿的嘴裡直～火. Flames kept coming out of the magician's mouth. (B) 1) brave danger or hardship. ～雨 brave the rain. 2) forge, imitate. ～名 use someone else's name. 3) heedless. ～然 recklessly.

    冒失 **máushr** (SV) be unthinking, reckless. /他太～了當着陪審員就要賄賂法官. He was reckless enough to try bribing the judge in front of the jury.

    冒險 **mausyǎn** (VO) take a risk. /我不願意冒這個險了. I no longer want to take this risk. (SV) be risky. /從這條路走太～了. It's too risky to go by this route.

茂 **màu** (B) luxuriant, flourishing. 繁～ be thick, abundant, luxuriant (of flowers, plant life).

    茂盛 **màushèng** (SV) be thick, abundant, luxuriant (of flowers, plant life).

帽 **màu** (B) 1) <-子> hat, cap. (M頂 **dǐng**). 大禮～ top hat. 2) <-儿> head of a bolt, screw. ～釘 rivet.

梅[楳] **méi** (B) <-子> plum (M顆 **kē**). 酸～ sour plum. s

    梅花 **méihwā** (N) 1) <-儿> plum blossom (M朵 **dwǒ**; 枝 **jř**). 2) plum tree (M棵 **kē**). 3) club (in cards).

眉 **méi** (B) eyebrow. ～筆 eyebrow pencil.

    眉毛 **méimau** (N) eyebrow (M隻 **jř**, 條 **tyáu**).

沒[没] **méi** (FV) 1) do not have, do not possess. /我～錶. I don't have a watch. /我～朋友了. I don't have friends anymore. 2) there is not. /院子裡～樹. There are no trees in the yard. /牛奶都～了,你明天得買了. There's no milk; you'll have to buy some tomorrow. (CV) not as . . . as. /這個～那個好. This one isn't as good as that one. (RE) indicates finishing up, using up. 賣～了 be sold out; 吃～了 be eaten up. (B) 1) used before FV, did not (before 有 **yǒu** can mean either did not or do not). /他去了,我～去. He went, but I didn't go. /我昨天～抽煙. I didn't smoke yesterday. /我～有錢. I didn't (or I don't) have the money. 2) used before FV, have not (yet). /他從三月就～給我寫信. He hasn't written me since March. (PT) 1)～. . . 了 preceded by a NU-M of time have not . . . for a certain length of time. /他三天～來了. He hasn't been here for three days. 2) 還～. . . 呢 have not . . . yet. /他還～去呢. He hasn't gone yet. →沒 **mwò**.

    沒法子 **méifádz** (SV) be at a loss, stymied. /我太太不肯離婚,所以我真～. My wife doesn't want a divorce, so I'm completely at a loss.

    沒法儿 **méifǎr** = 沒法子 **méifádz**.

    沒關係 **méigwānsyi** (VO) matter very little, be unimportant. /他來不來都～. Whether he comes or not is unimportant. (IE) That's all right. /A: 對不起明天我不能來. B:～. A: I'm sorry but I can't come tomorrow. B: That's all right.

    沒轍 **méijé** (SV) be at a loss, stymied. /我簡直～. I am really at a loss.

    沒甚麼 **méishémma** (IE) That's all right. or It's nothing. /A: 謝謝你. B:～. A: Thank you very much. B: That's all right. /A: 你摔着了嗎? B:～. A: Are you hurt? B: It's nothing.

    沒想 **méisyǎng** (A) unexpectedly. /我們到了那儿,天～陰了. The sky unexpectedly grew cloudy when we arrived there.

    沒錯儿 **méitswòr** (IE) 1) I won't (don't worry). /A: 明天別忘了帶錢. B:～. A: Don't forget to bring the money tomorrow. B: I won't. 2) There's no doubt about it.

/～, 誰是他幹的. He did it,
there's no doubt about it.
没有 **méiyou** (P) used at the
end of a sentence in which 了 **le** or
着 **je** is added to the main verb, indicates a question. /他那張畫掛
着～? Is his painting hanging up?
(CV) not as . . . as. /我～你高.
I'm not as tall as you. (AV) 1) did
not. /昨天他～來. He didn't
come yesterday. 2) have not (yet).
/因為他～來, 我們現在還不
能開會. Since he hasn't come yet,
we can't start the meeting. (IE) No,
not yet. /A: 天晴了～? B: ～.
A: Has the sky cleared? B: No, not
yet.

玫 **méi** (B) ↓.
玫瑰 **méigwèi** (N) 1) rose (M
朵 **dwǒ**; 枝 **jī**). 2) rose bush (M 棵
kē).

煤 **méi** (N) coal (M 塊 **kwài**).
煤氣 **méichì** (N) gas (as in a
gas stove). ～燈 gas lamp.
煤球儿 **méichyóur** (N) briquette
(made of powdered coal).
煤油 **méiyóu** (N) kerosene.
煤油燈 **méiyóudēng** (N) kerosene lamp.

每 **měi** (SP) each, every. ～一個人
everyone; ～次 each time. (B) every
time, whenever. ～逢 on each occasion.

美 **měi** (SV) 1) be beautiful, fine, artistic. /那個女孩子～極了.
That girl is really beautiful. 2) be
too elated, overjoyed, proud (lp).
/你別～了. Don't be so over-
joyed. (N) beauty. 自然～ natural
beauty. (B) 1) America. ～金 American dollar. 2) good. ～德 virtue.
t
美國 **měigwo** (PW) (in) the
United States (of America).
美麗 **měilì** (SV) be beautiful.
美滿 **méimǎn** (SV) 1) be perfect (of a relationship, life). /他
們的婚姻很～. Their marriage
is perfect. 2) be happy (of a married couple). /他們兩人在一
起過得很～. Those two are very
happy together.
美人 **měirén** (N) beauty (a
woman).

美容院 **měirúngywàn** (N)
beauty parlor (M 家 **jyā**).
美術 **měishù** (N) fine art. ～
家 artist; ～館 art gallery.
美意 **měiyì** (N) kind thought,
kindness. /謝謝你的～. Thank
you for your kindness.

妹 **mèi** (B) younger sister. ～夫 brother-
in-law (younger sister's husband).
妹妹 **mèimei** (N) younger sister.

謎 **mèi** (B) ↓. →謎 **mí**.
謎儿 **mèr** (N) 1) riddle. 打一
個～ tell a riddle; 猜～ solve or
guess a riddle 2) reverse side of a
coin, tails.

們 **men** (B) 1) plural ending for 我 **wǒ**,
你 **nǐ**, 他 **tā**, 咱 **dzá**. 我～ we, us; 你
～ you (plural); 他～ they, them; 咱
～ you and I, we, us. 2) optional
plural ending for certain nouns denoting persons when no definite number of people is mentioned. 學生～
students; 孩子～ children

悶 **mēn** (SV) 1) be stuffy, close. /這
間屋子很～. This room is
very stuffy. 2) be muffled (of a
sound). /他說話的聲音很～.
His voice is muffled. (FV) steep
tea. /那個茶還得～一會儿.
That tea should steep a while longer.
→悶 **mèn**.

門[门] **mén** (N) 1) door (M 扇 **shàn**). 2)
<-儿> doorway, gateway, entrance
(M 道 **dàu**). (M) 1) <-儿> for
courses in school. 一～課 a course.
2) <-儿> line of work, field of
study. /幹我們這～的發不了
財. We can't make money in our
line of work. 3) <-儿> set of relatives. 兩～親戚 two sets of relatives. 4) for cannons. 一～砲 a cannon.
門診 **ménjěn** (FV) see patients
(at one's office). /張大夫上午～,
下午出診. Dr. Chang sees
patients in his office in the morning
and makes house calls in the afternoon.
門口儿 **ménkǒur** (PW) 1) at
the door, by the door. /我家～有
兩棵樹. There are two trees by
the door of my house. 2) area in
front of a door, doorway. /他站在

~敲門. He stood at the door knocking.

門牌 **ménpái** (N) doorplate.

門栓 **ménshwān** (N) bolt (on a door).

悶 **mèn** (SV) 1) be stuffy, close. /這屋子很~. It's very stuffy in this room. 2) be bored. /你一個人在這儿不~嗎? Aren't you bored here all by yourself? →悶 **mēn**.

燜 **mèn** (FV) simmer with just a little liquid. ~肉 simmer meat, simmered meat.

夢〔梦〕**mèng** (N) dream (M場**chǎng**). 做~ to dream.

夢見 **mèngjyan** (RC) dream about, dream that. /我~我家裡的人了. I dreamt about the people back home. /我~他結婚了. I dreamt that he got married.

夢想 **mèngsyǎng** (FV) daydream, imagine, dream about. /你別~發財了. Don't dream about being wealthy.

猛 **měng** (SV) 1) be fierce, violent. /那夜的風雨很~. There was a violent storm that night. 2) be potent (as medicine). /這種藥很~. This kind of medicine is very potent. (B) suddenly. ~省 suddenly recall.

猛孤釘的 **měnggudīngde** (A) suddenly (lp). /火車~站住了. The train stopped suddenly.

猛烈 **měnglyè** (SV) 1) be violent, powerful. /風雨~地吹打. The storm raged violently. /敵人的砲火很~. Enemy fire is very heavy. 2) be potent (as medicine). /醫生給我的藥很~. The medicine the doctor gave me is very potent.

猛然間 **'měngránjyān** (A) suddenly, unexpectedly. /我~想起來我忘了鎖門了. I suddenly remembered that I had forgotten to lock the door.

謎 **mí** (B) riddle, conundrum. ~語 riddle. →謎 **mèi**.

迷 **mí** (FV) 1) be very fond of, crazy about. /他很~那個電影明星. He's crazy about that movie star. 2) captivate, fascinate, possess. /她的聲音~了很多人. Her voice has captivated many people. /他

叫鬼給~了. He was possessed by an evil spirit. (RE) indicates being lost. 走~了 lose one's way. (B) 1) fan, enthusiast. 球~ ball fan. 2) bewilder. ~糊 be muddled.

迷路 **mílù** (VO) lose one's way, get lost. /你可別迷了路. Don't get lost.

迷信 **mísyìn** (N) superstition. (SV) be superstitious.

米 **mǐ** (N) rice (uncooked). (M粒**lì**, 顆**kē**). (B) grain. 小~ spiked millet. (M) meter. 一百~短跑 hundred-meter dash *s t*

米飯 **mǐfàn** (N) rice (cooked).

蜜 **mì** (N) honey.

蜜蜂 **mìfēng** (N) honeybee.

蜜蜂窩 **mìfēngwō** (N) beehive.

蜜餞 **mìjyàn** (N) fruit preserves. (AT) preserved in heavy syrup. ~菠蘿 preserved pineapple.

密 **mì** (SV) be dense, thick, close together. /樹葉很~. The foliage is very dense. /這個網子織得很~. This net is very closely woven. (B) 1) secret, confidential. ~談 private conversation 2) intimate, close. ~友 close friend.

密切 **mìchyè** (SV) be close (of a relationship). /他們的關係很~. They have a very close relationship.

密碼 **mìmǎ** (N) <-ル> code, cipher.

秘 **mì** (B) secret. ~方 secret recipe.

秘密 **'mìmì** (SV) be secret, confidential. /那件事很~不能在這儿談. That matter is very secret; we can't talk about it here. (N) secret. (A) secretly, confidentially. /我~給了他兩百塊錢. I secretly gave him two hundred dollars.

秘書 **mìshū** (N) secretary.

mian *see* **myan.**

miao *see* **myau.**

mie *see* **mye.**

民 **mín** (B) 1) inhabitant of a country. 國~ citizen, national. 2) civil (not criminal). ~庭 civil court. 3) civil (as opposed to military). ~防 civil defense.

民兵 **mínbīng** (N) militia.

民族 **míndzú** (N) race, ethnic group, people. 大和～the Japanese people.

民法 **mínfǎ** (N) civil law (M 條**tyáu**).

民主 **mínjǔ** (N) democracy. (SV) be democratic.

民眾 **mínjùng** (N) 1) the people. /政府應當尊重～的權利. The government must respect the rights of the people. 2) people (in general) (M群**chyún**). /一大群～在市政府門前示威. A large group of people is demonstrating in front of the mayor's office.

敏 **mǐn** (B) keen, clever. ～銳be alert, sharp.

敏捷 **mǐnjyé** (SV) 1) be quick, nimble. /他做事很～. He is very nimble in doing things. 2) be alert (of one's mind, thinking). /他的思想很～. He is quick-witted.

名 **míng** (M) <u>for persons whose names might be listed or recorded some-where, as in a newspaper or file.</u> /有四～學生受傷了. Four students were wounded. (B) 1) <-子, -儿> name. ～片 calling card. 2) famous. ～醫 famous medical doctor. 3) reputation. 壞～bad reputation.

名字 **míngdz** (N) name.

名聲 **'míngshēng** (N) reputation.

名望 **'míngwàng** (N) good reputation (of a person).

名義 **'míngyì** (N) official title, status. /他在他工作的地方是什麼～? What's his official title where he works? /我用教授～來的美國. I came to the United States as a professor.

名譽 **'míngyù** (N) reputation.

明 **míng** (B) 1) bright. ～月 bright moon. 2) clear. ～證 clear evidence. 3) comprehend. 聰～be intelligent. 4) openly. ～説speak openly. 5) next <u>day, year, morning, evening</u>. ～晨 tomorrow morning.
　　　　　d　t

明白 **míngbai** (FV) understand. /我～你説的話. I understood what you said. (SV) be perceptive. /他是個～人. He's a perceptive

person. /你怎麼這麼不～呢! How come you are so dense?

明確 **míngchywè** (SV) be clear and definite, precise. /他給的指示不夠～. The instructions he gave were not precise enough. /請你再説的～一點. Please state it more definitely.

明礬 **míngfán** (N) alum.

明後天 **mínghòutyan** (TW) 1) tomorrow or the day after tomorrow, in a day or two. /他～來. He will come in a day or two. 2) tomorrow and the next day. /～是最後兩天了. Tomorrow and the next day are the last two days.

明亮 **mínglyàng** (SV) be clear and bright. /這個小孩的眼睛很～. This child has clear, bright eyes.

明瞭 **'mínglyǎu** (FV) understand. /我不～你的意思. I don't understand what you mean.

明年 **míngnyan** (TW) next year. /他～就畢業了. He's graduating next year.

明顯 **míngsyǎn** (SV) be obvious.

明信片 **míngsyìnpyàn** (N) postcard (M張**jāng**).

明天 **míngtyan** (TW) tomorrow. /～又是另一天了. Tomorrow is another day. /他～來. He's coming tomorrow.

明儿 **myár** = 明天**míngtyan**.

明儿個 **myárge** = 明天**míng-tyan**.

命 **mìng** (N) 1) life (the time something is alive) (M條**tyáu**). /海龜的～很長. The sea turtle has a very long life /貓有九條～. A cat has nine lives. 2) fate, destiny. /這是我的～. This is my fate. (B) order, command. 奉～ receive an order.

命令 **mìnglìng** (N) order, command (M道**dàu**).

命運 **'mìngyùn** (N) fate, destiny. /別盡靠～. Don't rely too much on fate.

mo *see* **mwo.**

謀 **móu** (FV) find <u>a job</u>. /現在～職業很難. It's very hard to find a job these days. (B) 1) a plot, plan. 奸～ treacherous plot. 2) to plan, plot. ～算 devise, scheme.

謀殺 **móushā** (FV) murder (<u>by</u> <u>plotting</u>). /聽説他是被他手下的人~的. It was reported that he had been murdered by his subordinates.

謀生 **móushēng** (VO) make a living. /為了~我們都得做事. We all have to work in order to make a living.

某 **mǒu** (B) a certain <u>person or thing</u>. ~部長 a certain cabinet minister; ~處 a certain place.

模 **mú** (B) ⊦. →模 **mwó**.

模子 **múdz** (N) mold, die.

模樣 **múyang** (N) <-ㄦ> facial appearance, face. /那女孩子的~不壞,但是身裁不好. That girl has a nice face, but not a good figure.

畝[亩] **mú** (M) Chinese acre (<u>about</u> $\frac{1}{6}$ <u>acre</u>).兩百~地 two hundred Chinese acres of land.

牡 **mǔ** (B) male (<u>of animals or plants</u>). ~牛 ox.

牡丹 **mǔdan** (N) peony (M 朵 **dwǒ**,枝 **jr̄**,棵 **kē**).

母 **mǔ** (AT) female (<u>of animals</u>). ~牛 cow. (B) 1) mother. 祖~ grandmother; 乳~wet nurse. 2) letter of the alphabet, sound. ~音 vowel; 字~ letter of the alphabet, alphabet.

母親 **mǔchin** (N) mother.

母鷄 **mǔjī** (N) hen.

木 **mù** (SV) 1) be numb, without feeling. /我的兩條腿都~了. Both my legs are numb. 2) be dumbfounded, stunned. /他一聽那個消息就~在那ㄦ了. When he heard the news, he just stood there stunned. (B) <頭> wood (M塊**kwài**). ~器 wooden furniture.

木工 **mùgūng** (N) 1) carpenter. 2) carved wood.

木匠 **mùjyang** (N) carpenter.

木料 **mùlyàu** (N) wood, timber (M塊**kwài**).

木炭 **mùtàn** (N) charcoal (M塊**kwài**).

目 **mù** (B) 1) eye. ~力 vision. 2) item. 節~program, item on a program.

目標 **mùbyāu** (N) objective, target.

目前 **mùchyán** (TW) 1) at present. /~没問題,明年就不敢説了. There aren't any problems at present, but I don't dare say how it'll be next year. 2) the present time. /~是最困難的一個時期. The present time has been the most difficult period.

目的 **mùdi** (N) aim, objective, purpose. /這個工作有什麽~. What is the purpose of this work?

目錄 **mùlu** (N) table of contents (M篇 **pyān**).

幕 **mù** (M) act <u>of a play</u>. 第一~the first act of a play. (N) stage curtain. (B) screen. 銀~movie screen; 煙~smoke screen.

募 **mù** (FV) raise, collect, <u>money,</u> <u>troops</u>. ~兵 raise troops. /他們~了很多錢. They raised a lot of money.

募捐 **mùjywān** (VO) take up a collection, raise money <u>through</u> <u>voluntary contribution</u>. /那個舞會是為慈善~開的. This dance is being held to raise money for charity.

牧 **mù** (B) tend animals (<u>as a shepherd</u>). ~牛 tend cattle.

牧師 **mùshr** (N) pastor, minister, preacher (<u>Christian</u>).

摸 **mwō** (FV) 1) grope for (<u>lit. or fig.</u>). ~電門 grope for a light switch. /這ㄦ的情形我還没~熟呢. I still haven't grasped the situation here. 2) feel <u>or</u> touch <u>with the</u> <u>hand</u>. /別~你的傷口. Don't touch that sore of yours. 3) sneak in <u>or</u> out. /他~到敵人的陣地裏去了. He sneaked into the enemy's encampment.

模 **mwó** (B) 1) model, pattern. 楷~ model, good example. 2) indistinct, ambiguous. ~稜 indecision. →模 **mú**.

模範 **mwófàn** (N) model, example <u>of what is good</u>. ~住宅 model apartments. /我們應當以他為~. We should take that student as our model.

模糊 **mwóhu** (SV) be blurred,

indistinct, not clear. /這本書印得很～. The printing in this book is blurred.

横型 **mwósyíng** (N) scale model in three dimensions.

磨 **mwó** (FV) 1) grind, sharpen. ～刀 sharpen a knife. 2) pester. /這孩子老～我. This child is always pestering me. 3) dawdle. /別～了, 快點兒作. Don't dawdle; do it more quickly. 4) rub. /牛在樹上～它的背. The cow is rubbing its back on the tree. →磨 mwò.

蘑 **mwó** (B) mushroom. 口～ mushroom (a variety that originally came from Inner Mongolia).

蘑菇 **mwógu** (N) mushroom. (SV) 1) be a slowpoke. /她真～. She is really a slowpoke. 2) be fussy. /別那麼～了, 就拿這個吧！ Don't be so fussy; take this one. (FV) pester. /他跟我～了半天. He pestered me for a long time.

抹 **mwǒ** (FV) 1) smear on, apply. ～口紅 put on lipstick. /小孩～了一牆的墨水. The children smeared ink all over the wall. 2) wipe off. ～桌子 wipe off a table; ～眼淚 wipe away tears. →抹 mwò.

抹子 **mwǒdz** (N) trowel (M把 bǎ).

脈 mwò→脈 mài.

抹{磨2)} **mwò** (FV) 1) smooth out plaster, putty. /你最好趁着水泥還沒乾的時候～. You'd better smooth out the cement while it is still wet. 2) turn a vehicle around. /這條街太小, 我不能在這兒～車. This road is too narrow; I can't turn the car around here. →抹 mwò.

沒{没} **mwò** (FV) inundate. /大水～了房子了. The flood inundated the houses. (B) 1) confiscate. ～收 confiscate 2) disappear. 出～ appear and disappear; 沉～ sink into water. 3) decline. ～落 be ruined. →沒 méi.

磨 **mwò** (FV) grind, mill. /他把豆子磨成粉了. He ground the beans into powder. (N) millstone (M盤 pán). →磨 mwó, 抹{磨} mwò.

末 **mwò** (SP) last of a series. ～一個 the last one. (B) 1) <-儿, -子> dust, powder. 粉筆～儿 chalk dust. 2) end. ～尾 in the end。

末了儿 **mwòlyǎur** (SP) last of a series. ～一個 the last one; ～一回 the last time. (TW) 1) the very last, the very end. /到了～他才明白. He didn't catch on until the very end. 2) at last, in the end. /他們～把他捉住了. They caught him at last.

墨 **mwò** (N) 1) ink stick (M塊 kwài). 2) ink. (B) 1) black, dark. ～綠 dark green. 2) Mo Ti (contracted form of 墨翟 mwòdí). ～家 Moism, Moist. t

墨盒儿 **mwòhér** (N) ink box (metal box with ink-soaked cotton pad).

墨水 **mwòshwěi** (N) <-儿> ink. 紅～ red ink.

莫 **mwò** (B) not. ～若 cannot do better than. t

莫非 **mwòfēi** (A)q could it be that, is it possible that. /～你是來找我的? Could it be that you're looking for me? /～你不喜歡你太太了? Could it be that you don't like your wife anymore?

莫明其妙 **mwòmíngchí'myàu** (SV) 1) be completely baffled. /我對那件事情～. I'm completely baffled about that. 2) be confusing, baffling. /那本書寫得真是～. That book is really confusing.

棉{綿} **myán** (AT) cotton-padded. ～褲 cotton-padded trousers. (B) cotton. ～子油 cottonseed oil.

棉襖 **myánǎu** (N) cotton-padded jacket (M件 jyàn).

棉布 **myánbù** (N) cotton cloth.

棉花 **myánhwa** (N) cotton (the plant or the sterilized variety).

棉紗 **myánshā** (N) cotton yarn.

棉絮 **myánsyù** (N) cotton wadding.

綿{絲} **myán** (B) 1) soft, downy. 軟～ ～的 be soft. 2) continuous, prolonged. ～延 extend over a period. →棉{綿} myán.

綿子 **myándz** (N) silk wadding.

綿羊 **myányáng** (N) sheep (M隻 jr̄, 群 chwún).

勉 **myǎn** (B) 1) exert, force, <u>oneself</u>. ～力 exert one's strength. 2) urge. ～勵 encourage, incite.

勉強 **myǎnchyáng, myánchyǎng** (SV) 1) be reluctant, unwilling. /這件事情他做得很～. He did this very reluctantly. 2) be unconvincing, insufficient, <u>as a reason</u>, <u>answer</u>. /你的理由很～. Your reasons are unconvincing. (A) barely. /他～可以生活. He's barely able to make a living. (FV) force, compel. /要是他不願意去,你不要～他. If he doesn't want to go, don't force him.

免 **myǎn** (FV) eliminate, dispense with. /這些禮節我們就～了. Let's dispense with the formalities. (B) free from. ～稅 be exempt from taxes; ～票 free pass.

免得 **myǎnde** (FV) save someone from an inconvenience. /你要是去～我去了. If you go, it will save me a trip. (AV) avoid <u>doing something</u>. /我明天不來～石亚見他. I'm not coming tomorrow so I'll avoid meeting him.

麵(麥刂)(面)**myàn** (N) 1) flour. 2) noodle (M 條 **tyáu**, 根 **gēn**). (SV) be mushy (of fruits). /這個蘋果真～. This apple is very mushy.

麥麵包 **myànbāu** (N) bread (M 塊 **kwài**).

麥麵子 **myàndz** = 麵儿 **myàr**.

麥麵粉 **myànfěn** (N) flour.

麵條儿 **myàntyáur** (N) noodle (M 條 **tyáu**, 根 **gēn**).

麵儿 **myàr** (N) powder. 磨成～ grind into powder; 藥～ powdered medicine.

面{画}**myàn** (M) 1) for mirrors. 一～鏡子 a mirror. 2) <u>for flags</u>. 一一～旗子 a flag. 3) page <u>of a book, newspaper, etc</u>. /請翻到第十～. Please turn to page ten. 4) <-儿> side. 這～ this side. (B) 1) <-儿> surface. 海～ surface of the sea. 2) <-儿> part, side. 外～ outside, the outside part; 左～ (on) the left side; 前～ in front, the front part. 3) face to face. ～談 talk face to face. 4) face. ～紗 veil. <u>SF of</u> 麵 **myàn**.

面前 **myànchyán** (PW) (the <u>area</u>) in front. /他走到我～哞

了我一口. He walked up to me and spit on me. /你～就有一個電話. There's a telephone right in front of you.

面子 **myàndz** (N) 1) face, social standing, prestige. 失～ lose face. /你的～不小. You have a lot of prestige. 2) honor, favor. /你真給我～. You're doing me a great honor. 3) width <u>of textiles</u>. /這個料子的～太窄. The width of this material is too narrow.

面積 **myànji** (N) surface area, area. /這個地方的～很大. This place covers a huge area.

面目 '**myànmù** (N) 1) facial appearance, face. /她的～很清秀. She has a pretty face. 2) nature, behavior. /他生氣的時候真～都露出來了. When he got angry he revealed his true nature.

面儿 **myàr** (N) 1) the right side of a piece of material. 2) the outside material of a lined garment.

描 **myáu** (FV) 1) make a tracing, trace. /把那張畫儿～下來. Please trace that picture. 2) write *or* paint over, retrace. ～眉 paint eyebrows. /寫字別～. When you write characters, don't ever go over your strokes.

描寫 '**myáusyě** (FV) depict, describe, <u>in detail, realistically</u>. /他的表情我～不出來. I can't describe his expression.

瞄 **myáu** (FV) aim. /～準了再放槍. Aim accurately and then shoot.

苗 **myáu** (B) 1) <-儿> sprout, shoot (M 棵 **kē**, 根 **gēn**). 麥～ wheat sprouts. 2) <-儿> offshoot, jet. 火～ jet of flame; 礦～ vein of ore. 3) progeny. ～裔 descendant. 4) <-子> Miao person. ～語 Miao language. 5) vaccine. 痘～ smallpox vaccine.

苗條 '**myáutyǎu** (SV) be slender and graceful (of a person).

秒 **myǎu** (M) second (<u>of time or of an angle</u>). 一分二十～ one minute and twenty seconds; 十五度三十～ fifteen degrees and thirty seconds.

廟{庙}**myàu** (N) 1) temple, monastery

(M 座 dzwò). 2) shrine (M 座 dzwò). 土地~ shrine for the earth god.

滅[灭] **myè** (FV) 1) go out (as lights, a fire). /燈~了. The lights went out. 2) extinguish, put out. ~火 put out a fire. 3) destroy completely, annihilate, a country. /他們把那個小國~了. They completely destroyed that small country. (RE) indicates extinguishing, putting out. 刮~ blow out (as the wind would a candle).

    滅亡 **myèwáng** (FV) destroy completely, annihilate, a country. /秦朝在公元前二零七年就~了. The Ch'in Dynasty fell in 207 B.C.

哪[呐] **na** (P) 1) fusion of 呢 **ne** and 啊 **a**. /你怎麼不吃~？ Why haven't you eaten yet? 2) usually used in place of 啊 **a** when the preceding word ends in the sound "n." /怎麼這麼難~! This is so difficult! →哪 **nǎ**.

拿[拏] **ná** (FV) 1) take, bring. /請你把這個花瓶~到客廳去. Please take this vase into the living room. /他給你的錢你~了嗎? Did you take the money he gave you? /請你把那本書~給我. Please bring me that book. 2) hold, grasp. /怎麼~筷子才對? What is the proper way to hold chopsticks? 3) seize, capture, arrest. /我們兩個星期就把敵人的首都~下來了. We captured the enemy capital in two weeks. /我們幫助警察去~賊吧. Let's go help the policeman catch the thief. 4) earn a salary. /你一個月~多少錢? How much do you earn a month? 5) make things difficult for, give someone a hard time. /你別~我. Don't give me a hard time. 6) eat away at (and thus destroy something, as acid, insects). /樹葉子叫蟲子~的都黃了. The worms have eaten away at the leaves so that they've all turned yellow. (CV) with. /你~這把刀切肉吧. Chop the meat with this knife. (PT) 1)~...當...regard someone as. /我~他當我的親兄弟. I regard him as my brother.

2)~...當...mistake something for. /我~糖當鹽了. I mistook the sugar for salt.

哪[那] **nǎ, něi** (SP)q which, what. /你要~個? Which one do you want? /他說的是~國話? What language is he speaking? (PT) 1)~...都 (or 也) any. /你~天來都可以. You can come any day. /~個我都不喜歡. I don't like any of them. 2)~...~...whichever. /你~天方便就~天來. Come whichever day is convenient for you. →哪 **na**.

    哪裏 **'nálǐ** (PW)q = 哪兒 **nǎr**. (IE) 1) Thank you (in reply to a compliment). /A: 你這套衣服真漂亮. B: ~~. A: Your dress is so pretty. B: Thank you. 2) You're welcome. /A: 謝謝你. B: ~~. A: Thank you. B: You're welcome. 3) It doesn't matter. or That's all right. /A: 啊呀! 我踩了你一腳, 真對不起. B: ~~. A: Oh, I'm sorry. I stepped on your toe. B: That's all right.

    哪怕 **nǎpà** (A) no matter how, even though. /~錢再多, 也是不夠花的. No matter how much money you had, you would still feel it's not enough. /~你潤, 她還是不會嫁給你的. Even though you're rich, she still won't marry you.

    哪兒 **nǎr** (PW)q where. /你到~去? Where are you going? /這個故事在~發生的? Where does this story take place? (A)q how. /你~能這麼固執呢? How can you be so stubborn? (PT) 1)~...都 (or 也) everywhere, anywhere. /我到~都碰見他. I meet him everywhere I go. /~我都不想去. I don't want to go anywhere. 2)~...~. Wherever. /你想上~就上~. Go wherever you want to go.

    哪兒的話 **nǎrdehwà** (IE) That's not true. or Don't give me that. or Oh, come now. /A: 你不來我家吃飯一定因為我飯做得不好. B: ~. A: I bet you didn't come to my house for dinner because I don't cook very well. B: That's not true. or Oh, come now. /A: 有你這麼漂亮的女孩子在我們班上, 真是我們的光榮. B: ~. A: It's really a great honor to have such a beautiful girl as you in our class. B: Don't give me that.

哪樣儿 **nǎyangr, něiyangr** = 哪麼樣儿 **němmayangr.**

哪麼 **němma** (PW)[q] used after CV such as 往 **wǎng,** 望 **wàng,** 從 **tsúng,** 朝 **cháu,** 向 **syàng,** which direction, what direction. /他是從～來的? Which direction did he come from? (A)[q] how, which way. /這本字典～用? How do you use this dictionary?

哪麼樣儿 **němmayangr** (A)[q] how, in which way. /～做好? Which is the best way to do it?

那 **nà, nèi** (SP) that. /～時候我在場. I was there at that time. /～個皮包是我的. That purse is mine. (N) that (thing). /～是我女朋友的照片. That's my girl friend's photograph. (A) 1) used at the beginning of a sentence, in that case, then, if so. /A: 你如果不去看電影我也不去了. B: ～我就去吧 A: If you don't go to the movies, I won't go. B: In that case, I'll go. 2) used before SV, how . . . it (he, she, etc.) is. /他～胖啊! How fat he is! 3) used before FV, . . . so much. /一家子～哭啊! The whole family grieved so much!

那邊 **nàbyan, nèibyan** (PW) <一儿> 1) that direction. /我就住在～. I live in that direction. 2) there. /～有人等我. Somebody's waiting for me over there.

那裡 **nàli** = 那儿 **nàr.**

那麼 **nàmma, nèmma** (A) 1) used before FV, in that way, like that. /這事不能～辦. It can't be done that way. /這個字應當～寫. This character should be written like that. 2) used before SV, to such an extent, so, that. /我不能吃～多. I can't eat that much. 3) used at the beginning of a sentence, in that case, then, if so. /A: 她打電話來說她不來了. B: ～我們就不必再等了. A: She called and said she's not coming. B: In that case, we needn't wait any longer. (PW) used after CV such as 從 **tsúng,** 望 **wǎng,** 往 **wàng,** 朝 **cháu,** 向 **syàng,** that direction. /他是從～來的. He came from that direction. (SP) such a . . . as that. /不錯，有～一本儿書. Yes, there is such a book. (PT) 有 (*or* 跟) . . . ～ . . . as . . . as . . . . /她有我～高. She is as tall as I am. /美國飯沒有中國飯～好吃. American food isn't as good as Chinese food.

那儿 **nàr, nèr** (PW) 1) that place. /我們約好在～見面. We'll meet each other at that place. 2) there. /～沒有樹. There aren't any trees there.

那樣儿 **nàyangr, nèiyangr** = 那麼樣儿 **nèmmayàngr.**

那麼樣儿 **nèmmayàngr** (A) 1) used before FV, in that way, like that. /你～做，絕不會成功. You definitely won't succeed if you do it like that. 2) used before SV, to such an extent, so, that. /你為什麼～不客氣? Why do you have to be so impolite?

納 **nà** (B) 1) pay, give. ～糧 pay taxes in grain. 2) receive. 出～ cashier, cashier's work. *t*

納稅 **nàshwèi** (VO) pay taxes. /你今年納了多少稅? How much did you pay in taxes this year?

捺 **nà** (N) <一儿> stroke slanted to the right (in Chinese calligraphy). (B) press down. ～住 press down firmly.

奶[嬭] **nǎi** (N) 1) milk. 羊～ goat's milk; ～粉 powdered milk. 2) breast. (FV) breast-feed, nurse. /她在臥室裡～孩子呢. She's in the bedroom nursing the baby.

奶奶 **nǎinai** (N) paternal grandmother.

奶頭 **nǎitóu** (N) <一儿> nipple.

耐 **nài** (B) endure, bear. 忍～ endure; ～久 be durable.

耐心 **nàisyīn** (N) patience. (SV) be patient. /請你～點儿吧! Please be patient.

難[难] **nán** (SV) be difficult, hard. /這個問題太～了，一時不能解決. This problem is too difficult to be solved immediately. (FV) present someone with a problem, ask something too difficult. /你別～我了. Don't present me with such a problem. /你的問題把我～倒了. Your question stumped me. (AV) be difficult to, hard to. ～説 be difficult to say. (B) be unpleasant to, bad to. ～喝 taste bad (of a liquid). →難 nàn.

難吃 **nánchī** (SV) be unpleasant to eat, taste bad. /魚肝油很～. Cod liver oil tastes awful.

難道 **'nándàu** (A) it couldn't be . . . could it, really (in questions of surprise). /～連五分錢你都没有嗎? You really don't have even five cents? /～你認識他? It couldn't be that you know him (could it)?

難怪 **'nángwài** (A) no wonder . . . . /北部下雪了,～今天怎麼冷. No wonder it's so cold today; it snowed up north. (FV) be hard to blame someone. /這也～你不去. It's hard to blame you for not going.

難過 **nángwò** (SV) 1) be sad, unhappy, sorry. /聽説他父親去世了,我很為他～. I heard that his father passed away. I feel very sorry for him. /他很～,因為没考上大學. He's very unhappy because he didn't pass the college entrance exam 2) be uncomfortable. /我的鼻子堵住了,很～. My nose is stuffed up and it's very uncomfortable.

難看 **nánkàn** (SV) be ugly, repulsive.

難免 **nánmyǎn** (AV) can't help doing something. ～出錯兒 can't help making mistakes. /你如果見了她,也～愛她的. When you see her, you won't be able to help falling in love with her either. (SV) be difficult to avoid, inevitable. /戰爭恐怕很～. Perhaps war is inevitable.

難受 **nánshòu** (SV) 1) be sad, unhappy, sorry. /他走了我很～. He's gone so I'm feeling very sad. /聽説你的女朋友和你絕交了我很～. I'm sorry to hear that you and your girl friend broke up. 2) be uncomfortable. /我頭痛了兩天,真～. I've had a headache for two days and am really uncomfortable.

難聽 **nántīng** (SV) 1) be unpleasant to listen to, sound terrible. /這首歌太～了. That song is awful to listen to. 2) be annoying (to

hear). /你的話真是太～了. The remarks you made were really annoying.

難為情 **nánwéichíng** (SV) embarrassed. /他覺得很～. He felt very embarrassed.

難聞 **nánwén** (SV) be unpleasant to smell, smell bad. /這種藥很～. This medicine smells awful.

南 **nán** (L) south. 城～ (the area) south of the city; ～風 south wind; 朝～走 go south. t

南邊 **nánbyan** (PW) <ール> 1) (in) the south part or area. /這個宿舍男生住～,女生住北邊. Boys live in the south part of this dormitory, girls in the north. 2) to the south of. /學校～是一個工廠. There's a factory to the south of the school.

南方 **nánfāng** (PW) (in) the south. /～產米. Rice is grown in the south. /～比北方暖一點ル. The south is warmer than the north.

南瓜 **nángwā** (N) pumpkin.

男 **nán** (AT) male (of humans). ～孩ル male child, boy, son. (B) 1) son. 長～ eldest son. 2) man. ～女平等 equality of men and women.

男人 **'nánren** (N) 1) man. 2) husband (not very polite).

難[难]**nàn** (B) 1) disaster. ～民 refugee. 2) difficulty. 克～ overcome difficulties. →難 nán.

nao *see* nau.

撓 **náu** (FV) scratch. ～癢癢 scratch an itch. /貓把我的手～了. The cat scratched my hand.

腦[脑]**nǎu** (B) <-子> brain. 大～ cerebrum; ～門子 forehead.

腦袋 **nǎudai** (N) head (on the body).

腦筋 **nǎujīn** (N) mind, brains. /他～很好. He has a good mind. /他没～. He doesn't have any brains.

惱[恼]**nǎu** (FV) be mad at, annoyed with, somebody. /請別～我吧. Please don't be mad at me. (SV) be mad, angry, annoyed. /你罵他妹妹他很～. He's mad because you said bad things about his younger sister.

惱怒 **nǎunù** (N) anger. /別激起他的～. Don't arouse his anger. (SV) be mad, angry. /他～的時候不喜歡別人對他説話. He doesn't like people to speak to him when he is angry.

鬧(鬧) **nàu** (FV) 1) make noise, make a fuss. /請你們不要再～了好不好? Would you please cut out the noise? 2) get something (no matter what). /明年我也～一輛新車. I'll get a new car next year, no matter what. 3) end up with. /我～了一身債. I ended up with a lot of debts. 4) be disturbed by, suffer from, something. ～饑荒 suffer from famine;～賊 be disturbed by a burglar. /他現在正～眼睛呢. He has eye trouble now. 5) in RC, indicates a change of condition with general causal meaning, not specifying the precise method by which the change is brought about. ～清楚 understand clearly;～錯 be mistaken about;～壞 spoil. (SV) 1) be disturbing, noisy. /街上很～. It's very noisy in the street. 2) be naughty. /這孩子～極了. This child is extremely naughty.

鬧着玩兒 **nàujewár** (FV) tease, make fun. /我跟你～呢. I was just teasing you.

鬧鐘 **nàujūng** (N) alarm clock (M 架 **jyà**, 座 **dzwò**).

呢(呢) **ne** (P)q used at the end of a sentence after a noun, how about, what about. /我想去看電影,你～? I think I'll go to a movie. How about you? /我的大衣～? How about my coat? or Where's my coat? (P) 1) used at the end of a choice-type or question-word interrogative sentence. /你倒底告訴不告訴我～? Are you going to tell me or not? /我們怎麼辦～? What can we do about it? 2) used to mark a pause after a suppositional clause or noun. /如果天氣好～,我們就去野餐,不好～,只能在家裡吃了. If the weather's good, we'll go on a picnic; if not, we'll just eat at home. /錢～倒是有,只是他太吝嗇. He certainly has the money, but he's very stingy. 3)

used at the end of sentences containing FV which are often preceded by the adverb 正 **jeng**, indicates that the action is going on. /他(正)洗澡呢. He's taking a bath. /他在客廳裡等你～. He's waiting for you in the living room. (PT) 1) 還沒 (or 不)... not... yet. /我還沒吃飯～. I haven't eaten yet. /我還不知道～. I don't know yet. 2) 還在... ～ still going on. /他還在生氣～. He's still angry. →呢 **ní**.

哪 **něi** →哪 **nǎ**.

內 **nèi** (B) 1) inner, internal, inside. ～部 the inside of an organization, inner part;～地 interior of a country; ～戰 civil war. 2) within a time limit. /我必須在三天～完成這件工作. I have to finish this work within three days. 3) wife. ～姪 nephew (wife's brother's son). t

內科 **'nèikē** (N) medical department or clinic (in a hospital, for general treatment of diseases or injuries).

內容 **nèirúng** (N) substance, content, of something. /他演説的～很充實. The content of his speech was quite substantial. /他説的話沒有～. What he said was pointless.

那 **nèi** →那 **nà**.

嫩 **nèn, nwùn** (SV) 1) be tender, delicate. /這肉很～. This meat is very tender. /她的皮膚又滑又～. Her skin is smooth and delicate. 2) be light (of color). /這件衣料的顏色太～了. The color of this material is too light. 3) be inexperienced. /做這件事他還嫩了點. He is still too inexperienced to do this.

能 **néng** (AV) can, be able to. /我不～告訴你. I can't tell you. /我想我不～在九點鐘趕到. I don't think I'll be able to make it at nine o'clock. (SV) be capable. (N) energy (in physics). 原子～ atomic energy. (B) ability. 才～ talent; 無～ not be any good at anything.

能幹 **nénggàn** (SV) be capable, able. /他太太很～. His wife is very capable.

能夠 **nénggou** (AV) can, be able to. /你一個月～省下多少錢來? How much can you save in a month? /這一點錢不～做什麼. You can't do anything with such a small amount of money.

能力 **néngli** (N) ability.

能耐 **néngnai** (N) ability. (SV) be capable, smart. /我沒有你～. I'm not as smart as you are.

膿 **néng** →膿 **núng**.

濘 **nèng, ning** (SV) be muddy. /下過雨以後路上～得很. After it rains the road is very muddy. →濘 **ning**.

弄 **nèng** →弄 **nùng**.

泥 **ní** (N) 1) mud, clay. 2) dirt, grime (on one's body or on clothing) (lp). (FV) plaster. ～牆 plaster a wall. (B) mashed vegetable or fruit. 土豆ル～ mashed potatoes. →泥 **nì**.

　泥水匠 **níshwěijyàng** (N) mason.

呢 **ní** (B) <-子> woolen material (M 塊 **kwài**). ～大衣 wool coat. →呢 **ne**.

你 **ní** (PN) 1) you (singular). 2) used before a noun, your (singular). ～太太 your wife.

　你們 **nímen** (PN) 1) you (plural). 2) used before a noun, your (plural). /～客廳真漂亮. Your living room is very pretty.

泥 **nì** (FV) fill up a crack or a seam. /你先得把牆上的縫ル都～起來. You must fill up the cracks in the wall first. →泥 **ní**.

　泥子 **nìdz** (N) putty.

膩 **nì** (SV) 1) be greasy, oily. /這盤炒肉～得很. This fried meat is awfully greasy. 2) be boring, dull. /這種工作做久了真～. It's really boring doing this work for very long. 3) be bored, tired of something. /她老說沒完我～死了. I'm bored to death with her constant talking. (FV) pester. /這個孩子老～我. This child is always pestering me. /他不給你錢,你就跟他～. If he won't give you the money, you just keep pestering him.

　膩人 **nìrén** (SV) be boring. /這

件事情很～. This matter is terribly boring.

nian see nyan.

niang see nyang.

niao see nyau.

nie see nye.

您 **nín** (PN) you (singular) (h).

寧[寍,寧寧][宁] **níng, nǐng*** (B) 1)* rather than. ～肯 would rather. 2) peaceful. 安～ be peaceful and quiet. 3) Nanking. ～綢 silk from Nanking. (PT)～...也... would rather... and.... /我～死也不投降. I would rather die and not surrender. or I would rather die than surrender. /我～晚了,也得洗一個澡. I'd rather be late and take a bath. or I'd rather be late than not take a bath. t

　寧可 **níngkě, nǐngkě** = 寧願 **níngywàn**.

　寧願 **níngywàn, nǐngywàn** (AV) would rather, prefer to, do something. /我～要這個,不要那個. I prefer to have this rather than that. (FV) would rather. /我～你去,不願意他去. I'd rather have you go; I don't want him to go.

檸 **níng** (B) ↓.

　檸檬 **níngméng** (N) lemon. ～水 lemonade.

凝 **níng** (FV) congeal, jell. /那碗雞湯已經～成凍了. That bowl of chicken soup has congealed. (B) freeze. ～結 freeze.

擰 **nǐng** (FV) 1) wring. /把衣服～一～. Wring out the clothes. 2) pinch. /你別～我. Don't pinch me. →擰 **nǐng**, 擰 **nìng**.

擰 **nǐng** (FV) 1) screw on a bottle cap, screw in a screw. /你能把那個瓶子蓋ル～下來嗎? Can you unscrew the cap on that bottle? 2) twist. /你把我的胳膊～疼了. You twisted my arm and hurt it. 3) go wrong (lp). /自從他來了,什麼事都～了. Ever since he came, everything has gone wrong. (SV) 1) be at odds, incompatible (lp). /最近他們兩個人～了. Thos two have been at odds lately. ~擰 níng, 擰 nǐng.

擰 nǐng (SV) be stubborn. ~擰 níng, 擰 nǐng.

濘 nìng→濘 nèng.

寧 nǐng→寧 níng.

niu *see* nyou.

no *see* nwo.

nong *see* nung.

nü *see* nyu.

奴 nú (B) slave. ~才 slave.
  奴隸 'núlì (N) slave.

努 nǔ (B) exert, strive. ~傷 be injured through over-exertion. *t*
  努力 nǔlì (SV) be diligent. /他讀書很~. He studies very diligently. (AV) try hard to do something. /他~忘記他的往事. He tried hard to forget his past. (VO) do one's best, work hard. /我已經努了力了. I've done my best. (N) effort. /我的~都沒有結果. All my efforts were fruitless.

nuan *see* nwan.

nüe *see* nywe.

nun *see* nwun.

濃 núng (SV) 1) be heavy, thick. /他的眉毛很~. He has heavy eyebrows. /救火員在~煙裡跑來跑去的. The firemen ran in and out of the thick smoke. /希飯太~了. The congee is too thick. 2) be strong (of coffee, tea, a flavor, odor). ~香 strong perfume. /這種食品的味道很~. This kind of food has a very strong flavor. /這咖啡太~. This coffee is too strong. 3) be strong, great (of one's interest). /他對下棋的興趣很~. He has a great interest in chess.
  濃厚 'núnghòu (SV) be strong, great (of one's interest). /他對學中文的興趣很~. He is greatly interested in learning Chinese.

膿 núng, néng (N) pus.

農[農][农] núng (B) agriculture, farming. ~人 farmer. *t*

農場 núngchǎng (N) farm.
農夫 núngfū (N) farmer.
農具 núngjyù (N) farm implement (M件 jyàn).
農民 núngmín (N) peasant, farmer.
農村 núngtswūn (N) small village surrounded by farms, rural area (in contrast to urban districts). ~生活 rural life.
農業 núngyè (N) agriculture.
農業社 núngyèshè (N) farmers' cooperative.

弄 nùng, nèng (FV) 1) do. /我幫你~吧. I'll help you do it. 2) straighten, fix. /請你把窗簾~一~. Will you please fix that curtain? 3) repair, fix. /我的表壞了, 你能~嗎? My watch is broken; can you fix it? 4) get something (no matter what). /我會~一點錢來的. I'll get some money, no matter what. 5) fool with, fuss with. /他老~他的指甲. He is always fooling with his fingernails. /別~你小弟弟. Leave your little brother alone. 6) in RC, indicates a change of condition with general causal meaning, not specifying the precise method by which the change is brought about. ~皺 get something wrinkled; ~清楚 understand clearly. ~倒 knock something over. (B) sub-lane, branch lane (used in addresses) 中山路三巷六~九號 9, Sub-lane 6, Lane 3, Chungshan Road.

暖[煖]nwǎn (SV) be warm. /這件大衣很~. This coat is very warm. /天氣漸漸地~了. The weather is gradually getting warmer. (FV) warm something. /把酒~一~. Warm up the wine.
  暖氣 nwǎnchì (N) warm air, heat.
  暖氣爐 nwǎnchìlú (N) <-子> radiator (for steam heat).
  暖和 nwǎnhwo (SV) be nice and warm. /春天的氣候真好, ~但不熱. Spring weather is really pleasant. It's nice and warm, but not hot. (FV) become warm. /你先坐會儿, 等~過來再出去. Sit down and warm up first before going out again.
  暖水壺 nwánshwěihú (N) thermos jug.

暖水瓶 **nwánshwěipíng** (N) thermos bottle.

挪 **nwó** (FV) shift, move. /我們把桌子~到那屋去吧. Let's move the table into that room.

懦 **nwò** (B) weak, timid. ~夫 weak person, coward.

懦弱 **nwòrwò** (SV) be weak, cowardly.

嫩 **nwùn** 一嫩 **nèn**.

年 **nyán** (M) year. /我在紐約住了三~. I lived in New York three years. (B) 1) year. 閏年 leap year; 去~ last year. 2) the New Year. 過~ celebrate the New Year. 3) age. 老~ old age; 青~ youth.

年輕 **nyánchīng** (SV) be young (of a person). /我~的時候也很愛玩. When I was young I liked to have fun too.

年青 **nyánchīng** = 年輕 **nyánchīng**.

年紀 **nyánjì** (N) age (of people).

年級 **nyánjí** (M) grade in school, year in high school, college. 一~ freshman year; 二~ sophomore year. /你念幾~了? What grade are you in? or What year are you?

年鑑 **nyánjyàn** (N) yearbook, annual report (M 本 **běn**).

年齡 **nyánlíng** (N) age (of people).

年歲 **nyánswèi** (N) 1) age (of people). 2) year's harvest. /今年的~很好. This year's harvest was very good.

年頭兒 **nyántóur** (N) 1) (business) year. /這個~不好. This has been a bad year. 2) time, era, days. /這~過日子不容易. It's hard to earn a living these days. /那~人人都闊. In those days everybody was rich.

黏〔粘〕 **nyán** (SV) be sticky. /漿糊不~了. This paste isn't sticky anymore.

碾〔輾〕 **nyǎn** (FV) roll over something with a roller. ~米 roll rice (in order to remove the outer shell). (B) <-子> roller. ~路機 steam roller.

念〔唸(FV)〕 **nyàn** (FV) 1) read out loud. /請你把這封信給我~~. Please read this letter to me. 2)

study. ~物理 study physics. (B) 1) think of. 掛~ miss someone. 2) thought. 觀~ concept.

念頭 **nyàntou** (N) <-ㄦ> idea, thought (for future action). /她已經打消和她丈夫離婚的~了. She discarded the idea of getting a divorce from her husband. /你可別動怪~. Don't get any funny ideas.

娘〔孃〕 **nyáng** (N) mother, mamma. (B) girl, young lady. 姑~ maiden.

鳥〔鳥〕 **nyǎu** (B) <-ㄦ> bird (M 隻 **jī**). ~獸 birds and beasts.

尿〔溺〕 **nyau, swei**＊ (N)＊ urine. 撒~ urinate. (FV) urinate. ~炕 wet the bed. /這個小孩把新地氈~了. The child urinated on the new rug.

捏 **nyē** (FV) 1) hold tightly between the thumb and other fingers. /那個小娃娃手裡~了一張照片. The little child is holding a picture in his hand. 2) mold, shape. /他會~泥人. He knows how to mold clay figures. 3) pinch. /你為什麼~我? Why did you pinch me? (M) pinch. 一~鹽 a pinch of salt. (B) fabricate. ~造謠言 spread a rumor.

牛 **nyóu** (N) cow, bull, ox (M 頭 **tóu**, 隻 **jī**). s

牛奶 **nyóunǎi** (N) cow's milk.

牛排 **nyóupái** (N) steak (M 塊 **kwài**).

牛肉 **nyóuròu** (N) beef.

扭 **nyǒu** (FV) 1) turn or twist the head or body around. /他~過頭來. He turned his head. 2) swing one's hips, sway in walking. /瞧她那~勁ㄦ的! Look at the swing she's got! 3) twist, wrench. /我下樓的時候把腳~了. I twisted my ankle coming down the stairs. 4) wring. /先把拖把~乾再用. Wring out the mop before you use it.

紐〔鈕〕 **nyǒu** (B) <-子, -ㄦ> button (on clothing or on a device) (M 顆 **kē**). ~扣 button (on clothing); 電~ button (electric, as on a doorbell). t

女 **nyǔ** (AT) female (of humans). ~司機 female cab driver. (B) 1) daughter. 小~ daughter (when referring to one's own daughter); ～公子 daughter (somebody else's). 2) woman. 男～平等 equality of men and women.

女兒 **nyǔer** (N) daughter.

女工 **nyúgūng** (N) 1) female worker. 2) needlework.

女孩子 **nyǔháidz** (N) 1) girl. /那個～很漂亮. That girl is very pretty. 2) daughter. /我的～還很小. My daughter is still very small.

女人 **'nyǔrén** (N) 1) woman. 2) wife (not very polite).

女士 **'nyǔshr̀** (N) lady. (B) used after surnames, Miss, Mrs. 張～ Miss or Mrs. Chang.

女婿 **nyǔsyu** (N) son-in-law.

虐 **nywè** (B) cruel. ～待 ill-treat.

瘧[疾] **nywè** (B) malaria. ～蚊 malaria mosquito. →瘧 **yàu**.

o see e.

嘔 **ou** (P) used at the end of a sentence to call attention to, or to warn of, a situation. /下雪天路滑,慢點開車～. It's snowing and the road is slippery; drive slowly. →嘔 **ǒu**. cf 嘍 **lou**.

哦 **óu** →哦 **é**.

嘔 **ǒu** (FV) throw up, vomit. /他暈船把吃下的東西都～光了. He got seasick and threw up everything he ate. →嘔 **ou**.

嘔吐 **ǒutù** (FV) throw up, vomit. 他～了半天. He kept throwing up.

藕 **ǒu** (N) lotus root (M 根 **gēn**).

偶 **ǒu** (B) 1) accidental. ～性 fortuity, chance occurrence. 2) image (of a person). ～像 idol; 木～ puppet. 3) spouse. 配～ spouse. 4) even (of numbers). ～數 even number.

偶爾 **óuěr** (A) occasionally, once in a while. /我們～在一起吃吃飯. We occasionally have dinner together.

偶然 **ǒurán** (A) 1) all of a sudden, suddenly. /我～想起今天和他有約會. All of a sudden I remembered that I have a date with him today. 2) accidentally, by chance. /我們～在電影院裡遇見. We

met in the movie theater accidentally. 3) occasionally, once in a while. /他～到我家來吃飯. He came to our house to eat once in a while. (N) accident, chance thing. /我認識他完全是一種～. My getting to know him was completely an accident.

哦 **òu** (I) Oh, I see. / A: 這就是我昨天沒來的原因. B:～. A: This is why I didn't come yesterday. B: Oh, I see. →哦 **é**.

趴 **pā** (FV) 1) lie on one's stomach. /我們～在地下放槍. We shoot lying on the ground. 2) lean on. /她～在我肩上哭. She leaned on my shoulder and cried.

趴下 **pāsya** (RE) indicates falling face down. 打～ be knocked down; 摔～ trip and fall flat; 累～ fall down with exhaustion.

耙 **pá** (B) <-子> rake (M 把 **bǎ**).→耙 **bà**.

爬 **pá** (FV) 1) crawl, creep. /這個小娃娃才七個月就會～了. This baby is only seven months old but she can already crawl. 2) climb. ～山 climb a mountain.

怕 **pà** (FV) 1) be afraid (of). /我～蛇. I'm afraid of snakes. /我～他病了. I'm afraid he's ill. 2) cannot stand, cannot endure. /我真～這種熱天. I really can't stand this hot weather. (SV) be frightened, scared. /我昨天晚上一個人在家～得要命. I was home by myself last night and was frightened to death. (A) probably. /他～不來了. He probably won't come. /今天怕會下雨吧. It'll probably rain today. (AV) fear to. /我怕游泳. I'm afraid to swim.

拍 **pāi** (FV) 1) pat. /我不喜歡人～我的頭. I don't like people to pat me on the head. 2) clap. ～手 clap the hands. 3) bounce. ～球 bounce a ball. 4) take a picture. ～照片 take a picture. 5) send a telegram. ～電報 send a telegram. 6) fawn on. /他最愛～有錢人. He likes to fawn on rich people.

(M) beat in a measure of music.
/這歌是四~的. This song has four beats to a measure.

拍子 **pāidz** (N) 1) racket, paddle. 網球~tennis racket; 蒼蠅~ fly-swatter. 2) beat (of music). 打~beat time to music. /按着~跳舞. Dance to the beat of the music.

拍掌 **pāijǎng** (VO) applaud, clap one's hands. /她唱完以後, 聽眾大聲~. After she sang, the audience applauded loudly.

拍賣 **pāimài** (FV) auction. /這張椅子~了五塊錢. This chair was auctioned off at five dollars.

牌 **pái** (N) 1) <-子,-ル> signboard, placard (M塊**kwài**). 2) mahjong piece, dominoe, card, square playing piece (M張**jāng**). 3) game of mahjong, cards, etc. (M圈**chwān**). /讓我打幾~. Let me play a few games. (B) 1) <-子,-ル> brand. 名~ good brand. 2) <-ル> metal plate (M塊**kwài**). 車~ license plate.

排 **pái** (FV) 1) arrange in a row or column, line up (lit.or fig.). /請你把椅子都~起來. Would you please arrange the chairs? /今天的節目已經~好了. Today's program has been arranged. 2) be lined up (as people, cars). /電影院門口正~了很多人買票. There are many people lined up in front of the theater buying tickets. 3) rank someone. /他~在前三名. He is ranked among the top three. 4) discharge, eject, get rid of. /汽車後面那條管子是用來~氣的. The pipe in the back of the car gets rid of the exhaust. 5) rehearse. /今天晚上我們~第三幕. We'll rehearse the third act this evening. 5) set type. /社會新聞還沒有~. The type for the social column hasn't been set yet. (N) platoon. (M) row. 第一~ the first row. (B) 1) steak. 牛~ steak. 2) anti-. ~外 be anti-foreign. →排**pái**.

排版 **páibǎn** (VO) set type. /排這本書的版要一個星期. It will take a week to set type for this book.

排球 **páichyóu** (N) 1) volleyball (the game) (M場**chǎng**, 次**tsz**). 2) a volleyball (M隻**jr**).

排字 **páidz** (VO) set type. /他忙了一天才排了兩行字. He was busy all day and only set two lines of type.

排長 **páijǎng** (N) platoon leader.

排列 **páilyè** (FV) arrange in a line or column. /我該怎麼~這些書呢? How should I arrange those books?

排演 **páiyǎn** (FV) rehearse. /這齣戲我們排演過三次了. We've rehearsed this play three times. (N) rehearsal (M次**tsz**).

排 **pái** (B) 1. →排**pái**.
排子 **páidz** (N) row of logs or boards. ~車 cart; 冰~sledge.

派 **pài** (FV) 1) assign something, appoint someone. /我的上司~了我一個很重要的工作. My boss assigned me a very important job. /政府~他做駐美大使. The government appointed him ambassador to the United States. /我~我的女佣人來你家取吧. I'll send my maid to your house to get it. 2) charge, levy. ~稅 levy taxes. /公路局~每家出五塊錢修那條路. The highway department charged every house five dollars to pave that road. 3) distribute. /請你替我把這些書~給學生們. Please distribute these books to the students for me. (M) 1) clique, party, group, with common feeling and purpose. /開會的時候工人分成三~. At the meeting, the workers divided into three groups. 2) school of thought, art, etc. /這一~的學者很少. Few scholars belong to this school of thought. (B) 1)-ism, -ist. 浪漫~ romanticism; 樂觀~optimist. 2) clique, party. 黨~ political party. t

派出所 **pàichūswǒ** (N) police station (branch office, not the main headquarters).

攀 **pān** (FV) make friends with (having ulterior motives). /他老想~一個闊朋友. He always tries to make friends with rich people. (B) 1) climb up. ~登 climb up. 2) involve, implicate. ～扯 implicate someone.

盤{槃 (N)}〔盌〕 pán (N) <‑ㄦ,‑子> tray, platter, plate, dish. (FV) 1) coil up. /她把辮子～在頭頂上了. She coiled the pigtail up on her head. 2) move something big and heavy. /五個人才能把這架鋼琴～下樓去. It will take five people to move the piano downstairs. 3) transfer, sell, a business. /我去年就把那小店～給別人了. I sold that little store to some other people last year. (M) game of chess, cards. 一～棋 a game of chess. (B) market price. 開～ start bidding.

盼 pàn (FV) 1) wish, hope, expect. /～他早來信. I hope he'll write soon. /我正～着朋友. I'm expecting a friend right now. (B) look. 左顧右～look around.
盼望 pànwàng (FV) 1) wish, hope. /我～他們兩人結婚. I hope those two will get married. 2) long for. /他很～你. He longs for you very much. (N) hope.

判 pàn (FV) 1) sentence someone. /法官～了他十年監禁. The judge sentenced him to ten years in prison. 2) make a decision on a law case. /這樁案子已經～了. The case has been decided.
判斷 'pàndwàn (FV) judge, ascertain, evaluate. /他要～我們兩人誰對. He'll have to judge which one of us is right. /這顆鑽石的價值沒有人能～. Nobody can judge the value of this diamond. (N) judgment, evaluation.
判斷力 pàndwànlì (N) ability to make judgments. /他那個人沒～. He has no ability to make judgments.
判決 pànjywé (FV) make a decision on a law case. /這樁謀殺案太複雜了,法官～不了. This murder case is so complicated that the judge can't make a decision on it. (N) decision (in court).

旁 páng (AT) other, different. ～人 other people. (B) side. ～門 side door; 兩～ both sides; ～觀 be a spectator.

旁邊 pángbyān (PW) <‑ㄦ> (by) the side of, (the area) near. /我家～有一個教堂. There's a church near my house. /路～停着許多汽車. Many cars stopped by the side of the road.

螃 páng (B) ↓.
螃蠏 pángsye (N) crab (M 隻 jŕ).

胖 pàng (SV) be fat (of a person). /他比去年～了很多. He is much fatter than he was last year.
胖子 pàngdz (N) 1) fat person. 2) fatty (nickname).

pao see pau.

泡 pāu (SV) 1) be thick and soft, fluffy. /這床棉被很～. This quilt is very thick and soft. 2) be swollen. /她哭得眼睛都～了. She cried so long her eyes are all swollen. (M) for bowel movements, urine. 一～大便 a bowel movement. →泡 pàu.

抛 páu (FV) 1) throw. /請你把那本書～給我. Please throw me that book. 2) abandon, desert. /她～了丈夫和孩子去和別人結婚了. She deserted her husband and children to marry another man.
抛錨 páumáu (VO) 1) drop anchor. /我們要在這裏～. We'll drop anchor here. 2) break down (as a car). /我們的汽車在路上～了,所以來遲了. We are late because our car broke down on the way.

刨 páu (FV) 1) exclude, subtract. /～了我還有多少人? How many people are there, excluding me? 2) dig. /我們～一個坑把他埋了吧. Let's dig a hole and bury him there. →刨 bàu.

炮 páu (B) decoct medicine from herbs. ～製 decoct medicine. →炮 bāu, 炮 pàu.

跑 pău (FV) 1) run. /我沒你～得快. I can't run as fast as you. 2) run away, escape. /那個賊是從窗戶～的. The burglar escaped through the window. 3) go. /你～那儿去了? Where did you go? (RE) indicates running away. 嚇～ frighten away.

跑馬場 **páumǎchǎng** (N) racing park, raceway (for horse racing only).

跑道 **pǎudàu** (N) 1) racetrack. 2) runway (for airplanes). (M條**tyáu**).

泡 **pàu** (FV) 1) steep, soak. ～茶 steep tea. /在水裡～一會再洗就容易了. Soak it in water for a while and then it'll be easier to wash 2) be together. /我跟他～了一個下午. He and I were together the whole afternoon. 3) pester. /你不給我錢我就跟你～了. I'll keep pestering you until you give me the money. (N) 1) <ㄦ,-子> bubble. 2) <-ㄦ> blister. 3) <-ㄦ,-子> light bulb. →泡**pāu**.

砲(礮)**pàu** (N) 1) gun, cannon, artillery (M尊**dzwún**, 座**dzwò**, 門**mén**). 2) cannon (piece in Chinese chess) (M隻**jī**). (M) shot of a gun. 發兩～ fire two shots.

砲彈 **pàudàn** (N) artillery shell (M發**fā**).

砲臺 **pàutái** (N) 1) gun platform (M座**dzwò**). 2) fort.

炮(爆)(B)}**pàu** (N) 1) gun, cannon, artillery (M尊**dzwūn**, 座**dzwò**, 門**mén**). 2) cannon (piece in Chinese chess) (M隻**jī**). (M) shot of a gun. 發兩～ fire two shots (B) firecracker. 鞭～ firecracker. →炮**bāu**, 炮**páu**.

炮仗 **pàujang** (N) firecracker (M掛**gwà**, 串**chwàn**).

哑 **pēi** (I) bah (expression of contempt). /～, 胡說八道! Bah, that's nonsense!

賠 **péi** (FV) 1) pay damages, pay for something spoiled or broken. /洗衣店把我的大衣弄壞了, 所以～了我一件新的. The dry-cleaners ruined my overcoat, so they paid for a new one. 2) lose money in business. /他～了一萬塊錢只好關店了. He lost ten thousand dollars, so he had to close his store.

賠不是 **péibúshr** (VO) apologize. /你得給他賠個不是. You should apologize to him.

賠償 **péichǎng** (FV) make up a loss, pay for something lost or damaged. /我要～你的損失.

I'll pay for your losses. (N) indemnity, reparation.

賠罪 **péidzwèi** (VO) apologize. /你向他賠個罪. Apologize to him.

培 **péi** (B) 1) bank up. ～土 bank up with dirt. 2) nourish, cultivate. ～育 raise animals, plants.

培養 **péiyǎng** (FV) 1) stimulate, nourish, cultivate (as one's interest). ～人材 stimulate talented people. /我想～一點讀書的興趣. I want to cultivate an interest in reading. 2) raise, grow. ～細菌 grow bacteria.

陪 **péi** (FV) keep someone company. /我今天下午來～你. I'll come and keep you company this afternoon. (CV) along with, with. /她願意～我去歐洲旅行. She's going along with me to Europe.

陪襯 **'péichèn** (FV) complement, enhance, brighten up. /這個衣服得用一個紅裡子～. This dress needs a red lining to brighten it up. (N) accessory (decoration).

配 **pèi** (FV) 1) find something to match or fit something else. /這塊料子不夠, 我得去～一點. This piece of material isn't big enough; I'll have to find some more to match it. 2) mate. /我家的波斯貓和隔壁的暹邏貓～了. My Persian cat mated with my neighbor's Siamese cat. 3) allot. /我們每個人～了三天的糧食. Each of us was allotted three days' food. (SV) be a good match. /他跟他太太不～. He and his wife aren't a good match. (AV) be qualified to, fit to. /他不～做我們的領袖. He is not qualified to be our leader. (CV) next to, with. /粉的～淺藍很好看. Pink goes well with light blue.

配合 **pèihe** (SV) be a good match, go well together. /這兩個顏色很～. These two colors go very well together. (FV) be coordinated. /他們兩個人的工作～得很好. The work those two do is well coordinated.

配角兒 **pèijyǎur, pèijywéer** (N) 1) subsidiary or supporting role. 2) subsidiary or supporting actor.

佩 **pèi** (B) 1) wear at the waist. ～刀 wear a sword. 2) admire and respect. 欽～ admire and respect. *t*

   佩服 **pèifu** (FV) admire and respect. /我很～他的學問. I admire and respect his knowledge.

噴 **pēn** (FV) 1) spurt, puff. /噴泉向空中～水. The fountain spurts water into the air. /烟自～着很濃的烟. The chimney is puffing very dense smoke. 2) spray. /她～了很多香水在頭髮上. She sprayed a lot of perfume on her hair. →噴 **pèn**.

   噴氣機 **pēnchìjī** (N) jet plane (M 架 **jyà**).

   噴霧器 **pēnwùchì** (N) atomizer (M 具 **jyù**, 架 **jyà**).

盆 **pén** (N) <-子,-ㄦ> basin, bowl, tub, pot. 臉～ washbowl; 澡～ bathtub; 花～ flowerpot.

噴 **pèn** (B) puff. ～香 be very fragrant (lit. puffingly fragrant). →噴 **pēn**.

   噴嚏 **pènti** (N) sneeze. /我打了好幾個～. I sneezed many times.

烹 **pēng** (FV) simmer in a pan with sauce after searing. /這個蝦還得～幾分鐘. The shrimp need to simmer for a few minutes more. (B) to cook. ～飪 cooking.

棚 **péng** (N) <-子,-ㄦ> 1) tent. 2) shed.

朋 **péng** (B) friend, companion. ～黨 clique.

   朋友 **péngyou** (N) friend.

捧 **pěng** (FV) 1) hold something out or up in both hands. /新娘～着一束玫瑰花從走道中走來. The bride is coming down the aisle holding a bouquet of roses. 2) praise, flatter, fawn on. /別把他～得太高了. Don't praise him too much. /他喜歡～有錢人. He likes to fawn on rich people. 3) be the patron of (a performer, actor, etc.). ～戲子 be the patron of an opera performer. (M) for amounts of something one can carry with the hands cupped together. 一～米 a double handful of rice.

碰撞 **pèng** (FV) 1) knock, bump. /他～了我一下. He bumped me.

/我的頭～了一個疙. I bumped my head and it made a lump. 2) touch. /別～我 Don't touch me. 3) run into, meet accidentally. /我剛才在街上～到一個老朋友. I just ran into an old friend of mine on the street.

   碰巧 **pèngchyǎu** (A) <-ㄦ> by chance, by accident. /我～今天沒帶錢. It just so happened that I didn't bring any money today.

   碰見 **pèngjyan** (RC) run into, meet accidentally. /我昨天在公園～他和他女朋友. I ran into him and his girl friend in the park yesterday.

   碰運氣 **pèngywùnchi** (VO) try one's luck. /在這兒找不到事到紐約去碰碰運氣. I can't find any work here, so I'm going to try my luck in New York.

匹疋 **pī**, **pǐ*** (M) 1) for horses. 一～馬 a horse. 2) for horsepower. 一百二十五～馬力 one hundred and twenty-five horsepower. 3)* bolt of cloth. 一～布 a bolt of cloth.

披 **pī** (FV) drape or put something over one's shoulders. /有點冷,你最好～一件毛衣. It's a little chilly; you'd better put a sweater over your shoulders. /她～着長而黑的頭髮. She wears her long black hair down over her shoulders.

批 **pī** (FV) 1) write down one's opinion, comment on, a document (of a higher official). /請你把這個文件給～一～? Would you please write down your opinion of this document? 2) mark an examination paper. ～考卷 mark an exam. (M) 1) batch. 一～新書 a batch of new books. 2) group of people. 一～學生 a group of students. (B) 1) annotation, note. 眉～ notes at the top of a page. 2) wholesale. ～進 buy wholesale.

   批發 **pīfā** (N) wholesale. /我們做～. We do business wholesale. (FV) sell wholesale. /香烟工廠把香烟～給商人. The cigarette company sells cigarettes to the merchants wholesale.

   批准 **pījwǔn** (RC) approve, sanction, ratify. /你的請求已

經～了. Your request has been approved. /美國還沒有～那個條約呢. The United States hasn't ratified that treaty yet.

批判 **pīpàn** (FV) criticize (c). /他把那本書～得很厲害. He criticized that book very strongly. (N) critique. /康德的純理性～ Kant's *Critique of Pure Reason*.

批評 **pīping** (FV) criticize. /我不喜歡～人. I don't like to criticize people. (N) criticism. /我願意接你的～. I'm willing to accept your criticism.

劈 **pí** (FV) split. /我的指甲～了. My fingernail split. (B) right on. ～臉一掌 slap someone right across the face. →劈 **pí**.

皮 **pí** (N) 1) <-ㄦ> skin, hide, peel, bark (M張 **jāng**, 塊 **kwài**). 2) <-子> leather (M張 **jāng**, 塊 **kwài**). 3) <-子> fur (M張 **jāng**, 塊 **kwài**). 4) <-子,-ㄦ> cover of a book. (SV) 1) be stale, not crisp. /花生～了. The peanuts aren't crisp any more. 2) be naughty, unmindful of scolding. /那個孩子很～. That child is very naughty. (B) sheet metal. 銅～copper sheeting. s t

皮襖 **píáu** (N) fur-lined gown (M件 **jyàn**).

皮球 **píchyóu** (N) ball (leather or rubber).

皮帶 **pídài** (N) leather belt (M根 **gēn**, 條 **tyáu**).

皮膚 **pífu** (N) skin (of a person).

皮鞋 **písyé** (N) (leather) shoe (M隻 **jŗ**, 雙 **shwāng**).

疲 **pí** (B) tired, exhausted, weary. ～倦 be tired and sleepy.

疲乏 **pífá** (SV) be tired, fatigued. /工作了一天之後,我很～了. After a day's work, I'm very tired.

疲勞 **píláu** (SV) be tired, fatigued. /我昨天一天沒睡,很～. I didn't sleep a wink last night, so I'm very tired.

脾 **pí** (N) spleen.

脾氣 **píchi** (N) 1) temper. /他的～很壞. He has a bad temper. 2) temperament. /我們的～不同. Our temperaments are different.

啤 **pí** (B) ㄣ. t

啤酒 **píjyŏu** (N) beer.

劈 **pí** (FV) 1) pull apart something with the hands. /那個孩子把我的眼鏡～了. That child pulled my glasses apart. 2) divide into several parts, split (fig.). /我們把利錢～三份ㄦ. We split the profit three ways. →劈 **pí**.

劈柴 **píchái** (N) firewood, kindling.

匹 **pí**→匹 **pí**.

譬 **pí** (B) give an example. ～喻 analogy; ～方說 for example.

譬如 **pírú** (A) for example. /～我就不喜歡他. I, for example, don't like him.

屁 **pí** (N) gas (in the stomach). 放～ give off gas (from the rectum). (B) useless, stupid. ～話 nonsense; ～事 useless thing, unimportant matter.

屁股 **pígu** (N) 1) buttocks. 2) rear end of a thing. 船～ stern of a boat.

pian *see* **pyan**.

piao *see* **pyau**.

pie *see* **pye**.

拼 **pīn** (FV) 1) fight with all one has (fig). /明天你敢來開會我就跟你～了. If you dare come to the meeting tomorrow, I'll fight you with all I've got. 2) piece something together. /太碎了就～不起來了. If it's in too many fragments, it can't be pieced together. 3) spell a word. /這個字我不會～. I can't spell this word.

拼命 **pīnmìng** (VO) fight with all one has (fig). /你不給我錢我跟你～. If you don't give me the money, I'll fight you with all I've got. (A) to the utmost, desperately, very hard. ～念書 study very hard.

拼音字母 **pīnyīndzmŭ** (N) alphabet.

貧 **pín** (SV) be garrulous, gabby. /這個人的嘴真～. He is really gabby. (B) poor。～窮 poverty.

貧民 **pínmín** (N) poor people.

品 **pĭn** (B) 1) goods, stuff. 貨～ merchandise; 食～ foodstuffs; 農產～ agricultural products. 2) quality.

上 ~ superior quality. 3) rank, grade, of pre-Republic officials. — ~ first rank. 4) personality, character. ~格 personality, character. (FV) sample, judge the quality of something. ~ 茶 sample tea.

品質 **pǐnjŕ** (N) 1) quality. 2) character (of a person).

品行 **pǐnsying** (N) behavior, conduct. /他的~好極了. His conduct is excellent.

乒 **pīng** (ON) bang. /~~~ 響了三鎗. Three shots went bang bang bang.

乒乓球 **pīngpāngchyóu** (N) 1) ping-pong ball. 2) ping-pong (the game) (M 盤 **pán**).

蘋〔苹〕**píng** (B) ⸴.

蘋果 **pínggwǒ** (N) apple (M 隻 jŕ).

瓶 **píng** (N) vase. (M) bottle, jar. 一 ~ 牛奶 a bottle of milk. (B)<子⸴ 一ル > bottle, jar. 酒 ~ wine bottle.

憑〔凭〕**píng** (FV) 1) depend on. /計劃能不能實現全~你了. Whether or not this plan can be carried out depends completely on you. 2) lean on. /他正~着欄杆看月亮呢. She's leaning on the railing looking at the moon. (CV) 1) due to the fact that, since. /~我是你哥哥所以要管你. Since I'm your older brother, I can tell you what to do. 2) according to, basing on. /你~什麼說這句話? What are you basing this statement on? (B) 1) basis, evidence. ~據 evidence; 文 ~ diploma. 2) followed by a noun, who, what (showing surprise or disbelief). /A: 我想把帝國大廈買下來. B: ~你? A: I plan to buy the Empire State Building. B: Who, you?

平 **píng** (SV) 1) be level, flat. /那邊的地很 ~. The ground over there is level. 2) be smooth. /這條路很 ~. This road is very smooth. (FV) 1) put down an uprising, pacify. /內亂已經 ~ 了. The civil disorder has been put down. 2) weigh. /~ 一下這塊銀子有多重. Weigh this piece of silver and see how heavy it is. (B) 1) equal, just, fair. 公 ~ be just; 不 ~ be un-

fair. 2) peaceful. 和 ~ peace, be peaceful. 3) common, ordinary. ~ 民 common people. 4) Peiping (contracted form of 北平 **beiping**).

~劇 Peiping opera. 5) level tone (in Chinese). ~聲 level tone. t

平安 **píngān** (SV) 1) be safe, secure. /打仗的時候住在山上比較 ~. In wartime living in the mountains is safer. 2) be peaceful. /鄉村生活很 ~. Country life is peaceful.

平常 **píngcháng** (SV) be common, ordinary. /一月掙四五百塊錢是很 ~ 的. Earning four or five hundred dollars a month is quite common. (A) normally, ordinarily, usually. /我 ~ 不大出門. I usually don't go out much.

平等 **píngděng** (SV) be equal (of people). /你相信所有的人都 ~ 嗎? Do you believe that all men are created equal? (N) equality.

平分 **píngfēn** (FV) divide equally. /我的錢讓他們三個人給 ~ 了. My money was equally divided among those three persons.

平衡 **pínghéng** (SV) be balanced, in equilibrium. /收入跟支出不 ~. Income and expenditures don't balance. (N) balance, equilibrium.

平靜 **píngjìng** (SV) be peaceful and quiet. /這個地方很 ~. This place is very peaceful and quiet.

平均 **píngjyūn** (AT) average, mean. /今年的 ~ 濕度比去年低. The average humidity is lower this year than last year. (SV) be equal. /我們的工作分配得很 ~. The work has been equally divided among us. (A) 1) on the average. /我 ~ 每天只睡六個鐘頭. I sleep only six hours a day on the average. 2) equally. /把這塊餅給他們 ~ 分一分. Divide this cake up equally among them. (FV) average up. /把這些數目 ~ 一下. Average up these figures, please.

平穩 **'píngwěn** (SV) be steady, smooth. /車走的很 ~. The car rides very smoothly.

平原 **píngywán** (N) plain (M 片 **pyàn**).

評 **píng** (FV) 1) judge, umpire. /我們兩個人誰對請你 ~ 一 ~.

You judge which of the two of us is right. 2) comment on, criticize. /我只聽了半齣戲所以沒有法兒～. I can't criticize that play because I've only seen half of it. (B) criticism, review. 書～ book review.

評論 pínglwùn (FV) discuss critically. /他們幾個人在一起就愛～政事. Whenever those people get together, they like to discuss politics. (N) 1) editorial. 2) commentator's *or* critic's piece in a publication. (M篇pyān).

po *see* pwo.

撲[扑]pū (FV) 1) spring, pounce. /老虎～到他身上,他就昏倒了. The tiger sprang at him and he fainted. 2) apply (of face powder). /她在臉上輕輕地～了一層粉. She lightly applied some powder to her face. t

撲克牌 pūkèpái (N) 1) playing card (M副fù, 張jāng). 2) poker (the game) (M盤pán).

撲通 pūtūng (ON) sound of something dropping into water. /他～一聲跳進水裏. He jumped into the water with a splash.

鋪 pū (FV) 1) spread out *or* over. ～地毯 spread out a rug. /請你在那張桌子上～一張桌布. Please put a tablecloth on the table. 2) pave. /公路局現在～那條路呢. The highway department is paving that road now. →鋪pù.

鋪蓋 pūgai (N) bedding (M牀chwáng).

葡 pú (B) ↓. t
葡萄 pútau (N) grape (M顆kē; ↓都嚕dūlu; 串chwàn).

僕[仆]pú (B) servant. 男～ male servant.
僕人 'púren (N) servant.

樸 pú→樸pǔ.

菩 pú (B)↓. t
菩薩 púsa (N) 1) bodhisattva. 2) statue *or* image of Buddha. (M位wèi, 尊dzwūn).

譜 pǔ (FV) score, arrange, music. /他把那個歌又～了一下兒. He rearranged that song. (B) 1) list, chart. 家～ genealogy; 光～spec-

trum. 2) manual, guidebook. 食～ recipe book; 棋～ guidebook for playing chess; 歌～ book of songs.

譜兒 pǔr (N) 1) stylishness, style (lp). /她的～很大. She has a lot of style. 2) standard, something to go by, plan. /因為我一點～也沒有,所以很着急. I'm worried because I don't have anything to go by.

樸[朴]pǔ, pú (B) unadorned, plain. ～實 be unadorned.

樸素 púsù, púsu (SV) be simple, plain, (of dress or one's life). /那位小姐穿的很～. That girl dresses very simply.

普 pǔ (B) universal, general. ～天下 all over the world. t

普遍 pǔbyàn (SV) be prevailing, widespread. /教育不夠～. Education isn't sufficiently widespread. (A) generally. /英文程度～很低. The level of English is generally very low.

普通 pǔtūng (SV) be common, ordinary. /花十塊錢買雙鞋是很～的事. Spending ten dollars on a pair of shoes is quite common. (A) usually, commonly. /我～一天抽十隻香烟. I usually smoke ten cigarettes a day.

普通話 pǔtūnghwà (N) 1) Mandarin language in ordinary use and incorporating dialectal peculiarities. 2) standard Mandarin (c).

瀑 pù (B) ↓.
瀑布 pùbù (N) waterfall.

堡 pù→堡bǎu.

鋪[舖](B)} pù (N) bed (M張jāng). (B) <-子> store, shop (M家jyā). 肉～ butcher shop. →鋪pū.

坡 pwō (B) <-子,-兒> slope. 山～ mountain slope.

潑 pwō (FV) 1) toss, throw, liquid out of a container. /她把一盆水～在院裏了. She threw a basinful of water out into the yard. 2) spill. /小心別把湯～了. Be careful not to spill the soup. (SV) be shrewish. /那個女人～極了. That woman is really shrewish.

婆 pwó (B) 1) old woman. 老太～ old

woman; 巫 ~ old witch; 接生 ~ mid-wife.　2) husband's mother. ~ 媳
mother-in-law and daughter-in-law.
3) grandmother. 外 ~ maternal
grandmother.　*t*

　　婆婆 **pwópwo** (N) 1) mother-in-law (husband's mother).　2) grand-mother.

簸 **pwǒ** (B) ↓. → 簸 **bwǒ**, 簸 **bwò**.

　　簸籮 **pwǒlwo** (N) oblong, shallow basket.

破 **pwò** (SV) 1) be damaged, broken,
worn out, torn. ~ 衣裳 torn *or* worn-out garment; ~ 房子 damaged house.
/ 我這雙鞋快 ~ 了. This pair
of shoes of mine is almost worn out.
2) be lousy. ~ 電影 lousy movie.
(FV) 1) break a record. / 他 ~ 了世
界跳遠紀錄. He broke the
world broad-jump record.　2) break
a large bill. / 你能 ~ 這張十塊
錢的票子嗎? Can you break this
ten dollar bill?　3) have a cut, tear,
hole. / 我的襪子上 ~ 了一個
洞. My sock has a hole in it.　4)
wreck a scheme, break a spell. / 我
可以 ~ 他的妖法. I can break
his magic spell.　(RE) indicates the
disclosure or revealing of something.
看 ~ see through something (fig.);
說 ~ disclose orally.

　　破產 **pwòchǎn** (VO) go bank-rupt. / 他已經破了產了. He
has already gone bankrupt.　(N)
bankruptcy. 宣佈 ~ declare bank-ruptcy.

　　破壞 **pwòhwài** (FV) 1) ruin,
destroy. / 他們設法 ~ 敵軍的
武力. They tried to destroy the
enemy's military power.　2) spoil
a plan. / 他想 ~ 我的婚事. He
wants to spoil my marriage plans.
3) say bad things about. / 他在我女
朋友面前 ~ 我. He said bad
things about me to my girl friend.　4)
violate an agreement, etc. / 他 ~
校規被罰了. He violated the
school regulations and was punished.

片 **pyān** → 片 **pyàn**.

篇 **pyān** (M) < -ㄦ > 1) for formal
speeches or writings. 一 ~ 文章 an
article; 一 ~ 演講 a speech.　2)
leaf of a book, page (including both
sides). / 這一 ~ 被撕掉了. This

page is torn.　3) section of a book.
第二 ~ section two.

偏 **pyān** (SV) be inclined to one side,
leaning. / 往左推一推, 有點 ~.
Push it to the left; it's leaning a
little.　(A) perversely. / 他 ~ 不
睡覺. He perversely refused to
sleep.

　　偏見 **pyānjyàn** (N) prejudice.
(SV) be prejudiced. / 這個人很
~. This person is very prejudiced.

　　偏偏 **pyānpyān** (A) 1) perverse-ly. / 他 ~ 等我病的時候來.
He came just when I got sick.　(lit.
He perversely waited until I was
sick to come).

便 **pyán** (B) ↓. → 便 **byàn**.

　　便宜 **pyányi** (SP) be cheap, in-expensive, reasonable in price.
/ 這輛車很 ~. This car is really
cheap.　/ 這價錢相當 ~. This
price is pretty reasonable.　(FV) let
someone off easy. / 這次我 ~ 你,
再有這事我就殺掉你. This
time I'll let you off easy. If it ever
happens again, I'll kill you.　(N) ad-vantage. / 這件事沒有什麼 ~.
There's no advantage to this.

騙 **pyàn** (FV) 1) swindle, cheat. / 他
~ 了我一百塊錢去. He cheated
me out of a hundred dollars.　2)
fool, joke with, someone. / 我 ~
你呢. I was just fooling you.

　　騙子 **pyàndz** (N) swindler.

片{片} **pyàn**, **pyān*** (M) 1) < -ㄦ > slice,
thin piece. 一 ~ 西瓜 a piece of
watermelon; 一 ~ 橘子 a piece of
orange; 一 ~ 麵包 a slice of bread.
2) expanse. 一 ~ 大海 a broad ex-panse of ocean; 一 ~ 陽光 an ex-panse of sunshine.　(FV) slice. / 我
在 ~ 肉呢. I'm slicing the meat.
(B)* < -子, -ㄦ > sheet, card (M 張
jāng). 照 ~ photograph; 賀年 ~ New
Year's greeting card.

　　片ㄦ **pyàr** (N) size of things
which take the measure 片 **pyàn**.
/ 這片麵包的 ~ 太厚了. This
slice of bread is too thick.　(M) ↑
(M) 1).

漂 **pyāu** (FV) float on water. / 汽油
在水上 ~. There's gasoline
floating on the water. → 漂 **pyǎu**,
漂 **pyàu**.

飄(飃)**pyāu** (FV) float <u>in the air or on</u> <u>water</u>. /雪花在空中～,葉子在 水上 ～. There are snowflakes floating through the air and leaves floating on the water.

漂 **pyǎu** (FV) bleach. /這牀被單要 ～一～. This sheet needs to be bleached. →漂 **pyāu**,漂 **pyàu**.

漂 **pyàu** (B) ⌐. →漂 **pyāu**,漂 **pyǎu**.

    漂 亮 **pyàulyang** (SV) be handsome, pretty, attractive, polished. /那個男孩很～. That boy is very handsome. /這是一套很 ～的衣服. This is a pretty dress. /他説話～極了. He talks beautifully.

票 **pyàu** (N) 1) <-子,-ル> ticket. 2) vote. (M張**jāng**). (FV) perform as <u>an amateur in Chinese opera</u>. /我 去年～了兩齣戲. Last year I performed in two operas. (M) <u>for</u> <u>large business transactions and pur-</u> <u>chases</u>. 一～買賣 a large business transaction. (B) 1) stamp. 郵 ～ postage stamp. 2) <-子> bank note (M張**jāng**). 滙 ～bank draft; 支 ～ check. 3) document, certificate. 捕 ～warrant; 傳 ～summons. 4) hostage. 綁 ～kidnap.

撇 **pyē** (FV) 1) desert, abandon. /他 把他的孩子～了. He deserted his children. 2) skim <u>something off</u> <u>the surface of a liquid</u>. /把湯上 漂着的油～掉. Skim off the grease floating on top of the soup. →撇**pyě**.

    撇 下 **pyēsya** (RC) leave behind, desert. /他死的時候～ 了兩個孩子. He left two children behind when he died. /她～丈 夫和孩子去嫁別人. She deserted her husband and children to marry another man.

撇 **pyě** (FV) 1) throw. /不要往湖 裡～石頭. Don't throw stones into the lake. 2) cry (lp). /這孩 子要 ～ 了. The child is about to cry. →撇**pyē**.

    撇 嘴 **pyédzwěi** (VO) turn the corners of one's mouth down <u>to</u> <u>show contempt for someone</u>. /他 看見我來了就把嘴一撇. When he saw me coming, his face took on a disdainful expression.

撇 ル **pyěr** (N) stroke slanted to the left (<u>in Chinese calligraphy</u>). (M) <u>for moustaches</u>.兩～鬍子 a moustache.

qi *see* **chi.**

qia *see* **chya.**

qian *see* **chyan.**

qiang *see* **chyang.**

qiao *see* **chyau.**

qie *see* **chye.**

qin *see* **chin.**

qing *see* **ching.**

qiong *see* **chyung.**

qiu *see* **chyou.**

qu *see* **chyu.**

quan *see* **chywan.**

que *see* **chywe.**

qun *see* **chyun.**

兒[ル] **-r, er** (B) 1) added to certain elements primarily to form nouns. 鳥 ～ bird; 一大張畫 ～a large painting; 一朵花 ～a flower. 2) added to certain nouns or measures <u>to make diminutives</u>. 水果刀 ～ small fruit-knife. 3) added to certain <u>noun compounds to show the second</u> <u>noun is a part of or belongs to the</u> <u>first</u>. 茶壺蓋 ～ teapot lid; 電燈 泡 ～ electric light bulb. 4) added <u>to certain elements to form TW or</u> <u>PW</u>. 明 ～ tomorrow; 這～here. 5) added <u>to a few verbs in local Peiping</u> <u>without changing their meaning</u>. 玩 ～ play; 翻～get angry; 顛～run away. → 兒 **er.**

日 **r̀** (B) 1) day <u>of the month</u>. 生 ～ birthday; 禮拜～Sunday. 2) day- time. ～ 夜 day and night. 3) <-頭> sun. ～ 光 sunshine, sunlight. 4) Japan (<u>contracted form of</u> 日本**rběn**) ～俄戰爭 Russo-Japanese War. *t*

    日 子 **r̀dz** (N) 1) date. 定 ～ set a date. 2) day (<u>used when referring</u> <u>to a particular day</u>). 結婚的～ wedding day; 洗衣服的～wash day. 3) time. /～過的真快. Time is really going by fast.

日記 rìjì (N) diary (M 本 běn).
日曆 rìlì (N) calendar (M 份 fèn).
日蝕 rìshŕ (N) solar eclipse.

然 rán (B) 1) stative verb- or adverb-
forming suffix. 必 ~ certainly; 顯
~ be obvious, obviously. 2) so, thus.
要不~ if not, otherwise. *t*
　　然而 ránér (A) nevertheless,
but, yet. /我不喜歡那個方法，
~又沒有別的辦法. I don't
like that way of doing it, but there's
no alternative.
　　然後 ránhòu (A) afterward,
subsequently, then. /你等我説
完了~你再説. Wait until I'm
done talking, then you can have your
say.

染 rǎn (FV) 1) dye. /這件衣裳可
以~成黃的嗎？ Can this dress
be dyed yellow? 2) acquire a bad
habit. /他最近~了很多壞習
慣. He's acquired a lot of bad habits
lately. (B) be infected. ~病 catch a
disease.

嚷 rāng (B) ↓. →嚷 rang.
　嚷嚷 rāngrang (FV) 1) shout.
/你為什麼~？ What are you
shouting for? 2) blab, blurt out, a
secret (lp). /你不要到處~.
You don't have to blab this all over.

嚷 rǎng (FV) shout, call out. /他~
救命啊! He shouted "Help!"
/你~什麼？ What are you shouting about? →嚷 rāng.

讓(让) ràng (FV) 1) yield to, give in to.
/你應該~你弟弟一點. You
should give in to your younger brother
a little. 2) let someone have something for a price. /你要喜歡我
的狗我可以按原價~給你.
If you like my dog, I'll let you have
him for the original price. 3) reduce, lower, a price. /這個價錢
已經是我的本錢了，我不能
再~了. This price is what I had
to pay; I can't lower it any further.
4) offer food, cigarettes, etc. /我
想你不喜歡這個牌子，所以
我不~你. I don't believe you like
this brand, so I won't offer you any.
5) usher or bring someone in. /你
怎麼把他~到我的卧房來了？
How could you bring him into my bedroom? 6) move out of the way. /請

你~一~我好過去. Would you
please move so I can get by? 7)
cause, make. /你別~你母親着
急. Don't make your mother worry.
8) let, allow. /~他去吧. Let
him go. /我母親不~我抽烟.
My mother doesn't let me smoke.
(CV) by (marking the agent). /他~
他父親罵了一頓. He was given
a scolding by his father. *t*
　　讓步 ràngbù (VO) concede, compromise, yield. /我對他已經讓
了很大的步了. I've already com-
promised with him a lot.

rao *see* rau.

饒 ráu (FV) 1) spare. ~命 spare someone's life. 2) forgive, excuse, a
person. /他絕不會~你的. He
certainly won't forgive you. 2) give
something free or as a bonus. /你
要買三個我就~一個. If you
buy three, I'll give you one free.
3) take, have, some more. /菜很
多，再~一點. There's plenty of
food; have some more. 4) get someone involved in something. /他們
吵架把我也~在裡邊了. They
got me involved in their dispute. (B)
abundant. 富~ be plentiful. (PT)
~…也 (or 還)… even though
…(still)…. /~他告訴十回
了，我還記不住. Even though
he's told me ten times, I still can't
remember. *t*
　　饒恕 ráushù (FV) forgive, excuse, a person. /你説我能~他
嗎？ Do you think I should forgive
him?

繞(绕) ráu (FV) 1) go around (move in a
circle around something). /我們
圍着湖邊~了一圈. We went
around the lake once. 2) detour.
/前面沒有橋，我們得~過去.
The bridge is out ahead; we'll have
to detour around it. 3) wind something around something. ~線 wind
thread. /一條蛇~在樹上. A
snake had wound itself around a
tree. 4) confuse. /你的話把我
~住了. What you said confused
me.

惹 rě (FV) 1) stir up, cause, make.
/他~了很多禍. He caused a
lot of trouble. /他故意~我笑.

He purposely made me laugh. 2) tease, annoy. /你別～他, 他已經醉了. Don't annoy him; he's drunk.

熱[热] rè (SV) be hot, uncomfortable, warm. (FV) heat, warm. /把酒～一～. Heat the wine. (N) 1) heat. /我受不了這種～. I can't stand this heat. 2) fever. /他有～沒有? Does he have a fever? (B) 1) warm, earnest. ～忱 warm-heartedness. 2) popular, fashionable. ～門貨 popular merchandise.

  熱愛 rèài (FV) love ardently, be crazy about. /他～祖國. He loves his country. /他～橋牌. He is crazy about bridge.

  熱情 rèchíng (SV) 1) be passionate. /他對他太太很～. He's very passionate about his wife. 2) be devoted. /他對朋友很～. He is very devoted to his friends.

  熱烈 'rèlyè (SV) be lively (of a party, meeting, etc.). /昨天開會的情形很～. Yesterday's meeting was a lively one. (A) exuberantly, fervently. /他們～慶祝勝利. They celebrated the victory exuberantly.

  熱鬧 'rènàu (SV) be lively, bustle with noise and excitement. /香港的街上很～. The streets in Hong Kong bustle with noise and excitement. /除夕晚會很～. That was a lively New Year's Eve party. (N) <-ㄦ> noise and excitement. /她不喜歡～. She doesn't like noise and excitement.

  熱心 rèsyīn (SV) be enthusiastic, earnest. /他對教會很～. He is a very enthusiastic church-goer. (A) enthusiastically. /他～服務. He performs his duties enthusiastically. (N) enthusiasm.

rén (N) 1) person, human being, man. 法國～ Frenchman. /～有兩條腿. A human being has two legs. 2) someone. /我聽～說你結婚了. I heard someone say that you got married. 3) personality. /那位小姐～很好. That young lady has a very nice personality.

  人家 rénjya (N) 1) others, other people. 2) I myself (emphatic, as in a complaint). /你都拿走了,

～吃什麼? You've taken everything, what am I going to eat? (B) 1) that or those respectable or esteemed . . . . /賻賻～編字典的多有學問! How learned those esteemed lexicographers are! 2) added to nouns indicating age groups, as adults, children, etc., all. /小孩子～不許抽烟. All children are forbidden to smoke. /姑娘～不應該那麼粗魯. Young ladies shouldn't be so rude.

  人家ㄦ rénjyār (N) household, family. /這個村子裡有多少～? How many families are there in that village?

  人們 rénmen (N) people (belonging to a certain group). /在那個公司裡～都不喜歡他. All the people in the company dislike him.

  人民 rénmín (N) people (of a country).

  人民幣 rénmínbì (N) currency issued by the People's Bank of China.

  人民解放軍 rénmínjyěfàngjyūn (N) People's Liberation Army (c).

  人人 rénrén (N) everybody (used only as a subject or transposed object). /～都去. Everybody will go. /他把～都得罪了. He has offended everybody.

任 rén (B) s t →任 rèn.

忍 rěn (FV) 1) endure, tolerate, stand. /我昨天在他的沙發上～了一夜. I endured last night on his sofa. 2) hold back, control, one's emotions or reactions. /我～着沒笑出來. I controlled myself and didn't laugh.

  忍耐 rěnnài (N) patience. (FV) endure, tolerate, stand. /我簡直不能再～了. I simply can't stand any more.

  忍受 rěnshòu (FV) endure, tolerate, stand. /在這種情形下, 我簡直沒法子～. Under those conditions, I simply couldn't stand it.

認[认] rèn (FV) 1) identify. /警察叫我去～那個賊. The police asked me to identify that thief. 2) admit, confess to. /他～了罪了. He confessed to the crime. 3) be resigned to the fact that. /他不還我錢我～了. I'm resigned to the fact that he's not going to pay me back. 4) make <u>someone an honorary relative</u>. /為了不交房租,我～我的房東當乾媽. In order to avoid paying rent, I made the landlady my honorary mother. (B) 1) recognize, know. ./～不出來 Cannot recognize. 2) insert. ～針 thread a needle. ～鐙 put <u>one's feet</u> into stirrups.

認得 rènde (FV) be acquainted with, know. /我早就～他. I knew him a long time ago. 2) recognize. /你還～我嗎? Do you still recognize me?

認真 rènjēn (SV) be conscientious, serious. /你何必太～呢? Don't be so serious. (A) seriously, conscientiously. /他～念書. He studies very conscientiously.

認可 rènkě (FV) approve. /雖然他不～,可是他也沒辦法. Although he doesn't approve, there still isn't anything he can do. (N) approval.

認識 rènshr (FV) 1) be acquainted with, know. /我不～他. I don't know him. 2) recognize, know. /我才～兩千字. I only know two thousand characters. (N) understanding. /我對原子彈沒有什麼～. I have no understanding at all of the atomic bomb.

認輸 rènshū (VO) admit defeat, give up. /我看你～吧. I think you should give up.

認為 rènwei (FV) think, feel. /你～怎麼樣? How do you feel about it?

任 rèn (FV) let, allow. /你～他自己做去. Let him do it all by himself. (M) term <u>of office</u>. /他做了三～市長. He has been mayor for three terms. (B) 1) duty, responsibility.責～ duty, responsibility. 2) employ, appoint. ～免 hiring and firing. 3) official position, office. 上～ take over an official post. 4) bear, endure. ～勞 bear hard work. (PT) 1)～...還... no matter ...still.... /～我怎麼勸,她還是哭. No matter how much I comfort her, she still cries. 2)～...也 (or都)... no matter <u>who, what, how, etc.</u>..., still.... /他～什麼都不吃. He won't eat

anything. (lit. No matter what it is, he won't eat it.) s t →任 rén.

任何 rènhé (SP) any. ～三個人 any three people; ～時間 any time.

任務 rènwu (N) mission, assignment (M件 jyàn,樁 jwāng).

扔 rēng (FV) 1) throw. ～球 throw a ball. /他把錢～在獻金箱裡. He threw some money into the collection box. 2) throw away, get rid of. /我想你這個電視機還是～了吧. I think you had better get rid of this television set.

仍 réng (A) still, yet, as before. /我～編那本字典. I'm still working on that dictionary.

仍舊 réngjyòu (A) still, as before. /他～沒改. He still hasn't changed any.

仍然 réngrán (A) still, yet, as before. /他～不聽你的話. He's still not paying attention to what you say.

刃 rèn (B) knife. 利～ sharp knife.

刃儿 rèr (N) cutting edge. /～已經鈍了. The edge is already dull.

ri see r.

rong see rung.

揉 róu (FV) rub, massage, knead. ～麵 knead dough. /不要用手～眼睛. Don't rub your eyes with your hands.

柔 róu (SV) 1) be soft (<u>of light, color, or sound</u>). /這個燈光很～. This lighting is very soft. 2) be gentle, mild (<u>of one's temperament</u>). /他脾氣很～. He's a mild-tempered person.

柔和 róuhwo (SV) 1) be soft (<u>of light, color, sound</u>). /光線很～. The lighting is very soft. 2) be gentle, mild (<u>of a person or one's temperament</u>). /他太太脾氣～極了. His wife is very mild-tempered.

肉 ròu (N) 1) flesh, meat (M塊kwài). 瘦～ lean meat. /他身上沒什麼～,他得吃維他命. He doesn't have much meat on him; he should take vitamins. 2) pulp (<u>of fruit</u>). /這個果子的～不能吃. You can't eat the pulp of this fruit. (SV) be slow in movement, sluggish (lp). /他的性子很~. He's very slow by nature.

如 **rú** (FV) be as good as. /你什麼地方~他? In what respects are you as good as he? (B) 1) according to. ~期 according to schedule. 2) like, as. ~此 like this. 3) if. 假~ if, supposing.

如果 **'rúgwǒ** (A) if. /你~不吃藥,你的病就好不了. You won't get well if you don't take the medicine.

如何 **rúhé** (A)q how. /你~能拿他當朋友呢? How can you treat him as a friend?

如今 **rújīn** (TW) nowadays, these days. /~比不了從前了. There's no comparison between the past and nowadays. /我~不抽煙了. I'm not smoking these days.

如意 **rúyì** (SV) be satisfied. /我最近不大~. I haven't been very satisfied lately.

乳 **rǔ** (B) 1) breast. ~腺 mammary gland. 2) milk. 馬~ mare's milk. 3) suckling. ~虎 tiger cub.

乳房 **rǔfáng** (N) breast (anat.).

入 **rǔ** (FV) 1) get something stuck. /他把腳~在泥裡了. He got his foot stuck in the mud. 2) pass something secretly, slip. /他~給那個警察十塊錢. He slipped that policeman ten dollars. 3) leave something somewhere deliberately. /我不知道我把我的錶~在那兒了. I don't know where I left my watch. 4) stick someone with something, palm something off on someone. /他把賬單~給我就走了. He palmed the bill off on me and took off. → 入rù.

入 **rù** (FV) enter a school, join an organization or group. ~黨 join a political party. /我今年秋天~大學. I'm entering college this fall. (B) income. 收~ income. → 入rù.

入會 **rùhwèi** (VO) join a society, association, club, etc. /你是那年入的會? What year did you join the association?

入籍 **rùjí** (VO) be naturalized

(adopted as a citizen). /他入了美國籍了. He is a naturalized American citizen.

入教 **rùjyàu** (VO) become a member of a religious faith. /他入了天主教了. He became a member of the Catholic faith.

入伍 **rùwǔ** (VO) enlist in the armed services. /我已經入了三年伍了. It's already been three years since I enlisted.

褥 **rù** (B) <-子> mattress, bedding (M 牀chwáng). ~單子 bed sheet.

ruan see **rwan**.

rui see **rwei**.

run see **rwun**.

容 **rúng** (FV) 1) allow, let. /~我說一句話. Allow me to say a word. 2) tolerate. /他不能~人. He can't tolerate people. 3) hold, contain. /這閒屋子可以~二十人. This room can hold twenty people. (B) 1) facial appearance. 笑~ smiling face. 2) perhaps. ~或 perhaps.

容量 **rúnglyàng** (N) volume, cubic content, capacity.

容易 **rúngyì** (SV) be easy. /吃飯可真不~. It's really not easy to make a living. (A) easily. /你~生病嗎? Do you get sick easily? /這件事~說不~做. This is more easily said than done.

溶 **rúng** (B) dissolve, melt. ~媒 a solvent.

溶解 **rúngjyě** (FV) melt, dissolve. /糖在熱水裏很容易~. Sugar will dissolve easily in hot water.

榮[荣] **rúng** (B) 1) flourishing. 繁~ be prospering. 2) glorious. 光~ glory, be glorious.

榮幸 **rúngsyìng** (SV) be honored (used in polite statements). /我們很~今天張先生來給我們演講. We are very honored to have Mr. Chang come to speak to us today.

ruo see **rwo**.

軟[輭] **rwǎn** (SV) 1) be soft, yielding (lit. or fig.). /這個墊子很~. This cushion is really soft. /他的心很~. He is very soft-hearted.

2) be weak. /我看見那個老虎我的腿都～了. When I saw that tiger, my legs got very weak. 3) be inferior in quality. /這個貨今年的成色比去年～多了. The quality of this product this year is quite inferior to that of last year.

軟和 **rwǎnhwo** (SV) be soft, yielding, to the touch. /這塊草地很～. This grass is very soft.

軟弱 **rwǎnrwò** (SV) be weak (of a person) (lit. or fig.). /他病剛好所以身體還很～. He just recovered, so he's still very weak. /你不應該這麼～. You shouldn't be so weak.

鋭 **rwèi** (B) sharp. 尖～ be sharp-pointed.

弱 **rwò** (SV) be weak. ～國 weak nations. /他的身體很～. He (lit. His health) is very weak. (FV) lose a colleague by death. /原子科學家又～一個. The atomic scientists have lost another of their colleagues. (B) added to fractions, less than. 三分之二～ less than two-thirds; 五點六～ less than five and six-tenths.

若 **rwò** (A) if. /你～不去,我也不去. If you're not going, I won't go either. t

若是 **rwòshr** (A) if. /～他來就好了. If he comes, that'll be good.

閏 **rwùn** (B) intercalary. ～年 leap year.

閏月 **rwùnywè** (N) intercalary month in the lunar calendar.

仨 **sā** (N) three of something (a fusion of the NU 三 **sān** and the M 個 **ge**. /你給我～. Give me three. (B) three people. 哥兒～ three brothers. /他們～都是美國人. Those three are all Americans.

撒 **sā** (FV) 1) let go, set free, release from the hand. /我捉住一個鳥又把它～了. I caught a bird and then let it go. 2) pass out, distribute. /他站在街上～廣告. He was standing in the street, passing out advertisements. 3) urinate. ～尿 urinate. t →撒 **sā**.

撒謊 **sāhuǎng** (VO) tell a lie.

/他撒了一個大謊. He told a big lie.

撒開 **sākāi** (A) <-ㄦ> unrestrainedly, to one's heart's content, to the full. /菜很多,你～吃吧. There's plenty of food; eat your fill of it.

撒 **sǎ** (FV) scatter. ～種 sow seed. → 撒 **sā**.

灑[洒] **sǎ** (FV) 1) sprinkle, scatter. ～水 sprinkle water. /給那條狗～點蚤子藥. Sprinkle some flea powder on the dog. 2) spill. /我的酒都～了. My wine spilled.

腮[顋] **sāi** (N) 1) part of the cheek below the cheekbone. 2) gill of a fish.

腮幫子 **sāibāngdz** (N) part of the cheek below the cheekbone (lp).

塞 **sāi, sēi*** (FV)* 1) block, stop up. /我的鼻子～住了. My nose is stopped up. 2) slip something forcibly into a narrow slot or opening. /他把一把十塊錢的票子～在我手裡頭了. He slipped a bunch of ten-dollar bills into my hand. (B) <-子,-ㄦ> cork, stopper. 活～ piston. →塞 **sài**.

塞 **sài** (B) strategic pass. 要～ stronghold. →塞 **sāi**. t

賽 **sài** (FV) 1) compete, compete in. ～高爾夫 compete in a game of golf. /我們兩個人～,看誰快. Let's compete and see who's faster. 2) be as good as, rival. /那個人的個兒～金鋼. That man's size rivals King Kong's. t

賽球 **sàichyóu** (VO) compete in or have a ball game. /明天他們～嗎? Are they having a ball game tomorrow? (N) ball game (M 場 **cháng**).

賽馬 **sàimǎ** (VO) 1) hold a horse race. /今天賽了八次馬. There were eight races held today. 2) play the horses. /他明天又要去～了. He's going to play the horses again tomorrow. (N) 1) horse race (M 場 **cháng**). 2) horse racing.

賽跑 **sàipǎu** (VO) run a race. /今天我們賽了兩次跑. We ran two races today. (N) footrace.

三{叁,弍} **sān** (NU) three. 兩～天 two

or three days. (B) third. ～馬路 Third Avenue.

三角儿 **sānjyǎur** (N) triangle. ～戀愛 love triangle.

三角形 **sānjyǎusyíng** (N) triangle (*geom.*).

三輪車 **sānlwúnchē** (N) pedicab (M輛 **lyàng,** 部 **bù**).

三月 **sānywè** (N) 1) (in) March. 2) the third month of the lunar calendar.

傘[伞] **sǎn** (N) umbrella, parasol (M把 **bǎ**). (B) parachute. ～兵 paratroops.

散 **sǎn** (FV) 1) fall to pieces, come apart. ／這個木頭盒子～了. This wooden box fell apart. 2) break up (of a group). ／那個戲班儿～了. That troupe broke up. (B) 1) medicinal powder. 強胃～antacid powder. 2) fragmentary. ～工 odd job. →散 **sàn.**

散 **sàn** (FV) 1) distribute, pass out. ／請你把傳單～一～. Please pass out the handbills. 2) dismiss, break up (as a meeting). ／～隊！ Dismissed! (military command). ／會什麼時候～? When will the meeting break up? 3) fire, dismiss, an employee. ／我昨天把他～了. I fired him yesterday. (B) dispel sorrow, worry, etc. ～悶 dispel one's cares. →散 **sǎn.**

散開 **sànkai** (RC) break up, disperse (as a crowd). ／下雨了, 所以人都～了. It started raining, so everyone dispersed.

桑 **sāng** (B) mulberry. ～葚儿 mulberry (fruit). *t*

桑樹 **sāngshù** (N) mulberry tree (M棵 **kē**).

嗓 **sǎng** (B) 1) <-子> throat. 氣～ trachea. 2) <-子> singing voice (M條 **tyáu**). 3) <-儿> voice. 啞～ hoarse voice.

sao *see* sau.

臊 **sāu** (SV) be smelly, stink (of urine). ／這個小便池真～. This urinal really stinks. →臊 **sàu.**

嫂 **sǎu** (B) 1) <-子> sister-in-law (older brother's wife). 二～ sister-in-law (second oldest brother's wife). 2) your (used to refer to a friend's

wife) (h). ～夫人 your wife.

嫂嫂 **sǎusau** (N) sister-in-law (older brother's wife).

掃[掃][扫] **sǎu** (FV) 1) sweep, brush away. ／你把廚房～了嗎? Did you sweep the kitchen? 2) sweep, rake (fig.). ／那個胖子用眼睛向飯桌一～. The fat man gave the dinner table a sweeping glance. ／他們用機關槍向樹林子～了一陣. They raked the forest with machine-gun fire. (B) wipe out. ～除 exterminate. →掃 **sàu.**

掃地 **sǎudi** (VO) sweep the floor *or* ground. ／我三個禮拜沒～了. I haven't swept the floor for three weeks.

掃興 **sǎusying** (VO) spoil someone's fun, be a kill-joy (lit. sweep away pleasure). ／這個人老愛掃別人的興. This guy is a kill-joy. (SV) be disappointed. ／他覺得很～. He's very disappointed.

掃[掃][扫] **sàu** (B) broom. 竹～把 bamboo broom. →掃 **sǎu.**

掃帚 **sàujou** (N) broom (M把 **bǎ**).

臊 **sàu** (FV) embarrass. ／你別～他了. Stop embarrassing him. (SV) 1) be ashamed. 2) be bashful. (B) shame. 沒～ be shameless. →臊 **sāu.**

澀[涩] **sè** (SV) 1) be tart. ／這個柿子很～. This persimmon is very tart. 2) be rough (to the touch), not glossy. ／打過蠟了, 地板怎麼還這麼～呀? The floor has been waxed; how come it still feels so rough? (B) harsh, unpolished (of speech or writing). 艱～ crude.

色 **sè** (B) 1) color. 紅～ red color. 2) looks, appearance. 氣～ complexion; 景～ scenery. 3) kind, type. 各～人等 all kinds of men. 4. quality. 足～ pure (of gold or silver). 5) sexual passion. 好～ be lustful. →色 **shǎi.**

色彩 **sètsǎi** (N) bias. ／那個報紙有～. That newspaper is biased.

塞 **sēi** →塞 **sāi.**

森 **sēn** (B) 1) forest. 2) awesome. ～嚴 awe-inspiring. *t*

森林 **sēnlín** (N) forest, jungle (M 片 **pyàn**).

沙{砂 (N)} **shā** (N) <-子> sand, gravel. (SV) be hoarse, raspy. *s t*

沙發 **shāfā** (N) sofa (M 套 **tàu**, 張 **jāng**).

沙灘 **shātān** (N) beach (M 片 **pyàn**).

殺[杀] **shā** (FV) 1) kill, murder. /他們隨便～人. They kill people at will. 2) tighten a belt. /我們從現在起應該～緊褲帶. We must tighten our belts from now on. 3) add up. /你的賬～了嗎? Did you add up your accounts? 4) brake, stop, a vehicle. /你為什麼看見紅燈不～車? Why didn't you stop the car when you saw the red light? 5) sting, hurt (of medicine or a wound). /這個瘡口～的很厲害. This wound hurts a lot. (B) 1) reduce. ～價 reduce a price. 2) fight (in a battle). ～敗 defeat.

紗 **shā** (N) gauze, sheer cloth. /鐵～ wire screening; ～布 gauze.

啥 **shá** (N)*q* 1) what (d). /你要～? What do you want? 2) used after negative verbs, anything (d). /我不要～. I don't want anything. 3) what for, for what reason (d). /客人都走了,你還做～點心呢. The guests are all gone; what are you making refreshments for? (PT) 1) ～...都(*or* 也) every (d). /現在～都想吃. I feel like eating everything now. 2)...～...～ whatever (d). /你要～拿～吧. You take whatever you want.

傻[傻] **shǎ** (SV) be silly, foolish. /你別這麼～了. Don't be so foolish. (A) without control, stupidly, senselessly. /他對着鏡子～笑. He's looking in the mirror and laughing stupidly.

傻子 **shǎdz** (N) fool, simpleton.

篩 **shāi** (FV) sift, strain. ～沙子 sift sand; ～金子 pan gold. (B) <-子> sieve, strainer. ～籮 strainer.

色 **shǎi** (B)<-儿> color. 掉～ fade. → 色 **sè**.

曬[晒] **shài** (FV) sun something. /衣裳還沒乾呢,多～一會吧. The clothes are still not dry; leave them out to sun a while longer. (SV) be sunny and hot. /這個地方太～. It's too sunny and hot here.

曬臺 **shàitái** (N) porch, balcony.

山 **shān** (N) hill, mountain (M 座 **dzwò**). 上～ climb a mountain. *t*

山坡 **shānpwō** (N) <-儿> slope of a hill.

山羊 **shānyáng** (N) goat (M 隻 **jr̄**).

山藥 **shānyau** (N) yam.

衫 **shān** (B) 1) shirt. 絨線～ sweater. 2) gown, robe. 長～ man's long gown.

搧{煽}[扇] **shān** (FV) fan. /用扇子給我～～. Fan me a bit. (B) agitate, stir up. ～動 arouse.

刪 **shān** (FV) delete, skip, leave out, part of some written material. /我把那段～了. I've deleted that paragraph.

閃 **shǎn** (FV) 1) flash. /那光一～就過去了. That light flashed once and then went out. 2) dodge, evade. /他～到一邊儿去了. He dodged to one side. (N) lightning. /打了兩個～. Lightning flashed twice.

閃電 **shǎndyàn** (N) lightning.

扇 **shàn** (M) for doors, windows. 一～窗戶 a window. (B) <-子> fan (hand variety) (M 把 **bǎ**). 電～ electric fan. SF of 搧 **shān**.

善 **shàn** (B) 1) good, virtuous. ～人 good people. 2) be good at. ～忘 be good at forgetting. *t*

膳[饍] **shàn** (B) meal. ～宿生 boarding student.

膳費 **shànfèi** (N) cost of food, board (M 份 **fèn**).

贍 **shàn** (B) supply, give. ～養 support, provide for.

贍養費 **shànyǎngfèi** (N) alimony (M 份 **fèn**).

商 **shāng** (N) quotient. /拿五除十～是二. If you divide ten by five, the quotient is two. (B) 1) commerce, trade. ～船 merchant ship. 2) businessman, merchant. 進口

~ importer. 3) discuss, consult. 磋差 ~negotiate. *d s*

商場 **shāngchǎng** (N) arcade, emporium (M所 **swǒ**, 座 **dzwò**).

商店 **shāngdyàn** (N) business establishment, shop (M家 **jyā**, 開 **jyān**).

商量 **shānglyang** (FV) discuss, talk over. /我得跟他 ~ ~ 這件事情. I've got to talk that matter over with him.

商人 **shāngrén** (N) merchant, businessman.

商業 **shāngyè** (N) business. ~ 學校 business school; ~ 區 business district.

傷[仿] **shāng** (FV) hurt, injure (lit. or fig.). /那個爆炸 ~ 人了嗎? Did that explosion injure anybody? /你何必 ~ 他的感情呢? Why do you have to hurt his feelings? (N) injury, wound (M塊 **kwài**, 處 **chù**). (SV) be sick of something or someone. /我對看電影都 ~ 了. I'm sick of going to the movies. (B) 1) suffer from illness. ~ 暑 suffer from sunstroke. 2) grieving, sad. ~ 慘 be sad, mournful.

傷風 **shāngfēng** (VO) catch a cold, have a cold. /去年冬天我傷了好幾次風. I had numerous colds last winter. (N) cold.

傷寒 **shānghán** (N) typhoid fever.

傷心 **shāngsyīn** (SV) be grieved, heartbroken.

晌 **shǎng** (B) noon, midday. ~ 覺 noon-time nap.

晌午 **'shǎngwǔ** (TW) (at) noon. /現在已經過了正 ~ 了. It's already past noon. /我 ~ 來. I'll come at noon.

賞 **shǎng** (FV) give a reward to a person of lower rank. /校長 ~ 了我一枝鋼筆. The principal gave me a fountain pen as a reward. (B) 1) praise. 獎 ~ praise. 2) enjoy the beauty of. 欣 ~ appreciate.

賞識 **'shǎngshr̀** (FV) be appreciative of someone lower in rank or of his work. /老板很 ~ 我的工作. The boss is very appreciative of my work.

尚 **shàng** (B) 1) still. ~ 能 still able to.

2) esteem. ~ 武 militarism, esteem of military power. *t*

尚且 **'shàngchyě** (A) even, still, yet. /他 ~ 不知道, 你更不用説了. Even he doesn't know it, to say nothing of you.

上 **shàng** (DV) 1) come *or* go up. ~ 山 come *or* go up a mountain; ~ 梯子 climb a ladder. 2) go somewhere. ~ 學 go to school. /你 ~ 那兒啊? Where are you going? 3) get on a conveyance, board. ~ 船 board a boat. 4) apply, smear on. /我又 ~ 了一道漆. I applied another coat of paint. 5) serve (as a course of a meal). /先 ~ 湯. Serve the soup first. 6) impose taxes. ~ 捐 impose taxes. 7) tighten a spring, wind. ~ 鐘 wind a clock. 8) record. ~ 帳 record in an account. 9) submit something to a superior. /他給他的上司 ~ 了一個報告. He submitted a report to his boss. (RE) 1) up, up on. /他走 ~ 台就昏了. He fainted as soon as he got up on the stage. 2) indicates the starting of an action. /他吃 ~ 飯了. He's already started to eat. 3) indicates joining tightly. 鎖 ~ lock up; 關 ~ close up. (L) 1) up, above. 往 ~ 看 look up; 樓 ~ upstairs; ~ 游 (in) the upper part of a river. 2) on. 桌子 ~ on the table; 往 ~ 貼 paste on. 3) in, concerning. 事實 ~ in fact; 數學 ~ in mathematics. (SP) 1) higher, upper. ~ 兩班 the upper two grades (in school). 2) past. ~ 三個月 the past three months.

上邊 **shàngbyan** (PW) <-ル> 1) the top, upper surface. /桌子 ~ 有一個花瓶. There's a flower vase on top of that table. 2) above, up there. /~ 有兩個人. There are two people up there. /我 ~ 還有很多人呢. There are a lot of people above me. 3) upper part *or* area of something. /梯子的 ~ 壞了. The upper part of the ladder is broken. (N) <-ル> higher-ups (lp). /這是 ~ 説的. That's what the higher-ups said.

上千 **shàngchyān** (VO) be close to a thousand. /他的薪水上八千. His salary is close to eight thousand.

213

上 去 shàngchyu (RE) up (there). 推 ~ push something up (there). (RC) go up. /没有電梯,我們上不去. There's no elevator, so we can't go up.

上 當 shàngdàng (VO) be swindled, be taken in, fall into a trap. /我不會再上你的當. I won't be swindled by you again.

上 帝 shàngdì (N) God (in monotheistic religions).

上 凍 shàngdùng (VO) freeze. /河已經上了凍了. The river has already frozen.

上 級 shàngjí (N) superior.

上 課 shàngkè (VO) 1) go to class. /我三天没~了. I haven't gone to class for three days. 2) start (of a class). /早就上了半天課了,你怎麼還不去呀? The class started a long time ago; how come you haven't gone yet?

上 來 shànglai (RE) up (here). 爬 ~ climb up (here). (RC) come up. /你上得來嗎? Can you come up?

上 面 shàngmyan = 上邊 shàngbyan.

上 訴 shàngsù (FV) appeal (legal). /我想要向高等法院 ~. I will now appeal to the supreme court.

上 算 shàngswàn (SV) be a bargain, worth it. /一塊錢買這麼多~. This much for a dollar is really a bargain.

上 下 shàngsyà (PW) 1) from top to bottom. /這個樓~都住着人. There are people living on every floor of this building. 2) top and bottom. /這個盒子的~都掉了,没有用了. The top and bottom of this box are broken, so it's useless. (B) following NU-M, about, approximately. 十塊錢~about ten dollars.

上 學 shàngsywé (VO) go to school. /你怎麼還~呢? How come you're still going to school?

上 司 shàngsz (N) boss.

上 頭 shàngtou = 上邊 shàngbyan.

上 操 shàngtsāu (VO) take part in physical exercise, go to military drill. /他上了三年操他還不認識左右. He has gone to drill

for three years, and still he doesn't know right from left.

上 萬 shàngwàn (VO) be close to ten thousand. /遊行的人上了萬了. There were close to ten thousand marchers.

上 午 shàngwǔ (TW) 1) forenoon, morning. /~是一天最好的時候. The morning is the best part of the day. 2) in the morning. /我~去. I'll go in the morning.

shao see **shau**.

燒 shāu (FV) 1) burn. ~拉坂 burn trash. /他的房子~了. His house burned down. 2) cook (broil, fry, bake, etc.) (d). ~飯 cook a meal. 3) have a fever. /他還~不~了? Does he still have a fever? 4) make someone lose his head. /那些錢把他~的不知道做什麼好了. The money has made him lose his head so that he doesn't know what was what. (N) fever. 發 ~ have a fever.

燒 餅 shāubing (N) thick, flat biscuit or cake with sesame seeds on top, usually eaten for breakfast.

稍 shāu (A) a little, slightly. /我比你~高一點. I'm a little taller than you.

稍 微 shāuwēi (A) just a little. /~買一點兒. Buy just a little. /你~擦一擦就行了. Just rub it a little and it'll be O. K.

勺{杓} sháu (N) frying pan (M把bǎ). (M) one percent of a 升 shēng (Chinese dry quart). 木 ~ wooden ladle.

勺 子 sháudz = 勺兒 sháur.

勺 兒 sháur (N) spoon (M把bǎ).

芍 sháu (B) peony. 白 ~ white root of the peony (used as medicine).

芍 藥 sháuyau (N) peony (M枝jr, 朵dwǒ;棵kē).

少 shǎu (SV) be few, scarce. /這兒好人~. Good men are scarce here. /很~人不知道. There are few people who don't know it. (FV) lack, be missing. /我~了三塊錢. I'm missing three dollars. /這件事情~你不行. This matter cannot be managed without you. (A) 1) less, not so much. /~說話. Talk less. 2) seldom, rarely. /他很~來. He rarely comes. (B) for a little while. ~坐 sit down for a while. → 少 **shàu**.

少陪 **shǎupéi** (IE) Excuse me (said to guests when one has to leave the room).

少數儿 '**shǎushùr** (N) the minority of any group. 佔~ be in the minority.

少 **shàu** (B) 1) junior, minor. ~尉 second lieutenant. 2) young. ~婦 young married woman. → 少 **shǎu**.

少年 **shàunyán** (N) 1) youth, young person. 2) one's youth.

少年先鋒隊 **shàunyánsyān-fēngdwèi** (N) Young People's Pioneer Group (c).

少先隊 **shàusyāndwèi** (N) Young People's Pioneer Group (short form of 少年先鋒隊 **shàunyánsyānfēng-dwèi**) (c).

哨 **shàu** (FV) sing, call (of a bird) (lp). /他養的那個鳥儿不會~. That bird he raised can't sing. (B) 1) <-子,-儿> whistle. ~箭 whistling arrow. 2) sentry, guard. 放~ to station sentries.

賒 **shē** (FV) buy or sell on credit. /我想~兩磅肉,可是他不給我. I want to buy two pounds of meat on credit, but he won't sell it to me on that basis.

奢 **shē** (B) extravagant. ~侈 be lavish.

奢望 **shēwàng** (N) expectations. /我不敢有那麼大的~. I don't dare expect that much.

舌 **shé** (B) <-头> tongue (M條 **tyáu**). ~尖 tip of the tongue; 饒~ be loquacious.

折 **shé** (FV) 1) be broken into segments. /棍子~了. The stick is broken. 2) lose money in business. ~本 lose capital. SF of 摺jé, 襵jé. → 折jé, 折jé.

蛇 **shé** (N) snake (M條 **tyáu**).

捨[舍] **shě** (FV) give something as charity. /紅十字會現在~衣裳哪. The Red Cross is giving out clothes now. (B) give up, part with. ~命 give one's life for some ideal.

捨不得 **shěbude** (RC) hate to part with. /我~她. I hate to

part with her. (AV) hate to. /他~花錢. He hates to spend money.

捨得 **shěde** (RC) be able to bear parting with someone or something. /你~你的孩子嗎? Can you bear parting with your child? (AV) bear to. /你~把你的房子賣了嗎? Can you bear to sell your house?

舍 **shè** (B) 1) building. 宿~ dormitory. 2) my, our (when referring to relations, usually younger than oneself). ~弟 my younger brother. SF of 捨 **shě**.

舍下 '**shèsyà** (PW) (at) my home or house (used in a polite answer to a question about where one lives) (h). /A: 您府上是...? B: ~在北平. A: Where is your home? B: My home is in Peiping. /請到~吃杯茶. Would you come to my house for a cup of tea? /~人太多. There are lots of people at my house.

社 **shè** (B) 1) organization, group. 旅行~ travel bureau; 合作~ co-operative. 2) commune (contracted form of 人民公~ **rénmíngūngshè**) (c). ~隊 commune production team.

社會 **shèhwèi** (N) society. ~問題 social problem; ~學 sociology.

社會主義 **shèhwèijùyì** (N) socialism.

社交 **shèjyāu** (N) social activities. /他的~很廣. He's very active socially.

社論 **shèlwùn** (N) editorial (M 篇 **pyān**).

社評 **shèpíng** (N) editorial (M 篇 **pyān**).

社員 **shèywán** (N) 1) member of an organization. 2) member of a commune (c).

設 **shè** (FV) establish, found. /他們在那儿也~了一個分行. They're establishing a branch there too. (B) supposing. ~若 if.

設備 **shèbei** (N) equipment (as apparatus, furnishings, appliances).

設法 **shèfǎ** (VO) think of some way to do something. /你給我~吧. Think of a way for me. (AV) try to. /你給我~借一百塊錢. Try to borrow a hundred dollars for me.

設計 **shèjì** (FV) design. /這所房子是誰~的? Who designed this house? (N) design.

誰 **shéi, shwéi** (PN)��۹ 1) who. /~來了? Who came? /他跟~説話呢? To whom is he talking? 2) preceded by a negative verb, anyone. /我没跟~説話. I didn't speak to anyone. 3) someone. /你要找~嗎? Are you looking for someone? /他老説~~給他錢. He's always saying that someone gave him money. (PT) 1)~...都 (or也) anyone, everyone. /~都喜歡他. Everybody likes him. /~來我都不歡迎. No matter who comes, I won't welcome him. /他説的話~都聽不懂. Nobody understands what he's saying. 2)~...~... whoever. /~有錢~買. Whoever has money will buy it.

申 **shēn** (B) 1) state, inform. ~報 report to a superior. 2) Shanghai. ~曲 Shanghai song. *t s*

申請 **shēngchǐng** (FV) apply for. /我的手槍還没~執照呢. I still haven't applied for a license for my pistol.

申請書 **shēngchǐngshū** (N) application (official document) (M 件 **jyàn**, 份 **fèn**, 張 **jāng**, 封 **fēng**).

申斥 **shēnchr** (FV) reprimand. /他~了我一頓. He reprimanded me. (N) reprimand. /這不是他第一次受我的~了. This isn't the first time he's received a reprimand from me.

伸 **shēn** (FV) stretch a part of the body, reach. /你能(把手)~到這儿來嗎? Can you reach this far? (B) 1) straighten out, redress, some wrong. ~'寃 redress wrongs. 2) state. ~訴 complain.

參(葠,蔘) (B)ﾞ(参) **shēn** 1) ginseng (a kind of medicinal herb). 高麗~Korean ginseng. 2) seaslug. 刺~trepang. →參 **tsān**.

身 **shēn** (M) <-ㄦ> for suits, outfits (of clothing). 一~制服 a uniform. (B) 1) <-子> body. 周~ the whole body; 機~fuselage. 2) person (in grammar). 第三~單數. third person singular. 3) position, quali-

ty. ~分 position, rank, quality; ~為 in the capacity of.

身段 **shēndwan** (N) <-ㄦ> 1) bodily shape, figure. /她~長得很好看. She has a swell figure. 2) business (in drama).

身子 **shēndz** (N) 1) ﾞ(B) 1). 2) health. 3) pregnancy. 有~ be pregnant.

身量 **shēnlyang** (N) <-ㄦ> height of a person. /他~很高. He's quite tall.

身體 '**shēntǐ** (N) 1) body. 2) health.

深 **shēn** (SV) 1) be deep (lit. or fig.) /井很~. The well is very deep. /這本書太~了. This book is too deep for me. 2) be dark (of a color).

深刻 **shēnkè** (SV) be deep, profound. /他給我的印象很~. He made a deep impression on me.

神 **shén** (N) deity, god, goddess (M 位 **wèi**). 愛~ goddess of love. (SV) be remarkable, fantastic. /這傢伙好~了. This guy is fantastic. (B) 1) <-ㄦ> expression. 眼~expression in the eyes. 2) attention. 留~ pay attention. 3) divine, holy. ~權 divine right.

神氣 **shénchi** (SV) be successful and content. /他現在真~. He's really successful and contented now. (N) appearance, carriage, bearing, looks, manner, air. /那個人~十足. That person's manner is pretentious.

神父 **shénfu** (N) Catholic priest.

神經 **shénjīng** (N) 1) nerves (M根 **gēn**). 2) insanity. (SV) be insane, crazy (lit. or fig.). /他已經~了. He went insane. /你怎麼這麼~! You are really crazy!

神經病 **shénjīngbìng** (N) insanity. (SV) be insane, crazy (lit. or fig.).

神色 **shénsè** (N) facial expression, countenance. /他的~不對. He doesn't seem quite normal (lit. His facial expression is not right).

甚[什] **shén** (B) ﾞ. →甚 **shèn**.

甚麼 **shémma** (N)ᵍ 1) what. /你要~? What do you want? 2)

used after a negative verb, anything. /我不要～. I don't want anything. 3) what for, for what reason. /客人都走了,你還做～點心呢. The guests are gone; what are you making refreshments for? (B) such as, things like. /～別針啊,項鍊啊,她都不喜歡. She doesn't care for things like brooches or necklaces. (PT) 1)～...都(or也) every. /～人都能去. Everybody can go there. /我～都不想吃. I don't feel like eating anything. 2)...～...～ whatever. /你要～拿～吧. You take whatever you want. 一沒甚麼 **méishémma**.

沈 **shěn** (B) s. SF of 瀋 **sén**.

嬸 **shěn** (B) <-子,-ㄦ> aunt (father's younger brother's wife).

審[审] **shěn** (FV) try a person or a case. /明天還要～一件謀殺案. I still have another murder case to try tomorrow. (B) investigate, examine.～核 scrutinize.
    審查 **shěnchá** (FV) examine, look over. /我負責～所有的申請. I'm in charge of examining all applications.
    審判 **shěnpàn** (FV) try a person or a case (legal term). /法官都不願意～那件案子. None of the judges wants to try that case.
    審問 **shěnwèn** (FV) examine, interrogate, try, a person. /三個法官～那個小賊. The thief was tried by three judges.

瀋[沈] **shěn** (B)～.
    瀋陽 **shěnyáng** (PW) Mukden.

甚 **shèn** (B) very. ～好 very good; ～大 very big. 一甚 **shén**.
    甚至 **shènjr** (A) even to the extent that, so...that. /他忙的～好幾夜沒睡覺. He was so busy that he didn't even go to bed for several nights.

聲[声] **shēng** (M) <-ㄦ> for sounds. /我聽見一～炮响. I heard the sound of a cannon going off. (B) 1) <-ㄦ> sound, voice.～浪 sound wave. 2) tone of a Chinese syllable. 平～ level tone. 3) initial consonant of a syllable.～母 initial (in phonetics). 4) declare.～稱 state publicly. 5) reputation.～名 fame.

聲明 **shēngmíng** (FV) declare, announce. /他正式～他不是候選人. He announced officially that he was not a candidate. (N) announcement.
    聲望 **shēngwang** (N) fame, prestige.
    聲音 **shēngyin** (N) sound, voice.

牲 **shēng** (B) domestic animal. 畜～ domestic animal.
    牲口 **shēngkou** (N) livestock (M頭tóu, 匹pǐ, 隻jr).

升{昇 (FV) 1) 2), 陞 (FV) 2)} **shēng** (FV) 1) ascend, rise. /氣球～起來了. The balloon rose. 2) raise, hoist. ～旗 hoist a flag. 3) promote. /他～了工頭了. He's been promoted to foreman. (N) <-子> Chinese quart box (31.6 cubic inches, used for measuring grain and the like). (M) Chinese dry quart. 三～米 three quarts of rice.

甥 **shēng** (B) sister's child. ～女 niece (sister's daughter).

生 **shēng** (FV) 1) give birth to. /她～了一個十磅九兩的女兒. She gave birth to a ten-pound nine-ounce girl. 2) be born. /我～在日本. I was born in Japan. (SV) 1) be raw, unripe. ～菜 raw vegetables. /這個蘋果還～着呢. This apple is still unripe. 2) be unfamiliar, strange. /我對這個地方還很～呢. I'm still not familiar with this place. (B) 1) become, develop. ～銹 become rusty. 2) produce, put forth. ～火 start a fire; ～利 make a profit. 3) life. 謀～ make a living; ～死 life and death. 4) student. 女～ female student. t
    生病 **shēngbing** (VO) get sick, be ill. /我從來沒生過病. I've never been sick.
    生產 **shēngchǎn** (FV) 1) have a baby. /他太太快～了. His wife is going to have a baby soon. 2) produce. /那個工廠今年什麼都沒～. That factory hasn't produced anything this year. (N) 1) production. ～方法 methods of production. 2) childbirth.
    生產隊 **shēngchǎndwèi** (N) production team (c).
    生成的 **shēngchéngde** (A) from birth. /他～就那麼懶. He's

been lazy like that from birth.

生氣 **shēngchì** (N) spirit, vitality. /這個組織沒有~. This organization has no vitality. (SV) be angry. /他已經不~了. He's not angry anymore. (VO) get angry. /你還生我的氣嗎? Are you still angry at me?

生活 **shēnghwó** (N) 1) life. 日常 ~ everyday life. 2) livelihood, living. 謀 ~ make a living. (FV) live. /他~的很快樂. He lives very happily.

生長 **shēngjǎng** (FV) 1) be born and raised. /他~在中國. He was born and raised in China. 2) grow. /這種植物在水裡~. This kind of plant grows in water.

生力軍 **shēnglìjyūn** (N) fresh troops, reinforcements (M 支 **jr**).

生命 **shēngmìng** (N) life (as opposed to death). /那個星球上沒有~. There's no life on that planet.

生日 **shēngr** (N) birthday. 過 ~ celebrate a birthday.

生物 **shēngwù** (N) living things.

生物學 **shēngwùsywé** (N) biology.

生意 **shēngyì** (N) business. /他做什麼~? What is his business? /~好不好? How's business?

繩(繩)**shéng** (B) <-子,-ㄦ> rope, string (M條**tyáu**,根**gēn**). 絲 ~ silk cord.

省 **shěng** (FV) save, economize on. /這樣我~了很多時間. I save a lot of time this way. (SV) be frugal, sparing. /他用錢很~. He's very frugal with his money. (N) province, state. 最大的一個 ~ the biggest province. (B) abridged. ~ 略 ellipsis, omit. → 省 **syǐng**.

省的 **shěngde** (AV) save, avoid. /現在攢一點兒錢~以後沒錢用. Put away some money now and avoid being broke later on.

省會 **shěnghwèi** (N) provincial capital, state capital.

省長 **shěngjǎng** (N) provincial governor, state governor.

省着 **shěngje** (A) sparingly. /我們的油快沒有了,~點兒用吧. The oil is getting low, so use it sparingly.

月勝(肸)**shèng** (FV) 1) win a battle, war, or game. /這次比賽誰~了? Who won this race? 2) defeat someone. /我~了他了. I defeated him. (B) 1) superior. ~過 surpass. 2) scenic beauty. ~地 scenic spot.

勝利 **shènglì** (FV) win, be victorious. /他們倒底~了. They won in the end. (N) victory.

剩(賸)**shèng** (FV) have left, be left. /還~一碗飯. There's still one bowl of rice left. (AT) left-over, surplus. ~貨 surplus goods.

剩兒 **shèngr** (N) something left over. /你的五塊錢還有~沒~? Do you have anything left of your five dollars?

盛 **shèng** (B) 1) abundant. ~宴 sumptuous feast; ~開 be in full bloom. 2) cordial, hearty. ~情 kindness; ~意 goodwill. → 盛 **chéng**.

聖 **shèng** (B) 1) holy, sacred. ~水 holy water. 2) sage, saint. 孔 ~人 Confucius. 3) great master. 樂 ~ great master of music. **t**

聖誕 **shèngdàn** (B) holy birth. 耶蘇 ~ Christmas, birthday of Jesus; 孔子 ~ birthday of Confucius.

聖經 **shèngjīng** (N) the Bible (M 本 **běn**).

shi *see* **shr**.

收 **shōu** (FV) 1) receive. /昨天我~了十封信. I received ten letters yesterday. 2) accept. /我沒~他的禮物. I didn't accept his money. 3) collect, gather. ~租 collect rent. /莊稼還沒~呢. The crops still haven't been harvested. 4) put away, keep. /你把那個合同~在那兒了? Where did you put that contract? (B) close, bring to an end. ~口 closing of a wound.

收成 **shōucheng** (N) harvest.

收割 **shōugē** (FV) harvest. /稻子才~了一半. Only half of the rice has been harvested.

收割機 **shōugējī** (N) reaping machine, reaper.

收工 **shōugūng** (VO) quit work (at the end of a day). /我們今天下午五點就~了. We quit work at 5 P.M.

收穫 **shōuhwo** (FV) 1) harvest. /麥子已經～了. The wheat has been harvested. 2) gain from doing something. /這次旅行我～了不少的寶貴經驗. I gained a lot of precious experience from this trip. (N) 1) crop. 2) result. /你這次實驗有什麼～嗎? Did you get any results from this experiment?

收入 **shōurù** (N) income. (FV) make, earn, money. /你一個月～多少錢? How much do you earn a month?

收生 **shōushēng** (VO) serve as a midwife, perform a delivery. /這個月他收了三次生. She served as a midwife three times this month.

收拾 **shōushr** (FV) 1) put in order, straighten up, make ready. ～屋子 straighten up a room; ～行李 pack baggage. 2) repair, fix. ～汽車 fix a car. 3) teach someone a lesson (fig.). /我得好好地～～他. I'll teach him a lesson all right.

收攤兒 **shōutār** (VO) gather up wares (as a peddler gathers up wares at the end of a day). /那個賣水果的每天八點鐘～. That fruit vendor gathers up his wares at eight o'clock every evening.

收藏 **shōutsáng** (N) collection (of objects). /他的～很丰富. His collection is huge. (FV) collect something valuable. /他～了很多古畫. He has collected many ancient paintings.

收條 **shōutyáu** (N) <-ㄦ> receipt (M張jāng).

收音機 **shōuyīnjī** (N) receiving set (radio) (M架jyà).

熟 **shóu, shú** (SV) 1) be ripe. /蘋果還沒～呢. The apples aren't ripe yet. 2) be done, cooked. /肉～了. The meat is done. 3) be familiar with. /這個地方我也不～. I'm not familiar with this place myself. (B) 1) thoroughly, deeply. ～思 ponder; ～睡 sleep soundly. 2) processed, refined. ～鐵 refined iron.

熟練 **shóulyàn, shúlyàn** (SV) be skillful, well trained. /這一段蕭邦他彈的很～. He plays this Chopin piece skillfully. /他的

技術很～. His technique is very skillful.

熟識 **shóushr, shúshr** (SV) be well acquainted. /我跟他不大～. I'm not too well acquainted with him.

熟習 **shóusyí, shúsyí** (SV) be familiar with a process, a matter, etc. /我對這兒的情形還不～呢. I'm still not familiar with the situation here. (FV) familiarize oneself with. /你最好先把這件事情～～再跟他談. You'd better familiarize yourself with this matter before you talk to him.

手 **shŏu** (N) 1) hand (M隻jī; 雙shwāng). 2) <-ㄦ> good hand, expert (M把bă). /做這種事他是一把～. He's a good hand at this type of thing. 3) participant (in work or a game). /我們打牌缺一把～. We're short one player for a card game. (M) hand (in playing cards). /他有一～好牌. He has a good hand. (B) man. 投～ pitcher; 凶～ murderer.

手邊 **shŏubyān** (PW) <-ㄦ> 1) place right next to someone. /那個煙灰缸就在你～呢. That ash tray is right beside you. 2) on hand, within reach. /我～沒有現錢. I don't have any cash on hand.

手錶 **shŏubyău** (N) wristwatch (M隻jī).

手鎗 **shŏuchyāng** (N) pistol, revolver (M把bă, 枝jī).

手段 **shŏudwan** (N) 1) method, means, steps to be taken. /他對付這件事情很有～. He knows very well what steps to take in handling this matter. 2) devious device, indirect method. /這個人很喜歡用～. He likes very much to use indirect methods to get what he wants.

手電 **shŏudyàn** (N) flashlight.

手電燈 **shoudyàndēng** (N) flashlight.

手工 **shŏugūng** (N) handicraft.

手工業 **shŏugūngyè** (N) handicraft industry.

手掌 **shŏujăng** (N) palm (of the hand).

手巾 **shŏujin** (N) 1) towel. 2) handkerchief. (M塊kwài, 條tyáu).

手指頭 **shŏujŕtou** (N) finger. 大～ thumb.

手紙 **shǒujř** (N) toilet paper (M張**jāng**;捲**jywǎn**).

手絹儿 **shǒujywàr** (N) handkerchief (M條**tyáu**,塊**kwài**).

手榴彈 **shǒulyóudàn** (N) hand grenade (M隻**jr̄**,枚**méi**).

手儿 **shǒur** (N)↑(N) 2). (M) 1) method, technique. /你這～不怎麼樣. Your technique is nothing special. 2) trick, gimmick. /他真有兩～. He has quite a few gimmicks.

手術 **'shǒushù** (N) operation (surgical) (M次**tsz̀**). 動～perform an operation *or* have an operation.

手心 **shǒusyīn** (N) palm (of the hand).

手續 **'shǒusyù** (N) procedure, series of actions *or* processes, red tape. /借錢的～很麻煩. The red tape you have to go through to borrow money is very annoying.

手套 **shǒutàu** (N) <-儿> glove, mitten (M隻**jr̄**; 雙**shwāng**,副**fù**).

手提箱 **shǒutísyāng** (N) hand luggage (M隻**jr̄**).

手頭 **shǒutóu** (N) one's financial situation. (A) on hand, within reach. /夜裡我～老預備着手電筒. I always have a flashlight within reach at night.

手腕 **shǒuwàn** (N) 1) <-儿> wrist. 2) craftiness. 有～ be crafty.

手藝 **'shǒuyì** (N) skill in working with the hands. /那個廚子的～不錯. That cook has quite a bit of skill.

首 **shǒu** (M) for poems. 一～詩 a poem. (B) 1) head (on the body). ～級 head. 2) chief, principal. ～相 premier, prime minister. 3) beginning, first. ～次 first time.

首都 **shǒudū** (N) capital of a country.

首飾 **shǒushr** (N) ornament, piece of jewelry (M件**jyàn**).

'守 **shǒu** (FV) 1) defend, guard. /派誰去～那個城? Whom should we send to defend that city? 2) keep a secret, promise. /她不能～秘密. She can't keep a secret. 3) stick to a rule, principle. /你應當～規矩. You should stick to the rules.

守着 **shǒuje** (FV) be next to, near. /你～井可得小心一點. Be careful, you're near the well.

'守財奴 **shǒutsáinú** (N) miser.

'守衛 **shǒuwèi** (FV) stand guard over, defend. /我們派了很多兵～那個地方. We sent a lot of soldiers to defend that place.

'受 **shòu** (FV) 1) receive, take. ～教育 receive an education. /你～了他的錢,你當然不能逮他. Since you've taken his money, you naturally can't have him arrested. 2) undergo, endure. ～批評 undergo criticism. /他的態度我～不了. I can't endure his attitude. (CV) by (marking the agent). /他～人騙了. He was swindled by someone. (B) used before FV to form SV, not bad to. ～看 be easy on the eyes.

'受到 **shòudàu** (RC) suffer, receive. /他～很大的打擊. He suffered a great blow.

'受累 **shòulèi** (VO) be troubled, bothered. /對不起叫您～. I'm sorry to have troubled you.

'受刺激 **shòutsz̀ji** (VO) receive a mental shock. /他受了很大的刺激. He has received a terrific mental shock.

'受委屈 **shòuwěichyu** (VO) get a raw deal, receive unjust treatment. /他受了很大的委屈. He really got a raw deal.

瘦 **shòu** (SV) 1) be thin (of people, animals). /他越來越～了. He's getting thinner and thinner. 2) be lean. ～肉 lean meat. 3) be tight. /這雙鞋太～. This pair of shoes is too tight.

瘦子 **shòudz** (N) 1) thin person. 2) skinny (nickname).

售 **shòu** (B) sell. ～價 selling price; ～貨員 salesman.

售票員 **shòupyàuywán** (N) ticket seller.

獸[兽] **shòu** (B) animal. 野～ wild animal; ～醫 veterinarian.

壽[寿] **shòu** (B) 1) long life. 福～ good fortune and long life. 2) life. ～命 life. 3) birthday. ～禮 birthday gift. 4) funerary. ～衣 cerement.

壽險 **shòusyǎn** (N) life insurance.

獅 **shr̄** (B) <-子> lion (M隻**jr̄**,頭**tóu**). 石～ stone lion.

蝨[虱] **shr** (B) <-子> louse (insect) (M 隻 扪) 水 ～wood louse.

施 **shr** (B) 1) give as charity. ～醫 treatment without charge; ～藥 give out medicine without charge. 2) put into effect (of laws, regulations, etc.). ～行 put into effect. 3) apply, spread, spray. ～水 water a field, plants. s

 施 肥 **shrféi** (VO) put on fertilizer, fertilize. /如果你施一點 肥,這花會開得更好. If you put on a little fertilizer, these flowers will bloom much better.

失 **shr** (B) 1) lose. ～物 lost property; ～眠 have insomnia. 2) miss, err. ～當 be improper (of conduct). 3) lose control. ～手 accidentally (lit. losing control of the hand). → 不 失 bushr.

 失 敗 **shrbài** (FV) 1) be defeated. /敵軍終於～了. The enemy was finally defeated. 2) fail. /他考大學～了,很傷心. He failed the college entrance exam, so he's very unhappy. (N) 1) defeat. 2) failure. (M:次tsz̀).

 失 常 **shrcháng** (VO) deviate from normal, be abnormal. /他的 神經～了. He's not in his right mind.

 失 去 **'shrchyù** (FV) lose. ～信 心 lose confidence.

 失 蹤 **shrdzūng** (VO) disappear without a trace. /他忽然～了. Suddenly he disappeared completely from view.

 失 禮 **shrlǐ** (SV) be impolite. /他昨天很～. He was very impolite yesterday. (VO) make a faux pas. /你覺得我失了什麼禮了 嗎? Did I make any faux pas? (IE) Excuse my bad manners.

 失 守 **shrshǒu** (FV) fall, be captured (of a place). /昨天晚上 那個城～了. That city fell to the enemy last night.

 失 信 **shrsyìn** (VO) break one's word. /我從來沒失過信. I've never broken my word.

 失 望 **shrwàng** (SV) be disappointed.

 失 業 **shryè** (VO) lose one's job. /他已經失了三年業了. It has been three years since he lost

his job. (B) unemployment. ～問 題 unemployment problem.

 失 約 **shrywē** (VO) fail to keep an appointment. /對不起,昨天 跟您～了. I'm sorry I didn't keep my appointment with you yesterday.

詩 **shr** (N) poem (M首 **shǒu**, 篇 **pyān**). ～ 人 poet.

 詩歌 **shrgē** (N) rhyming verse (M首 **shǒu**, 篇 **pyān**).

 詩集 **shrjí** (N) collection of poems of one poet (M部 **bù**, 本 **běn**).

 詩選 **shrsywǎn** (N) anthology of poems (M部 **bù**, 本 **běn**).

濕[溼][湿] **shr** (SV) be wet, damp, humid. ～度 humidity. /我的鞋～了. My shoes are wet. /這種天氣又 ～又熱,很難受. The weather is hot and humid and it's very uncomfortable.

師[师] **shr** (M) division (m). (B) 1) teacher. 老～ teacher. 2) specialist. 工程～ engineer; 律～ lawyer; 醫 ～ physician.

 師傅 **shrfu** (N) 1) teacher. 2) specialist. (B) used politely after surnames of people performing some special role in society, as a barber, carpenter, tailor, cook, etc.

 師長 **shrjǎng** (N) 1) teacher. 2) divisional commander.

石 **shŕ** (B) <-頭> stone, rock (M 塊 **kwài**). ～像 stone statue. → 石 **dàn**. s

 石板 **shŕbǎn** (N) stone slab, slate.

 石碑 **shŕbēi** (N) stone monument with an inscription (M座 **dzwò**).

 石膏 **shŕgāu** (N) plaster, plaster of Paris, gypsum.

 石灰 **shŕhwēi** (N) lime (chem.).

 石榴 **shŕlyou** (N) pomegranate.

 石棉 **shŕmyán** (N) asbestos.

 石油 **shŕyóu** (N) petroleum, kerosene.

時 **shŕ** (B) 1) time. 古～ ancient times; 有～ sometimes. 2) hour. 計～給 薪 pay by the hour. 3) o'clock. 清 晨七～ seven o'clock in the morning. 4) current. ～價 current price. (PT) ～...～... sometimes... sometimes.... ～好～壞 sometimes good sometimes bad. → 不時 bùshŕ.

日寺常 **shŕcháng** (A) often. /他~來看我. He often comes to see me.

日寺期 **shŕchī** (N) period of time. /戰爭~東西很貴. Things are expensive during a period of war.

時代 **shŕdài** (N) age, era. 中古~ the Middle Ages; 我的學生~ my student days.

日寺候 **shŕhou** (N) 1) time, hour. /你甚麼~到的? What time did you arrive? 2) time, free time. /他已經等了很多~了. He's been waiting for a long time.

日寺間 **shŕjyān** (N) time, free time. /我沒有~和你爭辯. I have no time to argue with you.

時局 **shŕjyú** (N) current situation (political or military). /~變更得很快. The current situation is changing very fast.

時髦 **shŕmáu** (SV) <-ㄦ> be fashionable, stylish. /這種髮型很~. This hair style is very fashionable.

日寺評 **shŕpíng** (N) editorial (M 篇 pyān).

日寺日寺刻刻 **shŕshŕkekè** (A) all the time. /開車的時候~都得小心. When you're driving you have to be careful all the time.

日寺日寺 **'shŕshŕ** (A) from time to time, often. /一定~都有變化. There are bound to be changes from time to time.

時事 **shŕshr** (N) current events.

時興 **shŕsyīng** (SV) be fashionable, popular. /在一九二八的時候,麻將在美國很~. Mahjong was quite popular in the U. S. in 1928. (FV) be popular, in fashion. /今年冬天~白大衣. White coats are in fashion this winter.

日寺運 **shŕyùn** (N) luck, fortune.

食 **shŕ** (N) animal food. 貓~ cat food. (B) 1) food. 零~ snack; ~品店 food store. 2) eat. ~量 capacity to eat; ~蟻獸 anteater.

食堂 **shŕtáng** (N) 1) dining hall (M間 jyān). 2) restaurant (M 間 jyān, 家 jyā).

食物 **'shŕwù** (N) provisions, foodstuffs.

實[寔][实] **shŕ** (AT) solid (not hollow). /這裡面是~的還是空的? Is it solid inside or hollow? (B) 1) sincere. 誠~ honest. 2) real, true. ~值 real value; ~得 net income; 其~ in fact, as a matter of fact. 3) fruit. 結~ bear fruit.

實在 **shŕdzài** (A) really, actually. /我~不能再喝了. I really can't drink any more. (SV) 1) be honest. /那人很~,你可以信賴他. That man is very honest; you can trust him. 2) be real, true. /~情形沒有人知道. Nobody knows the real situation.

實話 **shŕhwà** (N) truth (M 句 jyù). /說~,我真不知道. To tell the truth, I don't really know.

實際 **shŕjì** (SV) 1) be practical. /他的建議很~. His suggestion is very practical. 2) be materialistic. /現在很多女孩子都很~. Nowadays many girls are very materialistic. (A) actually. /你的收入~並不少. Actually your income isn't bad. (N) reality.

實力 **'shŕlì** (N) strength, power. /敵人的~不如我們. The strength of the enemy is not equal to ours.

實現 **shŕsyàn** (FV) come true. /他的話都~了. Everything he said came true.

實行 **shŕsyíng** (FV) put into effect. /你什麼時候~你的計劃? When are you going to put your plans into effect?

實用 **shŕyùng** (SV) be practical, useful. /你的計劃現在不~. Your plan isn't practical at present.

識 **shŕ, shr*** (B) 1) know, recognize. ~貨 know the quality of goods. 2)* knowledge. 常~ general knowledge, common sense.

識字 **shŕdz** (VO) be literate. /他們多半都不識字. Most of them are illiterate.

十[拾] **shŕ** (NU) ten. ~個人 ten people. (M) ten. 二~人 twenty people. (B) 1) tenth. ~馬路 Tenth Avenue. 2) used before the numbers one through nine to form the numbers eleven through nineteen. ~一 eleven; ~二 twelve; ~三 thirteen; etc.

十字 **shŕdz** (N) cross-mark (similar in function to an X-mark but in the shape of a cross). 紅~會 Red Cross. /畫一個~. Make a cross-mark.

十字架 **shŕdzìjyà** (N) cross, crucifix.

十二月 **shŕèrywè** (TW) 1) (in) December. 2) the twelfth month of the lunar calendar.

十分 **shŕfēn** (A) completely, very. /那件事你做得～成功. You did that very successfully.

十一月 **shŕyīywè** (TW) 1) (in) November. 2) the eleventh month of the lunar calendar.

十月 **shŕywè** (TW) 1) (in) October. 2) the tenth month of the lunar calendar.

拾 **shŕ** (FV) 1) find accidentally. /我在街上～了五塊錢. I found five dollars in the street. 2) pick something up. /那個針太小,我～不起來. That needle is too small, I can't pick it up. →十{拾}shŕ.

拾掇 **shŕdou** (FV) 1) repair, fix. /我這雙鞋得拿去～～. This pair of shoes needs to be repaired. 2) straighten out. /把箱子～～. Straighten out (the things in) that box. 3) fix someone. /我們得～他一頓. We'll fix him.

什 **shŕ** (B) 1) ten. ～一 one-tenth. 2) miscellaneous. 家～ various utensils. SF of 甚 **shén**. t

始 **shŕ** (B) begin. ～祖 most remote ancestor.

始終 **shŕjūng** (A) 1) all the time, from beginning to end of a period of time. /他進來以後～沒說一句話. He hasn't said a word all the time he's been here. 2) at all. /我～不明白他為什麼要退學. I don't understand at all why he left school.

使 **shŕ** (FV) 1) use. /我能不能～～你的打字機? May I use your typewriter? 2) make, cause. /我可以～他高興. I can make him happy. /他真～我生氣. He really makes me mad. (CV) with. /我不喜歡～鉛筆寫字. I don't like to write with a pencil. (B) envoy. 大～ ambassador; 天～ angel.

使得 **shŕde** (SV) be all right. /你想這個計劃～嗎? Do you think this plan is all right? (FV) 1) can use. /這錢你～. You can use this money. 2) make, cause.

/那個消息～我傷心了幾天. That news made me sad for several days.

使壞 **shr̀hwài** (VO) play a dirty trick. /他給我～. He played a dirty trick on me.

使喚 **shr̀hwan** (FV) 1) manipulate, use. /你會不會～筷子? Can you use chopsticks? 2) boss someone around. /他老～人. He always bosses people around. 3) handle, manage, servants. /他很會～佣人. He can handle servants very well.

使勁 **shr̀jìn** (VO) use strength. /我不能再～了. I can't use any more strength. (A) with all one's strength, hard. /你把門～推一推. Push the door hard.

使命 **'shr̀mìng** (N) mission, assignment.

使用 **shr̀yùng** (FV) use, make use of. /這個機器已經不能～了. This machine cannot be used anymore.

屎 **shǐ** (N) movement, stool. 拉～ defecate. (B) secretion (d). 眼～ secretion from the eyes.

室 **shǐ** →室 **shr̀**.

史 **shǐ** (B) history. 歷～ history (in general); 思想～ history of human thought; 經濟～ economic history. s

士 **shr̀** (N) scholar (piece in Chinese chess). (B) 1) scholar, gentleman. 學～ Bachelor of Arts, B.A.; 博～ doctor, Ph.D.; 戰～ warrior. 2) non-commissioned officer. 下～ corporal.

士兵 **shr̀bīng** (N) enlisted man, soldier.

世 **shr̀** (B) 1) world. ～運 world athletic meet. 2) generation. ～交 friendship of many generations. 3) age, time. 今～ the present age.

世界 **shr̀jyè** (N) the world.

柿 **shr̀** (B) <-子> persimmon. ～餅 dried persimmon.

市 **shr̀** (N) 1) municipality, city. 天津～ the city of Tiantsin; ～長 mayor. (B) 1) market. ～價 market price. 2) Chinese standard system of weights and measures. ～尺 Chinese standard foot.

市場 **shr̀chǎng** (N) market, marketplace.

市區 **shr̀chyū** (N) business district of a city, downtown.

事 **shr̀** (N) <-ㄦ> 1) matter, affair, thing, business (M件**jyàn**). /這件～能不能等到下禮拜做？ Can this matter wait until next week? /我有一件～要告訴你. I have something to tell you. /不關你的～. It's none of your business. 2) job, work. 找～ look for a job. 3) trouble. 惹～ make trouble.

事情 **shr̀ching** (N) 1) matter, affair, thing, business (M件**jyàn**). /今天下午我沒有什麼～. I don't have anything to do this afternoon. 2) job, work. 3) trouble. /他現在出了～了. He's in trouble now.

事故 **shr̀gù** (N) trouble. /他還不來是不是發生了什麼～？ He still hasn't come. Could he have had some trouble?

事實 **shr̀shr̀** (N) fact.

事業 **shr̀yè** (N) 1) business on a large scale. /他把錢都投資在那件～上了. He invested all his money in that business. 2) undertaking, enterprise, task. /他的～很發達. That enterprise of his has been very successful.

試 **shr̀** (FV) try, try out, try on. /～～看你做的了做不了. Try and see whether you can do it or not. /我要～一～那雙鞋. I would like to try on that pair of shoes. (B) examine, test. 口～ oral exam; 筆～ written test.

試手 **shr̀shǒu** (VO) try something out. /我想拿這根高爾夫球棒～. I want to try out this golf club.

試驗 **shr̀yàn** (FV) test, run experiments on, try out. /一種新的殺蟲藥已經～成功了. A new kind of insecticide has been successfully tested. /我～了你教給我的方法,也不行. I've tried the method you taught me, but it didn't work either. (N) experiment.

似 **shr̀** (B) ↓. →似 **sz̀**.

似的 **shr̀de** (P) 1) used after verbal expressions with or without 像 **syàng**, 好像 **hǎusyàng**, 彷彿 **fǎngfu**, 似乎 **sz̀hu**, or 跟 **gēn**, as if. /他老有病～. He always looks as if he's ill. /我(好像)在那兒見過你～. It seems as if I've met you somewhere before. 2) used after nominal expressions with or without 像 **syàng**, 好像 **hǎusyang**, 彷彿 **fǎngfu**, or 跟 **gēn**, be the same as, be like. /他的臉馬～. He has a face like a horse. /他瘦的(跟)個猴ㄦ～. He's skinny as a monkey.

是 **shr̀** (FV) used between two nominal elements, be (is, are) (negated with 不 **bù** only, never 沒 **méi**). /我～學生. I'm a student. /今天～幾號? What day is today? /這本書不～他寫的. This book isn't the one he wrote. (B) 1) used before elements of a sentence to emphasize them. /這本書我～昨天買的. I bought this book YESTERDAY. /～他叫我來的. It was HE who asked me to come. /這個歌ㄦ～我聽會了的,沒人教我. I learned that song by just HEARING it; no one taught me. 2) used before elements of a sentence and stressed, it is true that. /東西～貴. (**Dūngsyi 'shr̀ gwèi**.) It's true that things are expensive. /他～沒看見我. (**Tā 'shr̀ méikànjyàn wǒ**.) It's true that he didn't see me. 3) added to adverbs without changing their function or meaning. /雖然～下雨,可是我還～得去. Even though it's raining, I still have to go. /也許～他不願意說. Maybe he doesn't like to speak. 4) every, any. /那種事～人就會做. Anyone can do that kind of thing. (IE) Yes. /A: 他來了很久了吧. B: ～. A: He's been here a long time now. B: Yes, he has. (PT)...～..., 可是 (or 不過)...... all right (or sure it is...) but.... /好～好可是我不喜歡. It's good all right; I just don't like it. /做～做完了,可是不一定好. It's finished all right, but that doesn't necessarily mean it's good. →不是 **búshr**.

是的 **shrde** (IE) Yes. /A:他來了很久了吧．B:～． A: He's been here a long time. B: Yes, he has.

是非 **shrfēi** (N) 1) right and wrong. /他不懂～． or 他不明～． He can't tell right from wrong. 2) gossip. /這儿～太多． There's too much gossip here.

是 **shr** (B) →鑰匙 **yàushr**. →匙 **chŕ**.

適[适] **shr** (B) appropriate, suitable. 合～ be appropriate, suitable.
適當 **shrdàng** (SV) be proper, suitable. /他穿的不太～． What he wore wasn't very proper.

室 **shr, shŕ** (B) room. 課～classroom; 臥～bedroom.

式 **shr** (B) 1) model, style, pattern. 新～ modern style. 2) <-子> formula. 圖解～ graphic formula.

勢[势] **shr** (B) 1) momentum. 權～power. 2) situation, tendency。時～ current situation.
勢力 **'shrlì** (N) power, influence. /他有很大的～。 He has a great deal of influence.
勢利 **shrlì** (SV) be snobbish.

視 **shr** (B) look. ～力 power of vision; 輕～ look down on someone or something.
視察 **shrchá** (FV) make an inspection tour of, inspect. /昨天教育局的人到我們學校來～． People from the Board of Education came and inspected our school yesterday.

釋 **shr** (B) 1) release, set free. 開～ liberate. 2) explain. 解～explain. 3) Shakyamuni (contracted form of 釋加牟尼 **shrjyāmwoní**). Buddhism.
釋放 **shrfàng** (FV) release a prisoner. /誰把戰俘都～了？ Who released all of the prisoners?

識 **shr** →識 **shŕ**.

書[书] **shū** (N) book (M 本 **běn**, 冊 **tsè**; 套 **tàu**, 部 **bù**). (B) 1) letter, statement. ～信 letter; 證明～certificate. 3) write. ～法 calligraphy; 草～ running style of handwriting; 代～ write for another.
書包 **shūbāu** (N) book bag, satchel.

書店 **shūdyàn** (N) bookstore.
書記 **shūjì** (N) clerk, secretary.
書籍 **shūjí** (N) books. /這個圖書館的～很全． This library has all kinds of books.
書架 **shūjyà** (N) bookshelf, bookcase.
書面 **shūmyàn** (AT) written. ～答覆 written answer.

輸 **shū** (FV) lose money in gambling, a game. /我～了五塊錢． I lost five dollars (in gambling). /我～給他一盤棋． I lost a game of chess to him. (B) transport. ～送 transport.

梳 **shū** (FV) comb. /她正～她的頭髮呢． She's combing her hair. (B) <-子> comb (M 把 **bǎ**). 木～ wooden comb.

叔 **shū** (B) 1) father's younger brother. 2) husband's younger brother.
叔父 **shūfù** (N) uncle (father's younger brother).
叔母 **shūmù** (N) aunt (wife of one's father's younger brother).
叔叔 **shūshu** (N) 1) uncle (father's younger brother). 2) brother-in-law (husband's younger brother).

舒 **shū** (B) 1) relax. ～坦 be relaxed and comfortable. 2) expand, stretch out. ～展 be opened, expanded. s t
舒服 **shūfu** (SV) 1) be comfortable. /這張牀很～． This bed is really comfortable. 2) feel well. /我有點不～． I don't feel very well.

疏 **shū** (B) 1) remove obstruction. ～濬 dredge (as a river). 2) careless, negligent. ～失 be careless. 3) sparse. ～散 disperse. 4) distant. 親～close and distant relatives.
疏遠 **shūywǎn** (SV) be estranged. /我們兩個人越來越～了． We have become more and more estranged.

熟 **shú** →熟 **shóu**.

贖 **shú** (FV) redeem, ransom. /我把我當的表～回來了． I redeemed the watch I pawned. /用支票～那個孩子成不成？

Can the child be ransomed by check?

贖 罪 **shúdzwèi** (VO) make up for one's offense, atone for one's sins. /我情願花二百塊錢贖我的罪. I prefer to pay two hundred dollars to make up for my offense. /你多念一點儿經,贖贖你的罪吧. You should pray more to atone for your sins.

暑 **shǔ** (B) summer heat. 中 ～ suffer from the heat *or* sunstroke.
暑假 **shǔjyà** (TW) (during) the summer vacation.

署 **shǔ** (B) 1) board, commission. 衛生 ～ Board of Health. 2) assign, appoint. 部～ assign positions to people. 3) to sign. ～ 名 sign one's name, signature.

屬[属] **shǔ** (FV) 1) belong to, be a part of, be under the control of. /越南從前 ～ 中國. Vietnam formerly belonged to China. /物理～自然科學. Physics is a part of natural science. 2) be born under the zodiacal sign of.... /他 ～ 狗. He was born under the zodiacal sign of the dog. (B) 1) member of a family. 遺 ～ surviving members of a family. 2) genus, family. 貓 ～ cat family. 3) subordinate, dependent. ～ 民 subject (person); 西～摩洛哥 Spanish Morocco. (PT) ～... 管 belong to, be under the control of. /所有的移民局都～司法部管. All immigration offices are under the control of the Department of Justice.
屬 於 '**shǔyú** (FV) 1) belong to, be under the control of, be a part of. /處女島～美國. The Virgin Islands belong to the United States. 2) be tantamount to. /我看你這種行動就～瘋狂. I think that your actions are tantamount to insanity.

數[数] **shǔ** (FV) 1) count. /請你 ～ 一～. Please count them. 2) be considered the best in a group. /我們這些人裡就～你了. You are considered the best one of all of us. (B) scold, reprimand. ～ 罵 scold. →數 **shù**.

數[数] **shù** (B) 1) <-儿> number, figure. 得 ～ sum. 2) several. ～ 年 sever-

al years. 3) fate, destiny. 氣 ～ fate, destiny. →數 **shǔ**.
數 目 **shùmu** (N) number, amount. /你數一數這些～. Count up these numbers. /這個 ～ 還不夠. That amount still isn't enough.
數 學 **shùsywé** (N) mathematics.

樹[树] **shù** (N) tree (M棵**kē**).
樹 枝 **shùjr** (N) branch of a tree (M枝**jr**).
樹 林 **shùlín** (N) <-子> forest, woods.
樹 皮 **shùpí** (N) bark.

漱 **shù** (FV) rinse one's mouth, gargle. /你嗓子痛可以用鹽水～一～. If you have a sore throat, gargle with salt water.
漱 口 **shùkǒu** (VO) rinse one's mouth, gargle. /飯後應該 ～. Rinse your mouth after meals.

豎[竖] **shù** (FV) set up vertically, erect. 他們在門前～了一根旗桿. They set up a flagpole in front of the door. (N) <-儿> verticle stroke (in Chinese calligraphy). (AT) vertical. ～ 坐標 vertical axis.

shua *see* **shwa**.

shuai *see* **shwai**.

shuan *see* **shwan**.

shuang *see* **shwang**.

shui *see* **shwei**.

shun *see* **shwun**.

shuo *see* **shwo**.

刷 **shwā** (FV) 1) brush. /你的鞋該～了. Your shoes need brushing. 2) whitewash. /這閒屋子是我自己 ～ 的. I whitewashed this room myself. 3) cut a class. /今天的法文我 ～. I cut French class today. 4) give someone the brush-off, flunk someone (in school) (lp). /他叫學校給 ～ 了. He was flunked by the school. /他的女朋友把他 ～ 了. His girl friend gave him the brush-off. (B) <-子,-儿> brush (M把**bǎ**). 牙 ～ toothbrush.
刷 牙 **shwāyá** (VO) brush the teeth. /你每頓飯以後都要 ～. You should brush your teeth after every meal.

226

耍 **shwǎ** (FV) play with, juggle. ～ 刀 juggle swords.

衰 **shwāi** (B) decline, decay. ～ 老 be feeble.
　衰敗 **shwāibài** (FV) decay, decline. /到十五世紀封建制度就～了. The feudal system declined after the fifteenth century.
　衰弱 **shwāirwò** (SV) be weak (physically), poor (of health). /他的身體越來越～了. His health is getting poorer and poorer.

摔 **shwāi** (FV) 1) throw down. /他一生氣就把書～在地上了. He got angry and threw the book down on the ground. 2) fall (of persons, animals). /他～了一下子,腿就傷了. He fell down and hurt his leg. 3) drop and break. /我～了一個茶杯. I dropped a teacup and it broke. →甩{摔} **shwǎi**.

甩{摔} **shwǎi** (FV) 1) shake with a jerk to one side. /他一～毛筆～了我一臉墨. He shook the brush and got ink all over my face. 2) jilt, let down, forsake. /他把她～到一邊去了. He jilted her.

拴 **shwān** (FV) fasten something to something else. /他船～在碼頭旁邊. Fasten the boat to the dock.

霜 **shwāng** (N) frost (M場 **chǎng**, 層 **tséng**). 下～ have a frost.

雙(双) **shwāng** (M) pair, couple. 一～鞋 a pair of shoes. (B) double, two. ～人床 double bed. →雙 **shwàng**.
　雙親 **shwāngchīn** (N) parents.

爽 **shwǎng** (B) crisp, invigorating. ～利 be brisk.
　爽直 **shwǎngjŕ** (SV) be straightforward. /他的脾氣很～. He has a very straightforward manner.
　爽快 **shwǎngkwai** (SV) 1) be happy. /今天我覺得很～. I feel very happy today. 2) be straightforward. /他的性格很～. He has a straightforward personality.

雙 **shwàng** (B) ↓. →雙 **shwāng**.
　雙生 **shwàngsheng** (N) twins (M 對 **dwèi**).

誰 **shwéi** →誰 **shéi**.

水 **shwěi** (N) water. 雨～ rain water. (M) washing of a garment. /這件襯衫洗了三～了. This shirt has gone through three washings. (B) 1) <-ル> juice, liquid. 橘子～ orange juice; 藥～ medicine (in liquid form). 2) river 湘～ the Hsiang River.
　水泵 **shwěibèng** (N) water pump.
　水車 **shwěichē** (N) waterwheel for irrigation. 2) water cart.
　水份 '**shwěifèn** (N) water content of anything. /這個果子～很多. This fruit is very juicy.
　水管子 **shwéigwǎndz** (N) water pipe, drainpipe.
　水果 **shwéigwǒ** (N) fruit.
　水坑 **shwěikēng** (N) pool of stagnant, muddy water.
　水庫 **shwěikù** (N) reservoir.
　水泥 **shwěiní** (N) cement.
　水平 **shwěipíng** (N) 1) level (instrument). 2) standard, average. ～以上 above average.
　水平儀 **shwěipíngyí** (N) level (instrument).
　水瓢 **shwěipyáu** (N) calabash water ladle.
　水獺 '**shwéitǎ** (N) otter.
　水彩畫 **shwéitsǎihwà** (N) <-ル> watercolor picture (M 張 **jāng**).
　水土 **shwéitǔ** (N) climatic conditions.
　水桶 **shwéitǔng** (N) water bucket.
　水銀 **shwěiyín** (N) mercury (metal).
　水源 **shwěiywán** (N) source of a river.

睡 **shwèi** (FV) 1) sleep. /他在地板上～了好幾晚. He slept on the floor for many nights. 2) lie on something. /他～在草地上看書. He's lying on the ground reading a book.
　睡覺 **shwèijyàu** (VO) sleep. /我昨天晚上沒睡好覺. I didn't sleep well last night. /他睡了一天的覺. He slept all day.

稅 **shwèi** (N) tax, duty, customs impost (M 道 **dàu**). 抽～ levy a tax; 上～ pay a tax *or* duty.

説 **shwō** (FV) 1) say, speak, talk. /他

不會～英文. He can't speak English. 2) talk about. /我們正說他,他就來了. We were just talking about him when he came. 3) scold. /我～了他幾句. I scolded him a bit. →不說 bùshwō.

說服 'shwōfú (FV) persuade, convince. /没人能～他. Nobody can convince him.

說話 shwōhwà (VO) say, speak, talk. /他們兩人說了半天話了. Those two have talked for a long time.

說明 shwōmíng (FV) explain, illustrate. /請你給我～這個機器的用法. Would you please explain how this machine operates?

說明書 shwōmíngshū (N) 1) book of directions, technical manual (accompanying a machine or apparatus). 2) synopsis of a play or movie. (M 本 běn, 張 jāng, 份 fèn).

順 shwùn (FV) smooth down. /她用手～一～她的頭髮. She smoothed down her hair with her hand. (SV) 1) be fluent, smooth (of speaking or writing). /這個句子念着很～. This sentence reads very smoothly. 2) be successful, lucky. /這兩年他做買賣很～. He's been successful in business the past couple of years. (CV) <着> along. /你～那條河走就可以到了. You can get there by following that river. (B) obey. ～民 obedient people.

順着 shwùnje (CV) ⊦ (CV). (FV) let someone have his way. /他是一個病人,你～他一點兒吧. He's a sick man; let him have his way a little bit.

順利 shwùnlì (SV) be prosperous, going well. /一切都～嗎? Is everything going all right? (A) without difficulty, smoothly. /他～達成他的使命了. He fulfilled his responsibilities without difficulty.

順手 shwùnshóu (A) on one's way to doing something else. /你出去的時候～關上門. Would you close the door on your way out?

順從 'shwùntsúng (FV) be unquestioningly obedient to. /他很～你的意思. He is unquestioningly obedient to what you say.

順眼 shwùnyǎn (SV) be appealing or pleasant to the eye. /有的新樣子看着很～,有的不～. Some of the new styles are appealing to the eye, some of them aren't.

si see sz.

song see sung.

搜[蒐] sōu (FV) search, search for. /警察挨家都～了. The police searched from door to door.

搜集 sōují (FV) obtain, collect. /我已經～了很多證據. I have collected a lot of evidence. /他在～論文的資料. He's collecting materials for his thesis.

搜尋 sōusyun (FV) search, search for. /警察在～什麽? What are the police searching for?

餿 sōu (SV) be sour, spoiled (of watery or oily foods). /給他留的牛奶～了. The milk which was being saved for him has gone sour.

俗 sú (SV) be unrefined, vulgar, in poor taste. /他穿的衣服很～. The clothes he wears are in poor taste. (B) custom, usage. 風～custom.

俗氣 súchì (SV) be unrefined, vulgar, in poor taste. /他說話很～. His language is vulgar.

速 sù (B) speed. ～記 to write shorthand, shorthand.

速度 sùdu (N) speed, velocity.

素 sù (SV) be simple, plain (of taste, dress). /她穿的很～. She is simply dressed. (B) 1) vegetarian. ～菜 vegetarian food. 2) habitually. ～常 usually. 3) element. 要～ important element.

塑 sù (FV) build, model, in clay, wax. /他～了一個很大的聖母. He built a huge model of the Virgin Mary.

塑像 sùsyàng (VO) make or build a statue. /他塑了很多人像. He has made many statues. (N) statue.

宿 sù (B) 1) lodge for the night. 借～ ask for a night's lodging. 2) old. ～將 aged general. 3) in the past. ～日 former days. →宿 syǒu.

宿舍 sùshè (N) dormitory.

suan see swan.

sui *see* **swei.**
sun *see* **swun**
suo *see* **swo**

松 **sūng** (B) pine tree. ~針 pine needle. SF of 鬆 **sūng.** *t*
松鼠 **sūngshǔ** (N) <-ㄦ> squirrel (M隻jī).
松樹 **sūngshù** (N) pine tree (M棵kē).

鬆[松] **sūng** (SV) 1) be loose, not tight. /我的鞋帶~了. My shoelaces are loose. 2) be fluffy, light (of a cake). 3) be easygoing, not strict. /我們先生相當~. Our teacher is rather easygoing. (FV) loosen. /把那個螺絲~一~. Loosen that screw a little bit.

悚 **súng** (SV) be cowardly (extremely impolite, almost profane) (lp). /你看他這個~像! Look at him, the coward! (lit. Look at his cowardly look!)

送 **sùng** (FV) 1) give. /他~了我一支筆. He gave me a pen. 2) send, deliver. /你要的書我明天給你~去. I'll send you the book you want tomorrow. /他出去~貨去了. He went out to deliver the goods. 3) see someone off. /我要到機場去~一個朋友. I'm going to the airport to see a friend off. 4) escort someone. /我~你回去好不好? How about my escorting you home? 一不送 **búsùng.**
送殯 **sùngbìn** (VO) attend a funeral and follow the coffin. /我昨天給他~去了. I attended his funeral yesterday.
送禮 **sùnglǐ** (VO) give someone a present. /他生日你送什麼禮? What are you giving him for his birthday?
送行 **sùngsyíng** (VO) see someone off. /我們給他~吧. Let's see him off.

suo *see* **swo.**

酸 **swān** (SV) 1) be sour tasting. /這個梨很~. This pear is very sour. 2) be sore, ache. /我的腿很~. My legs ache. 3) be sour (fig.). /他結婚你幹嗎這麼~呢? Why be so sour about his getting married? 4) be pedantic. /我們的歷史教授~得不得了. The

history professor is very pedantic. (N) acid. (B) distressed. 辛~ be grievous.

算 **swàn** (FV) 1) calculate, compute, figure out. /請你~一~我該你多少錢. Please figure out how much I owe you. 2) include. /我們班上~我一共有五個中國人. There are five Chinese students in our class including me. /你為什麼不~他? Why don't you include him? 3) be regarded as (often followed by 是 **shr̀**). /這個~(是)他的了. This is regarded as his.
算了 **swànle** (IE) Let it go. *or* Don't worry about it. *or* Forget about it. /A:你的書我找不着了. B:~. A: I can't find that book of yours. B: Don't worry about it. /幾塊錢丟了就~. It's only a few dollars and they're gone, so just forget about it. (P) used at the end of a sentence, indicates a suggestion or mild command. /我們就走着去. Let's walk there.
算盤 **swànpan** (N) abacus.
算術 **swànshù** (N) arithmetic.

蒜 **swàn** (N) garlic (M棵kē,頭tóu).

尿 **swei**→尿 **nyàu.**

雖[虽] **swēi** (A) although, even though. /我~不認識他,我還借給他錢. Even though I don't know him, I still lent him some money. (PT) ~...可(是).... although, even though. /他~沒請我,可(是)我也要去. Even though he didn't invite me, I'm still going to go.
雖然 **swēirán** = 雖 **swēi.**

隨[随] **swéi** (FV) 1) let something be. /反正沒法辦,你就~它吧. You can't do anything about it, so why don't you just let it be. 2) be up to someone. /去不去~你. Whether you go or not is up to you. (CV) <着> with, along with. /我得~着他去歐洲. I've got to go to Europe with him. (B) any, all. ~處 anywhere, everywhere. (PT) 1)~...都(or 也 or 全 or 還是) no matter what, how, where, etc. /~你逃到那兒,我都能找着你. No matter where you go I'll get you just the same. 2) ~...~... do one thing while

229

doing <u>another</u>. ～説～笑 laugh while talking. 3) ～...～... whenever. /我的錢～到手～花. Whenever I get hold of money, I spend it.

隨便 **swéibyàn** (SV) 1) be informal. /他的衣服穿得很～. The way he dresses is very informal. 2) be improper (<u>of behavior</u>). /那個女孩子的行為太～了. That girl's behavior is quite improper. (A) according to one's desires, as one pleases. /請你～坐. Please sit anywhere you like. *or* Please make yourself at home. (FV) be up to <u>someone</u>. /～你吧. It's up to you. (VO) do whatever one wishes. /隨你的便吧. You do whatever you wish. (PT) ～... 都(*or*也 *or* 全 *or* 還是) no matter what, how, where, etc. /～你給我多少錢,我都不賣. No matter how much you give me, I'm not going to sell.

隨和 **swéihe** (SV) be agreeable, easy to get along with. /他這個人可真～. He is really easy to get along with.

隨時 **swéishŕ** (A) at any time. /你～都可以來. You can come any time you like.

隨員 **swéiywán** (N) attaché (lowest diplomatic rank).

隧 **swéi** (B) tunnel.
隧道 **swéidàu** (N) tunnel (M條 tyáu).

碎 **swèi** (SV) be in bits and pieces (as when something is smashed). /這個杯子摔得很～. This cup is broken to bits.

歲〔歲〕〔岁〕 **swèi** (M) year of age, year old. /他幾～了? How old is he? /他已經二十五～了. He's already twenty-five years old. (B) year. ～入 annual income.
歲數 **swèishu** (N) age. /你多大～了? What is your age?

繐 **swèi** (B) <-子,-儿> braid, tassel, fringe. 絲～ silk braid.

縮 **swō** (FV) 1) shrink. /這些衣服洗了以後就～了. These clothes shrank after being washed. 2) draw back, withdraw. /那條蛇～回

洞裡去了. That snake withdrew into its hole. (B) reduce, decrease. ～短 shorten.

鎖 **swŏ** (FV) 1) lock. /我忘了～車了. I forgot to lock the car. 2) chain up. /把那個猩猩～起來. Chain that gorilla up. 3) do a lock stitch on. /那個裁縫連～釦眼都不會. That tailor can't even do a lock stitch on a buttonhole. (N) lock (M把**bă**).

所 **swŏ** (M) <-儿> for houses. 兩～房子 two houses. (B) 1) that which. ～存的貨 those goods which are stored. 2) place. 廁～ lavatory. 3) office, bureau, institute. 衛生～ public health office.
所謂 **swŏwèi** (AT) the so-called, what is called. ～專家 the so-called experts; ～北美洲 what is called North America.
所以 **swŏyĭ** (A) 1) therefore, so. /昨天下雨,～冷了. It rained yesterday so it's cold now. 2) the reason why .... /我～不教你去,因為你太小. The reason why I won't let you go is because you are too young.
所有的 **swŏyŏude** (B) all. ～人 all people.

孫 **swūn** (B) grandchild. ～子 grandson.
s
孫女 **swūnnyu** (N) granddaughter.

損 **swŭn** (SV) 1) be cruel, unkind. /他們對待犯人的法子～極了. Their method of treating prisoners is extremely cruel. 2) be sarcastic. /你說話別這麼～. When you speak, don't be so sarcastic. (FV) be sarcastic with (lp). /他老～我. He's always sarcastic with me. (B) 1) damage, injure. ～毀 damage. 2) loss. ～益 profit and loss.
損害 **swŭnhài** (FV) damage. /發大水的時候～了很多莊稼. During the flood, lots of crops were damaged. (N) damage.
損失 **swŭnshŕ** (FV) suffer the loss of, lose. /上次戰爭兩國都～了很多人力和財力. During the last war, both countries suffered losses of lives and capital. (N) loss. 精神～ loss of spirit; 賠償～ pay for damages.

筍{笋} **swǔn** (N) bamboo shoot (M棵kē).

瞎 **syā** (FV) be blind, go blind. /他～了一隻眼. He is blind in one eye. (A) nonsensically, blindly, aimlessly. ～説 talk nonsensically. /他滿處儿～跑. He wandered all over aimlessly. (SV) be tangled. /線～了. The thread is tangled.
    瞎子 **syādz** (N) blind person.

蝦{虾} **syā** (N) shrimp (M隻jī). →蛤{蝦} **há**.

匣 **syá** (B) <-子,-ル> small box. 手飾～ jewelry box.

狹 **syá** (B) narrow. ～軌鐵路 narrow-gauge railroad.
    狹義的 **syáyìde** (A) in a narrow sense. /～説只有漢語才算中國話. In a narrow sense, only the language of the Han race is considered Chinese. (N) narrow interpretation. /這個定義有兩種説法～跟廣義的. This definition has both a narrow and broad interpretation.

夏 **syà** (B) summer. ～布 summer linen (material). (M) summer. /這個草帽儿我已經帶了兩～了. I've already worn this straw hat for two summers. *d s t*
    夏季 **syàjì** (TW) (in) the summer. /這些樹～開花,秋季結果實. These trees bloom in the summer and bear fruit in the fall. /～是戶外活動的季節. Summer is the season for outdoor activities.
    夏天 **syàtyan** (TW) (in) the summer. /我～要到海邊儿去渡假. In the summer I'm going to the beach for a vacation. /去年的夏天不如今年熱. Last summer wasn't as hot as this summer.

下 **syà** (DV) 1) come *or* go down. ～樓 come *or* go downstairs. 2) get off a conveyance. ～飛機 get off a plane. 3) leave, get out of. ～學 get out of school. 4) come down (of rain, etc.). /現在～電子了. It's hailing now. 5) have, give birth to (of animals), lay eggs. ～狗 have puppies. 6) put something into something. /他把他太太的酒裡～了毒藥了. He put poison into his wife's drink. 7) issue, send

out, an order. ～命令 issue an order. 8) play a board game. ～棋 play chess. 9) go from a developed area to a less developed area. ～鄉 go to the country. 10) get food or drink down by taking a small amount of something tasty along with it. /他用沙丁魚～飯. He uses sardines to get his rice down. (RE) 1) down. /他走～台就昏了. He fainted just as he came down from the stage. 2) indicates holding, containing (in potential RC only). 坐不～ cannot seat so many people. 3) indicates fixing, finalizing an action. /他死了留～很多錢. He died and left a lot of money. (L) 1) down, below. 往～看 look down; 樓～ downstairs; ～舖 lower berth. 2) under. 樹～ under a tree. 3) off, away. 往～揭 tear off. (SP) 1) lower. ～兩班 lower two grades (in school). 2) next, coming. ～禮拜 next week.
    下巴頦儿 **syàbakēer** (N) chin.
    下邊 **syàbyan** (PW) <-ル> 1) bottom, lower surface. /桌子～有一塊口香糖. There's a piece of chewing gum stuck to the bottom of the table. 2) lower part *or* area of something. /這個牆的～是藍的. The lower part of this wall is blue. 3) under, below (lit. *or* fig.). /～有三個人. There are three people below. /我～還有兩個掃地的. There are two cleaning men under me. (N) <-ル> lower ranks (lp).
    下去 **syàchyu** (RC) go down, descend. /他是從這儿～的. He went down from here. (RE) 1) indicates motion down there. /誰把他推下池子去的? Who pushed him into the pool? 2) indicates the continuation of a motion. /這樣做～不會有好結果的. You won't get anywhere if you keep on doing it this way.
    下地 **syàdì** (VO) 1) get out of bed (as a patient after a long illness). /沒完全好以前你不能～. You can't get out of bed until you've recovered completely. 2) be born (as a baby). /昨天晚上小孩已經～了. The baby was born last

night. 3) go to work in the fields.
/北方的農夫每天六點鐘就
～了. Farmers in the north go to
work at six o'clock.

下 子 **syàdz** = 下儿 **syàr**.

下 葬 **syàdzàng** (VO) be buried.
/他已經下了葬了嗎? Has he
already been buried?

下 工 夫 **syàgūngfu** (VO) put
time and energy into some task,
work hard. /他下了不少的工
夫. He has put a lot of time and
energy into it.

下 級 **syàjí** (N) lower ranks,
subordinates.

下 降 **syàjyàng** (FV) descend,
come down. /我們現在已經～
到五千尺了. We have descended
to five thousand feet. /他的熱度
已經～了. His temperature has
come down.

下 課 **syàkè** (VO) get out of
class. /我下了課就去找你.
I'll see you as soon as I get out of
class.

下 來 **syàlai** (RC) come down.
/快從樹上～. Come down from
that tree quickly. (RE) indicates
motion down here. /你順着這個
梯子爬～吧. Climb down on this
ladder.

下 面 **syàmyan** = 下邊 **syàbyan**.

下 儿 **syàr** (M) time (one instance). /他踢了我一～. He
kicked me three times.

下 手 **syàshǒu** (VO) take action
in order to accomplish something.
/你什麼時候～啊? When are
you going to take some action?

下 雪 **syàsywě** (VO) snow. /這
個禮拜下了三場雪. It has
snowed three times this week.

下 頭 **syàtou** = 下邊 **syàbyan**.

下 午 **syàwǔ** (TW) (in) the
afternoon. /他～總是出去. He
often goes out in the afternoon. /我
們在一起消磨了一個愉快的
～. We spent a pleasant afternoon
together.

下 雨 **syàyǔ** (VO) rain. /已經
下了三天雨了. It's been
raining for three days now.

下 獄 **syàyù** (VO) send someone to prison. /法官把那個賊
下了獄了. The judge sent the

thief to prison. /他被捕～了.
He was arrested and sent to prison.

嚇[吓]**syà** (FV) frighten, scare. /你別
～你小弟弟. Don't scare
your little brother.

嚇唬 **syàhu** (FV) intimidate.
/你別～我. Don't you intimidate
me.

先 **syān** (A) first, earlier. /我們～
吃再去買東西. Let's eat first,
then go shopping. /昨天晚上他
～睡的. He went to bed earlier
than I did last night. (B) 1) ancestor. 祖～forefathers, ancestors.
2) my late (referring to deceased
family members who are older than
oneself). ～父 my late father; ～夫
my late husband. 3) preceding. ～
例 precedent. t

先 前 **syānchyán** (TW) (in) former times, (in) the old days, before.
/我～比他還闊. I was richer
than he before. /～比現在好.
The old days were better than now.
/他～在這儿,不過已經走了.
He was here before, but he's already
left.

先 進 **syānjìn** (N) leader, front
runner, vanguard. (AT) leading,
advanced. ～國家 advanced country.

先 生 **syānsheng** (N) 1) sir
(in direct address). /～,您貴姓?
Sir, may I ask your name? 2)
teacher. 3) husband. 4) gentleman.
那位老～ that old gentleman. (B)
used after surnames, Mr. 王～ Mr.
Wang.

鮮 **syān** (SV) be delicious (of savory
dishes). /這碗湯真～. This
soup is really delicious. (B) fresh,
new. 新～be fresh; ～果 fresh fruit.
一鮮 **syǎn**, 鮮 **syàn**.

鮮 艷 **syānyàn** (SV) be fresh
and beautiful (as of flowers, colors).
/這個花儿很～. This flower
is so fresh and beautiful.

鹹[咸]**syán** (SV) be salty. /這個菜太
～了. This food is too salty. (B)
salt-, salted. ～魚 salted fish; ～
水湖 salt-water lake.

鹹 菜 **syántsài** (N) salted, preserved vegetable, pickled vegetable.

閒[閑]**syán** (SV) 1) be free, idle. /他現在很~. He's free now. (N) <-ㄦ> free *or* leisure time. /他每天不得~. He doesn't have any free time all day. (A) idly, leisurely. /我們在街上~逛. We were wandering around the streets. (B) 1) unoccupied, vacant. ~ 房 vacant house. 2) unrelated. ~ 事 other person's affair.

弦[絃]**syán** (N) 1) string of a musical instrument or a bow (M根**gēn**). 2) spring (mechanical). 鐘 ~ clock spring. 3) hypotenuse (geom.). (B) 1) chord (musical). 和 ~ be in harmony with an instrument. 2) quarter moon. 上 ~ first quarter moon.
 弦 子 **syándz** (N) plucked stringed instrument (M把**bǎ**).

險 **syǎn** (SV) be dangerous, risky. (B) danger. 遇 ~ be in danger.
 險 些 **syǎnsye** (A) nearly, almost. /他~死了. He nearly died.

顯[显]**syǎn** (SV) be noticeable. /骨髒的那塊很~. That spot of dirt is very noticeable. (B) 1) manifest. ~ 出 來 reveal, make clear; ~ 示 display, show. 2) illustrious. ~ 達 be prominent, well known.
 顯 白 **syǎnbai** (FV) show off something. /他~他有錢. He likes to show off his wealth.
 顯 明 **syǎnmíng** (SV) be obvious, clear. /情形還不太~呢. The situation still isn't very clear.
 顯 微 鏡 **syǎnwéijìng** (N) microscope (M架**jyà**).

鮮 **syǎn** (B) rare. ~ 少 very few. t → 鮮 **syǎn**, 鮮 **syàn**.

縣[县]**syàn** (N) hsien.
 縣 長 **syànjǎng** (N) magistrate of a hsien.

線[綫]**syàn** (N) 1) thread. 2) wire. 3) line. (M條**tyáu**, 根**gēn**). (B) clue, trace. ~人 stool pigeon.
 線 索 '**syànswo** (N) trace, clue, trail. /這個案子已經有~了. There are already some clues in this case.

限 **syàn** (FV) set a limit for someone, limit someone to. /我~你本星期六完工. I'll limit you to Saturday to get the thing done. (N) time limit. /我給你三天~. I'm giving you a three-day time limit. (PT)以...為 ~ set ... as a limit. /我們以十塊錢為~. We set ten dollars as the limit.
 限 制 **syànjr** (FV) set a limit, limit someone to. /我~他一天用三塊錢. I limited him to three dollars a day. (N) limit, restriction.

現[見]**syàn** (A) when something is needed, as required. /我們到了那ㄦ~買吧. Let's get there and buy it when we need it. (AT) ready. ~錢 ready cash; ~貨 merchandise on hand. (B) 1) reveal. ~ 露 disclose. 2) present, current. ~價 current price.
 現 成 的 **syànchéngde** (N) ready-made thing.
 現 代 **syàndài** (AT) present, modern. ~ 文明 modern civilization.
 現 在 **syàndzài** (TW) (at) the present time, now. /他~已經長大了. He's grown-up now. /~比過去好. Present times are better than past.
 現 象 **syànsyàng** (N) phenomenon.

獻[献]**syàn** (FV) offer, present, contribute. /他把這塊地~給政府了. He presented this land to the government.

陷 **syàn** (FV) sink down (as into mud). /兩隻腳都~到泥裡去了. Both feet sank into the mud. (B) 1) ensnare, trap. ~'害 involve someone in trouble. 2) capture. 淪 ~ 區 enemy-occupied territory.

鮮 **syàn** (B) ↓. →鮮 **syàn**, 鮮 **syàn**.
 鮮 華 **syànhwo** (SV) be bright and pleasing (of colors). /紅的跟綠的擱在一塊可真~. Red and green are really a pleasing combination.

箱 **syāng** (M) box, case, chest, trunk. 兩~酒 two cases of wine. (B) <-子> box, case, chest, trunk (M隻**jr**).

相 **syāng** (B) mutually, each other. ~ 消 cancel each other. →相 **syàng**.

233

相差 **syāngchà** (FV) differ. /這兩個數目～不多. These two figures don't differ by much.

相襯 **syāngchèn** (SV) 1) match (as colors). 2) be a good match (of people). /他們兩口子不太～. That couple isn't a good match.

相當 **syāngdāng** (SV) be suitable, proper. /他的工作對他很～. His job is just right for him. (A) quite. /這個東西～不錯. This thing's quite good.

相等 **syāngděng** (FV) be identical, equal. /這兩個三角形～. These two triangles are equal.

相對 **syāngdwèi** (AT) relative (contrasted with absolute). /世界上的事都是～的,沒有絕對的. Everything in the world is relative, nothing is absolute.

相反 **syāngfǎn** (SV) be the opposite of, contrary to. /我的意思跟你正～. My opinion is just the opposite of yours.

相仿 **syāngfǎng** (SV) be similar, about the same. /他們兩個人的歲數～. Their ages are about the same.

相符 **syāngfú** (SV) be in agreement. /他說的話跟事實很不～. What he says isn't in agreement with the facts.

相合 **syānghé** (SV) be in agreement. /你的意思跟我很～. We (lit. Your ideas and mine) are very much in agreement.

相近 **syāngjìn** (SV) be very similar, closely related in characteristics. /這兩個字的意思很～. These two words are very similar in meaning.

相信 **syāngsyìn** (FV) believe, trust. /我～他是一個好人. I believe he's a good person.

相似 **syāngsz̀** = 相仿 **syāngfǎng**.

相同 **syāngtúng** (SV) be the same, identical. /那兩隊的制服完全～. The uniforms of those two teams are exactly the same.

鄉[鄉,鄉] **syāng** (N) rural unit under the jurisdiction of a hsien. (B) 1) country, rural. ～村 village. 2) native place, home town. 回～ return to one's native place; 同～ fellow townsman.

鄉下 **syāngsya** (PW) (in) the country. /～有很多樹. There are lots of trees in the country. /～的空氣很新鮮. Country air is refreshing.

香 **syāng** (SV) 1) be fragrant, aromatic. /這種花很～. These flowers are very fragrant. 2) smell good (of food). /這個炸雞很～. This fried chicken smells good. 3) be popular (of commodities). /這種啤酒在美國很～. This kind of beer is very popular in America. 4) be on good terms. /他們兩個人最近又～了. The two of them have been on good terms again lately. 5) be sound (of sleeping), hearty (of eating). /最近我老睡的不～. Lately I haven't been sleeping soundly. /他吃飯老是這麼～. He always eats this heartily. (N) incense (M枝 jř, 根 gēn).

香蕉 **syāngjyāu** (N) banana (M根 gēn, 條 tyáu).

香味儿 **syāngwèr** (N) aroma.

香油 **syāngyóu** (N) 1) sesame oil. 2) fragrant or aromatic oil.

廂[廂] **syāng** (N) box (in the theatre). /我訂了兩個～. I've reserved two boxes. (B) 1) adjacent. 城～ the city and adjacent area. 2) side. 這～ this side. 3) body (of a car). 車～ car body.

廂房 '**syāngfáng** (N) room adjacent to a main building (M間 jyān).

鑲 **syāng** (FV) 1) set, mount, jewels and the like. ～假牙 mount false teeth. /我想用一顆珠子～這個戒指. I would like a pearl set in this ring. 2) trim, edge. /她用鹿皮～袖口. She trimmed the cuffs with deerskin.

詳 **syáng** (B) 1) in detail. ～談 talk something over in detail; ～情 detailed information. 2) know. 不～ be unknown.

詳細 **syángsyì** (SV) be detailed. /他的報告寫的很～. His report was very detailed. (A) in detail. /我們得～談談. We must talk it over in detail.

降 **syáng** (FV) 1) surrender. /敵人

已經～了. The enemy has sur-rendered. 2) control. /這個孩子太鬧只有他舅舅能～他. This child is very naughty; only his uncle can control him. →降 **jyàng**.

想 **syǎng** (FV) 1) think, think about. /他～了一～. He thought for a minute. 2) miss, think of. /我一點都不～他. I don't miss him at all. 3) suppose, guess. /我～他不來了. I guess he's not coming. (AV) want to, plan to, feel like. /他老～到那儿去. He's always wanted to go there. → 不想 **bùsyǎng**, 沒想 **méisyǎng**.

想出 **syǎngchu** (RC) think up. /我實在想不出什麼好法子. I really can't think up any good way.

想法 **syǎngfa** (N) way of think-ing, view.

想法子 **syǎngfádz** = 想法儿 **syǎngfǎr**.

想法儿 **syǎngfǎr** (VO) think of a way, try, to do something. /我們得想個法儿. We have to think of a way. /請你～把窗戶開開. Try to think of some way to open the window. or Try to open the window.

想盡 **syǎngjìn** (RC) think of all the possibilities. /所有的答案都～了,可是他還說不對. I've thought of every possible answer, but he keeps saying I'm wrong.

想家 **syǎngjyā** (VO) be home-sick. /我從來沒想過家. I have never been homesick.

想象 **syǎngsyàng** (FV) imagine. /你可以～那個時候的情形. You can just imagine the state of af-fairs at that time. (N) imagination.

想要 **'syǎngyàu** (AV) want to, plan to, feel like. /他～做什麼呢? What does he want to do?

響[響,響][向] **syǎng** (FV) 1) sound, ring. /門鈴～了. The door bell rang. /我的汽車喇叭不～了. The horn in my car doesn't work any more. 2) make a sound, say a word (d). /你說什麼他也不～. It doesn't matter what you say, he won't say a word. (SV) be loud. /他說話的聲音很～. His voice is very loud.

響亮 **syǎnglyàng** (SV) be loud

and clear. /他的聲音～. His voice is loud and clear.

響儿 **syǎngr** (N) sound. /剛才你進來我沒聽見～. When you came in a moment ago I didn't hear a sound.

響應 **syǎngyìng** (FV) respond. /他提議造一所醫院,可是沒有人～. He suggested building a new hospital, but nobody responded.

享 **syǎng** (B) enjoy. ～福 have a happy life.

享受 **syǎngshòu** (FV) 1) enjoy oneself. /他很會～. He really knows how to enjoy himself. 2) have a privilege or right. /你可以～全部會員的權利. You have full membership privileges. (N) enjoy-ment, pleasure.

嚮[嚮,嚮][向] **syàng** (B) 1) guide. 2) in-clined. ～往 to desire.

嚮導 **syàngdǎu** (N) guide (per-son).

相 **syàng** (N) 1) physiognomy. /看相的說我的～很好. The physi-ognomist says that my physiognomy is promising. 2) photograph, picture (M張 **jāng**). 3) premier (piece in Chinese chess comparable to a bishop). (B) 1) examine. ～機 ex-amine a situation. 2) <～儿> facial expression. 做怪～make faces. 3) cabinet minister. 首～ premier, prime minister. →相 **syāng**.

相貌 **'syàngmàu** (N) looks (of a person). /他的～長的很好. She's very good-looking.

相片 **syàngpyàn** (N) photograph, picture (M張 **jāng**).

相聲 **syàngsheng** (N) comic stage dialogue (M套 **tàu**).

向 **syàng** (FV) 1) face. /這間屋子～東. This room faces east. 2) show partiality toward, take some-one's side. /你們吵架我誰都不～. I'm not taking anybody's side in this argument of yours. (CV) <～着> toward. /那輛車～我開來了. That car is moving toward me. /～前走. Go forward. (B) 1) habitually in the past. 一～ up to now. 2) inclination. 志～ ambition.

向來 **'syànglái** (A) always. /他～不喜歡吃甜的. He's

never liked to eat sweet things.
向 日 葵 **syàngrkwéi** (N) sun-
flower (M朵 **dwo**;棵 **kē**).

項 **syàng** (M) 1) article (of formal
documents). 第一節第三 ~ section
one, article three.　2) item (of business). 一~事情 an item of business.　(B) 1) nape of the neck. ~
鍊 necklace.　2) item (in accounting).
進 ~ income.　s

巷 **syàng** (B) <-子> lane, alley (M條
tyáu). ~戰 street fighting; 中山路
三~十號 No. 10, Lane 3, Chung-
shan Road.

象{象} **syàng** (N) 1) elephant (M隻**jī**).
2) elephant (piece in Chinese chess
comparable to a bishop).　(B) image.
現 ~ phenomenon; 印 ~ impression.
SF of像 **syàng**.
象 棋 **syàngchí** (N) Chinese
chess (M付 **fù**, 盤 **pán**).

像[像] **syàng** (FV) look like, resemble.
/他~他母親.　He resembles his
mother.　(SV) be alike. /這兩張
畫儿很 ~ .　These two pictures
are very much alike.　(N) picture,
portrait (M張 **jāng**).　2) statue (M
尊 **dzwūn**).　(B) such as, like. /~
這種飯我才不吃呢.　I won't
eat food like this.　(PT) ~...似
的 as if, be the same as. /他高興
的~瘋了似的.　He's so happy,
it's as if he were crazy. /他的腰
~一個桶似的.　He has a waist
like a barrel.

橡 **syàng** (B) 1) oak. ~椀子 acorn.　2)
rubber tree. ~膠 rubber.
橡 皮 **syàngpí** (N) 1) rubber.
2) eraser.　(M塊 **kwài**).

消 **syāu** (B) 1) abolish, diminish. ~
除 exterminate.　2) consume. ~費
consume, consumption; ~夏 spend a
summer.　2) be necessary. 不 ~
說 need not say; 只~三天 only three
days are necessary.
消 遣 **syāuchyan** (FV) amuse
oneself, have fun. /我們今天晚
上到那儿去~~?　Where can
we go tonight to have some fun? (N)
amusement.
消毒藥 **syāudúyàu** (N) disin-
fectant.

消 防 隊 **syāufángdwèi** (N) troop
of fire fighters, fire brigade.
消 化 **syāuhwa** (FV) digest.
/我的胃不能~太油的東西.
My stomach can't digest food that's
too greasy.　(N) digestion.
消 極 **syāují** (SV) be negative.
/他的態度很 ~ .　He has a very
negative attitude.
消 滅 **syāumyè** (FV) destroy,
annihilate. /我們想法子~敵
人的勢力.　We're trying to find
a way to destroy the power of the
enemy.
消 息 **syāusyi** (N) information,
news. /你們有什麼好~嗎 ?
Do you have any good news?

削 **syāu, sywè** (FV) peel with a knife.
~鉛筆 sharpen a pencil. /請你
給我~一個蘋果.　Please peel
an apple for me.　(B) reduce, cut
down. ~減 reduce, cut down.

銷 **syāu** (B) 1) melt. ~鎔 smelt.　2)
sell. ~貨額 rate of selling.　3)
finish. 撤~ cancel, annul.　4) destroy. ~滅 obliterate.
銷 路 **syāulù** (N) market or
demand for some product. /這個
貨的~現在不好.　There isn't a
very good market for this commodity
right now.

小 **syău** (SV) (when used before a noun,
a diminutive 儿**er** is often added to
the noun) 1) be small, little. ~屋
儿 small room. /那個數目很 ~.
That amount is very small.　2) be
young. /~老虎儿 tiger cub. /他
還~哪.　He's still young.　3) be
trivial, insignificant. /這件事
情很~.　This matter is very trivial.　(N) concubine.　(B) my, our (h).
~店 my shop.
小 便 **syăubyàn** (FV) urinate
(euphemistic; lit. small convenience).
/你不能在街上就 ~ .　You can't
go to the bathroom right in the street.
(N) urine.
小 氣 **syăuchi** (SV) 1) be petty,
small. /你要不跟他說話那就
~ 了.　It would be petty of you not
to talk to him.　2) be stingy. /他連
小費都不給未免太 ~ 了.
His not giving any tip at all is being

a bit too stingy. 3) be unstylish, lacking elegance, gaudy. /這件衣服的樣子很～. This dress isn't stylish.

小道儿 **syǎudàur** (N) 1) small, narrow path. 2) shortcut. (M 條 **tyáu**). 抄～ take a shortcut. (B) stolen. ～貨 stolen goods.

小兒科 **syǎuérkē** (N) pediatrics (the branch of medicine or the department in a hospital).

小費 **syǎufèi** (N) tip (given to a waiter, etc.).

小孩子 **syǎuháidz** = 小孩儿 **syǎuhár**.

小孩儿 **syǎuhár** (N) child.

小影子 **syáuhwǒdz** = 小影儿 **syáuhwǒr**.

小影儿 **syáuhwǒr** (N) young man.

小傳 **syǎujwàn** (N) biography (M 本 **ben**, 篇 **pyān**).

小姐 **syáujye** (N) 1) young lady, miss. 2) daughter (h). /你有幾位～? How many daughters do you have? (B) used before surnames, Miss. 劉～ Miss Liu.

小看 **syǎukàn** (FV) look down on, belittle, consider someone or something as unimportant. /別～人. Don't look down on people. /他太～這件事了. He considers this matter too unimportant.

小麥 **syǎumài** (N) wheat (M 粒 **lì**, 棵 **kē**).

小米 **syáumǐ** (N) <-儿> yellow millet (M 粒 **lì**).

小朋友 **syáupéngyou** (N) child, little friend.

小聲儿 '**syǎushēngr** (A) in a low voice, softly. /你～一點説, 人都睡着了. Please speak a little more softly, people are asleep.

小時 **syǎushr** (M) hour. 兩～ two hours.

小數點儿 **syǎushùdyǎr** (N) decimal point.

小説 **syǎushwō** (N) <-儿> 1) novel (M 部 **bù**, 本 **ben**). 2) fiction.

小心 **syausyin** (FV) beware of, be careful of. /你得～他. Beware of him. /你得～你的錢包. You must be careful of your wallet. (SV) be careful. /～點別

摔着. Be careful, don't fall. (A) carefully. /你得～開車. You must drive carefully.

小學 **syǎusywé** (N) primary school, grade school.

小偷儿 **syǎutōur** (N) sneak thief.

曉(暁) **syǎu** (B) 1) morning, dawn. 破～ daybreak. 2) know. ～示 proclaim.

曉得 **syǎude** (FV) know, know of (d). /我不～他是誰. I don't know who he is.

校 **syàu** (B) 1) school. 學～ school. 2) field grade officer. 少～ major (army or air force), lieutenant commander (navy). →校 **jyàu**.

校長 **syàujǎng** (N) principal, president (of a school).

笑 **syàu** (FV) 1) smile, laugh. /他～了又～. He laughed and laughed. 2) laugh at. /他常常～人家的錯. He's always laughing at people's mistakes.

笑話 **syàuhwa** (FV) laugh at, ridicule. /我唱得不好, 別～我. I can't sing, so don't laugh at me. (N) <-儿> 1) joke. 2) ridiculous situation, a laugh. /他會比我好? 真是～! He's better than I? That's a laugh! (SV) be ridiculous. /太～了, 我那儿能叫你給錢? That's ridiculous. How can I let you give me money?

笑容 '**syàurúng** (N) smiling expression, smile.

效(効傚) (B) 1) ⎫ **syàu** (N) effect. /那個藥有什麼～嗎? Does that medicine have any effect? (B) 1) imitate. 仿～ emulate. 2) devote. ～命 devote one's life to.

效法 '**syàufǎ** (FV) imitate, follow. /我們應該～他的榜樣. We must follow his example.

效果 '**syàugwǒ** (N) result, effect, of any cause. /你説這句話, 不會有什麼～. What you said won't have any results.

效率 **syàulyù** (N) efficiency.

歇 **syē** (FV) 1) rest. /我們～一～吧. Let's rest a minute. 2) stop. /我們那個買賣已經～了.

We've stopped that business of ours. *t*

些 **syē** (NU) few, some. 這～張桌子 these few tables. (M) amount, lot. 這一～書 this lot of books. (B) used after SV, a bit more, a little. /他的病輕～了. He's (lit. His sickness is) a little better now.

蝎 **syē** (B) <-子> scorpion (M 隻jī).

協[协] **syé** (B) join, participate. ～助 assist in managing something; ～定 agreement.
　協商 **syéshāng** (N) mutual agreement. (FV) discuss together. /那件事情我們得～一下. We have to discuss that matter together.

鞋 **syé** (N) <-子> shoe (M 隻jī; 雙 **shwāng**).

斜 **syé** (SV) be slanted, tilted. /那根柱子有點～. That pillar is a little tilted. (FV) 1) tilt, slant. /請你往左～一～. Please tilt it to the left a little. 2) turn something sideways. /把這張桌子～過來. Turn this table sideways.

叶 **syé** (B) to rhyme. ～韻 make something rhyme. SF of 葉 **yè**.

寫[写] **syě** (FV) write, describe in writing. /請你把名字～在這兒. Please write your name here. (B) sketch, draw. ～生 draw living objects.
　寫字 **syědż** (VO) write (characters *or* words). /他不會～. He can't write. /我不會寫這個字. I don't know how to write this character.
　寫作 **syědzwò** (FV) write (as a novelist). /那位小說家每天都～. That novelist writes every day. (N) creative writing.

血 **syě** → 血 **sywě**.

謝 **syè** (FV) 1) thank. /這件事你別～我, 你得～他. Don't thank me for this, thank him. 2) fade, wither. /花都～了. The flowers have all withered. (B) decline. ～絕 refuse. *s t*
　謝謝 **syèsye** (FV) thank. /他

應當～我們大家. He should thank all of us. (IE) Thank you.

卸 **syè** (FV) 1) unload, unhitch an animal. /貨還沒～呢. The goods haven't been unloaded yet. 2) throw off, get rid of. /你絕對～不了責任. You simply can't get rid of responsibilities.

懈 **syè** (B) remiss, lax. 鬆～ be negligent.
　懈怠 **syèdai** (SV) be listless. /他作事情很～. He does his work listlessly.

洩[泄] **syè** (B) leak out. 排～ excretion.
　洩漏 **syèlòu** (FV) disclose something, let information out. /是誰～的那個消息? Who let that information out?

解 **syè** (B) s. → 解 jyě, 解 jyè.

西 **syī** (L) west. 城～ (the area) west of the city; 向～跑 go toward the west; ～門 west gate. (B) occidental, western. ～式 western style. *t*
　西北 **syīběi** (L) northwest. 城～ (the area) northwest of the city; 望～飛 fly to the northwest; ～角 northwest corner.
　西邊 **syībyan** (PW) <-ル> 1)(in) the west part *or* area. /城的～很高. The west part of the city is very high. /美國的～有很多草原. There are many prairies in the west part of the United States. 2) west of something. /我家的～是一個醫院. There's a hospital west of my house.
　西方 **syīfāng** (PW) 1) (in) the west. 到～去 go to the west. 2) the West (Western nations collectively).
　西服 **syīfú** (N) western dress *or* clothing (M件 jyàn; 套 tàu).
　西瓜 **syīgwa** (N) watermelon.
　西紅柿 **syīhúngshr̀** (N) tomato.
　西南 **syīnán** (L) southwest. 中國～ (the area) southwest of China; 往～走 go to the southwest; ～角 southwest corner.
　西西 **syīsyī** (M) cubic centimeter.

吸 **syī** (FV) 1) inhale, breathe in. /我想到外面去～一點新鮮

空氣. I'm going outside and get a breath of fresh air. 2) absorb, soak up. /這張吸墨紙不能~墨水了. This piece of blotting paper won't absorb any more ink. (B) attract. ~鐵石 magnet.

吸墨紙 syímwòjr (N) blotter (M張 jāng).

吸收 syíshōu (FV) 1) absorb (lit. or fig.). /這種料子~水嗎? Does this material absorb water? /你教得太多,學生能~嗎? You covered so much. Can the students absorb it all? 2) take members into an organization. /他們~了很多新會員. They took in a lot of new members.

吸引力 syíyǐnlì (N) power of attraction (of a magnet, someone's personality, etc.).

膝 syí (B) knee.

膝蓋 syígài (N) kneecap.

稀 syí (SV) 1) be sparse, thin. /他的頭髮很~. His hair is very sparse. 2) be thin, diluted (of liquids). /這個湯太~. The soup is too thin. (B) 1) rare. ~罕 be infrequent. 2) very. ~破 be tattered.

稀薄 syíbáu (SV) be thin (of air). /山頂的空氣很~. The air at the top of the mountain is very thin.

稀奇 syíchí (SV) be rare, strange, uncommon.

稀飯 syífàn (N) congee (rice gruel).

稀少 syíshǎu (SV) be scarce, sparse. /中國西北的人口很~. The population in the northwest part of China is very sparse.

犧[牺]syí (B) ↓.

犧牲 syíshēng (FV) sacrifice. /他甚至於~了他的性命. He even sacrificed his life. (N) sacrifice.

希 syí (B) 1) rare, infrequent. ~客 rare visitor. 2) hope for, desire. ~圖 scheme for. t

希罕 syíhan (SV) be rare, uncommon. (FV) care about. /誰~你的錢? Who cares about your money?

希望 syíwàng (FV) hope. /我~他能來. I hope he'll be able to come. (AV) hope to, wish to. /他一直~有錢. He is always hoping to become rich. (N) hope.

錫 syí (N) tin. 2) pewter. t

蓆[席] syí (B) <-子> woven mat (M張 jāng, 領 lǐng).

席 syí (N) banquet, feast (M桌 jwō). (B) seat. 主~ chairman. s SF of 蓆 syí.

媳 syí (B) daughter-in-law. 兒~ daughter-in-law.

媳婦 syífu (N) <-儿> 1) daughter-in-law. 2) wife. 3) young married woman.

習[习] syí (B) 1) practice. ~字 practice writing. 2) habit. 惡~ bad habit.

習慣 syígwàn (N) custom, habit. (FV) be accustomed to something. /他已經~他的工作了. He's already accustomed to the work.

熄 syí (FV) extinguish, put out. ~火 put out a fire. /請你把燈~了. Please turn off the light.

喜 syǐ (B) 1) like. ~愛 delight in. 2) happy, joyful. 新~ Happy New Year; ~酒 wedding feast.

喜鵲 syǐchywe (N) magpie (M隻 jr).

喜歡 syǐhwan (FV) like. /我~她. I like her. (AV) like to. /這個孩子~哭. This child likes to cry a lot. (SV) be glad, happy.

喜劇 syǐjyù (N) 1) comedy. 2) play with a happy ending. (M齣 chū; 幕 mù).

喜事 syǐshr (N) happy affair, happy occasion (M件 jyàn).

洗 syǐ (FV) 1) wash, clean. /你多少天~一回頭髮? How often do you wash your hair? 2) shuffle cards, etc. /這回該我~牌了. It's my turn to shuffle the cards. 3) develop film. /我沒有暗房所以不能~. I can't develop it because I don't have a darkroom. 4) massacre. /土匪把整個村子給~了. The bandits massacred the whole village. (B) 1) expunge, wipe out. ~ 冤 avenge a wrong. 2) baptize. ~ 禮 baptism.

洗 澡 **syǐdzǎu** (VO) take a bath. /我每天洗兩個澡. I take two baths every day.

洗澡房 **syǐdzǎufáng** (N) bathroom (M 間 jyān).

洗澡盆 **syǐdzǎupén** (N) bathtub.

系 **syì** (N) department (in a university or college). 歷史 ~ Department of History. /這個大學有三十多個 ~. This university has more than thirty departments. (B) system. 太陽 ~ solar system. SF of 係 **syì**, 繫 **syì**.

系 統 **'syìtǔng** (N) system, organization worked out in detail, coherence. /他說話沒有 ~. He speaks incoherently.

細 **syì** (SV) 1) be thin, slender. /她的腰很 ~. She has a very slender waist. 2) be fine, fine-grained, delicate. /這個紗很 ~. This gauze is very fine. /她的皮膚很 ~. Her skin is very delicate. 3) be detailed. /他描寫得很 ~. He described it in detail. 4) be careful (in the way one thinks). /他的心很 ~. He has a careful mind. (A) minutely, carefully, in detail. /我們得 ~ 談一談. We must talk it over in detail. (B) unimportant, small. ~ 節 small point. t

細 情 **'syìchíng** (N) details, particulars.

細 緻 **syìjr** (SV) 1) be fine, delicate. /這張畫兒畫的很 ~. This painting is delicately done. 2) be keen (of one's mind). /她的心思很 ~. She has a keen mind.

細 菌 **syìjyūn** (N) bacteria.

細 目 **syìmù** (N) details, particulars.

細 膩 **syìnì** (SV) 1) be delicate and smooth. /她的皮膚很 ~. Her skin is very delicate and smooth. 2) be careful (in the way one thinks).

細 心 **syìsyīn** (SV) be meticulous, careful /管錢的人一定得 ~. People who handle money must be extremely careful.

戲(戲)(戏) **syì** (N) play (M 齣 chū; 幕 mù; 臺 tái). (B) jest, sport. ~ 弄 make fun of.

戲 子 **syìdz** (N) actor, actress (impolite).

戲 法 儿 **syìfǎr** (N) magician's trick.

戲 劇 **syìjyù** (N) dramatic works or art.

戲 院 **syìywàn** (N) theater (M 家 jyā).

繫(系) **syì** (FV) haul up or let down (as by a rope). /救火隊把他們從窗戶 ~ 下去. The firemen let them down through the window. (B) 1) attach, tie. 聯 ~ connect. 2) remember. ~ 念 be anxious about. → 繫 jì.

係(系) **syì** (B) 1) related. 關 ~ relationship, relevance. 2) be. 確 ~ 實情 it really is the case.

新 **syīn** (SV) be new. /這張桌子還很 ~ 呢. This table is still quite new. (A) newly, recently. /這是我 ~ 學的. I learned this recently. (B) newly married. ~ 郎 bridegroom.

新 年 **syīnnyán** (TW) (on) New Year's Day. /我 ~ 來. I'll come on New Year's Day. /明天就是 ~ 了. Tomorrow is New Year's Day. (N) the new year. 過 ~ celebrate the new year.

新 鮮 **syīnsyan** (SV) 1) be fresh (of produce, flowers, meat, and the like). 2) be refreshingly and attractively new (in style). 3) be strange, odd. /你這句話真 ~. Your remark struck me as odd.

新 聞 **syīnwén** (N) news (M 篇 pyān, 段 dwàn).

心 **syīn** (N) 1) heart. /我 ~ 碎了. My heart is broken. 2) mind. /你 ~ 裡想什麼呢? What's on your mind? (B) 1) center, middle. 圓 ~ center of a circle. 2) <-子> stuffing, filling (d).

心 病 **syīnbìng** (N) 1) troubled conscience. 2) heart disease.

心 情 **'syīnchíng** (N) mood. /現在他 ~ 不好. He's in a bad mood right now.

心 地 **'syīndì** (N) disposition.

/那個人的～很好. That person has a good disposition.

心臟 **syīndzàng** (N) heart (the organ).

心慌 **syīnhwāng** (SV) be nervous, restless, uneasy. /我考試的時候很～. I was very nervous while I was taking the exam.

心理 **syīnlǐ** (N) 1) intention. /我摸不清他的～. I don't know what his intentions are. 2) psychology. 兒童～ child psychology.

心事 **'syīnshr̀** (N) something weighing on one's mind (M件 **jyàn**). /他今天好像有～似的. He seems to have something on his mind today.

心思 **syīnsz** (N) 1) thought. /這個人～太多. This person thinks too much. 2) desire, interest. /誰有～管別人的事? Who's interested in bothering with other people's affairs?

心疼 **syīnténg** (FV) be deeply distressed about someone one loves. /不管我多受罪我母親也不～我. No matter how much I suffered, my mother didn't feel distressed about me. (SV) be distressed. /花幾個錢他就～極了. It pains him to spend money.

心願 **'syīnywàn** (N) desire, wish (M件 **jyàn**, 椿 **jwāng**). /這算了了我一件～. This serves to fulfill a desire of mine.

辛 **syīn** (B) 1) bitter, acrid. ～辣 be pungent. 2) toilsome. 艱～ be difficult, difficulty; ～勤 be industrious, hard-working *s t*

辛苦 **syīnku** (SV) be toilsome, tiring. /那事兒太～了,我不幹. That job is too tiring; I'm not going to do it. (N) hardship, toil, trouble.

/這一點～算什麼? What does a little hardship like this matter? (IE) You must be tired (polite greeting to a person who has just returned from a business trip).

薪 **syīn** (B) 1) firewood. 柴～ firewood. 2) salary. 月～ monthly salary.

薪金 **syīnjīn** (N) salary.
薪水 **syīnshwei** (N) salary.

欣 **syīn** (B) joy, delight. 歡～ rejoice, be joyful.

欣賞 **'syīnshǎng** (FV) admire, enjoy, appreciate. /我很～這地方的風景. I enjoy the scenery here a great deal. (N) appreciation. 音樂～ music appreciation.

信 **syīn** (N) 1) letter (M封 **fēng**). 2) <ㄦ> message, news. (FV) 1) believe in. /那人什麼宗教也不～. That person doesn't believe in any religion. 2) believe, trust. /我不～他的話. I don't believe (*or* trust) what he says. (B) free, aimless. ～口胡說 talk at random.

信封兒 **syīnfēngr** (N) envelope.

信紙 **syīnjř** (N) stationery, writing paper (M張 **jāng**; 本 **běn**).

信件 **'syīnjyàn** (N) mail, letters. /今兒來了很多的～. There was a lot of mail today.

信任 **syīnrèn** (FV) trust. /我的上司很～我. My boss trusts me a lot. (N) trust.

信箱 **syīnsyāng** (N) mailbox (to which mail is delivered).

信心 **syīnsyīn** (N) faith, confidence.

信筒 **syīntǔng** (N) mailbox (from which a mailman gathers mail).

信仰 **'syīnyǎng** (FV) believe, have faith in, a religion, principle. /他～佛教. He believes in Buddhism. (N) belief, faith.

信用 **syīnyung** (N) 1) trustworthiness. /這個人很有～. He's very trustworthy. 2) credit. /他的～很好,所以銀行敢借給他錢. His credit is good, so the bank is willing to lend him money.

星 **syīng** (N) star, planet (M顆 **kē**). 火～ Mars. (B) <ㄦ,-子> small particle. 火～ spark.

星期 **syīngchī** (N) week. 上～ last week; 這個～ this week; 下～ next week. (B) weekday. ～一 Monday; ～六 Saturday.

星期日 **syīngchǐr** (TW) (on) Sunday. /這個～是他的生日. This Sunday will be his birthday. /我們下～去吧. Let's go next Sunday.

星星 **syīngsying** (N) star (M顆 **kē**).

興[兴] **syīng** (FV) 1) be popular, be in fashion. /今年～長裙子. Long

skirts are in fashion this year.
2) permit, allow, let. /他不～我
走. He won't let me go. (B) 1) prosper. ～隆 prosperity. 2) begin,
start. ～建 begin construction. *t*
→興**syíng**.

興奮 **'syíngfèn** (SV) 1) be overjoyed. /他妹妹在賽美會中贏了,
所以他很～. His sister won
the beauty contest, so he's overjoyed.
2) be excited. /他越說越～了.
The more he talks the more excited
he becomes.

月星 **syíng** (SV) smell (of fish or raw
meat). /魚市場～得很,我不愛
去. The fish market smells so bad
I don't like to go there.

行 **syíng** (SV) 1) be OK, all right. /十
塊錢就～了. Ten dollars will be
all right. 2) be smart, capable.
/這班學生有幾個很～. Some
students in this class are quite smart.
(B) 1) perform, do. ～商 do business. 2) moving, traveling. ～人
passerby, pedestrian; ～星 planet.
～旅 traveler. 3) natural element. 五
～ the five elements (which are 金
jīn, 木 **mù**, 水 **shwěi**, 火 **hwǒ**, 土
tǔ). 4) semi-cursive script. ～草
semi-cursive script and grass writing →行**háng**.

行車表 **syíngchēbyǎu** (N) timetable (for trains or buses) (M張**jāng**,
份 **fèn**).

行動 **syíngdùng** (N) 1) action,
move. /對於他的侮辱你要採
什麼～? What action will you take
about the humiliation he caused?
2) movement. /我的～不自由.
I have no freedom of movement.

行好 **syínghǎu** (VO) perform
good deeds (usually used in asking
for charity or other such help).
/您行行好吧! equivalent to anything from Brother, can you spare
a dime? to Will you do your part in
furthering this charitable enterprise?

行政 **syíngjèng** (AT) executive.
～院 the Executive Yüan (branch of
the Chinese Central Government in
Taipei). ～人員 executive personnel. (N) administration. /這兒的
～辦得很不好. The administration here is not efficient.

行李 **syínglǐ** (N) luggage, baggage (M件**jyàn**).

行禮 **syínglǐ** (VO) 1) perform
the proper acts of courtesy. 行軍
禮 salute (with hand, rifle, etc.).
2) hold a ceremony. /明天他們結
婚幾點鐘～? What time is their
wedding being held tomorrow?

行為 **'syíngwéi** (N) conduct.
/他的～很壞. His conduct is
very bad. (B) act. 犯罪～ criminal act.

行醫 **syíngyī** (VO) practice
medicine. /我行了五年醫了.
I've practiced medicine for five years.

行營 **'syíngyíng** (N) field headquarters (m).

形 **syíng** (N) shape, form. 臉～ shape
of one's face. /那個盒子是什麼
～的? What shape is that box?

形容 **'syíngrúng** (FV) describe.
/我們常用花～女人的美麗.
We often use flowers to describe the
beauty of a woman.

形勢 **'syíngshr̀** (N) 1) appearance *or* condition of things. /看這
～我們要賠本兒. According to
the way things look, we will lose our
basic investment. 2) topographical.
～圖 topographical.

醒 **syíng** (FV) 1) wake up. /他還沒
～呢. He hasn't awakened yet.
2) become sober, sober up. /他醉
了兩天,現在～了. He was drunk
for two days but he's sober now.

省 **syíng** (B) 1) examine. 自～ self-
examination. 2) visit. ～親 visit
one's parents. →省**shěng**.

擤 **syíng** (FV) blow one's nose. /你得
使勁～一～. You had better
blow your nose hard.

杏 **syíng** (B) <子,ㄦ> apricot. ～乾
dried apricot.

杏花 **syínghwā** (N) <ㄦ> apricot blossom (M朵 **dwǒ**; 枝 **jr̄**).

杏仁 **syíngrén** (N) <ㄦ> almond.

杏樹 **syíngshù** (N) apricot tree
(M棵**kē**).

性 **syíng** (B) 1) quality, characteristic
(of things). 特～ special characteristic; 藥～ effect, potency (of medicine). 2) <子,ㄦ> nature, innate

quality, temperament (of people). 人
～ human nature; 個 ～ character,
temperament. 3) capacity, power.
可能 ～ possibility; 記 ～ memory;
悟 ～ power of comprehension.
4) used after nouns, changes them to
descriptive words. 政治 ～ political;
教育 ～ educational; 全國 ～ nation-
wide. 5) sex. 女 ～ female sex.

性情 **syìngchíng** (N) temperament, disposition.

性格 **'syìnggé** (N) character of
a person.

性急 **syìngjí** (SV) be impetuous,
impulsive.

性質 **syìngjr** (N) nature, property, of something. /這個問題的
～ 我還沒弄清. I haven't figured
out the nature of the problem yet.

性命 **syìngmíng** (N) life. /他
有 ～ 危險. His life is in danger.

姓 **syìng** (FV) be surnamed. /我 ～ 張.
My surname is Chang. (N) <-儿>
surname.

姓名 **syìngmíng** (N) full name.

興[兴] **syìng** (B) interest, pleasure. ～
致 interest; 高 ～ be happy. → 興
syìng.

興趣 **syìngchyu** (N) interest.
/他沒有 ～ 看書了. He has no
interest in reading.

幸 **syìng** (B) fortunate. ～ 而 fortunately; 不 ～ unfortunately.

幸福 **syìngfu** (SV) be happy.
/他們婚後生活很 ～. After they
got married they were very happy.
(N) happiness.

幸虧 **syìngkwēi** (A) fortunately.
/～ 他沒受傷. Fortunately he
didn't get hurt.

幸運 **'syìngyùn** (SV) be lucky.
/你真 ～ 有那麼一個有錢的爸
爸. You're lucky to have such a rich
father.

修 **syōu** (FV) 1) build. ～ 房子 build a
house. 2) repair. /我會 ～ 錶. I
can repair watches. 3) trim, pare.
～ 指甲 trim fingernails. /我得把
照片的四周都 ～ 掉,才能放進
鏡框. I have to trim off the four
sides of the picture before I can get
it into the frame. (B) 1) long. ～
眉 long eyebrows; ～ 竹 tall bamboo.
2) study. 自 ～ educate oneself or

study period or hour (in school).
3) revise. ～ 訂本 revised edition.
4) cultivate. ～ 身 self-cultivation.
t

修補 **syōubǔ** (FV) fix, repair,
by darning or patching. /你們 ～
輪胎嗎? Do you fix flats?

修改 **syōugǎi** (FV) alter, revise. /假如這件衣裳不合身我可以
給您 ～. If this dress doesn't fit you,
I can alter it for you. /這篇文章
得 ～ 了才能發表. This arti-
cle has to be revised before it can be
published.

修理 **syōulǐ** (FV) fix, repair.
/我下午要把汽車送去 ～. I
have to have my car fixed this afternoon.

修養 **syōuyǎng** (N) 1) culture.
文學 ～ literary culture. 2) self-
cultivation. (FV) cultivate, try to
improve. /我們應當 ～ 自己.
We should try to improve ourselves.

休 **syōu** (FV) divorce one's wife. /他
把他太太給 ～ 了. He divorced
his wife. (B) 1) cease, desist. ～ 戰
armistice; ～ 學 drop out of school.
2) rest. 退 ～ retire from a job.

休假 **syōujyà** (VO) take a vacation or furlough. /今年夏天我要
休三個禮拜的假. I want to
take three weeks' vacation this summer.

休息 **syōusyí** (FV) rest. /我
想 ～ 一下. I want to rest a while.

休養 **syōuyǎng** (FV) recuperate.
/他現在在鄉下 ～. He's now in
the country recuperating.

羞 **syōu** (FV) 1) blush. /她 ～ 的低
下了頭. She blushed and lowered
her head. 2) make someone feel
ashamed, embarrass. /別再說
話 ～ 我了. Don't say anything
more that will embarrass me. (B)
shame. 沒 ～ be shameless.

宿 **syōu** (M) night (lp). /我打了兩
～ 牌. I played cards two nights in
a row. → 宿 **sù**.

袖 **syōu** (B) <-子> sleeve (M 隻 jî; 對
dwèi). ～ 扣 cuff; 長 ～ long sleeve.

鏽[鏽][锈] **syòu** (SV) be rusty, corroded.
/刀 ～ 了. This knife is rusty. (N)
rust (M 層 **tséng**).

虛 **syū** (SV) be poor (of health). /他身體很～. His health is very poor. (B) 1) false, unreal. ～名 false reputation;～偽 be false, hypocritical. 2) empty, insubstantial. 空～ be empty, emptiness;～榮 vanity. 3) in vain, without effect. 光陰～度 pass time in vain. 4) humble. 謙～ be humble.

虛心 **syūsyīn** (SV) be meek, humble. /他對人很～. He is very humble toward people. (A) without prejudice, with an open mind. /他～學習. He approaches learning with an open mind.

需 **syū** (B) need. 急～品 urgently needed things.

需要 **syūyàu** (N) necessity. (FV) need. /我～一輛新車. I need a new car. (AV) need to. /我～跟你談一談. I need to talk it over with you.

許 **syǔ** (FV) 1) allow, permit, let. /她母親～她喝酒, 可是我母親不～我. Her mother allows her to drink but my mother doesn't allow me to. 2) promise somebody something. /我～我妹妹一件新衣服當生日禮. I promised my younger sister a new dress for her birthday. 3) be engaged to someone (of a girl, an arrangement made by the parents). /我女兒已經～人了. My daughter is engaged. (A) perhaps, probably. /他～病了. He is probably sick. (B) 1) praise. 稱～ praise. 2) very. ～久 a very long time. s

許多 **syǔdwō** (N) many things. /我也管不了～. I can't be concerned about so many things. (AT) many, much. ～人 many people; ～錢 a lot of money.

許可 **syǔkě** (FV) permit. /他～你去, 你才能去呢. You can go only if he permits you to. (N) permission.

許可證 **syǔkějèng** (N) permit (M張**jāng**).

畜 **syù** (FV) store up. ～'電 charge (as a battery). (B) rear, breed, domestic animals. ～馬 breed horses. → 畜 **chù**.

婿 **syù** (B) son-in-law. 女～ son-in-law.

勳(勛) **syūn** (B) 1) merit, distinguished service. 功～ distinguished service. 2) decoration, medal, award. 受～ receive a medal.

勳章 **syūnjāng** (N) decoration, medal, award, for any kind of merit.

尋(尋) **syún** (B) search for, look for. ～人 search for someone; ～死 attempt or commit suicide (lit. search for death).

巡(廵) **syún** (B) to patrol. ～邏 to patrol; ～夜 patrol at night. (M) round of drinks. 再喝一～ drink one more round.

巡警 **syúnjǐng** (N) policeman.

訓 **syùn** (FV) admonish, give someone a lecture. /他做錯了事, 他父親正～他呢. His father is giving him a lecture about his wrongdoings. (B) 1) instruction. 受～ receive training. 2) expound. ～話 comment on.

訓話 **syùnhwà** (VO) make a speech to subordinates. /連長向他的部下～. The company commander made a speech to his subordinates. (N) speech.

訓練 **syùnlyàn** (FV) train, drill. /他正～他的狗呢. He's training his dog. (N) training.

胸 **syūng** (B) thorax, chest. ～骨 sternum.

胸口 **'syūngkǒu** (N) space between the lungs, center of the chest. /他～痛. He has a pain in his chest.

胸脯 **syūngpú** (N) <-兒> breast, chest.

兇(凶) **syūng** (SV) 1) be violent. /風吹的很～. The wind is blowing very hard. 2) be cruel, fierce. (B) 1) unlucky, unfortunate. ～年 year of famine. 2) murder. ～手 murderer.

兇惡 **syūngè** (SV) be evil and cruel.

兄 **syūng** (B) older brother. 令～ your older brother.

兄弟 **syūngdi** (N) 1) younger brother (lp). 2) I (in speeches).

兄弟 **syūngdì** (N) older and younger brothers, brothers.

雄 **syúng** (B) 1) male (of lions, chickens). ～鷄 rooster; ～獅 male lion. 2) ambitious. ～心 ambition. 3) strong. ～偉 be big and strong. *t*
　　雄壯 **syúngjwàng** (SV) 1) be strong, robust (of people). 2) be spirited, lusty (of songs, poems, speeches).

熊 **syúng** (N) bear (M 隻 jī). *s*

宣 **sywān** (SV) be light, fluffy. /這塊蛋糕很～. This cake is very fluffy. (B) proclaim, declare publicly. ～言 declaration.
　　宣佈 **sywānbù** (FV) announce formally (that). /今天大會已經～閉幕了. Today the conference has already announced its adjournment. /他們兩人在舞會中途～訂婚. They announced their engagement in the middle of the dance.
　　宣傳 **sywānchwán** (FV) spread propaganda, advertise. /這種新香烟已經～很久了. This new brand of cigarette has been advertised for a long time. (N) propaganda.
　　宣戰 **sywānjàn** (VO) declare war. /1941年美國對日本～. The United States declared war on Japan in 1941.
　　宣判 **sywānpàn** (FV) announce a decision in court, announce a verdict. /法官～他無罪. The judge announced that he was not guilty. /這個案子還没～呢. No verdict has been given in this case yet.

選[选] **sywǎn** (FV) 1) elect, vote for. /我要～他當會長. I'm going to vote for him for chairman. 2) select, choose. /隨你～一個方便的時間. Choose whatever time is convenient for you.
　　選擇 '**sywǎndzé** (FV) choose, select. /你可以在這幾本書裏～. You may choose from these few volumes.
　　選舉 **sywánjyǔ** (FV) elect. ～國會議員 elect a congressman. (N) election.

玄 **sywán** (SV) be impossible, absurd. /他説的話太～了. What he said was very absurd. (B) 1) abstruse. ～學 metaphysics. 2) dark in color. ～色 black color.

靴[鞾] **sywē** (B) <子> boot (M 隻 jī; 雙 shwāng). 皮～ leather boots.

學[学] **sywé** (FV) 1) learn. /我想～英文. I want to learn English. 2) study. /他是～音樂的. He is studying music. 3) imitate. /他會～我的簽名. He can imitate my signature. 4) mock. /他老～人,叫人討厭. He always mocks people. It's really annoying. (B) 1) branch of learning. 心理～ psychology. 2) school. 退～ quit school. 2) learning. ～術 learning.
　　學會 **sywéhwèi** (N) academic society.
　　學生 **sywésheng** (N) student.
　　學校 **sywésyàu** (N) school.
　　學習 **sywésyí** (FV) 1) study. /他很勤奮的～. He studies diligently. 2) learn. /我想～速記. I would like to learn shorthand. (N) study, learning. 政治～ political study.
　　學位 **sywéwèi** (N) academic degree.
　　學問 **sywéwen** (N) learning, knowledge. /他的～很博. He's a person of very wide learning.
　　學員 **sywéywán** (N) student of an institute.
　　學院 **sywéywàn** (N) school or college within a university, institute.

尋[寻] **sywé** (B) *t*. →尋 **syún**.
　　尋摸 **sywéme** (FV) 1) wander around looking for something (as in window shopping). /我到街上給你～～,有没有你要的東西. I'll have a look around downtown to see if I can find the things you want. 2) search for something with the intention of purchasing it. /我想～一輛舊汽車. I'm thinking of looking for an old car.

血 **sywě, sywè, syě*** (N)* blood. 流～ bleed. (B) blood relationship. ～親 blood relatives.
　　血統 **sywétǔng, sywètǔng** (N) blood relationship. /他們倆是一個～. Those two are blood relatives.

雪 **sywĕ** (N) snow (M場**chǎng**). 下～ snowfall.

　　雪白 **sywĕbái** (SV) be snow-white.

　　雪花膏 **sywĕhwāgāu** (N) cold cream *or* vanishing cream (M瓶 **píng**).

血 **sywè** →血**sywĕ**.

司 **sz** (N) governmental bureau. (B) manage, control～法 judicature.

　　司機 **szjī** (N) 1) operator of a vehicle, driver, chauffeur. 公共汽車～ bus driver.

　　司令 **szlíng** (N) commander of a military unit.

　　司令員 **szlíngywán** (N) commander (army) (c).

思 **sz** (B) 1) think of.～鄉 think of home. 2) thought, idea.～潮 flood of ideas.

　　思想 **szsyǎng** (N) thought, way of thinking.

私 **sz** (B) 1) private, personal.～產 private property. 2) partial, selfish.無～ impartial, unselfish. 3) illicit, illegal, contraband.～貨 smuggled goods;～酒 illegal home brew, moonshine.

　　私人 **szrén** (N) staff selected with favoritism. (AT) personal, private.～房間 private room.

　　私生子 **szshēngdz** (N) illegitimate child.

　　私事 **szshr** (N) private *or* personal affair (M件**jyàn**).

　　私下裏 **szsyàli** (A) in private, in secret. /他～賄賂他. He secretly bribed him.

絲 **sz** (N) silk. (M) trace, bit. 一～笑容 a trace of a smile. (B) ＜ㄦ＞ thread. 鐵～ wire; 肉～ meat cut into slivers.

撕 **sz** (FV) tear, rip. /她看過那封信以後就～了. After reading that letter, she tore it up.

斯 **sz** (B) ⊦. *t s*

　　斯文 **szwen** (SV) be genteel, refined. /他很～. He is very genteel.

死 **sz** (FV) die. /他祖父昨天～了. His grandfather died yesterday. (SV)

be dull. /她眼睛～～的. Her eyes are dull. /我不喜歡他,因為他太～了. I don't like him, because he's too dull. (A) stubbornly. /他～不認錯. He stubbornly refused to admit his fault. (N) death. ～裡逃生 escape from death; peaceful death. (RE) 1) indicates fastness. /那個窗戶已經釘～了. That window has been nailed fast. 2) indicates dying. 打～ beat to death. (B) dead. ～胡同 dead-end street.

　　死了 **szle** (P) used after a SV, indicates an extreme condition. /那個女孩子難看～. That girl is extremely ugly. /我高興～. I'm extremely happy.

　　死尸 **szshr** (N) corpse (M具 **jyù**).

　　死刑 **szsyíng** (N) capital punishment.

　　死亡 **szwáng** (FV) die. /那次車禍～了兩個人. Two people died in that auto accident. (N) death. 沒有～ there is no death.

四 **sz** (NU) four.～把椅子 four chairs. (B) fourth.～樓 fourth floor.

　　四周 **szjōu** (PW) (on) four sides, all directions. /我家房子的～都有圍牆. There are walls around the four sides of my house. /～都是他的仇人. He has enemies everywhere.

　　四月 **szywè** (TW) 1) (in) April. 2) (in) the fourth month of the lunar calendar.

似 **sz** (B) as if, seem, like. 相～ alike, similar. →似**shr**.

　　似乎 **szhu** (A) seemingly. /問題～不那麼簡單. It seems that the problem isn't so simple. /她比你高一點儿. She seems a little taller than you. /他們在一起～很高興. They seemed happy together.

他 **tā** (PN) 1) he, she. /～是一個詩人. He (*or* She) is a poet. /請你告訴～我不能去. Please tell him (*or* her) that I can't go. 2) used before a noun, his, her. /～妹妹跟我同學. His (*or* Her) younger sister is my schoolmate. (B) other. 其～ the rest of, other.

他們 **tāmen** (PN) 1) they. /~ 上學去了. They went to school. /我要去看 ~. I want to visit them 2) used before a noun, their. /~家客人很多. There are many guests at their house.

她 **tā** (PN) 1) she. /~畫畫儿畫得 很好. She can paint very well. /我不喜歡 ~. I don't like her. 2) used before a noun, her. /~父 親送~來的. Her father accompanied her here.

它[牠] **tā** (PN) 1) it. /把~放在那儿 才好呢? Where shall I put it? 2) used before a noun, its. /那貓真 可憐~尾巴叫狗咬掉了. The poor cat! Its tail was bitten off by a dog. (B) other. 其~the rest, other.

塌 **tā** (FV) 1) collapse, fall to pieces. /這個橋快~了. This bridge is about to collapse. 2) sink down. /這個地板很壞, 有的地方鼓出來,有的地方~ 下去. This floor is no good. In some places it slopes up, and in other places it has sunk down. 塌實 **tāshr** (SV) be calm, peaceful. /他們一家人過得很 ~. Their whole family lives peacefully.

塔 **tǎ** (N) pagoda, tower (M座**dzwò**). *t*

踏 **tà** (FV) 1) step on or in something. /我~着一個蟲. I stepped on a bug. /我没留神,一脚~進水裏 了. I was careless, and stepped in some water. 2) pedal. ~三輪車 pedal a pedicab. (B) walk, stroll. ~月 walk in the moonlight; ~雪 walk through the snow.

擡[抬] **tái** (FV) 1) lift, carry (done by two or more people). /請你來幫我 ~一~這張桌子. Please help me lift this table. 2) raise a price. ~價 raise a price. 擡槓 **táigàng** (VO) argue. /你 老愛跟我~. You always like to argue with me.

臺[檯棓](B) 3)[台] **tái** (N) platform, stage. (M) 1) for plays or operas. 一~戲 a play. 2) for machines. 一~機器

a machine. (B) 1) balcony. 涼 ~ porch. 2) station (not railroad or bus). 電 ~ broadcasting station; 氣 象 ~ weather station. 3) table. ~ 布 tablecloth; 梳粧~vanity table, dresser. 4) Taiwan (contracted form of 臺灣 **táiwān**). ~大 Taiwan University.

太 **tài** (A) 1) too, excessively. /這~ 貴,我買不起. This is too expensive; I can't afford to buy it. 2) very, quite. /我~高興了. I'm very happy. 太平 '**tàipíng** (SV) be peaceful (free of fighting). /打完了仗就 ~. After the war things will be peaceful again. (N) tranquillity. 太太 **tàitai** (N) 1) married woman. /她是一位~. She's a married woman. 2) wife. /我~ 不在家. My wife isn't home. (B) used after a surname, Mrs. 王~ Mrs. Wang. 太陽 **tàiyang** (N) the sun. /~ 出來了. The sun is out.

態[态] **tài** (B) attitude, manner. 憨~ innocent manner. 態度 **tàidu** (N) attitude (of people).

灘[滩] **tān** (N) 1) sandy shore. 海~ seashore. 2) rapids. (M) 1) pool 一~ 血 a pool of blood. 2) blob 一~泥 a blob of mud.

貪 **tān** (SV) be avaricious, covetous. /他那個人很~. He's a greedy and avaricious fellow. (FV) be greedy for, long for. /我什麼都 不~. I'm not longing for anything. 貪贓 **tāndzāng** (VO) take bribes. /他貪了好幾回贓. He has taken many bribes.

攤[摊] **tān** (FV) 1) spread things out (as for a display). /他把他的畫一 張張地~在桌上. He spread his paintings out on the table, one by one. 2) share a financial burden. /需要多少錢?我們~吧. How much money will it take? Let's all chip in. (B) <子,-儿> stand for vending. 報~newspaper stand; ~ 販 vendor.

彈 **tán** (FV) 1) pluck a stringed instrument, play the piano or organ. ～鋼琴 play the piano. 2) flick. /把你大衣上的土～一～. Flick the dust off your coat. 3) hurl, eject. /跳板把他～到半空中去了. The diving board hurled him into the air. 一彈 dàn.

彈簧 tánhwáng (N) coiled spring (M根gēn).

彈性 'tánsyíng (N) 1) elasticity. /橡皮有很大的～. Rubber is extremely elastic. 2) flexibility (of laws, regulations, rules, etc.). /這條法律的～很大. This law is very flexible.

彈壓 tányā (FV) quiet, quell (by troops in times of crisis—official term). /他們請警察來～. They called the police to come and quell the disturbance.

談 tán (FV) talk, discuss, chat. /我要跟你～一～. I want to talk with you.

談話 tánhwà (VO) talk. /我們談了半天話. We talked for quite a while. (N) talk, statement. 發表～ make a statement.

談論 'tánlwùn (FV) talk about something. /他們在～時事. They are talking about current events.

談判 tánpàn (FV) confer about, negotiate. /兩國在～怎麼訂那個商約. The two countries are conferring about the establishment of a commercial treaty. (N) negotiation. 開～ start negotiations.

痰 tán (N) spittle, phlegm. 吐～to spit.

坦 tăn (B) 1) level, flat. 平～ be level, flat. 2) at ease. ～然 be at ease (of mind or manner). t

坦白 'tănbái (SV) be frank, open. /他說話很～. He talked very frankly. (FV) confess (c). /你非把這件事情～一下不可. You have to confess frankly about this matter.

坦克 tănkè (N) tank (m)(M輛lyàng).

毯 tan (B) <子> blanket (M張jāng, 條tyáu). 地～rug, carpet.

探 tàn (FV) 1) investigate, search out. /他們正在全力～那件案子. They are investigating that case exhaustively. 2) visit, inquire after. ～病 inquire after a sick person. 3) lean out, lean toward. /她～身欄杆外對他揮手. She leaned over the railing and waved to him. (B) <子> spy. 偵～ detective.

探險 tànsyǎn (VO) seek adventure, go in search of adventure. /他們到北極去探過兩次險. They went to the North Pole twice in search of adventure. (N) adventure.

探詢處 tànsyúnchù (N) information desk.

探聽 tànting (FV) find out about, get information about. /請你～～他的口氣. Find out what his opinions are.

探頭兒 tàntóur (VO) rubberneck at, stick one's head in or out, stick one's head out. /他從窗戶探出頭兒來看一看. He stuck his head out of the window to take a look. /他探着頭兒聽那兩人說悄悄話. He leaned forward to hear what those two were whispering about.

炭 tàn (N) charcoal. (B) carbon. ～氣 carbon dioxide; ～酸鈉 sodium carbonate.

趟{蹚躺}tāng (FV) wade through water. /他～着水過了那條河. He waded across the stream. 一趟tàng.

湯 tāng (N) soup. s

糖 táng (N) 1) sugar. 2) candy (M塊kwài).

堂 táng (M) class (as a period of time). /今天我上了一～英文. I had an English class today. (B) 1) hall, room. 講～lecture hall; 教～church. 2) prefix used to indicate cousins of the same surname. ～姐 older female cousin of the same surname. 3) polite term for another person's mother (h). 令～ your mother.

倘{儻}tăng (B) if. ～或 supposing.

倘若 tăngrwò (A) if. /～下雨, 我就不去. If it rains, I won't go.

躺 tăng (FV) lie down. /我很疲倦, 想

~ 一 ~ . I'm very tired and want to lie down for a while.

躺椅 **tángyǐ** (N) sofa *or* lounge chair, <u>with back or arms or both,</u> <u>long enough to lie down on</u> (M把**bǎ**, 張**jāng**).

趟(蹚踼) **tàng** (M) <-ㄦ> 1) trip, time. /我今天已經去過三~學校了. I have already made three trips to school today. /我到那儿去過幾 ~ . I went there several times. 2) column, row. 一~桌子 a row of tables. 一趟 **tāng**.

燙 **tàng** (SV) be scalding hot, burning hot. /湯太~了, 先別喝. The soup is too hot. Don't eat it now. (FV) 1) scald. /我~了手了. I scalded my hand. 2) iron. /我得自己~衣服 . I have to iron my own clothes. 3) get a permanent. /她去~頭髮去了. She went to get a permanent. 4) warm <u>something</u>. ~ 酒 warm wine; ~奶 heat a bottle (lit. heat milk).

tao *see* **tau.**

掏(搯) **tāu** (FV) 1) dig. /他用小刀在牆上~了一個洞 . He dug a hole in the wall with a small knife. 2) take out, pull out. /他從口袋裡~出錶來一看, 說, "啊! 我要遲到了." He took his watch out of his pocket and said, "Oh! I'll be late!" 3) grope, feel, <u>through the contents of a con-</u> <u>tainer with a small opening, trying</u> <u>to find something</u>. /他的球掉到洞裡去了, ~了半天也沒~出來. His ball fell into a hole. He felt around in there for quite a while but couldn't find it.

桃(核) **táu** (B) <-ㄦ,-子> peach (M隻**jī**). ~核 peach stone.

　桃花 **táuhwā** (N) <-ㄦ> peach blossom (M朵**dwǒ**; 枝**jī**; 棵**kē**).

　桃樹 **táushù** (N) peach tree (M棵**kē**).

逃 **táu** (FV) escape, flee. /他從監獄裡~走了. He escaped from prison.

　逃兵役 **táubīngyì** (VO) evade a draft *or* levy. /他逃過兩次兵役 . He evaded the draft twice.

　逃難 **táunàn** (VO) leave a

troubled place, flee from calamity. /打仗的時候我們逃過很多次難 . We fled several times during the war.

淘 **táu** (FV) 1) wash, rinse, <u>rice</u>. /米~過了沒有? Has the rice been washed? 2) clean out <u>drains, wells</u>. ~ 井 clean out a well. (B) to pan. ~ 金 pan for gold.

　淘汰 **táutài** (FV) weed out, eliminate. /沒用的人都被~. Useless people get weeded out.

討 **tǎu** (FV) 1) ask for, beg for. /他來~我欠他的賬 . He came to ask me for the money I owed him. 2) marry <u>a woman</u> (d). /他還沒~太太呢 . He hasn't married yet. (B) discuss. 研 ~ study and discuss.

　討債 **tǎujài** (VO) ask for the return of a loan. /~比捐款還難. It's even harder to ask for the return of a loan than it is to solicit a free contribution.

　討論 **tǎulwùn** (FV) discuss. /我們已經~過這問題了. We have discussed this problem already. (N) discussion.

　討厭 **tǎuyàn** (SV) be annoying, disgusting. /他的樣子很~. His manner is very disgusting. (FV) dislike. /我~他 . I dislike him.

套 **tàu** (FV) 1) put on, slip on. /外邊冷, 你最好~一件外套 . It's cold outside; you'd better put on a coat. 2) cover, envelop, put <u>something in-</u> <u>side something</u>. /把枕頭~在套子裡 . Put the pillow in the pillowcase. 3) use <u>the layer tint method</u> <u>(in printing)</u>. /這還得~一層色 This needs to be given another layer of color. 4) harness <u>a horse</u>, hitch up a cart. ~ 馬 harness a horse. /車已經~好了 . The cart is hitched up. 5) trick <u>a person into</u> <u>telling the truth</u>. /我拿話~她的秘密 . I coaxed out her secret. 6) imitate, copy. /他做詩盡~前人的體裁 . He always imitates former poets' styles of writing. (B) <-ㄦ> covering, wrapper. 手~ gloves; 外 ~ overcoat; 枕頭~pillowcase. (M) set 一~杯子 a set of cups; 一~衣服 a suit of clothing.

特 **tè** (B) 1) special. ～價 special price; ～徵 special feature. 2) specially. ～定 specially appointed. *t*

特別 **tèbyé** (SV) be special, uncommon, distinctive. /這種髮型很～. This hair style is very special. /藍色的玫瑰花真是太～了. A blue rose is really very uncommon. (A) especially, particularly. /他對人很好,～是對我. He's very good to people, especially to me.

特點 **tèdyǎn** (N) special characteristic, special feature, of people or things.

特殊 **tèshū** (SV) be special, exceptional. /這個情形很～. This situation is exceptional. /這筆錢有～用處. This money has a special use.

特性 **tèsyìng** (N) special trait, characteristic.

特為 **tèwèi** (CV) especially for something. /我～這件事情來的. I came especially on account of this. (A) specially, purposely. /我～去看他,結果他不在家. I especially went to see him, but he wasn't home.

特務 **tèwu** (N) 1) secret police. 2) spy.

騰 **tēng** (FV) steam, heat up by steaming. /把飯～一～再吃. Heat up the rice before you eat it. /你的眼睛用熱毛巾～一～就好了. Your eye will be better if you apply a hot compress. →騰 **téng**.

疼 **téng** (FV) love, dote on, people. /他很～他的女兒. He dotes on his daughter. (SV) be sore, painful. /我的腿很～. My legs are sore. /我頭很～. I have a headache.

疼痛 **téngtùng** (N) pain, soreness.

藤(籐) **téng** (B) <子> 1) climbing plant, vine (M根 gēn,棵 kē,條 tyáu).長春～ ivy. 2) rattan, cane.～椅 rattan chair.

騰 **téng** (FV) 1) move things out to make room. /把這盒子～出來. Empty this box. /給客人～一間屋子吧. Let's clear out a room for the guest. 2) make time for. /我得

～出點功夫來做自己的事. I have to make some time to do my own things. (B) mount.～空 soar; ～雲 mount a cloud. →騰 **tēng**.

梯 **tī** (B) <子> 1) ladder. 軟～ rope-ladder. 2) stairs. 樓～ stairs.

剔 **tī** (FV) 1) scrape off. ～牙 pick the teeth. /這塊骨頭上還有些肉沒有～下來. There's still some meat that hasn't been scraped off this bone. 2) pick out and get rid of something. /把壞的水果～掉吧. Let's pick out the rotten fruit and get rid of it.

踢 **tī** (FV) 1) kick. /馬～了他一下. The horse kicked him. 2) kick out. /他叫公司給～出來了. He was kicked out by his company.

提 **tí** (FV) 1) carry, lift with the hand, below shoulder level. /她下樓的時候輕輕地～起她的長裙. As she came downstairs, she lifted her long gown a little. 2) mention, bring up. /過去的事情還～它做什麼? Why should we mention what is past? /開會的時候他～了兩個問題. During the meeting he brought up two questions. 3) remind. /要是我忘了請你～我一～. If I forget it, please remind me. 4) draw out, take out, money. /我要到銀行去～一點錢. I'm going to the bank to draw out some money. →提 **dī**.

提案 **tían** (VO) make a motion (in a meeting). /今天他提了一個案. He made a motion today. (N) proposal, motion (in a meeting).

提包 **tíbāu** (N) small suitcase, handbag, briefcase (M隻 jī).

提琴 **tíchín** (N) violin (M隻 jī).

提出 **tíchu** (RC) 1) bring up, set forth. /他提不出什麼好意見. He can't give any favorable opinion. 2) take out, draw out, money. /昨天我才從銀行～一百塊錢來,今天就沒有了. I just took one hundred dollars out of the bank yesterday, and today it's all gone.

提前 **tíchyán** (FV) move a scheduled event to a time earlier than that originally planned. /他們的婚期～了. Their wedding date

has been moved up. /我們得~
開會. We've got to start the meeting earlier than we'd planned.
　提早 tízǎu (FV) move a scheduled event to a time earlier than that
originally planned. /還有一個星
期才是他的生日.不過我們~
給他慶祝. His birthday will be a
week later, but we moved the celebration ahead for him.
　提防 tífang (FV) beware of,
take precautions against. ~扒手
guard against pickpockets. /你得
~他來報仇. You must take pre-
cautions against his revenge.
　提高 tígāu (FV) raise (a standard, salary, etc.). ~警覺 increase
vigilance; ~待遇 raise a salary.
/這地方的人的知識水準已經
~了. The intellectual level of the
people here has been raised.
　提貨單 tíhwòdān (N) bill of
lading (M張 jāng).
　提箱 tísyāng (N) suitcase (M
隻 jī).
　提議 tíyì (VO) make a motion
at a meeting, etc. /開會的時候
我得提一個議. When the meet-
ing is held I'll make a motion. (FV)
suggest. /我~我們今天去游
泳. I suggest that we go and swim
today. (N) suggestion, proposal.

堤{隄} tí, dī (N) dike, dam (M條 tyáu,
道 dàu).

題 tí (FV) 1) write something on something. /中國畫家喜歡在他們
的畫上~詩. Chinese painters
like to write poems on their paintings. 2) mention, talk about. /別
再~它了吧! Let's not mention
it anymore. 3) remind. /你要是
不~我.我根本不會想起來.
If you hadn't reminded me, I would
never have remembered it. (N)
problem, exercise (M道 dàu). /我
還有幾道數學和物理~沒做.
I still have some mathematics and
physics problems left undone. 2) topic (M道 dàu). /這三道作文~,你
們隨便選一道. You may
choose any one of those three composition topics.
　題目 tímu (N) 1) title. /這本
書的~是"紅樓夢". The title

of this book is "Dream of the Red
Chamber." 2) heading. /這一章的
~是"語言的功用". The head-
ing of this chapter is "The Function
of Language." 3) problem, exercise.
數學 ~ mathematics problem. /這
個~很難解決. This problem is
quite difficult to solve. 4) topic.
/我還沒有想好講什麼~. I still
haven't decided what topic I'm going
to discuss. 5) subject. /這門課
的~是世界史. The subject of
this course is World History.

蹄{蹏} tí (B) <子> hoof (M隻 jī). 豬~
pig's feet.

體{体}{体} tǐ (B) 1) body. 人~ human
body; ~溫 temperature of the body.
2) physical. ~能 physical fitness;
~檢 physical examination. 3) style.
文~ style of writing; 字~ style of
writing Chinese characters. 4) consider. ~恤 sympathize with; ~帖
be considerate.
　體格 tǐgé (N) physique.
　體會 tǐhwèi (FV) comprehend,
understand (by feeling). /我能~
他說那句話的意思. I can make
out what he meant by saying that.
　體重 tǐjùng (N) weight (of people).
　體諒 tǐlyang (FV) have consideration for, sympathize with. /他
從不~人. He never has consideration for others.
　體面 tǐmyan (SV) 1) be pretty,
handsome. /她長得很~. She's
quite pretty. 2) be decent, in good
taste. /他們的婚禮辦的很~.
Their wedding ceremony was in good
taste. (N) honor.
　體裁 tǐtsái (N) style, fashion,
pattern, format, usually having to do
with writing or formal speaking.
　體操 tǐtsāu (N) calisthenics,
physical exercise, drill.
　體統 'tǐtǔng (N) dignity.
　體育 tǐyù (N) 1) physical training, physical education. 2) athletic
sports.

替 tì (CV) for someone. /請你~我
把這封信寄了行不行? Would
you please mail this letter for me?
(FV) take the place of, substitute
for someone. /我不能參加開會,

你能～我麼？ I can't go to the meeting, can you take my place?

替 工 **tǐgūng** (N) substitute (worker). /他走了,找一個～吧. He's gone, so find a substitute for him.

剃(薙) **tì** (FV) shave. /我一天不～, 鬍子就好長了. If I didn't shave for a day, my beard would grow quite a lot.

tian *see* **tyan.**

tiao *see* **tyau.**

tie *see* **tye.**

聽(听) **tīng** (FV) listen to. /好好～我說. Listen to me carefully. 2) hear. /我～不清楚. I can't hear clearly. (M) tin. 一～香烟 a tin of cigarettes. *t*

聽 差 **tīngchāi** (N) porter, doorman, male servant.

聽 眾 **tīngjùng** (N) audience, listeners.

聽 見 **tīngjyan** (RC) hear. /你聽得見嗎？ Can you hear it? /這是什麼音樂？我從來没～過. What music is that? I've never heard it before.

聽 說 **tīngshwō** (FV) hear it said that . . . , hear that . . . . /我～他早就到歐洲去了. I heard that he went to Europe a long time ago. /～臺灣冬天不下雪. I hear that there's no snow in the winter in Taiwan.

廳(厅) **tīng** (B) 1) department of a provincial government. 教育～ department of education of a provincial government. 2) hall, room. 飯～ dining hall; 客～ living room.

停 **tíng** (FV) 1) stop. ～火 cease fire. /這雨不知要到幾時才～. I don't know when the rain will stop. 2) stay. /我在這儿只能～兩天. I can only stay here for two days. 3) park, berth. /這裡可以～車. It's all right to park the car here. /船在港灣裡～了一個月. The ship has been berthed in the harbor for a month.

停 止 **tíngjř** (FV) stop doing something. /從明天起我們就～工作了. We will stop working, starting tomorrow.

停 頓 **'tíngdwùn** (FV) be stopped for the time being. /競選的活動已經～了. The election campaign has been stopped for the time being.

停 戰 書 **tíngjànshū** (N) armistice (signed document) (M張 **jāng**, 份 **fèn**).

挺 **tǐng** (FV) 1) straighten up (physically). /那個軍官叫士兵們把胸～起來. The officer ordered the soldiers to throw out their chests. 2) hold on (fig.). /這點傷不要緊,我還可以～一～. This wound is all right, I still can hold on a while. (SV) be straight and stiff. /你看他站得多～. See how straight he stands. (A) pretty, fairly. /這本書～好. This book is pretty good. (M) for machine guns. 一～機槍 a machine gun.

tong *see* **tung.**

偷 **tōu** (FV) steal. /我的脚踏車叫人～了. My bicycle was stolen. /他家很有錢,可是他常～同學的東西. His family is rich, but he always steals things from his schoolmates. (A) on the sly. /他～看過你的信. He read your letter on the sly.

偷 懶 **tōulǎn** (VO) shirk, loaf on the job. /他從來没偷過懶. He has never loafed on the job. /我太累了,得偷個懶歇歇. I'm so tired that I want to snatch a rest. (SV) be lazy. /別～,你的工作還没做完呢. Don't be lazy. You haven't finished your work yet.

偷 偷 的 **tōutōude** (A) stealthily, secretly. /他～跑出教室去了. He sneaked out of the classroom. /他剛才～看你女朋友來的信. He has just read your girl friend's letter on the sly.

頭(头) **tóu** (N) head (of a body). (SP) 1) first. ～一次 the first time; ～一個人 the first person; ～等 first class. 2) with NU-M of time ago, before. ～天 the day before; ～一年 the year before. (M) 1) for some domestic animals. 一～牛 a cow; 一～羊 a sheep. 2) for some vegatables. 一～白菜 a head of cabbage; 一～大蒜 a stalk of garlic. (B)

1) <-儿> front end. 車～ the front part of the car; 月～ first part of the month. 2) added to the localizers 上 shàng, 下 syà, 前 chyán, 後 hòu 裡 lǐ, 外 wài, forms PW. 上～ on top, above, upper part or area; 裡～ inside; 外～ outside; 後～ in back, the back part or area 3) added to FV to form nouns used with 有 yǒu or 沒 méi, interesting to do. /這本書沒看～. There is nothing interesting to read in this book. /他有什麼說～? What is there interesting to say about him? 4) noun suffix. 石～ stone; 木～ wood; 兆～ omen; 苦～ sufferings.

頭髮 tóufa (N) hair (on the human head) (M 根 gēn).

頭巾 tóujīn (N) scarf, turban (M 條 tyáu).

頭裏 tóulou (PW) (in the) place in front of, ahead of (in a line). /他本來走在我們～的, 怎麼我們到了他還沒到? He was ahead of us. How come we've arrived here and he still hasn't? /～沒有別人了. There's no one ahead.

頭儿 tóur (N) 1) boss. 2) end (of a street). /這條街我走到～了. I've come to the end of the street. (B) 1) side. 那～ the other side. 2) side, party. 兩～ both parties. 3) remnant. 烟～ cigarette butt; 布～ remnant of material.

投 tóu (FV) 1) drop. /敵機在我們城裡～了很多炸彈. The enemy's airplanes dropped a lot of bombs on our town. /請你把這封信～到信箱裡去. Please mail this letter. (lit. Please drop this letter into the mailbox.) 2) throw. /他～海自殺了. He threw himself into the sea and committed suicide. 3) go to a place to live. ～宿 go to an inn. /他父母都已經死了, 所以～到舅舅家去了. His parents were both dead, so he went to live in his uncle's house. (B) 1) submit. ～降 surrender; ～稿 submit an article to a newspaper or magazine. 2) project. ～影 projection. 3) fit in with. 情～意合 in harmony with feelings and intentions.

投標 tóubyāu (VO) enter a bid for a contract. /我不打算投這個標了. I no longer want to enter a bid for this contract.

投資 tóudz (VO) invest money. /你能不能再投一點儿資? Can you invest a little more money? (N) investment.

投機 tóujī (SV) 1) be speculative. ～事業 speculative business; ～份子 opportunist. 2) be congenial. /他們談得很～. They talked very congenially. (VO) 1) take a chance. /他最喜歡～. He likes to take chances. 2) speculate (financially). /他最近做股票又投了兩次機. Recently he speculated on stocks two more times.

投票 tóupyàu (VO) vote, cast a vote. /你說他投誰一票? Whom do you think he will vote for?

投降 tóusyáng (FV) surrender. /我寧死也不～. I would rather die than surrender. (N) surrender.

透 tòu (FV) 1) pass through, penetrate. /這所房子造得很好, 冬天寒氣～不進來. This house is very well built, so in the winter the cold can't come in. 2) reveal. /別把我們的計劃～給人知道. Don't reveal our plan to others. /他叫我來給你～一個信儿. He asked me to convey the message to you. (RE) indicates penetration or permeation. /我的鞋都濕～了. My shoes are all wet. /他一刀把桌子都扎～了. He stuck a knife through the table.

透氣 tòuchì (VO) <-儿> let air pass through or penetrate, air, something. /我們到院裡去透點氣去. Let's go out in the yard for a breath of air. /把氈子擱在外頭透點儿氣. Put the blanket out to air. (SV) be ventilated. /這間屋子很～. This room is well ventilated.

透風 tòufēng (VO) <-儿> breeze passes through. /這個門縫儿～. The wind is leaking through the seams of the door. /這間屋子一點風也不透. This room is airtight.

透光 tòugwāng (VO) let light penetrate, let light escape or pass through. /這個窗帘很好, 不會～. This drapery is very good. It won't let light penetrate. /這個照

相機～. 不能用了. That camera has a light leak, you can't use it.

透 了 **tòule** (P) used after SV, utterly, extremely. 笨 ～utterly stupid. /有意思～. It's extremely interesting.

擦 **tsā** (FV) 1) wipe, rub. /拿熱手巾～一把臉吧? Would you like to wipe your face with a hot towel? /別用髒手～眼睛. Don't rub your eyes with your dirty hands. 2) clean, polish. ～地板 clean and polish the floor; ～桌子 clean the table; ～鞋 polish shoes. 3) erase. /鉛筆寫的很容易～掉. Things written by pencil are easy to erase. 4) apply, put on. ～藥 put on medicine; ～粉 put on facial powder. (A) nearly. /天～黑的時候, 蚊子很多. At dusk (lit. when it is nearly dark), there are many mosquitoes.

擦洗 **tsāyǐ** (FV) clean by wiping with water and a rag. /請你把這把椅子～～. Please wipe this chair off.

猜 **tsāi** (FV) guess, guess that. /我～他不能來了. My guess is that he can't come. /我來～你這個謎兒. I'll try to guess your riddle. (B) suspect. ～疑 be in doubt.

纔[才] **tsái** (A) 1) not until, then and only then. /我今年～到美國. It was not until this year that I came to the United States. /你得先請請我, 我～告訴你哪. You have to treat me first, then I'll tell you. 2) followed by NU-M expression, only (indicating less than what is expected). /現在～八點鐘還早得很. It's only eight o'clock, still very early. /～五塊錢嗎? 真便宜. Is it only five dollars? That's really cheap. 3) actually, on the contrary (contrary to expectation). /你以為他傻嗎? 他～不傻呢! You thought he was foolish? On the contrary, he isn't. (PT) 要是 ... ～...呢. If ... it would be .... /他要是來～怪呢. It would be strange if he were to come.

纔剛 **tsáigāng** (A)剛纔 **gāngtsái**.

才 **tsái** (N) talent. /他很有～. He has a lot of talent. (B) ability. ～德 talent and virtue. SF of 纔**tsái**.

才幹 **tsáigàn** (N) ability, gift, talent. /他很有～. He has a lot of talent.

裁 **tsái** (FV) 1) cut out a pattern. /我會縫衣服, 就是不會～. I can sew, but I don't know how to cut out a pattern. 2) cut down, reduce, personnel. /最近我們公司～了不少人. Recently our company has laid off quite a lot of employees. (B) 1) decide. 仲～ arbitrate. 2) regulate. 制～ restrict.

裁縫 **tsáifeng** (N) tailor.

裁判 **tsáipàn** (FV) 1) act as referee, arbitrate in some matter. /我們賽球王先生～. Mr. Wang will be the referee in our ball game. 2) make a decision on, decide. /法官一天～好幾樁案子. The judge makes decisions on many cases in a day. (N) 1) referee. 2) arbitration. 3) decision (legal).

材 **tsái** (N) coffin (M 口 **kǒu**). (B) 1) material. 木～ timber. 2) ability, capacity. 人～ man of outstanding ability.

材料 **tsáilyàu** (N) 1) <-儿> material for building, sewing, cooking; or for preparing a report, speech, piece of writing, etc. /我的論文還沒找好～. I still haven't found enough materials for my thesis. 2) personnel (human material). /他不是個讀書的～. He isn't scholarship material.

財 **tsái** (B) wealth. ～主 wealthy man; ～政 financial administration.

財產 **tsáichǎn** (N) assets, property (M 份 **fèn**).

財閥 **'tsáifá** (N) tycoon, financial big shot.

採[采] **tsǎi** (FV) pick, gather. ～茶 pick tea-leaves; ～花 pick flowers. (B) choose, select. ～擇 adopt (as a policy).

採取 **'tsǎichyǔ** (FV) 1) assume an attitude. /你不應當～這種態度. You shouldn't assume this kind of attitude. 2) adopt a form of government, a scheme of operation. /中國的礦業現在～西方的方法. The mining industry in China is adopting Western methods.

採訪 **tsǎifǎng** (FV) gather <u>news, information</u> (as a reporter does). /他專門～地方新聞. He gathers local news only.

採購 **tsǎigòu** (FV) purchase for a group or organization. /政府派我到美國～通訊器材. The government sent me to the United States to purchase communications equipment.

採納 **tsǎinà** (FV) accept <u>a proposal, point of view.</u> /他們沒～我的意見. They didn't accept my idea.

採用 **tsǎiyùng** (FV) adopt and put into use. /你～什麼方法? What method have you adopted? /你們學校～那本教科書? Which textbook is your school using?

采 **tsǎi** (B) bright color. 多～ colorful. <u>SF of 採**tsǎi**.</u>

踩[踹] **tsǎi** (FV) step on. /噢!你～了我腳了. Ouch, you stepped on my foot! /當心,別～水. Be careful not to step in the water.

菜 **tsài** (N) 1) vegetable (M棵**kē**). ～園 vegetable garden; ～油 vegetable oil. 2) dish (<u>of food</u>) (M樣**yàng**, 道**dàu**). ～單 menu. /這樣～真好吃. This dish is really delicious.

參[叅] **tsān** (B) 1) take part in, participate in. ～戰 participate in a war; ～政 participate in politics. 2) refer, consult. ～看 refer. →參**tsēn**, 參**shēn**, 參**tsēn**.

參觀 **tsāngwān** (FV) visit <u>a place in order to see the facilities or activities there.</u> /很多人從遠處來紐約～世界博覽會. Many people came from faraway places to New York to visit the World's Fair.

參加 **tsānjyā** (FV) 1) join, participate in, take part in. /我可不可以～你們的討論? May I join your discussion? /我沒有～上次的演出. I didn't participate in the last performance. 2) attend. /對不起,我不能～你的婚禮. I'm sorry I can't attend your wedding.

參考 **'tsānkǎu** (FV) 1) consult <u>books, documents, etc., as references.</u> /請你把筆記借我～～.

Please lend me your notes to use as a reference. 2) consider. /你可以～一下我的意見. You might consider my opinion. (N) reference. ～書 reference book; ～資料 reference materials.

參謀 **tsānmou** (FV) serve in an advisory capacity, give advice. /我來給你好好～一下. Let me give you some good advice. (N) staff (m).

餐 **tsān** (B) meal. ～廳 dining room; ～館 restaurant. (M) <u>for meals.</u> 一～飯 a meal.

餐巾 **tsānjīn** (N) cloth napkin <u>used at a dinner table</u> (M條**tyáu**, 張**jāng**, 塊**kwài**).

慚[慙] **tsán** (B) be ashamed. 大言不～. be unashamed of bragging. ～色 blushing.

慚愧 **tsánkwèi** (SV) be ashamed. /我覺得非常～,別人都進大學了,只有我考不上. I feel so ashamed. Everybody else is in college, but I can't pass the entrance exam.

蠶[蚕] **tsán** (N) silkworm (M條**tyáu**).

蠶豆 **tsándòu** (N) lima bean, broad bean (M顆**kē**).

殘 **tsán** (FV) wither, fade. /花已經～了. The flowers have already withered. (B) 1) cruel, ruthless. ～殺 ruthless massacre; ～暴 cruel. 2) remnant. ～餘 remnants; ～生 the remaining years of one's life.

殘廢 **tsánfèi** (N) cripple, deformed person. (FV) be crippled. /他～了. He's crippled.

殘酷 **tsánkù** (SV) be cruel, ruthless. /他們對戰俘很～. They are ruthless toward prisoners of war.

殘忍 **tsánrěn** (SV) be cruel, ruthless. /對動物不應該這麼～. You shouldn't be so cruel to animals.

慘[惨] **tsǎn** (SV) 1) be miserable. /他死後,他的家人生活過得很～. After he died, his family had a miserable life. 2) be terrible. /我輸～了. I lost terribly (<u>in gambling</u>). (IE) tragic. /～了. It's tragic (<u>usually used by students for any bad state of things</u>).

蒼 **tsāng** (B) 1) dark green. ～松 green pine trees; ～山 green mountains. 2) light blue ～天 azure sky. 3) hoary, greyish. ～白 pale, greyish-white (of the hair or face).

　　蒼蠅 **tsāngying** (N) fly (insect) (M 隻 jǐ).

倉 **tsāng** (N) shed, barn, storage place. ～庫 warehouse, place of storage.

舟倉 **tsāng** (N) cabin (on a ship).

藏 **tsáng** (FV) hide, conceal. /你～在那儿我也找得到你. No matter where you hide, I can find you. /你把我的皮包～在那儿了? Where did you hide my purse? (B) amass, hoard. 儲～store up; ～書 book collection; ～書 art collection; 冷～preserve in ice. →藏 **dzàng**.

操 **tsāu** (FV) 1) drill, exercise. ～兵 drill troops. /我們～了一個早上, 累極了. We drilled for a whole morning. We were very tired. 2) speak with a kind of language or accent. /他～着法國口音, 我一句也不懂. He spoke with a French accent. I didn't understand a word. (B) restraint imposed upon oneself. 節～integrity.

　　操場 **tsāuchǎng** (N) exercise-ground, drill-field.

　　操縱 **tsāudzùng** (FV) dominate, control, manipulate. /他～股票的市場. He controls the stock market.

　　操練 **tsāulyàn** (FV) drill (m). /我們每天要～兩個鐘頭. We have to drill for two hours every day.

　　操心 **tsāusyīn** (VO) worry over something. /他交女朋友的事你做母親的操什麼心呢? As a mother, why should you worry about his having a girl friend? (SV) be worried. /我為那事很～. I am very worried about that.

草(艸) **tsǎu** (N) grass, straw, herb, weed. (SV) be cursive in writing. ～字 running-hand characters. /他的字很～, 我認不得. His handwriting is very cursive. I can't make it out. (B) draft. ～約 a draft treaty.

　　草地 **tsǎudì** (N) lawn, meadow, pasture land.

草帽 **tsǎumaù** (N) straw hat (M 頂 dǐng).

草鞋 **tsǎusyé** (N) straw sandals (M 雙 shwāng, 隻 jǐr).

測 **tsè** (B) 1) guess, estimate. 推～infer; 猜～guess. 2) measure. ～光表 light meter. →不測 **bútsè**.

　　測量 **tsèlyáng** (FV) survey. /他們在～這儿的地形. They are surveying the topography of this place. (N) survey.

厠(廁) **tsè** (B) rest room, toilet. 厠所 **tsèswǒ** (N) rest room, bathroom, toilet (M 間 jyān).

冊 **tsè** (M) volume (of a book). 第一～Volume I. (B) <-儿> booklet, pamphlet. 手～handbook, manual; 相～photo album.

參[参] **tsēn** (B) ‡. →參 **tsān**, 參 **shēn**.

　　參差 **tsēntsz** (B) be asymmetrical. ～不齊 be uneven, not uniform.

噌 **tsēng** (FV) scold. ～他一頓 give him a scolding.

曾 **tséng** (A) have . . . before (for action completed in the past). /我～見過他. I've met him before. /我們～談過這個問題. We have discussed this question before. →曾 **dzēng**.

　　曾經 **tséngjīng** (A) have . . . before (used only in the affirmative, showing that an action was completed in the past). /我們～是很好的朋友, 但是現在不好了. We were very good friends once, but not anymore. /我～學過唱京戲, 但沒學好. I studied Chinese opera before, but I didn't learn it well.

層[层] **tséng** (M) 1) layer. 一～油漆 a coat of paint; 一～灰塵 a layer of dirt. 2) story, floor. 三～樓 three-story building. 3) for reasons or meanings. 兩～用意 two reasons.

蹭 **tsèng** (FV) 1) brush against, scrape against. /門剛漆過, 別～它. The door was just painted. Don't brush against it. 2) graze. /飛機飛得很底, 都快～着房頂了. His plane flew so low that it almost grazed the roof.

湊 **tsòu** (FV) 1) gather, put together. /幾時我們~在一起玩玩. Let's get together sometime and have fun. /我們大家~錢買一輛車吧. Let's pool money to buy a car. 2) approach, draw near to. /別人不喜歡他,他還硬~過去. Other people don't like him but he persistently attaches himself to them.

湊巧 **tsòuchyǎu** (A) by chance. /我昨天去看你,~你不在家. Yesterday I came to visit you. You happened not to be home. /他向我借錢,我~有. He wanted to borrow money from me and I happened to have it.

湊合 **tsòuhwo** (FV) 1) put up with, get along with, <u>materials or situations inferior to those desired</u>. /那房子雖不好,我還可以~. Though that house isn't any good, yet I can put up with it. /地方不好,請您~一夜吧. This place isn't good. Please make the best of things and stay here for tonight. /這個就~了. This will do. 2) cater to <u>someone</u>. /我這麼做完全是~你. I'm doing it this way just to please you. (A) <u>making things do.</u> /我找不到別的鋼筆了,你就~用這支吧. I can't find any other pen for you. Try to make do with this one.

粗(麤) **tsū** (SV) 1) be thick, wide <u>in diameter</u>, large <u>in girth</u>. /我家門口有兩棵很~的柱子. In front of my house there are two very large pillars. /他的腰真~. His waist is really big. /他氣得臉紅脖子~. He was so angry that his face turned red and his neck became thick. 2) be coarse, rough. /這件衣服做工很~. This clothing is very roughly made. /她長得很好看,但是皮膚太~. She is good looking, but her skin is too coarse. /他的眉毛比你的還~. His eyebrows are even bushier than yours. 3) be rude, vulgar. /他是一個~人. He is a vulgar person. /不要說~話. Don't talk vulgar language.

粗魯 **tsūlu** (SV) be rough, crude (fig.). /你的動作太~了. Your actions are too rough. /這種~的態度很討厭. Such crude manners are disgusting.

粗心 **tsūsyīn** (SV) be careless. /你做事不能太~. You can't be very careless while doing things. (N) carelessness.

粗糙 **tsūtsāu** (SV) be rough, coarse. /這個桌面很~. The surface of the table is very rough. /這些傢俱做得很~. This furniture is roughly made.

粗野 **tsūyě** (SV) be coarse and vulgar, unrefined (<u>of a person or one's language</u>).

醋 **tsù** (N) vinegar. (B) jealousy. 吃~ be jealous of. /他吃我的~. He is jealous of me. /他的~勁兒很大. He is very jealous.

葱 **tsūng** (N) scallion (M 根**gēn**, 棵**kē**). 洋~ onion.

聰(聰) **tsūng** (B) clever, astute. ~慧 intelligent.

聰明 **tsūngming** (SV) 1) be clever, smart, wise. /這個計劃真是太~了. This plan is really very smart. 2) intelligent, brilliant. /你的女兒真~. Your daughter is really intelligent.

從(从) **tsúng** (CV) 1) from (a time or place). /你~那兒來的? Where did you come from? /我從三點鐘就來了. I have been here since three o'clock. 2) from (a point of view). /~我的觀點看來,這問題並不簡單. From my point of view, this problem isn't simple. /~這方面講他是對的. Speaking from this aspect, he is right. (PT) 從...到 from ... to. ~家到學校 from home to school. ~早到晚 from morning to night.

從前 **tsúngchyán** (TW) (in) the past. /~我們連吃的都不夠,現在至少不會挨餓了. Before we didn't even have enough food; now at least we don't go hungry. /我希望能把~忘掉. I wish I could forget the past.

從今以後 **tsúngjīnyǐhòu** (A) from now on. /~我決不抽煙了. I'm not going to smoke from now on.

從來 **tsúnglái** (A) customarily (in the past). /他~就沒好好的念書. He has never been accustomed to studying very hard. /他~就住在這兒. He's always

257

lived here. /我～沒見過他. I've never met him.

從新 **tsúngsyīn** (A) again. /請你～寫一遍. Please write it once more. /我的論文得～寫過. I have to write my thesis all over again.

躥 **tswān** (FV) make a leap *or* sprint. /這個河我一～就能過去. I can jump over this stream.

催 **tswēi** (FV) hurry, press. ～房租 press for rent. /請別～我. Please don't hurry me.

啐 **tswèi** (FV) spit. /別往地上～唾沫. Don't spit on the floor.

搓 **tswō** (FV) 1) rub the hands. /他急得直～手. He was so anxious that he kept rubbing his hands together. 2) twist by rolling between the hands. /請你把這兩條破布～成一根繩子. Please twist these two strips of rag into a rope.

銼 **tswò** (FV) file. /她在～指甲. She's filing her fingernails. (N) <-子> file (metal) (M把**bǎ**).

錯 **tswò** (SV) be wrong. /這回是我～了. This time I'm wrong. (N) <-ㄦ> mistake, error. (A) by mistake. /對不起,我～怪你了. I'm sorry I blamed you by mistake. (B) make a mistake. ～過 miss (a chance). →不錯 **bútswò**.

　　錯誤 **tswòwu** (N) mistake.

村{邨}**tswūn** (B) <-子-ㄦ> village (M座 **dzwò**). ～姑 young village girls.

蹲 **tswún** (FV) jar, strain, an arm or leg by coming down on something stiffly. /我把腳～了. I jarred my leg. →蹲**dwūn**.

存 **tswún** (FV) 1) deposit money, check as baggage. /把我們的錢～在銀行去吧. Let's deposit our money in the bank. 2) store. /我～了很多糧食以備荒年. I've stored up a lot of grain in order to have food in time of famine. 3) keep for someone. /我要到別處去,這些東西請你替我～着. I'm going somewhere else; please keep these things for me.

存 在 **tswúndzài** (FV) continue to exist, continue to be alive. /那個問題已經不～了. That problem no longer exists. (N) existence. ～主義 existentialism.

寸 **tswùn** (M) Chinese inch. /他比我高三～. He is three inches taller than I am.

詞 **tsź** (N) 1) <-ㄦ> word (as a linguistic unit; could be one or more syllables). 2) part of speech (M種 **jǔng**). /這個字在這句話裏是什麼～? What part of speech is this word in this sentence? 3) poem of unequal lines with fixed tonal patterns (M首 **shǒu**, 闋 **chywè**). 4) lyrics. /這個歌ㄦ是他作的～. He wrote the lyrics for this song. (B) <-ㄦ> 1) words, speech. 説～ words of explanation. 2) line in a play (M句 **jyù**). 台～ dialogue in a play.

　　詞典 **tsźdyǎn** (N) lexicon, dictionary (M本 **běn**).

辭{辤}詞 (N) 1) 2) 3) (B) 2) 辭 **tsź** (FV) 1) resign, quit. /我把銀行的事情～了. I resigned from my job at the bank. 2) discharge, fire, people from a job. /我把他～了. I fired him. 3) decline. /他請我做校長,可是我～了. He asked me to be the school principal, but I declined. (N) 1) <-ㄦ> word (as a linguistic unit; could be one or more syllables). 2) part of speech (M種 **jǔng**). 形容～ adjective. 3) lyrics. (B) 1) bid farewell. ～別 say goodbye and part. 2) words, speech. 祝壽～ congratulatory speech given at a birthday party. →不辭 **bùtsź**.

　　辭呈 **'tsźchéng** (N) resignation (document) (M張 **jāng**). /他把～送上去了. He handed in his resignation.

　　辭謝 **tsźsyè** (FV) decline with thanks. /我已經把他的邀請～了. I've already declined his invitation with thanks.

　　辭行 **tsźsyíng** (VO) say goodbye to someone staying behind. /我到那ㄦ跟他～去. I'm going over there to say goodbye to him. /我跟你辭了三回行了,可是還沒走. I have already said goodbye to you three times, but I'm still here.

磁 **tsź** (B) magnetic. ~極 magnetic pole. 一瓷{磁}**tsź**.

磁實 **tsźshr** (SV) be solid, firm, strong (of things). /他書念的很~. He does solid work in his studies. /這個地板很~. The floor is very firm.

瓷{磁}**tsź** (B) porcelain, china. ~器 chinaware.

慈 **tsź** (SV) be kind, benevolent, merciful. /他的心很~. He is very kind. (B) mother (of oneself). 家~ my mother.

   慈善 **'tsźshàn** (SV) be charitable, benevolent. ~機關 charitable organization. /他對窮人很~. He is very charitable toward the poor.

次 **tsź** (M) time, occurrence. 第二~ second time. (B) 1) next in order. ~日 the next day; ~要 second most important. 2) order. 順~ in order, in succession. (SV) be inferior, no good. /這本書真~. This book is really no good. /他開車開得真~. He drives atrociously.

   次序 **'tsźsyù** (N) scheduled order of events, proper order, proper procedure.

刺 **tsź** (N) 1) thorn, splinter, sliver (M根**gēn**). 2) fishbone (M根**gēn**). (FV) stab, pierce. /蜜蜂~了我的手了. The bee stung my hand. /強盜~了他一刀. The thief stabbed him with a knife. (B) 1) kill. 行~ assassinate; ~客 assassin. 2) be unpleasant. ~眼 be harsh to the eyes, be unpleasant to the eyes; ~耳 unpleasant to the ears, piercing to the ears.

   刺刀 **tsźdāu** (N) bayonet, dagger (M把**bǎ**).

   刺激 **tsźjī** (FV) 1) upset, shock. /這個消息把他~得很厲害. This news upset him very much. /別再~他了. Don't upset him anymore. 2) stimulate. /咖啡可以~神經. Coffee can stimulate one's nerves. (SV) be exciting. /那個歌很~. That song is very exciting. (N) 1) shock. /他受過很大的~. He received a great shock. 2) stimulation, excitement.

伺 **tsź** (B) wait on, serve, people. 服~ serve a person.

伺候 **tsźhou** (FV) wait on, serve, people (as in a restaurant). /為什麼沒有茶房~我們呢? How come there isn't any waiter here to serve us? /他有好幾個佣人~他. He has several servants to wait on him.

禿 **tū** (SV) 1) be bald. /他才二十七歲,但是頭都~了. He is only twenty-seven years old, but his head is bald. 2) be blunt, worn out. /這支毛筆已經~了. This writing brush is already worn out. /鉛筆~了. The pencil isn't sharp anymore.

   禿嚕 **tūlu** (FV) 1) fall off. /他的褲帶斷了,褲子都~到腳面上了. His belt broke, and his trousers fell down to his ankles. 2) fray. /我的毛衣~了. My sweater is frayed. (RE) 1) indicates insufficiency, exhaustion of something. /我的錢花~了. My money has run out. 2) indicates letting something slip. /他跟我談天的時候說~了. He made a slip while he was chatting with me.

突 **tú** (FV) protrude. /他很近視,眼睛都~出來了. He is so nearsighted that his eyes protrude. (B) 1) sudden. ~如其來 come suddenly. 2) break. ~出重圍 break through a siege. 3) offend. 衝~ clash. *t*

   突擊 **tújī** (FV) raid, attack by surprise. /昨晚上敵軍~我們. Last night the enemy attacked us by surprise. (N) surprise attack.

   突然 **túrán** (A) suddenly. /他沒告訴我們就~走了. He left suddenly without telling us. (SV) be sudden. /這件事情太~了. This thing was awfully sudden.

圖{圖}{图}**tú** (N) diagram, chart, illustration (M張**jāng**). (FV) wish for, aim at. /你不要盡~舒服. You shouldn't just aim at comfort. /她嫁他完全是~他的錢. She married him only because of his money. (B) 1) map (M張**jāng**). 天文~ star map; 地形~ topographical map. 2) plan (M張**jāng**). 草~ rough sketch-plan; 斷面~ section plan. *t*

   圖案 **túàn** (N) design, drawing, pattern, usually made with straight, sharp lines (M 張 <u>jāng</u>). ～ 畫 design drawing as a type of art distinct from pictorial drawing.

圖 釘 **túdǐng** (N) <儿> thumbtack (M 顆 **kē**).

圖 畫 **túhwà** (N) picture, drawing, illustration (M 張 **jāng**).

圖 章 **tújāng** (N) personal name seal (M 顆 **kē**).

圖 書 **túshū** (N) 1) books (a collection). 2) illustrated book.

圖 書 館 **túshūgwǎn** (N) library.

塗[涂] **tú** (FV) 1) shade in. /這張畫還要 ～ 一層顏色呢. This picture has to be shaded once more. 2) smear, daub. ～口紅 apply lipstick; ～藥 put on or apply ointment. 3) erase, cross something out. /這一頁 ～ 得都看不清了. This page has been erased, so that it's difficult to read. 4) muddle. 糊 ～ be muddled, foolish.

徒 **tú** (B) 1) follower, disciple. 學 ～ apprentice. 2) vagrant, bum. 賭 ～ gambler; 匪 ～ bandit, robber; 奸 ～ rogue. 3) in vain. ～ 勞 labor in vain. 4) empty, bare; ～ 手 empty-handed, without any weapon at hand.

徒 步 **túbù** (A) on foot. /他們要 ～ 到組約去. They are planning to make a journey to New York on foot.

徒 弟 **túdì** (N) apprentice.

徒 刑 **túsyíng** (N) prison term. /他被判了五年 ～. He was given a five-year prison sentence.

屠 **tú** (B) slaughter. ～殺 slaughter, to butcher.

屠 戶 **'túhù** (N) butcher.

土 **tú** (N) 1) earth, soil. /把這些種子種在 ～ 裡. Plant these seeds in the earth. 2) dust, dirt. /你看我鞋上盡是 ～. See, there is dirt all over my shoes. (SV) be rustic, uncouth. /他的樣子 ～ 得很. His manner is very uncouth. (B) 1) be local. ～話 local dialect; ～ 產 local products. 2) territory. 國 ～ territory of a country. *t*

土 地 **tǔdì** (N) land.

土 豆 儿 **tǔdòur** (N) potato.

吐 **tù** ～吐 **tù**.

吐 **tù**, **tǔ*** (FV) 1)* spew forth, spit out. /別 ～ 在地上. Don't spit on the floor. 2) vomit, throw up. /我暈船, 吃了東西要 ～. I am seasick. If I eat anything, I will throw up.

吐 沫 **tùmwo** (N) saliva.

兔[兔] **tù** (B) <子,儿> rabbit, hare (M 隻 **jī**). ～缺 harelipped.

tuan *see* **twan**.

tui *see* **twei**.

tun *see* **twun**.

通 **tūng** (FV) 1) be open, free. /這個水管不 ～ 了. This water pipe isn't blocked anymore. /這條路不 ～. This road isn't open. or This road is a dead end. 2) connect with, go to. /我家後院 ～ 着他家. My back yard connects with his house. /這條路 ～ 那個村子. This road goes to that village. (SV) 1) be logical. /他說的話不 ～. What he said is illogical. 2) be well learned. /他德文已經 ～ 了. He has a thorough knowledge of German. (RE) indicates penetrating, getting through to. 說不 ～ not get through to someone by talking; 想不 ～ be unable to come up with an answer. (B) 1) all, complete, whole. ～ 身 the whole body. 2) general. ～例 general rule; ～常 generally. → 通 **tùng**.

通 告 **tūnggàu** (FV) announce. /～ 大家八點鐘開會. Announce to everybody that the meeting will be at eight o'clock. (N) announcement, bulletin, notice (M 張 **jāng**).

通 過 **tūnggwò** (FV) 1) go through. /火車 ～ 那個村子. The railroad goes through the village. 2) be passed as a motion in a meeting. /那個議案 ～ 了. That bill has been passed.

通 知 **tūngjī** (FV) inform, notify, let someone know. /請你 ～ 他明天要開會. Please inform him that we are going to hold a meeting tomorrow. /你搬家以前一個月 ～ 我們就行了. It would be all right if you let us know a month before you move out. (N) notice, information.

通 票 **tūngpyàu** (N) through ticket (M 張 **jāng**).

通 信 **tūngsyìn** (VO) communicate by letter. /你們常～嗎？ Do you write each other often? (N) 1) letters from the readers (in the newspaper).～欄 letters-to-the-editor column. 2) news dispatch.

通信處 **tūngsyìnchù** (N) mailing address.

通 行 **tūngsyíng** (FV) 1) be open to traffic (as a road, pass, frontier). /這條路夜裏不～. This road is not open to traffic during the night. 2) current and accepted (as of currency). /美金在歐洲可以～. American money can be accepted in Europe.

通 行 證 **tūngsyíngjèng** (N) pass (permit to enter or exit) (M張**jāng**).

通 訊 **tūngsyùn** (N) 1) news dispatch. 2) letter (to the editor).

通 訊 處 **tūngsyùnchù** (N) mailing address.

通訊社 **tūngsyùnshè** (N) news agency (M家**jyā**).

通訊員 **tūngsyùnywán** (N) reporter, press correspondent.

通 通 **tūngtūng** (A) thoroughly, completely. /票～賣完了. The tickets were completely sold out. /他～拿走了. He took away absolutely everything.

同〔仝〕**túng** (A) together. /我們是～ 來的. We came together. (CV) with. /你～我去嗎？ Are you going with me? (SV) be the same. /這兩個字～音不～義. These two words are the same in pronunciation, but different in meaning. (B) used between two nouns, and, as well as. 英文～中文 English and Chinese languages.

同 情 **túngchíng** (FV) sympathize with, show sympathy for. /我 ～你. I sympathize with you. (SV) be sympathetic about. /我對他的 遭遇很～. I was very sympathetic about his calamity. (N) sympathy.

同 志 **túngjr̀** (N) comrade.

同 盟 國 **túngménggwó** (N) allied country.

同 人 **túngrén** (N) equals, one's peers, one's colleagues.

同 時 **túngshr̀** (A) 1) at the same time. /他們～來的. They ar-

rived at the same time. 2) and yet, on the other hand. /你說喜歡那 個人,可是～你又說他不好. You say you like that fellow, and yet you say he's no good. 3) and, also, as well as. /他會彈琴～也會唱 歌. He can play the piano as well as sing.

同 事 **túngshr̀** (N) colleague, fellow worker. (VO) be a colleague of someone. /我們同了三年事. We have been colleagues for three years.

同 學 **túngsywé** (N) classmate, fellow-student. (VO) be in the same school with, be a schoolmate of. /我跟他同了三年學. I was in the same school with him for three years.

同 樣 **túngyàng** (A) 1) nevertheless, still. /我的車雖然舊,跑 起來～快. Although my car is old, it still runs fast. 2) as...as. /他書念得跟你～好. He is as good a student as you are. (AT) the same. /他們兩人穿～大小的 衣服. Those two wear the same size clothes.

同 意 **túngyì** (FV) consent, agree. /我～你的意思. I agree with you. (AV) consent to, agree to. /他～不去了. He agreed not to go. (N) agreement, consent. /你 得先得到他的～. You must first get his consent.

銅 **túng** (N) copper, brass, bronze. ～ 版 copper plate; ～像 bronze statue; ～釦子 brass button.

童 **túng** (B) 1) child. ～年 childhood; ～ 心 childish disposition; ～工 child-labor. 2) virgin. ～男 virgin boy; ～女 maiden.

童 子 軍 **túngdž̩jyūn** (N) boy scout.

桶 **tǔng** (N) <-子,-儿> bucket, keg, cask (M隻**jř**).

統 **tǔng** (B) 1) govern, rule. ～治 rule. 2) whole, all. ～共 all, entirely, totally. 3) succession. 傳～ tradition; 正～ true succession.

統 計 **'tǔngjì** (N) statistics.

統 制 **'tǔngjr̀** (FV) control, dominate, politically, socially, or economically. / 郵政局,電話局,鐵路局等等由政府~. The post office, the telephone system, the railway system, etc., are all controlled by the government.

統統 **túngtǔng** (A) all without exception (d). /他們~走了. They all left.

統一 **túngyī** (FV) unify. /秦始皇在公元前二二一年~中國. The Ch'in Emperor unified China in 221 B.C. (SV) be in accord, be the same. /大家的意見很~. Everybody is of the same opinion. (N) unity.

筒 **tǔng** (B) 1) <子,儿> large cylinder, tube. 信~ mail box. 2) circles (in mahjong). 二~ two of circles.

捅 **tǔng** (FV) 1) poke at, poke into. ~火 poke a fire. /他用手指頭~我一下儿. He poked me with his finger. 2) reveal a secret. /誰把這個祕密給~了? Who gave away the secret? 3) stab (lp). /他們在電梯裏把那個人給~了. They stabbed that man in the elevator.

痛 **tùng** (SV) be painful, sore. /我的頭很~. My head aches a lot. (B) 1) intensely, extremely, severely, deeply. ~罵 scold severely. 2) ache. 牙~ toothache.

痛苦 **tùngkǔ** (SV) be sad, bitter. /聽了那個消息他很~. Upon hearing that news he was very sad. (N) bitterness, sadness.

痛快 **tùngkwai** (SV) 1) be happy, satisfied. /看他挨打我就~. I feel happy when I see him being beaten up. 2) be unreserved, act without hesitation, be straightforward. /他做事很~. He is very straightforward in doing things. 3) be clear, not blocked (as one's nose or throat). /我的鼻子很不~. My nose is congested.

通 **tùng** (M) instance of doing something. /我們吵了兩~. We quarreled twice. →通 **tǔng**.

tuo see **two**.

團(团) **twán** (FV) crumple up. /別把那張紙~了. Don't crumple up

that piece of paper. (M) 1) ball of yarn, string, etc. 一~絲 a ball of silk. 2) hunk of clay, mud. 一~泥 a hunk of clay. 3) for happiness, joy, friendliness. /他一來就把我們的一~高興破壞了. As soon as he came, our happiness was spoiled. 4) for messiness, disorder. 一~糟 a mess. (N) regiment. /又調走了兩個~. Two more regiments were transferred away. (B) 1) round. ~扇 circular fan. 2) affiliate. ~結 unite; ~圓 reunited (of a couple, or parents and children). 3) group, party. 集~ group.

團長 **twánjǎng** (N) regimental commander.

團結 **twánjyé** (FV) unite. /~大家的力量,一定可以救國. If we unite everybody's power, we certainly can save our country. (SV) unified. /他們幾個人很~. Those people are very unified.

團體 **twántǐ** (N) group, organization.

圓員 **twánywán** (N) member of a group or organization.

推 **twēi** (FV) 1) push. /我~不開這個門. I can't push the door open. 2) elect, select. /我們~他為代表. We elected him as our representative. 3) make excuses in order not to do something. /他請我吃飯,叫我給~了. He asked me to dinner, but I made excuses and declined. /他明明是不理我,還~說沒看見. It was obvious that he didn't want to speak to me, but he made excuses for not seeing me. 4) postpone a date. /我們考試的日期從十五號~到二十號了. The date of our exam has been postponed from the twentieth to the fifteenth. 5) shift on to somebody else. /你~我,我~你,倒底誰該負責? We pass the buck to one another. Who's responsible anyway? 6) cut, clip, hair, lawns. ~頭 clip hair. (B) 1) to reason, deduce. ~論 to infer, a deduction. 2) promote, expand. ~行成人教育 promote adult education.

推動 **twēidùng** (FV) 1) put into action, promote. /我沒法~這個

計劃. I have no way to put this plan into action. 2) propel. /這條船是用原子能～. This ship is propelled by atomic energy.

推子 **twēidz** (N) clippers (barber's) (M把 **bǎ**).

推翻 **twēifān** (FV) overthrow, upset. /孫中山先生～滿清政府成立中華民國. Dr. Sun Yatsen overthrew the Ch'ing Dynasty and founded the Republic of China. (RC) push over. /小心別把桌子～了. Be careful not to push the table over.

推廣 **twēigwǎng** (FV) promote, expand. /我們得～成人教育. We have to promote adult education.

推銷 **twēisyāu** (FV) promote the sales of, sell in a high pressured manner. /我最討厭推銷員到家裏來～貨物. I hate more than anything to have salesmen come to my house to sell things.

推測 **twēitsè** (FV) predict that, predict a situation. /我～他不會來. I predict that he won't come. (N) prediction. /那不過是一種～. That's only a prediction.

推辭 **twēitsź** (FV) decline, refuse an offer, honor, etc. /這一點禮物是表示我的敬意的請你不要～. This little present is to express my respect to you; please don't refuse it.

推諉 **twēiwěi** (FV) 1) make excuses. /凡是人託他辦事,他總是～. Whenever people ask him to do something, he always makes excuses. 2) make excuses for the fact that. /他～他沒錢. He made excuses for the fact that he had no money.

腿 **twěi** (N) 1) <ㄦ> leg. 2) thigh (M 條 **tyáu**).

退 **twèi** (FV) 1) withdraw, retire, retreat, move back, give way. /敵軍已經～出城去了. The enemy troops have retreated from the town. /後面有車,別～. There's a car behind you, so don't back up. 2) fade (of color). /這件大衣的顏色都～了. This coat's color is all faded. 3) return money, merchandise, gifts. /我～了一門課,學校應該～我一百塊錢.

I dropped a course, so the school should refund a hundred dollars to me. /那本書不好,我要～掉. That book is no good; I want to return it to the book store.

退讓 **twèiràng** (FV) give in courteously. /你不能老～. You can't always be giving in.

拖 **twō** (FV) 1) drag, drag along (on the ground). /她的長裙子～在地上. Her skirt is dragging on the floor. 2) put off, delay, procrastinate. /這件事情又～了兩天. This matter has been delayed again for a couple of days. 3) mop. /請你把地板～一～. Will you please mop the floor?

拖拉機 **twōlājī** (N) tractor (M 架 **jyà**, 輛 **lyàng**).

拖延 **twōyán** (FV) delay, put off. /要是我們老這樣～,恐怕做不完了. If we delay like this, I'm afraid we'll never get the job done.

脫 **twō** (FV) 1) take off clothes, etc. /把大衣～了吧. Take off your coat. 2) get out of, escape from, get away from. ～險 escape from danger. /假如他們把我抓到,你也～不了. If they get me, you won't be able to get away either. 3) shed, cast off. /昨天我曬了一天太陽,今天就～皮了. I sunbathed all day yesterday so my skin is peeling today. 4) miss, omit. /這一段～了幾個字. There are a few words missing in this paragraph.

脫掉 **twōdyàu** (RC) 1) take off clothing. /我還得～一件衣裳. I must take off another article of clothing. 2) avoid responsibility, involvement. /你反正脫不掉責任. Anyway, you can't avoid the responsibility.

脫離 **twōlí** (FV) break off, cease. ～父子關係 break off a father-son relationship. /他的病已經～危險期了. His illness has passed the critical stage.

托{託}(FV) 3) 4)} **twō** (FV) 1) carry, support on the palm. /她手裡～着一個盤子. She carried a tray on her palm. 2) lay something underneath something. /在紙下面～一張複寫紙. Lay a piece of carbon paper underneath the paper. 3) entrust, ask someone to take care of something for one as a favor, commit to the care of. /我有一點事要～你辦. I have something I want to ask you to do for me. /這事我～你了. I'll entrust you with this matter. /他把財產都～我管了. He entrusted all his property to me. (B) 1) <子,儿> tray. 茶～ tray for carrying teacups. 2) use something as a pretext. ～故 make an excuse. t

托兒所 twōérswǒ (N) nursery school (M 家 jyā, 所 swǒ).

托付 twōfu (FV) entrust someone with something. /我們把那件事～給他了. We entrusted him with this work. /你～～他. Have him take care of it.

托福 twōfú (VO) very polite and high-toned answer to a greeting, implying that one is well because of the benign influence of the person spoken to. /A: 您好啊? B: 托您的福 or ～～! A: How are you? B: I'm fine, thanks. /我們都挺好,托您福. We're all well, thanks.

馱 twó (FV) carry on the back (of an animal, not a human). /那頭驢馱了兩筐菜. The donkey has two baskets of vegetables on its back. /用驢把菜～到市上去. Take the vegetables to market on the donkey's back.

妥 twǒ (SV) 1) be safe, secure. /這樣辦很～. It's quite safe to do it this way. 2) be reliable. /這個人很～,你可以信任他. That person is very reliable; you can trust him. (RE) indicates settlement of something. /價錢已經說～了. The price has already been settled.

妥當 twǒdàng (SV) 1) be safe, secure. /錢交給他管很～. It's safe to give him the money to take care of. 2) be reliable. /我的用人很～. My servant is very reliable. (RE) indicates settlement of something. /事情已經辦理～了. That thing has already been settled.

妥靠 twǒkàu (SV) be reliable, dependable (of a person). /他年紀太輕,所以不太～. He is too young, so he isn't too reliable.

唾 twò (B) saliva. ～液 saliva.

唾沫 twòmwo (N) saliva, spittle.

吞 twūn (FV) 1) swallow. /這藥丸我～不下去. I can't swallow this pill. 2) appropriate illicitly. /我們捐來的款子叫他給～了. The money we raised was embezzled by him. (B) repress one's emotion. 忍氣～聲 hold back one's temper and keep silent.

天 tyān (N) 1) day. 三～ three days. 2) sky. 藍～ blue sky. 3) Heaven, divinity. ～意 the will of God. 4) <儿> weather. /今儿～很好. The weather is nice today. (B) 1) season. 春～ spring season. 2) natural, inborn. ～資 natural ability; ～良 natural goodness.

天邊 tyānbyar (PW) <儿> 1) horizon. 2) the ends of the earth. /你逃到～我也能找到你. Even if you go to the ends of the earth, I'll track you down.

天氣 tyānchi (N) weather.

天花 tyānhwā (N) <儿> smallpox.

天真 tyānjēn (SV) be innocent, natural, unaffected (of a person or his behavior).

天井 tyānjǐng (N) courtyard in a compound.

天主 tyānjǔ (N) God (Roman Catholic term). (B) Roman Catholic. ～教 Catholicism; ～堂 Catholic church (building).

天空 tyānkūng (PW) (in) the sky. /～有一片白雲. There is a white cloud in the sky. /～是藍色的. The sky is blue.

天亮 tyānlyàng (A) at daybreak. /我們～就可以走. We can go at daybreak.

天秤 'tyānpíng (N) balance, scales, with two trays hanging from a beam (M 架 jyà).

天然 tyānrán (AT) natural, untouched, not artificial. ～風景 natural scenery.

天上 **tyānshang** (PW) (in) the sky, the heavens. /~有雲彩.- There are clouds in the sky. /一顆慧星從~過去了. A comet passed through the heavens.

天生 **tyānshēng** (A) naturally, by nature. /她~漂亮. She is naturally beautiful. /他~是聾子. He is a dummy by nature.

天使 **tyānshř** (N) angel (Christian term).

天線 **tyānsyàn** (N) aerial, antenna (M條 **tyáu**, 根 **gēn**).

天才 **'tyāntsái** (N) genius, talent. /他有~. He has talent. /他們以為他們的孩子是個~. They think their child is a genius.

天天 **tyāntyān** (A) every day. /他~到我家來. He comes to my house every day.

天文 **tyānwén** (N) astronomy.

添 **tyān** (FV) add, obtain, additional personnel, money, materials, etc. /我們~了點新傢俱. We've added some new furniture. /他們新~了一個孩子. They just had a baby. (lit. They just added a baby to the family.) /天冷,你~點衣服吧. It's cold, you'd better put on some more clothes.

田 **tyán** (N) field, cultivated land, farm (M塊 **kwài**, 畝 **mǔ**). (B) rural, agricultural. ~莊 farmhouse. s

田地 **tyándì** (N) 1) arable land (M塊 **kwài**). 2) difficult straits. /你怎麼弄到這步~? How did you get into such a mess?

填 **tyán** (FV) fill in, fill up. ~表 fill out a form. /得用多少沙才能~得上那個坑呀? How much sand should be used to fill in that ditch?

甜 **tyán** (SV) be sweet. ~酸肉 sweet and pungent pork. /她說話很~. She talks very sweetly.

甜瓜 **tyángwa** (N) muskmelon.
甜蜜 **tyánmí** (SV) be pleasant, sweet. /那時候的回憶很~. The recollections of that time are very sweet.

舔 **tyǎn** (FV) lick, lap. /那條狗老~我的臉. That dog always licks my face.

挑 **tyāu** (FV) 1) carry on the shoulder with a pole. /他每天得~兩桶水. He has to carry two buckets of water every day. 2) choose, select, pick out. /把壞的蘋果~出來吧. Let's pick the rotten apples out. /你給我~一個好的. Choose a good one for me, please. (M) carrying-pole load (two filled baskets or buckets carried on a pole). 一~水果 a carrying-pole load of fruit; 一~水 a carrying-pole load of water. (B) <子,-儿> carrying pole with two baskets or buckets. 一挑 **tyāu**.

挑選 **tyāusywǎn** (FV) select, pick out. /他們~我來做這樁事. They selected me to do this job.

挑剔 **tyāutī** (SV) be choosy, particular. /他對衣服很~. He's very particular about clothes. (FV) find fault with someone. /我一說話他就~我. Whenever I speak he finds fault with me.

條[条] **tyáu** (M) 1) for long, narrow things. 一~河 a river; 一~街 a street or road; 一~絲帶 a ribbon. 2) article in a newspaper, magazine, or document. 一~新聞 a news story; 美國憲法第三~ Article 3 of the U.S. Constitution. 3) for some animals and crawling things. 一~狗 a dog; 一~牛 a cow; 一~蟲 a worm. (B) 1) <子,-儿> note, short message (M張 **jāng**). 便~ brief note. 2) <子,-儿> stripe, band. 星~旗 stars and stripes. 3) <儿> long, narrow thing. 麵~ noodle.

條件 **tyáujyàn** (N) terms, conditions.
條款 **tyáukwǎn** (N) article in a treaty or other document (M條 **tyáu**).
條約 **tyáuywē** (N) treaty.

調 **tyáu** (B) 1) stir up, mix. ~色 mix colors (for painting); ~漿糊 make paste by mixing powder in water and stirring. 2) regulate, tune. ~弦 tune a stringed instrument; ~整 regulate; ~音 to tune. 3) provoke. ~情 flirt with; ~皮 naughty, artful. 一調 **dyàu**.

調羹 **tyáugēng** (N) spoon (M隻 **jr**, 把 **bǎ**).

調劑 tyáují (FV) 1) add variety to. /你每天工作,也該看看電影～～. You work every day; you ought to add variety to your life by going to the movies. 2) rationalize, regulate. /我們應該把人事～一下. We should shift our personnel around. (N) change of routine.

調停 tyáuting (FV) mediate, act as an intermediary, in the settlement of difficulties. /你為什麼不出來給他們～～? Why didn't you come out and mediate between them? /中國和日本打仗,瑞士出來～. Switzerland acted as an intermediary during the war between China and Japan.

笤 tyáu (B) broom. ～把 long-handled broom.

笤帚 tyáushu, tyáujou (N) broom (M 把 bǎ).

挑 tyáu (FV) poke, probe. ～刺 dig out a splinter. (B) provoke, stir up. ～逗 provoke emotion. →挑tyāu.

挑撥 tyǎubwo (FV) provoke, cause bad relations between, people. /他們兩人被人～打起架來了. Those two were stirred up by someone, and have started to quarrel.

挑戰 tyǎujàn (FV) challenge to battle, provoke a fight. /你敢向他～嗎? Do you dare challenge him? (N) challenge. /我接受他的～了. I accepted his challenge.

跳 tyàu (FV) 1) jump, leap, hop. /你～得過去嗎? Can you jump over? 2) pulsate. /我高興得心～. My heart is throbbing with joy. /他的心～得很快. His heart beat very fast. 3) skip a line, row, column. /你～了一行. You skipped a line.

跳板 tyàubǎn (N) 1) diving board. 2) gangplank (M塊kwài).

跳蚤 tyàudzàu (N) flea (M 隻jř).

跳高兒 tyàugāur (FV) do the high-jump. /今天我們要～. We are going to do the high-jump today. (N) high-jump.

跳舞 tyàuwǔ (VO) dance. /我們跳了一整晚的舞. We danced for a whole night. (N) dancing. /我很喜歡～. I like dancing very much.

跳遠 tyàuywǎn (VO) <-儿> do the broad-jump. /今天我跳了個鐘頭的遠. I did the broad-jump for two hours today. (N) broad-jump.

貼 tyē (FV) 1) stick something to, paste something onto. /我把新相片都～好了. I have finished pasting in all the new photographs. 2) pay an additional amount. /你～他點錢他也許就幹了. If you give him some more money, he will probably do it. 3) pay out money from one's own pocket. /這次到華盛頓去開會,我～了兩百塊錢. I paid two hundred dollars out of my own pocket when I went to the meeting in Washington this time. (CV) <着> against, close to. /油漆還沒乾呢,別～着門站. The paint still isn't dry; don't lean against the door. (B) settled. 妥～ be well arranged.

帖 tyē (B) 1) smoothly. 妥～ settled. 2) submit. ～服 be submissive. →帖tyě, 帖 tyè.

帖 tyě (B) <-子,-儿> card, note (M 張 jāng). 請～ invitation card. →帖tyē, 帖 tyè.

鐵[鉄,鐡,鐡] tyě (N) iron (the metal). (B) firm, rigid, strong. ～漢 strong man, strong-willed man; ～定 decide definitely; ～軍 strong army.

鐵板 tyěbǎn (N) sheet iron (M 塊kwài).

鐵軌 tyégwěi (N) iron rail, railroad rail (M條tyáu).

鐵甲車 tyějyǎchē (N) armored car (M輛lyàng).

鐵架子 tyějyàdz (N) andiron (M付fù,對dwèi).

鐵匠 tyějyang (N) blacksmith.

鐵路 tyělù (N) railroad (M 條 tyáu).

鐵鍁 tyěsyān (N) shovel (M把 bǎ).

帖 tyè (N) book of model calligraphy (M 本 běn). →帖 tyē, 帖 tyě.

哇 wa (P) used in place of 啊a, when the preceding word ends in the sound u, au, or ou. /誰去買肉～? Who's going out to buy the meat? →哇wā.

挖 **wā** (FV) 1) dig. /～了三十尺才見水. They dug thirty feet into the ground before they found water. /～一個坑把這個樹種起來. Let's dig a hole in the ground and plant this tree. 2) scoop out, dig out. ～眼睛 gouge out the eyes. /他從地裡～了很多花生. He dug a lot of peanuts out of the field. 3) take, snatch, personnel away from a firm or institution. /那個新成立的大學～去我們兩位教授. That newly-founded college took two of our professors away.

娃 **wá** (B) 1) baby, child. 胖～儿 a fat baby. 2) pretty girl, "babe." 嬌～ pretty girl.
　娃娃 **wáwa** (N) 1) baby. 2) doll. 泥～ clay doll.

瓦 **wǎ** (N) roof tile (M塊 **kwài**, 片 **pyàu**). (AT) earthenware, clay. ～盆 earthenware basin. *i*
　瓦匠 **wǎjyang** (N) mason.
　瓦斯 **wǎsz** (N) gaseous substance.

瓦 **wà** (FV) plaster tiles on something. /找個人來把房頂～上瓦. Get somebody to plaster tiles on the roof. →瓦 **wǎ**.

襪(袜) **wà** (B) <子> sock, stocking (M 隻 jī, 雙 **shwāng**). 毛～ woolen stocking *or* sock.

歪 **wāi** (SV) be crooked, askew, tilted. /旗桿又～了. The flagpole is tilted again. (FV) lean to one side, tip. /請你向左～一～. Please lean to the left a little bit. (A) at an angle. /他～戴着帽子. He wears his hat at an angle. (B) wicked. ～念頭 bad idea. →歪 **wǎi**.

歪 **wǎi** (FV) twist *or* turn (as of a leg, ankle, foot, etc.). /我把脚～了. I turned my ankle. →歪 **wǎi**.

外 **wài** (L) outside. 向～跑 run outside; 國～ outside the country; ～蒙古 outer Mongolia. (A) externally. 這個藥只能～用. This medicine can only be used externally. (B) 1) foreign. ～貨 foreign goods. 2) with certain kinship terms, indicates relatives by marriage. ～姪 wife's nephew.

外邊 **wàibyan** (PW) <儿>
1) outer surface of something. /我的衣服～不髒裏邊很髒. The outside of my clothes is clean, but the inside is dirty. 2) area outside something. /房子的～很乾淨. The area outside the house is very clean. 3) outside. /～沒有人了. There's no one outside.
　外祖父 **wàidzǔfù** (N) grandfather (maternal).
　外祖母 **wàidzúmǔ** (N) grandmother (maternal).
　外公 **wàigūng** =外祖父 **wàidzúfù**.
　外國 **wàigwó** (N) foreign country.
　外行 **wàiháng** (N) dilettante, layman. (SV) be ignorant. /對那個問題我很～. I'm rather ignorant about that subject.
　外號 **wàihàu** (N) <儿> nickname.
　外科 **wàikē** (N) 1) surgery. 2) surgical department.
　外面 **wàimyan** =外邊 **wàibyan**.
　外婆 **wàipwó** =外祖母 **wàidzúmǔ**.
　外甥 **wàisheng** (N) nephew (sister's son).
　外孫 **wàiswūn** (N) <子> grandson (daughter's son).
　外頭 **wàitou** =外邊 **wàibyan**.

彎(弯) **wān** (FV) bend. /我的腿不能～了. I can't bend my leg. (SV) be bent, curved, curly (of hair). /那根管子太～了，水都流不過去了. That pipe is so bent that water can't flow through it. (B) <子儿> curve. 轉～ turn a corner.

豌 **wān** (B) ↓.
　豌豆 **wāndòu** (N) pea (M顆 **kē**, 粒 lì).

完 **wán** (FV) finish, complete. /等我～了這件事就去. I'll go as soon as I finish this work. /電影還沒～呢. The movie isn't finished yet. /我～了. I'm through. (RE) indicates completion, finishing. 用～ use up *or* finish using. (B) perfect, complete. ～備 be fully equipped, prepared.
　完成 **wánchéng** (FV) finish, complete. /這件工作限你三十

天～. You should finish this work within thirty days.

完全 **wánchywán** (SV) be complete. (A) perfectly, entirely, completely. /他～不懂英文. He doesn't understand English at all.

完了 **wánle** (IE) Thank you, that's all (used at the end of a speech).

頑 **wán** (B) 1) foolish, stupid. 愚～ stupid and dull. 2) obstinate ～疾 persistent ailment. 3) mischievous. ～童 mischievous boy.

頑強 **wánchyáng** (SV) be stubborn, obstinate. /他的態度很～ His attitude is very obstinate. (A) obstinately. /敵人～抵抗. The enemy resists obstinately.

頑固 **wángu** (SV) be obstinate, stubborn. /他的思想很～. His way of thinking is very stubborn.

頑皮 **wánpí** (SV) be naughty, mischievous. /這個孩子～的不得了. This child is extremely mischievous.

玩 **wán** (B) 1) play. 遊～play, sightseeing. 2) despise. ～忽 underestimate and neglect. 3) curio, antique. 珍～ precious curios.

玩兒 **wár** (FV) 1) amuse oneself (with), play (with). ～球 play ball; ～牌 play cards. /他坐在草地上～樹葉子. He's sitting on the lawn playing with the fallen leaves. 2) keep, raise, collect, something as a hobby. /他～熱帶魚. He raises tropical fish.

玩具 **wánjyù** (N) toy.

玩耍 **wánshwǎ** (FV) play. /孩子們在院子裡～. The children are playing in the front yard.

玩笑 **wánsyàu** (N) joke, prank. (FV) play a prank on, joke with, someone. /你別跟我～. Don't joke with me.

玩意兒 **wányèr** (N) 1) toy. 2) skill, talent, of a performer on the stage. 3) thing. 新鮮～new thing. 4) jerk (the person). /他是什麼～? What kind of a jerk is he?

丸 **wán** (B) <子,-儿> 1) pill, small ball (M 顆 **kē**, 粒 **lì**). 藥～ medicine in pill form; 彈～ bullet. 2) <子> meatball. 魚～湯 fish-ball soup.

碗{匜} **wǎn** (N) bowl, cup (M 隻 **jī**). 茶～ teacup.

晚 **wǎn** (SV) be late. /天儿～了. It's getting late. /我今天起～了. I got up late today. (B) 1) evening, night. ～課 evening class; 昨～ yesterday evening. 2) latter. ～母 stepmother; ～輩 younger generations.

晚飯 **wǎnfàn** (N) evening meal, supper.

晚年 **wǎnnyán** (TW) later years of one's life. /他～很可憐. The later years of his life were very wretched.

晚上 **wǎnshang** (TW) (in the) evening. /我～來. I'll come in the evening. /～比早上好. The evening is much better than the morning.

萬{万}**wàn** (A) used before negative expressions, absolutely. /你～不可去. You absolutely may not go. (M) ten thousand. 三～人 thirty thousand people. (B) all. ～能刀 all-purpose knife. s t

萬歲 **wànswèi** (IE) 1) hurrah. /～～! Hurrah, hurrah! 2) long live.... /女皇～! Long live the queen.

萬萬 **wànwàn** (M) hundred million. 六～ six hundred million. (A) used before negative expression, absolutely, by all means. /你～別跟他説. You absolutely must not tell him.

萬一 **wànyī** (A) in case, if by any chance. /～他不給錢,我就給. I'll pay in case he doesn't.

忘{亡}**wáng** (B) ı. →忘**wàng**.

忘八 **wángbā, wángba** (N) 1) tortoise. 2) cuckold.

往 **wǎng** (CV) toward, in the direction of. /他～海邊去了. He went in the direction of the beach. /你～那儿去? Where are you going? /～好裡做 work toward improvement. ～好處想 think about the good side of it. (B) past, formerly. ～日 in bygone days; ～時 formerly, in the past. →往**wàng**.

往後 **wǎnghòu** (TW) from now on, in the future. /這些錯誤～你不要再犯了. Don't repeat your mistakes again in the future. /我到現在還這麼窮,對～也不存希望了. I've been so poor up to now that I don't have any hope for my future either.

往年 **wǎngnyán** (TW) 1) in the past. /～那個國家的出生率很低. In the past that country has had a very low birth rate. 2) the years gone by. /～是我一生中最快樂的一段了. The years gone by were the happiest period of my life.

往往 **wǎngwǎng** (A) sometimes. /他～為一些小事生氣. He sometimes gets mad for some very unimportant reason. /金錢～使人喪失氣節. Money sometimes makes a man lose his integrity. /他對大事都處理得很好,但～對小事猶豫不決. He handles important things very well, but is sometimes indecisive about small problems.

網[网] **wǎng** (N) <子> net. 鐵絲～wire netting; 漁～fish net; 髮～hair-net; 蜘蛛～spider's web; ～球tennis.

忘 **wàng** (FV) forget. /我～了去了. I forgot to go. →忘**wàng**.

忘記 **wàngjì** (AV) forget to. /千萬別～帶錢來. Don't forget to bring money with you. (FV) forget. /他把過去的事都～了. He forgot all about the past.

望 **wàng** (CV) toward, in the direction of. ～東走 go eastward. (B) 1) hope, expect. 希～hope. 2) visit. 看～pay a visit. 3) look toward. 瞭～look down at from a distance. 4) fame. 名～prestige.

望遠鏡 **wàngywǎnjìng** (N) field glasses, telescope (M架 **jyà**).

妄 **wàng** (B) 1) absurd, fantastic. ～誕 be fantastic. 2) false. ～證perjury. 3) rash. ～動 act rashly.

妄想 **'wàngsyǎng** (AV) hope in vain to. /你別～娶她了. Don't have any pipe dreams about marrying her. (N) wishful thinking, vain hopes.

旺 **wàng** (SV) 1) be flourishing, prosperous. /他的買賣做得很～. He does a flourishing business. 2) be

strong, fierce (fig.). /火～極了. The fire is extremely fierce.

旺盛 **wànshèng** (SV) be flourishing, prosperous. /那個軍隊的士氣很～. That army's morale is flourishing.

威 **wēi** (B) 1) imperious, severe. ～儀 dignified manner; ～望 prestige; 發～ show severity. 2) threaten. ～脅 intimidate. t

威風 **wēifeng** (SV) be awe-inspiring, impressive. /他騎在馬上～極了. He was very impressive, riding on a horse. (N) awe-inspiring appearance of a person.

危 **wēi** (B) 1) danger. ～急 be dangerous and urgent; ～害 endanger. 2) lofty. ～樓 lofty building.

危險 **wēisyǎn** (SV) be dangerous, critical. /大雪的時候開車很～. It's very dangerous to drive in a snow storm. (N) danger.

微 **wēi** (B) tiny, small, slight. ～生物 microbes; 顯～鏡microscope.

微風 **wēifēng** (N) breeze, light wind (M陣 **jèn**).

圍 **wéi** (FV) 1) wrap around. /他～了一條毯子. He wrapped a blanket around himself. 2) surround, enclose. /警察把那所房子～起來了. The police surrounded that house. 3) besiege. /敵人把城～起來了. The enemy besieged the city. (M) span equal to that of both arms outstretched. 十～大的樹 a tree with a circumference of ten such spans. (B) 1) <子> rampart. ～壘 rampart. 2) <子> curtain hung before a table or chair. 桌～ curtain hung before a table. 3) woman's measurements. 三～ the three measurements.

圍脖兒 **wéibwór** (N) scarf, muffler (M條 **tyáu**).

圍牆 **wéichyáng** (N) wall enclosing something (M道 **dàu**).

圍裙 **wéichyun** (N) apron (M條 **tyáu**).

圍巾 **wéijīn** (N) scarf, muffler (M塊 **kwài**, 條 **tyáu**).

為{爲}[为] **wéi** (FV) be. /在中國十寸～一尺. In China, ten inches is one foot. (B) 1) <u>before a noun and after a verbal expression</u>, as. /我尊他 ～老師. I regard him as my teacher. /他們推他～主席. They elected him as chairman. 2) do, behave, act. 行～ behavior; ～善 perform good deeds. (PT)～...所.... be ... ed by .... /他是～朋友 所賣. He was sold out by his friend. →為 wèi.

為難 wéinán (FV) make trouble. /他們想盡法子～我. They think of every way to make trouble for me. (VO) be in a difficult position. /這個問題真叫我為了許 多難. You really put me in a difficult position by asking this question.

為人 wéirén (N) character. /我不喜歡他的～. I don't like his character. (FV) behave properly. /他不知道怎麼～. He doesn't know how to behave properly.

唯(惟)wéi (B) only. 不～ not only.

唯心主義 wéisyīnjǔyì (N) idealism.

唯物主義 wéiwùjǔyì (N) materialism.

唯一 wéiyī (AT) only, sole. /他是我們公司～會說英文的 人. He is the only one in our company who can speak English. /這是 我～的一本書. This is the only book I have.

維 wéi (B) maintain, hold together. ～ 繫 fasten together, maintain, <u>a relationship</u>. t

維持 'wéichŕ (FV) maintain, keep up, hold together. /他負責～ 會場裡的秩序. He's responsible for maintaining order during the meeting. /他的薪水不夠他 ～生活. He doesn't make enough money to maintain a living.

違 wéi (B) disobey, oppose. ～法 disobey the law; ～背 act contrary to, disobey.

違反 wéifǎn (FV) violate, be against. /他開車常常～交通 規則. He often violates traffic regulations when he drives. /不要 ～他的意思. Don't be against him.

委 wěi (FV) appoint, depute. /上面～

了他一個市長. The superiors appointed him mayor. (B) 1) abandon, give up. ～棄 discard. 2) really, indeed. ～實 truly.

委屈 wěichyu (SV) be wronged, feel grievances. /他覺得很～. He feels that he's been wronged. (FV) wrong <u>someone</u>, treat <u>someone</u> unjustly. /你為什麼～我? Why do you treat me unjustly? (N) grievance, raw deal. /我不能忍受這 種～. I can't stand this kind of raw deal.

委托 wěitwō (FV) 1) entrust, ask <u>someone</u> to do <u>something</u>. /我們 ～他交涉那件事. We entrusted him to negotiate that matter. 2) entrust <u>something to someone or someone with something</u>. /我把我 所有的財產～給他了. I entrusted all my belongings to him. (N) mandate.

委婉 wěiwǎn (SV) be indirect, amiable. /他的態度很～. He has an amiable manner. /他的話 說得很～. He talked very indirectly.

委員 wěiywán (N) 1) member of a committee. 2) commissioner.

委員會 wěiywánhwèi (N) committee, commission.

尾 wěi (M) for fish. 一～鯉魚 a carp. (B) 1) tail. 馬～ pony tail; 雞～酒 會 cocktail party. 2) end. 首～ beginning and end; 船～ stern of a boat; 巷～ end of a lane. →尾 yǐ.

尾巴 wěiba (N) tail (M 條 tyáu).

偉 wěi (B) great, heroic. ～人 great man; 魁～ large <u>physically</u>.

偉大 wěidà (SV) be great. /他的人格很～. He has a great personality.

位 wèi (M) 1) <u>for persons</u> (h). 三～小 姐 three young ladies. 2) <u>for digits in a number</u>. 六～數 figure with six digits. (B) 1) <子> seat. 客～ guest seat. 2) position. ～次 sequence, order; 學～ academic degree.

位置 wèijr (N) position. /這 個桌子～不對. This table isn't in the right position. /他在那個 機關～很高. He has a very high position in that organization.

為{爲}{为} **wèi** (CV) <着> for the benefit of, for, <u>something or someone</u>. /我~你才來的. I came only for you. /我~大家做的那件事. I did that for the benefit of everybody.
—為 **wéi**.
　　為了 **wèile** =為 **wèi**.
　　為什麼 **wèishémma** (A)�q why, for what reason. /你~打他? Why are you hitting him?

衛{衞}{卫} **wèi** (B) protect, guard. 自~ self-defense; 防~ protect.
　　衛兵 **wèibīng** (N) guard, sentry (m).
　　衛生 **wèishēng** (SV) be hygienic, sanitary. /向地下吐痰很不~. It's very unsanitary to spit on the ground. (N) hygiene, sanitation. 有礙~ be dangerous to health, unsanitary.
　　衛星 **wèisyīng** (N) satellite. 人造~ man-made satellite; ~國 satellite country.

喂{餵,飼}(FV)} **wèi** (FV) feed (<u>a child, an animal</u>). /我得~馬去. I must go feed the horse. /小孩哭了,應該~他了. The baby is crying, you should feed him now. (I) Hello, Hi. /~,~,~,~,電話壞了吧! Hello, hello, hello, hello! This telephone must be broken. /~,你上那兒去啊? Hi, where are you going?

胃 **wèi** (N) stomach.
　　胃口 **wèikou** (N) appetite. /我今天沒有~. I have no appetite today. /這個東西不對他的~. This isn't to his taste (lit. or fig.).

味 **wèi** (M) 1) <u>for medicine</u>. /這個藥方有五~藥. This prescription is made up of five medicines. 2) <u>for courses</u>. 兩~菜 two courses. (B) <儿> 1) taste, flavor. ~覺 sense of taste. 2) <儿> smell, odor (M 股 **gǔ**). 香~ perfume, fragrance.

未 **wèi** (B) not yet. ~成年 not yet of age.
　　未必 **wèibì** (A) not necessarily. /他~來. He may not necessarily come.
　　未婚妻 **wèihwūnchī** (N) fiancée.
　　未免 **wèimyǎn** (A) rather, more or less. /這個東西很好,可是

/~太貴了. This thing is quite good, but rather too expensive.

溫 **wēn** (FV) 1) warm up cold things. ~酒 warm wine. /請你把這碗剩菜~一~. Will you please warm up this bowl of leftovers? 2) review studies. /昨天晚上我沒~功課. I didn't review the lesson last night. (B) 1) temperature. 體~ body temperature. 2) warm. ~泉 hot spring. 3) gentle, mild. ~柔 be gentle. s t
　　溫度 **wēndù** (N) temperature. 試~ take <u>someone's</u> temperature; ~表 thermometer. /他的~很高. He has a high temperature.
　　溫和 **wénhé** (SV) 1) be amiable, gentle (<u>of a person</u>). /他的脾氣很~. He's very amiable. 2) be warm (<u>of climate</u>).
　　溫和 **wēnhwo** (SV) be moderately warm (<u>of things</u>). /這杯水剛才很燙,現在已經很~了. This glass of water was hot before, but it's only moderately warm now.
　　溫習 **'wēnsyí** (FV) review (<u>of studies</u>). /我得把數學~~,因為明天考試. I have to review mathematics, because there's an examination tomorrow.

瘟 **wēn** (B) epidemic. 牛~ cattle plague.
　　瘟疫 **wēnyì** (N) plague (<u>disease</u>).

文 **wén** (SV) be classical (<u>of literature or writing</u>). /他寫的信太~了,所以我看不懂. His letter was too classical, so I couldn't understand it. (B) 1) literature. ~科 liberal arts curriculum. 2) civil, civilian. ~官 civil servant. 3) language. ~法 grammar; 英~ English. 4) essay, article, writing. 作~ composition. 5) culture. ~化 culture. 6) elegant. ~靜 be graceful.
　　文字 **wéndz** (N) 1) written language, script. 中國~ Chinese script. 2) phraseology. /他的~很好. His phraseology is very good. /這篇文章的~很美. The phraseology of this article is beautiful.
　　文化 **wénhwà** (N) culture.
　　文化館 **wénhwàgwǎn** (N) museum.

文火 **wénhwǒ** (N) low flame, low heat, for cooking.

文章 **'wénjāng** (N) 1) article, essay (M 篇 **pyān**). 2) implication. /他那句話裡一定有～. There must be some implication in what he said.

文明 **wénmíng** (N) civilization. (SV) be civilized. /你～一點好不好? How about being a little more civilized?

文選 **wénsywǎn** (N) prose anthology (M 本 **běn**, 部 **bù**).

文學 **wénsywé** (N) literature.

文學士 **wénsywéshř** (N) bachelor of arts.

文雅 **'wényǎ** (SV) be cultured, well bred, genteel, elegant (of a person).

文藝 **wényì** (N) literature and fine arts.

聞 **wén** (FV) smell, sniff. /我一～ 就知道那是好酒. As soon as I smelled it, I knew it was good wine. (B) 1) information. 新～ news; 傳～ rumor. 2) hear. ～訊 hear the news. 3) famous. ～人 famous man.

蚊 **wén** (B) <子> mosquito (M 隻 **jř**).

蚊帳 **wénjàng** (N) mosquito net (M 床 **chuáng**).

穩[穩] **wěn** (SV) 1) be steady. /那輛車 走的很～. That car rides very smoothly. 2) be even-tempered (of a person). /我哥哥做事～極了. My older brother goes about things very calmly. (A) definitely, doubtlessly, certainly. /這場官司你 ～打贏. You'll doubtlessly win the law case. (RE) indicates stability. /請你站～一點. Stand still, please.

穩當 **wěndang** (SV) 1) be secure, safe. /錢存在銀行比較在家 裡更～. It is safer to put your money in the bank than to keep it in your house. 2) be steady, firm. /我的工作相當～. My job is pretty steady. 3) be reliable. /他 那個人做事很～. He is reliable in doing things.

穩固 **wěngù** (SV) be firm, stable. /這個根基打得很～. This foundation (physical, financial, of human relationships, etc.) has been built very firmly.

問 **wèn** (FV) 1) ask, inquire about. /別～那麼多問題. Don't ask so many questions. 2) interrogate. /你就～他好了,別打他. Just interrogate him, don't beat him up. (B) send regards to someone. ～好 send regards to someone.

問安 **wènān** (FV) extend greetings to someone older or to a superior. /請你替我向令尊～. Please give my greetings to your father.

問候 **wènhou** (FV) give regards to, greet. /請你替我～他. Give him my best regards.

問詢處 **wènsyùnchù** (N) information desk.

問題 **wèntí** (N) 1) problem. /目前有很多～得解決. There are quite a few problems before us that have to be solved. 2) question. /他問的～我都答不上來. I can't answer any of his questions.

窩 **wō** (N) nest, burrow, hive, or other home of animals, birds, or insects. 鳥～ bird's nest; 蜂～ beehive. (FV) 1) bend something. /別把照 片～了. Don't bend the picture. /我的胳臂～了. My arm was twisted. 2) harbor someone or something. ～匪 harbor a robber.

窩兒 **wōr** (N) small cavity. 酒 ～ dimple; 胳肢～ armpit.

窩頭 **wōtóu** (N) bread made of corn flour, shaped like a beehive.

我 **wǒ** (PN) 1) I. 2) used before a noun, my. ～哥哥 my brother. (B) our. ～軍 our army; ～國 our country.

我們 **wǒmen** (PN) 1) we (the person spoken to might not be included). /～學校明天放假,你們呢? We'll have a day off from school tomorrow, how about you? /～什麼 時候走? Where are we going? 2) used before a noun, our. ～校長 our principal.

握 **wò** (B) hold fast. 掌～ control, grasp.

握手 **wòshǒu** (VO) shake hands. /從前中國不興～. Formerly, it was not fashionable to shake hands in China.

臥 **wò** (FV) lie in a prone position (usually of animals). /狗在門口～著

呢. The dog is lying by the door. /他能叫那條獅子～在地上. He can make that lion lie down on the ground. (B) sleeping. ～房 bedroom; ～車 sleeping car; ～舖 berth (in a sleeping car).

屋 **wū** (B) 1) <子,儿> room (M間 **jyàn**). ～門 door of a room. 2) house (d). 造～ build a house.

烏 **wū** (B) 1) crow or rook. 白頭～ white-headed crow. 2) black. ～雲 black cloud; ～梅 black plums; ～木 ebony; ～賊 cuttlefish. t

　　烏龜 **wūgwēi** (N) 1) black tortoise. 2) cuckold.

　　烏黑 **wūhēi** (SV) be jet black. /她的頭髮～. She has jet black hair.

　　烏鴉 **wūyā** (N) crow (M隻 **jī**).

無[无] **wú** (B) 1) without. ～恥 shameless. 2) no matter, regardless. 事～大小 no matter whether the issue is big or small.

　　無產階級 **'wúchǎnjyējí** (N) proletarian class.

　　無期徒刑 **wúchītúsyíng** (N) life imprisonment.

　　無罪 **wúdzwèi** (SV) be innocent, be guiltless. /我早就知道他～. I knew he was innocent a long time ago.

　　無非 **wúfēi** (A) only. /他～又來借錢. He is only coming to borrow money again. /他～是一個小孩子. He is only a child.

　　無軌電車 **wúgwěidyànchē** (N) trolley-bus (M輛 **lyàng**).

　　無精打采 **'wújīngdǎtsǎi** (SV) be in low spirits, depressed. /你為什麼老是這麼～呢? Why do you always look so depressed?

　　無論 **wúlwùn** (A) no matter, regardless of. /～你到那儿,錢老是重要的. No matter where you go, money is always important. (PT) ...也 (or都).... no matter ...still.... /你～說什麼話,他也(都)不聽. No matter what you say, he still won't listen.

　　無聊 **wúlyáu** (SV) 1) be bored, uninterested. /我今天覺得很～. I feel very bored today. 2) be boring, dull. /星期六不出去玩儿多麼

～呀. How boring it is not to go out and have fun on Saturdays. /他真～. He's really boring.

　　無數 **wúshù** (AT) countless. ～年代 countless years.

　　無所謂 **wúswǒwèi** (SV) be of no importance, not matter. /你給我錢不給我錢都～. Whether you give me the money or not isn't important. /他來不來～. It doesn't matter whether he comes or not. (IE) It's all right. or So so. /A: 昨天的電影怎麼樣? B:～. A: How was the movie yesterday? B: So so. /A: 你喜歡咖啡嗎? B:～. A: Do you like coffee? B: It's all right.

　　無線電 **wúsyàndyàn** (N) radio (M架 **jyà**).

　　無效 **wúsyàu** (FV) be invalidated, not in effect. /從四月一日起,這條法律就～了. Starting April first, this law will be ineffective. /我的護照已經～了. My passport has been invalidated.

　　無從 **wútsúng** (B) not knowing where to start doing something. ～說起 not know where to start telling; ～下手 not know where to start something; ～知道 no way of knowing.

　　無味 **wúwèi** (SV) be dull, uninteresting. /他說話真～. His talk is really uninteresting.

　　無謂 **wúwèi** (SV) be aimless, pointless. /別做～的犧牲. Don't make pointless sacrifices.

　　無疑 **wúyí** (A) certainly, definitely, doubtlessly. /這件事情～是他幹的. He definitely did it.

　　無意的 **wúyìde** (A) unintentionally, not on purpose, without knowing. /我～把他給得罪了. I unintentionally offended him. (N) unintentional act. /我把你的帽子拿走是～. I didn't mean to take your hat away. (Lit. My taking your hat away was an unintentional act.)

　　無意中 **wúyìjūng** (A) unintentionally, accidentally. /我是～在公園裡碰見他的. I accidentally met him in the park.

　　無用 **wúyùng** (SV) be useless. /我沒想到他會這麼～. I never expected he would be so useless.

梧 **wú** (B) ↓.

梧 桐 **wútúng** (N) sterculia platanifolia (M棵**kē**).

午 **wǔ** (B) noon. 晌~noontime; 上 ~ morning; 下 ~afternoon; 正 ~ high noon.

午 飯 **wǔfàn** (N) lunch (M 頓 **dwùn**).

午 後 **wǔhòu** (TW) (in) the afternoon. /他~到這儿來. He'll be here in the afternoon. /~比午前長一點. The afternoon is longer than the morning.

武 **wǔ** (B) 1) martial, military. ~夫 warrior;~備 armaments. 2) fighting.動~fight; ~力 force of arms. s

武 器 **wǔchì** (N) weapon, arms (M件 **jyàn**).

武 官 **wǔgwān** (N) military attaché.海軍~naval attaché.

武 裝 **wǔjwāng** (N) arms.全付 ~ fully armed. (FV) take up arms, arm. /因為戰事緊急.連農民都~起來了. Because the military situation was critical, even the farmers all took up arms.

武 術 **wǔshù** (N) art or technique of fighting, with or without weapons. /他練過幾年~. He has practiced fighting techniques for a few years.

舞 **wǔ** (N) dancing.跳~to dance;土風 ~ folk dancing. (FV) 1) wield. ~ 劍 wield a sword. 2) dance. /我們都會~龍燈. We all know how to do the dragon dance.

舞 蹈 **wǔdǎu** (N) 1) the dance (as an art-form). 2) dancing.

侮 **wǔ** (B) insult, demean. 自 ~ demean oneself.

侮 辱 **wǔrù** (FV) insult. /我不能叫他們~你. I can't let them insult you. (N) insult.

五 **wǔ** (NU) five.~條牛 five cows. (B) fifth. ~馬路 Fifth Ave.

五 金 **wǔjīn** (N) 1) the five metals (金**jīn**, 銀**yín**, 銅**túng**, 鐵**tyě**, 錫**syī**). 2) metal. ~行 hardware store.

五 一 **wǔyī** (TW) (on) May Day. /很多國家都以~為勞工節. Many countries consider May Day a workers' holiday. /他們~放假.

They're going to have a holiday on May Day.

五 月 **wǔywè** (TW) 1) (in) May. /~是一年當中最好的一個月. May is the best month of the year. /我~去. I'll go there in May. 2) (in) the fifth month of the lunar calendar.

搗(捂)**wǔ** (FV) cover, conceal (especially with the hand). /電影到了太恐怖的時候.他就用手~著眼睛. When the movie got too frightening, he put his hands over his eyes. /這儿有味儿.把鼻子~起來. Hold your nose, it smells awful here.

惡 **wù** (B) loathe. 可 ~ be mean, hateful. →惡 **è**, 惡 **è**.

霧(雾)**wù** (N) fog, mist, vapor. /昨晚上~很濃. There was a dense fog last night.

霧 氣 **wùchi** (N) mist.

物 **wù** (B) matter, substance, thing.萬 ~ all things.

物 產 **wùchǎn** (N) natural resources and products.

物 質 **wùjr** (N) substance, matter. ~享受 material comforts.

物 件 **wùjyàn** (N) <儿> item, thing, object, article. ~單 inventory of items.

物 理 **wùlǐ** (N) physics.

誤(误)**wù** (FV) 1) be behind schedule, late. /今天火車又 ~ 了. The train is behind schedule again today. 2) fail to make, miss, a train, boat, plane, etc. /我把飛機~了. I missed the plane. 3) spoil, bungle. /他把我最後的機會給~了. He's spoiled my last chance. (B) by mistake.~犯 offend unintentionally; ~認 mistakenly recognize.

誤 會 **wùhwei** (FV) misunderstand. /你不要~他. Don't misunderstand him. (N) misunderstanding.

務(务)**wù** (B) 1) affair, business. 家 ~ domestic affair. 2) must, necessarily.~須 by all means.

務 必 **wùbì** (A) without fail, of necessity. /這封信請您~給帶到. Please deliver this letter without fail.

xi *see* **syi.**

xia *see* **sya.**

xian *see* **syan.**

xiang *see* **syang.**

xiao *see* **syau.**

xie *see* **sye.**

xin *see* **syin.**

xing *see* **sying.**

xiong *see* **syung.**

xiu *see* **syou.**

xu *see* **syu.**

xuan *see* **sywan.**

xue *see* **sywe.**

xun *see* **syun.**

呀 **ya** (P) used in place of 啊 **a** when the preceding word ends in the sounds **ei, ai, yu, e, o,** *or* **a.** /你是誰~? Who are you? (ON) a creaking sound. /門~地一聲就開了. The door opened with a creaking sound. (I) my goodness! /~! 我忘了帶錢了. My goodness, I forgot to bring the money with me!

押 **yā** (FV) 1) borrow money on something, mortgage. /他把他的房子~了三萬塊錢. He mortgaged his house for thirty thousand dollars. 2) hold in custody. ~解 send in custody. /他叫警察局~了兩天. He was held by the police for two days. 3) bet in a number game similar to roulette. /我~單數. I bet on odd numbers. (B) to sign, make a cross (as a signature). 畫~ sign a document.

鴨 **yā** (B) <子> duck (M 隻 **jī**). 烤~ roast duck.
　　鴨蛋 **yādàn** (N) duck egg.

壓 [压] **yā** (FV) 1) press down. /你那封信~在書底下了. Your letter is under the book there. 2) suppress, quell a riot or revolt. /他們~不住這次的叛變. They could not suppress the revolt. 3) hold onto a document, without taking any action on it, table. /他把很多文件~

着不辦. He is holding many documents without taking any action. (B) pressure. 血~ blood pressure.
→軋 [壓] **yà.**
　　壓力 **yālì** (N) pressure (lit. or fig.).
　　壓迫 **yāpwò** (N) oppression. (FV) oppress. /所有的獨裁者都~老百姓. All dictators oppress the people.

牙 **yá** (N) tooth. 門~ incisor (M 顆 **kē**). (B) brokerage. ~行 licensed broker. *t*
　　牙齒 **yáchř** (N) tooth (M 顆 **kē**).
　　牙子 **yádz** (N) 1) decorative edge. 2) broker.
　　牙粉 **yáfěn** (N) tooth powder.
　　牙膏 **yágāu** (N) toothpaste (M 筒兒 **tŭngr**).
　　牙兒 **yár** (M) section, portion of round-shaped fruit or cake. 一~西瓜 a portion of watermelon; 一~橘子 a section of orange.
　　牙刷 **yáshwā** (N) <子,-兒> toothbrush (M 把 **bǎ**).

芽 **yá** (B) <子,-兒> sprout, bud. ~豆 bean sprouts.

啞 [咂][啞] **yǎ** (SV) be hoarse (of a voice). /我的嗓子~了. I lost my voice. (B) <子> mute, dumb. ~劇 pantomime; ~鈴 dumbbell (for exercise).
　　啞吧 **yǎba** (N) mute (person who can't speak).

雅 **yǎ** (SV) be elegant, refined, in good taste. /那間屋子佈置的很~. The decoration of that room is in very good taste. *t*

軋 [壓] **yà** (FV) crush, roll over and press down. /車~人了. The car has run over someone. →軋 **gā.**
　　軋根兒 **yàgēr** (A) from the very beginning, in the first place. /我~就不願意. I didn't like it from the very beginning.
　　軋花機 **yàhwājī** (N) cotton gin.

咽 **yān** (B) throat. ~喉 throat, a narrow pass. SF of 嚥 **yàn.** →咽 **yé.**

烟 [菸][煙] **yān** (N) 1) <兒> smoke (M 股 **gǔ**). 2) tobacco, cigarette (M 包 **bāu**; 袋 **dài**; 枝 **jī**; 條 **tyáu**) (B) opium. ~槍 opium pipe.
　　烟子 **yāndz** (N) soot.

烟袋 **yāndài** (N) pipe (for smoking) (M 根 **gēn**, 隻 **jř**, 桿 **gǎn**).

烟筒 **yāntung** (N) chimney.

腌(醃) **yān** (FV) salt, preserve <u>something</u> by adding salt. /我~了兩磅肉. I have salted two pounds of meat.

淹 **yān** (FV) submerge, flood. /房子都叫水~了. All the houses were flooded.

胭(臙) **yān** (B) rouge. ~粉 rouge and powder.

　　臙脂 **yānjr** (N) rouge (M 盒兒 **hér**).

燕 **yān** (B) 1) name of an ancient feudal state. 2) Peiping region. →燕 **yàn**.

沿 **yán** (FV) edge, trim, a dress. /她在衣服上~了一道花邊. She trimmed the dress with lace. (CV) <着> extending along, bordering. /我們的船只能~海岸走. Our ship can only skirt the shore. (B) brim, edge. 帽~ hat-brim. →沿 **yàn**.

顏 **yán** (B) 1) color. 2) face, complexion. 容~ countenance. s

　　顏料 **yánlyau** (N) 1) pigment, paint (for painting pictures). 2) dye (for dyeing clothes).

　　顏色 **'yánsè** (N) color.

　　顏色兒 **'yánshǎr** = 顏色 **'yánsè**.

研 **yán** (FV) grind, rub fine. /把這個藥~成細末. Grind this medicine into powder. (B) study, research. ~討 study and discuss.

　　研究 **yánjyou** (N) 1) study, research. 2) knowledge. /他對數學很有~. He has a profound knowledge of mathematics. (FV) study, do research. /他~印度歷史. He's doing research on Indian history.

延 **yán** (FV) postpone. /這個會又~到下禮拜了. This meeting was again postponed until next week. (B) prolong. 推~ procrastinate. t

　　延長 **yáncháng** (FV) prolong, extend. /我們的合同又~了兩年. Our contract has been extended for another two years.

嚴(严) **yán** (SV) 1) be airtight, water-tight. /瓶子蓋的很~. The bottle is covered very tightly. 2) be strict, rigorous. /我們的規矩不太~. Our regulations are not very strict. s t

　　嚴格 **yángé** (SV) be strict, rigorous. /海關的檢查不算~. The inspection by the customs cannot be regarded as strict. (A) strictly. /~說起來,這個就不能用. Strictly speaking, this can't be used.

　　嚴重 **yánjùng** (SV) be serious, weighty, critical. /這種情形很~. This situation is very serious.

　　嚴厲 **yánlì** (SV) be stern, strict. /我父親對我們很~. My father is quite strict with us.

　　嚴密 **yánmì** (SV) be thorough. /他們的保護很~. Their protection is quite thorough.

　　嚴肅 **yánsù** (SV) be serious, solemn. /會場裡的氣氛很~. The atmosphere of the meeting was very solemn.

鹽(塩)(盐) **yán** (N) salt. (B) salt (chem.) 硫酸~ sulfate.

言 **yán** (B) 1) speech. 發~權 right to speak. 2) word. 三~兩語 a few words.

　　言語 **yányu, ywányi** (FV) make remarks, say something (lp). /他沒~. He didn't say a word. /你出去的時候請你~一聲兒. Please tell me when you go out.

　　言論自由 **yánlwùndzòu** (N) freedom of speech.

眼 **yǎn** (N) 1) eye (M 隻 **jř**). 2) <-兒> hole. 打一個~ drill a hole. (M) 1) for wells. 一~井 a well. 2) for an instance of looking at something. /他瞪了我一~. He gave me a dirty look. 3) a beat (in music). /京戲裡邊一板分四~. There are four beats in a measure in Chinese opera.

　　眼前 **yǎnchyán** (TW) (at) this moment. /~是最值得記憶的了. This is a moment well worth remembering. /~就有一個機會. There's a chance at this moment. (PW) (the area) before one's eyes. /我把那本書放在他的~了. I put that book right in front of his eyes. /~什麼都沒有. There's nothing in front of me.

眼 光 **yǎngwāng** (N) <ル> insight, vision. /他很有~. He has real insight.

眼 睛 **yǎnjing** (N) eye (M 隻jr; 對 **dwèi**).

眼 鏡 兒 **yǎnjingr** (N) glasses (M付fù). 戴 ~ wear glasses.

眼 淚 **yǎnlèi** (N) teardrop (M 滴 **dī**).

眼 皮 **yǎnpí** (N) <ル> eyelid.

眼 兒 **yǎr** (B) eyelet, hole. 鼻子 ~ nostrils; 耳朵 ~ auditory canal; hole through an ear pierced for earrings.

演 **yǎn** (FV) 1) perform (in), act (in). ~電影 act in a movie. /她很會 ~. She really can act. 2) put on, show, demonstrate. ~電影 run a movie. /那齣戲今天不 ~ 了. That play is not being put on today. (B) 1) state, tell. 講~ make a speech. 2) practice. 操~ practice military exercises. 3) develop, extend. ~繹法 deductive method.

演 變 **yǎnbyàn** (FV) develop, unfold. /我們看這個情形怎麼 ~. We'll watch and see how this affair develops. /我沒想到事情 ~成這種樣子了. I didn't expect that the matter would develop to such a degree. (N) development. 歷史的~ the unfolding of history.

演 講 **yǎnjyǎng** =演說 **yǎnshwō**.

演 說 **yǎnshwō** (FV) make a speech. /他~了三個鐘頭. His speech lasted three hours.

演 習 **yǎnsyí** (FV) rehearse, practice. /沒開幕以前,我們先 ~一次. Before the play opens we'll have a rehearsal. (N) maneuver, rehearsal.

演 戲 **yǎnsyì** (VO) perform (in) an opera *or* a play. /今天晚上我們要演一齣新戲. We will put on a new play tonight. /你演那齣戲? What play are you acting in?

演 員 **yǎnywán** (N) actor, actress.

掩 **yǎn** (B) 1) cover, hide something from view. ~蔽 conceal, cover over. 2) <着> ajar. /門~着呢! The door's ajar.

掩 護 **yǎnhù** (FV) serve as a protective cover for. /飛機~艦隊. Planes are flying cover for the fleet.

掩 飾 **'yǎnshr̀** (FV) conceal something by speaking or action. /他用話~他的錯兒. He covered up his errors by talking.

硯 **yàn** (B) ink-slab. ~水盒 small vessel to hold water for use on an ink-slab.

硯 台 **yàntai** (N) ink-stone (M 塊 **kwài**).

燕 **yàn** (B) <子,ル> a swallow (M 隻jr). ~窩 swallow's nest (used in bird's nest soup). →燕 **yān**.

沿 **yàn** (B) bank of a river or a well. 河~ riverside; 井~ mouth of a well. →沿 **yán**.

嚥[咽] **yàn** (FV) swallow, gulp. /我把我的假牙~了. I swallowed my false teeth.

驗[驗] **yàn** (FV) test, check upon. /請你把這個試管裡的血~一~. Please test the blood in this tube. (SV) be fulfilled, come true. /他的話現在已經 ~ 了. His prediction is coming true now.

雁[鴈] **yàn** (N) wild goose (M 隻jr).

陽[阳] **yáng** (B) 1) sun. ~曆 solar calendar. 2) open, exposed. ~溝 open drain. 3) cut in relief. ~文 character cut in relief. 4) this world, this life. ~間 the mortal world. 5) positive. ~電 positive electricity. 6) virile member. ~痿 impotence.

陽 光 **yánggwāng** (N) sunlight.

洋 **yáng** (N) ocean. 太平~ Pacific Ocean. (B) 1) foreign, abroad. ~貨 imported goods; 出~go abroad. 2) dollar, money. /不靈退~. Your money back if not satisfactory. 3) extensive. ~溢 widespread.

洋 灰 **yánghwēi** (N) cement.

羊 **yáng** (N) sheep, goat (M 隻jr,頭tóu; 群 **chwún**).

羊 肉 **yángròu** (N) mutton, lamb (as food).

楊 **yáng** (B) poplar *or* aspen. 白~ white poplar. *s*

楊柳 **yánglyǒu** (N) willow (M 棵**kē**).

楊梅 **yángméi** (N) strawberry.

楊樹 **yángshù** (N) poplar or aspen (tree) (M棵**kē**).

癢[痒]**yǎng** (SV) be itchy, ticklish. /我的眼睛很~. My eyes itch. /他一看見錢手就~. When he sees money he itches to get his hands on it.

養[养]**yǎng** (FV) 1) give birth to a child. /昨天她~了一個女兒. She gave birth to a daughter yesterday. 2) raise children, flowers, domestic animals, etc. /你還~雞嗎? Do you still raise chickens? 3) support a family or a member of a family. /誰~他們的母親? Who supports their mother? 4) rest, recuperate from illness, convalesce. ~傷 recuperate from a wound. /你回家去~幾天. Go home and rest for a couple of days. (B) 1) maintain. ~路 maintain the road. 2) nourish. ~精神 nourish mental energy. 3) foster. ~母 foster-mother.

養活 **yǎnghwo** (FV) support people by providing food, shelter, and other necessities of life. /他~一家子人. He's supporting a whole household of people.

氧 **yǎng** (B) oxygen. ~化汞 mercuric oxide.

氧氣 **yǎngchì** (N) oxygen.

仰 **yǎng** (B) 1) <着> facing up. ~頭 raise one's head. /他喜歡~看睡. He likes to sleep on his back. 2) expect. ~望 hope, desire; 久~ hoped very long to.

樣[样]**yàng** (B) <子,-儿> 1) appearance, shape. 式~ pattern, model. 2) sample. ~本 specimen copy. 3) manner. 這~ in this manner. (M) <-儿> 1) kind, sort. /我們今天有六~菜. Today we have six different dishes.

樣品 **'yàngpǐn** (N) sample.

樣式 **yàngshr** (N) style, pattern, model.

yao *see* **yau**

邀 **yāu** (FV) invite. /他~我跟他到

紐約去. He invited me to go to New York with him.

邀請 **yāuchǐng** (FV) invite. /沒人~我. Nobody invites me.

要 **yāu** (B) 1) force, compel. ~挾 coerce. 2) demand. →要**yàu**.

要求 **yāuchyóu** (FV) demand. /我~他說明理由. I demanded that he give me the reason. (N) demand.

腰 **yāu** (N) waist. (B) 1) midsection of something. 山~ halfway up a mountain. 2) <子> kidney (organ or food). 豬~ pig's kidney.

腰帶 **yāudài** (N) belt worn at the waist (M條**tyáu**).

約 **yāu** (FV) weigh something, weigh out some quantity of something. /請你給我~一斤麵. Weigh me out a catty of flour. *t* →約**ywē**.

謠 **yáu** (B) 1) ballad. 童~ children's songs. 2) rumor. 造~ fabricate and spread rumors.

謠言 **yáuyan** (N) rumor. /他老造~. He's always starting rumors.

謠傳 **yáuchwán** (A) according to rumor. /~他不來了. According to rumor, he's not going to come. (N) rumor.

搖 **yáu** (FV) shake, rock, swing to and fro. ~頭 shake the head. /別~了, 小孩已經睡着了. Stop rocking, the baby has already gone to sleep.

搖晃 **yáuhwang** (FV) wave, swing, shake. /別再~那棵樹了, 葉子都快掉了. Don't shake the tree again, its leaves are all starting to fall off.

咬 **yǎu** (FV) 1) bite. /狗~人不是新聞, 人~狗才是新聞. If a dog bites a man, it's not newsworthy, but if a man bites a dog, it's news. 2) incriminate an innocent person by giving false testimony. /那個犯人亂~好人. That criminal wantonly implicated the innocent. 3) bark (of a dog). /狗直~. The dog barks all the time.

要 **yàu** (FV) 1) want. /你~什麼? What do you want? 2) ask for. /你

為什麼老跟我～錢? Why do you always ask for money from me? 3) accept. /他給我,我沒～. He gave it to me, but I didn't accept it. 4) order food in a restaurant. /我～了兩客餃子. I've ordered two portions of *chiaotzu*. (AV) will. /火車～來了. The train will be here soon. 2) need to, should. /你～努力作事. You need to work hard. 3) want to. /我～洗澡. I want to take a bath. (A) if. /你明天～能來多好. It would be very nice if you could come tomorrow. (B) important. ～事 important business. 一要 yāu.

要不然 yàuburán (A) otherwise. /我得早點兒去,～我就趕不上火車了. I have to leave a bit early, otherwise I won't make the train. (PT) 不是...就是...～.... If not ... then ... or ... . /他不是睡覺,就是喝酒,～就玩兒. If he's not sleeping, then he's drinking or fooling around.

要不是 'yàubushr (A) if not. /今天～你來,我已經死了. If you hadn't come today, I would have been dead already. (PT) ～...就是.... If not ... then ... /你來,就是我去. If you're not coming, then I'll go.

要強 yàuchyáng (SV) be ambitious. /他太不～了. He is not ambitious at all.

要賬 yàujàng (VO) collect accounts *or* debts. /我不是跟你～來了. I didn't come to collect the money you owe me.

要緊 yàujǐn (SV) be important.

要麼 yàuma (A) 1) if that's the case. /～,你明天不必來了. If that's the case, you need not come tomorrow. 2) perhaps, maybe. /你～忘了. Perhaps you forgot. (PT) 1) ～...～.... either ... or.... /～他忘了,～他不知道. Either he forgot, or he doesn't know. 2) 不是...就是...～.... If not ... then ... or else.... /他不是下棋,就是打牌,～喝酒. If he's not playing chess, then he's playing cards, or else drinking.

要人 'yàurén (N) important people (usually referring to high-ranking government officials).

要是 yàushr (A) if, in case. /～他能來就好了. It will be nice if he can come. /他～來,我們就得預備好了. We should be prepared in case he comes.

藥[葯] yàu (N) medicine, drug (M顆 kē, 粒 lì, 丸 wán; 付 fù, 劑 jì). (B) 1) chemical compound. 火～ gunpowder. 2) to poison. ～老鼠 to poison rats.

藥房 yàufáng (N) drugstore, pharmacy, dispensary in a hospital.

鑰[鈅] yàu (B) key. 鎖～ key.

鑰匙 yàushr (N) key (M把 bǎ).

瘧[疟] yàu (B) ʈ. 一瘧 nywè.

瘧子 yàudz (N) malaria (M場 chǎng). 發～ have malaria recur.

耶 yē (B) ʈ. *t*

耶穌 'Yēsū (N) Jesus. ～教 Protestant Christianity.

椰 yē (B) 1) ＜子＞ coconut. ～樹 coconut palm. 2) savoy. ～菜 savoy cabbage.

噎 yē (FV) choke, block (in the throat). /慢點兒吃,留神別～了. Eat slowly, be careful not to choke.

爺[爷] yé (B) 1) grandfather. 2) father. ～娘 father and mother. 3) used after a surname, Mr. 張～ Mr. Chang. 4) god. 兔兒～ rabbit spirit.

爺爺 yéye (N) grandpa.

野 yě (SV) 1) be wild, untamed. ～象 wild elephant. /這個女孩子真～. This girl is really wild. 2) be uncivilized, crude. /他說話～極了. He speaks very crudely. (FV) gallivant around. /他到那兒去～去了? Where have you been gallivanting to? (B) 1) country, wilderness. ～茶館 country teahouse. 2) scope, sphere. 視～ field of vision. 3) covetous. ～心 mad ambition.

野蠻 yěmán (SV) 1) be uncivilized, barbaric. /五百年前這個部落還很～呢. This tribe was still quite barbaric five hundred years ago. 2) be rude. /你為什麼對我這麼～? Why are you so rude to me?

野獸 yěshòu (N) wild animal (M隻 j̄r).

野餐 **yětsān** (FV) have a picnic. /我們就在這兒~罷. Let's have our picnic here. (N) picnic.

野外 **yěwài** (PW) (in) the open country. /~有很多野花. There are a lot of wild flowers in the open country. /我不喜歡~. I don't like open country.

也 **yě** (A) 1) also, too. /你去,我~去. If you go, I'll go too. 2) <u>used after a QW and before a negative expression</u> any, no matter what, how, who, etc. /他什麼~不會. He can't do anything. /我什麼~做不好. I can't do anything well. 3) <u>used after a supposition and before a negative expression</u> still, yet, however. /我死~不能承認. Even if I have to die, I still won't admit it. 4) <u>used after a condition alone, by itself.</u> /熱~把他熱死了. The heat alone can kill him. 5) at all. /他~不笨,為什麼做這種事? He isn't stupid at all; why did he do this? (PT) 1) 連... ~.... even. /他連早飯~沒吃. He didn't even eat breakfast. 2) 就是...~.... even. /就是你給我錢,我~不去. I won't go even if you pay me. 3) ~...~.... (both)...and.... /~有好的, ~有壞的. There are both good ones and bad ones. /飯~做好了, 客人~來了. The dinner is ready, and the guests are here. 4) ~...~... either...or.... /你去~好,我去~好. There will be no difference whether you go or I go. 5) 不但...~.... not only...but also... /她不但漂亮,~聰明. She's not only pretty but smart. 6) 不管...~.... no matter...still.... /不管他是誰,~別叫他進來. No matter who he is, don't let him in. 7) 雖然(or固然)...~.... though, however. /我雖然(or固然)沒錢,我~要買. I want to buy it though I don't have the money. t

也不知道 **yěbujīdàu** (A) no one knows, who knows. /~今天下雨不下雨. No one knows whether it will rain or not today.

也不是 **yěbushr** = 也不知道 **yěbujīdàu**.

也就 **yějyòu** (A) 1) as well, instead. /你要是沒有現款,支票~行了. If you haven't the cash, a check will do as well. 2) sufficiently. /你能上大學,~很好了. It's satisfactory enough that you could get into college. 3) only, just. /這種筆~值一塊錢. This kind of pen is only worth a dollar.

也就是 **yějyòushr** (A) only, just only. /~你願意幹這個. You're the only one who's willing to do this.

也就是說 **yějyòushrshwō** (IE) in other words. /他叫我自己買, ~,他不管. He told me to buy it myself. In other words, he doesn't want to bother with it.

也許 **yésyǔ** (A) maybe, perhaps, probably. /他~病了. Maybe he's sick.

咽 **yè** (B) stifled sob. 哽~cry. <u>SF of</u> 嚥**yàn**. →咽**yān**.

葉(叶)**yè** (B) 1) <子,儿> leaf. ~柄 stem of a leaf. 2) period, age. 明朝中~ (in) the middle period of the Ming Dynasty. s

業(业)**yè** (B) 1) business. 實~industry. 2) profession, occupation. 律師~ legal profession. 3) property. ~主 property owner.

業務 **'yèwù** (N) business matters.

頁(页)**yè** (B) leaf, page (both sides). 活~筆記本 loose-leaf notebook. (M) page. /我念了三百多~書. I have read over three hundred pages of that book.

夜 **yè** (N) evening, night. /這是一個安靜的~. This is a quiet night.

夜裡 **yèli** (TW) at night. /他們~掃街. They clean the streets at night. 2) nighttime. /~是一天最安靜的時候. Nighttime is the quietest part of the day.

醫(医)**yī** (FV) 1) treat an illness or a patient. /現在誰給你~哪? Who's treating you now? 2) heal, cure. /這種病沒人能~. Nobody can cure this illness. (B) 1) healing art, medicine. ~科 medi-

cal course <u>in a school.</u> 2) doctor.
獸～ veterinarian.

醫 生 **yīsheng** (N) medical doctor.

醫 院 **yīywàn** (N) hospital (M
家 **jyā**).

衣 **yī** (B) 1) clothes. 大～ overcoat.
2) <子> covering. 砲～ tarpaulin
<u>for covering artillery;</u> 糖～sugar
coating.

衣 服 **yīfu** (N) garment, clothes
(M件 **jyàn**; 套 **tàu**).

衣 裳 **yīshang** (N) garment,
clothes (M件 **jyàn**; 套 **tàu**).

依 **yī** (FV) 1) agree with. /現在他們
都～我了. All of them agree with
me now. 2) forgive. /我～你才
怪呢. It would be very strange if I
forgave you. (CV) according to.
/我們～你的計劃辦. We'll do
it according to your plan. (B) depend on. ～賴 rely on.

依 照 **'yījàu** (CV) according to.
/我們一定～你的話去做.
We'll certainly do it according to
what you say.

依 靠 **yīkàu** (FV) depend on.
/你不能老～別人. You can't
always depend on other people.

一{壹} **yī** (**yí** <u>before a toneless syllable or
one with a fourth tone;</u> **yǐ** <u>before a
syllable with a second or third tone</u>).
(NU) 1) one (<u>directly after SP, or a
verb with M, the unstressed</u> — <u>is often
dropped</u>). ～把椅子 a chair. /這(～)
條街很寬. This street is quite
broad. /他是(～)個好人. He's a
good man. 2) <u>used before a borrowed
measure,</u> whole of, all. ～縣的人 people of the whole county. 3) each, every.
～磅五毛錢 fifty cents per pound.
/～車坐六個人. Each car will
seat five people. (A) 1) <u>indicates
the completion of an action in one
movement.</u> /我說完了,他把頭
～點. After I finished talking, he
nodded. 2) <u>used between two verbal
expressions,</u> and. /他抬頭～看,
天都黑了. He raised his head
and saw that the sky had grown dark.
(B) 1) first. ～號 number one; ～流
first class; 星期～ Monday. 2) all,
together. ～路 all along the route.
3) same. /我們～車走吧. Let's

ride in the same car. 4) <u>used in the
middle of a reduplicated verb,</u> a
little. 等～等 wait a little. 5) <u>used
between the SP</u> 這 **jèi**, 那 **nèi** <u>and a
verb,</u> the way in which. /瞧他這
～樂. Look at the way he laughed.
(PT)～...就.... as soon as ....
/我～看就知道了. As soon as
I looked, I knew.

一 般 **yìbān** (AT) general, average. ～學生 the average student.
(A) <u>used before SV,</u> equally, the
same. /他們兩個人～高. Those
two are the same in height.

一 半 **yíbàn** (N) <儿> half.
/我的年齡是他的年齡的～.
My age is half of his. (A) partly,
half. /這孩子～像父親,～像
母親. This child partly resembles
his father and partly resembles his
mother.

一 輩 子 **yíbeidz** (N) lifetime.
(A) all one's life. /他～都沒結
婚. He was unmarried all his life.

一 邊 儿 **yìbyār** (A) <u>used before
SV,</u> equally, the same. /我們倆
人～高. We both are the same
height. (PT) 1)跟...～... as
... as .... /我跟他～高. I
am as tall as he is. 2)～...～
.... do something while <u>doing something else.</u> /他～走着～唱. He
sings while walking.

一 起 **yìchí** (A) together. /我
們～吃飯吧. Let's eat together.
(N) the same place. /他們在～
呢. They're at the same place.

一 齊 **yìchí** (A) together, all at
once. /我們～去看電影儿吧.
Let's go to the movies together.

一 切 **yíchyè** (N) everything.
/～都很好. Everything is fine.
/他～都不管. He doesn't care
about anything (<u>lit</u>. He doesn't care
about everything).

一 帶 **yídài** (B) <u>used after SP</u>
這 **jèi**, 那 **nèi**, <u>or PW</u> region, area.
上海南京～ Shanghai-Nanking re-
gion.

一 定 **yídìng** (A) certainly, definitely, without fail. /他～去
He'll certainly go. /他～走了.
He must have gone. (SV) be certain.
/那件事情～了嗎? Is that thing
certain?

一 多 半 yìdwōbàn (A) <儿>
1) for the most part. /上月我們～
吃 麵. We ate noodles for the
most part last month. 2) probably,
most likely. /今天～下雪. It'll
probably snow today. (N) <儿> the
greater half. /我太太的薪水佔
我們收入的～. My wife's salary
makes up the greater half of our income.

一 點 儿 yìdyǎr (N) a little,
some. /請你吃～. Please eat
some. /他～也不會. He can't
even do a little. → 有一點儿 yǒu-
yìdyǎr.

一 概 yígài (A) without exception.
/他們的信我～不回. I refuse
to answer their letters without exception.

一 共 yígùng (A) in all. /我們
～有多少人？ How many of us
are there in all?

一 會 儿 yìhwěr (A) in a little
while. /我～去. I will go in a little
while. (N) a little while. /～也比
沒有好. A little while is better
than no time at all. → 不一會儿
búyìhwěr.

一 直 yìjŕ (A) 1) so far. /我～
沒吃. I haven't eaten so far.
2) straight on, forward. /我要～
做到十二點. I will work straight
through to 12 o'clock. /我們～走.
We'll go straight forward.

一 致 yíjŕ (SV) be consistent,
the same, in agreement. /他們的
意見不～. Their ideas are not in
agreement. (A) all in the same way,
all in agreement. /國會～通過
那個議案. Congress passed that
bill unanimously.

一 口 氣 yìkǒuchì (A) <儿> in
one breath, in one gulp (lit. or fig.).
/這杯酒太多,你別～喝完.
This glass of wine is too much for you
to drink in one gulp. /這件事～
做不完. This thing can't be done
in one sitting.

一 塊 儿 yìkwàr (A) together.
/我們～到我家去吧. Let's go
to my house together. (N) the same
place. /我們住在～. We live
at the same place.

一 來 yìlái (B) preceded by SP
這 jèi, 那 nèi 這麼 jèmma, 那麼

nèmma, once something is done in a
certain way, just because of something. /那～他什麼都看不見
了. Once that happened he couldn't
see anything. /那麼～他就病了.
Just because of that he became sick.
(PT) 1)～...二來.... in the
first place ..., in the second place
.... /我沒錢,二來我不願
意. In the first place I don't have
any money, and in the second place
I don't have any desire to do it.
2)～...就.... easily, at the drop
of a hat. /～他就哭. He cries
easily.

一 律 yílyù (SV) be uniform,
all the same. /這儿的薪水都是
～的. The pay here is uniform.
(A) all. /這儿的房子～是紅的.
The houses here are all red.

一 時 yìshŕ (A) 1) right then,
at that moment. /那是我～糊塗.
That was because I was confused at
that moment. 2) for a while. /我們
～還不能走. We can't leave for
a while.

一 下 子 yísyàdz = 一下儿 yí-
syàr.

一 下 儿 yísyàr (A) all of a
sudden, in a moment. /～他就昏
過去了. All of a sudden he fainted.
/他來了,～又走了. He came,
and in a moment he left again.

一 向 yísyàng (A) always in the
past, uniformly in the past. /他～
不愛說話. He's always been somewhat taciturn.

一 些 yìsyē (B) some. ～人 some
people.

一 同 yìtúng (A) together. /他
們～做工. They work together.

一 樣 yíyàng (SV) be the same.
/這兩本書不～. These two books
are not the same. (A) used before
SV, equally, to the same degree.
/這兩輛車～好. These two cars
are equally good. (PT) 1)跟...～.
be the same as. /她跟她姐姐～.
She is the same as her sister. 2)跟
...～.... be as ... as ....
/這本書跟那本書～貴. This
book is as expensive as that one.

一 月 yíywè (TW) 1) (in) January. 2) the first month of the lunar
calendar.

遺 **yí** (B) 1) leave behind. ～產 inherited property. 2) involuntary excretion. ～精 have a nocturnal emission.

遺傳 **yíchwán** (FV) transmit, pass something down in a family biologically. /他的病是他母親～給他的. His disease was transmitted to him by his mother. (N) heredity.

遺囑 **yíjǔ** (N) last will and testament (written or verbal).

遺失 **yíshr̄** (FV) 1) get lost (of a thing). /我的護照～了. My passport got lost. 2) lose. /我把我的文憑～了. I lost my diploma.

遺書 **yíshū** (N) note or letter written just before one's death (M封 **fēng**).

姨 **yí** (B) 1) <-儿> maternal aunt. 2) wife's sister. 小～子 sister-in-law (wife's younger sister). 3) concubine. ～太太 concubine.

儀(儀) **yí** (B) 1) model, standard. 禮～ etiquette. 2) scientific apparatus. 六分～ a sextant.

儀器 **yíchì** (N) apparatus, instrument, small tool like a drafting tool, medical instrument, etc. (M 付 **fù**).

儀式 **'yíshr̀** (N) ceremonial proceedings.

疑 **yí** (B) suspect, doubt. ～案 doubtful case; 多～ be very suspicious.

疑惑 **yíhwo** (FV) suspect that. /我～他沒做那件事. I suspect that he didn't do it. (N) doubt, suspicion. /你還有什麼～嗎? Do you still have any doubts?

疑心 **yísyīn** (FV) suspect, suspect that. /我～是他偷的. I suspect that it's he who took it. /我很～他. I'm very suspicious of him. (N) suspicion.

疑問 **'yíwèn** (N) doubt, question. /我還有一個～呢. I still have a question.

胰 **yí** (B) 1) pancreas. 2) <子> soap (M塊 **kwài**). ～皂 soap.

尾 **yǐ** (B) tail. 馬～儿 horse-tail hair. →尾 **wěi**.

尾巴 **yǐba** (N) tail (of an animal) (M根 **gēn**, 條 **tyáu**).

以 **yǐ** (CV) 1) by means of, using, with. /所有的價錢都～美金計算. All the prices are in American dollars. 2) because of, on account of. /～你的身份不應該買這樣的房子. You shouldn't buy this kind of house, because of your status. (B) used before localizers, forms compounds indicating direction, time, or location. ～東 to the east. (PT) 1)～...為.... use such-and-such as, take such-and-such to be, consider such-and-such to be. /你～什麼為根據說這句話? On what grounds are you making that statement? 2)～...而論 as far as someone or something is concerned, as for. /～資格而論,他就不夠. As for qualifications, he just doesn't have enough.

以前 **yíchyán** (TW) 1) formerly. /我～不喝酒. Formerly, I didn't drink. 2) the past. /～比現在好的多. The past is much better than now. (B) 1) in front of something. 桌子～ in front of the table. 2) used after NU-M indicating a period of time, ago. 三年～ three years ago. 3) used after a TW, before. 新年～ before New Year. 4) used after a verbal expression with or without 沒 **méi**, before. /(沒)吃飯～得洗手. You must wash your hands before eating.

以後 **yíhòu** (TW) 1) afterward. /～怎麼樣了? What happened afterward? 2) the future. /～會比現在好一點儿的. The future will be better than present. (B) 1) behind something. 房子～ behind the house. 2) used after NU-M, indicating a period of time, later. 五天～ five days later. 3) used after a TW, after. 新年～ after New Year. 4) used after a verbal expression, after. /我們吃了飯～就去看戲. After we finish our supper, we're going to a show.

以免 **yímyǎn** (A) so as not to. /請再查一遍～錯誤. Please check it once more, so as not to make mistakes.

以及 **yíjí** (B) and, as well as. 中國,美國,法國～日本China, the United States, France, and Japan.

以來 **yǐlái** (B) 1) preceded by

expressions of time, for a certain period of time. /這三年～我沒説過一句中國話. I haven't spoken a single word of Chinese for three years. 2) After a clause, since doing such-and-such. /我到美國～就吃過兩回中國飯. Since I got to America I have only eaten Chinese food twice. (PT)自從... ～. since a given date which is relatively long ago. /自從去年三月～,我就沒抽煙. I haven't smoked since last March.

以内 yǐnèi (B) 1) used after N, inside of something, within. 佔領區～ within the occupied area. 2) used after NU-M, less than, within a given figure. 三十塊錢～less than thirty dollars.

以上 yǐshàng (TW) so far, up to now. /我～説的話都明白了嗎? Have you understood what I've said so far? (B) used after N, above (an object or in rank). 科長～人員 all staff above section chief; 水平線～ above the horizon. 2) used after NU-M, more than, over.五塊錢～ more than five dollars.

以下 yǐsyà (TW) from now on, just after. /我～就要講這個故事了. From now on, I'm going to tell this story. (B) 1) used after N, below, under (something or in rank). 連長～ below captain in rank; 地面～ under the ground. 2) used after NU-M, less than, under, below a given figure. 三十度～ below thirty degrees.

以外 yǐwài (B) 1) used after N, outside of something, beyond. 長城～ beyond the Great Wall. 2) used after NU-M, more than, over. 三十磅～ over thirty pounds.

以為 yǐwei (FV) 1) assume (often to be proved wrong later). /我～是你呵. I thought that was you. 2) consider, think, be of the opinion that. /我～還是不去好. I think it's better not to go.

yǐ (B) already.業～ already.
已經 'yǐjǐng (A) already. /我～見過他了. I've already met him.
已然 yǐrán (A) already. /他～死了,你不用再説了. Since he's

already dead, there's no use in your saying anything more.

椅 yǐ (B) <子> chair (M把bǎ,張jāng). 摇～ rocking chair.

益 yì (B) profit. ～蟲 insects which are helpful to man.
益處 yìchu (N) benefit, advantage.

義[义]yì (B) 1) right conduct. ～士 righteous man. 2) loyal, faithful. ～犬 faithful dog. 3) meaning. 字～ meaning of a word. 4) free and open to all. ～學 public school. 5) false, not real. ～齒 false teeth.
義務 yìwu (N) duty, responsibility. (AT) free, open to all. ～教育 free education. (A) without pay. /她替人家～看孩子. She does baby-sitting for people free.

藝[艺]yì (B) 1) skill. 手～ handicraft. 2) art.～員 artist, actor, performer.
藝術 'yìshù (N) art. (SV) be artistic. /這本書的封面很～. This book's cover is very artistic.
藝術家 yìshùjyā (N) artist.

意 yì (B) 1) idea, thought. 主～ plan, way to solve problems. 2) meaning. 本～ original meaning. 3) intention. 無～ not on purpose. t
意志 'yìjr̀ (N) will, will power. /這個人的～很堅强. He has a strong will.
意見 'yìjyàn (N) opinion, point of view. /我們兩個人～不合. We two don't agree.
意料 'yìlyàu (FV) expect that. /我～他不會來. I expect that he won't be able to come. (N) expectation.
意思 yìsz (N) 1) meaning. /這個字的～是什麽? What is the meaning of this word? 2) intention, opinion. /我絕對沒存那個～. I absolutely didn't have that intention. 一不好意思 bùhǎuyìsz, 有意思 yǒuyìsz.
意外 yìwài (N) something impossible to anticipate, something unanticipated or accidental.
意義 'yìyì (N) significance, meaning, purport.

億[亿]yì (M) one hundred million.

議 yí (B) discuss. ～院 parliament.
　　議案 yíàn (N) 1) motion in parliamentary procedure. 2) bill in a legislative body.
　　議決 yíjywé (FV) reach a decision through discussion. /我們 ～每個人繳五塊錢. We made a decision that each person pay five dollars. (N) decision.
　　議論 yílwun (FV) talk about, discuss. /他們都～這件事情. They were all talking about this matter. (N) talk, discussion.
　　議員 yíywán (N) representative in a governing body, senator, member of parliament.

因 yīn (B) 1) because. ～事 because of certain affairs. 2) reason, cause. 近～ immediate cause.
　　因此 yīntsž (A) because of this, hence, therefore. /我沒請他,～他很不高興. I didn't invite him, therefore he is very disappointed.
　　因為 yīnwei (A) because. /今天我沒出門,～天冷. I didn't go out today, because it was cold. (PT) ～...所以. because. /～我住的地方太吵,所以得搬家. Because the place I live in is too noisy, I have to move.

音 yīn (N) 1) sound (in phonetics). 2) note (in music). (B) 1) sound (in general).回～ echo. 2) news, information. 佳～ good news.
　　音符 yīnfú (N) musical note (written).
　　音樂 yīnywè (N) music.

陰[陰][阴] yīn (SV) 1) be cloudy. /天～了. The sky has gotten cloudy. 2) be crafty, devious. /他～極了. He is extremely crafty. (FV) deceive. /他常常～人. He often deceives people. (B) lunar. ～曆 lunar calendar. 2) closed, concealed, secret. ～謀 secret scheme. 3) incised. ～文 inscription in intaglio. 4) the other world.～間 Hades. 5) negative. ～電 negative electricity. 6) female organ. ～戶 female organ. 7) shade, shadow. 樹～ shade of a tree.
　　陰涼 yīnlyang (SV) be cool and shady. /這個地方真～. It's very shady and cool here.

陰涼儿 yīnlyángr (N) shade. /太陽太曬,我們到～去吧. The sun is too hot. Let't get in the shade.
　　陰險 yīnsyǎn (SV) be crafty, devious.
　　陰天 yīntyān (VO) be cloudy, become overcast, get cloudy. /現在陰了天了. It's gotten cloudy now. (N) cloudy day.

殷 yīn (B) 1) abundant, flourishing. ～商 wealthy businessman. 2) attentive. ～切 be concerned about. d s
　　殷勤 'yīnchín (SV) be courteous, polite, attentive. /主人招待我們很～. The host treats us very courteously.

銀 yín (N) silver (the element). (B) 1) <-子> silver (the material). ～盤子 silver tray. 2) money. 定～ deposit put down on something. (AT) silver-colored. ～頭髮 silvery hair.
　　銀行 yínháng (N) bank (M 家 jyā).

隱[隱][隐]yín (B) hide. ～名 conceal one's name.
　　隱瞞 yínmán (FV) cover up, conceal from. /你的秘密我們都知道了,你就不必～了. We know your secret, you don't have to hide it.

引 yín (FV) 1) quote someone. /我～了一句他說的話. I quoted a sentence of his. 2) lead, guide, someone or something somewhere. /你把他～到那儿去了? Where are you leading him? 3) attract people. /他在公園裡演講,～了很多人. He spoke in the park, and and attracted a great many people. 4) arouse people's attention or interest. /這麼少的錢～不起他的興趣. This sum is too small to arouse his interest.

飲 yín (B) drink. ～酒 drink wine. →飲 yǐn.
　　飲料 yínlyàu (N) beverage.

印 yìn (N) seal, chop, stamp (M 顆 kē). 蓋～ put a seal or a stamp on a piece of paper. (FV) 1) print. /你要～多少份請帖? How many invitations do you want printed? 2) make an impression on a surface by pressing something on it. /他在那塊沒乾的洋灰地上～了一個腳印兒. He made a footprint on that wet cement. (B) <-子,-兒> mark, trace. 手～ fingerprint. *t*

印地安人 **yìndì'ānrén** (N) American Indian.

印刷 **yìnshwā** (FV) print. /我們不會～彩色圖片. We can't print colored illustrations.

印象 **yìnsyàng** (N) impression. /你的～不對. You have the wrong impression.

飲 **yìn** (FV) water <u>animals</u>. /我去～我的馬去. I'm going to water my horse. →飲 **yǐn**.

英 **yīng** (B) 1) brave, heroic. ～勇 be brave; ～豪 hero. 2) talented. ～才 talent. 3) England. ～法 England and France; ～尺 a foot (<u>English measuring standard</u>). *t*

英國 **Yīnggwó** (N) England.
英雄 **yīngsyúng** (N) hero. (SV) be heroic.

櫻 **yīng** (B) cherry. ～花 cherry blossom.

櫻桃 **yīngtau** (N) cherry (M 粒 lì, 顆 kē).

應[应] **yīng** (FV) promise. /我～了她一份禮物,還沒給呢. I promised her a present, but I haven't given it to her yet. (B) ought, should. ～得的 ought to get. →應 **yìng**.

應當 **yīngdāng** (AV) ought to, should. /你～去看看他. You should go visit him.

應該 **yīnggāi**=應當 **yīngdāng**.

應用 **yīngyùng** (FV) actually use, put in practice. /我們能不能～這個方法? Can we actually use this method?

贏 **yíng** (FV) win <u>money, a contest</u>, etc. ～錢 win money. /那個籃球隊～了? Which basketball team won?

營[营] **yíng** (N) 1) camp, encampment. 紮～ encamp; 集中～ concentration <u>camp</u>; ～房 cantonment, garrison; 夏令～ summer camp. 2) battalion. (B) manage. 經～ manage, operate. 私～的買賣 private business (<u>lit.</u> privately managed business).

營長 **yíngjǎng** (N) battalion commander.

營盤 **yíngpán** (N) encampment, barracks (M 座 **dzwò**).

營業 **yíngyè** (FV) run a business. /禮拜天我們照常～. We do business as usual on Sunday.

迎 **yíng** (CV) facing, against, toward. /～着風騎車很難. It's very difficult to ride a bicycle against the wind. (B) meet, welcome. ～客 welcome a guest; ～敵 encounter the enemy.

迎接 **'yíngjyè** (FV) receive *or* welcome <u>someone</u>. /他們到飛機場去～那個電影明星去了. They went to the airport to welcome that movie star.

影 **yíng** (B) 1) <-子,-兒> shadow. 黑～ black shadow. 2) <-子,-兒> image. 倒～ inverted image. 3) photograph. 攝～ take a picture; 電～ (cinema) film.

影響 **yíngsyǎng** (FV) influence, affect. /地震～天氣. Earthquakes affect the weather. /這件事～了很多人. This affair has influenced a lot of people. (N) influence, effect.

影印 **yíngyìn** (FV) photolithograph. /他們把很多珍版書都～了. They photolithographed a lot of rare books.

應[应] **yìng** (FV) 1) answer, respond, reply. /我叫了半天沒人～. I yelled a long time, but nobody answered. 2) turn out to be true. /那個預言家的話都～了. That soothsayer's words have turned out to be true. →應 **yīng**.

應酬 **yìngchou** (FV) entertain, visit, greet, <u>someone for the sake of courtesy or because of some social obligations</u>. /我得～～他. I have to entertain him. (N) social intercourse, social responsibility. /這兩天～很多,我都忙不過來了. Recently there have been too many social activities for me to get to all of them.

應付 **yìngfu** (FV) deal with, cope with <u>people, a situation</u>. /這麼多困難,他怎麼能～的了? There are so many difficulties. How can he deal with all of them?

應驗 **yìngyàn** (FV) come true, turn out to be true. /他所說的話都～了. Everything he said came true.

硬 **yìng** (SV) 1) be hard (to the touch). /這個麵包很～. This bread is very hard. /這塊牛肉太～了. This piece of steak is too tough. 2) be stiff. /領子不夠～. The collar isn't stiff enough. 3) be obstinate, uncompromising. /他的態度很～. His attitude is extremely unyielding. (A) uncompromisingly, stubbornly. /他～說他沒錢. He stubbornly insisted that he had no money.

yong *see* **yung**.

憂[忧]**yōu** (B) be worried, grieved. ～慮 be worried; ～鬱 be melancholy, be depressed.
　　憂愁 **yōuchóu** (SV) be distressed, sad, melancholy. (N) sadness, melancholy.

優[优]**yōu** (B) 1) excellent, superior. ～勢 superiority. 2) actor, player. ～伶 actor *or* actress.
　　優待 **yōudài** (FV) treat someone well. /他們對佣人很～. They treat their servants very well.
　　優點 **yōudyǎn** (N) good point, good feature.
　　優越 **yōuywè** (SV) be superior, outstanding.

唷 **yōu** (I) used to indicate surprise, Oh. /～, 原來是你啊! Oh, it was you!

悠 **yōu** (FV) swing. /泰山從這棵樹～到那棵樹去. Tarzan swung from this tree to the other. (B) far-reaching. ～久 be long (of time); ～遠 be far.
　　悠韆儿 **yōuchyer** (N) swing (M 架 **jyà**).

油 **yóu** (N) oil, fat, grease. 2) paint, varnish. 3) oil (fuel). 汽～ gasoline; 煤～ kerosene. (FV) paint, varnish. /那所房子外面儿～成綠的了. The outside of that house was painted green. (SV) be cunning, slippery. /他那個人～極了. He is very slippery.

油漆 **yóuchī** (N) paint, lacquer, varnish. (FV) paint. /我家正在～房子. We are having our house painted.
　　油燈 **yóudēng** (N) oil lamp (M 盞 **jǎn**).

由 **yóu** (FV) <着> rest with someone (of any matter). /這件事不能～你. This matter doesn't rest with you. (CV) 1) from. /我剛～紐約來. I just came from New York. 2) by a place. /我～他家門口儿經過. I passed by the door of his house. 3) by a person. /這件事應該～你辦理. This affair should be handled by you. (B) cause, means. 理～reason; 無～no reason.
　　由於 '**yóuyú** (A) because, since, due to. /～天氣不好, 我們不能去旅行了. Since the weather is no good, we can't travel.

郵[邮]**yóu** (B) post, mail. ～箱 mailbox; ～戳 postmark.
　　郵差 **yóuchāi** (N) mailman.
　　郵遞員 **yóudìywán** (N) mailman (c).
　　郵電局 **yóudyànjyú** (N) postal telegraph office (c).
　　郵件 '**yóujyàn** (N) mail. /郵差什麼時候來收～? When will the mailman come to collect the mail?
　　郵局 **yóujyú** (N) post office.
　　郵票 **yóupyàu** (N) postage stamp (M 張 **jāng**).

游[游2]} **yóu** (B) 1) swim, float. ～水 to swim. ～絲 floating gossamer threads. 2) travel, roam. 遠～ travel to a distant place; ～覽 go sight-seeing; ～蕩 wandering. 3) section of river. 下～ lower reaches of a river. 4) saunter. 閒～ saunter. *s*
　　游客 **yóukè** (N) tourist, excursionist.
　　游歷 '**yóulì** (FV) make a trip (as a tourist), travel, tour. /他～過很多地方. He has traveled to many places.
　　游戲 **yóusyì** (N) game. 做～ play games. (FV) play. /孩子們在花園裡～. The children are playing in the garden.
　　游行 **yóusyíng** (FV) parade. /他們舉着國旗在街上～.

They carried a national banner as they paraded through the streets. (N) parade.

游藝會 **yóuyìhwèi** (N) gathering for entertainment (as in a school).

游泳 **yóuyǔng** (VO) swim. /我游了一天泳. I swam for a whole day. (N) swimming.

游泳池 **yóuyǔngchŕ** (N) swimming pool.

游園會 **yóuywánhwèi** (N) garden party (M次**tsż**).

尤 **yóu** (B) ↓. s t

尤其 **yóuchí** (A) especially. /大家都很生氣,～我母親. Everybody is getting angry, especially my mother.

猶[犹] **yóu** (B) ↓. t

猶疑 **yóuyí** (SV) be hesitant. /我對這件事很～,不知怎麼做好. I'm rather hesitant about this matter, I don't know what's best.

友 **yǒu** (B) friend. 朋～ friend; 好～ good friend.

友善 **yǒushàn** (SV) be friendly. ～的態度 friendly manner. /他跟我很～. He is very friendly to me.

友誼 **yǒuyí** (N) friendship.

有 **yǒu** (negated by 沒 **méi** only, never 不 **bù**). (FV) 1) have. /他～八個孩子. He has eight children. /這個房子沒～窗戶. This house doesn't have any windows. /我～飯吃. I have food to eat. 2) there is, there are. /～問題嗎? Are there any questions? /～一本書你得看. There's a book you must read. (A) before NU-M, with or without SV following. about, approximately. /他～三十歲. He's about thirty. /樹～五尺高. The tree is about five feet tall. (B) followed by a noun, forms SV. ～錢 be rich; ～學問 be well-learned. (PT) 1) ～. . .那麼. . .as . . .as . . . /他沒～他太太那麼能說. He is not as talkative as his wife. 2) ～那麼. . . as . . .as that, so. /他～那麼高嗎? Is he that tall?

有辦法 **yǒubànfa** (SV) be good at something. /他對做買賣很

～. He's really good at doing business.

有邊兒 **yǒubyar** (SV) be likely (of a possibility). /我的獎學金～了. It's likely that I'll get the scholarship. (VO) take shape. /我們的計劃現在有一點邊兒了. Our plan is beginning to take shape.

有碴兒 **yǒuchár** (VO) have ill feeling, have a score to settle. /他們兩個人早就～了. There has been ill feeling between those two for a long time.

有的 **yǒude** (AV) have something to. /他這回可～玩兒了. This time he has something to play with. (B) with or without N following, some. /這些答案裡～不對. Some of these answers are wrong answers. (PT) ～. . .～. . . . some . . . some . . . . /～是紅的,～是白的. Some are red and some are white. /～人吃飯,～人喝酒. Some people eat, some people drink.

有的是 **yǒudeshŕ** (FV) have a lot of something. /這種衣服我～. I have a lot of clothes like these. /緬因州～龍蝦. There are a lot of lobsters in Maine.

有點兒 **yǒudyǎr** (A) somewhat, a bit. /今天～冷. It's a bit cold today.

有種 **yǒujǔng** (SV) be brave, have guts. /你要是～,你就把我殺了. If you have guts, kill me.

有兩下子 **yóulyǎngsyàdz** (SV) have a way with something, be pretty good at something. /他做飯～. He's pretty good at cooking. /他很～. He's not bad at all.

有名 **yǒumíng** (SV) be famous, prominent.

有人 **yǒurén** (B) some people, certain people. ～説 some people say.

有時候 **yǒushŕhou** (A) <-兒> sometimes, occasionally. /他～抽烟. He smokes occasionally.

有心 **yǒusyīn** (AV) intend to, wish to. /我～給你五塊錢,可是我也沒有. I wish to give you five dollars, but I don't have any money myself. (VO) have the intention. /你有沒有這種心? Do you intend to or not? (SV) be determined. /這個人很～. He's very determined.

有一點儿 **yǒuyídyar** = 有點儿 **yǒudyǎr**.

有一手儿 **yǒuyìshoǔr** (SV) be pretty good <u>at something</u>. /他真～. He is not bad at all. (VO) have an illicit relationship with. /我疑心他跟他的秘書～. I suspect that he's carrying on with his secretary.

有意思 **yǒuyìsz** (SV) be interesting. /那個小孩儿很～. That child is very interesting. (VO) be interested in. /你對李小姐有什麼意思嗎? Are you interested in Miss Lee?

有一天 **yǒuyìtyan** (TW) once upon a time, on a certain day. /～我遇見老張了. One day I ran into my old buddy Chang.

有用 **yǒuyùng** (SV) be useful.

右 **yòu** (L) right. 山～ right side of the mountain, to the right of the mountain; ～耳 right ear; 從～到左 from the right to the left. /往～走. Go to the right. (SV) be rightist (<u>politically</u>). /他的思想很～. His way of thinking is very rightist. (PT) 1) 左...～... over and over again. /他左跟我說,～跟我說. He talked with me over and over again. 2) 左也...～...either way. /左也不行,～也不行. It won't do either way.

右邊 **yòubyan** (PW) <-儿> 1) on the right. /我一看,～沒有人. When I looked, there was no one on the right. 2) the right side, part *or* area <u>of something</u>. /箱子的～壞了. The right side of the box is broken.

右傾 **'yòuchīng** (SV) be rightist (<u>politically</u>). ～份子 rightist element.

右面 **yòumyan** = 右邊 **yòubyan**.

又 **yòu** (A) 1) again (<u>repetition of an action</u>). /他～來了. Here he comes again. /我～忘了告訴他了. I forgot to tell him again. 2) and then. /他喝了很多咖啡,～喝了點儿茶. He drank a lot of coffee, then some tea. 3) <u>used before a negative expression or a question to make it more emphatic</u>. /我～不知道今天下雨. I didn't know at all that it was going to rain today. /他～知

道什麼? What on earth does he know? 4) and also. /他人很聰明～漂亮. He is very clever, and good looking too. (B) <u>used between a whole number and a fraction</u>, and, plus. 一～三分之一 one and one third. (PT) ～...～... not only, but also. /這儿的東西～便宜～好. Things here are not only inexpensive but also good.

幼 **yòu** (B) young. ～童 child.

幼兒園 **yòuérywán** (N) kindergarten (M所 **swǒ**).

幼稚 **yòujr** (SV) be childish, immature. ～園 kindergarten. /我太太很～. My wife is quite childish.

愚 **yū** (B) stupid. ～人 stupid person.

愚笨 **yūbèn** (SV) be stupid, slow in learning. /那個人很～,教他什麼都學不會. That person is quite stupid. No matter what you teach him, he can never learn it. (N) foolishness.

愚蠢 **yūchwǔn** (SV) be foolish, stupid. /自殺是很～的. Committing suicide is very foolish. (N) stupidity, foolishness.

於 **yú** (CV) for, toward, with reference to. /這～你有什麼好處呢? What advantage is it to you? /這件事～我有很大的關係. This is a life and death matter for me. (B) than. 多～ more than; 少～ less than.

於是 **yúshŕ** (A) thereupon, then. /～我告訴他了. Then I told him.

魚 **yú** (N) fish (M 條 **tyáu**).

魚網 **yúwǎng** (N) fish net (M 張 **jāng**).

愉 **yú** (B) be happy. ～悅 joyful.

愉快 **yúkwài** (SV) 1) be pleasant. /那裡的空氣很～. The atmosphere there is very pleasant. 2) be happy. /我近來很～. I've been very happy lately. (N) happiness.

榆 **yú** (B) elm. ～莢 elm-seed.

榆樹 **yúshù** (N) elm tree (M棵 **kē**).

娛 **yú** (B) amuse, give pleasure to. 自～ amuse oneself.

娛樂 **yúlè** (N) amusement,

yǔ yǔ

recreation. ～場 place of amusement. /晚上有什麼～嗎? Is there any recreation (scheduled for) this evening?

雨 yǔ (N) rain (M陣 jèn, 場 chǎng). /昨天下～了. It rained yesterday.
雨衣 yǔyī (N) raincoat (M 件 jyàn).
雨傘 yúsǎn (N) umbrella (M 把 bǎ).

與 [5] yǔ (CV) with, concerning. /那件事～我沒什麼關係. That matter has nothing to do with me. /我～他沒什麼可説的了. I have nothing to talk with him about now. (B) and. 父～子 father and son.
與其 yǔchí (A) rather than. /～送給他,還是自己留着吧. You'd better keep it for yourself, rather than giving it to him. (PT) ～...不如... rather than... it's better to. /～你去,不如我去. Rather than having you go, it'd be better if I went.

語 yǔ (B) 1) speech, talk. ～病 speech defect; ～調 tone of voice. 2) language, dialect. 英～ English language; 粵～ Cantonese dialect.
語法 yǔfǎ (N) grammar.
語文 yǔwén (N) 1) spoken and written language. 2) language and literature.
語言 yǔyán (N) spoken language. ～學 linguistics.

輿 yǔ (B) ↓.
輿論 yúlwùn (N) public opinion. /～攻擊他,攻擊的很厲害. Public opinion condemns him quite vigorously.

預(豫) yù (B) beforehand. ～付 pay in advance.
預備 yùbei (FV) 1) prepare, get ready. /你的生日禮物我早就～了. I got your birthday present ready a long time ago. /你得～一篇演講. You have to prepare a speech. 2) plan. /他們～訂婚了. They plan to get engaged. /你～幾時走? When do you plan to go? (N) preparation.
預防 yùfáng (FV) take preventa-

tive measures against. /我們應當～不景氣. We should take preventative measures against inflation.
預計 yùjì (FV) anticipate that, figure that. /我們～我們的工作五月裡可以做完. We anticipate that our work will be finished in May. /我們～五個人可以做這事. We figure that five people can do this job.
預料 'yùlyàu (FV) 1) predict. /這件事情我早就～到了. I predicted this event long ago. 2) predict that. /我～他不會來. I predict that he won't come. (N) prediction.
預算 yùswàn (FV) make advance plans or calculations. /我～五天之內一定能到那儿. I calculated that I would surely be able to get there within five days. (N) budget.
預先 yùsyān (A) beforehand. /你應該～看一看. You ought to take a look at it beforehand.

玉 yù (N) jade (M塊 kwài).
玉米 yùmi (N) corn (the plant, the ear, or the kernel) (M棵 kē; 個 ge; 粒 lì).
玉米麵 yùmimyàn (N) corn meal.
玉蜀黍 yùshúshǔ = 玉米 yùmi.

遇 yù (B) meet, run into. ～難 meet with misfortune; ～險 run into danger.
遇到 yùdau (RC) meet, run into. /我剛才在街上～一個朋友. I just met a friend on the street. /他又～困難了. He's running into difficulties again.
遇見 yùjyan (RC) meet, run into, someone or something. /我在那個宴會裡～很多熟人. I met many familiar people at that party. /昨天我們的船～大風了. Our boat ran into heavy winds yesterday.

芋 yù (B) yam. 山～ sweet potato.
芋頭 yùtou (N) taro.

浴 yù (B) bathe. 沐～ bathe, take a bath; ～盆 bathtub.
浴室 yùshř (N) bathroom (M 間 jyàn).

獄 yù (B) prison, jail. 入～ be put in prison.

育 **yù** (B) 1) give birth to. 生～give birth to. 2) bring up, raise. ～蠶 rear silkworms. 3) nourish. 教～ educate, education.

育嬰堂 **yùyīngtáng** (N) foundling home.

yuan *see* **ywan**.

yue *see* **ywe**。

暈 **yūn** (SV) 1) be dizzy. /我覺的有點兒～. I feel a little dizzy. 2) be reckless. /你怎麼這麼～呢? How could you be so reckless? (RE) indicates fainting. 嚇～了faint from fright. →暈 **yùn**.

暈倒 **yūndǎu** (RC) faint, pass out. /他又～了. He fainted again.

雲[云] **yún** (N) cloud (M塊**kwài**, 片**pyàn**).

雲彩 **yúntsai** (N) cloud (M塊 **kwài**, 片 **pyàn**).

勻 **yún** (FV) spare time, money, effort, space. /你能不能～點兒時間和我討論那個問題? Can you spare some time to discuss that problem with me? /你～點兒地方讓我坐行嗎? Can you spare a little more room, so that I can sit down? (SV) be balanced, even, evenly distributed. /顏色畫的很～. The color is spread on very evenly.

允 **yǔn** (B) allow, consent. ～諾to assent, to promise.

允許 **yúnsyǔ** (FV) permit, allow. /我～你們抽煙. I'll allow you to smoke. (N) permission.

暈 **yùn** (B) 1) be sick (of motion-sickness). ～船 seasick; ～車 carsick; ～飛機airsick. 2) halo. 月～ lunar halo. →暈 **yūn**.

運[运] **yùn** (FV) ship, transport, convey, goods, products, etc. ～費 freight. /貨物已經～到了. The goods have already been shipped. /我還沒決定是不是請人幫我～傢俱呢! I haven't decided whether or not I'm going to hire people to move the furniture. (B) 1) fate, luck. 好～ good luck; 壞～bad luck. 2) revolve, turn around. ～轉 to revolve.

運氣 **yùnchi** (N) luck. /他的～不錯. He has good luck.

運動 **yùndung** (FV) 1) exercise. /剛吃過飯別～. You shouldn't exercise right after eating. 2) try to get a job by using improper personal influence. /他現在想～一個差事. He's trying to get a job by using improper personal influence. 3) work on someone. /我得先～～他. I have to work on him first. (N) 1) physical exercise. 2) a movement. 勞工～ labor movement.

運動場 **yùndùngchǎng** (N) 1) stadium. 2) athletic field.

運河 **yùnhé** (N) canal (M條 **tyáu**).

運輸 **yùnshū** (N) transportation. ～公司 moving company; ～機transport plane. (FV) transport, ship. /這個東西太大,沒法兒由飛機～. This thing is too big to be transported by plane.

運輸業 **yùnshūyè** (N) transportation business.

運用 **yùnyùng** (FV) use, utilize. /你可以～私人的款項. You may use private funds. (N) use, utilization. 勞力的～ utilization of labor.

熨 **yùn** (FV) press *or* iron clothes. /我有很多衣服要～. I have a lot of clothes to iron.

熨斗 **'yùndǒu** (B) iron (for ironing clothes) (M把**bǎ**).

醞[酝] **yùn** (B) brew, ferment. ～酒 brew liquor by fermentation.

醞釀 **yùnnyàng**, **yùnràng** (FV) be brewing (of a situation). /那樁叛亂已經～很久了. There's been a revolt brewing for some time. (N) fermentation.

擁[拥] **yūng** (FV) crowd. /總統一下飛機, 新聞記者就都～上來照像 As soon as the president got off the plane, the news reporters crowded forward to take pictures of him. (B) support. ～戴領袖support a leader.

擁抱 **yūngbàu** (FV) hug, embrace. /他～着他太太接吻. He embraced his wife and kissed her. (N) hug, embrace.

擁護 **yūnghù** (FV) 1) support a government, leader. /我們～政府的政策. We support our government's policy. 2) back <u>someone</u> in <u>doing something</u>. /我們～你做班長. We're backing you to be the representative of our class. (N) support (<u>for a government or leader</u>).

踴(踴)**yŭng** (B) ↓.
   踴躍 **yŭngywè** (SV) be enthusiastic and numerous. /今天投票的人很～. Today the voters are enthusiastic and numerous. (A) enthusiastically. /請～參加. Please join in enthusiastically.

勇 **yŭng** (B) be brave, courageous. ～氣 bravery.
   勇敢 **yúnggăn** (SV) be brave.

永 **yŭng** (B) forever, perpetual. ～生 eternal life.
   永不 **yŭngbù** (A) never (<u>not used for past action</u>). /他～說謊. He never tells a lie.
   永久 **yúngjyŏu** (A) perpetually, eternally, permanently. /我不打算～住在這儿. I don't plan to live here permanently.
   永遠 **yúngywăn** (A) 1) perpetually, eternally, permanently. /他們就這樣～分開了嗎? Will they be apart like this forever? 2) always. /他～遲到. He always comes late.

用 **yùng** (FV) 1) use, utilize. /你可以～我的傘. You can use my umbrella. 2) have a <u>smoke</u>, <u>drink</u>, <u>meal</u>, etc. /請您～點儿點心. Please have some refreshments. (N) use, utility. /這個東西沒有什麼～. This thing doesn't have much use. (CV) using, with, making use of. /他～鉛筆寫字. He writes with a pencil. (AV) need to, have to. /我～去嗎? Do I need to go? /你不～操心. You don't have to worry. (B) expenditure. 零用 pocket money. (PT) 拿...當...～. use ...as.... /你可以拿報紙當傘～. You can use a newspaper as an umbrella.
   用不着 **yùngbujáu** (AV) need not. /你～買. You needn't buy it. (RC) have no need for <u>something</u>. /這本書我～. I have no need for this book.

用處 **yùngchu** (N) use, useful feature.
   用功 **yùnggūng** (FV) put in effort. /他研究這個問題用了不少功. He put a lot of effort into studying this problem. (SV) be studious, hard-working. /學生都很～. All the students are very diligent.
   用盡 **yùngjìn** (FV) use up, use all of. /我～我的力量幫他的忙. I used all my power to help him.
   用人 **yùngren** (N) servant.
   用心 **yùngsyīn** (VO) apply one's mind, use <u>one's</u> brains. /他做這件事用了不少的心. He really used his head when he did this. (SV) be diligent, careful. /他寫字很～. He writes very carefully. (A) diligently, carefully. /你得～念書. You'd better study diligently.
   用意 **yùngyì** (N) purpose, intention, underlying <u>and sometimes</u> <u>concealed</u> motive. /我說這句話沒什麼～. I didn't have any ulterior motive in saying that.

冤(寃)**ywān** (FV) cheat, fool, deceive. /我叫人給～了. I've been tricked. /我不～你. I wouldn't fool you. or I'm not kidding. (SV) 1) be wronged, cheated. /我覺的很～. I feel I've been wronged. 2) be not worthwhile. /花十塊錢買這個太～了. It's not at all worthwhile to pay ten dollars for this thing. (B) 1) grievance, wrong. 申～ redress a grievance. 2) rival. ～家 enemy.
   冤枉 **ywānwang** (FV) do injustice to, wrong, <u>someone</u>. /你別～我. Don't wrong me. (SV) 1) be cheated, wronged. /那筆錢他們說是我偷的,我覺的～極了. I feel very wronged by their saying that I stole the money. 2) be not worthwhile. /花兩百塊錢住這種房子很～. It's not worthwhile to pay two hundred dollars to live in a place like this. (N) wrong, grievance.

圓{元(M), (B) 1)} **ywán** (SV) 1) be round, circular. /月亮～了. The moon is full. 2) be mellifluous. /他的嗓子很～. His voice is mellifluous. 3) be smooth, personable, <u>in</u>

doing things. /這人做事很～.
He is a glad-hander. (FV) cover up,
make excuses. /昨天我說了一個
謊,請你替我～一～. Yester-
day I told a lie; please cover up for
me. (M) for currency. 一～港幣
one Hong Kong dollar. (B) 1) currency. 美～ American currency.
2) interpret, explain. ～夢 interpret
a dream.

圓 圈 儿 **ywánchywār** (N) circle
(geom.).

圓 規 **ywángwēi** (N) compasses
(for drawing circles).

圓 滑 **'ywánhwá** (SV) be smooth,
overly tactful. /他太～了. He's
very smooth.

圓 滿 **'ywánmǎn** (SV) be just
right in every aspect. /他的婚姻
很～. His marriage is ideal. (A)
satisfactorily. /那件案子現在
已經～解決了. That case has
been solved satisfactorily.

原 **ywán** (A) originally. /這件事情
我～不應該做. I shouldn't have
done this in the first place. (B)
1) origin, source. ～主 original owner. 2) excuse, forgive. ～宥 to excuse. 3) plain. 草～ prairie.

原 版 **ywánbǎn** (N) original copy,
original edition, of some book or
document.

原 子 **ywándž** (N) atom.

原 子 彈 **ywándždàn** (N) atomic
bomb (M顆 **kē**).

原 子 能 **ywándžnéng** (N) atomic
energy.

原 則 **ywándzé** (N) principle (M
條 **tyáu**).

原 稿 **ywángǎu** (N) <-儿> original draft of a manuscript.

原 故 **ywángu** (N) reason, cause.
/他不能來有兩個～. He has
two reasons for not being able to
come.

原 價 **ywánjyà** (N) original cost,
original price (commercial term).

原 來 **ywánlái** (A) 1) originally,
at first. /我～不喜歡喝茶. I
didn't like to drink tea at first. 2)
actually. /～是你啊! It actually
was you!

原 路 **'ywánlù** (N) the route one
came by. /他從～回去了. He
returned by the same route.

原 諒 **'ywánlyàng** (FV) forgive
a person for his offences. /請你
～我. Please forgive me. (N)
pardon, forgiveness.

原 料 **ywánlyàu** (N) raw material.

原 先 **ywánsyān** (A) at first,
previously. /他～是一個陸軍
上尉. Previously he was a captain
in the army. /我～不喜歡他.
At first I didn't like him.

原 文 **'ywánwén** (N) 1) words
actually used by a person being quoted.
/～不是這麼寫的. The original
words didn't read that way. 2) language in which something was originally
written. /舊約的～是希伯
來文. The original language of the
Old Testament was Hebrew.

原 因 **ywányīn** (N) cause, reason.

緣 **ywán** (N) affinity. /我們沒有～.
We just can't get along (lit. We have
no affinity.). (B) 1) reason. ～起
original cause. 2) edge. 邊 ～edge.

緣 故 **ywángu** (N) cause, reason.

元 **ywán** (B) 1) foremost, primary. ～
年 first year of an era; 一首 leader of
a country. 2) origin. 一一～論 monism
(philos.). 3) era. 公 ～ Christian era.
d 一圓{元} **ywán**.

元 旦 **ywándàn** (TW) (on) New
Year's Day.

元 帥 **ywánshwài** (N) marshal
(high ranking military officer).

員 **ywán** (B) 1) person who has certain
specific duties. 教～ teacher; 收票
～ ticket collector. 2) personnel. 幹
～ able personnel; 復～ demobilization.
3) member of an organization. 會～
member of a club.

園[园] **ywán** (B) <子> garden, orchard.
果 ～ fruit orchard; 公 ～ public park.

園 丁 **ywándīng** (N) gardener.

遠[远] **ywǎn** (SV) be far away, distant.
/我家離學校不～. It's not far
from my home to school. (FV) keep
away from someone or something.
/他人很危險,你最好～着他一
點儿. He is quite dangerous, you'd
better keep away from him. (A) by
far, far and away. /他～比你聰
明. He is far more clever than you.

院 **ywàn** (B) 1) <-子.-儿> yard, court-yard. ～落 courtyard. 2) institution. 醫～ hospital; 法～ court of law. 3) hall <u>open to the public</u>, public place. 電影～ movie theatre. 4) **yúan** (<u>any one of the five independent branches of the Chinese government</u>). 立法～ Legislative **Yúan**.

     院長 **ywànjǎng** (N) head <u>of an institution or a branch of the govern-ment</u>.

願[愿] **ywàn** (FV) hope, wish. /我～你們兩個人永不分離. I hope you two will never be separated. (N) vow. /我有一個～還沒了. I still have a vow not fulfilled. (B) volition, desire. 心～ one's heart's desire; 情～ voluntarily.

     願意 **'ywànyi** (AV) be willing to. /我～參加遊行. I am willing to participate in the parade.

怨 **ywàn** (FV) complain, grumble, <u>against someone or about something</u>. /這件事情我不～你. I'm not blaming you for this. (B) resentment. 埋～ resent.

約 **ywē** (FV) 1) invite, ask. /我～他吃午飯. I invited him to lunch. 2) reduce <u>fractions</u>. /請你～一～這個分數. Please see if you can reduce this fraction. (A) approx-imately. /昨天的客人～有兩百多位. There were around two hundred guests yesterday. (B) 1) <u>usually in RC</u>, make <u>an appointment</u>. ～好 set up an appointment. 2) con-tract, agreement, treaty. 條～ treaty; 立～ deed a contract. 3) restrain, bind. ～束 limit, restriction. 4) Testament (<u>of the Bible</u>). 新～ New Testament. *t* →約**yāu**.

     約定 **ywēdìng** (AV) agree to, decide to. /我們～三點鐘見. We agreed to meet at three o'clock.

     約會 **'ywēhwèi** (FV) invite. /我們～很多人. We invited a lot of people. (N) appointment. 定～ make an appointment.

樂[乐] **ywè** (B) music. *s* →樂**lè**.

     樂器 **ywèchi** (N) musical instru-ment (M件**jyàn**).

     樂隊 **ywèdwèi** (N) orchestra, band (M隊**dwèi**).

岳[嶽2)] **ywè** (B) 1) wife's parent. 2) mountain. 山～ mountain. *s*

     岳父 **ywèfù** (N) father-in-law (wife's father).

     岳母 **ywèmǔ** (N) mother-in-law (wife's mother).

月 **ywè** (N) month. 上～ last month; 正～ January. (B) moon. ～光 moon-light.

     月份牌儿 **ywèfenpár** (N) cal-endar (chart, not <u>system</u>).

     月季花 **ywèjìhwā** (N) <-儿> rosa Indica (M朵**dwǒ**).

     月亮 **ywèlyang** (N) moon.

     月蝕 **ywèshŕ** (N) lunar eclipse.

越 **ywè** (B) pass over, exceed. ～牆 go over a wall; ～界 encroach. (PT) ～...～.... the more ... the more. /他～說～生氣. The more he talked the madder he got.

     越發 **'ywèfā** (A) more than be-fore. /他～着急了. He's more worried than he was before.

     越獄 **ywèyù** (VO) make a jail break. /他越過兩次獄. He broke jail twice.

     越來越 **ywèlaiywè** (A) getting more and more .... /他的病～壞. His illness is getting worse and worse.

za *see* **dza**.

zai *see* **dzai**.

zan *see* **dzan**.

zang *see* **dzang**.

zao *see* **dzau**.

ze *see* **dze**.

zei *see* **dzei**.

zen *see* **dzen**.

zeng *see* **dzeng**.

zha *see* **ja**.

zhai *see* **jai**.

zhan *see* **jan**.

zhang *see* **jang**.

zhao *see* **jau**.

zhe *see* **je**.

zhei *see* jei.

zhen *see* jen.

zheng *see* jeng.

zhi *see* jr.

zhong *see* jung.

zhou *see* jou.

zhu *see* ju.

zhua *see* jwa.

zhuai *see* jwai.

zhuan *see* jwan.

zhuang *see* jwang.

zhui *see* jwei.

zhun *see* jwun.

zhuo *see* jwo.

zi *see* dz.

zong *see* dzung.

zou *see* dzou.

zu *see* dzu.

zuan *see* dzwan.

zui *see* dzwei.

zun *see* dzwun.

zuo *see* dzwo.

ENGLISH TO CHINESE

A (AN). Where English has **a** or **an** before a noun specifying merely an indefinite example of the item named by the noun, Chinese has sometimes the unmodified noun, sometimes the noun preceded by yī plus a measure; after a verb, the measure alone may replace the yī-plus-measure combination. / Is there a shoe store near here? (Jèr) 'fùjìn yǒu syé'pù ma? / That's a female cat. Nà shr̀ 'mǔmāu. / This is a book. Jèshr̀ 'shū. / Give me a book to read. Géi wǒ yìběr 'shū kàn. / A Mohammedan may have four wives. Yíge 'hwéihwei kěyi chyù 'sz̀ge tàitai.

(Each, per) is shown by order of sentence elements, sometimes with mei (each) plus a measure. / These eggs are fifty cents a dozen. Jèisyē jī'dzěr shr̀ 'wǔmáu chyán yì'dá. *or* Jèisyē jī'dzěr 'měiyìdá 'wǔmáu chyán.

ABDOMEN. dùdz.

ABLE. (Competent) néng dzwò shr̀, nénggan, yǒu běnshr, yǒu néngnai. / He's a very able assistant. Tā shr̀ ge hěn 'nénggan de 'jùshǒu. / We need three hundred able men immediately. Wǒmen 'jíkè yàu yùng 'sānbǎige néng dzwò 'shr̀ de rén.

Be able to. *See* **CAN**.

ABOUT. (Concerning) gwānyu, jyǎng. / This book is about international relations. Jèiběn 'shū jyǎngde shr̀ gwójì 'gwānsyì. / He's writing a book about Napoleon. Tā 'jèngdzai 'syě yìběn °jyǎng (°gwānyu) Nápwò'lwúnde 'shū.

(Almost) chàbudwǒ, chàbu'dwǒ jyòu, jyòu, kwài. / Dinner is about ready. 'Fàn jyòu 'dé(le). / The time is about up. 'Shr̀hou chàbu'dwǒ °jyòu (°kwài) 'dàu le. *or* 'Kwài dàu 'shr̀hour le.

(Approximately) chàbudwǒ, chyánhòu, dzwǒyòu, shàngsyà. / He was about five miles from home. 'Tā lí 'jyā chàbu'dwǒ 'wǔyīnglǐ dì. / This place is about fifty miles from the city. 'Jèige 'dìfang lí 'chéng yǒu 'wǔshryīnglǐ dzwo'yòu.

(Around) dàuchu dōu. / There were books about the room. Wūdzli dàuchu dōu shr̀ shū. / About face! (lit.) Syàng hòu 'jwǎn! *but* / She did an about face. (fig.) is expressed as She suddenly changed. Tā hūrán byànle.

Be about to 'kwài yàu . . . le, jyòu yàu . . . le. / The train is about to leave. Hwǒ'chē °'kwài yàu (°jyòu yàu) 'kāi le.

How about . . . . dzěmmayàng(r). / How about lunch? Jūng fàn dzěmmayàng(r)? **or** expressed as Is lunch ready? Jūng fàn déle ma? / How about it? Dzěmmayàng?

ABOVE. (Spatially) °dzài (°dàu, °tsúng) . . . °shang, (°shàngbyan, °shàngbyar, °shàngmyan, °shàngmyar, °shàngtou). / The plane is flying above the clouds. Fēi-'jī dzài 'yúntsai'shàngbyan 'fēi. / He can't keep his head above water. (lit.) Tā dzài 'shwéili bùnéng bǎ 'tóu 'lǒudzai shwěi 'shàngbyar. (fig.) is expressed as He can't cope with it. Tā 'yìngfubù'lyǎu.

(Numerically) yǐshàng. / He's above forty. Tāde 'nyánji dzài 'sz̀shryǐ'shàng.

(In the foregoing) yǐshàng, chyánmyan. / What's mentioned above isn't correct. 'Chyánmyan swǒ 'shwō de bú'dwèi.

Above all dzwèi yàu'jǐn de shr̀. / Above all, remember to be on time. Dzwèi yàu'jǐnde shr̀ yàu 'jìjùle shǒu 'shr̀ kè.

Be so far **above** lí . . . yǒu . . . 'gāu; 'gāuchū (rise above). / How far above sea level are we? Wǒmen 'jèr lí hǎi'myàn yǒu dwō 'gāu? / We're eight thousand feet above sea level now. Wǒmen syàndzài 'gāuchu hǎi'myàn 'bāchyān'chr̀.

Other English expressions. / He's above average height. is expressed as He is taller than the average man. Tā bǐ yì'bānrén 'gāu. / He's above doing anything like that. is expressed as He doesn't attempt to do such things as that. Tā bú'jŕyu dzwò 'nàyàngde shŕ. or as He isn't capable of doing such things as that. Tā(shŕ) bú'hwèi dzwò 'nàyàngde 'shŕde. / He's above suspicion. is expressed as He's definitely reliable. Tā jywédwèi kě kàu.

See also BEYOND.

ABSENT. chywēsyí; often expressed as not arrive búdàu, méidàu. / Three members were absent because of illness. Yǒu 'sānwèi hwèi'ywán yīn'bìng chywē'syí. / He's absent today. Tā 'jyēr méi'dàu.

ACCELERATOR. jyāsùbǎn, yóumén, yóumér.

ACCENT. jùngyīn. / Where's the accent in this English word? Jèige 'Yīngwén'dżde 'jùngyīn dzài 'nǎr?

(With source specified) 'kǒuyīn, . . .yīn. / He speaks English with a Russian accent. Tā shwō 'Yīngwén dài 'Ègwo 'kǒuyīn. / He speaks with a Cantonese accent. Tā shwō'hwà dài 'Gwǎngdūngyīn.

To accent jyājùng, shwōde jùngsye. / Accent the first word of this sentence. 'Jèijyù hwàde 'tóuyíge dż jyā'jùng. / The first word of this sentence should be accented. 'Jèijyù hwàde 'tóuyíge dż 'yīngdang shwōde 'jùngsye.

ACCEPT. 'jyēshòu, shōu, 'shōusyà. / Germany accepted the terms of the treaty. Tyáu'ywēlide 'tyáujyan Dégwo dou jyē'shòule. / Has the school accepted you as a student? Sywé'syàu 'shōule nǐ le ma? / He accepted the money I gave him. Tā 'shōusyale wǒ 'gěi tade 'chyán. / Do you accept American money? is expressed as Does this place use American money? 'Jèige dìfang yùng 'Měigwochyán ma? / Have you accepted the invitation? is expressed as Have you agreed to go? Nǐ 'dāyìng 'chyùle ma?

ACCIDENT. Expressed verbally as have an accident chūshŕ; or the action may be expressed more specifically with such verbs as jwàng, chwàng (run into), fān (overturn), etc. / We had a car accident yesterday. Dzwótyan wǒmende chì'chē °chūshŕ le (°fānle, °chwàngrén le).

By accident (without appointment) ǒurán. / We met them by accident. Wǒmen gēn tāmen ǒurán 'yùjyanle.

ACCOMPANY. (As a companion) péi, gēn . . . yíkwàr; (follow) gēnje; (to a definite place) sùng; (for protection) bǎuje, hùsùng. / I accompany him to school every day. Wǒ tyāntyān °péi tā(°gēn tā yíkwàr) dàu sywésyàu chyu. / The mayor was accompanied by two guards. Yǒu lyǎngge bǎu'byāude °péije (°gēnje, °bǎuje) shŕjǎng. / You should accompany him to the door. Nǐ yīnggāi °'sùng (°'péi) tā dàu ménkǒu. / It was I who accompanied him to the hospital. Shŕ 'wǒ °sùng (°péi) tā dàu yī'ywànde. / The flag ship was accompanied by a group of fighter planes. (Yǒu) yìfendwèi jàndòujī °bǎuje (°hùsùng) chíjyàn. / May I accompany you home? Wǒ kéyi sùng nǐ hwéi jyā ma?

Be accompanied by fùje. / His letter was accompanied by a receipt. Tāde 'syìnli fùje yìjāng shōu'tyáu.

ACCOMPLISH. dádàu, dzwòdau, wánchéng. / He accomplished his purpose quickly. Tā hěn 'kwàide dádau 'mùdì. *or* Tā hěn 'kwàide jyou 'dzwòdaule tā 'syǎng yàu dzwò de. / He's already accomplished his mission. Tā yǐjing wán'chéng le tāde 'rènwù le.

Accomplish something yóuswǒchéngjyou. / A man should accomplish something during his life. Yíge 'rén yì'shēng dzǔng 'yīngdang yǒuswǒchéngjyou.

Not accomplish anything yīwúswochéng. / He hasn't accomplished anything. Tā yìwúswǒ'chéng.

Be an accomplished . . . shr̀ ge hén yǒu chéngjyou de . . . . / He's an accomplished musician. Tā shr̀ ge hén yǒu chéngjyou de yīn ywè'jyā.

ACCORDING TO. ànjau, ànje, gēnjyu, jyù, yījau. / According to my orders, I must leave tomorrow. Yījau mìnglìng, wǒ 'míngtyan 'bìsyū déi 'dzǒu. / According to the latest rumor, there will be a change in policy. 'Gēnjyu dzwèi'jìn de 'yáuchwán, jèng'tsè yàu yǒu 'byàndùng. / According to the weather report, it'll rain tomorrow. Jyù tyānchi bàu'gàu 'míngtyan yàu syà'yù.

ACCOUNT. (Financial) jàng, 'jàngmù. / Have you figured out the account? 'Jàng 'swàn-chulai méiyou? / The company's accounts were in good order. Gūng'szde 'jàngmù hěn 'chīngchu.

(In a bank) hùtóu. / Do you have an account with this bank? Nǐ dzai jèige yín-'háng you 'hùtóu ma? / How much money is there in your account? <u>is expressed as</u> How much money do you have in the bank? Nǐ yín'hángli you dwōshau chyán?

(Explanation) . . . 'shwō de. / His account is different from hers. 'Tā shwō de gēn 'tā shwō de bùyí'yàng.

On account of yīn (formal). / The game was postponed on account of rain. Bǐ-'sài yīn'yǔjàn'chī.

On no account 'wúlwùnrúhé bu. / On no account should you mention the subject in his presence. Nǐ dzài tā 'myànchyán 'wúlwùnrúhé bùnéng 'tídau 'jèige wènti.

To account for jyěshr̀. / How do you account for that situation? 'Jèijǔng chíng-sying ní 'dzěmmayàng 'jyěshr̀?

ACCOUNTANT. kwàijishr̀.

ACHE. téng; <u>nominal expressions plus</u> téng <u>are used to express an ache in any part of the body;</u> **have a headache** 'tóuténg; **have a toothache** 'yáténg; **have a stomach ache** 'dùdzténg, 'wèiténg; <u>etc.</u> / I have a toothache. *or* My tooth aches. Wǒ 'yáténg. / My head doesn't ache any more. *or* I don't have a headache any more. Wǒ 'bùtóu-téng le. / Have you got a headache? Nǐ 'tóuténg ma?

ACID. (Chemical) swān. / That solution contains acid. Nèige 'rúngyè lǐtou yǒu 'swān. / Be careful! That's nitric acid. Syàusyīn 'dyǎr! Nèi shr 'syāuswān.

(Of the nature of an acid) swānde. / You shouldn't eat so many acid foods. Nǐ bùyīngdāng 'chr̄ nèmma dwō swānde dūngsyi.

Acid remarks 'jyānswān'kèbwóde hwà. / He made many acid remarks. Tā shwōle hǎusyē 'jyānswān'kèbwode hwà.

ACORN. syàngshùdzěr.

ACRE. yīngmǔ. / How many acres does your farm have? Nǐde núng'chǎng yǒu 'dwōshau yīng'mǔ.

ACROSS. (In combination with verbs) gwò; go **across** gwòchyu; come **across** gwòlai; **walk across** dzǒugwolai, dzǒugwochyu; **run across** pǎugwolai, pǎugwochyu; <u>etc.</u> / Walk across the bridge. Dzǒugwo chyáu °chyu (°lai).

Across <u>the street, road, river, etc.</u> from . . . dzài . . . °'dwèigwò (°'dwèimyàn,

° 'dwèimér, last term only for a street). / The restaurant is across the street from the hotel. Fàn'gwăr dzài lyú'gwăn 'dwèimér.

ACT. (Resolution of a governing body) yìjywéàn; -fă in compounds such as Child Labor Act Túnggūngfă. / The Child Labor Act is no longer in force. Túnggūng'fă yĭjing wú'syàu le. / It'll take an act of Congress to change that. is expressed lit. as It'll take Congress to change that. Jèige děi yóu Gwóhwèi lai găi.

(Of a play) mù; the third act 'syìdedì'sānmù.

In the act of 'jèngdzài. / He was caught in the act of stealing. Tā jèngdzai tāu dūngsyi de shŕhòu bèi ren 'dăijaule.

To act (in a play) yănsyì; (perform on a stage) byáuyăn. / They act well. Tāmen yăn'syì yănde hén 'hău. / He acted very well. Tā byáu'yănde hén 'hău.

(Do) dzwò, bàn, gàn. / I'm prepared to act on your suggestion. Wó 'jwŭnbèi ànje nĭde 'jyànyì chyu 'dzwò. / Now is the time to act. Syàn'dzài shŕ 'gàn de shŕhou le. / When will this matter be acted on? 'Jèijyàn shŕ 'shémma shŕhou 'bàn ne?

(Conduct oneself, behave) is expressed with the noun jyŭdùng action; **act like . . .** syàng . . . shŕde. / He's acting in a suspicious way. Tā 'jyŭdùng kě'yí. / He's been acting strangely lately. 'Jìnlai tāde 'jyŭdùng hĕn chĭ'gwài. / Don't act like a child. Byé syàng ge 'háidz shŕde. / He acts like a child. is expressed as His actions are childish. Tā jyŭdùng 'yòujr.

Act as, act in one's place dài'lĭ, dàitì. / Who'll act in your place after you're gone? Ní 'dzŏule 'shwéi dài'lĭ? / He acted as my substitute. is expressed as He represented me in performing the matter. Tā dàiti wŏ dzwò nèijyan 'shŕ.

ACTION. (Movement) 'dùngdzwò. / There's a lot of action in that movie. Nèige dyàn-'yĭngrlide 'dùngdzwò hĕn 'dwō.

(Military) jànshŕ. / There's no action on the western front. Syī'syàn wú jàn-'shŕ.

(Person's behavior) jyŭdùng, 'syíngwéi. / His actions show his character well. Tsúng tāde 'syíngweishang hĕn 'kàndechū tāde 'syìnggé lai. / His actions have been strange lately. 'Jìnlai tāde 'jyŭdùng hĕn chĭ'gwài.

Be in action jìnsyíng. / The plan is now in action. Jèige jìhwa jèngdzai jìnsyíng.

Put into action shŕsyíng. / The plan sounds good, but how are you going to put it into action? Jèige 'jìhwà 'tīngje hăusyàng bú'tswò, kĕshr dzĕmma néng shŕ'syíng a?

ACTIVE. (Of a child) hwópwo. / His son is very active. Tāde 'érdz hĕn 'hwópwo.

(In political or social life) ' hwódùng, 'hwóywè. / The communist element hasn't been active lately. Gùngchăn'fèndz 'jìnlai bútài ° 'hwódùng (° 'hwóywè).

(Of exercise) 'jĭlyè. / This sort of exercise is too active for a little boy. 'Jèijŭng'yùndùng dwèi yige syău'hár yŏu dyăr tài jĭlyè. / I don't feel like doing anything active. is expressed as I don't feel like moving. Wŏ búywànyi 'dùngtan.

Active life. / He leads an active life. (political) Tā 'jège rén hĕn 'hwódùng. (general) Tā dzwò de 'shŕ hĕn 'dwō. (sarcastically, meaning that he seeks publicity) Tā hĕn chū 'fēngtou.

ACTOR. (Drama) chàngsyìde, syìdz; (drama or movies) yănywán. / Mr. Smith takes part in the play, but he is not an actor. Sž syānshēng 'tsānjyā yăn 'syì, kĕshr tā 'búshr yige chàng'syìde.

ADDRESS

ACTUAL. shŕdzàide, shŕjì(de); in some compounds shŕ *or* jēn; **actual cost** shŕjyà; **actual situation** shŕchíng, jēnchíng, jēnsyàng. /What's the actual cost of this book? Jèibĕr 'shūde °shŕ'jyà (°shŕ'dzàide 'jyàchyán) shŕ 'dwōshou? /The actual damage isn't heavy. Shŕ'jì 'swŭnshr bú'jùng. /The actual situation in this matter isn't clear yet. 'Jèige shŕde °jēn'chíng (°jēn'syàng, °shŕ'chíng) hái bù'míngbai ne.

ACTUALLY. shŕjìshang, jēn. /Actually, he's wrong. Shŕjìshang tā 'tswòle. /He actually came! Tā 'jēn láile!

ADD. jyā. /Add water to the soup. 'Tāngli jyā dyar 'shwĕi. /You have to add this figure to the others. Nĭ dĕi bă'jèige shùmu °jyādzài (°jyādàu) 'nèisye shùmu shang. /Add it to my bill. is expressed as Figure it onto my bill. Swàndzai wŏde 'jàngshang.

Add together 'jyādzài yí'kwàr. /Add those two numbers together. Bă 'nèilyăngge shùmu 'jyādzài yí'kwàr.

Add up jyāchilai. /Add up this list of figures. Bă jèiháng shùmu 'jyāchilai.

Add up to. /How much does the account add up to? is expressed as The account altogether is how much? 'Jàng 'gùng dzŭng shŕ 'dwōshau?

Adding machine jìswànjī.

ADDITION. (Result of adding). /Is my addition correct? is expressed as Have I added (calculated) correctly? Wŏ °'jyāde (°'swànde) 'dwèi budwèi?

(Thing added). /The bathroom is an addition to the house. is expressed as The bathroom was added later. Syĭdzău'fáng shŕ 'hòulai jyāde.

(Person added). /We need many additions to our staff. is expressed as We must add personnel. Wŏmen 'syūyàu 'dzēngjyā hĕn dwō rén'ywán. or as We must add quite a few people. Wŏmen dĕi 'tyān bù'shăude rén.

In addition chútszyĭ'wài; **in addition to** chúle . . . (yĭ'wài). /Do you need anything in addition? Chútszyĭ'wài nĭ 'hái yàu 'shémma? /In addition to her original demands, she also wants a car. Chúle tā 'bĕnláide 'yāuchyóu (yĭ'wài), tā 'hái yàu yílyàng chì'chē.

ADDRESS. (Place) dìfang; (place at which some function is to be held) dìdyăn; (on an envelope) dìjŕ; (place of residence or business) jùjŕ; (mailing address) tūngsyìnchù. /Send the package to this address. Bă jèibāu 'dūngsyi sùngdau 'jèige dìfang chyu. /The wedding will be held at this address. Jyé'hwūnde dì'dyăn jyòu dzài 'jèr. /What address shall I put on this letter? Jèifēng 'syìnde °dì'jŕ (°tūngsyìnchù) yīngdāng 'dzĕmmayàng 'syĕ? /My address is. . . . Wŏde jù'jŕ shŕ. . . .

(Formal talk) yánjyăng, yănshwō; **give an address** *see* **To address** *below.* /I have to listen to an address tonight. Wŏ jīntyān 'wănshang dĕi tīng yíge °yán'jyăng. (°yánshwō). /The President is going to give an address tomorrow. Dàdzŭng'tŭng 'míngtyan yăn'shwō.

To address yánjyăng, yănshwō; (of a superior speaking to subordinates) syùnhwà. /The principal addressed the students. Syàu'jăng syàng 'sywésheng yăn'shwō. /The officer addressed his men. 'Gwān'jăng dwèi 'bùsyà syùn'hwà.

Address a communication. /To whom should I address this letter? is expressed as To whom should this letter be written? Jèifēng'syìn yīngdāng 'syĕgei 'shei?

Address A as B yĭ B chēnghu A. /I should address you as uncle. Wŏ yīngdāng yĭ làu'bwó 'chēnghu nín. /Mr. Jang should be addressed as Manager Jang. is expressed as Mr. Jang's title is Manager Jang. 'Jāngsyānshengde dzwŭn'chēng shŕ 'Jāngjīng'lĭ.

303

ADMIRAL. hǎijyūn 'jyànggwān; rear admiral hǎi'jwūn 'shàu jyàng; vice admiral hǎi-'jyūn 'jūng jyàng; full admiral hǎijyūn 'shàng jyàng.

ADMIRE. (Respect) pèifu, jìngpèi. /I admire the Chinese people. Wǒ hěn 'pèifu Junggworén.

(Enjoy) 'syīnshǎng. /I'm admiring the sights. Wǒ dzài 'syīnshǎng 'fēngjǐng.

ADMISSION. (Price of entrance) 'pyàujyà. /How much is the admission? 'Pyàujyà shr̀ 'dwōshau?

ADMIT. chéngrèn. /He himself admitted it quite frankly. Tā 'dzjǐ tǎnbáide chéng-'rèn le. /He admits no mistake. Tā búchéng'ren 'tswèr.

Admit someone shōu (formal); °syǔ (°jyàu) . . . jìnlai. /Not a single school would admit him. Ywànyi 'shōu tǎ de sywé'syàu 'yíge yě 'méiyou. or Méiyǒu yíge sywésyàu ywànyì shōu ta. /Don't admit them! Búsyǔ tāmen 'jìnlai! or Byé 'jyàu tāmen 'jìnlai! /Ask for me and you'll be admitted. is expressed as Say you're looking for me and you'll be able to go in immediately. Nǐ 'shwō jǎu 'wǒ jyòu kéyi jyàu ni 'jìnchyule. /When were you admitted to the university? Nèige dàsywé shémma shŕhou shōude nǐ?

ADOPT. (A child) bàu, lǐng; (where adoption is within the family) 'gwòjì. /They are going to adopt a son from the foundlings' home. Tāmen yàu tsúng yùyíng'táng °'bàu (°'lǐng) yige nán'háidz. /His uncle has adopted him. Tā yǐjing 'gwòjǐgei ta 'shūshu le.

(Take over and use) tsǎichyǔ, tsǎinà, tsǎiyùng. /We've decided to adopt this method. Wǒmen jywé'dǐng tsǎi'chyǔ 'jèige bànfa. /I can't adopt your plan. Wǒ bùnéng tsǎi'yùng nǐde 'bànfa.

ADULT. 'chéngnyánrén, chéng'nyán de rén (formal); 'dàrén (informal). /An adult may be mentally quite immature. Yíge 'chéngnyánrénde 'sz̄syǎng kěnéng hěn 'yòujr. /Children must be accompanied by adults. Syàu'háidzmen bìděi yǒu 'dàrén 'gēnje. /Adults have to pay the tax. Chéng'nyán de rén děi nà'shwèi.

Be (or Become) an adult chéngrén, chéngnyán. /He's not yet an adult. Tā hái méichéng'rén.

ADVANCE. (Progress) jìnbù. /What advances have been made in medicine? 'Yīsywé yǒu shémma jìn'bù?

(In battle) jìnjǎn. /No advance has been made by the enemy troops. 'Díjyūn wú jìn'jǎn.

In advance syān, yù, yùsyān. /Let me know in advance if you're coming. Nǐ rúgwo 'lái de hwà, chǐng 'syān 'gàusung wo yísyàr.

Be advanced (promoted) shēng; be advanced in grade shēngjí; be advanced in official position shēnggwān; be advanced to a certain position 'shēngdàu. /He's about to be advanced. Tā jyòu yàu 'shēngle. /You can be advanced for excellent service. Nǐde 'chéngjì 'hǎu, jyòu kéyi 'shēng. /He's recently been advanced to foreman. Tā 'dzwèi'jìn shēngdau gūng'tóurle.

To advance money (informal) syān jyègei; (formal) yùjr̀. /Could you advance me some money? Nǐ néng 'syān 'jyègei wo dyǎr 'chyán ma? /He asked the company to advance him $150. Tā yàu tsúng gūng'sz̄ 'yùjr̀ 'yìbǎi'wǔshrkwài 'chyán.

Advance prices jǎngjyàr. /Prices will be advanced after six o'clock. 'Lyòu-dyǎnjūng yǐ'hòu jyòu yàu jǎng'jyàr.

ADVANTAGE. lì; have advantages yǒulì; have disadvantages yǒubì. /This is to your advantage. 'Jèige 'dwèi ni yǒu'lì. / This method has advantages and disadvantages. 'Jèige fāngfa yǒu'lì yě yǒu'bì. / Since you have the advantage of a better position, I can't compete with you. is expressed as Since your position is better than mine, I can't compete with you. Yīnwei 'nǐde dìwèi bǐ 'wǒde 'hǎu, wǒ méi'fár 'gēn ni jìngjēng.

ADVERTISE. (Have a notice appear in a newspaper) dēngbàu; (put an ad in a paper) dēng gwǎnggàu; (pass out notices or handbills) sàn gwǎnggàu, sàn chwándān; (post bills) tyē gwǎnggàu, tyē chwándān. / They're advertising in the paper for a teacher. Tāmen dēng'bàu jēng pìn yíwèi jyàu'ywán. / They've already advertised three times in the paper. Tāmen 'yǐjīng dzài 'bàushang dēngle 'sāntsz gwǎng'gàu le. / This store is advertising a big three-day sale. Jèige 'pùdz dēng gwǎng'gàu shwō dàjyǎn-'jyà san'tyān.

(Make known or conspicuous) fābyǎu; gūngbù (make public); 'sywānchwán (make public with fanfare). / If they're making progress the government will advertise it. Yàushr tamen yǒu jìn'bù, jèngfù yídìng hwèi °'sywānchwánde (°gūng'bùde, °fābyǎude). / He likes to advertise his feelings. Tā hěn 'syǐhwan fābyǎu tāde 'yìjyàn.

ADVERTISEMENT. gwǎnggàu. / A full-page advertisement costs a lot of money. Yìjěngjāng de gwǎng'gàu děi hěn dwōde 'chyán. / I saw your advertisement. Wǒ 'kànjyan nǐ'dēng de gwǎng'gàu le.

ADVICE. chywàngàu, jūnggàu, yìsz. / Your advice has worked well. Nǐde jūng'gàu hěn yǒu'syàu. / I can't act on your advice. Wǒ bù'néng ànje nǐde 'yìsz 'dzwò. / I won't accept your advice. Nǐde chywàn'gàu wǒ bujyēshòu. / My advice is to leave here immediately. is expressed as I advise that you leave here immediately. Wǒ 'chywàn nǐ 'gánjǐn 'líkai jèr.

ADVISE. jǔjāng, shwō, chywàn. / I advise against going. Wǒ jǔ'jāng bú'chyù. / What do you advise me to do? 'Nǐ shwō wǒ 'yīngdang 'dzěmmayàng 'bàn? / I advise you to take a rest. Wǒ 'chywàn ni 'syōusyi yísya.

Be advised of 'jyēdau . . . de 'syāusyì. / His parents have been advised of his disappearance. Tāde jyā'jǎng yǐjing 'jyēdau tā shī'dzūng de 'syāusyi le.

AERIAL. tyānsyàn.

AFRAID. pà, hàipà. / Don't be afraid! Byé hài'pà!

Be afraid of dzàihu, pà. / I'm not afraid of you! Wǒ °bú'dzàihu (°bu'pà) ni! / He's not afraid of anything. Tā 'shémma dōu bú'pà.

Be afraid that jywéde, kǔngpà. / I'm afraid it's too late. Wǒ jywéde tài 'wǎnle! / I'm afraid I can't go. Wǒ kǔng'pà bunéng 'chyù.

Be afraid to pà. / I'm afraid to go out at night alone. Wǎnshàng wǒ pà 'dàndù chūchyù.

AFTER. yǐhòu; hòu (most usually after one-syllable nouns). / Can you see me after dinner? Nǐ 'fàn'hòu néng 'jyàn wo ma? / Come any time you like after nine. 'Jyǒudyán yǐ'hòu swéi'byàn 'shémma shr hou 'lái. / Wait until after I come back. Děng wǒ 'hwéilai yǐ'hòu (dzài 'shwō).

(Modeled on) fǎng, fǎngsyàu, fǎngjàu, fǎngje. / This dress is designed after a Parisian style. Jèijyan yīfu dzwò de 'yàngdz shr fǎng 'Bālí'shr.

(Next in order). / What's the next street after this? is expressed as What's the name of the next street? 'Syàyityáu jyē jyàu shémma 'míngdz? or as The next one is what street? 'Nèibyar shr shémma 'jyē?

After all dàudǐ, jyōujìng, búlwùnrú'hé. / You're right, after all. Dàu'dǐ hái-shr 'nǐ 'dwèi. / After all, why do you object? Nǐ jyōu'jìng 'wèi shémma fǎn'dwèi? / After all, don't forget that he saved your life once. Búlwùnrú'hé, byé 'wàngle tā 'tséngjīng 'jyòugwo nǐde 'mìng.

After that, afterwards hòulai. / What happened after that? 'Hòulai 'dzěmma yàng?

After this tsúngjīnyǐ'hòu, tsúngtsž, yǐhòu. / After this, please let us know in advance. °Tsúngjīnyǐ'hòu (°Tsúngtsž yǐhòu) chǐng 'syān 'tūngjr wǒmen.

Be after (search for) jǎu; (pursue) jwēi. / The police are after him. Sywún-'jǐng 'jǎu ta ne. / There are three girls after him. Yǒu 'sānge 'gūnyang 'jwēi ta ne.

Day after day, year after year, etc. yi'tyānyǐ tyānde, yǐ'nyányǐ nyánde, etc. / He worked on it day after day. Tā yǐ'tyānyǐ'tyānde 'dzwòsyachyu. but / We tried store after store. is expressed as We tried all of the stores one after another. Jèisye pùdz wǒmen yǐgeyǐgede dōu dzǒubyànle.

AFTERNOON. 'syàwǔ, 'gwòwǔ, hòubantyan, syàbantyan, wǔhòu. / I'm leaving in the afternoon. Wǒ 'syàwǔ 'dzǒu. / It came yesterday afternoon. 'Jèige shr̀ dzwótyan 'syàwǔ 'láide. / Can you come this afternoon? Nǐ 'néng bunéng 'jīntyan syàwǔ 'lái?

AFTERWARD(S). yǐhòu, hòulai; dǐsya (only if referring to following events in a story or on a program). / What happened afterwards? ° Yǐ'hòu (° 'Dǐsya) 'dzěmmayàngle ne? / See me afterwards. is expressed as After it's over come see me. Wánle yǐ-'hòu lái 'kàn wo.

AGAIN. dzài, yòu. / Try once again. 'Dzài 'shr̀ yísyà. / I hope to see you again later. Yǐ'hòu dzài 'jyàn. / Here I am again. Wǒ 'yòu láile. / I hope to see you again. (formal) is expressed as Later there may be an occasion. 'Hòu hwèi yǒu-'chī.

Again and again, time and time again 'yítsž 'yòu yí'tsžde, 'dzwǒ yítsž 'yòu yí'tsžde, and the same expressions with byàn instead of tsž; wúshùtsž. / I could do this again and again. 'Jèige wǒ 'kéyi yítsž 'yòu yí'tsžde 'dzwò. / I've told you again and again. Wǒ dzwǒ yítsž 'yòu yí'tsžde 'gàusu ni. / He tried time and time again. Tā 'shr̀le wúshù'tsž.

Never again dzài yě bū-, yùng búdzài, yǔngywǎn bú'dzài. / Never again will I make that mistake. Wǒ 'dzài yě bú'fàn 'nèijùng tswòr le.

AGAINST. (Detrimental to) dwèi . . . búlì, yú . . . búlì. / His looks are against him. Tāde syàng'màu °dwèi tā (°yú ta) bú'lì.

(Facing, near) dwèi, jèng dwèi, chùng. / Our house is built against the sea. Wǒmende 'fángdz shr̀ chùngje 'hǎi 'gàide.

(Contrasted with) dwèi. / The bill was passed by 150 votes against 100. Yì'àn yǐ 'yìbǎi'wǔshr dwèi 'yìbǎipyàu tūng'gwòle.

Against wind, storm chyāng(je), dǐng(je), yíng(je). / It isn't exactly easy to run against the wind. Chyángje fēng 'pǎu búdà 'rúngyì.

Against wind, rain, storm, snow, gunfire màu(je). / They went ahead against the storm. Tāmen màuje fēng'yǔ wǎng'chyán dzǒule.

Against the stream, the current, current opinion, wind nì. / A boat goes much slower against the current than with the current. 'Chwán 'nìshwěi 'dzǒu, bǐ 'shwǔnshwěi mànde 'dwō. / His thinking is against current opinion. Tāde 'sžsyǎng shr̀ 'nìje shr̀'dàide cháu'lyóude.

306

Against one's will myǎnchyǎng. /He came against his will. Tāmyǎn'chyáng 'láile.

Be against (of subordinate to higher authority) fǎnkàng. /Those soldiers are against the government. 'Nà shr̀ fǎn'kàng 'jèng'fǔ de jyūn'dwèi.

Be against (attack a person, policy) 'gūngjī. /He wrote an article against the president. Tā 'syěle yìpyàn 'wénjāng 'gūngjī dàdzǔng'tǔng.

Be against a person gēn . . . dzwòdwèi, búsyàngje. /He's against me. Tā 'gēn wo dzwò'dwèi. or Tā bú'syàngje wǒ.

Be against a person, policy, etc. fǎn, fǎndwèi. /I'm against war! Wǒ fǎn'jàn! /Is everyone against him? Dà'jyā dōu fǎn'dwèi ta ma?

Be against a proposal, idea bú dzànchéng. /Are you for or against the proposal? Nǐ shr̀ 'dzàncheng háishr̀ 'búdzàncheng jèige tí'yì?

Be against the law fànfǎ, wéifǎ, wéifàn 'fǎlyù, wéifàn 'fǎlyù. /That's against the law. 'Nà shr̀ °wéi'fàn 'fǎlyù (°etc.).

Bring action against gàu, kùnggàu. /He brought action against me. Tā bǎ wo gěi 'gàule.

Go against one's conscience bèije. /I'd never go against my own conscience. Wǒ 'jywé bùnéng bèije 'lyǎngsyīn.

Lean against kàu, yǐ. /He's leaning against a tree. Tā 'yǐje yìkē'shù 'jànje. /Lean it against the wall. Kàudzai 'chyángner.

Talk against gěi . . . shwō hwàihwà. /He was talking against you. Tā gěi ni shwō hwài'hwà láije.

Work against time gǎnje dzwò. /We worked against time in meeting the deadline. Wǒmen 'gǎnje dzwò wèideshr̀ kéyi àn shr̀hou dzwò 'wán.

AGE. (Year of age) swèi, swèishu, nyánji; (formal) 'nyánlíng; (in the Western sense) shr̀dzúnyánlíng, shr̀dzàide nyánlíng; (in the Chinese sense a person becomes one year of age upon birth and one's age increases by one at the turn of each year; if someone is born in December, then in January, it being the following calendar year, he becomes two years old) lyǎng swèi; (age required for admission to a school) rù'sywényánlíng; (age required for admission to the armed forces) fú'yì nyánlíng. /What is your age? (to a child less than ten) Nǐ 'jīnnyan jǐ'swèile? (to someone in the teens) Nǐ 'jīnnyan shŕjǐ'swèile? (to an adult) Nǐ 'jīnnyan dwōshau'swèile? (to an older person, very politely) Nín 'jīnnyan gāu'shòule? (to anyone; rather brusque) Nǐ dwō-'dà le? (if Western or Chinese age is in question one would first ask) 'Jūnggwo swèishu haishr̀ 'wàigwo swèishu? /What is your actual age? Nǐ shr̀ 'dzàide 'nyánlíng shr̀ dwōshau? /Sex and age make no difference. 'Syìngbyé túng 'nyánlíng bú-'lwùn. /Excitement isn't good for a man of my age. Syàng 'wǒ jèmma dàswèishùde rén, bùyìng'dāng tài 'syìng'fènle.

(Era) shŕdài. /This is the age of invention. Jèshr̀ fā'míngde shŕ'dài.

The aged (people) shàng swèishu de rén, yǒu 'nyánji de rén, 'lǎunyánrén, shàng 'nyánji de rén. /We should aid the aged and the poor. Wǒmen yīng'dāng 'bāngjù °shàng 'swèishù de rén (°etc.) gēn 'chyúngrén.

To age lǎu. /He's aged a great deal lately. Tā 'jìnlai lǎu'dwōle.

AGENT. (Person) 'dàilǐrén; (store) jīnglǐ(dyàn). /We must find an agent in every large city for our new merchandise. Měige 'dàchéngli dōu děi 'jǎu yige dàilǐrén 'dàisyāu dzámende 'syīn'hwò. /We're the sole agent for this make of radio. 'Jèige páidzde wúsyàn'dyàn(shōuyīn'jī) wǒmen shr̀ 'dújyājīng'lǐ.

(Representative) dàibyǎu. / Your agent has already called on me. Nǐde dài-'byǎu yǐjing lái 'jyàngwo wǒ le.

(Official) bànshr̀de. / I'm a government agent. Wǒ shr̀ tì 'jèngfǔ bàn'shr̀ de.

(Means) ywándùnglì. / Chance was the sole agent. 'Jīhwei shr wéi'yīde ywán-dùng'lì.

AGO. chyán, yǐchyán. / Two years ago I was in America. 'Lyǎngnyán chyán wǒ dzài 'Měigwo. / I was here two months ago. 'Lyǎngge ywè yǐ'chyán wǒ dzài 'jèr láije.

A while ago gāng . . . yǐhwěr. / I got here a while ago. Wǒ gāng 'dàu yǐhwěr. / He left a while ago. Tā gāng 'dzǒu(le) yǐhwěr.

Long ago dzǎujyou, hěn jyǒu yǐchyán. / He left long ago. Tā 'dzǎujyou dzǒu le. / That happened long ago. Nèi shr hěn jyǒu hěn jyǒu yǐchyánde shr̀ching.

Not very long ago bùhěn 'jyǒu yǐ'chyán.

AGREE. (Be in accord) syāngfú; (have the same opinion) túngyì; (be the same) yíyàng, syāngtúng. / The two statements don't agree. Lyǎngjyù'hwà °búsyāng'fú (°bùyí-'yàng). / We agree on everything. Wǒmen wán'chywán túng'yì. / Their ideas agree to some extent. Tāmende 'yìjyàn yǒu syē syāng'túngde dìfang.

Agree to something 'jyēshòu. / I agree to your terms. Wǒ 'jyēshòu nǐde 'tyáujyàn.

Agree with an idea or proposition 'dzànchéng. / Do you agree with me? Nǐ 'dzàncheng (wǒde 'yìsz) ma?

Agree with one (of food) is expressed as **agree with one's stomach** hé 'wèikǒu. / This food doesn't agree with her. Jèijǔng 'shr̀wù bùhé tā 'wèikou.

Agree with one (of life, environment, work, etc.) 'héshr̀, fú. / This kind of life doesn't agree with me. Jèiyangde shēnghwó dwèi wǒ bùhéshr̀. / She was afraid that the climate wouldn't agree with her. Tā 'pà bù'fú shwěi'tǔ.

AGRICULTURE. (Farming) núngyè; (as field of study) 'núngsywé.

AHEAD. chyán, chyánbyan, chyánbyar, chyántou, chyánmyan, chyánmyar. / Go straight ahead. Yì'jŕ wàng 'chyán dzǒu. / Look ahead. Wàng'chyán kàn. / The car ahead of us has stopped. Dzài wǒmen 'chyántoude chē 'tíngjùle.

Be ahead (in a game) yíng(je); in other instances often expressed as not to have fallen behind méilàsya. / Who's ahead? Shwéi 'yíngje ne? / I'm ahead in my work. Wǒde 'gūngdzwo méi'làsya. / He's way ahead of his class. is expressed as He's left his classmates far behind. Tā bǎ tāde túng'bānde 'làde hěn 'ywǎn. but / It's pretty hard to say just what's ahead of him. is expressed as It's pretty hard to say what his future prospects are. Tāde chyán'tú hěn nán'shwō.

Get ahead gǎngwochyu. / I tried to get ahead of Jāng. Wǒ syǎng gǎngwò lǎu Jāng chyù. but / I want to get ahead. Wǒ syǎng shàngjìn.

AID. bāng (máng). / Let me aid you. Ràng wo lái 'bāng ni ('máng).

(Of a charitable organization or the government) 'jōujì, 'jyòujì. / The government aids refugees. Jèngfǔ °'jōujì (°'jyòujì) nànmín. / The Red Cross is soliciting funds to aid the victims of the calamity. 'Húngshŕdz̀'hwèi yàu jywān'chyán 'jyòujì 'nànmín.

Financial aid jyǎngsywéjīn (money for study); yánglǎujīn (pension); jyòujìjīn (compensation); bǔjùjīn, jīntyé (subsidy).

Foreign aid wàiywán.

AIM. (Goal) mùbyāu, mùdi. /His aim is to finish writing this book. Tāde °mùbyāu (°mùdi) shr bǎ jèibèn shū 'syéwán.

(Ambition in life) jr̀syang. /His aims are high. Tāde 'jr̀syang hěn 'dà.

To aim a weapon myáu, myáujwǔn. /Aim higher. Wàng 'shàng 'myáudyar. or 'Myáude 'gāudyar. /Aim the gun this way. meaning in this manner 'Jèmmayàng myáu'jwǔn.

(Plan) 'dǎswàn, syǎng. /What do you aim to do? Nǐ 'dǎswàn dzwò 'shémma? /Enemy troops aim to capture the town. 'Dírén syǎng bǎ 'chéng 'gūngsyàlai.

Aim at jr̀je . . . shwō. /Who is your remark aimed at? Nǐ shr̀ 'jr̀je 'shwéi shwōde? but /What are you aiming at? is expressed as What do you mean? Nǐ shr̀ shémma'yìsz?

AIR. (Atmosphere) 'kūngchì; (sky, weather) 'tyānchì. /I'm going out for some fresh air. Wǒ yàu 'chūchyu 'hūsyī dyǎr 'syīnsyān 'kūngchì. /The air is clear today. 'Jīntyān 'tyānchì hěn shwǎng'kwài.

(Sky) tyān. /The swallows are soaring in the air. 'Yàndz dzài 'tyānshang 'fēi.

(Manner) tàidu. /But her air reveals that she's lying. Kěshr tāde 'tàidu 'syánchulai tā shr̀ dzài sā'hwǎng.

By air (for passengers) dzwò fēijī; (for freight or mail) yùng fēijī; (for mail) yùng hángkūng'syìn. /I want to go by air if possible. Rúgwo 'kěnéng, wǒ syǎng dzwò fēi'jī chyù.

Be airtight búlòu'chì.

Be on the air gwǎng'bwō. /This radio station hasn't been on the air for three days. Jèige wúsyàn'dyàn'tái yǒu 'sāntyān méi gwǎng'bwōle.

Open-air lùtyān. /They've built an open-air theater. Tāmen 'gàile yíge lùtyān syì'ywándz.

To air (of a room, etc.) bǎ . . . jyàu 'fēng 'chwēi(yichwēi), bǎ . . . tūng(yitūng) 'fēng; (of oneself or clothes, thoroughly) (bǎ . . .) tòufēng; (of bedding, clothes, etc.) lyàng. /Would you please air the room while I'm out? Wǒ 'chūchyu yǐhòu chǐng ni bǎ jèige 'wūdz jyàufēng 'chwēi yichwēi. /You should air your fur coat every now and then. Nǐ 'yīngdang 'shŕcháng bǎ nǐde pídà 'yī 'tòu yitòu 'fēng. /To prevent mildew, you should air it every day. Rwòshrsyǎng jyàu 'jèige dūngsyi bù shēngméi, nǐ 'yīngdang 'měityān 'lyàng ta yí'tsz̀.

(Of opinions) shwōchulai. /He aired his opinions among the students. Tā bǎ tāde yìjyan dzài sywésheng myànchyan 'shwōchulaile.

AIRCRAFT CARRIER. hángkūngmǔ'jyàn.

AIRFIELD. fēijīchǎng.

AIR FORCE. kūngjyūn.

AIRMAIL. hángkungsyìn; **by airmail** yùng hángkūng'jì.

AIRPLANE. fēijī. /There are three airplanes in the sky. Yǒu 'sānjyà fēi'jī dzài 'tyānshang 'fēi. /How long does it take by airplane? Dzwò fēi'jī chyù děi 'dwōshau 'shŕhou?

AIRPORT. fēijīchǎng.

AISLE. dzǒudàu.

ALARM. (Danger signal) jǐngbàu; **air-raid alarm** kūngsyī jǐng'bàu, (first signal) yùbèi jǐng'bàu, (second signal) jìnjí jǐng'bài, (all-clear signal) jyěchú jǐng'bàu; **fire alarm** hwójǐng. / What was that alarm for? 'Nèige jǐng'bàu shr̀ wèi 'shémma?

    Alarm clock 'nàujūng. / Set the alarm clock for six. Bǎ 'nàujūng shàngdau 'lyòudyǎnjūng.

    To alarm jǐngdùng. / The noise alarmed the whole town. 'Shēngyīn jǐng'dùng chywán 'chéng.

    Be alarmed hwāng, jǐnghwǎng. / Don't be alarmed. Byé 'hwāng. *or* Byé jǐng'hwāng.

    Be alarming kějǐng 'jyàu rén hàipà. / The situation is quite alarming. 'Chíng-shr̀ hěn °kějǐng (°jyàu rén hàipà).

ALBUM. jìnyàntsè(dz); **photograph album** syànpyārběndz, jàusyàngběr; **record album** chàngpyārběndz.

ALCOHOL. (Medicinal) hwǒjyǒu; (liquor) jyǒujīng.

ALE. màijyǒu.

ALGEBRA. dàishù.

ALIEN. 'wàigworén, wàichyáu.

ALIKE. syāngtúng, yíyàng. / If the cases were all alike, we wouldn't need to discuss them. Yàushr 'chíngsyíng dōu syāng'túng dehwà, wǒmen jyòu 'yùngbujáu tǎu-'lwùnle. / These places are all alike. Jèisyē dìfang dōu yí'yàng.

    (Same way). / We treat all the visitors alike. is expressed as We treat all visitors as equals. Wǒmen dwèi 'swóyǒude yóu'kè yīshr̀'túngrén.

    Look alike kànjesyàng, kànje yíyàng. / They look alike. Tāmen lyǎngge rén °kànje'syàng (°kànje yíyàng).

ALIVE. Usually expressed by hwó *or* hwóje (to live); (of people) dzài. *See* LIVE. / This fish is alive. Jèige 'yú °hwóje ne (°shr̀'hwóde). / Is she still alive? Tā shr̀ bushr̀ hái 'dzài? / Get him dead or alive. is expressed as Seize him, his life or death doesn't matter. Dǎu ta, sž'hwó búlwùn.

    Be alive to dzài dífangje, dzài fángbeije. / I am very much alive to the danger Wǒ lǎu dzai dífangje.

    Be alive with jǐng shr, mǎn shr (preceded by an adverb such as láilaichyu-'chyùde, 'kētóupèng'nǎude, etc.). / This place is alive with crackpots and halfwits. Jèige 'dìfang láilaichyu'chyùde jǐng shr bàn'fēngr gen bèn'dàn. / The station was alive with soldiers. Hwǒchē'jànlì 'kētóupèngnǎude mǎn shr bīng.

    Come alive with 'hūran byàncheng. / She came alive with passion. Tā 'hūran byàncheng hěn 'rèchíng le.

    Keep alive (fig.) ràng . . . lǎu jywéje. / The war kept the hatred alive. Nèitsz dǎ'jàng ràng tāmen lǎu jywéje yǒu'chî.

ALL. dōu, chywán, 'chywándōu (must be used in front of verbal expressions); <u>also</u>
<u>expressed with</u> yíchye (of things), dàjyā (of people), swóyǒude (of things or people),
fán (every) *or* fánshr (all those who are) (which all require one of the first three
words directly before the verb). / Please don't take all my money. Chíng ni byé bǎ
wǒde chyán °dōu (°etc.) nádzǒu. / All of us know him. Wǒmen dou 'rènshr ta.
/ He knows all of us. Wǒmen, ta dou 'rènshr. / Let's all go. Wǒmen dàjyā dōu
chyù ba. / I gave him all of my money. Wǒ bǎ wo swó'yǒude chyán dou gěi tā le.

(The whole) yi . . . yìjěng . . . / She cried all night. Tā kūle yi'jěngyè. / I
have been waiting all day long. Wǒ děngle yi'tyān le.

(Entirely) dōu. / It's all over now. 'Yǐjīng dōu 'gwòchyule. *or* Dōu 'wánle.
or Dōu 'lyǎule.

All <u>followed by a clause which modifies it</u> jyòu, jř. / This is all there is.
'Jyòu yǒu jèi'syē. *or* 'Jyòu shr jè'yàngr. *or* Dōu 'dzài jèr le. / All you have
to do is write a check. Nǐ jyòu kāi yijāng jř'pyàu, jyòu 'sying le. / All I know
is he is stupid. Wǒ 'jyòu jřdau tā 'bèn. / All I can say is he is honest. Wǒ 'jyòu
néng shwō ta hen 'chéngshr. *but* / All I said was true. Wǒ 'shwō de dōu shr
'jēnde.

All along tsúng 'chǐtóur, tsúng 'chǐchū. / He's known it all along. Tā tsúng
'chǐtóur jyòu 'jřdàu(le).

All around chywán . . . dou. / I've looked all around the city. Chywán'chéng
wǒ dōu kàn'byànle.

All-around chywánnéng, chywántsái. / He's an all-around athlete. Tā shr
yige °chywánnéngde (°chywántsáide) 'yùndùng'jyā.

All at once 'hūrán(jyān) jyòu, 'tūrán(jyān). / All at once something happened.
'Hūránjyān jyòu chūle 'shřle.

All but jīhu děng'yú. / He's all but dead. Tā jīhu děng'yú 'sžle.

All kinds of shémma(yàngrde) . . . dōu. / We sell all kinds of things. Wǒmen
shémma dōu mài. / It takes all kinds (of men). 'Shémmayàngrde(rén) dōu 'yǒu.

All the better gènghǎule. / If that's true, all the better. Rúgwo shř 'nàyàng,
dāngrán gèng 'hǎule.

All the same méiyou shémma 'fēnbye, dōu shř yí'yàngde. / You can take
either car, it's all the same. Nǐ swéi'byàn dzwò 'nǎlyàng chē, méiyou shémma
'fēnbye. / It's all the same to him. Dzài tā ('syīnli) dōu shř yí'yàngde. *but*
/ But I hate you all the same. Wǒ 'háishr 'hèn ni.

All the time lǎushř, dzǔngshř. / He does it all the time. Tā °'lǎushř (°dzǔng-
shř) dzèmma dzwò.

All the way yí'lù. / He ran all the way. Tā yí'lù 'pǎuje chyù de.

If at all rúgwo . . . (dehwà). / I'll be there before eight, if at all. Wǒ rúgwo
chyù dehwà, bādyǎn yǐ'chyán 'dàu.

In all yígùng. / How many are there in all? Yí'gùng yǒu 'dwōshau?

Not all (of) . . . (some of . . .) bù (*or* méi) *plus* dōu, chywán, *or* 'chywándōu.
/ Not all of us like to do it. Wǒmen bu'dōu syǐhwan 'dzwò. / I don't want to buy all
the books. <u>meaning</u> I only want some of them. Nèisye 'shū, wǒ bùdōu yàu 'mǎi.

Not at all 'gēnběn . . . bu, yì'jř . . . méi, 'wánchywán . . . bu, shř'jūng . . .
méi, 'yìdyǎr yě bu. / I don't know him at all. Wǒ 'gēnběn bú'rènde tā. / I didn't
speak at all. Wǒ yì'jř méishwō'hwà. / Don't you know it at all? Nǐ 'wánchywán bù-

'jŕdàu ma? / Haven't you been here at all? Nǐ shŕ'jūng méi'láigwo ma? / I'm not at all tired. Wǒ 'yìdyǎr yě bú'lèi.

Special expressions in English. / (Thank you.) Not at all! 'Méiyou shémma! / That's all there is to it. Búgwǒ rú'tsż. or Jyòushr 'jèmmaje jyòu 'wánle. / He isn't all there. Tā you yìdyǎr fēngfēngdyāndyānde. / All right. I'll go. Hǎule. Wǒ dzǒu.

ALLEY. hútùng(r), syǎusyàngr.

ALLIANCE. túngméng, lyánméng; form an alliance jyēméng.

ALLIGATOR. èyú.

ALLOW. (Permit) jyàu, ràng (informal); syǔ, jwǔn (formal). / She won't allow me to go. Tā °bú'ràng (°bújyàu, °bùsyǔ, °bùjwǔn) wo 'chyù. / They allow you fifty pounds of baggage without extra charge. Jwǔn myǎn'fèi dài 'wǔshrbàngde'syíngli.

(Leave) fàngchulai. / Allow one inch on the waistcoat. Bèi'syīn 'fàngchu yí-'tswùnlai.

(Figure in) dǎchulai. / Allowing a tenth for breakage, you can still make some profit. Jyòushr 'dǎchu 'shŕfēnjr'yīde swǔn'hàulai, 'hái kéyǐ 'yǒude 'jwàn ne.

Allow for (make allowances for) tǐlyàng. / You must allow for his youth. Nǐ děi tǐ'lyàng tā 'nyánchīng.

Allow so much for (pay, or loan on security). / How much will you allow me for this? 'Jèige nǐ 'dǎswàn gěi wo 'dwōshau chyán?

ALLY. (Country) yǒubāng.

ALMANAC. nyánjyàn; (chronicles) lìshū, dàshŕjì.

ALMOND. syìngrérsyìngrén.

ALMOST. 'chàbudwō, 'chàyìdyǎr, 'jīhū. / He almost died. Tā °'chàbudwō (°'chàyì-dyǎr) 'sżle. or Tā 'chàyìdyǎr méi'sż.

(With reference to time) jyòu, kwài. / I'm almost done. °'Jyòu (°'Kwài) 'wánle. / We're almost there. °'Jyòu (°'Kwài) 'dàule.

ALONE. 'dzjǐ, 'yígerén, jŕ yǒu... / Can you do it alone? Nǐ 'dż jǐ néng 'dzwò ma? I came alone. Wǒ shŕ 'yíge rén 'láide. / You alone can help me. Jŕ yǒu 'nǐ néng 'bāng wo. / I'm all alone in the world. Wǒ 'gūshēn 'yìrén. / I'm all alone here. Jyòu wǒ yíge rén dzàijèr. but / Leave me alone! 'Líwo 'ywǎndyǎr! or Byé jāu wo! or Byé 'rě wo! or Byé 'gwǎn wo! or Nǐ gwǎnde'jáu ma!

ALONG. yán. / A fence runs along the road. Yán 'lù yǒu yídàu 'líba. / The submarine coasted along the shore. Chyǎnshwěi'tǐng yánje hǎi'àn màn'mārde dzǒu.

Along with gēn, túng, hé. / Come along with me. 'Gēn wo lái. / Put it along with the others. Bǎ 'jèige °túng (°gēn, °hé) 'byéde fàngdzai yí'kwàr.

Get along. / How are you getting along? Nǐ 'jìnlái 'dzěmma yàng? or Nǐ 'jìnkwàng rú'hé? / Are you getting along all right together? Nǐmen ('lyǎnggerén) syāng'chù hái 'hǎu ma?

Take along dài. / How much baggage should I take along? Wǒ yīngdang dài 'dwōshau syíngli?

ALPHABET. dz̀mǔ.

ALREADY. yǐjīng. / I'm late already. Wǒ 'yǐjīng 'wanle.

(Unexpectedly soon) 'jyūrán yǐjīng. / Are you finished already? Nǐ 'jyūrán yǐjīng dzwò'wánle (ma)?

ALSO. yě. / I'd also like to have that one. Wǒ ('túngshŕ) yě syǎng yàu 'nèiyige.

(In addition, furthermore) yòu, hái, dzài jyāshang. / There was a policeman there also, so what could I do? °'Yòu (°'Hái, °Dzài 'jyāshang) yǒu ge jǐng'chá; nǐ shwō, wǒ néng yǒu shémma bànfa ?

See also **TOO.**

ALTHOUGH. 'swéirán (often followed in the next part of the sentence by kěshr *or* búgwò); or sometimes expressed with kěshr *or* búgwò without 'swéirán. / Although there were three of them against me, I wasn't at all afraid. 'Swéirán tāmen (shŕ) 'sānge rén dǎ wǒ 'yíge, (kěshr *or* búgwò) wǒ yi'dyǎr yě bú'pà. / They still see each other often, although they've been divorced. Tāmen ('swéirán) líle 'hwūn, kěshr 'hái cháng jyàn'myàr.

(Except that) búgwò. / I'll be there, although I may be late. Wǒ yí'dìng 'dàu nàr, bú'gwò wǒ 'syūhwèi 'wǎn yìdyǎr.

See also **THOUGH.**

ALTITUDE. gāudù.

ALWAYS. (Past, present and future) dzǔng(shŕ), lǎu(shŕ). / Down south the weather is always bad. 'Nánbyan 'tyānchi 'dzǔngshr bù'hǎu. / Are you always so busy? Nǐ 'lǎushr jèmma 'máng ma? / I am not always here. Wǒ 'búshr °lǎu (°dzǔng) dzài jèr.

(In the past, since some remote point of time) 'syànglái, 'tsúnglái, yìjŕ, yísyàng. / In China New Year's Day has always been a holiday. Dzài Jūnggwo syīnnyán nèityān syànglái fàng'jyà. / This train always runs on time. Jèilyè 'chē °syànglái (°'tsúnglái) búwù'dyǎn. / He's always been like that. Tā yì'jŕ shŕ 'nàyàng. / Having always had a very easy life, he doesn't know what hardship means. Tā °yì-'syàng (°yìjŕ) 'gwòde shŕ 'shūfu r̀dz, bù'jŕdàu 'shémma jyàu chŕ'kǔ.

(From now on) yǔngywǎn. / Always remember to be on time. Yǔng'ywǎn jì-'jùle shǒu shŕ'kè.

Not always bùyídìng dōu (shŕ). / Crows aren't always black. 'Wūyā bùyidìng dōu shr 'hēide.

See also **EVER, OFTEN, NEVER.**

AMBASSADOR. dàshŕ.

Ambassador to . . . jù . . . dà'shŕ. / He used to be the U. S. Ambassador to China. Tā tsúngchyán shŕ Měigwó jù Jūnggwó dàshŕ.

AMBULANCE. jyòuhùchē.

AMENDMENT. syōujèngfǎàn.

AMERICA. (The continent) 'Měijōu; **North America** Běi'měijōu; **South America** Nán-'měijōu. **United States of America** Měilì'jyānhéjùnggwó *or* Měigwo.

AMERICAN. (Pertaining to the United States) Měigwo(de). / This is an American movie. Jè shr̀ 'Měigwo dyàn'yǐngr.

    American (person) Měigworén. / He's an American. Tā shr̀ 'Měigworén.

AMONG. (In the midst of) dzài . . . lǐ(tou), dzài . . . dāngjūng. / Look among the papers. Dzài wénjyànli jǎu. *or* Dzài wénjyàn dāngjūng jǎu. / Choose among these. Dzài jèisyē dāngjūng tyāu. / You are among friends. is expressed as We all are not outsiders. Dzámen dōu búshr̀ 'wàirén. / It's nice to be among friends. is expressed as To be together with friends is nice. Gēn péngyǒu dzài yǐkwàr hěn yǒu'yìsz.

    (In the number or class of) dzài nèi, shr̀ chíjūngjr̄'yī. / He was among those that were killed in the plane crash. Nèitsz fēijī chū'shr̀ sz̆le hǎusyē rén; tā °dzài nèi (°shr̀ chíjūngjr̄'yī). / Fifty passed the exam and he was among them. Kǎu'shr̀, yǒu wǔshŕge rén jí'géle; tā °dzài nèi (°shr̀ chíjūngjr̄'yī).

    (In shares to each of). / They divided the food up among themselves. Nèisyē 'chr̄de dūngsyi, tāmen bǐ'tsz̆ 'fēnle.

    (By the joint action of). / They were quarreling among themselves. Tāmen bǐ'tsz̆ chǎu'jyà láije.

AMOUNT. (Numerical sum) shùmu; (quantity) shùlyang. / This isn't the right amount. 'Jèige °shùmu (°shùlyang) bú'dwèi.

    Total amount dzǔng shù. / What's the total amount? Dzǔng shù shr̀ dwō shǎu?

    To amount to swàn, děngyú. / My knowledge of Chinese doesn't amount to much. Wǒ 'dǔng de Jūnggwo'hwà búswàn 'dwō. / The work he did amounts to nothing. Tā dzwò de gūng °děngyú (°swàn) báidzwò. / What does the bill amount to? is expressed as How much is this bill in all? Jèibǐ 'jàng yí'gùng shr̀ 'dwōshau (chyán)?

AMUSE. (Of a child) hǔng. / Try to amuse the children. Syǎng'fár hǔng 'háidz.

    (Of an adult) gěi . . . dòu'syàur, gěi . . . kāikāi 'syīn, (jyàu) . . . jywéde kě-'syàu. / Tell them a story to amuse them. Shwō ge 'syàuhwar, gěi tāmen °dòudou 'syàur (°kāikāi 'syīn). / What she says amuses me very much. Tā shwō de 'hwà wǒ jywéde kě'syàu.

    Amuse oneself jyěmèr, 'syāuchyǎn. / How do you amuse yourself? Nǐ 'dzěm-mayàng jyě'mèr? *or* Nǐ dzwo shémma 'syāuchyǎn?

    Be amusing kěsyàu, yǒuchyù(r)(de). / Do you find this comedy amusing? Nǐ 'jywéde jèige syì'jyù kě'syàu ma? / Tell them an amusing story. 'Gěi tāmen shwō ge yǒu'chyùrde 'gùshr.

AMUSEMENT. yúlè; or expressed as **amuse** kāisyīn. / Are there many amusements here? Jèr yǒu shémma yú'lè ma? / Where can you go around here for amusement? Jèr yǒu 'shémma dìfang kéyi chyù kāikāi 'syīn?

    Place of amusement kě'wár de dìfang. / Are there many places of amusement here? Jèr 'yǒu méiyou kě'wárde dìfang?

ANATOMY. 'jyěpōusywé (the branch of study).

ANCHOR. máu; **weigh anchor** bámáu, chǐmáu; **cast anchor** syàmáu, pāumáu.

AND. (Between nouns) gēn, hé, túng; hàn (local Peiping). / The room had only a bed, a table, and a chair. 'Wūdzli jǐ yǒu yíge 'chwáng, yìjāng 'jwōdz, gēn yìbǎ 'yǐdz. / You and I have a lot in common. Nǐ túng wo syāng'jìnde dìfang hěn 'dwō. / The guests included bankers and lawyers. Láide kèrenlitou yǒu yínháng'jyā °gēn (°etc.)

lyu'shr. *but* /There are doctors and doctors. is expressed as There are all kinds of doctors. Yǒu gèshrgè'yàngde 'yīshēng. /I walked miles and miles. is expressed as I walked I don't know how many miles. Wǒ 'dzǒule bùjrdàu 'dwōshou 'lǐ le. /She waited for days and days. is expressed as She waited I don't know how many days. Tā 'děngle °bùjrdàu 'dwōshou 'tyān °le (°'hǎusyē 'tyān le).

And between nouns in English is often not expressed by a separate Chinese word: **father and mother** fùmǔ; **mother and child** mǔdž; **man and wife** fūfù; **brothers and sisters** dìsyungjyě'mèi; **table and chairs** jwōyǐ.

(Between adjectives) ywè . . . ywè. /She's getting prettier and prettier. Tā ywè lái ywè hǎukàn. But when followed by a time expression as You're getting better and better every day. Nǐ ('jēnshr) yì'tyān bǐ yì'tyān jyàn 'hǎule.

(Between verbs). /I called and called, but no one answered. Wǒ 'jyàule 'yòu jyàu kěshr 'méiren dā'shēngr. /I can wash and shave at the hotel. Wǒ kěyi dzai fàn'dyànli syǐlyǎn (gēn) gwāhúdz.

(Between clauses) in a sentence like He saw me and I ducked down again. *or* He came and then I left. and is not expressed in Chinese. Instead, one says When he saw me I ducked down again. *or* After he came I left. *or* He came, I left. either showing the relation between the two parts of the sentence more explicitly, or else not showing it at all.

(If . . . then). /Say one word and you're a goner! Chū yì'shēngr nǐ jyòu méi-'mìngle! or expressed as If you want to live, you'd better keep quiet. Nǐ yàushr yàu'mìng nǐ jyou byé chū'shēngr.

And so swǒyi, yǐntsž. /And so he quit. 'Swǒyi tā jyou tsź'jrle.

And so forth 'děngděng(de), shémmade. /I need towels, soap, and so forth. Wǒ 'syūyàu 'shǒujīn, 'yídz, °'děngděngde dūngsyi (°'shémmade).

And that érchyě. /He speaks English, and that almost as a native. Tā hwèi shwō 'Yinggwohwà, ér'chyě shwōde 'chàbudwō gēn dāng'dìrén yí'yàng.

And then jǐn gēnje (immediately after); yǐhòu, ránhòu (secondly, after that); *plus* jyou if the event is in the past, dzai if the event is in the future. /Cough loudly, and then enter. Dàshēngde 'késou yìshēng, 'ránhòu dzài 'jìnchyu. /Look all around and then close the door. 'Jōuwéi 'kànyikàn, jǐn 'gēnje bǎ 'mén 'gwān-shang.

And yet kěshr, 'búgwò. /And yet he did that to me! °Kěshr (°Búgwò) tā 'gěile wo 'nèmmayísyàdz! /Such an intelligent man, and yet he does a thing like that! 'Nèmma tsūngmíngde rén kěshr 'gànchu 'nèijǔng shř lai!

Both . . . and . . . yòu . . . yòu . . . . /He's both dull and boring. Tā yòu 'hútu yòu tǎu'yàn.

Come and lái . . . yi . . . . /Come and see. Nǐ lái 'kànyikàn.

Go and chyù . . . yi . . . . /Go and ask when the train leaves. Nǐ chyù 'wènyi-wèn hwǒ'chē 'shémma shŕhou 'kāi.

Try and 'shř yishř, syǎngfár. /Try and see him tomorrow. Syǎng'fár 'míng-tyan chyù °'kàn ta (°'kànyikàn ta). /Try and do it. is expressed as Try and see. 'Shřyishř kàn.

ANESTHETIC. máyàu, mádzwèiyàu.

ANGEL. (Protestant) tyānshř; (Roman Catholic) tyānshén.

ANGLE. jyǎu(r).

ANGRY. shēngchì, nù, chì. / He became very angry. Tā °'dà nù (°dà chì, °chìjíle). / What are you angry about? Nǐ 'wèishémma shēng'chì?

Be angry at nǎu, gēn . . . shēng'chì. / Are you angry at him? Nǐ 'shr̀ bushr̀ 'nǎule ta le? *or* Nǐ 'shr̀ bushr̀ 'gēn tā shēng'chì le?

ANIMAL. (Member of the animal kingdom) dùngwu; (wild) yěshòu; (as contrasted with human 'rénlèi) 'chùlèi, chùsheng. / An amoeba is a kind of animal, not a plant. Byànsyíng'chúng shr̀ yìjǔng'dùngwu, búshr̀ 'jŕwù. / The children went to the zoo to see the animals. 'Háidzmen dàu dùngwu'ywán chyu kàn yě'shòu chyule. / He called me an animal. Tā 'gwǎn wo jyàu °'chùlei (°'chùsheng).

(Livestock) shēngkou. / Do you have any animals? Nǐ yǒu jùng'dìde 'shēngkou ma?

ANKLE. jyǎuwàndz, jyǎuwàr.

ANNOUNCE. bàugàu (report); sywānbù (formally); gūngbù (declare). / That news was announced on the radio. Nèige syīnwén shr̀ wúsyàndyàn bàugàude. / The government has announced the budget for next year. Jèngfǔ yǐjīng °sywānbù (°gūngbù) míngnyande yùswànle. / They just announced that they're engaged. Tāmen gāng 'sywānbù dìng'hwūnle.

ANNOUNCEMENT. tǔnggàu; bùgàu (on a bulletin board).

ANNOUNCER. (Broadcasting) gwǎngbwōywán.

ANOTHER. (Different) lìng(wài)yi . . . , byé(de), lìng(wài)yi . . . byé(de). / I don't like this room; may I have another? Wǒ busyǐhwan 'jèijyan wūdz, wǒ kéyi yàu lìng- wài yijyān (byéde) ma? / That's another matter. Nà shr lìng('wài) yijyàn ('byéde) 'shr̀. / Tomorrow another man will come. 'Míngtyān yǒu °'byérén (°'lìng yige rén) lái.

(Additional) yòu, dzài, hái (with or without lìng(wài) before the verb). / Please give me another cup of coffee. Chǐng ni dzài 'gěi wǒ yibēi kā'fēi. / He gave me another five dollars. Tā lìng('wài) you gěile wǒ wǔkwai 'chyán. / Who can think of another method? Shéi néng °'dzài syàngchu ge 'fádz lái. or meaning . . . a different method . . . °'lìng syàngchu ge 'fádz lái.

Another day gwòtyān, gwò, jityān, gwò lyangtyān; one day . . . , another day . . . yìtyān . . . , yìtyān . . . *or* jīntyān . . . , míngtyān . . . . / Let's talk about it another day. 'Gwò (ji) tyān 'dzài shwō ba. / One day he's all smiles; another day he'll pull a long face on you. Tā °yìtyān (°jīntyān) 'mǎnlyǎn 'syàurúngr, °yìtyān (°míngtyān) jyou hwèi yǐ'lyǎn bùgàu'syìng.

One after another. / They died one after another. Tāmen 'yíge gēnje yíge de dōu 'sžle.

One another bǐ'tsž, hùsyàng. / They saw one another frequently. Tāmen bǐ'tsž cháng jyàn 'myàn. / They're trying to shift the responsibility to one another. Tāmen °hù'syàng (°bǐtsž) 'twēitwō.

One way or another. / He makes enough to live on one way or another. Tā 'dzǔng néng syàng 'fár jèng'chyán 'hwóje.

ANSWER. (Respond to a question) dá, 'hwéidá. / I can't answer that question. Nèige wèntí wǒ °bùneng 'hwéidá (°bùnéng dá, °dábulyau, °hwéidábulyau, °dábuchulai, °hwéidábuchulai).

(When one's name is called) dāying. / When he calls your name, don't answer. Tā jyàu nǐ míngdz de shŕhou, byé dāying.

(Of a letter) hwéisyìn, syě hwéisyìn. / Please answer my letter. Chǐng gěi wǒ °hwéisyìn (°syě hwéi'syìn).

Answer a telegram dǎ 'hwéidyàn.

Answer the phone jyē dyànhwà.

Answer by mail yùng shūmyàn hwéidá. / I'll answer him by mail. Wǒ yùng shūmyàn hwéidá tā.

Answer (to) gēn . . . syáng'fú. / That man answers (to) your description perfectly. Nèige rén gēn nǐ 'shwōde jèng syáng'fú.

Be answered yìng'yàn. / Your prayer has been answered. °Nǐde chǐ'chyóu (°Nǐde dǎugàu) yìng'yànle.

An answer (to a phone call or telegram) 'hwéidyàn; (to a letter) 'hwéisyìn. / We have already received an answer. Wǒmen yǐjīng shōudàu °hwéidyàn le (°hwéisyìn le).

(Reply) 'hwéidá. / He gave a poor answer. Tāde hwéidá bu'hǎu.

(To a mathematical problem or to a question) dáàn. / The answers are at the back of the book. Dá'àn dzài shū'hòutou.

ANTARCTIC. Nán'jíjōu; (ocean) Nánbīngyáng.

ANTENNA. (Radio, television) tyānsyàn; (feelers) chùjyǎu.

ANTHOLOGY. (Of prose) wénsywǎn; (of verse) shr̄sywǎn.

ANTIDOTE. jyědúyàu.

ANUS. gāngmén.

ANXIOUS. Be anxious about dyànji. / I've been anxious about you. Wǒ 'cháng 'dyànjije nǐ.

Be anxious (to) hěn syǎng, 'jíyu yàu, jáují. / I'm anxious to go there. Wǒ 'hěn syǎng dàu 'nǎr chyu. / He's anxious to know the results of the exam. Tā 'jíyu yàu 'jr̄dàu kǎu'shr̄de jyē'gwǒ. / But his father is still more anxious. Kěshr tā 'bàba °bǐtā 'hái (°'gèng) jáu'jí.

ANY. nǎyi (*or* něiyi) . . . dōu, 'rènhé . . . dōu, shémma (. . . dōu); or not expressed by a separate word. / Any policeman can direct you. 'Něiyíge syún'jǐng dōu néng 'gàusung ni dzěmma 'dzǒu. / Any school teaches that subject. 'Rènhé sywé'syàu dōu jyāu 'nèimén 'gūngkè. / Any job is better than none. 'Shémma shr̄ yě bǐ 'méishr̄ 'chyáng. / Any time will do. Swéi'byàn 'shémma shr̄hou dōu 'syíng. / Do you have any money? Nǐ yǒu 'chyán méiyou? / Do you have any more? Nǐ 'hái yǒu ma? / I don't have any. (Wǒ) méi 'yǒu. / Do you like any of these girls? Jèisyē 'gūnyangli yǒu nǐ 'syǐhwānde ma? / If you want any more, say so. Yàushr 'hái (syǎng) 'yàu jyòu shwō 'hwà. *but* / If any man can climb that mountain, he can. 'Nèidzwò shān, jǐyàu rén néng 'shàngdechyu 'tā jyòu shàngdechyù. *or* 'Nèidzwò shān, 'ta yàushr shàngbu'chyù jyòu 'meiyou rén néng 'shàngle.

Not . . . any 'shémma °dōu (°yě) bu-, (lyán) yi . . . dōu bu-, yidyǎr yě bu-, dōu bu-, *etc.* / I don't feel any pain. 'Yìdyǎr yě bù'téng. / I won't sell it at any price. °'Dwōshau chyán (°'Shémma jyàchyan) wǒ dōu bú'mài.

Anyone, anybody shwéi °dōu (°yě), 'shémma rén °dōu (°yě); anyone at all 'búlwùn shwéi. / Anyone can say that. 'Shwéi dōu hwèi 'shwō. / I don't want to see anybody. Wǒ °'shwéi (°'shémma rén) yě bú'jyàn. /Anyone at all can tell you. 'Búlwùn shwéi dōu néng 'gàusung ni.

Anything 'shémma dōu; **anything at all** 'búlwun shémma. /Anything you have will be all right (in a store). Nǐ 'màide 'shémma dōu 'syíng. /I'll give you anything but this letter. Wǒ 'shémma dōu néng 'gěi ni, 'jyòushr bùnéng gěi ni jèfēng 'syìn. *but* /Is there anything for me? Yǒu 'wǒde dūngsyi ma? (in a post office) Yǒu 'wǒde syìn ma? /Can't anything be done? 'Nándàu yìdyǎr 'bànfa yě 'méiyou ma?

Anything but. /He's anything but a miser. Tā 'jywé búshr ge shǒutsái'nú. /I'll do anything but that. Jywé'dwèi bugan 'neige. /He's anything but a hero. Wúlwùnrú'hé dzǔng 'bùnéng shwō tā shr ge 'yīngsyung.

Anywhere rènghòu dìfang, shémma dìfang °dōu (°yě). /You can buy it anywhere in town. Nǐ nénggòu dzài chénglǐ rènghòu dìfang máidàu tā. /I'm not going anywhere. Wǒ shémma dìfang °dōu (°yě) búchyù.

ANYWAY. héngshù, dzǔng, háishr, fǎnjèng. /You don't have to phone him; he'll be here anyway. Yùngbu'jáu dǎ dyàn'hwà, °héngshù (°fǎnjèng) tā shr dàu jèr lai de. /You'll get paid anyway, so why worry? Nǐ 'dzǔng hwèi nájáu 'chyán de, dzěmma hái bùfàng'syīn ne? /It's raining, but we'll go anyway. Syàje 'yǔ ne, 'búgwò wǒmen háishr 'chyù.

APART. (of distance) gé. /Those posts are six feet apart. Nèisye gāndz gé lyòuchr (yǒu) yíge.

Keep apart 'fēnkāi. /Keep the children apart. Bǎ 'háidzmen 'fēnkai.

Keep oneself **apart from** lí . . . hěn 'ywǎn, 'dwǒje . . . . /He always kept apart from us. Tā 'lǎushr 'lí wǒmen hěn 'ywǎn. *or* Tā lǎu 'dwǒje wǒmen.

Take something **apart** bǎ . . . 'chāikāi. /Take this alarm clock apart. Bǎ nàu'jūng 'chāikāi.

Tell apart fēnbyan. /How do you tell them apart? Nǐ 'dzěmmayàng 'fēnbyàn tāmen?

Set apart for 'tèwèi. /This building is set apart for the orphans. 'Jèige lóu shr 'tèwèi gū'ér gàide.

APPEAR. (Be published) chū, chūbǎn. /The paper appears every day. Bàu'jř 'měityǎn 'chū. /When is his latest work going to appear? Tā dzwèi 'jìnde 'jùdzwò 'jǐshř chū-'bǎn?

(Come into view) chūsyàn. /A submarine suddenly appeared before our ship. Yíge chyānshwěi'tǐng 'hūrán dzài wǒmen 'chwánde 'chyánbyar chū'syànle.

(In a play) yǎn. /She appeared as the heroine in that play. Dzài nèichu syìli tā 'yǎnde shr nyǔyǐngsyūngde jyǎur.

(In a play or theater) chūyǎn. /When did she appear at the Golden Theater? Tā jǐshř dzài 'Hwángjīn dàsyì'ywàn chū'yǎn de?

(In court) chūtíng. /The defendant didn't appear in court. Bèi'gàu méi chū-'tíng. /That judge will not appear in court today. Nèige fǎgwān 'jīntyan bùchū'tíng.

Appear to be fǎngfú kànje syàng, hǎu 'syàng . . . (shrde). /This appears to be correct. Jèige 'fǎngfú 'dwèile. /He appears to be very sick. Tā °hǎu 'syàng (°kànje syàng) 'bìngde hěn 'lìhài (shrde).

APPEARANCE. (Looks) yàngdz, wàimàu, wàibyǎu. /Her appearance is pleasing. Ta °yàngdz (°wài'màu, °wàibyǎu) hěn pyàulyang. (with emphasis on natural features)

Tā'jǎngde jyàurén 'syǐhwān. (with emphasis on make-up) Tā'dǎbande jyàurén 'syǐhwān. /Don't judge people by their appearance. Bù 'kě yǐ 'wài'màu 'chyǔrén. *but* /Try to improve your appearance. is expressed as Concentrate on make-up a little bit. Hǎu'hāurde 'dǎban yísyà.

Have the appearance of. *See* Appear to be *under* **APPEAR.**

Keep up appearances. /He keeps up appearances. Tā 'wéichŕ 'myàndz. /He keeps up a good appearance. Tā 'lǎushŕ hěn tǐ'myànde.

Make an appearance. *See* **APPEAR.**

APPENDIX. (Anatomy) mángcháng; (in a book) fùlù.

APPLE. 'píngwǒ. /Chinese apples have thinner skins than the American variety. 'Jūnggwo píngwǒ bǐ 'měigwode 'pyér 'báu.

APPLICATION. (Written) shēnchǐngshū; rùsywé °shēnchǐngshū (°jr̀ywàn'shū) (for a school). /Your application has been received. Wǒmen yǐjing 'shōudau nǐde shēnchǐngshūle. /Your application must be accompanied by two letters of introduction. Nǐde shēnchǐngshūlǐ děi 'fùje lyǎngfēng jyèshàu'syìn.

(Of medicine). /This medicine is only for external application. 'Jèige yàu jŕ néng 'wài yùng. *or* 'Jèige yàu jŕshŕ 'shàngde, búshŕ 'chŕde.

(Use, for a practical purpose) is expressed verbally with yīngyùng (to actually use). /The application of his theory is very simple. Tā nèige lǐlwùnde yīng'yùng hěn jyǎndān.

Application blank shēnchǐng'shū byǎu'gé; (in a library, for a book) jyèshūdān.

Oral application 'kǒutóu chǐng'chyóu. /Will an oral application do? 'Kǒutóu chǐng'chyóu 'syíng ma?

APPLY. (Have bearing) yīngyùng. /In this case this rule doesn't apply. Dzài 'jèijyànshŕshang, jèityáu 'gwēijyu bùnéng yīng'yùng.

(Place in contact) shàng. /Apply the glue first. Syān shàng jyāushwěi. /Apply the ointment carefully. Nèige yàu'gāur 'syǎusyīnje 'shàng. *but* /Apply a hot compress every two hours. Měi 'lyǎngdyǎn jūng yùng rè'shǒujīn 'tēng yísyà.

Apply oneself jwānsyīn. /He applies himself in his work. Tā hěn jwānsyīn dzwòshr̀.

Apply for chǐngchyóu, shēnchǐng. /He is qualified to apply for a pension. Tā yǒu dzgé °chǐng'chyóu (°shēn'chǐng) yǎnglǎujīn le.

Apply for a position (particularly but not always by indirect methods) móu 'chāishr̀. /I want to apply for that position. Wǒ syǎng 'móu nèige 'chāishr̀.

APPOINT. (General) pài; (to an office) rènmìng. /I appointed him to represent me. Wǒ pài tā dàibyǎu wo. /He was appointed treasurer. Tā bèi °'pài (°'rènmìng) dzwo 'kwàiji. *or* Rénjya 'pài tā dāng 'kwàiji.

APPRECIATE. (Of art, scenery, etc.) 'syīnshǎng. /You should learn to appreciate music. Nǐ 'yīngdang sywéje syīnshǎng yīnywè.

(Of a favor or kindness) 'gǎnjī. /I appreciate your help very much. Wǒ hěn 'gǎnjī nín bāngmáng.

(Of characteristics such as talent, ability, etc.) shǎngshŕ. /He really appreciates your ability. Tā jēn shǎng'shŕ nǐde tsái'gàn.

(Recognize) lyáujyě. /I can appreciate your difficulty, but there is nothing I can do. Wǒ hěn lyáu'jyě nǐde nánchu, kěshr wǒ méibànfa.

APPROACH. (Method) fádz. /Am I using the right approach? Wǒ yùng de 'fádz 'dwèi budwèi?

(Entrance) jìnkǒur; byār in such compounds as approach to a bridge chyáubyār. /The approaches to the bridge are under repair. 'Chyáu 'lyǎngbyānde jìn'kǒur jèngdzài 'syōuli.

To approach líje °jìn (°bùywǎn). /The camel caravan is approaching. Lwòtwo-'dwèi 'líje hěn 'jìn le.

(Of an enemy) bījìn. /The enemy is approaching from three directions. 'Dírén (yóu) 'sānmyàn bī'jìnle.

Approach a person about something jǎu. /Is it all right to approach him about this matter? Gwānyu 'jèijyàn shr̀ wǒ 'kéyi bukéyi 'jǎu yijǎu tā?

Be approaching is expressed as arriving soon kwài dàu. /We're approaching the end. 'Kwài dàu 'tóurle.

APPROVE. (Of higher authority) pījwǔn. /Make a draft of your plans and send them in; I'll approve them. Nǐ bǎ nǐde 'jìhwà ní ge 'gǎudz 'jyāujìnlai, wǒ jyòu pī'jwǔn.

Approve of 'dzànchéng, 'byǎushr̀ syǔkě. /I don't approve of his conduct. Wǒ bú'dzànchéng tāde 'syíngwéi. /His father hasn't approved of his engagement to that girl. Tā gēn nèiwèi nyǔ'shr̀ dìng'hwūn, tā 'fùchin hái méi 'byǎushr̀ syǔ'kě ne.

Be approved (by a group) 'tūnggwò. /Has this plan been approved? Jèige 'jìhwà yǐjing 'tūnggwole ma?

APRICOT. syìngr; (the tree) syìngshù.

APRIL. 'sżywè.

APRON. (Clothes) 'wéichyún.

ARCH. (Architectural term) hú; (arched doorway) gūngmén, 'gūngsyíngde 'mén; (of the foot) jyǎugǔ.

ARCHEOLOGY. 'kǎugǔsywé.

ARCHITECT. jyànjùshr̀, jyànjù gūngchéngshr̀.

ARCHITECTURE. (Construction) 'jyàn jù gūngchéng; (science) 'jyànjùsywé.

ARCTIC. Běijíde (dìfang); (ocean) Běijíhǎi.

AREA. (Size) myànji. /The area of my lot is much larger. Wǒde dìde 'myànji dà dwōle.

(Region) (yídài) dìfang. /You can't find gold in this area. Nǐ dzài jèi (yídài) 'dìfang jǎubujǎu jīndz.

(Field of interest) fāngmyàn. /He has no interest in things in that area. Tā dzài nèifāngmyàn méi syìngchyu.

ARGUE. chǎu (noisily); 'byànlwùn, jēngbyàn (seriously); táigàng, chyǎngbyàn (dog-matically); chyántsź dwó'lǐ (dogmatically, with plays on words for the sake of winning). / What are they arguing about? Tāmen dzài 'chǎu shémma ne? / They're arguing about the methods of treating war criminals. Tāmen jēng'byàn de shř dwèidai 'jànfànde 'fāngfa. / Now he's arguing dogmatically. Tā 'nàshř °chyǎng-'byàn (°'chyángtsź dwólǐ). *but* / There's no use arguing any more. is expressed as What else is there that can be said? 'Hái yǒu shémma kě'shwōde ne? *or* 'Hái yǒu shémma kě'byànde ne?

(Quarrel) chǎudzwěi. / He likes to argue with people. Tā 'ài 'gēn rén chǎu-'dzwěi.

(Appeal to one's reason) jyǎnglǐ. / You can't argue with him. is expressed as What use is there arguing with him logically? Gēn 'tā jyǎng'lǐ yǒu shémma 'yùng?

Argue something out bǎ . . . 'byànchū ge jyē'gwǒlai, bǎ . . . byàn chū ge shwěi'lwǒshř'chū lai. / We must argue this out. Dzámen bǎ jèige 'wèntí děi °'byànchū ge jyē'gwǒlai (°etc.).

Argue someone out of bǎ . . . shwōde bú . . . ; argue someone out of something *or* into something shwō'fú. / We argued him out of quitting. Wǒmen 'bǎ ta 'shwōde bùtsź'jřle. *or* Wǒmen shwō'fúle tā le; tā bùtsź'jř le.

ARGUMENT. (Disputation) is expressed verbally as to argue. *See* **ARGUE.** / He got into quite an argument with his wife. Tā gēn tā 'tàitai chǎu'dzwěi 'chǎude hěn 'lìhai. / Let's not have an argument about this. Dzámen bú'bì wèi 'jèige jēng'byàn. / How can you get the best of an argument with a pretty woman like her? Nǐ gēn 'tā nèmma hǎu'kànde 'nyǔrén jēng'byàn 'dzěmma néng 'yíng ne?

(Reasons offered in proof) lǐ, lǐyóu. / I don't follow your argument. Nǐ 'shwō de °'lǐ (°lǐ'yóu) wǒ bú'dà 'míngbai.

ARITHMETIC. swànshù.

ARM. (Of the body) bǎngdz, gēbe; (of a chair, etc.) fúshou. / My arm hurts. Wǒ °'bǎngdz (°'gēbe) téng. / My arms are longer than yours. Wǒ bǐ'nǐ °bǎngdz (°'gēbe) cháng. / The arm of this chair is broken. Jèibǎ yǐdzde fúshou 'hwàile.

Arm in arm 'kwàje 'gēbe, lāje shǒu. / They went away arm in arm. Tāmen °kwàje 'gēbe (°lāje shǒu) 'dzǒule.

At arm's length. / You'd better keep him at arm's length. Nǐ 'dzwèi hǎu lí tā ywǎn dyar.

With arms folded chāje 'gēbe. *but* / They looked on with folded arms. meaning with arms in the sleeves of the Chinese upper garment. Tāmen syòu'shǒupáng'gwān.

With open arms. / They welcomed him with open arms. Tāmen rè'lyède 'hwānyíng ta.

Arms (weapons) wǔchi, chyāngsyè. / This division is completely outfitted in arms and equipment. Jèi'shřde wǔ'chì jwāng'bèi hěn 'chywán.

Be armed (carry or have arms) dài. / All personnel must be armed. Swǒ-'yǒude rénywán dōu děi dài wǔchì.

To arm someone bǎ . . . wǔ'jwāngchilai. / Arm all the farmers. Bǎ 'núngrén dōu wǔ'jwāngchilai.

Other English expressions. / The arms of the law can't reach him. Tā syāuyàu fǎwài.

ARMISTICE. (Document) tíngjànshū; **conclude** (*or* make) **an armistice** tíngjàn.

ARMOR. (For body) kwēijyǎ; (for a vehicle or battleship) jwāngjyǎ, tyějyǎ.

321

ARMY. (In contrast to Navy) lùjyūn. / The American Army is bigger than the American Navy. Měigwo 'Lùjyūn'rénshù bǐ 'Hǎijyūnde 'dwō.

(As a force in the field) jyūndwèi. / There are no such men in the army. Jyūn-'dwèili 'méiyou 'nèmma yàngde rén.

(Armed forces or major subdivision thereof) jyūn; the Seventh Army dìchījyūn.

Send an army to . . . pài'bǐng dàu . . . chyu, pàijyūn'dwèi dàu . . . chyu, chū'bǐng dàu . . . chyu. / First the United States sent an army to Iceland. 'Měigwo 'syān °pài'bǐng (°etc.) dau Bīng'dǎu chyu.

Serve in the Army dzài jyūndwèili fúwù. / Have you ever served in the Army? Nǐ dzài jyūndwèili fúgwowù ma?

AROUND. (Approximately) dzwǒyòu, shàngsyà. / I'll be there around nine o'clock. Wǒ 'jyǒudyǎn'jūng dzwǒ'yòu 'dàu nèr.

Around something is expressed as something's **circumference** . . . jōuwéi. / How many miles is it around this lake? Jèige 'húde jōu'wéi yǒu dwōshau 'lǐ?

Around preceded by such verbs as walk, go, run, etc. wéije . . . , ràuje . . . . / We walked around the lake twice. Wǒmen wéije 'hú 'dzǒule lyǎng'chywār. / We'll have to detour around the town. Wǒmen děi 'ràuje 'chéng 'dzǒu. *but* / Turn around! (facing me) 'Jwàngwolai! (facing away from me) 'Jwàngwochyu!

Other expressions in English. / Are there any soldiers around? 'Jèr yǒu'bīng ma? / It's somewhere around the house. Jyòu dzài jyāli. / I'll have to look around for it. Wǒ děi 'jǎu yijǎu. / Look around you. °Sź'syà (°Jōu'wéi) 'kàn yikàn. / The store is just around the corner. 'Pùdz gwǎi'wār jyòu 'shr. / See you around. Hwéijyàn. *or* Hwéitoujyàn. *or* Dzàijyàn.

ARRANGE. (Put objects in a special order) bǎi. / How're you going to arrange the (things on the) table? 'Jwōdzshangde dūngsyi nǐ dǎ'swan 'dzěmmayang 'bǎi? / How would you arrange these flowers? Nǐ 'jywéde jèisyē 'hwār 'dzěmmayang 'bǎi hǎu?

(Plan) syǎngfádz. / I can arrange to have the book sent to you. Wǒ kéyi syǎngfádz bǎ shū gěi nǐ sùngchyu.

(Of furniture, etc.) ānpai. / How are you planning to arrange the tables? Jèisyē 'jwōdz nǐ syǎng 'dzěmma 'ānpái?

(Of small items in a row, usually books or cards) mǎ. / Who arranged the books? Gwǎn mǎ'shùde shr 'shwéi?

(Straighten out) shōushr, jěngli; (local Peiping) shŕdou, gwēijou, gwēijr. / Please arrange the things on your desk. Chǐng ni bǎ nǐ 'jwōdzshangde dūngsyi °shōushr (°etc.) yí'syà.

(Take care of) nùng, bàn, bàntwǒ. / Let me arrange this! 'Wǒ lái nùng 'jèige ba! / Can you arrange this for me? 'Jèige nǐ néng 'gěi wo 'bàn yí syàr ma? / It was arranged long ago. 'Dzǎu jyòu bàn'twóle.

(Of affairs, matters) 'lyàulǐ, 'chùjr, 'bànlǐ, ānpai. / He didn't arrange that matter well. 'Nèijyàn shr tā °'chùjrde (°ānpáide, °etc.) bùdé'dàng.

(Of a game, appointment, etc.) ywē. / The athletic committee has arranged a game for us. Tǐ'yùwěiywán'hwèi tì wǒmen 'ywēle yíge bǐ'sài.

(Of a schedule) pái. / Who's going to arrange the basketball schedule? 'Shwéi gwǎn pái lán'chyóubǐ'sàide 'tsźsyu?

(People) pái, 'páichéng, páilyè. / Arrange the children in two rows. Bǎ 'háidzmen 'páichéng lyǎng'háng.

(Prepare) 'yùbèi, jwŭnbèi, ānpai. /Everything has been arranged. Yí'chyè dōu yǐjing 'yùbèi'hǎule.

(Passage, tickets) dìng. /Can you arrange passage on the boat for me? Nǐ 'néng bunéng tì wo dìng yíge chwán'wèi?

Arrange for a job 'ānjr̀, 'ānchā. /Can you arrange for him to take this position? Nǐ néng 'bǎ ta °'ānjr̀le (ānchāle) ma?

Arrange with a person gēn . . . °'shānglyang (°'dìnggwei). /Have you arranged things with him? Nǐ gēn tā °'dìnggweihǎule ma (°'shānglyang'hǎule ma? /Wait until you've arranged things with him. 'Děng nǐ gēn ta 'shānglyang'hǎule 'dzài shwō ba.

ARREST. dǎi, dēi. /The police arrested two men. Syún'jǐng 'dǎile 'lyǎngge rén. /The police are arresting people all over town. Jǐng'chá dzài chywán'chéng dàu'chù °dǎi'rén ne (dēi'rén ne).

Arrest someone's **attention** ràng . . . jù'yì. /That hat will certainly arrest his attention all right. Nèige 'màudz jwūn 'kéyi ràng tā jù'yì.

Be arrested bèipǔ. /Why have you been arrested? Nǐ 'wèishémma bèi'pǔ?

Be under arrest. /You're under arrest! is expressed as Let's go to the police station. Dàu jǐngchájyú chyu.

ARRIVE. (At a place) dàu. /When will we arrive in New York? Wǒmen jǐshŕ kéyi dàu Nyǒu'ywē?

(At a decision or conclusion) dédàu, yǒu. /Did you arrive at a conclusion? Nǐ °dédàule (°yǒule) yíge dìng 'lwùn ma? /We have arrived at a decision. Wǒmen yǐjing °dédàule (°yǒule) yíge jywédìng.

ARROW. jyàn; shoot an arrow shè jyàn.

ART. měishù (includes hwèihwà painting, dyāukè sculpture, 'jyànjù architecture). /He came here to study art. Tā dàu 'jèr lai sywé měi'shù.

(More inclusive term) yìshù; the useful arts shǒu'yì; industrial arts gūngyì; liberal arts program wénkē; liberal arts school wénsywéywàn. /Drama is one of the arts. 'Syìjyù shŕ yìjǔng yìshù.

(Skill in performance) chyǎu'myàude 'fāngfa. /There's an art to it. Yǒu chyǎu'myàude 'fāngfa.

The art of self-defense chywánshù, wǔshù, gwóshù.

Art gallery měishùgwǎn (for display purposes only); hwàláng (for display and sale purposes).

ARTERY. (Blood vessel) (dà)dùngmài.

ARTHRITIS. gǔjyéyán.

ARTICLE. dūngsyi; in compounds wù, pǐn, wùpǐn; article of food yìjǔng 'shŕwù; article of merchandise shāngpǐn; toilet articles hwàjwāngpǐn. /Did they distribute any articles of clothing? Tāmen fā 'chwānde dūngsyi meiyou? /I have no articles of value to declare. Wǒ 'méiyou shémma jŕdé yì'bàude dūngsyi.

(In a document) tyáu, syàng, tyáukwǎn. /Article Three isn't clear to me. Dì'sāntyáu wǒ bú'dà míngbau.

(Written composition) wénjāng. /There was an article about this in the newspaper. Bàu'jr̆shang 'tséngjĭng yŏugwo yìpyān wén'jāng lwùn dau 'jèijyàn shr̀.

ARTILLERY. (Weapons) (da)pàu; (branch of service) pàubĭng.

ARTIST. (General) yìshùjya; (painter) hwàjya; (sculptor) dyāukèjyā; (a calligrapher, rated highly as an artist in China) shūfājyā. / The artist is painting a picture. Yìshùfā'jyā dzài hwà 'hwàr ne.

AS. (To the same degree in which; in the same manner in or with which) jàu(je), syàng, ànjàu, àn(je); or expressed with indefinite question words or adverbs in two clauses, such as dzĕmma . . . , dzĕmma . . . ; shémma . . . , shémma . . . ; jèmma . . . , jèmma . . . . / Do it as he does. Jàuje 'tāde bànfa lai 'bàn. / It is to be done as before. Syàng yĭ'chyán nèmma 'bàn. / He did as promised. Tā ànjàu tā 'dāyìngle de dzwòle. / Do as you're told. Dzĕmma 'gàusung nĭ de, nĭ jyou dzĕmma 'bàn. / Leave it as it stands. Ywánlai shr̆ shémma yàngr, jyou hái shr shémma yàngr. / I wish you had left them as they were. Hai bùrú nĭ bugwăn jyòu syàng yĭchyan nà yàngr ne. / Things are bad enough as it is. is expressed as In this manner, things already are bad enough. Jyòu °'dzĕmmaje (°'jèiyàngr) yĭjing gòu 'dzāu de le. / It's "hwà" as in "hwà hwàr," not as in "shwō hwà." is expressed as It's the "hwà" of "hwà hwàr," not the "hwà" of "shwō hwà." Shr 'hwà hwàrde 'hwà, bushr 'shwō hwàde 'hwà.

(Since) yīnwei, jì. / I must go as it is late. Wŏ fēidei 'dzŏu le, yīnwei tyān yĭjing bu'dzăn le. / As we've already refused the offer, let's stick to that answer. Dzámen jì 'hwéi le rénjya le, jyou byé găi'dzwĕi le.

(During the time that) de shr̆hou, yìbyār . . . yìbyār. . . . / Count the people as they enter. Rén 'jìnlai de shr̆hou, 'shŭje yidyăr. / As he read a book, we talked. Tā kànje shū de shrhou women tán hwà ne. / All the way he prayed as he went. Tā yí 'lùshang yibyār 'dzŏu yibyār 'dăugàu.

(In the capacity of) dāng, yĭ. / As a musician he's a flop but as a politician he'll be tops. Tā dāng 'yīnywejyā shr ge èrwu'yăn; bugwò dāng 'jèngkè hwei shr dì'yīlyóude. / He was famous as a painter. is expressed as He was famous for his painting. Tā yĭ hwà 'hwàr chū'míng. / They employed her as a secretary. Tāmen 'gù tā dāng 'shūjì.

(In giving ratios and proportions) dĕngyú (equals). / Three is to nine as six is to eighteen. Sān bĭ jyŏu dĕngyú lyòu bĭ shr̆bā.

As . . . as °yŏu (°syàng) . . . °nèmma (°jèmma); gen . . . °shrde (°yíyàng(de)) (when two people or things are being compared). / He's as tall as his father. Tā 'jàngde yŏu tāde 'fùchin nèmma 'gāu le. / If he works as quickly as I do, he's in. Tā yàushr 'dzwòde syàng 'wŏ jèmma kwài, jyou jyàu ta 'gàn ba. / This is not as good as that. Jèige méiyou nèige nèmma hău. / He talks as much as his wife. Tā gen ta tàitai yiyàngde 'nèmma ài shwō. / It will take as long as three months. Dĕi (yòu) sānge 'ywè nèmma 'jyŏu.

As . . . as (stressing no matter how much) bùgwăn plus a question word. / As strong as he is, he won't be able to stand it. Bugwăn ta dwōma jyèshr, ta hai shr shòubujù. / As low as the price may go, I still won't buy it. Bugwăn jyàchyán dwōma dī wŏ hái shr bùmăi.

As . . . as can be -jíle. / He is as poor as can be. Ta chyungjíle.

As . . . as ever plus a verb. / He is as great a painter as ever lived. is expressed as He is an unprecedented painter. Tā shr yíwèi kūngchyánde hwàjyā.

As long as jr̆yàu. / You may stay here as long as you behave. Nĭ jr̆ yàu hăuhāurde, dāi 'dwōshou shr̆hour, dou 'syíng.

As soon as yi . . . jyou. /We'll start planting as soon as it stops raining. Yǔ yíjù dzámen jyou syà 'jūngdz.

Other expressions using as . . . as. /As far as I can see, he's out. is expressed as As I see it, he's out. °Jyù (°Jàu) wǒ 'kàn, tāswàn 'wánle. /I'll go with you as far as the door. is expressed as I'll accompany you to the door over there. Wǒ 'péi nǐ 'dzǒudau mén nar. /He'll pay as much as a thousand dollars for it. is expressed as He'll pay up to a thousand dollars to buy it. Tā hwèi 'chūdau yì'chyānkwai chyán lai mǎi.

As a matter of fact shwōjēnde, chíshr̀. /As a matter of fact I don't like him. °Shwōjēnde (°Chíshr̀) wo busyǐhwan ta.

As a result (of) (yīnwei) . . . jyégwǒ. /As a result of his unfriendliness we didn't go. Yīnwei ta bu'kèchi, jyégwo wǒmen méi'chyù.

As a rule jàu gwēijyu, píngcháng. /As a rule we don't take anyone's check. Jàu 'gwēijyu wǒmen 'shéide jrpyàu ye bù'shōu.

As against (compared to). /The expenditure amounts to ten thousand dollars this year as against nine thousand last year. is expressed as The expenditure this year was ten thousand dollars, last year nine thousand dollars. Jrchū 'jīnnyan shr yiwànkwai, 'chyùnyan shr jyou'chyán.

As if, as though hǎusyàng . . . (shrde). /He acts as if he thinks he's the officer in charge. Tā nèi 'yàngr hǎu'syàng jywéje dz'gèr shr jǔgwǎn jǎng'gwān shrde. /It isn't as if he were destitute. is expressed as He certainly isn't destitute. Tā °bìng (°yòu) 'búshr dzěmma 'chyúngde mei'fár le.

As of, as from a date tsúng . . . chǐ. /The contract starts as of January first. 'Hétung tsúng yíywè yǐhàu 'chǐ yǒu syàu.

As to, as for jr̀yu. /There's no doubt as to who will be elected. Jr̀yu shwéi dāng sywǎn yǐjing méiyǒu yíwèn le. /As for that, I don't know. Jr̀yu 'nèige, wǒ yìdyǎr ye bùjr̀'dàu.

As well (in addition) lyán . . . yě, ye. /Take this as well. Lyán 'jèige ye 'náje ba. or Jèige ye 'náchyu ba.

As . . . was saying. /As I was saying just now, he's hopeless. is expressed as I was just saying, he's hopeless. Wǒ gāngtsái 'shwōgwo, 'jèige ren mei 'jyǒur le.

As . . . would say . . . yǒu jyu hwà. /As Americans would say, "It ain't hay." Měigwo ren yǒu jyu hwà, "Búshr gān 'tsǎu."

Be the same as gēn . . . yiyang. /This is the same as that. 'Jèige gēn 'nèige yi'yàng. /That's the same as before. 'Jèige gen yǐchyán yi'yàng. /He doesn't speak as other people do. is expressed as He doesn't speak the same as other people. Tā shwō'hwà gēn 'byéren buyi'yàng.

Be used as dàng . . . yùng. /It may be used as a knife. Kéyi dàng 'dāudz yùng.

Just as yě . . . nèmma. /I can walk just as far without being tired. Wǒ yě néng 'dzǒu nèmma dwō de 'lù bu'jywéje 'lèi. /This is just as good. Jèige 'yě nèmma hǎu.

May as well jr̀hǎu, jì nèmmaje . . . jyou (used in the beginning of the sentence). /If it's really like that, we may as well forget all about it. Yàu 'jēnshr syàng nèmma yàng, dzámen 'jr̀hǎu dàngdzwo méi nèmma hwéi 'shèr ba. /You may as well go. Jì 'nèmmaje nǐ jyou 'chyù ba.

Regard A as worthy, good, etc. jywéje, náje . . . dàng. /He doesn't regard this thing as worthy of his attention. Tā jywéje jèijyàn 'shèr bù'jŕde yi'bàn. *or* Tā bunáje jèijyàn shèr dàng hwéi 'shèr.

So . . . as lyán . . . °dōu (°yě). / He can't be so foolish as to believe that. Tā buhwèi 'shǎdau lyán'nèige dōu 'syìn ba.

So as to 'wèideshŕ, hǎu. / We are placating him like that so as not to make a scene. Wǒmen 'nèmma hǔngje tā °wèideshŕ (°hǎu) 'byé nàu gei ren 'kàn.

Such as (like) syàng . . . (děngděng). / Books, such as dictionaries, encyclopedias, "Who's Who," and so forth, are called reference books. Syàng dź'dyǎn a, bǎikēchywán'shū a, "Míngrénsyàu'jwàn" a, děngděng de shū, dou jyàu 'tsānkǎushū. / People such as you require special treatment. Syàng 'nǐ jèiyangr de rén děi 'lingyankàn'dài.

Take (*or* **Treat**) **A as** (if it were) **B** ná A dàng B *or* ná A dàng (dzwò) plus such verbs as dài, kàn, etc. as B; dài A gēn B shŕde. / They treat him as a member of the family. Tāmen ná tā dàng yijyā 'rén nèmma 'dài ta. *or* Tāmen 'dài tā gēn yìjyā 'rén shŕde. / They treated it as a problem. Tāmen ná jèige dàng (dzwo) yige wèntí kàn. / Take it as a joke. Ná jèige dàng (dzwo) 'syàuhwar kàn ba.

Use A as B ná A dàng B yùng. / We can use that rock as a table. Wǒmen kěyǐ 'ná nèikwai shŕtou dàng jwōdz 'yùng.

ASBESTOS. shŕmyán.

ASH. (Tree) yángshù; (wood) yángmù; (residue of fire) hwēi; (residue of a cigarette) yānhwēi.

ASHAMED. tsánkwèi, hàisàu, hàisyōu; (embarrassed) bùhǎu'yìsz; (have a sense of shame) jŕ syōuchŕ. / I am ashamed to have done the job so poorly. Jèijyàn shŕ wǒ méidzwòhǎu hěn tsán'kwèi. / As old as you are, don't you feel ashamed? 'Jǎngle nèmma 'dà le, nán'dàu hái bùdǔng de °hài'sàu (°hài'syōu)? / I was ashamed to ask for his help. Wǒ bùhǎu'yìsz chǐng ta bāng'máng. *or* Jyàu ta bāng'máng, wǒ hěn tsán'kwèi. / Aren't you ashamed of yourself? Nǐ bùjŕ syōu'chŕ ma?

ASK. (Inquire of) wèn. / May I ask you a question? Wo kéyi wèn nín ge wèntí ma? *or* Chǐng 'wèn? / Did you ask him his first name? Nǐ 'wèn tā jyàu shémma 'míngdz le ma? / Ask him if he can come. 'Wèn tā néng bunéng 'lái.

(Request, demand) yàu. / I went to that store and asked to see their diamonds. Wǒ dàu nèige 'pùdzli chyu yàu tāmen 'gěi wǒ jīngàngshŕ kàn kan. / You can have it for the asking. Nǐ yí 'yàu jyòu 'gěi nǐ. / How much are you asking for that (in a shop)? Nèige nǐ yàu 'dwōshau chyán?

Ask someone to do something chǐng; (more politely or pleadingly) chyóu. / Ask him to come tomorrow. Chǐng tā míngtyan 'lái. / May I ask you to buy a book for me? °Chǐng (°Chyóu) nín géi wo 'mǎi yiběr 'shū, hǎu ma? / I have to ask you to excuse me. Wo 'děi °chǐng (°chyóu) nín 'ywánlyàng (wo).

Ask about dǎtīng, wèn. / Mr. Jang is asking about that. Jāng Syānsheng dzai °dǎtīng (°wèn) nèijyan shŕching ne.

Ask about someone wèn . . . hǎu. / He asked about you. Tā wèn nín 'hǎu.

Ask for yāuchyóu. / He asked for a raise. Tā yāu'chyóu jyā'syīn.

Ask for someone jǎu. / Who asked for me? Shéi jǎu wǒ le? / The police are asking for him. Jǐng'chá dzài 'jǎu tā ne.

ASLEEP. Be asleep *or* **fall asleep** shwèijáu. / He's fallen asleep. Tā shwèi'jáule.

/ I must have been asleep. Wǒ yí'dìng shr̀ shwèi'jáule.

ASPARAGUS. lúngsyūtsài, lúswǔn.

ASPIRIN. āsẓpǐ'líng.

ASSIST. bāng. / Who assisted you? 'Shwéi 'bāng ni láije?

See also **AID, HELP.**

ASSISTANT. 'jùshǒu, jùlǐ.

ASSURE. shwō . . . yí'dìng. / He assured us that he would be there. Tā shwō tā yí'dìng 'dàu.

Assure you that (formal) dān'bǎu, gǎn 'bǎu, gǎn dān'bǎu. / I can assure you that he's the man for the job. Wǒ dān'bǎu 'tā dzwò 'nèijyàn shr̀ hěn hé'shr̀.

ASTHMA. chìchwǎnbìng.

ASTRONOMY. 'tyānwénsywé.

ASYLUM. (Refuge) bìnànswǒ, shōurúngswǒ; (mental hospital) fēngrénywàn; (for orphans) gūérywàn; (political) jēngjr̀pìhù.

AT. **At** a place (specifying position) dzài (situated at); dàu (arrive at); if the specification of place is first in the sentence there may be no word for at. / He is at his office. Tā dzai gūngshr̀'fáng ne. / I'll be at home. Wǒ yídìng dzai jyā. / There are lots of people at the railway station. (Dzài) hwǒchējàn nèr̀ yǒu hěn dwō rén. / I had dinner at Changs' last night. Dzwótyan wǎnshang wǒ shr dzai Jāngjyā chr̄de fàn.

At a place or thing (specifying place from which) tsúng. / Start at the beginning. Tsúng tóur °kāishr̀ ((in talking) °shwōchǐ, (in doing) °dzwòshr̀).

At a rate or price, expressed in various ways, none of which contains a direct translation of **at**. / They're producing cars at the rate of 1000 per day. Tāmen yìtyan dzàu yìchyānlyàng chìchē. / These apples are usually sold at a price of fifty cents a dozen. Jèisye pínggwo píngcháng mài wǔmáu chyán yìdá.

At a time (specifying time when) dzài, which is often omitted; at noon (dzài) shàngwǔ *or* (dzài) jūngwǔ; at night (dzài) yèli; at the beginning of something (dzài) . . . chǐtóur de shr̀hou; at the end of something (dzai) . . . 'wán de shr̀hou; at that time *or* moment nèige shr̀hou. / It rings twice a day, at noon and at midnight. Yìtyān syǎng lyǎngtsź, jūngwǔ yítsź, bànyè yítsź. / Please be there at 10 A. M. Chǐng ni dzàuchen shŕdyǎn jūng yídìng dàu nèr̀. / At that moment I couldn't think of an answer. Nèige shr̀hou wǒ syǎngbuchū ge hwéidá lai. / You may do it at any time (you please). Nǐ shémma shr̀hou dzwò dōu syíng.

At an age, expressed without a separate word for **at**. / He became a professor at (the age of) twenty-three. / Ta èrshrsānswèi jyòu dāng jyàushòu le.

At something (implying participation in) °dzài (°jèng, °jèngdzai) . . . ne. / He's at dinner now. Tā °dzài (°jèng, °jèngdzai) chr̄ fàn ne. / Two years ago those two countries were at war. Lyǎngnyán yǐchyán nèilyǎngwó °dzài (°jèng, °jèngdzai) dǎ jàng ne.

At following verbs, specifying direction in which or place to which, is usually expressed by a single Chinese verb which covers the meaning of the verb of the English sentence and the meaning **at**, *see below*.

Aim at myáujwěr, myáujwǔn, chyáujwǔn. / Aim at that light and fire. Myáu-jwěr (°Myáujwǔn, °Chyáujwǔn) nèijǎn dēng kāichyāng.

Arrive at (of a place) dàu; (of a decision) tánchulai, shānglyangchulai, dédau, dádau. / He arrived at the border. Tā dàu byānjyè le. / We haven't arrived at a decision yet. Wǒmen hái méi °tánchulai (°shānglyangchúlai, °dédau, °dádau) yíge jyelwùn ne.

Guess at tsāi. / I'm just guessing at it. Wǒ búgwo shr tsāi ne.

Laugh at syàu, 'syàuhwà. / They're laughing at me. Tāmen (dzai) °syàu (°'syàuhwa) wǒ ne.

Look at kàn, chyáu, chǒu, chùng . . . kàn, wàng . . . kàn. / What are you looking at? Nǐ (dzai) °kàn (°chyáu, °chǒu) shémma? / The photographer says, "Please look at the lens." Jàusyàngde shwō "Chǐng °kàn jìngtóu (°chùng jìngtóu kàn, °wàng jìngtóu kàn)."

See also specific verbs for other combinations with **at**.

At any rate wúlwùn rúhé, dzěmmaje, bùgwǎn dzěmmayàng. / At any rate you have to admit that she is good-looking. °Wúlwùn rúhé (°etc.) nǐ děi chéng rèn tā hěn hǎukàn.

At all costs wúlwùn rúhé, bùgwǎn dzěmmaje, 'bùgwǎn dzěmmyàng, dzěmmaje. / We must do it at all costs. °Wúlwùn rúhé (°etc.) dzámen yě děi dzwò.

At best dzwèihǎu yě búgwò shr . . . / At best it's only a moderately good university. Nèige sywésyàu dzwèihǎu yě búgwò shr yige hái bútswòde dàsywé.

At one's best dzwèihǎu. / He is at his best in telling jokes. Tā shwō syàuhwàr dzwèihǎu.

At ease dzòrán; 'shàusyī (military command). / He is never at ease in talking with his mother-in-law. Tā gēn ta jàngmunyáng shwōhwà de shŕhou dzǔng búdzòrán. / At ease! 'Shàusyī!

At first chǐchū, chǐtóur, yìchǐchū de shŕhou, yìchǐtóur de shŕhou. / At first we didn't like this place. Wǒmen °chǐchū (°chǐtóur) bùsyǐhwan jèige dìfang. *or* °Yìchǐchu (°Yìchǐtóur) de shŕhou, wǒmen bùsyǐhwan jèige dìfang.

At last (in a context indicating relief after a long wait) kě. / So you are here at last! Nǐ 'kě láile! / At last the train's arrived! Hwǒchē'kě dàule! / At last I'm allowed to talk! 'Kě syǔ wǒ shwō jyù hwà le!

At last (in a context indicating finality) jyēgwǒ, dàulyǎur, dàutóur. / At last he won. °'Jyégwǒ (°Dàu'lyǎur, °Dàu'tóur) shr 'tā yíngle.

At least 'jŕshǎu, 'dǐngshǎu, 'dzwèishǎu. / He's at least six feet tall. Tā °'jŕshǎu (°'dǐngshǎu, °'dzwèishǎu) yǒu lyòuchŕ gāu. / It'll take at least three days. 'Jŕshǎu (°'Dǐngshǎu, °'Dzwèishǎu) děi sāntyan.

At (some) length bàntyan, hěn jyǒu. / He spoke about it at some length. Nèi-'shèr tā shwō le °bàn'tyan (°hěn jyǒu).

At most 'jŕdwō, 'dǐngdwō, 'dzwèidwō. / He is at most six feet tall. Tā °'jŕdwō (°'dǐngdwō, °'dzwèidwō) yǒu lyòuyīngchŕ gāu.

At once lìkè (jyou), lìshŕ (jyou), syàndzài, jèjyòu. / I'll leave at once. Wǒ °lìkè (°lìshŕ) jyou dzǒu. *or* Wǒ °syàndzài (°jèjyòu) dzǒu. / Can you come at once? Nǐ néng °lì'ke jyòu lai ma (°lìshŕ jyòu lái ma, °syàndzài jyòu lái ma)? / I'll be there at once. Wǒ °lìkè jyou (°lìshŕ jyòu, °syàndzài jyòu) dàu. / He handed the money over at once. Tā °lìkè jyou (°lìshŕ jyòu) bǎ chyán dìgwòchyule. / When he heard that, his face at once broke out in a big smile. Tā yì tīngjyan nèige °lìkè jyou (°lìshŕ jyòu) mǎnlyǎnde syàurúngr.

At the same time túngshŕ, dzài jèige shŕhou; (concessive) késhr ne. /You think it over at the same time. 'Túngshŕ nǐ °syǎng yisyáng (°kǎulyùkaulyù, °pán- swàn pánswàn). /At the same time, he might've done it. Késhr ne, yèsyu shr tā gànde.

At times yǒu(de) shŕhou. /At times I'm doubtful. Yǒu(de) shŕhou wǒ yǒu dyǎr hwáiyì.

At will swéibyàn, swéiyì, yàu . . . jyou . . . /They come and go at will. Tāmen °swéibyàn (°swéiyì) chūrù. /He comes here at will. Tā 'yàu dàu jèr lái 'jyòu dàu jèr 'lái.

So many **at a time** is usually expressed with yítsź one time, or a similar phrase, with no word corresponding to **at**. /One question at a time. Yítsź jŕ néng °wèn yíge wèntí (°yòu yíge rén wèn). /He ran up the steps two at a time. Tā yíbù tyàu lyang- dèngde pàushàngchyùle. /Hey! One at a time, please! 'Hèi! Yígeyi'gède lái! or expressed negatively as Don't come all at once that way! Byé nèmma yíkwàr lái!

Be at a loss to do something. /I'm at a loss to understand it. Nèige shèr °wǒ yìdyar yě bùmíngbai (°hǎu wú tóusyù).

Be frightened (or surprised) **at** something, where **at** indicates **when** and also because of, calls for a change in method of expression. /He is frightened at the sight of the police. is expressed as When he sees the police he gets frightened. Tā chyáujyàn le jǐngchá syǐnli hěn hàipà. /I was surprised at the large size of the footprint. is expressed as That footprint's being so large made me jump a bit. Nèige jyǎuyèr dàde jyàu wǒ syàle yityàu.

Be good (fair, bad, etc.) **at** doing something is expressed without any equivalent for **at**, usually with the parts of the sentence in the opposite order from that found in English. /He's clever at magic tricks. is expressed as He does magic tricks cleverly. Tā byàn syìfàr byànde tǐng chyǎude. /He is quick at lettering. is ex- pressed as He letters quickly. Tā syě měishùdz syěde tǐng kwàide. /I'm not good at that. is expressed as I do that, I'm not so good. Dzwò nèige wǒ búdà °syíng (°hwèi).

Be still at it hái jyēje dzwò. /Are you still at it? Nǐ hái jyēje dzwò ma?

Not at all yìdyǎr . . . °yě (°dōu) °méi-(°bù-). /I haven't any money at all. Wǒ yìdyǎr chyán yě méiyou. /He couldn't do it at all. Tā yìdyǎr yě búhwèi. or Tā wánchywán búhwèi. but /Not at all! Byé kèchi! or Búswàn shémma! or Méishémma! or Syǎu yìsz!

ATHLETE. yùndùngywán.

ATHLETICS. 'yùndùng.

ATMOSPHERE. (Air in any locality) 'kūngchì, chì; (mass of air surrounding the earth) dàchì.

ATOM. ywándž; atomic bomb ywándždàn; atomic energy ywándžnéng.

ATTACHÉ. (Civilian) swéiywán; (military) wǔgwàn.

ATTACK. (Advance and attack; military) jìngūng, gūngjī. /We've already attacked the enemy position. Wǒmen 'yǐjing °jìn'gūng (°gūngjī) 'díjyūnjèn'dìle.

(Censure) 'gūngjī; (viciously or without regard to truth) hwěibàng, mà. /The morning paper has an editorial attacking the governor. Dzǎu'bàu yǒu yìpyān shè- 'píng gūngjī shěngjǎng. /Someone's attacked him for accepting bribes. Yǒu'rén 'mà tā tān'dzāng.

(Begin to work on) jáushǒu. / Let's attack that problem from this angle. Nèige 'wèntí dzámen tsúng 'jèi'fāngmyàn jáu'shǒu ba.

An attack (of illness) yitsz ... bìng. / I had a heart attack last year. 'Chyùnyán wo déle yitsz 'syīndzàngbìng.

ATTEMPT. shr̀. / That was the first time she had attempted to cook. Nà shr̀ tā dì-'yítsz 'shr̀je dzwò'fàn. / He attempted suicide once. is expressed as He was killing himself once, but he didn't die. Tā 'yǒu yítsz dz̀'shā, kěshr méi'sz̀.

Attempted murder móu'shāwèi'swéi.

An attempt. / That was his first attempt at English composition. is expressed verbally as That was the first time he tried to write English. Nà shr tā dìyī tsz̀ shr̀ syě 'Yīngwén. / An attempt was made on his life. is expressed as Someone was attempting to murder him. Yǒu rén yàu 'tsz̀ ta láije.

See also TRY.

ATTEND. (Of a patient) gěi ... kàn'bìng (for illness, not for minor ailments or child-birth). / What doctor attended you? 'Nèige 'dàifu gěi ni kànde 'bìng?

Attend a funeral. *See* FUNERAL.

Attend a meeting dàuhwèi, °lái (°chyù) kāihwèi. / Did you attend the meeting? Nǐ dàu'hwèile ma? *or* Nǐ chyù kāi'hwèile ma?

Attend to bàn. / I have something to attend to. Wǒ yǒu yijyàn 'shr̀ děi 'bànyi-bàn.

ATTENTION. Pay attention jùyì (focus one's attention on); lyóusyīn, yùngsyīn (be attentive, be careful). / No one pays attention to me. Méi rén jù'yì wo. / Pay attention to what he says. Tā 'shwō de 'hwà yàu lyóu'syīn 'tīng.

Stand at attention lìjèng. / The soldiers stood at attention. 'Bīng lì'jèngle.

AUDIENCE. (If listening) 'tīngde rén, tīngjùng; (if watching) 'kàn de rén, gwānjùng.

AUDIT. (To attend) pángtīng. / I'm just auditing this class. Wǒ dzài jèi'bānlǐ páng-'tīng ne.

Audit accounts chájàng. / He audits accounts for that company. Tā tì nèige gūng'sz̀ chá'jàng.

AUDITOR. (Of a class or course) pángtīngshēng; (of accounts) chájàngywán.

AUDITORIUM. dàlǐtáng.

AUGUST. 'báywè *or* 'báywè.

AUTHOR. (Professional) 'dzwòjyā; (of a certain work) jùjě, dzwòjě.

AUTHORITY. chywánbing. / What authority do you have to do this? Nǐ yǒu shémma 'chywánbing lái 'jèmma bàn?

(Permission) syǔkě. / On whose authority did you do that? Nǐ 'nèmma bàn déle 'shwéide syǔ'kěle?

Be an authority on yánjyōu ... de chywán'wēi. / He's an authority on Chinese history. Tā shr yánjyōu Jūnggwo lìshr̀de chywán'wēi.

Authorities dāngjyú (governmental); dìfānggwān (local); fùdzérén (in general).

/I want to speak to the authorities. Wǒ yàu túng °dǎng'jyú (°etc.) 'gwānjau yisya.

AUTOBIOGRAPHY. dżjwàn.

AUTOCRACY. jwānjr'jèngtǐ, jwānjrjèngjr̀.

AUTOMOBILE. chìchē; when the context is clear one uses simply chē vehicle. /My automobile broke down. Wode 'chē 'hwàile.

AUTUMN. chyōutyan, chyōujì. /I hope to stay through the autumn. Wǒ 'syīwàng néng dzài 'jèr gwò 'chyōutyan. /The autumn here is quite warm. 'Jèige dìfang chyōu-'jì hěn 'nwǎnhwo.

AVALANCHE. sywěbēng, shānbēng; have an avalanche is expressed as a mountain of snow slides down sywé'shān 'bēngle; or as a mountain of ice slides down bīng'shān 'bēngle; or as the mountain slides down shān bēngle.

AVENUE. mǎlù, lù, dàlù, dàjyē. /Take me to 246 Third Avenue. Dàu 'sānmǎ'lù 'èrbǎi'szshr'lyòu hàu.

    Avenue of escape shēnglu, chūlu. /That'll open up an avenue of escape for him. 'Nà jyòu 'gěi ta 'kāichu yìtyáu °shēnglu (°chūlu) láile.

    See also **ROAD, ROUTE, STREET.**

AVERAGE. (Mean value) píngjyūnshr̀, píngjyūn °fēnshur (°fēr). /The average for this exam is very low. Jèitsz kǎu'shr, píngjyūn °fēnshur (°fēr) hen 'dī. /What's the average of these numbers? Jèisye shùmude píngjyūn'shr̀ shr shémma?

    On the average píngjyūn. /I go to the movies on the average of once a week. Píngjyūn wǒ měilǐbài kàn yìtsz dyàn'yǐngr. /In this town there is, on the average, one car to every three persons. Jèige 'chéngli, píng'jyūn, sānge ren yǒu yìlyàng chì'chē. /On the average, the class's grades are lower than before. is expressed as This class's average is lower than before. Jèibān 'sywéshengde píngjyūn °fēn-shur (°fēr) bǐ shàngyibān 'dī.

    Average (medium). /He's below average height. is expressed as He's shorter than people in general. Tā bǐ yì'bān rén 'ǎi.

    To average píngjyūn. Average this column of figures for me. Tì wǒ bǎ 'jèiyihángde shùmu píng'jyūn yisya. /Average his grades and they're better than anyone else's. Tāde fēnshur píngjyūnchilai bǐ byéren dou 'hàu.

    Average out. /It averages out in the end. Dàule mwò'lyǎur jyou 'méiyou chūrù le.

AVIATION. hángkūng; (the study) 'hángkūngsywé.

AVOCATION. fùyè.

AVOID. (General term) dwǒ, 'dwǒkai. /He avoided her. Tā 'dwǒ ta. /You simply can't avoid him. Jyǎn'jr̀ dwǒbu'kāi ta.

    (Of a thing, of doing something) 'bìmyǎn. /Avoid (doing) that at all costs. Wúlwùnrú'hé yàu 'bìmyǎn 'nèige.

AWAIT. děng. /We await your reply. Wǒmen 'děng nǐde 'hwéisyìn.

    See also **WAIT.**

AWAKE

AWAKE. syǐng. /Are you still awake? Nǐ 'hái 'syǐngje ne ma? *or* Nǐ 'hái méishwèi-'jáu ne ma? /Stay awake tonight. Jīntyan 'yèli byé shwèi'jyàu. /I was awake most of last night. <u>is expressed as</u> I hardly closed my eyes last night. Wǒ 'chàbudwō yí'yè méibì'yǎn.

Be wide awake jǐngsyǐng. /You'd better stay awake throughout the night. Nǐ yí'yè yàu jǐng'syǐngje.

See also **WAKE.**

AWAY. Be away (from one's usual territory) chūmén, chyùle, dzǒule; (from home) búdzàijyā. /Have you been away? <u>is expressed as</u> Did you go away? Nǐ chū'ménle ma? /He's away at school. Tā dàu sywé'syàu chyùle. *or* Tā shàng'sywé chyùle. /He's away in the country. Tā syà'syāng chyùle. /He's been away for three months now. Tā 'dzǒule yǒu 'sānge 'ywè le. /He's away (from home). Tā búdzài'jyā.

Be away (by such and such a distance) lí . . . (place) yǒu . . . (distance). /It's thirty kilometers away. Lí 'jèr yǒu 'sānshr gung'lǐ.

<u>Expressions like</u> **go away, take away, move away,** <u>and other such expressions are in Chinese compound verbs with</u> chyù, dzǒu, *or* kāi <u>as the second element. Combinations not given below will be found under the appropriate verb entry.</u> /Please take this away. Chǐng bǎ 'jèige °'náchyu (°'nákai). /My work's too important, I can't go away. 'Shr̀ tài yàu'jǐn, wǒ bùnéng 'líkāi. /They carried the wounded soldier away. Tāmen bǎ shāng'bīng tái'dzǒule. /He looked away. Tā 'nyòugwò 'tóu chyùle. /Go away! Chū chyù! *or* 'Dzǒu ba! *or* (very emphatic and slangy) 'Kwài gěi wo 'gwǔn!

AWFUL. hěn búsyìng(de), hěn hwài. /An awful accident happened yesterday. 'Dzwótyan 'chūle yíjyàn hěn bú'syìngde 'shr̀. /We've been having awful weather. 'Jìnlai 'tyānchi hěn 'hwài. *but* /That's awful! *or* What an awful shame! is expressed as That's really too bad! Jēn dzāu'gāu! <u>or as</u> That's really face-losing! Jēn 'dyǒurén! <u>or as</u> You're really out of luck! Jēn dǎu'méi! <u>or as</u> What is there to say? Jèi háiyou shémma kě shwō de.

Look awful hěn bùhǎu'kàn. /He looked awful. Tā 'myànsè hěn bùhǎu'kàn.

AWFULLY. hěn, jēn, 'fēicháng, dǐng. /He's awfully boring. Tā 'fēicháng tǎu'yàn.

AWNING. péngdz.

AX. fǔ(dz).

AXIS. jóusyīn; (mathematics) jóusyàn; (of the earth) dìjóu.

AXLE. chējóu, jóu.

BABY. háidz, hár, syǎuháidz, syǎuhár. /The baby's crying. Syǎu'hár (dzài) 'kū ne. /She's sewing baby clothes. Tā jèng dzai °'dzwò (°'féng) syǎu'hár chwān de 'yīfu.

(The youngest) dzwèi syǎude. /She's the baby of our family. Tā shr̀ wǒmen jyāde dzwèi 'syǎude.

(Small) syǎu. /He is my baby brother. Tā shr̀ wo 'syǎu dìdi.

To baby hǔng, dàng shr̀de syǎu'hár 'dài. /Don't always baby her, or you'll spoil her. Nǐ byé lǎu °'hǔngje tā (°dàng syǎu'hár shr̀de dài tā), bù'rán nǐ hwèi 'bǎ tā gwàn'hwàile.

BACHELOR. dānshēnhàn, dúshēn('nán)ren, gwānggwèr.

> **Bachelor of arts** 'wénsywéshr̀, 'wénsywé sywéshr̀.

> **Bachelor of science** 'lǐsywéshr̀, 'lǐsywé sywéshr̀, 'kēsywéshr̀, 'kēsywé sywéshr̀.

> **Bachelor's degree** 'sywéshr̀.

BACK. (Upper part, human) jínyang; (upper part, human or of an animal) bèi; (small of the back, human) yāu. /My back itches. Wǒde 'jínyang 'yǎng. /Scratch my back. Géi wo 'jwājwa 'bèi. /Strap the saddle tightly, or the horse's back will be hurt by the rubbing. Bǎ mǎ'āndz kwǔn'jǐnle, bù'rán hwèi bǎ mǎ 'bèi mwó'pwòle. /He fell from the roof and broke his back. Tā tsúng fáng'dǐngshang 'dyàusyalai bǎ 'yāu shwāi'hwàile.

> (Of a chair, etc.) bèr. /This chair has a high back. Jèibǎ 'yǐdz de 'bèr hěn 'gāu.

> (Space behind anything) hòubyan, hòubyar, hòumyan, hòumyar, hòutou. /There's a flower garden at the back of the house. Fángdz 'hòumyan yǒu yíge hwā-'ywár.

> (Reverse side) bèimyar, fǎnmyar. /The photo is attached to the back of the letter. Syàng'pyàr dzài 'syìnde 'bèimyar. /Look at the back (the other side). Kànkan 'fǎnmyar.

> **Back to back** bèidweibèi. /They sat back to back. Tāmen bèidweibèi dzwòje.

> **Behind** someone's **back** dzài . . . bèi'hòu. /They talked about her behind her back. Tāmen dzài tā bèi'hòu shwō tā syán'hwà.

> **To back** someone in an election sywǎn. /We're backing him in this election. Jèitsz sywǎnjǔ wǒmen 'dōu sywǎn tā.

> **Back** a request 'dzànjù. /We'll back him in his request. Tā chǐng'chyóu de 'shr̀ wǒmen yí'dìng 'dzànjù.

> **Back down** ràngbù. /You're winning, why back down? Nǐ jàn shàng'fēng ne, hébì yàu ràng'bù?

> **Back into** twēidau. /She backed into the garage. Tā bǎ chì'chē twēidau chē'fángli chyùle.

> **Back out** of a promise 'shwōle bú'swàn, 'twēichū. /You shouldn't back out. Nǐ bùnéng 'shwōle bú'swàn. /You can't back out now. Syàn'dzài nǐ bùnéng 'twēi-chūle.

> **Back (up)** a vehicle dàu. /Please back your car (up) slowly. Chǐng ni 'màn dyar dàu 'chē.

> **Be back** (return) hwéilai. /I'm glad you're back. Nǐ 'hwéilaile, wǒ hěn gāu-'syìng.

> **Give back** hwángei. /Give it back to me! 'Hwángei wo!

> **Hold** something **back** lyóu, bukěn shwō, búgàusung. /Tell everything; don't hold anything back. 'Chywán 'shwōchulai; 'shémma yě bùsyǔ 'lyóu. *but* /Holding back on me, eh? Yǒu 'hwà 'wèishémma bú'gàusung wǒ? /Why did you hold that back? (not tell it all) Nǐ 'dzěmma bù'dōu 'shwōchulai ne? (purposely conceal some facts) Nǐ 'wèi shémma bùkěn 'shwō? /The buyers held back. 'Mǎi de rén bùkěn jyā'jyàr.

> **Hold** someone **back** lánhweichyu, 'lánjù. /They held the people back. Tāmen bǎ 'rén 'lánhweichyule. /I couldn't hold him back, he was so angry. Tā chì'jíle, wǒ méinéng 'lánjù tā.

> **Move back** (wǎng 'hòu) twēi. /The crowd all moved back. 'Rénrén dōu wàng 'hòu twēi.

Pay back hwángei, hwán. /We must pay back what we owe him. Wǒmen 'chyàn tā de jyou děi 'hwán tā.

Repeat back dzài 'shwō yíbyàn. /Repeat the numbers back to me. Wǒ 'shwō de nèisyē 'shùr 'nǐ dzài 'shwō yíbyàn, wǒ 'tīngting.

Send back 'twèihwei. /Send this back; I don't want it. Bǎ 'jèige 'twèihweichyu, wǒ bú'yàu.

BACKBONE. jíjwēi, 'jínyanggǔ.

BACKGROUND. (Historical) 'láilì, bèijǐng. /The background of this war is very complicated. 'Jèitsz̀ 'jànjēngde bèi'jǐng hěn 'fúdzá. /He has a dubious background. Tā 'láilì bù'míng.

(Visual) dyěr, bèijǐng. /Doesn't it look nice against a purple background! 'Pèishang shēn'dzsède 'dyěr 'dwōmma hǎu'kàn a! /The background of this painting is most beautiful. Jèijang 'hwàrde bèijǐng tài 'měi le.

In the background (not prominent) dzài hòutái, 'ānjūng. /He dominates the party, but remains in the background himself. Tā 'tsāudzùng dǎng'wù, kěshr 'běnrén 'dwǒdzai hòu'tái. /He's still active in the background. Tā hái dzài 'ānjūng hwó'dùng.

BACON. syánròu (smoked or salted meat).

BACTERIA. wēishēngwù, syìjyūn.

BAD. hwài, bùhǎu. /He does all sorts of bad things. Tā shémma hwài 'shèr dōu 'gàn. /His grades are bad. Tāde 'chéng jì °hěn 'hwài (°hěn bù'hǎu). /That's bad. or That's a bad thing to do. 'Nèmmaje bù'hǎu. /Here's some bad news. Jèige 'syāusyi búdà 'hǎu. /We've had some bad weather lately. 'Jìnlai jèrde 'tyānchi búdà 'hǎu. /The weather's pretty bad. 'Tyānchi hěn 'hwài.

(Of work or conditions) dzāu. /The management is pretty bad. Gwǎn'lǐde hěn 'dzāu.

(Of parts of the body) yǒubìngde, hwàile de. /That's his bad arm. Tā 'nèige gēbe shr̀ yǒu'bìngde. but /This is my bad ear. meaning totally deaf Wǒ 'jèige 'ěrdwo tīngbu'jyàn.

(Of money) jyǎde (counterfeit); bùnéng dwèi'syàn (of a check); **bad check** 'kūngtóujr̄'pyàu. /This doesn't look like a bad coin to me. 'Jèige chyán 'wǒ kànbuchu shr̀ 'jyǎde lai. /That's a bad check. 'Nèijāng jr̄'pyàu °bùnéng dwèi'syàn (°shr 'kūngtóujr̄'pyàu).

(Unskillful) bùhǎu, bùsyíng, bùchéng; (of calligraphy or painting) bùhǎukàn, búshryàngr. /His ideas are good but the presentation is bad. Tāde 'yìsz bú'tswò, kěshr 'shwōde 'fāngfǎ bù'hǎu. /His handwriting is bad. Tā 'syěde búshr'yàngr.

(Serious, severe) 'lìhài, jùng. /He has a bad case of TB. Tāde 'fèibìng hěn 'jùng. /He has a bad case of jitters. Tā (hài) 'pàde 'lìhài.

From bad to worse ywè 'lái ywè °'hwài (°pwò, °dzāu); °'hwàide (°'pwòde, °'dzāude, °'bìngde) ywè 'lái ywè 'lìhài. /His affairs went from bad to worse. Tāde 'shr̀ching ywè 'lái ywè °'hwài (°dzāu).

Be bad for dwei . . . yǒuhài or (limited to stomach or eyes) shāng. /This food is bad for you. 'Jèijǔng dūngsyi 'chr̄le °dwei nǐ yǒu'hài (°shāng'wèi). /It's bad for your eyes to go to too many movies. Dyàn'yǐng kàn'dwōle shāng 'yǎnjing.

334

Be in a bad humor. / He is in a bad humor today. Tā 'jīntyan yǒu dyǎr °bu-shwùn'syīn (°bu'tùngkwai).

Be in pretty bad shape, be in a bad way (of clothes, houses, etc.) 'pwòlànbù'kàn le; (of machinery, etc.) 'hwàide búsyàng 'yàngdz, 'hwàide bù'chéng 'yàngdz; in these expressions hwài may be replaced by pwò (of clothes), dzàu (of situations), or bìng (of patients). / My car is in pretty bad shape. Wǒde 'chē 'yǐjing 'hwàide bùchéng 'yàngdz le.

Bad luck. / Don't do that; it's bad luck. Byé 'nèmmaje; bù'jílì. / It's bad luck to say that. Shwō 'nàyàngde hwà bù'jílì.

Bad manners. / In China that's not considered to be bad manners. Dzài 'Jūng-gwo 'nà bú'swàn °shr'lǐ (°méiyou 'lǐmàu).

Bad mistake. / He made a bad mistake. is expressed as He made a big mis-take. Tā °chūle (°fànle) ge 'dà tswò.

Bad temper. / He has a bad temper. Tā 'píchi hěn °'hwài (°'dà).

Bad times (financial) bù'jǐngchì. / Times are bad. Shèhwèi bu'jǐngchì.

Feel bad jywéde bushūfu. / I feel bad. Wǒ jywéde bu'shūfu.

Feel bad about (feel sorry) jywéde nángwò. / I feel bad about his death. Tā sžle wǒ jywéde hěn nán'gwò.

Go bad hwài; (of fruits, vegetables, etc.) hwài, làn; (of oils and foods cooked with shortening) hwài, hā(la); (of rice, bean curd, etc.) sōu. / The machine's gone bad. 'Jīchi 'hwài le. / The apple's gone bad. 'Pínggwǒ 'làn le. / The butter's gone bad. Hwáng'yóu 'hā(la) le. / The bean curd has gone bad. Dòufu 'sōu le.

Smell bad (of food) chòu; (of air) yǒuwèr. / The fish smells bad. 'Yú 'chòu le. / The air in the room smells bad. 'Wūdzli(de kūng'chì) yǒu'wèr. / There's a bad smell somewhere. Yǒu yìgǔdz 'wèr. / He has bad breath. Tā 'dzwéilǐ yǒu'wèr.

Taste bad bushrwèr, buhǎuchr̄. / This meat tastes bad. Jèige 'ròu °bushr 'wèr (°buhǎuchr̄).

Other English expressions. / It's not a bad idea. Yìsz bú'tswò. / That's too bad! (general) 'Jè shr dzěmma 'shwōde! or (unsympathetic) Hwó'gāi!

BAG. 'kǒudài; (syǎu) kǒudar; (small bag with a drawstring) 'hébāur; bag of something 'kǒudài, dàidz, dàr, kǒudar; burlap bag mádài; flour bag myàn kǒudar; sandbag shānáng, shādài. / Will that bag hold it all? Nèige 'kǒudài chywán jwāngde'syà ma? / He bought a small leather bag to keep his tobacco in. Tā 'mǎile ge syǎu pí kǒudar jwāng yān'sz̄. / He can carry three bags of flour on his back. Tā néng 'bēi 'sānkǒu-dai 'myàn(fěn). / A bag of flour costs fifteen dollars now. Syàn'dzài °yídàr (°yì-'kǒudài, °yìkǒudar, °yí'dàidz) 'myàn mài shŕwǔ'kwài.

(Hand luggage) shǒutíbāu. / Where can I check my bags? Shǒutí'bāu tswún 'nǎr?

(Of hunting). / We made a good bag today. is expressed as The result of hunt-ing wasn't bad. 'Jyēr dǎ'lyède 'chéng jì bú'hwài.

Bag and baggage swǒyǒude 'jyādangr. / He moved in, bag and baggage. Tā bǎ 'swǒyǒude 'jyādangr 'dōu bānlaile.

Holding the bag. / He left us holding the bag. is expressed as He made us get caught but he himself ran away. Tā bǎ wǒmen 'syàndzai 'lǐtou, dž'jǐ kě 'pǎule. / You're going to leave us holding the bag; you can't get away with it. is expressed as You gave us all the trouble; that's not O. K. Nǐ 'gwāng jyàu 'wǒmen wéi'nán a; 'nà kě bù'syíng.

To **bag** (bring down) 'dǎsyà(lai). /He bagged ten ducks. Tā 'dǎsyàlai 'shŕjŕ yādz.

(Swell out) gǔchulai. /His trousers bag at the knees. Tāde kù'twěr dzài gēle'bàr nèr 'gǔchūlaile.

Other English expressions. He let the cat out of the bag. is expressed as He told all. Jyàu tā gěi shwō'pwòle. /It's in the bag! is expressed as No question! Méi 'wèntí!

BAGGAGE. syíngli; (bedding only, frequently an item of baggage in China) pūgaijywǎr, **baggage car** syínglichē; **baggage room** syínglifáng; **baggage check** syínglipyàu. /I want to send my baggage on ahead. Wǒ yàu bǎ wode 'syíngli syàn yùn'dzou. /How many pieces of baggage have you? Nǐ yǒu 'jǐjyàn syíngli? /Take my baggage up to my room. Bǎ wode pūgai'jywǎr nádau wǒ 'wūr chyu.

Check baggage °dǎ (°chǐ) syínglipyàu, gwà páidz. /These three pieces of baggage are to be checked; I'll take the rest along with me. 'Jèisānjyàn shŕ dǎ syíngli'pyàu de; 'shèngsyàde wǒ swéishēn 'dàije.

BAIL. (Money to release someone from arrest) bǎushŕjīn.

To **bail** someone out bǎuchulai. /We bailed him out of jail. Wǒmen bǎ ta 'bǎuchulaile.

Bail water out yǎuchulai, kwǎichulai. /We bailed the water out of the boat. Wǒmen bǎ chwánlide 'shwěi 'yǎuchulaile.

BAIT. (For catching fish) yúshŕ.

To **bait** (tempt). /They used prizes to bait customers. Tāmen yùng 'jyǎngpǐn lái 'yòuhwo gùkè.

(Lead on). /They baited him all evening. is expressed as All night long they made a fool of him. Tāmen gēn tā 'kāile yìwǎnshangde wánsyàu.

Bait a hook shàng yúshŕ.

BAKE. (Cook in dry heat) kǎu. /Was this bread baked this morning? Jèige myàn'bāu shŕ jīntyan 'dzǎuchen 'kǎude ma?

(Prepare baked goods) °dzwò (°kǎu) 'dyǎnsyīn. /Do you bake every day? Nǐ 'měityān °dzwò (°kǎu) 'dyǎnsyīn ma?

(In the sun) shài. /I baked in the sun all day. Wǒ 'shàile yìjěngtyān tàiyang.

Baking powder fāfěn.

BAKERY. myànbāufáng (Western-type bakery); dyǎnsyinpù (Chinese-style pastry shop); shāubingpu (a bakery which sells a kind of bread called bǐng and similar breads).

See also **BREAD, CAKE, COOK.**

BALANCE. (Scales) chèng (large); tyānpíng, děngdz (small). /Weigh it on the balance. Yùng °'chèng (°'děngdz, °'tyān'píng) °'chěng yicheng (°'yāu yiyāu).

Bank balance (deposit) tswúnkwǎn. /What's my bank balance? Wǒ (yín'hángde) tswún'kwǎn 'hái yǒu 'dwōshau?

(Remainder) 'shèngsyàde. /Pay one-third down and the balance in monthly installments. 'Syān gěi sānfēnjr'yī, 'shèngsyàde àn 'ywè 'gěi.

Balance of power shŕli jyūn'děng. /Their policy is to keep the balance of power in Europe. Tāmende jèng'tsè shŕ yàu bǎu'chŕ 'Ōujōude shŕli jyūn'děng.

In the balance. /His fate hung in the balance. is expressed as His fate is to be decided in this desperate moment (time of hanging by a hair). Tāde 'chyántú jyòu dzài jè 'chyānjyūnyì'fàde shŕhou lái jywé'dìng.

Keep one's **balance** (while standing) jànwěn; (while walking) dzŏuwěn. /Even standing still I can't keep my balance on such a narrow bridge. Dzài nèmma 'jǎide 'chyáushang wǒ lyán 'jàn yě jànbu'wěn. /That drunk can't keep his balance. Nèige hē'dzwèile de rén dzǒubu'wěn.

Lose one's **balance** wāi; (local Peiping) jāiwai. /I lost my balance and fell off the step. Wǒ yǐ 'wāi jyòu 'shwāidau tái'jyēr 'syàbyar chyùle.

Strike a balance jéjūng. /A balance was struck between old ways and modern methods. Tāmen bǎ 'syīn 'jyòu lyangjǔng 'fádz jé'jūng le.

To balance fàngpíng. /Balance the shoulder-pole on your shoulder. Bǎ 'byǎndan dzài jyān'bǎngrshang fàng'pingle.

(Of a pole on the shoulder with loads hanging down from each end) tyāuping, dānping. /Balance the pole (and load) on your shoulder. Bǎ 'tyāudz tyāu'pingle.

(Of an account) chū'rù syāng'fú; **not be balanced** chū'rù bù'fú. /Does this account balance? Jèibǐ jàng chū'rù syāng'fú ma? /This account isn't balanced. Jèibǐ 'jàng chū'rù bù'fú.

Balance each other (in weighing) píngjyūn, pínghéng, syāngděng, syāngchèn. /The two weights balance each other. 'Lyangbyānde 'jùnglyàng °syāng'děng (°etc.).

Balance each other in strength shŕ'jyūnlì'dí. /I'd say that the two teams balance each other. Jyù wǒ 'kàn, jèi'lyangdwèi shŕ'jyūnlì'dí.

Be balanced (be compensated for) chéngwolai. /He makes some mistakes but that's balanced by his speed. Tā 'yǒude shŕhou chū'tswòr, kěshr tā dzwò 'shŕ 'kwài, swóyi 'chéngwolaile.

BALCONY. (On the outside of a building) yángtái; (of a theater) bāusyāng.

BALE. (As of cotton) bāu.

BALL. chyóu(r). /He rolled the string into a ball. Tā bǎ 'shéngdz 'ràuchéngle yíge 'chyóu.

(A dance) tyàuwǔhwèi. /At the ball they danced until very late. Dzài tyàuwǔ-'hwèili tāmen yì'jr 'tyàudau hěn 'wǎn.

(In names of ball games) chyóu. /Do you want to play baseball, football or basketball? Nǐ yàu wár 'bàngchyóu, 'dzúchyóu, háishr 'lánchyóu?

Play ball dǎchyóu(r), wárchyóu. /They played ball all afternoon. Tāmen 'dǎle yì'syàwǔ de 'chyóu. but /What if he won't play ball with us (cooperate)? Tā bùgēn wǒmen 'hé'dzwò dzěmma 'bàn ne?

All balled up. /He got all balled up. Tā ràu 'húdūle.

BAMBOO. júdz; bamboo shoot júswǔn, swǔn.

BANANA. syāngjyāu.

BANDIT. tǔfěi, 'chyángdàu.

BAND. tyáu; (stripe) dàur; rubber band hóujyēr, syàngpíchywār. /The room was trimmed with a blue band near the ceiling. Jèi wūdzli kàu fáng'dǐng yǒu yìtyáu lán-

'dàur. / Put an iron band around this box. Ná tyě'tyáu bǎ jèige 'syāngdz 'gūshang. / Can you get me a box of rubber bands? Nǐ néng 'gěi wo mǎi yìhér °hóu'jyěr (°syàng-pí'chywǎr) ma?

(Instrumental group) ywèdwèi. / The band played marches and led the parade. Ywè'dwèi dzòuje jìnsyíng'chyù lǐngje rén yóu'syíng.

(Group) yìchywún(rén), yìhwǒdz. / A band of soldiers marched down the road. Yǒu °yìchyún (°yìhwǒdz) bīng dzai lùshang yóu'syíng.

To band together héchilai, tsòudau yí'kwàr. / They banded together to hire a guide. °Tāmen 'héchilai (°Tāmen tsòudau yí'kwàr) 'jǎule ge syǎng'dǎu.

BANDAGE. bēngdài; (gauze) 'shābù; (elastic) sūngjǐn bēngdài; (adhesive tape) syàng-pígāu.

BANK. (Shore) àn, hé byǎr. / The river overflowed its banks. 'Hé 'màngwò lyǎng'àn chyùle. / He swam to the bank. Tā fùdau hébyǎr chyule.

(Heap or pile) dwēi. / There's a bank of snow outside the gate. Dàmér 'wài-byan yǒu yìdwēi 'sywě.

(For money) yínháng; **banker** yínhángjyā. / The bank will exchange our money. Yín'háng kéyi ba dzámende 'chyán 'hwànle.

Open a bank account kāi ge hùtóu. / I'd like to open a bank account. Wǒ syǎng kāi ge 'hùtóu.

Bank note pyàudz, chāupyàu.

To bank money tswún. / We should bank this money. Wǒmen yīngdāng bǎ jèisye 'chyán tswún dàu yín'hángli chyu.

Bank a fire fēngshang. / Please bank the fire with ashes so it will burn slowly. Chǐng bǎ 'hwǒ yùng 'hwēi fēngshang hǎu jáude 'màn.

Bank a plane wāi. / He banked the airplane when he turned. Tā 'jwàn de shŕ-hou bǎ fēi'jī 'wāile yísyàr.

Bank on. / I'm banking on a better job. is expressed as I trust I will be able to find a better job. Wǒ syāngsyìn wǒ néng jàujàu yíge gèng hǎude shŕ.

BANQUET. yànhwèi.

BARBER. lǐfǎjyàng, tìtóude; lǐfǎshŕ (polite way of addressing a barber); **barbershop** lǐfǎgwǎn, tìtóudyàn. / Please direct me to a barbershop. Chǐng ni 'gàusung wo nǎr yǒu lǐfǎ'gwǎn.

BARGAIN. (Cheap things) 'pyányi(de) dūngsyi, pyányi hwò; (specially priced things) jyàn jyàde °dūngsyi (°hwò). / You'll find many bargains there. Nǐ yí'dìng kéyi dzài 'nèr chyáujyan hěn dwō 'pyányi(de) dūngsyi. / Tomorrow is bargain day at this store. is expressed as Tomorrow this store will have a big sale. Míngtyan jèige pùdz dǎ jyǎnjyà.

(Agreement) shwōhǎule de. / According to our bargain you were to pay half in advance. is expressed as What we agreed on was that you were to pay half in advance. Dzámen shwō'hǎule de nǐ 'syān gěi yíbàr 'chyán. / They made the best of the bargain. is expressed as Although they're not satisfied, they are doing all they can. Tāmen swéirán bumǎnyì, kěshr hái jìn'lì chyù dzwò.

Be a bargain 'pyányì. / This book was a great bargain. Jèibèn 'shū 'mǎide jēn 'pyányi.

At a bargain. /He got it at a bargain. <u>is expressed as</u> He bought it very cheaply. Tā mǎide hěn pyányi.

Make a bargain. /I'll make a bargain with you. <u>is expressed as</u> If it's to be that way I have a condition to make. Yàushr 'nèmmaje, wǒ yǒu ge 'tyáujyàn.

To bargain hwánjyà(r), jyǎngjyà(r). /We bargained with the man a long time before buying. Wǒmen méi'mǎi yìchyán gēn tā 'hwánle bàntyan 'jyàr. /They bargained for the house. Tāmen wèi nèige 'fángdzde shr̀ching jyǎng'jyàr. *or* Tāmen jyǎng'fáng'jyàr.

BARK. (Of a tree) shùpí.

To bark (of a dog) jyàu.

(Of people) rāngrang. /He does nothing but bark at his children. Tā dwèi tā háidz rāngrang.

BARLEY. dàmài(dz).

BARN. (For grain only) tsāngfáng. /The barn was filled with hay and grain. Tsāng-'fáng lǐtou 'chywán shr̀ gān'tsǎu gēn 'lyángshr.

See also **STABLE.**

BAROMETER. chìyābyǎu, chíngyùbyǎu. /The barometer reads 28 and is rising. Chìyā'byǎu shr̀ èrshr'bā bìngchyě 'hái wàngshàng 'jǎng.

BARRACKS. bīngyíng, 'yíngpán; (buildings) yíngfáng.

BARREL. tǔng(dz). /Those barrels are full of apples. Nèisye tǔng(dz)li jwāng mǎnle pínggwǒ. /The truck was loaded with barrels of beer. Dzàijùngchì'chēshang 'jwāngle bùshǎu'tǔng 'píjyǒu.

(Of a gun) chyānggwǎr, chyāngshēn, pàugwǎn, pàushēn. /Clean out the barrel of this rifle. Bǎ jèi'chyāngde chyāng'gwǎr 'tsāyitsa.

BARRIER. (Of any kind, lit. or fig.) dzǔai, jàngài.

BASE. (Of a statue, tower) dzwòr; (foundation) jī, jīchu, gēnjī; (of a mountain or hill) shānjyǎu, shāngēr. /The base of the statue was still there. Jèige 'syàng de 'dzwòr hài dzài nèr ne. /His orchard extends to the base of the hill over there. Tāde gwǒ'ywándz yì'jŕ dàu shān'gēr nàr.

(Military) gēnjyùdì, jīdì. /Telephone to the base for instructions. Dǎ dyàn-'hwà dàu gēnjyù'dì chǐng'shr̀. /Let's visit the naval base. Wǒmen chyù tsān'gwán hǎijyūn jī'dì ba.

Be base (morally low) bēibǐ. /His actions are consistently base. Tāde syíngwéi lǎu shr̀ hěn bēibǐ.

Be baseless háuwú 'gēnjyú. /His accusations are baseless. Tāde kùng'gàu háuwú 'gēnjyù.

Be based on yǐ . . . wéi 'gēnjyú, yùng . . . wéi 'gēnjyú, gēnjyù . . . dzwòde. /His report is based on the available statistics. Tāde bàu'gau shr̀ yǐ syàn'yǒude tǔng'jì wéi 'gēnjyú. *or* Tāde bàu'gau shr̀ 'gēnjyù syàn'yǒude tǔng'jì 'dzwòde. *but* /His success is based on honesty. <u>is expressed as</u> His success is because of his honesty. Tā chéng'gūng shr̀ yīnwei tā 'chéngshr.

BASEBALL. bàngchyóu.

BASEMENT

BASEMENT. dìyìndz.

BASIN. pén, shwěipén, lyǎnpén; (of a river) péndì.

BASKET. kwāngdz, lándz, lŏudz, lŏur. / Put the groceries in this basket. Bǎ 'dzáhwò fàngdzai jèige 'lándzli. / Buy a basket of oranges. Mǎi yìlŏur 'jyúdz lai. / He brought a basket of fruit. Tā 'dàilai yìkwāng(dz) shwěi'gwŏ.

BASKETBALL. lánchyóu.

BAT. (Animal) 'byānfú, byǎnfú; (club) bàng; (in baseball) chyóubàng.

BATH. (Bathroom) (syǐ)dzǎufáng. / Does this room have a bath? Jèige 'fángjyān dài syǐdzǎu'fáng ma?

(Bathtub) dzǎupén. / Please fill the bath half full. Bǎ dzǎu'pénli fàng yíbàr 'shwěi.

(Public bath) (syǐ)dzǎutángdz. / He's gone to the bath. Ta dàu dzǎu'tángdz chyù syǐ'dzǎu chyule.

Take a bath syǐdzǎu. / Where can I take a bath? Wǒ dzài 'nǎr kéyi syǐdzǎu?

Bathrobe 'yùyī.

Bathtowel (syǐdzǎu yùngde) dà máujin.

BATHING SUIT. fùshwěiyī, yóuyǔngyī.

BATTERY. (Electric) dyànchŕ, dyànpíng; (military) lyán. / The battery in my car is low. Wǒ chēlide °dyàn'chŕ (°dyàn'píng) kwēile.

A battery of tests yilyánchwànde kǎushŕ.

Assault and battery ōudǎ.

BATTLE. jàn, jàng; fight a battle dǎjàng, jyāujàn, dzwòjàn; meet in battle (of several armies) hwēijàn; battle situation jànjyú. / That battle came to a draw. 'Nèi yijàng °'dǎle ge píng'shǒu (°bù'fēn shèng'fù). / The Battle of Gettysburg stopped the northern advance of the Confederate Army. °Gettysburg yǐ'jàn (°Gettysburg 'nèitsz̀hwēi'jàn) dzǔ'jŕle Nán'jyūnde 'běijìn. / That was a great sea battle. 'Nèi shŕ yítsz̀ 'dà hǎi'jàn. / That battle was fought at the river. 'Nèiyijàng shŕ dzài nèige 'hénèr 'dǎde. / These soldiers haven't seen battle yet. Jèisyē 'bīng hái méi °'jyàngwo (°'jīnggwo) 'jàng ne. / He fell in battle. is expressed as He died fighting. Tā dzwò'jande shŕhou sž̌le.

Battle of wits dòujŕ. / The discussion turned into a battle of wits. Jèitszde tǎulwùn byàncheng tāmen lyǎngge rén dòujŕ le.

Battleground jànchǎng.

Battleship jànjyàn, jǔlìjyàn

BAY. wān; (specifically of the sea) hǎiwān. / The bay made a good harbor. Jèige hǎi'wān shŕ yíge hěn 'hǎude gǎng'kǒu. / The boat sailed into the bay. Jèige 'chwán kāijìn 'wān chyùle.

At bay. / The dogs had the bear at bay. Nèisye 'gǒu jwēi nèige 'syúng jwēidau'dǐle. / He kept his enemies at bay. is expressed as He guarded against the enemy's approach. Tā 'fángbèije dírén bùràng tāmen jyē'jìn.

BAYONET. tsz̀dāu, chyāngtsz̀dz.

BE (AM, ARE, IS, WAS, WERE, BEEN, BEING). Followed by a noun (denoting merely classification) shr̀; (indicating profession or function) dzwò, dāng (only the latter if the function is that of a soldier). /We're American soldiers. Wǒmen shr̀ 'Měigwo bīng. /She's an old hag. Tā shr̀ ge lǎu 'gwàiwu. /When I was a soldier things were different. 'Wǒ dāng'bīng de shŕhou bú'jèmmaje. /He's a lawyer. Tā °shr̀ ge (°dāng, °dzwò) lyù'shr̀. /They asked him to be chairman. Tāmen 'chǐng ta °dāng (°dzwò) jǔ'syí. *but* /Be a good boy and bring it to me. is expressed without any word for **be**: 'Hǎu háidz, géi wo 'nágwolai.

Followed by an adjective (denoting temporary or relative description) the Chinese stative verb is used without any separate word for **be**; (denoting general classification) shr̀ . . . de. /The sky is blue. (at the moment) 'Tyān hěn 'lán. (statement of a general truth) 'Tyān shr̀ 'lánde. /He's OK. 'Tā 'jēn °bù'hwài (°bú'tswò). /I'm thirsty. Wǒ 'kě le. *or* Wǒ hěn 'kě. /Be careful! 'Syǎusyīn dyǎr! /Are you ready? Yùbei'hǎule ma? But in some cases the specific words other than be call for a special expression in Chinese. /Be sure to be there. Yí'dìng yàu 'dàu ner. *or* Byé bú'chyù! *or* Byé bú'dàu! /Be calm! 'Chénjùle 'chì! *or* Byé 'hwāngjang! *or* Byé jāu'jí! /Be natural! *or* Be yourself! 'Dżdzrán'ránde! *or* Byé 'jwāngmudzwò'yàngde! /Do be careful! 'Kě yàu 'syǎusyīnje! *or* 'Chyānwàn 'syǎusyīnje!

Followed by an expression of place dzài; (if there is an idea of arriving) dàu. /When I was in Peiping I went to see the Imperial Palace. Wǒ dzài Běi'píng de shŕhou chyù 'gwànggwo Gù'gūng. /The books are on the table. 'Shū dzài 'jwōr shang. /He wasn't home when we called. Wǒmen chyu 'jǎu ta de shŕhou tā búdzài 'jyā. /Be here at nine tomorrow. 'Míngtyan 'jyǒudyǎn 'dàu jèr.

Be . . . -ing (referring to action going on at the time of speaking or at some reference point of time) often jèng(dzai) *or* dzài before the verb, frequently with an adverb of present time before it; sometimes (also, or instead of dzài) je added to the verb or ne at the end of the sentence, or both. /What're you doing? Dzwò 'shémma ne? /I'm winding my watch. Shàng'byǎu ne. *or* Wǒ jèngdzai shàng'byǎu ne. /They're eating dinner right now. Tāmen 'jèng chŕje 'fàn ne. /He was reading when I entered the room. Wǒ 'jìnchyu de shŕhou tā dzài nèr kàn'shū ne. *or* (putting the other part of the sentence first) Tā 'jèng kànje 'shū wǒ jyou 'jìnchyule.

Be . . . -ing (referring to an event in the future) yàu *or omitted*. /I'm going to Chungking tomorrow. 'Míngtyan wǒ yàu dàu 'Chúngchǐng chyù.

Be to do something, expressed with a word such as děi have to, etc. /You are to report to the captain at nine this morning. Jyér 'dzǎuchen 'jyǒudyǎn nǐ děi chyù jyàn chwán'jǎng. /You and Mr. Chou are to work together in this. 'Jèige shèr °'nǐ děi (°yàu 'nǐ) gēn 'Jōu Syānsheng yí'kwàr dzwò.

There is, there are, there were, etc. yǒu. /There's a pebble in my shoe. Wǒ 'syéli yǒu ge shŕtou'dzěr. /There're several other things I want to say. Wǒ 'hái yǒu jǐjyàn 'shr̀ děi shwōshwo. /There were thirteen at the dinner party. Chŕ 'fàn de shŕhou yǒu shŕ'sānge rén dzài 'dzwò. /There isn't any more sugar. Méiyou 'táng le. /Is there any more sugar? 'Hái yǒu'táng ma? /Aren't there any other ways to do this? Hái yǒu 'byéde fádz ma?

Other English expressions. /Be seeing you! 'Hwéitóu 'jyàn! *or* Hwéi 'jyàn! /Be that as it may, we cannot accept the proposal. Swéiran rútsż, wǒmen 'háishr bunéng 'jyēshòu jeige jyàn'yì.

For other specific combinations of **be** and another word, refer to the other word.

BEADS. jūdz; string of beads °yíchwàr (°yíchwàn) 'jūdz.

BEAK. dzwěi, nyǎudzwěi.

BEAM. (Building support) lyáng, fánglyáng; (of light) yídàu 'gwāng, yídàu gwāngsyàn; (radio) dyànbwō; (of a pair of scales) chénggǎr; (width of a ship) chwánfú.

> **To beam.** /He beamed with delight. is expressed as His face showed delight. Tā lyǎnshang hěn gāu'syìngde yàngdz. *or* Tā myànyǒusyìsè.

BEAN. dòudz; **string bean** byǎndòu, dòujyǎur; **lima bean** tsándòu; **soya bean** dàdòu *or* hwángdòu (the most important kind in China); **black bean** hēidòu; **kidney bean** yāudòu; **bean curd** (made from soya beans) dòufu.

> **Spill the beans** gei shwōchūlai. /I wonder who the hell spilled the beans! Wǒ bù'jŕdàu shr něige hwún'dàn gei 'shwōchulaide!

> Other English expressions. /He doesn't know beans about math. is expressed as He hasn't the least knowledge of math. Tā dwèi 'shùsywé yi'dyǎr budǔng.

BEAR. (Animal) syúng.

BEAR (BORE, BORNE). (Of a tree) jyē; (of an orchard) chū; (of humans or animals) shēng, yǎng; (of animals only) syà. /This pear tree doesn't bear any fruit. Jèikē 'líshù bùjyē 'gwōdz. /This orchard bears good peaches. Jèige gwǒ'ywándz chūde 'táur hen hǎu. /She's borne three children. Tā 'shēnggwo 'sānge 'háidz. /The cat bore many litters. Nèige 'māu syàle hen dwō syǎu 'māur.

> (Endure) rěn, rěnde; (only in the potential form) 'shòudelyǎu; 'rěndejù. /He bore the pain in silence. Tā nèmma 'téng de shŕhou, 'rěnje méichū'shēngr. /I can't bear to see them leave. Wǒ bù'rěnde kàn tāmen 'dzǒu. /I can't bear it any more. Wǒ 'dzài yě shòubu'lyǎu le. /I can't bear his attitude any more. Tāde 'tàidu jyàu wo 'dzài yě rěnbu'jù le.

> **Bear** oneself (demeanor). /She bears herself well. is expressed as Her bearing is good. Tāde fēngdù hen hǎu.

> **Bear a grudge** bu . . . ywánlyang. /He always bears a grudge. is expressed as He never forgives others. Tā tsúng'lái bukěn ywánlyang byéren.

> **Bear a signature.** /This document bears the signature of the president. is expressed as This document has the signature of the president. Jèige wénjyànshang yǒu dzung'tǔngde chyāndz.

> **Bear arms** káng. /All men who can bear arms must become soldiers. Néng káng 'chyāng de rén dōu děi chyù dāng'bīng.

> **Bear evidence** *or* **witness** dzwò jèngren. /He bore witness against me. Tā dzwò 'jèngren fǎndwèi wo.

> **Bear responsibility** fùdzé. /I had to bear the responsibility of his mistake. Shŕ 'tāde 'tswòr, kěshr 'wǒ děi fù'dzé.

> **Bear the expense** 'dānfù. /The government bears the expense of foreign aid. Jèng'fù dānfù wài'ywánde 'fèiyung.

> **Bear weight** 'jīndejù. /This board won't bear your weight. Jèi 'bǎndz jīnbu'jù nǐ.

> **Bear in mind** jìju. /Bear in mind what I told you. Jìju wo gàusung ni de 'hwà.

> **Bear out** jèngshŕle. /This bears out my prediction. Jèiyàng, wǒde yù'lyàu jèngshŕle.

> **Bear with.** /I bore with him through hardships. is expressed as I suffered with him through hardships. Wǒ gēn tā yí'kwàr chŕkǔ.

Have bearing upon yǒu gwānsyi. / This has bearing upon our previous statement. Jèige gen wǒmen yǐchyán 'shwō de yǒu 'gwānsyi.

BEARD. (Any facial hair including mustache, whiskers, etc.) húdz (of humans and of goats). / It's that man with a long beard! Shr̀ nèige cháng 'húdzde!

Grow a beard (naturally) jǎng húdz; (intentionally) lyóu húdz. / I didn't realize you were old enough to grow a beard. Wǒ méisyǎng'dàu nǐ yǐjing dzěmma 'dà le, dou jǎng 'húdz le. / He grew a fuzzy beard in twenty days. 'Èrshrtyānli tā 'lyóule yì'dzwěide 'húdz.

In the literary language rán means hair growing from cheeks and jaw, syū means a short beard from the chin, hú refers to hair on the chin just below the lower lip, and tsz̄ means hair on the upper lip. Some colloquial expressions borrowed from the literary language use these words; a man with a beautiful beard měirán'gūng.

BEARING. (Direction) 'fāngsyang; (relationship) gwānsyi; (demeanor) see BEAR. / Let's not lose our bearings. Byé dyōule fāngsyàng. or Byé dzòuswò le lù. / The ship is off its bearing. Chwán dzòuswòle fāngsyàng le. / His going home has no bearing on his failure to pass the examination. Tā hwéijyā gēn tā kǎushr̀ bùjígé méi'gwānsyi.

BEAST. yěshòu.

BEAT. (Of music) pāidz; (in referring to a traditional song) bǎn, bǎnyǎn. / The beat of music wasn't clear. Yīn'ywède 'pāidz bù'chīngchu. / He is singing off beat. Tā 'chàng de °bǎnyǎn bu'dwèi (°dzǒubǎn le).

(Of a drum) gǔdyǎr. / Follow the drumbeats. Gēnje gǔ'dyǎr.

(Of a policeman) dwàn, dwàr. / Chang patrols this beat at night. 'Jèiyídwàr 'yèli gwēi Lǎu'jāng syúnlwó.

To beat dǎ; (with a stick) chyāu; (with a whip) chōu; (with a flat surface, such as the palm of the hand) pāi. / Please beat this carpet. Chǐng bǎ jèige dì'tǎn °'dǎ yidǎ (°'chyāu yichyāu). / Beat the egg before putting it in. Syān bǎ jī'dzěr dǎ yidǎ dzai 'fàngjinchyu.

(To win) yíng; or expressed with shū lose. / Who beat whom? Shéi 'yíngle? or Shéi 'shūle? / He beat me at a game of chess. Tā 'yíngle wo yìpán 'chí. or Wǒ 'shūgei ta yìpán 'chí.

(Be better than) bǐ . . . 'hǎu, gǎndeshàng. / Nothing can beat it. 'Méiyou bǐ jèige 'hǎude. or 'Shémma dou gǎnbu'shàng jèige.

(Of the heart) tyàu. / His heart was beating regularly. Tā 'syīn 'tyàude hěn 'yún.

(Of a record) dǎpwò 'jìlù. / He beat the world swimming record. Tā dǎpwòle shr̀jyè yóuyǔng'jìlù le.

Beat a drum dǎ gǔ, chyāu 'gǔ. / He sure can beat that drum. Tā dǎ 'gǔ dǎde 'jēn hǎu.

Beat a retreat (withdraw) chètwèi. / The army beat a retreat. Jyūndwèi chètwèile.

Beat time dǎ 'pāidz; (in referring to a traditional song) pāibǎn. / He beat time with his foot. Tā yùng 'jyǎu °dǎ pāidz (°pāi'bǎn).

Beat around the bush ràuje 'chywār 'shwō. / Don't beat around the bush. Nǐ búyung ràuje'chywār 'shwō. or is expressed as If you have something to say, say it directly. Yǒu hwà jyou 'jŕ shwō.

Beat back, beat off bǎ . . . °dǎdzǒu (°dǎpǎu, °dǎtwèi). / He beat off the dogs with a stick. Tā yùng 'gwùndz bǎ 'gǒu dǎ'pǎule. / Has the enemy been beaten back yet? 'Dírén bèi dǎ'twèile ma?

Beat up dǎ yídwùn; **get beaten up, get a beating** 'āi yídwùn 'dǎ. / He was beaten up by a gang of hoodlums. Tā jyàu yìchyún lyóumáng gěi 'dǎle yí'dwùn. / He got beat up. Tā 'āile yídwùn 'dǎ.

Other English expressions. Let's beat it! 'Chǔchyu ba! *or* Dzǒu'kāi ba! / Beats me! Wǒ bujř'dàu! / I'm beat. Wǒ jīnpíli'jìn le.

BEAUTIFUL. hǎu, měi; (pleasing to the eye) hǎukàn; (pleasing to the ear) hǎutīng; (specifically of a person) jàngde hěn °'hǎu (°pyàulyang, °hǎukàn, °měi). / What a beautiful day! 'Tyār dwō 'hǎu a! / The scenery there is quite beautiful. Nèrde 'jǐngjř hěn 'hǎu. / The scenery is very beautiful. 'Jǐngjř hěn 'měi. / This picture is very beautiful. Jèijāng hwàr 'hwàde hěn hǎu'kàn. / She has a beautiful voice. Tā chàng 'gēer chàngde hěn hǎu'tīng. / His wife is a beautiful woman. Tā 'tàitai 'jàngde hěn °'hǎu (°etc.).

BECAUSE. yīnwèi, (yīnwei) . . . swóyi . . . / He didn't come because he got sick. Tā yīnwei 'bìngle méi'lái. *or* Tā méilái, yīnwei ta 'bìngle. *or* Tā (yīnwei) 'bìngle, swóyi méi'lái. / I didn't buy it because of the high price. Yīnwei 'jyàchyan tài 'gāu wǒ méi'mǎi.

Because of this (that, it) yīntsž. / He treats people so thoughtfully; I like him all the more because of that. Tā 'dài rén hěn 'jōudau, wǒ yīn'tsž 'gèng 'syǐhwān ta.

BECOME (BECAME). chéng, 'byànchéng. / He became famous overnight. Tā 'mǎshàng jyòu 'chéngle 'míng le. / She's borrowed it so many times that it's become hers (sarcastic). Tā 'jyègwò nèmma dwō 'tsž, jyé'gwò jyou 'byàncheng 'tāde le.

(Changing to a higher status) chéng, dāngshang, shēngdau, dzwò. / He became a professor at only twenty-nine. Tā èrshr'jyòuswei jyòu °'chéngle (°etc.) jyàu'shòu le.

(Reach an age) dàu. / When he became twenty-one he left home. Dàule èrshr-'yīswèi tā jyou 'líkai 'jyā le.

(Be suitable to) wèi . . . hǎukàn, wèi . . . pyàulyang. / That color is very becoming to you. Jèige 'yánsè wèi ni hěn hǎu'kàn. / That red dress becomes her. 'Húng yīshang tā 'chwǎnje tèbyé 'pyàulyang.

Often not expressed with a separate Chinese verb, but le is used at the end of a sentence to express change of status. / The secret has gradually become known. Jèige 'bìmì jyan'jyànde gěi 'rén 'jřdàule. / This invention will become more and more important as time goes on. Jèige fā'míng yǐ'hòu ywè 'lái ywè 'jùngyau le. / What became of them? Tāmen 'hòulai dzěmma'yàng le? / What's become of the original plan? 'Ywánláide 'jìhwà syàndzài dzěmma'yàng le?

BED. chwáng. / I want a room with two beds. Wǒ yàu yìjyān yǒu 'lyǎngge 'chwáng de 'wūdz. / When I came in he was lying in bed. Wǒ 'jìnlai de shŕhou tā dzai chwángshang 'tǎngje ne.

(Base, foundation) tái. / The machine is set in a bed of concrete. 'Jīchi 'āndzai 'shwěinǐ'táishang.

Go to bed shàngchwáng, shwèi(le). / He's already gone to bed. Tā 'yǐjing °shàngchwángle (°shwèile).

Make a bed pū(shang) chwáng. / My bed hasn't been made. Wǒde 'chwáng méi'pū. / Please make my bed. Chǐng bǎ wǒde 'chwáng 'pūshang.

Put someone to bed. / Put the child to bed. Dài 'háidz chyu shwèi'jyàu ba.

Bedbug chòuchung.

Bedclothes (sheets or bedspread) chwángdāngz; change a bed hwàn chwángdāndz. / When was this bedcloth last changed? Jèige chwáng'dāndz shr̀ 'shémma shŕhou 'hwànde?

Bedroom wòshr̀, wòfáng. / Let's make this the bedroom! 'Jèijyān dzwò 'wòshr̀ ba!

Flower bed hwārtán, hwārtái. / The chrysanthemums in the flower bed are blooming. Hwā'táishangde 'jyúhwār 'kāile.

River bed hédàu. / Follow the old river bed for two miles. Shwùnje jyòu hé'dàu dzǒu èrlǐ 'dì.

BEDDING. pūgai, 'bèirù.

BEE. mìfēngr; bumblebee hwángfēng, mǎfēng.

Beehive mìfēngwō, fēngwō.

Make a beeline. / He made a beeline for home. is expressed as He rushed straight home. Tā yì'jŕ 'gǎnhwei 'jyā chyule.

BEECH. (Tree) 'jyǔshù; (wood) jyǔmù.

BEEF. nyóuròu. / This piece of beef is tough. Jèikwài nyóu'ròu hěn 'lǎu. / I'll take the roast beef. Wǒ chr̄ kǎunyóu'ròu. / The market has fresh beef today. 'Jīntyan 'shr̀shàng yǒu 'syīnsyan nyóu'ròu.

Beefsteak nyóupái, nyóu(ròu)pá.

To beef (complain) bàuywan. / What're you beefing about? Nǐ 'bàuywan shémma?

BEER. 'píjyǒu.

BEET. húngtsàitóu, dǐlwóba.

BEFORE. (In time past, previously) yǐchyán, tsúngchyán. / I'd never been there before. Wǒ yǐ'chyán méi'dàugwo nèr. or Wǒ tsúng'chyán méi'chyùgwo.

(Earlier, sooner) dzǎujyou. / We should have done this long before. Wǒmen 'dzǎujyou yīngdāng 'chyù. / We should have done it this way before. Wǒmen 'dzǎujyou gāi 'jèmma bàn.

(Preceding in time) yǐchyán; (sometime) budàu, dàubulyǎu; before Christ, B.C. ('syīlì)jìywán'chyán. / Come before two o'clock. Lyǎngdyǎn jūng yǐ'chyán lái. / Don't come before two o'clock. Budàu lyǎngdyǎn byé'lái. or Lyǎngdyǎn yǐ'chyán byé'lái. / The telegram should come before evening. Wǎnshang yǐ'chyán, dyàn'bàu jyou yīngdang 'dàule. or 'Dàubulyǎu 'wǎnshang, dyàn'bàu jyou yīngdāng 'dàule. / Before that time she lived alone. Nèige shŕhou yǐ'chyán, tā'yíge rén jù.

(In front of a person) (dzài) ... 'myànchyán. / He was taken before the judge. Tā bèi 'dàidau shěnpàn'gwān myànchyán chyule.

(In front of a thing) (dzài) ... °'chyánbyan (°'chyánbyar, °'chyántou). / Who's standing before that tree? 'Shéi dzài 'shù chyántou 'jànje ne? or 'Shù chyántou 'jànje de shr̀ 'shéi?

(Confronting) 'mùchyán, dāngchyán, syàndzài. / The question before us is a hard one. °'Mùchyánde (°etc.) 'wèntí hěn nán 'bàn.

(Preceding in order) syān. / Business before pleasure. 'Syān dzwò 'shr̀, 'hòu wár. / Do this before anything else. 'Syān bǎ 'jèige 'dzwòle.

(Previous to the time when) (méi) . . . °yǐchyán (°jr̄chyán) (both the negative and affirmative translate the same way); or expressed with jyòu then or tsái then and only then. / I'll telephone you before I start. Wǒ (méi)dùng'shēn yǐ'chyán, gěi nǐ dǎ dyàn'hwà. / He left before he'd eaten breakfast. Tā (méi)chr̄ dzǎufàn yǐ-'chyán, jyou dzǒu le. / I can't leave before I finish this. Wǒ (méi)dzwòwán yǐ'chyán, bunéng'líkai. / They hadn't been married a month before they quarreled. Tāmen jyé'hwūn méiyou yíge 'ywè jyòu chǎu'dzwèi le. / It was midnight before he came back. Tā bàn'yè tsái 'hwéilai.

Before long kwài, bùjyòu jyòu, yìhwěr jyòu. / They'll come before long. Tāmen °'kwài (°etc.) 'láile.

BEG. (For something) yàu; (for alms) hwàywán. / The children begged for pennies. Syǎu'hár yàu 'chyán. / The man came to the door to beg for food. Tā dàu mén'kǒur lái yàu 'fàn. / That monk comes once a month begging from door to door. Nèige 'héshang 'měiywè lái yǐ'tsz̀ āi 'mér hwà'ywán.

Beg someone **to** chyóu. / They begged us to help them. Tāmen 'chyóu wǒmen 'bāng tāmen.

Beg someone **to stay** wǎnlyóu (especially in the sense of not leaving a job). / We begged him to stay on. Wǒmen wǎn'lyóu ta laije.

Beg to differ. / I beg to differ with you. Dwèibu'chǐ. Wǒ bunéng gēn nín túng'yì.

Beg one's **pardon.** / I beg your pardon. (for a social error) Dwèibu'chǐ. or Dwèibu'jù. (for a misunderstood remark, requesting repetition) Chǐng (ni) dzài 'shwō (yítsz̀).

BEGGAR. yàufànde, jyàuhwādz, hwādz.

BEGIN. (Start) 'kāishr̄; also expressed with the particle le because the beginning of an action is a kind of change of status; sometimes expressed with . . . chǐ . . . laile or . . . chǐlaile. / We must begin work right away. Wǒmen děi lìkè °'kāishr̄ 'gūngdzwò (°gūngdzwò le). / This building was begun many years ago. Jèige 'jyànju hǎudwō-'nyán yǐ'chyán jyou kāishr̄ 'dzàu le. / It's beginning to rain. Dyàu 'dyǎr le. or Syà'yǔ le. / Right away they began to fight. Tamen lì'kè jyòu 'dǎchi jyà laile. / He began to cry. Tā kūchilaile.

(Do the first part of an action) is expressed with syān (first). / I'll begin by reviewing last week's lesson. Wǒ syān wēnsyí 'shànglǐbàide 'gūngkè. / He began the report with a long quote. Tāde bàugàu 'syān láile yídà'dwàn yǐnjèng 'byérende hwà. / Let's begin with soup. 'Syān shàng 'tāng.

(Of a performance) kāiyǎn. / The performance begins at 8:30 P.M. Wǎnshang 'bādyǎn sānshr̄ kāi'yǎn.

Begin at (with, from) tsúng . . . chǐ. / Begin at the second chapter. Tsúng dì-'èrjāng 'chǐ.

Begin with dìyī. / To begin with, he's too old. Dì'yī, tā tài 'lǎu.

Not begin to yì'dyǎr °dōu (°yě) bu. / The supply doesn't begin to meet our requirements. Hwò 'láide yì'dyǎr dōu bú'gòu.

Beginning kāi'shr̄de shŕhou, chǐ'tóurde shŕhou. / Did you get there at the beginning? °Kāi'shr̄ (°Chǐ'tóurde) shŕhou nǐ dzai nèr ne ma? or expressed

<u>verbally as</u> When it started did you get there? Yǐ kāi'shr̄ ni jyou dàule ma?

From the beginning kāitóu, tsúng 'chǐtóur; from beginning to end tsúng 'tóur dàu 'lyǎur, tsúng 'tóu dàu 'wěi. / He's been wrong right from the beginning. Tā tsúng 'chǐtour jyou 'tswò le. / He was in charge of the job from beginning to end. Tā tsú ⁺óur dàu 'lyǎur yi'jr̄ 'gwǎn jèijyàn 'shr̄.

BEHIND. (dzài) . . . hǒumyan, hòubyan, hòubyar, hòutou. / The car is parked behind the house. 'Chē 'tíngdzai 'fángdzde 'hòubyar. / Their seats are behind ours. 'Tāmende 'dzwòwèi dzài wǒmende 'hòumyan.

Behind <u>in many verb groups is expressed with</u> syà <u>as a resultative ending,</u> **leave behind** rēngsya, dyǒusya or (intentionally) lyóusya; **fall behind** or **leave behind** làsya, etc. / We had to leave our trunk behind. Wǒmen děi bǎ 'syāngdz 'rēngsya. / He left his home behind him. Tā 'dyǒusya 'jyā 'dzǒule. / He's fallen behind in his work. Tā 'gūngdzwo 'làsyale bù'shǎu. / Have you left anything behind? Nǐ 'làsyale shémma 'dūngsyi méiyou?

Be behind (support) 'hòutou yǒu rén (jr̄chr̄), ('hòutou yǒu rén) 'jr̄chr̄. / There are tremendously powerful groups behind him. Yǒu hěn yǒu'lìlyangde twánti 'jr̄chr̄ ta. / Someone must be behind this. Hòutou yídìng yǒu rén ('jr̄chr̄).

Be behind (in the sense of scheming) dzài hòutou tsāudzùng. / Someone must be behind this. Yídìng yǒu rén dzài hòutou 'tsāudzung. / Who's behind this? Jèijyàn shr̄ shr̄ shwéi dzài 'hòutou 'tsāudzùngde?

Be behind (be the reason for) shr̄ . . . ywángu. / He leaves his house at one every morning I wonder what's behind it. Tā měityan yèli 'yìdyǎnjūngde shr̄hou 'lǐkai jyā. Wǒ bujr̄'dàu shr̄ 'shémma 'ywángu.

Be behind time or **behind schedule** wùdyǎn. / The train is behind time. Hwǒ'chē wù'dyǎn le.

BELIEVE. (Sincerely but not religiously) syìnli syǎng, syǎngsyìn. / I personally believe that what he said is right. Wǒ °'syìnli 'syǎng (°syǎngsyìn) tā 'shwō de 'dwèi.

(Think, suppose) jywéde, syǎng. / Do you believe he's sincere? Nǐ 'jywéde tā 'chéngshr ma? / I believe he's gone. Wǒ syǎng tā 'dzǒule.

<u>The indefinite answer</u> I believe not or I don't believe so <u>depends on the question.</u> / (Has he gone?) I believe not. (Tā'dzǒule?) 'Méiyou ba. or 'Hái méi'dzǒu ba. / (Did he do it?) I don't believe so. ('Tā dzwòde?) Búshr 'tā ba. / (Did that really happen?) I believe not. ('Jēnde ma?) Bú'hwèi ba. or Méiyou 'nèmma hwéi 'shr̄ ba. / (Is that yours?) I believe not. ('Nǐde?) 'Dàgài 'búshr. or Wǒ syǎng 'búshr.

Believe (in) (with firm conviction) syìn. / Do you believe what he told us? Nǐ 'syìn tā 'gàusung wǒmen de ma? or Tā 'shwō de nǐ 'syìn a? / Do you believe in God? (Roman Catholic) Nǐ syìn tyān'jǔ ma? (Protestant) Nǐ syìn shàng'dì ma? / What religion do you believe in? Nǐ syìn shémma 'jyàu?

Believe in <u>certain ethics or moral conduct</u> jywéde (bu)yīnggāi. / I don't believe in cheating old people. Wo jywéde bùyīnggāi chǐfu lǎurén. / I believe in studying hard. Wǒ jywéde yīng'gāi yùng'syìn nyàn'shū.

Believe me. (wǒ shwō) byé búsyìn. / Believe me! You were cheated. Byé bú'syìn, nǐ shr̄ bèi 'pyànle. / Believe me! This is expensive. Wǒ shwō jèige 'gwèi, nǐ byé bú'syìn.

Make-believe jyǎjwǎng / It's just make-believe. 'Búgwò shr̄ jyǎ'jwǎngje

BELL. (Large) jūng; (small) líng, língr, língdang. / That bell is cracked. Nèikǒu 'jūng 'lyèle. / This bell won't ring. Jèige 'língdang bù'syǎng le.

Ring a bell (by striking) dǎlíng, dǎjūng; (by moving with the hand) yáulíng; (by pulling a bell-cord) lā líng, lā língr, lā jūng; (by pushing a button) èn língr. / Has the bell rung yet? 'Jūng °dǎgwolema (°dǎgwo 'jūng le ma, °dǎgwo 'líng le ma, °yáugwo 'líng le ma, °líng syǎngle ma)? On shipboard time is marked by (ringing) a bell every half-hour. Dzài 'chwánshang měi'bàndyǎn jūng 'dǎ yi hwéi 'jūng. / The bell rings half an hour before services. Dzài dzwòlǐ'bài yi'chyán 'bàndyǎn jūng dǎ-'jūng.

Bellboy fàndyànlǐ °násyínglide (°kāiménde).

Bell tower jūnglóu.

Doorbell ménlíngr; (electric) dyànlíng. / The doorbell is ringing. Mén'língr 'syǎng le.

BELLIGERENT. (Country participating in a war) jyāujàngwó.

BELLOWS. (For producing a stream of air) 'fēngsyāng.

BELLY. (Of a person) dùdz; (of a plane) fēijī dùdz.

BELONG. (Be properly or comfortably at a place). / I don't belong here. is expressed as I don't fit in. Wǒ dzài 'jèr bùhé'shr̀. or as I'm an outsider. Dzài 'jèr wǒ shr̀ 'wàiren. or as I'm looked on as an outsider. Tāmen jèr ná wo dàng 'wàiren 'kàn. / This flower vase doesn't belong here. is expressed as This flower vase shouldn't be put here. Jèige hwā'pyéngr bù'gāi fàng 'jèr. / This book belongs on that shelf. is expressed as This book should be put on that shelf. Jèiběn 'shū gāi 'gēdzài 'nèitséng 'jyàrshang.

Belong to (be a member of a political party) shr̀; (be a member of an organization) shr̀ . . . ywán. / He belongs to the Nationalist Party. Tā shr̀ °Gwómíndǎng (°Gwómíndǎng(de) dǎngywán). / He belongs to the YMCA. Tā shr̀ Chīngnyánhwèi hwèiywán.

Belong to (be the property of or under the control of) shǔyú. / That island belongs to China. Nèige 'dǎu shǔyú 'Jūnggwo.

Belong to or **in** a place or family (be property of or customarily be kept at) shr̀ . . . de. / Does this book belong to you? Jèiběn 'shū shr̀ 'nǐde ma? / Do you belong to the Hwang family? Nǐ shr̀ Hwángjyade rén ma? / This old chair belongs in the kitchen. Jèibǎ 'pwò 'yǐdz shr̀ chú'fánglide.

BELOW. (In a lower place) syàbyan, syàbyar, syàmyan, syàmyar, 'dǐsyà. / We can see people below. Wǒmen 'kàndejyan °'dǐsyàde (°etc.) rén. / Try the floor below. Dàu 'syàmyan 'nèitséng lóu chyushr̀shr̀. / Watch out below! 'Syàmyar lyóu'shén! / Who has the room below me? Wǒ 'dǐsyà nèijyān 'wūr 'shwéi 'jù?

(Lower on a page or graduated scale) yǐsyà. / The temperature here gets below zero. Jèrde 'tyānchi hěn 'shǎu lěng dau líng'dù yǐ'syà. / What he said is quoted below. Yǐ'syà shr̀ 'tā shwōde.

(Lower in rank) ('jyējí) dī. / A colonel is below a brigadier in rank. Shàng'syàu bǐ shàu'jyàng ('jyējí) 'dī.

(Less than). / He's below average height. is expressed as He, compared to the average person, is short. Tā bǐ yì'bānrén 'ǎi.

Below deck dzài 'tsānglî. / He works below deck. Tā dzài 'tsānglî dzwò'gūng.

Be given below rúsyà. / The chart is given below. Byǎu'gé rú'syà. In a Chinese text, running from top to bottom and from right to left, the equivalent phrase is The chart is given to the left. Byǎu'gé rú'dzwǒ.

BELT. dàidz, dàr; (at the waist) yāudài; (for trousers) kùdài *or* kùyāudài; (for a skirt) chyúndài; (of leather, for any use) pídài; (for a machine) pídài, lwúndài; life belt jyòushēngdài. / Do you wear a belt or suspenders? Nǐ jì yāu'dài háishr jì bēi'dài? / We need a new belt for this machine. Jèijyà 'jīchi děi yàu yìtyáu 'syīnde lwún'dài.

(An area with certain characteristics or properties yídài('dìfang), 'dìdai. / This is the cotton belt. 'Jèi yídài('dìfang) chū 'myánhwa. *or* 'Jei shr chū 'myánhwade 'dìdai.

To tighten one's belt. / All you can do is tighten your belt a bit. Nǐ jr̄ néng bǎ kùyāu'dài lēi'jǐn yìdyǎr.

BENCH. (cháng)bǎndèng, (cháng)dèngdz.

BEND (BENT). wān. / You've bent this too much. Nǐ bǎ 'jèige 'wānde tài 'lìhài le. / How much will this rod bend without breaking? Jèige 'gwùndz néng wāndau shémma chéng'dù hái bù'shé?

(Submit) 'chyūfú. / He won't bend a bit under any pressure. Dzěmma yàng 'bǐ ta, tā 'yě bù'chyūfú.

Bend down (over) wānsyachyu, wānsyalai, wānyāu. / You'll have to bend down to get through here. Nǐ děi wānsya 'yāu lai tsái néng tsúng 'jèr 'gwòchyu. / He walks bent over. Tā wānje 'yāur 'dzǒu. / The doctor bent over the patient. Nèige 'dàifu wānje 'yāu kàn nèige bìngren.

Bend something into 'wānchéng. / Bend this wire into a circle. Bǎ jèityáu dyàn'syàn wāncheng ge 'chywār. / He bent the rod into a hook. Tā bǎ tyétyáu wānchengle yíge 'gōur.

Be bent (over) (of a person) wānyāu(r). / He's bent with age. Tā 'lǎude dōu wānle 'yāule.

A bend wār. / Follow the bend in the river. Shwùnje héde 'wār 'dzǒu.

BENEATH. (dzài) . . . 'dǐsyà. / He was buried beneath the tree. Tā 'máidzai shù 'dǐsya le.

Be beneath (in the social scale) bǐ . . . 'dī. / She is far beneath him. Tāde °jyāshr (°dìwei) bǐ 'tā dīde 'dwō.

Be beneath one to do shr̄ . . . shēnfèn. / I don't feel it's beneath me to do this work. Wǒ bùjywéde 'dzwò jèijyan 'shr̄ching 'shr̄ wǒde 'shēnfen.

Be beneath one's dignity. / It's beneath his dignity to say something like that. Tā shwō 'nèiyàngrde'hwà °yǒushr̄ 'dzwǔnyán (°yǒushr̄ 'shēnfèn). Both of the foregoing are literary phrases often quoted.

Look on someone as **beneath** one syǎu 'kàn, kànbuchǐ. / Don't look on these people as beneath you. Byé syǎu 'kàn jèisyē 'rén. *or* Byé kànbuchǐ jèisye rén.

BENEFIT. 'hǎuchù. / The new law gives us very little benefit. Jèige 'syīnde fǎlyù dwèi wǒmen yìdyǎr 'hǎuchù yě 'méiyou.

(Performance or affair for raising funds) yìwushr̄ (a play); tszʹshànyóuyì'hwèi (party, variety show); tszʹshàntyàuwǔ'hwèi (dance).

To benefit dwei . . . yǒu'lì. / Whom does that law benefit? Nèityáu fǎlyù dwèi 'shwéi yǒu'lì ne?

Benefit from yǒusyàu (have good results). / We benefited from the medicine. Jèige 'yàu wǒmen 'chr̄le hěn yǒu'syàu.

BENT. syǐhwan. /He has a bent for art. Tā syǐhwan 'yìshu.

Be bent wǎnle de. /He fastened the papers together with a bent pin. Tā yùng wǎnle de 'jēn bǎ 'jř dōu 'byéchilaile.

Be bent on yí'dìng yàu, jř syǎng, yígejyèrde 'syǎng. /In spite of everything he is bent on going. Wúlwùnrú'hé tā yí'dìng yàu 'chyù. /He's bent on making money. Tā jř 'syǎng jwàn'chyán.

See also BEND.

BERTH. (Sleeping place) wòpù; (for a ship) dìngbwòchù, tíngbwòchù.

BESIDE. (By the side of a person) dzài . . . 'shēnbyār. /The boy stood beside his mother. Syǎu nán'hár jàndzai tā 'mǔchin 'shēnbyār.

(By the side of a thing) dzài . . . 'pángbyār. /The boy stood beside the table. Syǎu nán'hár jàndzai 'jwōdz 'pángbyār.

(By the side of a thing and leaning on it) kàuje. /Please put the suitcase beside the bureau. Bǎ jèige 'syāngdz kàuje yī'gwèi 'fàng.

Be beside oneself. /He's beside himself with anger. Tā 'chìde 'lìhài. or expressed as He's so angry he's changed color. Tā 'chìde 'lyánse dōu 'byànle. /He's beside himself with joy. is expressed as He's out of his mind with joy. Tā 'lède fā'kwáng.

Be beside the point. /That's beside the point. 'Jèi shr 'lìng yíjyan shèr. or 'Jèi wèi'myǎn líle 'tíle. /His answer was beside the point. Tā swó'dáfēiswó'wèn.

BESIDES. (In addition to) (chúle) . . . yǐ'wài, chúle . . . lìng'wài, 'wài . . . hái, lìng'wài hái. /Others must help besides me. Chúle 'wǒ yǐ'wài 'byéren yě děi bāng'máng. /We need more besides these. Chúle 'jèisyēer lìng'wài hái děi 'yàu. /What do you have besides this? Tsž'wài nǐ 'hái yǒu 'shémma? /What do you want besides this? Nǐ lìng'wài hái yàu 'shémma?

(Other than) lìng. /I hate the work; you'll have to get someone besides me. Wǒ bù'syǐhwān jèijyàn 'shr̀; nǐ 'lìng 'jǎu rén ba.

(Moreover) érchyě 'yě, 'dzài jyāshang, yòu. /I'm not feeling well; besides, I haven't time. Wǒ bú'dà 'shūfu; érchyě 'yě méiyou 'gūngfu.

BEST. (Superlative of well *or* good) dzwèi hǎu(de), dǐng hǎu(de); dzwèi in such expressions as best looking dzwèi hǎu'kàn(de), best qualified dzwèi héshr̀, etc. /I work best in the morning. Wǒ dzǎuchen dzwò 'shŕching dzwòde dzwèi 'hǎu. /This car is the best looking. Jèilyang chē shr dzwèi hǎu'kànde. /He's the best qualified for this job. Tā dzwò jèijyan shr̀ dzwèi hé'shr̀. /The best work was done by the young men. Dzwèi hǎude gūngdzwò dōu shr nyán'chīngde rén 'dzwòde.

Best man (at a wedding) bànláng, nánbīnsyāng.

Best part of one's life hwáng'jīnshŕdài, jèng dāng'nyánde shŕhou.

The best (top grade) (dzwèi) shàngděngde. /We want only the best. Wǒmen jyòu yàu (dzwèi) shàng'děngde. *but* /Let's hope for the best. is expressed as Don't be too pessimistic. Búbì tài bēigwān. /Is that the best you can do? is expressed as Can't you do a little better? Nǐ bùnéng dzài dzwò 'hǎu yìdyǎr ma?

(Utmost) jìnlìde, jìnlyàng, jìn . . . . /Do your best. Jìn'lìde 'gàn. /We must make the best of the situation. Dà'jyā děi jìn'lìde gàn tsái 'syíng. /Make the best of the time you have. Jìn'lyàng lìyùng shŕ'jyan. /I'll do my best for you. Wǒ jìn-'lìde géi ni 'bàn yíbàn. /Do it to the best of your ability. Nǐ jìn'lìde dzwò ba. or Jìn nǐde 'lìlyang dzwò ba.

At best °dzwèi 'hǎu (°jr̀'dwō, °dìng'dwǒ) yě bú'gwò. /At best he's a dirty politician. Tā °dzwèi 'hǎu (°etc.) yě bú'gwò shr̀ ge fú'bàide jèng'kè.

Be at one's best déchǐ'swǒdzāi. /He's at his best when he plays baseball. Tā dǎ 'bàngchyóu de shŕhou, jyou déchǐ'swǒdzāi le.

Get the best of pyàn, 'jàn . . . de 'pyányi. /We must be careful that he doesn't get the best of us. Wǒmen děi 'syǎusyīn dyar, °byé 'ràng ta 'pyàn le (°byé 'ràng ta 'jàn dzámende 'pyányi).

BETTER. bǐ . . . 'hǎu, gènghǎu, hái hǎu, hǎude dwō, 'hǎudyǎr(de). /I can't do better than this. Wǒ 'dzwòde dzài bùnéng bǐ 'jèige hǎule. /Show me a better way. Nǐ yǒu bǐ 'jèige hái'hǎude 'fádz ma? /They did much better after they'd had some experience. Tāmen yǒule jīng'yàn yǐ'hòu dzwòde 'gènghǎule. /We'll be better off if we move. Wǒmen 'líkai jèr yí'dìng hǎude 'dwō. /I want a better room than this. Wǒ yàu yǐjyān 'hǎu dyǎrde 'wūdz. /Is this any better? (thing) 'Jèige 'hǎu dyǎr ma? (way) 'Jèmmaje 'hǎu dyǎr ma? /Better late than never. Wǎn dàu dzǔng bǐ budàu hǎu.

(Of a sick person) jyànhǎu. /The doctor says he's (getting) better. 'Dàifu shwō tā jyàn'hǎu.

Better and better ywè 'lái ywè 'hǎu. /His makrs are getting better and better. Tāde fēnshu ywè 'lái ywè 'hǎu.

The better part of dwōbàn. /It took him the better part of a month to do it. Tā 'dzwòle dwō'bànge'ywè tsái dzwò'hǎude.

The . . . the better ywè . . . ywè 'hǎu. /The sooner you go there the better it will be. Nǐ ywè 'dzǎu 'chyù ywè 'hǎu.

For better or for worse hǎudǎi. /I have to stick out this job for better or for worse. Bùgwǎn hǎudǎi wǒ'háishr děi dzwò jèijyan 'shr̀.

Know better. /You should know better than to do anything like that. Nǐ bù'gāi dzwòchu 'jèiyàngrde'shèrlai.

Get the better of chǐfu, jàn . . . de 'pyányi. /He'll try to get the better of you. Tā syǎng'yàu 'chǐfu ni. *or* Tā syǎng'yàu jàn nǐde 'pyányi.

(Had) **better** gāi, yīnggai. /I('d) better go. Wǒ gāi 'dzǒu. /I('d) better go now. Wǒ gāi 'dzǒule. *but* /Better not suggest it. 'Jèige shr̀ yǐ bù'tíwéi'myàu.

BETWEEN. (In the space which separates) . . . (°gēn, °hé, °túng) . . . jr̄jyān; **between X and Y** X (°gēn, °etc.) Y jr̄jyān. /There aren't any large cities between Los Angeles and San Francisco. Lwòshān'jī Sānfán'shr̀ jr̄'jyān méiyou 'dàchéng.

(In the interval which separates) . . . dàu . . . jr̄jyān; **between X and Y** dàu Y jr̄jyān. /It happened between six and seven o'clock this morning. Jīntyan 'dzǎuchen 'lyòudyǎn dàu 'chīdyǎn jr̄'jyān chūde 'shr̀. /I'll meet you between six and seven. Dzámen 'lyòudyǎn dàu 'chīdyǎn jr̄jyān 'jyàn. *or* Dzámen lyòu'chīdyǎnjūng 'jyàn.

(The) **Z between X and Y** X (°gēn, °hé, °túng) Y jr̄jyānde Z. /The treaty between Germany and Russia was broken. 'Dégwó (°gēn, °etc.) 'Égwo jr̄jyānde tyáu-'ywē dzwò'fèi le.

Between them (us, you) meaning jointly °tāmen (°wǒmen, °nǐmen) dàjyāhwǒr; meaning separate *or* divide bǐtsž. /They killed six ducks between them. Tāmen dàjyā'hwǒr 'dǎle 'lyòujr̀ yě'yādz. /We mustn't let anything come between us. Wǒmen bǐ'tsž bù'yīngdang yǒu 'rènhé wù'hwèi.

(In) **between** jūngjyàr. /He lives five miles down the road and there are no houses (in) between. Tā 'jù de dìfangr lí 'jèr yǒu 'wǔlǐ 'dì, jūng'jyàr méiyou 'byéde fángdz.

Choose between tsúng . . . lǐtou tyāu. / It was difficult to choose between the colors. Tsúng nèilyǎng ge 'yánsè lǐtou hěn nán'tyāu. / You must choose between the two. Nǐ'yīngdang tsúng lyǎngge lǐtou tyāu 'yíge.

Come between (physically) jyéju, dǎngju; (emotionally) shāng 'gǎnchíng. / We nearly caught up with him, but the traffic came between. Wǒmen chàbu'dwō 'jwēi-shang tā le, kěshr 'hòulai 'chē shémmade bǎ wǒmen 'jyéjule. / Don't let him come between us. (physically) Byé ràng tā dzai women dāng'jūng 'dǎngju women. (emotionally) Byé yīnwei 'tā shāngle wǒmende gǎnchíng.

Divide something between fēn, fēngei. / Shall we divide it between us? Dzámen dà'jyā bǎ 'jèige 'fēnle, 'hǎubuhǎu? / He divided his property between his two sons. Tā bǎ tsái'chǎn 'fēngei lyǎngge 'érdz le.

Other English expressions. / He's always eating between meals. Tā 'lǎu chr líng'shr. / This is just between you and me. 'Jèhwà yě jyou shr dzámen 'lyǎrén 'shwō. or Jège bùnéng ràng 'wàirén 'jr dàu. / He can't distinguish between right and wrong. Tā shr'fēibù'míng. or Tā 'jèige rén bùnéng 'fēnbyàn shr'fēi. / Between you two I think this can be done. Yǒu 'nǐmen lyǎ, wǒ syǎng jèige 'shèr bànde-'chéng. / There's no comparison between those two men. Tāmen 'lyǎngge rén 'dzěmma néng °bǐ (°syāng'tí 'bìng'lwùn) ne?

BEYOND. (On the farther side of) °dzài (°dàu) . . . 'nèibyan, nèibyar; (having passed a point) gwòle; (forward) wàngchyán. / The address you want is beyond the river. Nǐ jǎu de 'dìfang shr dzài 'hé nèibyar. / The ship has gone beyond the horizon. 'Chwán yǐjing dzǒu dau shwěipíng'syàn 'nèibyan chyule. / Are there any more streets beyond this one? Gwòle 'jèityáu jyē hái yǒu 'jyē ma? / There aren't any more inns beyond this village. Gwòle jèige 'tswēr jyou méiyou kè'dyàn le. / We can't go beyond this point. Wǒmen bùnéng 'dzài wàng'chyán dzǒule.

(Farther away, yonder) chyánmyan(de). / We looked to the mountains beyond. Wǒmen 'kàn 'chyánmyande 'shān. / There's nothing beyond. 'Chyánbyar méiyou 'dūngsyile.

Beyond control gwǎnbulyǎu. / These circumstances are beyond our control. Jèisye shr wǒmen gwǎnbulyǎu.

Beyond doubt háuwúyíwènde. / He is beyond doubt the killer. Tā shr 'syūng-shǒu yǐjing shr háuwúyíwènde le.

Beyond help méijyou. / When we arrived he was beyond help. Děngdau wǒmen 'dàule de shŕhou tā 'yǐjing méi'jyoule.

Beyond hope. / He's so ill that he's beyond hope. Tā 'bìngde nèmma 'lìhai háubu'lyǎule.

Beyond measure dà'jíle. / His contribution to this organization is beyond measure. Tā dwèi jèige dzǔjrde gùngsyan dà'jíle.

Beyond one's comprehension. / This is totally beyond his comprehension. 'Jèige tā 'dzěmma néng °'dǔng (°lyáu'jyě)? / It's beyond me. Wǒ 'jēn °bùjŕdàu (°bù'míngbai, °'syǎngbuchū) shr 'dzěmma hwéi 'shr.

Beyond one's expectations. / It's beyond my expectations. Wǒ jēn méi'syǎng dàu. or 'Chūhu wǒde yì'lyàu jŕ'wài.

Beyond one's means. / She's living beyond her means. Tā 'hwā de bǐ 'jèng de 'dwō.

Beyond one's power chūle . . . 'nénglì fàn'wéi. / That's beyond my power now. 'Nèige yǐjing chūle wǒde 'nénglì fàn'wéile.

Beyond one's reach. / That's beyond my reach. (lit.) 'Nèige wǒ °gòubu'jáu (°gòubu'dàu). (fig. in the sense of not being qualified for something) Wǒ gòubu'shàng 'nèige.

BIBLE. Shèngjīng.

BICYCLE. dzsyíngchē, jyǎutàchē. / He rides a bicycle to work. Tā 'chí dzsyíngchē shàng'bān.

BID. (kěn) chū, gěijyàr. / How much would you bid for this? 'Jèige nǐ kěn 'chū 'dwōshau chyán? / Who bids five dollars? 'Shwéi kěn 'chū 'wǔkwài? / Who was it that bid five dollars? Chū 'wǔkwài de shř 'nǎyiwèi? / He bid only five dollars for the rug. Nèityáu dǐ'tǎn tā gěi'jyàr jř gěile 'wǔkwài chyán. / I don't want to bid too high. Wǒ gěi'jyàr bú'ywànyi gěide tài 'gāu. or Wǒ bù'kěn chū 'dàjyàr.

(To order) jyàu, shwō. / We must do as he bids us. Tā 'jyàu dzámen dzěmma 'dzwò, dzámen jyòu 'děi dzěmma 'dzwò. / He wouldn't do as I bid him. Wǒ jyàu tā 'nèmma dzwò, tā bú'gàn. or Tā bú 'ànje wǒ 'shwōde 'dzwò.

Enter a bid tóubyāu. / The bid he entered was too low to get the contract. Tā tóu'byāu tóude tài'dīle, swóyǐ méi'dédàu nèige hétung.

BIG. dà. / Their big game is on Saturday. Tāmen lǐbài'lyòu yǒu yítsz 'dàbǐ'sài. / Is this big enough? 'Jèige gòu 'dà bugou 'dà?

(Boastfully). / He acts big. Tā hěn °dž'dà (°'jyāuàu, °'shénchi). / He talks big. Tā shwō 'dà hwà.

Big shot, bigwig (derogatory) 'dàrénwu. / He thinks he's a big shot. Tā 'jywéde tā shř ge 'dàrénwu. / Some bigwig's going to talk at the meeting. Yíwèidàrénwu yàu dàuhwèi yǎn'jyǎng.

Bighearted 'chǐlyang dà. / He is bighearted. Tāde 'chǐlyang hěn 'dà.

Other English expressions. / What's the big idea? Nǐ 'shémma yìsz? or (fighting talk) Nǐ 'dǎswàn 'dzěmmaje?

BILL. (To be paid) jàngdār, **pay a bill** hwánjàng, fùjàng; **send a bill** kāijàng. / The bill includes both labor and materials. 'Gūng hé 'lyàu dōu dzài jèijàng jàng'dār lǐtou. / We must pay the bill today. Wǒmen 'jīntyan 'bìsyū děi °hwánjàng (°fùjàng).

(Paper money) (chyán) pyàudz, (chyán) pyàur. / Can you change a five-dollar bill? Nǐ néng 'pwò (yìjāng) 'wǔkwài chyán de 'pyàudz ma? / I only have twenty-dollar bills. Wǒ 'jř yǒu 'èrshrkwàide 'pyàudz.

(Theater program) 'jyémù(dār), syìdār, syìbàudz. / What's on the bill at the theater this evening? Jyēr 'wǎnshang syì'ywǎndzli yǒu shémma 'jyému. / What does it say on the bill? Syì'dārshang dzěmma 'shwōde?

(Proposed law) yìàn. / The bill will be voted on by Congress. Gwó'hwèi yàu bǎ jèige yì'àn fù 'byǎujywé. / We don't have enough votes to pass the bill. Wǒmende 'pyàushù bú'gòu tūnggwò jèige yì'àn de.

(Of a bird) dzwěi. / The bird held a worm in its bill. 'Nyǎur 'dzwěili dyàuje yìtyáu 'chúngdz.

Bill of exchange hwèipyàu.

Bill of fare tsàidān.

Bill of lading tíhwòdān.

To bill kāijàng. / They'll bill us after sending the goods. Tāmen bǎ 'dūngsyi 'sùnglai yǐ'hòu dzài °kāi'jàng lai (°kāi jàng'dār(lai)). /Bill me at this address. Bǎ jàng'dǎr gěi wo kāidau 'jèige dìfang chyu.

BILLBOARD. gwǎnggàupái.

BILLFOLD. <u>Usually of leather, and so usually called</u> pí'bāu, pí'jyādz; <u>but also</u> chyán'bāu, chyán'jyādz.

BILLION. shŕwànwàn.

BIND (BOUND). kwǔn, kwúnchilai. /Bind him up. Bǎ ta 'kwúnchilai. /His hands are still bound. Tāde 'shǒu hái 'kwǔnje ne.

(Of a wound) gwǒ. /That wound was bound up too tightly. Shòu 'shāngde dìfang gwǒde tài 'jǐn le.

(Of books, magazines, etc.) jwāngdīng, dīngchilai. /The book was bound in leather. 'Shū shŕ yùng 'pídz 'jwāng'dīngde. /The magazines aren't bound yet. Dzá'jŕ hái méiyou 'dīngchilai ne.

(Put under legal obligation). /Both parties are bound by the contract. 'Shwāng-fāng shòuhétung syànjr.

Bind <u>someone</u> to <u>something</u> bǎngdzai, kwǔndzai. /Bind him to the post. Bǎ tā °'bǎngdzai (°'kwǔndzai) 'jùdzshang.

Bind together bǎngshang, kwǔnshang. /Bind his hands together. Bǎ tāde 'shǒu 'bǎngshang.

See also BOUND, TIE.

BINDING. (Of a book) jwāngdīng. /The binding of this book is rather poor. Jèiběn shū de 'jwāngdīng butài 'hǎu.

BIOGRAPHY. jwànjì, (syǎu)'jwàn.

BIOLOGY. 'shēngwùsywé.

BIRD. nyǎur. /The bird flew into the tree. 'Nyǎur fēidau 'shùli chyùle. /What kind of a bird is this? 'Jèi shŕ shémma 'nyǎur?

Early bird chǐdzǎurde.

Queer bird gwàiwu. /He's a queer bird. Tā shŕ ge 'gwàiwu. <u>or expressed as</u> He's very queer. Tā hěn 'gwài.

Birds of a feather túnglèi; (good or bad) yí'lèi de rén; (bad) 'húpénggǒu'yǒu *or* húchyúngǒudǎng. *but* /Birds of a feather flock together (good or bad). 'Wùyī-'lèi'jyù.

<u>Other English expressions.</u> /(Who told you?) A little bird told me. (Shéi 'gàusung nǐ de?) Nǐ béng 'gwǎn le. /Kill two birds with one stone. Yì'jyǔlyǎng'dé. *or* Yì'jyànshwāng'dyāu. /A bird in the hand is worth two in the bush. Dàu 'shǒuli tsái 'swàn.

BIRTH. (As an event). /They announced the birth of their son. Tāmen 'gàusung dàjyā, tāmen °'déle (°'shēngle) yige érdz.

(Background). /The Governor was a man of humble birth. is expressed as The Governor's background is quite humble (*or* quite poor and low). Shěng'jàngde 'chūshēn hěn 'pínhán.

354

By birth. /Are you an American by birth? Nǐ shr̀ 'Měigwo °'shēngde (°shēng 'rén) ma?

Date of birth. /What's the date of your birth? Nǐ shr̀ 'shémma shŕhou 'shēng de? *or* Nǐ 'shémma shŕhou 'shēngr̀?

Give birth to yǎng, shēng; (for animals only) syà. /She's just given birth to twins. Tā gāng 'yǎngle yídwèi 'shwàngsheng. /My cat gave birth to six kittens. Wǒde 'māu syàle lyòujr̄ syǎu māu.

BIRTHDAY. 'shēngr̀; (when wishing someone a happy birthday) bài'shòu bài'shòu (not said to children). /Happy Birthday! Bài'shòu bài'shòu!

Celebrate a birthday (anyone's) gwò 'shēngr̀; (older person's) dzwòshòu; (with entertainment) bàntánghwèi; (40th, 50th, 60th, etc.) dzwò jěngshòu; **celebrate** one's **fiftieth birthday** dzwò 'wǔshŕ jěng'shòu.

BISCUIT. syǎumyànbáu; (cracker or hard flat cookie, usually British) bǐnggān, bǐnggǎr.

BIT. (Tool) dzwàn. /I need a bit to drill a hole with. Wǒ 'syūyau yíge 'dzwàn hǎu dǎ'yǎr.

(Of a bridle) jyáudz. /This bridle doesn't have a bit. Jèige 'lúngtou méiyou 'jyáudz. *but* /He took the bit between his teeth. Tā jywé'dìng kāishr̄ yǎu'yá 'gàn.

Bit (of) dyǎr; (small piece of material thing) syǎukwàr. /I only want a little bit. Wǒ 'jř yàu yì'dyǎr. /It doesn't make a bit of difference. (lit.) Yìdyǎr 'fēnbye yě 'méiyou. (if said with personal feeling) Méiyou 'gwānsyi. *or* Wǒ bú'dzàihu. /They only had a bit of cake left. Tāmen jř 'shèngsyale yi'syǎukwàr dàn'gāu. *but* /May I give you a bit of advice? Nǐ 'ywànyi buywànyi tīng wo yìjyù 'hwà?

A bit more . . . , a bit . . . er . . . (yì)dyǎr. /They arrived a bit later than the others. Tāmen 'dàude bǐ 'byéde rén 'wǎndyar.

Bit by bit yìdyǎryìdyǎr(de). /We learned about it bit by bit. Jèijyàn'shr̀ wǒmen shr̀ yìdyǎryì'dyǎr 'tīnglaide.

Bits (small broken pieces) swèikwàr; (very small broken pieces) 'fēnswèi. /He broke the candy into bits. Tā bǎ 'táng 'bāichéngle swèi'kwàr. /The whole house was blown to bits. Jěnggèr 'fángdz 'jàde 'fēnswèi.

BITE (BIT). yǎu; (by an insect) dīng. /Did you get bitten? Nǐ āi 'yǎu le ma? *or* Nǐ āi 'dīng le ma? /I was bitten by a mosquito. 'Wéndz °'yǎule wo yì'kǒu (°'dīngle wo yikǒu). /Does this dog bite (people)? Jèi 'gǒu 'yǎu rén bùyǎu?

(Of fish) shànggōu(r). /The fish are biting well today. 'Yú 'jīntyan shàng'gōu shàngde hěn 'hǎu.

(Freeze). /His ears were bitten by the frost. Tā bǎ 'ěrdwo 'dùng le.

Bite into kěn. /Don't bite into the orange skin. Byé 'kěn jyúdz'pí. /He bit into the apple. Tā kěn 'pínggwo.

Bite off 'yǎusyà °lai (°chyù). /The dog bit some flesh off his leg. Tāde 'twěi jyàu 'gǒu 'yǎusya yíkwài 'ròulai.

A bite, bite of kǒu. /I have two bites on my arm from a mosquito. Wǒde 'gēbe jyàu 'wéndz dīngle lyǎng'kǒu. /I just took one bite of the apple. Wǒ jř 'yǎule 'yìkǒu 'pínggwo. /I haven't had a bite all day. is expressed as I haven't had a thing to eat all day. Wǒ yìtyānli yìdyǎr 'dūngsyi dōu méichr̄ ne.

(Of fish). /I haven't had a bite all day. is expressed as Not a single fish bit all day. Yìjěng'tyande gūngfu lyán 'yìtyáu yú dōu méilái shàng'gōur.

Biting (caustic) kèbwo. / She often makes biting remarks. Tā shwō 'hwà 'chángcháng hěn 'kèbwo.

Biting cold. / It's a biting cold day. 'Jīntyan 'lěngde syàng 'dāudz 'lá shr̀de.

BITTER. (Taste) kǔ. / Quinine tastes bitter. Jīnjīnàshwāng hěn 'kǔ. / This coffee is too bitter. Jyā'fēi tài 'kǔ.

(Deep) shēn. / After the war they still continued in their bitter hatred. 'Jàng dǎ'wánle kèshr tāmen bǐ'tsz̄ jr̀'jyànde shēn'chóu 'bìng méiyou jyàn'syàu.

(Implacable). / They are bitter enemies. Tāmen 'lyǎ chóu'shēn sz̀'hǎi.

(Painful). / He's had some bitter experiences. Tā 'shòule °syē 'kǔ (°syē 'dzwèi).

A bitter pill to swallow jyàu 'rén °nán'kān de 'shr̀ (°nán'rěn de 'shr̀).

Utter bitter words chū ywànyán, bàuywàn.

Bitter cold lěngjíle. / It's bitter cold out today. 'Jīntyan wàitou lěng'jíle.

Bitter end. / They fought to the bitter end. Tāmen pīn'mìng 'pīnle ge nǐsz̄wǒ-'hwó. / He held himself back to the bitter end. Tā yì'jr̄ rěndau 'dǐ.

Bitter quarrel. / He had a bitter quarrel with his brother. Tā gēn tā 'gēge dà 'chǎule yì'jyà.

Bitter wind. / A bitter wind was blowing. 'Fēng 'gwāde yòu 'lěng yòu 'lìhai.

BLACK. (Dark) hēi, àn. / The night was very black. 'Yèli 'tyān hěn °'hēi (°àn). / The room is pitch black. Wūdzli chī'hēi.

(Color of an object) hēi, chīng; **black ink** hēimwò'shwěr. / Many black clouds began to come up. Hǎudwō 'hēiyúntsai 'shànglaile. / Do you have a black dress? Nǐ 'yòu méiyou °'hēi (°chīng) 'yīfu a? / She has black hair. Tāde tóufa shr 'hēide.

(Color of bruised skin) chīng. / He got a black eye from someone. Tāde 'yǎnjing nèr jyàu 'rén dǎ'chīngle.

(Unpromising) 'àndàn, hēiàn. / Their future is black. Tāmende 'chyántú hěn 'àndàn.

(Morally bad) hwài, bùhǎu. / He's not as black as he's painted. Tā 'méiyou rén 'shwōde nèmma 'hwài.

A black look. / He gave me a black look. Tā 'dēngle wo yì'yǎn.

Black sheep (of a family) bàijyādzěr; (of any other group) hài'chyúnjr̄'mǎ. / He's the black sheep of our family. Tā shr̄ wǒmen 'jyāde bàijyā'dzěr. / We have a black sheep in our midst. Wǒmen yìchyún 'rénli yǒu yíge hài'chyúnjr̄'mǎ.

Black and blue chīngjǔng. / He was beaten black and blue all over by someone. Tā (ràng 'rén) 'dǎde chywán'shēn chīng'jǔng.

In black and white (written down, printed) 'hēijr̄ syě bái'dz̀, hēijr̀bái 'dz̀de syěsyalai. / I want it put down in black and white. 'Jèige děi hēijr̀bái'dz̀de 'syě-syalai. / Do you want it in black and white? Nǐ yí'dìng yàu °hēijr̄ syě báidz̀ ma (°'syěchulaide ma, °'yīnchulaide ma)?

Black (mourning clothes) syàu. (Note that the color of mourning clothes in China is white). / She's worn black (mourning clothes) since her husband died. Tā dz̀tsúng tā 'jàngfu 'sz̄le yǐ'hòu yì'jr̄ chwān'syàu. (Since the period of mourning for different relatives is rigorously prescribed in China, this sentence would be said only of a Westerner in China or possibly of a Chinese Christian.)

To black out (keep dark) bútòugwāng; (eliminate) 'túchyù. / The house must be blacked out by dark. Hēi'tyān yǐ'hòu 'wūdzli bùnéng tòu'gwāng. / This line should be blacked out. Jēihǎng dž děi 'túlechyu.

BLACKSMITH. tyějyang.

BLADDER. 'pánghwáng, 'pánggwāng, swēipau.

BLADE. (Razor) dāupyàr, dāupyàn; (of a knife) dāukǒu; **a blade of grass** yìgēr tsǎu.

BLAME. (Hold responsible) gwài. / You must blame the driver for our being late. Lái'wǎnle 'jèijyàn shř, nǐ děi 'gwài kāichǐ'chēde. / If anything goes wrong, you can't blame me. Yàushr chūle 'chàr, bùnéng 'gwài wǒ.

(Shift the responsibility unjustly to) lài, (bǎ 'tswòr) twēigei. / You can't blame others for the mistakes you made yourself. Nǐ dž'jǐ chū de 'tswòr bùnéng twēigei 'byéren. / He blamed us (unjustly) for the accident. Tā chū'shřle lài 'wǒmen.

Be to blame (be responsible). / Who's to blame for this? Shř 'shwéide tswòr? *or* 'Shéi yīnggai fù 'dzérèn?

Take the blame dānchéng, dāndāng. / One should have the courage to take the blame for what one does. Yíge 'rén děi gǎn'dzwò gǎn'dāng. / He took the blame for their mistake. Shř 'tāmende 'tswòr, kěshr 'tā gěi dān'chéngle. / I take all the blame for this mistake. Jèige 'tswòr wǒ 'yíge rén 'dāndāng.

BLANKET. tǎndz; (wool) máutǎn(dz).

To blanket. / Snow blanketed the ground. Dì(shang) dōu ràng sywě gěi 'gàijule. / The river bank was blanketed in fog. Hé'ànshang 'syàde dōu shr 'wù.

BLESS. (°gěi, °tì) . . . jùfú. / The priest blessed us. Shénfu tì wǒmen jù'fú.

(Bestow blessings on) bǎuyòu. / God bless you! Shàngdì 'bǎuyòu nǐ! *or* (after someone sneezes) Yìbǎi'swèi!

(In strong thanks). / Bless you for doing this! Gǎnjībú'jìn! *or* Fēicháng gǎnsyè!

Be blessed with tszgei, yǒufú. / He's blessed with a good temper. Tāde 'píchi 'hǎu, °shř tyān'tszde (°'jēn shř yǒu'fú).

BLIND. syā, syāyǎn; (partially) yǎnjing hwài. / He was too blind to read letters. Tā 'syāde lyán 'syìn dōu kànbu'chīngle. *or* Tā 'yǎnjing 'hwàide, lyán 'syìn dōu kànbu 'chīngle. / He's blind in one eye. Tā 'syāle 'yìjř yǎnjing. / Are you blind? (lit. or fig.) Nǐ syā'yǎnle ma? *or* Nǐ 'yǎnjing 'syā le! / Don't be a blind follower. Byé máng-'tsúng. *or* Byé 'syā gēnje 'rén 'pàu.

Blind person syādz, syāle'yǎnde rén. / We helped the blind person across the street. Wǒmen bāngje nèige 'syādz gwò'jyē láije. *or* Wǒmen 'lǐng nèige 'syādz gwò'jyē láije. In China the blind live by begging or by fortune-telling. A blind fortune-teller is called swàn'mìngde syānsheng.

Blind alley sžhútùngr. / This is a blind alley. Jè shř yìtyáu sžhú'tùngr. / He ran up a blind alley. Tā 'dzǒude shř yìtyáu sžhú'tùngr. *or* (fig.) Tā pèng'bìle.

Be blind to rènbuchīng, fēnbuchū, bùmíng, bùjřdàu. / He was blind to the (true) facts. Tā rènbu'chīng shř'shř. *or* Tā bù'míng jēn'jyà. *or* Tā fēnbu'chū shémma shř 'jēnde, shémma shř 'jyǎde. / I'm not blind to her shortcomings. Tāde nèisyē 'dwǎnchu, wǒ 'búshr bù'jřdàu.

To blind <u>someone</u> nùngsyā; (by striking) dǎsyā; (by puncturing) chwōsyā. /He was blinded in the accident. Nèitsż chū'shř tā bǎ 'yǎnjing nùng'syàle.

(Dazzle) kànbujyàn. /The lightning blinded me for a while. Dǎ'shǎnde shŕhou wǒ 'yǒu yihwěr 'shémma dōu kànbu'jyàn.

Blind (on a window) chwānghu lyár, chwānghu lyándz. /Please pull down the blinds. Bǎ chwānghu 'lyár 'lāsyalai.

BLISTER. (Of skin) shwěipàu(r); (of wood) pàu.

To blister chū pàu, jǎng pàu. /If I don't wear gloves, my hands will blister. Yàushr wǒ búdài shǒu'tàu, wǒde shǒu jyòu °chū'pàu (°jǎng pàu).

BLIZZARD. kwángfengdàsywě, dàfēngsywě.

BLOCK. (Solid piece of) kwài. /The door was propped open with a block of wood. Mén 'kāije ne, yǒu yíkwài mùtou dìngje ne.

(In a city, meaning the distance between two streets) yìtyáujyē. /I live a block away from the post office. Wǒ jùde (dìfang) lí yóujèngjyú yìtyáu jyē.

To block dǎngju. /Don't block the doorway. Byé bǎ ménkǒu dǎngju.

BLOOD. syě <u>also pronounced</u> sywè, sywě. /After the accident there was blood on the ground. Chūshr yǐ'hòu 'dìshang yǒu 'syě. /Blood flowed from the wound. 'Sywè tsúng 'shāngkǒu 'lyóuchulai le.

(Of race, lineage) sywě. /He has some French blood in him. Tā yǒu 'Fāgwo sywě.

In cold blood hěnsyīn. /They murdered him in cold blood. Tāmen 'shā tā de shŕhou, jēn shŕ hěn'syīn syà'shǒu.

Have a blood test yànsyě. /Have you had your blood test yet? Nǐ 'yàngwo 'syě le ma?

Lose blood lyóusyě, chūsyě. /He lost a good deal of blood. Tā 'lyóule hěn dwō 'syě.

Blood pressure sywěyā, syěyā. /I have high blood pressure. Wǒde sywě'yā hěn 'gāu.

Blood relatives sywěchīn.

Blood type syěsyíng. /What's your blood type? Nǐde syě'syíng °shŕ 'shémma (°'něijǔng)?

Bloodshot syěsěr, húngsěr. /His eyes were bloodshot. Tā 'yǎnli yǒu syě'sěr.

<u>Other English expressions.</u> /He has blood on his hands. (lit.) Tā 'shǒushang yǒu'syě. (fig.) Tā 'hàigwo rén. /He's a hot-blooded individual. Tāde 'p%&íchi hěn 'dà. *or* Jèige rén ài shēng'chì. *or* Jèige rén bùhǎu'rè. *or* Jèige rén ai fā 'píchi. /His blood was up. Tā hěn shēng'chì. /Freedom is bought with blood. Dż'yóu shŕ lyóu'syě 'hwànlaide. /Blood is thicker than water. 'Chīnchi 'dzǔng shŕ syàngje 'chīnchi.

BLOTTER. syīmwò'jř, chŕmwò'jř.

BLOW (BLEW, BLOWN). (Of wind) gwā. /The wind blew hard. 'Fēng 'gwāde hěn 'lìhai. /The wind has been blowing all night. 'Fēng yǐjing 'gwāle yí'yè le. /The wind will blow hard tonight. 'Fēng jīntyan 'wǎnshang yí'dìng hwèi 'gwāde hěn 'lìhai.

(Of an instrument, bugle-call, horn, whistle, with the mouth) chwēi; (by pressing a button) èn; (by pulling a cord) lā. / They blow taps at eleven o'clock. Tāmen shŕ'yī dyǎnjūng chwēi syīdēng'hàu. / Blow the horn three times when you come. Nǐ 'lái de shŕhou èn 'sānsyàr 'lāba. / Has the whistle blown? Lā 'byéer le méiyou?

Blow a bubble chwēipàur, chwēichi yíge 'pàur lai.

Blow one's nose syǐng 'bídz; (to get ride of mucus) syǐng 'bítì. / He blew his nose loudly. Tā hěn dà 'shēngrde 'syǐng bídz.

Blow away gwāpǎu, chwēipǎu. / This tent's going to blow away. Jèige 'jàng-peng kwài jyàu 'fēng gwā'pǎule. / My hat blew away. Wǒde 'màudz gěi chwēi-'pǎule.

Blow down chwēidǎu. / That tree blew down. Nèikē 'shù jyàu 'fēng gěi chwēi'dǎule.

Blow on _something_ (to cool it) chwēilyáng; (to warm it) chwēinwǎnhwo. / You can blow on your soup to cool it. 'Tāng nǐ 'chwēiyichwēi jyǒu 'lyángle. / You can blow on your hands to warm them. Nǐ kéyi bǎ nǐde 'shǒu chwēi'nwǎnhwole.

Blow out (of a tire) jà. / That old tire blew out. 'Lǎu chē'dài jàle.

Blow out _a light_ chwēimyè. / Blow the candle out before you go. Nǐ 'dzǒu yǐ'chyán bǎ 'là chwēi'myèle.

Blow over (of a storm) gwāgwochyu, 'gwāwán. / This storm will blow over soon. Jèi jèn 'fēng 'kwài °'gwāgwòchyule (°gwawánle).

Blow over (of trouble, situation) 'fēngcháugwochyu, 'gwòchyù, nàugwochyu. / Wait until all this blows over. 'Děngje 'jèige 'fēngcháu gwòchyu 'dzài shwō. _or_ 'Děngje jèijyàn 'shŕ 'gwòchyu 'dzài shwō. _or_ 'Děngje jèijyàn 'shŕ 'nàugwochyu 'dzài shwō.

Blow up (explode) jà, bēng, jàlyè, bēnglyè, jàhwài. / Be careful that it doesn't blow up (from inner pressure or from the outside). 'Syǎusyīn byé 'jyàu tā 'jàle. / The enemy will try to blow up the bridge. 'Dírén syǎngyàu bǎ 'chyáu 'jàle. / The (steam) boiler blew up. Chǐ'gwō 'jàle.

Blow up (of a storm) chǐfēng. / A storm may blow up this afternoon. Jīntyan 'syàwǔ yésyu hwèi chǐ'fēng.

Blow up _a tire_ (inflate) dǎchilai, dǎ'dzúle 'chì. / Please blow up this tire for me. Chǐng ni bǎ jèige chē'dàidz °'dǎchilai (°gěi dǎ'dzúle 'chì).

A blow (shock, setback) dǎji. / His wife's death was a big blow to him. Tā tàitai sǐle dwèi tā shŕ yíge hěn dàde 'dǎji. / Can he stand the blow? Jèiyàngrde-'dǎji tā shòude'lyǎu ma? / He suffered a terrible blow. Tā 'shòule yíge 'dà'dǎji. / If things go that way wholesale trade will receive a terrible blow. 'Nèmmaje pī'fāde 'shāngjyā yàu 'dà shòu 'dǎjile.

(A forcible stroke with some instrument) is expressed verbally as to give a blow dǎ yísyàdz, dǎ yísyàr, (with the fist) dǎ yìchywán, (with the palm) dǎ yìbā-jang, (with a stick) dǎ yígwùndz, (with a sword) kǎn yìdāu, (with the back of a sword) dǎ yì'dāubèr; or as receive a blow aī yísyàdz plus all the above with aī substituting dǎ. / He gave him a terrific blow on the head. Tā lìlihài'hāide dzài tā tóushang dǎle °yisyàdz (°yìchywán, °etc.). / He suffered a blow on the chin. Tā lyǎnshang 'aīle °yìchywán (°etc.).

Strike the first blow 'syān °syàshǒu (°dùngshǒu) (oratorical). / We must strike the first blow. 'Wǒmen děi 'syān syà'shǒu. / He was the one who struck the first blow. Shŕ tā syān dùngshǒu de.

Come to blows. / They came to blows. (with hands) Tāmen dùngchi 'shǒu lái-ile. (with fists) Tāmen dùngchi 'chywántou láile. (general) Tāmen 'dǎchi 'jyà láile.

BLUE. lán, 'lánsè, 'lánshǎr. / Blue was in vogue last year. 'Chyùnyan 'lánsè shŕ-'syīng. / Give me a blue one. Wǒ yàu °'lánshǎrde (°'lánde). / It's that book with a blue cover. Shŕ nèiběn 'lánpyérde 'shū. / This shade of blue is very pleasant. 'Jèijǔng lán(shǎr) °hěn 'róu (°bútsž'yǎn). / She always wears blue. Tā 'lǎu chwān 'lánde. / Do you have any blue ink? Nǐ yǒu 'lánmwò'shwěr ma?

Dark blue 'shēnlán; (very dark) 'dzàngchīng. / Have this dyed dark blue. Bǎ 'jèige rǎncheng 'shēnlánde. *but* / Do you have a darker shade of blue? (in this garment or material) 'Dzài 'shēndyǎrde 'hái yǒu ma? *or* Nǐ yǒu bǐ 'jèige dzài 'shēndyǎrde ma?

Light blue 'chyǎnlán.

Sky blue 'tyānlán.

Out of the blue hūránjyān jyòu. / He arrived out of the blue. Tā hū'ránjyán jyòu 'láile.

Blue bloods (nobility) gwèidzú.

Blueprint (method) shài lántú; (actual design on paper) lántú, lánběn.

Bluebook (government document) lánpíshū.

Be *or* **feel blue, have** *or* **get the blues** nánshòu, bùgāusyìng, bútùngkwai, 'mèndeheng. / After his family left he felt blue. Tā 'jyālide rén 'dzǒule yǐ'hòu tā °yǒu yìdyǎr nán'shòu (°jywéde mèndeheng). / Why're you blue this morning? Nǐ jīntyan 'dzǎuchen 'wèi shémma °bùgāu'syìng (°bútùngkwai)? / I get the blues when it rains. Syà'yǔ de shŕhou wǒ 'lǎu bú'tùngkwai.

BOARD. (Of wood or other material) bǎndz, bǎr; **ironing board** °tàng (°yùn) 'yīfu de 'bǎndz; **bulletin board** bùgàubǎn; **blackboard** hēibǎn. / We need some boards to make the top of the box with. Wǒmen děi yàu jikwài 'bǎndz hǎu dzwò hédz'gàr.

(For chess or checkers) chípán. / I still had three men left on the board. (Dzài) chí'pánshang wǒ 'hái 'shèngsya 'sānge 'dzěr.

(Meals) bāufàn; (cost of meals) shànfèi. / Is the board good there? Nèrde bāu 'fàn hái kěyi 'chŕ ma? / His scholarship includes room and board. Tāde jyǎng-sywé'jīnli 'bāukwò 'sùfèi gēn 'shànfèi.

(Official body) wěiywánhwèi (usually an especially appointed commission); -jyú, -shǔ, -chù, with preceding elements indicating the function, is used for regularly constituted parts of the government; **board of examiners** (of a school) 'kǎu-shŕwěiywán'hwèi *or* (governmental) 'shěncháwěiywán'hwèi; **board of trustees** (of a school) syàudǔnghwèi *or* (of a business) dǔngshŕhwèi. / The Board of Health has issued new regulations. 'Gūnggùng'wèishēng wěiywán'hwèi gūngbùchu syīn 'gwēi-dzé laile.

On board (dzài) 'chwánshang or with name of other vehicle replacing chwán boat; **get on board** shàng. / This boat has a fugitive on board. (Dzài) jèijr 'chwán-shang yǒu yíge táu'fàn. / The whistle has already blown to get on board. Yǐjing lā'byéer jyàu rén 'shàngchyùle.

To board (eat or serve meals) chŕ bāufàn, bāufàn. / Have you ever boarded at her house? Nǐ dzai tā 'jyā, bāugwo fàn ma? / How many people does she board? Dzài tā 'nèr chŕ bāu'fàn de yòu 'dwōshau rén?

(Get on a vehicle or boat) shàng. / Can we board the train early? Wǒmen kéyi 'dzǎudyǎr shàng hwǒ'chē ma?

Board up yùng mù'bǎn 'jēshang. / The front is all boarded up. Chyán 'myàr dōu yùng mù'bǎn 'jēshangle.

BOAT. chwán; (in some compounds, mostly military) tǐng, jyàn. / He'll take the boat for America soon. Tā kwài yau dzwò 'chwán dàu 'Měigwo chyù le. / The boat trip will take five days. 'Chwán děi 'dzǒu 'wǔtyān. / We can cross the river in this boat. Wǒmen kéyi dzwò jèityáu 'chwán gwòhé. / Will this small boat hold all five of us? Jèityáu °syǎu'chwán (°syǎu'chwár) jīnde'jù dzámen 'wǔge rén ma? / The enemy has five gunboats. Diren yǒu 'wúsou pàu'jyàn.

Be in the same boat. / We're all in the same boat. (not necessarily unhappy) Wǒmende 'chíngsying syāng'túng. *or* Wǒmende 'dzāuyù yí'yàng. (of an unfortunate situation) Wǒmen shr̀ túng 'bìng syāng 'lyán.

Go boating hwáchwán, yáuchwán. / We went boating. Wǒmen hwá'chwán chyùle.

BODY. shēn, shēndz, 'shēntǐ. / This soldier has a healthy body. Jèige bīngde °'shēndz (°shēnti) hen jyàn'kāng. / He has a red rash on his body. Tā 'shēnshang yǒu yikwai húng'bān. / His legs are too short for his body. Tā 'shēn 'cháng 'twěi 'dwǎn.

(Corpse) sžshr̄. / They buried the two bodies in one grave. Tāmen bǎ lyǎng-jyù 'sžshr̄ máidzai yí'kwàr le.

(Of a car) chēshēn.

(Main part of a speech) 'nèirúng. / The body of his speech was technical. Tā yǎn'jyǎngde 'nèirúng hěn 'jwān'mén.

Body of men yìchyún rén.

Body of troops yídwèi bīng (in formation) *or* yìchyún bīng (not in formation).

Body of water yípyàn shwěi.

In a body chywán'tǐ (dōu). / They left in a body. Tāmen chywán'tǐ dōu 'dzǒule.

Legislative body lìfǎjīgwān.

Political body jèngjr̀twántǐ.

Other English expressions. / They couldn't keep body and soul together. is expressed as They were so poor that they didn't have food to eat. Tāmen 'chyúngde mei 'fàn chr̄.

BOIL. jǔ. / Please boil the egg two minutes. Bǎ jì'dzěr jǔ 'lyǎngfēn jūng. / We want boiled potatoes for dinner. Wǒmen 'wǎnfàn yàu chr̄ jǔtu'dòur.

(Of water or other liquids) kāi, gwǔn. / In a few minutes the water will boil. Dzài dāi jifēn'jūng 'shwěi jyòu 'kāi le. / The engine (i.e., the water in the engine) is boiling. Jīchi lǐtou de shwěi 'rède dōu gwǔn le.

(Be angry) shēngchì. / That remark made me boil. 'Nèijǔng hwà hěn jyàu wo shēng'chì.

Boil away, boil dry jǔgān. / Don't let the pot boil dry. Byé jyàu ('húlide) 'shwěi jǔ'gān le.

Boil down. / It all boils down to this. °'Jyǎndānde shwō (°Jř́jyélyǎu'dàngde shwō, °Gǎn'tswèide shwō, °Gwěi'chí, °Nàule gwěi'chí) shr̀ 'jèmma yìhwéi 'shr̀. / What does all this boil down to? 'Jèige jyòu'jìng shr̀ 'dzěmma hwéi 'shr̀?

Boil over pū. / The coffee's boiling over. Kā'fēi kāide 'pūchulaile.

A boil (infection) bāu; (festered and open) chwāng. / He's suffering from boils. Tā jǎng'chwāngle. / This boil is painful. Jèige 'bāu hěn 'téng.

BOILER. (On a steam engine) chỉgwō, jēngchỉgwō; (for hot water) rèshwěigwō, rè-shwéisyāng.

BOLD. dǎndz dà. /He's always bold in the face of danger. Yǒu 'wéisyǎnde shŕhou, tā dzǔng shr 'dǎndz hen 'dà.

(Forthright) màusyǎnde. /They followed a bold policy. Tāmen 'tsǎichyǔle hěn màu'syǎn de 'bànfa.

(Forward) méiyou 'lǐmau, búkèchi, lyǎnpi hòu, maushr. /I can't stand bold people. Wǒ shǒubu'lyǎu méiyou 'lǐmàu de rén. /She's a little too bold with strangers. Tā dzai 'shēngrén myǎnchyán, yǒu yidyar tài 'màushr.

Be bold enough to gǎn. /He was bold enough to go in alone. Tā gǎn 'yíge rén 'jìnchyu. /He was bold enough to talk back to the (school) principal. Tāde 'dǎndz °hěn 'dà (°jēn 'dà, °jēn gòu 'dàde), gǎn gēn syàu'jǎng jyàng'dzwěi.

BOLT. (For a nut) lwósž (shwān); (door fastener) ménshwāndz; (of cloth) yī°kwǔn (°jywǎn, °jywǎr) bù.

BOMB. jàdàn.

To bomb hūngjà. /Five enemy planes came to bomb us yesterday. Dzwótyān yǒu wǔjyà dí'jǐ lai hūng'jà wǒmen.

BOMBER. hūngjàjī.

BOND. (Surety, bail) dānbǎu, yájīn.

Savings bond (government) jèngfǔ jàichywàn.

Bonds (securities) gūngjài(pyàu).

BONE. gútou, gǔtou; in compounds gǔ, **leg bone** twěigǔ, **cow bone** nyóugǔ or nyóu-gǔtou. /Those are made of bone. Nèisye shr yùng 'gútou 'dzwò de. /Cut the bone from this meat. Bǎ 'gútou 'tíchuchyu. /I feel chilled to the bone. 'Lěngdau 'gútou-li chyule. (or simply Wǒ lěng'jíle.) /In the accident he broke two bones. Chū'shr de shŕhou tā 'shéle lyǎnggěr 'gútou.

(Of fish) tsž. /A fish bone caught in his throat. Yìgěr yú'tsž 'chyǎdzai tā 'sǎngdzlile.

To bone a fish bǎ 'tsž 'tyāuchuchyu. /Has this fish been boned? Jèityáu yúde 'tsž 'tyāuchuchyule méiyou?

Special English expressions. /He made no bones about what he wanted. Tā yí 'shànglai jyòu 'shwō tā 'yàu shěmma. or Tā yì'dyǎr méiràu'wǎr. /I feel it in my bones that he isn't coming. is expressed as I feel that he certainly is not going to come. Wǒ 'jywéde tā yí'dìng bù'lái le. /I have a bone to pick with you. is expressed politely as I have to mention something to you. Wǒ yǒu yíjyàn 'shŕ děi gēn ni 'tí yitǐ.

BOOK. (A literary composition) shū; (bound volume, either blank or containing data) běndz, běr; **telephone book** dyànhwà běndz. /I want a book to read on the train. Wǒ yàu yìběn 'shu hǎu dzài hwǒ'chēshang 'kàn. /Keep your accounts in this book. Bǎ nǐde 'jàng jìdzai jèige 'jàng'běrshang.

Book of tickets cheng'běrde 'pyàu. /A book of tickets will save you money. Chéng'běrde 'pyàu 'pyányi syē.

Book collector tsángshūjyā.

Bookcase shūjyàdz (open shelves); shūgwèi, shūchú (closed).

Book end shūjyādz.

Bookmark shūchyāndz *or* shūchyār.

Bookselling trade shūyè.

Bookstore shūpù, shūdyàn.

To book someone yā. / He's been booked by the police. Tā ràng jǐng'chá yāchilaile.

Book passage dìng . . . pyàu. / I have booked my passage to London. Wǒ yǐ-jing 'dìngle dàu Lwúndwūn chyùde shwán'pyàu le.

BOOKKEEPER. gwǎnjàngde.

BOOKKEEPING. bùjì.

BOOKLET. syǎutsèdz.

BOOT. sywēdz.

BOOTH. (In a market) tāndz, tsài tān(dz); (telephone) dyànhwà 'gédz; (in a restaurant) hwǒchēdzwòr.

BORDER. (Between countries, provinces, states, cities, countries, etc.) jyāujyè; (between countries) gwójyè; (area near the border line) byānjìng; (of a piece of cloth, etc.) byār.

BORN. Be born shēng, shēngsya(lai). / Their child was born last March. (in this calendar year) Tāmende syǎu'hár shr jǐnnyan 'sānywè 'shēng de. *or* (in a previous calendar year) 'chyùnyan 'sānywè 'shēng de. / Were you born in America? Nǐ shr dzài 'Měigwo 'shēngde ma? *or* Nǐ shr 'shēngdzai 'Měigwo de ma? / When was he born? Tā shr 'shémma shrhou 'shēng de? (also may mean When did she give birth?) / He was born rich. Tā 'shēngsyalai jyou yǒu'chyán. *or* Tā shēngdzai yǒu'chyán rénjyāli.

See also BIRTH.

BORROW. jyè. / May I borrow this book overnight? 'Jèibén shū wǒ 'jyèchyu 'míng-tyan 'dzǎuchen 'hwán, 'syíng busyíng?

In telling someone that he may borrow something the polite expression is take it and use it. / You may borrow my umbrella to get home. Nǐ kéyi 'dǎ wǒde yǔ'sǎn hwéi'jyā.

Borrow from gēn . . . jyè. / He's borrowed money from the bank. Tā gēn yín'háng jyè'chyánle.

BOTANY. 'jŕwùsywé.

BOTH. lyǎng . . . dōu. / Both roads will take you into the town. 'Lyǎngtyáu 'dàur dōu tūng chéng'lǐ. / I'll buy both of those books. 'Nèilyǎngbén 'shū wǒ dōu 'mǎi. / We've asked both soldiers to come. 'Lyǎngge bīng wǒmen dōu 'chǐngle. / I can't take both. 'Lyǎngge wǒ bùnéng dōu 'yàu. / Both of us saw it happen. Wǒmen 'lyǎngge rén dōu 'dāngchǎng 'chyáujyànle.

(With things that come in pairs). / He lost both his shoes. Tā 'lyǎngjŕ 'syé dōu 'dyōule. *or* Tā yìshwāng'syé dōu 'dyōule. / Both sides fought hard. Shwāng-

'fāng 'dǎde hěn 'lìhai. *but* /He lost both pairs of shoes. Tā 'lyǎngshwāng 'syé dōu 'dyōule.

Both X and Y (nouns) X (gēn) Y . . . dōu. /Both boys and girls play here. 'Nánhár nyǔhár dōu dzài 'jèr 'wár.

Be both X and Y (adjectives) yòu X yòu Y. /It's both good and cheap. 'Yòu 'hǎu 'yòu 'pyányi.

BOTTLE. 'píngdz, píngr; <u>in combinations</u> píng; **milk bottle** nyóunǎipíng; **water bottle** shwěipíng. /The bottle broke in my suitcase. 'Píngdz dzài wǒde 'syāngdzli °'pwòle (°'lyèle, °'swèile). *but* /He can't stay away from the bottle. <u>is expressed as</u> He can't keep from drinking. Tā 'bùnéng bùhē'jyòu. *or* Tā fēi hējyòu bùkě.

Bottle of píng, píngdz, píngr. /This bottle of milk was delivered this morning. Jèipíng nyóu'nǎi shr 'jīntyan 'dzǎuchen sùnglai de. /He drank the whole bottle of milk. Tā bǎ yì jěng 'píngdzde nyóu'nǎi dōu 'hēle. /I'd like a bottle of ink. Wǒ yàu yìpíngr mwò'shwěr.

To bottle jwāngdau 'píngdzli. /They bottle the water and sell it. Tāmen bǎ-'shwěi jwāngdau 'píngdzli 'mài.

BOTTOM. dǐsya, dyěr. /The potatoes in the bottom of the sack are all rotten. Kǒu'dài 'dǐsya de tǔ'dòur dōu 'lànle. /I can't reach the bottom. (with the hand) Wǒ gòubu-'jáu 'dyěr. (in swimming) Wǒ yóu bu'dàu 'dyěr. /There were tea leaves at the bottom of the cup. Chábēi 'dyěrshang yǒu chá'yè. /The ship went to the bottom. 'Chwán chén'dyěrle.

(Base, support) dzwèr. /The bottom of this chair is broken. Jèijāng 'yǐdzde 'dzwèr 'hwàile.

(Buttocks) pìhu, pìgu. /The child fell on its bottom. Syǎu'hár shwāile ge 'pìhudwěr.

At bottom chíshr̂. /At bottom there's nothing unusual. Chí'shr̂ 'bìng méiyou shémma lyǎubu'dé de. /At bottom he's honest. Chí'shr̂ tā hěn 'chéngshr̂.

Be at the bottom of <u>something</u> jǔshr̂. /I'll bet you she's at the bottom of this. Dzámen 'dǔ dyǎr shémma; 'wǒ shwō yí'dìng shr̂'tā jǔ'shr̂ de.

Get to the bottom of <u>something</u> chá ge shwěi'lwòshr̂'chū, chèdǐ 'chá yichá. /His actions are so strange that we must get to the bottom of them. Tāde jyú'dùng hěn 'gwài; wǒmen děi °'cháge shwěi'lwòshr̂'chū (°chèdǐ chá yichá).

Bottoms up (in drinking) <u>is expressed as</u> dry the cup gānbēi.

BOULDER. dàshr̂tou.

BOULEVARD. dàmǎlù.

BOUND. **Be bound by** <u>something</u> shòu . . . jyūshù. /He is bound by convention and can't change his ways. Tā shòu chwán'tǔng jyūshù, bùnéng gǎibyan tāde 'tàidù.

Be bound (for) <u>a place</u> dàu . . . chyù, chyù, shàng. /I'm bound for the park. Wǒ dàu gūng'ywán chyu. /Where are you bound? Nǐ dàu 'nǎr chyu? *or* Nǐ shàng 'nǎr? /Are you bound for America? Nǐ shr̂ chyù 'Měigwo ma?

Be bound to yídìng (yàu), yǐ'dìng děi, fēiděi . . . bù'kě, bùnéng bū, bìdìng (yàu). /He's bound to be late. Tā yí'dìng wǎn 'dàu. /He's bound to fail. Tā °bǐ'dìng (°yídìng) shr̂'bài. /My luck is bound to change. Wǒde 'yùnchi yí'dìng hwèi 'jwànde.

Be bound up with. /His success is bound up with politics. Tā swóyi chéng-'gūng gēn 'jèng'jr̂ běi'jǐng yǒu gwānsi.

Be bounded by. / The valley was bounded by high mountains. Jèige shān'gǔ szjōu'wéi chywán shr̀ gāu'shān. / The United States is bounded on the north by Canada. 'Měigwode 'běibyan gēn Jyāna'dà jyāu'jyè.

To bound tyàu. / The ball bounded back to his hand. 'Chyóur tyàuhwéi tā-'shǒulichyule.

In one bound yítyàu. / He jumped to the other side in one bound. Tā yí 'tyàu jyou 'tyàudau 'nèibyar chyule.

On the . . . bound tyàu chilai de shŕhòu. / Try to catch the ball on the first bound. Dzài 'chyóur dì'yítsż 'tyàuchilai de shŕhou jyòu syǎng'fár 'jyéjù.

Bounds (limits, boundary). / His pride has no bounds. Tā jyāu'àude 'lyǎubu-'dé. / The ball fell out of bounds. 'Chyóu 'pǎudau 'wàibyan chyule.

BOUNDARY. (Between countries) 'gwójyè; (any geographical dividing line) 'byānjyè.

Boundary line 'jyèsyàn.

See also **BORDER.**

BOW. jyūgūng. / She bowed several times in front of the Buddha. Tā 'dwèije fwósyàng 'jyūle háujǐge 'gūng.

A bow. / He made a long, sweeping bow. is expressed as He bowed very deeply. Tā 'jyūle yīge hěn shēn de 'gūng.

BOW. (Weapon) gūng; **bow and arrow** 'gūngjyàn.

(Made of ribbon, string, etc.) hútyějyé, jyédz; **bow tie** lǐngjyé, lǐnghwār.

(Used with an instrument) gūngdz.

(Forward part of a vessel) chwántóu (of a ship); fēijītóu (of a plane).

BOWEL. (Intestine) chángdz; **move the bowels** làshr̄, dàbyàn.

BOWL. wǎn; **a bowl of rice** yìwǎn fàn.

BOWLING. (Game) (dǎ)dìchyóu.

BOX. (Container) hédz, syádz, syāngdz; in compounds héer, syár, syāngr, gwèi, hé, syá, syāng; (large box) dàhédz; (large paper box for packing) dàjr̄hédz; (large wooden box) dàmùtousyádz; (jewel box) shǒushr̄ 'syádz; (small money box) chyán-syāngr, chyánsyár; (large money box) chyángwèi. / We need a larger box for packing. Wǒmen děi yùng yige 'dàdyarde'hédz lái 'jwāng dūngsyi. / We can break up this box to make a fire. Wǒmen kéyi bǎ jèige 'hédz chāile shēng'hwǒ. / Fill up that box for me. Gěi wo bǎ nèige 'hédz jwāng'mǎnle. / Please put it in a box. Fàngdzai yíge 'syádzli 'hǎule. / This candy is cheaper by the box. Jèi 'táng lwùn 'syár mǎi 'pyányi. / She ate a whole box of candy. Tā 'chr̄le yījěng'héerde 'táng.

(In a theater) bāusyāng. / We took a box at the theater. Wǒmen dzài syì-'ywándzli dzwòde shr̀ bāu'syāng.

To box (in sports) dǎchywán. / Do you like boxing? Nǐ syǐhwan dǎ'chywán ma? / He boxes well. Tā dǎ 'chywán 'dǎde hěn 'hǎu.

(Put in boxes) jwāng(dzai) 'héerli, jwāngsyár, jwāngsyāng. / Box up what is left. 'Shèngsyade dōu jwāng(dzai) 'héerli. / I had a hundred pounds boxed in one hour. Wǒ 'yìdyǎn jūngli jwāng'syár jwāngle yìbǎi'bàng.

365

Be (*or* Come) boxed dàisyár. / The cheap candy isn't boxed. 'Pyányide tǎng búdài'syár.

BOXCAR. yǒu'dǐng'hwòchē.

BOY. nánháidz, nánhár (nán (male) is omitted when it is not necessary to specify sex). / Boys grow fast. Nán'hár 'jǎngde 'kwài. / That boy is growing fast. Nèige 'háidz 'jǎngde hěn 'kwài. / My boy doesn't do that. 'Wǒ nèige háidz bú'nèmmaje. / They have two boys and a girl. Tāmen yǒu, lyǎngge 'nánhár, 'yíge 'nyůhár. / Boys and girls! Come here! 'Háidzmen, dàu 'jèr lai! / Boys will be boys. Nán'háidz hái shr nán 'háidz.

(Servant or help) cháfang (in a hotel); pǎutángrde (in a restaurant); hwǒji (in a restaurant or store); tīngchāi(de) (in a home). / Please send a boy up for our luggage. 'Dǎfa yíge 'cháfang shànglai gěi wǒmen ná 'syíngli. / Boy, please bring me some ice water. °'Hwǒji (°'Pǎutángrde), ná dyàr bīng'shwěi lai. / He's serving as a boy in that house. Tā dzài nèi'jyār dāng tīng'chāide. In calling to a servant, Boy!, use the servant's full name, such as 'Lǐ Shēng, *or*, for a male servant, use lǎu and the surname lǎu'Lǐ. It is customary to ask a servant what his name is so that you can use it; ask him Nǐ 'jyàu shémma? *or*, more politely, Nǐ gwèi'syíng?

(Exclamation). / Boy oh boy! What a night! Hǎu'jyāhwo, jèi yì'wǎnshang! The boys (meaning grown-ups) tāmen yì hwǒdz. / The boys are having a game of poker tonight. Tāmen yì'hwǒdz jyēr 'wǎnshang dǎ 'púkèpái.

Boys' school. / That's a boys' school. Nà shr ge 'nánsywé'syàu.

BRACE. (Prepare something to resist) bǎuhù (protect). / The wall was built to brace the building against high winds. Dzwò nèidau 'chyáng wèideshr bǎuhù jèiswǒ 'fángdz, yùfáng gwā dà'fēng.

(Prepare oneself to resist) jwūnbei. / He braced himself for the argument he knew would follow. Tā dwèi kěnéng fā'shēng de wèn'tí yǐjing dzwòle jwūnbei le.

A brace tyějyàdz.

BRACELET. jwódz, shǒujwó, shǒulyàr.

BRAID. (Of hair) byàndz; (woven band) (yìlyǒur)'byānjrde dàidz.

To braid byān byàndz; (specifically of hair) shū byàndz. / She likes to braid her hair in the summertime. 'Syàtyande shrhou, ta ywànyi °'shū (°'byān) yige byàndz.

BRAIN. nǎudz.

BRAKE. já; (technical term) jrdùngchì. / The brakes gave out halfway through the trip. Dzǒu yíbàrde shrhou 'já hwàile.

Brakeman (railroad) gwǎnjáde.

To brake a vehicle tsǎijá, shāchē. / He didn't brake soon enough going around the curve. Jwǎnwārde shrhòu tā méiláidejí °shāchē (°tsǎijá).

BRAN. kāng, fūpí.

BRANCH. (Of a tree) shùchàdz, shùjrdz, shùjēr, dàjrdz, syǎujēr, syǎushùjēr. / The bird is on that highest branch. 'Nyǎu dzài dzwèi 'gāude shù'jērshang. / Several big branches blew off in the wind. Hǎujige shù'chàdz dōu gwā'dwànle.

(Of a family) jr, fáng. / Our branch of the family is poor. Wǒmen 'jèiyìjr hěn 'chyúng. / Our branch of the family lives in the western part of the house. (Specifically Chinese, referring to. the typical situation in which one of a man's sons, with his wife and servants and children, live in the western part of the house.) Wǒmen jēi'fáng jù dzài syīywànr.

(Of a river) jīlyóu. / No, this is only a branch of the river. 'Búshr, jè jrshr yìtyáu 'jīlyóu.

(Of the service) jyūn (the type of military organization such as the army, navy or air force); bīngjǔng, bīngkē (a part of a military organization. / What branch of the service are you in? Nǐ dzài něi jyūn (fúwù)? / Which branch are you in? Nǐde °bīng'jǔng (°bīng'ke) shr shémma?

(Of study or learning) kē, jǔng. / Optics is a branch of physics. 'Gwāngsywé shr wù'lǐsywéde yì°'kē (°jǔng).

If a business or official organization has branches at various locations, the terms for them follow the pattern post office yóujèngjyú; branch post office yóujèng-'fēnjyú or (short form) 'fēnjyú; east branch (west branch, etc.) (yóujèng)'dūngjyú, etc. Names of other such organizations end with a different element from jyú; this other element is used as jyú is above. / Get the stamps at the branch post office. Dàu (yóujèng)'fēnjyú chyù mǎi yóu'pyàu. / You can read the newspapers at the branch library across the street. Nǐ kéyi dzài dwèi'gwèrde túshū 'fēngwǎn kàn'bàu. / We are going to open a new branch (of a commercial firm) in New York City. Wǒmen yàu dzài Nyóuywe kāi yige °fēndyàn (°etc.).

To branch off from lí, líkāi. / We branched off from the main road. Wǒmen 'lí(kai)le 'dàlùle. / When he gives a speech he always branches off from his subject. Tā yǎn'shwō de shrhou 'chángcháng lí 'tí.

Branch out into dǎrù. / That company has branched out into oil now. Nèige gūng'sz yǐjing dǎ'rùle 'yóuyè le.

BRAND. (Of a product) páidz.

BRANDY. báilándì(jyǒu).

BRASS. (hwáng)túng.

BRASSIERE. nǎijàur.

BREAD. (Western-style bread or rolls) myànbāu. / We need two loaves of bread. Wǒmen děi yǒu 'lyàngge myàn'bāu. / I must slice the bread. Wǒ děi bǎ myàn'bāu 'chyēchéng 'pyàr.

Bread is not a part of the Chinese diet. The equivalent staple is some variety of rice fàn or wheat product myàn, the former being prevalent in the south, the latter in the north. Baked products which more or less resemble Western bread or other things called bread (corn bread, etc.) are bǐng, dàbǐng shortened dough in a flat, thin, round shape, baked on a griddle; shāubǐng smaller with sesame seeds on top; fāmyànbǐng with yeast; gwōbǐng a thick variety; jīyóubǐng with small pieces of pork fat; jūyóubǐng with lard; tsūnghwārbǐng with slices of scallion in it; báubǐng unshortened and very thin. Breadlike products made by steaming are mántou raised with yeast; hwājywǎr same as mántou but in a roll shape; wō(wo)tóu steamed corn bread.

Bread and butter (a living). / How does he earn his bread and butter? Tā 'jrje shéme chr 'fàn?

BREAK (BROKE, BROKEN). If something breaks of itself, the terms are pwò hwài (get out of order, become useless); lyè (to crack); swèi (break to bits, disintegrate); shé *or* dwàn (to break into segments, of any long object); sàn (to come apart). If something or someone breaks something, the terms are resultative compounds of which the second elements are the above, the first elements expressing the method or means of breaking, as dǎ (by striking a blow); dzá (by striking a blow with a heavy object); chyǎu (by a light sharp blow); shwāi (by dropping); pèng (by colliding with an object); tī (by kicking); yā (by squeezing down from above); jǐ (by squeezing, or by pressure from inside); lā (by pulling); chōu (by jerking sharply); twēi (by pushing); rēng (by throwing); shwǎi (by swinging and shaking); dǒulou (by shaking or swinging back and forth); jywē (by applying a bending force to the two ends of a long object); bāi (by applying a bending force to other than a long object); nùng more general, not specifying exact method. These first parts may also combine with the second elements dàu *or* chéng as the equivalent of English break something into so many pieces or such-and-such a shape, *or* break something to such-and-such a degree. Some of these combinations would not call for the English word break, but rather for some other word such as fracture, destroy, crack. There are also other less common words and combinations. Some of the above are illustrated below. / Be careful not to break this. 'Syǎusyīn byé bǎ 'jèige °'dzále (°'dǎle, °'shwāile, °'pèngle, °pèng'hwàile, °etc.). / The waiter broke three plates when he fell. °Pǎu'tángrde (°'Hwǒji) 'shwāile yìjyāu, 'dzále sānge 'pándz. / Does it break easily? Hěn 'rúngyi °'hwài ma (°'sàn ma, °etc.)? / Who broke the window? 'Shéi bǎ 'bwōli dǎ'swèile? / He fell down and broke his leg. Tā bǎ 'twēi shwāi'shéle. / He fell down and broke his nose. Tā bǎ 'bídz shwāi'pwòle. / The cup didn't break when I dropped it. 'Bēidz 'dyàu 'dìsya méi'swèi. / I broke the cup when I dropped it. 'Bēidz jyàu wo shwāi'pwòle. / Has the car broken down already? 'Chē 'yǐjing 'hwàile ma? / His health has broken down. Tā 'shēnti 'hwàile. / The car didn't break down until yesterday. 'Chē yì'jř dàu 'dzwótyan hái méi'hwài. / Please break off a piece for me. 'Bāi yìkwàr 'gěi wo. / The ice is breaking up. 'Bīng 'lyèle.

(Of dikes, dams, or teeth) bēng. / I've broken a tooth on this candy. Jèikwài 'táng jēn 'yìng, bǎ wǒde'yá gěi 'bēngle. / The dike broke. Nèige 'tí 'bēngle.

Break an engagement jyéchú hwūnywé. / Her parents broke her engagement. Tāde fù'mǔ gěi ta bǎ hwūn'ywē jyé'chúle.

Break a date shřywē. / He's broken his date. Tā shřywēle.

Break a promise. / He won't break his promise. Tā bú'hwèi 'shwō le bú'swàn.

Break camp 'báyíng. / We're going to break camp tonight. Jīntyan 'wǎnshang 'bá'yíng.

Break the ice. / They were very formal until somebody broke the ice with a joke. Tāmen chǐ'syān hěn 'jyūshù, 'hòulai yǒu 'rén shwō le yíge 'syàuhwar jyòu bǎ chén'mènde 'kūngchi gěi dǎ'pwòle.

Break the law 'fànfǎ. / We mustn't break the law. Wǒmén bù'yīnggai 'fàn'fǎ.

Break one's journey 'tíngyísyàr. / He must break his journey in order to see the cathedral. Tā dzài bàn'lù děi 'tíngyísyàr hǎu chyù kàn nèige jyàu'táng.

Break one's neck (fig.). / I'll break your neck! Wǒ bǎ nǐde 'nǎudai kǎnsyàlai! *or* Wǒ fēi 'dzòu nǐ bukě!

Break someone's **heart** jēn jyàu . . . °shǎng'syīn(°nángwò). / It really breaks my heart. Jēn jyàu wo °shǎng'syīn (°nángwò).

Break down (refute) bwōdǎu. / They broke down his argument. Tāmen bǎ tāde lǐyóu gěi bwō'dǎule.

Break down (take apart) 'chāikāi. / Break down this gun. Bǎ'chyāng 'chāikai.

Break into a house 'jǐngdau . . . li. /A thief may break into the house. Yésyu yǒu 'dzéi hwèi 'jǐndau 'fángdzli chyu.

Break (off) relations nàufàn, twō lí 'gwānsyi; jywéjyāu (between friends). /He broke off with his father. Tā gēn tā fùchin nàufàn le. /He broke off relations with his family. Tā gēn tā 'jyā twō lí gwānsyi le. /They've broken off relations. Tāmen jywé'jyāule.

Break out (of fire) chǐ, jáu. /The fire broke out about midnight. 'Hwǒ shř 'bànyè 'chǐde. /A fire broke out near here yesterday. 'Dzwótyan jèli 'fùjìn jáu 'hwǒle.

Break out (of war) 'dǎchǐlai. /We hope war won't break out. Wǒmen 'syīwàng jàng 'dǎbuchǐlái.

Break out with a skin disease chū . . . . /The child is breaking out with measles. Syǎu'hár chū 'jěndzle.

Break out of jail ywèyù. /Someone broke out of jail. 'Dzwótyan yǒu'rén ywè'yù.

Break up a crowd bǎ . . . 'gǎnkai, 'sànkāi. /Break (it) up! 'Sànkai! /Break up these demonstrators. Bǎ nèisye shř'wēide rén 'gǎnkai.

Break up (of ice) jyědùng. /The ice is breaking up. 'Bīngjèngdzài jyě'dùng.

A break. /Let's give him a break. meaning Let him try again. 'Gěi ta ge 'syīn 'jīhwei ba. or 'Dzài gěi ta ge 'jīhwei ba. or Jyàu ta 'dzài 'shřyishř. or meaning Give him a chance. 'Gěi ta ge 'jīhwei ba. /The breaks were against us. Wǒmen bùdzǒu'yùn.

BREAKFAST. dzǎufàn, dzǎudyǎn. /Have you had breakfast yet? Dzǎu'dyǎn 'chřgwole ma? /What do you have for breakfast? Dzǎu'fàn °chř (°yòu) 'shémma?

BREAST. rǔfáng, syūng(púr).

BREATH. (Mouthful of air) yìkǒu chì. /Hold your breath to stop the hiccups. 'Byē yìkǒu 'chì jyòu bùdǎ 'géer le. /Now take a deep breath. Syàn'dzài shēn'shēnde syī yìkǒu 'chì.

Breath of air yìdyǎrfēng. /There isn't a breath of air today. 'Jyèr yìdyǎr 'fēng ye 'méiyǒu.

Be out of breath 'chwǎnbuchū 'chyèr lai. /She ran up the hill and was out of breath. Tā 'pǎushang 'shān chyu pǎude 'chwǎnbuchū 'chyèr lai le.

Catch one's breath chwǎnchì, chwǎnchyèr. /Let's stop here and catch our breath. Dzámen dzài 'jèr 'tíng hwèr hǎu chwǎn kǒu 'chyèr. /We stopped to catch our breath. Wǒmen jàn'jùle 'chwǎnchwan 'chyèr.

Have bad breath 'dzwěili yǒu 'wèr, kǒuchòu.

Save one's breath. /You might as well save your breath. Nǐ yùngbu'jáu 'shwō shémma le. or Nǐ 'hái bù'rú bù'shwō shémma ne.

BREATHE. chwǎnchū 'chyèr lai. /He'd been running so hard he could hardly breathe. Tā 'pǎude tài 'lìhàile, jyǎnjř 'chwǎnbugwò 'chyèr láile.

(Exhale and inhale) hūsyī. /He's breathing regularly. Tā hū'syī jèng'cháng.

(Disclose). /Don't breathe a word of this to anyone. 'Jèige gēn 'shwéi yě byé 'shwō.

Breathe freely 'chwǎnchwan 'chyèr. /Now that he's gone we can breathe freely again. Tā kě 'dzǒule, women kéyi 'chwǎnchwan 'chyèr le.

369

Breathe hard 'chwǎn. / She was breathing hard from climbing the stairs. Tā shàng lóu'tī shàngde jŕ 'chwǎn.

Be breathing (showing presence of life; as of an injured person) ('bídz) yǒuchyèr. / He's still breathing. Tā ('bídz) hái yǒu'chyèr ne.

Have a breathing spell 'syē yisyē. / When do we have a breathing spell? Wǒmen 'shémma shŕhou néng 'syē yisyē?

BREEZE. syǎufēng(r), wēifēng(r).

BRICK. jwān; a brick of . . . yíkwài, yíkwàr. / He bought bricks and built the chimney himself. Jèige 'yāntung shr tā 'dżji mǎi 'jwān gàide. / This wall is made of brick. Jèige 'chyáng shr 'jwānde. / He chopped up a brick of ice to keep the meat cold. Tā bǎ yijěngkwài bīng chyāusweile bīng 'ròu.

Bricklayer wǎjyang.

BRIDE. syīnnyángdz.

BRIDEGROOM. syīnláng.

BRIDGE. chyáu. / This boat can go under the bridge. Jèijŕ 'chwán kéyi tsúng chyáu-'dǐsya 'gwòchyu. / We must go around; the bridge is out. Dzámen děi 'ràuje dzǒu, yīnwei 'chyáu 'hwàile.

(Of a ship) chwánchyáu; (of a warship) jyànchyáu. / The bomb fell on the bridge. Jà'dàn lwòdzai chwán'chyáushangle. / Can you see the captain on the bridge? Nǐ 'kàn-dejyàn °jyàn'jǎng dzài jyàn'chyáushang nàr ma (°chwán'jǎng dzài chwán'chyáushang nàr ma)?

(For false teeth) (jyá'yáde) chyǎdz. / The dentist says I need a new bridge for that false tooth. Yá'yī shwō wǒ nèige jyǎ'yá děi hwàn yige 'chyǎdz. / That dentist does excellent bridge work. Nèige yá'yī syāng jyǎ'yá hěn yǒu 'gūngfu.

(Of the nose) bílyángdz, bílyángr. / His nose has a low bridge. Tāde bí'lyángdz dī.

(Game). chyáupái; or the English word itself is used; play bridge dǎ 'chyáupái or dǎ 'bridge.

Burn bridges (fig.). / He burned his bridges behind him. Tā nà shŕ pwò'fúchén-'jyòule. or Tā nà shr bèichéng yíjànle.

To bridge (a gap) bǔchūng. / The new legislation helped to bridge the gaps in aid to the unemployed. Jèige syīn fǎ'àn bāngju (wǒmen) bǔchūng dwèi shŕyè de rén de 'jyòují.

BRIEF. dwǎn. / I've written him a brief note. Wǒ gěi ta 'syěle yìfēng 'dwǎn 'syìn. / Please make your speech brief. Nǐ yàn'shwō a, 'dwǎn yidyǎr 'syíng busyíng?

In brief dzūngér'yánjŕ, jyàn'dwànjyé'shwō, 'jyǎndānde shwō. / In brief, our plan is this. Dzūngér'yánjŕ, wǒmende 'jìhwà shŕ 'jèmmayàng.

A brief (summary) gāngyàu; (outline) dàgāng. / Send me a brief of that document. Nèige wén'jyàn (ching ni) gěi wo sùng ge gāng'yàu lai.

To brief bǎ'yàudyǎn . . . shwō, 'jyǎndānde shwō. / The instructor briefed the students on the program for this term. Nèige jyàu'ywán bǎ jèisywé'chī kècheng de 'yàudyǎn gēn sywésheng 'shwōle. / The squadron leader has already briefed the flyers on combat plans. Jūngdwèi'jǎng yǐjing bǎ dzwòjàn'jìhwa 'jyǎndānde gēn jyàshr'ywán shwōle.

BRIEFCASE. gūngshr̄bāu, gūngshr̄ pí'bāu; (for a student) shūbāu.

BRIGHT. (Of light, or of things that reflect light) lyàng. / This mirror isn't bright enough. Jèimyàn 'jìngdz búgòu 'lyàng. / The sunlight is quite bright. Tàiyang 'gwāng hĕn 'lyàng.

(Of colors) chyăn, syānyàn, syānmíng. / This flower is bright yellow. Jèijŭng 'hwār shr̀ chyăn'hwáng sè. / The colors aren't bright enough. 'Yánsè bú'gòu °syān'yànde (°syān'míngde).

(Of a fire) wàng. / What a bright fire! Hwŏgwāng dwó'wàng a!

(Of a person) tsūngming, năudz kwài. / He's a bright boy. Tā shr̀ ge 'tsūngming 'háidz. or Tā 'jèige háidz hĕn 'tsūngming. / He wasn't bright enough to catch the idea. Tāde 'năudz búgòu 'kwàide, swóyi tīngbu'dŭng.

(Of prospects) shwùnlì, kéyi lè'gwān. / The prospects are bright enough. Chyán'tú gòu shwùn'lìde. or Chyán'tú hĕn kéyi lè'gwān.

(Of weather) hăutyār. / We'd better wait for a bright day. Dĕng hău'tyār 'dzài shwō ba.

Bright and cheerful gāusyìng. / Everyone was bright and cheerful at the wedding party. Lái tsānjyā hwūnlìde rén dōu hĕn gāu'syìng.

Bright ideas hău fádz, hău júyi. / Do you have any bright ideas? Nǐ 'yŏu méiyou °hău 'fádz (°hău 'júyi)? / Don't give me your bright ideas. Byé 'hú chū 'júyi.

BRING (BROUGHT). dài; or expressed by the use of lái after ná and other verbs meaning carry (see **CARRY**). / I've brought more clothes than I need. Wo 'yīfu dàide tài 'dwōle. / The father brought the children a present. 'Fùchin gĕi 'háidz 'dàile jyàn 'lĭwu. / May I bring a friend with me? Wŏ kéyi dài yíwei 'péngyou lái ma? / He asked someone to bring me word that he's not coming. Tā twō 'rén dài 'hwàr lai, shwō tā 'bù'láile. / How many matches should I bring? Wŏ 'yīngdāng ná dwōshau yáng'hwŏ lai? / Please bring me that book. Chĭng ni gĕi wo bă nèiben 'shū 'nálai.

(To a waiter) lái alone. / Waiter! Bring another bowl of rice! 'Hwŏji! 'Dzài lái wăn 'fàn! / Bring me a glass of water. is expressed as Pour and bring a glass of water for me. Gĕi wo 'dàu bēi 'shwĕi lai.

(Cause someone to come). / What brings you to town? Nǐ wèi'shémma jìn'chéng láile? or Nǐ gàn 'shémma jìn'chéng lái a? / What brings you here? Nǐ gàn 'shémma lái le? or (slangy) 'Năjèn 'fēng bă ni 'chwēilaile? / What (important matter) brings you to town? Yŏu shémma 'yàujĭnde 'shr̀ ràng 'nǐ jìn'chéng lai?

Bring about (cause to take place) 'shr̀ yīnwei . . . de 'gwānsyi. / The shortage of water was brought about by the lack of rain. Shwĕi 'chywē shr̀ yīnwei 'yŭ bú'gòude gwānsyi. / The cold wave brought about a snow storm. Dàfēng'sywĕ shr̀ yīnwei hán'lyóude gwānsyi.

Bring action against (legal) gàu. / He brought action against you. Tā 'gàu ni le.

Bring someone **around** or **over** (convince) chywàngwolai, 'shwōde 'jwănle 'yì le, shwōfú. / At first they didn't agree but we brought them around. Tāmen chí'chū bú'dzànchéng, 'hòulai wŏmen jyòu bă tāmen °'chywàngwolaile (°'shwōde 'jwănle 'yì le). / We brought him over to our point of view. Wŏmen 'bă tā shwō'fúle.

Bring back (or in or out, etc.) is expressed by a resultative compound with dài (or ná, etc., see **CARRY**) as the first element and hwéilai (or jìnlai or chūlai, etc.) as the second element. / Please bring the book back with you. Chĭng nǐ bă 'shū °'dàihweilai (°'náhweilai). / Bring him in. (of a prisoner or stranger) Bă ta 'dàijinlai. / Bring in the food. Bǎ 'chřde nájinlai. / He brought out several books for us to look at. Tā náchu jǐběn 'shū lai ràng wǒmen 'kàn.

Bring before a court. / I'll certainly bring this before the court. 'Jèijyàn shř wǒ y í'dìng děi °dzài fǎtíng chǐ'sù (°dàu fǎtíng chyù jyějywé).

Bring a subject **forward** (*or* up) tíchulai. / If you have any suggestions bring them forward. Nǐ rúgwo yǒu shémma 'yìjyàn chǐng 'tíchuali. / I'll bring the plan up at the next meeting. Syà'tsż kāi'hwèi de shŕhou, wǒ jyou bǎ jìhwa 'tíchulai.

Bring in something. *See* **Bring back** above.

Bring (in) money, profits dé, jwàn, néng 'mài, yǒu . . . de shōu'rù. / This transaction will bring in a large profit. Jèijwàng 'mǎimài kéyi °dé bùshǎude 'lì (°'jwàn bùshǎude chyán). / How much does this bring in the market? 'Jèige dzài 'shŕshang néng 'mài 'dwōshau chyán? / It brings (him) in three hundred dollars a month. Tā měi'ywè yǒu 'sānbǎiywánde shōu'rù.

Bring (in) an audience syīyǐn. / This speaker ought to bring (in) a big crowd. Jèiwèi jyǎng'yànde 'yīngdang néng syí'yǐn bùshǎu tīng'jùng.

Bring on (*or* about) a calamity rěchu 'hwòlai; **bring on** (*or* about) a crisis *or* an accident rěchu 'shěrlai.

Bring on a cold jyàu . . . jāu'lyáng; **bring on a fever** jyàu . . . fā'shāu. / This bad weather will bring on many colds. 'Tyānchi jèmma 'lěng yí'dìng jyàu bù'shǎurén jāu'lyáng.

Bring out something. *See* **Bring back** above.

Bring out qualities, characteristics. / The emergency brought out all his good qualities. is expressed as When the emergency came all his good qualities came out. Dàule jǐnyàu gwāntóu de shŕhou tāde 'hǎuchù dōu 'syānchulaile.

Bring out a play chūyǎn, yǎn. / They're getting ready to bring out a new play. Tāmen 'jwǔnbèi chū'yǎn yìchū 'syīnde 'syì.

Bring someone **to** (from a faint) jyòu(syǐng)gwolai. / Cold water will bring him to. Kéyi yùng lyáng'shwěi bǎ ta 'jyòu(syǐng)gwòlai.

Bring someone **to his senses.** / You must bring him to his senses. Nǐ děi 'jyàu ta 'míngbaigwolai.

Bring someone **to do** something chywàn. / I can't bring him to do it. Wǒ 'chywàn bùlyǎu ta 'dzwò nèige. *or* Tā bù'tīng wǒ 'chywàn.

Bring . . . to bear on yùng . . . gūng . . . , yùng . . . chyù 'gàn. / They brought all the fire to bear on that fort. Tāmen yùng chywán'bùde pàu'hwǒ gūng nèige pàu-tái. / You must bring all your attention to bear on this. 'Jèijyàn shř nǐ děi yùng chywánfù 'jīngshén chyù 'gàn.

Bring pressure to bear on bī. / Can't you bring some pressure to bear on him? Nǐ 'néng bunéng 'bi ta yisyà? / They brought a lot of pressure to bear on him but he wouldn't budge. Tāmen 'bi ta bide hěn 'lìhai, kěshr tā yì'dyǎr yě bù'kěn twēi-'ràng.

Bring tears to one's eyes. / That music brought tears to her eyes. Nèige 'chyǔr bǎ ta 'gǎndùngde dou 'lyóulèile.

Bring up a child dàidà, yǎngdà, yǎngchilai. / They didn't bring their children up carefully. Tāmen méi hǎuhaurde bǎ 'háidz dài'dà. / Their grandmother brought them up. Tāmen shř dzǔ'mǔ °'yǎngchilai de (°yǎng'dà de).

Be unable to bring oneself **to do** something gànbu chū lai. / I can't bring my-self to do that sort of thing. 'Nèiyàngde shěr wǒ gànbu'chūlái.

BROADCAST. gwǎngbwō. / The news was broadcasted all over the world. Syīnwén 'gwǎngbwō dàu shr̀jyè 'gè 'chù.

Radio broadcast wúsyàndyàn gwǎng'bwō. / That one radio broadcast influenced a great many people. Nèiyige wúsyàndyàn gwǎngbwō yíngshǎngle hěn dwō rén.

BROKE. / He's dead broke. is expressed as He doesn't have even one penny. Tā 'yíge dzěr yě 'méiyǒule.

BRONZE. chīngtúng.

BROOK. syǎuhé(er).

BROOM. (With a long or short handle) tyáuchu; (made by tying branches together) sàuchu.

BROTHER. (General term) older brother gēge; younger brother dìdi; brothers dìsyung, syūngdì. / They are two brothers. 'Tāmen shr̀ lyǎng °'dìsyung (°syūngdì). (polite term) your older brother lǐngsyūng; your younger brother lǐngdì; my older brother jyāsyūng; my younger brother shèdì.

Brother in the sense of a fellow-member of an organization is not part of Chinese culture, except that in certain Chinese secret societies the term 'dàgē is used for a fellow-member; where Western lodges are found, English terms are used.

BROW. méimau, yǎnméi, méi.

BROWN. 'dzūngshǎr, jěshr, 'hèsè; but instead of these, the closest equivalents, the Chinese usually classify what English calls brown as shades of other colors; if yellow is predominant hwáng, 'hwángshǎr; if red is predominant húng; if green is predominant 'chàsè, 'cháshǎr; chestnut brown 'lìdzshǎr. / I like the brown bag better than the black one. Wǒ 'kàn, (nèige) 'hwáng chyán'bāu bǐ (nèige) 'hēide 'hǎu. / The brown is too dark. Jèige 'hwángshǎr tài 'shēnle.

(Of skin). / The sun made his skin brown. Tā 'shàide jēn 'hēi.

Brown bread hēimyànbāu.

Brown shoes hwángsyé.

Brown sugar húngtáng.

To brown (in cooking). / Brown the meat first. Nǐ syan jyānyijyān ròu.

BRUISE. (yíkwài) chīng, dž.

BRUSH. shwādz. / You may use this brush to brush your hair. Nǐ kéyi yùng jèibǎ shwādz 'shwā 'tóu. / I need a new brush to paint the walls with. Wǒ děi yàu yìbǎ 'syīnde 'shwādz hǎu shwā 'chyáng. / Please scrub this sink with a brush. Bǎ jèige 'pen yùng 'shwādz shwā'gānjing.

(Underbrush) shùkēdz. / The workmen are cutting the brush. 'Gūngrén dzài jyàu shù'kēdz ne.

(Chinese writing implement) (Jūnggwo)bǐ, máubǐ. / He doesn't know how to write with a brush. Tā bú'hwèi yùng máu'bǐ syě 'dž.

(Artist's brush) hwàbǐ.

To brush (with a brush) shwā; (with a duster) dǎn; (with a cloth) tsā; (by accidental glancing contact) húlu, pèng. / I must brush my teeth. Wǒ děi shwā 'yá. Please brush these clothes for me. Bǎ jèisyē 'yīfu 'shwā yisyar. / I've brushed off the top of the table. Jwō'myàr wǒ yǐjing °'dǎngwole (°'tsāgwole). / I brushed the plate off the table and broke it. Wǒ bǎ 'pándz 'huludàn 'dìsya chyùle, jyòu (dǎ) 'swèile.

Brush against tsèng. / I brushed against the paint. Wǒ tsèngchī le.

Brush aside. / He brushed my protests aside. Wǒ 'shwōle 'bàntyan, °tā jyǎn'jŕ 'dàngdzwò ěrbyān 'fēng (°tā chywán búdzài'yì).

Brush away hūngpǎu. / He brushed away the fly. Tā bǎ 'tsāngying hūng'pǎule.

Brush off (fig.). / She got brushed off. *or* She got the brush-off. Tā āi 'shwāle.

Brush past tsènggwochyu, dzǒugwochyu, tsāgwochyu. / She brushed past us without seeing us. Tā tsúng wǒmen 'shēnbyar 'tsènggwochyu, kěshr méi'kànjyan wǒmen.

Brush up on 'wēnsyí. / I'm brushing up on my French. Wǒ dzài 'wēnsyí Fà-'wén.

BUBBLE. pàur; **soap bubble** yídzpàur.

BUCKET. shwěitǔng.

BUCKLE. kǒudz, dàikòu.

BUD. hwā gūdu, hwālěi.

To bud (of flowers, trees, etc.) fāyá. / The trees are already budding. 'Shù yǐjing 'fāyá le.

BUDGET. yùswàn. / The committee discussed the budget for the following year. (Nèige) wěiywánhwèi tǎulwùnle °míngnyande (°syànyándùde) yùswàn.

To budget. / We must budget our money very carefully every month. Wǒmende chyán, tā měige ywè (dou) děi syǎusyinde yùswàn yisya.

BUG. chúng, chúngr, chúngdz.

BUILD. (Of a bridge) dzàu, syōu, jyà; (if very simple) dā. / They built a bridge across the bay. Tāmen dzài hǎi'wānshang °'dzàule (°syōule, °jyàle) yídzwò'chyáu.

(Of a house or building) gài, dzàu, syōu. / The men are building a new house. Tāmen °'gài (°etc.) yìswěr 'syīn 'fángdz.

(Of a foundation of a building) lì, dzàu, dzá, syōu. / The foundation is well built. Dì'jī 'lìde 'hǎu.

(Of a pillar, column, lighthouse) dzàu, lì, syōu. / They built a memorial column for him. Tāmen wèi tā 'lìle yíge jìnyàn'tǎ.

(Of a wall) chìchyáng. / They are building a wall around the garden. Tāmen dzài hwāywárde sžbyār 'chìle yídàu 'chyáng.

(Of a city wall, fortification) jù, dzàu, syōu. / It took 50,000 men to build that city wall. 'Jù nèige chéng'chyáng yùngle 'wǔwàn rén.

(Of a barricade) lánchilai. / They've built a barricade across the street. Tāmen yùng 'dūngsyi bǎ'lù 'lánchilaile.

(Of a plane or ship) dzàu. / The ship was well built. 'Chwán 'dzàude hěn 'hǎu.

(Of a fire) shēng, lúngchilai. / Please build a fire in the fireplace. Bǎ bì-'lúde 'hwǒ 'lúngchilai. / We need someone to build a fire. Wǒmen 'syūyàu yíge rén shēng 'hwǒ.

(Of a nest) dā. / The birds are building a nest in the tree. 'Nyǎu dzài 'shù-shang dā 'wō.

Build up (fill with buildings). / This region wasn't built up yet when I first came. Wǒ chū 'dàu de shŕhou jèige 'dìfang °hái méifā'jǎncheng jèi'yàngr ne (°hái méi byàncheng jèmma 'rènau ne).

Build (up) a business 'jīngyíngchilai, dzwòchilai, dzwòchuchyu. / His business was built up in thirty years. Tāde 'mǎimai shr yùngle 'sānshrnyán 'dzwòchilaide.

Build (up) an empire jyànlì dìgwó. / It took Japan 70 years to build (up) her empire. Ř'běn yùngle 'chīshrnyán tsái jyànlì chǐ dìgwó lái.

Build up a reputation làu ge hǎu'myéngr, 'shùlì shēng'wàng. / He's trying to build up a reputation. Tā syǎng tì 'dzjǐ làu ge hǎu'myéngr. *or* Tā jyé'lì yàu (gěi 'dzjǐ) 'shùlì shēng'wàng. *but* / That restaurant is trying to build up a reputation. Nèige fàn'gwar syǎng 'dzwò chū ge 'páidz lái.

Build on something (add to it, using it as foundation). / He took a simple story and built on it until it became a long novel. Tā bǎ yíge hěn jyǎn'dānde 'gùshr kwòjǎn chéngle yìběn 'chángpyān syǎu'shwērle.

Built-in (in the wall) dzài 'chyángli dzwò'hǎule de. / The room has a built-in bookcase. Jèijyān 'wūdzli yǒu dzài 'chyángli dzwò'hǎule de shū'jyàdz. *but* / He bought a radio with a built-in antenna. Tā 'mǎile yíge 'lǐtou dài tyān'syànde wúsyàn-'dyàn(shǒuyīn'jī).

Build (physique). / He has a good build. Tāde 'tǐgé hěn 'hǎu.

BUILDING. (Two stories or more) lóu; (residence) fángdz; (tower) tǎ; 'jyànjù (used where in English one might say structure). / Both offices are in the same building. 'Lyǎngge gūngshr̀'fáng dōu dzài 'yídzwò 'lóuli. / What building is that? 'Nèige lóu shr̀ 'shémma? / That building with a spire is a church. Nèige yǒu tǎ'jyārde 'jyànjù shr̀ ge lǐbai'táng.

BULB. (Electric) (dyàn)dēngpàur; (plant) gūdwor.

BULL. gūngnyóu.

BULLET. dǔdàn, chyāngdàn, chyāngdzěr.

BULLETIN. (Notice) tūnggàu, 'gàushr̀; (published statement of an organization) gūnggàu; (of a school) jyǎnjāng; (of a government organization) gūngbàu.

BUMP. (Raised place; as on the head) bāu.

To bump (hit) pèng, chwàng, jwàng. / His car bumped the car in front. Tāde 'chē °pèng (°chwàng, °jwàng) dzài 'chyántoude chēshang le.

Bump into (meet by accident) pèngjau, pèngjyan. / I bumped into him this morning. Wǒ jīntyān dzǎushang 'pèngjau tā le.

BUNCH. bǎ(r) (of something bunched in the hand, or for vegetables like celery that are sold in bunches, not by weight); kwǔn, kwěr (for a bunch with a band around it, like tobacco leaves); chwàr (for keys); 'dùlu (for a bunch of things joined at one end but loose and randomly arranged at the other, like grapes, keys); chyún (for a group of human beings or animals). A bunch of dirty crooks yìchyún hwàidàn. / I'll take two bunches of flowers. Wǒ yàu 'lyǎngbǎr 'hwār. / She's lost a bunch of keys. Tā bǎ yíchwàr 'yàushr 'dyōule. / How much is this bunch of grapes? Jèi yìdùlu 'pútau 'dwōshau chyán?

To bunch together 'jyùdzai yí'kwàr, 'jǐdzai yí'kwàr. / The passengers were all bunched together. Chèng'kè dōu (gěi) 'jyùdzai yí'kwàrle. *but* / The shots were all bunched together. Chyāng'dzěr dōu 'dǎdau yí'kwàr chyùle.

Bunch together at a place jyùdau, jyùdzai, jǐdau, jǐdzai. / The passengers were all bunched together at the front end of the car. Chèng'kè dōu (gěi) °'jyùdau 'chē 'chyántoule (°'jǐdau 'chē'chyántou le).

BUNDLE. (Of anything) kwǔn, bāu.

BUREAU. (Furniture) yīgwèi, gwèidz. *See* OFFICE.

BURGLAR. dzéi.

BURST. (Break open) bēng; (crack or split open) lyè; both may be used as a resultative ending with suitable verbs. / She was so fat that when she put on the dress she burst the seams. Tā tài 'pàng le, nèijyan 'yīshang ta yi 'chwān, jyou °lyèle (°bēngle) fèngr le. / In the winter the pipes freeze and burst. Dūngtyan 'gwǎndz 'chángchang dùnglyèle. / There's too much stuff in that bag; it's going to burst. Nèige 'kǒudaili dūngsyi tài 'dwō, kwài chēnglyè le.

(With a bang) bàu, fàngpàu. / The child's balloon has burst. Nèige 'háidzde chì'chyóu 'bàule. / The tire was so old that it burst easily. Chē'dài 'lǎude yì 'lái jyou fàng'pàu.

(Of a bomb) jà. / A bomb had burst in the next block. 'Pángbyār nèityáu 'jyēshang yǒu yige jà'dàn 'jàle.

(Of flowing water or a water barrier) jywékǒu, kāi kǒudz; (of a dike or dam) bēng. / The river burst its banks. 'Hé °kāi 'kǒudz le (°jywé'kǒule). / Last year the dam burst. 'Chyùnyan 'já kāi 'kǒudz le. *or* 'Chyùnyan 'já 'bēngle.

(With emotion). / He's bursting with anger. Tā 'chìde kwài rěnbu'jù le. / She burst °into tears (°out crying). Tā rěnbu'jù le, jyou 'kūchilaile. *or* Tā hūrán 'dà 'kū.

Burst into hūrán jìn, měngránjyān jìn, chwǎngjìn. / He burst into the room. Tā 'chwǎngjin nèijyan wūdz chyùle. *or* Tā 'měngranjyān 'jìnle wūdz le.

Burst into flame hūrán 'jáuchi 'hwǒ lai. / The airplane burst into flame. Fēi'jī hūrán jáuchi 'hwǒ laile.

Burst out (suddenly) hūran . . . chū. / The children came bursting out of the school. Nèisye 'háidzmen hūran dou tsúng sywé'syàuli °'pǎuchulaile (°'chwǎngchulaile).

Burst out of something chū. / The contents were bursting out of the trunk. 'Syāngdzli dūngsyi dwōde dou chūlaile.

A burst 'lyède dìfang, lyè kǒur le. / Did you find the burst in the water pipe? 'Gwǎndz 'lyè °de dìfang (°de lyèkǒur) nǐ 'jǎujáule méiyou?

Burst of jèn. / There was a burst of applause after his speech. Tā yǎn'shwō yi 'wán jyou 'hūrán láile yijèn pāi'shǒude shēngyin. / There was a burst of gunfire in the street yesterday. 'Dzwótyan 'jyēshang yǒu yijèn 'pàushēng.

BURY. mái (people or objects); āndzàng (quite polite); be buried rùtǔ, syàdzàng (people only). / The dog is burying the bone. 'Gǒu dzài 'mái 'gǔtou. / They'll bury the body tomorrow. 'Míngtyan °jyòu 'máile (°rù'tǔ, °syà'dzàng, °ān'dzàng). / They buried him yesterday. Tā shr̀ 'dzwótyan syàde 'dzàng.

(Perform burial rites for) jǔchr̆ . . . dzàng'lǐ. / They want a priest to bury the child. Tāmen yàu chǐng yíge 'shénfù lái jǔchr̆ 'háidzde dzàng'lǐ.

Bury alive hwómái. / They buried him alive. Tāmen bǎ ta 'hwó'máile.

Bury at sea hǎidzàng. / Did they bury him at sea? Tāmen shr̀ bǎ ta hǎi'dzàng le ma?

BUSY

Be buried in (absorbed). /He's buried in his work. Tā mái'tóukǔ'gàn ne.

Be buried under *or* among (be hidden) yādzai. /My passport was buried under the other papers. Wǒde hù'jàu 'yādzai 'byéde wén'jyàn 'dǐsyale.

BUS. (City or suburban) gūnggùngchìchē; (long-distance) chángtúchìchē. /Where can I catch the bus? Wǒ dzài 'nǎr néng shàng gūnggùngchì'chē? /We want to go by bus. Wǒmen 'dǎswàn dzwò chángtúchì'chē chyù. /Does a bus go to that town? Chángtúchì'chē 'dàu nèige 'chéng ma?

Bus driver (polite term) sżjī; (impolite if used in direct address) kāichēde. /The bus driver will tell you where to get off. Sż'jī hwèi 'gàusung ni yīngdang dzài 'nǎr syàchē.

BUSH. (syǎu)shù.

Beat around the bush ràuje chywār shwō. /He beat around the bush instead of getting right to the point. Tā (lǎu) ràuje chywār shwō, bushwōdau běn tí.

Be bushed bǎ . . . lèisz. /That trip left me bushed. Nèitsż lyǔsyíng bǎ wǒ nùngde lèisz le.

BUSINESS. (Buying and selling, trading, commerce) mǎimai; (commerce, used in compounds) shāng; (affairs, matters, work) shr̀; (the business world, businessmen as a group) shāngjyè; **big business** dà'shāngjyā, (particularly finance) tsáifá. /They're selling their business. Tāmende 'mǎimai yàu °chū'shǒu le (°dàu'shǒu le, °dǎu-'shǒu le). /He's in business. Tā dzwò 'mǎimai. *or* Tā shr̀ dzwò 'mǎimai de. *or* Tā jīng'shāng. *or* Tā shr̀ 'shāngrén. *or* Tā dzài 'shāngjyè. /Will your son join the business? is expressed as Is your son coming to help? Lìng'láng yàu lái bāng-'máng ma? or as Is your son coming to work? Lìngláng yàu lái dzwò'shr̀ ma? /What's his business? Tā shr̀ dzwò'shémma de? /An important part of a dentist's business is to pull teeth. Yá'yīsheng dzwò de 'shr̀li bá'yá shr̀ hen 'jùngyàude.

(A branch of study) shāngkē. /He's studying business. Tā °sywé (°nyàn) 'shāngkē.

(Affairs) shr̀, shèr. /It's your business to keep the staff satisfied. Jyàu swǒyǒude rén'ywán dōu mǎnyì shr̀ 'nǐde shr̀. /Can you understand this business? 'Jèiyàngde shèr °nǐ 'dǔng ma (°nǐ 'hwèi ma, °nǐ hwèi 'dzwò ma)? or Nǐ 'kàn, 'jè shr̀ 'dzěmma yihwei 'shèr a? /He told us to mind our own business. Tā 'jyàu wǒmen 'shǎu gwǎn syán'shèr. *or* Tā shwō wǒmen gwǎnbu'jáu. /That's my business; you can't interfere. Nà shr̀ 'wǒde shr̀, nǐ gwǎnbu'jáu. /Let's settle this business right away. Dzámen bǎ jèijyàn 'shèr syàn'dzài jyou 'lyǎule ba.

Have no business doing something. /He had no business asking such questions. 'Jèiyàngde wèn'tí °tā píng 'shémma lái 'wèn (°tā gwǎnbu'jáu)? or Tā jyàn'jr̀ shr̀ dwō'dzwěi. or Gēn ta wú'gwān de shr̀ tā búbì wèn.

Business college 'shāngyè jwǎn'mén sywé'syàu.

Business conditions shāngchíng, shāngyè chíng'kwàng, shāngyè jwàng'kwàng.

Businessman 'shāngrén, jīngshāngde, 'shāngjyā.

Business school 'shāng°yè (°kē)sywé'syàu.

Business section (of a city) 'shāngyèchyū, dàjyē, 'rènau dìfang.

BUSY. (Of a person) máng, yǒushèr; (harshly) méigūngfu. /I was busy all day. 'Mángle yī'tyān. /This morning I was too busy to read the newspaper. Wǒ jīntyan 'dzǎuchen tài 'mángle, méinéng kàn 'bàu. /When he called I was busy eating. Tā 'lái de shŕhou wǒ jèng 'mángje chŕ 'fàn ne. /He's busy. (occupied) Tā jèng 'máng

377

ne. *or* Tā hěn 'máng. *or* Tā yǒu'shèr. *or* (speaking harshly) Tā méi'gūngfu. /He's always busy. Tā 'lǎushr 'máng. *or* Tā 'lǎushr yǒu'shèr. *or* Tā 'lǎushr méi'gūngfu. /He's too busy to see anybody. Tā 'mángde méi'gūngfu 'jyēdai rén.

(Of a place) rènàu. /They live on a busy street. Tāmen jùdzai yìtyáu hěn 'rènau de 'jyēshang.

(Of a telephone) yǒu rén jyàu. /The operator says that the line is busy. Jyēsyànshēng shwō yǒurén 'jyàu.

BUT. kěshr, dànshr; or often expressed by a pause. /It wasn't me but my brother that you met. Nǐ 'jyàngwo de bùshr 'wǒ, shr wǒ 'gēge. /It's not that I don't like him as a person, but I just can't work with him. 'Bùshr wǒ'syǐhwan tā jèige 'rén, shr wǒ bù'néng gēn ta yìkwèr gùng'shr. /This is right, but that is wrong. 'Jèige 'dwèile, kěshr 'nèige tswòle. /I thought I could go, but I can't. Wǒ 'syān yǐ'wéi wǒ néng 'chyù ne, dànshr syàn'dzài bùnéng 'chyùle.

(Except) chúle . . . (yǐ'wài), 'jr yǒu, jyòuhwèi. /The library is open every day but Sunday. Túshū'gwǎn chúle syīngchī'r (yǐ'wài) 'měityān dōu 'kāi. /We could do nothing but wait. Chúle 'děngje méiyou byéde'fǎr. /Who can do it but you? *or* Who but you could have done it? Chúle 'nǐ hái yǒu 'shéi ne? /They have no meat but chicken. Tāmen 'jr yǒu 'jīròu. /She does nothing but grumble. Tā 'chéngtyān jyòu hwèi bàuywàn.

(Except that) 'búgwò. /We can go with you but we will have to come back early. Gēn ni 'chyù dàushr 'kéyi, 'búgwò wǒmen děi 'dzǎudyar 'hwéilai. *but* /It never rains but it pours. (lit.) Búsyà'yǔ dzé'yǐ, yí 'syà jyòushr (chīngpén) 'dàyǔ. (fig.) Bùchū'shr dzé'yǐ, yì 'chū jyòushr bùdé'lyǎu.

(Exclamation) kě. /Lord, but it's cold! Lǎu'tyānyé, kě 'jēn gòu 'lěngde!

But for. /I would have drowned but for him. Yàu 'búshr 'tā 'jyòu wo wǒ jyòu 'yānsǐle.

All but . . . jyòu shèng . . . °bū (°méi), jr̆ yǒu . . . °bū (°méi), jr̆ shèng . . . °bū (°méi). /All are ready but you. Jyòu shèng 'nǐ hái méi yùbèi'hǎu.

All but did something jyòu shèng bū, jr̆ shèng bū, chàdyǎr bū. /He was so nervous that he all but wrecked the machine. Tā 'hwāngde jyòu shèngle méi bǎ jīchi 'hwěile.

BUTCHER. (Meat seller) màiròude.

Butcher shop ròupù; since Mohammedans eat lamb and do not eat or handle pork, one often says jūròu'pù *or* jūròu'gàng for a butcher shop that sells pork, and yángròu-'pù *or* yángròu'chwángdz for a butcher shop that sells lamb.

BUTT. (of gun) chyāngbàr; (of cigarette) yāntóur.

BUTTER. nyóuyóu, hwángyóu.

Peanut butter hwāshēngjyàng, hwāshēngyóu.

To butter mwǒ °hwángyóu (°nyóuyou). /Shall I butter your toast? Kǎumyàn-'bāushang, nǐ 'yàu buyàu mwǒ hwáng'yóu?

BUTTERFLY. húdyé, hútyěr, hútyèr, fúdyè, fútyěr, fútyèr.

BUTTON. nyǒudz, nyǒukòur, kòudz, kòupàndz, kòupàr, nyǒupàr. Chinese buttons consist of two parts, made of thread; one contains a loop, one ends in a knot. The last three terms given apply to the whole set, and similarly to the Western-style button and buttonhole. / This button has come off. Jèige 'nyǒudz 'dyàule. / Do you have a button like this one? Nǐ 'jèr yǒu gēn jèige yí'yángde nyǒu'kòur ma? / I've lost two buttons. Wǒ dyōule lyàngge 'kòudz.

(Emblem) hwēijāng. / He's wearing a Red Cross button. Tā 'dàile yíge 'Húngshŕdz̀'hwèide hwēi'jāng.

Press a button (electrical) èn dyànmén. / When I pressed the button the light went out. Wǒ yí èn dyàn'mén 'dēng 'myè le.

Push a (bell) **button** ènlíngr. / When you want to use the elevator, just push the button. Yàu yùng dyàn'tī de shŕhou, èn'língr jyòu 'syíng le.

Buttonhole kòumér.

To button (up) kòushang (used with kòupàr or Western buttons); jìshang. / Button (up) your overcoat. Bǎ nǐde dà'yī 'kòushang. / Button (up) your collar. Bǎ 'lǐngdz 'jìshang.

BUY (BOUGHT). mǎi. / Have you bought your ticket yet? (Nǐ) 'pyàu 'mǎile ma? / I bought these shoes in London. Wǒ jèisyē 'syé shŕ dzài Lwún'dwūn 'mǎide. / Did I buy the right thing? Wǒ 'mǎide 'dwèi budwèi? / I'll buy our tickets tomorrow. Wǒ 'míngtyan yí'dìng bǎ 'pyàu 'mǎi le.

(Bribe) mǎitūng. / You can't buy the police in this town. 'Jèi chéngde syún-'jǐng nǐ shr bùnéng yùng'chyán lái mǎi'tūngde.

Be bought (take, receive a bribe) bèishōumǎi. / He can be bought quite easily. Tā hěn rúngyi bèishōumǎi.

Buy up (chywán, dōu) °'mǎilái (°'mǎichyu). / All the trucks have been bought up by the government. 'Swǒyǒude °dzàijùngchì'chē (°kǎchē) dōu jyàu 'jèngfǔ 'mǎichyule.

Buy out (chywán, dōu) mǎigwolai. / He bought out his partners. Tā bǎ 'byérénde 'gǔdz dōu 'mǎigwolaile.

A buy. / That's a good buy. is expressed as That is worth buying. 'Nèige 'mǎide hěn 'jŕ.

BY. (Location) dzài . . . pángbyār, dzài . . . yi'byār, dzài . . . °jèr (°nàr); kàu (be next to). / The hotel is by the sea. Lyǘ'gwǎn kàu 'hǎi. / Stand by the window. Kàu 'chwānghu 'jànje. / Come and sit by me. Lái dzwò dzai 'wǒ jèr. / Sit by him. Dzwò dzai 'tā nàr. / He's sitting by my side. Tā dzwò dzai wǒ 'pángbyār. or Tā dzài wǒ 'pángbyār 'dzwòje. or Tā kàuje wo 'dzwòje. / He stood by me. (lit.) Tā 'jàn dzai wǒ °pángbyar (°yì'byār). or Tā dzài wǒ 'pángbyār 'jànje. or Tā 'kàuje wo 'jànje. (fig.) Tā yì'jŕ °'bāng wǒ (°'syàngje wǒ, °dzài 'wǒ jèibyar).

(Motion past an object) tsúng . . . gwò(lái or chyù) with some verb of motion before gwò. / He passed by me. Tā tsúng wǒ 'shēnbyar 'dzǒugwochyule. / The bus went by without stopping. Gūnggùngchì'chē méi'tíng jyòu 'kāigwochyule.

(According to) ànje, jàuje. / We need a map to go by. Wǒmen ànje yì'jāngdìtú dzǒu tsái 'hǎu. / He's not playing by the rules. Tā bú'ànje 'gwēijyu lái.

By a quantity (in buying) lwùn. / Do you sell this by the pound? Nǐ 'jèige lwùn 'bàng mài ma? / No, by the piece. Búshr, shr lwùn 'gèr.

By a means of transportation (if a passenger) dzwò; (if traveling on a horse, bicycle, or anything else one straddles) chí. / He came to this country by boat. Tā shŕ dzwò'chwán dàu 'jèr láide. / Can we get there by rail? Wǒmen dzwò hwǒ'chē kéyi 'dàu(nèr)ma?

By a means of communication, or transportation for freight yùng, tsúng, yóu.

/ Send this by mail. Bǎ 'jèige (yóu yóujèng'jyú) 'jìchyu. / Send this letter by air-mail. Bǎ 'jèige yùng hángkūng 'jìchyu. / This merchandise came by sea. Jèi hwò shr tsúng hǎilù 'yùnláide.

By someone or something who causes an event jyàu, ràng, bèi. / He was struck by lightning. Tā °jyàu (°ràng, °bèi) 'léi dǎle. / The thief was shot in the leg by the police. Nèige syàu'tōurde 'twěishang °jyàu (°ràng) jǐng'chá (gěi) 'dǎle yì'chyāng. / He was beaten up by a gang of hoodlums. Tā °jyàu (°ràng) yìchyúnwúlài (gěi) 'dǎle (yídwùn). or expressed as follows without any of the above words: / This book was written by a Frenchman. Jèibén 'shū shr yíge 'Fàgwo rén 'syěde. / His speech was written by someone I know. Tāde yǎn'shwō 'gǎudz shr wǒ 'rènshrde yíge rén (gěi ta or tì ta) 'syěde.

By an instrument yùng. / This wood was sawed by a machine. Jèige 'mùtou shr yùng 'jīchi 'jyùde.

By (on or before) a time. / He should have been here by now. Tā syàn'dzài yīngdāng 'dàule. or 'Jèige shŕhou tā gāi 'dàule. / I must leave by next week. Wǒ jŕ'wǎn 'syàlǐbài('lǐtou) děi 'dzǒu. / Please return these clothes by Saturday. Jŕ'wǎn lǐbài'lyòu bǎ 'yīshang 'sùnghweilai. / I must finish this by tomorrow. 'Jèige wǒ 'míngtyan fēiděi dzwò'wán bù'kě.

By (during) a time. / He sleeps by day and works by night. Tā 'báityān shwèi-'jyàu, 'yèli dzwò'shŕ.

By a period of time (in renting or paying) àn. / It's rented by the hour. Àn 'jūngdyǎr 'dzū.

By so much excess. / He's taller by three inches. Tā 'gāu sān'tswùn. / This board is thicker than the other by a couple of inches. 'Jèikwài 'bǎndz bǐ 'nèikwài 'hòu ji'tswùn. / Of those two, he's the taller by half an inch. 'Tāmen lyǎngge rénli, 'tā gāu bàn'tswùn. / The winning horse beat the next by a length. Nèipí dé tóujyǎng de mǎ bǎ dì'erpīmǎ 'làle yìmǎ('shēndz nèmma)ywǎn.

By oneself (alone) 'dzìjǐ, (dzìgěr) dzìjǐgěr, 'yígerén. / He did that by himself. 'Nèige shr tā °'dzìjǐ (°dzìgěr, °dzìjǐ'gěr, °'yíge rén) 'dzwòde.

By accident (or chance) méisyǎngdàu, (óuěr) 'pèngshàng (bump into). / This happened purely by accident. Wán'chywán shr méi'syǎngdàude 'shr. or 'Jèihwéi shèr °'jēn shr 'yìdyǎr yě méi'syǎngdàu (°wán'chywán chūhū 'yìwài, °yìdyǎr yě 'búshr gù'yì). / We met by chance the other day. 'Nèityān wǒmen'lyǎ 'pèngshangle. / Some inventions have come by chance. Yǒude fā'míng shr 'óuěr 'pèngshangde.

By profession jàu jŕ'yè lái shwō. / She's a model now by profession. Jàu tā syàn'dzàide jŕ'yè lái shwō, tā shr ge mwótè'ér.

By surprise. / The rain caught me by surprise. Wǒ méi'syǎngdàu hwèi syà-'yǔ. or Hūrán syàchi'yǔlaile, bǎ wo gěi 'lwúnle.

By the way hèi or wǒ 'syǎngchilaile.

By someone's remark. / What did you understand by his remark? Nǐ 'míngbai tā 'wèishémma shwō 'nèijùnghwà ma? or Tā 'nèijyùhwà nǐ 'míngbai tāde 'yìsz ma? / What do you mean by that remark? Nǐ ('jèijyùhwà) shr shémma 'yìsz?

By (means of) . . . ing jŕje, jyèje, kàuje. / He makes a living by selling apples. Tā 'jŕje mài 'pínggwo gwò rdz. / He made his pile by selling that stuff. Tā (kàuje or 'jyèje) mài 'nèijǔng dùngsyi fāde 'tsái.

By order of fèng . . . de (mìng)lìng. / By order of the police (department). Fèng jǐng'chátīngde 'lìng. or Fèng jǐngchá'jyúde (mìng)lìng.

By virtue of (because of). / He passed his tests with honors by virtue of his intelligence. Tā kǎu'shr kǎude hen 'hǎu, shr yīnwei tā hen 'tsūngming. / The job was finished on time by virtue of his hard work.   Yīnwei tā dzwò'shr hen nu'lì swóyi jèijyàn shr̀ tsái ànchī dzwò'wánle.

By way of (route) °tsúng (°dǎ, °yóu) . . . 'nèityau lù.   / They went by way of the Cape of Good Hope.   Tāmen yóu Hāuwàng'jyāu 'nèityáu lù 'dzŏude.

By and large tsúng dà'tǐshang 'kàn.   / By and large the results were satisfactory.   Tsúng dà'tǐshang 'kàn, 'jyēgwǒ hái 'hǎu.

By far.   / This is by far the best hotel in town.   'Jè shr̀ jèr dzwèi 'hǎude lyǔ-'gwǎn, bǐ 'byéde hǎude 'dwō. *or* 'Jèrde lyǔ'gwǎn 'jèijyā bǐ 'byéde dōu hǎude'dwō. *or* 'Jèrde lyǔ'gwǎn shǔ 'jèijyā dzwèi 'hǎu le. *or* 'Jèrde lyǔ'gwǎn 'jèijyā 'ywán bǐ 'byéde 'hǎu.

Day by day yi'tyān bǐ yi'tyān(de).   / I grow fonder of her day by day.   Wǒ 'yi'tyān bǐ yi'tyān de 'syǐhwan tā le.

Do well by dài . . . hǎu, 'dwèiyu . . . hǎu.   / He did well by those kids.   Tā dài nèisyē'háidz hen 'hǎu.

Near by dzwǒjìn, 'fùjìn.   / Is there a restaurant nearby?   °Dzwǒ'jìn (°Fùjìn) yǒu fàn'gwǎr ma?

One by one yíjyànyí'jyànde, yíge'yígède, yíkwàiyí'kwàide, etc.; two by two lyǎngge'lyǎnggede, etc.   / We'll take these matters up one by one.   Jèisyē 'shr̀ dzámen yíjyànyí'jyànde 'bàn.

Stand by.   / They told me to stand by (wait prepared).   Tāmen jyàu wǒ yùbèihǎu 'děngje.

X by Y (dimensions).   / The room is ten feet by twelve feet.   Jèijyan 'wūdz shr̀ 'yíjàng 'kwān, 'yíjàng'èrchr̀ 'cháng.   / This picture frame is nine by nine (inches).   Jèige jìng'kwàngr shr̀ 'jyŏutswùn jyàn'fāng.

BYLAW. syìdzé.

BYPASS. (Passage to one side) syǎulù, syǎudàu(r).

To bypass (detour around) bù'jīnggwò.   / On my next trip I'm going to bypass Washington.   Syàtsz̀ wǒ bùjīnggwò Hwáshèngdwùnle.

CAB. (Taxi) chū'dzūde chì'ché, chū'chāichǐ'chē, líng'gùde chì'chē; often simply called chichē *or* chē.

(On a locomotive) sz̄jīshr̀.

CABBAGE. yángbáitsài; **celery cabbage** báitsài (a Chinese vegetable which is similar to cabbage).

CABIN (On ship or plane) tsāng; **first-class cabin** tóuděng tsāng; **second-class cabin** èrděng tsāng, fángtsāng.

(Pilot's cabin on a plane) sz̄jīshr̀.

(Small rough-built house) syǎu wūr, syǎu fángdz.

CABINET. (Cupboard) gwèidz, chú; (for dishes) wǎngwèi, wǎnchú.

(Of a government) nèigé.

CABLE. (Steel) tyělǎn; (fiber) dà shéngdz; (undersea) hǎidǐdyàn'syàn.

(Message) (hǎidǐ)dyàn'bàu; **send a cable** °fā (°dǎ) (hǎidǐ)dyàn'bàu.

To cable *See* send a cable *above*.

CAGE.　lúngdz;　bird cage nyǎulúngdz.

CAKE.　(Pastry) <u>general terms</u> dyǎnsyin, gāudyǎn; Western-style cakes and pastries yángdyǎnsyin, (including any sweet eatables) tyánshr̃. <u>Designations for specific types of cake end in the following elements:</u> (cakes made with yeast-rising dough, but not in flat and round shape) gāu; (flat and round cakes) bǐng; (cakes made with especially shortened dough) sū; (cakes in a finger shape, but smaller than ladyfingers) tyáur. <u>Some specific types are</u> **date cake** dzǎurgāu; **egg cake** dàngāu *or* tsáudz gāu; **nut cakes** (made with rice flour, in thin oblong slices) yúnpyàngāu; (made with sesame seeds) mábǐng; **almond cake** syǐngrérbǐng; **mooncake** (make especially for the moon festival on the fifteenth day of the eighth month of the lunar calendar) ywèbing; **shortened almond cake** syǐngrérsū; (cake so fragile that it breaks as it enters the mouth) dǎukǒusū; (fried finger-cakes made with rice flour) jyāngmǐtyáur. / I want a catty (Chinese pound) of egg cake. Gěi wǒ 'ná yìjīn tsáudz'gāu. / What kind of cake do you have? Nǐ 'jèr gāu'dyǎn dōu yǒu shémma'yàngrde? / I'd like some cake with my coffee. Wǒ syǎng 'dyǎnsyin gēn jyā'fēi yí'kwàr chr̃. / Do you have fish cakes? Nǐmen yǒu yú 'bǐngr ma?

　　　　Cake of (hunk, piece) kwài. / Could I have a towel and a cake of soap? Wǒ 'kéyi bukéyi yàu yìtyáu 'shǒujin gēn yíkwài 'yìdz?

　　　　To cake nǐng, nǐngshang; (dry) gān; (dry into lumps) gāncheng 'kwàr. / The oil caked in the cold weather. Tyār 'lěng, 'yóu 'nǐngshangle. / The mud caked. Ní 'gān le.

CALENDAR.　'lìfǎ (calendric system); lunar calendar 'yīnlì, <u>also called</u> old calendar 'jyǒulì *or* discarded calendar 'fèilì; solar calendar 'yánglì, <u>also, since its adoption by the National Government, called</u> official calendar 'gwólì *or* Western calendar 'syīlì *or* official international calendar 'gūngli *or* new calendar 'syīnlì; Mohammedan calendar 'Hwéilì *or* Hwéihweilì. <u>In the Chinese lunar calendar a year is divided into twenty-four solar periods, determined by the days on which the sun enters the first or the fifteenth degree of a zodiacal sign. The periods are called</u> jyé *or* jyéchi. / April 18, 1908 (of the Western calendar) corresponds to the eighteenth day of the third month of the thirty-fourth year of the Kuanghsü period. 'Yánglì yījyǒu líng'bānyán 'sżywè shr̃'bā(hàu) shr̃ 'yīnlì Gwangsyù sānshr̃'sżnyán 'sānywè shr̃'bā(r̃). / A Chinese family usually celebrates two New Year's Days per year, one by the solar calendar and one by the lunar calendar. 'Jūnggwo rénjyār chángcháng gwò 'lyǎngge nyán, gwò yíge 'yánglì nyán, yòu gwò yíge 'yīnlì nyán. / In the lunar calendar seventeen intercalary months are added every nineteen years. 'Yīnlì měi shr̃'jyǒunyánli jyā shr̃chíge rwùn'ywè. / In the lunar calendar a month is either twenty-nine or thirty days. Yīnlì yíge 'ywè yǒude yǒu èrshr̃'jyǒutyān, yǒude yǒu 'sānshr̃tyān. / This country has a different calendar. 'Jèigwóde 'lìfǎ gēn 'byéde gwóde bùyí'yàng. / What year is this by the Western calendar? 'Jīnnyan shr̃ 'syīlì 'shémma nyán?

　　　　(Device to show the date) r̃'lì, ywèfēnpár (on wall or desk); 'hwánglì *or* syànshū (in booklet form, with both lunar and solar dates, sometimes more like an almanac).

　　　　(Schedule). / What events are on the calendar this month? <u>is expressed as</u> What business is there this month? 'Jèige ywè 'dōu yǒu shémma 'shr̃?

CALF.　(Of a cow) syǎumǔnyóu(r).

　　　　(Leather) syǎunyóu(r)pí.

　　　　(Of the leg) syǎutwěi, syǎutwěr.

CALL.　(Use as a term of address) jyàu; (formal) chēnghu. / What shall I call her?

(ordinarily). Wǒ 'jyàu ta 'shémma ne? / Call her by her given name. Jyòu 'jyàu tā 'míngdz hǎu le. / What shall I call her (under more formal circumstances)? Wǒ 'dzěmma 'chēnghu ta ne? / You may call her Aunt Chou. Nǐ 'chēnghu ta 'Jōu bwó-'mǔ ba. / In China, husbands and wives never call each other "dear" or "darling" in public. Dzài 'Jūnggwo, fūchī jr̄'jyān méiyou dzài 'byérén 'myànchyán bǐtsž yùng "dear," "darling," 'jèijǔng 'chēnghude. / Some couples call each other by their given names. 'Yǒude fūchī bǐ'tsž 'chēnghu yùng 'míngdz.

(Give a name to) jyàu. / What do you call this in Chinese? 'Jūnggwo hwà 'jèige jyàu 'shémma?

(Classify person or object as such-and-such) °chēng (°jyàu)... wéi...; (classify oneself as) 'dzmíng wéi.... / Some people call him an old China hand. Yǒu 'rén 'chēng ta wéi Jūnggwo'tūng. / He calls himself an old China hand (presumptuous). Tā 'dzmíng wéi Jūnggwo'tūng.

(Awaken) jyàu, jyàusyǐng. / Please call me at 7 A.M. Míngtyan dzǎuchen 'chīdyǎn jūng 'jyàu wo.

(Summon) jyàu, hǎn, jāuhu. / Someone's calling you. Yǒu rén 'jyàu nǐ. / I didn't call you. Wǒ méi'jyàu nǐ a. / Would you call a porter for me? Nǐ gěi wǒ °jyàu (°hǎn) ge jyàu'háng syíng ma? / Call him back (said after he's started to leave). °'Hǎn (°Jyàu) ta 'hwéilai. or Bǎ ta °'hǎnhwéilai (°jyàuhwéilai). / Try calling his name once. Nǐ °'jāuhu (°etc.) ta yìshēng 'shr̄shr̄.

Call someone a certain name shwō... shr̄.... / No? Didn't you just call him a fool? 'Méiyou ma! Nǐ 'bùshr̄ gāng shwō tā shr̄ ge hwún'dàn ma?

Call something big, small, cheap, etc. jywéde, shwō. / I don't call this cheap. Wǒ 'bìng bu'jywéde jèige 'pyányi. / I don't call her cheap. Wǒ 'bìng bu'jywéde tā 'chīngtyau. / Someone called her cheap. Yǒu 'rén shwō tā 'chīngtyau.

Call a meeting jāuji... 'hwèi(yì). / How about calling a special meeting tomorrow? 'Míngtyan jāuji yíge línshr̄ 'hwèiyì 'hǎu buhǎu? but / A meeting was called for March third. 'Dìngde shr̄ sānywè 'sānhàu kāi'hwèi.

Call a meeting to order 'sywānbù kāi'hwèi. / The chairman is calling the meeting to order. Jǔ'syí jèngdzai 'sywānbù kāi'hwèi.

Call people to a meeting jāuji... kāihwèi. / You should call the members to a special meeting to discuss this matter. Nǐ yīnggāi 'jāuji hwèi'ywán kāi yíge línshr̄ 'hwèiyì tǎu'lwùn jèijyàn 'shr̄.

Call someone's **attention** to chǐng... jù yì, chǐng... lyóu syīn °tīng (°kàn) (addressing an audience). / I want to call your attention to this. 'Jèijyàn shr̄ chǐng 'jūwèi lyóusyīn °'tīngje (°jùyì). / May I call your attention to this letter, sir? Jèifēng 'syìn chǐng 'nín lyóusyīn 'kànkan?

Call my or our **attention** to 'tūngjr̄. / Please call our attention to any errors you find. Rúgwo yǒu 'tswòr dehwà, chǐng ni 'tūngjr̄ wǒmen yìshēng.

Call someone's **bluff** yíwèn... jyou wèn'lòule. / He said he was out of money, but I called his bluff. Tā shwō tā méi 'chyán le, kěshr̄ wǒ yí'wàn jyou bǎ ta gěr wèn'lòule.

Call someone **names** mà... yídwùn. / He was so angry that he began calling them names. Tā chì'jíle, 'màle tāmen yídwùn. / You shouldn't have called him names in the first place. Dì'yī, nǐ bùgāi 'mà ta.

Call at someone's **house** dàu... jyā chyu. / I'll call at his house later. Wǒ 'dāi hwěr dàu ta 'jyā chyu.

Call after someone hǎn; (running and calling) jwēije hǎn. / He called after me. Tā jwēije 'hǎn wǒ.

CALL

Call someone **back** (gěi . . .) dǎ 'hwéidyàn, (gěi . . .) hwéi dyàn'hwà. / Your friend said he would call back later. Nǐde 'péngyou shwō tā 'dāi hwĕr hwéi dyàn'hwà.

Call for (require) 'syūyàu, děi. / What does this plan call for? Jèige 'jìhwa 'syūyàu shémma? / This matter calls for prompt attention. Jèijyàn 'shr̀ děi 'kwài bàn.

Call for a person (come to meet and accompany) (lái or chyù) °jyē (°jǎu). / Can you call for me at the hotel? Nǐ néng dàu lyǔ'gwǎn lai 'jyē wo ma?

Call for a person (shout to) hǎn. / He's calling for you. Tā 'hǎn ni ne.

Call for a thing (come and fetch) (lái or chyù) 'chyǔ. / He'll call for it later. Tā 'dāi hwĕr lái 'chyǔ.

Call for help yàu rén chyù °'jyòu (°'bāng) hǎn jyòu'mìng, rǎng jyòu'mìng. / He's calling for help. (out of danger) Tā yàu 'rén chyù 'jyòu ta. or (in doing something) Tā yàu 'rén chyù 'bāng ta. / They didn't hear him call for help. Tāmen méi-'tīngjyan ta °hǎn (°rǎng) jyòu'mìng.

Call in (remove from circulation) 'shōuhwéi, wàng'hwéi shōu. / These notes are being called in. Jèisyē 'pyàudz jèng wàng hwéi 'shōu ne.

Call in a person (summon) chǐng . . . lái. / If you don't get well, call in a specialist. Nǐde 'bìng rúgwo hái bù'hǎu, 'gǎnjǐn chǐng yíwèi jwān'ménde 'dàifu lái.

Call off (cancel) chyǔsyāule, méiyǒu le. / The game has been called off this afternoon. Jyēr 'syàwǔ de bǐ'sài °méi'yǒu le (°chyǔ'syāule).

Call off names, call a roll dyǎnmíng(dz). / Who's to call the roll today? 'Jyērge 'shéi dyǎn'míng? / He wasn't present when the roll was called. Dyǎn'míngde shŕhou tā méi'dàu. / Has my name been called off? 'Dyǎndau wǒde 'míngdz méiyou?

Call on (visit) (lái or chyù) °jyàn (°kàn, °jǎu). / I'll call on him later. Wǒ 'gwò yìhwĕr chyù 'jyàn ta. / The insurance agent called to see you this afternoon. Mǎibǎu'syànde 'syàwǔ lái 'jyàn ni laije. / Someone called on you while you were out. Nǐ 'chūchyu de shŕhou yǒu rén lái 'jàugwo ni.

Call on (make a formal visit) 'bàifǎng, bàiwang. / The ambassador called on you. Dà'shr̀ lai 'bàifǎng ni láije. / I'm going out to make a call. Wǒ yàu 'chūchyu °'bàifǎng (°bàiwang) yíge rén.

Call on someone to do something chǐng, jyàu. / My friend was called on to make a speech. Yǒu 'rén chǐng wǒ 'péngyou yǎn'jyǎng. / They called on me to make a speech. Tāmen chǐng wo yǎn'shwō.

Call out reserves jāuji, dùngywán, jēngdyàu. / That country has called out all its reserves. Nèige gwó'jyā yǐjing bǎ yùbèi'bīng dōu 'jāujile.

Call someone (up) gěi . . . dǎ dyànhwà, jǎu . . . . / I intended to call him up, but I forgot. Wǒ 'běnlái syǎng 'jǎu ta, kěshr 'wàngle.

Be called away (temporarily) jyàudzǒu. / Someone called him away just a moment ago. Yǒu 'rén gāng bǎ ta jyàu'dzǒule.

Be called away (transferred). / I expect to be called away soon. Wǒ bu'jyǒu yěsyǔ hwèi dyàudau 'byéde dìfang chyù.

Be called down (informal) āi (yídwùn) °shwō (°tsēng, °mà); (formal) shòu shēnchr. / I was late and got called down for it. Wǒ yīnwei wǎn 'dàu 'āile yídwùn 'shwō. / When the company commander went to see the divisional commander he got called down. 'Lyánjǎng jyàn 'shŕjǎng de shŕhou shòule yídwùn 'shēnchr.

A call (of an animal) jyàu, jyàuhwan. / Can you imitate the call of an owl? Nǐ hwèi 'sywé yè'māudz 'jyàu ma?

(On the telephone) dyànhwà; **make a call** °dǎ (°jyàu) dyànhwà; **put through a call** tūng dyànhwà, jyàutūng. /Were there any calls for me? Yǒu wǒde dyàn'hwà ma? /Please put the call through right away. 'Gǎnjǐn jyàu'tūngle.

A close call. /That was a close call! 'Hèi! Jēn 'syǎn! or Hǎu'jyāhwo, syǎn-'jǐle!

Be on call jr̄bān. /The doctor will be on call all night. 'Dàifu jěng'yè jr̄'bān.

Be within call yǐ'jāuhu jyou 'lái.

Bugle call hàushēng, lǎbashēng.

Telephone call *see* **a call** (on the telephone) *above.*

CALM. (Of people) 'jènjǐng, °tsūngrúng (°'tsúngrúng), wěn, yì'dyǎr yě bù'hwāngjang. /That girl is very calm. Nèige nyǔháidz hěn 'jènjǐng.

(Of wind, water, etc.). /The sea is calm after the storm. Fēng 'tíngle, làng yě 'syǎu le. /The sea was calm about half the voyage. Yí'lùshang 'chàbudwō yǒu yí'bàr shr̄ méiyou fēng'làng de. /It was a calm voyage. Chwán 'dzǒude hěn 'wěn. /It's been calm all afternoon. Yì'jěng syàwǔ 'yìdyǎr fēng yě méiyǒu.

Keep calm byé hwāng, wěnjùle. /Keep calm everybody! 'Jūwèi byé 'hwāng! or Dà'jyā wěn'jùle!

To calm (down) 'ānjìngsyàchyù; (of children) hǔng, hǔngǎu; (of adults) chywàn-hǎu, 'ān wèi; (from crying) chywànde bùkū; (from being angry) chywànde bùshēngchì. /The children were frightened, so we sang several songs to calm them. 'Háidzmen 'syàjaule, swǒyi wǒmen chàngle jige 'gēer 'hǔng tāmen. /We did our best to calm her down. Wǒmen syǎng 'fár bǎ ta chywàn'hǎule. or Wǒmen syǎng 'fár 'ānwei ta. /We've just done our best to calm her down and now you make her cry again! Wǒmen 'hǎu 'rúngyi bǎ ta chywànde bù'kūle, 'nǐ yòu lái bǎ ta 'rède 'kūchilaile! /It took her some time to calm down. Tā gwòle 'bàntyān 'tsái 'ānjìngsyàchyude.

CAMEL. lwòtwo.

CAMERA. jàusyàngjī, (jàu)syàngsyádz.

CAMP. bīngyíng; (en route) lùyíng.

CAMPHOR. jāngnǎu, cháunau.

CAMPUS. syàuywán.

CAN (COULD). The various meanings of **can** are most often expressed by the verbs hwèi, kéyi *and* néng. Generally speaking, hwèi has the connotation have the skill to, know how to, kéyi be permitted to *and* néng be able *or* permitted to. However, their usage is not clear-cut and in some cases all three could be used to express the same idea. Resultative compounds in the potential form are also used. The differences can be shown as follows: /I can do it. meaning know how to Nèige wǒ 'hwèi. *or* 'Nèige wǒ °'kéyi (°neng) 'dzwò. *or* meaning am qualified to take it on and finish it 'Nèige wǒ dzwòde'lyǎu. *or* 'Nèige wǒ bànde'dàu. *or* meaning am qualified to do it 'Nèige wǒ 'syíng. *or* 'Nèige wǒ néng 'bàn. *or* 'Nèige wǒ néng 'gwǎn. *or* meaning am of the mind to do it, though it is cruel or harsh 'Nèige wǒ dzwòde'chū. *or* 'Nèige wǒ gànde'chū. *or* Wǒ néng syà'shǒu. /I can't do it. meaning I don't know how to 'Nèige wǒ bú'hwèi. *or* meaning am not equipped to 'Nèige wǒ dzwòbu'lyǎu. *or* meaning can't make a successful try 'Nèige wǒ bànbu'dàu. *or* in refusing a favor, *or* meaning make out a plan, *or* conclude a transaction 'Nèige wǒ bùnéng 'bàn. *or* 'Nèige wǒ bù'syíng. *or* meaning can't take on someone else's responsibility 'Nèige wǒ bùnéng 'gwǎn. *or* meaning can't be harsh enough to 'Nèige wǒ dzwòbu'chū(lai). *or* 'Nèige wǒ gànbu'chū(lai). *or* Wǒ bùnéng syà'shǒu.

(Examples with hwèi). /Can you speak English? Nǐ hwèi shwō 'Yīngwén ma? /You can't mean that, can you? Nǐ 'búhwèi shr̀ 'nèige yìsz ba! *or* Nǐ 'shwōde bú-'hwèi shr̀ 'jēnsyīnhwà ba!

(Examples with 'kéyi). /Can I help you in your work? Wǒ 'kéyi bukéyi bāng ni 'dzwò yísyàr? /Can you give me some help here? Nǐ 'kéyi bukéyi 'bāng wo yísyàr 'máng? /You can go now if you wish. Nǐ syǎng 'dzǒu de hwà, syàndzài kéyi 'dzǒu le.

(Examples with néng). /Can you direct me to a bank? Wǒ yàu 'jǎu yíge yín-'háng; (nǐ néng 'gàusung wo) dzěmma 'chyù(ma)? /You can't go swimming in this lake. Nǐ bùnéng dzài jèige 'húli fù'shwéi. /Can't we have these windows open? Dzámen bùnéng bǎ 'jèi jige 'chwānghu dǎ'kāi ma?

(Examples with resultative compounds in the potential form). /He can't see without his glasses. Tā méiyou yǎn'jìngr kànbu'jyàn. /(Can you see it?) Yes, I can see it. Wǒ kànde'jyàn. /I can even see that flagpole. Lyán nèige chí'gān wǒ dōu kànde'jyàn. /I can't see his point. Tā 'jyōujing shr̀ 'dzěmma ge 'yìsz, wǒ kànbu'chūlái.

(A word for **can** is sometimes not included in Chinese). /I don't see how that can be true. Wǒ jyòu kànbuchū'lái °'dzěmma néng 'jēn yǒu 'nàmma yìhwei 'shèr (°'nèige dzěmma hwèi shr̀ 'jēnde). *or* Wǒ 'jywéde bú'hwèi 'shr̀ yǒu chí'shr̀. /He can't read or write. Tā bùshr̀ 'dz̀. *or* (emphatic or impolite) Tā syā'dz̀ bù'shr̀. /I can't understand French. Wǒ bù'dǔng 'Fàwén.

CAN. (Container) gwàr; gwàntou (also means canned food). /Is this fruit out of a can? Jèi 'gwǒdz shr̀ 'gwàntoude ma? /Give me a can of soup. Gěi wo yígwàr 'tāng.

Can opener kāi'gwantoude, kāidz, gwàntou 'kāidz.

To can jwāng gwàntou (pack food in cans); dzwò 'gwàntou (manufacture canned goods). /Both factories can pineapple. Jèilyǎnge gūng'chǎng dōu°jwāng (°dzwò) bwōlwó gwàntou.

Canned gwàntou(de). /Do you have any canned vegetables? Nǐ 'yǒu méiyou 'gwàntou chīng'tsài?

CANAL. yùnhé.

CANARY. (bái)yùnyǎu(r), jīnsz̄chywè.

CANCER. dú'lyóu(bìng); **contract cancer, grow a cancer** jǎng dúlyóu.

CANDIDATE. (For an elective office) 'hòusywǎnrén; (a person next in line for a position) 'hòubǔrén.

CANDLE. là, làjú; (specifically Western style) yánglà, yànglàjú.

CANDLESTICK. là(jú)tár, làtái; (with a prong over which fits a hole bored in the end of the candle) làchyār.

CANDY. táng, tánggwǒr.

CANE. (For walking) gwùndz, gwǎigwèr, shǒujàng.

Sugar cane gānje.

CANNON. (dà)pàu.

CANOE. yóuchwán, syǎuchwán.

CANTEEN. (For water) shwěihú; shwěitǔng (both ends open but stopped up with something).

(For recreation) jyùlèbù.

CANVAS. fánbù; (for an artist's use) hwàbù.

CAP. byǎnmàu; (with a visor) shétoumàu(r). /He was wearing a cap. Tā 'tóushang dàile dǐng byǎn'màu. /Where'd you put my cap? Nǐ bǎ wǒde shétou'màur fàng 'nǎr le?

(Cover for a small object) gàr. /Put the bottle cap on. Bǎ píngdz'gàr 'gàishang.

CAPE. (Garment) dǒupeng (full size); pēijyān (short).

(Of land) dìjyǎu(r), tǔjyǎu(r).

CAPITAL. (Of a province or state) shěngchéng; (of a country) shǒudū, jīngchéng.

(Money invested) 'běnchyán, běr.

Capital letter dà(syě)dzìmǔ.

Capital punishment sžsyíng.

CAPITALIST. dzběnjyā.

CAPITOL. yìywàn.

CAPSULE. (Medicine) yàuwán(dz), wányàu, jyāunáng, yàupyér.

Space capsule tàikūngtsāng.

CAPTAIN. (Of a ship) chwánjǎng. /The captain commands the men on his ship. Chwán-'jǎng gwǎn tā 'chwánshang de rén.

(Of a team) dwèijǎng. /Let's choose a captain. Dzámen 'sywǎn ge dwèi'jǎng ba. /The captain led his teammates into the game. Dwèi'jǎng dàije dwèi'ywán tsān-jyā bǐ'sài.

(Navy rank) shàngsyàu. /That's Captain Davis of the U. S. Navy. Nèiwèi shř Měigwo 'hǎijyūn shàng'syàu 'Davis syānsheng.

(Of a naval vessel) jyànjǎng. /He's captain of a destroyer. Tā shř yíge chyū-jú'jyànde jyàn'jǎng.

(Army rank) shàngwèi. /The soldier saluted the captain. 'Bīng syàng shàng-wèi jìng'lǐ.

(Of a company, battery, troop) lyánjǎng. /Who's the captain of that company? 'Nèilyán lyán'jǎng shř 'shéi?

CAPTIVE. (Prisoner) fúlwǒ.

CAR. (Wheeled vehicle, general) chē; (automobile) chìche, chē; **streetcar** dyànche; **railroad car** hwǒchē; **baggage car** syínglìchē; **dining car** fànchē; **freight car** hwòchē; **sleeping car** wòchē. /Would you like to ride in my car? Nǐ 'ywànyi dzwò wǒde 'chē ma? /Which car goes downtown? 'Něiyílyàng 'chē dàu chéng'lǐ chyù?

CARAVAN. (Of camels) °yílòu (°yídwèi, °yíchwànde) 'lwòtwo; (of trucks, particularly military) yílyè (jyūnyùng) 'chē.

CARBON. (Element) tàn; (collected in a gasoline engine, chimney, etc.) yóuyāndz.

CARBON PAPER. fùsyějr.

CARBURETOR. tànhwàchì, tànhwàwù.

CARD. kǎpyàn, kǎpyàr; (postal) míngsyìnpyàn; (playing) (jr)pái; (calling) míngpyàn.

CARDBOARD. jrbǎn, jrbǎr, mǎfènjr, jrkéer.

CARE. (More or less impersonally) gwǎn, gwǎnjáu; (with more feeling) gwǎnsyīn. /What do you care? meaning Is it your affair? 'Ní gwǎnde'jáu ma? or Ní 'gwǎn ne? or Yùngde'jáu 'ní gwǎn? or meaning Does it affect you? Ai 'ní shémma 'shr le? or meaning What's it to you? Yú 'ní yǒu shémma 'gwānsyi? or Yú 'ní yǒu shémma syǎng'gān? or meaning Why should you worry about it? 'Ní °gwānsyīn shémma ne (°hébì gwānsyīn ne, °gwǎn shémma ne)? or meaning How could you care? 'Ní dzěmma hwèi gwānsyīn ne? /I may never come back. But what do you care? Wǒ 'yěsyǔ hwéibu'lái le. 'Búgwò 'ní shr 'búhwèi gwān'syīn de! /I don't care. 'Méiyou wǒde 'shr. or 'Búshr wǒde 'shr. or Yú 'wǒ 'méiyou 'gwānsyi. or 'Wǒ gwānbu'jáu. or Yú 'wǒ yǒu shémma syǎng'gān? or Wǒ bù'gwǎn. or Wǒ bu'dzàihu. /I do care! Wǒ 'dzěmma gwānbu'jáu? or Wǒ fēi'gwǎn bù'kě! or Wǒ 'dzěmma bugwǎn'syīn ne? or Wǒ 'dzěmma néng bù'gwǎn ne? /Who cares? 'Shéi yě gwǎnbu'jáu? /You needn't care a bit. Nǐ yì'dyǎr yě buyùng 'gwǎn. /He cares a lot. Tā hěn gwān'syīn. /He doesn't care a bit. Tā yì'dyǎr yě bùgwǎn'syīn. /He may go anywhere he likes for all I care. Tā 'ài shàng 'nǎr 'shàng nǎr, wǒ tsái gwānbu'jáu ne. /I don't care what he thinks. Wǒ bu'gwǎn tā dzěmma 'syǎng. or Tā 'ài dzěmma 'syǎng jyou dzěmma syǎng, wǒ tsái bù'gwǎn ne. /I don't care (even) if it is so. Jyòu'shr nèmma-je wǒ yě bù'gwǎn. /I still don't care. Wǒ 'háishr bù'gwǎn.

(If something happens) dzàihu, jyèyì. /Do you think they'll care if we're late? Dzámen yàushr 'wǎnle dehwà ní 'jywéde tāmen hwèi °'dzàihu (°jyè'yì) ma?

Care for (like) syǐhwan. /I don't care for this book. Wǒ bu'syǐhwan jèiběn 'shū. /Don't you care for him even a little? Nǐ yì'dyǎr yě bu'syǐhwan tā ma? or Nǐ jyōujìng 'yǒu yìdyǎr 'syǐhwan ta méiyou?

Care to do something syǎng, ywànyi. /We could go to the movies, but I don't care to. Wǒmen kàn dyàn'yěngr chyu dàushr 'kěyi; búgwò wǒ bù'syǎng chyù.

Care (worry). /He doesn't have a care in the world. Tā yì'dyǎr fán'syīnde shr yě méi'yǒu. /It's family cares (that are worrying him). Shr tā 'jyāshr fán'syīn. /He has too many cares. Tā fán'syīn de shr tài 'dwō le.

(Aid). /Where can I get immediate medical care? Wǒ yàu lì'shr 'jǎu ge 'dàifu, dàu 'nǎr chyù 'jǎu ne?

Care of . . . (of mail) chǐng . . . 'jwǎn. /He addressed the letter care of Mr. Chang. Tāde 'syìn chǐng 'Jāng syānsheng 'jwǎn.

Do with care, give care to (jyā) 'syǎusyīn, lyóushén. /Please do this with great care. Dzwò 'jèige de shŕhou chǐng tè'byé jyā 'syǎusyīn. or Chǐng chyán'wàn 'syǎu-syīn dyǎr 'dzwò. /You should give more care to what you are doing. Nǐ dzwò'shr de shŕhou děi 'dwō lyóu dyǎr 'shén.

Leave something **in** someone's **care** jyāu, 'jyāugei . . . (gwǎn), 'jyāugei . . .

388

'lyàulǐ, jyàu . . . lái 'lyàulǐ. / I'll leave this in your care. 'Jèige wǒ jyāugei 'nǐ le. / He left it in my care. Tā 'jyàu wǒ lái 'lyàulǐ. / I'll leave my valuables in your care. Wǒ jr'chyánde dūngsyi 'jyāugei nǐ 'gwǎn ba.

　　Leave children in the care of gwēi . . . 'yǎng. / The children were left in the care of their grandfather. 'Háidzmen gwēi dzǔ'fù 'yǎng le.

　　Take care of people 'jàulyàu, jàugu, jàuying. / There was no one to take care of the children. 'Méiyou rén 'jàugu jèsye 'háidz. / You take good care of him, don't you? Nǐ 'jàuying tā 'jàuyingde jēn 'hǎu, á?

　　Take care of guests jàuhu, 'jàudài. / You take care of the mayor; I'll look out for the rest. 'Nǐ 'jàuhu shr'jǎng, wǒ gwǎn 'byérén.

　　Take care of things jùyi, dzàiyi, kān, bǎugwǎn, 'jàulyàu. / He doesn't take care of his things at all. Tā 'dzjǐde 'dūngsyi yì'dyǎr yě bujù'yi. / Take care of my money for me. Géi wo 'kānje dyǎr 'chyán.

　　Take care of yourself (exclamation) 'dwōdwō bǎu'jùng.

　　Take care to do something kě chyānwàn. / Take care not to hurt his feelings. Kě chyān'wàn byé jyàu ta nán'gwò. / Take care to have enough money with you. 'Chyán kě chyān'wàn dài'gòule.

CAREFUL. 'syǎusyīn, dāngsyīn; (meticulous, attentive to detail) dzsyi, syisyīn; (mindful, conservative, regardful) jǐnshèn, shènjùng; (attentive, heedful, alert, watchful) lyóushén, lyóusyīn, yùngsyīn; (attentive, respectful) 'jōudàu; (attentive to one's own needs) jyǎngjyou; (careful in dealing with things) dzàiyi; (attentive about or to) jùyi; (on guard against) dīfang; (take care of oneself) bǎujùng. / Be careful in your work. Dzwò 'shr yàu °'syǎusyīn (°dāngsyīn, °dzsyi, °syisyīn, °jǐshèn, °shènjùng, °lyóusyīn, °yùngsyīn, °'jōudàu, °jùyi). / You've got to be careful in dealing with people. Dài 'rén děi yàu °'syǎusyīn (°dāngsyīn, °jǐnshèn, °shènjùng, °'jōudàu, °jùyi). / You've got to be careful in dealing with your employees. Yùng 'rén yàu °'syǎusyīn (°dāngsyīn, °dzsyi, °jǐnshèn, °shènjùng, °yùngsyīn, °jùyi). / Be careful of your conduct. Dwèi dz'jǐde 'syíngwéi děi °'syǎusyīn (°dāngsyīn, °jǐnshèn, °shènjùng, °lyóushén, °jùyi, °bǎujùng). / Be careful with your clothes (don't wear them out too quickly). Chwān 'yīfu děi °'syǎusyīn (°dāngsyīn, °dzsyi, °syisyīn, °jǐnshèn, °shènjùng, °lyóushén, °lyóusyīn, °yùngsyīn, °dzàiyi, °jùyi). / Be careful with him. Nǐ °'syǎusyīn (°dāngsyīn, °lyóushén, °lyóusyīn, °jùyi, °dīfang) ta. / Be careful not to break this. 'Syǎusyīn (°Dāngsyīn, °Lyóushén, °Lyóusyīn) byé bǎ 'jèige 'shwāi le. / Accidents occur when people aren't careful. 'Rén yàushr °bù'syǎusyīn (°bùdāngsyīn, °bùlyóu'shén, °bùlyóusyīn, °búyùngsyīn, °bújùyi, °bùdīfang) de hwà jyòu hwèi chū'shr. / Give this matter your careful attention. Jèijyàn 'shrchíng ni 'tèbyé jù'yi.

CAREFULLY. Expressed with the various words listed under **CAREFUL,** often followed by de. / He laid the eggs carefully in the basket one by one. Tā hěn 'syǎusyīnde 'yígèyigède bǎ jīdàn fàngdzài lándzlǐ. / You must work carefully. Nǐ děi °dāngsyīnde (°syǎusyīnde) dzwò'shr. / Handle the dishes carefully. °Dāng'syīn (°Lyóu'shén, °Syǎu'syīn) yidyǎr ná jèisye pándz. / Spend your money carefully. Yùng 'chyán děi °'syǎusyīn (°dz'syi, °jǐn'shèn, °shèn'jung, °dzài'yi). / Listen carefully. Jùyi 'tīng a.

CARGO. hwò, 'hwòwù.

CARPENTER. mùjyang.

CARPET. dìtǎn.

CARRIAGE. (Horse-drawn) mǎchē; (if open) chǎngchē, chǎngpéngchē; (if enclosed) jyàuchē. / Let's take a ride in a carriage. Dzámen dzwò mǎ'chē 'ràu yísyàr.

(Bearing) 'shénchì (appearance); fēngtsǎi (gait); 'tàidù, 'jyǔjř (conduct). / He has the carriage of a soldier. Tāde °'shénchì (°fēng'tsǎi, °'tàidù, °'jyǔjř) hěn 'syàng ge 'jyūnrén. *or* Tā hěn yǒu 'jyūnrénde °'shénchì (°fēng'tsǎi, °'tàidù, but not °'jyǔjř).

CARRIER. (Ship that carries planes) hángkūngmǔ'jyàn, fēijīmu'jyàn.

CARROT. húnglwóbwo, húlwóbwo.

CARRY. 1. In the meaning convey, transport, bear, support, hold up, Chinese distinguishes a number of different methods of carrying. A sentence with one of these words which implies motion toward the speaker may have in the nearest English equivalent sentence the word bring; if motion away from the speaker is implied the English may have take; hence all information below is relevant to the treatment of the English words bring and take.

(Most general word) ná. / It was carried away by two waiters. I yǎngge 'cháfang ná'dzǒule. / He carried it with him. Tā ná'dzǒule. / What are you carrying in your hand? Nǐ 'shóuli 'náje de shř 'shémma?

(General, meaning take *or* bring along while going through some other motion) dài. / He carried it with him. 'Nèige tā dài 'dzǒule. / Are you carrying arms? Nǐ dàije 'chyāng ne ma?

(In the hand, with arm held down along the side of the body) dīle, dīlou, dīlyou, tí. / The porter will take charge of carrying the bags. Jyǎu'háng gwǎn °'dīle (°etc.) 'syāngdz.

(In the hand(s), with arms chest-high stretched out part way) dwān. / He carries trays in the dining hall. Tā dzài shř'tángli dwān 'pándz.

(In the hand(s), with arms stretched overhead) jyǔ, twō. / The soldier is wading across the brook, carrying his rifle over his head. 'Bīng °jyǔje (°twōje) 'chyāng tāng 'shwěi gwò'hé.

(In palm(s) face up, with the edges pressed together or not, forming a bowl shape) péng, twō. / That bronze statue depicts a man carrying a child in his hand. Nèige túng'syàng 'shóuli twōje yige syǎu'hár. / The two women carried the tray on their palms. Lyǎngge 'nyǔrén yùng shǒu'jǎng twōje nèige 'pándz. / He was carrying a handful of rice. Tā 'shóuli péngje yìbǎ 'mǐ.

(With thumb and finger pinched together, or with tweezers) nyē. / The four men carried the flag by the corners. Nèige 'chídz tāmen 'sżge rén 'yíge nyēje 'yíge jyǎur 'dzǒu.

(Between two fingers other than the thumb, or between an arm and the side of the body) jyā. / He carried the papers between his fingers. Nèijāng 'jř tā yùng shǒu'jřtou 'jyāje 'dzǒu. / He's carrying a couple of books under his arm. Tā 'jyāje lyǎngber 'shū.

(Supporting with the arm(s)) jyà. / They carried the drunk out. Tāmen bǎ dzwèi'gwěi 'jyàchuchyule.

(By making a hook with a finger, or at the elbow or wrist) gōu. / You can carry the bag by using your finger as a hook. Nèige 'dàidz, kéyi yùng shǒu'jřtou 'gōuje.

(On shoulder or neck or high on the back) káng. / I can't carry this bag. Wǒ kángbu'dùng jèige 'kǒudai.

(On the back) bēi. / Carrying the child on his back, he went upstairs. Tā bēije syǎu'hár shàng'lóu.

(On the head) dǐng. / He's carrying a basin of water on his head. Tā 'tóushang dǐngje yìpén 'shwěi.

(Carry something that hangs from some part of the body or the clothing, particularly if it hangs by a strap) gwà, kwà. / He carries a ring of keys on his belt. Tā yāu'dàishang gwàje yíchwan 'yàushr. / He carries a pistol at his side. Tā 'yāuli kwàje yìgan shǒuchyāng. / He went away carrying the bag (hanging by a strap from his arm). Tā bǎ'kǒudài dzài 'gēbeishang 'gwàje dzǒude.

(In a pocket, or in one's clothes) chwāi. / The boy was carrying two cricket containers in his pockets. Syǎu'hár chwāije lyǎngge 'gwōgwòr 'húlùr.

(In a pocket made by folding the lower part of a long gown upward) dōu. / He walked off, carrying the rice in the skirt of his gown. Tā bǎ 'mǐ yùng dà'gwàr dōu-'dzǒule.

(On a pole held horizontally, resting on a man's shoulder or on the shoulders of two men, fore and aft) dān, tyāu. / The peddler was carrying two baskets slung from either end of a pole. Mài'dūngsyide °dānje (°tyāuje) ge 'tyāur.

(On one end of a pole, holding the other end) tyāu. / He entered the room carrying a snake on one end of a bamboo pole. Tā yùng jú'gāndz tyāuje gēn 'chángchung jyou 'jìnlaile.

(On one end of a pole held vertically) dǎ. / Carrying a large flag, he led the student procession. Tā 'dǎje gǎn dà'chí 'lǐngje 'sywésheng yóu'syíng.

(Lift up and carry, when done by two or more people) tái. / They carried the sick man to the hospital. Tāmen bǎ 'bìngrén táidau yī'ywàn chyule. / They carried the sedan chair with a swinging motion. Tāmen bǎ 'jyàudz táide nèmma 'yōuje dzǒu. / They carried him here in a sedan chair. Tāmen yùng 'jyàudz bǎ ta 'táilaile.

(Same as tai but with arms stretched down to lift) dǎ. / Two men carried away a large barrel of wine (with arms stretched down). Lyǎngge rén 'dǎje yídàtǔng 'jyǒu dzǒule.

(Of a horse, mule, donkey, camel) twó. / A mule can carry more than a donkey. 'Lwódz bǐ 'lyú 'twóde dūngsyi 'dwō. / Two army mules can carry one piece of mountain artillery. 'Lyǎngjī jyun'lwó kéyi 'twó 'yìmén shān'pàu.

(Of a vehicle, animal, boat, plane, pipeline) yùn. / Does this railroad carry freight? Jèityau tyě'lù yùn'hwò buyùn? / This pipeline carries enough oil to supply these states. Jèige 'gwǎndz yùnde 'yóu gòu 'jèjishěng 'yùngde. / One plane carries passengers and another carries the luggage. 'Yíjyà fēi'jī yùn chèng'kè, 'yíjyà yùn 'syíngli.

(Of a vehicle, boat, plane) jwāng, dzài. / That car can carry twenty tons. 'Nèilyang chē kéyi °jwāng (°dzài) èrshr'dwùn.

Be able to carry (pulling some vehicle) lādedùng *or* (pushing it) twēidedùng. / Can you carry that much on your cart? Nèmma 'jùng nǐ lāde'dùng ma?

2. Other meanings of carry.

(Be sufficient to get someone somewhere) néng jyàu. / Five dollars will carry you there. Yǒu 'wǔkwài chyán jyou néng 'jyàu ni 'dàu nèr. / Bluffing has carried him to his present position. Jìng kàuje chwēi'nyóu jyūran néng jyàu ta dàu 'jīntyan jèige 'dìwei.

(Conduct sound) chwán. / Water carries sound faster than air. 'Shwěi bǐ 'kūngchì chwán 'shēngyīn chwánde 'kwài.

(Of posture). /He carried his head high. Tā 'yángje tóur 'dzŏu. /The captain carries himself well. Chwán'jǎngde 'shénchì hěn 'hǎu.

(Take care of) yŏu. /That store carries our account. Nèige 'pùdz yŏu wŏmen-de 'jàng.

(Persuade, move) 'gǎndùng. /The speech carried the crowd. Yǎn'jyǎng hěn 'gǎndùng rén.

(In arithmetic) jìn. /Nine plus five plus eight is twenty-two; write two, carry two. 'Jyŏu jyā 'wǔ jyā 'bā, èrshr'èr; syě 'èr, jìn èr.

(Have in stock) mài. /Do you carry men's shirts? Nǐmen mài 'nánrén chwān de chèn'shān ma?

(Of an election) déshèng. /He carried thirty-two states this time. Jèitsz̀ jìng'sywǎn tā déjàule sānshrèrjŏu.

Carry weight (authority) yŏu 'lìlyàng. /His remarks carried great weight. Tāde 'hwà hěn yŏu 'lìlyang.

Carry off (win, take) dé. /Who carried off the first prize? 'Shwéi 'déle °tóu-'jyǎng le? or (in a lottery) °tóu'tsǎi le?

Carry on (an inherited business) 'jyēje dzwò. /He's been carrying on the business since his father retired. Tsúng tā 'fùchin twèi'syŏu(le) yǐ'hòu, tā jyou 'jyēje bǎ 'mǎimai 'dzwòsyachyule. /Can you carry on from here? Nǐ néng tsúng jèr jyē-je 'dzwò ma?

Carry someone **back to** (remind someone of) jyàu . . . 'syángchilai. /That poem of yours carried him back to the days when he was courting his wife. Nǐ nèishou 'shr jyàu ta 'syángchilai gēn ta 'tàitai chyóu 'hwūn de shŕhou le.

Carry something **through** (completion) bàndau dǐ. /Do you think you can carry it through? Nǐ 'syǎng nǐ néng 'bàndau 'dǐ ma?

Be able to carry (support) jīndejù. /How much weight will this bridge carry? Jèige 'chyáu jīnde'jù dwōme 'jùng? or expressed as What's this bridge's load limit? Jèi chyáu de dzàijùng'lyàng shr̀ 'dwōshau?

Be carried (of a motion) 'tūnggwò. /His motion was carried. Tāde tí'yì 'tūng-gwòle.

Be carried out shŕsyíng. /When will this new ruling be carried out? Jèige 'syīn 'gwēidìng jǐshŕ shŕ'syíng?

CART. 'dàchē (drawn by one or more horses or mules); jyàuchē, jyàuchēer (with a framework for a covering, for passengers); 'péngdzchē (with a shade above it); chē in combinations; ox cart nyóuchē; mule cart lwódzchē. /He'll bring the groceries in a cart. Tā hwèi bǎ dzá'hwò yùng 'chē 'sùnglai.

To cart yùng chē followed by a verb of moving. /The sand was carted away. 'Shādz shr̀ yùng 'dàchē 'yùnchyude.

CARTOON. mànhwà(r); (borrowed from English) kǎtūng(hwàr).

CARTRIDGE. hwóyàutǔng(r), dànyàutǔng(r); (entire projectile) dz̀dan.

CASE. (Container) hé, hédz, héer, syádz, syár (usually small, of any material, but not flexible); syāngr, syāngdz, syāng (large box or crate); bāu(r) (of soft material); tàur (of soft material and sheath-like); pencil case chyānbǐbaur, chyānbǐhéer; case for eyeglasses (if of soft material) yǎnjyèngrtàur, (if hard) yǎnjyèngrhéer; bookcase (with a door) shūgwèi, (without a door) shūjyàdz; showcase or display case gwèidz, (with a glass top) bwōli 'gwèidz. /I lost my cigarette case. Wǒ bǎ yān'héer 'dyōule. /He sent us a set of silver in a beautiful case. Tā sùngle wǒmen yítàu dāu'chā, dàije yíge hěn hǎu'kàn de 'syádz. /Don't take the bottles out of the case. Byé bǎ 'píngdz tsúng 'syāngdzli 'náchulai. /I received a case of oranges. Wǒ 'shōudàule yìsyāng 'jyúdz.

(Legal) àndz, gwānsz; (set of facts for one side of a case) 'ànyóu; *or* expressed with measures jyàn; (if detailing successive crimes at a single place) tsz̀; (if detailing simultaneous crimes at different places) chù. /Who's handling this case? 'Shéi bàn jèige 'àndz. /He's lost his case. Tā 'gwānsz dǎ'shūle. /He presented his case well. Tā bǎ 'ànyóu 'chénshùde 'tyáutyáu yǒu'lǐ. /Yesterday there were two cases of robbery. 'Dzwótyan yǒu 'lyǎng°jyàn (°chù) chyáng'àn. /Are there many cases of robbery in this city? 'Chénglǐ chyáng'àn 'dwō ma?

(Medical). /The doctor's out on a case. is expressed as The doctor has gone out to see a sick person. 'Dàifu 'chūchyu kàn 'bìngren chyùle.

(Typographical): uppercase (capitals) 'dàdz̀mǔ; lowercase (small letters) 'syǎudz̀mǔ.

By the case chéngsyāngde, jěngsyāngde, lwùnsyāngde. /This fruit is exported by the case. Jèige shwěi'gwo shr̀ chéng'syāng wàng 'wài 'yùnde.

In case meaning if yàushr, 'rúgwǒ, yù; (just) in case meaning on the long chance 'wànyī, yìfáng 'wànyī; just in case meaning because there may be need *or* use for it yèsyu 'yùngdejáu. /Wait for me in case I'm late. Wǒ yàushr 'wǎnle de hwà, 'děng wo yìhwěr. /In case you don't know, ask Information. Nǐ rúgwǒ bùjr̀'dàu, wèn 'Wènsyùnchù. /In case there's a fire, walk, don't run. Yù yǒu hwǒ'jǐng, màn'mārde dzǒu, byé 'pǎu. /Take warm clothes in case the weather is cold. Dàije dyǎr 'nwǎnhwo 'yīfu ba, 'wànyī 'tyār 'lyánge ne. /It may not rain but you'd better take an umbrella just in case. 'Yǔ yèsyu syàbu'chǐlái, búgwò 'dǐng hǎu háishr bǎ yǔ'sǎn 'náje, yìfáng 'wànyī. /You'd better take it along, just in case. Nǐ 'háishr 'dàije jèige, yèsyu 'yùngdejáu.

In any case bú'lwùn dz̄emma'yàng(r), wú'lwùnrú'hé. /In any case I would follow his advice. Bú'lwùn dz̄emma'yàng wo yàu 'ànje tā'shwō de chyù 'dzwò. /In any case I don't want to go. Wú'lwùnrú'hé wo bùsyǎng 'chyù.

In that case *or* if that's the case rúgwǒ shr̀ 'nèmma hwéi shr̀ dehwà.

Make out a case (legally or otherwise) 'byànhù. /You'll have no trouble making out a case for yourself. Nǐ tì 'dz̀jǐ 'byànhù, jywé bu'hwèi yǒu shémma 'kwùnnan.

Other expressions in English. /That's not the case! 'Búshr̀ 'nèmma hwéi 'shr̀! /She's a sad case! Tā 'jēn kě'lyán.

CASH. (Contrasting with credit) syànchyán, syànkwǎn. /I'll sell it for cash. 'Jèige dūngsyi wǒ yàu mài 'syànchyán. /I can make a cash payment. Wǒ 'kéyi gěi 'syànchyán. /All purchases are on a cash basis. 'Syànchyán jyāu'yì gài bù shē'chyàn.

(Money) chyán. /Is there any cash in the drawer? 'Chōutìli yǒu'chyán ma?

(Small change) 'língchyán. /I haven't enough cash with me; may I pay you tomorrow? Wǒ 'shēnbyar dàide 'língchyán bú'gòu, 'míngtyan hwán ni 'syíng busyíng?

To cash hwàn, dwèisyàn, chyǔ. /Will the manager cash a traveler's check? Jīng'lǐ néng 'hwàn jèijāng lyǔ'syíng jr̀'pyàu ma? /I think I can cash it for you. Wǒ syǎng wǒ 'néng gěi ni 'hwàn. /Will you cash a check for me? Jèijāng jr̀'pyàu nǐ néng gěi wo dwèi'syàn ma? *or* Wǒ ná yìjāng jr̀'pyàu, gēn ni 'hwàn yìdyǎr 'chyán 'syíng busyíng? /I must go to the bank to cash a check. Wǒ jyòu děi dàu yín'háng 'chyù yítàng, chyù chyǔ jāng jr̀'pyàu.

CASHIER. chūnàywán, gwǎnjàngde.

CASKET. gwāntsai.

CAST. (Of metal) jù. / They cast plates from liquid iron. (if large) Tāmen yùng rúng-'tyě jù tyě'bǎn *or* (if small and thin) (tyě)'páidz.

    Cast <u>people for a play</u> fēn'pèi (yǎn'ywán), sywǎn. / He's casting a group of amateurs for that show. Tā jèngdzài 'fēnpèi nèisyē pyàuyŏu lái 'yǎn nèichū 'syì. *or* Tā 'sywǎnle syē pyàu'yŏu yǎn nèichū 'syì.

    Cast a horoscope swàn ge mìng. / Let's cast a horoscope. 'Dzámen swàn ge 'mìng ba.

    Cast a net sā wǎng. / The fisherman cast his net. Dǎ'yúde sā 'wǎng. / He pulled up a cartload at one cast of the net. Tā 'yìwǎng 'dǎde gòu jwāng yì'chē de.

    Cast a shadow jàuchu yǐngdzlai. / The weak light casts a weird shadow on the wall. 'Gwāng hěn 'rwò, dzài 'chyángshang 'jàuchulai de 'yǐngdz gwài kě'pàde.

    Cast anchor pāumáu, tóumáu, syàmáu. / We'll cast anchor at daybreak. Wǒmen 'tàiyang 'chūlai de shŕhou pāu'máu.

    Cast ballots tóupyàu. / How many people cast ballots today? 'Jīntyan tóu'pyàude yŏu 'dwōshau rén?

    Cast dice jŕ shǎidz. / Watch his hand when he casts the dice. Tā jŕ ('shǎidz) de shŕhou 'kànje tāde 'shŏu.

    Cast light 'shèchu gwāng. / The spotlight cast a cone of light on the stage. Húgwāng'dēng dzài 'táishang 'shèchu yíge ywánjwēi'syíngde 'gwāng lai.

    Cast the lead (or line, in fishing) rēng jwèr, pyě jwèr. / Cast the lead farther out. Bǎ jwèr 'dzài °rēng (°pyě) 'ywǎn dyar.

    Cast <u>someone</u> into prison syàyù. / He was cast into prison for beating up a judge. Tā yīnwei 'dǎle ge fǎ'gwān syà'yù le.

    Cast off (of a ship) kāichwán. / The captain says we're ready to cast off. Chwán-'jǎng shwō wǒmen jyòu yàu kāi'chwán le.

    Be cast ashore 'pyāudàu 'ànshang. / He was cast ashore after five days. 'Wǔ-tyān yǐhòu tā pyāudau 'ànshang láile.

    Be cast for (of ballots) dé (number) 'pyàu. / How many ballots were cast for their candidate? Tāmende hòu'sywǎnrén yí'gùng déle 'dwōshau pyàu?

    Be cast in <u>such-and-such a role</u> dāng, chyù. / Who was cast in the leading role? 'Shwéi 'dāngde jǔ'jyǎu?

    A cast (for a broken bone) shŕgāu. / His broken arm was placed in a cast. Tā 'shéle de gēbei yùng shŕ'gāu 'bāuchilaile.

    (Of a show) (dēngchǎng)yǎn'ywán. / The cast (of players) has not been chosen yet. Dēngchǎng yǎn'ywán hái 'méiyou fēnpéi'hǎu.

    Cast-off (discarded) yàu rēng de, bú'yàule de. / They want to take our cast-off clothing. Tāmen yàu bǎ wǒmen yàu 'rēng de 'yīfu ná'dzŏu.

CASTOR OIL. bìmá(dž)'yóu.

CASUALTIES. sžshāng, shāngwáng.

CAT. māu. / Our cat keeps the mice away. Wǒmende 'māu bǎ 'lǎushǔ 'syàde bùgǎn lái 'nàu. / They've got a tomcat, a she cat, and a litter of kittens. Tāmen yŏu yìjŕ 'gūngmāu, yìjŕ 'mǔmāu, hái yŏu yìwō 'syāumāur. / When you scratch a cat under its chin it purrs. Gěi māu 'bwódz dǐsya jwā'yǎngr, 'māu jyòu dǎ 'hūlu. / Lions and tigers belong to the cat family. Shr̄dz gēn 'láuhǔ shr̀ 'shǔyú māu'kē de.

Catcalls dàuhǎur. / The catcalls angered the actor. Yǒu'rén jyàu dàu'hǎur, bǎ chàng'syìde gěi chì'hwài le.

Special expressions in English. / They're leading a cat-and-dog existence. (specifically of husband and wife). Tāmen 'gūmulyǎ lǎu bàn'dzwēi. / A cat has nine lives. The equivalent Chinese saying is: / A cat has seven lives, a dog has eight. 'Māu you 'chīmíng, 'gǒu yǒu 'bāmíng.

CATALOGUE. 'mùlù; (in book form) mùlù 'běndz, mùlùběr; (sent out by a school) shwōmíngshū, jyǎnjāng.

CATCH (CAUGHT). (With one's hand or legally) ná, dǎi, děi, dēi, dzwō, jwā; or any of these plus jù giving the meaning catch and hold on to or catch and stop. / The police are trying to catch the criminals. Syún'jǐng dzài syàng'fár °ná (°dǎi, °děi, °etc.) nèisyē 'fànrén. / The police caught two of them. Syún'jǐng °náju (°dàiju, °děiju, °etc.) 'lyǎ le. / We caught two thieves last night. Wǒmen dzwórge yèli °náju (°etc.) lyǎ 'dzéi.

Catch a child doing mischief 'chyáujyàn, 'dēiju, 'dǎiju. / Don't let your mother catch you doing that. Nǐ gàn 'nèige byé jyàu nǐ 'mā 'chyáujyàn. / You'll get caught if you do that again. Nǐ yàu 'dzài gàn 'nèige jyou yàu jyàu 'rén 'dēijule.

Catch someone running (just in fun) děi, dēi. / See if you can catch me! 'Kàn nǐ néng 'děi wo ma! or Jyàu ni děi!

Catch someone by grasping part of his body or clothes jyōu, 'jyōuju. / Catch him by his ear! 'Jyōuju tāde 'ěrdwo!

Catch a disease dé; (of a cold) jāulyáng. / I think you must have caught the flu. Wǒ syǎng nǐ yi'dìng shr̀ 'déle lyóusyíng(sying) gǎn'màu le. / There's danger of catching the flu in this weather. 'Jèijǔng tyānchi hěn 'rúngyi dé jùng shāng'fēng. / I caught a cold over the weekend. Wǒ jōu'mwòde shŕhou jāu'lyángle.

Catch a missile flying through the air 'jyē(jù). / Here, catch this! 'Hèi! 'Jyēje! or 'Hēi! 'Jyējù! or 'Jyē jèige! / The boy caught the ball. Syǎu'hár bǎ 'chyóur 'jyējùle.

Catch a vehicle scheduled at a certain time gǎn, 'gǎnshàng. / Hurry up if you want to catch the bus. Nǐ yàu syǎng gǎn gūnggùngchì'chē kě děi 'kwài dyǎr le. / I have to catch the 5:15 train. Wǒ děi 'gǎn wǔdyǎn shŕ'wǔ de 'chē.

Catch a word or a name tīngchīngchu. / I didn't catch his name. Wǒ méitīng-'chīngchu tā 'míngdz shr̀ shémma.

Catch an insect (with a swatter or insecticide) dǎ, 'dǎjáu; (with fly paper) jān, 'jānju, 'jānshàng; (by hand) 'dzwàn(jù), 'jwā(jù), 'chāu(jù).

Catch one's breath chwǎn (yì)kǒu 'chyèr.

Catch one's eye yǐn 'rén jù'yì. / The neckties in the window catch one's eye. 'Chwānghulide lǐng'dài hěn yǐn 'rén jù'yì.

Catch fire jáu, jáuhwǒ, jáuchi 'hwǒlai. / The car caught fire when it turned over. 'Chē 'fānle de shŕhou jáuchi 'hwǒ láile. / The wood's so dry that it will catch fire easily. 'Mùtou 'gānde yì 'dyǎn jyou 'jáu.

Catch fish (with a net) dǎ; (with a rod) dyàushanglai. / They caught a lot of fish with one cast of the net. Yì'wǎng dǎle hěndwōde 'yú. / They caught twelve fish. Tāmen 'dyàushanglai shŕ'èrtyáu 'yú.

Catch hold of something in order to move it (if the thing is at rest) 'nájù, 'dzwànjù; (if the thing is already lifted) 'táijù. / Catch hold of the other end and we'll move this. 'Dzwànjùle 'nèitóur dzámen hǎu bǎ 'jèige 'nwókai.

Catch sight of 'chyáujyàn. / If you catch sight of him, let us know. Nǐ 'rúgwǒ 'chyáujyàn ta dehwà, 'gàusung wǒmen yì'shēng.

Catch the fancy of <u>some group of people</u> dzài . . . li shr'syīngchilai. / This has caught the fancy of the women. 'Jèige dzài 'nyúrénli shr'syīngchilaile.

Catch on <u>to an idea, suggestion</u> sywéhwèi, míngbai. / We told him how and he caught on quickly. 'Jīng wǒmen 'yì jr'dyǎn ta hěn 'kwàide jyòu sywé'hwèi le. / Do you catch on? Nǐ 'míngbaile ma?

Catch on (of a fashion, habit) (shr)'syīngchǐlái. / This fashion caught on very recently. Jèige 'yàngdz shr dzwèi'jìn tsái shr'syīngchilai de.

Catch onto <u>a rope or part of a man's body, or clothing</u> 'jyōu(jù). / Catch onto this rope. 'Jyōujùle jèi 'shéngdz. / Catch onto his arm. 'Jyōuju tāde 'gēbei.

Catch up <u>with</u> (having fallen behind) 'jwēishàng, 'gǎnshàng, 'gǎnshàngchyu. / We're behind and are trying to catch up. Wǒmen lwò'hòule, dei 'gǎnshangchyu. / Since I walked faster than he did, I soon caught up with him. Yīnwei 'wǒ bǐ ta 'dzǒude 'kwài, wǒ yì 'hwěr de gūngfu jyòu 'jwēishàng ta le. / Go on ahead and I'll catch up with you. Nǐ 'syān dzǒu ba, yì'hwěr jyòu 'jwēishang nǐ.

Get caught <u>by traffic or in a traffic jam.</u> / I got caught in a traffic jam. 'Chē dōu 'jǐshàngle, wǒ bùnéng 'dzǒu le.

Get caught <u>in the rain.</u> / He got caught in the rain. Tā jyàu 'yǔ gěi 'lwúnle.

Get caught <u>in a trap</u> (of animals). / The mouse got caught in the trap. (snapping-type trap) 'Hàudz jyàu 'jyādz 'jyājùle. (wire trap) 'Hàudz jìnle 'kwāngdz, chūbu-'láile. (box trap) 'Hàudz °jìnle 'hédz, chūbu'lái le (°dzài 'hédzli 'dàijule, °gwān-dzai 'hédzli le).

Get caught <u>in a trap</u> (of a human being falling for a scheme). / He got caught in their trap. Tā 'shàngle tāmende chywān'tàur le.

Get caught <u>in a room, etc</u>. / He got caught in the room. (shut up in) Bǎ tā 'gwāndzai 'wūdzli le. (surprised by someone's arriving) Bǎ tā 'dǔdzai 'wūdzli le.

Get caught <u>by something closing, as a door</u> jǐ, 'jǐjù, yǎn, 'yǎnjù. / My hand was caught in the door. Wǒde 'shǒu jyàu 'mén gěi 'jǐle. / The door caught his sleeve. 'Mén bǎ tāde 'syòudz 'jǐjule.

Get caught <u>under something pressing down</u> (of something that moves only up and down) 'yā(jù); (of something that moves horizontally) 'nyǎn(jù), 'yā(jù). / My foot was caught under the leg of the table. Wǒde 'jyǎu jyàu °jwǒdz'twěr 'yājùle. or under the wheel of the car. °chē'lwúndz 'nyǎnjule (or yājùle).

Get caught <u>by a ring or loop-shaped object</u> 'gwàshàng, 'tàushàng. / His neck got caught (in the loop). Tāde 'bwóer gěi 'tàushangle.

Get caught <u>by a hook-shaped object</u> gōu, 'gōushàng, 'gōujù.

Get caught <u>by any hook-shaped object so that the thing caught hangs down</u> gwà, 'gwàshàng 'gwàjù.

Get caught and torn gwǎ, gwǎpwò. / My coat got caught on that hook and was torn. Wǒde shàng'yī jyàu nèige 'gōur gěi gwǎ'pwòle.

A catch (on a door, etc.) 'chāgwār, chāsyāu. / The catch on the door is broken. Mén 'chāgwār 'shéle.

Play catch rēng 'chyóur wár. / Let's go play catch. Dzámen rēng 'chyóur wár chyù ba.

Special expressions in English. / That's his catch word. 'Nèi jyòushr tā 'lǎu ài 'shwō de 'hwà. / But there's a catch to it. Kěshr 'lǐtou 'hái yǒu ge 'wèntí. / We'll have to catch as catch can for the time being. Wǒmen mù'chyán jr̀ 'hǎu bù-'gwǎn sānchiērshr'yīde 'néng dzěmmaje jyòu 'dzěmmaje.

CATERPILLAR. 'máu(mau)chúng.

CATHOLIC. (Person) Tyānjǔjyàutú, Syìntyānjǔ'jyàude rén; (quality) tyānjǔjyàude; Catholicism Tyānjǔjyàu.

CATTLE. nyóu.

CAULIFLOWER. (yáng)tsàihwār.

CAUSE. yīn in such forms as the following: **cause of death** sžyīn; immediate cause jìnyīn; ultimate (remote) **cause** ywǎnyīn; **cause and effect** yīngwǒ; (reason) ywányīn, ywányóu, ywángu. / Can you explain the cause for the delay? Dān'wù le de ywán'yīn nǐ néng (gěiwo) 'jyǎng yijyǎng ma? / That's not the cause, that's the result. 'Nèige búshr 'ywányīn, nèi shr̀ jyé'gwǒ. / The cause of his death was heart failure. Tāde sž'yīn shr̀ 'syīndzàng shwāi'rwò.

(A movement, great purpose) jèngyì (good cause). / He died for a good cause. Tā wèi jèng'yì 'sžde.

To cause trouble, unpleasantness rě, rěchu(lai), néngchu(lai). / He caused a lot of trouble for us. Tā'gěi wǒmen °'rěle hěn dwō 'shr̀ (°'rěchu hěn dwō 'shr̀ lai).

Cause an accident chū, 'fāshēng. / What caused the accident? Shr̀ dzěmma 'chūde shèr?

Cause . . . to (be) ràng, jyàu. / Sorry to cause you any inconvenience. Dwèi-bu'jù, jyàu ni 'máfan.

CAVE. (shān)dùng.

CEDAR. (Tree) 'bǎishù; (wood) bǎimù.

CEILING. wūdǐngdz; (if of paper) 'dǐngpéng. / There's a crack in the ceiling. Wū-'dǐngdz yǒu ge lyé'wér. / Can you reach the ceiling? Nǐ gòude'jáu 'dǐngpéng ma? / All the rooms have high ceilings. is expressed as All the rooms are very high. Swǒyǒude 'wūdz dōu hěn 'gāu.

(Aeronautical). / The airplanes are flying despite the low ceiling. 'Swéirán 'yúntsai hěn 'dī, fēi'jī 'réngjyòu 'fēi.

Ceiling price gwānjyà. / The salesman is asking more than ceiling prices. Mài 'dūngsyi de rén yàu de 'chyán bǐ 'gwānjyà 'gāu.

CELEBRATE. jìnyàn; (formal) chìnghè, chìngjù. / What holidays do you celebrate? Nǐ 'dōu jì'nyàn 'nèi jǐge jyà'chī? / Let's celebrate. Dzámen děi chìng'hè.

Celebrate the memory of chúngbài, dzànměi. / People in general celebrate the memory of their heroes. Yì'bānrén chúng'bài yīng'syúng.

CELEBRATION. (Large formal party) chìngjuhwèi. / They had a big celebration. Tāmen 'kāile yíge hěn dàde chìngjù'hwèi.

CELERY. chíntsài.

CELL. (In a jail) jyānfáng; (unit of protoplasm) syìbāu.

CELLAR. dìjyàu, dìyìndz; (for wine) tsángjyŏushr̀.

CELLOPHANE. tòumíngjr̆, bwōlijr̆.

CELLULOID. jyăsyàngyá (lit. false ivory).

CEMENT. (Not clearly distinguished from concrete) yánghwēi, shwĕiní, shwĕiméndīng.

CEMETERY. féndì; (public) gūngmù.

CENSOR. (An official) jyănchágwān, yùshr̀; (one who censors mail) jyăncháywán.

To **censor** jyănchá.

CENSUS. (Data) rénkŏutŭng'jì, rénkŏudyàu'chá; (of individuals) hùkŏu; (of families) hùjì.

CENT. yìfēn(chyán); three cents sānfēn chyán; ten cents yìmáu chyán; fourteen cents yìmáu 'sż(fēn chyán); fifty-seven cents wŭmáuchī(fēn chyán); . . . cents NU-fēn (chyán) (for amounts less than ten cents), NU-máu (chyán) (for ten cents or multiples of ten cents), NU-máu-NU(fēn chyán) (for multiples of ten cents plus one to nine cents). /Got a four-cent stamp? Yŏu 'sānfenchyánde yóu'pyàu ma? /I don't have a cent. Wŏ yìfēn chyán yĕ méiyŏu.

CENTER. jūngsyīn; (center point) jūngsyīndyăn, 'jèngdāngjūng. /Aim for the center of the target. Wàng 'băde jūng'syīn 'myáu. /At the center of the pool is a fountain. Dzài 'chŕdzde 'jèngdāngjūng yŏu yíge pēn'chywán.

Center of a circle 'ywánsyīn. /A radius (of a circle) is the straight line from the center to any point of the circumference. Tsúng 'ywánsyīn dàu ywán'jōushang rèn'hé yì'dyăn de 'jŕsyàn jyàu bàn'jìng.

Center of gravity 'jùngsyīn.

Industrial center 'gūngyè jūng'syīn; mining center 'kwàngyè jūng'syīn; etc. /Isn't this city an industrial center? Jèi'chéng 'búshr ge 'gūngyè jūng'syīn ma?

To center (put at the center) jèng, bùwāi; (in photography) dwèijèng. /This way it'll center right. 'Jèmmaje jyòu °'jèngle (°bù'wāile). /You didn't center (the shot) right. Nĭ méibă 'jìngtóu dwèi'jèng le. /That's not centered right. Wāile yìdyăr.

Center on (of thoughts, attention) jíjūng. /The attention of that crowd is centered on the policeman. 'Nèichyún rénde yăn'gwāng 'chywán jí'jūngdzài jĭng'chá shēnshang le. /All his thoughts were centered on her. Tā swóyŏude sż̄syăng 'dōu jí'jūngdzài 'tā shēnshang le.

CENTRAL. (Governmental; in contrast to local or provincial) 'jūngyāng. /Formerly the central government was in Nanking. Tsúng chyán Jūngyāngjèngfŭ dzài Nánjīng.

(Most important) dzwèi'jùngyàude. /He's left out the central point. Tā méi-'tí dzwèi 'jùngyàu de yì'dyăn.

Central office dzŭngjyú, dzŭngchù, dzŭngháng, depending for the second element on the official designation of the particular office.

Central location. /This hotel has a central location (near the stores). Jèige lyŭ'gwăn lí syŭ'dwōde 'pùdz dōu 'jìn.

Central (telephone term) dzŭngjyú. /Central doesn't answer. Dzŭng'jyú 'méi rén gĕi 'jyē dyàn'hwà.

CENTURY. 'shṛjì.

CERTIFICATE. 'jèngshū, jèngmíngshū, jèngmíng wén'jyàn.

CHAIN. lyàndz; **watch chain** byăulyàr, byăulyàndz; **gold watch chain** jīnbyăulyàr; **iron chain** tyĕlyàndz, tyĕlyàr. /Must I put a chain on the dog? Wŏ 'fēi dĕi bă 'gŏu yùng 'lyàndz 'swŏchilai ma? /A link of this chain is broken. Jèigēn 'lyàndz yŏu yíge 'hwándz 'lyèle.

Chain of events shṛ'shṛde yăn'byàn. /I haven't kept up with the chain of events. Wŏ méi'dé jī'hwèi lyóu'yì shṛ'shṛde yăn'byàn.

Chain of stores *or* **restaurants** lyánhàu. /He operates a chain of restaurants. Tā 'kāile hău 'syēge fàn'gwăr, 'dōu shṛ lyán'hàu.

Chain bridge swŏchyáu.

Mountain chain shānmài.

To chain (up) swŏ, swŏchilai. /The dog was chained up all night. 'Gŏu 'swŏle yí'yè. /Then he was chained up. Rán'hòu 'bă ta gĕi 'swŏchilaile.

CHAIR. yĭdz. /This is a more comfortable chair. 'Jèibă yĭdz 'bĭjyău 'shūfu dyăr. /Please sit down on this chair. Chĭng dzwò(dzai) jèibă 'yĭdz(shang).

(Chairman) jŭsyí. /Will the chair permit such a motion? Jŭ'syí hwèi 'jyēshòu 'jèiyàngde tí'yì ma?

(Professorship) jyăngdzwò. /That chair was established especially for him. Nèige jyăng'dzwò shṛ 'jwān wèi 'tā shède.

Take the chair dāng jŭsyí. /The meeting began with the president taking the chair. Hwèi'jăng dāngle jŭ'syí, sywānbù kāi'hwèi.

Sedan chair jyàu(dz).

CHALK. (In natural state; geological term) báiè; (for writing) fēnbĭ.

CHAMBER. (Sleeping room) 'wòshṛ.

(In machinery terms) shṛ; **firing chamber** 'dànshṛ. /The firing chamber of this gun is empty. (technical military) Jèigăn 'chyāng de 'dànshṛ shṛ 'kūngde. (less technical) Jèigăn 'chyāng méi'jwāng dz'dàn.

Chamber of commerce shānghwèi. /The chamber of commerce holds regular meetings. Shāng'hwèi àn'chī kāi'hwèi.

Chamber pot yèhú, nyàupén, nyàupér. /The chamber pot is kept in the washstand. Yè'hú dzài syĭlyăn'gwèide 'lĭmyan.

CHAMBERMAID. nyŭyùngren.

CHANCE. (Opportunity) 'jīhwèi. /He has no chance to get ahead. Tā méiyou °wàng 'chyán jìn de 'jīhwei (°'shēng de 'jīhwei). *but* /Give me a chance to explain. Ràng wo jyĕ'shṛ yísyàr. /Give him a chance. Gĕi ta ge 'jīhwei ba.

(Hope, prospect) 'syīwàng. /I believe you have a good chance to succeed. Wŏ syàng'syìn ni chéng'gūng de 'syīwang hĕn 'dà. /He stands a good chance to win. Tā hĕn yŏu 'yíng de syīwang. /Is there any chance of catching the train? 'Hái yŏu 'syīwang gănshang hwŏ'chē ma?

(Lottery ticket) tsǎipyàu.

Be a chance that yésyu hwèi, yésyu néng. / There's a chance that he may be alive. Tā 'yésyu hwèi hái 'hwóje. / I came because I thought there might be a chance of buying a pack of cigarettes here. Wǒ syǎng 'yésyu dzài 'jèr néng mǎidau yìbāu-'yān, 'swóyi láile.

Game of chance (yìjǔng)dǔ'bwó.

Meet by chance 'yùshàng, (ǒu'rán) 'péngshàng. / I met him by chance. Wǒ gēn ta shr̀ 'yùshangde. (*See also* **To chance upon.**)

Take chances màu'syǎn, dà'yì. / Don't take any chances. Byé màu'syǎn. *or* 'Yìdyǎr byé dà'yì.

Take a chance 'pèng yipèng 'yùnchi. / Let's take a chance on staying here. Dzám 'pèng yipèng 'yùnchi, 'jùsya ba. / He decided to take a chance, and bingo, he won the jackpot! Tā syǎng 'pèng yipèng 'yùnchi, shwéi 'jr̀dau 'yísyàdz jyòu 'dōu gěi 'yíngle chyùle.

Take a chance (try once) 'shr̀ yísyàr. / He may not be in, but we'll take a chance (and go on the possibility that he is). Tā 'yésyu méidzài 'jyā, dzáman kéyi 'shr̀ yísyàr.

To chance upon. / He chanced upon that invention. Tā 'nèige fā'míng shr̀ ǒu-'rán 'péngshangde.

CHANGE. (Alter, convert) gǎi (change partially or gradually, as by repentance, or as a rug fades and changes color when exposed to the sun); byàn (change radically, sometimes suddenly and into a state hardly recognizable, as water to ice, or magically, as a witch to a dog); hwà (change from one physical state to another, but only in the direction of solid to liquid, or liquid to gas, not vice versa). These words occur in compounds with combined meanings as gǎi'byàn *or* byàn'hwà; with any of the three chéng may be used as a post-verb to give the meaning **change into,** *or* dàu to give the meaning **change to** a degree, an extent. Examples of most of these follow. / I changed two lines in your manuscript. Nǐde 'gǎudz wǒ gěi 'gǎile lyǎng'háng. / You must change your bad habits. Nǐde hwài'máubing °děi 'gǎi yigǎi (*or* (more seriously) °fēi 'gǎi bù'kě). / Habits are hard to change. Syígwan hěn nán'gǎi. / You've changed; you're a man now. Nǐ 'byàncheng ge 'dàrén le. / He's changed. Tā 'byàn le. / The ghost mopped his face and changed into a beautiful woman. Nèige 'gwěi bǎ 'lyǎn yì-'mwǒ jyou 'byànchengle ge pyǎulyangde 'nyǔrén. / She suddenly changed into a large white cat. Tā 'hūrán 'byànle ge dà bái'māu. / Do you expect the weather to change today? Nǐ 'jywéde 'jīntyan hwèi byàn 'tyār ma? / In the evening the clouds change color constantly. Hwáng'hwūnde yúntsai shŕshŕ byàn 'shǎr.

(Exchange) hwàn. / The minister will be changed for another. Bù'jǎng yàu hwàn 'rén le. / If the government is bad, change it. 'Jèngfǔ bù'hǎu, 'hwàn ge 'syīnde. / Let's change the color of this room. Dzámen bǎ jèige 'wūdzde 'yánsè 'hwàn yihwàn, 'hǎu buhǎu? / I think I'll go back to the store and change this. Wǒ syǎng 'dzài dàu 'pùdz 'chyù yitàng bǎ 'jèige 'hwànle. / Ten of their servants have been changed already. Tāmen 'yǐjing hwànle 'shŕge 'dìsyarén le. / We have to change trains at the next station. Dzámen syà'jàn děi hwàn 'chē. *but* (in changing from one type of vehicle to another) / You'll have to change to a bus at Cambridge. Nǐ děi dzài Jyàn'chyáu 'gǎi dzwò gūnggùngchì'chē.

Change money hwan. / Can you change these bills for me? Nǐ 'tì wo 'hwàn yísyàr jèisyē 'pyàudz, kéyi ma? / Do you change American money (into your currency)? Nǐmen dwèi'hwàn 'Měigwo chyán ma?

Change appearance gǎi 'yàngr. / This place hasn't changed any since you left. Dztsúng nǐ 'dzǒule yǐ'hòu, 'jèr 'yìdyǎr yě méigǎi'yàngr. / You've changed a lot

400

since I last saw you (general, of appearance, habits, speech, or anything). Nǐ gēn wǒ 'shàngtsž 'kànjyan nǐ de shŕhou 'gàile hěn dwōyàng.

Change a date. / They've changed the date. Tāmen °'gàile (°'hwànle) ge 'ŕdz. / Would you like to change the date? Nǐ syǎng °'gǎi (°'hwàn, °'lìng tyāu lìt. again choose) ge 'ŕdz ma?

Change clothes (of style) gǎi; (to a different outfit) hwàn. / He changed to wearing Western-style clothes. Tā 'gǎi chwān 'syīfú le. / He changed into a new suit. Tā 'hwànle yìshēn 'syīn yīfu. / I've got to change. Wǒ děi hwàn 'yīshang. / She's changing her clothes now. Tā syàndzài 'jèngdzài hwàn 'yīfu ne.

Change hands dǎu'shǒu, hwàn'jǔr. / The hotel has changed hands several times. Lyǔ'gwǎn °'dǎugwo háuji'tsž shǒu le (°'hwànle háujige 'jǔr le).

Change one's mind °gǎi (°byàn) 'júyi; (of loyalty, or in a love affair) byàn-'syīn. / I thought of staying, but I've changed my mind. Wǒ 'běnlái syǎng dzài jèr 'dāije, kěshr wǒ gǎi 'júyi le. / When a woman changes her mind there is no way to prevent it. 'Nyǔrén byànle 'syīn, méi 'fár wǎn'hwéi. / She changes her mind every minute. is expressed as Her mind isn't fixed; one minute it's this way, the next minute it's that way. Tāde 'syīn bú'dìng; yìhwěr 'jèmmaje yìhwěr 'nèmmaje de.

Change one's tune °hwàn (°gǎi, °byàn) 'kǒuwěn. / He used to talk against the governor, but now he's changed his tune. Tā tsúngchyán 'fǎndwèi shěng'jǎng, kěshr syàn'dzài 'hwànle 'kǒuwěn le.

A change (act of changing) is expressed in terms of the verbs given above. / There'll be a change in the political setup. Jěng'jyú yàu chǐ 'byànhwà. / No changes are allowed after the merchandise leaves the store. 'Hwòwù chū'mén, gài bútwèi-'hwàn. / I don't see any change in your appearance, but your voice has changed a lot. Nǐde 'myànmàu wǒ kànbu'chū shémma gǎi'byàn lai, kěshr 'shēngyin 'gǎile hěn 'dwō.

(Chemical) hwàsywé byàn'hwà. / A chemical change took place. 'Chǐle hwàsywé byàn'hwà le.

For a change. / Let's have shrimp for a change. Dzámen chǐ tsž dà'syā hwànhwan 'kǒuwei. / Let's go north this year for a change. Dzámen 'hwàn yihwàn 'dìfang, 'jīnnyan shàng 'běibyar chyù ba.

Change (money of lower denomination) líng'chyán; (money returned to the purchaser in excess of the cost of an article purchased); jǎu de chyán, jǎuhweilai de chyán. / Do you have any change? Nǐ yǒu líng'chyán ma? / Here's your change. 'Jè shŕ °jáugei ni (°jǎuhweilai) de 'chyán.

CHANNEL. (Deep part of a stream) 'héchwáng; (ditch) gōu; (strait) shwěidàu, hǎijyá, hǎisyá.

CHAPTER. (Of a book) (yì)jāng(shū); (of an organization) fēnhwèi.

CHARACTER. (Qualities) pǐnsying. / I was disappointed in his character. Wǒ dwèi tāde pǐngsying bùmǎn'yì. / He's a man of great character. Tāde pǐnsying hěn 'hǎu.

(Person) 'rénwù (in a book); jyǎur (on the stage). / Who are the principal characters in the book? 'Shūli 'jyǔyàude rénwù dōu yǒu 'shéi? / He's a character actor. Tā 'jwān chyù 'yílùde 'jyǎur.

(Person who stands out). / He's quite a character. Tā nèi ge rén hěn tè'byé. *or* Tā 'hěn shŕ ge 'rénwù. / That person is a familiar character here. meaning Everyone here knows him. Dzài 'jèikwàr tíchi 'tā lai, 'shéi dōu 'jŕdau. *or* 'Jèi-yídài de dìfang dōu 'rènshr ta. or meaning Everyone here knows he's odd. Tā dzài 'jèikwàr shŕ ge rén dōu 'jŕdau de 'gwàiwu.

(Unit of the Chinese writing system) dz̀. / Please read these characters for me. Chǐng bǎ jèisyē 'dz̀ gěi wo 'nyàn yisyar.

A man of strong character yìjř'jyānchyángde rén, gèsyìng hěn 'chyángde rén.

Be in character (gēn . . . jèige rèn) syāng'chèn. / That new hat of hers is really in character. Tāde 'nèidǐng syīn'màudz gēn tā nèige rén syāng'chèn.

Be out of character syàng byànle ge 'rén shřde, gǎile cháng'tài le. / His fit of anger was out of character. Tā nèi yìfā 'pichi syàng byànle ge 'rén shřde.

Have no character, be without character 'píngfán. / His face has no character. Tāde 'lyǎn hěn 'píngfán.

CHARCOAL. tàn.

CHARGE. (Accuse someone) gàu. / I charge this soldier with insubordination. Jèige 'bīng, wǒ 'gàu ta bùfú'tsúng.

(Of money) yàuchyán, swànchyán; **charge extra** jyāchyán. / They charge for any added service. Lìng'wài jyàu tāmen dzwò 'shémma tāmen 'dōu yàu 'chyán. / You've charged me too much. Nǐ 'dwō swàn wo 'chyán le.

(Attack, military) 'gūngjī, chūngfēng. / The soldiers are preparing to charge the enemy. 'Bīng jwǔn'bèi °'gūngjī 'dírén (°syàng 'dífāng chūng'fēng).

(Of a bull, etc.) chwànggwo (lai *or* chyu). / Watch out or the bull will charge us. Dāng'syīn, 'nyóu yàu 'chwànggwòlai.

Charge someone with a crime. / What crime is he charged with? is expressed as What is his type of crime? Tāde dzwèi'míng shř shémma? *or* Tā shř shémma dzwèi'míng? / You can charge him with anything you like, but can you back it up with facts? Nǐ 'ài 'jyā tā shémma dzwèi'míng dōu 'syíng, 'búgwò nǐ yǒu 'jèngjyù ma?

Charge a battery (dzài dyàn'chřli) chūng 'dyàn. / Have you charged the battery for me? Nèige dyàn'chř chūng'dyànle méiyou?

Charge something to an account (with record kept by the store) jìjàng; (by verbal agreement without record) shē. / Charge this to Mr. Liu's account. Jèige jì 'Lyóu syānshengde 'jàng.

Open a charge account (and get an account book held by the purchaser) lì jédz.

A charge (legal) expressed with dzwèi crime *or* dzwèimíng type of crime. / What's the charge? Shémma dzwèi'míng? *or* 'Wèile shémma? / On what charges was he held? Tā gěi 'yàchilai shř 'fànle 'shémma dzwèi? / You can't make up charges against people. Nǐ bùnéng swéi'byàn jyā 'rén dzwèi'míng. / He pleaded guilty to the charge. Tā chéng'rèn tā yǒu'dzwèi. *but* / He pleaded guilty to the charge of speeding. Tā chéng'rèn tā 'kāide tài 'kwài le.

(Monetary). / Is there any extra charge for this service? is expressed as Do you want to charge extra? 'Jèmmaje 'yàu buyàu 'jyāchyán? / There's no extra charge. 'Búyùng 'jyāchyán. *or* Myǎn'fèi. *or* 'Buyàuchyán.

Be in charge shř gwǎn'shřde; (formal) shř fùdzérén; (official) shř (jǔgwǎn) jǎng'gwān. / Who's in charge here? (general) 'Shwéi shř jèr gwǎn'shřde? (military) 'Shwéi shř jèrde(jǔgwǎn)jǎng'gwān? (formally, expecting the person in charge to answer) 'Nǎ yíwèi shř 'jèrde fùdzé'rén? *or* 'Nǎ yíwèi shř jǔgwǎn jǎng'gwān? *or* Wǒ gēn 'nǎ yíwèi shwō'hwà?

Be in charge of gwǎn, °gwēi (°shǔ) . . . gwǎn. / He's in charge of this office. Jèige 'dìfang gwēi tā 'gwǎn. *or* Tā gwǎn jèige dìfang.

Be in charge of a class 'dānrèn. / The class Mr. Wang is in charge of is grumbling about him. 'Wáng syānsheng 'dānrèn de nèibān 'sywésheng 'bàuywàn tā le.

Be in <u>someone's</u> charge °gwēi (°shǔ) . . . gwǎn; (for safekeeping) °'jyāugěi (°'gwēi) . . . bǎu'gwǎn. / These documents were in your charge, weren't they? Jèisyē wén'jyàn 'búshr̄ gwēi 'nǐ bǎu'gwǎnde ma? / He's in your charge from now on. Tsúng 'jīn yǐ'hòu tā gwēi 'nǐ 'gwǎn le. / He's in your charge, not mine. Tā °gwēi (°'shǔ) 'nǐ 'gwǎn, 'méiyou 'wǒde shr̄.

Put <u>someone</u> in charge jyàu . . . 'gwǎn, jyāugěi . . . 'gwǎn. / Who put him in charge of that matter? 'Nèijyàn shr̄ shr̄ 'shwéi jyàu ta 'gwǎnde?

Put <u>someone</u> in <u>someone's</u> charge bǎ . . . jyāugěi . . . gwǎn. / I'll put him in your charge. Wǒ 'bǎ ta jyāugei 'nǐ gwǎn.

Take charge (of) gwǎn; (formal) fù . . . dedzérèn, 'jàugù, 'jàulyàu. / Who took charge after he left? Tā 'dzǒule yǐ'hòu shr̄ shwéi 'gwǎn? / You take charge of that section. Nǐ 'jàugù 'nèibùfen(de'shr̄).

Take charge of <u>doing</u> gwǎn. / You take charge of entertaining that crowd. Nǐ gwǎn jāu'dài nèiyì'bāng. / You take charge of feeding the babies. 'Nǐ gwǎn wèi syǎu'hár.

CHARM. (Of scenery) (jǐng'jr̄) hěn měi. / The lakes here have great charm. Jèisyē 'hú de jǐng'jr̄ hěn 'měi.

(Devilish attractiveness) mwóli. / Your eyes have great charm. Nǐde 'yǎnjing yǒu hěn 'dàde mwó'li. *See also* **Be charming.**

(Talisman) fǎshù, syéshù. / That lama from Tibet claims he has a charm. Nèige Syī'dzàng lái de 'lāma dž'chēng yǒu (mí'rénde)fǎ'shù. / They say he can use a charm to kill people. Tāmen shwō tā néng yùng syé'shù 'shārén.

To charm jyàu . . . jáu'mí, jyàu . . . shén'hwún dyān'dǎu, jyàu . . . 'ài. / She can charm any man. Tā néng jyàu 'rénrén jáu'mí. / Any man who looks at her is charmed. 'Nánrén 'kàn jyan ta dōu hwèi °jáu'mí de (°shén'hwún dyān'dǎu de).

Be charming (of a person) °jyàu (°'tǎu)'rén 'syǐhwān, jyàurén ài; (be enchanting) mírén; (of a child only) shr̄ ge mírén'jīng. / His sister is very charming. Tāde 'mèimei hěn 'tǎu rén 'syǐhwan de. / What a charming child! Jèige 'háidz 'dwōma jyàurén 'syǐhwan! *or* Jèige 'háidz jyān'jr̄ shr̄ ge mírén'jīng! / She has a charming personality. Tā hěn jyàu rén 'syǐhwan.

Be charmed by (a thing or a person) <u>is expressed as</u> appreciate 'syīnshǎng. / We were charmed by the beautiful sights. Wǒmen hěn 'syīnshǎng nèige dìfang de 'jǐngjr̄.

CHART. byǎu, yǐlǎnbyǎu, túbyǎu; (of land) dìtú; (mariner's) hǎitú, hánghǎitú.

CHASSIS. (Of car, truck) chēpán, chēpár, dǐpár.

CHAUFFEUR. (Courteous) szjī, jīshr̄; (less polite) kāichēde, (chì)chēfu.

CHEAP. 'pyányi, jyàn. / Do you have anything cheaper than this? Nǐ yǒu bǐ 'jèige 'pyányi dyǎr de ma? / Do you have a cheap room for rent? Nǐ yǒu 'pyányide 'wūdz chū'dzu ma? / Are the rates cheap at this hotel? Jèige lyǔ'gwǎnde 'jyàchyán 'pyányi ma? / He usually goes for cheap things. Tā 'píngcháng 'ài mǎi °pyányi'hwò (°'jyàn-hwò). / This is for sale cheap. 'Jèige 'jyànjyà chū'mài.

(Undignified) yǒu'shr̄ shēn'fèn, 'fēili fěi'chìde; (low-class) syàjyàn. / He looked cheap in those clothes. Tā 'chwānde 'fēili fěi'chìde. *or* Tā chwānde 'nèiyàngr de 'yīshang°('syǎnde) 'fěili fěi'chìde (°'syǎnje syà'jyàn, °yǒu'shr̄ shēn'fèn).

(Showy but unsound, of things) is expressed as second-grade tsz̀děngde or as not good búshr 'hǎude. / That's a cheap watch. 'Nèi shr tsz̀'děngde 'byǎu. or Nèige 'byǎu búshr 'hǎude.

Cheap trick. / He played a cheap trick on me. Tā 'gěi wo 'shr̄le (yì)hwéi 'hwài.

Feel cheap (jywéde) yǒu'kwèi, (jywéde) bùhǎu'yìszde. / His kindness made me feel cheap. Tā dàiwo jèmma 'hǎu, jyàu wo 'jywéde yǒu'kwèi.

CHECK. (Receipt) shōujyù; (made of metal) páidz, pár; (of cardboard) pyàndz, pyàr; (of paper) tyáudz, tyáur. / Be sure to keep this check. Chyān'wàn 'lyóuje jèige 'páidz. / Give your check to the baggage man. Bǎ nǐde 'pár jyāugei nèige gwǎn 'syíngli de rén.

(For money) jr̄pyàu; **traveler's check** lyǔsyíng jr̄'pyàu; **blank check** kùngtou jr̄'pyàu; **checkbook** jr̄pyàu 'běndz, jr̄pyàubě̌r; **make out a check** kāi jr̄pyàu. / I'll send you a check in the morning. Wǒ míngtyan 'dzǎuchen bǎ jr̄'pyàu gěi ni 'sùng-chyu. / Who shall I make the check out to? Wǒ jèijāng jr̄'pyàu yīngdang kāigei 'shwéi?

(Small mark to draw attention) gōur. / Put a check beside each price. Měiyàng jyàchyán pángbyar dǎ yíge 'gōur.

To check (stop by law) jìnjr̄. / Such lawlessness should be checked. Jèijǔng bù'fǎde syíng'dùng yīnggai jìn'jr̄.

(Examine for accuracy) dwèi. / Have you checked those sheets? Nèi jijāng 'jr̄ nǐ 'dwèi(gwo)le ma? / Check these (documents) for me. Gěi wo 'dwèi yidwèi.

(Look at officially) yàn, chá. / They're ready to check our passports. Tāmen 'yǐjing yùbèi'hǎule yàu yàn wǒmende hù'jàu le.

(Take a look at) 'kàn yikàn. / Please check the oil in my car. Chǐng 'kàn yikàn wǒ 'chēli de 'yóu 'gòubugòu.

(Leave for safekeeping) tswún. / Check your hat and coat here. Bǎ nǐde 'màudz gēn dà'yī tswúndzai 'jèr. / Where can I check my baggage? Wǒ dzài 'nǎr kéyi bǎ 'syíngli 'tswúnchilai?

(Put a check mark on) jì, hwà, gōu. / Check the items that are important. Bǎ 'yàujǐnde dōu °'jìsyalai (°'hwàchilai, °'gōuchulai).

Check oneself (in doing something) 'tíngjù; (in speaking) 'rěnjù. / He was about to speak, but checked himself. Tā 'gāng yàu kāi'kǒu yòu 'rěnjùle.

Check speed (slow down) mànsyalai. / The car checked its speed as it went around the corner. Chī'chē gwǎi'wār de shŕhou 'mànsyalai yìdyǎr.

Check something against . . . gēn . . . 'dwèi yidwèi, yùng . . . 'dwèi yidwèi. / Check these figures against that table. Jèisyē 'shùr yùng nèige 'byǎu 'dwèi yidwèi.

Check in at a hotel, etc. dēngjì. / Have you checked in at the hotel? Nǐ 'yǐ-jing dzài lyǔ'gwǎn dēng'jìle ma?

Check in at an office, headquarters, etc. bàudàu. / At this office we check in at nine o'clock. Dzài jèige gūngshr̄'fáng wǒmen shr̄ 'jyǒudyǎn jūng bàu'dàu.

Check out dzǒu. / I'm checking out; please have my bill ready. Wǒ yàu 'dzǒu le; chǐng bǎ 'jàng 'swànchulai. / Sign here when you check out. 'Dzǒude shŕhou dzài 'jèr chyān'míng.

Check <u>baggage</u> **through to** <u>a place</u> gwà'páidz 'yùndau . . . . / I want this suitcase checked through to New York. Wǒ yàu bǎ jèige syāngdz gwà'páidz yùndau Nyǒuywē chyu.

Check up on (investigate) dyàuchá. / They're checking up on your records now. Tamen 'jèngdzài dyàu'chá nǐde lyǔ'lǐ ne.

Check with (be in agreement with) gēn . . . yí'yàng. / Does this timetable check with the new schedule? Jèige syǐnchē'byàu gēn syǐn dìng de 'shŕjyān yǐ'yàng buyí-yàng?

Check with <u>someone</u> wèn, 'wèn yiwèn. / I must check with the manager first. Wǒ děi 'syān 'wèn yiwèn jǐng'lǐ. / I've check with the police bureau; it's no go. Wǒ 'yǐjing 'wènle jǐngchá'jyú le; bùsyíng.

Other English expressions. / Check! (in chess) Jyāng! <u>or meaning</u> correct 'Dwèi!

CHECKERS. (Game) chí; (pieces used) chídzěr; **play checkers** syàchí.

CHEEK. Expressed with lyǎn face <u>with measure</u> byǎr; <u>also</u> sāibāngdz, sāi, dzwěi-bàdz; left cheek 'dzwǒlyǎn, 'dzwǒsāi, 'dzwǒbyārde°lyǎn (°sāi'bāngdz, °dzwěi'bàdz) (for right cheek substitute yòu for dzwǒ); **cheekbone** 'chywángǔ. / He has a birth-mark on his cheek. Tā (yìbyar)'lyǎnshang yǒu kwài'jì. / I think it's his left cheek. Wǒ syǎng shŕ tā 'dzwǒsāishang. / His cheek is swollen from a toothache. Tā yá-'téngde ('bànbyar)'lyǎn dōu 'jǔngle. / She had a lot of rouge on her cheeks. Tā 'lyǎnshang 'tsāle bù'shǎude 'yānjr.

Tongue in cheek. / He had his tongue in his cheek when he said it. Tā shwō 'nèisyē shèr 'ywán ni ne. <u>or</u> Tā 'shwōje 'wár ne. <u>or expressed as</u> While saying it he traced the character "no" with his foot. Tā 'shwō de shŕhou jyàu 'dǐsya hwà 'bùdzèr.

CHEERFUL. (Of a person) kwàihwo, shwǎngkwai, tùngkwai, gāusyìng. / He has a cheerful personality. <u>or</u> He's always cheerful. Tā 'jèige rén 'lǎu nèmma °'kwài-hwo (°gāu'syìng, °'shwǎngkwai, °'tùngkwai). / They're cheerful donors. Tāmen jywān'chyán hěn °'tùngkwai (°'shwǎngkwai). / You seem very cheerful this morning. Nǐ jyēer 'dzǎuchen hǎu 'syàng shŕ gāu'syìng.

(Of a room) lyàngtang. / What a cheerful room! Jèijyān 'wūdz jēn 'lyàngtang!

(Of a color) syānmíng, syānyàn. / Pink is a cheerful color. Fěn'húng jèijǔng 'yánsè hěn syān'míng.

(Sarcastic). / That's a cheerful thought! Nǐ kě 'jēn hwèi shwō 'jísyáng hwà!

Cozy and cheerful. / The fire makes the room cozy and cheerful (both warm and comfortable). Jèige 'hwǒ bǎ 'wūdz nùngde yòu 'nwǎnhwo yòu 'shūfu.

CHEESE. (nyóu)nǎibǐng; (from the English word) chìsz.

CHEF. 'dàshŕfu, chúdztóur.

CHEMICALS. hwàsywépǐn; chemical products hwàsywéjr̀'pǐn; **medicinal chemicals** hwàsywé yàu'pǐn.

CHEMIST. hwàsywéjyā, hwàsywéshŕ.

CHEMISTRY. 'hwàsywé.

CHERRY. (Fruit) yǐngtau; (tree) 'yǐngtaushù; (wood) yǐngtaumù.

CHESS. (Game) 'syàngchí; **play chess** syà 'syàngchí; **chessman** (syàng) chídzěr.

CHEST. (Part of body) syūng, syūngpúr; (lower part only) syīnkǒu(r).

(Box) gwèi(dz), syāng(dz); **chest of drawers** chōutǐgwèi; **chest of seven drawers** (yíge)'chǐtǐ'gwèi (similarly with any number of drawers).

CHESTNUT. lìdz.

CHICKEN. jī; (male) gūngjī; (female) mǔjī; (young) syǎujyēr; (meat) jīròu; (if shredded) jīsz̄; (boned and diced) jīdyēngr; (cooked whole) jēngjī, chywánjī; **chicken breast** 'jīsyūngpúr. / Does this farmer raise chickens for their eggs? Jèige 'núngfū yǎng'jī 'wèideshr̄ syà'dàn ma? / Roast chicken isn't on the menu tonight. Jyēer 'wǎnshang tsài'dāndzshang 'méiyou °kǎu'jī (°shāu'jī).

CHICKEN POX. 'shwěidòur. / His younger brother has just had chicken pox. Tā dìdi gāng chūle 'shwěidòur.

CHIEF. (Familiar term of address for one's superior) tóur; (formal) jǎnggwān; dwèijǎng for the chief of an organization whose designation ends in dwèi; (of a clan) dzújǎng; (of a tribe, as among the Mongols or the Miaos) chyóujǎng, shǒulǐng; **chief of police** jǐngchá'jyú jyú'jǎng; **chief of staff** tsānmóujǎng or (of the U. S. A.) tsānmóudzǔng'jǎng; **chief of a department under the chief of staff** shǔjǎng, as in chief of ordnance 'bīnggūngshǔ shǔ'jǎng; chief engineer 'dzǔnggūngcheng'shr̄. / Our chief is quite lenient. Wǒmende 'tóur hěn 'sūng. / Who's your chief? Nǐmende jǎng'gwān shr̄ 'shwéi? / He's the chief of a mountain tribe. Tā shr̄ 'shānli yǐdzú'rénde chyóu-'jǎng. / The firemen reported to their chief. Syāufáng'dwèi syàng tāmende dwèi-'jǎng bàu'dàu.

(Main) jǔyàu(de); sometimes dzwèi followed by a stative verb. / What's your chief complaint? (sickness) Nǐde jǔ'yàude bìng'jēng shr̄ shémma? (otherwise) Nǐ dzwèi bùmǎn'yìde shr̄ 'shémma? / What are the chief points of interest here? Jèr dzwèi yǒu'yìsz de dìfang dōu dzài 'nǎr?

CHILD. háidz, syǎuhár. / They took the child with them on the trip. Tāmen lyǔ'syíng dàije 'háidz. / He's acting like a child. Tā 'nèmma yàng syàng yíge 'háidz shr̄de a.

(In formal phrases) értúng; **child psychology** értúng syīn'lǐ(sywé), **child welfare** értúng fúlì.

CHIMNEY. yāntung. / Smoke is coming out of the chimney. 'Yān tsúng 'yāntung 'màuchulai. or 'Yāntung màu 'yān. / I want this chimney repaired. Wǒ yàu 'syōulisyōuli jèige 'yāntung.

(Of a lamp) ('yóudēng)dēng'jàur. / Where's the chimney for the lamp? Dēng'jàur dzài 'nǎr?

CHIN. syāba'kéer; often one simply says lyǎn face. / I cut my chin while shaving. Wǒ gwā'lyǎn de shrhou bǎ °'lyǎn (°syāba'kéer) gwā'pwòle.

Chin strap (of a helmet) (gāng'kwēide)'dàidz; (of a hat) màudàr.

Keep one's chin up. / Keep your chin up! Syǎngkāi dyǎr!

CHOCOLATE. chyǎukelǐ (transliteration of the English word); **chocolate candy** kǒukoutáng, chyǎukelǐ'táng.

CHOICE. Expressed with verbs meaning choose as tyāu or sywǎn. / What choice is there? Yŏu shémma kĕ'tyāude? /Do we have our choice of rooms? Wŏmen kéyi swéi-'byàn tyāu fáng'jyān ma? or Yŏu 'fángdz kĕ'tyāu ma? / Take your choice. 'Tyāu ba. or Nĭ 'tyāu hău le. or 'Ai năige 'tyāu năige. /After all, he's the peoples' choice. Bùgwăn dzĕmma shwō, tā shr rén'mín 'sywănde. /My first choice is red; second, black. Dì'yíge wŏ tyāu 'húngde, chítsz shr 'hēide. is expressed as I like red best and black next best. Wŏ dzwèi 'syĭhwan 'húngde, chí'tsz shr 'hēide. /He's the man of her own choice. Nèi shr tā 'dzjĭ 'tyāude rén. but /I had no choice in the matter. Wŏ méiyou 'byéde bànfa. or Wŏ jřhău 'nèmmaje.

Choice (select) hĕn hăude, dzwèi hăude. /I've just heard a choice bit of news. Wŏ gāng 'tīngjyan yíjyàn hĕn hău'wár de syīn'wén. /This is the choice part of the meat. Jè shr ròude dzwèi 'hău de yí'bùfen.

CHOKE. (On a gasoline motor) (kūng)chĭmén.

CHOLERA. hŭlyèlā, hwŏlwàn.

CHOOSE (CHOSE, CHOSEN). (General) tyāu; (persons or books) sywăn. /I chose these books carefully. Jèisyē 'shū wŏ °'sywănde (°'tyāude) hĕn 'syăusyin. or Wŏ °tyāu (°sywăn) jèisyē 'shū hĕn 'fèile dyăr 'syīn. / They were unable to choose between the candidates. Dzài jèi'lyàngge hòubŭ rén'sywăn lĭtou tāmen bùnéng jywé'dìng sywăn 'nèige. /You can choose a leader from among yourselves. Nĭmen kéyi 'sywăn yíge lĭng'syòu. /I have to choose the lesser of two evils. Wŏ jř'hău tyāu nèige 'bĭjyàu 'hău yìdyăr de le. /I've chosen the black hat. Wŏ 'tyāule nèige 'hēi màudz le. /What is there to choose? Yŏu shémma kĕ'tyāude? /How many titles have you chosen from the book list? Tsúng nèige shū'dāndz nĭ 'tyāuchu 'dwōshau 'jŭng lai? /If you choose the red, I'll take the black. Yàushr nĭ tyāu nèige 'húngde, wŏ jyòu yàu nèige 'hēide. /Which one do you choose? Nĭ °tyāu (°yàu) 'nèige?

(Especially of a hotel) tyāuhău, jāuhău. /Have you chosen a hotel for the night? Jīntyan 'wănshang nĭ 'yĭjing jău'hăule lyŭ'gwăn méiyou?

Choose to syăng, dădìngle 'júyì. /I chose to remain in my room. (mild) Wŏ syăng háishr dzài'jyā bù'chūchyu 'hău. (strong) Wŏ dă'dìngle 'júyì, 'jyòushr bù-'chūchyu.

CHOW MEIN. chăumyàn.

CHRISTIAN. (Protestant) jīdūtú, syīnyesū'jyàude, syīnjīdū'jyàude; (Catholic) syīn-tyānjŭ'jyàude. /Is there a Christian church in town? Jèige chéngli 'yŏu méiyou Jīdūjyàu jyàu'táng?

CHRISTMAS. Shèngdànjyé, Yésū Shēng'dàn. /Merry Christmas! Gūng'hè shèng'dàn! or Shèngdàn kwàilè!

CHROMIUM. kèlwómĭ; (element) gè.

CHRYSANTHEMUM. jyúhwār, jyŏuhwār.

CHUNK. kwài, kwàr.

CHURCH. jyàutáng, lĭbàitáng.

Go to church to worship (Protestant) dzwò lĭbài; (Catholic) wàng mĭsa.

CHUTE. (Steep slide) 'syégwăr.

(Parachute) jyànglwòsăn.

407

CIGARETTE. yān, yānjywǎr, jřyān, syāngyān. /Have a cigarette. Chōu °jř(°gēr) 'yān ba. /Do you carry American cigarettes? Nǐmen mài 'Měigwoyān ma?

Cigarette case yānhéer. /I've lost my cigarette case. Wǒ bǎ yān'héer 'dyōule.

CIRCLE. (ywán)chywǎr. /Draw a circle. Hwà yíge ywán'chywǎr. /The sign has a red circle on a white field. 'Jǐhàur shř bái'dyershang (yǒu) yíge húng 'chywǎr.

(In city streets) ywánchǎng. /Let's meet at Columbus Circle. Wǒmen dzai Gēlwún'bù Ywán'chǎng 'jyàn ba.

(Of friends, etc.) (large) yìbāng; (small) jige. /I have a small circle of friends here. Wǒ 'jèr yóu jige 'péngyou.

(Government, educational, etc.) jyè. /He's known only in scholastic circles. Tā jř dzài 'sywéjyè yǒu dyǎr 'míng.

Go around in a circle (wéije) . . . ràu ('chywǎr); (if number of times is speci- fied) ràu . . . chywǎr, ràu . . . dzàur; (if the motion is flying, running, etc.) fēi . . . chywǎr, pǎu . . . chywǎr, etc. /We drove around in a circle. Wǒmen kāije 'chē ràu'chywǎr. /We drove around in a circle three times. Wǒmen kāije 'chē wéije ràule 'sān°chywǎr (°dzàur).

To circle see Go around in a circle above. /The plane circled around the field several times. Fēi'jǐ dzài fēijǐ'chǎng shàngtou 'fēile háuji'chywǎr.

(Make a circular mark around) yùng (ywán) 'chywǎr °'gōuchulai (°'chywān- chulai). /Please circle the words that are misspelled. Chǐng bǎ pǐn'tswòde dž yùng ywán'chywǎr 'gōuchulai.

CITIZEN. gūngmín; sometimes expressed with rén person. /I'm a citizen of the United States. Wǒ shř 'Měigwo gūng'mín. /What country are you a citizen of? Nǐ shř 'nǎ yìgwó de 'rén?

CITY. chéng (theoretically, a city with a city wall, of any size). shř (either a city on the governmental level of a syàn (county), directly under the provincial government, or one on the governmental level of a province, directly under the national govern- ment). /How far is the nearest city? Dzwèi 'jìnde chéng lí'jèr yǒu 'dwōywǎn? /I never lived in the city until this year. Wǒ 'jīnnyan yǐ'chyán méidzài chéngli jùgwo. /The whole city was aroused by the news. 'Syāusyi hūng'dùng chywán 'chéng.

(In contrast with country, rural area) chéngshř. /She's not accustomed to city life. Tā méi'gwògwàn 'chéngshř 'shēnghwó. or Tā dzài 'chénglǐ méi'gwògwàn.

CIVIL. (Of citizens) gūngmín(de). /The governor pays great attention to civil liberties. Shěng'jǎng hěn jù'yì °gūngmín chywán'lì (°gūngmín dž'yóu).

(Nonreligious or nonmilitary) pǔtūng(de), pǔtūng'rénde, mínshř(de). /He was married by a civil ceremony, not by a religious ceremony. Tā ànje pǔ'tūng yí'shř jyēde 'hwūn, búshr ànje dzūng'jyàu yí'shř.

(According to civil law, not criminal law) mínfǎ, mínshř; civil code mínfǎ, 'mínshřfǎ'gwēi.

(Polite) kèchi, yǒu lǐmàu. /At least he was civil to us. Tā dwèi wǒmen jř- 'shǎu hái °swàn 'kèchi (°yǒu lǐ'màu).

Civil authorities 'mínshř dāng'jyú; civil officials wéngwǎn. /The civil authori- ties must be consulted about this. 'Jèige děi gēn 'mínshř dāng'jyú tǎu'lwùnle tsái 'syíng.

Civil engineering 'tǔmù'gūngchéng; civil engineer 'tǔmùgūngchéng'shř.

Civil rights gūngchywán. / The judge has deprived him of civil rights. Fǎgwān chr̄dwóle tāde gūng'chywán le.

Civil service (personnel) gūngwùywán. / Has he ever been employed in civil service? Tā 'dānggwo gūngwù'ywán ma?

Civil war nèilwàn, nèijàn; the Civil War (U. S. A.) 'Měigwo Nán'Běi Jàn'jēng.

CLAIM. shwō (say); sywān'bù (shwō) (proclaim); dz̀chēng (profess). / The government claims the mineral rights. Jēngfǔ sywān'bù kwàngchywán gwēi jēngfǔ. / He claims to have a copy of that book. Nèige 'shū tā 'dz̀jǐ shwō 'tā yǒu yìběr. / He claims that the traffic delayed him. Tā shwō lùshang hěn 'jǐ, swóyi °'wǎnle (°'wùle jūngdyǎr). / He claims to be your relative. Tā 'dz̀jǐ shwō tā gēn nǐ °yǒu (°shr̀) 'chīnchì. / He claims to be a specialist. Tā dz̀'chēng shr̀ 'jwānyjā.

(Pick up) lǐng. / Where do I claim my baggage? Wǒ dzài 'nǎr lǐng wǒde 'syíngli?

A claim (demand) 'yāuchyóu. / They have no claim on us. Tāmen méi 'lǐyóu lái gēn wǒmen 'yāuchyóu shémma. / You can't justify your claims. Nǐde 'yāuchyóu méiyou 'gēnjyù.

(Indemnity) péichángfèi. / The insurance company paid all claims against it. Bǎusyǎn 'gūngsz̄ bǎ swóyǒude péicháng'fèi dōu °'gěile (°'fùle).

File a (legal) claim for chéng (yíge) 'jwàngdz yāuchyóu. / I wish to file a claim for damages. Wǒ yàu chéng yíge 'jwàngdz, (shr̀) yāuchyóu péicháng 'swǔnshr̄(de).

CLASS. (Sort, kind; general term) jǔng, lèi. / Don't associate with that class of people. Byé gēn 'nèijǔng rén 'láiwang.

(Grade, quality) děng; first class (on a boat) tóuděngtsāng; (on a train) tóuděng chē; (in a theater) tóuděng dzwòr; second class with èr instead of tóu in the preceding. / These accommodations are first class. Jèisye shè'bèi jēn děi swānshr̄ gāu'děng. / Give me one second-class ticket to Chungking. (Gěi wǒ) yìjāng chyù Chúng'chīng de 'èrděng'pyàu.

(Style). / This bar has class. Jèi jyǒu'gwǎr hěn 'jyàngjyǒu.

(Social level) 'jyējí, jí, děng; the higher classes gāu'jí, gāu'děng; moneyed class yǒu'chyán 'jyējí; propertied class yǒu'chǎn 'jyējí; middle class jūng'chǎn 'jyējí; moneyless class wú'chǎn 'jyējí, 'chyúngrén; low class syà'jí, dī'jí. / The educated class is supporting this measure. 'Jr̄shr jyējíde rén 'dzànchéng jèige 'bànfa.

(Class or course in a particular subject) yìmén(gūng)'kè, yìbān (gūng)'kè; a class session, class period yìtáng 'kè. / I have a class at nine. Wǒ 'jyǒudyǎn yǒu 'kè. / I must go to (my) class. Wǒ děi chyù shàng°'kè (°'bān). / Wait until after the class. Děng syàle °'kè (°'bān) 'dzài shwō. / How many classes are you teaching a week? meaning how many different courses Nǐ 'yíge lǐ'bài jyāu °'jǐmén gūng-'kè (°'jǐbān gūng'kè)? meaning how many class periods Nǐ 'yíge lǐ'bài jyāu 'dwō-shau °dyǎn'jūng (°'táng 'kè)?

(Students of a single year) bān, jí, 'nyánjí; (of special schools) chī. / He's one class higher. Tā 'gāu yì°bān (°'nyánji, °'jí). / The freshman class is bigger than it was last year. 'Jīnnyan de 'yīnyánjíde sywésheng bǐ 'chyùnyan de 'dwō. / The class of 1928 held a reunion dinner. Yìjyǒuèr'bābān bìyè'shēng 'kāile ge jyù-tsān'hwài. / He's a graduate of the fourteenth class of the Central Military Academy. Tā shr̀ 'Jūngyāng Jyūn'syàu dìshr̄'sz̀chī bì'yède.

Classroom kèshr̀, kèshr̀, kètáng, jyàngtáng.

Classmate túngbān(de), túngjí(de), túngchǐ(de).

Be classed as swànshr, 'fēndzai . . . 'lèi. / These can be classed as finished. 'Jèisyē kéyi °swànshr 'wán le (°fēndzai dzwò'wán de 'nèilèili).

CLAY. (Mud) ní, (dirt) (nyán)tǔ. / This kind of clay can be made into porcelain. 'Jèijǔng ní kéyi dzwò 'tsź. / Brick is made of clay. 'Jwān shr̀ yùng 'ní dzwòde. / The Chinese sometimes used to print cheap books with type made of clay. 'Jūng-gwo rén yǐ'chyán yìn 'pyányi shū, 'yǒude shŕhou yùng yìjǔng yùng 'ní dzwòde hwó-'dž. / The clay roads are impassable because of the rain. Tǔ'lù yīnwei syà'yǔ bù-'tūng le.

CLEAN. 'gānjìng. / Can you give me a clean towel? Yǒu 'gānjìng 'shǒuyin ma? / The hotels here are kept unusually clean. Jèrde lyǔ'gwǎn 'shǒushrde tè'byé 'gānjing.

(Free from obscenity) bùtsū, bùyě. / The new play is clean and amusing. Syīn 'pái de jèichu hwà'jyùli de 'tsér hěn dòu'syàur, kěshr 'yǐdyǎr yě bù'tsū.

(Free of guilt). / My hands are clean in the matter. Wǒ gēn 'nèijyàn shr̀ 'yǐdyǎr 'gwānsyi yě 'méiyǒu. / I wash my hands clean of the whole thing. Tsúng'jīn yǐ'hòu wǒ gēn 'jèijyàn shèr wán'chywán dwàn'jywé 'gwānsyi.

Clean cut, clean break. / That's a clean cut (wound). Nèi shr̀ yǐ'jŕ jìnchyu de 'shāng. / It's a clean break (of bone). 'Gútou 'dwàn de dìfang hěn 'jěngchí. / He has a clean-cut face. Tāde 'lyǎn 'jǎngde hěn °píng'jèng (°dwān'jèng). / She has a clean-cut face. Tā 'méichīngmù'syòude. / They made a clean break. Tāmen wán-'chywán dwàn'jywé 'gwānsyi le.

Clean lines. / The new cars have clean lines. Syīn'chēde 'shr̀yang méiléng-méi'jyǎurde hěn shwǎng'mù.

Clean record. / The prisoner doesn't have a clean (criminal) record. 'Fànrén 'búshr 'chūfàn.

Clean sweep. / He made a clean sweep of the old plans. Tā bǎ 'ywánláide 'jìhwà wán'chywán 'gàile. / He made a clean sweep of the prizes. Jyǎng'pǐn jyàu 'tā náde yìsǎur'gwāng.

Sweep (Rub, Wash, etc.) **clean** is expressed with compounds 'gānjìng as the second element, the first element specifying the manner or method of cleaning, as sǎu'gānjìng **sweep clean;** tsā'gānjìngle **rub clean;** etc. / He didn't sweep the floor clean. Dì'bǎn tā méisǎu'gānjìng. / Rub the car clean with that piece of cloth. Yùng nèikwài 'bù bǎ 'chē tsā'gānjìngle. / You can wash it clean with water. Yùng 'shwěi kéyi syǐ'gānjingle. / The rain washed the street clean. Yǔ'shwěi bǎ 'jyē chūng-'gānjìngle.

To clean is expressed as in the preceding paragraph or by single verbs which specify the method of cleaning, as sǎu sweep, tsā rub, syǐ wash, etc. / He's cleaning the car. Tā syǐ 'chē ne. / We spent all day cleaning the windows. Wǒmen yùng jěng yìtyān de gūngfu tsā 'chwānghu.

Clean with a broom 'dǎsǎu. / Has the maid cleaned the room? Lǎu'mādz bǎ 'wūdz 'dǎsǎule méiyou?

Clean with a feather duster yùng 'dǎndz 'dǎn. / She only cleaned it with a feather duster. Tā jr̀ yùng 'dǎndz 'dǎnle yìsyàr.

Clean house (lit.) dǎsǎu 'wūdz; (fig.) °chǐng'chú (°táu'tài) fúhwà fèn'dž. / The new adminstration will begin by cleaning house. Syīn gwān dàu'rèn syān yàu °chǐng-'chú (°táu'tài) 'fúhwà fèn'dž.

Clean out chǐnglǐ. / I'll look for it when I clean out my trunk. Wǒ chǐng'lǐ 'syāngdz de shŕhou 'jǎu yìsyàr.

Clean up (wash up) 'syǐ yisyǐ, syǐshǒu. /I'd like to clean up before dinner. Méichr̄'fàn yǐ'chyán wǒ syǎng 'syān 'syǐ yísyàr 'shǒu.

Clean up (straighten up) shōushr. /The room needs cleaning up for a new guest. Jèijyān 'wūdz děi 'shōushr yísyàr, yǒu 'syīn fáng'kè yàu 'bānjìnlai.

Clean up (finish) dzwòwán. /You may go home when you clean up the work. 'Shr̀ching dzwò'wánle yǐ'hòu, nǐ kéyi hwéi'jyā.

CLEAR. (General term) chīngchu. /His voice was clear over the radio. Tāde 'sǎngyīn dzài wúsyàn'dyànli hěn 'chīngchu. /I don't have a clear idea of what you mean. Nǐde 'yìsz wǒ búdà °'chīngchu (°'míngbái). /This seat has a clear view of the stage. 'Jèige dzwòr kàn syì'tái kéyi 'kànde hěn 'chīngchu.

(Of the sky or weather) chíng, syàngchíng. /The sky is clear tonight. Jyēr 'wǎnshang 'tyān °hěn 'chíng (°syàng'chíng). /The weather has been clear all week. Tyān 'chíngle yíge lǐ'bài le.

(Of water) chíng. /The water is clear and deep. Shwěi yòu 'chíng yòu 'shēn. /The spring is clear as crystal. Chywánshwěi 'chíngde °syàng 'shwěijīng shr̀de (°kéyi 'kàndau dyěr).

(Of the head) 'chíngsyǐng. /Try to keep a clear head. Syǎng'fár bǎu'chr̀ 'chíngsyǐngde 'tóunǎu.

(Of handwriting or copy) yì'bǐyí'hwàrde hěn 'chīngchu.

(Of a road freed from obstructions) hǎudzǒu. /Is the road clear up ahead? 'Chyánbyarde 'lù hǎu'dzǒu ma?

(Understandable). /Is it clear? 'Míngbai bumíngbai? or 'Dǔng budǔng? or 'Míngbaile ma? or 'Dǔngle ma?

(Of profit). /It is clear profit. Shr̀ chwún'lì. or Shr̀ 'jìngdéde.

To clear (remove obstructions from) expressed with bǎ and an appropriate resultative compound. /Have they cleared the cars from the road? Tāmen bǎ lùshangde chī'chē dou lā'dzǒule. /We can clear the enemy from this region in three days. Wǒmen néng dzai sāntyān yǐ'nèi bǎ jèige dìfangde 'dǐren gǎn'dzǒu.

(Miss). /The boat cleared the rock by inches. Nèijǐ 'chwán gwò 'yánshr̀ de shr̀hou 'líje bùji'tswùn. /The plane barely cleared the treetops. 'Fēijī 'fēigwòchyu de shr̀hou 'chàdyār jyòu 'tsèngjau shù'jyār. /Can we clear that bridge? (pass over) Chyáushang gwòde'chyù ma? (pass under) Chyáusya gwòde'chyù ma?

Be cleared (of physical obstacles). /The road has been cleared. Lù 'méiyou 'jàng ài le. or Lù 'tūng le. or Lù 'gwòdechyú le. /The track has been cleared (of other trains). Byéde 'chē dōu 'ràngkaile.

Be cleared (of legal obstacles or requirements). /All my debts are cleared. Wǒde 'jàng dōu hwán'chīng le. /The ship has been cleared. Chwán 'chūkou shǒu'syù °bàn'chīngle (°(yǐjing) 'lyǎu le). /The account has been cleared. Swàn 'chīng le. /The passport has been cleared. (issued) Hù'jàu°bàn'hǎule (°'fāsyalaile). (checked by foreign authorities) Hù'jàu °jyǎn chá'wánle (°'fǎhweilaile).

Be cleared (of a title) méiyou °'wèntí (°'jr̄jyé) chyán dōu fù'chīng le; (of a title or deed cleared by the authorities) shr̀ húngchì; (of a document passed by higher authorities) pījwúnle.

Be cleared (of wooded land) kāichulaile, kāihǎule.

Be cleared (of checks). /We must wait until the checks are cleared. Wǒmen dzǔng děi 'děng jr̄'pyàu chá'chīngle yǐ'hòu dzài 'shwō.

Clear away. /Ask her to clear away the dishes. 'Jyàu tā bǎ 'dyédz 'shōuchilai.

Clear off. /Ask her to clear off the table. 'Jyàu tā bǎ 'jwōdz 'shōushrle.

Clear out (empty). /Please clear out this bureau. 'Chǐng nǐ bǎ jèige 'gwèidz 'téngchulai.

Clear out (leave). /When the police came he had already cleared out. Jǐng'chá dàule, tā 'yǐjǐng °'pǎule (°'líkaile, °'dzǒukaile).

Clear out stock. /Wait until we have cleared out the stock. Děng 'tswún hwò dōu màï'wánle dzai 'shwō. or Děng 'tswún hwò 'chǐng yiching dzài 'shwō.

Clear up (explain). /Would you mind clearing up a few points for me? Yǒu jichù nǐ 'gěi wǒ °'jyěshr̀ yísyàr (°'jyǎng yijyǎng) 'kéyi ma?

Clear up (settle). /I want to clear up some affairs before I go. Wǒ méidzǒu yǐ'chyán yǒu jijyàn 'shr̀ děi 'chǐnglǐ yísyàr.

Clear (up or off) (of weather) chíng. /The skies are clearing now. Yàu 'chíng (tyān)le. /It may clear up this afternoon. Jyēr 'syàwǔ 'tyān yěsyǔ hwèi 'chíng. We will leave as soon as the weather clears up. 'Tyār yǐ 'chíng wǒmen jyou 'dzǒu. /The fog has cleared off. Wù 'sànle.

Special expressions in English. /He cleared his throat and continued to speak. Tā 'késule yísyàr yòu 'jyēje shwōsyachyu. /His frank statement cleared the air. Tā shwō de 'hwà hěn tǎn'bái, bǎ jǐnjāngde kūng'chǐ nùng hwǎn'héle. /Clear (the deck) for action. Jwǔn'bèi kāijàn. /It was clear out of reach. Jyān'jŕ 'gòubujáu. /Keep clear of politics. Byé gēn 'jènjr̀ 'fāshēng 'gwānsyi. or 'Dwǒkāi 'jèngjyè. or Gēn 'jèngjr̀ lí 'ywǎndyar. /Keep clear of in-laws. 'Chǐnchǐ ywǎnli 'syāng. /He's in the clear. Tā méiyou 'shèr. or Méiyou 'tāde 'shèr. or Gēn tā 'méiyou 'gwānsyi. /His name has been cleared. Tāde míngyù nùng'chǐngle. /He's been cleared (of an accusation in court). Sywān'gàu wú'dzwèile.

CLERK.
(Salesman in a store) hwǒji; (more formal) dyànywán. /The clerk is looking up the price. Nèige 'hwǒji dzài nar chá jyà'chyán shr̀ 'dwōshǎu.

(Accountant or bookkeeper, not necessarily highly trained) gwǎn'jàngde (syānsheng), 'syānsheng; (more formal) 'kwàijì.

(Employee, in a somewhat responsible position) 'jŕywán; (otherwise) 'gùywán.

(Secretary) 'shūjì; (typist) dǎ'dżywán; (copyist) 'lùshr̀, 'shànsyěywán.

(Court recorder) shūjigwān. /The clerk kept on file all the records of this court. Běn'ywànde 'jìlù dōu gwēi shūji'gwān fēn'lèi bǎu'gwǎn.

Chief government clerk dzǔngwù'sź sź'jǎng, dzǔngwù'kē kē'jǎng, dzǔngwù'chù chù'jǎng. The chief clerk of any government division the word for which ends in X is X-jàng.

Desk clerk gwèi'táishangde rén.

To clerk dzwò or dāng plus the appropriate noun for clerk. /She hasn't had much experience in clerking. Tā °dzwò (°dāng) 'shūjì de 'jǐngyàn méiyou 'dwōshǎu.

CLEVER.
'tsūngmíng, líng, 'línglì. /The kid is pretty clever. Syǎu'hár tǐng °'tsūngmíng (°'líng, °'línglì). /That's a clever horse. Nèipǐ 'mǎ jēn 'tsūngmíng. /It was clever of you to think of that. Nǐ néng 'syǎngchū 'nèige lai, jēn shr̀ 'tsūngmíng.

(Skillful, talented) chyǎu. /That carpenter is very clever. Nèige mùjyàng hěn 'chyǎu.

(Of a move, play, or maneuver) hǎu, myàu, chyǎu, chyǎumyàu, jīling. (lit.)

/Your friend made a clever chess move. Nǐ nèiwèi 'péngyou dzǒule yí'bù hǎu 'chí. /He made a clever bridge play. Tā jèijāng 'pái 'chūde 'myàu. /He made a clever move. Tā jèiyí 'bù 'dzǒude jēn °'jīling (°'myàu, °chyǎu'myàu, °'chyǎu, °'hǎu). (fig.) /He made a clever move. Tā jèi'shǒur 'wárde 'myàu.

CLIMATE. chìhou. /The climate here is similar to that in Italy. Jèrde 'chìhou hěn-syàng 'Yìdà'lì. /I'd like to visit a warmer climate. is expressed as I'd like to visit a warmer place. Wǒ 'syǎng dàu yíge 'nwǎnhwo yìdyǎrde 'dìfang chyu.

CLIMB. shàng. /I prefer not to climb stairs. Wǒ bú'ywànyì shàng lóu'tī.

(Using both hands and feet, or involving other difficulties; crawl, creep) pá. /I haven't climbed Mount Lu. Wǒ méi'págwo 'Lúshān. /The plane began to climb rapidly. 'Fēijī pá'gāur 'páde hěn 'kwài.

(In society or rank) wàng 'shàng dzwān, wàng 'shàng pá; (only of an official position) shēnggwār. /He's trying hard to climb to (worm his way into) a higher position. Tā yíge'jyèrde syǎng wàng 'shàng dzwān. /He is trying hard to climb to a higher office. Tā yíge'jyèr syǎng shēng'gwār.

Climb down pásyalai, syàlai. /Tell that lineman to climb down. 'Gàusu nèige 'shŕdwo dyàn'hwà de rén ('pá)'syàlai.

A climb is expressed verbally as in the second paragraph. /You will find the climb steep and difficult. Nǐ 'dàu nàr jyòu 'jŕdàu yòu 'jŕ yòu 'nánpá. /Is it much of a climb to the top? Yàu 'pádàu 'dyēngrshàng chyu shŕ bushŕ hěn chŕ'lì?

CLOCK. jūng; tower clock 'dàjūng; table _or_ mantel clock 'dzwòjūng; hall clock 'lì-jūng; alarm clock 'nàujūng. /What time does your clock say? Nǐde 'jūng jǐ'dyǎn le? /Before I went to bed, I set the clock for seven. Wǒ méishwèi yǐ'chyán bǎ 'nàu-jūng °shàng(°bwō)dàu 'chīdyǎn. /We've set the clock by the radio. Wǒmen shr gēn wúsyàn'dyàn bàu'gàu de jūngdyǎr 'dwèide.

To clock (record time used) jì shŕhou. /We'll clock you while you do this. Nǐ dzwò 'jèige, wǒmen gěi ni jì 'shŕhou.

See also **O'CLOCK.**

CLOSE. (Most general terms) gwān, gwānshang, gwānmén, shàngmén, shàngbàr; sometimes expressed negatively as not open bùkāi. These same terms sometimes cover the meanings close out and close up. /Close the door. Gwān'mén. _or_ 'Gwān-shang 'mén. _or_ Bǎ 'mén 'gwānshang. /Why don't you close the drawer? Nǐ 'dzěm-ma bù bǎ 'chōuti 'gwānshang? /The zoo closes at six P.M. Dùngwù'ywán wǎnshang 'lyòudyǎn gwān'mén. /It closed before one o'clock. 'Yìdyǎn jūng yǐ'chyán jyou 'gwānle. /That bookshop closed long ago. Nèige shū'pù 'dzǎujyou gwān'mén le. /That store down the street is closing out. Jyē 'nèibyàrde nèige 'pùdz yàu gwān'mén. /Today is Sunday; the library is closed all day. Jyèr lǐbài'r; túshū'gwǎn yì'tyān bù'kāi. /The museum is closed every evening after six. Bwówù'gwǎn 'měityan 'wǎn-shang 'lyòudyǎn yǐ'hòu jyou bùkāi'mén le. /They close up the store at six. Tāmende 'pùdz shr 'lyòudyǎnjūng °shàng'mén (°shàng'bàr). /They close up promptly at sun-down. 'Tàiyang yí 'lwò jyou shàng'mén le.

(Without barring or locking) yǎn, yǎnshang. /Close the door, but don't bar or lock it. Bǎ 'mén 'yǎnshang, kěshr byé 'chāshang, yě byé 'swǒshang.

(By official order) fēng. /That store was closed. Nèige 'pùdz fēngle 'mén le.

Close a box, trunk, etc. gàishang, gwānshang; (if the cover is hinged) héshang, yǎnshang. /Close the box. Bǎ 'héer °'gàishang (°'gwānshang). _or_ Bǎ hédz'gàr °'gàishang (°'gwānshang). /Close the suitcase. Bǎ shǒutí'syāng °'gàishang (°'gwān-shang, °'héshang, °'yǎnshang). _or_ Bǎ shǒutísyāng'gàr °'gèishang (°etc.). /Close the trunk, but don't lock it.   Bǎ dà'syāngdzde 'gàr 'héshang, kěshr byé 'swǒ.

Close a deal chéngjyāu. /The deal was closed this morning.   Jèipyàur 'mǎimai jyēr 'dzǎushang °chéngde 'jyāu (°chéng'jyāude).

Close a knife héshang, gwānshang. /Please close the knife after using it. Syǎu'dāur yùng'wánle jyòu °'héshang (°'gwānshang).

Close a safety pin byéshang, byéhǎu. /Have the safety pin closed before you give it to the baby to play with.   Bǎ byé'jěr 'byéshang dzài gěi háidz 'wár.

Close a bottle (with a cork) sāishang; (with a cap) gàishang.

Close a letter or speech, expressed with mwòlyǎur end, conclusion. /I'll close this letter with some gossip.   Mwòlyǎur syě dyǎr jèrde 'syánhwà. /He closed the speech with a prayer.   Tā(de) yǎn'shwō mwò'lyǎur dzwòle ge 'dǎugàu.

Close a road lánju. /Let's close the road here.   Dzámen dzài 'jèr bǎ 'lù 'lánju. /The road is closed.   is expressed as The road is not open.   Tsž'lù °bù-'tūng (°bùtūng'syíng).

Close a school (if unscheduled and temporary) tíngkè; (for a regular holiday) fàngjyà; (permanently) tíngbàn, gwānmén. /The school is closed today.   Sywé'syàu jyēr tíng'kè. or (for a holiday) Sywé'syàu jyēr fàng'jyà. /The school is closed for the summer vacation.   Sywé'syàu fàng shǔ'jyà le. /That school was closed because of a deficit.   Nèige sywé'syàu yīnwei 'kwēikung °tíng'bàn le (°gwān'mén le).

Close a stall or stand shōu tār. /That stall closes at seven.   Nèige 'tāndz 'chīdyǎn jyou °'shōu le (°shōu'tār le).

Close an account jyē or swàn followed by jàng account, bill, debt; chyǔ followed by chyán money. /I intend to close my account before I leave.   Wǒ (méi) 'dzǒu yǐ'chyán syǎng chyu °bǎ 'jàng 'jyēle (°bǎ 'jàng 'swànle, °bǎ 'chyán 'chyǔle).

Close an office, particularly a branch office shōu, jyēshù, chyǔsyāu. /Our Hankow branch was closed.   Wǒmen Hànkou fēn'hàu yǐjīng °jyē'shùle (°chyǔ'syāule, °'shōule).

Close the eyes hé, héshang, bì, bìshang. /He closed his eyes before he said that.   Tā °bìshang (°hèshang) 'yǎn tsái 'shwōde. or Tā °bìyǎn (°hé'yǎn) tsái 'shwōde.

Close the eyes to something (fig.). /Don't close your eyes to such matters. Jèiyàngde 'shèr nǐ bùnéng (jyǎ)'jwāng °kànbu'jyàn (°bùjř'dàu, °bù'gwǎn).

Close something tight gwānjǐn, gwānyán. /He didn't close the door tight.   Tā méibǎ 'mén °gwān'yánle (°gwān'jǐnle).

Close up ranks. /Close up! (if marching) Gēn'jǐn yidyǎr! or 'Gēnshangchyu! or Byé dzài 'hòutou 'làlaje! (if standing still) Āi'jǐn yidyǎr! or Wàng °'chyán (°'hòu, °'dzwǒ, °yòu, depending on the direction of motion which will fill the gaps) 'nwó yin- wó!

Close up on, close on, close in (get nearer). /They're closing in on him. Tāmen jyàn'jyānde lí ta 'jǐn le. /They're closing in.   Tāmen 'líde ywè 'lái ywè 'jǐn le.

Be closed (of a legal case) lyǎule, lyǎujyéle. /The case is closed.   Jèige 'àndz °'lyǎule (°'lyǎu'jyéle).

Behind closed doors. /The people are frightened and are hiding behind closed doors.   Rén dōu 'syàde gwān'ménbǐ'hùde 'dwōchilaile.

A close. /At the close of the meeting, everyone left.   is expressed as When the meeting was over everyone left.   'Hwèi 'wánle de shŕhou, dà'jyā dōu 'dzǒule.

/ By the time the exhibition came to a close, it was already snowing. is expressed as
When the exhibition concluded, it was already snowing. Jǎnlǎn'hwèi bǐ'mù de shr̄hou,
yǐjīng 'syàchi 'sywě láile. / The year is drawing to a close. is expressed as This
year will soon be finished. 'Jèiyìnyán kwài 'wán le.

The close (of a letter, speech, article, etc.) mwòlyàur.

CLOSE. (Near) lí . . . jìn. / The hotel is close to the station. Lyǔ'gwǎn lí hwòchē'jàn
hěn 'jìn.

(Of air in a room) mēn. / The air is very close in this room. Jèige 'wūdzli
mēnde'hěn.

(Of a vote). / The vote was very close. Tāmende 'pyàushù chàbu'dwō. / He
won by a close vote. Tā 'chà dyǎr sywǎnbu'shàng.

Close call. / That was a close call! Hǎu 'sywán le! or Jēn 'syǎn! / The car
didn't hit me, but it was a close call. Chìchē méi'jwàngjau wǒ, búgwo °jyǎnjr̄ shr̄
'chà yidyǎr (°'jīijīhū méi'jwàngshang, °'chà dyǎr méi'jwàngshang).

Close friend hǎu péngyou, chīn'jìnde péngyou. / I'm staying with some close
friends. Wǒ syàndzài 'jùdzai °jige hǎu 'péngyou 'jyā (°jige chīn'jìnde 'péngyou
'jyā).

Close neighbor línjyu. / They're close neighbors of ours. Tāmen shr̄ wǒmende 'línjyu.

Close relative chīnrén; (including other comparatively close relatives) jìnchīn.
/ Do you have any close relatives here? Dzài 'jèr yǒu °chīnrén (°jìn'chīn) ma?

Give something **close attention** 'tèbyé jù'yì. / Please give this your close attention. 'Jèige chǐng nǐ 'tèbyé jù'yì.

CLOTH. (of cotton, rarely of wool) bù; (of cotton only) bùlyàur; (material) lyàudz,
lyàur; (clothing material) 'yīlyàur; (cotton sheer, lace, gauze, yarn) 'myánshā, 'shā-
lyàur; (cotton or silk sheer, lace, gauze, yarn) shā; (finest cotton sheer) chányìshā;
(cotton crepe) yángjòu, jòushā; (wool) nídz, 'nílyàur; (angora) 'máurúng, rúngbù;
(velvet) rúng, 'sz̄rúng; (felt) jāndz; (raw silk) sz̄; (silk) chóudwàn; (fine silk) chóudz; (satin) dwàndz; (linen) 'mábù; a cloth bù; dust cloth 'jǎnbù, 'mábù; **tablecloth**
jwōbù. / Wipe off the car with a clean cloth. Bǎ'chē yùng 'gānjing 'bù 'tsā yitsā.
/ Do you have better quality (cotton) cloth? Nǐmen yǒu 'hǎudyàrde 'bù méiyou?
/ Where do you keep your dust cloths? Nǐ bǎ 'jǎnbu 'fàngdzai nǎr? / Change the tablecloth. Hwàn yíkwai jwō'bù. / This cloth is half cotton and half silk. Jèijūng 'lyàudz
shr̄ bàn'sz̄bàn'myánde. / Silk cloth is more expensive than wool. 'Chóudwàn(lyàudz)
bǐ °'nídz (°'nílyàur) hái 'gwèi.

CLOTHE. chwān. / You have to keep warmly clothed in this climate. Jèijūng 'tyānchi
nǐ 'yīngdāng chwān'nwǎnhwole. / He needs this money to feed and clothe his family.
Tā yàu jèi 'chyán hǎu 'gūng tā yìjyā chr̄ 'chwān.

CLOTHES. yīshang, yīfu, chwānde (chwānde means simply what is worn); **evening
clothes** yèlǐfú. / What clothes shall I wear? Wǒ yīngdāng 'chwān shémma °'yīshang
(°'yīfu)? / I want these clothes dry-cleaned. Jèijijyàn 'yīfu 'gānsyǐ. / I found this
in the clothes closet. Jè shr̄ dzài gwà 'yīfu de syǎu'wūrli 'jǎujaude. but / Clothes
make the man. is expressed as Clothes make the man as the saddle makes the horse.
'Rén pèi 'yīshang 'mǎ pèi 'ān.

CLOUD. yún, 'yúntsǎi. / It got chilly when the sun went behind the clouds. Yúntsai bǎ
'tàiyang 'jē chilai yǐ'hòu, tyār 'lyángle dyǎr. / The plane is flying above the clouds.
'Fēijī dzài yúntsai 'shàngmyan fēi.

(Fig.). / The car left in a cloud of dust. Chē kāi 'dzǒu de shŕhou 'yángchi yijèn 'chéntu lai. / Clouds of dense smoke are coming out of the chimney. Yǐ'twán-yǐtwánde 'núng yān jèng tsúng 'yāntungli 'màuchulai. / The grasshoppers came in clouds. 'Hwángchúng yí'pyànyípyànde 'fēigwolai. / One of the partners is a practical man, but the other has his head in the clouds. Tāmen lyǎ dā'hwǒ; yǒu 'yíge bàn-'shŕ hěn chyè shŕ; 'nèige a, jyǎn'jŕ shŕ ge °húdū'chúng (°húsź'lwànsyǎngde, °bú chyèshŕ'jǐ).

Cloudy day *or* sky 'yīntyān.

Be cloudy (of the memory). / The facts are clouded in my memory. 'Shŕchíng-de 'jīnggwò wǒ jìde búdà 'chīngchu le. (of thinking) / His mind was clouded by age. Tā shàngle 'swèishur le, °'syīnli nèmma 'mwómwohuhūde (°'syīnli búdà 'míngbai le).

Cloud up (of the sky) yīn(shanglai); (with word sky expressed) chǐyún. / Just after we started (eating) on the picnic, it began to cloud up. Wǒmen 'gāng chŕchi yě'tsān lai de shŕhou, tyān jyou 'yīnshanglai le. / It's starting to get cloudy. Tyān °yàu 'yīn le (°chǐ'yún le, °yàu 'yīntyān).

To cloud (darken). / His face clouded when I mentioned this man's name. Wǒ tíchi 'jèigerénde 'míngdz de shŕhou, tā lyǎn lìshŕ jyou 'chénsyalaile.

CLUB. (Weapon) gwùndz, bàngdz, chwéi, chwéidz, bàngchwei; **wooden club** 'mùchwéi; **iron club** 'tyěchwéi; policeman's club jǐnggwùn, jŕhwēigwùn. / The policeman was forced to use his club. Jǐng'chá bù'déyǐ tsái yùngde °'gwùndz (°'bàngdz, °jǐng'gwùn, °jŕhwēi'gwùn). / The girls beat the wet clothes with clubs to clean them. Nèisyē nyǔ-'háidz bǎ shŕ 'yīshang yùng 'bàngchwei °'chyāu (°'chyāudǎ, °dǎ) gānjìng le. *but* / He uses a rifle as a club. is expressed as He strikes with a rifle. Yùng chyāng'bàr dǎ.

(Organization) hwèi, shè; (for dancing, gambling, or political activities) jyùlè-bù. / Are you a member of the club? Nǐ shŕ '°hwèiywán ma ('°shèywán ma)? / Our club will meet next Thursday. °Běn'shè (°Běn'hwèi) syàlǐbài'sź kāihwèi. / The tennis court is reserved for club members. Wǎngchyóu'chǎng shŕ wèi hwèi'ywánmen yùngde.

(Suit in cards) 'méihwār. / I bid one club. Wǒ jyàu yíge 'méihwār. / He took the trick with the ace of clubs. Tā ná méi'hwār 'áisz yíngde.

Clubfooted dyǎnjyǎur.

To club someone yùng 'chwéidz dǎ yǐ'chwéi. / The police said the victim had been clubbed over the head. 'Swúnjǐng shwō shòu'hài de rén jyàu rén yùng 'chwéidz dzài tóushang dǎle yǐ'chwéi.

COAL. méi; **hard coal** 'yìngméi; **soft coal** 'yānméi, 'yārméi. / The fire needs more coal. Jèihwǒ děi tyān 'méi. / I want to order a ton of coal. Wǒ yàu jyàu yìdwūn 'méi. / This room is heated by a coal stove in winter. Jèijyān 'wūdz dūngtyan shēng de shŕ 'méi lúdz. / That's a coal-burning furnace. Nèige lúdz shāu'méi. / The ship will stop at that port to take on coal. Chwán yàu tíngdzài nèige 'hǎikǒu shàng-'méi.

(Ember) shāu 'húngle de méi. / Some (red-hot) coals fell from the grate. Yǒu jikwàr shāu 'húngle de 'méi tsúng tyě'bǐdzshang °'dyàusyalaile (°'lòusyalaile).

COARSE. (Not fine) tsū. / This cloth is too coarse. Jèi bù tài 'tsū. / The only flour he had was very coarse. Tā jŕ yǒu yìjǔng hěn 'tsūde myàn'fěn. / His hands are coarse from hard work. Tāde shǒu 'yīnwei dzwò kǔ'gūng swóyi hěn 'tsū.

(Vulgar). tsū, yě, 'tsūyě, 'tsūsú. / This lady was offended by his coarse manners. Tā jyǔjǐ 'tsūyě, rěde jèiwei 'tàitai hěn bùgāu'syìng. / His language was coarse and abusive. Tā shwō de 'hwà yòu 'yě yòu 'tswūn.

COAST. àn, hǎiàn. / So far we have seen only the coast. Jǐ dàu 'jèige shŕhou wǒmen kànjyan de jǐ shŕ hǎi'àn. / The ship sails down the coast. Chwán yánje'àn dzǒu. / Follow the coast road to Boston. Shwunje hǎiàn dà'lù dàu Bwōshŕ'dwūn. (fig.). / Let me know when the coast is clear. (if the point is that no one is in the way) Chyáuchyau 'nèr, méi 'rénde shŕhou, 'gàusung wǒ. (if the point is that some particular person is not in the way) 'Chyáuje dyǎr, tā yǐ 'dzǒukāi jyòu 'gàusung wǒ. (if the point is that the danger is over) °Děng shèr 'gwòle (°Děng shèr píng'jìng-syachyu le, °Děng méiyou 'wéisyǎn le), jyòu 'jŕhwèi wǒ.

To coast lyōu. / Let's try coasting down this next hill. Dzámen 'shŕshŕ lyōu-syà chyánbyarde shān'pwōr chyu.

COAT. 'shàngyī, 'dàyī; suit coat 'shàngyī; **overcoat, topcoat** 'dàyī, dàchǎng, wàitàur; **raincoat** yǔyī. / You can go without a coat in this weather. Jèijǔng 'tyār yùngbujau chwān 'dàyī. / You will need a heavy coat for winter. 'Dūngtyār nǐ dzǔngděi yòu yíjyàn 'hòudàyī. / The pants and vest fit, but the coat is too small. 'Kùdz gēn kǎn-'jyǎr dàu hé'shŕ, búgwò 'shàngyī tài syǎu.

(Layer) tséng; (of paint only) dàu. / This room needs another coat of paint. Jèi wūdz 'hái děi shàng yídàu 'yóuchī.

To coat (cover with a layer) shàng <u>plus the layer of substance</u>; (with paint, mud, molasses, or some other sticky substance, using the hand or a brush) 'mwōshang yìséng . . . , 'tsāshang yìséng . . . , 'túshang °yìséng . . . (°yídàu with 'yóuchī only); (paper with paste) 'húshang yìséng . . . ; (paper with gum, glue, or mucilage) 'jānshang yìséng . . . ; (with splashed mud) 'jyàn(shang) yìséng . . . . / The car was completely coated with mud. Chìchē 'wàibyar mǎn'mārde yìséng 'ní.

(Of the tongue) tāi. / My temperature is above normal and my tongue is coated. Wǒ yòu 'shāu, 'shétoushang yě yòu 'tāi.

COFFEE. 'jyāfēi, 'kāfēi, jyāfēichá, kāfēichá; a pound of coffee yíbàng 'jyāfēi. / I'd like a second cup of coffee, please. Chǐng nǐ dzài gěi wǒ yìbēi °'jyāfēi (°'kāfēi). / Will you have your coffee now or later? Nǐ syàn'dzài yàu 'jyāfēi, háishr 'děng yi-hwěr? / Would you like to drop in for a cup of coffee? Lái 'dzwǒdzwò hē bēi'jyāfēi 'hǎu buhǎu? / Please give me finer-ground coffee. Wǒ yàu mwòde 'syì yidyarde 'jyāfēi. / Do you have any coffee(-flavored) ice cream? Ni you dài jyāfēi'wèr de bǐngji'líng ma?

COIN. fúbì, chyár (less than a dollar in value). / I just gave a coin to the porter. Wǒ gāng gěile jyǎu'háng yíge °chyár (°fú'bì). / Could you give me some coins for this bill? Jèijāng 'pyàudz nǐ kéyi bukéyi gěi wǒ 'hwànchéng °fú'bì (°syǎu 'chyár, °'máuchyár)? <u>or other terms indicating the denomination of the coins desired.</u> / Let's toss a coin to decide. Dzámen rēng ge 'chyár lai (kànkan shr 'dzěr shr 'mèr, dzài) jywé'dìng ba.

To coin <u>money</u> jù (chyán); (fig.) jwàn (chyán). / The government needs to coin more money. 'Jèngfu yīnggāi dwō 'jù syē chyán. / Businessmen are coining money right and left. 'Mǎimàirén syàn'dzài hěn jwàn'chyán.

(Invent). / He coined that phrase himself. Tā nèijyu 'hwà shr °'dùjwàn (°tā 'dzìjǐ 'byànde).

COLD. lěng, lyáng (lyáng usually means cool, but when referring to air or drinks it means cold); **cold cuts** lyáng ròu, lěng hwūn. / The weather has grown cold. 'Tyān-chì 'lěng le. / Is it too cold for you in this room? Nǐ 'jywéde dzài jèjyān 'wūdzli tài 'lĕng ma? / This drink is not cold enough; please put some more ice in it. Jèi 'hē de dūngsyi (or name the particular drink) búgòu 'lyáng; dzài fàng dyăr 'bīng. / It feels cold in here. 'Jèi lĭbyār yŏu dyăr 'lyáng. / The nights are getting cold. 'Yèlĭ ywè 'lái ywè 'lĕng le.

(Not friendly). / After that incident, he grew cold toward us. Dztsúng 'nèijyàn shŕ 'fāshēng yĭ'hòu, tā dwèi wŏmen hĕn 'lĕngdàn. / We received a cold welcome. 'Rénjyā °bùdzĕmma 'dàijìng wŏmen (°méidzĕmma 'hwānyíng).

A cold (illness). / I feel that I'm coming down with a cold. Wŏ 'jywéde wŏ jáu'lyáng le. / Do you have something for a head cold? Nĭmen yŏu jŕ 'shāngfēng de 'yàu ma?

The cold. / Let's go in and get out of the cold. Dzámen 'jìnchyu ba, byé dzài jèr 'dùngje.

Other expressions in English. / He did it in cold blood. (of serious matters, such as murder) Tā hĕnsyīn sya'shòu. (of a less serious matter) Tāde shŏu'dwàn jēn 'là. or Tā jēn shŕ yìdyăr bùlyóu'chíng. / When the new jobs were assigned, he was left out in the cold. Pài syīn 'chāishŕ de shŕhou, bă ta gĕi °'pyēsyale (°'shwăi-le). / The blow knocked him cold. Yí'syàdz bă ta 'dăde °'hwūngwochyule (°'yūng-wochyule). / He got cold feet. Ta syàde 'swōhwéichyule. or Tā syàde wàng 'hwéi-syali swō. or Tā dăr 'syău le. or Tā dăn'chywè le. / He got cold feet about coming. Tā bùgăn 'lái le.

COLLAR. lĭngdz. / I take a size fifteen collar. Wŏ yùng shŕ'wŭhàurde 'lĭngdz. / Do you want your collars starched or soft? Lĭngdz 'jyāng bujyāng?

To collar. / They collared him after a short chase. Tāmen jwēile bù'ywăr jyòu bă ta °'jwājule (°'dĕijule).

COLLECT. (Receive) shŏu; (gather) lyăn. / Tickets are collected at the gate. Rù'mén shŏu'pyàu. or Dzài dàmén'kŏur shŏu'pyàu. / Who'll collect the money? Shwéi shŏu-'chyán ne? or 'Shwéi gwăn shōu 'chyán? / He is in charge of collecting the contribu-tions at all church services. Mĕitsz dzwò lĭ'bài de shŕhou tā gwăn shŏu'chyán. / We need more men to collect taxes. Shŏu'shwèi hái dĕi 'jyā rén tsái 'syíng. / How much money has been collected so far? Chyán'lyănle yŏu 'dwōshău le? / The person who collects rent is here. Shŏu'dzū de rén 'láile. / Someone at the door says he's collecting old clothes for charity. Mén 'wàitou yŏurén shwō shr gĕi 'chyúngrén lyăn jyòu 'yīshang de.

(Of a bill, debt, etc.) shōuchyán, shōujàng, yàuchyán, yàujàng, chyú(chyán). / The laundry man is here to collect the bill. Syĭ'yīfude lái yàu'chyán le. / In China debts are collected on New Year's Eve. Jūnggwo nyándĭ de shŕhou yàu'jàng. / They'll go to your home to collect it. Nèige tāmen yĭ'hòu dàu nĭ 'jyā chyu 'chyú.

(Accumulate, as a hobby or by research) 'shōutsáng, 'sōují; dzăn (used only for hobby collecting, or meaning to save money). / I am interested in collecting stamps. Wŏ 'syĭhwān °'shōutsáng (°'sōují, °dzăn) yóu'pyàu. / He has collected a lot of evidence. Tā 'sōujíle hĕn dwōde 'jèngjyù.

(Of mail) chyú. / When is the mail collected here? 'Jèr 'syìn shémma shŕhou (yŏurén lái) 'chyú?

(Come together) jyù; (gather around) wéi. / A crowd collected around the acci-dent. Chū'shŕ de dìfang °wéile (°'jyùle) yìchyún 'rén. / A large crowd collected there to hear him. Yídàchyún 'rén jyùdzài nàr 'tīng tā. but / He collected about ten children and opened a primary school. Tā shōule shŕlaige syău'hár kāile ge syăusywé.

(Of dust) jī. / Dust has been collecting on that shelf for years. Nèige 'jyàdz 'jīle hăusyē'nyánde °'chéntŭ (°'tŭ).

(Of thoughts) 'kǎulyù yisyar, 'kǎulyùkǎulyu, 'syǎng yisyǎng. /Give me a chance to collect my thoughts. Ràng wǒ °'kǎulyù yisyar (°'kǎulyùkǎulyù). or Rúng wǒ 'syǎng yisyǎng.

(Regain). /He collected his courage and made the final dash. Tā 'gǔle gǔ yǔng'chì jyòu 'pǎugwochyle.

Collect oneself bùhwāng, jèndìng, lěngjìng, bù'hwāngjāng, bùhwāngbù'mángde, 'džrán, 'dždzránrande. /He was comewhat confused at first, but collected himself quickly. Tā 'chǐtóur yǒu dyǎr mwòmíngchí'myàu shrde, kěshr yǐhwěr jyòu °bu-'hwāng le (°jen'dìng, °etc.).

Send something collect. /Send it collect. 'Nèibyār gěi'chyán. or 'Shōude rén gěi'chyán.

Wire someone collect. /Please wire (me) collect. Dyàn'bàuchyán °gwēi (°yóu) 'wǒ °fù (°gěi).

COLLECTION. Expressed verbally as collect. See COLLECT. /Mail collections are at 9 A.M. and 3 P.M. 'Shàngwǔ 'jyǒudyǎn, syàwǔ 'sāndyǎn chyù'syìn. /The library has a famous collection of books on America. Túshū'gwǎn shòutsáng de gwānyú Měijòude shū hěn yǒu'míng. /They took up a collection after the meeting. Hwèi 'wánle yǐhòu tāmen shōule yítsž 'chyán. /May I see your collection of rare books? Gwèigwǎn(shòutsáng)de shànběn'shū kéyi 'kàn yikan ma? /His collection of Ming porcelain has been auctioned. Tā °shòutsáng de (°sōuji de) Míngchau 'tszchǐ yǐ-jīng pāi'màile.

COLLEGE. (An institution higher than high school, lower than the university; or a college or school within a university) sywéywàn; (university or institution beyond high school) 'dàsywé; (technical school of college standards) jwānmén'sywésyàu; college of arts wénsywéywàn; college of sciences lǐsywéywàn; college of arts and sciences wénlǐsywé'ywàn; college of political science and law fǎjèngsywé'ywàn; college of engineering gūngsywéywàn. /There is a famous college in our town. Jèi 'chéngli yǒu yíge hěn yǒu'míngde °'dàsywé (°sywé'ywàn). /Where did you go to college? Nǐ 'dàsywé dzài 'nǎr shàngde? or Nǐ dzài nǎr nyànde 'dàsywé? /He has had two years of college. Tā dzài 'dàsywéli 'nyàngwo lyǎngnyán 'shū. /Lots of college students come here. Hěn dwōde dàsywé'shēng dōu lái 'jèr.

College degree sywéwèi. /He didn't get his college degree. Tā méi 'déjau sywé'wèi. /He has a college degree. Tā 'dàsywé bì'yè le. or Tā shr ge 'dàsywé bìyè'shēng.

COLOR. shǎi, shǎr, 'yánsè, 'yánshǎi, 'yánshǎr. /We have this pattern in several colors. Jèiyàng 'hwàrde wǒmen yǒu hǎujijǔng °'yánshǎrde (°'shǎide, °'yánsède, °etc.). /Write down the color of your hair, eyes, and complexion. Bǎ nǐ 'tóufa, 'yǎnjing, gēn 'pífūde 'yánsè syědzài 'jèr. /What color eyes does she have. Tā yǎn-'jūr shémma °'shǎrde (°'shǎide, °'yánsède, °etc.). /In China the color of the hair and eyes is rarely used for identification. Dzài 'Jūnggwo hěn shǎu yùng 'tóufa gēn yǎn'jūrde 'yánshǎr lái 'byànbyé rén. /Once you get out in the air, your color will improve. Nǐ chūchyu 'tòutou 'chyèr yǐhòu, 'yánsè jyòu hwèi hǎu'dwō le. /That color is too bright. Nèige 'yánsè tài 'syānle. /Do you have anything that is of a lighter color? Yǒu yánsè 'chyǎn yìdyǎr de ma?

(Vividness, brightness). /The flowers added color to the table. Yǒu nèmme yìpén 'hwār syànde 'jwōrshang 'rèrenaunàude.

Colors (flag) chí; (of a nation) gwóchí; (of a regiment) twánchí.

To color (blush) húng. /Her face colored. Tā lyǎn 'húngle.

(Give color to). / She wants the walls colored green. is expressed as She wants a green-colored wall. Tā yàu 'lyùyánshaide chyáng.

(Misrepresent). / The news in that paper is generally colored to suit the publisher. Nèige 'bàuli de 'syīnwén 'chángcháng °dài 'sètsǎi (°yǒu pyān'jyàn). / He colored his report a bit to protect you. Wèile 'wéihù nǐ tā bǎ bàu'gàu syěde gēn shř'shř yǒu dyǎr chū'rù.

Colored person (negro) hēirén, hēijūngrén.

COLORFUL. (Including many colors). / Her clothes are colorful. Tāde 'yīshang °'yánsè hěn dwō (°yǒu hěn dwō 'shǎr).

Too colorful (gaudy, too loud). / Her clothes are too colorful. Tāde 'yīshang °wǔ'yánlyòu'sède (°tài 'hwā).

(Adventurous; of life). / He led a colorful life. (of an old man) Tā yí'bèidz hěn bùpíng'fán. (of a young man) Tā gwò de 'shēnghwo bùpíng'fán.

COLUMN. (Shaft, pillar) jùdz; in combinations jù; stone column shřjù. / You can recognize his house by its white columns. 'Chyántou yǒu dàbái'jùdz de jyòu shř tā 'jyā. / Whose statue is on top of that column? 'Jùdz 'dǐngr shang shř shéide 'syàng.

Memorial column (obelisk) jìnyànbēi, jìnyàntǎ.

(Of smoke) gǔdz. / I wonder where that column of smoke comes from? Nèigǔdz 'yān yěbúshr tsúng 'nǎr láide.

(Formation) 'dzùngdwèi. / The soldiers marched in a column of twos. Bīng 'páije èrlù'dzùngdwèi chyán'jìn.

(Of print) háng. / There are two colums per page. Měi'yè lyǎng'háng.

(Regular feature in a newspaper). / His column on foreign affairs appears in twenty newspapers. Tāde gwójì 'shřpíng 'dēngdzài 'èrshrjijyā 'bàushang.

COMB. lúngdz, 'lúngshū, shūdz, 'mùshū; (fine-toothed) bǐdz. / I left my comb on the dresser. Wǒ bǎ °'lúngdz (°'lúngshū, °etc.) gēdzài shūjwǎng'táishang le. / She always wears several combs in her hair. Tā 'tóushang lǎu dàije háujige 'lúngdz.

(Honeycomb) fēngwō. / They have honey in jars, but not in combs. Tāmen jèrde fēng'mì shř 'píngdz jwāngde, méiyou dzài ywánláide fēng'wōli de.

To comb lúng, shū. / My hair needs combing. Wǒ děi 'lúnglúng tóu. or Wǒde 'tóufa děi 'shū yishu le.

(Search thoroughly) dzài . . . jīlegā'lárde 'jǎu. / We had to comb the city to find him. Dzài chywán'chéngli jīlegā'lárde jǎu tsái bǎ ta 'jǎujaude.

COME (CAME). (Specifying motion toward or to the speaker's position) lái; (specifying motion not toward the speaker's position) chyù; (definitely indicating arrival) dàu, often with lái or chyù later in the sentence. / Coming! (Wǒ) jyòu 'lái! or (Wǒ) jyòu 'chyù! (depending on whether the speaker speaks in terms of his position as he says it or in terms of the position he will have after the motion is done). / He came before nine. Tā 'jyǒudyǎn yǐ'chyán °'láide (°'dàude). / Did you come at nine? meaning Was nine o'clock one of the times that you came? Nǐ shř 'jyǒudyǎn 'láigwo yǐ'tsz ma? but meaning Was it at nine o'clock that you came? Nǐ shř 'jyǒudyǎn 'dàude ma? / He's come before. Tā yǐ'chyán láigwo. / They came after him (or after he did). Tāmen shř dzài tā yǐ'hòu láide. / Some letters came in the mail today. 'Jīntyan yǒu'syìn láile. or 'Jīntyan láile jǐfēng 'syìn. / When did he come? Tā 'jǐshř 'láide? / Come forward! Dàu 'chyánbyan lái!

420

(Followed by a word like here *or* home that specifies the terminus of the motion) dàu . . . °lái (°chyù); <u>if the motion is a return to a place from which one has come earlier</u> hwéi . . . °lái (°chyù). / Come here! Dàu 'jèr lái! often shortened to 'Jèr lái! / Why not come home with me for dinner tonight? Gēn wǒ hwéi'jyā chyu chr̄'fàn, 'hǎu buhǎu?

(Specifying position in some series). / She comes first. <u>is expressed as</u> The first one is her. 'Tóuyíge shr̀ 'tā. / Your turn comes next. <u>is expressed as</u> Next it will revolve to you. 'Syàyíge lwúndau 'nǐ. / It comes at the end of the book. <u>is expressed as</u> That is at the end of the book. Nèige dzài shūde mwò'lyǎur. / When does Easter come this year? <u>is expressed as</u> When is Easter this year? Fùhwó'jyé jǐnnyan shr̀ 'nèityān?

(Meaning be available *or* be produced) yǒu. / Does this cloth come in other colors? Jèige 'bù yǒu 'byéde 'yánshǎrde ma?

(Specifying future time). / The time will come when everyone will be literate. <u>is expressed as</u> Sooner or later there will be a day when everyone will be literate. 'Dzǎuwǎn yǒu 'nèmma yìtyān, rénrén dōu shr̀'dz.

Come plus an infinitive (specifying purpose) lái. / He'll come to see you. Tā yàu °lai 'kàn ni (°'kàn ni lai, °lai 'kàn ni lai). / They came to listen to the radio. Tāmen (lai) tīng wúsyàn'dyàn laile. / I've come to ask about a room. Wǒ (lai) 'dǎting 'fángdz laile.

Come about (happen) chéng, dàu. / How did all this come about? 'Dzěmma jyòu chéng 'jèiyangr le? *or* Dzěmma chéngle 'jèmma ge 'jyúshr̀? *or* Dzěmma dàule 'jèmma ge 'dìbù?

Come across <u>something</u> (cross over something towards the speaker) gwò (. . . lái); wàng . . . 'jèibyar lái. / The car's coming across the bridge now. Chī'chē jèng wàng 'chyáu 'jèibyar lái le.

Come across <u>something</u> (find) kànjyan, yùjyan. / Let me know if you come across anything with my name on it. Nǐ yàushr °'kànjyan (°'yùjyan) shémma 'dūngsyi yǒu wǒ 'míngdz de, chǐng ni gàusung wo yìshēngr. *but* / Come across! (fork over) Náchulai! *or* Gěi wo! (confess or inform) Shwōchulai! *or* Gàusung wo!

Come after (come to get) chyǔ, ná, lǐng (if a thing); jǎu (if a person); ná děi (if a person, in the sense of arresting); <u>all of these are preceded by</u> lái. / I've come after my passport. Wǒ lái °'chyǔ (°'ná, °'lǐng) wǒde hù'jàu laile. / They came after him. Tāmen lái 'jǎu ta.

Come along <u>something</u> (follow a route) dzài . . . lái. / Whose car is that coming along the road? Dzài'dàurshang wàng 'jèr lái de nèilyàng 'chē shr̀ 'shéide? *but* / Come along! (hurry up) 'Kwài dyǎr! *or* Kwàije! *or* 'Kwài lái! *or* 'Kwài dzǒu!

Come along (come also, accompany) yě lái, yě chyù, gēnje. / Mind if we come along? Wǒmen °'yě chyù (°'gēnje), nǐ 'dzàihu ma?

Come along (develop). / Everything is coming along well, thanks. <u>is expressed as</u> Everything is quite smooth, thanks. Yí'chyè dōu hěn 'shwùnlì, twó'fú. / How's your work coming along? <u>is expressed as</u> How is your work progressing? Nǐ 'gūngdzwò jìn'syíngde dzěmma'yàng le?

Come around (to our place) *see* **Come up, Come over.**

Come around <u>a corner</u> dzài . . . 'gwǎigwolái. / He just came around the corner. Tā 'gāng dzài 'jyējyǎur nèr 'gwǎigwòlái.

Come around (recover from illness) jyǎn hǎu. / She was very sick, but she's coming around now. Tā 'syān bìngde hěn 'lìhai, kěshr 'yǐjing jyàn 'hǎu le.

Come around to <u>a point of view</u> gēn . . . yí'jr̀ le. / He disagreed for a while, but now he's come around to our point of view. Yǒu yí'jèndz tā hěn 'byènyou, kěshr syàn'dzài tā 'yǐjing gēn 'wǒmende 'yìjyan yí'jr le.

Come away from a place lí . . . dzǒu, líkai. / Come away from there! 'Líkai nàr! *or* 'Dzǒukai!

Come back (return) hwéilai (sometimes hwéichyu). / Hey! Come back here! 'Hèi! 'Hwéilai! / I'll come back in a minute. Wǒ 'jèjyou 'hwéilai. *or* Wǒ yì'hwěr jyòu 'hwéilai.

Come back. / He retired ten years ago but he's now trying to come back (*or* make a come-back). 'Shrnyánchyán tā jyòu bú'gàn jèige le, kěshr syàndzài 'yòu syǎng °'gàn (°'dzài lái).

Come back to a place hwéi . . . lái, 'hwéidàu . . . lái. / I hope to come back to China often. Wǒ 'syīwang 'chángcháng néng hwéi(dau) 'Jūnggwo lai.

Come back to (be recalled by) syǎngchilai. / Suddenly it all came back to me. 'Hūránjyān wǒ dōu 'syǎngchilaile.

Come before a meeting (arise, be considered) tíchulai, tǎulwùn. / That question will come before the meeting this morning. Nèige 'wèntí jyēr 'dzāuchen kāi'hwèi hwèi °'tíchulai (°'tǎu'lwùnde).

Come before (in arrangement or protocol) dzài . . . 'chyánbyan. / The Secretary of State comes before the Secretary of Defense. Gwówùchīng dzài Gwófángbù Bùjǎng 'chyánbyan.

Come beyond expectations. / The results came far beyond our expectations. is expressed as The results were much better than the expectations. °'Jyēgwǒ (°'Chéngjì) bǐ 'yùlyàu de 'hǎude 'dwō.

Come by a route °yóu (°tsúng, °dǎ) . . . lái. / He's coming by the shorter route. Tā shr yóu 'jìndàur wàng 'jèr lái ne.

Come by, come past gwò, 'gwòlái, dǎ jèr gwò. / I was just coming by and thought I'd drop in. Wǒ jèng da jèr 'gwò, swóyi 'jìnlai 'kàn yikàn.

Come by (*or* past) a place 'lùgwò, 'jīnggwò, dǎ . . . 'gwò, tsúng . . . 'gwò. / He comes by our house every morning at this hour. Tā 'měityān 'dzāuchen jèige 'shŕhou °'lùgwò wǒmen 'jyā (°'jīnggwò wǒmen 'jyā, °'dǎ wǒmen 'jyā 'gwò, °tsúng wǒmen 'jyā 'gwò).

Come by (acquire) 'dédàu, lái. / How did you come by this? 'Jèige nǐ 'dzěmma 'dédàude? / How did he come by all that money? Tā 'nǎr láide nèmma syē 'chyán?

Come close to doing something *See* **Come near.**

Come down 'syàlái; (if from upstairs) syà'lóu lái; (if from further north; *see* Come up). / Come down here and we'll talk it over. °'Syàlai (°Syà'lóu lai), dzámen hǎu 'tántan.

A come-down. / His new job is quite a come-down. is expressed as He's really taken a lower position Tā 'jēnshr dǐ'jyòule.

Come down from a place tsúng . . . lái (in Chinese one omits the down idea) / I came down from Peiping by plane this morning. Wǒ 'jīntyan 'dzāuchen tsúng Běi-'píng dzwò fēi'jī láide.

Come down from a higher position tsúng . . . syàlái. / When he came down from the platform the crowd gathered around to congratulate him. Tā tsúng 'tái-shang 'dzǒusyàlái de shŕhou, dà'jyāhwǒr bǎ ta 'wéishàngle.

Come down off. / Come down off your high horse! (referring to haughty talk) Byé 'chwēile! *or* Shǎu 'chwēi dyǎr ba! (but said about facial expressions or about actions) Byé 'nèmma 'shénchi le! *or* Shǎu 'shénchi yìdyǎr ba!

Come down on someone (with a verbal attack) mà, 'jŕwèn; (with a physical attack) dǎ. /He came down on him sharply. Tā 'màde ta hěn 'lìhai. /They came down on him as soon as he sat down. Tā 'gāng yí dzwòsya, tāmen jyou °'jŕwèn ta (°'mà ta, °'dǎ ta).

Come down with a disease dé. /I think I'm coming down with the flu. Wǒ 'dàgài shr̀ 'déle jùngshāng'fēng le.

Come forward to do something *see* **Come out.**

Come from a place tsúng . . . lái; (in the sense of having that place as one's original home) tsúng . . . lái. /Do you come from America? Nǐ 'shr̀ bushr̀ tsúng 'Měigwo láide? /How long did it take you to come from America this time? 'Jèitsz̀ tsúng 'Měigwo lái 'yùngle 'dwōshau shŕhou?

Come from a family, stock, etc. /He comes from a very old family Tā shr̀ yíge 'shr̀jyāde 'hòudài.

Come in (enter a place) 'jìnlái. /I just saw him come (*or* coming) in. Wǒ gāngtsái 'kànjyan ta 'jìnlai. /Won't you come in and have a drink? 'Jìnlái 'hē dyǎr 'shémma. /Come (on) in! 'Jìnlái! *or* (more politely) Chǐng 'jìn! /This is where I came in. Wǒ jyòushr dzài 'jèr 'jìnlaide. or expressed as I ought to leave. Gāi 'dzǒule.

Come in (of money) 'shōujìnlái, jìn. /The money due us is coming in slowly. (of debts) Wàibyarde 'jàng jèng dzài màn'mārde 'shōujìnlai. (of other funds) Nèisyē 'kwǎndz jèng dzài yì'bǐyìbǐde 'jìn, búgwò 'mǎndyǎr.

Come in (in expressions other than the above). /Where do I come in? meaning Where do I speak (*or* start to act)? (as on the stage) 'Wǒ dzài 'nǎr 'chājìnchyu? meaning Where in the line do I fit? (as in a parade) 'Wǒ dzài 'nǎr jyā'rù? meaning What part of it am I supposed to do? (as when plans are being drawn up) 'Wǒ dzwò 'shémma ne? *or* Wǒ gàn 'shémma ne? meaning Why'd you leave me out of consideration? *or* What do I get out of it? 'Wǒ bǎi 'nǎr ne? *or* Wǒ dzài 'nǎr 'bǎi ne? /Where does the joke come in? is expressed as Where's the funny part? 'Nǎ yìdyǎr shr̀ kě'syàude? *or* Kěsyàude dìfang dzài 'nǎr? /When did this style come in? °'Jèijǔng 'jwāngshù (°'Jèige yàngr) 'shémma shŕhou 'syìngchilaide?

Come in for something (be the butt or object of) jǎuje jyàurén . . . . /He came in for a lot of kidding. Tā 'jǎuje jyàurén °'wǎku (°gēn ta kāi wán'syàu).

Come in handy 'yùngdejáu. /This tool will come in handy during the trip. Jèijyàn 'jyāhwo dzài 'lùshang jyòu 'yùngdejáule.

Come into a place jìn, 'jìnlái. /He just came into the house. Tā gāng jìn 'wūdz láile.

Come into money (acquire; the verb depends on the context). /He came into a lot of money after the lawsuit. Nèisyē 'chyán shr̀ tā dǎ'gwānsz 'dàlaide.

Come into play (*or* effect) shŕsyíng. /When your plan comes into play, there will be no more profit for those scoundrels. Nǐde 'jìhwa yì shŕ'syíng, jèichyún hwún'dàn jyòu 'lāubujáu shémma le.

Come into power 'dédàu, dāng. /The revolutionists came into power. Gémìngdǎng °dédàule jèngchywán (°dāng'chywán).

Come into sight (*or* view) chū, syànchulai, kàndejyàn. /The ship came into sight over the horizon just a minute ago. Nèityáu 'chwán 'gāng tsúng tyān'byārshang 'syànchulai.

Come loose sūngle. /The knot came loose. Jǐde 'kòur 'sūngle.

Text

Come near (approach) dzŏu (*or* pau or another verb of motion) 'jìn yidyăr. /Wait until he comes near. Dĕng tā dzŏu 'jìn yidyăr.

Come near doing something, **come near to** (*or* close to) doing something 'chà-dyăr (méi). /I came near throwing the thing at him. Wŏ 'chàdyăr (méi)nà nèige 'cháuta °'jwāigwochyu (°'kăngwochyu).

Come off (be removable) hwó; (by being lifted) násyalai; (by falling) dyàusyalai; (by other means) the appropriate verb plus syàlai. /Is this lid fastened or does it come off? Jèige 'gàr °'hwóde ma (°'náde'syàlai ma)? /We can't use the table because a leg has come off. Jèijāng 'jwōdz yŏu ge 'twĕr 'dyàusyalaile, swóyi bùnéng 'yùng.

Come off (happen) gwòle, wánle. /Has the high hurdle race come off yet? Gāulán 'pău'°gwòle ma (°'wánle ma)?

Come off expressed with 'jyēgwŏ result. /How did it come off? 'Jyēgwŏ dzĕm-mà'yang? /The concert came off as we expected. Yīnywèhwèide 'jyēgwŏ gēn wŏmen 'yùlyàu yí'yàng. /He came off a loser. Tā 'jyēgwŏ shř 'bàile.

Come on (begin) lái. /A storm came on before we got home. Wŏmen méidàu-'jyā yĭ'chyán, láile yíjèn 'kwángfēngbàu'yŭ.

A (*or* The) **come-on.** /Is she giving us the come-on (signal to approach)? Tā nà shř jyàu dzámen chyù jău tā chyu ma? /The cheap camera in that store is a come-on. Nèige pùdzlide 'pyányi jàusyàngjī shr 'jău rén chyu măi 'dūngsyi.

Come on stage dēngtái, chūtái. /When she came on stage the lights went out. Tā °dēng'tái (°chū'tái) de shŕhou 'dēng 'myèle.

Come out (exit, *or* appear) 'chūlái. /Come on out! 'Chūlái ba! /The sun didn't come out all day. 'Tàiyang yĭ'tyān méi'chūlai.

Come out (appear, other than of the sun) 'syānchūlái. /If you put lemon juice on the paper, the invisible writing will come out. Yàushr ná 'níngméng'jŕdz sháng-dzai nèijāng 'jŕshang, syàndzài kànbu'jyànde 'dz jyòu 'syānchūlái.

Come out (grow) chū. /A rash came out on his face. Tā 'lyănshang chū °húng-'dyăndz (°húng'bān).

Come out (be published; of a news account) dēng; (of a publication) 'chūlái, chūbăn. /The story hasn't yet come out in the papers. Nèidwàr 'syīnwén 'bàujŕ-shang hái méi'dēng. /When is that book coming out? Nèibĕn'shū 'shémma shŕhou °'chūlai (°chū'băn)? /When is the next issue of that magazine coming out? 'Syàyìchī 'shémma shŕhou °'chūlai (°chū'băn)?

Come out (be extracted, eliminated or made to disappear) bá, básyalai (of a tooth); lá, lásyachyu, bùlyóu (of a sentence or word to be deleted); tsāsyachyu (by rubbing); méile (be eliminated); other conditions call for other verbs plus syàlai *or* syàchyu. /That tooth's got to come out. Nèige 'yá dĕi 'bá(syàlai). /That sentence has got to come out. Nèijyù 'hwà dĕi 'lásyachyu. /If you put lemon juice on the cloth, the grease spot will come out. 'Bùshangde nèikwài yóu'dyăndz yùng 'níngméng-'jŕdz yĭ 'tsā jyòu °'tsāsyachyule (°'méile).

Come out a certain way is expressed with 'jyēgwŏ result. /Everything came out all right. Yíchyè 'jyēgwŏ hái dōu bú'tswò. /It (a calculation) didn't come out right. is expressed as The figure is wrong. 'Shùr bú'dwèi.

Come out against °sywàn'bù (°shwō) 'făndwèi. /The governor came out against the bill. Shĕng'jăng °sywàn'bùle (°shwōle) 'făndwèi jèige yì'àn.

Come out of a place tsúng . . . 'chūlái. /He came out of the room. Tā tsúng 'wūdzli 'chūlai.

COME

Come out on top yíng. /Who came out on top in the election? 'Sywǎnjyǔ 'jyēgwǒ 'shéi 'yíngle?

Come out (or forward) to do something chūlái. /No one came out to put in a word for him. Lyán 'yíge chūlai 'gěi ta shwō jyù'hwà de yě 'méiyou.

Come out with (information) shwōchulai; (a statement) 'sywānbù, shwō; (a suggestion) tíchulai; (object of money) náchulai. /At long last he came out with it. Dàu'lyǎur tā °'shwōchulaile (°'náchulaile). /He came out with a denial. Tā °'sywān- bù (°shwō) méi 'nèmma hwéi 'shèr. /He came out with a good suggestion. Tā 'tí- chu(lai) yíge hěn 'hǎude 'yìjyan.

Come over (or around) lái kàn. /We have friends coming over this evening. Jyèr 'wǎnshang yǒu 'péngyou yàu lái 'kàn wǒmen.

Come over something tsúng . . . gwòlái. /Who's that coming over the hill? Nèige tsúng 'shānshang 'dzǒugwolaide shr 'shéi?

Come over (take possession of). /What's come over you? Nǐ shr 'dzěmma le?

Come past see Come by.

Come short of. /He came short of what we expected. Tā jyàu wǒmen shr'wàng.

Come through something (motion) tsúng . . . 'dzwānchulai. /The train's coming through the tunnel. Hwǒ'chē tsúng shān'dùngli 'dzwānchulaile.

Come through (arrive) gwòlai, dàu, lái. /The mail can't come through. 'Yóu- jyàn °gwòbu'lái (°'dàubulyǎu, °'láibulyǎu).

Come through (survive) hǎule, méishèr le, gwòlai. /The operation was seri- ous, but he came through. Shǒushù hěn 'wéisyǎn, búgwò °tā 'yǐjing 'hǎu le (°tā 'yǐjing méi'shèr le, °jèige 'gwān tā swàn 'gwòlaile).

Come to (from a faint) 'hwǎnsyīnggwòlái, syǐnggwolai. /The woman who fainted is coming to. 'Yūngwochyu de nèige 'nyǔrén 'yǐjing màn'mārde (hwǎn)'syǐnggwolai le.

Come to (a place) dàu . . . lái; (a person) dàu . . . jèr lái, dàu . . . nèr lái. /When did you come to China? Nǐ 'shémma shŕhou dàu 'Jūnggwo láide? /He came to you, didn't he? Tā dàu 'nǐ jèr láile, 'búshr ma? or Tā lái 'nǐ jèr, 'búshr ma? /Come to me. Dàu 'wǒ jèr lái. or (if the speaker will be elsewhere when the coming takes place) Dàu 'wǒ nàr chyù.

Come to (amount to) yí'gùng shr. /The bill comes to two dollars. 'Jàng yí- 'gùng shr 'lyǎngkwài chyán.

Come to (result in) dàu, or expressed with 'jyēgwǒ result. /Who knows what all this will come to? Shéi 'jr̄dau 'jyǎnglái dàu 'dzěmma ge 'dìbu? or Shéi 'jr̄dàu 'jyǎnglai 'jyēgwǒ dzěmma'yàng? or Jèisyē 'shèr 'jyǎnglai 'chéng ge shémma 'jyē- jyú hěn nán 'yùlyàu. /Has it come to this? Dàule 'dzěmma ge 'dìbu le ma?

Come to a conclusion 'dédàu. /How did you come to that conclusion? Nèige 'jyēlwùn nǐ 'dzěmma 'dédaude?

Come to an understanding 'dédàu yìjǔng lyàng'jyě, shwōhǎule. /I think we'll be able to come to an understanding soon. Wǒ 'syang wǒmen bù'jyǒu jyòu kéyi °'dédàu yìjǔng lyàng'jyě (°shwō'hǎule).

Come to a head (of a boil or pimple) jǎngjyār, chūtóur; (of a situation) dàu 'jǐn yàugwān'tóu. /The boil has come to a head. Nèige 'gēde °'jǎngchy 'jyār láile (°'chūle 'tóurle). /When things come to a head, he'll dodge the issue. Děng dàule 'jǐn yàugwān'tóu, tā jyòu yàu 'twèitwō le.

Come to an end. /It's a pity all this came to an end. Kě'syǐ bái 'fèile yìhwéi 'shèr.

425

Come to blows dùngchǐ 'chywántou lai. / They came to blows. Tāmen dùngchǐ 'chywántou láile.

Come to pieces (of something composed of parts) sǎn; (of a single but fragile thing) swèi. / It'll come to pieces if you touch it. Yí 'pèng jyòu °'sǎn (°'swèi).

Come to believe (*or* think, etc.). / I've come to believe that he didn't do it. is expressed as Now I'm somewhat of the belief that it wasn't he who did it. Wǒ syàn-'dzài yǒu dyǎr syāng'syìn 'búshr tā 'gànde le. / Come to think of it, it does look suspicious. is expressed as With careful thinking, it does look suspicious. 'Dzǎyì 'syǎng yisyǎng, 'shr yǒu dyǎr kě̌yí. / How did you come to think of this? is expressed as How did you think of this? Nǐ 'dzěmma syǎngdau 'jèige de?

Come true dwèile, 'yìngyànle. / Everything he predicted came true. Tā 'yù-lyàudàu de yíjyànyíjyànde dōu 'dwèile. *or* Tā 'shwō de nèisye 'hwà yíjyànyíjyànde dōu 'yìngyànle.

Come under something tsúng . . . dǐsya gwò. / The boat's coming under the bridge. 'Chwán jèng tsúng 'chyáu dǐsya 'gwò ne.

Come under (be subject to) àn . . . lái 'bàn. / What regulations does this come under? 'Jèige àn 'něijǔng 'fǎgwēi lái 'bàn?

Come up (from a lower position) 'shànglái; (if from downstairs) shàng 'lóu lai. / Come up here and we'll talk it over. °'Shànglái (°Shàng 'lóu lai), dzámen hǎu 'tántán. *or* (if from farther south, in which case the idea of up is omitted in Chinese) expressed as Come to where I am and we'll talk it over. Shàng 'wǒ jèr lai, dzámen hǎu 'tántán.

Come up (present itself) yǒu. / This problem comes up every day. Jèige 'wèntí tyān'tyārde yǒu.

Come up (of the sun) is expressed as come out 'chūlái. / The sun's come up. 'Tàiyang 'chūlai le.

Come up (of things planted) chū, jǎngchulai. / Our tomatoes didn't come up this spring. Wǒmende syīhúng'shr jǐnnyán méi°'chū (°'jǎngchulai).

Come up (*or* around *or* over) to a person's residence or place of business) lái. / Come over and see me some night. 'Něityān 'wǎnshang lái 'kànkan wo. / Won't you come up and have some tea? Lái hē bēi 'chá, 'hǎu buhǎu?

Come up (of something eaten) tù. / My dinner came up. Wǒ 'tùle.

Come up something (proceed along) dzài . . . °'dzòugwòlái (°'gwòlái, °etc.). / He came up the walk limping a bit. Tā dzài syǎu'dàurshang 'dzǒugwolai de shŕhou yǒu dyǎr 'chywé.

Come up from a place; Chinese omits the idea of up and says come from tsúng . . . lái. / I came up from Chungking on the early plane. Wǒ tsúng Chúng'chǐng dzwò 'dzǎubārde fēi'jī láide.

Come up on one (of something eaten) wàng 'shàng yàng. / My dinner keeps coming up on me. Wǒ 'chŕ de dūngsyi jŕ wàng shàng 'yàng.

Come upon (find) 'dédàu. / I came upon the answer by accident. Wǒ shr pèng-'chyǎu 'dédàu jèige dá'àn de.

Come within (fall within the range of) dzài . . . yǐ'nèi. / Does this come within the terms of our agreement? Jèige dzài dzámen shwō'hǎule de 'tyáujyàn yǐ'nèi ma?

. . . **to come** in the following expressions: in time to come yǐ'hòu, 'jyānglái; in the years to come yǐ'hòu jǐ'nyánli, 'jyānglái jǐ'nyánli.

Coming specifying future time: this coming Saturday is expressed as this week's

Saturday 'jèige lǐbài'lyòu *or* 'běnlǐbài'lyòu; **this coming Tuesday** is expressed as this week's Tuesday 'jèige lǐbài'èr *or* 'běnlǐbài'èr, or as next week's Tuesday 'syà-lǐbài'èr, depending on what day it is as one speaks.

Other English expressions. / How are things coming? Dzěmma'yàng le? / Easy come, easy go. 'Láide rúngyi, 'chyùde rúngyi. / How come? 'Dzěmma ne? *or* 'Dzěmma hwéi 'shèr? / How come YOU weren't there? Dzěmma jyòushr 'nǐ méi-'dzài nàr ne? / Come, now, don't try to frighten me! 'Swànle ba, byé 'jǐng syǎng 'syàhu wo le! / Come come! Do you think I'll bite a second time? 'Hèi! Wǒ 'hái néng shàng 'lyǎngtsz̀ 'dàng ma?

COMFORT. (Physical)。 / This bed was not built for comfort. is expressed as This bed is not comfortable. Jèige'chwáng bù'shūfu.

(Material). / The Red Cross saw to their comfort. is expressed as The Red Cross took care of them. 'Húngshŕdz'hwèi 'jàugu tāmen.

(Relief). / The medicine didn't give me any comfort from the pain. is expressed as The medicine didn't relieve the pain at all. Jèige 'yàu 'yìdyǎr bùjř'téng.

Comforts. / They lack many comforts. is expressed as They don't have many things. Tāmen hǎusyē 'dūngsyi dōu méi'yǒu.

To comfort jyàu . . . gāu'syìng, 'syīnli kéyi 'dé dyar 'ānwèi. / This news may comfort you. Jèige 'syāusyī yěsyǔ jyàu nǐ gāu'syìng yìdyar. *or* Nǐ 'tīngjyan jèige yěsyǔ 'syīnli kéyi 'dé dyar 'ānwèi.

COMFORTABLE. shūfu. / This chair is soft and comfortable. Jèibǎ 'yǐdz yòu 'rwǎn yòu 'shūfu. / Were you comfortable sleeping here? Dzài jèr 'shwèide hái 'shūfu ma? / He makes a comfortable living. Tā gwò de řdz hěn 'shūfu.

COMFORTABLY. Expressed with shūfu **comfortable.** / He's living comfortably. Ta (de 'řdz) 'gwòde °'shūshufufúrde (°hěn 'shūfu).

COMMAND. (Order) jyàu; (more officially) 'mìnglìng. / He commanded his son to break the engagement. Tā °jyàu (°'mìnglìng) tā 'érdz jyěchú hwūn'ywē.

(Take charge of) tǔngshwài, 'shwàilǐng, 'jŕhwēi, gwǎn, dài, lǐng, dàilǐng. / He commands (*or* is in command of) fifteen destroyers. Tā °tǔng'shwài (°shwài-'lǐng, °'jŕhwēi, °'gwǎn, °'dài, °'lǐng, °dài'lǐng) shŕ'wǔř chyūjú'jyàn. / This expedition is commanded by an old general. Jèige 'ywǎnjēng'jyūn °shù (°'gwēi) yíge lǎu'jyāngjyūn °dài'lǐng (°'tǔng'shwèi, °etc.). / The three divisions which he commands suffered heavily. Tā °'gwǎnde (°'dàide, °etc.) sān'shŕ 'rén 'swǔnshŕ hěn 'jùng. / He commands the nineteenth division. Dìshŕ'jyǒu 'shŕ °gwēi (°'jyāugei) ta °'dài (°'gwǎn, °etc.).

(Evoke). / He commands respect. Tā jyàurén bùnéng bù'dzwūnjùng.

Command a view. / That hill commands an excellent view of the city. is expressed as On that hill you can see the whole city. Dzài nèige 'shānshang kànde-'jyàn chywán'chéng.

Be commanded (be ordered) fèngmìng. / We were commanded to take to the lifeboats. Wǒmen fèng'mìng shàng jyòushēng'chwán.

A command (an order) mìngling. / Has he issued his command? Tāde 'mìng-ling 'fāsyalai 'méiyou?

(A charge; military) various expressions as illustrated below. / He was relieved of his command. Tā gāng chèle 'jŕ. / A new officer has taken command of the troops. 'Syīnláide °sz̀'lìng (°jāng'gwān) jyē'rèn le. / Have you ever served under his command? Nǐ 'gēngwo tā ma? *or* Nǐ dzài tā nèr dzwǒgwo 'shř ma?

(Mastery). /Does he have a good command of English? (spoken) Tā 'Yīngwén 'shwōde 'hǎu ma? (written) Tā 'Yīngwén 'syéde 'hǎu ma?

Be in command of is expressed as in paragraph two above. /He is in command of fifteen destroyers. Tā °tǔng'shwài (°shwài'lǐng, °'jřhwèi, °gwǎn, °dài, °lǐng, °dài'lǐng) shř'wǔjř chyūjújyàn.

Officer in command, commanding officer jǔgwǎnjǎng'gwān, jǎnggwān, szlǐng, jřhwèi, szlǐnggwān, jřhwēigwān. *See also* **COMMANDER**. /Who is the commanding officer? Jèige 'dìfang °shwéi shř (jǔgwǎn)'jǎnggwān (°shwéi shř 'szlǐng, °shǔ shwéi 'gwǎn)?

COMMANDER. (Military) is expressed with jǎng preceded by the designation of the unit commanded company commander lyánjǎng, battalion commander yíngjǎng, etc. /He was transferred to another division to be the commander. Tā dyàudàu 'lǐng yi-'shř dzwò shř'jǎng.

Commander (navy rank) ('hǎijyūn)jūng'syàu; lieutenant commander ('hǎijyūn) shàu'syàu.

Commander in chief dzǔngszlǐng, jǔshwài, tǔngshwài, dàjyǎng, dàywánshwài, dàjyǎngjyūn.

COMMERCE. shāng, 'shāngyè, 'mǎimài, màuyì, 'shāngwù. /This port is a center for foreign commerce. Jèige hǎi'kǒu shř °jìnchūkǒu 'mǎimàide jūng'syīn (°jìn-chūkǒu 'shāngyède jūng'syīn, °jìnchūkǒu 'shāngwùde jūng'syīn, °'gwójì màu'yìde jūng'syīn).

Department of Commerce 'Shāngyèbù.

Chamber of Commerce 'Shānghwèi.

See also **BUSINESS**, **TRADE**.

COMMITTEE. wěiywánhwèi. /Who is on the committee? Shéi dzài wěiywán'hwèili? /There is a committee meeting tonight. Jyěr wǎnshang wěiywán'hwèi kāi'hwèi.

Committee member 'wěiywán.

Committee chairman wěiywánjǎng, 'jǔsyí ('wěiywán).

Foreign Affairs Committee Wàijyāu Wěiywán'hwèi.

COMMON. (General). /How common is this practice? Jèijǔng 'bànfǎ hěn 'pǔtūng ma? /It is common knowledge that you can't believe everything he says. Shwéi dōu 'jřdau tāde hwà bù 'wánchywán kě'kàu. /A common saying is that ... (Yǒu) yíjyù °'súyǔ (°'súywěr, °'súhwàr), jyòushř ....

(Ordinary) píngchángde (of a style or thing); píngfán, píng (of a person); common alley cat hěn píng'chángde 'māu; made of common material píng'chángde 'yǐlyàudz 'dzwòde; man of no common ability fēicháng 'nénggànde rén. /He says this is the century of the common man. Tā shwō jèi shř °píng'mínde 'shŕdài (°lǎu-bǎi'syìngde shŕdài).

(Shared). /These laws are for our common good. Jèijǔng fǎ'lyù shř wèi dàjyā 'hǎu. /It was done by common consent. Shř dàjyā túng'yì tsái nèmma 'bànde.

In common. /The two have nothing in common. Nèi'lyǎ yìdyǎr yě bùyí'yàng. /Have they any trait in common? Tāmende 'syìngching yǒu syāng'túngde dìfang ma?

Common sense chángshř, 'jyànwén, 'jyànshř. /He lacks common sense. Tā cháng'shř bú'gòu. *or* Tā 'jyànwén bù'gwǎng. *or* Tā 'jyànshř 'chà yidyar. *but* /If other problems arise, use your common sense. Yàushř yǒu 'byéde wèntí de'hwà, nǐ chyáuje 'bàn hǎu le.

COMMUNICATION. (Message, official) 'gūngwén. / The messenger brought two communications from headquarters. Chwánlìng'bīng tsúng sžlìng'bù dàilái lyǎngjyàn-'gūngwén.

(Means of communicating) 'jyāutūng; land communication lùshang'jyāutūng; sea communication hǎishàng'jyāutūng; communication center 'jyāutūng jūng'syīn; *but* rail communication tyědàu 'yùnshū. /Our communication lines have been broken by storms. Wǒmende jyāutūng'syàn jyàu 'kwángfēngbàu'yǔ gěi dwànle. / The only means of communication is by radio. is expressed as We can only use a radio to communicate. Jř yǒu yùng wúsyàn'dyàn kéyi tūng'syìn.

Ministry of Communications Jyāutūngbù.

Be in communication tūng syāusyi, tūngsyìn. /We have not been in communication with them. Wǒmen méiyǒu gēn tāmen °tūng 'syāusyi (°tūng'syìn).

COMMUNITY. (Place, area) dìfang, dài. /How many families are living in this community? °Jèige 'dìfang (°Jèiyí'dài) yǒu dwōshǎu 'jyā? / The whole community is behind this plan. is expressed as All the people of this area are behind this plan. °Jèi'dìfangde rén (°Jèiyí'dàide rén) chywán 'dzànchéng jèige 'bànfǎ.

(Areas with definite limits, often used to mean community) syàn (district *or* country); syāng, jèn (subdivisions of a syàn); bǎu (subdivision of a syāng *or* jèn, equal to about 100 families); jyǎ (ten families); chéng (a city, usually walled); syāng (suburb of a city); jèn (large town); jwāng (small town or large village); tswūn (village); jyē (street); chyū (district of a city).

Community center dàhwèitáng, gūnggùnghwèi'táng, 'dìfanggūngswǒ.

Community Chest gūngyìjywān, tsžshànjywān.

COMPANION. túngbàrde. / That old lady was traveling with a companion. Nèige lǎu-'tàitai yǒu ge túng'bàrde.

Be companions dzwòbàr. /We were companions on the trip. Wǒmen yí'lù dzwò'bàr.

Companion (matching). / There is a companion picture to this one. Jèijāng 'hwàr hái yǒu ge 'dwèr ne. / There are three companion pictures to this one. Hái yǒu 'sānjāng gēn 'jèijāng shř °yí'tàu (°yí'fù, °yífùsžshàn'píng).

COMPANY. (Visitors, guests) 'kèrén. /I'm expecting company tonight. Jyēr 'wǎnshang yǒu °'kèrén lái (°'rén lái 'jǎu wǒ).

(Companions). /You are known by the company you keep. is expressed with literary quotations as One who is near red gets red, one who is near black gets black. Jìn'jūjě'chř, jìn'mwòjě'hè. *or* Look at one's friend and you know one's person. Gwān chí'yǒu ér jř chí'rén.

(Companionship). /I find him very good company. Wǒ hěn 'syǐhwān gēn tā °'láiwǎng (°'jyāuwǎng, °dzwò 'péngyou). /He is poor company. Gēn tā 'láiwǎng méi 'yìsz.

(Business firm) gūngsž; hàu (confined to certain uses); jyā (house); also expressed by dyàn, háng and other terms that occur as the last syllable of firm names. / This company (of ours) was founded 157 years ago. °Běn'hàu (°Syǎu'hàu, °Běn'dyàn, °Běn'háng, °etc.) shř yìbǎiwǔshr'chīnyán chyán kāi'bànde. /What company do you represent? Bǎu'hàu? *or* Bǎu'hàu shř 'nèijyā? /We will have to order

429

this from the Tri-Star Company. Jèige wŏmen dĕi tsúng Sānsyǐng Gūngsz̄ syàn'dìng.

(Theatrical). / The leading actor is good, but the rest of the company is poor. Bāndzlide 'jŭjyǎu hĕn hǎu, 'byéde rén bù'syíng.

(Military) lyán. / A battalion has three companies. Yì'yíng yŏu sān'lyán. / The captain will review his company tomorrow. Lyán'jǎng míngtyān jyǎn'ywè chywán'lyán. / We have a company of engineers here. Dzài jèr °yŏu yìlyán 'gūngbīng (°yíge gūngbīng'lyán).

Keep someone **company** gen . . . dzwò'bàr. / Would you stay a little longer and keep me company? Nǐ 'ywànyi dzài 'dāihwer gēn wo dzwò'bàr ma?

COMPARATIVELY. / Comparatively speaking, this hotel isn't bad. *or* This hotel is comparatively good. is expressed as Compare this hotel with others and you can't call it bad. Jèige lyǔ'gwǎn gēn 'byéde yì'bǐ, yě 'bìng búswàn 'hwài. *or* Jèige lyǔ-'gwǎn gēn 'byéde 'bǐjyàuchí'lái, yě hái búswàn'hwài.

COMPARE. bǐ, 'bǐjyàu, 'bǐjyàu. / We compared the two methods and chose this one. Wŏmen bǎ lyǎngjǔng 'fāngfǎ bǐjyàule yísyàr, jywé'dìng yùng 'jèige. / This hotel doesn't compare with others I have stayed in. Jèige 'lyǔgwǎn gēn wŏ 'jùgwòde 'bǐ chà'ywǎnle. / Compare these two. Jèilyǎ nín 'bǐ yibǐ. / How can this one be compared with yours? 'Jèige dzĕmma néng gēn 'nǐ nèige 'bǐ ne? / His book is awfully dull compared to yours. Tā nèiben 'shū (yàushr 'nálai) gēn 'nǐ nèiben 'bǐ jyou °swŏránwú'wèi le (°syànde hĕn méiyou 'yìszde). / He's a dwarf compared to the captain. Tā gēn lyán'jǎng (jàn yíkwar) yì'bǐ syàng ge syǎurén'gwór shr̀de. / They don't compare. Bùnéng 'bǐ. *or* Jèige gēn 'nèige bùnéng 'bǐ. *or* Jèige bùnéng (nálai) gēn 'nèige 'bǐ.

COMPARISON. Expressed verbally as compare. *See* **COMPARE.** / They asked us to make a comparison. Tāmen jyàu wŏmen 'bǐ yísyàr. / There is no comparison between the two towns. Lyǎngge 'chéng gēnbĕn bùnéng 'bǐ. / It doesn't bear comparison. Yì'bǐ jyòu °bù'syíng le (°'chà le, °'syànchulai le). / In comparison with that one, this isn't a bad bargain. Gēn 'nèige yì'bǐ, mǎi 'jèige búswàn 'shàngdàng.

COMPASS. (For determining direction) jr̄nánjēn; (navigator's) 'lwópán. / A compass will be useful on your trip. Nǐ lyǔ'syíng de 'shr̄hou yŏu ge jr̄nán'jēn hǎudyǎr. / The ship's compass was broken. 'Chwánshangde 'lwópán 'hwài le.

(For drawing a circle) ywángwēi, lyǎngjyǎugwēi. / This circle was drawn with a compass. Jèige 'chywār shr yùng °'ywángwēi (°lyǎngjyǎu'gwēi) 'hwàde.

(Scope). / The compass of his work was limited. Tā gūng'dzwò de 'fànwéi hĕn syǎu.

COMPLAIN. (Mildly) bùmǎnyì, shwō; (violently) chǎu, nàu, dǎ'jyà; (by shouting) rǎng, rǎngrang; (by mumbling) dūnang, 'dúdunāngnángde; (to an authority about a person) gàu; (to an equal about a person) shwō; (about something) ywàn, 'bàuywàn. / What are you complaining about? Nǐ yŏu shémma bùmǎn'yìde 'dìfang? / She left work early, complaining of a headache. Tā dzău °'dzŏu (°syà'bān) de, shwō shr̀ tóu'téng. / We complained to the manager about the poor accommodations. Wŏmen gēn jīng-'lǐ shwō 'shèbèi tài °'chà (°bù'syíng, °'hwài). *or* 'Shèbèi tài 'hwài le, wŏmen gēn 'jīnglǐ °'chǎule yí'dwùn (°'dǎle yídwùn 'jyà, °'nàule yí'dwùn, °'rǎngle 'bàntyān, °'rǎngrangle 'bàntyān). / She's always complaining. Tā 'dzŭngshr̀ bùmǎn'yì. *or* Tā 'lǎushr̀ 'bàuywàn jège 'bàuywàn nàgede. *or* Tā 'lǎushr̀ °'dúdunāng'nángde (°dūnang, °shwō) jège yě bù'hǎu nèige yě bù'hǎu. / I'm not complaining about you. Wŏ búshr̀ shwō 'nǐ. *or* Wŏ búshr̀ ywàn'nǐ. / He complained about you (about your work). Tā wèile nǐ dzwòde 'shèr 'shwō nǐ láije. / He complained to the manager about you. Tā gēn jīng'lǐ 'shwō ni laije. *or* Tā dàu jīng'lǐ nàr 'gàu ni laije.

430

COMPLETE. (Finish) wán, dé, hǎu, chéng, dǐng. These words are placed after the word which specifies the thing or action which is completed. hǎu implies the satisfaction given in the completion; dǐng refers to something being settled. / Be sure to complete the work before you go home. Méihwéi'jyā yìchyán, yí'dǐng yàu bǎ jèige 'shèr °dzwò'wánle (°dzwò'hǎule, °dzwò'chéngle). / Is it completed? (of a piece of writing) Syěhǎule ma? / Have you completed the organization? 'Gáidzǔ 'wánle ma? / The preparations were completed. Dōu °'jwǔnbèi (°'yùbèi) 'hǎule.

Be complete (finished) is expressed as above. / The plans are not yet complete. 'Jìhwà hái méi °'níhǎu (°'nídǐng, °níchéng).

(Full, entire) 'wánchywán, chywán, 'chywándōu, dōu, 'swóyǒude (dōu or chywán). / This machine does the complete operation (all the work). Swóyǒude 'shèr jèijyà 'jīchì dōu dzwò'wánle. / Please make a complete list of your books. Chǐng bǎ nǐ swóyǒude 'shū kāi yíge 'dāndz. / This is the complete list of the names of persons arrested. Bèi 'dàipǔ de rénde 'míngdz dōu dzài jèijāng 'dāndzshang. or Jèijāng 'dāndzshang 'kāide shr 'swóyǒude 'dàichyùde rénde 'míngdz. / That's a complete victory for them. Tāmen 'dédàule chywán'shèng.

(Thorough). / As a soldier, he's a complete flop. Tā dāng 'jyūnrén, jyǎn'jr °yìtwán'dzāu (°búshr nèmmage 'tsáilyàur, °bù'chéng, °bù'syíng).

COMPOSE. (Of something in writing) syě, dzwò. / He composes poems. Tā syě'shr. or Tā dzwò'shr. / He composes music. Tā dzwò'pǔ.

(To calm, quiet). / Compose yourself! Byé 'hwāngjang!

Be composed of yóu . . . 'héchéngde.

COMPOSITION. (Musical) 'yīnywè (music); ywèpǔ (musical score). / What compositions will the orchestra play tonight? Yīnywè'dwèi jyēr 'wǎnshang 'yǎndzòu shémma 'yīnywè? / Whose compositions will be played tonight? Jyēr wǎnshang 'dōu shr yǎndzòu 'nǎsyě rénde °yīnywè (°ywè'pǔ).

(Graphic) 'bùjyú. / The composition of the painting seems defective. Nèijāng hwàrde 'bùjyú hǎusyàng yǒu dyǎr 'máubing.

(Literary) wén; a composition yìpyān wén; class in English composition 'Yīngwén dzwòwén'bān; composition book dzwòwénběr.

(Chemical) chéngfen. / The chemist will analyze the composition of this metal. Hwàyàn'shr yàu °'hwàyàn (°'yánjyōu) yísyàr jèijǔng 'jīnshǔde 'chéngfen.

(In printing) páibǎn. / The printer will need a week for composition. Yìn'dz de rén dzǔng děi yùng yíge lǐ'bài lái pái'bǎn.

CONCERN. (Involve) yǒu gwānsyi. / This concerns you. Jèi gēn nǐ yǒu 'gwānsyi. / Which people were concerned in this matter? Jèijyàn 'shèr dōu shr gēn 'shéi yǒu 'gwānsyi? or Jèijyàn 'shrli dōu yǒu °'shwéi (°'shémma rén)? / This doesn't concern me. Jèi yúwǒ wú 'gwān. or Jèige gēn 'wǒ méiyou 'gwānsyi.

(Be interested in) dzàihu, gwǎn. / I'm not concerned with the details. Wǒ °bú'dzàihu (°bú'gwǎn) °syǎude 'dìfang (°syǎu'jyémù).

Concern (worry). / She is showing a great deal of concern over her husband. Tā °'syānchulai (°'syānje) dwèi tāde 'jàngfu hěn 'gwānsyīn. or 'Kànshangchyu tā dwèi tāde 'jàngfu hěn 'gwānsyīnde 'yàngdz.

(Involvement or interest) shèr or expressed verbally. / She said it was no concern of hers. Tā shwō °méi tāde 'shèr (°búshr tāde 'shèr, °tā bù'gwān, °tā 'gwānbujáu). / Is it any concern of yours? Nǐ 'gwǎndejáu ma? or (more mildly) Yǔ 'nǐ yǒu shémma 'gwānsyi?

431

(Business) 'măimài, gūngsz̄, 'shāngdyàn, pùdz, chù, dìfang. ('shāngdyàn *and* 'pudz <u>also mean</u> store, shop; chù *and* 'dìfang <u>simply mean</u> place.) /How long have you been with this concern? Nǐ dzài °jèr (°jèige'dìfang) dzwò'shr̄ yŏu dwō-'jyŏule? *or* Nǐ dzài jèige °gūng'sz̄ (°'shāngdyàn, °'pùdz, °'măimài) °dzwòle (°dāile) dwōshău 'shŕhou?

CONCERNING. 'gwānyú. /Nothing was said concerning this matter. 'Gwānyú jèijyàn 'shèr̀ méi 'tí. /I have a question concerning these tickets. 'Gwānyú jèijijāng 'pyàu wŏ yŏu °ge 'wèntí (°dyăr bù'míngbaide 'dìfang).

CONCERT. yīnywèhwèi. /Is there to be a concert tonight? Jyēr 'wănshang yŏu yīn-ywè'hwèi ma? /We must allow time to pick up the concert tickets. Dzámen dzūng-dĕi °'lyóusya (°'ywénsya, °'téngsya) 'shŕhou hău chyù chyŭ yīnywèhwèide 'pyàu.

CONDITION. (State) yàngdz, yàngr. /You are in no condition to leave the house. Nǐ 'nèmmage yàngdz bùnéng 'chūchyu. *or* Nǐ bìngde 'nàyàngr bùnéng 'chūchyu. /The house was in poor condition. Fángdz kwài 'yàu kwă de 'yàngdz.

(Stipulation). /I will accept the offer on three conditions. Wŏ yŏu sānge 'tyáu-jyàn, dōu 'héle wŏ jyòu 'dāying. /I will go on the condition that I pay my own way. Yàushr jyàu wŏ 'dzjǐ chū'chyán wŏ jyòu 'chyù.

(Circumstances; social, political, financial, etc.) 'chíngsyíng, jwàngkwàng, 'chíngkwàng, syíng; financial conditions 'tsáijèng jwàngkwàng; business conditions 'shāngchíng, 'shāngyè chíng'kwàng. /She said she would not attend under any con-ditions. Tā shwō tā dzài 'rènhé chíngsyíng jr̄syà yĕ bú'chyù. *or* Tā shwō tā 'dzĕmma yĕ bú'chyù.

Be in condition (of persons) jwŭnbèihău, 'shēntǐ jwŭnbèi'hău; (of things) 'jwŭn-bèitwŏ'dàng, néng 'yùng, kéyi 'yùng. /The athletes are not in condition. Yùndùng-'ywán méi jwŭnbèi'hău. *or* Yùndùng'ywánde 'shēntǐ méi jwŭnbèi'hău. /The tanks are not in condition (for combat). Jàn'chē méi °jwŭnbèitwŏ'dàng (°bùnéng 'yùng, °bùkéyǐ 'yùng).

Good condition. /The porcelain arrived in good condition. 'Tsźchǐ hău'hāurde 'yùndàule. *or* 'Tsźchǐ yùndàule, yǐdyăr méi'hwài.

Mental condition 'syīnlǐ jwàng'kwàng, 'syīnlǐ jwàng'tài.

Physical condition shēndz, 'shēntǐ, 'tǐgé.

Be conditioned by. /His decision was conditioned by his religious beliefs. Tāde 'jywédìng shr̀ shòu tā 'dzūngjyàu syìnyăngde yíng'syăng. /The quality of the work is conditioned by the time limit. Gūngdzwò 'hăuhwài dĕi kàn 'yŏu méiyou 'shŕjyānde 'syànjr̀.

CONDUCT. (Lead) lǐng, dài, dău, 'dàilǐng, 'lǐngdău. /A guide will conduct the party through the art museum. Yíge syăng'dău hwèi 'lǐngje rén dzài chénlyè'swŏli 'ràu yisyar. *or* Yŏu jāudàiywán dàije dzài mĕishù'gwănli 'dzŏu yichywār. /Conducted tours leave from here. Dău'yóu tsúngjèr chū'fā.

(Of electricity). /We need a wire to conduct electricity to the barn. Wŏmen dĕi yàuyìgēr dyàn'syàn hău bă 'dyàn tūngdàu tsāng'fángli chyu.

(Manage) gwăn. /Who conducted the business in his absence? Tā méi dzài de 'shr̀hou shwéi gwăn 'shr̀?

(Music) 'jr̄dău. /Who conducts the symphony tonight? Shéi jr̄dău jyēr wăn-shangde jyāusyăng'ywè?

(Behave). /He conducted himself well during the meeting. Kāi'hwèi de 'shŕ-hou tāde 'tàidu hĕn bú'tswò.

Conduct (behavior) syíngwei; (general or usual) pǐnsying. / The children's conduct was satisfactory. 'Háidzmende 'syíngwei hěn hǎu. / His conduct is beyond criticism. Tāde 'pǐnsying méiyou kě 'pīpíngde.

(Management). / The conduct of the business affairs should be honorable. Dzwò-'mǎimài yīngdāng °'gwēijyǔ (°'gwēigweijyu'jyǔde). / They constantly criticized the conduct of the war. Tāmen 'láushr̀ 'pīping 'jànshr̀ jr̀'hwēide bù'dédàng.

CONNECT. (Join) jyē. / Please connect these wires to the battery. Bǎ jèijityáu 'syàn jyēdau dyàn'pínshang. / Operator, please connect me with . . . . Gěi wǒ jyē . . . . / All trains connect with busses at the station. Swǒyou hwǒ'chē dàu'jàn de shŕhou dōu yǒu 'gūnggùngchi'chē 'jyē.

(Associate). / I always connect war with Napoleon. Wǒ yì syǎngdàu dǎ'jàng jyou syǎngdàu Nápwò'lwún.

Be connected. / What firm are you connected with? Bǎu'hàu shr̀ 'něijyā? / He's connected with an oil company. Tā dzài yíge 'yóu gūngsz̄ dzwò'shr̀. / The families are connected by marriage. Tāmen lyǎng'jyār °shr̀ 'chīnchi. or (if the daughter of one family is married to the son of the other) °shr̀ 'chīngjya. or °yǒu chyúndài 'gwānsyi.

CONNECTION. (Relation) gwānsyi. / I don't understand the connection between their statements. Wǒ bù'míngbai tāmen nèilyǎngjyù 'hwà de 'gwānsyi. / I don't get the connection. Jèi gēn 'nèige wǒ °'kàn (°'tīng)buchulái shr̀ dzěmma ge 'gwānsyi. / Is there any connection between the two cases? Jèilyàngge 'àndz 'bǐtsz̄ 'yǒu méiyou 'gwānsyi? / It seems that his answer does not have any connection with what you asked. Tāde 'hwà gēn nǐ 'wèn de hǎusyàng méiyou yìdyǎr 'gwānsyi. or Tā hwéidá nǐ de 'hwà hǎusyàng °swǒ'dá fēi swǒwèn (°'wén búdwèi 'tí, or (rude) °'lyúchwún búdwèi mǎ'dzwěi).

(Physical). / There is a loose connection somewhere in the engine. 'Jīchi yǒu dìfang 'sūng le. / The telephone operator gave us a bad connection. Jyēsyàn'shēng méibǎ syàn jyē'hǎu.

(Traveling). / The connections for that town are very poor. Dàu nèige 'chéng chyù de shŕjyān'byǎu páide hěn bù'hǎu. / You make connections at the next station. Dàule 'syàjàn hwàn'chē.

(Business). / These people have extensive business connections. Jèisyē 'rén gēn hěn dwō 'mǎimai dōu yǒu 'lyánlwò.

(Family). / I'm not clear about their family connections. Wǒ bù'míngbai tāmen 'jyālide 'gwānsyi. or Tāmen shr̀ dzěmma ge 'chīnchi, wǒ búdà 'chīngchu.

CONSENT. (Agree) dāying, kěn. / Has he consented? Tā 'dāyingle ma? or Tā 'kěnle ma? / When asked to stay, he consented. Yì 'lyóu tā, tā jyou °'dāyingle (°'kěnle).

Consent (approval, permission) syúkě. / His consent is absolutely necessary. Yí'dìng děi yǒu tāde syú'kě tsái 'syíng. / If he is under age, the consent of his parents is required. Tā 'rúgwǒ shàng wèi 'chéngnyán tā 'jyājàngde syú'kě shr̀ bì-'syúde. or Tā 'yàushr hái méi'chéngnyán jyòu děi dé tā 'fùmǔde syú'kě. / He won't give his consent. is expressed as He won't agree. Tā búhwèi 'dāyingde.

CONSIDER. (Think about and discuss) 'kǎulyù; (investigate, look into) 'yánjyōu; (think, regard) syǎng; (be concerned with) gù, 'gùlyù. / We are considering all angles of your proposal. Wǒmen 'jèngdzài tsúng 'gè fāngmyàn °'kǎulyù (°yánjyōu) nǐ tí de nèijyàn'shèr. / Have you ever considered it from that angle? Nǐ tsúng 'nèifāngmyàn °'kǎulyùgwo ma (°'yánjyōugwo ma, °'syǎnggwo ma)? / He considers too many angles and then never acts. Tā 'láushr 'gùlyù tài dwō, jyégwǒ 'shémma yě bú'bàn. / I wouldn't consider him for the job. Nèige 'wèijr̄ wǒ kàn tā bùhé'shr̄. *or* Wǒ syǎng tā bùnéng dzwò nèige 'shr̄. / He never considers the feelings of others. Tā 'yŭngywǎn bú'gù byérén dzěmma 'syǎng. *or* Tā yí'syàng bùgwǎn byérén 'shòudelyǎu 'shòubulyǎu. *or* Tā yí'syàng bútǐ byérén 'syǎng yisyǎng.

(Take into account). / Considering his youth, he has achieved a great deal. Àn tāde 'nyánjì lái shwō, tāde 'chéngjyòu hěn kě'gwǎn.

CONSIDERATION. (Examination). / We'll take the matter under consideration. Jèijyàn 'shr̄ wǒmen 'kǎulyùkǎulyù.

(Regard). / The hotel manager showed us every consideration. Lyǔgwǎn 'jīnglǐ 'jàugùde hěn 'jōudàu. / Don't you have any consideration for other people's feelings? Nǐ 'nándàu(shwō) °yìdyǎr yě bù'gwǎn byérén dzěmma 'syǎng ma (°'jyòu bú'tǐ byérén 'syǎngsyǎng)?

(Compensation). / He will probably expect a consideration for his services. Tā 'dàgài syǎng 'dé dyǎr 'bàuchou. / We present this to you in consideration of your services. Nín gěi 'dzwòle dzěmma yē 'shr̄, 'jè jyòushr wǒmende yìdyar 'yìsz.

CONSIST. Consist of yǒu. / The meal consists of fish, vegetables, and tea. Nèidwèn 'fàn yǒu 'yú, chǐng'tsài gēn 'chá. / What does this consist of? Jèili dōu yǒu 'shémma?

CONSTANT. yìjr̄, lǎu, lǎushr̄. / Constant rains made the roads very muddy. Yìjr̄ 'syàyǔ bǎ 'lù 'nùngde mǎn shr̄ 'ní. / The constant noise kept me awake all night. °Yì'jr̄ (°Lǎu, °'Lǎushr̄) yǒu 'shēngyin, chǎude wǒ yī'yè méishwèi'jáu. *or* 'Shēngyin 'lǎushr̄ bù'tíng, chǎude . . . .

CONTAIN. yǒu; . . . lǐ shr̄ (refers to the total contents). / What does this package contain? Jèige 'bāurlǐ shr̄ shémma? / It contains three items. 'Lǐtou yǒu 'sānyàng dūngsyi. / The trunk contains (is packed full of) clothing. 'Syāngdzli 'jwāngde shr̄ 'yīfu. / The newspaper contains some interesting reports. Bàushang yǒu jisyàng yǒu'yìszde 'syīnwén. *or* Bàushang 'dēngle syēge yǒu'yìszde 'syāusyi. / How many liters does a gallon contain? Yì'jyālwún yǒu 'dwōshǎu 'gūngshēng? / How many catties of rice are contained in a standard burlap bag? Yìbāu'mǐ °shr̄ (°yǒu) dwōshau 'jīn?

(Restrain). / You must learn to contain your temper. Nǐ děi 'sywéje 'gwǎn nǐde 'píchi. *or* Nǐde 'píchì, nǐ děi 'lyànsyíje 'yājr dyar. / He contained himself throughout the quarrel. Dǎ'jyà de shŕhou tā yìjr̄ °búdùng 'shēngsè (°'píngsyīnjìng'chìde).

CONTENT. (Substance). / I don't understand the content of this letter. Wǒ bù'míngbai jèifēng 'syìnde 'nèirúng.

Contents. / The contents of your trunk must be examined. 'Fēidei 'jyānchá yísyàr nǐ 'syāngdzlide 'dūngsyi. / Do you know the contents of this box? Nǐ 'jr̄dau jèige hédzlǐbyār 'jwāngde shr̄ 'shémma ma?

CONTENT. (Satisfied) mǎnyì, jŕdzú; (willing) 'gǎnsyīn. / He was content with the price we offered him. Wǒmen gěi tāde 'jyàr tā hěn °mǎn'yì (°jŕ'dzú). / He's content with his lot. Tā hěn °mǎn'yì (°jŕ'dzú). / I am not content with those arrangements. Nèijǔng 'bànfa wǒ bùmǎn'yì. / I am not content to pay that price. Wǒ bù'gǎnsyīn gěi nèmma syē 'chyán. *or* Chū nèmma dàde 'jyàchyan wǒ yǒudyǎr bù'gǎnsyīn.

CONTEST. (Competition) jìngsài, bǐsài, jìngjēng. / He participated in an essay contest. Tā tsān'jyāle yige lwùnwér °jìng'sài (°bǐsài). / The winner of this contest will get a prize. Jèitsz °bǐ'sài (°jìngsài) yíngde rén dé 'jyǎng. / There was a bitter contest in the elections. 'Sywǎnjyǔ de shŕhou jìng'jēng hěn 'jǐlyè.

CONTEST. (Dispute) 'kànggàu (of legal decisions); jēng (of other things). / The judge's decision is being contested. Yǒurén 'kànggàu fǎgwānde 'pànjywé. / I'll contest your claim to the property. Nǐ shwō 'chǎnyè shr̀ 'nǐde; wǒ yí'dìng gēn ni 'jēng. / He is preparing to contest every inch of the ground. Tā 'yùbei pīn'mìng chyu 'jēng, yíbù bú'ràng. / His candidacy is not contested. Tā dzwò 'hòusywǎnrén méi rén gēn ta 'jéng. / This is the point being contested. 'Jēng de jyòu shr̀ 'jèidyǎn.

CONTINUALLY. 'lyánsyùbú'dwànde, 'jyēlyánbù'tíngde, yìjř. / He talked in his sleep continually for an hour. Tā shwō 'mènghwà °yì'jř (°'lyánsyùbú'dwànde, °'jyēlyán-bù'tíngde) shwōle 'yìdyǎn jūng.

CONTINUE. (Go on) jyēje, or expressed as not stop méitíng. / You may continue (talking) now. Syàn'dzài kéyi jyēje 'shwōsyachyu. / We'll continue (working) from here. Wǒmen dzài jèr jyēje 'dzwòsyachyu. / I want to continue (walking) on to the city. Wǒ syǎng 'jyēje dzǒudàu 'chénglǐ. / They continued his pay until he died. 'Jŕdàu tā sž̀ tāmen méi'tíng tāde 'syīn.

(Resume). / The entertainment will continue after a ten-minute intermission. Yóu'yì 'syōusyi 'shŕfēnjūng yǐ'hòu jì'syù byǎu'yǎn.

Be continued 'dàisyù, 'wèiwán. / The novel has been continued for seven issues and still isn't finished. Nèipyān syǎu'shwōr dēngle chī'chī, hái méi'dēngwán. / The story will be continued in the next issue. °Běn'wén (°Jèige syǎu'shwōr) syàchī 'syùdēng.

CONTROL. gwǎn. / The assistant manager controls the expenditures. Fù'jīnglǐ gwǎn yíchyède 'kāijr̄. / She is good at controlling children. Tā hwèi gwǎn 'háidz. / Can you control your men? Nǐde 'rén nǐ 'gwǎnde°jù (°lyǎu) ma? but / You must learn to control your temper. Nǐ děi 'lyànje byé fā 'píchi.

Control (power to control) is expressed verbally as above. / The control of the business has passed to the son. 'Mǎimài gěi tā érdz 'gwǎn le.

Have control over gwǎn. / He has control over three sections. Tā gwǎn sān-'bùfende 'shr̀.

Be beyond control gwǎnbulyǎu, jyàubulyǎu. / This child is beyond all control. Jèige 'háidz 'gwǎnbulyǎu le. / The fire is beyond control now. Hwǒ 'jyǒubulyǎu le.

Be in control gwǎn. / He is in control. Tā gwǎn'shr̀.

Be out of control gwǎnbujù; or expressed as develop trouble chū máubing. / The mob is out of control now. Nèichyún rén 'gwǎnbujù le. / The plane seems to be out of control. 'Fēijī fǎngfu chū 'máubing le.

Be under control. / Everything is under control. Méiyou shémma °'bùdélyǎu de (°'lyǎubudé de, °jūshr̀ rú'yì).

Be under the control of gwǎn; jŕsyáyú (directly under the jurisdiction of). / This office is under the control of the Army Service Forces. Běn'jyú shǔ 'Hòu-fāng-Chínwù'bù gwǎn. / This municipality is under the control of the Executive Ywan. Běn'shr̀ jŕsyá'yú Syíngjèngywàn.

Bring under control (of people) jyàu . . . ānjingsyalai; (of a fire) jyòu. / He wasn't able to bring the crowd under control. Tā méifǎr jyàu 'nèichyun rén 'ān-jingsyalai. / The fire was brought under control. 'Hwǒ shr̀ yǒu 'jyòu le. / The fire can't be brought under control. 'Hwǒ shr̀ méi'jyòu le.

Controls. / Are all the controls in order? 'Jīchī dōu 'líng ma? / Would you mind taking over the controls for a while? Nǐ lái °'kān (°'gwǎn, °kāi if referring to a plane, train or large machinery) yìhwěr, dzěmma'yàng.

435

CONVENIENT. fāngbyan; <u>also other indirect expressions</u>. / The bus service here is convenient. Jèrde 'gūnggùngchî'chē hěn 'fāngbyan. / Come whenever it is convenient for you. 'Shémma shŕhou 'fāngbyan jyòu 'lái. *or* 'Shémma shŕhou néng 'lái, jyòu 'lái. / Transportation is convenient here. Jèr 'jyāutung 'fāngbyan. / Only if it is convenient for you. Jřyàu 'nǐ °fāngbyan (°bùwéi'nán). / What place would be most convenient for us to meet? Dzámen dzài 'nǎr jyàn hǎu? / The accident was a convenient way for him to get out of it. °'Jènghǎu (°'Chyàchyǎu) chūle 'shèr, jyàu tā yǒu 'hwà shwō.

CONVERSATION. <u>Expressed verbally as</u> **converse** tán (hwà), lyáu (tyār), shwō (hwà). / We had a bit of a conversation. Wǒmen 'tánle °yìhwěr (°yìtán). / On the train I fell into conversation with a stranger. Dzài hwǒ'chēshang wǒ gēn yíge 'shēngrén °'lyáuchilaile (°'shwōchi 'hwà laile, °lyáuchi 'tyār laile, °'tánchilaile). / I had a long conversation with the boss. Wǒ gēn dzámende 'tóur 'tánle °yíjèn (°bàn'tyān, °hěn 'jyǒu). / I overheard a conversation about it. Wǒ 'tīngjyan rén 'shwōgwo.

COOK. dzwòfàn *or* dzwò <u>plus the particular kind of food cooked</u>. / Start cooking the dinner now. Dzwò'fàn ba. / He knows how to cook. Tā hwèi dzwò'fàn. / How do you want your meat cooked? Nèige 'ròu °dzěmma 'dzwò (°nǐ yàu dzěmma 'dzwòde)? / He can cook several special dishes. Tā hwèi dzwò jiyàng hǎu 'tsài. / He cooked all day long in the kitchen. Tā dzài 'chúfángli °dzwò'fàn dzwòle 'yìjěngtyān (°dzwòle yìtyān'fàn). / Sometimes the mistress cooks. <u>is expressed as</u> goes to the kitchen. 'Yǒude shŕhou tàitai 'dzjǐ syà 'chúfáng.

    (Fig.). **What's cooking?** ('Chūle) shémma 'shèr?

    Cook <u>in particular ways</u> (boil, in water or soup) jǔ; (bake, roast) kǎu; (roast over an open fire, barbecue) shāu; (pour in liquid and simmer after frying or searing) pēng; (deep-fry) já; (pan-fry; vegetables, pieces of meat, etc.) chǎu; (flat slices, eggs, etc.) jyān; (steam) jēng; (apply heat to evaporate water) kàu. / This needs to cook a little longer. 'Hwohour děi 'dà dyar. *or* Jèige 'hái děi (dwō) °'jǔ hwěr (°'jǔ yijǔ, or substitute any of the other terms for jǔ).

    Cook up <u>a story</u> dzōu, byān, 'syādzōu, 'syàbyān. / They cooked up a story for us. Tāmen °syàdzōule (°'syàbyān, °'dzōule, °'syānle) ge 'hwàr yàu 'pyàn dzámen. / That's a fantastic story they cooked up. Nèi shr tāmen °'húdzōude (°'syàdzōude), jyàu rén hěn nán'syìn.

    Cookbook pēngrènfǎ, jyǎng pēngrèn'fǎ de 'shū, shŕpǔ.

    Cooking <u>is expressed verbally as</u> **to cook** dzwòfàn. / The secret of Chinese cooking is in the correct use of soya sauce. Dzwò 'Jūnggwo fàn de 'mìjywé shr̀ yùng 'jyàngyóu yùngde 'défǎ.

    (As part of domestic science) 'pēngrèn. / Is there a cooking class? Yǒu pēngrèn'bān ma?

    Cooking time hwǒhour.

    A cook dzwòfànde, chúdz; (professional; polite terms) 'dàshŕfu, 'chúshŕfu; (chief chef) jàngsháude; (assistant chef) bāngsháude; (apprentice chef) sywétúde; (cook's helper, mess boy) dǎdzárde; (in the army) 'hwǒfu; <u>or expressed verbally as above</u>. / This is a specialty of our cook. Jèi shr wǒmen 'chúdzde náshǒu'tsài. / We must hire a cook. Wǒmen děi 'gù ge dzwò'fànde. / My younger sister is an excellent cook. Wǒ 'mèimei °'hěn 'hwèi dzwò'fàn (°dzwò'tsài dzwòde hěn'hǎu).

COOL. lyáng. / It gets pretty cool here toward evening. 'Wǎnshang jèr tǐng 'lyáng. / The water is pretty cool (for swimming). Shwěi yǒu yìdyǎr °'lyáng (°'lěng).

Cool <u>and comfortable</u> 'lyángkwài. / This is the coolest room in the house. Jèi shr jèiswǒ 'fángdzli dzwèi 'lyángkwàide 'wūdz. / Wait until I change into something cooler. Děng wǒ 'hwàn jyàr 'lyángkwàidyǎrde 'yīshang.

Keep <u>something</u> cool jyàu . . . 'lyángkwài, jyàu . . . bú'jr̀yu rè, jyàu . . . bú're. / Let's keep the house cool by shutting all the windows. Dzámen bǎ 'chwānghu chywán 'gwānshang hǎu jyàu 'fángdzli °'lyángkwài (°bú'jr̀yu tài 're).

Keep cool (of temper) rěn. / I tried to keep cool when he insulted me. Tā 'mà wo de shr̀hou wǒ jyé'lìde °'rěnje (°búdùng shēng'sè). / It was impossible for me to keep cool when he said that. Tā shwōle 'nèige wǒ jyou °'rěnbujùle (°bùnéng dzài 'rěn le).

To cool <u>something</u> lyàng. / Don't let this soup cool too long. Byé bǎ jèige 'tāng lyàng tài 'jyǒu le.

Cool off <u>something</u> see To cool <u>above</u>. / Let it cool off a bit before you eat it. 'Lyàng yihwěr dzai 'chr̄.

Cool off (of people) lyángkwài. / Let's go out on the porch and cool off. Dzámen dàu lyáng'táishang chyu 'lyángkwài yísyàr.

COPPER. túng; copper coin 'túngchyán; copper plate 'túngbǎr; <u>etc</u>. / The chest is lined with copper. Syāngdz'lyěr shr̀ 'túngde. <u>or</u> Syāngdz 'lǐtou 'syāngje yìtséng túngpyàr (sheet copper). / Bring me three feet of copper wire. Gěi wo 'sānchr̄cháng de °'túngsz̄ (°'túngsěr).

COPY. (By writing) chāu; (in facsimile or by tracing) myáu; (by typing) dǎ; (by photography) yìn, syǐ; (or if the plate is ready for prints to be made) 'jyāyìn, 'jyāsyǐ. / Copy each character exactly as it is written. Bǎ měige 'dz̀ °jàu'yàngr 'chāusyalai (°jàu ywán'yàngr yìdyǎrbú'chàde 'chāusyalai). / Copy that painting for me. Bǎ nèijāng 'hwàr gěi wo 'myáu yìjāng. / Copy it (by tracing) on a thin piece of paper. Yùng 'báujr̄ 'myáusyalai.

(Imitate) 'jàuje. / She copies the new styles of clothes in the movies. Tā dzài dyàn'yǐngshang 'kànjyanle syīn'yàngrde 'yīshang jyou 'jàuje dzwò. / They like to copy new American styles. Tāmen 'syǐhwan jàuje 'Měigwo 'shr̀yàng 'dzwò.

A copy (if it consists of several sheets) (yí)fèr; (if it consists of one sheet) (yì)jāng; (if it is bound) (yì)běr; <u>etc</u>. / Do you have a copy of this morning's newspaper? Nǐ yǒu yífèr jyēr 'dzǎuchende 'bàu ma? / This is a brand new copy (book). Jèiběr shr̀ jǎn'syīnde.

(Imitation) jyǎde; <u>or expressed as</u> model on fǎng. / This is a copy of a very expensive style. Jèi shr̀ fǎngje yíge hěn 'gwèide yàngdz 'dzwòde. / That's a copy, not the original painting. Nèijāng hwàr shr̀ °fǎngde (°'jyǎde), búshr̄ ywán'láide nèijang.

Make a copy <u>is expressed with the verbs given in paragraph one plus the terms for</u> a copy <u>above</u>. / Make ten copies of this report. (by hand) Jèige 'bàugàu °chāu 'shr̀fèr (<u>or</u> (by typing) °dǎ 'shr̀fèr). / Make ten copies of this print. Jèijāng 'syàng-'pyàr °'jyāyìn (°'jyāsyǐ, °yìn, °syǐ) 'shr̀jāng.

Copy (manuscript) gǎudz. / Copy has been sent to the printer. 'Gǎudz yǐjing 'sùngdau yìnshwājyú chyùle.

CORDIAL. (Of social acts) kèchi(de). / The host gave us a cordial welcome. 'Jǔren hěn 'kèchide 'jyēdài wǒmen. <u>or</u> 'Jǔren 'jyēdài wǒmen 'jyēdàide hěn 'kèchi. / He gave us a cordial invitation to his birthday party. Tā gwo'shēngr (chǐng'kè) gěi wǒmen °syěle fēng hěn 'kèchide 'syìn chǐng wǒmen chyù (an invitation by letter). <u>or</u> °syàle ge hěn 'kèchide 'chǐngtyě (an invitation by card).

(Hearty). / This plan met with a cordial reception at the meeting. Kāi'hwèi de shŕhou jèige 'jǐhwà dàjyā yǐ 'tǐng dōu hěn 'dzànchéng.

A cordial (liqueur). / He offered us a glass of cherry cordial. Tā gěile wǒmen 'měirén yìbēi yǐngtau'jyǒu.

CORN. 'yùmǐ, lǎuyùmi, bàngdz. / They planted corn in some fields and wheat in others. Tāmen dzài jikwài 'dìlǐ 'jùngde shŕ lǎu'yùmi, 'byéde 'dìli jùngde shŕ 'màidz. / The corn for the chickens is kept in this bin. Gěi 'jīchŕ de lǎu'yùmi chéngdzài jèige 'pénli.

    Ear of corn yíge lǎu'yùmi.

    Grains of corn 'yùmǐ, yùmǐlyèr.

    Cornmeal yùmǐmyàr, bàngdzmyàr.

    A corn (if it is painful) 'jǐyǎn; (if it is not painful) jyǎngdz. / He said that those shoes hurt his corns. Tā shwō nèishwāng 'syé °'mwó (°'gè) tāde jyǎu'jǐyǎn.

    To corn (with salt or in brine) yān; **corned beef** yānnyóuròu, syánnyóuròu.

CORNER. (Of an object) jǐjyǎur, -jyǎu, -jyǎur. / One corner of the box was broken open. 'Hédz yíge jǐ'jyǎur 'lyèkaile. / He hit his head on the corner of the table. Tā ba 'tóu pēngdzai jwōdz'jyǎurshang le. / The sender's address is put at the upper left corner of the envelope. Fā'syìnrén 'jùjŕ, syědzai dzwōshàng'jyǎur. / You may sit over in that corner. Nǐ kéyi 'dzwòdzai nèige jǐ'jyǎur nèr.

    (Of a room) <u>is expressed as above, or if the idea of hiding or getting away from the crowd is included, use</u> 'gālár. / The man you want is sitting in that corner. Nǐ 'jǎude nèige rén dzài nèige 'jǐjyǎur nèr 'dzwòje. / He hid himself in a corner. Tā dwòdzai yige 'gālár.

    (Of a street) 'jyējyǎur, 'jyēkǒur, gwǎi'wǎr de 'dìfang. / Let's meet at the corner of 96th and Broadway. Dzámen dzài Jyǒushr'lyòujyē gēn Bwólǎu'hwèilù °'jyēkǒur (°jyējyǎur, °gwǎi'wǎr de dìfang) nèr jyàn. / Please let me off at the next corner. Wǒ dzài 'syàyige 'jyēkǒur nèr syàchyu. / Stop at that corner. Dzài nèige gwǎi'wǎr de dìfang 'tíngsya. / This is a corner lot. Jèikwài 'dì dzài 'jyējyǎurshang.

    (Difficult or embarrassing position). / His line of argument drove me into a corner. Tā nèijǔng 'shwōfǎr °jyàu wǒ gwài nán (yǐ)wéi'chíngde (°jyàu wǒ méifǎr 'hwéidá, °bīrén 'bǐde tài'jǐn).

    To corner (drive into a corner). / The thief was cornered at his mother's house. Syǎu'tóur dzài tā'māde jyāli'jyàu rén °gěi 'děijau le (°bǐde méilù 'dzǒule, °dǔjùle, °'bǐjùle). / He was cornered (in an argument). Tā (jyàu rén) °gěi 'děijaule (°bǐde méihwà 'shwō le, °dǔde méihwà 'shwōle).

    (Get a monopoly of). / Some people have cornered the supply of cigarettes. Yǒu'rén ba jr'yān 'twúnjǐchilaile.

CORRECT. (Right) dwèi. / Is this the correct address? Jèige 'jùjŕ 'dwèi ma? / He got the correct answer to the (nonmathematical) problem. Nèige 'wèntí tā jyějywéde 'fāngfa hěn 'dwèi. / He got the correct answer to the (mathematical) problem. Nèige 'swàntí tā dá'dwèile. or Nèige 'wèntí tā 'swànchulaile. / Your answer is not correct. Nǐde dá'àn bú'dwèi. or Nǐ 'dáde bú'dwèi. / How many correct answers did you get? Nǐ dá'dwèile jǐge ('swàntí)?

    (Proper). / What is the correct dress for this ceremony? Wèi 'jèijyàn shèr yīngdāng chwān 'shémma?

    To correct gǎi; (of manuscripts or copy) jyàu, jyàudwèi. / Please correct my mistakes in French. Chǐng bǎ wǒ 'Fàwénde 'tswòr 'gǎi yigǎi. / The teacher has corrected the examination papers. 'Syānsheng 'yǐjǐng bǎ kǎu'jywàr °gǎi'wánle (°kàn-'wánle). / That has been corrected. Nèige yǐjǐng 'gǎigwole.

(Reprove). / She was constantly correcting the child. Tā lǎu 'shwō tāde syǎu-'hár 'dzèmmajr bú'dwèi, 'nèmmajr bú'dwèide.

CORRECTION. Generally, verbal expressions are used. *See* CORRECT. / Please make the necessary corrections. Chǐng bǎ 'gāi gǎide 'dìfang dōu 'gǎilou. / Correction of the proofs will take three hours. 'Jyàudwèi 'gǎudz dèi yùng sānge jǔng-'tóu. / Behavior like this needs correction. 'Lèisz jèiyàngrde 'jyúdung syúyàu 'jyàujeng. *or* Syàng jèiyàngrde 'syíngwei dèi 'gǎi.

COST. jŕ, dèi. / What does this article cost? Jèi 'dūngsyi °jŕ (°dèi) 'dwōshau chyán? / How much will it cost to have this watch repaired? Jèige 'byǎu syǒuli yísyàr dèi yùng 'dwōshau chyán?

(Nonmonetary). / His recklessness cost him his life. °Tā lǎu 'bùgwǎnbú'gùde (°Tā (yīnwèi) lǎu bù'syǎusyīn dyar, °Tā yīnwei bùkèn 'syǎusyin, °Tā 'tài dàyile), °jyou bǎ 'mìng 'sùngle (°yīntsz bǎ 'mìng sùngle, (°nèmma) sùngde 'mìng).

Cost (financial expense) 'jyàchyán, jyàr. / He buys clothes without regard for the cost. Tā mǎi 'yīfu bùgwǎn °'jyàchyán shŕ 'dwōshau (°'jyàr shŕ 'dwōshau). / The cost is too great. 'Jyàchyán tài °'dà (°'gāu). *or* 'Jyàr tài 'gāu. / The cost of living is rising. 'Shēnghwó 'fèiyùng 'jŕ wàng shàng 'jǎng.

(Nonfinancial price). / The cost is too high. 'Dàijyà tài 'gāu.

(Sacrifice). / Think of the cost of human lives! Chǐng 'syǎngsyang dèi °sz 'dwōshau rén (°'syīsheng 'dwōshau rén'mìng, °yùng 'dwōshautyáu 'mìng lái 'hwàn)! / He succeeded at the cost of some pain and suffering. Tā 'shòule syē 'dzwèi, chŕle syē 'kǔ, kèshr 'chéngle. / They won the battle at a tremendous cost. Jèijàng tāmen 'shèngle, kèshr 'swúnshŕ chí'jùng. / He finished his book at the cost of his health. Tā shū swàn syè'wánle, kèshr bǎ 'shēndz 'dzāutale.

(What was paid earlier). / He was forced to sell his stock (merchandise) at less than cost. Bǐ de tā bǎ 'tswúnhwò péije 'bèrde 'màile. / This hospital sells medicine at cost. Jèige yǐ'ywànde 'yàu shŕ ànje 'ywánjyàr mài.

At any cost, at all costs bùgwǎn 'dàijyà dwō 'gāu, bùgwǎn 'syīsheng dwō 'dà. / He was determined to see the reorganization through at all costs. Tā 'jywédìng yàu bǎ 'gǎidzǔde 'shǒusyù bàn'wánle, °bùgwǎn 'dàijyà dwō 'gāu (°bùgwǎn 'syīsheng dwō 'dà). / Carry out these instructions at any cost. Jàuje 'syùnlìng chyu bàn, bùgwǎn 'syīsheng (yǒu) dwō 'dà.

COTTON. (Raw) 'myánhwā. / This country imports two million tons of cotton a year. Jèige 'gwó měinyán 'jìnkǒu de 'myánhwā yǒu èrbǎi'wàndwūn.

(Medical) 'yàumyánhwa. / Wipe away the blood with cotton. Bǎ 'syè yùng 'yàu-myánhwa 'tsāchyu.

(Cloth) bù, myánbù. / She bought a couple of yards of cotton. Tā mǎile lyǎng-mǎ °myán'bù (°'bù). / Printed cottons are in style this spring. °Yìnhwārde myán-'bù (°Yìnhwār'bù) 'jìnnyan 'chwūntyan hěn 'shŕsyìng. / She had on a cotton dress and a pair of white cotton stockings. Tā chwānle yìshēn (myán)'bù'yīfu gēn yìshwāng báimyánsyàn 'wàdz.

(Thread) syàn. / Please give me a spool of white cotton (thread). Gěi wo yìjóur bái'syàn.

COUGH. késou. / The baby has been coughing all night. Syǎu'hár késoule yì'wǎnshang.

(Of a motor) pūchr. /We must be out of gas because the motor is coughing. Wŏmen yí'dìng shr méi 'yóu le 'yīnwei 'jīchì jr 'pūchr.

A cough késou; or expressed verbally as in paragraph one. /Does he have a cough? Tā yŏu 'késou méiyou? /A cough from him warned me. Tā 'késoule yì-shēng, jyàu wŏ 'syăusyin. /Do you have something that's good for a cough. Nǐ yŏu 'shémma néng jr 'késou ma?

COULD. (Referring to ability) néng, or a resultative compound in the potential form. /He did everything he could think of. Tā néng 'syăngdaude dōu 'dzwòle. /When could you start working? Nǐ 'shémma shrhou néng °'kāishr dzwò 'gūng (°chǐ'tóur)? /He could get here if he wanted to. Tā 'syàng lái jyòu 'néng lái. /Who could have thought of that? 'Nèige shéi 'syăngdedàu ne?

(Referring to social propriety) néng, găn. /I couldn't think of taking such a gift. Dzèmmayàngde 'lǐwù °wŏ dzèmma néng 'shòu ne? or °wŏ bùgăn 'shòu. /I couldn't do it! meaning It's too much of an honor for me. Bùgăn'dāng!

(Referring to possibility) hwèi. /Who could have called while I was out? Wŏ 'chūchyu de shrhou yŏu shwéi hwèi 'láigwò ne? but /I don't know what the trouble could be. Wŏ mwōbuchīng shr dzèmma ge 'máubìng.

(Asking permission) kéyi, néng, syíng. /Could I look at this, please? Wŏ 'kéyi 'kàn yikan jèige ma? or Néng jyàu wo 'kàn yisyàr 'jèige ma? or Jèige wŏ 'kàn yikan 'syíng ma?

COUNT. (Compute, enumerate) shŭ. /Please count your change. Chǐng nín bă 'jǎu-hwéilai de 'chyán 'shŭ yísyàr. /Count this for me. Gěi wŏ 'shŭ yishŭ. /Have the towels been counted? 'Máujīn 'shŭgwòle ma?

(Include). /There are fifteen people here, counting the guests. Jèr lyán 'kèren dōu 'swànshang yŏu shr'wŭge rén. /The bill is five dollars, not counting the tax. Jàng shr 'wŭkwàichyán °'jyājywàn dzài'wài (°bú'swànshang 'jyājywàn).

(Consider). /I count myself lucky to be here. Wŏ néng dzài 'jèr jēn 'swànshr 'yùnchì.

(Matter). /I'm in a great hurry; every minute counts. Wŏ yŏu 'jíshèr; 'yìfēn-jūng dōu bùnéng 'dānwu. /In this broad outline, the details don't count. Jèijūng 'tsūfēnde dà'gāng, 'syăujyé'mù °méiyou 'gwānsyì (°búdà 'jùngyàu, °búdà 'yàujǐn). /He doesn't count. Tā 'wúgwān 'jǐnyàu. or Tā 'swànbulyau shémma. or Shŭbujáu 'tā.

Count on (a person) kàu; (a thing happening) 'yǐwéi. /We are counting on you. Wŏmen chywàn kàu 'nǐ le. /We can count on him. Tā 'kàudejù. /Don't count on a reply too soon. Byé yǐwéi hěn 'kwàide jyòu hwèi yŏu 'hwéisyìn.

A count (nobleman). /What is the proper address for a count? 'Hóujywé dāng-'myàr dzèmma 'chēnghu?

(A charge). /He was convicted by the court on three counts. 'Făywàn dìng tā sān°syàng (°tyáu) 'dzwèi(míng).

(Act of counting) is expressed verbally as to count shŭ. /The boxer got up on the count of nine. Dă'chywánde dzài shŭdàu dì'jyòusyàr de shrhou 'jànchilaile.

Take a count gwò shù(r). /The count has not yet been taken. Hài méigwò 'shu(r) ne.

COUNTRY. (Nation) gwó. /What country were you born in? Nǐ shēngdzài 'něigwó? /What country are you a citizen of? Nǐ shr něigwó rén? /How long have you been in this country? °Nǐ dzài 'jèr (°Nǐ dzài ... gwo) yŏu 'dwōshău nyán le.

440

/The whole country is behind him. 'Chywángwó 'rénmín yíjr̄ 'yūnghù tā.

(District). /This is good wheat country. meaning it produces good wheat Jèiyi'dàide 'màidz hèn 'hǎu. or meaning it is good land for wheat Jèiyídài jùng 'màidz hèn 'hǎu. /We haven't yet visited the mountain country. Wǒmen hái méi 'dàugwo yǒu'shān de'dìfang.

(Rural region) syāngsya. /I'm going to the country for the weekend. Wǒ yàu dàu 'syāngsya chyu gwò 'jōumwò. /The country air will do you good. 'Syāngsyade 'kūngchi dwèi nǐ yídìng hèn 'hǎu. /The country roads are in bad shape. 'Syāngsyade 'lù dōu 'hwài le.

COUPLE. (Two) lyǎng, lyǎ. /I want a couple of eggs. Wǒ yàu lyǎngge 'jīdzěr.

(Few) jǐ. /There are only a couple of pieces left. 'Shèngsyade jr̄ jyòu yǒu jǐ'kwàr le.

(Pair). /Those two make a very nice couple. Tāmen lyǎ hèn shr̄ yí'dwèr. /We are inviting several couples for dancing this evening. Wǒmen jyēr 'wǎnshang chǐngle jidwèr 'rén lái 'tyàuwǔ.

To couple gwà, lyán. /The private car has been coupled to the last car. Nèilyàng 'jwānchē °'gwà(°lyán) dzài 'mwòyílyàng'chē 'hòutou le.

COURAGE. (The quality) 'yǔnggǎn, 'yǔngchì; (daring, or a specific act of courage) dǎndz, dǎnlyàng. /Courage is a virtue. °'Yǔnggǎn (°Yǒu 'dǎnlyàng) shr̄ yìjǔng 'désying. /That's courage for you. Chyáu 'rénjyade 'dǎndz. or Chyáu 'rénjyade 'dǎnlyàng. or Chyáu rénjya dwōma 'yǔnggǎn. or Nà 'jēn swàn yǒu 'dǎnlyàng. /He showed courage in saying what he did. Tsúng tā nèmma 'jr̄chéngbú'hwèi kéyi 'kànchulai °tā yǒu 'yǔngchi (°tā 'gǎndzwò gǎn'dǎng). /He has the courage to talk back to that man. Tā 'jyūrán °yǒu 'dǎndz (°gǎn) gēn nèige rén jyàng'dzwèi. /He has the courage of his convictions. Tā 'jywéje nèmmaje 'dwèi, jyòu gǎn nèmma °'bàn (°'shwō). but /Keep up your courage. Byé hwēi'syīn.

COURSE. (Direction) lùsyàn; (of a boat or airplane) 'hángsyàn. /The plane is flying a straight course. 'Fēijīde 'hángsyàn 'bǐjr̄. or 'Fēijī yì'jr̄ syàng 'chyán 'fēi ne. /The captain (of a ship) says we will have to change our course. Chwán'jǎng shwō wǒmen děi gǎibyàn °lù'syàn (°'hángsyàn). /He must either change his course or go back. Tā bùshr̄ gǎi ge lù'syàn, jyòushr̄ děi wàng 'hwéi dzǒu.

(Of action). /That's the proper course. Nèi shr̄ jèngdāngde 'shǒusyù. /That's the best course. Nèi shr̄ °'shàngtsè (°dzwèihǎude 'fádz). /That's the only course open to me. Wǒ jr̄ néng 'dzèmmaje. or Wǒ jr̄ néng dzǒu 'jèiyìtyáu 'lù. or Wǒ méiyou 'byéde 'fádz.

(Of a river). /The course of the river has been changed by the dam. Já bǎ 'hédàu gěi 'gǎile.

(Golf). /When is the course open for golf? 'Chyóuchǎngshang 'shémma shr̄hou néng dǎ 'gāuěr'fú?

(Part of a meal) dàu; **main course** dàjyàr, 'dàtsài, 'jǔtsài. /What do you want for the main course? °Dà'jyàr (°'Dàtsài, °'Jǔtsài) syǎng chr̄ 'shémma? /There were six courses to the dinner. Yǒu 'lyòudàu tsài. /How much is the five-course dinner? Yítsān 'wǔdàu tsài shr̄ 'dwōshau chyán?

(Of instruction) kē, 'kèchéng. /He never finished the medical course. Tā 'yīke tsúnglái méinyàn'wán. /What courses are being offered in chemistry? Hwàsywé'syì dōu yǒu shémma 'kèchéng?

As a matter of course 'dāngránrú'tsž. /He takes everything as a matter of course. Tā yǐwéi shémma 'shèr dōushr̄ 'dāngránrú'tsž.

In due course. /You will be nòtified in due course. Dàu 'shŕhou jwŭn 'gàusung ni.

In the course of. /I heard from him twice in the course of the year. Wǒ 'yìn-yánli 'jyēdàugwo tā lyǎngfēng 'syìn.

Of course 'dāngrán, 'džrán. /Of course I know what you mean. Wǒ 'dāngrán 'míngbai nǐde 'yìsz. /There will be a small charge for this service, of course. Jège 'džrán děi shōu dyǎr 'shǒusyù'fèi.

COURT. (Courtyard) ywàndz. /We have several rooms facing the court. Wǒmen yǒu hǎujǐjyān 'wūdz dōu shŕ 'chùngje 'ywàndz de. /Dogs are not allowed in the court. Bùsyu gǒu jìn 'ywàndzli lai.

(Game area) chǎngdz. /This court is too wet for a game. Chǎngdz tài 'shŕ.

(Judicial body) 'fǎywàn (referring to the place); 'fǎtíng (referring to the session). /When will the court be in session? 'Fǎywàn shémma shŕhou 'kāitíng? /I have to attend court to pay a fine. Wǒ děi dàu °'fǎywàn (°'fǎtíng) chyù jyǎu yìbǐ 'fákwǎn. /The court is adjourned. is expressed as The judge has adjourned the session. Shēnpàn'gwān twèi'tíng le.

(Royal residence). /The ambassador has not yet been received at court. Dà-'shŕ hái 'méiyou dzài 'hwánggūng 'jyējyàngwo ne.

To court a girl. /He used to court her years ago. Dwōnyán yǐ'chyán tā gēn tā 'jyǎnggwo 'lyànài. or Hǎusyēnyán'chyán tā 'jwēigwo tā.

(Invite). /You're courting trouble by making such a remark. Nǐ shwō nèijǔng 'hwà shŕ 'džjǎu 'máfan.

COVER. (Lid or cover that belongs with the thing that is covered) gàr, gài; trunk cover syāngdzgàr; cover of a teapot cháhúgàr; cover of a bottle (bottle cap, not cork) píng-dzgàr; etc. /There is a cover that goes with it. Jèige hái yǒu ge 'gàr ne. /Where are the covers for these boxes? Jèisyē 'hédzde 'gàr ne?

(Shaped like an inverted bowl, not not necessarily airtight) jàu, jàur.

(Sheath, fitted case) tàu, tàur; pillow cover (pillowcase) jěntoutàu; bedroll cover rùtàu; chair cover yǐdztàur. /The room must be cleaned and the covers removed from the furniture. Jèi 'wūdz děi hǎuhǎurde 'shōushr yisyàr, yǐdz'tàur yě dōu děi 'jàile.

(Binding) pí, pyér, myàr; book cover shūpí, shūpyér, shūmyàr, fēngmyàr; magazine cover dzájrpyér, dzájrde fēng'myàr. /The cover of this book has been torn off. Jèiběr 'shūde 'pyér dyàule. /The design on the cover of that book is really a masterpiece. Nèiběn 'shū °shū'pyér shangde (°fēng'myàrshangde) 'túan jēn shr 'jyédzwò. /Do you want it with a cloth or paper cover? Shū'pyér yàu 'bùde yàu 'jŕde? or 'Yàu °'bùmyàr (°'bùpyér) yàu °'jŕmyàr (°'jŕpyér)? /The title on the cover is embossed in gold. °Shū'pyérshangde (°Shū'myàrshangde) 'byāutí shŕ gúchulaide 'jīngdzèr. but /I read the book from cover to cover. Wǒ bǎ jèiběr 'shū tsúng 'tóur dàu 'lyǎur kànle yíbyàn.

(Mail). /Send it under separate cover. Lìng jwāng ge syìn'fēngr.

(For a bed) bèi (quilt); tǎndz (blanket); bèidāndz (sheet). /I didn't have enough covers last night. Wǒ dzwór 'wǎnshang °bèi (°'tǎndz) méigài'gòu.

(Shelter). /That building served as a better cover than we thought it would. Méisyǎng'dàu dzài nèige 'lóuli 'dwǒje bǐ 'byéchùr 'chyáng. /Take cover! 'Dwǒchilai! /Let's take cover under that tree. Dzámen dzài nèikē shù 'dǐsya 'dwǒ yidwǒ. /They took cover under that tree. Tāmen dzài nèikē shù 'dǐsya 'dwǒje. or Tāmen dwǒdzài nèikē shù 'dǐsya.

Under cover. /He carried out his plan under cover. Tā jàuje tāde 'jìhwà °'ànjūng (°àn 'dìli, °'tōuje, °bújyàu rén 'jr̄dàu) jyou dōu 'bànle. /He's been under cover for a year. Tā °'dwŏle (°'dwŏchilai) yŏu yì'nyán le. *or* Tā °'tsángle (°'tsáng-chilai) yŏu yì'nyán le. /He did it under cover of darkness. Tā °dwŏdzai (°tsáng-dzai) hēi'dyèrli 'gànde. *or* (at night) Tā dzài 'yèli 'gànde.

Cover girl fēng'myàr měi'rér.

To cover (spread on, cover a flat surface) pū. /The floor was completely covered by a large rug. Kĕje wūdzde 'dìshang 'pūle yíkwài dàdì'tǎn. /The floor is covered with a mat. 'Dìshang pūje 'syí. /They used fine silk to cover the bottom of the trunk. Tāmen dzài 'syāngdz'dyèrshang pū 'chóudz. *or* Tāmen yùng 'chóudz pū syāngdz'dyèr. /The mattress won't even cover a small bed. 'Rùdz lyán 'syǎuchwáng dōu 'pūbumǎn. /Cover the road with gravel first. Syān dzài 'lùshang pū yìtséng 'shr̄tou'dzèr.

(Spread over, cover an object or a person) gài; (specifically with a cloth, paper or similar flexible materials so that all of something is covered) méng; (specifically the body or a part of the body) dài (the head), pēi (the back), gwŏ, wéi (the entire body); (with something that drapes over the edges) jàu. /That hole should be filled, not covered. Nèige 'kūlung dĕi 'tyánshang, bunéng shwō shr̄ 'gàishang jyou 'swānle. /It's best to have the well covered. Jĭng 'gàishang dyar tsái 'hǎu. /Cover him with the quilt. Ná 'bèi gĕi ta 'gàishang. *or* Gĕi ta 'gàishang 'bèi. /Cover the bowl with this book. Ná jèiben 'shū bǎ wǎn 'gàishang. /He's too tall and the quilt is too short; when his head is covered, his feet stick out. Tā tài 'cháng, bèi tài 'dwǎn; 'gàishang 'tóu, lóuje 'jyǎu. /Cover the pot if you want to boil the water. Yàu syáng bǎ shwĕi jǔ'kāile dĕi bǎ hú 'gàishang. /Cover the pot with the lid. Ná 'gàr bǎ hú 'gàishang. /Cover it with a tablecloth; then it won't show. Ná jwō'bù °méngshang (°'gàishang) jyou kànbu'jyàn le. /Tack a calendar there to cover the stain. Ná fèn ywèfen-'pái yùng èn'dĭngr dĭngdzai nèr, hau bǎ nèikwai 'dzāngde dìfang 'gàishang. /Those girls cover their heads with veils. Nèisyē 'nyǔrén ná méngtóu'shā méngje 'tóu. /You can make a tracing by covering it with a piece of thin paper. Ná jāng báu'jr̄ °'méngshang (°'jàushang, °'pūshang) jyou kéyi 'myáusyalai le. /Cover his eyes (blindfold him). Bǎ tāde 'yǎn 'méngshang. /Cover the dough with a wet cloth and wait until it rises. Ná kwài shr̄'bù bǎ myàn 'méngshang, dĕngje 'fāchilai. /They covered the dead man's face with a handerchief. Tāmen yùng shǒu'jywàr bǎ sžrénde lyǎn °'méngshangle (°'gàishangle). /Keep your head covered in this weather. Jèi-jǔng 'tyānchi dzwèi hǎu 'tóushang dài dyar 'dūngsyi. /She covered herself with a blanket. Tā °'pēije (°'gwŏje, °wéije, °méngje, °gàije) tyáu 'tǎndz. /Cover the sofa (with a sofa cover) before you dust the room. Bǎ 'shāfā 'jàushang dzài dǎn ('wūdz). *or* (with newspapers or similar materials for protection) Bǎ 'shāfā 'gài-shang dzài . . . . /She wears a satin gown but covers it with a cotton one. Tā chwān de shr̄ 'dwànpáur, 'wàitou kěshr̄ 'jàuje jyàn bù'gwàr.

(Cover with the hand or hands) wǔ. /He covered it with his hands. Tā (yùng-'shǒu) 'wǔje. /Don't cover it up (with your hand). Byé 'wǔje. /There was a letter on the desk; she covered it with her hands and asked me to guess who it was from. Shū'jwōrshang yŏu yìfeng 'syìn; tā bǎ syìn 'wǔje jyàu wo tsāi shr̄ shwéi 'syěde. /The child covers his eyes with his tiny hands and says, I'm gone! Syáu'hár yùng syǎu'shǒur bǎ 'yǎnjīng 'wǔshang, jyou 'shwōla, "Wŏ 'méi le!" /When the guns are fired he covers his ears with his hands. Fàng'pàu de shŕhou tā wǔje 'ĕrdwo. /She covers her mouth with her hand, then giggles. Tā wǔje 'dzwěr 'gērgērde 'syàu.

(In order to imprison, protect, preserve, etc.) kòu. /They caught a frog and covered it with a large bowl. Tāmen 'dǎile ge 'háma, ná ge wǎn 'kòushangle. /He covered the butterfly with a (bag-shaped) net. Tā ná 'dōur bǎ hú'tyěr 'kòujule. /Cover the sugar so the flies won't get at it. Bǎ 'tang 'kòushang byé jyàu 'tsāng-ying 'dzùng.

(To avoid light or curious stares) jē. /He covered his face with a newspaper (as on the beach) and went to sleep. Tā ná 'bàujr̆ 'jēshang 'lyǎn, jyou shwèi'jáule. /He covered his face with a newspaper when he left the court. Tā tsúng 'fǎywàn chūlai de shŕhou ná 'bàujr̆ 'jēje lyǎn.

(Conceal from sight) dǎng. /He hung the mirror there to cover a black spot on the wall. Tā bǎ 'jìngdz gwàdzai nèr 'wèideshr bǎ 'chyángshangde hēi 'dyǎndz 'dǎngshang. /Put the vase here to cover the cigarette burn. Bǎ hwā'píng fàng 'jer hǎu bǎ yān shāulede 'dìfang 'dǎngshang.

(With dirt, sand or gravel, but not by actual burial) máishang. /They covered the gun with sand. Tāmen ná 'shādz bǎ 'chyāng 'máishangle. /Cover it with earth. Ná 'tǔ 'máishang.

(Include or go over). /This book covers the subject pretty well. Nèijyàn 'shèr jèibĕn 'shū jyǎngde hĕn 'syángsyi. /He covered all angles of the problem in 45 minutes. Tā yùngle sz̀shr'wǔfēn jūng bǎ nèige wèntíde 'gèfāngmyàn 'jyǎngle yi-jyǎng. /I've covered a lot of ground today. Wǒ jīntyān 'jyǎngle bushǎu 'shèr (in speaking or discussing). or Wǒ 'jīntyān 'dzǒule bushǎu 'lù (in physical traveling). /The train covers the distance in two hours. 'Kwàichē dzǒu lyǎ jung'tóu jyou 'dàu. /I believe that covers everything. Wǒ syǎng 'gāi shwō de dōu 'shwōle.

(Handle). /A new salesman has been taken on to cover this territory. Gùle yíge syīnde twēisyāu'ywán gwǎn jèiyídài 'dìfang. or Syīn 'gùle ge rén dzài jèiyí-'dài 'twēisyāu.

(Threaten). /He had us covered with a revolver. Tā ná shǒu'chyāng bǐje wŏmen.

(Protect). /Are you covered by insurance? Nǐ yǒu bǎu'syàn ma? /Artillery covered the enemy's retreat. 'Dírén 'twèichywè de shŕhou °yǒu (°yùng) 'pàuhwǒ 'yǎnhù. /The bombers are covered by fighters. Hūngjà'jī yǒu jàndòu'jī 'yǎnhù.

Cover up mistakes, crimes, etc. (by keeping people ignorant of something bad) mán; (conceal from higher authorities) 'méngbì; (conceal by making alterations in the unpleasant facts) 'yǎnshŕ; (by confusing others) 'ménghwùn, mēng, hwùn; (of something which is not necessarily bad) 'jēgài, 'jēyǎn. /Can we ask him to cover up for us? Chǐng tā gĕi °'jēgàijēgài (°'jēyǎnjēyǎn) 'syíng ma? /He tried to cover up his own obvious mistakes by confusing others. 'Míngmíngshr̀ tā dz̀jǐde 'tswòr, kĕshr tā syǎng °'hwùngwochyu (°'mēnggwochyu, °ménghwùnde byérén 'kànbuchu-'lái). /He's only trying to cover up his embarrassment when he acts so nonchalant. Tā nà mǎnbú'dzàihude yàngdz bú'gwòshr yàu rén 'kànbuchu'lái tā 'syīnli dwōma bù'ān. /He carefully covered up all his mistakes. Tā bǎ tāde 'tswòr mánde hĕn 'dz̀syi. /He acts as if he has something to cover up. Tā nèmma 'jējeyǎn'yànde hàu'syàng you dyǎr 'shèr dĕi mán 'rén shrde. /He used his high social position to cover up (as a cover for) his crimes. Tā yùng tā dzài shè'hwèishang 'gāugwèide 'dìwei lái 'jēyǎn tā fàn'dzwèide 'syíngwéi. or Tā jìng gàn 'hwàishèr; tā dzài shè-'hwèishangde 'dìwei búgwòshr 'nálai yǎnrénérmù. /He did that to cover up. is expressed as He did that to prevent people from knowing. Tā jè shr búyàu rén jīrdàu.

Be covered with is expressed with various terms meaning is all. /He was covered with blood (he was all blood). Tā mǎn'shēn dōu shr 'sywè. /He was covered with mud. Tā °mǎn'shēn (°chywán'shēn) dōu shr 'ní. or Tā nùngle yìshēn 'ní. /His face was covered with mud. Tā mǎn'lyǎn dōu shr 'ní. or Tā 'lyǎnshang chywán shr 'ní. /The car was covered with mud. Mǎn'chēshang dōu shr 'ní.

COW. nyóu. /The milk comes from their own cows. Nyóu'nǎi shr tāmen dz̀jǐde 'nyóude. /The cows are milked at six. is expressed as The milking is done at six. 'Lyòudyǎnjūng jǐ'nǎi.

To cow (intimidate). /I felt somewhat cowed in his presence. Dzài tā 'gēn-chyar wǒ 'jywéde yǒudyar dǎn'chywè.

COWARD. dǎr'syǎude rén; (a chicken-hearted person) 'jīdǎndz. /He's a coward. Tā shr °dǎr'syǎuderén (°'jīdǎndz).

COWARDLY. dǎrsyǎu, dǎndz hěn 'syǎu, méi dǎndz, syǎudǎr, dǎnchywè. /He gave up the fight in a cowardly manner. Tā méi dǎndz jyòu rèn'shū le.

CRACK. (A split) 'lyèwén, 'lyèwér, wèn (if the sides are still together); 'lyèkǒur, 'lyèfèngr, fèngr (if the sides have separated); hwōkǒudz, kǒudz (crack in a large object, which allows something to come through). /This crack must be repaired. Jèityáu °'lyèwén (°'lyèwér, °wèn, °'lyèkǒur, °'lyèfèngr, °'fèngr) yídǐng děi 'syōuli. or Jèige °hwō'kǒudz (°'kǒudz) yídǐng děi 'dùle. /The crack in the dike is getting wider. °Tí(°Dī)shangde hwō'kǒudz ywè lái ywè 'dà. or Tíshang kāi de 'kǒudz ywè lái ywè 'dà.

(Sharp sound). /I thought I heard the crack of a rifle. Wǒ 'fǎngfu 'tīngjyàn yi'shēngr 'chyāngsyǎng shrde.

(Wisecrack). /I don't mean that as a dirty crack. Nèijyù 'hwà wǒ bìng méi-you hwài'yìsz. /He made a crack about her looks. Tā ná tāde lyǎn 'kāi wánsyǎu laije.

(Try). /Would you like to take a crack at the job? Nǐ syǎng 'shr yísyàr ma?

(Expert). /She is a crack typist. Tā shr ge hěn hǎude dǎ'dzde. or Tā dǎ'dz hǎu'jíle.

To crack something is expressed with any number of resultative compounds which may be constructed from the following. For the first element, expressing the way in which the cracking is done, use yā (press down on); jyā (press on two sides); jǐ (press on two or more sides); dzá (crush with a heavy object); chyāu (give a light, sharp blow); pèng (collide with); jwàng (swing something against hori-zontally). For the second element, expressing the result, use kāi (open); pwò (be broken); swèi (be shattered); lyè (be cracked); or expressions such as chū 'lyèwér (be cracked but still holding together), chéng lyǎngbàr (be cracked to pieces). /If we can't open the safe any other way we'll have to crack it open. Bǎusyǎn'syǎng 'yàushr kāibu'kāi dehwà wǒmen jyou děi 'dzákāi. /This is a tough nut to crack. (lit. of a walnut) Jèige 'hétou jēn 'yìng, jǐbu'pwò. or Hěn nán'bàn.

Crack a joke shwō 'syàuhwar. /He cracked several jokes before beginning the speech. Tā yǎn'shwō yǐchyán syān shwōle hǎujige 'syàuhwar.

Crack up (crash) is expressed as crack something above. /I was afraid that the driver would crack up the car. Wǒ 'pàde jyòushr kāi'chēde hwèi bǎ 'chē jwàng-'hwàile. /The plane cracked up near the landing field. 'Fēijī dzài jyànglwò'chǎng 'fùjìn shwāi'hwèile.

Cracked ice swèi bīng. /Could you send some cracked ice to my room? Sùng dyǎr swèibīng shanglai syíng busyíng?

CREAM. (Top milk) nǎiyóu, nǎipí. /Do you take cream with your coffee? Nǐ hē kā'fēi yàu °nǎi'yóu ma (°nǎi'pí ma)?

(Choice part) 'dzwèihǎude. /Only the cream of the candidates will be accepted. Jǐ chyǔ 'hòusywǎnrénli 'dzwèihǎude. or Jǐ yǒu 'dzwèihǎude tsái chyǔdeshàng. /We were shown only the cream of the crop. Jyàu wǒmen 'kàn de jǐ shr °'dzwèi-hǎude. or (if referring to a literal crop) °dzwèihǎude 'jwāngjya.

(Medicinal) yàugāu, gāudzyàu. /Apply this cream twice a day. Jeige °yàu'gāu

(°gāudz'yàu) měi'tyān shàng 'lyǎngtsź. / Do you have any facial cream? Nǐ yǒu tsā-'lyǎn de yàu'gāu ma?

Cold cream sywěhwǎrgāu.

Be cream-colored 'yáshǎr(de). / The walls are cream-colored with a blue border. Chyáng shř 'yáshǎrde dài 'lánbyār.

CREATURE. 'hwówù(r) <u>or, if a particular type of creature is intended, a specific term is used.</u> / If you keep a living creature you must feed it. 'Yǎushr yǎng 'hwówù(r) jyǒu děi 'wèi. / The poor creatures (meaning kittens) haven't been fed. Kě'lyánde syǎu'māur héi méi'wèi ne.

(Detestable person) jyāhwo, dūngsyi. / Who is that creature at the information desk? Dzài wènshř'chù de nèige °'jyāhwo (°'dūngsyi) shř 'shwéi?

CREDIT. (In finance, loans) 'syìnyùng; **credit loan** 'syìnyùngdài'kwǎn. / His credit is very good. Tāde 'syìnyùng hěn 'hǎu. / His credit is bad. Tā méiyou 'syìnyùng. *or* Tā 'syìnyùng °búda 'hǎu (°hěn 'hwài).

(Balance). / The books show a credit of five dollars in your favor. 'Jàngshàng hái 'tswúnje nín 'wǔkwài chyán.

(Honor) gūnglau; **give** <u>someone</u> **credit** gwēi'gūngyú, (praise) chēngdzàn, (if an underling) 'kwājyǎng. / The credit is entirely his. 'Gūnglau chywán shr 'tāde. / He takes the credit, but we get the blame. 'Gūnglau shř 'tāde, 'tswǒr shr 'dzámende. / They give him credit for his foresight. Tāmen chēng'dzàn tā yǒu syān-'jyànjr'míng. / The commander-in-chief gives him credit for his quick decision. Dzūngsž'lìng 'kwājyǎng tā pàn'dwànde 'kwài. / The president gives him credit for doing that. Tā dzwò nèijyàn 'shèr 'dzūngtǔng hěn 'kwājyǎng ta. / They gave the doctor credit for curing him. Tāde 'bìng wánchyán jr'hàule, tāmen shwō dōu shr nèige 'dàifude 'gūnglau. / He takes all the credit. Tā 'dzjǐ shwō dōu shr tāde 'gūnglau. *or* Tā wánchywán gwēigūngyu tā 'dzjǐ. / He took credit for the planning, though others did the work. 'Swéiran shèr dōu shr 'byérén 'dzwòde, kěshr tā shwō chóu'bèide 'gūnglau shř 'tāde.

(Source of praise). / He is a credit to his profession. Tā wèi 'túngyè °'dzēng-gwāng (°'jēnggwāng).

(Academic) sywéfēn, sywéfēr. / He needs three more credits in order to graduate. Tā hái děi nyàn 'sānge sywé'fēr tsái néng bì'yè.

(In buying). / His credit is good anywhere. Tā dzài 'nǎr dōu néng jì'jàng. / The manager said that my credit is good. 'Jīnglǐ shwō wǒ 'kěyǐ jì'jàng.

On credit búyùng fù syànkwǎn. / They are willing to sell the furniture on credit. Tāmen 'ywànyi bǎ 'jyājyù 'màigei women, búyùng fù 'syànkwǎn.

Buy on credit jì'jang. / Will they let us buy on credit at this store? Jèi'pùdz néng jyàu women jì'jàng ma?

To credit (honor). / We have to credit him with finding it. Jèige néng 'jǎujau, °women děi gwēi'gūngyú 'tā (°women 'bùnéng bù'shwō shř 'tāde 'gūnglau).

CRIME. (Case) àndz. / The police are investigating the crime. Jǐng'chá jèngdzài 'dyàuchá nèige 'àndz.

(Offense) 'ànchíng. / This is a serious crime. 'Ànchíng jùng'dà.

(Violation of law) <u>is expressed verbally as</u> **commit a crime** fànfǎ, fàndzwèi. / He committed a crime. Tā fàn'fǎ le. *or* Tā fàn'dzwèi le. / What is his crime? Tā fànde shémma °'dzwèi (°'fǎ)? *or* Tāde 'dzwèimíng shř 'shémma?

(Criminal activity) fànfǎde shèr, bufǎ syíngwéi. / Crime has decreased since the declaration of martial law. 'Sywānbù jyèyán'lǐng yǐhòu, °fàn'fǎ de shèr (°bùfǎ syíngwéi) 'shǎule.

(Disgraceful act) kěchǐ, búdwèi, kěhèn, tǎuyàn (mild terms); gāisz, gāishā, dànǐbú'dàu (strong terms). / It's a crime! °Jēnshr (°'Jyǎnjr) °kě'chǐ ˉ(°bú'dwèi, °etc.). / The way they run these busses is a crime! 'Gūnggùngchì'chē bànlǐdàu dzèmmage 'dìbu jyǎnjr shr °gāi'sz (°etc.).

CROP. jywāngjya; (yield) shōucheng. / They get three crops a year. Tāmen yì'nyán shōu 'sāntsz jwāngjya. / How are the crops around here? (in regard to growing conditions) Jèr fùjìnde 'jwāngjya dzèmma'yàng? (in regard to yield) Jèr fù'jìnde 'shōucheng dzèmma'yàng? / The farmers expect a good crop this year. 'Núngrén pànje 'jǐnnyan shōucheng 'hǎu.

A crop of (a yield of) shōude; (a growing crop of) jǎngde; (specifying one of several in a period of time) tsz. / That's a good crop of wheat. (growing) 'Jīnnyan màidz 'jǎngde hěn 'hǎu. (harvested) (Nèitsz) (shōude) 'màidz hěn 'hǎu. / The price of land is high here because it yields three crops of wheat a year. Jèr dìjyà 'gāu, yīnwei yì'nyán kéyi shōu 'sāntsz màidz.

A crop of (fig.) jèn. / A new crop of rumors grew up after the conference. Hwèi 'wánle yǐ'hòu, yíjèn 'yáuyán yòu 'chǐlaile.

To crop up fāshēng or expressed with dwō many. / Many new questions are sure to crop up. Hěn dwōde 'syīn wèntí yí'dìng hwèi fā'shēng. or 'Chyáuje ba, °'shèr hái (°'wèntí hái) 'dwō jene.

CROSS. (Religious symbol) shŕdzjyà (lit. a framework shaped like the character for shŕ, meaning ten). / Do you see that church with the big cross on the steeple? Nǐ 'kànjyàn 'jyārshang yǒu ge dàshŕdz'jyà de neige lǐbài'táng le ma?

(Crisscross mark) chār (X-shaped); shŕdzèr (+-shaped). / Put a cross on the map to show where we are. Dzài dì'túshang °dǎ (°hwà) ge 'chār hǎu 'jrchūlai wǒmen dzài 'nǎr. / If you can't sign your name, make a cross instead. Nǐ yàu búhwèi chyān'míng, hwà ge shŕ'dzèr yě 'syíng.

(Hybrid). / The mule is a cross between the horse and the donkey. 'Lwódz shr 'mǎ gēn 'lyú 'pèichulaide.

To cross gwò. / Cross the street on the green signal. Dēng'lyù de shŕhou gwò 'jyē. / Where can we cross the river? Wǒmen dzài nǎr kéyi gwò 'hé?

Cross one's fingers. / Keep your fingers crossed! is expressed as Hope for us to succeed. 'Syīwàng wǒmen chéng'gūng ba! / I've got my fingers crossed. is expressed as My heart's in suspense. / Wǒ sywánje ge 'syīn. or as I'm worried. Wǒ hěn 'dān'syīn.

Cross one's mind. / It never crossed my mind that he would object. Wǒ 'tsúng-lái méi'syǎngdàu 'tā hwèi fǎn'dwèi.

Cross someone's path. / I've never happened to cross his path. Wǒ 'tsúnglái méi'yùjyàngwo tā.

Cross out lá(sya)chyu, hwà(sya)chyu, 'hwàdyàu. / Cross out the items you don't want. Bǎ nǐ bú'yàude dōu °'lásyachyu (°'lále chyu, °'hwàsyachyu, °'hwàdyàule).

CROWD. (Mob or set) chyún, ('dà)syē, bāng, hwǒdz (all these terms are measures; hwǒdz and bāng imply a certain amount of organization); rén, dà'dwèide rén. / A crowd gathered on the street corner. Jyē'kǒurshang 'jyùle °yì'chyún rén (°yì'bāng rén, °yì'hwǒdz rén, °yí('dà)sye, °('hǎusyē)rén). / Let's follow the crowd. Dzámen 'gēnje °rén (°dà'dwèide rén) 'dzǒu ba. / He runs around with a different crowd. Tā

447

gēn lǐng °yǐ'bāng rén (°yǐ'hwǒdz rén, °etc.) 'hwùn. / That's a smart crowd. °Nèi-'hwǒdz (rén) (°etc.) hěn 'hwāshàu. / This is a mixed crowd. °Jèi'chyún rén (°etc.) hěn 'dzá. / He is running around with a bad crowd. Tā gēn °yìchyún (°etc.) °'hwài-rén láiwang (°'húpénggǒu'dǎng láiwang).

To **crowd** (push forward) yūng; (press from all sides) jǐ. / More and more people crowded into the square. Jìjìn 'chǎngdz lái de rén ywè 'lái ywè 'dwō. / Don't crowd me! Byé 'jǐ wo! / The people crowded against the window to look in. Rén dōu °'yūngdzài (°'jǐdzài) 'chwānghu nàr wàng lǐ 'chyáu. / The theater was crowded to capacity. Syì'ywándzli jǐ'mǎnle rén.

CRUEL. (Physically; of a person, when the cruelty is apt to result in death or mutilation) 'tsánrěn; (of an act or of treatment) hěn, kù; be cruel to 'nywèdài. / The kidnappers were very cruel to the child. Bǎng'pyàurde 'nywèdài nèige 'bāngchyude syǎu'hár láije. or Bǎng'pyàurde dài nèige 'bānchyude syǎu'hár dàide tǐng °'tsán-rénde (°'hěnde, °'kùde).

(Severe, of laws or punishments) yán. / The punishments under the new laws are less cruel than under the old. Syīn fǎ'gwēi dìng de 'chěngfá méiyou yǐ'chyán nèmma 'yán.

(Of remarks) kèbwo, swǔn; be cruel to wāku. / I didn't pay any attention to his cruel remarks. Tā nèijǔng kèbwo 'hwà wǒ jr̄jr̄bù'lǐ. or Tā shwō de 'hwà hěn °kèbwo (°'swǔn), kěshr wǒ méi'lǐ ta. or Tāde 'hwà 'wāku rén 'wākude hěn 'lìhai, kěshr wǒ méi'lǐ ta.

CRUSH. Expressed with numerous resultative compunds which can be constructed from the following elements. For the first element, describing the way in which the crushing is done, use yā (apply steady pressure from above); jǐ (press from two or more sides); yà (crush by moving or rolling pressure); dzá (give a heavy blow); pèng (collide); etc. For the second element, describing the result, use pwò (be broken); hwài (be broken or ruined); sž (die); byǎn (be flat); swèi (be shattered); lyè (crack); sǎn (be in parts); byè (be dry, flat, empty); etc. See also **BREAK, CRACK**. / The package was crushed in transit. 'Bāugwǒ yun de shŕhou °jǐ'hwàile (°'jǐ'byǎnle, °etc.). / I want this crushed hat repaired. Wǒ syǎng bǎ jèige 'yàhwàile de 'màudz shōu-shrshōushr. / We were nearly crushed (to death) while leaving the theater. Wǒmen chū syì'ywándz de shŕhou 'chàdyǎr (méi)'jǐsž.

(Broken in spirit). / We were crushed by the announcement. Wǒmen 'tīngjyàn bàu'gàu yǐhòu, jēn shr̄ 'shāngsyin'jíle. / The telegram contained crushing news. Dyànbàude 'syāusyi hěn 'hwài.

A crush (crowd). / There was a crush when they opened the gates. Dàmén yì 'kāi dà'jyā °lwàn'jǐ (°yìyūng ěr'rù).

(Infatuation). / She has a crush on that actor. Tā °jyàu (°ràng) nèige 'syìdz gěi míjùle. or Tā 'míshangle nèige 'syìdz le. or Nèige 'syìdz jyàu tā °jáu 'míle (°rù 'míle).

CRY. (Weep) kū; (cry loudly) háu; (wail and weep) háutáu dà'kū. / The baby cried all night. Syǎu'hár °jūle (°háule) yí'yè. / She cried when she heard the news. Tā tīngjyàn nèige 'syāusyi yǐ'hòu, 'kūle yìchǎng. / She cried loudly. Tā háutáu dà'kū.

(Of animals) jyàu(hwan), háu. / The dog cried for a while. Gǒu °'háule (°'jyàu-hwanle) yìhwer. / You can hear the gulls crying from this window. Nǐ tsúng jèige 'chwānghu kěyǐ tīngjyan hǎi'ōu 'jyàuhwàn.

(Shout) hǎn. / Stop him! she cried. Tā dàshēng 'hǎn, Byé jyàu ta 'pǎule!

Cry out 'jyàuhwan, hǎn. / The pain was so great that he cried out. Tā téngde jr̄ 'jyàuhwan.

A cry (shout) is expressed verbally as to shout hǎn. / There was a cry of "Man overboard!" Yǒurén 'hǎn, "Yǒurén dyàu chwán wàitou chyùle!"

Have a good cry kū yǐ'chǎng. / She had a good cry and felt better. Tā 'kūle yǐ'chǎng hǎu 'dwōle.

Far cry. / The accommodations are a far cry from what we wanted. Jèrde 'shèbèi gēn wǒmen yàu de syāngchà tài 'ywǎn le.

CUP. bēi, bēidz; in some cases wǎn meaning bowl, and jūng or jūngr, meaning a small bowl, may be used; teacup chábēi, cháwǎn, chájūng. / This cup is not full. Jèige bēi(dz) bù'mǎn. / I have to buy more paper cups. Wǒ děi 'dwō mǎi dyǎr jǐr'bēidz. / Will you have a cup of coffee? Nǐ syǎng hē bēi 'jyāfēi ma? / Whoever wins the race this afternoon will get the cup. (trophy cup) Jyèr 'syàwǔde bǐ'sài shéi 'yíng shǒi dé nèige °jǐnyàn'bēi (or victory cup) °yōushèng jǐnyàn'bēi, or (gold cup) °jīn'bēi, or (silver cup) °yín'bēi). / He keeps the silver cups he won enclosed in a glass case. Tā bǎ tā 'déde yín'bēi dōu yùng 'bwōlijàur 'jàuje.

To cup. / You can light the cigarette if you cup your hands around the match. Nǐ yùng shǒu (bǎ yáng'hwǒr) °'wǔ(°'jàu)je dyar jyòu 'kéyi (bǎ'yān) 'dyǎnjáule.

CURE. (Make well) 'jr̄hǎu, 'kànhǎu, 'yǐhǎu (resultative compounds); if the person cured is not mentioned, jr̄ or kàn or yǐ may be used alone (kàn is said only of a person, as a doctor; jr̄ and yǐ are said of a person or a treatment). / We can trust the doctor to cure him. Wǒmen kéyǐ jr̄je jèige 'dàifu bǎtā °'jr̄hǎule (°'kànhǎule, °'yǐhǎule). / That can't be cured by medicine. 'Nèige búshr 'yàu néng jr̄de 'hǎude. / That can't be cured by medicine alone. 'Nèige bùnéng gwāng kàu 'yàu lái °'jr̄ (°'yǐ). or 'Nèige gwāng kàu 'yàu shr̄ °'jr̄buhǎude (°'yǐbuhǎude). / Who cured him? Shéi bǎ tā jr̄'hǎule de? or 'Shéi gěi 'jr̄de? or Shéi gěi 'kànde?

(Correct). / This will cure him of that (bad) habit. Jèige 'kéyi bǎ tāde 'máu-bìng °'gǎigwolai (°'jr̄gwolai, °'jr̄hǎule, °'gwǎngwolai).

(Prepare or preserve according to a formula) 'páujr̄ (of herbs, hides, tobacco); 'péijr̄, 'péigān (over a slow fire); shài, 'shàigān (in the sun); syūn (with smoke); jyā táng 'páujr̄ (with sugar); 'mǐjyàn (with syrup). / They cure tobacco in these buildings. Tāmen dzài jèijige 'lóuli 'páujr̄ 'yàntsǎu.

Cured ham hwǒtwěi.

A cure (remedy) jr̄de fár, jr̄de 'fádz, jr̄de 'fāngfa, 'jr̄lyáu, lyáu, jr̄ ('jr̄lyáu and lyáu are more formal). / Is there a cure for this disease? Jei bìng yǒu fár 'jr̄ ma? / There is no cure for that. Nèige 'bìng méi fár 'jr̄. / I have a cure for that. Nèige wǒ yǒu ge fár 'jr̄. or Nèige 'wǒ you ge fāngfa lái 'jr̄. / Would the water cure do him any good? Yùng shwěi °jr̄ de 'fāngfa (°'jr̄), dwèi tā néng yǒu shémma 'hǎuchù ma? / The title of this book is "Cures for Common Colds." Jèi-běn shūde 'míngdz shr̄ "Pǔtūng Shāngfēng Jr̄lyáufǎ."

CURL. (Form ringlets, as of hair) jywǎn; curl one's hair jywǎn 'tóufa or (in a beauty) parlor) tàng 'tóufa. / She curls her hair every night. Tā tyān'tyān wǎnshàng jywǎn 'tóufa. / She went to the beauty parlor to have her hair curled. Tā chyù měirúng-'ywàn tàng 'tóufa.

Curl up (of the body) chywán. / The dog curled up and went to sleep. Gǒu chywánchilai jyòu 'shwèijáule.

A curl (lock of hair) yíjywǎr 'tóufa.

(Spiral). / A curl of smoke is coming out of the chimney. Yìlyǔ 'yān tsúng 'yāntungli (wànwanchyu'chyūde) chūlaile.

CURRENT. (Of water) lyòu. / Does this river have a strong current here? 'Hé dzài jèr de 'lyòu 'dà bu'dà?

(Of electricity) dyàn, 'dyànlyóu; **direct current** jŕlyóu'dyàn; **alternating current** jyāulyóu'dyàn. / My electric current has been cut off. Wǒ nèr méi 'dyàn le. *or* Wǒ nèr de 'dyàn °'tíngle (°'chyāle). / The current passes through here and is connected into that room. 'Dyànlyóu dǎ jèr 'gwò, yòu 'tūngdàu nèijyān 'wūli. / What kind of current do you have here? Nǐ jèr yùng shémma 'dyàn?

Be current (circulating). / This story is now current in many papers. Jèijyàn shř hǎusyē 'bàushang °dōu 'yǒu le (°'dà'dēng).

(Present). / What is the current value of the franc? 'Fàláng syàndzài shémma 'hángshr? / I have no time to pay attention to current events. Wǒ méi 'gūngfu jùyì 'shŕshŕ 'syīnwén. / I read that in the current issue of the magazine. Wǒ shř dzài jèiyì'chĭde dzá'jŕshang kànjyànde. *or* Wǒ shř dzài dzwèijìn yì'chĭde dzá'jŕshang 'kànjyànde.

CURSE. (Swear at) mà. / The beggars cursed us because we didn't give them anything. Yàu'fàrde màle wǒmen yídwùn 'yīnwèi wǒmen méi'gěi tamen shémma.

(Afflict). / We were cursed with bad weather the whole trip. °Jēn dǎu'méi (°Wǒmen 'yùnchi jēn 'hwài), yílù 'hwàityār.

A curse (profanity) is expressed in terms of the verb **to curse** mà. / All he did was mutter a few curses. Tā jŕ 'màle jishēngr. *or* Tā syǎushēngr 'màle jijyù(jyē) jyòu °'wán le (°'swàn le, °'lyǎu le).

(Torment). / The mosquitoes were a curse. 'Wéndz jēn tǎu'yàn. *or* 'Wéndz jēn jyàu rén shòu'dzwèi.

(Evil spell). / They say the house has a curse on it. Tāmen shwō nèiswǒr 'fángdz nàu'gwěi. *or* Tāmen shwō nèi shř ge 'syūngjái.

CURTAIN. (In a house) lyár. / I want curtains for all the windows. Wǒ měige 'chwānghu dōu yàu chwānghu'lyár. / Pull the curtain shut. Bǎ lyár 'lāshang.

(In a theater) mù. / Drop the curtain. Bǎ mù 'lāsyalai. / The curtain goes up at eight-thirty. Syì 'bādyǎn'bàn °kāi'mù (°'kāichǎng, °'chĭshř).

(Fig.). / There was a curtain of smoke over that area. 'Nèibyar 'wūyānjàng-'chĭde. *or* 'Nèibyar jyàu 'yān dōu 'jàushangle. *or* 'Nèibyar jyàu 'yān gěi 'jějule.

CUSTOM. (Habitual practice of a group or locality) 'fēngtǔ'rénchíng, 'fēngsú. / I'm not yet familiar with the local customs. Běndìde °'fēngtǔ'rénchíng (°'fēngsú) wǒ hái bú'dà shóu.

(Habitual practice of an individual or family) gwēijyu (regulation); but more commonly expressed as often *or* always dzǔng *or* lǎu *or* 'chángcháng. / Is it your custom to eat breakfast early? Nǐ dzǎu'fàn dzǔng shř 'chŕde hěn 'dzǎu ma?

Customs (inspection at the border) hǎi'gwān jyàn'chá, hǎi'gwān jyàn'yàn; (tax imposed at customs) 'shwèichyán, shwèi; **customs inspector** hǎi'gwān chá'ywán, hǎi'gwānjì'chá, cháshwèide, hǎi'gwānshang chá'shwèide; **custom house** hǎigwān; (rate of) customs *or* income from customs 'gwānshwèi. / We were delayed by customs. Wǒmen 'yīnwei °hǎi'gwān jyàn'chá (°'hǎi'gwān jyàn'yàn) swǒyǐ 'dānwùle. / Is there a customs inspection at the border? 'Byānjyè ner yǒu °hǎi'gwān jyàn'chá ma (°hǎi'gwān jyàn'yàn ma, *or* (an inspector)°chá'shwèide ma)? / Do we have to pay customs on this? Jèige wǒmen yě děi °jyāu 'shwèichyán ma (°shàng'shwèi ma)? / The customs on this sort of thing are awfully high. 'Jèijǔng dūngsyi 'gwān-shwèi hěn 'jùng.

450

Custom-made 'dǐngdzwòde. / He wears oǹly custom-made clothes. Tā 'gwāng chwān dǐngdzwò de 'yīfu.

Custom tailor tsáifeng.

CUT. 1. (Sever, gash, incise, divide into parts, etc., with an edged instrument) is expressed with various specific terms depending on how the cutting is done; (most general) lá; (chop with a heavy instrument, swinging it with the arm) kǎn; (cut by slicing) chyē; (slice thin, as meat) pyàn; (cut into and then slide through; split; trim) pī; (chisel) dzáu, dzá; (carve) kē, dzáu; (amputate, cut off, or to cut grain) gē; (cut with a fodder knife) já; (with a sharp point) hwà, hwá; (with scissors) jyàn; (with a saw) jyù; (with a rotating saw or blade) sywàn; or sometimes expressed with fēn divide. / He cut himself with a pocket knife. Tā ná syǎu'dāur bǎ 'shǒu lále. / He cut his chin while shaving. Tā gwā 'lyǎn de shŕhou bǎ 'syàba 'lále. / You can use a diamond to cut glass. Kéyi yùng jīngāng'shŕ lá 'bwōli. / I cut my hand while I was cutting up the vegetables. Wǒ chyē 'tsài de shŕhou bǎ shǒu 'lále. / They have cut most of the trees for firewood. Tāmen bǎ 'shù chàbùdwō dōu 'kǎnle 'wèideshŕ shāu'hwǒ yùng. / Cut the meat into slices. Bǎ 'ròu chyēchéngle sēr. / Cut off a thin slice of the beef. Bǎ 'nyóuròu 'pyànsya yípyàr lai. / Cut the board in two. Bǎ 'bǎndz pīchéng 'lyǎngkwài. / Cut this stalk of bamboo into strips. Bǎ 'júdz pīcheng 'tyáur. / Use a chisel and a hammer to cut off a piece. Ná 'dzáudz gēn 'chwéidz °'dzáusya (°dzásya) yíkwài chyu. / He cut a design on the piece of wood. Tā dzài 'mùtoushang °'kēle (°'dzáule) ge 'hwār. / They use a sickle to cut the grass. Tāmen yùng 'lyándāu 'gētsǎu. / During the operation the doctor used seven kinds of scalpels to cut out the tumor. Syíng'shǒushù de shŕhou 'dàifu yùngle 'chījǔng 'dāudz bǎ nèige 'lyóudz °'gēsyalaide (°'lásyalaide). / The cake was dry and did not cut easily. Dàn'gāu gān le bùhǎu 'chyē. / They used a fodder knife to cut up the rice stalks to feed the cow. Tāmen ná 'jádāu bǎ 'dàutsǎu °'jále (°'chyēle) wèi 'nyóu. / Cut here (with scissors). Dzài jèr 'jyānkāi. / They cut the board in two. Tāmen bǎ mù'bǎr jyùcheng lyǎng'bàr. / They cut the wooden ball with a lathe. Tāmen dzài sywàn-'chwángdzshang sywànle ge 'mùtóuchyóur. / Shall we cut the cake now? Syàndzài fēn dàn'gāu hǎu ma?

Cases in which there is a choice of several of the above words. / He cut his hand when he fell. Tā 'shwāi de shŕhou bǎ 'shǒu °lále (°gwále, °hwále, °hwàle). *or* Tā 'shwāi de shŕhou bǎ 'shǒu °lále (°etc.) ge 'kǒudz. / Cut off all the loose ends. Bǎ 'swèitóur dōu °'jyànsyachyu (°'lásyachyu, °'dwòsyachyu, °etc.).

Cut a gash or furrow hē, hwō.

Cut paper or cloth tsái. / Fold the paper and cut at the folded edge. Bǎ jŕ 'dyéchilai, dzài dyé de 'dàur nàr 'tsái.

Cut cloth jyé. / This piece of cloth can be cut in two. Jèikwài 'bù kéyi °'jyécheng (°'tsáicheng) lyǎngkwài.

Cut hair lǐ, jyǎn; (with clippers) yùng 'twēidz twēi'tóu. / I must get my hair cut. Wǒ děi °'lǐfà le (°'jyǎnfǎ le).

Cut flowers. / These flowers were cut from our garden. Jèisyē 'hwār shŕ ywándzli °'chyāsyàlaide (°'jāisyàlaide, °'jyǎnsyàlaide).

2. Other uses of **cut**.

(Shorten, reduce). / The movie had to be cut in several places. 'Pyàndz yǒu 'jǐchù bùnéng bù'jyǎnle chyù. / The report had to be cut down to half its length. Bàu'gàu °'lásya yí'bàr chyù (°'syāusya yí'bàr chyù, °'syāuchyu yí'bàr, °'jyǎn-chyù yí'bàr, °'chyù yí'bàr). / We are trying to cut down expenses. Wǒmen jèng-dzài syǎng'fǎr °'shěng'chyán (°'shǎu yùng'chyán, °'jyéshěng dyar, °'jyǎnshěng dyar). / These prices will be cut next month. Syàywè jèisyē 'jyàr dōu yàu 'làu.

(Dig). / They are cutting ground for a new building. Tāmen jèngdzài pwò'tǔ gài syīn'fángdz.

(Ignore). / They are old friends, and I didn't mean to cut them. Tāmen shř wǒde 'lǎupéngyou; wǒ 'bìng búshř yàu bù'lǐ tāmen.

Cut <u>cards</u> dǎu, yāu. / Have these cards been cut? Pái °'dǎule (°'yāule) ma?

Cut <u>a class</u>. / He had to cut the class in order to meet us. Tā wèi 'jyē wǒmen °'shwāle yìtáng 'kè (°nèitáng 'kè méi'shàng). / During the term he cut two lectures. Yí'jìde gūngfu tā yǒu 'lyǎngtáng kè méi'tīng.

Cut <u>a figure</u>. / Their ambassador cut a big figure at the conference. Tāmende dà'shř dzài kāi'hwèi de shŕhou tǐng 'shénchì.

Cut <u>corners</u>. / The job will take five days, four days if we cut corners. Dzwò 'jèige hwór děi 'wǔtyān, (yàushr) jyā'jǐn dehwà 'sżtyān yě kěyǐ 'wán.

Cut <u>loose</u>. / When the president got there, they cut loose and raised the roof. Dzǔngtǔng 'dàule, tāmen 'dàhǎndà'jyàude lái 'hwānyíng.

Cut <u>short</u>. / Our trip was cut short by the bad news. Wǒmen 'tīngjyànle (nèi-jyānshèr) jyòu 'méidzài wàng chyán 'dzǒu. / His speech was cut short by the news. Tā 'tīngjyànle (nèige) jyòu méidzài wàng syà 'shwō.

Cut <u>across</u>, cut <u>through</u>. / It will save time to cut across the field. Tsúng 'chǎngdzli 'chwāngwòchyù °shēng 'shŕhou (°chāu'jyèr, °'jìndyar). / When we are in a hurry we cut through the park. Wǒmen 'mángde shŕhou jyòu tsúng gūng'ywánli 'chwāngwochyu.

Cut <u>in</u> (interrupt). / We were talking very quietly until he cut in. Tā méidǎ'chà yǐchyán wǒmen shwōhwà 'shēngyin hěn syāu.

Cut <u>in</u> (of cars). / He was going slow, and we cut in ahead of him. Tā dzǒude 'màn, wǒmen jyòu bǎ tā 'gǎngwochyule. / He's cutting in and out of traffic to get ahead. Tā jèng nèmma 'ráuláiràu'chyùde wàng chyán 'chyǎng.

Cut <u>off</u> (disconnect). / The flood has cut off all communication with that town. Yīnwei dà'shwěi 'nèige dìfang swǒ'yǒude 'jyāutung dōu dwàn le. / Operator, I've been cut off! Wèi! Dyànhwàsyàn 'dwànle!

Cut <u>out</u> (eliminate). / He used to have a good business but was cut out by competition. Tā 'mǎimài yǐchyán bú'tswò laije; 'hòulái jyàu 'rén gěi 'chyánggwòchyule. / Tell them to cut out the noise. Jyàu tāmen 'syāu dyar shēngr. / Cut it out! (of actions) Byé 'nèmmaje!

Cut <u>through</u> see Cut across.

Cut <u>up</u> (be disorderly). / Have the children been cutting up? 'Háidzmen 'fǎn-láije méiyou? or 'Háidzmen hú'nàu láije méiyou?

Be cut out for <u>something</u>. / He is not cut out for studying languages. Tā sywé 'yǔyán búdà hé'shř.

A cut (wound) kǒudz, kǒur, 'shāngkǒur. / The cut in my finger is nearly healed. Wǒ shǒu'jŕtoushang 'lá de nèige 'kǒudz kwài 'hǎu le.

(Of meat). / When you buy pork you have to specify what cut you want; for example, shoulder, ham, and so on. Mǎi 'jūròu de shŕhou nǐ děi 'shwō nǐ yàu tsúng 'nǎr lásyalaide ròu, pìrú 'jǒudz, hòu'twěr, shémmade. / What other cuts do you have? Hái yǒu 'byéde dìfang 'lásyalaide(ròu)ma? / We are having cold cuts for supper. Jyēr wǎnshang chŕ 'chángdz hé ròu'dùngr.

(Of clothes). / She always wears clothes of the latest cut. Tā yǔng'ywǎn chwān dzwèi mwó'dēngde yīfu. or Tā 'chwān de 'yīfu lǎu shř 'dzwèi syīnshřde.

/I'd rather have a suit of loose cut. Wǒ ywànyî yàu 'féiyidyǎrde 'yīfu.

(Reduction). /He asked us to take a salary cut of ten per cent. Tā jyàu wǒmen shǎu 'ná 'shŕfēnjŕ'yīde chyán. *or* Tā jyàu wǒmen jyǎn 'shŕfēnjŕ'yīde 'syīn.

(Illustration). /We're making a cut of your latest photograph for our next issue. Nǐde 'jàusyàng wǒmen yàu dzwò ge 'túngbǎn 'dēngdzài 'syàyìchī. /There are three cuts in the book. Jèběn 'shūli yǒu 'sānjāng chā'tú.

(A share). /Did all of them get their cut? Tāmen 'dōu fēn'dàule ma? /When the deal was finished they asked for their cut. Jyāu'yì shwōhǎule, tāmen jyòu yàuchi °'yùngchyán laile (°'tāmen nèr'fèr laile).

DAILY. (Day by day, referring to a continuous process) yì'tyānyìtyānde. /He is getting better daily. Tā yì'tyānyìtyānde jyàn'hǎu. *or* Tā 'yìtyān bǐ 'yìtyān jyàn'hǎu.

(Every day, referring to a repeated action) 'měityān, tyāntyan. /He comes daily. Tā °'měityān (°'tyāntyan) lái. /An inspection of the passports is made daily. °'Měityān (°'Tyāntyan) jyǎn'chá hù'jàu. /He makes a daily news broadcast. Tā °'měityān (°'tyāntyan) dzài wúsyàn'dyànli bàu'gàu syīn'wén.

Daily newspapers are usually called either morning papers dzǎubàu *or* evening papers wǎnbàu. /There are two (evening) dailies published in this town. Jèi 'chéngli yǒu 'lyǎngjǔng wǎn'bàu. /Morning dailies in New York are put on sale the night before. 'Nyǒuywē 'měityān chūde dzǎu'bàu tóutyan 'wǎnshang jyou 'mài le. but in the names of some papers ŕ'bàu; The World Daily 'Shŕjyè Ŕ'bàu.

DAMAGE. (Physically) dzǎuta, hwěi, nùnghwài; (by collision) jwànghwài; (by a sharp blow or by something falling) dzáhwài; (and other resultative compounds; *see* **BREAK**). /He damaged my car. Tā bǎ wǒde 'chē °'dzǎutale. (*or* °nùng'hwàile, °gěi 'hwěile, °jwàng'hwàile). /The car was damaged. Chǐ'chē °'hwěile (°jwàng'hwàile). /The hail damaged the wheat crop. Báudz bǎ 'jwāngjya dōu dzá'hwàile.

Damage (physical, general) expressed verbally as above; (physiological) shòushāng. /He did a lot of damage to our furniture. Tā bǎ wǒmende jyājyu 'dzǎu-tade bù'chīng. /He did a lot of damage in our factory. Tā dzài wǒmende gūng-'chángli nùng'hwàile hěn dwō 'dūngsyi. /What kind of damage? Nùng'hwàile 'nǎr le? /How was the damage done? Dzěmma nùng'hwàide? /How much damage? Hwàidau dzěmma ge 'dìbu? /He cannot climb stairs, because of the damage done to his heart. Tāde 'syīn shòugwo 'shāng, swóyi bunéng pá lóu'tī. /There was permanent damage done to his right arm. Tāde 'yòu gēbei shòude 'shāng hǎubu'lyǎu le.

(Physical or otherwise) dzǎutade, 'swǔnshŕ. /How much damage was done? 'Swǔnshŕ 'dwōshau? *or* 'Swǔnshŕ 'dà budà? *or* 'Swǔnshŕ yǒu 'dwō jùng? *or* 'Dzǎu-tade 'lìhai bulìhai? /He has done enough damage around here. Tā bǎ jèr 'dzǎu-tade gòu °'chyáude le (°'shòude le). /He did a lot of damage to the name of our factory. Tā jyàu wǒmen gūng'chǎngde 'míngyu shòu hěn 'dàde 'swǔnshŕ. *or* Tā bǎ wǒmen gūng'chǎngde 'míngyu 'dzǎutade bù'chīng. /Serious damages were suffered on the east coast (newspaper style). 'Dūngàn 'swǔnshŕ °'chíjùng (°'hěn-jùng). /The damage is done. 'Yǐjing nùngcheng jè'yàngr le. *or* 'Shēngmǐ yǐjing 'jǔcheng shóu'fàn le.

Pay damages péi, 'péicháng 'swǔnshŕ, péichyán. /He'll have to pay damages to the owner of the car. Tā děi 'péicháng chē'jǔde 'swǔnshŕ. /You'll have to pay damages for this. Jèige nǐ děi °'péi (°péi'chyán). /I'll sue you for damages. Wǒ chyù 'gàu ni, jyàu ni 'péi.

DANCE. tyàu, tyàuwǔ; dance a certain kind of dance *or* dance so many dances tyàu. . .

453

'wǔ. / They used to dance on the stage. Tāmen yǐ'chyán dzài wǔ'táishang tyàu'wǔ. / I don't dance. Wǒ bú'hwèi tyàu'wǔ. / He only knows how to dance the fox trot. Tā 'jř hwèi tyàu húbù'wǔ. / Let's dance some more. 'Dzài tyàu 'hwěr ba. *or* 'Dzài tyàu hwěr 'wǔ ba. / They danced three dances. Tāmen tyàu'wǔ tyàule sān'tsz̀. *or* Tāmen tyàule 'sāntsz̀ 'wǔ.

(Jump about) tyàu, bèng, 'lwàntyàu. / The little girl was dancing with joy. Nèige syàu'hár °'lède jř 'tyàu (°'lède jř 'bèng, °gāu'syìngde jř 'tyàu, °gāu'syìngde jř 'bèng, °'lède yítyàuyí'bèngde, °'lède lwàn'tyàu).

A dance, dancing tyàuwǔ, wǔ; (formal) wǔdǎu; **dancing girl** wǔnyǔ; **dancing partners** wǔbàr; **sword dance** wǔdāu, wǔjyàn; **snake dance** wǔshé; **tea dance** cháwǔ. / The next number is a very slow dance. Syàyìtsz̀ tyàu'wǔ, yīnywe hen 'màn. / Any dance music among these records? Jèisyē 'pyāndzli yǒu tyàu'wǔ yīnywè ma? / The next dance is a long one. 'Syàyíge 'wǔ hěn 'chéng. / They're dancing partners. Tāmen shr wǔ'bàr. / The dancing teacher in this school is a foreigner. Jèige sywé-'syàu jyāu °wǔ'dǎu (°'tyàu'wǔ) de syānsheng shr ge 'wàigworén.

(A party for dancing) tyàuwǔhwèi. / There's a dance at the YWCA tonight. Jyēr 'wǎnshang 'Nyǔchīngnyán'hwèi kāi tyàuwǔ'hwèi.

DANGER. 'wēisyǎn (*or* 'wēisyān); **the danger** 'wēisyǎnde 'dìfang. *See also* **DANGER-OUS.** / The danger is this, that. . . . 'Wēisyǎnde 'dìfang dzài 'jèr, jyòushr. . . . / The only danger is that he might forget himself and talk with a native accent. °Jř yǒu 'yíyàng 'wēisyǎn (°Wéi'yīde 'wēisyǎn) jyòushr tā wú'yìjūng yěsyǔ 'shwōchu běn'dìrende 'kǒuyīn lai. / There wasn't any danger to speak of. 'Méiyou shémma lyàubudé de wēisyǎn. *or* 'Méiyou shémma 'wēisyǎn 'jřde yìtí de. / There are going to be plenty of dangers, but I won't mind. 'Wēisyǎn yí'dìng bù'shǎu 'kěshr 'wǒ bú'dzàihu. / Would he be able to face real danger unflinchingly? Dàule 'jēn 'wēisyǎn de shŕhou, tā néng bùdǎn'chywè ma? / That's the real danger. 'Nà tsái shr jēn-'jèng 'wēisyǎnde dìfang ne. / There lies the real danger. Jēn'jèngde 'wēisyǎn dzài 'nàr. / Danger lurks in every corner. 'Dàuchù dōu hwèi yǒu 'wēisyǎn.

In danger; out of danger. / He's in danger. Tā yǒu 'wēisyǎn. / The patient is still in danger. 'Bìngrén 'hái yǒu wēisyǎn. / The patient is out of danger now. 'Bìngrén méiyou 'wēisyǎn le. *or* 'Bìngrén 'chūle 'wēisyǎn le. / When we're out of danger, I'll let you know. Děng °'chūle wēisyǎn (°'méiyou wēisyǎn le) wǒ jyou 'gàusu nǐ. / He's in danger of losing his life. Tā yǒu 'syìngmìngde 'wēisyan. *or* Tā jèngdzài 'shēngsz̀gwān'tóu. / That company is in danger of being surrounded. 'Nèilyán yǒu bèi bāu'wéi de 'wēisyǎn. *or* 'Nèilyán hěn °'wēisyǎn (°'jīnjí), yěsyu hwèi ràng rén 'bāuwéi. / The country is in danger. 'Gwójyā jèng dzài wéi'jíde shŕhou. *or* Gwó'nàn dāng'chyán.

(Less serious). / We're in danger of being late. Kwài yàu 'wǎn le. *or* Yàu 'wǎn le. *or* Yěsyu hwèi 'wǎn le.

Special expressions in English. / He sensed the danger in the dark. Hēigūlung-'dūngde tā 'jywéje yǒu dyǎr 'bú'myàu. / Don't shirk dangers. Búyàu lín'nàn gǒu-'myan. / He's a danger to peace. Tā shř ge 'hwògēn. *or* Tā shř ge dǎu'lwànfèn-'dz.

DANGEROUS. (Perilous) 'wēisyǎn, syǎn, sywǎn. / That's a dangerous game. Wár 'nèige hěn °'wēisyan (°'syǎn, °'sywǎn). / It is dangerous to swim here. Dzài 'jèr 'fúshwěi yǒu dyǎr °'sywǎn (°'syǎn, °'wēisyǎn). / It's no more dangerous than what I went through last time. Bìng bùbǐ 'shàngtsz̀ 'wēisyǎn. / That's a dangerous undertaking. Dzwò 'nèiyàngde shř °yǒu dyǎr 'syǎn (°yǒu 'wēisyǎn, °syǎndehěn).

(Bad, serious) 'wēisyǎn, and other expressions. / Is her condition still danger-ous? °Tāde 'chíngsying (°Tā 'bìngde) 'háishr hěn °bùhǎu ma (°'wēisyǎn ma)? / That's a dangerous remark. Nèijyù hwà shwōle °yǒu 'hàichù (°bù'hǎu). *or* Shwō

454

nèiyàngde 'hwà hěn 'wéisyǎn. / That's a dangerous habit. Nèijǔng 'syígwàn yǒu 'hài.

(Of a person or animal). / He's a dangerous character. (unreliable) Nèige rén bùkě'kàu. (smooth but mean) Nèige rén hěn 'yīnsyǎn. (can stand watching) Nèige rén děi 'dǐfangje dyar. (bad) Tā shr̀ ge 'syàurén. (extremely dangerous) Tā shr̀ ge 'èrén. (desperate) Tā hwèi hài 'rénde. or Tā hwèi shā 'rénde. or Tā hěn 'syūng. (needs special watching) Děi tè'byé 'syǎusyinje ta. or Děi tè'bye 'dǐfangje ta. (violently desperate) Tā 'chyúngsyūng jí'è. (violently desperate and ruthless) Tā shr̀ 'shārénbùjǎn'yǎnde 'mwówáng. / That's an extremely dangerous criminal you're going to deal with. Nǐmen yàu 'bàn de shr̀ ge 'shārénbùjǎn'yǎnde 'syūngshou. / That's a dangerous wild animal. Nèige yěshòu °hěn 'syūng (fierce) (°hěn 'lìhai, or (can harm people) °néng shāng 'rén, °néng hài 'rén, or (can eat people) °néng chr̄ 'rén). / He's a dangerous person to associate with. Gēn tā 'láiwang °děi 'dǐfangje dyar (°hwèi yǒu 'wéisyǎn(de), °hěn 'syǎn, °hwèi chū'shèr(de), °hwèi re'hwò(de).

DARE. (Have the nerve to do something) gǎn. / Do you dare take the responsibility? Nǐ gǎn 'dān jèige 'dzérèn ma? / Do you dare go there alone? 'Nǐ 'gǎn 'yíge rén chyù 'nèr ma? / Don't you dare! 'Nǐ 'gǎn! / Don't you dare move! Nǐ gǎn 'dùng! / Don't you dare move it! Nǐ gǎn 'dùng! or 'Jèige nǐ gǎn 'dùng yidùng kàn! / Don't you dare take it. Nǐ gǎn 'ná! / Let me see if you dare take it! Nǐ gǎn 'nána géi wo 'chyáuchyau! / I didn't dare leave the baby. Wǒ méigǎn 'líkāi syǎu'hár. / How dare you! Nǐ hǎu 'dàde 'dǎndz! / How dare you say that to me! Nǐ hǎu 'dàde 'dǎndz, ('jyūrán) 'gǎn gēn wo tí 'nèige!

(Challenge) jyàng. / My friends dared me to go, so I went. Wǒde 'péngyoumen 'jyàng wo 'chyù. or Wǒde 'péngyoumen shwō wo bugǎn 'chyù; wǒ jyou 'chyùle. but in the present, jyàng is not used. / I dare you to go into that haunted house. Nèige nàu'gwěide 'fángdz, wǒ shwō nǐ bugǎn 'jìnchyu.

Take a dare chr̄jyàng. / He always takes a dare. Tā 'dzǔngshr chr̄'jyàng.

DARK. (Without light) hēi; (may not be totally dark) àn. Only hēi is used with tyān to refer to the darkness of the sky at night. / Wait until it gets dark. Děng tyān 'hēileje. or Děng tyān 'hēile dzài shwō. or Děng tyān 'hēi dyar dzài shwō. / It's too dark outside. Wàitou tài 'hēi. / It gets dark earlier and earlier. Tyān 'hēide 'ywè lái ywè 'dzǎu. / Dark clouds are looming ahead. 'Chyántou hēi yúntsai 'shànglaile. / This place is very dark. Jèige dìfang °hěn 'hēi (°hěn 'àn, °'hēigulung-'dūngde, °'chīhēi, °'chyùhēi, °'jēn hēi, °'hēijene, °hēi'jíle, °hēide'hěn). or expressed as . . . so dark that you can't see your hand in front of your face. . . . 'hēide shēn'shou bújyàn'jǎng. or as . . . so dark that you can't see anyone. . . . 'hēide 'kànbujyàn 'rén. / When you come into a very dark room suddenly, you can't see anything for a while. 'Hūrán 'jìnle °hěn 'ànde 'wūdz (°hěn 'hēide 'wūdz, °'chīhēide 'wūdz, °'chyùhēide 'wūdz), 'yǎnjing yǒu yìhwěr 'shémma dōu kànbu'jyàn.

(Of a color) shēn, jùng unless special terms for dark shades of a color are used. / His house is a dark brown. Tāde 'fángdz shr̀ °'shēnhwángshárde (°'dzūngsède). Other terms for dark brown, more commonly used, are copper color 'túngshár; bronze color gǔ'túngshár; tea color 'cháshár; pigliver color jū'gǎnshár. / This color is too dark. Jèige 'shar °tài 'shēn le (°tài 'jùng le). / I want a darker shade of this color. Wǒ yàu jèige 'shǎr, kěshr dzài °'jùng (°'shēn) yidyǎr.

Darkness is expressed with the various terms given above for **dark**. / At midnight the darkness was complete. 'Dàule bàn'yè jyou 'chywán hēi le. / The wires were cut and we were left in darkness. Dyàn'syàn 'jyàu rén gěi 'jyǎnle, jěng'gèr dōu 'hēi le. / The reasons for going were kept in darkness. Méishwō 'wèi shémma dàu nèr chyù. or Wèi 'shémma dàu nèr 'chyù, shéi yě méi'gàusu. or Chyù 'nèr de 'ywángù, 'méiyou fā'byǎu.

Darkroom hēiwūdz, ànshr̀.

In the dark (lit.). / That place is hard to find in the dark. Nèige 'dìfang °méi 'dēng (°'hēigulung'dūngde, °mwō(je) 'hēr, °chǐ'hēide, °chyù'hēide) hěn 'nán 'jǎu. *or* Nèige 'dìfang yèli °mwōje 'hēr (°'hēigulung'dūngde) hěn 'nán 'jǎu.

In the dark (fig.). / My friend has kept me in the dark about his movements. Wǒde 'péngyou 'yìjr̀ méi'gàusung wǒ tā shr 'dzěmma bànde. / I'm completely in the dark about it. Jèihwéi shr̀ 'shéi yě méi'gàusungwo wo. *or* Wǒ 'wánchywán °bùjr̀'dàu (°bù'syǎude) jèihwéi 'shr̀.

(Adverse). / Those were dark days for me. 'Nèi shŕhou wǒ hěn 'tsǎn. *or* 'Nèi shŕhou wǒ jèngdzai °dǎu'méi (°dzǒu bèi'dzèr, °'nànjūng).

DATE. (On the calendar) tyān; (month and day) <u>NU</u>-ywè <u>NU</u>-hàu; (day of the month) <u>NU</u>-hàu; (within the first ten days of the month) chū-<u>NU</u>; (within the second ten days of the month) shŕ-<u>NU</u>; (within the third ten days of the lunar month) èrshr̄-<u>NU</u>; (of an event) 'r̀dz; (formal) r'chī; **what date** (local Peiping) jyér <u>or expressed as</u> when dwōhwer *or* dwōdzen; (referring to a year) -nyán. / What's the date today? It's the tenth. Jīntyan 'jǐhàu? 'Shŕhàu. / What's the date today? It's the tenth of March. Jīntyan 'jǐywè 'jǐhàu? Jīntyan 'sānywè 'shŕhàu. / What's the date today? It's the third (lunar calendar). Jīntyan chū'jǐ? Jīntyan chū'sān. / What's the date today? It's the fourteenth. Jīntyan 'nǎyityān? *or* Jīntyan 'nèityān? *or* Jīntyan 'jyér le? *or* Jyér (shr̀) 'jyér? *or* Jīntyan shŕ'jǐ? Jīntyan shŕ'sz̀(hàu). / What is the date (of something)? (Shr̀) 'nǎyityān? *or* (Shr̀) 'nèityān? *or* (Shr̀) jyér? *or* (Shr̀) 'dwōhwer? *or* (Shr̀) 'dwōdzen? / Has the date been set? (especially of a wedding) Dìngle 'r̀dz le ma? *or* R'chī dìng le ma? / What is the date on that letter? Nèifēng 'syìnshang 'syède °r'chī (°'r̀dz) shr̀ 'nǎyityān? *or* Nèifēng 'syìn shr̀ 'nǎtyān syède? / The date of coronation has been advanced. Syíng jyāmyan'lǐ de r'chī tí'chyán le. / Under this line write the date of your arrival. Dzài jèityáu syàn 'dǐsya syě nǐ 'dàu jèr de r'chī. / The date on the letter is Jan. 12, 1964. Syìnshang 'syède r'chī shr̀ yījyǒu lyóusz̀ nyán 'yíywè shŕ'èr hàu (°r̀). / The date of their marriage has not been set. (Jyē'hwende'r̀dz hái méidìng'hàu. *or* 'Nátyan jyē'hwēn hái méidìng'hàu. / There are three dates to be remembered. Yǒu 'sānge 'r̀dz děi jìje. / What were the dates of your employment at the bank? Nǐ yì'chyán dzài yín'háng dzwò 'shr̀ shr̀ °tsúng 'nèityān 'chǐ dàu 'nèityān 'jr̀ ('tsúng 'shémma shŕhou 'chǐ dàu 'shémme shŕhou)? / What is the date of your birth? (including year) Nǐ shr̀ 'nǎyinyán 'jǐywè 'jǐr shēng-'rén? *or* (not necessarily including year) Nǐ shr̀ 'jǐshŕ shēng'rén? *or* (informal) <u>is expressed as</u> / When is your birthday? Nǐ 'shēngr̀ shr̀ °'dwōhwer (°'nèityān, °'jyér)? / What is the date (year) of Confucius' birth? 'Kǔngdz 'nǎnyán 'shēngde? / Do you know the dates of Confucius' birth and death? 'Kǔngdzde 'shēngdzú 'nyánywe nǐ jŕdau ma? / What is the date of the founding of the Chinese Republic? 'Jūnghwamín'gwó 'nǎinyán chéng'lìde?

(Fruit) dzǎur. / How much per pound are these dates? 'Dzǎur shr̀ 'dwōshau chyán yí'bàng?

(Appointment) 'ywēhwèi. / I have a date for noon today. Wǒ 'jīntyan 'shǎng-wu yǒu yíge'ywēhwèi.

(Appointment with a girl or fellow). / Who do you have a date with this evening? Nǐ jīntyan 'wǎnshang gēn shéi 'chūchyu? / I haven't had a date in a year. Wǒ yì'nyán méi'gēn rén 'chūchyu le.

At an early date (very soon in the future). / I'll do it for you at an early date. Gwò syē 'shŕhou wǒ géi ni 'bàn. / The game was temporarily postponed, but will be played at an early date. Bǐ'sài jànshŕ yán'chǐle, kěshr bù'jyǒu hwèi jyǔ'syíngde.

At an early date (very long ago). / This building has been here from an early date. Jèidzwò 'lóu shr̀ hěn 'jyǒu yǐ'chyán gàide.

Out-of-date, dated jyòu, 'lǎushŕde, 'jyòushŕde, gwòshŕde; 'chénfǔ (only of ideas, customs, etc.). / He drives an out-of-date car. Tā kāi yílyàng- °'jyòu ('jyòu-shŕde, °'lǎushŕde, °gwò'shŕde) chē. / Her clothes seem out-of-date. Tā 'chwān de 'yīfu hǎu'syàng shŕ °gwò'shŕ le (°'lǎushŕde; (with 'jyòu, meaning old and worn) °'jyòushŕde). / His books are dated now. Tāde 'shū gwò'shŕ le. / His style of danc-ing dates him. meaning it's old-fashioned. Tā tyàuwǔde °'yàngdz (°'dzshŕ) gwò'shŕ le. or meaning One can tell when he learned to dance. Kàn tā tyàuwǔ de 'yàngdz jyou jŕdau tā shémme shŕhou 'sywéde.

To date (until now) 'jŕ dàu syàn'dzài, 'jŕ dàu 'jīntyan. / We have not heard from him to date. Wǒmen 'jŕ dàu syàn'dzài yě méi'jyējau tāde 'syāusyi.

Up to date. / Let's make a new edition and bring it up to date. Jèibèn shū dzá-men 'dzai chū yì'bǎn, bǎ dzwèi'jìnde shèr jyājinchyu. / I'm not up to date on this subject. Jèijyàn 'shŕ de syīn 'fājàn wǒ hái bùjŕ'dàu. / This will bring you up to date. Děng wǒ gàusule ni 'jèige, nǐ jyou dōu 'jŕdau le. / His ideas are not up-to-date. Tā 'szsyàng °'chénfǔ (°hěn 'jyòu). / Try to get up-to-date information. Syàng-fár 'dédau dzwèi'jìnde 'syāusyi.

To date syě . . . ŕdz. / The letter was dated April 10. Syìnshang syěde 'ŕdz shŕ 'szywè 'shŕhàu. or Syìnshang syěje 'szywè 'shŕhàude 'ŕdz. or expressed as The letter was one written April 10. 'Syìn shŕ 'szywè 'shŕhàu 'syěde. / You forgot to date your letter. Nǐ 'syìnshang méisyě 'ŕdz.

(Go out with a boy or girl). / He's been dating her regularly. Tā 'cháng dài tā 'chūchyu.

Date from. / The Great Wall dates from the Ch'in Dynasty. Cháng'chéng 'Chíncháu jyou 'yǒu le. / This custom dates from the American pre-Revolutionary days. Jèjǔng 'fēngsu shŕ Měigwo Gé'mìng yǐ'chyán °chǐde (°yǒude.)

Be dated up méi gūngfu. / I'm all dated up this week. Wǒ jèige lǐ'bài méi 'gūngfu.

DAUGHTER. 'nyuér, 'nyǔháidz; (local Peiping) gūnyang; (polite) syáujye; (old polite term) 'chyānjīn. / He has one son and two daughters. Tā yǒu 'yíge 'érdz 'lyàngge 'nyuér. / This is my youngest daughter. Jèi shr wǒ dǐng 'syàu de 'nyǔháidz. / That's Mr. Li's eldest daughter. Nèi shr 'Lǐ syānsheng de 'dà gūnyang. / The lady has a beautiful daughter. Nèiwèi 'tàitai yǒu yíwèi 'hěn hǎu'kàn de 'syáujye. / How old is your daughter? Nín jèiwei 'chyānjīn jīnnyan 'jǐswèi le?

DAY. tyān; (in a few combinations only) ŕ; (a specific day) ŕdz; (formal) ŕchī; (as opposed to night) báityan, bái ŕ; day and night jòuyè; (a period of twenty-four hours) yíjòuyè; every third day gé 'lyàngtyān, jyē 'lyàngtyān; in a day or two yìlyàng'tyān °yì'nèi (°li); in a few days ji'tyān, jityānli, 'bùjityár; day before yesterday chyán-tyan, (local Peiping) chyár(ge); day after tomorrow hòutyan, (local Peiping) hòur(ge); some day or one of these days 'dzǔng yǒu nèmma yì'tyān, jyàng'lái dzǔng; the other day 'nèityān; one day yǒu yìtyān; for days on end jyélyán hàusyē'tyān; some other day 'gàityān, yǐhòu; the next day dì'èrtyān; on the day of maturity mǎn'chǐde nèi-'tyān, mǎn'chǐde ŕdz; D-day Dzwò'jàn Dìyí'ŕ; the Day of Judgment 'Shŕjyè Mwò'ŕ; days of grace kwānsyàn ŕ'chī. / The day is breaking. 'Tyān °'míng le (°kwài 'lyàng le). / He works days. Tā 'báityan dzwò'gūng. / He worked a whole day. Tā dzwòle yì'jěngtyānde 'gūng. / He worked on it day and night for two weeks. Tā jòu'yèbù-'tíngde gànle lyǎ lǐ'bài. / We spent three days in the country. Wǒmen dzài 'syāngsya jùle 'sāntyān. / A day has twenty-four hours. Yì'tyān yǒu èrshr'sz'syāushŕ. / One day he said to me, "From this day on I'm going to come every other day." 'Yǒu yìtyān tā gēn wo 'shwō, "Tsúng 'jīntyan 'chǐ wǒ 'gé yìtyān 'lái yitsz." / What day of the week is today? 'Jīntyan lǐbài'jǐ? / What day of the month is today? Jīntyan 'jǐhàu? / He's paid by the day. Tāde 'gūngchyán °àn 'tyān (°lwùn 'tyān) 'swàn. / He's paid every day. Tāde 'gūngchyán 'měityān yǐ'fā. /It's only a day('s journey) away now. Jr̆ yŏu 'yìtyānde 'lù le. /It's three years to the day today. Dàu 'jīntyan jěng 'sān-nyán. /One day she says yes, the next day she says no. 'Yìtyān tā shwŏ 'syíng, ('lǐng) yìtyān yòu shwŏ 'bùsyíng. /Has she named the day yet? Tā dìngle 'r̆dz le ma? /That's a day to be remembered. 'Nèityān wŏmen dĕi 'lǎu 'jìjie. or 'Nèi shr bùnéng 'wàng de °yì'tyān (°ge 'r̆dz). /I'll give you a day's grace. Géi ni kwān'syàn yì'tyān. /All employees work an eight-hour day. 'Swŏyŏude 'gùywán 'měityān gūng-dzwò 'bāsyǎushŕ. /My day begins at seven o'clock. meaning I start work at seven o'clock. Wŏ 'měityān 'chīdyan jūng kāi'shŕ dzwò 'shŕ. /This is the day of the celebration. 'Jīntyan shr̆ 'chīngjùde 'r̆dz.

(The day of some special occasion) jyé, sometimes r̆ not used for traditional Chinese occasions; **Father's Day** Fùchin'jyé; Mother's Day Mǔchin'jyé. /Christmas day is a holiday. Shèngdàn'jyé (nèi'tyān) fàng'jyà. /Today is Memorial Day. Jīn-tyan shr̆ 'chīngmíng'jyé. /Today is Lantern Day. 'Jyēr Dēng'jyéer. /The Mayor announced that today is Free China Day. Shr̆jǎng sywān'bù jīntyan shr̆ Dz̀yóu-Jūnggwó-r̆. but /I arrived on New Year's Day. Wŏ shr Dànyánchū'yī 'dàude. or Wŏ shr Syīn'nyán nèityan 'dàude.

(Era, epoch, period, time). /They're still using that to this day. Tāmen syàn-'dzài hái yùng 'jèige ne. /That custom is practiced to this day. 'Nèige 'fēngsu dàu syàn'dzài hái 'yòu ne. /That's the fashion of the day. Nèi shr rú'jīn dzwèi lyóu-'syíng de 'shr̀yàng. /Present-day customs differ greatly from those of the old days. Syàn'dzàide 'fēngsú syí'gwàn gēn yǐ'chyán 'dàbùsyāng'túng. /In America people don't realize such poverty exists in this day and age. Dzài 'Měigwo yì'bānrén syàng-budàu syàn'dzài hái hwèi yŏu rén 'jèmma 'chyúng. /The writers of those days had to pay for the printing of their own books. Nèi 'shŕhou de dzwòjyā syĕle 'shū dĕi dž'jǐ ná chyán chyū 'yìn. /He was a clever boy in his school days. Tā shàng'sywé de shŕhou hĕn 'tsūngming. /Ah, the good old days! Hái shr 'nèige °nyán'tóur (°shŕhour, °shŕhou 'hǎu)! /He's seen better days. Tā 'dāngnyán 'gwògwo 'hǎu r̆dz. /He's had his day. Tā 'yǐjing gwò'shŕ le. /The days of our oppression are num-bered. 'Dwèi wŏmende yā'pwò 'méiyou °jìtyān le (°dwōshau shŕhour le). /This is the day of air transportation. Rú'jīn shr̆ 'hángkūngyùn'shūde 'shŕdài. /Let's stop work and call it a day. Byé 'dzwò le, yòu swàn 'gwòle yi'tyān.

See also **DATE**.

DEAD. sžde, sž-; **be dead** sžle (not used in polite reference to a person's death). /Two dead horses lay there. Nèr 'dǎuje 'lyǎngpǐ sž'mǎ. /They suffered the loss of 5,000 men, including dead, wounded, and captured. Tāmen swǔnshrle 'wǔchyān rén 'bǎukwò 'sžde, 'shāngde, gēn 'fúlwóde. /He's dead all right, and no mistake. Méi-'tswòr, yí'dìng shr 'sžle. /Over my dead body! Chúfēi wŏ 'sžle! or Nǐ dĕi 'syān bǎ wŏ 'dǎsž! or 'Jywédwèi bù'syíng!

(Polite circumlocutions). /His father is dead. Tā 'fùchin °'yǐjing chyù'shr̆ le (°bú'dzài le, °'gùchyùle, °'gwòchyùle).

(Dull). /It's terribly dead around here in the summer. 'Syàtyande 'shŕhou jèr hĕn méi'yìsz. /The movie was pretty dead. Dyànyǐngr 'syāngdāng gān'dzàu (wú'wèi).

(Complete, completely). /I'm dead tired. Wŏ lèi'jíle. or Wŏ 'lèiszle. /The car stopped dead. Chi'chē jěng'gèer 'tíngjùle. /Are you dead certain you can do it? Nǐ 'jwŭn 'jrdàu nǐ néng 'dzwò ma? /She fell in a dead faint. Tā 'hwūngwochyule. /He's dead set against this plan. 'Jèige 'jìhwà tā °shr̆'jūng (°yíge'jyèrde) fǎn'dwèi. /Whatever we say to him, he's dead set against this plan. Jèige 'jìhwà wúlwùn 'dzěm-ma gēn ta shwō, tā háishr fǎn'dwèi. /Come to a dead stop! Jànju! /He came to a dead stop. Tā jěng'gèer 'jànjule. or Tā yìdyǎr yě bú'dùng le.

(Obsolete, outdated). /That insurance law is dead. Nèige bǎusyǎn'fǎ 'yǐjing °shr̆'syàu le (°wú'syàu le).

(Inoperative). / The battery is dead. Dyàn'chŕ méi dyàn le. / The furnace is dead. 'Lúdz 'myèle.

(Heavy and useless). / This trunk is so much dead weight. Jèige 'syāngdz yòu 'chén yòu méi'yùng.

Dead end street szhútùngr.

Shoot dead, strike dead, beat dead, etc. expressed with resultative compounds describing the type of action in the first element, and using sž as the second element. / They shot him dead with only one bullet. Tāmen 'yìchyāng bǎ ta dǎszle. / Hang him till he's dead. Bǎ ta dyàusz. *or* Bǎ ta 'jyáusz.

Dead (dead people) szde; **monument to our honored dead** jèn-wángjyànshŕ-bēi.

See also **DEATH, DIE.**

DEAF. lúng; (local Peiping) bèi, chén. / He's a little deaf. Tā ('ěrdwo) yǒu dyǎr °'lúng (°'bèi, °'chén). / He's stone deaf. Tā 'ěrdwo jěnggèer 'lúng le. *or* Tā 'lúngde shémme dōu tīngbu'jyàn. / He's deaf in the left ear. Tā 'dzwǒěrdwo yǒu dyǎr 'lúng. / He doesn't go to concerts because he's deaf. Tā 'ěrdwo lúng, 'swóyi bú'chyù tīng yīnywè'hwèi. / He became deaf lately. Tā 'jìnlai 'lúng le. / The poor child was born deaf and dumb. Nèige 'háidz jēn kě'lyán, 'shēngsyalai jyou yòu 'lúng yòu 'yǎ.

Deaf man lúngdz.

(Intentionally unhearing). / He is deaf to my requests for help. Wǒ chyóu ta bāng'máng, tā 'jwāng tīngbu'jyàn.

DEAL (DEALT). (Business) mǎimai, 'jyāuyì. / They said the deal was off. Tāmen shwō nèipyàur 'mǎimai °bùnéng chéng'jyāu le (°'hwángle). / He made a lot of money on that deal. °Nèitsz 'jyāuyì (°Nèipyàur 'mǎimai) tā 'jwànle bù'shǎu chyán. / Did you close that deal? °Nèitsz 'jyāuyì (°Nèipyàur 'mǎimai) 'chéngle ma?

(Agreement). / It's a deal! 'Syíng, °'jyòu nèmmaje ba (°jyòu nèmma 'bàn ba). *or* Dzámen °shwō'hǎule a (°kě shwō'hǎule), 'jyòu nèmmaje. / If they make a deal with each other we're lost. °Tāmen 'yàushr ('bìtsž) shwō'hǎule (dehwà) (°Tāmen 'yàushr ('bìtsž) 'lyánhéchilai), 'dzámen jyou °chwēi le (°swàn 'wán le). / I made a deal with him. Wǒ gēn tā °shwō'hǎule (°shwō'chéngle).

(Treatment). / You can expect a square deal from him. Tā yí'dìng bú'hwèi gēn ni 'shwǎ hwǎ'tóu. *or* Tā yí'dìng búhwèi tswò 'dài nǐ de. / The workmen say they got a raw deal. 'Gūngrén shwō 'tāmen °ài 'kēng le (°shòu 'pyàn le, °chŕ 'kwēi le).

(Amount). / A good deal remains to be done. Gāi dzwò de hái °hěn (°tǐng) 'dwō ne. / I haven't a great deal of money to spend. Wǒ méi dwōshǎu chyán kě 'hwā. / I smoke a good deal. Wǒ 'chōuyān 'chōude hěn °'lìhai (°'dwō).

To deal (inflict). / The regulation deals a severe blow to my plans. Jèijǔng 'gwēijyu gěi wǒde 'jìhwà yíge hěn 'dà de 'dǎjī. / That kind of rule dealt a severe blow to the morale here. 'Nèijǔng 'gwēijyu jyàu jèr 'gūngdzwòde 'jīngshen hěn 'shòu 'dǎjī.

(Of cards) fā. / Who dealt this hand? 'Jèitsž shŕ shwéi fāde 'pái? / Whose deal is it? Gāi 'shwéi fā pái le? / It's your deal. Gāi 'nǐ fā 'pái le. *but* / Deal me in (in cards or otherwise). Bǎ wǒ 'swànshang. *or* Swàn 'wǒ 'yíge. *or* Jèi-'pái wǒ yě 'lái.

Deal in (sell) mài. / That merchant deals in smuggled wine. Nèige dzwò-'mǎimaide mài sž'jyǒu.

Deal with (do business) dzwò mǎimai, yǒu 'jyāuyè. /We don't deal with him any more. Wǒmen búdzài gēn tā °yǒu 'jyāuyì le (°dzwò 'mǎimai le).

Deal with (treat) dài. /He dealt fairly with me. Tā dài wo °'syāngdāng 'gūng-ping (°hái 'gūngping, °hái bú'hwài).

Deal with (handle a person or situation) yìngfu, dwèifu. /That man is hard to deal with. Nèige rén hěn nán °'yìngfu (°'dwèifu). /He dealt with the situation superbly. 'Nèijyàn shèr tā 'yìngfude jēn 'hǎu. /To deal with that kind of person you need a little finesse. 'Dwèifu 'nèijǔng rén děi yùng dyǎr 'shǒudwàn. /That boy is hard to deal with. Nèige 'háidz 'jēn °nán dwèifu (°nán 'bàn, °nán gwǎn).

Deal with (have charge over) gwǎn. /This office deals with passports. 'Jèige 'jīgwǎn shr̀ gwǎn hù'jàu de.

DEAR. (Beloved). /My (oldest) sister is very dear to me. Wǒde 'dàjyě gēn wǒ 'dzwèi hǎu.

(Term of endearment). No special term is used in Chinese. The idea is expressed in the use of a personal name or a relationship term.

Oh dear kě 'lyǎubude, jēn dzǎu'gāu, jè shr dzěmma 'shwōde. /Oh dear, we're late again! °Kě 'lyǎubude (°etc.), (women) yòu 'wǎn le!

DEATH. Most expressions include sž **die**. /His father met a strange death. Tā 'fùchin 'sžde hěn 'líchí. /The death of the manager threw the whole company out of gear. Jīnglǐ yì 'sž, jēng'gèerde gūng'sž yǒu dyǎr jwā'syā. /His death was announced in the papers. 'Bàushang dēngje tā sž de 'syāusyi. /He was condemned to death by the military court. Jyūnshrfǎ'tíng pàn tā 'sžsyíng. /Even death is better than this. 'Sžle dōu bǐ 'jèmma 'hǎu. *or* Jyòushr 'sž yě bǐ 'jèmma hǎu.

In the following, sž is not used. /It's a matter of life and death. Jèige shèr 'gwānsyi rén'mìng. *or* Jèi shr̀ jyòu'mìngde 'shr̀. or expressed with sž Jèi shr̀ 'shēng sž gwān'tóu. /He isn't going to die a natural death. Tā hwèi bùdé shàn'jūng-de. /I'm sorry to hear of the death of your friend. Wǒ 'tīngshwō nǐde 'péngyou bú'dzài le; wǒ hěn nán'shòu. /He'll fight you to the death. Tā hwèi gēn nǐ pīn-'mìngde.

Death notice 'fùwén, bàusāng tyědz.

. . . **to death** (killed by some means) is expressed by resultative compounds in which the first element is a word showing the method of killing (shāu burn, dǎ hit, etc.), and the second element is sž. /He was burned to death. Tā 'shāuszle. /They whipped him to death. Tāmen ná 'byāndz bǎ tā 'dászle. /I'm bored to death. Wǒ nì'szle. *or* Wǒ 'nǐde yàu'mìng.

DEBT. (Financial obligation) jàng, jài, gāide °chyán (°jàng, °jài), chyànde °chyán (°jàng, °jài); lāde °jàng (°'jài) (local Peiping). /How are you going to pay debts? °Nǐde nèisyē 'jàng (or 'jài) (°Nǐ gāi de 'chyán, °Nǐ gāi de 'jàng, °Nǐ gāi de 'jài, °Nǐ chyàn de 'chyán, °Nǐ chyàn de 'jàng, °Nǐ chyàn de 'jài, °Nǐ lā de 'jàng, °Nǐ lā de 'jài) dzěmma 'hwán ne? /I'll try to pay these debts by the end of the month. Wǒ syǎng'fár dzài ywèdǐ yǐ'chyán °bǎ 'jàng (°bǎ nèijibǐ 'jàng, °bǎ nèisyē 'jàng) 'hwánle.

(Non-financial obligation) chíng. /I owe him a debt of gratitude. Wǒ 'jēnshr 'chyàn tā bùshǎu 'chíng. *See also* **OWE**.

National debt (general) gwójài; (internal) gūngjài; (payments owed to foreign countries) wàijài.

Be in debt chyàn jàng, chyàn jài, chyàn chyán; chyàn 'rén °jàng (°jài, °'chyán);

or use gāi <u>instead of</u> chyàn; *or* (local Peiping) lājàng, lājài. /Are you in debt now? Nǐ syàn'dzài °chyàn jàng (°etc.) ma?

DECEMBER. shr'èrywè; (lunar calendar) 'làywè.

DECIDE. (Make up one's mind) 'jywédìng, °'nádìng (°'dàdìng) 'júyì. /I've decided to go to the theater. Wǒ 'jywédìng (yàu) chyù 'tīng syì. /Wait until he's decided. Děng tā °'jywédìngle (°'nádìngle 'júyì, °'dàdìngle 'júyì) dzài 'shwō. /He can't decide which one to take with him. °Tā 'jywédìngbu'lyǎu (°Tā bùnéng 'jywédìng, °Tā 'ná-budìng 'júyì, °Tā 'dàbudìng 'júyì, °Tā yóuyí bù'jywé, °Tā yóuyí bú'dìng) dàu'dǐ shr̀ dài 'něige. /We're still undecided as to which road to follow. Dàu'dǐ shr̀ dzǒu 'něiyáu 'lù, wǒmen háishr °'jywédìngbù'lyǎu (°bùnéng 'jywédìng).

(Judge) pàn, dwàn, dìng, 'pàndwàn, 'pàndìng, 'dwàndìng; (only legal) pànjywé. /The referee decided in their favor. Tsáipàn'ywán °dìngde (°'pàndwànde, °etc.) shr̀ °tāmen 'yíngle (°tāmen 'dwèi le, °tāmende 'fèr). /The Supreme Court decided in his favor. Dzwèigāufǎ'ywàn °'dwànde (°etc.) shr̀ tā 'yíngle. *or* Dzwèigāufǎ'ywàn °'dwàndìngle (°etc.), shr̀ 'tā yíng. /The judge decided fourteen cases today. Fǎ'gwān °pànle (°'dwànle, °pàn'jywéle) shr̀'szge 'àndz.

(Solve) 'jyějywé. /It isn't easy to decide that question. Nèige 'wèntí bù'róng-yì 'jyějywé.

Decided, decidedly yídìng, 'dāngrán, méi 'wèntí, búyùng wèn. /His height gave him a decided advantage in the game. Tāde 'gèr nèmma 'gāu dǎ'chyóurde shr̀-hou °yí'dìng (°'dāngrán) jàn 'pyányi. /He's decidedly the better of the two. Tāmen 'lyǎ rénli °méi'wèntí (°etc.) shr̀ 'tā hǎu.

Deciding (most important) 'dzwèi jǔ'yàude, 'dzwèi 'yàujǐnde. /The expense was the deciding factor. 'Kāisyau tài 'dà shr̀ °'dzwèi jǔ'yàude 'ywángù (°dzwèi 'yàujǐnde 'ywángù).

DECISION. (Act of making up one's mind) <u>expressed by verbal forms.</u> (When any number of persons is involved) jywédìng; (when specifically more than one is involved) shwōhǎu, 'shānglyang'hǎu, shānglyangchu(lai). /We haven't come to a decision yet. Wǒmen hái 'méiyou jywé'dìng 'dzěmmayàng 'dzwò. *or* Wǒmen háiméishwō'hǎu ne. *or* Wǒmen hái méi'shānglyang'hǎu ne. *or* Wǒmen hái méi'shānglyangchū ge 'jyē-gwǒ lái ne. /We'll follow your decision. Nǐ 'dzěmma jywé'dìng, wǒmen jyou °jàuje (°dzěmma) 'bàn. *See also* **DECIDE.**

(Verdict) pànjywéde. /The decision of the court will be announced tomorrow. <u>is expressed as</u> How the court decided will be announced tomorrow. Fǎ'ywàn dzěm-ma pàn'jywéde 'míngtyan kéyi sywān'bù.

(Determination, persistence). /He showed great decision in carrying out the plan successfully. Tā jàuje nèige jìhwa 'bànde hěn 'hǎu, tsúng jèr kéyi 'kànchu tā °yǒu jywé'syīn (°yǒu 'gwǒdwàn, °néng 'jyānchŕ dàu'dǐ, °néng yǎuje yá 'gàn, °búshr 'yóuyíbù'jywéde rén).

DECK. (Of a ship) jyábǎn, chwánmyàn, chwánmyàr, tsāngmyàn, tsāngmyàr; below deck tsāng(li). /The deck is very slippery. Jyábǎn hěn 'hwá. /Let's go up on (the) deck. Dzámen dàu °jyá'bǎn(°etc.)shang chyù ba. /Let's go below deck. Dzámen dàu 'tsāngli chyù ba. *or* Dzámen syà 'tsāng ba.

(A particular deck) (dì) NUtséng('tsāng). /Our stateroom is on the third deck. Wǒmende 'fángjyān shr̀ dzài dì'sāntséng('tsāng).

(Cards) fù. /Do you have a deck of cards? Nǐ yǒu yí'fù pái méiyou?

On deck (ready). /We're usually on deck early in camp. Wǒmen lù'yíng de shr̀hou, lǎu shr̀ yìchīng'dzǎur jyou dōu jwǔnbèi'hǎule chyù 'gūngdzwò.

461

To **deck** (decorate) <u>expressed by a specific verb in Chinese</u>. / The building was decked with flags for the occasion. Wèi 'jèijyàn shr̀ 'lóushang gwà'mǎnle 'chídz. / She was decked out with cheap jewelry. Tā 'dàile yǐ'shēnde 'jyǎ 'shǒushr.

DECLARE. (Say, claim) 'rènwéi, shwō. / The newspapers are declaring that he's innocent. 'Bàujr̆de píng'lwùn °'rènwéi (°shwō) tā méi 'dzwèi.

(Legal verdict) sywāngàu. / The court declared him guilty. Fǎ'tíng sywān'gàu tā yǒu 'dzwèi.

(Announce) 'sywānbù. / The two countries have declared an armistice. Nèilyǎngge 'jyāujàn'gwó sywān'bù tíng'jànle. / The company has declared a dividend. Nèige gūng'sz̄ 'sywānbù yàu 'fēn húng'lǐ.

(At customs) bàugwān, bàu. / Must I declare these goods at the customs? Jèisyē 'hwò yídìng děi °bàu'gwān ma (°chyù hǎigwān 'bàu ma)? / You must declare everything in your possession at the customs. Yǒu 'shémma dōu děi 'bàu-(gwān). *or* Dzài 'hǎigwān nàr yǒu 'shémma dōu děi 'bàu.

Declare war sywānjàn. **declaration of war** sywānjànshū. / Russia (has) declared war on Germany. 'Egwo °dwèi (°syàng) Dégwo sywān'jàn le.

Declare <u>oneself</u> byǎushr̀, 'sywānbù. / He declared himself against that kind of law. Tā 'tséngjīng °byǎu'shr̀ (°'sywānbù) tā fǎn'dwèi nèijǔng 'fǎlyù.

DEED. (Action) shr̀. / The soldier was decorated for a brave deed. Nèige 'bīng dzwòle yíjyàn yǔnggǎnde 'shr̀, swóyi lǐng °jyǎng'jāng (°syūn'jāng).

(Of property) chì, chìjr̆; **official deed** húngchì; **privately drawn deed** báichì. / I received the deed from my lawyer. Jèijāng chì wǒ shr̀ tsúng wǒ 'lyùshr̄ nèr shǒudàu de.

(Behavior) 'syíngwéi. / They should be held responsible for their deed. Tāmen yí'chyède 'syíngwéi 'yīngdāng gwēi tāmen dz̀'jǐ fù'dzé.

Register a deed shwèichì; (local Peiping) shwùnchì. / He went to the magistrate's office to register a deed. Tā dàu syànjèng'fǔ chyù shwèi'chì chyule.

To deed (transfer) rànggei. / The land was deeded to its new owner. 'Nèikwai 'dì 'rànggei nèige syīn dì'jǔ le. *but* / The land was deeded to his son (by inheritance). Nèikwài dì °'lyóugei (°'yílyougei) tā 'érdz le.

DEEP. (Lit. and fig.; but see exceptions below) shēn; (mentally) 'shēn(kè). / That's a deep well. Nèi shr ge 'shēn jǐng. *or* Nèige 'jǐng hěn 'shēn. / That well is the deepest. 'Nèige 'jǐng 'dzwèi shēn. / This lake is very deep. Jèige 'hú shēn'jǐle. / The mine is half a mile deep. Jèige 'kwàng yǒu bànlǐ 'dì shēn. / Is the wound very deep? 'Shāngkǒu 'shēn bushēn? / They dug deeper and deeper into the mine. Tāmen dzài 'kwànglǐ wāde 'ywè lái ywè 'shēn. / They dug deeper and deeper into that subject. Nèige 'wèntí tāmen yánjyoude 'ywè lái ywè 'shēn. / Take a few deep breaths and you'll feel better. 'Shēnshēnde chwǎn jìkǒu 'chì nǐ yídìng 'jywéde hǎu-'dwòle. / Beyond them are deep forests. Tāmen 'chyánbyar shr̀ hěn 'shēnde shù-'líndz. / The hotel is deep in the mountains. Fàn'dyàn dzài shēn'shānli. / The sky was a deep blue. Tyān shr̀ shēnlán 'shǎrde. / He studied deep into the night. Tā nyàn 'shū nyàndau 'shēnjīngbàn'yè. / He has given the question deep study. Tā bǎ nèige 'wèntí 'yánjyoude hěn °'shēn(kè) (°'dz̀syǐ). / That subject is too deep for me. Nèige 'wèntí 'wèi wǒ tài 'shēn le. *but* (as noted above). / That doctrine is very deep. Nèige 'dàuli hěn 'àumyàu. / That family is always deep in debt. Nèi'jyār rén lǎushr̀ 'chyàn bùshǎu 'jàng. / He is a man of deep feelings. Tā shr̀ yíge 'gǎn-chíng hěn 'jùngde rén. / His voice is a lot deeper than it used to be. Tāde 'sāngmér bǐ yǐchyán °dǐ'dwōle (°'tsū'dwōle).

DEFEAT. bàijàng; or may be expressed by verbal forms bài, dàbài, dǎ bàijàng. / This defeat decided the whole war. Jèitsz bài'jàng 'yǐngsyàng chywán'jyú. *or* Jèiyi'bài jyou jěng'gèer kwǎle. / They suffered repeated defeats. Tāmen lyánje °'bàile háuji'tsz̀ (°dǎ'bàile háuji'tsz̀, °dǎle háuji'tsz̀ bài'jàng).

To defeat (in battle) bǎ . . . dǎ'bài; **be defeated** bàile, dǎbàile, dǎ bàijàng le. / We defeated the enemy. Wǒmen bǎ 'díren dǎ'bàile. / They were defeated three times (in a row). Tāmen 'jyēlyán (dǎ)bàile 'sāntsz̀. *or* Tāmen dǎle 'sāntsz̀ bài-'jàng. (without emphasis on the defeats being consecutive) Tāmen 'jyēlyán dǎle 'sānge bàijàng.

(In sports) bǎ . . . 'yíngle; **be defeated** shūle. / We defeated our opponents in the last game. Wǒmen 'shàngyítsz̀ bǎ 'dwèifāng 'yíngle. / They were defeated three times. Tāmen 'shūle 'sāntsz̀.

(Work against). / They're defeating their own purposes. Nà shr̀ 'dzsyāng 'máudwùn.

(Dispose of). / We defeated their plans at one stroke. Wǒmen 'yí'syàdz jyou bǎ tāmende °'jìhwà (°'yīnmóu) 'pwòhwàile.

DEFEND. (Against physical attack) 'fángshǒu, shǒu, 'bǎuwèi. / That position is well defended. Nèige 'jèndì °'fángshǒude hěn 'hǎu (°'shǒude hěn 'hǎu, °'bǎuwèide hén 'hǎu). / They decided not to defend the city. Tāmen 'jywédìng °'bùshǒu (°'bùbǎuwèi, °'bùfángshǒu, °'fángchì) nèige 'chéng. / That boxer has a strong attack but he can't defend himself well. Nèige dǎ'chywánde hwèi 'gūng, búhwèi 'shǒu. *See also* **PRO-TECT**, take care of under **CARE**.

(Against verbal attack) °tì (°gěi) . . . 'byànhù; 'tì (°gěi) . . . dǎ 'gwānsz (used only when speaking about court defense); fángbèi (prevent). / He should get a lawyer to defend him. Tā yìng'dāng chǐng yíge 'lyùshr̄ lai 'tì tā °'dǎ 'gwānsz (°'byànhù). / He issued the report to defend his reputation. (against attacks already made) Tā fāchu nèige 'bàugàu lai, wèide shr̀ gěi tā dz̀'jǐde 'míngyù lái 'byànhù. (against possible attacks) Tā fāchu nèige 'bàugàu lai, wèide shr̀ 'fángbèi yǒurén 'gūngjǐ tāde 'míngyù. / She always defends him. Tā lǎu tǐ tā 'byànhù. *or* Tā lǎu 'hùje tā shwō 'hwà. / He said it in that way to defend himself. (against past accusations) Tā 'nèmma shwō shr̀ wèi dz̀'jǐ 'byànhù. (against possible attacks) Tā 'nèmma shwō shr̀ °'fángbèi yǒu rén 'shwō tā (°'dīfángje yǒu rén 'shwō tā, °gěi dz̀'jǐ lyóu 'dìbu, °yàu 'dǔju 'byérénde 'dzwěi).

DEFENSE. (National) gwófáng. / He has a job in a defense plant. Tā dzài yíge 'gwó-fáng 'gūngyè gūng'chǎng dzwò 'shr̀. / The defenses of the country have stood the test. 'Gwófáng 'gūngdzwò bànde 'hǎu, yǐjīng jèng'shŕle.

(Physical protection). *See also* **DEFEND**, **PROTECT**, take care of under **CARE**. / We lost the game because of our poor defense is expressed verbally as We lost the game because we defended poorly. Wǒmen 'shūle, 'yīnwèi 'shǒude 'bùhǎu.

(Legal). / The defense rested its case. 'Bèigàu fāngmyàn 'tíngjr̄ 'byànhù, 'jìnghòu sywān'pàn. / The lawyer summarized the defense for the accused in only three minutes. 'Lyùshr̄ wèi 'bèigàu 'byànhù jr̄ 'shwōle 'sānfēn jūng, jyou 'wánle.

Self-defense. / He said it in self-defense. / Tā shr̀ dz̀'wèi tsái 'nèmma 'shwōde. / What can you say in your defense? Nǐ yǒu 'shémma °kě'shwōde (°'hwà shwō)?

DEFINITE. yídìngde, dìng, jwǔn; **definitely** yídìng, dìng, jwǔn. / Can you name a

definite date? Nǐ néng 'shwōchulai yíge yí'dìngde 'r̀dz ma? / Nothing is definite.
'Shémma dōu méi'dìng ne. / He was definite in his refusal. Tā shwō tā yí'dìng
°bú'gàn (°'jyùjywé). / That's definitely not mine. Nèi °yí'dìng (°'jwūn) búshr̀ 'wǒde.
/ He says definitely that it's yours. °Tā yí'dìng (°Tā yi'kǒu yàu'dìngle) shwō shr̀
'nǐde. / He says that it's definitely yours. Tā shwō nèi °yí'dìng shr̀ 'nǐde (°méi-
you 'wèntí shr̀ 'nǐde). / When can you give me a definite answer? Nǐ 'shémma shŕhou néng gěi wǒ ge °'jwūnhwàr (°yí'dìngde 'hwéihwà)? / Is that a definite answer?
Dzámen 'yìyánwéi'dìng le ma? / Now this is a definite agreement, and no backing
out! Dzámen 'yìyánwéi'dìng, 'bùnéng fān'hwéi! / I can't say definitely. Wǒ hái
bùnéng shwō°'jwūnle (°'dìngle). / The plans for the trip aren't definite. Lyǔ'syíng
'jìhwà hái méi°'dìng (°dìng'jwūn, °dìng'hǎu).

(Precise). / This sentence doesn't have a definite meaning. Jèijyu hwàde
'yìsz °'hánhanhū'hūde (°dzài lyǎngkějr̀'jyān). / He never answers definitely. Tā
'hwéidá de 'hwà lǎushr̀ °dzài lyǎngkějr̀'jyān (°'hánhanhū'hūde). or Tā lǎu bùkěn
'tùngtungkwāi'kwārde °shwō ge 'jwūnhwàr (°'dāying).

DEGREE. (Unit of measurement) dù. / A centigrade thermometer is a thermometer
which divides the range from the freezing point of water to its boiling point into 100
degrees. Bǎidù'byǎu shr̀ yìjǔng hánshǔ'byǎu, tsúng shwěide 'jyēbīngdyǎn dàu 'fèidyǎn 'fēncheng yìbǎi'dù. / At night the temperature sometimes drops forty degrees.
Yǒu'shŕhou 'yèli yí'jyàng jyàng 'szshrdù. or . . . drops to forty degrees below zero.
. . . yí'jyàng jyàngdau líng(dùyi)syà 'szshrdù. / The pilot recorded the degrees of
latitude and longitude. Nèige jyàshr̀'ywán bǎ 'jīngwěidù 'jìsyalaile. / The lines form
an angle of 45 degrees. Lyàngtyáu 'syàn 'chéng yíge szshrwǔdùde 'jyǎu. / 20° 35'
59" N., 118° 10' 0" E. Běi'wěi èrshrdù, 'sānshrwǔ'fēn, 'wǔshrjyǒu'myǎu; dūng-
'jīng 'yìbǎi'shrbā'dù, shr̀'fēn, líng'myǎu.

(Extent). / What degree of progress have you made in English? Nǐ 'Yīngwén
'yǐjing jìnbùdau shémma 'chéngdù le? / That book is useful only to a small degree.
Nèiběr 'shūde 'yùngchu bú'dà. or Nèiběr 'shū yǒu dyǎr 'yùng, kěshr bú'dà. / I
don't know to what degree you are interested in this. Wǒ bujr̄'dàu ni dwèi 'jèige you
'dwō dà 'syìngchyu. / The workmen have reached a high degree of efficiency. 'Gūng-
rénde 'syàulyù yǐ'jīng hěn 'gāu le. / You'll have to use your own judgment to a certain degree. °Yí bùfen (°Yǒude 'shr̀, °Yǒude 'shŕhou) ni děi dž'jǐ 'jywédìng.

(Academic) 'sywéwèi; B.S. (degree) lǐ'sywéshr̀ ('sywéwèi); LL.B. (degree)
fǎ'sywéshr̀ ('sywéwèi). / What degrees have you received? Nǐ dé de dōu shr̀ 'shémma 'sywéwèi? / He holds a B.A. (degree). Tā yǒu 'yíge wén'sywéshr̀ ('sywéwèi).

The third degree yùngsyíng; (if condemning it) yùng 'fēisyíng. / He wouldn't
confess until after they gave him the third degree. Méiyou yùng'syíng yǐchyán tā
°bùkěn chéng'rèn (°bùkěn 'jāu). / It's illegal to use the third degree to get a confession. Yùng 'fēisyíng jyàu rén rèn'dzwèi shr̀ fēi'fǎde.

First degree murder 'yùmóu 'shārén. / He's accused of first degree murder.
Tāde 'dzwèimíng shr̀ 'yùmóu 'shārén.

By degrees. See also **GRADUALLY.** / He's getting well by degrees. Tā jyàn-
'jyànde 'hǎu le.

DELAY. 'dāngé; 'dānwù (usually refers to a more serious or irreparable delay); be
delayed is expressed as be late wǎn, bùdzǎu. / He delayed me. 'Tā jyàu wo 'wǎnde.
or Wǒ wǎn le, shr jyàu 'tā (gěi) 'dāngéde. / She blames her parents for delaying
her marriage. Tā 'mánywàn tā dyē'ma °bǎ tāde 'jūngshēndà'shr̀ gei 'dānwùle (°bú-
jyàu ta 'dzǎu jyē'hwūn). / She blames her parents for delaying her marriage two
weeks. Tā 'mánywàn tā dyē'ma bǎ tāde 'hwūnchī 'dāngéle lyǎngge lǐ'bài. / Don't
delay the child's education. Byé 'dānwùle háidz shàng'sywé. or Byé jyàu háidz
shàng'sywé shàng'wǎnle. / The air raid delayed the train two hours. Hwǒ'chē jyàu

'kūngsyí °'dāngéle (°'dānwùle) lyǎngge jūng'tóu. *or* Hwǒchē 'yīnwèi 'kūngsyí 'wǎn-le lyǎngge jūng'tóu.

(Postpone) 'jǎnchǐ. /We'll delay the trip a week. Wǒmen 'jywédìng bǎ 'lyǔ-syíng 'jǎnchǐ yíge lǐ'bài.

Don't **delay** is expressed as hurry up 'gǎnjǐn, 'kwài yidyǎr. /Don't delay sending the letter. °'Gǎnjǐn (°'Kwài yidyǎr) bǎ 'syìn 'sùngchyu.

Delay (detention) is expressed verbally with 'dāngé to **delay**. /The delay caused us to miss the train. Nèmma yì'dāngé jyàu wǒmen bǎ chē 'wùle.

DELICIOUS. hěn hǎuchǐ. /This candy is delicious. Jèige 'táng hěn hǎu'chǐ. /They served us a delicious supper. Tāmen 'gěile wǒmen yídwùn hěn hǎu'chǐde 'wǎnfàn.

DELIGHT. (Please) gāusyìng. /The play delighted everyone. Nèige 'syì jyàu dàjya-'hwǒr tǐng gāu'syìng.

Delight in 'syǐhwān, ài. /He delights in teasing her. Tā 'syǐhwān 'dòu tā. *or* Tā (hěn) ài 'dòu tā.

Be delighted. /I'd be delighted! Hǎu'jíle. /I'll be delighted to have you come. Nǐ néng 'lái, hǎu'jíle. /I'll be delighted to oblige you. Kéyi gěi nín 'bàn. *or* (more politely) Yǒu 'jǐhwèi gěi 'nín syàu'láu, jēnshr 'chyóujǐ bù'dé. /I'll be de-lighted to help you out. Jèige shr wǒ 'kéyi 'dāying. /I was delighted with the trip. Jèitsž 'chūchyu 'wárde hěn 'hǎu.

Delight (something giving pleasure) gāusyìngde 'shr, ài dzwò de 'shr. /Buy-ing clothes is her greatest delight. Mǎi 'yīfu shr tā °'dzwèi gāu'syìngde 'shr (°'dzwèi ài dzwò de 'shr).

DELIVER. (Send, bring) sùng. /The mailman delivers the mail at nine o'clock. Sùng-'syìnde 'dzǎuchen 'jyǒudyǎn lái sùng 'syìn. /Do you deliver? 'Nǐmén gwǎn 'sùng ma? /Please deliver these packages to my hotel. Bǎ jèisyē 'bāugwo 'sùngdau wǒde lyǔ'gwǎn. /It'll be delivered Monday. Syīngchī'yī sùng'dàu.

(Produce orally). /The professor delivered a course of ten lectures. Jyàu-'shòu 'lyánje °gěile (°jyángle) shŕge 'yǎnjyǎng. /The jury delivered its verdict. Péishěn'ywán 'yǐjīng bǎ tāmen shěnchá de jyé'gwǒ 'sywānbùle.

Deliver a child. /The doctor was called on to deliver two babies last night. 'Dàifu dzwór 'wǎnshang 'chǐng chuchyu 'lyǎngtsž gěi ren °shòu'shēng (°jyē'shēng).

Deliver the goods. /He promised to do it for us, but he couldn't deliver the goods. Tā 'dāyìng tì wǒmen 'bàn, kěshr méigěi bàn'dàu.

DEMAND. (If a person demands) yí'dìng yàu, 'fēi yàu... bù'syíng (*or* jyàu may be substituted for yàu if the demand is made upon another person); shwō děi.... /When she was sick she demanded that we visit her every day. Tā 'bìng de shŕhou, °yídìng yàu (*or* jyàu) wǒmen 'tyāntyar chyù 'kàn ta (°'fēi jyàu wǒmen 'tyāntyar chyù 'kàn ta bù'syíng, °shwō wǒmen děi 'tyāntyar chyù 'kàn ta). /He demands immediate payment. Tā shwō 'chyán lì'kè děi 'hwán tā. *or* Tā shwō děi lì'kè hwán tā 'chyán. *or* Tā yí'dìng yàu lì'kè hwán ta 'chyán. *or* Tā 'fēi yàu lì'kè hwán ta 'chyán bùsyíng.

(If a country demands) 'yāuchyóu. /Germany demanded that France supply men for labor in Germany. Dégwo 'yāuchyóu Fàgwo 'pài rén dàu 'Dégwo chyu dzwò-'gūng. /Germany demanded several billion francs from France as indemnity. Dégwo gēn 'Fàgwo 'yāuchyóu jishŕ'wànwàn fàlángde péi'kwǎn.

(If a situation demands). /This matter demands your immediate attention. 'Jèijyàn shr nǐ (°yí'dìng) děi lì'kè 'bàn (°'fēiděi lì'kè bàn (bù'syíng)).

A demand has no set expression in Chinese. /His constant demands get on our nerves. Tā jěngtyān 'máfan rén 'jēn yǒu dyǎr jyàu 'rén tǎu'yàn ta. /They make many demands on our time. Tāmen 'jànle wǒmen 'bùshǎu 'shŕhou. /The library isn't big enough to supply the demand for books. Túshū'gwǎnde shū búgòu °'yùng (°'gùngyìng).

Be in demand. /This is in demand now. Syàn'dzài 'yàu 'jèige de hěn 'dwō. /He was in great demand as a speaker. 'Chǐng tā yǎn'jyǎng de hěn 'dwō.

DENTIST. 'yáyī, 'yákēyīsheng, 'yákēdàifu. /Is there a good dentist around here? Jèr yǒu 'hěn hǎude °'yáyī (°etc.) 'méiyou?

DENY. fǒurèn, bùchéngrèn. /He denies he was ever a member of that party. Tā °fǒu-'rèn (°bucheng'rèn) tā 'jyārùgwo nèige 'dǎng. /The prisoner denies all the charges. 'Fànrén bùchéng'rèn yǒu'dzwèi.

(Technically, in law). /The judge asks the prisoner, "Are you going to deny these charges?" 'Fǎgwān wèn 'fànrén shwō, "Nǐ hái bù'jàu ma?"

Other English expressions. /I couldn't deny him such a small favor. 'Jèmma dyǎr 'syǎu shèr wǒ 'bùhǎu'yìsz bù'dāying tā. /She never denied herself anything. Tā dz'jǐ °'yàu (°'syǎng) dzěmmaje, jyou 'fēi dzěmmaje bù'kě. or Tā dz'jǐ syǎng 'mǎi shémma, jyou 'fēi mǎi bù'kě.

DEPARTMENT. (General) bùfen, 'bùmén, -bù, -chù. /What department does he work in? Tā dzài °'nèibùfen (°'nèige bùmén) dzwò 'shŕ? /He works in the accounting department. Tā dzài °'kwàijichù (°'kwàijibù) dzwò 'shŕ.

(Of the government) -ywàn, -bù, -tǐng, -chù, -sz̄, -kē, -dzǔ, -jyú, etc.; State Department Gwówùywàn, Wàijyāubù; Defense Department Gwófángbù; Department of Finance (federal) Tsáijèngbù, (provincial) Tsáijèngtǐng; Police Department (provincial) Jǐngwùchù, (municipal) Jǐngchájyú; Fire Department Syāufángjyū, Syāufángdwèi.

(Of a university) -syì; Department of Psychology Syīnlǐsywésyì.

(Of a store) -bù; children's clothing department túngjwāngbù; stationery department wénjyùbù; department store bǎihwǒgūngsz̄. /I'm going to a department store to do some shopping. Wǒ dàu yige bǎihwǒgūng'sz̄ chyu mǎi 'dūngsyi.

DEPEND. Depend on (trust to something) kàu. /We have to depend on the radio for our news. Wǒmen 'yàusyǎng 'dédau syīn'wén jř néng 'kàuje wúsyàn'dyàn.

Depend on (be determined by) děi kàn, děi chyáu. /My plans depend on the weather. Wǒde 'jìhwà děi °'kàn (°'chyáu) 'tyānchi dzěmma'yàng. /Our trip depends on whether we can get a passport. Wǒmen 'chyù bu'chyù děi 'kàn hù'jàu 'nádedàu nábu'dàu. /That depends on what she says. Děi °'kàn (°'chyáu) tā 'dzěmma shwō. /It depends on him. Děi °kàn (°chyáu) 'tā dzěmma'yàng. /That depends. Kàn chíngsying. or Děi 'kàn yikan (dzài 'shwō). or Děi 'chyáu yichyáu (dzài 'shwō).

Depend on (rely on a person to do something) jřje, jřwang, jřwangje. /Don't depend on me alone. Byé jìng °jřwangje (°etc.) 'wǒ. /You can't depend on just a child to do all the housework for you. 'Jyālide 'shèr byé gwāng °'jřwangje (°etc.) yige syǎu'háidz 'dōu gěi nǐ 'dzwòle. /He thinks he'll depend on that son-in-law of his to help him. Tā syǎng °'jřwangje (°'kàuje) tā nèige 'nyǔsyù lai 'bāng tā.

Depend on (consider someone reliable) is expressed either by saying someone is dependable, using resultative compounds with kàu, or by saying that someone is certain about a person. /You can't depend on him. or He can't be depended on. Tā kàubu'jù. or Tā bùkě'kàu. /Can I depend on his keeping his promise? Tā dāying de 'hwà °kàude'jù ma (°kě'kàu ma)? /You can depend on him to see the thing

through. °Tā 'jwǔn (°Tā yí'dìng) hwèi bǎ jèijyàn 'shèr bàndàu'dǐde. *or* Tā 'jywé
buhwèi méibàn'wán jyou bù'gwǎnde. / You can depend on him to spill the beans.
Jwǔn méi'tswòr, yǐ yǒu 'shèr tā yí'dìng dou gěi 'shwōchuchyu.

DEPTH. (Physical) shēn; (mental) 'shēn(ke). / The well is fifty feet in depth. Jǐng yǒu
'wǔshŕchř 'shēn. / Measure the depth with this stick. Yùng jèiger 'gwèr 'lyáng
yilyàng yǒu dwō 'shēn. / He has great depth of mind. Tāde 'sz̄syǎng hěn 'shēn(kè).
/ That music shows great depth of feeling. Nèige 'yīnywè °byǎushrde 'gǎnching hen
'shēn(kè). or meaning It moves people very much. °hěn dùng 'rén.

(Interior space, as of a hall, stage, etc.) jìnshen. / Because of its depth the
stage can accommodate a large cast. Syì'táide 'jìnshen hěn 'shēn, kéyi 'rúngsya
hěn 'dwōde yǎn'ywán.

Out of (or Beyond) **one's depth.** / I feel out of my depth when I talk to him. Hé
'tā tán hwà, wǒ jyǎn'jŕ 'jywéde wǒ yí'chyàurbù'tūng. / I don't go beyond my depth.
(lit., in swimming) Wǒ yí'dìng búfùdau 'tài shēnde dìfang chyu. (fig., of physical,
mental or other difficulties) Wǒ búdzwò chāugwo wǒ nénglì fànwei yíwàide shř.

DESCRIBE. (By telling about) 'shwō yishwō, shwōchulai, shwōgei. . . 'tīngting; (by
writing or telling about) myáusyě; (by picturing in words) 'syíngrúngchulai. / Describe the kind of work you have been doing. Nǐ dōu dzwògwo shémma 'shř °shwō
yishwō wǒ 'tīngting (°shwōgei wǒ 'tīngting). / Can you describe his appearance?
Tā 'jǎngde shémma 'yàngr nǐ néng 'shwōchulai ma? / Describe his appearance.
Bǎ tā 'jǎngde shémma 'yàngr géi wo °'shwō yishwō (°'myáusyě'myáusyě). / I
can't describe it. Nèige wǒ 'syíngrúngbuchū'lai. / I can't describe it; it's too hor-
rible. 'Tài kě'pà le; wǒ jyǎn'jŕ 'syíngrúngbuchū'lái. / You can feel it but you can't
describe it. Syīnli 'jywédechū'lái, kěshr 'syíngrúngbuchu'lái. / He described her
perfectly. Tā bǎ tā 'syíngrúngde jēn'syàng.

DESERT. (Waste region) shāmwò, shāmwòdì. / The desert begings a few miles beyond
the town. °Chéng 'nèibyar (°Lǐ 'chéng) (méi) jilǐ 'dì jyòu shr shā'mwò. / We will
soon have to cross a desert region. Wǒmen bù'jyou jyòu děi 'gwò shāmwò'dì le.

DESERT. (Leave, run away) líkai, pǎu, dzǒu; táu (escape). / The woman deserted
her husband. Nèige 'nyǔren líkai tāde 'jàngfu le. or (local Peiping) Nèige 'nyǔren
ba ta 'jàngfu 'shwàile. or Nèige 'nyǔren tsúng jyāle °'pǎule (°'dzǒule). / The
crew deserted the ship. Nèige hǎiywán tsúng 'chwánshang 'táule. / That member
deserted the party. Nèige dǎng'ywán gēn dǎng twō'líle. / That soldier deserted.
Nèige bīng °'táule (°'pǎule).

Be deserted (of a place) méi rén le, rén dou dzǒule, kūngle. / The town
was completely deserted when we got there. Wǒmen 'dàu nèr de shŕhou, nèige
dìfang °rén dou 'dzǒule (°méi 'rén le). / At midnight the streets have a deserted
look. Dàule bàn'yè jyēshang °méi 'rén le (°kànje hěn 'syāutyáu, °hěn 'lěngjìng).

Deserter (military) táubīng. / A deserter is shot if caught. Táu'bīng jwōjule,
jyòu chyāng'bì.

DESERVE. yīngdāng dé, gāi dé; also other expressions shown below. / Such a steady
worker deserves better pay. Syàng 'tā nèmma 'chínjinde rén °'yīngdāng (°gāi) dé
'gāu yidyǎrde 'syīnshwei. / You deserve it! (something bad) 'Gāi! or Hwó'gāi!
(something good) 'Yīngdāng rú'tsz̄. or Jèmmaje 'dwèile. / He deserves it. (something bad) Tā 'gāi nèmmaje. (something good) 'Nèmmaje tsái jyàu 'gūngping.
/ He doesn't deserve it. Nà 'shŕdzai bù°'gūngping (°'dwèi). / It's my mistake; I
deserve it. Shŕ wǒde 'tswòr; méide 'ywàn. / I don't deserve it. (bad treatment)
Wǒ 'ywàndeheng. or 'Ywānwang wǒ le. (overly good treatment) Wǒ ('shŕdzai) bú-
'pèi. or Wǒ ('shŕdzai) bùgǎn'dāng.

DESIGN. (Pattern) 'hwāyàng. / The tablecloth has a simple design in the center. Jwŏ-'bùde dāng'jūng yŏu yìdyàr 'hwāyàng.

(Purpose). / What's your design in going that way? Nǐ wàng 'nèmma dzŏu °shr̀ (°yŏu) shémma °'yìsz (°'mùdì)?

Paint designs hwà túanhwàr. / She's an expert in painting designs. Tā shr̀ hwà túan'hwàr de jwan'jyā.

To design (make a plan) shèjì. / He is good at designing (making general plans). Tā shè'jìde hèn 'hǎu. *or* Tā hěn 'hwèi shè'jì. / He is working on the design for (*or* He is designing) a new machine. Tā jèngdzai shè'jì, syǎng dzàu yíge syǐnde 'jǐchi. / The architect is designing an addition to the building. Jyànju'shr̄ jèngdzai shè'jì, syǎng bǎ 'lóu jyēchuchyu yǐdwàn.

(Make a drawing) hwà 'tú(àn), °hwà (°jr̀) shèjì'tú, *or* (if a blue print) hwà yì-jāng lán'tú. / Draw a design (for this). Hwà yijāng °tú(àn) (°etc.). / He's drawing the design for the new machine. Tā syǎng dzàu yige syǐnde 'jǐchi, jèngdzai hwà tú(àn).

(To pattern). / She designs her own clothes. Tā 'yīfude 'yàngdz shr̀ dz̀'jǐ °'syǎngchūlaide (°'shè'jìde).

DESIRE. syǎng yàu, 'syīwàng. / What do you desire most of all? Nǐ 'dzwèi °syǎng 'yàu (°'syīwàng) de shr̀ 'shémma?

A desire (for something in particular) yìsz; (for luxuries, etc.) 'yùwàng. / He's expressed a desire to meet you. Tā yŏu °syǎng 'jyàn nǐ de 'yìsz (°'yìsz 'jyàn ni). / My desires are easily satisfied. Wŏde 'yùwàng hěn 'rúngyì 'mǎndzú.

See also **WANT, LIKE.**

DESK. (For writing or studying) shūjwōr; (in an office) bàngūngjwōr; (counter as in a hotel) gwèitái. / Hand your application to the secretary at that desk. Bǎ nǐde 'chǐng-chyóushū 'jyāugei dzài °gwèi'tái nèr de gwǎn'shr̀de *or* (depending on the kind of desk) °bàngūng'jwōr nèrde bàn 'shr̀ de rén). / Leave your key at the desk. Bǎ 'yàushr 'jyāugei gwèi'tái nèr.

(For a section, or department, even if located at one desk) -bù, -chù; **information desk** wènshr̀chù. / Ask at the information desk over there. Dàu 'wènshr̀'chù chyu 'dǎtīng.

City desk (newspaper) 'běndì syǐn'wén (byānjì)'bù.

DESTROY. (General) hwěi; but often expressed with resultative compounds, the first element describing the manner of destruction, such as shāu (by fire), chūng (by washing away), hūng *or* jà (by explosion), etc., and the second element using such words as hwěi destroy, wán finish, gwāng stripped, hwài ruined, tā caved in, etc. / This delay will destroy our chances of success. Jèiyì'dānwù bǎ wŏmen 'chéng-gūngde jīhwèi dōu 'hwěile. / The town was entirely destroyed. Chywán'chéng dōu gei hwěile. / The dam was destroyed by floods. Dàshwěi bǎ 'dī gei chūng'hwěile. / That house was destroyed by fire. Nèiswŏ fángdz jyàu hwŏ °shāu'wánle (°shāu-'tāle, °shāuhwěile, °etc.). / That building was destroyed by gunfire. Nèige lóu bèi pàu °hūng'hwěile (°jà'hwàile).

(Military) hwěimyè. / First destroy their tanks. Syān hwěi'myèle tāmende 'jǎnchē.

Destroy evidence hwěi, 'syāumyè. / He destroyed all the evidence. Tā bǎ 'jèngjyù dōu °'hwěile (°'syāumyèle).

DESTRUCTION. Expressed verbally as destroy hwěi, hwěimyè. *See* **DESTROY.**

/ The destruction of the bridge held us up for an hour. Chyáu 'hwĕile, 'dānwùle wŏmen yíge jūng'tóu. / The flood caused a lot of destruction. 'Húngshwĕi 'hwĕile hĕn dwō de 'dūngsyi. / The destruction of the enemy fleet is our chief task. Wŏmende jŭyàu 'rènwù shr̆ 'hwĕimyè 'dírénde 'jyàndwèi.

DETAIL. (Minor point) 'syăude dìfang, 'syău jyému, 'syău shr̆. / The battalion commander demands great attention to detail. Yíng'jăng hĕn jù'yì °'syăude dìfang. (°'syău jyému). / That's a mere detail. Nèige shr̆ 'syăushr̆ yí'dwàn.

(Particular) dzáshr̆. / The details of the trip will be arranged by the guide. Lyŭ'syíngde 'dzáshr̆ yóu 'syăngdăuywán 'gwăn.

(Military). / I sent out a detail of six soldiers to take charge. Wŏ pàile 'lyòuge 'bīng chyu 'tányā.

In detail syì, 'syángsyìde, syìsyíde. / The story is too long to be in detail here. 'Hwà tài 'cháng le, bùnéng °'syì shwō (°syì'syìde shwō, °'syángsyìde shwō). but / He loves to talk about his travels in great detail. Tā yì 'shwōchi tā 'dàugwode 'dìfang lai jyou °méi'wán (°méi'tóur).

Details 'syángsyìde 'chíngsyíng. / Today's paper gives further details. Jyēr 'bàushang dwō 'dēngle dyăr 'syángsyìde 'chíngsyíng. / No details have been given out as yet. 'Syángsyìde 'chíngsyíng hái méi'fāchulai.

To detail pài. / Policemen were detailed by the police chief to hold back the crowd. 'Jĭngchájyú'jăng pài syún'jĭng chyu 'tányā kàn 'rènàur de rén.

DETERMINE. (Decide, resolve, settle) 'jywédìng; (expressing more of the sense of come to a decision) dìng. / We must try to determine the best course of action. Wŏmen dĕi °'jywédìng (°'dìng) yíge 'dzwèi hăude 'bànfa. / This matter is to be determined by the chief of staff. 'Jèijyàn shr̆ dĕi yóu tsānmou'jăng lái °'jywédìng (°'dìng). / We determined to stay on until the end. Wŏmen °'jywédìng (°dìng'hăule) 'jyānchŕ dàu'dĭ. / The subject of the lecture is already determined. 'Yănjyăngde 'tímù 'yĭjīng °'dìngle (°'jywédìngle).

(Calculate) swàn(chulai). / Can you determine the exact height of that hill? Nĭ néng 'swànchulai nèige 'shān jyóu'jìng yóu dwō 'gāu ma?

Be determined (unwavering, obstinate). / She is determined to have her way. Tā sz̆'nĭng. or Tā 'fēi yàu jàuje tā dz̆'jĭde 'yìsz bù'kĕ. or Tā 'yàu dzĕmmaje jyou 'fēi dzĕmmaje bù'kĕ. or Tā yì'sĕr yàu 'ànje tā dz̆'jĭ syăngde lái bàn. or Tā yì'dyăr bù'kĕn ràng 'rén. / She is determined to get back her child. °Tā yì'sĕr (°Tā nádìngle júyì, °Tā yí'dìng) yàu bă tāde 'háidz 'yàuhweilai. or Tā 'fēi yàu bă tāde 'háidz 'yàuhweilai bù'kĕ. or Tā bùbă tāde 'háidz 'yàuhweilai bùsz̆'syīn. / They had a determined look about them when they came. Tāmen 'lái de shŕhou hău'syàng hĕn yóu jywé'syìnde 'yàngdz. (of soldiers going into battle) Tāmen lái de shŕhou yóu yìjŭng shr̆'sz̆rú'gwēide 'yàngdz. (of an angry mob) Tāmen láishr̆ syūng'syūng.

Be determined by (depend on) dĕi 'kàn... dìng, dĕi 'chyáu... dìng. See also DEPEND. / My answer will be determined by what happens today. Wŏde 'hwéidá dĕi 'kàn 'jyērde 'chíngsying lái 'dìng.

Determining factor 'gwānjyàn. / What is the determining factor in this case? Jèige 'àndzde 'gwānjyàn dzài 'năr?

DEVELOP. (Of strength, skill) lyàn. / His skill is well developed. Tāde 'gūngfu lyànde hĕn 'shēn. / These exercises will develop the strength of your fingers. Jèisyē 'lyànsyi kéyi 'lyàn nĭ shŏu'jŕtóude 'jyèr.

(Of plans) 'jìnjăn, jìnsyíng, bàn. / Are your plans developing to suit you? Nǐde jǐhwà ⁰'jǐnjǎnde (⁰jǐn'syíngde, ⁰'bànde) hái rú'yǐ ma?

(Of film) syǐ. / Can you develop these films right away? Nǐ néng lǐ'kè bǎ jèige jyāu'jywǎr 'syǐchulai ma?

(Invent) fāmíng. / Our research men have developed a new process. Wǒmen jèr dzwò 'yánjyǒu gūngdzwò de rén fā'míngle yǐjǔng 'syǐnde 'fāngfǎ.

Develop into chéng (that which precedes chéng describes the method); 'syé-chéng (by writing); 'fājanchéng (by expansion); 'jǎngchéng (by a process of growth). / He developed a simple story into a two-volume affair. Tā bǎ yíge hěn 'jyandānde 'gùshr 'syéchengle 'lyǎngdàběnde 'shū. / He developed his store into the largest in this town. Tā bǎ tāde 'pùdz fā'jānchengle jèr dzwèi dàde 'mǎimai le. / The girl developed into a great beauty. Nèige 'syǎu'gūnyang 'jǎng cheng yige yǒu'míngde měi'rér le.

DIAMOND. (Gem) jīngāngshr, jīngāngdzwàr, dzwànshr. / Where are diamonds produced? Nǎr chūchǎn ⁰'jīngāng'shr (⁰etc.)? / He gave her a diamond engagement ring. Tā 'sùnggei tā yíge 'dzwànshrde 'dìnghwūn 'jyèjr. / One large diamond and several small ones are mounted on that ring. Nèijr 'jyèjrshang syāngje yǐkwài dà dzwàn'shr, hái syāngje jikwài 'syǎudyǎr de. / He's put his diamonds in the safe. Tā bǎ tāde ⁰jīngāng'shr (⁰etc.) 'gēdzai bǎusyǎn'syāngli le.

(Suit in cards) 'fāngkwàr. / Did you bid two diamonds? Nǐ 'shr bushr jyàu 'lyǎngge fāng'kwàr? / I think he has a flush in diamonds. Tā 'dàgàishr nále yǐshǒu 'fāngkwàrde 'túnghwār.

(Baseball). / There is enough room here for a diamond. Jèi 'dìfang 'gòu yíge bàngchyóur 'chǎngdz.

DICE. shǎidz. / There are several games you can play with dice. ⁰Jr (⁰Wár) 'shǎidz yǒu háujige ⁰'jrfa (⁰wár fa). / O. K. Let's play the dice game your way. Hǎu ba, jr 'shǎidz jyou jàu 'nǐde 'fǎdz jr ba.

Other expressions in English. / No dice. Bù'chéng.

DICTIONARY. (With items listed by single characters) dzdyǎn; pocket dictionary syǒu-jēndz'dyǎn; (an old term for a dictionary of characters) dzhwèi. / Where do you keep your dictionaries? Nǐ bǎ dz'dyǎn 'fàngdzai nǎr le? / Do you have a small Chinese-English dictionary? Nǐ yǒu 'syǎuběrde Hàn'yǐngdz'dyǎn ma?

(With items listed by words and compounds) tsźdyǎn; dictionary of chemical terms 'hwàsywé tsź'dyǎn; dictionary of personal names 'rénmíng tsź'dyǎn; dictionary of place names 'dìmíng tsź'dyǎn; military dictionary 'jyūnyǔ tsź'dyǎn.

DIE. sž. Like the English word die, sž is often replaced by euphemisms when referring to the death of some person. / I'm not afraid to die. Wǒ búpà 'sž. / He died a pauper. Tā sžde shrhou ⁰'chyúngde yàu'fàn (⁰méi 'fàn chr). / He died of starvation, but left ten thousand dollars for a decent funeral. Tā shr 'èszde, kěshr lyóusya yí'wànkwai chyán hǎu 'chūge dà'bìn. / I'm not going to die. (will not) Wǒ bú'hwèi sžde. (don't want to) Wǒ búywànyi 'sž. / How did he die? Tā shr dzěmma 'sžde? / He died of illness. Tā shr 'bìngszde. / He died of an operation. Tā ⁰gē'bìng (⁰lá-'bìng, ⁰dùng'shǒushù) sžde. / He died of a tumor. Tā jǎng 'lyóudz sžde. / He died of rabies. Tā shr jyau 'fēnggǒu 'yáuszde. / Over twenty people died in yesterday's plan crash. Dzwótyan fēi'jǐ chū'shr sžle 'èrshrdwo rén. / He died of overeating. Tā shr 'chēngszde. or Tā chr dwō le 'chēngszle. / He died of intoxication. Tā shr 'dzwèiszde. / He died of overwork (or exhaustion). Tā 'lèiszde. (fig.) / He died laughing. Tā 'syàuszle. / I just about died laughing when I heard about it. Wǒ 'tīngjyan yǐ'hòu 'chà dyǎr méi'syàusz.

(Euphemisms, like the English pass away) tszshř, syàshř, chyùshř, gwòchyu, gùchyu, búdzài, dzwǒgǔ; (Taoist terms) 'syānchyù, 'syānshř; (referring to the exact time of death) yànchǐ, dwànchǐ; referring to relatives who have died, syān- is prefixed to the relationship term. /When did your father die? (not asking the precise moment) Lìng'dzwūn jǐ'shř °tsź'shřde (°syà'shřde, °bú'dzàide, °'syānshřde, °gùchyude, °etc.); or (asking the precise moment) °yànde 'chǐ, (°'dwànde 'chǐ)? /My father died three years ago. 'Syānyán 'sānnyánchyán tsź'shřde. or Wǒ 'fùchin 'sānnyánchyán 'gwòchyude. or Jyāfù shr sānnyánchyán chyù'shřde. etc. /He died at two o'clock this morning. Tā 'jīntyān 'dzǎuchen 'lyǎngdyǎn 'yànde chǐ.

(Terms less polite than sž, but not actually insults) jyàn 'yánwáng (meet the kings of Hades, a Buddhist reference); yí'mǐng gwēi'yīn (go to Hades); (quoted at end of obituaries) 'wūhu'āidzāi (shàng 'syāng); wán(le), méi(le).

(Very rude terms) wánshř dàjí, wárwán; to stare dèngyǎr; be stiff-legged shēntwěr. /He died after a short illness. (normal statement) Tā bìnglc 'méiji'tyān °jyou 'sžle (or (polite) °jyou 'gùchyule, °etc., or (less polite) °jyou 'wūhu'āidzāile, °etc., or (very impolite) °jyou wár'wánle, °etc.).

(In line of duty and while in action) 'jènwáng, jànsž; (naturally, but while on official duty) yīn'gūng syùn'jř. /He died in action. Tā 'jènwángle. or Tā jàn'sžle. /He died in line of duty (natural death). Tā yīn'gūng syùn'jř le.

Die off màn'mārde 'dōu sžle. /The old inhabitants are dying off. Jèrde 'lǎurén màn'mārde 'dōu sžle.

Die out (lit., as of animals) sžgwāng; (of a family) sžjywé. /The deer have almost died out around here. Jèr fù'jìnde 'lù dōu kwai sž'gwāngle. /His family has died out. Tā yi'jyārén sž'jywéle. /The old families here are all dying out. Jèr ywányǒude 'rénjyār kwai 'dōu sžgwāngle. (fig.) /The custom of wearing vests is dying out. 'Chwān kǎn'jyār yǐ'jīng kwai °bùshř'syīng le (°gwò'shř le).

Be dying to 'hèn bunéng, hèn bude. /I'm dying to meet him. Wǒ °'hèn bunéng (°'hèn bude) lì'kè jyou 'rènshr tā. /She's dying to find out what he said. Tā °'hèn bunéng (°'hèn bude) lì'kè jyou 'jřdàu tā shwō 'shémma láije.

(Fig. uses). /After she came in, the conversation died out. Tā 'jìnlai yǐ'hòu, 'méirén shwō 'hwà le. /The noise of the train died away in the distance. Hwǒ'chē dzǒu'ywǎnle, 'chēshēng jyou tīngbu'jyàn le. /The motor died before we got to the top of the hill. Méidau 'shāndingr yǐ'chyán, (chēde)'jǐchi °bú'dùng le (°'tíng le). /The racket died down when the teacher came in. 'Syānsheng 'jìnlai yǐ'hòu, dà'jyā dōu 'ānjìng le. /After dinner we'll let the fire die down. Chřwánle 'fàn, wǒmen jyau 'hwǒ dž'jǐ 'myèle. /We know the truth now, but old stories die hard. Syàn'dzài wǒmen jřdàu shř 'dzěmma yìhwéi 'shř le, kěshr nàsyē 'yáuyán yǐ'shř hěn nán 'syāumyè. /He's a die-hard. (a compliment) Tā shř ge 'jyānchřdàu'dǐde rén. (an insult; lit. He's like a bull.) Tā shř ge 'nyóusyìngdzde rén. or Tā shř ge 'dzwānnyóu'jǐjyaude rén. or meaning not adaptable Tā jèige rén 'sžsyīn'yǎr.

DIFFERENT. (Comparing things) bùyíyàng, bùsyāngtúng. /He's quite different from what I expected. Tā 'gēn wǒ syīnli 'syǎng de hěn °bùyí'yàng (°bùsyāng'túng). /He's different (from others). Tā gēn 'byéren bùyí'yàng. /He's different (from what he used to be). Tā gēn yǐ'chyán hěn bùyí'yàng. /These two seem to be the same, but they're really different. Jèilyǎngge kànje hǎu'syàng °syāng'túng (°yí'yàng), chí'shř 'bùyíyàng.

(Individualistic) gēn 'byéde bù'túng. /This wine has a really different flavor. Jèi jyǒude 'wèr gēn 'byéde bù'túng.

(Varying with each individual) yi-M . . . yi-M . . . , bù'túng. /Different people tell different versions of the incident. Nèijyàn 'shèr °yírén yígè 'shwōfa (°yíge rén shwō yíyàngr, °'chwánshwō bù'yī, °'gèrén 'shwōfǎ bù'túng). /Different manufacturers have their own car styles. Chǐ'chē, yíge gūng'chǎng you yíge gūng'chǎng-de yàngdz.

(Another) lìng(wài) . . . yi-M . . . , hwàn . . . yi-M . . . . /A different person might have considered it an insult. Yàushr °'lìng('wài) yige rén (°'hwàn yige rén) yěsyǔ hwèi 'jywéde nèi shr 'mà tā ne. /He seems to be a different person now. Tā hǎu'syàng °'hwànle ge rén shrde (°byàncheng 'lìng(wài) yige rén shrde). or Nà 'nǎr shr 'tā ya, jyàn'jǐr chéngle 'lìng(wài)yige 'rén le. /That's a different person. Nà shr 'lìng(wài) yige rén. or Nà 'yòu shr (lìng'wài) yíge rén le. /Let's have someone different. Dzámen 'hwàn yíge rén ba. or Dzámen 'lìng(wài) jǎu ge rén ba. /That's a different story. Nà shr 'lìng(wài) yihwéi 'shèr.

(Separate) not expressed directly in Chinese. /I saw him three different times today. Wǒ 'jīntyān 'kànjyan tā 'sāntsz. /I went to three different book stores trying to find the right book. Wèile yàu jǎu nèiběr 'shū wǒ 'pǎule 'sānjyā shūpù.

DIFFICULT. (Not easy) nán, bù'rúngyi; (requiring effort) fèishr. /The lessons are getting more and more difficult. 'Gūngkè 'ywè lái ywè 'nán. /It's difficult for me to say it to his face. Dāng tā 'myàr wǒ hěn 'nán shwōchu 'kǒu lai. /I'm in a difficult position now. Syàn'dzai wǒ 'jēngdzai wéi'nán. /That job is difficult. Nèijyàn shèr hěn nán 'bàn. /I've always found him difficult to talk with. Wǒ yí'syàng jywéde hěn 'nán gēn tā shwō 'hwà. /He's difficult to work with. Hěn 'nán gēn tā gùng'shr. /Don't leave all the difficult problems to me. Byé bǎ °'nántí (°'nánde, °'nánde wèntí) dōu 'lyóugei wǒ. /It's difficult to understand what he means. Búdà 'rúngyi 'míngbai tāde 'yìsz. /I won't make it difficult for you. Wǒ búhwèi 'jyàu nǐ wéi-'nán. /It was an awfully difficult job explaining this to that blockhead. Gěi nèige hwún'dàn bǎ jèige jyěshr'chīngchule jēn fèi'shr. /That design is difficult to draw. Hwà nèige 'túan hěn fèi'shr. /He's a difficult person to reason with. Gēn tā jyǎng-'lǐ hěn fèi'shr.

(Troublesome, of a person) dǎulwàn, húnàu, hújyǎu, syānàu, hújyǎumánchán. /He's being difficult on purpose. Tā gù'yì °dǎu'lwàn (°etc.). /Don't be difficult! 'Byé °'syā'nàu (°etc.).

DIFFICULTY. (In accomplishment) 'nánchù, 'kwùnnán, kwùnnánde 'dìfang, wéi'nánde 'dìfang. /The difficulty of the job is greater than he thinks. Nèijyàn shrde 'nánchù bǐ tā 'syàngde nán 'dwō le. /I have my own difficulties. Wǒ yǒu dzìjǐde 'nánchù. /What seems to be the difficulty? Kwùnnánde 'dìfang dzài nǎr?

(Troublesome situation) 'nánshr, nángwān. /Any difficulty can be overcome if one keeps on working. Yàushr 'jyānchǐr dàu'dǐ shémma °'nánshr 'dōu néng bàn'hǎule (°nán'gwān dōu néng gwòde'chyú).

(Financial troubles) 'kwùnnán, wéinán; be in (financial) **difficulty** jǐn. /I have my own difficulties. 'Jīngjì fāngmyàn wǒ dzì'jǐ yě shr hěn 'jǐnde. /He is in financial difficulty. Tā wèile 'chyán jēngdzai wéi'nán. or 'Syàndzài tā 'shóuli hěn 'jǐn.

(Problem) wèntí. /If he had saved his money he wouldn't be having these difficulties. Tā dāngchū 'yàushr bǎ chyán 'shěngsyalai dehwà, tā syàn'dzài jywé bu'hwèi yǒu jèisyē wèn'tí.

(Trouble) shr(ching). /He's always getting into difficulties. Tā °lǎu (°'cháng-cháng, °'shrcháng) chū'shr.

(Disagreements, quarreling). /We're having difficulty with him. Wǒmen 'jèng-dzai gēn tā °dǎ'jyà ne (°chǎu'dzwěi ne). or Wǒmen syàn'dzài jèng gēn ta °'hěn budwèi'jyèr (°nàu 'byènyou ne).

DIG. (With hands or paws, or with a pick or mattock, but not with a shovel or spade,

and not when digging a hole) páu. / They're digging the earth with a mattock. Tāmen
yùng gău páu 'tŭ ne. / The dog dug up the bone. Gŏu bă mái de 'gútou 'páuchulaile.
/ These potatoes are ready to dig now. Jèisyē tŭ'dòur kéyi 'páuchulaile.

Dig a hole, ditch, trench, well, etc. (with a shovel, spade, or other tool; ex-
cavate) wā, kāi, jywé. / Dig this hole a little deeper. Bă jèige 'kēng wā 'shēn
dyăr. / They dug a tunnel under the river. Tāmen dzài hé'dĭ 'dĭsya °'wā (°'kāi)le
yige dĭ'dùng. / They dug a canal three hundred miles long. Tāmen °'wā (°'kāi,
°'jywé; see below)le yityáu 'sānbailĭ 'cháng de yùn'hé. / They dug a ditch there.
Tāmen dzài 'nàr °'wā(°'kāi, °'jywé)le yidàu 'gōu. / We can't get through because
they're digging up the pavement. Wŏmen 'gwòbuchyù 'yīnwei tāmen bă 'jwāndàu
°'wāchilaile (°'jywéchilaile).

Dig down into something in order to get something out wā. / They dug up a
chest full of gold and silver and jewels. Tāmen 'wāchulai yí'syāngdzde 'jīnyín jū'bău.
/ Dig up some asparagus. Wā dyăr lúngsyū'tsài. / We'll have to dig up this apple
tree and put it over there. Wŏmen dĕi bă jèige pínggwŏ'shù 'wāchulai 'nwódau
'nèibyar chyù.

Dig ground for the foundation of a building pwò(tŭ). / They're going to start
digging today. Tāmen 'yùbei 'jyér pwò 'tŭ.

Dig in (reach into something to get something or to remove an obstacle) tāu.
/ Gentlemen, dig in your pockets! Nímen dĕi tāu yāu'băur!

Dig in (fortify). / How long will it take your company to dig in (military)? Nĭ
'nèilyán rén °jwūnbei (°'bùjr) 'fángyù'gūngshr dĕi yùng 'dwōshău 'shŕhou?

Dig in (work hard). / It's a hard job, but he's digging right in. 'Shŕching hĕn
'nán, 'kĕshr tā jēn pīnmíng 'gàn.

Dig into (investigate) 'dyàuchá; (do research on) yánjyou. / I've been digging
into the history of that town. Wŏ 'jèngdzai °'dyàuchá (°'yánjyou) nèige 'chéngde
lì'shr. / They dug into his private affairs, but found nothing to point to as a fault.
Tāmen °dyàuchá (°dătīng) tāde 'sžshr, kĕshr 'méijăuchu shémma kéyi 'jŕjáide lai.
but / He's digging into his books for some material. Tā 'jèngdzai 'shūli jău 'tsáilyaur ne. / He's digging into the books. / Tā 'bàuje shū 'sž nyàn.

Dig up (find out) jăuchulai. / See what you can dig up about him. 'Gwānyu tāde
'shr 'chyáu nĭ néng 'jăuchu 'shémma lai.

A dig (physical) expressed with the verb meaning **give** someone a dig tŭng, chŭ.
/ If he starts talking too much, give him a dig in the ribs. Tā yàushr 'shwō hwà
'shwōde tài 'dwōde shŕhou, kéyi °'tŭng tā (°'chŭ tā) yí'syà.

(Verbal) expressed with the verb meaning **take digs at** mà. / That editor is always taking digs at the mayor. Nèige jŭ'bĭ lău 'mà shŕ'jăng.

DINE. chŕ fàn. / They're dining with the Ambassador tonight. Tāmen jyér 'wănshang
°gēn (°péije) 'dàshŕ (yíkwàr) chŕ 'fàn. / We always dine out on Sundays. Wŏmen
'lĭbaityān 'lăushŕ 'chūchyu chŕ 'fàn. *but* / They wined and dined him but in the end
he made complete fools out of them. Tāmen chĭng tā 'dà chŕ 'dà hē kĕshr dàule
'mwòlyăur tā 'bă tāmen °'pyànge (°'shwăge) búyí'lèhu.

Diner, dining car fànchē. / There's no diner on this train. Jèilyè hwŏ'chēshang
méiyou fàn'chē.

Dining room (at home) fàntīng; (in a hotel) shŕtáng, tsāntáng, tsāntīng.
/ Bring another chair into the dining room. Dzài (lìng'wài) bān yibă 'yĭdz dàu fàn-
'tīng chyu. / We use this room as a dining room. Wŏmen ná jèijyān 'wūdz dàng
'fàn'tīng. / The dining room closes at 10. °Shŕ'táng (°'Tsān'táng, °'Tsān'tīng)
shŕdyan gwān 'mén.

DINNER. fàn, wǎnfàn. / Dinner's ready! Fàn dzwò 'délōu. *or* Chr̄ 'fàn lōu. / We are giving a dinner in his honor next Friday. Wǒmen syàlǐbài'wú chǐng ta chr̄ (wǎn) 'fàn. / Won't you come over and have dinner with us tomorrow night? Nǐmen 'míng-tyan 'wǎnshang néng lái túng wǒmen chr̄ (wǎn)'fàn ma? / I have a dinner engage-ment tonight. Jyèr 'wǎnshang wǒ yǒu °fàn'jyú (°ge chr̄fànde 'ywēhwèi). / Has the dinner bell rung? (Chr̄)'fànlyéngr 'syǎngle 'méiyou?

DIRECT. (Without anyone or anything in between) 'jr̄jyē 'yìjr̄, jr̄jyēlyǎudàng. / I shall make a direct appeal to the colonel. Wǒ yàu °'jr̄jyē (°'yìjr̄) chyu 'chyóu shàng'syàu. / His answers are always direct and to the point. Tāde 'hwéidá yí'syàng shr̄ 'jr̄jyē-lyǎu'dàng.

(Straight, not roundabout) jìn. / This is the most direct route to the city. 'Jèi shr̄ dàu 'chéngli chyù dzwèi 'jìnde yityáu lù.

(Exact) jèng. / The result is the direct opposite of what we expected. 'Jyēgwǒ gēn wǒmen 'syǎng de 'jèng syǎng'fǎn.

(Forthright) jr̄, 'gēngjr̄, 'jèngjr̄, 'chéngkěn. / He has always been direct and honest with me. Tā 'dwèi wǒ yísyàng dōu hěn 'chéngkěn. / He's a direct person. Tā hěn 'jr̄. *or* meaning just and straightforward Tā hěn 'jèngjr̄. *or* Tā dzwò shr̄ shwō 'hwà 'búhwèi ràu'wār.

Direct descendant 'dísyì. / She is a direct descendant of Confucius. Tā shr̄ 'Kǔngdzde 'dísyì.

To direct (inform). / I was directed to wait until he returned. Yǒu'rén 'jyàu wǒ 'děng tā 'hwéilai.

(Guide). / Can you direct me to the post office? Chǐng'wèn, dàu yóujèng'jyú chyu dzěmma 'dzǒu?

Direct a play dǎuyǎn. / Who's directing the play? Jèige 'syì 'shéi dǎu'yǎn ne?

Direct attention. / May I direct your attention to rule No. 3? Chǐng nǐ 'kàn yikan dì'sān tyáu.

Direct traffic 'jr̄hwēi chēmǎ, 'jr̄hwēi jyāu'tūng. / Ask the policeman who's directing traffic. Wèn nèige °jr̄hwēi chēmǎ de (°'jr̄hwēi jyāu'tūng de) jǐng'chá.

DIRECTION. (Course). / Since he came the work has taken a new direction. 'Dztsúng tā láile yǐ'hòu, 'gūngdzwòde 'fāngjēn 'gǎile.

(Instructions for getting somewhere) dzǒude lù, lùsyàn. / Here are the direc-tions for finding my house. 'Jèi shr wàng wǒ 'jyā chyu dzǒude 'lù. / Follow the directions printed in the guidebook. 'Ānje yóulǎnjr̄'nánshang gěide lù'syàn 'dzǒu.

(Instructions for doing something). / Are there any directions (with it)? Yǒu 'méiyou shwōmíng'shū? / This booklet gives all the directions for using this machine. Jèige 'jīchǐde yùngfǎ dōu dzài jèibēr shwōmíng'shūli. / Can you give me some directions on how to use this? Chǐng nǐ gěi wǒ 'jyángjyang jèige dzěmma 'yùng, syíng ma? / Better follow the divisional commander's directions. Dzwèi hǎu shr̄ 'dzūnjàu shr̄'jǎngde 'syùnlìng bàn. / Please give me some directions. Chǐng 'jr̄dyǎnjr̄dyǎn. *or* 'Chǐng 'dwōdwō 'jr̄jyàu. *See also* **COMMAND.**

(Guidance) 'lǐngdǎu. / They have made great progress under his direction. Dzài tāde 'lǐngdǎujr̄'syà tāmen hěn yǒu 'jìnbù.

In a certain direction (location) dzài . . . byār; (involving motion toward) wàng . . . byār; (facing) chùng(je) . . . byār. / The village is a mile away in that direction. Tswūn'jwāngr dzài 'nèibyār yǒu yìlǐ 'dì. / He went in that direction. Tā wàng 'nèibyār chyùle. / He went in an easterly direction. Tā wàng 'dūng(byār) chyùle. / Look out! He's coming in our direction! Hèi! Tā 'chùngje 'dzámen (jèibyār) láile. /He's aiming in our direction! Duck! Tā 'chùngje 'dzámen (jèi-byār) myǎu ne! Kwài 'dwǒ! /He went in the direction of that house. Tā wàng 'nèiswǒ 'fángdz nèibyār chyùle.

From all directions tsúng °sżbyār (°sżmyàr). /They came from all directions. Tāmen shr tsúng °'sżbyār (°sżmyàr) laide.

In different directions. /They went in different directions. Tāmen 'gè dzǒu yìtyáu 'lùr le. *or* Tāmen 'gè dzǒu 'gède le.

DIRECTLY. (Exactly) jèng. /The post office is directly opposite the theater. Yóu-jèngjyú jeng 'dwèije syìywándz.

(Straight) 'yìjr, 'jŕjyē. /Let's go directly to the hotel. Dzámen °'yì'jŕ (°jŕjyē) chyù lyǔ'gwǎn ba.

DIRTY. (Soiled) dzāng, bùgānjing. /These dirty clothes must be sent to the laundry. Jèisyē 'dzāng 'yīfu děi °'sùngdàu 'syǐyīfáng chyù 'syǐ le (°'sùngchyu 'syǐ le). /The floor of my room is dirty. Wǒ 'wūdzde °dǐ(°dìbǎn)hěn °'dzāng (°bù'gānjing). /I've never seen a hotel as dirty as that. Wǒ 'syànglai méi'kànjyàngwo °'nèmma dzāngde lyǔ'gwǎn (°yíge lyǔ'gwǎn nèmma 'dzāng). /Don't get my clothes dirty. Byé bǎ wǒde 'yīshang nùng'dzāngle.

Dirty joke dzāng syàuhwar. /He's telling dirty jokes. Tā shwō dzāng 'syàu-hwar ne.

Dirty story hwài syǎushwō, hwai gùshr, hwài shŕ, 'fén shū. /Don't let such dirty stories fall into the hands of the children. Byé 'ràng jèijung °hwài syǎu-'shwō (°'fén shū) làudzai háidzmende 'shóuli. /Don't listen to that sort of dirty story. Byé 'tīng nèijǔng °hwài gùshr (°etc.).

Dirty trick. /That was a dirty trick he played on us. Tā nèitsz 'jēn shr 'gěi wǒmen shŕ'hwài le. /That's a dirty trick. (mild) Jēn 'hwài. *or* Jēn táu'chì. (seriously) 'Wèimyǎn tài 'swǔn le! *or* 'Hàirén bù'chyǎn! *or* Jēn 'chywē'dé!

Give somebody **a dirty look** 'dèngle . . . yiyǎn. /He gave us a dirty look. Tā 'dèngle wǒmen yì'yǎn.

DISAPPEAR. (From sight) (kàn)bujyàn le. /The man disappeared over the hill. Nèige rén 'gwòle shānjyār yǐ'hòu, jyou (kàn)bu'jyàn le. /It's going to disappear soon. Děng yihwěr jyou (kàn)bu'jyàn le.

(From a place) méi ('yǒu) le. /The old houses are disappearing from the city. 'Chénglǐde lǎu 'fángdz màn'mārde méi ('yǒu) le.

(Socially). /He disappeared three years ago. Sānnyán'chyán °tā shŕ'dzūngle (°jyou 'méi rén jŕdau tā dàu nǎr 'chyùle).

DISAPPOINT. shŕwàng, sǎusyìng, bumǎnyì. /The new play was rather disappointing. Nèige gāng 'shàngyande syì °'bìng bùhǎu (°'yǒu dyar jyàu rén shŕ 'wàng). /I was disappointed with the results. 'Jyégwǒ jyàu wǒ 'hěn °bùmǎn'yì (°sǎu'syìng, °shŕ'wàng). /Please don't disappoint me by not coming. 'Byé bùlái, jyàu wǒ sǎu-'syìng. /He is awfully disappointing to us. Tā 'jēn jyàu rén hěn shŕ'wàng. /We're disappointed in you. Nǐ 'jyàu wǒmen shŕ'wàng.

DISCOVER. (Find) 'jǎujáu, fāsyàn. /We have discovered a new restaurant that's very good. Wǒmen 'jǎujaule yíge 'tǐng hǎude fàn'gwǎr. /Was Columbus the first to discover America? Gēlwún'bù shr °'jǎujáu (°fā'syàn) 'Měijōu de 'tóuyige rén ma?

(Invent, develop) fāmíng, 'yánjyōuchulai. /He discovered a new process for making glass. Tā °fā'míngle (°'yánjyōuchuláile) yìjǔng 'syīn fádz lai dzwò 'bwōli.

(Find out by investigation) 'dyàuchá. / There is no truth in the story, so far as I can discover. Jyù wǒ 'dyàuchá de 'chíngsying, lai 'shwō, nèijyàn shř 'háuwú 'gēnjyù.

DISCUSS. (Talk about) 'tán (yìtán); (consult about) shānglyang; (debate about) tǎulwùn. / There are lots of things left to discuss. 'Hái yǒu hǎu'syē shř děi °'tán yìtán (°'shānglyang, °'tǎulwùn). / Let's discuss this questions first. Dzámen 'syān °'tǎulwùntǎulwùn 'jèige wèntí (°'bǎ 'jèige wèntí 'tǎulwùnlou). / We were just discussing our plans. Wǒmen 'jèngdzai °'tǎulwùn (°'shānglyang, °'tán yìtán) wǒmende 'jìhwà.

DISCUSSION. Expressed verbally with 'shānglyang (discuss), tán (talk about), 'tǎulwùn (debate about). / We reached our decision after a long discussion. Wǒmen °'tánle (°'tǎulwùnle, °'shānglyangle) bàn'tyān tsái yǒu 'jyēgwǒ. / There will be a discussion period after the lecture. Jyǎng 'wánle yǐ'hòu, yǒu yí'dwàn shŕhou 'tǎulwùn.

A discussion meeting tǎulwunhwèi.

DISEASE. bìng; **contagious disease** chwánrǎnbìng. / That disease is quite easy to catch. Nèijǔng 'bìng hěn 'rúngyì °'jāusheng (°'rǎnshàng). / The disease rate here is very low. Jèr měi'nyán hài'bìngde rén hěn 'shǎu.

DISH. pándz, dyédz. If several kinds of dishes are referred to, pándz and dyédz mean small plate, and the other kinds have their own terms. See under each kind. / He dropped the dish and broke it. Tā bǎ °'pándz (°'dyédz) shwāi'pwòle.

(Type of food) tsài. / What is your favorite dish? Nǐ dzwèi 'syǐhwan 'chř de tsài shř 'shémma?

Dishes (all dishes and utensils needed for cooking and serving) pándz 'wǎn shemmade; **wash the dishes** syǐ wǎn. / We'll have to buy dishes (all kinds). Pándz 'wǎn shemmade 'dōu děi 'mǎi le. / Let me help wash the dishes. Wǒ lái 'bāng nǐ syǐ wǎn.

To dish out food chéng; (serve in quantities) kāi(fàn). / The cook dished out the food on our plates. 'Dàshrfu bǎ tsài 'chéngdzai wǒmende 'pándzli le. / The cook is dishing out the food now. 'Chúdz 'jèngdzai chéng 'tsài ne. / The canteen will start dishing out the food at six o'clock. 'Jyūnrén jyùlè'bù 'lyòudyǎn °kāi'fàn (°'chīshŕ kāi'fàn).

Other expressions in English. / He can dish it out but he can't take it. °Tā 'gwāng hwèi jàn 'pyányì (°Tā 'gwāng hwèi 'chīfu rén), dz̀'jǐ chř dyǎr 'kwēi jyou shǒubu'lyǎu le.

DISLIKE. tǎuyàn, bù syǐhwan. / I dislike him very much. Wǒ hěn tǎuyàn tā. or Wǒ hěn bù 'syǐhwan tā. / I dislike traveling by boat. Wǒ °bù'syǐhwan (°tǎuyàn) dzwò chwán lyù'syíng. / I dislike interruptions when I'm concentrating. Wǒ syǎng 'shèr de shŕhou bù'syǐhwan yǒu rén dǎ'jyǎu. / I dislike interruptions when I'm talking. Wǒ shwō 'hwà de shŕhou bù'syǐhwan you rén °dǎ'chà (°chā dzwèi). / Your strong dislike of him is just prejudice on your part. is expressed verbally as Nǐ nèmma °bù'syǐhwan tā (°tǎuyàn tā) shř nǐ dz̀'jǐ pyān'syīn. / I can't explain my dislike for that city. is expressed as I can't explain why I dislike that city. Wǒ 'shwōbuchulái wèi 'shémma wǒ tǎuyàn nèige 'chéng.

DISPOSE. (Arrange in a certain order) pái. / The soldiers were disposed in a thin line. Bǎ 'bīng páichéngle 'sānbīng'syàn le.

Dispose of (settle) bàn. /We still have some business to dispose of. Hái yǒu hǎusye 'shǐ °děi 'bàn ne (°méi'bàn ne).

(Get rid of) mài (sell); rēng (throw away); tsáng (hide); 'jr̆jrbù'lǐ, búdalǐ, bù-'lyǎu 'lyǎujr (ignore). /They will leave as soon as they dispose of the furniture. Tāmen bǎ 'jyājyu 'màile yǐ'hòu, jyou 'dzǒu. /Where can we dispose of the garbage? 'Lājǐ 'rēngdau 'nǎr chyu? /Where did he dispose of the corpse? Tā bǎ 'szshī tsáng dzai 'nǎr le? /He disposed of our objections in short order (as with a shrug of the shoulders). Wǒmen 'fǎndwèide 'dìfang tā °'jr̆jrbù'lǐ (°búda'lǐ, °bù'lyǎu 'lyǎu-jr).

Dispose of a person dǎfa(dzǒu). /Let's think of a way to dispose of that fellow. Dzámen syǎng ge 'fár bǎ nèige 'jyāhwo 'dǎfa('dzǒu)le ba.

Be disposed (mentally inclined). /He was disposed to take things too seriously. Tā jèige rén 'szsyīn'yǎr. or Tā jèige rén ài jyàu 'jěr. or Tā 'wǎngwǎng bǎ 'shr-ching 'kànde tài 'yánjùng.

Be well disposed toward 'dzànchéng. /I found him well disposed toward our suggestion. Tā hěn 'dzànchéng wǒmende jyànyì.

DISTANCE. Sometimes translated by jyùlí but more commonly by expressions including ywǎn far and other terms. See also DISTANT. /What is the distance to Kunming? Tsúng 'jèr dàu 'Kwūnmíng de jyù'lí you 'dwōshǎu lǐ? or 'Kwūnmíng lí 'jèr yǒu dwō 'ywǎn? but /We can cover the distance in three hours. Wǒmen yùng 'sānge jūngtóu de 'gūngfu jyou kéyi 'dàudelyǎu.

(Coolness of manner). /The distance in her manner is caused by shyness. Tā 'yīnwei 'myǎntyǎn 'swóyi tàidù (syǎnje) °hěn 'lěngdàn (°'lěnglěngdàn'dànde, °'lěng-bujyěrde). /I wanted to be friends with him, but he always kept at a distance. Wǒ syang 'gēn tā dzwò 'péngyou, kěshr tā °'hǎuwú 'byǎushr (°'lěngbujyěrde, °'lěng-lēngdàn'dànde). /Keep him at a distance. Gēn tā 'shǔywǎndyǎr. /Since our argu-ment he keeps his distance. 'Dztsúng wǒmen bàn'dzwēi yǐ'hòu, °tā bù'lǐ wo le (°ta 'dwǒje wo).

At (or from) a distance lǎu 'ywǎn. /You can see the tower from a distance. Lǎu 'ywǎn jyou 'kéyi kànjyàn nèige 'tǎ. or Nèige 'tǎ nǐ tsúng lǎu ywǎn jyou 'kàn-dejyàn. /At a distance the building seems attractive. °Nèige 'lóu tsúng 'ywǎnchù kàn (°Nèige 'lóu lǎu ywǎnde 'kànje) hái bú'tswò. but /Keep at a distance. Lí 'ywǎn dyǎr. or 'Líkāi yǐdyǎr.

To outdistance (leave behind) làsya; (pass) 'kāigwò. /We can easily outdistance them. Yàusyǎng bǎ tāmen °'kāigwochyu (°'làsya) hěn 'rúngyì.

In the distance. /The plane disappeared in the distance. is expressed as The plane disappeared in the sky. 'Fēijǐ 'fēidau 'tyānbyǎr bú'jyàn le.

DISTANT. (Far away) ywǎn; a distant view ywǎnjǐng. /My brother lives in a distant part of the country. Wǒ 'gēge 'jùdzai °'lí jèr hěn 'ywǎnde yíge 'dìfang (°yíge 'dì-fāng lí jèr hén 'ywǎn). /She is a distant relative of mine. Tā shr̆ wǒde ywǎn'chīn. but /The river is five miles distant. Hé 'lí jèr yǒu wǔlǐ 'dì (nèmma 'ywǎn).

(Cool in manner) 'lěngdàn. /She seems very distant today. Tā jyér 'fǎngfu (dàirén) tǐng 'lěngdàn shr̆de.

In the distant future jyānglái yǒu yǐ'tyān. /Some time in the distant future I may learn to read Chinese characters. 'Jyānglái yǒu yìtyān wǒ yěsyǔ sywé Rèn'dż.

In the distant past 'shànggǔde shr̆hou. /It was said that in the distant past people wore nothing but leaves. Tǐng'shwō dzài 'shànggǔde shr̆hòu, rénmen jyou chwān shù'yèdz.

See also FAR, AWAY.

DISTRIBUTE. (Divide among) fēn, fā. / The food and clothing will be distributed among the refugees. Wǒmen 'yàu bǎ 'yīfu hé 'shŕpǐn °'fēngei (°'fāgei) nàn'míng.

(Spread out) sǎ, bwō. / Distribute the seed evenly over the ground. Bǎ 'jǔngdz 'píngjwūnde °'sǎdzài dìshang (°'bwōdzai dìlǐ).

DISTRIBUTION. (Passing out to many people) expressed as to distribute fēn. / When is the first distribution of mail? 'Syìn 'tóuyitsž shémma shŕhou 'fēn?

(Spreading of many things in their places) expressed with to distribute 'fēnpèi. / The distribution of population in this country is uneven. 'Gwónèi 'rénkou 'fēnpèide bù'jyūn.

(Handing out in shares) expressed as release fàng. / He is in charge of the distribution of relief. Tā 'gwǎn fàng'jèn.

DISTRICT. (General vicinity) 'dìdài, dìfang. / The town is in a mountainous district. Nèi chéng shŕ dzài yige shān 'dwō de °'dìdài (°'dìfang).

(Administrative subdivision) chyū. / The city is divided into ten administrative districts. Jèige 'chéng 'fēnchéngle shŕge ('syínjèng)'chyū.

(Administrative unit in China, something like a county) syàn. / The Chinese Republic was divided into 28 provinces and two border regions; the provinces were divided into about 2,000 districts. 'Jūnghwámín'gwó tsúng'chyán fēn èrshr'báge 'shěng hé lyǎngge 'byānchyū; jèièrshrbà'shěng yòu 'fēnchéng lyǎngchyānlaige 'syàn.

DISTURB. (Move or derange objects) nùnglwàn, dùng. / Someone's disturbed my papers! Yǒurén °'dùng (°'nùng'lwàn) wǒde 'wénjyàn laije!

(Call; as after a nap) jyàu. / I don't want to be disturbed until ten. Shŕdyǎn yǐ'chyán byé 'jyàu wǒ.

(Bother) jyǎu, nàu, chǎu. / Don't disturb me again until this is done. Jèige méi'wán yǐchyán, 'byé dzài lái °'jyǎu (°'nàu, °'chǎu) wo. / Don't disturb them (from sleep). Byé bǎ tāmen °nàu'syǐngle (°chǎu'syǐngle, (if no noise is made) °jyǎu'syǐngle).

(Alarm, excite) 'jǐngdùng. / Don't disturb the others. Byé 'jǐngdùng 'byérén.

Be disturbed (emotionally) jāují, syīnli lwàn, syīnli fán, 'syīnli nán'gwò. / I'm disturbed to hear that news. Wǒ 'tīngjyan nèige 'syāusyi yǐ'hòu, °yǒu dyǎr jāu'jí (°'syīnli yǒu dyǎr 'lwàn, °'syīnli hěn nán'gwo, °'syīnli 'fándeheng). / She's easily disturbed. Ta °yìlái jyou (°hěn 'rúngyi °jāu'jí (°'syīnli 'lwàn, °'syīnli fán, °'syīnli nán'gwò, °fā'hwāng). / This is disturbing news. Jèige 'syāusyi jyàu rén °jāu'jǐ (°'syīnli 'lwàn, °etc.).

DITCH. gōu. / There is a ditch on each side of the road. Dàu lyǎng'páng yǒu 'gōu. / The car fell in the ditch three kilometers up the road. Chì'chē dzài 'lù 'chyánbyàr sān'gūnglǐde 'dìfang dyàudzai 'gōuli le.

Irrigation ditch gwàngàichyú, chyú, or (if it is small) gōu.

Other expressions in English. / Let's ditch these people and have some fun. / Dzámen °'dwōkai (°'shwǎikai) jèisyē rén hǎu wárde 'tùngkwai dyar.

DIVIDE. fēn; **divide equally** 'píngfēn, 'jyūnfēn. / Divide the money among you. Nǐmen bǎ 'chyán 'fēnle ba. / Here the river divides into two streams. Hé dzài jèr 'fēncheng lyǎng'tyáu ('jīlyóu). / A road divides the town (into two parts). 'Yìtyáu 'lù bǎ chéng fēncheng 'lyǎngbù. / Let me divide it for you. (Ràng) 'wǒ lai gěi nǐmen 'fēn. / On the question of taxes Congress (is) divided into two camps. 'Gwānyu 'jywānshwèi 'wèntí gwóhwèi 'fēncheng lyǎng'pài. / The committee (was) divided on the question of taxes. 'Gwānyu 'jywānshwèi 'wèntí wěiywán'hwèi 'fēncheng lyǎng'pài.

(Watershed) shānjí; **Continental Divide** fēnshwěi lǐng. / The hotel is on the divide between the two valleys. Lyǔ'gwǎn shr̀ dzài shān'jǐshang.

Divided by; X divided by Y X bèi Y chú, X yùng Y chú, Y chú X. / 14 divided by 2 equals 7. Shr̀'sz̀ bèi 'èr chú dé 'chī. *or* Shr̀'sz̀ yùng 'èr 'chú dé 'chī. *or* Er chú shr̀'sz̀ dé 'chī.

DIVISION. (Section) 'bùfen, 'bùmén. / What division of the office do you work in? Nǐ dzài 'gūngshr̀'fángli nǎyi'bùfen dzwò 'shr̀? *or* Nǐ dzài 'bànkūngtīngde nǎyi'bùmén bàn'gūng?

(Disunity) 'fēnfēn, bùyī, bùyījr̀. / There was a division of opinion on that subject. 'Gwānyu nèige 'wèntí °'yìlwùn 'fēnfēn (°'yǐjyan bù'yī, °'yíjyan bùyí'jr̀). / There's a division of authority in that office. Dzài nèige gūngshr̀'fángli °'bùshr 'yíge rén 'gwǎnshr̀ (°'shr̀ chywán bùtǔng'yī).

(Military) shr̄. / Three infantry divisions were sent. 'Pàichyùle sānge 'bùbīngshr̄.

(Mathematical) 'chúfǎ. / The children haven't started division yet. 'Háidzmen hái 'méisywé 'chúfǎ (ne).

DO (DID, DONE). 1. (Perform, accomplish) dzwò; nùng *or* néng (less formal); gǎu (colloquial); bàn (manage); gàn (implying mental ability, energy, or effort); wán, dzwòwán (finish); **do something this way, that way** *or* **which way** is expressed by °dzěmma (°jěmma, °němma, °dzěmma) **with or without** je **plus** °dzwò (°nùng, °gǎu, °bàn, °gàn). / What sort of work does he do? Tā dzwò shémma 'shr̀? / What is he doing? Tā °dzwò (°etc.) 'shémma ne? / How do you do this? 'Jèige dzěmma °dzwò ne (°bàn ne, °nùng ne, °gǎu ne)? (gàn is not used here, but might be used in the following sentence.) / How did you ever do it? 'Jèige nǐ dzěmma 'gànde? / Are you going to do it or not? Nǐ 'jyòujing shr̀ 'gàn bugàn? / He's doing three men's work here. Tā 'yíge rén dzài jèr dzwò 'sānge rén de 'shr̀. / The secretary does her work well. Jèige 'nyǔ'shūji dzwò 'shr̀ dzwòde hen 'hǎu. / He didn't do his work well. Tā 'dzwòde 'bùhǎu. / He didn't do that job well. Nèige shèr tā méidzwò'hǎu. / It certainly was his doing. Méi 'tswòr, 'jwǔnshr 'tā gàn de. / He's doing his duty. Tā 'dzwò tāde 'shr̀ ne. *or* Tā nashr jìn 'tāde 'dzéren. / He does odd jobs for people around here. Tā gěi 'jèikwàrde 'rén °dzwò 'línghwó (°dzwò língswèi-'shèr, °dzwò língchība'swèide 'shèr, °dzwò 'dzáshèr, °dà'dzár). / Well done! Dzwòde °'hěn hǎu (°hǎu'jíle). / Is this the right thing to do? Jèige 'shèr shr̀ 'gāi dzwò de ma? / Is this the right way to do it? Jèijyàn shr̀ °'gāi jěmma dzwò ma (°'jěmma dzwò 'dwèi ma)? / If he can do it, so can I. 'Tā yàu néng 'gàn nèige, 'wǒ yě néng. / You'd better do as you're told. 'Dzěmma 'gàusung nǐ de jyou dzěmma °'bàn (°'dzwò, °'nùng). / I am busy. You do it. Wǒ hěn 'máng. Nǐ 'dzwò ba. / If you think I didn't do it right, you do it! Yàushr nǐ yǐwéi wǒ 'dzwòde bu'dwèi, °'nǐ dzwò yidzwò 'kàn (°'nǐ shr̀ yishr̀ 'kàn)! / Let me see you do it. Nǐ 'dzwò yihwei gěi wǒ 'kànkan. / You can't do it that way. Nǐ 'bùnéng °'nèmmaje (°'nèmma dzwò). / Whatever he does, you do it too. 'Tā dzěmmaje, 'nǐ yě dzěmmaje. *or* 'Tā dzěmma 'bàn, 'nǐ yě dzěmma 'bàn. / Now that you've done it, how do you feel? Syàndzài nǐ 'yǐjīng °'bàn'hǎule (if it was good; if bad, °'bàn'dzàule) syīnli jywéje dzěmma'yàng? / Now you've done it! (scolding). Nǐ 'kàn! Nǐ dōu °nùng-'hwàile (°'nùng'dzàule). / How is your brother doing at his new job? Nǐde 'gēge 'jèige 'syīn shr̀ching 'dzwòde dzěmma'yàng? / He's doing pretty well. Tā 'nùngde hěn 'hǎu. *or* Tā 'nùngde hái bú'tswò. / Something should be done about the high price of meat. Ròu 'dzěmma gwèi 'yīnggāi 'syǎng dyar 'bànfa. / My pen won't work; what did you do to it? Wǒde 'gāngbǐ bùnéng 'yùngle; nǐ 'dzěmma °'nùng laije (°'hwòhwo laije)? / See what you've done! 'Kàn nǐ 'nùng de! *or* 'Kàn nǐ 'hwòhwo de! *or* 'Kàn nǐ 'nàu de! / He's a hard man to do business with. Gēn 'tā °'lái'wǎng hěn 'nán (°dǎ 'jyāudài hěn 'nán, °'gùngshr̀ hěn 'nán, °'dzwò 'mǎimai hěn 'nán). /It's not done yet. Hái méi'wán. /All my lessons are done. Wǒde 'gūngkè chywán dzwò'wánle. /I can't leave before the job is done. Shèr méi'wán wǒ bùnéng 'dzǒukai. /It's only half done. Gāng dzwòle yí'bàr.

2. When some other word can easily be used in place of **do**, specifying the type of action more accurately, use the word in Chinese that corresponds to the more specific English word; e. g., for **do the dishes** use wash the dishes. /Do (tie) the package up good and tight. Bǎ 'bāufu °gwǒ'hǎule, gwǒ'jǐnle (°gwǒde hǎu'hāurde, jǐn'jyèrde). /The maid wants to do (put in order) this room now. Syàndzài nyǔ'dǐsyàrén yàu °'shr̀dau (°'shǒushr) jèijyān wūdz. /On a bad road like this I can't do (drive) more than twenty miles an hour. 'Jèmma hwài de 'lù wǒ 'yìsyǎushr̀ bùnéng 'kāigwo 'èrshr̀lǐ. /This car only does (goes) twelve miles to the gallon. Jèige 'chē yì'jyālwún jr̀ dzǒu shr̀'èryīnglǐ. /I'd better do (read, study) tomorrow's history lesson now. Wǒ syàn'dzài 'háishr °'nyànnyàn (°'yùbeiyùbei) myérde lǐ'shr̀ (nèitáng 'kè) ba. /Could I help you do (wash, wipe) the dishes? Wǒ 'bāng ní °syǐ (°tsā) 'dyédz 'hǎu ma? /Where can I get this laundry done (washed)? Jèisyē 'yīshang dzài 'nǎr syǐ 'hǎu ne? /He is doing (writing) a magazine article on local customs. Tā 'jèngdzai syě yìpyān 'gwān yú dāngdì 'fēngsu syí'gwànde 'wénjang, yàu dzài yíge dzá'jr̀shang 'dēng. /This variety of melon does (grows) better in sandy soil. 'Jèijūng 'gwā dzài 'shādìli 'jǎngde hǎu. /If we get caught, we'll have to do (sit) at least five years. 'Yàushr 'dzámen jyàu rén 'děijau₂ jyòu děi jr̀shǒu dzwò 'wǔ nyán jyàn na. /She does (fixes) her hair up in a knot. Tā bǎ 'tóufa dzài 'tóushang 'shūle yíge 'jyǒur. /She's getting her hair done (professionally) for the party. Tā yīnwèi yàu chǐng 'kè dàu meirúng'ywàn chyule. /I've got to go downtown and do (buy) a little shopping. Wǒ děi jìn'chéng chyu mǎi dyǎr 'dūngsyi.

3. When **do** is used as a substitute for another word earlier in the sentence, Chinese repeats either the first word or some other word which is to be emphasized. In comparison, **do** is not expressed. /If you want to ask any questions, do it now. 'Yàushr nǐ yàu 'wèn shémma₂ syàn'dzài jyou 'wèn hǎu le. /He drinks wine the way I do water. Tā 'syàng wo hē 'shwěi shr̀de nàmma hē 'jyǒu. /He gets up early and so do I. Tā 'chǐde 'dzǎu; wǒ yě 'chǐde 'dzǎu. /Who was it who saw him? I did. Shr̀ 'shéi kànjyande ta? Shr̀ 'wǒ. /Did anyone see him? I did. Shéi 'kànjyan ta le? 'Wǒ kànjyanle. /I've always written home every week, and I still do. Wǒ yí'syàng gěi 'jyāli 'yíge lǐ'bài syě 'yìfēng 'syìn; 'syàndzài 'háishr °jèiyàngr (°dzěmmaje). /We have to pay more than you do for cigarettes. 'Wǒmen mǎi yān'jywǎr děi bǐ nǐ °'hwàde 'dwō (°'dwō chū'chyán). /He works harder now than he did last year. Tā syàn'dzài bǐ 'chyùnyán mài 'lìchi màide 'dwō dyar.

4. As an auxiliary verb in questions (does he go), negatives (he doesn't go), and emphatics (he does go), **do** is expressed respectively by an interrogative form, a negative word, or an emphatic word. /Do you like the food here? Nǐ 'syǐhwan 'jèrde 'fàn ma? /Does he live here? Tā jù 'jèr ma? /What do you want? Nǐ yàu 'shémma? /Why did he say that? Tā 'wèi shémma shwō 'nèige? /Did you want to see me now? 'Shr̀ bushr nǐ yàu syàndzài 'jyàn wo? /I don't want to trouble you. Wǒ bú'ywànyì 'máfan nǐ. /Why doesn't he like this hotel? Tā 'wèi shémma bù-'syǐhwan jèige lyǔ'gwǎn? /Didn't you have enough to eat? Nǐ méichr̀'bǎu ma? /I didn't say I liked him. Wǒ 'méishwō wǒ 'syǐhwan tā. /Don't lean out the window. Byé dzài 'chwānghu ner 'tànchuchyu. /In that case, don't do it. Yàushr 'nèmmaje, jyou béng 'gàn hǎu le. meaning Let it go. 'Nàmma jyou 'swàn le ba. or, meaning If you don't do it, that's your tough luck. 'Àigànbú'gàn. /But we DO want you. 'Búgwo wǒmen 'shr̀ jēn yàu nǐ ('búshr̀ 'jyǎde). /I do wish we could finish today. Wǒ 'jēnshr̀ 'pànje 'jīntyān néng dzwò'wán. /No matter what you say, I did see the man. Bù'gwǎn nǐ 'shwō shémme, wǒ 'shr̀ 'jyànle tā le. /You did say it! Nǐ 'shr̀ shwō-gwo!

5. Combinations of **do** with other words as **do good, do well,** etc. /He has

done a lot of good. Tā 'dzwòle hěn 'dwō de 'hǎu 'shr̀. (See 1 above.) / It will do you good. Yú nǐ yǒu 'hǎuchù. / But it didn't do me any good. 'Wǒ kě 'méidédau shémma 'hǎuchù. or Yú 'wǒ keshr méi shémma 'hǎuchù. or (if referring to medicine) 'Wǒ yùngle kě méi shémma 'syàu. / The drug does some good, but it's not a cure. Yàu yǒu dyǎr 'syàu, búgwo bùnéng 'wánchywán jr̀'hǎule. / It won't do any good to complain to the police. Gēn jǐng'chá 'bàuywàn 'méiyou shémme 'yùng. / A vacation will do you lots of good. Syēsye 'jyà hwèi gěi nǐ bù'shǎu 'yíchu. / He did pretty well by me. Tā 'dài wǒ hěn 'hǎu. / I see the army's done pretty well by you. Hē! Jyūn'dwèi 'dài nǐ hái bú'hwài. or Hē! Nǐ dzài jyūn'dwèi dāide hái bú'hwài. / He did pretty well for himself in politics. Tā dzài 'jèngjyè °gànde (°hwùnde) hěn 'hǎu. / He's out of danger now and is doing as well as can be expected. Tā méi 'wéisyan le, 'yíchyè dōu hái 'shwùnlì.

Do one's best jìnlì (dzwò or other verb). / I'll do my best to have it ready on time. Wǒ yàu 'jìnlì dàu 'shŕhou gěi 'yùbeichulai. / Do your best; that's all. Nǐ jìnlì 'dzwò jyou 'shr̀ le.

Do harm hài, shòuhài, yǒu hwàichu. / Will it do any harm if we talk the matter over? 'Tántan nèijyàn 'shr̀ yǒu shémma 'hwàichu ma? / His unfriendly report did our work a lot of harm. Tā nèige bàu'gàu gěi wǒmen shwō hwài'hwa laije, jyàu wǒmende 'gūngdzwò °dà shòu 'yǐngsyang (°shòu'hài bù'chyán). / The new tax has done a lot of harm to retail trade. Syīn'shwèi 'yǐjīng jyàu 'syǎumǎimai 'shòule bù'shǎude 'hài le. or Syīn'shwèi bǎ 'syǎumǎimai 'hàide bù'chyán. / He did us a lot of harm by refusing to testify for us. Tā bùkén tì wǒmen dzwò 'jyànjèng °jyàu wǒmen shòu'hài bù'chyán (°jyàu wǒmen dàshòuchí'hài, °jēn 'hàile wǒmen le).

Do away with chyǔsyāu. / They plan to do away with most of these regulations. Tāmen 'dǎswàn chyǔ'syāu yídàbàrde 'gwēijyu.

Do out of. / He did me out of ten dollars. Tā 'nùngle wǒ 'shŕkwài chyán chyu.

Do with (dispose of, use) bàn. / What can I do with the leftover vegetables? meaning How can I use them? or Where shall I throw them out? 'Shèngsyade 'tsài wǒ dzěmma 'bàn?

Do with (use, welcome). / We could do with several more people to come and help us. Dzài 'lái jige rén bāng'máng, yě hǎu.

Have something **to do with** (be related to) yǒu gwānsyi. / That has nothing to do with the question. 'Nèige gēn 'jèige wèn'tí méi'gwānsyi.

Do without. / Can you do without this pencil for a while? Nǐ néng 'dāi hwer dzài yùng 'jèijr̄ chyān'bi ma? / If we can't get fresh fruit, we'll have to do without. Yàu mǎibu'jáu 'syāngwǒdz, wǒmen jyou 'jr̀hǎu bù'chr̄. / I can't do without you. Méi 'nǐ bù'syíng. / We can't do without him. 'Wǒmen jèr méi 'tā °bù'syíng (°'bànbulyǎu).

Make something **do** tsòuhwo, dwèifu, jyāngjyan. / We'll have to make this do. Jèige méi fádz, jr̀hǎu °tsòuhwo (°etc.).

Will do (be O. K.) syíng, chéng, tsòuhwo, dwèifu, jyāngjyou. / Do you think this color will do? Nǐ jywède jèige 'yánsher 'syíng ma? / That'll do all right for us, but she's more particular. 'Wǒmen kéyi 'tsòuhwo, kěshr 'tā hen 'tyāuti. / That'll do! meaning It's OK. 'Syíng le. or 'Chéng le. or 'Hǎu le. or 'Yǒu le. or meaning It's enough. 'Gòu le. (or sarcastically) 'Déle ba. or 'Swànle ba! or 'Dzěmma 'méi'gòu a? or 'Hái bú'gòu ma? or Nǐ hái yǒuwán méi'wán a? / That'll do now; no more of that! Hái bú'gòu ma? Byé dzài °nèmmaje le (°'shwō le)!

6. Other English expressions. / Someone do something! 'Kwàije! 'Kwàije! / Yes, do! Hǎu'jíle! / I do! (Shr̀) 'jēnde! / I do (take this woman, etc.). Shr̀. / Well, I do. (spoken with emphasis on I) 'Wǒ kě 'nèmmaje. or 'Wǒ . . . (with

specific indication of what is done). /Do I? 'Wǒ? /Did I? meaning Did I say it? Shr̀ 'wǒ shwōde ma? or meaning Did I do it? Shr̀ 'wǒ nùngde ma? /Oh, I did, did I? Wǒ °'shr̀ nèmmaje laije (°'shr̀ . . . laije, °'shr̀ . . . le with specific indication of what is done) á! /Easy does it. (be careful) 'Syǎusyīnje. or (slower) 'Màn dyar. or (more lightly) Chǐng dyar. or (don't get excited) Byé 'hwāng. or Byé jāu'jí. /Do or die! Bú'nèmmaje jyou 'sz̆! /How do you do? 'Nǐ hǎu! or (when meeting somebody for the first time) Jyǒuyǎngjyǒu'yǎng.

Done (cooked, finished) done for, done in, done with. See DONE.

DOCTOR. (Medical) yīsheng, dàifu. /He's a doctor. Tā 'shr̀ ge °'yīsheng (°'dàifu). /Will you please send for a doctor? Láu nǐ 'jyà chyù 'jǎu ge 'dàifu lai. /Is there a doctor in the house? Dzài jèiyiwūdz rénli you °'dàifu (°'yīsheng) ma? /May I introduce Dr. Fáng. 'Jèiwèi shr̀ 'Fáng dàifu.

Doctor of Philosophy 'bwóshr. /He is a Ph.D. Tā shr̀ ge 'jésywé 'bwóshr. /May I introduce Dr. Féng. Lái, wǒ gei ni 'jyèshaujyèshau. 'Jèiwèi shr̀ 'Féng bwóshr.

To doctor (treat medically) jr̀. /I'm doctoring myself for a cold. Wǒde shāng-'fēng wǒ dz̀'jǐ 'jr̀ ne.

Doctor up. /The documents appear to have been doctored up. Jèijyàn 'gūng wén 'kànshangchyu hǎu'syàng yǒu rén gěi °dzwòle 'jyǎ le (°'gǎigwo). /The editor really doctored up the story for publication. 'Byānjí bǎ nèidwàr syīn'wén 'pūjāngde hěn 'dà.

DOG. gǒu. /Have you fed the dog? Wèi 'gǒule ma? or Gǒu 'wèile ma? /Please take the dog out for a walk. Dài gǒu 'chūchyu 'dzǒudzǒu.

Doghouse gǒuwō; be in the doghouse (fig.) shr̄chǔng. /He's in the doghouse now. Syàndzài tā shr̄'chǔng le.

Dog-tired lèipāsya. /They came in dog-tired after sightseeing all day. Gwàng-le yì'tyān tāmen dōu lèi'pāsyale.

Go to the dogs. /He used to be successful, but now he's going to the dogs. Tā yǐ'syàng hěn dé'yì, kěshr 'syàndzài °'twēitáng le (°'làudau le, °dǎu'méi le, °lè-'pwò le). /He thinks the world is going to the dogs. Tā syǎng 'jèige 'shr̀jye jyàn-'jr shr̀ hwún'jàng.

To dog bǐ. /They say they'll dog him until he gives in. Tāmen shwō yàu bǎ tā 'bǐdau °bù'dāying bù'jr̆ (°tā 'dāyingle wéi'jr̆, °tā 'dāyingle tsái swàn 'wán.

DONE. For most uses, see DO; the following are uses of DONE not common to DO.

(Cooked) déle, dzwòhǎule; well done shóu, hwǒhou dà; half done 'bànshēng-bù'shóude. /In ten minutes the rice will be done. 'Shŕfēn'jūngnèi fàn jyou °'déle (°dzwò'hǎule, °nùng'hǎule). /I want the meat well done. 'Ròu dzwò'shóu yidyǎr. or 'Ròu dzwòde 'hwǒhou 'dà dyar. /I don't want the meat well done. Ròu 'byé dzwòde 'hwǒhou tai 'dà le. or Ròu dzwòde 'hwǒhou 'syǎu dyǎr. /It was only half done when he served it. Hái 'bànshēngbù'shóude jyou gěi wǒmen 'dwānshanglaile.

Done for swàn wánle, swàn lyǎule, swàn wárwánle, swàn hwèile. /These tires are done for. Jèiji'tyáu 'chēdai °swàn 'wánle (°etc.). /If the boss finds this out I'm done for. Tóur yàu 'cháchulai, wǒ jyou swàn 'wánle.

Done in lèiszle. /I'm done in, working in all this heat. Dzài jèmma 'rètyārli 'gūngdzwò, wǒ 'lèiszle.

Done with shr̄wán, yùngwán. /Are you done with these scissors? Nǐ °shr̄'wán (°yùng'wán) jèibǎ 'jyǎndz le ma?

DOOR. mén, mér. / The dining room has two doors. 'Jèige fàn'tīng yǒu lyǎngge 'mén. / The china closet has two glass doors. Jwāng 'tsźchǐde 'gwèi yǒu lyǎngge 'bwōli mér. / Please open the door for me. Láu'jyà tì wǒ 'kāikai 'mén. or Láu'jyà gěi wǒ bǎ mén 'kāikai. / His house is three doors down the street from ours. Dǎ 'wǒmen jer wàng 'nèibyar 'shǔ, dì 'sānge dàmén jyòu shr tā 'jyā. or 'Tā jyā gēn 'wǒmen 'jyēje 'lyǎngge dàmén.

Outdoors (dzài) wàibyan. / Let's have the game outdoors. Dzámen dzài 'wài-byan 'wár ba.

Other English expressions. / If he gets insulting, show him the door. Tā 'yàu-shr 'wūrǔ rén jyou °chǐng tā 'chūchyu (°jyàu tā 'chūchyu, °bǎ tā 'gǎnchuchyu, (vulgar) °jyàu ta 'gwǔn). / His remarks closed the door to further discussion. Tā 'nèmma yìshwō, °jyou 'chále (or (local Peiping) °'yùngbujáu dzai 'tánle).

DOUBLE. (Twice as much) dwō(. . .)yibèi, jyābèi. / His income was double what he expected. Tāde shōu'rù bǐ tā 'yùlyàude dwō yí'bèi. / I'll double his offer. Wǒ jyā-'bèi chū'chyán. or Wǒ bǐ 'tā gěide 'chyán jyā'bèi. / He doubled my offer. Tā bǐ 'wǒ dwō 'chū yí'bèi de 'chyán. or Tā yàu bǐ wǒ dwō 'gěi yí'bèide 'chyán. / If you lose, you lose double. Nǐ yàu 'shūle, nǐ shūde jyou děi jyā'bèi. / Double (in bridge)! Jyā'bèi! / Redouble! Jyā'bèide jyā'bèi! but / Double the order! Jàu 'yàngr dzài 'yàu yí'fèr! or Jàu 'yàngr dwō 'lái yí'fèr! / He's doubled his capital in two years. Tā lyǎng'nyánde 'gūngfu jyou bǎ 'běnchyán 'jwànhweilaile.

(Involving two of something) lyǎng; double room lyǎngge rén jùde fángjyān, shwāng rénfangjyān; double bed shwāng ren chwáng. / May I have a double portion (two parts) of ice cream? 'Bīngjīlíng wǒ 'kěyǐ lái 'lyǎngfèr ma? / The double doors (lit. two-fan gate) open onto the terrace. Nèi 'lyǎngshàn 'mén 'chùngje 'shài-tái 'kāi. but / You must be seeing double. Nǐ yí'dìng shr °yǎn'lǐle (°yǎn'hwāle).

(Pair of) shwāng. / That word has a double meaning. Nèi shr yíge 'shwāng-gwān 'dzèr. / There's a double-track railroad between the two towns. Jèilyǎ chéng 'jrjyánde tyě'lù shr 'shwāng'gwěide. / et's play doubles. Dzámen dǎ 'shwāngdǎ ba. / The Double Tenth is the national holiday of the Republic of China. Shwāngshŕ-'jyé shr Jūnghwámín'gwóde gwóchìng'r.

(Of life). / He's leading a double life. Tā 'yánsyíng bù'fú. or 'Tā 'jyǎmàu wéi'shàn. or meaning He's keeping a mistress. Tā 'yǒu ge °'syǎugūng'gwǎn (°'wài'jyā).

To double (of fists). / He doubled his fists in anger. Tā 'chìde jŕ 'dzwàn 'chywántou.

Double (back) hwéi. / The burglar must have doubled on his tracks. Dzéi yí'dìng shr dzǒu 'ywánlù hwéichyule. / The road doubles back toward town. Jèityáu 'lù 'jwànhweilai hái hwéidau 'chéngli.

Double up. / There's only one room, so we must double up. Jŕ yǒu 'yìjyān 'kūng fáng, dzámen lyǎ rén děi jù yí'kwàr.

One's double. / He looks enough like you to be your double. Tā 'jǎngde 'syàng nǐ 'syàngdehěn, 'kéyi dzwò nǐde 'tǐshēn.

Other expressions in English. / He's doubled up with pain. Tā 'dùdz 'téngde °'wānje yāu (°'máuje yāu, °'jŕbuchi 'yāu lai). / Double time, march! 'Pǎubù, 'dzǒu!

DOUBT. (Not believe) búsyìn; doubt someone (suspect) 'yísyīn; but when saying doubt that . . . you have to say suspect that . . . not . . . , using a negative; not to doubt that

. . . (believe certainly) syāngsyìn . . . . /I don't doubt that in the least. Wǒ syāng-'syìn yí'dìng shŕ 'nèmma hwéi 'shèr. /I doubt if he meant it that way. Wǒ 'yísyìn tāde 'yìsz 'búshr nèmmaje. *or* Wǒ bú'syìn tā yǒu 'nèige yìsz. /I'm beginning to doubt his intentions. Syàn'dzài wǒ 'yǒu dyǎr °'yísyìn tā 'bùhwái hǎu'yì le (°bú-'syìn tā shŕ 'shànyìde le). /I don't doubt him at all. Wǒ yìdyǎr yě bù'yísyìn tā. /I don't doubt that he meant it. <u>meaning</u> what he said about the past. Wǒ syāng'syìn tā nà shŕ jēnsyìn'hwà. <u>meaning</u> what he threatened. Wǒ syāng'syìn tā 'jēn °yàu 'nèmmaje (°hwèi 'gàndechu'lái). / I doubt if the story is true. Wǒ 'yísyìn 'méiyǒu nèmma yi'hwéi shŕ.

Have doubts about <u>expressed as above</u>. /I still have some doubts about him. Wǒ 'hái yǒu dyǎr °'yísyìn ta (°bùnéng syāng'syìn tā).

No doubt yídìng, wúyíde, wúyíwèn. /There's no doubt about it. 'Háuwúyí'wèn. /No doubt the train will be late. Hwǒchē yí'dìng wùdyǎn.

Without doubt 'dāngrán. /Without doubt he's the best man for the job. Wèi dzwò nèijyàn 'shŕ jāu'syāng tā 'dāngrán shŕ dzwèi 'héshŕde rén.

Be in doubt bùyídìng. /The result is still in doubt. 'Jyēgwǒ hái bùyí'dìng.

Be in doubt about bù'jwǔn jŕdàu. /When in doubt about the enemy's intentions, it's best to strike first. Bù'jwǔn jŕdau 'dírénde lái'yìde shŕhou, háishr 'syānsyà-'shǒuwéi'chyáng.

DOUBTFUL. /I'm doubtful about when he plans to come. °Wǒ 'búdà 'jŕdàu (°Wǒ bù'jwǔn jŕdau) tā 'dàswàn 'shémma shŕhou lái. /It's doubtful whether he'll get well. Tā bùyí'dìng hǎude'lyǎu. *or* Tā 'yěsyǔ hǎubu'lyǎu le.

(Not beyond reproach) bùkěkàu, kàubujù. /The guides here are of doubtful character. 'Jèrde 'syāngdǎu 'dōu °bùkě'kàu (°kàubu'jù).

See also **DOUBT.**

DOWN. (To a lower place) syà. /Come down from there! 'Syàlai! /Step down! 'Syàchyu! /Sailing downstream is much faster. 'Syàshwéi dzǒude 'kwàide 'dwō. /Down! (lowering something) Dzài wàng °'syà dyar (°'dǐ dyar)! *See also* **LOWER.** / Lie down! (to a dog) 'Tǎngsya! /Sit down. 'Dzwòsya. *or* (in a greeting or invitation) Chǐng 'dzwò. /Is this elevator going down? Jèige 'dyàntī shŕ wàng 'syà chyù ma? /The shop went (sank) down with all hands, five miles offshore. Lyàn 'chwán dài 'rén dzài lí 'àn 'wǔlǐ dì de 'dìfang 'chénsyachyule. /Put on the brakes, or the car will roll down the holl. 'Gǎnjǐn tsǎi 'já, bùrán chē yàu 'gwǔnsya 'shān chyule. /This thing moves up and down. Jèige dūngsyi °yǐ'shàngyǐ'syàde (°shàng-syàde, °shàngshàngsyà'syàde) dùng. /He stepped down from the porch. Tā tsúng 'lyángtáishang 'dzǒusyalaile. /Swallow it down. 'Yànsyachyu. /Put that thing down. Bǎ nèige °'gēsya (°'fàngsya). /The price is going down. 'Jyàchyan dzài wàng syà °'làu (°'jyàng). *or* (without syà) 'Jyàchyan kàn 'làu. /Wait until the price has come down a little. Děngdau 'jyàchyan 'làusya dyǎr lai dzài 'shwō. /The balloon is coming down. Chìchyóu jèngdzai wàng syà °'làu (°'jyàng). /The mercury (in the thermometer) is coming down. Hánshǔ'byǎu dzài wàng syà °'làu (°'jyàng). /The sun is just going down. 'Tàiyang jèng wàng sya 'làu ne. /The sun has gone down. 'Tàiyang 'làule.

When the place or terminus is specific, **down** is not usually expressed separately. /Put the suitcase down there. Bǎ 'syāngdz °'gēdzai nèr (°'fàngdzai nèr). /The mercury went down to zero. Hánshǔ'byǎu làudau 'língdù le.

(Of directions or geographical locations) <u>the Chinese say **go down** only when the motion is actually downhill or away from Peiping; otherwise use go up, as we sometimes do in English, or neither.</u> /I went down (downhill or from Peiping) to Tientsin last week. 'Shànglibài wǒ syà 'Tyānjǐn le. /In the winter I go down (up) to Shanghai.

'Dūngtyande 'shŕhou wǒ shàng 'Shànghǎi. / I saw him walking down the street. Wǒ 'kànjyan tā wàng jyē 'neitóur dzǒu. / He lived down south two years. Tā dzài 'nánfāng jùle lyang'nyán. / It's way down that way. Dzài 'nèibyar 'ywǎnje ne. / They live down by the river. Tāmen 'jùdzai kàu hé'byàr nèr. / He comes down here once a week. Tā měilǐ'bài dàu jèr lái yí'tsż.

(Unfortunate). / Don't hit a man when he's down. Byé 'chǐfu dǎu'méide rén. / They used to be well off, but they're down and out now. Tāmen jyā yǐchyán hěn 'kwò, syàn'dzài °bàile (°bù'syíng le).

Down is sometimes expressed with syà when a physically lower place is not referred to. / Write down your address. Bǎ nǐde jù'jř 'syěsyalai. / The police took down his statement. Syún'jǐng bǎ tāde kǒugung 'jìsyalaile.

Down is not expressed at all in some cases, usually those in which it may also be omitted in English. / He fell down. Tā 'dǎule. / He lost his balance and fell down. Tā °shwāi'dǎule (°dyē'dǎule, °'shwāile, °'dyēle) ge 'jyāu. / He tripped and fell down. Tā °'bànle (°'hwále) ge 'jyāu. / He fell down on the floor. Tā 'dǎudzai dì'bǎnshang le. / She is loaded down with packages. Tā 'bàule yí'dàdzwēi 'dūngsyi.

Be down on (be disgusted with) tǎu yàn; (attack verbally) gūngji, mà. / The others are down on him because he can't keep his temper. 'Tāmen hěn tǎu'yàn tā 'yīnwèi tā jìng fā'píchì.

Boil down to, cut down to swǒdwǎn. / This report needs to be boiled down to half its length. 'Jèige bàu'gàu děi swǒ'dwǎn yí'bàr. / It boils down to this. 'Jyándwàn 'jyéshwō shř 'jèmmaje. or (local Peiping) 'Gwēile bāu'dzwēi shř 'jèmmaje.

Burn down shāuhwěi, shāutā. / The building has burned down. Jěng'gèr lóu dōu °shāu'hwěile (°shāu'tāle).

Calm down lěngjìng syalai. / I'll talk to you after you calm down. Děng nǐ 'lěngjìng syalai wǒ dzài 'gēn nǐ 'shwō. / Calm down! meaning Don't be excited! Byé 'hwāng! or meaning Don't be noisy! Byé 'chǎule!

Come down with (catch) jāu. / I'm coming down with a cold. Wǒ jāu'lyáng le.

Get down to. / Let's get down to work. Dzámen hǎu'hǎurde 'gàn yísyàr.

Go down (lose in card games) shū. / We went down two on the last hand. Shàng-yibǎ 'pái, wǒmen shūle °'lyǎngwǔn (°'lyǎngfù).

Pay down, pay . . . down (make the first payment) 'tóu(or 'dǐ)yítsż (syān) °'jyāu . . . (°'fù . . . , °'syà . . .) with 'dǐng chyán only; (pay cash) fù'syàn; or any of the other combinations plus -de chyán; or (deposit to reserve something) 'tóuyítsż 'jyāude 'dǐngchyán. / How much is the down payment? is expressed as How much must be paid down? Dìyítsż děi °jyāu (°fù, °syà) 'dwōshǎu ('dǐng)chyán? or Syān °jyāu (°fù) 'dwōshau 'chyán? or 'Syànchyán syān °jyāu (°fù) 'dwōshau? or 'Dǐng-chyán shř 'dwōshau? / They want half (paid) down and the rest in monthly installments. Tāmen yàu yí'bàr fùsyàn, 'shèngsyade àn 'ywè fēn 'chī gěi. or Tāmen 'syān yàu yí'bàr chyán, shèng- . . . . / You must pay five dollars down. Dǐ'yítsż nǐ děi °jyāu (°fù) 'wǔkwài chyán.

Up and down (back and forth). / He was walking up and down the room. Tā dzài 'wūli °'láihwéide 'dzǒu (°'dzǒuláidzǒu'chyù).

Up and down (better and worse). / Business goes up and down. 'Mǎimai yǒu 'péi yǒu 'jwàn. / He has his ups and downs. (emotionally, physically, financially, etc.) Tā yǒu shŕhou 'hǎu yǒu shŕhou 'hwài.

To down (consume) expressed with an appropriate verb plus syàchyu. / He downed (drank) his drink quickly. Tā bǎ 'jyǒu hěn 'kwàide 'hēsyachyule.

Down (of a bird) rwǎnmáur; **swan's down** tyānérúng. / This pillow is filled with swan's down. Jèige 'jěntou lǐtou 'jwāngde shř °'tyānéde rwǎn'máur (°tyāné-'rúng).

DOZEN. dá. / Please give me a dozen eggs. Gěi wǒ yídá jǐ'dzěr.

(Indefinite quantity). / There are dozens of people in line already. Yǐ'jīng yǒu hǎusyē rén °jàn'pái le (°'páicheng cháng'lúng le).

DRAFT. (Drawing power of a chimney) **have a draft** tūngfēng, tòuchyèr. / This chimney doesn't have enough draft. Jèige 'yāntung 'búda °tòu'chyèr (°tūng'fēng).

(Regulator to a furnace, fireplace, etc.) fēng mér. / Please open the draft of the furnace. Bǎ lúdzde fēng'mér kāikai.

(Breeze) fēng(kǒu). / I'm sitting in a draft. Wǒ dzwòdzai fēng'kǒushang le. / There's a draft here. Jèr yǒu 'fēng.

(Tentative sketch or outline) tsǎugǎur; **make a draft** meaning rough *or* first draft chǐ tsǎu, °dǎ (°chǐ) tsǎugǎur, ní gǎu. / He has made a draft of his speech. Tā bǎ 'yǎnjyǎng °'dǎle (°'chǐle) ge tsǎu'gǎur. / A draft has been made of it (but not in final form). Yǐjǐng chǐ 'tsǎu le. / Do you have a draft of your plan? Nǐde 'jìhwà yǒu ge tsǎu'gǎur ma? (but formally, a first draft is tsǎuàn.) / This is the first draft of the Constitution. Jèi shr 'syànfǎ dì'yítsz tsǎu'àn.

(Displacement, of a boat) chřshwěilyàng but not commonly used; replaced more frequently by **have a draft of** . . . chř . . . shwěi. / This boat has a draft of six feet. Jèige 'chwán chř shwěi 'lyòuchř. *or* Jèige 'chwán chř 'lyòuchřde 'shwěi. / What's the draft? Chř 'dwōshau shwěi? *or* Chřshwěi'lyàng shř dwōshau?

Bank draft hwèipyàu. / The bank will cash this draft for you. Nǐ jèijāng hwèi-'pyàu yín'háng kéyi gěi nǐ dwèi'syàn. / This draft is drawn on the Central Bank of China. 'Jèi shr yìjāng 'Jūngyāngyín'hángde hwèi'pyàu.

To draft (draw) hwà. / The plans were drafted in the engineer's office. Jèi tú shř dzài gūngchéng'shř nèr 'hwàde.

(Draw up a plan, a lecture, a document, etc.) ní, nǐ, nì, syě. / The plan of the offensive was drafted in the Pentagon Building. 'Gūngjǐde 'jìhwà shř dzài Wǔ-jyǎudà'shàli °níde (°'nì'dìngde, °ní'hàude). / The committee is drafting a message of welcome. Wěiywán'hwèi jèngdzai °syě (°nì) 'hwānyíng'tsź.

Be drafted (for military service) jēng; **draft board** bǐngyìjyú; **draft laws** bǐng-yìfǎ. / He's due to be drafted next month. Tā 'syàywè yàu bèi 'jēng chyù °'dāng-bīng (°fúbīng'yì). / The draft has taken half our men. is expressed as Half of our men have been drafted. Wǒmen jèr yíbàrde 'rén yǐjǐng bèi 'jēng chyu 'dāngbīng chyule.

DRAW (DREW, DRAWN). (Pull, drag, haul) lā; (only stationary things) jwài. / Two horses are used to draw that cart. Nàilyang 'chē yùng 'lyǎngpǐ ma 'lā. / Have you seen a dog-drawn cart? Nǐ 'jyàngwo 'gǒu lā de chē ma? / It took six horses for them to draw that piece of stone out. Tāmen yùng 'lyòupǐ mǎ bǎ nèikwai 'shřtou 'jwàikāide. / Draw it tight. Lā'jǐnle. *or* Jwài'jǐnle.

(Pull out from) chōu; (pull out using force) bá; (take out from a container with a small opening) tāu; (withdraw) twèi; (pull in) swō. / He drew out a piece of paper from the pile. Tā tsúng yǐdwēi 'jřli 'chōuchu yì'jāng lai. / Draw the sword out and look at the blade. Bǎ 'dāu °chōu (°bá, °lā)chulai, 'chyáuchyau nèige 'rèr. / He drew a piece of paper out of his pocket. Tā tsúng kǒu'dàrli 'tāuchu yìjāng 'jř lai. / He drew his hands out of his pockets. Tā bǎ 'shǒu tsúng kǒu'dàrli 'twèi chulaile. / Don't draw back your hand. Byé bǎ 'shǒu °'chōu (°'swō)hweichyu. / The turtle drew in its head. Nèige wūgwēi bǎ 'tóu 'swōjinchule. / When he drew out a knife, I shot him. Yīnwéi tā syān bá 'dāudz, 'swóyi wǒ ná 'chyāng 'dǎ tā.

(Of air or smoke) syī, chōu; (but referring to a chimney) tūngchyèr. /When it was over he drew a deep breath. 'Wánle yī'hòu, tā shēn'shēnde °'syīle (°'chōule) yìkǒu 'chì. /This pipe draws well. Jèige 'yāndǒu hěn hǎu'chōu. (syī would not be used here.) /This pipe doesn't draw. Jèige 'yāndǒu °'chōubujin 'yān lái (°'syībujin 'yān lai, °syību'jáu, °chōubu'jáu, (it is clogged) °'dǔjùle). /When the wind is in this direction the chimney draws well. Fēng wàng 'jèibyar gwā de 'shŕhou 'yāntung hěn tūng'chyèr. /The chimney doesn't draw well. 'Yāntung budà tūng-'chyèr.

(Attract) jāu . . . , yǐn . . . , 'jāuyǐn . . . , jyàu . . . ; the construction with each is cause someone to do something; (of a magnet) syī; draw a crowd or be a drawing card jyàu dzwòr. /This concert is sure to draw a big crowd. Jèige yīn-ywè'hwèi yídìng néng °jyàu 'dzwòr (°'jāu (or yǐn, or 'jāuyǐn or 'jyàu) hěn 'dwō rén lai ('tīng)). /Her little hat drew a lot of attention. Tā nèidǐng syǎu'màur hěn °'jāu (or 'yǐn or 'jāuyǐn or 'jyàu) rén jù'yi (°'jyàu rén 'kàn, °'jyàu rén 'chyáu). /She wears that on the street just to draw attention to herself. Tā chwānje 'nèige shàng'jyē jyou shř yàu °'jāu (or 'yǐn or 'jāuyǐn or 'jyàu) rén jù'yi (°jyàu rén dwō 'chyáu tā lyǎngyǎn). /His remark drew applause from the audience. Tā 'nèijyu hwà jyàu 'tīng de rén gǔ'jǎng. /The magnet draws these pieces of iron toward it. 'Syī-tyě'shŕ bǎ jèisye 'tyě kwàr 'syīgwolai.

(Take out money) chyǔ, chyǔchu. /I'll have to draw fifty dollars out of the bank. Wǒ děi tsúng yin'háng chyǔ wǔshrkwài 'chyán. /I've drawn most of my money out of the bank. Wǒde 'chyán chàbudwō dōu tsúng yín'háng 'chyǔchulaile. /You're overdrawn. Nǐ 'chyǔ de chyán gwòle 'shùr le. or expressed as Your deposit is insufficient. Nǐ 'tswún de chyán bú'gòu le.

(Collect interest) shēng. /I'm letting my money draw interest. Wǒ bǎ 'chyán 'tswúnchilai shēng °'lì (°'syī, °'lìsyī).

(Make pictures, maps, etc.) hwà. /Everybody can draw (pictures). 'Rénrén dōu néng hwà 'hwàr. /Won't you please draw me a map of the route? Nǐ 'néng bunéng bǎ lù'syàn gěi wǒ 'hwàchulai? /Draw a map. Hwà yìjāng dì'tú. /Draw a tiger. Hwà yíge 'hǔ. /Draw a circle. Hwà yíge ywán'chywār. /Draw a line here. Dzài 'jèr hwà yìtyáu 'syàn. /The officer drew a map. 'Jyūngwān 'hwàle yìjāng dì'tú.

Draw a blank pèngbì (run into a wall); pèng dǐngdz (run into a nail) báifèi 'shŕ (exert effort in vain). /He drew a blank everywhere he looked. Ta 'dàuchù °pèng 'bì (°'dǐngdz). /I drew a blank there. Wǒ 'pèngle ge 'dǐngdz. or Wǒ pèng-'bì le. or Wǒ 'báifèile yìhwéi 'shŕ.

Draw blood (bleed) lyóusyě, chūsyě. /The scratches were deep enough to draw blood. Jwāde hěn 'shēn °lyóu (°chū) 'syě le.

Draw conclusions 'dédàu jyē'lwùn, or expressed with 'kànfǎ (point of view), or 'jyànjyě (opinion). /They drew different conclusions from the same facts. Tsúng yí'yàngde 'shŕchingshang tāmen 'dédaule bù'túngde jyē'lwùn. /What conclusion can you draw from that? Tsúng 'nèijyan shř shang 'kàn, nǐ 'dédàu de jyē'lwùn shř 'shémma? /Each one will draw a different conclusion. 'Gèrén °dédàu de jyē'lwùn (°'kànfa, °'jyànjyě) bù'túng.

Draw the line. /You have to draw the line somewhere. (between right and wrong) 'Shŕfēi dzǔng děi 'fēn yisyàr. (set a limit) Dzǔng děi hwà ge 'jyèsyàn. /I draw the line right here! Wǒ jyòu'tszdǎ'jù! or Wǒ dàu 'jèr wéi'jř! or 'Nèm-maje wǒ jyou bú'gàn le!

Draw lots or straws chōu (tyáur), chōu (chyār), jwā (jyōur), nyǎn (jyōur). /Let's draw straws to see who goes first. Dzámen chōu 'tyáur kàn 'shwéi syān

487

'dzǒu. / He drew a winning number. Tā 'chōude hǎumǎr 'jùngle. / Would you like to draw for partners? Dzámen yíge rén 'chōu yijang 'pái, ná 'páide dà'syǎu lái dìng 'shéi gēn shéi yì'byǎr, hǎu buhǎu?

Draw water dǎ(shwěi); (with a rope) syì. / Go out and draw a bucket of water. 'Chūchyu 'dǎ yìtǔng 'shwěi lai. / The rope they use for drawing water is too short. Tāmen °syì (°dǎ)'shwěi yùng de 'shéngdz tài 'dwǎn. / They drew him out of the well with a rope. Tāmen yùng 'shéngdz bǎ tā tsúng 'jǐngli 'syìshanglaile.

Draw so much **water** chī shwěi. / On this river a boat has to draw less than three feet. Dzài 'jèityau 'héli chwán chī'shwěi bùnéng 'gwò 'sānchī.

Draw back twèi. / Suddenly he drew back into the shade. 'Hūrán tā twèihwei hēi'yéngrli chyule. / The enemy drew back to his second line of defense. Dírén 'twèidau dì'èrtyáu 'fángsyàn.

Draw into (enter) jìn. / The train is just drawing into the station. Hwǒ'chē gāng jìn 'jàn.

Draw near or to kwài(dàu) le. / The train is drawing near the station. Hwǒ-'chē kwài dàu 'jàn le. / The time is drawing near. Kwài dàu 'shŕhou le. / The campaign is drawing to a close. 'Jìngsywǎn kwài 'jyéshù le. but / Draw near the fire. Kàu hwǒ 'jìn dyar.

Draw out (encourage) yǐnje, yǐnchu. / I did my best to draw him out. Wǒ syǎng-'jìnle 'fāngfa °'yǐnje tā shwō 'hwà (°bǎ tāde 'hwà 'yǐnchulai).

Draw up (drive up and stop) kāigwo, kāidau. / Just then a car drew up. 'Jèng-dzai nèi shŕhou yílyang chì'chē 'kāigwolaile.

Draw up an object lāgwo, lādau. / Draw up that table. Bǎ (nèijāng) jwōdz 'lāgwolai. / He drew the blanket up under his chin. Tā bǎ 'tǎndz lādau syàbakéer ner le.

Draw up a report syě. / As soon as I get the information I'll draw up a report. Wǒ 'dédau 'tsáilyau yǐ'hòu, 'lìshŕ syě yíge bàu'gàu.

A draw (in games, etc.) 'píngshǒu (between sides); **end in a draw** píng, °'méi (°bù)fēn shèng'fù. / The game ended in a draw. 'Jyēgwǒ °'píngle (°méifēn shèng'fù). / They fought to a draw. Tāmen 'dǎle ge °'píngshǒu (°bùfēn shèng'fù). but (in Chinese chess) / It's a draw. Shŕ 'héchi. or 'Héle. / The opposing team won the draw. Wèi tyàur 'byǎr jwā'jyǒur 'dwèifāng 'yíngle.

Drawback 'dwǎnchù. / That's his drawback. Nèi shr tāde 'dwǎnchù.

Drawbridge 'dyàuchyáu.

DRAWER. 'chōutì. / My passport is in the top drawer. Wǒde hù'jàu shŕ dzài 'tǒu-yìtséng 'chōutìli. / This drawer is stuck. Jèige 'chōutì °'kāibukāi (°'lābuchu'lái, °'jwàibuchulái, °gwānde sž'jǐn). / Pull out that drawer. Bǎ nèige 'chōutì °'lā (°'chōu)chulai.

Drawers (garment) 'chènyī. / He advised me to wear heavy drawers. Tā 'chywàn wǒ chwān 'hòude chènyī.

DRAWN. See DRAW, except for the following uses in which draw is impossible.

Long drawn-out. / This will be a long drawn-out battle. Jèiyí'jàng děi 'dǎ syē 'rdz.

Drawn with pain. / Her face was drawn with pain. Tā 'lyǎnshang 'dàije hěn 'tùngkǔde 'yàngdz. or 'Téngde tā 'lyǎn dōu gǎile 'yàngr le. or Téngde tā 'yǎuyá lyě'dzwěi.

DREAM. mèng. /I had a strange dream last night. Wǒ dzwór 'wǎnshàng 'dzwòle yíge hěn chí'gwàide 'mèng. /It could happen only in a dream. Jr̄ you 'mèngli tsái hwèi yǒu 'nàyangde shr̀. /That's only a dream. 'Búgwo shr̀ ge 'mèng. /In the dream I seemed to have walked miles and miles. Dzài 'mèngli wǒ °hǎusyàng (°'fǎngfú) dzòule 'hěndwōhěn'dwōde 'lù.

To dream dzwòmèng, mèngjyàn. /Last night I dreamed I was home. Dzwór 'wǎnshang wǒ 'mèngjyan dzài 'jyāli. /I dreamed of you. Wǒ 'mèngjyan 'nǐ le. /I've been dreaming (thinking) about buying a car. Wǒ 'dzwòle 'bùshǎu 'rdz mǎi 'chē de 'mèng le.

Daydream. /Don't waste time daydreaming. Byé °'húsyǎng le (°'húsz̄lwàn-'syǎng le).

Other expressions in English. /I wouldn't dream of doing that. Wǒ 'jywé bu-hwèi gàn 'nèige. /Their new house is a dream. 'Tāmende syīn 'fángdz jēn shr̄ shwōbu'chūde 'hǎu.

DRESS. (Woman's garment) yīfu, yīshang. <u>These words may also refer to clothing in general, and so may designate other garments as well. The measure jyàn, however, specifies a single garment rather than an outfit; and since most other garments have special terms, these will usually be understood to mean</u> **a dress.** /She wants to buy a new dress before she leaves. Tā yàu dzài méi'dzǒu yǐ'chyán mǎi yíjyàn syīn °'yīfu (°'yīshang). /That looks like a cool dress. Nèijyàn °'yīfu (°'yīshang) 'kàn-shangchyu hěn 'lyángkwài.

(Clothing, style). /She appeared in students' dress. 'Chūlaide shŕhou tā °chwānje 'sywésheng 'yīfu (°chwānje 'sywésheng 'jwāng, °yìshēn 'sywésheng 'jwāng-shù, °yìshēn 'sywésheng 'dàbàn).

(Formal) lǐfú; (military) 'jyūnlǐfú, chywǎnfù jyūnjwāng. /The reception is a dress affair. Tsānjyā 'hwānyíng'hwèi děi chwān lǐ'fú. /It's a dress parade. Jèi-tsz̀ yóu'syíng yàu chwān°'jyūnlǐfú (°chywánfù jyūn'jwāng). /You have to go in full dress. Nǐ 'chyù de shŕhou, děi chwān °chywānfùjyūn'jwāng (°'jyūnlǐfú).

To dress (put on clothes) chwān (put on, wear, must be followed by a word for clothes); **get dressed** 'dàbàn (includes toilet preparations and all the trimmings). /I'm not dressed yet. Wǒ hái méichwān'hǎu 'yīfu ne. /We've got to dress (put on evening clothes) for the occasion. 'Jèitsz̀ dzámen děi chwān lǐ'fú. /I'll have to dress up to go there. Wǒ děi 'chwānshang lǐ'fú tsái néng chyù 'nèr. /It took her a whole hour to dress. Tā 'jěng 'yùngle yíge jūng'tóu tsái 'dàbàn'hǎu.

(Decorate) jwāngshr. /They dress the store windows in the evening. Tāmen 'wǎnshang bǎ 'chwānghu 'jwāngshrchilai.

(Treat medically) shàngyàu. /When was this wound dressed? Jèige 'shāng shr̀ 'shémma shŕhou °'shàngde 'yàu (°bāuchilaide)?

(Of poultry) <u>In China, only live poultry is retailed;</u> **dressing** <u>must be expressed by more detailed words, such as</u> slaughter dzǎi; pluck twèi, <u>etc.</u> /Does he sell dressed chickens? Tā mài dzǎi'hǎule twèi'gānjingle de 'jǐ ma? /You have to dress the chicken yourself. Nèijr̄ 'jǐ nǐ děi dz̀'jǐ chyu 'dzǎi, dz̀'jǐ chyù twèi'gānjing le.

DRILL. (Boring tool) dzwàn. /They need another drill. Tāmen děi dzài yàu yíge 'dzwàn. /The bit in this drill has got to be changed. Jèibǎ dzwànde 'tóur děi 'hwànle.

To drill (bore) dzwǎn, kāi (open); dzáukai (punch open, drill with considerable force). /The dentist has to drill (a hole in) this tooth. Yá'yī děi bǎ jèige 'yá dzwǎn yíge 'kūlung. /The engineers are planning to drill a tunnel. Gūngchéng'shr̄ dzài 'jĭhwà °kāi yíge 'swéidàu (or (especially through rock) °dzáukai yíge 'swéidàu, or (with a machine drill) °yùng 'jĭchĭ kāi yíge 'swéidàu). / They are drilling for oil (opening an oil well). Tāmen dzài kāi yóu'jĭng.

(Train or practice) lyàn followed by a term designating the persons trained, as drill soldiers lyàn 'bĭng; or designating the thing practiced as drill in typing lyàn dă'dz̆; drill in a military sense is either practice drilling lyàn'tsāu, or go to drill shàng'tsāu. / He'll drill us in typing every day. Tā měi'tyān jyàu wǒmen lyàn dă-'dz̆. / The officer is drilling his men. Jyūn'gwān dàije tāde 'bĭng lyàn'tsāu ne. / We drill every day on that field. Wǒmen měi'tyān dzài 'nèige tsāu'chǎngshang lyàn 'tsāu. / They're tired of drilling. Tāmen lyàn 'tsāu lyàn'nìle. / The soldiers have (go to) drill at 8 A.M. and 2 P.M. 'Bĭng (měi'tyān) 'dzǎuchen 'bādyǎn gēn 'syàwu 'lyǎngdyǎn shàng 'tsāu.

DRINK (DRANK, DRUNK). hē. / Drink plenty of water. 'Dwō hē 'shwěi. or 'Hē hěn dwō 'shwěi. / Don't drink too much at the party. Fù'hwèi de shŕhou shǎu 'hē dyǎr. / He drinks too much (liquor). Tā hē 'jyǒu hēde tài 'dwō.

  Drink to (toast). / Let's drink to your speedy return. 'Jù nĭ 'dzǎu dyǎr 'hwéi-lai.

  A drink. / May I have a drink of water? is expressed as I want a little water to drink. Wǒ yàu dyǎr 'shwěi hē. or Wǒ syǎng hē dyǎr 'shwěi.

  (Liquor) jyǒu. / Can I bring you a drink? Yàu 'jyǒu ma? or Lái bēi 'jyǒu hǎu buhǎu?

DRIP. dĭ, dĭda. / His clothes are dripping wet. Tāde 'yīshang shŕde jŕ dĭ(da) 'shwěi. / Let it drip for a while. Dzài 'dĭ yihwĕr.

DRIVE (DROVE, DRIVEN). (Operate a vehicle) gǎn (if horse-drawn); kāi (if mechanical). / He drives a cart. Tā gǎn 'chē. or Tā shŕ ge gǎn'chēde. or Tā gǎn 'mǎchē. / The car was driven by a woman. Nèige 'chē shŕ ge 'nyǔrén 'kāide. / Can you drive a truck? Nĭ hwèi kāi 'dzàijùngchē ma? / I don't know how to drive (a car). Wǒ búhwèi kāi 'chē. / Let's drive (a car) out into the country. Dzámen kāi chē dàu 'syāngsya chyù ba.

  (Take a person somewhere in a vehicle) dài (coming or going); sùng (going only); jyē (coming only). / I'll drive you over. Wǒ °'sùng (°'dài) nĭ chyu. / I can call for you and drive you back. Wǒ kéyi chyù 'jǎu nĭ, bǎ nĭ °'jyē(°'dài)hwei-lai. / The boss drove me home in his new car. Wǒde 'shàngsz yùng tāde 'syīnchē bǎ wǒ 'sùnghwéi 'jyā chyule.

  (Hammer) dĭng. / Drive the nail into the wall. Bǎ 'dĭngdz dĭngdau 'chyángli chyu.

  (Screw) nĭng. / Drive the screw straight. Bǎ lwósz'dyĭngr nĭng'jèngle. / I can't drive this screw in. Jèige lwószdyĭngr wǒ nĭngbu'jĭnchyu.

  (Force to do something) bĭ; (urge, hurry) tswēi; and other less direct ways of saying it. / Hunger drove him to stealing. Jīhán 'bĭde tā dzwò 'dzéi or Tā °'chyúng-de (°'ède) dzwò 'dzéi. or Tā °'chyúngde (°'ède) méi'fár le, jyou 'bèi 'bĭde dzwò 'dzéi. / The foreman drives the workmen continually. Gūng'tóur lǎu °'tswēi-je (°'bĭje) gūngrén dzwò'gūng.

  Drive away, drive out, etc. gǎn; (by force; impolitely, impatiently) hūng, (local Peiping) nyǎn. / They drove him out. Tāmen bǎ tā °'gǎnchuchyule (°'hūng-chuchyule, °'nyǎnchuchyule). / Drive the dogs away. Bǎ gǒu °'hūng(°gǎn)dzǒu. / He's using a fan to drive the flies away. Tā yùng 'shàndz °gǎn (°hūng) 'tsāng-yíng ne. / They drove the cattle this way. Tāmen bǎ 'nyóu gǎndau 'jèibyar laile. / The crowd was driven back. Nèichyún 'rén gěi °'gǎn(°hūng)hweichyule. / The cows were driven to pasture. Bǎ nyóu gǎndau tsǎu'dǐli chyule. *but* / The soldiers drove (fought) the enemy back. Jyūndwèi bǎ 'dírén 'dǎhweichyule.

Drive (road) mǎlù. / The drive goes around the lake. Nèityáu mǎ'lù shr̀ 'wéije hú'byār dzǒu.

(Vigor, energy). / He has a lot of drive. Tā hěn yǒu °gǔdz 'gànjyèr (°'jīngshen).

(In tennis, golf, etc.) chōu. / He has a powerful drive. Tā 'chōu chyóu chōude hěn °'yǐng (°'chùng).

(Concerted effort put forth) yùndung. / The town is staging a drive to raise money for the poor. Nèige dìfang 'jèngdzai 'jyǔsyíng mù'jywān 'yùndùng gěi 'chyúng rén jywān 'chyán.

Go for a drive. / Would you like to go for a drive in my car? Nǐ 'ywànyi dzwò wǒde chē 'chūchyu °'wár yiwár ma (°'dōudōu'fēng ma)?

Other English expressions. / He drives a hard bargain. (lit.) Tā jyǎng'jyàr jyǎngde tài 'kè le. (lit. or fig.) Tā jǐng yàu jàn 'pyányi. / We made our way home through a driving rain. Wǒmen 'màuje yíjèn 'bàuyǔ hwéi 'jyāde. / What are you driving at? Nǐ °shr̀ (°'yǒu) shémma 'yìsz?

DRIVER. (Of a coach or cart) gǎnchēde; (of a motor-driven vehicle) sz̄jǐ, kāichēde, 'chēfū. / He's a cart driver. Tā shr̀ ge gǎn'chēde. / Where's the driver of this car? °Sz̄jǐ (°Kāichēde, °'Chēfū) nǎr 'chyùle?

DROP. (Fall) dyàu. / The pencil dropped out of my hand. 'Chyānbǐ tsúng wǒ 'shóuli 'dyàuchuchyule. / Something dropped on his hat. 'Yǒu dyǎr shémma 'dyàudzai tā 'màudzshangle. / Let it drop. Jyàu jèige 'dūngsyi dǐjǐ 'dyàu.

(Let fall, set aside) rēng (throw); pyē (fling); lyàu (set aside, leave); dyōu (let go, lose); gē (put); fàng (place); or appropriate combinations with syà (down), or kāi (away). / I dropped the letter in the street. Wǒ bǎ 'syìn dyōudzai dà'jyēshang le. / Drop the letter in the box. Bǎ 'syìn gēdzai syìn'syāngli. / Drop anchor! Dyōu'máu! or Pāu'máu! or Syà'máu! / Drop the anchor overboard. Bǎ 'máu rēngdzai 'shwéili. / I can't just drop my work and go with you. Wǒ bùnéng bǎ wǒde shèr °'dyōusya (°'lyàusya, °'pyēsya, °rēngsya, °'gēsya), jyou gēn ni 'dzǒu. / Why don't you drop her? Dzěmma nǐ bùbǎ tā °'dyōukai ne (°'pyēkai ne)? / Let's drop the subject for the time being. Dzámen bǎ jèijyàn shèr °'gēsya (°'fàngdzai yǐ'byār, °'dyōukai, °'lyàusya) yǐ'hòu dzài 'shwō. or Dzámen jàn'shŕ 'syān bùtǎu'lwùn °jèige 'wèntí (°jèijyàn 'shèr).

(Fall down, fall over) pāsya. / The messenger dropped from exhaustion. Sùngsyìnde lèide 'pāsyale.

(Go down, of temperature) jyàng. / The temperature dropped very rapidly. 'Wēndù 'jyàngde hěn 'kwài.

(Omit) chyǔsyāu. / Drop every other letter and you can read the code. Fān dyàn'mǎr de shŕhou 'jyē yíge 'dzèr °chyǔ'syāu yige (°nyàn yige).

A drop of fluid dǐ. / There isn't a drop of water left. Lyán yǐ'dǐ 'shwěi yě méi'yǒu le. / Put two drops of medicine in a glass of water. Yìbēi 'shwéili dǐ 'lyǎngdǐ 'yàu (jyou 'gòule). / Just a few drops. 'Bùgwo jǐ'dǐ. / Put in a few drops. Jr̀ 'gē jǐ'dǐ. *but* / A few drops of rain fell. 'Dyàule jige yǔ'dyǎr.

Other English expressions. / If I don't pay my dues I'll be dropped from the club. Wǒ 'rúgwǒ bùjyāu hwèi'fèi, 'hwèili jyòu yàu bǎ wǒ kāi'chúle. / From the second floor there is a drop of twenty feet to the ground. Dì'èrtséng lóu lí 'dǐ yǒu 'èrshrchǐ gāu. / Please drop me (off) at the corner. Wǒ dàu lù'kǒur nèr 'syàlai.

/Drop in to see me tomorrow. Míngtyān lái 'jyàn wǒ. /I dropped off to sleep immediately. Wǒ lǐ'kè jyou shwèi'jáule. /She dropped a hint that she wanted to go. Tā 'hwàli dàije yàu 'dzǒude 'yìsz. /Lemon drops are my favorite candy. Wǒ dzwèi 'syǐhwan chř níng'méng táng'chyóur. /He'll fight at the drop of a hat. Tā 'dùng budùng jyòu dǎ'jyà.

DROVE. (Herd) chyún. /There was a drove of cattle crossing the road. Yǒu yìchyún 'nyóu tsúng jèityau lù jer héngje 'chwāngwochyule.

See also **DRIVE.**

DROWN. (Die by drowning) yānsz. /Many people have drowned at this beach. Jèige hǎi'byārshang 'yānszgwo bùshǎu 'rén. /You shouldn't have drowned the kittens. Nǐ bùyǐng'gāi bǎ nàsyē syǎu'mǎur 'yānsz.

(Covered with water) yān. /The field was drowned out by the spring rains. Jèipyàn 'dì jyàu 'chwūntyande 'yǔshwěi gěi 'yānle.

Drown out (of sound) gài, yā. /The noise drowned out his remarks. 'Dzá-lwànde 'shēngyīn bǎ tāde hwà °gàijùle (°'yāsyachyule).

Drown one's sorrows. /He's just trying to drown his sorrows. Tā búgwò shř syǎng syāu'chóu jyòu shř le.

DRUG. yàu; (intoxicating drug, sleep-producing drug, or anesthetic) 'míyàu, 'méngyàu; (paralyzing drug or local or general anesthetic) 'máyàu; **poisonous drug** 'dúyàu, yǒu-'dúde dūngsyi; **to drug** syà °yàu (°etc.); **drugstore** yàufáng; (Chinese medicine store) yàupù. /This drug is sold only on a doctor's prescription. Jèige 'yàu děi yǒu 'dàifu kāi 'fāngdz tsái néng 'mài. /Opium is a (medical) drug. Yǎ'pyàn shř yìjǔng 'yàu. /Opium is a (poisonous) drug that has ruined I don't know how many people. Yǎ'pyàn shř yìjǔng yǒu'dúde dūngsyi, bùjřdàu hwēile 'dwōshǎu rén le. /He's a drug addict. is expressed as He has the habit. Tā yǒu 'shřhau. or expressed by a pun meaning both addict and recluse. He's a gentleman of peculiar habits. Tā shřge 'yǐnjyūn'dz.

To drug is expressed as **give a drug** gěi . . . °yàu (°etc., see above) *or as* **put a drug into something** bǎ . . . syà °yàu (°etc.). /They drugged his coffee. Tāmen bǎ tāde jyā'fēili 'syàle 'yàu le. /They drugged him. Tāmen gěi tā °'míyàu chřle (°'méngyàu chřle, °'máyàu chřle, °'dúyàu chřle (depending on the kind of drug). /He thought he'd been drugged. Tā 'jywéje yǒu rén gěi tā shàng °'méngyàu (°etc.) le.

Other expressions in English. /I felt drugged with sleep. Wǒ kwùn'jíle. /This year grapes are a drug on the market. 'Jīnnyan 'pútau 'kě jēn 'dwō.

DRUM. (Percussion instrument) gǔ; **sound of a drum** 'gǔshēng, 'gǔsyǎng; **drummer** gǔshǒu, chyāugǔde, dǎgǔde; **drumbeat** gǔdyǎr. /Please don't give our boy any more drums for Christmas. Yǐhòu Shèngdàn'jyé chyān'wàn byé dzài sùnggei wǒmen nèige háidz 'gǔ le. /This drum needs fixing. Jèige 'gǔ děi 'syōulisyōuli le. /We have eight drums, but no drummer. Wǒmen yǒu 'báge gǔ kěshr méiyou °hwèi 'chyāu de (°hwèi 'dǎ de, °gǔ'shǒu, °chyāu'gǔde, °dǎ'gǔde). /Can't you hear the drums yet? Nǐ hái 'tīngbujyàn 'gǔsyang ma? /The drums are fading out. Gǔ'shēng jyàn'jyānde syǎudau tīngbu'jyàn le. /He can't follow the beat of the drums. Tā 'gēnbushàng gǔ-'dyǎr.

(Container). /They unloaded six drums of gasoline. Tāmen 'syèle 'lyòutǔng chì'yóu.

To drum (tap) chyāu. /Please stop drumming on the table. Chǐng nǐ 'byé chyāu 'jwōdz.

Drum into. /These rules have been drummed into me. Nàsyē 'gwēijyū wǒ 'tīngle bùjŕdàu yǒu 'dwōshau hwéi le. *or* Tāmen bǎ nèisye 'gwēijyū 'lyǔtszsān-'fānde 'shwōgei wǒ 'tīng.

Drum up. /He's trying to drum up trade. Tā dzài nèr syǎng 'fár °'jānglwo 'mǎimai ne (°'lā 'mǎimai ne).

DRUNK. (Be intoxicated) dzwèi, hēdzwèile. /He got drunk. *or* He's drunk. Tā °dzwèile (°hē'dzwèile). /He gets drunk every night. Tā 'měityān 'wǎnshang dōu hē'dzwèile. /He looks like he's drunk. Tā 'hǎusyàng shŕ °dzwèile shŕde (°hēdzwèile 'jyǒu shŕde, °dà 'hēle yí'jèn le).

(Fig.). /He's hard to work with because he's drunk with power. Gēn tā hěn 'nán gùng'shŕ, yīnwèi tā °ài 'déyi wàng'syíng (°tài 'báhù, °yǒu dyǎr 'syǎurén dé-'jŕ). /They were drunk with joy at the outcome of the trial. Shěn'pànde 'jyēgwǒ ràng tāmen °'hwānsyǐde 'lyǎubùdé (°'hwānsyiszle, °hwānsyǐde yàu'sž).

A drunk (person) dzwèigwěi. /We had trouble with a drunk. Yíge dzwèi'gwěi gēn wǒmen dǎu'lwàn laile.

DRY. (Not wet) gān, bùshŕ; (not damp) bùcháu; **keep dry** from rain méilínjau, méilwúnjau. /Change into some dry clothes. 'Hwànshang dyǎr °gān yīshang (°bu'shŕde yīshang). /Are your clothes dry? Nǐde yīshang gānle ma? /These towels are still damp; get some dry ones. Jèisyē 'shǒujin hái 'cháu ne; ná dyǎr °'gānde lai (°bù'cháude lai). /I wore a raincoat and kept dry. Wǒ 'chwānje yǔ'yī laije, °'shēnshang méi'shŕ (°lǐtou méi'línjau, °'lǐtou méi'lwúnjau). /The streets are dry now. 'Jyēshang syàndzài 'gānle. /The well's gone dry. Jèige 'jǐng 'gānle.

(Of weather) hàn, dwǎn 'yǔ(shwěi), chywē 'yǔ(shwěi) (arid); **dry air** gānshwangde kūng'chǐ. /It's been a dry summer. Jīnnyan 'syàtyān hěn °'hàn (°dwǎn 'yǔ(shwěi), °chywē 'yǔ(shwěi). /After the long rains this dry air feels swell. Syàle 'jèmmasyē shŕhou de 'yǔ le, jèijǔng 'gānshwangde kūng'chǐ jyàu rén jywéde jēn 'shūfu. /The weather is very dry there. is expressed as It doesn't rain very often there. Nèige dìfang bùcháng syàyǔ.

(Thirsty) ke. /I'm dry; let's have a drink. Wǒ yǒu dyǎr 'kě, dzámen 'hē dyǎr shémma ba.

(Not giving milk). /The cow has been dry a month. Jèityóu 'nyóu yíge 'ywè °méi 'nǎi le (°bùchū 'nǎi le).

(Not sweet) bùtyán. /I'd like a good dry wine. Wǒ yàu bù'tyánde hǎu 'jyǒu.

(Boring) 'gāndzàuwú'wèi. /The lecture was so dry that I walked out. Yǎn'jyǎng 'gāndzàuwú'wèi, wǒ jyou 'dzǒule.

Dry land àn, lùdì. /It's good to be on dry land after such a long voyage. Dzài 'shwěishang dzǒule jèmma 'jyǒu, yíshàng °'àn (°'lù'dǐ) jēn 'shūfu.

To dry (by fire or heat) kǎu, hūng, kǎugān, hūnggān; (in the sun) shài, shàigān; (by airing) lyàng, lyànggān; (in the wind) chwēi, chwēigān. /Have your clothes dried out? (by fire) Nǐde yīshang °kǎu'gānle ma (*or* (by heat) °hūng'gānle ma, *or* (by sun) °shài'gānle ma, *or* (by airing) °lyàng'gānle ma, *or* (by the wind) °chwēi'gānle ma)? /Dry yourself by the fire. Nǐ dàu 'hwǒ nèr chyù 'kǎu yikǎu. /The paint dried in five hours. is expressed as The paint was dry in five hours. Yóuchǐ 'wǔge jūngtóu jyou 'gānle. /Every summer this stream dries up. is expressed as Every summer this stream is dry. Yídàu 'syàtyān jèityáu hé jyou 'gān le.

(Wipe; dishes) tsā. /Who's going to dry the dishes? Shéi lái tsā 'dyédz?

Dry up (stop talking). /Tell him to dry up. Jyàu tā byé 'shwō le. *or* Jyàu tā byé 'dāudau le. *or* Jyàu tā jù'dzwèi ba.

Dried (dehydrated; of foods) gār. /Give me a pound of dried apples. Gěi wǒ yíbàng 'pínggwǒ'gār.

DUCK. (Fowl) yādz. / My father brought home three ducks. 'Fùchin dàile 'sānjr̄ 'yādz hweilai. / We're having roast duck for dinner. 'Wǎnfàn wǒmen chr̄ °'kǎuyādz (°'shāuyādz). / Don't walk like a duck waddling along. Dzǒu'lù byé syàng yige 'yādz 'jwǎi a jwǎide. / A duck quacks. 'Yādz 'gwā'gwāde 'jyàu.

(Cloth) 'fānbù, 'syéwénbù. / Lots of summer clothes are made of white duck. 'Syàtyānde 'yīshang hěn dwō shr̄ °'bái fǎn'bù (°'bái syéwén'bù) dzwòde. / He's wearing white ducks. Tā chwānde shr̄ °'báibù (°'bái fǎnbù, °'bái syéwén'bù) 'kùdz.

To **duck** (lower the head or body quickly) dǐtóu. / Duck your head! 'Dǐ yidǐ 'tóu ba!

(Plunge in and quickly withdraw) twēi, èn. / Let's duck him in the lake. Dzá-men bǎ tā 'twēidau °'húli chyu ba (or (in the water) °'shwéili chyu ba). or (hold under water a while) Dzámen bǎ tā 'èndzai 'shwéili 'gwàn ta yisyàr. but / He took a quick duck in the lake. Tā 'yísyàdz jyou 'dzwānjìn 'húli chyùle.

(Get away from). / Let's duck him. Dzámen bǎ tā 'shwǎikai ba. or Dzámen 'dwōkai tā ba. / Let's duck out of here. Dzámen tōu'tōurde 'chūchyu ba. or Dzá-men 'lyōuchuchyu ba. or Dzámen 'dwōchuchyu ba.

DUE. (Owed) gāi, chyàn; (overdue, to a person) méifàgei. / I have three weeks' pay due me. Wǒ hái yǒu 'sānge lǐ'bàide °'syīnshwei (°'gūngchyan, °'syàng) méi'fàgei wǒ ne. or Hái °'gāi wǒ (°'chyàn wǒ) 'sānge lǐ'bàide °'syīnshwei ne (°'gūngchyán ne, °'syang ne). or Wǒ hái yǒu 'sānge lǐ'bàide °'chyàn'syīn (°'chyàn'syàng).

(Deserved). / Gratitude is due him. °'Yīnggāi (°'Yīngdāng) 'gǎnjī ta. / Grati-tude is due these retired veterans who defended our country. Jèisyē 'bǎuwèi 'gwó-jyā de 'twèiwǔ 'jyūnrén, wǒmen °yīnggāi (°yīngdāng) 'gǎnjī. / Respect is due these men. Jèisyē rén wǒmen 'yīnggāi 'dzwūnjìng. or Jèisyē rén 'jŕde wǒmen 'dzwūn-jìng. / We should pay him due respect for his courage. Tāde 'yǔngchì °'jŕde wǒmen 'pèifu (°wǒmen 'yīngdāng 'pèifu). / I pay him due respect. is expressed as He deserves my respect. Tā 'jŕde wǒ 'dzwūnjìng. or as I respect him. Wǒ hěn 'dzwūn-jìng tā. or as I pay him as much respect as he is worth. Wǒ syàng'dāngde 'dzwūn-jìng ta. / With due respect for your learning, I can't agree with you on this point. Nǐde 'sywéwèn wǒ hěn 'pèifu, búgwo 'jèiyìdyǎn wǒ bùnéng gēn nǐ túng'yì. or Wǒ búshr bú'pèifu nǐde 'sywéwèn, búgwo 'jèiyìdyǎn wǒ gēn nǐde 'yìjyàn bùyí'yàng.

(Straight, in one direction) yìjŕ. / Go due west and you'll hit the river. Nǐ yì'jŕ wàng'syī dzǒu jyou dàu 'hébyār le.

Be due, come due (with the thing due as object) (yǐng)gāi jyāu, yàu jyāu; (arrive) yīngdāng dàu; (arrive at the day, with the thing due as subject) dàu chī, dàu r̀dz; **be overdue** gwò chī, gwò r̀dz. / The rent will be due again next Monday. Syà lǐbài'yī yòu °gāi (°yàu) jyāu 'fángchyan le. / The train is due at noon. Hwǒ-chē 'yīngdāng 'jūngwǔ 'dàu. / The rent was due five days ago. 'Fángchyan 'wǔtyān yǐ'chyán jyou ('yīng)gāi 'jyāu le. / Your report is due tomorrow. Nǐde bàu'gàu 'míngtyān gāi 'jyāu le. / Your note will be due soon. Nǐde 'jyèywē kwài °dàu 'chī le (°dàu 'r̀dz le). / Your insurance payment is overdue. Nǐ gāi 'jyāu de bǎusyǎn-'fèi yǐjing gwò 'chī le. or Nǐde 'bǎusyǎn 'yǐjīng 'gwòle jyāu'kwǎnde 'r̀dz le.

Due to. *See* **BECAUSE.** / His death was due to malaria. Tā (yīnwei) fā'yàudz 'sž̀de. / His failure is due to overcautiousness. Tā (yīnwei) tài dǎr'syǎule, swǒyǐ tsái shr̄'bài de. or Tā shr̄'bàide 'ywányīn shr̄ 'tài dǎr'syǎu le.

One's due. / You must give a person his due (treat him fairly). Dài 'rén děi 'gūngpíng. / You have to give each person his due. is expressed as Treat a per-son the way you judge him. Dài rén 'hǎu'hwài, děi fēn 'rén lái. or as Each person has his good points and his bad points. 'Shéi dōu yǒu 'chángchu, yǒu 'dwǎnchu.

Dues hwèifèi. / The dues are five dollars a year. Hwèi'fèi shr̀ 'wǔkwài chyán yì'nyán.

DULL. (Not sharp) dwùn; (of an edge only) búkwài, méi rèr; (of a point only) bùjyān; (edge only, when it is bent) jywǎnle 'rèr le; (edge only, when it is chipped) bēnle 'rèr le. / This knife is dull. Jèibǎ 'dāu °dwùnle (°bú'kwài, °yǒu dyǎr 'dwùn (a bit dull), °búdà (°bùhěn) 'kwài (a bit dull), °méi 'rèr le). / This needle is awfully dull. Jèige 'jēn °hěn 'dwùn (°hěn bù'jyān).

(Of light or colors; general descriptions) fāhwēi, fāwū, búlyàng, 'àn(dàn), 'wū-chīmā'hēide; (technical definitions) dull green 'hwēilyù(shǎr); dull red 'hēihúng(shǎr); (pig-liver color) jūgānshǎr. / That's a sort of dull green. Nèi shr yìjǔng bú'lyàngde 'lyùshǎr. / That green is too dull. Nèijǔng 'lyùshǎr tài °'àn(dàn) le (°bú'lyàng le, °fā'hwēi le, °'wūchīmā'hēide, °fā'wū le). / The floor is painted a sort of dull red. Dì'bǎn 'yóude shr yìjǔng °'hēi'húngshǎr (°jū'gānshǎr). / They have only a dull light to see by. Tāmende 'dēng °bú'lyàng (°hěn 'àn(dàn), °'wūchīmā'hēide).

(Of day or sky) 'hwūnchénchénde, 'yīnchénde. / If it's a dull day, let's not go. Tyār yàushr °'hwūn(°'yīn)chénchénde, dzámen jyou byé 'chyù.

(Of sound) 'tài bú'tswèisheng, bēng a 'bēngde, pū'tūngputūngde. / The dull thumping of that drum depresses me. Nèige 'gǔ chyáude °'tài bú'tswèisheng le (°bēng a 'bēngde, °pu'tūngputūngde), jyau rén 'tīngje 'mèndeheng.

(Of pain). / She feels a dull pain in her chest. Tā jywéje syūng'kǒu mènbujìde 'téng. / It's a dull sort of pain. 'Téng, kěshr bú'lìhai.

(Of persons; uninteresting, stodgy, foolish) dāi, mù, shǎ, nyé, °'dāi(°'mù, °'shǎ, °'nyé)le gwǎngjìde, °'dāi (°etc.)bujìde, yǒu dyǎr °'dāi (°etc.), fā°'dāi (°etc.), méi'yìsz; (in studying) bèn, bùtsūngming; (of speech) méiyìsz, 'dāiban. / He's dull. 'Tā nèige rén °méi'yìsz (°'mùbujìde, °'shǎlegwǎngjìde, °etc.). / Their son is a dull student. 'Tāmen nèige háidz nyàn 'shū hěn °'bèn (°bù'tsūngming). / His talk is very dull. Tā shwō 'hwà shwōde °hěn méi'yìsz (°hěn 'bèn, °hěn 'dāiban). / Our neighbors are nice but dull. Wǒmende 'jyēfang 'rén hái bú'hwài, 'jyòushr °méi shémma 'yìsz (°yǒu dyǎr fā'nyé, °etc.).

(Of an event) méiyìsz, méijìn, 'kě jyàu rén 'mènszle. / What a dull evening! 'Jèiyi'wǎnshang °'jēn méi'yìsz (°jēn méi'jìn, °'kě jyàu rén 'mènszle).

Dull thud (resonant) 'bēngde yi'shēng, 'pēngde yi'shēng; (heavy) pū'tūng yi'shēng; (of a flat thing) pā'jìde yishēng; (as a pail of water on the ground) 'pūde yi'shēng; (as cards on a table) kwā'chā yi'shēng; (as a door closing) gwā'dā yishēng; (as a door closing in an empty place) kwāng'dāng yishēng, gwāng'dāng yishēng, 'gwāngde yi'shēng. / The book hit the floor with a dull thud. Shū 'bēngde yi'shēng jyou dyàudzai dì'bǎnshang le.

To dull (something) bēn, nùngdwùnle. / Don't cut the nail with the knife; it'll dull the blade. Byé ná 'dāudz lá 'dīngdz; děng yihwěr bǎ 'rèr °'bēnle (°nùng'dwùnle).

Dull one's appetite (seriously) bǎ 'wèikou nùng'hwàile; (mildly) jyàu . . . 'bùsyǎng chr̄ 'dūngsyi. / A cigarette might dull my appetite. Chōu'yān yěsyǔ 'hwèi jyau wǒ 'bùsyǎng chr̄ 'dūngsyi le. / I think that drug dulled my appetite. Wǒ syǎng nèige 'yàu bǎ wǒde 'wèikou nùng'hwàile.

DURING. (Of a period that has to be specified at some length; not regular units) (dzài . . . de shŕhou the addition of dzài puts more emphasis on the particular period; during the day báityan(li); during the night (dzài) yèli; during a year yìnyánli. / I met him during the last war. 'Shàngtsz dàjànde shŕhou wǒ 'rènshrde ta. / It was during the last war that I met him. Wǒ 'rènshr tā shŕ dzài shàngtsz dà'jànde shŕhou. / We were close friends during school days. Wǒmen dzài sywé'syàu de shŕhou °shŕ hěn 'hǎude péngyou (°'hěn 'shóu). (In this sentence the dzài goes with sywé'syàu, not with the whole construction.) / He eats five times during the day. Tā 'báityan chř 'wùtsż.

DUST. tǔ, chéntǔ; (only in the air or settled on furniture) 'hwēichén. / She swept the dust under the rug. Tā bǎ 'tǔ dōu sǎudau 'dǐtǎn 'dǐsya chyule. / The car raised a cloud of dust. Chǐ'chē °'yángchilai (°jywánchilai) yíjèn °'hwēichén (°chén'tǔ). / Look at the coat of dust on the window sill! 'Chyáu chwānghu'társhang nèitséng °'tǔ (°chén'tǔ)! / The bureau has collected a layer of dust as thick as a silver dollar. 'Gwèishangde °'tǔ (°'chén'tǔ, °'hwēichén) 'jǐde yǒu yǐkwài 'chyán nèmma 'hòu. / Dust shows clearly in a beam of sunlight. 'Hwēichén dzài yídàu ř'gwāngli syàndè hěn 'chīngchu. / The dog must have rolled in the dust. Gǒu yí'dìng shř dzài °'túli (°'chéntúli) dǎ'gwěr laije.

Bite the dust. / The enemy sniper in the tree bit the dust. meaning tumbled down Nèikē 'shùshang 'tsángje de nèige 'díbīng °'dǎsyalaile (or meaning was killed °'dǎszle, or meaning was wounded °'dǎshāngle).

To dust (with a duster) dǎn, dǎnpu; (with a cloth) tsā, 'gāntsā. / Please dust my desk. (Ná 'dǎndz) bǎ (wǒde) 'jwōdz °'dǎnyidǎn (°'dǎnpudǎnpu). or (Yùng'bù) bǎ (wǒde) 'jwōdz °tsā yitsā (°'gāntsā yisyar).

DUTY. (Natural, common responsibility) 'běnfèn, yǐng'jìnde 'běnfèn, 'běnfènli 'yīnggāi dzwòde 'shř. / It's your duty as a citizen to buy bonds. Mǎi gūng'jài shř nǐ dzwò gūng'mín yǐng'jìnde 'běnfèn. / To help one's younger brother is one's duty. Bāng dż-'jǐde 'dìdi shř 'běnfènli 'yīnggāi dzwòde 'shř.

(Social; under specific circumstances, duty toward others) 'dzérèn, 'yìwù. / It's your duty to have your children educated. Jyàu nǐde 'háidzmen shòu 'jyàuyù shř °nǐde 'dzérèn (°nǐ yǐngjìnde 'yìwù).

(Particular duty in a job) 'gūngdzwò, shèr; 'rènwù (military). / What are your duties as a secretary? Nǐ dāng 'shūjì dōu °yǒu shémma 'gūngdzwò (°dzwò shémma 'shèr)? / Answering the phone is one of my duties. Tīng dyàn'hwà yě shř wǒde 'shèr. / It's not my duty to clean the wastebaskets. Dàu fèi'jř 'búshr 'wǒde shèr. / What is the duty of the officer of the day? Jřřgwānde 'rènwù shř 'shémma?

(Customs). / How much duty on this tobacco? 'Jèijǔng yān shàng 'dwōshǎu 'shwèi?

Go off duty 'syàgūng, 'syàbān, 'wánshèr. / I go off duty at 5:30. Wǒ 'wǔdyǎnbàn °syàgūng (°syàbān).

Go on duty 'shàngbān. / I go on duty at 8:30. Wǒ 'bādyǎnbàn shàng'bān.

Be on duty 'jřbān. / Who's on duty now? Syàndzài 'shéi jřbān?

EACH. měi, yǐ; for emphasis 'měiyi; less often gè. / How many beds are there in each room? 'Yìjyān 'wūdz yǒu 'jǐjāng chwáng? / Issue three of these to each person. 'Jèige, měi'rén gěi 'sānge. / Please give me one sheet from each pile (of papers). 'Měiyi'dwēili chǐng nǐ 'gěi wǒ yì'jāng / I want one copy of each of the books on this book-list. Jèijang shū'dārshangde shū, wǒ 'měijǔng yàu yìběr. / Please give me one of each kind. 'Yíyàngr 'lái yíge. or Wǒ 'yíyàngr 'yàu yíge. / Each of these men has his own peculiar temperament. 'Jèisyē rén 'gè(rén) yǒu gè(rén)de gwài'píchi. / Each country has its own customs. 'Gègwó you gègwóde 'fēngsu. or 'Yìgwó yǒu yìgwóde 'fēngsu. or 'Gèchù'fēngsu bù'túng.

(Apiece) yí'gè. / These apples are a penny each. 'Jèisyēge 'pínggwo yifēn 'chyán yí'gè.

Each of us (you, them) wǒmen (nǐmen, tāmen) °měirén (°gèrén).

Each other bitsz, hùsyāng; <u>or indirect expressions</u>. /We don't understand each other. Wǒmen bǐ'tsz bù'mínglyǎu. *or* (if the misunderstanding is one of language) Wǒmen shwōde 'hwà bǐ'tsz bunéng 'dǔng. / They're accusing each other in court. Tāmen dzài 'fǎtǐng hùsyāng 'gàufā. / They just look at each other. <u>is expressed as</u> They're facing one another and looking. Tāmen 'gwāng dzài ner 'dwèije 'kàn. /They're killing each other! (of a fist fight) Tāmen pīnle'míngle dǎ'jyà!

See also **EVERY**.

EAGER. (Want very much) 'hěn syǎng. /I am eager to meet your friends. Wǒ 'hěn syǎng jyànjyan nǐde 'péngyou. /He's eager to learn. Tā 'hěn syǎng sywé. /I'm eager to get home. <u>is expressed as</u> I want to get home as early as possible. Wǒ yàu 'dzǎu dyar dàu'jyā. (but note the following, when the action has already taken place): /He has been quite eager to learn so far, but we'll have to wait and see. <u>is expressed as</u> Up to now he's exerted a great deal of effort in learning, still we must wait and see what it will be like. Tā dàu syàn'dzài 'sywéde háishr hěn chǐ'jyèr, yǐ'hòu dzěmmayàng jyòu děi 'dzǒuje 'chyáu le.

EAR. ěrdwo. /My ear hurts. Wǒ 'ěrdwo téng. /He pricked up his ears as soon as they lowered their voices. Tāmen shwō'hwà de 'shēngyin 'gāngyi 'dīsyachyu, tā jyòu 'jīlengje ěrdwo yàu 'tīng. /She spoke something in his ear and he smiled. Tā dzài tā ěr'byānshang 'syǎushēngr shwōle dyǎr mar, tā wēi'wēide yísyàu.

(Head of grain) swèr; *but* **ear of corn** yùmǐbàngr. /The ears of wheat are nearly ripe. Mài'swèr kwài 'shóu le. *or* 'Màidz kwài syóu'swèr le.

An ear for music. /I don't have an ear for music. <u>is expressed as</u> I don't understand music when I hear it. 'Yīnywè wǒ 'tīngbù'dǔng. <u>or as</u> /I don't know how to enjoy music. Wǒ 'búhwèi 'syīnshǎng 'yīnywè.

An ear to the ground. /He keeps his ear to the ground. <u>is expressed as</u> He's very careful to learn other people's opinions. Byérénde 'yìjyàn, tā hěn 'lyóusyīn yàu 'jīrdau.

A deaf ear. /He turned a deaf ear to all their pleas. <u>is expressed as</u> He pretended he didn't hear what they pleaded. Tāmen 'dzěmma chyóu tā jyóushr 'jwǎng tīngbu'jyàn.

All ears. /Go on with your story; I'm all ears. <u>is expressed as</u> Continue with what you were saying; I'm here listening. 'Jyēje 'shwōsyachyu ba, wǒ jèr 'tīngje ne.

Burning ears. /Were your ears burning last night? Dzwór 'wǎnshang nǐ 'ěrdwo °fā'shāule ma (°fā'rèle ma)? (In Chinese this means either that someone was talking about you or that someone was thinking about you.)

EARLY. (Sooner than expected or sooner than normal) dzǎu. /You are early. 'Dzǎu a. /Am I too early? Wǒ °'láide (°'dàude) tài 'dzǎu le ma? /He always arrives early. Tā 'láushr 'dzǎu dàu. /It's still early. Hái 'dzǎu ne. /He arrived very early today. 'Jīntyan tā dzǎu'dzāurde jyòu 'dàule. /Be sure to get here as early as possible. Yí-'dìng dzǎu'dzāurde 'chǐlai a. *or* 'Chǐlaide 'néng dwō 'dzǎu jyòu dwō'dzǎu. *or* 'Chǐlaide ywè 'dzǎu ywè 'hǎu. /I'll be there early. Wǒ yí'dìng 'dzǎu dyǎr 'dàu. /Please call me early Láujyà 'dzǎu dyǎr jyàu wǒ. /You are two minutes early. Nǐ 'dzǎule 'lyǎngfēn jūng. *or* Nǐ 'tài dzǎu le, 'dzǎule 'lyǎngfēn jūng. /Let's not get there too early. Wǒmen byé °'chyù(de) (°'dàu(de)) tài 'dzǎule. /He's been arriving earlier than before. Tā 'láide bǐ yǐ'chyán 'dzǎu(dyǎr) le. /Let us have an early reply from you. Chǐng 'dzǎu °dyǎr 'dáfù (°dyǎr 'hwéidá, °gěi 'hwéisyìn, °lái 'hwéisyìn). /Spring is early this year. 'Jīnnyan 'chwūntyān láide 'dzǎu.

(First of two or more) dzǎu, 'tóuyī, dìyī. (In combinations such as these, dzǎu often refers to morning, rather than merely to first.) /What time does the early show

begin? (morning show) °'Dzǎuchǎng 'dyànyǐngr (or, meaning the first show in the afternoon or evening °'Tóuyichǎng 'dyànyǐngr, °Dǐ'yīchǎng 'dyànyǐngr) 'jǐdyǎn jūng 'kāishř?
/ Has the early mail come? (morning mail) 'Dzǎubān de syìn 'láile méiyou?

    (First part of) often dzǎu, but also expressed by other terms; early life 'dzǎu-
nyán, 'syǎu shŕhou; early morning 'chīngdzǎu, 'dàdzǎu; early evening pàngwǎn.

    Early in (a certain period) gāng . . . bù'jyǒu (with a verbal expression enclosed);
or expressed as in the early years of . . . 'chūnyán. / He went to school early in the
Chinese Republican period. Tā Míngwó 'chūnyán shàngde 'sywé. / He was wounded
early in the war. Ta shr gāng kāi'jàng bù'jyǒu shòude 'shāng.

    Early in the afternoon (hardly past noon) 'gāng gwò 'jūngwǔ. / The boat docked
early in the afternoon. Chwán kàu 'mǎtou de shŕhou, 'gāng gwò 'jūngwǔ.

    Early in the day dzǎuchen. / The boat docked early in the day. Chwán 'dzǎuchen
kàude 'mǎtou.

    Early in the evening (not long after dark) tyān 'gāng hēile bù'jyǒu. (used in sen-
tences as with early in the afternoon.)

    Early in the month ywèchū; in the early months 'tóujige'ywè.

    Early in the morning (very early, 5 or 6 A.M.) 'chīngdzǎu, 'dàdzǎu; (about 7 to 9
A.M.) dzǎuchen.

    Early in the season 'chūX or 'Xchū (X represents the name of a season); (for
spring and fall only) 'dzǎuX, gāng dàu 'Xtyān de shŕhou, gāng rù 'Xtyān de shŕhou.
Or use the term for the first month of any season, which in the lunar calendar is two
months before the corresponding month in the Western calendar.

    Early in the year (in January and February) 'Jēng èrywèli; (spring) chwūntyan;
(not long after the passing of the year) nyánchū, 'gāng gwònyán bù'jyǒu; early in 1968
'yījyòulyòu 'bā nyán 'gāng gwònyán bù'jyǒu (or with either of the other phrases after).

    See also **SOON**.

EARN. (Financially, be paid) jèng (of wages, salary, and fees only); jwàn (also of profit).
/ How much do you earn a week? Nǐ yíge lǐ'bài °jèng (°jwàn) 'dwōshau chyán? / The
boy earned fifty cents by mowing the lawn. 'Nèige háidz twēi'tsǎu jèngle 'wǔmáu
chyán. / He didn't earn that wealth; he inherited it. Tāde chyán 'búshr 'dzjǐ 'jèng-
laide; shr 'chéngshòulai de.

    (Fig. merit) sometimes translated by words meaning deserve, sometimes by
literary expressions. / He earned his reputation. Tā 'míngfùchí'shr. or Tā 'míng-
bùsyū'chwán. or Tā 'shŕdzài 'pèi shòu rén nèmma 'chēngdzàn. / He didn't earn his
reward. Tā 'wúgūngshòu'shǎng. or Tā shòu 'nèiyàngde 'shǎng yǒu dyǎr bú'pèi.
/ His behavior earned him the respect of everyone. Tāde 'syíngwéi 'rénren dōu 'pèifu.

EARTH. (As a planet) dìchyóu. / The earth is mostly covered with water. Dì'chyóushang
'dwōbàn shř 'shwěi.

    (Ground) dì. / There are many treasures buried in the earth. °Dì'dìsya (°Dì-
'lǐtou) máije 'hěn dwò 'bǎubei.

    (Dirt) tǔ. / These holes must be filled with earth. Jèisyē 'kūlung děi ná 'tǔ
°'dùshang (°'tyánshang). / There is a thin layer of earth on top of the rock. 'Yánshŕ-
shang yǒu báu'báude yìséng 'tǔ.

    (World) 'shřjyè (the inhabited world); tyāndìsya (that which is under heaven);
'rénjyān (among men). / There is nothing on earth like it. °'Shřjyèshang (°Tyān'dìsya,
°'Rénjyān) (jyòu) 'méiyǒu 'jèiyàngrde °'shř (°'dūngsyi).

On earth (added for emphasis). /What on earth is that? (showing merely surprise) 'Āiya! 'Nà jyàu 'shémma a? *or* 'Āiya! 'Nà shr̀ ge 'shémma ya? (showing disapproval) 'Hāi! 'Nà jyàu 'shémma a? /What on earth did you do that for? (mild) Nǐ 'dzěmma 'nèmmaje a? (with strong disapproval) Nǐ 'nèmmaje dàu'dǐ shr °'dzěmmage 'yìsz a (°'wèide 'shémma)? /Who on earth could have seen that far ahead? °'Shéi yòu (°Shémma rén) néng 'jyànde 'nèmma 'ywǎn ne? /Where on earth did you buy that? 'Āiya 'nǎr mǎi de?

Back to earth *or* down to earth. /The trip was very pleasant, but now we have to get back to earth. 'Jèiyítsz̀ lyǔ'syíng wárde hěn gāu'syìng; syàn'dzài kě děi °'gāi gàn shémma 'gàn shémma le (°shōu'syīn le). /Oh, come back to earth! <u>meaning</u> Stop dreaming! 'Hāi! 'Byé dzwò'mèng le. <u>or meaning</u> Let's talk sense 'Hāi! Shwō jèng'jǐng de. *or* 'Hāi! Shwō jēn'gé de. /He has a down-to-earth attitude. Tā hěn 'shr̀shr̀ chyóu'shr̀ de.

EASILY. (Without difficulty) 'rúngyì, bùnán, bùféishr̀, *or* bu <u>plus other words for</u> difficult *or* hard. /It's easily done. Hěn 'rúngyì. *or* Bùféi'shr̀. /I learned it quite easily. Wǒ 'rúngrungyì jyòu sywé'hwèile. *or* Wǒ sywéde hěn 'rúngyì. *or* Wǒ sywéde bùféi'shr̀ /I learned how to ride a bicycle quite easily. Wǒ sywé chí 'dz̀syíngchē sywéde °'hěn rúngyì (°'hěn bùféi'shr̀). *or* Wǒ 'rúngrúngyì'yìde jyòu °bǎ chí 'dz̀syíngchē sywé'hwèile (°sywé'hwèile chí 'dz̀syíng'chē le). /He doesn't make friends easily. Tā °bù'rúngyì (°hěn 'nán) jyāu 'péngyou. *or* (with the additional idea that he doesn't care to) Tā bù °'chǐngyì jyāu 'péngyou (°'swéisweibyan'byànde jyāu 'péngyou).

(Beyond question). That is easily the best I've seen. <u>is expressed as</u> Among all I've seen, that is much better than the others. Dzài wǒ swǒ'jyàngwo de 'lǐtou, 'nèige bǐ 'byéde dōu 'hǎude 'dwō.

(Very possibly) hěn 'kěnéng. /We are expecting him, but he could easily be late. Wǒmen dzài jèr jèng 'děngje tā 'lái, kěshr̀ °tā hěn 'kěnéng lái 'wǎnle (°tā 'jyòusyǔ hwèi lái 'wǎnle).

See also EASY.

EAST. dūng; east end dūngtóur; southeast dūngnán; northeast dūngběi; Far East Dūngfāng, Ywǎndūng; Near East Jìndūng. /An east wind usually comes up in the afternoon. 'Píngcháng 'syàwǔ °chǐ (°gwā) 'dūngfēng. /Where do I turn east? Wǒ dzài 'nǎr wàng 'dūng gwǎi? /We get most of our tea from the East (the Orient). Wǒmen hē de 'chá °'dwōbàn (°'dàbàn) dōu shr̀ tsúng 'Dūngfāng lái de. /The plane is north by east of the airport now. Jèige 'fēijī syàndzài shr̀ dzài fēijīchǎngde běiwēidūngde fāngsyàng.

(Indicating a part or area) dūngbù, dūngbyār, dūngfāng. /I lived in the east (part of a certain country) for ten years. Wǒ dzài °'dūngbù (°etc.) °jùle (°jùgwo) 'shr̀nyán.

(Indicating an area beyond a border) dūngbyār; (to the) east of . . . dzài . . . (de) dūngbyār. /It's just east of the highway. (Nèi) jyòu dzài gūnglù(de) 'dūngbyār yìdyār.

EASTERN. dūng; eastern Asia dūngyǎ; eastern China 'Jūnggwode 'dūngbù; the Near Eastern question 'Jìndūng 'wèntí.

The Eastern Church Syīlàjyàu.

See also EAST.

EASY. (Not difficult) 'rúngyì, bùnán; (requiring little effort) bùféishr̀. In a few combinations, hǎu (good) is used. /English would be easy for you. Nǐ sywé 'Yīngwén yīngdāng hěn 'rúngyi. /It looks easy, but actually it's quite complicated. 'Kànje rúngyi, chí'shŕ hěn 'máfan. /He is easy to see or to approach. Tā 'rúngyi jyàn. /It isn't so easy as that. 'Méi nèmma 'rúngyi /Bicycling is easy to learn. Chí-'dzsyīngchē °'rúngyi (°'hǎu) sywé. /He's easy to deal with. Tā 'rúngyi dádyan. or Tā 'hǎu bàn. /Is it easy? Nèige 'rúngyi ma? or Nèige 'rúngyi bùrúngyi. /It's very easy. 'Hěn 'rúngyi. or Yì'dyǎr yě bù'nán. /It's easier said than done. °'Shwōje (°'Kànje) rúngyi, 'dzwòchilai jyòu 'nán le.

(Comfortable) shūfu; **easy chair** 'shūfude 'yǐdz. /He leads an easy life. (in regard to physical comforts) Tā 'gwòde hěn 'shūfu. (in regard to mental attitude) Tā 'syīnli hěn 'shūfu.

(Of writing). /He writes in an easy style. Tā 'syěde °'hěn 'lyóulì (°'hěn 'tūngshwùn).

(Not harsh, hurried, etc., especially in such expressions as take it easy). /Take it easy! or Easy! meaning Don't hurry. Byé 'máng! or Màn'mārde! or meaning Don't be excited! Byé 'hwāng! or Byé 'hwāngjāng! or Byé jānghwang! or 'Chénjùle 'chǐ! or meaning Don't be noisy! Byé 'nàu! or Byé 'chǎu! /Easy does it! meaning Go slowly! Màn'mārde! or meaning Be careful! 'Syǎusyīnje dyar! or Lyóu'shen dyǎn! /Let's take things easy (slowly). Dzámen màn'mārde dzwò. /His manners are free and easy. Tā ('tàidù) hěn °syāusǎ (°'dàfāng, °'swéibyàn, °'bùbǎi 'jyàdz, °'dzrán). /Go easy on the sugar; it's hard to get. 'Shěngje dyar °yùng 'táng (°'chŕ'táng); hěn nán 'mǎidàu ne. /Take it easy on your sprained ankle. Nǐ 'nyòule de 'jyǎu yàu °'shǎu yùng (°'syǎusyīnje). /She's easy on the eyes. Tā 'jǎngde hěn shwùn'yǎn.

Easygoing. /Their boss is very easygoing. (good-natured) Tāmende 'tóur °'hěn hǎu shwō'hwàr (°'píchì 'hěn hǎu, °hǎu 'píchyèr, °hěn 'héchi, °'syīn hěn 'kwāndàde).

Easy street. /He has been living on easy street since his father died. Tā 'fùchin yǐ 'sž, tā jyòu 'gwòchǐ 'shūfu 'ŕdz laile.

See also **HARD, DIFFICULT.**

EAT (ATE, EATEN). (As a particular action, or to eat a particular thing) chŕ. /I want something to eat. Wǒ yàu 'chŕ dyǎr 'dūngsyi. or Wǒ 'yàu dyǎr 'chŕde 'dūngsyi. /Did you eat that? 'Nèige nǐ shŕ 'chŕ le ma? /Have you really eaten that? Nèige nǐ 'jēn 'chŕle ma? /Are these good to eat? meaning Do they taste good? 'Jèisyē 'dūngsyi °hǎu 'chŕ ma (°hái 'chŕde ma, or meaning Are they edible? °'néng chŕ ma, °'chŕde ma)? /He likes to eat it raw. Jèige tā ài °chŕ 'shēng de (°'shēng(je) chŕ). /They ate up everything. Tāmen 'dōu gěi chŕ'gwāngle.

(To have a meal) chŕfàn, occasionally chŕ alone. /Where shall we eat after the show? Kàn'wánle dyàn'yǐng dàu 'nǎr chŕ'fàn ne? /Have you eaten? Chŕ'gwò (fàn) le ma? /We take turns eating. Wǒmen 'lwúnbār chŕ'fàn. /Shall we eat out tonight? Jyēr 'wǎnshang 'chūchyu chŕ('fàn), 'hǎu ma? /Are we going to eat out tonight? Jyēr 'wǎnshang wǒmen dzài 'wàitou chŕ'fàn ma?

(Fig.). /What's eating you? Nǐ 'dzěmma la? or Nǐ shēng 'néiméndz 'chì a? or Nǐ wèi'shémma 'byènyou? /She is eating her heart out. Tā 'shàngsyīn'jíle.

Eat up (damage, destroy). /The rifle barrel was eaten up with rust. Chyāng-'gwǎndz dōu 'syòude bùchéng'yàngr le. /The clothes were eaten up by moths. 'Yī-shang jyàu 'chúngdz dōu gěi °'chŕle (°'dǎle).

EDGE. byār, byān (most general term; refers particularly to the area near the edge or the side surface; see also below). /It is on the edge of town. Dzài chéng'byārshang.

/She moved the glass from the edge to the center of the table. Tā bǎ bwōli'bēi tsúng jwōdz'byār nar nwódau dāng'jūng chyule. /Don't fall over the edge of the rock. Byé tsúng shŕtou'byārshang 'dyàusyàchyu. /Keep away from the edge of the platform. Lí 'táibyār 'ywǎn dyar.

(Boundary) 'byānjyè. /How far is the edge of town? Dàu jèige chéngde 'byānjyè yǒu 'dwō ywǎn?

(Long, narrow side of a flat, thin object; side surface) byār, byān; often expressed as line along the border of a surface léngr (or léng, or, in combinations, sometimes 'lénger). /The edge of the glass is very sharp. °Bwōli'byār (°Bwōli-'léngr) hěn 'kwài. /The first cars that were made had many edges and corners. 'Tóu yīpī chē dzwòchulai de léng'jyáur hěn dwō.

(Of a cliff, bank, etc.) yàr. /There are rails on the edge of the cliff. Yánshŕde °'yàrshang (°'byārshang) yǒu 'lángān.

(Of a book) kǒu. /The book has gilt edges. Shū'kǒu shŕ 'jīnde. or Shū shŕ 'jīnbyàrde. but /The book was placed on its edge (standing upright); he picked it up and laid it flat. Shū syānshr 'shùje de; tā 'náchilai gěi fàng'píngle.

(Extended edge of a roof; eave) fángyár, wūyár.

(Cutting edge of a blade) rèr, dāukǒu. /The edge of this razor is too dull. Jèige 'gwālyándāude °'rèr tài 'dwùn (°dāu'kǒu tài 'dwùn).

Have the edge on someone. /A has the edge on B. A bǐ B 'chyáng. or B bù-'rú A. /I think you have the edge on me, at least in foreign languages. Wǒ jywéje nǐ 'jŕshǎu 'wàigwoyǔ bǐ wǒ 'chyáng. or Wǒ jywéje wǒ 'jŕshǎu 'wàigwoyǔ bù'rú nǐ.

Put an edge on (for the first time) kāi'kǒu; (to sharpen) mwó. /I want an edge put on this blade. meaning I want it sharpened. Gěi wǒ 'mwómwo jèibǎ 'dāu. /This knife has not yet had an edge put on it. Jèibǎ dāu hái méi kāigwo 'kǒu.

Take the edge off (weaken). /That piece of bread only took the edge off my hunger. Jèikwài myan'bāu jŕ jyěle wǒ yi'dyǎr 'è. /Your statement took the edge off his enthusiasm. Nǐ nèmma yǐshwō jyàu tāde 'syīn 'lěngle yí'bàr.

Be on edge. /His nerves have been on edge for days now. (from excitement) Tā 'syīnli °fā'dzàu (°'jētengle, °'fánde hwang) yǒu syē'ŕdz le. or (from impatience) Tā 'syīnli °jáu'jí (°'jíde hwang, °búnàifán, °búnàifár) 'yǒu syē'ŕdz le.

To edge (press; as in a crowd) jǐ. /I edged my way to the front of the room. Wǒ (syéje 'shēndz) jǐdàu wūdz 'chyánbyar chyùle. /I just edged in. Wǒ yǐ'jǐ jyòu 'jǐnchyule. /The man edged through the crowd. Nèige rén dzài rén'dwēili ('pyānje shēndz or 'syéje shēndz) jǐdàu wūdz 'chyánbyar chyùle. /He edged into the crowd unnoticed. Tā 'shénbùjŕ 'gwēibùjywéde jyòu 'jǐjǐn nèi'chyún 'rénli chyùle.

Edge along (to go slowly and carefully along the side of a building, a wall, etc.) 'lyōuje . . . 'byār dzǒu, 'shwùnje . . . 'byār dzǒu, 'kàuje . . . byār dzǒu; pǎu or other verbs of motion can be used instead of dzǒu. /The soldiers edged along the buildings while the bullets were flying in the street. Bīng dōu °'shwùnje (°'lyōuje, °'kàuje) lóu'byār dzǒu, nèi shŕhou 'dždàn dzài 'jyēshang 'lwàn fēi. /The child edged along the wall and went out of the room. Syàu'hár °'lyōuje (°'shwùnje, °'kàuje) chyáng'byār jyòu °'dzǒu (°'lyōu) chūchyule. /The thief edged away along the wall. Dzéi 'lyōuje chyáng'byār pǎule.

EDUCATION. 'jyàuyù; **department of education** (in a school) 'jyàuyùsyì; **mass education** 'mínjùng jyàu'yù, 'píngmín jyàu'yù; **adult education** 'chéngnyán jyàu'yù, 'pǔtūng jyau'yù. /Where did you receive your education? Nǐ dzài 'nǎr °shòude jyàu'yù (or meaning Where did you go to school? °shàngde 'sywé, or meaning Where did you study? °nyànde 'shū)? / How much education have you had? Nǐ 'shòugwo °shémma (°dwōshǎu) jyàu'yù? or expressed as What schools have you entered? Nǐ 'rùgwo shémma 'sywésyàu? or as How much have you studied? Nǐ 'nyàngwo 'dwōshǎu 'shū?

Other than formal schooling is expressed as experience 'jīngyàn; benefit 'yìchù; or knowledge jŕshr. / Going out with her is an education in itself. Gēn 'tā chūchyu 'wár °jyàu rén 'dé hěn dwō 'jīngyàn (°jyàu rén 'dé hěn dwō 'yìchù, °kéyi 'jǎng hěn dwō 'jŕshr, °jyòushr ge dé 'jyàuyù de 'jīhwei).

EFFECT. (Final result; result as opposed to cause; or an indirect and incidental result) 'jyēgwǒ; **cause and effect** 'ywányīn hé 'jyēgwǒ, or (fixed combinations) 'yīngwǒ, 'chyányīnhòu'gwǒ. / Let's examine the cause and effect of this incident. Dzámen 'yánjyouyan'jyōu jèijyan shŕde °'yīngwǒ (°'ywányīn hé 'jyēgwǒ, °'chyányīnhòu'gwǒ). / What do you think the effect of his speech will be? Nǐ 'jywéje 'tāde jyǎngyǎn hwèi dzài rén'syīn yǒu 'shémma yàngde 'jyēgwǒ ne?

(Immediate, direct or intended result, usually desirable) 'syàulì, or sometimes expressed as potency lìlyang; (particular effect of a specific action) 'syàugwǒ; (an experimentally proved result) 'syàuyàn; syàu alone is used only in negative or indefinate expressions. / His speech had a great deal of effect. or His speech was very effective. Tāde 'yánjyǎng hěn yǒu 'syàuli. / The full effect of this medicine hasn't been felt yet. Jèige yàude °'syàulì (°'lìlyang) hái méi'wánchywán °'jyàn(°'syǎn)chulai ne. / What is the effect of this medicine? Jèige 'yàu yǒu shémma 'syàuli? / What will be the effect of this medicine (when it is applied)? Jèige 'yàu yǒu shémma 'syàuyan? / What was the effect of this medicine? Jèige 'yàu yǒu shémma 'syàugwǒ? / Will this medicine have any effect? Jèige 'yàu yǒu'syàu méiyou? / His speech had exactly the desired effect. Tā yǎn'jyǎngde 'syàugwǒ 'jèng gēn 'ywánlái 'syǎng de yì-'dyǎr bú'chà.

(Of a law, etc.) syàu, except in the phrase 'shr̄syíng **be put into effect.** / The law will take effect (or go into effect) a week from today. Jèityáu 'fǎgwēi 'chītyān yǐ'hòu jyòu °yǒu'syàu le (°shēng'syàu le). / When does this regulation go into effect? Jèige 'gwēidzé 'shémma shŕhou 'chī °yǒu'syàu (°shēng'syàu). / The new law is not in effect yet. Syīn 'fǎlyù hái méi 'shr̄syíng ne. / The law is still in effect. Nèige 'fǎgwēi hái 'yǒu'syàu. / The law is no longer in effect. Nèige 'fǎgwēi yǐjǐng °'wú-'syàu le (°'shr̄'syàu le).

(Influence) 'yǐngsyǎng; **good effect** 'hǎuchù; **bad effect** 'hwàichù. / The effect of climate on these plants is tremendous. Jèisyē 'jŕwù shòu 'chīhòude 'yǐngsyǎng hěn 'dà. / You can see the effect of the mountain air on him. Shānshangde 'kūngchì dwèi tāde 'yǐngsyǎng kěyǐ 'kàndechulái. / Living in these places has many bad effects on the children. Dzài jèisye 'dìfang jù dwèi syǎu'hár yǒu hěn dwō 'hwàichù.

(For) **effect.** / I'm not doing this for effect. Wǒ bìng 'búshr yàu 'syànbai. / She's wearing those clothes for effect. Tā chwān 'nèijǔngde 'yīfu jyòu 'wèide shr yàu °'yǐn rén 'jù'mù (°syǎnnùng'syǎnnùng, °chū 'fēngtou). See also **SHOW OFF.**

In effect (really; for all practical purposes) 'shŕdzài 'shwōchǐlai, 'chíshŕ. / His career began, in effect, when he was twelve. °'Shŕdzài'shwōchilai, (°'Chíshŕ) tāde 'shr̄yè shr tsúng shŕ'èrswèi kāi'shr̄de.

No effect is expressed by one of the terms discussed in paragraph two, or by others covering a wider range of meaning. / This medicine had no effect at all. Jèige 'yàu yǐ'dyǎr °'syàulì (°'syàuyàn, °'syàu) yě 'méiyou. or meaning It was no use. Jèige 'yàu yǐ'dyǎr 'yùngchu yě 'méiyou. or meaning It was no help. Jèige yàu 'szháuwú'bǔ. or Jèige 'yàu 'wúyìyú'shr. or Jeige 'yàu yǐ'dyǎr yě bújì'shr. or meaning It didn't cure. Jèige 'yàu yǐ'dyǎr yě bújŕ'bìng.

Take effect (begin to show results) chī dzwòyung, yǒu dùngjing; shànglai (said of the potency of the substance). / The medicine is beginning to take effect (*or* is taking effect); I can feel it. 'Jèige yàu yǐjǐng °chǐ 'dzwòyung le (°yǒu 'dùngjing le); wǒ jywédechū'lái. / These drinks are beginning to take effect. Jèige 'jyoujyèr shànglaile.

Effects (possessions) dūngsyi. / His personal effects are still in his room. Tāde 'dūngsyi hái dzài tāde 'wūdzli ne.

To effect bàn. *See also* **DO**. / He effected the change without difficulty. Jèitsż 'gǎibyàn tā 'bànde hěn 'shwūnli.

See also **RESULT**.

EGG. (Of any bird) dàn, dàr; **chicken egg** 'jīdàn, jīdzěr, 'báigwǒr (lit. white fruit, local Peiping) or when chickens are mentioned elsewhere in the sentence, dàn *or* (local Peiping) gwǒr; **scrambled eggs** 'chǎujīdàn; **boiled eggs** 'jǔjīdàn; **poached eggs** 'wōjīdàn, wò'gwǒr. / There are four eggs in the swallow's nest. Yàndz'wōli yǒu 'szge 'dàr. / How much are eggs by the dozen? °'Jīdàn (°Jī'dzěr) 'dwōshǎu chyán yì'dá. / That hen laid two hundred eggs last year. 'Nèijī jī 'chyù nyán 'syàle 'èrbǎige 'dàn. / Those eggs are for hatching (chicks). Nèisyē 'dàn shř 'fū syǎu'jyēr de. / I like fried eggs. Wǒ 'syǐhwān °'jyānjīdàn (°'jágwǒr, °hébāu'dàn). / I'd like two poached eggs in my soup. 'Tāngli °wǒ lyǎ 'gwǒr (°wǒ 'lyǎngge jī'dàn).

A bad egg (lit.) 'chénjīdàn (stale); syèle 'hwángr de jīdàn (bad to the point where the yolk and the white mix); 'chòujīdàn (rotten).

A bad egg *or* **good egg** (of a person). / He's a good egg. is expressed as He's not bad. Tā jèige rén hěn °'hǎu (°bú'hwài, °bú'tswò). / He's a bad egg. is expressed as in English Tā shř ge °hwài'dàn (°'hwàidūngsyi, °'hwàijūng). *or* Tā 'búshř ge 'hǎurén. or expressed as Don't associate with him. 'Byé gēn tā 'láiwang.

All one's eggs in one basket. / He failed because he put all his eggs in one basket. is expressed as He didn't understand the teaching that a wise rabbit has three holes, so he couldn't succeed. Tā bùdǔng 'jyǎutùsān'kūde 'dàuli, swóyi bùnéng 'chénggūng. or as He depended on just one tree to hang himself, so what could he do? Tā jǐng jrje 'yīkē shùshang 'dyàusž, nà dzěmma 'syíng ne? / He's putting all his eggs in one basket. is expressed as He's betting all his chips at once. Tā nà shř 'gūjù °yí'jr (°yì'jr).

To lay an egg (fig.). / The comedian laid an egg. Nèige 'chǒur shwōle jyù'hwà, méirén °'lǐhwèi (°'syàu).

To egg on chywàn, 'gǔdùng; (local Peiping) tswāndeng. / He was egged on by his friends. Tāde 'péngyoumen °'chywànde (°'gǔdùngde, °'tswāndengde) tā nèmmaje.

EIGHT. bā; **one eighth** 'bāfēnjr'yī; **the eighth** dìbā.

EIGHTEEN. shŕbā; **one eighteenth** shŕ'bāfēnjr'yī; **the eighteenth** dìshŕbā.

EIGHTY. 'bāshŕ; **one eightieth** 'bāshŕfēnjr'yī; **the eightieth** dì'bāshŕ.

EITHER. (One of) něiyi . . . dōu. / Does either of these roads lead to town? Jèi-'lyǎngtyáu lù 'néiyityáu dōu 'tūngdàu 'chénglǐ ma? / Either one will do. ('Lyǎnggeli) 'nèiyige dōu °'chéng (°'hǎu, °'syíng). *but* / Either way will do. Dzěmmaje dōu 'syíng. *See* **ANY**.

(Both) 'lyǎng . . . dōu. / There were trees on either side of the road. Nàtyáu 'lùde 'lyǎngbyār 'dōu yǒu 'shù láije.

(Negative of also) yě. / If you won't go, I won't either. 'Nǐ yàu bú'chyù, 'wǒ yě bú'chyù le.

Either . . . or . . . in Chinese two degrees of emphasis are distinguished: if the choice is a matter of indifference, **either X or Y** is expressed as X Y(de) dōu, (hwòshr) X hwòshr Y (dōu), (hwójě) X hwójě Y (dōu), (dōu being used only in cases where both can be used in English); if the choice is urgent, (yàushr) 'bu . . . , (háishr) 'jyòu . . . ; also (definitely) 'bu . . . , . . . 'jwùn. / Either today or tomorrow will do. 'Jyēr 'myér(de) 'dōu chéng. or (Hwòshr) 'Jyēr hwòshr 'myér dōu chéng. / You may fill it out with either pen or pencil. 'Tyán de shŕhou yùng 'gāngbĭ 'chyānbĭ 'dōu syíng. / I shall leave either tonight or tomorrow morning. (it doesn't matter which) Wŏ °hwòshr (°hwójě) jyēr 'wănshang dzŏu, °hwòshr (°hwójě) míngrge 'dzău-shang dzŏu. (definitely one of the two) Wŏ jyēr 'wănshang bùdzŏu, míngrge 'dzăn-shang jyou jwŭn dzŏu. / Either you go there or he does. Búshr 'nĭ chyù, jyòushr 'tā chyù. or Nĭ hé tā nĭmen 'lyăngge rén lĭtou 'dzŭng děi yŏu 'yíge 'chyù de. / Either you marry her, or you drop her entirely. Nĭ bù'chyù tā jyòu děi 'dwànkāi. or Nĭ 'bùgēn tā jyē'hwūn, jyòu byé gēn tā 'hăo. / Either take it or leave it. 'Búyàu jyou 'byé 'syăng yàu. / There is no middle ground; you either go the whole way or stop right now. Méiyŏu lyăng'kěde 'bànfa; nĭ yàushr 'bùsyăng gàndàu'dĭ, háishr 'jyòutsz dă'jù wéi'myàu.

ELECT. sywăn; 'sywănjyŭ; (less formal) jyŭ, twēi. / Have you elected a chairman? Nĭmen °'sywănle (°'sywănjyŭle, °'jyŭle, °'twēile) jŭ'syí le ma?

   Be elected 'dāngsywăn. / Who was elected president? Shéi 'dāngsywăn dzŭng-'tŭng le?

   President-elect 'dāngsywăn 'syàrénde dàdzŭng'tŭng. / The President-elect will speak tomorrow. °'Dāngsywăn 'syàrénde dàdzŭng'tŭng (°Hái méiyou jyòu'jŕ de 'syīn dàdzŭng'tŭng) 'míngtyān jyăng'hwà.

ELECTRIC. dyàn; **electric power** or **electricity** 'dyànchì; **electric power** or **electric current** (used to operate something) 'dyànlì; **electric range** 'dyànlùdz. / Are there electric lights? Yŏu 'dyàndēng ma? / His girl friend sent him an electric razor. Tāde 'nyŭpéngyou 'sùngle tā yíge yùng'dyàn de gwālyăn'dāu. / It's electric (electrically operated). Shŕ yùng'dyàn de. / He received an electric shock. Tā jyàu 'dyàn 'dăle. / He got the electric chair. (punishment executed) Tā dzwò dyàn'yĭdz le. (sentence passed) Tā pàn de shŕ dzwò dyàn'yĭdz. / Is the electric train still opera- ting? 'Dyànlìhwŏ'chē hái 'tūng ma? / Is the electric train still running (at this hour)? 'Dyànlìhwŏ'chē hái °'dzŏuje ne ma (°'yŏu ma, °'kāije ne ma)?

ELEVEN. 'shŕyī; **the eleventh** dìshŕ'yī; **one eleventh** shŕ'yīfēnjŕ'yī.

   Eleventh hour kwài dàu 'shŕhou le, dàule mwò'lyăur le. / At the eleventh hour he starts to worry. °Kwàidàu 'shŕhou le (°Dàule mwò'lyăur le) tā fāchi 'chóu laile.

ELSE. (Other) usually byé(de), often with hái in the same sentence; if hái occurs, byé (de) is sometimes omitted. / There is no one else here. Jèr 'méiyou 'byéren. / Everyone else has gone. 'Byérén chywán 'dzŏule. / What else can we do? 'Hái yŏu shèr ma? or Hái yŏu 'byéde ma? or Hái yŏu 'byéde shèr kě'dzwò de ma? or Hái yŏu 'byéde 'făr ma?

   (Otherwise) ('yàu) bùrán, 'fŏudzé. / How else can I manage? is expressed as If not that way, then how? Bú'nèmmaje nĭ jyàu wŏ 'dzěmmaje? or Yàubu'rán wŏ 'dzěmma 'bàn ne? / Hurry, or else we'll be late. 'Kwài dyăr, °'fŏudzé (°'yàu bù-'rán) wŏmen jyòu 'wăn le. / You do as I tell you, or else! °Wŏ dzěmma 'shwō nĭ dzěmma dzwò (°Wŏ 'jyàu nĭ dzěmmaje nĭ 'jyòu dzěmmaje), °yàubù'rán na, 'hm (°'fŏudzé a, 'hm)!

EMPIRE. 'dǐgwó. / They discussed the history of the British Empire. Tāmen 'tǎulwùn 'Yīngdǐgwóde lǐ'shr̆ (láije).

EMPLOY. (To use; of persons or tools) yùng; (use a tool) shr̆; (of servants only) 'shr̆hwàn; (hire) gù; (polite; of lawyers, etc.) chǐng; **be employed** (work) dzwòshr̆, (especially of labor) dzwògūng. / How many workers are employed here? Jèr yùngje 'dwòshǎu °rén (°'gūngrén (laborers))? / We used to employ five hundred workers. Wǒmen yǐchyan yùnggwo 'wǔbairén. / We plan to employ about 1,000 men. Wǒmen 'yùbei °yùng (°gù) yǐ'chyānrén. / They have employed all the workers available. 'Néng dzwò'gūng de rén tāmen 'dōu °'yùngle (°'gùle chyule). / He knows how to employ people to the best advantage. Tā 'hěn hwèi yùng'rén. / He employs a flock of servants. Tā °'yùngje (°'shr̆hwànje) yǐchyún 'dǐsyarén. / He's trying to employ the services of a good lawyer in an advisory role. Tā 'hěn syàng chǐng ge hǎu 'lyùshr̆ dzwò 'gùwèn. / We were fortunate in being able to employ his help. Wǒmen 'syǐngkwēi néng chǐngdàu 'tā lái bāng'máng. / Are you employed here? Nǐ dzài 'jèr °dzwò'shr̆ ma (or (of labor) °dzwò'gūng ma)? / By whom are you employed? is expressed as Where (or For whom) do you work? Nǐ dzài 'nǎr dzwò'shr̆? or Nǐ gěi 'shéi dzwò-'shr̆?

EMPTY. (Of contents other than people) kūng; (emptied to make space) kūngchulai, téngchulai, 'téngjǐng; **an empty house** (yǐswǒr) 'kūngfángdz; **empty space** (on the ground) 'kūngdǐ, kùngr. / Do you have an empty box? Yǒu 'kūng(de)hédz ma? / The room is empty now (of furniture, etc.). Wūdz °'kūngle (°'kūngchulaile, °'kūngchulaile, °'téngchulaile, °'téngjǐngle). / The room is almost empty. Wūdzli °'kūngkungdung-'dùng de (°'kūngkūngrú'yě). or Wūdz 'jyànjr̆shr̆ °'kūngde (°'kūngje). / The trunk is empty. Syāngdz shr̆ 'kūngde. / The trunk is (still) almost empty. Syāngdz 'jyànjr̆ (shr̆) °'kūngde (°'kūngje). / The trunk is (already) empty. Syāngdz °'kūngchulaile (°'kūngchulaile, °'téngchulaile). / He came with an empty stomach. Tā 'kūngje dùdz láide. or Tā 'kūngdùr láide.

(Of people; no people in it; everyone gone out; etc.). / Is this an empty (unoccupied) room? Jèijyān 'wūdz °'méirén 'jù ma (°'yǒurén 'jù ma, °'yǒu méiyou rén 'jù)? / The theater was empty in five minutes. Syǐ'ywándzlide rén 'wǔfēnjūngde gūngfu jyòu 'dōu dzǒu'jǐngle.

Empty-handed 'kūngshǒu, 'kūngje shǒu. / He came back empty-handed. Tā °'kūngshǒu (°'kūngje shǒu) hwéilai de.

Empty-headed (silly) shǎ, 'shǎule ge syǐn'yǎr; (stupid) húdu, bèn.

Empty talk 'kūnghwà. / That's just empty talk. Nà shr̆ 'kūnghwà.

Empty threats. / He always makes empty threats. Tā lǎushr °'kūng (°jyǎ-'jwāngr) 'syàhu rén, syàhu 'wánle jyòu 'swàn le. or Tā lǎushr 'shwōde hěn 'syūng, kěshr shwò'wánle jyòu 'swàn le. or expressed as He always thunders, never rains. Tā lǎushr 'gāndǎ'léi 'búsyà'yǔ. / He made a few empty threats. Tā 'kūng syahule ji'jyù jyòu 'swàn le. or Tā jyǎ'jwāngrde 'syàhule ji'jyù jyòu 'swàn le.

To empty (or be emptied in proper constructions). There are several types of constructions, depending on the nature of the action or of the contents, as follows.

When all the contents of a container are emptied (by taking them out) náchulai, náchuchyu, nájǐng(le), náde 'gānganjǐng'jǐng de; (by lifting and carrying them out) tái instead of ná in the same constructions; (by moving them out; as furniture) bān instead of ná in the same constructions; (by chasing living beings out) gǎn instead of ná in the same constructions; or use other verbs with meanings such as throw, carry, etc., in the same constructions. / The room was emptied of everything. Wūdzlide 'dūngsyi dōu bān'jǐngle. / Empty everything out of the trunk. Bǎ 'syāngdzlide 'dūngsyi dōu °'náchulai (°'chǐngchulai, °etc.).

When a container is emptied and room is being made for other contents téngchulai, kùngchulai, kūngchulai. See above. /Can you empty these things? (containers) Nǐ néng bǎ jèisyē 'dūngsyi °'kūngchulai (°'téngchulai, °'kùngchulai) ma?

When either containers or their contents are emptied, and the emptying is done in a particular way: (by inverting or tipping) dàu, dàuwán(le), dàujìng(le), dàu'gānjìng(le); (by suspending in an inverted position and letting it drip, as a sieve) kùng instead of dàu in the same constructions; (by letting it drip, drop by drop) dǐ instead of dàu in the same constructions; (by flowing or letting it flow) lyóu instead of dàu in the same constructions; (by letting it out) fàng instead of dàu in the same constructions; empty into 'dàudzài, 'kùngdzài, 'dǐdzài, 'fàngdzài, 'fàngdàu, 'lyóudàu; (lyóu is used only of a container, and only with jyàu as co-verb; the other words are used of container or contents, with bǎ as co-verb). /Empty the ash tray (ashes) here. Bǎ 'yānhwēi 'dàudzài jèr. /Empty all the ash trays. Bǎ 'yāndyér dōu 'dàule. /Empty the garbage (can) in that bag. Bǎ 'tūngdzlide 'dzāngdūngsyi 'dàudzài 'kǒudaili. /Can you empty these things? (contents or containers) Nǐ néng bǎ jèisyē 'dūngsyi °'dàule ma (or by letting the contents out) °'fàngle ma)? /The bottle is empty (of something that dripped out). Píngdz kùng'wánle. or Píngdz 'kùngde yǐ'dǐ yě méi'you le. or Píngdz 'dǐde 'gānganjìng'jìng de. /Empty all the cod-liver oil out of the bottle (by letting it drip). Bǎ nèige píngdzlide 'yúgānyóu kùngde °'gānganjìng-'jìng de (°'gānjing le). /This oil tank empties in about five minutes. Jèige yóu'tǔng dàgài dzài 'wǔfēnjūng yǐ'nèi kéyi °lyóu'jìngle (°fàng'wánle, °etc., with lyóu and fàng). /This stream empties into a big lake. Jèityáu 'hé lyóudàu yíge dà'hú lǐtou chyù.

ENCLOSE. (Insert in an envelope) fù, 'fēngdzài . . . , 'jwāngdzài . . . . /Enclose this with the message. Bǎ 'jèige gēn 'syìn °'jwāngdzài 'yíge syìn'fēngrli (°'fēngdzài yíge syìn'fēngrli). or Bǎ 'jèige 'fùdzài 'syìnfēngrli. /The money you requested is enclosed. Nǐ yàu de 'chyán jàu'shùr 'fùdzài jèfēng 'syìnli.

(To surround) wéi(chilai), chywān(chilai). /The property is enclosed by a fence. Jèikwài 'dì sżjōu'wéi chywānchǐláile. or Jèikwài 'dì °yǒu (°ná, °yùng) yídàu 'dwǎnchyáng °'wéije (°'chywānje). /Our house is enclosed on four sides by tall buildings. Wǒmende fángdz 'sżmyàr jyàu 'gāulóu °wéichǐláile (°'chywānchǐláile).

ENCOURAGE. 'gúlì; (to encourage someone to do something) 'myǎnlì; (to encourage by praising) 'kwājyǎng. /He encouraged us to go ahead. Tā 'gúlì wǒmen 'gànsyachyu. /She should have discouraged the child from saying that sort of thing; instead, she encouraged him. Tā 'gēnběn jyou yīnggāi 'gwǎnje dyar háidz 'bújyàu tā shwō 'nèiyàngrde 'hwà, kěshr (háidz 'shwō de shŕhou) tā 'fǎndàu 'kwājyǎng tā. /So far he hasn't encouraged us to do it this way. Jŕdàu syàn'dzài tā bìng 'méiyou 'gúlì wǒmen yùng 'jèige fāngfa 'dzwòsyachyu. /So far he hasn't ventured to encourage us to do it this way. Jŕdàu syàn'dzài tā 'bùkěn 'gúlì wǒmen yùng 'jèige fāngfa 'dzwòsyachyu. but /Do you feel more encouraged now? meaning Do you feel better? Syǐnli 'hǎu dyǎr le ma? or meaning You're not hesitating anymore? Búnèmma fā'chù le ba? or meaning You're not depressed anymore? Búnèmma fā'chóu le ba?

Not encourage (discourage) is expressed as dislike bùsyǐhwan, búywànyi; or as discourage someone from doing something gwǎn . . . bújyàu. /We do not encourage that conduct here. is expressed as We don't like people to do that sort of thing here. Wǒmen jèr bù'syǐhwan rén 'nèmmaje dzwò 'nèiyàngrde 'shŕ. /Don't encourage the child to say that! is expressed as In managing the child, don't let him say that kind of thing. 'Gwǎnje dyar háidz 'byé jyàu tā shwō 'nèiyàngrde 'hwà.

END. (Of something long and narrow) tóur. /You hold this end and I'll take the other. Nǐ 'náje 'jèitóur; wǒ chyù ná 'nèitóur. /Stretch it at both ends. 'Dzwànje 'lyǎngtóur °yǐ'chēn (°yí'dèn). /He searched from one end of the street to the other. Tā tsúng

jyē 'jèitóur 'jǎudàu 'nèitóur. / Is this the end of the street? Jyē dàu tour lema?
or Jěi shŕ jyēde jĭntóur ma? / It's at the very end of the street. Dzài jèityáu
'jyēde jĭn'tóurshang.

(Of something pointed) jyār. *See also* **POINT**. / Use the sharp end. Yùng
nèige 'jyār. or Yùng 'jyānde nèitóur. / The crab caught the end of the-dog's tail.
'Pángsyè bǎ 'gǒude yĭba'jyār 'jyājule.

(Of something rectangular or irregularly shaped) byān, byār, tóur. / That end
of the building is not finished. Fángdz °'nèibyār (°'nèitóur) méi wán'gūng ne. / This
end of the island is rocky. 'Dǎude °jèitóur (°'jèibyār) dōu shŕ dà'shŕtou. / Put the
blue label on this end. Bǎ 'lánjř'tyáur 'tyēdzai °'jèibyār (°'jèitóur). / Put blue la-
bels on both ends. Bǎ 'lánjř'tyáur 'tyēdzai 'lyǎngtóur. or Lánjř'tyáur 'lyǎngtóur
'dōu 'tyēshang. / Stand it on this end. Lĭchilai de shŕhou, jyàu 'jèitóur °cháu'syà
(°dzài 'dĭsya). *but* / Stand it on end. is expressed as (Bǎ jèige) 'lĭchilai.

(Result) 'jyēgwǒ, 'jyējyú. / It's going to be quite unpleasant in the end. °'Jyēgwǒ (°'Jyējyú) 'jwūn búhwèi jyàu rén gāu'syĭng de. / Who knows what the end will
be? 'Shéi jŕdàu hwèi dàu 'dzěmma ge °'jyēgwǒ (°'jyējyú)? or 'Shéi jŕdàu °'jyēgwǒ
(°'jyējyú) hwèi 'dzěmmayàng? / The end will certainly be awful. °'Jyēgwǒ (°'Jyējyú,
°'Wán de shŕhou, see below) 'jwūn yàu dzāu'gāu. / Their marriage came to an unhappy end. Tāmende 'hwūnyin 'jyējyú hěn bù'hǎu.

(Conclusion, ending) (mwò)lyǎur; (last part of the time) dzwèi'hòu(de shŕhou);
(conclusion of a story, etc.) shōuwěi; (ending time) 'wán de shŕhou, 'jyēshù (de
shŕhou); in some combinations dǐ; sometimes expressed verbally by wán, lyǎu,
'jyēshù, 'lyǎujyú all meaning to come to an end. / I read the book from beginning
to end at one sitting. Wǒ yí'chyèr bǎ jèiběn 'shū °tsúng 'tóur kàndàu 'lyǎur
(°tsúng chĭ'tóur kàndàu mwò'lyǎur). / At last the end is in sight. 'Kě kwài
yàu 'wán le. or 'Kě dàu le °kwài 'wán de shŕhou (°kwài 'jyēshù de shŕhou). / Is
there an end to it? Hài yǒu 'wán ma? or Hái yǒu'tóur ma? or Hái yǒu ge 'wán de
shŕhou ma? / I don't like the ending. Wǒ bù'syĭhwān °mwò'lyǎurde nèidwār (°nèige
shōu'wěi). / Will you stay with us to the end? Nǐ 'ywànyì gēn wǒmen yí'kwàr gàndàu
'dǐ ma? / She slept to the end of the show. Tā yì'jŕ shwèidàu °sàn'chǎng de shŕhou
(°dyàn'yĭng yǎn'wánle). / There is an end to everything. 'Shémma dōu yǒu ge 'wán
(de shŕhou). / I'll pay you at the end of the month. Wó ywè'dǐ hwán nǐ. / I'll pay you
at the end of one month. Wó ywè'tóur hwán nǐ. / He ended by saying, "This is the
end." Tā °dzwèi'hòu (°mwò'lyǎur) shwō de shŕ, "'Wánle."

(Objective). / To what end (for what) are you working so hard? 'Dzèmma mài
'lìchi °wèile (°wèide shŕ) 'shémma? / This is only a necessary means to the end.
Jèi 'búgwo shŕ wèi 'dádàu nèige 'mùdí 'děi yùng de 'shǒudwàn.

(Referring to death). / His father came to an unhappy end. Tā fùchin chyùshŕ
de shŕhou hěn 'tsǎn. *See also* **DEATH**.

Loose ends. / Matters are still at loose ends. Shèr hái méi dzwò'wán ne.
or Shèr hái bùnéng 'jyēshù ne. or Shèr hái méi 'wánchywán 'lyǎu ne. / A few
loose ends remain to be cleared up. Hái 'shēngsya 'dzǎshr děi °nùng'wán (°'chĭnglǐ-
chĭnglǐ). / He always leaves some loose ends for me to clear up for him. Tā dzwò-
'shŕ lǎu 'shēng dyar °'dzǎshr (°'língtour) yàu wǒ gěi ta dzwò.

Make ends meet chūrùsyāng'dǐ. / It'll be hard to make ends meet that way.
'Nèmmaje 'chūrùsyāng'dǐ jyòu hěn 'nán le.

No end. / He'll give you no end of trouble. Tā hwèi méi'tóurde máfan nǐ.
/ We had no end of trouble on the trip. Wǒmen yí'lù °'jĭng chū'shèr (°'jĭng chū
'máfan'shèr). / We had no end of trouble with him on the trip. Tā yí'lù °jĭng dǎu
'máfan (°jĭng jyàu rén fèi'shŕ).

507

Odds and ends (objects) 'língchǐbā'swèide dūngsyi; (matters) 'língchǐbā'swèide shŕ. /The room is full of odds and ends. Wūdzli 'mǎn dōu shŕ 'língchǐbā'swèide dūngsyi. /We keep him to take care of the odds and ends. Wǒmen jyàu tā 'dzàijèr hǎu 'jàugwǎn 'língchǐbā'swèide 'shŕ.

Put an end to, make an end of (abolish) chyǔsyāu; (forbid) 'bùsyǔ; (stop) 'jènyā-syachyu; (finish) lyǎu. /As soon as the new director came, he put an end to that nonsense. Syīn jǔ'rèn yídàu jyòu °bǎ 'nèige chyǔ'syāule (°'bùsyǔ nèmma hú'nàu le). /He put an end to the riot. Tā bǎ 'lwàndz gěi °jènyāsyachyule (°'lyǎule). /He put an end to their fight by pointing out the cause of the misunderstanding. Tā bǎ 'lyǎng-byār 'wùhwei de 'ywángu jyě'shŕle yísyàr °tāmen jyòu 'bùdǎ'jyà le (°jyòu 'gěi tāmen 'héle).

Rear end or end of the line jǐn'hòutóu. /You've got to go to the end of the line. Nǐ yàushŕ jàn'pái děi dàu jǐn'hòutóu chyu. /Look! He's standing at the end. 'Kàn a! Tā dzài °mwò'lyǎur nar ne (°'mwòmwolà'lyǎur nèr ne, °jǐn'hòutou ne).

This is the end (the last straw) 'jè kě bù'syíng le.

To end something dzwòwán or other words for dzwò; dzwòchéng; (conclude) dzwòjyě; (stop) tíng; (of work) búdzwòsyachyu; (come to a stop) 'wéijr; see also expressions in paragraph five. /The work will be ended next month. Jèige shèr syàywè °dzwò'wán (°dzwòchéng). /His whole project ended in nothing. Tā jěng'gèrde 'jìhwà 'gǎule bàn'tyān °'jyěgwo 'yìchǎng'kūng (°dàu'tóulai shŕ 'yìchǎng'kūng, °dàu'lyǎur yě méi 'gǎuchu shémma lai, °'méi shémma 'jyěgwo jyòu 'wán le). /He ended the book with a proverb. Tā dzài shūde mwò'lyǎur 'yùngle jyu 'chéngyǔ dzwò'jyě. or Tāde shū 'mwoyíjyù hwà 'yùngle jyù 'chéngyǔ. /When does the performance end? 'Syì shémma shŕhou (yǎn) 'wán? /There's no telling how this will end. (Shéi yě) bùjŕdau 'jèige (jyānglai) °dzěmma 'jyěshù (°dzěmma 'lyǎujyú, °dàu'lyǎur dzěmma-yàng, °dàu'tóur dzěmmayàng, °'wán de shŕhou shŕ ge shémma yàngdz). /The enterprise ended with his death. Nèijyàn shŕ tā yǐ 's̄z jyòu °'wánle (°'lyǎule, °'jyěshùle, °méi'jyēje 'dzwòsyachyu, °'tíngle). /The history of ancient Europe ends with the fall of the Roman Empire. Ōujōu'shànggǔshŕ dàu 'Lwómǎ'dìgwó 'myèwáng wéi'jŕ.

ENEMY. (Personal) 'chóurén. /We are enemies. Wǒmen shŕ 'chóurén. or Wǒmen yǒu'chóu.

(In war; a single individual or the group) 'dírén; enemy nation 'dígwó; enemy national or enemy alien 'díchyáu. /Where is the enemy? 'Dírén dzài'nǎr ne? /Are there any enemy nationals here? Jèr yǒu °'díchyáu (°'dígwó 'chyáumín) ma?

ENERGY. (Potential power, especially mental) jīngshen; (a capacity for work) 'gànjyèr. /He is a man of energy. or He is full of energy. Tā 'jèige rén hěn yǒu °'jīngshen (°ge 'gànjyèr).

(Expended power) jīngshen; (mind and strength) 'jīnglì; (strength) jyèr, jìn; (strength) lìchi. /A lot of energy will be needed in this work. Jèige 'gūngdzwò hěn fèi °'jīngshen (°'jīnglì, °'jyèr, °'jìn, °'lìchi). /His energy is waning gradually. Tā °'jīngshen (°'jīnglì, °'lìchi) jyàn'jyànde 'shwāisyachyu le. /His energy seems to be unlimited. Tāde °'jīngshen (°'jīnglì, °'lìchi) hǎusyàng yùngbu'wán shŕde.

ENGINE. (Motor; general term for any power-driven machine; automobile motor) 'jīchǐ; (technical term; especially for an airplane motor) 'fādùng'jī; (rare) 'yǐnjǐng; diesel engine 'cháiyóu fādùng'jī. /One engine on the airplane stopped. Fēijīde 'yíge fādùng-jī 'tíngle. /My engine needs repairing. Wǒde 'jīchǐ děi °'syōulile (°'shōushrshōushr-le). /Can someone fix an automobile engine? Shéi hwèi 'syōuli chǐchē 'jīchi?

(Locomotive) chētóu, 'jīchē. /The train has two engines. Jèilyè 'chē yǒu 'lyǎngge °chē'tóu (°'jīchē). /Does it have a steam or electric engine? Nèilyè 'chēde °chē'tóu (°'jīchē) shr yùng 'jēngchî háishr yùng 'dyàn?

ENGINEER. (One whose profession is engineering) gūngchéngshr; **electrical engineer** dyǎnjî gūngchéng'shr; **mechanical engineer** 'jīsyè gūngchéng'shr; **civil engineer** 'tǔmù gūngchéng'shr; **hydraulic engineer** 'shwěilî gūngchéng'shr; **aeronautical engineer** hángkūng gūngchéng'shr. /What kind of an engineer are you? Nǐ shr °'nǎyikēde (°'nǎyiménde) 'gūngchéng'shr?

(In government employ) 'jìshr; **chief engineer** jíjèng.

(In army service; individual or group) 'gūngbīng; **a regiment of engineers** yìtwán 'gūngbīng. /I am a Pfc., 3rd Co. Engrs. Wǒ shr 'Gūngbīng Dì'sānlyánde 'yīděngbīng. *or* Wǒ shr 'Gūngsānlyánde 'yīděngbīng. /I'm Major Swūn, 17th Engrs. Wǒ shr 'Gūngbīng Shŕ'chītwánde 'Swūn Shàusyàu. /I am a Captain in the Engineers, U.S. Army. Wǒ shr 'Měigwo 'Lùjyūn 'gūngbīng shàng'wèi.

(Of a train) kāichēde, szjî. /The engineer brought the train to a stop. Nèige °kāi'chēde (°sz̄'jī) bǎ chē 'tíng'jùle.

Engineering (as a subject of study) 'gūngkē. /I was in the engineering department in the military academy. Wǒ dzài 'jyūngwān sywé'syàu nyàn de shr 'gūngkē.

To engineer. /He engineered the building from beginning to end. Nèige 'lóu (tsúng shè'jî dàu'lyǎur) chywán shr tā 'yìshǒu 'jyāndzàu de. /He engineered his scheme successfully through a good deal of opposition. Tāde 'jìhwà yǒu hěn'dwō rén 'fǎndwèi, kěshr tā gěi 'shūtūngde tūng'gwòle. /Who engineered the robbery? Jèige 'chyàngàn °shr 'shéi chūde 'júyi (°shéi shr 'jǔmóu, °shr shéi'jǔdùng de, °shr shéijú'shr de, °shr shéi'jìhwa de)? /He engineered (planned) the whole thing. 'Dōu shr 'tā °chū de 'júyî (°'jìhwà de).

ENGLISH. (Of England) Yīnggwo(de); **English** (made) 'Yīnggwo dzwò de, 'Yīnggwo dzàu de. /Do you like English cigarettes? Nǐ 'syǐhwān 'Yīnggwo 'jřyān ma? /She likes English china. Tā 'syǐhwān °'Yīnggwo dzwò de (°'Yīnggwo dzàu de) 'tszchî. /Is this of English make? Jèi shr °'Yīnggwo dzwò de ma (°'Yīnggwo dzàu de ma)? /This is English merchandise. Jèi shr 'Yīnggwo hwò. /He's English. *or* He's an Englishman. Tā shr 'Yīnggwo rén. /He married an Englishwoman. Tā 'chyǔ de shr °'Yīnggwo tàitai (°'Yīnggwo rén). /His actions are English, but he talks like a German. Tā 'jǔdùng syàng 'Yīnggwo rén, kěshr shwō'hwà syàng 'Dégwo rén. /He's English all over. Tā jēng'gèrde Yīnggwo 'pàitour. /He came of pure English stock. Tāde 'sywètǔng shr 'chwún Yīnggwo 'jǔng de. *or* Tāde 'dzǔsyān 'dōu shr 'Yīnggwo rén.

(The English language) 'Yīngwén, 'Yīnggwo hwà. /Do you speak English? Nǐ hwèi shwō 'Yīngwén ma? *or* Nǐ 'hwèi búhwèi shwō 'Yīnggwo hwà? /He is in the English Department. Tā dzài 'Yīngwénsyî. /He can read and write English. Tā 'Yīngwén hwèi 'shwō hwèi 'syě. /English is not difficult. 'Yīngwén bùnán. /His English is excellent. Tā 'Yīngwén °'chéngdu hěn 'shēn (°hǎu'jíle). /He speaks (English) with an English (British) accent. Tā shwō de 'Yīngwén dài °'Yīnggwo 'kǒuyīn (°Yīnggwo 'dyàur).

ENJOY. In general, an action is described and followed by yǒu yìsz, yǒu 'chyùwèi, yǒuchyùr; sometimes hěn hǎu. /Are you enjoying yourself? 'Wárde hái °yǒu 'yìsz (°yǒu 'chyùwèi, °yǒu'chyùr) ma? /I enjoyed myself very much. Wǒ wárde 'hěn hǎu. or simply 'Hěn hǎu, 'hěn hǎu. /Did you enjoy his speech? Tā 'jyǎngde nǐ 'tīngje °yǒu 'yìsz (°yǒu 'chyùwèi, °yǒu'chyùr) ma? /I didn't enjoy it at all. Yì-'dyǎr °yìsz (°chyùwèi, °chyùr) yě méi'yǒu. /How do you manage to enjoy yourself (lit. how do you entertain yourself) staying home alone every evening. 'Tyāntyar wǎnshang 'dǯjǐ dzài'jyā dāije °dzwǒ shémma 'syāuchyǎn (°dōu ná shémma jyěmèr)?

In polite formulas such as I hope you enjoyed yourself the Chinese say nothing of the sort, but rather apologize for being bad hosts. / I hope you enjoyed the party (or the dinner, etc.). is expressed as We treated you half-heartedly. 'Dàimànde 'hěn. / I hope you enjoyed the dinner. is expressed as I'm sorry; there was not enough prepared or nothing fit to eat. Dwèibu'jù, 'jīntyān méi °dzěmma 'yùbei (°shemma kě'chŕde). or as I'm sorry; you didn't eat well. Dwèibu'jù, nín dōu 'méichŕ 'hǎu ba. / I hope you enjoyed the party. is expressed as I'm sorry; you didn't have a good time. Dwèibu'jù, nín dōu 'méiwǎr'hǎu ba. The proper answer to these statements, I enjoyed myself very much, would be Hǎu 'shwō, hǎu 'shwō. or 'Hěn hǎu, hěn hǎu. or (if a party) Wǒ wǎrde 'hěn °hǎu (°yǒu 'yìsz, °yǒu 'chyùwèi, °yǒu'chyùr). or (in any situation) Byé 'kěchi.

To enjoy doing something (like to) ài, hǎu, 'syǐhwān. / He enjoys eating good food. Tā (hěn) °'ài (°'hǎu, °'syǐhwān) chŕ (hǎude). / He enjoys kidding people. Tā °'ài (°etc.) gēn rén 'dōuje wár.

Enjoy good health is expressed as health is good. / He enjoys good health as a rule. Tā 'shēntǐ yí'syàng hěn 'hǎu.

Enjoy life syǎnglè, syǎngfú, 'syǎngshòu. / He knows how to enjoy life. Tā hwèi °syǎng'lè (°syǎng'fú, °'syǎngshòu).

ENOUGH. (Sufficient) gòu; (only of eating one's fill) bǎu. / Do you have enough money? Nǐ 'chyán 'gòu ma? or Nǐ 'chyán 'gòu bugòu? / Is that enough (of anything)? 'Gòu-le ma? / That's enough! 'Gòu le! or meaning Don't say any more. Byé 'pín le. or Byé 'shwō le. / Have you had enough? 'Gòule ma? or (of a beating) Nǐ 'fú bùfú? or (of exertion, bad luck, etc.) Nǐ shòu'gòule ma? / I've had enough (food). Wǒ chŕ'bǎule. or Wǒ chŕle ge 'jyǒudzúfàn'bǎu.

(Rather) hěn. / He seemed glad enough to do it. Tā (hǎusyàng) 'hěn gāusying 'dzwǒ shrde. / He's willing enough. Tā hěn 'ywànyì.

ENTER. (Come, or go, into a place) jìn, 'jìndau . . . lǐ; jìn may be preceded by a verb specifying the type of action, whether walking, running, driving, etc., in which case the combination means enter by X or X in, as 'dzǒujìn, enter by walking or walk in. Any of these expressions may be followed by lái or chyù, depending on whether the motion is toward or away from the speaker. / We might as well enter now. Dzámen 'bùfáng 'syàndzài 'jìnchyu ba. / The boat is entering the harbor. Chwán 'jèngdzai °jìn hǎi'kǒu (°jìn'gǎng). / You enter here. Tsúng 'jèr °jìnlai (°jìnchyu). / My orders from the chief are that no one is allowed to enter this room unescorted. 'Shàngtou yǒu 'hwà, méiren 'gēnje 'shéi yě bùneng 'jìn jèijyan 'wūdz. / He entered on foot. Tā dzǒujìnlaide. / When you enter a cave, it takes a little while before you can see. °Jìn'dùng (°Jìndau 'dùngli lai, °Jìndau dùngli chyu) yǐ'hòu děi 'dāi hwer tsái kànde'jyàn.

(To join an organization) jìn, rù; (go to, of a school) shàng. / When did you enter the army? Nǐ 'shémma shŕhou °jìnde (°rùde) jyūn'dwèi? / Do you plan to enter a university? Nǐ °'yàu (°'dǎswàn) °jìn (°rù, °shàng) dà'sywé ma?

(To list or write in) syějin; (fill in) tyánjin; (report in) bàujin. / Your name was entered yesterday. Nǐde 'míngdz shŕ 'dzwór °syě (°tyán, °bàu) jìnchyude.

(To register) bàumíng. / Who is entered in the race? Nèige sài'pǎu 'shéi bàu-míng le? / He entered his name as a candidate. Tā bàule 'míng le, yàu dzwǒ 'hòusywǎnrén.

(Join) 'tsānjyā, 'jyārù. / He entered the discussion without introduction.

Yě méirén 'jyèshàu, tā 'dzjǐ jyòu °'tsānjyā (°'jyārù) 'tǎulwùn le.

ENTERTAINMENT. 'yúlè, kě'wár de dìfang, kě'syāuchyǎn de dìfang. /Is there any entertainment in this town? Chéng 'lǐtou yǒu shémma °'yúlè (°kě'wár de dìfang, °kě'syāuchyǎn de dìfang) ma?

An entertainment (show put on for amusement; amateur performances) 'yóuyǐhwèi. /When does the entertainment begin? 'Yóuyǐhwèi shémma shŕhou chǐ'tóur? /Is the entertainment good? (if the person questioned is a performer) Nèige 'yóuyǐhwèi 'wárde 'hǎu ma? (if the person questioned has seen it) Nèige yóuyǐhwèi yǒu-'yìsz ma?

ENTIRE. (Whole, as a unit) jěng'gèrde . . . °dōu (°chywán); sometimes yī . . . °dōu (°chywán). /His entire attitude is wrong. Tā jěng'gèrde 'tàidù dōu 'tswò le. /He spent his entire fortune on her. Tā bǎ tā jěng'gèrde 'jyāchǎn 'chywǎn hwādzai 'tā shēnshang le. /This requires your entire attention. Jèige nǐ děi bǎ jěng'gèrde 'syīn dōu 'yùngshang. *or* Jèige nǐ děi 'chywánshén'gwànjù. /The entire trip was pleasant. Yí'lù dōu jyàu rén 'tùngkwai. /His entire family came. Tā °'chywánjyā (°'yījyā) dōu láile.

(Pertaining to everything, distributively) 'swóyǒude; or a sentence with alto-gether yígùng. /Is this the entire cost? (the cost of everything). Yí'gùng dzèmmasyē 'chyán ma? *or* 'Swóyǒude 'fèiyùng dōu dzài'nèi ma?

ENTIRELY. (Completely) 'wánchywán. /It's entirely up to you. 'Wánchywán děi nǐ 'dzjǐ dǎ 'júyi. /He's entirely reliable. Tā 'wánchywán kě'kàu.

ENTRANCE. (Place to enter) 'rùkǒu, mén; or a sentence including an expression mean-ing enter. *See* ENTER. /Where is the entrance? 'Rùkǒu dzài 'shémma dìfang? *or* 'Mén dzài'nǎr? *or* Tsúng 'nǎr jìnchyu? /Is the entrance closed? °'Rùkǒu (°'Mén) 'gwānle ma?

(Act of entering). *See also* ENTER. /Is there an entrance fee? 'Jìnchyu yàu-'chyán ma? *or* Jìnchyu yàu mǎi'pyàu ma? *or* Yàu rù'chǎngfèi ma? /Her sudden entrance took us by surprise. Tā 'hūránjyān yí 'jìnlai, wǒmen 'chywán syàle yí-'tyàu. /What an entrance she staged! Tā nèi yí'jìnlái de 'jyèr jēn jyàu ge 'dzúle!

(Of a performer) chūchǎng. /Everyone applauded the actor's entrance. Nèige 'yǎnywán chū'chǎng de shŕhou °'rén chywán gǔ'jǎng (°'dàjyāhwǒr 'chywándōu pāi-'shǒur).

ENVELOPE. syìnfēngr. /This envelope has the wrong address. Jèige syìn'fēngrshang syěde °dì'míngr (°dì'jǐr) 'tswò le. /I need a larger envelope for this letter. 'Jèifēng syìn wǒ děi yùng yíge 'dàdyàrde syìn'fēngr.

EQUAL. (In mathematics and some other circumstances) děng; to be equal syāngděng; to equal 'děngyú. /Two times two equals four. 'Èr chéng 'èr děngyú 'sž. or ex-pressed as Two times two amounts to four. 'Èr chéng 'èr dé 'sž. /This angle equals that angle. 'Jèige jyǎu 'děngyú 'nèige jyǎu. /These two angles are equal. Jèi'lyǎngge jyǎu syāng'děng. /They are of equal (official) rank. Tāmen 'gwānjyē syāng'děng. /A lieutenant in the navy is equal in rank to a captain in the army. 'Hǎijyūn 'shàngwèi gēn 'lùjyūn 'shàngwèi gwānjyē syāng'děng.

In general, in comparing two or more things, use yíyàng the same; píng(děng) fair and equal; other expressions meaning same; other roundabout expressions; sometimes one of the expressions listed above. /We traveled at equal speeds. Wǒmen 'dzǒude °yǐ'byār kwài (°yì'bān kwài, °yí'yàng kwài). /Adjust the three wheels to rotate at equal speeds. Jyàu jèi'sānge lwúndz jwànde °yì'bān kwai (°yí'yàng kwài,

511

°yĭ'byārkwài). (byār is used only with kwài.) or in technical language Jĕi'sānge 'lwúndz yàu 'tyáujĕngdàu 'sywǎnjwàn de 'súdù syāng'dĕng. / These two bottles are equal in size (or are equally large). Jĕi'lyàngge 'píngdz °yĭ'bān dà (°yĭ'bār dà, °yĭ'yàng dà). / Divide this into two equal parts. Bǎ jèige °'fēnchéng yí'yàngde 'lyàngfèr (°'fēnchéng syāng'dĕngde 'lyàngfèr, °'fēnchéng lyǎng'dĕngfèn, or expressed as Divide it into halves. °'fēnchéng yí'bàr yí'bàr, or expressed as Divide it equally. °'píngfēn le). or expressed as Divide it into matching parts. 'Dwèi'bàr fēnle. / Divide this into three equal parts. Bǎ jèige 'fēnchéng °yí'yàngde 'sānfèr (°syāng-'dĕngde 'sānfèr). / All men should have equal rights. 'Swǒyǒude rén dōu 'yīnggāi yǒu °yí'yàngde 'chywánlĭ (°'píng'dĕngde 'chywánlĭ).

To equal (to correspond to in other terms or in another system) shr̀. / How much does that equal in American money? 'Nèige °hé (°'héchéng, °'swànchéng) 'Mĕigwo chyán shr̀ 'dwōshǎu?

(Come up to) usually gǎnshang. / We'd been behind in the game, but we equalled their score. Bǐ'sài de shŕhou 'syànshr 'tāmende fēn shŭr 'dwō; 'méidwōdà'hwèr °wǒmen jyòu 'gǎnshangle (or meaning overtook °wǒmen jyòu 'jwēishangle, or meaning the two sides become even °lyǎngbyār jyòu 'píng le). / His record will be hard to equal. Tāde 'jìlù bùrúngyi 'gǎnshang. / It will be hard to find someone equal to him. °Gēn 'tā yí'yàngde rén (°Syàng 'tā nèiyàngrde rén) 'bùhǎujǎu. or 'Hěn nán jǎujáu 'gǎndeshang 'tā de rén.

Equal to (able to bear) shǒudelyǎu. / I don't feel equal to the trip. Dzǒu 'jèiyí-tàng wǒ pà (wǒ) 'shǒubu'lyǎu.

Equal to (qualified for, able to do). / Do you think he is equal to such a job? Nǐ jywéje 'tā °'pèidzwò (°'dzwǒdelyǎu, °'dāngdechǐ, °'dāndechǐ) 'jèmma yàngde 'shr̀ ma?

An equal; be one's equal. In the negative, Chinese usually uses superior instead of equal; in most cases verbs are used, bǐ compare with; dwèi, pèi match. / He doesn't think of anyone here as his equal. Tā jywéje 'jèr °shéi yě 'bǐ tā bú-'shàng (°shéi yě 'bǐ tā bǐbú'shàng, °shéi yě 'bùnéng gēn tā 'bǐ, °'méirén bǐde'shàng tā, or (of physical strength) °'shéi dōu 'bùshr tāde'gèr, or (of social or other rank) °'shéi dōu bǐ tā 'dǐ). / His mother thinks he ought to marry his equal. Tā 'mǔchin jywéje tā gāi 'chyǔ ge 'méndānghù'dwèi de. / Do you regard her as his equal? Nǐ jywéje 'tā 'pèide'shàng tā ma?

ERROR. tswòr, tswèr; or expressed verbally as tswò make a mistake, or as búdwèi not right. / Pardon me; my error. °Dwèibu'jù (°Dwèibu'chǐ), °wǒ tswò le (°shr̀ 'wǒde tswèr). / Look for errors and check them with a red pencil. Bǎ °'tswèr (°'tswòde dìfang, °bú'dwèide dìfang) 'jǎuchulai, yùng 'húngchyānbǐ yǐ'gōu. / Please try not to make any errors. Láu'jyà, lyóu dyǎr 'shén, byé chū'tswòr. / Some errors are unpardonable. 'Yǒude tswòr 'bùnéng 'ráushù. / There seems to be an error in the bill. Jèige jàng'dārshang hǎusyàng °yǒu ge 'tswèr (°yǒu dyǎr 'tswèr, °'tswò le, °búdà dwèi).

ESCAPE. The noun is usually expressed verbally as below. but / We had a narrow escape. is expressed as We almost had it. Wǒmen chà 'dyǎr. or as We were in great danger. Wǒmen 'syànde 'hěn.

To escape (get away or to get away from physically, escape in flight) táu, 'táupǎu, 'táudzǒu, táutwō, 'táukāi, 'táubǐ; (get away from, hide from) 'dwōkāi, 'dwōbǐ; (run away from) 'pǎukāi, 'pǎudzǒu; (get away) twō, 'twōkāi; (escape from danger) twōsyǎn; (leave) 'twōlí; (**escape as a refugee**) bìnàn. / Where can we escape to? 'Táudàu 'nǎr chyù ne? / Is there any way to escape from the prison? Tsúng 'jyānyùli yǒu fǎr °'táu (°'táupǎu, °'táuchūchyu) ma? / There is no way to escape

bombings. 'Hūngjà 'méifǎr °'dwǒbi (°'dwǒkāi, °'táukāi, °'pǎukāi). /Did anyone
escape? Yǒu °'táule (°'pǎule, °táu'pǎule, °táu'dzǒule) de ma? /Where can we escape the crowds? <u>is expressed as</u> Where shall we go to avoid the crowds? Dzámen
dàu nǎr °'dwǒkāi (°'dwǒdwo) jěyǐ'chyún yǐchyúnde rén ne? <u>or, if the situation seems</u>
<u>hopeless,</u> as With all these crowds, where can one escape? Jěyǐchyún yǐchyúnde rén
'nǎr dwǒde'kāi a? /He escaped with his life. Tā swàn 'táule 'mìng le. /You can't
escape the consequences. Nǐ °'twōbukāi (°'twōlíbùlyǎu) 'gwānsyi. /Did the criminal
escape? Nèige 'fànrén °'pǎule (°'táule) ma?

(Get away mentally). /He took to drinking for escape. Tā wèile jyě'mèr hēchi
'jyǒu láile. /He went to live in the mountains to escape from worldly worries. Tā
dàu 'shānshang chyù 'jù hǎu °'táukai (°'dwǒkai, °'twōlí) 'chénshr̀de 'fánnǎu. /Her
face is familiar, but I can't think of her name. Wǒ 'kàn tā hěn myàn'shú, kěshr
'syàngbùchí tā 'míngdz lai.

ESPECIALLY. (Unusually or most of all) 'yóuchí(shr̀), tèbyé(shr̀); dzwèi (limited in use,
not occurring before shr̀). /I want this one especially. Wǒ °'yóuchíshr̀ (°'tè'byé,
°'dzwèi) syǎng yàu 'jèige. /Everybody must give, especially you. 'Shéi dōu děi 'gěi,
°'tè'byéshr̀ (°'yóuchíshr̀) 'nǐ. /It is this child especially who needs correction. 'Jèige
háidz °'dzwèi (°'yóuchíshr̀, °'tè'byé) děi 'gwǎn. /That is an especially unpardonable
mistake. °'Tè'byé shr (°'Yóuchíshr̀) 'nèige tswòr shr̀ bùnéng 'ráushù de. or 'Nèige
tswòr shr̀ 'dzwèi bùnéng 'ráushù de. /Cantonese food is especially good. 'Gwǎngdūng
'fàn °'yóuchí (°'tè'byé, °'dzwèi) 'hǎuchr̄.

(Particularly) tèbyé. /This dish is made especially for you. 'Jèidyér tsài shr̀
tè'byé wèi 'nǐ dzwò de. /This was arranged especially for you. Jèige shr̀ tè'byé
wèi 'nǐ yùbei de.

ESTABLISH. (Of an organization) shè, 'shèlì, 'chénglì; (especially of a government or
church) 'jyànshè; (especially of a business, school, or other organization) 'kāibàn;
(to found; not used of a branch) 'chwàngbàn. /A new government was then established.
Yǐ'hòu jyòu °'shèle (°'shèlìle, °'chénglìle, °'jyànshèle) yíge 'syīn jèng'fǔ. /The
new government was established at the old capital. 'Syīn jèng'fǔ 'shèdzài 'jyoudū.
or Dzài 'jyoudū °'shèlìle (°'chénglìle, °'jyànshèle) 'syīn jèng'fǔ. /Our business
was established forty years ago. Běn'hàu shr̀ 'sz̀shrnyán'chyán °'shèlìde (°'chénglìde,
°'kāibànde, °'chwàngbànde). /We also established three branches in this town.
Wǒmen yòu dzài běn'shr̀ °'shèle (°'shèlìle, °'chénglìle, °kāibànle) 'sānge 'fēnhàu.

(Of an account) lì jédz; (colloquial, only for an account in a bank) kāi 'hùtóu(r).
/I should like to establish an account. Wǒ yàu lì yíge 'jédz. or (if a banking account)
Wǒ yàu kāi yíge 'hùtóur.

(Of a reputation, especially in government or military exploits) 'lìsya 'gūngmíng,
'lìsya 'míngshēng, chéngmíng, bǎ 'shēngmíng lì'dìng; be **established** (as to reputation) chéngle. /You might be able to establish a reputation for yourself. Nǐ 'yěsyǔ
néng °'lìsya dyǎr 'gūngmíng (°'chéng ge 'míng). /Establish a reputation first, and
then carry out your plans. °'Syān bǎ 'shēngmíng lì'dìngle (°'Syān 'lìsya ge 'míngshēng), dzài jàuje nǐde 'jìhwa chyù 'bàn. /He was established after that write-up.
Tāmen nèmma yì 'pěng tā, tā swàn 'chéngle.

(Of a brand of merchandise) chwàng(chuchyu). /That brand is established.
Nèige 'páidz 'chwàngchuchyule.

(Of residence) jùsyalai. /Are you comfortably established here? Nǐ dzài jèr
'jùsyalai jywéje 'shūfu ma?

(Prove a fact or claim) jèngmíng, jèngshr̀. /His presence was established by
several witnesses. Tā 'dāngshr̀ dzài'chǎng, yǐjīng yǒu 'hǎujige 'jèngrén ₍jèng-
'míngle (°jèng'shr̀le). /Can you establish your claim? Nǐde 'hwà néng yǒu fádz
°jèng'míng (°jèng'shr̀) ma?

EVEN. (Level) píng; (smooth and level) 'lyōupíng; **be even with** píng *or* lyōu <u>in some combinations</u>; gēn . . . píng, gēn . . . chí. /Is the surface even? 'Myàrshang 'píng ma? /The water in the river is nearly even with the top of the dikes. Héli de 'shwěi °gēn 'ànshang de dǐ kwài 'píngle (°kwài píng'tsáu le). /Fill it with water almost even with the rim. Dàu de'shwěi chàbudwō °'lyōubyārlyōuyàr de (°gēn 'kǒur 'píngje, °gēn'kǒur 'chíje).

(Constant; of motion) yún; **at an even speed** (of vehicles, etc.) ('píng)wěn. /The train traveled at an even speed. Hwǒ'chē dzǒude °'kwàimàn hěn 'yún (°hěn 'wěn, °hěn 'píngwěn). /The wheel turned at an even speed. Lwúndz 'jwànde °'kwàimàn hěn 'yún (°hěn 'wěn, °hěn 'píngwěn). /His heartbeat is even. Tā syīn 'tyàude hěn °'yún (°'wěn, °'píngwěn).

(Impartial; of distribution) 'píngjyūn, 'jyūnyún. /There was an even distribution of food. 'Lyángshŕ 'fēnpèide hěn °'píngjyūn (°'jyūnyún).

(Calm; of disposition) 'hépíng, 'wěnjùng. /He has an even disposition. Tā hěn 'hépíng. *or* Tā hěn 'wěnjùng. *or* Tāde °'píchí (°'syīngdz, °'syìngching) hěn °'hépíng (°'wěnjùng).

(Equal, well-balanced) yíyàng, chí, jyūn. /The two teams were almost even in strength. Jèi'lyǎngdwèide 'lìlyàng °'chàbudwō (°'chàbudwō yí'yàng, *or* (not one up, one down) °'bùsyāng shàng'syà, °hěn 'chí). *or* Jèi'lyǎngdwèi 'chàbudwō 'shŕjyūnlì-'dí.

(Neither in debt to the other). /This check makes us even. 'Fùle jèijāng 'jŕpyàu °jyòu shéi yě bù'gāishéi le (°dzámen jyòu chǐng'jàng le, °jyòu 'lyǎng bù'gāi le).

(Exact; of a number) jěng *or* 'gānghǎu <u>before a verb</u>. /When the last couple arrived, we had an even dozen. 'Nèilyǎngge rén 'dàule yǐ'hòu, wǒmen jyòu °'jěng (°'gānghǎu) yǒu shŕ'èrge rén.

(Divisible by two) shwāng; <u>but in mathematics</u> ǒu. /Does it make any difference whether this game is played by an odd or even number of people? Wár 'jèige de 'rénshù 'dānshùr 'shwāngshùr 'dōu syíng ma? /Four is an even number. 'Sz̀ shr̀ 'ǒushù ('shwāngshù).

Even (for emphasis) <u>usually expressed by an emphatic word both before and after the word to be emphasized, though sometimes only one occurs. Those occurring before are</u> jyòushr indeed, **even if;** lyán including, also; 'swéirán **even though.** <u>Those occurring after the word emphasized, and just before the verb are</u> yě also; dōu, yě . . . dōu all, altogether, also; hái(shr) still, furthermore; gèng still, more; yě(shr) still, also. /Even the little children caught cold. °Lyán (°'Jyòushr) syáu'háidzmen yě dōu jāu'lyángle. /Even he didn't go. °Jyòushr (°Lyán) 'tā °yě (°dōu) 'méi'chyù a. /Even he will say no to your request. °Jyòushr (°Lyán) 'tā dōu 'bùkěn 'dāying de. /He'll refuse even his own mother, let alone you. Jyòushr tā 'dzjǐde 'mùchin (chyóu tā) tā yě búhwèi 'kěn de, 'hékwàng 'nǐ ne? /Yes, even you have to go. 'Dwèile, °jyòushr (°lyán) 'nǐ yě děi chyù. /He can do even better if he tries. Tā yàushr 'yùngsyīn dzwò, jyòu néng 'dzwòde °hái (°gèng) 'hǎu dyar ne. /They don't just wear coats; they even wear neckties. Tāmen 'búdàn chwān 'shàngyī; °hái (°'èrchyě, °'jyūrán) 'jǐ lǐng'dài ne. *or* Tāmen 'bùjŕ chwān 'shàngyī; lyán lǐng'dài °dōu (°yě) 'jǐje ne. /The clothes were dirty even after (even though) they were washed. Jèisyě 'yīfu (swéirán *or* jyòushr) 'syǐle, 'háishr 'dzāng. /Even so, I don't agree with you. Jyòushr 'dzèmmaje, wǒ yě bú'dzànchéng nǐ. /Even so, I couldn't swing him around. (fig.) Lyán 'dzèmmaje, wǒ hái bùnéng bǎ tā 'shwōde 'hwéisyīnjwàn'yì le ne. /Even if we left early, it would take an hour to get there. Wǒmen 'jyòushr chyùde 'dzǎu, yě děi dzǒu yǐ'dyǎnjūng tsái néng 'dàu nèr ne. /He can't do it even if he tries. Tā 'jyòushr 'syǎng gàn, yě 'gànbu'chéng. /I must say he's a good man, even though I don't like him. 'Swéirán wǒ bù'syǐhwān tā, wǒ yě dèi shwō tā shř yíge 'hǎurén.

To even (make equal) (general) néngchí, nùngchí; (with scissors) jyǎnchí; (with a knife) láchí. Similar resultative compounds can be constructed with other meanings of even, using many of the Chinese equivalents as second members. / Please even the sleeves of this coat. Láujyà, bǎ wǒ jèijyàn 'yīfude(lyǎngjř) 'syǒudz °nèng'chí le (°nùng'chí le, °'jyǎnchí le).

Even the score (catch up with) gǎnshang, jwēishang. / Let's even the score. Dzámen °'gǎnshang (°'jwēishang) 'tāmen.

Break even (just meet expenses) gāng gòu 'kāisyāu; (just make enough to eat) gāng gòu 'chřde, (local Peiping) gāng gòu 'jyáugu; (no profit or loss) 'bùpéi bú'jwàn. / His business doesn't make much; he just breaks even. Tāde 'mǎimài 'méijwàn dwōshǎu 'chyán; yě jyòushr °gāng gòu 'kāisyāu (°gāng gòu 'chřde, °gāng gòu 'jyáugu, °'bùpéi bú'jwàn).

Get even (get revenge) bàuchóu. / I'll get even with you sooner or later. 'Dzǎuwǎn wǒ yàu 'bàu jèige 'chóu. or expressed with the proverb For a gentleman to get revenge, even ten years is not too late. 'Jyūndž bàu'chóu, 'shŕnyán bù'wǎn.

EVENING. wǎnshang: in compounds wǎn, yè; **this evening** jyēr wǎnshang; **last evening** 'dzwótyān wǎnshang, 'dzwór wǎnshang; **tomorrow evening** °'míngtyān (°'mingr, °'myér) wǎnshang; **two evenings ago** 'chyántyān wǎnshang; **three evenings ago** 'sāntyān yǐchyán de 'wǎnshang. / He comes in about this time every evening. Tā 'měityān wǎnshang bāngje 'jèige shŕhou dàu. / She feels pretty lonesome during the day, but worse in the evening. Tā 'báityan yǐjīng 'gòu mènde le, 'wǎnshang 'gèng nán'gwò. / What time does the evening show begin? °'Yèchǎng (°'Wǎnchǎng) shémma shŕhou kāi'shř? / He attends an evening school. Tā shàng 'yèsyàu. but / Good evening! as a greeting is just How are you? Nǐ hǎu? or Nín hǎu? or Hǎu a?

EVENT. (Happening) shř; **a happy event** 'syǐshř. / I always try to keep up with current events. Wǒ 'syǎnglái hěn 'jùyì 'shŕshř. / It's an important event in her life. Dzài tā yì'shēngli jèi shř jyàn °'dàshř (°hěn 'jùngyàude 'shř). / In this town the arrival of a foreigner is an event. Dzài 'jèige 'dìfang dàule yíge 'wàigwo'rén dou shř yíjyàn °'dàshř (°'syīnsyan'shř). but / A thing like that couldn't happen in the normal course of events. Dzài píng'chángde 'chíngsying jř'syà, 'jèijùng 'shř shř 'chūbulái de.

(Item on a program) syàng, 'jyémù. / What's the next event? Syà °yí'syàng (°'yíge'jyémù) shř 'shémma?

In any event 'wúlwùnrúhé, dzěmmaje, 'bùgwǎn dzěmmaje, 'fǎn jèng. / I'll be there waiting for you in any event. 'Bùgwǎn dzěmmaje wǒ yě 'dzài nar děng nǐ.

In the event of 'yàushr . . . . / In the event of an accident, please notify my father. Wǒ 'yàushr chūle 'shř chǐng nǐ 'tūngjr wǒ 'fùchin yīshēngr.

EVER. (At any time at all; said of past events or customary actions) gwo. / Have you ever done it this way? Nǐ dzěmmaje nùnggwo ma? / Have you ever been in America? Nǐ (yǐchyán) 'dàugwo 'Měigwo ma? / Have I ever met you before? Dzámen yǐ'chyán 'jyàngwo ma? / Have I ever told a lie? Wǒ shwōgwo 'hwǎng ma? / I hardly ever play cards. is expressed as I have hardly ever played cards. Wǒ jyǎn'jŕde 'méi-dzěmma 'wárgwo 'pái. or Wǒ 'yísyàng 'méi dà 'wárgwo 'pái. / He seldom if ever is on time. Tā 'jyānjŕ 'měian'shŕhou 'dàugwo. or expressed as If he is ever on time, it is most unusual. Tā jyòushr 'yǒudeshŕhou àn'shŕhou 'dàu, nà yěshr 'bùcháng 'yǒu de 'shř.

(At some time in particular; said of present or future events, wishes, questions, etc.) yŏu . . . de shŕhou; yŏu . . . (when the words following yŏu refer to an event). /Will that woman ever stop wrangling? 'Nèige 'nyŭrén yě yŏu ge bù'chǎubú'náu de 'shŕhou ma? /Is she ever home? Tā yŏu dzài 'jyā de 'shŕhou ma? /Could a thing like that ever happen? Yŏu chū 'nèiyang shŕ de shŕhou ma? or Yŏu 'nèiyangrde shŕhou ma? /Will there ever be a chance like this again? 'Hái néng 'dzài yŏu syàng 'jèiyàngrde 'jīhwei ma? /If you ever find it, let me know, will you? °Nǐ yàushr 'jǎujáule (°Nǐ yàushr yŏu ge 'jǎujáude shŕhou), jyòu gěi wŏ ge 'syèr; 'syíng ma? /Do you think he'll ever change? Nǐ syǎng tā yŏu ge 'gǎi(de shŕhou)ma? /Will he ever believe in you again? Tā 'háiyŏu syǎng'syìn nǐ de shŕhou ma?

(Before; especially in than ever) yǐchyán. /I like this more than ever. Wŏ bǐ yǐ'chyán gèng 'syǐhwān jèige le. /He is drinking more than ever. Tā bǐ yǐ'chyán hěde 'gèng dwō le.

(Used only for emphasis) ne, a, ya, na. /Why did I ever get into this? Wŏ dzěmma hwèi dàule °'jèibù 'tyándǐ ne (°jèmma ge 'dìbù ne)? /Why did I ever say that? Wŏ nàshr 'dzěmmale, 'dzěmma shwō 'nèiyangrde 'hwà a? /How did you ever hit on such a plan? Nǐ 'dzěmma 'syǎngdàude 'nèmmage 'fár ne? /How did you ever find out? Nǐ 'dzěmma 'jŕdàude a?

Ever since tsúng, 'dztsúng. /I've been taking it easy ever since she left. 'Dztsúng tā 'dzŏule (yǐ'hòu), wŏ jyòu 'yŏuyóudz'dzài de. /I've left this alone ever since he said that. 'Dztsúng tā 'nèmma yǐ'shwō, wŏ jyòu méi'gwǎngwo jèige.

See also NEVER.

EVERY. měi, yī; for emphasis 'měiyi; gè in certain limited compounds as gèrén everyone, gègwó **every country**; or expressed by the reduplication of certain nouns, as 'tyāntyan **every day**, 'nyánnyan **every year**; or by a question word plus dōu; if the emphasis is collective rather than distributive, swŏyŏude plus dōu or chywán or (stronger) chywán'dōu altogether before the verb. /Every person gets three dollars. 'Měirén °dé (°ná) 'sānkwàichyán. /He knows every man, woman and child in the village by name. Jèige 'tswūndzlide °'měiyíge 'nánrén, 'nyŭrén, syǎu'háidz (°'nánnyulǎu'shàu, °yíge'yígede) tā dōu 'jyàudechū 'míngdz lai. /I see him every day. Wŏ 'měityān 'kànjyan ta. /It rains every day. 'Tyāntyān syà'yǔ. /Every year there's been a flood. °'Měinyán (°'Nyánnyán) fā'shwéi. or 'Yǐnyán fā 'yítsż 'shwéi. /Every time I see him he's busy. 'Měitsż wŏ 'kànjyan tā de shŕhou, tā °'lǎushr (°dōushr, °'dzŭngshr) nèmma 'máng. /Every dynasty has its founders. °'Měicháu (°Gè'cháu) dōu yŏu 'kāigwóde rén'wù. /Every time he makes the same mistake. °'Měihwéi (°'Měitsż, °'Hwéihwéi) chū yíyàngrde 'tswòr. /Every village has a school. Měige 'tswūndz yŏu ge sywé'syàu. or 'Gège tswūndz dōu yŏu ge sywé'syàu. or 'Yíge tswūndz yŏu 'yíge sywé'syàu. /Every bill is marked. 'Měijāng (chyán'pyàudz) shang dōu °yŏu (°jìle) 'jìhàur.

Every kind of gè'jŭngde, 'gèshŕge'yàngrde, gèjŭng'yàngrde, 'jŭngjŭngde. /I've given him every kind of opportunity to make good. Wŏ 'gěile ta 'gèshŕgè'yàngrde 'jīhwei ràng ta 'chéng dyàr 'shŕ.

Every other (skipping one) 'jyēyì plus a measure; (all but this one) 'byéde- . . . dōu. /They have movies here every other day. Jèr 'jyēyìtyān 'yǎn yìhwéi dyàn'yingr. /Take every other book, from left to right. Tsúng 'dzwŏ dàu 'yŏu 'jyē yìběr 'ná yì-'běr.

Every now and then, every once in a while 'sāntyānlyǎng'tóurde. /He takes a drink every now and then. Tā 'sāntyānlyǎng'tóurde hē dyǎr 'jyŏu.

See also EACH.

EVERYBODY. 'měirén, 'měiyíge rén,· 'rénrén, shéi, 'dàjyā, <u>all followed by</u> dōu;
(in formal statements) 'swóyoude rén dōu; *or* dōu <u>alone</u>. /Did everybody have a
good time? 'Dàjyā dōu wárde yǒu 'yìsz ma? *or* (if referring to a meal) Dōu chr̄-
'hǎule ma? /I'm willing if everybody else is. Dàjyā dōu 'ywànyì de hwà wǒ yě
'swéije. /Nearly everybody likes the climate here. Chàbudwō °'měiyíge rén (°'rénrén) dōu 'syǐhwan jěrde °'tyānchi (°'chìhou). /Is everybody here? 'Dōu dzài jěr
ne ma? *or* °'Swóyoude rén (°'Dàjyā) 'dōu dzài jěr ne ma? /Everybody does it;
why shouldn't I? 'Rénrén dōu nèmma dzwò, dzěmma 'wǒ jyòu bùyǐng gai ne? /Not
everybody enjoys this kind of music. 'Jèyàngrde 'yīnywè búshr̀ °'rénrén (°'shéi,
°'měiyíge rén) dōu °ài'tīng (°néng 'syīnshǎng).

See also **EVERY.**

EVERYTHING. (When referring to objects of all sorts) swóyoude 'dūngsyi, 'měiyíjyàn
dūngsyi, 'shémma (dūngsyi), <u>all followed by</u> dōu; <u>when referring to all objects or</u>
<u>actions of a particular sort replace</u> dūngsyi <u>in the above by the particular word for</u>
<u>the object or action</u>. /I want to see everything you have about engineering. Wǒ yàu
'kànkan nǐ jěr 'swóyou gwānyú 'gūngchéng de °'dūngsyi (°'shū). /He lost everything when his ship was sunk. Tāde chwán 'chénle de shr̄hour tā °'swóyoude dūngsyi
dōu 'dyōule (°'shémma (dūngsyi) dōu 'dyōule, °'jyànjyàr dūngsyi dōu 'dyōule,
°'dūngsyi dōu 'dyōule). /Everything is expensive these days. 'Jìnlái 'shémma
dūngsyi dōu 'gwèi. /Everything in the house is insured. Jèige 'fángdzli °'měijyàn
dūngsyi (°'jyànjyàr dūngsyi, °shémma dūngsyi, °swǒ'yǒude dūngsyi, °shémma)
'dōu bǎule 'syǎn le. /We can't all do everything. Wǒmen 'bùnéng 'měi (yíge)rén
'shémma('shr̀chíng) 'dōu hwèi 'dzwò. /An officer should be able to do everything his
men can do. 'Shr̄bīng hwèidzwò de 'gwānjǎng jyòu 'yīnggāi 'dōu hwèi.

It means everything (it's most important). /In this business a good start means
everything. Gàn 'jèige 'dzwèi yàu'jǐnde shr̀ yàu chǐ'tóur chǐde 'hǎu.

See also **EVERY.**

EVERYWHERE. 'chùchù, 'dàuchù, 'gèchù, 'nǎr, <u>all followed by</u> dōu; dōu <u>plus a re-</u>
<u>sultative compound with the ending</u> byàn. /I've looked everywhere for it. Wǒ °'dàuchu
(°'chùchù, °'gèchù, °'nǎr) dōu 'jáule. *or* Wǒ 'dōu jǎu'byànle. /Everywhere he
goes he is welcome. Tā °'dàuchù (°'gèchù, °dàu 'nǎr) dōu 'shòu rén 'hwānyíng.

See also **EVERY.**

EXACT. (Precise, accurate) 'jwǔnchywè; . . . yě bú'chà, <u>where the words which precede</u>
<u>specify a division, detail, or characteristic of the thing referred to</u>; (of news, infor-
mation, etc.) 'jèngchywè, 'chywèshr̀; <u>or sometimes expressed with</u> jèng **exactly**.
/This answer is only approximate, not exact. 'Jèige 'hwéidá 'bùgwòshr dàgài'chí,
bìng 'búshr °'jwǔnchywè de (°'yìdyǎr yě bú'chà). /The exact location of the city is
29° 34' N., 106° 35' E. 'Jèige chéngde 'jwǔnchywè 'dìwèi shr̀ 'běiwěi èrshr̄'jyoudù
sānshr̄'szfēn, 'dūngjīng 'yìbǎilíng'lyòudù sānshr̄'wǔfēn. /Are these figures exact?
Jèisyē 'shùr 'jwǔnchywè ma? /These are his exact words. Jèi shr̀ tā 'shwō de,
'yíge dz̀ yě bú'chà. /Tell me his exact words. Tā 'dzěmma shwōde, nǐ 'yígedz̀
yě bú'chàde shwōgei wǒ 'tīngting. /This is an exact reproduction of the original
edition. Jèi shr yíge fānyìnběn, gēn ywánbǎn yìdyar yě bú'chà. /Is that information exact? Nèige 'syāusyi °'jèngchywè ma (°'chywèshr̀ ma)? /We live in the
exact center of town. Wǒmen jùdzài shéng'lǐde 'jèng dāngjūng. /That's the exact
solution. Nèmma jyějywé 'jèng dwèi.

(Correct) . . . yě bú'tswèr, <u>used as</u> yě bú'chà <u>above</u>; bùchūtswèr. /His work
is very exact. Tā dzwò'shr̀ °'yìdyǎr yě bú'tswèr (°'bùchū'tswèr).

EXACTLY. jèng; (whole, with no fractions) jěng; (in questions) dàudǐ, 'jyòujǐng; (in comparisons) jyǎnjŕ, jěng, <u>followed by</u> syàng. /We both arrived at exactly the same time. Wǒmen 'jěnghǎu 'túngshŕ dàude. /That's exactly the amount he gave me. Nèi 'jèng shr tā géi wǒ de nèige 'shùr. *or* Tā géi wǒ de 'jyòu shr 'nèmmasyē. /It's exactly four-thirty. °'Jěng (°'Jěng) 'sźdyǎn'bàn. /That's exactly what I want. Nèi 'jèng shř wǒ 'yàude. /Exactly what do you mean? Nǐ °'jyōujǐng (°dàu'dǐ) shř shémma 'yìsz? /He walks exactly like his father. Tā 'dzǒulù °jyǎn'jŕ (°jèng) syàng tā 'dyě shřde. *or* Tā 'dzǒulù jyǎn'jŕ gēn tā 'dyě yí'yàng. /This coat is exactly like mine. Jèijyàn dà'yī °jyǎn'jŕ (°'jèng) syàng wǒde. /That's exactly it! *or* Exactly! 'Jèng dwèi! *or* 'Jyòu shr 'nèmmaje! *or* 'Yídyǎr bú'chà! *or* Kě bú'shŕ ma!

EXAMINATION. <u>Most of the terms listed below also mean</u> **examine.**

(Physical, by eyes or instruments) 'jyǎnchá, 'jyǎnyàn; **reveal by examination** cháchulai. /He is still under examination. Tā hái dzài 'jyǎnchá. /How did your (physical) examination come out? Nǐ ('jyǎnchá shēn'tǐ) °'jyǎncháde (°'jyēgwǒ) dzěmma'yàng? /The examination of the (contents of the) trunk revealed nothing. 'Syāngdzlǐde 'dūngsyi 'jyǎnchále, °méi'kànchu (°méi'cháchu) shemma lai. *or* 'Syāngdzlǐde 'dūngsyi méi'cháchu shemma lai. /You ought to have a thorough physical examination. Nǐ děi dzwò yìhwéi 'syángsyî 'tǐge °'jyǎnchá le (°'jyǎnyàn le).

(Investigation) 'kǎuchá, 'shěnchá, 'yánjyōu. /I have made a careful examination of the situation. Wǒ 'yǐjǐng bǎ jèige 'chíngsyíng 'dzsyîde °'kǎuchále (°'shěnchále, °'yánjyōule) yísyar.

(Test) kǎude, kǎushř (the verb is kǎu); **pass an examination** kǎushangle, 'jígé le; **civil service examination** 'wén gwānkǎu'shř. /How did you make out in your examinations? °Nǐ 'kǎude (°Nǐde 'kǎushř) °dzěmmayàng (°'jyēgwǒ dzěmma'yàng)? /The students are taking examinations now. Sywéshēng syàndzài yǒu kǎu'shř. *or* Sywéshēng jèng dzai 'kǎu ne.

EXAMINE. (Look over carefully) 'jyǎnchá, chá, yàn, 'jyǎn yàn; <u>sometimes</u> (for perfunctory examinations) kàn, chyáu. /The police went to examine their passports. 'Jǐngchá chyù °'jyǎnchá (°'jyǎn yàn, °'chá, °'yàn) tāmende hù'jàu chyule. /Let me examine your passport again. Wǒ 'dzài °kànkan (°chyáuchyau) nǐde hù'jàu. /Has the doctor examined you yet? 'Dàifu °'jyǎnchá (°'jyǎn yàn, °'chále, °'yànle) nǐ le ma? <u>or simply</u> °'Jyǎnchá (°'Jyǎn yàn) 'gwòle ma?

(Investigate) 'yánjyōu; (with particular care) 'kǎuchá, 'shěnchá; (with deep thought) 'kǎulyù; (by merely looking around) 'chákàn. /We should examine the claims made on both sides. Wǒmen 'yīnggāi bǎ 'lyǎngbyārde hwà dōu °'yánjyouyánjyou (°'kǎulyùkǎulyù, °etc.). /The police are examining the circumstances of the accident. 'Chūshř de 'chíngsyíng, 'jǐngchá jèngdzài °'yánjyou (°'kǎuchá, °'shěnchá, °'chákàn).

(To question in court) shěn, wèn, 'shěnwèn. /When examined in court, he denied everything. Dzài °'tángshang (°gwò'tíng) °'shěn tā (°'wèn tā, °'shěnwèn tā) de shŕhou, tā dōu méi'chéngrèn.

EXAMPLE. (Illustration, case in point) 'bǐfāng (the example given may be authentic or hypothetical); lìdz (only if the example given is authentic). /Let me give you an example. Wǒ géi nǐ ge °'bǐfāng (°lìdz) ba. /There are many such examples in history. Lìshŕshang yǒu hěn 'dwō syàng jèiyangrde 'lìdz. /His speech was very interesting because he made good use of examples from everyday life. Tāde jyǎngyǎn'hěn yǒuyìsz, yīnwei yùng řcháng shēnghwóde 'lìdz 'yùngde hěn hǎu.

(Specimen, sample; for purposes of study and imitation) 'lìtí; (for purposes of comparison) yàngdz; <u>or sometimes expressed indirectly.</u> /Study the example carefully and answer the questions the same way. Bǎ 'lìtí 'dzsyî kànle; swǒyǒude 'wèntí dōu jàu'yàngr 'hwéidá. / Show me an example of his writing. Tā 'syě de dūngsyi gěi wǒ °ge 'yàngdz kànkan (or meaning a bit °'ná dyar lai (or 'ná ge lai) kànkan). / Is this a typical example of his work? is expressed as Is all his work like this? Tā dzwò de 'dōu 'jèiyàngr ma? / This painting is a good example of his art. is expressed as This painting will illustrate his art. 'Jèijāng hwàr 'hěn kéyi 'dàibyǎu tā hwà-'hwàr de 'gūngfu. or Tsúng 'jèijāng 'hwàr jyou 'kéyi 'kànchu tā (hwà'hwàr)de 'gūngfu lai. / This is (an example of) how the machine works. Jèige 'jīchi 'dzèmmaje °'dùng (°'yùng, °'kāi, °'shř).

(Precedent) 'bǎngyàng; (only in a voluntary sense) 'byǎushwài; or sometimes expressed indirectly. / You ought to set an example for the others. Nǐ děi gěi 'byérén dzwò °ge 'bǎngyàng (°ge 'byǎushwài). / The way he is treated will be an example for the others. (good or bad) 'Tā jèijyàn shř a, jyou shr ge 'bǎngyàng. or (bad; a warning) Jě jyou shr 'shāyījǐng'bǎi. / He ought to be made an example of. (good or bad) Děi ná 'tā lai dzwò ge 'bǎngyàng. or (a warning) Děi ná 'tā lai 'jǐngjyèjǐngjyè 'byérén.

For example 'bǐfang(shwō), jyúlǐshwō, jyǔ ge 'lǐdz shwō. / For example, if you come late, you will be punished. °'Bǐfang(shwō) (°Jyúlǐshwō, °Jyǔ ge lǐdz shwō) yàushr nǐ lái'wǎnle, jyou děi āi 'fá.

EXCELLENT. hǎujíle, 'jēn hǎu. / That was an excellent dinner. Nèidwùn fàn °jēn hǎu (°hǎujíle). / He is an excellent tennis player. Tāde 'wǎngchyóu dǎde °'jēn hǎu (°hǎujíle). / She gave an excellent performance last night. Dzwér 'wǎnshang tā yǎn de °'jēn hǎu (°hǎujíle).

EXCEPT. (Excluding; occurs initially only) 'chúle . . . (yǐwài); (if it were not that, if it had not been that; occurs initially only) yàu'búshr; (only for, just that; occurs after the general statement) jyòushr, 'jyòu yǒu, jřshr, 'jř yǒu. See JUST. / Everything was fine except one thing. Chúle 'yíyàngr (yǐwài), 'dōu hǎu. or 'Dōu hǎu, °'jyòushr (°'jyòu yǒu, °'jřshr, °'jř yǒu) 'yíyàngr °'bùhǎu (°'chàdyar, °bújyàu rén 'mǎnyì, or other expressions meaning bad). / There are no rooms available except on the top floor. Chúle jǐn'dǐngrshang yǐ'tséng 'méiyǒu 'kūngfáng. / There is no way out except giving him what he wants. 'Chúle tā 'yàu shémma 'gěi tā shémma (yǐ'wài), jyou 'méiyou 'byéde fár. or expressed as There's no other way; give him what he wants. 'Méiyou 'byéde fár; tā 'yàu shémma 'gěi tā shémma hǎu le. / I don't have any reason except that I don't like him. 'Chúle wǒ 'bù'syǐhwān tā (yǐ'wài), 'méiyou shémma 'lǐyóu. or expressed as There's no reason; I just don't like him. Shémma 'lǐyóu yě méi'yǒu; wǒ 'jyòushr bù'syǐhwān tā. / I would have been here much sooner except for some trouble on the way. Yàu'búshr dzài 'dàurshang 'chúle dyàr 'máfan, wǒ 'dzǎu jyou kéyi 'dàule. / I like the book pretty well except for the last two chapters. 'Jèiběr shř, 'chúle dzwèi'hòu lyǎng'jāng wǒ 'dōu hěn 'syǐhwān.

EXCEPTION. lǐwài; or expressed indirectly. / There's an exception to everything. 'Shémma shř 'dōu yǒu lǐ'wài. / That's an exception. Nèi shř lǐ'wài. or expressed as That doesn't count. 'Nèi bú'swàn. / We allow no exceptions for anyone. is expressed as We treat everyone the same way. Wǒmen jèr 'shéi dōu 'yílyù 'kāndài. / Make an exception (for him) this time. 'Jèitsž swàn lǐ'wài hǎu le. or expressed as Allow him to do it that way this time. 'Jèitsž 'ràng tā nèmmaje hǎu le. / However, I'll make an exception in your case. 'Kěshr, 'jèitsž °'swàn le (°'swàndzwò lǐ'wàile). or expressed politely as In your case it calls for different treatment. 'Kěshr ('nínhe), 'nín jèitsž 'yǒu dāng 'byélwùn le.

EXCHANGE. (To trade one thing for another) hwàn. / I'd like to exchange this book for another one. Wǒ syǎng ná 'jèiběr shū 'hwàn yìběr ('byéde). / Could I exchange this (for something else)? Jèige syú 'hwàn ma? or Jèige 'hwànhwan 'syíng busyíng? or Jèige 'hwàn 'byéde, 'syíng busyíng?

(Interchange mutually) 'jyāuhwàn. / Prisoners of war are going to be exchanged within a year. 'Fúlwǒ dzài yǐ'nyán yǐnèi 'jyāuhwàn. / I've been exchanging information with your friend. Wǒ gēn nǐde 'péngyou °'jyāuhwànle bù'shǎude 'syāusyi (or talking with him) °'tánle tán. / They exchanged ideas before reaching a decision. Dzài 'méi'jywédǐng yǐ'chyán tāmen 'jyāuhwàn 'yìjyan láije. / Would you exchange with me? Dzámen 'jyāuhwàn, nǐ 'ywànyi ma? or expressed as Would you exchange yours for mine? (See above.) Nǐ ywànyi °ná 'nǐde hwàn 'wǒde ma (°ná 'nǐ nèige hwàn wǒ 'jèige ma)?

In exchange for hwàn or an indirect expression. / Would you like to give me your tickets in exchange for this fountain pen? Nǐ'ywànyi °ná (°yùng) nǐde 'pyàu lái 'hwàn jèigwǎn 'dzláishwěi'bǐ ma? / I'll give you this book in exchange for your tie. Wǒ géi ni jèiběr 'shū hwàn nǐde lǐng'dài.

Rate of exchange 'hwèilyǔ, hwèidwèilyǔ, 'hwèidwèide 'hángshr. / What's the rate of exchange today? Jyērde °'hwèilyǔ (°'hwèidwèi'lyǔ, °'hwèidwèide'hángshr) (shǐ) 'dwōshǎu?

EXCITE. Chinese uses no general terms, but specifies several ways in which a person becomes excited, as by happiness, anger, etc.

To **excite.** / Don't excite him (an animal or person). (by intentional or unintentional teasing; with pleasant or unpleasant results) Byé 'jāu ta. or (by intentional teasing, kidding, or nagging; with pleasant or unpleasant results) Byé 'dòu ta. or (by irritating) Byé 'rě ta. / Don't excite the patient. or Don't let the patient get excited. (cross, angered) Byé jyàu 'bìngrén °jāu'jí (or angered) °shēng'chì, or (too happily excited, as by good news) °tài gāu'syìng le, or (too dangerously excited; a medical term not widely understood) °tài 'syìngfèn le). / The book is too specialized to excite (draw out) popular interest. 'Jèiběr shū tài jwān'mén le, bùnéng 'yǐnchǐ 'pǔtūngrénde 'syìngchyu.

Be **excited.** / The kids were excited (very happy) when you said you would take them to the circus. Nǐ shwō yàu dài 'háidzmen chyù kàn 'mǎ'syǐ laije, jyàu tāmen 'syǐhwān °'jíle (°de 'lyàubudé). / The excited mob (like madmen) threatened to break in. Nèichyún rén fā'fēng shrde yàu 'chwǎngjinlai. / Don't get excited! is expressed as Be calm! 'Wěnje dyar! or as Don't be impatient! Nǐ syān byé jāu'jí! or as Don't be agitated! Nǐ syān byé 'hwāng! or as Don't get angry! Nǐ syān byé °'hwǒr (°'shēng'chì). or as Go slowly. Màn'mār lái. or Màn'mān lái.

Be **exciting.** / That was an exciting story. (moving) Nèige 'gùshr hěn °dùng-'rén (or (interesting) °you'yìsz). or Nèige 'gùshr jyàu rén 'tīngle dùng'syīn. / Isn't it exciting? 'Dwō yǒu 'yìsz a?

EXCUSE. (Pardon, forgive; or in expressions of politeness) the Chinese expressions fit narrower contexts than the English. Thus the equivalents of **excuse me** are as follows: (most general, also usable in most of the more specific contexts stated below) dwèibuchǐ, dwèibujù; (if preceding a request for information made to a stranger) jyégwǎng, chǐngwèn; (if preceding a request for a favor) láujyà; (in extremely formal circumstances) hěn bàu'chyàn; (less formal apology for a shortcoming) 'ywánlyàng. / Excuse me; where's the railroad station? Jyè'gwǎng; hwǒchē'jàn dzài 'nàr? / Excuse me; didn't you say ten cents at first? Chǐng'wèn; nín chǐ'syān shwō de búshr 'shrfēn chyán ma? / Excuse me; would you move over a bit? Láu'jyà; 'nwónwór 'syíng ma? / Excuse me; please repeat that. °Dwèibuchǐ (°Láujyà); chǐng nín dzài shwō °yitsz (°yǐhwéi). / Excuse me for appearing in informal clothes this evening. (Wǒ) hěn bàu'chyàn, jyèr 'wǎnshang chwǎnje 'byànyī jyòu 'láile. / Excuse me for coughing. Chǐng 'ywánlyàng wo, wǒ yǒu dyǎr 'késou. / Please excuse my bad Chinese; I'm just learning the language. Chǐng 'ywánlyàng, wǒ 'gāng sywé 'Jūnggwo hwà, shwōbù-'hǎu.

EXPECT

Less often, where English may have **excuse me,** the following two expressions are used: byé 'syáuhwa don't hold me up to ridicule; byé jyàngwài don't feel outraged. /You'll have to excuse the way the house looks. Nín byé 'syáuhwa, wǒmende 'wūdz 'lwànchǐbā'dzàude. /Please excuse me! The child doesn't have any manners. Chǐng byé jyàn'gwài! 'Háidz bùdǔng 'lǐmàu.

EXERCISE. (Bodily movement) 'yùndùng. /In a job like this, it's hard to get enough exercise. Jèiyàngrde 'gūngdzwò 'yùndùng 'tài bú'gòu.

(Particular set of motions) 'dùngdzwò. /Each exercise should be performed fifty times. Měiyíge 'dùngdzwò děi dzwò 'wǔshrhwéi.

(Problem) 'syítí. /Do all the exercises at the end of the lesson. Bǎ 'jèikè shū 'hòumyànde 'syítí 'dōu dzwò le.

Graduation exercises bì'yèhwèi, bìyè dyǎn'lǐ. /The graduation exercises will be held at 10 o'clock. °Bìyèhwèi (°Bìyè dyǎnlǐ) dzài shŕdyan jūng °kāi (°'jyǔsyíng).

To exercise (do exercises) 'yùndùng. /You ought to exercise at least three times a week. Yì'syīngchī nǐ jŕshǎu děi 'yùndùng sāntsż.

(Practice) 'lyànsyí (yùng). /You ought to exercise your new vocabulary. Nǐ 'yīngdāng 'lyànsyí (yùng) nǐde 'shēngdz.

(To use) yùng, or indirect expressions. /He has exercised a good deal of ingenuity in this matter. Dzài nèijyàn 'shrchingshang tā °yùngle bùshǎude 'syīn fǎdz (°yùngle bùshǎude 'chyǎujāur). /Exercise care in handling that horse. 'Shŕ 'nèipi mǎ děi °jyā 'syǎusyīn (°'tèbyé yùng'syīn).

(Of a horse) lyòu. /We exercised the horses twice a day. Wǒmende 'mǎ 'yìtyān lyòu 'lyǎnghwéi. /He went out to exercise the horse. Tā lyòu 'mǎ chyule.

EXIST. (Have being) yǒu, 'tswúndzài. /I doubt if such a person exists. Wǒ 'búsyìn yǒu 'dzèmma ge rén. or 'Shrjyèshang 'nǎr yǒu 'jèyàngr rén? /Such conditions shouldn't be allowed to exist in our neighborhood. Wǒmen jèr syàng 'jèiyangde chíngsyíng bùyīngdang °yǒu (°'tswúndzài).

(Sustain life) hwó. /He existed on water and fish only. Tā jyòu kàu chŕ 'yú (gen) hē 'shwěi hwóje. /Who can exist on such a meager ration? Jyòu fēn 'jèmma dyàr dūngsyi °jyàu rén dzèmma 'hwóde'lyǎu ne (°shéi hái hwódesya'chyù ne)? /How does he manage to exist on what he makes? Tā jèngde 'nèidyǎr chyán dzèmma °hwóde'lyǎu ne (°gòu 'chŕde ne, °gòu chŕ'fàn ne)?

EXPECT. (Think, suppose) syǎng /When do you expect the train will get in? Nǐ syǎng hwǒchē shémma shŕhou jìn'jàn? /I expect you had a hard time finding this house. Wǒ syǎng nǐ 'jǎudàu jèiswor fángdz hèn 'kwùnnan ba.

(Think of in advance) syǎngdàu only with a negative preceding; 'yǐwéi only without a negative preceding. /I never expected to see him again. Wǒ 'tsúnglái méisyǎng-'dàu néng 'dzài jyànde'jáu tā. /It's more than I expected. Méisyǎng'dàu yǒu 'jèmma dwō. /He gave me more than I expected. Méisyǎng'dàu tā gěi wǒ jèmma dwō. /It's easier than I expected. Wǒ 'ywánlái 'yǐwéi °méijèmma 'rúngyi (°bǐ 'jèige 'nán).

(Want) syǎng yàu. /Does he expect a tip? Tā 'shŕ bushŕ syǎng 'yàu syǎu'fèi? /Well, what did you expect? Hái 'syǎng yàu dzèmmaje ne?

(Count on something happening) dǎswan, syǎng. /You can't expect good weather here at this time of the year. Dzài 'jèige 'jyéchili, 'béng °'dǎswan (°syǎng) 'jèige dìfang 'néng yǒu 'hǎutyār.

521

(Count on someone for something) 'jr̆wàng. / Don't expect too much of him. Byé 'tài 'jr̆wàng tā. / I never expected such gratitude from him. Wŏ 'tsúnglái °méi- 'jr̆wàng (°méi'syàngdàu) tā néng 'dzèmma 'baudá wŏ. / You have no right to expect him to have everything done for you. Nĭ 'bùgāi 'jr̆wàng 'rénjyā gĕi nĭ 'shémma dōu dzwò'hăule.

(Hope for) 'syīwàng. / Don't expect too much. Byé 'syīwang °tài dwō (°tài 'gan).

(Wait for) dĕng, hòu. / I'll expect you at six. 'Lyòudyăn jūng wŏ °'dĕngje nín (°'hòuje nín).

As well as can be expected gēn 'syàngsyàngde yíyang 'hău. / He's doing as well as can be expected. Tā 'syàndzài dzwòde gēn 'syàngsyàngde yíyàng 'hău.

EXPENSE. kāisyău, fèiyung; *or expressed as* money chyán *preceded by a word meaning* use, spend, *etc.* / I'd like to do it, but I can't afford the expense. Wŏ 'dzwŏ dàushr syàng dzwŏ, búgwò °'kāisyău (°'fèiyung) tài dà, °wo chūbu'chĭ (°chūbu'chĭ nèmmasye 'chyán). / The expense is more than I can afford. °'Fèiyung (°'Kāisyău) tài 'dà, wŏ 'dānfubu'chĭ. *or* Yùng'chyán tài 'dwō, wŏ 'dānfubù'lyău. / I must cut down expenses (economize a little). Wŏ dĕi 'jyànshĕng dyăr. *or* Wŏ dĕi °'shău yùng dyăr)°'shău hwā dyăr) 'chyán. / He built the whole thing at his own expense. Jĕng'gĕrde 'dōushr tā °yùng tā 'dz̆jĭde chyán 'gàide (°'dz̆jĭ chūchyán 'gài de, *or* expressed as digging into his own pocket. °'dz̆jĭ tāu yāu'baur gàide). / I don't want to go to much expense for this party. Wŏ 'jèitsz̆ chĭng'kè 'bùsyăng °hwā (°yùng, °chū) 'tài dwōde chyán. / Please don't go to any expense on my account. Byé wèi 'wŏ °hwā (°yùng) 'chyán. *or meaning* don't bother Byé wèi wŏ tài fèi'syĭn le.

Other English expressions involving **expense(s)** are expressed by appropriate Chinese equivalents compounded with -fèi; **expense account** bāngūngfèi; **daily expenses** ryungfèi; **incidental expenses** línshr̆fèi; **miscellaneous expenses** dzáfèi, dzáyùngfèi, língyùngfèi *or* líng'yùngchyán; **traveling expenses** (paid by an organization) chū'chāifèi, chēmáfèi; (paid by oneself or others) 'lyufèi; **household expenses** jyāyùngfèi. / He gets a straight salary and expenses in this job. Tā jèige shr̆ching 'jĕngsyĭn yĭ'wài hái yŏu chū'chāifèi.

At one's expense (other than financial). / We had a good laugh at his expense. Tā gànle jyàn 'shă shèr, jyàu wŏmen 'dàsyàu. *or* Tā gĕi wŏmen dòu'syàur laije.

EXPERIENCE. (Time spent and knowledge gained; general term) 'jīngyàn; (with resulting good judgment) 'jyànshr̆; (contacts with people, "getting around") shr̆myan. / He has had a good deal of experience. Tā hĕn yŏu °'jīngyàn (°'jyànshr̆). *or* Tā 'jyàn gwo hĕn dwō 'shr̆myan. / I've learned by experience that this is the best way. °Jyù (°Jàu) wŏde 'jīngyàn wŏ 'jr̆dau jèi shr̆ 'dzwèihăude 'bànfa. / What experience do you have? Nĭ yŏu 'dwōshău 'jīngyàn? *or* Nĭ dōu 'dzwògwo 'shémma 'shr̆? / Is experience necessary? Yídĭng yàu yŏu 'jīngyàn ma? / You might take that as an opportunity to gain some experience. Ná 'nèige dàng °ge dé'jīngyàn de 'jīhwei (°ge jàng'jyànshr de 'jīhwei) bùyĕ 'hău ma? *or* Nèmmaje jăngjang 'jyànshr bùyĕ 'hău ma? *or* (to someone young) 'Nèmmaje jyànjyan 'shr̆myan bùyĕ 'hău ma? / I haven't had much experience with cars. *meaning* haven't learned much about Chĭ'chēde 'shr̆ wŏ °bù'shòushr (*or meaning* don't know much about °bù'jr̆dàu shémma, °'méiyŏu shémma 'jīngyan).

(Particular thing experienced) expressed indirectly. / That was really an experience! is expressed as That really wasn't lived through in vain. Nèi jēn méi'bái gwò! / I'll never forget the experience I had last night. Wŏ 'yŭngywăn 'wàngbulyău dzwér 'wănshang nèijyàn 'shr̆. / I'll never forget the bitter experience I had last night. Dzwér 'wănshang 'shòude 'dzwèi wŏ 'dzài yĕ bùnéng 'wàng. / I'll never forget the pleasant experiences I had with their family that summer. Wǒ gēn 'tāmen jyā yíkwàr °'jùde (°'wárde) nèiyí'syàtyan 'jēn shr̀ 'kwàihwo; wǒ 'yūngywan wàngbu'lyǎu.

In all one's experience 'tsúnglái, 'yísyàng, 'syànglái. / In all my experience I've never seen such a thing happen. Wǒ °'tsúnglái (°'yísyàng, °'syànglai) méi 'jyàngwo jèyàngrde 'shr̀.

To experience (undergo, meet up with) 'yùjyàn; yǒu (have). / We may experience some difficulties. Wǒmen hwèi 'yùjyàn syēge 'kwùnnan. / We've never experienced such a debacle. Nèmma wéi'nánde shr̀ wǒmen jèr 'syànglái °méi'yùjyangwo (°méi-'yǒugwo).

EXPERIENCED. Yǒu 'jīngyàn, yǒu 'jyànshr̀, jyàn(gwo) 'shr̀myan; (be expert; *see also* EXPERT) dzàiháng. / I am experienced in this. Jèige wǒ °yǒu 'jīngyàn (°yǒu 'jyàn-shr̀). / He's as inexperienced as a ten-year-old. Tā gēn ge 'shr̀swèide 'háidz shr̀de nèmma °méi'jīngyàn (°méi'jyànshr̀, °méijyàn gwo 'shr̀myan, °méijǐnggwo 'jèn). / He's quite experienced in this sort of thing. Jèijǔng 'shr̀ tā °hěn dzài'háng (°hěn shr̀ ge 'hángjya, °hěn yǒu 'jīngyan, *or* (an old hand) °shr̀ ge 'lǎushǒur). / He's quite inexperienced in this sort of thing. Jèijǔng 'shr̀ tā °méiyǒu 'jīngyàn (°méi-'jīngyàngwo, *or* (inexpert) °shr̀ 'wàiháng, °'búdzài'háng, °méi'jyàngwo).

EXPERT. (Specialist) 'jwānjyā, jwān'ménde rén; (in the trade, practiced) dzàiháng; (one who is expert) 'nèiháng; **be expert** nèiháng; (experienced) yǒu'jīngyàn; (an old hand) 'lǎulyànde; (expert in . . .) . . . 'jīng; (good at, skillful) hǎu. / He is considered an expert in his field. Rén 'dōu shwō tā dzài 'tā nèihángli shr̀ ge 'jwānjyā. / He's an expert in that kind of work. Nèijǔng 'shr̀ tā °shr̀ ge 'nèiháng (°hěn 'nèiháng, °hěn yǒu 'jīngyàn, °(hěn) dzài'háng). / The experts decided the documents were a forgery. 'Jwānjyā 'dwàndìng nèisyē 'wénjyàn shr̀ 'jyǎde. / He is an expert at all kinds of games. Wár shémma tā dōu 'wárde °'jīng (°'hǎu). / I need some expert advice. Wǒ děi 'chǐngjyàu °'jwānjyā (°jwān'ménde rén, °yǒu'jīngyànde). / We need an expert mechanic for this job. Jèige 'shr̀ching děi jàu °ge 'hǎu jīchi'jyàng (°ge yǒu'jīngyànde jīchi'jyàng, °ge 'lǎulyànde jīchi jyàng) lái dzwò.

EXPLAIN. (Make clear) jyǎng; (speak; of mental problems only) shwō; (clarify; especially of a misunderstanding) 'jyěshr̀; or any of these three as the first element of a resultative compound of which the second element is míngbai *or* chǐngchu. / Could you explain how this machine works? Jèige 'jīchi dzěmma 'shr̀ gěi wǒ 'jyǎng yijyǎng syíng ma? / He can explain anything (clearly) in ordinary language. Shémma tā 'dōu néng yùng píng'chángde hwà °jyǎng'míngbai le (°'jyǎng'chǐngchu le, °shwō'míngbai le, °shwō'chǐngchu le, °'jyěshr̀'míngbai le, °'jyěshr̀'chǐngchu le, °'jyǎngde (*or* 'shwōde *or* 'jyěshrde) 'míngmíngbái'báide (*or* 'chǐngchingchu'chǔde)). / He explained and explained, but still nobody understood. °Tā 'shwōle yòu 'shwō (°Tā 'shwōlái shwō'chyù) kěshr̀ 'hái méirén 'dǔng. (or substitute jyǎng *or* 'jyěshr̀ for shwō in every case.) / It's hard for me to explain what that word means. Nèige dz̀de 'yìsz hěn nán °shwō'míngbai le (°jyǎng'chǐngchu le, °'jyěshr̀'míngbai le, °etc., °'jyǎngde (etc.) jyàu rén 'míngbai, °'jyěshrde (etc.) jyàu rén 'tǐngde 'chǐngchu). / I can explain everything. Wǒ lái °'shwōshwō (°'jyěshrjyěshr) jyòu 'dōu míngbai le. / Let me explain (a misunderstanding). °Wǒ lái (°'Tīng wǒ) 'jyěshrjyěshr. / Let me explain it to him. 'Jèige shr̀ ràng 'wǒ lai gēn tā °'shwōshwō (°'jyěshrjyěshr, °'jyǎng-jyang).

(Justify, make excuses for) expressed indirectly. / Explain yourself. 'Dzěmmale? / Can you explain your behavior last night? Nǐ dzwér 'wǎnshang shr̀ 'dzěmma le? or expressed as Do you dare tell about it openly? Nǐ gǎn bǎ dzwér 'wǎnshangde 'shr̀ching gūngkāide 'shwōshwō ma?

EXPRESS. (Say in words) shwō, shwōchulai; (talk about) tán; **express oneself** shwō (hwà); <u>also some indirect expressions.</u> /I want you to feel free to express your opinions. 'Ywó shemma 'hwà 'swéibyan °tán (°shwō, °shwōchulai). /He expressed a desire to join the new political party. Tā shwō syǎng 'jyārù 'syīn jèng'dǎng le. /He expressed his opinion very clearly in a few words. Tā yùng ji'jyù hwà bǎ tāde yì-'jyàn shwōde hěn 'chīngchu. /I have difficulty expressing myself in Chinese. <u>meaning</u> I can't express what I mean. Wǒ shwō 'Jūnggwo hwà °'bùnéng 'syǎng 'shémma 'shwō shémma, <u>or meaning</u> It's an effort to express the meaning clearly. °Yàu bǎ 'yìsz shwō'chīngchu le hěn fèi 'shr̀). /You can express yourself clearly if you use plain words. Nǐ yàushr yùng píng'cháng shwō de 'hwà, jyòu kěyǐ shwōde jyàu rén °'míngbaile (°'dǔng). /He doesn't know how to express himself. Tā 'búhwèi shwō-'hwà. *or* Tā 'yǒuhwà bù'jr̀dàu dzěmma 'shwō. *or* Tā 'yǒuhwà búhwèi 'shwō.

Express (system for transportation of parcels, etc.) 'jwǎnyùngūng'sz (company). /Is it quicker to send this by mail or express? Bǎ 'jèige sùngchyu shr̀ 'yóujèng'jyú kwài, háishr 'jwǎnyùngūng'sz kwài?

Express (train) (fast train) 'kwàichē; (super-express) 'tèbyé'kwàichē. /Is the next train an express or a local? 'Syàyitang 'chē shr̀ 'kwàichē háishr 'mànchē? /Does the express train stop here? Jèr 'kwàichē tíng ma? /Can I get an express train here? Jèr yǒu 'tèbyé'kwàichē ma?

EXPRESSION. (Manner of statement) (shwōde)hwà. /That sounds like an expression of his. Nèige 'tīngje hǎu syàng shr̀ tā shwō de 'hwà.

(Facial appearance) 'lyǎnsè, lyǎnshangde 'shénchi. /I can tell what you're thinking by your expression. Wǒ kàn nǐde °'lyǎnsè (°'lyǎnshangde 'shénchi) jyòu 'jr̀dàu nǐde 'syīnshr̀.

(Token) yìsz; <u>this may include by implication the thing expressed,</u> as **an expression of love, an expression of gratitude,** etc. /I give you this book as a small expression of my gratitude. Sùng nín jèiběr 'shū búgwo shr̀ ge 'syǎu yìsz.

(Feeling) 'byǎuchíng, yìsz; **without expression** 'szbulajǐde. /He plays the piano without much expression. Tāde gāng'chín tánde °'méi shémma 'byǎuchíng (°'szbulajide, °méi shémma 'yìsz).

EXTEND. (Be extensive, reach a distance) <u>expressed indirectly by expressions of distance, definitions of limits, etc.</u> /This road extends for miles in that direction. <u>is expressed as</u> That end of the road is far away. 'Jèityáu 'lù wàn 'nèitóur 'ywǎnle chyùle. /This farm extends for many miles to the east. <u>is expressed as</u> The eastern boundary of this farm is many miles away. Jèige núng'chǎng 'dūngbyar yǒu 'hǎusyē lǐ'dì ywǎn. /The battle line extends (lit. is long) from the mountains to the coast. Jàn'syàn hěn 'cháng, tsúng'shān dàu'hǎi.

(Lengthen) 'yáncháng; (add; followed by what is added) jyā. /The enemy extended his line along the river to the coast. 'Dírén bǎ jàn'syàn yánje hé'àn 'yáncháng-dau hǎi'byārshang chyule. /They plan to extend the railroad to the coast next year. Tāmen 'dàswàn 'gwònyán bǎ 'jèityáu tyě'lù 'yánchángdàu hǎi'àn. /They extended the fence to enclose the lake. Tāmen bǎ 'chyáng 'jyāle yídwàn, bǎ 'hú °'chywān (°'tàu)jinlaile.

(Postpone the date of expiration) jǎnchǐ. /I'd like to get this visa extended. Chǐng bǎ 'jèige hù'jàu jǎn'chǐ. /I'd like to get this visa extended to next June. Chǐng bǎ 'jèige hùjàu jǎn'chǐ dàu Lyòuywe. /I'd like to get this visa extended for three months. Chǐng bǎ 'jèige hùjàu jǎn'chǐ 'sānge 'ywè.

(Offer) gěi. /May we extend to you our heartiest congratulations? 'Gěi nín dàu'syǐ.

EXTRA. (In addition) <u>expressed adverbially by</u> 'lìngwài; (special) 'géwài, wài; (of an extra amount or number) dwō; <u>expressed verbally by</u> jyā add; <u>sometimes both adverb and verb occur.</u> /Do I get extra pay for this job? Wǒ dzwò jèige 'shŕching °'géwài 'jyāchyán ma (°yǒu 'lìngwài 'jyāde chyán ma, °yǒu jyā'jǐ ma, °yǒu wài'jyā de chyán ma)? or Wǒ dzwò °'jèijyàn shŕ (°'jēngsyīn jŕ'wài, °'gūngchyán jŕ'wài) hái gěi 'chyán ma? /How much extra pay do you get for doing this? Nǐ dzwò 'jèige dé 'dwōshau wài'jyā de chyán? /We must put in some extra time in order to finish this on time. Děi ('géwài or 'lìngwài) jyā'gūng tsái néng bú'wùchǐ ne. /You probably need only five tickets, but I'm giving you a few extra. Nǐ dàgài 'wǔjāng pyàu jyòu 'gòule, búgwò wǒ °dzài (°lìng'wài) dwō 'gěi nǐ jijǎng.

(Special) 'tèbyé, 'géwài. /Pay extra attention to this. Jèige °'tèbyé (°géwài) lyóu'shén.

(Superfluous) fùyude; **have extra** fùyu. /Do you have an extra pencil you could lend me? Nǐ yǒu 'fùyude chyān'bǐ 'jyègěi wǒ yì'jŕ ma? /I have two extra blankets. Wǒ 'fùyu 'lyǎngtyáu 'tǎndz.

An extra (an actor without an assigned part); **be an extra** pǎu 'lúngtàu. /He was an extra for years before he got his first part. Tā 'pǎule hǎuji nyán 'lúngtàu yǐ'hòu, tsái 'dāngde 'pèijyǎur.

(Unscheduled edition) hàuwài. /They put out several extras on V-E day. 'Ōujōu jàn'shèngde nèityān tāmen chūle 'jitsż hàu'wài.

EXTREME. (Excessive, very great) <u>is expressed with the various forms for</u> extremely. *See* **EXTREMELY**. /Such an operation is necessary only in extreme cases (of illness). 'Jèiyàngde 'shǒushù jŕ yǒu °'lìhai'jílede (°'jílìhaide, °'jísyūngde, °'dǐngsyūngde, °'dǐnglìhaide, °'fēicháng lìhaide, °'jíchi 'lìhaide, °shŕfèn'lìhaide, or other combinations with syūng instead of 'lìhai) 'bìng tsái 'yùngde'jáu. /He was reduced to extreme poverty. Tā 'hòulai °chyúng'jíle (°chyúng'tòule, °lèpwò'jíle). /He is in extreme danger. Tā 'jíchi 'wéisyǎn. or Tā 'wéisyǎn 'jíle. <u>or expressed as</u> He is in danger to the 10,000 degree. Tā 'wéisyǎndàu 'wànfēn le. /This is an extreme case. <u>is expressed as</u> This isn't frequent. 'Jèige búshr 'chángyǒu de. <u>or as</u> This isn't often seen. 'Jèige bù'cháng jyàn.

(Radical) gwòfèn. /She is extreme in her tastes Tā syǐhwān shémma, jyòu 'syǐhwànde gwò'fèn.

An extreme. /We never have any extremes in temperature here. <u>is expressed as</u> It's never too hot nor too cold. Jèr 'tyānchì syànglai méiyǒu 'tài lěng 'tài rède shŕhou. <u>or as</u> It's mild. Jèr 'tyānchì syànglai hěn 'wēnhé.

Go to extremes gwòfèn; <u>or in cases in which the meaning is appropriate, the expressions described above may be used.</u> /Let's not go to extremes. Wǒmen byé tài 'nèmmaje le. or Wǒmen byé (tài) gwò'fèn lou. /You may tease him, but don't go to extremes. 'Dòudou tā bú'yàujǐn, 'kě byé dòude °'tài 'lìhai lou (°('tài) gwò'fèn lou). /If he goes to extremes in this matter, you'll have to let him learn his lesson. 'Jèijyàn shŕ tā yàushr 'bànde gwò'fèn le, nǐ jyòu děi gěi tā ge 'jyàusywun.

Go from one extreme to the other <u>is expressed as</u> change extremely byànde hěn 'lìhai. /He always goes from one extreme to the other. Tā 'lǎushr byànde hěn 'lìhai, yí'byàn jyòu 'byànde °'jèng syāng'fǎn (°tsúng 'jèitóur dàu 'nèitóur). /He went from one extreme to the other and married a chorus girl. Tā 'byànde 'tài 'lìhai le; 'chyǔle ge wǔ'nyǔ.

EXTREMELY. ... 'jíle, dǐng ... , 'fēicháng ... , 'shŕfēn ... , 'jíchi ... ; (too, very) tài ... ; <u>with some stative verbs</u>, jí ... ; <u>with</u> chyúng poor <u>and</u> hwài bad, ... tòu. /This weapon is extremely useful in jungle warfare. Jèijǔng 'wǔchì dzài 'sēnlínjànde shŕhou °'yùngchu dà 'jíle (°'fēicháng yŏu'yùng, °'dǐng yŏu'yùng). / This is an extremely serious crime. Jèi shŕ jídàde dzwèi. *or* Jèi shŕ 'jíjùnde 'àndz. *or* Jèi shŕ fēicháng jùngdàde àndz. *or* 'Jèi shŕ 'dǐngdàde 'dzwèi. *or other combinations with* 'shŕfen, 'jíchi, dǐng, 'fēicháng. / He is extremely sensitive about his baldness. Tā °'fēicháng (°'shŕfen, °'jíchi, °tài) 'jǐhwèi rén shwō tā 'tū. / That was an extremely bad movie. Nèige dyànyǐngr hwài'tàu le.

EYE. (Organ of vision) yǎnjing; in compounds and some phrases yǎn or occasionally yǎr; before the eyes yǎnchyán; **cross-eyed** 'dòuyǎr; **left eye** 'dzwǒyǎn; **right eye** 'yòuyǎn; **eyelash** yǎnmáu; **eyebrow** yǎnméi; **eyeball** yǎnjūr (used also in referring to the color of eyes). / My eyes are tired. Wǒ 'yǎnjǐng lèi le. / Small type hurts the eyes. 'Syǎudzèr shāng 'yǎnjing. / Open your eyes wide. Bǎ 'yǎnjing jēng'dàlou. / Close your eyes. 'Bìshang 'yǎnjing. / This eyewash will relieve the strain on your eyes. Yùng 'jèige syǐ'yǎnyàu'shwěi kéyǐ jyàu 'yǎnjǐng 'shūfu. / It's right before your eyes. 'Jyòu dzài nǐyǎn'chyán ner. / I have something in my eye. Wǒ 'yǎnjǐnglǐ 'jìnchyu dyǎr 'dūngsyi. / He is blind in one eye. Tā 'yìjr 'yǎnjǐng syāle. / He is nearsighted in his left eye and astigmatic in the right. Tā 'dzwǒyǎn 'jìnshr, 'yòuyǎn 'sàngwàng. / He is cross-eyed. Tā shŕ 'dòuyǎr. / Her eyelashes and eyebrows were burned, but her eyes weren't hurt. Tā yǎn'máu yǎn'méi dōu 'shāule, kěshr 'yǎnjing hǎu'hǎurde. / One of his eyes (eyeballs) is false. Tā yǒu yíge 'jyǎyǎnjūr. / His eyes are blue. Tāde yǎn'jūr shŕ 'lánde. *or* Tā shŕ 'lányǎnjūr. / Have you got anything good for a black eye? 'Yǎnjing nar dǎ'chīngle, 'yǒufár 'jr ma? / It's invisible to the naked eye. 'Ròuyǎn bùnéng 'kànjyan.

(Small round hole) yǎr; (of a needle) jēnyǎr; **hook and eye** gōur, gōudz. / The eye is squeezed shut; I can't hook it. Yǎr 'jǐjǐnle; wǒ 'gōubujinchyu. / This coat fastens at the neck with a hook and eye. Jèijyan wài'yī lǐngdz ner shŕ yùng 'gōur gōushangde.

Be all eyes is expressed with kàn look. / The boy was all eyes. Syǎu'hár kànde chū 'shér le. *or* Syǎr'hár 'mùbujwǎn'jīngde kàn.

Catch one's eye ràng ... 'kànjyan followed by a pronoun referring to the subject. / I've been trying to catch your eye for the last half hour. Yǒu 'bàndyǎn jūng le wǒ syǎng'fár ràng nǐ 'kànjyan wǒ.

Close one's eyes to (pretend not to be able to see) 'jwāng kànbu'jyàn. / He closes his eyes to his pupils' mischievous pranks. 'Sywéshengmen táu'chǐ tā 'jwāng kànbu'jyàn.

Give someone the eye gen ... fēiyǎr. / She gave me the eye, but I went right by. Tā gēn wo fēi'yǎr, kěshr wǒ méi'lǐ ta.

Have one's eye on chyáushang. / He has his eye on that position. Tā 'chyáushangle 'nèige 'wèijr le.

Have a good eye (aim). / He has a good eye. Tā hwèi myáu'jwǔn.

Have a good eye for yǒu 'yǎnlì. / He has a good eye for horses. Tā kàn'mǎ hěn yǒu 'yǎnlì.

In one's eyes (opinion). / In the eyes of his parents he's a little angel. Tāde dyē'mā kě 'ná tā 'dàng ge bǎu'bèr kàn ne.

Keep an eye on kàn, chyáu. / Keep an eye on him. 'Kānje tā dyar. *or* 'Chyáuje tā dyar. / Be sure to keep an eye on the children. 'Chyānwàn °'kānje dyar (°'chyáuje dyar) háidzmen.

Keep an eye out for lyóushén. / Keep an eye out for escaped prisoners. Yǒu 'fúlwǒ 'táule, 'lyóu dyar 'shén.

Make eyes at. /Don't make eyes at married women. is expressed as Don't fish for married women. Byé dyàu jyēle 'hwūn de 'nyǔren.

My eye tsái'gwài ne. /Hasn't she been kind to you? Kind, my eye! Tā bushr 'dài nǐ hěn 'hǎu ma? 'Tā dài'wǒ hǎu? Tsái'gwài ne!

Pull the wool over one's eyes jyàu . . . 'shàng . . . dàngde, jyàu . . . 'shǒu . . . 'pyànde. /His suave manner is likely to pull the wool over your eyes. Tā nèijǔng 'tǎurén syǐhwān de yàngr hwèi jyàu nǐ °'shàng tāde 'dàng de (°'shǒu tāde 'pyàn de).

See eye to eye is expressed in various ways as points of view being the same. See SAME. /I don't see eye to eye with you on this question. 'Jèige wèntí wǒ gēn 'nǐde kànfǎ °bù'túng (°bùyí'yàng). /They don't see eye to eye on much of anything. Tāmen 'jǐhū 'shémma shr̀ dōu °'yí'jyàn bù'hé (°bùtúng'yǐ). or 'Jǐhū 'shémma shr̀ tāmende 'kànfǎ dōu °bù'túng (°bùyí'yàng). /We do see eye to eye, don't we? 'Dzámen kànfǎ °yí'yàng (°syàng'túng), 'dwèi ma? or 'Dzámen 'yì'jyàn syàng'hé, 'dwèi ma?

Set eyes on 'kànjyàn. /I never set eyes on her before in my life. Wǒ 'jèibèidz 'tóuyǐhwéi 'kànjyàn tā. or Wǒ 'tsúnglái méi'kànjyan gwo tā.

With one's eyes open míng'míngde 'jr̄dau. /He did it with his eyes open. Míng-'míngde 'jr̄dau a. /His eyes were open all right, but he married her anyway. Tā míng'míngde 'jr̄dau, kěshr̀ 'hái gēn tā jyē'hwūn le. compare /That'll open his eyes. 'Nèi jyòu 'jyàu tā 'míngbaile.

With one's eyes shut 'húlihú'dūde. /He went into that marriage with his eyes shut. Tā 'húlihú'dūde jyòu jyē'hwūn le.

With dry eyes (not crying). /She went through the funeral with dry eyes. Syíng dzàng'lǐ de shŕhou tā yì'dyǎr méi'kū.

To eye or **have one's eyes on** something or someone pyāu, byāu, kàn. /He's been eyeing me for the last half hour. Tā (nà 'yǎnjing) °pyāu wǒ pyāule (°'byāu wǒ byāule, °'kàn wǒ kànle) 'bàndyǎn jūng le.

FACE. (Physical features) lyǎn, lyǎr; in certain fixed expressions myàn, myàr, as dāng °myàn (°myàr) **right to one's face**, myàn°shóu (°shú) **have a familiar face**, myànshēng **have an unfamiliar face**, lòu 'myàr **show one's face**; 'myànmàu (appearance). /When he gets angry his face gets red. Tā yì shēng'chì, 'lyǎn jyou 'húng. /His face is oval. Tā shr̀ ge 'édànlyǎr. /His face is pockmarked. Tā 'lyǎnshang yǒu 'mádz. or Tā shr̀ ge 'mádz. /What an ugly face! 'Nèi lyǎr hǎu °'hánchenle (°nán'kànle, or (fierce) °'syūngsyàng)! /Lie on the bed face down. Lyǎn cháu 'syà pāje. /He was laid on the bed face up. Tāmen bǎ tā lyǎn cháu 'shàng gēdzai 'chwángshang. /Ever since she lost her job she's been going around with a long face. 'Dz̀tsúng tā bǎ shèr dyōule, °tā 'lyǎnshang jyou méi'dàigwo syàu'rúngr (°tā jyou 'láu běngje ge 'lyǎn, °tā jyou 'láu kūsangje ge 'lyǎn, or (pouting) °tā jyou làu jywēje 'dzwěi). /He said it with a straight face. Tā 'běngje lyǎn shwōde. /I'd call him that right to his face. Wǒ jyòu 'dāngje tāde 'myàr nèmma 'mà ta. /He has an intelligent face. Tā myànmàu hěn 'tsūngmíng. or expressed as He looks intelligent. Tā 'jǎngde 'yàngdz hěn 'tsūngmíng. /His face looks familiar to me. Jèi rén wǒ kànje myàn'shóu. /His face is unfamiliar to me. Jèi rén wǒ kànje myàn'shēng. /How can you look me in the face (with a shameless face) and say that? Nǐ dzěmma néng 'tyánje lyǎn shwō syà'hwàr a? but /Can you look me in the face and say that (is the truth)? Nèi shr̀ shŕ'hwà ma? /He's so ashamed that he doesn't dare show his face. Tā ('sàude) °bùgǎn lòu'myàr le (or meaning doesn't dare to see people °bùgǎn jyàn 'rén le, or meaning doesn't have the face to see people °'méilyǎr jyàn 'rén le).

(Surface, side) myàr. /I can't see the face of the clock from here. Jūngde 'jèngmyàr wǒ tsúng 'jèr chyáubu'jyàn. / The face of the coin has been rubbed almost smooth. Chyán yǒu'dzèrde nèimyàr kwài mwó'gwāngle. *but* / A poem was inscribed on the face of the cliff. 'Yáishang 'kèje yishǒu 'shr̄.

(Honor, social prestige) lyǎn, myàndz; **lose face** is expressed with the foregoing, or also as dzāi gēntou (fall flat). / He felt that he had lost face when you said that to him in front of people. Nǐ dāngje 'byéren gēn tā shwō nèijyù 'hwà de shŕhou, tā jywéje °dyōu'lyǎn le (°dzāi 'gēntou le, °hěn méi 'myàndz). / When you said "No!" to him like that, it made him lose face. Nǐ 'nèmmaje gēn tā shwō "Bùsyíng," jyàu tā 'jywéje hěn °dyōu'lyǎn (°méi 'myàndz). / You should have helped him save face, and not have said that to him in front of others. Nǐ yīnggāi gěi tā lyóu dyǎr 'myàndz, 'bùgāi nèmma 'dāngje 'rén shwō tā.

Face down (not of people) kǒuje; **face up** fānje. / Put your cards on the table face down. Bǎ pái 'kǒuje fàngdzai 'jwōrshang.

Face to face myàndwèi'myàrde. / They sat through the meeting face to face, but neither one would say a word to the other. Kāi'hèide shŕhou tāmen myàndwèi'myàrde dzwòje, kěshr yì'jŕ shéi yě bù'lǐ shéi. / Let's get together and talk the whole thing over face to face. Dzámen 'jyù yijyù, °myàndwèi'myàrde (°'jŕjyē, lit. directly) bǎ 'jèijyan shèr 'dzsyî 'tán yitán.

Come face to face with (fig.) yùjau, pèngjau. / Suddenly we came face to face with a difficult problem. Hūrán wǒmen °'yùjaule (°'pèngjanle) yíjyàn nán 'bàn de 'shr̄.

Make a face lyédzwěi; dzwò gwéilyǎr. / He made a face when he tasted it. Tā 'chángle yìkǒu, jŕ 'lyé'dzwěi (°dzwò gwéilyǎr). / Stop making faces at me. 'Byé gēn wǒ dzwò gwéi'lyǎr.

In the face of dzài . . .de shŕhou. / He remains cool in the face of great danger. Dzài dzwèi wéi'syǎn de shŕhou tā hái néng bù'hwāng.

On the face of it tsúng byǎu'myànshang kàn. / His idea seems to be absurd on the face of it. 'Tā jèige 'júyi tsúng byǎu'myànshang kàn hǎusyàng shr̄ bù'tūng shŕde.

Face card dài rén'tóur de pái.

Face value. / This bank note is still worth its face value. is expressed as This banknote can be exchanged according to its face value. Jèijāng 'pyàudz 'hái néng ànje pyàu'myàr °hwàn'chyán (°dwèi'syàn). or as There is no discount on this bank note. Jèijāng pyàudz háishr bùjébúkòu. / Don't take his word at its face value. Tāde 'hwà °déi dǎ 'jékòu (°'bùnéng 'chywán syìn).

Be faced (covered on the outside) 'wàimyàr shr̄ followed by the material. / The building is faced with red brick. Jèige lóu 'wàimyàr shr̄ yìtséng 'húngjwān.

Be faced (hemmed) yánshang . . . byǎr. / She had the collar and cuffs faced in red. Tā bá 'lǐngdz gēn syòu'kǒur dōu yánshang húng'byǎr.

To face (physically) chùngje, °háuje (of position); syàngje (of position or motion); dwèije (especially of facing a counterpart). (When speaking of one person facing another or others) kàn is often added.). / Turn around and face the wall. 'Jwǎngwochyu °chùngje (°cháuje) 'chyáng. / Our windows face the street. Wǒmende 'chwānghu °syàngje (°chùngje, °cháuje, °dwèije) dà'jyē. / He lives in the house facing ours. Tā jù wǒmen dwèi'mérde nèiswǒr 'fángdzli. / Suddenly he turned his head and faced her. Tā 'hūrán jwǎngwo 'tóu lai °'cháuje (°'chùngje) tā kàn.

(Meet or deal with) yìngfù. / You must face this difficulty with courage. Nǐ yìngfu jèijung 'kwùnnan, déi yóu 'yǔngchi. / You should face your troubles like a man. Nǐ 'yìngfù jèisyē 'nán 'shr̄ yīnggāi syàng ge 'nándzhàn 'dàjàngfu tsái chéng.

but / He faced death unflinchingly. is expressed as When he was about to die the color of his face didn't change. Tā lín sž 'myǎnbugǎi'sè. *or* Tā lín 'sž 'syíngsèbú-'byàn.

(In military commands) syàng . . . 'jwǎn. / About, face! Syàng 'hòu 'jwǎn! / Left, face! Syàng 'dzwó 'jwǎn! / Right, face! Syàng 'yòu 'jwǎn!

Face the music. / I guess I'd better go home and face the music. Wó syáng wǒ háishr hwéi'jyā āi 'shwō chyu ba.

FACT. (The real situation) 'jēnshr, 'jēn yǒu de shr, 'shŕdzàide chíngsying; or expressed adjectivally by jēnde (true); or expressed adverbially by jēn (really) or similar adverbs. / Is this a fact or is it just your own opinion? 'Jèi shr °'jēnshr (°'jēn yǒu de shr, °'shŕdzàide chíngsying), háishr nǐ dž'jǐde 'yìjyan? / Is that a fact? Shr 'jēnde ma? *or* 'Jēnde ma? *or* 'Jēn yǒu nèmma hwéi 'shr ma? *or* Nèijyàn 'shrching shr 'jēnde ma? / Tell him the facts. Bǎ 'shŕdzàide 'chíngsying 'gàusung ta. or expressed as Whatever there is tell him. 'Yǒu shémma jyou gēn tā 'shwō shémma. or expressed as What you actually saw tell him. Bá nǐ 'chīn yǎn 'kànjyan de shr gàusung tā.

(In a legal case) 'shrshŕ, 'shrchíng, 'jēnsyàng, 'chíngyóu. / Do you understand the facts in this case? Jèige 'àndzde °'shrshŕ (°'shrchíng, °'jēnsyàng, °'chíngyóu) nǐ dōu 'chīngchu ma?

(Situation, referring to something already mentioned) shr, shèr, shrching; **the fact that** . . . . . . nèijyàn shr, . . . jèijyàn shr; or simply omitted. / That fact makes no difference to me. 'Nèijyàn shr wo bú'dzàihu. / What about the fact that you were late for work today? (What do you have to say about it?) Nǐ 'jīntyan chŕ'dàu, (jèijyàn shr), ní dzěmma °'shwō ne (*or* (What are you going to do about it?) °'bàn ne)?

(Something assumed to be true). / His facts (what he says) are definitely open to question. Tā 'shwō de (nèisyē shr) 'dōu °bújyànde shr 'jēnde (°yǒu kě'yíde dìfang).

The facts of life (the way things are) rénshēng. / Those are the facts of life. Rénshēng jyòu shr jè'yàngr. *but* / It's time he learned the facts of life. meaning sexual facts. Wǒmen gāi gěi ta 'jyǎngjyang le. *or* Tā yīnggai 'kāikai 'jŕshr le.

As a matter of fact *or* **in fact** chíshŕ. / As a matter of fact, I couldn't go if I wanted to. Chí'shŕ wǒ jyòushr yàu chyù °hái chyùbu'lyǎu ne (°yě chyùbu'lyǎu). / In fact, he's a Ph.D. Chí'shŕ tā hái shr ge 'bwóshr ne.

FAIL. (Not succeed) bu *or* méi with a verb (usually néng or some other verb expressing ability), or a resultative compound with bu. / I failed to convince him. Wǒ °'méinéng jyàu tā 'syìn (°bǎ tā shwō'fúle). / I failed to find him. Wǒ méijǎu'jáu tā. / I still fail to see the point of your argument. Wǒ hái méitīngchu'lái nǐ 'shwō de 'jyōujìng shr shémma 'yìsz. / I tried to do it alone, but failed. Wó 'běnlai syǎng dž'gěr dzwòde, búgwò °bù'syíng (°bù'chéng, °méibàn'dàu, °dzwòbù'lyǎu, °bànbú'dàu).

(Of crops) (not good) bùhǎu. / The crops failed last year. Chyùnyán 'shōuchéng bù'hǎu.

(Of business) dǎu (fall); péi (lose money); gwānmén (close doors); pwòchǎn (go bankrupt); a negative with dzwòchéng *or* dzwòhǎu (not succeed). / His business failed. Tāde 'mǎimai °dǎule (°péile, °gwān'mén le, °pwò'chǎn le, °'méidzwò'chéng, °'méidzwò'hǎu).

(In school) bùjígé. / Five students in the class failed. Nèi'bān yóu 'wǔge sywésheng 'bùjí'gé.

(Of a sick person) yàu bù'syíng le; (getting worse and worse) bìngde 'ywè lái ywè 'lìhai. / The patient is failing rapidly. 'Bìngrén kwài yàu bù'syíng le.

Fail a person. / I won't fail you. Wǒ 'shwō dzěmmaje 'jyòu dzěmmaje. *or* Wǒ 'shwōle jyòu 'swàn. / I won't fail to help you out of this jam. Nǐ 'jèijyàn shr̀ wó 'jwǔn géi nǐ 'bàn. / He failed me when I needed his help most. Wǒ syūyàu tā bāng-'máng de shr̀hou tā méi'bāng wǒ. / This rifle of mine never fails me (it is accurate). Wǒ 'jèigǎn chyāng °hén 'jwǔn (°'shwō dá nǎr jyou dá nǎr). / Words fail me. Wó 'yǒu hwà 'shwōbuchū'lái.

Without fail yi'dìng (děi), 'fēi (děi) . . . bu'kě; or expressed with a double negative. / Be there without fail. Nǐ yí'dìng děi chyù. *or* 'Byé bú'chyù. / I'll finish the work without fail. Wǒ yí'dìng déi bǎ jèige 'shr̀ dzwò'wán. *or* Wǒ 'fēi (déi) bǎ jèijyan shr̀ dzwò wán bu'kě.

FAINT. (Lose consciousness) hwūn le, yūn le, hwūngwochyu, yūngwochyu; (fig.) 'syà yí'tyàu. / Someone fainted. Yǒurén 'hwūngwochyule. *or* Yǒurén 'yūngwochyule. / You'll faint when you hear this. Nǐ 'tīngjyan jèige děi 'syà yí'tyàu.

(Dizzy and weak) hwūn, yūn, yùn (said of tóu head). / I feel faint. Wǒ 'tóu yóu dyǎr 'hwūn. *or* Wǒ (yóu dyǎr) 'tóuhwūn. *or* Wǒ yóu dyǎr 'yùn.

(Weak, of color) dàn. / The color is too faint. Shǎr tài 'dàn.

(Not distinct, of ideas, etc.) constructions with yǐng shadow, *or* yìnsyang impression. / I have only a faint idea of what you said. Nǐ 'shwō de wǒ 'yíngyǐngchāu-'chǎude jìde yǐdyǎr. / I don't have the faintest idea of what you're talking about. Nǐ shwō de hwà wǒ yǐdyár °'yǐngr dōu mwōbu'jáu (°yìnsyang dou méiyou).

Be fainthearted °dǎndz (°dán, °dár) °syǎu (°chywè). / He's a fainthearted individual. Tā dár 'syǎu. *or* Tā dǎn 'chywè. *or* Tā 'dǎndz tài 'syǎu.

FAIR. (Just, honest) gūngping, gūngdau. (Only gūngping is used of people's treatment of each other; only gūngdau is used of a price; some more general expressions are also used.) / That's a fair way to say it. 'Nèmma shwō hěn °'gūngping (°'gūngdau). / They made a fair distribution. Tāmen fēnde hěn °'gūngping (°'gūngdau). / He always treats me fairly. Tā dài wǒ 'lǎushr °hěn 'gūngping (°hén 'hǎu). or expressed as He never cheats me. Tā 'syànglái bù'chǐfu wǒ. / That's a fair price. Jyàchyan hěn 'gūngdau. / Give me a fair price and I'll let you have it. Géi ge 'gūngdau jyàr wǒ jyòu 'mài. / They said he wasn't playing fair (lit. or fig.). Tāmen shwō tā °bù-'gūngping (°bùgūngdau, *or* (wasn't being reasonable) °bùjyǎng'lǐ, *or* (wasn't going according to the rules) °bújàu 'gwēijyu bàn'shr̀).

(Moderately good). / The work is only fair. 'Dzwòde °píng'cháng (°bú'tài hǎu yě bútài 'hwài, °'hái hǎu, °hái kéyi).

(Moderate in size). / He has a fair chance of winning. Tā 'yíngde jīhwèi °bù-'syǎu)°syàngdāng 'dà).

(Moderate in amount). / Give me a fair amount of it. Géi wǒ de byé tài 'dwō yě byé tài 'shǎu. *or* 'Bùdwōbù'shǎude géi wǒ dyar jyòu 'syíng le. *or* 'Byé géi wǒ tài'shǎu lou.

(Light in color) bái (of complexion); chyǎn (of hair); a fair-haired baby 'chyánshǎr tóufa de háidz. / Her complexion is fair. Tade 'pífu hěn 'bái.

(Of weather) hǎu, chíng. / Is the weather fair? Tyānchi 'hǎu ma? *or* Tyānchi 'chíng ma? / The weather is going to be fair tomorrow. Míngrge shr̀ 'chíngtyān. *or* Míngrge tyānchi 'hǎu. / Fair and warmer (weather report). 'Tyānchíng shāu 'nwǎn.

Fair and square. / The contest must be fair and square. Bǐsài yídìng děi gūngpíng. *or* Bǐsài bùnéng °yóu jyǎ (°nàugwěi).

A **fair** jí (a sort of market day, held at regular intervals); 'bwólǎnhwèi (a modern, large-scale exposition); **the New York World's Fair** Nyǒuywē shř 'Shřjyè 'Bwólǎn'hwèi. / Are you going to the fair? Ní gǎn'jí chyu ma? / There isn't any fair today. 'Jyèr 'méiyou 'jí a. / He bought it at the fair. Tā dzài 'jíshang mǎide.

FALL (FELL, FALLEN). (Drop) dyàu; làu, lwò, lè (especially of things falling of their own accord). / Did you hear something fall? Ní 'tīngjyàn yǒu 'dūngsyi 'dyàusyalai ma? / The leaves are beginning to fall. Shù'yèr kāishř °'làule (°'dyàule). / The lid fell off. 'Gàr dyàule. / When the curtain fell, he came to the front of the stage. Mù 'làusyalai de shŕhou tā dzǒudàu tái 'chyántou laile. / He fell into the well. Tā 'dyàu dzài 'jǐngli le. / This letter would cause trouble if it fell into the hands of those people. 'Jèifēng'syìn 'rúgwǒ lwòdzài nèisye rén 'shǒuli hwèi 'nàuchu 'lwàndz lai. / He fell out of the boat. Tā tsúng 'chwánshang °'dyàuchuchyule (°'dyàusyachyule).

(By stumbling or tripping) shwāi, dyē; **fall over** <u>something</u> jyàu . . . bàn yi-'jyāu. / Where did you fall? Ní dzài 'shémma dìfang shwāi'dǎule de? / I fell down. Wǒ shwāi'dǎule. or Wǒ shwāile yì'jyāu. or Wǒ dyēle yì'jyāu. / I fell over a chair. Yǐdz bǎ wǒ 'bànle yì'jyāu. or Wo shwāidzài 'yǐdzshàng le. / He died from falling. Tā shř 'shwāiszde.

(Go lower, of prices and other things) dǐ, làu; dyē (only used of a price falling). (Only dǐ is used of a voice falling in pitch or volume.). / The stock market fell slightly today. 'Jīntyān 'gǔpyàu 'hángshř °'dǐ le (°'làule, °'lwòle, °'lèle) yì'dyǎr. / His voice fell when he mentioned her name. Tā tídàu tā 'míngdz de shŕhou, 'shēngyīn 'dǐsyachyule.

(Be overthrown in war) bèi gūng syàn; shŕshǒu. / The city fell last week. Nèige chéng shř 'shàngywè °shŕshǒude (°bèigūngsyànde).

(Be inherited by) gwēi, lyóugei. / His property falls to his wife. Tāde 'tsáichǎn °gwēi (°lyóugei) tā 'tàitai.

(Shine on; of light) 'jàudzài. / The sunlight fell directly on his book. 'Tàiyang-'gwāng jèng jàudzài tāde 'shūshang.

(Occur, as of accent on a word) dzài. / Where does the accent fall on this word? Jèige dzde 'jùngyīn dzài 'nǎr?

(Occur on a date) shř. / Christmas falls on Monday. Shēngdànjyé shř lǐbài'yī.

Fall asleep shwèijáu. / Did you fall asleep? Ní shwèi'jáule ma?

Fall back on kàuje; (depend on) jřje. / We can always fall back on our savings. Dzámen 'dzǔng néng °kàuje (°jřje) dzámende tswún'kwǎn lái 'gwò.

Fall back (to) chè, chètwèi. / The enemy fell back twenty miles. Díren wàng hòu chètwèile 'èrshrlǐ. / They fell back to the village. Tāmen °chètwèi (°chè) dàu 'tswūndzli chyùle.

Fall behind (in). / He's fallen behind in his payments. Řdz 'gwòle tā hái méijyāu chyán. or Tā méi 'àn shŕhou jyāu'chyán.

Fall down on the job. / He won't fall down on the job. Tā 'búhwèi dzwòbù'hǎu.

Fall due dàuchī. / The rent falls due next Monday. Fáng'dzū syàsyīngchī'yī dàu'chī.

Fall for míshang. / Boy, I really fell for her! 'Hǎujyàhwo, wǒ 'jēn 'míshang tā le. but (of words) / His story sounded convincing, so I fell for it. Tāde hwà 'tīngje hén yóu'lǐ, swóyi wǒ °jyou 'syìn le (°'syìnyǐwéi 'jēn le, °shàngle 'dàng le, °shǒule 'pyàn le).

Fall in(to). / Fall in! Jàn'pái! *or* (military command) Jí'hé! / They fell into line. Tāmen jànde yì'páiyì'páide. / I've fallen into the habit of reading newspapers on the train. Wǒ dzài 'chēshang kàn 'bàu, yǐjing chéngle 'syígwànle. / All these documents will fall into three classes. Swó'yǒude jèisyē 'wénjyàn kéyi 'fēnchéng 'sānlèi.

Fall in love. / They fell in love with each other at first sight. Tāmen yíjyàn °chǐng'syīn (°jūng'chíng). / He fell in love with her. Tā 'àishang tā le.

Fall off. / His income has been falling off lately. Tāde 'shōurù 'jìnlai °jyàn 'shǎu le (°ywè lái ywè 'shǎu le).

Fall on. / They fell on the food as though they were starving. Tāmen 'chyǎngje chī hǎu'syàng 'dwōshau shǐhou méichī 'fàn shìde.

Fall out. / Fall out! Sàn'dwèi! / They used to be good friends, but now they've fallen out because of some woman. Tāmen ywán'lái shì 'hǎu péngyou, kěshr syàn-'dzài wèile ge 'nyǔren °'dǎchiláile (°'nǎule).

Fall short of. / The dinner fell short of our expectations. °Nèidwùn fàn 'bùrú (°Nèidwùn fàn 'méiyǒu) ywán'lái 'syǎngde nèmma 'hǎu.

Fall through. / The plans for the park fell through. Dzàu gūng'ywán de 'jìhwà °méi'chéng (°'chwēile).

Fall to. / He fell to work cheerfully. Tā 'gāugausyìng'syìngde dzwòchǐ 'shì laile.

Fall to pieces. / This typewriter is ready to fall to pieces. 'Jèijyà dǎdž'jī swéi'shì kéyǐ 'sàn.

Fall under. / All those expenses will fall under the same heading. Swóyǒude 'kāisyāu 'dōu kéyi °lyèdzài (°fàngdzài) yísyàngli.

Fallen arches. / He wears special shoes because he has fallen arches. Tā chwān tè'byéde syé 'yīnwei tāde jyáu'jǎng yóu dyǎr 'píng.

A fall (act of falling) is expressed verbally as in the first two paragraphs above. / Be careful, it's a bad fall if you slip. 'Syāusyīn dyǎr; °jèr hěn 'gāu (°jèr hěn 'shēn), 'dyàusyachyu kě 'bùshr 'wárde. / She had a bad fall last winter. Tā 'chyùnyán 'dūngtyān nèihwéi 'shwāide bùchīng.

A fall (precipitation) jèn. / We were delayed by a heavy fall of snow. Wǒmen ràng yíjèn dà'sywě gěi 'dānwule.

(In prices) is expressed verbally as in paragraph three above. / Let's wait for a fall in prices before we buy. Dzámen děng 'jyàchyán °dǐ (°lǎu) syàchyu dzài 'mǎi. *or* Wǒmen děng dyě'jyà de shrhou dzài 'mǎi.

(Autumn) 'chyōutyān. / I'll be back next fall. Wǒ 'chyōutyān 'hwéilái. / Is that your new fall outfit? Nèi shr nǐ 'chyōutyānde 'syīn yīshang ma?

Falls (waterfall) 'pùbù. / There are a lot of falls on this river. Jèityáu 'hé yóu hěn dwō 'pùbù.

FALSE. (Not true, not genuine) jyǎ (not used for statements or ideas). / Is this true or false? Jèi shr 'jēn shr 'jyǎ? / Is this real or false? Jèi shr 'jēnde shr 'jyǎde? / She can't get used to her false teeth. Tā yùngbu'gwàn tade jyǎ'yá. / This drawer has a false bottom. Jèige 'chōutide dyěr shr 'jyǎde.

(Not right) búdwèi, tswò(le), 'bùshr nèmma hwéi 'shèr; (of a way of saying or thinking) bú'jèngchywè; also several more specific expressions. / That's a false statement. 'Nèmma shwō bú'dwèi. *or* 'Nèmma shwō jyòu 'tswòle. *or* Nèige 'shwōfa yǒu'tswèr. / His account of the accident is all false (not deliberately). Tā shwō de chū'shr̀de 'chíngsying 'chywán °bú'dwèi (°'tswòle, °'búshr nèmma hwéi'shèr). / He gave me a false (wrong) answer. Tā 'géi wo de hwéidá °bú'dwèi (°'tswòle, or (entirely false) °'chywán 'tswòle, °yí'dyár bú'dwèi, °'chywán búshr nèmma hwéi 'shèr, °'wánchywán méi nèmma hwéi 'shèr, or (local Peiping) °mán'nǐng). / Many people get false ideas from movies. Hěn 'dwō rén yīnwei kàn dyàn'yǐngr déle °bú'jèng-chywède sz̄'syǎng (°'hwāngmyòude sz̄'syǎng). or (get fooled by the movies) Hěn'dwō rén shòu dyàn'yǐngrde 'pyàn. or Hěn'dwō rén shàng dyàn'yǐngrde 'dàng. / One false step and you're washed up. (lit.) 'Yī shr̄'dzú chéng 'chyángǔ 'hèn. or (fig.) Nǐ yíbù dzǒu'tswòle jyòu 'yúngywǎn bùnéng fān'shēn le. / Don't blame him because of his one false step. Byé 'yīnwei ta dzǒu'tswòle 'yíbù jyòu 'gwài tā. / Don't get any false ideas. (suspicions; perhaps including plans) Byé dwō'syín. or (meaning impressions; often used as a joke) Byé syāngrù fēi'fēi.

(Deliberately deceptive). / That's a false (lying) statement! Nǎ shr̀ 'syāshwō! or 'Nèmma shwō jyòushr wèi pyàn'rén! or 'Nèi shr̀ 'syāhwàr! or 'Nèi shr̀ 'húshwōbā'dàu! or 'Nèi shr̀ wú'jǐjr̄'tán! or Nèi 'búshr 'shr̄hwà! / He gave a false (falsified) account of the accident. Tā bǎ chū'shr̀de 'chíngsying °'shwōle yí'byàn, kěshr shwōde 'búshr 'shr̄hwà (°'shwōle yí'byàn, dōu shr̀ 'húdzōude, °'shwōle yí-'byàn, dōu shr̀ 'syāshwōbā'dàu, °syā'dzōule yítàu'hwàr, °'húshwōbā'dàude shwōle yíbyàn). / She got the job under false pretenses. Tā nèi 'shèr shr̀ 'pyànlaide. or Tā jǎu nèige 'shr̀ de shr̄hou, °shwō 'syāhwàr laije (°méishwō 'shr̄hwà, °shwōde búshr 'shr̄hwà, °shwō'hwǎng laije, °pyàn'rén laije).

False alarm. / The rumor turned out to be a false alarm. 'Jyēgwǒ shr̀ 'yáuyán. or 'Jyēgwǒ 'méi nèmma hwéi 'shèr. / The fire engines were called out on a false alarm. Jyòuhwǒ'dwèi tīng'shwō you dìfang jóuhwǒ le; chūchyu yí'kàn, °shr 'jyǎde (°'yǒurén 'syūbàu, °'yǒurén dáu'gwěi).

FAMILIAR. (Acquainted with) shóu, bùshēng; (recognize) rènshr, rènde; **unfamiliar** bùshóu, shēng, búda 'rènshr or búda rènde or (strange) (kànje) hěn 'gwài. / I'm not familiar with him. Wǒ gēn tā bù'shóu. or Wǒ gēn tā 'búda 'rènshr. / He looks familiar. Tā hěn myàn'shóu. / His face doesn't look at all familiar to me. Tā yí-'dyár yě búmyàn'shóu. / It's good to see a familiar face. Kànjyan ge 'shóurén jēn jyàu wǒ gāu'syìng. / I'm not familiar with the place or the people. Wǒ °'rénshēng-'dìbù'shóude (°réndìshēngshū). / That word (or character) is not quite familiar (or quite unfamiliar) to me. 'Nèige dz̀ °hén yǎn'shēng (°wǒ kànje hěn 'gwài, °wǒ 'búda 'rènde). / After you've become familiar with the people here, they're quite friendly. Děng tāmen gēn nǐ 'shóu le, hwèi 'hěn héchide.

(Accustomed to) shúsyi; (negative) bùshúsyi, búda 'jr̄daude. / I'm not yet familiar with your customs. Nǐmen jèrde 'fēngsú wǒ hái °'bù'shúsyi ne (°búda 'jr̄dau ne, or (not acquainted with) °bù'shóu ne). / After a while our system will be familiar to you. 'Gwò syē shr̄hou wǒmende 'bànfa nǐ jyòu °'shúsyi le (°'shóu le).

(Common). / Tall buildings have become a familiar sight nowadays. 'Syàndzài 'gāulóudà'shà °'dàuchù dou 'kànde'jyàn (°'rén dōu jyàn'gwànle, °rén 'jyànle bùjywéje yǎn'shēngle, °rén 'jyànle méi shéme'syīchi le).

Get familiar (be intimate) lājìnhu, yǒu 'shēnjyǎn; (take undue liberties) syānàu(de). / Don't get too familiar with them. 'Byé gēn tāmen °tài lā'jìnhu (°tài 'shóu lou, °yǒu shēnjyāu). / If you aren't careful with him, he's likely to get familiar. Nǐ yàu bù'syǎusyinje tā dyar, tā hwèi gēn nǐ syā'nàude. or 'Byé gēn tā tài 'shóu le, tā ài syā'nàu.

FAMILY. Three rather subtle distinctions may be observed:

1. jyā (which also means home) is the family as a group of people living to-

gether, a household, but without any particular emphasis on its social unity. / She
has to work to support her family. Tā děi dzwò 'shr̄ (tsái néng) yǎng'jyā. / This
farm has been in their family for seven hundred years. Nèikwài 'dì dzai 'tāmen
jyāli yǒu 'chībǎinyán le. / Which are the leading families of the town? Jèrde 'dàjyār
dōu shr̄ 'něi jijyā? / That temper of his is a family trait. Tā yǐ'jyā 'dōu shr̄ nèmma
dàde 'píchyi. / That's a family heirloom. Nèi shr̄ (wǒmen) chwán'jyājr̄'bǎu. or
(inherited from ancestors) Nèi shr̄ (wǒmen) 'dzúchwánde.

2. 'jyālide rén is the family as several related individuals, the members of the
family; hence also yǐ'jyā(dz) de rén (the whole family). / He has a large family.
Tā 'jyāli rén 'dwō. or Tā 'jyāli rénkǒu 'dwō. or Tā yǒu yí'dàjyādzde 'rén. / His
whole family came. °Tā 'chywánjyā (°Tā'yǐjyā, °Tāyǐjyāde rén) 'dōu láile. / Her
family always comes first in her mind. Tā syīnli láu 'syǎngje tā 'dzǐjǐ 'jyā de rén.
/ We're just one big, happy family. Wǒmen yí'dàjyādz rén °'yìtwán hé'chī (°'héhémù-
'mùde, °hěn 'hémù). or (sarcastic) 'Wǒmen jyā 'nà tsái jyàu 'hémù ne! or
'Dzámen jyā dzěmma 'hémù a?

3. 'jyātíng refers to the family as a closely knit social unit. / The Chinese have
very strong feelings for family ties. 'Jūnggwo rén 'jyātíng gwān'nyàn hěn 'jùng.
/ There are fewer large families as industrialization progresses. 'Gūngyè ywè 'fādá,
'dàjyātíng jyou 'ywè lái ywè 'shǎu. / He has family troubles. Tā 'jyātíng jr̄jyàn
°jǐng nàu'shr̄ (°de 'shr̄ búshwùn'syīn, °de 'shr̄ bùrú'yì). / He is on good terms with
his family. Tā gēn tā 'jyātíng jr̄jyàn 'chǔde 'hǎu. / Small families are now in vogue.
Syàndzài 'shr̄syíng 'syǎujyātíng.

In some cases, the family is referred to indirectly by speaking of outsiders as
'wàirén. / He is almost one of the family. Wǒmen 'bùnà tā dàng 'wàirén kàn.
/ When the family is alone, we eat in the kitchen. is expressed as When there are no
outsiders, we eat in the kitchen. Méi 'wàiren de shr̄hou wǒmen dzài chú'fángli chr̄-
'fàn. / Keep it in the family. is expressed as Don't sell it to an outsider. Byé jyàu
'wàirén 'déchyu. or as Don't tell it to an outsider. Byé jyàu 'wàirén 'jr̄dàu. or as
Family skeletons should not be exposed outside. Jyā'chǒu bùkě wài'yáng.

(Of animals and birds) wō (nest; litter, brood, etc.). / There's apparently a
family of weasels living under the front porch. 'Lángdz 'dǐsya yí'dìng yǒu yìwō
'hwángshǔ'láng.

FAMOUS. yǒumíng, yǒu 'míngchì, chūmíng; **become famous** chéngmíng, chūmíng.
/ He is quite famous. Tā 'hén yǒu'míng. or Tā 'hén yǒu 'míngchì. / This road is
famous for its view. 'Jèityáu lù yǐ 'fēngjǐng 'háu °yǒu'míng (°chū'míng). or 'Jèityáu
lù chū'míngde 'fēnjǐng 'háu. / His book made him famous. Nèiběn 'shū jyàu tā
°chū'míng le (°chéng'míng le). or Tā yīnwei nèiběr 'shū ér yǒu'míng.

FAR. (Distant) ywǎn. / Don't go far. Byé dzóu'ywǎnle. or Byé wàng 'ywǎnlou 'chyù.
/ Do you live very far from the station? Nǐ jù de lí chē'jàn 'hén ywǎn ma? / Is it
far away? Lí jèr 'ywǎn ma? or Lí jèr 'ywǎn buywǎn? / How far are the mountains?
'Shān (lí jèr) (yǒu) 'dwōywǎn? / Have you ever been in the Far East before? Ní
'yǐchyán dàugwo Ywǎn'dūng ma? / He is in a car far ahead of us. Ta dzài wǒmen
'chyántou 'hěn ywǎnde yíge 'chēli. / We heard, far off in the distance, a ship's
whistle. Ywǎn'ywǎnde tīngjyan yǒu 'chwán lā'byér. but / This tunnel goes pretty
far (deep) down. Jèige °'swéidàu (°'dìdàu) hěn 'shēn. / He kicked the ball far (high)
into the air. Ta bǎ 'chyóu tīde hěn 'gāu. / His house is on the far (other) side of
the woods. Tāde 'fángdz dzài shù'líndzde 'nèibyār.

Far be it from me. / Far be it from me to criticize, but I think you should use
that word more carefully. is expressed as I'm not qualified to criticize, ... Chí
'shr̄ wǒ 'méi dzge lái 'pǐpíng, bǔgwo wǒ 'jywéje nǐ yùng 'nèige dzèr de shr̄hou
yīng'gāi 'syǎusyīn dyar.

Farfetched lí 'tí ywǎn (far from the subject); méi lǐ (makes no sense). / That argument is pretty far-fetched. 'Nèmma ge 'shwōfar lí 'tí tài 'ywǎn le. / What she said is too farfetched. Tāshwōde tài méi 'lǐle.

Far more . . . bǐ . . . de dwō, ywán bǐ . . . . / This is far more important than that. 'Jeige bǐ 'nèige yàu'jǐnde 'dwō. *or* 'Jèige 'ywán bǐ 'nèige yàujǐn.

Farsighted (lit.) 'ywǎnshr̄yǎn; (fig.) jyànde ywǎn, yóu 'ywǎnjyàn. / Are you nearsighted or farsighted? Nǐ shr̄ 'jìnshr̄yǎn háishr 'ywǎnshr̄yǎn? / Their plans proved to be farsighted. Jyēgwǒ jèng'míngle tāmende 'jìhwà yóu 'ywǎnjyàn.

As far as. (lit.) / We walked together as far as the gate. Wǒmen yí'kwàr dzǒudàu dà'ménnar. (fig.) / As far as I'm concerned, you do as you please. °'Gwāng ná 'wǒ lái shwō (°Yíwǒ 'gèren ér'lwùn) nǐ 'ài dzěmmaje jyòu dzěmmaje. *or* (rude) Nǐ 'ài dzěmmaje 'jyòu dzěmmaje, 'wó gwǎnbu'jáu. / This is a good idea as far as it goes. Jyòu 'shr̄ lwùn 'shr̄, 'jèige júyi hái bú'hwài.

By far. / She is by far the best cook we ever had. Tā bí wǒmen yǐ'chyán gùde 'chúdz hǎude 'tài dwō le. *or* Yǐ'chyán wǒmen gùde 'chúdz 'ywǎn bùrú tā. / He is by far the better of the two. 'Tāmen lyǎli 'tā °chyángde 'dwō (°hǎudwōle).

Few and far between. (lit.) / In this country gasoline stations are few and far between. 'Jèige dìfang mài chǐ'yóu de hén 'shǎu, bingchyě 'líde yé 'ywǎn. (fig.) / Men like that are few and far between these days. Mù'chyán syàng tāmen nèiyàngrde rén jēn shr̄ °tài 'shǎu le (°'fèngmáulín'jyáu).

Other English expressions. / So far so good. Dāu syàndzai wéijr̄, °'hái kéyǐ (°hái bútswò, °dōu tíng hǎu). / That young fellow will go far. 'Nèige °háidz (°syáu-'hwǒdz) °'chyánchéng ywǎn'dà (°yóu chyántu). / The meeting lasted far into the night. 'Hwèi yǐjr kāidàu ban'yèli. / This joke has gone far enough. Jèige 'wánsyàu kāide 'gòu lǐhaide le. / Are you feeling well now? No, far from it. Nǐ syàn'dzài 'jywéje 'hǎu le ma? 'Hài! Tsái 'bù ne. *or* 'Hài! Yǐ'dyǎr dōu bù'hǎu. / It's far from perfect, but it will do. Jèige 'chàde hěn 'dwō, búgwò kéyi 'tsòuhwoje yùng. / That's not far from wrong. Nèige °chàde (°'tswōde) bú'tài °dwō (°lǐhai).

FARM. (Field) tyán; (land) dì; (farmed land) jùngde dì; (large-scale farm) núngchǎng. / A brook runs through their farm. Yǒu yidàu hé'gōudz tsúng tāmende °'tyáli (°'dìli) 'lyóugwochyu. / He owns the farm now. Syàn'dzài (tājùngde) nèikwài °'dì (°'tyán) shr̄ 'tāde le. / This farm seems to be well taken care of. Jèikwài °'dì (°'tyán) jùngde 'hǎu. *or* Jèige núng'chǎng 'jǐngyíngde hén 'hǎu. / They're short of farm hands. Tāmen 'gùbujáu 'rén jùng'dì. *or* Tāmen jùng'dìde rén bu'gòu. *but* / They have a chicken farm. is expressed as They raise chickens. Tāmen yǎng'jī. / Have you ever lived on a farm? is expressed as Have you ever lived in the country? Nǐ dzài 'syāngsya jùgwo ma? / Have you ever lived in a farmhouse? is expressed as Have you ever lived in a farmer's house? Nǐ dzài jùng dì de rénjyāli 'jùgwo ma? *or* Nǐ dzài núngrén jyāli 'jùgwo ma?

To farm jùng(dì), gēng(dì); (local Peiping) jīng(dì). / Their family has been farming the same piece of land for generations. Tāmen jyā 'hǎusyēdài dāu °jùng (°gēng, °jīng) nèi'yíkwài 'dì. *or* Tāmen jyā °jùng (°gēng, °jīng) 'nèikwài 'dì yóu 'hǎusyē'dài le. / Their family has been farming for generations. Tāmen jyā °jùng'dì (°gēng'dì, °jīng'dì) °'jùngle (°gēngle, °'jīngle) háuji'dài le.

Farm out 'jìyǎng. / He farms out his children. Tā bǎ 'háidz dōu °'jìyǎngdzài 'byéren 'jyāli (°jìdzài 'byéren jyāli 'yǎngje).

FARMER. (As a social class) 'núngrén. / The farmers want to be left alone by the government. 'Núngrén 'búywànyì jyāu 'jèngfú 'gwǎn. / Farmers and industrial laborers must cooperate. 'Núngrén gēn 'gūngrén děi hé'dzwò tsái 'syíng.

(As an occupation) 'jwāngjyarén, jùngdǐde, 'núngrén; 'syāngsyarén (those who live in the country); núngfu (rarely used); **be a farmer** shŕ plus any of the above or jùngdǐ. / The farmers bring their vegetables to town every morning. °'Jwāngjyarén (°Jùng'dǐde, °'Syāngsyarén) 'tyāntyan 'dzăuchen bă 'chīngtsài dàidau 'chéngli lai. / My (maternal) uncle is a farmer. Wŏ 'jyòujyou °wù'núng (°jùng'dǐ, °shŕ ge 'núngrén, °shŕ ge 'jwāngjyarén, °shŕ ge jùng'dǐde, °shŕ ge 'núngfu, °shŕ ge 'núngrén).

FARTHER. (More distant) ywăn with another word such as still hái or again dzài elsewhere in the sentence. / How much farther do we have to go? 'Hái děi dzŏu 'dwōywăn? or expressed as How much road is there still? 'Hái yŏu 'dwōshău lù? / His house is farther away than mine. 'Tājyā bí 'wŏjyā líde hái 'ywăndyar. / Move the chair a little farther from the fire. Bă 'yǐdz nwóde lí 'hwŏ 'dzài ywăndyar. / The farther he goes the less homesick he becomes. Tā 'ywè dzŏude 'ywăn, ywè 'bùsyăng'jyā. but / The post office is farther down that way. (still that way) 'Yóujèng'jyú 'hái dzài 'nèibyar ne. or (still ahead) 'Yóujèng'jyú 'hái děi wàng 'chyán dzŏu. / They went toward the farther (other) side of the park. Tāmen wàng gūngywán 'nèibyar chyùle. / Bring your car a little farther up. Bă nǐde 'chē wàng chyán dzài 'kāiyidyar.

(Not referring to distance). / He never got farther than grade school. Shàngle 'syăusywé yǐ'hòu tā 'dzài yĕ méishàng'sywé.

See also **FAR.**

FASHION. shŕsyīng; (showing disapproval) shŕmáu. (Both of these terms are stative verbs, meaning be in fashion, be the fashion, be fashionable). / Is it the fashion here to wear straw hats? Jèr shŕ'syīng dài tsău'măur ma? / During the last few years women have given up the fashion of wearing long dresses. 'Jìnjinyánlai 'nyŭ rén bùshŕ'syīng chwān 'cháng 'yīfu le. / We don't try to keep up with all the latest fashions here. Wŏmen jèr 'bùjyăng shŕ'máu. / Long hair has gone out of fashion. Syàn'dzài 'bùshŕsyīng 'chángtóufa le. or Syàn'dzài 'chángtóufa °bùshŕ'syīng le (°bùshŕ'máu le).

(Manner). / He has a habit of rubbing his hands together in this fashion. Tā yŏu ge 'máubing, ài 'dzèmmaje tswō'shŏu.

Set the fashion. / They set the fashion. is expressed as They lead at the head. 'Tāmen lǐng'tóur. or as Everyone imitates them. 'Dàjyā dōu 'sywétāmen. / The dancing girls here set the fashion in dress. is expressed as The dancing girls here lead in the way of dressing. Jèrde 'wúnyŭ lǐng'tóur găi 'yīshang 'shŕyang. or as Everyone imitates them in manner of dress. Jèr 'dàjyā dōu sywé 'wúnyŭde 'jwāngshu.

FAST. (Speedy, quick) kwài. / If you get a fast train you can get there in two hours. Dzwò 'kwàichē lyàngge jūngtóu jyou 'dàu. / You're setting too fast a pace for the others. Nǐ dzwòde tài 'kwài le, 'byérén 'gēnbu'shàng. / Tell him about the new rules, and make it fast. 'Kwài dyar bă syīn 'gwēijyu 'gàusu ta. / Not so fast, please! Láu'jyà, byé nèmma 'kwài! or (slower) Láu'jyà, 'màndyar. / Hurry as fast as you can. or The faster the better. Ywè 'kwài ywè 'hău. / It can be done as fast as you want. 'Yàu dwō kwài 'néng dwō 'kwài. / My watch is ten minutes fast. 'Wŏde byău 'kwài 'shŕfēn jūng. / Your watch is fast too. 'Nǐde byáu 'yĕ kwài le.

(Permitting fast movement). / The horses have a fast track today. is expressed as The horses can run fast on the track. 'Jyĕrde 'chăngdz má păude 'kwài. / This is a fast (tennis) court. is expressed as You can run fast on this court. Dzài 'jèige (wăngchyóu) 'chăngdzshang kéyi 'păude 'kwài.

(Tight) jǐn; dùng (used in the negative). / Hold it fast. Jǐn'jǐnde 'dzwànje. / He held it fast. Tā dzwànde hén 'jǐn. / Make the boat fast. Bă chwán shwān'jǐnle.

/ The ship was stuck fast in the mud. Chwán yūdzai 'níli dùngbu'lyàu le. / Stand fast. Jànje byé'dùng.

(Strict) jǐn, yán. / We don't have any hard and fast rules here. Wǒmen jèr méiyǒu shémma tài 'jǐn de 'gwēijyu. or (severe) Wǒmen jèr méiyou shémma hěn 'yán de 'gwēijyu.

(Permanent, of color) bùrúngyi 'dyàu, bùrúngyi 'twèi. / Are these colors fast? Jèisyē 'yánshǎr rúngyi °'dyàu ma (°'twèi ma, °bùrúngyi 'dyàu, °bùrúngyi 'twèi)? / This color is fast. Jèi shǎr bùrúngyi °'dyàu (°'twèi).

(Of friends). / They are fast friends. Tāmen 'láiwang hen °chín (°jìn). or Tāmen 'jyāuchíng hěn 'shēn. or Tāmen shr̀ 'hǎupéngyou.

(Of sleep) shóu, shŕdzai, sž. / I was fast asleep. Wǒ 'shwèide hěn °'shóu (°'shŕdzai, °'sž).

(Of people) expressed as like to play àiwár. / He travels in fast company. Tā gēn yìchyún ài 'wárde rén 'láiwǎng. / She's too fast to suit me. Tā 'tài ài 'wár le, jyàu wǒ 'búdà 'syǐhwān.

To fast (abstain from food; entirely) jìnshŕ (usually used by Catholics); (stop eating, go on a hunger strike) jywéshŕ; (stay away from meat, fowl, and fish) chŕjāi (a Buddhist expression). / Are you fasting? or Are you keeping the fast? Nǐ jèngdzài jìn'shŕ ne ma? / He often fasts for days on end. Ta 'chángcháng jywé'shŕ hǎu-'syētyān. / She is fasting. Syàndzai tā chŕ'jāi ne.

FAT. (Of animals) féi. / This is a nice fat chicken for roasting. 'Jèijŕ féijǐ 'kǎuje chŕ 'hǎu. / This pork is too fat. Jèikwài 'jūròu tài 'féi le.

(Of people) pàng; (politely) fāfú. / I'm getting too fat, don't you think? Wǒ tài 'pàng le, nǐ shwō 'shr̀ bushr̀? / You're getting a bit fat. Nín fā'fúle. / He is getting fat again. Ta yòu pàng le.

Fat (part of the flesh) féirou. / This piece of pork has too much fat on it. Jèikwài 'jūròu 'féirou tài dwō.

(Vegetable or animal fat used for cooking) yóu (also means oil). / What is the best fat for frying? 'Jyān dūngsyi yùng shémma 'yóu dzwèi 'hǎu?

FATHER. (kinship term) fùchin; (somewhat more intimate term) bàba, dyē, dyēdye; (wife's father) ywèfù, jàngren; (husband's father) gūnggung; (polite term) your father lìngdzwūn; my father jyāfù, jyāyán; my late father syānfù, syānyán.

(Priest) 'shénfù.

To father. / He fathered the whole idea. Jèige 'júyi chywán shr̀ 'tā chū de.

FAULT. (Mistake; does not stress the idea of blame) tswò, tswèr; (wrongdoing, something worthy of blame) búshr. / Sorry, it's my fault. Dwèibú'jù, shr̀ 'wǒde °tswò (°tswèr, °'búshr). / I can't be blamed for other people's faults. 'Wǒ bùnéng gěi 'byérén dān 'búshr. or 'Byérénde 'tswèr 'bùnéng gwài 'wǒ. / It's nobody's fault but your own. Shr̀ nǐ 'dzjǐde tswèr, °gēn 'byérén méi 'gwānsyi (°búshr 'byérende tswǒr).

(Defect, in a person) 'dwānchù; (bad habit) 'máubìng. / In spite of her faults, she is easy to get along with. Tā 'swéirán yǒu syēge 'dwānchù, kěshr °'rén hěn 'swéihe (°'rúngyi syàng'chù). / His worst fault is that he talks too much. Tā 'dǐng hwài de 'máubìng jyòushr °ài shwō'hwà (°shwō'hwà tài 'dwō).

(Defect, in something material) 'máubìng, 'chywēdyǎn. / The collapse of the bridge was caused by a fault in one of the beams. Chyáu 'dǎule shr̀ yīnwei yǒu yìgēn-'lyáng yǒu °'máubìng (°'chywēdyǎn).

537

Find fault tyāutswèr, tyāu máubing, tyāuti; (with maximum effort) 'chwēimáu-chyóu'tsź. /You're always finding fault. Ní 'lǎushr °'tyāuti (°tyāu'tswèr, °'chwēimáuchyóu'tsź). /I don't mean to find fault with you, but that won't do. Wǒ °'búshr chéng'syīn 'tyāu nǐde 'tswèr (°'búshr gù'yǐde 'tyāu nǐde'tswèr, °'búshr 'chwēimáuchyóu'tsź), 'búgwo 'nèmmaje 'jēnshr bù'chéng.

FAVOR. (Kindness, privilege) in statements, myàndz (honor); in questions, the idea is expressed in words such as chǐng (request, please), chyóu (beg, ask very politely), láujyà (please). /As a great favor, he let me use this camera for a day Tā géi wó 'hǎudàde 'myàndz, bǎ jèige jàusyàng'jī jyàu wǒ nálai 'yùng yìtyān. /I want to ask you a favor. Wǒ yóu dyǎr shř 'chyóu nǐ. /Would you do me a favor? Chyóu nǐ dyǎr 'shř, 'syíng busyíng? or Láu'jyà gěi 'dzwò dyǎr 'shř, 'syíng busyíng? or (Wó) yǒu yíjyàn 'shř chyóu nǐ.

(Gift, especially at a party) 'lǐwù. /What shall we give as favors at the children's party? Syǎu'hár lái 'wár de shŕhou dzámen géi dyǎr 'shémma lǐwù hǎu ne?

In one's favor (be of benefit) yú . . . yǒu'lì; (enable one to gain an advantage) jyàu . . . jàn 'pyányi. /That's a point in your favor. Nèidyǎn yú 'ní yǒu'lì. or (grudgingly) Nèi jyàu 'nǐ jàn 'pyányi. /That's in my favor. Nèi yú 'wó yǒu'lì. or Nèi jyàu 'wǒ jàn 'pyányi.

In favor of (to the advantage of) yíng, jànsyàn. /The result was 5 to 3 in favor of our team. Jyēgwǒ wǔ dwèi 'sān, 'wǒmen nèidwèi °yíngle (°jàn'syān).

Be in favor of 'dzànchéng. /I'm in favor of immediate action. Wǒ 'dzànchéng jǐkè'bàn.

To favor (prefer) syàngje. /Which side do you favor? Nǐ 'syàngje 'něibyar?

(Deal gently with) 'búdà 'gǎnyùng. /He seems to be favoring his right leg. Tā 'hǎusyàng 'búdà 'gǎnyùng yòu'twèi shŕde.

FAVORITE. (Held in special regard) is expressed with 'dzwèi syǐhwān or dzwèi ài like best; also dzwèi or dǐng with other verbs similar in meaning to syǐhwān and ài. /Red is my favorite color. Wǒ 'dzwèi syǐhwān de shř 'húngshǎr. /Who is your favorite movie actress? 'Nyúmíng'syīngli nǐ 'dzwèi syǐhwān 'něige? /This is the children's most favorite book. Jèibén 'shū syǎu'háidzmen 'dzwèi °ài (°syǐhwān) 'kàn.

The favorite (in a race, match). /The favorite (horse) dropped out of the race early. 'Dàjyā jywéje yàu 'yíngde mǎ 'méipǎu 'dwō ywǎn jyòu 'làdzai 'hòutoule. /He was the favorite. 'Tā shř rénren shwō'shwō'syǐhwānde.

Be a favorite is expressed with various terms for like best, see paragraph one above. /The boy is his father's favorite. Jèi háidz shř tā 'fùchin dzwèi °'syǐhwānde (°'àide, °'téngde, °'chǔngde). /He's the favorite of the boss. Dzài 'tóur nar 'tā dǐng 'húng. or Tóur dǐng 'syǐhwān tā. or Tā shř 'tóurde 'húngrén (lit. red person, used for favorite in this sense).

FEAR. (Emotion) is expressed verbally as to fear or as be afraid hài'pà, pà. /His actions were strongly influenced by fear. Tāde nèisyē 'jyúdùng 'dwōbàn 'dōu shř yīnwei ('syīnli) hài'pà. /He doesn't know the meaning of fear. Tā 'bùdǔng 'shémma jyàu hài'pà. /He always has that fear in his mind. Tā 'syīnli lǎu shr °'pà (°hài'pà). /There's no fear of anything like that happening. 'Shémma dōu bu'pà.

For fear (of) (afraid in a very weak sense, with no actual fear) kǔngpà, pà. /He went to the station early for fear of missing the train. Tā dzǎu'dzāurde shàng chē-'jànchyùle, yīnwei (kǔng) 'pà 'wùle 'chē. /I hurried home for fear I'd miss you. Wǒ kwài'kwārde hwéi'jyā lai, yīnwei (kǔng) pà 'jèitsż jyànbu'jáu nǐ.

To fear <u>something or someone</u>, **fear that, fear to** pà; (be anxious about) wèi . . . dān'syīn; **not to fear** <u>is also expressed as</u> put the mind at rest fàng'syīn. / Never fear! He'll take care of you. <u>is expressed as</u> There's nothing to be afraid of . . . . 'Méi shémma kě'pàde. 'Tā hwèi jàuying nǐ de. <u>or as</u> Don't be scared . . . . °'Byé (°'Búyùng) hài'pà . . . . / I don't fear for myself, but I'm worried about them. Wǒ dàu 'búshr wèi wǒ 'dzjǐ dān'syīn, wǒ shr wèi 'tāmen dān'syīn. *or* Wǒ 'dzjǐ 'méi shémma kě'pàde, wǒ shr pà 'tāmen yǒu shémma 'chàtswò. / I can say this without fearing anything. Jèige wǒ 'kéyi 'fàngsyīn dà'dànde shwō. *or* Wǒ 'dzèmma shwō, yidyǎr dōu bu'pà.

FEATHER. máu (especially soft feathers that can be used for stuffing); língdz (especially larger feathers with a good-sized shaft); *but* **chicken feathers** <u>are always called</u> 'jīmáu <u>unless referring to a long tailfeather</u>. / They make dusters out of chicken feathers. Tāmen ná 'jīmáu dzwò 'dǎndz. / Peacock feathers are long and colorful. 'Kǔngchyè 'língdz yòu 'cháng yòu yǒu 'háujijǔng 'yánse. / Her new hat has a red feather on it. Tāde 'syīnmàudzshang 'chāje yìgen °'húngde 'língdz (°'húngmáur).

Light as a feather 'jēn chǐng. / This coat is as light as a feather. 'Jèijyàn dà yī 'jēn chǐng.

<u>Other expressions in English.</u> / If he could get his book published, it would really be a feather in his cap. Tā yàushr néng bǎ tā nèibén shū chūle'bǎn, °'jēn kéyi 'jyāu àu yísyar (°nà jēn kéyi dz'háu). / Birds of a feather flock together. <u>is expressed as</u> Everything goes with its own kind. 'Wùyǐlài'jyù.

FEBRUARY. 'èrywè.

FEEL (FELT). (Touch, handle, grope) mwō. / Feel it. Isn't it smooth? 'Mwō yimwō. Búshr hěn 'gwānghwarde ma? / He felt her head with his hand. Tā ná shǒu 'mwōle mwō tāde 'tóu. / It looks like leather and feels like leather, but it isn't. Kànje syàng 'pídz, mwōje 'yě syàng 'pídz, kě jyòushr 'búshr 'pídz. / He felt for the light switch. Tā 'mwōje jàu dyàn'mén. / It was so dark I had to feel my way around the room. Dzèmma hēi, wó děi °mwōje 'hēr dzǒu (°mwōje 'syǎr dzǒu). / I felt his pulse. Wǒ 'mwōle mwō °tāde 'mài (°tāde 'mwò). *but* / The doctor is feeling his pulse (technical medical term). 'Dàifu gěi tā °hàu'mwò ne (°hàu'mài ne).

(Weigh in the hand) dyān (by holding on the palm); dīlou (by suspending ᶠrom the hand); tái (by lifting); nwó (by moving); <u>these terms are usually reduplicated as,</u> 'dyān(yi)dyān, etc. / He put the coin on his palm to feel how heavy it was. Tā bǎ 'chyán gēdzai shǒu'jǎngshang dyāndyan yǒu 'dwō jùng. / Feel how heavy this chair is. 'Jèibá yǐdz nǐ °'dīloudīlou (°'tái yitái, °'nwó yinwó) kàn yǒu 'dwōjùng. / This box feels heavy. Jèige 'syádz 'dyānje hěn 'chén.

(Perceive, be aware of, have feelings about, think) jywéje, jywéde, gǎnjywé. / I feel a pain here. Wǒ °'jywéje (°etc.) wǒ 'jèr téng. / I feel the need of a little exercise. Wǒ °'jywéje (°etc.) wo syūyau dyar 'yùndung. / I never feel the cold. Wó lǎu jywébuchu lěng lai. / How do you feel about this? Jèi 'nǐ °jywéje (°etc.) dzèmma'yàng? / I felt that this would be a bad move. Wǒ °'jywéje (°etc.) dzèmma bàn bù'hǎu. / I've never felt such heat. Wǒ yísyàng 'méi °jywéje (°etc.) dzèmma 'règwo. / I felt tired last night. Dzwó 'wǎnshang wǒ °jywéje (°etc.) hěn 'lèi. / I feel sure he'll come. 'Wǒ jywéje (°etc.) tā yí'dìng lái. / It feels like (it's going to) rain today. 'Jyēr °jywéje (°etc.) yàu syà'yǔ shrde. / Does the room feel cold to you? Jèijyān wūdz shr nǐ °jywéje (°etc.) 'lěng ma? / Do you know how it feels to have a hangover? Nǐ jrdau jyóu'syǐng de shŕhou shr rén °jywéje (°etc.) 'dzèmmayàng ma? / I feel pretty well. °Wǒ jywéje (°Wǒ 'shēnshang) hěn 'shūfu. / I felt a little disturbed by this affair. Jèijyan shr tā jyàu wo syīnli(jywéje) °bùgāusyǐng (°bùshūfu, °bùtùngkwài). / I feel a little tired. Wǒ jywéje yóu dyǎr 'lèi. / Do you feel hungry?

Nǐ jywéje 'èle ma? /I feel as if I'm going to get sick. Wǒ jywéje syàng yàu yǒu-bìng shŕde. /I feel certain of it. °Wǒ 'jywéje (°Wó syǎng) yí'dìng shř 'nèmmaje(le). /I feel like I've been cheated. Wǒ jywéje hǎu syàng wǒ 'shàngle 'dàng le. /I feel like a fool. Wǒ 'jywéje syàng °ge 'shǎdz shŕde (°ge 'húdu'chúng). /I feel very strongly about women smoking (that it's bad). 'Nyúrén syǐ'yān wǒ jywéje 'hěn bùhǎu.

Feel like (want to) 'ywànyî, syǎng. /Do you feel like taking a walk? Nǐ °'ywànyî (°syǎng chyù) °'sànsanbù ma (°'lyǒudalyǒuda ma)? /I feel like (having) another beer. Wǒ syǎng dzài 'hē bēi pí'jyou.

Feel out. /Let's feel out the situation before we do anything more. Dzámen 'kànkan 'chíngsying dzài dzǒu 'syà yíbù.

Get (or have) **the feel of** ... ... 'shóu; ... 'shúsyi; ... 'désyīnyǐng'shǒu; ... jywéje 'dzrán. /If you keep on practicing you'll get the feel of it. Nǐ yàushr bú-'dwànde 'lyànsyí jyou °'shóu le (°'shúsyi le, °'désyīnyǐng'shǒu le, °jywéje 'dzrán le). /I still don't have the feel of it. 'Jèige wǒ hái °bù'shóu ne (°méi'shúsyi ne, °bùnéng 'désyīnyǐng'shǒu ne, °bùnéng jywéje 'dzrán ne).

Other expressions in English. /This city didn't feel the full force of the hurri-cane. meaning it died down first 'Dàfēng dàu 'běnchéng de shŕhou 'yǐjīng 'búlìhai le. or meaning the center didn't come here 'Dàfēng dzài 'běnchéng yě jyǒushr 'shāuje yìdyǎr'byǎr. /I really feel for you. Wó hěn 'chyāngwàje ni. or Wó hěn 'dyànjije nǐ.

FELT. (Compressed wool or fur) jāndz. /Is this felt or cloth? Jèi shr 'jāndz hái shr 'bù? /He has an old felt hat that he always wears in the rain. Tā 'yóu dǐng 'jyòu jān'màu, 'yí syà'yǔ jyou 'dài.

See also **FEEL.**

FEVER. (High body temperature) shāu; **have a fever** fāshāu. /Do you have a fever? Nǐ fā'shāu ma? /His fever is going down. Tāde 'shāu °'dǐle dyǎr le (°'twèile dyǎr le). /His fever went down. Tā méiyou 'shāu le. or Tā twèi'shāu le. or Tā shāu 'twèile.

(In names of diseases) rè, rèbìng, rèjèng; **as scarlet fever** syīnghúngrè; **yellow fever** hwángrèbìng, hwángrèjèn; **hay fever** kūtsāurè. /He nearly died of yellow fever a year ago. Tā 'yìnyánchyán dé 'hwángrè'jèng 'chàdyǎr (méi)'sǎle.

(Fig.). /The good news put them all into a fever of excitement. 'Nèige hǎu 'syàusyi jyàu tāmen 'shŕfēn gāu'syìng.

FEW. (With emphasis on the fact that there are some, though not many) ji-M. /We asked him to say a few words at the meeting. Wǒmen chǐng tā dàu'hwèi 'shwō jǐjyù 'hwà. /A few of these books are torn. Jèisyē shūli 'yǒu jiběr sžhwàile. /I want to stay a few days. Wǒ yàu 'jù jityān. /I'd like to borrow a few of your cups. Wó syǎng gēn nǐ jyè jige 'wǎn yùng. /I know only a few words. Wǒ jyòu jŕdau ji'ge dzèr. /Say it over a few more times. 'Dzài shwō jibyàn.

(With emphasis on the fact that there are not many, though there are some) 'méi ji (followed by a measure); bùdwō, (hén) shǎu. /Few people realize it, but it's true. 'Jèi shěr shŕ 'jēnde, 'bùgwò °'méi jige rén 'jŕdàu (°'jŕdàude rén bù'dwō, °'jŕdàude rén hén 'shǎu). /Very few children draw as well as he does. 'Méi jige háidz néng syàng 'tā hwàde nèmma 'hǎu. or Syàng 'tā hwàde nèmma 'hǎu de háidz °bù'dwō (°hén 'shǎu). /Few of them like the idea. 'Tāmen nèisyē rénli 'syǐhwān 'jèige bànfa de °hén 'shǎu (°'bù'dwō). /Fewer people come here every year. Lái 'jèr de rén 'yì-nyán bǐ yì-nyán 'shǎu. /The fish in this river are few and far between. 'Jèi héli 'yú hěn 'syǐshǎu.

Quite a few bùshău, hĕn dwō, hĕn bùshău. /Quite a few people objected. 'Făndwèide rén °bù'shău (°hĕn 'dwō, °hĕn bù'shău).

FIELD. (Tract of land) dì; with measure kwài. /Let's cut across this field. Dzámen tsúng jèikwài 'dì 'chwāngwo chyù ba. /That's a fine-looking field of corn. Nèi yí-'dì lău'yùmĭ 'jăngde jĕn hău.

(For playing) chăngdz, tsāuchăng. /The teams are coming onto the field. Bĭ-'sài de rén jèng wàng 'chăngdzli 'pău ne.

(For other purposes) -chăng; **magnetic field** tszlĭchăng, tszchăng; **airfield** fēijīchăng; **battlefield** jànchăng, (more properly) 'jàndì.

(In combat) 'jàndì, jàn chăng. /He is a correspondent who spent months in the field with the troops. Tā shr̆ ge 'syīnwénjì'jĕ, dzài °'jàndìli (°jàn chángli) gēn shr̆'bīng dzài yí'kwàr gwòle 'háujige 'ywè.

(Sphere, range) yánjyōude 'fànwéi (range of study); men mér (specialty or course of study); háng (profession). /Political questions aren't in my field. 'Jēngjr̆ wèntí búdzài 'wŏ yánjyou de 'fànwéi yĭ'nèi. /He's the best man in his field. 'Tā °nèi'hángli (°nèi'mérli) tā 'dzwèi hău. *but* /They were out of our field of vision. Wŏmen kànbu'jyàn tāmen. /What is your field? (What do you study?) Ni nyàn °'nĕimér (°'shémma, °'yánjyou 'shémma)?

(On a flag) dyèr. /Their flag has white stars on a blue field. Tāmende 'chídz shr̆ lán 'dyèrshang yŏu 'bái syēngr.

(Away from base of operations) wàibyar. /He is doing field work now. *or* He is working in the field now. Tā pàidau 'wàibyar °chyùle (*or* (collecting materials) °'sōují 'tsáilyàur chyùle, *or* (doing investigation) °dyàu'cháchyule, *or* (excavating) °fā'jywéchyule).

Field correspondent jàndìjìjĕ.

Field hospital yĕjàn yī'ywàn.

FIERCE. (Of persons or animals) syūng; (of animals, in some combinations) mĕng. /Is your dog fierce? Nĭde gŏu 'syūng busyūng? /This is a fierce dog. Jèi shr̆ yìtyáu mĕng 'gŏu. /He has a fierce-looking face. Tāde lyăn kànje hĕn 'syūng. *or* Tā lyăn you 'syūng syàng. /He gave me a fierce look. Tā dwèi wó 'lyănshang hĕn 'syūng. *or* Tā hĕn'hénde 'dēngle wŏ yiyăn.

(Of actions or characteristics) lìhai, syūng. /How can you stand that fierce heat all day? Rède 'nèmma 'lìhai nĭ yì'jēngtyān dzĕmma shòude'jù a? /You're going to come up against fierce competition. Hwéi yŏu rén gēn nĭ 'jēngde hĕn °'lìhaide (°'syūngde).

FIFTEEN. shŕwŭ; one fifteenth shŕ'wŭfēn jr 'yī; the fifteenth dìshŕwŭ.

FIFTH. One fifth 'wŭfēn jr 'yī; the fifth dìwŭ.

FIFTY. 'wŭshŕ; one fiftieth 'wŭshŕfēn jr 'yī; the fiftieth dì'wŭshŕ.

Fifty-fifty. /We'll split fifty-fifty. Dzámen dwèi'bàr fēn. *or* Dzámen'lyă 'píngfēn. *or* Dzámen lyăngge rén 'jyūnfēn. *or* 'Nĭ yí'bàr, 'wŏ yí'bàr. *or* Dzámen 'èryityān dzwò'wŭ ba.

FIGHT (FOUGHT). (Between individuals, physically) dăjyà; (especially start to fight) dùng'shŏu (dă'rén); (especially in combinations or when the type of fighting is described) dă; (with the fists) dùng chywántou; **fight back** hwéishŏu. /People are fighting in the street. 'Jyēshang yŏurén °dǎ'jyà (°'dáchilaile). / Have you been fighting with the boy next door again? Nǐ 'yòu gēn jyè'byĕrde háidz dǎ'jyà la ma? / They fought with their fists. Tāmen dùngchi 'chywántou laile. / They fought and kicked each other for an hour. Tāmen °'chywándájyàu'tīde (°'lyántīdài'dǎde) dǎle yĭdyǎn 'jūng de 'jyà. / What can I do if he doesn't fight back? Tā yàu °'bùhwéi'shŏu (°'bùgēn wó 'dǎ) wó dzěmma 'bàn ne? / What could I do? He wouldn't fight back. Tā °'bùhwéi-'shŏu (°'bù gēn wó 'dǎ), wó yŏu shémma 'fádz ne?

(Verbally) chǎujyà, cháudzwěi, (curse) mà(chilai); (generally) dǎjyà. / He and his wife are forever fighting. Tā gēn tā tàitài 'lǎushr °chǎujyà (°cháu'dzwěi, °syāng mà, °dǎjyà).

(In court) dǎ; (argue, contend) jēng; (explain reasons) jyánglǐ; all are said of a lawsuit gwānsz; the combination dǎ gwānsz is also possible. / I intend to fight that suit to the bitter end. Nèige 'gwānsz wó yí'dĭng yàu dǎudàu'dǐ. / I intend to fight them on that suit. Dǎ nèige 'gwānsz de shŕhou, wó yàu gēn tāmen °'jēng yijēng (°jyángjyang 'lǐ).

(In war) dǎjàng, sometimes 'jàndòu, dzwòjàn; (in combination) dǎ. / China and Japan have been fighting since 1931. 'Jūnggwo gēn R'běn tsúng yījyŏusān'yīnyán chǐ jyŏu dǎ'jàngle. / He fought through the worst campaign. 'Dǐng lìhai de nèi yí'jàng tā yě dzài nàr 'dǎ láije. / The enemy has fought on flat land rather than in the mountains. Dírén yí'jŕ dzài píng'ywánshang °dǎ'jàng (°jàn'dòu, °dzwò'jàn), 'bùkěn dàu 'shānlùshang chyu. / They fought up the beach to the railroad. Tāmen tsúng hǎi'àn dǎ dàu tyě'lù nar.

(In most of the above senses, but with emphasis on the vigorous life-or-death nature of the fight) pīnmìng. / We must all unite in fighting the common enemy. (Of a nation) Dzámen děi 'lyánhéchilai gēn dzámende °'dírén pīn'mìng (or (of a person) °'chóurén pīn'mìng).

Fight about, fight over, fight for wèi . . . plus most of the words used above. / I think I'm right, but I'm not going to fight about it. Wó syǎng 'wó yŏu'lǐ, búgwo wó 'bùsyǎng chyù wèi nèige °'jēng (°dǎ'jyà, °dǎ 'gwānsz, °pīn'mìng, °cháu'dzwěi).

Fight against (fig.). / You've got to fight against that habit of yours. is expressed as Concerning that habit of yours, you must bite your teeth and change it. Nǐ nèige 'máubìng ní déi yǎuje 'yá gwǎngwolai. / They're fighting against (trying hard to get rid of) malaria. Tāmen 'jyélǐ yàu 'chǎnchú 'nywèji.

Fight off (in combat) dǎtwèi; (in personal inner struggle) yǎuje 'yá plus a negative and a verb. / They fought off the enemy. Tāmen bǎ 'dírén dǎ'twēile. / I was very sleepy, but I fought it off. Wó kwùn'jíle, kěshr yǎuje 'yá méi shwèi.

Fight it out (in speaking of others) fēn ge shèng'fù, dǎ ge 'tùngkwài; (including oneself) dǎdàudǐ, pīnmìng; (to the death) dǎ ge 'nísžwŏ'hwó. / Stand back and let them fight it out. 'Dwŏkāi dyar jyàu tāmen °'fēn ge shèng'fù (°dǎ ge 'tùngkwai). / We're going to have to fight it out with them. Wŏmen děi gēn tāmen °dǎdàu'dǐ (°pīn'mìng, °dǎ ge 'nísžwŏ'hwó).

A fight (physical struggle) is expressed verbally as in the first paragraph above. / They had a fight. Tāmen 'dǎle yí'jyà. or Tāmen dǎ'jyà láije. / Let's not start a fight. Dzámen byé dǎ'jyà. or Dzámen byé 'dáchilai. / He started the fight. Tā 'syān dùngde 'shŏu. / How did the fight come out? Dǎde 'jyēgwŏ rú'hé?

(Verbal) 'chwúnshé; or more commonly expressed verbally as in paragraph two above. / They had a fight. Tāmen cháu'dzwěi laije. or Tāmen bítsž dwèi 'mà laije. / I'm afraid we're going to have a fight about this. 'Jèi shèr 'kŭngpà °dzámen déi yŏu yì̀fān 'chwúnshé.

(Boxing) dǎchywán. / How was the fight last night? Dzwótyan 'wǎnshangde dǎ-

'chywán dzĕmma 'yàng? / I went to the fight last week. Wǒ 'shànglǐbài chyù kàn dǎ-'chywán chyùle.

Put up a good fight (in competition) hǎuhǎurde dǎ; (in argument) jēngjr. / When we compete with the third team (in a basketball game) tomorrow, let's put up a good fight. Míngrge gēn dì'sāndwèi sàichyóu de shŕhou, dzámen hǎu'hǎurde dǎ yìchǎng. / At the debate yesterday he put up a good fight, but he lost. Dzwótyan byànlwùn de shŕhou tā 'jēngjrde hěn lìhai, kěshr 'shūle.

FIGURE. (Numeral) shù̀r. / These figures don't add up right. Jèisyē 'shù̀r jyādzaiyí-'kwàr bú'dwèi. / Those figures show that the population is decreasing. Tsúng nèisyē 'shù̀rshang kéyi kànchu syàndzài 'rénkou jyàn'jyànde 'shǔa le. / Delete that figure. Bǎ nèige shù̀r 'shānchyu.

(Shape; human) shēntsái, shēndz; _or sometimes not expressed._ / She has a nice figure. Tā shēn'tsái jǎngde 'hǎu. _or_ Tā'shēndz jǎngde °hǎu'kàn (_or_ (slender) °'myáutyáu, °'syìlyou, _or_ (ample) °'fēngmǎn, _or_ (shapely) °'línglúng, _or_ (good looking) °'shwùn'yǎn). / What a figure! (nice) ('Shēndz) jǎngde 'jēn hǎu'kàn! _or_ (ugly) ('Shēndz) jǎngde 'jēn nán'kàn. / I have to watch my figure. Wǒ déi 'syāusyīnje, byé tài 'pàng le.

(Personage) 'rénwù, 'yàurén, yàu'jǐnde 'rénwù, 'dàrénwù, 'shēnshr̀. / He's a very important figure in this town. Tā shr̀ jèige dì'myàrshangde 'yàurén. _or_ Tā shr̀ 'jèi dìfang °hěn yàu'jǐn de rénwù (°de 'dàrénwu, °de 'shēnshr̀). / He cut a fine figure in national politics. Tā dzài 'jēngjr̀wù'táishang dzjí gàude chéngle ge 'rénwù le.

(Small statue) syàng; (human) syàurér. / How do you like that little bronze figure? Nèige °syǎu túng'syàng (°dz̀túngde syǎu'rér) nǐ 'syǐhwān ma?

(Illustration) tú. / Figure 7 shows the parts of a machine gun. Dì'chītú shr̀ jīgwān'chyāngde língjyàn.

(Computation) 'swànsywé. / Are you good at figures? Nǐ 'swànsywé hǎu ma?

Figure of speech bǐfang, 'bǐyù. / I didn't mean it that way; it was only a figure of speech. Wǒ 'búshr nèige 'yìsz; nèi búgwò shr̀ ge °'bǐfang (°'bǐyù).

To figure (compute) swàn. / Figure up how much it amounts to. Swàn yiswàn yí'gùng dwōshǎu (plus chyán if money is referred to).

(Judge) kàn. / I figure it's about time we were going. Wǒ kàn dzámen gāi 'dzǒule. / I figure we can get it done in time. Wǒ kàn dzámen dàu 'shŕhou 'kéyi dzwò'wán.

(Plan, predict) 'dǎswàn, swànji, dǎ swànpan; (think) syǎng; (guess) tsāi; (form an idea) dǎ 'júyì. / He figured it wrong. Tā 'dǎswàntswòle. _or_ Tā 'tsāitswòle. _or_ Tā 'swànjitswòle. _or_ Tā 'syǎngtswòle. _or_ Tā dǎtswòle 'júyi le. _or_ Tā dǎtswòle 'swànpan le.

Figure in. / This didn't figure in my plans. Jèige méi bǎ wode jìhwà dǎjìnchyu.

Figure on dǎswàn, swànji, jìhwa; (think) syǎng. / How did you figure on going? Nǐ dǎswàn 'dzĕmma chyù a? / That's something I hadn't figured on. Wǒ méi 'syǎngdàu 'jèige. _or_ Wǒ méi 'swànjidàu 'jèige. / There are a lot of things we must figure on. Yǒu hěn dwō shr̀ wǒmen děi °'jìhwa (°'syǎngsyang).

Figure out (by guessing) tsāichulai; (by thinking) syǎngchulai; (by calculation) swànjichulai; (by looking) kànchulai. / I couldn't figure out what he was going to do. Wǒ °'tsāibùchūlai (°'syǎngbùchūlai, °'swànjibùchūlai) 'tā yàu dzĕmma'bàn. / I can't figure him out. Wǒ °'tsāibùjáu (°'kànbùchūlai) tā shr̀ 'dzĕmmayàng yige rén. / Can you figure out this problem? (mathematics) 'Jèige tí nǐ hwèi 'swàn ma? _or_ (not mathematics) °Jèige 'wèntí (°Jèijyàn 'shŕ) ní 'syǎngdechū ge 'bànfa lái ma?

FILL. Chinese uses resultative compounds in almost all cases; the first element indicates the type of action, the second element indicates the result. The second element
is usually mǎn full, but sometimes, especially when speaking of filling up holes,
shàng is used, corresponding to up in fill up; in a few cases only shàng is used.

(Of a hole or gap) tyánshang, tyánmǎn (especially of vertical holes); sāishang,
sāimǎn (plug up; of vertical and horizontal holes); dǔshang (stop up; especially stop
up the opening; of vertical and horizontal holes); bǔshang (patch up). / Fill up the
holes in the road with gravel. Bǎ 'lùshangde 'kēng yùng swèishŕtou °'tyánshang
(°tyán'mǎnle). / They filled up the well with earth. Tāmen ná 'tǔ bá 'jǐng °'tyánshangle (°tyán'mǎnle, °'dǔshangle). / This cavity (in a tooth) will have to be filled
pretty soon. Jèige 'yákūlung dèi kwàidyar °'tyánshang (°'bǔshang, °'dǔshang). / The
ditch has been filled in. Nèige 'gōu yǐjīng tyánshangle. / That cave has been filled
in. Nèige 'dùng yǐjīng 'dǔshangle.

(Of a gap, fig. left by the absence of a person) bǔ(shang). / There are several
jobs here that need to be filled. Jèr 'yóu jige °'wèijŕ (°'chywē é) °déi 'bǔshang
(°hái 'méi rén bǔ). / All the jobs are filled now. 'Swóyǒude °'wèijŕ (°'chywéé) dōu
'bǔshangle. / I'm just filling in here temporarily. Wǒ 'búgwo dzài jèr 'bǔ ge lín-
shŕde 'chywē.

(Of space on paper) búmǎn, tyánmǎn; syě (write); (fill completely) bǔshang,
tyánshang (fill with something); **fill in** or **fill out** tyán. / Fill up that space (as in a
newspaper). Bǎ nèikwài 'kùngbái °bú'mǎnle (°tyán'mǎnle). / Fill (up) that space
with this story. Ná 'jèidwàr 'syīnwén bǎ nèikwài 'kùngbái °'tyánshang (°'bǔshang).
/ Fill out the blanks first. Syān bǎ 'dǎndz dōu °'tyánshang (°'tyánle). / Fill in your
name and address here. (Bá) Nǐde 'syìngmíng jù'jŕ °tyándzai (°syědzai) 'jèr.

(Of a container) the second element is usually mǎn; the first may be dàu (pour),
jwāng (pack, contain) or chéng (contain, especially of a mass). / That bottle is
filled (up) with hot water. Nèige 'píngdzli jwāng'mǎnle rè'shwěi. / Fill this bottle
full of hot water. Bǎ jèige 'píngdz °jwāng'mǎnle (°dàu'mǎnle) rè'shwěi. / Fill up
his cup first. Syān gěi 'tā dàu'mǎn yibēi. / They filled his bowl with rice. Tāmen
gěi tā 'chéngle yǐ'mánwǎn 'fàn. / His pocket is all filled up with candy. Tāde kǒu-
'dàili jwāng'mǎnle 'táng le. or Tā 'jwāngle yìkǒu'dàrde 'táng. / There isn't enough
rice to fill three bowls. Fàn búgòu chéng sān'wǎn de. / Fill 'er up (with gas).
Jwāng'mǎnle. or Dàu'mǎnle. or Jyāmǎnle.

(Of an area filled with objects) the second element is mǎn, unless such an expression as the whole occurs, in which case no second element is needed; some of the
verbs used as first elements are bǎi arrange in order; gē, fàng put; pū, gài cover;
ān set up; tíng park a car. / The sofa just about fills that end of the room. Shā'fā
jyāng'jyāngrde bǎ wūdz nèitóur bái'mǎnle. / They filled the shelves with odds and
ends. Tāmen dzài 'jyàdzshang °bái'mǎnle (°gē'mǎnle, °fàng'mǎnle) 'língswèide
dūngsyi. / He filled the room with antiques. Tā bàile yǐ'wūdzde gǔ'wán. / He filled
the room with electric lamps. Tā ānle yǐ'wūdzde dyàn'dēng. / This rug will fill up
the living room (floor). Jèikwài 'dǐtǎn kéyi bǎ kètīngde dì'bǎn pū'mǎnle. / The parking place is filled with out-of-town cars. Tíngchē'chǎng tíng'mǎnle wài'láide 'chē.

(Of a space filled with people) the second element is mǎn; first elements are
dzwò (by sitting); jàn (by standing); jǐ (by crowding together); jyù (by gathering together); jù (by living). / The theater was slowly filling with people. Syì'ywándz màn-
'mārde dzwò'mǎnle rén le. / The hall was filled with people standing there listening.
'Tīngli jàn'mǎnle rén dzài nàr 'tīng. or 'Tīngli °jǐ (°jyù) 'mǎnle rén, dōu 'jàndzài
nàr 'tīng. / The barracks are filled with recruits. 'Yíng'pánli jù'mǎnle 'syīnbīng.
or 'Syīnbīng bǎ 'yíngpán dōu jù'mǎnle.

Be filled with without the means being specified mǎn and other expressions; see FULL. /The room is filled with smoke. Yǐ'wūdzli 'mǎn shř 'yān.

Have one's fill (of food) bǎu; (of an experience, etc.) gòu. /Have you had your fill of it? (food) 'Bǎule ma? (otherwise) 'Gòule ma? /Don't be bashful; go ahead and eat your fill. 'Byé bùhǎu'yìsz; 'chřba, chřde bǎu'bǎurde.

FINAL. (Last) mwòlyǎur(de), 'dzwēihòu(de) followed by a numeral or demonstrative and a measure before the noun. /This is the final lecture of the semester. Jèi 'shř 'běnchī °'dzwēihòude (°mwò'lyǎurde) °yìtáng 'kè le (°yì'bān le). /Did you go to the final lecture of the semester? 'Běnchī 'dzwēihòu nèitáng 'kè nǐ 'dàule ma?

(Definite) yídìngde, dìnghǎule, jywédìngle (already decided); néng dǐng de (determinable). /This is final, you don't have to say any more. Jèige yǐjing °dìng-'hǎule (°jywé'dìngle), nǐ búyùng dzài'shwōle. /There's nothing final about it yet. (already decided; as of a plan) 'Jèi shř hái 'méiyou yí'dìngde 'bànfa ne. *or* (determinable, as of something now happening) 'Jèi shř jyē'gwò dzěmma'yàng hái bùnéng 'dìng ne.

(Beyond appeal; legal) 'bùnéng °'kànggàu (°shàng'sùle). /The decision of the Supreme Court is final. 'Dzwēigāufǎ'ywàn °pàn'jywé de 'bùnéng 'kànggàu (°pàn jywé yǐ'hòu, jyou 'bùnéng shàng'sùle).

(Leaving nothing to be said or done). /Is that final? meaning absolutely necessary. 'Fēi nà yàngr bù'kě ma? or meaning Is there any other way? 'Hái néng yǒu 'byéde 'bànfǎ ma? or meaning Can it be discussed? Hái néng 'shāng lyang shāng lyang ma? or meaning It's settled, then? 'Yǐyánwéi'dìng le, ā? /His word is final. meaning What he says goes. 'Tā shwō 'dzěmmaje 'jyou děi 'dzěmmaje.

Final examination 'dàkǎu; (of a semester) 'chīkǎu, chī'jūngkǎushř; (of a school year) 'sywényán kǎushř; (for graduation) bì'yè kǎushř. /Did he pass his French final? Tā 'Fàwén °'dàkǎu (°etc.) jí'géle ma?

Final outcome jyēgwǒ, jyéjyú. /You can already tell what the final outcome is going to be. °Jyē'gwǒ (°Jyē'jyú) shémma 'yàngr yǐjǐng 'kàndechū'lái le.

Finals (in competition) 'jywésài. /He was eliminated before he got to the finals. Tā 'jywésài yǐ'chyán jyou 'syàchyule. *or* Tā 'méidàu 'jywésài jyou 'syàchyule.

FIND (FOUND). Chinese uses several verbs depending on the means of discovery. Resultative compounds are often used. The first element indicates the type of action, the second indicates completion of action. The second elements -chūlai, -dàu, -jáu are not always interchangeable and must be used each with its own particular verbs.

(General) jǎu, jǎujau, jǎudau, jǎuchulai. /They looked everywhere for him, but couldn't find him. Tamen 'dàuchù 'jǎu tā kěshr jǎubu'jáu. /When you find him, tell him there is nothing for him to worry about anymore. 'Jǎujau tā de shŕhou, 'gàusu tā yíchyè dōu kéyi fàng'syīnle. /They found him. Tāmen bǎ tā 'jǎujaule. /Put everything back where you found it. Dzài nǎr 'jǎujaude hái dōu 'gēhwéi 'nǎr chyu. *or* Dzài 'shémma dìfang 'jǎujaude hái dōu 'gēhwéi nèige 'dìfang chyu. /Did you find it? 'Jǎujaule ma? /Where did you find it? (Dzài) 'nǎr jǎujaude? /Could you find him for me? Nǐ néng 'tì wǒ bǎ tā 'jǎujau ma? /Find him and bring him here. Bǎ tā 'jǎulai. /You can find faults in anyone. Nǐ yàu 'jǎu dehwà dzài shéi shēnshang dōu 'jǎudechū 'máubing lai.

(Accidentally) shř, shŕjau, jyàn, jyànjau. /I found a coin in the street. Wǒ dzài 'jyēshang °shŕle (°jyànle, °shŕjaule, °jyànjaule) yíge 'chyán. /I found this five-dollar bill in the street. Jèijāng 'wǔkwàichyánde 'pyàudz shř wǒ dzài 'jyēshang °shŕde (°jyànde, °shŕjaude, °jyànjaude).

(By turning things up or over) fān, fānjau, fānchulai. /I found this five-dollar bill in that book. Jèijāng 'wǔkwàichyánde 'pyàudz shř wǒ dzài nèiběr 'shūli °'fān-jaude (°'fānchulaide).

(Discover) kànjyan. /I found a note on my desk. Wǒ dzài wǒ shū'jwōrshang kànjyan yíge tyáur. /I found a book missing from the shelf. Wǒ kànjyan shū'jyàr-shang °'dwǎnle (°'shǎule, °'dyōule) yìběn 'shū. /Who found the body? 'Shřshou shř 'shéi °'kànjyande (°'jǎujaude)? /I found her staring at me. Wǒ kànjyan tā (dzài nǎr) 'dèngje yǎn 'chyáu wo ne. /I found her writing a letter. Wǒ 'kànjyan tā 'syě syìn ne.

(By visual examination) kànchulai. /I found five mistakes on one page. Dzài 'yìpyǎrshang wǒ 'kànchulai 'wǔge 'tswòr. /I found many mistakes in that book. Dzài 'nèiběr shūli wǒ 'kànchulai 'hǎusyě 'tswòr.

(By experience or perception) jywéde, jywéje, fājywé. /We've always found this place peaceful. Wǒmen yí'syàng °jywéde (°jywéje) jèr hěn 'ānjing. /If you ever find yourself in a tight spot, call on me. Nǐ 'yì jywéje méi'bànfa le, jyòu jáu 'wǒ hǎu le. /I found the book interesting. Wǒ °'jywéje (°fājywé) jèiběn 'shū hén yǒu 'yìsz. /I found him quite a bore. 'Wǒ °jywéde (°jywéje) tā 'jēn jyàu rén °'nǐwei deheng (°'tǎu'yàn).

(By thinking) syǎng, syǎngchulai. /How did you ever find such an illuminating word to describe him? Nǐ 'dzěmma syǎngchu 'dzèmme chyàdangde 'dzèr lái 'syíngrung tā? /He couldn't find anything to say. Tā 'syǎngbuchu 'hwà lai 'shwō le. /I haven't found a solution yet. Wǒ hái méi'syǎngchu ge 'bànfa lái ne. /Can you find an answer to this problem? Jèijyàn shèr nǐ 'syǎngdechū ge 'bànfa lai ma? /I've found the best answer to it. Wǒ 'syǎngchulaile yige 'dzwèi hǎude 'bànfa. /Let's try to find a way out. (to solve a problem) Syǎng ge 'jyějywéde 'bànfa ba. (to avoid embarrassment). Syǎng ge syà'táide 'bànfa ba. or (to a place) Jǎu yìtyáu 'lù hǎu 'chūchyu.

(Through scientific research) yánjyouchulai (by studying); shřyanchulai (by experimenting). /They found a new drug. Tāmen 'yánjyouchu yìjǔng 'syīnyàu lai. /They found a new way to cure diabetes. Tāmen °'shřyanchu (°'yánjyouchu) yìjǔng syīn'fádz lái jř 'tángnyàu'jèng.

(By exploration) 'fāsyàn. /They found gold in those streams. Tāmen dzài nèisyē 'héli °'fāsyàn (°'jǎujau, °'kànjyàn) 'jīndz le.

(By digging) jywéchulai, wāchulai. /They found gold in those mountains. Tāmen dzài nèisyē 'shānli °'jywéchu (°'wāchu) 'jīndz laile.

(By searching, research, investigation or diagnosis) (jyǎn)chá, ('jyǎn)cháchulai, chájau. /They found a gun in his trunk. Tāmen dzài tā 'syāngdzli °'cháchulai (or, with meanings given above °'jǎujaule, °'fānjaule, °'fānchulai) yìgǎn 'chyāng. /I found this word in that dictionary. Wǒ shř dzài nèiběn dz'dyǎnshang bǎ jèige 'dz 'cháchulaide. /The doctor found him to be a mental case. Dàifu °'jyǎncháchulai (°'cháchulai, °jèng'míngle) tā yǒu 'shénjīng'bìng.

In some cases find may be interpreted in more than one of the above ways, and is not translated at all. /They found him already dead. Tā 'yǐjīng 'szle. /I found her sick in bed. 'Tā jèng bìngdzai chwángshang. /When I got home I found my brother waiting for me. Wǒ dàu 'jyā de shřhou, tsái 'jřdau, 'gēge dzài nàr 'děng wǒ ne.

(Of a court) (prove) 'jèngmíng; (decide) pàn. /The court finds him guilty of murder. 'Fǎywàn 'jèngmíngle tā shr 'syūngshou. or 'Fǎywàn 'pàn tā yǒu 'shārén-'dzwèi. /The court found him innocent (or not guilty). 'Fǎywàn 'pàn tā °'méiyou 'dzwèi (°'wúdzwèi).

Find oneself. /I think he'll find himself someday. (know himself) Wǒ syǎng 'dzúng yǒu yìtyān tā néng jrdau tā 'dzǐjǐ shr 'dzěmma hwéi 'sher. (understand himself) Wǒ syǎng tā 'dzúng yǒu yìtyān néng 'dzǐjǐ 'míngbaigwolai. *or* Wǒ syǎng 'dzúng yǒu 'nèmma yìtyān tā hwèi dzǐjǐ 'jywéwu de.

Find the mark (lit.) dǎjùng, dǎjáu, 'dǎshàng; (fig., of something said) shwōjáu. / The bullet found its mark. 'Nèichyáng °dǎ 'jùngle (°dǎ'jáule, °dǎshàngle). / Your accusation really found its mark. 'Nǐ nèijyù hwà 'jēnshr shwō'jáule.

Find out (by asking) dǎting, dǎtingchulai, wèn, wènchulai, wènjau; (by obtaining information or material) déjau. / Find out all about him. Bǎ tāde 'dǐsyì dōu °'dǎtingchulai (°wènchulai). / How much did you find out? Ní 'dǎtingchulai 'dwōshǎu le? *or* Ní 'wènchulai 'dwōshǎu le? *or* Ní 'déjau dwōshau 'tsáilyau?

Lost and found department 'Shr wùbǎugwǎn'chù.

FINE. (Very good) hǎu <u>and combinations</u>; *see* **GOOD**. / That's fine! 'Hǎu! *or* Hǎu-'jíle! / We gave him the finest watch. Wǒmen gěi tā yìjǐ 'dzwèihǎude 'byǎu. / I had a fine time last night. Wǒ 'dzwéi 'wǎnshang wárde °hén 'hǎu (°hěn 'kwàihwo, °hén yǒu'yìsz). / That's a fine job for him. Tā dzwò nèige 'shr, dwèi 'tā hǎu'jíle. / He has a fine disposition. Tā 'píchi 'jēn hǎu. / I'm feeling fine, thanks. 'Syèsye, (wo jywéde) hén 'hǎu. / It's a fine day today. 'Jyēr tyār 'jēn hǎu. / That's a fine way to put it. Nèi hwà 'nèmma shwō °'hén hǎu (°hěn 'dwèi, °hěn 'wánjwǎn, °'jēn hwèi shwō'hwà a). (also sarcastically) / That's fine! (*or* A fine thing!) I lend you money to eat and then you spend it all on her! Wǒ jyègei nǐ 'chyán, wèide shr jyàu ni chr fàn yùngde. 'Hǎu (a)! Nǐ 'dōu hwādzài 'tā shēnshang le. / That's a fine way to treat a friend! Hǎu! Dài 'péngyou 'nèmma ge dàifar!

(Thin) syì. / You can draw finer lines with a hard pencil. Ná 'yìng chyānbǐ hwà de 'syàn kéyi 'dzài syì dyar. / There are some fine hairs on her shin. Tā syáu'twěishang yǒu syē 'syìmáur. / This thread is too fine for sewing on buttons. 'Jèige syàn féng 'kòudz tài 'syì le.

(Sharp) jyān. / Don't sharpen it to such a fine point. 'Byé syáude 'dzěmma jyān a. / I'd like a fine-pointed one, please. Wǒ yàu ge 'jyānde.

(Powdery) syì. / The pharmacist ground the drug into fine powder. °Yàujì'shr (°Mài'yàude) bǎ yàu 'yánchéng °syì'myǎr (°hěn syìde 'myǎr).

(Subtle, in detail) syì. / There is no need of making such fine distinctions. 'Búyùng fēnde 'dzěmma 'syì. *or* 'Búyùng fēn 'dzěmma 'syì. *or* 'Búyùng dzěmma 'syìfēn.

(Expert; of workmanship) syì, jīng, chyǎu. / What fine workmanship! °'Dzwòde (°Jèi 'gūng) 'jēn °syì (°jīng, °chyǎu).

(Acute; of musical ear) líng, 'língmǐn. / She has a fine ear for music. Tā 'ěrdwo tīng 'yīnywè hěn °líng (°'língmǐn).

Fine arts 'měishù; **museum of fine arts** 'měishùgwǎn.

Fine gold 'chwúnjīn.

A fine fákwǎn; **pay a fine** jyāu (yìbǐ) fá'kwǎn. / If he's convicted he'll have to pay a stiff fine. Yàushr tā bèi'pàn yǒu 'dzwèi, tā děi jyāu yìdàbǐ fá'kwǎn. / I paid a five-dollar fine. Wǒ jyāule 'wǔkwài chyán de 'fákwǎn. / You may pay the fine now or have your case tried in court. Nǐ hwòshr syàndzài jyāu 'fákwǎn, hwòshr dàu 'fǎywàn chyu gwò'táng.

To fine fá. / He was fined five dollars. °Tā fále (°Fále tā, °Tā bèi'fále) 'wǔkwài 'chyán.

FINGER. shǒujrtou; <u>especially in combinations</u> jr; <u>sometimes</u> shóujr; **index finger**

'shŕjř, 'ềrjř; **middle finger** 'jŭngjř; **fourth finger** 'wúmíngjř (nameless finger); **little finger** 'syáujř, syáushŏu'jŕtou, syáu mujř, syáumugễr; **fingernail** shŏu'jřjyă, jřjya-'gàr. /He has six fingers on each hand. Tā lyàngge shŏu 'dōu yŏu 'lyòuge shŏu-'jŕtou. *or* Tā shř lyòu'jềr. /I cut my thumb and middle finger opening that can. Wŏ kāi 'gwāntou de shŕhou bă 'dàjř gēn 'jŭngjř 'lá le. /Watch out or you'll burn your fingers. (lit.) 'Syāusyĭn dyar byé 'shāule shŏu'jŕtou. (lit. or fig.) Dāng'syĭn dyar byé 'tàngle shŏu'jŕtou. (fig.) Dāng'syĭn dyar, °byé 'dżtáu'kŭchř (°byé 'dżsywún 'fán'nău). /You can count them on your fingers. Jén shř 'chyūjŕkě'shŭ. (Unlike Westerners, who start with a closed fist and count to five by sticking out the fingers, the Chinese start with the hand open and bend the fingers one at a time until the fist is closed, then count from 6 to 10 by sticking out the fingers again, so that they can count to 10 on each hand.)

Snap the fingers dá fēidz. /Don't snap your finger at me. Byé gēn wŏ dá 'fēidz.

To finger (yùng shŏu'jŕtou) mwō. /She fingered (felt with her fingers) the material appraisingly. Tā yùng shŏu'jŕtou mwōle mwo yĭlyàur kàn °shř shémma 'chéngse (°hău bu'hău).

Other expressions in English. /I know there is a mistake somewhere, but I can't put my finger on it. Wŏ 'jŕdau 'yŏu ge dĭfang 'tswò le, búgwo 'jŕbuchū'lái. /I'm sure I know his name, but I just can't put my finger on it. Wŏ 'jŕdau tā jyàu shémma °'jyòushr syàngbuchu'lái(°shwōbuchu'lái, °jyàubushang'lái). /Don't let him slip through your fingers. Byé bă tā 'fànggwochyu. /He had a fine opportunity, but he let it slip through his fingers. Tā yŏugwo yíge 'hău jīhwei, kěshr °'tswògwo-chyule (°'fànggwochyule). /He had all that information at his fingertips. 'Dżềmma dwōde shèr tā 'dōu jìde, 'yàu shwō 'shémma dōu shwōdeshàng'lái. /He always keeps some spicy jokes at his fingertips. Tā yŏu jige nềi yàngrde 'syàuhwàr dzài dzwĕi'byārshang, 'yàu shwō jyòu shwō.

FINISH. <u>Chinese usually uses resultative compounds.</u> The first element indicates the <u>action being finished, such as</u> dzwò do, make, nùng make, syě write, shwō speak, <u>and any number of others.</u> The second element indicates completion wán, lyău, chéng (usually of a piece of work), hău (complete and well done), bău (of eating only), <u>and some others. When the type of action is not specified, the second element may be used alone. Occasionally, when the action is the important thing, only the first element occurs.</u> /Let's finish this job tonight. Dzámen jyēr 'wănshang bă jềi shèr °nùng'wánle ba (°dzwò'wánle ba, *or* (rush) °gàn'wánle ba). /Wait until he finishes eating. Děng tā °chř'wánle je (°chř'hăule je, °chř'băule je). /Don't hurry; finish what you're doing. Búyùng 'máng; °syān bă ni dzwò de 'shř dzwò'wánle (°dzwò-'wánle dzai 'shwō, °bă ni syàndzài dzwò de 'shř dzwò'wán dzài 'shwō). /Have you finished the book yet? Nềiběr 'shū °kàn'wánle (°nyàn'wánle, °yùng'wánle) ma? /I'll be with you as soon as I finish this drink. Wŏ hē'wánle jềibēi 'jyou, jyou 'lái. /It's finished. Yĭjīng 'wánle. /There's only a little bit left; finish it up. (of food) Shèng 'nèmma dyăr le, °dōu 'chřle ba (*or* (of drink) °dōu 'hēle ba, *or* (of work) °dzwò'wánle ba, °nùng'wánle ba, *or* (mowing a lawn) °twēi'wánle ba, °etc.). /I'd like to borrow your paper if you're finished with it. 'Bàu nĭ kàn'wánle de hwà, 'wó syàng jyèlai 'kànkan. /The maid has finished making the beds. Lău'mādz bă chwáng dōu °pū'hăule (°pū'wánle). /The carpenter has just finished the cabinet. 'Mùjyang 'gāng bă 'gwềidz °dzwò'chéngle (°dzwò'wánle, °dzwò'hăule). /When she finishes talking, wake me up. Tā shwō'wánle de shŕhou, bá wŏ jyàu'syĭngle. /You can never finish it that way. 'Nèmmaje nĭ jyou 'yúngywăn °dzwòbu'wánle (°méi ge 'wánle, °dzwòbu'chéng le).

<u>When speaking of finishing in a certain order (first, last, etc.) Chinese uses</u> wán *or* dàu, <u>or names the position alone.</u> /He finished first. Tā 'tóuyíge 'wánde.

or Tā 'tóuyíge 'dàude. *or* Tā syān 'wánde. *or* Tā dì'yī. *or* (in a race) Tā 'pǎu dì'yī. / He finished last. Tā mwò'lyǎur wánde. *or* Tā dzwèi'hòu wánde. *or* Tā shr̀ 'dàushǔ dì'yī. *or* Tā shr̀ mwò'lyaurde 'yíge. *or* Tā dzài 'jǐnhòutou. *or* (in an examination) Tā kúngbǎng.

(Give a desired surface effect) chī (with lacquer); yóu (with lacquer, varnish, oil); dǎmwo (with sandpaper); shàngshǎr (with paint). / This table is finished nicely. Jèige jwōdz °'chīde hǎu (°'yóude hǎu, °'dǎmwode 'hǎu, °shàng'shǎr shàngde hǎu). / How would you like it finished? is expressed as What kind of lacquer? Shàng 'shémma 'chī? or as Do you want it lacquered? Shàng 'chī búshàng? or as Do you want lacquer added? Jyā 'chī bù'jyā? or as How many coats of lacquer? Shàng 'jǐdàu 'chī? or as What color? Yàu 'shémma shǎrde? or as Do you want it polished? Yàu búyàu 'dǎmwo?

Finish someone bǎ . . . 'jyéshū, bǎ . . . de tái 'chāile, bǎ . . . dá'dǎu; (specifically by affecting possessions) bǎ . . . nèng'gwāng, bǎ . . . nèng'jǐng, bǎ . . . nèng-'kūng, bǎ . . . nèngde 'yìgānèr'jǐng, bǎ . . . 'shóulide 'dōu nèngchulai; **be finished** (of a person) wán, chwēi, lyǎu, wárwán, 'wánshr̀dà'jí, (very vulgar) wándàn (these are usually preceded by swàn, meaning to consider as, be as good as, and are usually followed by le.). / That finished him. 'Nèmma yìlái jyòu bǎ tā °'jyéshūle (°-de tái 'chāile, °dá'dǎule, °nèng'gwāngle, °nèngde 'yìgān èr'jǐng le, °'shóulide 'dōu nèngchulaile). *or* 'Nèmma yìlái tā jyòu swàn °'wánle (°'chwēile, °'lyǎule, °etc.) / He's finished. Tā swàn °wánle (°'chwēile, °'lyǎule, °etc.). / He's finished as a politician. Dzài 'jèngjr̀ wú'táishang tā swàn °'chwēile (°etc.).

FIRE. (Flames) hwǒ; **build a fire** shēnghwǒ; **light a fire** dyánhwǒ. / Fire! Fire! Jáu-'hwǒle! Jáu'hwǒle! *or* Chí'hwǒle! Chí'hwǒle! / Build a good fire. Hǎu'hǎurde shēng ge 'hwǒ. / It's very hard to build a fire when there are cross winds. Fēng lwàn °'chwēi (°'gwā) de shŕhou 'hwǒ hěn nán 'shēngde'jáu. / I can't get this fire going. 'Jèi hwǒ wǒ shēngbu'jáu. *or* 'Jèi hwǒ wó dyǎnbu'jáu. / They built a fire to warm their hands. Tāmen shēngle ge 'hwǒ lai kǎu 'shǒu. / Will you light the fire? Ní bǎ 'hwǒ 'dyǎnjau. / He likes to relax with a fire in the fireplace and all the lights out. Tā syǐhwan bǎ 'dēng dōu 'syīle, dzài bìlúli °shēngje (°dyǎnje, °jáuje) 'hwǒ, nèmma 'dāije yǎng'shén. / The fire is going strong. 'Hwǒ jáude hěn 'wàng. / Let the fire go out. Ràng hwǒ 'syīle ba. *or* Ràng hwǒ 'myèle ba. / That building burned down in a fire. 'Nèige lóu (ràng) 'yìbǎ 'hwǒ gei shāu'gwāngle. / The fire lighted up the whole town. 'Hwǒgwāng bǎ yì'chéng dōu jàu'lyàngle. / How much fire insurance do you carry? Ní bǎule 'dwōshau chyánde hwó'syǎn? / This material doesn't catch fire easily. Jèijǔng 'tsáilyàur 'bùrúngyi jáu'hwǒ.

Be on fire jáu. / The basket's on fire. 'Kwāngdz 'jáule.

Catch fire jáuhwǒ. / The rug caught (on) fire and burned the house down. Dì-'tǎn syān °'jáule (°shāuchilaile), 'hòulai bǎ 'fángdz yě 'shāule.

Set fire to . . . , set . . . on fire fànghwǒ, bǎ . . . dyán'jáu, bǎ . . . shāu'jáu, bǎ . . . 'shāu . . . . / That was no accident; someone set the house on fire. 'Nèi tsái búshr °'ǒuránde (°yì'wàide) shr̀ne; jwǔnshr yǒu rén fàng'hwǒ bǎ fángdz 'shāule de. / The people set fire to their own homes before leaving. Nèisyē rén bǎ 'dz̀jǐde 'fángdz °dyán'jáule tsái 'dzǒude (°dyán'jáule hwǒ tsái 'dzǒude, °shāu'jáule tsái 'dzǒude, °'shāule tsái 'dzǒude, °'fànghwǒ 'shāule tsái 'dzǒude). / Set fire to that haystack at midnight. Dàule 'yèli shŕèr'dyǎn bá tsǎu'dwēi dyán'jáule.

Fire alarm jyòuhwójǐngbàu.

Firebug (arsonist) fànghwǒde.

Firecracker pàujyú.

Fire station jyòuhwǒdwèi, syāufángdwèi.

Fireman jyòuhwŏde, syāufángdwèi, 'syāufáng'dwèide rén, (one who tends a fire) 'hwŏfú.

To fire (bake, of pottery, etc.) shāu. / They're firing bricks. Tāmen shāu 'jwān ne. / They fire the pottery in primitive ovens. Tāmen yùng 'jyòushr lúdz shāu 'tsźchî.

(Of guns) kāihwŏ (to open fire); kāichyāng (with small arms); kāipàu, fàngchyāng, fàngpàu (with artillery); 'shèjî (shoot); **gunfire** 'pàuhwŏ, 'chyānglíndàn'yŭ. / Wait until they open fire. Děng tāmen 'syān kāi°'hwŏ (°'chyāng, °'pàu). / Don't fire! (not in military connection) Byé fàng'chyāng! / Fire! (military) 'Shèjî! / Cease firing! 'Tíngjř shèjî! / He fired a couple of shots in our direction. Tā 'chùngje wŏmen °'fàngle (°'kāile) lyǎng(sān)'chyáng. / They were under fire for three days and nights before they attacked. Dzài 'gūngjî yǐ'chyán tāmen dzài °'chyānglíndàn-'yúli (°'dírén pàuhwŏ jřsyà) áule 'sāntyān sān'yè.

(Keep a fire going) tyān hwŏ; (with coal) tyān méi. / Fire the boiler. Chĭgwō děi tyān hwŏ. / They're firing the furnace. Tāmen jèng tyān méi ne.

(Discharge from employment) tsź, tsái, shwā (local Peiping), and some indirect expressions. / That man was fired last week. Nèige rén 'shànglĭbài (jyàu 'rénjya) gei °'tsźle (°'shwāle, °tsáile). or Nèige rén 'shànglĭbài jyàu 'rénjya chĭng tā 'dzŏule. / You can fire him, can't you? Nĭ 'tsźle tā, bù'syíng ma? or Nĭ jyàu tā jywǎn 'pūgai bújyou 'wánle ma? or (vulgar) Nĭ jyàu tā gwŭn'dàn bújyou 'wánle ma?

(Of something said). / I'm ready. Fire away. Wŏ 'tĭngje ne. Nĭ 'shwō ba. / They fired a lot of caustic questions at him. Tāmen wènle tā °syē hén 'swŭnde 'wèntí (°syē hén 'wākurénde 'wèntí, °syē hén 'kèbwóde 'wèntí).

Other expressions in English. / Better be careful; you're playing with fire. Syāu'syĭn dyar ba, °nèi 'búshr 'wárde (°nà shr jàu 'dzwèi shòu, or (of a person) °nèige rén 'rèbude, or (of a thing) °nèige shř 'dzwòbude, or (of an action) °nĭ 'nèmmaje hwèi rè'hwŏde, °nĭ 'nèmmaje hwèi chū'shèrde, °nĭ 'nèmmaje shr 'méibĭngjǎu'bĭng, °nĭ nèmmaje shř 'méishèrjǎu'shèr). / Where's the fire? (lit.) 'Nǎr jáu'hwŏle? or (fig.) Jíde shř 'shémma? or 'Mángde shř 'shémma? or 'Hwāng ge shémma 'jyèr? / That's fighting fire with fire. Nèi shř yĭdúgūng'dú. / He's out of the frying pan and into the fire. Tā 'yĭpwŏ wèi'píng 'yĭpwŏ yòu 'chĭ. or Tā 'fúwú-shwāng'jř 'hwòbùdān'syíng. / The scheme has been hanging fire for weeks now. 'Nèi shèr nèmma °'sywánje (°'gēje) yŏu háujige lĭ'bài le. / They were fired with enthusiasm about the plan by his speech. Tāde yán'jyǎng jyàu tāmen dwèiyu nèige 'jĭhwà hén °rèsyĭn (°shàng'jĭn). / How does it feel to be under fire? (fig.) Byéren 'pĭping nĭ, nĭ jywéde dzěmma'yàng.

FIRM. (Solid) jyēshr, dzwòshr, láukau; (tight) jĭn; (hard) yìng; (steady) wěn; also negatives of words meaning weak, soft, etc. / The ground is firmer here. 'Jèr dì °'yìng dyar (°'bùnèmma 'rwǎn, °'bùnèmma wàngsya 'syàn). / This chair is not firm. 'Jèibá yĭdz °bù'jyēshr (°bú'dzwòshr, °bù'láukau, °bù'wěn, °jř 'hwódung). / Make sure the plank is firm before you walk on it. 'Jwŭn jřdau bǎndz gē °'láukaule (°wēnle), dzài dzài 'shàngtou 'dzŏu. but / He was on firm ground in his argument. Tā shwō de °hén yóu'lĭ (°hén yŏu 'gēnjyù, °dōu shr 'shřshřdzài'dzàide 'chíngsyíng).

(Tight; of grip) jĭn, szjĭn(de), °yùng (°shř) dàjyèr. / Don't use too firm a grip on the wheel. 'Lwúndz 'byé dzwànde 'nèmma °jĭn (°sź'jĭnde). or 'Lwúndz 'byé shř 'nèmma dàde jyèr lái 'dzwànje.

(Strict) yán, 'rènjēn. / I intend to be very firm in enforcing that rule. Wŏ yàu jàuje 'nèityáu gwēijyu 'rènjēn 'bànlĭ. or (of a law) Fàn 'nèityáu 'fǎlyù de wŏ 'yídĭng 'yĭfǎ 'yánchéng 'jywé bù'kwāndài. / He is very firm in enforcing that rule. Tā jàuje 'nèige gwēijyu 'hěn rèn'jēnde bànlĭ. or 'Nèityáu 'fǎlyù tā 'bànde hěn °'yán

(°rèn'jēn). / You have to be firm with children. Gwǎn 'háidzmen děi °'yán (°'shwō shémma jyòu 'shŕ shémma).

(Insistent) jyānchŕ. / We must take a firm stand in this matter. 'Jèijyàn shŕ dzámen °děi 'jyānchŕdàu'dǐ (°yǐ'dyár yě 'bùnéng 'ràng). / He's very firm about his ideas. Tā 'jyānchŕ tā dż'jǐ de 'yìjyan, (yì'dyár yě bùkěn 'ràng). or Tā yí'dìng yàu ànje tā 'dżjǐ de'yìjyan lái 'bàn.

(Of belief or conviction; in a religious sense) hěn syìn; (in other senses) jywéje (feel) and similar expressions plus some expressions including the idea of necessity or rightness; see NECESSARY, RIGHT. / I'm a firm believer in it. (religiously) Wǒ hěn 'syìn jèige. (otherwise) Wǒ jywéde jèige °'jēn dwèi (°shŕ wéi'yíde bànfa). / He's a firm believer in heaven and hell. Tā hěn 'syìn yǒu 'tyāntang yǒu 'dìyu nèmma yì'shwō. / He's a firm believer in letting people alone. Tā jywéje 'bùgwǎn 'byérénde 'shŕ shŕ 'dwèide. or Tā jywéje bùyǐnggāi gwǎn 'byérénde shŕ. / It is my firm conviction that we should take immediate action. Jyù 'wǒ kàn dzámen fēi 'lìshŕ jyòu 'gànchǐlai bù'kě. or Jyù 'wǒ kàn dzámen yí'dìng děi lìshŕjyou 'gànchǐlai. or Wǒ 'jywéde wǒmen děi lì'kè 'tsáichyù syíng'dùng.

A firm (company, corporation) jyār, gūngsz̄; (store) pùdz; your firm (polite) gwèigūngsz̄, bǎuhàu; (office of professional people such as accountants, lawyers, etc.) shŕwùswǒ; law firm lyùshŕ shŕwù'swǒ. / Whose firm do you represent? (polite) °Bǎu'hàu (°Gwèigūng'sz̄) shŕ 'něijyā? or Nǐ shŕ 'něijyār de? or Nǐ shŕ 'něige gūng'sz̄ de? or Nǐ shŕ 'něige 'pùdz de?

FIRMLY. (Tightly, solidly) . . . (de)°jǐn (°jyēshr, °dzwòshr, °láukau, °wěn). / The boat has been firmly secured. Chwán 'shwānde °hén'jǐn (°hěn'jyēshr, hěn 'láukau). / Have the chair nailed firmly. Bǎ 'yǐdz dìng °'jyēshr le (°'dzwòshr le, °láukau le, °'jǐn le). / Hold it firmly. Nájǐnle. or Dzwàn'jǐnle. or (steady) Ná'wěnle.

(In a determined manner) 'chywèshŕde. / I told him firmly not to do that anymore. Wǒ 'chywèshŕde gàusung tā bú'yàu dzài nèmma dwzò le. / The teacher spoke very firmly to him. Jèige lǎushr hěn 'chywèshŕde gēn tā shwō.

FIRST. (Preceding or happening before all others) dìyī, tóu(yi), tóu, chū, sometimes only yi; (each of these is followed by a measure). / Do you remember the way you stared at me the first time I came here? Nǐ 'jìde wǒ °'tóuyihwéi (°'dì'yítsz̀, °'tóutsz̀, °'chūtsz̀) dàu jèr nǐ 'dèngje yǎr 'chóu wǒ de nèi'yàngr ma? / This is my first trip to China. Wǒ jèi shŕ °'tóuyitsz̀ (°'tóutsz̀, °dì'yítsz̀, °'chūtsz̀) shàng 'Jūnggwo. / The first day she came here to work she looked like a child. Tā °'tóuyityān (°dì-'yītyān) shànggūng (lái de shŕhou), 'kànshangchyu 'jyānjŕ shŕ ge syàu'háidz. / Is this his first offense? Tā jèi shŕ 'chūfàn ma? or Tā jèi shŕ °'tóuyitsz̀ (°etc.) fàn-'dzwèi ma? / This is only the first step. Jèi 'búgwo shŕ °'chūbù (°'tóuyíbù, °dì-'yíbù, °(gāng)chǐ'tóurde yíbù, °(gāng)chǐ'shŕde yíbù, °'gāng jáushǒu 'bànde yíbù). / The first step is the hardest. Yīchǐ'tóur 'dzwèi nán. or Gāng kāi'shŕ 'dzwèi nán. or 'Tóuyíbù 'dzwèi nán. or 'Chūbànde shŕhou 'dzwèi nán. or (proverb) 'Fánshŕ 'tóunán. or (lit., of a baby) Syàu'hár dzǒu 'tóuyí'bù de shŕhou 'dzwèi nán. / It's the first house after you turn the corner. 'Gwǎile wār °'tóuyìjyār (°'tóuyìswŏr 'fángdz) jyòu 'shŕ. / That's the first good news we've had for a long time. 'Dzèmma syē 'shŕhou le jèi shŕ dì'yítsz̀ tīngjyàn 'hǎu syāusyi. / The first good rainstorm will wash it off. 'Yí syà 'dàyǔ jyòu hwèi 'chūngsyàchyude. / He's always the first one to complain. Tā 'lǎushr °dì'yíge (°'tóuyíge, or (leading) °lǐng'tóur) 'bàuywan de. / He was the first one there. Tā shŕ °'tóuyíge (°dì'yíge) dàude. or meaning He got in first (sports competition). Tā °pǎu (°dé) dì'yī.

(Before anything else) syān. / I have to go to the store first. Wǒ děi 'syān dàu 'pùdzli chyù. / Put first things first. 'Gāi syān dzwò de jyòu 'syān dzwò. or Yǒu 'syānhòu 'bùdzòu, 'bùnéng 'lwàn lái de. / First, let me ask you this. Wǒ 'syān wèn nǐ 'jèige. or is expressed as The first thing I want to ask you is this. °'Tóuyí-yàngr (°'Tóuyísyàng, °Dì'yíjyàn shr̀) wǒ yàu 'wèn nǐ de shr̀ 'jèige.

(At the beginning of something continuous) when . . . first . . . . . . gāng . . . de shŕhou; or, instead of gāng, use chū, gāngyǐ, chǐ'tóur, yǐchǐ'tóur, 'chwàng (usually with bàn), etc. (chǐtóur is sometimes used without a verb following). /When we first came here, there was only one store. Wǒmen °'chū-(°gāng-)dàu de shŕhou, jèr jř yǒu 'yíge pùdz. /When the firm was first established, there was only one secretary. 'Gūngsz̄ °'chwàngbàn (°'gāng kāibàn, °chǐ'tóur, °'yǐchǐ'tóur, °'gāngyí bàn, °'chūbàn) de shŕhou, jř yǒu 'yíge 'shūjì. /He was way behind when the race first started. °'Gāngpǎu (°'Gāngyǐ pǎu, °Chǐ'tóur pǎu, °Yǐchǐ'tóur pǎu, °Tsáiyǐ 'pǎu, °'Chū'pǎu) de shŕhou, tā làdzài 'hòutou láije.

The first (of a month) 'yíhàu (solar calendar); chūyī (lunar calendar). /I get paid on the first. Wǒ °'yíhàu (°chū'yī) lǐng'syīn. /He'll arrive on the twenty-first. Tā èrshr̀'yíhàu dàu.

At first chǐsyān, chǐchū, chǐ'tóurde shŕhou. /I didn't like him at first. Wó °chǐ'syān (°chǐ'chū, °chǐ'tóurde shŕhou) bù'syǐhwān tā.

At first sight (either lit. of seeing or fig. of hearing, etc.) yī plus a verb; some-times yī is preceded by gāng, jà, or mèng, and the verb followed by de shŕhou. (See also above.) /I knew he was a crook at first sight. °Wǒ yí 'kànjyàn tā (°Wǒ gēn tā yí jyàn'myàn, °Wǒ 'tóuyítsz̀ kànjyan tā) jyòu jŕdàu tā 'bùshr̀ hǎu'rén. /The idea is really much better than it looks at first sight. 'Jèige bànfǎ °yī 'tīngjyàn (°'gāngyī 'tīngjyàn, °'jàyī 'tīngjyàn, °'mèngyī 'tīngjyàn, °yí 'kànjyàn, °gāngyí 'kàn, °jàyí 'kàn, °mèngyí 'kàn) de shŕhou 'bùdzèmma 'hǎu; chǐ'shŕ shr̀ 'hén hǎude.

First aid 'chūlyáu, jíjyòufǎ, jyòu'jífǎ.

First class (travel) 'tóuděng. /I always travel first class. Wǒ chū'mér de shŕhou lǎushr dzwò 'tóuděng.

First class, first rate, first grade. (See BEST.) /These are first-class stockings. Jèi 'dōu shr̀ °dzwèi shàngděngde (°dzwèihǎude) sz̀'wàdz. /He gave a first-class performance. Tā yànde 'jēn hǎu. or Tā yànde 'shŕdzài hǎu. /He's a first-rate comedian. Tā shr̀ °dǐyī'lyóu (°'dzwèihǎu) -de 'chóujyǎur.

FISH. yú; freshwater fish 'héyú, 'hélide 'yú; lake fish 'húyú, 'húlide yú; saltwater fish 'hǎiyú; fresh fish 'syānyú. /Do you like (to eat) fish? Ní 'syǐhwān chr̄ 'yú ma? /I caught a fish. Wǒ 'dyàushanglai yìtyáu 'yú. /How many fish did you catch? (implying that there were probably few) Nǐ dyàushang °'jǐtyáu yú lai (or (implying many) °'dwōshǎutyáu 'yú lai)? /What kind of fish do you have? Ní yǒu 'shémma-yàngrde 'yú? or Nǐ 'dōu yǒu 'shémma yú? /What would be the best way to cook the fish? Yú 'dzěmma dzwò 'hǎu? or expressed as What is the best way to eat fish? Yú 'dzěmma chr̄ 'hǎu? /They have a fish pond. Tāmen yǒu ge 'yǎngyú'chŕ.

To fish (catch fish) 'dyàuyú (by hook); (yùng 'wǎng) 'dǎyú (by net); 'chāyú (by spear); 'dǎiyú (by hand); but to catch (a) fish (succeed in catching) dyàujuan yú, dyàushang yú, dǎjau yú, chājau yú, dǎijau yú. /They make their living by fishing. or They are fishermen. Tāmen shr̀ dǎ'yúde. or Tāmen dǎ'yú wéi'shēng. or Tāmen dǎ'yú gwò 'r̀dz. /Do you want to go fishing? Chyu dyàu'yú chyu 'hǎu buhǎu? /Are you allowed to fish here? Jèr syǔ dyàu'yú ma?

Fish for (feel for) mwō, māu. /He fished through his pockets for keys, but couldn't find them. Tā 'jèige kǒudàr 'nèige kǒudàr de mwō 'yàushr, 'dzěmma mwō yě 'méimwō'jáu. or Tā yàu jǎu 'yàushr, kǒudàr 'dōu mwō'dàule yě méimwō'jáu. or Tā shēn'shǒu dau tā 'kǒudàrli chyu mwō 'yàushr, jige kǒudàr 'dōu mwō'dàule yě méimwō'jáu.

Fish for (try to get) is expressed as have in mind syǎng, want yàu, try tàn, and other similar verbs, plus another verb. / She's fishing for information. Tā jēng syǎng dǎtīng 'shěr ne. *or* Tā nà shř °yàu 'dǎtīng shř 'dzěmma hwéi 'shěr (°'tàntīng 'syāusyi ne, °yàu 'dédàu dyǎr 'syāusyi, °'tàntīng 'kǒuchǐ laile). / He's always fishing for compliments. Tā 'lǎu syǎng 'dé rén 'chēngdzàn. *or* Tā 'lǎu ài gù'yǐde dzwò dyǎr shemma hau jyàu rén 'kwǎjyang.

Fish out, fish up mwōchulai; *see also* FIND, PULL, TAKE, etc. / He fished a picture of his son out of his wallet. Tā tsúng chyán'jyǎdzli °'mwōchu (°'jǎuchu) yìjāng tā érdzde syǎng'pyǎr lai. / The puppy fell into the brook, but we fished him out. Syǎu'gǒu dyàudzài 'héli le; 'wǒmen bǎ tā °'jyòuchulaile (°'jyòushanglaile, °'lāchulaile, °'lāshanglaile). / I was hunting in the toolbox for a hammer, but fished up this screwdriver. Wǒ dzài 'hédzli jǎu 'lángtou, kěshr °mwōjau (°jǎujau) dzěmma yige gǎnjwěi.

FIT. (Be the right size, be suitable) héshř; (just right) jēng héshř, gāng héshř, jēng hǎu, gāng hǎu; (be contained in) gēsya, bǎisya, fàngjinchyu, etc. (*See* PUT and other appropriate words.) / It fits you perfectly. Wèi 'nǐ °jēng hé'shř (°etc.). *or* (of clothes) 'Nǐ chwānje °jēng hé'shř (°etc.). *or* (of a job) 'Nǐ dzwò °jēng hé'shř (°etc.). *or* (of a chair) 'Nǐ dzwò(shang) °jēng hé'shř (°etc.). / Does it fit all right? Hé'shř ma? / These shoes don't fit. 'Jèishwāng syé bù hé'shř. / We're missing the piece that fits in here. Dzài 'jèr °gē('fàng)de'syà de nèikwàr jǎubu'jáule. / This picture just fits this space. Jèijāng 'hwàr 'gwàdzai jèr °jēng 'hǎu (°etc.). *or* 'Jèijāng hwàr °'jēng (°'gāng) hǎu dzài jèr 'gwà(de) 'syà. / This typewriter just fits in that cardboard box. 'Jèijyà dǎdz'jǐ dzài nèige 'jřsyāngdzli °gāng hǎu 'gēsya (°gāng háu bǎisya, °gāng hǎu 'fàngjinchyu, °jēng 'bǎidesyà, °'gējinchyu (*or* 'fàngjinchyu *or* 'bǎijinchyu) jēng hé'shř). *or meaning* That box just fits this typewriter. Nèige 'jřsyāngdz 'gāng hǎu °'rúng(de)sya (°'gēdesya, °'bǎisya, °'bǎidesya) nèige dǎdz'jǐ. / Have you got a key to fit this lock? Yǒu 'kāidekāi jèibá 'swǒ de 'yàushr ma? *or* 'Jèibá swǒ nǐ yǒu hé'shřde yàushr ma? but (of a description) / The description fits you perfectly. °'Syíngrúngde (°'Myáusyéde, °'Shwōde nèige lyànde 'yàngdz) gēn 'nǐ 'yìmú yí'yàngr de.

(Equip, put on) ān. / I want to have a new lock fitted on the door. Wó syǎng dzài 'ménshang 'ān bǎ 'syīnswǒ. / The plane is being fitted with the best instruments. Fēijīshang 'ānje 'dzwèi hǎu de 'yíchì. / The ship is being fitted out with all the latest gadgets. 'Chwánshang 'ānje dzwèi 'syīnshř de líng'jyàr.

Fit someone in (to a schedule). / The doctor's very busy today, but he'll try to fit you in somewhere. Dàifu jyēr 'hěn máng, búgwò tā dzǔng hwèi 'yún ge shřhou 'kàn nǐ de.

Fit in with gēn . . . hé'shř, gēn . . . 'chèn, gēn . . . 'pèishang. / That chair won't fit in with the rest of the furniture. Jèibá 'yǐdz gēn byéde jyājyu °bùhé'shř (°bú'chèn, °'pèibu'shàng).

Be fit (be suitable for a certain purpose) héshř, syāngyí, and many indirect expressions. / What kind of work is he fit for? Tā dzwò 'shémma yàngrde shř °hé'shř (°syāng'yí). / The food here isn't fit to eat. 'Jèrde fàn °'bùshr 'rén chřde (°jyàu rén 'chřbusyà'chyù, °bù'yíyu rén 'chř, °'rénchřle bùhé'shř, °'chřle bù-'hǎu, °'chřle bùsyāng'yí). / I'll do whatever you think fit. 'Nǐ jywéje °'dzěmmaje hé'shř (°gāi 'dzěmma dzwò), wǒ jyou dzěmma 'dzwò. / He may act as he sees fit. 'Tā jywéje °'gāi dzěmmaje (°'dzěmmaje hǎu) jyòu kéyi 'dzěmmaje. *or* Tā yàu 'dzěmmaje dōu 'syíng.

Be fit (physically suited) 'tǐgé gòu . . . *or* néng . . . (followed by what the person is fit for); tǐgé hégé (physically qualified). / He was classified as not fit (*or* unfit) for front-line duty. Tā 'fēndzai 'tǐgé °'búgòu (°buhégé) dàu 'chyánsyàn dzwò'jàn de nèi'lèili. / He was classified as fit for front-line duty. Tā 'fēndzai °'néng (°'tǐgé gòu, °tǐgé hégé) dàu 'chyánsyàn dzwò'jàn de nèi'lèili.

Be fit (healthy) 'tǐgé hén hǎu, 'shēndz hén hǎu, 'shēntǐ hén hǎu. / I feel pretty fit. (Wǒ jywéje) wó °'tǐgé hén hǎu (°etc.).

A fit (spasm) jèn, jèndz; **have a fit** (lit.) chōu yíjèn . . . , (fig.) is expressed with words meaning to become angry, as shēngchì. / He had an epileptic fit one morning. Yǒu yìtyān 'dzǎushang tā 'chōule yíjèn ('yángjyǎur) 'fēng. / Every time I mention her name he has a fit. Wǒ 'yǐ shwō 'nèige nyurén de míngdz tā jyòu °chǐ'jí (°shēng'chǐ, °'nǎule, °'tóuténg). / In a fit of anger he swore and swore. Tā 'yíjèn 'dànù 'màle yòu 'mà. / In a fit of energy he cleaned his desk inside and out. Tā 'hūrán yí'jèndz mài'jyèr bǎ tāde 'jwōdz tsúnglǐdàu'wàide dōu 'shōushr'gānjingle.

FIVE. wǔ; one fifth wǔfēnjryī; the fifth dìwǔ.

FIX. (Repair) syōuli, shōushr (also means put in order); (patch up) 'syōubǔ, bǔ; also resultative compounds of these plus hǎu, etc. / Can you fix this watch? Néng bǎ jèige 'byǎu °syōuli'hǎule ma (°shōushr'hǎule ma)? / Who can fix my car? Shéi néng géi wo °'shōushr (°'syōuli) chǐ'chē. or Shéi néng bá wǒde chǐ'chē °syōu(li) 'hǎu (°shōushr'hǎu). / We fix flats. Wǒmen °'syōubǔ (chǐchē) lwún tāi (°bǔ dài). / We're having a little trouble now, but it will be all fixed up soon. (of actual repairing) Wǒmen jèr syàn'dzài 'chūle dyàr 'máubing, yǐ'hwěr jyou °'shōushr'hǎule (°'syōuli-'hǎule, or (of any kind of trouble) °'hǎule).

(Set in order) usually shōushr. / I was just fixing up my room. Wǒ 'jēngdzai 'shōushr 'wūdz.

(Establish) dìng; (physically, make unmovable) dìngjù, dìngsž; (be unmovable, fixed) sž(de); (definite) gùding, yídìng. / You fix the date. 'Nǐ dìng ge 'rdz. / All these prices are fixed by the government. Jèisyē 'jyàchyan 'chywán shr 'jēngfu 'dìngde. / This part of the machine moves, but the rest is fixed. Jīchi jèi 'bùfen shr 'hwóde, byéde dōu shr °'sžde (°dìng'jùle de, °dìng'sžle de). / These aspects show a fixed relationship with the weather. 'Jèisyē 'chíngsyíng gēn 'tyānchi 'dōu yǒu °gù-'dìngde 'gwānsyi (°yí'dìngde 'gwānsyi). but / I'm trying to fix that impression in my mind. Wǒ 'jēngdzài yàu bǎ 'nèijyù 'hwà 'jìdzai 'syīnli. / He has fixed (stubborn) ideas. Tā syīnli yóu hěn 'gùjrde 'jyànjyé. or Tā 'yǒude dìfang sžsyīn'yǎr. or Tā 'gāngbìdž'yùng.

(Prepare, as food) dzwò. / I have to fix something to eat. Wó děi 'dzwò dyar dūngsyi chř. / I'll fix a drink for you. Wó géi nǐ dzwò °dyar 'hē de (°dyár 'jyòu hē).

Fix someone or something **up** (take care of) géi . . . plus a specific expression for the favor done. / I'll fix you up. 'Wǒ géi nǐ bàn. / I'll fix you up for the night. 'Wǒ géi nǐ jǎu dìfang gwò'yè. / Can you fix me up with a place to sleep? (arrange a place) Nǐ néng géi wo nèng ge dìfang 'shwèi ma? or (find a place) Nǐ néng géi wó jǎu ge dìfang 'shwèi ma? or Wó syáng jǎu ge dìfang 'shwèi, nǐ néng (géi wǒ) bàn ma? / I'll fix it up with the mayor. meaning talk it over to a satisfactory conclusion Wǒ géi nǐ gēn shř'jǎng chyù °shwō chyù (or meaning merely talk it over °'shwō yishwō kàn, or meaning explain it °'jyǎng yijyǎng kàn).

Fix a person. / I'll fix him. Wǒ 'gwángwan tā. or expressed as I'll get him into an embarrassing situation. 'Wǒ kéyi 'shōushr tā yísyàdz.

Fix a race, a match 'ānjūng 'tsàutsùng. / No wonder that horse won; the race was fixed. 'Gwàibudé 'nèipímǎ 'yíngle ne; páumá yǐ'chyán yǒurén 'ānjūng 'tsāudzùng.

Fix blame. / They don't know where to fix the blame. Tāmen 'bùjrdàu °shř 'shéide 'tswòr (°gwài 'shéi (hǎu)).

Fix the eyes *or* **attention.** /His eyes were fixed on the door. Tā 'lyáyǎn °'dèngje (°yǐ'jr̄ chǒuje, °'mùbujwǎn'jǐngde chǒuje) 'mén nar. /I want you to fix your attention on this card in my hand. Dàjyā jù'yi °kànje (°chǒuje, °chyáuje) wǒ 'shǒuli jèijāng 'pái.

Fix on, fix upon (decide on) dǐng, 'dìnggwēi. /Let's fix on that one. Dzámen jyou °'dǐngle (°'dìnggwēi) yàu 'nèige 'hǎule. /We finally fixed upon the 28th as the best day for the meeting. 'Jyēgwǒ °dǐng (°dìnggwēi) èrshr'bāhàu kāi'hwèi dzwèi 'hǎu. *but* /Her mind is fixed on getting that hat. is expressed as She certainly wants to get that hat. Tā °yǐ'sérde (°yǐ'dǐngde) syáng mǎi 'nèige 'màudz. *or* Tā 'fēi yàu mǎi 'nèige 'màudz bù'kě.

A fix (predicament). /He got himself into a terrible fix. Tā 'dz̀'jí °rěle 'hwò 'méifár 'lyàu le (°nùng de 'syàbulái 'tái le, °nùngde 'méi bànfa two'shēn le, °nùngde 'chǐhǔnán'syà le, *or* (dilemma) °gàude 'dzwǒyǒu wéi'nán le).

FLAG. chí, chídz, (informally) chyér; national flag 'gwóchí; school flag 'syāuchí; (etc. with other compounds). /The Chinese flag is known as "Blue sky, bright sun, all the ground red." Jūnggwo gwó'chí jyàudzwo 'chīngtyān báir̄ mǎndi'húng. /The American flag has three colors. 'Měigwode gwó'chíshang yǒu 'sānge shǎr. /Did you see that red flag? Nǐ chyáujyan °húng'chí (°húng'chyér, °húng chídz) le ma? /That's a white flag. Nèi shr̄ bái'chí. /They're putting up white flags. Tāmen chě bái'chí le. *or* (surrender flags) Tāmen gwàchí tóu'syángde'chídz le. /Raise the flag. Gwà'chí. *or* Shēng'chí. *or* Bǎ 'chídz 'chěshangchyu. *or* Bǎ 'chídz 'lāshangchyu. *or* (formal) 'Shēngchí. /Lower the flag. Bǎ 'chídz 'chěsyalai. *or* Bǎ 'chídz 'lāsyalai. *or* (formal) Jyàng'chí.

To flag (stop by a signal) jyàu . . . 'tíng(sya). /The stationmaster flagged the train. (with a flag) Jàn'jǎng yùng 'chídz jyàu 'hwǒchē 'tíngle. /Can you flag a passing truck? Nǐ néng jyàu yǐlyàng gwò'lùde 'dàkāchē 'tíngsya ma?

(Fade, lag). /Public interest flagged after a while. 'Gwòle syē shŕhou 'dàjyāde °syīn dōu 'lěngle (°'syìngchyu 'jyǎnle) yǐdyǎr.

FLAME. hwǒ, hwǒmyáur, 'hwǒyán. /The flames sprang up as high as the ceiling. °'Hwǒ (°Hwǒ'myáur, °'Hwǒyán) 'tswānde yǒu fáng'dǐng nèmma 'gāu. /The flames flared out in all directions. °'Hwǒ (°Hwǒ'myáur, °'Hwǒyán) 'sz̀syali lwàn 'pū. /Heat it in the flame. Dzài °'hwǒli (°hwǒ'myáurshang) 'kǎu. ('hwǒyán is not used here.)

Be in flames jáu, jáuchilai, jáuchi 'hwǒ lai. /By that time the whole house was in flames. Dàu 'nèi shŕhou jěng'gěrde 'fángdz dōu °'jáule (°'jáuchilaile). /The car turned over and burst into flames. Chē 'fānle, 'hūrán °'jáuchilaile (°jáuchi 'hwǒ laile).

Flame up 'jáuchilai, chǐ hwǒmyáur, wàngchilai. /He blew on the fire until it flamed up. Tā bá hwǒ 'chwēide °'wàngchilaile (°'jáuchilaile, °chǐle hěn 'dà de hwǒ'myáur).

See also **FIRE.**

FLASH. (A burst of light) shǎn; also expressed verbally as to flash (as of lightning) dáshǎn. /Did you see that flash of lightning just now? Nǐ 'kànjyan gāng 'dǎde nèige 'shǎn le ma? /A bright flash of lightning was followed by a loud crack of thunder. 'Dǎle yige hěn 'lyàngde shán yǐ'hòu, gēnje jyou 'dǎle yige 'dàléi.

(An instant) 'yísyàdz; (in the twinkling of an eye) yìján'yǎnde gūngfu. /It's all over in a flash. °'Yísyàdz (°Yìján'yǎnde gūngfu) jyou °'dōu gwòchyule (°wán le).

Flashlight shǒudyàn'dēng. /The battery in this flashlight is weak. Jèige shǒudyàn'dēng de dyàn'chŕ méi dyàn le.

555

News flash syāusyi. / An important news flash has just been received. 'Gāng jyēdàu yíge 'jùngyàude 'syāusyî.

To flash (shine a light) jàu. / Flash the light in this corner. 'Jàu yijàu jèige 'jyǎur.

(Emit, gleams). / Her diamonds flashed dazzlingly in the light. Tāde dzwànshř dzài 'gwāngli yǐ'shǎnyǐ'shǎnde (jēn hǎu 'kàn).

(To spread, of news). / In a few minutes the news had been flashed over the whole country. (spread by telegraph) Jǐfēn'jūngli 'nèishèr jyou °yùng dyàn'bàu 'chwánbyàn 'chywángwó le (or (spread by radio) °'gwǎngbwòde 'chywángwó 'dōu jřdaule).

(Pass like a flash). / An idea just flashed through my mind. Wǒ 'syīnli 'gāngtsái 'hūrán yí'dùng, syàngchū ge 'júyi lai.

FLAT. (Level) píng. / His house has a flat roof. Tāde fáng'dǐng shř 'píngde. / He has flat feet. Tāde jyáudǐ shř 'píngde. / Put the flat side against the wall. Bǎ 'píngde nèimyàr kàu 'chyáng fàng. / Is the country flat? Dì 'píng bupíng? or meaning Are there flat plains? Shř píng'ywán búshr?

(Thin and flat) byǎn, 'byǎnpíng. / What's in that flat package? Nèige 'byǎn(píng) de bāugwoli yǒu 'shémma?

(Deflated) byě(le). / The car has a flat tire. 'Chē yǒu ge lwún'tāi byěle. but / We fix flats. is expressed as We repair tires. Wǒmen 'syōubù lwún'tāi.

(Tasteless) 'chīngdàn, méiwèr, méiyǒu 'wèidau, bùjūng chř, 'píngdànwú'wèi. / The food lately has been pretty flat. 'Jìnlái fànshr hěn °'chīngdàn (°méi'wèr, °méiyou 'wèidau, °bùjūng 'chř, °'píngdànwú'wèi).

(Uninteresting) méiyìsz, 'píngdànwú'wèi. / Her conversation is flat. Tā shwōde 'hwà tīngjie °méi'yìsz (°'píngdànwú'wèi).

(Decisive) expressed with definitely 'jywédwèi. / He published a flat denial of the charges. Tā dēngbàu shwō 'gūngjí tā de jídyǎn tā 'jywédwèi 'bùchéng'rèn.

(Established) yídìngde. / Can you give me a flat price? Dōu swàn yí'kwàr shwō ge yí'dìngde jyàchyán.

(Low in pitch) dyàumér dǐ, búgòu dyàu'mér. / Her high notes are a little flat. Tā chàngde 'gāuyīn yǒu dyǎr búgòu dyàu'mér. / He has a flat voice. Tāde dyàumér 'dǐ.

Fall flat (lit.) shwāidǎu, shwāipāsya, shwāi ge dàmǎ'pā; (fig.) shřbài (fail) or a more specific expression. / He fell flat on his face. Tā shwāidǎule. or Tā shwāile ge dàmǎ'pā. or Tā shwāi'pāsyale. / My plan fell flat. Wode jìhwà 'shřbàile. / My prize joke fell flat. is expressed as no one laughed Wǒ 'dzwèi dòu'génde 'syàuhwàr °'méirén 'lǐhwēi (°méirén 'syàu).

A flat (one-floor apartment) yìtséng 'lóu. / I rented a flat. Wǒ dzūle yìtséng 'lóu.

Flatiron 'yùndǒu, 'làutye.

FLOOR. (Of a room or house) dì; (wooden only) dìbǎn. / Put it on the floor. Gēdzài 'dìshang. or Gēdzài dì'bǎnshang. / I just swept the floor. °'Dì (°Dì'bǎn) wǒ gāng 'sǎule yísyàr. / They're waxing their floor. Tāmen jèng gěi dì'bǎn dǎ'là ne. / The floor squeaks. Dì'bǎn 'gējrgējrde 'syǎng. / The floor of the cave is damp. Dùnglide 'dìshang fā'cháu.

(Story of a building) lóu. / What floor are you on? Nǐ dzài dì'jǐ'tséng lóushang?

or Nǐ dzài 'jǐlóu? *or* Nǐ dzài 'něitséng 'lóushang? /We live on the third floor. Wǒmen jùdzài 'sāntséng 'lóushang. *or* Wǒmen jù dì'sāntséng lóushang. *or* Wǒmen jù 'sānlóu. *or* Wǒmen jù 'sāntséng lóu.

Have the floor (speak; in a meeting) jyǎng, shwō hwà. /He still had the floor, and the chairman just yawned. Tā 'hái dzài nar °jyǎng ne (°shwō hwà ne), jǔ'syí jŕ dǎ 'hāchi.

To floor (stump) <u>a person</u> bǎ . . . 'nánjù. /The problem floors us. 'Nèi shèr kě 'jēn bá wǒmen 'nánjule.

(Knock down a person) bǎ . . . dǎ'pāsya, bǎ . . . dá'dǎu; (knock out) bǎ . . . dǎ(de) 'hwūngwochyu, bǎ . . . dǎ(de) 'yūngwochyu. /Do you think you can floor him with one blow? Nǐ jywéje nǐ néng 'yǐchywǎn bǎ tā °dǎ'pāsya (°dá'dǎule, °dǎ(de) 'hwūngwochyu, °dǎ(de) 'yūngwochyu) ma?

FLOUR. myànfěn; (white wheat flour) 'báimyàn; (when specifying the grain of which it is made) myàndz, myàr, fěndz. /Flour is three dollars a sack. °Myàn'fěn (°'Báimyàn) 'sānkwàichyán yí'dàr. /Sprinkle the fish with flour, and fry. Bǎ 'yú sāshang 'báimyàn dzài 'jyān. /Millet flour is too sticky. 'Syǎumǐmyàr tài 'nyán. /Rice flour is good for steamed dumplings. 'Dàmǐmyàr jēng 'bāudz hǎu. /It's first ground into flour. 'Syān mwòchéngle °'myàndz (°'myàr, °myàn'fěn, °'fěndz).

FLOWER. hwā, hwār. /The plum blossom is China's national flower. °'Méihwā (°'Méihwār) shǐ 'Jūnggwode 'gwóhwā. /He likes to raise flowers. Tā ài °jùng'hwār (°yǎng'hwār).

FLY (FLEW, FLOWN). (Of birds, planes, etc.) fēi. /The birds have flown south. Nyǎur dōu fēidau 'nánbyar chyule. /The young bird can't fly yet. Syǎu'nyǎur hái °búhwèi 'fēi ne (°fēibu'dùng ne). /This plane can fly 300 miles per hour. Jèige fēi'jǐ yìdyǎn jūng néng fēi 'sānbái'lǐ. /The higher you fly the harder you fall. 'Fēide ywè 'gāu, 'dyēde ywè 'jùng. /The bird flew into that tree. Nyǎur fēidau 'nèikē 'shùli chyùle.

(Ride in a plane) dzwò fēi'jǐ °chyù (°lái), fēi. /He flew down to Brazil. Tā °dzwò fēi jǐ dàu (°fēidau) Bā'syī chyùle. /I am going to fly to America tomorrow. Wo míngtyān fēi 'Měigwó.

(Pilot a plane) kāi fēijǐ, fēi. /He flew down to Brazil (as a pilot). Tā °kāi fēi'jǐ dàu (°fēidau) Bā'syī chyùle. /She's just learning to fly a plane. Tā gāng dzài sywéje kāi fēi'jǐ.

(Run fast) syàng fēi shrde 'pǎu, 'fēi shrde 'pǎu. /She flew down the street that way. Tā (syàng) 'fēi shrde wàng jyē 'nèitóur 'pǎu.

(Flutter) pyāu. /Her hair is flying around her face. Tāde 'tóufa dzài tā 'lyǎnshang °'pyāuláipyāuchyùde (°lwàn 'pyāu). /The flag was flying in the breeze. 'Chídz dzài 'fēngli °'pyāuje (°'pyāuyáng, °'pyāudàng).

Fly a <u>flag</u> (on a pole) gwà; (holding it) dǎ. /What flag are they flying? Tāmen °'gwàje (°'dǎje de shǐ) 'shémma chídz?

Fly a <u>kite</u> fàng. /Kite flying is a good sport for children. Syǎuhár fàng !fēngjeng yǒu 'yìchu.

Fly at (start a fight with). /They flew at each other. Tāmen 'dǎchilaile. /She flew at me as though I'd said something awful about her. 'Tā nèmma °'mà wǒ (°'gūngjǐ wǒ), 'hwó syàng wǒ shwōle tā shémma hwài'hwà shrde.

Fly into a temper fā 'píchi. /There's no need to fly into a temper. 'Yùngbujáu 'hūrán fāchi 'píchilai.

Fly off the handle. /He flies off the handle at every little thing that happens. Yĭ 'chū dyar shémma 'syáushèr tā jyòu °jywéje bùdé'lyău le (°'jíde bùdé'lyău, °'jíchilaile, °'jíde yàu'mǐng, °nău ge 'tyānfāndǐ'fù).

Let fly (words). /He let fly (with) a few choice remarks. Tā 'dàmàle jǐjyù. *or* Tā pwòkŏudà'mà.

On the fly (hurrying). /I was late and caught the train on the fly. Wŏ 'dàude 'wăn le dyar, 'jíjimángmángde 'gāng gănshang hwŏ'chē. /I caught the ball on the fly. Chyóur 'fēije de shŕhou wó gĕi 'jyējaule.

Fly (insect) tsāngying, yíngdz. /The flies around here are terrible. °'Jèikwàrde 'tsāngying (°'Jèi 'yíngdz) tàuyàn'jíle.

FOLLOW. (Be behind, be after) gēnje, dzài 'hòutou 'gēnje, gēnshang; of events in time X follows Y is expressed as Y yǐ'hòu (gēnje *or* jyēje) X. /This dog followed me all the way home. 'Jèige gŏu gēnje wŏ yǐ'jŕ dzŏudau 'jyā. /Don't look now, but I think there's someone following us. 'Byé hwéitou kàn; wŏ jywéje yŏurén °'gēnje dzámen ne (°dzài dzámen 'hòutou 'gēnje ne, °'gēnshang dzámen le). /The hot weather was followed by several days of rain. Tyānchì 'rèle yíjèn yǐ'hòu °gēnje (°jyēje) 'syàle jityān 'yǔ. *or* Tyānchi 'rēgwole, (jǐn) °'gēnje (°'jyēje) jyou 'syàle jityān 'yǔ. /Follow the leader. 'Gēnje 'lǐngsyòu (dzǒu). /Follow the guide. 'Gēnje dài'lùde dzǒu. /Follow him. 'Gēnje tā ('dzǒu). or meaning Get closer to and then follow. 'Gēnshang tā. /He's following in his father's footsteps. Tā gēnje tā 'fùchin de 'jyǎubŭr dzǒu.

(Imitate) sywé. /Follow him. Gēn tā 'sywé. /He's (deliberately) following in his father's footsteps. Tā 'sywé tā 'fùchin ne.

(Obey) 'fútsúng, tīng . . . de hwà. /Follow your leader. 'Fútsúng 'lǐngsyòu. *or* Tīng 'lǐngsyòude 'hwà.

(Go along a road, a river, etc.) shwùnje. /Follow this road until you come to the river. 'Shwùnje jèityáu 'lù yǐjŕ dàu 'hé ner.

(Go according to instructions) jàuje, ànje. /Just follow these instructions step by step and you can bind the book yourself. 'Jyòu °jàuje (°ànje) jèige shwōmíngshū 'yíbùyíbùde 'dzwò, 'dzjǐ jyòu kéyi bă shū jwāngdǐng'hăule. /Be sure to follow these instructions exactly. 'Chyānwàn 'wánchywán °jàuje (°ànje) jèr 'shwō de bàn, yǐ'dyár yě bunéng 'tswò.

(Understand) dŭng, tīngdŭng, tīngmíngbai, tīngchīngchu. /I can't quite follow your arguments. Nǐ 'byànlwùn de nei jidyàn wŏ °bùdŭng (°tīngbudŭng, °méitīngdŭng, °méitīngmíngbai). /Do you follow me? Wŏ shwō de nǐ °'dŭngle (°etc.) ma?

(Be the logical conclusion). /From what you just said this doesn't necessarily follow. Jàu nǐ 'gāng shwō de, 'bújyànde jyou yí'dìng dĕi °'dzèmmaje. *or* °'jèiyangr.

(Keep track of news or events such as ball games, etc.) jùyì, 'lyóushén. /I haven't been following the news much lately. 'Jìnlai wŏ 'méidà jù'yì syīn'wén. *or* 'Jìnlaide syāusyi wŏ 'méidà lyóu'shén. /I follow the baseball games every year. Wŏ mĕinyán dwèi 'bàngchyóu de 'syāusyi dōu hĕn jù'yì. or meaning I go to baseball games every year. Wó 'mĕinyán dou kàn 'bàngchyóu.

Follow suit 'gēnje . . . yě . . . . /You're supposed to follow suit and play a heart too. Nǐ yīnggāi 'gēnje 'yě chū húng'syīn tsái 'dwèi. /They left early and we followed suit. Tāmen dzŏude hén 'dzău, wŏmen gēnje 'yé dzŏule.

Follow out jàu(je) . . . bàn (or another verb meaning do). /We decided to follow out your suggestion. Wŏmen jywé'dìng 'wánchywán jàu 'nǐ shwō de chyù 'bàn.

Follow up chè'díde bàn, bàn dàudí, 'cháwèn 'chīngchu. / They try to follow up every case. 'Měijyàn shr̀ tāmen dōu syǎng yàu °chè'díde bàn (°bàndàu'dí, °'cháwèn-'chīngchule).

Following (after one already mentioned) dì'èr-M, syàyi-M, dísya yi-M. / This took place the following day. Dì'èrtyān chūde 'jèijyàn shr̀. / We shall talk about it in the following class. Jèige wǒmen °'syàyitáng (°dièrtáng) dzài tán ba.

Following *or* as follows (coming next) yǐsyà, 'dísyà, 'hòumyàn, rúsyà. / The following sentence is a quotation from Confucius' Analects. °Yǐ'syà (°'Dísyà, °'Hòumyàn) yíjyù hwà shr̀ tsúng 'Lwúnyǔli yǐnde. / My reasons are as follows. °Yǐ'syà (°'Dísyà) shr̀ wǒde jige 'lǐyóu.

FOOD. (A meal or cooked rice) fàn, tsài; (anything edible) chr̄de 'dūngsyi, 'chr̄de; (food prepared in quantity) hwǒshr, fànshr; (foodstuffs) lyángshr. / Is the food good there? Nàrde °'fàn (°'tsài, °'fànshr, °hwǒshr) 'hǎu ma? *or* Nàr 'chr̄de 'hǎu ma? / Is that food? Shr̀ 'chr̄de dūngsyi ma? *or* Shr̀ 'chr̄de ma? / He went to buy some food. Tā chyù mǎi 'tsài chyùle. / There was no food to be found. Jàubujáu 'chr̄de dūngsyi. / The people need food, not sympathy. Rénmén 'yàude shr̀ °'chr̄de (°'lyángshr), 'bùshr hǎu'tǐngde 'hwà. / They've had no food for three days. Tāmen 'sāntyan °méichr̄ fànle (°méiyǒu 'dūngsyi chr̄ le). / Food should be kept clean. 'Shŕwù yàu 'chīngjyé. / I like Chinese food. Wǒ hěn ài chr̄ 'Jūnggwo °fàn (°tsài).

(For animals or birds) shŕ. / I give them this kind of fish food. Wǒ yùng 'jèijǔng yúshŕ wèi yú.

Food for thought. / This news gives us food for thought. Jèige 'syāusyi dzámen děi °'džsyǐ syǎngsyang (°'dzwómedzwóme).

FOOLISH. shǎ, húdu, bùdǔngshr̀; (in actions or words) húnàu, syānàu; (in words only) húshwō, syāshwō, 'húshwōbā'dàude; (like a fool) 'shǎlishǎ'chǐde, syàng ge 'shǎdz shŕde; (be a fool) shr̀ ge- plus one of the following 'shǎdz, shǎ'gwā (vulgar); shǎ'dàn, hwún'dàn; (foolhardy) 'shásyǎudz; (muddleheaded) 'húduchúng. / I was foolish (or I was a fool) to believe what she said. Wǒ jēn °'shǎle (°'húdule), syìnle 'tāde hwà le! / Don't be foolish! Byé hú'nàu le! *or* Byé syā'nàu le! *or* Byé hú'shwō le! *or* Byé syā'shwō le! *or* Byé 'húshwōbá'dàude le! or meaning Don't be a fool! Byé shr̀ ge 'shǎdz. *or* Byé bùdǔng'shr̀! etc. / I said a very foolish thing. Wǒ shwōle jyù °'hěn shǎde hwà (°'hěn húdude hwà, °bùdǔng'shr̀ de hwà). / I did a foolish thing. Wǒ dzwòle jyàn °'shǎshèr (°'húdushèr).

FOOT. (Part of body) jyǎu. / You're stepping on my foot. Ní tsǎije wǒde 'jyǎu ne. My feet hurt. Wǒ jyǎu'téng. / Are your feet cold? Nǐde jyǎu 'lěng ma? / They carried him out feet first. Tāmen bǎ tā 'táichūchyule, jyǎu cháu'chyán. / He always has his feet on the ground. (only fig.) Tā lǎushr 'jyǎu tà shŕdǐ de dzwòshr̀. *or* Tā dzwòshr̀ de shŕhou, lǎushr 'jyǎu tà shŕdǐ.

(Bottom) in some cases jyǎu; otherwise 'syàtóur; the foot of the mountain 'shānjyǎu. / Put your coat at the foot of the bed. Bǎ nǐde 'yīshang fàng dzài chwáng-'jyǎur ner. *but* / He was sitting at the foot of the stairs. Tā dzwò dzài lóu'tǐde 'syàtóur.

(Twelve inches) chr̄. / The wall is a foot thick. Jèige 'chyáng yǒu yì'chr̄ hòu. / She's five feet two. Tā yǒu 'wúchr̄'èr. / There's a six-foot drop here. Jèr wǎsyàle lyòu'chr̄ chyù. *or* Tsúng jèr wàng syà shr̀ 'lyòuchr̄. / He's over six feet tall. Tā yǒu 'lyòuchr̄dwō gāu. / That building is about 200 feet high. Nèige 'fángdz yǒu 'èrbǎidwōchr̄ 'gāu.

On foot (walking) dzǒuje; (informal) bùnyǎr. / We came on foot. Wǒmen bù-'nyǎr láide. *or* Wǒmen dzǒuje láide.

FOR

Back on one's feet. /After that illness it took her a long time to get back on her feet again. is expressed as . . . a long time before she could start walking again. Tā yăngle háu'jyou tsái néng 'chĭlai dzŏu'dùng. /A good rest will put him back on his feet again. is expressed as After a good rest he will return to normal. Hău'hăur 'syōusyi yísyàr, tā jyou hwèi 'hwēifù ywán'jwàng le. /Did he ever get back on his feet (start up again) after his store failed? Tā 'pùdz 'dăule yĭhòu, you 'chĭláile ma? /He was badly in debt for a while but he's back on his feet again now. Tā 'gāigwo bùshău 'chyán, búgwo syàndzài dōu 'hwánchĭngle.

Put one's foot down gwángwan. /This has gone far enough; I'm going to put my foot down. 'Yĭjĭng búsyàng 'yàngdz le; wŏ fēi 'gwán gwan bù'kĕ le.

Put one's foot in it shř dž'jăude. /I really put my foot in it that time. Nèitsž wŏ jēn shř dž'jăude.

Stand on one's own feet. /He's old enough to stand on his own feet now. Tā yĭjĭng 'dàle, yĭnggāi néng dž'lĭ le.

Foot the bill fùjàng, gĕichyán. /Who's going to foot the bill? Shéi fù'jàng? or Shéi gĕi'chyán?

FOR. (On behalf of) gĕi; (instead of, in place of) tì. /Can't you get someone to do this for you? 'Jèige ní 'jàu ge rén °géi ni (°tì ni) 'dzwò, 'syíng busyíng? /Who does he work for now? Tā gĕi 'shéi dzwò 'shř ne? /He's a salesman for our company. Tā géi wŏmen gūng'sž dāng shòuhwŏ'ywán. /I couldn't be there, so he did my work for me. Wŏ méinéng 'dàu, swóyi tā 'tì wŏ dzwòle.

(Because of) 'yīnwei followed by a verb; 'wèile or sometimes yĭ followed by a verb or noun. /I kept quiet for fear of trouble. Wŏ yīnwei pà 'máfan swóyi méi'shwō shémma. /She did it for her mother's sake. Tā 'wèile tā 'mŭchin tsái 'nèmmaje de. or Tā 'nèmmaje shř wèile tā 'mŭchin de ywángu. /He did a stretch for burglary. Tā °wèile (°'yīnwei) tōu dūngsyi syàgwo 'yù. /This restaurant is noted for its good food. Jèige 'gwăndz yĭ 'tsài 'hău chū'míng.

(Adapted to) wèi, gĕi. /Is this textbook for children or adults? 'Jèijŭng 'jyàu-kèshū shř °wèi (°géi) syáu'hár (yùng)de háishr °wèi (°gĕi) 'dàrén (yùng)de? /That movie is not for children. 'Nèige dyàn'yĭng 'búshr °wèi (°gĕi) syáu'hár kànde.

(In honor of) wèi. /We're giving a dinner for him. Wŏmen yàu wèi 'tā chĭng hwéi 'kè.

(With reference to) yú, dwèi. /This is good for you. Jèi °'yú nĭ (°dwèi nĭ) yŏu 'yìchù. /As for me, I don't care what you do. °Jřyú 'wŏ a (°Dwèi wŏ shwō), ní 'dzĕmmaje yĕ méiyou 'wŏde shř. or 'Wŏ a, wŏ bùgwán ní 'dzĕmma 'bàn.

(Throughout; of time or space) expressed only in the designation of time or distance. /He stayed for an hour. Tā 'dàile yĭdyăn'jŭng. /That'll be enough for the time being. Nèige 'jànshř 'gòule. or Nèige gòu 'jànshř yùngde le. /That'll be enough for three days. Nèige gòu 'sāntyānde le. /Go straight ahead for ten miles. Wàngchyán yĭ'jř dzŏu 'shřlĭ. /The road goes straight for about a mile, and then curves. Lù chàbudwō yŏu 'yĭlĭ'dĭ shř 'bĭjřde, rán'hòu jyòu gwăi'wārle.

(In favor of) 'dzànchéng. /Are you for or against it? 'Jèige nĭ shř 'dzànchéng háishr 'făndwèi?

For good. /He's gone for good. (from a place) Tā 'bùhwéilái le. (from a job) Tā 'líkāi jèr le.

For now syàndzài. /That's all for now. Syàndzài 'méiyou 'byéde le.

For once jèitsž. /For once I don't agree with you. 'Jèitsž wŏ gēn nĭde 'yĭjyan bùyí'yàng.

For one thing jyòu ná 'jèige lái shwō. / For one thing, he doesn't know the language of the place. Jyòu ná 'jèige lái shwō ba, tā 'bùdǔng 'nèige dìfangde 'hwà.

For the first time tóuyitsž. / For the first time, he was stumped. Tā nèi shŕ °'tóuyihwéi (°'tóuyitsž) jyàurén gěi 'wènjule.

In a large variety of other expressions, **for** occurs in fixed combinations with other words. A few of these are listed below. For others see the words with which **for** is combined.

Be hard for nán. / Is it hard for you to do this? 'Nǐ dzwò jèige jywéje 'nán ma?

Be in for trouble °jwún déi (°yí'dǐng yàu) yǒu 'máfan. / You're in for some trouble. Ní °'jwún děi (°yí'dǐng yàu) yǒu 'máfan. *or* Jèi 'máfan nǐ swàn °'táubu'kāi le (°'dwǒbu'kāi le).

Be time for. / It's time for us to go home. Dzámen gāi hwéi 'jyā le. *or* Dàule dzámen gāi hwéi 'jyā de shŕhou le.

Do something **for** so much. / I wouldn't do it for any amount of money. Gěi 'dwōshǎu chyán wǒ yě bú'gàn.

Do something **for a living** dzwò . . . °wéishēng (°shēngyì). / What does he do for a living? Tā °dzwò (°yǐ) 'shémma wéi'shēng? *or* Tā dzwò 'shémma 'shēngyì?

Know something **for a fact** jŕdau shŕ 'jēnde. / Do you know it for a fact? Jèige nǐ 'jŕdau shŕ 'jēnde ma?

Pay so much **for** something hwā. / How much did you pay for this? Jèige nǐ 'hwāle dwō shau 'chyán? / I paid three dollars for this. Wó mǎi 'jèige hwāle sankwài 'chyán.

There is so much **for each** (*or* every) . . . . (měi) NU-M . . . °yǒu (°déi gwǎn). / There are two pairs of shoes for each person. (available) 'Měirén kéyǐ yóu 'lyǎng-shwāng syé. *or* (issued) 'Měirén líng 'lyǎngshwāng syé. / There are only four rifles for every five soldiers. Méi'wǔge bīng tsái yǒu 'sžgǎn chyāng. / There are fifty prisoners for each M.P. Měi'yíge 'syànbīng déi gwǎn 'wǔshrge fú'lwǒ.

Use something **for** yùng. / What do you use for firewood? Nǐ yùng 'shémma shāu'hwǒ. *or* Nǐ shāude shŕ 'néijǔng 'pǐchái.

FORBID (FORBADE, FORBIDDEN). 'bùjwǔn, 'bùsyǔ, 'jìnjř. / Smoking is forbidden in the barracks. 'Yíng nèi °'bùjwǔn (°'bùsyǔ, °'jìnjř) syǐ'yān. / They forbade him to leave his house. Tāmen °'bùjwun (°'bùsyǔ, °'jìnjř) tā tsúng tā jyā 'chūchyu. / I forbid you to enter that door again. °'Bùjwǔn (°'Bùsyǔ, °'Jìnjř) nǐ 'dzài jin nèige 'mér(le).

Other expressions in English. / Heaven forbid! (of a possibility) 'Nà kě bù-'syíng! *or* 'Nà kě bù'hǎu! *or* 'Nà kě bùdé'lyǎu! *or* (of something past) Dzěmma 'nèmje a?

FORCE. (Strength) lìlyang, lì, jyèr. / I had to use a good deal of force to crack that walnut. Wǒ °yùngle 'hǎu dàde 'lìlyang (°shŕle 'hǎu dàde 'jyèr) tsái bǎ nèige 'hétau 'jǐkai. / Force is always applied at one end of a lever. Gàng'gǎr dzǔngshr dzài 'yìtóurshang °yùng'lì (°shŕ'jyèr). / The mill is turned by the force of the wind. 'Jèige mwò shŕ °yùng (°jyèje) °'fēnglì (°'fēngde lìlyang) 'jwànde. or expressed as This is a windmill. Jèi shŕ 'fēng mwò. / Many trees were torn up by the force of the storm. Fēngde 'lìlyang hěn 'dà, bǎ 'hǎusyē shù gwā'dǎule.

(Physical compulsion, often with violence) is expressed verbally as **use force** dùngyìngde, dùngwǔ, dùngshǒu; **by force** yìng; also many verbs with meanings such as push, pull, strike, etc. / The police had to use force to make him come. 'Jǐngchá děi gēn tā dùng 'yǐngde, tā tsái 'láide. *or* 'Jǐngchá dùngle 'shǒu tsái bǎ tā 'dàilaide. / We took the drunk home by force. Neige dzwèi'gwéi wǒmen °'twēije (°'jwàije, °'jyōuje) tsái bǎ tā nénghwéi'jyā chyude. *or* Nèige dzwèi'gwéi sȟr wǒmen 'yǐng gěi 'nénghwéi'jyā chyude. / I'm afraid we'll have to use force. 'Kǔngpà dzámen °búdùng'yǐngde bù'syíng (°děi dùngwǔ). *or* (against the person addressed) 'Nèmmaje wǒmen 'jr̄ hǎu lái 'yǐngde le.

(Military action) 'wǔlǐ, bīng. / Some say that diplomacy must be backed by force. Yǒurén shwō 'wànjyāu déi yǒu °'wǔlǐ (°'bīng) dzwò hòu'dwùn.

(Strength of an argument) lǐlyang, lǐ. / I admit the force of your argument. Wǒ 'chéngrèn 'nǐ shwō de hwà hén yǒu °'lǐlyang (°'lǐ).

(Legal validity) syàu, syàuli (each is used in special combinations). / His decrees have the force of law. Tāde 'mìnglìng gēn 'fǎlyù yǒu 'túngděngde 'syàuli. / When did that come into force? Nèige shr̄ tsúng 'shémma shŕhou chǐ yǒu 'syàude? / My insurance is still in force. Wǒde báusyǎn hái yǒu 'syàu.

Force of habit. / I go there from force of habit. Wǒ dàu 'nàr chyù shr'yīnwei chyù'gwànle.

Police force 'jǐngchá. / How large is the police force? Yǒu 'dwōshau jǐngchá?

In force (in large numbers). / The students turned out in force. 'Sywésheng °'láide hěn 'dwō (°'chyùde hěn 'dwō, °'dàdwèichū'mǎ).

Armed forces (especially the army) 'jyūndwèi; (military personnel) 'jyūnrén; (land, sea, and air forces) 'lù'hǎi'kūngjyūn. / Civilians must back up the armed forces in a war. Dǎ'jàng de shŕhou rén'mín děi 'jyélǐ bāngje °jyūn'dwèi (°'jyūnrén). / Which branch of the armed forces were you in? Tsúng'chyán nǐ dzài 'nǎr fú'yì, 'lùjyūn, hǎijyūn, háishr 'kūngjyūn?

To force (compel) bī, chyángpwò; (by urging) myánchyǎng; **be forced** *also* bù-'dé bu-. / I was forced (by them) to sign the check. (Tāmen) 'Bīde wǒ bù'dé búdzài jr̄'pyàushang chyān 'dż. *or* Nèi shr̄ (tāmen) 'bīje wǒ dzài jr̄'pyàushang chyānde 'dż. *or* Tāmen chyángpwo wǒ 'dzài jr̄pyàushang chyānde 'dż. / We were forced to change our tactics. Wǒmen bù'dé bù'gǎibyàn °jàn'shù (°fāng'jēn). / We finally forced him to admit that he did it. Dzwèi'hòu wǒmen bǎ tā 'bī de 'chéngrènle 'shr̄ tā gàn de. *or* Wǒmen chyáng'pwò tā chéngrèn shr̄ ta 'gànde. / They forced a confession out of him. Tāmen 'bīje tā 'jāu de ('kǒugùng). / Don't force yourself to eat it if you don't want to. Chr̄bú'syà byé °'myánchyǎng (*or* (see second paragraph above) °'yǐng chr̄). / Don't force him to eat. Byé myánchyǎng tā chr̄. / He forced himself to swallow the drug. Tā bǎ 'yàu °'myánchyǎng (°'yǐng) 'chr̄syachyule. / His laugh sounded somewhat forced. Tā syàude 'tīngje yǒu dyár 'myánchyǎng.

(Apply physical strength) yùnglǐ, yùngjyèr, shr̄jyèr. / Don't force it because you might break it. Byé °yùng'lǐ (°yùng'jyèr, °shr̄'jyèr) yīnwei ni kéméng bǎ tā nùng'hwàile.

(Break open; with a heavy object) 'dzákāi; (with an ax) 'pīkāi; (by swinging a heavy object) 'jwàngkāi; *etc.; see* BREAK. / The door has been forced. 'Mén jyàu rén gěi °'dzákāile (°'pīkāile, °'jwàngkāile). / The lock has been forced (broken). 'Swǒ jyàu rén gěi °'dzá'hwàile (°nyǒu'hwàile).

Force one's way is expressed with such verbs as jǐ press; chwǎng crush; dǎ fight plus second elements, such as jìn in *or* gwò through. / We may have to force our way in. Dzámen yésyù děi °(yǐng) 'jǐjìnchyu (°'dǎjìnchyu, °'chwǎngjìnchyu). / We forced our way through the crowd. Wǒmen tsúng nèichyún 'rén li °(yǐng) 'jǐgwochyude (°'chwǎnggwochyude).

Forced landing. / The plane made a forced landing. Fēi'jī bèi 'pwò jyàng'lwò.

FOREIGN. (Of foreign origin) wàigwo(de); in some combinations yáng; in identifying one of several foreign countries, gwó alone is used; foreign countries 'gwójyā. / He studied at a foreign university. Tā dzài 'wàigwo shàngde 'dàsywé. or Tā 'dàsywé shr̀ dzài 'wàigwo 'nyànde. / Do you speak any foreign languages? Nǐ hwèi shwō °'wàigwo hwà (°yánghwà) ma? or Nǐ 'dōu hwèi shwō 'nájǐ gwóde hwà? / These are all foreign goods. Jèi 'dōushr̀ °'wàigwo hwò (°'yánghwò). / That's a foreign custom. Nèi shr̀ 'wàigwo °gwēijyu (°fēngsu). / Which foreign country do you mean? Nǐ shr̀ jr̀je 'nèigwó shwōde? / Not all foreign countries are represented in the conference. 'Jèitsz̀ 'hwèiyì búshr̀ 'swóyǒude gwójyā 'dōu yǒu dài'byǎu de. / He has a thick foreign accent. Tā 'wàigwo kǒuyin hěn 'jùng. or Tā shwōhwà yǒu wàigwó kǒuyin. / He likes to travel in foreign lands. Tā syǐhwàn dàu 'wàigwo chyu lyǔ'syíng. / He acquired many foreign manners. Tā sywéle bù'shǎude °'wàigwo 'gwēijyu (°'wàigworén-de 'jyúdung). / His manners look quite foreign to me. Wǒ kàn tāde 'jyújr̀'dùngdzwò °hěn (yǒu) 'wàigwo chyèr (°'wàigwojyèr hěn 'dà (or 'dzú), °'wàigwo pàitóur hěn 'dà (or 'dzú), °hěn 'yángpài, °'yángchyèr 'shr̀dzú). / He is foreign born. Tā shr̀ dzài 'wàigwo shēngde 'rén.

(With foreign reference) 'gwówài; in some combinations, especially official titles, wài; foreign trade 'gwówài màu'yì; foreign trade commission 'gwówài màuyì-'jyù; foreign propaganda (to, not from foreign countries) 'gwówài 'sywānchwán, but (from foreign countries) 'wàigwo(de) 'sywānchwán; Ministry of Foreign Affairs Wàijyāubù; foreign policy 'wàijyāu 'jèngtsè; in foreign service dzwò 'wàijyāu'gwān; foreign affairs 'wàijyāu; foreign exchange wàihwèi; foreign resident wàichyáu; foreign residence (dzai) wàigwode dìjr̀.

(Strange). / His manners are foreign to me. Wǒ dwèi tāde 'jyújr̀'dùngdzwò hěn kàn bu'gwàn. or Wǒ kàn tāde jyújr̀dùngdwò °hěn syàng 'wàiláide rén (°hěn syàng 'wàishēngrén, °hěn chí'gwài, °hěn tè'byé).

(Unknown, unclear). / The whole procedure is foreign to me. Jěng'gèrde 'bànfa wǒ dōu °bùjr̀'dàu (°bù'chǐngchu, °bù'míngbai, °'mwōbujáu 'mér).

(Different from). / His suggestion is completely foreign to what we had in mind. 'Tā shwō de gēn 'wǒmen syǎngde 'wánchywán °bùyí'yàng (°shr̀ 'lyǎngjyàn 'shèr, °búshr̀ 'yíjyàn 'shèr).

FOREIGNER. 'wàigwo rén.

FORGET (FORGOT, FORGOTTEN). wàng, wàngji; (not be able to remember) syǎngbuchǐ-lai, bújǐde. / I forgot (to bring) it. Wǒ 'wàngle. or Wǒ 'wàngjile. or Wǒ 'wàngji 'dàilaile. / It's raining, and we forgot to close the windows. Syà'yǔ le; wǒmen 'wàng-(ji)le bǎ 'chwānghu 'gwānshangle. / I'll never forget what you just did for me. Nǐ 'tsái géi wǒ 'bànde jèijyàn 'shèr wó 'yǔngywǎn °'wàngbu'lyǎu (°'búhwèi 'wàngde, °'bùnéng 'wàngde). / We forgot that you were coming. Wǒmen bǎ nǐ 'láide jèijyàn shèr °gèi 'wàng(ji)le (°chywán wàng le). / She's forgotten all her two years of Chinese. Tā bǎ 'lyǎngnyánde 'Jūngwén 'dōu °wàngle (°wàngjile, °wàng'jǐngle, °wàngde 'gānganjìng'jǐngde le). / I've forgotten his name. Wǒ °'wàngle (°'wàngjile, °bú'jǐde, °'syǎngbuchǐlai) tā 'jyàu shémma le. or Wó bǎ tāde 'míngdz gěi 'wàngle. / Don't forget! Byé 'wàng le! but / Oh, forget it! 'Búswàn shémma. or Swàn le. or 'Méishémma; swànle ba. or 'Béng tí le. or 'Syǎushr̀ yìjwàng, 'swànle ba.

FORK. (Eating utensil) chādz; sometimes chār; in compounds chā; tuning fork 'yīnchā. / He's learning to eat with a knife and fork. Tā jèng 'sywéje yùng 'dāudz 'chādz chr̀'fàn.

(Fork-shaped thing) chàdz, chàr; in combination chà; fork of a tree shùchàdz;

fork in the road 'chàdàu. /He was sitting in a fork of the tree. Tā dzài shù'chàr nar dzwòje. /Go left when you get to the fork in the road. Dàule yǒu 'chàdàu nàr, dzǒu 'dzwòbyar nèityáu 'lù. /Did you see that forked lightning? Nèi shǎn fēn'chàr nǐ 'kànjyan le ma?

FORM. (Make, organize) chéng <u>as the second element in a resultative compound; the first element indicates the type of action used in forming; also</u> (of establishing a group for some purpose) 'chénglì. /They formed a long line to get tickets. Tāmen 'jànchéng yì'pái háu mǎi 'pyàu. /Can you form two triangles with five matches? Nǐ néng ná 'wugēn yánghwǒr 'bǎichéng 'lyǎngge sān'jyǎur ma? /They formed a new political party. Tāmen 'dzǔjr(chéng)le yíge 'syīn jèng'dǎng. /They're going to form a new cabinet. Tāmen yàu °'dzǔjr(chéng) (°'chénglì) yíge 'syīn nèi'gé. /A theory has been formed. Chénglìle yige ywánlǐ.

(Develop, of an idea) syǎngchulai; (draft) 'nǐchū, níding, níhǎu; (decide on) dìng. /A plan was slowly forming in his mind. Tā dzài syīnli màn'mānde syǎngchū yíge 'jìtsè lai. /I haven't formed an opinion on the subject yet. 'Nèijyàn shr wǒ hái méi 'syǎngchu ge 'yìjyàn lái ne. /They formed a plan but didn't dare to let people know about it. Tāmen °'syǎngchūlai (°'nǐchūle, °ní'dìngle, °ní'hǎule, °'dìngle) ge 'bànfa, kěshr 'bùgǎn jyàurén 'jrdau.

A form (shape, appearance, model) yàngdz, yàngshr, yàngr; (an established format) 'géshr. /His arguments were the same, only he presented them in a different form. Tāde 'yìsz shr yí'yàngde; búgwò tā 'hwànle ge °'yàngdz (°'yàngshr, °'yàngr) lái °'shwō jyòushr le (or if the arguments were written rather than spoken) °'syě jyòushr le). /Give me a form to follow. Géi wǒ ge 'yàngdz °hǎu 'jàuje syě (°'bǐje syě). /This document is not written according to the proper form. Jèijyàn 'gūngwén búshr °'ànje (°'jàuje) 'géshr syěde. /Is this a different character or just another form of the same character? Jèi shr 'lìng yíge dzèr, háishr ywán'láide nèige dzèr °hwànle (°gǎile) yíge °'yàngdz (°'yàngshr, °'yàngr) syě? but /This article is not yet in its final form. 'Jèipyān 'wénjāng °hái méidìng'gǎur ne (°'gǎudz hái méidá-'hǎu ne, °hái shr tsáu'gǎur ne).

(Way of doing something) <u>verb plus fǎ</u> or fǎr. /This word has two written forms; the meaning and pronunciation are the same, only there are two ways of writing it. Jèige dz yǒu 'lyǎngge 'syéfǎ; 'yìsz gēn 'nyànfǎ dōu yí'yàng; jr yǒu 'syéfǎ bù-'túng.

(Physical form) 'dzshr, yàngdz, 'shēndwàn. /I play a reasonably good game of tennis, but my form is terrible. Wó dǎde 'wǎngchyóu hái 'búswàn 'hwài; búgwo °dzshr (°'yàngdz, °'shēndwàn hěn nán kàn).

(Style, written) 'tǐtsái, 'géshr; <u>the phrase in the form of is also often translated by verbal expressions, for which see the first paragraph above.</u> /Put your suggestions in the form of an official letter. Bǎ nǐde 'yìjyàn °yùng gūng'hánde 'tǐtsái syěchulai (°'syěchéng yìfēng gūng'hán). /He printed his findings in the form of a dictionary. Tā bǎ tā 'yánjyōude 'jyégwǒ °yùng tsź'dyǎnde 'tǐtsái 'yìnde (°'yìnchéng yìběn syàng tsź'dyǎn shrde nèmma yìběn 'shū). /Copy it down according to that form. Ânje nèige géshr 'chāusyàlai. but /Have this bound in book form. Bǎ jèige 'jwǎngdìng chéng 'shū. /All questions must be submitted in written form. 'Wèntí dōu déi 'syěchulai dzài 'jyāujìnchyu.

(Ceremony) 'yíshr; (outward ceremony without appreciation of meaning) wàibyǎu, wàiyàngr, myàndz; (regulations) 'syíngshr; (custom) gwēijyu; (etiquette) lǐ, lyěr. /The prayer meetings here are conducted only as a matter of form. 'Jèrde 'chídǎu 'hwèi búgwò shr yìjǔng 'yíshr. /They attended the prayer meetings only as a matter of form. Tāmen dàu 'chídǎu'hwèi chyu 'búgwò shr wèile °wài'byǎu (°wài'yàngr, °'myàndz) jyòushr le. /Elections in this town are conducted only as a matter of form.

'Jèige dìfang de sywán'jyǔ búgwo shr̀ °wèile 'syíngshr̀ (°jàu 'gwēijyu) 'bùnéng bú-'bàn jyòushr̀ le. / As a matter of form you have to fill out these blanks. Jèi °búgwo shr̀ 'gwēijyu (°shr̀ wèile 'syíngshr̀shangde wèn'tí); ní déi bǎ jèisyē byǎugé dōu 'tyánle. / You have to bow to elders as a matter of form. Ní déi gěi 'jǎngbèr syíng-'lǐ, nèi 'jyòushr̀ nèmmage 'lyěr. / It's considered bad form if you leave her party early. Tā chǐng'kè, yàushr̀ nǐ 'dzáu dzǒu, byérén jywéje nǐ bùdǔng 'lǐmàu.

(A blank) 'byǎugé. / Did you fill out all the forms? 'Byǎugé dōu tyán 'hǎu le ma?

(A mold) múdz; (large wooden framework, as for cement) jyàdz.

Form letter 'yìnchulaide syìn.

Form of government 'jèngtǐ. / Do you think this is the best form of government? 'Nǐ jywéje jèi shr̀ 'dzwèi hǎude 'jèngtǐ ma?

Be in good form hěn gāu'syìng. / He was in good form and kept us amused all evening. Tā hěn gāu'syìng, yì 'wǎnshang jyàu wǒmen jywéje 'gwài yǒu'yìsz de.

FORMER. (Earlier) expressed as **formerly** yǐchyán (before the verb); (of a person, ex-president, etc.) 'chyánrèn; **in former times** 'wǎngr̀, 'wǎngnyán, 'chyánsyē shŕhou, tsúngchyán, 'lǎunyánjyān, yǐchyán. / He is a former student of mine. Tā yǐ'chyán shr̀ wǒde 'sywésheng. *or* Wǒ yǐ'chyán 'jyāugwo tā. / The former presidents of this university had all been lawyers. °'Jèige dàsywe yǐ'chyán de syàu'jǎng (°'Jèige dàsywéde 'chyánrèn syàu'jǎng) 'dōu dānggwo 'lyùshr̀. / He is a former president of this university. Tā shr̀ jèige 'dàsywéde chyánrèn syàu'jǎng.

(First). / Of your two suggestions I think I prefer the former. Nǐ tíchu de 'lyǎngge bànfa wǒ rènwéi °'tóuyíge 'hǎu (°nǐ 'syān shwō de nèige 'hǎu).

See also **FIRST**.

FORMERLY. yǐchyán, tsúngchyán. / Formerly he was president of our university. °Yǐchyán (°Tsúngchyán) tā dānggwo 'běnsyàude syàu'jǎng. / Formerly it was he that gave the orders. °Yǐchyán (°Tsúngchyán) shr̀ 'tā fā mìnglìng de.

FORT. (Fortification with mounted guns) pàutái, 'bīngyíng, 'yíngpán, 'jyūnshr̀ jīdì. / The old fort is at the top of the hill. Jyòu °pàu'tái (°'bīngyíng, °'yíngpán, °'jyūnshr̀ jīdì) dzài shān'dǐngshang.

FORTH. (After verbs). *See* **OUT**.

And so forth (etc.) déngděngde (plus dūngsyi of articles, shr̀ of affairs, dìfang of places, etc., or with nothing added, all of which may be followed by chywán and a verb). / I need a whole new outfit: shoes, ties, hat, suit, and so forth. Wǒ děi 'dálǐdàu'wàide 'chywán hwàn le, °shémma 'syé a, lǐng'dài a, 'màudz a, 'yīshang a, déng'děngde 'chywán děi 'hwàn (°'syé, lǐng'dài, 'màudz, 'yīshang, déng'děngde (dūngsyi) 'chywán děi 'hwàn). / They went sight-seeing and saw the museum, the library, the park, and so forth. Tāmen chyù 'gwàng chyu le, °kànle 'bwówù'gwǎn, 'túshū'gwǎn, gūng'ywán, déng'děngde 'dìfang (°shémma 'bwówù'gwǎn a, 'tushū'gwǎn a, gūng'ywán a, déng'děngde 'dìfang 'chywán kànle).

Back and forth (coming and going, coming and returning) láihwéide, 'láilaihwéi-'hwéide; (first one way, then the other, with a verb expressing the action) . . . lái . . . 'chyù(de); (especially of rhythmic actions) yì'láiyì'wǎngde. / He kept walking back and forth. Tā yì'jŕ nèmma °lái'hwéide 'dzǒu (°'láilaihwei'hwéide 'dzǒu, °'dzǒulái-dzǒu'chyùde). / He made several trips back and forth between his house and his office before he found his money. Tā tsúng tā 'jyāli dàu tā dzwò'shr̀de nàr 'lái'hwéide jǎule háujǐ 'tàng tsái bǎ chyán 'jǎujáude. / They sent the letter back and forth, but he never got it. 'Nèifēng 'syīn 'jwǎnláijwǎn'chyù yě 'méijwǎndàu tā 'shǒuli. / They hit the ball back and forth for a long while. Tāmen bǎ 'chyóur ('ní) 'dǎgwolái('wó) dǎgwo'chyùde dǎle bàn'tyān. *or* Tāmen bǎ 'chyóur °'dǎgwolái 'jyēhwéi'chyù de (°yǐ'láiyǐ'wǎngde) dǎle bàn'tyān. / They insulted each other back and forth for hours. (with something of a humorous turn) Tāmen 'yǐláiyǐ'wǎngde 'dwèimàle bàntyān. *or* Tāmen hùsyāng màle bàntyān.

FORTY. 'sz̀shŕ; one-fortieth 'sz̀shrfēnjr'yī; the fortieth dǐ'sz̀shŕ.

FORWARD. (To the front) dàu °'chyánbyan (°chyántou), syàng chyán, wàng chyán. / Come forward. Dàu 'chyánbyan lái. *or* Syàng chyán lái. *or* Wàng 'chyán °lái (°'lái). / You go forward and take a look. Nǐ dàu 'chyántou chyù kànkan. / Don't take a step forward. Byé wàng chyán dzǒu yíbù. / Forward, march! Kāi'bù 'dzǒu! *or* Chǐbù dzǒu!

Backward(s) and forward(s). *See* back and forth under FORTH.

Bring forward (fig., suggest) tíchulai. / Finally he brought forward a new suggestion. Mwò'lyǎur tā 'tíchule ge 'syīnbànfa lai.

Come forward 'chūlai. / No one came forward to confess. 'Shéi yě bù'chūlai 'chéngrèn.

Look forward to (await) děng, děngje; (hope that) pànje. / I'll look forward to your letters. Wǒ 'déng nǐ lái 'syìn. / I'm looking forward to that day. Wǒ pànje °'nèityān kwài dàu (°'yǒu nèmma yìtyān). / I am looking forward to meeting him. Wǒmen děngje 'jyàn tā le.

To forward 'jwǎn. / Would you please forward this letter? Chǐng nǐ 'jwǎnyijwǎn jèifēng syìn. / Please forward my mail to this new address. Chǐng bǎ wǒde 'syìnjyàn 'jwǎndàu jèige 'syīn dìjǐr chyu。

A forward (player in certain games) chyánfēn; left forward dzwǒfēng; right forward yòufēng.

FOUND. (Establish) lì, jyànlì; (especially of a country) kāi. / He founded a new dynasty. Tā lìle ge 'syīncháudài. / He was one of those who founded the nation. Tā shr̀ yíge 'kāigwó ywánsyún.

Be founded jyànlide, lìde, shède, 'chwǎngbànde, 'shèlìde; (opened) 'kāibànde, kāide. / That republic was founded three years ago. Nèige gùnghégwó °shr̀ sānnyán yǐ'chyán 'jyànlì de (°'kāigwó 'sānnyánle). / Our company was founded in the first year of the (Chinese) republic. 'Běnhàu shr̀ 'míngwó 'ywánnyán °shède (°'chwǎngbànde, °kāide, °kāibànde). / That college was founded in 1908. Nèige 'dàsywé shr̀ 'yǐjyǒulíng'bā nyán °'chwǎngbànde (°'shèlìde, °'kāibànde).

See also FIND.

FOUR. sz̀; one fourth 'sz̀fēnjr'yī; the fourth dìsz̀.

FOURTEEN. shŕsz̀; one-fourteenth shŕ'sz̀fēnjr'yī; the fourteenth dèshŕsz̀.

FREE. (Not enslaved, unrestricted) dz̀yóu. / We are free people. Wǒmen shr̀ dz̀'yóu de rén. / This is a free country. meaning not a dependency Jèi shr̀ 'jèngjr̀ dz̀'yóude 'gwójyā. or meaning The people have freedom Jèi shr̀ jyǎng 'mínchywán de 'gwójyā. *or* Jèi shr̀ yíge mín'jǔ (de) gwójyā.

(Untied) bùkwǔn(je), 'swéibyàn dùng. / This robe will keep the baby warm and also leave his arms free. 'Jèijyàn yīshang syǎuhár 'chwǎnje nwǎnhwo, 'érchyě gēbe kéyǐ °'swéibyàn dùng (°bù'kwǔnje).

(Having leisure) yǒu gūngfu; (with nothing to do) syándzai, syánje; (finished) ... wánle; (having no business) 'méi(you) shèr; (not busy) 'bùmáng. /When will he be free? Tā 'shémma shŕhou °yǒu 'gūngfu (°'syándzai, °bàn'wán 'shŕ)? /Are you free now? Syàndzai °yǒu 'gūngfu le ma (°'shŕ dōu 'wánle ma)? /I'm free now. Wǒ 'syàndzai °yǒu 'gūngfu le (°'méishèr le, °'bùmáng le, °'syánje ne). /Wait until I'm free. Déng wó °yǒu 'gūngfu (°'syánje de shŕhou, °shèr dōu 'wánle, °méi-'shèr de shŕhou) dzài 'shwō. /I don't have any free time today. Wǒ 'jīntyan yí'dyǎr °gūngfu yě méi'yǒu (°syán'kùngr yě méi'yǒu). or Wǒ 'jyér yí'tyān budé'syár.

(Without cost) 'báigěide, 'báisùngde, 'búyàuchyán, 'búyùng (gěi or hwā)chyán, myǎnfèi. /This is a free sample. Jèi shŕ °'báigěi dzwò 'yàngdz de (°'báisùng dzwò 'yàngdz de, °myǎn'fèi dzwò yàngdz de). /This is free of charge. Jèi 'búyùng gěichyán. or Jèi 'búyàuchyán. or Jèi shŕ bái'sùng de. or Jèi shŕ 'báigěi de. /He never lets a chance go by to get something free. Yǒu °'búyùng'chyán jyòu 'déde'dàude (°'báigěide, °'báisùngde), tā 'méiyou bú'yàu de shŕhou. but /Do you have any free tickets? Yǒu myǎn'pyàu ma? or Yǒu 'búyùng hwāchyán 'maide 'pyàu ma? /The food is free of charge. Chŕde dūngsyi °búyàu chyán (°myǎnfèi, °búyùng hwāchyán).

Free and easy. /He has a free and easy way of doing things. Tā dzwòshr hěn 'dzŕrán yí'dyár yě bù'hwāng.

Free-for-all. /It ended in a free-for-all. 'Jyégwǒ dàjyā °dáchǐ 'jyà lai le (°'lwàn dǎ le yí(jèn) 'jyà).

Free from or **of** (not having) méiyou or any other negative plus verb combinations. /The product is guaranteed (to be) free from defects of any kind. Jèijǔng dūngsyi °'dānbǎu (°'gwánbǎu) 'rèn shémma 'chywēchyàn yǐ méi'you. /He is free of trachoma. Tā méiyou shā'yǎn. /When the money arrived, he was free from worry. Chyán yi'dàu, tā jyòu 'bùjāu jí le.

Free of tax or duty °méiyou (°myǎn) ... shwèi. /Cigarettes are free of import duty. Jŕyān °méiyou rùkǒushwèi (°myǎn rùkǒushwèi, °búyùng shàngshwèi). /This article is tax free. Jèijyan dūngsyi myǎn 'shwèi.

Feel (or **Be**) **free to** (bù'jyūshu or swéibyàn) ... dōu syíng. /Feel free to do whatever you like. Nǐ 'swéibyàn dzwò shémma dōu syíng. or Búyàu 'jyūshū dzwò shémma dōu syíng. or meaning Do whatever you like, without restraint °'Ài (°'Syáng) dzěmmje, 'jyòu dzěmmaje, byé 'jyūshū. /He's free to leave at any time. Tā 'shémma shŕhou yàu 'dzǒu, °dōu 'syíng (or as Whenever he wants to leave, let him go. °jyòu 'ràng tā 'dzǒu).

Let someone go free bǎ ... fàng, jyàu ... dzǒu; (forgive) bǎ ... rán; (not hold as prisoner) buyā. /They held him for three hours and then let him go free. Tāmen bǎ tā yàle 'sāndyǎn jūng, yòu bǎ tā 'fàng le. /They let him go free. Tāmen °bǎ tā 'fàng le (°bǎ tā 'ráu le, °jyàu tā 'dzǒu le, °'méi bǎ tā 'yāchilai).

To free (release) fàng. /They're freeing the prisoners. Tāmen bǎ 'chyóufàn dōu fàng'dzoule. /When will he be freed? Tā 'shémma shŕhou 'fàngchulai? but /You're freed from all responsibility. 'Méiyou nǐ °shémma'shèr le (°de 'dzéren le).

Other English expressions. /Did you do it of your own free will? Jèi 'wán-chywán shŕ nǐ 'dzjǐ dzwò'jù gànde ma? or Jèi shŕ nǐ 'dzjǐ 'chínggān ywàn'yì de bànde ma? or meaning were others managing Nǐ gàn 'jèi shèr, 'yǒu méiyou 'byérén 'júshŕ? /Will you give me a free hand in the matter? 'Jèi shèr 'shŕ bushŕ 'wán-chywán yóu wǒ dzwò'jù? or meaning May I do as I please? 'Swéi wó 'dzěmma bàn dōu 'syíng?

FREEDOM. Most of the expressions are verbal; see **FREE.** /Only when there is free-dom of speech can there be a true democracy. Yǒu 'yánlwùndz'yóu tsái néng yǒu 'jēnjèngde 'mínjǔjèng'jŕ. /That doesn't leave me much freedom of action. 'Nèmma yilái jyòu jyàuwó °'hǎu dwō shèr bùnéng 'dʒjǐ dzwò'jǔ le (°bànshr̄ 'tài búdʒ'yóu le). meaning That limits me too strictly. 'Nèmma yilái jyòu bá wǒ syànjrde tài 'yánle. / The neighbors' children were also given freedom of the house. 'Línjyūde 'háidzmen 'yě kéyǐ dzài 'wǒmen jyāli 'swéibyàn 'wár. / His painting shows a freedom from conventions. Tsúng tā hwàde 'hwàr kéyǐ kànchulai, tā °'bùkěn 'syúngwēidǎu'jyùde (°néng 'dúchū'syīntsái). / When the prison term was up, he was given his freedom. 'Túsyíng 'r̄chǐ 'mǎn le, tā jyòu bèi 'fàngchulaile. / In the United States, church properties enjoy freedom from taxation. Dzài 'Měigwo, jyàu'hwèide 'chǎnyè 'dōu búyùng shàng'shwèi.

FREQUENT. (Often) chǎng (occurs before the verb); sometimes 'chǎngchǎng, (hěn) dwō. / I was a frequent visitor here. 'Jèr wó yǐchyán 'chǎng lái. / There was a frequent exchange of letters between them, but only for a while. Yǒu yí'jèndz tāmen 'chǎng tūng'syìn. / He is a frequent visitor. Tā shr̄ ge 'chǎng lái de 'kèren. / The rainstorms have been more frequent than usual this year. 'Jīnnyán bí 'wǎngnyánde yǔ syàde 'dwō.

To frequent chǎng lái. / This restaurant is much frequented by artists. 'Jèige gwǎndz 'yìshùjyā chǎng lái.

FRESH. (Newly produced, not stale or canned) syīnsyan. / Are these eggs fresh? Jèisyē 'jīdàn 'syīnsyan ma? / Let's go out and get some fresh air. Dzámen 'chūchyu syǐ dyǎr 'syīnsyan kūng'chì chyu. / I like fresh peas better than canned. 'Wāndòu wǒ ài chr̄ 'syīnsyande, 'búài chr̄ 'gwàntóude.

(New, recent) syīn (before noun or verb); gāng (before verbs only). / Let's open a fresh deck of cards. Dzámen 'dǎkāi yífù 'syīnpái ba. / That was a fresh deck of cards. 'Nèi fù pái °'gāng (°'syīn) dǎkāide. / That's fresh paint. 'Yóuchī shr̄ °'gāng (°'syīn)shàngshangde. or (not dry yet) 'Yóuchī hái méi'gān ne. / He's fresh out of school. Tā °'gāng (°'syīn) líkāi sywé'syàu.

(Not salty) dàn; fresh-water 'dànshwěi; fresh-water fish dànshwěiyú.

(Full of energy) yǒu 'jīngshén. / After all this work he seems as fresh as when he started. Dzwòle 'nèmmadwō 'shèr tā 'hái syàng gāng chī'tóur nèi 'shr̄hou nèmma yǒu 'jīngshen.

(Impertinent). / Don't be fresh! 'Byé táu'chì. or 'Gwēijyu dyǎr. or 'Byé hú'nàu. or Byé méiyou 'lǐmàu.

(Improperly playful). / He got fresh with her. Tā gēn tā nàuje 'wár lai je. or Tā gēn tā hú'nàu lai je. or Tā gen tā kāile ge 'wánsyàu.

FRIDAY. syīngchīwǔ, lǐbàiwǔ.

FRIEND. péngyou. / We're old friends. Wǒmen shr̄ 'lǎu péngyou. / He's a good friend of mine. Tā shr̄ wǒde 'hǎu péngyou. / Only intimate friends were invited. 'Chǐngde jr̄ yǒu °dzwèi'jìnde péngyou (°'jyāuchíng 'shēnde 'péngyou, °hěn 'chǐnjìnde péngyou). / You're not my friend. (seriously) Nǐ 'búgòu 'péngyou. (as a joke) Ní 'dzěmma bú-'syàngje wǒ a! / A friend in need is a friend indeed. Yùngde'jáu de shr̄hou tsái 'syàndechū 'jēn péngyou lai. or (a comparable Chinese proverb) 'Sywěli sùng'tàn de 'tsái swàn 'péngyou.

Be friends (with) shr̄ péngyou, syànghǎu, 'láiwǎng, yǒu jyāuching. / They're no longer friends. Tāmen bùsyàng'hǎu le. or Tāmende 'jyāuching 'dwàn le. or Tāmen bù'láiwǎng le. / Are you still friends with him? Nǐ gēn tā hái °shr̄ 'péngyou ma (°syàng'hǎu ma, °'láiwǎng ma)? but / Let's be friends. meaning Let's not disagree. Dzámen 'byé nàu 'yìjyan. or meaning Let's not fight. Dzámen 'byé dǎ'jyà. or meaning Let's not be angry at each other. Dzámen 'byé bǐtsz shēng'chì.

Make friends jyāu 'péngyou 'jyāuwǎng dzwò 'péngyou. /I want to make friends with him. Wo yàu gēn ta °jyāu 'péngyou (°'jyāuwǎng, °dzwò'péngyou). /He makes friends easily. Tā'rúngyî gēn rén °jyāu 'péngyou (°etc.)

FRIENDLY. héchi, héaǐ (courteous as well); hǎu (good); chīnyìn (intimate); lā jìnhu (try to gain friendship). /He seemed friendly towards you. Tā hǎusyàng gēn ní hěn 'héchi. /He's too friendly towards you. Tā hǎusyàng gēn ní hěn 'héchi. /He's too friendly towards them. Tā gēn tāmen tài 'héchi le. or Tā dài tāmen tài 'hǎu le. /She is a very friendly girl. Tā shr yíge hěn 'héaǐde nyǔháidz. /He's too friendly with them. Tā gēn tāmen 'tài °lā'jìnhu le (°'chīnjìn le). /Don't get too friendly with him. Byé gēn tā tài 'jìnhu. /This dog is friendly. Jèige 'gǒu gēn rén 'hǎu. /This dog is friendly with anyone. Jèige 'gǒu gēn 'shéi dōu 'hǎu. /Our country has always had friendly relations with yours. 'Dzámen lyǎnggwó 'bāngjyāu yísyàng hén 'hǎu. /He has a very friendly smile. Tā 'syàurúng hěn 'héchi de. or (meaning kindly, of an old person) Tā 'syàurúng hěn 'tszshàn de.

FRIENDSHIP jyāuching, 'yǒuyî. /Our friendship is the only thing that matters. Dzámen-de °'jyāuching (°'yǒuyî) shr 'dzwèi yàu'jǐn de. /Our long friendship came to an end. Wǒmen 'dwō °nyánde'jyāuching (°nyán de 'yǒuyî) °swàn 'lyǎu le (°tsúngtsz 'dwàn le).

See also **FRIEND.**

FROM. (Of motion in space or time) tsúng; sometimes dǎ; (of motion in space only) chǐ. /Where did you come from just now? Ní 'gāng °tsúng (°dǎ, °chǐ) 'nǎr lái? /I just came from home. Wǒ gāng °tsúng (°dǎ, °chǐ) 'jyāli lái. /Where do you come from? Ní shr tsúng 'nǎr lái de? or expressed as Of what place are you? Ní shr 'nǎrde rén? /I can't reach it from here. Wǒ tsúng 'jèr gòubu'jáu. /The smell comes from beyond the river. Nèige 'wèr shr tsúng hé 'nèibyārgwòlaide. /I took a pencil from your drawer. Wǒ tsúng ní 'chōutili nále yìgwàn chyān'bǐ. /Choose any one from those three. Tsúng nèi'sānge li 'swéibyàn 'tyāu yíge. /Look out from here. Tsúng 'jèr wàng 'wài kàn. /He took it from my hand. Tā tsúng wó 'shǒuli náchyu de. /I got the news from him. Wǒ tsúng tā nar 'tīnglai de. /I got this from the corner store. Jèi shr tsúng gwǎi'jyāurde nèige 'pùdzli 'mǎi de. /I brought it from America. Wǒ tsúng 'Měigwo 'dàilai de. /Take a clean glass from the cupboard. Tsúng wǎn-'jyàdzshang ná yíge 'gānjǐng bēidz lai. /Take the coat from the hook. Bǎ 'yīshang tsúng 'gōurshang 'násyalai. /I took it from the table there. Wǒ tsúng 'jwōdzshang nálaide. /The shot came from the top of that hill. 'Nèi yì chyāng shr tsúng nèi shān'dǐngshang 'fàng de. /These country people are from the mountains. Jèisyē 'syāngsyàrén shr tsúng shānli lái de. /The tax the merchants pay comes from you and me too. Shāngrén nà de 'shwèi yě shr tsúng 'ní wǒ 'shēnshang chū de. /I pulled the carpet out from under her feet. Wǒ shr tsúng tā jyáu 'dǐsya bǎ dì'tǎn 'chōuchulaide. /The chair slipped out from under him. 'Yǐdz tsúng tā 'pìgu dǐsya °'hwáchūchyule (°'lyōuchūchyule, °'hwákāile, °'lyōukāile). /The children slipped away from the house one by one. 'Háidzmen 'yíge yíge de tsúng 'jyāli lyōuje dzǒule. /It takes three days to go from here to Peiping. Tsúng jèr dzǒudàu 'Běipíng yàu 'sāntyān. /He ran from his house to the post office. Tā tsúng tā 'jyāli pǎudàu 'yóujèng'jyú chyu. /It's bad from beginning to end. Tsúng 'tóur dàu 'lyǎur dōu bù-'hǎu. /It took him exactly twenty-five years to rise from a street sweeper to the mayor's office. Tā tsúng (dāng)sǎu'jyē(de) dàu dzwò shr'jǎng 'jěng yùngle èrshr-'wǔnyán. /We lived in Peiping from 1901 on. Tsúng 'yījyǒulíng'yīnyán 'chǐ, wǒmen jyòu jùdzài 'Běipíng. /From now on there isn't anything to worry about. 'Tsúngjīn yǐ'hòu kéyí fàng'syīnle.

(Of distance) lí. /It's a three-day trip from here. 'Lí jèr dzúng yǒu 'sāntyān de 'lù. or Tsúng jèr déi dzǒu 'sāntyān. /How far is it from here? 'Lí jèr dwō ywǎn? /Do you live very far from the station? Ní 'jùde lí chē'jàn hén 'ywǎn ma?

/He lives ten miles from town. 'Tā jùde dìfang 'lí chéng 'shŕlǐ. /I'd like to live miles away from town. Wǒ ywànyi 'jùde líchéng 'hén ywǎn.

(Of gifts, mail, etc.) from X is expressed as X plus a verb; or as X plus de. /That's from home. (sent) !Jyāli sūnglái de. or (mailed) 'Jyāli jìlái de. /That's from me. Nèi shr 'wǒ sùng de. or Nèi shr 'wǒ jǐ de. or (given) Nèi shr 'wó gěi de. /I got a letter from my brother. Wǒ 'jyēdàu wǒ 'gēge °syéde (°syégéi wǒ de) yìfēng 'syìn. /She got her temper from her father. Tāde 'píchì shŕ °tā 'fùchin 'chwángěi tā de (°tsúng tā 'fùchin nar 'dé lai de). /She got her money from her aunt. Tāde 'chyán shŕ °tā gū'mā gěi tā de (°tsúng tā gū'mā nar(de)láide). /He built a house with the profits from that transaction. °Tā dzwò (°Tsúng) 'nèipyàur 'mǎimaijwàn de 'chyán nálai gàile yìswòr'fángdz. /I won't take money from anybody. is expressed as Whoever gives me money, I don't want it. 'Shéi gěi wǒ chyán wó yě bú'yàu. /I won't take such insulting remarks from anybody. is expressed as Whoever says such things, I won't take it. 'Shéi gěi wǒ 'jèiyàngrde hwà 'tīng, wó yě 'bùnéng 'ràng. or 'Shéi nèmma 'mà wǒ 'dōu bù'syíng. /I got it from him. (a thing) Shŕ 'tā géi wǒde. or Wǒ tsúng 'tā nar 'ná de. or (information) Wǒ gēn (°tsúng) 'tā nar sywé de. or Shŕ 'tā gàusung wǒ de. or (a disease or something inherited) Shŕ 'tā chwán géi wǒ de. /Who is that letter from? Shŕ 'shéi lái de 'syìn?

(As a result of) 'yīnwei (. . . , 'swóyǐ). /He was tired and nervous from overwork. Tā yīnwei dzwòshŕ tài 'dwō, swóyǐ yòu lài yòu 'syīnshén bú'dìng de. /He got the disease from exposure in the rain. Tā yīnwèi jyàu 'yǔ lwúnjaule déde 'bìng. or Tā jyàu 'yǔ lwùnjaule, °tsúng 'nàr déde 'bìng (°'nèmma déde'bìng). but /He suffers from (has) high blood pressure. Tā (yóu) sywěyā'gāu(de'bìng).

(According to) jàu, ànje, tsúng . . . lái 'kàn. /From what he says, I don't think we should go. °Jàu (°Ànje) 'tā nèmma shwō de, wó syǎng dzámen háishr 'byé chyù ba. /That's all right from your point of view, but I'll have to take the blame if anything goes wrong. °Jàu (°Ànje) 'nǐde kànfa nèmmaje 'búyàujǐn, búgwò yàushr yǒule 'tswòr, 'wó děi āimà. /What is your opinion of him, judging from what he said? °Tsúng tā shwō de 'hwàli lái 'kàn (°Tīng tā shwō de 'hwà), nǐ jywéje 'tā jèige rén 'dzěmmayàng?

(In defining limits of numbers) from X to Y (definitely between X and Y) dzài X yǐ'shàng Y yǐ'syà (and similar expressions); (anywhere between X and Y) (tsúng or dzài) X dàu Y; (about X or Y) XY. /There were from five to six hundred people in the audience. 'Tīngde rén °dzài 'wúbǎi yǐ'shàng 'lyòubái yǐ'syà (°dzài 'wúbǎi dàu 'lyòubǎi jřjyān, °yóu wǔlyòu'bǎi). /This is for the use of children from eight to twelve years old. Jèi shř gěi (tsúng) 'bāswèi dàu shř'èrswèide syǎuhár yùngde. /There are from ten to fifteen thousand men in a division. Yìshř yǒu 'yíwàn dàu yíwàn'wǔchyān rén. /It's anywhere from 30 to 40 miles from here. Lí'jèr 'sānsž-shŕlǐ. or Lí'jèr yǒu 'sānshrdwō'lǐ 'sžshrláilǐ. /This car will cost anywhere from seven to eight hundred dollars. Jèilyang 'chē děi chìbābǎikwai chyán.

From day to day tyāntyān, 'yìtyānyì'tyānde. /The situation changes from day to day. 'Chíngsyíng °tyāntyān (°'yìtyān yì'tyānde) yóu 'gǎibyàn.

From door to door āije mér. /He sells soap from door to door. Tā āije 'mér de mài 'yídz.

From house to house āije jyār. /He sells soap from house to house. Tā āije 'jyār de mài 'yídz.

From time to time 'jyēchángbù'dwǎrde. /He comes home drunk from time to time. Tā 'jyēchángbù'dwǎrde hē 'dzwēile.

FRONT. chyán. /He served for three months at the front lines. Tā dzài chyán'syàn-shang fúwùle 'sānge 'ywè. /We can both get front seats. Dzámen lyǎ 'dōu néng dzwò 'chyánpái. /Someone's knocking on the front door. Yǒurén °chyāu 'dàmér ne (°dzài 'chyánmér nar 'chyāu ne).

The front 'chyánmyàr, 'chyánbyàr, 'chyántou. /The front of the house is painted white. Fángdz 'chyánmyàr shwāde shř 'báishǎr. /The table of contents is in the front of the book. 'Mùlù dzài shū °'chyánbyàr (°'chyánmyàr, °'chyántou). /I want a room in the front. Wǒ yàu jyān 'chyánbyārde 'fángjyān. or expressed as facing the street Wǒ yàu jyān lín'jyēde 'fángjyān.

In front of dzài ... 'chyánbyàr, dzài ... 'chyántou; (in the presence of) 'dāngje ..., dzài ... myànchyán, dzài ... gēnchyán. /A big crowd is standing in front of the post office. Yí'dàchyún rén dzài 'yóujēngjyú 'chyánbyar 'jànje ne. /Who was that sitting in front of you at the movies? Kàn dyàn'yǐngr de shřhou, nǐ °'chyánbyan (°'chyántou) dzwòde shř 'shéi? /Don't say that in front of others. 'Nèige 'búyàu dāngje 'byérén 'shwōchulai. or 'Nèige 'búyàu dzài 'byérén °myànchyan (°gēnchyan) 'shwōchulai.

To front (face) ... chyán (byàr) °shr (°lín), syàng ... kāi, cháu ... kāi, chùng(... kāi). /The house fronts the river. Ménchyán jyòushr 'hé. or Fángdz chyánbyàr °shř (°lín) 'hé. or expressed as The door opens facing the river. Fángdz °chùng (°cháu) 'hé kāi'mér.

FRUIT. 'shwéigwǒ (juicy fruits); gwǒdz, gwǒ, gwǒr (includes also nuts). /Oranges are my favorite fruit. 'Shwéigwǒli wǒ 'dǐng syǐhwàn 'jyúdz. /Do you have any fresh fruit? Yǒu 'syīnsyān shwéigwǒ ma? /That tree bears a non-edible fruit. 'Nèike shù jyē de gwǒdz bùnéng 'chř. /What kind of fruit does that tree bear? 'Nèikē 'shù jyēde shř 'shémma gwǒr? or meaning What kind of a tree is it? Nèi shř shémma shù? /I like dried fruit. Wǒ syǐhwan 'gāngwǒ. but /Kindness always bears fruit. (of business) meaning Kindness produces wealth. 'Héchì shēng'tsái. or (in general; a proverb) 'Shànyǒu'shànbàu.

(Results) 'jyēgwǒ. /His success is the fruit of long years of hard work. 'Tā 'gūngchéngmíng'jyòu, nà shř tā 'dwōnyán 'syīnkǔde 'jyēgwǒ.

FULL. (Filled) mǎn, often as second element of a resultative compound; but of a person filled with food, bǎu. /Give me a full glass of water. Gěi wǒ yì'mǎnbēi shwěi. /That bottle is full of hot water. Nèige °'píngdzli (°'dàidz) °mǎn'mànde 'jwāngje rè-'shwěi (°jwāng'mǎn rè'shwěi le). /The parking lot is full of out-of-town cars. Tíngchē'chǎng tíng'mǎnle wài'láide 'chē. /I'm full; I can't eat any more. Wǒ chř-'bǎule, bùnéng dzài 'chřle. /There's a full enrollment (of a school, army, etc.). Míng'é yǐjīng 'mǎnle.

(Containing many) 'mǎn dōu shr, chywán shr, dōu shr, 'chywán dōu shr, yǒu (or other appropriate verbs) 'hěn dwō, yóu hǎusyē, all of these expressions are followed by what the subject is full of. /That book is full of mistakes. 'Nèiběr shūli °'chywán shr (°'chywán dōu shr, °'dōu shr, °'mǎn dōu shr) 'tswòr. or 'Nèiběr shū yóu °'hěn dwō tswòr (°'hǎusyē tswòr). /This plan is full of holes. Jèige 'bànfali yóu 'hěn dwō dìfang syàngde bù'jóudau.

(Of rooms, vacancies, etc.) mǎn as a second element; chywán or dōu before a verb. /Do you have any vacant rooms? They're all full. Yǒu 'kùngfáng ma? Wǒmen jèr °jù'mǎnle (°'chywán jùshang 'rén le, °'fángjyān dōu yǒu rén 'jùje).

(Complete) jěnggèrde, jěng, chywán; (in detail) 'syángsyì; (fully) 'wánchywán. /The papers carry a full account of the incident. 'Bàujř shang bǎ 'nèijyàn shř °'wánchywán 'dēngchulaile (°'jěng'gèrde 'dēngchulaile, °shwōde hěn 'syángsyì). /That was a full day's work. Nèi shr chywán'tyānde gūngdzwò. /Are you working full-time? Nǐ syàndzài shř bushř dzwò 'jěnggūng ne? /Are you a full-time student? *or* Do you study full-time? Nǐ shř jěng'gèrde shŕhou dōu nyàn shū ma?

(Entire) yígùng (altogether; comes before a verb). / This is far from the full amount you owe me. Jèi bǐ nǐ yí'gùng gāi wǒ de hái 'chàde'dwō ne.

In full chywán, dōu. / He paid the debt in full. °Tāde 'jài (°Tā 'jyè de chyán) °'chywán (°'dōu) °hwánle (°hwánshangle, °hwán'chǐngle).

To the full (one hundred percent) 'shŕfēn. / I enjoyed the dinner to the full. 'Jèidwùn fàn wǒ chřde 'shŕfēn mǎn'yì. or meaning I ate to my heart's content. 'Jèidwùn fàn wǒ 'chřle ge 'syǐnmǎnyì'dzú.

FUN. There is a wide variety of meanings and translations in the following sentences, but the most common expressions contain words such as wár to play, yìsz interest, syàu to laugh. / I think fishing is a lot of fun. Wǒ jywéje dyàu'yú hén °yǒu 'yìsz (°yǒu 'chyùwei, °yǒu'chyùr, °hǎu 'wár). / He's a lot of fun. (enjoyable) Tā hén °yǒu 'yìsz (°yǒu 'chyùwei, °yǒu'chyùr, °hǎu'wár, or (amusing) °hwèi 'dòurén 'syàu, °hwèi 'yǐnrén 'syàu, °hwèi gěirén dòu'syàur, °hwèi gěirén kāi'syǐn). / He's no fun at all. Tā nèi rén 'yìdyǎr 'yìsz (°'chyùwei, °'chyùr) yě méiyǒu. or Tā nèi rén 'yìdyár yě 'bùhǎu 'wár. / We're just having a little fun. meaning not being serious about it Wǒmen jè shř nàuje 'wár. or meaning playing, not working Wǒmen jèng dzài jèr 'wárne. / We were just starting to have a little fun when that killjoy came in and broke it up. Wǒmen 'gāng wárde °yóu dyǎr 'yìsz le (°yóu dyǎr 'chyùr le, °yóu dyǎr gāu'syǐng le, °chǐle dyǎr'jyèr), nèige 'tǎuyàn'gwěi 'jǐnlai géi 'jyàule. / Let's step out and have some fun. Dzámen chūchyu °'wárwar ba (°hǎu'hǎurde 'wárwar ba). / Let's try it just for fun. Dzámen 'shřyishř, 'jřdàng nàuje 'wár. or Dzámen 'wár yiwar kàn. / He hid her pocketbook just for the fun of it. 'Tā bǎ tāde chyán'dàr tsángchilaile, °nèi 'búgwo shř gēn tā nàuje 'wár (°yàu gēn tā 'kāi ge 'wànsyàu). / They're making fun of him. (ridiculing him) Tāmen 'syàuhwa tā ne. or (amusing themselves with him) 'Tāmen ná tā °kāi 'wànsyàu ne (°kāi'syǐn ne, °'dòuje 'wár, °dòu'syàur, °'shwǎje 'wár, °chyǔ'leěr). or Tāmen 'dòuje tā 'wár. / Don't make fun of my pronunciation. Byé 'syàuhwa wǒde 'kǒuyǐn a. / We had a lot of fun. Wǒmen wárde °hǎu'jíle (°yǒuyìsz'jíle). / Have fun! I'll see you tomorrow. is expressed only as See you tomorrow. Míngtyan jyàn.

FUNERAL (General, covering everything from death to burial) 'báishř, 'sāngshř; (covering only funeral rites) 'sāngyí, 'sānglǐ. Other expressions are verbal rather than nominal; the chief ones are 'bàusāng (to send out obituary notices containing information about the funeral); rùlyàn (to hold the ceremony of putting the deceased into the coffin); kāidyàu (to hold a ceremony to allow friends and relatives to pay their last respects to the deceased); nyànjǐng (to engage Buddhist priests or others to conduct funeral services); shàngjì (to offer funeral sacrifices); chìchì (to hold a ceremony on the forty-ninth day after death); chūbin (to take care of everything connected with the funeral, or just to hold the funeral procession from home to graveyard); 'fàsùng (to conduct the body in the funeral procession from home to graveyard); fàsāng (to hold the funeral procession from home to graveyard); andzàng (to inter); shǒulíng (to hold a wake); 'dyàusāng, dyàusyàu (to come and console and mourn, of people outside the family); sùngbin (to follow the bier to the graveyard and be present at the interment); 'gūngdzàng (to hold a funeral ceremony for an eminent person with local authorities and the general public participating); 'gwódzàng (to hold a state funeral for someone, financed and conducted by the national government). / They're having a funeral but they don't know how to do it properly. Tāmen jèng 'dzài nàr bàn °'sāngshr (°'báishř), kěshr yǐ'dyár yě bù'dǔng sàng'lǐ. / He said he wanted to have a big funeral when he died. Tā 'shwǒgwo dzài 'sž de shŕhou 'chū ge 'dàbin. / We're going to attend a funeral tomorrow. Wǒmen 'míngtyan chyù °dyàu'sāng (°dyàu'syàu, °sùng'bin). / The day of his funeral was rainy. Tā °chū'bin de (°'fàsungde, °fà'sāngde, °an-'dzàngde) 'nèityan syà'yǔ láije.

Funeral home bǐnyígwǎn.

FUNNY. (Laughable, amusing) yǒu yìsz, dòusyàur, dòugén, jàusyàur; kěsyàu (sometimes not a compliment); and related expressions. / That's the funniest clown I've ever seen. Wǒ 'syànglái méi jyàn gwo syàng 'tā nèmma °dòu'syàurde (°yǒu'yìszde, °dòu'génde, °néng jyàurén 'syàude, °néng jaurén 'syàude, °néng dòurén 'syàude) 'chǒur. / He says some awfully funny things. Tā shwō de 'hwà °jāu rén 'syàu (°dòu rén 'syàu, °hěn dòu'gén, °hěn dòu'syàur, °hěn jau'syàur, °hén kě'syàu, °hén yǒu'yìsz). / He can tell very funny jokes. Tā hwèi shwō °hěn dòu'génde'syàuhwar (°hén yǒu'yìszde syàuhwar). / It was supposed to be serious, but it turned out to be awfully funny. Nèi 'běnlái shr hěn 'yánjùngde, kěshr nùngde hén kě'syàu. / I saw a very funny show last night. Dzwér 'wǎnshang wǒ kànle °ge hěn dòu'génde (°ge hěnjáu'syàude) 'syì. / You mean that funny little man? Nǐ shwōde shr nèige 'jǎngde hén °kě'syàude (°hǎu'syàude) nèige 'áidz ma? / The one with the very funny nose. Shr 'bídz jǎngde hén °kě'syàude (°jáu'syàurde, °hǎu'syàude) nèige. / The joke isn't funny at all; it's the way he tells it. Nèige 'syàuhwar yì'dyár yě °búdòu'gén (°bùkě'syàu, °méi'yìsz, °etc.), shr tā'jyǎngde hǎu. / It's not funny anymore. 'Búnèmma kě'syàu le. *or* 'Búnèmma jāu'syàur le. *or* 'Nèmmaje jyòu méi 'yìszle. or meaning It's been overdone. Tài gwò'hwòrle. *or* Nèmmaje jyòu tàu'yànle.

(Peculiar). / I have a funny feeling in my stomach. Wǒ 'dùdzli jywéje yǒu dyǎr 'bú dà 'hǎu. / I have a funny feeling that something is going to happen. Wǒ 'syīnli jr'dùng, 'syàng yàu yǒu shémma 'shèr shr̀de. / Funny, but I can't seem to remember. Chí'gwài (°'Gwàile, °Jēn 'gwài, °Jēn chí'gwài, °'Hǎu chí'gwàile, *or* (implying that it didn't happen) °'Jèishèr 'shénle, °'Jèi shèr yǒu'gwěi), wǒ dzěmma bú'jìde ne? / He is awfully funny about other people talking to his wife. is expressed as He doesn't like other people talking to his wife. Tā bùsyǐhwan byéren gēn tā tàitai shwō'hwà.

FUR. pídz; in combinations pí (these terms also mean skin *or* leather); (as material in a garment) 'pílyàur, 'pílyàudz, pítǔngdz; furs 'píhwò, pídz. / She always wears a fur coat, even in warm weather. 'Nwǎnhwo tyār tā'yě chwān 'pídàyī. / That fur looks like seal. Nèi syàng shwéi'tàpí. / What kind of fur do you want, lamb, Persian lamb, fox, or squirrel? Yàu néijǔng 'pídz; 'yángpí, dž'gāu, 'húlipí, háishr 'hwēishǔr? / What kind of fur do you want to line the satin gown? Nèige 'dwànpáur gwà 'shémma pídzde 'lyěr. / Can you make a fur coat for me? Nǐ néng géi wǒ 'dyàu jyàn pídàyī ma?

(The hair of fur) (pídzde)'máur. / This fur is very soft. Jèige pídzde 'máur jēn 'rwǎnhwo. / This fur comes in natural colors or dyed. Jèijǔng pídzde 'máur yǒu 'ywánshàrde yǒu 'rànde.

FURNISH. (Supply with furniture) one of the following verbs plus jyājyu furniture: jr̄, 'jr̀bàn (supply oneself with); mǎi (buy); yǒu (have, be furnished with); dài (be furnished with); gwǎn (be taken care of in respect to). / I haven't furnished my new apartment yet. Wǒ 'syīn dzū de dìfang hái °méiyǒu (°'méijr̄, °méi 'jr̀bàn) 'jyājyu ne.

(Supply with furniture and all other necessities and ornaments) 'shèbèi, bǎishe, 'chénshè. / This room is very well furnished. 'Jèijyàn wūdz °'shèbèi hěn 'chywán (°'chénshè hén 'jyǎngjyou, °'bǎishe hén 'jyǎngjyou).

(Provide) yǒu (have); gwǎn (take charge of); gěi (give); chū (supply as one's share); yùbei (prepare); gwǎn mǎi (take charge of buying); nálai (bring); etc. / The hotel will furnish you with everything you need. Nǐ yàu 'yùng shémma, fàn'dyànli dōu °'yǒu (°'gwǎn). / We furnish sheets and towels (free of charge). Wǒmen gwǎn chwáng'dāndz gēn 'shǒujīn. / You furnish your own soap. 'Yídz 'dzbèi. / If you furnish the paper, I'll print them for you. Nǐ yàushr °chū 'jr̄ (°gwán 'jr̄, °'yùbèi

573

'jř, °gwǎn mái 'jř, °gěi wo 'jř, °ná 'jř lái), wǒ jyou géi nǐ 'yǐn. / The police
department will furnish two guards. Jǐngchájyú °pài (°géi) lyǎngge bǎu'byāude.

Furnished room °yǒu (°dài, °gwǎn) 'jyājyu de wudz. / I want a furnished
room. Wǒ yàu yǐjyān °yǒu (°dài, °gwǎn) 'jyājyu de wūdz.

FURNITURE. 'jyājyù; (tables and chairs; usually referring to old-fashioned things)
'jwōyǐ; **living room furniture** kè'tǐngde 'jyājyu; **furniture store** jyājyùdyàn, jwōyǐpù.
/ I want to buy some furniture. Wo yàu °'máu (°'jř) dyǎr 'jyājyu.

See also **FURNISH.**

FURTHER. (More) dzài before the verb; sometimes dwō *or* dzài 'dwō; in a few cases
hái, also before the verb. / Let's walk a little further. Dzámen dzài 'dwō dzǒu dyar.
or Dzámen dzài dzǒu 'ywān dyar. / If you come any further I'll shoot. Nǐ yàu 'dzài
°dzǒu 'jǐn yidyar (°dzǒu 'yíbù, °'jǐn yíbù), wǒ jyou kāi'chyāngle. / Do you want to
discuss this matter further? 'Jèi shèr nǐ hái syāng °'dzài (°'dwō) tán yitán ma?
/ Don't you want me to make further investigations? Nǐ 'búywànyi jyàu wǒ °dzài 'jǐn
yíbù 'chá (°dzài 'shēn yíbù 'chá, °(dzài) 'dwō chá) yichá ma? / Let's go ahead
without further arguments. Wàng syà 'dzwò ba, 'byé dzài 'jēng le. / Are there any
further instructions? 'Hái yǒu 'hwà ma? *or* 'Hái yǒu yàu 'fēnfude ma?

To further yóu °hǎuchù (°bāngju). / His work furthered the development of this
matter. Tā 'dzwòde 'shŕching dwèi jèijyan shŕchingde 'fājǎn yóu °'hǎuchù (°'bāngju).
but / You must further your education. Nǐ hái děi nyàn'shū.

FUTURE. (In time still to come) yǐhòu (henceforth); 'jyānglái (about to come); wèilái
(not yet come). / Try to do better in the future. Yǐ'hòu syāng'fár dzwò 'hǎu dyar.
/ If anything like this happens in the future, call me first. °Yǐ'hòu (°'Jyānglái) dzài
yǒu jèi yàngr de shèr, 'syān tūngjŕ 'wǒ. / That astrologist pretends to know all of
the future (events). 'Nèige swàn'gwàde 'dzjǐ shwō néng jŕdàu yǐ'chyè °jyāng'láide
(°wèi'láide, °yǐ'hòude) 'shŕ. / He might be the future president. Tā kěnéng shŕ
°jyāngláide (°wèiláide) dzúng'tǔng.

In the near future bùjyǒu, 'gwòbulyǎu dwōshǎu 'shŕhou. / Things are going to
blow up in the near future. °Bù'jyǒu (°'Gwòbulyǎu dwōshǎu 'shŕhou) 'nèi shèr jyǒu
yàu 'nàuchǐlai le.

(Prospects, prospective; road ahead) 'chyántú; (journey ahead) 'chyánchéng;
(hope) 'syīwàng; (something to hope for) syāngtour. / The future of that industry is
uncertain. 'Nèijǔng gūngyè 'chyántú 'bùgǎn shwō 'dzěmmayàng. / This affair ruined
his whole future career. 'Jèijyan shèr bǎ tā °'jyānglái de 'shŕyè chywán (°'chyántú
jěng'gèrde, °'chyánchéng jěng'gèrde) 'hwěile. / This job has no future. 'Jèige shèr
'méi shémma °'syīwàng (°'syāngtour).

Bright future chyán'tú ywǎndà, chyán'tú gwāngmíng, chyán'tú wúlyàng.

GAIN. (Obtain; as an object or objective) dé (especially in certain combinations); (reach)
dàu; (occupy) jàn; (win from an enemy) dégwolai, dwógwolai; (add, gain more) jyā;
and some indirect expressions. / The victory was gained at a tremendous cost of lives.
'Jèitsz dé'shēng swùnshŕle hěn 'dwō rén. / Now that he has gained the upper hand,
he'll be relentless. Tā syàndzài 'déle 'shŕ le, 'kě jyou yàu bùrúng'chǐng le. / He
gained a lot of votes by his last speech. Tā 'shàngtsz jyǎng'yǎn °jyàuta 'dwō déle
(°gěi tā 'jyāle) bù'shàude 'sywǎnjyǔ'pyàu. / His sincerity gained everybody's confidence. Tā hěn 'chéngshr, swóyi 'dé rén'syìn. *or* Tā 'chéngshrde 'jyàu rén 'dōu
'syìren ta. *or* Tā hěn 'chéngshr, swóyi 'rén dōu 'syìnren ta. / He has not yet
gained his objective. Tā hái 'méidédau tāde 'mùdi. / The soldiers have gained the

hill beyond the town. meaning reached Nèisyē 'bīng dàule chéng 'nèibyār de nèige 'shānshang le. or meaning won Nèisyē 'bīng bǎ chéng 'nèibyārde nèige 'shān °'jànle (°'dégwolaile, °'dwógwolaile).

(Make profit; in business) dé, jwàn; each followed by lǐ (profit), chyán (money), or 'lǐchyán. / He lost all he had gained for the year through speculation. Tā yīnwei tóu'jī bǎ yī'nyán jwànde 'chyán dōu 'péichuchyule. / How much did he gain last year? Chyùnyán tā 'déle dwōshǎu °lǐ (°chyán, °'lǐchyan)?

(Catch up, in a race or game) yàu 'gǎnshangle, yàu 'jwēishangle; **gain on** is expressed with the above two phrases and also (jyàn'jyànde 'lí . . .) lǐde 'jǐnle (of lit. distance only). / He's gaining (in distance or points). Tā yàu °'gǎnshangle (°'jwēishangle). / He's gaining on us. (distance only) Tā (jyànjyànde 'lí wōmen) lǐde 'jǐn le. or (distance or points) Tā yàu °'gǎnshanglaile (°'jwēishanglaile). / No. 6 (horse) is gaining on No. 2. Dì'lyòuhàu ('mǎ) yàu °'gǎnshang (°'jwēishang) dì'èrhàu le. or Dì'lyòuhàu ('mǎ) jyàn'jyànde 'lí dì'èrhàu lǐde 'jǐn le.

(Improve in health) hǎu. / The doctor reports that the patient is gaining rapidly. 'Dàifu shwō nèige 'bīngrén 'hǎude hěn 'kwài.

Gain ground (lit.) chyánjìn; (of one's own side only) yǒu 'jìnjyán; (fig.) déshr̀, or indirect expressions. / We are gaining ground (in battle). Wǒ'jyūn °yǒu 'jìnjǎn (°jyàn'jyànde chyán'jìn). / The enemy is gaining ground. 'Dírén dzài chyán'jìn. / The idea is gaining ground among us. Nèijǔng 'sz̄syáng dzài 'wǒmen jèr °jyàn-'jyànde dé'shr̀ le (or meaning is prospering °jyàn'jyànde 'syīngchilaile). or expressed as The number of people who believe it is increasing. 'Syìnde rén jyàn'jyànde 'dwōchilaile.

Gain time 'hwǎn yihwǎn, 'dwō dé dyǎr 'shŕjyān, 'dwō dé dyǎr 'gūngfu. / The attack was postponed to gain time for preparation. 'Gūngjī jǎn'chǐ le wèideshr °'dwō dé dyǎr 'shŕjyān (°'dwō dé dyǎr 'gūngfū, °'hwǎn yihwǎn) °hǎu (°lái) 'jwǔnbèi. / The enemy's request for a truce is just to gain time for putting up a stronger defense. 'Dírén chyóu'hé búgwo shr̀ yàu °'hwǎn yihwǎn (°'dwō dé dyǎr 'shŕjyān) lai 'jyāchyáng 'fángyù. / His double-talk is just to gain time for a good excuse. Tā nèmma syà'dǎudau búgwo yàu 'hwǎn yihwǎn, hau 'syǎng jyù 'hwà shwō.

Gain weight jǎngbàng. / He's determined not to gain weight. Tā jywédìng 'bùjǎngbàng.

Gain back 'hwēifù(le); (only of health) fùwán(le). / A week in the country will help you gain back your health. Dzài 'syāngsya jù 'yíge syīng'chī jyou kéyi jyàu nǐde 'shēntǐ °'hwēifule (°fú'ywánle). / All the lost ground has been gained back. 'Dyōule de dìfang dōu °'hwēifúle (°déhweilaile).

Gain(s) (winnings in a game) yíngde; (money) yíngde 'chyán; (points) yíngde fēr; (chips) yíngde chóu'mǎr. / On the last hand I lost all my gains. 'Shàngyìbǎ pái wǒ bǎ °'yíngde (°'yíngde 'chyán, °'yíngde 'fēr, °'yíngde chóu'mǎr) 'dōu shūchuchyule.

(Advantage; profit) lǐ, lǐyì, hǎuchu. / Their loss is our gain. 'Tāmende 'swǔnshr̄, jyòushr 'wǒmende 'lìyì. / He's interested only in personal gain. Tā jǐr gù (tā) 'dz̀jǐde °'lìyì (°'hǎuchu).

(Increase) 'dzēngjyā. / There has been a recent gain in the population of the city. 'Jìnlái 'jèige chéngde 'rénkǒu 'dzēngjyāle.

GAME. (Contest) is usually expressed in Chinese by a verb-object form as **play a game.** The general expression is dzwò'yóusyì but this is limited in use. The verb wár alone is also used. More often a specific verb of playing is used with the appropriate kind of game as the object, such as dǎ wǎngchyóu play tennis; dǎ pái play cards; syà chí play chess or checkers; etc. / That's a good game for children. Nèijǔng 'yóusyî syǎuhár °dzwò (°wár) tǐng hǎu. / Let's play a game. Wǒmen 'wár dyar shémma ba. / He plays all sorts of games well. Tā wár 'shémma dou wárde bú-'tswò. / I'm a little off my game today. (general) Wǒ jīntyan °wárde bùsyíng (or (of tennis) °dǎ wǎng'chyóu dǎde bù'syíng, or (of chess) °syà 'chí syàde bù'syíng, °etc.). / He plays a good game. (general) Tā wárde hěn hǎu. or (of tennis) Tā dǎ wǎng'chyóu dǎde hěn hǎu. (of cards) Tā dǎ 'pái dǎde hěn hǎu. (of chess or checkers) Tā syà 'chí syàde hěn 'hǎu.

(Fun, as opposed to work) (nàuje) wár. / He thinks of his work as a game. Tā ná tā dzwò de 'shèr °dàng (nàuje) 'wár shr̀de (°búdàng 'shèr).

(Athletic meet) yùndùng hwèi; **Olympic games** shr̀jye yùndùng'hwèi, 'gwójî yùndùng'hwèi; **the autumn games** 'chyōujî yùndùng'hwèi.

(Trick, intention, shady dealing) is translated by many indirect expressions and proverbs. / I saw through his game. is expressed as I could see through his chess moves. Tā 'dzǒu de nèijibù 'chí wǒmen 'dōu 'kàndechulái. or (closely correspond-ing to the English) Tā 'wárde °nèi'jāur (°nèi'shǒur, °lyǎng'jāur, °lyǎng'shǒur, °jijāur, °ji'shǒur, °nèiyítàu, °hwā'jāur, °'bǎsyi, °syî'fǎr) wǒ 'dōu kàn°'chwānle (°'tòule). or Tāde °gwèi'jî (°syīn'yǎr, 'júyi, 'shǒudwàn) wǒ 'dōu kàn °'chwānle (°'tòule). / Does anyone know what his game is? Yǒu rén 'jr̀dau tā °yàu dzǒu 'nèibù'chí ma (°dǎ de shr̀ dzěmma ge 'júyì ma, °wárde shr̀ 'shémma 'bǎsyî ma, °yàu yùng 'shémma 'shǒudwàn ma, °yàu 'shr̀ 'shémma syīn'yǎr ma, °'húluli 'màide shr̀ shémma 'yàu ma)? / I can play that game too. (lit. or fig.) Nèige 'wǒ yě 'hwèi. or (fig. only) meaning That's a game two can play. 'Nèmmaje shéi bú-'hwèi a. / I don't play that sort of game. Wǒ 'búgàn 'nèige yàngrde shr̀. or Wǒ 'búgàn 'nèijǔng 'shr̀. / It takes two to play that game. (lit.) 'Nèige děi 'lyǎ rén 'wár. or (fig.) expressed as A single palm can't make any noise clapping. Gūjǎngnán-'míng. / When their secret was discovered, they realized the game was up. Tāmende 'mìmi 'syèlòule, tāmen 'jr̀dau (tāmen) °swàn 'wánle (°swàn 'lyǎule, °swàn 'chwēile, °wárwánle, or (vulgar) °wán'dàn le).

(Occupation) is usually expressed by a verb, as gàn, nùng (do). / How long have you been in this game? Nǐ °gàn (°nùng) 'jèige yòu 'dwōshau 'shríhou le? / He plays a dangerous game. Tā 'gàn de shr̀ °'syānshr̀ (°hěn 'wéisyǎn). / That's a dangerous game. Nài shr 'syānshr̀. or 'Nèige hěn 'wéisyan. or (lit. or fig.) Wár 'nèige tài 'wéisyǎn.

(Animals) yěshòu (in wild state); 'yěwèr, 'yěwèi (as food). / Is there any big game near here? Jèr 'fùjìn yǒu shémma yě'shòu ma? / This restaurant serves game in season. Jèige fàn'gwǎndz °'yìngshrílwùn'jyérde mài 'yěwèi (°yǒu 'yìng-shrílwùnjyérde 'yěwèr).

(Games as toys) wányèr. / Do you sell games here? Nǐmen jèr mài 'wányèr ma?

A game (of) (one particular instance of its being played) tsź, chǎng, hwéi; (chess only) pán. / We have time for one more game. Hái kéyi °'dzài (°'dwō) °wár yí'tsź (°'wár yì'chǎng, °'wár yì'hwéi, or (of chess) °'syà yì'pán).

Play the game fairly, lit. or fig. / He doesn't play the game. Tā 'búàn 'gwēijyu 'lái. or Tā 'ài shwǎ hwā'jāur. or Tā bùjyúchi.

Win or **lose a game** yíng (win), shū (lose). / Our team won five games to their three. Wǔ bǐ sān, wǒmen 'yíng. / You've lost the game. Nǐ 'shūle.

Be game (plucky). / Their team put up a game fight. 'Tāmen nèi'dwèi dǎde hai °jēn mài 'lìchi (°'jēn pīn'mìng, °yì'dyǎr búsyè'chì, °yìdyǎr bù'hánhu, °yǒu 'yùngchì, °jēn yǒu yì'gǔdz 'gànjyér). / They were game to the end. Tāmen °yǐjr̀ (°dàu'lyǎur) méisyè'chì. or Tāmen 'fèndàu'dǐ.

(Ready and willing). / I'm game for anything. Wǒ 'dzěmmaje dōu 'syíng. *or* 'Wǒ hǎushwǒ'hwàr.

GARDEN. ywándz, -ywár, -ywán. / These flowers are from our own garden. 'Jèisyē hwār shr̀ tsúng wŏmen 'dzjǐde hwā'ywár °'chyālaide (°'jāilaide). *or* 'Jèisyē hwār shr̀ wŏmen 'dzjǐde hwā'ywárli 'chū de. / The vegetable garden is behind the garage. Tsài'ywándz dzài 'chēfáng 'hòutou. / How do I get to the botanical gardens? Dàu 'jŕwù'ywán chyù 'dzěmma 'dzǒu? / Are the gardens open to the public? (of private gardens) 'Hwāywár syǔ rén 'jr̀nchyu ma? *or* (of public gardens) 'Gūngywán 'kāile ma?

To garden jùngywándz; (raise flowers) jùnghwār; (raise vegetables) jùngtsài. / He spends all of his free time gardening. Tā bǎ tā 'swóyǒu kùngsyánde 'shŕjyān 'dōu yùnglái °jùngywándz (°jùnghwār, °jùngtsài).

GAS. (Not a liquid or solid; technical term) 'chìtǐ, chì, chyèr. / Various gases have been tested for this purpose. 'Yǐjīng 'shŕyànle 'gèjŭngde 'chìtǐ, kàn 'nǎjŭng hé'yùng. / In its normal state hydrogen is a gas. 'Chīngchì 'chángtài shr̀ 'chìtǐ. / The gas escaped from the balloon. Chì'chyóude 'chì dōu 'pǎule. *or* Chì'chyóu °lòu'chì le (°'dzǒu'chì le). / Let the gas out before you work on it. Syān bǎ 'chì °'sāle (°'fàngle), dzài 'syōuli.

(Gasoline) yóu, chìyóu. / He still had enough gas for a ten-mile ride. Tāde (chì) 'yóu 'hái gòu dzǒu 'shŕyǐng'lǐ de. / Let's stop at the next station and get some gas. Dàu 'syàyige jàn nar 'tíngsya °'jyā (°'tyān) dyar 'yóu ba.

(Anesthetic) méngyàu. / Did the dentist give you gas? 'Yáyīsheng gěi ni shàng méng'yàu le ma?

(In the stomach) -chì used only with wèi for stomach; otherwise Chinese merely refers to the stomach (dùdz) aching. / He was doubled over with gas. Tā °'wèichì (°'dùdz) 'téngde, °wānchì 'yāu láile (°'jŕbuchì 'yāu láile).

Coal gas *or* **natural gas** méichì. / Turn off the gas. Bǎ méi'chì 'gwānshang. / The gas in the kitchen knocked him out. Chú'fánglide méi'chì 'bǎ tā gěi syūn-'tāngsyale. / He was poisoned by gas. Tā jyàu méi'chì syūnjau le. *or* Tā jùngle méi'chì le. / They did all their cooking on a gas stove. Tāmende 'fàn dou shr dzai 'méichì lúdzshang 'dzwòde. / The gas exploded. 'Méichì 'jàle.

Poison gas dú'chì. / The enemy hasn't used poison gas yet. 'Dírén hái 'méiyùng dú'chì ne.

GATE. (General, but especially the entrance gate in a high fence surrounding a house) dàmén; (in an ordinary fence) jàlarmér; (in a city wall) chéngmén. / The crowd poured out through the gate. Dà'hwŏr tsúng dà'mén nèr 'yūngchūchyule. / He closed the gate behind him on his way out. Tā chū'mén de shŕhou bǎ dàmén 'dàishangle. *or* Tā 'dzǒu de shŕhou bǎ dà'mén 'gwānshangle. / There are two stone lions outside the gate. 'Dàmén 'wàitou yǒu lyǎngge 'shŕtou 'shr̄dz.

(Of a dam) já (which also means the entire dam). / When the water rises too high they open the gates. 'Shwěi yàushr jǎngde tài 'gāu le, tāmen jyou bǎ 'já kāikai.

(Receipts). / The gate totaled $4,000. is expressed as Altogether they sold $4,000 worth of tickets. Mén'pyàu yígùng 'mǎile 'szchyānkwài 'chyán. / The game drew a gate of 3,000. is expressed as For this game they sold 3,000 seats *or* tickets. 'Jèi yìchǎng chyóur mǎile 'sānchyān°ge 'dzwòr (°-jāng 'pyàu).

Gatekeeper kān 'mérde, ménfángr; **guard at the gate** kān'mérde; (if police) ménjǐng.

GATHER. (Pick up from here and there; put in order) gwēijr, shōushr; (hurriedly throwing things together) lyǎnba (local Peiping). / He gathered up his things and left. Tā °'gwēijrgwēijr (°'shōushrshōushr, °lyǎnbalyǎnba) tāde 'dūngsyi, 'náje jyou 'dzǒule. / Gather up the papers and put them in order before you leave. Bǎ 'jr °'gwēijrgwēijr (°'shōushrshōushr, °gwēijr'hǎulè) dzài 'dzǒu.

(Pick up from the ground or floor) shr, jyán. / Gather up those papers (from the floor) and put them in the drawer. Bǎ 'nèisyē 'jr °'jyánchilai (°'shrchilai), shōudzai 'chōutili. / He's out gathering dry branches for a fire. Tā chūchyu °'jyǎn (°'shr) gān jrdz chyule, hau 'lǔng ge 'hwǒ.

(Pick up to put in one place) lyǎn. / Gather the dirty clothes together and pile them on the floor. Bǎ 'dzāng yīfu °'lyánchilai (°'lyǎndzai yí'kwàr, °'lyǎndau yí'kwàr), dwēidzai 'dìshang.

(Put into a pile or piles) dwēi. / He gathered the dry leaves into piles. Tā bǎ gān 'yèdz 'dwēile ji'dwēr.

(Assemble by any method; of people, things, water, etc.) jyù; (of people only) 'jyùjí, 'jíhé, 'hwēihé. / Gather the people together and make an announcement. Bǎ rén °'jíhéchilai (°'jyùjíchilai, °'jyùdzai yí'kwàr, °'jyùdau yí'kwàr, °'hwēihédau yí'kwàr), 'sywānbù yísyàr. / Let's gather the specialists together and hold a meeting. Bǎ 'jwānjyā 'jyùdzai yí'kwàr kāi ge 'hwèi ba. / All the talented people have been gathering there for years. Nèige 'dìfang 'réntsái jyùjíle hǎusyē 'nyán le. / He gathered a crowd around him. Tā 'jyùle yìchyún 'rén 'wéije ta. / A crowd gathered around him. °'Wéije ta (°'Dzài tā 'jōuwéi) 'jyùle yìchyún 'rén. or Yìchyún 'rén 'jyùdzai °'tā 'sɀjōu'wéi (°'nàr bǎ ta 'wéichilaile). or Yǒu yìchyún 'rén 'wéije ta.

(Pick (up) or collect flowers, nuts, etc.) jāi, chyā. / She gathered enough flowers from the garden to fill all these vases. Tā °'jāi (°'chyā) de 'hwār gòu bǎ jèisyē 'píngdz dōu chā'mǎnle de.

(Accumulate) jī. / Dust gathers on window sills. is expressed as Window sills collect dust. Chwānghu'társhang jī 'chéntu jǐde hen 'dwō.

(Take in the arms) bàu, lǒu. / He gathered the two boys in his arms and said "Don't cry anymore." Tā bǎ lyǎ 'háidz °'bàu-(°'lǒu)chilai, shwō, "Byé 'kūle!"

(Of cloth with thread) chōujǐn, shōujǐn. / Her sleeves are gathered at the cuff. Tāde 'syòudz syòu'kǒur shr °chōu-(°shōu)'jǐnle de.

(Infer). / I gather you don't like him. (from the way you look) °Kàn'yàngr (°'Kàn jèige 'yàngr, °Kàn 'nǐ nèige 'yàngr) nǐ 'bú da 'syǐhwan ta. or (from my observation) 'Jyù wǒ 'chyáu (°'kàn), nǐ 'bú da 'syǐhwan ta. or (from what I hear) Jyù wǒ 'tīngjyàn de, nǐ 'bú da 'syǐhwan ta.

(Of mental faculties) gú(-chilai) (courage); dá(-chilai) (wits, etc.). / She gathered all her courage and walked in. Tā gúchi 'yǔngchilai, jyòu jìnchyule. / She gathered all her wits to talk her husband out of it. Tā dáchi 'jīngshenlái, bǎ tā 'syānsheng shwōde gǎile júyi le.

Gather in shōu. / They're gathering in the crops. Tāmen shōu 'jwāngjya ne.

Gather speed 'kwàichilai, ywè 'dzǒu ywè 'kwài. / The car slowly gathered speed. Chē màn'mārde 'kwàichilaile. or Chē jyàn'jyànde ywè 'dzǒu ywè 'kwài.

GENERAL. (Of all, not local or particular) píngcháng(de), pǔtūng(de), yìbān(de); in some combinations pǔ-. / The general public is often misled by unscrupulous journalists. Yì'bān rén cháng jyàu bùjyǎng'lǐ de syīnwénjì'jě gěi 'pyàn le. / This is not a book for specialists; it's for the general reader. Jèiběn 'shū búshr gěi jwān'jyā kànde; shr wèi °'píng'cháng rén (°pǔ'tūng rén, °yì'bān rén) kànde. / They hold a general election every year. Tāmen 'měinyán pǔ'sywǎn yí'tsź. *but* / That is for the general welfare of the people. Nà shr wèi 'dàjùngde lìyì.

(Existing extensively) 'dàjyā(de) (of everyone); 'dwōshù rén(de) (of a majority); 'dàdwōshù rén(de) (of a large majority); <u>when followed by a verb</u> 'dàjyā (may be followed by chywán *or* dōu), 'dwōshù(rén), 'dàdwōshù(rén); dà (greatly). / By general consent, the doorman was paid a month's extra wages when he left. Kān'mérde 'dzōu de shŕhou 'dwō gěile tā 'yíge ywè de 'gūngchyan; 'nèi shr̀ 'dàjyā túng'yì de. / The general opinion is that he is right. °Dà'jyāde (°'Dwōshù rénde, °'Dàdwōshù rénde) 'yìjyàn shwō tā 'dwèi le. / There is a general feeling of uneasiness about the future. 'Syàngdau jyāng'láide shr̀ dàjyā °'chywán (°'dōu) jywéje syīnli bù'ān. / There was general confusion. Dà'jyā °dōu (°chywán) 'lwànchilaile. / There was general confusion in the station. Chē'jànshang 'dà lwànchilaile.

(Miscellaneous) dzá. / She's been doing general office work. Tā 'dzwò de shr̀ °'dzáshr̀ (°gūngshr̀'fánglide 'dzáshr̀). / You can get almost anything at the general store. Dzài 'dzáhwò'pùli chàbu'dwōde 'dūngsyi 'dōu mǎide'dàu.

(Vague) dzǔng. / "Far East" is a general term for eastern Asiatic countries. °'Ywǎndūng" shr̀ Dūngyà 'gègwóde 'dzǔngmíng. / "Furniture" is the general term for chairs, tables, beds, etc. °'Jyājyù" shr̀ 'yǐdz, 'jwōdz, 'chwáng 'déngdengde 'dzǔngmíng.

(Not in detail; in broad outline) <u>is translated by a number of different expressions,</u> <u>depending on the noun, as</u> 'jyānmíng (brief and clear, of such things as instructions); tūng (in summary); **general history** tūngshr̀. / The general instructions are brief, but not clear. 'Jyānmíngde 'syùnlìng °'jyàn ér bù'míng (°jyànde 'dōu bù'míngbai le).

(Usual) 'píngcháng, chángcháng. / As a general rule the meetings are held here. 'Hwèi °'píngcháng (°'chángcháng) dzài 'jèr 'kāi.

General idea (not too clear) dàgài(chí); (a shadow, vague idea) yǐngdz, dàgài *or* dàjr̀ (probably) <u>followed by a verb</u>; (more or less) 'dwōshǎu, 'dwōdwōshau'shǎude <u>followed by verb.</u> / I have a general idea of the problem. Jèige wèn'tí wǒ °'jr̀dau ge dà'yì (°'jr̀dau ge 'dàgài('chí), °'jr̀dau ge 'yǐngdz, °'dàgài('chí) 'jr̀dau dyǎr, °dà'jr̀ 'jr̀dau dyǎr, °'dwōshǎu 'jr̀dau dyǎr, °'dwōdwoshǎu'shaude 'jr̀dau dyǎr).

General outline dàgāng, 'gānglǐng, 'gāngyàu. / Here's the general outline; we can learn the details later. Jè shr̀ ge °dà'gāng (°'gānglǐng, °'gāngyàu); 'syángchíng yǐ'hòu dzài 'shwō.

In general (looking at it in general) dà'tǐshang kàn; (taking it in general) dà-'gàide shwō, dàtǐshang shwō, dàgài'chí ér 'lwùn, dàgài'chí 'shwōchilai; (referring to all points mentioned) 'dzǔngér'yánjr̀, 'dzǔngchilai 'shwō. / In general, the outlook is bright. 'Chyántú °dà'tǐshang kàn (°dàigài'chí shwōchilai) hái 'hǎu. / In general, things are all right. °Dà'tǐshang shwō (°Dàgài'chí ér 'lwùn) 'chíngsying hái 'hǎu. / In general, these three points are irrelevant to the question. °'Dzǔngér'yánjr̀ (°'Dzǔngchilai 'shwō) jèi 'sāndyǎn dōu yú 'běntí wúgwān.

A general (of the military) (collective term for general officers) 'jyānggwān; (title for any such officer if his exact command is not known) 'jyāngjyūn; (usual title for any such officer, named by his command) shr̀jyǎng (divisional commander), jyūn-jyǎng (army commander); **major general** shǎujyàng; **lieutenant general** jūngjyàng; **inspector general** dzǔngjyān (in the armed forces).

(Of the civil service and civilian organizations) <u>may be expressed by</u> dzǔng *or* jyǎng; consul **general** dzǔng'lǐngshr̀; **secretary general** mìshūjyǎng; **inspector general** (police) dūchájyǎng; **general manager** dzǔngjīnglǐ.

GENEROUS. (Opposed to stingy) dàfang. / He's certainly generous with his money.

(implying either approval or disapproval) Tā hwā'chyán 'shŕdzài shŕ °'dàfang (or meaning free-spending and not too approving °shǒu'dà, °shǒu'sùng). / That's really generous of you. (referring to something done to the speaker) Nǐ °'syīnyǎr (°'syīn) jēn 'hǎu. or (referring to something done to someone else) Nèi 'jēn shr syíng'hǎu a. or Nín 'jēn shr 'kwānhúngdà'lyàng. or Nín 'jēn shŕ 'dàfang. / It pays to be generous. °Dàfang (°'Kwānhúngdà'lyàng) 'yǒuhǎuchu. or is expressed with the liter-ary quotation Generosity to others is generosity to oneself. Yǔ'rénfāng'byàn, dz-'jǐfāng'byàn.

(Not strict). / Be generous; don't always pick on his faults. °'Dàfang dyǎr ba (°'Bāuhan dyǎr ba, °'Dài rén 'kwān dyǎr ba, °'Hòudau dyǎr ba, °'Dé rúng rén de 'dìfang jyou 'swànle ba, °'Dé ráu rén de 'dìfang jyou 'swànle ba, °'Jēngje yíge 'yǎn 'bìje yíge 'yǎn ba, °'Syíngsying 'hǎu ba); byé 'jìng tyāu 'rénjyàde 'tswòr. / He's very generous toward his subordinates. Tā 'dài tā 'shòusyàde rén °hěn 'kwānhúng dà'lyàng (°hěn 'hòudau, °yìdyǎr bu'kèbwo, °lǎu 'jēngje yíge 'yǎn 'bìje yíge 'yǎn de, °hěn 'kwān, °hěn kwān'dà, °hěn néng 'kwānrúng, °hěn néng 'bāuhan, °hěn 'jūnghòu).

(Abundant or ample). / That restaurant serves generous portions. Jèige fàng-wǎndz gěide hěn 'dwō. / That cocktail had a generous amount of liquor in it. Nèige jǐwěi'jyǒuli yǒu hǎu'syē jyǒu. / Notice the generous cut of this coat. Nín 'kàn jèige 'gwàdz °tsáide dwō 'sūng a (°tsáide dwōma sūngsungkwānkwàrde).

GENTLE. (Light, soothing, mild) chǐng; (of hands) wěn. / The nurse has very gentle hands. Jèige 'kānhùde 'shǒu hěn °'chǐng (°'wěn). / The tap on the door was so gentle that we hardly heard it. °Mén 'chyāude hěn 'chǐng (°Chyāu'ménde shēngr 'chǐngde) wǒmen 'jīhu méitǐng'jyàn.

(Slow or moderate; of a current) màn, hwǎn. / He was rowing against a gentle current. 'Shwěi lyóude hěn ᵛ'màn (°'hwǎn), tā 'dzwòje chwán wàng 'shàng 'hwá.

(Soft and moderate; of a breeze) 'wēnhé, chǐng. / There is a gentle breeze from the south. Chǐ 'nán chwēilaile yíjèn 'wēnhéde 'fēng. or Chǐng'chǐngde 'chwēilaile yíjèn 'nánfēng.

(Of a person's attitudes and actions) 'wényǎ (refined, elegant); 'ānsyáng (com-posed); 'lǎushŕ (docile); (specifically of innate nature) 'wēnróu (warm and gentle). / Professor Liu is well-liked by every student because his manner is very gentle. 'Sywésheng dou syǐhwan 'Lyóu Jyàushòu, yīnwei tāde 'tàidu hěn 'wényǎ. / He always talks in a gentle manner (in a composed manner). Tā shwō 'hwà de shŕhou dzǔngshr dàije 'ānsyángde tàidu. / He is a gentle old soul. Tā shr ge 'lǎushŕren. / She is like her mother in that she is very gentle. Tā syàng tā 'mǔchin shŕde hěn 'wēnróu.

(Of an animal; tamed, docile) 'lǎushŕ, tǐnghwà. / We'll let you ride this old horse; she's the gentlest one we have. Nǐ chí 'jèipǐ lǎu 'mǎ ba; 'wǒmen jèr 'jyòushr 'jèipǐ hái °'lǎushŕ (°'tǐng'hwà).

GENTLEMAN. (Well-bred man) 'jēngjǐng(rén), 'jyūndzrén; be **gentlemanly** (of a person) 'jēngjǐng, (of actions) jèng. / Can't you act like a gentleman? Nǐ 'néng bunéng °'jēngjǐng dyǎr (°'jēngjengjǐng'jǐngde) ne? / He's no gentleman. Tā bú'jēngjǐng. or Tā 'búshr ge 'jēngjǐngrén. / He doesn't act like a gentleman. Tā 'jyùjŕ 'busyàng ge 'jēngjǐngrén. or Tā 'syíngwéi bú'jèng. or Tā méijèng'syíngr. / He's a gentleman of the old school. Tā shr yíge lǎu'pàrde 'jyūndzrén.

(Polite term of address or reference) is expressed by the measure wèi used with or without 'syānsheng. / A gentleman called this morning (not on the phone). Jyēr 'dzǎushang yǒu yíwèi 'syānsheng láigwo. / Who is that gentleman? 'Nàyiwèi shŕ 'shéi? / Ladies and gentlemen! 'Jūwèi! or 'Gèwèi!

GENTLY. (Lightly, mildly, tenderly) chǐngchǐngde. /She pushed the child gently. Tā bǎ syǎu'hár chǐng'chǐngde yì'twēi. /The doctor lifted his arm gently. Dàifu chǐng-'chǐngde bǎ tāde shǒu 'náchilai.

GEOGRAPHY. dìlǐ. /The geography of this region has been studied thoroughly. 'Jèiyídài 'dìfangde dìlǐ yǐjing 'yánjyòude hěn chè'dǐ le. /He studied geography for three years. Tā nyànle 'sānnyán dìlǐ. /Any specialist in geography ought to know geology as well. Dìlǐsywé jwān'jyā 'yě děi dǔng dì'jrsywé. /How many maps are there in your geography book? Nǐ nèiběr dìlǐ (shūli) yǒu 'dwōshaujāng dì'tú?

GET (GOT, GOTTEN). 1. Get plus a noun.

(Receive) 'shōudàu, 'jyējáu; **get word** or **news,** also désyìn. /When did you get my letter? Nǐ 'shémma shŕhou °'jyējáude (°'shōudàude) wǒde 'syìn? /I got this book last week. 'Jèibén shū wǒ 'shànglǐbài 'shōudàude. /He got word that his father had died. Tā 'déle 'syìn shwō tā 'fùchin 'gwòchyule. /Did you get any news from home? is also expressed as Did any news come from home? 'Jyāli lái'syìn le ma? or 'Jyāli yǒu 'syìn lái ma? /I got this from my father. (as a gift) Jèi shr wǒ 'fùchin °géi wo de (or (as a legacy or inherited characteristic) °lyóugei wǒ de).

(Receive money) ná(dàu), dé(dàu); (of regular pay) jwàn. /He gets fifty dollars a week. Tā 'yíge syǐng'chī °ná (°dé, °nadàu, °dédàu, °jwàn) 'wǔshrkwài chyán.

(Obtain or acquire by means of) (bringing) nálai; (finding) jǎulai; (asking for) yàulai; (buying) mǎilai; (borrowing) jyèlai; (any means) nùnglai; **get back** chyúhweilai. /Wait till I get my hat. 'Děng(yìhwěr,) wǒ bǎ 'màudz nálai. /I'll go and get the book tomorrow. Nèibèr 'shū wǒ 'myéngr chyù °'nálai (°'yàulai, °'mǎilai, °'jyèlai, °'chyúlai). /Can you get me another pencil? Nǐ néng dzài géi wo jǎu yìjr chyān'bǐ lái ma? or 'Dzài lái yìjr chyān'bǐ, syíng ma? or 'Dzài °jǎu (°yàu, °ná, °'nùng) yìjr chyān'bǐ lai, syíng ma?

(Fetch a person) bǎ plus the person, followed by one of the following: (by asking him) 'chǐnglai; (by calling him; not very polite) 'jyàulai; (by finding him) 'jǎulai; (by dragging him) 'lālai; etc., with other verbs of action. /Go and get him. Chyù bǎ ta °'chǐnglai (°etc.)

(Find as a job; reach, as a person by phone) jǎujáu, jǎudàu. /Did she get a job? Tā °'jǎujau (°'jǎudau) 'shèr le ma? /I couldn't get him by phone. Wǒ dǎ dyàn'hwà jǎu bu'jáu ta.

Get a disease jāu(shang), chwán(shang). /Aren't you afraid of getting a cold? Nǐ bú'pà jāu'lyáng ma? /Aren't you afraid of getting that disease? Nǐ bú'pà °'jāushang (°'chwánshang) nèijǔng 'bìng ma?

Get a meal dzwò'fàn. /When are you going to get dinner? Nǐ 'shémma shŕhour dzwò'fàn?

Get a person (catch) bǎ ... dǎijù; (wound) bǎ ... dǎ'shāng; (kill) bǎ ... dǎ'sž; (hit) bǎ ... 'dǎjáu. /They got him. Tāmen bǎ ta °dǎijùle (°dǎ'shangle, °'dǎ'sžle, °'dǎjáule). /The blow got him on the chin. 'Yísyàdz dǎjau tāde 'syàba 'kédz le.

Get a person (leave him without a comeback) bǎ ... wèn'jù(le), jyàu ... 'dábushàng'lái(le), jyàu ... méi'hwà shwō(le), bǎ ... 'wènde °méihwà shwō(le) (°'jāngkǒujyè'shé(le), °'dábushàng'lái(le). /You've got me there. 'Jèisyàdz kě °bǎ wo wèn'jùle (°jyàu wǒ 'dábushàng'láile, °jyàu wǒ méi 'hwà shwō le). /They got him that time. Tāmen 'nèisyàdz kě bǎ ta wèn'jùle. or Tāmen 'nèisyàdz bǎ ta 'wènde °'jāngkǒujyè'shé le (°'dábushàng'lái, °méi 'hwà shwō le).

Get a person (annoy) jyàu ... followed by 'nǐwei, 'nǐfan, tǎu'yàn, tǎu'syán; or expressed as annoy to death kě bǎ ... nǐ 'sžle, kě jēn tǎuyàn'sžle. /What gets me is the way he cracks his knuckles. Tā nèmma 'en 'shŏushangde gŭtóu'jyér 'gābēr-'gābērde 'syang, jyàu rén °nǐwei (°etc.).

Get a person (ruin) bǎ . . . hwěi. / The opium habit finally got him. 'Dàyān'yǐn dàu'lyǎur bǎ ta 'hwěile.

Get someone to do something is expressed by one of the following: jyàu, ràng; chǐng (invite); chywàn (persuade); lā, jwài (compel by pulling); dyàu (by a trick); etc. / Can you get him to come to the theater? Nǐ néng syang 'fár °ràng ta (°chywàn ta, °etc.) shàng syì'ywándz lái ma?

Get a divorce líhwūn. / They got a divorce. Tāmen 'jèngshr lí'hwūn le.

Get a (mental) shock chr̄'jīng. / He's going to get the shock of his life when he sees her. Tā yí 'kànjyan ta hwèi 'dà chr̄ yì'jīng de.

Get the idea or get (understand) it dŭng; (be clear about) míngbai; (see clearly) kànchulai; (think clearly) syangchulai; (feel the implications of) mwōchīngchu; (know) jr̄dau; (hear clearly) tīngchulai. / Do you get the idea? Jèige 'yìsz nǐ °'dŭngle (°'míngbaile) ma? or Jèige 'yìsz nǐ °'kànchulai (°'syangchulai, °mwō'chīngchule) shr̄ 'dzĕmma hwéi 'shèr le ma? or Nǐ 'míngbaile ma? or Nǐ 'jr̄dau shr̄ 'dzĕmma hwéi 'shr̄ le ma? / I don't get it. (Wŏ) °bù'dŭng (°bù'míngbai, °méi'tīngchulái) shr̄ 'dzĕmma hwéi 'shèr.

Get the right answer dádwèi, dáchulai, shwō'dwèi, nùng'dwèi; (of a mathematical calculation) 'déde 'shùr 'dwèi. / You still haven't got the right answer. Nǐ 'hái méi °dá'dwèi ne (°shwō'dwèile ne, °nùng'dwèile ne, °'dáchulai ne). or Nǐ 'déde 'shùr hái bú'dwèi ne.

Get a station or a place on a radio wúsyàn'dyàn 'tīngdàu. / Can you get Tokyo on your radio? Nǐde wúsyan'dyàn 'tīngdedàu Dūng'jīng ma?

Get so much of something per unit measure. / I can get twenty-two miles a gallon with this car on the open highway. Wŏ 'jèilyàng chē dzài dà'lùshang yì'jyālwún-(chǐ'yóu) kéyi dzŏu èrshr̄'èrlǐ. / I can get three dozen oranges for a dollar at that store. Nèijyā pùdz 'sāndǎ jyúdz tsái mài yí'kwài chyán.

Get so many years imprisonment °pàn (°nùng, °làu, °nàu) ge . . . nyán jyān-'jīn. / He got ten years. Ta °'nùngle (°'làule, °etc.) ge 'shr̄nyán jyàn'jīn. / He may get ten years. Tā yésyŭ °'pàn (°yàu 'nùng, °etc.) ge 'shr̄nyán jyàn'jīn.

2. **Get** plus an adjective or expression of action; usually expressed by an adjective plus -le or by a verb. / His feet got wet. Tā 'jyǎu 'shr̄le. / He got tired of waiting. Tā 'dĕngde bù'nàifán dzài 'dĕng le. / She got sick. Tā 'bìngle. / He got thin. Tā 'shòu le. / He got hurt. Tā shòu'shāng le. / The train got under way at last. (began moving) 'Hòulai hwŏ'chē yě jyòu °'kāile (or (began to gather speed) °'kāichǐlaile, °'dzŏuchǐlaile). / Get busy! 'Gāi dzwò shémma kwài 'dzwò ba! or meaning Hurry up! 'Kwàije dyǎr!

Get going (command) 'dzŏu, dzŏukai, dzŏu ba.

Get murdered (fig.). / Someone's going to get murdered if we don't get paid today. 'Jyér yàu 'bùfā'chyán a, děi 'chū ge 'rénmìng 'àndz.

Get ready (for something to happen) yùbèi hǎule; (for a visitor, or to go) jwúnbèi hǎule; (to go) 'shŏushr hǎule. / I'm sure she's gotten everything ready for the guests. Wŏ gǎn shwō tā gěi kèren 'shémma dōu °yùbèihǎule (°jwúnbèihǎule). / He likes to get ready early. Tā syǐhwan dzǎu °yùbèihǎu (°jwúnbèihǎu, °shŏushrhǎu).

Get rid of a person 'dwŏkāi, bǎ . . . 'shwǎikāi, bǎ . . . 'dyōusya, bǎ . . . 'dǎ-fādzŏu; (kill) bǎ . . . 'néngsz. / How can we get rid of him? (in what way) Wŏmen néng dzĕmma syangfár °'dwŏkai ta (°bǎ tā 'dyōusya, °bǎ tā dǎfā'dzŏu, °'nùngsz)?

GET

Get rid of a thing (sell) mài, chūshǒu; (throw away) rēng; (give away) sùngrén. /I got rid of my car while prices were high. Chèn 'jyàchyán 'gāu deshŕhou wǒ bǎ 'chē °'màile (°chū'shǒule). /He got rid of all his old books. Tā bǎ tāde jyòu'shū dōu °'màile (°'rēngle, °sùng'rénle).

Get rid of a disease. /I can't get rid of this cold. is expressed as This cold doesn't get better. Jèitsz shāng'fēng °lǎu bù'hǎu (°lǎu 'hǎubulyǎu, °lǎu 'jŕbu'hǎu, °'shāngchǐlai méi'tóur le).

3. Get plus a noun followed by a preposition or adjective or adverb; often constructions with bǎ, jyàu, or ràng.

Get something wet, dirty, etc. bǎ . . . nùng plus an appropriate resultative ending. /I don't want to get my feet wet. Wǒ pà bǎ 'jyǎu nùng'shŕle. /I got my dress dirty. Wó bǎ 'yīfu nùng'dzāngle.

Get something across. /I was finally able to get the meaning across. Dàu'dǐ wǒ bǎ nèige 'hwàr °ràng tāmen tǐng 'míng baile (°'tóugwochyule).

Get someone down. (intentionally or unintentionally, pleasantly or unpleasantly) Tā 'jyàu wo 'shǒubulyǎu. or (intentionally) Kě 'jyàu ta bǎ wo mwó'hwàile.

Get something going. /He'll be able to get the work going. 'Tā néng °jyàu (°ràng) jèige 'gūngdzwò 'jìnsyíngde hěn 'shwùnli. or 'Tā néng bǎ jèige 'shèr 'bànde shwùn'shǒu le.

Get something in. /Get the report in tomorrow. 'Míngtyan bǎ bàu'gàu 'jyāujìnchyu. /Please get the clothes in before it rains. 'Chènje 'yǔ hái méi'syà bǎ (lyàngde) 'yīfu °nájìnlai (°'shōujìnlai, °'lyǎnjìnlai) ba.

Get something in(to). /Get this into your head! (listen well) Hǎu'hǎurde 'tīngje! or Yùng'syīn 'tīngje! or Nǐ 'dǔng bu'dǔng a? or Nǐ 'byé dzài 'húdújele! (remember well) Nǐ hǎu'hǎurde 'jìje. /Do you expect to get all these things in(to) your suitcase? Nǐ syǎng bǎ 'nèmma syē dūngsyi 'dōu °'fàngjìn (°'gējin, °'sāijin) nǐde shǒutí'syāngli chyù ma?

Get something off. /I can't get my shoe off. Wǒ 'syé 'twōbusyà'láile.

Get something open. /I can't get this drawer open. Jèige 'chōutì wǒ °kāibu'kāi (°dǎbu'kāi, °néngbu'kāi, °nùngbu'kāi, °'lābuchū'lái, °'lābu'dùng).

Get something out (of). /Get that thing out of the house! Bǎ 'nèige dūngsyi °'rēngchuchyu (°'nùngchuchyu, °'néngchúchyu)! /Get that dog out of the house! Bǎ nèige 'gǒu °'hūngchúchyu (°'gǎnchuchyu, °dǎchuchyu, °'jyàuchuchyu)! /He tried to say the man's name, but couldn't get the words out before he died. Tā 'jyélì yàu 'shwōchu 'nèige rénde 'míngdz lai, kěshr 'méinéng 'shwōchulai jyòu dwànle 'chìle.

Get a point or message over. /I finally got the point over. Wǒ 'dàu'lyáur ràng °ta (°tāmen) 'míngbàile.

Get something there or here. /You can get a letter there by Monday. is expressed as A letter you mail today will get there Monday. Syìn nǐ 'jyēr fā, syīngchī'yī °nénggòu 'dàu nèr (°jyòu 'dàu nèr le). /Can you get the pictures here by next week? 'Jèisye jàupyàn nǐ 'néng bu néng dzài 'syàsyīngchī sùnglai?

Get things or people together. /We'll get all the papers together before the meeting. Kāi'hwèi yǐ'chyán wǒmen děi bǎ 'wénjyàn 'shōudau yí'kwàr. /Can you get everybody together for a meeting? Nǐ kéyi bukéyi bǎ dàjyā 'jyùdzai yíkwàr kāi ge 'hwèi?

4. Get plus a preposition or an adverb.

Get along. /How are you getting along? 'Jìnlai 'dzěmyàng? /Oh, he gets along.

583

Tā a, 'hái 'gwòdechyù. /I'll get along somehow. (manage to survive) Wǒ 'dzǔng néng (yǒu'fár) 'gwòdechyù. or (in work) Wǒ 'dzǔng hwèi yǒu'fár 'bànde. /He's getting along in years. Tā 'lǎu le. or Tā shàng 'nyánjì le. /It's late; I'd better be getting along. Bù'dzǎule, wǒ děi 'dzǒu le. /Those two don't get along. Tāmen °'lyǎ (°'lyǎnggerén) °'yǐjyàn bù'hé (°'bù'hé, °'hébulái, °'shwōbudàu yí'kwàr). /I get along with him very well. Wǒ gēn tā °'hěn héde'lái (°'hwùnde tǐng bú'tswōde).

Get anywhere, get somewhere. /We're not getting anywhere doing the work this way. 'Dzèmma ge bànfa °'bànbu'tūng (°'bái fèi'jìn).

Get around (of a person). /He gets around a lot. (is very active) Tā hěn 'hwódùng. or Tā 'gèchùr 'pǎu. or (in order to get ahead) Tā °'bēndzǒude (°'dzwānyíngde) 'lìhai. /Get around a bit; don't just sit at home and complain about everything. 'Gèchùr 'dzǒudzou; 'byé jìng 'dzwòdzài 'jyāli °'hāishēngtàn'chǐde (°'bàuywàn'jèige'bàuywàn'nèigede). /For an old man, he gets around very well. Tā 'nèmmadà'swèishùr le, 'twèijyàur °jēn 'líng (°hái swàn hěn 'líng, °jēn 'yìnglang). /He'll be able to get around in no time at all. Jì'tyār tā jyòu néng gēn 'hàurén yíyàngde °'dzǒu a 'pǎude le (or (especially of a child) °'tyàu a 'bèngde le). /Oh, I get around! is expressed as I hear things. Hà! Wǒ 'syāusyi 'língtūng. or as I've had experience. Hà! 'Wǒ shr̄ 'gwòlairén. or 'Wǒ dzǒude'dìfangr kě 'dwōle. or 'Wǒ chr̄le 'dwōshauwǎn'fànle ne. /He gets around. Tāshr yǒu 'jīngyànde. or Tā 'fùyǒu 'jīngyàn. or Tā jyàngwo °'shr̄myàn (°'chǎngmyàn). or Tā 'shémma méi'jyàngwo? or Tā shr 'dzǒubyàn'jyànghúde rén. or Tā 'syāusyi 'líng.

Get around (of a story). /The story will get around in a little while. 'Nèige shr̄ching yǐ'hwěr jyòu hwèi °chwán'byànle (°'chwánde 'shéi dōu 'jr̄daule, °chwánchūchyule). /The story got around that he was an enemy agent. 'Yǒurén shwō tā shr̄ ge 'dírénde 'jyāndyé.

Get around plus a noun. /That girl certainly gets around him. Nèige 'nyǔháidz jēn náde'jù ta. /Can you get around that regulation (in this case)? 'Jèijyàn shèr (jàu 'gwēijyu shr̄ bù'syíngde, búgwò) néng °'tūngrung (°'tūngrung bàn'lǐ, °'tūngrungdegwǒ'chyù) ma? /Can you get around it for me? Láujyà gěi °'tūngrungtūngrung, syíng ma (°'tūngrung yísyàr, 'syíng ma, °'tūngrung bàn'lǐ, syíng ma)?

Get at. /I can't get at my luggage. (can't reach it) Wǒ 'gòubujáu wǒde 'syíngli. or Wǒ 'syíngli nábu'dàu. /Our fortifications were so strong that the enemy couldn't get at us. Wǒmen 'fángyùde hěn 'jyāngù, 'dírén 'dǎbudàu wǒmen 'jèrlai. /Someday I'll get at the real reason. Wǒ 'dzǔng yǒu 'nèmma yìtyān bǎ jèige nèng(de) °'míngbaile (°'míngmíngbai'báide, °'chǐngchule, °'chǐngchǐngchu'chǔde).

Get away. /I'd like to go, but I'm afraid I can't get away. Wǒ °'ywànyi (°'syīnli syǎng) 'dzǒu, 'búgwò kǔng'pà °dzǒubù'lyǎu (°dzǒubù'kāi). /We chased him for two blocks, but he got away. Wǒmen 'jwēile ta 'lyǎngtyáu'jyē (nèmma'ywǎn), kěshr tā °'háishr 'pǎule (°'pǎude méi yǐngr le). /I want to get away from this place. Wǒ yàu °'dwǒkāi (°'líkāi) jèige 'dìfang.

Get away with. /He gets away with murder. Tā (jyòushr) 'shāle 'rén yě méi'shèr. /I'm sure I can get away with it. Wǒ 'jwǔn jr̄dàu wǒ °'búhwèi chū shémma 'wèntí de (°méi'shèr, °'bújr̄yu chū'shr̄).

Get back (return) hwéi(lai); (retrieve) 'náhwéilai. /When did you get back? Nǐ 'shémma shŕhou 'hwéilaide? /Did you get your umbrella back? Nǐde yǔ'sǎn 'náhwéilaile ma? /Let's get back to the dormitory. Dzámen 'hwéi sù'shè ba. /Let's get back home. Dzámen hwéi'jyā ba. /Let's get back to town. Dzámen hwéidàu chéng'lǐ chyù ba. /Let's get back to the original question. Dzámen háishr 'hwéidàu běn'tíshang lái ba.

Get back at. /How can I get back at him? Wǒ yǒu 'shémma fǎr yě gěi 'tā lái yí'syàdz ne? or (more seriously) Wǒ yǒu 'shémma fǎr 'bàufù yísyàr ne?

Get by (pass) gwòchyu (may be preceded by a verb such as lyōu sneak). /Can I get by the guard? Kān'mérde néng ràng wo 'gwòchyu ma? *or* (slip by) Kān'mérde nàr wǒ néng 'tōuje 'lyōugwòchyu ma? /Let me get by. Ràng wo 'gwòchyu.

Get by (get along). /I'll get by if I have a place to sleep. Wǒ 'yǒu ge dìfang 'shwèi, jyòu °'chéng (°'syíng). /Do you think I can get by with it? Nǐ shwō wǒ °'léng (°'yǐng, °'jyòu) nèmje °syíng busyíng (°gwòdechyù ma)?

Get in (to a place) jìn. /What time did you get in last night? Dzwór 'wǎnshang nǐ 'jǐshŕ °'jìnlaide (°'jìnchyude)? /How did he get in? 'Tā dzěmma °'jìnlaide (°'jìnchyude)? /What time does the train get in? Hwǒchē 'shémma shŕhou jìn'jàn?

Get in (be elected) sywǎnshangle. /Did your candidate get in? 'Nǐ yàu jyǔde 'hòusywǎnrén 'sywǎnshangle ma?

Get into something. /Get into the house! 'Jìnchyu. *or* Dàu 'wūli chyù. *but* /He got into the car. Tā shàng'chē le.

Get into (of clothes) chwān. /It will take me only a minute to get into my bathing suit. 'Yóuyǔng'yī wǒ yì'hwěrde gūngfu jyòu kéyi 'chwānshangle.

Get off. /Get off the grass. is expressed as Don't step on the grass. 'Byé tsǎi tsǎu'dì. /I want to get off at the next stop. Wǒ 'syàyíjàn 'syàchyu. /Get off your high horse! 'Byé nèmma 'shénchi le. *or* Byé 'chwēi le. *or* Byé chòu'měi le. Byé 'jwǎi le. *or* Byé jwǎng'swàn le. /He got off to a flying start. Tā chǐ'tóur 'chǐde hěn °'kwài (°'málì). *or* (in working) Tā dùng'shǒu jyòu 'gànchilaile. *or* (in running) Tā sā'twěi jyòu 'pǎu. /He got off with very light punishment. Tā 'fáde hěn 'chīng, 'jēnshŕ 'pyányi tale.

Get on (mount) shàng. /Don't get on the train yet. Syān byé shàng'chē ba.

Get on (of time). /It's getting on toward twelve o'clock. 'Kwài shŕ'èrdyǎn le.

Get on one's nerves. /That whistling gets on my nerves. Nèmma chwēi'shàur jyàu wǒ ('syīnli) 'fándehwang.

Get out (publish). /They are getting out a new book on the subject. Tāmen yàu chū yìběr jyǎng 'jèigede 'syīn'shū.

Get out (of) usually expressed with chū; (of a vehicle) syà. /Get out of this house! (impolite) (Gěi wǒ) °'gwǔnchūchyu (°'chūchyu)! *or* (urgent, as in case of fire) Kwài 'chūchyu! /We mustn't let this news get out. Dzámen kě 'bùnéng bǎ jèige °'chwánchūchyu (°'jyàurén 'jŕdàule, °'syēlòule). /How did you ever get out of it? (escape) Nǐ 'dzěmma °'táu(°'pǎu)chūlaide? *or* (avoid doing something) Nǐ 'dzěmma 'dwǒkāide? /Three men got out of the car. Sānge rén syà le che le.

Get meaning **out of.** /What did you get out of his lecture? Nǐ 'tīng tā yǎn'jyǎng yǐ'hòu °yǒu shémma syīn'dé (°'déjau shémma le ma)?

Get profit **out of.** /What do I get out of it? Yú 'wǒ yǒu shémma °'hǎuchu (°'yíchu) ne? /How much did you get out of the deal? (money) 'Nèiyísyàr nǐ °'jwànle (°'lāule) 'dwōshǎu? *or* (advantage) 'Déjau shémma 'hǎuchu le?

Get over. /I got over my cold quickly. Wǒ 'jèitsz shāng'fēng hǎude hěn 'kwài. /You feel badly now, but you'll get over it. Mù'chyán yǒu dyǎr nán'shòu, 'gwò syē 'shŕ jyòu 'hǎu le. /I can never get over it (forget it). Wǒ 'yǔngywǎn bùnéng 'wàngde. /She got over it in a short while. Tā 'gwòle hwěr jyòu °'hǎu le (°'bùněmmaje le, °'wàngle, °yě jyòu 'swànle). /How did you get over that difficulty? ('Nèmma nánde shŕ) Nǐ shŕ dzěmma °'bànde (°'lyǎude) ne? *or* 'Nèmmayàngde 'nángwān nǐ dzěmma 'gwòlaide ne?

Get to a place dàu; **get there** dàu nèr. /We have to get to the station by five o'clock. Wǒ děi 'wúdyǎn jūng dàu chējàn. /I'll get there in an hour. Wǒ dzài yì-'syǎushŕ yǐ'nèi 'dàu nèr.

585

Get together. / Let's get together at my house tonight. Jyēr 'wǎnshang dzài wǒ 'jyāli 'jyùhweijyùhwei. / They never seem to get together on anything. Tāmen hǎu-'syàng shémma 'shř yě °nùng(°shwō, °gǎu)bu'dàu yí'kwàr.

Get up. / I get up at seven every morning. Wǒ 'měityān 'dzǎuchen 'chīdyǎnjūng 'chǐlai. / Get up from that chair! 'Jànchǐlai! / They're getting up a party. Tāmen 'jěngdzài °'yùbeije (°'shānglyangje, °'dǎswànje) chǐng (yǐ)hwéi'kè.

GIFT. 'lǐ(wù) (somewhat formal); or expressed with verbs such as sùng send, gěi give.
/ This is a gift (from someone to me). Jèi shr 'rénjyā °'sùnggei wo de 'lǐ(wù) (°sùnggei (or 'sùng or 'gěi) wo de). / This is a gift from him (to me). Jèi shr tā 'sùnggei wo de 'lǐ(wù). (or alternates as above). / This is a (little) gift for you (from me). Jèi shr °'sùnggei (°'gěi, °'sùng) ni de ('yìdyǎr 'dūngsyi). or 'Jèi dyǎr dūng-syi shř °'sùnggei (°etc.) ni de. or 'Jèi shr yìdyǎr 'syáu'yìsz (a small token). / Here is a gift for you (from someone else). Jèr yǒu géi 'nǐ de 'lǐwù. or Jèr yǒu dyǎr 'dūngsyi, shř gěi 'nǐ de. etc. / We must send them some sort of gift. Yí'dìng děi 'sùng tāmen dyǎr °'lǐ(wù) (°shémma, °'dūngsyi) tsái 'hǎu. / Whose gift is that? (to whom) 'Nèi shr gěi 'shéi de? or (from whom) 'Nèi shr 'shéi °'gěide (°sùngde)? / Thank you for your Christmas gift. 'Syèsye nín 'Shèngdàn'jyéde 'lǐwù. or 'Syèsye nín a! Shèngdàn'jyé °'jyàu nín fèi'syīn le (°nín hái 'sùng dūngsyi). / That's a free gift. 'Nèi shr bái'gěi de. / I wouldn't have it even as a gift. °Bái'gěi (°Bái'sùng) wǒ yě bú'yàu.

(Talent) 'tyāntsái; be gifted tyānshēng, tyānfù. / He has a gift for drawing. Tā yǒu hwà'hwàrde 'tyāntsái. or Tā tyān'shēngde hwèi hwà'hwàr. / She's very gifted musically. Tā yǒu 'yīnywède 'tyāntsái. / To be able to sing like that is a gift. 'Chàngde 'nèmma hǎu 'jēnshr °'tyāntsái (°tyān 'shēngde, °tyān'fùde).

GIRL. nyǔháidz; nyǔ in other combinations; syáujye, gūnyang (both mean especially young lady). / The new baby is a girl. 'Syīnshēngde syàu'hár shr °'nyǔde (°ge 'syáujye, °ge 'gūnyang). / It's a girl again. 'Yòu shr ge °'nyǔde (°'gūnyang, °'syáu-jye). / Are there any pretty girls in town? Chéng 'lǐtou 'yǒu méiyou 'pyàulyangde °nyǔ'háidz (°'syáujye, °'gūnyang)? / She's quite a girl. (complimentary or insulting) Hǎu('lǐhaide)yíwèi °'syáujye (°'gūnyang) le. or 'Nèiwèi °'syáujye (°'gūnyang) a °'jēn shr ('lìhai) (°jēn 'lyàubude). / I just got a letter from my girl (friend). Wǒ 'gāng jyédàu wǒ nyǔ'péngyou yǐfēng'syīn. / We pay our (hired) girl fifty dollars a month. Wǒmende °nyǔ'yùngrén (°nyǔ'dǐsyarén, or, if older °lǎu'mǎr) 'měiywè 'wǔshŕkwài chyán. / Jimmy certainly made a hit with the girls here. Lǎu'jāng jyàu jèrde °nyǔ'háidz (°'nyǔrén) dōu 'syǐhwan ta. / Well, girls, it's time to go. (including both married and unmarried women) 'Hēi! 'Tàitai'syáujyemen, dàu 'shŕhour le, gāi 'dzǒule. or (unmarried women only) 'Syáujyemen, gāi 'dzǒu le.

GIVE (GAVE, GIVEN). 1. (Transfer, present; general term) gěi. / This watch was given to me by my mother. Jèige 'byǎu shr wǒ 'mǔchin gěi wǒ de. / Who gave you this? Jèi shr 'shéi gěi nǐ de? / Was this given to you by someone I know? Gěi nǐ 'jèige de rén wǒ 'rènde ma? / Give him a dollar. 'Gěi tā yíkwài 'chyán. / I'll give you five dollars for it. 'Nèige dūngsyi wǒ gěi nǐ 'wǔkwai chyán. / They gave him a very large room. Tāmen gěi tā yǐjyān 'hǎudàde 'wūdz. / They gave him a job. Tāmen 'gěile tā ge 'shèr dzwò. / Give him a letter of introduction. Gěi tā yìfēng jyèshàu-syìn.

With the thing given expressed by a verb in Chinese, gěi is followed by the person to whom it is given or for whom it is done. / They gave him a raise. Tāmen gěi tā jyā 'chyán le. / They gave him a raise of $50. Tāmen gěi tā jyāle 'wǔshŕkwai chyán. / We're planning to give him a farewell party. Wǒmen syǎng chǐng'kè, gěi tā jyàn'syíng. / They gave him a birthday party. Tāmen gěi tā gwò 'shēngr. / Give him an injection. Gěi tā dǎ yìjēn. / Give him a promotion. Gěi tā 'shēng yí'jí. / Give him a recommendation (verbal). Gěi tā shwō jyù hǎu'hwà. / Give him some help. (Gěitā) Bāngbang 'máng.

(Hand over, to someone present) 'dǐgěi; (to someone absent) 'jyāugěi. / Please give me the letter. Láu'jyà bǎ 'syìn 'dǐgěi wǒ. (But, when referring to something that was to be brought, Chinese usually asks, more politely, Did you bring it with you? Nèifēng 'syìn nǐ 'dàiláile ma?) / Give this letter to him and be sure to get a receipt. Bǎ jèifēng 'syìn jyāugěi tā; yí'dìng yàu ge shōu'tyáur.

Give someone a disease 'chwángěi. / I don't want to give you my cold. Wǒ shāng'fēng le, kě byé 'chwángěi nǐ.

Give a present sùng, gěi, 'sùnggěi. See also **GIFT**. / This watch was given to me by my friends. Jèige 'byǎu shr̀ wǒ 'péngyou °sùng (°gěi, °sùnggěi) wǒ de. / What did he give you for your birthday? Nǐ 'shēngr̀ tā °'sùng (°'gěi, °'sùnggěi) nǐ shémma le?

Give a name chǐ. / The baby hasn't been given a name yet. Syǎu'hár hái 'méi- (gěi)chǐ 'míngdz ne. / They gave him a nickname. Tāmen gěi tā 'chǐle ge wài'hàur.

2. (Cause, allow) usually jyàu; (of trouble) jǎu, tyān; occasionally expressed indirectly. / Too much noise gives me a headache. is expressed as Too much noise causes my head to ache. 'Chǎude tài 'lìhai le jyàu wǒ 'tóuténg. / The heat gave me a headache. 'Rède (jyàu) wǒ 'tóuténg. / Tell him the story; it ought to give him a laugh. Bǎ nèige 'syàuhwàr 'gàusu ta; yí'dìng hwèi jyàu tā 'dàsyàude. / It's guaranteed to give you satisfaction. 'Jwǔnbǎu jyàu nǐ mǎn'yì. / They give you your money's worth at this restaurant. is expressed as What they give you makes you feel it's worth it. 'Jèige gwǎndz gěide'dūngsyi jyàunǐ 'jywéje °gòu'běr (°hěn shr̀hwèi, °méi'báihwā 'chyán). or as The service they give you . . . . 'Jèige gwǎndz 'tszhoude jyàu nǐ . . . . / Don't give the child too much freedom, or you'll spoil her. 'Byé jyàu syǎu'hár tài swéi'byàn le, hwèi gwàn'hwài le. or Syǎu'hár yàu yàu 'gwǎnje dyàr, 'bùrán hwèi gwàn'hwàile de. / Give him a taste of it, and he'll demand it all the time. Jyàutā yí'chángjau 'tyán tóur, tā jyòu 'yàuchilai méi'wán le. / Give him an inch, and he'll take a mile. or Give him a finger, and he'll take the whole hand. is expressed as If he gets an inch he'll advance a foot. Tā dé'tswǔnjìn'chř. / He gave us no end of trouble. Tā gěi wǒmen °'jǎule (°'tyānle) bù'shǎude 'máfan.

3. When followed by a noun in many cases is expressed in Chinese by a verb which has the meaning **give** only in certain contexts, or which is equivalent to the entire English phrase. When gěi is included in these cases, it can usually be translated by to or for. Some indirect expressions are also used.

(Contribute to charity) shě, 'shr̀shě. / They gave many things to the poor. Tāmen ('shr̀)shěle hěn dwō 'dūngsyi gěi 'chyúngrén. / They gave a good deal of money to the (Buddhist) monastery. Tāmen gěi 'myàuli (shr̀)shěle bù'shǎude 'chyán.

Give a speech jyǎng, yǎnjyǎng. / Who's giving the main speech? Shr̀ 'shéi jǔ- 'jyǎng ne?

Give information (tell, say) gàusung, gàusu, shwō. / They gave me the wrong information. Tāmen 'gàusung wǒ °de bù'dwèi (°'gàusu'tswòle). / He gave me the wrong time. Tā °'gàusu wǒ (°'shwō) de nèige 'shŕhou bú'dwèi. / Sorry, I gave you the wrong directions. 'Dwèibuchǐ, wǒ °'shwōde bú'dwèi (°shwō'tswòle, or (the wrong direction of the compass) °shwō de 'fāngsyang bú'dwèi, °shwōde 'fāngsyang 'tswò le). / Did he give a reason? Tā shwōle ge 'lǐyóu méiyou? or is expressed as Did he explain? Tā 'jyěshrle ma? but / Can you give me the time, please? is expressed as What time is it, please? °Láu'jyà (°Jyè'gwāng). °'Shémma shŕhou le (°Jǐ'dyǎn le)?

Give mileage. / This gas will give you 15 miles to the gallon. is expressed as If you use this gas, you can go 15 miles on a gallon. Yùng 'jèijǔng chǐ'yóu yǐ'jyālwǔn keyi dzǒu shŕ'wǔ yǐnglǐ.

Give a hand (gěi . . .) 'bāngbang 'máng, bāng. / Give me a hand, will you? (Gěi wǒ) 'bāngbang 'máng, syíng ma? or Bāng wǒ yísyàr, 'syíng ma? or 'Bāng wǒ yìbǎ 'shǒur, syíng ma?

Give a light. / Will you give me a light? (Do you have a match?) Yǒu yáng'hwǒ ma? or (May I borrow a match?) Jyè gēn yáng'hwǒr syíng ma? or (May I use a bit of fire?) Jyè dyǎr 'hwǒr shŕshr syíng ma?

Give a performance (shàngyǎn; (go on stage) dēngtái. / The first performance will be given Tuesday. Tāmen syīngchī'èr dì'yítsž °shàng'yǎn (°dēng'tái).

Give a scream °hǎn (°jyàu) yìshēng. / She gave a loud scream. Tā °'dàhǎnle (°'dàjyàule) yì'shēng.

Give heat nwǎnhwo (be warm). / The fireplace gives a lot of heat. 'Jèige lúdz hěn 'nwǎnhwo.

Give one or someone **an idea.** / What gave you that idea? is expressed as How did you think of that? Nǐ dzěmma 'syǎngdàude 'nèmma ge 'fár? or as Where does that kind of talk come from? 'Nǎr láide 'nèmmayàngde hwà? or as It wasn't so! (No such thing) 'Méi nèmmahwéi'shèr! / What you just said gives me an idea. Nǐ 'nèmma yì'shwō jyàu wǒ 'syǎngchū ge 'fár lai.

Give one's time 'yúnchū 'gūngfu. / We've come to ask you to give a part of your time to a good cause. Yǒu yíjyàn syíng 'hǎude shr̀; wǒmen lái chyóu nín 'yúnchu dyǎr 'gūngfu lai 'bāngbang 'máng.

Give orders gwǎnrén, jŕshr rén (both mean order people around); syà mìngling. / He likes to give orders, but doesn't enjoy following them. Tā ài °gwǎn rén (°'jŕshr 'rén), búài 'shòu rén °'gwǎn (°'jŕshǐ). or Tā ài syà 'mìngling, kěshr 'dzìjǐ bùkěn jàu'bàn.

Give permission jwǔn. / He gave me permission to go. Tā jwǔn wǒ 'dzǒu de. / I was given permission to stay until midnight. Wǒ chǐng'jwǔnle, kěyi 'dāidàu bàn-'yè.

Give service. / This clock has given good service. (has stood use) 'Jèige jūng hěn jīn'yùng. or (has been used many years) 'Jèige jūng yùngle 'hǎusyē nyán le. / He has given the best years of his life to that job. Tā 'bànbèidzde 'jīnglì 'dōu yùng-dzài 'nèijyàn 'shr̀shang le. / My old coat still gives me good service. Wǒ nèijyàn 'jyòu dàyī hái néng 'chwān ne.

Give a damn. / I don't give a damn. Wǒ tsái bú'dzàihu ne. / Who gives a damn? 'Shéi dzàihu?

4. Combinations of **give** and a preposition, and a few other fixed phrases.

Give away. / That old coat was given away long ago. (See 1 above.) Nèige 'jyòu dàyī 'dzǎu °gěile (°sùnggěile) 'rén le. / Who gave away the bride? is expressed as Who acted as head of the bride's family? Jyè'hwūn de shr̀hou dzwò syīn'nyángdzde jyā'jǎng de shr̀ 'shéi? / Don't give away my secret. 'Jèidyǎr('mìmi) byé gěi wǒ °'shwōchuchyu (°'ràngrang'chuchyu). or 'Byé géi wǒ 'syèle 'dǐ.

Give back 'hwán(gěi). / Please give me back my pen. Láu'jyà bǎ 'bǐ hwán wǒ. / I'll give it back to you in an hour. Wǒ 'yìdyǎnjūng yǐ'nèi jyòu 'hwán nǐ. / When he gave it back to me, it was in even better shape than when I lent it to him. 'Jèige tā 'hwánlai de shr̀hou, bǐ 'jyèchyu de shr̀hou hái 'jěngchí.

Give birth to shēng, dé. / She gave birth to a baby boy. Tā °shēngle (°déle) ge

'nánháidz. /The results of the experiment gave birth to a new idea. Tsúng 'shr̄yàn
de 'jyēgwǒ °shēngchu yìjǔng 'syīn jyànjyě lai (°'dédàu yìjǔng 'syīn fāngfa).

Give in (admit failure) rènshū. /After a long argument I finally gave in. 'Byàn-
lwùnle bàn'tyān wǒ 'jyēgwǒ rèn'shūle.

Give off is expressed indirectly or by chū, fāchulai, or yǒu. /This flower
gives off a strange odor. is expressed as The odor of this flower is strange. Jèijǔng
'hwār de wèr hěn 'tèbyé. or 'Jèijǔng 'hwār °yǒu (°'chū) yìjǔng gwài'wèr. or
'Jèijǔng 'hwār 'fāchu yìjǔng gwài'wèr lai.

Give out (issue) fā; (distribute) sàn. /Who gave out the tickets? 'Shéi gwǎn
fā mén'pyàu láije? or 'Shéi °fāde (°sànde) mén'pyàu? /News of the battle casualties
won't be given out for several days. 'Gwānbīng 'sz̄shāng 'míngtsè děi 'gwò jǐtyān
tsái 'fābyàu ne.

Give out (be all gone) méiyǒule. /My supply of ink is giving out. Wǒde mwò-
shwér kwài méi'yǒule.

Give out (fail in operation) bùchéngle, bùsyíngle, bùjūngyùng le. /His heart
gave out. Tāde 'syīndzàng °bù'chéng le (°bùjūng'yùng le, °bù'syíng le).

Give up (stop trying). /I tried hard, but I had to give up. Wǒ 'dzěmma nùng
yě bù'chéng, 'jr̄hǎu fàng'shǒu le. /Finally we gave up trying. 'Jyēgwǒ wǒmen
°jyòu budzài 'nùngle (°'rèn le, °rèn'shū le, or (knew there was no way) °'jr̄dau
méi'fárle, or (let go) °jyòu fàng'shǒu le).

Give up something jyāuchulai. /They had to give up the stolen goods. Tāmen
méi'fár, jr̄hǎu bǎ dzāng 'jyāuchulai. but /Our maid gave up her job. Wǒmende
nyúgūngrén °'dzǒule (°bú'gànle, °tsź'shr̄le, °chǐngchǎng'jyà le). /He was so ill the
doctor gave up hope for him. is expressed as He was so terribly ill that the doctor
said there was no cure. Tā bìngde 'jēn lìhai dàifu 'dōu shwō °meifár 'jr̄le (°méiyǒu
jyòu le).

Give up a person. /After their quarrel she gave him up. (brushed him off)
Tāmen 'chǎule yíjèn 'dzwèi yǐhòu, nèige 'nyúrén jyòu °'shwāle tā le (or (flung him
away) °'shwāile tā le, °bǎ ta 'shwāle, °bǎ ta 'shwāile). /When he was half starved,
he gave himself up. (to the police) Tā 'ède méi'fár le jyòu °dz̀'shǒu le (or (to the
enemy) °tóu'syángle, or (to fate) °'jr̄hǎu děng 'sž le).

Give way (break down, fail). /The bridge gave way. (couldn't stand the strain)
Chyáu jīnbu'jùle. or (broke down) Chyáu 'hwàile. or (collapsed) Chyáu 'tā le. or
(broke into two or more parts) Chyáu °'shéle (°'dwànle). or (fell on one side) Chyáu
'dǎule. or (leaned to one side without falling) Chyáu 'wāile. /Be careful; that step
might give (way) under your weight. Lyóu dyǎr shén; nèige tīdz yěsyǔ jīnbu'jù ne.

Give way (get out of the way; retreat) wàng hòu 'twèi; (step back) 'ràngkai.
/The crowd gave way. Nèichyún 'rén °wàng hòu 'twèile (°'ràngkaile).

Give. /The elastic has a lot of give. Jèige 'sūngjǐn'dǎr 'jǐndejù 'chēn.

Give-and-take. /It was a matter of give-and-take. (a fair exchange) Nèi shr̄
'gūngpíng jyāu'yì. or (no one got the worst of it) 'Shéi yě méichr̄'kwēi. /Marriage
is a matter of give-and-take. 'Fūfu jr̄'jyān děi néng 'rúngrèn.

GIVEN. See **GIVE** except for the following uses of **given** not common to **give.**

(Certain) yí'dìngde, dìng'hǎule de, shwō'hǎule de. /I have to finish this in a
given time. Wǒ děi dzài °yí'dìngde (°dìng'hǎule de, °shwō'hǎule de) 'shr̄jyānlǐ bǎ
'jèige dzwò'wánle.

(Supposing; under) dzài . . . jr̄'syà. /Given such a situation, what else could I do? Dzài 'jèiyàngr 'chíngsyǐng jr̄'syà, wǒ hái néng yǒu 'byéde 'bànfǎ ma?

(In the habit of) 'chángcháng . . . . /He's given to making rash statements. Tā shwō'hwà 'chángcháng shwōde tài °'lǔmǎng (°'mǎngjwàng). *or* Tā shwō'hwà chángcháng °bùlyóu'shén (°bù'syǎusyǐn). *or* Tā chángcháng 'bùgwǎn 'sānchiēr̄shr̄'yǐde jyou 'shwōchulaile.

Be given to understand. /I was given to understand that I'd get a raise in a month. is expressed as From what I heard there was the understanding that I'd get a raise in a month. Wǒ 'tīnglai de 'hwàrli yǒu 'yíge ywè yǐ'nèi yàu gěi wǒ jyā'chyán nèmma yǐ'shwō.

Given name míngdz. /What is his given name? Tā 'míngdz jyàu 'shémma?

GLAD. gāusyǐng; but when **glad** in English is primarily for politeness Chinese usually has some other polite expression. /I'm glad to hear you're better. Wǒ 'tīngshwo nǐ jyàn 'hǎu le hěn gāu'syǐng. /I sensed that they were not glad to see you. Wǒ jywéje tāmen jyàn nǐ de 'shŕhou 'búdà gāu'syǐng. /I'm glad to see you. 'Syìng'hwèi, syìng-'hwèi! /Gee, am I glad to see you! 'Āi'yà! Nǐ 'láide 'jēn 'hǎu. /I'm very glad to meet you. 'Jyǒuyǎng, jyǒu'yǎng. /I'm glad you warned me. 'Dwōsyè nǐ 'jřjyàu. *or* 'Dwōsyè nǐ 'gàusu wǒ.

GLASS. (A substance) bwōli. /I cut my hand on a piece of glass. Wǒ jyàu 'bwōli °bǎ 'shǒu 'lále (°lále 'shǒu le). /I cut myself on a piece of glass. (in answer to How did you cut yourself?) Wǒ dz̀'gěr ná 'bwōli 'láde. *or* (in answer to What happened?) Wǒ dz̀'gěr bù'syǎusyǐn, jyàu 'bwōli 'lále. /Be careful of the pieces of broken glass on the floor. Lyóu'shén, 'dìshang yǒu °bwōli 'chádz (°'shèibwōli ('chádz)). /The library keeps his manuscripts under glass. (in a glass case) Túshū'gwǎn bǎ tāde shǒu'gǎur °bǎutswundzài bwōli'gwèili (*or* (covered with glass) °yùng 'bwōli(jàur) jàuje). /These roses were grown under glass. Jèisyē 'méigwèihwār dōu shr̄ yùng bwōli'jàuje jǎngde. /That's made of glass. Nèi shr̄ 'bwōli dzwòde. /I bought a glass vase. Wǒ mǎile yíge °bwōli 'hwāpyéngr (°'bwōli (dzwò)de 'hwāpyéngr).

Drinking glass (the object) bwōlibēi; (a measure) bēi. /I knocked a glass off the table. Wǒ bǎ yíge 'bwōli'bēi tsúng 'jwōrshang 'pèngsyàchyule. /May I have a glass of water? Láu'jyà gěi wǒ yìbēi 'shwěi.

Eyeglasses yǎnjyèngr, yǎnjìngdz. /I wear glasses only for reading. °Wǒ kàn-'dzèrde (°Wǒ kàn'shūde) shŕhou tsái dài °yǎn'jyèngr (°yǎn'jìngdz).

Field glasses wàngywǎn jìng. /I want to buy a pair of field glasses. Wǒ yàu mǎi yíjyà 'wàngywǎn'jìng.

Looking glass jìngdz.

GLORIOUS. (Illustrious) 'gwāngrúng(de). /Our country has a glorious history. Wǒmen-de 'gwójyā yǒu yíge hěn 'gwāngrúngde 'lìshř.

(Beautiful) 'měilì; (colorful) 'tsǎnlàn; (of weather) hǎu. /The leaves have glorious colors at this time of year. 'Nyánnyan jèi shŕhou shù'yèdzde 'yánshar jēn °'měilì (°'tsǎnlàn). /This is certainly a glorious day. 'Jīntyan 'tyānchi jēn 'hǎu.

GO (WENT, GONE). 1) Denoting simple motion, without indication of direction, destination, or purpose, dzǒu (means walk when used with other verbs); dùngshēn (to get a move on); líkai (leave a place). /Let's go. Dzámen 'dzǒu ba. *or* Dōu 'dzǒu a。 /It's time to go. Gāi 'dzǒu le. *or* Gāi 'dzǒuje le. *or* Dàule gāi 'dzǒude shŕhou le. *or* Dzámen gāi dùng'shēn le. *or* Dzámen gāi 'líkai jèr le. /When did he go? Tā shémma shŕhou °'dzǒude (°dùngde 'shēn, °'líkaide)? /He's gone. Tā 'yǐjīng 'dzǒule. /There goes the man we've been talking about. Nàr 'dzǒuje de 'nèige 'rén 'jyòushr dzámen gāngtsái 'shwōde nèige. or expressed as There he is. 'Jyòushr 'nèige rén! /You go first. or Go ahead. Nǐ 'syān dzǒu yíbù. /He went on ahead. Tā 'syān dzǒude.

2. Indicating direction, destination, or purpose of going, chyù. (Compare COME. When direction or destination is expressed, chyù is usually at the end of the sentence; when purpose is expressed, the thing to be done usually follows chyù.) /Is he going (to some place)? 'Tā chyù ma? or Tā chyù buchyù? /Where are you going? °Shàng (°Dàu) 'nǎr chyù? /We're going the same way. Dzámen dàu 'yíge dìfang chyù. or (with no destination in mind) Dzámen dzǒu 'yìtyáu lù. /He went that way. Tā wàng 'nèibyar chyule. /The road goes due south. Jèityáu 'lù wàng 'jèngnán chyù. /He won't go. (somewhere) Tā 'bùkěn 'chyù. or (he won't leave) Tā 'bùkěn 'dzǒu. /Let's go for a walk. Dzámen chyù °'lyòudalyòuda (°'dzǒuyidzǒu). /He went swimming. Tā fù'shwěi chyule. or (if already back) Tā fù'shwěi chyu laije. or Tā chyù fù'shwěi láije. /Go and see it. Chyù 'kànkan chyù. /Go and ask her. Chyù 'wènwen tā chyu. or (defiantly) Nǐ 'wèn tā chyu ba. /Now see what you've gone and done! 'Kàn nǐ chyù 'gànde jèjyàu 'shémma shèr! /Since her husband died, she hasn't gone out much. Tā 'jàngfu sǐle, tā jyòu 'méidà 'chūchyu 'wárgwo. /I'm going out to dinner. Wǒ 'chūchyu chr̄'fàn. /He went from Peiping to Nanking. Tā tsúng 'Běipíng dàu 'Nánjīng chyùde. /She's gone upstairs to get her hat. Tā dàu lóushàng 'chyù ná tā 'màudz chyùle. /He went downstairs just a minute ago. Jǐfen jūng yǐchyán tā dàu lóudǐsya chyùle.

3. When a word indicating a more specific variety of motion can be substituted for go, Chinese uses the more specific word; with màn slow and kwài fast Chinese often uses no word for the motion itself. /Go slow! (walking or in general 'Màn dzǒu! or (running) 'Màn dyar pǎu! or (driving) 'Màn dyar kāi! or (general) 'Màn dyar! or Byé nèmma 'kwài! /Let's get going! (especially of working) Dùng-'shǒu a! /Ready! Get set! Go! Jàn'hǎu! Yù'bèi! 'Pǎu! /The time goes very fast. °'Shŕjyan (°'Ŕdz, °etc.) 'gwòde jēn 'kwài. /The train is certainly going fast. Jèige 'hwǒchē °'kāide (°'dzǒude) jēn kwài.

4. (Be done away with, finished, spent, sold) Chinese uses the more specific terms. /This rule must go (be abolished). 'Jèige gwēijyu děi chyǔ'syāu. /Everything they had went (was burned up) in the fire. Nèitsź jáu'hwǒ tāmen swǒ'yǒu de 'shémma dōu °shāu'wánle (°shāu'gwāngle). or Nèitsź jáu'hwǒ bǎ tāmen shǎule ge °'jīnggwāng (°shémma dōu méi'shèng). /All his money would be gone (spent) by this time. Dàu 'jèi shŕhou 'dàgài tāde 'chyán °gāi hwā'gwāngle (°gāi hwā'wanle, °gāi hwā'jīngle, °hwāde 'shèngbusya shémma le). /The brandy is all gone (used up). Báilán'dì °dōu yùng'wánle (°dōu 'méile, °yì'dyǎr méi'shèng, °yì'dǐ yě méi'yǒu le). /The pain is gone (stopped). Syàndzai bù'téng le. or 'Téng yǐjīng 'jŕ le. /They're all gone. (sold) 'Chywán mài'wánle. or (bought) 'Chywán °gěi rén (°jyàurén, °'màichyule, °mǎi'gwāngle). /They're going at a dollar apiece. (Here sold is not expressed.) Yíkwài 'chyán °yì'tyáur (°yíge, °yì plus another appropriate measure).

5. (Be or become something) is expressed by a stative verb or by other indirect expressions. /Let him go hungry. Jyàu tā 'èje ba. /He went crazy. Tā 'fēng le. /I'll go crazy if this keeps up. Yàu 'lǎu jèyàngr wǒ 'jēn yàu 'fēng le. /He went blind. Tā 'syā le. /Everything has gone wrong. 'Shémma shŕ dōu °'tswò le (°mǎn'nǐng °chū 'tswòr, chū lóudz). /Things were going pretty well until he came along. 'Ywánlai shèr hěn 'shwùnlì; tā yǐlái jyòu chū 'lóudz le. /This meat has gone bad. Ròu 'hwài le. /The well has gone dry. Jǐng 'gān le. /I hope the incident will go unnoticed. 'Syīwàng 'méi rén 'lǐhwèi tsái 'hǎu. /They're still going strong. Tāmen háishr 'jyèr hěn 'dzú de.

6. (Be, but not become, referring to the character or details of something) shŕ or indirect expressions. /So the story goes. (as told) Jyòushr 'jèmma yǐhwéi shèr. or (so people say) 'Rénjyā nèmma 'shwō. /The story goes like this. Shŕ 'jèmme

yìhwéi shèr. *or* (if fiction) Nèige 'syàuhwàr shř 'dzěmma shwōde. /How does that tune go? Nèige 'dyàur dzěmma 'chàng? *or* Nèige shř dzěmma ge 'dyàur? /As writers go these days, he's not exceptional. 'Jèi nyántóur mài 'wénjangde 'dōu (shř) nèiyàngr; (tā yě búshr lì'wài).

7. (Be placed, fit in) Chinese uses the specific terms. /That chair goes in the corner. 'Nèibǎ 'yǐdz °fàngdzai (°gēdzai, °bǎidzai) nèige jǐ'jyàur nar. /Will that umbrella go in your suitcase? 'Nèibǎ sǎn nǐde 'syàngdzlǐ °jàude'syà (°fàngde'kāi) ma? /Is that umbrella to go in your suitcase? 'Nèiba sǎn shř bushr fàng nǐ 'syàngdzli de?

8. Going to do something yàu . . . . /The roof is going to fall in one of these days. Fáng'dǐngdz 'dzǎuwǎn (yǒu yìtyān) yàu 'tāsyalai.

9. Combinations in which the idea of motion is not included.

Go ahead (polite) meaning you first, please (nín) chǐng; meaning you may do it syíng, hǎu, kéyi, 'jyòu nèmmaje ba. /Go ahead (and eat). 'Chr̄ ba. /Go ahead (and write). 'Syě ba. /Go ahead (and talk). 'Shwō ba. /I'll go ahead then. (and do as we agreed) 'Nèmmaje wǒ 'jyòu nèmma 'bàn le.

Go around (be enough for all). /There's barely enough to go around once. 'Gāng gòu jwàn °'yìdzǎur de (°'fēn de).

Go back on shř'syìn, fānhwěi, 'shwō(le) bú'swàn (all these mean fail to keep faith and may be preceded by a verb or by gēn plus a personal noun). /Don't go back on your word. Byé shř'syìn. *or* Byé fān'hwěi. *or* Byé 'shwōle bú'swàn. /He won't go back on his promise. Tā 'dàyingle jyòu 'búhwèi °shř'syìn de (°fān'hwěide, °'shwōle bú'swàn de).

Go by (act according to) ànje . . . 'bàn, jàuje . . . 'bàn; (use) yùng. /Those are the rules we go by. Wǒmen 'jyòu °ànje (°jàuje) 'nèisyē 'gwēidzé lái 'bàn. /He goes by a false name. Tā yùng yíge 'jyǎ míngdz.

Go down (be defeated) dǎbài(le); (be passed on) 'lyóuchwán(de). /Their best troops went down before ours. 'Jyòushr tāmen 'dzwèihǎude jyūn'dwèi 'yě jyàu wǒmen dǎ'bàile. /That speech will go down in history. Nèige 'yǎnjyǎng yǐ'dǐng hwèi dzài lì'shřshang 'lyóuchwán de.

Go far. /A man like that should go far in politics. Syàng nèmma ge rén dzwòchǐ 'gwār lai yīnggāi 'chyántúwú'lyàng.

Go in for (like). /I don't go in for that sort of thing. 'Nèijǔng shř wǒ bù-('syǐhwān) 'gàn. /He goes in for loud ties. Tā ài 'hwāhwa lǐng'dài.

Go in with (do together). /Would you like to go in with me on this proposition? Jèijyàn shř nǐ 'ywànyi °gēn wǒ 'hébàn (°'jyārù) ma?

Go into business. /He's planning to go into business after the war. Tā 'dǎswàn jàn'hòu dzwò 'mǎimai.

Go into a subject. /Let's not go into (talk about) that subject now. Syàndzài dzámen syǎn byé °'shwō (°tán, °tǎulwùn) 'nèige.

Go off. /The rifle went off by accident. Chyāng dzǒu'hwǒ le. /He went off on a tangent. Tā hú'nàuchilai le. /The play went off well. Syǐ yǎn de hén hǎu.

Go on (continue) . . . syàchyu; (start) . . . chǐlai; (as an exclamation) 'déle ba, 'lādǎule ba. /He went right on talking. Tā 'jyēje 'shwōsyachyule. /I can't go on like this. °Wǒ 'dzěmma syàchyu (°'Hwósyàchyu, °'Twōsyàchyu), kěbù'syíng. /He went on a rampage. Tā syā'nàuchilai le. /Go on! You can't fool anyone. 'Déle ba! *or* Lādǎule ba! Nǐ 'shéi yě ywānbu'lyǎu. *but* /What's going on here? Shémma 'shř? *or* 'Dzěmma la?

Going on (approaching an age) kwài. / He's going on fifty. Tā kwài wǔ'shŕ le.

Go out (be extinguished) myè(le); (of fashion) gwòshŕ, bùshŕsyīng. / Suddenly the lights went out. Dēng 'hūrán 'dōu myèle. / That song will go out with the war. Dǎ 'wánle 'jàng, nèige 'gēr jyòu yàu °gwò'shŕ de (°'bùshŕ'syīng de).

Go over (succeed) chénggūng. / Do you think this song will go over? Nǐ syǎng jèige 'gēer néng chéng'gūng ma?

Go over (change one's position, lit. or fig.). / He went over to their side. Tā 'pǎudàu 'tāmen nèibyar chyùle.

Go over *or* go through. / Let's go over this carefully once. (discuss) Dzámen 'dzsyî °'tǎulwùn yí'byàn (*or* (search or check) °'chá yíbyàn, *or* (proofread) °'jyàudwèi yíbyàn).

Go through (be successful) chénggūng; (receive, undergo) shòu. / Do you think your application will go through? Nǐ syǎng nǐ 'jǎu de nèige shŕ néng chéng'gūng ma? / The soldiers went through severe training. 'Bīng 'shòude 'syùnlyàn hěn 'yán.

Go through with (do to the end) dzwòdàu 'tóur de. / She'll never go through with it. Tā 'búhwèi dzwòdàu 'tóur de.

Go to (attend) shàng. / What school do you go to? Nǐ 'shàng de shŕ 'nèige sywé-'syàu?

Go to (be given to) gěi. / A fifty-dollar prize will go to the best student. Yǒu 'wǔshŕywánde 'jyǎngjīn gěi dzwèihǎude 'sywésheng.

Go to bed. / It's time to go to bed. Gāi 'shwèi le. *or* Gāi shàng'chwáng le.

Go to press. / It has already gone to press. 'Yǐjīng fù'yìnle.

Go to pieces (fig.) swèi. / She went to pieces when her husband died. Tā syānsheng yìsž tā syīn dōu 'swèile.

Go to the devil. / Go to the devil! 'Gāi 'sž! *but* / We told him to go to the devil. Wǒmen bǎ tā 'màle yídwùn.

Go under a name yùng. / He goes under an assumed name. (false name) Tā yùng 'jyǎmíngdz. (pen name) Tā yùng 'bǐmíng.

Go up (in price) jǎng jyàr. / Apples have gone up. 'Pínggwo jǎng'jyàr le.

Go together *or* go with (associate with) syānghǎu. / They have been going with each other (*or* going together) for years. Tāmen syāng'hǎu 'yǒu syē nyán le.

Go with (match) pèi. / These curtains don't go with the other furnishings. 'Jèisyē chwāng'lyár gēn 'byéde 'jyājyù 'dōu °bú'pèi (°'pèibu'shàng).

Go with (of foods). / Dried shrimp go well with wine. 'Gān syāmi jyòu jyǒur hǎu 'chŕ.

Go without (get along without). / If there isn't enough meat, someone will have to go without. Yàushr 'ròu bú'gòu, 'yǒurén jyòu 'méide 'chŕ. / You'll have to go without it. Nǐ 'méiyǒu jyòu 'jŕhǎu °'méiyǒu ba (°'swānle).

Let go (release). / Don't let go of the rope. Byé bǎ 'shéngdz °'fàngkai (°sūng-'shǒu, °'sākai 'shǒu). *or* 'Dzwànje 'shéngdz. / Let go of my hand. Byé 'dzwànje wǒde'shǒu.

Let go (release or pardon). / Let him go. 'Ráule ta ba. *or* Jyàu tā 'dzǒu ba.

Let it go at that 'Jèmmaje jyòu 'swànle ba. *or* 'Béng dzài 'tíle.

Let oneself go. / He'd have a better time if he'd let himself go. 'Tā syǎngde'kāi dyar, jyòu 'tūngkwai 'dwō le.

10. <u>Nominal expressions</u>. / He's on the go day and night. Tā 'hēisya 'báirde 'gàn. / Let's make a go of it. Dzámen bǎ 'jèige 'bànde hǎu'hāurde.

GOD. (Common Protestant term) Shàngdì, <u>but some Protestants use</u> Shén; (Roman Catholic) Tyānjǔ; (the name Jehovah) Yēhéhwá; (Buddhist, Taoist, Confucian) Tyān (heaven). / The minister gave thanks to God. 'Mùshr 'gǎnsye Shàng'dì. / God knows what we'll be doing next. 'Tyān jrdau 'syàtsz gàn 'shémma ne. (Some Christians may avoid using Tyān here, but it is not universally considered irreverent, even in orthodox circles. However, when a Christian says this with a theological meaning, he would say Shàng'dì jrdàu . . . .) / Oh, my God! (reverent, not profane, Protestant) Shàng'dì a! <u>or expressed as</u> Heavens! Tyān a!

(An idolized person) shén, shénsyan, ǒusyàng. / His admirers have made a god of him. 'Chúngbài 'tāde 'rén bǎ tā dàng °'shén(syan) kàn (°ǒusyàng).

By God <u>no exact equivalent in Chinese</u>. / By God, I'm not going to let him get away with that. Hn! Wǒ 'kě bùnéng 'ráule ta. *or* Wǒ fāshr 'jywé bùnéng jyàu tā 'nèmmaje jyou 'swàn le.

GOLD. jīndz, jīn; **solid gold** *or* **pure gold** 'chwénjīn(de), 'dzújīn(de), 'chrjīn(de); **made of gold** 'jīndz dzwòde, jīnde; **gold watch** jīnbyǎu; **gold watch chain** jīnbyǎulyàr, 'jīn-(byǎu)'lyàndz; **gold coins** 'jīnbì, 'jīnhwò; **gold coin** *or* **gold** (money) 'jīnchyán; **gold thread** jīnsyàn, jīnsz, jīnsēr; **gold leaf** jīn 'yèdz; **gold standard** 'jīnběnwèi; **overlaid with gold** 'bāujīn; **gold-plated** (metal) 'dùjīn; **gold-painted** (woodwork) 'jwāngjīn, 'tújīn; **gold** (color) 'jīnsè, 'jīnshǎr; <u>and many other such compounds</u>. / These dishes are solid gold. Jèisyē 'pándz shr °'chwúnjīnde (°'dzújīnde, °'chrjīnde). / How much is that gold ring? Nèige jīn'jyèjr 'dwōshau chyán? / He can't be bought with gold. °'Jīndz (°'Chyán) 'mǎibu'dùng tāde 'syīn. / The dome was painted gold. Ywán'dyēngr túde 'jīnshǎr. / The frame was done in gold. Kwāngdz shr °'tújīnde (°'jwāngjīnde). / The box was inlaid with gold lines. 'Hédzshang 'syāng('chyán)je jīn'sz. / Their flag is blue and gold. Tāmende 'chídzshang 'lánde gēn 'jīnde 'lyángshǎr. *or* Tāmende-'chíshang shr 'lán hé'jīn 'lyángshǎr. / It has silver stripes on a gold background. Shàngtou shr 'yíndàur 'jīndyèr. / Do you have this in gold (color)? 'Jèige yǒu 'jīnshǎr de ma?

Gold mine (fig.). / You've got a gold mine in that idea. Nǐ nèige 'fádz hwèi jyàu nǐ fā'tsái de.

Goldbricking mwótseng, dwǒlǎn. / Soldier, cut out the goldbricking! °Lǎu-'syūng(°Túng'jr)byé °'mwótseng le (°dwǒ'lǎn le).

GOOD. 1. (Of outstanding quality) hǎu; (not bad) búhwài, bútswò. <u>In some cases more specific adjectives are used.</u>

(Of direct judgment). / Good! (approving something already said or done) Hǎu! *or* 'Hěn hǎu! *or* Búhwài! *or* 'Jēn hǎu! *or* 'Jēn bútswò! <u>etc.</u> (approving a request, meaning, You may *or* I will) Hǎu! *or* Hǎuba! *or* Chéng! *or* Syíng! *or* Kéyi. *or* 'Jyòu nèmmaje ba. / That one is good. *or* There's a good one. 'Nèige °hǎu (°bú-'hwài, °bú'tswò). / That's very good. 'Hěn hǎu. *or* 'Jēn hǎu. *or* Hǎude 'hěn. *or* 'Dǐng hǎu. *or* 'Tǐng hǎu. / That one is very good. 'Nèige °'jēn búhwài (°'hěn búhwài, °hǎude 'hěn). / That one is not so good. 'Nèige 'búdà hǎu. *or* 'Nèige 'bútài hǎu. *or* 'Nèige 'chà dyar('jīn). *or* 'Nèige hěn 'tsz. / That one is neither good nor bad; it is what you'd call so-so or medium. Nèige yě bù'hǎu yě bú'hwài; kéyi shwō shr 'búgwò rú'tsz, 'búshàngbú'syàde. Jèige hěn chà'jīn. / That's a good one! *or* That's good! (of a true or fictitious story) 'Shwōde 'hǎu. (of a fictitious story only) 'Byànde 'hǎu. *or* 'Dzōude 'hǎu. (ironically) <u>meaning</u> What a tall one! Hǎu 'húshwō bā'dàu le! *or* Syā'bāi! / That will be good for him (will teach him a lesson). 'Nèi shř 'wèi tā 'hǎu. / Good for you! <u>meaning</u> You did the right thing. 'Jēn hǎu! *or* Jēn 'chéng. *or* Jēn 'syíng. *or* 'Jēn dwèi. *or* 'Yǒuníde. <u>or meaning</u>, I didn't think you could do it. ('Jyúrán) °nèng'hǎule (°'chéngle, °'syíngle, °'dwèile).

(Referring to a specific object). / Is the milk still good? Nyóu'nǎi méi'hwài ma? *or* (not sour) Nyóu'nǎi méi'sōu ma? *or* Nyóu'nǎi hái 'hǎuje ne ma? / He gave me good advice. Tā gàusu wǒ yíge hěn hǎu de 'fádz. *or* Tā 'jyāugěi wǒ de'bànfa 'hěn hǎu. / This is a good meal. 'Jèidwùn fàn °'hěn hǎu (°'jēn hǎu, °'hǎude 'hěn). / Are those mushrooms good to eat? Nèisyē 'mwógu hǎu 'chr̄ ma? / The medicine is good for you. Jèige 'yàu yú nǐ yǒu °'hǎuchù (°'yíchù). / He's got a good body. Tā 'shēndz bú'hwài. *or* (strong, healthy) Tā 'shēndz hěn 'jwàng. *or* (local Peiping) Tā yǒu ge 'hǎu shēndz'gur. / Does he have a good brain? <u>is expressed as</u> Is he bright? Tā rén 'tsūngmíng bùtsūngmíng?

(Referring to persons in general). / He's a good man. Tā 'hěn hǎu. *or* (especially of innate character) Tā shr̄ ge 'hǎu rén. *or* Tā 'wéirén 'hěn hǎu. *or* (of ability) Tā hěn jūng'yùng. *or* (of reliability) Tā hěn kě'kàu. / He's not a good man. Tā °'bùhǎu (°etc.). / He's no good. (innately) Tā búshr̄ 'hǎu rén. (for a job) Tā 'méiyǒu'yùng. *or* Tā bù'chéng. *or* Tā bù'hǎu. *or* Tā bù'syíng. / Be good. *or* Be a good boy. Hǎu'hǎurde! / He's a very good child. Jèi háidz 'hěn hǎu. *or* (likable) Jèi háidz jyàu rén °'syíhwān (°'ài, °'téng). *or* (obedient) Jèi háidz hěn °'tīng'hwà (°'tīng'shwō).

(Referring to persons in their treatment of others). / She's very good with children. Tā dài 'háidz hěn 'hǎu. *or* (kind) Tā dài 'háidz °hěn 'tsź̄shàn (°hěn 'réntsź). *or* (she likes them) Tā hěn °'ài (°'téng) syǎu 'háidz. *or* (children like her) Syǎu 'háidz dōu °'ài (°'syíhwān) ta. / He has always been good to his family. Tā yí'syàng dài tā 'jyāli de rén hěn 'hǎu. *or* (to his children) Tā °dài 'dznyǔ (°bǎ 'dznyǔ 'jyàuyude) 'hěn hǎu. / He's very good to people who come for help. 'Shéi lái 'chyóu tā, tā 'dōu hǎu'hǎurde 'jyēdài. / It's good of you to think of us. <u>is expressed as</u> Many thanks for thinking of us. Dwō'syè nǐ 'dyànjije wǒmen. *or* Nǐ 'jēn hǎu, hái nèmm'a 'dyànjije wǒmen.

(Referring to persons as good in a certain profession, field, or way of life.) / He's a very good mechanic. Tā jèige'jīchìjyàng °hěn 'hǎu (*or* (capable) °hěn yǒu 'běnlǐng, °hěn 'chéng, °hěn 'syíng). *or* Tā shr̄ ge hǎu 'jīchìjyàng. / He's a good writer. Tā syě 'wénjang syěde 'hǎu. <u>or expressed as</u> His writings are good. Tā 'wénbǐ hěn 'hǎu. / He's not a very good mechanic. Tā jèige 'jīchìjyàng bú'tài hǎu. *or* Tā 'búshr̄ ge 'dǐnghǎude 'jīchìjyàng. / He's a good doctor. Tā shr̄ ge 'hǎu yīsheng. *or* Tā jèige 'yīsheng 'jēn hǎu. *or* Tā jr̄'bìng 'hěn yǒu 'běnlǐng. / He could have been a good politician. Tā yàushr̄ dzwò ge 'jèngkèr, yí'dìng bú'hwài. / He's a good Christian. Tā shr̄ ge 'hǎu(de)jīdū'tú. *or* (earnest) Tā syìn'jyàu hěn 'jēn. *or* (pious) Tā syìn'jyàu syīn hěn 'chéng. / Do you call that being a good Christian? Nèi yě jyàu jīdū'tú ma? / He's a good soldier. Tā shr̄ ge 'hǎu jyūnrén. *or* 'Tā jèige 'jyūnrén hěn 'hǎu. / He's a good man for the job. Tā dzwò 'jèi shr̄ hěn °hé'shr̄ (°syàng'yí).

(Special combinations). / Wait until he's in a good humor before asking him. Děng tā °gāu'syìng (°syīnli 'tùngkwai) de shŕhou dzài wèn tā. / He's not in a good humor today. Tā jyèr °bùgāu'syìng °('syīnli) bú'tùngkwai, °(syīnli) bú'dz̄dzai). / Who do you get your good looks from? Nǐ jǎngde 'nèmma hǎu, swéi 'shéi a? / She's good-looking. Tā jǎngde hǎu 'kàn. / Don't waste your good money on it. Hǎu'hǎurde 'chyán °'byé yùngdzài 'nèi shàngtóu (°byé 'nèmma hwā). / They're making good money. Tāmen 'hěn jwàn'chyán. *or* Tāmen 'jwànchyán hěn 'dwō. / The teacher is a good-natured old man. Lǎu 'syānsheng 'wéirén hěn °héǎi (°hòudàu, °'wēnhòu, °héchì). *or* Syānsheng shr̄ ge hěn °'héǎi (°etc.) de lǎu'tóur. / He's good-tempered. Tā 'píchi hěn 'hǎu. / They keep things in good order. Tāmen bǎ

595

GOOD

'dūngsyi 'shōude °hěn yǒu 'tszsyu (°hěn yǒu tyáuli, °yǒutyáuyǒu'lǐde). /It's a good thing you came early. Nǐ lái'dzaule 'hǎu a. *or* (lucky for you) °'Kwēile (°'Syìngkwēi) nǐ lái'dzǎule. /It would be a good thing for him to go away to school. Tā yàushr shàng'sywéchyu tsái 'hǎu. /Of course he's interested in your idea; he knows a good thing when he sees it. Tā 'dāngrán jywéje nǐ nèige 'fádz bú'hwài le; tā °shř shŕ'hwǒde (°'dǔngde hǎu'hwài). /Of course he likes your idea; he wouldn't let a good thing like that slip through his hand. Tā 'dāngrán syǐhwān nǐde 'fádz le; nèmma hǎu de 'fádz tā 'jywé búhwèi 'fànggwochyude. /One good turn deserves another. (proverbial) 'Shàn yǒu 'shàn bàu. /Let's ask him; he's got a lot of good sense. Wènwèn 'tāba; tā °'syīnli hěn 'míngbai (°shř ge 'míngbai rén). /Did you have a good time? Wárde 'hǎu ma? *or* Wárde 'tùngkwai ma? *or* Wárde yǒu'yìsz ma? /Do you have good soil for farming? Nǐmen nàr 'dìtǔ °'féi (°jùng 'jwāngjya 'syíng) ma? /Put in a good word for me. Gěi wǒ 'shwō jyù hǎu 'hwà.

2. (Outstanding in quantity or thoroughness) often hǎu, but also many other expressions, depending on the circumstance. /Give him a good talking-to. Bǎ tā hǎuhǎurde shwō yí'dwùn. *or* Bǎ tā hěn'hěnde shwō yídwùn. /Let's give this matter a good going-over. Dzámen bǎ 'jèijyàn shř °chè'dǐde (°'hǎu'hǎurde) 'yánjyou yísyàr.

(Fully, at least). /It's a good eight miles. Yǒu 'bālǐdwō dì. /We waited a good hour. Wǒmen 'děngle yì'dyǎndwōjūng.

Good deal, good many. /The operation gave me a good deal of pain. °Shǒu'shù (°'Láde, °Kāi'dāu) °'téng'jíle (°hěn 'téng, °hǎu'téng, °'téngjrne). /A good many people don't like him. °'Hǎudwōrén (°'Hěndwōrén) 'bùsyǐhwān tā. /I haven't seen him for a good while. Wǒ °'hǎu jyǒu (°'hěn jyǒu) méi 'kànjyàn tā le.

3. In combinations with other words.

Be as good as jyǎn'jŕ jyòu swàn . . . . /The job is as good as done. Jèijyàn 'shř jyǎn'jŕ jyòu swàn'chéngle. /He's as good as elected right now. Syàndzài tā 'yǐjīng jyǎn'jŕ jyòu swàn 'sywǎnshàngle. *but* /He's as good as his word. Tā 'bùshř'syìn. *or* Tā shwō de hwà 'méiyǒu bú'swànde.

Be good at (know how to) hwèi . . . ; (be an expert) . . . shř 'nèiháng, . . . shř 'hángjyā. /He's very good at that sort of thing. 'Tā 'hěn hwèi nèiyàngrde 'shř. *or* 'Nèiyàngrde shř tā shř °'nèiháng (°'hángjyā). /He's only good at talking. Tā 'jŕ hwèi shwō'hwà. *or* 'Jŕ yǒu shwō'hwà tā shř °'nèiháng (°'hángjyā). /Are you good at this sort of thing? usually, for courtesy's sake, Chinese says Do you have any experience in this? Dwèiyú 'jèiyàngrde 'shř yǒu 'jīngyàn ma? or, if said by a superior, expressed as Do you have confidence in yourself to do this? Nǐ dzwò 'jèijùng shř yǒu 'bǎwò ma? or, said by a superior, as Can you do this well? Nǐ dzwò 'jèijùng shř 'dzwòde 'hǎu ma? *or* (referring to something of no great importance) 'Jèijùng shèr nǐ 'hwèi ma?

Good and . . . . is expressed by doubling an adjective. /Make the tea good and strong. 'Chá chǐde °núng'núngde (°yàn'yànde).

Good for. /That watch is good for a lifetime. 'Jèijř byǎu kéyi yùng yí'bèidz. /This fur coat is still good for several seasons. 'Jèijyàn 'pídàyī hái kéyi chwān 'hǎu jǐ'jyèr ne. /He's good for the damages to your car. Nǐde 'chē yǒu 'shémma swǔnshr tā 'dōu péide'chǐ. /He's sort of a good-for-nothing. Tā shř nèijǔng méi 'yùng de rén. *or* Tā shř ge 'fèiwù. *or* Tā shř ge 'fèiwù 'dyǎnsyīn.

Have a good mind to 'syīnli 'hěn yǒu dyǎr syǎng; **had a good mind to** 'chà dyǎr. /I have a good mind to go with you. Wǒ 'syīnli 'hěn yǒu dyǎr syǎng 'gēn nǐ 'dzǒu. /I had a good mind to leave her there. Wǒ 'chà dyǎr méi 'bùgwǎn tā jyòu 'dzǒule.

4. In greeting and exclamations. /Good day. *or* Good-bye. Dzàijyàn. *or* Dzàihwèi. /I'll say good-bye now. Dzámen dzài'jyàn le. *or* (if parting for a long

time) 'Jyòutsź gàu'tsźle. /If you do that again, it'll be good-bye for you. Nǐ yàu
'dzài nèmmaje a, nà nǐ jyòu swàn chǐng cháng'jyà le. /Good heavens! *or* Good
Lord! *or* Good night! *or* My goodness! Hǎu jyàhwo! *or* 'Jè shř dzěmma 'shwōde!
/Good morning. *or* Good afternoon. *or* Good evening. (general greeting) Hǎu a?
or Nín hǎu? *or* Nǐ hǎu? /Good morning (only). Dzǎu a? /Good night. Míngtyan
jyàn. *or* 'Myéngr jyàn. *or* 'Myár jyàn. /Good old Jones! (referring to him when
he's absent) 'Háishr rénjyā Lǎu 'Jōu. *or* (greeting him) Jè 'búshr Lǎu 'Jōu ma!

5. Nominal uses.

Be to the good (of winnings) <u>expressed in the verb</u> yíng; (of benefits) yǒu 'yíchù,
yǒu 'hǎuchù, yóulì. /At the end of the poker game I was eight dollars to the good.
'Pūkěpái dǎ'wánle, wǒ 'yíngle 'bāywán. /Whatever he brings us is all to the good.
'Wúlwùn tā gěi wǒmen dài shémma lai 'dōu yǒu °'yíchù (°'hǎuchù, °'lì).

Do (any or some) **good** yǒuyùng, yǒu 'hǎuchù, yǒu 'yùngchù. /I'd like to go and
see him, but what good would it do? Wǒ 'hěn syàng chyù 'jyàntā, búgwǒ yǒu shémma
°yùng ne (°'hǎuchù ne, °'yùngchù ne)? *but* /He's always going around doing good for
people. Tā 'lǎushr 'gēchù 'pàuláipàu'chyùde °'bāngjù rén (°gěi rén bàn'shr, °syíng-
'hǎu).

For good. /Let's fix it for good this time. <u>is expressed as</u> Let's fix it well in
order to save labor. Jèitsź dzámen nùngde hǎu'hǎurde, hǎu °yǐ'hòu shéng'shr.
/She's gone for good. <u>is expressed as</u> She's gone and won't return. Tā 'dzǒule,
'bùhwéilaile. /Is she gone for good? <u>is expressed as</u> Will she return? Tā hái 'hwéi
lai ma? <u>or as</u> Won't she return? Tā 'bùhwéilaile ma?

For one's (own) **good** 'wèi . . . 'hǎu, 'wèi . . . yǒu 'yíchù, 'wèi . . . yǒu 'hǎuchù.
/This is for your own good. Jèi shr 'wèi nǐ 'dzjǐ °'hǎu (°yǒu 'yíchù, °yǒu 'hǎuchù).

Up to no good. /They're up to no good. Tāmen dzàinàr °'méi 'hǎushèr (°'gàn-
buchu 'hǎushèr lai, °dǎu shémma 'gwěi ne, °'gwěigu shémma ne).

Make good. /I'm sure he'll make good. (accomplish something) Wǒ jrdàu tā
(néng) °'chéng dyǎr shémma (°yǒu (dyǎr) 'chéngjyòu, °'dzwòchu dyar mar lai, *or*
(become famous) °chéng'míng). /I'm sure he'll make good in business. Wǒ jrdàu
tā dzwò 'mǎimài yǐ'dìng dzwòde 'hǎu. /If I break it, I'll make good the damage.
Yàushr wǒ gěi nùng'hwàile, wǒ yí'dìng 'péi(cháng). /He always makes good his
promises. Tā 'dāying de °jyòu 'jwǔn bàn (°'méiyǒu bú'swànde shrhou).

See also BETTER, BEST.

GOODS. 'hwòwu (-hwò in compounds); (things) dūngsyi; (merchandise) shāngpǐn;
foreign goods yánghwò, wàigwo hwò. /This store has a large stock of goods. Jèige
'pùdz lǐtou yǒu 'hěn dwō'tswénhwò. /This store sells all sorts of goods. Jèige
'pùdz mài 'gè shrgè 'yàngr de °'hwòwu (°'shāngpǐn, °'dūngsyi).

GOVERNMENT. 'jèngfǔ; **central government** 'jūngyāng 'jèngfǔ; **federal government**
'lyánbāng 'jèngfǔ; **local government** 'dìfāng 'jèngfǔ; **provincial** (*or* state) **government**
'shěng jèngfǔ; **district government** 'syàn jèngfǔ; **coalition government** 'gè'dǎng'pài
'lyánhé('dzǔjrde) 'jèngfǔ; **one-party government** 'yìdǎngjwān'jèngde 'jèngfǔ; **the United**
States Government 'Měigwo('lyán bāng)'jèngfǔ. /All governments will have to cooperate in this matter. 'Swǒyoude 'jèngfǔ dwèiyú 'jèijyànshr 'yīngdāng hé'dzwò.
/He works for the government. Tā gěi 'jèngfǔ dzwò'shr. /He is a government
employee. Tā shr 'jèngfǔde 'gùywán. /He is a government official. Tā shr ge
'gwān. /He is an important official in the government. Tā shr 'jèngfǔde 'yàurén.
/Put your money into government bonds. Chǐng mǎi 'jèngfǔ 'gūngjài °'pyàu
(°'chywàn). /That's an example of good government. 'Hǎude 'jèngfǔ 'yīnggāi dzwò
de 'shr, 'jèi jyòushr ge 'lìdz. *or* 'Hǎu 'jèngfǔ 'yīnggāi dzwò 'nèiyàngrde shr.

Form of government 'jèngtǐ; constitutional (form of) government lì'syànjèng'tǐ; democratic (form of) government 'mínjǔ'jèngtǐ; republican (form of) government 'gùnghéjèngtǐ; monarchist (form of) government 'jyūnjǔ'jèngtǐ; dictatorial *or* fascist (form of) government 'dútsái 'jèngtǐ. / This country has a republican form of government. 'Jèigwó(de 'jèngfǔ) shr̀ 'gùnghé 'jèngtǐ.

Power *or* control over the government 'jèngchywán. / The people have control over the government. 'Rénmín you 'jèngchywán.

GRAB. jwā; (in order to pull) jyōu. / She reached out her hand and grabbed the end of the rope. Tā shēn'shǒu chyu °'jwā (°jyōu) shéngdz'tóur. *or* Tā 'shēnshǒu bǎ shéngdz'tóur °'jwājaule (°'jyōujaule).

(Take hold of and hold tightly) 'jwājù, 'jyōujù; (if the thing has already been held loosely) 'dzwànjù. / She grabbed the broom handle and pulled. Tā yǐ'bǎ °'jwājù (°'jyōujù, °'dzwànjù) tyáushu'bàr jyòu 'dèn. / He said he could grab the end of the rope in one try. Tā shwō tā yǐ'bǎ jyòu 'kěyi °'jwājù (°'jyōujù) nèige shéngdz'tóur. / She reached out to grab the end of the rope, but couldn't make it. Tā shēn'shǒu chyu °'jwā (°'jyōu) shéngdz'tóur, kěshr °'méijwā'jù (°méijyōu'jù).

(Pick up in the hand) chāuchilai, náchilai, shŕchilai, láuchilai, jwāchilai. / She grabbed a broomstick and let him have it. Tā °'chāuchi (°'shŕchi, °etc.) 'tyáushulai 'dǎle ta yí'dwùn.

(Move quickly to accept an offer or opportunity). / He grabbed at the offer. is expressed as He accepted immediately. Tā lì'kè jyòu 'dāyingle. or as The minute it was offered he accepted it. Tā yì 'shwō jyòu 'kěn le.

See also HOLD.

GRADE. (Class of things of one quality) děng; **best grade** 'shàngděng, dzwèi gāu děng; **high grade** 'gāuděng; **medium grade** 'jūngděng; **low grade** 'syàděng; **cheaper grade** 'tsz̀děng. / We buy the best grade of silk. Women mǎi 'shàngděng 'chóudz. / This is a cheaper grade of yarn. Jèi shr 'tsz̀děngde rúng'syàn.

(Class in school) 'nyánjí; in some cases bān, which is not used in numbering grades, except when counting from the highest. / What grade do you teach? Nǐ jyāu 'nèibān? *or* Nǐ jyāu 'jǐnyánjí? / He's in the second grade now. Tā dzài 'èrnyánjí.

(Marks in school) fēnshur. / He received the highest grades in the class. Tā dzài 'tā nèi 'bānlǐ 'fēnshur °'dzwèihǎu (°'dzwèi gāu).

(Slope) pwōr; (degree of slope) 'pwōdù, chǐngsyé dù; upgrade (of a road) 'shàng-pwōrlù; downgrade 'syàpwōrlù. / The railroad has a 3 per cent grade. 'Tyělùde 'pwōdù shr̀ 'bǎifēnjr̀'sān. / There is quite a steep grade on the other side of the hill. Shān 'nèibyār °de'pwōdù hěn 'dōu (*or* (dangerous) °de'pwōr 'syànde hěn). *but* / The car had trouble making the grade. 'Jèige chē shàng'shān de shŕhour hěn chŕ'lì.

Make the grade (fig. come up to standard) gǎnde'shàng; (succeed) chéngde'lyǎu. / If you work hard, you can make the grade. Nǐ yàushr 'dwō mài dyar 'lìchi, jyòu néng °'gǎnde'shàng (°'chéngde'lyǎu).

On the downgrade (fig.). / Business has been on the downgrade for the last month. 'Shēngyì tsúng 'shàngywè chǐ °'yìtyān bùrú yì'tyān (°'ywè lái ywè 'dzāu, °'měikwàngyùsyà).

On the upgrade (fig.). / Business is on the upgrade. 'Mǎimài °'hěn you 'chǐsè (°'yìtyān bǐ yìtyān 'hǎu, °hěn 'fādá, °'jēngjēngr̀'shàng).

To grade (without specifying how) fēn děng, fēn 'děngjí; (to classify) fēn-; **grade according to** . . . 'àn(je) . . . °'fēnchūlái (°'fēnkāi, °lái fēn, °'fēn), fēn . . . ; **grade according to size** fēn dàsyǎu, 'àn(je) dà'syǎu 'fēnchūlái, etc.; **grade by quality** fēn hǎuhwài, etc.; **grade by length** fēn chángdwǎn, etc.; **grade by thickness** fēn hòubáu,

etc.; grade by depth *or* closeness in relationship fēn shēnchyǎn, etc.; **grade into so**
many classes 'fēnchéng <u>NU</u> °'dĕng (°'jǔng (kinds), *or* °'lèi (kinds), *or* °'dwēi
(piles)). /Oranges are graded by size and quality. 'Jyúdz dōu shr̀ 'ànje 'dàsyǎu gēn
hǎu'hwài °'fēnchūláide (°'fēnkāide, °lái 'fēnde, °'fēnde). /Grade these eggs by size.
Bǎ jèisyē jī'dàn àn dà'syǎu °'fēnkāi (°'fēnchūlai). /Grade these eggs into three sizes.
Bǎ jèisyē jī'dàn àn dà'syǎu 'fēnchéng sān °'dĕng (°'jǔng, °'lèi, °'dwēi). /These eggs
must be graded by size. Jèisyē jī'dàn dĕi °'fēn dà'syǎu (°'àn dà'syǎu 'fēnkāi).

(Level) nùngpíng, píng. /The laborers graded the land. 'Gūngrénmen bǎ
nèikwài'dì °nùng'píngle (°'píngle yìpíng). /The land has been graded. Nèikwài 'dì
°'píng le (°nùng'píngle).

GRAIN. (Wheat, corn, etc.) wǔ'gǔdzá'lyáng (of all kinds); lyángshr (harvested); gǔdz,
gǔdz (an amount of any kind of grain not to be used for food; also, especially millet);
lyáng in combinations. /This year the grain crop is much better than the tobacco
crop. 'Jīnnyán shōu de °'lyángshr (°wǔ'gǔdzá'lyáng) bǐ yān'yèdz 'chyángde 'dwō.
/These trucks are designated for transporting grain. 'Jèisyē kǎ'chē shr̀ yùn 'lyángshr de. /Grain merchants had a good year last year. °'Lyángshāng (°'Mài wǔ'gǔdzá-
'lyáng de) 'chyùnyán 'mǎimài bú'hwài. /This is pure grain alcohol. Jèijǔng jyóu-
'jīng shr̀ 'chwún yùng 'lyángshr 'dzwòde. /This grain is being saved for seed. Jèisyē °'gǔdz (°'gǔdz) lyóuje dzwò °'jǔngdz (°'jǔngr).

(Small particle) lì, lyèr; **a grain of rice** yílì mǐ. /I got most of the sand out
of the spinach, but there are a few grains left. Wǒ bǎ 'bwōtsailide 'shādz chàbudwō
'dōu 'dóulóuchūchyule, kĕshr hái 'shèngle °ji'lì (°ji'lyèr).

(Small amount) yìdyǎr. /There isn't a grain of truth in what he said. 'Tā shwō
de °yì'dyǎr (or, more emphatic °yì'dǐngdyǎr) 'jēnhwà dōu méi'yǒu.

(Of wood) wén, wér. /This wood has a beautiful grain. 'Jèige 'mùtou de 'wér
hĕn hǎu 'kàn. /What a fine-grained pipe! Jèige yān'dǒu 'wén dwō 'syì a!

Go against the grain. /Does loud conversation go against the grain with you?
is expressed as Do you dislike loud conversation? Nǐ shr̀ °bù'syǐhwān (°'nǐwei,
°'tǎuyàn) 'dàshēngr shwō'hwà ma? or as Does loud conversation make you displeased?
'Dàshēng shwō'hwà shr̀ jyàu nǐ °bù'syǐhwān ma (°'nǐwei ma, °'tǎuyàn ma, *or* make
you irritated? °'byènyou ma)?

GRAMMAR. wénfǎ; **good grammar** is expressed with tūng clear *or* shwùn using proper
word order or with both of these 'tūngshwùn; **bad grammar** is expressed with bùtūng
unclear *or* bùshwùn using poor word order. /I've never studied English grammar.
Wǒ 'tsúnglái méi'sywégwo 'Yīngwén wén'fǎ. /Do you have a good grammar (book)
for a beginner? Nǐ yǒu méiyou wèi chūsywéde rén yùng de wén'fǎ, yàu hǎu yidyǎr
de? /He has bad grammar in Chinese. Tā shwō de 'Jūnggwo hwà wén'fǎ °'bù'tūng
(°bú'shwùn).

GRAND. (Splendid) jēn 'hǎu. /It's grand weather for tennis. Jèige 'tyánchi dǎ wǎng-
'chyóu 'jēn hǎu. /He's a grand old man. 'Nèiwèi 'lǎu syānsheng jēn 'hǎu. *or*
(implying great virtue, good reputation, and advanced years) Tā 'jēn shr̀ 'dégāuwàng-
'jùng. *or* Tā jēn shr̀ ge 'dégāuwàng'jùng de lǎu syānsheng.

(Luxurious). /They live in very grand style. Tāmen hĕn 'shēchr̀. *or* Tāmen
'páichǎng hĕn 'dz̀. *or* Tāmen 'jyāli hĕn 'jyǎngjyóu.

(Complete). /What is the grand total? 'Dzǔngshùr shr̀ 'dwōshǎu? *or* 'Dzǔng-
jyē shr̀ shémma 'shùr?

GRANDFATHER. (General term) **paternal grandfather** dzǔfù; **maternal grandfather** wàidzǔfù; (somewhat more intimate term) **paternal grandfather** yéye, gūnggung; **maternal
grandfather** lǎuye, wàigūng.

GRANDMOTHER. (General term) **paternal grandmother** dzúmŭ; **maternal grandmother** wàidzúmŭ; (somewhat more intimate term) **paternal grandmother** năinai, pwópwo; **maternal grandmother** lăulau, wàipwó.

GRANT. (Of permission or a request) is expressed as to permit jwŭn (rather formal); ràng (informal); 'dăying jyàu; be **granted** gàusyalai (only of a request for leave). / Did they grant him permission to leave? (no matter who asked permission for him) Tāmen °jwŭn (°'ràng, °'dăying jyàu) tā 'dzŏu (le) ma? or (specifically at his own request) Tāmen dăying tā jyàu tā dzŏu(le) ma? / Did they grant him his request for a leave? Tāmen °'jwŭn (°'ràng, °'dăying) tāde 'jyà le ma? or Tā gàu'jyà tāmen °'jwŭnle ma (°rèn'kĕ le ma, °'dăying tā le ma)? / Was he granted leave? Ta gàijyà gàusyaláile ma? / They granted him a three-day leave. Tāmen °'jwŭnle (°etc.) tā 'sāntyan jyà.

(Give) gĕi; (especially of government appropriations) 'bwōgĕi. / The government granted the school $10,000 for research. 'Jēngfu (bwō)gĕi sywésyàu yí'wànkwài chyán, dzwò 'yánjyōu 'gūngdzwò.

Granted that . . . 'chengrèn . . . 'búgwò, jyòu swàn . . . yĕ. / Granted that we were late, still you had no reason to be so mad about it. Jyòu 'swàn wŏmen 'wăn le, nĭ yĕ 'fànbushang 'nèmma jāu'jí a. or Wŏmen 'chéngrèn wŏmen 'wăn le, búgwò nĭ 'fànbushang 'nèmma jāu'jí a. / Granted that you're right, still that's not the way to say it. Jyòu 'swàn nĭ 'dwèi le, yĕ 'bùgāi nèmma 'shwō a. or Wŏ 'chéngrèn nĭ 'dwèi le, 'búgwò nĭ 'bùgāi 'nèmma shwō'hwà.

Take something **for granted** (no need to ask) 'yùngbujáu 'wèn; (know, of something that turned out as expected) jīrdau; (think, of something that didn't turn out as expected) yĭwei, dăje; (suppose, with the tentativeness sometimes implied by the English phrase) jywéje. None of these is normally expressed when referring to future actions of the person addressed; the idea is then expressed by 'yídìng (certainly), which is also used with the above constructions. / I take it for granted that you'll be there. Nĭ shr 'yídìng 'dàude. / I take it for granted that he'll be there. 'Yùngbujáu 'wèn le, tā shr 'yídìng 'dàude. or (tentatively) Wŏ 'jywéje tā shr 'yídìng 'dàude. / I never thought to ask whether you were coming; I just took it for granted. Wŏ méi-'wèn nĭ 'láibulai, yīnwei wŏ °'dăje 'yùngbujáu 'wèn (nĭ) le ne (or (if the person came as expected) 'jīrdau nĭ 'yídìng hwèi 'láide, or (if the person didn't come as expected) °'yĭwei (or 'dăje) nĭ 'yídìng hwèi 'lái ne). but / You take too much for granted. (friendly advice) Nĭ 'jèige rén °'tài 'bŭkĕn shēn'jyòu (°'rénjyā shwō 'shémma dōu 'rènyĭwéi 'jēn, °tài 'dàyì, °tài 'māhu, °tài 'māmahu'hūde, °'shémma dōu bù'dzsyì 'syàngsyang). or (rebuke) Nĭ 'jĭngyàu jàn 'pyányi. or Nĭ 'wèimyăn tài 'chīfù 'rén. or Nĭ 'yĭwéi 'shéi dōu hău 'chīfu shrde.

A grant (gift) gĕi de(kwăndz); (especially governmental) bwō de(kwăndz), 'jīntyē. / The school is supported by a government grant. Jèige sywé'syàu de jīng'fèi shr 'kàuje °'jēngfu 'gĕi de 'kwăndz (°'jēngfu 'bwō de 'kwăndz, °'jēngfúde 'jīntyē).

GRASP. Grasp or **grasp at** an object, see GRAB, HOLD.

To **grasp** an idea is expressed as to understand míngbai, dŭng, jīrdau. / He grasped the idea at once. (from something said) Tā °yì 'shwō (or (from something written) °yí 'kàn) jyòu °'míngbai le (°'dŭngle, °dōu 'jīrdaule).

Have a good **grasp** of °dŭngde (°jīrdàude, °'yáujyĕde) hĕn 'tòuchè. / He has a good grasp of the subject under discussion. Tău'lwùnde 'tímù tā °'dŭngde (°'jīrdàude, °'lyáujyĕde) hĕn 'tòuchè.

GRASS. tsău; (ground with grass growing on it) 'tsăudì; grassland 'tsăudì, (grazing ground) dàtsauywán. / Who's going to cut the grass? Shéi chyù °kăn (°gē) 'tsău? / Keep off the grass. 'Búyàu dzŏu 'tsăudì. or Byé dzài 'tsăudìshang 'dzŏu. / They often play on grass courts. Tāmen 'chángchang dzài 'tsǎudǐshang dǎ'chyóu. /These grasses grow best in a dry climate. Jèisyē 'tsǎu dzài 'chǐhòu gān'dzàu de dìfang 'jǎngde 'dzwèi 'hǎu. /Don't let grass grow under your feet. Cháng 'hwódùngje dyar. *or* 'Byé dāi'lǎnlou.

GRATEFUL. 'gǎnsyè, · gǎnjí. /I am extremely grateful for all you've done. Nǐ dwèi wǒde 'hǎuchu wǒ °'fēicháng gǎnjí (°'fēicháng gǎnsyè, °'gǎnjíbú'jìn). /I am grateful to you for your help. Nǐ bāng wǒde 'máng, wǒ hén 'gǎnsyè nǐ. *or* 'Méng nǐ bāng'jù, 'gǎnjíbú'jìn.

GRATITUDE. gǎnjí, gǎnsyè. /I don't know how to express my gratitude. Wǒ bújŕdau dzěmmayang byaudá wode °'gǎnjì (°'gǎnsyè). /That's gratitude for you! is expressed as That's certainly conscienceless! Jyàn'jŕ shr méi'lyǎngsyīn!

   Show gratitude bàudá. /That's his way of showing you his gratitude. Tā 'nèi shr yàu 'bàudá 'bàudá nǐ a. *or* (sarcastically) Tā 'nèmmaje jyòu swàn 'bàudá nǐ le.

GRAY. hwēi(shǎr) (de); (of the sky) yīn. /Gray goes well with red. Hwēi gēn 'húng °'pèidelái (°'pèichilai hěn 'hǎu). *or* 'Hwēishǎr gēn 'húngshǎr hěn 'chèn. /It is a gray stone building. Nèi shŕ yídzwò 'hwēi(shǎr)de shŕtou 'gàide 'lóu. /She has gray eyes. Tā yǎn'jū shŕ 'hwēide. *or* Tā shŕ 'hwēiyǎn'jū. /Her eyes are bluish-gray. Tāde yǎn'jūr 'hwēili dài 'lán. /The sky was gray all morning. (Tyān) 'yīnle yì-'dzǎushang. *or* 'Tyān yìdzǎushang dōu 'yīnje. *or* Yì'dzǎushang 'tyān nèmma 'yīnchenchende.

   To gray (of hair) bái. /He's graying fast. Tā 'tóufa 'báide jēn 'kwài. *but* /He's graying at the temples. is expressed as His temples are getting streaked. Tā 'lyǎngbìn 'bān le.

GREAT. (Outstanding). Chinese has no single word with this wide range of meaning, but emphasizes the particular quality referred to by some emphatic word. Before words indicating an occupation or calling, Chinese uses simply dà *or* 'wěidàde. Elsewhere, an adjective meaning good, bad, important, etc., is emphasized by saying dà..., 'tǐng..., hěn..., ...jíle; or emphasis is expressed elsewhere in the sentence. /He's a great statesman. Tā shŕ ge °'dà (°'wěidàde) 'jèngjŕ'jyā. /He's a great inventor. Tā shŕ ge °'dà (°'wěidàde) 'fāmíng'jyā. /He's a great man. (very good) Tā shŕ ge 'dà hǎu'rén. *or* Tā jèige rén °hǎu'jíle (°'shŕfen 'hǎu). *or* (very famous) Tā jèige rén 'hěn yǒu'míng. *or* Tā shŕ ge °'wěirén (°'dàrénwu). /He's a great speaker. Tā 'hěn °hwèi (°'néng) 'yǎnshwō. *or* Tā shŕ ge 'dà 'yǎnshwō'jyā. /He's a great scoundrel. Tā shŕ ge 'dà °hwàirén (°hwàidàn). *or* Tā dǐng búshr ge 'dūngsyi le. /He's a great talker. (endless, but not necessarily boring) Tā 'shwō-chilai °'tāutaubù'jywéde (°jyòu 'méi'tóur). or meaning He loves to talk. Tā 'lǎu ài shwō 'hwà. /He was a great favorite with everybody. 'Rénrén dōu 'syǐhwan tā. /That was a great day in my life. (happy, successful) Nèi shŕ wǒ yí'bèidzli °'tǐng dé'yìde (*or* important) °'tǐngyàu'jǐnde, *or* (memorable) °'tǐng jyàu wǒ 'lyóulyànde) yí'tyān. /The conference accomplished great things. Jèitsz hwèi'yì 'jyěgwó 'fēicháng 'hǎu. /They're great friends. Tāmen shŕ °'tǐnghǎude (°hěn 'chǐnjìnde) 'péngyou. *or* Tāmen lyǎ 'hǎu'jíle (°'hǎuje ne). /I was in great pain. Wǒ 'nèi shŕhou °'téng-'jíle (°'téngsz le). /It was a great injustice. Nèi 'jēnshr (tài) °bù'gūngping(le) (°'ywānwang(le)). /That was a great help! Nèi kě 'jēn yǒu'yùng! *or* (sarcastically) 'Nèi kě yǒu shémma 'yùng a? *or* 'Nèi jyàu yǒu'yùng, tsái 'gwài de ne! /There's a great difference between these two men. 'Tāmen lyǎ °'chàbyé (°'fēnbyé) hěn 'dà. *or* 'Tāmen lyǎ yǒu 'hěnbù'túngde dìfang. /That'll make a great difference. Nà kě jyòu °'dà bù'túng le (°'dà bùyí'yàng le, °'chàde'ywǎn le). /That's great news. 'Nèi kě °hǎu'jíle (°'jēn hǎu). /That's great! Hǎu'jíle! *or* ('Nèi kě) 'Jēn hǎu!

   Great big (of things) dà, hǎu dà de, hěn dà de, tǐng dà de, yòu'kwānyòu'dàde (wide and big); (of persons or things) gāu dà de, 'gāugaudà'dàde, 'yòugāuyòu'dàde;

(tall and big, of persons only) 'kwéiwĕi. /He owned a great big house. Tā yŏu yĭswor °'dàfángdz (°'hăudàdefángdz, °etc.). or Tā yòu'gāuyòu'dàdefángdz. /He's a great big fellow. Tā (shŕ ge) °yòu'gāuyòu'dà(derén) (°gāu'dà(de rén), °etc.) or Tā (shŕ ge)hĕn 'kwéiwĕi(derén). /They brought in a great big coffin. Tāmen 'táilaile yíge yòu'kwānyòu'dàde 'gwāntsai.

    Great deal, great many hĕn dwō (much or many); 'hăusyē (many only); in exclamations dwōshau. /He caused a great deal of trouble for us. Tā gĕi wŏmen °'rĕle hĕn 'dwō de 'máfan (°'dwōshàu 'máfan a)! /A great many people don't know the difference. °'Hĕn dwō (°'Hăusyē) rén bùjŕdàu jèige 'fēnbyé. or 'Bùjŕdau 'jèige 'fēnbyé de rén °'dwōje ne (°'dwōlechyule, °dwō'jíle).

GREEN. (Of color) lyù, lyùshăr, lyùde. /Bring me my green sweater. Bă wŏ lyùmáuyī 'nálai. /The book cover is green. Shū'pyér shŕ 'lyùde. /Green is not becoming to her. 'Lyùshăr 'pèi tā °'bùhé'shŕ (°'bùhău'kàn). or Tā chwān 'lyùde 'bùhău'kàn.

    (Of plant life) chīng; **green grass** chīngtsău, 'lyùtsău; **green vegetables** chīngtsài, dài'lyùshărde chīng'tsài; **fresh green** (color) 'chīngtswèi, 'syīnlyù; **evergreen** chángchīng shŕ; **green tea** (leaves) 'chīngcháyè, 'lyùcháye. /They passed miles of fresh green countryside. Tāmen gwòle 'hău syē lĭ 'dì, 'dòushr °'syīnlyùde (°'chīngtswèide) 'tyányĕ.

    (Unripe) fāchīngde (lit., still green); shēng (lit., not ripened); 'bànshēngrde (half ripe). /Don't eat green apples or you'll get sick. 'Byé chŕ °'shēng (°fā'chīngde, °'bànshēngrde) pínggwŏ, hwèi 'bìngde. but /That wood won't burn well; it's still green. 'Nèikwài 'mùtou bùhău 'jáu; hái 'lyùje ne.

    (Inexperienced) shēng (also means unripe); (not having experience) 'méiyou 'jīngyàn; **green hand** (at doing something) 'shēngshŏur. /When I first came, I was green at selling. Wŏ tsái 'lái de shŕhou, dzai mài 'dūngsyishang °'méiyou 'jīngyàn (°'hĕn shŕ ge 'shēngshŏur, °hĕn 'shēng). /He's still green at it. Tā 'hái °shŕ ge 'shēngshŏur ne (°'shēng ne). or Tā hái yŏu dyar °wài'háng (°'lìba).

    Green with envy. /He's green with envy. is expressed as He is extremely jealous. Tā 'tsùjyèr 'dà le. or as He was so jealous that his face turned half green and half white. Tā 'jìdùde 'lyànshang chīngyíkwàibáiyíkwàide.

    A green (grass-covered land) 'tsăudì; (park) gūngywán; (in golf) chăngdz, chyóuchăng. /The drought has ruined the green. Jèitsz 'hànde bă °chyóuchăng (°'chăngdz) gĕi 'hwĕile.

    Greens chīngtsài; **turnip greens** lwóbwo'yèr, lwóbwo'yēngr, lwóbwo'yīngdz. /Let's buy some greens for dinner. Măi dyăr 'chīngtsài hău dzwò wăn'fàn.

GRIEF. Expressed verbally with nángwò suffer or shāngsyīn be unhappy. /Her grief over the death of her husband is pitiful indeed. Tā 'jàngfu 'szle, tā °nán'gwò de (°shāng'syīnde) 'jēn kĕ'lyán. /We have deep sympathy for her in her grief. Tā °nèmma nán'gwò (°'nèmma shāng'syīn) jyàu 'wŏmen yĕ hĕn nán'shòu. or expressed as Her suffering such an unfortunate thing makes us sympathetic. °Tā dzāule (°Tājyā 'chūle) 'nèmma °bú'syīngde shŕ (°yàngr de 'shŕ) °'jyàu wŏmen 'hĕn nán-'shòu (°'jēn jyàu wŏmen 'jywéje tā kĕ'lyán).

GRIND (GROUND). (By rubbing two things together) mwó. /They ground the ax to a sharp edge. Tā bă fŭdz mwóde hĕn kwài. /The optician grinds his own lenses. Dzwò yănjīngrde dzjĭ mwó jìngdz. /The stone is almost ground smooth. Jèikwài shŕtou chàbudwō °mwóping (°mwó 'gwāng) le. /First I must grind some ink off the ink stick. Wŏ dĕi syān °mwó (°yán) dyăr mwò.

(By rubbing two things together, such as millstones or mortar and pestle, with something hard in between) mwò; (for small amounts) yán. / We grind our coffee by hand. Wŏmen yùng shŏu (yáu jĭchi) mwò kāfei. / They are using the small millstones to grind beans. Tāmen yùng syǎumwòr mwò dòudz ne. / The pharmacist ground the medicine into powder. Yàujìshr̄ bǎ yàu °yánchengle (°mwòchengle) mwòr.

(By a screw-action machine; of something soft as meat) jyǎu; **meat grinder** jyǎuròujĭ. / Grind the meat into hamburger. Bǎ'ròu jyǎuchéng ròu'mwèr. / Please have the meat ground for me. Chĭng bǎ'ròu gěi jyǎu le.

Grind the teeth yǎu yá (yǎu also means bite). / He grinds his teeth in his sleep. Tā shwèi 'jyǎu de shŕhou yǎu'yá.

Ground glass (rough-surfaced glass) 'máubwōli. / The windows are of ground glass. 'Chwānghushang shr̄ 'máubwōli.

Special expressions in English. / He has an ax to grind, you may be sure. Méi-'tswòr, tā yŏu 'tāde 'ywánge. / Learning any language is a long grind. Sywé 'shémma 'yǔyán dōu děi 'syà hěn 'dà de 'gūngfu. / During examinations he turns into a grind. 'Kǎushŕde shŕhou tā 'byànchéng yíge hěn yùng'gūng de rén. / He grinds out three songs a day. 'Yìtyānli tā 'tsòuchū 'sānge 'gēer lai.

GRIP. (A strong hold) 'shŏujyèr; **loosen one's grip** fàngshŏu, sūngshŏu; **break one's grip** bāikai 'shŏu; **vise-like grip** (lit. tiger-head pincers) hǔtóu chyán. / He has a powerful grip. Tā'shŏujyèr hěn 'dà. / He was holding the rifle with a vise-like grip. Tā dzwàn 'chyāng dzwànde syàng 'hǔtóu'chyándz shŕde. / He didn't loosen his grip on the man's throat until the man was dead. Tā chyāje nèige rén de 'sǎngdz, yìjŕ chyā'szle tsái °fàng'shŏu (°sūng'shŏu).

(A strong hold; fig.). / He has the whole nation in his grip. Tā bǎ 'chywángwó 'tǔngjŕde hěn 'yán. or 'Chywángwó 'dōu dzài tā 'jǎngwò jŕjūng.

(Handle) bàr. / The grip of the revolver is broken. 'Shŏuchyāngbàr 'hwài le.

(Suitcase) shŏutí bāu. / I have a clean shirt in my grip. Wŏ shŏutí'bāuli yŏu jyàn 'gānjĭng 'chènyī.

To grip. See HOLD, GRAB.

Come to grips with a person jwā, jyóu; **come to grips** with a subject jwāju. / They argued for hours, but never really came to grips with the central issue; but they did come to grips with each other. Tāmen 'chǎule bàn'tyān, 'shéi yě méi'jwāju jèng'tí; kěshr tāmen bĭtsz °'jwā (°'jyóu) chilaile.

Gripping. / It was a gripping speech. Yǎn'jyǎng jyǎngde jyàu rén °ài 'tīng (°bù'néng búyùng'syīn 'tīng).

GROUND. (Surface of the earth) dìshang; (land) dì; (particular place) dìfang; (soil) tǔ. / The ground was very rocky. 'Dì shang yŏu 'hěn dwō 'shŕtou. or 'Nèidai 'dìfang, 'dōu shr dà shŕtou. / This ground is not rich enough for a good crop. °Jèige 'tǔ bù-'féi (°Jèikwài dì 'búgòu 'féi de), 'jùngbuchu hǎu 'jwāngjya lai.

(Background, as on a flag) dyèr, dìdz. / The flag has white stars on a blue ground. Chí shr̄ °'lán dyèrshang (°'lándìdz 'shàngtou) yŏu syē'báisyēngr.

Cover ground. / My men covered the covered the ground thoroughly (lit. searched everywhere). 'Wŏde rén 'yĭjĭng dzài jèi yi °'dài (°'dwàn, °'pyàn) 'dìfang 'dōu jǎu 'byànle. / If I drive, I can cover a lot of ground (lit. a great distance) in one day. Yàushr wŏ kāi'chē, yìtyān néng 'kāide hěn 'ywǎn. / He covered the ground thoroughly. (in a speech) Tā (bǎ jèijyàn 'shr̄) shwōde °hěn 'syángsyì (°hěn 'tòuchè, °dōu shwō-'dàule, °'dōu shwō'byànle). or (in research) Tā bǎ gwānyu jèijyàn shr̄de 'tsáilyàu dōu °jǎudàu le (°jǎu'byànle).

603

From the ground up. / He changed the entire personnel from the ground up (from bottom to top in rank). Tā tsúng 'syā dàu 'shàng bǎ rén 'dōu hwànle. / He changed everything from the ground up (not in special rank). Tā shémma dōu gěi 'gàile.

Hold one's ground. / He held his ground against all opposition. (didn't give in) Nèmma 'fǎndwèi tā, tā yě méiràng'bù. / Hold your ground! (don't retreat, fight it out, etc.) Byé 'twèi! *or* Yìdyǎr byé 'twèi. *or* Ná'dǐngle 'júyì, yì'dyǎr byé 'ràng. *or* Búyàu ràng'bù. *or* 'Jǎnjùle 'jyáu, yì'dyǎr byé'ràng.

On dangerous ground, on solid ground (in an argument). / You're on dangerous ground when you say that. Nǐ 'nèmma ge 'shwōfǎr °'jànbu'jù (°bù'láukàu, °yì'bwō jyòu 'dǎu). / He was (standing) on solid ground when he made that argument. Tā 'shwōde nèi'dyǎn hěn °'yǐng (°jànde 'jù, °nán bwō'dǎu ta).

Grounds (logical basis) 'gēnjyù. / What grounds do you have for saying that? Nǐ 'nèmma shwō yǒu shémma 'gēnjyu? / You have grounds for your opinions. Nǐde 'yìjyàn 'dōu yǒu 'gēnjyu.

Grounds (gardens) 'ywándz. / A gardener takes care of the grounds. 'Ywándz yǒu ge °hwār'jyàng (°kàn'ywándzde) 'jàuguje.

(Area used for a particular purpose) chǎng(dz). / The circus grounds are on the east side. Mǎ'syìchǎng(dz) dzài 'dūngbyar.

Coffee grounds jār. / Rinse out the coffee grounds. Bǎ kāfēi'jār náshwěi 'chūngsyachyu.

To ground (of electricity) is expressed as **connect the ground wire** ān(shang) dì'syàn. / Is the radio grounded? Wúsyàn'dyàn ānle dì'syàn méiyou?

Be grounded, run aground (of a boat) gēchyǎn (le). / The boat has run aground. Chwán gē'chyǎn le.

Be grounded (of a plane) is expressed as **can't begin to fly** 'bùnéng 'chǐfēi. / The plane was grounded by bad weather. Yīnwei 'tyānchi bù'hǎu, fēijī 'bùnéng 'chǐfēi.

Be grounded in (have a good background in) dǎ 'gēndǐ, dǎ'gēnjī. / They are well grounded in history. Tāmen (dwèiyu) lì'shǐ, (dǎde) °'gēndǐ (°'gēnjī) hěn °hǎu (°jyēshr).

Ground floor (of several floors) dì'yìtséng lóu; (of two) lóusyà. / I don't want a room on the ground floor. Wǒ búyàu °dì'yìtséng lóu de (°lóu'syàde) 'fángjyān.

GROUP. (Of people) chyún, dwēi, dzwēi; (more informally, especially of a group or crowd of people who happen to be together) chyúr; (a group with a common characteristic or interest) hwǒr, hwǒdz, bāng; (a closely-knit organized group) 'twántǐ; (a well-organized group, a party) dǎng; (an organization or society) hwèi; (a group or division within an organization) pài; (a group or section for discussion or work) dzū. All these except 'twántǐ and hwèi are measures. / A group of men stood in the street and watched. °Yì'chyún rén (°Yì'dwēi rén) dzài 'jyēshang 'jànje 'chyáu. / Don't associate with that group. 'Byé gēn °'nèichyún (°'nèihwǒdz °'nèibāng) rén 'láiwang. / They will be hard to deal with if they form a group. Tāmen 'jyēchéng °yì'dǎng (°'yíge twán'tǐ) jyou 'bùhǎu 'yǐngfu le. / They organized themselves into a group. Tāmen 'jyēchéng °yì'dǎng (°'yíge 'twántǐ, °'yíge 'hwèi). / They belong to another group. Tāmen shr 'lìng yì'dǎng de (°ge 'hwèi de, *or* (within a larger organization) °'pàide). / There are different groups in the party. 'Dǎnglǐtou yǒu 'pài. / The party was divided into several groups over the controversy. 'Jèijyàn shr yì'dǎngde rén 'yìjyàn bù'hé, 'fēnchéngle ji'pài. / Let's divide the members into three groups to discuss these three items. Dzámen bǎ hwèi'ywán fēnchéng sān'dzǔ lái 'tǎulwùn jèi 'sānjyàn 'shr̀. / The group met every Wednesday. 'Nèige hwèi měi Syīngchī'sān 'jyùhwèi yí'tsz̀. / They went out in groups of two or three. Tāmen 'sā yī'chyún 'lyǎ yī'hwěr de jyòu 'dzǒule.

(Of things) dwēi, dzwēi; (pile) lwò; (set) tàu; (of moving objects that can be scattered) chyún; (technical, of an air force) dwēi; syē (several) may be used when grouping is expressed in the verb. / That's a beautiful group of trees. Nèi yídwēi 'shù hěn hǎu'kàn. / The textile design has groups of red squares on a white background. Nèijǔng bù de 'hwāyàngr shr̀ 'báidyèrshang yǒu yī'dzwēiyídzwēide húng fāng'kwàr. / He arranged the cards into groups of four. Tā bǎ 'pái 'fēnchéngle 'szge °yí'lwò (°yī'dzwēi). / How many buildings are there in that group? Nèi °yí'tàu (°yī'dwēi) yǒu 'dwōshàuswǒr 'fángdz. / How many planes are there in that group? (non-technical) Nèi yīchyún fēi'jīli yǒu 'dwōshǎu 'jyà? / How many planes are there in a group? (technical) Yī'dàdwēi yǒu dwōshǎu jyà fēi'jī? / You'll have to memorize this group of letters in the given order. 'Jèisyē dz̀'mùr nǐ děi 'jàuje ywán'láide 'tsz̀syu'lyán-chǐlai 'jìdzai 'syīnli.

To group (divide into groups) 'fēnchéng yī'dzǔyídzǔde; or instead of dzǔ use lèi (class), dwēi, lwò, tàu, dwēi, pài. / Group the words according to meaning. Bǎ jèisyē 'dz̀ ànje 'yìsz̀ 'fēnchéng °yī'dzǔyídzǔde (°yí'lèiyíleide).

Group together (by organization) lyánchilai, 'lyánhéchilai, 'jēchéng °yíchī (°yìtwán); (informally, of people) 'jyùdzai yíkwàr, hé lǔnglai; (put together, of things) 'hédzai yíkwàr. / They grouped together to resist him. Tāmen °'lyánchilai (°'lyán-héchilai, °'jyēchéng yíchī, °'jyēchéng yìtwán) lái 'gēn tā 'dǐkàng. / Those cards can be grouped together. Nèisyē 'kǎpyàn kěyǐ 'hédzai yíkwàr.

GROW (GREW, GROWN). (Become larger physically) jǎng. / She grew two inches in six months. Tā 'lyòugeywèli 'jǎngle 'lyǎngtswùn. / He's six feet tall and still grow-ing. Tā yǒu 'lyòuchǐ'gāu le, 'hái(dzai) 'jǎng ne. / Weeds grow fast. 'Yětsǎu jǎngde 'kwài. / He grew to his full height before he was eighteen. Tā 'méidàu shr̀'bāswèi jyòu 'jǎngde nèmma 'gāu le. / Trees grow tall near the river. Hè'byārde 'shù jǎngde 'gāu. / His daughter is growing up rapidly (growing into an adult). Tāde 'nyuér hěn 'kwài de jyòu yàu 'jǎngchéng 'rén le. *but* / He has let his beard grow for two days. Tā 'húdz lyóule 'lyǎngtyān le.

(Raise crops) jùng. / These farmers grow fruit. Jèisyē 'núngrén 'dōu jùng 'gwǒmùshù.

(Increase in respect to some characteristic) is occasionally expressed by le *or* de after the verb describing the characteristic, but more commonly by such construc-tions as jyànjyànde . . . by degrees, *or* ywē . . . ywē . . . the more . . . the more . . ., or by the resultative ending chǐlai. / Hasn't she grown fat! Tā 'jǎngde 'hǎubu'pàng a! *or* Tā (jǎngde) 'pàngchilaile! *or* Tā °'ywē lái (°'ywèjǎng) ywē 'pàng! *or* Tā jǎng'pàngle. / The crowd grew rapidly. Nèichyún rén yíhwérde 'gūngfu °ywē 'jyù (°'ywèlái) ywè 'dwō. / He grew careless. Tā (jyàn'jyànde) °'dàyìchilaile (°'bùnèmma 'syǎusyīn le). / He's growing old. Tā jyàn'jyànde 'lǎu le. / After a while he grew used to the change in climate. Syīnde 'chìhou tā °jyàn'jyànde (°'ywè lái ywè) 'jywéje 'gwànle. / He grew away from his family. Tā °jyàn'jyànde (°'ywèlái ywè) gēn tā 'jyālide rén 'shēngfenle. *or* Tā gēn tā 'jyālide rén °jyàn'jyànde (°'ywèlái ywè) 'shēngfenle. / That song is growing in me. Wǒ 'ywè lái ywè 'syǐhwan nèige'gēr le. / The taste for liquor has been growing on him. Tā jyàn'jyànde 'ài hē'jyǒu le. *or* Tā 'ywè lái ywè ài hē'jyǒu le. / A new political group is growing up here. 'Jèr yǒu yíge 'syīnde °jèng'dǎng (°'jèngjr̀ twán'tǐ) °'hwódùngchǐlaile (°'fājǎnchǐlaile). / His business has grown rapidly. Tāde 'mǎimài °'chǐláide (°'fājànde) hěn 'kwài.

Be full-grown jăng chéng le. / This dog is full-grown. Jèige gŏu 'yíjing jăng chéng le.

Be grown, grown-up jăng dà, jăng chéng 'dàren, shř ge dàren. / My son is quite grown-up now. Wŏde 'érdz syàn'dzài jyàn'jŕde 'jăngchéng 'dàren le. / Wait until he's grown-up. Děng tā jăng 'dàle dzài 'shwō ba. / He's a grown man (an adult) now. Tā syàn'dzài shř ge 'dàren le.

GROWTH. (Production by growing). / We forced our way through the thick growth (dense forest) of pines. Wŏmen dzài 'mìmichén'chénde sūngshù'líndzli yìng 'chwǎnggwo-chyule. / He has a two-day growth of beard. is expressed as He hasn't shaved for two days. Tā 'lyàngtyān méigwā'lyǎn le.

(Abnormal mass of tissue on the body) 'chwāng. / He has some sort of growth on his neck. Tā 'bwódzshang jǎngle ge 'chwāng.

GUARD. (Defend or watch a person or place) kān(je); (referring to a place only) 'bǎshŏu-(je). / Soldiers guard the place day and night. Dàbīng 'hēisya'báirde °'kānje (°'bǎ-shŏuje) nèige 'dìfang. / Guard the prisoner carefully. Hǎu'hǎurde kānje nèige 'chyóufàn. / They guarded the fallen bridge until the police came. Chyáu 'tāle; tāmen 'jàn ner 'kānje děng 'syúnjǐng 'láile tsái 'dzŏude. / They guarded the bridge very closely. Nèige 'chyáu tāmen °'bǎshŏude (°'kānde) hěn °jǐn (°'yán, °'yánmì).

(Be careful about) syǎusyīn, lyóu'shén, dìfang. / You'd better guard your words. Shwō hwà děi °syǎusyīn dyar (°lyóu dyǎr'shén, °'dìfangje dyar).

Guard against 'dìfang(je) (take precautions against); 'fángbèi(je) (prepare for); 'yùfáng (try to prevent); or expressed as be careful, see paragraph two. / This is just to guard against burglary. Jèi 'búgwo shř °'fángbèije (°'yùfáng, °'dìfangje) 'bú jyàu rén 'tōu. / They tried to guard against the spread of disease. Wèile °'yùfáng (°'fángbèi) jèige 'chwánrǎn'bìng, 'bújyàu 'nàuchilai, tāmen 'hěn mài 'lìchi laije.

A guard (a person who guards) 'wēibīng (military, especially bodyguard); jàn-'gǎngde (military, police, or civilian guard on duty); bǎ'mérde, kān'mérde (guard at a door or gate); mén'jǐng (police guard at a door or gate); kān . . . de (a guard over . . .); bodyguard bǎu'byāude, 'hùwèi. / There are always two guards at the entrance. Dà'mén nar 'lǎu yŏu 'lyàngge °'wēibīng (°'jàn'gǎngde, °bǎ'mérde, °kān'mérde, °mén-'jǐng). / He has two guards who accompany him everywhere. Tā dàu nǎr chyu dōu yŏu 'lyàngge °bǎu'byāude (°'hùwèi) 'gēnje. / They hired a guard for the house. Tāmen 'gùle ge °kān'fángdz de (°rén kān 'fángdz).

(Protective device) bǎusyǎn plus the type of object used for protection. / He has a guard on his pin so that he won't lose it. Tāde byé'jēnshang yŏu bǎusyǎn'hwár, hǎu 'bújŕyu 'dyōu. / There's a guard on the machine to keep the blade from cutting anyone. 'Jīchīshang yŏu bǎusyǎn'bǎr, hǎu jyàu dāu'rèr 'lábujáu 'rén.

Lifeguard jyóushēng'ywán.

Mudguard 'dǎngní'bǎn.

Be off one's guard (not on the alert) 'shūhu, sūngsyè, 'jīngshen bú'gwànjù. / For a moment he was off his guard. or For a moment his guard was down. Yŏu nèmma yìhwěr tā °méilyóu'shén (°bútài 'syǎusyīn, °'sūngsyèle yísyàr, or (against a person or attack) °'dìfangde 'chàdyar). / You can never catch him off guard. Tā 'chùchù °lyóu'shén (°'syǎusyīn), 'méi ge jyàu ni 'dèijau de shŕhou. or Nǐ 'yàusyǎng 'jǎu tā °bùlyóu'shén (°bù'syǎusyīn, °'shūhu, °'jīngshen bu'gwànjù) de shŕhou, 'nà kě méi'yŏu.

Be on guard is expressed as guard against above. / She's always on guard against me. Tā 'lǎu nèmma 'dìfangje wŏ. / We had to be on guard constantly. Wŏmen 'yǐshŕyí'kè děi °'dìfangje (°'fángbèije). or meaning We had to be careful. Wǒmen 'yǐshŕyíkè °děi 'syǎusyǐnje (°děi lyǒu'shěn).

GUESS. tsāi, tsāijau; syǎng (think, suppose); kàn (see, decide from appearances). /Just guess! or I'll let you guess. Nǐ 'tsāi(yi)tsai (kàn). /Guess who it is. Nǐ 'tsāi shŕ 'shéi. /Let me guess. Ràng wǒ °'tsāi(yi)tsai (°'syǎng syang). (kàn). /I guess he's sick. Wǒ °syǎng (°kàn, °tsāi) tā 'bìngle. /Let's see if you can guess. 'Kàn nǐ tsāide'jáu ma? /You won't guess right anyway. Nǐ 'dzěmma yě tsāibu'jáu de. /Did you guess the end of the story? Jèige gùshr 'jyēgwǒ dzěmmayàng, nǐ 'tsāijaule ma? /Can you guess my age? Nǐ 'tsāidejáu wǒ dwǒ'dà ma? /How did you ever guess it? Nǐ dzěmma 'tsāijáule ne? /You'd never guess it! or Who could ever guess it? 'Shéi syǎngde'dàu °a (°ne)! /You guessed wrong. Nǐ tsāitswòle. or Bú'dwèi, bú'dwèi! but /You guessed it! 'Dwèi le! or (of a thing) 'Jyòu shr 'nèige! or (of something abstract) 'Jyòu shr 'nèmmaje.

A guess is expressed verbally as above. /I'll give you three guesses. Rúng nǐ tsāi °'sānhwéi (°'sāntsž, °'sānsyàr). /That was a good guess. Tsāide 'hǎu. /I'd say there were twenty-five divisions, but that's just a wild guess. Wǒ shwō yǒu 'èrshrwǒshrrén, búgwo jèi shr °syǎ'tsāi jyòu 'shŕle. /One guess is as good as another. 'Fǎnjèng shr 'tsāi. but /Your guess is as good as mine. is expressed as I don't know either. 'Wǒ yě bù'jŕ'dàu. or as Whatever you guess is O.K. by me. Nǐ 'dzěmma tsāi dōu 'syíng. /It's anybody's guess. is expressed as No one knows for sure. 'Shéi yě bù'jwǔn jŕdàu.

GUEST. 'kèrén; (an invited guest) 'chǐnglái('jù)de ('kè)rén (with jù means a guest who stays overnight or longer); be a guest at . . . dzài . . . 'jù; invite someone as a guest chǐng ('kè)rén, or (to stay) chǐng . . . jù. /The hotel does not permit guests to keep dogs. Jèige lyǔ'gwǎnlǐ 'bùsyǔ 'kèrén °yǎng (°dài) 'gǒu. /When the guests arrive, you answer the door. 'Kèrén 'dàu de shŕhou 'nǐ chyù kāi'mén. /Don't ever do that again when there are guests. Yǒu 'kèrén de shŕhou 'bùsyǔ 'dzài nèmmaje le. /How many guests did you invite? Nǐ chǐngle 'jǐge (kè)rén? /How many guests did you invite to stay? Nǐ chǐngle 'jǐge (kè)rén lái 'jù? /I was (only) a guest at his house. Wǒ dzài 'tā jyā °shŕ 'kèrén (°'jùgwo). or Tāmen 'chǐng wǒ chyù 'jùgwo. /I was a guest at his house for three days. Wǒ dzài tā 'jyā jùgwo 'sāntyān. or Tā chǐng wǒ dzài tā 'jyā jùle 'sāntyān. /I was a guest at his house last week. 'Shànglǐbai wǒ dzài 'tā jyā 'jùlaije.

Guest of honor jǔkè.

Honored guest gwèibīn.

GUIDE. (Physically) lǐng, dài. /He guided the group through the woods. Tā °'lǐngje (°'dàije) nèisyērén gwòde shù'líndz. /A trained dog guided the blind man through the traffic. 'Syàdz dzài dà'jyēshang 'dzǒu de shŕhou, yǒu ge 'syùnlyànchūlai de 'gǒu °lǐngje (°dàije).

(Mentally or otherwise) is expressed as be guided by ànje, jàuje (go according to); 'tsānkǎuje (referring to); píng (rely on); tīng (listen to). These words are usually followed by a verb of motion or action. /Don't be guided by his advice. 'Byé tīng tāde °'hwà (°'sōu júyi). or Byé °ànje (°jàuje) tāde °'hwà (°'sōujúyi) 'dzǒu. /This schedule will guide you in planning your work. Nǐ kěyǐ °ànje (°jàuje, °'tsānkǎuje) jèige shŕjyān'byàu lai 'dìnggwei dzwòshr de syàn'hòu. but /Try not to be guided by your own personal feelings in this matter. Jèijyàn 'shèr yàu 'syǎusyǐnje; byé 'gǎnchíngyùng'shŕ.

A guide (one who guides) 'syǎngdǎu; (one who leads the way through difficulties) lǐng lùde, dài lùde. /The guide took me around. 'Syǎngdǎu 'lǐngje wǒ dàu 'gèchù chyù 'kàn. /You must have a guide to go through enemy territory. Gwò 'díjìng děi jǎu °ge 'syǎngdǎu (°ge lǐng'lùde, °ge dài'lùde, *or* (lit., someone to guide) °rén 'lǐngje, °rén 'dàije).

(Something acting as a guide) is expressed verbally as in paragraph two above. / Let your conscience be your guide. Ping 'lyǎngsyīn 'dzwǒ, jyǒu 'syíng.

(Device for steadying or directing a moving part) gwǎntour.

Guidebook (for a city, etc.) 'yóulǎnjř'nán; (of instructions) shwōmíng shū. / Where can I buy a guidebook to the city? 'Jèrde 'yóulǎnjř'nán dzài 'nǎr mǎi?

GUILTY. (Suffering from guilt) yǒu'kwèi. / I have a guilty conscience. Wǒ 'syīnli yǒu-'kwèi. / He has a guilty look. is expressed as He looks as if he had a guilty conscience. Tā 'hǎu syàng 'syīnli yǒu'kwèi. or as His expression isn't right. Tā 'shénchi bú-'dwèi. or as He's skulking around. Tā nèmma 'gwéigweiswèi'swèide. or as He looks as if he had done something bad. Tā 'hǎusyàng 'dzwòle shemma hwài 'shèr shřde.

(Legal term) yǒudzwèi; plead guilty 'chéngrèn; or expressed verbally with gàn do. / Is he guilty? Tā yǒu'dzwèi ma? or 'Shř tā 'gànde ma? / He's guilty, all right. 'Jwùnshr tā 'gànde. / Guilty or not guilty? Nǐ 'chéngrèn bù'chéngrèn? or 'Shř bushř nǐ 'gànde? / Guilty. (to the first version of the previous sentence) 'Chéngrèn. or (to the second) Shř. / Not guilty. (to either version) Wǒ 'méigàn nèige. or 'Búshr wǒ. / The prisoner was found guilty. 'Shénchá 'jyēgwǒ 'fànrén yǒu'dzwè. or expressed as The crime of which he was accused was verified. 'Fànrén-(de) 'dzwèijwàng jèng'shřle.

Be guilty of something (be to blame for) yǒu . . . 'dzwèi; (specifically of commit-ting a crime) fàn . . . 'dzwèi. / What am I guilty of? 'Wǒ yǒu 'shémma 'dzwèi? or Wǒ fànle 'shémma dzwèi le? / I'm not builty of anything. Wǒ yì'dyǎr dzwèi yě °méi'yǒu (°méi'fàn). / He's guilty of burglary. Tā fànde shr 'tōuchyèdzwèi.

GUN. (Small arms) chyāng with measures gǎn, jř, gēn; machine gun 'jīgwānchyāng. / He spends a lot of time cleaning his gun. Tā dzài tsā'chyāng shang yùng de 'shřhou 'hěn bù'shǎu.

(Cannon) pàu with measures mén, dzwūn. / Every gun on the ship had been put out of action by enemy bombs. 'Chwánshang 'swǒyǒude 'pàu dōu jyàu 'dírénde jà'dàn 'jàde bùnéng 'yùng le. / The ship fired a salute of 21 guns. is expressed as The ship fired 21 sounds of a gun. 'Chwánshang fàngle èrshr'yīshēng °'pàu (°lǐ'pàu).

Stick to one's guns. / He couldn't prove his point, but he stuck to his guns. Tā bùnéng 'dz`ywánchí'shwō, kěshr lǎu 'jyānchř dzjǐde 'yǐjyàn.

To gun for (fig.). / He's gunning for you. Tā jèngdzai 'jǎuje ni yàu gēn nǐ °swàn'jàng (°dǎ'jyà ne).

HABIT. 'syígwàn; good habit hǎu 'syígwàn; bad habit hwài 'syígwàn, 'máubìng. / I'm trying to break myself of this habit. Wǒ 'jèngdzài syàng bǎ 'jèige máubing 'gǎile ne. / It's a good habit to get up early. Dzǎu'chǐ shř ge 'hǎu syígwàn. / That's a bad habit. Nèi shř ge °'máubìng (°'hwài máubìng, °'hwài syígwàn). / While I was abroad I got into that habit. Wǒ dzài wàigwo de shřhou 'yǎngchéngle nèmma ge 'syígwàn. / Don't get into such a habit. Byé 'yǎngchéng 'nèmma ge 'syígwàn. / I've never gotten into the habit of smoking. Wǒ méi'yǎngchénggwo 'chōuyān de 'syígwàn.

Be in the habit of (to do something habitually) is expressed as always lǎushr or as love to ài or as always love to 'lǎuài. / I'm in the habit of sleeping late on Sundays. Wǒ yí'dàu lǐbài'tyān °lǎushr (°ài, °'lǎuài) chǐde hěn 'wǎn de.

HAIR. (On a human head) tóufa, fǎ; haircut lífǎ, lǐfà; hairdo fǎshř, tóufáde yángdz;

hairdresser lǐfàshī. /What color is her hair? Tā 'tóufa shṛ shémma 'yánshar de? /All his hair turned white. Tāde 'tóufa 'dōu bái le. or Tā 'báifàtsāng'tsāng le. /Look at that fuzzy-haired boy! Kàn nèige háidz, yìtóu 'rúnghūhurde'tóufa. /There is a hair on your coat. Nǐ 'yīfushang yǒu yìgēn 'tóufa. /You should have had your hair cut shorter. Nǐde 'tóufa yīnggāi jyǎn 'dwǎn dyar. /I like her hairdo. Wǒ syǐhwan tā tóufa 'shūde nèige 'yàngr. but /Want your hair (head) washed? 'Syǐtóu ma?

(On the temples) bìn, bìnjyǎu, bìnjyǎur.

(On other parts of the body) 'hánmáu, hánmaur (fine hair); máu, máur (coarse or thick).

(On animals) máu, máur; (very soft hair) rúng, rwǎnmaur; (near the mouth) húdz, syūdz. /Feel the fuzzy hair on this dog! Nǐ 'mwōmwo jèigegǒude 'máur, 'rúnghūhurde.

Hang by a hair hěn 'wéisyǎn. /His life hangs by a hair. Tāde'syìngmìng °hěn (°jēn) 'wéisyǎn. /The situation is hanging by a hair. 'Chíngsyíng °hěn (°jēn) 'wéisyǎn. or is expressed as The situation is like a thousand 40-pound weights hanging by one hair. 'Chíngsyíng jēn shr 'chyānjyūnyí'fà.

Miss by a hair. /His shot just missed by a hair. Tā nèiyi'chyāng chà yì'dǐdǐdyǎr méi'dǎjáu wǒ.

HALF. bàn (bàr after numbers only); in some cases, expressed as not all, not finished, etc.; half a mile 'bànlǐ dì; half dollar 'bànkwàichyán, 'wǔmáu chyán. /Give me a half pound of pork. Gěi wǒ bàn'bàng 'jūròu. /Bring home half a pound of butter. 'Dàihwéi bàn'bàng hwáng'yóu lai. or Hwéi'jyālai de shŕhou dài bàn'bàng hwáng'yóu. /This shirt will take a yard and a half of material. Jèijyàn chèn'shān děi yùng yìmǎ'bànde 'lyàudz. /I'll be back in a half hour. Wǒ bàndyán 'jūng yǐ'nèi jyòu 'hwéilai. /I've been waiting the last half hour. Wǒ děngle yǒu bàndyán 'jūng le. /I got this at half price at a sale. 'Jèige, wǒ shŕ dzài jyǎn'jyàr de shŕhou 'bànjyà maide. /I bought a half interest in that store. Nèige 'pùdzde 'běnchyán yǒu wǒ yí'bàr. /I'll give him half of my share. Wǒ bǎ wǒde nèi'fèr fēngěi ta yí'bàr. /The enemy's fighting efficiency was reduced by half. 'Dírénde 'jàndòu'lì 'jyǎnle yí'bàn. /Your half is larger than mine. (of an object) Nǐ nèi bàn'lǎ bǐ °wǒde (°wǒ jèibàn'lǎ) dà. (of something abstract) 'Nǐnèibàr bǐ °'wǒde (°wǒ jèibàr) dwō. /It's only half done (finished). Gāngwánle yí'bàr. or Hái chà yí'bàr méi'wán ne. /That's only half true (or only a half truth). Nèige bù'wánchywán shŕ 'jēnde. /The meat is only half done. Ròu hái 'bànshēngbàn'shóude ne (°'bànshēngr ne, °méishóu'tòu). /I was half afraid (a little afraid) you weren't coming. Wǒ yǒu dyar 'yísyīn nǐ 'bùlái le. /I said it half jokingly. Wǒ shŕ 'bànshwōbàn'syàude 'shwōde. or Wǒ 'shwō de shŕhou yí'bàn shŕ kāi 'wánsyàu. /This way it'll cost only half as much. Jèmmaje jyòu 'shǎu chū yí'bàrde chyán. /He's not half as clever as his wife. Tāde 'tsūngmíng lyán tā 'tàitai yí'bàr dōu 'gǎnbushàng. /I was lying on the couch half asleep (nodding). Wǒ jèngdzài tǎng'yǐshàng °chùng'dwǒr (°'mímihu'hǔde, °méishwèi'jáu, °'bànsyīngbàn'shwèide). /He's been only half awake all day. Tā yì'jēngtyān nèmma 'bànsyīngbàn'shwèide. /I have half a mind to chuck the whole thing and scram. Wǒ hěn syǎng yìshwài'shǒu jyòu 'dzǒukai. /He's doing it halfheartedly. Tā dzwòde 'hěn búrè'syīn. /He's half cracked. Tā shŕ ge bàn'fēngr. /I'll be there at half past eight. Wǒ bādyán'bàn dàu 'nèr. /Shall I cut this in half? Wǒ bǎ jèige 'chyēchéng lyǎng'bàr hǎu ma?

Go halves with someone. /Will you go halves with me? Dzámen lyǎ dwèi'bàr dzěmmayàng? or Dzámen lyǎ dwèibàr'fēn dzěmmayàng? or Dzámen lyǎ píng'fēn dzěmmayàng? or Dzámen lyǎ jyūn'fēn dzěmmayàng?

HALL. (Passage or entrance) gwò dàur. /Please wait in the hall. Chǐng dzài gwò'daur 'děng. /It's the second door down the hall. Shwùnje gwò'dàur dzŏu, dì'èrge mér.

(Assembly room) lǐ táng. / There were no seats, so we stood at the back of the hall. 'Yīnwei méi'dzwòr le, 'swŏyǐ wŏmen 'jàndzài lǐ'táng 'hòubyār.

(Public building) tǐng, fǔ. / His office is in City Hall. Tāde gūngshř'fáng shř dzài °Shřjěng'tǐngli (°Shřjěng'fǔli).

Reception hall kètǐng, hwèikèshř.

Hall in such places as the old Imperial Palace, large monasteries, etc., is expressed with dyàn (also means court, courtyard); main hall 'dàdyàn; front hall 'chyándyàn. / The emperor used to receive foreign diplomats in this hall. Tsúngchyán 'hwángdì dzài 'jèige dyànli jyējyàn 'wàigwó 'shřchén. / The Buddhist monks are chanting the liturgy in the main hall. 'Héshang dzài 'dàdyànli nyàn'jǐng ne.

HAMMER. (Relatively small) chwéidz; (relatively large) lángtou. / Could I borrow a hammer? Jyè °'chwéidz (°'lángtou) shř yishř 'syíng ma? or Jyè °'chwéidz (°'lángtou) yùng yiyùng 'syíng ma?

To hammer chwéi, dǎ; (with repeated sharp blows) chyāu. / Someone is hammering at the door. Yŏurén 'dàshēng °chyāu'mén (°dǎ'mén). / He hammered him with his fists. Tā ná 'chywántou °'chwéi ta (°'dǎ ta). / The blacksmith hammered horseshoes out of that piece of iron. 'Tyějyàng ná nèikwai 'tyě °dǎchéngle (°chwéi-chéngle) mǎ'jǎng le. (fig.) / I tried in vain to hammer it into his head that that's no way to treat people. Wŏ syǎng'jìnle fár jyàutā míngbai 'nèmma dài 'rén bù'syíng, kèshr dzěmma shwō tā yě bù'tǐng.

HAND. (Part of the body) shŏu. / Where can I wash my hands? Wŏ dzài 'nǎr kéyi syísyi 'shŏu? / What's that in your hand? Nǐ 'shŏuli 'náje de shř 'shémma? or Nǐ 'shŏulide nèi shř 'shémma? or (grasped) Nǐ 'shŏuli 'dzwànje de shř 'shémma? / Take him by the hand. 'Lāje tāde 'shŏu. / I shook hands with him and left. Wŏ gēn tā lā'shŏu yǐ'hòu jyòu 'dzŏule. / His hand shakes. Tāde 'shŏu fā'chàn. / He made this with his own hands. Tā 'dzjǐ 'dùngshŏu dzwòde. or Tā 'chīnshŏu dzwòde. / He is waiting for him, hat in hand. Tā 'shŏulǐ náje 'màudz 'děng tā.

(Applause) is expressed as clap hands gǔjǎng, pāishŏu. / The audience gave her a big hand. 'Tīngjùng gěi tā 'rèlyede °gǔjǎng (°pāi'shŏu). / Give him a hand, please! 'Dàjyāpāi'shŏu!

(In cards) shŏu or bǎ used as a measure with pái; or in some cases simply pái. / This is the worst hand I've had all evening. Jèi shr wŏ 'yìwǎnshang 'dzwèihwài de °yìshŏu 'pái (°yìbǎ'pái). / Let's play out this hand. 'Jèibǎ pái dzámen dǎ'wánle ba. / Don't look at my hand. Byé 'kàn wŏde 'pái. / I've been having bad hands all evening. Wŏ 'yìwǎnshang ná 'hwàipái. or Wŏ 'yìwǎnshang náde 'pái °dōu 'bùhǎu (°yì-'bǎyǐ'bǎde dōu nèmma 'hwài). / What a hand! (good or bad) 'Hǎu yìbǎ'pái le! or 'Nèmma yìbǎ'pái!

(Pointer) jēn, jēr; hour hand 'shřjēn, 'syǎujēr; minute hand 'dàjēn, 'dàjēr; second hand 'myǎujēn, 'myǎujēr. / The hour hand is broken. °'Shřjēn (°'Syǎujēr) 'shéle. / Both hands are broken. 'Lyǎngge jēn 'dōu shéle. / The minute hand is bent. 'Dàjēr wānle. / Watch the second hand moving. Kàn nèige 'myǎujēr 'dùng.

(Worker) 'gūngrén, -gūng and other expressions depending on the situation. / I worked a couple of years as a farm hand. Wŏ dzài dìli gěi 'rénjya dzwòle lyǎngnyán'hwór. / He is a farm hand. Tā shř ge °'chánggūng (°'dwàngūng). / He's one of the hands (not on a farm). Tā shř ge °dzwò'hwór de (°dǎ'dzár de, °'gūngrén). / The ship sank with all hands. Lyán'chwándài'rén 'dōu chénle. / We are short of hands. or We are shorthanded. Wŏmen 'chywērén.

610

(Style of writing). /He writes in a round hand. Tā ·syě'dž (syěde) hěn 'ywánrwùn. *or* Tāde 'bǐfǎ 'ywánrwùn. /Is this signature in his hand? Jèige 'dž shř tā 'chyānde ma? *or* Jèige 'dž shř tā chyānde °'míngma (°'dž ma)? *or* 'Jèige shř tā 'chǐnbǐ 'syěde ma?

A free hand. /Do you have a free hand? meaning Can you help me? Nǐ yǒu °kùng (°gūngfu) ma? /I don't have a free hand in this. Jèige shèr bù'chywán yóu wǒ dzwò'jǔ. *or* Jèige shèr 'yǒu rén chè'jǒu.

By hand shǒu, yùngshǒu. /All this sewing had to be done by hand. Jèisyē 'hwó dōu shř 'shǒugūng dzwò de. /You've got to do it by hand. 'Fēidei yùng 'shǒu lái dzwò bù'kě.

Change hands hwànjǔr, hwàn dūngjya, 'dǎushǒu. /The business has changed hands. 'Mǎimài °hwànle 'dūngjya le (°'dǎule 'shǒu le, °hwàn'jǔr le). /The store had changed hands. 'Pùdz °hwànle 'dūngjya le (°etc.).

Clap one's hands pāi shǒu, gǔjǎng. See also this entry under (Applause).

Eat out of someone's hands (fig.). /I can make him eat out of my hands. Wǒ kéyi bǎ ta 'gwǎnde 'jyàu tā dzěmma je tā 'jyǒu dzěmma je.

Firsthand, secondhand, etc. 'jŕjyē, 'jyànjyē; secondhand store 'jyòuhwò-'dyàn. /I got this information firsthand. Jèige 'syāusyi wǒ shř 'jŕjyē 'délaide. /I got this information secondhand. Jèige 'syāusyi wǒ shř 'jyànjyē 'délaide. *but* /It's secondhand. (old) Shř 'jyòude. *or* (used) Shř 'yùnggwode. *or* (worn before, of clothes) Shř 'chwāngwode.

Give *or* **lend a hand** bāng, bāngmáng. /Would you lend me a hand in moving that furniture? Nǐ néng 'bāng wǒ bān yísyàr 'jyājù ma? /Give him a hand. 'Bāng ta yǐsyar ('máng) ba. /Lend me a hand. Lái 'bāngbang 'máng.

Hand in hand (closely related). /Science and the standard of living go hand in hand. 'Kēsywé gēn 'shēnghwo 'chéngdù yǒu 'lyándàide'gwānsyi. but lit. /They came in hand in hand. Tāmen 'shǒulāje'shǒur jyòu 'jǐnlaide.

Hand over hand. /He pulled himself up by the rope, hand over hand. Tā °'dǎuje 'shǒu (°'dzwǒyishǒu 'yǒuyishǒude) pá 'shéngdz, jyòu 'páshang chyule.

Hands off. /Hands off! is expressed as Don't touch! Bùsyǔ mwò! *or* Byé dùng shǒu! or as Take your hands away! Bǎ 'shǒu nákāi! but in a fig. sense, meaning Don't get messed up in that. 'Yùngbujáu 'nǐ gwǎn. *or* 'Shéi yě bùsyǔ 'gwǎn. /My advice is, hands off (fig.). Yǐ 'wǒ kàn a, 'byé 'gwǎn.

Hands up (command) jyúchi 'shǒu lai, yǔshǒu.

Have a hand in yǒu . . . °yí'fèr (°'yí'shǒur); yǒu . . . de fèr, yǒu. . . dzài °'lǐtou (°'lǐbyar). /Did you have a hand in this? 'Jèijyanshèr yǒu °'nǐde 'fèr méiyou (°nǐ dzài 'lǐtou ma)? /You could see he had a hand in this (in a bad sense). Nǐ 'kéyi 'kànchulai yǒu 'tā dzài 'lǐbyar (dǎu'lwàn). /It's obvious that he had a hand in this. (in any sense) Míng'syǎnde jèi 'lǐtou yǒu 'tā °yí'fèr (°yí'shǒur, *or* (in a bad sense) °shř'hwài).

Have one's hands full. (fig.) /He certainly has his hands full with that new job. Tā dž'tsúng yǒule nèijyàn 'syīn shèr yǐ'hòu 'jēn shř 'mángde 'lìhai. (lit.). /He had his hands full of papers. Tā 'lyǎshǒulǐ náde 'chywán shř 'jř. *or* Tā 'jwāle lyǎng-'dàbǎ 'jř.

Have one's hands tied. /My hands were tied. (lit.) Wǒde 'shǒu 'kwǎnje ne. *or* (fig.) Wǒ 'bùnéng 'džyóu. *or* Wǒ 'jēn shr méi'fár.

In hand, out of hand. /The situation is well in hand. 'Yíchyè shwùn'lǐ. *or* 'Bànde hěn °dé'shǒu (°'désyīnyìng'shǒu). /The crowd got out of hand. 'Nèichyún rén 'gwǎnbú'jùle. /Don't let the students get out of hand. Byé jyàu 'sywésheng dzàu-'fǎn.

In one's hands (in one's charge). / The affair is in my hands. 'Jèige shèr gwēi 'wǒ gwǎn le. /I'll leave the whole matter in your hands. is expressed politely as I'll transfer it over to you. Nêmma wǒ jyòu bǎ 'jèijyàn shèr 'chywán ˙jyāugěi 'nǐ le. *or* (even more polite) Nêmma 'yíchyè bǎi'twō le. *or* (to a subordinate) Nemma 'jèijyàn shèr yóu 'nǐ fù'dzé chyù 'bàn.

Fall into one's hands 'làudzai shǒuli. /Don't let this (either an object or an affair) fall into their hands. Byé jyàu 'jèige 'làudzai 'tāmen shǒuli.

Lay one's hands on. /Wait until I lay my hands on him! Děng wǒ 'děijau tā dzài 'shwō. *or* (fig. only) Děng tā 'làudzai 'wǒ shǒulǐ dzài 'shwō.

On hand. /He's never on hand when I want him. Wǒ yàu 'yùng tā de shŕhou, tā dzǔng bú'dzài. /There is only one battalion on hand. °'Gēnchyán (°'Yǎnchyán) 'jŕ yǒu yì'yíng rén. /I have only a small amount on hand. (meaning money) Wǒ 'shǒu °tóur (°byār) jŕ yǒu bù'dwō de chyán (or use other words for chyán if one refers to something other than money).

On one's hands, off one's hands. /I've got a lot of work on my hands today. 'Jīntyān wǒ('shǒulí)'gāi dzwò de shŕ hěn 'dwō. /I still have her on my hands. is expressed as I can't get rid of her. Hái yǒu 'tā wǒ 'méifár 'dǎfa. or as She is still my responsibility. Hái yǒu 'tā wǒ děi 'gwǎn ne. /I'm glad I got that off my hands. Bùgwǎn nèige le 'jēn 'shūfu. or expressed as I'm glad it's finished. Bǎ 'nèige nùng'wánle 'jēn shūfu. or as I'm glad it's been turned over to someone else. Bǎ 'nèige 'twēichuchyu bù'gwǎnle 'jēn shūfu.

On the other hand. /As you say, he's a good man; but on the other hand he hasn't had much experience. Nǐ 'shwōde 'hěn dwèi; kěshr, tsúng lìng yí fāngmyàn 'kàn, tā 'chywēfa 'jīngyàn. /Yes, he did cuss you out; on the other hand, you weren't entirely in the right yourself. Bú'tswò, tā 'shŕ 'mà nǐ láije; búgwò 'fāngwolaishwo ne, 'nǐ yě yǒu 'bùshŕ a.

On the right-hand side dzài (nǐ)'yòubyar; **on the left-hand side** dzài (nǐ)'dzwǒ-byar. /The house is on your left-hand side as you go up the street. Nǐ wàng jyē 'nèibyar dzǒu, nèiswǒr 'fángdz (shŕ) dzài nǐ 'dzwǒbyar.

Wash one's hands of. /I wash my hands of the whole thing here and now! 'Jèijyàn shèr tsúng'tsž wǒ 'dzài bú'gwǎn le. *or* Wǒ gēn 'jèijyàn shèr jyòu'tsž 'dwànjywé 'gwānsyì. *or* (of something evil) Tsúng'tsž yǐ'hòu wǒ syǐ'shǒu bú'gàn le.

Hand brake 'shǒujá.

Handcar (railroad) shǒuyáuchē.

Handcart shǒutwēi chē.

Hand drill shǒudzwàn.

Hand grenade shǒulyóudàn.

To hand (to give, of small objects conveyed by hand) 'dǐgěi, gěi, náchulai. /Will you hand me that pencil? Bǎ nèijŕ 'chyānbǐ 'dǐgěi wǒ. /Hand it over! 'Gěi wǒ! *or* 'Náchulai! *or* 'Gěi wǒ 'náchulai!

(Tell). /Don't hand me that sort of stuff. Nèijǔng hwà 'byé gēn 'wǒ shwō. *or* 'Nèijǔng hwà gēn 'wǒ 'shŕbu'shàng. *or* Nǐ 'dāng wǒ shŕ 'shéi a, gēn wǒ shwō 'nèijǔng hwà.

Hand it to (give credit to) pèifu. /You've got to hand it to him for this. 'Jēn děi 'pèifu tā. *or* 'Tā jèi yi'shǒur 'shŕdzài kéyi 'pèifu.

Hand down (by inheritance, or referring to a secret or a recipe, etc.) chwán; (referring to an object, as clothing, given by one person to another) gěi. / The recipe has been handed down in our family for generations. Jèige 'dzwòfǎr dzài 'wǒmenjyā 'chwánle hǎu jǐ'dài le. *or* Jèi shr 'wǒmen jyā'chwánde 'dzwòfǎr. / It was handed down from our ancestors (may refer to an object). Shr̀ wǒmen 'dzǔsyān chwánsyalaide. / This is a hand-me-down from my brother. Jèi shr̀ 'gēge gěi 'wǒ de.

Hand in. / I'm going to hand in my resignation tomorrow. (to a higher authority) Wǒ 'míngtyān bǎ tsź'chéngr °dǐshangchyu (*or* (not specifying to whom) °'jyāujǐnchyu). / My report has been handed in. (to a higher authority) Wǒde bàu'gàu °chéngshangchyule (*or* (not specifying to whom) °jyāujǐnchyule).

Hand out (distribute) sāchuchyu, sànchuchyu. / Take these tickets and hand them out. Bǎ jèisyē'pyàu °'sāchuchyu (°'sànchuchyu).

Hand over jyāu(chulai), 'jyāudài, 'yíjyāu, 'jyāugěi. / Hand him over to the police. Bǎ tā 'jyāugěi 'jǐngchá. / He handed over all his documents. Tā bǎ 'wénjyàn °'yíjyāule (°'jyāudàile). / He is just now handing over his office to the new mayor. Tā jèngdzài gēn 'syīn'jǎng bàn 'jyāudài.

HANDLE. (Affect with the hand) 'mwōswō, 'māsā (touch); nwó, dùng, bān (move); ná (pick up); 'syānùng, 'lwàndùng, hwǒ hwo, nǎje wár (handle carelessly); yùng (use). *See also* **CARRY, HOLD, USE, MOVE.** / Look at it all you want, but don't handle it. 'Dzěmma kàn dōu 'syíng, kě byé °'mwō (°'māsā, °'dùng, °'náchilai, °etc.). / Handle with care. °'Bān (°'Ná, °'Nwǒ, °'Yùng, °etc.) de shŕhou °lyóu'shén (°yàu 'syǎusyīn). / That child must have handled it. Yídìng shr̀ nèige 'háidz °'māsā (°'mwōswō, °'ná, °dùng °'nǎje wár, °'nùng, °'syānùng, °'lwàndùng, °'hwǒhwo) láije. (Each is more serious than the preceding.) / Don't handle the watch like that; you might break it. Byàu byé 'nèmma °'mwōswō (°'māsā, °'syānùng, °etc.); 'nèmmaje hwèi nùng'hwàile. / When you handle a priceless thing like that, you've got to be careful. Dzài 'shǒulǐ nǎje nèmma yàng de 'wújyàjř'bǎu, bù'néng bù'syǎusyīn.

(Manage, control) gwǎn. / Can you handle the students? Nǐ 'gwǎndejù 'sywé-sheng ma? / Students nowadays are hard to handle. 'Jèige nyántóur 'sywésheng nán 'gwǎn. *See also* **CONTROL.**

(Operate; of tools; weapons, etc.) yùng, shř; (of a car) kāi; (of sharp weapons) shwǎ. / He can handle any kind of firearm. Tā shémma yàngr de 'chyāngpàu dōu hwèi °'yùng (°'shř). / He handles the car very well. Tā chē 'kāide hěn 'hǎu. *or* Tā kāi'chē kāide hěn 'hǎu. / He shouldn't be allowed to handle the sword the way he does, or he'll get hurt. 'Bùyīnggāi jyàu tā 'nèmma shwǎ 'dāu; tā hwèi bǎ tā 'dżjǐ 'lájaude. / This car handles well. Jèige 'chē hěn hǎu 'kāi. / This machine handles easily. Jèige 'jīchi hěn hǎu °'yùng (°'shř).

(Deal with) 'chǔjř, yìngfu, 'bànlǐ. / He handled the situation well. Tā °'chǔjřde (°'yìngfude, °'bànlǐde) hěn dé'dàng.

(Deal in) mài. / We don't handle that brand. Wǒmen bú'mài nèige 'páidz de.

A handle bàr. / This hoe needs a new handle. Jèibǎ 'chú děi hwàn ge ('syīnde) 'bàr.

HANDSOME. (Good-looking) hǎu, búhwài, bútswò, 'pyàulyàng, hǎukàn, měi; <u>any of these may be preceded by</u> jǎngde <u>referring to appearance</u>. / I don't think he's very handsome. Wǒ jywéde tā 'bùdzěmma °'pyàulyàng (°etc.).

(Generous) hěn hǎu, bútswò; (of money) hěn dwō, bùshǎu; (of price) hěn dà. / He made me a handsome offer for my farm. Wǒ nèikwài 'dì tā °gěile ge hěn hǎu de 'jyàr (°chūde 'jyàr hěn 'dà).

HANG (HUNG). (Fasten or suspend something) gwà; (with a tack) èn; (with a nail) dǐng, dǐng; (with paste) jān, hú, tyē. /I am hanging pictures. Wǒ gwà 'hwàr ne. / They cleaned the room and hung the curtains. Tāmen shǒushrwánle 'wūdz jyou gwà chwānghu 'lyándz. /He hung a sign on the hook. Tā dzài 'gōurshang gwàle yíge 'páidz. /My coat was hanging on the wall a minute ago. Wǒde dà'yī dzai chyángshang gwàje laije. /Is that your hat hanging on the hook? Dzài gōurshang 'gwàje de neige 'màudz shr 'nǐde ma? / The lantern was hanging in front of the house. Dēng dzai fángdz 'chyánbyar 'gwàje. /Hang it on the wall with a thumbtack. Ná èn'dǐng èndzai 'chyángshang. /Hang it on the wall with a nail. Ná 'dǐngdz °'dǐngdzai (°'dǐngdzai) 'chyángshang. /Call in a paperhanger to hang the wallpaper. Jyàu yíge byàuhú'jyàng lai hú 'chyáng(jř).

(Naturally) chwéi. / There are several bunches of bananas hanging on the tree. Yóu ji'dūlu syāng'jyàu dzài 'shùshang 'chwéije. or 'Shùshang 'chwéije ji'dūlu syāng-'jyàu. / The fruits are hanging down. Jyēde 'gwǒr wàng syà 'chwéije. / The students stood in front of the principal with hands hanging down (a mark of respect). Sywésheng dzài syàujǎng 'chyántou chwéishǒu 'jànje.

(Install) ān. /Hang the door (on the hinges). Bǎ mén (yùng hé'yè) 'ānshang.

(Drape something over something) dā. / They propped up a bamboo pole and hung the dyed threads over it to dry. Tāmen 'jřchi yǐgēn jú'gāndz lai, bǎ rǎnle de 'syàn 'dādzai shàngtou 'lyàng.

(Of clothes) is expressed with píng (smooth); hé'shř (fit). / The dress hangs well on you. Jèijyan 'yīfu chwāndzai nǐ 'shēnshang hěn °'píng (°hé'shř). / She made the skirt hang better by shortening the waist a little. Tā bǎ 'chyúndz 'yāu ner 'shōujinchyule dyar, chwānje jyou °píng le (°hé'shř le).

(Securely from a freely pivoting point) dyàu. /A medal was hanging from the chain. Yíkwài jīn'páidz dyàudzai syàng'lyàrshang. /He hung the hammock between the trees. Tā bǎ dyàu'chwáng dyàudzai shùshang le.

(Of a person's death) dyàu; jyǎu (as legal punishment; death brought about by strangling). /He hanged himself. Tā shàng'dyàu le. or Tā sywán'lyáng dž'jǐnle. /He died by hanging. Tā shř 'dyàuszde. or (as legal punishment) Tā shř 'jyáuszde. / The man will be hanged for his crime. Nèige rén 'fàn de °'dzwèi děi 'jyáusz (°dzwèi gāi 'jyǎu, °shř 'jyǎudzwèi).

(Suspend from a part of the body is expressed in Chinese by verbs meaning carry). /He has a string of fish hanging from his left index finger. is expressed as He is carrying a string of fish with his left index finger. Tā yùng 'dzwǒshǒude 'shřjř 'gōuje yíchwàr 'yú. /She came back with a basket hanging from her left elbow, and carrying a huge watermelon with both hands. is expressed as She came back carrying a basket on her left elbow, ... Tā 'hwéilai de shřhou, dzwǒgēbwo'jǒurshang kwàje ge 'lándz dzài lyàngjr 'shóuli 'bàuje ge dà 'syīgwā. See CARRY.

Hang one's head dī tóu, chwéi tóu, tái tóu with a negative. /He hung his head and sneaked away. Tā 'dīje tóu jyou 'lyōule. /Whey are you hanging your head? Nǐ wèi 'shémma °'chwéitóusàng'chǐde (°'chwéije tóu, °'dīje tóu, °bùtái 'tóu a)?

Hang around (wait) děng, bùdzǒu; (walk back and forth) 'dzǒuláidzǒu'chyù; (stay) 'lyóulyán, dāije; (walk around) jwànyou; (mix in the crowd; make a sort of living) hwùn. /He's always hanging around the racetrack. Tā yùng'ywǎn shr dzài pǎumǎ-'chǎng nèr 'hwùn. /Hang around a while. Dzài jèr 'děng hwěr, byé 'dzǒu. /Some suspicious people are hanging around their neighborhood. Tāmen nèr fù'jìn yóu jige kě'yí de rén dzài nàr °jwànyou (°'dāije, °'dzǒuláidzǒu'chyù). /He hangs around that joint every night. Tyāntyan 'wǎnshang tā dzài 'nèige dìfang 'dāije. / They already hinted to him that he's not wanted, but he still hangs around. Tāmen 'yǐjing 'tòugwo bú'yàu tā de 'yìsz le, kěshr tā hái 'lyóulyánje bùkěn 'dzǒu. /Why you're still hanging around her is beyond me. Nǐ 'hái dzài 'tā gēnchyan nèmma 'jwànyou, wǒ jēn 'syǎngbuchū shř 'dzěmma ge 'dàuli.

Hang on (hold tightly; by pulling) lā, chēn, dèn, jwāi; (by holding fast to) jwài, jyōu; (in one's arms) bàu; (in the hand) jwā, dzwàn; <u>all are used with resultative endings</u> jǐn *or* jù. /Hang on (as to a rope). Lā'jǐnle. *or* Lā'jùle. /I hung on as tight as I could. Wǒ 'jyòu néng °'lāde (°'chēnde, °'dènde, °'jwàide, °'jyōude, °'bàude, °'jwāde, °'dzwànde) 'nèmma jǐn. /She hung on to his arm and screamed. Tā 'jyōuje tāde 'gēbwo jyou dà'jyàuchilaile.

Hang on (depend on). /Everything hangs on his decision. Yí'chyè dōu děi kàn tā 'dzěmma jywé'dǐngle.

Hang on to (don't spend) byé hwā lou; (don't lose) byé dyōu lou; (watch) hǎu-'hǎurde 'kānje; (keep) hǎu'hǎurde 'shǒuje。 /Hang on to this money. Jèige 'chyán °byé 'hwā lou (°byé 'dyōu lou, °hǎu'hǎurde 'kānje, °hǎuhǎurde 'shǒuje).

Hang out (from a window) tànchu, shēndau. /Don't hang out the window. Byé bǎ 'shēndz °'tànchu (°'shēndau) chwānghu 'wàibyār chyù.

Hang out *see* **Hang around** <u>above</u>. *but* /That's a place where thieves hang out. Nèi shř dzéi'wō.

Hang over <u>someone</u>. /The fear of losing his job hangs over him like a sword. Tā 'pà jyàu rénjya gěi 'tsź le; 'jèijyan 'shèr dzài tā 'syīnshang 'sywánje syàng yìbǎ 'dāu shřde.

Hang up gwàchilai, gwàshang. /Hang up your hat and coat. Bǎ nǐde 'màudz gēn dà'yī gwàchilai ba. /He hung up (the telephone receiver) on me. Tā méidēng wǒ shwō'wán jyou bǎ dyàn'hwà 'gwàshangle.

Hang up <u>a lantern</u> sywán. /They hung up lanterns and festoons to celebrate the Double-Tenth Festival. Tāmen 'sywándēng jyē'tsǎi 'chǐngjù °Shwāngshř'jyé (°Gwó-chǐng'r̀).

The hang of it (knack). /Now you're getting the hang of it. <u>is expressed as</u> You've found the door by groping. Nǐ 'kě mwōjau 'mér le. /You have to use your head to get the hang of it. Nǐ děi 'fèi dyar 'syīnsz tsái 'mwōdejáu 'mér le. /Did you get the hang of it? Nǐ 'mwōjau 'mér le ma? <u>or meaning</u> the trick Nǐ déjau jèige 'jywéchyàur le ma? <u>or meaning</u> the idea Nǐ dǔngde jèige 'yìsz le ma? <u>or meaning</u> the method Nǐ 'míngbai jèige 'fádz le ma? /I can't get the hang of it. Wǒ 'mwōbujáu 'mér. *or* Wǒ 'débudàu 'jywéchyàur. *or* Wǒ bù'dǔngde shř shémma 'yìsz. *or* Wǒ bù'míngbai shř dzěmma ge 'fádz.

<u>Other English expressions</u>. /Hang it all! Tǎu'yàn!

HAPPEN. <u>Most commonly expressed by a verb</u> (usually yǒu there is *or* chū come out, occur) <u>plus shř</u> *or* shèr affair, event, a happening; <u>in short phrases the verb is often omitted</u>. /What happened? 'Dzěmma le? *or* 'Dzěmmahwéi 'shèr? *or* (Yǒu) 'shémma shèr. *or* (Chūle) 'shémma shèr. /What happened while I was gone? Wǒ dzǒule yǐ-'hòu °yǒu (°chūle) shémma 'shř láije? /Nothing happened at all. 'Méi shèr. *or* 'Méi shémma. *or* 'Shémma shř yě 'méiyǒu. /Plenty happened! 'Shèr kě 'dwōje ne. /Nothing ever happens around here! 'Jèr jyàn'jr̀ 'shémma shèr yě 'méiyǒu! /Think of it! All these things happened in (that) five minutes. Nǐ 'syǎngsyang! 'Jèmma dwō de 'shèr dōu 'chūdzài nèi 'wǔfēn 'jūngli. /Were you there when the accident happened? Chū'shèr de 'shřhou nǐ 'dzài nèr ma? /How did it happen? Shř 'dzěmma hwéi shèr? *or* 'Dzěmma gàude? /It happened this way. Shř 'jèmma hwéi shř. /So it happened THAT way! 'Ywanlái shř 'nèmma hwéi shř a. /Did it really happen that way? 'Jēn shř 'nèmma yàng de yǐhwéi 'shř ma? /So it really happened! Ywánlái 'jēn yǒu nèmma hwéi shř a! /How could such a thing happen?

'Dzĕmma hwèi yŏu 'jèmma yàng de 'shř? /What happened to you? Nǐ 'dzĕmma le? /I just knew it would happen to me this way. Wŏ 'dzău jyŏu jywéde yàu 'jèmmaje. /Everything happens to me. 'Shémma 'shèr dōu jyàu'wŏ pèngshangle. /What happened to this typewriter? 'Jĕijyà dădz̀'jǐ jè shř 'dzĕmmale? /What happened to the man who found the body? 'Tóuyige kànjyan 'shřshou de nèige rén dzĕmma 'yàngle ne? /A wonderful thing happened to me last night. 'Dzwór wănshang wŏ yŏu yíjyàn dà'syíde 'shèr. /A thing like that WOULD happen to me now! 'Jèige shŕhou 'pyān-pyān °yŏu (°jyàu wŏ 'pèngshang, °jyàu wŏ 'yùjyan) 'nèiyàng de 'shèr. /I couldn't help it; it just happened. 'Jyòu nèmmaje le 'mwō, 'wŏ yŏu shémma 'fár ne? or expressed as It wasn't intentional. Wŏ 'búshr gù'yìde. or Jè 'wánchywán shř gān-'chyău le, 'wŏ méifár. /Could anything ever have happened so opportunely? Néng yŏu 'nèmma 'chyău de('shř) ma?

Happen to, happen that (just at that time) jèng gānshang; (fortunately or by chance) jèng hău, jèng chyău; (unluckily) (jèng) bù chyău; (not as usual) kĕ; sometimes the idea of chance is implied rather than expressed. /It happened that they were having a marriage ceremony. Jèng 'gānshang tāmen bàn 'syǐshř. /It happens that we can't do anything about it. Jèng 'gānshang wŏmen yìdyăr 'bànfa yĕ 'méiyŏu. /It happened that I was called away at the time. Jèng °'gānshang (°'chyău) nèige 'shŕhou wŏ yŏu 'byéde shř, bú'dzài nàr. /It happened that we were all there. Jèng °'hău (°'chyău, °'gānshang) nèige 'shŕhou wŏmen 'dōu dzài nàr. /I happen to be the man you've been looking for. Jèng °'hău (°'chyău) 'wŏ jyòushr nǐ yàu 'jău de nèige rén. or Nǐ yàu jăude 'nèige rén (jènghău) jyòu shř 'wŏ. /Did you say that you happened to be there when the shot was fired? Nǐ 'shř shwōgwo fàng'chyàngde shŕhou nǐ jèng 'gānshang 'dzài nàr ma? /I happened to meet him on the street once. Yŏu yí'tsž wŏ dzài 'jyēshang °'yùjyanle (°'pèngjyanle) tā. /I happened to bump into him in a crowd. Wŏ dzài yí'dàchyún rénli ('jèng chyău) 'pèngjyan tā le. /I happen to agree with you this time. 'Jèitsž wŏ kĕ gēn 'nǐde yìjyan syāng'túng. /That happens to be Mr. Wang. 'Nèige rén a! Kĕ'chyău 'jèng shr Wáng Syānsheng. /How did you happen to find me? Nǐ 'dzĕmma jăuje 'wŏde? or Dzĕmma nèmma 'chyău nǐ jyòu bă wŏ 'jăujáule.

HAPPINESS. (The emotion) kwàilwo, kwàilè; (technical) lè; or expressed by stative verbs meaning be happy. /Happiness lessens with age. Rén ywè 'dà ywè nán 'jywédechu 'kwàilwolai. /Contentment breeds happiness. Néng jř'dzú, jyòu 'kwàile. /The Chinese regard happiness as one of the seven emotions; these emotions are pleasure, anger, sorrow, happiness, love, hate, and fear. 'Jūnggwo rén yǐ 'lè wēi 'chǐ'chíng jr'yǐ; chǐ'chíng jyòu shr 'syǐ, 'nù, 'āi, 'lè, 'ài, 'wù, 'jyù.

(Good luck, good fortune). /He knows how to enjoy happiness. Tā shř hwèi syăng'fú de rén. /Let's drink to your happiness. Hē (bēi)'syǐjyŏu. /Here's to your happiness. (a toast) Dà'syǐ, dà'syǐ. /Here's happiness to you! 'Jūshř rú'yì. /Happiness can't last. 'Hăushř wú'cháng. /I've never had much happiness. Wŏ méi-syăngjáu shémma 'rénshēng lè'chywèr. /Next year you'll have great happiness coming to you. (especially of marriage) 'Míngnyán dà'syǐ. or (general) 'Míngnyán nín °'yùnchi 'hău (°jyāu 'hăuyùn, °'syǐshř chúng'chúng, °'fúsyīnggāu'jàu).

See also **HAPPY.**

HAPPY. 'kwàilè, 'kwàilwò, kwàihwo, gāusyìng; (of dogs or children) sāhwār; (be contented) jřdzú; (be satisfied) 'mănyì; (be successful) 'déyì; (be lucky) dzŏuyùn, yùnchǐ hău, yŏufú, syàngfú; (be pleased with) syǐ, syǐhwan, hwānsyi. /I don't feel happy about it. Wŏ bìng bùjywéde gāu'syìng. /Oh, those happy days! Hāi! 'Nèi shŕhou 'dwóma 'kwàihwo! /You don't look happy these days. Jèisyē 'řdz nǐ 'hău-syàng búdà 'kwàihwo. /If you don't feel too happy when you're successful, then you won't be too depressed when you aren't. 'Déyìde shŕhou búyàu 'tài gāu'syìng, 'shř-yìde shŕhou jyòu 'búhwèi 'tài nán'shòu le. /He's always happy. Tā lăushr 'kwàihwode. / This is the happiest day of my life. Jè shř wǒ yì'shēng 'dzwèikwàile de yì'tyān. *or* Wǒ yìshēngli 'méiyou yì'tyān syàng 'jèmma 'kwàile de.

(Smiling). / Look at his happy (smiling) face! Kàn tā nèmma °'méikāiyǎn- 'syàude (°'yìlyǎn 'syàurúngr)! *or* Kàn tā 'lède 'bǐbushang 'dzwěr!

Happy-go-lucky. / He's a sort of happy-go-lucky person. Tā shř ge 'lètyānpài- de rén.

Happy ending. / The movie had a happy ending. 'Pyāndz mwò'lyǎur shř ge 'dàtwánywán.

Many happy returns 'jūshř rú'yì.

See also HAPPINESS.

HARBOR. (Port) 'gǎngkǒu, gǎng. / New York is a natural harbor. 'Nyǒuywē shř ge 'tyānránde 'gǎngkǒu. / What's the difference between a commercial harbor and a naval base? 'Shānggǎng gēn 'jyūngǎng yǒu 'shémma 'fēnbyé? / All the harbor facilities were destroyed. 'Gǎngkǒude 'gūngshř dōu 'hwěile.

To harbor (give shelter to) tsáng. / Do you know it's against the law to harbor an enemy in your house? Nǐ 'jřdàu bǎ 'dírén tsángdzai nǐ 'jyāli shř fàn'fǎ ma?

Harbor a grudge 'jìhèn, 'hwáihèn, jì . . . de 'chóu. / I don't harbor a grudge against him anymore. Wǒ bú °'jìhèn (°'hwàihèn) tā le. *or* Wǒ bújì tāde 'chóu le.

HARD. (Not soft) yǐng, bùrwǎn. / I don't like to sleep on a hard bed. Wǒ bù'syǐhwān shwèi 'yǐng chwáng. / Sitting on that hard chair all day certainly tires one out. Dzài nèige 'yǐng yǐdzshang dzwò yì'jěngtyān, 'shéi yě hwèi jywéje 'lèi de. / You'd better change to a hard pencil; soft lead smears easily. Háishr hwàn ge 'yǐng chyānbǐ 'hǎu; rwǎn chyān rúngyì 'dzāng. / We burn hard coal. Wǒmen shāu 'yǐngméi. / This is made of hard wood. Jèi shř 'yǐngmù dzwòde. / The ground becomes hard in winter. Dàule 'dūngtyan 'dì jyǒu 'yǐng le. / This wood is hard enough for wood carving. Jèijǔng 'mùtou yǐngde kéyi dzwò mù'kè yùng. / You can drive over fifty miles an hour if the road is hard. Lù'myàn yàushr 'yǐngde, jyǒu kéyi kāi 'gwò yìdyan jūng 'wǔshřlǐ. / After the first few miles they came to a hard road. Dzǒule jǐlǐ'dǐ yì'hòu tāmen 'shàngle yìtyáu 'lù, lù'myàn shř 'yǐngde. / Don't wash clothes in hard water. Byé dzài 'yǐngshwěilǐ syǐ 'yīfu. / The water here is hard; it has too high a mineral content. 'Jèrde shwěi 'yǐng; hánde 'kwàngjř tài 'dwō. / The ice cream didn't freeze hard. Bīngjǐ'líng méidùng °'tszshr (°'jyēshr, °'yǐng). / Wait until the river is frozen hard. Děng hé dùng °'yǐngle (°'jyēshrle, °'tszshrle).

(Not easy) nán, bù'rúngyì, búyì, 'syīnkǔ, máfan; (requiring energy or effort) fèishř, fèilì, fèijìn, chřlì; (requiring mental effort) fèisyīnsz; or in a few cases bùhǎu. / I had a hard time getting here. Wǒ 'fèile 'bàntyān 'shr tsái 'dàu jèr. / It's hard to say. Hěn 'nán shwō. *or* Bù'hǎu shwō. or expressed as It's hard to predict. Hěn 'nán 'yùlyàu. *or* Bùhǎu 'yùlyàu. / Don't make it so hard for me. Byé jyàu wǒ wéi'nán. / It's hard to make a living. Chř'fàn °bù'rúngyì (°bú'yì, °hěn 'nán). / No job is too hard for him. Tā dzwò 'shémma dōu bùwéi'nán. / Isn't this job too hard for him? Tā dzwò 'shémma dōu bùwéi'nán? / Isn't this job too hard for him? Tā dzwò 'shémma dōu bùwéi'nán? 'Jèijyàn shř jyàu 'tā dzwò bú'tài nán dyǎr ma? / This mathematics prob- lem is hard to solve. 'Jèige tí 'jyěchilai hěn fèi'syīnsz. / Farming is hard. Jùng'dì °búshr 'rúngyìde shř (°bú'yì, °hěn 'nán, °hěn chř'lì, °hěn 'syīnkǔ). / This kind of box is hard to make without the right tools. Méiyou hé'shřde 'jyāhwo, jèijǔng 'hédz °bùhǎu'dzwò (°hěn nán'dzwò, °'dzwòchǐlai hěn fèi'shř, °'dzwòchǐlai hěn fèi'lì, °'dzwòchǐlai bù'rungyì). / If you like hard work, there is plenty here. Nǐ yàushr 'syǐhwān dzwò fèijìnde 'hwór, jèr 'yǒude 'shř. / This job is hard to tackle. Jèijyàn 'shř dzwòchilai hěn °fèi'shř (°fèi'syīnsz, °fèi'jìn, °fèi'jyèr, °fèi'lì, °'nán). / It looks easy, but it's really quite hard. 'Kànshangchyu 'rúngyì, 'dzwòchilai jyòu 'nán le. / The work gets harder and harder. Gūngdzwò 'ywè lái ywè °'nán (°bù'rúngyî, °'máfan, °chr̄'lî, °etc.).

(Strenuous; of work) shr̄jǐn, shr̄jyèr, màilîchi, chūlî; (of trying to do something) fèi . . . jǐn, fèi . . . 'lîchi, fèi . . . jyèr; <u>also compare some of the expressions in the previous section.</u> / He is a hard worker and does a good job. Tā dzwò'shr̄ hěn mài 'lîchi, érchyě 'dzwòde yě hěn 'hǎu. / He gets ahead because he works hard. Tā dzwò'shr̄ kěn chū'lî, swóyi néng dzǒudàu 'byérén 'chyántou chyu. / He tried hard to do it right, but failed. Tā 'fèile hěn 'dà de jǐn syǎng bǎ 'nèige dzwò'dwèile, 'kěshr méi'chénggūng. *or* Tā 'hěn syǎng dzwòde'hǎu, kěshr °fèile hǎu 'dà de 'lîchi (°'báifèile hěn 'dàde 'jyèr) yě bù'syíng.

(Tight) jǐn. / He tied the rope into a hard knot. Tā bǎ 'shéngdz dǎle yíge hěn 'jǐn de 'kòur.

(Strict) yán, jǐn; (severe) hěn. / We have no hard and fast rules here. 'Wǒmen jèr 'méi shémma hěn °'yán (°'jǐn) de 'gwēijyù. / Hard rules are hard to apply. Tài °yán (°jǐn) de 'gwēidzé nán 'syíng. / He's hard on people. Tā dàirén tài °'yán (°'jǐn, °'hěn).

(Harsh; of words). / Those are hard words. Nèisyē 'hwà °hěn 'syūng (°hěn 'swǔn, °hěn 'kèbwo, °yǒu dyǎr gwò'fèn).

(Hurt; of feelings). / No hard feelings? Shèr 'gwòle jyòu 'swàn le, hǎu ma? *or* Byé 'jîdzài 'syīnshang, hǎu ma? / I know he left with some hard feelings. Wǒ 'jr̄dau tā 'dzǒu de shŕhou 'syīnli °hěn bú'tùngkwai (°hwái'hèn).

(Of rain, snow, etc.). / It was raining hard when he left the house. Tā 'líkai jyā de shŕhou, yǔ 'syàde hěn °'dà (°'jǐn, °'lîhai).

(Of persuasion). / Don't press him too hard. Byé 'bǎ tā 'bīde tài °'jǐnle (°'jíle).

(Of physical condition). / He's been training for two months and is hard as nails. <u>is expressed as</u> . . . like a small iron ball. Tā 'lyànle yǒu 'lyǎngge ywè le, °gēn ge syǎu tyě'dǎr shrde (<u>or as</u> . . . trained to where he's like iron. °lyànde syàng 'tyě dǎ de shŕde, <u>or as</u> . . . trained so that his body is solid. °lyànde 'shēndz hěn 'jyēshr).

Be hard on fèi. / He's hard on shoes. Tā chwān'syé hěn 'fèi.

Hard of hearing. / You'll have to speak louder, because he's hard of hearing. Nǐ děi 'dà dyǎr shēngr 'shwō, tā 'ěrdwo yǒu dyǎr °'bèi (°'lúng).

Hard up (short of cash). / He's always hard up before payday. Yí 'kwàidàu fā'chyán de nèi 'jǐtyān tā jyòu °hěn 'jyūng (°hěn 'jǐn, °shǒu 'dísya hěn 'jǐnde).

HARDLY. (Only, just) gāng X . . . jyòu Y; tsái X . . . jyòu Y (X and Y must include a verb). / He had hardly begun to speak when he was interrupted. Tā 'gāng yǐ'shwō de shŕhou, jyòu 'jyàu rén gěi 'chākāile. *or* Tā °'gāng (°'tsái) kāi'kǒu, jyòu gěi 'chàgwochyule.

(Scarcely) 'chàdyǎr, 'jīhū, 'jyǎnjŕ (almost) <u>plus a negative or a word meaning the opposite of the English; also other expressions.</u> / There were hardly any people there when the picture started. 'Dyànyǐngr 'kāi de shŕhou, °'jyǎnjŕ 'méi jige (°'jīhu méiyou) rén. / I could hardly believe my eyes when I saw him. Wǒ 'gāng yí'kànjyan tā 'chàdyǎr yǐwéi wǒ kàn'tswòle rén le. / I could hardly believe my eyes when I saw the food on the table. Wǒ yí'kànjyan jwōrshang 'bǎi de chr̄shr, 'jīhu 'yǐwéi wǒ °kàn'tswòle (°yǎn'líle, °shr̄ dzwò'mèng ne). Hardly any people came. 'Jīhu 'méiyou rén 'lái. / He hardly ever shows up anymore. Tsúng 'nèitsż yǐ'hòu, tā 'jyǎnjŕ búlòu'myàr le. / You can hardly expect me to believe what he just said. Tā'gāngtsai

HAVE

shwō de 'hwà nǐ °syǎng 'wǒ néng 'syìn ma (°'búyàu yǐwéi wǒ hwèi 'syìn de, °'fàng-syǐn, wǒ 'búhwèi 'syìnde). /You can hardly expect me to be taken in like that. Nǐ syǎng 'wǒ 'nèmma 'rúngyì 'pyàn ma? /It's hardly right to say that about him. 'Nèmma 'jyànglwùn tā búda 'dwèi. /You can hardly blame him for losing his temper. Bùhǎu 'gwài tā fā 'píchi de. or Dzěmma néng 'gwài tā fā 'píchi ne? /You can hardly call him a scholar. Tā 'chēngwéi 'sywéjě búdà 'pèi.

(Barely) búdàu. /He's hardly twenty. Tā hái 'búdàu 'èrshrswèi.

HAT. màudz. /Where can I buy a hat? Wǒ yàu mǎi 'màudz, °dzài 'nǎr mǎi hǎu (°dàu 'nǎr mǎi ne)? or 'Nǎr yǒu mài'màudzde?

HATE. hèn. /She hated her husband because he had left her. Tā 'hèn tā 'jàngfu, yǐn-wei tā bǎ tā 'rēngsyale. /They hate him because he worked them to death. Tā 'bǐ tāmen dzwògūng tài 'jǐn le, swóyi tāmen 'hèn tā. /They hate her because she is more intelligent than they. Tā bǐ tāmen 'jīngming, swóyi tāmen 'hèn tā. /He hates that family because they forced his father to commit suicide. Tā 'hèn nèi 'jyā de rén, yǐnwèi tāmen bǎ tā 'fùchin 'bǐde dž'shāle. /She hates you for saying that. Nǐ shwō 'nèige láije, tā jyòu 'hèn nǐ le.

(Milder dislike) bù'syǐhwān. /I hate to get up in the morning. 'Dzǎushang wǒ bù'syǐhwān 'chǐlái.

Hate (hatred) is expressed verbally as above. /Hate is anger perpetuated. Shēng'chì shēngde méi'wán le, nà jyòushr 'hèn. /You could see hate in her eyes. Tā 'yǎnli dàije 'hèn de yìsz.

HAVE (HAS, HAD). (Possess) is often directly translated by yǒu; sometimes indirectly translated by other verbal expressions; in describing physical characteristics the pattern N (jàngde) (hěn) SV is used. /I have two tickets to the theater. Wǒ yǒu 'lyǎngjāng syì'pyàu. /Do you have any brothers or sisters? Nǐ yǒu 'dìsyūng jyě-'mèi ma? /He has a dog. Tā yǒu jijř 'gǒu. /He has a fine library. Tā yǒu 'hěn dwō 'hǎu shū. /I have a lot on my mind. Wǒ 'syīnli yǒu hěn dwō 'shr. /What do you have in your hands? Nǐ shǒuli °yǒu (°nájě) shémma? /He has a bit of a southern accent. Tā °dài (°yǒu) dyar 'nánfang 'kǒuyin. /He has big feet. Tā jyǎu (jàngde) hěn 'dà. /He has a funny nose. is expressed as His nose grows funny. Tāde 'bídz jàngde kě'syàu. /I have a headache. is expressed as My head hurts. Wǒ tóu 'téng. /I have a slight headache. Wǒ yǒu yidyar 'tóuténg. or Wǒ tóu yǒu yidyar 'téng. /I have a terrible headache. Wǒ 'tóu téngde hěn 'lìhai. /He has a sore foot. Tā jyǎu téng. or Tā yǒu yijr jyǎu téng. or Tā yijr 'jyǎu yǒu dyar 'téng. /He has tuberculosis. Tā yǒu fèi'bìng. but /May I have one? Wǒ kéyi °'yàu (°'lái) yige ma? /Let me have a look. Ràng wo 'kàn yikàn.

(Keep) various expressions, usually with dzài. /I had the gun under the pillow the whole night. Jēng 'yè chyāng dōu dzài 'jěntou 'dǐsya. /I had him with me the whole evening. Yì'wǎnshang tā dōu gēn 'wǒ dzài yí'kwàr. /They're going to have a guest staying with them for some time. 'Tāmen nèr kwài yàu °yǒu ge 'kèrén lái 'jù syē shrhou (°lái ge 'kèren 'jù syē řdz).

(Take along) dài. /I had some money with me. Wǒ ('shēnshang) 'dàije dyar 'chyán laije. /I had my dog with me when I went there. Wǒ dàije 'gǒu chyùde. /I had my gun with me when I came downstairs. Wǒ dàije 'chyāng syàde 'lóu. or Wǒ syà'lóu de shrhou dàije 'chyāng laije. /I had a gun with me all the time. Wǒ yì'jř dàije 'chyāng laije.

(Give birth to) shēng; or more commonly expressed by euphemisms. /Is she going to have a baby? is expressed as Does she have happiness? Tā yǒu'syǐ le ma? or as Has she conceived a child? Tā yǒu syǎu'hár le ma? or as (medical) Is she

619

pregnant? Tā yǒu'yùn le ma? *or* (local Peiping) Tā yǒu le ma? /When is she going to have the baby? Tā 'jǐshŕ shēng syǎu 'hár? or expressed as When will she reach the month? Tā 'jǐshŕ dzwò 'ywèdz? /My wife is going to have a baby. Wǒ 'tàitai yàu shēng 'háidz le.

(Eat) chŕ. /Let's have dinner at six o'clock. Dzámen 'lyòudyǎn jūng chŕ 'fàn ba. /Have you had dinner yet? Chŕ 'fàn le ma? /Please have some more. Chǐng dzài °chŕ (°lái) yidyar ba.

(Drink) hē. /I've had one drink too many. Wǒ 'dwō hēle yidyǎr. /Do have another cup of coffee. Dzài °'hē (°'lái) bēi 'kā'fēi ba.

(Take lessons) sywé. /I have piano lessons twice a week. Wǒ 'měilǐbài sywé 'lyǎngtsż gāng'chín.

(Permit) usually syǔ. /I won't have noise in this room any longer. 'Dzài bùsyǔ dzài 'jèijyan wūdzli 'chǎu le. /I won't have it! 'Bùsyǔ 'nèmmaje. *or* 'Bùnéng 'nèmmaje.

(Before a verb, indicating past time or completed action) le *or* gwo (negative forms are méi *or* méi . . . gwo, but never méi . . . le except with a time expression of duration used before méi; 'méiyou is sometimes used by southerners, and always as the negative alternative or a question); sometimes expressed by a phrase ending in de; when a specific time is indicated, there is often no additional expression. /Have you read this? Jèige nǐ kàn'wánle °ma (°méiyou)? /I've read it. 'Kànle. *or* Kàn-'wánle. /I've read it three times. Wǒ 'kàngwo 'sānbyàn le. /I haven't read it. Méi'kàngwo. *or* Méi'kàn. or sometimes, (by southerners) Méiyou 'kàn. /Has he gone home? Tā ('yǐjīng) hwéi'jyā le ma? *or* Tā hwéi'jyā le méiyou? /He hasn't come for three years. Tā sānnyán méilái le. /Has he taken the medicine? Tā chŕ 'yàu le méiyou? /I have lived here twelve years. Wǒ dzài 'jèr (jùle) shŕ'èrnyán le. /What I have done, I have done. 'Yǐjīng nèmmaje le, jyou 'swàn le. /Has he done his job well? Tāde shŕ 'dzwòde hǎu buhǎu? /He has had his day. Tā gwò'shŕ le. /I have known her since kindergarten days. Tsúng yòujŕ'ywánde shŕhou wǒ jyou 'rènde ta. /I've been watching him since he came in. Tsúng tā yǐ'jìnlai wǒ jyou 'dǐngje tā.

(Experience) various expressions according to the situation. /I had a hard time buying it. 'Jèige wǒ mǎide hěn fèi'shŕ. *or* Jèige wǒ 'fèile hǎusyē shŕhou tsai mǎijaude. /I had a wonderful time. Wárde °hěn 'hǎu (°jēn yǒu'jìsz).

Have a word with. /May I have a word with you? Wǒ yǒu 'hwà yàu gēn ni 'tántan?

Have it in for. /They'll have it in for us if we do that. Yàushr 'jèmmayàng tāmen 'búhwèi 'ráu wǒmende.

Have it out (argue). /It's better to have it out now than later. Háishŕ syàndzài shwō'míngbaile hǎu. *or* (proverbial) Syān syǎurén hòu'jyūndz ba.

Have in mind. /I have in mind a vacation in Hong Kong. Wǒ dǎswan dàu Syānggǎng shōujyà chyu. /When I asked about schools, I had my son in mind. Shr 'wèile wǒ érdz dǎting sywésyàude shŕching.

Have something clearly in mind 'jŕdàu hěn 'chīngchu. /I have the idea clearly in mind. Nèige wǒmen 'jŕdàude hěn 'chīngchu. *or* Nèige wǒ 'jŕdàude 'chīngchingchu-'chūde.

Have someone do something jyàu. /I'll have two men here tomorrow to cut down the trees. Myér wǒ jyàu 'lyǎngge rén lái kǎn'shù. /I had him do it. Wǒ jyàu 'tā dzwòde. /I had him do it over and over again. Wǒ jyàu tā 'yíbyàn yòu yí'byànde dzwò. /He has the laundry do his shirts. Tā jyàu syǐ'yīfude syǐ tāde chèn'shār.

Have something done bǎ. . . . /Have this cleaned thoroughly. Bǎ 'jèige 'dždz-syǐ'syǐde tsā'gānjingle. /I'll have the room ready for you in fifteen minutes. Yǒu shr̄-'wǔfēn jūng wǒ jyou bǎ 'wūdz gěi nǐ 'shōushrchulaile. /He had the driver discharged. Tā bǎ kāichēde gěi·'tsáile. /He had all the cards marked as you told him. Tā bǎ 'pyàndz dōu jàu nǐ 'shwō de nèiyàngr hwà'hǎule. *but* /I have my teeth cleaned twice a year. Wǒ 'měinyán syǐ 'lyǎngtsz̄ yá. /I had it made to order. Nèi shr̄ wǒ dìng-'dzwòde.

Have to (must) děi, yi'dìng děi; *or, more emphatic,* bu. . . busyíng, fēi. . . busyíng, fēi. . . bu'kě, fēiděi . . . (busyíng *or* bukě), bunéng bu; not have to bùyí-'dìng děi, 'bu . . . yě 'syíng, 'bu . . . hǎu, búbǐ. /I had to leave early. Wǒ děi 'dzǎu dzǒu. /She has to go home now. Tā děi hwéi'jyā le. /I simply had to hit him. Wǒ bù'dǎ ta bù'syíng. *or* Wǒ fēi 'dǎ tā bù'syíng. *or* Wǒ 'bùnéng bù'dǎ tā. *or* Wǒ bù'dǎ tā nǐ 'jyàu wo 'dzěmmaje ne? /Do I HAVE to have tickets? 'Fēiděi yǒu 'pyàu (bu'kě) ma? /Do you HAVE to say that? Nǐ 'fēi nèmma shwō bù'syíng ma? *or* Nǐ yí'dìng děi nèmma shwō ma? *or* (sarcastically) Nǐ 'dzěmma jyou 'fēi dwō 'dzwěi bù'syíng ne? *or* Nǐ 'dzěmma jyou 'fēiděi 'shwōchulai ne? /Does he have to wear patent leather shoes? Tā °'fēiděi (°yí'dìng děi) chwān 'chǐpísyé ma? *or* Tā 'bùchwān 'chǐpísyé bù'syíng ma? /She had to say yes. Tā bù'néng bù'dāying. /You don't have to do anything you don't want to. Nǐ búywànyi dzwò de jyou 'béng dzwò, hǎu le. /You don't have to come. Nǐ 'bùlái yě 'syíng. *or* (impatiently) Nǐ 'bùlái jyou 'bùlái ba. /You don't have to pay me now. Nǐ 'syàndzài 'bùhwán yě 'syíng. *or* Nǐ 'búbǐ 'syàndzài jyou 'hwán wo. /I don't have to go, do I? Wǒ 'búshr̄ yí'dìng děi 'chyù ba? *or* Wǒ 'búchyù yě 'syíng ba, nǐ 'shwō ne? /You don't have to be that polite. Nǐ 'búbǐ 'nèmma 'kèchi. *or* Nǐ 'yùngbujáu 'nèmma 'kèchi.

Other expressions in English. /Let him have it! is expressed as Give it (something) to him. 'Gěi ta! /Have it your way then. is expressed as We'll do it your way. °Yǐ (°Swéi) 'nǐde yìsz 'bàn, hǎule.

HAY. tsǎu (also means grass and straw). /They saw field after field of hay. Tāmen yí'kàn, 'nǎr dōu shr̄ 'tsǎu. *or* Tāmen 'kànjyan yí'kwàiyíkwàide'dìli 'dōu shr̄ 'tsǎu.

Other expressions in English. /Let's make hay while the sun shines. is expressed as While there's a chance, let's hurry and do it. 'Chènje yǒu 'jīhwèi, dzámen 'gǎnjǐn kwài'gàn. or as Don't let this chance slip away. Byé 'tswǒgwòle jèige 'jīhwei. /If we don't leave now, what other time are we waiting for? or by the use of a comparable saying 'Tsžshr̄ bù'dzǒu 'gèngdài 'héshr̄? /I'm tired; let's hit the hay. Wǒ 'lèi le; shwèi'jyàu ba.

HE (HIM, HIS). tā; *or* tā is often lengthened to tā 'nèige rén *or* tā nèige 'nánren; or sometimes one just says that person nèige 'rén; him tā; his tā, 'tāde. /Who is he? 'Tā shr̄ 'shéi? /If anyone can do it, he can. (Yàushr) 'rén néng 'dzwò de shr̄, 'tā jwǔn néng 'dzwò. /I've seen him once. Wǒ 'kànjyangwo tā yí'tsz̄. /Oh, HIM! Òu, 'tā a! /Give this to him. Bǎ jèige gěi 'tā. /I saw him last week. Wǒ 'shànglǐbài 'kànjyan ta le. /This is his hat. Jèi shr̄ 'tāde màudz. /Do you have his address? Nǐ yǒu tāde 'jùjr ma? /His father was a minister. Tā 'fùchin shr̄ ge 'mùshr̄. Compare SHE.

(Used to specify sex) nánren, nánde (for human beings); gūngde (for animals). /It's a HE. Shr̄ ge 'nánren. *or* Shr̄ ge 'nánde. *or* (of an animal) Shr̄ ge 'gūngde. /It's a he-goat. Shr̄ ge'gūngyáng.

Himself. *See* SELF.

HEAD. (Part of the body) tóu; or, in certain localities, nǎudai. /My head hurts. Wǒ 'tóu téng. /He shook his head and left. Tā yáu'tóu jyou 'dzǒu le. /He's raising his head. Tā 'táichi 'tóu lai le. /He nodded his head in recognition. Tā dyǎn'tóu le.

/He turned his head that way. Tā chùngje 'nèibyar 'nyŏutóu. /I fell head first. Wŏ 'tóu cháu 'syà 'shwāisyachyule. /The child's head is covered with dust. Nèige háidz °'tóu(°'nǎudai)shang 'chywán shř 'tǔ. /The head of that monkey is almost human. Nèige 'hóudz de 'tóu jyǎnjř syàng 'rénde.

(Unit) tóu (in counting cattle); rén (in counting people). /How many head of cattle are there on the farm? 'Chǎngshang yǒu 'dwōshǎu tóu'nyóu? /At ten dollars per head (person) that would amount to seventy-five million dollars. 'Měirén 'shŕkwài chyán jyòushr 'chīchyān'wǔbǎi'wàn.

(Of vegetables) kē. /We need two heads of cabbage. Wŏmen děi yàu 'lyǎngkē bái'tsài. The cabbage is ten cents a head. 'Yángbáitsài yľ'máu chyán yľ'kē.

(Top) gàr. /We'll have to knock in the head of the barrel. Tǔngdz'gàr yí'dǐng děi 'dzásyàchyù.

(Top or front) chyánbyar, dìyī; (of a page) chľtóur. /You are at the head of the list. Nǐ dzài 'míngdār jǐn 'chyánbyar. /The mayor was at the head of the procession. Shŕ'jǎng dzài dwèi 'chyánbyar lǐngje. /The boy is at the head of his class in school. Jèige 'háidz dzài tā 'bānli dì'yī. /Begin at the head of this page. Dzài jèi 'pyār-shang tsúng chľ'tóur nyàn.

(Source) fāywándǐ. /How far is it to the head of the river? (Jèityáu'hé) lí 'fāywán'dǐ yǒu 'dwōywǎn?

(Top person) jyājǎng (of a family); jǔshŕde (of an organization). /Who is the head of the family? Jyā'jǎng shŕ shéi? /I want to speak to the head of the organiza-tion. Wǒ yàu jyàn jǔ'shŕde.

(of workmen or an informal group) tóur, lǐngtóur. /Mr. Wáng is the head man. Wáng syānsheng shŕ °'tóur (°'lǐng'tóurde).

(Of a nail, pin, tack, etc.) tóu, tóur. /We want some nails with larger heads. Wŏmen yàu tóur 'dà dyǎr de 'dīngdz.

Head over heels. (lit.) /He fell out of the car head over heels. Tā tsúng 'chē-shang 'dyàuchuchyu de shŕhou, 'fānle jige 'gēndou. (fig.) /My friend is head over heels in love. Wǒde 'péngyou jèng dzai °'lyàn'ài lyànde 'hwǒrède (°'rèlyàn de shŕ-hou, or (of a man only) °'bàidǎu 'shŕlyou'chyúnsyà).

Out of one's head fēng(le). /That man is positively out of his head. 'Nèige rén jyǎn'jŕ shŕ 'fēng le.

Over one's head (beyond one's understanding) 'mwŏmíngchímyàu. /That prob-lem is over my head. Nèige wèn'tí wǒ 'mwŏmíngchľ'myàu.

Come to a head. /Matters are coming to a head. Dàule 'jǐnyàugwān'tóu le. or 'Shŕchíng 'dzài bùnéng 'twōle. or 'Shŕchíng dàule 'fēi bàn bù'kě de shŕhou le. /When did this trouble come to a head? Jèige 'lwàndz 'shémma shŕhou 'nàu'lǐhaile de?

Go over one's head (to a higher authority) ywègwo . . . chyu. /It may be neces-sary to go over his head on this. 'Jèijyàn shŕ, yěsyǔ děi 'ywègwo tā chyu.

Go to one's head. /The success has gone to his head. Tā yǒu dyǎr 'déyìwàng-'syíng.

Have a good head 'běnlǐng, 'tsáigàn. /He has a good head for business. Tā yǒu dzwò 'mǎimai de °'běnlǐng (°'tsáigàn).

Hit the nail on the head. /You hit the nail on the head that time. 'Nèitsz nǐ kě shwō'jáule. or 'Nèitsz nǐ shwōde jèng 'dwèi.

Keep one's head bùhwāng, 'lěngjìng, 'jènjìng; **lose one's head** hwāng, 'húdū.

/Everyone kept his head in the excitement. Dzài 'jǐnjāng de shŕhou, dàjyā dōu °hěn 'lěngjǐng (°hěn 'jěnjǐng, °méi'hwāng). /Everyone lost his head. Dàjyā dōu °hwāng le (°'húdū le, °'bùjŕdàu dzěmma 'bàn le). /She got angry and lost her head. Tā °jíde (°chǐde) 'húdu le.

Keep one's head above water. /He can hardly keep his head above water. Tā dzài 'shwěili dzǐjǐ jyǎnjŕ 'táibuchǐ 'tóu lai. *or* (fig.) Tā 'jyǎnjŕ dzgùbù'syá.

Make head or tail of °'māu (°'mwō) chǐng. /I can't make head or tail of the story. Wǒ °'māu (°'mwō) buchǐng shŕ 'dzěmma hwéi shŕ。

Put heads together 'jyùjǐnghwèi'shén. /Let's put our heads together and figure it out. Dzámen 'jyùjǐnghwèi'shénde 'yánjyōu yíshàr.

Take it into one's head. /The maid suddenly took it into her head to leave. Nyǔ-'syàrén 'hūrán °syǎng (°yàu) °'dzǒu (°bú'gàn). *or* Nyǔsyàrén 'fēi yàu 'dzǒu (bù'kě).

Turn someone's **head** (make one conceited). /His flattery turned her head. Tā bǎ tā 'kwāde 'wàngchí swǒ'yǐle. *or* Tā yíjèn hwāyánchyǎu'yǔ bǎ tā 'shwōde 'gàile 'júyǐ le.

Head-on. /It was a head-on collision. Jěng 'chwàngshang. *or* (of vehicles only) Chē'tóu °pèng (°jwàng, °chwàng) chē'tóu.

Head wind. /A head wind all along the way delayed our arrival. is expressed as We were heading into the wind the whole way, so we were late. Yí'lù 'dǐngje 'fēng, swóyi 'wǎndàude.

Heads (in tossing a coin) dzèr. /Heads I win, tails I lose. Yàushr 'dzèr, wǒ jyòu 'yíng; 'mèr, wǒ jyòu 'shū.

To head (be the leader of) dāng tóur. /He heads the corporation. Tā dzài nèige gūngszlǐ dāng tóur. /He heads the discussion. Tā dāng nèige tǎulwùn hwèi de tóur.

(Move or face in a direction) shàng (go); hwéi (return); wàng, syàng (go toward); chùngje, dǐngje (face toward). /Where are you headed? 'Nǐ shàng 'nàr? /It's about time for me to head home. 'Dàule wǒ gāi °hwéi'jyā (°wàng 'jyā dzǒu) de shŕhou le. /I saw the plane heading east. Wǒ 'kànjyan nèijyà fēi'jǐ °syàng (°wàng) 'dūng fēi. /He is heading that way. Tā 'jèng °wàng (°syàng, °chùngje) 'nèibyar °'dzǒu (*or* (if he is in a rush) °'pǎu). /The pilot headed the plane into the wind. Jyàshr'ywán bǎ 'fēijǐ °'chùngje (°'dǐngje) fēng 'kāichyule.

Head off. /Head him off! is expressed as Stop him! Bǎ tā 'jyéjù! *or* Bǎ tā 'lánju! *or as* Force him to go in another direction! Jyàu tā byé wàng 'nèibyar chyù!

HEALTH. shēndz, 'shēntǐ (both also mean body, bodily condition), 'jyānkāng; (technical) wēishēng; (in) good health 'jyānkāng. /How is your health? Nǐ °'shēndz (°'shēntǐ) dzěmmayàng? *or* Nǐ 'jyānkāng dzěmmayàng? /If you keep on that way you'll ruin your health. Nǐ yàu 'làu nèmmaje, jyòu bǎ 'shēndz nùng'hwàile. /You should guard your health. °'Shēndz (°'Shēntǐ) yàu °bǎu'jùng (°'bǎuchŕ 'jyānkāng, °jyǎng wēi'shēng). /He's in good health. Tā °shēndz (°shēntǐ) hěn 'hǎu. or meaning in sound health Tā °'shēndz (°'shēntǐ) hěn 'jyēshr. *or* Tā hěn 'jyānkāng. /This is the Public Health Bureau. Jèi shŕ 'Gūnggùngwèi'shēng'jyú. /It's good for your health. Jyàu nǐde 'shēndz 'hǎu. *or* Jyàu nǐ °'jwàng (°'chyángjwàng). /She has been in poor health lately. Tā jǐnlai 'shēndz búdà 'hǎu. /Health is appreciated only after it is lost. Dàule 'bújyānkāng de shŕhou rén tsái 'jŕdàu °'jyānkāng (°'shēndz) 'dwōma yǐnggai 'àisyǐ. *but* /Here's to your health! 'Jìng nǐ yì'bēi! *or* 'Fúshòukāng'níng! *or* 'Jìng nǐ yìbēi 'fúshòukāng'níng!

HEALTHY. (Strong) jwàng; (well) hǎu; (sound) jyēshr, tszshr. /I feel healthy enough.

Wǒ 'jywéde wǒ shēndz gòu °ʼjwàng de (°ʼhǎude, °ʼjyēshrde, °ʼtszʹshr). /He's healthy. Tā (shēndz) hen °ʼjwàng (°ʼchyángjwàng, °ʼhǎu, °ʼjyēshr, °tszʹshr). *or* Tā hěn 'jyànkāng. *or* Tā 'méiyou 'bìng. /You look healthier now. °Nǐ 'shēndz (*or,* (referring to facial color) °Nǐʼchǐshǎr, °Nǐʼlyǎnshǎr) kànshangchyu hǎu 'dwō le. *or* Nǐ 'jīngshen hǎu 'dwō le. (fig.) /The pupils showed a healthy respect for their teacher. Sywésheng hěn 'dzwūnjing tāmende 'syānsheng.

(Conducive to health). /This isn't a healthy climate to live in. Jèr de 'chìhou 'rén jùje bùsyāng'yí. /This isn't a healthy job. 'Jèige shèr yú 'jyànkāng yǒu'hài. *or* Dzwò 'jèige shèr dzwò'chángle jyàu 'shēndz bù'hǎu. /This is a healthy sport. 'Jèijǔng 'yùndung jyàu rén 'shēndz 'chyángjwàng. /This is a healthy place to be in. Jèige 'dìfang dàije °ʼyú rén yǒu'yí (°ʼyú rén syāng'yí, °jyàu rén yǒu 'jīngshen, °jyàu rén 'kāngjyàn, °jyàu rén 'shēndz hǎu, °jyàurén 'dwō hwó jinyán).

HEAP. dwēi (Peiping pronunciation dzwēi); **small heap** dwēr. /Heaps of sand dotted the yard. 'Ywàndzli yǒu yìʼdwēiyìʼdwēide 'shǎdz. /Throw all this stuff in the rubbish heap. Bǎ 'jèisyē dōu 'rēngdàu 'lāsyiʼdwēishang chyu. /What is that canvas-covered heap? Yùng 'fānbù gàije de nèiʼdwēi shr shémma? /The children piled sand into small heaps. Syǎu 'hár bǎ 'shǎdz dwēide yìʼdwēryìʼdwērde.

To heap dwēi. /The table was heaped with all kinds of food. 'Jwōdzshang dwēi- 'mǎnle 'gèshrge'yàngrde 'chrde. /Heap everything onto the bed. Dōu dwēidzài 'chwángshang hǎu le. /I just can't heap any more on the table. 'Jwōrshang 'dzài yě dwēibu'syà shémma le. *or* Jwōrshang nèiʼdwēi dzài yě bùnéng 'jyā shémma le. *but* (fig.) /That's heaping insult upon insult. Nèi shr jyāʼbèide 'chǐfù rén.

Heaping (full) mǎnmānde. /He put two heaping teaspoons of sugar in his coffee. Jyāʼfēilǐtou tā 'fàngle mǎn'mānde lyǎngsháur 'táng.

HEAR (HEARD). (Simple perception) 'tīngjyàn; (more specifically clear perception) tīngchǐngchu. /I hear someone coming from there. Wǒ 'tīngjyàn yǒu'rén tsúng 'nàr lái. /Did you hear anything? Nǐ 'tīngjyànle dyǎr 'shēngyīn ma? /Can you hear it? Nǐ 'tīngdejyàn ma? /Do (*or* Did) you hear it? Nǐ 'tīngjyànle ma? /I just heard the telephone ring. Wǒ gāng 'tīngjyàn dyàn'hwà syǎngle. /I hear a scratching sound. Wǒ tīngjyànle 'kwāchakwachāde 'shēngyīn. /I can't hear a thing. Wǒ shémma dōu 'tīngbujyàn. /I didn't hear a thing. Wǒ 'shémma dōu méi'tīngjyan. /All you can hear is his endless prattle. Nǐ 'jr néng tīngjyàn tā 'yíge rén de'shēngyīn, dzài nàr syā'shwō. /He pretends that he didn't hear me. Tā 'jwāng tīngbujyàn. /I can't hear you very well. Wǒ tīngbu'chǐngchu nǐ 'shwō de shr shémma.

(Listen to, listen for) tīng. /I hear good music every night. Wǒ 'měityān 'wǎnshang tīng hǎu 'yīnywè. /Hear me to the end. Nǐ 'tīng wǒ shwō'wánle. /I heard an interesting story yesterday. Wǒ dzwór 'tīngle yídwàr hěn yǒu'yìszde shèr. /Let me hear the arguments from both sides. 'Lyǎngbyārde 'lǐ dōu 'jyǎnggěi wǒ 'tīngting. /Hear ye, hear ye! 'Tīng a! 'Tīng a!

(In court) shěn. /The judge hears different kinds of cases every day. Fǎ'gwān 'měityān shěn gèjǔng 'àndz. /The case was heard in open court. Nèijyàn 'àndz dōu shr 'gūngkāi 'shěnde.

(Of news). /What do you hear from home? Jyāli yǒu 'syèr ma?

Hear that, hear of tīngshwō. /I hear that the play was a success. Wǒ tīngshwō 'syì hěn chéng'gūng. /I never heard of such a thing. 'Jèige wǒ 'tsúnglái méitīng- 'shwōgwo. *or* Nǎr yǒu 'nàyàngde shr. *or* (emphatic) Nà jēn 'chǐyǒutszʹlǐ. /I never heard of him. Jèige rén 'méitīngjyàn 'shwōgwo.

Not hear of (not stand for). /They offered to put me up for the night, but I wouldn't hear of it. Tāmen 'lyóu wǒ 'jùsya, wǒ °bú'gàn (°méi'tīng).

HEART. (Physical) 'syĭndzàng. / He has a weak heart. Tā 'syĭndzàng yŏu dyăr 'shwāi-rwò. / His heartbeat is weak today. Jyērge tā 'syĭndzàng yŏu dyăr 'rwò. / He has heart disease. Tā yŏu 'syĭndzàngbìng.

(Emotional) syĭn. / She has a soft heart. Tā syĭn 'rwăn. / His heart is in the right place. Tā 'syĭn hău. *or* Tāde 'syĭn jăngde 'jèng。 / He wears his heart on his sleeve. (complimentary) Tā 'syĭnjŕkŏu'kwàide. *or* Tā shŕ ge °'jŕsyĭnyăr (°'jŕsyĭncháng) de rén. *or* Tā 'yìjyúyí'dùng dōu néng jyàu rén 'kàndechū tāde 'syĭnshŕ lai. (not complimentary) Tā jèige rén bù'shēnchén. *or* Tā 'syĭ'nù syíngyú'sè. / Don't lose heart. Byé 'hwēisyĭn. / My heart was in my mouth when I said that. Wŏ shwō nèijyù hwà de shŕhou, °'tísyĭndyàu'dănde (°'jĕng'gèrde syĭn 'sywánje). / He's a man after my own heart. Tā gēn wŏ 'syĭntóu'yìhé. *or* 'Jèige rén 'jēn jyàu wŏ 'syĭhwān. / At heart he is really a nice fellow. Chí'shŕ tā nèige rén 'syĭndĭ hĕn 'hău. / He broke her heart when he left. Tā 'dzŏu de shŕhou 'jēn jyàu tā shàng'syĭn. / His mother died of a broken heart while he was serving the sentence. Tā dzài'jyàn de shŕhou tā 'mŭchin shàng'syĭn szde. / It does my heart good to see them happy. Tāmen gāu'syìng 'wŏ syĭnli yĕ hĕn 'tùngkwài。 / Don't take it to heart. Byé 'tài gēdzai 'syĭnshang. *or* Byé 'tài rèn'jēn. / His dog and his gun are the things nearest his heart. Tā syĭnli 'dzwèi ài de shŕ tāde 'gŏu gēn tāde 'chyāng. / He has no heart. Tā syĭn 'hĕn. *or* Tā 'hĕnje ne. *or* Tā jèige rén 'méiyou 'chíngyì. *but* / Have a heart. 'Syíngsying'hău ba.

Other expressions relating to emotions. / I haven't the heart to do it. Wŏ bù-'rénde. / I haven't the heart to leave him here unattended. Wŏ bù'rénde bă tā 'lyàu-sya jyòu 'dzŏu. / Do you have the heart to treat him that way? Nĭ 'nèmma dài tā syĭnli 'rénde ma? *or* Nĭ néng 'rénsyĭn 'nèmma dài tā ma?

(Heart-shaped figure) syĭn, táu. / Give me the box of candy with the heart on it. Gĕi wŏ nèi 'hédzshang dài °'syĭn (°'táu) de 'táng.

(Suit in cards) húngtáur. / I bid two hearts. Wŏ jyàule 'lyăngge húng 'táur.

(Central part) jūngbù; (precise center) jēngdāngjūng, 'jūngsyĭn, jūngsyĭndyăn. / The store was located in the heart of town. 'Pùdz shŕ dzài chéngde °'jēngdāng'jūng (°'jūngsyĭn('dyăn), °'jūng'bù).

By heart bèi. / He learned the poem by heart。 Tā bă 'shŕ 'bèisyalaile.

Get at the heart of. / I intend to get at the heart of this matter. Wŏ yàu 'jŕdàu jèijyàn shŕ °'dàudĭ (°'jyōujìng) shŕ 'dzĕmma hwéi shŕ. *or* Jèijyàn shŕ wŏ yí'dìng yàu 'chèdĭ chá'chĭngle. *or* Jèijyànshŕde 'dĭsyì wŏ yàu 'dōu jŕdau le.

HEAT. (Hotness) rè (used mostly as a noun in scientific statements, otherwise as a stative verb); also rèjyèr. / Heat can be produced by rubbing. Mwótsā néng shēng 'rè. / Iron is a better conductor of heat than stone. Tyĕ bi 'shŕtou rúngyi chwán 'rè. / The (degree of) heat must be as high as 1000° centigrade. Rè'dù dĕi gāudau băidubyău yì'chyāndù. / You can feel the heat from here. Tsúng 'jèr nĭ jyou jywédechu 'rè lai. / I can't stand the heat in this room. Jèige °'wūdz tài 'rè (°'wūdzde 'rèjyèr) wŏ shŏubu'lyău. / In July the heat is intense. 'Chíywè rède 'lìhai. / There is more heat in this place than necessary. Jèr 'yùngbu'jáu dzèmma 'rè.

(Of a heating system) hwŏ, or expressed verbally by shēng hwŏ, shēng lúdz, shēng nwǎnchĭ; **steam heat** nwǎnchĭ. / There isn't any heat in this radiator. Nwǎnchĭ lúdzli méiyou nwǎn'chĭ. / They haven't had any heat there for three days now. Tāmen nèr 'sāntyān méishēng °'hwŏ (°'lúdz, °nwǎn'chĭ) le. / You provide your own heat. Shēng 'hwŏ, nĭ dzìjĭ gĕi chyán. / Our house has no heat as yet. Wŏmen jyā hái méi-shēng °'hwŏ (°'lúdz, °nwǎn'chĭ) ne. / What kind of heat do you have? Nĭmen jyāde °'hwŏ (°'lúdz, °nwǎn'chĭ) shāu shémma. / That building has oil heat. Nèige lóulide

°'hwǒ (°lúdz, °nwǎn'chǐ) shāu yóu. / The heat should be turned on. Gāi shēng 'hwǒ le. *or* Gāi kāi nwǎn'chǐ le.

(Of a race). / He qualified in the first heat, but lost out in the final race. Tā 'yùsài chyǔshangle, kěshr 'jywésài shūle.

To **heat** (of food) rè, wēn. / I'll heat up the soup for you. Wǒ bǎ 'tāng gěi ni °rère (°wēnwen).

(Of water) dzwò shwěi; (up to a boil) dzwò kāishwěi. / Let's heat some water and make tea. Wǒmen 'dzwò dyar kāi'shwěi chǐ dyǎr 'chá.

(Of a building) shēng hwǒ, shēng lúdz, shēng nwǎnchǐ. / This place hasn't been heated yet. Jèige 'fángdz méi shēng 'hwǒ ne. / This house is hard to heat. is expressed as This house uses much heat. Jèige fángdz yàu syàng 'nwǎnhwo hěn fèi 'hwǒ.

Heat an iron shāu làutye (over a fire); chāshang dyànyùndǒude chāsyāu (with electricity). / She heated the iron. (over a fire) Tā bǎ làutye 'shāushangle. *or* (with electricity) Tā bǎ dyànyùndǒude chā'syāu 'chāshangle.

Other expressions in English. / They had a heated argument. Tāmen 'jēngbyànde hěn lìhai. / They hit each other in the heat of the argument. Tāmen 'byàndàu hěn 'jíde shŕhou 'dáchilaile. *or* Tāmen ywè 'jēng ywè 'chǐ jyou dáchilaile.

HEAVY. (Of weight) jùng, chén. / Is that too heavy for you? Tài °'chén (°'jùng) le ma? / How heavy you are! Nǐ jēn °'chén (°'jùng). / How heavy is this? Jèige yǒu dwō-(ma) °'chén (°'jùng)? / That's a heavy trunk. Nèige 'syāngdz hěn °'chén (°'jùng). / Heavy industry depends on coal and iron. 'Jùnggūngyè yàu 'kàuje 'méi gēn 'tyě. / We need the support of your heavy artillery unit. Wǒmen děi yóu nǐmende 'jùngpàu-dwèi 'yǎnhù.

Other uses are sometimes expressed as large dà; much dwō; (of sleep only) chén; or other indirect expressions. / He was tired and fell into a heavy sleep. Tā 'lèi le; °'hūhu dà shwěichǐlaile (°shwèide hěn 'chén, °shwèide hěn 'sź). / He is a heavy sleeper, so he couldn't have heard it. Tā shwěi'jyàu hěn 'chén, swóyi 'búhwèi tīngde'jyànde. / His eyes are heavy with sleep. (for want of sleep) Tā 'kwùnde °yǎn-jing 'jēngbukāile (°yǎn'pí fā'chén). *or* (because he just woke up) Tā 'shwèide 'yǎn-jing 'mwōmwohu'hǔde. / In the morning there was a heavy rain. 'Dzǎuchen syàle yíjèn 'dàyǔ. / There will be a heavy vote if the weather is good. Tyānchi 'hǎu, tóu-'pyàu de rén jyòu 'dwō. / The heavy strain these last few days is beginning to tell on him. 'Jèi jityān 'tài 'jǐnjāng le, bǎ tā 'lèide dōu dài'syàngrle. / That was a heavy meal. (too much of everything) Nèidwùn'fànchŕde 'jēn dwō. *or* (too much fat) Nèidwùn 'fàn tài 'yóunì le. / He is a heavy buyer. Tā 'mǎide 'dwō. / He is a heavy gambler. Tā 'dǔchilai jyòu syà 'dà jùdz. *or* Tā hàu'dǔ. / Use a soft pencil to draw these heavy lines. Jèi jityáu 'tsū syàn yùng 'rwǎn dyǎr de chyàn'bǐ hwà. / This dough is still heavy. 'Myàn hái méifǎ'hǎu. / His heavy features attract attention. Tāde 'tsūbènde 'yàngdz 'jāurén jù'yì. / Are you a heavy drinker? Nǐ hē'jyǒu hěde 'lìhai ma? / He is well known for his heavy drinking. Tā yǐ hējyǒu hěde lìhai chū-míng. / My duties are heavy this week. Wǒ 'jèige lǐ'bài 'shèr tǐng °'dwō (°'lèi, °'fèisyīn, °chŕ'lì). / It is a heavy problem. Wèn'tí hěn °'máfan (°'fùdza). / This book is heavy reading. Jèiběr 'shū 'kànchǐlai °'tǐng fèi'jìn (°hěn nán). / Traffic is heavy today. 'Jīntyan 'lùshang hěn 'jǐ. *or* 'Jīntyan chē hěn 'dwō.

HEEL. (Back of the foot) jyǎuhòugen, jyǎugēn. / I cut my heel on a sharp stone. Yíkwài jyān 'shŕtou bǎ wǒ °jyǎu'hòugen (°jyǎu'gēn) 'lále. / Something is hurting my heel. Yě búshr 'shémma 'dūngsyi jŕ 'gè wǒ jyǎu'hòugen.

(Back of a shoe, etc.) hòugen, hòugēr. / My shoes are worn down at the heels. Wǒ syé de 'hòugen 'mwósyachyùle. / There are holes in the heels of these socks.

'Wàdzde °'hòugen (°hòu'gēr) pwòle. / Put heels on (the shoes). Ān (syé)'hòuger.
or Hwàn ('syé)'hòuger. / Darn the heels. Bǔ (wàdz)'hòuger.

(Cad). / He's a heel. Tā shř ge 'syǎurén.

Cool one's heels. / He's been cooling his heels outside the office since noon.
Tā tsúng 'jūngwǔ jyòu dzài mén 'wàitou 'děngje. / Let him cool his heels for a
while. Jyàu tā 'děngdeng.

Take to one's heels. / He took to his heels when I said, "Hey!" Wǒ yìshwō,
"Dēi!" Tā jyòu 'pǎule.

To heel (of a ship) wāi. / The ship heeled as it made the turn. Chwán 'wāije
jwǎnde 'wār。 / The ship heeled and turned over. Chwán 'wāide 'fānle.

HEIGHT. (By measurement) gāu. / What is the height of those hills? (Nèisyē)'shān
yǒu 'dwō gāu? / This plane can fly at a great height (*or* at great heights). Jèijyà
fēi'jī kěyǐ 'fēide 'hěn 'gāu.

(Limit) dzwèi . . . de shŕhou. / He has reached the height of success. Tā
yǐjīng 'dàule dzwèi dé'yǐ de shŕhou le. / There is a Chinese proverb, "The height of
success must be followed by a decline." 'Jūnggwo yǒu jyù'súhwàr: "Shèng'jí bì'shwāi."

Heights (hills, high places) shān, 'gāudì. / His house is on the heights west of
the town. Tā jyā dzài chéng 'syībyar shānshang. / He suffered no loss during the
flood because his house is on the heights. Tā jyā dzài °'shānshang (°'gāudìshang),
swóyi fā'shwéide shŕhou méi'yānjáu.

HELLO. / Hello! How are you? 'Dzěmmayàng? (more frequent) *or* 'Hèi! Nǐ 'hǎu ma?
or 'Ā! 'Hǎu ma? / Hello! (on the telephone) 'Wài! *or* 'Wèi! *or* 'Èi! *or* 'Ài!

HELP. (Assist, give assistance to) bāngmáng; (help do something, or help financially)
bāng, bāngjù; (help a number of people financially) 'jōujì; (help financially in an
emergency) jyòu; (help a number of people financially in an emergency) 'jyòujì; (help)
physically in an emergency) jyòu, jyòumìng; (be of use) yǒuyùng; (of medicine) jř,
gwǎn, 'gwǎnjř. / Can someone help? 'Shéi 'bāngbang 'máng? *or* 'Shéi 'bāng yìba
'shǒur? *or* Yǒu 'rén ma? / Help! Jyòu'mìng ou! *or* Jyòu'mìng a! *or* Jyòu'mìng!
/ Please help me. Láu'jyà, °'bāng syar 'máng (°'bāngbang 'máng, °'bāng yìba
'shǒur). / Please help him hold this up. Láu'jyà, 'bāng tā 'táije dyar. / Can you
help me get out? °Bāng wo (or, meaning pull me °La wo) yì'bǎ, wǒ hǎu 'chūchyu.
/ Help him up. °Bāngje (°Fújie) tā 'shàngchyu. / I helped him a good deal. Wǒ hěn
'bānggwo ta. / Won't you give something to help the poor? Nín 'shě dyàr shémma
'jōujì 'chyúngrén, syíng busyíng? / Can you help him? (financially) Nǐ 'bāng tā
yísyàr 'syíng busyíng? *or* Nǐ néng 'bāng tā dyar 'chyán ma? *or* (physically) Nǐ
'fú tā yìbǎ 'syíng busyíng? *or* Nǐ néng 'bāngbang tāde 'máng ma? / Can you help
him finish it? Nǐ néng 'bāngje tā nùng'wánle ma? / Help me put away the books.
Bāng wǒ bǎ 'shū 'shōushr chilai. *or* Bāng wǒ 'jyánjyan shū. / I was just helping
her wash dishes. Wǒ gāng'tsái bāng tā syǐ'wǎn laije. / Come and help! 'Lái bāngbang 'máng! *or* Lái 'bāng yìba 'shǒu. / Come help lift it. Gwòlai 'bāngje 'táitai.
/ I helped that old man cross the street. Wǒ °'bāngje (or, by leading him °'lǐngje,
or, by holding his arm °'jyàje, °'fújie, °'chānje) nèige lǎu'tóur gwo'jyē laije. / Help
the old lady across the street. 'Bāngju jèige lǎu'tàitai gwo 'jyé. *or* Bǎ lǎu'tàitai
fú (°chān, °lǐng, °jyà) gwo 'jyē chyu. / I would have drowned if he hadn't come to
help me. Yàu búshr tā lái 'jyòu wo, wǒ jyou 'yānszle.

(Prevent). / Sorry, it can't be helped. Dwèibu'chǐ, °méiyou 'fádz (°'méi fǎr
'bàn). / Well, it just can't be helped. 'Hài! 'Méi fǎr 'bàn a! / I can't help it. 'Wǒ
méi 'fǎr. *or* 'Wǒ yǒu shémma 'fǎr ne? / I can't HELP it (of weeping or anger).
is expressed as I can't hold it back any longer. Wǒ 'rěnbu'jù le. / I couldn't help

but tell him. Wǒ 'jřhǎu 'gàusung ta le. or expressed as I couldn't hold it back any longer. Wǒ rěnbu'jù le, jyou 'gàusung ta le.

(Serve). /Help yourself. Dž'jǐ lái byé 'kèchi. /Help yourself to some more rice. Nǐ dž'jǐ lái 'chéng fàn.

Help (aid) is expressed verbally as in the first paragraph above. /Do you need any help? Yàu rén bāng'máng ma? /I need your help. Fēi yǒu 'nǐ lái bāng'máng tsái 'syíng. or Wǒ gēn nǐ gàu'bāng laile. or expressed as I can't get along without you. 'Wǒ jer méiyou 'nǐ bù'syíng. or as I can use you. Wǒ yùngde'jáu nǐ. /When I need your help I'll let you know. Wǒ yùngde'jáu nǐ de 'shřhou jyou 'gàusu nǐ. /Whenever you need any help from me (can use me), let me know. Nǐ 'shémma shř-hou yùngde'jáu wo, jyou shwō 'hwà. /The stricken area needs immediate help. 'Dzāichyǔde nàn'mín děi lìkè 'jyòuji. /He needs some (financial) help. Děi 'bāng tā dyar 'chyán. or Děi 'bāngbang tā. /It's a help. is expressed as It's useful. Yóu dyǎr 'yùng. /He'll be a big help. Tā 'hěn néng bāng'máng. /He's no help at all. Tā jyàn'jř °'méiyou'yùng (°shř ge 'fèiwu).

(Persons who help). /It's difficult to get help these days. 'Rújīn hěn nán jǎu °'yùngrén (°dǐsya'rén). /Our help didn't show up this morning. Wǒmen 'yùng de rén jyēr 'dzǎuchen méi'lái. /I want to hire some help. Wǒ syǎng 'gù ge °bāng'mángrde (or meaning an odd-job man °dǎ'dzárde, or meaning a short-term laborer °'dwǎn-gūng, or meaning a seasonal laborer °'chánggūng, or meaning a boy °syǎu'hár).

(Military). /Help will come in two days. 'Lyǎngtyānli jyòubīng néng 'dàu. /Help came too late. Jyòubīng 'dàule, yǐjīng 'wǎnle.

HEN. (Fowl) mǔ jī. /He has a rooster and several hens. Tā yǒu yìjř 'gūngjī, jǐjř-'mǔjī.

Hen party. /It's strictly a hen party. Nèige 'hwèi °dōushr (°jř yǒu) 'nyǔrén. or Nèige 'hwèi 'jywédwèi 'búyàu 'nánrén.

HER (HERS). See **SHE.**

HERE. (In this place) jèli, jèher, 'jège dìfang, 'jèige dìfang; (especially in Peiping) jèr; (this locality) jèikwar; all preceded by dzài when at this place is meant. /Meet me here at six o'clock. 'Lyòudyǎn dzài 'jèr gēn wǒ jyàn'myàr. or Dzámen 'lyòu-dyǎnjūng dzài 'jèr jyàn. /Stand here and don't move. Nǐ jàndzài 'jèr, byé 'dùng. /We've never had any snow here. 'Wǒmen °jèr (°jèli, °jèige 'dìfang, °jèikwàr) 'tsúnglái méi 'syàgwo 'sywě. /We don't have anyone here by that name. 'Wǒmen jèr 'méiyou rén jyàu 'nèige míngdz de. /We have a man here who answers your description. Wǒmen jèr 'yǒu ge rén syàng nǐ 'shwō de nèige 'yàngr. /We've had no electricity here for three days. 'Wǒmen °jèr (of, if a town, etc. °jèikwàr) 'sāntyan méiyou 'dyàn le. /Here's the book (in this place). Shū dzài 'jèr. /Your hat is here. (Nǐde)'màudz dzài 'jèr. /Come here. Dàu 'jèr lái. or Lái 'jèr. or 'Gwòlai. /Here I am! (over here, not there) (Wǒ dzài)'jèr ne! /There's something for you here. 'Jèr yǒu dyǎr 'dūngsyi shř 'nǐde. /Here it is. Dzài 'jèr ne. but /Here's your hat. (when handing it to a person) is expressed as Your hat. Nǐ 'màudz. /Here's something for you. is expressed as This is to be given to you. 'Jè shr gěi 'nǐ de. /Here is a man who has never complained about anything. is expressed as This man . . . . 'Jèiwèi 'syànglái méi'bàuywàngwo shémma.

(At this point, at this time) tsž. /Here's where I draw the line. Wǒ jyòu 'tsž wéi'jř.

(Exclamatory). /Here, take this! Èi, 'náje 'jèige. or 'Èi, gěi nǐ 'jèige. /Here, let me help you. 'Wǒ lái (gěi nǐ nùng). /Here, watch me do it. 'Lái a, kàn 'wǒde. /Here! (Look here!) This isn't right! 'Hèi! or 'Èi! 'Jèkě bú'dwèi. /Look here! See what I got! 'Kàn a! Kàn 'jè shr shémma. /Now, look here! You can't do that to me! 'Hèi! *or* 'Èi! 'Nǐ bùnéng 'nèmma dài wǒ. /Here I am! <u>meaning</u> I've come. Wǒ 'láile. /Well, here we are (in a mess). Wǒmen jyòu 'dàule 'jèige dìbu le. /Here I am, without a cent, while they dine and make merry. Chyáuchyau 'wǒ, yíge 'dzěr yě 'méiyou; chyáuchyau 'tāmen ne, yòu 'chī yòu 'wár de. /Here you are. <u>meaning</u> This is what you wanted. 'Jèi jyoushr nǐ 'yàu de. /Here you are, holding the bag. Chyáuchyau 'nǐ, 'dzài jèr shǒu'dzwèi. /Here it is. <u>meaning</u> Look at it. Nǐ 'chyáuchyau. /Here goes! Chyáu 'jèi shǒur de.

(For emphasis). /My friend here will take you to the station. Wǒ (jèiwèi) 'péngyou kěyǐ 'sùng nǐ dàu chē'jàn. /Now, take Mr. Wáng here. I'm sure he wouldn't do it. Jyòu ná (jèr jèiwèi) 'Wáng syānsheng shwō ba. Wǒ 'jwǔn jīdàu 'tā búhwèi de.

(Present). /Here! 'Dàu! or 'Yǒu! or 'Dzài! /Only six of the men answered, "Here!" Chí'jūng jǐ yǒu 'lyòuge rén dá '"Dàu!"

Here and there. /The stores are scattered here and there throughout the city. 'Pùdz dzài chéng'lǐ 'dàuchu dōu 'yǒu. /He looked here and there and left without a word. Tā 'jèr kànkan, 'nàr kànkan, 'yíjyùhwà yě méi'yányu jyòu 'dzòule.

Be neither here nor there. /That's neither here nor there. <u>is expressed as</u> What's been said has no relation to the main point. Jè yú 'běntí méiyǒu 'gwānsyi. <u>or as</u> The problem still isn't solved. 'Wèntí háishr 'jyějywébù'lyǎu.

HIDE (HID, HIDDEN). (Conceal) tsáng; hide <u>oneself</u> tsáng, dwǒ. /He hid his money in a bureau drawer. Tā bǎ 'chyán 'tsángdzài yíge gwèidz 'chōutǐlǐ le. /He hid it somewhere. Nèige tā 'tsángchǐlaile. /Have you hidden anything? Nǐ 'tsángle shemma láije ma? or Nǐ yǒu shemma 'tsángchilaide ma? /Look! He seems to be hiding something. Kwài 'kàn! Tā yǒudyǎr 'tsángtsangyan'yànde. or Tā dzài nar 'tsáng-shémma ne. /The men are hiding in those woods. Rén dōu °'tsángdzài (°'dwǒdzài) nèipyàn shù'líndzlǐ le. /He hid himself under the bed. Tā °tsángdzài (°dwǒdzài) chwáng'dǐsya le. /Go and hide! Kwài 'tsángchilai! or Kwài 'dwǒchilai! /Hide it under the blanket. 'Tsángdzài tǎndz 'dǐsya.

(Keep from sight by an obstruction) dǎng, jē. /The sign hides the view. 'Páidz °'dǎngjùle (°'jējùle). /This tall building hides everything from view. Jyàu jèige lóu °'dǎngde (°'jēde) 'shémma dōu kànbu'jyàn.

(Of emotions) jē. /He became cross just to hide his embarrassment. Tā nèmma shēng'chì búgwò shr yàu jē'syōu.

A hide (animal skin) 'shēngpídz, 'shēng-X-'pí <u>where X is the name of an ani-mal</u>; cowhide 'shēngnyóu'pí. /They are selling hides in the market. Tāmen dzài 'jíshang mài 'shēngpídz.

Save one's hide. /He did that to save his own hide. Tā nèmma 'gàn shr yàu lín'nàn góu'myǎn.

HIGH. (By measurement) gāu; (not low) bùdī. /That's high enough. Nèi jyou °'gòu gāude le (°'búswàn 'dīle). /The building is eight stories high. 'Lóu yǒu 'bātséng gāu. /Hang it high. 'Gwàde gāu'gāurde. /Hang it higher. Dzài gwà 'gāu dyar. /This is as high as I can reach. Wǒ 'gòude bùnéng bǐ 'jèige dzài 'gāu le. or Wǒ 'jī néng gòudau 'jèr. /The mountains are so high that their tops are always snow-capped. Shān 'gāude 'dyěngrshang lǎu jàuje 'sywě. /It's always the other mountain that looks higher. (proverb) 'Jèshān 'wàngje 'nàshān 'gāu. /The highest mountain peak has never been reached by man. 'Dzwèi gāu de (shān)'fēng hái méiyou rén 'dàugwo. /He climbed up so high that we couldn't see him. Tā wàng shàng 'pá, 'gāude wǒmen dōu kànbu'jyàn tale. /The temperature will be pretty high today. Jīntyān 'wēndù yídìng hwèi hěn 'gāu. /She sang a high note. Tā chàngle yíge hěn

629

'gāude 'yīn. / Your voice is too high. Nǐ 'shēngyin tài 'gāu. / He is in a higher class. (in school) Tāde bān 'gāu. (in native ability) Tā 'běnlǐng 'gāu dyar. (in acquired skills) Tā 'shǒuyî 'gāu dyar. (socially) Tā 'dîwèi 'gāu dyar.

(Of price) gāu, dà, gwèi. / This price is too high. Jèige jyàr tài °'gāu (°'dà, °'gwèi).

(Of hopes) gāu, dà. / Don't let your hopes fly too high. Byé °bàuje (°tswúnje) 'tài °dà (°gāu) de 'syīwàng. or (more emphatic) Byé 'wàngsyàng (tyān'kāi).

(Of speed) is expressed as fast kwài. / How high a speed will this car reach? 'Jèige chē kéyi kāi 'dwō kwài? / At high speeds it's likely to develop engine trouble. Kāide 'kwài de shŕhou, 'jǐchi hwèi chū 'máubìng.

High above (dzài) . . . 'shàngbyar. / We were high above the clouds. Wǒmen dzài 'yúntsai 'shàngbyar.

High and dry (fig.). / She was left high and dry. Bǎ tā gěi jěng'gèrde °'pyē-kaile (°'pyēsyale).

High and low nǎr dōu, 'shémma dìfang dōu. / I looked high and low, but couldn't find it. Wǒ 'nǎr dōu 'jǎule, 'jyòushr jǎubu'jáu. or Wǒ 'shémma dìfang dōu jǎu-'byànle, yě méijau'jáu.

High-class 'gāuděngde; (expensive) gwèi; (wealthy, of people) kwò, bù'chyúng. / A high-class restaurant serves the same food, but charges extra for the atmosphere. 'Gāuděngde 'gwǎndzli 'fàn bìng 'bújyànde tèbyé 'hǎu, búgwo jyèje 'shèbei é'chyán. / This is a high-class restaurant. Jèige 'gwǎndz 'gwèi. / This is a high-class neigh-borhood. 'Jèikwar 'jùde dōu shŕ 'kwòrén. or 'Jèikwar 'chyúngrén jùbu'chǐ.

High grade hǎu; or expressed as of high quality °'chéngshǎi (°'chéngse) °hǎu (°gāu). / This is high-grade silver. Jèige 'yíndz °'chéngshǎi (°chéngse) °'hǎu (°'gāu).

High-handed jwānjř, bàdau, bàchi. / He is too high-handed to suit me. Tā tài °jwān'jř (°'bàdau, °'bàchi), jyàu wǒ bù'syīhwan.

High jump tyàugāur.

High-minded (having high principles) 'fēngdu bù'sú, 'jwāngjùng; (proud) àuchi, jyàuau. / He's a high-minded person. Tā 'fēngdù bù'sú. or Tā hěn 'jwāngjùng. / He's too high-minded. Tā tài °'àuchi (°'jyàuau).

High-powered (of force) dà; (of horsepower) dà, gāu. / This air-rifle is high-powered. Jèige chǐ'chyāng lìlyang hěn 'dà. / This is a high-powered engine. Jèige 'jǐchi 'lìlyang hěn 'dà. / This car is high-powered. Jèilyàng 'chē 'mǎlì hěn °'gāu (°'dà).

High-ranking officers 'gāují jyūngwàn.

High-strung 'shénjǐng 'jǐnjāng. / He's too high-strung to be a good driver. Tā 'shénjǐng tài 'jǐnjāng, kāi 'chē 'búhwèi kāide 'hǎude.

High tide jǎngcháu, shàngcháu. / Let's wait until high tide. Děng °jǎng'cháu (°shàng'cháu) dzài shwō.

High time. / It's high time you came. Nǐ 'láide kě 'jēn búswàn 'dzǎu. / It's high time you did something about it. Kě 'jēn gāi 'bàn le. or Nǐ 'bànde kě jēn búswàn 'dzǎu le.

High wind ('fēicháng) 'chyángde fēng. / The airplanes met high winds. Fēi'jī 'yùjyanle 'fēicháng 'chyángde fēng.

The high courts 'gāujífǎ'ywàn.

Highest respect is expressed verbally as respect most highly dzwèi 'dzwūnjǐng. /He commands the highest respect in his circle. 'Tā nèi chywārli de rén dzwèi 'dzwūnjǐng tā.

Be in high spirits gāusyìng. /Why is he in such high spirits today? Tā 'jīntyān wèi 'shémma jèmma gāu'syìng?

Have a high opinion of pèifu. /I have a high opinion of him. Wǒ hěn 'pèifu tā.

To high-pressure is expressed by a proverb meaning make flowers fall from heaven by talking shwōde 'tyānhwālwàn'jwèi, or as talk someone into bǎ . . . 'shwōde . . . , or as persuade someone that nothing will do but to . . . 'fēi chywàn . . . bù'kě. /The salesman high-pressured him into buying a high-priced car. 'Màichēde shwōde 'tyānhwālwàn'jwèi, jyègwǒ bǎ tā shwōde mǎile lyàng 'tǐng gwèide 'chē. or 'Màichēde bǎ tā 'shwōde mǎile lyàng 'tǐng gwèide 'chē. or 'Màichēde 'fēi chywàn tā mǎi lyàng 'tǐng gwèi de 'chē bù'kě, 'jyègwǒ tā 'mǎile.

High (gear) is expressed as third dìsān or as fast kwài. /He shifted into high. Tā dǎudau dì'sāndau jǎ. or Tā gǎidau 'kwàijǎ le.

A new high. /Prices have reached a new high. Wùjyà 'yòu wǎng 'shàng jǎngle yisyàr. or 'Dūngsyi yòu jǎng'jyàr le.

HILL. shān, 'syǎu shān, 'ǎi shān (shān also means mountain; the other terms are used only to contrast the meaning). /We must cross a range of hills before we reach the mountains. Wǒmen dǎu 'gāushān yǐ'chyán děi gwò yídàu °'syǎu (°'ǎi) shān. /What is beyond the hills? Shān 'hòubyar yǒu 'shémma?

(Slope, road on a hill) shān, pwō, pwōr, shānlù. /That's a bad hill. Nèige °pwō (°'pwōr, °shān, °shān'lù) hěn 'dòu. /That hill is icy. Nèige °'shānshang (°shān'lù, °pwōr) hěn 'hwá.

HIM. See HE.

HIS. See HE.

HISTORY. lìshǐ, shǐ. /The history of this country is very interesting. 'Jèi gwó de lì'shǐ yǒu °'yìsz (°'chywèr). /This picture has quite a history. Jèijāng 'hwàr yǒu syāng'dāngde lì'shǐ. /He is writing a history of historiography. Tā jèngdzài syě yìběn 'shǐsywé'shǐ. /He wrote several works on the history of printing. Tā 'syěle jiběn gwānyu 'yìnshwā'shǐ de 'shū. /His field is history. meaning He's studying history. Tā shǐ nyàn lì'shǐ de. or meaning He's majoring in history. Tāde 'jùsyōu-kē shǐ lì'shǐ. or meaning He teaches history. Tā jyāu lì'shǐ. or meaning He works on history professionally. Tā jr 'shǐsywé.

HIT. (General term; can be used in almost any connection) dǎ; (hit with a sharp blow) chyāu; (hit with a heavy blow, especially with something in the hand) dzá; (especially with a hammer, fist, or club) chwéi; (especially with a hammer, and with downward motion) dzáu; (hit by throwing, or hit and cut with a sword) kǎn; (by throwing) rēng, pyě, jywāi; (by colliding) pèng, jwàng; (with an arrow) shè; (by bombing) jà; or expressed with resultative compounds, with one of the above words as the first element, and one of the following for the second: jùng, jáu (hit the mark); kāi (open, broken); hwài (broken); swèi (to pieces); dàu (reach); shāng (wound); sz (dead); etc.; sometimes a second object, yídwùn (a number of blows) or yísyà, yísyàr (a blow), or a numeral, plus the object used in hitting is added; be hit by also jùng. /He hit her. Tā 'dǎ tā. /He hit her head with his fists. Tā ná 'chywántou °'dǎ (°'chwéi, °'dzáu) tāde 'tóu laije. /He hit her with a hammer. Tā ná 'chwéidz °'chwéi (°'dǎ, °'dzáu, °'chyāu) tā. /He hit her with a piece of stone (in his hand). Tā ná yíkwài 'shŕtou

°'dǎ (°'dzá, °'dzáu, °'chyāu) tā. / He hit her with a piece of stone (by throwing it). Tā ná yǐkwài 'shŕtou 'kǎn tā. or Tā ná yǐkwài 'shŕtou jàuje tā °'kǎnle (°'rēngle, °'jwāile, °'pyěle) chyùle. / He hit her face once with his palm. Tā 'dǎle tā yǐ'bājang. / He held him against the wall with his left hand and hit him several times with his right fist. Tā yùng 'dzwǒshǒu bǎ tā 'ēndzai chyángshang, yùng 'yòuchywántou °'dǎle (°'chwéile, °'dzáule) tā yǐ'dwùn. / He hit the man and made him cry. Tā bǎ nèige rén dǎkūle. / He hit the thief so his nose bled. Tā bǎ dzéi dǎde bídz lyóu'sywě le. / He hit me with his umbrella and I hit him back with my fist. Tā dǎle wǒ yǐ'sǎn, wǒ dǎle tā yǐ'chywán. / The (deaf) mute hit the lama with his trumpet, and the lama hit back with his sole (fish). (a popular tongue twister) 'Yǎba dǎle 'lama yǐ'lǎba, 'lǎma dǎle 'yǎba yǐ'tǎma. / He hit me, and I hit back. Tā yi'chywán dǎgwo'lái, wǒ yě yi'chywán dǎgwo'chyù. / The ball hit the wall and bounced back to my hand. Chyóur °'dǎ(°'pèng)dàu 'chyángshang, yòu °'pènghwei (°'hwéidau) wǒ 'shǒuli. / He was trying to hit the nail, but hit his own finger instead. Tā yàu dzá 'dīngdz, 'kěshr bǎ dž'jǐde shǒu'jŕtou dzále. / The blacksmith hits the iron with a hammer. 'Tyějyang ná 'chwéidz dǎ'tyě. / He hit the clock with a hammer and broke it to pieces with one blow. Tā ná 'chwéidz bǎ 'jūng 'yísyàdz jyou dǎ'swēile. / I hit my knee against the door. Wǒ géle'bàr °'jwàngdzai (°'pèngdzai) 'ménshangle. / The door suddenly opened and hit him in the face. 'Mén yi'kāi °'pèng (°'jwàng) le tāde 'lyǎn le. / He was hit by a streetcar, but fortunately didn't get under the wheels. Tā jyàu dyàn'chē °'pèngle (°'jwàngle), kěshr jyàu'syǐng méi 'yàjau. / Did the ball hit him? Chyóur 'dǎjau tā le ma? / He was hit by a bullet. Tā 'jùngle yǐkē 'dždàn. or Tā jùng'dàn le. / Let's see if you can hit that tree. Kàn nǐ °'dǎde'jáu (°'kǎnde'jáu) nèikē 'shù ma. / If you can hit that coin with this one, you get both. Nǐ yàushr néng ná 'jèige chyár bǎ 'nèige chyár 'dzáshang, 'lyǎ chyár nǐ 'dōu 'yíngle chyu. / He hit the bull's-eye. Tā dǎ'jùngle húng'syīnle. / You might get hit if you stand in the open. (by bullets) Nǐ dzài 'kùngdìshang jànje yěsyǔ hwèi jyàu °dž'dàn 'dǎjau (or (by a bomb) °jà'dàn 'jàdau). / You hit it! 'Jùngle! / He hit the deer with an arrow. Tā (yùng 'jyàn) 'shèjau nèige 'lù. / He hit the ball so hard that it sailed out of the park. Tā nèiyí-'bàng jyèr 'jēn dzú, bǎ chyóur dǎde fēidau 'chǎngdz 'wàitou chyu le.

(Shine brightly upon). / The light hit his eyes and made him blink. Gwāng °'jàuje (°'hwǎng, °'shèdau) tāde yǎn, jyàu tā jŕ'jǎme.

Hit hard (affect severely) jyàu . . . nán °'shòu (°'gwò). / The news hit me very hard. Tīngjyan nèige 'syāusyi jyàu wǒ 'hěn nánshòu. / The death of her son hit her so hard that she never left her sick bed. Tā érdz nèiyi'sž jyàu tā 'syǐnli 'hěn nán 'gwò, tsúng nèi shŕhou 'chǐ tā yǐ'jŕ méichǐ'chwáng.

Hit it off (get along well). / They hit it off well from the beginning. (of friendship only) Tāmen yǐjyànrú'gù. or (of friendship or love at first sight) Tāmen yí'jyànchǐng-'syǐn.

Hit on (find) syǎngchulai, dàu. / How did you hit on that? (mentally) Nǐ dzěmma 'syǎngchulaide? / I just hit on that pun. Nèige shwāng'gwānde hwàr shŕ wǒ 'ǒurán syǎng'dàude.

Hit the jackpot. / He hit the jackpot (won first prize, as in a lottery). Tā jùngle tóu'tsǎi le. or Tā 'dàyíng.

A hit (a blow striking the object aimed at) is expressed verbally as above. / He made just four hits. Tā °jyòu (°jŕ) 'dǎjaule 'szsyàr. / It's a hit! (baseball) Dǎ-'jùngle! or Dǎjaule!

(Not a miss). / It's a hit! 'Jùng le!

(Success) shòu hwānyíng. / The movie was a hit. Nèige 'pyāndz shòu hwān-'yíng. or expressed as It made a lot of money. Nèige 'pyāndz jwàn chyán. / He made a hit with her family. Tā hěn shòu tā 'jyāli rén 'hwānyíng. or Tā 'jyāli rén yíjyàn'myàn jyou dōu 'syǐhwan tā.

Hit-or-miss. /He works in a hit-or-miss fashion. Tā dzwò'shr °tài 'mǎngjwǎng (°tài 'měng, °'yǒu dyǎr syā'měng, °yǒu dyǎr syā'pèng). /It was sort of hit-or-miss, but he was lucky. Búgwò shr °syā'měng (°syā'pèng) kěshr tā jyou °'měngshangle (°pèngshangle).

HOLD (HELD). 1. <u>Chinese distinguishes a number of different methods of holding. The most general verb corresponding to</u> hold <u>is</u> ná, <u>which also means</u> carry. <u>Almost all of the other numerous words meaning</u> carry <u>may also be used to mean</u> hold (see **CARRY**). <u>Just a few of these are listed here, along with some words which are not used when one speaks of carrying something from one place to another.</u>

(General term) ná. /Will you hold this package a minute for me? Jèige 'baur nǐ gěi wǒ 'ná hwer, syíng ma?

(Between thumb and finger, or with tweezers) nyē. /He held the snake by its tail in his fingers and shook it. Tā nyēje 'chángchūng 'yǐba'jyār, jŕ 'dǒulou.

(Grip in the fist) dzwàn. /He is holding a fistful of sand. Tā 'dzwànje yǐbǎ 'shādz. /He held both ends of the iron rod and bent it in one twist. Tā 'dzwànje tyě- 'gwùndzde lyǎng'tóur yǐ'jywē jyòu jywē'wǎnle.

(Grip in the fist or hand used only with a certain few objects) bǎ. /The captain held the tiller in one hand, and a long pipe in the other. Chwánjǔ 'yǐshǒu bǎ'dwò, 'yǐshǒu náje ge 'hàn yān'dài.

(With the palms face up, especially when pressed together to form a bowl shape) pěng. /He did not have any container for the rice, so he could only hold it in his hands. Tā 'méiyou dūngsyi 'chéng mǐ; jŕ hǎu ná shǒu 'pěngje.

(In the hand, with arm partially outstretched) dwān. /He held the tray with both hands while the other man piled dishes on it. Tā lyáshǒu 'dwānje yíge twō'pár, 'lìng yige rén wàng shang lwò 'pándz 'dyédz. /He held the gun level and faced me. Tā 'chùngje wǒ píng'dwānje chyāng.

(In the hand, with arm stretched out) twō. /He held the tray balanced in one hand. Tā 'yǐjŕ shǒu 'twōje twō'pár.

(In the hand, with arm stretched overhead) jyǔ. /He held up his hat as if he were going to put it on. Tā jyǔje 'màudz hǎu'syàng yàu dàishang shrde. /He held the flag and walked ahead of the parade. Tā jyǔje dà'chí dzài 'dàdwèi 'chyánbyan 'dzǒu. /Hold up your right hand. Jyǔ 'yòushǒu. or Bǎ yòushǒu jyǔchǐlai.

(In the arms, in an embrace) lǒu, bàu (bàu may also include lifting up, as of a baby). /They stood there and looked at each other for a while, and then he suddenly held her in his arms. Tāmen jàn nàr 'bǐtsz dwèi'kànle yǐhwèr; tā 'hūrán yísyàdz bǎ tā °'lǒu (°'bàu)dzài 'hwáili le. /They held each other in a clinch while the referee tried to break them up. Tāmen jǐn'jǐnde °'lǒuje (°'bàuje), 'nèi shŕhou tsáipàn'ywán shŕjyèr yàu bǎ tāmen 'fēnkāi. /He held her (a baby) in his arms and she stopped whimpering. Tā bǎ tā 'bàuchilaile, tā jyòu bù'kūle. /Hold the baby and burp her. 'Bàuje háidz 'jyàutā dǎ ge 'gér. /Hold the baby on your lap. Bǎ syǎu 'hár gēdzài dz'twèishang 'bàuje. /Hold me tight! Bàu'jǐn le!

(Support with the arms) jyà, chān, fú. /Hold him or he'll fall. °'Chānje (°'Jyàje, °'Fúje) tā dyǎr, yàubùrán tā hwèi 'tǎngsya.

2. **Hold** <u>meaning</u> contain <u>is expressed according to the nature of the things contained.</u>

(General terms) rúng, jāu, <u>resultative compounds with</u> kāi, syà, lyǎu. /That box can hold all this rice and then some. Jèisyē 'mǐ, nèige 'syāngdz 'dōu rúngde'syà, hái yǒu'yú ne. / Can your pocket hold all these things? Nǐde kǒu'dàr néng °rúng (°jāu) jêmma dwō 'dūngsyi ma?

(Of things in liquid or granular form) jwāng, chéng, resultative compounds with syà, lyǎu. / This bottle holds a thousand cubic centimeters. Jèige 'píngdz néng °chéng (°jwāng, °rúng) yì'chyān lìfānggūng'fēn. / That box can't hold all this rice. Nèige 'syāngdz °'chéngbusyà (°'chéngbulyǎu) nèmma dwō 'mǐ.

(Of things that are put in the container one by one, packed or arranged) jwāng, gē, fàng, resultative compounds with kāi, syà, lyǎu. / Will this box hold all these books? Jèige 'syāngdz, nèisyē 'shū dōu °'jāudekāi (°'jwāngdesyà, °'gēdesyà, °'fāngdelyǎu, °etc.) ma? / One box won't hold all those books. 'Nèmma syē shū yíge syāngdz 'gēbusyà. / You'd be surprised how much a woman's pocketbook can hold. Nǐ yàu 'jr̄dàule 'nyūrénde kǒu'dàrli néng gē 'dwōshǎu dūngsyi nǐ jyòu dèi 'syà yí-'tyàu. / Our garage can hold three cars. Wǒmende 'chēfáng °rúngdesyà (°gēdesyà, °fāngdesyà, °tíngdesyà, °etc.) 'sānlyàng 'chē.

(In a limited space, or arranged for artistic purposes) bǎi, pái, gē. / That shelf holds fifty books in two rows. 'Nèitséng shū'jyàr, yàushr fēn 'lyàngpái, kéyi °bǎi (°gē) 'wǔshrbèn 'shū.

(Of persons in an auditorium, hotel, etc.) dzwò; (specifically of passengers) dā, dzài. / The car holds five people. 'Jèilyàng chē néng dzwò 'wǔge rén. / Will the car hold one more? Chē néng dzài °dzwò (°jāu, °rúng) 'yíge rén ma? / It can't hold one more as fat as you. Syàng 'nǐ nèmma 'pàng de yíge jyòu °rúng (°dzwò)bu-syàle. / This plane can hold thirty-five passengers. Jèige 'fēijǐ °kéyi dā (°kéyi dzài, °'dzwòdelyǎu, °etc.) 'sānshr'wǔge 'kèrén。

(Of liquor in a person). / How much can he hold? Tā néng hē 'dwōshǎu? or Tāde 'lyàng °dzěmmayàng (°dwōma dà)?

3. Miscellaneous verbal meanings.

(Stand the strain of weight, support) 'jǐndejù. / Will this bridge hold? Jèige 'chyáu 'jǐndejù ma? / How much weight will the bridge hold? 'Chyáu néng 'jǐndejù 'dwōjùng? / Will this chair hold me? Jèibǎ 'yǐdz 'wǒ dzwòshang 'jǐndejù ma? or Jèibǎ 'yǐdz 'wǒ dzwòde'syà ma? / Will this nail hold the picture in place? Jèige 'dǐngdz 'jǐndejù jèijāng 'hwàr ma?

(Remain fast). / That knot will hold. Nèige 'kǒur °'kāibulyǎu (°hěn 'jǐn).

(Restrain; suppress with the hands) 'jyōujù, 'lājù; (with a rope in the hands) 'lājù, 'chyānjù; (with a rope tied to something) 'shwānjù; (detain, not let go) 'kǒujù, 'lyóujù, 'kòusyà, 'lyóusyà, yāchilai, kānchilai, gwānchilai, 'bùsyǔ (tā) 'dzǒu, 'bújyàu (tā) 'dzǒu; (stop by obstructing the way) 'lánjù, 'jyéjù, 'dǎngjù. / You hold him while I get my gun. Nǐ bǎ tā °'jyōujù (°'lājù, °'lánjù, °'jyéjù, °'dǎngjù), dèng-wǒ bǎ 'chyāng nálai. / Hold that horse! Bǎ mǎ °'lājù (°'chyānjù, °'jyōujù, °'shwān-jù, °'lánjù, °'jyéjù, °'dǎngjù)。 / When that little boy wants to go somewhere, there's no holding him. Syau 'hár yàu syàng 'shàng nǎr 'pǎu, jyòu 'méifár bǎ tā 'lājù. / He's being held by the police. Tā jyàu jǐngchá °'kǒujùle (°'lyóujùle, °'yāchǐlaile, °'kānchǐlaile, °'gwānchǐlaile). / Hold your horses! Byé jáu'jí. 'Máng shémma?

(Keep) tswúnje, lyóuje; (keep safely) shōuje; (keep from going out, as a document) kōu, yā, gē. / She held the check for a long time. Tā bǎ jr̄'pyàu °'kōule (°'yāle, °'gēle) hǎu syē 'r̀dz. / We'll hold the letter for you. Wǒmen bǎ 'syìn gěi nǐ °'tswúnje (°'lyóuje, °'shōuje).

(Believe and maintain) 'yǐwéi, yí'dìng shwō. / They held that the earth was flat. Tāmen °yí'dìng shwō (°'yǐwéi) dì'chyóu shr̀ 'píngde.

(Judge) pàn (in court); otherwise shwō. / The court held him guilty. Fǎ'ywàn pàn tā yǒudzwèi. / The police held him responsible for the accident. Jǐng'chá shwō (jèitsż chūde 'shř) shř 'tāde tswòr. *but* / We'll hold you responsible if it turns out otherwise. Yàushr 'búnèmmaje, jyòu 'dōu shř 'nǐde tswòr.

(Of a meeting, etc.) usually kāi; (hold ceremonies) syíng. / The meetings of the club are held once a week. 'Měi lǐbài kāi yítsż 'hwèi. / When will the wedding be held? 'Jǐshŕ syíng 'jyēhwūn'lǐ?

(Of a rule) néngyùng, jàndejù, yùngbushàng. / The rule won't hold in this case. 'Jèijyàn shř, nèityáu 'gwēijyu 'yùngbu'shàng. / The rule he proposed holds. Tā jyàn'yǐ de jeige 'gwēijyu °jànde'jù (°néng 'yùng).

(Retain a position or office) dzài rèn. / He held office for a long time. Tā dzài 'rèn bùshǎu 'nyán.

(Keep a job) dzwòcháng, dāijù. / There must be some reason why he can't hold a job. Tā nèmma 'nǎr dōu °dāibu'jù (°dzwòbu'cháng) yí'dìng yǒu ge 'ywángù.

(Have possession of) shǒu. / They held the land under a ten-year lease. Dzài 'dzūchǐde 'shŕnyánli jèi 'dǐ shǒu 'tāmen.

(In music) lā. / She held the high note for a long time. Nàge gāuyīn tā 'lāle hěn 'cháng.

4. Verbal phrases.

Hold one's attention. / He holds your attention. Tā jyàu rén °ài 'tīng (°'tīngje 'chǐjyèr). / The teacher couldn't hold our attention. 'Syānsheng 'jyǎngde °méi'jìn (°'wújīngdǎ'tsǎide, °jyàu wǒmen 'tīngje bùchǐ'jyèr).

Hold one's breath. / Hold your breath. Byé chūchǐ. *or* 'Bǐjù (yì)kǒu'chǐ. / Hold your breath until I say OK. Bǐje 'chǐ, děng wǒ shwō 'hǎu le, dzài chūchǐ. / Everybody held their breath when she missed a rung of the ladder. Tā dzài 'tīdzshang 'yìjyǎu tsǎi'tszle, syàde 'rénren 'bǐje(yi)kǒu 'chǐ.

Hold one's head high. / He holds his head high in spite of all. Kěshr tā hái néng 'mǎnbú'dzàihu. / He can hold his head high in any group. Tā dàu 'nǎr dōu néng 'pángrwòwú'rén.

Hold it (command) meaning don't move byé dùng, or meaning don't leave byé dzǒu, or meaning stop 'dàjù, or meaning hold that pose 'jyòu nèmmaje byé'dùng.

Hold the lead. / Our team held the lead to the end. Wǒmen 'dwèi déde 'fēr yì-'jŕ dzài 'chyántou. / Can we hold the lead from now on? Dzámen 'néngbunéng yì'jŕ bújyàu tāmen 'gǎngwochyu?

Hold the line (telephoning) byé gwàshang. / Would you please hold the line a minute? 'Chǐng nǐ byé 'gwàshang.

Hold one's tongue. / Hold your tongue! meaning don't start to speak Byé 'shwō! or meaning stop speaking Byé 'shwō le!

Hold water (fig., of reasoning) 'chūngdzú; (of a plan) 'twǒdàng. / Your arguments won't hold water. Nǐ shwō de 'lǐyóu bù'chūngdzú. / Your plan won't hold water. Nǐde 'bànfa búda 'twǒdàng.

Be held in respect. / He is held in great respect by his fellows. Tā nèi'dǎng de rén dōu tǐng 'dzwūnjìng ta.

Hold oneself ready. / He held himself ready for all emergencies. Tā 'yíchyè 'dōu yǒu 'jwǔnbèi.

Take *or* **grab hold of** jwā. / He reached out and grabbed hold of his collar. Tā 'yìbǎ bǎ tāde 'lǐngdz 'jwājule.

Hold back. /I wanted to go but held myself back. Wǒ běnlai yàu 'chyù, kěshr 'hòulai wǒ 'gwǎnje wǒ 'dżjǐ méi'chyù. *or* Wǒ syīnlǐ 'syǎng chyù láije, búgwò yǎuje 'yá méi'chyù. /Hold that crowd back. Bǎ něichyún rén 'lánhwéichyu. *or* 'Byé jyàu něichyún 'rén shàng'chyán lai. /He held me back. (lit.) Tā bújyàu wǒ 'gwòchyu. *or* (lit. *or* fig.) Tā bǎ wǒ 'lánjùle.

Hold forth tǎulwùn. /The professor has been holding forth for an hour about some scientific theory. Jyàu'shòumen tǎulwùn yǐjǔng kēsywé 'ywánlǐ, tǎu'lwùnle 'yídyǎnjūng.

Hold in (of feelings) rěnje. /I was simply furious, but I held it in until he had left. Wǒ syīnlǐ chì'jíle, kěshr 'rěnje 'jŕ dàu tā 'dzǒule。

Hold off (delay) táng. /The butcher wants us to pay our bill, but maybe we can hold him off for a few days。 Mài'ròude syǎng yàu'chyán, búgwò dzámen yěsyǔ néng dzài 'táng lyǎngtyān.

Hold on ná, dzwàn, etc., see paragraphs above for other specific words. /Hold on! meaning Don't let go. 'Dzwànje. *or* 'Náje. etc. *or* Byé fàng'shǒu. or meaning Wait a moment! 'Děng yihwěr! /Hold on to me when we cross the street. Gwò'jyēde shŕhou, 'lāje wo dyar. /Why don't you hold on to (keep) that house until prices rise? Nǐ wèi'shémma bùděng 'jyàchyan 'jǎngle dzài mài'fáng ne? /Try to hold on (keep going) a little longer. Dzài 'rěn yihwěr. /Hold on (stop) and let me explain that. Nǐ syān tǐng 'wǒ shwō.

Hold out. /They held out against all odds. Tāmen °'sžbúfàng'shǒu (°'sžbùkěn-'ràng). /They held out longer than I thought. Méisyǎng'dàu tāmen néng 'nèmma 'chéndejù 'chì.

Hold over. /Let's hold this over until the next meeting. Jèige dzámen děng 'syàtsž kāi'hwèi dzài 'shwō ba. /The movie will be held over an extra week. Nèige 'pyāndz hái dzài 'dwō yǎn yìsyīng'chì。

Hold together sǎn with a negative or some expression implying almost. /This coat has been mended so much it will hardly hold together. Jèige wài'tàur 'bùleyòu-'bùde dōu yàu 'sǎn le. /The box was barely holding together after the trip. Dzǒule yí'dzǎur, nèige 'hédz jyǎn'jŕ jyòu yàu 'sǎn le. *but* /Let's hold together to the end. Dzámen 'twánjyē dàu'dǐ.

Hold up (support) jyà, fú, chān. /She's such a poor skater that we had to hold her up to keep her from falling. Tā lyōu'bīng 'jyǎnjŕ bù'syíng, hái děi rén °'jyàje ne (°'fúje ne, °'chānje ne).

Hold up (stop). /The work was held up for three weeks. Gūngdzwò 'dānggēle 'sālǐbài. *but* /What's holding up traffic? is expressed as Why isn't everything moving? 'Dzěmma dōu bù'dzǒu le? *or* 'Dzěmma dōu bú'dùng le?

Hold up (endure) 'dǐngde, dingbujù. /He held up well under the strain. Nèmma-yàng nán de shŕ tā 'jyūrán néng 'dǐngdejù.

Hold up (rob) chyǎng; (on the road) jyé. /I was held up last night. Wǒ dzwór 'wǎnshang jyàu 'rén gěi °'chyǎngle (°'jyéle).

5. Nominal uses.

(A grip) is expressed verbally as in paragraph one above. /He lost his hold and fell. Tā °'tūlu shǒule (°'jwābujùle, °'jyòubujùle, °'dzwànbujùle), jyòu 'dyàusyà-chyùle.

(Influence). /Say, what hold does he have on you? meaning Why do you believe in him so implicitly? Hèi! Nǐ dzěmma 'nèmma 'mísyìn tā? *or* (implying that there is a cause for blackmail) Nǐ yǒu shémma 'dwǎnchu jyàu tā 'nájule ma?

(Below decks in a ship) tsāng(li). / The boat carried planes on the deck, and all sorts of merchandise in the hold. Chwán 'myànshang dzài fēi'jǐ, 'tsángli jwāng de shř 'gè jǔng de 'hwòwù.

HOLE. kūlung, dùng; or, if the hole is quite round and regular yǎr. / There is a hole in that glove. Shǒu'tǎurshang °yǒu (°pwòle) yíge °'kūlung (°'dùng). / His hat was shot full of holes. Tāde 'dàlǐmàushang 'dǎle hǎusyē 'kūlung. / The mouse ran into his hole. 'Hǎudz dzwān °'dùngli (°'kūlungli) chyù le. / Are there any holes in the screen? Shā'chwāngrshang yǒu °'kūlung (°'dùng) ma? / Drill a hole two inches deep in these tables. Dzài jwōdz 'jèr dzwàn ge 'lyǎngtswùnde °'kūlung (°'dùng, °yǎr).

(In the ground) kēng, kēngr. / They dug a hole and planted the tree. Tāmen °'wā (°'páu) le ge 'kēng bǎ shù 'jùngshangle. / They dug a deep hole and buried the gold. Tāmen °'wā (°'páu) le ge 'shēn kēng bǎ jīndz máile.

Other expressions in English. / She suddenly found herself in a hole financially. Tā 'húrán jŕdàule tā ('dzjǐ) 'kwēikùngle bù'shǎu. / The trip made a big hole in her funds. 'Jè yitàng °'hwāle (°'pwòfèile) tā bù'shǎu chyán. / He picks holes in everything I say. Búlwùn wǒ shwō 'shémma, tā dzǔng tyāu °'tswòr (°'yǎr). / He's a square peg in a round hole. Tā yùngdzài 'nàr bùhé'shř. or Tā bù'yíyú dzwò 'nèige. / That restaurant is just an old hole. Nèige fàn'gwǎr 'pwòlànbu'kàn.

HOLIDAY. (Time off from work) fàngjyà (also means have a holiday, be a holiday; lit. give time off); (the specific day) fàngjyà'r; a holiday of so many days NU-tyānjyà; holiday period 'jyāchī. / Is today a holiday? Jyēr fàng'jyà ma? / When does the holiday season begin? Fàng'jyà tsúng 'něityān 'chǐ? / October tenth is a holiday in China. 'Shŕywè 'shŕhàu dzài 'Jūnggwo shr fàngjyà'r. / Sunday is a holiday. Lǐbài'r fàng'jyà. / I want to take a holiday for a few days. Wǒ syǎng gàu 'jǐtyān'jyà. / I'll see you during the holiday(s). Dzámen 'jyāchīli 'hwèi. or Dzámen fàng'jyà de shŕhou 'jyàn.

However, the modern Western concept of a holiday as a vacation is recent in China and is common only in government circles, schools, and Western-style business concerns. In other circles, a holiday is really a festival, and is called jyé. The three main festivals (all by the lunar calendar) are the fifth day of the fifth month (wǔywèjyé or dwānwú), the fifteenth day of the eighth month (bāywèjyé or 'jūnchyōu), and the turn of the year (gwònyán). / We passed the New Year's holiday season (old festival) by feasting several days. Wǒmen gwò'nyán 'dà chřle ji'tyān.

HOME. (Referring only to the building; house) fángdz, jáidz. / They have a beautiful home in the country. Tāmen dzài 'syāngsyà yǒu yǐswǒr hěn 'hǎu de °'fángdz (°'jáidz). / Whose home is this? Jèi shř 'shwéide °'fángdz (°'jáidz)?

(Including other associations) jyā (also means family in some cases); (polite forms) your (honorable) home 'fǔshàng; my (humble) home 'shèsyà, 'bǐyù. / Where is your home? My home is at No. 15 Sun Yat-sen Road. Nǐ 'jùdzài nǎr? Wǒ °'jùdzài (°jyā dzài) 'Jūngshān'lù shř'wǔhàu. or (polite) 'Fǔshàng dzài 'nǎr? 'Bǐyù 'Jūngshān'lù shř'wǔhàu. / How many persons are there in your home? (polite) Fǔshàng yǒu 'dwōshàu rén? / There are five persons including me in my home. (polite answer) 'Shèsyà lyán wǒ 'wǔkǒu rén. / This is my home. Jè shř wǒde 'jyā. / Here is my home. Wǒ 'jyā dzài 'jèr. or Jèr shř wǒde 'jyā. / Come to my home tomorrow evening at six. Myér 'wǎnshang 'lyòudyǎn dàu wǒ 'jyā lai. / I have to go home. Wǒ děi hwéi'jyā le. / He'll drive me home. Tā kéyi kāi'chē sùng wǒ hwéi'jyā. / See her home, will you? 'Sùng tā dàu'jyā, á? / I was at home all day yesterday. Wǒ 'dzwótyān yì'jěngtyān dzài 'jyā. / They are at home every Wednesday evening (to receive guests). Tāmen 'dìnggwēide shř měi 'syīngchī'sān 'wǎnshang dzài 'jyāli jyēdài 'péngyou. / This is just like home cooking. Jèige hěn syàng 'jyāli dzwò de

637

'fàn. / This is home cooking (plain style). Jèi shr̀ °'jyācháng'fàn (°'byànfàn). / Make it a sort of home atmosphere. 'Nùngde jyàu rén 'jywéje syàng dzài 'jyāli shr̀de. / He makes all his guests feel at home in his place. Dzài 'tā nar 'shéi dōu gēn dzài dz̀jǐ 'jyāli shr̀de nèmma swéi'byàn. *but* / Make yourself at home. Byé kèchi. *or* Búkèchi. *or* Dzài 'jèr gēn dzai 'dz̀jǐ 'jyālǐ shr̀de.

(Place to stay). / You can always find a home with us (live with us). 'Wǒmen jèr nǐ 'jǐshr̀ yàu 'jù, jyòu lái 'jù.

(Native). / He went back to his home state. Tā hwéi tāde běn'shěng chyule. / My home state is California, but now I'm living in New York. Wǒ shr̀ Jyājōu rén, búgwǒ syàn'dzài jùdzài 'Nyǒuywē. / Where is your home town? (polite) Gwèi'chù shr̀ °shémma 'dìfang (°'nǎ yǐchéng)? *or* (common) Nǐ shr̀ °'nǎchéngde (°'nǎrde) rén? / My home town is Tàiywán. (polite) °Bì'chéng (°Bì'chù) Tàiywán. *or* (common) Wǒ shr̀ Tàiywǎnde rén.

(Institution for the poor, old, sick, etc.) ywàn; **old people's home** lǎurén ywàn; **orphans' home** gúérywàn. / There is a home for old ladies up on the hill. 'Shānshang yǒu ge jwàn shōu 'nyǔrén de 'lǎurén'ywàn.

(Of birds, animals, etc.) wō (nest); <u>and other expressions.</u> / This tree is the home of a family of squirrels. Jèikē 'shùshang yǒu yì'wō sūng'shur. / Several squirrels make this tree their home. Yǒu jige sūng'shur dzài jèikē 'shùshang dā'wō. / This is the home of a delicious kind of carp. 'Jèige dìfang chū yì'jǔng hǎu'chrde 'lǐyú.

Bring (*or* **Drive**) **home.** / He drove his point home. Tā °'shwōde (°'jyǎngde) jùng'kěn. *or* Tā 'yǐyǔ pwò'dì. *or* Tā °'shwōde (°'jyǎngde) hěn 'jùng kěn'chǐ. / He brought home the point that the enemy is tough. Tā bǎ 'dírén hěn 'syūng jèi yǐ'dyǎn °shwōde (°jyǎngde) hěn °'tòuchè (°'chīngchu, °'míngbai).

Home-grown dz̀jǐ jùngde. / Are these vegetables home-grown? Jèisyē 'chīng-tsài shr̀ dz̀'jǐ jùngde ma?

HONEST.

HONEST. (Upright or frank) 'chéngshr̀, 'lǎushr̀; <u>or expressed as</u> not being capable of lying 'búhwèi shwō 'syāhwàr de, 'búhwèi shwō 'hwǎng de, 'búhwèi sā 'hwǎng de. / Is he honest? Tā rén 'chéngshr̀ ma? *or* Tā shr̀ ge 'chéngshr̀ rén ma? *or* Tā shr̀ ge 'búhwèi shwō 'syāhwàr de rén ma? / Here is an honest man. Let's have his opinion. Tā shr̀ ge °'lǎushr̀ rén (°etc.), dzámen wènwen 'tā ba. / He has an honest face. Tā lyǎn 'jǎngde hěn syàng ge °'lǎushr̀ (°'chéngshr̀) rén.

(Fair to all concerned) 'gūngdàu, 'gūngpíng. / That's an honest bargain. Nèige jyàr hěn °'gūngdàu (°'gūngpíng).

(Exact; of weight) jwǔn. / That scale gives honest weight. Nèige 'chèng 'fēnlyàng hěn 'jwǔn. / I don't believe your scale gives honest weight. Wǒ jywéje nǐ nèige 'chèng °'fēnlyàng bù'jwǔn (*or* (if a buyer thinks the scale reads high) °'syǎu, *or* (if a seller thinks the scale reads low) °'dà).

(Really). / Honest? (Shr̀) 'jēnde ma? / Honest, I didn't say anything. (Shr̀) 'jēnde; wǒ yíjyù 'hwà yě méi'shwō.

Be honest *or* **speak honestly** shwō 'shr̀hwà. / Tell me honestly what you think of that plan. Shwō 'shr̀hwà, nǐ 'jywéje nèige 'bànfa 'dzěmmayàng? / Be honest with me and I'll see that your name is kept out of it. Nǐ gēn wǒ shwō 'shr̀hwà, wǒ jyou 'bú bǎ nǐde 'míngdz °'lyèdzai 'lǐtou (°'tíchulai). / Women are usually not honest about their age. 'Nyǔrén yi tí 'dz̀jǐde 'nyánlíng chángchang °bùkěn shwō 'shr̀hwà (°'mánje dyar).

HONEY. mì; fēngmî (lit. bee honey, used especially of prepared honey as eaten); honey-bee 'mîfēngr. /I'd like some bread and honey. Wǒ syǎng chr̄ dyǎr myàn'bāu gēn fēng'mî. /The clover is full of bees gathering honey. 'Dīngsyáng'shùshang jǐng shr̄ 'mîfēngr dzài nar tsǎi 'mî. (fig.) /That's a honey of a dress. Nèi'yīfu kě jēn 'pyàulyáng. /She's a honey. (looks only) Tā jēn hǎu'kàn.

HONOR. (In the sense of personal glory, personal privilege) is expressed verbally as (jywéje) rúngsyìng, lóulyǎn, yǒumyàndz, 'tǐmyàn, or frequently expressed in round-about ways. /What an honor to be invited to dinner by the governor! Shěngjǔ'syí chǐng chr̄'fàn dwōma °yǒu'myàndz (°'tǐmyàn). /It is a real honor to be asked to speak to such a learned audience. (as a comment about the fact) Rénjya 'chǐng chyu gēn 'nèmma yǒu 'sywéwèn de rén yǎn'jyǎng 'jēnshr °lóu'lyǎn (°'tǐmyàn). or (as an introduction to the speech) meaning gives me great pleasure Gēn 'jūwèi 'jèmma yǒu 'sywéwen de rén tántan, 'shr̄dzai shr̄ jyàu wǒ jywéje rúng'syíng. /I consider it a great honor to be elected president of this association. Chéng jūwèi 'sywǎnjyǔ wǒ dzwò běn'hwèide hwèi'jǎng, jyàu wǒ jywéde shr̄dzai shr̄ hěn rúng'syíng. (Or, each time wǒ occurs in the above sentence, substitute 'syūngdì or 'bǐrén which are more modest forms). /He has won great honors. Tā 'hěn lóu'lyǎn. or more commonly expressed as People praise him. Tā 'hěn shòu rén 'chēngdzàn. or Tā 'hěn shòurén 'kwājyǎng. or 'Rénren dōu shwō tā 'hǎu.

    Honors (at school, etc.). /He expects to graduate with honors. meaning among the highest few Tā syǎng yàu bì'yè de shr̄hou dzài 'tóuji'míngli. or meaning with prizes Tā syǎng yàu bì'yède shr̄hou dé'jyǎng.

    A man of honor. /You are a man of honor. Nǐ shr̄ ge 'jyūndz. or Nǐ shr̄ ge 'hǎu rén.

    In someone's honor. /We gave a birthday party in his honor. Wǒmen 'chǐngle syē rén lai 'gěi tā gwò 'shēngr̀.

    On one's honor. /I swear on my honor. Wǒ píng 'lyángsyīn chǐ'shr̀.

    Your honor is expressed with the person's official title. /Would your Honor (to a judge) please repeat that? Chǐng 'Shěnpàngwān 'dzài shwō yítsz̀.

    Be an honor to wèi . . . °dzēng'gwāng (°jēng'gwāng). /He was an honor to his country. Tā wèi 'gwó °jēng'gwāng (°dzēng'gwāng). /He is an honor to his family. Tā wèi 'ménhù dzēng'gwāng. or (colloquial) Tā gěi 'jyāli lóu'lyǎn.

    Do the honors the specific job to be done is expressed in the Chinese. /You do the honors tonight at the banquet. meaning be the speaker Jyēr wǎnshangde yàn'hwèi nǐ shwo jijyu 'hwà. /Let me do the honors (pay the bill). Ràng 'wǒ chǐng. or 'Wǒ chǐng ba. or Ràng 'wǒ dzwò 'dūngdau. or 'Wǒ dzwò 'dūngdau ba. or (local Peiping) 'Wǒ hwèile ba.

    To honor someone is expressed with chǐng invite; gěi, sùnggei give. /They honored him with a gift for his hard work. Tā dzwò 'shr̄ hěn mài'lìchì, tāmen 'sùnggei ta yige 'lǐwu. /They gave a dinner to honor us. Tāmen 'chǐng wǒmen chr̄ 'fàn. or Tāmen shè'yàn 'kwǎndài wǒmen.

    (Accept for payment). /We can't honor this check. 'Jèijāng jr̄'pyàu wǒmen bùnéng 'shōu.

    Feel honored. /I feel honored to meet you. is expressed as I've heard of you for a long time. Jyǒuyǎng'jyóu'yǎng.

HOOK. gōudz, gōur. /Is there a hook to hang my coat on? Yǒu gwà 'yīfu de 'gōudz ma? /That stick has a hook at one end. Nèigēn 'gwèr yǒu yì'tóur yǒu ge 'gōur. /We went fishing with a hook and line. Wǒmen dàije yú'gōur gēn yú'gār jyòu dyàu-'yú chyule. /This dress is fastened with hooks and eyes. Jèijyàn 'yīfu yùng 'gōudz 'jìshang.

(In boxing). /He gave him a left hook to the jaw. Tā yùng 'dzwŏshŏu yì'chywán 'dǎdzài 'nèige rén de ('yòu)yá'chwángshang。

By hook or crook. /He'll get the job by hook or crook. Tā 'búlwùn 'dzěmmaje yě yàu bǎ nèige 'shèr 'chyǎngdàu 'shŏuli. *or* Tā 'wèile chyǎng 'nèijyan shèr bùdzé shŏudwàn.

Hookup. /He spoke on a coast-to-coast hookup. Tā (dzài wúsyàn'dyànshang shwō) de 'hwà chywángwó 'gèdyàntái dōu 'gwāngbwō.

To hook (fasten with a hook) gōu(shang), kòu(shang). /Help me hook this. Bāngje wŏ bǎ jèige °'gōushang (°'kòushang). /This dress buttons, it doesn't hook。 Jèisye 'yīfu shř yùng °'kòur (°'kòudz) 'kòude; 'búshř yùng 'gōudz de. /He hooked his arm around the post. Tā yùng 'gēbei bǎ jùdz °'gōujule (°'bàujule)。

(In fishing) dyàu(shang). /I hooked a big fish. Wŏ 'dyàushang yìtyáu 'dà yú lai.

HOPE. (Expect, desire) 'syīwàng; (especially desire) 'pànwàng; (especially expect, depend on) 'jřwàng; (expect, think, plan on) dǎje, 'dǎswàn, 'yǐwéi; (wait and see) děngje chyáu. /I hope you can come. Wŏ °'syīwàng (°'pànwàng) nǐ 'néng lái. /I hope it will turn out all right. Wŏ °'syīwàng (°'pànwàng) jèige shèr 'bùchū 'lwàndz. /There is nothing to hope for. Yìdyǎr °'jřwàng (°'syīwàng) yě méi'yŏu. /I hope to go back to school. Wŏ 'syīwàng hwéi sywé'syàu chyu. /Let's hope for the best. Děngje 'chyáu ba. /We had hoped that after he came the situation would improve. Wŏmen 'ywánlái °'syīwàng (°'pànwàng, °'jřwàng, °'dǎswàn, °'dǎje, °'yǐwéi) 'tā yǐ 'lái jèishèr jyòu hwèi 'hǎude. /We hoped you would come. Wŏmen °'dǎje (°'dǎswàn-je) nǐ hwèi 'láide.

Hope (desire, expectation) 'syīwàng, 'jřwàng; or expressed verbally as above. /There is still hope. Hái yŏu dyǎr °'syīwàng (°'jřwàng). /There is still hope that he'll change his mind. Děngje 'chyáu ba, tā 'yésyǔ hwèi 'hwéisyīnjwǎn'yì. /I don't see any hope in this job. Jèige shèr wŏ jywéje °'méi shémma 'syīwàng (°méi shémma 'jřwàng, °méi shémma kě 'syīwàng de, °méi shémma kě 'jřwàng de). *but* /The new player is the only hope of the team。 is expressed as The whole team is depending on that new player. Jèi yídwèi jyòu °'chyáu (°'jřje) nèige 'syīnláide sywǎn-'shŏu (dzěmma'yàng) le.

Give up hope is expressed as be disheartened 'hwēisyīn. /Don't give up hope. Byé 'hwēisyīn. /He gave up hope. Tā 'hwēisyīn le.

HORN. (Of an animal) jǐjyau; jyǎu preceded by the name of the particular animal, as goat's horn yáng'jyǎu. /Be careful, the bull has sharp horns. Lyóu'shén, nyou 'jǐ-jyau 'jyānje ne. /This is made of horn. Jèi shř nyóu'jyǎur dzwò de. /The two bucks locked horns (fought with heads bull-fashion). Lyǎ 'lù dǐng'nyóur ne.

(Wind instrument) hàujyǎu; (trumpet) lǎba. /Horns were once used by the Mongolian Army. Yǐchyán 'Měnggu jyūn'dwèili yùng hàu'jyǎu. /Don't blow that horn so much. Byé lǎu chwēi 'lǎba.

Horn in (interfere). /I don't like to horn in. Wŏ bú'ywànyi gwǎn 'syánshř.

HORSE. mǎ. /Where can I get a horse? Wŏ dzài 'nǎr néng jǎuje yìpǐ 'mǎ? /Take care of my horse. °'Chyáuje (°'Kānje, °'Jàuyīngje) dyǎr (wŏde) 'mǎ. /Let's go to the horse races. Dzámen kàn °sài'mǎ (°pǎu'mǎ) chyù ba. /Saddle the horse. 'Bèi mǎ.

Horse-drawn carriage 'mǎchē; horse-drawn cart *or* wagon 'dàchē 'mǎlǎde'chē.

Special expressions in English. /He works like a horse. Tā chyúng mài lǐchi. /He was up on his high horse. Tā 'ywewǔyáng'weide. or Tā 'jřgāuchǐ'yangde. /You're putting the cart before the horse. Nǐ nà shr 'chǐngjùng dàu'jř. or Nǐ nà shř 'chyánhòu dyān'dǎu. or Shřching 'búshr nèmma 'bànde。

HOSPITAL. 'yǐywàn. /Where is the hospital? 'Yǐywàn dzài 'nǎr? /You will have to go to the hospital. Nǐ děi jìn 'yǐywàn.

HOST. 'jǔrén; **act as host** dzwò 'jǔrén, dzwòdūng, chǐng(kè); **perform the duties of a host** 'jāudài. /The host sits here, and the honored guest sits there. 'Jǔren dzwò 'jèr, 'gweìkè dzwò 'nèr. /I'm the host. Wǒ shř 'jǔren. /I'll act as host today. Jyēr 'wǒ dzwò °'jǔrén (°'dūng). or Jyēr 'wǒ chǐng('kè). /Who is the host? Nǎwei shř 'jǔren? or Shéi 'chǐng(kè)? /You are a wonderful host. Nǐ 'jāudàide 'jēn jōudau.

HOSTESS. 'nyújǔrén; **act as hostess** dzwò 'nyújǔrén; **perform the duties of a hostess** 'jāudài. /Who is the hostess? 'Shéi shř nyújǔrén? /She's a wonderful hostess. Tā 'jāudàide 'jēn jāudau. /My younger sister will act as hostess. Wǒ 'meìmei dzwò 'nyújǔrén.

HOT. (High in temperature) rè. /Do you have hot water? Nǐmen jèr yǒu 'rè shwei ma? /This is too hot. (Jè) 'Tài rèle. /I want a hot dinner. Wǒ syǎng chř 'rède. /The motor is running hot. 'Jǐchi 'rè le. /His forehead is hot. Tā nǎu'méndz °fā-'rè (or, meaning is burning up °fā'shāu). /The sun is (shining) awfully hot today. Jyēr 'taiyang °shàide jēn 'rè (or (harsh) °hěn 'dú, or (shines like fire) °shàide syàng 'hwǒ shřde). but /The water must be boiling hot. Děi 'kāije de 'shwei. or Shwei děi 'gwēnkāi.

(Pungent) là. /I don't like hot foods. Wǒ 'búài chř 'làde. /Is this pepper hot? Jèige 'chínjyāu 'là búlà?

(Violent, of temper) bàu. /He has a hot temper. Tā 'píchi hěn bàu.

HOTEL. (Western style, with dining room) fàndyàn. /Where is the hotel? Fàn'dyàn dzài 'nǎr?

(Other hotels, high grade) lyǔgwǎn. /Are there any other hotels? Yǒu 'byéde lyǔ'gwǎn ma? /I'm looking for a cheap hotel. Wǒ jèngdzài jǎu yíge 'pyányide lyǔ-'gwǎn.

(Inn, guest house) kèjàn, jànfáng, kèdyàn.

(Country inn) syǎudyàr.

HOUR. (Sixty minutes) dyǎn(jūng) (dyǎn, a measure, refers particularly to the point of time, not the space of time; it may be used without jūng only when it is clear that time is being talked about); jūngtóu, syǎushř. /I'll be back within an hour. Wǒ 'yíge °jūng'tóu yǐ'nèi (°syǎu'shř yǐnèi) hwéilai. or Wǒ 'yìdyǎn jūng yǐnèi 'hwéilai. /I'll be back in about an hour. Wǒ 'gwò yíge °jūng'tóu (°syǎu'shř) 'hwéilai. or Wǒ 'gwò yìdyǎn 'jūng 'hwéilai. /A day has twenty-four hours. Yìtyān yǒu èrshr'sż °dyǎnjūng (°gejūng'tóu, °ge syǎu'shř). /That city is about four hours from here by plane. °'Nèige dìfang lí 'jèr (°Dàu 'nèigedìfang chyù) dzwò fēi'jǐ yàu °'sżge jūng'tóu (°'sżge syǎu'shř, °'sżdyǎn jūng). /The big clock struck the hour. Dà'jūng dǎ'dyǎnle. /Wait a quarter of an hour. Děng yí'kè jūng. /Wait a half-hour. Děng 'bàndyǎn jung. or Děng 'bànge jūng'tóu. /Wait an hour and a half. Děng yíge'bàn jūng'tóu. but /We are open twenty-four hours (all day, all night). Wǒmen 'jěngtyān jěng'yè kāije.

(Time, more generally) shřhou. /Are you available at all hours? Nǐ 'shémma shŕhou dōu 'fāngbyàn ma? / When do you take your lunch hour? 'Shémma shŕhou shř nǐ chř wǔ'fàn de shŕhou? *or* 'Shémma shŕhou chř wǔ'fàn?

(A long time) 'bàntyān. / We waited for hours. Wǒmen děngle °hǎu 'bàntyān (°'hǎu dà 'bàntyān, °'hǎu jidyǎn jūng).

(Academic unit) sywéfēn; (hours per week) dyǎnjūng. / How many hours of French are you taking? Nǐ nyàn 'jǐge sywé'fēn de 'Fàwén? *or* Nǐ 'Fàwén yíge lǐ-'bài 'jǐdyǎn jūng?

Every hour on the hour měi dyǎn 'jūng yi tsž dzài . . . dyǎn。 / The train leaves every hour on the hour。 Hwǒ'chē 'měidyǎn'jūng yí'tsž, dzài 'jèngdyǎn 'kāi. / The train leaves every hour on the half hour. Hwǒ'chē 'měidyǎnjūng yí'tsž, dzài 'bàn-dyǎnshang 'kāi.

Late hours. / He keeps late hours. Tā °bàn'gūng bànde (°syà'bān syàde) hěn 'wǎn.

Working hours. / This is after working hours. 'Syàndzài yǐjīng 'búbàn'gūng le. *or* 'Syàndzài yǐjīng 'gwòle syà'bānde shŕhou le. / You'll have to see me during working hours. Nǐ děi dzài wǒ bàn'gūng de shŕhou lái 'jyàn wǒ.

Hourglass lòu.

Hour hand twànjēn.

Other English expressions. / He's the man of the hour. (favorite) Tā shř yí-'shŕde 'húngrén. *or* (important) Tā shř yì'shŕde 'yàurén.

HOUSE. (Dwelling place) fángdz; occasionally fáng. / I want to rent a house. Wǒ děi 'dzū yǐswǒr 'fángdz. / They sold their house. Tāmen bǎ 'fángdz 'màile. / This house has three courtyards arranged one behind another. Jèiswǒr 'fángdz yǒu sān'jǐn. / All the houses are packed together in the city. Chéng'lǐde 'fáng dōu 'jǐdzài yí'kwàr.

(Household) jyā; imperial house 'hwángjyā, 'hwángshř; royal house 'wángfǔ; noble house 'gwèidzú. / The whole house turned out to greet him. Chywán'jyā dōu chūlai 'hwānyíng tā. / Eighty generations of the house of K'ung have lived in this city. 'Kǔngjyā dzài 'jèige chéngli jùle 'bāshr'dàile. / He was formerly a servant in the imperial house. Tā tsúng chyan shr °hwángjyālide (°'hwángshřlide) yige yùngrén. / This is from the collection of a noble house. Jèi shř tsúng yǐjyā 'wángfúli 'chūlaide. / He is a descendant of a noble house. Tā shř 'gwèidzúde 'hòuyi. / I'm not used to keeping house for others. Gěi 'byérén gwǎn jyā'shř wǒ yǐchyán méi 'dzwǒgwo. / We made a house-to-house search. Wǒmen āi'jyā(r)de 'sōule.

(Audience). / The whole house enjoyed the play. Lái 'kàn de rén 'dōu jywéje syǐ 'hǎu. *or* (formal) 'Chywántǐ'gwānjùng dōu hěn 'syīnshǎng nèichū 'syì. / We had a full house. Mǎn'dzwòr le. *or* Màile ge 'mǎndzwòr.

(Legislative) 'yǐywànywàn; House of Representatives 'Jùngyǐywàn; member of the House of Representatives 'Jùng(yǐywàn)yǐ'ywán. / The law was just passed by the Upper House. 'Jèityáu 'fǎàn 'Shàngywàn 'gāng tūng'gwò.

Movie house dyànyǐngywàn. / Let's go to the movie house around the corner. Dzámen chyù jǐ'jyǎur nèrde dyànyǐng'ywàn ba.

Housing. / Can you provide housing for all of us? Nǐ néng gěi wǒmen 'chywán-dōu jǎujau 'dìfang 'jù ma? *or* Nǐ néng gūnggěi wǒmen dàjya jù de fángdz ma?

To house. / Where are the visitors to be housed? 'Kèrén jùdzài 'nǎr? / We can house your car in the barn. Wǒmen 'kéyi bǎ nǐde chē gē dzài 'tsāngfángli.

See also HOME.

HOW. (In what way) dzĕmma, dzĕmma'yàng. /How shall I do this? 'Jèige 'dzĕmma dzwò? /How did you do it? (of an affair) Nĭ 'dzĕmma bàn'chéngde? *or* (of an object) 'Jèige 'dzĕmma dzwòde? /How did he get here? Tā dzĕmma 'láide? /How does this sound to you? 'Jèmma shwō nĭ 'tīngting (dzĕmma'yàng)? /How do you feel? Nĭ jywéde dzĕmma'yang? /How do you like your new house? Nĭ jywéde syīn'fángdz dzĕmma'yàng? *or* expressed as Are you satisfied with your new house? Syīn'fángdz (ni) mǎn'yì ma? /How do you like her for a mother-in-law? 'Nèige rén dāng nĭde 'jàngmǔ'nyáng dzĕmma'yàng? /How do you sell this, by the pound or by the piece? Jèige 'dzĕmma mài, lwùn 'bàng háishr lwùn 'gèer? /No matter how I try I still can't say it right. Wǒ 'dzĕmma shwō dōu shwōbu'dwèi.

(The way, like this, like that) jèmma, dzĕmma, nèmma. /This is how he walks. Tā 'jèmma dzǒu. /That's how the accident happened. Jyòu shr 'nèmma chūde 'shr̀. /That's how I would interpret your remark. Nĭ 'nèijyu 'hwà wǒ jywéde jyou shr 'nèmma ge yìsz.

(To what extent) dwō(ma), dwó(ma); **how long** (spatial length) 'dwō(ma) cháng, 'dwó(ma) cháng, (length of time) 'dwō(ma) jyǒu, 'dwó(ma) jyǒu, dwōshau 'shŕhou (also translated as how soon). /How tall are you? Nĭ (yǒu) °'dwō(ma) gāu (°'dwó(ma) gāu)? /How wide is this table? Jèige jwōdz (yǒu) °'dwō(ma) kwān (°'dwó(ma) kwān)? /How long is this piece of cloth? Jèikwai bù (yǒu) °'dwō(ma) cháng (°'dwó(ma) cháng)? /How long have you waited? Nĭ dĕngle 'dwōshau shŕhou le? /How soon can you finish (reading) the book? Jèibĕn shū nĭ 'dwōshau shŕhou néng kàn'wán?

(In exclamations) dzĕmma 'nèmma, dzĕmma, dzĕmma 'jèmma, dwō(ma), dwó(ma). /How beautiful she is! Tā °dwō(ma) (°etc.) hǎu'kàn a! /How kind of you! °Dzĕmma 'nèmma (°etc.) 'kèchi a! *or* Nĭde 'syīn °dzĕmma nèmma (°etc.) 'hǎu a! /How smart he is! Tā °dzĕmma 'nèmma (°etc.) 'jīling a!

How many dwōshau; (if the expected answer is less than ten) jĭ-M. /How many people came? Yǒu °'dwōshau (°'jĭge) rén láile? *or* Láile °'dwōshau (°'jĭge) rén? /How many copies do you want? /Nĭ yàu °'jĭfèr (°'dwōshaufèr)?

How much dwōshau. /How much rice do you want? Nĭ yàu 'dwōshau fàn? /How much (money) did he give? Tā gĕile 'dwōshau chyán?

How often *see* **OFTEN.**

How is it that (why) wèi 'shémma, dzĕmma. /How is it that you didn't come? Nĭ °wèi 'shémma (°dzĕmma) méi'lái?

Know how hwèi. /Do you know how to swim? Nĭ hwèi fú'shwĕi ma?

Show someone **how** jyāu. /Show me how to tie that knot. 'Jyāu wǒ 'jì nèige 'kòur.

Special expressions in English. /How do you do? Nĭ 'hǎu? /How are you getting along? 'Jìnlái 'dzĕmmayàng? *or* Jìnlái 'hǎu a? *or* Yísyàng 'hǎu a? *or* Dzĕmma ge 'hǎufar? /How about you? 'Nĭ dzĕmmayàng? *or* 'Nĭ ne? /That's a fine how-do-you-do! Dzĕmma 'hǎu a! *or* Dzĕmma 'bàn ne! *or* 'Jēnshr dzwò'là! *or* 'Jēnshr 'méifár 'bàn! *or* 'Jēn jyàu rén wéi'nán! /How is that? meaning How can that be? 'Dzĕmma hwéi shèr? or meaning I didn't catch it. Nĭ shwō 'shémma laije? /How come? 'Dzĕmma ne?

HOWEVER. (In whatever way) °dzĕmma (°bùgwǎn ... 'dzĕmma) ... °yĕshr (°dzŭngshr, °dzĕmma, °dōu). /However you do it, do it well. Bùgwǎn nĭ 'dzĕmma dzwò, 'dzŭng-shr dĕi dzwòhǎu. /However you tell him, he won't listen. Bùgwǎn nĭ 'dzĕmma gàusu tā, tā 'dzŭngshr bù'tīngde. /However you do it, it won't be right. Nĭ dzĕmma dzwò, °dzĕmma (°dōu) búdwèi.

(To whatever degree) (bùgwǎn) °dwōma (°dzĕmma) ... °yĕ (°'dzŭngshr,

°'háishr, *or* (more emphatic) °'jyòushr). /However ungrateful he is, I still treat him the same way. Bùgwǎn tā 'dwōma méi 'lyángsyīn, wǒ háishr jàu 'yàngr dài tā. /However cold it gets, I still won't wear my fur coat. Tyān 'dwōma lěng wǒ yě 'bùchwān pídà'yī. /However persuasive you are, I just won't go. 'Bùgwǎn nǐ shwōde 'dwōma hǎu'tīng, wǒ °'jyòushr (°yě, °'yěshr, °'háishr, °'dzǔngshr) bú'chyù.

(Nevertheless, yet) <u>is expressed as</u> although this is said 'jǐngwǎn nèmma 'shwō; <u>or as</u> but, still kěshr ne; <u>or as</u> although this is so 'swéirán rútsz̀; <u>or as</u> no matter what you say bùgwǎn 'dzěmma shwō; etc. /However, he's still better than anyone else. 'Jǐngwǎn nèmma 'shwō, tā háishr bǐ 'shéi dōu 'chyáng a.

HUMAN. (Pertaining to man) rénde, ren. /The human skull is much larger than the monkey's. Rénde'nǎugǔ bǐ hóudzde dàde 'dwō. /The human mind is quite unfathomable. Rén'syīn nán'tsè. /Will the human race become extinct? 'Rénlèi yě hwèi 'syāumyè ma?

<u>In many sentences there is no direct equivalent.</u> /It's only human to make mistakes. <u>is expressed as</u> We're all people, no one can help making mistakes. 'Dōu shr̀ 'rén, 'shwéi néng méi 'tswò̀r? /I'm only human. <u>is expressed with the quotation</u> A human being who is not a sage, how can he avoid mistakes? 'Rénfēi'shēngsyán 'shúnéngwú'gwò? /It's not human to make people do such things. <u>is expressed as</u> Can one who does that sort of thing be called a human being? Jyàu rén dzwò 'nèijǔng shr̀ de háishr 'rén ma?

Human (being) rén. /This food isn't fit for human beings. Jèi 'bùshr̀ 'rén chr̄de. /There were more animals than humans on the island. Nèige 'dǎushang 'yěshòu bǐ 'rén dwō.

HUMOR. (Amusing quality) <u>is sometimes translated with the transliteration</u> 'yōumwò; <u>though is most often expressed indirectly.</u> /Humor carried too far becomes sarcasm. 'Yōumwò gwò'fèn le jyòu byàn'chéngle fēng'tsz̀ le. /I don't see any humor in the situation. <u>is expressed as</u> I don't think the situation is amusing at all. Wǒ 'bìng bù jywéde 'jèijǔng 'chíngsying kě'syàu. /He's full of humor. <u>is expressed as</u> What he says makes people amused. Tā shwō'hwà hěn °dòu'gén (°dòu'syàur). <u>or as</u> He's amusing, both in speech and action. Tā hěn 'hwájī.

Sense of humor. /Keep your sense of humor. <u>is expressed as</u> It's just kidding, don't take it seriously. Kāi 'wánsyàu, byé rèn'jēn. *or* (of a situation) <u>as</u> One laugh and it's over. Yí'syàu jyòu 'gwòchyule. *or* (of a serious situation) <u>as</u> Be sure you don't flare up. Chyānwàn byé fā'pīchi.

To humor hǔng. /You'll have to humor him. Nǐ děi 'hǔngje tā.

HUNDRED. bǎi; one one-hundredth 'bǎifēnjr'yī; the hundredth dìyìbǎi.

(A great many). /Hundreds of refugees left the stricken area. Hěn 'dwō nàn-'mín líkaile 'jāichyu le. /I've come across that word a hundred times. 'Nèige dz̀ wǒ 'jyànle °bù'jr̄dau 'dwōshau tsz̀ le (°'hǎu syē 'hwéi le).

HUNGRY. è. /I'm hungry. Wǒ 'èle. /I'm a little hungry. Wǒ yǒu dyǎr 'è. /Are you hungry AGAIN? Nǐ dzěmma 'yòu è le? /The child seems hungry. Syǎu 'hár hǎusyàng 'è le.

(Craving). /He's hungry for knowledge. <u>is expressed as</u> His anxiety to learn is very strong. Tā chyóu'sywé de syīn hěn 'cháng. /She's hungry for love. <u>is expressed as</u> With her whole heart she wants someone to love her. Tā 'mǎnsyīn syǎng yǒurén ài tā.

HUNT. (Chase game) dǎlyè; dǎ <u>plus other objects, such as</u> lù deer, húli fox. /Do you like to hunt? Nǐ syǐhwan dǎ'lyè ma? / They are out hunting deer. Tāmen chūchyu dǎ 'lù chyule. / Good hunting! is expressed as Get more than usual! Dwō 'dá jige!

(Search for someone) sōu, jǎu; or expressed with jwēi (harry), gǎn (chase). / They hunted the fugitive from city to city. Tāmen bǎ dzéi 'jwēide pǎudau 'jèige chéng pǎudau 'nèige chéng. / How long have they been hunting for the criminal? Nèige 'fànrén, tāmen 'jǎule 'dwōshau shŕhou le?

(Search for something) sōu, jǎu; (search for something by turning over things) fān. / What are you hunting for? Nǐ jǎu 'shémma ne? / I hunted high and low and couldn't find it. Wǒ 'nǎr dōu 'fānle, jyòushr jǎubù'jáu. / Try to hunt up that telephone number. Syǎng 'fár bǎ nèige dyànhwà hàu'mǎr 'cháchulai.

Hunt down jǎujau, jwājǔ, dēijǔ. / They hunted him down. Tāmen bǎ tā °'jǎujaule (°jwājule, °dēijule).

Hunt up (invent) 'byānchu, 'dzōuchu, 'dzǎuchu. / He could always hunt up an excuse. Tā dzǔng néng °'byānchu (°dzōuchu, °dzǎuchu) yige 'lǐyou lai.

A hunt is expressed verbally as above. / Are you going on the hunt? Nǐ chyu dǎ'lyè ma? / I made a thorough hunt for the missing bracelet; guess where I found it? Nèige 'dyóule de 'jwódz wǒ 'nǎr dōu jǎu'byànle; nǐ 'tsāitsai dzài 'nǎr jǎujaude?

Hunter (sportsman) dǎ'lyède; (professional) lyèhù.

HURRY. (Move faster) kwàije, gǎnje, mángje, gǎnmáng, gánjǐn, gǎnkwài. / Hurry up! (in general) 'Kwàije! or 'Kwàidyar. or (if the person is running or walking; already moving) °Dzǒu (°Pǎu, °Yáu, °Kāi) 'kwàidyar. or (if the person is just thinking or talking) 'Kwài (je)dyar °'shwō (°'syǎng, °'shóushr). or 'Gánjǐn bàn. or 'Gǎnmáng bàn. or Gǎn'kwài bàn. / Let's hurry or we'll be late. 'Kwài(je)dyar ba, bùrán jyòu 'wǎn le. / Hurry! Hurry! 'Kwàije! 'Kwàije! / Don't hurry. Byé 'máng. or expressed as Slow down. 'Màndyar. / They hurried all the way home. Tāmen yílù 'gǎnje hwéi'jyā le. or Tāmen hwéi'jyā de shŕhou yílù 'gǎnganmáng'máng de.

(Make haste in doing something) gǎn. / We're hurrying to have this done before five o'clock. Wǒmen 'gǎnje yàu dzài 'wǔdyǎn yǐchyán dzwò'hǎule. / Hurry and have this typed in half an hour. Dzài 'bàndyǎnjūngli bǎ jèige 'gǎnchulai. or 'Kwàije bǎ jèige dzài 'bàndyǎnjūngli 'dǎchulai.

(Cause to move quickly) tswēi, jyàu . . . 'kwàidyǎr, gǎnlu. / Hurry them out of here. is expressed as Tell them to hurry out. Jyàu tāmen 'kwài dyǎr 'chūchyu. or as Urge them to hurry and go. 'Tswēije tāmen jyàu tāmen 'kwài wán le hǎu 'dzǒu. or (if the process is quite involved) as Hurry up the process of getting them out. 'Kwài dyǎr bǎ tāmen 'dǎfā'dzǒule ba. or (if you're chasing them out) Kwài bǎ tāmen 'gǎnchuchyu. / Hurry him up a bit. 'Tswēitswei tā. or Jyàu tā 'kwàidyar. / If you hurry him too much, he can't turn out a good job. Nǐ yàushr 'gǎnlu 'gande tài 'jǐn le, tā jyòu bùnéng dzwòde 'hǎu. / Don't hurry the decision. is expressed as Don't hurry; discuss it slowly. Byé 'máng, màn'mànde 'shānglyang. / Time is short. Can you hurry up the packing? is expressed as There isn't much time. Can you hurry to pack? Méiyou dwōshau 'shŕhou le. Néng bunéng 'kwàidyar 'shóushr?

A hurry is expressed verbally. / What's the hurry? 'Máng shémma? / I'm in a hurry. Wǒ tǐng 'máng. / We were surprised that he was in such a hurry. Wǒmen méisyǎng'dàu tā hwèi 'nèmma 'mángmangdau'dāude.

Hurried. / That's a hurried job. Nèige 'dzwòde tài °'kwài le (°gǎnlùle).

Hurry-up. / This is a hurry-up job. is expressed as This must be done quickly. Jèige děi 'kwài dzwò.

HURT. (Injure or wound) shāng, but the use of this word alone as a verb is limited;

more commonly expressed with shòu shāng receive an injury *or* get hurt. /How many were hurt? Shāngle 'jǐge rén? /I hurt a muscle. Wǒde 'jīn shòu 'shāngle. *or* Wǒ shāngle 'jīn le. *or* Wǒde 'jīn 'shāngle. /I hurt the bone. Wǒ 'gútou shòu 'shāng le. /Was anyone hurt? Yǒurén shòu 'shāng le ma? /Where were you hurt? meaning on what part of the body Nǐ 'nǎr shòu 'shāng le? or meaning Where were you when you got hurt? Nǐ dzài 'nǎr shòude 'shāng? *or* Nǐ shòu 'shāng de shŕhou jàndzài 'nǎr?

(Pain) téng. /My arm hurts. Wǒ 'gēbei téng. /It hurt badly. Téngde 'lìhai. *or* 'Hěn téng. *or* 'Jēn téng. *or* Téngde bùnéng shwō 'hwà le. or expressed as It hurt so that I groaned. Téngde jŕ 'āiyou. or expressed as It hurt so that I grit my teeth. Téngde yǎu'yá. /Where does it hurt? 'Nǎr téng?

(Offend, distress) shāngsyīn, (syīnli) nán'shòu, 'syīnli bùhǎu'gwò, 'syīnli 'byènyou, shēngchì. /I hope your feelings aren't hurt. Nǐ 'búhwèi jywéje °shāng-'syīn ba (°nán'shòu ba, °shēng'chǐ ba). *or* Nǐ syīnli 'búhwèi °bùhǎu'gwò ba (°'byènyōu ba). /This hurts me more than it does you. Jèi jyàu wǒ bǐ 'nǐ hái °nán-'shòu (°bùhǎu'gwò). /Whenever I think of his ingratitude, it hurts. Yǐ 'syàngchǐ tā 'dwōma méi'lyángsyin lai, jyou jyàu wǒ °nán'shòu (°shāng'syīn, °syīnli bùhǎu-'gwò, °etc.).

(Have a bad effect on) shòu swǔnshr, shòu 'yǐngsyǎng. /This will hurt business. 'Nèmmaje hwèi jyàu 'mǎimai shòu °'swǔnshŕde (°'yǐngsyǎng).

(Matter) 'yàujǐn. /Will it hurt if I'm late? Wǒ 'wǎn dyǎr 'yàujǐn búyàujǐn?

HUSBAND. (General term) jàngfu; (informal, colloquial) 'nánrén. /A husband has his responsibilities. 'Jàngfu yǒu 'jàngfude'dzérèn. *or* Dzwò 'jàngfu de yǒu 'jàngfude 'dzéren. /Some husbands pamper their wives. 'Yǒude'jàngfu °'gwànje 'chǐdz (°bǎ 'tàitai gwàn'hwàile). /Don't pamper your husband. Byé bǎ °'jàngfu (°'nánrén) gwàn'hwàile.

(Of a particular person; polite term) syānsheng; (limited to Mainland China) 'àirén; (common terms, rarely used to refer to the husband of the woman spoken to) 'nánrén, yémen, jǎnggwèide, dāngjyāde; (vulgar and insulting) hàndz; or, when talking to or about a wife, refer to the husband by his title, such as shopkeeper jǎnggwèide. When acquainted with the family, always refer to the husband by his given name or by his relation to the person addressed (your brother, your cousin, etc.). Do not ask a woman if her husband is living; get such information, when it is necessary, by some indirect method, such as asking her one of the following questions: What does your husband do? °'Syānsheng (°Nǐde 'jàngfu) dzwò shémma 'shr? *or* Where is your husband? Nín 'syānsheng dzài 'nǎr? *or* (if you know the family) Lùdūng (or whatever his name is) dzài 'nǎr? /Her husband is a good-for-nothing. Tā(de) 'syānsheng bùchéng'tsái. *or* (very insulting) Tā(de) 'hàndz bùchéng'tsái. /Who's her husband? Tāde 'syānsheng shr 'shéi? /Does your husband like this color? Jèijǔng 'yánshǎr nín 'syānsheng 'syǐhwan ma? /He thinks that no man on earth is worthy of being her husband. Tā 'jywéje 'shŕshang 'méi rén 'pèi °dāng tāde 'jàngfu (°'chyǔ ta). /What kind of a husband would you like to have? Nǐ 'syǎng 'jyà ge 'shémma yàng de rén? /My husband is not home. 'Syānsheng búdzài 'jyā. *or* Wǒmen dāng'jyāde 'chūchyùle.

Husband and wife fūfù, 'fūchī, lyángkǒudz, gūmulyǎ; **husbands and wives** 'lǎuyé (gēn) 'tàitai, 'syānsheng (gēn) 'tàitai. /Husband and wife should live harmoniously. Fū'fù gwò 'rdz yàu °'hémù (°'héhemù'mùde). /Husbands and wives shouldn't sit together. °'Lǎuyé (°'Syānsheng) gēn 'tàitai bùyīngdang dzwòdzai yíkwàr.

I (ME, MY, MINE). wǒ; **me** wǒ; **my** *or* **mine** wǒde (de is sometimes dropped before nouns; in polite speech referring to one's own relatives). / She phoned me but I wasn't home. Tā gěi wǒ dǎ dyàn'hwà laije, kěshr wǒ méidzài 'jyā. / I gave him mine. Wǒ bǎ 'wǒde gěile tā le. / Mine is better than yours. Wǒde bǐ 'nǐde 'hǎu. / He is a friend of mine. Tā shr wǒ(de) 'péngyou. / My pen leaks. Wǒ(de) bǐ lòu mwò 'shwěr. / My bank pays a higher interest. Wǒ (tswúnchyán de) yín'háng gěi de 'lìchyán 'dwō dyar. / My feet hurt. Wǒ(de) 'jyǎu téng. / The wife of the president of my school is very stern. Wǒ sywésyàu syàu'jǎngde 'tàitai hěn 'lìhai. / My three students are very good. Wǒ(de) jèi'sānge sywésheng 'dōu hen 'hǎu. / You can imagine my annoyance! Nǐ 'syǎngsyang wǒ yǒu 'dwōma 'byènyou ba!

   Myself *see* **SELF**.

ICE. bīng. / Put some ice in the glasses. Dzài 'bēidzli 'gē dyǎr 'bīng. / Is the ice thick enough for skating? Bīng 'dùngde néng lyōu le ma?

   Break the ice (break up a stiff atmosphere) bǎ jyāng'jyú dǎ'pwòle. / She broke the ice by telling a joke. Tā 'shwōle ge 'syàuhwà, jyou bǎ nèige jyāng'jyú gěi dǎ-'pwòle. or expressed as She told a joke and immediately everyone was less stiff and formal. Tā 'shwōle ge 'syàuhwà dǎ'jyā jyou 'bùnèmma 'jyāng le.

   Icebox bīngsyāng; (electric) dyànbīngsyāng.

   Ice cream bīngjilíng.

   Ice water bīngshwěi, bīng'jèn lyángkāi'shwěi.

   Iced bīng; (cool) lyáng. / Let's order iced drinks. Dzámen yàu dyǎr 'lyáng dūngsyi 'hē ba.

   Put on ice bīngshang, gēdzai 'bīngshang. / Put the meat on the ice right away. 'Gǎnjǐn bǎ 'ròu 'bīngshang.

   To ice (cool with ice) bīng. / This orange juice ought to be iced. Jèige 'jyúdz-'shwěi 'yīnggai 'bīng yibīng.

   (Put frosting on) 'nùngshang yī'tséng táng'pyér. / Ice the cake as soon as it's cool. Dàn'gāu yī 'lyáng jyou děi bǎ nèitséng táng'pyér 'nùngshang.

IDEA. (Thought, suggestion) 'júyì; (understanding) 'jyànjyě; (meaning, opinion) yìsz; (viewpoint, opinion) 'yìjyàn; (point of view) 'kànfǎ; (plan) 'bànfǎ, fádz, fāngfar or, colloquial, jāur. / He has an idea for making money. Tā yǒu yíge °'fāngfar (°'fádz, °'bànfǎ) jwàn'chyán. / Say, I have an idea! Hēi, wǒ 'syǎngchū yíge 'jāur lai! / Do you have any ideas on the subject? Dwèiyú 'jèijyàn shr nǐ yǒu shemma 'yìjyan ma? or Gwānyu jèijǔng 'wèntí nǐ yǒu shémma 'jyànjyě? / That's a good idea. Nèige 'júyì bú'tswò. / What's the big idea? Nǐ shr shémma 'yìsz? / Was this party your idea? Jèidwùn 'fàn shr nǐde 'júyì ma? / His idea is that the war will be over quickly. Jyù tāde 'kànfǎ 'jàng hwèi hěn 'kwàide jyòu dǎ'wán le.

   Other expressions in English. / Don't you give him any ideas now! is expressed as Don't you teach him bad things. Nǐ jyou byé 'jyāu ta 'hwài le! / He hasn't an idea in his head. is expressed as He doesn't understand anything. Tā 'shémma yě bù'dǔng. / I had an idea this would happen. is expressed as I knew before that it would be this way. Wǒ 'dzǎu jyou 'jrdau yàu 'jèiyàngr. / I haven't any idea where he is. is expressed as I don't know at all where he is. Tā dzài 'nǎr wǒ lyán 'yǐngr yě bùjr'dàu. / The idea is to get there early. is expressed as The best thing is to get there early. 'Dzwèi hǎu shr 'dzǎu dyǎr 'dàu nèr. / That's the idea! 'Jyòu shr 'nèiyàngr! or Jyòu děi 'jèmeje! or 'Dwèi le!

IDEAL. (Aim, model) 'jǐsyàng, syǎng yàu dzwò(dàu)de. / He has very high ideals. Tā 'jǐsyàng hěn 'gāu. / His father has always been his ideal. Tā yī'jǐ syàng yàu dzwò yíge syàng tā 'fùchin nàyàngrde 'rén. *or* Tā yǐ'jǐ jywéje tā 'fùchin shř shřjyè-shang 'dzwèi hǎude rén.

Be ideal (existing only in the imagination) 'lǐsyǎngde; (model) mwófàn; (best) dzwèi hǎu; (nothing better) 'dzài hǎu 'méiyou le. /His ideal woman is too hard to find. Tā 'lǐsyǎngde 'nyǔrén 'tài nán 'jǎu le. /He's an ideal student. Tā shř ge 'mwófàn'shēng. /He is the ideal man for the job. 'Tā dzwò nèijyàn 'shèr °'dzài hǎu 'méiyou le (°dzwèi 'hǎu). /A situation like that would be ideal. 'Nèmmaje kě jyou hǎu'jíle.

IF. °yàu(shr) (°rwòshr, °'rúgwǒ) . . . (dehwà); <u>often omitted, the if-clause coming first in a sentence</u>; **even if** *see* EVEN. /If I had any suggestions, I'd give them to you. 'Yàushr yǒu shémma 'yǐjyàn dehwà, wǒ yí'dìng hwèi 'gàusu ni. /Stop me if you've heard this before. Nǐ yàushr 'tīnggwo jèige jyou byé 'ràng wo dzài wǎng syà 'shwō le. /If anyone asks for me, say I'll be right back. Yǒu 'rén 'jǎu wo, nǐ shwō wǒ jyòu 'hwéilai. /What if it rains? °'Yàushr (°'Rwòshr) syà'yǔ ne?

(Whether) /See if there's any mail for me. 'Kànkan yǒu wǒde 'syìn méiyou. *or* 'Kànkan 'yǒu méiyou wǒde 'syìn. /I don't know if he's left yet. Wǒ bù'jřdàu tā 'dzǒule 'méiyou. /Ask her if she's coming with us. Nǐ 'wènwen ta 'shř bushř yàu 'gēn women chyù.

As if gēn . . . shřde; (the appearance of it seems) °'sżhu (°hǎu'syàng) . . . shřde. /He walks as if he were crippled. Tā dzǒu'dàur gēn ge 'chywédz shřde. /She talks as if she were a movie star. Tā shwō 'hwà gēn ge dyàn'yǐng míng'syīng shřde. /He talked as if he had been there. Tā 'shwō de yàngdz °'sżhu (°hǎu'syàng) tā 'dàugwo nàr shřde. /As if you didn't know! (sarcastically) Hǎu'syàng nǐ bùjř'dàu shřde! *or* (local Peiping) Nǐ hǎusyàng méishr'rér shřde!

If only. /If today were only payday! <u>is expressed as</u> If today they gave out pay, it would be swell. 'Yàushr jyèr fā'syīn °dwō 'hǎu a (°jyou 'hǎu le). /If she'd only stop talking! Tā byé nèmma 'syùsyudāudāude le! /If he had only come home earlier, nothing would have happened. Tā yàushr 'dzǎu dyǎr 'hwéilai dehwà, yě jyou méi 'shèr le.

ILL. bìng; (uncomfortable, not well) bùshūfu. /He has been seriously ill. Tā 'bìngde hěn 'lìhai láije. /Are you feeling ill? Nǐ 'jywéde bù'shūfu ma?

Ill at ease (shy, nervous) fāmáu; (timid) 'jyūnǐ; (unnatural) bú'dzrán; (restrained, held back) 'jyūshù; (uncomfortable) bùshūfu. /He always feels ill at ease at formal affairs. Dzài yige 'jèngshrde chǎnghé, ta lǎu 'jywéde hen 'jyūshù.

IMAGINE. (Suppose) syǎng (think); jywéde (feel). /I imagine the shops will be open. Wǒ °'syǎng (°jywéde) 'pùdz hwèi kāi'mér. /I imagine so. Wǒ °'syǎng (°jywéde) °shř ba (°'shřde, °'dwèi ba).

(Produce by the imagination) yǐwéi; <u>or expressed as</u> think syǎng. /You're just imagining things. Nà 'jřshr 'yǐwéi shř 'nèiyàngr. *or* Nà 'jřshr nǐ nèmma 'syǎng ér'yǐ. /She imagined there was someone in the room. Tā °'yǐwéi (°'jywéde) 'wūrli yǒu yíge 'rén. /He imagined himself the ruler of the world. Tā yǐwéi shř shř'jyè 'bàwáng. /I can't imagine what you mean. Wǒ 'syǎngbuchū nǐ shř 'shémma 'yìsz. /I can't imagine him doing that. Wǒ 'jēnshř 'syǎngbudàu tā hwèi gàn 'nèige. /Just imagine you're on a boat. Nǐ bǐ'yàn 'syǎng nǐ dzài 'chwán shang shřde. /Imagine living in a place like that! (of a desirable or undesirable place) Jùdzài 'nèmma ge dìfangr, nǐ 'syǎngsyǎng kàn. *or* (of an undesirable place only) <u>is expressed as</u> How could anyone live in a place like that! Dzěmma 'néng 'jùdzài 'nèmma ge 'dìfang!

IMMEDIATE. (Foremost) mùchyánde. / This is our immediate problem. Wǒmen mù-'chyánde 'wèntí shř 'jèige. / Our immediate job is to fill up the swamp. Wǒmen mù'chyán syān děi bǎ shwěi'kēng 'tyánshang.

(Directly following) dzwěichūde; **the immediate future** dzwěi'jìn. / The immediate result was not what they expected. Dzwěi'chūde 'jyēgwǒ 'chūhu tāmen yù-'lyàujr'wài. / We don't know what's going to happen in the immediate future. Wǒmen bùjř'dàu dzwěi'jìn hwèi dzěmma'yàng.

(Urgent) jǐnjíde. / The need is immediate. Jèi shř jǐn'jíde shř.

(Nearest). / There is a river in the immediate neighborhood. is expressed as There is a river right in the neighborhood. Yǒu yídàu 'hé 'jyòu dzài 'fùjìn. / There's no school in the immediate vicinity. is expressed as There's no school in the neighborhood here. Jèr 'fùjìn méi sywé'syau. / Our immediate neighbors live in a big house. is expressed as Our next door neighbors have a big house. Wǒmen jyè'byàrde rén yǒu yìswǒr 'dà fángdz.

(Occurring at once). / We must take immediate action. is expressed as We must do it immediately. Wǒmen bì'děi mǎ'shàng jyòu 'dzwò. / There was an immediate rise in prices. is expressed as Things immediately rose in price. 'Dūngsyi lì'shř jyou jǎng'jyàr le.

IMMEDIATELY. jyòu; lìkè, lìshř, mǎshàng, 'gǎnjǐn, kwàikwārde, all followed optionally by jyòu. / You'd better go home immediately. Nǐ 'háishr °lì'kè jyòu (°kwài'kwārde) hwéi'jyā ba. / We heard the news immediately after it happened. Jèijyàn 'shèr yǐ fā'shēng, wǒmen jyòu 'déjau 'syāusyi le.

IMPORTANT. 'yàujǐn, 'jùngyàu; (grave, serious) 'yánjùng; (extremely significant) 'lyǎubùdé; (of people; famous, esteemed) yǒumíngde, or (powerful, influential) yǒu-'shřlide. / I want to see you about an important matter. Wǒ yǒu yíjyàn 'yàujǐnde 'shřching děi 'jyàn ni. / There were no important letters in the mail. 'Láide 'yóujyàn lǐtou 'méi shémma 'yàujǐnde 'syìn. / He's never accomplished anything very important. Tā méi'dzwò shémma 'lyǎubudéde 'shř. / Why is she going around looking important? meaning Whey does she think she is important? Tā gàn'má 'yǐwéi 'dzjǐ tǐng 'lyǎubùdé shřde? / He's the most important man in the municipal government. Tā shř shř'jèngfùli dzwèi 'yàujǐnde 'rén. / He was the most important man in town. Tā shř jèi 'chéngli dzwèi °yǒu'míngde (°yǒu'shřlide) rén.

IMPOSSIBLE. 'bùsyíng, 'bùchéng, bànbùdàu, dzwòbùdàu, bùkěnéng. / According to my point of view, it's impossible. 'Jyù wǒ 'kàn °bùsyíng (°'bùchéng, °etc.). / That's an impossible task. 'Jèi shř dzwòbù'dàude 'shř. / Don't try to do the impossible. °Bànbù'dàude (°Bùkěnéngde) 'shř jyòu 'byé bàn.

(Unendurable, obnoxious; of a person) yàumíng. / She's impossible! Tā 'jēn shř yàu'míng. / She's an impossible snob. Tā jyāu'àude yàu'míng.

Be impossible for one bù'néng, bulyǎu, jyàn'jr ... bū. / It's impossible for her to come. Tā 'láibulyǎu. or Tā bùnéng lái 'jyàn ni. or Tā méi 'fár lái 'jyàn ni. / It was impossible for me to understand that book. Nèiběr 'shū wǒ jyàn'jr shř kànbu'dǔng.

It's impossible to ... méifár. / It's impossible to describe the scene. Jyǎn'jr méi'fár 'myáusyě nèige 'jǐngjr. / It's impossible to get there except by plane. 'Chúle dzwò fēi'jī yǐ'wài méi'fár néng 'dàu nèr.

IMPROVE. (Get better) hǎule; (of a situation; take a turn for the better) jyànhǎu, (progress) yǒu jìnbù; (of a neighborhood; become more desirable) syàngyàngr; (of someone's work; show progress) jǎngjìn; (of social behavior; change) gǎile, (be softened) héhwǎnle; and other expressions depending on the subject. / Do you think his health has improved? Nǐ 'jywéde tā 'hǎu yǐdyǎr le ma? / The war situation has improved a lot. Jàn'jyú °hǎude'dwō le (°hěn jyàn'hǎu, °hěn yǒu jìn'bù). / This neighborhood has improved a lot. Jèi yí'dàide rén °syàng'yàngr 'dwō le (°hǎu'dwō le). / Has his work improved? Tā dzwò'shēr °jǎng'jìnle (°'hǎu dyar le) ma? / His manners have improved a lot. Tāde 'tàidu °'gǎile bù'shǎu (°hé'hwǎnde'dwō le, °hǎude'dwō le).

(Make better) gǎilyáng, dzēngjìn, dzēngjyā; (of a house) jyànsyīn. / To what extent have they improved the soil? Tāmen bǎ jèikwài 'dǐde tǔ'rǎng gǎi'lyáng dwōshau le? / They've really managed to improve their product. Tāmen jyū'rán bǎ chū'pǐn gǎi'lyángle. / They're trying to improve the efficiency of the work. Tāmen 'jèngdzài syàng'fǎr dzēng'jìn 'gūngdzwò 'syàulyù. / They haven't made any attempt to improve the house. Tāmen méibǎ 'fángdz jyàn'syīn.

Improve on something (change) gǎi; (add the finishing touches) syōugǎi. / Can you improve on my dissertation? Nǐ 'néng bǎ wǒde lwùn'wén °'gǎi yigǎi (°syōu'gǎi yí'syàdz) ma? / The picture is so beautiful it can't possibly be improved on. is expressed as The picture is painted so well there are no points that can be improved on. Nèijāng 'hwàr 'hwàde hǎude méi shémma kěsyōu'gǎide 'dìfang le.

IN. (Physical location, participation in a group) (dzài) . . . °li (°'lǐtou). / There's no heat in my room. Wǒ 'wūdzli méi 'hwo. / The dress is in that pile of clothes. Nèijyàn 'yīfu dzài nèidwēi 'yīfuli. / Is he in the Army? Tā shr dzài jyūn'dwèili ma? / There are fifty members in the club. Jèige jyùle'bù lǐtou yǒu 'wǔshŕge hwèi-'ywán.

(Using as a medium) yùng. / Write it in ink. Yùng mwò'shwěr 'syě. / Say it in English. Yùng 'Yīngwén 'shwō.

(At, concerning). / Are you good in arithmetic? is expressed as Is your arithmetic good? Nǐde 'swànsywé 'hǎu buhǎu?

(During a period of) . . . de shŕhou. / He broke it in anger. Tā shēng'chì de shŕhou bǎ nèige dǎ'pwòde.

(Engaged in) dzwò. / He's in business for himself. Tā gěi 'dzjǐ dzwò 'mǎimai.

(Location in time) . . . de shŕhou; sometimes not expressed directly. / It gets hot here in the daytime. Jèr 'báityan (de shŕhou) 'rè.

(Within a period of time) °dzài (°yùng) . . . de shŕhou, dzài . . . yǐ'nèi, or sometimes just the term for the period of time. / I can finish this in a week. Yíge lǐ'bài wǒ néng dzwò'wán jèige. or Wǒ yùng yíge lǐ'bàide shŕhou néng dzwò'wán jèige.

(After a period of time) gwò . . . ; or often just the term for the period of time. / You can begin this in one hour. Gwò yíge 'jūngtóu, nǐ jyou kéyi 'dzwò jèige le. / I'll be back in a week. Wǒ yíge lǐ'bài jyou 'hwéilai.

(Marking resultant state) chéng as a postverb. / Cut it in half. Bǎ nèige 'chyēcheng lyǎng'bàr.

Be in is often expressed as have entered °jìn (°rù, or sometimes °shàng) . . . le. / His boys are all in college. Tāde 'háidzmen dōu °jìn (°rù, °shàng) 'dàsywé le.

Be in (general) dzài; (at home) dzài 'jyā. / Is the doctor in? 'Dàifu dzài ma? / My husband isn't in. Wǒ 'syānsheng búdzài'jyā.

For other combinations, such as come in, go in, put in, etc., see the verb.

INCH. tswùn. / How many inches are there in a foot? Yìchř 'yóu jǐtswùn?

Every inch (every bit) 'swŏyŏude . . . dōu. /I used up every inch of cloth. 'Swŏyŏude 'bù dōu jyàu wo yùng'wánle. /We covered every inch of ground looking for it. Wŏmen 'swŏyŏude 'dìfang dōu jǎu'dàule.

To inch along gūng, nwó, tsèng. /The traffic is just inching along. Chēlyàng yí'bùyí'bùde wàng 'chyán °'gūng (°'nwó, °'tsèng).

Other expressions in English. /The bullet missed him by inches. is expressed as The bullet almost hit him. Nèige chyáng'dzér chà'dyǎr jyòu 'dǎje ta. /He was beaten within an inch of his life. is expressed as He was almost beaten to death. Tā chà'dyǎr jyàu rén 'dǎsz.

INCLINE. (Lean) syé, pyān, wāi. /Doesn't that tower incline to the right? Nèige 'tǎ 'shř bushř syàng 'yòu °'syé (°'pyān, °'wāi)?

(Tend to) yóu dyǎr (be a little); cháng (often); syíhwān (like to). /He's inclined to be late. Tā cháng 'wǎn. /He's inclined to boast. Tā 'syíhwan shwō dà'hwà. /She's inclined to stoutness. meaning either She's on the stout side. or She's apt to get fat if she's not careful. Tā yóu dyǎr 'pàng. /He's inclined to act queerly. Tā yóu 'dyǎr 'fēngfēngdyān'dyānde. /I'm inclined to believe you. Wŏ 'yóu dyǎr 'syìn ni le. or expressed as I think I can believe you. Wŏ 'syǎng wŏ 'hwèi syāng'syìn ni.

An incline pwōr. /How steep is the incline? Nèige 'pwōr yŏu dwō 'dŏu?

INCLUDE. (Within a whole) bāukwò; (have) yŏu; (have in a container) chéng, jwāng; (be counted in) swàndzai °lǐtou (°nèi), dzài °lǐtou (°nèi), dzài . . . jr'nèi. /All his friends were included in the party. Tā 'swŏyŏude 'péngyou dōu dzài bèi'chǐng jr'nèi. /We're going to include the most common words in this dictionary. Wŏmen jèibèr dz'dyǎnli bāu'kwò 'swŏyŏude dzwèi cháng'jyàn de 'dzèr. /His criticism included some very unkind remarks. Tāde 'pīping lǐtou yŏu hǎusyē 'hwà tǐng nán'tǐng. /This chest includes all the tools you need. Jèi 'syádzli °'chéngje (°'jwāngje) 'swŏyŏude nǐ yàu 'yùng de 'jyāhwo. /Be sure to include him at your dinner party. Chǐng'kè de 'shřhou byé 'wàngle bǎ 'tā swàndzài °'lǐtou (°'nèi). /My name wasn't included on the list. Wŏde 'míngdz búdzài míng'dār jr'nèi.

Including . . . lyán . . . dzài'nèi. /This is the price, including tax. 'Jyàchyan lyán 'shwèi dzài'nèi. /He sold everything he owned, including his car. Tā bǎ 'swŏyŏude 'dūngsyi dōu 'màile, lyán 'chē dzài'nèi.

INCREASE. (Become greater) dàle; (become more) dwōle. /His power is increasing all the time. Tāde 'shřli ywè 'lái ywè 'dà. /His power has increased a lot. Tāde 'shřli dà'dwōle. /The demand for refrigerators has increased a great deal. Yàu dyànbǐng'syāng de bǐ yi'chyán dwō'dwōle. /The population has increased by fifty percent. 'Rénkŏu 'dwōle 'bǎifēnjrwǔ'shŕ.

(Make greater) dzēngjyā (add to). /You must increase production. Nǐ děi dzēng'jyā chǎn'lyàng. /The population has been increased by fifty percent. 'Rénkŏu dzēng'jyāle bǎifēnjr'wǔshŕ.

(Of taxes) jyāle, jyājùngle (get heavier); tígāule (get higher).

(Of prices) jǎngle (rise); tígāule (get higher).

An increase (growth) is expressed verbally as above. /There was a sudden increase in prices. 'Hūrán jyòu jǎng'jyàr le. /Do you expect an increase in salary? Nǐ syǎng tāmen yàu gěi ni jyā'syìn ma?

INDEED. (In reality) jēn. /She's very sick indeed. Tā 'bìngde 'jēn shř hěn 'lìhai. /There are, indeed, some people who disagree. 'Jēn yŏu syē 'rén bú'dzànchéng.

(Exclamation). /Indeed! (either for surprise or disbelief) 'Jĕnde! /Indeed not! meaning Certainly not! 'Dāngrán 'bù!

INDEPENDENT. (Of nations or people) dúlî. /Korea became independent after World War II. 'Hángwó dzài diĕrtsz̀ dàjàn yî'hòu jyòu dúlîle. /I used to have an allowance, but now I'm financially independent. Wŏ tsúng'chyán 'lĭnggwo jānyăng'fèi, syàn'dzài wŏ dz̀'jĭ 'jĭngjî dú'lî le.

(Of people only) 'búyùng chyóu'rén (not need to ask other people for things); 'yùngbujáu kàu'rén (not need to depend on people); néng dz̀'lî le (be able to stand on one's own feet); 'gèsying hĕn 'chyáng (of personalities; have a strong personality). /Those farmers are completely independent. Néisyē jùng'dĭde yî'dyăr dōu 'búyùng chyóu'rén. /You're getting pretty independent. Nĭ syàn'dzài 'yùngbujáu kàu'rén le. or Syàn'dzài nĭ hĕn néng dz̀'lî le. /He's an independent fellow; he never takes anyone's word for anything. Tā jèige 'rén 'gèsying hĕn 'chyáng, gàn 'shémma yĕ bùtĭng 'byérén de 'hwà.

(Separate). /Her interests are independent of her husband's. is expressed as Her interests and her husband's aren't the same. Tāde 'syìngchyu gēn tāde 'jàngfude bùyî'yàng. /This company is completely independent of that one. is expressed as This company has no connection at all with that one. Jèige gūng'sz̀ gēn 'nèige 'yĭdyăr 'gwānsyi dōu 'méiyou. /She has an independent income. is expressed as She has her own income. Tā yŏu tā 'dz̀jĭde shŏu'rù.

INDICATE. (Point out) jř̄chulai. /The policeman indicated the way traffic was to go. Syún'jĭng 'jř̄chūlai chēlyàng 'yĭngdang wàng 'nĕibyār 'dzŏu.

(Show) syănje (tend to show); syănchulai (show definitely); shwōmíng (explain); 'byăushř̀ (express); jèngmíng (prove); jùmíng. /This indicates that he has nothing to do with it. Jèige kéyi jèngmíng 'méi tā shémma shř̀. or 'Jèmma kànlai méi tāde 'shèr. /The results of the examination indicated that the class had really studied. Jèige kău'shř̀ de 'jyēgwŏ 'syănchūlai chywán'bānde 'rén dōu jēn'jèng nyàn'shū láije. /This pointer indicates the room temperature. Jèige jyàn'tóur 'wèideshř̀ °shwō-'míng (°'byăushř̀, °'jř̄chūlai) 'wūdzlide wēn'dù yŏu dwō 'gāu. /A footnote is indicated by an asterisk. Syĭng'hàur shř̀ 'byăushř̀ °'hòutou (°syàbyar) yŏu ge 'jùr.

(State) shwō. /Indicate briefly your experience in this kind of work. 'Jyăndānde 'shwōshwo nĭ dwèi 'nèijŭng 'gūngdzwòde 'jĭngyàn.

(Mean). /What is that symbol supposed to indicate? is expressed as That symbol has what meaning? Nèige 'jîhaur shř̀ shémma 'yìsz̀? /His rash might indicate measles. is expressed as His body has red spots on it, perhaps it's measles. Tā 'shēnshangde húng'dyăr 'yĕsyŭ 'jyòushř̀ 'jĕndz.

(Show with a mark) jùmíng. /Indicate which of these jobs you'd prefer. Jù-'míng nĭ 'syĭhwān 'nèijŭng 'shr̄ching.

INDUSTRY. gūngyè. /Steel is one of the main industries here. Gāng'tyĕ shř̀ jèr 'jŭyàu gūng'yède yî'jŭng. /How fast has heavy industry developed here? Jèrde 'jùnggūng'yè fā'jănde yŏu dwō 'kwài?

INFLUENCE. (Effect) 'yĭngsyăng. /His travels had a tremendous influence on him. Tā 'yóuli de 'jĭngyàn dwèiyu ta yŏu hĕn 'dàde 'yĭngsyăng. /You can see the influence of the French painters in his work. Nĭ 'kéyi 'kànchūlai 'tā hwà de 'hwàr shř̀ 'shòule 'Fàgwo hwà'jyāde 'yĭngsyăng. /Your friendship has always been a good influence on him. Tā gēn nĭ dzwò'péngyou °yú tā hĕn yŏu 'hăuchù (°déle bù'shăude 'yíchù). /I don't think he's a very good influence on you. is expressed as I think you can't learn anything good with him. Wŏ 'jywéde gēn 'tā yĭkwàr 'sywébulyău 'hăude.

(Power) 'shr̆lì. / The church has a big influence in politics here. 'Jèrde jyàu-'hwèi dzài jèng'jyèli hĕn yŏu 'shr̆lì.

To influence (persuade) chywàn; (draw into something) lā; (talk into) 'shwèishwō. / I'm not trying to influence you. Wŏ bìng'búshr yàu lái 'shwèishwō ni. / She influenced him to stay. Tā bă ta 'chywànde 'dàisyale.

Be influenced by shòu . . . de jr̆pèi, °bèi (°shòu) . . . dzwóyòu. / We are often influenced by sentiment. Wŏmen 'wăngwăng shòu 'gănchíngde jr̆pèi. / He was influenced by her. Tā shr̆ bèi tā dzwóyòude. / Try not to be influenced by his flattery. is expressed as Try not to listen to (or believe in) his flattery. 'Byé °'tīng (°'syìn) tā nèitàu hwāyánchyău'yŭ.

INFORM. (Notify, orally or by a written message) tūngjr; (tell) gàusu. / They informed him that his brother had died. Tāmen °'gàusu (°'gàusung, °'tūngjr) ta tā 'gēge 'gwòchyùle. / I was not informed in time. Tāmen 'gàusu wo de tài 'wănle.

Be well informed (know a lot) °'dŭngde (°'jr̆dau) hĕn 'dwō. / He is quite well informed on the subject. 'Gwānyu jèige 'wèntí tā 'dŭngde hĕn dwō.

INFORMATION. (News) syāusyi; also various other expressions, as illustrated in the following sentences. / Can you give me some information? Nĭ néng 'gàusu wo dyăr 'syāusyi ma? or expressed as Can you advise me? Nĭ néng 'jr̆dyănjr̆dyan wŏ ma? / I want some information about train schedules. Wŏ syăng °'jr̆dau (°dàtīngdăting) hwŏ'chēde jūng'dyăr. / We haven't had any information about him in a long time. Wŏmen hĕn'jyŏu méi'jyēje tāde syāusyile. or expressed as We haven't had any word from him in a long time. Wŏmen hĕn 'jyŏu méi'jyēje tāde 'yīnsyìn le. / The information he gave me was wrong. is expressed as What he told me was wrong. Tā gàusung wo de 'tswò le.

Information desk wènsyùn'chù.

INK. mwòshwĕi, mwòshwĕr. / She uses green ink. Tā yùng 'lyŭ mwò'shwĕr. / Please use ink. Chĭng ni yùng mwò'shwĕr 'syĕ. or expressed more naturally as Please write with a fountain pen. Chĭng ni yùng 'gāngbĭ 'syĕ. or as Please write with a Chinese brush. Chĭng ni yùng 'mwòbĭ 'syĕ.

To ink. / Don't ink the pad too heavily. is expressed as Don't pour too much ink on the stamp pad. 'Byé dzài yìnshăi'hédzli dàu tài 'dwō mwò'shwĕr.

Ink in yùng mwò'shwĕr 'túshang. / Ink in the letters on the sign. Bă páidz-shangde 'dzèr yùng mwò'shwĕr 'túshang.

INQUIRE. (Ask about) wèn, 'dăting. / I want to inquire about rooms. Wŏ yàu °'dătīng-dăting (°'wènwen) 'fángdz. / Several people stopped to inquire what was going on. Yŏu 'hăujĭge 'rén 'jànjùle 'wèn shr̆ 'dzĕmma hwéi 'shèr. / He inquired about you, and I said you were fine. Tā 'dătīng ni láije, wŏ 'gàusung ta nĭ tĭng bú'tswò。

Inquire into (investigate) 'dyàuchá; (study) yánjyou. / A committee was appointed to inquire into the matter. 'Yĭjing 'dzŭjrle 'yíge wĕiywán'hwèi 'wĕideshr̆ 'dyàucha jèijyàn 'shr̆. / Let's inquire into the truth of the matter. Dzámen lái 'yánjyouyánjyou dàu'dĭ shr̆ 'dzĕmma yìhwéi 'shr̆. or Dzámen dĕi bă jèijyàn 'shr̆ 'dyàucha'chīngchule.

INSECT. 'kwūnchúng (scientific name for insect class); chúngdz, chúngr (colloquial for insect, bug, or worm). / Are there any poisonous insects here? Jèr yŏu 'yŏudú-de 'kwūnchúng ma?

INSIDE. -li, lĭtou, lĭmyan, lĭbyan. / May I see the inside of the house? Wŏ 'kéyi 'kànkan fángdz 'lĭbyar shr̆ shémma 'yàngr ma? / The inside of the overcoat is red.

Dà'yǐ lǐbyar shr̀ 'húngshǎrde. / The fruit looked good, but the inside was rotten. Jèige 'gwǒdz 'kànje hěn 'hǎu, kěshr 'lǐtou 'lànle. / She kept on the inside of the sidewalk. Tā dzài byàn'dàushang kàu 'lǐbyar 'dzǒu. / Let's go inside. Dzámen dàu 'lǐtou chyù ba. / Leave it inside. 'Gēdzai 'lǐtou 'hǎu le. / Inside the house, everything was in confusion. Dzài wūdz 'lǐbyār, shémma dōu tǐng 'lwànde.

An inside job. / The theft must have been an inside job. is expressed as This must have been done by (their) own people. Jèi yí'dìng shr̀ dz̀'jǐde 'rén 'gànde. or as This must have been done by the people inside. Jèi yí'dìng shr̀ 'lǐbyārde 'rén 'gànde.

Inside of (within; of a time) (dzài) . . . yǐ'nèi. / I think I can have it done inside of five minutes. Wǒ 'syǎng wǒ 'wǔfēn jūng yǐ'nèi kéyi bǎ 'nèige dzwò'wánle.

Inside out fǎn; **turn inside out** fāngwolai. / Your sweater's on inside out. Nǐ bǎ máuyǐ chwān'fǎnle. / Turn the coat inside out. Bǎ 'yīshang 'fāngwolai.

INSIST. fēi 'shwō . . . (bu'kě), 'háishr shwō. / I insist that I know nothing about it. Wǒ haishr shwō wǒ wán'chywán bùjr'dàu. / He insists that you're wrong. Tā fēi 'shwō nǐ 'tswòle (bu'kě).

Insist on fēi yàu . . . (bu'kě), 'háishr yàu, yi'dìng yàu, 'jyānchŕ(je) yàu, (local Peiping) sz̀chǐbái'lyē(de) yàu, yǐ'sěr(de) yàu. / Why do you insist on going? Nǐ 'wèishémma °'fēi yàu (°etc.) 'chyù? / He insists on knowing more about it. Tā yǐ'sěrde yàu 'dwōjrdau dyǎr. / He insisted on paying. Tā yi'dìng yàu gěi 'chyán.

INSTANT. yìhwěr. / Don't wait an instant. 'Yìhwěr yě béng 'děng. / Let me know the instant he arrives. is expressed as When he arrives, please tell me immediately. Tā yí 'dàu de 'shŕhou, chǐng ni lì'kè 'gàusu wo.

In an instant, this instant (or other expressions meaning immediately) lìkè, 'gǎnjǐn, dāngshŕ, lìshŕ, mǎshàng. / He was ready in an instant. Tā lì'kè jyòu 'yùbei'hǎule. / Come this instant. is expressed as Come right now. 'Gǎnjǐn 'lái. or Syàn'dzài jyòu 'lái.

(Immediate). / The play had instant success. is expressed as The play was immediately successful. Jèichū 'syì lì'shŕ jyòu chū'míng le. / When the product was advertised, there was an instant demand for it. is expressed as When the product was advertised, people immediately wanted to buy it. Jèige 'dūngsyide gwǎng'gau yǐ 'dēngchūlái rén lì'kè jyòu yàu 'mǎi.

INSTEAD. (In the place of) tì (of someone); other indirect expressions. / He went instead of his brother. Tā tì tā 'gēge 'chyùde. / I was bawled out instead of him. Wǒ 'tì ta āile dwùn 'mà. / They decided to walk instead of ride. is expressed as They decided to walk, not ride. Tāmen jywé'dìng 'dzǒuje chyù, 'búdzwò 'chē. / Can I pay you later instead of now? is expressed as Is it all right to pay you later? Wǒ yǐ'hòu géi ni 'kéyi ma? or as Is it all right not to pay you right now? Wǒ jàn'shŕ syān 'bùgéi ni 'kéyi bù'kéyi?

(In its stead). / I don't want that; give me this instead. is expressed as I want this, not that. Wǒ yàu 'jèige, 'búyàu 'nèige. or as I don't want that; change it for this. Wǒ 'búyàu 'nèige le, hwàn 'jèige ba. / Would you like this instead? is expressed as Will this do then? Nèmma 'jèige 'syíng busyíng?

INSTRUMENT. 'yíchǐ; (tool) jyāhwo, 'yùngjyù, 'chǐjyù; (thing) dūngsyi. / The school bought lots of instruments for the chemistry lab. Sywésyàu mǎile hǎu'syē hwàsywé shŕyàn'shŕde yíchǐ. / That doctor used the latest surgical instruments. Nàwèi 'dàifu yùng dzwèi 'syīnshŕde 'wàikē °'yùngjyù (°'chǐjyù, °shŕde 'jyāhwo, °shŕde 'dūngsyi).

(Musical instrument) ywèchi; (know how to) **play an instrument** hwèi ywèchi, hwèi yǐnywè. / This store sells musical instruments. Jèige 'pùdz mài 'ywèchi. / Does anyone here play an instrument? Jèr yǒu 'rén hwèi °'ywèchi (°yǐn'ywè) ma?

(Means). / Money was the instrument by which he achieved his purpose. Tā bànchéngle nèi 'shèr °shr̀ yǐnwei tā kěn hwā'chyan (°dōu shr 'chyánde 'gūnglau).

INTEND. syǎng; (plan, but never viciously) 'dǎswàn. / What do you intend to do? Nǐ 'dǎswàn dzěmma 'yàng? or expressed as What plans do you have? Ní yǒu shémma 'jìhwa? / I didn't intend to hit him. Wǒ méichéng'syǐn syǎng 'dǎ ta. / He had intended to do harm to her. Tā 'syǎng 'bǎ ta gěi 'hàile láije. / I intended you to have it. Wǒ 'běnlái jyòu syǎng bǎ 'nèige 'géi ni. / Is this intended for me? is expressed as Is this mine? 'Jèi shr̀ 'wǒde ma?

INTEREST. (Share) fèr, gǔr. / Do you have an interest in the business? Jèige 'mǎimai lǐtou nǐ yǒu °'fèr (°'gǔr) ma?

(Legal claim) chywányí. / He hired a lawyer to protect his interest in the property. Tā 'chǐngle lyù'shr̄ lái bǎu'jàng tā dzài nèifèr 'chǎnyèlǐ de chywán'yí.

(Money return) 'lì(chyán), 'lìsyî. / How much interest does it pay? Gěi 'dwō-shau °'lìchyán (°'lìsyî)? / They pay 3% interest. Tāmen gěi 'sānfēn 'lì.

(Advantage) lìyi, hǎuchu (benefit). / He's only thinking of his own interests. Tā 'jr̀ shr̀ wèi tā 'dz̀jíde °hǎuchu (°lìyi) 'syǎng. / For your own interest, you ought to look into the matter. Wèi nǐ 'gèrén lìyi shè'syǎng, nǐ 'yīngdang 'chácha shr̀ 'dzěmma hwéi'shèr.

Be of interest (concern) syǎnggān, yǒu gwānsyi. / It's of no interest to me whether we win or lose. Shū'yíng gēn 'wǒ °bùsyǎng'gān (°méi 'gwānsyi). or expressed as Win or lose, I don't care. Shū'yíng wǒ búdzàihu.

Take an interest in (like) 'syǐhwān; (be enthusiastic about) dwèi . . . yǒu 'syǐng-chyu. / Do you take an interest in sports? Nǐ 'syǐhwan 'yùndung ma? or Nǐ 'dwèiyu 'yùndung yǒu 'syǐngchyu ma?

Interests (group) jyè. / The business interests in the city want a new bridge. Jèi 'chéngli de shāng'jyè 'chǐngchyóu 'dzàu yídzwò 'syǐn 'chyáu.

To interest someone. / That book didn't interest me at all. is expressed as I didn't think that book was interesting at all. Wǒ 'jywéde nèibēr 'shū 'yìdyǎr 'yìsz yě 'méiyou. / He tried to interest me in the property. is expressed as He wanted me to buy the property. Tā syǎng yàu wǒ 'mǎi °jèiswǒr 'fáng (°jèikwai 'dì).

Be interested in, same as **take an interest in** above. / I'm not interested in the problem. Wǒ dwèi nèige 'wèntí méiyǒu 'syǐngchyu. / Would you be interested in going to a movie? is expressed as Do you want to go to a movie? Nǐ °yàu (°syǎng) kàn dyàn'yǐng chyù ma? or as What do you say to going to a movie? Kàn dyàn'yǐngr chyù nǐ shwō 'dzěmma yàng? / Would you be interested in buying a second-hand car? is expressed as What about buying a second-hand car? Mǎi lyàng 'jyòu'chē dzěmma 'yàng?

INTO. jìn preceded by a verb of motion, as go or **walk into** dzǒujin (lai or chyu), **run into** pǎujin (lai or chyu), etc. / He went into the house. Tā dzǒujin 'wūdzli chyù le.

For special phrases as **get into trouble, break into pieces,** etc., see the other word.

INTRODUCE. (Introduce two people of about equal rank) jyèshau; (present someone to a superior) 'yǐnjyàn; or expressed as meet jyàn. / Have you two been introduced (to each other)? Yǒu 'rén 'gěi nǐmen 'jyèshaule ma? / Allow me to introduce you two. Wǒ lái gěi nǐmen 'jyèshau yísyàr. / Can you introduce me? Nǐ gěi wo 'yǐnjyanyǐn- jyan, syíng ma? / I'd like to introduce you to my father. Wǒ syǎng 'dài ni chyù 'jyànjyan wǒ 'fùchin.

(Propose) tíchulai. / Who introduced that law? Jèityáu fǎ'lyù 'shéi 'tíchulaide? / The bill has been introduced in Congress. Jèige fǎ'àn yǐjīng Gwó'hwèili 'tíchulaile.

(Start) is expressed as do something first kāi . . . fēngchi, tóuyige plus a verb. / She introduced the fashion of short hair for women. Nyǔrén jyan dwǎn tóufa de fēngchi shr̄ tā kāide. or Tā shr̄ tóuyige jyǎn dwǎn tóufa de 'nyǔrén.

(Present) chū, gěi; (present orally) shwōchulai. / He introduced a new problem for our consideration. Tā °'chūle (°'gěile, °'shwōchuláile) yíge'syīnde 'wèntí jyàu wǒmen 'syǎng.

INVENT. fāmíng. / Who invented this contraption? Jèige gwàiwán'yèr shr̄ 'shéi 'fāmíngde?

(Make up a story) dzōu, byān. / Did you invent that story? Nèige 'gùshr shr̄ 'nǐ 'dzōude ma?

INVITATION. (Written) chǐngtyě; (oral) is expressed indirectly. / I didn't receive your invitation. Wǒ méi'jyējáu nǐde chǐng'tyě. / Thanks for the invitation. is expressed as You're too kind, I'll certainly go. Nín tài 'kèchi le, wǒ yí'dìng dàu. or I'm sorry I can't go. Dwèibu'jù wǒ 'bùnéng 'dàu.

Be an invitation is expressed with chǐng request. / The applause was an in- vitation for him to sing another song. Dàjyā dōu pāi'shǒu 'chǐng ta dzài 'chàng yíge 'gēr.

INVITE. chǐng. / Who is invited for dinner tonight? Jyēr 'wǎnshang chr̄'fàn dōu yǒu 'shéi bèi 'chǐngle? / The speaker invited questions. Yǎn'jyǎngrde rén chǐng dà'jyā fā 'wèntí.

(Arouse) 'yǐnchǐ. / His painting invited a lot of criticism. Tāde 'hwàr 'yǐn- chile hěn 'dwōde 'pīping.

Invite trouble jǎu máfan. / You're just inviting trouble. Nǐ jēnshr jǎu 'máfan ne.

Look inviting ràng 'rén syǎng . . . (lit. move people's hearts). / The water looks very inviting. Jèige 'shwěi 'chyáuje hěn ràng 'rén syǎng 'syàchyu fù.

IRON. (Metal) tyě. / This stove is made of iron. Jèige 'lúdz shr̄ 'tyě dzwòde. / Go as far as the iron gate. Yǐjr̄ 'dzǒudàu tyě'mér nàr.

(Instrument for ironing clothes) làutye, yùndou; (specifically electric) dyàn- làutye. / Have you an iron I can borrow? Nǐ yǒu 'làutye méiyou, 'jyèwo 'yùngyung?

To iron tàng, làu, yùn. / Iron my dress carefully, please. Chǐng ni 'syǎusyīn yìdyǎr 'tàng wǒde 'yīfu. (fig.) / There are still a few problems to be ironed out. is expressed as There are still a few problems to be solved. Hái yǒu 'jǐge 'wèntí děi 'jyějywé yísyàr.

ISLAND. dǎu. / They swam out to the island. Tāmen 'fúdàu 'dǎu nèr chyùle.

ISSUE. (Publish) chū. / When was the paper issued? Jèige 'bàu shr̄ 'shémma shr̄hou 'chūde.

(Send out, distribute) fā. / A bulletin will be issued to each department in the university. Dà'sywéli měiyì'syì dōu 'fā yíge tūng'jr̄. / A new series of government bonds is being issued. Yìchì 'syínde 'jēngfugūng'jài gāng 'fāchūlai. / Our raincoats haven't been issued to us yet. Wǒmende yǔ'yì hái méi 'fāgěi women ne.

An issue (publication) chǐ (number, of a periodical); bǎn (edition or printing, of a newspaper, book, etc.). / The story was in the November issue. Nèige 'gùshr shr̄ dzài Shŕ'yīywè nèi'chǐli. / When does the next issue of the paper come out? Jèige 'bàude 'syàyì'bǎn 'shémma shŕhou 'chū?

(Problem, dispute) 'wèntí. / The issue is whether or not they'll be allowed to participate. 'Wèntí shr̄ 'syù busyǔ tamen chū'syí.

At issue. / What's the point at issue then? is expressed as What are you quarreling about then? 'Nèmma, nǐmen shr̄ 'wèi shémma 'chǎu ne? or as Then what are you arguing about? 'Nèmma, nǐmen 'jēngde shr̄ 'něiyì'dyǎn ne?

Make an issue of (raise a question about) 'jēngjŕ. / He insists on making an issue of the problem. 'Gwānyu nèige 'wèntí tā 'fēi yàu 'jēngjŕ yísyàr bù'kě. / I don't want to make an issue of it. Wǒ bú'ywànyi 'jēngjŕ 'něiyìdyǎn.

Take issue with (oppose) fǎndwèi. / Why do you always take issue with what I say? 'Wèishémma wǒ 'shwō shémma nǐ fǎn'dwèi shémma?

IT. (As a substitute for a noun) is not expressed when the noun is elsewhere in the sentence; when the noun is not in the sentence, it is usually not expressed but may be by using jèige or nèige plus the noun. / This suit is nice, but it costs too much. Jèityàu 'yīfu dàu bú'tswò, kěshr tài 'gwèi. / I don't like this book; it's too dull. Wǒ bù'syǐhwan jèiběr 'shū, tài 'gǎndzàu. / I like it. Wǒ 'syǐhwan. / Sell it. 'Mài le ba. / How long was the movie? It lasted two hours. Dyàn'yǐngr yǒu dwō 'cháng? °'Yǎnle (or (less natural) °Dyàn'yǐngr 'yǎnle, °Nèige dyàn'yǐngr 'yǎnle) yǒu 'lyǎ jūng'tóu. / Did the car work all right? No, it broke down. Chē 'dzòude 'hǎu ma? Bù'syíng, °bàn'dàur (°chē bàn'dàur, °nèige 'chē bàn'dàur) 'hwàile. / It's an hour late. (of a train, etc.) 'Wǎnle 'yíge jūng'tóu. / How's it going? Dzěmma'yàng?

(As a demonstrative) is expressed by jèi(ge) or nèi(ge); or is not expressed at all. / What is it? 'Nèi(ge) shr̄ 'shémma? or Shr̄ 'shémma? or Shémma? / Who is it? Nèi(ge) shr̄ 'shéi? or Shr̄ 'shéi? or Shéi? / I can't do it. Nèige gwǒ 'bànbulyǎu. or Wǒ 'bànbulyǎu.

(With the impersonal verb). / It's five o'clock. Shr̄ 'wǔdyǎn. or 'Wǔdyǎn le. / Is it raining? (Shr̄) syà'yǔ ne ma? / It's a beautiful day. Shr̄ ge 'hǎutyār. or 'Tyār jēn bú'tswò. / It snowed last night. Dzwór 'yèli syà'sywě le.

It is (or was) . . . which (or that or who) 'nèi jyòushr, shr̄. / It was that house that I saw yesterday. 'Nèi jyòushr wǒ 'dzwótyān 'chyáujyànde nèiswǒ 'fángdz. / It was a friend of mine who phoned. 'Shr̄ wǒ yíge 'péngyou 'dǎláide dyàn'hwà.

It is plus an adjective. / It's hard to get a ticket. is expressed as Getting a ticket isn't easy. 'Mǎijau 'pyàu kě jēn bù'rúngyi. / It's impossible to get there by tomorrow morning. is expressed as To get there by tomorrow morning is definitely impossible. Yàu 'syǎng míngr 'dzǎuchen jyòu 'dàu nèr 'gēnběn bùkě'néng. / Is it necessary for us to go? is expressed as Must we go? Dzámen 'fēiděi 'chyù ma?

Its (of children) tāde. / The baby's lost its rattle. Syǎu'hár bǎ ('tāde) hwā 'gǔr 'dyōule. In all other instances its is expressed as follows: If the noun for which its is a substitute is in the sentence, its is not expressed (unless the sentence is very long and there might be some ambiguity). If the noun is not in the sentence, its is either not expressed or is expressed by the noun plus de or (rarely) by tāde or 'dzjǐde (its own). / This city is famous for its parks. Jèige 'chéng yǐ gūng'ywán chū'míng. / The dog is chasing its tail. 'Gǒu dǎ'jwàr 'wár 'yǐba ne. / The dog led us to its master. Nèityáu 'gǒu bǎ wǒmen lǐngdàu tā 'jǔrén nàr chyù le. / I don't like its smell. (of a flower) Wǒ bù'syǐhwan nèige 'hwārde 'wèr. *or* Wǒ bù'syǐhwan nèige 'wèr.

JACK. (Tool) jyǔjùngjǐ, chǐjùngjǐ, chyānjin. / I need a jack to change my tire. Wǒ hwàn chē'dài děi 'yùng ge °jyǔjùng'jǐ (°chǐjùng'jǐ, °'chyānjin). *or* Gěi wǒ yíge jyǔjùng'jǐ hǎu 'hwàn chē'dài.

    To jack up (raise with a jack) bǎ . . . 'jrchilai. / You'll have to jack up the car. Nǐ děi bǎ 'chē 'jrchilai.

    Jack up prices wù'jyà tí'gāu; (without any reason) jyā'jyà méi 'dàuli. / At that time prices were jacked up. Nèitsz 'yǒude wù'jyà (jyàu tāmen) wú'gù tí'gāule. *or* Nèitsz 'yǒude 'dūngsyi jyā'jyà hěn méi 'dàuli.

JANUARY. (Modern calendar) 'Yīwè; (lunar calendar) 'Jēngywè.

JAR. (Container) gwàn, gwàr, gwàndz (usually a small jar); (specifically of glass) (bwōli) °píngr (°píngdz, °gwàr, °gwàndz). / I bought a jar of cherry preserves. Wǒ mǎile °yí'gwàr (°yì'píng) mǐ'jyànde 'yīngtau. / Those jars are for wine. Nèisyē 'tándz shr chéng 'jyǒude. / Pour the water in that jar. Bǎ 'shwěi dàudzai (shwěi) 'gāngli.

    To jar (jolt) jèn. / One jar and it will explode. Yí 'jèn jyou 'jà. / That drill jars my hand. Nèige 'dzwàn 'jèn wǒde 'shǒu. / That drill jarred out of my hand. Nèige 'dzwàn 'jènde wǒ nábu'jù le. / That drill jars on my nerves. is expressed as That drill jars so that my nerves can't stand it. Nèige 'dzwàn 'jènde wǒ 'syīnli shòubu'lyǎu.

    (Jolt up and down) dyān (at the end of a sentence dyānda); (jolt sideways) yáuhwang. / When you hold the bottle, be sure you don't jar it. Náje jèige 'píngdz de shŕhou, 'chyānwàn byé °'dyānda (°yáuhwang).

JEALOUS. 'jìdù, 'dùjì; (hate) hèn. / He is jealous. Tā ài °'jìdù (°'dùjì). / She is jealous of her husband's secretary. Tā 'jìdù tā 'jàngfude nyǔ 'shūjì. / They are jealous of him. Tāmen °'jìdù (°'hèn) tā. / His successes made them jealous. Tā tài dé'yì le jyàu 'tāmen yǒu dyǎr °'jìdù (°'hèn).

    Be jealous of (be watchful of) búfàngsūng (lit. not loosen). / Journalists must be jealous of their right of free speech. 'Syīnwénjyède rén dwèiyu 'yánlwùndz'yóu yì'dyǎr yě bùnéng fàng'sūng.

JELLY. (A food preparation) tángjyàng, gwǒdzjyàng. / I want bread and jelly. Wǒ yàu myàn'bāu 'gēn táng'jyàng.

    (Any jelly-like substance) dùngr. / It becomes a sort of jelly if you leave it in the icebox overnight. Dzài bīng'syāngli gē yí'yè jyòu chéngle 'dùngr le.

    Petroleum jelly fánshrlín'yóu.

    To jelly níng, níng (cheng) dùngr, chéng dùngr. / Wait until it has jellied, then put it away. Děng °'níngle (°níng(cheng) dùngr, °chéngle dùngr) dzài 'shōuchilai.

JEWEL. (Precious stone) bǎushŕ. / My watch has seventeen jewels. Wǒde 'byǎu yǒu shŕ'chīkwài bǎu'shŕ.

    (Ornaments) 'shǒushr; 'jēnjūbǎu'shŕ (pearls and other stones); 'jūbǎu'yùchì (pearls, jade and other stones); 'jēnbǎu, 'jūbǎu (jewelry and other precious things). / She has many jewels in that box. Tā nèige 'syádzli yǒu hěn 'dwō 'shǒushr. / I have no jewels worth declaring. Wǒ 'méiyou shémma jŕde 'bàu de °'shǒushr (°'jēnjūbǎu-'shŕ yíléide 'dūngsyi, °'jūbǎu'yùchǐ).

Jewelry (ornaments in general) shǒushr. / She wears a lot of jewelry. Tā 'dài hěn dwō 'shǒushr̀.

Jeweled syāng bǎu'shŕ de. / She has a beautiful pair of jeweled earrings. Tā yǒu yífù syāng bǎu'shŕ de ěr'jweidz, jēn hǎu'kàn.

JOB. (Piece of work) hwó (small; as repairing a car); gūng (any size); hwó and gūng both involve manual labor。 / That job took longer than I thought. Nèige °'hwó (°'gūng) syǎngbu'dàu yùng 'nèmma dwō shŕhou. / How many hands would this (large-scale) job require? Jèige 'gūng děi 'dwōshau rén 'dzwò?

(Permanent employment, or work that requires mental effort) shŕ. / He's looking for a job. Tā syǎng jǎu 'shŕ. / How many men does this job require? Jèijyàn 'shŕ yàu yùng 'dwōshau rén?

By the job 'bāugūng. / He is paid by the job. Tāde gūngchyán àn 'bāugūng swàn.

Do a good job hǎu'hǎurde 'dzwò, dzwòde hǎu'hǎurde; (if repairing) hǎu'hǎurde 'syōuli; (if washing) hǎu'hǎurde 'syǐ; etc. / They did a good job on my car. Wǒde 'chē tāmen °'syōulide (°'syǐde, °etc.) hěn 'hǎu.

Have the job of gwǎn (to be in charge of). / I have the job of washing the dishes. is expressed as I'm in charge of washing the dishes. Wǒ 'gwǎn syǐ 'wǎn.

JOIN. (Connect something) jyē; join hands lāshǒu. / Join these pipes together. Bǎ jèisyē 'gwǎn dz °'jyēshang (°jyēchilai). / Let's join hands. 'Lái, women lāje 'shǒu.

(Connect, come together) hé. / Where do the two roads join? is expressed as Where do the two roads meet and become one road? 'Lyǎngtyáu lù dzài 'nǎr 'héchéng 'yìtyáu?

Join a group 'jyārù, tsānjyā. / Do you want to join us? Nǐ yàu °'jyārù (°tsān-'jyā) ma? / He joined the Republican party several years ago. Tā °'jyārù (°tsān-'jyā) Gūnghédǎng yóu 'háujǐ nyán le.

Join the army 'jyārù jyūn'dwèi, dāngbīng, rùwǔ.

JOKE. syàuhwar. / He's always telling jokes. Tā lǎu shwō °'syàuhwar (°dòu'syàurde hwà).

Make a joke of something 'nùngchéng ge 'syàuhwar. / They made a joke of the whole thing. Tāmen jyàn'jŕ bǎ jèng'gèrde 'shŕ 'nùngchéngle ge 'syàuhwar le.

Play a joke nàuje 'wár, kāi ge 'wánsyàu. / I was only playing a joke on you. Wǒ 'búgwo shŕ gēn ni °nàuje 'wár láije (°kāi ge 'wánsyàu).

To joke shwō syàuhwar. / This is no time to joke. Jè 'búshŕ shwō 'syàuhwar de shŕhou a!

Joking matter nàuje wárde, shwōje wárde. / This is no joking matter. Jèi 'búshŕ °nàuje wárde (°shwōje 'wárde, °kāi wánsyàu de shŕ).

JOURNEY. lù; or expressed verbally with dàu arrive or dzǒu travel. / It's a three-day journey. Shŕ 'sāntyānde 'lù. or Děi dzǒu 'sāntyān tsái 'dàu. / Is it more than a day's journey? 'Yìtyān 'dàude'lyǎu ma? or 'Yìtyān néng 'dàu ma? / It is more than a day's journey. 'Yìtyān 'dàubu'lyǎu. or Děi dzǒu 'yìtyān 'dwō.

To journey lyǔsyíng. / They journeyed all the way to the east coast. Tāmen yì'jŕ lyǔ'syíngdàu 'dūngàn.

JOY. gāusyỉng, kwàile. / On hearing the news, she was filled with joy. 'Tīngjyan jèige 'syāusyi tā mǎn'syīn gāu'syỉng. / You could see the joy on their faces. Nǐ kàndechuláí tāmen měige rén dōu dàije yỉ'lyǎn °gāu'syỉng (°gāusyỉngde yàngdz). / Going to school is no joy. Shàng'sywé 'méi shemma °kwài'lè (°kěgāusyỉngde). *but* / I wish you joy in your marriage. 'Dàusyǐ, dàusyǐ.

Be a joy to jēn yǒuyỉsz, shř yíge lèdz, shr yỉlè'yě. / She is a joy to watch. Kànje 'tā shř yíge lèdz. / The book is a joy to read. Kàn jèibér shū shr yỉlè'yě. / He's a joy to be with. Gēn tā dzài yỉ'kwàr 'jēn yǒu 'yỉsz. / They're a joy to know. Rénshr tāmen 'jēn yǒu 'yỉsz.

JUDGE. (In a law court) 'fǎgwān (general, comprehensive term, indicating any law official); 'twēishř (any official who conducts trials and passes judgment); shěnpàngwān (one of three or more judges, each of whom is a 'twēishř, presiding over a serious case); shěnpàn jǎng (the chief judge of such a trial); ywànjǎng (chief justice of an established court-district, high or circuit, or supreme); tíngjǎng (head of one of the divisions, civil or criminal, of one of the established courts). / He is a judge. Tā shř ge 'fǎgwān. / Where is the judge? 'Twēishř dzài nǎr? *or* Ywàn-'jǎng dzài nǎr? *or* Tíng'jǎng dzài nǎr? / He is a judge in the circuit court. Tā shř 'gāudēng fǎ'ywàn de 'twēishř. / He is the (chief) district court judge. Tā shř 'dìfang fǎ'ywàn ywàn'jǎng. / Is the head of the civil court going to serve as the chief judge in this case? 'Jèige àndz shř bushř yóu ('mínshř fǎ'tíng) tíng'jǎng dzwò shěnpàn'jǎng? / The three judges agreed to postpone the trial of this case. 'Sānwèi °'twēishř (°'shěn-pàn'gwān) yỉ'jywé běn'àn 'yánchí dzài 'shěn. / The judge asked the prosecutor to repeat. °'Twēishř (°'Shěnpàngwān) chǐng 'jyǎnchágwān 'dzài shwō yíbyàn.

(In a contest) 'tsáipànywán, 'píngpànywán, 'gūngjèngrén. / The judges picked that bulldog as the winner in the show. °Tsáipànywán (°'Píngpànywán, °'Gūngjèngrén) 'pàndǐng nèige 'lǎuhǔgǒu °dì'yī (°dé 'tóujyǎng).

To judge (*or* Be a judge of) kàn, 'kànchū . . . lai; (judge by appearance) syàng; (make a final judgment about) 'pàndwàn; (judge critically) 'pīpíng; (understand) dǔng; and a few special expressions in certain cases. / He is a good judge of men. Tā kàn 'rén kànde hén 'jwǔn. *or* Tā néng 'kànchū rénde 'pǐn gé lai. or is expressed as He has a talent for knowing people. Tā yǒu 'jř rénjr'míng. (by facial physiognomy) Tā hwèi syàng 'myàn. / Don't judge him by that alone. Byé 'gwāng ànje nèi 'yíjyàn shř láí °'pàndwàn (°'kàn) tā. / Don't judge people too harshly. 'Pīpíng rén 'bùyīng-gāi tài 'kè le. / Don't judge people only by appearance. 'Kàn rén 'bùnéng 'gwāng kàn 'wàibyǎu. *or* (accept) Búyàu yỉ'màuchyǔ'rén. / He is a good judge of horses. *or* He can judge horses. Tā kàn 'mǎ kànde hén 'jwǔn. *or* Tā 'chángyú syàng 'mǎ. / I'm no judge of art. Wǒ 'búpèi 'pīpíng 'měishù. *or* Dwèiyú 'měishù wǒ shř 'wàiháng. / He is a good judge of art. Tā hén 'dǔngde 'měishù. *or* Tā 'dwèiyú 'měishù hén 'nèiháng. or expressed as He specializes in art. Tā 'jwānmén yánjyou 'měishù.

Judge (*or* Be the judge of) (decide about) 'jywédìng, kàn(chulai), dǐng, shwō, píng, dwàn, 'pàndwàn. / You be the judge of that. Nèige nǐ 'dzjǐ °lái (°chyù) 'jywédìng ba. / You'll have to judge it for yourself. Nǐ děi 'dzjǐ chyù °'kàn (°'jywé-dìng). / Can you judge who is right (and who is wrong)? Nǐ néng °'shwō (°'dǐng, °'jywédìng, °'píng yipíng, °'dwàn yidwàn, °'kànchulai, °'pàndwàn) shéi 'dwèi shéi 'tswò ma?

JUDGMENT. kànde; (in a particular case) 'kànfǎ; or expressed verbally by kàn *or* chyáu. / He always shows good judgment. Tā kànde hén 'jwǔn. *or* (of events) Tā kàn 'shř kànde hén 'jwǔn. *or* (of persons) Tā kàn 'rén kànde hén 'jwǔn. / The judgment he made was not very sound. Tāde 'kànfǎ búdà 'gāumíng. / In my judgment, you're doing the wrong thing. °Jyù 'wǒ kàn (°Jyù 'wǒ chyáu, °Yǐ 'wǒ kàn, °Yǐ 'wǒ chyáu, °Jàu wǒde 'kànfǎ), nǐ jège 'shr̀ °dzwòde bú'dwèi (°dzwò'tswòle).

(In court) pàn jywé, pànjywé shū. / How large was the judgment against you? Pànjywéshūshang shwō nǐ děi péi 'dwōshǎu chyán? or 'Fǎtíng jyàu nǐ péi 'dwōshǎu chyán?

Pass judgment syà 'dwànyǔ. / Don't pass judgment too quickly. Syà 'dwàn'yǔ °'búyàu tài kwài le (°yàu 'jēnjwo'jēnjwo).

JUICE. jr̄dz, jēr, jyāng, shwěi; (liquid, secretion) yè. / He is preparing some orange juice for us. Tā 'jēngdzai nèr gěi dzámen °'dzwò (°'jǐ, °'yà) °jyúdz'jēr (°jyúdz-'shwěi) ne. / Just squeeze it with your fingers and the juice will come out. Yǐ 'nyē, °'jr̄dz (°jēr, °shwěi) jyou chūlaile. / They take the juice from sugar cane and sell it to sugar manufacturers. Tāmen tsúng 'gānjē 'yàchu táng'jyāng lai màigei dzwò-'tángde. / Gastric juice contains acid. Wèi'yèli yǒu 'swān.

JULY. Chīywe. / July Fourth is the national birthday of the United States. 'Chīywe 'szhàu shr̀ 'Měigwode gwóchíng'r̀. / "Chīchī" is the shortened form of July Seventh in Chinese, on which day in 1937 the Sino-Japanese War began. "'Chīchī" jyòu shr 'Chīywè chīhàude 'jyǎnchēng; dzài 'yǐjyǒusān'chī nyánde 'nèityān 'Jūngr Jànshr̀ kāi-'shr̀de.

JUMP. <u>Chinese distinguishes three types of jumping; tyàu and (local Peiping) bèng refer to jumping or leaping in general, including jumping up and down and jumping involuntarily as when frightened; tswàn or (more colloquial pronunciation) tswan refer to jumping for a particular purpose, or jumping to reach an object or get to a place; pū refers to jumping more or less horizontally in order to grasp something, often</u> **jump at.** / He jumped onto the table. Tā 'tyàudàu 'jwōrshang chyule. / The tiger jumped at the deer. Láu'hǔ chùngje 'lù 'pūgwochyu. / Jump down. 'Tyàusyalai. or 'Tyàusya-chyu. (depending on where the speaker is). / The child jumped up and down with joy. Syǎuhár 'lède jr̀ °'tyàu (°'bèng). / The man jumped up and down with rage. Nèige rén 'chìde lwàn °'tyàu (°'bèng). / Jump! (for safety) 'Tyàu! (not bèng, tswan, or pū.) / See how high you can jump. °'Kàn (°'Chyáu) nǐ néng °tyàu (°bèng, °tswān) 'dwō gāu. / Jump over it. 'Tyàugwochyu. or 'Bènggwochyu. or 'Tswāngwochyu. (or lai instead of chyu). / Jump your horse over the fence. Jyàu nǐde 'mǎ tyàugwo nèige 'lan gān chyu. / He can jump up and reach the ceiling. Tā °yí'tyàu (°yí'tswàn) kéyǐ gòujau fáng'dǐngdz. / He jumped out the window. Tā tsúng 'chwānghu 'tyàuchu-chyule. / The girl is so short that she has to jump up to hang up her coat. Syǎu'gūn-yang tswóde děi 'tswānchilai tsái néng bǎ 'yīfu 'gwàshang. / You made me jump. Nǐ bǎ wǒ 'syàle yí'tyàu. or Nǐ 'syàle wǒ yí'tyàu. but / Suddenly he jumped up from his chair. Tā 'húrán tsúng 'yǐdzshang 'jànchilaile.

Jump at <u>an offer</u> (chance, etc.) °lì'kè (°'chyǎngje) jyòu 'dáyìngle. / He jumped at the offer. Tā °lì'kè (°'chyǎngje) jyòu 'dáyìngle.

A jump (distance). / It's quite a jump from one side of the brook to the other. <u>is expressed as</u> From this side of the brook to that side is not near. Tsúng hé 'jèibyar dàu hé 'nèibyar bú'jìn. / It's quite a jump from the main topic. <u>is expressed as</u> It's quite far from the main topic. Shwōde lí 'běntí tài 'ywǎn le. / He reached the door in one jump. <u>is expressed as</u> When he jumped he jumped to the door. Tā °yí'tswàn (°yí'tyàu, °yí'pū) jyòu °'tswāndàu (°'tyàudàu, °'pūdàu) 'mén nar le.

(Sudden rise). / There's been quite a jump in the temperature. 'Tyānchì 'húrán 're le. or 'Wēndù 'húrán °'gāu le (°'jǎngle).

Broad jump tyàuywǎn, tyàuywǎr.

High jump tyàugāu(r).

JUNE. Lyòuywe.

JUST. (Fair) 'gūngpíng, 'gūngjèng, 'jèngjŕ (of a person); 'gūngpíng, 'gūngdàu, dwèi (of decisions, judgments, or opinions). /Even his enemies admit he's a just man. Lyán tāde 'chóurén dōu chéngrèn tā jèige rén hěn °'gūngpíng (°'gūngjèn, °'jèngjŕ). /His decisions are always just. Tā 'pànde (°'dwànde, °'dìngde) shŕchíng dōu hěn °'gūngpíng (°'gūngdàu, °'dwèi).

(Deserved, particularly of punishment) gāi (nèmma 'fá), (nèmma 'fá hěn) 'dwèi, (nèmma 'dǎ hěn) 'dwèi; and other expressions meaning that punishment is right, that punishment is deserved, etc. /His punishment was just. Nèmma 'fá tā hěn 'dwèi. or Tā 'gāi nèmma 'fá. or Tā ('yīng)gāi shòu 'jèmmayàngde °'chéngfá (°'syíngfá).

(Accurate; fair) 'jwǔnchywè. /He gave a just account of what happened at the meeting. Tā bǎ nèitsz̀ kāi'hwèi de 'chíngsyíng 'bàugàude hěn 'jwǔnchywè.

(Legitimate, of claims, rights, reasons, etc.) (hěn) yǒulǐ, 'búshr méi'lǐ. We felt that he had a just claim to this piece of land. Wǒmen 'jywéje tā yàu jèikwài 'dì (yàude) °hěn yǒu'lǐ (°'búshr méi'lǐ).

(Exactly) jèng, dàudǐ, 'jyōujǐng, or occasionally jyòu. /Just what do you mean? Nǐ °dàu'dǐ (°'jyōujǐng) shr 'shémma yìsz? /Just how much do you want? Nǐ °dàu'dǐ (°'jyōujǐng) (shr) yàu 'dwōshǎu? /Just who do you think you are? Nǐ 'jywéje nǐ 'jyōujǐng shr lǎu'jǐ a? /That's just what I want. Nèige 'jèng shr wǒ 'yàude. /That's just the one I had in mind. Nèi jèng shr wǒ 'syīnli 'syǎng de nèige. /Just so! 'Jèng dwèi! /Just right! 'Jèng dwèi! or 'Jèng shr̀! /He must have everything just right. Tā yí'dìng yàu shémma shr̀ dōu shr̀ °'jèng 'hǎu (°'jèng dwèi tāde syīnsz). /You must do it just right or you'll spoil everything. Nǐ děi 'dzwòde °'jèng 'dwèi (°'yìdyǎr yě 'bú'chà) bùrán jyou 'chywán 'hwěi le. /That's just the trouble. 'Nánchù 'jèng dzài jèige 'dìfang. or Jèi 'jèng shr̀ jyàu rén wéi'nánde dìfang. /That's just the way it should have been done (but wasn't). Yàushr 'nèmmaje, jyou 'dwèi le. /Just that much will be enough. meaning exactly that much 'Jyòu nèmma 'syē jyòu 'gòu le.

(But a moment ago) gāng, tsái; **just a while ago** 'gāngtsái. /He won't know; he just came in. 'Tā búhwèi 'jŕdau; tā °'gāng (°'tsái) 'jìnlai. /They had just arrived here. Tāmen °'gāng (°'tsái) dàude. /Did you just come? (friendly question) 'Gāng lái a? or 'Tsái lái a? or (simple question, emphasizing just) Nǐ 'shr̀ bushr 'gāng lái? or Nǐ 'shr̀ bushr 'tsái lái? or (with surprise, sarcasm, or impatience) Nǐ 'tsái 'lái a? /He was here just a while ago. Tā 'gāng(tsái) 'dzài jèr laije. /You just said so yourself. Nǐ 'dz̀jǐ 'gāng nèmma 'shwō laije.

(By a small margin, barely) gāng, jǐjihū, chà'dyǎr jyou. /He just barely made the train. Hwǒ'chē tā 'gānggāng 'gǎnshang. /He just missed the train. Hwǒ-'chē, tā 'gānggāng 'méinéng 'gǎnshang. or Hwǒ'chē, tā 'jǐjihū 'gǎnshang. or (almost made it) Hwǒ'chē, tā chà'dyǎr jyòu 'gǎnshangle. /The bullet just missed him. Chyāng'dzěr 'gānggāng méi'dǎjau tā. or Chyāng'dzěr °chà'dyǎr jyòu (°'jǐjihū) 'dǎjau tā. /That's just enough for the three of us. (barely enough) Nèige dzámen 'sā 'gāng gòu.

(Only, nothing more than) búgwò (just and nothing but); 'jŕ(shr̀), gwāng, 'jŕyú (just and nothing further). /He's just a little boy. Tā 'búgwò shr̀ ge 'háidz. /He's just acting (or pretending). Tā nà shr̀ jwāng'swàn. /He's just trying to be smart. Tā nà búgwò shr̀ yàu 'syànnung syánnung. /He's just a crackpot. Tā 'búgwò shr̀ ge bàn'fēngr. /He just shook his head and said nothing. Tā 'gwāng (°'jŕyú, °'jŕshr) yáule yáu 'tóu, méi 'shwō shémma. /He just said that word and everyone understood what he meant. Tā °'gwāng (°'jŕshr, °'jŕ) shwōle nèi yíge 'dzèr, kěshr 'rénren dōu jŕdau tā shr̀ shémma 'yìsz.

JUSTICE

(Simply) jyòu, jyòushr. /I just won't let you do it. Wǒ 'jyòushr bú'jyàu nǐ 'nèmmaje. /I just don't understand! Wǒ 'jyòushr bù'dǔng ma! /Just a little bit! That's enough! 'Jyòu nèmma yǐ'dyǎr. 'Gòu la! *but* /Just a little lower! Hold it! (still a little lower) Dzài 'dǐ nèmma yǐ'dyǎndyǎr! Syíng la! /In that case, let's just pretend that we don't know who he is (and let it go at that). 'Nèmmaje ne dzámen jyòu 'jwāng bù'jřdàu tā shř 'shéi, hǎu le.

(Simply; used primarily for emphasis) 'jyǎnjŕ, jyǎnjŕ; kě (used especially in asking for something). /I'm just tired to death! Wǒ kě 'lèiszle! *or* Wǒ 'jyǎnjŕ 'lèiszle! /Just let me go there once! Kě 'jyàu wǒ 'chyù yihwéi ba. /I just don't understand. Wǒ jyǎn'jŕ bù'dǔng. /He's just a crackpot. (emphatic, with the implication that he should therefore be avoided) Tā 'jyǎnjŕ shř ge bàn'fēngr. *but* /Just you wait (and see)! Nǐ 'děngje 'chyáu ba.

Just, just as, just when (at that moment) 'jèngdzai . . . de shŕhou, 'gāng (yī), gāng, 'gānghǎu, 'gāngchyǎu. /Just as I was opening the door I heard a shot. 'Jèng-dzài wǒ kāi'mén de shŕhou, wǒ tīngjyàn 'pángde yǐ'chyāng. /Just as she was stipping into the bathtub the doorbell rang. Tā gāng 'màijìn 'dzàupénchyu, mén'lyéngr jyòu syǎngle. /He was just leaving when you came. Nǐ 'jìnlai de shŕhou, tā 'gāng dzǒu. /You were just coming in when he left. Tā 'dzǒu de shŕhou, nǐ 'gāng jìnlai.

Just about (almost) 'chàbudwō; *see* **ALMOST**.

Just as, just like (exactly as) jēn, jyǎnjŕ. (Either of these may be followed by syàng resembling, like; jyǎnjŕ is often followed by gēn . . . yǐ'yàng *or* 'jyòu shr . . . yǐ'yàng the same as.) /It turned out just as I told you. 'Jēn jyòu syàng wǒ 'gàusu nǐ de nèi'yàngr. /It was just like a dream. °'Jēn (°Jyǎnjŕ) syàng dzwò (le yíge) 'mèng shŕde. /It's just like spring. °'Jēn (°Jyǎn 'jŕ) syàng 'chwūntyān (shŕde). *or* Jyǎn'jŕ °jyòushr (°gēn) 'chwūntyān yǐ'yàng. /He walks just like his father. Tā 'dzǒulù °jēn (°jyǎn'jŕ) syàng tā 'dyē shŕde. *or* Tā 'dzǒulù jyǎn'jŕ °gēn (°'jyòu shr) tā 'dyē yǐ'yàng. *but* /I'm just as tall as you are. Wǒ gēn 'nǐ yǐ'bān 'gāu. *or* Wǒ 'bìng bù bǐ nǐ 'ǎi. /Do just as much as you can. 'Néng dzwò 'dwōshau, jyòu dzwò 'dwōshau.

If . . . just 'jřyàu (if only); *or* yàushr followed by some other expression for only. /If he would just say it, I would give him the money. Jřyau tā yǐ kāi'kǒu, wǒ jyou bǎ chyán gěi ta. /If he'd said just one more word, I'd have let him have it. Tā 'yàushr dzài shwō 'yíge dzèr, wǒ jyou bùnéng 'ráu ta le.

JUSTICE. (Fairness) is expressed by verb phrases; see **JUST** for various meanings and terms. /Don't expect justice from him. is expressed as Don't expect him to be just. Nǐ byé 'wàngsyǎng tā hwèi 'gūngpíng. /We must admit the justice of his demands. is expressed as We must admit that his demands are just. Wǒmen 'bùnéng bù'chéng-rèn tā 'yāuchyóu de yǒu'lǐ.

(A judge) fǎgwān tsáipàngwān.

Be brought to justice. /He will be brought to justice for his crimes. (general) Tā 'wéifēidzwòdǎide yí'dìng bùdé hǎu bàu. *or* Tā yí'dìng yǒu 'ègwànmǎn'yíngde yì'tyān. *or* (legal only) Tā fànle jèisyē 'dzwèi yídìng 'nán táu fǎ'wǎng. /He was brought to justice. Tā bèi sùngdau fǎywàn chyu le. *or* Tā fànle àn le.

Do justice to. /This work certainly doesn't do justice to your abilities. Jàu 'nǐde 'nénggàn lái shwō, dzwò 'jèiyàngde shř 'shŕdzài shř °'wěichyū le (°'dàtsái syǎu'yùng le, °chyū'tsái le, °'dǐjyóu le). *or* Nín dzwò 'jèiyàngde shř 'shŕdzài shř °'wěichyū le (°etc.). /Are you doing justice to his talents? Nǐ 'yùng tā yùngde dé-'dàng ma? *or* Jàu tāde 'tsáigàn lái shwō, nǐ 'shř bushr yǒu dyǎr 'wěichyu tā? /You're not doing justice to his talents. Nǐ 'dài tā 'wěimyǎn 'dàtsái syǎu'yùng le.

663

KEEP (KEPT). (Remain in good condition) is expressed as still be good hái hǎu'hāurde; or as still be edible hái néng chr̄; or as still be drinkable hái néng hē; or by a negative word with hwài be spoiled or swān be sour; or by resultative compounds with lyóu (keep in the sense of retain; see below) such as lyóubùjyǒu not (be able to) keep for long, lyóubujù or 'lyóudedàu (be able to) keep until. / Did the milk keep all right? Nyóu'nǎi hái hǎu'hāurde ma? or 'Nǎidz hái néng 'hē ma? or 'Nǎi méihwài ma? or Nyóu'nǎi méi'swān ma? / This milk won't keep until tomorrow. Jèige nyóu'nǎi 'lyóubudàu 'míngtyan (jyou hwài) le. / Meat won't keep for more than a week without refrigeration. Ròu bufàngdzai bǐng'syāngli, °lyóubújù (°jyou hwài le). but / The story will keep. Nei shèr yǐ'hòu dzài 'shwō.

(Retain in one's possession, save) lyóu (preserve); shōu (put away); tswún (keep on hand for future use, keep in stock, etc.). / I kept this book for you. 'Jèibén shū °wǒ géi ni 'lyóuje ne (°shr wǒ géi ni 'lyóuje de). / Let's keep this candy and eat it later. 'Jèi táng °'shōuchilai (°'shōuje, °'lyóuchilai, °'lyóuje, °'tswúnchilai, °'tswúnje) yǐ'hòu dzài chr̄ ba. / We kept the champagne for her wedding. Wǒmen bǎ 'syāngbīnjyǒu °'shōuje (°'lyóuje, °'tswúnje) děng tā jyé'hwūn de shŕhou dzài 'hē. / What do you keep in stock? Nǐ dōu tswúnle shémma hwò le? or expressed as What is all your stock? Nǐ dōu yǒu 'shémma 'tswúnhwò? / Do you want to keep this? 'Jèige nǐ syǎng °'shōuje (°'lyóuje, °'tswúnje) ma? / May I keep this picture? 'Jèijāng syàng'pyār wǒ 'lyóusya, syíng ma? or expressed as I want this picture, O.K.? 'Jèijāng syàng'pyār 'wǒ yàule, syíng ma? or as Let this picture be mine, O.K.? 'Jèijāng syàng'pyār swān 'wǒde le, syíng ma? / Do you keep (have) soap? Yǒu 'yídz ma? / Where do you keep (put) your stamps? Nǐde yóu'pyàu °gē (°fàng, °shōu) 'nǎr le? / I can't keep a fountain pen two weeks. is expressed as If I have a fountain pen, in two weeks it's lost. Wǒ 'yǒule dzláishwěi'bǐ, dàubùlyǎu lyǎ lǐ'bài jyou děi 'dyōu.

(Raise, tend) yǎng; (of a garden) jùng. / Do you keep chickens? Nǐ yǎng 'jī ma? / They keep chickens, draft animals, and bees. Tāmen yǎng 'jī, yǎng shēng-kou, hái yǎng 'mìfēngr. / Why don't you keep a garden? Nǐ wèi shémma bújùng 'ywándz ne?

(Detain a person) bǎ . . . 'dānwù, bǎ . . . 'lyóu, jyàu . . . dzài . . . 'dāi, jyàu . . . bùnéng 'lái. / I'm sorry to be late; the dentist kept me longer than I expected. 'Dwèibujù, 'láide 'wǎn le; wǒ méisyǎng'dàu yá'yīshēng °bǎ wǒ 'dānwule (°bǎ wǒ 'lyóule, °jyàu wǒ dzài nàr 'dāile) 'nèmma dà bàn'tyān. / What's keeping him? Tā yòu shémma 'shèr jyàu tā 'bùnéng 'lái ne? / What kept you? is expressed as What were you doing? Nǐ dzwò'shémma láije?

(Observe) shōu. / They keep all the Christian holidays. 'Swóyǒude Jīdūjyàu 'jyéchi tāmen 'dōu shōu. / If you keep the law, you ought to stay out of trouble. Nǐ yàushr °shóu'fǎ (or, not violate the law °'byé fàn'fǎ), dàgài jyou 'bújŕyu 'jāudzàrrě'hwòde le.

(Continue doing something or being a certain way) is expressed usually by constructions with lǎu (always), yìjŕ, búdwànde, yì'jŕbú'dwànde (continually), or jyēje (continue) before a verb of action, je following a verb of action or a negative word with a verb of opposite meaning. / Keep cool. (physically) Lǎu dzài 'lyángkwài dìfang dāije. or (mentally) is expressed as Keep your head. Byé 'hwāng. or 'Jènjìngje. or 'Wěnjùle 'syīn. (See also keep one's temper below.) / Keep cool, don't let them make you nervous. 'Wěnjùle 'syīn, byé jyàu tāmen bǎ nǐ °rě'jí le (°nùng'húdu le). / They built a fire to keep warm. Tāmen shēngle ge 'hwǒ hǎu °nwǎnhwo dyǎr (or, in order not to feel cold °'bújŕyu 'dùngdehwang). / Keep quiet. is expressed as Don't speak. 'Byé shwō 'hwà. or as Don't make any racket. Byé 'chǎu. or Byé 'nàu. or Byé 'rāngrang. or as Don't make a sound. 'Byé chū'shēngr.

or as Stop talking. Byé 'shwō le. or as Stop the racket. Byé 'nàu le. or Byé 'chǎu le. or Byé 'rāngrang le. /He keeps bothering me. Tā °lǎu (°bú'dwànde) 'máfan wǒ. /We kept telling her you'd come. Wǒmen yì'jrbú'dwànde 'gàusu tā shwō nǐ hwèi 'láide. / The policeman told us to keep moving. 'Jǐngchá jyàu wǒmen °byé 'jànju (°'dzǒuje dyǎr). /Keep trying. is expressed as Don't stop. Byé dǎ'jù. or 'Búyàu 'tíng. or Byé 'tíngju. or as Don't lose heart。 Byé hwēi'syīn. or as Continue working. 'Jyēje 'gànsyachyu. or as Continue calling. Jyēje 'jyàusyachyu. or as Continue searching. Jyēje 'jàusyachyu.

(Continue to have someone or something a certain way) is expressed with jyàu before someone, or bǎ before something. /Sorry to keep you waiting。 'Dwèibujù, jyàu nǐ 'děngle bàn'tyān. / This will keep him amused for a while. Jèi jyou kéyi jyàu tā °'wár (°'lǎushr) hwěr le. or Jèi jyou kéyi gòu tā 'wár hwěr de le。 /Keep him busy. Byé jyàu tā 'syánje. or 'Jyàu ta 'lǎu yǒu 'shèr dzwò. or (distract his attention) 'Jyàu tā 'mángbugwolái. or 'Jyàu tā 'mángde 'gù bugwolái. /Keep dinner warm for me. Byé bǎ 'fàn gěi wǒ nùng'lyángle.

Keep a diary jì rjì. /Do you keep a diary? Nǐ jì r'jì ma?

Keep a job. /He kept the same job for the last ten years. is expressed as He has done his job straight through for ten years. Tāde 'shèr yì'jr dzwòle 'shrnyán le. or as He has done that one job for ten years. Tā dzwò nèi 'yíge shèr dzwòle 'shrnyán le. /He can't keep a job. Tā dzwò 'shèr dàibu °'jù (°'jyou). or expressed as He can't work long. Tā dzwò 'shèr dzwòbu °'cháng (°'jyou).

Keep a promise or **keep one's word.** /You kept your promise. (congratulations) Nǐ jēn shr yánéryǒu'syīn na. /He always keeps his promise. Tā 'yánéryǒu'syīn. or Tā 'dàyingde jyou 'yídìng gěi °bàn'dàu le (°bànde'dàu). or Tā lǎu shr shǒu-'syīnde. or 'Tāde hwà 'kàude'jù. /I always keep my word. Wǒ 'shwōle jyou 'swàn.

Keep a secret. /Can you keep a secret? Nǐ néng 'shǒu mì'mì ma?

Keep accounts jìjàng. /Can you keep accounts? Nǐ hwèi jì'jàng ma?

Keep one's balance or **keep one's footing** (be able to stand firmly) jàndewěn; (be able to place the foot firmly) wěndejù 'jyǎu(bùr). /It's very hard to keep your balance on that tiny spot. 'Nèmma syǎude yíkwài 'dìfangshang 'jànje hěn nán °jànde-'wěn (°wěndejù 'jyǎu(bùr)). / The road was so slippery that I couldn't keep my footing, and I kept falling down. Lù tài 'hwá le, wǒ lǎu 'wěnbujù jyǎu'bùr, yì'jr shwāi 'gēndou.

Keep good time (of a timepiece) dzǒude jwǔn. /Does your watch keep good time? Nǐde 'byǎu dzǒude 'jwǔn ma?

Keep house (manage a house) gwǎnjyā; (take care of the housework) 'jàuying 'jyālide 'shèr; **keep house by** oneself (live by oneself) 'dzìjǐ gwò. /Who's keeping house for them? 'Shéi gěi tāmen gwǎn'jyā ne? or 'Shéi gěi tāmen 'jàuying 'jyālide 'shèr ne? / They're going to keep house by themselves. Tāmen yàu 'dzìjǐ gwò le.

Keep one's looks. /She's certainly kept her good looks all these years. Tā 'jēn hwèi 'báuyǎng, 'dzèmmasyé nyán le 'hái nèmma °'měi (°hǎu'kàn)。

Keep one's temper bùshēngchì, bùfā'píchi, rénsyachyu, rěnje, 'rěn yísyar, 'rěnjùle 'chì. /Keep your temper. 'Byé shēng'chì. or 'Byé fā 'píchi. or 'Rénsyachyu ba. etc.

Keep the change. /You may keep the change. is expressed as Don't bother bringing change. °Béng (°'Búyùng) jǎu'chyán le. or as That's for you. Nèige gěi 'nǐ le. or as That's yours. Nèige shr 'nǐde le. or as Keep that. Nèige nǐ 'lyóusya ba。

Keep time (of a timepiece) dzǒude jwǔn.

KEEP

Keep time (mark time with a beat) dǎ 'pāidz; **keep time to music** gēnje 'yīnywè dǎ 'pāidz; **keep time to a drumbeat** gēnje gǔ'dyǎr dǎ 'pāidz *or* (perfectly marking accented and unaccented beats) pāidade 'yóubǎnyǒu'yǎnde. /He kept time to the music with his fingers. Tā gēnje 'yīnywè yùng shǒu'jr̄tou dǎ 'pāidz.

Keep track of. /He changes jobs so often we have a hard time keeping track of him. Tā 'sāntyanlyǎng'tóurde hwàn 'shèr, wǒmen 'jyǎnjr̄ °gēnbu'shàng tā le (°bù-jr̄dàu tā 'shémma shŕhou 'dzài nǎr le).

Keep watch shǒu, kān. /I kept watch through the night. Wǒ 'shǒule yí'yè. *or* (in my turn) Shǒu'yè shr̀ wǒ jŕde bān. /I'll keep watch. 'Wǒ shǒuje. *or* 'Wǒ kānje. /You keep watch over the patient tonight. Jyēr 'yèli 'nǐ °shǒuje (°kānje) 'bǐngrén ba.

Keep at. /Keep at it. Byé dǎ'jù. *or* Jyēje 'gànsyachyu. *or* Dzài'jyēdzài'lǐ. /We kept at her until she told us. Wǒmen °bù'tíngde (°bú'jùde, °bú'dwànde) wèn tā yī'jŕ dàu tā 'shwōchulaile. *or* Wǒmen 'jyēgwǒ 'bǐde tā 'shwōchūlaile.

Keep someone away. /If the food is good you can't keep him away. 'Tsài yàushr hǎu'chr̄, nǐ 'hūng tā tā yě bù'dzǒu. /She keeps insulting him, but even that doesn't keep him away. Tā lǎu 'mà tā, kěshr jyòu 'nèmmaje tā 'háishr bùkěn °fàng'shǒu (°dǎ'jù, °'dzǒu, °'líkai).

Keep away. /Keep away from here. 'Byé dzài dàu 'jèr lái. *or* 'Lí jèr 'ywán dyar. /Keep away from her; she's a vicious gossip. °'Byé gēn ta láiwang (°'Dwǒje tā dyar, °Lí tā 'ywán dyar), tā 'nà tsái ài 'chwán syán'hwà ne.

Keep down. /He pretends to be helping the workers, but actually he wants to keep them down. Tā 'jwāngje gěi 'láugūng bāng'máng, shr̄'jǐshang tā shr̀ yàu °bǎ tāmen 'yāju (°'yājr̄ tāmen ne). /He's so sick that he can't keep anything down (*or* keep down anything) but water. Tā bǐngde 'jr̄ néng hē 'shwěi, chr̄le (byéde) 'shémma dōu 'tùchulai.

Keep from doing something. /We couldn't keep from laughing, he looked so funny. Wǒmen °méifǎr bú'syàu le (°'rěnbujù jyou 'syàule), tāde 'yàngr 'jēn kě'syàu.

Keep something or someone from. /You'd better put a bandage on to keep the dirt from getting into that cut. Nǐ lá'pwǒle de nar 'háishr °chánshang (°gwǒshang) dyǎr bēng'dài ba, hǎu byé °jyàu 'dzāng dūngsyi jìnchyu (°'jānshang 'dzāng dūngsyi). /The doctor quarantined the house to keep other people from getting the disease. Dàifu 'bùsyǔ rén dzài 'nèijyār chū'rù, wèideshr̀ 'búràng 'byérén °'chwánrǎnshang (°'jāushang) nèijǔng 'bǐng. /We wrote often to keep him from feeling blue. Wǒmen cháng gěi tā syě 'syìn, hǎu 'bújyàu tā 'syīnli nán'gwò.

Keep in. /I like to play the piano, but I'm so busy I can't keep in practice. Wǒ 'ài tán 'gāngchín, búgwò tài 'máng le, °méi gūngfu (°bùnéng 'jyēje) 'lyànsyi. /Keep in touch with me. Cháng gěi wǒ lái ge 'hwàr. *or* 'Jyēchángbù'dwǎrde gēn wǒ 'jyējye 'tóu. *or* Cháng 'gwānjau wǒ dyar. /We were furious at her, but we managed to keep in our feelings until she left. Tā jyàu wǒmen hěn shēng'chì, kěshr 'dzǐjǐ 'yāje yī'jŕ děng tā 'dzǒule. /This work keeps him in a great deal. Jèi shèr jyàu tā °lǎu děi dzài 'wūdzli dzwò (°'hěn shǎu 'chūchyu). *or* Tā dzwò 'jèi shèr lǎu děi 'gwāndzai 'wūrli. /I'm working on another job now, but I'm trying to keep my hand in the importing business at the same time. Wǒ 'lǐng yǒu ge 'shèr, búgwò wǒ 'hěn syǎng túng'shŕ hái °gànje (°bù'dyōukai) 'jìnkǒude 'shēngyi.

Keep off. /Keep off the grass. Byé dzài tsǎu'dìshang 'dzǒu. /They're doing that to keep people off the new cement path. Tāmen nèi shr̀ yàu 'jyàu rén 'byé dzài 'syīn 'yánghwèi'lùshang 'dzǒu.

Keep on. /Keep on the job. Byé bǎ nǐde 'shèr dyōu le. *or* Nǐde 'shèr yī'jŕ 'dzwòsyachyu ba. /Keep on the watch for him. *or* Keep on the lookout for him. Nǐ °hǎu'hāurde (°lyóuje 'shén) děngje tā 'lái.

666

Keep something **on.** /Keep your coat on. Byé 'twō. *or* 'Yīshang 'chwānje ba. /Keep your eyes on that man. Nǐ 'dǐngje dyar nèige rén. *or* Nǐ 'kānje dyar nèige rén. *or* Nǐ 'lyóu dyǎr 'shén kànje neige rén. /Keep your feet on the ground. Jàn 'wěn lou. *or* 'Lǐjù le 'jyǎu.

Keep out. /I'll try to keep out of trouble. Wǒ yí'dìng syǎngfǎr 'bùrě °'shr̄ (°'hwò). /We'll keep him out of mischief. Wǒmen yí'dìng búhwèi jyàu ta °rě'shěr de (°hú'nàu de, *or* (of children only) °táu'chǐ de).

Keep to. /Do I keep to the right or the left? Kàu 'dzwǒ dzǒu háishr kàu 'yòu dzǒu? /Keep to the subject, please. Byé lí 'tí.

Keep up. /Keep up the good work. Jàu 'jèiyàngr 'dzwòsyachyu ba. *or* (Dzwòde 'hǎu) 'lǎu nèmmaje tsái 'hǎu. *or* Jèi shr̄ 'hǎushěr, byé 'jyǎndwàn tsái 'hǎu. /Keep it up. Jyēje 'gànsyachyu. *or* Byé dǎ'jù. *or* 'Lǎu nèmmaje tsái 'hǎu. /We have to keep up appearances. Wǒmen 'bùnéng °'búgù (°'bùgwǎn) 'chǎngmyàn. *or* Wǒmen fēiděi 'gùchywanje dyǎr 'myàndz. /Isn't it expensive to keep up your car? °'Yǒu (°'Yàu) nèmma ge 'chē búfèi'chyán ma? *or* 'Cháng nèmma 'syòuli chē búfèi-'chyán ma? /I'll keep up my end of the bargain. 'Wǒ jèitóur dzèmma 'shwōde jwǔn °bànde'dàu (°jàu 'bàn). /They're trying to keep up the prices. Tāmenyàu bǎ 'jyàchyán 'wéichr̄jùle. *or* Tāmen yàu bújyàu 'jyàchyán 'làusyachyu.

Keep up with. /Do you have any trouble keeping up with the others? Nǐ °'gēndeshàng (°'gǎndeshàng) 'rénjyā ma? /Did you have any trouble keeping up with the others? Nǐ 'nèmma gēn tāmen 'bǐje, 'fèijyèr ma?

Keep (means of living) is expressed as enough for doing something (such as eating, using, etc.) gòu . . . de. /Does he earn his keep? Tā jwànde gòu °'gwòrde (°'chr̄de, °'yùngde) ma?

For keeps. /We're playing this game for keeps. is expressed as This is real gambling. Jèi shr̄ dǔ 'jēnde.

For keeps (permanently) is expressed with yǐjr̄. /We expect to stay here for keeps. Wǒmen syǎng yàu dzài 'jèr yǐ'jr̄ dāisyachyu.

KEY. (Lock opener) yàushr. /I have a pair of keys to that door. 'Nèige mén wǒ yǒu 'lyǎngba 'yàushr. /This key doesn't fit (can't open) that lock. 'Jèige yàushr kāibukāi nèiba 'swǒ.

(Solution; way of doing) bànfa; (way of translating, as a code) 'fānfǎ; (printed directions giving the key to something) shwōmíngshū; or expressed verbally by bàn, fān, and similar words. /I don't know the key to this code. Wǒ bujr̄dàu jèijung 'mǐmǎrde 'fānfa. *or* Jèijung 'mǐmǎr wǒ bùjr̄dàu dzèmma 'fān. /I don't know the key to this problem. Wǒ bujr̄dàu jèige 'wèntíde 'bànfa. *or* Jèige 'wèntí wǒ bùjr̄dàu dzèmma 'bàn. /Here is the key to this code. Jèijung 'mǐmǎr shr̄ 'jèmma °ge 'fānfa (°yàng 'fān). *or* Jè shr̄ jèijung 'mǐmǎrde shwōmíng'shū.

(Lever of typewriter, piano, etc.) jyàndz. /The piano keys are terribly stiff. Gāng'chín 'jyàndz fēicháng jǐn.

(In music) dyàu, dyàur. /The symphony is written in the key of G. Nèi jyāu-syǎng'chyǔ °'jǐdyàur (°yùng 'jǐdyàur syéde).

(Most important) dzwèi 'yàujǐnde. /He's the key man in the plant. Gūng'chángli tā shr̄ dzwèi yàu'jǐnde rén.

Keyed up děngje . . . syīnli hěn 'jǐnjāng, 'yísyīn děngje . . . . /He's all keyed up for his stage appearance. Tā děngje chū'tái, syīnli hěn 'jǐnjāng. *or* Tā 'yísyīn děngje yàu chū'tái le.

KICK. (With the foot) tǐ. /He kicked her. Tā 'tǐ tā láije. /Kick the ball! Tǐ 'chyóur!

(Of a hoofed animal kicking with hind feet) lyàu jywĕdz. /I hope this horse doesn't kick. Syīwang 'jèipǐ mǎ °búlyàu 'jywĕdz (°bùtǐ'rén).

(Gripe, complain) bàuywan; (find fault) tyāuti; (grumble) dūnang. /What are you kicking about? Nǐ nèmma 'bàuywan, shř wèile 'shémma? /What are you kicking about then? Nèmmaje nǐ yŏu 'bàuywan shémma ne?. /He's always kicking about something. Tā 'lǎu dzài nàr °'bàuywan (°'tyāuti, °'dūnang, °'bàuywan jèige bàuywan nèigede). or 'Tyāuti jèige °tyāuti nèige de (°'dū dunangnangde).

A kick (a recoil) hòudzwòlǐ; (to recoil) wàng'hòudzwò. /The kick of the rifle can hurt your shoulder. °'Bùchyāngde hòudzwò'lǐ (°'Bùchyāng wàng'hòu yǐ'dzwò) kěyǐ bǎ jyān'bǎng jwàng'shāngle.

Get a kick out of doing something yǐ... jyòu 'jywéje tǐng yŏu'chywèrde, tǐng gāu'syìngde, 'hěn syǐhwān..., 'tǐng syǐhwān..., 'tǐng ài..., 'hěn ài...; get a kick out of someone or something is expressed in the same way by stating the action enjoyed in connection with the person or thing. /He gets a big kick out of telling that story about the mayor. Tā yǐ'jyǎngchi shř'jǎngde nèidwàn 'gùshr lai jyòu 'jywéje tǐng °yŏu'chywèrde (°gāu'syìngde). or Tā °'hěn syǐhwān (°'tǐng ài) gàusung rén shřjǎngde nèidwàn 'gùshr.

Give a kick 'tǐ yǐjyàu, 'tǐ yísyàr. /He gave her a kick. Tā 'tǐle tā °yǐ'jyàu (°yísyàr). /Give it a kick and let it roll over this way. Nèige nǐ 'tǐ yǐ'jyàu jyòu 'gúlugwolai le. /That horse gave you some kick! Nèipǐ mǎ °'tǐle nǐ yísyàr 'hǎude (°'tǐde nǐ hěn bù'chǐng a)!

KID. (Young goat) syāu shānyáng, 'syāu yáng, 'syāu yángr, 'yánggāudz, 'gāuyáng. /That kid is always following the she-goat around. Nèijř 'syāu yángr lǎu 'gēnje nèijř 'mǔyáng.

(Leather) 'jǐpí. /She is very proud of her kid gloves. Nèifù 'jǐpí shŏu'tàur tā tǐng dé'yìde. or Tā 'tǐng déyǐ tā nèifù 'jǐpí shŏu'tàur.

(Child) syǎuhár, háidz; (children) syǎuhármen, háidzmen. /Send the kids to bed. Jyàu 'háidzmen chyù shwèi'jyàu ba.

To kid (joke) shwōje wár. /Are you kidding? Nǐ shwōje 'wár ba.

Kid someone ywān, dzwàn, pyàn, gēn... nàuje'wár. /Who're you kidding? Nǐ nàshř ywān 'shéi a? or Nǐ yàu °dzwàn (°pyàn) 'shéi a? /I was just kidding with him. Wǒ nà 'búgwò shř gēn tā nàuje 'wár.

KILL. (Put to death) 'néngsž; (murder) shā; or expressed with sž die alone; or with resultative compounds ending in sž when the specific means of killing is given. /Who killed him? 'Shéi shāde tā? or 'Shéi bǎ tā 'néngsžde. /How was he killed? Tā 'dzěmma sžde? or Tā jyàu rén dzěmma 'néngsžde? /This man was killed by a blow on the head. Jèige rén shř °jyàu rén dzài 'tóushang 'dǎle yísyàr 'dásžde (or by a gun °jyàu rén yùng'chyáng dásžde, or by being stabbed with a bayonet °jyàu rén yùng 'tsždāu 'tsžsžde, or by being strangled °'lèiszde, or by lightning °jyàu 'léigěi 'jǐsžde, or by being hit by a car °jyàu chē 'jwàngsžde, or by being smothered °'byē-sžde, °'mēnsžde, or by a falling rock °jyàu yǐkwài shřtou 'dzásžde, or by coal gas °jyàu méichǐ 'syūnsžde). /He kills a man as if he were killing a fly. Tā shā ge 'rén gēn 'néngsž ge 'tsāngying shřde. or Tā dásž ge 'rén gēn 'dásž ge 'tsāngying shřde.

(Fig.) is expressed with resultative compounds with sž as the second element, as (by laughter) 'syàusž; (by overwork) 'lèisž; (by pain) 'téngsž; (by boredom) 'mēnsž; (by noise) 'chàusž; etc. /You're killing me! (laughter) Nǐ kě jyàu wǒ 'syàusž le!

or (overwork) Nǐ kě bǎ wǒ 'lèisž le! / This is killing me! (overwork) Kě bǎ wǒ 'lèisž le. *or* (pain) Kě bǎ wǒ 'téngsž le. *or* (boredom) Kě bǎ wǒ 'mènsž le. <u>etc.</u>

(Eliminate, defeat) bǎ... 'yāsyachyu (suppress); bǎ... 'dwóchyu (rob, as of flavor); bǎ... 'hwěi (destroy); bǎ... chyǔ'syāu (eliminate); bùděng, bùfābyàu (not publish, as an article); bùbǎ... 'tíchulai 'tǎulwùn (not bring up for discussion). / Too much salt will kill the flavor. Gě 'yán tài 'dwō hwèi bǎ 'wèr °'dwólechyu de (°'yāsyachyu de, °'hwěile de). / The mayor killed their plan. Shř'jǎng bǎ tāmende 'jíhwà gěi °'yāsyachyule (°chyǔ'syāule). *or* Shř'jǎng méi bǎ tāmende 'jíhwà 'tíchulai 'tǎulwùn. / Let's kill that article. Nèipyān 'wénjang 'byé °děng (°fā'byàu) ba.

(Of time; pass, spend) gwò; (enjoy in a leisurely way) 'syāumwó, 'syāuchyǎn; **have time to kill** yǒu 'gūngfu méi'shèr, yǒu 'gūngfu 'syánje, yǒu 'gūngfu 'syánje méi'shèr. / Let's go to the park and kill a few hours. Dzámen dàu gūng'ywán chyù °'gwò (°'syāumwó, °'syāuchyǎn) jǐdyǎn'jūng ba. / We have four hours to kill. Dzámen yǒu 'sždyǎnjūng de 'gūngfu °méi'shèr (°'syánje, °'syánje méi'shèr).

The kill (act of killing) <u>is expressed verbally as</u> drop the raised hand syà syà-shǒu. / They closed in for the kill. Tāmen °'wéilǔnglái (°'bījìnlái) yàu syà syà-'shǒu.

(Animals killed in hunting) 'dászde, dǎjaude, shāle de. / The hunters brought home the kill. Dǎ'lyède bǎ 'dászde 'shòu dàihwéi 'jyāchyule.

Killer shā'rénde rén, shā'rénde 'syūngshǒu, 'syūngshǒu.

KIND. (Benevolent; of persons) hǎu (good); 'shànlyáng (philanthropic); héchi (mild, polite); 'wēnhòu (gentle and liberal); hòudau (generous); 'jūnghòu (faithful and liberal); 'tszbēi (compassionate); hǎuhǎurde (kindly in manner); kěn 'bāngju rén de, kěn gěi rén bāng'máng de (helpful). / He's a very kind man. Tā rén hěn °'hǎu (°'shànlyáng, °'héchi, °'wēnhòu, °'hòudau, °'jūnghòu, °'tszbēi). / He's the kindest person I've ever met. 'Méijyàngwo nèmma °hǎu'syínde (°'shànlyángde, °'héchide, °'hòudaude, °'jūnghoude, °'tszbēide) rén. / He's very kindhearted. Tā 'syīn hěn °'hǎu (°'shàn-lyáng, °'hòudau, °'jūnghòu, °'tszbēi). / Be kind to others. Dài 'rén yàu °hǎu'hǎurde (°'héchi, °'hòudau, °'jūnghòu, °yǒu 'tszbēisyīn). / Be kind to animals. Dài °'shēng-kou (°'syāu 'chùshengr) yàu °hǎu'hǎurde (°'tszbēije dyar). / You'll gradually find the people here very kind. Nǐ màn'mārde jyou jřdàu le, 'jèrde rén °'syīn hěn 'hǎu (°hěn 'héchi, °hěn 'hòudau, °'dài rén hěn 'hǎu, °hěn kěn 'bāngju rén de, °hěn kěn gěi rén bāng'mángde). *but* / You've been very kind. 'Jēn shr fèi'syīn le. *or* Fèi-'syīn, fèi'syīn. *or* Dwō'syè, dwó'syè. *or* Láu'jyà, láu'jyà.

Be kind enough to chǐng (*see also* PLEASE); (sarcastic) 'fáfa 'tszbēi, 'syíng-sying 'hǎu (ba). / Would you be kind enough to help me? Chǐng nǐ 'bāngbang 'máng. *or* Chǐng nǐ 'bāngjubāngju ba. *or* (sarcastically) Nín °'fáfa 'tszbēi (°'syíngsying 'hǎu ba), 'bāngbang wǒ ba.

Do a kind deed dzwò jyàn 'shàn shèr, dzwò jyàn'hǎu shèr, syíng ge hǎu. / Do a kind deed every day. 'Měityān 'dzwò jyàn °'hǎu shèr (°'shàn shèr). *or* 'Měityān 'syíng ge 'hǎu.

Give kindest regards 'wēnhòu (used for elders); wēnhǎur, dàihǎur, shāuhǎur. / Give my kindest regards to your family. 'Fùshang 'dōu tì wǒ °'wēnhòu (°wèn ge 'hǎur, °wèn yìshēng 'hǎur, °dài ge 'hǎur chyu, °shāu ge 'hǎur chyu).

Kind (sort) jǔng (especially of inherent type, as species); yàng, yàngr, jǔng-yàngr (especially of types distinguished by external characteristics as shape, form, mannerisms); pài (type); děng (grade); lù (of people distinguished by their way of life; also means road, way); lèi (class characterized by some point of similarity in all members); <u>when referring to actions,</u> **that kind** <u>may be expressed by</u> nèmma(je), **this kind** <u>by</u> jèmma *or* dzèmma, **what kind** *or* **any kind** <u>by</u> dzěmma. / What kind of

a person is he? Tā shr̄ °'shémmayàngrde (°dzĕmmayàngrde, °'dzĕmma) ge 'rén?
/That kind of person is hard to deal with. °'Nèijŭng (°'Nèiyàngr, °'Nèijŭng'yàngr,
°'Nèilèi, *or* of social class °'Nèidĕng) (de) rén hĕn nán °'yĭngfu (°'dwèifu, °'chán,
°'dŏu). /Do you have any more of this kind of paper? 'Hái yŏu °'jèijŭng (°'jèiyàngrde) jr̄ ma? /There are several kinds of people here. Jĕr yŏu °ji'jŭngde (°ji-
'lèide, °jijŭng'yàngrde, °ji'pàide) rén. /He's a different kind of person. Tā shr̄
°'lĭngyípàide (°'lĭngyíjŭngde, °'lĭngyílèide, °'lĭngyílùde) rén. /He's the same kind
of a man as Lincoln. Tā gen Lín'ken shr̄ yí'lèide rén. /This is the same kind of
work I did before. 'Jèishèr gēn wŏ yĭ'chyán dzwògwo de yí'yàng. /He's not my kind.
Tā gēn wŏ búshr °yí'pàide (°yí'lùde) rén. /This kind of book doesn't sell. °'Jèijŭng (°'Jèiyàngrde, °'Jèijŭng'yàngrde, °'Jèilèide) shū 'màibuchū'chyù. /This is a new
kind of glass. Jèi shr̄ yíjŭng 'syĭnbwōli. /What kind (species) of dog is he? Jèi gŏu
shr̄ shémma 'jŭngr de? *or* Jèi shr̄ 'nèijŭng 'gŏu? *or meaning* What is this kind of
dog called? 'Jèijŭng gŏu jyàu shémma 'míngdz? /I like all kinds of food. 'Gèjŭng
'chr̄shr̄ wŏ 'dōu ài chr̄. *or expressed as* I like all foods that people eat. 'Fán shr̄
'rén chr̄ de wŏ jyou ài chr̄. /He's an engineer or something of the kind. Tā shr̄
ge gūngchéng'shr̄, yàu 'búshr dehwà yĕ shr̄ (dzwòde) nèiyí'lèide shr̄. /So that's
the kind of friend you are! Nĭ 'ywánlái shr̄ °'nèmmayíjŭngde (°'nèiyàngrde, °nèmma-
yàngrde yíge) 'péngyou a! /I'll do nothing of the kind! 'Nèiyàng shèr 'wŏ tsái bu-
'gàn ne! *or* Wŏ °'jywé (°tsái, °'pyān, °'jyòu shr) bú'nèmmaje! /She's a journal-
ist of a kind. (sarcastic) Tā shr̄ 'nèmma yĭ'jŭngde 'syĭnwénjĭ'jĕ.

   In kind (in a similar way) jàuyàngr. /He answered the challenge in kind. Tā
jàu'yàngr 'hwéile yíjyù. *but* /Workers on farms here are not paid in money but in
kind (in produce). Jèr 'dĭli gù de rén bugĕi 'gūngchyán, °gĕi 'lyángshr̄ (°dĭli 'chū
shémma 'gĕi shémma).

   Kind of yìdyăr, dyăr. /It's kind of lonesome here. Jèr yŏu (yì)dyăr 'mèndeheng. /We're kind of busy right now. Wŏmen 'jèihwer 'yŏu dyăr 'máng. /Yes,
kind of! Éi, 'yŏu nèmma yìdyăr!

KINDLY. (Benevolent) see paragraph one under **KIND**. /He's a very kindly man. Tā
rén hĕn °hăo (°'shàn, °shànlyáng, °'hēchi, °'wēnhòu, °'hòudau, °'jūnghòu, °'tsź-
bēi).

   (In a kind manner) hăuhāurde; or is expressed as be kind. *See* **KIND**. /He
treats people kindly. Tā hăuhāurde 'dài rén. *or* Tā 'dài rén hĕn °hău (°shànlyáng,
°hēchi, °etc.).

   (Please) chĭng, láujyà. *See* **PLEASE**. /Kindly stop when your time is up.
'Dàule 'shŕhou jyòu chĭng °'tíngju (°'búyàu wàngsyà 'dzwò le). /Kindly mind your
own business. Láu'jyà, 'byé dwō gwăn syán'shèr. *or expressed as* I'll thank you to
mind your own business. 'Syèsye 'nín a, 'byé dwō gwăn syán'shèr. *or as* Don't
tire yourself out sticking your nose into other people's business. Nín 'shău gwăn
dyăr syán'shèr ba, °kàn (°lyóu'shén) 'lèijau.

   Take kindly to 'syĭhwān; or expressed as like to hear ài tĭng. /He didn't take
kindly to my advice. Wŏ 'chywăn tā 'búdà °'syĭhwān (°ài 'tĭng).

KINDNESS. 'ēndyăn, 'ēn (used of superiors or sarcastically); more commonly expressed
indirectly with words meaning kind. See **KIND**. /I can never forget your kindness.
°Nĭ dài wŏ 'nèmma hău (°Nínde 'ēndyăn) wŏ 'yŭngywăn wàngbu'lyău. /How can I
ever repay you for such kindness? Nín dài wŏ 'dzèmma hău, wŏ dzèmma 'bàudá
nín ne? /Her kindness knows no bounds. Tā dài 'rén hăudàu'jyā le. *or* Tā 'hòudàu-
jíle. /Even this is an exceptional kindness from him. Jyòu 'jèiyàngr dzài'tā 'yĭjĭng
shr̄ °dài rén tè'byé 'hău le (°dà'dade kāi'ēn le, °'tēēn le). /I appreciate your
kindness very much. Wŏ hĕn 'gănjĭ nĭ. *or* 'Gănsyè bú'jìn. *or* 'Jēn shr̄ fèi'syĭn le.
or Dwō'syè, dwō'syè.

KING. gwówáng, hwángdi. / This magazine has a picture of the king. Jèibĕr 'dzájȓ dēngle yìjāng °gwó'wángde (°hwángdide) syàng'pyār.

KISS. chīn(chin) (used especially of kissing children; public or indiscriminate kissing among adults, even as a merely friendly gesture or between relatives, is not generally approved in China); chīndzwĕr, jyēwĕn. / Let me kiss you, you precious little thing. (strictly confined to infants) Wŏ 'chīnchin nǐ, nǐ jèige syau bau'bĕr. / When they kissed on the screen, someone whistled. Tāmen dzài dyàn'yǐngli °chīn'dzwĕr (°jyē'wĕn) de shŕhou, yŏu rén 'chwēile yìshēng 'shàur.

    A kiss is expressed verbally as above. / He gave his mother a kiss on the cheek. Tā chīn tā mŭchinde 'lyǎn.

KITCHEN. 'chúfáng. / The kitchen is large and clean. 'Chúfáng yòu 'dà yòu 'gānjing. / From the kitchen window you can see the river. Dǎ chú'fángde 'chwānghu nar kéyǐ kànjyan 'hé. / Who is in charge of the school kitchen? Sywé'syàuli 'shéi gwǎn chúfáng?

KITTEN. syǎumāu, syǎumāur.

KNEE. bwōlegàr; 'syīgài, or sometimes 'chīgài (used most often technically as in medicine). / My knee hurts. Wŏ bwōle'gàr 'téng.

    (Of pants) expressed as above. / I tore a hole in the knee of my pants. Wŏ bǎ 'kùdz dzài bwōle'gàr nar gwāle ge 'kŏudz.

    On one's knees is expressed verbally as kneel gwèi. / On your knees! 'Gwèi-sya! / He was down on his knees begging. Tā 'gwèije 'chyóu.

KNIFE. dāu, dāudz; **carving knife** chyēròu'dāu. / Give me the big knife to cut the bread. Gĕi wŏ 'dàdāu lái chyē myàn'bāu.

    To knife ná 'dāudz lá. / He was knifed in a street fight. Tā dzài 'jyēshang dǎ-'jyà jyàu rén ná 'dāudz °'lále (or meaning and killed °'lászle).

KNOCK. (Bump) pèng; (more violently, usually accidental) jwàng. / Don't knock the table. 'Byé °pèng (°pèngjau) 'jwōdz. or Byé °'pèngdzài (°'jwàngdzài) 'jwōdzshang. / He was knocked down by a car. Tā jyàu chī'chē °pèng'dǎu (°jwàng'dǎu) le. / Be careful not to knock anything down. Syǎu'syīnje byé bǎ shémma dūngsyi 'pèngsyachyu. / He knocked his head against the wall. Tā 'tóu °jwàng(°pèng)dzài 'chyángshang le.

    (Rap or tap) chyāu; **knock on a door** chyāu mén, dǎ mén, jyàu mén (especially of shouting to have a door opened, but may be confined to persistent knocking). / Knock before you open the door. °'Chyāuchyau (°'Chyāuyisyar) °'mén dzài 'kāi (°dzài kāi 'mén). / Someone is knocking on the door. 'Yŏu rén °chyāu (°dǎ, °jyàu) 'mén ne. / He broke the glass rod by knocking it on the rim of the cup. Tā dzài wǎn'byārshang bǎ 'bwōligwèr °chyāu'dwànle (°'chyāudadwànle).

    (Strike or pound) dzá; (with sharp blows) chyāu; (with a hammer) chwéi; (punch or strike in order to break something from what it is fastened to) dzáu; (ram) dāu; (hit, especially with a missile) dǎ; (with a hard sharp blow) chyāuda; *see also* **HIT**. / Knock the bottom out of the barrel. Bǎ 'tŭngde 'dyĕr °'dzásyachyu (°'chyāusyachyu, °'chwéisyachyu, °'dāusyachyu). / Knock the box apart and burn it. Bǎ syádz °'dzákāi (°dzá'sānle) shāu'hwŏ. / They knocked all the legs off the table. Tāmen bǎ jwōdz-'twĕr dōu °'dzáusyachyule (°'dzásyachyule, °'chyāudasyachyule). / The book fell from the shelf and knocked him on the head. 'Shū tsúng 'jyàdzshang 'dyàusyalai, 'dzádzài tā 'tóushang le. / The bullet missed him and knocked a picture off the wall. Chyāng'dzĕr méi'dǎjau tā, bǎ chyángshang gwà de 'hwàr dǎ'dyàule.

671

KNOT

(In a motor) 'gāngdēng, 'gwāngdēng, 'gāngdāng, 'gēdēng, syǎng。 / The motor
is knocking, do you hear it? 'Jǐchǐ jŕ °'gāngdēng (°'gwāngdēng, °'gāngdāng, °gē-
dēnggēdēngde), 'tīngjyànle ma? / See what you can do to stop this motor from knocking. Nǐ gěi 'shōushr shōushr, byé jyàu 'jǐchǐ nèmma °'syǎng (°'gāngdēnggāngdēngde,
°'gwāngdēnggwāngdēngde, °'gāngdānggāngdāngle, °'gēdēnggēdēngde).

(Criticize) 'pīpíng. / They're always knocking the administration. Tāmen lǎu
'pīpíng jèng'fǔ.

Knock around (wander aimlessly) gwàng. / I've been knocking around town for a
couple of days. Wǒ dzài jèr 'gwàngle lyǎngsān'tyān le。

Knock someone **cold** bǎ . . . dǎ'hwūngwochyu, bǎ . . . dǎ'yūngwochyu, bǎ . . . dǎ-
'mēnggwochyu. / The punch caught him on the jaw and knocked him cold. Nèiyi'chywán
dǎdzài tā'syàba'kérshang, bǎtā °dǎ'hwūngwochyule (°dǎ'yūngwochyule, °dǎ'mēng
gwochyule).

Knock down (dismantle) chāi. / Knock down the scaffolding. Bǎ jyàdz 'chāi le.

Knock down (reduce; of a price) is expressed as reduce by a certain amount
jyǎn or jyǎnsyachyu; or as deduct a certain amount 'shǎuyàn (see knock off below).
/ Can't you knock down the price a couple of dollars? 'Jyàchyán hái néng °'jyǎnjikwài
(°'jyǎnsyàjikwài, °shǎuyàu jikwài) ma?

Knock someone **for a loop** (with charm; intentionally) bǎ . . . 'míju; (unintentionally) jyàu . . . jàu'mí; be knocked for a loop gěi 'míjùle, jáule 'mí le (mí in all of
these expressions means bewitch). / That gorgeous actress has knocked him for a
loop. Nèige 'pyàulyang nyǔ'syìdz 'kě jyàu tā jáule 'mí le. / He was knocked for a
loop. Tā gěi 'míjùle. or Tā jáule 'mí le.

Knock off (deduct) 'shǎu yàu, jyǎn, jyǎnsyachyu. / Knock a couple of dollars
off the price and I'll take it. °'Shǎu yàu jikwài chyán (°'Jyǎn jikwài chyán, °Jyǎnsyà
jikwài chyán chyu), wǒ jyòu 'mǎi.

Knock off (stop work) búdzwòle (not work anymore); dǎjù (stop); dzǒu (leave);
syàgūng (cease work, especially at the regular quitting time). / Let's knock off at
five o'clock. Dzámen 'wǔdyǎn °jyòu 'dzǒu ba (°jyòu byé 'dzwò le, °dǎ'jù ba,
°syàgūng ba).

Knock someone **out** (hit into unconsciousness) see **Knock** someone **cold** above.

Knock the bottom out of (fig.). / That knocked the bottom out of my plans. Wǒde
'jìhwà dzèmma yǐlái °'chywán wánle (°mǎn'níngle, °'chywán gěi twēi'fānle, °'wánchywán méi'yùngle, °jèng'gèrde dzá'gwōle, °'chywánchéngle pàu'yǐng le).

Be knocked out (exhausted) lèihwàile, lèipāsyale, méijyèrle. / He was knocked
out after playing tennis for only a little while. Tā dǎ 'wǎngchyóur dǎle yǐ'hwěr jyòu
°lèi'hwàile (°lèi'pāsyale, °méi'jyèrle).

Be knocked together (constructed hastily) gàide tǐng 'mǎhude, gàide tǐng 'háng-
hude; (boards taken and nailed up) ná 'mùtoubǎr °'dīngbashangde (°'dīngbashangde,
°'dzábashangde). / That garage is just knocked together。 Nèige 'chēfáng °gàide tǐng
'mǎhude (°búgwò shr ná 'mùtoubǎr 'dīngbashangde).

Other expressions in English. / I'll knock your block off. Wǒ bǎ nǐ 'nǎudài
'jyòusyalai. / They finally knocked some sense into his head. 'Jyégwǒ tāmen jyàu
tā 'míngbaigwolaile.

KNOT. (The place tied; especially a fastening) kòur; (especially an obstruction, which
may be a knot unintentionally tied, a knot tied to keep a rope from passing through a
hole, or simply a bump in the rope caused by a fault in weaving) 'gāda, gēda, gēde.
/ Can you untie this knot? Jèige 'kòur nǐ jyéde'kāi ma? / Could you untie this knot

for me? Láu'jyà gěi bǎ jèi'kòur 'jyěkāi? / There are a lot of knots in this rope. Jèige 'shéngdz yǒu 'hǎujǐge °'kòur (°'gāda).

(Hard mass, as in wood) jyēdz, gāda. / I can't saw through this knot. Jèige °'jyēdz (°'gāda) wǒ 'jyùbukāi.

(Group) dzwēi, chyún. / A knot of people gathered around the accident. Chū-'shèrde nàr jyùle °yǐ'dzwēi (°yǐ'chyún) rén。

(Nautical miles) (hǎi)lǐ. / This ship can make fifteen knots. Jèige 'chwán yī-'dyǎnjūng kěyǐ dzǒu shŕ'wǔ (hǎi) lǐ.

To knot jìkòur, jè gāda, dǎjyēr. / He knotted the rope securely. Tā bǎ 'shéngdz jǐn'jǐnde °jìle ge 'kòur (°jìle ge 'gāda, °dǎle ge 'jyēr).

KNOW (KNEW, KNOWN). (Be sure of or have knowledge about) 'jŕdàu, 'syǎudé. / I'm not guessing; I really know. Wǒ 'búshŕ 'tsāi; wǒ 'jēn °jŕdàu (°syǎude)。 / I know he's ill. Wǒ 'jŕdàu tā 'bìng le. / I knew something was wrong. Wǒ jyou 'jŕdàu °'chūle dyǎr 'shèr (°'yǒu dyǎr bú'dwèi). / Who knows? Shéi jŕ'dàu ne? / Who else knows? 'Hái yǒu shéi jŕdàu? / That's a known fact. Nèi shŕ 'yǐjǐng 'jŕdàu de shèr le. *or* 'Nèishèr 'yǐjǐng 'jŕdàu shŕ 'jènde le. / Wait until all the facts of the case are known. Děng 'ānchǐng dōu °'jŕdàu le (*or* clear °'chǐngchu le, °nèng 'mǐngbai le) dzài 'shwō. / Not that I know of. 'Wǒ bùjŕ'dàu. or expressed as I haven't heard. 'Méi-tǐngshwō. / What do you know? is expressed as Tell me all about everything. Yǒu shémma 'shèr a, shwōshwo wǒ 'tǐngting. *but* / What do you know! (surprise) A? 'Jyū ránrú'tsž! *or* (astonishment) 'Shéi syàngde'dàu? *or* (confirmation) A? Jēn-jyou 'nèmmaje! *or* (pleasure) 'Jēnchǐ'gwài.

(Be skilled in; know how to) hwèi; (have studied) sywégwo; (understand) dǔng. / He knows Arabic. Tā °'sywégwo (°dǔng, °hwèi, °hwèi shwō, °hwèi syě) Yàlā-'bwowén. / I don't know how to drive a car. Wǒ °búhwèi (°méi'sywégwo) kāi 'chē.

(Be acquainted with; be familiar with, well acquainted with) rènshr, rènde, gēn . . . shóu; (be friendly with) gēn . . . yǒu 'jyāuching; (be able to pick out) kànde-chulai. / Do you know him? Nǐ °'rènshr (°'rènde) tā ma? *or* Nǐ gēn tā yǒu 'jyāuching ma? *or* Nǐ gēn tā 'shóu ma? or meaning Do you have any knowledge about him? Nǐ 'jŕdàu jèige rén ma?

Know better than 'jŕdàu 'bùnéng. / He knew better than to tell his wife. Tā 'jŕdàu 'bùnéng gàusu tā 'tàitai. / You ought to know better than that. Nǐ yīnggāi 'jŕdàu 'bùnéng nèmmaje.

Know by sight. / I know him only by sight. is expressed as I've only seen him to know (be sure of) who he is. Wǒ búgwò 'kànjyàn tā jŕdàu tā shŕ'shéi jyou shŕle.

Know by name. / I know him only by name. is expressed as I have only heard his name. Wǒ búgwò 'tǐngjyàngwo tāde 'mǐngdz.

You know (comment added to a statement) búshr ma. / She's going to have a baby, you know. Tā yǒu'yùnle, 'búshr ma.

In the know. / He's in the know around there. is expressed as They haven't concealed anything from him. Tā 'méimánje tā. or as They let him know everything. Tāmen 'shémma dōu jyàu tā 'jŕdàu.

Knowing (giving the appearance of knowing all). / He gave her a knowing smile, as if to say, "I know all about it." Tā gēn tā nèmma yí'syàu, 'hǎusyàng shŕ shwō, "wǒ 'dōu jŕdàu." / His knowing smiles make his sister mad。 Tā lǎu nèmma 'syàu, hǎu syàng 'shémma dōu jŕdàu shŕde, jyàu tā 'mèimei hěn shēng'chì.

KNOWLEDGE. jŕshr, 'sywéwèn; or expressed indirectly by verbs meaning **know**.

673

See **KNOW.** / To the best of my knowledge, he didn't go. Jyù 'wǒ jr̄dàude, tā 'méi-chyù. / Do you have any knowledge of this matter? 'Jèi sher̀ nǐ yìˇdyǎr yě bùjr̄'dàu ma? / He has a tremendous amount of knowledge. Tā hěn yǒu 'sywéwèn. *or* Tāde jr̄shr hěn 'fēngfù. *or* Tā 'jr̄dàude hěn °'dwō (°'shēn). *or* Tā 'sywéwèn hěn 'shēn.

LABOR. (Work or effort) gūng; (stressing the activity) 'gūngdzwò; (a job) hwór; (handwork) 'shǒugūng. / Mining is very hard labor. Kāi'kwàng shr̀ hén °kǔde (°'jùngde) 'gūngdzwò. *or* 'Kwànggūng gūngdzwò hén °'kǔ (°chr̄'lì). or expressed as Being a miner is very hard. Dzwò 'kwàngkūng hén °'láukǔ (°chr̄'lì). / He was sentenced to three years' hard labor. Fá ta dzwò 'sānnyán kǔngūng. / How much did you pay for the labor on this, and how much for the materials? Jèiyàngr 'dūngsyide 'shǒugūng 'chyán ní gěile 'dwōshau, 'tsái lyàu chyán 'dwōshau? *or* Jèijyàn hwór 'gūng shr̀ 'dwōshàu (chyán), 'tsái lyàu shr̀ 'dwōshàu (chyán)? / This kind of labor is inhuman. 'Jèijúng 'hwór 'búshr 'rén gànde.

(Organized workers or pertaining to workers) 'láugūng. / Labor favors a six-hour day. 'Láugūng (fāngmyan) 'dzànchéng 'měityān °'gūngdzwò 'lyòusyǎushŕ (°dzwò 'lyòudyǎn'jùngde 'gūng). / He became a very powerful labor leader. Tā chéngle yíge 'hén yǒu 'shr̄lìde 'láugūng lǐng'syǒu. / Do you know the labor laws? Ní 'dǔngde láugūng'fǎ ma?

Be in labor (in childbirth) shēng háidz, shēngchǎn, fēnmyǎn. / She was in labor for nine hours. Tā °shēng 'háidz (°'shēngchǎn, °'fēnmyǎn) tsúng 'fādùng dàu 'shēng-syalai 'jīnggwòle 'jyǒuge jūng'tóu.

To labor (exert effort) kǔgàn; (struggle) fèndòu. / He labored under difficulties. Tā dzài hěn 'kwùnnande hwán'jìnglǐ °kǔ'gàn (°fèn'dòu). / He labored hard on it. 'Jèi 'shr̀ tā dzwòde hěn mài 'lìchì. *or* Wèi 'jèi shr̀ tā 'jēnshr hén kǔ'gàn.

(Elaborate). / Don't labor the point. Byé 'lǎu shwō jèiyidyǎn. *or* Byé chyúng 'dāudau jèi'yìdyǎn. *or* 'Byé jǐngdzài jèi'yìdyǎnshang chyúng 'dāudau.

Be labored (of breathing) fèijǐn (require strength). / His breathing is labored. Tā chwǎn'chyèr tíng fèi'jǐn.

LACK. (Be somewhat deficient, be somewhat deficient in) chà dyar, chyàn dyar, chywē dyar; (not have, be entirely lacking in) 'méiyou; (be short of) dwǎn; (be not enough; said of the thing lacked) búgòu; (be little; said of the thing lacked) (hén) shǎu; (be deficient in strength; said of the thing lacked) chàjǐn; also some indirect expressions. / He lacks the courage of his convictions. Tā °chyàn (°chywē, °chà) dyar 'jryán bù-'hwèide 'jīngshen. or expressed as When he has opinions he doesn't dare to speak them out. Tā 'yǒu °'júyì (°'jyànjyè) búdà gǎn 'shwōchūlai. / He lacks common sense. Tā 'rénchíng'shr̀gù °'dǔngde hěn 'shǎu (°'jr̄daude bú'gòu). *or* Tā 'rénchíng-'shr̀gùshang °chyàn dyar ('gūngfu) (°chywēdyar 'gūngfu, °'chàdyar ('gūngfu). ('gūngfu in these cases refers to the time spent in acquiring common sense). / Young pilots lack experience. Nyánchīngde jyàshr̄ywán °méi yǒu (°chywèfá, °chywēshǎu) jīngyàn. / He lacks tact. Tā 'yìngfurénshang °chà (°chywē, °chyàn) dyar ('gūngfu). *or* Tā 'yìngfurén de 'gūngfu °chà dyar (°chyàn dyar, °'bú'gòu). / His lack of knowledge was obvious. 'Nèige rén yí'kàn jyòu 'jr̄dàu méi shémma °'sywéwen (°'jr̄shr̀). / Nothing was lacking to make the party a success. Jèige 'yànhwèi 'chóubèide hěn 'jōudàu, bùchywē shémma. / The area was lacking in defenses. 'Jèiyídàide fáng'yùgūng'shr̀ °bú'gòu (°chà'jǐn). / He lacks emotion. Tā méiyou 'gǎnchíng. or expressed as He has no human feelings. 'Tā jèi rén 'mámùbù'rén. or as He is emotionally very cool. Tā dzài 'gǎnchíngshang hén 'lěng. or as His heart is harsh. Tā 'syīncháng hěn 'yìng.

A lack. / For lack of anywhere else to stay, I have to live in a hotel. is expressed as Since there's no other place to stay, ... Yīnwei 'méiyŏu byéde dìfang kĕ 'jù, wŏ 'jŕhău jù lyǘ'gwăn.

LADY. (Woman) tàitai (married); fūren (married; a somewhat politer term); **young lady** syáujye, *or* (in Peiping) gūnyang (apparently unmarried); nyán'chīngde 'tàitai (married); (as a term of address) 'nyŭshŕ; **ladies** (married and unmarried) 'syáujye 'tàitaimen. /Is that lady at the door your mother? Dzài mén'kŏurde nèiwèi lău-'tàitai shŕ ní 'mŭchin ma? /Do you wish to speak to the lady of the house? Nǐ yàu gēn (jèijyàrde) 'tàitai shwō'hwà ma? *or* Nǐ yàu jyàn wŏmen 'tàitai ma? /Let the ladies go first. Chǐng 'syáujye 'tàitaimen 'syān dzŏu. /She is a fine young lady. Tā shŕ yíge 'hĕn 'syánhwèide syáu'jyĕ. *but* /Ladies and gentlemen! Jūwèi lái'bīn.

(As a prefix indicating the female sex) nyǘ. /I have a lady friend. Wó yŏu yíge 'nyŭpéngyou.

(Well-bred woman) is expressed indirectly or by 'dàjyāgwēisyŏu. /She acts like a lady. Tā yŏu 'dàjyāgwēisyŏu de 'fēngdù. or expressed as She very much understands etiquette. Tā 'hén dŭng 'lǐjyé.

Lady-killer (fig.) syăubáilyăn.

Ladies' room nyŭtsè swŏ。

LAKE. hú. /I want to row around the lake. Wŏ yàu wéije 'hú °'hwá (°'yáu) yĭdzāur。 **The Great Lakes** 'Béimĕijōu Wŭdà'hú.

LAME. (Crippled) chywé, 'gwăilegwăilede; *or* (expressed as a noun; a cripple) chywédz; (clubfoot) dyānjyàur. /That little boy is lame. Nèi syău'hár shŕ ge °'chywédz (°dyān'jyàur). *or* Nèi syăuhár °'twĕi (°'jyău) yóu dyăr °'chywé (°'gwăilegwăilede). /He became lame after being hit by a car. Tāde twĕi jwàngchywéle.

(Sore and temporarily unable to move comfortably) °twĕi'swānde (°twĕi'téngde) dōu dzŏubú'dùngle, (dzŏulù) yǐ'chywéyǐ'gwăide, dzŏu'lù tǐng fèi'jyèr, yímài'bùr jyŏu 'téng. /I was lame after the horseback ride. Chímá yǐ'hòu wŏ °twĕi'swānde °twĕi'téngde) dōu dzŏubu'dùngle. *or* Wŏ chíwánle 'mă, °(dzŏu'lù) yǐ'chywéyǐ'gwăide (°dzŏu'lù tǐng fèi'jyèr, °yí mài'bùr jyŏu 'téng).

(Poor). /That's a lame excuse. Nèi 'lǐyóu tài 'chyānchyăng. *or* Nèmma shwō shéi 'syìn na? /That's a lame excuse for giving up. 'Yīnwei °'nèige (°'nèmmaje) jyŏu bú'gànle, shéi 'syìn ne?

To lame jyàu 。. . 'tsánfèi, (jyàu . . .) lău ge °'tsánji (°chywé'twĕi), jyàu . . . °twĕi (°'jyău) chywéle. /The fall lamed him for life. Tā nèi yí 'shwāi jyàu ta 'tsánfèile yí'bèidz.

LAMP. dēng; **kerosene lamp** 'méiyóudēng; **oil lamp** 'yóudēng; **gas lamp** 'méichìdēng; **safety lamp** báu'syāndēng; **electric lamp** 'dyàndēng. /Let's light the lamp. 'Dyàn-dēng ba. /Light the lamp. Bă dēng 'dyănjáw. /Blow out the lamp. Bădēng 'chwēile. /Turn up the lamp. Bădēng nyán'dàle. *or* (the lampwick) Bă dēng'nyăndz nyăn-'dàle. /Turn down the lamp. Bă °dēng (°dēng'nyăndz) nyán'syāule. /Turn on the lamp (of an electric lamp). Bă dēng 'kāikai. /Turn off the lamp. Bă dēng 'gwānle.

LAND. dì; (real estate) 'dìchăn, 'dìpí. /He inherited a great deal of land. Tā 'chéng-shòule syúdwō °'dìchăn (°'dì, °dìpí).

(Soil) tŭ, dì. /The land here is too poor for farming. Jèrde 'tŭ jùng'dì búgòu 'féi. *or* Jèrde 'dì bùnéng jùng 'dūngsyi.

(Nation) gwó; **native land** *or* **fatherland** 'dzŭgwó, gùsyāng. /He has a great love for his native land. Tā hĕn 'ài tā 'dzŭgwó. *or* Tā dwèi 'dzŭgwó yí'syàng hĕn rè'syìn. *or* Tā hĕn 'lyóulyàn 'gùsyāng.

(Shore) àn; (land in contrast to water) lùdî. / When do you expect to reach land? Nǐ shwō shémma 'shŕhou kéyǐ °kàu'àn (°jyànje lù'dî)?

(Rural territory) núngtswūn. / He always wanted to get back to the land. Tā dzúng syǎng hwéidàu núng'tswūn chyu. or expressed as He's always wanted to return to the happiness of country life. Tā dzǔng 'pànje néng 'chúng syǎng 'tyánywán jr̄ 'lè.

(Mainland) dàlù. / The United States mainland has forty-eight states. Měigwó dàlù yǒu szshrbā jōu.

To land (come to earth) làu, jyànglè, lèdî. / About a hundred planes take off and land here every day. Měityān yǒu yì'bǎiláijyà fēi'jǐ dzàijèr °'chīya 'làude (°yǒude chǐ'fēi yǒude jyàng'lè, °yǒude chǐ'fēi yǒude lè'dî, °chǐ'fēi jyànglè). / The pilot landed the plane at night. °Jyàshr̀'ywán (°Kāifēi'jǐde) dzài 'yèli bǎ fēi'jǐ °jyàng'lède (°lè'dîde).

(Fall) dyàu (drop); shwāi (slip or stumble); dzwò (sit down). / The car landed in the ditch. Chǐ'chē dyàu 'gōuli le. / Too many of my golf balls have landed in that pond. Wǒde gāuěrfū'chyóu hěn dwō dōu dyàudzài nèi shwěi'kēnglǐ le. / He slipped on the ice and landed with a thud. Tā dzài 'bīngshàng yì'hwá jyòu pā'jǐde yísyàr °'shwāidǎule (°'dzwònàrle).

(Catch; of fish) dēi, dǎi, 'dyàushanglai. / You should have seen the fish I almost landed. Wǒ chà'dyǎr °méi'dēije (°méi'dyàushanglai) de nèityáu 'yú, kě'syǐ nǐ méi-'kànjyàn.

(Of a contract) bàn'chéng, shwō'chéng. / I landed a big contract today. Wǒ jyēr °bàn'chéngle (°shwō'chéngle) yì̀jwāng dà 'mǎimai.

(Of a job) 'jǎujáu. / He finally landed a job. 'Jyēgwǒ tā 'jǎujáule ge 'shèr.

LANGUAGE. yǔyán (somewhat literary); hwà, shwōde 'hwà (spoken language); wéndz̀ or (in combinations) wén (written language). / Some nations have several spoken languages, and some have no written language. Yǒu 'jǐ gwó yǒu háujíjǔng 'yǔyán; yǒu 'jǐgwó méiyǒu 'wéndz̀. / Language is one of the things that distinguish human beings from animals. 'Rénlèi gēn 'chínshòu bùtúngde 'dìfang yǒu 'yǐdyǎn jyòushr rén °néng shwō'hwà (°yǒu 'yǔyán). / This is a textbook on the Japanese language, spoken and written. Jèibén jyàukē'shū jyǎngde shř °Rběn'hwà gēn Rběn'wèn (°dzěmma shwō Rběn 'hwà gēn dzěmma syě Rběn 'wén). / What languages do you know? Nǐ dōu °tūng (°hwèi) 'néijǐ 'gwó °wéndz (°'hwà)? / The baby speaks a language all her own. Jèi háidz shwōde 'hwà 'méirén 'dǔng. (fig.) / You have got to talk his language. is expressed as You have to talk the way he does. Nǐ děi ànje 'tāde shwō。 / We don't talk the same language. is expressed as We don't understand each other。 Wǒmen bùdǔng bítsž'shwōde.

(Way of speaking, words used) hwà; **use bad language** may be expressed by constructions with hwà, or also as sātswūn (of vulgar language) or mǎjyē (of profane or abusive language). / His language is terrible. Tāde 'hwà hěn 'tsū. / Try not to use bad language here. Dzàijèr néng bùshwō °'bùhǎu'tīngde hwà (°'dzānghwà, °'tsūhwà, °nán'tīng de hwà), jyòu 'byé shwō. or Dzài 'jèr lyóu'shén byé °sā'tswūn (°mǎ'jyē, °mà'rén).

LARGE. dà (of size); dwō, bùshǎu, hǎu syē (a large amount or number of); gāu (in number). / This room is not large enough. Jèi 'wūdz bùgòu 'dà. / I want a larger desk. Wǒ yàu ge 'dàdyǎrde shū'jwōr. / This is the largest building in town. Jèi shř jèr 'dzwèi dàde 'lóu (le). / He wants a larger share. Tā syǎng 'dwō yàu dyar. / He wants a larger share of responsibility. Tā syǎng 'dwō gwán dyǎr 'shèr. / A large crowd gathered to watch the fire. Chí'hwǒ de nàr jyùle °hǎusyē rén (°hěn 'dwō rén, °yídà'chyún rén) dzàinàr 'kàn. / Large quantities of ammunition can be shipped by plane. 'Dàlyàngde jyūnhwǒ kéyi yùng 'fēijī yùn. / He spent a large part of the time talking about politics. Tā °yùngle 'hǎusyē gūngfu tán (°tánle 'hǎu bàn-tyānde) 'jēngjr̄shangde shèr. / To a large extent we'll have to raise our own food. °Yí'dàbànde (°'Hǎusyē, °Hěndwōde) 'chr̄shr̄ déi wǒmen 'dz̀jǐ lái °bàn (°jùng). / The enemy has a large number of casualties. Díren sz̄shāngde shùmu hěn 'gāu.

At large (not imprisoned) is expressed as taking it easy outside the law 'syāu-yáufǎ'wài; or as has escaped pǎule. / The thief has been at large for two days. Syàutōur 'syāuyáufǎ'wài yǒu 'lyǎngtyān le. or Dzéi 'pǎule lyǎng'tyān le.

At large (as a whole) chywán. / The country at large is interested in the problem. 'Chywángwó 'dōu hěn 'jùyì jèige 'wèntí. / He's a congressman at large. Tā jèige 'syàyîwàn yǐ'ywán shr̄ 'dàibyǎu chywán'shěng de.

LAST. (Final(ly)) dzwèi 'hòu(de), mwò, mwò'lyǎur(de); 'dàushù dì'yī (first counting backwards); or expressed indirectly as there is only 'jr̄ yǒu, or as and then no more dzài 'méiyou le, etc. / I spent my last dollar for lunch. Wǒ bǎ °dzwèi 'hòu (°mwò-lyǎurde, °'mwò) yīkwài 'chyán 'hwādzai wǔ'fànshang le. / The last battle of the war was fought here. °Dzwèi 'hòu (°'Mwò, °Mwò'lyǎurde) yí'jàng shr̄ dzài 'jèr dǎde. / He's the last one left now. is expressed as There only remains he alone. 'Jyòu shèngsya tā 'yíge rén le. / She said she wouldn't marry him if he were the last man on earth. Tā shwō, jyòushr 'shr̄jyèshang °jr̄ (°jyòu) 'shèng tā 'yíge nánrén tā yěshr bú'jyà ta. / He was last. Tā shr̄ 'mwòyíge. or Tā shr̄ dzwèi 'hòude yíge. / He came last. Tā dzwèi 'hòu dàude. or Tā shr̄ dzwèi 'hòude yíge dàude. or Tā shr̄ 'mwòyíge dàude. or (on a list or in turn) Tā dzài dzwèi mwò'lyǎur ner. or Tā dzài 'dàushù dì'yī ner. / These were his last words before he died. Jè shr̄ tā méi'sz̀ yǐ'chyán dzwèi 'hòude jijyù 'hwà. / This is my last word. Jèi shr̄ wǒ dzwèi hòu yàu shwō de (jijyù 'hwà). or expressed as After speaking this time I'll say no more. 'Jèitsz shwōle yǐ'hòu wǒ jyou 'dzài bushwō le. / This is your last chance. Jèi shr̄ nǐ dzwèi 'hòude 'jīhwei le. or expressed as After this time there is no more such chance. 'Jèitsz yǐ'hòu 'dzài méiyǒu jèmma ge 'jīhwei le. or as There is only this chance. 'Jr̄ yǒu 'jèitsz 'jīhwei le. / That was the last straw. is expressed as That is simply impossible to bear anymore. Nà 'jyǎnjr̄ shr̄ 'bùnéng dzài 'rěn le.

(Most recent(ly)) dzwèijìn; 'shàng(yi) (of events, times); 'chyán(yi) (the former); jèi (this or these last); last night °'dzwór (°'dzwótyān) wǎnshang; the night before last 'chyántyān wǎnshang; last week 'shàng(ge) °lǐbài (°syīngchī); last month 'shàng-(ge) ywè; last year 'chyùnyán; last Monday (last Tuesday, etc.) shànglǐbài'yī or shàngsyīngchī'yī (shànglǐbai'èr or shàngsyīngchī'èr, etc.); the last few days 'chyán-jityān, 'jèijityān; the last few weeks 'chyánjige °lǐbài (°syīngchī), jèijige °lǐbài (°syīngchī); the last few months chyánjíge ywè, jèijige ywè; the last few years 'chyánjinyán, 'jèijinyán. / When were you in Chungking last? Nǐ dzwèi 'jìn shr̄ shémma shr̄hou? / The last movie I went to was two years ago. Wǒ 'shàngyitsz kàn dyàn'yǐngr shr̄ lyángnyán yǐ'chyán le.

(Most unlikely). / That was the last thing I expected him to do. is expressed as It was my opinion that he absolutely wouldn't do that. Wó 'yǐwéi tā 'jywé buhwèi 'gǎnchū 'nèijǔng shr̄ lai ne. or as I never thought he'd do that. Wǒ 'méisyǎng'dàu tā hwèi gǎnchu 'nèijǔng shr̄ lái.

At last kě, dàu'lyǎur; 'jyēgwǒ (the final result); dzwèi'hòu. / At last we found the place. Wǒmen °'kě (°dàu'lyǎur, °'jyēgwǒ, °dzwèi'hòu) bǎ nèige 'dìfang 'jǎujau le.

The last dzwèi mwò'lyǎur, 'mwòyíge, mwò'lyǎurde yíge. / He was the last to leave. Tā shr̄ °dzwèi mwò'lyǎur (°etc.) dzǒude.

The last of. / You haven't heard the last of it yet. <u>is expressed as</u> This isn't finished yet. Jèi shèr hái méi'wán ne. / You'll never hear the last of it. <u>is expressed as</u> You wait and see, it will never end. Nǐ 'chyáuje ba, 'chyè méi'wǎn ne. / I hope we've seen the last of her. <u>is expressed as</u> I hope this is the last time we see her. 'Syǐwàng jèi shr dzwèi'hòu yi'tsz chyáujyan ta. <u>or as</u> I hope that hereafter she won't trouble us anymore. 'Syǐwang yǐ'hòu tā 'dzài bùlái 'máfan dzámen le. <u>or as</u> I hope from now on we won't have any more dealings with her. 'Syǐwang tsúng-'tsž dzámen 'dzài bùgēn ta dǎ 'jyāudai le.

To the last yǐ'jŕ dàu dzwèi hòu; (to death) yǐ'jŕ dàu 'sž. / She believed to the last that her husband would be saved. Tā yǐ'jŕ dàu °dzwèi hòu (°'sž) hái 'yǐwéi tā 'jàngfu yǒu 'jyòur ne。

To last <u>is expressed by any verb followed by an expression of time</u>, especially yùng (be used or usable, use); jīn'yùng (stand use); dǐng, 'jŕchr (hold out); <u>last long</u> <u>may also be expressed simply by</u> jyǒu <u>or</u> cháng; <u>not last long</u> <u>may also be expressed</u> <u>as</u> one moment, then it's past yǐ'hwěr jyou 'gwò le <u>or as</u> one moment, then it's finished yǐ'hwěr jyou 'wán le. / How long does this ride last? 'Jèitang 'chē děi 'dzwò 'dwōshau shŕhou? / It lasted an hour. Yǒu yìdyǎn 'jūng (nèmma 'jyǒu). / The battle lasted five days。 Nèijàng dǎle 'wǔtyān. / Do you think you can last another mile? Nǐ jywéje °hái néng 'dǐng (°néng dzài 'jŕchr, (of running) °hái néng 'pǎu) yìlǐ 'dǐ ma? / It doesn't last very long. Nèi búhwèi °'jyǒude (°'cháng de). <u>or</u> Nèi yǐ'hwěr jyou 'gwòle。 <u>or</u> (of the effect of medicine) Yàude 'lìlyang °búhwèi 'jyǒude (°búhwèi 'chángde, °yǐ'hwěr jyòu 'gwòle). <u>or</u> (of pain) 'Téng yǐ'hwěr jyou 'bùténg le。 <u>or</u> (of someone's anger) Tā shēng'chì yǐ'hwěr jyou 'wán. / This chair won't last very long。 Jèibǎ 'yǐdz °'búhwèi jīn'yùngde (°yùngbu'chángde, °yùngbu-'jyǒude, °'yùngbulyǎu jityān jyou hwèi 'hwàide, °bu'jyēshr). / I didn't think my money would last me until today。 Wǒ méisyǎng'dàu wode 'chyán néng °'yùngdàu (°'hwàdàu) 'jyērge. / This butter will have to last us a week。 Jèidyǎr hwáng'yóu dzámen děi chŕ 'yíge lǐ'bài.

LATE. (Far advanced in time) wǎn, chŕ; **stay up late** dāide 'wǎn <u>or</u> áu'yè (suffer through the night). / It's getting awfully late. (Tyān) tài °'wǎn (°chŕ) le. / He keeps late hours. <u>or</u> He goes to bed late. <u>is expressed as</u> He goes to sleep late. Tā 'shwèide hén 'wǎn. / He sleeps late. <u>is expressed as</u> He gets up late. Tā 'chǐde hén 'wǎn. / Should we come at eight P.M. or later? Wǒmen shŕ 'yīngdāng 'wǎnshang 'bādyǎnjūng dàu, háishr dzài 'wándyǎr? / Don't stay up too late. Byé áu'yè. <u>or</u> Byé dāide tài 'wǎnle. <u>or</u> Byé shwèide tài chŕ.

(Tardy) wǎn; chŕ (used of arriving, with dàu, especially in school); wùle jūng-'dyǎr le (miss the hour); bùnéng àn 'shŕhou (dàu). / I'll be late if I don't take a taxi. Yàu 'búdzwò chì'chē chyù, wǒ jyòu °hwèi 'wùle jūng'dyǎrde (°wùle jūng'dyǎr le, °bùnéng àn 'shŕhou 'dàu le, °'wǎn le, <u>or</u> (for work or school) °chŕ'dàu le). / Don't be late at the theater. °Tīng'syì (°Kàn'syì) byé °chyù 'wǎn le (°'wǎn dàu).

(Recently deceased) 'gāngchyù' shŕde. / Your late Secretary of War was a fine man. 'Gwèigwó 'gāng chyù' shŕde 'lùjyūnbù bù'jǎng 'jēn shŕ ge 'hǎurén. / This is a picture of our late president。 Jèi shŕ yìjāng wǒmen 'gāngchyù' shŕde dzúngtǔngde syàng'pyàn.

Late at night <u>or</u> **at a late hour** 'shēnjīngbàn'yède. / You shouldn't have waked them up at such a late hour. Dzèmma °'shēnjīngbàn'yède (°'wǎn le, °chŕ le) nǐ-'bùgāi bǎ rénjya jyàu'syíngle de.

Late in life 'hǎudà 'swèishur le. / He learned to read and write late in life. Tā 'hǎudà 'swèishur le tsái sywéde 'nyànshūsyě'dž de.

Late in the day 'hòubànshǎngr, 'hòubàntyān, <u>or</u> (dusk, late afternoon) hwáng-'hwūnde shŕhou, bànhēichyǎr, bàn'hēide shŕhou, <u>or</u> (evening) 'wǎnshang. / It was late in the day when she came. Tā shr̀ °'hòubànshǎngr (°hòubàntyān, °hwáng'hwūnde shŕhou, °bàn'hēichyǎr, °bàn'hēide shŕhou, °wǎnshang) dàude. / The mountains are beautiful in the late afternoon. Shān dzài °hwáng'hwūnde shŕhou (°bàn'hēide shŕhou, °bàn'hēichyǎr) hén hǎu 'kàn.

Late show dzwèi'hòu yì'chǎng; (night show) 'yèchǎng. / It was the late show he went to. Tā kànde shr̀ °dzwèi'hòu yì'chǎng (°'yèchǎng).

Late summer (winter, etc.) °'syàtyān (°dūngtyān, °etc.) kwài 'wán le de shŕhou. / I always take my vacation in late summer. Wó 'lǎushr̀ dzài 'syàtyān kwài wán le de shŕhou syē'jyà.

Of late, lately 'jìnlái. / The news has been better of late. 'Jìnlai 'syāusyi 'hǎudyǎr le。

Latest dzwèihòude (final); dzwèijìnde (most recent); dzwèisyīnde (newest). / You can read the latest news in the evening paper. Ní kéyí dzài 'wǎnbàushang 'kàndàu °dzwèi'hòude (°dzwèi'jìnde, °dzwèi'syīnde) 'syāusyi. / This is the latest style. Jèige shr̀ dzwèi'syīnde yàngdz.

At the latest 'dzwèiwǎn, 'jŕwǎn búgwò. / You said you'd be here by five at the latest. Ní 'dzjí shwōde °'dzwèiwǎn (°'jŕdwō búgwò) 'wúdyǎn jwǔn 'dàu jèr.

LATTER. dìèr(ge), 'hòuyī(ge), hòutoude; hòu in some other combinations. / Of the two reports, I prefer the latter. Jèi lyǎ bàu'gàuli, wó 'jywéde dì'èrge 'háu dyǎr. / I said the latter, not the former. Wǒ 'shwō de shr̀ °dì'èrge, búshr dìyíge (°'hòuyíge, búshr 'chyányíge; °hòutoude nèige, búshr 'chyántoude nèige). / He was very successful in the latter part of his life. Tā 'hòubàn bèidz tíng dé'yì.

LAUGH. syàu. / We laughed and laughed. Wǒmen syàule you'syàu. / We laughed a lot about the matter. Wǒmen jywéde nèijyàn shr̀ hén kě'syàu.

Laugh at (make fun of) syàuhwa, syàu. / He was always afraid that people were laughing at him. Tā 'dzúng yǐwéi 'byérén dzài nàr °'syàuhwa (°'syàu) ta.

Laugh off yí'syàu jyòu °'swànle (°'gwòchyule). / When we found a mistake, he tried to laugh it off。 Wǒmen jǎujaule ge 'tswòr, tā syáng nèmma yí'syàu jyòu °'swànle (°'gwòchyule).

Laugh out of. / We laughed him out of his bad temper. Tā shēng'chì jyàu wǒmen 'lyánshwō dài'syàude 'hǔnggwòchyule.

No laughing matter. / It's no laughing matter. Yì'dyár yě 'bùkě'syàu. or 'Búshr nàuje 'wárde.

A laugh 'syàude shēngyīn. / He has a hearty laugh. Tā 'syàude shēngyin hěn 'dà.

Have a good laugh over something dàsyàu yí'jèn. / We had a good laugh over the matter. 'Nèi shèr jyàu wǒmen 'dàsyàule yí'jèn.

LAUGHTER. syàude shēngr (sound of laughing); 'syàude (action of laughing). / We heard loud laughter behind us. Wǒmen 'tīngjyàn 'hòubyǎr yǒu 'hāhā dà'syàude 'shēngr. / She shook with silent laughter. Tā 'syàude bùchū'shēngr, kěshr jŕ 'yáuhwang 'shēndz.

LAUNDRY. (Place where clothes are washed) syíyídyàn, syíyí(shang)fáng, syí'yí(shang)de nàr, syí'yí(shang)de dìfang; (Peiping) syíyídzwō. / These clothes are ready to go to the laundry. Jèisyē 'yīfu gāi sùngdàu syíyí'dyàn chyù le. / There's a lack of help in the laundry. Syíyí'fánglí chywē'rén.

(Clothes washed) 'syĭde yĭfu, 'syĭde dūngsyi. / My laundry just came back. Wŏ náchyu 'syĭde 'yĭfu 'gāng hwéi lai.

(Clothes to be washed) °gāi' syĭde (°yàusyĭde) yĭfu, °gāi' syĭde (°yàusyĭde) dūngsyi. / I've got to take my laundry out. Wŏ ké dĕi bá wŏ gāi 'syĭde 'dūngsyi 'sùngchūchyùle.

LAW. (Legal institutions) 'fălyù; făgwēi (rules and regulations); fádyăn (legal code); fă after one-syllable verbs and in many combinations; civil law mínfă; criminal law syíngfă; national law *or* law of the land gwófă, gwójyā'fălyù; international law 'gwójĭfă, 'gwójĭgūngfă; maritime law 'hăishàngfă; military law 'jyūnfă. / You'll have to obey the law. Ní dĕi shóu 'fă. / You can't expect to break a law and escape the consequences. Ní béng syăng °'fànle (°'wéile) fă hái néng 'syăuyáufă'wài. / He'll be punished according to the law. Yí'dĭng yàu yí'fă °bàn (°chùfen) ta. / It's against the law to park here. Dzàijèr tíng'chē °fàn'fă (°'wéi'fă). / Is there a law against speeding? is expressed as Is speeding against the law? °Kāi 'kwàichē (°Kāichē kāide kwài) fàn'fă ma? or as Is it forbidden to speed? Shŕ 'bùsyŭ kāi 'kwàichē ma? or as Is there a law prohibiting driving a car too fast? Shŕ yóu 'fălyù 'jĭnjŕ bă chē kāide tài 'kwài ma? / He is studying law now. Tā syàndzài °nyàn (°sywé) °'fălyù ne (°'făkē ne). / Who makes the laws in this country? Jèi gwóde °'fălyù (°'făgwēi, °'fádyăn) yóu 'shéi lái 'dĭng? or expressed as In whose hands is the legislative power of this country? Jèi gwóde 'lìfăchywán dzài 'shéi shŏuli? / Don't get into trouble with the law again. Byé dzài fàn'fă le. / I am a law abiding citizen. Wŏ shŕ ge shóu'făde láubăi'syíng. / He took the law into his own hands. is expressed as He didn't follow the law (*or* He didn't go through official procedure), (but) punished people himself. Tā °bùyí'fă (°bùjīng'gwān), 'dzjĭ jyòu °fă'rén (*or* (took revenge) °bàu'chóu). / My brother is practicing law. is expressed as My brother is a lawyer. Wŏ 'gēge dāng lyù'shŕ ne.

(Statement of invariable relationships) lĭ; **natural law** *or* **laws of nature** lĭ *or* tyānlĭ (especially in relation to man or life); 'dzrànlyù (in physics and other sciences); **law of averages** lĭ; **law of gravity** dìsyīnsyĭ'lĭ. / That's against the laws of nature. Nèi jyàn'jŕ shŕ bùhé °'lĭ (°tyān'lĭ, °'dzrànlyù). / According to the laws of nature (*or* of averages), this is bound to happen. Jàu'lĭ shwō, yí'dĭng hwèi 'dzèmmaje de. / Haven't you ever heard of the law of gravity? Nĭ 'nándàu 'méitīngjyàngwo °'dìsyīn yŏu 'syīlĭ nèmma yĭ'shwō ma (°dìsyīnsyĭyĭnlĭ ma)?

(Authority). / His word is law around here. is expressed as Everybody has to listen to his word here. Dzài 'jèr tāde hwà 'shéi dōu dĕi 'tīng. or as He dictates the affairs of this place. Tā °'dúdwàn (°'wŭdwàn) jèige dìfang de 'shrching.

Lay down the law (gĕi . . .) 'dĭng ge 'gwēijyu, jyàu . . . shŏu (establish a rule and make someone obey); (gēn . . .) 'ywēfăsān'jăng (literary quotation, meaning lit. make three stipulations). / He laid down the law to them. Tā gĕi tāmen 'dĭngle ge 'gwēijyu, jyàu tāmen 'shŏu. / My father laid down the law to me last night. Wŏmen làu 'yédz dzwér 'wănshang gēn wo 'ywēfăsān'jăng.

LAWYER. lyùshŕ. / Try to find a good lawyer to handle the case. Syăng'făr jău yíge hăude lyù'shŕ lái 'dă jèige 'gwānsz. / My brother is a lawyer. Wŏ 'gēge dāng lyù-'shŕ ne.

LAY (LAID). (Put) gē, fàng; băi (arrange, put in proper place). / Lay the book here. Bă shū °gē (°fàng, °băi) 'jèr. / Lay the baby on the bed gently. Bă syău'hár chīng-'chīngrde °fàng (°gē) dzai 'chwángshang. / All your clothes are laid out on the bed. Nĭde 'yĭfu 'dōu °gē (°fàng) (dzai) 'chwángshang le. / Lay the board down flat. Bă 'băndz °fàng'píng le (°gē'píng le, °'píngje fàngsya, °'píngje gēsya). / Lay those books down. (flat, not standing on end) Bă 'nèisyē shū °fàng'píng le (°etc., *or* (set them down any way) °'fàngsya, °'gēsya).

(Spread out) pū; (unfold or unroll and spread out) 'pūkāi, 'tānkāi, 'dǎkāi, *or* (to full length) 'pūjankāi; (spread out to cover) méng, jàu. / There was a Persian rug laid on the floor. Dìshang pūje 'Bwōsz dì'tǎn. / The floor was laid with linoleum. Dìshang pūje chǐ'bùdǐ'tǎn. / Lay that scroll on the floor for him to examine. Nèijywǎn dz'hwàr °pūdzai 'dìshang (°dzài 'dìshang 'pūkāi, °dzài 'dìshang 'dǎkāi, °dzài 'dìshang 'tānkāi) gěi ta 'kàn. / She laid a damp cloth over the bowl. Tā 'ná yíkwài 'shr̄bù °'méngdzai (°'jàudzai) 'wǎnshang. / A satin cover was laid on the table. Jwērshang °pūje (°méngje, °jàuje) yíkwài 'dwàndz. / He laid a cement path across his garden. Tā dzài 'ywǎndzli tsúng 'jèi tóur dàu 'nèi tóur pūle yìtyáu 'yánghwēi-'lù. / Laying concrete is backbreaking work. Pū °'yánghwēi (°'sānhétu) 'lèisz 'rén.

(Of bricks) chǐ; (if in a pile with a design) mǎ. / He didn't lay the bricks carefully. Tā 'méi bǎ jwān chǐ'hǎu. / He laid the bricks in a neat pile. Tā bǎ jwān má'hǎule.

(Of tiles) ān, shàng, chǐ. / He didn't lay the tiles evenly. Tā 'méi bá wǎ °ān'jěngchi (°ān'chǐ).

(Of a cornerstone) ān, lì. / The cornerstone was laid in 1900. Chyáng'jyàurde nèikwài 'shr̄tou shr̄ 'yījyǒulíng'língnyán °ānde (°'lìde).

(Of a keel) ān. / It took only two months to build this ship, from the time the keel was laid until it was launched. Nèi chwán tsúng ān lúng'gǔ dàu syà'shwěi yígùng 'lyǎngge ywè.

(Of a foundation) dǎ, dzá, gài, syōu; (fig.) dǎ, lì. / The foundation was laid forty years ago. 'Dìjī shr̄ 'szshr̄nyán 'chyán °dǎde (°dzáde, °gàide, °syōude). / He laid a solid foundation for the business. Tā bá 'mǎimaide 'gēnjī °dǎde (°'lìde) hěn °'láukau (°'jyēshr).

(Of eggs) syà. / This hen lays a lot of eggs. Jèige mǔ'jī syà hěn dwō'dàn.

(Of a wager or money in a wager) *see* **BET.**

(Of a tax) dìng (fix); jyā (add); shōu (put); jyàu rén shàng, yàu rén shàng (make people pay). / They laid a heavy tax on wool. Tāmen gěi máu'rúng °dìngle (°jyāle) hěn jùngde 'shwèi. / They laid a tax on everything. Tāmen 'shémma dōu °jyàu rén shàng'shwèi (°yàu rén shàng'shwèi, °shōu'shwèi).

(Of a trap) ān; shè (of a large or complicated device); syà (of a small device); syàshang, ānshang (only of a net); (fig., of a scheme) dìng, ānpai; or in some cases shè. / They laid a trap for that tiger. Tāmen °ānle (°shèle) ge °syàn'jǐng (°'lúngdz) yàu dǎi nèijr̄ 'láuhǔ. / We've laid a trap for that woodpecker. (if a net) Wǒmen yǐjīng °'syàshang wǎng le (°'ānshang wǎng le, °syàle ge 'wǎng, °ānle ge 'wǎng, *or* (if a loop) °syàle ge 'tàur, °ānle ge 'tàur, *or* (if a snapping trap) °syàle ge 'jyādz, °ānle ge 'jyādz) yau 'dǎi nèige 'běnder'mù. / They laid a trap for you. Tāmen °'shèle ge 'chywāntàur (°'shèle ge 'jìtsè, °'dìngle ge 'chywāntàur, °'dìngle ge 'jìtse, °'dìngle ge 'jāur, °'dìngle ge 'gwēijāur, or use 'ānpai instead of 'dìng) yàu °'hài ni (to hurt you, physically or otherwise) (°jyàu ni shàng'dàng (to take you in), *or* jyàu ni shànggōur (to trick you), *or* °jyàu ni chr̄'kwēi (to make you lose). or more commonly expressed as They intend to hurt you. Tāmen yàu (syàn)'hài ni.

Lay a hand on 'jān yijān, 'pèng yipèng, 'āi yiāi, 'dùng yidùng, 'mwō yimwō. / Don't you dare lay a hand on that child! Nǐ gǎn °'jān yijān (°etc.) nèige 'háidzde!

Lay a scene somewhere. / The scene of his last play is laid abroad. is expressed as The background (*or* scenery) of his last play is abroad. Tā dzwèi'jìn nèichū 'syì °yùngde 'bèijǐng (°chyú'jǐng) shr̄ dzài wài'yáng.

Lay one's cards on the table (lit. and fig.) tānpái. / It's time to lay your cards on the table. Shr̄ nǐmen tān'pái de shr̄hòule.

Lay claim to. / You'd better lay claim to the estate while you can. (of inheritance rights) Hái búchènje 'jèi shr̄hou 'gānkwài 'shēngmíng nèifèr 'chǎnyè °ní yǒu 'chywán lái 'chéngjǐ (*or* (of ownership) °shr̀'nǐ de)?

Lay emphasis on 'jùjùng, jyǎngjyou, dzài . . . tǐng °jù'yǐ (°'jyǎngjyou, °jù'yǐ). / They lay great emphasis on sports at this school. Tāmen jèige sywésyàu °hěn 'jùjùng 'yùndùng (°hěn 'jyǎngjyou 'yùndùng, °dzài yùndùngshang tǐng jù'yǐ).

Lay one's hand on (be able to find) néng jǎu, néng nálai, 'jǎudejáu, 'jwādejù, 'nádejù, yǒu'fár. / I think I can lay my hands on those papers right away. Wǒ syǎng wǒ 'lìkè jyòu néng bǎ nèisyē 'wénjyàn °'jǎujau (°'nálai). / The trouble is that you can't lay your hands on anything to prove that he did it. 'Wèntí jyòushr 'méifár lái jèngmíng shr̀ tā 'gàn de. 'Wèntí jyòushr °'jǎubujáu (°jwābujù, °'nábujù) yìdyǎr 'jèngjyu lái jèngmíng shr̀ tā 'gàn de.

Lay it on thick. / Don't you think he was laying it on a bit thick when he was describing that wonderful job of his? °Shr̀ bushr̀ (°Nǐ 'jywéde bujywéde) tā shwō tā 'dzjǐ dzwò 'shr̀ de shr̄hou 'chwēide tài 'lìhai le? *or* Shr̀ bushr̀ tā shwō tā 'dzjǐ dzwò 'dzèmma hǎu 'nèmma hǎude, 'shwōde yóu dyǎr °gwò'fèn (°gwò'hwǒr)? / Aren't you laying it on a little too thick? Nǐ 'wèimyǎn °chwēide (°shwōde) yóu dyǎr °gwò-'fènle ba (°gwò'hwǒrle ba, °tài 'lìhaile ba). or meaning Aren't you praising me too much? 'Gwòjyǎng, 'gwòjyǎng. *or* 'Bùgǎndāng, 'bùgǎndāng. *or* 'Nèmma shwō jyàu wǒ 'tài nányǐwéi'chíng le.

Lay plans 'dǎswàn, 'jìhwà, 'swànjǐ, dìng 'jìhwà, syǎng fádz. / They laid their plans carefully, but still failed. Tāmen °'dǎswànde (°'jìhwàde, °'swànjǐde, °dìngde 'jìhwa, °syǎngde 'fádz) hěn 'jǒudau, búgwo 'jyēgwǒ 'háishr bù'syíng.

Lay the blame on gwài, 'mánywàn, bǎ tswòr twēidàu . . . shēnshang. / Don't lay the blame on me. Byé gwài 'wǒ ya. *or* Byé 'mánywàn 'wǒ ya. *or* Byé bǎ tswòr twēidàu 'wǒ shēnshang a. or expressed as I can't be blamed. 'Gwàibujáu 'wǒ ya. *or* 'Mánywànbujáu 'wǒ ya. or as It wasn't my doing. Méi 'wǒde shèr a.

Lay aside *or* **lay away** (of an object) gēsya, fàngsya; (of a piece of work) gēsya, gēje, fàngsya, fàngje, lyóusya, lyóuje, lyàusya, lyàuje; (of something for future use) tswún(je), tswúnchilai, shōuchilai, lyóuje, *or* (of money only) jīsyu; *see also* **Lay up** below, and **Put aside** under PUT. / Lay aside your book and listen to me. °'Gēsya (°'Fàngsya) shū tǐng wo shwō'hwà. / If you can't do it now, lay it aside and do it later. Yàushr 'yǐshr̀ 'bùnéng 'dzwò jyòu 'lyóuje déng yǐ'hòu dzài shwō ba. / He laid aside a good sum of money. Tā °'tswúnle (°'tswúnje, °'jīsyu) bùshǎu(de) 'chyán. / Lay that aside for an emergency. Bǎ nèige °'tswúnchǐlai (°'tswúnchilai déng, °'shōuchǐlai lyóuje, °'shōuchǐlai déng, °'lyóuje déng) yǒu'shr̀de shr̄hou yùng ba.

Lay something before someone bǎ . . . 'tíchulai (jyàu . . . *or* dàjyā) 'tǎulwùn. / The chairman laid the plan before us. Jǔ'syí bǎ nèige 'bànfǎ 'tíchulai (jyàu wǒmen *or* dàjyā) 'tǎulwùn.

Lay down one's life jywānchyū, syīshēng, jìnjūng. / He laid down his life for his country. Tā wèi'gwó jywān'chyū.

Lay down the law *see* **LAW.**

Lay in a supply tswúnje. / We'd better lay in a supply of rice. Dzámen mái dyár 'mǐ tswúnje tsái 'dwèi.

Lay into someone bǎ . . . gěi 'dzòu. / They laid into him as though they'd kill him. Tāmen bǎ ta gěi 'dzòude gēn yàu bǎ ta gěi 'dzòusž shr̀de.

Lay off an employee kāi, tsái, sàn, dǎfadzǒu. / They laid off ten men today.

Tāmen jīntyan °'kāile (°tsáile, °'sànle, °'dǎfa'dzǒule) 'shŕge rén. / He was laid off. Tā (jyàu rénjyā) gěi °'kāile (°tsáile, °'sànle).

Lay open. / The blow laid open his skull. Nèi yísyàr bǎ tā °'tóu géi 'dǎpwòle (or (Peiping) °gěi kāi'pyáurle). / Eventually the whole scandal was laid wide open. Dàu'lyǎur nèijyàn °'chòusher (°dyǒu'rénde sher) °dàjyā 'hwěr 'dōu jŕdàu le (°'wánchywán gūng'kāile).

Lay someone **out cold** bǎ . . . géi dǎ °'mēn(°'yūn, °'mēng, °'hwūn)gwòchyu. / That sock on the jaw laid him out cold. Sāi'bāngdzshang nèi yì'chywán bǎ ta géi dǎ mēngwòchyule.

Lay something **to a cause** shwō . . . shŕ 'yīnwei . . . . / If he loses all his money, I'll lay it to his drinking. Rwòshr tā bǎ tāde 'chyán dōu 'hwāle dehwà, wǒ jyòu shwō 'wánchywán shŕ 'yīnwei tā hē'jyǒu.

Lay up (store away) shōuchilai, lyóuchilai, tswúnchilai; see also **Lay aside** above. / We have a lot of vegetables laid up for the winter. Wǒmen 'shōuchǐ bù'shǎude chǐng'tsài lai °wèide (°'wèile) °'dūngtyan chŕ (°hǎu gwò'dūng).

Lay hold of jyōuju, jwāju, dzwànju, lāju. / He laid hold of him. Tā bǎ ta 'jyōujule. See also **Take hold of** under **TAKE**.

Lay waste is expressed by resultative compounds whose second element is hwěi or hwài, or by bǎ . . . hwěile. / The whole region was laid waste by the storm. 'Jèiyídài 'wánchywán jyàu fēng gěi °gwā'hwěile (°gwā'hwàile). / The war laid waste many large cities. 'Jèitsź 'jànshr bǎ 'hǎusyē 'dàchéng dōu 'hwěile.

Be laid up (sick) bìng; (sick in bed) °bìng(°tǎng)dzai 'chwángshang. / He's been laid up with a cold all week. Tā shàng'fēng °bìngle yíge lǐ'bài (°bìng (°tǎng)dzai 'chwángshang yíge lǐ'bàile.

The lay of the land (lit.) 'syíngshr, dìsyíng. / From this hill you can see the lay of the land. Tsúng jèi 'shānshang 'kéyǐ 'kànjyàn °sżjōuwéide dìsyíng (°sżjōuwéide 'syíngshr). (fig.) / I'd like to get the lay of the land around here before I start work. Wǒ syǎng 'syān jŕdàu °'jèr shŕ dzěmma hwéi 'sher (°jèr dà'gàide 'chíngsying) dzài kāishŕ gūng'dzwò.

Layout géjyú. / I like the layout of this house. Wǒ syǐhwan jèige fángdz de géjyú.

LAZY. lǎn. / I'm too lazy to get up. (out of bed) Wǒ 'lǎnde 'chǐlai. or (from elsewhere) Wǒ 'lǎnde 'dùngtan. / Aren't you being a bit too lazy? Nǐ 'wèimyǎn tài 'lán dyǎr le ba. / You can't help being lazy in this hot weather. 'Jèmma rède tyār, rén 'dzrán fā'lǎn. / It's a very lazy way of doing things. 'Nèmmje jyǎn'jŕ shŕ tōu'lǎn. or Jèi shr 'lǎnfádz. / This (the way I'm doing it) is the lazy man's way. Wǒ jèi shŕ 'lǎnrénde 'lǎnfádz.

Lazybones lǎn'gútou. / That boy is a lazybones. Nèige háidz shŕ ge lǎn'gútou.

LEAD (LED). (Guide) lǐng (conduct, or lead by the hand); dài (conduct); chyān (of an animal, by a rope, or of people, by the hand); lā, jwāi, děn, jyōu (pull with force; see PULL). / Please lead us to the U.S. Consulate. Chǐng bǎ wǒmen °'dàidau (°'lǐngdau) 'Měigwo 'Lǐngshŕ'gwǎn chyu. / He led the people onward. Tā (dzài 'chyántou) 'lǐngje 'rénmín chyán'jìn. / He led us on a little further. Tā °lǐngje (°dàije) wǒmen 'yòu wàng chyán 'dzǒule dyar. / He led the child across the street by the hand. Tā °'lāje (°'chyānje, °lǐngje) syǎuhárde shǒu gwò'jyē. / He led the horse to the stable. Tā bǎ 'mǎ chyāndau mǎ'hàu chyule. / The dog led us to his master. Nèityáu 'gǒu bǎ wǒmen lǐngdau tā 'jǔrén nèr chyule. or expressed as

We followed the dog and found his master. Wǒmen gēnje nèityáu 'góu dzǒu, jyòu bǎ tā 'jǔrén 'jǎujaule.

(Be at the front of) dzài (. . .) 'chyántou lǐngje. / The general was leading the parade. 'Jyāngjyūn dzài 'dwèiwu 'chyántou lǐngje.

(Be ahead in a contest) dzài tóuli, dzài chyántou (in a race); yíng (by points in a game); dwō (by votes in an election). / Our horse is leading, but only by a neck. Wǒmende 'mǎ dzài 'tóuli, búgwò syáng'chà jř yǒu yì'dyǎr. / Our team is leading by seven points. Wǒmen jèidwèi 'yíngje chī'fēr ne. / He's leading by 2,000 votes. Tā bǐ 'nèige rén dwō 'lyǎngchyān'pyàu.

(Conduct; in music) lǐng, dài, jřhwēi. / He led them in singing. Tā °'lǐngje (°'dàije, °jř'hwēi) tāmen 'chàng. / I lead their band. Wǒ 'jřhwēi tāmende ywè'dwèi.

(Of a road, etc.) tūng (go through). / This road leads to the bridge. 'Jèityáu lù tūngdau 'chyáu ner. / Where does that road lead? 'Nèityau lù tūng 'nǎr? / It leads to Rome. Tūng Lwó'mǎ. *but* / This road leads to a dead end. (lit. and fig.) is expressed as If you follow this road, somewhere along the way it doesn't go through. 'Jèityáu lù 'dzǒuje dzǒuje jyou bù'tūng le. or as The other end of this road is a blind alley. 'Jèityáu lù 'nèitóur shř ge 'sžhú'tūngr.

(In cards) (syān) chūpái (put out a card); (syān) chū followed by the name of a card or suit. / Who leads? Gāi 'shéi (syān) chū'pái a? / Why did you lead spades? Nǐ wèi'shémma chū hēi'táur ne?

Lead a certain kind of life 'gwò de (řdz) . . . ; (as a way of making a living) dzwòde 'shř . . . . / He's leading a quiet life. Tā syàndzài 'gwò de (řdz) hěn 'ānsyán. / He leads an exciting life. Tā dzwò de 'shř hén 'jǐnjāng. or Tā 'gwò de (řdz) hěn 'rènau.

Lead the way 'syān dzǒu, dzài 'chyántou lǐngje (go first); lǐngtóur (be the leader). / You lead the way. Chǐng nǐ 'syān dzǒu. or Chǐng dzài 'chyántou 'lǐngje.

Lead astray (by setting example, perhaps unintentionally) yǐnhwài; (by teaching) dàihwài, jyáuhwài, lǐnghwài. / He led the child astray. Tā bǎ háidz dài'hwàile.

Lead someone on (get someone to do something) dòu, shwǎ. / He won't marry you. He's just leading you on. Tā 'búhwèi gēn nǐ jyē'hwūn. Tā nà shr °'dòuje (°shwǎje) ni wár ne. or expressed as Don't let him fool you, he's just putting a little candy in your mouth. Byé shàng tāde 'dàng, tā bugwo shr gěi nǐ ge táng 'tóur 'dyōuje.

Lead to (result in, or guide to, indirectly). / That plan is going to lead to disaster. Jàuje 'nèige fádz 'bàn, jwǔn 'dzāu. / The information supplied by that woman led to his hiding place. Ná nèige 'nyǔrén gěi de 'syāusyi dàng 'syànswǒ jyou bǎ tā 'dwòtsángde dìfang 'jǎujaule.

Lead someone to do something jyàu, chywàn, 'jřdǎu; (by deception) bǎ . . . pyàn. / I led him to change his plans. Shř 'wǒ °jyàu (°chywànde) ta gǎide 'júyì. or Tā gǎi 'júyì shř °'wǒ chywànde (°yīnwei 'wǒde ywángu). / He led the police to believe that he planned to run away. (intentionally or unintentionally) Tā jyàu jǐng'chá 'jywéje tā yàu 'pǎu shřde. or (intentionally) Tā gù'yìde jyàu jǐng'chá jywéje tā yàu 'pǎu shřde. or (by deception) Tā bǎ jǐng'chá 'pyànde yǐwei tā yàu 'pǎu le.

Lead up to (a conclusion or request) syǎng shwō, yàu shwō, syǎng yàu shwō (want to say); when the object is a word like this, that, or what, may be expressed as shř . . . 'yìsz. / What did his talk lead up to? Tāde hwà jyóu'jǐng shř 'shémma yìsz ne? or Tā jyóu'jǐng shř syǎng yàu shwō 'shémma ne? / He's trying to lead up to something. Tǐng tāde 'kǒuchì hǎusyàng yǒu shémma 'hwà yàu 'shwō shřde. / What are you leading up to? Nǐ jyóu'jǐng shr °'shémma yìsz (°syǎng shwō 'shémma ne)?

A lead (clue) 'syànswŏ; (suggested route) 'ménlù. / The thief hasn't been caught yet, but the police have some leads. Dzéi hái méidǎi'jáu ne, búgwò 'jǐngchá yóu dyǎr 'syànswŏ le. / When I was looking for a job, he gave me a lead. Wó jǎu'shèr de shŕhou, tā °'jŕdyan gěi wo (°gěile wo) yíge 'ménlù.

(In drama) 'jújyàur. / She had the lead in the play. Tā °chyù (°dzwò, °dāng, °shŕ) nèi 'syìlide 'jújyàur.

Follow one's lead gēnje (followed by a person and a verb of action); (of an example) jàuje . . . de 'bànfa (followed by a verb of action), or expressed as see someone do something or also do it thus kàn . . . yě nèmma . . . ; (of directions) tǐng . . . de °'hwà (°'jŕhwēi, °'dyàudung). / We followed his lead and entered by the window. Wŏmen 'gēnje tā (sywé), yé dǎ 'chwānghu jìnchyude. or Wŏmen jàuje 'tāde bànfa, 'yé dǎ 'chwānghu jìnchyude. or Wŏmen kàn 'tā dǎ chwānghu jìnchyude, 'yě nèmma jìnchyule. / They followed his lead in voicing opposition to my plan. Tāmen 'tǐng 'tāde °hwà (°jŕhwēi, °dyàudung), 'yé fǎndwèichi 'wŏde 'bànfa laile. / They always followed his lead. Tāmen 'lǎu 'gēnje tā 'dzŏu. or (imitate him) Tāmen 'lǎu gēn tā 'sywé. or (of directions) Tāmen 'lǎu tǐng tāde °'hwà (°'jŕhwēi, °'dyàudung). or (of example) Tāmen 'lǎu °jàuje 'tāde bànfa lai 'bàn (°kànje 'tā dzěmmaje tāmen 'yé dzěmmaje).

Take the lead see Lead the way above. / The guide should take the lead and direct us. °Dài'lùde (°Lǐng'lùde) 'yǐngdāng dzài °'chyántou (°'tóule, °'tóuli) °'jānglwoje dyǎr (°'jàuyingje dyǎr). / When we are together he always takes the lead. Wŏmen dzài yí'kwàr de shŕhou, 'lǎu shŕ tā lǐng'tóur.

Leading (outstanding) dzwèi hǎude (best); dìyī lyóu (first rate); dzwèi yōu-'míngde (most famous). / He's the leading chemist of our time. Tā shŕ rú'jīn dzwèi 'hǎude hwàsywé'jyā.

LEAD. (Metal) chyān. / Is this made of lead? Jèi shŕ 'chyān dzwòde ma? / The house is fitted with lead pipes. Fángdzli 'ānde shŕ 'chyān gwǎndz. / I prefer a lead pencil to a pen. Wó syǐhwan yùng 'chyānbǐ, 'bùsyǐhwan yùng 'gāngbǐ. / The lead in the pencil is broken. 'Chyānbǐ lǐtoude 'chyān shéle. / His left leg was packed with lead. is expressed as His left leg was shot quite a few times. Tā 'dzwŏtwěi bèi dǎle háuji-chyāng. (fig.) / My feet feel like lead. Wó jyǎu 'lèide jyǎn'jŕ 'táibuchǐ'lái le.

LEADER. (A person fitted to lead) 'lǐngsyòu. / He's a born leader. Tā tyān'shēngde jyou shŕ ge 'lǐngsyòu.

(Chief) lǐngsyòu (in a good sense, a leader of men); tóur (good or bad, especially in certain combinations, as dàtóurde vanguard or guide, dzéitóur leader of a gang, leader of bandits, ringleader); dǎngkwéi (leader of a party, usually bad); féishŏu (in a bad sense only; of bandits); platoon leader páijǎng. / He was the leader of the movement. (good) Tā shŕ nèipàide 'lǐngsyòu. or (bad) Tā shŕ nèi 'dǎngde dǎng-'kwéi. / We haven't caught the leader of the gang yet. Dzéi'tóur hái méi dǎi'jáu ne.

(Conductor; in music) 'jŕhwēi. / The leader of the band was a very tall man. Ywè'dwèide 'jŕhwēi °'gèr (°'shēnlyang, °'jǎngde) tǐng 'gāu.

Leadership 'lǐngdǎurénde 'néngli.

LEAF. (Part of plant) yèdz, yèr; yè in combinations; tea leaves cháyè, sometimes chá。 / I like to see the leaves on the trees turn color. Wó 'syǐhwan kàn ('shùshangde) shù-'yèdz byàn 'yánshar. / They're picking tea leaves. Tāmen dzài nèr tsǎi 'chá ne. / There are some tea leaves left in the cup. Wǎn'dyèrshang yóu jipyàn 'cháyè.

(Page) pyār. / Many leaves of this book are torn. Jèibèr 'shūli yóu bùshǎu 'pyār dōu 'chéle.

(Section of a table) bǎr. / Add another leaf to the table. 'Jwōdzshang dzài jyā yíkwài 'bǎr.

Gold leaf jīnjř, jīnyèdz.

Turn over a new leaf gǎigwò dz̀'syīn, 'syǐsyīngé'myàn. / If you don't turn over a new leaf soon, you'll be sorry. Nǐ 'yàushr bùgǎn'kwài °gǎigwò dz̀'syīn (°'syǐsyīn gé'myàn) dehwà, (jyāng'lái) 'dzúng yǒu hòu'hwèide nèmma yǐ'tyān.

LEAN. (Of an object) wāi, syé; (of a person leaning to see, hear, speak, etc.; to the side only) wāi(je) shēndz; (forward or to the side) tàn(je) shēndz; (to the side or back, turning at the same time) nyǒu(je) shēndz; (lean over or down, bending at the waist) wān(sya) yāu, máuyāu; (stretching the neck as if to see) tàn(je) tóur; (stretching the neck to see over something) bā(ba) tóur; (stretch the body in any direction) shēn(shen) yāu; (stretch forward) hāyāu; (backward, with face up) yǎng; 'pādzai (followed only by 'ĕrdwoshang, to lean over to talk into someone's ear). / The bookcase seems to be leaning over a little to this side. Shū'jyàdz hǎu syàng yóu dyǎr wàng 'jĕibyar °'wāi (°'syé). / He leaned over and whispered something to his wife. Tā °'wāije shēndz (°'tànje shēndz, °'nyǒugwo 'shēndz lai) gēn tā 'tàitai 'syǎushēngrde 'shwōle jijyù hwà. or Tā 'pādzai tā tàitai 'ĕrdwoshang 'syǎushēngrde 'shwōle jijyù hwà. / If you lean forward, you can see. Nǐ wàng 'chyán °tàntan 'shēndz (°tàntan 'tóur, °yí-'tàn), jyou néng 'kànjyànle. / He leaned over backward in his chair. Tā dzwǒdzai 'yǐdzshang wàng hòu 'yǎng. / He leaned over (or down) to pick up the baby. Tā °wānsya 'yāu lai (°yìmáu'yāur) bá syǎu'hár °bàuchilaile (°jyúchilaile).

Lean against (rest against, of an object) 'kàudzai . . . shang (on side or end); 'lǐdzai, 'kàuje . . . 'lǐ (on end only); 'dǐngdzai . . . shang, 'dǐngje (on end, with top touching); 'dǎudzai . . . shang (of something normally vertical). / Bring me the ladder that's leaning against the tree. Bǎ °kàudzai 'shùshang de (°dǐngdzai 'shùshang de, °lǐdzai 'shùner de) nèige 'tǐdz nálai. / The flagpole is leaning against the wall. 'Chígān ('yìtóur) dǎudzai 'chyángshang le.

Lean against or **lean on** (support oneself, of a person) yǐje, 'yǐdzai . . . shang, 'kàudzai . . . shang, bǎ 'shēndz 'kàudzai . . . shang (with the whole body); kàuje (less common; also means be close to and depend on); fúje, bá 'shǒu fúdzai . . . shang (with the hands or sometimes the arms); 'pādzai . . . shang (forward, with the arms or elbows or sometimes the hands); jǔje (on a stick or cane). / He leaned against the wall and tied his shoes. Tā °'yǐje chyáng (°'yǐdzai 'chyángshang, °bǎ 'shēndz kàudzai 'chyángshang) bǎ syé'dàr jìshangle. / He's leaning back in the chair. Tā dzwǒdzai 'yǐdzshang wàng 'hòu °'yǐje (°'kàuje). / Here, lean on this cushion. °Yǐje (°Kàuje) jèige 'dyǎr. or °Yǐdzai (°Kàudzai) jèige 'dyǎrshang. / As he leaned against the door to listen, it suddenly gave. Tā °yǐdzai (°bǎ 'shēndz kàudzai) 'ménshang 'tīng; 'hūrán mén °'yōukāile (°'dzjǐ kāile). / He leaned on my arm for support. Tā 'fúje wǒde 'gēbwo. or Tā °'yǐdzai (°'kàudzai) wǒde 'gēbwoshang. / He leaned on the table. (with hand or hands) Tā 'fúdzai 'jwōdzshang. or (with elbows or forearms) Tā 'pādzai 'jwōdzshang. / He leaned against the table. (with back, side, or leg) Tā °'yǐje (°'kàuje) 'jwōdz. / He has to lean on his cane to rest awhile before walking on. Tā déi jǔje 'gwèr 'syēhwer tsái néng dzài 'jyēje dzǒu.

Lean something **against** bǎ . . . 'kàudzai . . . shang, bǎ . . . 'lǐdzai, bǎ . . . 'dǐngdzai . . . shang; (on end, with part of the top extending above the point of support) bǎ . . . 'dādzai . . . shang (without bǎ . . . , this would refer to being supported horizontally at two points, as boards on a scaffold). / Lean the ladder against the wall. Bǎ tǐdz 'kàudzai chyángshang. / Lean the ladder against the eaves. Bǎ 'tǐdz 'shàng-byar dādzai fáng'yánshang. / Lean your head against the wall. Bá nǐde 'tóu kàudzai 'chyángshang.

Lean on (depend on someone or something) kàuje; (if depending on another person only, also) jřje, 'yǐkàuje, jàngje, 'yǐlài. / She leans on her mother in everything. Tā 'shémma dōu °'kàuje (°'jřje, °'yǐkàuje, °'jàngje, °'yǐlài) tā 'mǔchin. / I'll have to lean heavily on my memory. Wó děi kàuje wǒde 'jìsying.

Lean over backward (fig.) tài gwòfèn (overdo it); syàng'jǐn fár lai, jílǐ(de) (do all in one's power). / He leaned over backward to please her. Tā °syàng'jǐnle fár lai (°jí'lǐde) °'bǎjye (°'fèngchéng) tā. / He leaned over backward to make her like him. is expressed as To make her like him he was willing to suffer. Tā wèile 'tǎu tāde 'syǐhwan 'nǐngkě 'dzjǐ shòu'wèichyu.

Lean toward or lean in some direction (incline in opinion) 'pyānsyàng; lean toward the left in politics may also be expressed as yóu dyár 'dzwǒchǐng; 'jywéje . . . 'dwèi (feel that . . . is right). / He leans toward the left (in politics). Tā ('jēngjř 'szsyàng) °'pyānsyàng 'dzwǒbyar yìdyǎr (°yóu dyár 'dzwǒchǐng). / I've been leaning toward your viewpoint lately. Jìnlái wǒ ywè lái ywè 'jywéje 'nǐde 'yìjyàn 'dwèi.

Lean (not fat) shòu; tall lean person is also expressed as syīgāu'tyǎur. / I like lean meat. Wǒ 'syǐhwan 'shòuròu. / I'd like some lean meat. Géi wó dyǎr shòuròu. / Who's that tall lean individual over there? 'Nèibyār nèige °syīgāu'tyǎur (°yòu'gāu-yòu'shòude rén) shř shéi?

(Unproductive) 'bùhǎu (bad) preceded by a verbal expression describing the activity in question. / It's been a lean year for farmers. 'Jèiyǐnyán 'shōuchéng 'bùhǎu. / It's been a lean year for black market racketeers. 'Jèiyǐnyán 'hēishřde mǎimai 'bùhǎu.

LEAP. (General term) tyàu; (over a distance, to a higher level, or straight up) tswān; (more vertically than horizontally) bèng. / He leaped from the boat to the shore. Tā tsúng 'chwánshang °tyàudau (°tswāndau) 'ànshang chyule. / The horse leaped over the fence. Mǎ tsúng 'jàlarli °'bèng(°'tyàu, °'tswān)chūchyule. / He leaped out of the window. Tā tsúng 'chwānghu 'tyàuchuchyule. / He leaped to his death (from a high building). Tā tyàu'lóu dž'shāde. or Tā tsúng 'lóushang 'tyàusyalai °dž'jǐnde (°dž'shāde). / The thief leaped over the wall. Dzéi °tswān (°tyàu)gwo 'chyáng chyule. or Dzéi dǎ chyángshang °'tswān(°'tyàu)gwochyule.

A leap is expressed verbally as above. / He made a ten-foot leap. Tā °tyàule (°tswānle yǒu yí'jàng ywǎn. / The frog made a big leap. 'Háma 'tswānle yísyàr. but / It's a ten-foot leap across the brook. is expressed as The brook is ten feet wide. Hè'gōur yǒu yí'jàng kwǎn.

Leaps and bounds. / His fame increased by leaps and bounds. Tāde 'míngshēng chǐlaide jēn 'kwài.

Leap year rwùn nyán. / 1964 was a leap year. Yǐjyóulyòu'sz̀ shř rwùn'nyán.

LEARN. (Receive knowledge) 'jřdaujřdau; (by experience) chángchang (taste); (by suffering) shòudzwèi. / I want to learn all about this country. 'Jèi gwóde yí'chyè wǒ 'dōu syàng 'jřdàujřdàu. / Let him learn a lesson. Jyàu ta shòu dyǎr 'dzwèi yé 'hǎu. or Jyàu ta °'jřdàujřdàu (°'chángchang) nèige 'dzwèr yé 'hǎu.

(Acquire knowledge by studying) sywé; (by studying and practicing) sywésyi; (of a skill only) lyàn. / He learns quickly. Tā 'sywé shémma dōu 'sywéde hěn 'kwài. or Tā 'sywé dūngsyi hěn 'kwài. / That language is very difficult to learn. °'Nèi gwóde (°'Nèijǔng) hwà hěn 'nán sywé. / Are you learning how to type? Nǐ °'lyàn (°'sywé, °'sywésyi) dǎ'dž ne ma?

Learn by heart bèisyalai. / She learned the part by heart. Tā bǎ 'tsér dōu 'bèisyalaile.

Learn that or learn of or learn about is expressed as hear 'tīngjyàn, hear tell

LEARNED

'tīngshwō, or, in some cases know 'jŕdàu. /I didn't learn of his death until today.
Wǒ jŕdàu 'jīntyān tsái °'tīngshwō (°'tīngjyàn, °'jŕdàu) tā 'sžle. /I learned that he
had gone. Wǒ tǐng shwō tā yǐjing 'dzǒule. /I have to learn what you people are doing.
Wó děi 'jŕdau'jŕdau nǐmen gàn 'shémma ne.

    Learn the hard way. /He has to learn the hard way. Tā děi chŕ dyar kǔ tsái
'jŕdau.

LEARNED. (Erudite) yǒu sywéshr(de), yǒu sywéwen(de), bwó sywé(de). /He gives the
impression of being a learned man. °'Kàn tā (něi'yàngr) (°Tā nèiyàngr jyàurén
'jywéje tā) °hén yǒu'sywéwen shŕde (°hěn bwó'sywé shŕde). or (somewhat sarcastically) Kàn tā 'nèijǔng 'shénchǐ 'fāngfú shŕ ge 'syāngdāng °yǒu'sywéshr (°yǒu-
'sywéwen, °bwó'sywé) de rén.

LEARNING. (Erudition) sywéwen; **have learning** yǒusywéwen, bwósywé dwō'wén,
shòugwo 'jyàuyù. /The book shows a great deal of learning. Jèiběr shūli 'sywéwen
'dà le. /He has no learning to speak of. 'Tā nèige rén °'jēn shŕ 'bùsywéwú'shù
(°'méi shòugwo shémma 'jyàuyù, °'méi shémma 'sywéwen). /Learning is a life-
long project. Hwódau 'lǎu sywédau 'lǎu.

LEAST. (Smallest amount) dzwèi shǎu, dǐng shǎu; (less than all other people) bǐ 'shéi
dōu 'shǎu. /He worked the least but was paid the most. Tā dzwò de shèr 'dzwèi
shǎu, kěshr ná de 'chyán dzwèi 'dwō. /A got less than B, but C got the least. A
déde bǐ B shǎu; C déde °bǐ 'shéi dōu 'shǎu (°'dzwèi shǎu). /He was the one who
did the least work but got the most money. 'Tā jyou shr nèige bǐ 'shéi dzwòde shèr
dōu 'shǎu kěshr bǐ 'shéi náde 'chyán dōu 'dwō de nèige rén.

    (Smallest; in the smallest degree) dzwéi or dǐng (most) followed by a stative
verb or descriptive phrase of opposite meaning from that of the English. /The least
capable ones should be discharged at once. °'Dǐng (°'Dzwèi) °bù'syíngde (°bù-
chéngde, °méi 'bēnshr de) yīnggāi lǐ'kè jyou 'tsź le. /I like this one least of all.
Wó °'dǐng (°'dzwèi) bùsyǐhwān de shŕ 'jèige. /Of the four boys, he seemed to have
the least chance of success at that time. (of future possibilities) Nèi shŕhou nèi-
'sžge háidzli 'tā hǎusyàng shŕ °'dzwèi méiyǒu 'chūsyi de (or (of a particular
situation) is expressed as be entirely unable to do anything °'jywé chéngbulyǎu
shémma'shŕ de). /That's the least of my worries. is expressed as That is what is
most useless for me to worry about. 'Nèi shŕ wǒ 'dzwèi yùngbujáu 'chóu de. or as
I worry but little about that. 'Nèige wǒ dàu 'bùdzemma chóu. /I am least interested
in politics. Wǒ dwèi jèngjr 'dzwèi méisyǐngchyu.

    (Even a little) yì'dyǎr(...) (in negative sentences, yě or dōu usually follows
yì'dyǎr before the negative; a noun after least in this construction is usually an action
noun and often is expressed by a verb in Chinese). /He doesn't have the least concern
for his appearance. Tā yì'dyár yě bù'jyǎngjyou wài'byǎu. /He hasn't the least
consideration for other people's feelings. Tā yì'dyár °yě (°dōu) méiyou 'tǐlyàng
'byérénde °'syīn (°'yìsz). or Tā yì'dyár °yě (°dōu) bùgwǎn 'byérén shòude'lyǎu
shòubu'lyǎu. /If you had the least consideration for other people's feelings, you
wouldn't say that. Nǐ yàushr yǒu yì'dyár'tǐlyàng byérénde 'syīn a, ní °yě búhwèi
shwōchu 'nèijǔng hwà lai (°jyou búhwèi shwōchu 'nèijǔng hwà laile). /You haven't
the least chance of winning him over. is expressed as If you want to win him over,
it is definitely impossible. Nǐ yàu syǎng bǎ 'tā lāgwolai, nà shŕ 'jywé(dwèi)
(°'wànwān) bànbu'dàu de 'shŕ. /You haven't the least chance of doing that. is
expressed as If you want to do that it's definitely impossible. Nǐ yàu syǎng ¯nèmma-
je, nà shŕ °'jywé(dwèi) (°'wànwān) bànbu'dàu de 'shŕ.

    At least 'jŕ shǎu, 'dǐng shǎu; (as the least desirable thing) 'jŕ bújǐ; (in any
case) 'wúlwùnrú'hé; (no matter what) bùgwǎn dzěmma 'yàng; (to the least extent)

688

LEAVE

dzwèi dī syàn'dù. / The trip will take at least three days. Jèiyí'tàng 'jř sháu děi
yùng sān'tyān. / You might at least have written to me. Nǐ 'wúlwùnrú'hé yě °'gāi
(°'kéyi) géi wǒ lái fēng 'syìn. / He should at least let us know. Tā dzwèi dī syàn-
'dù yīnggai 'gàusung wǒmen yisya. *or* Tā jřbú'jǐ yě yīnggai 'tūngjr wǒmen.

Not in the least yǐ'dyár yě bu-. / I don't mind the noise in the least. Wǒ yǐ-
'dyár yě bú'dzàihu nèige 'shēngyin.

The least (one can do, etc.) is expressed as at least (see above). / That is the
least you can do. °Bùgwán dzémma'yàng (°'Jř shǎu, °'Jř bújǐ, °'Díng shǎu, °Dǐng
bú'jǐ, °'Wúlwùnrúhé) 'nèige ní dzǔng kéyi dzwò'dàule(ba).

The least possible is expressed by a stative verb or descriptive phrase in the
construction 'ywè . . . ywè 'hǎu. / This work has to be done in the least possible
time. 'Jèijyàn shèr děi kwài'kwārde gàn'wánle, °wánde 'ywè kwài ywè 'hǎu
(°fèide 'shřhour ywè 'shǎu ywè 'hǎu). *or* Jèige 'fēidéi gàn'kwài dzwòchulai tsái
'syíng, wánde 'ywè kwài ywè 'hǎu.

To say the least 'byéde 'búyùng shwō le; or expressed as at least (see above).
/ He made a brave attempt, to say the least. 'Jř shǎu tā 'gǎn nèmma 'gànle yisyar.
/ We were surprised, to say the least. 'Byéde 'búyùng shwō le, 'jř shǎu wǒmen
syàle yí'tyàu.

LEATHER. pídz *or* (especially in combinations) pí. / Is this saddle made of the best
leather? Jèige (mǎ) 'āndz shř yùng 'dzwèi hǎude 'pídz dzwòde ma? / This isn't
made of real leather. Jèi 'búshr 'jēn pídz dzwòde. / This book is bound in leather.
Jèiben 'shūde 'shūpyér shř °'píde (°'pídz dzwòde). / I gave her a leather bag. Wó
géi ta yige pí'bāu. / He bought a pair of leather gloves. Tā mǎile yífù 'píshǒu-
'tàur.

LEAVE (LEFT). (Let remain, including especially leave behind; of something or someone that was already there) lyóu(sya) (intentionally); shèng(sya) (so that some remains); là(sya) (go away without); dyōu(sya), lyàu(sya); or expressed indirectly.
/ He took all the money but left these jewels. Tā bǎ 'chyán dōu nádzǒule, kěshr bǎ
jèisyē 'shǒushř °'lyóusyale (°'làsyale, °'lyàusyale, °'dyōusyale). / We were left
behind. Bá wǒmen gěi °'lyóusyale (°'shèngsyale, °'làsyale). (*See also* **Leave
behind,** meaning outdistance, below.) / Leave him behind to watch things. 'Lyóusya
ta kānje 'dūngsyi. / I don't like him around; let's leave him behind. Wǒ bu'ywànyi
gēn ta dzài yí'kwàr; 'bǎ ta 'lyóusya ba (*or* (make him stay here) °jyàu ta dzài jèr
'dāije ba, *or* (not let him go along) °'byé jyàu ta 'gēnje, °'byé jyàu ta 'chyù). / I
left my hat in the restaurant. Wǒ bǎ 'màudz °'làdzai (°dyōudzai) fàn'gwarli le.
/ He left half a bowl of rice. Tā 'shèng(sya)le 'bànwǎn 'fàn. / Don't leave any rice
in your bowl. Wanli yǐ'dyǎr fàn yě 'búyàu 'shèng(sya).

(Put or cause to remain when leaving; of something that was not there before)
lyóu(sya). / Leave a note saying we called. Lyóu(sya) ge °'tyáur (°'dzèr) shwō
dzámen 'láigwòle. / He left a message for you. (if written) Tā géi ni lyóule ge
°'dzèr (*or* (verbal) °'hwàr). / We must leave a sentry here. Jèr děi 'lyóu ge rén
'kānje. / I left three dollars for him. Wǒ gěi ta 'lyóu(sya)le 'sānkwài chyán.

(Do something to something when leaving, or before leaving) is expressed by
saying what is done and adding the verb dzǒu. / He dragged the suitcase out of the
car and left it on the road. Tā bá shǒutí'syāng tsúng 'chēli 'jwàichulai, °fàngdzai
(°gēdzai, °rēngdzai, °dyōudzai) 'lùshang jyou 'dzǒule. / He left his desk clean.
Tā bǎ jwōdz shǒushr'gānjingle 'dzǒude. / He always leaves his desk clean. Tā 'láu
bǎ jwōdz shǒushr'gānjingle tsái 'dzǒu.

(For future reference or safekeeping, including especially leave with) gē, fàng,
tswún. / May I leave my books here for a while? Wó bǎ 'shū dzài jèr °'gē (°'fàng,

689

°'tswún) yǐhwěr, 'syíng ma? / May I leave my trunks with you? Wó bǎ 'syāngdz °gē (°fàng, °tswún) 'nǐ nèr, 'syíng ma? / May I leave it with you for a few days? Wó bǎ 'jèige dzài 'nǐ jèr °'tswún (°'gē, °'fàng) jityān, 'syíng ma? / I'll leave it with you then. 'Nèmmaje jyou °tswún (°gē, °fàng) 'nǐ jèr ba. or (permanently) 'Nèmma-je jyou 'lyóudzai nǐ jèr le. / I left three dollars with him. Wǒ °gē (°fàng, °tswún) tā nèr 'sānkwài chyán.

(Hand over for care or use, including especially leave with) jyāugei, lyóu, gē, fàng, tswún. / I left three dollars with him (to use in a certain way). Wǒ 'jyāugei tā 'sānkwài chyán. / I left two dollars with the next-door neighbors to pay the news-boy for me. °Wǒ 'jyāugei jyè'byěr (°Wǒ gěi jyè'byěr lyóule, °Wǒ tswúndzai (or gēdzai or fàngdzai) jyè'byěr nèr) 'lyǎngkwài chyán 'tǐ wǒ gěi sùng'bàude. / Leave the baby with us if you want to go. Nǐmen yàu syǎng 'chyù dehwà, bǎ 'háidz °jyāugei 'wǒmen ba (°lyóu(dzai) 'wǒmen jèr ba, °gē(dzai) 'wǒmen jèr ba, °fàng(dzai) 'wǒmen jèr ba).

(Bequeath, including especially leave to) 'lyóu(gei); (by a will) jyàu . . . 'chéng-shòu. / She will leave the house to her son. Tā yàu bǎ nèiswǒr 'fángdz lyóugei ta 'érdz. or Tā yàu jyàu tā 'érdz 'chéngshòu nèiswǒr 'fángdz.

(Be survived by) 'shēnhòu 'lyóusya, 'shēnhòu 'pyēsya. / He leaves a wife and three children. Tā 'shēnhòu 'lyóusya ge tàitai gēn sānge háidz. or Tā 'shēnhòu 'pyēsyale ge 'gwǎfu hé sā 'háidz.

(Let remain unchanged) is expressed by a negative word with a verb expressing a change, or by a verb indicating the status quo usually followed by -je; if it is an object that is left unchanged, lyóu is sometimes added; see also **Leave** someone **alone,** below. / They left all the lights on. is expressed as They didn't turn off a single light. Tāmen 'yíge dēng yě méi'gwān. / I left the door open. Wǒ méigwān 'mén. / He left everything as it was. is expressed as He didn't touch anything. Tā shémma dōu méi'dùng. or as When he left he put everything in its original place. Tā 'dzǒu de shŕhou 'shémma dōu jàu 'ywányàngr 'gēje. / He left his food untouched. Tā 'fàn yì'dyǎr dōu °méi'dùng (°méi'chŕ). / Leave everything as it is. 'Shémma dōu byé °'dùng (°'mwō). or Dzǒu de shŕhou 'shémma dōu jàu 'ywányàngr gē'hǎule. / Leave your coat off. °Byé (°Béng) chwān 'shàngyī le. / Leave your hat on. 'Dàije 'màudz ba. or °Byé (°Béng) jāi 'màudz le. / Many items were left for the next meeting. Hǎusyē 'shèr dōu méi fù byǎu'jywé, lyóuje děng 'syàtsż kāi'hwèi dzài 'shwō. / A great many things were left unsaid. (undiscussed) Hǎu'syē °hwà (°'shèr) dōu méi °'tí (or (not said for lack of time or opportunity) °dé 'jīhwei shwō, °yǒu 'jīhwèi shwō, °láide'jí shwō). / Let's leave it at that. Dzámen byé °gǎi (°'dùng) le. or 'Jyòu nèmmaje 'swàn le. / Let's leave the matter open. Jèi shèr °yǐ'hòu dzai jywé-'dìng ba (°bubì syàn'dzài jywé'dìng). / I left the door unlocked. Wǒ méiswǒ 'mén. / I left the door unlocked for you. (if you is stressed) Wǒ méiswǒ mén shr wèi 'nǐ. (if left unlocked is stressed) Wǒ gei ni 'lyóuje mén ne.

(Depart) dzǒu; (for some place) chyù. / I must leave now to catch that train. Wó kě 'jèn děi 'dzǒu le, háu 'gǎnshang nèitàng hwǒ'chē. / I'm leaving. Wǒ yàu 'dzǒu le. / He has left already. Tā 'yǐjīng 'dzǒule. or (gone to a place) Tā 'yǐjīng 'chyùle. / He has left for home. Tā hwéi'jyā chyùle. / I am leaving for school. Wǒ dàu sywé'syàu chyù.

(Depart from a place or person) °tsúng (°dǎ) . . . dzǒu; (especially permanently) 'líkāi; (leave the country) chū'gwó, chūyáng; (leave home) chū'mér (go out the door). / He left the station at seven and must be home by now. Tā 'chīdyǎnjūng °tsúng (°dá) hwǒchē'jàn dzǒude, 'jèi shŕhou yí'dìng dàu'jyā le. / I'm leaving this place. Wǒ yàu 'líkāi jèr le. / I'm going to leave you now. Wǒ yàu 'líkāi nǐ le. / He left home when he was sixteen. Tā shŕ'lyòuswèi °líkāide 'jyā (°tsúng (dǎ) 'jyāli dzǒude, °jyou líkāi'jyā le, °jyou tsúng (or dǎ) 'jyāli dzǒule). / I'm going to leave this country within a month. Wǒ yíge 'ywè yǐ'nèi yàu ᵒ'líkāi jèr (ᵒchū'gwó, ᵒchū'yáng). /This time he left home for good. Tā 'jèitsž ᵒ'líkāijyā (ᵒchū'mér) jyou 'bùhwéilai le. /I was forced to leave school. Wǒ shř bèi 'chyángpwò líkāi sywésyàude.

(Depart; of a train, bus, etc.) kāi. /The train leaves at six. Hwǒchē 'lyòudyǎn 'kāi.

(Quit a job) búdzwò le (stop doing); búgàn le (stop working; need not take an object); tsźjŕ (resign). /I'm leaving my job. Wǒ yàu bú'gàn le. or Jèi 'shèr wǒ yàu bú'dzwò le. or Wǒ yàu tsž'jŕ (bú'gàn) le.

(Desert a husband or wife) 'bùgēn . . . yíkwàr 'gwò le (stop living with); gēn . . . lí (separate or divorce); lí'hwūn (divorce); fēn'jyū (separation); or expressed as run off with someone (else) gēn rén 'pǎu(le). /She left her husband. Tā 'bùgēn tā 'jàngfu yíkwàr 'gwò le. or Tā gēn tā 'jàngfu 'líle. or Tā gēn rén 'pǎule. or Tā gēn tā jàngfu ᵒlí'hwūn (ᵒfēn'jyū) le.

Leave someone **alone** (not bother) bùgwǎn; bùlǐ (not do anything for); bùjyàu, bù'dájyàu (not disturb); ràng . . . ᵒ'yíge rén (ᵒ'džgér) nèng (let someone do something by himself); 'swéi . . . chyù (let someone do as he likes); . . . 'ài dzěmmaje, jyou 'jyàu . . . 'dzěmmaje (let someone do anything he pleases). /Leave me alone. Byé 'gwǎn wo. or (rude) Ní gwǎnde'jáu ma? or 'Chyù nǐ yǐ'byǎr chyù. /Leave him alone. Byé 'gwǎn ta. or Byé 'lǐ ta. or Byé 'jyàu ta. or Byé 'dájyàu ta. or 'Swéi ta chyù ba. or Tā 'ài dzěmmaje jyou ᵒ'jyàu ta dzěmmaje ba (ᵒ'swéi tā chyù ba). or Ràng ta ᵒ'yíge rén (ᵒdž'gér) nùng ba.

Leave someone **behind** (outdistance) là(sya); for other meanings see first paragraph above. /We were left behind. Wǒmen jyàu rén gěi 'làsyale. /We walked so fast that we left them far behind. Wǒmen dzǒude tǐng 'kwàide, bǎ tāmen ᵒ'làle háu (ᵒ'làde tíng) 'ywǎn.

Leave someone **cold** (unaffected) bú'jyàu . . . dùng'syīn, . . . bù'jywéde dzěmma'yàng. /That speech left me cold. Wǒ 'tīngle nèige 'yánjyǎng yǐ'hòu, yǐ'dyár yě ᵒbù'jywéde dzěmma'yàng (ᵒbú'jyàu wǒ dùng'syīn).

Leave something **out** làsya; bù'gējinchyu, bú'fàngjinchyu (not put in). /When you copy it, don't leave anything out. 'Chāude shŕhou 'shémma yě 'byé 'làsya. /Leave it out. ᵒBúyùng (ᵒByé) ᵒ'gējinchyu (ᵒ'fàngjinchyu).

Leave someone **out** byé bǎ . . . swànshang, bǎ . . . 'chúchuchyu, 'méi . . . shemma shŕ. /You can go and fight the police, but leave me out (of it). Nǐ chyù gēn jǐng'chá dǎ'jyà chyù, ᵒbyé bá 'wǒ swànshang (ᵒbá wǒ chúchuchyu, ᵒméi 'wǒ shemma shŕ).

Leave something **to** someone (of an action) jyàu followed by the person and a verb expressing the action; ràng (allow) in the same construction; ᵒ'gēje (ᵒ'lyóuje) děng (put or leave in someone's hands) in the same construction; (of a thing, by inheritance) see above under the meaning bequeath; lyóugei (save for). /Leave it to him! (sarcastically, meaning that's the way he does it every time or it never fails). Tā 'lǎu nèmmaje. or (manage) Jyàu 'tā ᵒ'gwǎn ba (or (do) ᵒ'nùng ba, ᵒbàn ba, or (wash, as dishes or laundry) ᵒ'syǐ ba, or (say) ᵒ'shwō ba, ᵒetc.). /Leave everything to me. 'Dōu jyàu 'wǒ gwǎn 'hǎu le. or 'Shémma dōu ràng 'wǒ lái hǎu le. or ᵒ'Gēje (ᵒ'Lyóuje) déng 'wǒ lái 'nùngba. etc.

Leave a way open or **out** is expressed with lyóu. /Leave a way open for him. Gěi ta 'lyóu ᵒge 'dìbù hǎu syà'tái (ᵒge 'twèishēnde 'dìbù, or (escape confinement) ᵒge 'lùr). /He always leaves himself a way out. Tā lǎu gěi dž'jǐ lyóu ge ᵒ'twèishēnde 'dìbù (ᵒ'twèishēnde 'lùr, ᵒsyà'táide 'dìbù).

Be left (remaining) hái with a verb, as hái yǒu (still are some) or hái dzài . . . (still at . . .); shèng(sya) (remaining); fùyu (be surplus); or expressed indirectly.

/Are there any tickets left for tonight? Jyĕr 'wǎnshangde 'pyàu °hái 'yŏu ma (°yŏu 'shèngsyade ma, *or* (surplus) °yŏu 'fùyude ma, *or* (unsold) °yŏu méi 'màichu-chyude ma, *or* (not given out) °yŏu méi'gĕichuchyude ma)? /All sold out; nothing left. Chywán 'màile; yĭ'dyǎr méi'shèng. /They've all gone; I'm the only one left. Tāmen dōu 'dzŏule; °'jyou shèngsya 'wŏ le (°'jŕyou 'wŏ hái dzài jèr).

Leave (vacation) jyà; ask leave gàujyà, chĭngjyà; be given leave fàngjyà; take leave syōujyà. /He asked for three months' leave from his job. Tā °'gàule (°chĭngle) sānge ywède 'jyà. /When he was on leave he came home. Tā °fàng'jyà (°syōu'jyà) de shŕhou, hwéi'jyā laile.

LEFT. dzwŏ, dzwŏbyar. /My home is over there on the left. Wŏ 'jyā dzài 'dzwŏbyar. /Take the other bag in your left hand. 'Nèige 'kŏudài yùng 'dzwŏshŏu 'ná ba. /Make a turn to the left at the next corner. Dzŏu dàu 'syàyíge jyē'kŏur wàng 'dzwó gwǎi.

(Politically) dzwŏchĭng, jĭlyè. /He's always been on the left politically. Tā yĭ'syàng shŕ 'szsyàng °'dzwŏchĭng (°hén dzwŏ). /This newspaper follows a leftist policy. Jèige bàujŕ de lwùndyàn °dzwŏchĭng (°hén dzwŏ, °jĭlyè).

LEG. twĕi; (or sometimes, especially informally, derogatorily, or of animals) twĕr. /My right leg hurts. Wŏ 'yòutwĕi 'téng. /One of the dog's legs is lame. Nèi 'gŏu chywéle yìtyáu °'twĕi (°'twĕr). /Try to buy a leg of lamb for dinner. Mái dyǎr yáng'twĕi chŕ wǎn'fàn.

(Of inanimate objects) twĕr; or sometimes twĕi. /I've torn the leg of my trousers. Wó bǎ kù'twér chĕle. /The leg of the chair is broken. Yĭdz'twĕr shéle. /Steady the table by putting some paper under that leg. Dzài 'nèityáu 'jwō(dz)twĕr 'dĭsyà dyàn dyǎr 'jŕ jyou hwǎngyou le.

(Stage in trip, etc.) dwǎr. /We're on the last leg of our journey. Jèi shŕ dzámen °'mwò yídwǎr 'lù le (°dzwèi'hòu yichéng le).

(Side of a triangle) yāu, byār. /Measure the legs of the triangle. 'Lyánglyang sānjyāusyíngde °lyǎng'yāu (°lyǎng'byār).

Not have a leg to stand on. /He didn't have a leg to stand on. is expressed as He is simply without basis for argument. Tā jyǎn'jŕ shŕ 'háuwú'dàulĭ. or as He has not a bit of reasonableness. Tā yĭ'dyǎr 'lĭyóu yĕ méi'yŏu.

On one's last legs kwài bù'syíng le; kwài wár'wán le (impolite). /He's on his last legs. Tā kwài wár'wán le. or Tā kwài bù'syíng le.

Pull one's leg pyàn, jyàu ... shàng'dàng. /He's trying to pull your leg. Tā syǎng °'pyàn nĭ ne (°jyàu nĭ shàng'dàng ne).

LENGTH. (Long dimension) chángdwǎn, chángli, chángsyali, but more often expressed indirectly by cháng (long). /What length boards do you need? °Mùtou'bǎr (°'Bǎndz) yāu 'dwō cháng de? /The length of the room is twice its width. Jèi 'wūdz 'cháng-(sya)li bĭ 'kwān(sya)li dwō yí'bèi. or (width is half the length) Jèi 'wūdz 'kwānsyali jŕ you 'chángsyalide yí'bàr. /What is the length of the table? Jwōdz cháng'dwǎn you 'dwō cháng?

(Distance) ywǎn (far); lù (road). /What is the length of the trip? (Dzŏu) °jèiyí'tàng (°'Jèiyílù) yŏu 'dwō ywǎn? or °Jèiyí'tàng (°Jèi yí'gùng) yŏu 'dwōshǎu 'lù?

(Piece measured in long dimension) jyéer. /We need more than one length of pipe. 'Yĭjyéer 'gwǎndz búgòu 'yùngde.

(Duration) syèshŕhou; syē plus a word for a unit of time, as day *or* year; referring to several hours as a long time 'dàbàntyān; as a long time in general jyŏu.

/We were surprised at the length of time you were away. Ní dzŏule °'nèmmasyē 'shŕhou (°'nèmmasyē tyān, °'nèmma dàbàntyān, °'nèmma jyŏu) wŏmen 'dōu jywéde tǐng chǐ'gwàide.

The length of (as long as) . . . jèmma 'cháng; (from one end to the other) °tsúng (°dǎ) . . . 'jèitóur dàu 'nèitóur. /He has a cut on his face the length of this pencil. Tā 'lyǎnshang lále yídàu 'kŏudz, yóu 'jèigwǎn chyānbǐ jèmma 'cháng. or Tā 'lyǎnshang lále jèigwǎn chyán'bǐ jèmma'chángde yídàu 'kŏudz. /He swam the length of the pool. Tā °tsúng (°dǎ) 'yóuyǔngchř 'jèitóur (yóudàu 'nèitóur. or Tā dzài yóuyǔng'chřli °dǎ (°tsúng) 'jèitóur yóudàu 'nèitóur.

At length (in great detail) 'syángsyángsyǐ'syìde, 'dzdzsyǐ'syìde, 'tsúngtóur dàu-'lyǎur. /He described his trip at length. Tā bǎ yí'lùde 'shř °'syángsyángsyǐ'syìde (°'dzdzsyǐ'syìde, °'tsúngtóur dàu'lyǎur) shwōle yíbyàn.

At arm's length. (lit.) /Hold the picture at arm's length to look at it. Bǎ gēbei shēn'jŕle náje jèijāng hwàr kàn. (fig.) /If you take my advice, you'll keep him at arm's length. Nǐ yàushr tīng 'wǒde hwà, °lí tā ywǎn'ywārde (°'dwòje tā dyar).

Go to any length 'shémma dōu gàndechū'lái. /They would go to any length to get what they wanted. Tāmen 'jŕyàu néng bǎ 'nèige dédàu 'shóuli, 'shémma dōu gàndechū'lái.

LESS. (Smaller amount, or to a smaller degree) shǎu (. . . yi)dyǎr; in comparisons as **A is less than B** is expressed by the patterns **A bǐ B shǎu, A méiyou B dwō,** or **A bùrú B dwō**; in comparisons involving less plus an adjective, is expressed by the comparison pattern in the negative, as **A is less interesting than B** is expressed as **A méiyou B yǒuyìsz** or **A bùrú B yǒuyìsz**; sometimes less plus an adjective is expressed as more plus an adjective of opposite meaning, as **less noise** may be expressed as more quiet ānjing yidyǎr; **the less . . . the less** and **less and less** are expressed by the patterns ywè . . . ywè shǎu, ywè shǎu ywe . . . , or ywè lai ywè shǎu. /Eat less but exercise more. Shǎu 'chř dyar, dwō 'yùndùng. /Less noise please. Láu'jyà, 'ānjing dyar. or (of verbal noises) Láu'jyà, 'shǎu rāngrang dyar. or Láu'jyà 'byé nèmma 'chǎu le. or Láu'jyà, 'byé nèmma 'rāngrang le. /I've always paid less for such things. is expressed as I've never paid so much for such things. Wó mǎi 'jèijǔng dūngsyi yí'syàng méi °'hwā(°'chū)gwo 'jèmma syē 'chyán. /You should talk less and think more. Nǐ yīngdāng 'shǎu shwō dyar hwà, 'dwō yùng dyar 'syǐn. /Give me less sugar this time. 'Jèihwéi 'shǎu °lái (°gěi wǒ) dyar 'táng. /I seem to be getting paid more now, but in reality, I'm getting less. Wǒ 'syàndzài ná de chyán hàusyàng 'dwō le, chǐ'shř wǒ 'jēn nádàude chyán °gèng 'shǎu le (°hái 'shǎu le ne, °hái 'méiyóu yǐchyán 'dwō ne, °hái 'bùrú yǐchyán 'dwō ne). /The less said about it the better. 'Jèige ywè 'shǎu °tí (°shwō) ywè 'hǎu. /We saw him less and less after that. Dǎ nèihwéi yǐ'hòu wǒmen °ywè lái ywè bucháng jyàn tā le (°jyàn tāde 'jǐhwei ywè lái ywè 'shǎu le). /He's less enthusiastic now (than before). Tā °méiyóu (°'bùrú) yǐ'chyán nèmma chǐ'jyèr le. or Tā 'búnèmma chǐ'jyèr le. /He's less intelligent than I thought. Wǒ méisyǎngdàu tā nèmma 'bèn. or °Wǒ jywéje (°Wǒ yǐwéi) tā (bǐ 'jèige) hái °'tsūngmíng (°'jīngmíng) dyar ne. /A square bottle takes less space than a round one in packing. Jwāng'syàngde shřhou (sz̀)'fāng píngdz bǐ 'ywán píngdz jànde 'dìfang 'shǎu. /I have less money than he. 'Wǒ de chyán °bǐ 'tāde shǎu (°'méi(yǒu) 'tāde dwō, °'méi(yǒu) tā nèmma 'dwō). /This game is even less fun than that one. Jèige yóusyì hái méiyou nèige yóusyì yǒu'yìsz ne. or Jèige yóusyì bùrú nèige yóusyì. /I have less money with me than I thought. Wǒ ywán'lái 'yǐwéi wǒde 'chyán bǐ jèige 'dwō ne. or Wó 'yǐwéi wǒ dài de 'chyán bǐ jèige 'dwō ne.

(Minus) jyǎn, 'jyǎnchyù, chyù; (in payment) mwō (deduct), bùgěi (not pay); in computing discounts, as **less 10%** may be expressed by using jyǎn, 'jyǎnchyù, chyù, or as (take) nine parts (dǎ) 'jyǒujé or (dǎ) 'jyǒukòu (and so on with other

693

multiples of ten). / Five less three is two. 'Wú °jyǎn (°chyù, °jyǎnchyù) 'sān °dé (°shèng, °děngyú) 'èr. / $ 75 less 20% discount would be $ 60. Chīshr'wǔkwài °chyù 'bǎifēnjrèr'shŕde jékou (°dǎ bājé, °dǎ bākou, °bājé, °bākou) °jyoushr (°shŕ, °jyou děngyú, °děngyú, °hái shèng, °hái you) 'lyòushrkwài. / $ 75 less 2% would be $ 73.50. Chīshr'wǔkwài °chyù (°jyǎn, °jyǎnchyù) bǎifēnjŕ'èr °jyoushr (°jyòu děngyú, °děngyú, °hái shèng, °hái you) chīshr'sānkwài'wǔ. / She'll pay the amount of the note for you, less interest. Tā syǎng tì ni 'hwán nèibǐ 'jàng, búgwo °'bùsyǎng gěi 'lìchyán (°syáng bǎ'lìchyán 'mwòle).

(Lacking) chywē(je), chyàn(je), chà(je), shǎu, dwǎn. / We have two divisions, less three battalions. Wŏmen (jèr) °chà (°chyàn, °chywē) sānyíng búdàu 'lyǎngshŕ rén. or Wŏmen (jèr) yǒu 'lyǎngge shŕ, kěshr °'chywēje (°'chyànje, °'chàje, °'shǎu, °'dwǎn) sānyíng.

Less than (not in comparisons of parallel things) búdàu (not up to); 'búgòu (not enough for); 'bùzú (not fully); méiyou (are or have not). / We have less than two divisions. Wŏmen jèr °'búdàu (°'búgòu, °bùzú) 'lyǎngshŕ rén. or Wŏmen jèr 'lyǎngshŕ rén hái °bú'dàu ne (°méi'you ne). / Less than a hundred people were at the play. Kàn'syìde °'búdàu yì'bǎi rén (°hái méiyou yì'bǎi rén ne, °lyán yì'bǎi rén hái bú'dàu ne).

No less than (at least) jrshǎu. / There were no less than a hundred people at the play. Kàn'syìde jrshǎu yǒu yì'bǎi rén. / He wants a position no less than that of associate professor. Tā syǎng °jŕ'shǎu (°jŕbují) dāng ge fùjyàu'shòu. or Bǐ fùjyàushòu dī de wèijr tā bùkěn jyòu.

Other expressions in English. / In less than no time it was all finished. °Yì-'jwányǎn (°Yì'jwányǎnde gūngfu, °Yìján'yànde gūngfu, °Yìjǎma'yǎrde gūngfu, °'Yísyàdz, °Yì'hwěrde gūngfu, °'Lìshŕ, °'Děngshŕ, °Mǎ'shàng, °'Dāngshŕ) jyòu dōu 'wánle. / I couldn't care less about what he just said. Tā gāng shwō de hwà wŏ yì'dyǎr ye bú'dzàihu.

LESSON. (Material to be learned, or assignment) 'gūngkè. / The boy is good at his lessons. Jèi syǎuhár 'gūngkè (dzwòde) tíng 'hǎu. / He has to finish his lessons before he can go out and play. Tā děi 'syān bǎ 'gūngkè dzwò'wánle tsái néng 'chū-chyu 'wár ne.

(Learning unit) kè. / The book is divided into thirty lessons. Jèiběn 'shū fēn 'sānshr kè. / This is lesson twelve. Jèi shŕ dìshŕ'èr kè.

(Instructive experience) 'jyàusyùn. / This failure should be taken as a lesson. 'Jèitsz shŕ'bài 'yīnggāi dàngdzwò yíge 'jyàusyùn kàn. / Let this be a lesson to you. Jèi shŕ gěi ni yíge 'jyàusyùn. / The experience taught him a great lesson. Tā °'jīngle nèmmajyàn 'shèr (°'shòule nèmmahwéi 'dzwèi, °'shàngle nèmma hwéi 'dàng, °chŕle nèmmahwéi 'kwēi) déle yíge hěn 'dàde 'jyàusyùn. / I'll teach you a lesson. Wŏ 'fēiděi 'jyàusyùn'jyàusyùn ni bù'kě. or (somewhat stronger) Wŏ 'fēiděi 'gwǎnjyàugwǎnjyàu ni bù'kě. but / You learned a lesson from that, didn't you? is expressed proverbially as No experience, no increase in wisdom, right? Bù'jīng yí'shr, bù'jǎng yí'jr, dwèi ma? or as Having had the experience, you learned a little about cleverness, eh? °'Shàngle hwéi 'dàng (°'Chŕle hwéi 'kwēi, °'Shòule hwéi 'dzwèi), swàn'sywéle dyar 'gwāi ba, á? or as Having had the experience, you quieted down a bit! 'Shàngle hwéi 'dàng 'lǎushrle ba!

Take lessons in something sywé (study). / He takes dancing lessons. Tā sywé tyàu'wǔ.

LET. (Permit; in a strong sense, used in negative statements or in questions or exclamations) jwǔn, syǔ (give permission); jyàu, ràng (allow); swéi, yóu, 'bùgwǎn (allow without interference); fàng (permit passage, let go, let loose); or expressed by

/We were surprised at the length of time you were away. Ní dzŏule °'nèmmasyē 'shŕhou (°'nèmmasyē tyān, °'nèmma dàbàntyān, °'nèmma jyŏu) wŏmen 'dōu jywéde tǐng chí'gwàide.

The length of (as long as) . . . jèmma 'cháng; (from one end to the other) °tsúng (°dǎ) . . . 'jèitóur dàu 'nèitóur. /He has a cut on his face the length of this pencil. Tā 'lyǎnshang lále yídàu 'kŏudz, yŏu 'jèigwǎn chyánbǐ jèmma 'cháng. *or* Tā 'lyǎnshang lále jèigwǎn chyán'bǐ jèmma'chángde yídàu 'kŏudz. /He swam the length of the pool. Tā °tsúng (°dǎ) 'yóuyŭngchŕ 'jèitóur (yóudàu 'nèitóur. *or* Tā dzài yóuyŭng'chŕli °dǎ (°tsúng) 'jèitóur yóudàu 'nèitóur.

At length (in great detail) 'syángsyángsyǐ'syìde, 'dźdźsyǐ'syìde, 'tsúngtóur dàu-'lyǎur. /He described his trip at length. Tā bǎ yí'lùde 'shŕ °'syángsyángsyǐ'syìde (°'dźdźsyǐ'syìde, °'tsúngtóur dàu'lyǎur) shwōle yíbyàn.

At arm's length. (lit.) /Hold the picture at arm's length to look at it. Bǎ gēbei shēn'jŕle náje jèijāng hwàr kàn. (fig.) /If you take my advice, you'll keep him at arm's length. Nǐ yàushr tīng 'wŏde hwà, °lí tā ywǎn'ywārde (°'dwòje tā dyar).

Go to any length 'shémma dōu gàndechū'lái. /They would go to any length to get what they wanted. Tāmen 'jŕyàu néng bǎ 'nèige dédàu 'shŏuli, 'shémma dōu gàndechū'lái.

LESS. (Smaller amount, or to a smaller degree) shǎu (. . . yi)dyǎr; in comparisons as **A is less than B** is expressed by the patterns A bǐ B shǎu, A méiyou B dwō, *or* A bùrú B dwō; in comparisons involving **less** plus an adjective, is expressed by the comparison pattern in the negative, as **A is less interesting than B** is expressed as A méiyou B yŏuyìsz *or* A bùrú B yŏuyìsz; sometimes **less** plus an adjective is expressed as **more** plus an adjective of opposite meaning, as **less noise** may be expressed as more quiet ānjing yidyǎr; **the less . . . the less** and **less and less** are expressed by the patterns ywè . . . ywè shǎu, ywè shǎu ywe . . . , *or* ywè lai ywè shǎu. /Eat less but exercise more. Shǎu 'chŕ dyar, dwō 'yùndùng. /Less noise please. Láu'jyà, 'ānjing dyar. *or* (of verbal noises) Láu'jyà, 'shǎu rāngrang dyar. *or* Láu'jyà 'byé nèmma 'chǎu le. *or* Láu'jyà, 'byé nèmma 'rāngrang le. /I've always paid less for such things. is expressed as I've never paid so much for such things. Wó mǎi 'jèijǔng dūngsyi yí'syàng méi °'hwā(°'chū)gwo 'jèmma syē 'chyán. /You should talk less and think more. Nǐ yīngdāng 'shǎu shwō dyar hwà, 'dwō yùng dyar 'syīn. /Give me less sugar this time. 'Jèihwéi 'shǎu °lái (°gěi wŏ) dyar 'táng. /I seem to be getting paid more now, but in reality, I'm getting less. Wŏ 'syàndzài ná de chyán hàusyàng 'dwō le, chí'shŕ wŏ 'jēn nádàude chyán °gèng 'shǎu le (°hái 'shǎu le ne, °hái 'méiyóu yǐchyán 'dwō ne, °hái 'bùrú yǐchyán 'dwō ne). /The less said about it the better. 'Jèige ywè 'shǎu °tí (°shwō) ywè 'hǎu. /We saw him less and less after that. Dǎ nèihwéi yǐ'hòu wŏmen °ywè lái ywè bucháng jyàn tā le (°jyàn tāde 'jīhwei ywè lái ywè 'shǎu le). /He's less enthusiastic now (than before). Tā °méiyóu (°'bùrú) yǐ'chyán nèmma chǐ'jyèr le. *or* Tā 'búnèmma chǐ'jyèr le. /He's less intelligent than I thought. Wŏ méisyǎngdàu tā nèmma 'bèn. *or* °Wŏ jywéje (°Wŏ yǐwéi) tā (bǐ 'jèige) hái °'tsūngmíng (°'jīngmíng) dyar ne. /A square bottle takes less space than a round one in packing. Jwāng'syāngde shŕhou (sz̀)'fāng píngdz bǐ 'ywán píngdz jànde 'dìfang 'shǎu. /I have less money than he. 'Wŏ de chyán °bǐ 'tāde shǎu (°'méi(yŏu) 'tāde dwō, °'méi(yŏu) 'tā nèmma 'dwō). /This game is even less fun than that one. Jèige yóusyì hái méiyou nèige yóusyì yóu'yìsz ne. *or* Jèige yóusyì bùrú nèige yóusyì. /I have less money with me than I thought. Wŏ ywán'lái 'yǐwéi wŏde 'chyán bǐ jèige 'dwō ne. *or* Wó 'yǐwéi wŏ dài de 'chyán bǐ jèige 'dwō ne.

(Minus) jyǎn, 'jyǎnchyù, chyù; (in payment) mwō (deduct), bùgěi (not pay); in computing discounts, as **less 10%** may be expressed by using jyǎn, 'jyǎnchyù, chyù, *or as* (take) nine parts (dǎ) 'jyŏujé *or* (dǎ) 'jyŏukòu (and so on with other multiples of ten). / Five less three is two. 'Wú °jyǎn (°chyù, °jyǎnchyù) 'sān °dé (°shèng, °děngyú) 'èr. / $ 75 less 20% discount would be $ 60. Chīshr'wǔkwài °chyù 'bǎifēnjr̄èr'shr̄de jékòu (°dǎ bājé, °dǎ bākòu, °bājé, °bākòu) °jyòushr (°shr̀, °jyòu děngyú, °děngyú, °hái shèng, °hái yǒu) 'lyòushrkwài. / $ 75 less 2% would be $ 73.50. Chīshr'wǔkwài °chyù (°jyǎn, °jyǎnchyù) bǎifēnjr̄'èr °jyòushr (°jyòu děngyú, °děngyú, °hái shèng, °hái yǒu) chīshr'sānkwài'wǔ. / She'll pay the amount of the note for you, less interest. Tā syǎng tì ni 'hwán nèibǐ 'jàng, búgwo °'bùsyǎng gěi 'lìchyán (°syáng bǎ'lìchyán 'mwòle).

(Lacking) chywē(je), chyàn(je), chà(je), shǎu, dwǎn. / We have two divisions, less three battalions. Wǒmen (jèr) °chà (°chyàn, °chywē) sānyíng búdàu 'lyǎngshr̄ rén. *or* Wǒmen (jèr) yǒu 'lyǎngge shr̄, kěshr °'chywēje (°'chyànje, °'chàje, °'shǎu, °'dwǎn) sānyíng.

Less than (not in comparisons of parallel things) búdàu (not up to); 'búgòu (not enough for); 'bùdzú (not fully); méiyǒu (are or have not). / We have less than two divisions. Wǒmen jèr °'búdàu (°'búgòu, °bùdzú) 'lyǎngshr̄ rén. *or* Wǒmen jèr 'lyǎngshr̄ rén hái °bú'dàu ne (°méi'yǒu ne). / Less than a hundred people were at the play. Kàn'syìde °'búdàu yǐ'bǎi rén (°hái méiyǒu yǐ'bǎi rén ne, °lyán yǐ'bǎi rén hái bú'dàu ne).

No less than (at least) jr̄shǎu. / There were no less than a hundred people at the play. Kàn'syìde jr̄shǎu yǒu yǐ'bǎi rén. / He wants a position no less than that of associate professor. Tā syǎng °jr̄'shǎu (°jr̄bujì) dāng ge fùjyàu'shòu. *or* Bǐ fùjyàushòu dī de wèijr tā bùkěn jyóu.

Other expressions in English. / In less than no time it was all finished. °Yī-'jwányǎn (°Yī'jwányǎnde gūngfu, °Yìján'yǎnde gūngfu, °Yìjǎma'yǎrde gūngfu, °'Yísyàdz, °Yì'hwērde gūngfu, °'Lìshr̄, °'Děngshr̄, °Mǎ'shàng, °'Dāngshr̄) jyòu dōu 'wánle. / I couldn't care less about what he just said. Tā gāng shwō de hwà wǒ yì'dyǎr ye bú'dzàihu.

LESSON. (Material to be learned, or assignment) 'gūngkè. / The boy is good at his lessons. Jèi syáuhár 'gūngkè (dzwòde) tíng 'hǎu. / He has to finish his lessons before he can go out and play. Tā děi 'syān bǎ 'gūngkè dzwò'wánle tsái néng 'chū-chyu 'wár ne.

(Learning unit) kè. / The book is divided into thirty lessons. Jèiběn 'shū fēn 'sānshr̄ kè. / This is lesson twelve. Jèi shr̄ dìshr̄'èr kè.

(Instructive experience) 'jyàusyùn. / This failure should be taken as a lesson. 'Jèitsż shr̄'bài 'yīnggāi dàngdzwò yíge 'jyàusyùn kàn. / Let this be a lesson to you. Jèi shr̄ gěi ni yíge 'jyàusyùn. / The experience taught him a great lesson. Tā °'jīngle nèmmajyàn 'shèr (°'shòule nèmmahwéi 'dzwèi, °'shàngle nèmma hwéi 'dàng, °chr̄le nèmmahwéi 'kwēi) déle yíge hěn 'dàde 'jyàusyùn. / I'll teach you a lesson. Wǒ 'fēiděi 'jyàusyùn'jyàusyùn nǐ bù'kě. *or* (somewhat stronger) Wǒ 'fēiděi 'gwǎnjyàugwǎnjyàu nǐ bù'kě. *but* / You learned a lesson from that, didn't you? is expressed proverbially as No experience, no increase in wisdom, right? Bù'jīng yí'shr̄, bù'jǎng yí'jr̄, dwèi ma? or as Having had the experience, you learned a little about cleverness, eh? °'Shàngle hwéi 'dàng (°'Chr̄le hwéi 'kwēi, °'Shòule hwéi 'dzwèi), swàn'sywéle dyar 'gwāi ba, á? or as Having had the experience, you quieted down a bit! 'Shàngle hwéi 'dàng 'lǎushrle ba!

Take lessons in something sywé (study). / He takes dancing lessons. Tā sywé tyàu'wǔ.

LET. (Permit; in a strong sense, used in negative statements or in questions or exclamations) jwǔn, syǔ (give permission); jyàu, ràng (allow); swéi, yóu, 'bùgwǎn (allow without interference); fàng (permit passage, let go, let loose); or expressed by saying that something is permitted néng, syǔ, or that it is O.K. syíng, chéng; or other indirect expressions. /He won't let me see his sister anymore. Tā °'bújyàu (°'bùràng, °'bùjwǔn, °'bùsyǔ) wǒ 'dzài chyù jǎu tā 'mèimei le. /He wanted to stay, but they won't let him. Tā syǎng °'bùdzǒu (°hái 'dāije), búgwo tāmen yí'dìng °bújyàu tā 'dzài nèr 'dāije (or (going to make him go) °jyàu ta 'dzǒu, or (won't retain him) °bù'lyóu ta). /Will the customs officials let us go through? Nǐ kàn hǎi'gwānshangde rén 'hwèi °jyàu (°ràng, °syǔ, °jwǔn, °fàng) dzámen 'gwòchyu ma? / Let him do it! 'Swéi ta (chyù) ba. or 'Yóu ta (chyù) ba. or 'Byé gwǎn ta le. or Ràng tā chyu 'nùng ba. or Jyàu'tā chyu 'nùng ba. /I won't let you! Wǒ bù'jwǔn ni! or Wǒ bù-'syǔ ni! or (very strong prohibition) Dǎ 'wǒ jer shwō, jyou °bù'syíng (°bu'chéng)! or (courteous protests) 'Byé nèmmaje! or 'Kě byé nèmmaje! or 'Bùnéng nèmma-je! or 'Bùsyǔ nèmmaje! or 'Hái yǒu 'nèmmaje de ma? or Nà kě 'búsyàng 'hwà le. or Nà jyou 'bùchéng 'hwà le. or 'Nǎrde 'hwà? or 'Byé dǎu'lwàn. or 'Byé hú'nàu. or 'Nèmmaje wó kě bù'dāying ni.

(Allow; in a weak sense, as used in affirmative statements or mild commands) jyàu, ràng; fàng (let go, let loose); let someone have is often expressed as give gěi; let me see is often expressed by wǒ kànkan, wǒ chyáuchyau; let someone know is often expressed as tell gàusu, gàusung; a negative with a word opposite in meaning to what follows let is sometimes used. / Let him try once. °Jyàu (°Ràng) 'tā °lái yisyar kànkan (°shr yishr). /Don't let the fire go out. 'Byé jyàu hwǒ 'myè le. /He let the cup fall from his hands and broke it. (unintentionally) Tā °bùhǎu'hǎurde náje 'wǎn (°méi bǎ 'wǎn ná'jùle) gei 'shwāi le. or (intentionally) Tā gù'yi °bùhǎu-'hǎurde náje 'wǎn (°bù bǎ 'wǎn ná'jùle) gei 'shwāile. /Don't let him get the better of you. Byé °jyàu (°ràng) ta 'jànle nǐde 'pyányi. /He always lets his dog run loose on the street. Tā 'lǎu jyàu gǒu 'swéibyàn dzài 'jyēshang pǎu. /Please let me have the menu. Bǎ tsài'dǎr dǐgei wo. /Please let me see the menu. Jyàu wǒ 'kànkan tsài'dǎr. or Wǒ 'chyáuchyau nèige tsài'dǎr. /I'll let you know. Wǒ yí'dìng (hwèi) °jyàu (°ràng) ni 'jrdàu de. or Wó yí'hòu 'gàusu nǐ. / The police let the burglar go. Jǐng'chá bǎ dzéi 'fàng le. / Let me see it. 'Wǒ kànkan. or °Ràng (°Jyàu, °Gěi) 'wǒ kànkan. / Let it stand. is expressed as Don't change it. 'Búyàu gǎi. or 'Byé gǎi. or Byé 'dùng. or as It's all right not to change it. Bù'gǎi hǎu le. or 'Búyùng gǎile. or Jyòu nèmma 'jè ba. or 'Jyòu nèmmaje 'swàn le. /Don't let me catch you again. Byé °jyàu (°ràng) wǒ 'dzài dǎijau ni.

Let it go (at that) swànle. /We'd better just let it go at that. 'Jyòu nèmmaje 'swànle ba. /He didn't mean it; just let it go (or pass). Tā 'búshr °yǒu'yìde (°gù'yìde, °chéng'syīnde), (gwòchyule) jyou 'swànle ba.

Let me see and other verbal delaying actions are expressed as **let me think and see** wǒ 'syǎngsyǎng kàn, or as wait a bit and see 'děng yiděng kàn, and similar constructions using verbs for think, calculate, etc. / Let me see; two by two, times fifty, that's two hundred square feet. Wǒ °'syǎngsyǎng kàn (°'swàn yiswàn), èr chéng 'èr, dzai chéng wǔ'shr; yigùng shr èrbǎifāng'chǐ. /Let's see; today is Tuesday; it must have been last Friday then. °Wǒ 'syǎngsyǎng kàn (°Wǒ 'swàn yiswàn °Wǒ 'kàn, or (don't rush me) °'Byé máng byé máng), 'jyèr shr syīngchī'èr; nemma nèi yí'dìng shr 'shàngsyīngchī'wǔ le. / Let me think for a while. Wǒ 'syǎng-yisyǎng. or Wǒ 'dzwómedzwóme. or Wǒ 'jwómejwóme. or Wǒ 'swànjiswànji.

Let's is expressed by ba at the end of a sentence with dzámen or wǒmen as the subject only if the reference is clearly to us; when the expression is a command rather than a suggestion, ba is not used. / Let's go to a show. Dzámen chyu kàn dyàn'yěngr ba. / Let's give him a little more time. Dzài dwō gěi tā dyar 'shrhou ba. / Let's leave it until tomorrow. Myéngr dzài 'shwō ba. / Let's face the facts. is expressed as The facts are displayed in front of us, let's see how we should go about it. 'Shrching dōu 'bǎidzai yǎn'chyán le, (kànkan) dzámen gāi dzěmma 'bàn ba. or as Let's look at it according to the facts. Dzámen ànje 'shrdzàide 'chíngsyíng lai °'kànkan (°'syángsyǎng) ba. / Let's see you do it. (without sarcasm) 'Chyáu-chyau 'nǐde. *or* 'Kànkan 'nǐde. *or* (with or without sarcasm) 'Nǐ láilai kàn. *or* 'Nǐ shr̀shr kàn.

Let alone (to say nothing of) hái shwō shémma <u>with</u> ne <u>at the end of the sentence</u>; jyòu béng 'tí le, gèng búyùng 'tí le, *or* gèng tánbu'dàu le <u>at the end of the sentence</u>; 'nǎr néng <u>with</u> a <u>at the end.</u> / I can't even speak Chinese well, let alone read it. Jūnggwo'hwà wǒ hái shwōbu'hǎu ne, °kàn (Jūnggwo)'shū jyòu béng 'tí le (°kàn (Jūnggwo)'shū gèng búyùng 'tí le, °kàn (Jūnggwo)'shū gèng tánbu'dàu le, °hái 'shwō shémma kàn (Jūnggwo)'shū ne, °'nǎr néng kàn (Jūnggwo)'shū a).

Let <u>something or someone</u> **alone** *or* **let** <u>something or someone</u> **be.** *See* **Leave** <u>someone</u> **alone,** <u>under</u> **LEAVE.**

Let <u>someone</u> **by** °ràng (°jyàu) . . . 'gwòchyu. / Let me by. Ràng wo 'gwòchyu. <u>or is usually expressed by a polite request similar to</u> Please Jyè'gwāng.

Let <u>something</u> **down** (by releasing) fàngsya. / Let down the curtain. Bǎ 'lyándz 'fàngsyalai. / She let her hair down. (lit.) Tā bǎ 'tóufa °'fàngsyalaile (°sānkāile). *or* (fig.) <u>is expressed as</u> She told all about it. Tā 'chywán dōu 'shwōchulaile.

Let down (relax efforts) 'sūngsyèsyachyu, syèchǐ, syèjǐn; 'syèdàisyachyu, mànsyachyu (slow down). / They let down in their work. Tāmen gàn'hwór °syèle 'jǐn le (°syè'chǐ le, °'sūngsyèsyachyule, °'syèdàisyachyule, °'mànsyachyule).

Let <u>someone</u> **down** (disappoint) dwèibuchǐ, dwèibujù; (seriously) jyàu . . . °shāng-'syīn (°hwēisyīn); (purposely) bǎ . . . gei 'shwǎ (le), bǎ . . . gei 'pyàn le; <u>or ex-pressed indirectly.</u> / They let him down badly. Tāmen kě 'jēn °dwèibu'chǐ tā (°'dwèibu'jù tā, °jyàu ta shāng'syīn, °bǎ ta gei 'shwǎ le, °bǎ ta gei 'pyàn le). / I won't let you down. Wó 'jwǔn °dwèide'chǐ (°dwèide'jù, °bú'pyàn) ni. *or* Wó 'jwǔn búhwèi jyàu nǐ shāng'syīn. *or* Wó 'jwǔn búhwèi 'pyàn ni de. / Do your best; don't let us down. Jǐnlǐ 'dzwò, byé jyàu women hwēi'syīn.

Let go (of) (release hold) bǎ . . . sākai, bùchéje, bùlǎje, bùjyǒuje; **let go of** <u>something is often expressed as</u> release (your) hand fàngshǒu *or* sāshǒu, <u>without the thing being held expressed.</u> / Don't let go of the rope until I tell you. Wǒ bùshwō 'hwà nǐ byé °bǎ 'shéngdz 'sākai (°'fàng'shǒu, °sā'shǒu). / Let go of my coat! Sā'shǒu! *or* Fàng'shǒu. *or* 'Byé °chéje (°lǎje, °jyǒuje) wǒde 'yīshang.

Let go (of) mài (sell); chūshǒu (let get out of one's hand). / Don't let go of your car yet. Nǐde 'chē syān byé °'mài (°chū'shǒu).

Let (oneself) **go.** / Let yourself go! <u>is expressed as</u> Don't be so self-conscious; relax. 'Byé 'pà jèige pà'nèigede. *or* 'Byé nèmma 'jyūjyushù'shùde. <u>or as</u> Be a little more active. 'Hwódùng dyar ba. *or* 'Hwópwoje dyar ba. <u>or as</u> Be less in-hibited. 'Sūngsung 'syīn ba. *or* 'Fàngsyīn dà'dande lai yísyàr ba. *or* (in crying) (Yàu 'kū, jyou) °Kū ge 'tùngkwai ba (°'Tùngtungkwāi'kwārde 'kū ba, °'Fàngshēng 'dà kū ba). <u>or as</u> Enjoy yourself to the full. 'Tùngtungkwār'kwārde °'lái yísyar ba (°'láilai, *or* (of playing) °'wárwar). *or* Shr̀'jyèrde 'láilai. *or* Pǐn'mǐngde 'láilai. *or* Búyàu 'mǐngde 'láilai. (*or* 'wárwar *or* 'lái yísyar ba *or* 'lái yísyàdz in place of 'láilai in any of these.) *or* (in dancing) °'Tùngtungkwār'kwārde (°Shr̀'jyèrde) 'tyàu yìhwéi. *or* (in speaking) Byé nèmma 'twǔntwuntu'tǔde. *or* 'Tùngtungkwār'kwārde 'shwō ba. *or* Yàu 'shwō jyou shwō ge 'tùngkwai. *or* 'Fàngsyīndà'dande shwō ba. / She took the news of his death calmly, but when she was alone she let (herself) go. Tā 'tīngjyan tā 'szyèr de shŕhou dàu hěn 'jènjǐngde, kěshr dàule méi'rénde shŕhou °'tùng (°dà'dārde) kūle yìcháng.

Let <u>someone or something</u> **in** °ràng (°jyàu) . . . °jìnlai (°jìnchyu); (of air) <u>also</u> tūng, jìn; (of light) tòu, jìn. / Let us in. Ràng wǒmen 'jìnchyu. / He won't let us in.

Tā °'búràng (°'bújyàu) wŏmen °jìnchyu (°jìnlai). / Let the dog in. Jyàu gŏu 'jìnlai. / Windows let in light. 'Chwānghu °tòu'gwāng (°tòu'lyàngr, °jìn'gwāng). *or* Yŏu 'chwānghu shř wèile yàu °tòu'lyàngrde (°tòu'gwāngde, °jìn'gwāngde). *or* °Tsúng (°Dǎ) 'chwānghu ner kéyi °tòujin 'gwāng lai (°yŏu 'gwāng jìnlai). / Windows let in air and light. Chwānghu shř tūng °'fēng (°'chyèr) tòu'lyàngrde. / That opening is to let in air. Nèige 'kŏur shř °jìn'chyèrde (°tūng'chyèrde, °tūng'fēngde, °jyàu kūng 'chì jìnlai de dìfang, °fàngjìn 'chyèr lai de). *or* °Tsúng (°Dǎ) nèige 'kŏur ner kéyi °'fàngjin 'chyèr lai (°jìn'chyèr, °tūng'chyèr, °jyàu kūng'chì jìnlai).

Let someone **in on** something gàusung, gàusu (tell); swānjinchyu, swānshang (include); tsānjyā (participate in). / I'll let you in on a little secret. Wŏ 'gàusung nǐ dyar mì'mì. / Let me in on the deal. Bǎ 'wŏ swānshang. *or* Bǎ 'wŏ yě 'swānjinchyu. *or* Ràng wŏ yě tsān'jyā. *or expressed as* There's surely a part for me! Yŏu 'wŏ yí'fèr, á!

Let oneself **in for** something. / Well, you let yourself in for it. 'Nǐ shř dž'jǎu. *or* 'Nǐ shř gàn'syìnlè'yì. *or* Nǐ jè shř dž'jǎude, hái yŏu shémma kě'shwōde.

Let loose (express anger fully) 'fādzwò, fā 'píchì, nàu 'píchì. / When he really lets loose, he can fight like mad. Tā 'jēn °'fādzwòchilai (°'fāchi 'píchì lai), kéyi nàude 'tyānfāndì'fùde. *but* / It seemed as though all hell had let loose. Hǎusyàng °'tyānfāndì'fù (°'tyāntādì'sywàn, °'háidàushān'bēng) shřde. / He let loose (with) a torrent of invective. Tā 'pwòkǒu dà 'mà. *or* Tā 'yíjèn 'chǒu mà. *or* Tā 'yíjèn 'dà mà.

Let someone **off** (a train, bus, etc.) °ràng (°jyòu) . . . 'syàchyu. / Please let us off at the next corner. Dàu 'syàyíge jyē'kǒur nèr ('tíngsyalai) ràng wŏmen 'syàchyu.

Let someone **off** (set free) fàng. / Will they let him off? Tāmen hwèi bǎ tā 'fàngle ma? *or* Tāmen hwèi 'fàng tā ma? *but* / He was let off with a light sentence. Pàn de tā bújùng, 'pyányi tā le.

Let off steam (lit.) sāchì fàngchì; (fig.) sāsā chyèr, jyéjyě hèn (of anger). / The locomotive is letting off steam. Hwŏchē'tóu °sā(°fàng)'chì ne. / He played a fast game of tennis to let off steam. Tā wèile yàu °sāsā 'chyèr (°sānsàn 'syīn) shř'jyèrde dǎle yìcháng wǎng'chyóu. / Their argument doesn't mean anything; they're just letting off steam. Tāmen °dá 'chǎudz (°cháu'dzwèi) bìng 'méi shémma; 'búgwo shř °sāsā 'chyèr (°jyéjyě 'hèn) jyou 'shř le. / Every once in a while he has to let off some steam. Tā gwò jityān jyou 'nàu yihwéi.

Let on (tell) shwō(chūlai); (to someone) 'gàusu . . . , °jyàu (°ràng) . . . 'jřdau; not **let on** is also expressed as feign ignorance jwāng bùjř'dàu. / He knew it all the time and never let on. Tā yì'jř jyou 'jřdau, kě 'jyòushr °'méishwōchulai (°'búgàusu 'rén, °'méigàusu 'rén, °'méijyàu rén (*or* wŏ, or any other person) jřdau, °méi ràng rén 'jřdau, °jwāng bùjř'dàu).

Let something or someone **out** fàng(chuchyu); (of water, let flow out) °jyàu (°ràng) . . . °'lyóusyachyu (°'lyóuchuchyu). / Will you let the dog out? Nǐ bǎ 'gŏu 'fàngchuchyu dzěmma'yàng? / Let the water out of the sink slowly. Bǎ shwěi màn-'mārde 'fàngle. *or* Jyàu shwěi màn'mārde °'lyóuchuchyu (°'lyóusyachyu).

Let up (stop) tíng, jù, 'syǎu dyǎr (le). / Do you think the rain will let up soon? Nǐ jywéje 'yǔ kwài °'tíng (°'jù, °'syǎu dyǎr) le ma? / The rain hasn't let up for two days. Yǔ bù'tíngde syàle yŏu 'lyǎngtyān le.

To let (may be rented) jāudzū, chūdzū, chūlìn. / The sign says "House to Let." Nèi páidzshang 'syěje: "'Jífang °jāu'dzū (°chū'dzū, °chū'lìn)." *See also* **RENT**.

Letdown méi'yìszde, méichyùrde, méijìnde; (also, of feelings, unhappy) bùgàu-'syìngde. / The point of the joke was an awful letdown. Nèige 'syàuhwa dǔngle yi'hòu tǐng °méiyìszde (°méi'chyùrde, méi'jǐnde). /I had an awfully letdown feeling when he said he wasn't coming. Tā 'yǐ shwō bù'lái jyàu wǒ jywéje tǐng °bùgāu'syìngde (°méi'yìszde, °méi'chyùrde, °méi'jǐnde).

LETTER. (Message) syìn; (official correspondence between two organizations) 'gūnghán; (official correspondence such as requests, applications, instructions, appointments, etc.) 'gūngshŕ, 'gūngwén (official documents). /Are there any letters for me today? 'Jyěr you wǒde 'syìn ma? /He wrote me a letter. Tā gěi wo syěle yìfēng 'syìn lai. /These are all business letters. Jèi dōu shŕ °'gūnghán (°jyàng dzwò'mǎimai shŕching de 'syìn). /We got a letter from the War Department. Wǒmen 'jyējáule Lùjyūn'bù láide °yíjyàn 'gūngshŕ (°yíjyàn 'gūngwén, °yìfēng 'gūnghán, °yìfēng 'syìn). /That's a personal letter for him. Nèi shŕ (gěi) tā de 'szsyìn. or Nèi shŕ gěi ta 'běnrén de 'syìn. /He was nice enough to give me a letter of introduction. 'Tā géi wǒ 'syěle fēng 'jyèshàu'syìn, 'jēn shŕ gòu 'myàndz.

(Of an alphabet) dzèr (also means a Chinese character); dzmúr (used for a letter of an alphabet in contrast to a character). /These letters are not very clear. Jèijige 'dzèr búdà 'chīngchu. /Have you learned all the letters of the alphabet? Nǐ (swó'yǒude) dz'múr dōu 'rèndele ma?

(The literal meaning) dz'myàrshangde'yìsz. /According to the letter of the law, it is possible to do that. Ànje 'tyáuwén dz'myàrshangde 'yìsz lái 'jyěshŕ, yàu 'nèmma bàn yě 'kéyǐ.

To the letter (in every minute and necessary detail). /I want these instructions followed to the letter. 'Jèisyē 'syùnlìngshangde 'hwà yàu 'wánchywán °'jàubàn (°'dzwūnshǒu). or for emphasis expressed as Even a little bit of these instructions may not be neglected. 'Jèisye 'syànlìngshangde'hwà 'yìszyǐ'háu yě 'bùnéng °'hūlywě (or (disobeyed) °'wéibèi, or (changed) °'gǎidùng). /He obeyed the law to the letter. is expressed as He looks upon every word in the law as sacred, and doesn't dare disobey. Tā bǎ 'fǎlyùshang měi yíge 'dzèr dōu kàndzwò 'jǐnkēyù'lyù shŕde, 'bùgǎn 'wéibei.

To letter syědzèr; (in artistic style) syě'yìshùdz, syé 'měishùdz; (on large signs) syě jāupai. /Letter the sign carefully. 'Páidzshangde 'dzèr yàu hǎu'hǎurde syě.

LEVEL. (Horizontal) píng. /Is Peiping on level terrain or on a mountain? Běi'píng shŕ dzài píng'dìshang háishr dzài °'shānshang (°shāndìshang)? /Is Szechwan level or mountainous? Sz'chwān 'dìshŕ 'píng bupíng? /The table is not level. Jwōdz °bù'píng (°méigē 'píng, °méifàng 'píng, °'twěr bù'píng). /Hold the basin level. Bǎ 'pén dwān 'píng le.

(Equal in height) chí (of the same kind of things; °yìbār(°yìbān)°'píng (same level) (°chí (same length or height or level of termination), °gāu (same height). /The book shelf is level with the top of the table. Shū'jyàdz gēn jwō'myàr °'chíje (°yìbār 'píng, °yìbār 'chí, °yìbār 'gāu). /The shrubs are clipped all to the same level. Syàu'shùr dōu jyànde yìbār °'píng (°etc.). /The river is level with the top of the dike. 'Héshwěi jǎngde gēn °dí (°tí) yìbār 'píngle.

Levelheaded. /He's levelheaded in emergencies. Tā yù 'shŕ 'jěnjǐng. or Tā yǒu'shěr de shŕhou tsúnglái °bùjwā'syā (°(syīnli) bù'hwāng, °(syīnli) bú'lwàn, °hěn 'jěnjìngde, °'bùhwāngbù'mángde).

One's level best. /He tried his level best. Tā 'jēn °mài 'lìchi (°shŕ 'jyèr) laije. or Tā yǐ'dyár yě °méishwǎhwá'tóu (°méishŕsyìn'yǎr, °méi'tōugūngjyàn-'lyàu).

Level (degree of attainment) chéngdù, jyědwàn. /This textbook is high school level. Jèiběn jyàukeshū shŕ 'jungsywéde chéngdù.

(Tool) shwěipíngchř. / A level would be handy. Yǒu ge shwěipíng'chř jyòu 'hǎule.

On a level *or* **on the same level** (fig.) chí, yíyàng, yìbān, yìbyār plus a word to indicate what is on the particular level, or in what respect the things are level. / The two classes are not on the same level of intelligence. 'Lyǎngbānde 'chéngdù °bù'chí (°bùyí'yàng). / Try to keep the work of the two classes on a level. (by teaching at the same speed) 'Lyǎngbānde 'gūngkè yàu jyāude °yí'yàng (°yì'bān) kwài tsái 'hǎu. *or* Syǎng fádz jyàu jèilyǎngbānde jìndu chíle.

On the level (of something said) jēnde (true); (of something said or done) búpyàn; (of a person) numerous expressions are used which are illustrated in the sentences below. / Is that tip on the level? Nèige 'syèrshr 'jēnde ma? / What I said is on the level. Wǒ shwō de °shr 'jēnde (°bú'pyàn ni). / I don't think he's on the level. Wǒ jywéje tā yóu dyǎr °bùchéngshr (°bú'jèngjř, °'jyǎ, °bùkě'kàu). *or* Wǒ jywéje tā °búshr 'jèngjǐngrén (°shr ge 'syàurén). / He's entirely on the level. Tā hěn °'chéngshr (°'jèngjř). *or* Tā hén kě'kàu. *or* Tā shr ge °'jèngjǐngrén (°'jyūndz). *or* Tā búhwèi jwāngjyǎ.

To level (to flatten by destruction) is expressed by resultative compounds, the first element containing the means of leveling and the second such words as píngle (leveled), gwāngle (destroyed), hwěile (be in ruins); **leveled place** 'hwāngdì (a wilderness), 'jyāutǔ (scorched earth). / The shelling leveled the town. Pàu bǎ chywán 'chéng dōu °hūng'hwěile (°dǎ'gwāngle, °hūng'píngle). *or* 'Pàu bǎ 'chéng 'hūngchéng yípyàn °'jyāutǔ (°'hwāngdì) le.

Be leveled (made horizontal) nèng píng; (by filling in earth) dyànpíng, tyánpíng; (by removing earth) chǎnpíng; (of wood, with an adz) bàupíng. / This slope has to be leveled. Jèige 'pwōr děi °dyàn'píngle (°tyán'píngle, °chǎn'píngle). / This road has to be leveled. Jèilù děi nèng'píngle.

LIBERTY. (Political) dzyóu; **liberty and equality** dz'yóu píng'děng; **civil liberties** 'mínchywán (rights). / This new law puts our civil liberties in danger. 'Syīnfǎlyù 'wēisyé 'mínchywán. / There is no absolute liberty. 'Méiyǒu 'jywédwèide dz'yóu.

(Legal) is expressed verbally as **obtain one's liberty** chūyù (get out of prison); fàngchulai (be set free). / The prisoner got his liberty. 'Chyóufàn 'yǐjīng °chū'yùle (°'fàngchūlaile).

Be at liberty (to do something) °kéyǐ (°néng) 'swéiyì (be able freely); néng (be able). / Are you at liberty to talk? Nǐ 'syàndzài kéyǐ °'swéibyàn (°'swéiyì) shwō-'hwà ma? / I'm not yet at liberty to talk. Wǒ hái bùnéng °'swéibyàn (°'swéiyì) shwō'hwà. *or* 'Yǒude hwà wǒ hái bùnéng °'shwōchūlai (°'jyǎngchūlai, °'gàusu rén).

On liberty (leave) fàngjyà 'chūchyu. / All the sailors are on liberty. Swóyǒude shwéishou dōu fàngjyà 'chūchyule.

Take the liberty (to do something) 'dàdànde (lit. with great courage). / May I take the liberty of making a suggestion? Wǒ 'dàdànde °shwō jyù'hwà (°chū ge 'júyì), syíng ma?

Take liberties 'swéibyàn (act freely); 'fàngsz (be unrestrained, disorderly). / He took too many liberties when he was here. Tā dzài 'jèr de 'shrhou tài °swéi-'byàn (°'fàngsz) le.

See also **FREEDOM, FREE.**

LIE. shwō °'jyǎhwà (°'hwānghwà, °'syǎhwàr, °hwǎng), sā hwǎng (ranging in meaning from giving false information to cheating); húshwōbádàu, húdzōu, húdzōubái'lyě, syáchě, syáshwǒ, 'byānde 'syāhwàr (ranging in meaning from relating false impressions to being slanderous). /Don't lie to me. Byé gēn wǒ °shwō 'jyāhwà (°sā 'hwǎng, °etc.). or expressed as Tell the truth. Shwō °'shŕhwà (°'jēnhwà). /There's no doubt he's lying about it. Tā 'nèi 'jwǔn shŕ °sā 'hwǎng ne (°etc.). /He's trying to lie his way out. Tā syǎng shwō ge 'syāhwàr jyou °'tánggwochyule (°'dǎnggwochyule, °méi tāde 'shèr le, °'dwǒgwochyule). /He wanted to put his mother's mind at ease, so he lied to her. Tā yàu jyàu tā 'mǔchin bùfán'syīn, swóyǐ shwōle ge °'syāhwàr (°etc.). /He's lying. Tā nèi shŕ °sā 'hwǎng ne (°shwō 'syāhwàr ne, °húshwōbá'dàu, °syā'chě, °byānde 'syāhwàr, °etc.).

A lie jyāhwà, 'hwǎnghwà, 'syāhwàr, hwǎng; or expressed by a negative and a word for truth, as búshr 'shŕhwà, búshr 'jēnhwà; or as no such thing happened °méi(yǒu) (°nàr yǒu) nèmma hwéi 'shèr; or as be false jyàde; or verbally as in the above paragraph. /What he said is a lie. Tā shwō de shŕ °'hwǎnghwà (°'syāhwàr, °'jyāhwàr, °'jyàde). /He never told a lie in his life. Tā 'píngshēng méishwōgwo yíjyù °'jyāhwà (°'hwǎnghwà, °'syāhwàr, °'hwǎng). or Tā 'píngshēng méisāgwo 'hwǎng. /He told a lie. Tā 'shwōle yíjyù °'hwǎnghwà (°etc.). /That's a lie! Nèi shŕ °húshwōbá'dàu(°etc.). or °'Nár yǒu (°Méi, °Méiyǒu) nèmma hwéi 'shèr. /Everything he says is a lie. Tā shwōde 'wánchywán shŕ °húshwōbá'dàu (°húdzōubài'lyě, °syā'chě, °syā'shwō, °hú'dzōude, °'jyàde, °hwǎng'hwà, °etc.). or Tā shwō de 'wánchywán 'méi nèmma hwéi 'shèr.

LIE (LAY, LAIN). (Assume a horizontal position; of human beings) tǎng, (Peiping) dǎu (on back or side); pā (face down); (of animals) wǒ (curled up); pā (head up or on the paws). /Don't lie on the damp grass. 'Byé tǎng dzài 'shŕde tsǎu'dìshang. /He lay on the sofa and took a rest. Tā tǎng dzài shā'fāshang 'syēle hwèr. /The soldiers just lay down on the ground and went to sleep. Bīng °tǎng (°dǎu) dzài 'dìshang jyou dōu shwèi'jáule. /Lie down (on back or side). 'Tǎngsya. /Lie down, face down. 'Pāsya. /You'd better lie down for a while. Nǐ 'táng hwèr ba. /I want to lie down for a few minutes. Wǒ syáng 'tǎngsya 'syē yihwèr. /Let him lie on his side only; don't let him lie face up or down. Jyàu tā °wāije(°shēndz) 'tǎngje, byé 'yǎngje yě byé 'pāje. /He was lying facing this way. Tā lyǎn cháu 'jèibyar tǎngje. /Lie down! (to a dog) 'Wòsya! or 'Pāsya! /The cat just lay there motionless with her eyes closed. Māu °'pā (°'wǒ) dzai nàr, 'bìje yǎr yì'dyár yě bú'dùng.

(Be located at) dzài; (after being put at) dzài . . . 'fàngje. /Most of the town lies on the east bank of the river. 'Dàbànge 'chéng dzài héde 'dūng °ànshang (°byar). /The book is lying on the table. Shū dzài 'jwōrshang (fàngje) ne.

(Be buried at) máidzai; or expressed as someone's tomb is at . . . de 'fén dzài. /His body lies in the International Cemetery. Tā 'máidzài 'Gwójìgūng'mù le. or Tāde 'fén dzài 'Gwójìgūng'mùli.

(Consist in) shǐ yīnwei (be because of); dzài (be located at); A lies in B may also be expressed as B shǐ A. /The appeal of this book lies in its humor. Jèiběr 'shū swóyǐ ràng rén 'syǐhwànde shǐ 'yīnwei 'syéde °hěn 'yōumwò (°'néng yǐn rén fā'syàu). /Therein lies his weakness. Tāde 'chywēdyǎn jyòu dzài 'nàr. or Nèi jyòu shǐ tāde 'chywēdyǎn.

Lie around syán, syán gwochyu, syán dāi, 'shémma yě bú'gàn (do nothing at all). /I've just been lying around all day. Wǒ yì'tyānde gūngfu °jyòu nèmma 'syán gwochyu le (°jyòu nèmma syán 'dāije láije, °'shémma yě méi'gàn). /He's been lying around all this time. Tā yì'jŕ jyòu nèmma °'syánje (°syán 'dāije, or (as a habit) °'yóushǒuhàu'syánde).

Lie down see first paragraph above.

Lie down on the job búgànle (stop working); bǎ shǐ 'lyàusya, bǎ shǐ 'rēngle. /He lay down on the job. Tā bú'gànle. or Tā bǎ shǐ °'lyàusyale (°'rēngle).

Lie idle (of a factory) 'tíngdwūn; **lie fallow** (of ground) hwāng, méijùng, méi-'jùng shemma, méirén jùng; (of other things, unused) méiyùng, (unmoved) méirén dùng. / The factory has been lying idle for a year. 'Gūngchǎng 'tíngdwūnle yǒu yí'nyán le. / This ground has been lying fallow for two years. Jèi dì yóu 'lyāngnyán °méi'jùng le (°méi'jùng shemma le). *or* Jèidì 'hwāngle lyǎng'nyán le. / This machine has been lying idle for two years. Jèige 'jīchi yóu 'lyāngnyán °méi'yùng le (*or* (unmoved) °méiren 'dùng le).

Lie in wait for byē, děng, tsángje děng. / It's there that the enemy's ships are lying in wait for us. 'Dírénde chwán shr dzài 'nàr °'byēje (°tsángje 'déng, °'děngje) wǒmen ne.

Lie low 'dwǒ yidwǒ, dwódwer (avoid trouble, hide); bùyányu (keep still). / You'd better lie low for a while. Nǐ 'jànshr °'dwǒ yidwǒ ba (°'dwódwer ba, °byé 'yányu).

LIFE. (Being or remaining alive, or behavior of organic matter) 'shēngmìng, mìng; in some combinations shēng; or expressed indirectly by live hwó *or* die sz̄. / Biology is the science of life. 'Shēngwùsywé shr 'yánjyou 'shēngmìngde kēsywé. / The Buddhists teach that killing even an ant is destroying life. 'Fwójyā shwō nùngsz̄ ge 'máyi yě shr °shā'shēng (°hài yìtyáu 'mìng, °hài yìtyáu 'shēngmìng, or expressed as is destroying a living thing °'hàisz̄ ge 'hwówùr, °'hàisz̄ ge 'hwójede dūngsyi). / He barely escaped with his life. Tā nèi shr °'szlǐtáu'shēng (°'húkǒuyú'shēng). *or* Tā jyou táuchū yìtyáu 'mìng lai. *or* Tā nèityáu 'mìng jyǎn'jr shr °'shrlaide (°'jyǎn-laide). / His life is hanging in the balance. Tā 'mìng bùjr̄dàu bǎude'jù bǎubu'jù. *or* Tā yésyu hwèi 'sz̄de. *or* Tā shr 'sz̄ shr 'hwó hái bùjr̄'dàu ne. / It's his life or mine. Búshr 'tā sz̄ jyoushr 'wó sz̄. *or* Búshr 'tā hwóje jyoushr 'wó hwóje. *or* Wǒ gēn 'tā pīn ge 'nísz̄wǒ'hwó. / His life depends on you now. Tāde 'mìng syàndzài 'nǐ 'shóuli le. *or* Tā 'hwódelyǎu 'hwóbu'lyǎu 'chywán kàu 'nǐ le.

(Way of living) 'shēnghwó; gwòde (passing time); hwóde (living); wárde (playing, of an enjoyable life); or expressed verbally as pass (one's) days gwò r̄dz, or as be dwelling jùje; also some indirect expressions. / Life in the country is dull. Dzài °chéng'wàitou (°'syāngsya) °jùje méi'yìsz (°jùje tǐng wú'lyáu, °gwò 'r̄dz méi'yìsz, °gwò 'r̄dz tǐng wú'lyáu). *or* °'Syāng(°'Núng)tswūn 'shēnghwó yi'dyár yě bú'rènau. / He can't get used to married life. Tā gwòbu'gwàn jyèhwūnde shēnghwó. / Their married life is very happy. Tāmen lyáng'kǒudz gwòde tíng °'hǎu (°'hémù). *or* Tāmen fū'fù jr̄jyān tǐng °'hémù (°'kwèile). / He leads a high life. Tā gwòde hěn 'shēchr̄. / He leads a simple life. Tā gwòde hén 'pǔsù. / He leads a busy life. Tā °jěng'tyān (°'yìtyān dàu'wǎnde) °'máng (°hěn 'mángde, °yóu hěn 'dwō shèr, °'mángje ne, °'láu yǒu'shèr, °'mángmangdau'dāude). / This is the life! 'Jè tsái jyàu °'hwóde (°'wárde) 'tùngkwai ne!

(The extent in time one lives) 'shēngpíng, 'píngshēng, yìshēng (the whole life up to the present); or expressed as until old dàulǎu; or as from youth (until adulthood) tsúng'syǎur (dàu'dà); or as straight through yìjr̄ (of the past); lifetime yíbèidz (a complete life); or in other indirect ways. / He was crippled all his life. Tā 'tsánfèile yí'bèidz. / He was (became) crippled for life. Tā làule ge yí'bèidzde 'tsánjí. / I've lived here all my life. Wǒ yì'jr̄ jù'jèr. *or* Wǒ tsúng'syǎur jyou jù-'jèr. *or* Wǒ tsúng'syǎur dàu'dà méidzài 'byéchùr jùgwo. *or* (of an old man whose life is complete) Wǒ dzài 'jèr jùle yí'bèidzle. or expressed as I grew up nowhere but here. Wó jǎng dzèmma'dà méidzài 'byéchùr jùgwo. or as I was born here and brought up here. Wǒ shr jèr 'shēngde jèr 'jǎngde. / You can't expect to have such a chance twice in a lifetime. 'Jèmmage 'jǐhwèi jèiyí'bèidz 'béngsyǎng 'dzài yǒule. / That's a lifetime job. 'Nèishèr kéyǐ dzwò yí'bèidz. *or* 'Nèige děi dzwò °yí'bèidz (°dàu'lǎu). / He can have that job for life if he wants it. Nèishèr tā syǎng dzwò yí-'bèidz dōu 'syíng. / He never told a lie in his whole life. Tā °yí'bèidz (°'shēngpíng,

°'píngshēng, °yī'shēng) méi'shwōgwo yíjyù 'hwǎnghwà. /He had a long and happy life. Tā yí'bèidz bú'dàn shòucháng bìngchyé syǎng'fú. *or* Tā 'fú'shòu shwāngchywán.

(Living things) is expressed as human beings rén, or as animals 'dùngwù, 'hwówùr, or as signs of human life 'rényān; or indirectly with a verb meaning live shēng, hwó, *or* grow jǎng; no life may also be expressed as not even a blade of grass lyán yígēn 'tsǎu dōu méi'yǒu; wild life 'yěshòu. /There was no life on the island. 'Dǎushang °méiyǒu 'rén (°méiyǒu 'hwówùr, °méiyǒu 'rényān, °méi dùngwu, °lyán gēn 'tsǎu dōu méi'yǒu). /No life can exist in such a place. 'Jèmma ge dìfang 'shémma dōu °hwóbu'lyǎu (°bùnéng 'shēng, °bùnéng 'jǎng). /There's a lot of wild life in these forests. 'Jèi yídài shù'lindzli yǒu bù'shǎude °'yěshòu (°fēichín, °fēichindzǒushòu).

(Biography) 'jwànjì (book-length); syǎujwàn (shorter); write a book on someone's life bǎ . . . de 'shēngpíng'shr̀jì syě yìbě̌n 'shū, syě yì'bě̌r . . . de 'jwànjì. /I'm reading the life of a great novelist. Wǒ jèng kàn yíge dàsyǎu'shwōrjyàde °'jwànjì (°syǎu'jwàn). /He wrote a book on the life of the President. Tā bǎ dzúngtǔngde 'shēngpíng'shr̀jì syěgwo yìbě̌n 'shū. *or* Tā syěgwo yì'bě̌r jèiwèi dzúng'tǔngde 'jwàn-jì.

A matter of life and death °'syìngmìngjyāu'gwānde (°'shēngsžjyāu'gwānde, °'rén mìngjyāu'gwānde) shr̀. /This is a matter of life and death. Jèi shr °'syìng-mìngjyāu'gwānde shr̀ (°etc.).

For the life of (one) yàule (. . . de) 'mìng. /I can't for the life of me understand this. Yàule (wǒde)'mìng, wǒ yě 'bùdǔng jèi shr̀ 'dzěmma hwéi 'shèr.

Full of life (of a person) (yǒu) jīngshen; 'hwópwóde, 'hwóbwóde, hwānshr (active); (of other things; as eyes) (yǒu) jīngshen, yǒushén. /The children seem full of life. Háidzmen tǐng °(yǒu) 'jīngshen (°'hwóbwōde, °'hwópwōde, °'hwānshr). /His eyes are full of life. Tā 'yánlí yǒu 'shén. *or* Tā 'yǎnjīng hen (yǒu) 'jīngshen.

Give one's life jywānchyū, jìnjūng, 'shāshēnchéng'rén, sàngmìng。 /He gave his life for his country. Tā 'wèigwó °jywān'chyūle (°jìn'jūngle, °'shāshēnchéng'rénle, °sàng'mìngle).

Life after death (as a concept) is expressed as after death there is a soul sž-'hòu yǒu 'hwún, sž'hòu yǒu 'línghwún, or as there is a heaven and hell yǒu 'tyāntáng 'dìyù, or as when the body dies the soul still lives 'shēndz 'sžle 'línghwún hái 'dzài. /Almost every religion teaches (that there is) a life after death. Chàbudwō °'shémma (°'nèijùng) 'dzūngjyàu dōu jyàu rén 'syìn 'sž'hòu yǒu 'línghwún (°etc.).

Lose one's life sž. /He lost his life in the flood. Tā shr fā'shwěi de shŕhou 'sžde.

Signs of life chyèr (breath); 'jr̄jywé (sensory reaction). /Are there still signs of life in the child? Syǎu'hár hái yǒu °'chyèr (°'jr̄jywé) méiyǒu? /There are still some signs of life in that man. Nèige rén hái yǒu yìkǒu 'chyèr.

Life imprisonment 'wúchī'túsyíng.

Life insurance rén'shòubáu'syǎn.

Life line (fig., supply line, etc.) 'shēngmìng syàn.

Life membership 'yúngjyǒuhwèi'ywán, jūngshēnhwèi'ywán.

Life preserver (the ring-shaped type) jyòushēngchywān; (the jacket, belt, or Mae West type) jyòushēngdài, jyòushengyī; lifeboat jyòushēngchwán; lifeguard jyòu-shēngywán.

Life span 'shòu(mìng), or expressed as may live kéyǐ hwó. /The average life span of a dog is ten years. Gǒu 'píngjyūn kéyǐ hwó 'shŕnyán. *or* Gǒu 'píngjyūnde shòumìng sȟr shŕnyán.

Night life. / There is very little night life in this town. Jèige 'chéngli °'yèli 'méi shémma 'rènau (°'yèli 'méiyǒu shémma kě'wárde dìfang, °de yèshēnghwó bùdzemmayàng).

Lives (persons) rén, 'rénmìng, mìng, 'syìngmìng. / Many lives were lost in the flood. Nàushwěi'dzàide shŕhou sžle bù'shǎu 'rén. / Peace was gained only through the loss of tens of millions of lives. 'Hépíng sȟr jǐ'chyānwàn °'rénmìng (°tyáu 'mìng, °tyáu'syìngmìng) 'hwānláide. / They saved two lives. Tāmen jyòule 'lyǎngtyáu 'mìng. *or* Tāmen jyòu'hwóle 'lyǎngge rén.

Other expressions in English. / He was the life of the party. 'Nèi tsž 'jyùhwèi jyàu 'tā nùngde tǐng °'rènaude (°yǒu'yìszde, °yǒu'chyùrde).

LIFT. (Raise) is expressed with numerous verbs (given below) which distinguish different ways of lifting; in some instances verbs meaning hold *or* carry are also appropriate (*see* **HOLD** *and* **CARRY**); these are most often in combination with directional expressions, such as -chilai (up); -shangchyu (up and away); -dàu . . . chyu (to a place); -chuchyu (out); -gwochyu (over); . . . gāu (high); also in combination with -de dung *or* -de chilai (be able to move); verbs meaning pull, push, *or* move also have the meaning lift in combination with -shangchyu *or* gāu.

(Most general term; of lifting with hands or arms above the shoulder) jyǔ. / Lift these boxes over the fence. Bǎ jèisyē 'hédz tsúng 'lángārshangnar 'jyǔgwòchyu. / Lift it up a little higher so I can reach it. Dzài jyǔ 'gāudyar, wǒ tsái 'gòude'jáu. (*or* Any of the verbs given below may be used for jyǔ here.)

(By two or more persons using their hands below the shoulder) tái, dā. / The trunk is full of books; I don't think one person can lift it. Yīsyāngdzli 'chywán sȟr 'shū; wǒ kàn 'yíge rén °tái (*or* dā *or* jyǔ)bú'dùng (°tái (*or* jyǔ)buchǐlaí). / Be careful when you lift him out; don't hurt him. Bǎ tā °tái(°dā)chùchyu de shŕhou yàu 'dwōjyā 'syǎusyīn; byé bǎ tā pèng'téngle. / They lifted the patient from the bed to the operating table. Tāmen bǎ 'bìngrén tsúng 'chwángshang °tái (°dā) dàu shǒushùtáishang chyule. / Help me lift this trunk, will you? Láu jyà, bāng wǒ °'dā(°tái)-yisyar 'syāngdz.

(Of raising one's own head, hand, or arm) yáng; (including feet also) tái. / He was too weak to lift his hand. Tā rwǎnde lyán 'shǒu dōu 'bùnéng °yángle (°táile, °jyǔle, °táichǐlaile, °jyúchǐlaile).

(In the arms) bàu. / Lift the baby up so he can see. Bá syǎuhár °'bàu(°jyǔ)-chilai hǎu jyàu tā kànde'jyàn. ·

(In the hand, especially with arm down and hand holding a handle) dǐlou, tí. / Lift the suitcase and see how heavy it is. Bǎ 'syāngdz 'tíchilai, kànkan yǒu dwō 'jùng.

(With both hands stretched forward, palms up, especially balancing something) dwān. / There are so many things on the tray that I can hardly lift it. 'Twōpárshangde 'dūngsyi tài 'dwōle, wǒ 'chàbudwō °dwān(°twō)buchi'laile.

(With both hands, palms up, especially of something that must be handled with care) twō. / Life his head up and give him a drink of hot tea. Bǎ tāde 'tóu twōchilai gěi ta bēi rè'chá hē.

(Onto the shoulders) káng. / The crowd lifted him to their shoulders. Dàjyā-'hwǒr bǎ ta °'káng(°jyǔ)chilaile. / He lifted the bag to his shoulder. Tā bǎ nèige kǒudai 'kángdzài jyānbǎngshang.

(With a crowbar or other lever) chyàu. / Lift the stone with a crowbar. Ná gēn tyě'gwùn bǎ 'shŕtou 'chyàuchilai.

(By picking up) ná. / That suitcase is too heavy for you to lift. Nèige syāngdz tài 'jùng, nǐ °ná(°jyǔ)bu'dùng.

(Of raising the corner or side of something, as a cover, curtain, or rug; only the following combinations with -kāi occur) 'syānkāi; 'jyēkāi (used of flexible things only if strength is required); 'dǎkāi (not used of flexible things). / Lift up the cover and see what's inside. °'Syānkāi (°'Jyēkāi, °'Dǎkāi) 'gàr kànkan 'lǐtou dōu yǒu-'shémma. / He lifted up a corner of the rug and swept the dirt underneath it. Tā bǎ dì'tǎn syānkāile ge'jyǎur, jyòu bǎ 'dzāngtu 'sǎujìnchyule.

(By pulling, pushing and other motions) lā, chě (pull); twēi (push); yùn (transport); néng, gúdu (get to move). / They had to lift the heaviest boxes with a pulley. Tāmen yùng hwá'chēr tsái ba dǐng'jùngde jǐge'syāngdz °lā(°chě, °ywùn, °néng, °gúdu)shàngchyu.

(To rise; as fog) sàn (disperse). / The fog lifted quickly. 'Wù hěn'kwàide jyòu 'sànle.

Not lift a hand (or finger) to do something yì'dyár yě bùbāng'máng. / She wouldn't lift a hand to help. Tā yì'dyár yě °méi(°bù'kěn)bāng'máng. / He won't lift his little finger to help unless there's something in it for himself. Yàushr tā'dżjǐ débudàu 'hǎuchù de hwà, tā yì'dyár yě 'bùkěn 'bāng byérénde 'máng.

Lift (upward force) (shàng)'shēnglì. / The plane didn't have enough lift to get off the ground. Fēi'jī shàng'shēnglì bú'gòu('dàde), swóyǐ 'méinéng °lí'dì (°fēichǐlai).

Give someone a **lift** (in a car) shwùn'byàn °dài (°sùng). / May I give you a lift? Wǒ shwùnbyàn 'dài ni chyu, hǎu buhǎu? / Someone gave him a lift to the station. 'Yǒurén kāi'chē bǎ ta shwùn'byàn 'dàidàu chē'jànchyude.

Give someone a **lift** (emotionally) jyàu . . . gāu'syìng (make happy); jyàu . . . 'jīngshén °yí'jèn (°'hwànfā, °jèndzwòchǐlai), bǎ . . . 'jīngshén °'tíchǐlai (°'jèndzwò-chǐlai) (encourage). / His letter really gave me a lift. Tā nèifēng 'syìn jyàu wo hěn gāu'syìng. / That speech of the general's gave the soldiers quite a lift. 'Jyāng-jyunde °tán'hwà (°sywùn'hwà) jyàu 'shr̄bīng'jīngshén °yí'jèn (°'hwànfā, °'jèndzwò-chǐlaile). or 'Jyāngjyunde °tán'hwà (°sywùn'hwà) bǎ 'shr̄bīngde 'jīngshén °'tíchǐlai (°'jèndzwòle) bù'shǎu.

LIGHT (LIT). 1. In relation to vision.

(Luminous energy) gwāng; sometimes expressed indirectly by saying something is bright lyàng, or (for lack of light) dark àn; a light-year yíge 'gwāngnyán; light waves 'gwāngbwō. / The velocity of light is 186,000 miles per second. 'Gwāngsù 'méimyǎu shr̄'bāwàn'lyòuchyānyīng'lǐ. / The light is reflected from that window. 'Gwāng shr̄ tsúng nèige (bwōli)'chwānghushang °'fǎnshè(°jàu)gwolai de. / A point of light shows up clearly in the deep darkness. °'Dīnghēide dìfang (°'Dīngàndē shŕhou, and other similar combinations) °yìsyīngrde (°yì'dyándyar, °yì'dyár) gwāng dōu syǎnde tǐng'lyàngde. / The soft light in the room made it cozy and restful. 'Wūlide 'gwāng tǐng 'róu, jyàu rén jywéje hěn 'shūfu, hén 'jìnchengde. / The light was so strong that he had to close his eyes. Nèige 'gwāng °hěn 'chyáng (°lyàng'jíle), 'jàude tā bù'dé bù bá 'yǎnjǐng 'bìshang. / The light on the snow was blinding. Sywé fàn-'gwāng, jàude (jyàu ren) 'jēngbukāi 'yǎn. or Sywě 'lyàngde jyàu rén 'jēngbukāi 'yǎn. / The light is bad in here. (of artificial light) Jèrde 'dēnggwāng °'búgòu 'lyàngde (°'tài 'àn). or expressed as It's not bright enough here. Jèr búgòu 'lyàngde. or as It's too dark here. Jèr tài 'àn.

(Brightness) lyàngde dìfang; or expressed with lyàng (be bright) alone. / There is a strong contrast between light and shade in that painting. Nèijāng 'hwàrshang bǎ 'lyàngde dìfang gēn °'àndē (°yǒu'yērde) dìfang 'hwàde tǐng chǐngchu. / There's some light here. Jèr yǒu dyǎr 'lyàngr. / That bulb doesn't give enough light. 'Nèige dyàndēng'pàur °búgòu 'lyàngde (°'gwāng búgòu 'lyàngde, °'gwāng búgòu chyáng).

(Source of artificial illumination) dēng; **electric light** 'dyàndēng; **light bulb** dyàndēng'pàur; **flashlight** shǒudyàn'dēng; **lighthouse** 'dēngtǎ; **headlight** 'chēshangde dàdēng. / Please turn on the light. Bǎ °'dēng (°'dyàndēng) kāikai. / Give me a light bulb. Géi wǒ yíge dyàndēng'pàur. / Did you turn off the lights? Ní bǎ dēng 'gwānshàngle ma? / We'll leave a light on in the hall. Gwò'dàurli lyóuge 'dēng ba. / I bought a flashlight and some batteries. Wó mǎile ge shǒudyàn'dēng, hái mǎile jǐge dyàn'chř.

(Something that causes to burn, especially for smoking) hwǒr (fire); yánghwǒr (match). / May I have a light? (Gēn nín) 'jyège hwǒr? *or* Nín yǒu yáng'hwǒr ma?

(Point of view). / I don't think you're looking at this thing in the right light. Wǒ jywéde °nǐ dwèi jèijyàn shř de 'kànfa bútài 'jèngchywè. *or* Gwānyu 'jèijyàn shèr wǒ jywéje °nǐ kàn'tswòle (°nǐ 'kànde búdà 'dwèi, °nǐde 'kànfa búdà 'dwèi, °nǐde 'kànfa 'tswòle).

Bring to light (by investigation) cháchulai. / The investigation brought many new facts to light. Nèmma yì'chá cháchule bù'sháu yǐ'chyán bùjř'dàu de shèr lai.

In the light of ànje, běnje. / I made my decision in the light of what you said. Wǒ shř 'ànje 'nǐde 'hwà °dǎde 'júyì (°jywé'dìngde).

See the light (fig.) míngbaigwolai (become clear); 'ràugwo nèige 'wār lai (turn the corner, get the point); dǔng (understand). / At last I've made you see the light. Wǒ dàu'lyàur ràng nǐ 'míngbaigwolaile. / He still hasn't seen the light. Tā 'hái bùdǔng.

Throw (some) **light on** is expressed by saying that after doing something one will understand 'míngbai dyǎr *or* 'dwōshǎu 'jřdau dyǎr (followed by an expression containing a verb); or as explain somewhat 'dwōshǎu 'jyángdyǎr (with a noun). / This article ought to throw a little light on the subject. Kànle jèipyàn 'wér dàgài kéyǐ °'míngbai dyar (°'dwōshǎu 'jřdau dyar) 'nèi shř dzěmma hwéi 'shèrle. *or* 'Nèijyàn shèr 'jèipyàn wérli yīnggāi 'dwōshau 'jyángle dyǎr.

To light (cause to burn, without flame, as an electric light) bǎ . . . 'dyǎnshang; (with flame or smoke, as a candle or pipe) bǎ . . . dyǎn'jáule. / Light the lamp as soon as it gets dark. Tyān yì 'hēi jyòu bǎ 'dēng dyǎnshang. / Light the candles. Bǎ 'làjú dyǎn'jáule. / Light up your pipe and stay awhile. Bǎ yān dǒur dyǎn'jáule °'dāihwěr (°'dzwòhwěr). or expressed as Smoke a pipeful of tobacco and stay awhile. Chōu °dàr 'yān (°kǒu'yān) dzwǒ 'hwěr.

Light up (make bright) bǎ . . . jàude 'lyàng; be lit up lyàng. / The candle lit up the table. °'Là bǎ 'jwōdz (°'Làjú jàu dzài 'jwōdzshang) jàude tǐng 'lyàngde. / The fire lit up the whole street like day. Hwǒ bǎ yìtyáu 'jyē jàude gēn 'báityān shřde (nèmma 'lyàng). / The house is all lighted up. Nèiswǒr 'fángdzli dēng tǐng 'lyàng.

Light up (fig., of eyes or face). / A smile lit up her face. Tā mán 'lyǎn 'syàurúngr. *or* Tā 'méikāiyǎn'syàude. / As soon as the children heard it, their eyes lit up in anticipation. Syǎu'hármen yì tǐng, dōu °'dēngje lyàngge yǎn (°bǎ 'yǎnjīng jēngdàle) 'dēngje.

Be light lyàng; (of morning only) míng. / That room is light and airy. 'Nèi wūr yě 'lyàng, 'kūngchì yě hǎu. / We can work outdoors as long as it's light. Jř yàu °tyān hái 'lyàngje (°hái yǒu 'lyàngr) wǒmen jyòu néng dzài 'wàitou dzwò'hwòr. / Wait until it's light. Děng tyān °'lyàngle (°'míngle) dzài 'shwō. / Wake me up as soon as it's light. Tyān yí 'lyàng jyòu 'jyàu wo.

(Pale) bái. / Her complexion is very light. Tā 'pífu hěn 'bái.

(Of colors) chyǎn. / The book has a light blue color. Shū'pyér shř 'chyǎnlán-

(shǎr)de. / He came in a light gray suit. Tā chwānje yítàu 'chyǎnhwēi(shǎrde) 'yī-shang láide. / I want this color, but in a lighter shade. Wǒ yàu jèige 'shǎrde, búgwò děi dzài 'chyǎn dyar. / A lighter color like silver would be better. °Dzài 'chyǎn dyarde shǎr (°Shǎr dzài 'chyǎn dyar) tsái 'hǎu, yín'hwēi jyòu 'syíng.

2. In relation to weight or feeling.

(Of weight only) chǐng. / Please take light packages with you. °'Chǐngdyǎrde 'baur (°'Fēnlyàng 'chǐngde 'baur) chǐng 'dzjǐ dàije. / Light artillery won't be enough. Jǐng kàuje °'chǐngpàu (or (small caliber) °'kǒujǐng 'syǎude pàu) bú'gòu. / This coat is very light (in weight). Jèijyan dà'yǐ hěn chǐng.

(Of blows, knocks, footsteps, etc.; said of their sound) (tǐng) chǐng(de); or expressed by chǐngchǐngde followed by a verb. / She's very light on her feet for such a heavy woman. Tā swéirán nèmma 'pàng, kěshr jyǎu'bùr tǐng 'chǐng(de). / He heard light footsteps in the yard. Tā tǐngjyàn 'ywàndzli °yǒu tǐng 'chǐngde jyǎu'bùr shēngyīn (°yǒu rén chǐng'chǐngde dzǒu'lù). / There was a light knock on the door. Yǒu rén chǐng'chǐngde chyāule yísyàr 'mén. or Yǒuren chyāule yísyàr 'mén, chyāu de 'shēngyīn tǐng 'chǐngde. / I heard a light scratching on the other side of the wall. Wǒ tǐngjyàn chyáng 'nèibyar yǒu rén chǐng'chǐngde dzài 'chyángshang 'jwāle yísyàr.

(Of losses) bújùng, bùdwō. / Our losses in the battle were light. Wǒmen dzài 'nèi yíjànglǐde °'swǔnshr (°'sżshàng) °bú'jùng (°bù'dwō).

(Of snow, rain, etc.) dyǎr, bú'dà(de), syǎu. / A light snow fell last night. Dzwér 'wǎnshang °syàle dyár 'sywě (°syàde 'sywě bú'dà). / It was only a light rain. Búgwò shr syáuyǔ.

(Of wind) chǐng, syǎu, wēi. / There's a light breeze. Chwēi yíjèn °chǐngfēng (°'syāufēng, °wēifēng).

(Of work) 'chǐngsung dyǎrde. / Our maid has not fully recovered yet; she can only do light housework. Wǒmende lǎu'mādz (bìngle) hái méiwánchywán 'hǎu; 'jǐr néng dzwò 'chǐngsung dyǎrde 'hwór.

(Of taxes) chǐng; (in comparison, lower) jyǎnchǐng(le), dǐ(le). / Our taxes are lighter this year. 'Jǐnnyánde 'shwèi °jyǎn'chǐngle (°'dǐle) bù'shǎu.

(Of food; in quantity) hén shǎu, bùdwō. / I had only a light lunch today. Wó 'shàngwu chǐde °hén 'shǎu (°bù'dwō). / Light meals are served during the flight. Fēisyíngde shŕhou °yóu 'dyǎnsyin chǐ (°'yóu dūngsyi chǐ késhr bù'dwō).

(Of food; in quality) rúngyi syāuhwa (easy to digest). / Eat light food for a few days. 'Jèi jǐtyān jyòu chǐ dyar rúngyi 'syāuhwa de dūngsyi. or expressed as Don't eat heavy stuff for a few days. 'Jèijǐ tyān °'byé (°'shǎu) chǐ 'yóunǐde dūngsyi.

(Of pastry) 'chǐde hǎu, 'fāde hǎu (well risen). / My cakes are lighter today than usual. Wǒ 'jyěr dzwò de 'dyǎnsyin bǐ píng'chángde °'chǐde (°'fāde) hǎu.

(Of sleep). / He fell into a light sleep. Tā dzài nèr dá'dwěr ne. / He is a light sleeper. is expressed as He can be easily waked up. Tā yi'chǎu jyòusyíng.

(Of punishment) chǐng. / He got off with a very light sentence. 'Fáde tā tǐng 'chǐngde (pyányi tā le). or 'Pànle tā hěn chǐngde túsyíng.

(Of moods) is expressed with gāu'syìng be happy, cheerful. / I'm in a light mood today. Wǒ 'jǐntyan tǐng gāusyìng.

(Of reading). / I prefer light reading after work. Syà'gūng yǐ'hòu wǒ ywànyi 'kàn °'búyùng fèi 'syīnsż de (°kéyǐ 'syāusyánjyě'mèrde, °'chǐngsūngdyarde, °syǎu-'shwōryílèide) shū.

Make light of. / He made light of the matter. Tā bǎ 'nèishèr kànde °tǐng 'chǐng

(°bú'jùngyàu). *or* 'Nèishèr tā jywéde °búyàu'jǐn (°'méi shémma 'gwānsyì, °shr̀ 'syàushèr yǐjwāng). *or* Tā 'méibǎ nèishèr °gēdzai 'syīnshang (°dàng hwéi 'shèr kàn). /He made light of the danger. 'Tā jywéde 'búdà 'wéisyǎn.

Light-headed (dizzy). /I feel a little light-headed. Wǒ jywéje °'yūnhuhude (°yóu dyǎr 'yùn).

Lighthearted. /He's always lighthearted. Tā 'lǎu shr̀ °'kwàikwaihwohwóde (°syàng 'syīnli méi shémma'shèr shr̀de, °'syīsyīhā'hāde).

3. **Other uses.**

To light (to come down and land) làu. /The birds often light on this tree. Nyǎur 'cháng làudzai jèikē 'shùshang.

LIKE. (Be attracted toward; of people) 'syǐhwān; ài (also means love, but may be used for like when speaking of an older person liking a younger person, etc.); <u>in some cases</u> kàndeshàng, shàngshr̀; jywéde . . . 'hǎu (or other words for good or, in the negative, for bad, etc.); (if the opinion is derived from appearances) kàn . . . 'hǎu (etc.); <u>other indirect expressions are also used, especially in the negative.</u> /She likes children. Tā hén °'syǐhwān (°'ài) syǎu'hár. /There are three young faculty members that the president likes very much. Jyàu'ywánli yǒu 'sānge nyán'chīngde, syàu'jǎng tíng °'syǐhwān(de) (*or* (due to respect for) °kànde'shàng(de), *or* (due to their qualities and abilities) °'shàngshr̀(de). /I like you as you are. <u>is expressed as</u> I like the way you are. Nǐ syàn'dzài jèiyàngr wǒ tíng 'syǐhwān. *or* Wǒ jywéje nǐ syàn'dzài jèiyàngr tíng 'hǎude. /He doesn't like her. Tā 'bùsyǐhwān tā. *or* Tā jywéde tā °'bùhǎu (°tǎu'yàn). *or* (stronger) Tā tǎu'yàn ta. *or* Tā 'kànbu'shàng tā. *or* Tā 'kàn ta °kànbu'shàng 'yǎn (°bùshwùn'yǎn, °bùjūng'yì). /I don't like her. Wǒ 'bùsyǐhwān 'tā (nèige rén). *or* Wǒ 'jywéje tā °'bùhǎu (°tǎu'yàn). *or* (stronger) Tā nèige rén °tǎu'yàn (°tíng tǎu'yànde). /I don't like her looks. (as she always is) Wǒ kàn ta búshwùn'yǎn. *or* Wǒ jywéje tā 'jǎngde °'chǒu (°bùhǎu 'kàn, °búshwùn-'yǎn, °nán 'kàn). *or* (as she looks just now) Tā nèige 'yàngdz °hǎu nán'kànle (°hén tǎu'yànde, °jyàu rén kànbu'shàng). *or* (she looks sick to me) Wǒ kàn ta yǒu'bìng le. *or* (she is sick, and looks seriously ill to me) Wǒ kàn ta bìngde hěn 'jùng.

Like each other hédelái, 'jìngjùng, 'chùde 'hǎu; (of two people in a stated mutual relationship) syānghǎu, (chùde) 'hǎu. /They like each other very much. Tāmen 'bǐtsz °hen hédelai (°'jìngjùng, °'chùde hén hǎu, °hén syānghǎu, °hén hǎu, °hǎujíle).

Like a thing 'syǐhwān (may be followed by a verb such as see kàn); ài (must be followed by a verb such as see kàn); °jywéde (°kànde if judged by appearance) . . . 'hǎu (or other similar words for hǎu); <u>also many indirect expressions.</u> /This is the kind of book I like. Wó 'syǐhwān °de jyǒu shr̀ (°kàn) jèijǔng 'shū. *or* 'Jèijǔng shū wó 'syǐhwān. *or* 'Jèijǔng shū wó °'syǐhwān (°ài) 'kàn. *or* Wǒ 'ài kàn 'jèijǔng shū. /Do you like this pen? Ní 'syǐhwān jèigwán 'bǐ ma? /I like your hat. Wǒ hén 'syǐhwān (kàn) nǐde 'màudz. *or* Wǒ 'jywéje nǐde 'màudz tíng hǎu'kàn. <u>or</u> <u>expressed as</u> Your hat is very good-looking. Nǐde 'màudz hén hǎu'kàn. /I don't like her hat. Wǒ jywéje tāde 'màudz 'bùhǎu'kàn. *or* Wǒ bù'syǐhwān tāde nèige 'màudz. /How do you like my new dress? Wǒde 'syīn yīshang nǐ °'jywéde (°kàn) °dzěmma'yàng (°'hǎu bùhǎu)? *or* Nǐ °'jywéde (°'kàn) wǒde 'syīn yīshang °dzěmma-'yàng (°'hǎu bùhǎu)? /I like the way she carries herself. Wǒ hén syǐhwān tāde 'jyújr̀'dùngdzwò. *or* Wǒ jywéje tā 'yìjyǔyí'dùng dōu tíng 'hǎu. /I don't like your work. Wǒ jywéje nǐ dzwòde °bù'chéng (°bù'syíng, °chà'jìn). /Do you like it? 'Syǐhwān ma? *or* 'Hǎu bùhǎu a? *or* Nǐ °'jywéde (°kàn) °'dzěmmayàng (°'hǎu bùhǎu)? *or* (of a taste) Nǐ chr̀je dzěmma'yàng? *or* Hǎu 'chr̀ ma? *or* (of a smell) Nǐ wénje dzěmma'yàng? *or* Hǎu 'wén ma? *or* (of looks) Nǐ kànje dzěmma'yàng? *or* Hǎu 'kàn ma? /I like it. Hǎu. *or* Syíng. *or* Chéng. *or* Bú'hwài. *or* Wǒ jywéje nèi

707

bú'hwài. *or* (of a taste) Hǎu 'chr̄. (etc.) /I don't like it. 'Wǒ jywéje 'bùhǎu. *or* Wǒ 'búdà 'syǐhwan. *or* (stronger) 'Bùhǎu. *or* 'Búdwèi. *or* Bù'syíng. /How do you like the food there? Nàrde fàn nǐ syǐhwan (chr̄) ma? *or* Nàrde fàn nǐ 'jywéde °dzěmma'yàng (°'hǎu buhǎu, °'hǎu chr̄ bùhǎu 'chr̄)? /Do you like fish? is expressed as Do you like to eat fish? °Nǐ 'syǐhwan (°Nǐ 'ài) chr̄ 'yú ma? /I like movies. is expressed as I like to see movies. Wó °'syǐhwan (°'ài) kàn dyānyǐng. *but* /Well, how do you like that! Jè 'wèimyǎn 'tài nánle. *or* Jè 'búshr̄ ('chéngsyīn) dǎu'lwàn ma? *or* 'Jēn méisyǎng'dàu. *or* 'Jēn méi syǎng'dàu hwèi 'dzěmmaje. *or* 'Jè kě 'jyàu rén dzěmma 'bàn ne.

Like to do something or have something done **ài, 'syǐhwan, 'ywànyì,** jywéje . . . 'hǎu, dwèi . . . yǒu syìngchyu. /I like to be with you. °Wǒ 'ài (°Wó syǐhwan) gēn ni dzài yí'kwàr. *or* Wǒ jywéje néng gēn ni dzài yi'kwàr tsái 'hǎu. /I like my hair cut short. Wó syǐhwan bǎ 'tóufa jyǎn 'dwǎnle. /He likes to show off. Tā ài syǎn 'běnshr̄. *or* Tā ài 'syànnéng tā dz̀'gěrde 'běnshr̄. /I like to hunt. °Wó syǐhwan (°Wǒ ài) dǎlyè. *or* Wǒ jywéje dǎlyè yǒu yìsz. *or* Wǒ dwèi dǎlyè yǒu syìngchyu. /He likes to take charge of things. Tā ài gwǎn 'shèr. /He doesn't like to read small type. Tā °'búài (°bù'syǐhwan) kàn 'syǎudzèrde shū. /He likes to be babied. Tā °'ywànyì (°'ài, °'syǐhwan) jyàu rén 'hǔngje tā. /He doesn't like to be ordered around. Tā 'búywànyì 'shòu rén °'gwǎn (°'jr̄shr̄). /He doesn't like to be called by that name. Tā búywànyì rén 'nèmma °jyàu ta (°chēnghu tā). *or* 'Nèmma °jyàu ta (°chēnghu tā) tā 'búài 'tǐng.

Would like (followed by a verb) 'ywànyì, (hěn) 'syǎng, (syǎng) yàu (want); (followed by a noun) (syǎng) yàu; also some indirect expressions. /I'd like to be with you. °Wǒ 'ywànyì (°Wǒ 'hěn syǎng) gēn ni dzài yí'kwàr. /Would you like to go there for me? Nǐ 'ywànyi tì wo 'chyù yi'tàng ma? /I'd like to see his face. Wǒ 'jēn °syǎng (°ywànyì) kànkan tāde lyǎn. /I'd like to, but I can't. Wǒ °'ywànyì dàushr̄ (°'syīnli) 'ywànyì, 'búgwo bànbu'dàu. /Would you like (to have) another cup of tea? Ní syǎng'dzài lai wan 'chá ma? /I'd like to have some pork. Wǒ (syǎng) yàu dyar 'jūròu. /Would you like this pen? (to have it) Ní syǎng yàu jèigwǎn 'bǐ ma? *or* (to buy it) Ní syáng mǎi 'jèigwan 'bǐ ma? /Would you like it? Nǐ 'ywànyì ma? *or* Ní dzěmma 'shwō ne? *or* Nǐ shwō dzěmma'yàng? /I'd like it. 'Ywànyì. *or* 'Kéyǐ. *or* Syíng. *or* Chéng. /I wouldn't like it a bit. Wǒ 'búywànyì nèmmaje. *or* Wǒ 'búgàn. /How would you like that? 'Nèmmaje nǐ yòu dzěmma'yàng ne? /I'd like nothing better. (of a thing) °'Nèige (*or* (of an action) °'Nèmmaje) 'dzài hǎu méiyǒule. /I'd like to have my hair cut. Wǒ yàu jyǎn 'tóufa。

Like (similar to) gēn . . . shr̀de, syàng . . . (shr̀de), syàng . . . yí'yàng; **like that** nèmma(je), 'nèiyàngr; **like this** dzěmma(je), 'jèiyàngr; **like what** 'dzěmma(je), shémma'yàngr. /He talks like a minister. Tā shwō 'hwà °gēn (°syàng) jyàng'dàu shr̀de. *or* Tā shwō 'hwà syàng ge 'mùshr̄. /People here are very much like Americans. 'Jèrde rén °gēn (°syàng) 'Měigwo rén shr̀de. *or* 'Jèrde rén hěn syàng Měigwo 'rén. /You look like your father. Ní 'jǎngde °syàng (°gēn) nǐ 'fùchin shr̀de. /You look exactly like your father. Ní 'jǎngde °gēn nǐ 'fùchinde 'múyàngr yì'dyǎr bú'chà (°gēn nǐ fùchin yíge 'yàngr, °syàng nǐ 'fùchin syàng'jíle, °syàng'jíle nǐ 'fùchinle). /I've never met anyone like him. Wǒ 'tsúng lái méi'pèngjyangwo syàng-'tā nèiyàngrde (rén). /He ran like mad. Tā 'pǎude gēn 'fēngle shr̀de. *or* Tā gēn 'fēngle shr̀de nèmma 'pǎu. /She's like a mother to him. Tā dài tā jyòu gēn 'mùchin dài 'érdz shr̀de. /Don't talk like that. Hwà 'búshr̄ 'nèmmashwō de. *or* Byé 'nèmma shwō'hwà ya. *or* Byé shwō 'nèiyàngrde hwà. *or* (polite) Jè shr̄ 'nǎrláide 'hwà a! /What is she like? Tā 'shémma yàngr? /Is it like this? (a thing) Shr̄ syàng °'jèige shr̀de (°'jèiyàngrde) ma? *or* Shr̄ 'jèiyàngrde ma? *or* (an action) Shr̄ 'dzěmmayàngr ma? /Oh, so it's like that! 'Nèmmaje, á?

And the like (and so forth) nèi yílèide °'dūngsyi (°'shèr).

Feel like (doing something) syǎng. /Do you feel like dancing? Nǐ syǎng tyàu-'wǔ ma? *See also* **FEEL**.

Look like 'chyáuje hǎu syàng, 'kànje hǎu 'syàng, kànyàngr, kàn jèiyàngr. /It looks like (it will) snow. 'Chyáuje hǎusyàng yàu 'syàsywě.

There's nothing like 'shémma yě 'bùrú, gǎnbu'shàng, bǐbu'shàng. /There's nothing like a good cup of hot tea. 'Shémma yě 'bùrú yìwǎn 'rèchá.

Something like 'chàbudwō (almost, about); . . . -de yàngdz (of that sort); dzwǒ- yòu, chyánhòu (more or less). /He paid something like $1,500 for that car. Tā mǎi nèilyàng 'chē hwàle 'chàbudwō yòu yìchyán'wúbǎidwōkwài chyán. /It may be some- thing like three o'clock when I get there. Wǒ 'dàgài (dǐng) 'sāndyǎnjūngde yàngdz 'dàu nàr. or °Wó yésyú (°Wǒ 'dàgài) děi 'sāndyǎn °dzwó'yòu (°chyán'hòu) tsái néng 'dàu nàr.

Other expressions in English. /As you like. Swéi'byàn. or 'Dzěmmaje dōu 'syíng. or 'Hǎuba. /That's more like it! 'Nèmmaje hái 'hǎudyar. or 'Nèmmaje 'syàng hwéi 'shèr. or 'Nèmmaje 'syàng jyù 'hwà. /Like heck you will! (expressing disbelief) Hm! Tsái 'gwài ne! or (a threat, like our Over my dead body) Hèi! Wǒde 'chywántou bù'dāying. or Dá 'wǒ jèr shwō jyòu bù'syíng.

Likes. /She doesn't hesitate to express her likes and dislikes. Tā 'syīnli dzěmma 'syǎng 'dzwéili jyòu dzěmma 'shwō. or Tā 'syīnjŕkǒu'kwài. or Tā dzwéi hěn 'jŕ. or Tā (syīnli) 'syǐhwān 'bùsyǐhwān yì'jŕ jyòu 'shwōchūlai.

LIKELY. (Probable) hwèi (may be); néng (can be). /Are we likely to arrive on time? ('Chyáu jèiyàngr) dzámen °'néng (°'hwèi) àn 'shŕhou 'dàu ma? /Is it likely to rain tonight? (Chyáu jèiyàngr) jyēr 'wǎnshang °'hwèi (°'néng) syà'yǔ ma?

Most likely or very likely 'dàgài; kǔngpà (fear that); 'dwōbàn, 'dwōbàr (in all probability). /The trip will most likely take three days. 'Chyù yítàng °'dàgài (°'dwōbàn, °'dwōbàr, °kǔngpà) déi dzǒu 'sāntyānde 'yàngdz. /We'll very likely be seen. ('Chyáu jèiyàngr) dzámen °'dàgài (°'dwōbàr, °'kǔngpà) yàu jyàu rén 'kànjyàn. /He most likely won't come. Ta °kǔngpà (°etc.) bùláile.

Most likely to succeed dzwéi yǒu'syīwangde 'rén. /He was the most likely to succeed according to his classmates. Tā túng'bānde jywéde tā shŕ dzwéi yǒu- 'syīwangde 'rén.

A likely story. /That's a likely story! 'Nèishwōde hái syàng 'hwà ma? or 'Nèishwōde búsyàng 'hwà! or °Hwèi (°Néng) yǒu 'nàyàngde 'shŕ!

LIMIT. (Control) 'ywēshù, 'gwǎnshù; be limited (restricted) yǒu'syàn, yǒu'syànjŕ; (controlled) shòu 'ywēshù, shòu gwǎnshù, shòu 'syànjŕ; (insignificant) 'méi shémma kě 'chyù de; (low) hěn 'dī. /The president's powers are limited by law. Dzǔng- 'tǔngde 'chywánlì shòu 'fǎlyùde °'ywēshù (°'syànjŕ). /His ability is definitely limited. Tā jèi rén 'tsáinéng °yǒu'syàn (°'méi shémma ké 'chyù de, °hěn'dī).

Limit to or be limited to (consist of nothing but) jŕ yǒu; (not exceed) búgwò; (not go beyond the range) bùchū 'fànwéi. /My interest is limited to history. °Wǒ hàusyǐde (°Wó 'syǐhàude, °Wó 'syǐhwānde) jŕ yǒu lì'shŕ. /Limit your speech to twenty minutes. Ní yán'jyǎng byé gwò 'èrshrfēn 'jūng. /Limit your remarks to the subject under discussion. Shwō de 'hwà búyàu 'chūle běn'tíde 'fànwéi.

A limit (restriction) (yídìngde) 'syànjŕ; (set amount) yí'dìngde 'shùr; or ex- pressed indirectly as at the most 'jŕ dwō or as only jŕ. /There's a limit to the amount of work I can do in one day. Wǒ yì'tyānli 'néng dzwò de 'shŕ yǒu yí'dìngde °'syànjŕ (°'shùr). or Wǒ yì'tyānli °'jŕ dwō (°jŕ) néng dzwò 'nèmmasyē 'shèr.

Have no limits or know no limit or there is no limit to méiyǒu ge 'byār, méiyǒu ge 'tóur. /There is no limit to his ambition. Tāde 'syǔngsyīn méiyǒu ge

°'byār (°'tóur). or expressed as He is never satisfied. Tā 'lǎu méiyou jr̄'dzúde shŕhou.

Up to a limit of dàu. / You may spend up to a limit of ten dollars. Nǐ 'kéyǐ 'hwādàu 'shŕkwài chyán (wéi'jr̄ or wéi 'syàn).

Speed limit is expressed indirectly. / The speed limit is 25 m.p.h. is expressed as Driving at most should not exceed 25 m.p.h. Kāide °'jr̄ dwō (°'dzwèi kwài) bùnéng ('chāu)gwò èrshr̄'wúlǐ yídyǎn 'jūng. or as A speed of 25 m.p.h. is the limit. 'Sùdù yǐ 'méisyǎushr̄ èrshr̄'wúlǐ wéi 'syàn. / What's the speed limit? is expressed as How fast is the fastest one can drive? Kāichē 'dzwèi 'kwài néng kāi dwō kwài?

Time limit is expressed by constructions including dìng (set) followed by chīsyàn or 'shŕ'hou or 'r̄dz. / We'll have to set a time limit for this job. Dzwò jèijyàn 'shèr dzámen (dzǔng) děi °'gwēidìng(°'dìnggwēi, °'dìng)chū ge 'chīsyànlai. or 'Jèijyànshèr dzámen (dzǔng) děi °'dìnggwēi (°'gwēidìng, °'dìng) ge dzwò'wánde °'r̄dz (°'shŕhou, °chīsyàn). or (more emphatic) Jèijyàn sher dzámen (dzǔng) děi 'dìngchū ge 'chīsyànlai, dàule 'shŕhou yí'dìng yàu dzwò'wán. / You must finish everything within the time limit. Shémma dōu děi dzài °yí'dìngde (°dìng'hǎulede, °shwō'dìnglede) 'chīsyànli dzwò'wán.

City limits chéngjyè, chéngde 'byānjyè; chéngde sz̀'wéi (the four boundaries); or expressed as the place where the city's controlled area stops °chéng (°shr̄) gwǎnde dìfang dōu dàu . . . wéi'jr̄; **outside the city limits** is also expressed as outside the city chéng'wài. / Where are the city limits? °Chéng'jyè (°Chéngde 'byānjyè, °Chéngde sz̀'wéi) (dōu) °dzài (°dàu)'nǎr? or °Běnshr̄ (°Běnchéng) gwǎn de 'dìfang dōu dàu'nǎr wéi'jr̄? / We're out of the city limits now. Wǒmen 'syàndzài °chūle chéng'jyè le (°'chūle chéngde 'byānjyè le, °yǐjīng dàule chéng'wài le).

Limited yǒu syàn; or expressed as small (see **SMALL**); or expressed indirectly in other ways. / They have a limited income. Tamen 'jìnkwàn °yǒu 'syàn (°bù'dwō, °hěn 'shǎu, °hěn 'syàu, °'méi dwōshǎu). / We have only a limited amount of time to finish this in. Dzámen 'méiyǒu dwōshǎu shŕhou jyòu déi bǎ jèige nèng'wánle. / She lived on a limited diet. (for reasons of health) is expressed as She could eat only a few things. Tā 'jr̄ néng chr̄ 'jǐyàngr dūngsyi. or as She was unable to eat many things. Tā 'hǎusyē dūngsyi dōu 'bùnéng 'chr̄. or (for reasons of poverty) is expressed as She ate very thriftily. Tā'chr̄de hěn 'shěng.

Other expressions in English. / This is the limit! Dàu 'tsz̀ wéi'jr̄. or Dàu 'jèr jyòu swàn 'jr̄yǐ'jìnyǐ le. or 'Dzài bùnéng °'rén le (°'shòule). / He's the limit! 'Jèijyāhwo 'jēn shr̄ shǎu 'yǒu. or 'Méi nèiyàngrde 'rén! or Tā 'jēn shr̄ gòu'chyáude le! / The sky's the limit. 'Dwōshau chyán dōu ké'yǐ.

LIMITATION. (Restriction) 'syànjr̄. / There are limitations on the amount of baggage a passenger may carry. 'Chéngkè 'syínglide 'fènlyàng yǒu 'syànjr̄.

(Deficiency or shortcoming) syàn; (lack) 'chywēdyǎn; (shortcomings) 'dwǎnchù; (insecure points) bù'twōde 'dìfang, bù'twōdàngde 'dìfang. / He has great limitations. Tāde 'néngli yǒu'syàn. or Tāde 'dwǎnchù hěn 'dwō. / Everyone should recognize his own limitations. is expressed as Everyone should know himself. 'Shéi dōu yīnggāi yǒu 'dz̀jr̄ jr̄'míng. / This plan has its limitations. Jèige 'bànfa yǒu °syē 'dwǎnchù (°syē 'chywēdyǎn, °bù'twō(dàng)de 'dìfang).

LINE. (Mark) syàn (especially fine, threadlike); dàur (usually wider). / Draw a line connecting these two points. Dzài jèi'lyángdyǎn jr̄'jyān hwà tyáu 'syàn 'lyánchǐlai. / Divide the court into two parts with a chalk line. Bá 'chǎngdz °yùng 'báidàur (°'hwà yìtyáu bái'syàn, °'dǎ yìtyáu bái'syàn, °'hwà yìtyáu bái'dàur, °'dǎ yìtyáu bái'dàur) dzài dāng'jūng 'fēnkai. or Bá 'chǎngdz dāng'jūng °yùng 'báidàur (°etc.) 'fēnkai. / I want a tablet with lines. Wǒ yàu °yìběr dài 'dàur de 'jr̄ (°yíge dài

710

'daurde jr'ber). /Sign on the dotted line. (Bǎ 'míngdz) chyāndzai 'syūsyànshàng.

(Electric or telephone wire) syàn; or expressed in terms of a telephone dyàn-'hwà. /The rebels cut the telephone lines. Pàntú bǎ dyànhwà'syàn gěi °'chyāle (°nèng'dwànle). or Pàntú 'bùjwǔn tūng dyàn'hwà le. /I'm sorry, the lines are all busy. Dwèibu'jù, 'jǐtyáu 'syàn dōu °'jànje ne (°yǒu rén 'jyàu, °'yùngje ne, °yǒu rén shwō'hwà ne). /The line's busy; she must be talking to someone else. Tāde dyàn'hwà °yǒu rén 'jyàu (°syàn jànje ne); tā yídìng shr gēn 'byérén shwō'hwà ne.

(Cord or rope) shéngdz (for rescue work); (for clothes) lyàng'yǐfu 'shéngdz; (for fishing) yúsyán, dyàu'yúde °syàn (°shéngdz). /Throw out a line! Bǎ 'shéngdz 'yìtóur 'rēngchūchyu! /Hang the clothes on the line. Bǎ 'yǐfu 'gwàdzai lyàng'yǐfu shéngdzshang. /Is your line strong enough to land a ten pound fish? Nǐde °yú'syàn (°dyàu'yúde syàn, °etc.) jǐnde jù yìtyáu 'shrbàng jùng de 'yúma?

(Series of objects, as cars or trees) lyòu, pái (measures). /There's a long line of cars ahead of us. Wǒmen 'chyántou yóu tǐng 'chángde °yílyòu (°yípái) 'chē. /How many people are ahead of you in the line? Nǐ jàn de °jèiyì'pái (°jèiyì'lyòu) 'chyántou yǒu 'dwōshǎu rén? /I had to stand in line to get this pack of cigarettes. Wó děi jàn'pái tsái mǎijáude jèibāu yān'jywǎr. /They formed a line in front of the post office. Tāmen dzài yóujèng'jyú 'chyántou jànchéngle yì'pái.

(Of type or writing) háng (a measure); refers to a vertical line in Chinese or a horizontal line in Western languages. /Don't skip a line when you write. 'Syěde 'shrhou yì'háng yě byé 'là. /Set these lines in smaller type. Pái jèiji'háng de shrhou yùng 'syǎuhàurde chyān'dž. /Leave out these five lines when you copy this. Nǐ 'chāu jèige de 'shrhou °bǎ 'jèiwǔ'háng 'chyùle (°bǎ 'jèiwǔ'háng chyú'syàule, °byé chāu 'jèiwǔ háng). /You left out five lines when you copied this. Nǐ chāu de °'lòule (°'làle, °'dyàule) 'wǔháng.

(Of poetry, or sometimes prose) jyù (a measure; means also sentence). /Do you know what poem these lines are from? Nǐ 'jrdàu jèijǐ'jyù shr tsúng něishǒu 'shrshang láide ma?

(In battle) syàn (used alone or in combinations). /The enemy has shortened its lines. 'Dírén 'swōdwǎn °'fáng(°'jèn, °'jàn)syàn le. /He saw action in the front lines. Tā 'shànggwo chyán'syàn.

(Of argument) is expressed by terms referring to method, as 'shwōfǎ way of talking, dzěmma how, etc. /What line of argument are you going to use to prove that? 'Nèige ní syǎng yùng °'shémma 'fāngfǎ lái 'shwō (°'dzěmma ge 'shwōfa tsái) néng jyàu rén 'syìn ne? /What line is the defense following? 'Bèigàu fāngmyàn °dzěmma 'shwō (°yùngde shr 'néijǔng 'shwōfǎr)?

(Of talk or action, meant to interest someone) yìtàu('hwàr); or expressed by saying someone knows how to talk hwèi shwō'hwàrde. /He has a good line. Tā 'tǐng hwèi shwō'hwàrde. or Tā 'jyànle shémma 'rén dōu jǒu yítàu 'hwàr. /Don't try that line with me. 'Yùngbu'jáu gēn 'wǒ °lái (°shwō, °shr) 'nèi yítàu.

(In transportation) lù (route); hàu (number, as of a bus); jyār, gūngsž (company); when referring to using or riding on a line, the expression is dzwò . . . -de followed by the name of the type of vehicle in question. /Which bus line do you use to go home? Nǐ hwéi'jyā shr dzwò °'něi'lùde (°'jǐhàude, °'néijyàrde, °'néige gūng-'sžde) 'gūnggùngchì'chē? /Have you ever traveled on this air line before? Nǐ 'dzwògwo jèige gūng'sžde fēi'jǐ ma? /This is one of the largest railroad lines in the world. Jèi shr 'shrjyèshang dzwèi dàdeyíge'dà tyělùgūng'sž. /That steamship line owns over a hundred liners. Nèige ('chwán)gūng'sž yǒu yì'bǎidwōjī 'dàchwán.

(Business or profession, specialty or sphere of interest) háng; (selling) mài . . . -de; (of study) sywéde, nyànde; in one's line is expressed by saying that the person is in the line nèihángde, or specializes in the thing gàn or 'jwānmén, or is a specialist 'jwānjyā or jyàng, or by saying that the thing is his specialty jwānménde or běnháng or ná'shǒude hǎu'syì or yǒu'náshǒude; out of one's line is also expressed by saying that the person is out of that line wàiháng, or is an outsider lìba or lìbatóu or ménwàihàn. / That's out of my line. or That's not my line. Nèi 'bùshr wó °'běnháng (°'sywéde, °'nyànde). or Nèige wǒ shr °ménwài'hàn (°wài'háng). / That's right in his line. Tā 'jèng shr °nèi 'háng de (°'gàn nèige de, °gàn nèihángde, °'jwānmén 'gàn nèige de, °gàn 'nèimérde 'jwānjyā). or 'Nèige tā hěn dzài'háng. or Nèi jèngshr tā °jwān'ménde (°běn'háng, °de ná'shóu hǎu'syì, °yǒu'náshǒude). / He's in the dry-goods line. Tā shr mài'bùde. / What is your line of work? Nǐ shr gàn °nèi 'hángde (°shémma de)? / We're in the same line. Wǒmen shr 'túngháng.

(Of goods) 'páidz (brand). / They sell a good line of radios. Tāmen mài de 'wúsyàndyànde páidz 'hǎu.

(Short letter) syìn; (a few words) jǐge dzèr. / Drop me a line if you have time. Yǒu 'gūngfu de shŕhou gěi wo °lái fēng 'syìn (°syé jǐge 'dzèr).

All along the line. / There will have to be improvements all along the line. Jěng'gèrde 'bànfa dōu déi 'gǎi. or Tsúng'shàng dàu'syà 'swóyǒude 'bànfa dōu děi 'gǎi. or Tsúng'tóur dàu'lyàu měiyí'bùde 'bànfa dōu déi 'gǎi.

Along the line(s) of (according to) běnje, jàuje, ànje; (similar to) gēn . . . °syàng'sz̀ (°hěn jìn, °chàbudwō). / They're working along the lines of my idea. Tāmen jèngdzài °'běnje (°'jàuje, °'ànje) 'wǒde 'yìsz lái 'dzwò. / That's along the line of what I meant. Nèi gēn 'wǒ shwōde 'yìsz °syàng'sz̀ (°hěn 'jìn, °'chàbudwō).

Come from a long line of is expressed indirectly. / He comes from a long line of doctors. Tā 'jyāli °'shŕdài (°bèi'bérde) syíng'yǐ. or 'Tā jyā syíng'yǐ °yǒu 'hǎusyē 'dài le (°shr dzǔ'chwánde).

Down the line (including everyone) is expressed indirectly in terms of each or all. / He shook hands all down the line. Tā °āije 'gèrde (°'yíge yígède) lā'shǒu, 'dōu lā'dàule. / Everyone got a raise, from the president on down the line. Tsúng jīng'lí chǐ yí'gè yígède chywán jyā'syīnle. or Tsúng'shàng dàu'syà °yí'lyù (°'chywán) jyā'syīn le. or Chywán'tǐ yí'lyù jyā'syīn le.

Get a line on (investigate) 'dyàuchá; (find out about by questioning) 'dǎtīng; **like to get a line on** (want to know about) syàng 'jŕdàu. / Get a line on his background. °'Dyàucháyàuchá (°'Dǎtīngdǎtīng) °tāde 'bèijǐng (°tā yǐchyán shr dzěmma'yàngrde ge rén). / I'd like to get a line on his ability. Wǒ hén syàng 'jŕdàu tāde 'bénlǐng rú'hé.

In line (aligned) dwèijwǔnle. / See whether the wheels are in line. 'Kànkan lwúndz shr bushr dwèi'jwǔnle.

In(to) line (working together properly) yí'jŕ syíng'dùng; (not disagreeing with each other) bǐ'tsz̀ búnàu 'yìjyàn; (under control) gwǎnjùle. / Try to bring the committee into line. 'Syàngfǎr jyàu 'hwěilǐde rén 'tsáichyù yí'jŕ syíng'dùng. / He managed to keep the whole party in line. Tā 'dzǔng swàn shr 'méijyàu 'dǎnglide 'rén bǐ'tsz̀ nàu 'yìjyàn. or Tā 'dzǔng swàn shr bá dǎnglide rén gwǎn'jùle.

In line for. / He was in line for a promotion. °Gāi 'lwún dàu (°'Syà yíge gāi shr) 'tā shēng('jí)le.

In line of duty. / He was wounded in line of duty. 'Tā shr yīn'gūng shòu'shāng. or 'Tā gwà'tsǎile (slang). / His brother was killed in line of duty. Tā gēge °sywùn-'gwóle (°jènwángle).

In the line of . . . yílèide. / Do you have anything in the line of old paintings? Gǔ'hwàr yílèide 'yǒu ma?

712

Line of fire hwǒsyàn; or expressed as the place where the fire power can reach 'hwǒlǐ gòude'dàu de dìfang. / Our troops were out of the enemy's line of fire. Wǒmende jyūn'dwèi °chūle 'dírénde hwǒ'syàn le (°dzài 'dírén 'hwǒlǐ gòubú'dàude dìfang le, °búdzài dírende shècheng yǐ'nèile).

Line of march dzǒu de lù'syàn. / The arrows on the map show our line of march. Dì'túshangde jyàn'tóur 'jrchūlai wǒmen dzǒu de lù'syàn.

Pipeline gwǎndz; (for oil) yóugwǎndz. / They built a huge pipeline to transport oil to the north. Tāmen ānle yítyáu 'dà yóu'gwǎndz, bǎ yóu wàng'běi yùn.

Production line jwāngpèisyàn. / Our production line is working smoothly now. Syàndzài wǒmende jwāngpèisyànshang méiyǒu kùngnanle.

Supply line jyāutūngsyàn, 'jyāutūnglù'syàn, jíyǎngsyàn (military). / Our supply lines are longer now. Wǒmende 'jyāutūnglù'syàn bǐ yǐ'chyán 'chángle.

To line up (form a line) see fourth paragraph above; (arrange in formation) báihǎule 'dwèi, jànhǎule 'dwèi, páihǎule 'dwài; (organize) jwúnbèi hǎu; **have lined up** (of a job) yǒu, 'jǎujáu(le), dìnggwei(le) jyàu . . . 'dzwò(le); (in mind) 'syīnli yǒu. / Line up the boys before we start. Bǎ 'háidzmen 'syān 'pái hǎule dzài 'dzǒu. or Syān jyàu 'háidzmen °jànhǎule (°páihǎule) 'dwèi dzài 'dzǒu. / I have everything lined up. Wǒ 'shémma dōu 'jwúnbèi 'hǎule. / Do you have anyone lined up for that job yet? 'Nèi shr̀ ní °yǒu (°jǎujau, °'syīnli yǒu) 'rén le ma? or 'Nèi shr̀ nǐ 'dìnggweile jyàu 'shéi dzwò le ma? / I had a job lined up. Wó 'jǎuje yíge shr̀.

Be lined with (have a line on each side) is expressed indirectly. / The street was lined with people watching the parade. °'Yánjyē (°'Jyēde lyáng'páng) °jàn'mǎnle (°yǐ'pái yí'lyòude 'dōu shr) kàn yóu'syíng de rén. / The walls are lined with books. Yán chyáng dōu shr̀ shū'jyàdz, shàngtou °bái 'mǎnle shū (°'jìng shr̀ 'shū).

Be lined with (have a lining of) shr̀ . . . -lyěrde, gwàde . . . -lyěr. / Her coat is lined with red. Tāde 'yīshang °shr̀ 'húnglyěr de (°gwà de shr̀ 'húnglyěr).

LINEN. (Type of cloth) 'syàbù (general term for Chinese types of linen); 'mábù (any cloth made of hemp or sometimes flax; likely to be a coarser, rougher cloth than Western linen); má'shā (lyàudz) (coarsely woven linen, or muslin); yáng'shā (lyàudz) (finely woven linen, or cambric). / Linen is fine, but expensive. °'Syàbù (°'Mábù, °Má'shā lyàudz, °Yáng'shā lyàudz) 'hǎu dàu shr̀ hǎu, kěshr tǐng 'gwèi. / You can buy nice linen handkerchiefs down the street. Nǐ 'kéyǐ dzài jyēshang mǎi dǐng hǎude yáng'shā shǒu'jywàr.

(House furnishings as sheets and tablecloths) is expressed as bedclothes and so forth chwángdāndz shémmade or as tablecloths and so forth jwōbù shémmade. / What laundry do you send your linen(s) to? Nǐ °chwáng'dāndz (°jwō'bù) shémmade sùng 'nǎr chyù 'syǐ?

LIP. (Part of the mouth) dzwěi chwún (when referring to the individual lips); dzwěi (when referring to the lips as the whole mouth); **upper lip** shàngdzwěi'chwún; **lower lip** syàdzwěichwún. / His lips and cheeks are swollen from frostbite. Tā dzwěi'chwún gēn lyǎn dùng'jǔngle. / I've been practicing lip reading. Wǒ jèng lyànje 'kàn rén 'dzwéi dzěmma 'dùng jyou 'jrdàu tā shwōde shr̀ shémma 'hwà. but / Keep a stiff upper lip. Chyěr yàu jwàng. or Chyěr yàu dzú. or 'Dǎr dà dyar.

(Of a pitcher) dzwěr. / The lip of the pitcher is broken. Shwéi'gwǎndzde 'dzwěr pwòle.

Lip service. / He gives only lip service to that principle. Gwà 'yángtóu mài 'gǒuròu. or Mán kǒu 'rényi dàu'dé. or Tā 'syīn kǒu bùyí'jr̀. or Tā 'kǒu'shr̀syīn-'fēi.

Lipstick chwúngāu, kǒu'húng. / She hasn't put on lipstick yet. Tā hái méitú °chwún'gāu (°kǒu'húng) ne.

LIQUID. (Substance in liquid form, as opposed to gas or solid) 'yètǐ; **liquid oxygen** 'yètǐ yāngchǐ. / Some gases change into liquids only at very low temperature and under tremendous pressure. Yǒude 'chìtǐ 'fēi děi nùngde 'hén lěng, dzài jyā 'hěn dàde 'yālì, tsái néng byàn 'yètǐ.

(Watery substance) shwěr. / What's this blue liquid? Jèige 'lánshǎrde 'shwěr shř shémma? / Take a teaspoonful of this liquid (medicine) every two hours. Jèige yàu'shwěr gé 'lyángdyǎn jūng 'chř yìtyáu'gēng. / Do you have liquid shampoo? Yóu syǐ'tóude (yídz) 'shwěr ma?

(Nonsolid foods). / Keep him on a liquid diet. Jyàu ta gwāng chř 'syǐde. *or* Byé jyàu ta chř 'gānde.

LIST. dāndz, dǎr. / This is a list of the materials I need. Jèi °dāndzshang (°dǎrshang) 'kǎide shř wó děi 'yàu de 'tsáilyàu. / Is my name on the list? °Dǎrshang (°Dāndzshang) yóu wǒde míngdz ma? *or* Míngdārshang yóu wǒde míngdz ma?

Make a list kāi dāndz, kāi dǎr. / Make a list of the things you lost. Bǎ dyōule de 'dūngsyi kāi ge 'dāndz.

List price dìngjyà. / The list price is $500, but I can let you have it for $ 450. Dìngjyà wú'bǎi búgwo wǒ szbáiwǔ jyou màigei nǐ.

Blacklist hēimíngdǎr.

To list kāi; syě (write); lyè (arrange); often expressed with these same verbs in resultative compounds, such as kāisyalai, kāichulai, lyèsyalai, syěsyalai, etc. / List their names on a separate sheet. Bǎ tāmende 'míngdz °kāidzai 'lìngyijāng jřshang (°'lìng kāi ge dāndz). / List their names in the letter. Ba tāmende míngdz kāidzai 'syìnli. / I have to list all the things. Wó déi bǎ swó'yǒude dūngsyi dou °'kāisyalai (°syěsyalai, °lyèsyalai, °kāi yijang dāndz).

LISTEN. tīng. / I like to listen to folk songs. Wǒ °'syǐhwān (°'ài) tīng 'míngē. / Listen! (Nǐ) 'tīng (yi)ting. *or* (urgent) 'Tīng a! *or* (keep listening) 'Tīngje! / I'm listening. Wǒ 'tīngje ne. / Listen for the sound of a bell. 'Tīngje dyar 'lyéngr syǎng. / I told him so, but he wouldn't listen. Wǒ nèmma 'gàusung tā de, 'kěshr tā bù'tīng. / Listen to what I have to say. (of a statement or opinion) Tīng 'wǒ lái shwō. *or* (of long instructions) 'Lyóusyīn 'tīngje, jèi shř hěn yàu'jǐnde hwà. / Now you listen to me. (in turn) 'Syàndzài tīng 'wǒ de. *or* (of a command) Nǐ 'tīngje! / My child wouldn't listen to me. Wǒde háidz butīng 'hwà. / He always listens to his wife. Tā lǎu tīng ta tàitaide hwà.

LITERATURE. (Literary productions) 'wénsywé. / The library has an excellent collection of English literature. Túshū'gwǎn dzài 'Yīngwén 'wénsywé fāngmyàn 'sōujíde °'jùdzwò hěn dwō (°hěn 'chywán). / He's going into literature. Tā yàu °'sywé (°'yánjyōu) 'wénsywé. / He's taking a course in the history of English literature. Tā 'sywǎnle yìmér 'Yīnggwo 'wénsywéshř.

(Writing on a certain subject) is expressed as books shū; **the literature of** (*or* on) . . . / . . . yílèide 'shū. / The literature on travel is extensive. Yóu'jì yílèide 'shū tīng 'dwō.

(Printed matter, general) jyǎnjāng (school bulletin); sywǎnchwánpǐn (commercial type).

LITTLE. (Small in size, of objects) syǎu; (of persons) shēntsáisyǎu, gèrǎi, gèr syǎu;

syǎugèr (short); shòusyǎu (short and thin); (of children) also syǎu; but note that syǎurén means a small (mean) person. /Give me a little piece of cake. Gěi wǒ yì-'syǎukwàr dàn'gāu. / This dress is for a little girl. Jèijyàn 'yīfu shr̀ wei °'syǎu (°'shēntsái'syǎude, °etc.) 'nyǔhár chwānde. /He is a little man. Tā 'shr̀ yige °shòusyǎude (°shēntsái syǎude) rén. or Tā 'gèr °ǎi (°syǎu). or Tā shr̀ syaugèr. /He wore a ring on his little finger. Tā dzài syáushǒu'jr̀toushàng dàije ge jyéjr.

(Unimportant) syǎu, bú yàu'jǐnde; yì'dyǎr dàde (lit., of even the smallest size). /He noticed every little mistake. °Tā shémma 'syǎutswòr (°Yì'dyǎrdàde tswòr tā yě, °'Tíng syǎude 'tswòr tā ye, °Tā bǎ búyàu'jǐnde 'tswòr) dōu 'kànchulaile.

(Not much) 'méi shémma, búdà, hén syǎu. /He has little influence there. Tā dzài nàr °'méi shémma 'shr̀lì (°'shr̀lì bú'dà, °'shr̀lì hén 'syǎu).

A little (in amount) (yì)dyǎr; sometimes expressed as a few jǐ plus a unit measure; (in the past) 'méi dwō jyǒu, 'méidwōshǎu 'shr̀hou; (later) (wǎn) 'yìbù; (in the future) 'hwéitóu, děng yísyàr, jyǒu; a little while yì'hwěr; a little way ji'bùr. / Take a little interest in your work. Dzwò'shr̀de shr̀hou yùng dyǎr 'syìn. / There's just a little of the cake left. Dàn'gāu jyǒu shèngle yì'dyǎr le. /I think she's a little drunk. Wǒ kàn tā yóu dyǎr 'dzwèi le. /I'll tell you what little I know about it. Wó swǒ'jr̀daude jèidyǎr dōu 'gàusung nǐ. /It won't do any harm to pamper her just a little. 'Chǔng ta (yì)dyǎr pà shemma? /He's a little worried. Tā yóu dyǎr °jāu-'jí (°'bùfàng'syīn, °dān(je)'syīn). /He pampers her a little too much. Tā 'chǔng tā 'chǔngde yóu dyǎr °tài 'lìhàile (°gwò'fèn le, °gwò'hwòr le). /He doesn't love her even a little. Tā yìdyár yě bú'ài tā. /I can speak a little French. Wǒ néng 'jyǎng jijyù 'Fàwén. or Wǒ néng 'shwō yìdyǎr 'Fàgwó 'hwà. /I'll come in a little while. Wǒ °yì'hwěr (°'hwéitóu, °děng yísyàr) jyǒu 'lái. /He came a little (while) after you did. 'Nǐ dàule yǐhòu °'méidwō jyǒu (°yì'hwěr, °gwòle yì hwěr, °gwòle 'méidwōshau shr̀hou) tā 'yě dàule. or 'Tā dàude bǐ nǐ wǎn °'yíbù (°nèmma yìhwěr). /I rode a little (while) yesterday. 'Dzwérge wǒ 'chíle hwěr 'mǎ. /I can walk a little way with you. Wǒ 'kéyǐ gēn ní 'dzǒu ji'bùr.

(Of activity, ability; not much or not well) is expressed as sometimes 'yǒude shr̀hou or as not much bùcháng, 'búdà; (said of someone else) bútài hǎu (not too well); (said of oneself) bùhǎu (not well); or 'māmahū'hūde (just so-so). /Does he play chess? Oh, a little. Tā hwèi syà'chí ma? Hwèi, 'búgwo bú'tài hǎu. or Tā syà'chí ma? Bù'cháng syà. or 'Búdà syà. or 'Yǒude shr̀hou syà. /I can shoot a little, but not well. Wǒ hwèi 'māmahū'hūde 'fàng lyǎng 'chyāng.

Little better than bǐ . . . 'chyángbulyǎu dwō'shǎu. /He's little better than a thief. Tā bǐ syǎu'tōur 'chyángbulyǎu dwō'shǎu. /His grades are little better than mine. Tāde fēnshu 'bǐ wǒde chyáng bulyǎu dwōshǎu.

Little by little (in separate bits) yì'dyǎryìdyǎrde; (gradually) jyànjyānde; (slowly) mànmārde. / Little by little the job's getting done. Shèr °jyàn'jyānde (°màn-'mārde, °yì'dyǎryìdyǎrde) jyǒu yàu dzwò'wánle.

LIVE. (Be or remain alive) hwó or expressed with a negative plus sž̌ die. /I don't know whether he's living or dead. Wǒ 'bùjr̀dàu tā shr̀ 'sž̌le háishr 'hwóje ne. /He lived to a ripe old age. Tā hwódàu 'hǎu dàde 'nyánjì. / Live and let live. 'Džjǐ hwóje yé děi jyàu 'byérén hwóje. /The doctor said the patient would live. 'Dàifu shwō 'bìngrén °'néng 'hwó (°'sž̌bulyǎu, or (has hope) °yǒu'jyǒur). /I hope we live to see this finished. Wǒ 'syīwang jèige 'néng dzài dzámen méi'sž̌ yǐchyán dzwò-'wánle. or Wǒ syīwang jèige 'wán de shr̀hou dzámen hái °'hwóje (°méi'sž̌, or (be on earth) °dzài'shr̀). /He's living on borrowed time. is expressed as He's living each day for itself. 'Hwó yityān swàn yì'tyān le. or as He has today but not tomorrow. Tā yǒu 'jīntyān méi 'míngtyān de le.

(Spend one's life) gwò plus a noun referring to time, as r̀dz days *or* yíbèidz lifetime; occasionally hwó in the same construction; see also **LIFE**. /He lived a happy life. *or* He lived happily. Tā 'kwàikwaihwó'hwérde gwòle °yi'shēng (°yí'bèidz). /He never really lived (well). Tā yí'bèidz méi'gwògwo °'shūfu 'r̀dz (°'hǎu r̀dz). /You've never really lived unless you've seen Peiping. is expressed as This life can be said to have been lived in vain unless . . . . Ni 'yàushr méi'kànjyàngwo Běi'píng, jèi'bèidz kě 'swàn shr̀ 'bái °hwóle (°gwòle).

(Dwell) jù. /Does anyone live in this house? Jèiswǒr 'fáng yǒu rén 'jù ma? /Where does he live? Tā 'jù nǎr? *or* Tā dzài nǎr 'jù? /I expect to live here for two months. Wǒ 'dàswàn dzài 'jèr jù 'lyǎngge 'ywè. /Their maid lives in. Tāmen nyǔ'yùngren jù dzài tāmen'jyā.

Live down. /It will take years to live down the gossip. is expressed as Wait and see; this rumor will be passed on endlessly. Ni 'chyáuje ba, 'jèidwàr yàuyan 'chyé yǒu rén 'chwán ne.

Live it up syǎngfú. /We'd better live it up while we can. Wǒmen 'néng syǎng-fú jyou syǎngfú ba.

Live off (a person) °'jr̀je (°'kàuje) . . . °'hwóje (°chr̄'fàn). /They've been living off his parents for years. Tāmen 'dwōshǎu'nyán le dōu shr̀ °'jr̀je (°'kàuje) 'lǎurénjyār °'hwóje (°chr̄'fàn).

Live on (of money) is expressed in terms of passing days gwò 'r̀dz or in terms of eating by chr̄ and other expressions. /He earns hardly enough to live on. Tā jēngde jyàn'jr̀ búgòu °gwò 'r̀dzde (°'gwòr, °'chr̄de, °'jyáugwer). /How can you live on that little salary? 'Syīnshwéi 'nèmma dyǎr, dzěmma gòu 'gwòde ne? /They live on $100 a month. Tāmen měiywè yùng yì'bǎikwài chyán gwò 'r̀dz.

Live on (of food) ('gwāng) chr̄ . . . hwóje; (to eat nothing but) 'gwāng chr̄ . . . . /I live on rice. Wǒ chr̄ 'mǐ hwóje. *or* Wǒ 'gwāng chr̄ mǐ. /How can you live on bread and water? Ni 'gwāng chr̄ myàn'bāu hē lyáng'shwěi, dzěmma néng hwóje ne?

Live up to. /He didn't live up to my hopes. is expressed as He disappoints me. 'Tā jyàu wǒ shr̄'wàng. or as I formerly had great hopes for him. Wǒ 'ywánlái dwèi ta 'syīwàng hěn gāu.

A living (income) jìn'kwǎn, shǒu'rù; **make one's living** doing something jr̀je . . . °gwò 'r̀dz (°hū'kǒu). /He makes a good living. Tā °jìn'kwǎn (°shǒu'rù) hěn 'fēngfù. /He makes his living selling books. Tā jr̀je mài 'shū °gwò 'r̀dz (°hū'kǒu).

LIVE. (Of biological life) expressed by constructions with hwó to live. /That's a live snake. Nèityáu 'chángchung °'hwóje ne (°shr̀ 'hwóde). /Buy some live fish. Mǎi dyar 'hwóyú.

(Of an electric wire) dài dyàn de, tūngje 'dyàn de, yǒu dyàn de. /Never touch a live wire. Yúngywǎn byé mwō dài 'dyàn de dyànsyàn.

(Of coals) shāuhúngle de, hái húngje de, hái jáuje de, hái méimyè de. /Roast it over live coals. Dzài shāu'húngle de 'méishang 'kǎu.

(Of ammunition) jēnde; shr̀ in the combination 'shr̀dàn a live cartridge *or* a live shell; or expressed by saying that it might explode hwèi jàde *or* has not yet exploded méi yùnggwo de. /They use live cartridges for practice. Tāmen yùng 'shr̀dàn dá 'bǎ. /That's a live shell. Nèi shr̀ °'shr̀dàn (°'jēnde pàu'dàn). *or* Nèige pàu'dàn °hwèi 'jàde (°shr̀ méi'yùnggwode).

(Of an issue) is expressed by saying that people really have the issue 'jēn shr̀ yǒu, or that the issue is not yet solved hái méi'jyějywé. /It's a live issue in some places. Hǎu'syē 'dìfang 'jēn shr̀ yǒu jèijǔng °'wèntí (°'máfan 'shèr). /It's still a live issue. Jèige 'wèntí hái méi'jyějywé.

LIVELY. (Of a person, in actions or disposition) hwópwo, hwóbwo, hwóbe. /She has a lively disposition. Tā hěn 'hwópwo.

(Vigorous; in emotions or actions connected with emotions, as hatred, fighting) 'jīlyè, lìhai. /She's a lively arguer. Tā 'byànlwùn de hěn °'jīlyè (°'lìhai). /They often get into lively arguments. Tāmen chángcháng tái'gàng, tàide hen 'lìhai.

(Inspiring; as of music or actions) 'syúngjwàngde. /The band played a lively march. Yīnywè'dwèi dzòule yíge hěn 'syúngjwàngde jìnsyíng'chyǔ.

(Vivid; of a description) 'yǒushēngyǒu'sède. /He gave a lively description of the scene. Tā bǎ nèige 'chíngsying 'syíngrúngde 'yǒushēngyǒu'sède.

(In a brisk manner). /Step lively! 'Kwàidyar 'dzǒu.

Make things lively for someone gēn . . . 'dáudǎu 'lwàn, gēn . . . 'nàu yinàu. /We'll make things lively for him when he comes back. Tā 'hwéilai de shŕhou 'dzámen děi gēn ta °'dáudǎu 'lwǎn (°'nàu yinàu).

LOAD. (Place something on or in a vehicle) jwāng, shàng plus the name of the thing being placed; (on an animal) bǎ . . . twó. /The men are loading hay onto the wagon. Nèibāng rén 'jèngdzài wàng 'chēshang °shàng(°jwāng)'tsǎu ne. /We've been loading (things) all morning. Wǒmen jwāng °'dūngsyi (°'hwò) jwāngle yi'dzǎushang le. /Load the packs on the mules. Bǎ 'bāu °'twódzài 'lwódzshang (°jyàu 'lwódz twó).

Load a vehicle jwāng plus the name of the vehicle being filled. /Are the men loading or unloading the vessel? Nèisyē rén 'jwāngchwán ne háishr 'syèchwán ne? /It's time to load the truck. Gāi jwāng'chē le.

Load a gun bǎ chyāng jwāngshang °'dzěr (°dž'dàn). /Load this gun for me. Bǎ jèigǎn chyāng géi wǒ jwāngshang °'dzěr (°dž'dàn).

Load someone **with work** géi . . . bù'shǎude shr dzwò. /They loaded us with work. Tāmen 'géile wǒmen bù'shǎude 'shr dzwò. or Tāmen jyau wǒmen dzwò de 'shèr 'tài dwō le.

Be loaded (of a gun) jwānghǎule, yǒu chyāngdzěr, yǒu dždàn. /The gun was loaded and ready for firing. 'Chyánglǐtou °jwāng'hǎule (°jwāngshang 'dzěr le, °'jwāngshang dž'dàn le, °yǒu 'chyāng'dzěr, °yǒu dž'dàn), swéi'shr kéyi 'fàng.

Be loaded (with) (of a vehicle) jwāng, dzài; (of an animal) twó; (of a person with arms loaded) bàu; (when the things are hanging down) is expressed as hang full (of) gwà'mǎn(le); **be fully loaded** may also be expressed as mǎn'dzàr(le). /His arms were loaded with books. Tā 'bàule yí'dà °dwēi (°bàu) shū. /The tree was loaded with Christmas presents. 'Shùshang gwà'mǎnle shēngdan'lǐ. /The boat is fully loaded with merchandise. Nèijŕ 'chwánli jwāng'mǎnle 'hwò le. or Nèijŕ 'chwánli jwāngde °mǎn'chwánde (°yì'chwánde, °yì'mǎnchwánde) hwò. /The mule is too heavily loaded. 'Lwódz twóde tài °'jùngle (°'chén le).

Be (or Get) **loaded** (intoxicated) hēdzwèile. /He got loaded again last night. Tā 'dzwótyan wǎnshang yòu hē'dzwèile.

A load is expressed verbally as above. /How heavy is the normal load? Píng'cháng néng °'jwāng (°'dzài, or (of an animal) 'twó) 'dwōshau 'dūngsyi? /How much of a load can that boat carry? Nèijŕ 'chwán néng °jwāng (°dzài) 'dwōshǎu °'dūngsyi (°'hwò, or (pounds) °'bàng, or (tons) °'dwùn, or (catties) °'jīn)? or Nèijŕ 'chwán dzài'jùng 'dwōshǎu? /The load weighs a hundred pounds. is expressed as It weighs a hundred pounds. Yǒu yì'bǎibàng 'jùng. /The load on the mule weighs a hundred pounds. Lwódz 'shēnshang °'twóje yǒu yì'bǎibàng jùngde 'dūngsyi (°'twóde yǒu yì-

'băi bàng (jùng)). / The plane is carrying a full load now. Fēijīshang °jwāngde (°dzàide) yǐjīng gòu'jùngde le. *or* Fēijīshang °'bùnéng dzài 'jùngle (°'mǎn le, °mǎn'dzàr le).

Work load gūngdzwò. / Our work load has been getting heavier. Wǒmende 'gūngdzwò ywè lai ywè dwō le.

LOCK. (Operated by key or combination) swǒ. / Do you have a lock for a trunk? Ní yǒu 'syāngdzshang yùng de 'swǒ ma? / The lock on the stable door is broken. Mǎ-'hàu ménshangde nèibǎ 'swǒ hwài le.

(A stopping device) syāusyer, 'jīgwān. / There's a lock on the gears to keep them from turning backwards. °'Lwúndzshang (°Chř'lwúnshang) yǒu °'syāusyer (°'jīgwān) 'bújyàu lwúndz wàng 'hòu °'jwàn (°'dzǒu).

(Of hair) -lyǒur; <u>sometimes expressed as</u> one hair yìsz̄. / She gave him a lock of her hair. Tā gěile ta yilyǒur 'tóufa. / She won't go out unless every lock of her hair is in place. Tā fēi déi bǎ 'tóufa 'nùngde 'yìsz̄ bú'lwàn, 'yàubùrán jyou bù-'chūchyu.

(Of a canal) já. / The second lock of the canal is under repair now. Yùn'héshang dì'èrdàu 'já jèngdzai 'syōuli.

To lock (of a lock operated by a key or combination) swǒ, bǎ . . . 'swǒshang, bǎ . . . swó'hǎule. / Be sure to lock the door when you leave. 'Dzǒude shŕhou byé 'wàngle °swǒ 'mén (°bǎ mén 'swǒshang, °bǎ mén swó'hǎule).

(Be immovable) <u>is expressed as</u> be stuck 'chyáshangle, 'chyǎshangle, kéjule. / The brakes locked. Já °'chyáshangle (°etc.).

Lock in a place 'jywāndzai, 'gwāndzai, 'swǒdzai; (without the place being expressed) 'jywānchilai, 'gwānchilai (*see also* Lock up below). / We locked the dog in the cellar. Wǒmen bǎ gǒu °'jywān(°'gwān)dzai dì'yǐndzlǐ le. / Lock the prisoners in their cells. Bǎ 'fànrén dōu °'gwānchilai (°'jywānchilai, °swǒdzai 'yùli, °'swǒdzai 'wūdzli).

Lock out (a person) swǒdzai 'wàibyar, bǎ 'mén 'swǒshangle, 'bújyàu . . . 'jìnlia; **be locked out** (intentionally) swǒdzai 'wàibyar, bǎ mén'swǒshàng jyàu . . . °jìnbulái (°jìnbu'chyù); (accidentally) swǒdzai 'wàibyar mén 'swǒshangle °jìnbu'chyù (°jìnbu'lái). / We locked him out. Wǒmen bǎ 'mén 'swǒshangle, °méi(°bú)jyàu ta 'jìnlai. *or* Wǒmen bǎ ta 'swǒdzai wàibyar le. / We forgot to take the key last night and were locked out. Wǒmen dzwór 'wǎnshang 'wàngle dài 'yàushr, °jìnbu'chyùle (°bèi swǒdzai 'wàibyar le).

Lock up a person jywānchilai, gwānchilai, kānchilai, yāchilai; (may also mean in chains) swǒchilai. / The prisoners were locked up. 'Fànrén dōu 'jywānchilaile.

Be locked together (interlocked) gwǎshangle, gōushanglc, chyáshangle, chyá-shangle. / The bumpers of the two cars are locked together. 'Lyǎnglyàng chēde báusyǎn'gàng °'gwǎshangle (°etc.).

LOG. (A cut tree) mùtou'jwāngdz, 'kǎnsyàlai de 'shù. / There's a log cabin. Yǒu yìswǒ mùtou'jwāngdz gàide 'fángdz. / The logs are tied into rafts and floated down the river. Jēng'kěde kǎnsyàlai de 'shù dōu kwǔnchéngle °mù'pái (°mù'fá), shwùnje 'hé pyāusyalaile.

(A record) jìlù. / There is a complete record of the storm in the ship's log. Nèitsz̄ dà'fēng chwánshangde jì'lùli jìde tǐng 'chywán.

To log (record) jìsyalai. / Don't forget to log the speed. Byé wàngle bǎ 'súdù 'jìsyàlai.

(Cut down trees) kǎnshù, fáshù. /When will they start logging? Tāmen 'shémma shŕhou chǐ'tóur °kǎn'shù (°fá'shù)?

LONELY. (Of a person) 'jìmwò, mèn, mèndeheng, 'gūdān. /Aren't you lonely without your friends? Nǐde 'péngyou 'dōu bú'dzài jèr nǐ °bú'mèndeheng ma (°bú'jìmwò ma, °bùjywéje 'mèn ma, °bùjywéje 'mèndeheng ma, °bùjywéje 'gūdān ma)?

(Of a place). /This must be a lonely place in the winter. is expressed as This place must be cold and quiet in the winter. 'Jèige dìfang 'dūngtyan yǐ'dìng hěn °'lěngjìng (or as sad and cold °'chǐlyáng).

LONG (In space) cháng; in a few cases dà (big) is used; a long way ywǎn (far). /The room is twenty feet long. Jèijyān wūdz °(yǒu) 'èrshrchǐ 'cháng (°'chángli yǒu 'èr-shr 'chǐ). /Longer ones are better. 'Cháng dyarde 'hǎu. /These are the longest ones we have. 'Jèi shr̀ wǒmen jèr 'dzwèi chángde le. /The longest river in China is called the Big River or the Long River; on foreign maps it's called the Yangtze River. Jūnggwo 'dzwèi chángde hé jyàu 'dàjyāng, yě jyàu 'chángjyāng, dzài 'yángwéndì'túshang jyàu "Yangtze River." /I need a long rope. Wǒ děi yàuyi tyáu 'cháng shéngdz. /It's a long story. 'Nèi hwà tíchilai kě °'cháng jene (°jyou 'cháng le). /The snake was as long as from here to the table. 'Shé yǒu tsúng 'jèr dàu nèige 'jwōdz nar nèmma 'cháng. /He gave me a long list of names to investigate one by one. Tā jyāugei wǒ °yí'dàlyòu rén'míngdz (°yí'dàdwēi rén'míngdz, °yíge hěn 'chángde rén'míng dāndz), jyàu wǒ yí'gèyígède chyù 'dyǎuchá. /It's a long way to the top of the mountain. Dàu shān'dyǐngrshang °tǐng 'ywǎnde (°'ywǎn jene, °'lù hěn 'ywǎn).

(In time) jyǒu; bàntyān (lit., half a day); sometimes expressed by the adverb chyě (for a long time); or expressed by dà or cháng with shŕhou or gūngfu, or by dwō or syē with shŕhou, gūngfu or other time-spent expressions, such as hěn 'dàde gūngfu, hěn 'dwōde shŕhou, hěn 'chángde shŕhou, hǎusyē 'gūngfu, hǎusyē'nyán, hěn dwō 'r̀dz, etc. Note that time-spent expressions usually occur after the verb. In expressions indicating a given period, as all night long yíyè, long is usually not expressed, though sometimes such expressions as nèmma 'jyǒu or nèmma dwō 'shŕhou, etc., are used. /How long? Dwō 'jyǒu? or Dwōshau 'shŕhou? or Dwō da 'gūngfu? or Dwōshau 'r̀dz? /Not long. Bujyǒu. or Budàde 'gūngfu. or Búda-'hwěr(de gūngfu). /Don't stay away too long. Byé 'líkai tài jyǒu le. /I haven't seen you for a long time. Wǒ hěn jyǒu méikànjyan ni le. or as Long time no see. Hěn jyǒu méijyàn. /The event happened a long time ago. Nèi shr °hěn jyóu (°hen 'dwō shŕhou, °hǎu'syēnyán) yǐ'chyánde shŕching. /He got there long after we did. Wǒmen dàu ner °bàn'tyān (°hén 'jyǒu, °hěn 'dwōde shŕhou) yǐ'hòu, ta tsái 'lái. /We can wait as long as you can. Nǐmen néng děng °dwō jyǒu (°dwōshau 'shŕhou, °dwō da 'gūngfu) wǒmen ye néng děng °dwō jyǒu (°dwōshau shŕhou, °dwō da 'gūngfu). /The play is three hours long. Jèichū 'syì děi yǎn sānge jūng'tóu. /The child cried all night long. Syǎuhár kūle yí'yè. /It may take as long as six months. Yésyú děi yùng 'lyòuge ywè (nèmma 'jyǒu). /It'll still be a long time before this job will be finished. Jèijyan 'shr hái chyě dei °'dzwò ne (°'dzwò syē shŕhou ne).

As long as (provided that, if; referring to something still uncertain or unfinished) 'jǐryàu; see also **IF**; also, especially when there is a time element present, the construction ... yǐ'tyān, ... yǐ'tyān is sometimes used in a conditional sentence. /As long as you're here, I'll have nothing to worry about. 'Jǐryàu 'nǐ dzài jèr, wǒ jyou 'méiyou kě'bùfàng'syīnde. or 'Nǐ dzài jèryǐ'tyān wǒ jyou kéyi °'fàng yìtyánde 'syīn (°yǒu yǐ'tyánde gūngfu búyùng tsāu'syīn). /You may play in the yard as long as it doesn't rain. Jǐryàu 'búsyà'yǔ, nǐmen °dzài 'ywàrli wár 'dwōshau shŕhou dōu 'syíng (°jyǒu dzài ywàrli 'wár hǎu le, °jyǒu dzài ywàrli 'wár ba).

As long as (since, referring to an accomplished fact) 'jǐrán, 'jǐshr, jì. /As long as you really want it, you can have it. Nǐ °'jìrán (°'jǐshr, °jì) 'jēn syǎng 'yàu, jyou swàn 'nǐde le. /As long as no one is asking you about it, you may as well keep quiet. Jǐ 'méirén 'wèn nǐ, ní yě jyou 'béng tǐ le.

Have a long face 'dāle 'lyǎn, yìlyǎn bùgāu'syìngde yàngdz, 'mánlyǎn dàije bùgāu'syìngde yàngdz, 'mánlyǎn dàije bú'tùngkwaide yàngdz. /Why has he got such a long face today? Tā 'jyērge dzěmma °'dāle je ge 'lyǎn (°yìlyǎn bùgāu'syìngde yàngdz)? or Tā 'jyērge dzěmma 'mánlyǎn dàije °bùgāu'syìngde (°bú'tùngkwaide) yàngdz?

In the long run 'jyēgwǒ, kàu'chánglou, wàng cháng le 'kàn. /In the long run the more expensive watch would be better. °'Jyēgwǒ (°Kàu'chánglou, °Wàng cháng le 'kàn) háishr 'gwèidyarde'byǎu shàng'swàn.

To long (yearn) hén syǎng (want badly); 'pànwàng (hope). /I long to finish that job. Wǒ °'hén syǎng (°'jēn shr 'pànwàngje) bǎ nèijyàn shèr bàn'wánle.

Other expressions in English. /So long! 'Hwéi jyàn!

LOOK. (Direct the eyes to see) kàn, chyáu; (especially of looking once, or a little) kànkan, chyáuchyau, 'kàn yikan, etc.; (with more specific meanings) lyóu 'shén (pay attention); jāu (search). /Look this way. Wàng 'jèr °kàn (°chyáu). /I have to look first. Wǒ děi syān °'kànkàn (°'chyáuchyau, °'kàn yikàn, °'chyáu yichyáu). /No harm in looking. 'Kànkan'búaishr. /I wasn't looking just at that moment. Jěnghǎu 'nèijèr wǒ °méi'kànje (°méi'chyáuje, °méilyóu'shén, °'yǐyǎn méichyáu'jyàn). /Did you look everywhere? Ní 'nǎr dōu °'kànle (°'jàule) ma? /Hey! Look! 'Hèi! Nǐ 'kàn! or 'Hèi! Nǐ 'chyáu! or 'Hèi! 'Kàn a! or 'Hèi! 'Chyáu a! or (Peiping) 'Hèi! 'Lōu yilou! or (especially when whispering) simply 'Hèi! /Look where you're going! 'Chyáuje dyar! or rudely expressed as Where are your eyes? 'Yǎnjing jáng 'nǎr chyule.

(Appear, seem) kànje; sometimes unexpressed, but the rest of the sentence in such cases usually includes some expression referring to external appearance, as lyǎnshang (face) or hǎukàn (good-looking); or expressed by kànshangchyu. /She looked angry when she said that. Tā 'shwō nèige de shrhour °'lyǎnshang hén bùhǎu 'kàn (°hǎu 'syàng tíng yǒu 'chì shrde, °lyǎnshang dàije shēng'chì de yangdz, °lyǎnshang dàije 'nùrúng). /How does this hat look to you? 'Jèidǐng'màudz °'dzěmmayàng (°'syíngbusyíng, °'syàngyàngr ma)? /It looks nice on you. 'Nǐ °chwānje (°dàije) 'tíng °shr ge'yàngrde (°hǎu'kànde). /You look very healthy. Nǐ 'kànje hén 'jyànkāng. /The food looks very appetizing. °Fàn (°Chrde) kànje hén hé'wèikou. /She looks very pretty today. Tā jīntyan °'kànje (°'dàbande) hén hǎu'kàn. or Tā jīntyan hén měi. /This hat looks good on you. Jèige mòudz nǐ dàije hǎukàn.

(In exclamations) hēi, 'āiyā, or not expressed. /Look who's here! 'Āiyā! or 'Hēi! Kàn 'shéi lái le! /Look who's talking (now)! (if the person talking, referred to as you or he, has no right to talk) °'Nǐ (°'Tā) dǔngshémma (yě 'syāshwō)! or °'Nǐ (°'Tā) yě pèi shwō'hwà! or Dzěmma 'shéi dōu néng shwō 'hwà ya! or (a proverb) Jě jyàu 'yǐpíngdz bùmǎn 'bànpíngdz 'gwàngdang. or (if the person talking has changed sides in an argument) Hēi, dzěmma 'ní yě gǎi le 'dzwèi le? or (if insincerity is suspected) 'Kǒushr syīn'fēi.

Look like °kànje (°cháuje) syàng; (of one person to another) jǎngde syàng. /It looks very much like snow. Chyáuje hǎu syàng yàu 'szàsywě. /He looks like a ghost. Tā kànje syàng ge'gwèi shrde. /You look very much like your father. Ní 'jǎngde hén syàng nǐ 'fùchin.

Look after kān (of children; also means to guard); (of an adult, affairs, etc.) 'jàulyàu, 'jàugwǎn, jàuying. /Did you get someone to look after the child? Ní 'jāujáu rén kān 'háidz le ma? or Ní 'jāujáu kān'háidzde le ma? /He's getting old and needs someone to look after him. Tā 'lǎule, déi 'yǒu ge rén °'jàuyingje (°'jàu-gwǎnje, °'jàulyàuje) dyar.

Look at is expressed as in paragraph one, and also by dīng, 'dèngje yǎn kàn (fix the eyes on); (especially of looking sideways, out of the corner of the eyes, stealthily, etc.) náyǎn 'lyōu yísyàr, 'lyáyǎr 'lyōu yísyàr, 'syéjeyǎn 'kànkan. / Look at the beautiful sunset! Ei! Nǐ kàn nà °wǎn'syá (°lwò'r) 'dwō hǎu 'kàn. / May I look at it? Ràngwǒ °'kànkan (°'chyáuchyau) 'syíng ma? / I enjoy looking at pictures. Wǒ 'hǎu kàn 'hwàr. / He looked at her for a long time without moving his eyes, as if he were in a trance. Tā °'dèngje yǎn (°'mùbùjwǎn'jīngde) °'kànje tā kànle (°'chyáuje tā chyáule, °'dīngje tā dīngle) bàn'tyān, 'háu syàng jáule 'mí shr̀de. or Tā 'sź̌dīngje tā kànle bàn'tyān, 'háu syàng jáule 'mí shr̀de.

Look ahead to *see* **Look forward to,** below.

Look around kànkan; (examine) chá(kàn). / I didn't buy anything, I was just looking around. Wǒ 'shémma dōu mei'mǎi, wǒ jyòu 'kànle kàn. / You'd better look around in back. Nǐ dzwèi hǎu dàu hòubyar chyù °kànkan (°chácha). / A detective looked around for quite a while but didn't find anything. Jēntàn chále bàn'tyān, kěshr 'shémma ye meijàu'jáu.

Look back (recollect) 'hwéi syǎng, syáng yǐchyánde shèr, syǎng 'jyòushr̀. / Looking back now, those years we spent together were the most memorable in my life. °'Hwéi syǎngchilai (°'Syáng syang yǐ'chyánde shèr, °Syángsyang 'jyòu shr̀), wǒmen dzài yí'kwàr gwò de nèisyē'nyán shr̀ wǒ 'jèibèidzli 'dzwèi kě'lyóulyànde. / Don't look back (on the past). 'Byé syáng yǐ'chyánde shèr.

Look down on kànbuchǐ, chyáubuchǐ, 'syǎu kàn, bǎ . . . kàn'dǐ, 'chǐngshr̀. / He felt that the people there looked down on him. Tā jywéje nàrde rén °kànbu'chǐ tā (°chyáubu'chǐ tā, °'syǎukàn tā, °bǎ ta kàn'dǐle, °chǐngshr̀ tā).

Look for jǎu. / We're looking for rooms. Wǒmen jǎu 'fáng ne. / What are you looking for? Nǐ jǎu 'shémma ne? / I'm looking for my keys. (Wǒ) jǎu 'yàushr ne. / I've looked everywhere for him, but no luck yet. Wó jǎu tā jǎu'byànle, hái méi bǎ tā jǎu'jáu ne. / He's always looking for trouble. Tā 'lǎu shr̀ °'méishr̀jǎu-'shr̀ (°'dztáu'kǔchr̄, °'dž̀'jǐ jǎu 'máfan, °dž̀'jǐ jǎu'shèr). or Tā 'láu rě'shr̀. or Tā 'láu (jǎu)rě 'shr̀fēi. / Are you looking for trouble? (a threat) Nǐ syáng jǎu 'máfan a! or Nǐ syáng dǎ'jyà a! / Aren't you looking for trouble? (friendly warning) Nǐ nà búshr °(dž̀jǐ) 'méishèr jǎu'shèr ma? or °dztáu'kǔchr̄ ma? or Nǐ nà búshr jǎuje yàu °chr̄'kwēi (°dǎ'jyà, °rě'shèr, °chū'shèr) ma?

Look forward to (wait impatiently for) 'pànje 'kwàidàu. / He's looking forward to the time when he'll finish college. Tā 'pànje 'kwài dàu 'dàsywé bì'yè de shr̀hou. / We're looking forward to our vacation. Wǒmen 'pànje 'kwàidàu fàng'jyàde shr̀hou.

Look here (forbidding) hèi, ei, or (mild warning) nǐ syángsyang, nǐ tīng 'wǒ shwō, nǐ tīng 'wǒde. / Look here! You can't do that! 'Hèi! 'Nà kě bù'syíng. or 'Ei! 'Bùnéng 'nèmmaje a! or Nǐ 'syángsyang 'nà dzěmma 'syíng ne? or Nǐ tīng °'wǒ shwō (°'wǒde), 'nèmmaje bù'syíng.

Look into (investigate) 'dyàuchá. / The police will certainly look into the robbery. Jǐngchá 'jyú yí'dìng hwèi 'dyàuchá nèijyàn 'chyǎngàn de.

Look on (as a spectator) kàn, dzài yì'byār kàn. / The others played, but he just looked on. 'Byérén 'wárde shr̀hou tā °gwāng (°dzài yì'byār) kànje.

Look on something as (consider) 'rènwéi, jywéje. / Her father looked on her marriage as unfortunate. Tā 'fùchin °'rènwéi (°'jywéje) tā 'jyàderén bùhé'shr̀.

Look out (exclamation) lyóushén, syǎusyīn, dāngsyīn, àn a.

Look out on (face) chùngje, dwèije; *see also* **FACE.** / The big window looks out on a flower garden. 'Dàchwānghu chùngje hwā'ywár.

Look over *see* **Look at** above.

Look to someone for help jřje, kàuje. / He always looked to his father for help. Tā lǎu shř 'jřje tā 'fùchin.

Look up someone jǎu, kàn. / Look me up sometime. Méishèr 'jáu wǒ lái. *or* 'Méishèr lái 'jǎujau wǒ. / I am going to look up a friend. Wǒ chyù °'kàn (°'jǎu) ge péngyou.

Look up (lift the head) 'táitóu. / He looked up quickly. Tā lǐ'kè bǎ tóu 'táichilaile. *or* Tā lǐ'kè 'táitóu yí'kàn.

Look up (find out) jǎujau; or expressed as examine chácha. / If you lose this card you can always look up my address in the phone book. Yàu bǎ jèijāng 'pyàndz 'dyōule, °dzǔng kéyi dzài 'dyànhwà'bèndzshang 'jǎujau wǒde 'jùjrde (°'chácha (or kànkan) 'dyànhwà'bèndz jyòu 'jǎujáu wǒde 'jùjrle). / Look it up in the train schedule. is expressed as Examine the timetable. 'Chácha 'hwǒ'chē shrjyàn'byǎu.

Look up to pèifu (admire); 'jìngjùng (respect). / I can't help looking up to him. Wǒ bù'néng bú °'pèifu (°'jìngjùng) tā. *or* Tā jēn jyàu rén °'pèifu (°'jìngjùng).

Looking up (improving). / Things are looking up. Jyàn 'hǎu. *or* Yóu 'chǐsè.

Look (appearance) yàngdz, syàngr, shénchi. / The house has a neat look. 'Jèiswǒr fángdz 'yàngdz ('kànje) tíng °'jēngchi (°'gānjing). / I don't like his looks. Wǒ bù'syǐhwān tāde °'yàngdz (°'syàngr, °nèijung 'shénchi). *or* 'Jèirén wǒ kànje 'búshwèn'yǎn. or expressed as Look at the way he looks. 'Chyáu tā nèige °'yàngdz (°'shénchi, °'syàngr). *or* (if he looks sick) Tāde 'yàngdz bùhǎu kàn, syàng °yòu'bìng shrde (or (if he looks sicker than expected) °bìngde hěn 'jùng). / I don't like the looks of this situation. Wǒ °kàn (°jywéje) °jèige 'chíngshr búdà 'dwèi (°dà'shr bù'hǎu, °jèige 'chíngsyíng yàu 'dzǎu).

Take (*or* Have) a look (at) *or* give someone a look is expressed verbally as in paragraph one. / Take a look from here. Tsúng'jèr °'kàn yikan (°'chyáu yichyau). / Take a good look. °'Dzsyì (°Hǎu'hǎurde) °'kànkan (°'chyáuchyau, °'dwànsyang-dwànsyang). / She gave him a nasty look. Tā hěn'hěnde °'dīngle (°'chǒule, °'kànle, °'chyáule, °'dèngle) tā yì'yǎn.

Take one look and ... °yí'kàn (°yí'chyáu) jyòu ... , °'kàn (°chyáu) yì'yǎn jyòu .... / He took one look and beat it. Tā °yí'kàn (°yì 'chyáu, °'kànle yì'yǎn) jyòu sya'pǎule.

LOOSE. (Not tight; of a fastening or grip) sūng, bù'jǐn; come loose 'sūng le, 'sūngkaile; be loose (because never tightened) is expressed by verbs meaning tie, nail, screw, pull, etc., in such constructions as ... de sūng, ... de bù'jǐn, méi ... 'jǐn; of a knot, also 'jǐde 'búshr 'szǎkóur (not tied in a tight knot); of a screw, also méi'nǐngdau tóur (not screwed to the head). / If that knot comes loose, the whole bundle will fall apart. Nèige 'kòur yàushr 'sūng(kāi)le, °kwèr (°bāur) jyou 'sǎn le. / The knot is loose, so it shouldn't be hard to undo it. Nèikòur °'jǐde hěn 'sūng (°'jǐde bù'jǐn, °'méijǐ'jǐn, °shr sūng'sūngrde 'jǐde, °'jǐde 'búshr 'szǎkóur), bùgāi 'nèmma nán 'jyě ya. / If the rope around the box is too loose, it will slip off. 'Hédzshangde 'shéngdz yàushr °kwùnde tài 'sūngle (°bǎngde tài 'sūng le, °bùchóu'jǐn le, °bùshóu'jǐn le), hwèi 'dyàusyalaide. / Put a loose bandage on his arm. Dzài tā 'gēbeshang °kwǔn ge sūng dyarde bēng'dài (°kwǔnshang bēng'dài 'byé kwǔn'jǐnle, °sūng'sūngrde kwǔn tyáu bēng'dài). / Doesn't that bolt seem loose? Nèige 'lwósz shr bushr °yóu dyǎr 'sūng le (°méi'nǐngdau 'tóur, °méi níng'jǐn)?

(Not connected tightly; as a wire) is expressed in the same way as above, but also come loose bù'jyēje le. / There must be a loose wire in the plug. Chā'syǎuli yŏu yìtyau syàn °'sūngkai le (°bù'jyēje le, *or* (not fastened tightly in the first place) °méiníng'jǐn).

(Not fitting in tightly, as a cork) sūng; tài 'syǎu (too small); sāibu'jù (can't plug up); sāibu'jǐn (can't plug tightly). / This cork is too loose. Jèige sāidz °tài 'syǎu (°sāibu'jù, °sāibu'jǐn). *or* Sāishang tài 'sūng.

(Not fitting tightly, as clothes) tài 'dà (too large); 'dà le (become large); 'fèi (too large a size); buhé'shr (not fitting); 'gwànglegwàngdāngde (le) (like a half-full bottle); all of these are preceded by 'chwānje (in wearing). / I've lost so much weight that my clothes are all loose. Wŏ 'shoude 'yīshang dōu chwānje °'dà le (°'féi le, °'gwànglegwàngdāngde le, °'bùhé'shr le).

(Not sewn on tightly, as a button) yàu 'dyàu (about to fall off); 'dālaje le (hanging by a thread); 'syàn dwàn le (a thread broken). / There's a loose button on your coat. Nǐ 'yīshangshang yŏu yíge 'nyŏudz °yàu 'dyàu le (°'dālaje le, °'syàn dwàn le).

(Not firm or rigid) hwó, hwódung, hwóyou (moving, wiggling); bù'láukau (insecure); hwàngyou (of a board) also chǐlaile (risen, buckled) *or* chyàuchilaile, yŏu dyar 'chyàuje (tipped up at one end). / He has a loose tooth. Tā yŏu yíge 'yá 'hwó-(dùng)le. / This plank is loose. (of a board laid to walk on, as a gangplank) Tyàu-'bǎn °'dāde bù'láukau (°'méidā'láukau). *or* Tyàu'bǎn yŏu dyar °'hwàngyou (°'hwó, °hwódung). *or* (of a board fastened down) Jèikwai °'bǎndz (°'bár) yŏu dyar °'hwó (°'hwódung, °'chyàuje). *or* Jèikwai 'bǎndz °'dīngdz sūng le (°'méidīng'láukau, °'dīngde buláukau, °'chyàuchilaile).

(Not tied up or shut in) fàngkai(le), 'fàngchuchyu(le). / Isn't that dog allowed to go loose? Nèi 'gŏu bunéng 'fàngkai ma?

(Individual, not packaged) lwùn plus a measure (by the piece); or expressed by the appropriate measure; or expressed as buy loose líng 'mǎi or as sell loose líng 'mài. / During the cigarette shortage some shopkeepers broke open the packages and sold the cigarettes loose. 'Jryān shǎu de nèi shŕhou, yŏude mài'yānde bǎ jēngbāur 'dǎkai °'líng mài (°lwùn 'gēr mài). / I bought some loose cookies. Wŏ mǎile jikwài bǐng'gān, shr °'líng mǎi de (°lwùn 'kwàrmaide). / He has some loose cigarettes in his pocket. Tā kŏu'dàrli yŏu jigēn 'yān.

(Out of order, disorganized; as papers) lwàn. / Look for it among the loose papers on my desk. Dzài wŏ 'jwōrshang lwàn'jřli 'jǎujau kàn.

(Of life) 'làngmàn, 'fàngdàng. / She leads a loose life. Tāde 'shēnghwo hěn °'làngmàn (°'fàngdàng).

Loose ends 'swěr, 'swèitóur. / Cut off the loose ends. Bǎ °'swěr (°'swèitóur) °'jyànsyachyu (°jyǎn'chíle). *but* / We are still at loose ends over the problem. is expressed as We still do not have a solution for this problem. Wŏmen dwèi jèijyān 'shrchíng hái méidedàu dáàn.

Loose talk. / What he said was all loose talk. Tā shwō hwà shwōde tài dwō.

Loose tongue. / She's known for a loose tongue. Tā shř chūle 'míngde hàu chwán hwà. *or* 'Shéi dōu jřdàu tā shwō 'hwà tài swéi'byàn.

Loose translation. / He made a loose translation from the original. Tā 'jřshr bǎ ywán'wénde dà'yì 'fānchulaile.

Loose weave jřde 'syǐde, jřde bú'mìde. / Get material with a loose weave. 'Lyàudz yàu jřde 'syǐ dyarde. *or* 'Lyàudz búyàu jřde 'mìde.

Cut loose (fig.) °fǎnde (°'nàude) gòu 'chyáude, °fǎnde (°'nàude) 'lìhai. / He certainly cut loose at that dance. Nèitsz kāi tyàuwǔ'hwèi tā 'fǎnde kě jēn gòu chyáu-de.

Turn loose 'fàngkai (untie); fàng'dzǒu (let out). /You'd better turn the prisoner loose. Nǐ dzwèi háu bǎ fànren dōu °'fàngkai (°'fàng'dzǒu).

LOSE (LOST). (Of objects) (bǎ . . .) dyōu . . . , (bǎ . . .) dyàu . . . ; or expressed by saying that the object is lost 'dyōule or is not seen bú'jyànle. /I've lost my fountain pen again. Wǒ 'you bǎ 'dz̀láishwéibǐ 'dyōule. or Wǒ dz̀láishwéi'bǐ 'you °dyōule (°'bú'jyànle). /Don't lose it. Byé 'dyōule. /Don't lose this negative. Byé bǎ jèidǐ-pyàn dyōule. /I've lost a gold ring somewhere. Wǒ bujŕdàu bǎ yíge jīn'jyèjŕ °'dyōu-(°'dyàu)dzai 'nǎr le.

(In a game or race) shū; (not necessarily last, but not first) méi'yíng, méi-'chyúshàng; (of horses only) méi'pǎushàng. /I lost. 'Wǒ shūle. /Our team lost. Wǒmen dwèi 'shūle. /My horse lost the race. Wǒde nèipi 'mǎ °méi'yíng (°méi-chyǔ'shàng, °méi'pǎu'shàng).

(In gambling) shū. /I lost five dollars. Wǒ 'shūle 'wǔkwai chyán. /I lost the most. 'Wǒ shūde 'dzwèi dwō. /He lost his shirt playing dice. Tā jŕ 'shǎidz ·shémma dou 'shūle (°'dōu shū'gwāngle, °'dōu shūchuchyule, °shūle ge 'jīnggwāng, °shūle ge 'yìgānèrjìng, °bǎ 'kùdz 'dōu shūle).

(In battle or war) dǎbài. /Their army can't afford to lose any more battles. Tāmende 'jyūndwèi 'bùnéng 'dzài dǎbài'jàng le. *See also* **DEFEAT.**

(Of battle casualties; in dead and wounded) 'swǔnshŕ, 'shāngwáng, sŕshāng。 /We lost 2,000 men in that battle. Wǒmen nèiyíjàng °'swǔnshŕle lyǎngchyānrén (°'shāngwang lyǎng'chyān).

(In an election) méisywǎn'shàng, lwòsywǎn. /He lost the election. Tā 'méi-sywǎnshàng. or Tā lwòsywǎnle. /That speech lost him the election. Tā méisywǎn-'shàng jyòu shr yīnwei nèitsz yán'jyǎng.

(In death; as a loved one) is expressed by saying that the person lost died 'gwò-chyule, etc. *See* **DIE.** /He lost his wife five years ago. Tā 'tàitai wǔnyán yǐchyán 'gwòchyule.

Lose someone (when trying to catch or follow him) is expressed as not see him anymore bú'jyàn . . 。 le; or as not see his shadow anymore bújyàn . . . de 'yěngr le; or by saying that the person disappeared bú'jyàn le; (when trying to get rid of him) bǎ . . . °'shwǎikai (°'dyōusya, °'jŕshrkai). /The police chased him all over until they lost him in a crowd. 'Jǐngchá 'dàuchùr 'jwēi ta, jwēidau 'rènau dìfang °'hǎusyē rén yǐ 'jǐ jyou bú'jyàn tā(de'yěngr) le (°'tā wàng rén'dwēili yǐ 'dzwān (or 'dwǒ) jyou bú'jyànle). /Can't we lose him somehow? Dzámen('nándaushwō) jyou 'méifǎr bǎ ta °'shwǎikai (°'dyōusya, °'jŕshrkai) ma?

Lose oneself (intentionally). /He lost himself in the crowd. Tā wàng rén-'dwēili yǐ °'dzwān (°'dwǒ) jyou bú'jyàn le.

Lose an opportunity bǎ 'jīhwèi °'tswògwochyu (°'dānwugwochyu). /You've lost a good opportunity by delaying. Nǐ yǐ 'dānwu bǎ yíge 'tíng hǎude jīhwèi (gěi) °'tswògwochyule (°'dānwugwochyule).

Lose control of is expressed indirectly, and in different ways when referring to different objects. /He almost lost control of the car. Tā kāi chī'chē de shŕhou chà 'dyǎr °gwǎnbuju (°'bǎbuju) dwò'lwér. /He lost control of the plane. Tā 'méifǎr bǎ fēijī 'jènggwolai. or Jèijyà fēijī tā tsǎudzùngbulyǎu le. /The police lost control of the mob. Nèiyí'dàchyún 'rén jǐng'chá °gwǎnbu'jù le (°'méifǎr 'gwǎn le). /Don't lose control of yourself. 'Gwǎnje nǐ dzìjǐ dyar. or Byé 'húdūle. or Yàu dzìjǐ nádìngle 'júyì. or Yau 'wěnjùle.

Lose face dyōu'rén, dyōu'lyǎn. /He lost face admitting that. Tā nèmma yì chéng'rèn, 'jēn °dyōu'rén (°dyōu'lyǎn).

Lose hope *or* **lose heart** hwēi'syīn. / Don't lose hope. Byé hwēi'syīn.

Lose patience shēng'chì, fā 'píchi. / My teacher lost patience with me. Wǒde 'syānsheng gēn wǒ °shēng'chì le (°fā 'píchi le).

Lose sight of is expressed in terms of watching *or* following and letting get away. / Don't lose sight of him. °'Dīngje tā dyar (°'Chyáuje tā dyar, °'Kànje tā dyar, °Yǐ'jŕ gēnje tā), byé jyàu ta °'pàule (°'dzǒukai, °'lyǒule).

Lose sleep (not be able to sleep) shwèibu'jáu, shr̄'myán; (not get enough sleep) shwèi'jyàu °bú'gòu (°chywējyàu). / I've been losing too much sleep lately. Wǒ 'jìnlái lǎu °shwèibu'jáu (°shr̄myán). *or* Wǒ 'jìnlái shwèi'jyàu °bú'gòu (°chywējyàu).

Lose the thread of an argument. / I lost the thread of his argument when you spoke to me. Wǒ jèng tīngje tā jyǎng tāde 'lǐyóu, 'nǐ nèmma yí shwō 'hwà gei dǎ'dwànle.

Lose time fèi 'gūngfu, dānwu 'gūngfu. / I don't want to lose any more time here. Wǒ bú'ywànyi 'dzài dzài jèr °fèi (°dānwu) 'gūngfu le.

Lose track of a person bujŕdau . . . dzài nǎr. / I've lost track of all my friends. Wǒde 'lǎupéngyoumen dzài 'nǎr wǒ 'dōu bujŕ'dàu le.

Lose weight 'shòu. / You've been losing weight, haven't you? Nǐ jìnlái 'shòule ba?

Lose one's accent (change from the former one) bǎ ywán'láide 'kǒuyin °'chyù-dyàu (°'gǎile, °'byànle); (change to the local one) bá 'kǒuyin °'gǎigwolai (°'byàngwo-lai). / He lost his accent within six months. Tā 'lyòuge 'ywèli jyou bá 'kǒuyin °chywán 'gǎigwolaile (°'byàngwolaile). *or* Tā 'lyòuge 'ywèli jyou bá ywán'láide kǒuyin chywán °'chyùdyàule (°'gǎile, °'byànle).

Lose one's balance méijàn'wěn, méitsǎi'jù. / He lost his balance and fell. Tā 'yíbù °méijàn'wěn (°méitsǎi'jù) jyou 'shwāile yì'jyāu.

Lose one's credit shr̄ 'syìnyung. / If I don't pay them now I'll lose my credit. Yàushr 'syàndzài bùbǎ chyán 'hwángei tāmen wǒ jyou shr̄le 'syìnyung le.

Lose one's head (be seriously confused) hwāng, 'hwāngjāng; (be temporarily mixed up) húdu; **lose one's head over** someone (emotionally) jyàu ◦ . . . gei °nùng-'míhule (°nùng'húdule, °nùng de 'shénhwúndyān'dǎu le). / Even during the worst of the battle he never lost his head. Jyòushr 'jànshr dzwèi bú'lìde shŕhour tā yě méi 'hwāng(jāng). / Don't lose your head. Byé 'hwāng(jāng). *or* Byé húdu le. / He lost his head over that woman. Tā jyàu nèige 'nyǔrén gei °nùng'míhule (°nùng'húdule, °nùngde 'shénhwúndyān'dǎu le).

Lose one's hold shŕ'shǒu, 'shǒuli 'hwá, méiná'jù, nábu'jù. / He lost his hold and broke the bowl. Tā °yǐ shŕ'shǒu (°'shǒuli yǐ 'hwá, °'yísyàdz méiná'jù) jyòu bá 'wán (gei) 'dǎle.

Lose one's job is expressed as one's job is lost 'dyōule, 'méile. / He lost his job. Tāde shèr °'dyōule (°'méile).

Lose one's mind fēng, shénjǐng shŕcháng. / She lost her mind after her husband died. Tā 'jàngfu sžle yǐ'hòu, tā °'fēngle (°shénjǐng shŕcháng le).

Lose one's reputation 'míngyùsǎudì. / He lost his reputation. Tā 'míngyùsǎudì.

Lose one's temper (be unable to forbear) rěnbu'jù; (get angry) (chì)jí; (burn up) hwǒr; all of these are usually preceded by jēn. / Finally I lost my temper and beat him up. Dzwèi hòu wǒ 'jēn °hwǒrle (°rěnbu'jùle, °jíle, °chì'jíle), jyou bǎ ta 'dzòule yí'dwùn.

Lose one's way, be lost (dzǒu)'míle 'lùr, (dzǒu)'tswò 'lùr, búrènde 'lùr le, dzŏu'níhule; **lose one's way home** búrènde 'jyā (le), 'jǎubujáu 'jyā (le). / Don't lose your way going home. Hwéi'jyāde shŕhour byé °dzŏu'míle (°dzŏu 'tswò) 'lùr. / The little boy lost his way. Syǎu'hár °búrènde 'jyā le (°jǎubujáu 'jyā le, °míle 'lùle, °dzŏu'míhule, °búrènde 'lùrle).

    Be lost (of an object) **'**dyōule, bú'jyànle (see above); (of a person) búrènde jyā le (*see also* Lose one's way, above); **be lost in thought** 'syāngde chū'shér le; (of lives) *see* **LIFE.** / Are you lost, little boy? Hèi, nǐ 'shŕ bushr 'búrènde 'jyā le? / He was lost in thought. Tā 'syāngde chū'sher le.

    Lost and found department 'shŕwùbáugwǎn'chù, 'shŕwùjāulíng'chù.

LOSS. Expressed verbally as **lose** except in a few cases; see under the appropriate paragraphs of **LOSE.**

    (By losing an object). / I want to report the loss of some jewelry. Wǒ yàu 'bàu 'dyōule dyár 'shǒushr.

    (In a game or race). / The team took all their losses lightly. Dwèi'ywán měitsz 'shū de shŕhou dōu 'bùdzěmma 'dzàihu.

    (In gambling). / My losses amounted to five dollars. Wǒ shūle 'wǔkwài chyán.

    (By death). / The loss of his wife was a great blow to him. Tā tàitai yǐ 'sž, tā shāng'syīnde 'lyǎubudé.

    (By burglary or robbery) expressed with the verb shŕ. / We are not responsible for the loss of personal property. (as worded on a sign) Yīwù gèdz lyóu'shén, rúyǒu yǐ'shŕ, gài búfù'dzé.

    (By destruction) 'swǔnshŕ; or expressed with the verb shāng *or* hwēi. / The drought caused a great loss of crops. Tyān'hàn °'swǔnshŕ (°'shāngle, °'hwēile) bù'shǎude 'jwāngjya. / There was a $5000 loss from the last fire. Shàngtse jáu'hwǒde swǔnshŕ yóu wǔchyānkwài chyán.

    (In business) 'péichyán, 'kwēikùng; or expressed with the verb péi (lose in business). / The company's books showed a loss over a period of several years. Gūng'sžde 'jàngshang 'jǐje 'hǎusyēnyán le lǎu shŕ °'péichyán (°'kwēikùng).

    (Of time). / There was no reason for the loss of time. 'Dānwule nèmmasyē 'shŕhou 'méi °'lǐyóu (°'dàulǐ). *or* °'Hěn kéyǐ 'búbì (°'Yùngbujáu, °'Fànbushàng) 'dānwu nèmmasyē 'shŕhou.

    Be at a loss to know yǐ'dyár yě bùjŕ'dàu; **be at a loss to explain** (*or* say, etc.) yǐ'dyár yě bùjŕ'dàu, 'jyǎnjŕ 'shwōbuchūlái, 'jyǎnjŕ shwōbu'shànglái. / I'm at a loss to know what to do. Wǒ yǐ'dyár yě bùjŕ'dàu 'dzěmmaje 'hǎu. / I'm at a loss to explain his absence. °Wǒ yǐ'dyár yě bùjŕ'dàu (°Wó 'jyǎnjŕ 'shwōbuchūlai, °Wó 'jyǎnjŕ shwōbu'shànglai) wèi'shémma tā méi'lái.

LOT. (Many) dwō, syē; háuji (quite a few but under ten). / There are a lot of cars parked in front of our school. Wǒmen sywésyàu 'chyántou tíngje °hěn dwō (°hǎusyē, °háuji) lyàng chì'chē. *or* Dzài wǒmen sywésyàu 'chyántou tíngje de chìchē kě dwō ne. / I still have lots of books at home. Wǒ jyāli hái yóu °hěn dwō (°hǎusyē, °háuji'běn) shŕ.

    (Much) is expressed as above; or before verbs as very hěn, tǐng, jēn, jìng, etc.; or after verbs as terribly 'lìhai or other appropriate words. / Put a lot of sugar in my coffee. Géi wǒde kā'fēili 'dwō gē 'táng. / It was lots of fun at the dance last night. Dzwór 'wǎnshang tyàu'wǔ °'tíng (°'hén, °'jēn, °'jēnshr) °yǒu'yìsz (°yǒu'chyùr, °hǎu'wár). / The cats make an awful lot of noise at night. 'Māu dzài 'yèli jìng 'jyàuhwan. *or* 'Yèli 'māu °chǎude (°nàude) 'lìhai. / He caused me a lot of trouble. Tā 'jǐng géi wó °rě'shr̀ (°rě'hwò). *or* Tā géi wó 'jǎule hěn dwo máfan.

A lot more, a lot . . . er (with or without a noun following) . . . de 'dwō; hái . . . hěn dwō. / She's a lot sicker than when I last saw her. Tā 'bìngde bí wǒ 'shàngtsz̀ chyáujyan tā de shŕhou jùngde 'dwōle. / We'll need a lot more food. Dzámen hái syūyàu hěn dwō 'chŕde dūngsyi.

A lot (plot of ground) dì. / He bought a lot near my house. Tā dzài wǒ 'fángdz páng'byār 'mǎile yíkwài dì.

(Group of people) chyún, 'hwǒdz, bāng, syē (*see* **GROUP**). / They're a fine lot of soldiers. Nèi(yi)°'chyún (°'hwǒdz, °'bāng, °syē) bīng bú'tswò.

(Group or package of things) fèr (division); dwēi, dzwēi (pile); kwěr (bundle); bāur (package); dár (stack). / I'll send the books in three different lots. Wǒ bǎ shū fēn °'sānbāur (°'sānfèr) sùngchuchyu. / The books were auctioned off by lots. Shū shr̀ °yī'dzwēiyìdzwēide (°'lwùn 'dwēi, °lwùn 'dzwēi, °yī'kwěryìkwěrde, °'lwùn 'kwěr) pāi'màide. / The powder is sold in hundred-pound lots. Nèijúng 'fēn °yī'bǎibàng yì'bāurde 'mài (°shr̀ chéng'bāur yì'bǎibàngyì'bǎibàngde 'mài, °shr̀ lwùn 'bāur mài 'měibāur yì'bǎibàng).

Draw lots (if they are slips of paper) chōu'tyáur, chōu'chyār; (if they are rolled into balls) jwā jyōur; (informal expressions) jwā dà'tóu, pyě'lán. / They drew lots to see who would go first. Tāmen °jwā'jyōur (°'chōu'tyáur, °chōu chyār, °jwā dà-'tóu) kàn 'shwei syān 'chyù.

LOUD. (In sound) dà; (of speaking) 'dàshēng; (of an explosion) hūngde, pāngde, gwāngde. / She has a loud, unpleasant voice. Tā °'sǎngmér (*or* (her speaking voice) °shwō-'hwà de 'shēngyīn, *or* (her singing voice) °'chàng de 'shēngyīn) yōu 'dà yòu nán-'tīng. / Please speak loud enough to be heard. 'Dàdyār shēngr 'shwō, hǎu 'ràng rén 'tīngjyàn. / Louder, please! 'Shēngyīn (dzài) 'dàdyar. / Don't talk so loud. Byé nèmma 'dàshēng shwō'hwà. / The music is too loud. Yīnywède shēngyin tài dà le. / There was a loud report after the flash. 'Gwāng yǐ 'shǎn 'gēnje jyòu shr̀ °'hūngde (°'pāngde, °'gwāngde) yì'shēng.

(Vigorous, as of criticism) dà, tùng, lìhai. / There were loud criticisms in the press. Bàu'jŕshang °'gūngjide (°'pīpingde) hěn 'lìhai. *or* Bàu'jŕshang °dà (°tùng) 'mà.

(Flashy, of clothes) 'hwāhwā(r)de, 'hwā, búsyàng ge 'yàngr; chyè (in poor taste). / His ties are always too loud. Tā swóyǒude lǐng'dài dōu tài 'hwāle. *or* Tā (dài)de lǐng'dài °'dōu (°'lǎu) (shr̀) nèmma °'hwāhwāde (°'hwāhwārde búsyàng ge 'yàngr, °chyè).

Out loud 'dàshēng; **not out loud** bú'dàshēng, yùng °syǎu'syāurde (°dǐdǐde) shēngyīn. / He said it out loud. Tā 'dàshēng °'shwōchulaide (°'rāngrangchūlaide). / Don't talk out loud. 'Byé 'dàshēng shwō'hwà. *or* Yùng °syǎu'syāurde (°dǐdǐde) shēngyīn shwō'hwà.

LOVE. Most of the cases in which **love** is used as a noun in English are translated by verbal expressions.

(Between persons, general) ài, 'syīhwān. / He loves you very much. Tā hěn °'ài (°'syīhwān) nǐ. / I simply love children. Wǒ jēn °'ài (°'syīhwān) syǎu'hár.

(Between elders and children involving close relationship) 'téng, ài, 'syīhwān. / Grandmother loves her grandson. Dzúmǔ °'téng (°etc.) tāde swūndz.

(Between children and parents) 'syàushwùn, 'syàujìng. / He loves his parents very much. Tā hěn °'syàushwun (°'syàujing) tā fùmǔ.

(Between brothers and sisters) °dài (°gēn) . . . 'gǎnchíng hǎu (or similar words in place of hǎu). /He loves his older sister. Tā 'gēn tā 'jyějyede gǎnchíng hén hǎu. (this also means He gets along very well with his older sister.) *or* Tā dài tā 'jyějye hén hǎu. *or* Tā 'gēn tā 'jyějye hǎu.

(Of things) 'syǐhwǎn. /I love big cars. Wǒ 'syǐhwǎn dà chē. /Children love their toys. Syǎuháidz 'syǐhwǎn tāmende wánjyù.

(Of one's country) àigwó. /He has a sincere love for his country. Tā yìsyīn àigwó. *or* Tā hén àigwó.

(Of certain action) ài, 'syǐhwǎn. /He loves to drive fast. Tā °ài (°'syǐhwǎn) kāi kwài chē. /Do all of the students love to study? 'Sywésheng dōu °'ài (°'syǐhwǎn) nyàn shū ma?

(Strong liking or habit; of an action) dwei . . . yóuyǐn. /He loves to sing. Tā dwèi chàng'gēr yóuyǐn. *or* Tā ài chàng'gēr. *or* Tā yǒu chàng'gērde yǐn.

Give *or* **send one's love.** /Give my love to all my old friends. Chǐng tì wǒ wèn 'swóyǒude lǎu'péngyou 'hǎu. *or* Jyànle lǎu'péngyoumen dōu tì wǒ wèn 'hǎur.

Fall in love (with) àishang. /They fell in love with each other. Tāmenlyǎ 'àishangle. /They fell in love at first sight. Tāmen yí jyàn'myàn jyòu 'bítsz àishangle.

LOVELY. (Of visual things) měi (beautiful); hǎukàn (good-looking); hǎu (good, of a view). /There's a lovely view from the bridge. Tsúng 'chyáu ner 'kàngwochyu 'jǐngjr °'hǎu'jíle (°'měijíle, °hén 'hǎu, °hén 'měi). /I've never seen such a lovely girl. Wǒ 'tsunglái méi 'kànjyàngwo 'jèmma °hǎu'kànde (°'měide) nyǔ'háidz.

(Of things heard) hàutīng. /Isn't that a lovely song? 'Nèige 'gēr 'dwō hǎu-'tīng a?

LOW. (Physically) dī (especially of level); ǎi (especially of vertical distance); some-times expressed as not high *or* not tall bùgāu; or as short dwǎn; or as small syǎu; or as down syà; or expressed indirectly; **low land** 'dīdì; **low coastline** hěn 'dīde hǎiànsyàn. /The ceiling is very low. Fáng'dǐngdz hěn 'dī. /The hill looks very low from here. Tsúng 'jèr kàn nèi 'shān hǎusyàng °tǐng 'dī (°tíng 'ǎi, °bù'gāu, °buhěn 'gāu) (shr̀de). /She prefers low-heeled shoes. Tā ài chwān 'hòugēr 'dīde syé. That plane is flying too low. Nèige fēi'jī fēide tài 'dī le. /This bed is too low. 'Chwáng tài °'ǎi (°'dī). /There is a low fence around the house. Fángdz jōuwéi yǒu yídàu °'dwǎn (°'ǎi, °'syǎu) chyáng. /Have you a room on a lower floor? 'Syà yìtséng yǒu fángjyān ma? /Please give me a lower berth. Gěi wo yíge 'syàpù. /She has a very low forehead. Tāde nǎu'méndz hěn 'dī. /Hang the picture a little lower. 'Hwàr dzài °gwàde 'dī dyar (°gwàde wàng'syà dyar, °gwàde wàng'syà dyar, °wàng'syà gwà dyar).

(Of tide) twèi jǐng, twèi wàn, làudàu dzwèi 'dīde dìfang; (of water level) is expressed as shallow chyán. /Low tide is at twelve today. Jyēr 'jūngwǔ shr̀er'dyǎn 'cháu(shwěi) °twèi 'jǐng (°twèi 'wán, °làudàu dzwèi'dīde dìfang). /The river was so low during the drought that several rocks never seen before stuck out. Nàu hàn'dzāi de shr̀hou 'héshwěi 'chyánde yóu jǐkwài yí'syàng kànbu'jyànde 'shr̀tou dōu 'lòuchu-laile.

(Of rank, position, grade, etc.) dī. /He's of lower rank. 'Tāde °'gwānjí (°'jyějí) 'dī. /He was in the lower grades then. 'Nèi shr̀hou tā dzài 'dī bānli.

(Of temperature) dī; or expressed in terms of being cold lěng. /The tempera-ture is very low today. Jyēr 'wēndù hěn 'dī. *or* Jyēr tíng 'lěngde.

(In pitch) dī, 'dī yín (of specific notes); dī, tsū (of someone's voice). /Sing low. Yùng 'dǐ yīn 'chàng. / The opera singer has a very low voice. Nèige 'syìdzde sǎng'yīn hěn °'dǐ (°'tsū).

(In volume) 'syǎu shēng(r), 'dǐ shēng(r). / Speak a little lower. 'Syáu dyǎr shēngr shwō. *or* Dǐ dyǎr shēngr shwō.

(Of marks) dǐ, hwài, 'bùhǎu. / He got low marks. Tā dé de 'fēr tǐng °'dǐde (°'hwài, °'bùhǎu).

(Of prices) dǐ; *or expressed as* low-priced pyányi; be(come) low(er) làu. / Would you consider the price low enough? Nǐ 'jywéde jèige 'jyàr gòu 'pyányide le ma? / This car is in the lower-priced group. 'Jèijŭng chē shr dzài °'pyányi chē (°'jyàchyán 'dǐde) nèi'lèili. / Prices will be lower again after the war. Dǎ'wánle 'jàng °shémma jyòu dōu 'pyányi le (°'jyàchyán jyòu 'làude).

(Of supplies) *is expressed as* almost used up kwài yùng'wánle; *or as* not much 'méidwō'shǎule. / Our gas is getting low. Dzámende chì'yóu kwài yùng'wánle. / We're low on sugar. Wǒmende 'táng °'méidwō'shǎule (°kwài yùng'wánle).

(Depressed) nánshòu, bùgāusyìng, bú'tùngkwài. / I'm low today. *or* I feel very low today. Wǒ 'jyērge hěn °nán'shòu (°bùgāu'syìng, °bú'tùngkwài).

(Vulgar) tswūn, yě. / He has a low type of humor. Tā shwō de 'syàuhwàr °'tswūnde (°'yéde).

Low *or* low-down (mean; of an action) *is expressed as* cruel kèbwo; *or as* not right méi'dàulǐ, bùjyánglǐ, búdwèi; (of a person) 'syǎurén; (of a person or action) 'chíyóutsź'lǐ; (vulgar) chywē'dé; **play a low(down) trick on** *someone is also expressed* as °chǐfu . . . chǐfude (°pyàn . . . pyànde) hěn °'lìhai (°'swūn, °méi'dàuli, °bú-'dwèide). / That was a low trick. °'Nèi'shǒur (°'Nèmma yí'shǒur) bànde 'tài °'kèbwo le (°méi'dàuli le, °bùjyáng'lǐ le, °bú'dwèi le, °'syǎurén le, °chíyóutsź'lǐ le). / It was a low-down trick to kick him out at this stage of the game. Dōu 'dzwòdàu 'jèige 'dìbù le, hái bǎ rénjyā kěidzǒule, 'wèimyǎn tài °'kèbwo le (°etc.). / He played a low trick on her. Tā °'chǐfu tā chǐfude (°pyàn ta pyànde) hěn °'lìhai (°swūn, °méi'dàuli, °bú'dwèide).

Have a low opinion of jywéje . . . °bù'hǎu (*or* (as to character) °tǐng 'syàjyàn, *or* (as to possibilities) °tǐng méi'chūsyide, °tǐng méi'běnshrde); *or* (despise) chyáubu'chǐ, bù dzemmayàng (nothing worthwhile). / I have a low opinion of him. Wǒ jywéje tā °bù'hǎu (°tǐng 'syàjyàn, °tǐng méi'chūsyide, °tǐng méi'běnshrde, °bù-dzemmayàng). / He has a low opinion of his staff. Tā chyáubu'chǐ tā 'shŭsyàde rén.

Lie low (remain in hiding) dwódwo. / You'd better lie low for a while. Nǐ dzwèi hǎu °dwódwo (°dwó jityan).

The lowdown. / Give me the lowdown. Géi wǒ jyǎng yijyǎng. *or* 'Gàusu wǒ 'tǐng yiting.

Low (gear) 'tóudàujá, yǐjá. / Put the car in low to climb the hill. Shàng'shānde 'shŕhou yùng °'tóudàujá (°yǐjá).

A low. / The temperature hit an all-time low. *is expressed as* The temperature has never been as low as this. 'Tyānchì yí'syàng méidzěmma 'lěnggwo.

LOWER. (Physically) *is usually expressed by* bǎ . . . *followed by a combination of an* action verb with syàlai *or* syàchyu; *some of the verbs so used are* làu fall *or* drop, lā, chě pull, fàng, gē put; **lower** by ropes 'syǐ. / Please lower the window. Láu-'jyà bǎ 'chwānghu °'làu(°'lā, °'fàng)sya dyǎr lai. / Lower the flag at sunset. R̄ 'lè de shŕhou °syà'chí (°jyàng 'chí, °bǎ chídz 'làsyàlai, °bǎ chídz 'chěsyàlai). / The crew slowly lowered the body into the sea. 'Shwéishóu bǎ 'shŕshou màn'mārde 'syìdàu 'háilǐchyule. / He lowered his head and didn't say a thing. Tā bǎ tóu 'dǐsya-

729

chyu, 'yìshēngr °bù'syǎng (°bù'yányu). *but* /He remained seated with his head lowered. Tā yǐ'jǐ dzwò nàr, °'dǐje (°'chwéije, °'dālaje) tóu.

Lower the voice (in speaking) °'dǐ (°'syáu) dyǎr 'shēngr shwō 'hwà. /Can't you lower your voice? Nǐ °'dǐ (°'syáu) dyǎr 'shēngr shwō 'hwà 'syíng ma?

LUCK. yùnchi; (in gambling) shǒuchi; (continuing) fúchi; **be in luck, have good luck** (at a particular time) dzǒu'yùn, dzǒu'húngyùn, dzóu hǎu'yùn *or* (always) yǒu-'fú(chi), 'fúchi dà, 'fúchi 'hǎu *or* (in gambling) shǒuchi (hén)hǎu; **be out of luck, not have good luck** budzǒu'yùn, dzǒu 'bèiyùn, dǎu'méi; **a sign of good luck** 'jíjàu. /He said his failure was entirely due to bad luck. Tā shwō tā méinùng'hǎu wánchywán shr̀ yīnwei 'yùnchi bù'hǎu. /I can't help it if you couldn't go; that's your hard luck. 'Nǐ bunéng 'chyù, wó yǒu shémma 'fǎr ne? Nèi shr̀ nǐ 'yùnchi bù'hǎu. /My luck won't last. 'Yùnchi 'dōu shr̀ yí'jèr. *or* Wó yě 'jyòu shr jèi °yǐ'shr̀de 'yùnchi hǎu (°yǐ'shr̀ dzǒu'yùn, °yǐ'shr̀de shǒuchi 'hǎu). /You're in luck. Nǐ 'yùnchi 'hǎu. *or* Nǐ jēn dzǒu'yùn. /I'm out of luck today. Wǒ 'jyēr °dǎu'méi (°bùdzǒu'yùn, °'yùnchi bù'hǎu, °'yùnchi bù'jyā). /That's supposed to be a sign of good luck. Nèi shr̀ 'jíjàu.

Good luck when wishing someone luck, has no set expression in Chinese. /Good luck! (to someone about to have a job interview or attempting to attain something) is expressed as I wish you success. Syīwang nǐ chénggūng. *or* (to someone about to take an exam) is expressed as I hope you pass. Syīwang ní kǎushang. or as I hope you pass the first in your class. Syīwang kǎu dǐyī. *or* (to someone who is going away) is expressed as Have a safe journey. Yílùpíng'ān. or as I hope you have a tail wind the entire journey. Yílùshwùn'fēng.

Just luck (good or bad) jěng 'chyǎu; (good only) jěng 'hǎu. /It was just luck that he happened along at that moment. Jěng °'chyǎu (°'hǎu) dzài 'nèi shrhou 'tā dàu nèr le.

Not just luck 'bìngfēi 'ǒurán. /This victory is not just a matter of luck. Jèitsz̀ °dǎ (°jàn)'shèngle 'bìngfēi 'ǒurán.

LUCKY. dzǒu'yùn, dzǒu'húngyùn, dzóu hǎu'yùn; also expressed with phrases involving the various words for luck (*see* LUCK); **be unlucky** budzǒu'yùn, dzǒu 'bèiyùn, dǎu-'méi. /Why you lucky dog! Nǐ jēn dzǒu'yùn! /I'm always unlucky. Wó dzǔngshr hén dǎu'méi. /You're always lucky. Nǐ shr̀ yǒu'fúde rén. *or* Nǐ 'fúchi °'dà (°'hǎu). /I was lucky last night; I won twenty dollars. Dzwór 'wǎnshang wó 'shǒuchi hén 'hǎu, yíngle èrshr'kwài.

LUMBER. 'mùtoubǎr, 'mùtou'bǎndz, mùbǎndz, 'mùlyàu. /Where can I buy lumber and nails? Wǒ dzài 'nǎr néng mái dyǎr 'mùtoubǎr gēn 'dīngdz? /We need lumber to build a garage. Wǒmen gài chē'fáng déi yàu °'mù(tou)'bǎndz (°'mùlyàu). /He's in the lumber business. Tā dzwò 'mùlyàu 'shēngyì.

To lumber (cut trees) tsǎi mùtou, fá mùtou, kǎn shù. /This company does its lumbering up the river. Jèige gūng'sz̄ dzài hé'shàngyóu °tsǎi 'mùtou (°etc.).

(Move clumsily) 'yíbùyíbùde °'jwǎi (°'nyǒu). /The elephant lumbered along. Dà'syàng 'yíbùyíbùde °'jwǎi (°'nyǒu).

LUNCH. (Noon meal) 'wǔfàn, 'jūngfàn, 'shàngwǔfàn, wǔtsān; **have lunch, eat lunch** chr̄ plus one of the above, or more commonly simply as eat chr̄'fàn. /It's almost time for lunch. Kwài dàu chr̄ 'wǔfàn de shrhou le. /What do you want for lunch? Nǐ 'shàngwǔfàn syǎng chr̄ 'shémma? /Will you have lunch with me? Nǐ 'néng gēn wǒ yí'kwàr chr̄ 'wǔfàn ma? *or* 'Jūngwǔ dzámen yí'kwàr chr̄'fàn hǎu ma?

A little lunch (snack) is expressed as eat a little bit chr̄ dyǎr 'shémma, chr̄ dyǎr fàn, etc. /How about a little lunch before going to bed? 'Chr̄ dyǎr shémma dzài 'shwèi ba.

LUNG. fèi. /I'll have to see a doctor about my lungs. Wó děi 'jyàn yíge 'dàifu 'yànyàn wǒde 'fèi. /When I breathe deeply, my lungs hurt. Wó shr̄'jǐn chwǎn'chǐ de shŕhou 'fèi jyòu 'téng.

MACHINE. 'jīchî. /She uses machines for washing and ironing clothes. Tā yùng 'jī-chi 'syǐ yīshang 'tàng yīshang. /Will the machine work? 'Jīchi néng 'yùng ma? /It's an electric machine. Shr̄ yùng 'dyàn de 'jīchi. /That machine is operated by hand. 'Nèi shr̄ yùng 'shǒu 'dùng de 'jīchi.

(Political) 'dzǔjr̄. /The machine is backing him in the election. Jèige 'dzǔjr̄ 'bāng tā jìng'sywǎn.

MAD. (Angry) shēngchî, nǎu, fā píchi; (crazy, rabid) fēng, fākwáng; (foolish) shǎ. /That's no reason to get mad. Byé wèi 'nèige °shēng'chî (°'nǎu le). *or* 'Yùngbujáu wèi 'nèige fā 'píchi a. /He must be mad to take such a chance. Tā 'jèyàng màu-'syǎn, jēnshr 'fēngle. /Watch out for the mad dog. 'Syǎusyīn fēng'gǒu. /That was a mad thing to do. 'Nàyàng 'gàn jēn 'shǎ.

Be mad at someone gēn . . . 'nǎu, nǎu . . . . /He's been mad at me for a long time. Tā °gēn wo 'nǎule (°'nǎu wo yǒu) 'hǎusyē shŕhou le.

Be mad about someone míshang. /She was mad about him from the very first. Tā tsúng yí jyàn'myàn jyòu 'míshang ta le.

Like mad syàng 'fēngle shŕde. /He drove like mad. Tā kāi'chē syàng 'fēngle shŕde.

MAGAZINE. dzájr̄; (illustrated news magazine) hwàbàu. /Where can I buy a magazine? Shémma 'dìfang kéyǐ mǎi dzá'jr̄? /That magazine comes out on Thursdays. Nèige hwà'bàu Lǐbài'sz̀ chū'bǎn.

(For munitions) dànyàukù; (of a rifle) dànsyá.

MAID. (Servant) nyǔ'yùngrén; lǎumādz (if married). /Where can I hire a maid? Shémma 'dìfang kéyǐ 'gù yíge nyǔ'yùngrén?

(Maiden) 'chùnyǔ.

Maid of honor nyǔ bīnsyàng.

Old maid lǎu'chùnyǔ. /Two old maids live there. Lyǎngge lǎu'chùnyǔ jùdzai nàr.

MAIL. (Materials transmitted) syìn; (postal system) yóujèng, yóu(jèng)jyú, sometimes yóu. /Did I get any mail this morning? Jīntyan 'shàngwǔ wó yǒu 'syìn méiyou? /The mail comes twice a day here. Jèr 'měityān sùng 'lyǎnghwéi 'syìn. /The mail was held up by the storm. Tyānchi bù'hǎu, syìn wùle 'dyǎn le. /The mail truck is late. Yóujèng'chē lái'wǎnle. /He promised to send the check by mail. Tā 'dáying tsúng yóu'jyú bǎ 'jr̄pyàu 'jìlai.

Mailbox shìngsyāng.

Mailman yóuchāi.

To mail jì. /Where can I mail this? Shémma 'dìfang kéyǐ 'jì jèige dūngsyi?

MAIN. (Most important) dzwèi 'yàujǐnde; (biggest or most prominent) dzwèidàde, sometimes dà, jǔyàude. /What's his main reason for wanting to leave? Tā yàu

731

'líkai jèr dzwèi °'yàujǐnde (°jǔyàude) 'ywányǐn shr̄ shémma? / Where is the main street? 'Dàjyē dzài 'nǎr?

Main (conduit) gwǎndz, dzúnggwǎndz, lùsyàn, 'gànsyàn。 / The water main has burst. Dz̀láishwěi 'dzúng gwǎndz 'hwàile. / The gas mains end at the city line. 'Méichǐ 'gwǎndz tūngdau 'chéng(shr̄de)'byārshang.

In the main dàjr̀. / I agree with him in the main. Wǒ 'dàjr̀ hé tā túng'yì.

MAINTAIN. (Keep up) bǎuchŕ, wéichŕ. / You'll need more coal to maintain that degree of heat. Nǐ yàu bǎu'chŕ 'nàyàngde wēn'dù děi 'dwō yùng yìdyǎr 'méi. / Those countries have maintained peace for twenty years. Nèisyē gwó'jyā 'wéichŕle 'èrshr̄- lainyánde hé'píng.

(Assert) gǎn shwō, 'jyānchŕ. / I maintain that I'm not at fault. Wó 'gǎn shwō wǒ méi'tswò. / How can you still maintain that? Nǐ 'dzěmma hái yàu 'jyānchŕ 'nèige?

Maintain a reputation 'bǎuhù. / He's always careful to maintain his good name. Tā 'lǎushr hén 'syǎusyīnde 'bǎuhù tāde 'míngyù.

Maintain a family yǎngjyā. / He needs more money to maintain a family. Tā yàu yǎng'jyā hái děi 'dwō dyǎr chyán.

MAKE (MADE). (Build, create) dzwò, dǎ, dzàu; often a more specific word, thus **make a hole** is expressed as drill a hole dzwān kūlung or chwāndùng. / He made a book- case for his room. Tā dzwòle yíge shū'jyàdz háu 'bǎidzài tā 'wūli. / Make a hole in this. Dzài'jèr chwān yíge dùng. or Dzài 'jèigeshang °'dzwān yíge 'kūlung (°dǎ yige yǎn).

(Add up to) yǒu, shr̄. / Twenty dollars per week makes about eighty dollars per month. 'Èrshrkwài chyán yíge lǐ'bài °jyou you 'bāshrdwōkwài chyán yíge 'ywè (°yíge 'ywè jyòushr̄ 'bāshr dwō kwài). / That makes the tenth truckload today. 'Jīntyan 'jèi shr dì'shrchē le.

(Attain a speed) dzǒu. / That car can make eighty miles an hour. 'Nèilyàng chē 'yìdyǎnjūng néng dzǒu 'bāshr lǐ.

(Be, function as) shr̄, dāng, dzwò. / He makes a good carpenter. Tā shr̄ ge 'hǎu 'mùjyang. / He'd make a good carpenter. Tā yàushr dāng 'mùjyang yí'dìng hén 'hǎu.

(Succeed in something, the something not always specified) expressed with néng followed by a specific verb, or by that verb in the potential form of a resultative compound. / Do you think a table this wide can make the doorway? Ní syǎng 'jèmma kwānde 'jwōdz °néng 'táigwò 'mén chyu ma (°nèige 'mén gwòde'chyù ma)? / Can you make it? Nǐ néng dzwò ma? or Nǐ dzwòde'lyǎu ma?

(Render someone successful). / The writer was made by his first book. is ex- pressed as This writer with his first book immediately became famous. Jèige 'dzwòjyā dì'yī̌běn shū jyòu chéngle 'míng le.

(Choose someone to perform a function) °jyǔ (°twēi, °sywǎn) . . . °dāng (°dzwò) . . . 。 / They made that man chairman. Tāmen jyǔ'tā dzwò jǔ'syí.

(Estimate that something is such-and-such) syǎng, gūmeje. / I make the height of the hill five hundred feet. 'Wó °syǎng (°gūmeje) jèige 'shān yǒu 'wúbǎichr̄ 'gāu. / I make it (the time) eight o'clock. Wó °syǎng (°gūmeje) syàndzài °shr̄ (°yǒu) 'bādyǎnjūng le.

(Cause one thing to be another, or to be a certain way). / Hard work made him a success. is expressed as He became successful through hard work. Tā shr̄ kǔ'gàn

732

°'gànchulai de (°chéng'gūng de). / He's making a success of his business. is expressed as His business he's carrying on very well. Tāde 'mǎimai dzwòde hén 'hǎu. / What made you sick? is expressed as How did you get sick? Ní 'dzěmma hwèi 'bìngle?

Make someone do something jyàu. / Don't make me do that. Byé 'jyàu wo dzwò 'nèige.

Make a destination dàu. / The train will make New York within two hours. Jèitàng 'chē lyǎngge jūngtou yǐ'nèi jyòu kéyǐ 'dàu Nyóu'ywē. / We can make our destination by evening. Wǒmen jyēr 'wǎnshang °néng 'dàu (°'dàudelyǎu).

Make a train (or bus, etc.) gǎnchē. / Do you think we'll make the train? Ní 'syǎng wǒmen néng 'gǎndeshàng hwǒ'chē ma?

Make money jwànchyán, jèngchyán, náchyán, shōuchyán, nùngchyán, nèngchyán. / How much do you make a week? Ní yíge lǐ'bài °jwàn (°jèng, °etc.) 'dwōshau chyán?

Make something big, good, red, etc. nùng or nèng followed by the proper stative verb; if a specific action is involved, the verb for that action replaces nùng or nèng. / Make the background blue. Bǎ 'dyēr °nùng'lánle (°tú'lánle).

Make someone happy, sorry, sad, etc. shǐ. / He makes me happy. Tā 'shǐ wǒ kwàilè.

Make a fire shēnghwǒ, bá 'hwǒ dyán'jáule. / Can you make a fire in this wind? Ní néng dzài jèige 'fēnglǐtou shēng'hwǒ ma?

Make a mistake nùngtswòle, nèngtswòle, chūtswòr, dzwòtswòle, dzwò tswòshǐ. / Someone made a mistake. Yídìngshr yǒu 'rén nùng'tswòle. / He hardly ever makes a mistake. Tā 'chàbudwō 'tsúnglai °'bùdzwò tswò'shǐ (°yě 'méichūgwo 'tswòr).

Make a point shwōchīngchu. / Has he made his point? Tā shwō'chīngchule ma?

Make a reputation yǒumíngle, chūmíng. / He made his reputation early in life. Tā dzài nyán'chīngde shǐhou jyòu °yǒu'míngle (°chū'míngle).

Make a score dé (nùng or nèng) 'fēnshù. / Who made the highest score? 'Shéi déde 'fēnshù dzwèi 'dwō?

Make (both) ends meet 'chūrùsyāng'dǐ or chūrùsyāng'fú. / It's hard to make both ends meet. 'Chūrùsyāng'dǐ shǐ hén bù'fúngyi. / We can't make both ends meet. Rùbùfú'chū.

Make one's living móushēng; **make** one's living on . . . jřje . . . °wéi'shēng (°chī). / How does he make his living? Tā 'dzěmmayang móu'shēng? or Tā 'jřje shémma wéi'shēng a?

Make peace jyǎnghé. / Are they willing to make peace? Tāmen 'ywànyi jyǎng'hé ma?

Make sense yǒu dàuli. / Does this make sense? 'Jèige 'yǒu méiyou 'dàuli?

Make time shěng shřhour, 'kwàidyǎr. / We can make time if we take the dirt road. Wǒmen yàushr dzǒu 'nèityáu 'tǔlù, jyòu °shéng dyǎr 'shřhour (°néng 'kwàidyǎr).

Make believe (that) (jyǎ)jwǎng. / She's only making believe she doesn't know. Tā (jyǎ)'jwǎng tā bùjř'dàu.

Make good a promise, offer, etc. / He always makes good his promises. is expressed as You can count on what he says. Tā shwōhwà 'swàn hwà.

Make for a place, expressed with a verb such as run pǎu, often with an adverb

733

such as quickly 'gánjǐn *or* kwài. / Let's make for that tall tree. Dzámen 'pǎudàu neìke 'dà'shù nèr ba. / The boys made for home at dinner time. 'Háidzmen chr̄'fàn de shŕhou 'gánjǐn wàng 'jyāli 'pǎu.

Make for (contribute to the possibility of). / Her company made for a pleasant afternoon. is expressed as That afternoon as soon as she came it rendered things very pleasant. Nèige 'syàwǔ tā yǐ 'lái gàn shémma jyòu tíng yǒu 'yìsz le.

Make off with chāudzǒule, tōudzǒule. / Don't make off with my book. Byé bá wǒde 'shū chāu'dzǒule. / They've made off with our books. Tāmen bá wǒmende 'shū tōu'dzǒule.

Make out a report, list, etc. dzwò. / It's time to make out our annual report. Wǒmen dzwò nyán'hàu de shŕhou 'dàule.

Make out a check, bill, etc. kāi. / Have you made the check out yet? Jr̄'pyàu yǐjing kāi'hǎule ma? / Please make out our bill. Chǐng ni bá wǒmende jàng'dār 'kāichulai.

Make out a form tyán. / Come back when you've made out this form. Bǎ jèige 'byǎu tyán'hǎule dzài 'hwéilai.

Make out (manage despite possible difficulties) 'bàndelyǎu, bàndechulai. / Don't worry; I'll make out. Byé 'jāují; wǒ 'bàndelyǎu. but / We'll have to make out with what we've got. is expressed as All we can do is do the best we can. Wǒmen jr̄ 'hǎu jìn wǒmende 'lìlyang 'dzwòsyachyu. / How did you make out with him (*or* her *or* the problem, etc.)? is expressed as What was the result? 'Jyēgwó dzěmma'yàng?

Make out (general) dǔng, míngbai; (understand when listening) tīngdǔng; (understand when looking) kàndǔng. / Can you make out what he means? Ní 'dǔng tāde 'yìsz ma? *or* Ní 'néng bunéng °tīng'dǔng (°kàn'dǔng) nà shr̀ shémma 'yìsz? / He couldn't make out the sign. Tā kànbu'dǔng nèige 'páidz.

Make clothing **over** gǎi. / She's having her old coat made over. Tā bǎ tāde 'jyòu dà'yī nàchyu 'gǎichyùle.

Make room for °ràngchu (°téngchu) . . . de 'dìfangr lái. / Can you make room for one more? Ní néng 'dzài °ràngchu (°téngchu) 'yíge rénde 'dìfangr lai ma?

Make up (after a quarrel) hǎule, nènghǎule, nùnghǎule. / Do you know whether they've made up yet? Ní 'jr̄dàu tāmen yǐjing °hǎule (°nèng'hǎule, °nùng'hǎule) méi-you?

Make up (use cosmetics) dǎban, dában. / She takes a lot of time to make up. Tā yùng 'hǎusyē 'shŕhour lái 'dǎban.

Make up a deficit 'tsòushàng, 'bǔshàng. / Collect all you can, and he'll make up the rest. Nǐmen 'jǐnlyàngde shōu'chyán ba, bú'gòude 'tā lái °'tsòushang (°'bǔ-shang).

Make up (prepare) 'yùbèi, jwǔnbèi, dzwò; or expressed as write syě, etc. / Did he make up the speech himself? Tāde yǎn'shwō shr̀ tā °'dzjǐ'yùbèide ma (°'jwǔnbèide ma, °'dzwòde ma)?

Make up (invent) syābyàn. / Is it true, or did he make that story up? Shr̀ 'jēnde ma, 'háishr tā syā'byàn de?

Make up (arrange print, etc.) byānhǎule. / The newspaper's already made up. 'Bàu yǐjing byān'hǎule.

Make up (prepare) 'yùbèi'hǎule. / We make up the payroll on the fifteenth of the month. Wǒmen dzài shŕ'wǔhàu bǎ 'syīnshwěi dōu yùbèi'hǎule.

Make up one's mind 'dǎdìng'jú yi, jywédìng. / My mind is made up. Wó yǐjing °'dǎdìng 'júyile (°jywé'dìngle).

Make up for péi; (of time) bǔshang. /He's willing to make up for his mistake. Tā 'ywànyi péi'tswèr.

A make (brand) páidz. /He has a car of an old make. Tā yǒu yílyàng 'lǎu páidzde chì'chē.

Makeup (cosmetics) hwàchwāngpǐng.

MAN.

MAN. (Human being) rén; (adult, not specifying sex) 'dàrén; (a male, not specifying age) 'nánrén. /Men have used that road for hundreds of years. 'Nèityáu 'lù 'rén yǐjing 'dzǒule 'jǐbǎi'nyán le. /I need a man to mow the lawn. Wǒ yàu 'jǎu yíge rén gěi wo twēi'tsǎu. /Is that man this boy's father? Nèige 'rén shr̀ jèige 'háidzde 'fùchin ma? /There are two men and three boys in the party. 'Nèichyún rénli yǒu 'lyǎngge 'nánrén, 'sānge nán'háidz.

(Manly person) hǎuhàn. /He spoke like a man. Tāde 'kǒuchi jēn syàng ge hǎu'hàn. /What a man he was! Tā 'jēnshr ge hǎu'hàn!

(Of male characteristics or for males) nán-. /Where's the men's room? Nántsè'swǒ dzài 'nǎr? /They've asked for a man cook. Tāmen yàu 'gù yíge 'nán-chúdz.

Man and wife fūfù. /Are they man and wife? Tāmen shr̀ fū'fù ma?

Man-to-man píng'lyángsyin, dǎkai tyān'chwāngr de. /We'll have to have a man-to-man talk about this. Dzámen 'lyǎ °píng'lyángsyin (°dǎkai tyān'chwāngr dè) bǎ jèijyàn 'shr̀ lái 'tántán.

To a man 'chywántǐyí'jr̀. /The committee voted for the bill to a man. Jèige 'àndz shr̀ 'wěiywán'hwèi 'chywántǐyí'jr̀ 'tūnggwò de.

To man a gun (be in charge of it) gwǎn fàngpàu; (go to operate it) chyù fàngpàu. /Man the guns! 'Yùbèi fàng'pàu!

Man a boat (work on it) dzài 'chwánshang dzwò'gūng. /Man the lifeboats! Shàng jyòushēng'chwán!

MANAGE.

MANAGE. (Succeed in doing something, handle successfully) is expressed by a verb meaning do (see DO), or by verbs with more specific meanings appropriate to the circumstances, as (of a car) kāi drive, (of packages, etc.) ná carry, etc., (of persons) dwèifu keep under control; the common combination can manage is expressed by resultative compounds made up of such verbs with -de'lyǎu or by the verb syíng can do; in the meaning be able to get along, can manage is expressed as have a way of doing yǒu bànfa. /Can you manage the horse by yourself? Nǐ 'dzìjǐ chí'mǎ °chíde'lyǎu ma (°néngde'lyǎu ma)? /Can you manage those packages by yourself? 'Nèisyē bāu 'dūngsyi nǐ 'nádelyǎu ma? /How did you manage to get these tickets? Jèisyē pyàu nǐ yùng 'shémma fádz nùnglaide? /I managed to see him twice last week. Wǒ shànglǐbài syǎng 'bànfar jyànle tā 'lyǎnghwèi. /They say he is difficult, but I think I can manage him. Dàjyā 'dōu shwō tā nán 'dwèifù, wǒ ké yǒu fádz dwèifu tā. /Oh, I'll manage. È, wǒ 'dzúng yǒu 'bànfa. /I can manage, thanks. Wó yǒu 'bànfa, 'syīnlǐng jyòu shr̀le.

(Control, have charge of) gwǎn, 'gwánlǐ; (especially of a store, shop, or business; also means manager) 'jīnglǐ. /Who manages this place? Jèige dìfang gwēi 'shéi gwǎn? /This place is well managed. Jèige dìfang °'gwǎnde (°'gwǎnlǐde, °'jīnglǐde) hén 'hǎu.

MANAGER.

MANAGER. gwǎnshr̀de, 'jīnglǐ. /Who's the manager here? Gwǎn'shr̀de shr̀ 'shéi? /I want to see the manager. Wǒ yàu 'jyàn yijyàn 'jīnglǐ.

MANNER. (Way) yàngdz. / He seems to be doing his work in an efficient manner. Tā bàn'shr̄ hǎusyàng hěn 'nénggande yàngdz. / He answered in a sharp manner. Tāde 'hwéidá hǎu'syàng hěn 'lìhàide yàngdz.

In a manner of speaking kéyǐ shwō. / In a manner of speaking she's a nurse, though she never got her certificate. Tā 'kéyǐ shwō shr̀ ge 'kānhù, 'swéirán tā méibǐ'yè.

Manners (politeness of behavior) lǐmàu; (customs) lǐjyé. / We must be careful of our manners when we go there. Wǒmen dàu 'nàr chyù děi jù'yǐ yìdyár lǐ'màu. / The manners in this country are different from ours. 'Jèige dìfangde lǐ'jyé gēn 'wǒmen nàrde bùyí'yàng.

Ill-mannered méigwēijyu. / That child across the street is ill-mannered. Jyē nèibyar nèige syǎuhár méi'gwēijyu.

Well-mannered yǒugwēijyu. / His son is well-mannered. Tā érdz yǒu'gwēijyu.

MANUFACTURE. dzwò, dzàu, jr̄dzàu. / What do you manufacture here? Nǐmen 'jèr jr̄'dzàu shémma? / How long does it take to manufacture this? 'Jèige dūngsyi yàu 'dwōshau shr̄hour dzwò'dé le? / They specialize in manufacturing light bulbs. Tāmen jwānmén dzàu 'dyàndēngpàur.

(Invent or make up) 'nyēdzàu. / He'll be able to manufacture a story for the occasion. Tā kéyǐ wèi jèijyàn 'shèr 'nyēdzàu yídwàn 'hwà.

MANY. dwō, hěn dwō, syǔdwō; a great many syǔsyǔdwō'dwōde. / I have many reasons. Wó yǒu 'syǔdwōde 'lǐyóu. / I have many things to do. Wó yǒu 'syǔdwō 'shr̀ yàu 'dzwò. / Are there many coming to dinner? Lái chr̄'fàn de rén 'dwō ma? / There weren't very many people at his house. Dzài tā 'jyāli de rén bù hěn 'dwō. / He knows a good many people in this city. Dzài jèige 'chéngli tā rènshr hěn dwō rén. / I called you a good many times yesterday. Dzwótyan wó 'jǎule ni 'hěn dwō 'tsź. / I've passed you on the street many a time. Wǒ dzài 'jyēshang 'pèngjyàngwo nín 'syǔdwō 'hwéi. / A great many people use that bank. 'Syǔsyǔdwō'dwōde rén gēn nèige yín'háng 'wǎnglái. / We have a great many things to do before we leave. Wǒmen 'dzǒu yǐ'chyán hái yóu 'syǔsyudwō'dwōde shr̀ yàu 'dzwò.

How many dwōshau. / How many tickets do you want? Nín yàu 'dwōshau pyàu? / I don't know how many of my friends will turn up this evening. Wǒ bùjr̄'dàu jyēr 'wǎnshang wó yǒu 'dwōshau péngyou hwèi'lái.

MAP. dìtú. / I want a map of China. Wǒ yàu yìjāng 'Jūnggwo dì'tú. / Can you show me the town on this map? Nǐ 'kéyǐ dzài dì'túshang bǎ jèige chéng 'jr̄géi wǒ 'kàn ma?

To map an area, etc. hwà, hwàchulai. / We want to map the coast. Wǒmen yàu bá hǎiàn'syàn 'hwàchulai.

(Plan a route) 'jìhwà. / The guide is mapping our route now. Lǐng'lùde dzài 'gēn wǒmen 'jìhwà 'lùchéng ne.

Map out (plan) dìng. / Have you mapped out your schedule yet? Nǐde 'shr̄jyān-'byáu yǐjing dìng'hǎule ma?

MARCH. (Walk in formation) dzǒu (when referring primarily to the walking motion); °páije dwèi (°bǎije dwèi, °páidwèi) dzǒu (with emphasis on formation); kāi instead of dzǒu in the same constructions (when leaving under orders); march by gwò in place of or after dzǒu or kāi in the same constructions. / They march the prisoners in the yard every morning. Tāmen 'měityān 'dzǎuchen jyàu 'fànrénmen dzài 'ywàn-dzli °páije (°bǎije) 'dwèi dzǒu'chywār. / Did you see the soldiers march by? Nǐ

736

kànjyàn 'jyūndwèi tsúng jèr °bǎije 'dwèi gwò ma (°'gwò ma, °'kāigwochyu ma)?

A march is expressed verbally by the same expressions given above. /We had a tough march this morning. Wŏmen jīntyān 'dzǎushang 'dzŏude 'jēn gŏu'shŏude. /They just came in from a twenty-mile march. Tāmen dzŏule 'èrshrlí 'lù 'gāng dàu jèr.

(Military music) jìnsyíngchyŭ. /The band started the concert with a march. Ywèdwèi 'kāichǎng dzŏule ge 'jìnsyíng'chyŭ.

(Month) Sānywè. /I plan to stay through March. Wó dǎswàn dzài jèr jùje, gwòle Sānywè dzài 'dzŏu.

MARK. (Written symbol, as a check) 'jǐhàur; (a check) gŏur; (a circle) chywār; (a line) 'dàur; make a mark °dǎ (°dzwò, °hwà, °syě) ge 'jǐhàur, dǎ ge 'gŏur, dǎ ge 'chywār, or expressed as to mark (with a check) gŏuchulai, gŏusyalai or (with a circle) chywānchulai or (with lines) hwàchulai or (as a note or record) jìsyalai. /Make a mark after the names of those present. Dzài 'dàu de rénde 'míngdzshang °dǎ ge 'jǐhaur (°dǎge 'gŏur, °dǎ ge 'chywār). /This bill has a mark on it. Jèijāng 'chyánpyàude shàngmyan yǒu ge 'jǐhàur. /Be sure your mark is on your laundry. Nín yàu 'syǐ de 'yīshangshang yí'dìng déi °dǎ (°hwà, °syě) ge 'jǐhàur. /The river has never gone higher than this mark. Héshwěi 'tsúnglái méiyou jǎng'gwò °jǐhaur (°'dàur gwò).

(Grade) fēr, fēnshu. /Your mark on the final exam is very important. Dà-'kǎude 'fēnshu hěn 'yàujǐn.

(Target) is usually expressed indirectly, but sometimes by mùdi or bǎ. /The shells fell wide of the mark. Pàu'dàn 'lwò de dìfang lí °mùdi (°'bǎ) tài 'ywǎn. or expressed as The shells didn't hit. Pàu'dàn méi'jùng. or as The deviation in firing was too great. 'Nèijīpàu 'fàngde 'pyānchā tài 'dà.

Be wide of the mark (of a guess, etc.). /His guess was wide of the mark. Tā tsāide 'tài chà le. or Tā tsāide kě 'jēn chàde °'tài ywǎn (°'tài dwō, °'ywǎnle chyù) le.

Miss the mark (fig.). /His answers missed the mark every time. is expressed as Every time he answered wrong. Tā 'měitsz̀ 'lǎushr °dá'tswòle (or didn't answer the question °'dáde búdwèi'tí, or didn't answer what was asked °'dáfēiswǒ'wèn).

Reach a mark (goal). /Do you think he'll reach the mark he has set for himself? Tā syǎng (jyānglái) dzwòdàu 'nèmma ge 'dǐ bu, 'nǐ jywéje tā 'dzwòde'dàu ma?

On your mark (command) jànhǎu. /On your mark; get set; go! Jàn'hǎu; yù-'bèi; 'pǎu! or expressed as One, two, three, go! 'Yī, 'èr, 'sān, 'pǎu!

To mark (with a check) gŏuchulai, gŏusyalai; (with a circle) chywānchulai; (with lines) hwàchulai; (as a note or record) jìsyalai; or expressed as make a mark see paragraph one. /I've marked the items I want. Wǒ 'yàude dōu °'gŏuchulaile (°'gŏusyalaile, °'chywānchulaile, °dǎle 'jǐhaurle). /I've marked the important parts of the notice. Wó bǎ jèige 'tūnggàude 'jùngyau 'bùfen yǐjǐng °'hwàchulaile (°'gŏu-chulaile, °'chywānchulaile, °dǎle 'jǐhaur). /Mark the names of those present. Bǎ 'dàule de rénde 'míngdz °'gŏuchulai (°'chywānchulai, °'gŏusyalai, °'jìsyalai). /I've marked your route on the map. Ní dzŏu de lùsyàn wó 'yǐjǐng dzài dì 'túshang géi nǐ 'hwàchulaile.

(Of examinations) dǎ fēr, dǎfēnshu; or expressed as look over kàn. /When will you have our examination papers marked? Nín 'shémma shŕhou kànwán wŏmen-de 'jywàndz? /Have you marked those examination papers yet? Nèisyē 'jywàndz dōu °dǎle 'fēr le ma (°dǎle 'fēnshu le ma, °kàn'gwòle ma)?

737

(Of prices on goods) bǎ . . . °syě(°jǐ, °byāu)shang 'jyàchyan. /We must mark these goods today. Dzámen 'jyēr déi bǎ nèisyē 'hwò °syě(°jǐ, °byāu)shang 'jyàchyan. /What price is marked on the tag? °'Pyàrshang (°'Párshang) °syě (°byāu) de 'jyàr shr̀ 'dwōshǎu?

Mark time until 'gānděngje, 'jǐngděngje; (waste time until) děngje . . . hàu 'shŕhou. /They're just marking time until their boat leaves. Tāmen 'děngje kāi-'chwán, dzài nàr hàu 'shŕhou ne. or Tāmen dzài nàr °'gānděngje (°'jǐngděngje) kāi'chwán ne. /They're marking time until he leaves. Tāmen dzài nàr °'gānděngje (°'jǐngděngje) tā 'dzǒukāi ne.

Mark down prices of goods jyǎn jyàchyan, jyǎnjyàr. /These coats have been marked down. Jèisyē 'dàyīde jyàchyán yǐjīng 'jyǎnle. /These are marked down prices. Jèi shr̀ 'yǐjīng 'jyǎnle de 'jyàr.

Mark up prices of goods jǎng jyàchyan, jǎngjyàr; or expressed indirectly. /He seems to have marked up his prices. Tāde dūngsyi 'hǎu syàng jǎngle 'jyàr le. or Tāde dūngsyi dìng de 'jyàchyan hǎu syàng °'jǎng le (°yàu de bǐ yǐchyán 'dwō le, °yàu de bǐ yǐchyán 'dà le).

Marked. /Business has shown a marked improvement this year. 'Jīnnyán 'mǎimai hěn jyàn 'hǎu.

MARKET. (Place to buy and sell) shr̀, shèr; (a country market held on certain days) jí; (the same, held on monastery grounds) myàuhwèi; (a market open at night in large cities) 'yèshèr; **market place** shr̀chǎng; **black market** 'hēishèr; **stock market** jyāuyì-swǒ. /The market is very lively today. Jyēr °'shr̀shang (°'jíshang, °myàu'hwèi, °'yèsher, °shr̀'chǎngli, °jyāuyì'swǒ) tǐng 'máng. or Jyēr °'shr̀shang (°etc.) 'mǎimai tǐng 'rènau. /These eggs were brought to the market this morning. Jèisyē jǐ'dzěr shr̀ jyēr 'dzǎushang tsái 'shàng'shr̀de. /When does the meat market open? Ròu shr̀'chǎng shémma shŕhou kāi'mén? /Is there anything new on the market today? Jyēr 'shr̀shang °'syīn dàule shémma 'hwòle ma (°yǒu shémma 'syīn hwò)?

(Sales field) 'syāulù; (customer) 'mǎijǔr. /This country is a good market for cotton cloth. Dzài jèige 'gwóli 'myánbù °'syāulù hén 'hǎu (°kéyǐ 'chàngsyāu). /He's trying to find a market for his product. Tā syáng gěi tā 'dzàu de dūngsyi jǎu °'syāulù (°ge 'mǎijǔr). /There's a heavy market in machinery here. Jèige dìfang 'jīchide 'syāulù hěn 'hǎu.

(Prices) hángshr. /The tea market is off today. 'Jīntyān 'cháyè méiyou 'hángshr.

Be in the market for (want to buy) yàu 'mǎi. /Are you in the market for a good car? Nǐ yàu mǎi lyàng hǎu chǐ'chē ma?

Do marketing, go marketing, or **go to market** (to buy) is expressed as buy things mǎi dūngsyi. /She does her marketing in the morning. Tā 'dzǎushang chyù mǎi 'dūngsyi.

To market goods is expressed as **send to market** sùngshang 'shr̀ chyu, sùngdàu 'jíshang chyù 'mài or as **send to sell** sùngchyu mài. /He will market his fruit this month. 'Jèige ywè tā yàu bá 'gwǒdz °sùngshang 'shr̀chyu (°sùngchyu 'mài, °sùngdàu 'jíshang chyù 'mài).

MARRIAGE. (Wedding) jyēhwūnlǐ; (of old traditional style) 'húngshr̀, 'syǐshr̀; **have a marriage** syíng 'jyēhwun'lǐ, bàn 'húngshr̀, bàn 'syǐshr̀; verbal expressions meaning **get married** or **marry** are also used. See **MARRY**. /The marriage will take place on March 1. 'Sānywè 'yīhàu °syíng 'jyēhwūn'lǐ (°bàn 'syǐshr̀). /They have had several marriages in their family within the last year. Tāmen jyā yì'nyánli bànle hǎujijyàn °'húngshr̀ (°'syǐshr̀). *or* Tāmen jyà jèi yí'nyánli 'gūnyang °chū 'méndz (°chū'jyà), 'érdz chyù 'syíferde, bànle 'hauji 'hwéi syǐshr̀.

(Married life) 'hwūnyīn. / Their marriage has been very successful. Tāmende 'hwūnyīn hěn 'méimǎn.

MARRY. (Of a woman) jyà, jyàgěi. / Is she going to marry him? Tā 'hwèi buhwèi 'jyà(gěi) tā?

(Of a man) chyù. / They say he married her for her money. Dà'jyā shwō tā 'chyǔ tā shr̀ wèile tāde 'chyán.

(Of the one performing the ceremony) gěi . . . jèng'hwūn. / When will he be able to marry us? Tā 'shémma shŕhour néng gěi wǒmen jèng'hwūn?

(Give a woman in marriage) bǎ . . . jyàgěi. / He married his daughter to an old friend. Tā bǎ tāde 'nyǔer 'jyàgei tāde yíge lǎu'péngyou.

Get married (of a couple or an individual) jyéhwūn; (of a man) chyù syífer; (of a woman) chū méndz, chūjyà; (in old ceremonies) gwòmén. / Do you know when she's going to get married? Nǐ 'jr̄dau bujr̄dau tā 'shémma shŕhou °jyé'hwūn (°chū mendz, °chūjyà)?

MASTER. (Of a household or servants) 'jǔrén; **master of the house** 'jǔrén *or* (man of the house) syānsheng, 'lǎuyé. / Who is the master of the house? 'Něi yíwèi shr̀ 'jǔrén? / Is the master of the house in? 'Syānsheng dzài'jyā ma?

Be master of a situation néng 'yìngfùdz̀'rú, néng 'tsǎudzùngdé'yì, bànde 'chyàdàu 'hǎuchù. / No matter what happens, he's always master of the situation. 'Bùgwǎn yùjyàn 'shémma shr̀, tā 'dōu °néng 'yìngfùdz̀'rú (°néng 'tsǎudzùngdé'yí, °bànde 'chyàdàu 'hǎuchù).

Master of the ship chwánjǔ, chwánjǎng. / The master of the ship has sailed the sea for many years. °Chwán'jǔ (°Chwán'jǎng) páu'hǎi pǎule 'hǎusyē 'nyán le.

Master of Arts 'Shwòshr̀, 'Wénkē 'shwòshr̀; **Master of Science** 'Lǐkē 'shwòshr̀.

In combinations, such as **master key**, dzǔng is used or the idea is expressed by a word for all, as chywán. / Where is the master switch? °'Dzǔngdyànmén (°'Dzǔng-kāigwān) dzài 'nǎr? / This is the master schedule. Jèi shr̀ 'dzǔngshŕjyān'byǎu.

To **master** a subject of studying jīngtūng, sywétūng, sywéhǎu. / He has mastered several languages. Tā jīngtūng 'hǎujigwó hwàle. / He mastered the language in a year. Tā bǎ nèigwóde hwà yìnyán 'jr̄nei jyòu sywétūngle. / I find this language difficult to master. Wǒ jywéje nèigwóde 'hwà hěn nán sywéde'hǎu.

Master one's feelings 'kùngjr̀. / You must master your feelings. Ní děi 'kùngjr̀ níde 'chínggǎn tsai 'syíng. / He cannot master his temper. Tā bùnéng 'kùngjr̀ tāde píchi.

MATCH. (Fire lighter) yánghwǒ, yánghwǒr; (in Peiping, also) chyùdēngr, yáng'chyǔ-dēngr; (in some other areas) hwǒ'chái. / Have you got a match? Yǒu yáng'hwǒ ma? / A box of matches, please. 'Gěi wo yìhé yáng'hwǒ.

(Equal of a person) 'dwèishǒu. / I'm no match for him. Wǒ 'bùshr̀ 'tāde 'dwèishǒu. / He met his match. Tā 'kě pèngjau 'dwèishǒu le.

(A contest) bǐsài. / Would you like to see a tennis match? Nǐ yàu kàn 'wǎng-chyóu bǐ'sài ma?

(Marriage). / She's making a good match. is expressed as The man she's marrying is suitable. Tā 'jyà de rén tǐng hé'shr̀. / He's making a good match. is expressed as He's marrying her; it's very suitable. Tā 'chyù tā tǐng hé'shr̀de.

To match (equal) 'gǎnshang . . . nèmma dwō *or* dà, or with other stative verbs, depending on whether the reference is to equaling in amount, size, speed, quality, etc.; yé yǒu instead of 'gǎnshang in the same constructions; gēn . . . yí'yàng dwō or etc. /Can we match their speed? Dzámen °'gǎndeshang (°yě néng yǒu) 'tāmen nèmma 'kwài ma? /He matched Jones's record for sales. 'Tā màide gǎnshangle °lǎu'Jōu màide nèmma 'dwō le (°gēn lǎu'Jōu màide yí'yàng dwō le).

(Be of the same set of pair) is expressed as be one set *or* be one pair (*see* SET, PAIR). /These gloves don't match. Jèilyǎngjr̄ shǒu'tàur 'búshr yí'fù. /This cup and saucer don't match. Jèige chábēi gēn chápár búshr yí'tàu.

(Fit together physically) dwèishang, dwèideshàng. /The broken edges don't match. 'Chár dwèibu'shàng.

(Be of the same kind) pèi, pèideshang. /Can you match this plate? Nǐ 'pèideshang jèige 'pár ma? *or* Nǐ néng 'pèi jèiyàngrde 'pándz ma?

(Be of the same color) (shr̀) yíge shǎr(de). /These two match. Jèi'lyǎngge dōu shr̀ yíge 'shǎr. /Do you have thread to match this? Yǒu 'jèishǎrde 'syàn ma?

(Harmonize, go together well) pèi; (in color) 'yánshǎr 'pèi, dwèi'shǎr. /His tie doesn't match his suit. Tāde lǐng'dài hé tāde 'yīshang °bú'pèi (°'yánshǎr bú'pèi, °búdwèi'shǎr).

Other English expressions. /I'll match you for it. is expressed as Let's flip a coin to see who pays (or other expressions instead of pays). Dzámen dǔ ge 'dzèrmèr kàn 'shéi gěi 'chyán.

MATERIAL. (For building, sewing, preparing a report, etc.) 'tsáilyàu; **raw material** 'ywánlyàu. /What materials do you need to make a bookcase? Nǐ dzwò shū'jyàdz yàu yùng shémma 'tsáilyàu? /Do you have enough of this material to make me a suit? Ní 'yǒu méiyou jèijǔng 'tsáilyàu gòu gěi wo dzwò yìshēn 'yīshang? /He's collecting material for a new book. Tā dzài jǎu 'tsáilyàu syě 'shū. /The factory is short of raw materials. Jèige gūng'chǎng 'ywánlyàu bú'gòu.

Writing materials wénjyù.

Material comfort wù'jr̀de syǎng'shòu. /They've never had much material comfort. Tāmen syànglai 'méiyougwo dwōshau wù'jr̀de syǎng'shòu.

Material witness jǔ'yàude 'jèngrén.

MATTER. (Material substance) wùjr̀, jr̀ (technical terms); or expressed as things in the world 'shr̀jyèshangde 'dūngsyi; specific kinds of matter are expressed by a stative verb with 'dūngsyi or by specific terms; néng, núng (pus or similar body secretion). /All matter has one of three forms: gas, liquid, or solid. 'Wùjr̀ 'syíngtǐ yǒu 'sānjǔng: 'chìtǐ, 'yètǐ, 'gùtǐ. *or* 'Shr̀jyeshangde 'dūngsyi yǒu 'sānjǔng: 'yàubujyòurshr 'chyèr, 'yàubujyoushr 'shwěr, 'yàubujyòushr shŕ'dzáurde. /All religions teach the existence of spirit as well as matter. 'Syóyǒude 'dzūngjyàu 'dōu shwō °yǒu-'jr̀ yé yǒu 'líng (°'wujr̀ yǐ'wài hái yǒu 'línghwún). /Many kinds of coloring matter are obtained from bark. Hěndwō dzwò 'yánlyàu de 'dūngsyi dōu shr̀ tsúng shù-'píshang 'chyǔchūlaide. /Pine trees secrete a sticky matter. 'Sūngshù chū yìjǔng °nyánde 'dūngsyi (*or* (sap) °'nyánjr̄).

(Affair) shr̀, shèr; sometimes expressed indirectly; matters (indefinite) 'shémma shr̀, shr̀ching. /Will you look into the matter? Jèijyàn 'shr̀ ní gěi 'chá (yi)cha ('syíng ma)? /I must settle some business matters. Wó yǒu jǐjyàn 'gūngshr̀ děi bàn'wánlou. /You take matters too seriously. Nǐ 'shémma shr̀ dōu (kànde) tài rèn'jēn le. *or* Ní bǎ 'shr̀ching dōu kànde tài °rèn'jēn le (°'sž le, °'yánjùng le, °'dà le). /You're only making matters worse. Ní fán bǎ 'shr̀ nèngde gèng °'dzāu le (°méifár 'bàn le). or expressed as You're simply giving people more trouble. Ní 'jyánjr shr̀ gěi rén 'tyān máfan. /It's a matter of no importance. 'Syàu shèr yì'jwàng. or 'Búshr shémma °yàu'jǐn shr̀ (°'dàshr̀, °'yánjùngde shr̀, °dàbu'lyǎude shr̀, °'jŕdegwān'syīnde shr̀, °'jùngyàude shr̀). /The matter is of absolutely no concern to me. Nèi shèr °gēn wǒ yì'dyǎr gwānsyi yě méi'yǒu (°wǒ yì'dyǎr yě gwānbu'jáu). /Bring the matter up tomorrow. °Jèijyàn shèr (°Jèige) 'myér dzài shwō. /Bring the matter to his attention. °Jèijyàn shèr (°Jèige) °yàu (°děi) jyàu 'tā jŕdàu. or Bǎ °jèijyàn shèr (°jèige) 'gàusu tā. /His health is a matter of great concern to the people of the whole world. Tā 'bìngde dzémma'yàng chywánshr̀'jyède rén dōu °'rènwéi shr̀ yíjyàn 'dàshr̀ (°hěn gwān'syīn, °jywéje hěn'jùngyàu, °jywéje yǒu 'gwānsyi).

A matter of course 'dāngránrú'tszde; or expressed as **of course** dāngrán, dz̀rán. /That's a matter of course. Nèi shr̀ 'dāngránrú'tszde. or °Dāng'rán (°Dz̀'rán) shr̀ nèmmaje.

(Take) **as a matter of course** gwànle, 'bùyǐwéi'chíle, 'rènwéi 'dāngrán le. /She accepts praise as a matter of course. Tā shòu rén 'gūngwei °'gwànle (°'bùyǐwéi'chíle, °'rènwéi 'dāngrán le).

A matter of life and death °'syìngmìngjyāu'gwānde (°'shēngsz̀jyāu'gwānde, °'rénmìngjyāu'gwānde) shr̀. /This is a matter of life and death. Jèishr °'syìngmìng-jyāu'gwānde (°etc.) shr̀.

A matter of opinion. /That's a matter of opinion. is expressed as People's opinions differ. 'Gèrén 'kànfa bù'túng.

As a matter of fact chíshr̀ (a); or expressed as simply 'jyǎnjr̀; or as let me tell you the truth gēn nǐ shwō 'shr̀hwà ba. /As a matter of fact, this should have been placed under your control in the beginning. Chí'shr̀ (a), 'jèi shèr yì chǐ'chū jyòu gāi ràng 'ní gwǎn. /As a matter of fact, she did go to college. Chí'shr̀ a, tā 'jēn shànggwo dà'sywé. /His handwriting is pretty bad; as a matter of fact, I can't read it at all. Tā syě de dz̀ jēn °'bùchéngsyíng (°'bùhǎu rèn), wó 'jyǎnjr̀ °rènbu-chū'lái (°kànbu'dǔng). /As a matter of fact, I didn't even know his name. Gēn ni shwō °'shr̀hwà ba (°chí'shr̀ a), wǒ lyán tā 'jyàu shémma yě bùjr̀'dàu.

Matter-of-fact or **in a matter-of-fact sort of way** is expressed as as if nothing were the matter syàng 'méi nèmma hwéi 'shèr shr̀de; or as not changing the attitude 'búdùng'syīnde; or as not changing the voice or expression 'búdùng'shēngsède; or as unperturbed 'bùhwāngbùmángde; or as not taking (it) as anything at all °nàje 'búdàng (°'bùnàje dàng) hwéi 'shèr. /Don't be so matter-of-fact about it! 'Byé nèmma °nàje 'búdàng (°'bùnàje dàng) hwéi 'shèr lái kàn! or 'Byé nèmma °syàng 'méi nèmma hwéi 'shèr shr̀de (°'búdùng 'syīn)! /He told me in a matter-of-fact sort of way that he had just won ten thousand dollars at the races. Tā °'bùhwāngbùmángde (°syàng 'méi nèmma hwéi 'shèr shr̀de, °'búdùng'shēngsède) gēn wǒ shwō tā 'gāngtsái dzài má'chǎng déle yí'wànkwài chyán.

Be a matter of (depend on) děi kàn. /It's a matter of how you look at it. Děi kàn ní dzémma ge 'kànfa. /That's a matter of how you say it. 'Nèi děi kàn dzémma 'shwō le. /It's a matter of timing. 'Shr̀hour děi kànde °'jwǔn (°jèng 'dwèi). /It's all a matter of time. (of how much time there is) Děi kàn yǒu 'dwōshǎu 'shr̀hou. or (of how much time it will take) Kàn děi yùng 'dwōshǎu 'shr̀hou le. or (for time to decide) Děi kàn 'shr̀jyān lái 'dìng. or expressed as This is a question of time. Jèi shr̀ 'shr̀jyān wèn'tí.

Just a matter of (depends only on). /It's just a matter of time. is expressed as above but may also be expressed as There isn't much time. 'Méi dwōshǎu shr̀hou le. or expressed as In a little while it will be known. 'Děng yiděng jyòu 'jŕdàule. /His death is just a matter of days. Tā 'hwóbulyǎu jǐ'tyǎr le. or Tā 'méi jǐtyǎrde 'hwó-tour le. *or* Tā yǎn'kànje jyòu kwài 'sž le. *or* Tā méi 'jǐtyār jyòu hwèi 'sžde.

For that matter (so far as this point is concerned) dzài 'jèi yìdyǎnshang; (even) jyòushr; (also) yě, lyán. /He said our work was no good, and we agreed with him, for that matter. Tā shwō wǒmen dzwò de 'shèr chà'jǐn; °dzài 'jèi yìdyǎnshang 'wǒmen gēn tā túng'yì (°jyòushr wǒmen yě 'gēn ta túng'yì).

No laughing matter. /That's no laughing matter. Nèi 'búshr °kě'syàude shèr (°yí'syàujyòu'lyàude) shèr. *or* 'Nèi 'shèr °hěn yàu'jǐn (°bùnéng 'chǐngshr, °bùnéng 'búdàng hwéi 'shèr, °bùnéng kàn'chǐngle).

(Postal) matter 'yóujyàn. /This package will have to go as first-class matter. Jèige 'bāugwǒ yí'dìng děi ànje 'yìděng 'yóujyàn °dzǒu (°jì).

Printed matter yìnshwāpǐn. /Do I have to declare printed matter? 'Yìnshwā-'pǐn yé děi 'bàu ma?

Reading matter kě'kàn de dūngsyi; dūngsyi if kàn is used elsewhere in the sentence; or expressed as books and magazines shū, dzájù. /This reading matter will last me a week. Jèisyē 'dūngsyi °'gòu wǒ kàn yíge syīng'chīde (°wó děi kàn yíge syīng'chī).

Subject matter jyǎng de shèr. /The subject matter of the book is interesting, but the presentation is dull. Nèiběn shū jyǎng de 'shèr tíng yǒu 'yìszde, búgwo 'syěde °nèmma 'szchenchénde (°nèmma 'mènchenchénde, °bù'shēngdùng).

The matter (the trouble, wrong, when not followed by with) shr or not expressed. /What's the matter? 'Shémma shr? *or* Yǒu 'shémma shr? *or* 'Dzěmma yǐhwéi shr? *or* 'Dzěmmale? /Nothing's the matter. 'Méi shémma shr. *or* 'Méi shèr. *or* Méi 'dzěmmaje.

The matter with is expressed as illness bìng; or as defect máubing; or as broken 'hwàile; or in other ways similar to those in the preceding paragraph. /Something's the matter with my stomach; I can't eat without getting a stomach-ache. Wǒ 'wèikou 'jwǔn shr yóu dyǎr 'bìng; 'yí chr dūngsyi jyòu 'téng. /There's something the matter with my car; it won't start. Chē kāibu'dùngle; jwǔnshr nǎr °yóu dyǎr 'máubing (°'hwàile). /What's the matter with you? Are you crazy? Nǐ jè shr 'dzěmma le? Nǐ °'fēng (°'shǎ, °'húdu) la! /There's nothing the matter with him that a good rest won't cure. Tā °'shémma bìng yě méi'yǒu (°hǎu'hāurde), 'syē hwer jyòu 'hǎu le. /There's nothing the matter with him that a good talking-to won't cure. 'Tā ya, 'shwō yídwùn jyòu 'hǎu le.

No matter (followed by what, whether, if, how, etc.) bùgwǎn, píng, swéi. /We've made up our minds no matter what you say. °'Píng (°'Bù'gwǎn, °'Swéi) ní 'dzěmma shwō, wǒmen fǎn'jèng shr ná'dìngle 'júyì le. /No matter whether he comes or not, we've got to leave. Bù'gwǎn tā lái bulái, wǒmen déi 'dzǒu le. /She wants that coat no matter what the cost. Tā 'fēi yàu mǎi nèijyàn dà'yī bùkě, bùgwǎn 'dwō dàde 'jyàr. *or* 'Bùgwǎn 'dwō gwèi, tā yě yàu 'mǎi nèijyàn dà'yī.

To matter is expressed in various indirect ways referring to importance or personal interest and concern. /It doesn't matter. 'Búyàujǐn. *or* 'Méi shémma 'gwānsyi. *or* 'Syǎushèr yì'jwāng. *or* 'Swànle. *or* 'Búshr shémma 'dàbu'lyǎude shr. *or* 'Yùngbujáu gwǎn. *or* 'Yùngbujáu tsǎu'syīn. /What does it matter how it's done, so long as it gets done in time? 'Gwǎn dzěmma 'bàn ne? *or* 'Gwǎn ta dzěmma 'bàn ne? *or* 'Dzěmma ge 'bànfa yǒu shémma 'gwānsyi? 'Jǐ yàu dàu shŕhou dzwò-'chéngle jyòu 'shŕle. /It matters a great deal to me what he says about you. Tā dzěmma shwō °'ní wǒ dōu tǐng gwǎn'syīnde (°'ní jyòu gēn shwō 'wǒ yí'yàng). /It matters a great deal to me whether he'll be there or not. Tā 'dàu yǔ bú'dàu tsúng 'wǒ jèr syàng 'tíng yǒu'gwānsyide. *or* (I'll have to do something about it) Tā 'dàu yǔ bú'dàu wǒ 'fēi gwǎn bù'kě.

MAY (MIGHT). (Possibly) 'yésyŭ. / That may be true. 'Nà yésyŭ shŕ 'dwèide. / I may go with you tomorrow night. Míngr 'wǎnshang wǒ 'yésyŭ 'gēn ni yí'kwàr chyù. / You might try to reach him at home. Nǐ 'yésyŭ kéyi wàng tā 'jyāli chyù 'jǎu ta. / I might be there. Wǒ 'yésyŭ hwèi 'lái. / You might have changed your mind if you'd heard all the facts. Nǐ yàushr 'jŕdaule 'swóyǒude shŕ'shŕ, 'yésyŭ hwèi gǎi-'byàn nǐde 'yìsz.

(In polite requests; formally, in their answers) 'kéyǐ, kéyi. / May I leave this with you? Wǒ 'kéyi bǎ 'jèige 'jyāugei nǐ ma? / May I have this dance? 'Jèi yítsz nín 'kéyi gēn wǒ 'tyàu ma? / Certainly you may. 'Kěyi.

May (month) 'Wǔywè.

MAYOR. (Of a city classed as a municipality) shŕjǎng; (of a city classed as a district) syànjǎng (more often translated into English as District Magistrate); (of a village) tswūnjǎng (often translated as village head man).

ME. *See* **I.**

MEAL. fàn with measure dwùn. / Where can I get a good meal? Shémma 'dìfang wǒ kéyi 'chr̄ yídwùn 'hǎu 'fàn? / I eat some of my meals at home. Yǒu jidwùn 'fàn wǒ dzài 'jyāli chr̄.

(Ground grain) myàn usually with the type of grain specified; **corn meal** bàngdz-myàr.

MEAN (MEANT). (To be defined or explained as; used with this, that, what, anything, etc.). / What does it mean? (what is its definition) Shr 'shémma yìsz? *or* (how is it to be explained) 'Dzěmma jyǎng? *or* (how is it to be stated *or* what is it in other words) Shŕ 'dzěmma ge 'shwōfar? *or* (what is it all about) Shŕ 'dzěmma hwéi shèr? Other usages are similarly constructed. / What does this word mean? Jèige 'dzèr shŕ 'shémma yìsz? / What does this small circle mean? Jèige syāu 'chywār °shŕ 'shémma yìsz (°'dzěmma jyǎng, °shŕ 'dzěmma ge 'shwōfar, °shŕ 'dzěmma hwéi shèr)? / Oh! So that's what it means! 'Òu! Shŕ 'nèmma °ge yìsz (°hwéi shèr) a! / That's what this word means, but it can't be used that way. Jèige dzèr 'shŕ nèige 'yìsz, búgwo 'yùng de shŕhou 'bùnéng nèmma 'yùng. / I heard what you said, but I don't understand what it means. (Nǐde 'hwà wǒ) 'tīngjyanle, kěshr 'bùdǔng shŕ shémma 'yìsz. / What does this word mean literally? Jèige dzèr bĕn-'shēn shŕ 'shémma yìsz? *or* Jèige dzèrde 'bĕnyì shŕ 'shémma? / What did this word mean originally? Jèige dzèr 'ywánláide yìsz shŕ 'shémma?

(Get across a meaning, or intend; of a person) is expressed by saying that what the person says **means** so-and-so, the expressions for which are the same as above; (intend) syǎng, yàu, 'syǎngyàu, 'dǎswàn, or expressed in terms of a person's intention yìsz, or indirectly, especially with a negative, as intentionally *or* with malicious purpose gùyìde, yǒuyìde, chéngsyīn, *or* (dropping the negative) as un-intentionally 'wúsyīnjūng or as carelessly méilyǒushén, bù'syàusyīn, or as an un-intentional mistake 'wúsyīnjŕ'gwò; (intend definitely) yí'dìng yàu. / That's not what he meant. (of meaning) Tāde 'hwàlitou méiyǒu 'nèige 'yìsz. *or* (of intention) Tā bìng 'búshr nèige 'yìsz. *or* Tāde 'yìsz 'búshr 'nèmma hwéi shèr. / What do you mean by that? Nèi shŕ 'shémma yìsz? *or* Nèi dzěmma 'jyǎng? *or* Ní syǎng yàu 'dzěmmaje? / What do you mean by saying that? (of meaning or intention) Nǐ shwō 'nèige yǒu shémma 'yìsz? *or* (of intention only) Nǐ shwō 'nèige °shŕ 'dzěmma ge 'yìsz (°nà shŕ syǎng yàu 'dzěmmaje, °nà shŕ 'dǎswàn 'dzěmmaje)? / Perhaps that's what he meant. Tā 'yésyŭ yàu shwō 'nèige láije. *or* Tā shwō de 'hwà 'yésyŭ shŕ °'nèmma ge (°'jèige, °'nèige) yìsz. / Do you mean this for me? °Ní syǎng (°Nǐde 'yìsz shŕ yàu) bǎ 'jèige géi 'wǒ ma? / Do you mean to see him before

you go? Nǐ 'shr̀ syǎng dzài °'dzóu (°'méidzóu) yǐ'chyán 'jyànjyan tā ma? /I meant
to do it yesterday, but I forgot. Wǒ ywánlái °'syǎng (°'dǎswàn) dzwér jyòu bǎ jèige
'dzwò le, yǐ'syàdz gěi 'wàngle. /I didn't mean to come today, but I had nowhere to
go. Wǒ °méi'dǎswan (°méisyǎng) 'jīntyān láide, kěshr wǒ 'méichǔr 'chyù. or Wó
běnlái °'dǎswàn (°syǎng) jīntyān bùláide, kěshr wǒ 'méichǔr 'chyù. /Please forgive
me; I didn't mean to do that. Dwèibu'jù; °wǒ búshr gù'yìde (°'jèi shr̀ wǒ 'wúsyīnjr̀-
'gwò). or Dwèibu'jù; shr̀ wǒ °'méilyóu'shén (°bù'syàusyīn) láije. /Don't get sore;
he didn't mean anything by that remark. 'Byé shēng'chì ba; tā nèijyù 'hwà yǐ'dyár
yě búshr °chéng'syīn (°gù'yìde, °yǒu'yìde) shwōde. /She means to have her way
about the party. Chǐng'kè de shr̀ tā yí'dìng yàu àn tā 'dzjǐde 'yìdz lái 'bàn.

(Refer to) shwō, 'jr̄je . . . shwō. /I didn't mean you. Wǒ búshr °shwō 'nǐ
(°jr̄je 'nǐ shwōde). /I do mean you! Wǒ 'jèngshr shwō 'nǐ. or Wǒ shwōde °jyòu
(°jèng) shr 'nǐ. /Which one do you mean? Nǐ shwōde shr̀ 'nèige? /That's not the
one I meant. Wǒ 'búshr shwōde 'nèige.

(Stand for; of a symbol) 'dàibyǎu. /The big circles mean field officers, the
small circles mean company officers. 'Dàchywār 'dàibyǎu 'syàugwān, 'syàuchywār
dàibyǎu 'wèigwān. /Every symbol of this kind means a thousand men. Měiyíge jèijǔng 'jìhaur 'dàibyǎu yì'chyān rén.

Mean (that) (of a condition or situation, to have the effect or meaning that) is
expressed as say shwō, be shr̀, or not expressed. /If he scowls at you, it means
you're in; if he's very friendly, you might as well go elsewhere to look for a job. Tā
yàushr 'dzòuje 'méitóu 'dèng nǐ, nèi jyòushr shwō tā yàu 'yùng nǐ; tā yàushr 'fēicháng 'héchi a, 'nà nǐ jyòu dàu 'byéchùr jǎu 'shèr chyù ba. /If I don't come before
noon, it means I can't come at all. Wǒ yàushr 'jūngwǔ hái méi'dàu, wǒ jyòu (shr̀)
°'bùlái le (°'bùnéng lái le). /If he comes, it'll mean trouble for us. Yàushr 'tā
lái a, 'dzámen kě jyòu yàu °yǒu 'máfan le (°'méiyǒu 'ānjing 'rdz le). /He means
that he wants you to give him a drink. (by his gestures or actions) Tā nàshr °yàu
hē'shwěi (°syǎng 'gēn nǐ yàu bēi 'shwěi hē). or (by his speech, as in another
language) Tā shwō de shr̀ syǎng gēn nǐ yàu bēi 'shwěi hē.

Mean a lot to. /This means a lot to me. Jèi gēn 'wó yóu 'hěn dàde 'gwānsyi.
or Tsúng 'wǒ jèr 'syǎng 'jèi shr̀ °'tǐng yàu'jǐnde shr̀ (°'dàshr̀).

Mean it, mean business, mean followed by a quotation of what one said is expressed by saying that the thing said is true jēn(de), the truth 'shr̄hwà, not said in
fun 'búshr shwōje 'wár or that when one says something it goes jyòu swānshùr or
more indirectly, by saying that someone must do something about it. /I mean it.
'Jēnde. or Shr̀ 'jēnde. or Wǒ shr̀ 'jēnsyīn 'hwà. or Wǒ 'shwōle jyòu swàn'shùr.
or expressed as If I say one, it's one; if I say two, it's two. Wǒ 'shwōyīshr̀'yī,
shwō'èrshr̀'èr. /When a woman tells you that she's twenty-one, she doesn't always
mean it literally. Yàushr yǒu 'nyǔrén gàusu nǐ tā shr̀ 'èrshr̀'yī swèi, nèi 'chángchang 'búshr °'jēnde (°'shr̄hwà). /When he tells you to do something, he means
business. Tā jyàu nǐ 'dzwò shemma de shr̄hou, 'búshr shwōje 'wár. /When I say
stop, I mean stop! Wǒ shwō byé 'dùng, nǐ jyòu 'bùnéng dzài 'dùng! or Wǒ shwō
'jànju, nǐ jyòu °děi 'jànju (°'bùnéng dzài 'dzǒu)!

Mean well, mean no harm shr̀ hǎusyīn, shr̀ hǎuyì, (bing) méiyǒu 'èyì(de),
'syīn hǎu, syīn hén 'hǎude. /He means well anyway. Tā 'wúlwùnrúhé shr̀ °hǎu-
'syīn (°'hǎu'yì). /He makes mistakes, but I'm sure he means well. Tā 'cháng nèng
'tswòle, búgwo tā °'syīn hǎu (°bìng méiyǒu 'èyì). /Don't worry about what he says;
he really means well by us. Tā ài 'shwō jyàu tā 'shwōchyu ba; tā dwèi 'dzámen
°shr̀ 'hǎusyīn (°shr̀ hǎu'yìde, °syīn hén 'hǎude, °shr̀ 'méiyǒu 'èyìde).

What does someone **mean by** . . . wèi'shémma, dzěmma. /What do you mean
by calling people names? °Ní 'dzěmma (°Nǐ wèi'shémma) mà'rén a?

Be meant for. / That remark was meant for you. (it meant you; see third paragraph above) Nèi jyù hwà shr̀ °'jr̀je 'nǐ shwōde (or (it was said for you to hear) °'shwōgěi 'nǐ tīngde, or (it was said because of you) °yīnwei 'nǐ shwōde). / He was meant for that job. is expressed as He's really suited to do that job. Tā dzwò 'nèi sher̀ 'jèng hé'shr̀. or as That job seems to have been made for him. 'Nèi sher̀ hǎu syàng wèi 'tā 'shède shr̀de. or meaning He was supposed to do that job, not this one. 'Běnlái 'pài tā dzwò 'nèijyàn shr̀. / They were meant for each other. (really a pair) Tāmen °'jèng (°'jēn) shr̀ °yí'dwèr (or (destined) °'ywánfer, °'tyānshēngdi'shède yí'dwèr, °'tyānshēngde yí'dwèr, °'chyánshr̀de 'yīnywán, or (sarcastically, of a couple that doesn't get along) °'ywānjyālù'jǎi, °'búshr 'ywānjya 'bújyù'tóu).

(Be) **mean** (fierce) syūng; (hot-tempered) syìngdz tǐng 'bàu(dzau) 'píchyer jēn °'lìhai (°'syūng, °hwài); (hard to manage) nángwàn; (difficult) nánbànde; (stingy) syǎuchi, 'lìnsè; (cruel, harsh) hěn, hěn'syīn; and similar expressions. / Be careful; that's a mean animal. 'Syǎusyīn dyar; nèige 'shēngkou °nán 'gwǎn (°hěn 'syūng, °'syìngdz tǐng 'bàu). / She's a pretty girl, but she has a mean temper. Tā jèiwèi 'syáujye 'jǎngde mǎn 'pyàulyang; kěshr °'píchyer jēn 'lìhai (°píchyer jēn 'syūng, °'píchyer jēn 'hwài, °tǐng nán'chánde, °tǐng bùhǎu'rěde, °'syìngdz tǐng 'bàudzau). / I'd borrow some of his books if he weren't so mean about them. Tā yàushr bú nèmma °'syǎuchi (°'lìnsè), wǒ jyòu gēn tā 'jyè jiběr 'shū le. / It was mean of him to put his child to bed without any supper, even if she had been misbehaving. Jyòushr háidz 'táu dyǎr 'chǐ, 'tā nèmma 'bùgěi 'fàn chr̄ jyòu jyàu 'háidz shwèi'jyàu yě 'wèimyǎn tài °'hěn le (°hěn'syīn le). / This is the meanest job I've ever done. Wǒ yí'syàng méi dzwògwo dzěmma °'máfande (°'bùhǎu'bànde, °nán'bànde, °'jyàurénwéi-'nánde) 'sher̀.

Feel mean (about having done something) jywéde méi'yìsz, jywéde bú'dwèi, jywéde °dwèibu'chǐ (°dwèibu'jù). / I felt mean about hurting her feelings that way. Wǒ jyàu tā 'nèmma nán'shòu, 'jēn shr̀ jywéde °méi'yìsz (°bú'dwèi, °dwèibu'chǐ tā, °dwèibu'jù tā).

No mean is expressed in ways similar to some of the above, as not small bùshǎu, not easy bùrúngyi, etc. / That mountain range is no mean obstacle. Yàu syàng 'gwò nèige shān'líng °'búshr 'rúngyide 'sher̀ (°'nánje ne, °'nánlechyù le).

The mean (average) 'píngjywūn. / The mean temperature here is 65°F. 'Tsz̀dì 'píngjyūn 'wēndù 'Hwáshr̀ 'lyòushr̀'wǔ dù.

The golden mean (as a teaching) 'jūngyūngjr̄'dàu. / Confucius is best known for his teaching of the golden mean. Hěn'dwō rén dōu jr̄dàu 'Kǔngdzde 'jūngyūngjr̄dàu.

Means (a method) fǎr or fa in combination with many verbs. / We've got to find some means of getting him out of here. Dzámen yí'dìng děi syǎng'fǎr bǎ tā sùngdau 'byéchùr chyu.

By all means yídìng, chyānwàn. / By all means look up my brother when you get to Peiping. Dàule Běi'píng °yí'dìng (°chyǎn'wàn) yàu jáu wǒ lǎu'dì chyu 'tántan, a!

By no means tsái, jywé, bìng followed by a negative. / That's by no means the end of the matter. 'Nèi sher̀ 'tsái méi'wán ne. or 'Nèi sher̀ 'tsái bùnéng swàn 'wánle ne. or 'Nei sher̀ °'jywé (°'bìng) bùnéng swàn 'wán le.

MEASURE. (Of linear dimensions) lyáng yilyang; (specifically of length) 'lyáng yilyang (kàn) yǒu 'dwō cháng; (of width) 'lyáng yilyang (kàn) yǒu 'dwō kwān; (of height) 'lyáng yilyang (kàn) yǒu 'dwō gāu; (in inches) 'lyáng yilyang (kàn) yǒu 'dwōshǎu 'tswùn (etc. for other units); (estimate by the eye) °gúlyang (°'gūjì, or in Peiping °gūme) yísyàr yǒu 'dwō cháng (etc. for other dimensions or by various units) or °'kàn yikàn (°'chyáu yichyáu) yǒu 'dwō cháng (etc.). / We'll have to measure the room before we buy the rug. Déi bǎ 'wūdz 'lyáng yilyang dzài mǎi dǐ'tǎn. / Measure it from here to there. Tsúng jèr dàu 'nàr lyáng yilyang yǒu 'dwō cháng. / Have you measured (yourself to see) how much cloth you'll need for the suit? Nǐ 'lyáng yilyang 'shēndz, kàn dzwò 'yìshēn děi yùng 'dwōshǎu 'bù le ma? / He measured the distance with his eye. Tā (syīnli) °'gūlyangle (°'gūjìle, °'gūmele) yísyàr yǒu dwō 'ywǎn. or Tā °'gūlyangle (°etc.) yísyàr yǒu dwōshǎu 'chr ywǎn. or Tā °'kànle kàn (°'chyáule chyáu) yǒu dwō 'ywǎn.

(Have linear dimensions of) is expressed only by stating the dimensions. / This kitchen measures sixteen by ten feet. 'Jèige chúfáng shr'lyòuchǐ 'cháng 'shrchǐ 'kwān. or 'Jèige chúfáng 'cháng(sya)li yǒu shr'lyòuchǐ, 'kwān(sya)li yǒu 'shrchǐ.

Measure (out) (a specific quantity) 'dàuchū (measure out and pour out of the measuring container); 'chéngchū (measure out and leave in the container). / First measure (out) a cup of sugar. Syān °'dàuchū (°'chéngchū) yìbēi 'táng lai.

A measure of capacity is expressed by specific words for such measures. / Take the rice in this peck measure. Bǎ 'mǐ ná jèige 'dǒu chéngje 'náchyu ba.

(Measurement of the circumference of part of the body) 'jōuwéi. / What's your waist measure? Nǐ 'yāu nar 'jōuwéi dwōshǎu 'tswùn?

(In music) pāi. / Begin singing after the four-measure introduction. 'Szpāi yǐ 'wán jyòu 'chàngchilai.

(Law) 'fǎlìng. / Taxes under the new measures will be very high. 'Syīn fǎlìng bǎ shwèi hwèi 'tíde hěn 'gāude.

In some measure 'dwōshǎu. / The mistake was in some measure my fault. Jèige tswèr 'dwōshǎu °gēn 'wó yǒu 'gwānsyi (°shr̀ yīnwei 'wǒ nàuchūlaide).

To a great measure yì'dwōbàr, yí'dàbufen. / The plan was his idea to a great measure. Nèige 'bànfa °yì'dwōbàr (°yí'dàbufen) shr̀ 'tā syǎngchūlaide.

Measures (methods of operation) fāngfa, 'shǒudwàn; **take strong measures** lái 'yìngde, yùng 'yìng (dyar)de 'shǒudwàn. / The doctor took measures to stop the bleeding. Dàifu yùngle syē 'fāngfa bá syě 'jřjù. / We'll have to take strong measures. Dzámen děi lái 'yìngde. or Dzámen děi yùng 'yìng dyarde 'shǒudwàn.

MEAT. ròu. / I want the meat well done. 'Ròu wó 'syǐhwan jáde °'tòu (°'lǎu) yìdyar.

(Of a nut) rér.

(Substance) 'nèirúng. / There's very little meat in that book. Nèiběn 'shū 'méiyou shémma 'nèirúng.

MEDICINE. yàu. / Did the doctor give you any medicine for your cold? Nǐ shāng'fēng, 'dàifu gěi ni 'yàu méiyou? / Are you taking medicine? Nǐ dzài chř 'yàu ma?

Practice medicine syíngyǐ. / He's practiced medicine here for twenty years. Tā dzài 'jèr syíng'yǐ syíngle 'èrshr'nyán le.

Study medicine sywéyǐ.

Take one's medicine (fig.) chř kǔtou. / You started the quarrel; now take your medicine. Shr̀ 'nǐ syān yàu 'chǎude; syàndzài nǐ 'dzjǐ chř 'kǔtou ba.

MEET (MET). (For the first time, especially by introduction) jyàn(myàn), jyànjyan-(myàn), hwèi(myàn), hwèihwei(myàn); often expressed with introduce jyèshau, 'yīn-jyàn. / I want you to meet her one of these days. 'Gwò lyǎngtyān wǒ jyàu nǐmen °jyànjyan (°'hwèige) 'myàn. or 'Gwò lyǎngtyān wǒ géi nǐmen °'jyèshau jyèshau (°'jyànjyan, °'yǐnjyan yǐnjyan). / I'd like you to meet my friend Mr. Lù. (expressed desire, with Mr. Lù not present) Wó syǎng géi 'nǐ gēn wǒde yíwèi syǐng 'Lù de péngyou °'jyèshau jyèshau (°'yǐnjyan yǐnjyan). or Wǒ ywànyi nǐ gēn wǒde syǐng 'Lù de péngyou °'jyàn yijyàn (°'hwèi yihwèi, °'jyànjyàn ('myàr), °'hwèihwèi'myàr). (actual introduction) Wǒ 'géi nǐmen °'jyèshau jyèshau (°'jyàn yijyàn, °'yǐnjyan yǐnjyan); jèi shr wǒde péngyou 'Lùsyānsheng. /When you've met and talked to him, you'll know what I mean. Déng nǐ gēn tā jyànle 'myàr, yǐ 'tán jyòu 'jīdau wǒ 'shwōde shr shémma 'yìsz le. /We've never met before, have we? Dzámen yǐ-'chyán °'méijyàngwo (°'méi hwèigwo) ba? /Have we ever met! Why, we were brought up together! Wǒmen 'hwèigwo méiyou! 'Hǎu! Wǒmen yí'kwàr jǎng'dàle de! /Come over here; I want you to meet a friend of mine. 'Gwòlai; wǒ géi nǐ 'jyèshau yíwèi 'péngyou. /I'd like to meet your friend. Wǒ hén 'syǎng °'jyànjyan (°'hwèihwei) nǐ 'nèiwèi 'péngyou. /We met once long ago. Wǒmen 'hǎu jyòu yǐ-'chyán °'jyàngwo (°'hwèigwo) yítsz ('myàr). /Haven't we met before? Dzámen dzài 'nǎr °'jyàngwo (°'hwèigwo) ba? /Have you two met before? Nǐmen 'lyǎngge rén yǐ'chyán 'hwèigwo ma? /I'm glad to meet you. is expressed as Long respected, long respected (your name). 'Jyóuyǎng, jyóuyǎng.

(Get together as prearranged; informal, mainly of just two people) jyàn, hwèi, (Peiping) pēngtóu; (informal, of more than two persons, when after meeting they go on elsewhere or do something) hwèichí, chyùchí; (formal, large-scale) 'jyùjí, jyùhwèi, kāihwèi. /I'll meet you (one person) there at eight. Dzámen 'bādyǎn dzài nǎr °'jyàn (°'hwèi, °hwèi'myàn, °jyàn'myàn, °pèng'tóu). /I'll meet you all there at eight. Wǒ 'bādyǎn 'dàunèr gēn nǐmen °jyàn'myàn (°hwèi'myàn, °hwèi'chí, °jyù-'chí). /We'll meet at his place at eight and then go to the meeting together. Dzámen 'bādyǎn dzài 'tā jyā °chyù'chí °jyù'chí, °jyù'jí, °hwèi'myàn), ránhòu yí'kwàr chyù kāi'hwèi. /We're going to meet next Tuesday (referring to a formal group). Dzámen 'syàsyǐngchǐ'èr °kāi'hwèi (°jyù'hwèi).

(Come across by chance) yùjyan, pèngjyan, sometimes kànjyan. /Did you meet anyone on the road? Dzài 'lùshang °'kànjyan (°'yùjyan, °'pèngjyan) shémma 'rén le méiyou?

(Receive; at a station, etc.) jyē, yíng; (go out of one's house to receive a visitor; a Chinese custom) 'yíngjyē; (welcome, formal) 'hwānyíng. /Is anybody going to meet them at the train? Yǒurén dàu °'chēshang (°chē'jàn) chyù °'jyē (°'yíngjyē, °'hwānyíng, °yíng) tāmen ma? /He came out to the gate to meet us. (informal) Tā dàule dà'mén nàr chyù 'jyē °wǒmen (or (formal) °'yíng wǒmen, °'yíngjyē wǒmen). /A bus meets the train outside the station. Hwǒ'chē 'dàu de shrhou, you 'gūnggùng-chì'chē dzài chējàn 'wàitou °'jyē (or (waiting) °'děng). /I've sent a car to meet him at the station. Wó 'dǎfāle yílyàng 'chē chyù dzài chē'jàn nàr °jyē (°'děng) tā.

(Of a court) kāitíng. /The court doesn't meet again until next week. Fǎ'ywàn syàsyǐng'chǐ tsái dzài kāi'tíng.

(Of a class) shàngkè. /This class meets every Monday and Thursday. Jèi'bān měisyǐngchǐ'yǐ hé syǐngchǐ'sz shàng'kè.

(Of rivers) hélyóu, hwèidzai yí'kwàr, hédzai yí'kwàr. /The two rivers meet below the city. Lyǎngtyáu 'hé dzài chéng 'nèibyar °hé'lyóu °hwèidzai yí'kwàr.

(Of roads; if two roads combine) 'héchéng 'yìtyáu 'lù, 'bìngchéng 'yìtyáu 'lù, 'hédzài yí'kwàr, 'bìngdzài yí'kwàr; (if two or more roads intersect) 'jyāuchā, 'jyāuchà; (if three roads meet at approximately 60-degree angles without intersecting) expressed as three-fork corner 'sānchàlù'kǒur. /The two roads meet three miles from here. (if they combine) Lí 'jèr 'sānli dì 'lyǎngtyáu 'lù °'héchéng (°'bìngchéng) 'yìtyáu 'lù. or (if they cross) Lí 'jèr 'sānli dì 'lyǎngtyáu 'lù °'jyāuchā (°'jyāuchà). /I'll meet you where the three roads meet. (if they all intersect at a point) Dzámen dzài 'sāntyáu 'lù 'jyāuchā de nǎr 'jyàn. or (if they come together without crossing) Dzámen dzài 'sānchàlù'kǒur nàr 'jyàn.

(Of areas) jyēshang, fēnjyè. / My field meets his at that fence. Wǒde 'dì gēn 'tāde dzài nèidàu 'líba nǎr °'jyēshang (°fēn'jyè). / Our two fields meet at that fence. Wǒmen 'lyǎngjyārde 'dì dzài nèidàu 'líba nǎr °'jyēshang (°fēn'jyè).

Meet bills fù. / We have only enough to meet this month's bills. Wǒmen 'gāng gòu fù 'jèiywède 'kāisyāu(de chyán).

Meet demands gěi; (only a demand for money) gěide'chǐ, gěide'lyǎu. / Can you meet their demands? Tāmen 'yàude nǐ 'dōu néng °'gěi ma (°gěide'chǐ ma, °gěide-'lyǎu ma)? / Did you agree to meet all their demands? Tāmen 'yàude nǐ 'dōu 'dá-ying 'gěi le ma?

Meet one's death is expressed as die sž. / She met her death in a street accident. Tā dzài 'jyēshang jyǎu'chē °'jwǎngsžde (°'yàsžde).

Meet someone **halfway** (compromise) gēn . . . jéjūng. / I'll meet you halfway; you pay for the dinner, but I'll buy the tickets for the show. OK? Wǒ gēn nǐ jéjūng ba, 'nǐ géi 'fànchyán, 'wǒ mái syì'pyàu, 'hǎu buhǎu?

Make ends meet. / He can barely make ends meet. is expressed as He barely manages to eat. Tā 'yě jyòushr gāng gòu 'jyáugūr. *See also* **MAKE.**

A meet hwèi. / Are you going to the swimming meet? 'Yóuyúng bǐsài'hwèi nǐ 'chyù buchyù?

MELT. hwà; (technical chemical term) rúng. / The ice in my glass has all melted. Wǒ 'bēidzlide 'bīng dōu 'hwàle. / The candy is melting from the heat. 'Táng 'rède 'hwàle.

Melt something bǎ . . . °gěi'hwàle (°nùng'hwàle). / Melt the chocolate first. Syān bá chyáugēlìtáng °gěihwàle (°nùng'hwàle). / The sun melted the candles. 'Tàiyang bǎ là °gěi'hwàle (°nùng'hwàle).

Melt away (of a crowd) sàn. / The crowd melted away when the police came. Jǐng'chá láile dà'jyā jyòu 'sànle.

MEMBER. hwèiywán; when referring to a member of an organization the specific name of which does not end in hwèi, hwèi is replaced by the element which is found at the end of the name of the organization, such as shè club, dwèi team, dǎng party, twán corps, etc. / What organizations are you a member of? Nǐ shr shémma 'hwèide hwèi'ywán? / Only members are allowed. Jwān wèi hwèi'ywán jr 'yùng. / I'd like to be a member. Wó 'syǎng dzwò hwèi'ywán. / He is a member of a literary club. Tā shr gè 'wényìshède shèywán.

MEMORY. jìsying; or expressed verbally as remember jǐ or as forget wàng, wàngji or as recall syangchilai. / My memory isn't very good. Wǒ 'jìsying °búda 'hǎu (°tīng 'hwài). / My memory for names isn't very good. Wǒ jǐ rén'míngdz lǎu jìbu-'jù. / His memory is bad (due to old age or some such condition). Tā ài 'wàng. or Tā 'lǎu ài 'wàng. or Tā 'lǎu jìbu'jù. / He has a clear memory of the accident. Nèi shèr tā 'jìde hěn 'chīngchu. / Do you have any memory of that? Nèige nǐ 'jì-de ma? / The old man lost his memory (entirely). Lǎu'tóur 'shémma dōu °'wàngle (°bú'jìdele, °jìbú'jùle). / That's never happened before to my memory. Jyù wǒ 'jìde de, yǐchyán 'méiyǒugwo 'dzèmmayàngde 'shèr. or Wǒ 'bújìde 'yǒugwo 'dzèmmayàngde 'shèr. / I'll certainly have pleasant memories of this town (of having lived here). Wǒ yí'dìng °'cháng jìde (°cháng syǎngchilai, °wàngbu'lyǎu, °bùnéng 'wàngji) dzài jèige dìfang jùde 'dwōme yǒu 'yìsz.

In memory of, in one's memory 'jìnyàn. / This tablet was put up in his memory. Jèige 'páidz shr wèi 'jìnyan tā de. / This monument is erected in memory of the men who were killed in action for their country. (a statement) Nèi shr 'jìnyan °'jèn-

wáng (°'wēigwójwān'chyū de) 'gwānbīng lì de 'bēi. *or* (an inscription) 'Jènwáng-
'jyàngshř 'jìnyan'bēi.

MENTION. (Speak) shwō; (bring up) tá, shwōchilai. / He didn't mention the price. Tā
méishwō 'jyàr. / Did the teacher mention my name? Syānsheng tí wǒde 'míngdz
méiyou? / Now that you mention it, (I remember) I did hear him say that. Nǐ nèmma
yì 'shwō, jyàu wó 'syǎngchilaile'tā 'jēn nèmma shwō láije. / Don't mention it in
his presence. Jèige dzài 'tā myànchyán kě byé 'shwō. / Don't mention it! 'Syàu
shèr, jŕbude yì 'tí. *or* Syàu yìsz. *or* 'Méi shémma.

MERCHANT. shāng, 'shāngrén, dzwò'mǎimaide. / Who are the leading merchants of
this town? Jèige dìfang °'dàshāngrén dōu shř 'shéi (°'dàshāngjyā dōu yóu 'nèiji-
jyār)?

　　Merchant ship *or* marines (shāng)chwán.

MERELY. Expressed as only 'búgwò *or* entirely 'wánchywán, 'chwúntswèi, *or* (with a
negative) yì'dyár yě. / This is merely a formality. Jèi 'búgwo shř °děi 'jǐng
dzèmma ge 'shǒusyù jyòu shřle (°jàu 'gwēijyu děi dzèmma 'bàn). / This is merely
red tape. Jèi 'búgwo shř 'lǐsyínggūng'shř jyòu 'shřle. / I ran into him merely by
chance. Wǒ 'pèngjyan tā 'wánchywán shř 'yùnchi. *or* Wǒ °yì'dyár yě ('wánchywán)
méisyǎng'dàu hwèi 'pèngjyan tā.

　　See also **ONLY, JUST.**

MESSAGE. (Oral) hwà; (written) syìn, syèr; (note) tyáur. / Is there a message for
me? Yǒu rén gěi wo lyóu'hwà méiyou? / I want to leave a message. Wǒ yàu lyóu
ge'tyáur. / Could you take a message? Láujyà, gěi tā lyóu ge 'hwàr, syíng ma?

　　(Significant idea) dàuli. / His book has a strong message. Tāde 'shūli yóu
hěn 'shēnde 'dàuli.

METAL. 'jīnshǔ, tyě (which usually means iron); **the metals** wǔjīn. / I'd rather have
the metal desk. Wǒ 'ywànyi yàu nèige 'tyějwōdz. / This is a dull metal. Jèijǔng
'jīnshǔ búlyàng.

METHOD. fádz, bànfa, fāngfa; **method of X-ing** X-fǎ *or* (if X is a longer expression
in Chinese) X-de 'bànfa. / Your method here is new to me. Nǐ 'jèige bànfa wó yǐ-
'chyán 'dàu bùjř'dàu. / I don't understand your method of bookkeeping. Wǒ bù'dúng
nǐ jì'jàng de 'fádz. / He's learning the language much quicker by this new method.
Tā yùng jèige 'syīn 'fádz sywé jèijǔng 'hwà bí yǐ'chyán sywéde 'kwàidwō le.

MIDDLE. (Of a space) dāngjyàr, dāngjūng, jūngjyàr. / You'll find them in the middle
room. Tāmen dōu dzài °dāng'jyàrde (°dāng'jūngde, °jūngjyàrde) nèijyān 'wūrli ne.
or Nǐ dàu °dāng'jyàrde (°etc.) 'wūrli jyòu 'jǎujau tāmen le. / It's in the middle of
the street. Dzài jyède °dāng'jūng (°dāng'jyàr, °jūng'jyàr) nèi 'kwàr. / Put the vase
in the middle of the table. Bǎ hwā'píng bǎidzài 'jwōdzde dāng'jūng. / He drove in
the middle of the road. Tā dzài 'lùde dāng'jūng nàr kāi'chē. / Take the middle road.
Dzǒu °dāng'jūngde (°jūng'jyàrde) nèityáu 'lù. / He parts his hair in the middle. Tā
'tóufa dzài dāng'jūng °fēnde (°fēnkāi). / The middle part of the Yangtze Valley is
very densely populated. 'Chāngjyānglyóu'yù dāng'jūng yidài rénkǎo hěn 'mì.

　　(Of an action) is expressed as just then (doing something) jèng, 'jèngdzài; or as
not finished méi . . . 'wán; or as half done . . . (dàu) yí'bàr, . . . dàu bàn'jyérshang.
/ I'm in the middle of packing. Wǒ °jèng (°'jèngdzài) dǎ 'syíngli. *or* Wó dǎ 'syíngli
'gāng dǎ °le yí'bàr (°dàu bàn'jyérshang). / In the middle of the battle our planes
arrived. 'Nèi jàng jèng °'dǎje (°dǎdàu yí'bàr de shŕhou) wǒmende fēi'jǐ dàule.

/Don't interrupt me in the middle of my work. Wǒ °'jèng (°'jèngdzài) dzwò'shèr, byé'jyáu wǒ. *or* Wǒ shèr jèng dzwòdàu °bàn'jyérshang (°yí'bàr), byé 'jyáu wǒ. /He broke off in the middle of a sentence. Tā yíjyù 'hwà °méishwō'wán (°shwōle yí'bàr, °shwōdàu bàn'jyérshang) jyòu bù'shwōle. /They called him away while he was in the middle of dinner. Tā °'jèng chřje 'fàn (°'jèngdzài chřje 'fàn, °chř'fàn gāng chřdàu yíbàr) tāmen jyòu bǎ tā jyàu'dzǒule.

Around the middle (of the body) is expressed by reference to the waist yāu *or* the belt dùdz. /He's put on weight around the middle. Tā 'yāu nar 'tsūle. *or* Tā 'dùdz 'dàchǐlaile. or more politely expressed as He's put on weight. Tā fā'fúle.

In the middle (involuntarily involved) is expressed as in the first paragraph above. /A fight started and I was right in the middle. Tāmen dǎchǐ 'jyà lai de shřhou °wǒ jèng dzài dāng 'jūng ne (°bǎ wǒ jyàdzài dāngjūng le, °etc.).

In the middle of (in the thick of, involved in) jyārù, dzài 'lǐtou gwǒje, 'gwǒdàu 'lǐtouchyu. /He always manages to get in the middle of a fight. Yǐ yóu dǎ'jyàde 'shèr tā jwùn °jyā'fù (°dzài 'lǐtou gwǒje, °'gwǒdàu lǐtouchyu).

Of middle height. /He's of middle height. Tā 'jūngděng 'shēnlyang. *or* Tā 'bùgāubù'aǐde.

Middle-aged 'jūngnyán. /He's middle-aged. Tā shř ge 'jūngnyán rén.

Middle class jūngděng'jyéji.

The Middle Ages Jūngshřjì.

The middle road *or* the middle course (not extreme). /Take the middle course. Yàu 'bùpyānbù'yǐ tsái hǎu. *or* Yàu syíng 'jūngyūngjř'dàu tsái 'dwèi.

MILE. yǐnglǐ; Chinese mile lǐ. /It's three miles away. Yǒu 'sānyǐnglǐ 'lù ywǎn. /The speed limit here is thirty miles an hour. Sù'dù 'méidyǎnjūng bùnéng gwò 'sānshr'yǐnglǐ.

MILK. (General) nǎi; (of a cow) nyóunǎi. /Is the milk fresh? Nyóu'nǎi 'syīnsyān busyīnsyān?

(Of a coconut) jř. /Will you help me get the milk out of this coconut? 'Bāng 'máng bǎ jèige 'yēdzde 'jř 'nùngchulai, hǎu ma?

Milkman sùngnyóunǎide.

To milk (of cows) jǐ nyóunǎi. /Do you know how to milk a cow? Nǐ 'hwèi buhwèi jǐ nyóu'nǎi? /Is it time to milk the cows? Shř 'jǐ nyóu'nǎi de shřhour ma? (fig.) /The officials milked the treasury year after year. Yǐnyányǐ'nyánde jř'ywánmen lōule bù'shǎu gūng'kwǎn.

MILL. (Machine) is expressed in compounds as X mill mwò 'X de jīchi. /Some stores have coffee mills. Yǒusye 'pùdzli you mwò °kāfēi (°jyā'fēi) de jīchi.

(Establishment for grinding, particularly grain) mwòfáng. /There's a flour mill the other side of the bridge. Chyáude 'nèibyan yǒu ge myàn'fēn mwò'fáng.

(Manufacturing plant) gūngchǎng; chǎng if type of plant is specified. /How many people work in the mill? Jèige gūng'chǎngli yǒu 'dwōshau rén dzwò'gūng? /They're building a new cotton mill on the edge of town. Dzài jèige 'dìfangde 'byānjìng tāmen syǎng yàu 'bàn yige 'myánhwā'chǎng.

Have been through the mill (fig.) gwòlaile, aúgwolaile. /He's been through the mill already and he knows what he's talking about. Tā shr 'gwòláirén, tā shwōde dōushr yǒu 'jīngyàn de hwà. /I've just been through the mill. 'Syàndzài wó 'dzǔng-swàn 'aúgwolaile.

To mill (grind) mwò. /The baker here mills his own flour. Jèrde dzwòmyàn-'bāude 'dżjǐ mwò'fén.

(Manufacture or produce) chū. /How much steel does that plant mill per month? Nèige gūng'chǎng yíge 'ywè chū 'dwōshau gāng?

Mill around or **about** 'jǐlái'jǐchyù, 'jwànláijwànchyù. /The crowd milled around waiting for the parade to begin. Nèichyún 'rén 'jǐlái'jǐchyù, 'děngje yóu'syíng 'kāishr.

MILLION. bǎiwàn.

MIND. (Mental faculty) nǎudz (brain); 'syīnsž (thinking power); 'syīnsywě (thinking activity); syīn (thoughts, concentration; also means heart); jìsying (memory); often expressed indirectly as think syǎng; **a quick mind** also 'jíjr or expressed as quick and clever jīlingde; **a good mind** also expressed as intelligent líng; also other indirect expressions. /He has a good mind. Tā °'nǎudz (°'jìsying) tǐng 'hǎu. or Tā °'syǎng de (°'syīnsž) tǐng °'syìmì (°'jōudau). or Tā hěn 'líng. /He has a very quick mind. Tā hěn 'jīlingde. or Tā 'syīnsž tǐng 'kwàide. or Tā hén yǒu 'jíjr. or Tā shémma 'shèr yí 'kàn jyòu jŕdàu syíng bu'syíng. or Tā 'syǎngde tǐng 'kwàide. or Tā shemma 'shèr yǐ 'syǎng jyòu yǒu 'bànfa. /He has a one-track mind. Tā syīnli lǎu 'ràubugwo 'wārlai. or Tā 'sžsyīn'yǎr. or Tā 'jìng dzwān nyóu'jǐjyau. /My mind isn't clear on what happened. Chū'shèr de 'chíngsyíng wǒ ('syīnli) búdà 'chīngchu. /His mind isn't on his work. Tā 'syīnli yǒu byéde 'shèr. or Tā 'jèijèr dzwò 'shèr 'syīnshén bú'dìng. /He doesn't keep his mind on his work. Tā dzwò 'shèr de shŕhou, 'syīnli yǒu byéde 'shèr. or Tā dzwò 'shèr °'syīnshén bú'dìng (°bùjwān'syīn, °bùhǎu'hǎurde). or Tā 'syīnbú'dzàiyān. /Keep your mind on your work. Yùng'syīn dzwò'shr̀. or Dzwò'shr̀ syīn yàu 'jwān.

A meeting of minds is expressed as a decision (on method) bànfa or as a conclusion 'jyēgwǒ or as agree túngyì. /Let's see if we can't reach a meeting of minds on this thing. 'Kànkan dzámen 'néng bunéng bǎ jèijyàn shèr 'shānglyang chū ge °'bànfa lai (°'jyēgwǒ lai). or 'Kànkan dzámen dzài 'jèijyàn shèrshang 'néng bunéng túng'yì.

Be out of one's mind or **lose one's mind** fēng. /She's practically out of her mind with worry. Tā °'chóude (°'jíde) jyǎn'jŕ yàu 'fēngle. /I thought I'd lose my mind with all that noise. Chǎude 'nèmma lìhai, dōu kwài bǎ wó chǎu'fēng le.

Be simple-minded shǎ. /He's a bit simple-minded. Tā yǒudyar 'shǎ.

Call to mind or **bring to mind** is expressed by saying that the person thinks of syǎngchilai. /That calls to mind a story I know. 'Nèmma yì shwō, wó 'syangchilai °ge 'syàuhwàr (or a true story) °yíjyàn 'shèr).

Change one's mind gǎi júyi; (not want it so) 'búywànyi nèmmaje. /I thought I'd go along with them, but I changed my mind. Wǒ 'ywánlái syǎng gēn tāmen yíkwàr 'gàn laije, kěshr 'hòulái °gǎile 'júyi le (°'búywànyi nèmmaje le).

Give someone a piece of one's mind °'shwō (°'mà) . . . yí'dwùn.

Have a mind of one's own. /He has a mind of his own. (of a child; a compliment) is expressed as He makes his own decisions. Tā 'nà tsái jyàu yǒu 'júyi ne. or as He can think of ways to do things. Tā tǐng néng 'dżjí syǎng 'bànfa de. or (of a child; not a compliment) expressed as He's disobedient. Tā bùtǐng'hwà. or (of an adult; a compliment) Tā hěn yǒu júyi. or expressed as He doesn't listen to what anyone says. Tā 'shéide hwà yě bù'tǐng. or as He doesn't listen to other people's advice. Tā bùtǐng rén 'chywàn. or as He's very stubborn. Tā rén tǐng 'nìngde. or as No matter what you say to him, he always follows his own advice. Píng ní 'dzěmma gēn tā shwō, tā láu yǒu yí'dìngjr̄'gwēi.

Have half a mind to or **have a good mind to** 'hén syǎng. /I've got half a mind to leave tomorrow. Wǒ 'hén syǎng 'myér jyòu 'dzǒu. /I've got half a mind to give him a good scolding. Wǒ 'hén syǎng °¹shwō (°¹mà) tā yí'dwùn. /I've got a good mind to quit. Wǒ 'hén syǎng bú'gànle.

Have one's mind set on yí'dìng yàu, 'jywédìng yàu, dǎ'dìngle 'júyi yàu, ná-'dìngle 'júyi yàu, 'yìsyīn yàu, fēi yàu . . . bù'kě. /She's got her mind set on going shopping today. Tā yídìng yàu 'jyèr chyù mǎi 'dūngsyi.

Have in mind (of a person) 'syīnli yǒu; (of a person; mean in saying something) jřje; (of an action; think about or plan) syǎng, 'dǎswàn. /Do you have anyone in mind for the job? Nèige 'wèijr nǐ °¹syīnli yǒu 'rén le ma (°syǎng gěi 'shéi ne)? or Nèige 'shèr nǐ syǎng °jyàu 'shéi dzwò a (°chū hé'shr̀de 'rén láile ma)? /Did you have her in mind when you said that? Nǐ shwō 'nèige de shŕhou shr̀ bushr̀ jřje 'tā shwō de? /What do you have in mind to do with him? 'Nèige rén nǐ °syǎng (°¹dǎswàn) yàu jyàu tā 'dzěmmaje? or 'Neige rénde shèr nǐ °syǎng (°¹dǎswàn) 'dzěmma bàn? /What did you have in mind? (to get or buy) Nǐ 'dǎswàn °yàu (°mǎi) 'shémma yàngr de?

Have something on one's mind yǒu syīnshr, 'syīnli yǒu 'shèr; (say) yǒu hwà. /What's on your mind? Ní yǒu shémma 'syīnshr? or Nǐ 'syīnli yǒu 'shémma shèr? or Ní syǎng 'shémma ne? /I think he's got something on his mind. Wǒ kàn tā °¹syīnli yǒu 'shèr (°yǒu 'syīnshr). /He's got something on his mind, but he hasn't spoken up. Tā you 'hwà 'meishwōchū'lái. /She must have had something on her mind today. Tā 'jīntyān yí'dìng shr̀ 'syīnli yǒu shémma 'shr̀laije. /I've got too much on my mind. Wǒ 'syīnli 'shèr tài 'dwō. or Jyàu wǒ dān'syīn de 'shèr tài 'dwō.

Keep in mind (of a thing) °gē(°fàng)dzài 'syīnshang (hǎule); (take care of) lyóu-'shén (hǎule); (remember) jì(de) or (not forget) 'búhwèi 'wàngle(de); (of a person, do something for) gěi . . . 'bàn yiban. /I'll keep it in mind. Wǒ 'jìde. or Wǒ 'jìje. or Wǒ 'búhwèi 'wànglede. or Wǒ lyóu'shén hǎule. or Wǒ °gē(°fàng)dzài 'syīnshang hǎule. /I'll keep you in mind. 'Nǐde shèr wǒ géi nǐ °¹lyóu dyǎr 'shén (°¹'bàn). or 'Nǐde shèr wǒ °fàng(°gē)dzài 'syīnshang hǎule.

Know one's own mind. /He doesn't know his own mind. Tā °nábú'dìng (°dǎbu-'dìng) júyi. or Tā 'yóuyíbù'jywé. or Tā lǎu °¹chóuchúbú'dìngde (°¹sānsyīnèr'yìde, °¹bùjr̄dàu dzěmmaje 'hǎu).

Make up one's mind is expressed by various constructions which include the element meaning determine dìng. /Have you made up your mind what to do about him yet? 'Nèige rénde 'shèr ní °¹syǎngchūle (°¹yǒule, °¹jywédìngle) yí'dìngde 'bànfa le ma? or 'Nèige rende 'shèr nǐ °dìng'hǎule (°syǎng'dìngle, °jywé'dìngle, °ná'dìngle 'júyi, °dǎ'dìngle 'júyi) yàu dzěmma 'bàn ma? /I've made up my mind to go, and nobody's going to stop me now. Wó 'yǐjīng °ná'dìngle 'júyi le (°dǎ'dìngle 'júyi le, °¹jwédìngle) 'fēi chyù bù'kě, 'shéi yě bùneng 'bújyàu wo 'chyù.

Not be able to get one's mind off or **off one's mind** or **out of one's mind** ('syīnli) lǎu °nyànjije (°¹dyànjije, °¹dyànnyanje, °¹syǎngje, °¹gwànyanje, °wàngbu'lyǎu) or (of a thing, thinking over) lǎu 'pánswàn or (of a person) lǎu 'chyāngwàje. /I can't get my mind off my office work at night. Dàule 'yèli, wǒ 'syīnli haishr lǎu 'nyànjije 'gūngshr̄'fánglide 'shèr. /I can't get her out of my mind. Wǒ ('syīnli) lǎu 'dyànjije tā.

Slip one's mind is expressed by saying that the person forgets (gěi) wàng. /I planned to do it, but it slipped my mind. Wó °¹dǎswàn (°¹syǎng) dzwò laije, kěshr yísyàdz (gěi) 'wàngle.

To one's mind (from one's point of view) jyù . . . kàn, . . . jywéje, . . . kàn. / To my mind, the job will take at least a week. °Jyù 'wŏ kàn (°'Wŏ jywéje, °'Wŏ kàn) jèi shèr 'jr̀sháu dĕi yìsyĭng'chĭ tsái dzwòde'wán. / To my mind he seems sort of simple. °'Wŏ jywéje (°Jyù 'wŏ kàn, °'Wŏ kàn) tā yŏudyar 'shăbujyērde.

To mind (take charge of; of persons or things) kān, jàuying; (of persons) gwăn; (of things) 'jàulyàu. / Mind the store for me while I go to lunch, will you? Láu'jyà, wŏ chyù chr̄'fàn de shŕhou, géi wŏ °'jàuyingje dyar (°'kānje dyar, °'jàulyàuje dyar) 'pùdz. / Will you mind the baby for a while? Nĭ géi wŏ °'kān (°'gwăn, °'jàu-ying) yìhwér syău'hár, syíng ma? / Mind your own business. is expressed (mildly) as Mind other people's business less. 'Sháu gwăn °'byérende 'shèr (°'syànshèr). or (more strongly) as Why should you mind (this)? Nĭ 'gwănde'jáu ma? or as What's it to you? °Āi (°Yóu) 'nĭ shémma 'shèr?

(Obey; of obeying a person) tīnghwà, tīng . . . de'hwà; hău (be good); shŏu (of obeying laws). / Mind your mother. Tīng nĭ 'mŭchinde 'hwà. or Mŭchin shwō de 'hwà yàu 'tīngje. / The child won't mind anybody. Syău'hár gēn 'shéi dōu bùhău. / He doesn't mind. Tā bùtīng'hwà. / You have to mind the laws when you drive here. Dzài 'jèikwàr kāi'chē °déi shŏu 'gwēijyu (°dĕi shóu'fă, °bùnéng bùshŏu 'gwēijyu).

(Be careful) 'syāusyīn; (watch out for) chyáuje, 'kànje, dĭfangje. / Mind how you cross the street. Gwò'jyē de shŕhou 'syāusyīnje dyar. / Mind the traffic when you cross the street. Gwò'jyē de shŕhou °'chyáu(°'kàn, °'dĭfang)je dyar 'chē a 'mă de.

(Care about or dislike; of active dislike) (syīnli) 'dzàihu, (syīnli) bú'ywànyi; **not mind** (be agreeable) is expressed as not matter (see **MATTER**) or as be OK syíng. / Are you sure you don't mind? Nĭ 'jēn bú'dzàihu ma? / Do you mind work-ing with him? Nĭ gēn 'tā yíkwàr dzwò'shr̀ °syīnli 'ywànyi ma (°syīnli 'dzàihu budzàihu)? / I wouldn't mind taking the trip alone, except that I don't have enough money with me. Wŏ 'dzgér chyù yìtang dàu °búyàu'jĭn (°yĕ 'méi shémma), 'búgwo wŏ 'shēnshang dài de 'chyán búgòu'hwāde. / I don't mind going alone. Wŏ dz̀'gér chyù, jyòu dz̀'gér chyù ba. or Wŏ dz̀'gér chyù yĕ 'méi shémma. or 'Méi °gwānsyi (°shémma), wŏ dz̀'gér chyù 'hăule. / Would you mind working over there for a few minutes? Láu'jyà dàu 'nèibyār chyu dzwò hwer, 'syíng busyíng?

Never mind. / Never mind. meaning It isn't important. 'Búyàujĭn. or Swānle. or 'Méi shémma. or 'Méi shèr. or meaning You don't have to do it. 'Búyùng gwănle. or (said in a sour way) Hău ba. or 'Bùgwăn jyòu bù'gwăn ba. or 'Āi gwăn bù'gwăn ba. / Never mind that. 'Nèi yùngbujáu nĭ tsáu'syīn. / Never mind what THEY say. 'Byé gwăn 'tāmen dzĕmma shwō. or 'Béng 'lĭ 'tāmen. or Tāmen dzĕmma 'shwō jyòu jyàu tāmen 'shwōchyu ba. or Tāmen 'ài dzĕmma shwō, dzĕmma 'shwō ba. or 'Swéi tāmen dzĕmma 'shwōchyu ba.

MINE. (Belonging to me) see **I.**

(Of minerals) kwàng; **X mine** X'kwàng. / Who owns this mine? Jèige 'kwàng shr̀ 'shéide? / We get our coal from the mines around here. Wŏmende 'méi shr̀ 'fùjìnde méi'kwàngli láide.

(Rich source; fig.). / He's a mine of information. is expressed as He knows everything. Tā 'shémma dōu 'jr̄dau. / This book is a mine of information. is ex-pressed as This book contains a great many facts. Jèibĕn 'shūli yóu hĕndwōhĕn-'dwōde shr̀'shŕ. / He's a mine of information about this locality. is expressed as He's a map. Tā shr̀ ge dìlĭ'tú.

To mine a mineral, expressed as produce such-and-such a mineral product chū . . . 'kwàngwù or as open (or operate) such-and-such a mine kāi . . . 'kwàng.

/What do they mine around here? 'Jèr 'chū shémma 'kwàngwù? /This company has mined iron here for years. Jèige gūng'sż dzài 'jèr kāi tyě'kwàng kāile hǎusyē 'nyán le.

MINUTE. (One-sixtieth of an hour) jūng with measure fēn; (one-sixtieth of a degree) fēn. /I'll be back in five minutes. Wǒ 'wǔfēnjūng jyòu 'hwéilai. /They can't wait more than twenty minutes. Tāmen 'jř néng 'děng 'èrshrfēnjūng. /The ship is five degrees and forty minutes off its course. 'Chwán 'dzǒude gēn hángsyàn 'chàle 'wǔdù 'sżshrfēn.

(Short period of time) hwěr. /He'll only be a minute. Tā 'jř yàu yì'hwěr. /We can only see you for a minute. Wǒmen 'jř néng gēn nín tán yì'hwěr。 /Can you give me a minute of your time? is expressed as Do you have some leisure so I can have a word with you? Nín yǒu 'gūngfu ma? Wǒ 'gēn nín shwō yíjyù 'hwà.

The last minute 'línlyǎu, mwò'lyǎur. /Don't leave everything to the last minute. Byé bǎ 'shémma dōu 'děngdàu °'línlyǎu (°mwò'lyǎur) tsái dzwò.

The minute (that) yī . . . jyòu . . . . /Call the hotel the minute you get home. Nǐ yi hwéi'jyā, jyòu gěi lyú'gwǎnli dǎ dyàn'hwà. /You'll know the house the minute you see it. Nǐ yí 'kànjyan nèige 'fángdz jyòu 'rènde le.

Up to the minute dzwèijìnde. /The news in this paper is up to the minute. Jèige bàu'jřlide 'syīnwén shr dzwèi'jìnde.

Minutes (of a meeting) 'jìlù. /Who's taking the minutes of the meeting? Kāi-'hwèi 'shé jì 'jìlù? /Have the minutes of the last meeting been read yet? 'Shàngtsż kāi'hwèide 'jìlù yǐjing 'nyànle méiyou?

MINUTE. (Very small) syǎu. /It's hard to read the minute print in this book. 'Shū-shangde syǎu'dż hěn nán nyàn. /The engineer knows every minute detail of the new machine. Jèige syīn 'jīchr rèn shémma 'syǎu dìfangr gūngchíng'shr dōu dǔngde.

MIRROR. jìngdz. /Is there a mirror in the bathroom? Dzǎu'fáng yǒu yímyàn 'jìngdz ma?

Be mirrored 'fǎnjàu. /The trees on the bank are mirrored in the lake. 'Húbyān 'shùmùde 'dàuyǐng 'fǎnjàu dzai 'shwéili.

MISS. (With a missile or bullet) is expressed by negative forms of dǎjùng, dǎjáu, jùng; (by collision) jwàng, 'jwàngjáu, jwàngshang; **miss by** a certain distance °dǎde (°jwàngde) chàle . . . or °dǎde (°jwàngde) lí . . . yòu . . . . /He missed twice, but he finally made a hit. 'Lyǎngsyàr dōu méidǎ'jáu, dì'sānsyàr ké °'dǎshàngle (°'dǎ-jáule, °'jùngle). /The truck just missed (hitting) the boy. 'Dàchī'chē °chà'dyǎr (°chàyi'dyǎr, °syànyi'dyǎr) (méi)bǎ syǎuhár 'jwàngle. /His shot missed the bird by at least five feet. Tā nèi chyāng 'dǎde (nàr) lí 'nyǎur 'jřshǎu yóu 'wúchř. /His shot missed by at least five feet. Tā nèichyāng dǎde 'jřshǎu chàle 'wúchř.

(Not hear, or not understand) expressed by negative forms of tīngjyàn (hear) or tīngdǔng, tīngmíngbai, tīngchīngchu (hear with understanding) or tīngchīngchu (hear clearly) or dǔng, míngbai, chīngchu (have an understanding). /I missed that last remark. 'Gāng shwō de nèijyù 'hwà wǒ méitīng'jyàn.

(Not see, or not find) expressed by negative forms of 'chyáujyàn, 'kànjyàn (see) or 'jǎujáu (find); **don't miss** (seeing) byé °'wàngle (°yàu 'jìje, °yàu) 'kànkan. /I missed you at the meeting last night. Dzwér 'wǎnshang kāi'hwèi wǒ méi °'chywáu-jyàn (°'jǎujau nǐ). or expressed as Hey! How come you weren't at the meeting last night? Hēi! Dzwér 'wǎnshang nèige 'hwèi ní dzěmma méi'dàu a? /I missed him at the hotel, so I went on to the station. Wǒ dàu lyú'gwǎnli méi °chyáujyàn (°'jǎujau) tā; (wǒ) jyòu yǐ'jŕ dàu chē'jàn chyùle. or expressed as When I got to the hotel he had already left, so . . . . Wǒ dàu lyú'gwǎn de shŕhou tā yǐjīng 'dzǒule; . . . . /Don't miss seeing the Confucian temple when you get to that town. Dàule 'nèige 'dìfang, yí'dìng byé °'wàngle (°yàu 'jìje, °yàu) kànkan Kúngdz'myàu. /It's just around the next corner; you can't miss it. 'Yì gwǎi'wār jyòu 'shŕ; 'méi ge jàubu-'jáude.

(Fail) see **FAIL, SUCCEED.** /You can't miss. (of physical aim) (Nǐ) yí'dìng °dǎde'shàng (°dǎde'jáu, °dǎde'jùng). or (of finding something) (Nǐ) yí'dìng jǎude-'jáu. or (because of a suggested procedure) (Nǐ) yí'dìng °bànde'hǎu (°bànde'dàu, °néngde'chéng). or (because of personal ability) 'Nǐ yídíng °bànde'hǎu (°néng'chéng, °chéng'gūng). Or all of these alternants may be used in a construction such as (Nǐ) yí'dìng búhwèi dǎbu'shàng de. or (you must not miss this time) 'Jèitsz nǐ kě 'bùnéng bàn'dzǎu le.

(Be lonesome without) is expressed as think of syǎng. /I'll miss you. Nǐ 'dzǒule wǒ yí'dìng yàu 'syǎng nǐ de. /She missed him very much. Tā 'syǎng tā syǎngde 'lìhai.

(Be at a loss without). /I miss my car. is expressed as My car's not being here is a great inconvenience. Wǒ 'chē bú'dzài jèr hěn bù'fāngbyan. /We certainly missed you while you were sick. (we were helpless) 'Nǐ nèmma yí 'bìng wǒmen °tǐng jwā'syàde (or (we didn't know how to do anything right) °dōu bùjŕdàu dzěmmaje 'hǎule). /I miss my library. is expressed as If my books were all here everything would be fine. Yàushr wǒde 'shū dōu dzài 'jèr °tsái 'hǎu ne (°dwō 'hǎu a).

Miss a chance fànggwochyu; **never miss a chance to** . . . 'méi ge shwō 'bū . . . de. /He never misses a chance to do a little business. 'Tā a, 'yì yǒu ge 'jīhwei dzwò dyár 'mǎimar, °'méiyǒu 'fànggwochyu de 'shŕhou (°'méiyǒu 'fànggwochyude nèmma yì 'shwō, °'méi ge shwō 'búdzwò de).

Miss a train (not make it) méi gǎnshang; (be delayed so that it can't be made) wù. /Do you think I'll miss my train? Nísyáng wǒ 'hwèi °gǎnbushang (°wùle) 'chē ma?

Miss something (worthwhile) is expressed as lose a chance shŕ ge jīhwei, or as what a pity (that someone wasn't there) kěsyǐ; **not miss anything** is expressed as it isn't interesting méi yìszde or as (someone's not being there) doesn't matter 'méi shémma or is all right dàuhǎu. /You sure missed something by not going with us. Nǐ jèitsz 'méi gēn wǒmen dàu nàr 'chyù 'jēn shŕ °'shŕle ge 'jīhwei (°kě 'syǐ). /Oh, you didn't miss anything by not going. Hāi! 'Búchyù °yě 'méi shémma (°dàu-'hǎu). or Hāi! 'Tǐng méi 'yìsz de.

Miss the mark when speaking 'jyǎngde ('wánchywán) °'bùjáu 'byānjì (°bùtyē 'tí, °búdwèi, °búshr nèmma hwéi 'shèr). /The speaker missed the mark completely. Yán'jyǎng de nèige rén 'jyǎngde 'wánchywán °'bùjáu 'byānjì (°bùtyē 'tí, °bú'dwèi, °búshr nèmma hwéi 'shèr).

Miss one's guess tsàitswòle, tsàide búdwèi; **unless I miss my guess** is expressed as as I see it jyù 'wǒ °chyáu (°kàn). /I missed my guess that time. Nèitsz wǒ tsàitswòle (°tsàide bú'dwèi). /Unless I miss my guess, we're going to run into some trouble. Jyù 'wǒ °chyáu (°kàn), dzámen yàu yǒu 'máfan shèr.

Be missing (lost) dyōule, bújyànle; (not able to be found) jàubujáule; (gone) 'méile shŕdzūngle; (not here) bú'dzài jèr; (not yet arrived) hái méidàu; **missing in action** is expressed as after the battle it was not clear whether he was dead or alive dzwò'jàn yǐ'hòu 'shēngsž bù'míng. /Is anything missing from your wallet? Nǐ chyán-'bāurlide dūngsyi yǒu °'dyōude ma (°bú'jyànle de ma)? /Yes, I'm missing my passport. 'Dwèile, wǒde hù'jàu 'bú'jyànle (°jàubu'jáule, °'méile, °'dyōule, °bú'dzài jèr). /Some of the crew on this ship are missing. Jèige 'chwánshang yǒu jǐge 'hǎiywán shr̄'dzūngle. /He was reported missing in action. Yǒu bàu'gàu shwō tā dzwò'jàn yǐ'hòu °'shēngsž bú'míng (°shr̄dzūngle).

A miss (failure to hit) is expressed verbally as above. /That was pretty close, but a miss is as good as a mile. °'Syàn kě 'jēn syàn (°'Sywán kě jēn 'sywán búgwo); 'jìshr méi °dǎ'jùng (°dǎ'jáu, °'jwàngjáu, °'jwàngshang) yě jyòu 'búswàn shémma le. /After two misses, he finally made a hit (fig.). 'Lyǎngtsž dōu méi'chéng; kěshr dàu-'lyǎur háishr °'chéngle (°'nèngshangle).

Miss (unmarried woman) **Miss** . . . . . . 'syáujye; (very formal) . . . 'nyǔshr̀; (of a teacher, also means Mr.) . . . syānsheng; when calling a waitress, etc., **miss** is not expressed, èi an exclamation used in getting someone's attention, is used; among the younger people of China, the English word **Miss** is sometimes used. /This is Miss Jones. (in making an introduction) Jèi shr̀ 'Jōu °syáujye (°nyǔshr̀, °syān-sheng). or (in answer to Who is this?) Wǒ syìng 'Jōu. or (in answer to Is this Miss Jones?) 'Wǒ jyòu shr̀. /We have three Miss Joneses here. Wǒmen jèr yǒu sānwèi °'Jōu syáujye (°'syáujye dōu syìng 'Jōu). /Miss Jones, come here. °'Jōu syáujye (°Miss Jōu), dàu 'jèr lái. /Will you please sit over there, miss? (Èi) 'chǐng nín °dzwòdzài 'nàr chyu (°dzài 'nèibyar dzwò).

MISTAKE (MISTOOK). tswòr; sometimes 'tswòwù, 'chàtswò, bú'dwèide difang; **make a mistake** tswò, chū ge tswèr; (in doing something) nèngtswò, nàutswò, nèngchū ge 'tswèr (etc., with other verbs meaning do); (in looking at something) kàntswò; (in recognizing someone) 'rèntswòle 'rén. /Sorry, my mistake. (in action) 'Dwèi-buchǐ, shr̀ °'wǒde tswèr (°wǒ 'tswòle). or (in mistaking identity) 'Dwèibuchǐ, wǒ rèn'tswòle 'rén le. /There must be a mistake somewhere. Yí'dìng shr̀ 'nár °yǒu ge 'tswèr (°yǒu dyǎr 'tswèr, °'tswòle, °'tswòle dyar, °yǒu (dyǎr) bú'dwèide difang, °yǒu 'tswòwù, °yóu dyǎr 'chàtswò). /There must be some mistake. Yí-'dìng °yǒu dyǎr 'tswèr ba (°nèng'tswòle ba, °nàu'tswòle ba, or (in identity) °shr̀ rèn'tswòle 'rén le ba). /Anyone could make such a mistake. 'Jèiyàngrde tswèr 'shéi dōu hwèi °'yǒu de (°'nèngdechū'lái de). /You must have made a mistake. Nǐ yí'dìng shr̀ °nèng'tswòle or (in identity) °'rèntswòle 'rén le ba. /He made a mistake. Tā chūle ge 'tswèr. or Tā nèngchule ge 'tswèr lai. or (he was completely wrong) Tā 'tswòle. or (in identity) Tā 'rèntswòle 'rén le. /What a terrible mistake to make! 'Dzěmma néng °dzwòchū (°nèngchū, °nàuchū, °bànchū) 'nèmma lìhaide ge 'tswèr lái a! or 'Dzěmma néng 'tswòdàu 'nèmma ge yàngr ne! /I made a terrible mistake. Wǒ 'nèngchu ge 'dàtswèr lai. /It's a case of mistaken identity. Shr̀ rèn'tswòle 'rén le. /That's a mistaken belief. Nèmma syǎng °bú-'dwèi (°jyòu 'tswòle). or Yàu syìn 'nèige jyòu 'tswòle. or Nèige syìn'tswòle. but /Make no mistake about it. is expressed as You can rest assured. Nǐ jyòu fàng'syīn ba. or as I'm telling you! Nǐ jyòu tǐng 'wǒde hǎu le.

By mistake is expressed as in the first paragraph or as carelessly méilyóushén, or as thoughtlessly 'méidžsyi 'syǎngsyǎng, or as not on purpose 'búshr gù'yǐde; **take** something **by mistake** nátswò. /Did you do it by mistake? 'Nǐ jè shr̀ °'méilyóu-'shén (°'méidžsyi 'syǎngsyang) nèng de ba. or Nǐ 'búshr gù'yǐde nèmmaje ba. /Did you take that by mistake? Nǐ 'shr̀ bushr kàn'tswòle, jyòu bǎ jèige'náchyule? or 'Nèige nǐ shr̀ bushr ná'tswòle?

To mistake a person's meaning (misunderstand) wùhwei, 'tswògwài. /Please don't mistake me. Byé 'wùhwei wǒde 'yìsz. or Byé 'tswògwàile wǒ.

(Misidentify) is expressed as in the first paragraph. /You can't mistake it. 'Jywé búhwèi yǒu'tswèr de. or 'Méitswèr. or 'Méi ge bu'dwèi de.

Mistake someone for someone else 'ná . . . dàng . . . , 'dǎng(je) . . . shr̀ . . . . /I mistook her for a friend of mine. Wǒ (kàn'tswòle 'rén le) 'dǎng(je) tā shr̀ wǒde ge 'péngyou ne. /They mistook me (*or* I was mistaken) for someone else. Tāmen ('rèntswòle 'rén le) dàng wǒ shr̀ 'lìngyíge 'rén ne.

MISTER (MR.). syānsheng. /Hello, Mr. Jones. 'Jōu syānsheng, ní 'hǎu? /Are you Mr. Jones? Nín shr̀ 'Jōu syānsheng ma? /Hey, mister! Hèi syānsheng!

MIX. (Combine ingredients) hwò; (stir) hwòlung, jyǎu. /Mix this flour with two cups of water. Jèige 'myàn jyājin lyǎngbēi 'shwěi chyù 'hwò. *or* Yùng lyǎngbēi 'shwěi lái hwò jèige 'myàn. /Don't mix too much sand with the concrete. Yáng'hwēili hwò de 'shādz byé tài 'dwōle. *or* Yáng'hwēili 'shǎu °hwò (°gē) dyar 'shādz. /You'll have to mix it with a large spoon. Ní děi ná 'sháur °'jyǎu yijyǎu (°'hwòlung hwòlung).

(Associate with people) láiwang, lālung; **mix well** hédelai, 'tándeshàng'lái, 'shwōdeshàng'lái; **not mix well** 'tánbushàng'lái, 'shwōbushàng'lái, 'gégébú'rù. /He mixes well with everybody. Tā gēn'shéi dōu °'hédelái (°'tán(*or* 'shwō)deshàng'lái). /He doesn't mix well. Tā gēn rén °'gégébú'rù (°'tán(*or* 'shwō)bushàng'lái).

Mix well (of foods) néng yí'kwàr chr̄, néng 'chānhechilai chr̄, néng 'héchilai yí'kwàr chr̄. /These two foods don't mix well. Jèi lyǎngyàngr dūngsyi 'bùnéng °yí'kwàr (°'chānhechilai, °'héchilai yíkwàr) chr̄.

Mix up (disarrange, get out of order) nènglwàn; **be all mixed up** lwànle; (of things) nènglwànle; (of a situation) 'lwànchǐbā'dzàude. /Who mixed up all these cards like this? Shéi bǎ jèisyē 'pyàndz nèngde jèmma 'lwàn? /These cards are all mixed up. Jèisyē 'pyàndz dōu °'lwànle (°nèng'lwànle). /What a mixed up mess! °'Hǎujyāhwo (°'Dzāugāu)! Dzěmma 'dzěmma 'lwàn a! *or* Nàude dzěmma 'lwànchǐbā-'dzàude a!

Mix up, get mixed up (confuse in identity) nàuhwǔn; *or expressed as* not be able to tell which is which °'fēnbukāi (°'fēnbuchǐng, °'nàubuchǐng, °'rénbuchǐng) . . . shéi shr̀ 'shéi (*or* of things) °'nèige shr̀ 'nèige, °shémma shr̀ shémma). /I always get those two brothers mixed up. Wǒ 'láu bǎ tāmen lyǎng 'dìsyūng nàu'hwǔnle. *or* Wó 'láu °fēnbukāi (°etc.) tāmen 'lyǎng 'dìsyūng shéi shr̀ 'shéi.

Mix up (confuse a person) bǎ . . . °nùng(°nàu, °jyǎu)'húdule, jyǎu. /Don't mix me up. Byé bǎ wǒ °nùng(°nàu, °jyǎu)'húdele. *or* Bye 'jyǎu wo. /Now you've got me all mixed up. Ní bá wǒ 'wánchywán nùng'húdule.

Get underlined _someone_ **mixed up in** bǎ . . . °'lā(°'nàu, °'gwǒ)jìnchyu. /Don't get me mixed up in your argument. 'Nǐmen 'chǎu, byé bá 'wǒ °'lā(°'nàu, °gwǒ)jìnchyu.

Be mixed (composed of different kinds of people). /That's quite a mixed crowd. (as to types) °Dàu de (°Nàrde) rén hěn 'dzá. *or* Nàr 'gèshr̀gè'yàngrde rén dōu 'yǒu. *or* Nàr 'shémma yàngrde rén dōu 'yǒu. *or* (as to sexes) °Dàu de (°Nàrde) rén 'nánnannyǔ'nyùde hěn 'dwō. *or* Nàrde rén 'nánnyǔ 'hwǔn dzá.

Mixed marriage. /Mixed marriages are common in Hawaii. Bùtúng'jǔngde rén jyē'hwūn dzài Tánsyāng'shān shr̀ 'chángshèr.

Mixed feelings. /She took the news with mixed feelings. (confused) Tā yǐ 'tīngjyàn nèige, 'syīnli °'lwànle (*or* with happiness and sadness) °'bēisyǐ jyāu'jí, *or* (with joy and fear) °yòu 'syǐhwān yòu 'pà, *or* (with anger and regret) °yòu 'chǐ yòu 'hèn, *or* (with love and hate) °yòu 'ài yòu 'hèn).

MODEL. (Small copy) mwósyíng. /He's making a model of the bridge. Tā dzài dzwò 'chyáude mwó'syíng. /Please show me a model of the boat. Láu'jyà bǎ nèige 'chwánde mwó'syíng géi wǒ 'kànkan.

(Form for imitation or copying) yàngdz, yàngr. /Give me a model to follow (for writing). Géi wǒ ge 'yàngdz °'jàuje (°'bǐje) syě. /Use this model for your writing. Ná jèige dzwò 'yàngdz lái °'jàuje (°'bǐje) syě.

(Style, type) yàngdz, yàngr, 'shr̀yàng; <u>a certain year's</u> model <u>may be expressed</u> <u>as</u> manufactured <u>in a certain year</u> . . . dzàude. /Is that your latest model? Nà shr̀ nǐmen dzwèi'syǐnde °'yàngdz (°'yàngr, °'shr̀yàng) ma? /This year's model has a lower body. 'Jīnnyán chē °'yàngr (°'yàngdz, °shr̀yang) chēshēn 'dīle dyar. /That car is last year's model. Nèilyàng 'chē shr̀ 'chyūnyán dzàude.

(Person who poses or mannequin) 'mwótèér. /She's an artist's model. Tā gěi 'hwàjyā dzwò 'mwótèér.

A model of good behavior <u>is expressed as</u> really well behaved 'jēn gwēijyu *or* (of a child) as better behaved than anyone else's children bǐ 'shéijyāde háidz dōu 'gwēijyu. /Their boy is a model of good behavior. Tāmende 'háidz °'jēn ('bǐ 'shéijyāde háidz dōu) 'gwēijyu.

A model <u>town</u> 'mwófàn. /Ours is a model town. Běn'shr̀ shr̀ 'mwófàn 'shr̀.

To model <u>clothes</u>. /She modeled the dress for us. <u>is expressed as</u> She put the dress on for us to see. Tā bǎ 'yīshang 'chwānshang géi wǒmen 'kàn laije.

Model <u>something</u> **after, be modeled after** °jàuje (°'bǐje, °ànje) . . . de. /American law is modeled after British law, while Continental law is modeled after old Roman law. 'Měigwo 'fǎlyù shr̀ °'jàuje (°'bǐje) 'Yīnggwo 'fǎlyù 'dìngde; Dà'lùfǎ'syì shr̀ °'jàuje (°'bǐje) 'Lwómǎ 'fǎlyù 'dìngde. /We're modeling our plans for the house after that picture. Wǒmen jèngdzài ànje nèijāng 'hwàr lái dìnggwei nèi 'fángdz dzěmma 'gài.

See also **FORM, EXAMPLE.**

MODERN. (Recent, of recent years) 'jìndài; **modern times** 'jìndài; **modern history** jìndài shr̀.

(Up-to-date) syīn (new); 'syàndài (present, current); 'syīnshr̀de, 'syàndàishr̀de, mwódēngde (referring to style). /Do you have anything more modern? 'Hái yóu bǐ jèige °'syīnshr̀de (°'mwó'dēngde) ma? *or* 'Syr̀yàng hái yǒu gèng'syīnde ma? /Are there any modern conveniences? 'Nèige dìfang yǒu 'syīnshr̀de 'shèbèi méiyǒu? *or* (of a house) <u>usually expressed as</u> Are there electric lights and running water? 'Nèige dìfang 'dyàndēng dz̀lái'shwěi dōu 'yǒu ma? /We're thinking of buying some modern furniture. Wǒmen 'dàswàn mái dyǎr °'syīnshr̀de (°mwó'dēngde) 'jyājyu.

MOMENT. (Short period of time) hwěr. /I'll be back in a moment. Wǒ yì'hwěr jyòu 'hwéilai. /We'll have your change in a moment. Wǒmen yì'hwěr jyòu jáugěi nín 'chyán. /Wait a moment. 'Děng yìhwěr.

(Instant) shr̀ jyān, shr̀hou. /I didn't have a single moment to myself. Wǒ 'dz̀-'jǐ 'yìdyǎr shr̀'jyān yě 'méiyǒu.

The moment (that) yì . . . jyòu . . . . /Let me know the moment he arrives. Tā yí 'dàu jyòu 'gàusung wǒ.

At a moment's notice yìdédau 'tūngjr jyòu . . . . /Be ready to leave at a moment's notice. 'Yùbèi'hǎule, yì dédau 'tūngjr̄, jyòu dùng'shēn.

At the moment yìshr̀. /I can't answer your question at the moment. Wǒ yì'shr̀ 'dábushàng nǐde 'wèntí lai.

MONDAY. Syīngchīyī, Lǐbàiyī.

MONEY. chyán. /Where can I change my American money? 'Měigwo chyán 'shémma dìfang kéyǐ 'hwàn? /Do you accept American money? Nǐmen yùng 'Měigwo chyán ma? /How much is that in American money? Yùng Měigwo chyán swàn shr̀ 'dwōshau chyán? /How much money do I owe you? Wǒ 'chyàn ni 'dwōshau chyán? /Do you have any money on you? Nǐ 'shēnshang yǒu 'chyán ma? / He has lots of money. Nèige rén 'hén yǒu 'chyán. / He's taking another job to make more money. Tā lǐng-'wài jāule ge 'shř, hǎu 'dwō jwàn dyǎr 'chyán.

MONTH. ywè; **one month** yíge ywè; **last month** shāng(ge)ywè; **next month** syà(ge)ywè. / How about joining us on a trip next month? 'Syàywè gēn wǒmen 'chūchyu lyǔ'syíng, 'hǎu buhǎu? / Can we rent this house by the month? Jèige 'fángdz kěyi àn'ywè 'dzū ma? / This job should be finished in a month's time. Jèige 'gūngdzwò kéyi yíge 'ywè dzwò'wán. / They never know where they'll be from month to month. 'Měige ywè tāmen dōu bùjř'dàu hwèi wàng 'nǎr chyù.

MOON. 'ywèlyàng. / Is there a full moon tonight? Jyērge 'wǎnshang 'ywèlyang hwèi 'ywán ma? / The moon is hidden behind the clouds. 'Ywèlyang gěi 'yúntsai 'jējule.

MORAL. (Ethical) 'dàudé; **not moral** bú'dàudé *or* (more colloquially) chywēdé; **moral standards** (of a community) 'fēnghwà, rénsyīn; **moral standards** (of an individual) *or* **moral character** is expressed in terms of character 'pǐnsyíng (being good) hǎu, (high) gāu, (upright) 'dwānjèng, (not upright) bùjèng, bùdwàn, etc. / That was hardly a moral thing to do. Nèmmaje 'wēimyǎn °chywē'dé (°bú'dàudé). / This will have a profound effect on moral standards. 'Jèige yǒu gwān 'fēnghwà. / The mayor was attacked on a moral issue when other methods failed. 'Gūngjí shř'jǎng de fāngfǎ 'dōu bù'chéngle, tāmen jyòu shwō tā 'pǐnsyíng °bú'jèng (°bù'dwān). / This is fundamentally a moral issue. Jèi 'gēnběn shř °'dàudéshangde (°'fēnghwàshangde) wèn'tí. / Let's forget the legal technicalities and get down to the moral issue. meaning Let's get down to the question of whether this is morally right or wrong. Dzámen byé gwǎn 'fǎlyùshang dzěmma 'shwō, syān kànkan jèi shèr 'dàudéshang shř °'hǎu shř 'hwài (°'dwèi hái shř 'tswò, °'dwèi hái shř bú'dwèi). or meaning Let's get down to how this question is related to the morals of society. Dzámen byé gwǎn fǎlyùshang dzěmma 'shwō, syān kànkan jèi shèr dwèiyu 'shèhwèi °'dàudéde (°rén-'syínde, °'fēnghwàde) 'gwānsyi ba. / Everybody knows him as a man of high moral character. 'Rénren dōu 'jywédé tā shř ge 'pǐnsyíng °'hǎude (°'dwānjèngde) rén.

A **moral** (lesson) jyàusyun, yìyi. / I don't get the moral of this story. Jèige 'gùshrde °'jyàusyun (°'yìyi) dzài 'nǎr wǒ 'méitīngchu'lái.

Be **without morals** is expressed as to be able to do anything (without restraint) 'shémma dōu dzwòdechū'lái. / She's a woman without morals. 'Tā jèige 'nyǔrén 'shémma dōu dzwòdechū'lái.

MORE. (In amount, as used alone or followed by a noun) dwō before a verb, often with dyǎr following; hái *or* dzài before a verb, with or without dwō(dyar) following; **much more** *or* **a lot more** dwōdwōde before a verb, hái *or* dzài before a verb with hěn dwō following; **need more, want more,** and similar expressions may also be expressed in terms of enough gòu *or* not enough búgòu *or* still need háichà, háidwǎn; comparisons with than which may be omitted in English are also not expressed in Chinese; for necessary comparisons, see below. / You should eat more (than you do). Nǐ yīnggāi 'dwō chř dyar. / I'll allow them more time, then. Nèmmaje wǒ jyòu 'dwō rúng tāmen dyǎr 'shřhou 'hǎule. / Can you get this man at the regular salary, or do you think he wants more? Nèige rén ní gěi tā jàu'lìde 'syīnshwei tā 'gàn bugàn? Nǐ jywéje tā 'hái syǎng 'dwō yàu ma? / How much more time do you need? 'Hái děi yàu 'dwōshǎu shřhou? / Do you need more time? 'Shřjyān 'gòule ma? *or* 'Shřjyān bú'gòu ba? / Won't you have some more? Hái 'yàu dyar me? *or* Dzài 'lái dyǎr ba? *or* Dzài dwō 'lái dyar ba? / I need more money (than I have on me). Wǒ 'shēnshang dài de 'chyán bú'gòu. / I need two dollars more. Wǒ °hái'chà (°hái-'dwǎn) lyǎngkwài chyán. / This one costs more. is expressed as This one is more expensive. Jèige 'gwèi(dyar).

(In degree, as used before an adjective) is expressed by the specific stative verb often followed by dyar; or by hái *or* dzài before a stative verb or verb; or, especially with the meaning **even more,** by gèng before a stative verb. /Which do you think is the more careful worker? Nǐ kàn nèige dzwòde yùng'syīn dyar? /I don't think I can afford a more expensive one. Wó syǎng wó 'mǎibuchǐ 'dzài gwèide le. /Which one is more important? Nèige ('gèng) yàu'jǐn ne? /I have a more important problem on my hands. Wǒ 'syàndzài 'jèng nèng yíjyàn 'gèng yàu'jǐnde 'shèr.

(In number, preceded by a numeral or other word indicating number) hái *or* dzài before a verb with a numeral following. / There are two more guests coming. 'Hái yǒu 'lyǎngge kèrén méi'dàu ne. /I'm going to stay three weeks more. Wǒ 'hái yàu 'dwō jù 'sānge syīng'chǐ. / There are a few more left. Hái 'shèngsya jǐge. or expressed as Those left are not many. 'Shèngsya de bù'dwō le. /Give me a few more, please. 'Dzài gěi wǒ jige ba. or Dzài 'lái jige. /Give me two more bottles, please. Láu'jyà, 'dzài géi wǒ 'lyǎngpíng. /I want two more. 'Dzài géi wó 'lyǎngge. or Wǒ 'hái yàu 'lyǎngge. or 'Dzài lái 'lyǎngge. / Try once more. 'Dzài lái yítsz̀. or 'Dzài shr̀ yísyàr. /I'd like to buy some more of these if you still carry them. Jèige yàushr hái 'yǒu dehwà, wó syǎng °'dwō (°dzài dwō) 'mǎi dyǎr.

Anymore (with a negative) dzài, 'dzài yě; (from now on) 'tsúngtsz̀. / Don't do that anymore. Byé 'dzài nèmmaje le! /I don't care anymore. Wǒ °'tsúngtsz̀ (°'dzài yě) bùgwǎn le.

More and more (as time goes by) ywè lái ywè . . . . / They got more and more out of control as time went by. Tāmen 'ywè lái ywè méifár 'gwǎn le. / They've been seeing more and more of each other lately. Tāmen 'jìnlái láiwǎngde ywè lái ywè °'mìchye (°'chīnmì, °'mì, °'dwō). / This place seems more and more beautiful every time I come here. is expressed as Each time I come, this place seems more beautiful than each (other) time. 'Jèige dìfang wǒ 'lái yítsz̀ bǐ yítsz̀ kànje 'hǎu.

More or less (of amount) shàngsyà, dzwǒyòu, yésyū 'dwō dyar yésyū 'shǎu dyǎr; (almost) chàbudwō; (in the main) dàjr̀; (probably) 'dàgài, or expressed by méi shemma or 'búhwèi shemma followed by a word with opposite meaning from that which follows **more or less.** / There were a hundred people there, more or less. Dàule yǒu yì'bǎi rén °shàng'syà (°dzwǒ'yòu). /It will take two months, more or less. Déi 'lyǎngge ywè °shàng'syà (°dzwǒ'yòu, °yésyū 'dwō dyar yésyú 'shǎu dyar. or Chàbudwō déi 'lyǎngge ywède gwǎngjǐng. /I believe that report is more or less true. Jyù 'wǒ kàn, nèige bàu'gàulide shèr °'dàgài (°'dà'jr̀) shr̀ °'jēnde (°'kě'syìnde). or Jyù 'wǒ kàn, nèige bàu'gàulide shèr °méi shémma 'jyàude (°'búhwèi yǒu shémma 'jyǎde).

More than . . . bǐ . . . dwō; **more . . . than . . .** bǐ . . . plus a stative verb; **more than** (followed by a numeral) is expressed by dwō (or, if the amount more than is less than ten, sometimes jǐ) after a numeral, or as dzài . . . yǐ'shàng; **much more than** . . . bǐ . . . dwōde 'dwō, bǐ . . . dwō'dwōle; **more than enough** 'dzúgòule or expressed as too much tài 'dwō; also expressed indirectly. / There were a hundred more there today than yesterday. 'Jyér bǐ 'dzwér dwō yǐ'bǎi. / Doing a good job is much more important than finishing quickly. Dzwòde 'hǎu 'ywán bǐ dzwòde 'kwài yàu'jǐn. /I dislike her too, perhaps even more than you do. 'Wó yé tǎu'yàn tā; yésyū bí nǐ 'hái tǎu'yàn tā ne. / They need more time than we did. 'Tāmen děi bí 'wǒmen yùng de 'shŕjyān 'dwō dyar tsái 'syíng. / There were more than a thousand people there. Dàule yǐchyān'dwō rén. or Dàu de rén dzài yì'chyān yǐ'shàng. /He's more than forty years old. Tā yǒu °'sz̀shrdwō (°'sz̀shrjǐ) swèr. or Tā dzài 'sz̀shr-swèi yǐ'shàng. / That's more than enough. 'Nèi yǐjǐng °tài 'dwō (°'dzúgòu) le. / This costs more than I expected. Nèige 'jyàr bǐ wǒ syīnli 'syǎngde 'gwèi. or Wǒ 'méisyǎng'dàu hwèi nèmma 'gwèi. but /I'd be more than willing to lend you ten, but I simply don't have it. Wǒ 'syàndzài 'méiyǒu 'shŕkwài chyán. Yàushr 'yǒu dehwà

°yǐ'dǐng jyègéi nǐ (°byé shwō 'jyè le, géi nǐ dōu 'syíng). / It was more luck than brains. is expressed as It depended entirely on luck, not at all on ability. Nèi shr kàu 'yùnchi 'yíng de, búshr 'jìng píng 'běnshr. / Don't bother fixing it; it's more bother than it's worth. is expressed as Don't bother fixing it; to expend that energy isn't worth it. Béng syǎngfǎr 'shōushr le; fèi 'nèige sher bù'jŕde.

More than ever, all the more, even more (than that) gèng. / After hearing you say the show was so good, I wanted to go more than ever. Tǐng nǐ shwō de nèichū syì 'nèmma hǎu, wǒ 'gèng syǎng chyù 'kànkan le. / I'd like to see him, but even more (than that) I'd like to see his daughter again. Wǒ 'syǎng chyù 'jyànjyan tā; wǒ yě 'gèng syǎng chyù 'dzài hwèidàu 'tāde nèiwèi 'syáujye. / I'd like to go to the show, but I want to go to this lecture even more. Wǒ dàu 'syǎng chyù kàn nèichū 'syì; búgwo wǒ 'gèng syǎng tǐng jèige yán'jyǎng.

More to something than you'd think and similar expressions are expressed indirectly. / There's more to his plan than you'd imagine at first sight. is expressed as There are many things about his plan that you can't see at first glance. Tāde 'bànfa 'yǒu syē dìfang 'jà yí 'jyàn kànbuchū'láide.

No more than, not any more than is expressed as in the first paragraph; when followed by numerals, often as not over búgwò; many indirect expressions are also used. / I don't care any more than you do. Wǒ 'bìng bùbǐ 'nǐ hái 'dzàihu a. / There were no more than fifty people in the whole town. Chywán'chéngli yě búgwò 'wǔshr-rénde yàngdz. / The price surely can't be more than ten dollars. 'Jyàchyán 'jywé búhwèi °gwòle 'shŕkwài chyán (°chāugwò 'shŕkwài chyán, °bǐ 'shŕkwài chyán hái 'dwō). / Don't do any more than you have time for. Nǐ dzwò'shŕ yàu 'kěje 'shŕhou dzwò, byé tǎn'dwō. / We're no more ready to start the work now than we were a year ago. Wǒmen 'háishr 'bùnéng 'dzwòbuchilai, jyǎn'jŕ gēn 'chyùnyán °yǐ'yàng (°méi shémma 'fēnbye). / He's paid $3,000 a year, but it's no more than he's worth. Tā 'yìnyánde 'syīnshwei 'sānchyānywán; yàu àn tāde 'běnlǐng lái shwō, bìng 'búswàn 'dwō.

The more . . . the plus an adjective in the comparative form ywè 'dwō ywè . . . ; the more . . . the more . . . ywè . . . ywè . . . . / The more I read it the madder I get. Jèige wǒ 'ywè kàn ywè 'chì. / The more I read it the less I understand. Jèige wǒ 'ywè nyàn ywè bù'dǔng. / The more the merrier. Ywè 'dwō ywè 'hǎu. / The more you eat the more you want. is popularly expressed as The more you chew it the tastier it gets. 'Ywè jyáu ywè 'syāng. or 'Ywè chŕ ywè chán. or 'Ywè chŕ ywè 'syāng chŕ.

Other English expressions. / They bit off more than they could chew. Tāmen nèi shr 'tāndwò'jyáubu'làn. or Tāmen 'jēn shr 'búdžlyàng'lì. / He's more fun than a barrel of monkeys. may be expressed lit., except that crowd chyún is used instead of barrel. Tā bǐ yìchyún 'hóudz hái néng dòu rén 'syàu. / What's more, I don't believe you. °'Dzài shwō ne (°'Hái yǒu yì'tséng, °Gèng 'jìn yíbù lái shwō ne, °Dzài 'jìn yíbù lái shwō ne), wǒ 'gēnběn bú'syìn nǐde 'hwà. / More power to you. is expressed as I certainly hope you succeed. Wǒ 'jēn pànwang nǐ bànde'dàu.

MORNING. dzǎuchen, dzǎushang; dzǎu in combinations. / I'll see you in the morning. Míngr 'dzǎuchen 'jyàn. / He slept all morning. Tā 'shwèile yì'dzǎushang. / Is there a morning train? Yǒu dzǎu'chē ma? / Shall I pick up a morning paper? Wǒ mǎi fèn dzǎu'bàu ba?

Good morning is expressed as it's early dzǎu a; or simply as hello nǐ hǎu.

MOST. (Greatest in quantity or degree, etc.) dzwèi or dǐng followed a stative verb; (when not followed by an adjective in English, and referring to amount) 'dzwèi dwō, 'dǐng dwō; at (the) most 'jŕ dwō, 'dzwèi dwō, 'dǐng dwō; the most I've ever seen

and similar expressions is expressed as I've never seen so much, etc. / This is the
most fun we've had in a long time. Wǒmen 'hausyē r̄dzli yàu swan 'jèitsz̀ wárde
'dzwèi °chǐ'jyèr (°yǒu'yìsz) le. / Which room has the most space? 'Nèijyān wūdz
°dǐng (°dzwèi) 'kwānchang? / Who has done the most work in this job? 'Jèijyàn shèr
'shéi chū de 'lǐ dzwèi 'dwō? / He's the most reliable person I've ever had. Wǒ
'yùnggwo de rénli tā dzwèi kě'kàu. / That is the most I can pay。 Wǒ °'jr̄ (°'dzwèi)
dwō néng chū jèmma ge 'jyàr. / That's the most I want to pay. Wǒ °'jr̄ (°'dzwèi,
°dǐng) dwō chūdau 'jèmma syē chyán. or often expressed as That's the price, it
can't be higher. 'Jyoushr 'nèmma ge jyàr, 'dzài bùnéng 'gāu le. / What's the most
you can lend me? 'Dzwèi dwō nǐ néng jyè wǒ 'dwōshau? / I can pay fifteen dollars
at the most. Wǒ °'jr̄ (°'dzwèi, °'dǐng) dwō néng chūdau shŕ'wǔkwài chyán.
/ Where's the most convenient place to meet you? °Dzài 'nǎr (°'Shémma dìfang) jyàn
nǐ dzwèi 'fāngbyan? / The train goes there, but you can go most easily by bus.
Nèige dìfang tūng hwǒ'chē, búgwo dzwò 'gūnggùngchìchē 'dzwèi shéng'shr̀. / The
hotel can hold three hundred guests at most. Lyú'gwǎn °jr̄ (°dzwèi) dwō (yě 'búgwo)
néng rúng 'sānbǎi rén. / This is the most beautiful photograph of a cat I've ever seen.
Wǒ 'tsúnglái méi jyàngwo gěi 'māu jàu'syàng jàude 'jèmma hǎu'kàn de.

(Almost all, a majority) is expressed as almost all chàbudwō °'dōu (°'chywán);
the greatest number of . . . all dà'dwōshùde . . . 'dōu; very nearly all jǐhū dōu.
/ Most people think he did the right thing. °Dà'dwōshùde rén (°Chàbudwō 'shéi,
°Chàbudwō 'rénrén) 'dōu jywéje tā bànde 'dwèi. / She's already been to most of the
stores in town. Jèige dìfangde 'pùdz tā 'chàbudwō 'yǐjīng °'dōu (°'chywán) dzǒu-
'byànle. or Jèige dìfangde'pùdz tā °jǐhū (°'chàbudwō) 'jyājyar dōu 'dàugwole. / He's
away from home most of the time every day. Tā jěng'tyānjya chàbudwō dōu °búdzài
'jyāli (°dzài 'wàitou).

(Very) jēn, hěn, tǐng, 'fēicháng, 'shŕfēn; (after an adjectival expression)
jíle, lìhai, hěn. / His talk was most interesting. Tā shwōde °'jēn (°'hěn, °tǐng,
°'fēicháng, °shŕfēn) °yǒu'yìsz (°yǒu'yìsz 'jíle, °yǒu'chyùrde 'lìhai, °yǒu'chyùrde
'hěn). / I found his manner most annoying. Wǒ kè jywéje tāde 'jyújr̀'dùngdzwò
°'tǐng (°'hěn, °'shŕfēn, °'fēicháng) jyàu rén 'nǐwei de.

For the most part dàjr̀, 'dwōbàn; or expressed indirectly. / I agree with your
plan for the most part. Nǐde 'jǐhwà wǒ dà'jr̀ dzàn'chéng. or expressed as There
aren't many places in which I disagree with your plan. Nǐde 'jǐhwà wǒ 'mèiyou dwōshǎu 'búdzànchéng de 'dìfang.

To make the most of is expressed indirectly. / We're not staying here long, so
let's make the most of our time. is expressed as We're not staying here long, so
let's not waste this chance. Dzámen dzài jèr 'dāibulyǎu dwō 'jyǒu, hái bú'chèn
jèige 'jǐhwei 'dà °gàn (°wár) yísyàr. / Let's make the most of the money we've got
left. is expressed as We'll have to use the rest of the money in the right place.
'Shèngsyade chyán dzámen děi 'hwāde 'shr̀ 'dìfangr tsái 'hǎu.

MOTHER. (In a human family) mǔchin; (somewhat more intimate terms) nyáng, mā;
(used by children) māma; your mother (terms used for special politeness) lǐngtáng,
lǐngtsź; my mother (terms used for special politeness) jyātsź, jyāmǔ; my mother
(if she is deceased) 'syāntsź, 'syānmǔ; stepmother (polite term) 'jìmǔ or (more
colloquial) 'hòunyáng; mother-in-law (wife's mother, polite term) 'ywèmǔ or (more
colloquial) 'jàngmǔnyáng, (husband's mother) pwópwo. / Mother wants you to go
home. °'Mǔchin (°'Māma, °'Nyáng) jyàu nǐ hwéi'jyā. / I'd like you to meet my
mother. (sometime) Wǒ syǎng yàu nǐ jyànjyan wǒ 'mǔchin. or (in an introduction)
Wǒ 'mǔchin. or Jè shr̀ jyā'mǔ. / Do you live with your mother? Nǐ gēn nǐ
'mǔchin yí'kwàr jù ma? / Did your mother tell you to come here? Shr̀ °nǐ 'nyáng
(°nǐ 'māma, °ní mǔchin, °lǐng'táng) jyàu nǐ dàu jèr 'láide ma?

(Among animals) is expressed indirectly by the verb give birth syà. / This one is the mother of the litter (of puppies). Nèi yǐwō syáu'gǒur shr̀ 'jèige gǒu 'syàde.

One's mother country 'bēngwó, gwó; (the country of one's ancestors) 'dzǔgwó.

One's mother tongue is expressed indirectly as speak natively 'běnlái shwō. / What is your mother tongue? Ní 'běnlái shwō °'něigwó (°neige dìfangde) 'hwà?

To mother someone is expressed as **care for as a mother** (treats a child) syàng 'mǔchin (dài 'érdz) shr̀de nèmma °'jàuying (°'jāuhu, °'kānhù). / She mothered him all through his illness. Tā bìngde shr̀hou, tā syàng 'mǔchin (dài érdz) shr̀de nèmma °'jàuying (°'jāuhu, °'kānhù) tā láije.

MOTION. (Movement) expressed with move dùng. / The motion of the boat has made me ill. Chwán 'dùngde ràng wo nán'shòu.

(A gesture) 'jāuhu. / He made a motion in my direction. Tā gēn wó dǎ 'jāuhū.

(Formal suggestion in a meeting) 'tíyi, tíàn. / I want to make a motion. Wó yǒu ge 'tíyi. / The motion was carried. Tí'àn yǐjīng 'tūnggwòle.

Motion picture dyànyingr.

To motion to someone gēn . . . dǎ 'jāuhū. / Will you motion to that bus to stop? Láu'jyà 'jāuhū nèi chīchē 'tíngsya. or Láu'jyà gēn neige kāichi'chē de dǎ 'jāuhu, jyàu tā 'tíngsya.

MOUNTAIN. shān; when contrasting with a hill gāushān. / How high is the mountain? Nèige 'shān dwō 'gāu? / It takes several days to cross through the mountains. Gwò jēidwàn 'shān děi 'hǎuji tyān. / We're spending a month in the mountains this summer. 'Jīnnyán 'syàtyan wǒmen dzài 'shānli jùle yíge 'ywè. / How do you like this mountain view? Ní 'ài buài jèige shān'jǐng? / He's living here for the mountain air. Tā jùdzai 'jèr 'wèideshr̀ 'shānshangde kūng'chì. (fig.) / I've got a mountain of work to do next week. 'Syàlǐbài wó yǒu yí'dàdwēide 'shr̀ yàu dzwò.

MOUTH. (Part of the body) dzwěi; in some combinations kǒu. / His mouth is a little crooked. Tā dzwéi jǎngde °yǒu dyar 'wāi (°buhěn'jèng). / He has a large mouth. Tā dzwéi hěn 'dà. / Don't put it in your mouth; it's dirty. Byé gēdzai 'dzwěili; tài 'dzāng. / He opened his mouth as if to say something. Tā 'jāngkai °dzwéi (°kóu) hǎu syàng yàu 'shwō shémma shr̀de. / He looks frightened, with his mouth open and his eyes staring like that. Tā 'jāng(je) °kǒu (°dzwěi) 'dèng(je)yànde nèi 'yàngr 'hǎu syàng tǐng hài'pà shr̀de.

(In constructions referring to speaking) sometimes kǒu; more commonly expressed in terms of speak shwō, or words hwà. / I didn't have a chance to open my mouth. Wǒ 'jyànjr̀ 'méi jǐhwei kāi'kǒu. / He kept his mouth shut like a clam. (over a period of time) Tā yì'jr̀ bùkěn shwō. or (didn't say a word) Tā 'yíjyù hwà yě bùkěn 'shwōchulai. or expressed as He kept his mouth like a bottle. Tā shǒu'kǒurú-'píng. / Why did you have to open your big mouth? Dzěmma ní jyòu 'fēi děi °shwō-'hwà (°'shwōchulai) bù'syíng ne? / He can't keep his mouth shut. Tā 'tswúnbuju 'hwà. or Tā 'yǒu hwà jyòu 'shwōchuchyu. or Tā 'yǒu shémma hwà 'dōu géi ní 'dōulouchuchyu. or Tā shwō 'hwà tǐng bù'syāusyin. / He couldn't keep his mouth shut. Tā 'fēi shwō bù'kě. or Tā 'yíge bù'syāusyin jyòu 'shwōchūchyùle. or Tā °'bùjr̀bù'jywéde (°'shǎbujǐde, °'húlihúdūde) gěi 'shwōchūchyùle. / You took the words right out of my mouth. Wǒ 'gāng yàu nèmma 'shwō. or Ní shwōde 'jēn dwèi. or Kěbú'shr̀ ma! / Don't put words into my mouth. Hēi! Nèi búshr̀ °wǒ 'shwōde (°wǒde 'yìsz). / The story was passed from mouth to mouth. Nèijyàn shèr °'chwán-ràngchuchyule (°chwán'byànle, °jèige(rén) chwán 'nèige(rén)de chwánde hén 'ywǎn. / The word was passed from mouth to mouth that a date had been set for the general strike. 'Dàjyā 'ānjūng °'chwánshwō (°bítsź 'gàusu shwō) dàbà'gūngde 'r̀dz yǐjīng 'dìngle.

763

MOVE

(Opening, place of emptying) kǒu, kǒur. / How far is it to the mouth of the
river? Dàu hé'kǒu nar yǒu 'dwōshǎu 'lù? / The dog stopped at the mouth of the cave.
Gǒu dàule dùng'kǒur nar jyòu 'jànjule. / Wipe off the mouth of the bottle. Bǎ píngdz
'kǒur tsā'gānjingle.

Other English expressions. / It makes his mouth water. (fig.) Jyàu tā 'chánde-
heng. or Jyàu tā kànje yǎn'chán. Jyàu tā kànje yǎr're. / Why are you so down in
the mouth? Ní 'dzěmma nèmma °bùgāu'syìngde 'yàngdz (°'chwéitóusàng'chìde)?

MOVE. (Change the location of something) nwó (general term); dùng (with the hand);
bān (of heavy things); also expressed by a wide variety of specific terms such as
lā pull, twēi push, kāi drive, ná carry in the hands, etc.; see these words and
others with similar meanings; these words are also used in combination with dùng
above; move something to a place is expressed with the above verbs plus -dàu; move
something away the above verbs plus -kāi or sometimes -dzǒu; be able to move
something dùngdelyǎu, nwódelyǎu, nwódedùng, bāndelyǎu, bāndedùng, or other
specific terms plus -dedùng. / Move the table away, please. Láu'jyà bǎ 'jwōdz
°'nwókai (°'bānkai, °'twēikai, °'lākai, °táikai, °'dākai, °etc.). / Move the table
over there, please. Láu'jyà bǎ 'jwōdz °'nwódàu (°etc.) 'nèibyar chyu. / He's going
to move the car around to the front of the house after dinner. Chīwánle 'fàn tā jyòu
chyù bǎ chē °'nwódàu (°'kāidàu) fángdz 'chyánbyar chyu. / Don't move these books.
'Jèisyē shū byé °'dùng (°nwókai, °nádzǒu). / These things are not to be moved.
Jèisyē 'dùngsyi °yì'dyar yě búyàu 'dùng (or (moved away) °byé bān'dzǒu). / I can't
move the table. 'Jwōdz wǒ °nwóbu'dùng (°'twēibu'dùng, °'lābu'dùng).

(Change one's position or posture, while remaining in the same general location)
dùng; move around (shift one's position restlessly) lwàn dùng, 'nwógwolái nwógwo-
'chyùde, 'dàibujù syánbu'jùde; (when sitting) dzwòbujù; (when standing) jànbujù.
/ Don't move! Byé 'dùng! / I can't move (a muscle). Wǒ bùnéng 'dùng. or Wǒ
'dùngbu'lyǎu ('jyèr). / Don't move around so much. Byé nèmma °lwàn 'dùng (°'nwógwolái nwógwo'chyùde, °'dàibujù syánbu'jùde, °dzwòbu'jù, °jànbu'jù).

(Change one's location or be in motion, of a person) 'nwódùng, dzǒu; (not stand)
bújàn; (not stay) bùdāi; move over 'nwó yinwó, 'nwókāi (dyar); move up (forward)
wàngchyán °nwó (°dzǒu); move closer (together) āijǐn(dyar), wàng yì'kwàr 'nwó-
(yinwó). / I can't move (from here). Wǒ 'nwóbukāi. or Wǒ bùnéng 'nwódùng. / Move
on! or Move along! 'Dzǒu(je dyar)! or 'Nwódùngje dyar! or Wàng chyán 'dzǒu!
/ The police kept the crowds moving. Sywúnjǐng jyàu rén °'nwódùngje (°wàng chyán
'dzǒu). or Sywúnjǐng búyàu rén °'jàndzai ner (°dzài nèr 'dāije). / Don't move
around so much. (from one place to another) Byé nèmma °'nwó(dàu)jèr nwó(dàu)-
'nèrde (°dzài'jèrdāihwer dzài'nèrdāihwerde, °'dzǒugwolái dzǒugwo'chyùde, °'dzǒuláidzǒu'chyùde).

(Be in motion, of a thing) dùng, dzǒu (changing location); kāi (of a vehicle);
(without changing location) dùng; (of wheels, turn) jwàn. / Don't get off the train
while it's moving. Chē °'dùng(°'dzǒu)je de shŕhou byé 'syàchyu. / The train is
really moving along! 'Hwǒchē jēn °'kāi(°'kwài)chilaile.

(Change residence) bān, bānjyā. / Do you know where they're moving to? Ní
'jŕdàu tāmen yàu wàng 'nǎr bān ma? / Are they going to move? Tāmen yàu bān'jyā
ma? / They've moved out of town. (to the suburbs) Tāmen 'bāndàu chéng'wài chyule.
or (elsewhere) Tāmen 'bāndàu 'byéchùr chyule. / Where can I find someone to help
me move? Yàu 'jǎu rén lái bāng wǒ bān'jyā, dàu 'nǎr chyu 'jǎu ne? / I've been
moving around all my life. Wǒ yì'bèidz °méidzài 'yíchùr dìfang 'dāijùgwo (°lǎushr
'bāndàujèr bāndàu'nèrde, °lǎushr 'bānláibān'chyùde). / When will the house be ready
for us to move in? Fángdz 'shémma shŕhou nùng'hǎule wǒmen hǎu 'bānjìnchyu?
/ We have to move out next week. Wǒmen 'syàlǐbài děi 'bānchuchyu.

764

(Make a motion, in parliamentary procedure) 'dùngyì, 'tíyì. /I move we adjourn. Wŏ °'dùngyì (°'tíyì) 'syàndzài sàn'hwèi. /I move that we accept him as a member. Wŏ °'dùngyì (°'tíyì) 'jyēshòu tā dzwò hwèi'ywán.

(Affect emotionally) 'gǎndùng, 'gánkǎi. /I was very much moved by what he said. 'Tāde hwà jyàu wó 'hěn shòu 'gǎndùng. or Tīngle 'tāde hwà jyàu wó 'hěn shēng 'gánkǎi. /He gave a moving speech. Tāde yán'jyǎng hén °'gǎndùng rén (°'jyàu rén shòu 'gǎndùng). /His speech moved the crowd to tears. Tīngle 'tāde 'hwà, nèisyē rén 'gǎndùngde lyóu 'lèi.

Move in (associate with) gēn ... láiwang. /They enjoy the fact that they move in the best circles. Tāmen 'hàu gēn 'shàngděng rén láiwang. /She's been moving in fast company lately. Tā 'jìnlái 'láiwangde 'dōu shr̀ syē ài'wár de rén. or Tā 'jìnlái 'jǐng gēn ài'wár de rén 'láiwang.

Move in on (get closer) lí ... jìn(dyar). /Move in on them so you can fire at close range. Lí tāmen 'jìn dyar, myáu'jwèr jyòu 'rúngyi dyar.

Be moving (busy, in action, etc.) is expressed as be busy máng, be doing gàn, bàn; (of matters or business) be much dwō, be fast kwài. /Things are really moving now. Jēn °'mángchǐlaile (°'gànchǐlaile). or Shèr (jēn) °'dwōchǐlaile (°'mángchǐlaile). /Things are moving much faster now. Shèr bànde kwài'dwōle. /The new director has really got things moving. 'Syīn jǔ'rèn kě 'jēn bǎ shèr nùngde °'kwàichilaile (°'mángchilaile).

A move (in games or fig.) bù; **the next move** (fig.) 'syàyíbù, syàyíjyan shr̀, or expressed as next dzài; also expressed verbally as move (in games) dzǒu, syà; (fig.) dzǒu, dùng, bàn, dzwò. /Whose move is it now? Gāi 'shéi dzǒu le? or 'Jèibù 'shr̀ (°'gāi) 'shéi dzǒu? /It's your move. Gāi 'ní dzǒu. /That was a wasted move. 'Nèiyíbù 'dzǒude méi'yùng. /He can't make a move without his secretary. Méiyòu tāde nèiwèi 'shūji tā °'yíbù yě bùnéng 'dùng (°'shémma yě bànbu'lyǎu, °'shémma yě bùnéng 'bàn). /He doesn't dare make a move at present. Tā syàndzài 'yíbù yě bùgǎn 'dùng. /I'm not going to ask him again; it's his move now. Wŏ búdzài 'wèn tā le; 'syàyíbù gāi 'tāde le. /Let me know before you make a move. Yàu 'dzwò shémma syān 'gàusu wŏ yì'shēng. /My next move is to go for the tickets. Wŏ °'syàyíbù (°'syàyíjyan shr̀, °'dzài jyou) gāi chyù mǎi 'pyàu le.

Be on the move (on the road) dzài lùshang; (moving around) dzǒudau 'jèr dzǒudàu nèrde, 'bānláibān'chyùde. /We've been on the move for the last month. Dǎ 'shàngywè wǒmen jyou °lǎu dzài 'lùshang (°dzǒudau 'jèr dzǒudau 'nèrde, °'bānláibān'chyùde).

Make a move (change one's position) 'dùng yidùngr. /If you dare make a move I'll shoot. Nǐ yàu gǎn dùng yi'dùngr wǒ jyòu kāi'chyāng.

MRS. tàitai; for the wife of a prominent man, particularly an official, one says 'fūrén Madame. /Hello, Mrs. Jones. How are you? 'Jōu tàitai, ní 'hǎu? /This is for Mrs. Jones. 'Jè shr̀ gěi 'Jōu tàitaide.

MUCH. (In amount) dwō, bùshǎu; (a measure) syē; not much bùdwō, méi'dwōshǎu; how much 'dwōshǎu; much of ... ... 'dwōbàn, ... 'dàbàn, or expressed as to a great extent syàng'dāngde. /Did you spend much last night? Dzwér 'wǎnshang hwā de chyán °'dwō ma (°'dwō budwō, °shr̀ bushr̀ tǐng 'dwōde)? or Dzwér 'wǎnshang shr̀ bushr̀ hwāle °'hěn dwō (°'bù'shǎude, °'hǎusyē) chyán? /Take as much as you like. Nǐ 'yàu dwōshǎu 'ná dwōshǎu. or Ní ywànyi 'yàu dwōshǎu jyòu 'ná dwōsháu hǎu le. /We don't have much time to spend here. Wǒmen dzài jèr 'dāibulyǎu 'dwōshǎu 'shr̀hou. /How much will it cost me? Wó děi chū 'dwōshǎu chyán ne?

/ I've done only that much up to now. Wǒ 'jŕ dàu syàn'dzài 'jyòu dzwòchūlai 'nèmma syē. / Much of what you say is true. Nǐ 'shwō de hwà °yìdwō'bàr (°'dàbàn) dōu 'dwèi. *or* Nǐ shwō de syāng'dāngde yóu'lǐ. / Much of what's written here is rubbish. Jèr syēde 'dwōbàn shŕ 'fèihwà.

(In degree) dà (with verbs); lìhai, syūng (awfully); <u>and other more specific expressions</u>; <u>not much</u> (with verbs) búdà, <u>and indirect expressions</u>; **much more** *or* **much** plus an adjective in the comparative form dwō; <u>too much</u> tài; **very much** (with verbs) hěn; **much rather** syǎng háishr . . . hǎu, nìng kě. / Was there much fuss about it? Nèi shèr nàude °'lìhai (°'syūng) ma? *or* Nèi shèr shŕ bushr nàude tǐng °'dàde (°'lìhaide, °'syūngde)? / Do you feel much pain? Nǐ téngde 'lìhai ma? / He's not much good at this sort of work. 'Jèijǔng shèr tā 'búdà °'hwèi (°'chéng, °'syíng, °dzwòde'lái). / I don't care very much for that. Wǒ 'búdà 'syǐhwan °'nèige (*or* (of an action) °'nèmmaje). / I don't care much about that (one way or the other). 'Nèige wǒ 'búdà 'dzàihu. / I don't have much faith in what they say. Tāmende 'hwà wǒ 'búdà °'syìn (°syāng'syìn, °néng 'syìn, °néng syìnde'jí). *or* Tāmende 'hwà wǒ jywéje 'búdà °kě 'syìn (°kě 'kàu, °kàude'jù). / I don't think that car is much of a buy. Wǒ jywéje 'nèilyàng chē °mǎije 'búdà shàng'swàn (*or* (not worth buying) °bù-'jŕde yǐ 'mǎi, °bùjŕ'dàngde 'mǎi). / I feel much better, thanks. Hǎu'dwōle, dwō 'syē. / This piece is much bigger. 'Jèi yíkwàr 'dàde'dwō. / This one is much more expensive. 'Jèige 'gwèide'dwō. / That's too much! (to bear) Nèi wèi'myǎn tài 'nán dyǎr le. *or* (excessive) Nèi wèi'myǎn tài gwò'fèn le. *or* (too improper) Nèi tài búsyàng'hwà le. / I'd very much like to go, but I can't. Wǒ 'hén syǎng 'chyù, 'búgwo wǒ 'bùnéng chyù. / I'd much rather stay home. Wó syǎng wǒ 'háishr dzài 'jyāli 'dāije hǎu.

Much of the time (often) cháng, chángchang, lǎu, jìng. / Do they travel much? Tāmen °cháng (°'chángchang) °chū'mér (°chūchyu lyǔ'syíng) ma? / Did they travel much when they were in Russia? Tāmen dzài 'Ègwo de shŕhou °'cháng(chang) chūchyu lyǔ'syíng ma (*or* (to many places) °dàu de 'dìfang 'dwō ma)? / Don't go out too much; you should do your homework once in a while. 'Byé °jìng (°lǎu) chūchyu 'wár, yě gāi dzài 'jyāli 'yùbei 'gūngke le.

(As) **much as** (although . . . very much) 'swéirán (. . .) hěn. / (As) much as I'd like to go with you, I'm afraid it's impossible. Wǒ 'swéirán 'hén syǎng gēn nǐmen 'chyù, shŕ'shŕshang kǔngpà bù'syíng.

Inasmuch as (since) jìshr. / Inasmuch as I've decided to go myself, I don't think you'll have to write that letter now. Wǒ 'jìshr 'jywédìng 'chǐndzŕ dàu nàr 'chyù-le, wǒ kàn nǐ jyòu 'béng syē nèi fēng 'syìn le.

So much the better gèng 'hǎu. / Well, if she's not coming, so much the better. Tā 'bùlái, gèng 'hǎu.

Other English expressions. / I don't think he's so much. Wǒ jywéje tā 'méi shémma(lyǎubu'chǐ de). *or* Wǒ bùjywéje tā °dzěmma'yàng (°dzěmma lyǎubu'chǐ). / Not much! (sarcastically) Tsái'gwài ne!

MUD. ní. / Don't step in the mud. Byé wàng 'níli 'tsǎi. / My car is stuck in the mud. Chǐ'chē °'syàndzai (°'sywàndzai) 'níli le. / My shoes are covered with mud. Wǒde 'syéshang 'mǎn shŕ 'ní.

MUSIC. yīn ywè. / Where's the music coming from? Yīn'ywède 'shēngyīn tsúng 'nǎr láide? / What kind of music do you like? Ní 'syǐhwan 'shémma yàngde yīn'ywè? / She's studied music for ten years. Tā 'sywéle 'shŕnyán yīn'ywè. / Who's giving the music course this year? 'Jīnnyán 'shéi jyāu yīn'ywè?

(Score) ywèpǔ(r). / Has the band received the music yet? Ywè'dwèi yǐjing 'nádàule ywè'pǔ ma? /I'd like to practice this music. Wó syǎng 'lyànlyan jèige °'pǔdz (°ywè'púr).

Face the music (fig.) shòu dzwèi. /It's your mistake; now you must face the music. Nǐ 'dzjǐ nùng'dzāule, syàndzài nǐ 'dzjǐ shòu'dzwèi ba.

MUST. děi; _or expressed with the adverbs_ yídìng, 'jwǔnshř. /We must do what we can to help him. Wǒmen děi jílì bāng tāde 'máng. /It's my party; you must let me pay. 'Wó chǐng'kè, ní děi ràng 'wǒ fù'jàng. /They were so nice to us; we must have them over. Tāmen dài wǒmen hén 'hǎu; wǒmen déi 'chǐngching 'tāmen. /The contract must be signed by the end of the month. Jèige 'ywè'nèi yí'dìng déi bǎ jèige 'hétung 'chyānhǎu. /If you must catch an earlier train, I'll see you to the station. Nǐ yàushr yí'dìng yàu dzwò 'dzǎuchē dzǒu, wǒ jyòu dàu chē'jàn chyù 'sùngsyíng. /He must be there by now. Tā 'jèige shŕhour yí'dìng dàu 'nèr le. /I must have left my wallet home. Wǒde pí'bāu 'jwǔnshř 'làdzai 'jyāli le. /It must be almost four o'clock. 'Jwǔnshř 'chàbudwō 'sżdyǎnjūng le. /This must be my room. 'Jèige wūdz °'dàgài (°'yīnggai) shř 'wǒde.

MY. _See_ I.

NAME. (Of a person; first name or given name) míngdz; (surname) syìng; (family nickname of a child) 'rúmíng, 'syàumíng; (name used only in school) 'sywémíng; _or expressed as_ call, be called, be named jyàu _or as_ address, be addressed as 'chēnghu; full name 'syìngmíng; pen name 'bǐmíng; nickname wàihǎur; courtesy name dž, hàu. /In a Chinese name, the surname comes first; e.g., in the name 'Hwáng Ān'lǐ, Hwáng is the surname and Ān'lǐ the given name. 'Jūnggwo °'rénmíng (°rénde syìngmíng) 'syìng dzài 'chyántou; 'bǐfang shwō, 'Hwáng Ān'lǐ jèige 'míngdz ba, 'Hwáng shř 'syìng, Ān'lǐ shř 'míngdz. /According to custom, a Chinese should never be addressed directly by his given name, except by superiors, elders or close friends. Ān Jūnggwo gwēijyu dāng'myàr jyàu rén, chúle 'shàngsz, 'jǎngbèr, gēn hěn hǎude 'péngyou yǐwài, bùnéng jyàu 'míngdz. /So there are also courtesy names. Swóyi yǒu 'dž a 'hàu de. /A Chinese usually has a formal name and several courtesy names. Yíge 'Jūnggworén chángchang yǒu yíge 'míngdz gēn jige 'dž a 'hàu de. /Some Chinese have only one name which they use throughout their lives. 'Yǒude Jūnggworén yí'bèidz jř yùng 'yíge míngdz. /When a man grows up, he should never be referred to by his childhood name, except sometimes by his elders. Yíge rén jǎng'dàle, chúle 'jǎngbèr, 'shéi dōu bùnéng jyàu tāde °'syàumíngr (°'rúmíng). /He may be called by his surname, as Mr. So-and-so. Kéyǐ jyàu tā °mǒu (°shémma shémma) syānsheng. /Please write your full name here. Chǐng bǎ °'míngdz (°'syìngmíng) syědzai 'jèr. /What is your name? (polite) Gwèi'syìng? _or_ (surname and given name) Gwèi'syìng, dà'míng? _or_ (only among highly educated people in very formal circumstances) Méi'lǐngjyàu? _or_ (courtesy name) °Tái'fù (°Dà'míng) dzěmma 'chēnghu? _or_ (to inferiors) Nǐ jyàu 'shémma míngdz? _or_ Nǐ 'syìng shémma, 'jyàu shémma? /My last name is Wèi and my first name is Mù'shř. °Bǐ-'syìng (°Wǒ syìng) 'Wèi, jyàu Mù'shř. /His name is 'Chywán Lù'chí. °Tā jyàu (°Tāde 'míngdz shř) 'Chywán Lù'chí. /His nickname is Shorty. Tāde wài'hǎur shř àidz. _or expressed as_ Everybody calls him Shorty. Rén dōu 'jyàu tā àidz. /They gave him a nickname. Tāmen gěi tā 'chǐle ge wài'hǎur. /I forgot his name. Tā °'míngdz (°'jyàu shémma) wó 'syàngbùchǐláile. /Let's give the baby a (formal) name. Dzámen gěi 'háidz chǐ ge 'míngdz ba. /I know him only by name. Wó jř 'tīngjyàngwo jèige 'rénde 'míngdz. /I know him by name. Wǒ 'jřdàu tāde 'míngdz. _or_ Wǒ 'jřdàu tā 'jyàu shémma. /I'm sorry I can't call you by name. Dwèibu'chǐ, 'táifu wǒ yǐ'shř °jyàubushang'láile (°syàngbùchǐláile).

(Of something other than a person) míngdz, -míng; (trade name) páidz; _or expressed by_ jyàu; _or in some cases not expressed at all._ /What's the name of your store? (polite) Bǎu'hàu shř 'něi jyā? *or* (ordinary conversation) Nǐmende 'pùdz °jyàu 'shémma (°shř 'něi jyār)? / What's the name of that store? 'Nèige 'pùdz °jyàu 'shémma (°shř 'shémma míngdz)? / What's the name of the street she lives on? Tā 'jùde nèityáu 'jyē °jyàu 'shémma (°shř shémma 'míngdz) laije? / The name of the book is . . . . 'Shūmíng shř . . . . *or* Jěibĕn 'shūde 'míngdz shř . . . . / The name of the boat is . . . . 'Chwánmíng shř . . . . *or* 'Chwánde 'míngdz shř . . . . / What's the trade name of that product? 'Nèijŭng 'dūngsyi shř shémma 'páidz de? / My dog's name is Spot. Wǒde gǒu jyàu Syǎuhwā.

(Reputation, fame) míng, 'míngyù, míngchi. / That product has a good name. 'Nèi dūngsyi hén yǒu'míng. / He's just trying to whitewash his father's name. 'Tā na búgwòshř yàu gěi tā 'fùchīnde 'míngyù 'syǐshwāsyǐshwā. / He's a lawyer who has made quite a name for himself. Tā shř ge 'lyùshř, (dżgér) gǎude 'hén yóu dyǎr 'míngchi le.

In name only yǒu'míngwú'shř; **be only a name** shř ge 'kūng míngdz. / He is head of the company in name only. 'Tā dāng jīng'lǐ yǒu'míngwú'shř. *or* Tā nèige jīng'lǐ °dāngde yǒu'míngwú'shř (°shř ge 'kūng míngdz). / He's a scholar in name only. 'Tā shř ge yǒu'míngwú'shřde 'sywéjě.

In the name of, in someone's **name** yùng . . . de míngdz, yùng . . . de míngyì. / I bought the property in her name. Jèikwài 'chǎnyè wǒ yùng 'tāde °'míngdz (°'míng-yì) mǎide. / He's been borrowing money in my name. Tā yùng 'wǒde °'míngyì (°'míngdz) °jyè 'chyán (*or* (without my consent) °'jāuyáujwàng'pyàn). *but* / Open the door in the name of the law! Wǒ fèng 'mìnglìng láide, kwài kāi'mén! / In the name of all that's holy! Dàu'dǐ! *or* 'Jyōujìng! / What in heaven's name did you do that for? Nǐ 'nèmmaje °dàu'dǐ (°'jyōujìng) shř 'dzĕmma hwéi 'shř a?

Call someone **names** (curse) mà. / He likes to call people names. 'Tā ài mà 'rén.

To name (give a name to) gěi . . . chǐ °'míngdz (°'míngr), (very formal) gěi . . . mìng'míng, (in a formal naming ceremony) mìng'míng, each may be followed by jyàu plus the name given. / In China a baby is never named after its parents (elders). Dzài 'Jūnggwo 'syǎuhár 'méiyou gēn °fùmú (°jǎngbèr) chǐ yí'yàngde 'míngdz de. / We named the dog Fido. Wǒmen gěi 'gǒu chǐle ge míngr, jyàu Féi'dòur. / I name you . . . (in a formal naming ceremony). Wǒ gěi nǐ mìng'míng, jyàu . . . . / Have you named the baby yet? Syǎu'hár chǐ'míngr le ma? *or* Nǐmen gěi syǎu'hár chǐ-'míngr le ma?

(Call by name) 'jyàuchu 'míngr lai, 'shǔchu . . . , 'shwōchu . . . . / Can you name all the basketball players? Lánchyóu chyóuywán dōu shř 'shéi, nǐ jyàudechu 'míngr lai ma? *or* Chyóuywánde 'míngdz nǐ dōu °'shǔdechulái (°'jyàudechulái, °'shwōdechulái) ma? / The burglar refused to name the men who had helped him. Syǎu'tōur 'bùkén bǎ bānggwo tā de rénde 'míngdz 'shwōchulai. / Just name one! Nǐ 'shwōchū 'yíge lai wǒ 'tīngting.

(Designate, select) shwō; (set) dìng; (choose) tyāu. / You name the day, and we'll have dinner together. Nǐ °'shwō (°'dìng, °'dìngwei, °'tyāu) ge 'řdz, dzámen hǎu yí'kwàr chř dwùn 'fàn. *or* Dzámen 'nèityān yí'kwàr chř dwùn 'fàn, °nǐ 'shwō 'řdz ba (°'řdz yóu 'nǐ shwō). / Name a price. Shwō yíge 'jyàr. / We asked him about a good place to eat, and he named several well-known restaurants. Wǒmen wèn tā 'nǎrde 'tsài hǎu, tā shwōle 'háujǐjyār yǒumíngde 'gwǎndz.

Other expressions in English. / I haven't a cent to my name. Wǒ yíge dzèr dōu 'méiyou. *or* Wǒ 'yìwénbu'míng. / He was named in the will. 'Yíjùshang 'tídàu tā le.

NARROW. (Of spatial dimension) jǎi, bùkwān; sometimes shòu *or* syī (thin), syǎu (small), jǐn (tight), bùgwǎng (not widespread). / This is a very narrow road. Jèityáu 'lù tǐng 'jǎi. / Be careful when you are on narrow roads. Dzài 'jǎilùshang dzǒu de shŕhou, yàu 'syǎusyǐnje. / The road gets narrow just beyond the bridge. 'Gāng yi gwò 'chyáu lù'myàr jyòu 'jǎi le. / This piece of cloth is too narrow. 'Jèikwài bù °tài jǎi (°búgòu 'kwān). / I don't want it that narrow. Wǒ 'búshr yàu 'nèmma jǎide. / The pants are very baggy and narrow at the cuffs. Kù'twěr dūluje, kù'jyǎur hén °'jǎi (°'shǒu). / Her eyebrows are narrow and long. Tāde 'méimau yòu 'syì yòu 'cháng. or expressed as She has willow-leaf eyebrows. Tā shr lyǒu'yèr méi. / She has very narrow shoulders. Tā jyān'bǎngr hén °jǎi (°'syǎu, °bù'kwān). / The waist of her skirt is very narrow. Tā 'chyúndz 'yāu ner hén °'jǎi (°'syì, °'syǎu, °'shǒu, °'jǐn). / These shoes are too narrow. 'Jèishwāng syé tài °'jǎi (°'jǐn). / He only had a narrow circle of friends. Tā 'péngyou hén 'shǎu. or Tā 'jyāuyóu bù- 'gwǎng.

(Literal) kǒuje dz̀'myàr, ànje dz̀'myàr. / His decision in this case showed a narrow interpretation of the law. Jèige 'àndz tā shr 'kǒuje 'jèityáu 'fǎlyùde dz̀- 'myàr 'dwànde. or Tā dwàn 'jèige àndz de shŕhou, shr 'ànje fǎlyùde dz̀'myàr 'jyěshŕde.

(Detailed and careful) 'dz̀syì. / A narrow scrutiny of the case is called for. Jèige 'àndz hái déi 'dz̀syì 'chá yichá.

(Of the mind, views, etc.). / She's a narrow-minded person. 'Tā nèige rén °syīn'jǎi (°'syīnyǎr hén 'jǎi, °'syīnyǎr hén 'syǎu, °bú'dàfang, °'syǎuchì, °'dùlyang hén syǎu, or (especially in thinking) °méi'jyànshr, °'jyànjyé hén 'dǐ, °'jyànjyé 'chyǎnbwó, or (prejudiced) °yǒu 'pyānjyàn, °'pyānsyīn'yǎr). / His views on the subject are very narrow. Dzài 'jèijyan shr̀shang tāde °'yǎngwǎng (°'kànfǎ, °'jyàn- jyé) hén °'pyān (°'jǎi).

Narrow escape. / We had a narrow escape yesterday. is expressed as We were in great danger. 'Dzwérge wǒmen °'syànde (°'sywánde) 'hěn. or meaning from death Dzwór wǒmen chà'dyǎr méi °bǎ 'mìng dyōu le (or meaning from being seen and caught °jyàu rén dǎijau).

To narrow down ('byàncheng) jyòu 'shèng (become); bǎ . . . °'swōjyǎndau (°'swōjyǎnchéng) (reduce). / The question narrows down to this; do you want to go, or don't you? Wèn'tí 'byàncheng jyòu 'shèng nǐ 'ywànyì búywànyi 'chyù le? / His suspicions have narrowed down to one person. Tā 'yísyīn de rén 'byàncheng jyòu shèng 'yíge le. / I've narrowed the possibilities down to two. Wó bǎ kěnéng'syǐng 'swōjyǎndau lyàngge le. / He narrowed down the possibilities. Tā bá kě'néngsyìngde 'fànwéi swō' syǎule. / He narrowed down the argument to three subjects. Tā bǎ byànlwùn 'tímùde 'fànwei 'swōjyǎnchéng 'sānge le.

NATION. gwó, 'gwójyā; the whole nation chywángwó, 'gwómín, chywángwó °'gwómín- (°derén); (with special reference to the people) 'mǐndzú. / Five nations were repre- sented at the conference. Nèige 'hwèi yóu °'wǔgwóde dài 'byǎu chū'syí (°'wǔge 'gwójyāde dài'byǎu chū'syí). / The whole nation will be affected by the new law. Chywán'gwó(derén or gwómín) dōu yàu shòu nèige 'syīnfǎlìngde 'yíngsyǎng. / It is our hope that this organization will embody all nations of the world. Wǒmen syīwang jèige dzǔjr néng bāukwò shr̀jyèsheng 'swóyǒude mǐndzú.

NATIONAL. (Pertaining to the political entity) gwó-. / Stand up when they play the national anthem. ('Yǎn)dzòu 'gwógēer de shŕhou, 'jǎnchilai.

(Pertaining to the political entity and its people) 'gwójyāde. / A national law gives all citizens the right to vote. Ànje 'gwójyāde 'fǎlyù 'swóyǒude 'gwómín 'dōu yǒu sywánjyǔ'chywán.

(Pertaining to the whole country distributively) is expressed by the noun 'chywángwó. / This is a matter of national importance. Jèijyàn shŕ gēn 'chywángwó yǒu 'gwānsyì. / He owns a national chain of restaurants. Tāde 'gwǎndz 'chywángwó dōu yǒu 'fēnhàu.

A national (a citizen) 'rénmín, 'gwómín. / The government requires all nationals to register in time of war. Dzài dǎ'jàng de shŕhou jèngfǔ jyàu 'swóyǒude °'rénmín (°'gwómín, °gūngmín) dōu 'dēngjì.

Nationalism 'míndzújǔ'yì, 'gwójyājǔ'yì.

Nationality (recorded in a census, etc.) gwójì. / What nationality are you? Nǐ shr 'něigwó gwó'jì. or Nǐ shr 'něigwó rén?

NATURAL. (Pertaining to the physical universe) 'dżrán. / He's studying natural science. Tā nyàn 'dżran'kēsywé.

(In accordance with nature, in a native state) 'tyānrán; **natural gas** 'tyānrán-'méichì. / The landscape has been left in its natural state, with none of the works of man added. Jèi shŕ 'tyānránde 'fēngjǐng, 'yìdyǎr 'réngūng yě méi'jyāgwo. / There is a natural waterfall there. Nèr yǒu yíge 'tyānránde pù'bù.

(Innate, in accordance with inborn nature) tyānshēngde; tyān only in the phrase 'tyāntsái **natural talent.** / He has a natural talent for painting. Tā tyān'shēngde hwèi hwà 'hwàr. or Tā yǒu hwà 'hwàr de 'tyāntsái.

(Normal) 'dżrán, 'dāngrán, both mean normally or of course. / It was a natural thing to say. °'Dżrán (°'Dāngrán) děi nèmma 'shwō le. / It was only natural for him to feel that way. Tā °dż'rán (°dāng'rán) hwèi 'jywéje nèmma yàngrde. / It's only natural that he didn't like it. Tā °dż'rán (°'dāngrán) búhwèi 'syǐhwānde.

(Real) jēnde. / The picture looks natural. Jèijāng 'hwàr kànje gēn 'jēnde shŕde.

(Unaffected) 'tyānjēn, 'dżrán, 'dàfāng, búhwèi jwāng'jyǎ, búhwèi 'jwāngmú-dzwò'yàngrde; (not bound by convention) bù'súchì, bù'jyūshù, 'syāusǎ, 'sàtwō. / He's a very natural person. 'Tā jèige rén °hěn 'tyānjēn (°hěn 'dżrán, °hěn 'dàfāng, °hěn 'syāusǎ, °bù'súchì, °etc.). / Be natural. 'Dżdzrán'ránde. or 'Dàdafāng'fāngde.

(Not violent). / He died a natural death. (of an old man, literary) Tā shŕ 'shòujūngjèng'chǐnde.

A natural. / He's a natural at (playing) tennis. is expressed as He plays tennis with natural talent. Tā dá 'wǎngchyóu yǒu 'tyāntsái. or Tā tyān'shēngde dá 'wǎngchyóu dǎ de 'hǎu.

NATURE. (System of the physical universe) Chinese uses only the combining form meaning natural(ly) 'dżrán. / Gravity is one of the laws of nature. 'Dìsyīn 'syǐlì shr 'dżrán'lyù jŕ'yì. / He won't take medicine; he says, "let nature take its course." Tā 'bù kěn chŕ 'yàu; tā shwō °'"děng ta 'dżjí hǎu ba (°'yàng yiyang dż'rán jyòu 'hǎu le)."

(Inborn nature) 'tyānsyìng; or expressions with the combining form meaning natural(ly) tyānshēngde. / It's not his nature to forget. Tā 'tyānsyìng °'búhǎu 'wàng (or (of hatred) °ài jì'chóu, or (of loyalty) °'jūnghòu). / It's not in his nature to be rude to his parents. is expressed as He's naturally respectful to his parents. Tā 'tyānsyìng hěn 'syàushwùn. or Tā tyān'shēngde 'syàujìng 'fùmǔ. or expressed as He's not naturally disrespectful to his parents (despite evidence to the contrary). Tā 'búshr tyān'shēngde bùkěn 'syàujìng 'fùmǔ de rén. / He's a lazy person by nature. 'Tā jèige rén °tyān'shēngde 'lǎn (°'tyānsyìng 'lǎndwò).

(Characteristic, of something other than a person) 'tèsyìng. /It's the nature of this metal to melt at a very low temperature. Jèijǔng 'dūngsyide 'tèsyìng shr dzài wēndù hěn 'dǐ de shŕhou jyòu kéyǐ 'hwà.

(Kind) jǔng, yàng(r) (measures meaning kind of); (hwéi) shr̀, syìngjr. /Has he explained to you the nature of your work? Nǐ 'yàudzwò de shr̀ °'néijǔng (°'shémma yàngrde) shr̀ tā dwèi ní 'jyǎnggwole ma? /What was the nature of the crime? Jèi-(jyàn) 'àndz(de'syìchíng) shr̀ dzěmma hwéi 'shr̀? or Jèi(jyàn) 'àndz shr̀ dzěmma ge 'syìngjr?

Good-natured. /She's a good-natured person. Tā píchì 'hǎu. or Tā jèi 'rén hǎu 'píchyer. or Tā jèi 'rén °tyān'shēngde (°'tyānsyìng) °'hòudau (°'jūnghòu).

NEAR. (Close in space or relationship) lí . . . jìn, lí . . . bùywǎn, jìn, bùywǎn. /The store is near the station. Pùdz lí hwǒchē'jàn hěn 'jìn. /Where is the nearest post office? Lí jèr 'dzwèijìnde 'yóujèng'jyú dzài 'nǎr? /He grabbed the arm of the man nearest him. Tā bǎ 'lí tā 'dzwèi jìn de nèige rénde 'gēbwo 'yìbǎ °'dzwǎnjule (°'lājule). /We walked near the river. Wǒmen dzài lí 'hébyār bù'ywǎn de nèr 'dzǒu laije. /He is a near relative of ours. (of the same surname) Tā shr̀ wǒmende jìn bènjyā. or (by marriage) Tā shr̀ ge 'jìnchīn. or Tā shr̀ ge hěn 'jìnde 'chīnchì.

(Close in time) kwài dàu; (almost, just before) 'chàbudwǒ, jyòu yàu 'dàu le; (be near at hand) . . . jyòu dàu. /It will be sometime near Christmas before he gets back. Tā děi °'kwài dàu (°'chàbudwǒ) Shèngdàn'jyé de shŕhou tsái néng 'hwéilai ne. /The time for the attack is near. Jìn'gūng de shŕjyān °jyòu yàu 'dàu le (°'shwō-hwà jyòu 'dàu, °'jányǎn jyòu 'dàu, °kwài 'dàu le).

(Soon, early) dzǎu. /We tried to get theater tickets, but the nearest date was two months off, so we didn't buy any. Wǒmen dǎswan mái jǐjang pyàu láije 'búgwò dzwèi 'dzǎude yě dzài 'lyǎywè yǐ'hòu, 'swóyǐ méi'mǎi.

(Closely resembling) 'syàng (dyǎr), gēn . . . chàbu'dwǒ. /This ring is nearer to what I had in mind. 'Jèige jyèjr gēn wǒ 'syīnli syàng 'yàu de hái 'syàng dyar. /We don't have that kind of tobacco, but this is the nearest thing to it. Wǒmen 'méi-yǒu nèijǔng yān'yèdz, búgwò 'jèige gēn nèige 'chàbu'dwǒ.

Near at hand (easily accessible) dzài shǒu'byārshang. /The documents are all near at hand. Nèisyē 'wénjyàn 'dōu dzài shǒu'byārshang.

Near here, nearby (in the neighborhood) (jèr) 'fùjìn, (jèr) 'dzwǒjìn, 'gēnchyǎr, bùywǎn. /Is there a hotel near here? Jèr °'fùjìn (°'dzwǒjìn) yǒu lyú'gwǎn ma? /We can get milk from one of the nearby farms. Fù'jìnde núng'chǎng nèr kéyǐ mǎi nyóu'nǎi. /There are several grocery stores nearby. °'Gēnchyǎr (°Fù'jìn, °Bù-'ywán) yǒu jijyā 'dzáhwò pùr.

Near miss. /It's a near miss. (Méi'jǔng, búgwò) °'pyànde bù'dwǒ (°'chàde bù'dwǒ, °'chàde hén 'shǎu, °chàbu'dwǒ (jyòu 'jǔng le), °'shāuwēi chà nèmma yì-'dyǎr jyòu 'shr̀ le).

Nearsighted 'jìnshr̀(de), (shr̀) jìnshr̀'yǎn. /He's nearsighted. Tā 'jìnshr̀. or Tā shr̀ jìnshr̀'yǎn. /He's so nearsighted that he can't see without glasses. Tā 'jìnshr̀de 'búdài yǎn'jìngr 'shémma dōu 'kànbu'jyàn.

To near (come near, get near, be nearly at) (lí . . .) jìnle, (lí . . .) bù'ywǎnle; (almost at) kwài dàu. /The boat is nearing land now. Chwán kwài dàu 'àn le. or Chwán lí 'àn bù'ywǎn (°hěn 'jìn) le. /We're nearing Chicago. Dzámen 'kwài dàu Jŕjyā'gē le. or Dzámen lí Jŕjyā'gē °'jìn le (°bù'ywǎn le).

NEARLY. kwài . . . , 'chàdyǎr jyòu . . . . See also **ALMOST.** /I nearly forgot how to get here. Wǒ °dōu kwài (°chà dyǎr jyòu) 'wàng le dzěmma láide le.

NECESSARY. (Essential) yí'dìng °yàu (°děi) . . . de, bǐděi . . . de; (stronger) 'bìsyū °yàu (°děi) . . . de, 'fēi(děi) . . . °bù'syíng de (°bù'chéng de, °bù'kě de), bu . . . °bùsyíng de (°bùchéng de); (referring to things that ought to be) 'yīngdāng . . . de. /He brought only the most necessary articles of clothing with him. Tā swéishēn 'dàide jŕyóu jǐjyàn °fēichwānbù'kě (°yí'dìng děi chwān, °bú'dài bù'syíng, °etc.) de 'yīshang. /I'll make the necessary arrangements. °'Yīngdāng (°Yí'dìng děi) bàn de 'shǒusyu dōu jyāu géi wǒ ba. /Do you have all the necessary evidence to prove the case? 'Jèige àndz °yí'dìng děi (°'bìsyū déi) 'yǒu de 'jèngjyu dōu 'chywán ma?

(Inevitable) is expressed verbally as fēi(děi) . . . bù'kě, yí'dìng yàu . . . . /The necessary result will be a great deal of confusion. 'Jyēgwǒ 'fēi chéng yìtwán'dzāu bù'kě. *or* 'Jyēgwǒ yí'dìng yàu nèng ge 'lwànchiba'dzāude.

It is necessary to . . . yí'dìng °yàu (°děi) . . . , bǐděi . . . ; (stronger) 'bìsyū °yàu (°děi) . . . , 'fēi(děi) . . . °bù'syíng (°bù'chéng, °bù'kě), bu . . . °bùsyíng (°bùchéng). /It will be necessary to have a passport to travel abroad. Dàu gwó'wài chyu lyǔ'syíng °yí'dìng déi (°bǐdéi, °'bìsyū déi) yǒu hù'jàu. (*or* yàu instead of děi) *or* Dàu gwó'wài chyu lyǔ'syíng °'fēi(děi) yǒu (°'méiyǒu) hù'jàu °bù'syíng (°bù'chéng). /It will be necessary to have everything checked carefully. °Yí'dìng yàu (°Yí'dìng děi, °Bǐ'syū dei, °Bǐděi) 'dzsyī 'chá yíbyàn. *or* Fēi(děi) 'dzsyī chá yíbyàn °bù'syíng (°bù'chéng, °'bùkě). *or* Bù'dzsyī chá yíbyàn °bù'syíng (°bù'chéng). /Is it necessary to make this trip? 'Jèitsz̀ 'fēiděi 'chyù ma? or expressed as Is it worthwhile? (may be sarcastic) 'Yùngdejáu dzǒu nèmma yí'tàng ma?

It is necessary for . . . **to** do so-and-so, put the word after for before any of the expressions in the paragraph above. /It is necessary for you to be here at eight o'clock. Nǐ °yí'dìng (°'bìsyū) °děi (°yàu) 'bādyǎn jūng 'dàu jèr. *or* Nǐ 'fēiděi 'bādyǎn jūng 'dàu jèr °bù'kě (°bù'syíng, °bù'chéng). *or* Nǐ 'bādyǎn jūng bú'dàu °bù'syíng (°bù'chéng).

NECK. (Part of the body) bwódz. /He has a scar on the back of his neck. Tā 'bwódz hòutou yǒu ge 'bāla. /He has a thick neck. Tā 'bwódz hěn 'tsū. /I've got a stiff (sore) neck. Wǒ 'bwódz téng. *or* Wǒ 'bwódz fā'swān.

(Collar) lǐngdz, lǐngr. /She wore a dress with a high neck. Tā chwān de nèijyàn 'yīshang 'lǐngdz hěn 'gāu. *or* Tā chwānle yìjyàn 'gāu lǐngrde 'yīshang.

(Narrow part of a bottle) kǒur. /Pick up the bottle by the neck. Bǎ 'píngdz 'náchilai de shŕhou, náje píngdz 'kǒur ner.

Neck and neck. /The two horses finished neck and neck. (even) Lyǎngpi 'mǎ °pǎule ge 'píng (*or* in a draw) °pǎule ge 'bùfēnshèng'fù, *or* (arrived together) °yí'kwàr dàu 'jyā).

Break one's neck. /I'll break your neck, if you don't give that back to me. Yàushr nǐ bu'hwángéi wǒ nèige 'dūngsyi, wǒ yàu ba ní 'dzái le.

Save one's neck. /Never mind about me. You'd better save your own neck. (think of a way out) Byé gwǎn 'wǒ le. Ní gěi dž'jǐ syǎng 'fádz ba. *or* (save your life) Nǐ 'džjǐ táu'mìng yàu'jǐn.

NEED. (Require something or someone) syūyàu, °děi (°yīng'gāi) °yǒu (°yùng); (have use for) 'yùngdejáu; do not need busyūyàu, búyung, yùngbu'jáu. /I need some money. Wǒ syū'yàn dyar 'chyán. *or* Wó děi 'yùng dyǎr 'chyán. /I think we need a man of your abilities. Wó syǎng wǒmen °syūyàu (°déi yǒu, °yīng'gāi yǒu) yiwèi syǎng 'nǐ dzěmma nénggande rén. /We need him badly. Wǒmen jer fēidéi yǒu 'tā bu'syíng. *or* Wǒmen hěn 'syūyàu tā. /They don't need me. Tamen °busyū'yàu (°yùngbu'jáu) wǒ. /If I need you, I'll let you know. Yàushr wǒ °'yùngdejáu (°'syūyàu) nǐ, wǒ lai 'jyáu nǐ. /I don't need money. Wǒ °busyū'yàu (°bu'yùng) chyán.

Need to do something or have something done syūyàu, yǒu . . . de bì'yàu, děi, gāi, yǐng'gāi, yǐngdāng, 'yùngdejáu. / These clothes need to be washed. Jèisye 'yīshang you 'syǐ yisyǐde bì'yàu. or Jèisye 'yīshang °déi (°gāi, °yǐng'gāi, °syūyàu, °yǐng'dāng) 'syǐ yisyǐ. / Do you need to leave now? Nǐ syūyàu syàndzài jyou 'dzou ma? / He needs to be taught a lesson. Ta syūyàu shòu dyar 'jyàusyun. / He needs to get a haircut. Tā děi 'líli fǎ le.

Need not, do not need to, need not have busyū'yàu, méiyou . . . de bì'yàu, buyǐng'dāng, buyǐnggāi, búbi, búyung, yùngbu'jáu. / You don't need to thank me. Nǐ °'búyung (°yùngbujáu, °búbi) 'sye wǒ. / She needn't have made such a fuss. Tā buyǐnggāi nèmma fā'píchi. / He needn't have slapped her. Ta běn'lái buyǐnggāi 'dǎ ta.

If need be bùde'yǐ, fēi nèmmaje bùkě, méi'fádz. / I'll go myself if need be. Yàushr °bùde'yǐ (°fēi nèmmaje bu'kě, °méi'fádz) wǒ jyou dz'jǐ chyù.

A need syū'yàu; or expressed verbally as chywē, chà (lack); bugòu (not enough); or as in paragraph one. / His needs are very simple. Tāde syū'yàu hén 'jyǎndān. / Take care of his needs. Tā 'chywē shémma chǐng nín 'jàuyingje dyar. / They have a need for clothing and medicine. Tāmen yòu chywē 'yīfu, yòu chywē 'yàupǐn. / There is a great need for cooperation. Dàjyāde hé'dzwò tài °'chà (°bu'gòu). / I don't see any need for me to go. Wǒ jywéde °yùngbu'jáu (°busyū'yàu) wǒ chyù. or Wǒ jywéde méiyou wǒ chyùde bì'yàu.

A friend in need. / You certainly are a friend in need. Nǐ 'jēn gòu °'péngyou (°'jyāuchíng). / A friend in need is a friend indeed is expressed as Only one who can be relied on can be called a friend. Néng kàude'júde tsái swàn 'péngyou. or as Only one who sends charcoal when it snows can be called a friend Néng 'sywélisùng-'tànde tsái swàn 'péngyou.

NEEDLE. (Sewing, hypodermic, phonograph) jēn; **magnetic needle** 'tszjēn, jǐnánjēn. / Do you have a needle and thread? Ní yǒu 'jēn gēn 'syàn ma? / She's lost a knitting needle. Tā dyōule yìgēn dǎ 'rúngsyàn de 'jēn. / Change the needle before playing that record. Syàn hwàn yíge 'jēn dzài chàng nèige 'pyāndz. / Does the needle point due south? °'Tszjēn (°Jǐnánjēn) jǐje 'jèng nán ma?

Pine needle 'sūngmáu. / We made a bed of pine needles. Wǒmen dzài 'dǐshang pūle 'sūngmáu dàng 'rùdz. / We slept on a bed of pine needles. Wǒmen 'dyànje 'sūngmáu 'shwèide.

To needle (heckle) bǐ. / Who needled him into this? 'Shéi bǎ tā 'bǐde 'jèmma-je le?

NEGLECT. Many indirect expressions are used with such meanings as not serious, careless, not put to heart, not do well, forget, not take care of, etc. / He's been neglecting his work lately. 'Jìnlái tā dzwò'shr °búshàng'jìn (°yòu dyàr 'syèdai, °búrèn'jēn, °bù'syǎusyīn, °bùlyóu'shén, °'syǐnbú'dzàiyàn). or 'Jìnlái tā méi bǎ tā dzwò de 'shr gēdzài 'syīnshang. or 'Jìnlái tā dzwò 'shr tài °'dàyi (°'shūhu, °'tsǎushwài). or 'Jìnlái tā yóu dyàr ná shr búdàng'shr dzwò. / He's been neglecting her. Tā 'jìnlái °búdà bǎ tā 'gēdzài 'syīnshang (°dwèi tā 'búdà shàng'jìn, °yóudyàr 'bù ná tā dàng hwéi 'shèr). / You'd better not neglect that infection. Nèige hwèi-'néng de 'dìfang byé °'dàyi (°'dānwù) le tsái 'hǎu. or Nèige hwèi'néng de 'dìfang °děi 'jǐ (°děi hǎu'hǎurde 'jǐ yijr, °děi syǎusyīn dyàr). / He's been neglecting his health. Tā dwèiyu shēntǐ tài 'dàyi le. / He's been neglecting his duties lately. 'Jìnlái tā 'bùhǎu'hǎurde 'dzwò 'gāi dzwò de shr. / Her parents neglected her education. Tāde 'fùmǔ 'dānwule ta, 'méi jyàu tā hǎu'hǎurde shàng'sywé. or Tāde 'fùmǔ bǎ tā nyàn 'shū de shèr gěi 'dānwule. / You've been neglecting your school work. 'Jìnlai nǐ 'gūngke 'méihǎu'hǎurde °nyàn (°'yùbei).

(Not do at all, forget). /I neglected to lock the door. Wǒ 'wàngle swǒ'mén le. *or* Wǒ tài °'dàyi (°'shūhu) le, méiswǒ 'mén. /He neglected to tell his boss that he'd borrowed some money. Tā yǐ °'shūhu (°'dàyi) °méi (°wàngle) bǎ tā jyè 'chyán de shèr gàusu tāde 'tóur.

Signs of neglect. / The house shows signs of neglect. is expressed as It seems as if nobody has taken care of this house. Jèige 'fángdz méi rén gwǎn'shr.

NEIGHBOR. 'línjyū, jyēfang; **next door neighbor** jyè'byěr(jùde). /He is our next door neighbor. Tā shr wǒmende °'jyēfang (°jyè'byěr). *or* Tā jù wǒmen jyè'byěr. /The neighbors formed a committee. Jyēfang dà'hwěr 'chénglìle yíge 'wěiywán'hwèi.

NEITHER. (Not one nor the other) . . . 'dōu bu . . . , . . . yě bu . . . (preceded by a noun, followed by a verb). /Neither statement is true. 'Lyángjǔng 'shwōfǎ 'dōu bú-'dwèi. *or* 'Nèige 'shwōde yě bú'dwèi. /Neither one of us can be there. Wǒmen lyǎ 'shéi °dōu (°yě) bùnéng 'dàu. *or* Wǒmen lyǎ 'dōu bùnéng 'dàu.

(Not either) 'yě bu . . . , 'yě méi . . . followed by a verb; if two parallel negations are expressed, yě is used with each; *see* **neither . . . nor** below. /If she isn't going to write, neither will I. 'Tā yàushr 'bùsyě 'syìn a, wó 'yě bu'syě. /He doesn't have any, and neither do I. 'Tā yě méiyǒu, 'wó yě méiyǒu.

Neither . . . nor yòu bu . . . yòu bu . . . , yě bu . . . yě bu, jì bu . . . yòu bu . . . . /She can neither sew nor cook. Tā °yòu (°yě, °jì) 'búhwèi dzwò 'yīshang, °yòu (°yě with yě, °yòu with jì) 'búhwèi dzwò'fàn. /I could neither see nor hear the speaker, so I left. Nèi yán'jyǎng de rén wǒ °yòu (°jì) 'kànbujyàn yòu 'tīngbu-jyàn, swóyǐ jyòu 'dzǒule. *or* Nèi yán'jyǎng de rén wǒ 'kàn yě 'kànbujyàn, 'tīng yě 'tīngbujyàn, swóyǐ jyòu 'dzǒule.

Neither here nor there (irrelevant; inconclusive). /That talk is neither here nor there. Nèisyē 'hwà (dōu) °'wúgwān'jǐnyàu (°'bùgwān'tùngyǎng, °méi'yùng, °'bújùng'kěn). *or* Nèi dōushr 'fèihwà.

NET. (Mesh) wǎng(dz); wǎng in combinations; **mosquito net** 'wénjàng. /The nets were loaded with fish. (Yú)'wǎngli °'jīngshr (°'chywánshr) 'yú. /The ball went through the net. Chyóur tsung wǎngdzli 'chwāngwochyule. /It's safer to sleep under a mosquito net in this climate. Dzài 'jèijǔng dìfang 'háishr dzài 'wénjàngli shwèi °'hǎu dyar (°'jyàu rén fàng'syìn).

Net (free of deductions) jìng; (actual) 'shŕjìshang (both go with verbs); **net profit** chwúnli; **net income** 'shŕjìshangde 'shōurù; **net weight** jìngjùng. /What was your net profit last year? Chyùnyan 'jìng °jwàn (°shèng) 'dwōshǎu chyán? *or* Chyùnyan 'chwúnlì dwōshǎu? /We made $3,000 net. Wǒmen jìng °jwàn (°shèng) 'sānchyān(ywán). /The net weight is two catties. 'Jìng jùng 'lyǎngjīn. /We made a net gain of ten yards. Wǒmen 'shŕjìshang wàng'chyán jìnle shŕ 'mǎ.

To net (of money) jwàn; (of other things) (jyàu . . .)dé. /The firm netted a good profit. Gūng'sz jwànle hěn'dwōde chyán. *or* Gūng'sz 'dà jwàn 'chyán. /The clever suggestion netted him a reward. Tā chū de 'fádz hěn 'chyǎu, jyàu tā déle 'jyǎng le.

NEVER. (Habitually not, including at present) bū . . . , méi(yǒu) . . . . /I never say such things. Wǒ 'bùshwō 'nèiyàngrde hwà. /When he starts talking he never stops. Tā 'yǐ shwōchilai jyòu °méi(yǒu) 'wán (°méi(yǒu) 'tóur, °bújù'dzwèi, °bújù'dzwěr, °bù'tíng).

(Habitually not, in past time only) 'syànglái bu, tsúnglái bu, 'yísyàng bu. /I've never said such things. Wǒ °'syànglái (°'tsúnglái, °'yísyàng) bùshwō 'nèi-yàngrde hwà.

(Not once, in past time only) ('gēnběn) méi, 'syànglái °bu (°méi) . . . . /I never said any such thing. Wǒ 'gēnběn 'méishwōgwo 'nèmmayàngrde 'hwà. /He never even opened the book. 'Nèiběn shū tā (gēn'běn jyòu) lyán 'běr dōu méi'dǎgwo. /I don't know why she's crying; I never even touched her. 'Wǒ bùjřdàu tā wèi shémma 'kū; wǒ °(lyán) 'āi dōu méi'āijau tā (°yě méi'āi tā méi'pèng tā de). /I've never felt better in my life. Wǒ yí'bèidz méi jèmma gāu'syìnggwo. or expressed as I feel swell. Wǒ 'shūfu'jíle. or as I'm not sick at all. Wǒ 'shémma bìng dōu 'méi-yǒu.

Never again jywé bu-, dzài bu-, dzài yě bu-, jywé búdzài, yí'dìng bu-, yí-'dìng búdzài; in imperatives, use 'búyàu or byé instead of bu. /I'll never go there again. Wǒ dzài (yě) bú'dàu nèr 'chyù le. or Wǒ °jywé (°yí'dìng) bú(dzài) dàu nèr 'chyù le. /Never do it again. 'Dzài byé 'nèmmaje le. or 'Yídìng °¹'búyàu (°¹'byé) 'dzài nèmmaje le.

NEW. (Not old) syīn; or expressed with gāng or tsái plus a verb. /This building is new. 'Jèige lóu °shř 'syīnde (°hěn 'syīn, °shř syīn 'gài de). or Jèi shř ge 'syīn lóu. /A new president has just been elected. 'Syīn dzúng'tǔng gāng 'sywǎnshangle. or Gāng 'sywǎnle ge 'syīn dzúng'tǔng. or Syīn 'sywǎnle ge dzúng'tǔng. /He bought a new car. Tā mǎile yílyàng syīn 'chē. /They have a new suite of furniture. Tāmen yǒu yítàu 'jānsyīnde 'jyājyu. /That's a new style. Nèi shř ge 'syīn shřyang. /The new man was cross-eyed. Syīn °¹'lái (°¹'dàu, °¹'hwàn) de nèige rén (shř ge) dòu'yǎr. /Do you have any new potatoes? Tǔ'dòu yǒu °¹'syīn syàlai de (°'gāng dàude) ma? /I'd like a new one. Wó syǎng yàu ge 'syīnde. /I like the new one better. Wó 'syīhwan nèige 'syīnde. /There will be a new moon next week. 'Syàlǐbài yǒu 'syīnywè. or 'Syàlǐbài jyou yàu chū ywè'yár le. but /Happy New Year! Bài-'nyán, bài'nyán!

(Different) hwàn(le) (changed, exchanged); lìng (another); also a few indirect expressions. /I'd like a new one (a different one). Wó syǎng yàu 'hwàn yige. /He bought a new car. (new to him, not necessarily newly made) Tā 'hwànle yílyàng 'chē. /After the operation he looked like a new man. Kāi'dàu yǐ'hòu tā 'kànshang-chyu °syàng 'hwànle ge 'rén shřde (°syàng 'lìngyíge rén shřde, or (doesn't look like himself) °bú'syàng tā le). /She got a new man. (servant) Tā hwànle ge °tīng-'chāide (°yùngren). or (lover or husband) Tā hwànle ge 'nánrén. /I feel like a new man. Wǒ 'jywéde °gēn (°syàng, °hǎu syàng) 'hwànle yíge 'rén shřde.

(Unfamiliar). /This place is new to me. is expressed as I just came to this place. 'Jèi dìfang wǒ °chū 'lái (°¹'syīn dàu). or as I never came to this place before. 'Jèi dìfang wǒ méi'láigwo. or as I'm not familiar with it. Wǒ 'jèiher hái bù'shóu ne. or as I'm green here. Wǒ 'jèiher hěn 'shēng ne. or Jèige dìfang wǒ hái 'rénshēngdìbù'shóude ne. /This is a new experience for him. 'Tā jèi shř °¹'chūtsž (°¹'tóuyi'hwéi, °kāi'hwūn, °¹'syīn kāi'chyàur). /I'm new at this kind of work. is expressed as I've done it before. 'Jèijǔng shř wǒ °méi'dzwògwo (°méi'gàngwo, °hǎishr wài'háng ne, °yóu dyǎr 'lìba, °shř ge 'ménwài'hàn). or as I'm not used to it. 'Jèijǔng shř wǒ hái °bú'gwàn ne (°bù'shóu ne, °hái méi'mwōjau 'mér ne).

NEWLY. syīn. /They're a newly wed couple. Tāmen 'syīn jyē'hwūn. or Tāmen shř 'syīnhwūn de 'fūfù. /The ground was covered with newly fallen snow. 'Dìshang 'pūje yitséng 'syīn syà de sywě.

NEWS. (News report) 'syīnwén; (information) syāusyi. /What's the latest news? Yǒu shémma 'syīnwén? or Yǒu shémma 'syīn dàu de 'syāusyi? /Here is the very latest news. Jèi shř 'gāng(dé)dàu de 'syīnwén. /What's the latest news about the election? Sywǎn'jyude 'shř °'gāng déle shémma 'syīn syāusyi méiyou (°'syàndzài dzěmma'yàng le)? /Who's going to break the news to him? 'Shéi chyù bǎ jèige 'syāusyi 'gàusu tā ne?

News to . . . . /That's news to me. Wǒ hái méi'tīngjyangwo ne. *or* Wǒ 'ywánlai 'bùjrdau yǒu 'nèmma hwéi shř. /That's no news to me. Nèi wó dzǎu °'tīngjyangwole (°'jrdàule, °syǎng'dàugwole).

Get news (personally) désyìn; (by mail or message) °jyējau (°'shōudàu) °syìn (°syàusyi). *See* GET.

NEWSPAPER. bàu, bàujř; (referring to the publisher or company) bàu gwǎn. /Do you have an evening newspaper? Ní yóu 'wǎnbàu ma? /What does the newspaper say? °'Bàushang (°Bàu'jřshang) dzěmma 'shwōde? /We have eleven newspapers in our library. Wǒmen túshū'gwǎnli yǒu shř'yí fèn °'bàu (°bàu'jř). /They're collecting old newspapers. Tāmen jēngdzài jyǎn 'jyòu bàu'jř ne. /He wrapped the bottle in newspapers. Tā bǎ 'píngdz ná 'bàujř 'bàushangle. /That newspaper is subsidized. °Nèijyā bàu'gwǎn (°'Nèige bàu'jř, °Nèige 'bàu) yǒu 'rén 'jīntyē. /This town has no newspaper. Jèige dìfang meiyǒu °bàu'gwǎn (°běn'dìde bàu'jř).

Newspaper boy bàutúng.

NEXT. (In a series of several things or times) 'syà(yī), 'dzài(yī); (below) 'dǐsyà; the next time 'syà(yí)tsž, dzài; next week 'syàlǐbài; next month 'syàywè; next year 'míngnyán; next Monday (Tuesday, etc.) syàlǐbài'yī *or* syàsyīngchī'yī (syàlǐbài'er *or* syàsyīngchī'er, etc.); the next few days (yǐ'hòu) jèijityān; the next few weeks (yǐ'hòu) jèijige °lǐbài (°syīngchī); the next few months (yǐ'hòu) jèijige ywè; the next few years (yǐ'hòu) jèijinyán. /Who's next in line here? Syà yíge shř 'shéi? *or* 'Syà yíge gāi 'shéi le? *or* 'Dǐsyà gāi 'shéi le? *or* 'Dzài yíge gāi 'shéi le? /You're next. 'Syà yíge gāi 'ní le. /I'll tell him that the next time I see him. Wǒ °'syà(yí)tsž (°'dzài) 'kànjyàn tā de shřhou bǎ nèige 'gàusu tā. /I've finished this questionnaire, and I'm ready for the next one. 'Jèige wèn'dá wǒ dōu dá'wánle; děngje dzwò 'syà yige ne. /The next train leaves in half an hour. 'Syà yítàng 'chē gwò 'bànge jūng'tóu kāi. /The next one is mine. 'Syà yíge jyòu shr 'wǒde. *or* 'Dzài yòu yíge, jyòu shr 'wǒde.

(After one thing or time) dìèr (the second); next in rank, next best chítsž. /I went home the next day. Dì'èr tyān wǒ hwéi 'jyā chyule. /He's next to the last. Tā 'dàushǔ dì'èr. /He's next in authority (*or* prestige, power, etc.). (merely second) 'Tā dzwò dì'èrbǎ jyāu'yǐ. *or* (after naming one) Chí'tsž shř 'tā. /That is the next best thing. Chí'tsž jyòu °shř (°shǔ) 'jèige °'hǎu le (°'bànfa hǎu le).

(Afterwards) rán hòu yǐhòu. /Next he put the letter in his pocket. Rán'hòu (°Yǐ'hòu) tā bǎ 'syìn °jwāng (°yē, °chwāi, °gē, °shōu) dzài tā kǒu'dàrlile. /What shall I do next? °Yǐ'hòu (°Rán'hòu) dzwò 'shémma ne? *or* 'Syà yíge dzwò 'shémma ne? *or* Dzwòwán 'jèige dzwò 'shémma ne?

(In location) 'pángbyār; (on that side) 'nèibyār; the next . . . 'pángbyār nèi(ge . . .), 'nèibyār nèi(ge . . .); next to . . . . . . (de) °'pángbyār (°'nèibyār); next-door jyèbyěr in the same constructions. /The next house is mine. °'Pángbyār (°'Nèibyār, °'Jyèbyěr) nèige 'fángdz shř 'wǒde. or expressed as Next time you pass a gate, that's our home. 'Dzài gwò yíge 'mér jyòu shr wǒmen 'jyā le. /Who lives next-door? °Jyè'byěr (°'Nèibyār) nèiswǒr 'fángdz 'shéi jù? /She sat next to me at the theater. Kàn'syì de shřhou 'tā dzwòdzài wǒ 'pángbyār. /We live next-door to the school. Wǒmen jùdzài sywé'syàude jyè'byěr.

Next to nothing. /She knows next to nothing about world affairs. 'Shřjyè 'dàshr tā °'jyǎnjr (°'chàbudwō) 'shémma dōu bùjr'dàu.

NICE. hǎu; sometimes more specific terms. /Did you have a nice time? Ní wárde 'hǎu ma? /I had a very nice time, thank you. Dwō syè, wǒ wárde hén 'hǎu. /I thought your friend was very nice Wǒ 'jywéje ní nèige 'péngyou hěn °bú'hwài (*or* (friendly) °'héchi, *or* (well-mannered) °yóu 'lǐmàu). /Everyone was very nice to us. 'Shéi dōu dài wǒmen (dàide) hén 'hǎu. /She wears nice clothes. Tā chwān °'hǎu yīfu (*or* (well-chosen) °'jyǎngjyou yīfu, *or* (expensive) °'gwèi yīfu). /It's nice and warm here. (really warm) Jèr jēn 'nwǎnwo. *or* (comfortable and warm) Jèr yòu 'shūfu yòu 'nwǎnhwo.

(Sarcastic). /This is a nice mess! 'Hǎu yìtwán 'dzāu le! /You certainly did a nice job of confusing things! Nǐde 'shǒudwàn 'jēn gāu a, 'dōu gěi néng'lwànle! *or* Nǐ 'jēn yóu 'běnshr, néngde 'nèmma lwànchībā'dzāude!

NIGHT. yèli; yè *in combinations*; **midnight** bànyè; **in the middle of the night** 'sānjīngbàn'yède; **night and day** 'hēiye'báirde, 'r̀yè. /He studies better at night. Tā 'yèli nyàn 'shū nyànde'hǎu. /These flowers bloom at night. Jèisyē 'hwār dōu dzài 'yèli kāi. /He spent the night on the train. Tā dzài 'chēshang gwòde 'yè. /I spent two nights there. Wǒ dzài 'nèr °jùle (°gwòle) 'lyǎng yè. /He snored all night. Tā °'jēngyè (°'yíyè) dǎ'hūlu. /He works nights. Tā 'yèli dzwò °'gūng (°'shr̀). /He does night work. *or* He works on a night shift. Tā dzwò °'yègūng (°'yèbān). /Did you sleep well last night? ('Dzwótyān) 'yèli shwèide 'hǎu ma?

(Evening) wǎnshang. /They're going to the movies tomorrow night. 'Míngtyan 'wǎnshang tāmen chyù kàn dyàn'yǐngr chyù.

Make a night of it. /Let's go to the play and then go dancing, and really make a night of it. Wǒmen 'syān chyù kàn 'syì, dzài chyù tyàu 'wǔ, 'tùngtùngkwàr'kwārde 'wár yiwǎnshang.

Good night (when parting to meet the next day) 'myéngr jyàn, 'míngtyanjyàn; (when parting for a longer time) dzàijyàn; (to someone sleeping in the same house) hǎu'hǎurde 'shwèi *or* (more politely) nín 'syēje ba.

NINE. jyǒu; **one-ninth** 'jyǒufēnjr̄'yī; **the ninth** dìjyǒu.

NINETEEN. shŕjyǒu; **one-nineteenth** shŕ'jyǒufēnjr'yī; **the nineteenth** dìshŕjyǒu.

NINETY. 'jyǒushŕ; **one-ninetieth** 'jyǒushŕfēnjr'yī; **the ninetieth** dì'jyǒushŕ.

NO. (In answer to a question) méiyou, búdwèi, bùsyíng; *or often expressed by repeating the verb of the question in negative form.* /No, I'm not going. Wǒ 'búchyù. /Have you eaten yet? No. 'Nǐ chrgwo 'fàn le ma? Méiyou. /May I go now? No. Wǒ 'kéyi dzǒule ma? Bùsyíng. /Is this the road to New York? No. 'Jèityáu shr̀ dàu Nyǒuywē chyù de 'lù ma? Búdwèi.

No . . . -er than someone, something, sometime bùbǐ *plus a stative verb.* /He's no better than she is. Tā bìng 'bùbǐ tā 'hǎu. *or* Tā yi'dyǎr dou bùbǐ ta 'hǎu. /The situation is no better than before. Chíngsying bùbǐ tsúng'chyánde 'hǎu. *or expressed as* The situation hasn't gotten any better. Chíngsying yi'dyǎr bujyàn'hǎu.

No . . . -er than followed by a numerical expression as a length of time, distance, height, etc. búdàu, búgwò. /He's been gone no longer (*or* more) than twenty minutes. Tā ('gāng) dzǒule búdàu 'èrshrfēn jūng. *or* Tā 'dzǒule búgwò 'èrshrfēn jūng. *or* (just twenty minutes) Tā 'dzǒule tsái yǒu 'èrshrfēn jūng. /He is no taller than six feet. Tā búdàu 'lyòuchr̄ gāu. *but* /He promised to be gone no longer than necessary. *is expressed as* He promised to return as soon as he was finished. Tā shwō shr̀ yiwánle lǐ'kè jyòu 'hwéilai.

No . . . -ing (not be allowed) bùsyǔ, bùjwǔn. /No swimming is allowed here. Jèr °bùsyǔ (°bùjwǔn) yóu'yùng. /There's no smoking here. Jèr °bùsyǔ (°bùjwǔn) chōu'yān. /That sign says "No Parking." Páidzshang 'syēje "Bùsyǔ Tíng'chē."

No longer bu . . . le. /He's no longer here. Tā 'búdzài jèr le.

No less than (at least) jr̃sháu. /There were no less than 200 men who volunteered to go. Jr̃'sháu yŏu 'èrbăi rén 'dàgàufèn'yŭng yàu 'chyù.

Have no, there is (or are) **no** 'méiyou. /We have no guns, no rifles, and not even enough swords. Wŏmen méiyou 'pàu, méiyou 'chyāng, lyán 'dāu dōu bugòu 'yùngde. /There are no women in the club. 'Hwèili méiyou 'nyŭrén. /There's no meat today. (there is none) 'Jīntyan méiyou 'ròu. or (none for sale) 'Jīntyan 'búmài 'ròu. or (eating it is not allowed) 'Jīntyan bùsyŭ chr̄ 'ròu. or (I don't want to buy any) 'Jīntyan °'búyàu (°'bùmăi) 'ròu. /I have no more to say. (nothing more that can be said) Méiyou 'byéde kĕ'shwō de le. or (that's about all) 'Yĕ jyou shr 'nèmmaje le. or (helplessly) Wŏ méi 'hwà shwō le. or (angrily) Wŏ 'dzài 'méide kĕ'shwō le. /There is no more. Méi'yŏu le! /There's no hope of our winning. Dzámen 'méiyŏu 'yíng de 'syīwang. or Dzámen 'búhwèi 'yíngde.

It (or This or That) **is no** búshr̄. /It's no small matter. 'Búshr̄ 'syău shr̄. or expressed as It's important. 'Gwānsyi hĕn 'dàde. /That's no joke! 'Bushr̄ 'wár de. or 'Búshr̄ shwōje 'wár de.

Other English expressions. /No sooner said than done. is expressed as As soon as it's said it's done. 'Shwōwánle yĕ 'dzwòwánle. or Shwō'hwà jr̃'jyān jyou dzwò'wánle. or 'Gāng shwōwánle jyou °'déle (°'chéngle). or as That's easy. 'Nà hăubàn. or as That can be done immediately. 'Măshàng jyou kĕyĭ 'chéng.

NOBODY. (Before a verb) 'méirén, 'shéi yĕ bu, 'dōu bu, 'chywán bu, 'chywándōu bu, 'shéi dōu bu; in past time méi instead of bu. /Nobody knows where he is now. 'Shéi °yĕ (°'dōu, °'chywán, °'chywándōu) bùjr̃dàu tā 'syàndzài dzài 'năr. or 'Méirén 'jr̃dau tā syàn'dzài dzài 'nĕr. /The policeman said that nobody was to leave the room. Sywún'jǐng shwō 'jèi wūdzlide 'rén °'dōu (°'shéi yĕ, °etc.) bùsyŭ 'chūchyu. /Nobody told me. 'Shéi °yĕ (°'dōu, °etc.) méi'gàusung wŏ. or 'Méirén 'gàusung wŏ.

There is nobody 'méi(yŏu)rén. /There's nobody here. Jèr 'méi(yŏu)rén. /There's nobody else here. Jèr 'méi(yŏu) 'byéren.

Other English expressions. /He's a nobody. 'Tā méiyŏu 'míngchi. or Tā shr̄ ge 'wúmíng syău'dzúr.

NONE. (Not one) dōu, chywán, 'chywándōu plus a negative (of things or persons, expressed after the noun in Chinese); or, emphasizing, not a single one yíge before the noun and a negative, with yĕ preceding the negative if the verb comes after the noun; shéi, 'shéi dōu plus a negative word (of people only). /They have none of the things you have. Syàng 'nĭde jèisyē 'dūngsyi 'tāmen °dōu (°'chywán, °chywándōu) méi'yŏu. /None of the men spoke to me. Méiyou 'yíge rén °'gēn wŏ shwō 'hwà (°'lí wŏ). or (Lyán) 'yíge 'lí wŏ de rén yĕ méi'yŏu.

(Not any) expressed only in the negative word. /He asked for some money, but we had none. Tā yàu 'jyè dyăr chyán, kĕshr̄ 'wŏmen °yĕ méi'yŏu (°'méide kĕ'jyè de).

None of that. /None of that! (talk) 'Bùsyú nĭ 'húshwō! or Byé 'syàshwō! or (action) 'Bùsyŭ 'nèmmaje! or 'Byé nèmmaje!

None the less 'swéiránrú'tsz̆ . . . háishr . . . , 'búgwo . . . háishr . . . . /The situation looks hopeless, but none the less we're determined to try. 'Jèi shèr 'kànje 'méi yìdyăr 'syīwang, °'búgwo (°'swéiránrú'tsz̆) wŏmen háishr yàu 'shr̃ yishr̃.

None the worse. /He was none the worse for the accident. Chūle hwéi 'shèr tā 'jyūrán °méi dzĕmma 'yàng (°hău'hăurde 'hái nèiyàngr).

None too . . . 'búdà . . . . /He was none too happy about it. Tā 'búdà gāusyìng nèmmaje. or Nèi shèr 'jyàu tā 'búdà 'tùngkwài.

Have none of it. / They told him of the plan, but he would have none of it. Tāmen bǎ nèige 'yìsz gēn ta 'tíle yìtí; tā °bú'gàn (°'wánchywán 'búdzàn'chéng, °'wán-chywán fǎn'dwèi, °jyù'jywéle).

NOON. 'jūngwǔ; (Peiping) 'shángwǔ; (in combination) wǔ. / I'll meet you in front of the hotel at noon. Dzámen °'jūngwǔ (°'shǎngwu) dzài lyúgwǎn 'chyánbyar jyàn. / It's exactly twelve noon. Jěngshr °'jūngwǔ (°'shǎngwu) shrèr'dyǎn. / He's arriving on the noon train. Tā dzwò de nèi'tàng hwǒché °jūngwǔ (°'shángwǔ) 'dàu.

NOR. *See* NEITHER.

NORTH (NORTHERN). běi; **northeast** dūngběi; **northwest** syīběi; **Northern Hemisphere** Běi Bànchyóu; **North Pole** Běi'jí; **North Star** Běi'jísyīng. / There's a strong north wind today. Jyēr 'běifēng gwāde hěn 'dà. / Which way is north? Něibyǎr shr 'běi a? *or* (straight north) Něibyǎr shr 'jèng běi a? / Go north to the bridge; then turn right. Wàng 'běi dzǒudàu(le) 'chyáu nèr (dzài) wàng 'yòu gwǎi.

(Indicating a part or area) běibù, běibyǎr, běifāng. / I'm from the north, but my friend is from the south. Wǒ shr tsúng °'běibù (°'běibyǎr, °'běifāng) láide, wǒde péngyou shr tsúng °'nánbù (°'nánbyǎr, °'nánfāng) láide.

(Indicating an area beyond a border) běibyǎr; (to the) **north of** . . . dzài . . . (de) běibyǎr. / The cemetery is just north of the monastery. 'Féndì jyòu dzài myàu(de) 'běibyar yì'dyǎr.

NOSE. (Physical organ) bídz; (in combinations) bí. / He has a large red nose. Tāde 'bídz yòu 'dà yòu 'húng. / The bridge of his nose is prominent. Tā 'bílyángdz hěn 'gāu. *or* Tā 'gāubílyángr. / The bridge of his nose is deep-set. Tā 'bílyángdz shr 'byěde. *or* Tā 'byěbílyáng. / Go blow your nose. Chyù syǐng 'bídz chyu. *or* Chyù bǎ 'bídz 'syǐng yisyǐng. / He talks through his nose. Tā 'bíyīn hěn 'jùng. / He is talking through his nose. Tā shwō 'hwà yùng 'bídz chū'shēngr. / Most dogs have sharp noses. Gǒu 'bídz °'jyān (°'líng). *or* (dogs can really smell) Gǒu néng 'wén.

(Of a plane) fēijīde jītóu. / The nose of that plane is pointed. Nèige fēi'jīde jī'tóu shr 'jyānde.

Led by the nose. / He led them by the nose. is expressed as Whatever he says, they listen. Tā 'shwō shémma tāmen 'tīng shémma. / You're just being led by the nose. is expressed as You're just following blindly. Nǐmen jè shr 'mángtsúng.

Count noses 'shǔyishǔ yǒu 'dwōshau rén. / Let's count noses. Dzámen 'shǔ yishǔ yǒu 'dwōshǎu rén.

To nose (of an airplane, train, car, etc.). / The plane nosed into the wind. Fēijī 'chùngje fēng jyòu 'fēidzǒule.

(Of an animal) wén. / The dog is nosing around (smelling everywhere) for the bone he buried. Gǒu dàuchùr 'wénje jǎu tā mái de 'gutou.

Other expressions in English. / He pokes his nose into everything. is expressed as He wants to manage everything. Tā 'shémma dōu yàu 'gwǎn. / She turned up her nose at him (wouldn't look at him). Tā kànbu'chǐ tā. *or* Tā chyáubu'chǐ tā. / That reporter has a good nose for news (knows how to get news). Nèige 'jìjě hěn hwèi °'tsǎifǎng (°'dzwān) 'syīnwén. / That's as plain as the nose on your face. 'Nèi shr °'syāneryì'jyàndê (°'syǎnrányì'jyàndê, °'míngmingbaibáide, °'míng'syàndê).

NOT. bù (bú before syllables with a fourth tone); méi before yǒu and in situations where the action had not, has not, or will not have started; byé, búyàu; béng, búyùng (local Peiping) <u>for imperatives</u>. /He's not going to be home today. Tā jyēr bùhwéi-'jyā. /I'm not busy right now. Wǒ 'syàndzài °bù'máng (°'méi shémma 'shèr). /Not everyone can go to college. 'Dàsywé búshr 'shéi dōu chyùde'lyǎu de. *or* Bùnéng 'měirén 'dōu shàng dà'sywé. *or* 'Búshr 'měirén 'dōu néng shàng dà'sywéde. /Not me. <u>meaning</u> It isn't me. 'Tsái búshr 'wǒ ne. <u>or meaning</u> I'm not going to . . . . Wǒ tsái bu . . . . <u>or meaning</u> I didn't . . . . Wǒ tsái méi . . . . /Tell him not to leave before seeing me. 'Gàusu tā méi'jyànjau wó yǐ'chyán byé 'dzǒukai. *or* 'Gàusu tā 'jyànle wǒ dzài 'dzǒu. /Not one person offered to help. Lyán 'yíge shwō yàu 'bāngbang'máng de yě méi'yǒu. /That's not so! 'Búshr nèmma hwéi'shr. *or* Bú-'dwèi. /Not that he isn't right; it's the way he expresses it that irritates me. Bìng 'búshr tā méi'lǐ; shǐ tā shwō de 'hwà bújùng'tǐng. /No, not that! Āiya! 'Kě byé 'nèmmaje a! /Not now (it can't be done now). Syàn'dzài bù'syíng. /Not so fast! Byé nèmma 'jí! *or* Byé nèmma jāu'jí! *or* Byé nèmma 'kwài! *or* (slower) 'Màn dyar! *or* 'Mànje dyar! /Whether he comes or not is nobody's concern. Tā 'lái 'bùlái shéi yé gwǎnbu'jáu. /He doesn't like it; that is, not much. Jèige tā bù'syǐ-hwān, ē, bu'dà syǐhwàn. /He's not in (at home). Tā búdzài 'jyā. /Not bad. Bú-'hwài. /Not a bit. (in answer to Are you tired?) Yǐdyár yě bú'lèi. (and so forth with other stative verbs substituted for lèi depending on what is asked). /Not at all. (in answer to thank you) 'Méishémma, 'méishémma. /Not a bad idea. Jèi °'fádz (°'júyì) bú'hwài. /Not so good. 'Búdà 'hǎu. /Not a soul. 'Yíge rén yě méi'yǒu.

NOTE. (Short letter) 'dwǎnsyìn, tyáur, syèr; (a word) dzèr. /We just had time to write a short note. Wǒmen 'jř yóu syě fēng 'dwǎnsyìn de 'gūngfu. /Drop me a note when you get there. 'Dàule lái °ge 'syèr (°ge 'dzèr, °fēng 'dwǎnsyìn). /Leave a note. 'Lyóu ge °'dzèr (°'tyáur).

(Formal communication) syìn, 'gūnghán. /He sent in a note of resignation. Tā syěle fēng tsź'jřde °syìn (°'gūnghán).

(Newspaper item) dwàr (a measure). /Today's paper has a note about the ship's arrival. Jyērde 'bàushang 'yǒu yídwàr shwō 'nèijř chwán 'dàule.

(Sound with steady pitch) yīn. /She sang the high notes very easily. Tā chàng 'gāu yīn yìdyǎr dōu 'búyùng fèi'jyèr. /That's a very high note. 'Nèige yīn 'hěn gāu.

(Written musical symbol) yīnhàu, yīnfú.

(Suggestion, implication) yìsz. /There was a note of anxiety in her voice. Tīng tā shwō 'hwà de 'shēngyīn 'hǎusyàng dài dyǎr jāu'jíde yìsz.

(Written record or observations) 'bǐjì; **take notes** jì bǐjì; **make a note of** jìsyalai; **take notes on** . . . . . . yóu jìchù 'dìfang 'jìsyalai. /His notes on the lecture are very good. 'Yǎnjyǎng 'bǐjì 'tā jìde 'hén hǎu. /Do you always take notes during the meetings? Kāi'hwèi de shŕhour ní 'lǎu jì bǐ'jì ma? /Make a note of the time he left. Tā 'shémma shŕhour 'dzǒude 'jìsyalai. /I took notes on that lecture. Nèige 'yánjyǎng yóu jìchù 'dìfang wǒ 'jìsyalaile. *but* /We compared notes (not necessarily written) on this case. °'Jèijyàn shèr (*or* legal case °'Jèige àndz) wǒmen °bǎ 'gèrén swǒjř-dàu de 'dwèijàule yísyàr (°'jyāuhwànle syar 'yìjyàn, °'tánle yitán, °'bǐtsž 'tsān-kǎule yísyàr).

Notes (for a speech, etc.) tsáugǎur, dǐgǎur (original draft, manuscript); 'dà-gāng (outline). /He can't give a speech without using notes. Tā jyáng'yǎn méiyǒu °dí'gǎur (°'tsáu'gǎur, *or* °'dàgāng) bù'syíng.

(Explanatory annotations) jù, jùr, 'syǎujùr, 'jùyě. /I have a copy of "Marco Polo" with notes. Wó yǒu yìběr dài 'jùr de "'Mǎkēbwōlwó" yóu'jì. /Read the notes. Kànkan °'jùr (°'syǎujùr, °'jùyě). /Who wrote the notes for that book? Nèiběn shūde 'jùr shŕ 'shéi syě de?

Bank note chyánpyàudz, chyánpyàur, pyàudz, pyàur.

Notebook 'bǐjǐ běndz. / That notebook is for chemistry. Nèige 'bǐjǐ běndz shr̀ jǐ 'hwàsywé de.

Promissory note 'jyèdzèr, 'dz̀jyù, 'jyèywē. / I took a promissory note for the amount of money he owed me. Tā 'gāi wǒ de chyán wǒ gēn tā yàule yǐjāng °'jyèdzèr (°'dz̀jyù, °'jyèywē).

To note (notice) kànchulai (see also NOTICE). / He noted that there was a mistake. Tā 'kànchulai yǒu ge 'tswèr.

Noted yǒumíng(de). / This restaurant is noted for its food. 'Jèijyā 'gwǎndz 'tsài hén yǒu'míng. / A very noted man sat opposite us. Dwèi'myàr dzwòje ge 'míngrén.

NOTHING. shémma yě, shémma dōu, yǐdyár yě plus a negative; or, if the affirmative uses yǒu as the verb, méi(yǒu) shémma; shémma and yǐdyár are often followed by nouns specifying what there is nothing of; simply méi(yǒu) plus the noun is also possible; and in some cases a simple negative sentence is used. / There is nothing for me to do. Wǒ 'méiyǒu shémma °'shr̀ching (°kě'dzwò de). or 'Méiyǒu 'wó kě-'dzwò de 'shr̀. or 'Méiyǒu 'shr̀ géi wǒ 'dzwò. / Nothing can be done about it. 'Méifár 'bàn le. or 'Méi fádz 'syǎng le. or 'Méiyǒu shémma 'fádzle. / There's nothing I can do about it. 'Wǒ méifár 'bàn. / Oh, nothing. (in answer to Why?) 'Búwèi shémma. or (in answer to What?) 'Méi shémma. or 'Búyàujǐn. / Oh, nothing; forget it. 'Méi shémma. or 'Búswàn shémma. or 'Syàushr̀ yìjwāng. or 'Búyàujǐn. or 'Gwòle jyóu 'swànle. / He said nothing about it to me. 'Jèishèr tā yǐ'dyár yě °méi'gàusu 'wǒ (°méigēn 'wǒ shwō). / Nothing ever happens around here! Jèr 'shémma shèr °dōu (°yě) méi'yǒu, jēn 'mèndehwāng. / She's pleasant, but there's nothing to her. Tā hén 'héchì, búgwò °méi'chywèr (°'méidà'yìsz). / Nothing doing! Bù'chéng! or Bù'syíng! / She means nothing to me. Tā yǐ'dyár yě búdzài wǒ 'syīnshang. or Tā gēn wǒ yǐ'dyǎr gwānsyi yě méiyǒu. / That's nothing to me. Nèi 'wǒ yǐ'dyár yě bú'dzàihu. or 'Nèi gēn 'wǒ yǐ'dyár gwānsyi yě méiyǒu. / That means nothing to me (has no meaning). 'Nèi wǒ yǐ'dyár yě bù'dǔng. / I've heard that story before, but there's nothing to it. 'Nèi shèr wǒ 'tīngjyàngwo; yǐ'dyár yě bù'jēn. / She's so thin that there's nothing to her (no strength). Tā 'shòude yǐdyǎr 'jyèr dōu méi'yǒule.

For nothing (in vain or free) bái. / We did the work for nothing. Dzámen 'bái °fèi'shèrle (°fèi'jyèrle). or Dzámen swànshr 'bái mánghele yíjèn le. or Dzámen swánshr 'bái °fèi'shèrle (°fèi'jyèrle). / He works there every day for nothing. Tā 'tyāntyan dzài nèr gěi rén 'bái dzwò 'shr̀. or Tā tyāntyan dzài nèr dzwò 'shr̀, shémma 'bàuchóu yě bú'yàu.

Nothing compared to, nothing like gēn . . . yǐ'bǐ kě chà'ywánle. / That's nothing compared to some things I've seen. 'Nèige gēn 'wǒ kànjyàngwo de nèisyē yǐ'bǐ kě chà'ywánle. / He's nothing like his father. Tā gēn tā 'fùchin yǐ'bǐ kě chà'ywǎnle.

Nothing less than 'jyǎnjr̀ jyòushr. / That's nothing less than a lie. Nà 'jyǎnjr̀ jyòushr shwō'hwàngle.

Think nothing of °bú'swàn (°bú'dàng) hwéi 'shèr. / He thinks nothing of driving seventy miles an hour. Tā ná yǐ'dyǎnjūng kāi 'chīshrlǐ °bú'swàn (°bú'dàng) hwéi 'shèr.

NOTICE. (Announcement) 'chwándān (handbill); syìbàudz (handbill or sign about a play); gwǎnggàu (advertisement). / Did you see the notices about the new play? Nèichū 'syīn syìde °syì'bàudz (°gwǎng'gàu, °'chwándān) nǐ 'kànjyanle ma?

(Posted announcement) gàushr. / The police posted a notice about the missing men. 'Jǐngchájyú chūle yíge 'gàushr, jàu nèijǐge shr̀'dzūng de rén.

(Notification) tūnggàu, bùgàu; (of an employee) is expressed verbally as dzau
. . . gàusu. / The factory will be closed until further notice. 'Gūngchǎng tíng'gūngle,
yǐhòu 'dzài kāi de shŕhou yǒu °tūng'gàu (°bù'gàu). / You will have to give your
employer two weeks' notice before you leave your job. Nǐ yàushr tsź'jŕ děi 'dzáu
lyǎngge 'syīngchī 'gàusu nǐ 'júgwǎn de rén.

(Act of observing) is expressed with the verb jìsyalai. / Was any notice taken
of his failure to attend the meeting? Tā méidàu'hwèi yǒu rén 'jìsyalaile ma?

At a moment's notice. / I can be ready at a moment's notice. Wǒ swéi'shŕ dōu
kéyi jwǔnbèi'hǎule.

Escape one's notice méi'lǐhwèi, méikàn'jyàn, méichyáujyàn. / That paragraph
escaped my notice the first time I read the preface. Wǒ 'tóuyìhwéi kàn nèipyān 'syù
de shŕhou, 'nèiyídwàr wǒ °méilǐ'hwèi (°méikàn'jyàn, °méichyáu'jyàn).

Serve notice shwō. / The store has served notice that all bills must be paid
tomorrow. 'Pùdz 'shwōle 'swóyǒude 'jàng 'míngtyān °děi yí'lyù hwán'chīng (°'dōu
děi hwán'chīng le).

Take no notice of méilǐhwèi, méilyǔhwèi. / We didn't take any notice of him.
Wǒmen °méi'lǐhwèi (°méi'lyǔ'hwèi) tā.

To notice (see) 'kànjyàn, 'chyáujyàn; (see and notice particularly) lǐhwèi,
lyǔhwèi; (pay attention to) 'jùyì; also expressed as escape notice or take notice.
/ I didn't notice the sign until you spoke of it. Nèige 'páidz °'nǐ bùshwō (°bùshr 'nǐ
shwō) wǒ °méijù'yì (°méichyáu'jyàn, °'jēn jyou méi'kànjyàn). / Did you notice that
his hand was trembling? Nǐ °'kànjyàn (°chyáujyàn) tā shǒu 'chànle ma?

NOVEMBER. Shŕ'yíywè.

NOW. (Right at this moment) 'syàndzài. / The doctor can see you now. 'Dàifu 'syàndzài kéyǐ 'jyàn nǐ le. / You'd better leave now, or you'll miss the train. Nǐ 'dínghǎu
'syàndzài jyou 'dzǒu, 'yàubùrán hwéitóu 'wùle 'chē le. / Now let's see what he's
going to do. 'Syàndzài kàn 'tāde le. / Now do you understand? Nǐ 'syàndzài 'dǔngle
ma? or 'Dǔngle ma? or 'Míngbaile ma?

(At this time) 'jèi shŕhour. / He ought to be here by now. Tā 'jèi shŕhòur
yīnggāi 'dàu jèr le. / From now on the work will be difficult. Tsúng °'jèi shŕhou
(°'syàndzài) chǐ, 'shŕching jyou yàu 'nánchǐlai le.

(In this case) 'jè ké. / Now what am I going to do? 'Jè ké dzěmmaje 'hǎu ne?
/ Now what? 'Jè ké dzěmma 'hǎu ne. or (meaning What next?) 'Yǒu yàu 'dzěmmaje?
/ Now we're sure to be late. Jè kě 'jēn yàu 'wǎn le.

(Sometimes expressed for stress only, with no meaning). / Now you listen to me!
Tīng 'wǒ shwō. or Tīng 'wǒ gàusu ni. or (somewhat angrily) 'Tīngje. or 'Syàndzài 'nǐ gāi tīng 'wǒde le. / You be careful, now! 'Syǎusyīn dyar, ā!

Now and then 'jyēchángbù'dwǎrde. / I see him now and then. Wǒ 'jyēchángbù-
'dwǎrde kànjyàn tā.

Now that (in light of the present situation) 'syàndzài; (once something else has
happened) yǐ before a verb. / Now that the rain has stopped, we can leave. 'Syàndzài
yǔ 'jùle, wǒmen kéyǐ 'dzǒu le. / Now that you mention it, I do remember seeing her.
'Nǐ dzèmma yǐ 'shwō, wǒ 'syángchǐlaile, wǒ 'kànjyàngwo tā.

Just now (just a moment ago) 'gāngtsái . . . (hái); see JUST. / I saw him on
the street just now. Wǒ 'gāngtsái dzài dà'jyēshang hái 'kànjyàn °tā le ne (°tā
láije ne).

NUMBER. (In a series) hàu, dì . . . hàu; (particularly with a modifier or after shémma) 'hàushù(r), (Peiping) hàumǎr, hàutóur; (particular figure) shùr; house number 'ménpái 'hàushù(r), 'ménpái hàu'mǎr, 'ménpái hàu'tóur; page number 'yèshù. /What is the number of your house? Nǐ jyā 'mén pái 'shémma °hàushu (°hàu'tóur, °hàu'mǎr)? or Nǐ jyā 'mén pái 'dwōshǎu 'hàu? /They changed all the numbers on this street. Tāmen bǎ jèityáu jyēde ménpái °'hàushur (°'hàumǎr, °'hautóur) 'dōu hwànle. /His street (or house) number is 409. Tā 'ménpái 'hàushu shr̀ 'sz̀líng'jyǒu. /I can never remember telephone numbers. 'Dyànhwà °'hàushu (°hàu'mǎr, °hàu-'tóur) wó lǎu jìbu'jù. /What is your telephone number? Nǐ 'dyànhwà dwōshǎu 'hàu? My telephone number is 3-6001. Wǒde dyàn'hwà hàushu shr̀ 'sānyòulínglíng'yī. /No, it's a large number, at least six digits. Jèi bú'dwèi. 'Nèige shùr hěn 'dà, 'jr̀shǎu yǒu 'lyòuwèi. /His room is on the fifth floor, but I've forgotten the number. Tāde 'fángjyān dzài 'wǔlóu; wǒ 'wàngle shr̀ 'dwōshǎu 'hàu le (°shémma hàushu le). /Room number, please? Dì'jǐhàu fàngjyān? /There is a number on the badge. 'Párshang yǒu ge 'hàushu. /It's a Western superstition to think of 13 as an unlucky number. Ná shr̀'sān dàng 'syūngshùr shr̀ syīyangrénde 'mísyìn. /He says 5 is his lucky number. Tā shwō 'wǔ jèige shùr dwèi 'tā hěn 'jílì. /Number 10 is the best player on the team. 'Nèi dwèili (dì) 'shr̀hàur dǎde 'dzwèi hǎu.

(Issue) chī. /The latest number of the magazine arrived today. Dzwèi'jìnde yì'chī hwà'bàu 'jyèrge dàule. /We missed three numbers of that weekly magazine. Nèige 'jōukān wǒmen chywēle 'sānchī.

(Performance on a program) syàng. /There were five numbers on the program. 'Jyémù yígùng yóu 'wǔsyàng.

A number of see **MANY.** /He owns a number of houses. Tā yǒu bù'shǎude 'fángchǎn. or 'Tā chèn °'hǎujiswòr 'fángdz (°'hǎusyē fángdz). /There's a large number of stores on this street. Jèityáu 'jyēshang yǒu °'hěndwōde (°'hǎusyējyār) 'pùdz. /Only a small number of men volunteered. Jr̀ yǒu 'bùjǐ'gèr rén 'dz̀ gàufèn-'yùng.

Numbers (of people) rén dwō. /They won the battle by sheer force of numbers. Nèiyíjàng tāmen jr̀ 'jàngje rén 'dwō dǎ'shèngde. but /Refugees came to America in large numbers (by large groups). 'Nànmín °yí'dàpīyí'dàpīde (°'chéngchyúndǎ-'hwōde) dàu 'Měigwo lái.

To number (assign serial numbers to) jyā °'hàushùr (°etc.); **be numbered** yǒu °'hàushùr (°etc.). /He numbered the pages carefully. Tā bǎ 'yèshù yí'yèyíyède 'jyāde hěn 'dz̀syi. /These are all numbered. 'Jèishang 'dōu yǒu °'hàushur (°hàu-'mǎr, °hàu'tóur). /These have all been numbered. Jèi dōu 'jyāle hàu'mǎr le. /Have these sheets numbered. Bǎ jèisyējāng 'jr̀ 'jyāshang hàu'mǎr.

(Total) yí'gùng shr̀, yí'gùng yǒu. /The population of this place numbered 2,000 in 1940. Jèige dìfang 'rénkǒu dzài 'yíjyòusz̀'língnyán yí'gùng °shr̀ (°yóu) 'lyǎng'chyān.

Other English expressions. /His days here are numbered. (on earth) Tā méi-'jyòurle. or Tā 'hwōbùlyáu jǐtyān le. or (in this place) Tā dzàijèr 'dāibùlyáu jǐ-'tyān le. or (impolite) Tā kwài gwǔn'dàn le. or Tā kwài jywàn 'pūgai le. /His number will be up pretty soon. meaning It will be his turn soon. Kwài 'lwúndàu 'tā le. or meaning His serial number (as in the draft) is not far off. Lí 'tāde hàu-'tóur bù'ywǎn le. or meaning His day is coming. 'Tāde 'r̀dz kwài 'dàu le. /I've got your number. Wǒ 'jr̀dàu 'nǐ shr̀ dzěmma hwéi 'shr̀. or Wǒ swàn °chyáu (°kàn)'tòu nǐ le.

NURSE. (A trained person) 'kànhù, 'kānhù, hùshr. /You need (to call in) a nurse. Nǐ déi chǐng ge °'kànhù (°'kānhù, °'hùshr). /When does the night nurse come? 'Yèbānde °'kànhù (°etc.) shémma shr̀hou °jyē'bān (°shàng'bān, °dàu'bān) ne?

/She's a graduate nurse. Tā shr̀ 'jèngshr̀ bi'yè de °'kànhù (°etc.). *or* Tā shr̀ 'hùshr'hwèide.

(For taking care of children) báumǔ, kānháidzde. / The children's nurse has taken them for a walk. °Kān'háidzde (°'Báu'mǔ) dàije 'háidzmen lyòu'wārchyu laije.

To nurse (take care of) jàuying(je), jàugu(je), 'fúshr̀(je). / They nursed him through his illness. Tā 'bìngje de shr̀hou tāmen yi'jr̀de °'jàuyingje (°'jàuguje, °'fúshrje) tā. / You need someone to nurse you. Ní déi 'yòu ge rén °'jàuyingje (°'jàuguje, °'fúshrje).

(Breastfeed) wèi; gěi . . . nǎi chr̄. / She was nursing the baby when I came in. Wǒ 'jìnlai de shr̀hou tā jèng °'wèi 'háidz ne (°gěi háidz 'nǎi chr̄ ne).

(Of a disease, wound, etc.) yǎng. / I'm nursing a cold. Wǒ shāng'fēngle, yǎngje ne.

(Of a grudge). / He's nursing a grudge against me. 'Tā gēn wǒ 'byèje yi'kǒu 'chr̄ ne. *or* Tā 'syīnli 'jèngdzài 'hèn wǒ. *or* Tā dzài nèr 'ywè syǎng ywè 'hèn wǒ ne.

(Help along) 'jyòuhu. / We had to nurse the fire (along) carefully to make it burn. Jèige hwǒ děi 'jyòuhuje dyǎr tsái 'jáudechilái ne.

NUT. (Hard-shelled seed or fruit) Chinese has no general term for nut in this sense. 'gāngwǒr may be used for (dry) **nuts,** but it may also mean dried fruit. The following are names of some varieties of nuts that are common in China: **peanut** dāhwāshēng, 'lwǒhwāshēng, hwāshēng; **Spanish peanut** (the small variety) 'syǎuhwāshēng; **hazelnut** jēndz; **chestnut** lìdz; **walnut** hétau, hétou; **lichee nut** 'lìjr̄. / Crack the walnut and eat the meat. Bǎ 'hétou dzákāi chr̄ hétou'rér. / He's eating peanuts. Tā chr̄ hwā-'shēng ne. / He's eating shelled peanuts (peanut meats). Tā chr̄ hwāshēng'rér ne. / That store sells candy and nuts. Nèige 'pùdz mài 'táng mài 'gāngwǒr.

(Counterpart of a bolt) lwósźmǔr. / The board is held in place by a nut and bolt. (Chinese says bolt and nut) 'Jèikwài 'bǎndz shr̀ yùng lwósź'dyēngr gēn lwósź'mǔr 'dìngjùde.

(Eccentric person). / He's a nut. is expressed as He's a strange thing. Tā shr̀ ge 'gwàiwu. or as He's a character. 'Nèijyàhwo jēn shr̀ kwài 'bǎubèi. or as He's somewhat abnormal. Tā 'fēnglifēng'chìde. or Tā shr̀ ge 'mwógu. or Tā shr̀ ge 'mwójeng. or as He's somewhat subnormal. Tā 'shǎlishǎ'chìde.

Nuts or **nutty** (insane). / If this keeps up, I'll go nuts. Yàushr 'lǎu dzèmma yàngr wǒ jyòu 'kwài °dé 'jīngshen'bìng le (°'fēng le, °dé 'shénjīng'bìng le). / It was driving him nuts. Nèi shèr jyàu tā 'jíde fā'fēng.

In a nutshell. / That's the story in a nutshell. 'Jyòushr 'dzèmma yìhwéi 'shèr. or °'Gwēilebāu'dzwēi (°'Jyǎndwàn'jyéshwō) jyòushr̀ 'dzèmma yìhwéidz 'shèr.

Other English expressions. / I thought the problem would be easy, but it turned out to be a hard nut to crack. (in mathematics) Wǒ 'ywánlái dǎngje jèige 'wèntí 'rúngyì swàn ne; 'shéi jr̄dàu 'dzèmma nán 'swàn a? or (a situation) Wǒ 'ywánlái dǎngje 'jèishèr hǎu 'bàn ne; 'shéi jr̄dàu jyàu rén 'dzèmma wéi'nán a? / Oh, nuts! (said to a person) Syā'bāi! or (said about something that has happened) 'Jè shr dzèmma 'shwōde. or Dzāu'gāu.

OBEY. shǒu, fútsúng, tǐng (. . . de)'hwà. / We must obey the law. Wǒmen yīng'dǎng shǒu'fǎ. / I can't obey that order. Nèige 'mìngling wǒ bù'néng fú'tsúng. / That car didn't obey the signals given by the policeman. Nèilyang 'chē méitǐng jīng'chá jr̀hwèi. / That child obeyed him immediately. Nèige háidz lì'kè jyou 'tǐng tāde 'hwà le.

OBJECT. (Be opposed) fǎndwèi; (not approve) búdzànchéng. /Will you object to his marriage? Tā jyē'hwūn; nǐ fǎndwei bùfǎndwei? /I hope you don't object to drinking. Wǒ 'syīwàng nǐ 'bùfǎndwèi hē 'jyǒu. /I won't object. Wǒ 'búhwèi búdzàn'chéng.

An object (thing) dūngsyi. /What's that object on the road? Dzài nèige 'dàurshangde shr shémma 'dūngsyi?

(Purpose) 'mùdì. /The object of the game is to hit the ball over the net. Jèijung 'yùndungde 'mùdì shr bǎ 'chyóur dǎgwo 'wǎngdz chyu.

(Something or someone arousing feeling). /I hate to be an object of sympathy. is expressed as I hate to have everybody pity me. Wǒ dzwèi 'hèn jyàu 'rénjya kě-'lyán wǒ. /The object of his affections is someone you know. is expressed as The person he loves you know. Tā 'ài de nèige rén nǐ 'rènshr.

OBLIGE. (Do a favor). /I am always glad to oblige you. is expressed as I'm glad to do anything for you at any time. 'Shémma shŕhou wǒ dōu 'ywànyi gěi 'nín dzwò shr. /Glad to oblige. Nǎrde 'hwà. or Méi shemma. /We asked him to sing for us, and he was glad to oblige. is expressed as We asked him to sing for us, and he very pleasantly agreed. Wǒmen 'chǐng ta géi wǒmen 'chàng yíge 'gēer, tā hěn gāu-'syìngde jyou 'dāyingle. /Please oblige us by coming early. is expressed as Please come early. Chǐng 'dzǎu dyǎr 'lái.

(Require). /His social position obliges him to entertain frequently. is expressed as A man in his social position has to entertain often. 'Tā nèijung 'dìwèide rén 'děi cháng chǐng'kè.

Be obliged (be grateful). /Much obliged. is expressed as Many thanks. Dwō 'syè dwō 'syè. or Syèsye. or Kě'tóu kě'tóu. /I'd be much obliged if you'd come early. is expressed as It would be very nice if you can come early. Nǐ 'yàushr néng 'dzǎu lái de'hwà nà kě tài 'hǎu le.

Be obliged to děi, 'fēiděi (. . . bù'kě), bù'dé bu-, bù'néng bu-; see also **have to** under **HAVE.** /Will I be obliged to attend the meeting? Wǒ 'fēiděi chyù kāi'hwèi (bu'kě) ma? /He's obliged to work nights. Tā 'děi °dzwò (°dǎ) yè'gūng. /After her husband's death she was obliged to go to work. Tāde 'jàngfu 'sžle yǐ'hòu tā bù-'dé búchyù dzwò 'gūng.

Feel obliged to jywéje . . . °'yīngdāng (°'yīnggāi). /He feels obliged to see her home. Tā 'jywéje tā 'yīngdāng sùng ta 'hwéichyu.

Not be obliged to méiyou . . . de °'yìwu (°bì'yàu). /I am not obliged to go. Wǒ méiyou chyù de bì'yàu.

OBSERVE. kàn, chyáu; (pay attention to) jùyì; (study closely) 'yánjyou. /Did you observe her reaction? Nǐ 'jùyì 'tāde 'fǎnyìng le ma? /He was careful not to be observed. Tā 'méiràng rén 'chyáujyan ta. /We can observe better from above. Wǒmen dǎ 'shàngmyar 'kànde 'gèng 'chǐngchu dyǎr. /The students were observing bacteria under the microscope. 'Sywéshengmen 'yánjyou jèige syànwéi'jìnglide wéishēng'chúng ne.

(Obey) (dzwūn)shǒu. /Be careful to observe all the rules. 'Swóyǒude gwēi'dzé 'dōu déi hǎu'hǎurde dzwūn'shǒu.

Observe a holiday gwòjyé, fàngjyà. /What holidays do you observe? Nǐmen dōu shr shémma 'shŕhour fàng'jyà? or Nǐmen dōu 'gwò shémma 'jyé?

OBTAIN. (Acquire) dé, 'dédàu; mǎi (buy); etc., depending on the means of acquisition. /All this information was obtained from his daughter. Jèisyē 'syāusyi dōu shr tsúng tā 'nyůér 'délaide. /We managed to obtain a favorable settlement. 'Jyēgwǒ bànde hái bú'hwài. / He was able to obtain the book at a very tiny bookstore. Tā dzai nèige syău shū'pù mǎijau nèiben 'shū le.

OCCASION. (Time) shŕhou, 'chǎnghé, shŕ; **big occasion** 'dàshŕ; **happy occasion** (as a wedding, birthday, etc.) 'syǐshŕ; **sad occasion** (a funeral) 'báishŕ. / Can this be used for all occasions? Jèige 'shémma 'chǎnghé dōu néng 'yùng ma? / This is a happy occasion. 'Jèi shŕ yíjyàn 'syǐshŕ. / It's always a big occasion when the whole family gets together. Chywán 'jyā 'tsòudzai yíkwàr, jēn shr yijyan 'dàshŕ. <u>or expressed</u> <u>as</u> When the whole family gets together, it's always bustling. Chywán 'jyāde rén 'tsòudau yí'kwàr de 'shŕhou yúng'ywàn shr hěn 'rènàude.

(Opportunity) jīhwei. / I haven't had occasion to attend to it. Wǒ 'hái méiyou 'jīhwei 'dzwò nèige ne. / There is no occasion for me to practice my French. Wǒ méi 'jīhwei lyànsyi wǒde Fǎ'wén.

(Cause, reason) 'lǐyóu. / There's no occasion for you to be angry. Nǐ méi 'lǐyóu shēng'chì.

To occasion (cause) jāu, rě. / Her appearance in public with that man occasioned a great deal of gossip. Tā gēn 'nèige rén lái, °'jāude (°rěde) dàjyāhwǒr jŕ shwō syàn'hwà.

OCCUPY. (Take up space or time) jàn. / The playground occupies three acres of land. Jèige yóusyì'chǎng 'jànle 'sānmǔ dì. *but* / He tried to occupy his time with reading. <u>is expressed as</u> He tried to spend his time by reading. Tā 'syǎng yùng kàn 'shū lai 'syāumwǒ shŕhou.

(Seize in a military action) jàn, jànlǐng (of a position or place); jànjyù (of a place only). / The enemy occupied the town. 'Dírén bǎ jèi 'chéng gěi jàn'lǐngle.

(Live in) jù. / What room do you occupy? Nǐ jùdzai 'něijyān wūdzli? / All our rooms are occupied. 'Wūdz chywán yǒu rén 'jùle. *or* Wūdz dou jù'mǎnle.

Occupy a position / What position do you occupy? <u>is expressed as</u> You are in what occupation? Nǐ shr shémma 'chāishr? <u>or as</u> What are you in charge of? Nǐ 'dānrèn °shémma 'jŕwu (°něi'bùfende 'shŕ)? / For the last ten years the position has been occupied by a woman. <u>is expressed as</u> For the last ten years a woman has done that job. Gwò'chyù 'shŕnyán nèige 'shèr shr yíge 'nyǔrén dzwò.

Be occupied yǒu shŕ (doing something); máng (be busy); méi 'gūngfu (have no time). / I'm occupied at present. Wǒ syàn'dzài °méi 'gūngfu (°etc.).

Be occupied (taken or reserved). / Every seat was occupied. <u>is expressed as</u> The seats were all full. 'Dzwò dōu 'mǎnle. / Is this seat occupied? <u>is expressed</u> <u>as</u> Has anyone reserved this seat? Jèige 'dzwòr yǒu 'rén 'dìngle ma? <u>or as</u> Has this seat got anyone (in it)? Jèige 'dzwòr yǒu 'rén méiyou?

OCEAN. yáng, dàyáng; <u>sometimes</u> dàhǎi big sea; **Pacific Ocean** Tàipíngyáng; **Atlantic Ocean** Dàsyǐyáng. / How far is this place from the ocean? Jèr lí dà'hǎi yǒu 'dwō ywǎn?

O'CLOCK. jūng <u>with measure</u> dyǎn, *or* dyǎn <u>alone</u> / The train leaves at seven o'clock. Hwǒ'chē 'chīdyǎn jūng 'kāi. / It's five o'clock. 'Wúdyǎn. *or* 'Wúdyǎn jūng.

OCTOBER. 'Shŕywè.

OF. **A of B** <u>equivalent in meaning to</u> **B's A** *or* **BA** <u>is expressed as</u> **B-de A** <u>or as</u> **BA**. / There's a hole in the roof of this house. 'Fáng'dyěngrshang yǒu ge 'dùngr. / I met a friend of yours yesterday. 'Dzwótyan wǒ 'pèngjyan nǐde yíwèi 'péngyou. / He's a man of means. Tā shr ge °yǒu'chyánde (°'kwò) rén. / Do you have a certificate of good health? Ní yǒu 'jyànkāng jèngmíng'shū méiyou? / I hate the taste of pickles. Wǒ bù'syǐhwan pàutsài de 'wèr. / The estimate of the cost will have to be revised. Jèige chéng'bènde 'gūjì déi 'gǎi yigǎi. / Do you have any books of short stories? Nín yǒu shémma dwǎn'pyan syǎu'shwōde 'shū ma? / Who's the driver of this car? 'Shéi shr̄ kāi jèige 'chē de? or expressed as Who drives this car? 'Shéi kāi jèige 'chē? or as Who's this car's driver? 'Shéi shr̄ jèilyàng 'chēde kāi'chēde? / This movie is a story of adventure. is expressed as This is an adventure movie. Jèishr̄ yíge tàn'syǎnde dyànyǐng.

A of B where A indicates a quantity or kind of B is usually expressed as A-B, where A is a measure and B a moun; in some cases the noun B is placed first, and the specification of quantity or kind comes later, expressed with a numeral plus a measure. / I want to buy a carton of cigarettes. Wǒ yàu 'mǎi yìtyáur yān'jywǎr. / Could I have a glass of water, please? Láu'jyà géi wo yìbēi 'shwěi, 'syíng busyíng? / A bottle of wine is served with the meal. Shàng'fàn de shŕhou shàng yìpyéngr 'jyǒu. / I want a pound of rice. Wǒ yàu yíbàng 'mǐ. / First put a coat of blue on the walls. 'Chyángshang 'syān shwā yídàu 'lánshàr. / Please give me a piece of that cake. Láu'jyà bǎ nèige dàn'gāu géi wo yí'kwàr. / A few of my belongings are missing. Wǒde 'dūngsyi yóu jijyàn 'dyōule. or Wǒde 'dūngsyi 'dyōule jijyàn. / Three of the prisoners escaped. 'Fànrén 'pǎule 'sānge. / I'll pay half of the bill. Nèige jàng-'dǎrshangde 'chyán wó gěi yí'bàr.

(Examples similar to those in the above paragraph in which the specification of quantity does not take the form of a measure). / He wasted a good deal of time. Tā 'dānwùle hen 'dwō 'gūngfu. / We'll need much more of this silk than we've got. Sz̄ bú'gòu. / None of us have ever been there. Wǒmen 'shéi yě méi'dàugwo nèr.

(Expressing time before an hour) chà . . . (búdàu) . . . -dyǎn; a quarter of eight chà yí'kè (búdàu)'bādyǎn, or, more often expressed as seven forty-five 'chīdyǎn sān'kè.

(Specifying the number included). / We made up a party of four. is expressed as The four of us made up a party. Wǒmen 'sz̄ge rén 'jyùhwēile 'jyùhwēi.

(Between city, state, etc., and the name of a particular city of state); the city of Peiping is expressed as Peiping city 'Běipíng'chéng; the province of Anhwei is expressed as Anhwei province 'Anhwēi'shěng.

In many combinations with other words, of has a special meaning. Such combinations should usually be looked for under one of the other words. The following are only a few examples of what may be involved.

Be afraid of pà. / There's nothing to be afraid of. 'Méi shémma kě'pà de.

Be built or made of a material yùng . . . °gǎi de(°dzwò de). / The house is built of stone. Jèige 'fángdz shr̄ yùng 'shŕtou 'gàide. / The cabinet is made of steel. Nèige jwèidz shr̄ yùng 'gāng dzwòde.

Be north (or south, etc.) of a place dzài . . . de °běibyar (°nánbyar, °etc.). / The hotel is six miles south of here. Lyú'gwǎn dzài jèrde nánbyar 'lyòulǐ.

Be within such-and-such a distance of lí . . . búdàu . . . . / We're within ten miles of our destination. Wǒmen lí nèige dìfang búdàu shr̄'yīnglǐ le.

On the other side of A A-de 'nèibyar. / My house is on the other side of the church. Wǒ 'jyā dzài jèige jyàu'tángde 'nèibyar.

On top of A A-shàng. / Put the package on top of the table. Bǎ jèige 'bāur fàngdzai 'jwōdzshang.

Die of A A sz̄de. / His father died of apoplexy. Tā 'fùchin shr̄ jùng'fēng 'sz̄ de.

787

Fall short of méi- . . . -dàu. /He fell short of his goal. Tā méi'dádàu tāde 'mùdù.

Hear of 'tīngshwō. /I've never heard of him. Wǒ tsúng'lái méi'tīngshwōgwo ta.

Know of 'jŕdau . . . shŕ °'shémma (°'shéi). /I don't know him personally, but I know of him. Wǒ bú'rènshr ta ('běnrén) kěshr wǒ 'jŕdau tā shŕ 'shéi.

OFF. (Away) is expressed with lí (from, away from) or dàu (until); or expressed with resultative compounds with -kāi as the resultative ending; move off 'nwókāi, 'dzǒukāi; stand off 'jànkāi; take off (away) 'nákāi; for fall off, get off, take off, send off, etc., see the verb. /How far off is it? Lí 'jèr yǒu dwō 'ywǎn? /The ship anchored three miles off shore. Jèige chwán pāu'máu de 'dìfang lí 'àn 'sānyīng'lǐ. /June is still three months off. °Dàu (°Lí) 'lyòuywè 'hái yǒu 'sānge 'ywè ne.

(Below standard) bùhǎu; off grade (secondary) tǐng tsz̀; (bad) bùhǎu, hwài le, bújì. /He sold us an off grade of eggs. Tā màigei 'wǒmende jǐ'dzěr °tǐng 'tsz̀ (°etc.). /It's an off year for crops. Jīnnyán 'shōuchéng bù'hǎu.

(Disconnected) see turn off, shut off, etc. /The power is off. is expressed as There's no power. Méi 'dyàn le. or as The power has stopped. Dyàn 'tíng le. or 'Tíng dyàn le.

(Missing) is expressed with dyàu (lose). /There's a button off your dress. Nín 'yīfushang yǒu yíge 'kòudz 'dyàule. or Nín 'yīfushang dyàule yíge 'kòudz.

(Wrong) is expressed with chà (differ). /His figures were way off. 'Tāde nèige shù(mu)'dz̀ °chà'dwō le (°chà'ywǎnle).

Off and on (sometimes) yǒushŕhou. /I've been studying off and on all year. Jèi yi'nyán lái wó yǒu'shŕhou nyàn 'shū, yǒu'shŕhou °'syēje (°bú'nyàn).

Off one's course (go on the wrong road) dzǒu 'tswòle 'lù le.

Have time off syējyà, fàngjyà, syōujyà. /I'm going to have a week off. Wǒ yàu syē yíge lǐ'bàide 'jyà.

Well off kwò (rich) jǐngkwàng hǎu; **badly off** kǔ (hardship). /How well off is he? Tā yǒu dwō 'kwò? or expressed as How much money has he? Tā 'chèn dwōshau 'chyán? /They're not so badly off. Tāmen 'méiyou nèmma 'kǔ. or Tāmen bútài 'kǔ.

OFFER. (Present for consideration). /She offered to preside at the meeting. is expressed as She volunteered to be chairman at the meeting. Kāi'hwèi de 'shŕhou tā gāufèn'yǔng dzwò jǔ'syí. /He offered to help us. is expressed as He wanted to help us. Tā 'yàu bāng wǒmende 'máng. /He offered us the use of his car. is expressed as He was going to lend us his car. Tā yàu bǎ 'chē 'jyègei wǒmen.

(Bid as a price). /I am willing to offer one hundred dollars for it. is expressed as I'm willing to pay out a hundred dollars to buy it. Wǒ 'ywànyì 'chū yì'bǎikwài chyán 'mǎi.

(Attempt to inflict). /Did they offer any resistance? is expressed as Did they try to resist? Tāmen dǐ'kàngle méiyou?

Offer one's congratulations dàu'syǐ. /May I offer my congratulations? Wó gěi 'nín dàu'syǐ.

An offer. /They made him an offer of a good job. is expressed as They gave him a good job (which he may or may not have taken). Tāmen yàu 'gěi ta yíge hǎu'shèr. /Will you keep the offer open? is expressed as Can you keep it for a while? Nín 'néng bùnéng géi wǒ 'lyóu syē 'shŕhou? /I'd sell the car if I had a good offer for it. is expressed as When someone gives me a good price, then I'll sell the car. Yǒu-'rén géi hǎu'jyàr, wǒ jyòu bǎ 'chē 'mài le.

OFFICE. (Place or room for business) gūngshr̄fáng, bàngūngshr̀. / I'll see you at the office tomorrow. Wǒ 'míngrge dzài gūngshr̀'fáng 'jyàn ni. / His office is to the left. Tāde gūngshr̀'fáng dzài 'dzwǒbyar.

(Office staff) jŕywán. / He arranged a picnic for the whole office. Tā géi chywán'tǐde jŕ'ywán 'bàngwo yí'tsz̀ yě'tsān.

(Department, bureau) 'jǐgwān; in compounds -jyú, -chǎng, -swǐ, -hwèi, and others, patent office jwānlǐjyú; post office yóujēngjyú. / All the government offices are having a holiday. Swóyoude 'jēngfǔ jǐgwān dōu fàng'jyà ne.

(Position, rank, title) 'míngyì; (responsibility) 'jŕwù; (term of office; or to hold an office) rèn. / What office does he hold? Tā shémma 'míngyì? or Tā 'dān-rèn shémma 'jŕwù? / He's been in office five years. Tā dzài 'rèn 'wǔnyán le.

Office hours bàngūng shr̄'jēn.

OFFICER. (Government or military) gwān, gwār; (of the police force) jǐnggwān or (policeman) syúnjǐng, jǐngchá; in addressing a policeman, call him 'syānsheng. / Were you an officer in the army? Nín 'shr̀ bushr̀ 'dānggwo jyūn'gwān? / Are you a police officer? Nín shr̀ jǐng'gwān ma? / Officer, can you tell me which street goes there? 'Syānsheng, dzóu 'nèityáu jyē tsái néng 'dàu ner?

(Of a club or similar organization) jŕywán, gànshr̀. / Yesterday the club elected its new officers. 'Dzwótyān nèige twántǐ bǎ syīn °jŕ'ywán (°'gànshr̀) 'sywǎnchulaile.

OFFICIAL. (Public, not personal) gūngjyade. / This is an official car. Jèi shr yílyàng 'gūngjyade chì'chē.

(Verified, authoritative) jèngshr̀de. / Is that an official order? Nèi shr̀ bushr̀ 'jèngshr̀de 'mìnglìng?

Official business gūngshr̀. / Is this official business? Jèi shr̀ bushr̀ gūng'shr̀?

Official news (from an official source) 'gwānfāng syāusyi; (verified news) 'jèngshr̀de syāusyi.

An official (government or military) gwān, gwār; (of a company or organization) jŕywán (usually clarified by mentioning the person's title or adding gāují). / He's a government official. Tā shr̀ dzwò 'gwār de. / Who are those officials? Nèisyē 'gwār dōu shr̀ 'shéi? / My cousin is a bank official. Wǒde byǎu'gē shr yínhánglide 'gāujíjŕ'ywán.

OFTEN. cháng. / Does this happen often? 'Cháng yǒu jèiyàngde 'shèr ma? / I've seen them together often. Wǒ 'cháng 'kànjyan tamen dzài yí'kwàr. / Does he come here often? Tā 'cháng lái ma? / Did he come to see you often? Tā 'cháng lái 'kàn ni ma?

How often 'dwōshautsz̀, 'jǐtsz̀. / How often did he come to see you? Tā lái 'kàngwo ní 'jǐtsz̀ le? or expressed as He came to see you once in how many days? Tā °dwōshautyān (°dwōshau shr̀hou) lài kàn ni yi'tsz̀? or as Did he come to see you often? Tā 'cháng lái 'kàn ni ma? / How often do the buses run? Gūnggùngchìchē °yì'tyān (°yìdyǎn jūng) kāi °'jǐtsz̀ (°'dwōshautsz̀)?

OIL. yóu. / What kind of oil is in that can? Dzài nèi 'gwàrli de shr̀ shémma 'yóu? / Please check the oil. is expressed as Please check whether my car has oil enough or not. Láujyà 'kànkan wǒ chēlide 'yóu 'gòu bugòu.

(In painting). /He does his best work in oils. is expressed as He paints oil paintings best. Tā hwà 'yóuhwàr 'hwàde 'dzwèi hǎu.

Oil painting yóuhwà(r).

Oil well yóujǐng.

To oil (rub on oil, apply oil) shàngyóu; (squirt oil on or into something) gàuyóu; (rub oil on something) tsāyóu. / The machine needs to be oiled. Jèige 'jīchi gāi gàu'yóu le.

OLD. (of people) lǎu; (of children) expressed as big dà; (really aged) shàng 'swèi-shùr, shàng 'nyánji. /His grandmother is a very old woman. Tāde 'nǎinai shr̀ ge hen 'lǎude lǎu'tàitai. or Tāde 'nǎinai shàng °'swèishur (°'nyánji) le. /I'm getting old. (if you're an adult) Wǒ 'lǎu le. /He's too old to be treated like a child. Tā 'yǐjing 'nèmma dà le, bùnéng dzài 'ná ta dàng syǎu'hár dài le.

(Of things; used, dilapidated) jyòu; (old but still good) lǎu; (ancient) gǔ. /Wear old clothes. Chwān 'jyòu yīfu. / This is a very old wine cup. Jèige jyǒubēi hén 'lǎu le. / This is a very old city. Jèi shr̀ dzwò 'gǔ chéng.

(Former) lǎu. /He's an old student of mine. 'Tā shr̀ wǒde 'lǎu 'sywésheng. /Is this the old type? Jèi 'shr̀ bushr̀ lǎu 'yàngrde?

(Mature) 'lǎulyàn. /He's old for his years. Tā 'swèishu 'búdà, 'kěshr̀ tíng 'lǎulyàn.

(In talking about age). /How old are you? (if said to a young person) is expressed as How big are you? Nǐ dwō 'dà le? or as How many years have you? Ní 'jǐswèi le? or (if said to an adult) as How big is your age? Nín dwō dà 'nyánjì? or as How big a number of years have you? Nín dwō dà 'swèishù le? or (if said to an old person) as How high is your age? Nín gāu'shòu? /I'm eighty years old. Wǒ 'bāshr̀ swèi le. or Wǒ 'bāshr̀ le.

An old hand láu shǒu. /He's an old hand at that. Tā 'bàn nèige 'shèi shr̀ ge láu'shǒu le.

Old age lǎunyán.

ON. 1. (On the surface of) . . . shang. /What's on the list? Jèige dāndzshang syěde shr̀ 'shémma? /Is chicken on the menu today? Jyēr de tsài'dārshang yǒu 'jǐ méi-you? / There were two pictures on the wall. 'Chyángshang yóu lyǎngjāng 'hwàr.

(Next to or facing) āi, kàu, chùng, syàng, dwèi, cháu, all plus je. /Do you have a room on the street? Nǐ 'yǒu méiyou °āije (°'kàuje, °etc.) dà'jyē de 'wūdz?

(In a direction) dzài. /It's on the left. Dzài 'dzwǒbyar.

(Included in) . . . li. /There's only one woman on the committee. Jèige wěi-ywán'hwèili jr̀ yǒu 'yíwèi shr̀ 'nyǔde. /Who's on the team? Jèige 'dwèili dōu yǒu 'shwéi?

(At a time). /Are you open on Saturday? is expressed as Are you open Satur-day? Nín lǐbài'lyòu kāi 'mér ma? The bell rings on the hour. is expressed as The bell rings when it reaches a whole hour. Jèige 'jūng měidàu 'jěng yíge jūngtóur de shr̀hou 'dǎ yí'tsz̀.

(From or on the basis of) tsúng. /I got this on good authority. Jèige 'syāusyi wǒ tsúng kě'kàude 'dìfang 'délaide.

(Concerning) gwānyu, dwèiyu, jyàng. /It's a book on animals. Jèishr yìběr °'gwānyu (°jyàng) 'dùngwù de shū. /What're your ideas on the subject? Nǐ dwèiyu jèige 'wèntí yǒu shémma 'yìjyàn?

(Resting on). / The car went around the corner on two wheels. is expressed as When the car turned the corner there were only two wheels touching the ground. Jèige chī'chē gwǎi jèige 'wār de shŕhou jŕ yóu 'lyǎngge 'lwúndz jāu'dì.

(Using as means of locomotion). / Can we go on foot? Wǒmen 'néng bunéng °'dzǒuje (°'twěije) chyù?

2. In a combination with a verb, where on means come to be in a position above and resting on something not specified, Chinese uses an appropriate verb of motion plus shang as postverb. / Climb on! 'Páshangchyu! *or* 'Páshanglai! / Jump on! 'Tyàushangchyu! *or* (if jump is said just for liveliness) 'Shànglai! / Is the coffee on? Jyā'fēi 'jùshàngle ma? *or* Bǎ kāfēi'hú 'dzwòshangle ma? / Is the pot cover on? Hú'gàr 'gàishangle ma?

In similar combinations, where the meaning is cause something to be on something not specified, Chinese uses as appropriate verb of handling plus shang as postverb or, occasionally, a different postverb, such as hǎu, indicating satisfactory completion of the action. / Have you got your shoes on yet? Nǐde 'syé yǐjing °chwān'hǎule (°chwānshangle) méiyou? / Put your coat on. Bǎ dà'yī 'chwānshang ba.

In combinations similar to the last, except that the object on which the thing handled comes to rest is specified and followed by shang. Dzài is generally used as the postverb. / Put it on the table. 'Fàngdzai 'jwōdzshang. / Put it on ice. Fàngdzai 'bīngshang. or expressed as Ice it. 'Bīngshang.

3. Combinations in which on has the force of resume *or* continue.

Be on (in process). / Is the race on yet? is expressed as Has the race already been started? Nèige bǐ'sài yǐjing kāi'shŕle ma? *or* Tāmen yǐjing 'sàichilaile ma?

Go on (continue or resume moving forward) 'háishr jyēje. . . dzǒu. / Let's go on toward the mountains. Dzámen 'háishr 'jyēje wàng nèige 'shān nèr 'dzǒu ba.

Go on . . . -ing jyēje, bùtíngde, búwànde. / Let's go on working hard. Wǒmen °'jyēje (°bù'tíngde, °bú'dwànde) kǔ 'gàn ba.

Keep on with 'jìsyù, jyēje, háishr. / Keep on with what you're doing. Nǐ °'jìsyù (°'jyēje, °'háishr) gàn nǐde 'hwór.

4. Miscellaneous combinations (for such combinations see also the word or words with which on is combined).

Be on (at the expense of). / This one's on me. 'Jèi ràng 'wǒ ba. *or* 'Wǒ hòu ba. *or* 'Wó gěi ba. / The drinks are on the house. 'Jyǒu dōu shŕ láu'bǎn jìngde. *or* 'Jyǒu chyán 'gwèishang 'hòu le.

Bring something on (cause). / What brought on this condition? 'Dzěmma 'nùngchéng 'jèiyàngr le ne? *or* 'Jèi shŕ dzěmma 'nàude?

Later on yǐhòu, gwò syē 'shŕhour. / Wait till later on. Děng °yǐ'hòu (°'gwò syē shŕhour) dzài shwō.

Move on (command) 'dzǒu a, 'dzǒukai.

On the contrary jèng syāngfǎn.

On credit. / Do you sell on credit? °'Gāije (°'Chyànje) 'syíng busyíng? *or* Kéyi °syě'jàng (°jì'jàng) ma?

ONCE. yìhwéi, yítsz̀, yíbyàn. / He feeds the dog once a day. Jèige 'gǒu tā yì'tyān wèi yí'tsz̀. / Try it just this once. Jyòu 'shr̀ jèiyí'hwéi. / I've seen him once or twice. Wǒ jyàngwo tā yìlyǎng'hwéi. / If you read it once, you'll never forget it. Ní 'jŕyàu bǎ jèige 'nyàngwo yíbyàn, jyou yúngywǎn wàngbù'lyǎu le.

(Formerly) tsúngchyán, tséngjīng. / I was in the army once. Wǒ 'tsúngchyán

791

dǎnggwo 'bǐng. / We lived near here once. Wǒmen 'tséngjǐng dzài jèr fù'jìn 'jùgwo.

Once . . . (then) yi . . . jyòu. / Once we get there you'll see how beautiful it is. Yí 'dàu nèr, nǐ jyou 'jřdau nèige 'dìfang dwōme hǎu'kàn le.

Once in a while yǒu(de) 'shř(hour), oúěr. / You might be nice to me once in a while. Ni yǒu 'shřhour yě dài wo 'hǎu dyǎr 'syíng busyíng? / I drink once in a while. Wǒ 'oúěr yě hē dyǎr 'jyóu.

At once (immediately) 'lìkè, mǎshàng, 'gánjǐn, gǎnkwài. / Come at once. Nǐ 'lìkè 'lái.

At once (at the same time) túngshř; (together) yíkwar. / Everyone was shouting at once. Dà'jyāhwǒr túng'shř 'rāngrang. / Everything always happens at once. Shémma 'shèr dōu 'tsòudau yí'kwàr le.

ONE. yi plus a measure. / Count from one to a hundred. Nǐ tsúng 'yī 'shǔdau yì'bǎi. / One or two will be enough. Yì'lyàngge jyou 'gòule. / One of us can buy the tickets while the others wait here. Wǒmen kéyi 'yíge rén chyù mǎi 'pyàu, 'byérén dzài'jèr 'děngje déle. / I have only one thought. Wǒ 'jř yǒu 'yíge 'nyàntou. or Wǒ 'syīnli 'jř yǒu 'yijyàn shř. / I have only one thought, and that's to go home. is expressed as With my whole mind I'm thinking of going home. Wǒ yì'syīn syǎng hwéi 'jyā.

(Some person not specified) rén or omitted. / One has to be careful with fire. (Rén) déi 'syǎusyīn 'hwǒjù.

(Referring to a single thing, but without specifying what) yi plus a measure, without a noun following, or a stative verb ending in de without a noun following. / You have two horses; will you give me one? Ni yǒu 'lyǎngpí mǎ; 'gei wǒ 'yìpí, 'hǎu buhǎu? / I prefer the more expensive one. Wó 'syǐhwan nèige 'gwèi dyǎr de. / I prefer more expensive ones. Wó 'syǐhwan 'gwèi dyǎr de.

One another bǐ'tsž. / It's up to us to protect one another. Wǒmen děi bǐ'tsž 'jàulyàuje dyǎr. or Chywán 'jàngje wǒmen bǐ'tsž 'jàuyingle.

One at a time or **one by one** yíge'yígede or with another measure replacing ge in the same pattern. / One at a time, please! Chǐng 'yígeyí'gèrde lái. / They came in one by one. Tāmen 'yíge'yígede 'jìnlaile.

ONLY. (Single, only existing one) wéiyīde, jínyǒude. / It's our only hope. Nà shř wǒmen wéi'yīde 'syīwàng le. / It's your only chance. Nà shř nǐ wéi'yīde 'jīhwèi le. / Am I the only one here? is expressed as Is there just me alone here? Jèr 'jř yóu wǒ 'yíge rén ma? / She's an only child. is expressed as Her family has just her alone. Tā 'jyā jyòu shř 'tā nèmma 'yígè.

(Merely, just, exclusively) jř, jyòu. See also JUST. / This is only for you. Jèi °'jř (°'jyòu) wèi 'nín de. / This seat is only big enough for one person. Nèige 'dzwòr 'jř néng dzwò 'yíge rén. / I only want a little. Wǒ °'jř (°'jyòu) yàu yì'dyǎr. / He was here only two weeks. Tā °'jř (°'jyòu) 'dzài jèr 'dāile 'lyá lǐ'bài.

(But) jyòushr. / I was going to buy it, only you told me not to. Wó 'běnlái yàu 'mǎi láije, jyòushr nǐ bú'ràng wó mǎi. / He wanted to help, only he didn't have time. Tā 'dàushr syǎng bāng'máng láije, jyòushr méi 'gūngfu.

Only . . . ago tsái. / He died only a month ago. Tā tsái 'sžle yíge 'ywè. / I got here only a moment ago. Wǒ 'tsái 'dàu jèr yì'hwěr.

Only too dāngrán, dz̀rán (naturally, of course). / I'm only too glad to help you. Wǒ °dāng'ran (°dz̀rán) 'ywànyi bāng nínde 'máng. / He was only too willing to agree. is expressed as That was unexpectedly good, and of course, he agreed. Nà jyàn'jř shř 'chyǒujřbu'dé, tā °dz̀rán (°dāng'rán) 'dāyingle.

If only see IF. / If you could only help me! Nín yàu néng 'bāng wo yí'syàr, dwō 'hǎu!

Not only . . . but also . . . yòu . . . yòu . . . , bú'dàn shr . . . érchyě 'yòu . . . .
/ It's not only snowing, but there's a wind, too. Yòu syà'sywě yòu gwā'fēng. *or* Bú-'dànshr syà'sywě érchyě 'yòu gwā'fēng.

OPEN. (Of a door, building, dining room, etc.) kāi (mér). / Open the door. Bǎ 'mén 'kāikai. / Open the door, please. Chíng bǎ 'mér 'kāikai. *or* Chǐng kāi 'mér. *or* 'Kāikai 'mér. / What time do you open shop? Nǐ 'pùdz shémma shŕhou kāi 'mér? / The store opens at ten o'clock. 'Pùdz shŕ 'shŕdyǎn jūng kāi ('mér).

(Begin; of a meeting) kāihwèi; (of a school) kāisywé. / When does school open this year? 'Jīnnyán sywésyàu 'shémma shŕhou kāi'sywé? / When will they open the meeting? Tāmen 'shémma shŕhou kāi 'hwèi?

(Of flowers) kāile, kāi. / I'd like some roses that haven't opened too far. Wǒ yàu jidwǒr méi'dàkāide méigwei'hwār.

Open something is expressed with various compounds containing kāi, the first element expressing the means of opening as **open a window** dǎkai 'chwānghu; **open a box** dǎkai 'hédz; **open a drawer** lākai 'chǒuti; **open a book** dǎkai shū, fānkai shū; **open a letter** °dǎkai (°chāikai) nèifēng 'syìn; **open one's mouth** jāngkai dzwěi, jāng dzwěi; **open one's eyes** jēngkai yǎn, jēng yǎn. (fig. wide-eyed). / The doctor told the child to open her mouth. 'Dàifu jyàu jèige 'háidz jāngkai 'dzwěi. / Open your eyes. Bǎ 'yǎn 'jēngkai. / That certainly opened my eyes to a few things. Nèi kě 'jēn ràng wo kāi 'yǎnle. *or* Jèihwéi kě ràng wǒ 'jŕdaule.

Open one's mouth (fig. to speak) kāi 'kǒu, jāng 'dzwěi. / He never opened his mouth. Tā yì'jŕ °méikāi 'kǒu (°méi jāng 'dzwěi).

Open into (*or* onto) cháu; (to face) chùngje. / There's a door opening into the garden. Yǒu yíge 'mén 'chùngje hwā'ywár. / What do the windows open onto? Nèisyē 'chwānghu 'chùngje 'neibyār?

Open up. / Open up! (open the door!) 'Kāikai! Bǎ mér 'kāikai. / He finally opened up and told us everything. is expressed as He finally couldn't hold it any longer, and told us everything. Tā dàu'lyǎur byébu'jù le, bǎ 'shémma dōu 'gàusu wǒmen le.

Be open (not closed up) is usually expressed with kāi (see first paragraphs). / Is the door open? Mén méi'gwān ba. *or* Mén 'shr bushr °'kāije ne? *or* °'chǎngje ne? / He came in through the open window. Tā 'tsúng nèige 'kāijede 'chwānghu 'jìnlaide. / Are you open on Sundays? Lǐbài'tyan nǐmen kāi mér ma? / The roses are fully open. 'Méigwèi'hwār dōu 'kāikaile. / The pipe is open at both ends. is expressed as The pipe has an opening at both ends. 'Gwǎndz lyǎng 'tóur dōu yǒu 'kǒur.

(Passable; of a road, pipe, river, communication line, or any passage that has been obstructed) tūngle. / This road is open to traffic. Jèityáu 'lù yǐjing °tūngle (°tūng 'chē le). *or* Nèityáu 'lù °néng (°syǔ, °'kéyi, °ràng) 'dzǒule. / Is the harbor open? Gǎng'wān 'kéyi 'jìnchyu ma? or meaning Is the harbor cleared of ice? Gǎng'wān kāi'dùng le ma?

(Frank, on the level) 'tǎnbái; (frankly) 'tǎnbáide. / I don't think he was really open with me. Wǒ 'syǎng tā gēn wo bùgǎn 'tǎnbái.

(Generally known) gūngkāide; also several expressions meaning everybody knows it. / That's an open secret. 'Nèi shr ge gūng'kāide mì'mì. *or* Nèijyàn 'shr °'rénrér (°'dàjyā, °'shéi) dōu 'jŕdau.

(Undecided) méi 'jyēgwǒ, méi jywédìng. / That's still an open question. Nèige 'wèntí hái méi °'jyēgwǒ (°jywé'dìng) ne. or expressed as No one's decided what to do about that yet. 'Nèige dàjyā'hwŏr hái bùjŕ'dàu dzĕmma 'bàn ne.

(Available, accessible). / Is the park open to the public? is expressed as Are people allowed to go in the park? Jèige gūng'ywán syŭ rén 'jìnchyu ma? / All our harbors are open to ships of neutral countries. is expressed as Neutral ships are allowed to come in all our harbors. Wŏmen 'swŏyŏude gǎng 'wān dōu 'syŭ jūnglì-gwóde chwán'jŕ 'jìnlai. / The contest is open to anyone. is expressed as Anyone can join this contest. Jèige bĭ'sài 'shéi dōu néng tsān'jyā. or as This is a public con-test. Jèige shŕ gūng'kāi bĭ'sài. / The job is still open. is expressed as There's still no one working on that job. Nèijyàn 'shŕ hái méi rén 'dzwò ne. / Is your offer still open? is expressed as That thing you mentioned, can we still do it? Nĭ 'shàng-hwéi 'tí de nèige 'shèr hái néng 'bàn ma? / The 23rd is still open, if you want to use the auditorium then. is expressed as If you want to borrow the auditorium, it's unoccupied the 23rd. Nĭ yàu syǎng 'jyè dàlĭ'táng, èrshr'sānhàu 'syánje ne. or as . . . it's all right the 23rd. . . . èrshr'sānhàu 'syíng. or as . . . it's still not taken for the 23rd. . . . èrshr'sānhàu hái 'kūngje ne. / There are several possibilities open. is expressed as There are several ways, any of them is all right. Yŏu 'háu-jijŭng 'bànfa, 'dzĕmmaje dōu 'syíng. / He's always open to reason. is expressed as He's always reasonable. Tā 'nèige rén hĕn jyáng'lĭ. / I have an open mind about it. is expressed as I have no prejudice at all about it. Wŏ dwèi 'nèige bìng 'méiyou shémma °'chéngjyàn (°'pyānjyàn).

Open air lùtyān. / The concert was given in the open air. Yīnywè'hwèi shŕ dzài lù'tyān 'yànde.

Open city (unfortified) búshèfáng chéng'shŕ.

Open country 'kūngkwàng 'dìfang.

Open fields kwàngyĕ.

Open wound (unhealed) méishōu'kŏurde shāng'kŏu.

Opening remarks is expressed as the remarks at the beginning chĭ'tóur jijyu 'hwà.

With open arms (affectionately, willingly) rèlyède, chéng'syīnchéngyìde. / They welcomed him with open arms. Tāmen hĕn °rè'lyède (°chéng'syīnchéngyìde) 'hwān-yíng tā.

OPERATE. (Manage, run; of machines that move through space) kāi; (use; of other machines) yùng, shŕ. / I don't know how to operate this car. Wŏ búhwèi 'kāi jèige 'chē. / Can you operate a sewing machine? Nĭ hwèi °'yùng (°'shŕ) féngyī'jī ma?

(Be running; be in use) (yŏu 'rén) 'yùngje, shŕje, kāije; (be in condition to run) néng yùng, néng shŕ, néng kāi; (of a factory) kāigūng. / The factory operates twenty-four hours a day. Gūng'chǎng 'ryè kāi'gūng. / Is this elevator operating? (in use) Dyàn'tī 'kāije ne ma? or Dyàn'tī yŏu ren 'yùngje ne ma? or (usable) Dyàn'tī néng 'kāi ma? / Is this machine operating? (in use) Jèige 'jīchi (yŏu 'rén) 'yùngje ne ma? or (usable) Jèige 'jīchi néng 'yùng ma?

(Act, work). / Just how would your plan operate? is expressed as Just how do you do it according to your method? Nĭde 'bànfa shŕ 'dzĕmmaje 'dzwò? or as What's the method of approach of your plan? Nĭde 'bànfa shŕ 'dzĕmma ge 'dzwòfar? / The plan operates to his advantage, of course. is expressed as The plan being used is advantageous to him, of course. Jèige 'bànfar 'dzwòchilai dāng'rán dwèi 'tā yóu hǎuchù.

(Use surgery) kāidāu, dùng 'shŏushù. / The doctor said he'd have to operate. 'Dàifu shwō tā dĕi °kāi'dāu (°dùng'shŏushù).

Operating room shŏushùjyān. / He was in the operating room two hours. Tā dzài shŏushùjyānli yóu 'lyǎ jūng'tóu.

OPERATION. (Movement, process; movements made by a person) 'dùngdzwò; (processes) 'bùdzòu; (steps) 'jyēdwàn; (procedure) 'shòusyù. /It takes three operations to do this. Dzwò 'jèige yòu sānge °'bùdzòu (°'jyēdwàn). *or* Dzwò 'jèige yòu 'sānjǔng 'shòusyù. /It involves too many operations. Nèmmaje bàn 'shòusyù tài 'máfan. /Everything could be done in one operation. is expressed as Everything could be done at one time. 'Swóyòude yí'syàr jyòu 'kéyǐ 'dzwòchulai.

(Surgical) shòushù. /Do I have to have an operation? Wǒ 'yídìng 'děi 'dùng yítsż shòu'shù ma?

Military operations 'jyūnshrsyíng'dùng. /They kept the military operations a secret. 'Jyūnshr syíng'dùng tāmen 'shòuje mì'mì laije. /He has been in many military operations. is expressed as He has many times fought in campaigns. Tā 'yǐjing dǎgwo 'háu jǐtsż 'jàng le.

Be in operation (running) *see* **OPERATE.** /Are the street cars in operation? Dyàn'chē 'kāije ne ma? *or* Yǒu dyàn'chē 'méi'you?

Be put into (Go into) **operation** shr̀syíng. /The plan will be put into operation immediately. Nèige 'jìhwa mǎshang jyòu yàu shr̀'syíng.

OPINION. 'yìjyàn, yìsz. /What is your opinion? Nínde 'yìjyàn dzěmma'yàng?

Have an opinion (think) jywéde. /I have a very good opinion of him. is expressed as I think he's quite good. Wǒ 'jywéde tā hěn bú'tswò. /I haven't a very good opinion of his ability. is expressed as I think he has no ability. Wǒ 'jywéde tā 'méishémma 'běnshr. /She has a pretty high opinion of herself. is expressed as She thinks that she's pretty good. Tā dz̀'jǐ 'jywéde dz̀'jǐ tǐng °bú'tswò shr̀de (°'lyǎubúchǐshrde).

OPPORTUNITY. jīhwei. /This is a big opportunity for you. 'Jèi shr̀ nǐde hǎu 'jīhwei. /When will you have an opportunity to see me? Nǐ 'shémma shŕhou néng yǒu 'jīhwei lái 'gàn wo? or expressed as When will you have time to come and see me? Nǐ 'shémma shŕhou néng yǒu 'gūngfu lái 'kàn wo? /Opportunities are scarce. Jīhwèi nán 'dé.

OPPOSITE. (That which is opposed) syāngfǎn. /That is just the opposite of what I meant. 'Nèige gēn wǒ shwōde 'yìsz 'gāng hǎu syāng'fǎn. /This is the opposite of what I expected. Gēn wǒ 'syīwàngde gāng'gāng syāng'fǎn. /He and his wife are exact opposites in looks and personality. is expressed as He and his wife are definitely not alike. Gēn ta 'tàitai jyàn'jr bùyí'yàng.

Opposite (facing) dwèije; **opposite side** dwèimyàn, dwèigwòr. /What's that opposite us? Dwèije 'jèr de 'nèige shr̀ 'shémma? *or* °Dwèi'myàr (°Dwèi'gwòr) shr̀ 'shémma? /The cemetery is just opposite the church. Fén'dì jyòu dzài lǐbài'tángde dwèi'gwòr. *or* Fén'dì jèng 'dwèije lǐbài'táng. /She sat opposite me at the table. Chr̄ 'fàn de 'shŕhou °'tā 'dzwòdzai wǒ dwèi'myàr (°tā 'dwèije wo 'dzwòje).

Opposite direction. /You should go in the opposite direction. Nǐ děi wàng dwèi'myàr dzǒu. or expressed as You should go that way. Nǐ děi wàng 'nèibyar dzǒu.

On opposite sides. /They live on opposite sides of town. is expressed as Of their two homes one is at one end of the city and one at the other end. Tāmen lyǎng-'jyā 'yíge dzài chéng 'jèitóur 'yíge dzài 'nèitóur.

OR. (Between choices in a choice-type question) háishr. /Shall I wait here or come back later? Wǒ dzài'jèr 'děngje 'háishr hwéi'tóu dzài 'lái? /Does he want carrots or peas? Tā shr̀ yàu hú'lwóba háishr yàu wān'dòu?

(Between two possible things in a statement, or question-word question) hwòshr, 'hwòjĕ. /Give me a pencil or a pen. Géi wo yij̆r 'chyānbĭ, hwòshr yij̆r 'gāngbĭ. /What is the aim or purpose, of this meeting? Jèitsz hwèi'yĭde 'dzūngjr °hwòshr (°'hwòjĕ) 'mùdĭ shr shémma?

(Between one number and another) no direct translation; one or two yĭlyăng plus a measure; two or three lyăngsān plus a measure. /Could I have two or three more cookies? 'Néng bunèng 'dzài géi wo lyăng'sānkwàr bĭng'gār?

(Otherwise) (yàu)bu'rán, 'fŏudzé. /Hurry, or we'll be late. 'Kwài dyăr, °(yàu)-bu'rán (°'fŏudzé) wŏmen jyou 'wăn le.

Either . . . or . . . meaning either way will do (hwòshr) . . . hwòshr . . . , (hwò-je) . . . hwòje; in most cases, dōu 'syíng or dōu 'kéyi may be used at the end of the sentence. /You may either go to New York or San Francisco. Nĭ hwòshr dau 'Nyóu-ywē chyù hwòshr dau Jyòujin'shān chyù, dōu 'syíng. /Give me either carrots or peas. Géi wo hú'lwóba hwòje wān'dòu, dou 'kéyi.

ORANGE. (Fruit) chéndz; (éasily peeled, as a tangerine) jyúdz; (large, sweet) mĭgān; (red-skinned) 'húngjyú. /How much are oranges? 'Chéndz 'dwōr chyán? /Do you have orange juice? Nĭmen yŏu °'chéndz'jĕr (°'chéndz'shwĕi, °jyúdzshwei) méiyou?

(Color) 'syĭnghwáng, 'jyúhwáng. /Her dress was orange. Tāde 'yĭfu shr °'syĭnghwángde (°'jyúhwáng'shăr).

ORDER. (Arrangement) tsż̇syu; in some order °āije (°ànje) . . . tsż̇syu. /These are not in the right order. Jèisye 'tsż̇syu budwèi. /What order should these papers be filed in? Jèisye 'wénjyàn yĭngdāng ànje 'shémma tsż̇syu fàngdzai dăng 'ànli? /Line up in order of height. Anje gāuăide 'tsż̇syu jàn'pái. /The names were listed in alphabetical order. 'Míngdz shr ànje Yĭngwén dż̇'mŭr de tsż̇syu 'páide.

(Discipline, orderliness) jr̆syu; law and order fājĭ. /You'll have to keep order in this hall. Dzài jèi dà'tĭngli nĭ dĕi 'wéichr̆ 'jr̆syu. /He has to see that law and order is observed. Tā 'gwăn 'wéichr̆ fă'jĭ.

(Command) 'mìnglìng. /Have you got your orders? Nĭ 'jyēdau 'mìnglìng le ma? /This is an order from the Captain. 'Jèige 'mìnglìng shr̆ dwèi'jăng 'syàde.

(List of things wanted) dìngdār. /The order was given to the purchasing agent. Nèige dìng'dār 'jyāugei bàn 'hwò de rén le.

By order of. /The new regulation was put into effect by order of the mayor. is expressed as The new regulation was ordered made by the mayor. Jèige 'syīn 'jāngcheng shr̆ shr̆'jăng syà'lìng 'dìngde.

Be in order (or Out of order) (of things in general) búlwàn, lwàn. /Everything on my desk was in order when I left. Wŏ dzŏu de shr̆hou jwōrshangde 'dūngsyi yi-dyár yĕ bu'lwàn. /These cards are out of order. Jèisye kăpyàn dōu 'lwàn le.

Be in order (or Out of order) (of machines). /Is the machinery in order? is expressed as Is the machine usable? Jèige 'jĭchi néng 'yùng ma? /The elevator is temporarily out of order. is expressed as The elevator is temporarily unusable. Dyàn-'tī jàn'shr̆ bunéng 'yùng. /Is the machinery out of order? is expressed as Is the machine broken? Jèige 'jĭchi 'hwài le méiyou?

Call to order. /He called the meeting to order. is expressed as He announced the beginning of the meeting. Tā sywānbù kāi 'hwèi le.

In order to 'wèideshr̆ (lái), ('wèideshr̆) lái. /I came all the way in order to see you. Wŏ láu'ywănde 'păulai jyou 'wèideshr̆ lai 'kànkan ni.

Made to order. /The suit was made to order. is expressed as The suit was custom made. Jèitau 'yīfu shr dìng'dzwòde. /A day like this is made to order. Jyērde 'tyār tài 'hǎule.

Put in order 'jénglǐ, pái. /Put these papers in order. Bǎ jèisyē wénjyàn 'jénglǐ yísyàr.

To order (command) syà mìngling, syàlìng. /He ordered them put under arrest. Tā 'syàle mìngling bǎ tāmen 'jwāchilaile. /Who ordered you to do this? is expressed as Who told you to do this? Shwéi 'gàusu ni dzwò 'jèige? or as Who made you do this? Shwéi °'ràng (°'jyàu) ni 'dzwò 'jèigede? /He was ordered to appear in court. is expressed as He was summoned by the court to go there. Fǎ-'ywàn chwán ta chyù dàu'tíng.

(Ask for₀ yàu, jyàu; (reserve) dìng. /You can order these things by mail. Nǐ 'kéyi syě 'syìn °yàu (°dìng) jèisye 'dūngsyi. /I ordered you a glass of wine. 'Wǒ géi ni 'yàule yìbei 'jyǒu. /You can order these things by telephone. Nǐ 'kéyi yùng dyàn'hwà °yàu (°jyàu, °dìng) 'jèisye 'dūngsyi. /I want to order some things. Wǒ yàu dìng dyǎr 'hwò.

Order a meal °dyǎn (°jyàu, °yàu) tsài; (if delivered to one's home) jyàu fàn. /Have you ordered yet? Ní dyǎn 'tsài le ma? /This is not what I ordered. Jèi 'búshr wǒ °'dìng de (°'yàu de, °dyǎn de).

Order around (hú) jr̄shr. /Stop ordering me around! Byé nèmma (hú) 'jr̄shr wo!

ORDINARILY. píngcháng. /Where do you ordinarily eat? Nǐ píng'cháng dzài 'nǎr 'chr̄ fàn? /I wouldn't ordinarily do this. Wǒ 'píngcháng bú'dzèmmaje. or Wǒ 'píng-cháng bù'gwǎn 'jèiyàngrde 'shr̀. /Ordinarily we can get cigarettes here. 'Píngcháng 'jèr mǎide'jáu 'yān.

ORDINARY. (Commonplace) píngchángde, pǔtūngde. /Just give me an ordinary room. Wǒ jyòu 'yàu yì'jyān píng'chángde 'wūdz. /They're very ordinary people. Tāmen shr̀ hěn píng'chángde rén.

(Usual). /Is this the ordinary route? is expressed as Is this the route people often go on? Jèi 'shr̀ bushr̀ 'cháng dzǒude lù'syàn?

Out of the ordinary (unusual, special) 'tèbyéde; (outstanding) chūsède. /Is this anything out of the ordinary? Jèi yóu dyǎr 'tèbyé ma? /I didn't notice anything out of the ordinary about him. Wǒ 'chyǎubuchūlái tā yǒu shémma chū'sède dìfang.

ORIGINAL. (First) ywánláide, dzwèichūde. /The original site of the house was over there. Dzwèi'chūde fáng'jr̀ shr̀ dzài 'nèibyar. /Our original plan had to be changed. Ywán'láide 'jìhwà bù'dé bù'gǎile.

(Not imitated) jēnde (real). /The original statue is in London. Nèige 'jēnde shr̀syàng shr̀ dzài Lwún'dwūn. but /Is that joke original, or did you get it somewhere? is expressed as Did you make up that joke, or did you get it somewhere? Nèige 'syàuhwar shr̀ nǐ 'byānde, háishr byéchu 'tīnglaide?

(New, novel) syīn. /That's an original idea. Nèige 'yìjyan shr °'syīnde (°byéren méi'shwōgwode).

(Not like the others) yǔjùngbù'túng, tèbyé. /His plan was quite original. Tāde 'jìhwa °hěn tèbyé (°yǔ'jùngbù'túng). /The style of that dress is very original. Nèi-jyàn 'yīfude 'yàngdz yǔjùngbù'túng.

Original manuscript ywángǎu. /Is this the original manuscript? Jèi 'shr̀ bushr̀ ywán'gǎu?

ORIGINALITY

An **original** (painting) jēnde hwàr; (book) ywánwén. /Where is the original of this painting? Jèijāng 'jēnde hwàr dzài 'nǎr ne? /I read the translation, not the original. Wǒ 'nyàngwo 'fānyîde, méi'nyàngwo 'ywánwén.

In the original (language) ywánwénde. /Have you read this book in the original? Jèiběr 'shū nǐ 'nyàngwo ywán'wénde ma?

ORIGINALITY. 'syīnchí. /His stories don't have enough originality to be published. Tāde syǎu'shwōr 'tsáilyaur méi shémma 'syīnchí, bu'jŕde chū'bǎn.

OTHER. (Remaining) chítāde, chíyúde. /Do you want to know the other reasons? Nǐ syǎng jŕdau chí'tāde 'ywángu ma?

(More, additional) byéde; sometimes expressed with hái; **other people** 'byérén, 'pángrén. /Sorry, I have other things to do. Dwēibu'jù, wó 'yóu dyǎr 'byéde 'shr̀. /If any other people come, say I'm busy. 'Yàushr yǒu 'pángrén 'lái dehwà, jyòu 'shwō wó hěn 'máng. /Have you any other books? Nǐ 'hái yǒu 'byéde shū méiyou? /What other things did he say? Tā 'hái shwō 'shémma láije?

The other of two nèi(ge). /Give me the other one. 'Gěi wo 'nèiyíge. /Use your other hand too. 'Nèijr̄ shóu yě 'shànglái ba. /What's on the other side of the mountain? Shān 'nèibyar yǒu 'shémma? /He waved to her from the other side of the street. Tā dzài jyē 'nèibyar chung ta jāu'shǒur. /I don't want this one, but the other. Wǒ 'búyàu 'jèige, yàu 'nèige. /I can't tell one from the other. is expressed as I can't tell which is which. Wǒ 'fēnbuchulái 'něige shr̀ 'něige.

Every other (alternating) 'jyē yíge, 'gé yíge. /Trains leave every other hour. Hwǒ'chē měi 'jyē yíge jūng'tóur kāi yí'tàng. but /Every other time (but this) he's come with us. is expressed as It's just this time he hasn't come with us. Tā jyòushr 'jèihwéi méi 'gēn wōmen 'lái.

On the other hand kěshr, búgwò. /On the other hand, he may be too busy to see you. Búgwò, tā 'yěsyu méi 'gūngfu 'jyàn nǐ.

Someone or other is expressed as I don't know who bù('jŕdau) shr̀ 'shéi. /Someone or other phoned you just now. Yě 'búshr̀ 'shéi gāng gěi ni dǎ dyàn'hwà láije.

Something or other is expressed as I don't know what bù(jŕdàu) shr̀ 'shémma. /He wrote something or other in his notebook. Tā 'dzài tā bǐjì'bérli yě 'búshr̀ 'syěle syě 'shémma. /He said something or other about meeting you. is expressed as He seems to have said he wanted to meet you. Tā 'fǎngfu 'shwōgwo yàu 'jyàn ni shr̀de.

The others (ones remaining) chitāde, chíyúde; (of people) 'byérén, jángrén, or sometimes expressed with tāmen. /The others you sold me were better. is expressed as This is not as good as the others you sold me. Nǐ 'màigei wo de jèige dūngsyi méiyou chí'yúde hǎu. /Where are the others? 'Byérén ne? /If the others come, say I'm busy. 'Tāmen yàu 'lái de hwà jyòu 'shwō wó hěn 'máng. /I told the others to meet us here. Wǒ gēn tāmen 'shwōde dzài jèr 'jyàn.

OUGHT. yīngdāng, yīnggāi, gāi; (certainly must) yídìng děi. /You ought to help your parents. Nǐ 'yīnggāi 'bāngjù nǐ fù'mǔ. /The cake ought to be done soon. Jèige dàn'gāu jyòu gāi 'déle. /He ought to leave before it rains. Tā yí'dìng děi dzài 'yǔ méi syàchilai yǐchyán 'dzǒu.

OUR, OURS. See WE.

OURSELVES. See SELF.

OUT. (From inside to outside) chū as a postverb with the proper main verb, or occasionally as a verb. / Take your tickets out! Bǎ 'pyàu 'náchulai! / Let's go out for a while. Dzámen 'chūchyu yǐ'hwěr ba. / Let the cat out. Bǎ 'māu 'fàngchuchyu. / The secret is out. Jèige mì'mì 'lòuchulaile. or expressed as Everyone knows the secret. Jèige mì'mì 'rén dōu 'jřdaule.

Be out so much money dwǎnle, chàle, chyànle, shǎule. / I'm out three dollars. Wǒ °'dwǎnle (°'chàle, °etc.) 'sānkwài chyán.

Be out for something syǎng, 'dǎswàn. / He's out for a fight. Tā °syáng (°'dǎswàn) dǎ'jyà.

Be out of (beyond). / It's out of my control. is expressed as I can't control that. 'Nèige wǒ °'kùngjř bu'jùle (°'kùngjř bù'lyǎule, °gwǎnbu'jùle, °gwǎnbu'lyǎule, °'méifár 'gwǎnle).

Be out of (minus) méi, méiyou; or expressed by saying that the thing is finished wánle, all sold màiwánle, etc. with other appropriate main verbs before wán. / We're all out of cigarettes. Wǒmen méiyou yān'jywǎr le. or Wǒmende yān'jywǎr dōu °'wánle (°chōu'wánle, °mài'wánle). / He's been out of work a long time. Tā hén 'jyōu méi 'shèn le.

Be out of step. / You're out of step. Nǐde 'bùfa °'lwànle (°'tswòle).

Be out of the question shř bànbu'dàude, shř bùkěnéngde. / My staying here is out of the question. Wǒ 'jùdzai jèr shř bànbu'dàude. / To take leave at this busy period is out of the question. Syàndzai jèmma 'máng de shřhou chǐng 'jyà shř bukě'néngde.

Be out to do something 'dǎswàn. / He's out to break the record. Tā 'dǎswàn dǎ'pwò jì'lù.

Come out or be out (be published) chū, chūbǎn. / When does the magazine come out? Dzá'jř 'shémma shřhou °'chūlai (°chū'bǎn)? / The new number of that magazine is out today. Nèige dzá'jř dzwèi 'jìnde yì'chī jyěr °'chūlaile (°chū'bǎnle).

Come out or be out (in bloom) kāi. / What flowers are out now? Syàn'dzài shémma 'hwār 'kāije ne?

Out-and-out jyǎnjř, wánchywán, jēn. / It's an out-and-out case of murder. 'Nèi jyǎn'jř shř yíjyàn móushā'àn. / You're an out-and-out liar! Nǐ wán'chywán shř sā'hwǎng!

Out of (because of). / Are you acting out of spite? is expressed as Do you want to take revenge? Nǐ shr yàu bàu'chóu ma? or as Is hate your reason? Nǐ shř 'wèile jyě'hèn ma? / I did it for him out of gratitude. is expressed as I did it for him because I owed him a favor. Wǒ 'yīnwei 'chyàn tāde 'chíng tsái nèmma 'bànde.

Speak out. / He wasn't afraid to speak out in the meeting. is expressed as At the meeting he really dared to speak. Tā dzài jèige 'hwèili hén 'gǎn shwō'hwà.

Vote someone out. / They voted him out. is expressed as They voted that they didn't want him. Tāmen byǎu'jywé bú'yàu ta le.

For other expressions containing out see the word or words with which out is combined.

OUTSIDE. wàimyan, wàibyar, wàitou. / Is it cold outside? 'Wàibyar 'lěng bulěng? / Wait outside. Dzài 'wàimyan 'děngje. / Step outside, and say that again! Dzámen shàng 'wàitou chyù, nǐ hái gǎn 'shwō ma! / Three of them sat in the front seat, with the boy on the outside. Tāmen 'sānge rén dzwòdzai 'chyántou, nèige 'nánháidz 'dzwòde kàu 'wàibyar. / I like the outside of the house very much. Jèi 'fángdz de 'wàibyar wǒ tíng 'syǐhwan. / The bowl is purple outside and blue inside. Nèige 'wǎnde 'wàibyar shř 'dźshǎr, lǐbyar shr 'lánshǎr. / We need the opinion of someone from the outside. Wǒmen déi 'jǎu yíge 'wàibyarde rén tīngting tāde 'yìjyàn. / Do you have an outside room? is expressed as Do you have a room facing the outside? Ní 'yǒu méiyou yìjyān cháu'wài de 'wūdz? / Isn't this outside your jurisdiction? is expressed as Doesn't this not belong to you to manage? Jèi 'búshr bù'gwēi nín 'gwǎn ma? or 'Jèige ní gwǎnde'jáu ma?

Outside of (besides, or except for) chúle . . . °yǐ'wài (°jr'wài). / I wouldn't trust anyone outside of you. Chúle 'ní yǐ'wài wǒ 'shéi dōu bú'syìn. / Outside of a few funny remarks his speech was very dull. Chúle jijyù dōu'génde hwà yǐ'wài, tāde yán'jyǎng hěn 'méi'yìsz. / Outside of the rent there's still the electric light bill to be paid. 'Chúle 'fángchyán yǐ'wài hái děi fù 'dyànchyán.

OVER. (In a higher position than; spatially) dzài . . . °shàngmyan (°shàngmyar, °shàng-tou, °shàngbyar). / His room is directly over mine. Tāde 'wūdz jyòu dzài ' wǒ wūdzde 'shàngtou. (fig.) / His speech was way over my head. is expressed as What he said was too deep; I couldn't understand it. Tāde 'hwà tài 'shēn; wǒ tīng bu'dǔng.

(In a higher position than; in authority) dzài . . . shàngtou, bǐ . . . gāu, or expressed by using a term which has the meaning of person in authority, such as 'shàng-sz, tóur, láubǎn, etc. / Is his position over yours in your company? Dzài nǐmende gūngszli, tāde dìwèi °bǐ nǐ gāu ma (°dzài nǐ 'shàngtou ma)? / How many bosses are over you? Ní yǒu 'dwōshau 'shàngsz? or Nǐde 'shàngbyar yǒu 'jǐge 'tóur a?

(Relative to someone in a lower position or with less power). / He has the power of life and death over those people. Tā 'dwèi nèisye rén yǒu 'shēngshājr'chywán. / We won a complete victory over them. is expressed as We beat them completely. Wǒmen bǎ tāmen wánchywán dǎ'bàile. / The commander-in-chief is over the whole army. Dzǔng'szlǐng shr chwánjyūn tǔng'shwài.

(Moving through a higher position than, spatially) gwò alone or as postverb with a main verb which implies motion over rather than motion through, as climb over something págwochyu. / I threw a stone over the wall. Wǒ bǎ yíkwài 'shŕtou 'rēng-gwò 'chyáng chyule. / How can I get over the river? Wó 'dzěmmayàng gwò 'hé ne? / The horse jumped over the gate. 'Mǎ 'tyàugwò 'mér chyùle.

(Moving from one position to another, not necessarily through higher points) gwò as verb or postverb. / We asked them over to play cards. Wǒmen 'chǐng tāmen ('gwò)lái dǎda 'pái. / Bring the chair over here. Bá 'yǐdz 'bāngwòlai.

(Along the surface of) dzài. / We were traveling over a very good road. Wǒmen dzài yìtyáu hén'hǎude 'dàurshang 'dzǒu láije.

(From vertical to horizontal) dǎu or 'tǎngsyà as postverbs. / Don't knock the lamp over. Byé bǎ 'dēng °pèng'tǎngsyale (°pèngdǎule). / Don't fall over the rock! is expressed as Don't let the rock trip you. Byé ràng 'shŕtou gěi 'bànle!

(Upside down) fān as postverb or verb; **roll over** dǎ ge gwěr. / Turn the eggs over. Bǎ jǐ'dzěr fān ge 'gér.

(Covering completely) dzài . . . °wàitou (°shàngtou). / Are you going to wear a coat over your sweater? Ní dzài máu'yī °wàitou (°shàngtou) hái yàu 'jàushang yíjyàn shàng'shēr ma?

(In a direction) wàng, syàng (for motion); dzài (for location). / It's ten miles over that way. Wàng 'nèibyar dzóu yǒu 'shŕlǐ'dì. / What's over there? Dzài nèi-byar shř 'shémma? / It's over there. Dzài 'nèibyar.

(From one person to another) **hand** something **over** dìgwolai, jyāuchulai. / Hand over the money! Bǎ 'chyán °'jyāuchulai (°'dìgwolai)!

(Through, in various parts of, in more or less detail) **go over** a problem yán-jyou, tán; **count over** shǔ °yí'dàur (°yí'gwòr, °yí'hwéi); **read over** nyàn yí'byàn;

look over 'kàn yikàn. / Let's go over the problem together. Dzámen yí'kwàr bǎ jèige 'wèntí 'yánjyouyánjyou. / We've been over this before. Jèi dzámen yǐjing 'tángwole. / He counted over the money. Tā bǎ 'chyán 'shǔle °yí'dàur (°yí'gwòr, °yí'hwéi). / They read over the terms of the contract. Tāmen bǎ hétúng de 'tyáu-jyàn 'nyànle yí'byàn. / May I look the house over? Ràng wo 'kàn yikàn jèiswòr 'fángdz, 'kéyi ma?

(Through a period of time) often expressed by a verb plus the postverb dàu such as **keep over** tswúndau; **stay over** dāidau; **hold over** (of a show) yǎndau, (of a meeting) kāidau, děngdau; etc. / How long will it be held over? Yàu yǎndau 'shémma shŕhour? / Can you stay over till Monday? Nǐ néng 'jùdau lǐbài'yī ma? / The matter must be held over until the next meeting. Jèijyan 'shŕ wǒmen děngdau 'syàtsz kāihwèi dzài 'shwō ba.

(Done). / It's all over now. °Syàn'dzài (°'Yǐjing) dōu °'wánle (°'gwòchyule, °jyě'jywéle, °jyé'shùle, °'hǎule, °méi'shèrle). / Let's get this over with. Dzámen bǎ 'jèige nèngwánle jyòu 'wánle. / The war is over. Jàn'shŕ °'wánle (°jyé'shùle). / When is the play over? 'Syì 'shémma shŕhou 'wán?

(More than) dwō, yǐshàng after a numerical expression; gwò as a verb or postverb; or expressed as and a little more hái'líng dyǎr, hái 'dwō dyǎr. / It'll cost over twenty dollars to have it fixed. 'Shōushr yísyàr děi °'èrshr'dwōkwài chyán (°èrshrkwài chyán yǐ'shàng). / Don't drive over forty miles an hour. Byé 'kāigwò 'szshŕ'lǐ. / She's over thirty, if she's a day. Tā 'dzěmmaje yě 'gwòle sān'shŕ le. / Is it over three miles from here to there? Tsúng 'jèr dàu 'nèr 'shŕ bushŕ 'chāugwò 'sānlǐ 'dì? / The meat weighs a little over five pounds. 'Ròu shŕ 'wǔbàng hái °'líng (°'dwō) dyǎr.

(Again) dzài; **over and over** láihwéide, yíbyànyí'byànde, . . . le 'yòu . . . , 'dzwò . . . 'yòu . . . . / Do it over. 'Dzài dzwò yíbyàn. or 'Dzài tsúng 'tóur 'lái yìhwéi. / He read it over and over. Tā láihwéide 'nyànle háujǐ'byàn. or Tā yíbyànyí'byànde 'kànle háujǐ'byàn. or Tā 'nyànle 'yòu nyàn. or Tā 'dzwò nyàn 'yòu nyàn.

(About, concerning) wèi, dwèi. / All that trouble over such a tiny thing! 'Swóyòude 'máfan jyòu wèi 'nèmma yìdyǎr 'dòurdàde 'shŕ! / They're fighting over some woman. Tāmen wèi nèige nyǔde 'dachilaile. / They quarreled over who should get the money. Tāmen wèile 'shéi yīnggai 'dé nèige 'chyán tái'gàng láije. / It's silly to fight over it. Wèi 'jèige 'jēn tài bù'jŕle. / We'll laugh over this some day. Jyāng'lái wǒmen dwèi jèijyan shŕ 'hwèi jywéde hén kě'syàu.

All over (in all parts of). / He traveled all over the country. °Jèi (°Nèi) 'gwóli gè'chùr tā dōu dzǒu'byànle. / I've been all over this part of the country. Jèi-yí'dàide dìfang wǒ 'chywán dōu 'dàugwo.

OVERLOOK. (Have a view from a high position). / This window overlooks the garden. is expressed as The window faces the garden. 'Chwānghu 'chùngje hwā'ywár. or as The garden is beneath the window. 'Chwānghu 'dǐsya shŕ hwā'ywár.

(Neglect; not notice) méilǐ hwèi, méilyǔhwèi, méi'kànjyàn; (not pay attention to) méilyòushén, méijùyǐ. / Here are some papers you overlooked. Jèisyē wénjyàn nǐ dàgài méilǐ'hwèi.

(Excuse). / I'll overlook your mistake this time. is expressed as I won't go any further with your mistake this time. Nǐ jèitsz chū'tswòr wǒmen °bù'jwēijyoule (or (excuse you) °'ywánlyàng nǐ ba, or (let you go) °fàng nǐ 'gwòchyu). or (if said by some high authority who is really relieving you of some punishment) as I forgive you your mistake this time. Nǐ jèitsz chū'tswòr wǒ 'ráule nǐ ba.

OVERSHOE. tàusyé.

OVERWEIGHT. Expressed verbally as **become overweight** gwòjùng. / He's twenty pounds overweight. Tā gwò'jùng gwòle yŏu 'èrshrbàng.

OWE. (Be obligated to give something) chyàn, gāi (of money); or in other cases expressed with yīngdāng ought to. / How much do I owe you? Wŏ °'chyàn (°'gāi) ni 'dwōshău chyán? / You owe me ten dollars. Nĭ °gāi (°chyàn) wo 'shŕkwài chyán. / I owe you an apology. Wŏ yīng'dāng géi ni dàu'chyán.

(Be indebted to) chyàn chíng. / He owes his friend a great deal. Tā 'chyàn ta 'péngyou bushău 'chíng. / I owe him a lot for his help. Wŏ 'chyàn ta bushău 'chíng yīnwei ta bāng wo 'máng laije.

(Have or possess because of someone or something) kàu, jàngje, dwōkwēi. ' / To what do you owe your success? Nĭ chéng'gūng 'kàude shr 'shémma? / I owe my life to you. Wŏ jīntyan hái hwóje, dwōkwēi 'nĭ.

Owe it to oneself. / You owe it to yourself to take a vacation. is expressed as You ought to take a vacation. Nĭ yīng'dāng syōu'jyà le.

OWN. (Possess) yŏu. / Do you own a typewriter? Ní yóu dădz'jĭ méiyou? / He owns seven houses. Tā yŏu 'chīswŏr 'fángdz. but in sentences where have would be unnatural in English / Who owns this property? is expressed as Whose property is this? Jèige 'chănyè shr 'shéide? / He owns this house. is expressed as This house is his. Jèiswŏr 'fángdz shr 'tăde.

One's own (belonging to oneself) dzìjĭde, dzìgérde; of **one's own** (by oneself, alone) 'yíge rén. / Are these your own things? Jèisyē 'dūngsyi shr nĭ dz'jĭde ma? / This is his own car. Jèi shr tā dz'gérde 'chē. / He has his own horses. Tā dz-'jĭ yŏu 'mă. / Can I have a room of my own? Wŏmen kéyi 'yíge rén jàn yìjyān 'wūdz ma?

Be on one's own (live on one's own efforts) dz'shŕchí'lì; (having one's own business) dz'jĭ dzwò 'măimai. / He's been on his own since he was sixteen. Tā shŕlyòu-swèi jyou dzshŕchí'lì le. / He is on his own now. Tā syàn'dzài dz'jĭ dzwò 'măimai.

OWNER. 'jŭrén; (possessor; legal term) swóyŏurén; in compounds jŭ or jŭr; landowner dìjŭ(r). / Who is the owner of the house? Fángjŭr shr 'shéi? / He's the owner of this copyright. Tā shr jèige băn'chywánde swóyŏu'rén. / The owner of the dog will be fined ten dollars. Jèijŭr gŏude 'jŭrén déi gĕi 'shŕkwài chyán fá'kwăn. but / Who's the owner of this car? is expressed as Whose car is this? Jèige 'chē shr shéide? / I am the owner. is expressed as It's mine. Shr wŏde.

PACK. (Put things in a container; said of the container) jwāng; (pack in a container; said of the things packed) jwāngsyàng; (pack in; followed by the name of the container) jwāngdzài; (pack in order) 'shŕdou, 'shōushr; (pack into the form of) 'dăchéng; (used only of baggage) dă; (bundle up) kwŭn; (make a bundle of) dákwĕr; (make a package of) dăbāu. / Hve you packed your trunk yet? Nĭ 'syāngdz jwāngle ma? / Have you finished packing yet? 'Syíngli dōu °dá'hăule ma (°'shŕdou'hăule ma, °shōushr-'hăule ma)? or 'Syāngdz dōu jwāng'hăule ma? / Start packing at once. Lì'kè jyòu chyù °shōushr (°'shrdou, °dă) ' syíngli ba. / He packed up his things and left. Tā bă 'dūngsyi °'shōushrchilai (°'shŕdouchilai, °jwāngdzài 'syāngdzli, °'dăchéngle syíngli'jywăr) jyòu (dài)'dzòule. / Have you packed up your books yet? Nĭ shū 'shōu-chilaile ma? or Nĭ shū °jwāng'syāngle (°dă'bāule, °dá'kwĕrle, °kwŭn'hăule) méi-you a? / I have a good deal of packing to do yet. Wŏ 'shōushr dūngsyi dă 'syíngli hái yóu hăusye 'shèr ne. or Wó yóu hăusyē 'syíngli dĕi shōushr. / The fruit will soon be packed in boxes for shipping. 'Shwéigwŏ 'jyòu yàu °jwāng'syāng yùn'dzŏu le (°jwāngdzài 'syāngdzli hău 'yùnchuchyu).

(Crowd of people in a space) jǐ. / The train was really packed this morning. Jyěr 'dzǎuchen 'chēli jēn 'jǐ. / The people packed into the train. Rén dōu 'jǐjin 'chēli chyule. / The room was packed with people. Wūdzli ji'mǎnle rén. / Several hundred men were packed into the boat. Hǎují'bǎi rén dōu 'jǐdau nèi yijīr chwánli chyule.

(Press together; as earth) yà. / They're packing the earth down firmly to make a strong foundation. Tāmen bǎ tǔ 'yàde hén 'jǐn, wèideshr dzá yíge hǎu gēnjī.

Pack someone **off** sùng. / He packed his wife off to the country. Tā bǎ 'tàitai 'sùngdau 'syāngsya chyùle.

Pack a wallop. / That letter really packs a wallop. Nèifēng 'syìn shwōde jēn yǒu °'jyèr (°'lìlyang). / He really packs a wallop (physically). Tā 'dǎrén dǎde hěn 'jùng. or Tā 'chywantou hěn °'yìng (°yǒu'jyèr, °yǒu 'lìlyang).

A pack (bundle) bāu; (load carried on the back) bēibāu. / The donkeys were carrying heavy packs. Lyú 'twó de bēi'bāu hén 'jùng.

(Set, of cards) fù, chùng. / Where is that new pack of cards? °Nèifù (°Nèi-chùng) 'syīnjīrpái dzài 'nǎr ne?

(Group) chyún. / A pack of wolves attacked our sheep. Yìchyún 'láng lái chīr wǒmende 'yáng laije.

A pack of lies. / His story is a pack of lies. 'Tā shwō de 'chywán shr syā-'hwà. or Nèi shr tā 'dzǒu de yítàu syā'hwà.

Ice pack bīng kǒudai. / That ice pack made him feel much better. Nèige bīng-'kǒudai jyàutā jywéde 'shūfu'dwōle.

PACKAGE. bāur; (if wrapped) bāugwǒ; (if wrapped with cloth) 'bāufu; (if a box) syāng-dz, hédz. / Has a package arrived for me? Wǒ yǒu ge °'bāur (°bāu'gwǒ) 'dàule méiyou? / Here's a package for you. Jèr yóu nǐ yíge °'bāur (°bāu'gwǒ, °'bāufu). or (paper box) Jèr yóu nǐ yíge °jīr'syāngdz (°jīr'hédz).

Package of something bāu (measure). / How much is a package of cigarettes? Yìbāu 'yān 'dwōshǎu chyán?

PAGE. (One side of a sheet) myàr; (one side or the entire sheet) yè; (term used most often in giving page numbers) yèr; (the entire sheet) pyār. / This book is 200 pages long. Jèibēr 'shū you èrbǎi °yè (°'yèr, °'myàr). or Jèibēr shū yǒu yìbǎi pyār. / The illustration is opposite page 101. Chā'tú dzài (dì)yīlíngyīyède bèi'myàr. / There is a footnote on page 10. Dì'shryè 'dǐsya yóu syāu'jùr. / Isn't there a page missing in this book? 'Jèibēr shū 'shr bushr 'dwǎnle yìpyār?

(Attendant) shr—yìng shēng.

To page someone jyàu, 'jāuhu. / If you want me, page me in the dining room. Nǐ 'yàushr 'jáu wǒ dehwà, jyàu rén dàu fàn'tǐng chyu °'jyàu (°'jāuhu) wǒ.

PAIL. tǔng; (for water only) shāu. / Put the rubbish in this pail. Bǎ °'lājī (°'dzāng-'dūngsyi) dàudzai jèige 'tungli. / Bring me a pail of water. Géi wǒ °ná (°dǎ) °yìtúng (°yìshāu) 'shwěi lai.

PAIN. téng (a stative verb meaning have pain, hurt). / I have a pain in my stomach. Wǒ 'wèi téng. / I have a pain in the back. Wǒ 'bèiténg. / Where is the pain? 'Nǎr téng? / The pain is gone. Téng 'jīr le. or 'Bùténg le. / Do you feel any pain? 'Téng ma? or Jywédechu 'téng lai ma? / This shouldn't cause you any pain at all. Jèige yì'dyár yě bù'téng. / The pain is unbearable. 'Téngde shòubu'lyǎu. / Labor pains come before childbirth. 'Shēngchán yǐ'chyán °dùdz yijènyijènde téng (°yǒu 'jèntùng).

(Mental anguish). / His drinking caused his mother a great deal of pain. Tā nèmma hē 'jyóu jyàu tā 'mǔchin(syīnli) hěn °nán'gwò (°nán 'shòu).

Take pains. / Take pains to do your work well. °Mài 'lìchi (°Shǐ'jyèr, °Jìn dyar'syīn) bǎ shèr dzwò'hǎule.

To pain is expressed as in the first paragraph. / The tooth pained so I couldn't sleep. 'Yá téngde wǒ 'shwèibujáu 'jyàu.

PAINT. yóu (also means oil). / There is wet paint on the door. 'Ménshangde yóuméi-'gān. / The house needs a new coat of paint. 'Fángdz děi 'chúngsyīn 'shàng yídàu 'yóu le.

To **paint** (cover with paint) shàngyóu; (brush on paint) shwāyóu; sometimes yóu. / They are painting. Tāmen 'jèngdzai °shàng'yóu (°shwā'yóu). / Paint the house white. Bǎ 'fángdz °shàng yídàu 'báiyóu (°yóu'báilou). / The house has been painted. Fángdz 'yóule. / The house was painted white. Fangdz yóu'báile.

Paint pictures hwà. / He paints very well. Tā hwà 'hwàr hwàde hén 'hǎu. / He painted a very good picture of his mother. Tā gěi tā 'mǔchin 'hwàle yìjāng 'syàng, hwàde jēn hǎu.

PAIR. Three measures are commonly used: shwāng for pairs of things that are identical, as chopsticks, socks, and shoes (not made differently in China for right and left); dwei or dwèr for pairs of things that match or are set opposite each other but are not normally identical, as a man and a woman, matching vases, eyes, ears; fù (also a set of more than two) for things that are similar and used together, but not necessarily identical, as glasses, gloves, earrings; in the case of some things as earrings either fù or dwei may be used; trousers and scissors and other inseparable objects that we sometimes call pairs are units in Chinese, and take unit measures. / Where can I get a pair of skating shoes? Wǒ yàu mǎi (yì)shwāng lyóu'bīng chwān de 'syé, dàu'nàrchyu mǎi? / He owns a fine pair of horses. Tā yǒu yídwèr háu 'mǎ. / He kept a pair of rabbits for breeding. Tā 'yàngle yídwèr 'tùdz wèideshr °lyóu'jǔngr (°syà 'syàuder). / You get two pairs of trousers with this suit. Jèitàu 'yīfu dài 'lyangtyàu 'kùdz. / Have you a pair of scissors? Ní yǒu yìba 'jyǎndz ma?

To **pair off** tsòu dwèr. / The boys and girls paired off for the dance. Nannyǔ-'háidz tsouhǎule 'dwèr tyàu'wǔ.

PAN. (Any cooking pan) gwō; (an earthenware or metal pan, usually without a handle, seldom used for cooking) pén, pér; **frying pan** chǎushǎu; **dustpan** (tǔ)bwòchi. / Put a cup of water in the pan. °Dzài (°Wàng) 'gwōli dàu yìbēi 'shwěi. / Put a pan of water on the stove. Nùng °yìgwō (°yìpén) 'shwěi gēdzai 'lúdzshang.

Pancake bǐng.

To **pan** (as gold) shāi (sift). / Those men are panning for gold. 'Nèisyē rén dzài nàr shāi 'jīndz ne.

Pan out chénggūng. / My scheme panned out well. Wǒde 'jìhwa hěn chéng-'gūng.

PAPER. (As material) jř; **writing paper** (for pen and ink) 'yángjř, 'yángsyīnjř; (thin bamboo paper) 'jújř; (other varieties) 'fángjř, 'lyánshŕjř, 'máubyānjř; **rice paper** (for writing Chinese with brush and India ink; a thick, durable variety used for decorative purposes) 'sywānjř; **wallpaper** hú 'chyáng de jř; **toilet paper** 'shóujř; **pad of paper** jřbèndz; **ruled paper** dài 'dàur de jř; **paper carton** jřsyāngdz. / Do you have some good writing paper? Ní yǒu hǎu °'yángjř (°'jújř) ma? or Ní yǒu háu syě 'dž de 'jř ma? / She wrapped up the package with heavy paper. Tā yùng 'hòujř bǎ bāu-'gwǒ 'bāuchilaile.

(Document) 'wénjyàn. / Some important papers are missing. Yǒu syē 'jùng-yàude 'wénjyàn bú'jyànle.

(Essay) wénjang. / He has written a paper on the production of rubber. Tā 'syěle yìpyān 'gwānyu 'jrdzàu syàng'pí de 'wénjang.

(Newspaper) bàu. / Where's the morning paper? °'Dzǎubàu (°'Dzǎuchende bàu) dzài 'nǎr?

On paper (not existing otherwise) 'byǎumyànshang, jr'shàngtánbǐng. / My profits were only on paper. Wǒ yě jyòushr 'byǎumyànshang 'jwànchyán. / Their plan is only on paper. Tāmende 'jìhwà búgwò shr jr'shàngtánbǐng.

Paper money (chyán)pyàudz; (if of foreign origin) yángchyán'pyàudz; (technically, as a medium of exchange) 'jrbì. / Could you give me coins for this paper money? Wǒ yùng jèijāng(yángchyán)'pyàudz gēn nǐ hwàn dyǎr líng'chyán syíng ma? / Paper money was first used in the Táng dynasty. Jr'bì dzwèidzǎu shr 'Tángchau kaishr 'yùngde.

Papers (identification) jèngjyàn, jèngmín'wénjyàn; (official orders) gūngshr; (procedure) shǒusyu. / You must see that your papers are in order before you can leave the country. Nǐ dei bǎ jèng'jyàn nùng'hǎule tsái néng chū 'gwó ne. *or* Ní děi bá 'shǒusyu dōu syān bàn'hǎulou tsái néng chū 'gwó ne.

To paper a room, walls hú. / This room hasn't been papered in five years. Jèi 'wūdz yǒu 'wǔnyán méi'hú le. / Paper the walls blue and the ceiling white. 'Chyáng-shang hú 'lánde(jr), fáng'dǐng(dz) hú 'báide.

PARALLEL. píngsyíng; **parallel lines** 'píngsyíngsyàn; except in mathematical discussion, these terms are not usually used. / These two lines are parallel. 'Jèilyǎngtyáu syàn °píng'syíng (°shr píng'syíng de). / Put the figures betweeen the parallel lines. is expressed as Put the figures between the two straight lines. Bǎ 'shùmu fàngdzài °'lyǎnghángde (°'lyǎngtyáu 'jrsyànde, °'lyǎngdau 'jrsyànde) jūng'jyàr nàr.

Parallel (of latitude) 'wēisyàn . . . dù. / That small island is located on the 34th parallel. Nèige syáu dǎu dzài 'wēisyàn 'sānshr 'sz dù shang.

(Comparison). / You can draw a parallel between these two events. Ná jèi'lyǎng-jyàn shèr yì'bǐ, kéyí 'bǐchū bùshǎu °yí'yàngde (°syāng'túngde, °syāng'syàngde) dìfang lai.

Parallel with (along) shwùnje, yánje. / The road runs parallel with the river. Lù shr °'shwùnje (°'yánje) hé dzǒu.

PARCEL. bāur, 'bāugwǒ, bāufu (package, wrapped); hédz, syádz (box). / I'm expecting a parcel from the store. 'Pùdz yàu géi wǒ sùng yige °'bāur (°etc.) lai.

(Amount; of land) kwài. / He bought a parcel of land. Tā 'mǎile yíkwài 'dì.

Parcel post dàng 'bāugwǒ; (at parcel rates) àn 'bāugwǒ. / Send it parcel post. °Dàng (°An) 'bāugwǒ jì.

To parcel out (distribute) 'fēnfā, fāchuchyu; (divide into portions) 'fēnpèi. / All the supplies have been parceled out. Dūngsyi dōu 'yǐjīng °'fēnfāle (°'fāchu-chyule). / Let's parcel these out before distributing them. Dzámen bǎ jèisyē 'dūng-syi 'fēnpèi'hǎule dzài 'fā.

PARDON. (In polite apologies). / Pardon me. *or* I beg your pardon. (for something to be said or done) Láu'jyà. *or* Jyè'gwāng. *or* (for something already said or done) Dwèibu'jù. *or* Dwèibu'chǐ. *or* Chíng nǐ 'ywánlyang. / Pardon me; let me pass. °Láu'jyà (° Jyè'gwāng); 'ràng yí bù.

(Forgive, remit penalty; said of a person) shè; (said of a crime or penalty)

myăn, 'shèmyăn. / He was pardoned by the president. Shr̀ dzúng'tŭng 'shède ta.
or Dzúng'tŭng bă tā 'shèmyănle. *or* Shr̀ dzúng'tŭng 'myănde tāde 'dzwèi. / The
governor pardoned the thief. Shéng'jăng bă nèige 'dzéide dzwèi °'myănle (°'shèmyănle).

PARENTS. (Father, mother) 'fùmŭ; (somewhat more formal) 'shwāngchīn. / Both my
parents are still living. Wŏ 'fùmŭ dōu 'dzài. *or* Wŏ 'shwāngchīn dōu 'dzài.
/ They're good parents. Tāmen shr̀ 'syánmíngde 'fùmŭ. or expressed as They
bring up children very well. Tāmen 'jyàuyù 'dznyŭ jyàuyude 'hén hău.

PARK. (Public land) gūngywán. / The city has many beautiful parks. 'Chéngli yóu
hău'syēge hău'kànde gūng'ywán. / We camped for two weeks in the National Park.
Wŏmen dzài 'Gwóligūng'ywánlĭ dā 'jàngpéng jùle 'lyàngge lĭ'bài.

　　To **park** a car tíng. / Where can we park (the car)? 'Nár syŭ tíng'chē? *or*
'Chē tíngdzài 'nár ne? / There's a parking lot over there. Nèr yŏu ge tíngchē-
'chăng. / Leave a parking space for others. Gĕi 'byéren lyóuchu 'tíngchē de 'dìfang lai. *or* Lyóuchu 'kùngr lai hău jyàu 'byéren (yè néng) 'tíngchē. / No parking!
'Bùsyŭ 'tíngchē!

　　(Leave something someplace) fàng. / You can park your things here. 'Dūngsyi
fàng 'jèr hău le.

PART. (Division) bùfen; (length, or one of several continuous parts) dwàr, dwàn;
(length, only physical) jyér; (a natural division or section, as of an orange) bàr;
(section, side; of a place) byàr. / We can divide the work into four parts. Wŏmen
kéyí bă 'gūngdzwò 'fénchéng 'szbùfen. / His part of the work isn't finished. Jèijyàn shèr °'tāde (°'tā gwănde, °'tā dzwòde) nèi °'bùfen hái méi'wán (*or* (if the
work was done in consecutive parts) °'yí'dwàr hái méi'wán). / He cut off part of the
rope. Tā bă 'shéngdz 'lāsyà °'yí'dwàr (°'yĭ'jyér) lai. / This part of the road is muddy. Jèi yídwàr 'lùshang °'yŏu 'ní (°'hĕn 'nèng). / The fence is part wood and part
stone. is expressed as The fence is wood for a distance, stone for a distance. 'Wéichyáng yídwar shr̀ 'mùtoude, °'yídwàr or, meaning one layer of each °'yíjyér shr̀
'shr̀toude. / What part of town do you live in? Nĭ jùdzài chéng 'nĕibyàr?

　　(Unit measurement) fèr. / Mix two parts vodka with one part lemon juice.
Dwèi 'lyăngfèr 'shāujyŏu 'yífèr níngméng'jèr.

　　(Some) yóude. / Part of this shipment of apples isn't good. 'Jèitsz̀ lái de
'pínggwŏ 'yóude 'bùhău.

　　(Role in a play) 'jyàusè, jyàur. / She played her part very well. Tā yăn 'nèige
°'jyàusè (°'jyàur) yànde 'hén hău.

　　(Dividing line in hair) fèngr. / The part in your hair isn't straight. Nĭ tóufa
'fèngr 'fénde bù'jŕ.

　　(Piece of a machine) 'língjyàr. / Where can I get some new parts for my car?
Nár yŏu mài 'chìchē'língjyàrde?

　　For the most part. / For the most part, this work is very pleasant. 'Jèi shèr
°'dà'tĭshang (°'dà'jŕ, °'yóu 'hăusyē dìfang) 'hĕn jyàu rén 'syĭhwan dzwò. / For the
most part, the weather has been nice this season. 'Dzŭngchilai shwō 'jèi yíjìde
'tyānchì hái bútswò. / For the most part, I enjoyed this book. Jèibĕn 'shūli yì-
'dwòbàr wŏ hái °'syĭhwan (°'ài kàn).

　　Take one's part syàngje (favor). / He always takes his brother's part in an
argument. Tā 'yì gēn rén 'byàn de shŕhou lăushr̀ syàngje tā 'gēge.

　　Take part in 'tsānjyā. / He refused to take part in the game. Tā 'bùkĕn
'tsānjyā bĭ'sài.

Parts (places) dài (region); dìfang (place). /I haven't traveled much in these parts for a long time. Wǒ 'hén jyou méidà dzài °'jèiyidài (°'jèisyē dìfang) 'yóulì le.

Part time expressed verbally as not work full time 'búdzwò 'jěnggūng or as work a half-day dzwò 'bàntyār; **part-time work** 'línggūngr, 'línghwór. /May I work part time?. Wǒ 'búdzwò 'jěnggūng syíng busyíng? or Wǒ dzwò 'bàntyār syíng busyíng? /Is there any part-time work available? Yǒu shémma °'línggūngr (°'línghwór) kě 'dzwò ma?

To part (separate) 'fēnkāi, fēnshǒu; 'fēn'dàuyáng'byāu (deliberately; somewhat poetic); 'fēndzài 'lyǎngbyār (divide). /We parted at the corner. Wǒmen dzài gwǎi-'jyǎur nar °'fēnkāile (°'fēn'shǒule). /Our ways parted three years ago. Wǒmen °'fēnkāi (°'fēn'shǒu, °'fēn'dàuyáng'byāu) yǒu 'sānnyándwō le. / The best of friends must part. 'Dzwèihǎude péngyou yě yǒu fēn'shǒu de shrhou. / The policemen parted the crowd. Jǐng'chá bǎ rén 'fēndzài 'lyǎngbyār.

Part with something chūshǒu, chūràng. /I wouldn't part with that book for any price. 'Nèiběr shū a, shwō 'shémma wó yě bùkěn °chū'shǒu (°chū'ràng).

Part with someone fēnshǒu. /I don't want to part with him. Wǒ bú'ywànyi gēn tā fēnshǒu.

PARTICULAR. Used to emphasize this, that or the; Chinese stresses jèi or nèi, and often adds the numeral yī. /I can't get a ticket for that particular train. Wó 'mǎibujáu 'nèi (yí)tàng chēde 'pyàu. /I can't get a ticket for the particular train I want to take. Wó 'mǎibujáu wǒ yàu dzwò de 'nèi (yí)tàng chēde 'pyàu. /I have to take this particular train. Wǒ fēi děi dzwò 'jèi (yí)tàng chē bù'kě. /That particular dress costs more. 'Nèijyàn 'yīfu bǐ 'byéde 'gwèi.

(Special) 'tèbyé, 'yóuchíshr; 'tèwèi (referring to intentions or possibilities); sometimes expressed merely by stress. /He has a particular dislike of sloppy persons. Tā tè'byé busyǐhwan 'lēliledēde rén. /I remember one fellow in particular. Yǒu 'yíge jyāhwo wǒ °tè'byé jide (°tè'byé wàngbu'lyǎu, °'yóuchíshr wàngbu'lyǎu). /Are you going anywhere in particular? Nǐ shr 'tèwèi yàu shàng nǎr 'chyù ma? /Is he a particular friend of yours? Tā shr ní 'hǎu péngyou ma?

(Fussy) jùyi, jyǎngjyou (especially about decorations and luxuries); (finicky) 'syán'jège 'syán'nàgede, 'tyāu(ti)de lìhai (disliking this and that). /He's very particular about his appearance. Tā 'hěn jùyi 'dǎban. or Tā 'hén jyǎngjyou 'dǎban. /He's very particular about manners. Tā 'hěn jùyi 'lǐmàu. or Tā 'hén jyǎngjyou 'lǐmàu. /You can't be too particular around here. Dzài 'jèr nǐ 'bùnéng tài °'jyǎngjyou le (°'nèmma 'syán'jège'syán'nàgede, °tyāu(ti)de lìhai).

Particulars (detail; of a situation) 'syìchíng, 'syángchíng, 'syángsyìchíngsyíng. /We haven't learned the particulars of the accident yet. Nèige shèrde °syìchíng (°'syángchíng, °'syángsyìchíngsyíng) wǒmen hái bùjr'dàu ne.

In every particular 'chùchùr, 'gèfāngmyàn, 'yàngyàngr. / The work is complete in every particular. °'Jèige gūng (°'Jèijyàn hwór) °'chùchùr (°'gèfāngmyàn, °'yàngyàngr) dōu dzwò'wánle.

PARTY. (Social gathering) Chinese has no single term that covers the range of meaning of the English term **party,** but the following expressions are useful: chǐngkè (invite guests); yǒu kèren (have guests); chǐng . . . chr'fàn (invite . . . to eat; have a dinner party for . . .); chǐng . . . dǎ'pái (have a card party for . . .); similarly with other kinds of parties; 'jyù yijyù, 'jyùhwei jyùhwei (get together); fàn jyú (more or less informal dinner party); yànhwèi (a very formal dinner party). /We're having a party. Wǒmen jèr yǒu 'kèren. /I gave a (dinner) party for him. Wó chǐng tā chr-'fàn. /We had a big party last night. Dzwér 'wǎnshang wǒmen °you (°chǐngle) hěn-'dwōde kèren. /Let's have a party for him before he goes. Tā 'méidzóu yǐ'chyán dzámen °'jyù yijyù (°'jyùhwei jyuhwei). /I went to a big dinner party last night. Wǒ 'dzwér wǎnshang °chyù (°tsānjyā) le yíchùr yànhwèi. *or* Wǒ 'dzwér wǎnshang yǒu ge fàn'jyú.

(Group of people) chyún. /A party of soldiers arrived by car. Yǒu yìchyún 'bīng dzwòje chì'chē láile.

(Political group) 'jèngdǎng; dǎng in combination. /Which party won the last election? 'Shàngtsż sywán'jyù 'nèige 'jèngdǎng 'yíngle?

(In negotiation, a lawsuit, drawing up a contract, etc.) fāng. /Both parties in the lawsuit failed to appear. 'Shwāngfāng dōu méi'chūtíng. /Both parties agreed. 'Shwāngfāng túng'yì.

(Participant) X is a party to (dzài) . . . li yǒu X *or* X dzài . . . li yǒu 'gwānsyi; party to a crime 'túngmóufàn, (legal) gùngfàng. /They couldn't prove that he was a party to the crime. Tāmen 'méinéng 'jèngmíng (dzài) nèige 'àndzli yǒu 'tā méiyou. *or* Tāmen 'méinéng 'jèngmíng tā dzài nèige 'àndzli 'yǒu méiyǒu 'gwānsyi. *or* Tāmen méiyǒu 'jèngjyù shwō tā 'jwùn shř túngmóufàn. *or* (legal) Tāmen 'wútsúng 'jèngmíng tā shř gùng'fàn.

PASS. (Go by) chāugwo, gwò. /He passed our car at a tremendous speed. Tā chāu gwò wǒmen 'chē de shřhou dzǒude kwài'jí le. /I pass the bank every day on the way to work. Wǒ 'měityān chyù dzwò 'shř de shřhou, 'lù gwò yín'háng. /We passed by the park. Wǒmen °dǎ (°tsúng) 'gūngywán 'pángbyār gwò. /We passed the building. Wǒmen °dǎ (°tsúng) 'lou nar gwò láije. /We passed by the building. Wǒmen °dǎ (°tsúng) lóu pángbyār gwòde. /We passed in front of the building. Wǒmen °dǎ (°tsúng) lóu 'chyántou gwòde. /We passed over the bridge. Wǒmen °dǎ (°tsúng) 'chyáushang gwòde. /The days pass quickly when you are busy. 'Mángde shřhou yì'tyānyìtyānde gwòde 'jēn kwài. /We passed several towns without stopping. Wǒmen gwòle 'hǎujige chéng yě méi'tíngsyalai.

(Encounter a person) 'pèngjyàn. /Did you pass him on the road? Nǐ dzài 'dàurshang 'pèngjyàn 'tā meiyou?

(Hand to) 'dìgwo. /Please pass (me) the bread. Láu'jyà, bǎ myàn'bāu dìgwolai.

(Send) sùng, yùn. /The supplies were passed up to the front. 'Jyūnsyū'pǐn °sùngdàu (°yùndàu) chyǎn'syàn chyule.

(Of an examination) jígé (in school); jīng (undergo). /Did you pass your examination? Ní 'kǎude jí'géle ma? /Did you pass? Nǐ jí'géle ma? /He has to pass a stiff test before he can go. Tā děi jīng hěn'yánde 'kǎushř tsái néng 'chyù.

(Approve, of legislation) 'tūnggwò. /The Senate passed the bill yesterday. Shàngyìywàn 'dzwótyān 'tūnggwò nèige 'yìàn. /It passed. 'Tūnggwòle.

(Not bid, in cards) bú'jyàu shémma. /I had a lousy hand and decided to pass. Wǒde'pái hěn 'hwài, swóyi 'jywédìng bú'jyàu shémma.

(Transfer by inheritance) chwán. /The title passes from father to son. Nèige 'jywéwèi lǎushr yóu 'fùchin chwán gěi 'érdz. *or* 'Jywéwèi °shř shř'syíde (°fù'dz syāng'chwan).

Let it pass swànle. /He shouldn't have said that, but let it pass. Tā 'bùyīngdāng 'shwō nèijǔng hwà, búgwò (gwòchyule jyòu) 'swànle ba.

Pass judgment on shwō . . . dzěmma'yàng, shwō . . . hǎu'hwài, and similar expressions depending on the nature of the judgment. /Don't pass judgment on his character until you know him better. °Nǐ hái 'búdà 'rènshr rénjyā de shřhou byé (°Ní 'děng gēn rénjyā 'shóu dyar dzài) shwō rénjyāde 'pǐnsyíng dzěmmayàng.

Pass sentence pàn dzwèi, dìng dzwèi. / The court passed sentence on him to-day. 'Fǎ ywàn 'jīntyān °'pànle (°'dìngle) tāde 'dzwèi le.

Pass time 'syāumwó. / He passed most of his time fishing. Tā bǎ 'gūngfu 'dwōbàn dōu 'syāumwó dzài dyàu'yúshang le.

Pass around (of a story) chwánchuchyu, (with the speaker as subject) 'chwán-shwō. / The story passed around that we were about to leave. Dàjyā 'chwánshwō wǒmen 'jyòu yàu 'líkāi °jèr(°nàr).

Pass away gùchyu, gwòchyù. / She said her mother passed away last week. Tā shwō tā 'mùchin shànglǐbài °'gùchyule (°'gwòchyule).

Pass off as chūng, 'hwùnchūng, 'màuchūng. / He tried to pass off an imitation as the real thing. Tā syǎng ná jyǎde °chūng (°'hwùnchūng, °'màuchūng) °'jēnde.

Pass out (distribute) sàn; (give free) sùng. / He's passing out handbills. Tā dzài nar 'sàn chwán'dān ne. / He passed out a free ticket to each soldier. 'Swó-yǒude bīng tā 'měirén sùngle yìjāng 'pyàu.

Pass out (faint) yūngwochyu; (lose consciousness from excessive drinking) dzwèidǎule, dzwèide 'bùsyǐngrén'shèr le. / When the gas escaped several people passed out. 'Méichi lòuchulai de shŕhou, 'hǎujǐge rén syūnde 'yūngwochyule. / If you give her another drink, she'll pass out. Nǐ dzài jyàu tā 'hē dyǎr, tā 'yídìng hwèi °dzwèi'dǎule de (°dzwèide 'bùsyǐngrén'shrle de).

Pass through gwò, 'chwāngwò, (press through) 'jǐgwò. / We passed through the park. Wǒmen °dǎ (°súng) 'gūngywán'lǐtou °'chwāngwochyu (°gwò). / How long will it take us to pass through the town? Dzámen °dǎ (°súng) 'chéngli ('chwān)gwò-chyu děi yùng 'dwōshau shŕhou? / We passed through the center of the town. Wǒmen °dǎ (°súng) chéng dàng'jūng (chwān)gwòchyude. / When we passed through the town we found it deserted. Wǒmen °'gwò nèige 'chéng (°dǎ nèige 'chéng gwò) de shŕhou kànjyan 'rén dōu 'pǎule. / We passed through the crowd with much effort. Wǒmen °dǎ (°súng) nèichyún rénli 'jǐgwochyu de shŕhou, 'hěn fèile dyǎr 'shèr. / Pass the rope through here and tie it. Bǎ 'shéngdz °dǎ (°súng) jèr 'chwāngwochyu 'jìshang. *but* / That manuscript has passed through several hands. Nèige 'gāudz 'hǎujige rén dōu 'kàngwole.

Pass up 'tswògwò, bǎ . . . 'tswògwochyu, bǎ . . . 'fànggwochyu. / You shouldn't pass up an opportunity like that. Nǐ 'bùyīngdāng tswògwò 'nèmma hǎude 'jīhwei. *or* Nǐ 'bùyīngdāng bǎ 'nèmma hǎude 'jīhwèi °tswògwochyu (°fànggwochyu).

A pass (a narrow passage) kǒudz. / You can't get through the mountain pass at this time of the year. 'Jèi shŕhou nèige shān'kǒudz gwòbu'chyù.

(Permit) jèng; (door pass) chūménjèng; (pass to go through a place) tūngsyíng-jèng; etc., with passes for other purposes. / You'll need a pass to get by the gate. Nǐ chū dà'mér děi yǒu chūmén'jèng.

PASSENGER. There is no exact equivalent in Chinese; under varying circumstances it is possible to use rén (person); kè (guest); 'chèngkè (riding guest). / Our car holds only five passengers. Wǒmende chē 'jř néng dzwò 'wǔge rén. / That railroad car is not used for passengers. 'Nèilyàng chē búshr °'kèchē (°dzài'kède). / Passengers are not allowed byond this line. 'Chèngkè dàu'tsź jř'bù.

PAST. (Gone by, in space or time) gwò(le) (a verb; also used in combination after verbs of motion, such as pǎu run, kāi drive). / The worst part of the trip is past. 'Dzwèi-hwàide nèi yídwàr 'lù yǐjīng 'gwòlaile. / Don't worry about a thing that's past. Yǐ-jīng 'gwòchyu de 'shř le, byé 'syǎng le. / Walk past the church and turn right. 'Gwòle lǐbài'táng wàng'yǒu gwǎi. / It's past noon; let's eat. 'Gwòle 'shàngwu le; dzámen chř'fàn ba. / We drove past his house on the way here. Wǒmen 'lái de shŕhou °dǎ (°tsúng) tā 'jyā nar 'gwòlaije. / I thought he was going to stop, but he ran right past. Wó 'yǐwei tā yàu 'jànju ne, 'shéi jr̃dau tā yǐ'jr̃ jyòu 'pǎugwochyule.

(Of time only) 'shàngtsz̀ plus a verb (the last time . . .); jèi (this just past); in the past tsúngchyán, yǐchyán, chyán plus a period of time, as past few years 'chyán-jinyán; 'wǎng plus nyán or r̃li; the past month 'shàngywè; the past year 'chyùnyán (see LAST); for the past month . . . le yíge 'ywè le (etc.). / We've been expecting rain for the past week. 'Shàng yíge syĩngchī wŏmen yǐ'jr̃ pànje syà'yǔ. or Wŏmen 'pànje syà'yǔ pànle 'yíge syĩng'chī le. / In the past it's been very difficult to get tickets. °Tsúng'chyán (°Yǐ'chyán, °'Chyán jige ywè, °etc.) 'hěn nán měijau 'pyàu. / The past election made him realize his mistakes. 'Shàngtsz̀ sywán'jyǔ jyàu tā 'míngbaile tā bàn de bú'dwèide 'dìfang.

The past, one's past tsúng'chyánde shèr, 'dāngnyánde shèr; (recorded history) lìshř, 'gùshř, 'dyǎngù; (remembered events) 'wǎngr̃de shr̃, yí'wǎngde shř, 'wǎng-shř; (past actions) 'lǎuhwàr, yǐ'chyán dzwògwo de shèr. / That city has a very interesting past. Nèige chéngde °tsúng'chyánde shèr (°'dyǎngù, °lì'shř, °'gùshr, °'dāngnyánde shèr) hěn yŏu'yìsz. / He's always haunted by his past. Tā °'dāng-nyánde (°tsúng'chyánde, °'wǎngr̃de, °yí'wǎngde) shr̃ 'lǎu jyàu tā 'syĩnli bù'ān. / He can talk about his past for days on end. Tā 'jyángchī tā °tsúng'chyánde (°yǐ'chyán dzwògwo de, °'dāngnyánde) shèr lai, 'dwòshau'tyān yě shwōbu'wán. or Tā 'jyáng-chī tǎde °'wǎngshř (°'lǎuhwàr) lai, 'dwòshau'tyān yě shwōbu'wán. / Whenever she thinks of the past she starts to weep. Tā yì 'syángchī 'dāngnyánde shř lai jyòu 'kū. / A great man doesn't talk about past glories. 'Hǎuhàn 'bùtán 'dāngnyán'yǔng.

PATH. 'syǎudàur, 'syǎulù. / Take the path that runs along the river. 'Dzŏu kàu hé-'byār de (nèityáu) °'syǎudàur (°syǎulù). but / Our paths had never crossed before that. Dzài nèijyàn shr̃ yǐ'chyán wŏ gēn tā yí'syàng méidǎgwo 'jyāudau.

PATIENT. rěn (used after néng, děi, etc., said especially of circumstances); yŏu 'nài-syin'fár (said especially of patience with people); 'rĕnnài, nài 'syĩndz, bùjāují. / He's a very patient man. Tā hěn néng 'rěn. or Tā hén yŏu 'nàisyin'fár. / He'd be a better teacher if he were more patient. Tā yòushr yŏu 'nàisyin'fár dehwà, yídìng jyàude 'hǎudyar. / He's a patient man to wait that long for her to say yes. Tā 'jēn néng 'rěn, děngle 'nèmma jyòu tā tsái 'dāyingde. / He's very patient with the children. Tā dài háidzmen °'hén yŏu nàisyin'fár (°yǐ'dyár yě bùjāu'jí). / You have to be very patient with talkative people like that. Gēn 'nèijǔng àishwō'hwà de rén 'hén děi °'rěnje dyar (°'rĕnnàije dyar, °'nàije dyar 'syĩndz, °yŏu 'nàisyin'fár). Be patient! 'Byé jāu'jí.

A patient 'bìngrén. / How's the patient this morning? 'Bìngrén jyēr 'dzǎuchen 'dzěmmayàng?

PATTERN. (Design) 'hwāyàng. / This rug has a nice pattern. 'Jèikwài dì'tǎnde 'hwā yàng hén hǎu.

(Model) yàngdz. / Where did you get the pattern for your new dress? Nǐ nèi-jyàn 'syĩn yīfude 'yàngdz shr̃ 'nǎr lái de?

To pattern oneself after 'syàufǎ. / I've tried to pattern myself after my father. Wǒ 'hén syǎng 'syàufǎ jyā'yán.

PAY (PAID). (Make payment for something) gěichyán, fùchyán, chūchyán, náchyán (especially an established amount). / I paid him three dollars. °Wó gěile (°Wŏ fùle) tā 'sānkwài chyán. / I haven't paid for it yet. Wŏ hái méigěi'chyán. or Wŏ hái méifù'chyán. / If you pay a blackmailer once, you have to pay and pay and pay. Yàushr yŏu rén °'é (°'jà, °'éjà) nǐ, nǐ 'yì géichī chyán lai jyòu méi'tóur le. or Yàushr yŏu rén °'éjà (°etc.) nǐ, nǐ gěile 'yítsz̀ chyán jyòu děi 'láu gěi. / Who will pay for our dinner? Dzámen 'chr̃fàn shéi °ná(°chū)'chyán?

810

PAY

(Spend) hwā, yùng, ná, plus chyán or a certain amount of money followed by mǎi (buy) or similar words; or simply the amount plus mǎi. / How much did you pay for your car? Nǐde 'chē shř °hwā (°yùng) 'dwōshau chyán mǎide? or Nǐde 'chē shř 'dwōshǎu chyán mǎide? / How much were you paid for your car? Nǐ nèi'chē °màile 'dwōshau chyán (°'dwōshau chyán mǎide)? / I paid five dollars for this watch. Jèige 'byáu wǒ °hwā (°yùng, °ná) 'wǔkwài chyán mǎide.

(Give as a price) chū. / How much do you want to pay for this? Jèige nǐ syǎng chū 'dwōshau chyán (lái mǎi)?

(Buy) any of the above; also mǎi; (dig in the pocket) tāu yāu'bāu. / You'll have to pay for your own ticket. Nǐ děi 'dżjí mǎi'pyàu. / You'll have to pay for it yourself. Nǐ děi 'dżjí 'mǎi (°chū'chyán, °ná'chyán, °gěi'chyán, °tāu yāu'bāu). / You can't get it for nothing; you have to pay for it. Jèige 'bùnéng 'bái géi nǐ; nǐ děi °gěi-'chyán (°náchu'chyán lai, °chū'chyán) tsái 'syíng. or Jèige 'bùnéng 'bái géi nǐ; nǐ děi °hwā'chyán (°yùng'chyán, °ná'chyán) mǎi.

(Give a salary or wage) fā . . . °syīnshwei (°'gūngchyán). / I pay my employees every Friday. Wǒde jŕywán, wó měi syīngchī'wǔ 'fāgěi tāmen °'syīnshwei (°'gūng-chyán).

(Of payments coming due regularly) jyāu (hand over). / I have to pay the rent every Monday. 'Měi syīngchī'yī wó děi jyāu fáng'dzū.

(Of bills, debts, loans) hwán (return). / The bills were paid up yesterday. Jàng 'dzwótyan dōu 'hwánle. / He pays his debts promptly. 'Tā gāi de 'jàng dōu shř 'shwō shémma shŕhou 'hwán 'jwǔn hwán. or Tā hwán'jàng hwánde hěn 'máli. / I'll be all paid up after (paying) one more installment. Dzài °gěi (°fù, °jyāu) 'yítsż wǒ jyòu hwán'chīng le. / The paid bills are listed in this column. 'Yǐjīng 'hwánle de jàng lyèdzài 'jèiháng. / Loan me a dollar now, and I'll pay you back Monday. Jyè wǒ yíkwài 'chyán, lǐbài'yī hwán nǐ.

(Of damages) péi. / You'll have to pay for it. Nǐ yídìng děi 'péi. or Nǐ fēi 'péi bù'syíng.

(Of gambling debts) 'shūgěi.

(Of taxes, duty, etc.) nà, shàng, jyāu, gěi, fù. / Pay your taxes or go to jail. °Búnà'shwèi (°Bushàng'shwèi, or (of regular payments) °Bùjyāu'shwèi) jyòu syà'yù. / How much import duty do you have to pay? Děi °nà (°shàng, °gěi, °fù) 'dwōshǎu chyánde 'jìnkǒushwèi?

(Be worthwhile) shàngswàn, héswàn, jŕde. / It doesn't pay to spend too much time on this work. Dzài jèijyàn 'gūngdzwòshang fèi tǐngdwō 'shŕhou °búshàng'swàn (°bùhé'swàn, °bù'jŕde). / It won't pay to settle now for cash. 'Jèi shŕhou mài syànchyán °búshàng'swàn (°bùhé'swàn, °bù'jŕde).

Be paid lǐng 'syīnshwei, gwānsyǎng, náchyán. / When are we going to be paid? 'Shémma shŕhou °gwān 'syǎng (°ná 'chyán, °lǐng 'syīnshwei)?

Pay a visit kàn . . . yisyàr. / We ought to pay him a visit before he leaves. Wǒmen 'yīngdāng dzài tā 'méidzóu yǐ'chyán chyù 'kàn tā yisyàr.

Pay for (fig.) hwán. / I'll make you pay for that! is expressed as I'll make you pay for this debt. Wǒ yidìng jyàu nǐ 'hwán jèibǐ 'jài.

Pay for itself bá 'běr 'jwànhwéilai, bá 'běnchyán 'jwànhwéilai. / This machine will pay for itself in no time. Jèijyà 'jǐchi 'búyùng dwōshǎu shŕhou jyòu kéyǐ bá °'běr (°'běnchyán) 'jwànhwéilai.

Pay (salary) syīnshwei; (wages) gūngchyan, gěi de chyán, jèng(de) chyán. / Is the pay good on your new job? Nǐde syīn shèr °gěi de (°jèng de) chyán 'dwō ma? or Nǐde syīn shèr °syīnshwei (°'gūngchyan) °'dwō (°'dà) ma?

PAYMENT. Expressed verbally; *see* **PAY.** / I have to make three monthly payments of ten dollars each. Wǒ jř néng 'yíge ywè °gěi (°fù, °hwán, °jyāu) 'shŕkwài chyán, yí'gùng °gěi (°etc.) 'sānge ywè. *or* Wǒ děi fù 'sānge ywède chyán, 'měitsž gěi 'shŕkwài.

PEACE. (National) 'hépíng, 'tàipíng; however, when speaking of peace as the ending of a present war, verbal expressions are used, such as 'bùdǎ'jàngle, 'jànshŕ 'wánle, 'méiyou 'jànshŕ; **peace treaty** 'héywē; **peace conference** 'hépíng hwèi'yì. / Do you favor a strong peacetime army? Nǐ 'dzànchéng dzài °'hépíngde (°'tàipíngde) shŕhou yáng hěn dwōde jyūn'dwèi ma? / It cost blood and sweat to win this peace. Jè shr wǒmen ná 'sywě'hàn délai de °'hépíng (°'tàipíng). *or* Jèitsž 'hépíng shŕ wǒmen ná 'sywě'hàn hwànlaide. / I hope peace will come soon. Wǒ 'pànwàng 'kwàidyar 'bùdǎ'jàng le. *or* Wǒ 'pànwàng 'jànshŕ kwàidyar 'wánle. / I'm going to buy a car as soon as peace comes. °'Yù dǎwánle 'jàng (°'Jànshŕ 'yǐ wán) wǒ jyòu mǎi lyang chǐ'chē. / He wants peace in our time. Tā syǎng jyàu 'dzámen jèibèidzli méiyou jànshŕ.

    (Domestic) expressed verbally by hémù meaning be harmonious; 'héhemù'mùde (harmonious, peaceful). / She always manages to have peace in her house. Tā 'láu bǎ 'jyāli nèngde 'héhemù'mùde. / Their family is always at peace. Tāmen 'jyāli hěn 'hémù. / There's no more peace in his home since his mother-in-law came. Tsúng tā jàngmu 'nyáng láile yǐhòu tā 'jyāli jyòu 'bú nèmma 'hémù le.

    Peace (and quiet) expressed verbally by ānjing, bùcháudzwěi, bùdǎjyà, sháu dǎjyà, shǎu cháudzwěi. / Can't we have a little peace (and quiet) around here? Dzámen jèr °sháu dǎ dyar 'jyà (°shǎu cháu dyar 'dzwěi, °'ānjing dyar) syíng busyíng?

PEN. (Writing implement) 'gāngbǐ (Western type); bǐ, 'máubǐ (Chinese type; actually a brush, but used for writing); **pen point** (Western) gāngbǐtóur, gāngbǐjyār; **fountain pen** 'dzláishwéi'bǐ; **ball point pen** yuán dź bǐ. / My pen is dry; can you spare some ink? Wǒ 'gāngbǐ méi'shwěrle; nǐ néng 'jyè wó dyǎr mwò'shwěr ma? *but* / It's from his pen. meaning He wrote it. Shŕ 'tā syě de.

    (Enclosure) jywàn (for pigs, sheep); lán (for cattle). / We'll have to build a larger pen for the pigs. Dzámen děi nèng yíge 'dàdyarde jū'jywàn.

    Pen name 'bǐmíng.

    To pen up (animals) jywān. / We keep the sheep penned up at night. Wǒmen 'yèli bǎ yáng 'jywānchilai.

PENCIL. chyānbǐ. / Will you sharpen this pencil for me? Láu'jyà gěi jèigēr chyān'bǐ syōusyou syíng ma? / I lost my pencil. Wó bǎ chyān'bǐ dyōule.

    To pencil ná 'chyānbí syě. / He penciled a short note. Tā ná 'chyānbí syěle jǐge 'dzèr.

PEOPLE. (Persons) rén. / Were there many people at the meeting? Dàu'hwèi de rén 'dwō ma? / You must consider other people's feelings (desires). Ní děi syǎngsyǎng 'byérén ywànyi bú'ywànyi. / Several people have asked that question. 'Yóu jǐge rén 'yě nèmma 'wèngwo wo.

    (Electorate) 'rénmín, 'mínjùng, láu'bǎisyìng. / This government is not well supported by the people. Jèige 'jèngfǔ bú'dà shòu °'rénmínde (°'mínjùngde, °láu-'bǎisyìngde) 'yūnghù.

    (Race) 'jǔngdzú; (kind of people) rén with measure jǔng. / The natives of this region are a distinct people. Jèi yídàide 'jyūmín °'dān (°'lìng) shŕ yì'jǔng rén. *or* Jèi yídàide 'jyūmín shŕ 'lìng yíge jǔngdzúde rén.

(Nation) gwó. / Many peoples will be represented at the conference. 'Jèitsz̀ 'hwèiyî yóu 'hěn dwō 'gwóde dài'byǎu chū'syí.

PER CENT. bǎifēnjr̄ <u>followed by the amount of per cent.</u> / The cost of living has gone up 10 per cent since last year. Ř̄chángshēnghwó 'fèiyùng bǐ'chyùnyán yǐjīng 'gāule bǎi fēnjr̄'shŕ. / What per cent? Bǎifēnjr̄'jǐ?

PERFECT. <u>There is no single word that expresses the idea of</u> **perfect,** <u>but the following expressions are used to convey the idea;</u> hǎu (good) <u>or some other stative verb plus</u> jíle, dàujyāle *or* dàu 'jídyǎnle (to the last detail); jeng (just) *or* jēn (really) <u>plus</u> hǎu <u>or another stative verb or a verb, or expressed with</u> hǎu *or* dà <u>and similar stative verbs plus a noun;</u> yì'dyǎr jár yě méiyǒu (no defects at all); yì'dyǎr tswòr yě méiyǒu (no mistakes at all); yi'dyár ke °'pīpíng (°'tyāuti) de (dìfang) yě méiyǒu; yìdyár 'bāuhan yě méiyǒu (beyond criticism); yì'dyǎr yě <u>plus a negative stative verb;</u> <u>also a few other indirect expressions.</u> / It's perfect! Hǎu 'jíle! *or* Hǎu dàu'jyāle! *or* Yì'dyǎr jár! *or* Yì'dyǎr tswòr yě méiyǒu! / They're a perfect match. 'Pèide 'jèng hé'shr̀. *or* 'Pèide hǎu 'jíle. *or* 'Jèng shr̀ yí'dwèr. *or* 'Jēn shr̀ yí'dwèr. *or* Pèidzài yí'kwàr yìdyǎr °kě 'pīpíng de (°etc.) yě méiyǒu. / He's a perfect scoundrel. Tā shr̀ ge 'dàhwài'dàn. *or* 'Tā jèi rén hwài'jíle. *or* 'Tā jèi rén jēn shr̀ 'hwùnjàng dàu 'jyāle. *or* Tā hwàide yì'dyǎr ké 'chyǔ de dìfang yě méiyǒu. / She gave a perfect performance. Tā yànde °jēn shr̀ hǎu dàu 'jídyǎnle (°hǎu'jíle, °hǎude dàu'jyāle). *or* Tā yànde yìdyár ke 'pīping de dìfang yě méiyǒu. *or* Tā yànde yìdyǎr °'bāuhan (°tswòr) yě méiyǒu. / He speaks perfect Chinese. Tā shwō 'Jūnggwohwà shwōde hǎi'jíle. *or* (like a native) 'Tā shwō de Jūnggwo hwà gēn 'Jūnggworén shwōde yí-yàng. / He's a perfect stranger to me. <u>is expressed as</u> I don't know him at all. Wǒ yì'dyǎr bú'rènshr tā. *or* Wǒ gēn tā 'sùbùsyàng'shr̀. / It's the perfect crime. Jèige 'àndz dzwòde yì'dyǎr 'pwòjàn yě méi'yǒu. / He did a perfect job of ridiculing him. Tā bǎ tā 'swùnde dàu 'jyāle. / It's a perfect caricature of him. Bǎ tā 'pīpíngde 'tǐwúwán'fú.

PERFORM. (On a stage) yǎn, byáuyǎn; (come on stage) shàngtái. / She performed very well. Tā °yǎnde (°byáu'yǎnde) hǎu'jíle. / Who performs next? 'Syà yímù shr̀ 'shéi °yǎn (°byáu'yǎn, °shàng'tái)?

(Carry out) shŕsyíng. / He promises, but doesn't always perform. Tā láu syǔywàn, kěshr bújyànde jwūn shŕ'syíng.

Perform an operation 'gěi rén °lá'bìng (°kāidāu). / The doctor is performing an operation. 'Dàifu 'jèngdzài 'gěi rén °lá'bìng (°kāi'dāu ne).

See also **DO.**

PERHAPS. 'yésyǔ, syǔ, hwòje; (I'm afraid that) (wǒ) 'kǔngpà. / Perhaps it'll rain today. Jyēr °yésyǔ (°syǔ yàu, °kǔngpà yàu) syà'yǔ. *or* Jyēr yésyǔ °yàu (°hwèi) syà'yǔ. *or* Jyēr 'hwòje hwèi syà'yǔ; yěwèike'jr̄. / Perhaps he forgot. °'Yésyǔ (°Kǔngpà) tā 'wàngle. *or* Tā °yésyǔ (°syǔshr, °'hwòje) 'wàngle. / Perhaps it was I who was wrong. °Yésyǔ (°Syǔ) shr̀ 'wǒ tswòle ba. *or* 'Hwòje shr̀ 'wǒ tswòle. *but* / I think perhaps you'd better take an umbrella. Wǒ kàn nǐ 'háishr dài bá 'sǎn hǎu. *or* Wǒ kàn nǐ (yésyǔ) dài bá 'sǎn tsái 'hǎu.

PERIOD. (Stretch of time) shŕhou. / He worked here for a short period. Tā dzài jèr dzwòle 'méi dwōshau 'shŕhou.

(Limited section of time) chī, dwàr (measures); 'shŕdài (noun). / The history of this town may be divided into three periods. Jèi dìfangde lì'shr kéyǐ fēnchéng °sān'chī (°sān'dwàr, °sānge 'shŕdài). / The first period is the most interesting. °Dì'yīchī (°Dì'yīdwàr) 'dzwèi yǒu'yìsz. / The Civil War period of American history serves as a good example. 'Měigwoshr̄li 'Nánběijàn'jēng °jèi yì'chī (°jèi yí'dwàr, °jèige 'shŕdài) kéyǐ 'nálai dzwò ge 'lìdz.

(Class hour) táng. /I have no classes the third period. Dì'sāntáng wǒ 'méikè.

(Punctuation mark) dyǎr (dot). /You forgot to put a period here. Nǐ jèr 'wàngle dyán'dyǎrle.

(That's all there is to be said) 'méiyou 'byéde kě 'shwō de. /He's no good, period. Tā 'búshr hǎurén, 'méiyou 'byéde kě 'shwō de.

PERMIT. (Written permission) syúkějèng; **special permit** tèsyújěng. /You'll have to get a permit to visit this factory. Nǐ déi 'lǐng yíge syúke'jèng tsái néng 'tsāngwān jèige gūng'chǎng. /They're issuing special permits to discharged soldiers. Tāmen jèngdzài fā twèiwǔ 'jyūnrén 'tèsyú'jèng ne.

To **permit** jyàu, ràng (allow without interference); syǔ, jwǔn (give authoritative permission); rúng (give a chance); **be permitted** syǔ, jwǔn, néng (be possible), syíng (be OK). /I won't permit you to go. Wǒ °bú'jyàu (°bú'ràng, °bù'syǔ, °bù'jwǔn) nǐ 'chyù. /He never permits me to speak. Tā bù'rúng wǒ shwō'hwà. /No one is permitted to enter this building. 'Jèidzwò lóu 'shéi yě °'bùsyǔ (°'bùjwǔn) jìnchyu. /Such behavior as theirs shouldn't be permitted. 'Bùgāi °jwǔn (syǔ) tāmen 'dzěmmaje. /I won't permit anybody to bully people around here. Dzài wǒjer 'shéi yě °bùsyǔ (°bùjwǔn, °bùnéng) 'chǐfu rén (dōu bù'syíng or wó bùnéng 'rúng).

PERSON. rén. /What sort of a person is she? Tā shr 'dzěmmayàngrde yíge rén? /She seems like a different person. 'Tā hǎu syàng °'byànle (°'hwànle, °shr 'lǐng) yíge 'rén shrde. /As a person he isn't bad. Tā yòushr 'rén búhwài. or Gwāng ná jèige 'rén lái shwō, tā bìng 'búhwài.

In **person** 'běnrén (oneself); 'chǐndz (personally); dāngmyàr (face to face); or combinations of these. /She's going to be here in person! 'Tā yàu dàu 'jèr lái, (shr) ('běnrén) 'chǐndz lái! /Please deliver this to him in person. (yourself) Chǐng nǐ 'chǐndz bǎ jèige sùngdàu 'tā nar chyu. or (to himself) Chǐng nǐ bǎ jèige sùng- dàu 'tā nar, dāng'myàr jyāugěi tā. /He came in person and handed me this. Tā 'běnrén 'chǐndz láide, dāng'myàr bǎ jèige 'jyāugěi wǒ de.

PERSONAL. 'dzjǐde, 'gèrénde; in a few combinations sz; **personal affairs** 'szshr; **personal property** (legal term) 'szchǎn. /Don't mix personal affairs with business. Búyàu bǎ 'szshr gēn 'gūngshr 'hwùndzài yi'chǐ. /He asked too many personal questions. Tā 'jìng wèn rénjyāde 'szshr. or Tā 'wèn rénjyāde'szshr wènde tài 'dwōle. /This is my personal opinion. Jèi shr wǒ °'dzjǐde (°'gèrénde) 'yìjyan. /Are these your personal belongings? Jèi shr nǐ 'dzjǐde dūngsyi ma?

PHOTOGRAPH. syàngpyār; **take a photograph** or **have a photograph taken** jàusyàng. /You'll need eight copies of a photograph of yourself. Nǐ 'běnrénde syàng'pyār déi yǒu 'bājāng. /I haven't had a photograph taken for months. Wó 'jǐge ywèli 'yìjāng syàng yě méi'jàu. or Wó yǒu 'háujige ywè méijàu'syàngle.

To **photograph** jàusyalai. /He photographed those fishing boats for the exhibit. Tā bǎ nèisyē 'yúchwán jàusyalaile, wèi ján'lǎn yùng.

PIANO. gāngchín. /He really knows how to play the piano. Tā jēn hwèi tán gāng'chín. or Tā tán gāng'chín tánde hén 'hǎu.

PICK. (Choose) tyāu; sywǎn, 'tyāusywǎn (with particular care). /You certainly picked a nice time to start an argument! Ní kě 'jēn hwèi tyāu 'shrhour bàn'dzwèi a! /I picked (successfully) a winner that time. 'Nèitsz wó kě 'tyāujaule ge 'yíngde. /He picked out a very nice bracelet to give to his wife. Tā 'tyāule yíjyàn 'hénhǎude 'jwódz 'sùnggěi tā 'tàitai. /He picked out two watches and had a hard time deciding which to buy. Tā tyāuchu 'lyǎngjǐr byāu lai; 'dzěmma yě nábudìng 'júyi mái 'nèige. /The captain picked me to do the job. Lyán'jǎng tyāu 'wǒ chyù dānrèn 'jèige 'chāishr.

814

or (sarcastically) Lyán'jǎng °'chyáushang wǒ le (°'kànshang wǒ le, °jēn 'shàngshr̃ wǒ) géi wǒ'dzèmma ge 'chāishr.

(Pluck) jāi (fruit, vegetables); chyā (flowers). / Are the tomatoes ripe enough to pick? Syīhúng'shr̃ kéyǐ 'jāile ma?

Pick one's teeth tí. / He knows he shouldn't pick his teeth in public. Tā 'jr̃dau tā 'bùyīngdāng dzài 'hěn dwō rén 'myànchyán tí 'yá.

Pick a fight dǎjyà. / Are you trying to pick a fight with me? Nǐ syǎng 'gēn wó dǎ'jyà ma?

Pick a lock (bá swǒ) 'bwōkāi; (with a lever) 'chyàukāi; (in any way) 'nèngkāi, 'gǔdukāi. / We'll have to pick the lock to get into the house. Wǒmen děi bá swǒ °'bwōkāi (°'chyàukāi, °syǎngfár 'nèngkāi, °syǎngfár 'gǔdukāi) tsái néng 'jìnchyu.

Pick on (annoy) 'chǐfu (chǐfu), gēn . . . jǎu'chár. / Pick on someone your own size. Yǒu 'néngnei, 'chǐfu chǐfu gēn nǐ gèr yí'byàrdàde. / Stop picking on him. Byé dzài 'chǐfu rénjyā le. *or* Byé dzài gēn 'rénjyā jǎu'chárle.

Pick to pieces. / They picked his arguments to pieces. Tāmen bǎ 'tā shwō de jídyǎn °'pīpingde 'yìwénbù'jr̃ (°'wánchywán bwó'dǎule).

Pick up an object jyǎnchilai, shr̃chilai. / Please pick up the papers. Láu'jyà bá 'jr̃ °jyǎnchǐlai (°shr̃chilai).

Pick up passengers děng rén 'shàng (wait for people to get on). / The bus is stopping to pick up passengers. 'Gūnggùngchì'chē yàu dzài jèr 'tíngsyalai děng rén 'shàng.

Pick up information 'tīngjyàn (unintentionally); 'dǎtīngdàu (intentionally). / He picked up some information while in town. Tā dzài chéng'lǐ de shr̃hou °'tīngjyànle (°'dǎtīngdàu) jǐjyàn 'shèr.

Pick up (a bargain) 'mǎijáu. / She picked up a good bargain yesterday. Tā 'dzwérge 'mǎijáule jyàn 'pyányi 'hwò.

Pick up speed kwàichilai. / The train will pick up speed in a minute. Yì'hwěr hwǒchē jyòu 'kwàichilai le.

A pick (a digging tool) gǎu. / The men were working with picks and shovels. Nèisye rén yùng 'gǎu gēn 'chǎndz dzwò'hwór.

Be picked *or* handpicked (specially chosen) is expressed verbally as in the first paragraph. / These are all picked men. Jèisyē dōu shr̃ °'tyāuchulai (°'sywǎnchulai, °'tyāusywǎnchulái) de 'jwàng'ding. / We have a handpicked group. Wǒmende jèisyē rén 'dōu shr̃ hén 'dǎsyide °tyāuchulaide (°sywǎnchulaide, °tyāusywǎnchulaide).

PIECE. The following measures are used: kwài, kwàr (chunk); jāng (sheet; also used of flat things not expressed in English as piece); jyàn, jyàr (of work, or an article of something made); bàr (natural section, as of an orange); dwàr, dwàn (section or paragraph or piece of music); pyān (written article); tyáu, gēn (a length); jyér (a section of length). The following nouns are also used: chádz, chár (small broken pieces); jādz, jàr (crumbs, ground pieces). / She cut each cake into six pieces. Tā bá 'měi yíkwài 'gāu dōu chyēchéngle °'lyòukwàr (°lyòu'syǎukwàr). / He owns a piece of land in the country. Tā dzài 'syāngsya yǒu yíkwài 'dì. / Write your name on this piece of paper. Bǎ nǐ 'míngdz syědzài jèijāng 'jr̃shang. / Tear off a piece of that paper for me. Nèige 'jr̃ géi wǒ 'sz̃ yíkwàr. / That's a fine piece of furniture. Nèijyàr 'jyājyu jēn bú'hwài. / That (porcelain) is a Ming piece. Nèijyàn 'tszchì shr̃ 'Míngchaude. / What is the name of that piece the orchestra is playing? Ywè'dwèi jèng dzòu de jèidwàn 'yīnywe jyàu 'shémma míngdz? / Maybe I can fix it with this piece of copper wire. 'Jèige wǒ yùng °jèityáu (°jèigēn) 'túngsēr 'yésyǔ néng nùng'hǎulou. / The stick was broken into two pieces. Gwùndz dwànchéngle 'lyǎngjyér. / He picked up all the pieces except this one. Tā bǎ °'swèikwàr (°'swèi-chádz) 'dōu jyǎnchilaile, jṛ yǒu 'jèikwàr 'làsyale. / That's a fine piece of work. (of a job) Jèijyàn 'hwó dzwòde 'hén hǎu. or (of a situation) Jèijyàn 'shṛ bànde 'hén hǎu. or (of working or a product) Nèige 'dzwòde 'hén hǎu. or (of writing) Jèige 'syéde 'hén hǎu. or Jèipyàn 'wénjāng syéde 'hén hǎu. or (of a book) Jèibén 'shū syéde 'hén hǎu. or (of a plan) Jèige 'dàswànde 'hén hǎu. / There's a piece missing from the tool shelf. Gē 'jyāhwo de jyàdzshang 'dwǎnle yíjyàr shémma. / There's a piece (part or thing) missing from this machine. Jèige 'jīchi 'dwǎnle °yíge 'língjyàr (°dyǎr 'dūngsyi).

A piece of one's mind yídwùn. / She gave him a piece of her mind. (to equals or superiors) Tā gēn tā 'chǎule yí'dwùn. or (to inferiors or equals) Tā bǎ tā °'shwōle (°'màle, °'gwǎnjyàule) yí'dwùn.

To pieces, go to pieces (shatter) swēi; (come apart) sǎn; (collapse) tā; (collapse mentally) lwàn; **break to pieces** resultative compounds with swēi as second element; see **BREAK**. / The bookcase just fell to pieces all at once. Shū'jyàdz 'hūránjyān jyòu °'sǎnle (°'tāle). / This shoe is going to come to pieces. Jèijṛ 'syé kwài yàu 'sǎnle. / The ball hit the fish bowl and broke it to pieces. Chyóur bǎ yú'gāng °dzá (°dǎ) 'swēile. / She just went to pieces after his death. Tā nèmma yì'sẓ jyàu tāde syīn dōu 'lwànle.

Timepiece (clock) jūng; (watch) byǎu; (stop watch) 'mábyǎu.

To piece together dwèishang, 'tsòudzai yí'kwàr, 'pīndzài yí'dwàr. / See if you can piece them together again. Kàn nǐ 'néngbunéng bǎ jèige dzài °'dwèishang (°'tsòudzai yí'kwàr, °'pīndzài yí'kwàr).

PIG. jū. / He raises pigs. Tā yǎng 'jū. / He eats like a pig. Tā 'chṛchilai gēn 'jū shṛde. or Tā chṛde gēn 'jū shṛde nèmma 'dwō.

PILE. dwēi (heap); lwò, mǎ (stack up neatly). / He piled the books on top of each other. Tā bǎ shū yì'bèryì'bèrde °'lwòchilaile (°'mǎchilaile, °'lwòchéng yí'lwò, °'mǎchéng yí'lwò, °'lwòle yídà'lwò, °'mǎle yídà'lwò). / Pile the books over there. Bǎ 'shū dōu gěi 'dwēi nèr.

A pile dwēi; dzwēi (local Peiping); lwò (a neat pile of). / He carried the pile of clothes into the bedroom. Tā bǎ °nèidwēi (°nèilwò) 'yīshang nádau wò'fáng chyùle.

See also **HEAP.**

PIN. (Fastener) jēn, jēr; **safety pin** (or any pin that has a fastening device) 'byéjēr; **bobby pin** chyǎdz; **hairpin** 'tóujēr. / If you haven't got a safety pin, a straight pin will do. Nǐ rúgwǒ 'méiyǒu byé'jēr, yùng dzwò'hwó de 'jēn yě 'syíng. / I need some hairpins and bobby pins. Wó děi yàu 'syēge 'tóujēr gēn 'chyǎdz. / She wore a silver pin on her coat. Tāde 'yīfushang 'byéle yíge 'yínde byéjēr.

To pin (fasten with pins) byé. / Pin some flowers on your hat. Bǎ'hwār yùng 'byéjēr byédzài nǐ 'màudzshang. but / Pin (nail) this notice on the bulletin board, will you please? Bǎ jèige 'tūnggàu dìngdzài gàubái'bǎnshang, láu'jyà, láu'jyà.

(Hold fast) yā. / The two men were pinned under the car. Lyǎngge rén 'yādzài chē'dǐsya le.

Pin someone down (mentally). / You can't pin him down to the facts. 'Méifár gēn tā jyǎngchu ge 'lyěr lai. / We couldn't pin him down to a definite agreement. Tā 'dzěmmaje yě 'bùkěn gēn wǒmen shwō'dìngle.

PINE. (Tree) 'sūngshù. / That tree looks like a pine to me. Wǒ kàn nèikē 'shù syàng 'sŭngshù. / Pines and cedars make good lumber. 'Sŭngshù gēn 'bǎishù dōu shr̄ 'hǎu mùlyàu.

(Wood) 'sŭngmù. / That pine table is not very strong. Nèige 'sŭngmù jwōdz 'búdà 'jyēshr̄.

Pine needles sūngjēn, sūngjér.

PINK. 'fěnhúng(shǎr).

PIPE. (Tube) gwǎndz. / There's a leak in that pipe. 'Gwǎndz 'lòule. *or* (water pipe) 'Shwéigwǎndz 'lòule. *or* (steam pipe) 'Chìgwǎndz 'lòule. *or* (gas pipe) 'Méichì gwǎndz 'lòule.

(For smoking) yāndǒu; (a long-stemmed Chinese pipe) yāndài; **water pipe** shwěiyāndài. / If you smoke a pipe, you'll have a hard time getting tobacco here. Nǐ yàushr̄ chōu °yān'dǒu (°yān'dài), 'jèr hěn nán mǎidàu yān'yèdz.

To pipe yùng 'gwǎndz 'yǐn. / I piped this water here from a spring a mile away. Jèrde 'shwěi shr̄ wǒ tsúng 'lí jèr yìlǐ 'dìde yíge 'chywánywán nèr yùng 'gwǎndz 'yǐngwolaide.

Other English expressions. / Pipe down! Byé 'rāngrang le!

PLACE. (Location) dìfang; or expressed with measures with and without dìfang as (general) ge dìfang, (spot) chù (dìfang), (region) dài (dìfang), (area) pyàn (dìfang), (section) dwàr. / Be sure to put it back in the same place. Byé 'wànglou 'gēhwéi 'ywánláide 'dìfang. / Is there any place to put the car? Yǒu gē 'chē de dìfang ma? / There's no parking place around here. 'Jèiher méiyou tíng 'chē de dìfang. / This place is ten miles from the railroad. 'Jèige dìfang lí chē'jàn yǒu 'shr̄lidǐ. / There's not a single tree in that place. °Nèige 'dìfang (°Nèi'dài dìfang, °Nèi'dài, °Nèi'kwàr, °'Nèiher, °Nàr) lyán 'yìkē shù yě méi'you. / We put a cordon around that place. Wǒmen jyàu rén bǎ nèige 'dìfang wéichilaile. / His place of business is near mine. Tā dzwò'sher de dìfang lí 'wǒ nèr tǐng 'jìn. / My place is very noisy. 'Wǒ °nèr (°nàr) hén 'chǎu. / We'll come to your place; OK? Wǒmen dàu 'nǐ °nèr (°nàr) chyù, 'hǎu ma? / We have a lot of trees on our place. 'Wǒmen nèige dìfang yǒu 'hàusyèkē 'shù. / They're looking for a good place to open a shop. Tāmen jèngdzai jǎu ge 'hǎu dìfang kāi 'pùdz. / There isn't a single place open now. Dàu 'jèi shr̄hou °'nàr (°'shémma dìfang) dōu gwānle 'mén le. *or* Dàu 'jèi shr̄hou méiyou 'yìjyār kāijede le. / This is hardly the place for dancing. Jèr 'jyánjr̄ búshr̄ tyàu-'wǔ de dìfang. / The play is weak in several places. Nèichù 'syǐ yǒu °'hǎujǐchùr (dìfang) (°háujǐ'dwàr) chà'jìn. / I've lost my place in the book I was reading. Wǒ 'wàngle shù kàndàu °'nàr le (°shémma 'dìfang le).

(Job) wèijr̄; (vacancy) chywē. / There are two places vacant in the office. 'Gūngshrfángli yǒu lyǎngge 'chywē. / I have no place for you here. 'Wǒ jèr méi-yǒu nǐde 'wèijr̄. / I got a place for you. Wǒ géi nǐ jǎule ge 'wèijr̄.

In place (where something belongs) ywán'láide dìfang, dzwèi hé'shr̄de dìfang; (fitted together) dwèishang(le). / Please put the books back in place. Chǐng bǎ 'shù fànghwéi ywán'láide dìfang chyu. / The chairs are all back in place. 'Yǐdz dōu bǎihwéi ywán'láide dìfang chyu le. / The pieces are all in place and yet there still seems to be something wrong. Yí'kwàryíkwàrde dōu 'dwèishangle, kěshr̄ 'hái syàng nǎr yǒu dyǎr 'tswòr shrde.

In the . . . place dì . . . , dì . . . dyǎn. / In the first place, we can't leave until the supplies arrive. Dì'yì(dyǎn) 'jyējì méilái yǐ'chyán wǒmen 'bùnéng 'dzǒu.

Out of place (not in the proper location) °gēde (°bǎide, °fàngde) 'búshr̄ 'dìfang. / This chair is out of place. Jèibǎ 'yǐdz °gēde (°bǎide, °fàngde) 'búshr̄ 'dìfang.

Out of place (inappropriate) bùsyíng, búdwèijyèr, bùchéng 'tǐtǔng, bùchéng 'yàngdz, búshr̀ 'yàngdz. / Your actions are out of place here. Nǐ 'nèmma yàngrde 'jyǔdùng dzài 'jèiher °bù'syíng (°etc.).

Put <u>someone</u> in his place. / Somebody should put you in your place. Jyòu 'chyàn yǒu rén °'jyàusyun nǐ yí'dwùn (°jyàu nǐ 'jr̄dau nǐ shr̀ ge lau'jǐ).

Take the place of (a person) tì (substitute for) <u>or indirect expressions such as</u> do one's work; (other than a person) <u>indirect expressions such as</u> be just as good, use as, etc. / Go and find someone to take his place. Chyù 'jǎu ge rén lái °'tì tā (°dzwò tā nèige 'shèr). / No one can take his place. Shéi yě 'tìbulyǎu tā. or Tāde 'shèr shéi yě °dzwòbu'lyǎu (°dānfubu'lyǎu, °dānrenbu'lyǎu). / Nothing can take the place of a good spanking to make a child behave. Jyàu syàu'hár tīng'hwà, 'shémma fár yě méiyou 'dzwòdzwoshr̄shŕde 'dǎ yídwùn 'hǎu. or Jyàu syau'hár tīng'hwà, shémma yě 'bùrú 'dzwòdzwòshr̄shŕde 'dǎ yídwùn.

Take place (happen) 'fāshēng, chū. See HAPPEN. / This must have taken place while I was away. 'Jèi shèr yí'dìng shr̀ dzài wǒ bú'dzài jèr de shŕhou °'fāshēng de (°'chū de).

To place (put) fàng(dzài), gē(dzài), bǎi(dzài). / The table can be placed over there for now. 'Jwōdz kéyǐ 'jànshr̄ °'fàngdzài (°'gēdzài, °'bǎidzài) 'nàr.

(Find employment for) gěi . . . jǎu(jáu) °'wèijr (°'shèr), 'wèijr . . . , ba . . . °'ānchā (°'ānjr), yǒu 'wèijr lái 'ānchā . . . , yǒu °'shèr (°'dìfang) lái 'ānchā. / They placed her in a large company as a secretary. 'Tāmen gěi tā dzài yìjyā 'dàgūngszli jǎule ge 'shūjide wèijr. / Could you place three people in your office? 'Nǐ nàr 'néng bunéng °'wèijr jèi'sānge rén (°bǎ jèi'sānge rén 'ānchā (or 'ānjr) jìnchyu)? / So many people are looking for jobs; how can I place them all? 'Dzèmma dwōde rén yàu jǎu 'shèr, wó nár yǒu 'jèmma dwōde °'wèijr (°'shèr, °'dìfang) lái 'ānchā tāmen ne? or 'Dzèmma dwōde rén yàu jǎu'shèr, wǒ dzèmma néng 'dōu gěi tāmen jǎujáu °'shèr (°'wèijr) ne?

(Identify). / I'm sure I've met him before, but I can't quite place him. Wó 'jwǔn jr̄dàu wó yǐchyán 'jyàngwo tā, 'kěshr wǒ bú'dà jìde tā shr̀ 'shéi le.

PLAIN. (Clear; of statement or arguments) chīngchu (especially of pronunciation); míngbai (understandable); <u>or expressed by saying that a person understands, for which the verbs are the two above</u> and also dǔng, 'lyáujyě or 'lyǎurán. / His argument was plain to me. Tā shwō de 'lǐyou 'wǒ tīngje hén °'chīngchu (°'míngbai). / I'll put it in the plainest language I can. Wǒ yùng dǐng 'rúngyi'míngbaide hwà lái 'jyǎng ba. / He made it perfectly plain that he didn't want to leave. Tā shwōde °'chīnchingchu'chǔde (°'míngmingbai'báide) tā 'búywànyì 'dzǒu. / He writes in a very plain style. Tā syě de dǔngsyi °hěn 'chīngchu (°hěn 'míngbai, °jyàu rén yíkàn jyòu néng 'lyáujyě, °yímù'lyǎurán).

(Clear; in other connections) míngbai, chīngchu, 'syānrán, 'syānéryì'jyànde, míngsyānje, yí'kàn jyòu(néng) 'jr̄daude, yì'tīng jyòu (néng) 'jr̄daude, yì'tīng jyòu (néng 'míngbaide, hái 'kànbuchu'lai ma (lit. can't you see through it); in plain sight dzài 'yǎnchyán (bǎije), 'shéi dōu 'kàndejyàn. / It's perfectly plain that that's the case. Jèi shr̀ 'syānéryì'jyànde shr̀. or Jèi shr̀ yí 'kàn jyòu néng 'jr̄dau de shr̀. or Jèi shr̀ yì 'tīng jyòu 'míngbai de shr̀. or °'Syānrán (°'Míng'syānje, °Míngmingbái'báide, °Chīngchingchu'chǔde) shr̀ nèmma hwéi 'shèr. or Yǎn'chyánde shèr hái kànbuchū'lái ma? / It's quite plain (or It's plain as day) that he isn't going to be a sucker. °'Syānrán (°Syānéryì'jyànde, °Míng'syānje, °Hái 'kànbuchū'lái ma, °Yí-'kàn jyòu 'jr̄dàu, °Yì 'tīng jyòu 'jr̄dàu) 'tā shr̀ 'búhwèi °shàng'dàngde (°dzwò 'ywāndà'tóude, °shòu'pyànde). / It's in plain sight. Jyòu dzài 'yǎnchyán (bǎije). or 'Shéi dōu 'kànde jyàn.

(Ordinary) píngcháng. / It's too bad she's such a plain-looking girl. Kě'syǐ tā

°'jăngde (°'myànmàu, °'syàngmàu) píng'cháng. / They are plain people. Tāmen shr̀ píng'cháng rén. / We have a plain house. Wŏmende 'fángdz °hĕn píng'chángde (°méi shémma jyăngjyou). *but* / He came from plain stock. Tā shr̀ píng'mínchū'shēn.

(Of design) 'sùjing, buhwāshau. / She wore a plain dress. Chwān de 'yīfu °hĕn 'sùjing (°'yìdyăr bù'hwāshau).

(Of color) sù (means plain white by itself, plain when used with words for other colors). / She wore a plain white dress. Tā chwānje °'sù yīshang (°hĕn 'sùde yīshang). / She wore a plain blue dress. Tā 'chwānje hĕn 'sùde 'lán yīshang.

(Of food) 'jyācháng (byàn)'fàn; (not fancy) 'méi shémma hwāyàngr. / That restaurant serves good plain food. Nèige 'gwăndzde fàn 'méi shémma hwāyàngr, kĕshr hău 'chr̄. *or* Nèige 'gwăndz(dzwò de) dōu shr 'jyācháng byàn'fàn.

A plain (level land) 'píngywán, 'dĭdĭ. / I've lived most of my life on the plains where trees and hills are scarce. Wŏ yí'bèidzli 'dwōbàr dōu shr̀ jùdzài °dĭdĭshang (°'píng'ywánshang), yĕ méi dwōshău 'shù, yĕ méi dwōshău 'shān. / There is a wide plain between the mountains and the coast. Tsúng 'shān nar dàu hăi'byār shr̀ yípyàn-'dài 'píngywán.

PLAN. (Intend) 'dăswàn, syăng, 'jìhwà. / Where do you plan to spend the summer? Nĭ °'dăswàn (°'syăng, °'jìhwà) dzài năr gwò'syà?

(Arrange) ānpai, 'jìhwà. / I planned the whole thing this way. 'Jèi shèr wŏ 'tsúngtóur dàu'lyăur 'dōu shr̀ dzèmma °'ānpaide (°'jìhwàde). *or* 'Jèi shèr 'yíbùyí-'bùde dōu shr̀ wŏ °'ānpaide (°'jìhwàde).

Plan on kàuje, 'jr̆wàngje. / You'd better not plan on it. Nĭ 'dzwèihău byé °'kàuje (°'tài jr̆wàngje) nèige.

A plan (intention) 'dăswàn, 'jìhwà; or expressed verbally as in the first paragraph above. / What are your plans for tomorrow? / Nĭ 'míngtyan yŏu shémma °'dăswan (°'jìhwà)? / I've made all my plans. Wŏ dōu °'dăswàn'haule (°'jìhwà-'haule).

(Arrangements) expressed verbally as in the second paragraph above. / All my plans are in good order. Wŏ dōu 'ānpai'hăule.

(Method) fádz, fāngfa, bànfa. / I've adopted a simple plan for disposing of such people. Yàu 'dăfa 'jèijŭng rén wŏ yŏu ge hĕn 'rúngyìde °'fádz (°'fāngfa, °'bànfa).

(Diagram) tú, 'túàn; (technical) shèjìtú. / Do you have a plan of the house? Nĭ yŏu jèi 'fángdzde °'tú (°'túàn, °shèjì'tú) ma?

PLANT. (Vegetation) Chinese has no general term, but several specific or descriptive terms. (grass or a grasslike leafy plant) tsău; (plant with thick wood-like stem or tree) mù the common opposite of tsău, not used independently; (a tree) shù; (a vegetable) tsài; (a flower) hwār; (something growing) jăngde; (something blossoming) kāi'hwārde; specific names of vegetable and flower plants are used but may be distinguished as whole plants by the measure kē (a single plant), pái (a row), dì (a patch), dwēi (a clump); plants (plant life) 'tsăumù, 'hwātsău'shùmù, 'hwātsău. / No plants will grow in this cold climate. Jèmma lĕngde 'chìhou °'tsăumù (°'hwātsău, °'hwātsău'shùmù) 'dōu hwóbu'lyău. / What kind of plants are these? 'Jèisyē shr̀ 'shémma °hwār (°tsău). / What is the name of that plant? 'Dìshang jăngde nèi jyàu 'shémma? *or* Nèi kāi'hwārde jyàu 'shémma? / Do you want cut flowers or a plant? Nĭ yàu yĭ'dwŏryì'dwŏrde hwār háishr yàu jĕng'kēde?

(Factory) chăngdz, gūngchăng. / The manager offered to show me around the plant. 'Jīnglĭ yàu dài wŏ dzài °'chăngdzlĭ (°gūng'chănglĭ) 'ràu yiràu.

To **plant** (of seeds or plants) jùng; (of plants or trees) dzāi; (sow seeds) syà-jŭngr. /The seeds I planted last week are just beginning to come up. Wŏ 'shàng-syīngchi jùng de 'dzěr gāng 'chūlai. /Early spring is the time for planting. 'Chū-chwūn shŕ °syà'jŭngr (°jùng'dzěr) de shŕhou. /I planted a cypress tree in our yard. Wŏ dzài ywàndzli °jùngle (°'dzāile) kē 'bǎishù.

PLATE. (Dish) pándz; (as a measure) pár. /Pass your plate and I'll give you some more food. Bǎ nǐ 'pándz dìgwolai wó géi nǐ jyā dyǎr 'tsài. /This plate of meat will be enough. 'Jèipár ròu 'gòule.

(License) páijàu. /Did you get the plates for your car? Nǐ de chē 'lǐngle pái-jàu le ma?

(Sheet of metal) . . . -bǎn. /The sides of the car have steel plates on them. Chēde lyǎng'byār yŏu gāng'bǎn.

To **plate** dù. /His watch is gold-plated. Tāde 'byǎu shŕ 'dùjīnde.

PLAY. (Amuse oneself) wár; (be at leisure) syán, syánwár; (do something in fun) nàuje wár; (engage in organized recreation) dzwò 'yóusyì. /The children are playing in the yard. 'Háidzmen dzài 'ywàndzli 'wár ne. /Don't play with fire. (lit.) Byé wár 'hwŏ. or 'Hwŏ búshŕ 'wár de. or (fig.) 'Nèi kě búshŕ 'wár de. /You've been playing around long enough. Nǐ °wárle (°syán'wárle, °syánle) bù'shǎu shŕhour le. /You mustn't take it to heart; he was just playing. Nǐ byé °'dzàihu (°wǎng 'syīnli chyù); tā nà shŕ nàuje 'wár.

(Compete) sài, 'bǐsài. /When are we going to play their team? Wŏmen 'shémma shŕhou gēn 'tāmen nèi dwèi °'sài (°'bǐsài)? /The teams had just started to play when it began to rain. 'Gāng sài(chilai) jyòu syà'yǔle.

(Of games) dǎ (tennis and other games in which a ball is hit; also cards); tī (games in which a ball is kicked); syà (chess and checkers); when no specific game is mentioned, wár may be used; see also **GAME**. /He plays a good game of tennis. Tā dǎ 'wǎngchyóur 'dǎde 'hěn hǎu. /He plays a good game of chess. Tā syà'chí syàde 'hěn hǎu. /He plays a good game. Tā 'wárde 'hěn hǎu. or Tā hén 'yŏu lyǎngshŏur. /We played a good game of tennis. Wŏmen nèicháng 'wǎngchyóu dǎde 'tíng hǎu.

(Of musical instruments) lā (played with a bow); tán (played with the fingers); chwēi (of wind instruments); dǎ, chyāu (of percussion instruments). /He plays the violin very well. Tā lā tí'chín lāde 'hěn hǎu. /He plays the piano very well. Tā tán gāng'chín tánde 'hěn hǎu. /He plays the trumpet very well. Tā chwēi 'lǎba chwēide 'hěn hǎu.

(Of music) dzòuywè. /Listen; the orchestra is playing now. 'Tīng a, ywè'dwèi dzòu'ywèle.

(Of a card in a card game) chū. /He played his high card. Tā 'chūde shŕ tāde 'dàpái. or Tā chū 'dàpái le.

(Act) yǎn; **play the part of** yǎn, dāng, chyù. /He plays the part of a villain (or traitor). Tā °chyùde (°dāngde, °yǎnde) shŕ ge °'hwàirén (°'jyānchén).

Play a joke kāi 'wánsyàu, kāisyīn, dǎ 'hāhar, dòusyàur. /He played a joke on us. Tā ná 'wŏmen °kāi 'wánsyàu (°'kāi'syīn, °dǎ 'hāhar, °dòu'syàur) laije.

Play fair with dài . . . 'gūngping, dài . . . 'gūng, dài . . . jyáng'lǐ. /He really doesn't play fair with me. Tā kě 'jēn dài wŏ bù'gūng(ping). or Tā dài wŏ 'jēn bùjyáng'lǐ.

Played out gěi lèi'hwàile, lèide méi 'jyèr le, lèide 'jīnpílì'jyé le. /After a hard day's work he's all played out. 'Dzwòle yìtyān 'lèihwór (bǎ) tā °gěi lèi-'hwàile (°lèide méi 'jyèr le, °lèide 'jīnpílì'jyé le).

Play up. / He plays up only the good points of the job. Tā 'gwāng °shwō (°jyǎng) nèi shèrde 'hǎuchù. *or* Tā 'gwāng ba nèi shèrde 'hǎuchù shwōde 'tyānhwārlwàn-'jwèi.

A play (drama) syî. / Are there any good plays in town? Chénglǐ syàndzài yǒu shémma hǎu 'syî ma?

Play (looseness) expressed verbally with sūng (be loose) *or* bùjǐn (not tight). / There's a lot of play in this rope. (tied around something) 'Jèigēn shéngdz 'kwūnde °bù'jǐn (°tài 'sūng). *or* (stretched in a straight line) 'Jèigēn 'shéngdz °'bēngde bùjǐn (°'lāde búgòu 'jǐnde, °hěn 'sūng, °tài 'sūng).

PLEASANT. (Of a person) 'héchì (friendly). / Your friend is a very pleasant person. Nǐ nèige 'péngyou hěn 'héchì.

(Of a person's manner) kèchi. / He asked me in a very pleasant way. Tā hěn 'kèchide wèn wǒ.

(Of appearance) syǐsying. / She has a pleasant face. Tā jǎngde hén 'syǐsying.

(Enjoyable) jyàu rén hěn gāu'sying. / Our work is very pleasant. 'Wǒmende shèr dzwòje jyàu rén hǎu gāu'sying.

(Enjoyable and interesting) yǒuyìsz, yǒuchywèr, gāusyìngde. / We had a very pleasant talk. Wǒmen 'tánde 'hén °yǒu'yìsz (°yǒu'chywèr °gāu'syìngde).

In many cases hǎu (good) is used. / It was a very pleasant day today. 'Jīntyān tyānchi hén 'hǎu. / We had a pleasant time. Wǒmen 'wárde hén hǎu.

PLEASE. (Be agreeable to) jyàu . . . 'syǐhwān, jyàu . . . 'hwānsyi; (make happy) jyàu . . . 'gāu'sying; (of something said) jyàu . . . ài 'tīng; or, instead of saying that something pleases someone, Chinese often say that a person likes something, using 'syǐhwān *or* hwānsyi. / Does this please you, or do you want something else? °Nǐ 'syǐhwān (°Nǐ 'hwānsyi) jèige ma, háishr syǎng yàu ge 'byéde? / He's pleased with it. Jèige tā 'syǐhwān. / What you said pleased him very much. 'Nǐde hwà jyàu tā hén °'syǐhwān (°'hwānsyi, °gāu'sying, °ài 'tīng).

(Satisfy) tszhou (serve); dwèifu (deal with). / She's a hard person to please. Tā nèige rén hěn nán °'tszhou (°'dwèifu).

(Wish). / Do as you please. 'Swéibyàn, swéibyàn. *or* Byé 'jyūshù. *or* 'Dzěmmaje dōu 'hǎu. *or* 'Dzěmmaje dōu 'syíng. *or* (impatiently) 'Swéi nǐde byàn.

(In requests) chǐng, láujyà. / Please shut the door. °Chǐng (°Láu'jyà) bǎ 'mén gwānshang.

PLENTY. (Many or much) hěn dwō, hǎusyē; (enough) gòu; (more than enough) (yǒu) fùyu. / I have plenty of matches. 'Wǒ jèr yánghwór hěn 'dwō. *or* 'Wǒ jèr yǒu °hǎu'syē (°hěn'dwō) yáng'hwór. *or* 'Wǒ jèr yáng'hwór hái yǒu 'fùyu. *or* Wǒde 'yánghwǒr gòu'yùngde. / There's plenty more in the kitchen. Chú'fángli hái yóu hǎu-'syē ne.

PLOW. lí, líba. / You need a heavier plow than this. Yùng de 'lí(ba) déi bǐ jèige 'jùng dyar.

To plow (of soil) gēngdì, jīngdì. / We started to plow early this spring. Wǒmen 'jīnnyán chwūntyān °gēng 'dì gēngde (°jīng 'dì jīngde) 'dzǎu dyar.

(Move through) jǐ (press); gǔng (nose along with up-and-down motion, as a boat); dǐng (push along with head down, as a bull). / He plowed his way through the crowd. Tā tsúng rén'dzwēili 'jǐgwochyule. / The ship plowed slowly through the waves. Chwán dzài 'làngtouli màn'mārde gǔng.

POCKET. (In clothes) kǒudàr, dōur; (only in a secretive sense) yāubǎur. /He put it in his pocket. Nèige tā 'gēdzai °kǒu'dàrli (°'dōurli) le.

(Of metal in the earth) kwàng. / They discovered a valuable pocket of silver. Tāmen jǎujáule ge 'kéyǐ chū hěn 'dwō yíndz de 'kwàng.

(Small) 'syòujēn, syòujēnde. / This is a pocket edition of the Bible. Jèiběr Shèng'jīng shr syòujen 'bǎn.

Air pocket chǐyā'dǐde dìfang. / The plane hit several air pockets. Fēijǐ 'pèng-shangle hauji'chù chǐyā 'dǐde dìfang.

Pocketbook (purse) píbāu; (paperbound) píngjwāngshr.

Pocketknife syǎudāur. /Do you have a pocketknife I can borrow? Nǐ yǒu yìbǎ syǎu'dāur jyè wǒ 'yùngyung ma?

To pocket bǎ . . . gēdzai °kǒu'dàrli (°'dōurli). /He paid the bill and pocketed the change. Tā bǎ 'jàng gěile yǐ'hòu, bá 'jǎuhweilai de chyán °'gēdzai kǒu'dàrli le (°'gēdzai 'dōurli le, or (cheating by so doing) °rùle 'dzìjǐde yāu'bāur le).

POEM. shr (also means poetry); tsź (poems of irregular meter); chyǔdz (verses for singing in a play). / This book contains all his poems. ('Swóyou) tā syě de 'shr 'dōu dzài jèiběr °'shūli (°'jídzli).

POET. 'shrrén; (a great poet) dà'shrjyā, dà'tsźjyā, dà'chyǔjyā. /A new collection of the poet's works will come out this summer. Nèige 'shrrénde 'syīnshr'jí 'syà-tyān chū'bǎn.

POINT. (Sharp end) jyār; (having a sharp point) jyānde. /He broke the point of his knife. Tā bǎ 'dāudz 'jyār gěi °nùng 'shéle (°'bènle). / The point of this pencil is not sharp enough. 'Jèigwan 'chyānbǐ ('shyōude) búgòu 'jyānde. or 'Jèigwan 'chyān-bǐ 'jyār hai tài tsū.

(Place) dìfang (see **PLACE**); **halfway point** jūngjyàr(de dìfang), dāngjūng (nar), dāng'jūngde dìfang. / The train stopped at a point halfway between the two stations. Hwǒ'chē dzài 'lyǎngjàn °jūng'jyàr(de dìfang) (°dāng'jūng nar, °dāng'jūngde dìfang) 'tíngsyale. / The enemy has fought to a point four miles from here. 'Dírén yǐjīng 'dǎdàu 'lí jèr 'sżlǐdi de 'dìfang. /At one point they were only ten miles from here. Dzài 'yíge dìfang tāmen lí jèr 'jr yǒu 'shrlǐ dì.

(Land jutting into water) jyǎur. / The boat we saw has sailed around the point. Wǒmen 'chyáujyàn de nèijr chwán 'yǐjīng 'ràugwo nèige 'jyǎur chyu le.

(Dot) dyǎn, dyǎr. / The decimal point in this number is in the wrong place. Jèi-ge shùrlide syǎushùr'dyǎr °dyǎnde 'búshr 'dìfangr (°dyǎn'tswòle dìfangle).

(Time) shŕhou; (stage, condition) dìbu. /At that point in the proceedings he suddenly got angry. Dàu 'nèi shŕhou tā 'hūrán fāchǐ 'pích lai le.

(Unit of scoring) fēn, fēr. /Our team made 23 points in the first half of the game. 'Wǒmen jèibyār dzài 'chyánbànchǎng déle èrshr'sān fēr.

(Degree) dù, dyǎn; **boiling point** 'fúdyǎn, 'fèidyǎn. / The thermometer went down ten points. Hánshú'byǎu jyàngle 'shŕdù. / The water was heated to the boiling point. Shwéi jǔdàu °'fúdyǎn (°'fèidyǎn) le.

(Of a compass) dzèr, dù (mark); 'fāngsyàng (direction). /He steered several points off the course. Tā bǎ 'dwò jwànde chàle °'háujǐge 'dzèr (°'háujidù).

(Detail) dyǎn. /We've gone over that point already. 'Nèidyǎn dzámen yǐjīng 'tángwole. /I disagree with your argument at every point. Nǐ swǒ 'shwō de wǒ méiyou 'yìdyǎn °túng'yì de (°dzán'chéng de). /Every point in your argument needs expanding a little. Ní swǒ shwō de 'něi yǐdyǎn dōu děi °dwō 'fāhwēi yísyàr (°'dzài shwōde 'syángsyi dyar).

(Characteristic, part) dìfang; **good points** 'hǎude dìfang, 'hǎuchù; **bad points** 'hwàide dìfang, 'hwàichu. / The book has its good and bad points. Jèiběn 'shū yóu 'hǎude dìfang yé yǒu 'hwàide dìfang. / Can you name just one good point about that book? 'Nèiběn shū nǐ néng jřchu 'yǐdyán 'hǎude dìfang lái ma? / He has many good points. Tā yóu 'hǎusyē 'hǎuchù. / Don't you think the job has any good points at all? 'Nándaushwō nǐ jywéje 'jèi shèr yǐ'dyár 'hǎuchù yě méi'yǒu ma?

(Of a story) jyéguyǎr (the critical spot); **get the point** °'tīngchū (°'kànchū) jyégu'yǎr lai, dǔng shř 'dzěmma hwéi 'shèr, (aim, application) dǔng shř jřje 'shémma shwōde. / His answer shows that he missed the whole point of the joke. Tsúng tāde 'hwéidáli kéyǐ kànchulai nèige 'syàuhwar de jyégu'yǎr tā °'méitīngchūlái (°'méikànchulai). Tsúng tāde 'hwéidáli kéyǐ kànchulai nèige 'syàuhwarde tā 'gēn-běn bùdǔng shř °'dzěmma hwéi 'shèr (°'jřje'shémma shwōde). / What's the point? Jyégu 'yǎr dzài 'shémma dìfang? or Shř 'dzěmma hwéi shèr? or (application) Shř 'jěje 'shémma shwōde? / That's just the point. Jyégu'yǎr jyòushr dzài 'nèige dìfang. or 'Jyòu shr 'nèmma hwéi 'shèr. / The point is this. 'Jyòu shr jřje 'jèige shwōde.

(Purpose) wèide; (desire) yàude. / Our point is to get the result quickly. Wǒmen °'wèide (°'yàude) jyòu shr 'gǎnkwài dzwò'wánlou. / What was the point of his doing that? Tā nà shř 'wèide shémma?

Point of view 'yǐjyàn; **from . . . point of view** (on . . . basis) tsúng . . . fāng-myan kàn, tsúng . . . fāngmyan lái'syǎng, or (on . . . opinion) °'àn(je) (°jàu) . . . yǐjyàn, °àn(je) (°jàu) . . . yìsz. / His point of view is nearly the same as mine. 'Tāde 'yǐjyàn gēn 'wǒde chàbù'dwō. / From his point of view the plan is, of course, im-possible. Tsúng 'tā nèi fāngmyan °kàn (°jáu'syǎng), 'jèige bànfa dž'rán shř 'dzwò-budéde. / From our point of view, it is the right thing to do. °Àn(je) (°Jàu) 'wǒmen-de °yǐjyan (°yìsz), 'yīnggāi dzěmma bàn.

Be on the point of 'jèngdzai yàu, 'jèng yàu, 'gāng yàu. / We were on the point of leaving when some visitors arrived. Wǒmen °'jèngdzài (°jèng, °'gāng) yàu dzǒu de shŕhou, 'kè láile.

Beside the point ('háu) bú'chyětí, ('háu) bùtyětí, gēn běn'tí méi 'gwānsyi. / That's an interesting statement, but it's quite beside the point. Nèijyù 'hwà hén yǒu'yìsz, kěshr °('háu) bú'chyětí (°('háu) bùtyě'tí, °gēn běn'tí méi 'gwānsyi).

Make a point of yídìng yàu. / He makes a point of dressing properly. Tā yí-'dìng yàu chwānde jěng'chí.

To the point 'jèngshr 'dìfangr, dwèijyèr, chyětí, tyětí. / His comments are always right to the point. °Tāde pínglwùn (°'Tā pípingde) 'lǎushr °hěn chyě'tí (°hěn tyě'tí, °jèng chyě'tí, °'jèngshr 'dìfangr, °jèng dwèi'jyèr).

To point (indicate direction) jř; **point out** jřchulai. / He pointed to where the house is located. Tā (yùng shǒu) 'jřje nèiswǒr 'fángdz nar. / The compass needle points (to the) north. Lwópán'jēn jřje 'jèngběi. / Point to the one you mean. Nǐ shwōde shř 'nèige, géi wǒ °'jřchulai (°'jř yijř). or Nǐ shwōde shř 'nèige, 'jř géi wǒ °kàn (°kànkan, °chyáuchyau). / Point out the place you told me about. Nǐ 'gàusung wǒ de nèige 'dìfang géi wǒ'jřchūlai.

(Aim) ná . . . chùng(je) (°wàng(je), °syàng(je), °dwèi(je); **be pointed** chùng-(je), wàng(je), syàng(je), dwèi(je). / Don't point the gun at me. Byé ná 'chyāng-kǒu 'dwèije 'wǒ. / The gun is pointed north. Pàu chùngje 'běibyār. or Pàu shř °wàng (°chùng, °syàng, °dwèi) 'běi myáude.

Point toward (indicate). / All the signs pointed toward a hard winter. 'Chyáu jèige °'yìsz (°'yàngr) jīnnyán 'dūngtyān hwèi tíng 'lěngde.

POISON. 'dúyàu, dú in combinations. / This medicine is poison if taken internally. Jèi'yàu búshr 'chr̄de, chr̄le hwèi jùng 'dú. / This is poison. Jèi shr 'dúyàu. / The enemy may attack with poison gas. Dírén hwòjě yàu yùng 'dúchì. *but* / He's poison. Tā shř ge 'dàirén. *or* Tā shř ge 'syàurén. *or* Tā shř ge 'hàichyúnjr'mǎ.

To poison gěi ... dú'yàu chr, syàdú, (if the victim died) bǎ ... 'dúsž̌le. / He tried to poison his mother. Tā syáng gěi tā mǔchin °dú'yàu chr̄ (°syà'dú). / She poisoned her husband. Tā bǎ tā jàngfu 'dúsž̌le. / The thief poisoned our dog. Dzéi ná 'dúyàu géi wǒmende gǒu chr̄le. *or* (so that it died) Dzéi bá wǒmende 'gǒu dúsž̌-le.

Be poisoned jùngdúle. / Our dog has been poisoned. Wǒmende gǒu jùng'dúle.

POLICE. jǐngchá, 'jǐnggwān; military police 'syanbǐng. / Call the police! °Jyàu (°Chǐng) °'jǐngchá (°syún'jǐng) lái.

To police syúnlwó, 'syúnchá. / During the war soldiers policed the streets. Dǎjàng de shŕhou yǒu 'jyūndwèi °syúnlwó (°syúnchá) 'jyēdàu.

POLICY. (Settled course to be followed) gwēijyu; (of a government) 'jèngtsè. / Our foreign policy has always been consistent. Wǒmende 'wàijyāu 'jèngtsè tsúnglái shř yí'gwànde. / It is the policy of our company never to cash checks. Wǒmen gūngsž̌de 'gwēijyu shř bùshǒu 'jřpyàu.

(Contract) dāndz. / I've just taken out another $5,000 insurance policy. Wǒ 'gāng yòu lǐngle yíge 'wǔchyānywánde báu'syàn dāndz.

POLITE. (Proper in action) yóu 'lǐmàu, jyáng 'lǐmàu, jyáng 'lǐjyé, dǔng 'gwēijyu; (according to etiquette) jàu 'gwēijyu, jàu 'lǐjyé, jàulǐ; be polite to ... 'gūngjing ... , dwèi ... yóu 'lǐmàu, gěi ... 'myàndz; not be polite 'búdà hǎu'yìsz *or* negative forms of the above. / They consider that polite. Tāmen jywéje 'nèmmaje shr °yóu 'lǐmàu (°jyáng 'lǐmàu, °jyáng 'lǐjyé, °dǔng 'gwēijyu). / He's very polite. Tā 'hén °yóu 'lǐmàu (°jyáng 'lǐjyé, °jyáng 'lǐmàu, °dǔng 'gwēijyu). / The polite thing to do is to open the packages at once. Jàu 'gwēijyu shř lì'kè bǎ bāur 'dǎkāi. / That is a polite expression. Jàu °'gwēijyu (°'lǐjyé, °'lǐ) gāi nèmma shwō. / He isn't very polite to her. Tā búdà 'gūngjing tā. *or* Tā dwèi tā méiyóu 'lǐmàu. *or* Tā hěn bùgěi tā 'myàndz. / I don't think it'd be polite for us to leave so soon. Wǒ jywéde 'jèmma kwài jyòu dzǒu °'búdà hǎu'yìsz (°tài méiyóu 'lǐmàu, °tài bùdúng 'lǐjyé).

POLITICAL. 'jèngjř; in combinations jèng; political circles 'jèngjyè; political party jèngdǎng; political rights 'jèngchywán, 'jèngjř 'chywánlì. / Every citizen has certain political rights. Měige 'gūngmín dōu 'kéyí 'syǎngshòu rwǒgān'jùngde °'jèngjř 'chywánlì (°'jèngchywán). / He's an authority in political science. Tā shř jèngjř-'sywé 'jwānjyā. *or* Yánjyòu jèngjř'sywéde tā shř ge 'chywánwēi. *or* (a student of) Tā shř nyàn 'jèngjř̌sywéde. / He is an important political figure. Tā dzài °'jèng-jyèli (°'jèngjř̌wútáishang) shř yíge hěn 'jùngyàude °'rénwù (°'jyàusè). *or* Tā shř ge °'jèngjyède ('jèngjř̌wútáishangde) 'yàurén. / What political party do you belong to? Ní 'shǔyú něi yíge jèng'dǎng ne?

POOR. (Not rich) chyúng. / Many poor people live in this neighborhood. 'Hǎusyē 'chyúngrén jùdzài jèi'fùjìn. / She doesn't like being poor. Tā 'bùkěn shòu'chyúng.

(Not good) bùhǎu; tsž (poor quality); chàjìn, chàdyar (something lacking); often more specific terms. / This soil is poor for roses. Jèijúng 'tǔ jùng 'méi-gwēihwār °tài 'tsž (°tài chà'jìn, °tài 'chàdyar, *or* (not rich enough) °bù-gǒu 'féide). / She gave a poor performance. Tā yǎnde °chà'jìn (°chàdyar, °búda 'hǎu). / That's a mighty poor excuse. Nèmmaje 'jyèshrde 'tài chà'jìnle. *or* Nèmmaje 'shwōde °tài méi'lǐ le (°jyàu 'shéi yě bùnéng 'syìn). / That's a poor example. Nèige 'bǐ de búdà 'dwèi. / The workmanship is rather poor. 'Gūng hěn tsz̀. *or* (rough) 'Gūng hěn 'tsāu. *or* Gūng hěn 'tsū. *or* (careless) 'Gūng hén 'mǎhu. / That's a pretty poor job. Nèige dzwòde °chà'jìn (°bù'hǎu, °méi'yìsz). / His health is poor. Tā 'shēndz bù'hǎu. / His poor eyesight explains why he retired so young. Tā nèmma 'nyánchīng'chīngrde jyòu twèi'syōule shr̀ 'yīnwei tā 'yǎnjing °bù'chéngle (°yàu 'syāle).

(Worthy of pity) is expressed as be pitiful kě lyán. / The poor fellow is blind. 'Jēn kě 'lyán; tā 'syāle.

The poor pínmín, chyúngrén. / We are taking up a collection for the poor. Wǒmen dzài tì pín'mín mù'jywān.

POPULAR. (Much liked) is expressed by indirect expressions which say that many people like something or do something or that something is often done. / He is the most popular mayor the city has ever had. Jèi dìfangde shr̀'jǎngli °tā 'dzwèi jyàu rén 'syǐhwān (°tā 'dzwèi shòu rén 'àidài, °dàjyā 'dzwèisyǐhwān tā). / This book is quite popular. Jèi běn 'shū hěn'dwō rén °ài (°'syǐhwān) 'kàn. / That song was very popular last year. Nèige gēr 'chyùnyán °hěn'dwō rén ài 'chàng (°'cháng tīng-de'jyàn, *or* (in vogue) °hěn shr̀'syīng). / It's a popular custom in China to have flowerpots in the courtyard. Dzài 'Jūnggwo rénjyāerde ywàndzli chángcháng bǎije yǒu hwā'pér.

(Of style of writing or speaking) sú, 'tūngsú. / This is not a bad book, in spite of its popular style. Jèiběr 'shū swéirán 'syěde hěn °'sú (°'tūngsú), búgwò hái bú'tswò.

(Of the people) 'rénmín. / No government can stand long without popular support. 'Rénmín bù'yǔnghù de jèng'fǔ chángbu'lyǎu.

Popular prices bùjyā'jyàr le (lit. not at increased prices). / The movie will be shown at popular prices pretty soon. Nèige dyàn'yǐngr gwò bùji'tyār jyòu 'bùjyā-'jyàrle.

PORCH. (On ground level) lángdz; (on roof level) lyángtái (a porch for airing) *or* shàitái (a sun porch).

PORT. (Harbor) kǒu, háikǒu, gángkǒu. / When do you expect the ship to get into port? Nǐmen kàn jèige 'chwán 'shémma shr̀hou néng jìn (hái)'kǒu?

(Harbor city) shānggǎng, shāngfù; (city along the coast) yán'àn de chéng. / This town is one of the principal Pacific ports. Jèi shr̀ 'Tàipíngyáng yán'àn de yíge °'dàchéng (°dàshāng'gǎng, °dàshāng'fù).

(Left side of a ship) chwán dzwǒbyar. / There's a man overboard on the port side of the ship. Chwán 'dzwǒbyar yǒu rén dyàu 'shwéili le.

(Kind of wine) 'húng pútáu jyǒu (red grape wine). / Port is my favorite wine. Wǒ dzwèi 'syǐhwān hē 'húng pútáu jyǒu.

PORTION. *See* **PART.** / You must take some portion of the responsibility. Nǐ 'dzúng děi fù yí'bùfende 'dzérèn.

POSITION. (Location) dìfang (*see* **PLACE**). / From this position you can see the whole city. Tsúng 'jèige dìfang kéyǐ kànjyàn 'chywán chéng.

(Posture) is expressed as the way in which one stands, sits, or lies, combined in various constructions; or by such words as jànje, standing, etc. / If you're not comfortable, change your position. Nǐ 'rúgwǒ bù'shūfu, hwàn ge 'yàngr °jànje (°dzwòje, °tǎngje). *or* (move a bit) Nǐ 'rúgwǒ bù'shūfu, 'nwónwo jyòu 'hǎu le.

(Situation) 'chíngsyíng (circumstances); 'dìwèi (high social position). / A man in my position has to be careful of what he says. Dzài 'wǒ jèujǔng dìwèi de rén shwō'hwà děi lyóu'shén. *or* Wǒ dzài 'jèijǔng chíngsyíng jr̀'syà shwō'hwà děi lyóu-shén. /He's in a similar position; he doesn't know what to do either. 'Tāde °chíng-syíng (°dìwèi) yě shr̀ yí'yàngde, méi 'bànfa. *but* /This places me in a very difficult position. is expressed as This makes things hard for me. 'Dzěmmaje jyàu wǒ hěn wéi'nán.

(Job) shèr, wèijr. /He has a good position with a wholesale house. Tā dzài yìjyāer 'pīfā'dyànli dzwò 'shèr, °nèi shèr hén 'hǎu (°nèi 'wèijr hén 'hǎu, °'dìwei hén 'gāu).

(Attitude) 'yìjyàn (opinion); kànfa (point of view). /What is your position in regard to this new law? Nǐ dwèiyù jèige 'syīn fǎ'gwēi °yǒu shémma 'yìjyàn (°shr̀ 'dzěmma ge 'kànfa)?

POSSESSION. (Property) 'jyādàng. /He gave away all his possessions before he went in the army. Tā méirù'wú yǐ'chyán bǎ 'jyādàng dōu sùng'rénle.

(Of a country) shǔdì. /This island is a possession of the United States. Jèige 'dǎu shr̀ 'Měigwode shǔ'dì.

Have in one's possession yǒu. /I have in my possession a book with your name on it. 'Wǒ nar yǒu 'shū, shàngtou yǒu 'nǐde míngdz.

Take possession of bǎ . . . 'jyēgwolai. /The new owner hasn't taken possession of the house. 'Syīn fáng'jǔ hái méi bǎ fángdz 'jyēgwolai.

POSSIBLE. (Within power of performance) is expressed by the verbs néng (be able to), syíng (be workable); or with resultative compounds using de. /Be here by nine, if possible. °Rúgwo 'syíng (°Yàushr bànde'dǎu) dehwà, jyòu dzài 'jyóudyǎn jūng 'dǎu jèr. /I'll come early if it's at all possible. 'Dànfán 'néng dzǎu 'dàu, wǒ yí-dìng dzǎu 'dàu. /Is it possible? meaning for something to be done (Néng) bànde-'dǎu ma? or meaning for something to happen Néng yǒu 'nàyàngrde shèr ma? *but* /It's possible but not probable. 'Nàyàngrde shèr 'yǒu dàushr 'yǒu, búgwo 'jèi búhwèi 'shr̀de.

(Of something that may happen) 'yésyǔ (perhaps); 'kéyǐ (it may be). /We'd better be prepared for a possible shower. Dzámen 'chyù de shŕhou 'fángbèije dyǎr ba, yésyǔ hwèi syà'yǔ. /It's possible that the letter will come today. Nèifēng 'syìn °yésyǔ (°kéyǐ) 'jīntyān dàu.

The best (*or* worst, etc.) **possible** dzwèi . . . de. /You'll get the best possible treatment. Yí'dìng yùng 'dzwèi hǎude 'fāngfa géi nǐ 'jr̀.

POST. (Of a fence) jùdz. /The fence needs some new posts. Jèidàu wéidz děi hwàn jǐge syīn 'jùdz le.

(Assigned place) gāng, 'gāngwèi, syùndì. /Those soldiers were arrested for being away from their posts. Nèisyē 'bīng yīnwei 'sžlí °gāng'wèi (°syùn'dì) bèi-'pǔde. /That soldier has to go to his post at the gate. Nèige 'bīng děi chyù dàu dà-'mén nar jàn'gǎng.

(Army camp) 'yíngpán (the place); 'yíngpánlide rén (the forces at the place). /The whole post has been notified of the change in rules. 'Syīn gǎi de 'fǎgwēi 'yǐjīng 'tūngjr̄le 'yíngpánli 'swóyǒude rén le.

(Job) chāishr (appointment); wèijr (position). /He has just been appointed to a new post in the government. Tā 'gāng dzài jèng'fǔli déle yíge 'syīn °chāishr (°wèijr).

Post office yóujèng jyú.

To post (put up) tyēdàu, tyēdzai (put on by sticking); 'gwàdzài (hang on); dìng-dzai (nail on). / Post it on the bulletin board. Bǎ 'jèige °tyēdau (°tyēdzai, °gwàdzài, dǐngdzài) bùgàu'bǎnshang chyu.

(Assign to a place) pài. / We posted a squad to guard that bridge. Wōmen pàile yǐ'pái rén chyù 'shǒu nèige 'chyáu. / Troops were posted to guard the bridge. 'Chyáu-shang pàile 'bīng chyù.

POT. hú; (pan) gwō. / She has a pot of tea ready for us. Tā gěi wōmen 'chīhǎule yìhú 'chá. / There's a pot of soup on the stove. 'Lúdzshang yǒu yìgwō 'tāng.

Flowerpot hwāpér. / There's a row of flowerpots on the porch. Lyáng'táishang yǒu yílyòu hwā'pér.

POTATO. tǔdòur, shānyaudòur; (terms not commonly used) shānyaudàn, fánshǔ.

POUND. (Unit of weight) bàng. / Give me a pound of tobacco, please. Gěi wǒ yíbàng yān'yèdz.

(Unit of money) 'yǐngbàng (British). / He owes me six pounds. Tā gāi wǒ lyòu'yǐngbàng.

To pound (hit) dǎ, chyāu; (with considerable force) dzá. / We pounded on the door for five minutes before they heard us. Wōmen °chyāu 'mén chyāule (°dǎ 'mén dǎle) yóu 'wǔfēn'jūng tsái yǒu rén 'tīngjyan. / They pounded the rock into small pieces. Tāmen bǎ 'shŕtou dzáchéngle swěi'kwàr.

POUR. (Cause to flow) dàu. / Please pour me a cup of tea. Láu'jyà gěi wǒ dàu yì-bēi 'chá (hē). / He poured all the water out of the pail. Tā bǎ tǔnglide 'shwěi dōu 'dàuchūchyule.

(Flow) chūng; (of people) jǐ, yūng, chūng. / The water was pouring through a little hole in the dike. 'Dīshang yǒu ge syāu 'kūlung, 'shwěi tsúng nàr 'chūngchu-laile. / The crowd poured out of the theater. Rén tsúng syì'ywándzli °jǐchūlaile (°yūngchūlaile, °chūngchūlaile).

(Rain hard) 'yǔ syàde tǐng 'dà. / Don't go out; it's pouring. 'Byéchūchyule; 'yǔsyàde tǐng 'dà. (fig.) / It never rains but it pours. 'Hwòbù'dānsyíng.

POWER. (Mechanical energy) 'lìlyàng; **electric power** 'dyànlì, dyàn; **hydraulic power** 'shwěilì, shwěi; **horsepower** 'mǎlì. / This machine has more power than that one. 'Jèige 'jīchi bǐ nèige 'lìlyàng 'dà. / This is run by electric power. Jèi shŕ yùng °'dyànde (°'dyànlìde). / Water is the cheapest source of power. 'Shwěilì dzwèi 'pyányi. / This factory uses a lot of electric power. 'Jèige gūng'chǎng yùng 'dyàn hěn 'dwō. / The power has been turned off. Dyàn 'tíngle. / How much power does this machine have? Jèige 'jīchi yǒu °'dwōdàde (°'dwōshǎu) 'mǎlì?

(Authority) chywán, chywánbing; (influence) shŕ, 'shŕlì; **come into power** may also be expressed as take office shàngtái, and **be in power** as be in office dzài 'táishang. / When he came into power he forgot all his promises. Tā 'yí °shàng'tái (°déle 'shŕ, °yǒule 'chywán, °yǒule'chywánbing) jyòu bǎ tā 'dàyingde 'dōu wàngle. / This party won't be in power much longer. Jèiyì'dǎng dzài 'táishang 'méi jǐtyār le. / The one who has the real power here is not an official. Jèi dìfang 'dzwèi °yǒu'chywán de (°yǒu 'shŕli de) 'bùshr ge 'gwār. / He has the real power. Tā yǒu 'shŕchywán. / What power does he have over you? (lit.) Tā yǒu shémma 'chywánbing lái 'gwǎn nǐ? or (fig., as of blackmail) Nǐ yǒu shémma 'bǎbing dzài tā 'shǒuli? / The mayor's power should be limited. Shŕ'jǎngde 'chywán(bing) yīng-gāi °yǒu 'syànjr (or (by legislation) °yóu 'fǎlyù lái syànjr, or (reduced) °dzài 'syǎu dyar).

827

PRACTICAL

(Ability) is expressed by the verb néng be able, or by resultative compounds with de or, in the negative, with bu. / I'll certainly do everything in my power. Wǒ 'néng bànde'daude jyou yí'dǐng bàn. / His powers of concentration are amazing. Tā 'jēnshr jyàu rén chí'gwài, dzemma néng 'nèmma jwān'syīn ne.

(Great nation) 'lyèchyáng. / Our nation is one of the world powers. Wǒ gwó shr shrjyè 'lyèchyáng jr'yī.

Powerhouse, power station fādyànchǎng.

See also FORCE, STRENGTH.

PRACTICAL. (Usable) is expressed by saying a thing is fit for use or that it can be done, using expressions such as kéyǐ yùng, kéyung, shryùng, jùngyùng, néng yùng, néng syíng, bàndedàu, yùngdeshàng, etc. / That was a very practical suggestion you made. 'Nǐ shwō de nèige 'fádz hen °kéyǐ 'yùng (°jūng'yùng, °ké'yùng, °shr'yùng, °'kéyǐ bànde'dàu, °'kéyi yùngde'shàng). / Is his idea practical? 'Tāde yìjyàn °ke'yùng ma (°néng 'yùng ma, °néng 'syíng ma)? / Your suggestion is good, but it isn't practical. Nǐ shwō de 'yìsz hén 'hǎu, 'búgwò °bùshr'yùng (°bùnéng 'yùng, °bùnéng 'syíng, °bànbú'dàu). / Your suggestion is good, but it isn't practical so far as this matter is concerned. Nǐ shwō de 'yìsz 'hǎu, 'búgwò °dzài 'jèijyàn shrshang bùnéng 'yùng (°dzài 'jèijyàn shrshang yùngbu'shang, °'jèijyàn shr bù'néng nèmma bàn, °yùngdzài 'jèijyàn shrshang bù'syíng). / His ideas are all impractical. 'Tāde júyì 'dōu °bùnéng 'yùng (°yùngbú'shàng, °bùshr'yùng, °bànbu'dàu, °bùnéng 'syíng). *or* (rude) Tā jìng chū 'sōujúyi. *or* Tā chūde'júyi chywán shr syā'nàu. *or* Tā jìng 'húchūjúyì.

(Sensible; of a person) dǔngshr, jrchywèr; (sarcastically) 'syànshr. / Your friend is a very practical man. Nǐ jèige'péngyou hén °dǔng'shr (°jr'chywèr, °'syànshr).

PRACTICE. (Perform repeatedly) lyànsyi, lyàn. / I need to practice a little more before I can take you on. Wó dei syān °'lyànlyan (°'lyànsyi lyànsyi) tsái néng gēn nǐ 'sài. / He's practicing the piano. Tā lyàn 'chín ne. *or* Tā jèng 'lyànsyi tán gāng-'chín ne.

Practice law is expressed as be a lawyer formally 'jèngshr dāng 'lyùshr. / How much longer do you have to study before you can practice law? Nǐ 'hái dei nyàn 'dwōshǎu shrhou tsái néng 'jèngshr dāng 'lyùshr.

Practice medicine is expressed as be a physician formally 'jèngshr dāng 'yī-shēng, 'jèngshr syíng'yī. / Are you an intern or are you practicing (medicine) now? Nǐ shr shr'syí ne háishr yǐjīng 'jèngshr °dāng 'yīshēng le (°syíng'yīle)?

Practice (training) expressed verbally as in paragraph one. / Chinese calligraphy requires constant practice before you can master the art. Syě 'Jūnggwodz dei °syà (°yùng, °fèi) 'gūngfu yì'jrbú'dwànde 'lyànsyi tsái néng syéde'hǎu ne. *but* / Practice makes perfect. 'Shóujūngshēng'chyǎu. *or* 'Shóunéngshēng'chyǎu.

(Professional work). / The new doctor has only a small practice. Nèiwèi 'syīn lái de 'dàifu, chǐng tā jr'bìng de rén bù'dwō.

Be in practice, put into practice (use) yùng; (make real) shr'syíng; (apply) shrsyíng; (act according to) jàu'bàn; (try out) shr (yishr). / His suggestion was put into practice immediately. 'Tā syǎng de 'bànfa lì'kè jyòu °'yùngshangle (°shr-syíngle, °'yùngle, °jàu'bànle). / A law becomes a useless document unless it is put into practice. 'Fǎlyù °'gē nar bú'yùng (°yǒule kèshr bùshr'syíng) jyòu chéngle 'jyùwén le. / Let's put your plan into practice and see whether it works. 'Nǐde fádz dzámen 'shr yishr kàn 'syíng busyíng.

Be out of practice 'yǒu syē shrhou méi . . . le. / I know how to play chess,

828

but I'm a little out of practice. Syà'chí wǒ 'hwèi dàushr 'hwèi, búgwò 'yǒu 'syē shŕhou méi'syàle.

In practice (in reality) shŕ'jìshang. / The law sounds harsh, but in practice it is very fair. Jèige 'fǎlyù 'tīngje hěn 'yán, °shŕ'jìshang hěn 'gūngpíng (°'yùngchilai jyòu jŕdàu shŕ hěn 'gūngpíngde le, °shŕ'syíngchilai jyòu jŕdau shŕ hěn 'gūngpíngde le).

Make a practice of, make it a practice to (always) 'syànglái, lǎu. / We make it a practice to get to work on time. Wǒmen °'syànglái (°lǎu) shŕ àn 'shŕhou shàng-'bān.

PRAY. 'chídǎu, 'dǎugàu; (ask for) chyóu. / They prayed for rain. Tāmen chyóu 'yǔ. / They prayed to heaven for forgiveness. Tāmen dǎu'gàu chyóu 'ráu.

PRAYER. 'dǎugàude; **the Lord's Prayer** Júdǎuwén. / The prayer was rather long. Dǎugàude yǒu yìdyǎr 'cháng.

PRECIOUS. 'gwèijùng, bǎubei (*also* a precious thing). / These jewels are very precious. Jèisye 'shǒushr hěn 'gwèijùng. / He regards it as being very precious. Nèige tā nàje dàng 'bǎubei shŕde. *or* Tā 'jywéje nèige hěn gwèijùng.

PREFER. (Followed by a noun) bǐjyàu 'syǐhwān, jywéje . . . háu dyǎr, háishr 'ài, háishr 'syǐhwān. / Whom do you prefer? Ní bǐjyàu 'syǐhwān 'shéi? *or* Ní jywéje shéi hǎudyar? *or* Ní háishr 'syǐhwān 'shéi? / I prefer this brand of cigarettes. Wó °bǐjyàu 'syǐhwān (°háishr 'ài) jèige páidzde 'yān. *or* Wǒ jywéje chōu jèige páidzde 'yān hǎudyǎr.

(Followed by a verb) 'chíngywàn, 'nìngkě, bǐjyàu 'syǐhwān. / I prefer to wait until the weather is cooler. Wǒ °'chíngywàn (°'nìngké) děng tyān 'léng dyǎr dzài 'shwō. / I prefer to eat fish. Wǒ °'chíngywàn (°'nìngkě, °'bǐjyàu 'syǐhwān) chŕ 'yú.

Prefer X to Y bǐjyàu 'syǐhwān X, búdà 'syǐhwān Y. / I prefer pork to beef. Wǒ bǐjyàu 'syǐhwān 'jūròu, búdà 'syǐhwān 'nyóuròu.

Prefer to X rather than Y °'nìngkě (°'chíngywàn) X, 'yě bu Y. / I prefer to see a movie rather than stay home with you. Wǒ °'nìngké (°'chíngywàn) kàn yì-'chǎng dyànyengr yě bù gēn ní dzài 'jyāli 'dāije.

PREPARE. (Get ready) 'yùbèi; (make careful preparations) 'jwǔnbèi; (make, as a report) dzwò. / I am preparing a report. Wǒ jèng °'dzwò (°'yùbèi, °'jwǔnbèi) yíge bàu'gàu ne. / They prepared to leave immediately. Tāmen 'yùbèihǎule, 'shwō dzǒu jyòu 'dzǒu. / He prepared a long and detailed report, and then didn't have a chance to present it at the meeting. Tā °dzwò'hǎule (°'yùbèi'hǎule) yíge hěn 'cháng hěn 'syángsyide bàu'gàu, kěshr 'méiyou 'jīhwei dzài hwèi'chǎngshang 'jyánggěi dàjyā 'tīng.

(Cook) dzwò. / That was a delicious meal you prepared. Ní 'dzwò de nèidwùn fàn 'jēn syāng. / That's not the way to prepare fish. Yú °búshr (°bunéng) 'nèmma dzwòde. *or* Nèi 'búshr dzwò'yú de 'fǎdz.

Be prepared for, be prepared to (expect) syàngdàu; (be qualified for) yǒu 'dzgé; (be able) néng. / I'm not prepared for this. 'Jèige wǒ méisyàng'dàu. *or* Dzwò 'jèige wǒ 'bùgòu 'dzgé. / I'm not prepared to say how many divisions of troops we have in China. Wǒmen dzài 'Jūnggwo yǒu 'jǐshr wǒ °'bùnéng 'shwō (*or* (shouldn't say) °'bùnéng 'shwōchulai, *or* (don't know) °bùjŕ'dàu, °méidé'chá).

Prepare someone **for** something. / You'd better prepare him for the news. Ní syān ná hwà 'kāidǎu tā yísyàr, dzài jyàu tā 'jŕdàu.

PRESENCE. (Being present). / My presence makes them happy. is expressed verbally as They see me and are very happy. Tāmen kànjyàn wó hěn 'gāusyíng. / His presence is not going to make any difference. is expressed as Whether he comes or not won't make any difference. Tā 'dàu bú'dàu 'méiyǒu 'gwānsyi.

Presence of mind. / He showed considerable presence of mind. (was not ruffled) Tā 'jēn néng 'jènjìng. *or* Tā 'jēn 'chǔjř'tàirán. *or* Tā 'jēn néng nèmma 'bùhwāng-bù'mángde. *or* Tā 'jēn néng yǐ'dyǎr bù'hwāngjang. *or* (knew what to do) Tā jēn 'jīling. *or* Tā 'jēn néng 'swéijíyìng'byàn.

In the presence of 'dāngje . . . de myàr, dzài . . . 'myànchyán. / This must be signed in the presence of three witnesses. Jèige 'fēiděi °dzài 'sānge 'jèngrén 'myànchyán (°'dāngje 'sānge 'jèngrénde myàr) chyān'dz tsái'syíng.

PRESENT. (Gift). *See* GIFT. / This watch was a present from my wife. Jèi 'byǎu shř wǒ 'tàitai °sùng (°géi, °sùnggéi) wǒ de.

(This time) 'syàndzài, 'jēngdzài (right now); 'jànshř, mùchyán, 'tszkè, 'tsž-shř, 'syànshř, 'jèi shřhou, 'jèijèr (this short period of time, temporarily); 'rújīn (the present as opposed to the past). / The present policy is to hire younger men. °'Syàndzàide (°'Mù'chyánde, °'Tszkède, °etc.) 'bànfa shř gù nyán'chīng dyarde rén. / The future cannot be any worse than the present. 'Jyānglái bù'gwán dzěmma yàng yě 'bùnéng bǐ °'syàndzài (°'tszkè, °mù'chyán) hái 'hwàidàu 'nǎr chyù. / That will be enough for the present. °'Jànshř (°'Mù'chyán, °etc.) swàn 'gòu le. / He's too busy to see you at present. Tā °'jèijèr (°'tszkè, °'tszshř, °'syàndzài, °etc.) tài 'máng, 'bùnéng 'jyàn nǐ.

To present (give) gěi, 'sùnggěi, sùng. *See* GIVE. / They presented him with a gold watch. Tāmen °'sùngle (°'gěile, °'sùnggěile) tā yíge jīn'byǎu.

(Offer to view) 'kànshangchyu yǒu. / This assignment presents many difficulties. 'Jèijyàn shř 'kànshangchyu hwèi yǒu bù'shǎude 'nánchù. / The soldiers presented a good appearance. Bīngde 'yàngdz 'kànshangchyu 'hén yǒu 'jīngshen.

(Submit) shwō (sya). / This report presents all the facts. Jèige bàu'gàuli °yí'jyànyíjyànde (°'jyànjyàn) shř 'dōu shwō'dàule.

(Perform; of a play) yǎn. / That play was presented by a group of young actors. Nèichū 'syì shř yìchyún 'chīngnyán yǎn'ywán 'yǎnde.

(Introduce). / Allow me to present Mr. McPherson. is expressed as I'll introduce you; this is Mr. Mǎ. Wó gěi nímen 'jyèshàu; 'jèiwèi shř 'Mǎ Syānsheng.

Be present (not absent) expressed by the verbs dàu (arrive) *or* dzài (be at). / There are five hundred people present. 'Dàule yǒu 'wúbǎi rén. *or* Yǒu 'wúbǎi rén °dàu'chǎng (°dzài jèr). / How many people are expected to be present? 'Dàgài yǒu 'dwōshau rén 'dàu?

PRESIDENT. (Of a republic) dzúngtǔng, 'dàdzúngtǔng; (of a republic governed by a committee of which the president is chairman) jǔsyí; (of a ywàn in the Chinese government) ywànjǎng; (of a school) syàujǎng; (of a business concern) 'jīnglǐ, dzúng-jīnglǐ, (especially of a bank) hángjǎng; (of a society or association) 'hwěijǎng.

Vice-president 'fù- plus any of the above terms.

PRESS. (Exert physical pressure) jǐ (squeeze, crowd); yā (apply weight to); èn (with finger or hand); yà (press down or with a roller); tsǎi (with foot). / The crowd pressed through the gates. Dàjyā'hwǒr °'jǐjìn (°'jǐchū) dà'mén °lái le (°chyù le). / The crowd pressed against the gates. Dàjyā'hwǒr jř jǐ dà'mén. / The baby pressed his nose against the window to watch his daddy watering the flowers. Syǎu'hár bǎ 'bídz jǐdzài 'chwānghushang kàn tā 'dyē jyǎu'hwār. / Keep the two pieces of wood pressed together until the glue dries. Bá lyǎngkwài 'mùtou °jǐdzài (°yādzài, °yà-dzài) yíkwǎr jŕdàu 'jyāu 'gān le. /Don't press too hard; that's where it hurts. 'Byé shř'jǐn 'èn; 'jyòu shr nàr 'téng. /When you press the piano key, a little hammer inside strikes the string. Nǐ yí èn gāngchínde 'jyàndz, lǐtou yǒu ge syāu 'chwéidzer jyòu chyāu nèige 'syán. /Press the button and see what happens. Èn yísyà 'lyéngr kànkan °dzěmmayàng (°yǒu shémma 'dùngjyengr). /Press the lever at this end. Èn gàng'gǎrde 'jèi tóur. /Press the handle down. Bǎ bàr 'ènsyachyu. or Bǎ bàr 'yàsyachyu. /Press the pedal down. Bǎ 'tǎbǎn 'tsǎisyachyu. /After the prints are washed, press them flat with this roller. 'Syàngpyār syǐchulai yǐ'hòu, ná jèige 'gwǔndz yà'pínglou.

(To iron) tàng, tàngpíng, yùn, yùnpíng, làu, làuping. /Have this suit pressed for me. Jèitàu 'yīshang géi wǒ °'tàng yitang (°'tàng'píng le, °'yùn yiyun, °yùn'píng le, °'làu yilau, °làu'píng le). /Where can I get my suit pressed? Yàu tàng 'yīshang, dàu 'shémma dìfang chyu? or Dzài 'hǎr kéyǐ tàng 'yīfu? or Nár yǒu tàng 'yīfu de?

(Force) bī. /If you press him a little further he'll talk. Nǐ yàushr 'bīde tā 'dzài °lìhai (°jǐn) dyar, tā jyòu 'shwō le. /They're pressing him for a definite answer. Tāmen 'bīje tā gěi ge 'jwǔnhwàr. /Don't press people too hard. Búyàu bī rén bīde tài °'lìhai le (°'jǐn le). or Bùnéng 'bīréntài'shèn. or 'Búyàu 'tài gǎnlou rén.

(Push or urge; an investigation) 'jwēijyōu, 'jwēiwèn. /I wouldn't press the matter any further if I were you. 'Wǒ yàu shř nǐ dehwà, jèijyàn shèr wǒ 'búdzài °'jwēijyōu le (°'jwēiwèn le). /The governor is pressing this matter too far. 'Jèi shèr shéngjǎng 'jwēijyōude tài °'yán le (°'jǐn le).

(Insist on) 'yìjŕbú'dwànde shwō. /He pressed the point until everyone got the idea. Tā bǎ 'nèijyàn shř 'yìjŕbú'dwànde shwō, 'jŕdàu 'dàjyā 'dōu míngbai le.

Hard pressed. /He was hard pressed for an answer. Tā jíde méiyou hwà kéyǐ 'hwéidá. or Tā jyàu rén 'bīde 'syàngbuchu fár lai 'hwéidá le.

Pressing yàujǐn (important); jí (urgent). /I have a pressing engagement elsewhere. Wǒ dzài 'byéchùr yǒu °ge yàu'jǐnde 'ywēhwèr (°jyàn 'jíshèr).

Press (newspapers, collectively) 'bàujyè. /This play was well received by the press. Nèichū 'syì 'bàujyè 'dōu shwō 'hǎu.

(Journalists) 'syīnwénjì'jě. /Will the press be admitted to the conference? Hwèi'yì syǔ 'syīnwénjì'jě jìnchyu ma?

(Machine for printing) yìndzjī, yìnshwājī. /Only trained men can operate this printing press. Jèijyà °'yìndzjī (°'yìnshwā'jī) fēiděi 'shòugwo 'syùnlyàn de rén tsái néng 'yùng.

(Machine for pressing) yàjájī (for punching, stamping, or applying steady pressure); **oil press** jáyóujī; **drill press** dǎyǎnjī; **hydraulic press** shwěiyājī (for applying steady pressure only).

Go to press. /This edition is ready to go to press. Jèiyì'bǎn kéyǐ °fù'yìn le (°'náchyu 'yìn le).

PRETTY. (Pleasing to the eye) hǎu kàn. /She is a very pretty girl. Tā jǎngde hén hǎu 'kàn.

(Pleasing to the ear) hǎu tīng. /That's a pretty tune. Nèige 'dyàur tíng hǎu 'tīng.

(Rather) hěn, tǐng. /I've been pretty busy since I saw you last. Wǒ 'dżtsúng 'shàngtsż jyàn ní yǐ'hòu, yìjŕ °hěn (°tǐng) 'máng láije.

PREVENT. (Keep someone from doing something) jyàu . . . bu, ràng . . . bū, búyàu . . . , búràng . . . plus a verb indicating what is to be prevented; bǎ . . . plus a verb which means stop such as láu, dǎng, lyóu, kān, tíng, jǐ, etc., followed by a proper post-verb, such as -jù, -hwéilái, -hwéichyù, -syálái, etc.; or expressed as . . . therefore not . . . , with 'yīntsž or 'swóyǐ as therefore. / Can you find a way to prevent him from leaving? Nǐ néng syǎng ge 'fǎr °jyàu tā 'bùdzǒu ma (°ràng tā 'byé dzǒu ma, °bújyàu tā 'dzǒu ma, °búràng tā 'dzǒu ma, °bǎ tā 'lánju ma, °bǎ tā 'lyóusya ma)? / The bad weather prevented the ship from arriving on time. 'Tyānchì 'bùhǎu, 'swóyǐ chwán °dàude 'wǎn le (°wùle 'dyǎn le, °'méinéng àn 'shŕhou 'dàu). / Your timely wink prevented him from spilling the beans. Nǐ jí'yǎr jǐde 'jèngshŕ 'shŕhou, °'méijyàu (°'méiràng) tā (bǎ nèige) gěi 'shwōchuchyu. or Nǐ jí'yǎr jǐde 'jèngshŕ shŕhou, °bǎ tā 'gāngyàushwō de nèige géi 'dǎnghweichyule (°'búràn tā jyòu bǎ nèige 'shwōchulaile). or Nǐ jí'yǎr jǐde 'jèngshŕ shŕhou, °jyàu (°ràng, °swóyǐ, °yīntsž) tā méi bǎ nèige gěi 'shwōchuchyu.

(Keep something from occurring) yùfáng, fángjǐr; or expressed as above. / We should try to prevent forest fires. Wǒmen 'yīngdāng 'syǎngfǎr °bújyàu (°búràng, °yùfáng, °fángjǐr) shù'líndz jáu'hwǒ. / The army prevented aggression. Jyūn'dwèi fángjǐrle chīn'lywè. or Jyūn'dwèi bǎ ('dírénde) chīn'lywè géi dǎngjule.

PRICE. jyàr, jyàchyán; (amount asked) yàu de chyán; **wholesale price** pī'fā de °jyàr (°'jyàchyán); **retail price** 'língmài de °jyàr (°jyàchyan); **sale price** 'mài jyàr, 'mài de jyàchyan; **fixed prices** (no bargaining) 'dìngjyàr, yídìngde jyàchyan; **prices** (of all things) 'wùjyà. / I like the rooms, but the price is too high. 'Wūdz dōu tíng'hǎude jyòushr °'jyàr tài 'gāu dyar (°'jyàchyan tài 'gāu dyar, °yàu de 'chyán tài 'dwō le). / This price is less than the cost. 'Mài jyàr bǐ 'běnchyán hái 'shǎu ne. or Jàu 'jèige °jyàr (°jyàchyan) lái mài hái 'búgòu 'běnchyán ne. / Prices are higher this year. 'Jīnnyande 'wùjyà 'gāule dyar.

PRIDE. (Gratification) expressed by the stative verb déyì be satisfied and other expressions. / He takes great pride in his work. Tā dzwò de dūngsyi tā 'dzjí hěn dé'yì. / The new park is the pride of the city. Yì'chéngde rén 'dōu jywéje nèi syīn 'kāi de gūng'ywán hén 'hǎu. or Yì'chéngde rén 'dōu kànje nèi syīn 'kāi de gūng-'ywán hen dé'yì de.

(Self-respect) dżdzwūnsyīn. / He hurt her pride. Tā shāngle tāde dżdzwūn-syīnle.

(Self-righteousness) expressed with àu be proud. / His pride won't let him admit he's wrong. Tā °'rén (°'syìngdz) hěn 'àu, 'bùkěn rèn 'tswòr. or Tā 'bùkěn rèn 'tswèr, yīnwèi tā 'syìngdz hěn 'àu.

(Haughtiness) jyāuàu. / Pride goeth before a fall. is expressed as Pride usually causes failure. Jyāuàu chángchang shŕ shŕbàide ywányīn.

To pride oneself dżfù, jywéje dżjǐde . . . hén 'hǎu. / He prides himself on his good judgment. Tā jywéje tā 'dżjí de 'yǎngwāng hén'hǎu. or Tā hěn dż'fù néng pàndwàn shŕfēi.

See also **PROUD.**

PRINCIPAL. (Most important) 'dzwèi yàu'jǐnde, jùyàude. / Cotton is the principal crop in this province. 'Myánhwa shŕ 'běnshěng °'dzwèi yàu'jǐnde (°jǔ'yàude) 'núng-chǎn. / This is his principal argument against your plan. Tā 'fǎndwèi 'nǐde nèige 'bànfa, shwōle jǐtyáu 'lǐyóu; 'jèishr 'dzwèi yàu'jǐnde yìtyáu.

A principal (head of a school) 'syàujǎng. / The principal called a teachers' meeting. 'Syàujǎng 'jāují 'jyàuywán kāi'hwèi.

(Participant in a legal case) 'dāngshŕrén. / The principals in the case were represented by their lawyer. Jèige 'àndzlide 'dāngshr̄rén yóu tāmende 'lyùshr̄ 'dàibyǎu chū'tíng.

(Sum of money) 'běnchyán, běr. / We'll need a principal of over $100,000. 'Běnchyán děi yàu 'shr̄wànywán yǐ'shàng. / Don't draw on your principal. Byé dùng 'běnchyán. or Byé dùng 'běr.

PRINT. (By printing press) yìn. / How much will it cost to print this? Jèige děi 'dwō-shau chyán lái 'yìn? or 'Yìn jèige děi 'dwōshau chyán? / Who printed this newspaper? Jèi 'bàu shr̄ 'shwéi yìn de?

(Write like type) yùng 'jèngkǎi syě (write in formal script). / Please print your name instead of writing it. Chíng bǎ 'míngdz yùng 'jèngkǎi syěchulai.

Be printed (published) 'yìnchulai, yìn'hǎu, yìndé, chūbǎn, dēng. / A printed notice will be sent out tomorrow. Yǒu ge °'yìnchulai (°'yìnhǎule) de 'tūnggàu 'míng-tyan fāchuchyu. / This letter was printed in yesterday's paper. Jèifēng 'syìn dēng-dzài 'dzwótyānde bàu'jr̄shang.

Printing shop yìnshwāswǒ.

Print (type) dzèr (characters). / The print in this book is too small. Jèiběr 'shūlide 'dzèr tài 'syǎu.

(Figured cloth) yìnhwārbù; **a print dress** 'yìnhwārbùde 'yīshang, 'hwāryīfu. / We're selling lots of prints this year. 'Jīnnyán wǒmen màile hěn 'dwōde 'yìnhwār-bù. / She wore a pretty print dress. Tā chwānle yíjyàn 'hén hǎukànde °'hwār yīfu (°'yìnhwārbùde 'yīshang).

(Printed picture) yìn de hwàr. / The museum of fine arts has a collection of famous prints and paintings. 'Měishù'gwǎnli yǒu hén yǒu'míngde 'hwàr, yǒu 'yìnde, yǒu 'jènde. / He collects old prints of sailing ships. Tā 'sōují 'jyòubǎn 'yìn de fānchwán 'hwàr.

(Photographic positive) 'syàngpyàn, syàngpyār; **make prints** °syǐ (°yìn) 'syàng-pyàn. / How many prints do you want from this negative? 'Jèijāng 'dǐpyàn nǐ yàu syǐ (°yìn) 'dwōshǎu jāng? / I'm going to have a few prints made. Wǒ yàu chyù °yìn (°syǐ) jijāng 'syàngpyār chyu.

Be out of print; be in print. / Is the book still in print? is expressed as Do the plates still exist? 'Jèi shū 'bǎn hái 'yǒu ma? / This book is still in print. 'Jèi shū 'méijywé'bǎn. / That book is hard to get because it's out of print. 'Nèiběr shū yǐjīng jywé'bànle swóyí 'hěn nán 'mǎijau.

Come out in print see **be printed.** / The president's speech has just come out in print. Dàdzúng'tǔngde yán'jyǎng 'gāng °'yìnchulai (°chū'bǎn).

PRISON. (Penitentiary) 'jyānyù, jyān, láu, yù, jyānláuyù. / He was sent from the local jail to the state prison. Tāmen bǎ tā tsúng 'dìfāng 'kānshóuswǒ jyědàu 'shěng 'jyānyù chyu le. / Put him in prison. Bǎ tā °gwāndzài (°sùngdàu) °'jyānli (°'láuli, °'jyānláu'yùli, °'yùli) chyu ba.

PRISONER. (Prison inmate) 'fànrén, 'chyóufàn. / A prisoner has just escaped and is headed this way. Yíge °'fànrén (°'chyóufàn) 'gāng °ywèle 'yù (°tsúng jyān'yùli 'pǎuchulaile), jèng wàng 'jèibyār dzǒuje ne.

(Captive) fúlwǒ; (of war) jànfú. / How many prisoners were taken during the last battle? 'Shàngtsz̄ dzwò'jàn de shŕhou, °fú'lwó (°jànfú) yǒu 'dwōshau?

Take someone **prisoner** fúlwǒ, dǎiju. / They took him prisoner. Tāmen bǎ tā °fú'lwǒle (°'dǎijule).

PRIVATE. (Not public; personal) 'dzjǐde, 'gèrénde, 'dz̀ . . . de with a verb; sz̄ in some

PRIZE

combinations; (not in front of people) bù'dāngje rén. / This is a private car. Jèi shr̀ 'dzyūngde 'chē. *or* Jèi shr̀ 'dzjǐ yùng de 'chē. / This is their private house. Jèi shr̀ tāmen 'dzjǐde fángdz. *or* Jèi shr̀ tāmende 'szrén jù'jái. / My private opinion is that the man is a thief. Wǒ 'gèrénde (°'dzjǐde) 'yìjyàn 'yǐwei 'nèige rén shr̀ ge 'dzéi. *or expressed as* I believe in my mind that the man is a thief. Wǒ 'syīnli jywé-je tā shr̀ ge 'dzéi. / I'd like to discuss this matter with you in private. Wó syǎng °'szsyàli (°bù'dāngje rén) gēn nǐ 'tán yitán jèijyàn shr̀. *or* Wó syǎng dzámen 'dzjǐ 'tán yitán jèijyàn shr̀.

A private (army rank) has no exact equivalent in Chinese, but syǎubīng or simply bīng may be used. / He was a private in the last war. 'Shàngtsz̀ 'shr̀jyè dà'jàn de shŕhou tā °shr̀ ge syǎu'bīng (°dāngde shr̀ 'bīng).

PRIZE. (Award) jyǎng; (money) 'jyǎngjīn. / There will be a fifty-dollar prize for the writer of the best short story. 'Shéi syède 'dwǎnpyān 'syǎushwōr 'dzwèi hǎu jyòu dé 'wǔshrywán °'jyǎngjīn (°de 'jyǎng). / The prize story was written by a friend of mine. Dé 'jyǎng de nèige syǎu'shwōr shr̀ wǒde yíge 'péngyou syède.

(Best) 'dzwèi hǎude. / That's the prize movie of the year, don't you think? Nǐ jywéde bùjywéde 'nèige dyàn'yěngr shr̀ 'jīnnyánli dzwèi hǎude.

To prize dwèi . . . gūjyà hěn gāu. / I prize this very highly. Wǒ dwèi jèige gūjyà hěn 'gāu.

Prized possession bǎubei. / This is one of my most prized possessions. Jèi shr̀ wǒde yíge 'bǎubei.

PROBABLE. Expressed with the adverbs 'dàgài, dwōbàn, 'dwōbàr; (not for certain) shwōbudìng, jŕbudìng. / It's possible but not probable that you'll see him on the train. Nǐ 'yésyǔ néng dzài 'chēshang 'pèngjyan tā, búgwò °'dwōbar (°'dàgài) shr̀ 'pèng-bujyàn de.

PROBABLY. 'dàgài, 'dwōbàn, 'dwōbàr. / He will probably go. Tā °'dàgài (°'dwōbàn, °'dwōbàr) chyu. / It's possible that you'll see him on the train, but you probably won't. Nǐ 'yésyǔ néng dzài 'chēshang 'pèngjyan tā, búgwò °'dàgài (°etc.) shr̀ 'pèngbujyàn de. / There will probably be a bad storm tonight. Jyēr 'wǎnshang °'dwōbar (°'dà-gài) shr̀ yàu 'gwādà'fēng 'syàdà'yǔ.

PROBLEM. (In mathematics) 'swàntí; (question; may refer to a problem in mathematics) 'wèntí; (difficulty) 'nánchù, nán'bànde dìfang, nán'bànde shr̀, wéi'nánde shr̀; (situation; which may be hard to solve, nán bàn, or easy to solve, rúngyì bàn, etc.) shèr. / It's a difficult problem to solve. Jèige °'swàntí (°'wèntí) 'hěn nán 'jyějywé. / There's no problem at all. Yì'dyǎr °'nánchù (°nán'bànde dìfang) yě méi'yǒu. / I have a problem here. 'Wǒ jèr yǒu °ge 'wèntí (°ge 'nánchù, °jyàn nán'bànde shr̀, °jyàn shèr jyàu wǒ wéi'nán). / I have a way to solve your problem. Nǐde °'wèntí (°'swàntí) 'wǒ yǒu ge 'fāngfa 'jyějywé. *or* 'Nǐ nèijyàn °wéi'nánde (°nán'bànde) 'shr̀ 'wó yǒu ge °'bànfa (°'fádz bàn). / That problem is easy to solve; why don't you do it like this? 'Nèi shèr °'hǎu bàn (°'rúngyì bàn, °'bùnán, °'bùnán bàn); ní 'dzèmma bú'dzèmmaje ne? / He's a problem child. Jèi háidz hěn nán °'bàn (°'gwǎn). *or* Jèi háidz 'méifár °'bàn (°'gwǎn). *or* Jèi háidz jyàu rén méi 'bànfa.

PROCEED. (Continue) jyēje, 'jìsyù (general) 'jàucháng (as usual); each of these must be followed by a verb describing the action continued. / After the interruption they proceeded with their work. 'Dǎnwùle yìhwér yr̄'hòu tāmen °'jyēje (°'jìsyù) dzwò-syáchyule. / Despite the bombing, he proceeded with his bath. Jà'dàn yìbyār 'làu-je, tā háishr °'jyēje (°'jìsyù, °'jàucháng) syǐ tāde 'dzǎu. / Our orders are to proceed to the bridge (when already advancing). 'Mìnglìngshang shwō jyàu dzámen 'jìsyù 'chyánjìn dàu 'chyáu nar.

834

(**Start out**) chyu̇ (of going from one place to another); <u>for other action</u> kāishr̄ <u>plus the specific verb describing the action started.</u> / Our orders are to proceed to the bridge (from a stationary position). 'Mìnglìngshang shwō jyàu dzǎmen dàu 'chyáu nar chyu̇. / Now we can proceed to lesson one. Wŏmen syàndzài 'kāishr̄ dìyīkè.

PROCEEDS. 'jìnkwǎn. / He sold his house and put the proceeds in government bonds. Tā bǎ fángdz 'màile, bǎ 'swóyŏude 'jìnkwǎn 'dōu mǎile gūngjài'pyàu le.

PRODUCE. (Manufacture) dzwòchu, dzàuchu, chū. / How many planes does that factory produce per month? 'Nèige gūng'chǎng 'yíge ywè °néng 'dzàuchu(lai) (°néng 'dzwò-chu(lai), °chū) 'dwōshǎujyà fēi'jī?

(Grow) jǎng (of crops); chū (of crops and other commodities); <u>or expressed by the noun</u> shōucheng (crop produced). / This soil ought to have produced better grapes than these. 'Jèijǔng túli 'yīnggāi °jǎngde (°chūde) 'pútau bǐ jèige 'hǎu a. / The farm ought to produce a good crop this year. 'Jīnnyán 'dìli jwāngjya 'yīnggāi jǎngde 'hǎu. *or* 'Jīnnyán 'dìli 'shōucheng 'yīnggāi bú'hwài. / This place produces raw silk. 'Jèige dìfang chū 'shēng'sz̄.

(Result in) shēng (give birth to, lit. or fig.); dé (said of 'jyēgwǒ, results); jyàu <u>plus a noun and verb; or expressed by the noun</u> 'jyēgwǒ (result produced). / All these are the effects produced by one cause. Jèisyē 'dōu shr̄ 'yíge ywányīn 'shēng-chulaide 'jyēgwǒ. / Well, it produced the right effect. 'Bùgwǎn dzěmmaje, (déde) 'jyēgwǒ bú'tswò. / This kind of news always produces a lot of excitement. Jèijǔng 'syāusyi 'dzǔngshr̄ jyàu ren hěn syīng'fèn.

(Present; as facts, evidence) náchu, shwōchu. / You have to produce the facts to prove your argument. Nǐ 'nèmma ge shwōfar děi °náchu 'jèngjyu lai (°yǒu 'jèng-jyu nádechū'lái) tsái 'syíng.

(Of a play) jǔbàn, yǎnchū; shwǎn (local Peiping). / How much will it cost to produce the play? °Jǔ'bàn (°Yǎn'chū, °Shwǎn) jèige 'syì děi 'dwōsháu 'běnchyán?

Produce (farm products) 'chūchǎn, 'núngpǐn, 'núngchǎn, núngchánpǐn. / There is no market for our produce. Wŏmende °'chūchǎn (°'núngpǐn, °'núngchǎn) méi 'syàulù.

PROFIT. (Financial) lì, lìchyán; (net profit) 'chwúnlì; **make a profit** jwàn (chyán). / The profits from the business will be divided equally. °Déle 'lì (°Déle 'lìchyán, °'Lìchyán, °Yŏu 'lì, °'Jwànlai de chyán) 'dàjyāhwǒr píng fēn. / How much profit did you make on that sale? Nèipàur 'mǎimai °jwànle (°'chwúnlì) 'dwōshau (chyán)? / I sold my car at a $50 profit. Wŏ mài 'chē jwànle 'wǔshrkwài chyán.

To profit (gain advantage) shàngswàn. / The store has profited (financially or otherwise) from its use of advertising. Nèige 'pùdz dēngle gwǎng'gàu yǐhòu hěn shàng'swàn.

Profit by (of personal benefit) yú . . . yŏu 'hǎuchù, dé ge 'jyàusyun. / I hope he profits by this experience. Pànwang tā 'jèitsz̀ dé ge 'jyàusyun. *or* Pànwang tā jīnggwo 'dzèmma yítsz̀ yú tā yŏu 'hǎuchu.

PROGRAM. (Schedule) jr̀syùdār, jr̀syùdāndz, jyémùdār. / The programs sell for a dime. °Jr̀syù'dār (°etc.) yì'máu chyán yì'fèr. / There are eight numbers on the program. °Jr̀syù'dāndzshang (°etc.) 'yí'gùng yŏu 'bāsyàng (°de 'jyémù yŏu bā-'syàng, °yŏu bāge 'jyémù).

(Period of entertainment or performances) <u>expressed indirectly by verbs such as</u> tīng (hear), kàn (see), <u>or any one of several specific verbs describing the type of performance, or not expressed at all; however, a radio program, as one item in a continuous series of entertainments, may be called</u> 'jyémù. / Are there any good programs on now? 'Syàndzài yǒu shémma °'hǎu jyémù (°kě 'tīng de, °kě 'kàn de)? /I enjoyed the program very much. Wǒ tīngde (°kànde) hěn gāu'syìng. /It will probably be a very good program. Nèige 'dàgài bú'hwài. /I thought he was going to be (perform) on the program. Wó 'yǐwei yǒu 'tā °yǎn ne (or (sing) °chàng ne, or (play the piano) °tán 'gāngchín ne, or (dance) °tyàu'wǔ ne, or (speak) °shwō'hwà ne, or (juggle) °shwā'chyóur ne, °etc.) or (without specifying) Wó 'yǐwei 'nèi lǐtou 'yǒu 'tā ne. /What's (on) the program for tonight? Jyēr 'wǎnshang dōu yǒu 'shémma? or expressed as What's going to be done? Jyēr 'wǎnshang dōu gàn 'shémma?

(A plan) 'chéngsyùbyǎu, jìhwàbyǎu. /He made out a program for his work. Tā dìngchulai yíge 'gūngdzwò 'chéngsyùbyǎu.

PROGRESS. (Advance) jìnbù, jìnjǎn. /We've progressed since those days. Wǒmen bǐ 'nèisyē rdz °jìn'bù (°jìnjǎn) 'dwō le.

(Continue some action) expressed by any verb of action, usually dzwò, or with je added to the verb, or with dwō more. /How are things progressing? 'Shèr dzwō-de dzěmma'yàng le?

Progress (advancement) jìnbù, jìnjǎn. /Our country has made a lot of progress lately. Wǒmende gwo'jyā 'jìnlái hén yǒu °jìn'bù (°jìnjǎn).

(Continuation of some action) expressed verbally as in paragraph two. /Are you making any progress with your report? Nǐ bàu'gàu dzwòde dzěmma'yàng le? or Nǐ bàu'gàu 'yǒu dwō 'syěle yìdyǎr ma? /Our work is still in progress, but it will soon be done. Wǒmende 'shèr 'hái °dzài nèr 'dzwò ne (°'jèng dzài 'dzwòje ne), búgwo 'kwài wán le.

PROMISE. shwō (jyāng'lái) yidìng . . . , syúgěi . . . , bǎujèng (guarantee); 'dāying (answer affirmatively). /This candidate promises higher wages if he is elected. Hòusywǎnrén shwō rúgwo tā dāng'sywǎn le, (jyāng'lái) yidìng bǎ 'gūngdz tígāu. or Hòusywǎnrén bǎujèng tā dāngsywán yǐhòu bǎ 'gūngdz tígāu. /My mother promised me a gold watch. Wó 'mǔchin °syúgěi wǒ (°shwō jyānglái yidìng géi wó mǎi) yíge jīn'byǎu. /I asked him to buy me a new car and he promised he would. Wǒ jyàu tā géi wó mǎi yige syīn chē tā 'dāyingle. /He promised to meet me here. Tā 'dā-yingle dzài jèr jyàn wǒ.

A promise shwō'hǎule de (shèr), ywē'hǎule de (shèr), ywēdìng; **break a promise** shrywē, shrsyìn. /A promise is a promise. Shwō'hǎule de (shèr), jyòu děi swàn. /You've broken your promise. Nǐ °shwō'hǎule de (°ywē'hǎule de) shr shémma láije nǐ °shr'syìnle (°méibàn'dàu).

(Indication of later performance) yǒuchyántú, yǒu . . . de 'syīwàng. /His future is full of promise. Tā jyānglái hén yǒu'chyán'tú. /Does my English show any promise? Wǒde 'Yīngwún yǒu méiyǒu sywé'hǎule de 'syīwàng.

PROMPT. (Quick) kwài; (quickly, immediately) lìshŕ, lìkè, 'dāngshŕ, 'děngshŕ; (on time) 'ànje shŕhou; (at the appointed time) 'shwō shémma shŕhou . . . °'jyòu (°'jwǔn) . . . . /She sent a prompt reply to my letter. Wǒde 'syìn tā °lǐ'shŕ (°lǐ'kè, °'dāng-shŕ) jyòu 'hwéile. or Wǒde 'syìn tā hwéide hěn 'kwài. /He's prompt in paying his debts. 'Tā jyè de chyán 'shwō shémma shŕhou hwán °'jyòu (°'jwǔn) hwán. or Tā hwán'jàng hwánde hěn 'kwài.

To prompt (remind) 'tísyǐng; (tell) gàusu. /Don't prompt him. Byé 'tísyǐng tā. or Byé 'gàusu tā.

(Cause). /What prompted you to say that? °Nǐ wèi'shémma (°Nǐ 'dzěmma jyòu) tíchǐ 'nèige láile?

PRONOUNCE. (Enunciate) fāyīn; shwō (say); nyàn (read). /How do you pronounce that word? Nèige dzèr ní 'dzěmma °fā'yīn (°shwō, °nyàn)?

836

(Declare) pàn (of a judge); shwō (say). / The judge pronounced him guilty of murder. 'Fǎgwān 'pàn tā shā'rén 'dzwèi. / When he was brought to the hospital, the doctor pronounced him dead. Bǎ tā táidau yī'ywànli yī'hòu, 'dàifu shwō tā yǐjīng 'sžle.

PROOF. (Evidence) 'jèngjyù. / What proof do you have that he is the man we want? Ní yǒu shémma 'jèngjyù shwō tā °'jyòu shr nèige rén (*or* (to arrest) °'jyòu shr dzá-men yàu 'dǎi de nèige rén)?

(In printing) jyàudwèi de 'gǎudz; **read proof** *or* **proofread** jyàu(dwèi) gǎudz. / Are you through reading the proof? 'Jyàuwánle ma? *or* 'Jyàudwèi 'gǎudz kàn-'wánle ma? / I've just finished proofreading my book. Wǒ 'gāng kànwánle wǒ nèibér 'shūde 'jyàudwèi 'gǎudz.

In proof of (kéyǐ) 'jèngmíng. / I have here some evidence in proof of his as-sertion. 'Wǒ jèr yǒu syē 'jèngjyù, kéyǐ 'jèngmíng tāde hwà shr 'dwèi de.

PROPER. (Correct according to custom; following custom) jàu, gwēijyù; (agreeing with custom) hé 'gwēijyù; (be right) dwèi; (ought) 'yīnggāi, gāi; (be permitted) néng, syǔ; **the proper time** shŕhou; **do the proper thing** 'syúngwēidǎu'jyùde. / What is the proper way to address a business letter? 'Mǎimai syìnshang de 'chénghū yīnggāi dzěmma syě? *or* 'Mǎimai syìnshang 'yīnggāi dzěmma yàng 'chēnghu? / The proper thing to do is to send some flowers. Jàu 'gwēijyù °shr (°'yīnggāi) sùng dyar 'hwār chyu. *or* 'Yīnggāi sùng 'hwār. *or* Sùng 'hwār tsái 'dwèi. / It's not proper. Nèmmaje bùhé 'gwēijyù. *or* Nèmmaje bú'dwèi. *or* Bù'gāi nèmmaje. *or* Bù'néng nèmmaje. *or* 'Bùsyǔ nèmmaje. / This will certainly be taken care of at the proper time. Jèige dàu 'shŕhou °jyòu 'bàn (°'jwǔn bàn). / He always does the proper thing. Tā 'lǎushr 'syúngwēidǎu'jyùde.

(In the strict sense). / His office is in a smaller building in the back, not in the building proper. Tāde bàn'gūng de dìfang dzài hòutou de 'syǎulóurli, 'búdzài °'jènglóuli (°'dàlóuli). / The city proper ends here; from here on it's suburbs. Chéng bén'shēn dàu 'jèr wéi'jŕ; 'gwòchyu jyòushr sž'syàng le. / The United States, proper, is divided into 50 states. Měigwó 'běnbù fēnchéng 'wǔshŕ 'shěng.

PROPERTY. (Possessions) dūngsyi (things); 'jyādàng(r) (family possessions). / The things on my desk are my own property. Dzài wǒ 'jwērshangde dūngsyi dōu shr wǒ 'dzjǐde. / You should be more careful in using other people's property. Yùng °'byérénde (°'rénjyade) dūngsyi yīnggāi 'dwō jyā 'syǎusyin.

(Real estate) 'chǎnyè (general); dì, 'dìchǎn (land only); fángdz (house), etc. / I own some property near the river. Wǒ dzài 'hé nar yǒu dyǎr °'chǎnyè (°'dì, °'dìchǎn).

(Attribute) 'syìngjŕ. / This salt has the property of absorbing moisture from the air. Jèijǔng 'yán yǒu 'syīshōu 'shwěifèn de 'syìngjŕ.

PROSPECT. (Expectation) chyántú; (chance) jīhwei. / What are your prospects for the future? Nǐ jyāngláíde chyántú dzěmmayàng? or expressed as Do you have any plans in the future. Nǐ yǒu shémma 'jyānglaide 'dǎswan ma? / There are no prospects in this job. Dzwò jèige 'shŕching méi shémma 'chyántú. / The prospect of a swim appeals to me. 'Néng yǒu nèmma ge 'jīhwei chyù 'fù hwéi 'shwěi, jyàu wǒ jywéje gāu'syìng.

(A prospective person for something). / I've been looking for someone to fill this job, but I haven't found any prospects yet. is expressed as . . . but I haven't found a person who wants the job. Wǒ yǐ'jŕ syǎng jàu rén 'bù jèige 'chywē, °kě-'shr 'yíge syǎng'gàn de hái méi'yǒu ne. or as . . . but I haven't found a qualified

837

person. ... °kĕshr 'yíge hé'géde hái méi'yŏu ne. / He's a good prospect (for buying). is expressed as He most probably will buy. Tā 'dwōbàn hwèi 'măide.

PROTECT. (Defend) 'bău̯hù; (take care of) 'báuyăng; protect **X** from **Y** (some English sentences which do not have this form are also expressed this way in Chinese) jyàu **X** 'bújřyu **Y** or **X** 'bújřyu jyàu ... **Y**, and similar constructions with jyàu or 'bú-jřyu, in which **Y** is a verb. / This law is designed to protect the poorer farmers. Jèige 'fălyù shř wèi 'bău̯hù 'chyúng dyàrde 'núngrén de. / I wear these glasses to protect my eyes. Wŏ dài jèifù yăn'jyèngr wèide shř 'báuyăng wŏde 'yănjing. / The dike protects the land from minor floods. Fā de 'shwĕi bú'dàde shŕhou, jèityáu dī kéyĭ jyàu dì 'bújřyu 'yān le. / This shield protects the worker from the flying sparks. Yŏu jèige 'dăngtour dzwò'hwórde jyòu 'bújřyu jyàu hwŏ'syīngdz 'shău̯jau le. / He hired a lawyer to protect his interests. (from loss) Tā chĭngle ge 'lyùshř hău̯ jyàu tā 'bújřyu °chř'kwèi (or (from being cheated) °shàng'dàng). / Put this oil on: it protects your hands from chapping. 'Tsāshang jèige 'yóu, shŏu jyòu 'bújřyu 'lyèle. / He sleeps in a mosquito net to protect himself from snakes. Tā dzài 'wénjàngli shwèi'jyàu, hău̯ jyàu 'chángchúng yău̯bu'jáu.

PROUD. (Exulting in) déyĭ and various indirect expressions; déyĭ is not used politely of oneself, one's own accomplishments or, in speaking to others, of members of one's own family; in these cases expressions of opposite meaning are more common. / He's proud of his promotion to the new position. Tā shēngdàu syīn 'wèijŕ hĕn dé'yĭ. / You must be very proud to have such a student. Yŏu 'nèmma ge °'ménshēng (°'sywé-sheng) dĕi 'dwōma dé'yĭ a. / I'm proud of this student of mine. Jèi shř wŏde dé-'yĭde 'ménshēng. / I'm proud that my country did the right thing. Wŏ jywéde 'bĭgwó jèngfŭ 'jèijyàn shř bànde hĕn 'dwèi. / I'm proud of you. (for yourself) Nĭ 'jēn hău̯. or (to a child) Nĭ 'jēn shř ge 'hău̯ háidz. or (for what you did) Dzwòde 'jēn hău̯. or Dzwòde 'jēn dwèi. or (for your abilities) Nĭ 'jēn chéng. or Nĭ 'jēn syíng. / I'm proud of my son. is expressed as He has some few possibilities. Wŏ 'jèige érdz hái 'yŏu dyăr 'chūsyi. / I feel very proud of myself for completing this task alone. is expressed as It's just luck that I finished this job alone, I'm not sure whether that's good. 'Hĕn jyău̯'syìng, wŏ 'yíge rén bă jèige dzwòwánle, kĕshr bù-jřdàu 'hău̯ buhău̯. or Wŏ 'yíge rén bă jèige dzwò'wánde, 'jyău̯syìngde 'hĕn.

(Haughty) àu, dz̀măn, 'jyău̯àu, jywé 'dz̀jĭ 'hău̯; or other indirect expressions. / He is a very proud person and would not ask for any help. Tā °'rén (°'syīngdz) hĕn 'àu, 'búywànyi chyóu 'rén. / She's become very proud since she inherited all that money. Tā dz̀túng 'chéngjîle nèibĭ 'chyán yĭ'hòu, °'jyàdz byànde hĕn 'dà (°băichi 'jyàdz laile, °'jyău̯àuchilaile, °nèmma 'chĭshŕlíng'rénle, °jywéje 'mĕide bùdélyău̯, or (vulgar expressions) °chóu'mĕide bùdé'lyău̯, °'nàge 'mĕi a). / Don't be too proud; you can always find someone better than yourself. Byé tài °dz̀'măn (°jywége 'dz̀jĭ 'hău̯, °'jyău̯àu); yàu jřdàu 'néngrén bèi'hòu yŏu 'néngrén.

PROVE. (Demonstrate) 'jèngmíng; or expressed as have proof yŏu °'jèngjyù (°'gēn-jyù); or as show people jyàurén 'jřdau. / I can prove that he didn't do it. Wŏ 'kéyĭ 'jèngmíng °tā 'méidzwò nèige (°nèi 'búshr 'tā gànde). / Can you prove your statement? Nĭde 'hwà yŏu °'jèngjyù ma (°'gēnjyù ma, °shémma 'jèngjyù ne, °shémma 'gēnjyù ne)? or Nĭ 'néng bunéng náchu 'jèngjyù lai 'jèngmíng nĭde hwà shř 'dwèide? / That proves nothing. 'Nèi 'bìng bunéng 'jèngmíng shémma. / It only proves that his mind is muddled. Jèi 'jř néng °'jèngmíng (°jyàu rén 'jřdàu) tā syīnli hĕn 'húdu.

(Turn out). / This disease might prove fatal. Jèijŭng 'bìng yésyŭ hwèi jř-'mìngde. / The letter proved to be a forgery. Nèifēng syìn 'jyégwo jřdau shř 'jyăde. / The movie proved to be very bad. Nèige pyāndz yí'kàn, tĭng 'dzàude. or (contrary to expectations) Nèige pyāndz 'jēn jyòu tĭng 'dzàude. or (for the producers) 'Nèige pyāndz yí shàng'yăn, 'jyégwó tĭng 'dzāu.

PROVIDE. (Supply) chū. *See also* **SUPPLY.** / If you provide the material, I'll build a garage for you. Nǐ rúgwo chū 'tsáilyau, wó gwān géi nǐ gài yíge chē'fáng.

(Stipulate) dìng. / The rule provides that you cannot leave the camp without permission. 'Gwēijyu 'dìngde shŕ 'méijǐng syú'kě 'bùnéng lí'yíng.

Provide against, provide for 'dǎswàn, 'swànji (plan for); syǎngdàu (think of); 'gùlyu'dàu (pay attention to). / My plan provides for that possibility too. 'Wǒde bānfali lyán 'nèige yě °'dǎswàn dzài lǐtou le (°'swànji dzài lǐtou le, °syǎng'dàule). *but* / Our (automobile) insurance provides also against the theft of our car. Wǒmen bǎu de 'chēsyānli, chē yàushr jyàu rén 'tōuchyule yě 'gwànde.

Provide with gěi (give). / We were provided with food enough to last two weeks. Géi wǒmen de 'lyángshr gòu yùng lyǎngsyīng'chǐde.

Provided (that) 'jŕyǒu, 'yàushr. / I'll come, provided (that) you come with me. 'Jŕyǒu nǐ gēn wǒ yí'kwàr lái, wǒ tsái 'lái. *or* Yàushr 'nǐ gēn wǒ yí'kwàr lái, (jŕyǒu 'nèmmaje) wǒ tsái lái.

Be provided for (of a person) yǒu'fèr (have a share); *or* yǒu with other nouns, as money. / The family was provided for in the will. 'Jyālide rén dzài yí'jùlǐ dōu yǒu'fèr.

PUBLIC. (All people) 'dàjyā (everybody); chywán'gwóde rén (all the people of the nation); and similar expressions with other place terms instead of gwó; gūng in combinations; **public park** 'gūngywán; **public telephone** 'gùnggùng dyàn'hwà; **public interests** 'gūnggùng'lìyi, 'gūngyì, 'dàjyāde 'lìyi; **public opinion** 'dàjyāde °'yìjyàn (°'gūnglwùn, °'yúlwùn). / There isn't enough public interest in the election. 'Jèitsž sywǎn'jyǔ °'dàjyā (*or* (if a national election) °chywán'gwóde rén, *or* (if a provincial election) °chywán'shěngde rén, °etc.) 'bùgòu °gwàn'syīnde (°yùngywède). / Public opinion is against him. 'Dàjyāde 'yìjyàn °bú'dzànchéng (°dōu 'fǎndwèi) tā. *or* 'Yúlwùn 'fǎndwèi tā. *or* 'Gūnglwùn 'dwèi tā bù'mǎn.

(Audience) is expressed as the people who hear a speaker 'tīng . . . de rén, the people who read a writer's writings 'kàn . . . syě de dūngsyi de rén, etc. / His program reaches a large public. Tīng tā de rén hěn 'dwō. / He writes for a small but select public. Kàn 'tā syě de dūngsyi de rén bù'dwō, 'búgwò shr yí'pàide.

In public dzài rén 'myànchyán (in front of people); dzài 'byérén 'myànchyán (in front of others). / That's not the way to behave in public. Dzài 'rén myànchyán bù'yīng'gāi nèmmaje.

Open to the public gūngkāide, 'shéi dōu néng (jìn)chyùde. / This library is only for members of the society; it is not open to the public. Jèige túshū'gwǎn jř wèi 'hwèiywán yùng, 'búshr °gūng'kāide (°'shéi dōu néng 'jìnchyude). / This meeting is open to the public. Jèige hwèi shr °gūng'kāide (°shéi dōu néng 'chyùde).

Public office 'jèngjyè. / He's held a public office for the last twenty years. Tā °dzwò'gwān (°dzài 'jèngjyè) yǒu 'èrshrnyán le.

Public officer gwān.

PULL. (Cause to move toward the force exerted) lā (draw); jwài (especially to start in motion by pulling); dèn (tug); chě (especially to pull sideways or with a ripping motion); bá (pull out by the roots or from something sticky); swō (contract, pull in); jyōu (grasp and pull, as hair). / We'll have to get a truck to pull this car out of the mud. Dzámen déi jàu lyàng 'dzàijùngchǐ'chē lai bǎ jèi 'chē tsúng 'nílǐ °'lāchulai (°'jwàichulai). / I'll pull while you push. Wǒ 'lāje nǐ 'twēi. / Pull the shades down. Bǎ chwāng'lyándz 'lāsyalai. / He pulled the blankets over his head. Tā bá 'tǎndz °'lāshanglai (°'lāgwolai), bǎ 'tóu gàishangle. / If you pull this cord, the driver will stop the bus. Nǐ yì °'lā (°'chě, °'jwài, °'dèn) jèi 'shéngr, kāi'chē de jyòu bǎ chē

°'tíngsyalai (°'tíngju). /However they pull at it, it won't move a bit. Tāmen 'dzěm-ma lā yě lābu'dùng. or Tāmen 'dzěmma jwài yě jyàibu'dùng. /This trunk is not well made; I just gave the handle a pull and it came off. Syāngdz tài bù'jyēshr; nèige 'bǎr wǒ yí °'jwài (°'dèn, °'chē, °'lā) jyòu 'dyàule. /Pull the door shut when you go out. 'Chūchyu de shŕhou 'shwùnshóu bǎ mén 'lāshang. /He pulled furtively at my coat with the idea of getting to speak to me in private. Tā 'tōuje °dèn (°ché) wǒde 'yīshang, 'yìsz shr̄ yàu gēn wǒ dàu 'bèijing dìfang chyu shwō'hwà. /If you give it too hard a pull, the rope will break. Nǐ yàushr 'tài shř'jìn °dèn (°chē, °jwài, °lā), shéngdz jyòu yàu °'shéle (°'dwànle). /This tooth has to be pulled. Jèi yá děi 'bá. /He's pulling weeds. Tā bá yé'tsǎu ne. /They pulled up the flowers by the roots. Tāmen bǎ 'hwār lyán 'gēr 'báchulaile. /The turtle pulled in its head and legs. 'Wūgwēi bǎ 'tóu gēn'twěi dōu 'swōjinchyule. /They're pulling each other's hair. Tāmen 'jyōuje tóufa dǎ'jyà.

(Tear, rip) chě (if it can be done with the hands); chāi(break). /We can pull the box apart for firewood. Dzámen kéyí bǎ 'syádz °'chāile (°'chāi'sǎnle, °'chěkāi) dàng 'pǐchai shāu. /They're going to pull it down and build a new one. Tāmen dǎ-swàn 'chāilou gài 'syīnde.

(Perform, as a trick) shř (use); often expressed indirectly. /He pulled a mean trick on me. Tā géi wó °shř'hwài láije (°'shř̌le ge 'dàhwài). /Don't pull any funny stuff. (serious warning) Byé shř 'gwěi jāur. or (friendly) Byé táu'chǐ. /He pulled a fast one that time. (of an action) Tā 'nèi jāur shř̌de 'chyǎu. or Tā 'nèihwéi nèng-de jēn 'myàu. or Tā 'nèishōur °shwǎde (°wárde) 'pyàulyang. or Tā 'nèitsź °shwǎde (°wárde) 'hwātóur 'tài chyǎu le. or (of something said) Tā 'nèige hwà shwōde 'tài °chyǎu le (°jǐling le). or Tā 'nèisyàr bǎ rén °'dzwànde (°pyànde) háu 'kǔ a.

Pull a knife dùng. /He pulled a knife on us, so we had to kill him. Tā gēn wǒmen dùng 'dāu, wǒmen bù'dé bù bǎ tā 'shā le.

Pull one's punches (in boxing) dǎde °bùshř'jìn (°búdài'jìn, or jyèr instead of jìn); (in speaking) shwō de 'hwà °méi 'lǐlyang (°méi'jìn, °méi'jyèr, °búdài'jìn, °bújùng'kěn, °chà'jìn) or 'gūngjíde °'búshr 'dìfang (°búdàu'jyā, °'lǐyou chà'jìn). /He pulls his punches. Tā 'dǎde °bùshř'jìn (°búdài'jyèr). or Tā shwō de 'hwà °méi 'lǐlyang (°etc.). or Tā 'gūngjide °'búshr 'dìfang (°'lǐyóu chà'jìn, °etc.).

Pull oneself together (settle the mind) dìngshén, dìngshér, dìngding shén, bǎ 'syīnshén 'dìngding; (quiet down) jēnjingsyachyu; (be no longer confused) syīn bú-lwànle; (recover) hǎule. /Pull yourself together and let's be on our way. °Dìngdìng 'shér (°Bǎ 'syīnshén 'dìng yidìng), dzámen gāi 'dzǒuje le. /Wait until he's pulled himself together. Děng tā °'jēnjingsyachyu (°hǎule, °syīn 'búnèmma 'lwàn le) dzài 'shwō. /After being stunned for a while he pulled himself together and walked on. Tā 'lèngle yìhwěr, ránhòu 'dìngle dìng 'shén, jyòu 'jyēje wàngchyán 'dzǒule.

Pull the wool over one's eyes (cheat) pyàn . . . , (fool completely) bǎ . . . 'pyànde °yí'lèngyílèngde (°'mwōmíngchímyàule). /He tried to pull the wool over my eyes. Tā syǎng 'pyàn wo láije. /He pulled the wool over her eyes. Tā bǎ tā 'pyànde °yí'lèngyílèngde (°'mwōmíngchí'myàu le).

Pull in (arrive) dàu; (enter the station) jìnjàn. /What time do you expect to pull into town? Nǐ 'dàgài 'shémma shŕhou dàu chéng'lǐ? /The train's just pulling in. Hwǒchē gāng °'dàu (°jìn'jàn).

Pull off (accomplish) dzwòchulai, bàndedàu, bànde chéng, 'gàndechu'lái. /It's a good idea if you can pull if off. Nǐ yàushr néng 'dzwòchūlai, yí'dìng bú'tswò.

Pull out (leave) kāi. /The train pulled out on time for once. Hwǒchē 'kě àn 'shŕhou 'kāile yǐhwéi.

Pull out (level off; of a plane that has been diving) 'gǎidàu 'píngfēi. /The plane pulled out of the dive at 2,000 feet. Fēijī wàngsyà 'jŕchūng dàu 'lyǎngchyānchǐ 'gāu nar jyòu 'gǎidau 'píngfēi le.

Pull over (drive to the side of the road) kāidàu 'byārshang chyu (including stopping); wàng 'byārshang kāi (remaining in motion). / Pull over to the curb and show me your driver's license. Kāidàu 'byārshang chyu, wǒ 'kànkan nǐde 'kāichē 'jŕjàu. / Pull over a bit. Wàng 'byārshang kāi yidyǎr.

Pull through (recover from illness or injury) hǎule, hǎudelyǎu. / She was pretty sick, and we were afraid she might not pull through. Tā bìngde tǐng 'lìhai, wǒmen 'yǐwei tā 'hǎubu'lyǎu le.

Pull up (stop) 'jànjù. / The car pulled up in front of the house. Chē kāidàu 'fángdz 'chyántou 'jànjùle.

Pull (influence) 'rénchíng (favors); 'ménlù (means of access); 'shŕlì (influence, power); **have pull** °yǒu (°twō) 'rénchíng, °yǒu (°dzǒu) 'ménlù, yǒu 'shŕlì; or expressed as ask favors of people twō'rén. / You have to have a lot of pull to get a job here. Nǐ děi °yóu tǐng 'dàde 'rénchíng (°twō bù'shǎude 'rénchíng, °'dzóu hěn 'dwōde 'ménlù, °twō bù'shǎu rén) tsái néng dzài 'jèr dé ge 'chāishr. / He has a great deal of pull at the municipal government. (as a member of it) Tā dzài 'shŕ jèng-'fúli hén yǒu 'shŕlì. or (as an outsider) Tā dzài 'shŕjèng'fúli yóu 'hǎusyē 'ménlù.

(Ascent requiring effort) expressed verbally by pá (climb). / This hill is a hard pull for an old car. 'Jèige shān 'gòu jèige 'lǎuchē 'páde.

PUNISH. fá, 'chǔfèn, 'chěngfá; (deal with) bàn; **be punished** (especially legal and physical) shòu syíngfa; (by natural suffering rather than inflicted punishment) shòu-dzwèi, shòusyíng, shòufá, shòu 'chufèn. / How are you going to punish him? Nǐ syǎng dzěmma °'fátā (°'chǔfèn tā, °'bàn tā)? / I think he's been punished enough. Wǒ jywéje °'fáde tā 'bùchíng le (°tā shòu de 'syíngfa 'bùchǐng le, °tā shòu de 'chǔfèn 'gòujùngde le). or Wǒ jywéje dzěmma °'fátā (°'chǔfèn tā, °'bàn tā) yǐjing 'gòujùngde le. or (by the natural consequences of his actions) Wǒ jywéje °tā jèige 'dzwèi shòude 'gòuchyáude le (°tā shòu de 'dzwèi 'búswàn 'shǎu le). / This crime ought to be punished more severely. (of a minor crime) °'Jèiyàngrde 'gwòfàn (°Jèi-yàngrde 'gwòtswǒ, °'Dzěmma yàng fàn'fá de shŕ) yīnggāi °'fáde (°'chǔfènde, °'bàn-de) 'dzài lìhai dyǎr. or (of a major crime) 'Jèiyàngrde 'dzwèichíng yīnggāi jyā °'jùngde (°'děngde) °'chěngfá (°'chǔfèn, °'fá, °'bàn).

PUNISHMENT. syíngfa (legal and physical); or expressed verbally, see PUNISH; or expressed indirectly. / This punishment is too severe. Jèige °'syíngfa (°'fáde, °'chǔfènde, °'bànde) tài 'jùng. / The punishment for this crime is death. Jèijùng dzwèide 'chǔfèn shŕ 'szsyíng. or expressed as This is a capital crime. Jèi shr 'szdzwèi. or as The violator of this law is given the death penalty. Fàn 'jèityáu 'fǎlyùde °shŕ 'szdzwèi (°chú 'szsyíng, °shòu 'szsyíng). / The car took a lot of punishment on its last trip. 'Jèi yitàng °'jēn gòu nèichē 'shòude (°jyàu chē shòule bù-shǎude 'dzwèi).

PUPIL. (Student) sywésheng; (disciple) 'ménshēng.

(Of the eye) 'yǎnrér, 'túngrér.

PURCHASE. mǎi. / I'm trying to purchase some land on this street. Wǒ jèngdzài syǎngfár dzài 'jèityáu jyēshang mái dyǎr 'dì.

Purchases (things bought) ('mǎi de) 'dūngsyi. / I have a few purchases to make in this store. Wó děi dzài 'jèi pùdzli mái jǐyàngr 'dūngsyi. / Please deliver these purchases for me. Láu'jyà bǎ °jèisyē 'dūngsyi (°wó 'mǎi de 'dūngsyi) géi wǒ 'sùngchyu.

PURE. (Unadulterated) chwún; <u>sometimes</u> jēn (real). / Pure gold should be heavier than this. 'Chwúnjīn bǐ jèige 'jùng. / The dress is pure silk. 'Yīfu shř °'jēnszde (°'chwúnszde).

(Unpolluted) gānjing(de) (clean); lǐngwo de (filtered; of liquids); <u>or expressed indirectly.</u> / Is the water pure enough to drink? Jèi 'shwěi shř °'gānjingde (°'lǐng-wo de)? or 'Shwěi néng 'hē ma? <u>or expressed as</u> Is the water drinkable? 'Shwěi °kéyi 'hē (°'hēde) ma?

(Sheer) 'wánchywán, 'gēnběn, jyǎnjŕ. / His statement is pure nonsense. Tā 'gēnběn shř °'húshwōbá'dàu (°'syàshwōbá'dàu). or (rather polite) Tā shwōde °'wánchywán méi'lǐ (°yìdyár 'lǐ yě méi'yǒu). or (very vulgar) Tā jyǎn'jŕ shř fàng'pi.

Pure and simple. / He's a pushover, pure and simple. Tā jyǎn'jŕ shř 'rúng-yi 'dwèifu. or Tā míng'bǎije shř ge 'rúngyi 'dwèifu de rén.

PURPLE. dž(de), 'dzshǎr(de), 'džsè(de).

PURPOSE. (Intention) 'yìsz 'mùdì; <u>or expressed indirectly with</u> wèi (because of), yàu (want, intend), 'wèide shř (in order to); <u>or without defining the purpose</u> syīn (heart), 'tswúnsyīn or 'jyūsyīn (heart, inner man). / What's the purpose of all this commotion? Jèr 'lwànlwantēngtēngde shř °wèi 'shémma (°wèile 'shémma, °yàu 'dzěmmaje, °shémma 'yìsz ne)? / What's the purpose of this visit (here)? Tā wèi 'shémma dàu jèr láide? or Tā dàu 'jèr lai shř °wèi 'shémma (°wèile 'shémma, °yàu 'dzěmmaje, °shémma 'yìsz ne)? / He is coming here for the purpose of starting a branch office. Tā 'láijèr °'wèideshř (°shř yàu, °yàu) 'lǐ yíge 'fēnhàu. / I know that his purpose is honorable. Wǒ jŕdàu tā °shř 'hǎusyīn (°de 'yìsz hén 'hǎu, °méiyǒu 'hwài yìsz, °'tswúnsyīn 'jèngdàgwāng'míngde). / His purpose is dishonorable. Tā °'tswúnsyīn (°'jyūsyīn) °bù'lyáng (°bú'shàn, °bú'jèng). or Tā 'yìsz bú'jèng. or Tā nèi 'búshr 'hǎu yìsz. or Tā 'bùhwái 'hǎuyì. / His sole purpose is personal gain. Tā 'wánchywán °shř 'szsyīn (°wèile tā 'dzjǐ).

On purpose chéngsyīn(de), gùyì(de); <u>in some cases</u> jīngyèr(de); (for a reason) yóuswǒwèi. / He did this on purpose. Tā shř °gù'yìde (°chéng'syīn, °jīng'yèrde) dzěmmaje. or Tā 'nèmmaje shř 'yóuswǒ'wèi. / He threw a monkey wrench into the works on purpose. Tā jè shr °'chéngsyīn (°gùyì) dǎu'lwàn. / I left my coat home on purpose. Wǒ °gù'yìde (°chéng'syīnde) bǎ wài'tàur gēdzài 'jyāli le. / I asked on purpose to see what you'd say. Wǒ °chéngsyīn (°gù'yì) wènde °wèideshř (°yàu) kàn nǐ dzěmma 'shwō.

Serve a purpose yǒu yìsz; yǒu yùng (have use); yóu hǎuchu (have benefit). / It serves no purpose to do it that way. Nèmmaje °méi'yùng (°méi'hǎuchù). or Nèmmaje méi 'shémma °'yìsz (°'mùdì). / What purpose does it serve to do it that way? 'Nèmmaje yǒu shémma °'yùng ne (°'hǎuchù ne, °'yìsz ne, °'mùdì ne)? <u>or expressed as</u> If that way, then what? 'Nèmmaje yòu °'dzěmmaje (°dzemma'yàng) ne?

Serve the purpose chéng, syíng, néngyùng (be satisfactory); myǎnchyáng yùng (be a necessary substitue); jyāngjyou (be a poor substitute); 'jànshr yùng . . . 'hǎu le (be a temporary substitute). / I guess this desk will serve the purpose until we get a new one. Wǒ kàn dzài wǒmen méinèngdau 'syīn jwōdz yǐ'chyán, °'jànshr yùng 'jèige (jwōdz) 'hǎu le (°'jèige yě jyòu 'jyāngjyoule, °'jèige yě jyòu 'jyāngjyouje ba, °'jèige yě jyòu 'myǎnchyáng 'yùngje ba, °'jèige yě 'chéng, °'jèige yě néng 'yùng, °'jèige yě 'syíng).

PURSE. (Moneybag; billfold) chyánjyādz; (bag) chyánbāur. / How much money do you have in your purse? Nǐ °chyán'jyādzli (°chyán'bāurli) yǒu 'dwōshau 'chyán?

(Prize money) 'yínglái de chyán jyǎngjīn. / The purse was divided evenly among the winners. 'Yínglái de chyán 'dàjyāhwǒr 'fēnle. / The purse for this fight (boxing) is $20,000. Jèi'chǎng 'chwánsàide jyǎng'jīn shř lyǎng'wànkwài chyán.

To **purse** (pucker) 'jywē. / He pursed his lips. Tā 'jywēje 'dzwěr.

PURSUE. jwēi (chase); gǎn (chase and drive). / He pursued the enemy as far as the river. Tāmen yǐ'jr bǎ 'dírén °jwēidàu (°gǎndàu) 'hé ner.

(Try to get) chyóu (ask for, seek). / Do you intend to pursue your education after your military service? Fú'bīngywè yǐhòu nǐ hái dǎswàn chyóu'sywé ma?

Pursue a course dzǒu . . . 'bù (take a step); 'tsáichyù 'bùdzǒu (adopt a procedure); and indirect expressions. / This is a dangerous course to pursue. Dzǒu 'jèiyíbù 'búdà kě'kàu. _or_ 'Tsáichyù 'jèijǔng 'bùdzǒu yǒu dyár 'syǎn. or expressed as This method is dangerous. 'Jèige 'bànfa yǒu dyár 'syǎn. or as To follow this method is dangerous. Jàu 'jèige fádz lái bàn yǒu dyár 'syǎn.

PUSH. (Shove) twēi; (with the head or with the end of something) dǐng; (impatiently) sǎngda; (from the side or to the side) 'bāla; (force aside, also means chase back) hūng. / Push the table over by the window. Bǎ jwōdz 'twēidàu kàu 'chwānghu ner chyù. / He pushed me out of the way and went right by. Tā bǎ wǒ °'twēikāi (°'sǎngda kāi, °'bālakāi), jyòu dzǒugwòchyule. / He pushed the dishes aside and laid a map on the table. Tā bǎ 'dyédz 'wànde °'bālakai (°'twēikai), jyòu bǎ dì'tú pūdzai 'jwōrshangle.

(Press) jǐ (of people); chyǎng (of a single person fighting his way through a crowd); chūng (with force, especially of an army); twēijìn (push ahead, as of an army); dǎ (by fighting). / The crowd pushed into the elevator. Rén 'jǐjìn dyàn'tīli chyù le. / There's room for everybody. Don't push. 'Yǒudeshr 'dìgangr. Byé 'jǐ le. / He was pushed to the front of the crowd. Tāmen bǎ tā 'jǐdàu 'chyánbyar chyu le. / The policeman pushed his way through the crowd to where the men were fighting. 'Jǐngchá dǎ 'réndwēili °jǐdàu (°chyǎngdàu) 'nèisyē rén dǎ'jyà de dìfang. / Our armies have pushed to within ten miles of the enemy's divisional headquarters. °'Wǒ jyūn 'twēijìndàu (°'Wǒ jyūn 'chūngdàu, °Wǒmende 'jyūndwèi wàng'chyán dǎdàu) lí 'dírénde 'shrbù búdàu 'shrlǐde dìfang. / The enemy attacked and advanced five miles, but were soon pushed back. 'Dírén jìngūng dǎgwolai 'wúlǐ, kěshr 'yísyàdz yòu géi 'dǎhwéichyule.

(Back a person) 'yùndùng, 'twēijyǔ. / He's being pushed for the mayor's office. 'Yǒu rén jèngdzài °'yùndùng, syǎng jyàu tā (°'twēijyǔ tā) dzwò shr'jǎng.

Push a claim to (contend for) jēng; (contend to the end for) 'jēngdàu 'dǐ. / I intend to push my claim to the land. Jèikwài dì wǒ yí'dìng yàu °'jēngde (°'jēngdàu-'dǐde).

Push someone **around** (treat roughly) chǐfu, 'bālalai 'sǎngdachyu. / I've been pushed around a good deal for the last three years. Wǒ jyàu rén °'chǐfule (°'bālagwolai 'sǎngdagwochyude) yǒu 'sānnyán le.

Push off (of a boat) líàn (leave the shore). / The boat pushed off from the shore. Chwán lí'ànle.

A push is expressed verbally as in the first paragraph. / Give the car a push for me, will you? Bǎ 'chē gěi wǒ °twēi (°'dǐng) yísyar dzěmmayàng?

Other expressions in English. / Don't push your luck. Byé tài 'tān le. _or_ Byé nèmma 'tānsyīn bù'dzú. _or_ 'Tānsyīn bùkě gwò'fèn. _or_ Búyàu 'tāndéwú'yàn. / It's a pushover. 'Nèi rúngyì. _or_ 'Nèi hǎu'bàn. _or_ 'Nèi 'méi shémma.

PUT. (Place, set) gē, fàng; (set in proper place, arrange) bǎi; (set in order, in proper places) shōu; (in one's pocket) chwāi; (insert) chā; (put on by rubbing) tsá; (leave something rather than taking it away) lyàu; (drive in, of a car into a garage, etc.) 'kāijìn; (put more, add) jyā. _See also_ PACK, LAY, SET, PLACE, POUR. / Put your suitcase over here. Bǎ nǐde shǒutí'syang °gē (°fàng) 'jèr. / Put the book back where you got it. Bǎ shū °'fànghwéi (°'gēhwéi, °'bǎihwéi) ywán'láide 'dìfang chyu. / Put the tools away when you're through with them. 'Jyāhwo yùng'wánle jyou °'shōuchilai (°'shōuhwéichyu, °'gēhwéichyu). / He put the knife in his pocket. Tā bǎ 'dāudz °'gēdzài (°'fàngdzài, °'chwāidzài) °kǒu'dàrli le (°'dōurli le). / Put the flowers in this vase and put the vase on the table. Bǎ hwār 'chādzài jèige hwā'píng li, dzài bǎ hwā'píngr °bǎidzài (°fàngdzài, °gēdzài) 'jwōrshang. / Put some of this salve on, and it won't hurt so much. °'Gēshang (°'Tsáshang) dyǎr jèige 'yóu, jyòu 'búnèmma 'téng le. / Put that chair down. Bǎ yǐdz °'gēsya (°'fàngsya, °'lyàusya). / Put the car in the garage. Bǎ 'chē kāijìn chē'fángli chyu.

(Print, as in a newspaper) dēng. / The notice was put on the front page. Nèige 'chǐshr dēngdzài 'tóuyìpyārshang le.

(Express or record) syě (in writing); shwō (in words). / The report puts the facts very clearly. Jèige bàu'gàu, 'nèijyàn shr °'shwōde (°'syěde) hǎn 'chīngchu. / Put it in another way. 'Lìng yùng ge 'fāngfa lái syě. or 'Hwàn jyùhwà lái shwō. / Put it in writing. 'Syěsyàlai.

Put an end to is expressed by a verb describing the thing stopped in the constructions méi . . . le, . . . 'méile, 'bùnéng dzài . . . le, dzài bu . . . le. / This news put an end to our hopes. °'Jèi syàdz (°'Dzèmma yìlái) °méi'syīwangle (°méi'jrwangle). or Yǐ 'tīngjyàn 'jèige syāusyi wǒmen jyòu 'jrdàu °méi'syīwangle (°'méi'jrwangle).

Put across (make clear) jyàurén 'míngbai; (put into action) 'syíngchūchyu; (make people think something can be used) jyàu rén jywéje kéyǐ 'yùng. / Can this idea be put across successfully? Jèige °'yìsz (°'fádz, °'bànfa) néng jyàu byé 'rén 'míngbai ma? or 'Jèige 'bànfa °'syíngdechū'chyù ma (°néng 'syíng ma, °néng jyàu rén jywéje kéyǐ 'yùng ma)?

Put aside money lyóusyalai (save); tswúnchilai (deposit); shōuchilai (put away). / She's been putting aside a little money each month. Tā 'ywèywě °'lyóusyà (°'tswúnchi, °'shōuchi) dyǎr 'chyán lai.

Put a price or value **at** an amount gū, dìng. / They put the value of the estate at fifty thousand dollars. Lyán 'fángdz dài'dì tāmen °gūle (°dìngle) 'wǔwànkwài chyánde 'jyàr. or expressed as Their estimated price is fifty thousand dollars. Lyán 'fángdz dài'dì tāmende 'gūjyà shr 'wǔwànkwài chyán.

Put down (quell) dǎpíng, jyàupíng, píng. / The revolt was put down with little trouble. Nèi 'lwàndz méifèi'shèr jyòu °dǎ'píngle (°jyǎu'píngle, °'píngle).

Put down (write) syěsyalai. / Put down your name and address. Bǎ nǐde 'míngdz gēn 'jùjr syěsyalai.

Put in (of time) dzwò (work). / How many hours did you put in at the office last week? Nǐ 'shàng yíge lǐbài yí'gùng dzài gūngshr'fángli dzwòle 'dwōshǎu shrhoude shr?

Put (affairs) **in order** 'lyàulǐ, 'lyàulǐchǐngchu, jěngli; (wind up) 'lyǎu yilyǎu, lyǎule; (set straight) 'jěngdwùn. / He's putting his affairs in order. Tā jèngdzài bǎ tāde 'shrching dōu °'lyàuli'chǐngchule (°'jěngli jěngli).

Put off (delay) 'chyānyán(je bú'bàn), wàngsyà twēi, 'gēje bú'bàn; (neglect) lǎhu; put off until 'dēng(dàu), 'chyānyándàu, 'twēidàu or 'gēdàu followed by an expression of time and a verb of action. / He likes to put things off and then rush them through hurriedly at the last minute. Tā 'cháng bǎ shr °'gēje bú'bàn (°'chyānyánje bú'bàn, °wàngsyà 'twēi), dàule mwò'lyǎur 'jíjimáng'mángde °'fúyán'lyàushr (°'tsǎushwài'lyǎushr, °má'mǎhū'hū jyòu 'swànle). / Let's put off the decision until tomorrow. Dzámen dēng 'míngtyan dzài dǎ 'júyì ba. / Don't put off until tomorrow what you can do today. 'Jīntyan néng'bàn de 'bùkě °'twēidàu (°'chyānyándàu, °'gēdàu, °'dēngdàu) 'míngtyan bàn. or 'Fán'shr bùkě °'lǎhu (°'chyānyán).

Put off a person táng (ward off); 'fúyǎn (placate temporarily); dǎng (stop). / Can't you put him off until we have time to think it over? Nǐ néng bunéng °'táng tā yitáng (°'fúyǎnje tā), hǎu jyàu wǒmen yǒu·'gūngfu °'pánswàn pánswàn (°'dzwómwo dzwómwo, °'syǎng yisyǎng)? or Nǐ néng bunéng °'fúyǎn tā syē 'shŕhou (°'táng tā syē 'shŕhou, °'táng yitáng tā), hǎu 'rúng wǒmen °'pánswàn pánswàn (°'dzwómwo dzwómwo, °'syǎng yisyǎng)? / Put him off for three days. °'Táng (°'Fúyǎn) tā 'sāntyān dzài shwō. / I can't put him off any longer. Wǒ 'dzài yě °'tángbú'jù (°'dǎngbú'jù, °'fúyǎnbú'jù) tā le.

Put on (assume) jyǎjwāng, jyǎjwāngr; (only of an accent in speech) jwāngchyāng; (act) jwāng. / That accent isn't real; it's just put on. Nèige 'kǒuyin 'búshŕ 'jēnde, yí'dìng shŕ °'jyǎ'jwāngrde (°'jyǎ'jwāngde, °'jwāng'chyāng ne, °'jwāngde).

Put on clothes chwān(shang) (of articles of clothing which a part of the body passes through); dài(shang) (of hats, gloves, ornaments); jì(shang) (of something tied, as a tie or belt); pēi(shang) (of an outer covering, as a cape); bēi(shang) (of suspenders); chā(shang) (of ornamental pins). / Wait until I put on my coat and hat. Déng wǒ chwānshang dà'yī dàishang 'màudz.

Put out a light myè, syí; (of electric light only) gwān. / Put out the lights before you leave. 'Méichūchyu yǐ'chyán bǎ 'dēng °'myè (°'syí, °'gwān) lou.

Put out (publish) chū. / This publisher puts out some very good books. Jèige yìnshū'jyú hěn 'chūle jíbén 'hǎu shū.

Put someone **out** gěi ... jàu 'máfan (trouble); bǎ ... de shèr dōu 'dānwùle (distract). / Don't put yourself out on my account. Byé yīnwei 'wǒ °'bá nǐ 'dzjǐde shèr dōu 'dānwùle (°'gěi nǐ 'dzjí jàu 'máfan).

Put something **over on** hǔ (intimidate); mēng, pyàn, dzwàn (cheat); jyàu ... shàng'dàng (take in). / You can't put anything over on him. Nǐ hǔbu'jù tā. or Nǐ béng syǎng °'mēngdelyǎu (°'pyàndelyǎu, °'dzwàndelyǎu) tā. or Nǐ mēngbu'lyǎu tā. or Nǐ pyànbu'lyǎu tā. or Nǐ dzwànbu'lyǎu tā. or Nǐ 'méifár jyàu 'tā shàng'dàng.

Put through (vote on and pass) tūnggwò. / The bill was put through (by) Congress last week. 'Nèige yìàn gwó'hwèi 'shànglǐbài yǐjīng tūng'gwòle.

Put through a telephone call tūng, dǎ, dǎtūng. / He put through a call to his home. Tā gēn tā 'jyāli °'tūngle (°'dǎle, °'dǎ'tūngle) yítsz̀ dyàn'hwà.

Put a question **to** wèn. / The question was put to the chairman. 'Nèi shèr yǒu rén wèn jǔ'syí láije.

Put someone **to bed** jyàu ... chyù shwèi'jyàu. / I have to put the kids to bed. Wǒ děi jyàu syǎu'hár chyù shwèi'jyàu.

Put someone **to death** bǎ ... 'néngsǎle; (shooting by an executioner) bǎ ... chyāng'bìle; **be put to death** jyàu rén 'néngsǎle; (be shot by an executioner) chyāng-bìle; (by legal execution) shòu 'sǎsyíng le. / He's already been put to death. Tā yǐjīng °'shòu 'sǎsyíng le (°'chyāng'bìle, °'jyàu rén 'néngsǎle).

Put someone **to expense** °'jyàu (°'ràng) ... hwā bù'shǎude chyán. / This will put me to considerable expense. Jèige yí'dìng yàu °'jyàu (°'ràng) wǒ hwā bù'shǎude chyán.

Put to good use (of money) 'búshŕ 'swéishwéibyàn'byànde hwā; yùngde 'jèng-dàng (use rightly); yùng dzài 'jèngchù (use in the right place). / You can be sure this money will be put to good use. Nǐ 'fàngsyīn, 'jèibǐ chyán °'jywé bunéng 'swéiswéi-byàn'byànde jyòu 'hwāle (°'yí'dìng yùngde 'jèngdàng, °'yí'dìng yùng dzài 'jèngchu).

Put someone **to work** jyàu ... dzwòchǐ 'gūnglai. / They put him to work as soon as he got there. Tā yí 'dàu tāmen jyòu jyàu tā dzwòchǐ 'gūng lai le.

Put up (build) gài; syōu (of an engineering project). / This building was put up in six months. Jèige 'lóu yùngle 'lyòugè ywède 'gūngfu jyòu °gài'déle (°gài'hǎule, °gài'chéngle).

Put up (accommodate). / Can you put up some extra guests for the night? 'NĬmen jèr yòu 'dìfangr 'dwō jāudài 'jige rén 'gwò yíyè ma?

Put up (supply, provide). *See* SUPPLY, PROVIDE.

Put up for sale chūmài. / The farm will be put up for sale this week. Núng-'chǎng jèilǐbài chū'mài.

Put someone up to jyàu . . . , 'tyáusu . . . ; jyāu . . . (rather polite). / Who put him up to that trick? Shr̀ 'shéi °jyàu (°tyáusude, °jyāu) tā nèmma shr̀'hwàide? *or* Nèige hwài 'jāur shéi 'jyāu gĕi tā de?

Put up with 'rěnshòu. / I can't put up with this noise any longer. Wǒ 'bùnéng dzài 'rěnshòu 'jèijǔng 'chǎujyèr le.

Be (*or* Feel) put out. / I feel quite put out about it. Nèijyàn shèr °ràng (°jyàu) wǒ jywéje °hěn bú'tùngkwai (°tǐng 'byènyou).

Stay put bùnwówōr (not move); hǎu'hāurde dzài . . . 'dāije (remain somewhere). / I'll stay put right here until you get back. Nǐ 'méihwéilai yǐ'chyán wǒ yí'dìng °bùnwó'wōr (°hǎu'hāurde dzàijèr 'dāije).

QUALITY. (Property) -syìng, 'syìngjr̀; more commonly have the property of is expressed as can *or* can be néng, 'kéyǐ; or with a resultative compound in the potential form; or as is shr̀. / Bamboo has three special qualities; lightness, strength, and elasticity. (technical) 'Júdz yǒu 'sānjǔng °'tèsyìng (°tè'byéde 'syìngjr̀); 'chīng, jyēshr, yǒu'tánsyìng. / This medicine has the quality of dissolving in water. 'Jèjǔng yàu °yǒu rúngjyè'syìng (°dzài 'shwéili 'hwàdekāi). *or* Jèjǔng yàu °kéyǐ (°néng) dzài 'shwéili 'hwàkai.

(Characteristic) dìfang (also means place); -chù commonly in combinations as good quality 'hǎuchù, 'chángchù *or* bad quality 'hwàichù, 'dwǎnchù. / She has many good qualities. Tā yóu hěn 'dwōde °'chángchù (°'hǎuchù). / He has many qualities that I like. Tā yóu hěn 'dwōde dìfang wó hěn 'syǐhwàn. *or* Wǒ 'syǐhwàn tāde dìfang hěn 'dwō.

(Grade) 'chéngshǎi (of things only, not workmanship); usually expressed simply by saying a thing is good hǎu, bad hwài, fine jūng *or* syì *or* (especially of workmanship) 'jīngsyì, coarse tsū *or* (especially of workmanship) 'tsūtsāu, secondary tsz̀; 'chéngshǎi may be described by any of these stative verbs or as high gāu *or* low dī; quality as opposed to quantity is sometimes expressed by jr̀. / There are different qualities of cloth. Bùde 'chéngshǎi bù'túng. *or* Bù yóu 'hǎu yóu 'hwài. *or* Bù yóu 'jīng yǒu 'syì. / The better quality is, of course, more expensive. (Chéngshǎi) 'hǎude dz̀'rán jyou 'gwèi. / If it's of good quality, quantity doesn't matter. Jr̀yàu 'hǎu, 'dwōshǎu méi 'gwānsyi. / We want (good) quality, not (large) quantity. Wǒmen yàude shr̀ °'jīng (°'hǎu), bùshr̀ 'dwō. / If the quality is good, I won't dicker about the price. Jr̀yàu °'hǎu (°'chéngshǎi hǎu, °dzwòde 'hǎu, °dzwòde 'jīngsyì, °'hwò hǎu), 'jyàchyánshang hǎu'shānglyang. / It's quality that's important, not quantity. Jwòjùng dzài 'jr̀, búdzài 'lyàng. / The quality of his work has improved a great deal lately. Tā 'jìnlái dzwòde hǎu'dwōle.

Tone quality 'shēngyīn.

QUANTITY. lyàng; but more commonly expressed by words such as dwō *or* syē many *or* much, shǎu few, syǎu small, dà large, etc. / He's neglecting quantity for quality. Tā búgù 'lyàng, 'jr̀ chyóu 'jr̀. *or* Tā yàu 'chéngshǎi hǎu, dzwò'dwōdzwò-'shǎude bú'dzàihu. / He hoarded a large quantity of good liquor. Tā 'twúnjǐle °'hǎusyē (°bù'shǎude) 'shàngdéng 'jyǒu. / They say there are (large) quantities of coal underground in this region. Yǒu rén shwō 'jèiyídài dì 'dìsya yóu °'hǎusyē (°bu'shǎu) 'méi.

QUARREL. dǎjyà (refers to angry quarreling, which may include blows); nàuchǎudz, nàu'yìjyàn (refer to violent disagreement); fānlyǎn (refers to serious dispute in which the participants have a close relationship); chǎujyà, cháudzwèi, dáchǎudz, bàndzwèi (refer to any kind of arguing); nàu, chǎu, 'rāngrang (refer to a noisy wrangling, as among children); jēng (about the same as the preceding, but may include more serious dispute). *See also* FIGHT. / What are they quarreling about? Tāmen wèi 'shémma dzài nèr °'chǎu (°chǎu'jyà, °cháu'dzwěi, °dá 'chǎudz, °bàn'dzwěi, °'rāngrang)? / The children are quarreling about what game they want to play. Syǎu'hármen bùnéng 'dìnggwei wár shémma 'hǎu, dzài nèr °'chǎuchilaile (°'chǎu ne, °'nàuchilaile, °'nàu ne, °'jēngchilaile, °'jēng ne, °'rāngrangchilaile, °'rāngrang ne). / He always quarrels with people. Tā 'làu gēn rén °chǎu'jyà (°etc.).

A quarrel is expressed verbally as above. / They haven't been friends since that quarrel. Tāmen 'dztsúng 'nèitsz °chǎu'jyà (°dǎ'jyà, °cháu'dzwèi, °nàu'chǎudz, °dá'chǎudz, °bàn'dzwèi, °nàu'yìjyàn, °fān'lyàn) yǐ'hòu jyou méi'hǎugwo. / They had a quarrel about some woman. Tāmen wèile ge 'nyǔrén °chǎu'jyà (°chǎule yítsz 'jyà, °etc.).

QUARTER. (Fourth) 'sżfēnjr̄- followed by a numeral indicating how many; **three quarters** sżfēnjr̄'sān. / Each son received a quarter of the estate. Měige 'érdz déle 'sżfēnjr̄'yíde 'jyāchǎn.

(Twenty-five cents) 'lyǎngmáu'wǔ(fēn chyán). / It costs a quarter to get to the theater. Dàu syì'ywándz chyu děi hwā 'lyǎngmáu'wǔ.

(Fifteen minutes) -kè (measure used with jūng). / The train leaves at quarter of three. Hwǒ'chē chà yí'kè sāndyǎn 'kāi. *or* Hwǒ'chē 'lyángdyǎn sān'kè 'kāi. / The train leaves at quarter after three. Hwǒ'chē 'sāndyǎn yí'kè 'kāi. / We waited there for three-quarters of an hour. Wǒmen dzài nèr 'děngle 'sānkè jūng.

Quarters (place to live) 'jùde (dìfang); (field headquarters) syíng'yíng. / His quarters are near the camp. °Tā 'jùde (dìfang) (°Tāde syíng'yíng) lí 'yíngpán bù-'ywǎn.

(Area) dìfang, with -chù as measure. / He has a very bad reputation in certain quarters. is expressed as The people of certain quarters speak very ill of him. 'Yǒu jichù 'dìfangde rén 'mà tā màde 'lìhai. or as . . . feel he is worthless. 'Yǒu jichù 'dìfangde rén jywéje tā 'búshr 'dūngsyi.

To quarter (divide into four parts) 'chyēcheng °sż'bàr (°sżfèr) (by cutting); for other methods of dividing substitute other verbs for chyē. / She quartered the apples. Tā bǎ 'pínggwǒ dōu 'chyēcheng °sż'bàr (°sżfèr).

Be quartered (stationed) 'jùjá. / The soldiers were quartered in an old house near the fort. Lí 'yíngpán bù'ywǎn, yǒu yìswór 'lǎu fángdz, bìng dou dzài nèr 'jùjá.

QUEEN. (Wife of a king) hwánghòu; (female ruler) nyǔwáng, nyǔhwáng. / This magazine has a picture of the queen. Jèibèr 'dzájr̄ dēngle yìjāng °hwáng'hòude (°nyǔ-'wángde, °nyǔ'hwángde) syàng'pyār.

QUESTION. (Inquiry or point of uncertainty) 'wèntí; (something asked) wènde; (the words of something asked) wènde hwà; (something someone wants to ask) yàu wènde, (yàu)'chǐngjyàude (more polite); (an unclear point) bù'míngbaide (dìfang), or often expressed verbally as to ask wèn; (want to find out about something from someone) yàu gēn . . . 'dǎtīng, (more polite) yàu gēn . . . 'lǐngjyàu, (yàu) chǐng . . . 'jr̄jyàu;

questions and answers 'wèntí dá'àn. /What you said is a statement, not a question.
Nǐ 'shwō de shr̀ nǐde 'yìjyàn, 'búshr ge 'wèntí. /Why don't you put it in the form
of a question? Nǐ 'bùrú bǎ jèige yùng 'wèntí lái 'wènwen. /Have you answered all
the questions? °'Wèn de (°'Wèntí) 'dōu dále ma? /What you said didn't answer my
question. Nǐ 'dá de búshr wǒ 'wèn de. /Do you understand my question? Wǒ 'wèn
de 'hwà nǐ 'dǔng ma? /What was your question: Nǐ wèn 'shémma laije? /Any
questions? Yǒu shémma °'wèntí (°yàu 'wèn de) ma? /If there are any questions,
raise your hand. Yǒu °'wèntí (°yàu 'wén de), jyou jyǔ'shǒu. /Would you like to
ask any questions? Ní yǒu yàu wèn de 'shr̀ ma? or Ní syǎng 'wèn shémma ma?
or Nǐ yàu 'wèn shémma ma? /I have a question here. (polite expressions) 'Chǐngjyàu, 'chǐngjyàu. or Wó yǒu yì'dyǎn °yàu 'chǐngjyàu de (°bù'míngbai de, °yàu
(gēn nín) 'lǐngjyàu, °yàu chǐng nín 'jr̀jyàu). or (neutral expressions) Wǒ jèr yǒu ge
'wèntí. or Wó yǒu yì'dyǎn yàu 'wèn de. or (impolite expressions) Wǒ 'wèn nǐ.
or Wǒ yàu 'wèn nǐ yíjyàn 'shr̀. /I want to ask you a question. (polite) Wó yǒu yìdyǎn bù'míngbai de dìfang, kéyǐ 'wèn ma? or Wó yǒu yì'dyǎn bù'míngbai de dìfang,
°gēn nín 'lǐngjyàulǐngjyàu (°chǐng nín géi 'jr̀jyàujr̀jyàu). or (neutral) Wǒ yàu gēn
nǐ 'dǎtīngdǎtīng. /They asked me a lot of questions about my past experience. Tāmen
°'pánwèn (°'wènláiwèn'chyùde wèn, °'dzwǒwènyòuwènde 'wèn) wǒ °dōu 'dzwǒgwo
shémma 'shèr (°de 'lyǔlǐ laije).

(Matter of doubt) 'wèntí. /Then the question of his qualification came up for
discussion. 'Hòulái 'tǎulwùndau tāde 'dzgé wèntí. /There is no question about his
ability. Tāde 'tsáigàn °'méiyǒu (°'bùchéng) wèntí.

(Problem) 'wèntí; often indirectly expressed by saying that something is hard
to do nán bàn; or easy to do rúngyi bàn, etc. See PROBLEM. /It's a question to
know what to do in this situation. 'Jèijǔng 'chíngsyíng hěn nán 'bàn. or Dàu 'jèige
'dìbu hěn nán 'bàn.

Beyond question (unquestionably) 'háuwú'yíwènde; (cannot be questioned) 'yùngbujáu 'wèn le. /His honesty is beyond question. Tā 'háuwú'yíwènde shr̀ yíge hěn
'chéngshr̀ de rén. or Tā hěn °'chéngshr̀ (°kě'kàu), nèi 'yùngbujáu 'wèn le.

Out of the question yí'dìng bù'syíng, 'jywédwèi bù'syíng. /It's out of the
question for me to leave the job. 'Yàu syǎng 'jyàu wó bǎ shèr 'rēngsya °yí'dìng
(°'jywédwèi) bù'syíng.

Without question yídìng, jwǔn. See also CERTAINLY. /He'll be there without
question. Tā yí'dìng dàu. or Tā 'jwǔn dàu.

To question someone 'pánwèn (ask many questions of); 'shěnwèn (by authorities;
of a person under arrest). /The prisoners will be hold for questioning. 'Fúlwo děi
'yāchilai °'shěnwèn (°'pánwèn).

Question something (doubt) 'yísyīn (suspect that); jywéje (feel that) followed
by a negative verb. /I question the sincerity of his speech. Wǒ °'yísyīn (°'jywéje)
tā 'shwōde 'búshr 'jēnsyīn'hwà.

QUICK. (General term) kwài; (quick and efficient) 'málì; (nimble, active) hwó, língbyan; or expressed adverbially as in a hurry gānkwài or as immediately 'gǎnjǐn,
'děngshr, lìke, 'dāngshr, mǎshàng; also other adverbial expressions. /Be quick
about it! 'Kwàije! or 'Kwài'kwārde! or Gěi wǒ °'gǎnjǐn (°lì'kè, °'dāngshr,
°'děngshr, °ma'shàng) jyou 'bàn. /His answer was quick and to the point. Tā 'hwéi-
dáde yòu 'kwài yòu 'chyàdang. /His hands aren't quick enough for this sort of work.
Dzwò 'jèijǔng shr̀ tāde 'shǒu búgòu °'kwàide (°'málìde). /He's certainly quick on
his feet! Tā °'pǎude (°'tyàudade, °'twěijyǎur) jēn °'kwài (°'hwó, °'língbyan)!

(Of temper) jí, dzàu, 'jídzàu. /She has a very quick temper. Tā 'píchì hěn
°'jí (°'dzàu, °'jídzàu).

Be quick to is expressed as one instant (or one look or one listen, etc.) immediately °'yísyàdz (°yí'kàn, °yí'tǐng, °etc.) jyou . . . le. / Don't be so quick to take offense. Byé nèmma 'yísyàdz jyou 'nǎule. / He was quick to catch on. Tā yì-sywé jyou 'hwèile. *or* Tā yì'tǐng jyou 'dǔngle. *or* Tā yí'kàn jyou 'míngbaile. *or* Tā 'yísyàdz jyou 'tǔngle.

Quick-witted, quick on the trigger 'syīnsz (tǐng) 'kwàide, syǎngde (tǐng) 'kwàide, (tǐng) jīlingde, (tǐng) 'línglide, yǒu 'jíjr̀. / He's pretty quick-witted; he'll always have an immediate answer for your questions. Tā °'syīnsz tǐng 'kwàide (°syǎngde tǐng 'kwàide, °tǐng jīlingde, °tǐng 'línglide, °hén yǒu 'jíjr̀); yì 'tíchi 'shémma lai, tā 'dōu néng lì'kè jyou 'hwéi nǐ yítàu 'hwà.

Cut someone to the quick jyàu . . . 'hěn bú'tùngkwai, gěi . . . dǎng tóu yí'bàng. / His statements cut me to the quick. Tā 'shwōde °jyàu wǒ 'hěn bú'tùngkwai (°gěi wǒ dǎng tóu yí'bàng).

QUICKLY. kwài, gǎnkwài; (immediately) 'gánjǐn, 'děngshŕ, lìkè, 'dāngshŕ, mǎshàng. / Shut the door, quickly! Bǎ mén 'gwānshang, °'kwàije dyar (°'kwàije, °kwài 'chyù)! *or* °'Kwài (°Kwài'kwārde, °Gǎn'kwài) bǎ mén 'gwānshang! / If we work quickly we can finish in two weeks. Yàushr wǒmen 'kwài dzwò lyǎngge syīngchī kéyǐ dzwò'wán. / He's a man who's able to make decisions quickly. Tā jèi rén 'shémma shŕ °'děngshŕ (°'dāngshŕ, °lì'kè °mǎ'shàng) jyou néng jywédìng. / I'll be there as quickly as I can. Wǒ dàu nèr néng 'dwō kwài jyou 'dwō kwài. / It was all over so quickly that I didn't even see it. underline{is expressed as} In one instant it was immediately over, I still hadn't seen it. 'Yísyàdz jyou 'wánle, wǒ hái méi'kànjyan.

QUIET. (Without noise or confusion) 'ānjìng, jìng; (only of a place) 'chīngjìng; (of profound stillness) 'chénjìng; (peaceful and quiet) 'píngjìng; (of a person, quiet in manner) 'szszwén'wén(de); or negatives of words meaning noisy dzwò'shēngr, chū'shēngr, chǎu, 'rāngrang *or* rowdy 'nàuhung *or* mischievous hú'nàu, táu'chǐ. / I live in a quiet neighborhood. Wǒ 'jù de nèi yídài hěn °'ānjìng (°'jìng, °'chīngjìng). / It's as quiet as night around here. Jèr °'ānjìngde (°'jìngde, °'chīngjìngde, °'chénjìngde) syàng dzài 'yèli shr̀de. / He's so quiet you would never know he's around. Tā 'ānjìngde nǐ tsúnglái bù'jywéde tā 'dzài jèr. / He's very quiet. Tā rén hěn 'ānjìng. *or* Tā 'lǎu °búdzwò'shēngr (°bùchū'shēngr). *or* Tā lǎu nèmma °'ānānjìng'jìngrde (°'szszwén'wénde).

(With little current) lyóude hwǎn, lyóude màn, lyóude bù'jí. / This stream isn't quiet enough. Jèige 'hégōurde 'shwěi lyóude tài 'jí. / It's very quiet two miles upstream, though. Wàng shàng dzǒu 'èrlǐ shwěi lyóude °'hwǎn'dwōle (°'màn'dwōle).

(Not bright, of colors) 'sù(shǎrde). / She always dresses in quiet colors. Tā lǎu shr̀ chwān 'sù(shǎrde) 'yīfu.

Quiet (silence) is expressed verbally as in the first paragraph. / We've learned to enjoy the quiet of the country. Wǒmen jyàn'jyànde néng 'lǐnghwèi syāngsya °'ānjìngde (°'chénjìngde) 'hǎuchù le.

To quiet (calm someone) bǎ . . . 'yāsyachyu, bǎ . . . 'jènjìngsyachyu. / His speech quieted the crowd. 'Tā nèi yìfān 'hwà bǎ rén dōu °'yāsyachyule (°'jènjìngsyachyule).

Quiet down. / Quiet down, please! 'Ānjìng dzar! *or* Byé 'chǎu le! *or* Byé 'rāngrang le! / He'll quiet down a bit when he grows up. underline{is expressed as} Wait until he's older and he won't be so rowdy. Děng tā 'dà dyǎr jyou 'bùnèmma °'nàuhung le (°hú'nàu le, °táu'chǐle).

QUIT. (Stop doing something). / Quit it! (making trouble) Byé dǎulwàn! *or* (being rowdy) Byé hǔnàu! *or* Byé húlài! *or* (talking nonsense) 'Byé syǎ'shwō le! *or* 'Byé syǎ'jyǎng le! *or* 'Byé hú'shwō le! *or* (talking) 'Béng shwō le!

(Stop work according to schedule) syàgūng. / I quit at five. Wǒ 'wǔdyǎn jūng syà'gūng.

(Leave something for a time) gēsya. / Why don't you quit what you're doing and come out for a walk? Nǐ 'wèi shémma bùbá nǐ dzwò de shèr 'gēsya, gēn wǒmen chūchyu °'dzóudzǒu (°'lyóudalyōuda)?

(Leave a job permanently) dzǒu, búgàn le, bǎ shr̀ching 'tszle, bǎ shr̀ching 'lyàusya jyou bú'gàn le. / He quit (his job) yesterday. Tā 'dzwór °dzǒule (°bú-'gàn le, °bǎ shr̀ching 'tszle, °bǎ shr̀ching 'lyàusya jyou bú'gànle).

(Surrender) tóusyáng; (ask for peace) jyǎnghé, chyóuhé. / The enemy refuses to quit. 'Dírén bùkěn °tou'syáng (°jyǎng'hé, °chyóu'hé).

QUITE. (With meaning ranging from somewhat to very) tǐng, hěn, syāngdāng, yóu dyǎr; (local Peiping) -je(de)ne. / The movie was quite good. Dyàn'yǐngr tǐng °'hǎu (°yóu-'yǐszde). or Dyàn'yǐngr hěn bú'hwài. / It turned out to be quite cold during the night. 'Jyēgwó 'wǎnshang °tǐng (°hěn, °syāngdāng, °yóu dyǎr) 'lyáng. / I live quite near here. Wǒ 'jù de 'lí jèr °tǐng 'jìn (°'hěn jìn, °'jìnjene). / He has quite a lot of money in the bank. Tā dzài yín'hángli 'hén yǒu jige 'chyán. / There were quite a few people there. 'Dàude rén hěn °'dwō (°bù'shǎu). or 'Dàule syāngdāng'dwōde rén.

Quite a plus a noun jen plus a description indicating goodness, badness, interest, etc. / That was quite an experience we had yesterday. 'Dzwórge dzámen °nèi'dwàr (°nèijyàn 'shèr) jēn °ké'yǐde a (or (all that could be asked for) °gòu'chyáude, or (all that could be borne) °gòu'shòude)!

Not quite (is still lacking) 'chà dyǎr, 'chà yidyǎr, 'chàbudwō (may be followed by jyǒu plus a verb); 'búda plus a stative verb. / That's not quite what I wanted. Jèige 'chà dyǎr. or (not quite right) Jèige búda 'dwèi. / It's not quite finished. or I'm not quite finished. 'Chà yidyǎr jyou 'wánle. or Chàbudwō jyou 'wánle. or 'Méiwán ne, hái 'chà dyar.

Not quite plus a numerical expression budàu. / It'll come to not quite five dollars. Yí'gùng budàu 'wǔkwai chyán. / I have been here not quite three months. Wǒ 'láile budàu 'sānge ywè.

Be quite sure that (in statements, meaning in all probability) 'dwōbàn; (in questions, meaning know for certain) 'jwǔn jr̀dàu, 'jēn jr̀dàu, or expressed as dare to say for certain 'jwún gǎn shwō, or as certainly jēnshr. / I'm quite sure I can go. Wǒ 'dwōbàn néng 'chyù. / Are you quite sure that you can't go? Nǐ 'jēnshr bùnéng 'chyù ma? / Are you quite sure that he's the guy? °Nǐ 'jwǔn jr̀dàu (°Nǐ 'jēn jr̀dau, °Nǐ 'jwún gǎn shwō) shr̀ 'tā ma?

Other expressions in English. / Quite so. or Oh, quite! Méi tswòr. or 'Hěn dwèi. or 'Jēngshr̀. or Yì'dyǎr bú'tswò. or 'Jyòushr 'nèmmaje. or Kě bú'shr̀ ma?

RACE. (A contest of speed; competition) bǐsài, in compounds sài- or pǎu-; race between persons sàipǎu. / The races will be held next week. 'Syà lǐ'bài °bǐ'sài (°sài-'mǎ, °sài'chē, °etc.). / Are you going to the (automobile) races this afternoon? Nǐ jyèr 'syàwǔ chyù 'kàn sài 'chē ma? / His horse won every race, is expressed as His horse won every time. 'Tāde mǎ hwéi'hwér 'yíng. / He made a lot of money on the horse races. is expressed as He bought tickets on the horses and won a lot of money. Tā mǎi mǎ'pyàu yíngle bùshǎude 'chyán. / It was a race for us to get to the station on time. is expressed as We had to rush not to miss the train. Wǒmen déi 'jǐnje 'gǎn tsái méi'wùle 'chē. or as We ran to the station to get the train. Wǒmen 'jǐnje 'pǎu dàu chē 'jàn tsái 'gǎnshàng 'chē.

(People of same ancestry) 'jǔng rén; **white race** báijǔngrén; **yellow race** hwángjǔngrén; **black race** hēijǔngrén; **red race** húngjǔngrén. / What is your race? Nǐ 'shǔyú 'něi 'jǔng 'rén? / The French and English belong to the same race. 'Yīnggworén gēn 'Fàgworén túng'jǔng.

Human race rénlèi; lèi means class or group and is found in compounds such as 'chùlèi (animal class) or 'nyǎulèi (bird class). / He's an enemy of the whole human race. 'Tā shr̀ chywán rén'lèide gūng'dí. / He hates the whole human race. is expressed as He hates absolutely everybody. 'Swóyǒude 'rén tā 'dōu hèn.

To race (have a contest for speed) sài, bǐ, bǐsài, chyǎngje (kàn shéi syān 'dàu). / I'll race you. Wǒ gēn nǐ 'sàisai. / The two boats raced into the harbor. Jèilyǎngjr̄ 'chwán 'chyǎngje 'kāijìn hǎi'gǎng chyùle. / I'll race you to that schoolhouse. is expressed as Let's see which of us runs to that schoolhouse first. Kàn dzámma 'lyǎ 'shwéi syān 'pǎudàu nèige sywé'syàu nar chyù.

(Go fast; of persons or animals) is expressed as run pǎu; (of vehicles) 'fēikwàide 'kāi. / The dog raced down the road. Gǒu dzài 'jyēshang jr̄ 'pǎu. / The car raced past the bridge. Nèilyàng 'chē 'fēikwàide 'kāigwo 'chyáu chyù le.

Race a motor or **engine**. / Why are you racing the engine? is expressed as Why are you making the motor go so fast? Nǐ 'wèishémma jyàu 'jīchi jwànde nèmma 'kwài?

RADIO. wúsyàndyàn; (receiving set) shōuyīnjī. / Do you have a radio here? Nǐ 'jèr yǒu wúsyàn'dyàn ma?

To radio (transmit a message by radio) yùng wúsyàn'dyàn 'dǎ lai (radio in) or 'da chūchyù (radio out). / The news was radioed to us. Jèige syāusyi shr̀ yùng wúsyàn'dyàn 'dǎláide.

RAILROAD. tyělù; (company) tyělùjyú; (train) hwǒche; **railroad track** hwǒchēdàu; **railroad station** hwǒchējàn. / A new railroad will be built soon. Yàu 'syōu yí'táu syīn tyě'lù le. / The railroad offers a cheap rate on Saturday. Tyělù'jyú gwēi'dìng lǐbài'lyòu chēpyàu jyǎn'jyà. / He works for the railroad. Tā dzài tyě'lùshang dzwò-'shr̀. / The railroad track is torn up beyond the city. Chéng 'nèibyarde hwǒchē'dàu 'chāile.

To railroad someone or something. / They railroaded the bill through the House. is expressed as They rushed and got the bill passed in the House. Syàyìywàn 'chyǎngje jyóu bǎ jèige yì'àn 'tūnggwòle.

RAIN. yǔ; **drop of rain** dyǎr; **rainstorm** 'bàuyǔ, dà'fēngyǔ, bàu'fēngyǔ, kwáng'fēngbàu'yǔ. / A light rain made the street wet. Yíjèn syǎu'yǔ bǎ jyēshang dōu jyāu-'shr̄le. / Only a few drops of rain have fallen. Gwāng 'dyàule jǐge 'dyǎr. / The rains started late this year. 'Jīnnyán yú'shwěi 'wǎn.

To rain syàyǔ, dyàu 'dyǎr. / It rained hard during the morning. 'Dzǎushang yǔ 'syàde hěn 'dà. / It's beginning to rain. Dyàu 'dyǎrle.

RAISE. (Elevate) kāi. / We'd better get in, they've raised the curtain. Dzámen 'jìnchyu ba, 'syǐ yǐjīng kāi'mùle. / How about raising that window a bit? Kai yidyǎr 'chwāng ba.

(Grow) jùng. / They raise wheat. Tāmen jung 'màidz.

(Of farm animals) yǎng. / He raises hogs. Tā yǎng 'jū.

Raise an army jāu, lyàn. / The country raised a large army. Jèi 'gwó °'jāule (°'lyànle) hěn 'dwōde 'bīng.

Raise a family yǎng. / They raised a big family. Tāmen 'yǎngle yí'dàjyādz.

or expressed as There are a lot of children in their family. Tāmen 'jyāli 'háidz hěn 'dwō. *but* /He was raised in China. Tā shr dzài 'Jūnggwō jǎng'dàle de.

Raise <u>money</u> jywān. /How large a sum did they raise? Tāmen yí'gùng jywānle 'dwōshau chyán?

Raise <u>a question</u> tíchulai. /He raised a very interesting question. Tā 'tíchulai yíge hén you'yìszde 'wèntí.

Raise <u>a flag</u> shēng, gwàchilai. /The soldiers raised the flag. Jèisyē 'bīng bǎ 'chídz °'shēngchilaile (°'gwàchilaile).

Raise <u>a price</u> jǎngjyàr, jyājyàr, bǎ 'jyàchyán tí'gāule. /He's raised the price of this book. Tā bǎ jèibér 'shūde 'jyàchyán tígāule. *or* Jèibér 'shū tā °jǎng'jyàrle (°jyǎ'jyàrle).

Raise <u>one's hand</u> jyúshǒu. /If you want a ticket please raise your hand. Shéi yàushr yàu 'pyàu dehwà, jyú 'shǒu.

Raise <u>one's hat</u> jāi màudz. /When she came by, he raised his hat. Nèige 'nyǚde gwòlai de shŕhou, tā bǎ 'màudz 'jāile.

Raise <u>wages</u> jǎng 'gūngchyán; **raise salary** jyāsyīn. /Should we raise their wages? Wǒmen 'yīnggāi gěi tāmen jǎng 'gūngchyán ma?

A raise (in pay) <u>is expressed as</u> **raise wages** *or* **salary** (see above). /He asked for a raise. Tā 'yāuchyóu °jyā'syīn (°jǎng'chyán).

RANGE. (Variety) <u>is expressed indirectly</u>. /What is his range of prices? <u>is expressed as</u> His prices go from how much to how much? /Tā nèr de 'jyàchyán shŕ tsúng 'dwōshau dàu 'dwōshau? /The store had only a small range of colors to choose from. <u>is expressed as</u> The store didn't have many kinds of colors to choose from. Jèi 'pùdz 'méiyou 'dwōshau °jǔng (°yáng r) 'yánshar kě 'tyāu de. /He has a wide range of interests. <u>is expressed as</u> The things he likes are many. Tā 'syǐhwān de 'dūngsyi hěn 'dwō. /His voice has a very wide range. <u>is expressed as</u> His voice can go high and low. Tāde 'sǎngdz néng 'gāu néng 'dī. /His voice has a very narrow range. <u>is expressed as</u> His voice when high can't go very high, and when low can't go very low. 'Tāde sǎngdz gāu yě 'gāubùshàngchyù 'dwōshǎu, 'dī yě 'dī búsyà'chyù dwō-'shǎu.

(Distance). /Are we out of range of hearing? <u>is expressed as</u> Can people hear us? Rén 'hái néng 'tīngdejyàn wǒmen shwō'hwà ma? /Wait till the wolf is within (firing) range and then shoot. 'Děngdàu láng dàule shèchéng yǐ'nèi dzài 'fàng. <u>or</u> (if you're the one who's moving) <u>expressed as</u> Wait till the gun can get the wolf, then shoot. Děngdàu 'chyāng 'gòude'jáu nèityáu 'láng de 'shŕhou dzài 'fàng.

(Grazing land) tsǎudì. /The cattle were turned out on the range. Nyóu dōu 'fàngchūchyù dzài tsǎu'dìlǐ ne.

(Area for practicing shooting) chǎng; **rifle range** báchǎng. /You can find him at the rifle range. Nǐ 'kéyǐ dàu bá'chǎng chyù 'jǎu tā.

(Of mountains) dàu. /We will cross the range of mountains tomorrow. Wǒmen 'myéngr yàu 'gwò jèidàu 'shān.

(Stove) lúdz. /Light the range. Bǎ 'lúdz 'lúngshang.

To range (be within the limits of). /Prices range from one to five dollars. <u>is expressed as</u> Prices go from one to five dollars. 'Jyàchyán shŕ tsúng 'yíkwài dàu 'wǔkwài.

(Wander). /Wolves range over this valley. Cháng yǒu 'láng dzài jèi shān-'gǔli °ráu (°páulái pǎuchyù).

RANK. (Row) pái; **form ranks** jàndwèi, páidwèi. / Only the front rank had guns. 'Jř yǒu 'chyánpáide bīng yǒu 'chyāng. / The soldiers formed ranks. Jèisyē 'bīng páidwēile.

(Position, title) jyēji. / He had the rank of captain. Tāde 'jyēji shř shàng'wèi.

(Class, grade) děng, lyóu. / That university is of the first rank. Nèige dà-'sywé shř °dì'yīděngde (°dì'yīlyóude, °jyá'děngde) sywé'fǔ. or expressed as That university is very good. Nèige dà'sywé shř díng'hǎude.

Come up from the ranks dāng'bīng chū'shēn, dǎ dāng'bīng 'shēngshanglai. / That major has come up from the ranks. Nèige shàu'syàu shř °dāng 'bīng chū-'shēn (°dǎ dāng'bīng 'shēngshanglaide).

To rank (grade). / How would you rank him in efficiency? is expressed as How well do you think he works? Nǐ 'jwède tā bàn'shř dzěmmayàng? / He doesn't rank very highly with me. is expressed as I don't regard him as worth much. Wǒ kàn tā °'méi shémma lyǎubu'dé (°'bùdzěmma'yàng).

(Be graded as) is expressed as be shř or count as swàn. / He ranks second in popularity among all the movie stars. Swǒ'yǒude 'dyànyǐngr míng'syīngli tā shř dì'èrge dzwèi shòuhwān'yíng de. / This city ranks high in importance. Jèige 'chéng 'swàn shř hěn jùngyàude 'yíge.

RAPID. kwài; or expressed adverbially with kwàikwārde, gǎnje, mángje, jǐnje. See **RAPIDLY, FAST, HURRY.** / He made a rapid journey. Tā °kwài'kwārde (°'gǎnje, °etc.) 'dzǒule yí'tàng. / There has been a rapid increase in population. Rén'kǒu dzēng'jyāde hěn 'kwài.

Rapids jílyóu; or expressed with shwěilyóu (current). / The rapids are stronger this year than last. Jīnnyánde °jí'lyóu (°shwěi'lyóu) bǐ 'chyùnyán gèng °'jí (°'dà).

RAPIDLY. kwài, kwàikwārde, gǎnje, mánje, jǐnje. / He walked rapidly away. Tā hěn kwài jyòu 'dzǒule. / He worked rapidly for a long time but still didn't finish. Tā gǎnje dzwòle bàn'tyān, kěshr hái méi dzwò'hǎu. / He spoke so rapidly I missed what he said. Tā shwōde tài kwài, kwàide wǒ meitīng chīngchu tā shwō de (shr shémma).

RATE. (Charge or fee) fèi, dz̄; (price) jyàr, 'jyàchyán; **special rate** yōudài. / The postage rate is six cents an ounce. °'Yóufèi (°'Yóudz̄) shř 'měiyí'lyǎng 'lyóufēn chyán. / He charges more than the regular rate. Tā 'yàude bǐ píng'chángde °'jyàchyán (°'jyàr)°dwō (°'dà). / Is there a special rate for this tour? Jèi yítsz̄ lyǔ-'syíng yǒu méiyǒu yōudài 'bànfǎ?

(Class, grade) děng. / This restaurant is definitely first rate. Jèige jywé-'dwèi shř dì'yīděngde fàngwǎr.

At any rate 'bùgwǎn dzěmmayàng. / He arrived here today; at any rate his baggage is here. Tā jīntyān 'dàule, 'bùgwǎn dzěmma'yàng, tāde 'syíngli 'dàule. / We think this is the best plan; at any rate we will try it. Wǒmen 'jywéde jèige 'jìhwa 'dzwèi hǎu, 'bùgwán dzěmma'yàng, wǒmen yàu 'shřshr kàn.

At the rate of. / You can pay for it at the rate of five dollars a week. is expressed as You can pay five dollars a week for this. Jèige nǐ 'kéyǐ 'měilǐbài 'fù 'wǔkwài chyán. / This car can go at the rate of sixty miles per hour. Jèilyàng 'chē 'měidyǎnjūng 'néng dzǒu 'lyòushr lǐ.

At this or **that rate** jàu 'jèiyàng. / The work is too much for one man; at this rate we will need other helpers. Jèijyàn 'shř 'yíge rén 'dzwòbùlyǎu, jàu 'jèiyàng, wǒmen 'hái déi 'jàu jǐge bāng'mángrde.

To **rate** (deserve) yǐng'dāng dé. / He rates a reward for that. Tā nèige yǐng-'dāng dé 'jyǎng de. / That exam paper rates an A. Nèibèr kǎu'jywàr yǐnd'dāng dé A.

(Rank). *See* RANK. / He was rated most popular man in his class. 'Tā dzài tā 'bānlǐtou 'swàn shr̀ yíge 'dzwèi shòurénhwàn'yíng de rén le.

RATHER. (A little) dyǎr, syāngdāngde. / It is rather cold on deck. Jyá'bǎnshang 'yǒu dyǎr 'lěng. / The play was rather long. 'Syì syāng'dāngde 'cháng. / It seems rather early to decide. Syàn'dzài 'jywédìng 'sz̀hū hái 'dzǎu dyǎr.

. . . **rather than** . . . (actually . . . not . . .) chí'shr̀ . . . bùnéng 'swàn . . . . / This is a small trunk rather than a suitcase. Chí'shr̀ jèige shr̀ yíge syǎu 'syāngdz bùnéng 'swàn tí'bāu.

Or rather (actually) chí'shr̀ ne. / I was running, or rather walking quickly. Wǒ 'pǎu láije, chí'shr̀ ne, wǒ jr̀ néng 'shwō kwài'kwārde 'dzǒu láije. / His mother, or rather his father, is foreign born. is expressed as His mother—no, it's his father—is foreign born. Tā 'mǔchin shr̀, 'bùshr̀, shr̀ tā 'fùchin shr̀ dzài 'wàigwo shēngde.

Would rather chíngywàn, háishr, syǎng, all expressing a rather mild prefer-ence; 'níngkě, expressing a strong preference, making a decision that may entail sacrifice, etc. / Would you rather come with us? Nǐ °chíng'ywàn (°'háishr 'ywànyi, °'syǎng) gēn wǒmen yíkwàr 'dzǒu ma? / I don't feel well and I'd rather stay at home. Wǒ 'jywéde bù'shūfu, °'háishr dzài jyā 'dāije ba (°'bùsyǎng 'chūchyù le). / We would rather stay at home than hurt her feelings. Wǒmen chíng'ywàn dzài'jyāli 'dāi-je, yě bú'ywànyi 'jyàu tā nán'shòu. / I'd rather have ice cream. Wǒ háishr yàu bīngjī'líng ba. / I'd rather die than do it. Wǒ 'níngké 'sž yě bú'gàn.

RAW. (Uncooked or unprocessed) shēngde; **raw silk** 'shēngsz̄; **raw cotton** myánhwa; **raw material** ywánlyàu. / She eats only raw vegetables. Tā jr̀ 'chr̄ 'shēngde chīng-'tsài. / This meat is nearly raw. Jèikwài 'ròu chàbu'dwō hai 'shēngje ne. / The raw material must be shipped in. Ywán'lyàu yídìng yàu 'yùnjìnchyù.

(Inexperienced) 'méiyǒu jīngyàn de; (new) syīn; (untrained) méi'shǒugwo 'syùn-lyàn de. / He had only raw soldiers to use for the work. Tā 'jr̀ yǒu °'syīnbīng (°'méiyǒu 'jīngyàn de bīng, °méi'shòugwo 'syùnlyàn de bīng) kě 'yùng.

(Sore; chapped) shānle; (scraped) mwópwòle. / Her face is raw from the wind. 'Tāde 'lyǎn jyàu 'fēng gwā'shānle. / The horse has a raw spot on its back. Mǎ-'bèishang mwó'pwòle.

(Damp and cold) yòu 'cháu yòu 'lyáng. / There's a raw wind today. 'Jyērde 'fēng yòu 'cháu yòu 'lyáng.

RAY. (Beam of light) yídàu gwāng, °yidàu (°'yìtyáu) gwāng'syàn; (a tiny sliver of light) yì'dyǎr lyàngr, yí'syànde gwāng. / If you turn the lights off, you can see a ray of light through that crack. Yàu bǎ 'dēng 'gwānshang jyòu kéyi kǎnjyan tsúng nèige 'fèngrli 'tòujinlai °yí'dàu 'gwāng (°yìtyáu gwāng'syàn, °yí'syànde gwāng, °yí'dyǎr lyàngr). / We couldn't see even a ray of light. Lyán °yí'syànde gwāng (°yí'dyǎr lyàngr) yě kànbu'jyàn.

A ray of hope yí'syànde 'syīwàng. / There is not a ray of hope that he will live. Tā jèi'tyáu 'mìng shr̀ yí'syànde 'syīwàng dōu 'méiyǒule.

REACH. (Make a motion toward, without much effort; reach for) 'shēnshǒu yàu 'ná; (reach for something in one's pocket) tāu; (reach for something, when it involves stretching and effort) gòu; (reach for and touch) gòudejáu. / He reached for his gun.

Tā tāu 'chyāng. *or* Tā 'shēnshǒu yàu ná 'chyāng. *or* Tā 'gòu tāde 'chyāng. /Can you reach the sugar? Nǐ 'gòudejáu nèi táng'gwàr ma?

(Extend to) dàu or in compounds -dàu; (touch) jān. /The garden reaches to the river. Jèige 'hwāywàr yi'jr̄ dàu hé'byār nèr. /His power reaches everywhere. Dàu'chù dōu 'yǒu tāde 'shr̄lì. *or* Tāde 'shr̄lì shēn'jǎngdàu 'gèchù. /This curtain reaches the floor. 'Jèige lyándz 'chángde jān'dìle. or expressed as This curtain hangs to the floor. 'Jèige lyándz 'chángde °dāledàu 'dìshang le (°dzài 'dìshang 'dāleje).

(Arrive at) dàu. /Your letter didn't reach me until today. 'Nǐde 'syìn 'jīntyān tsái 'dàu. /Tell me when we reach the city. 'Dàu nèi chéng de 'shr̄hou, 'chǐng nǐ 'gàusu wǒ yi'shēngr. /He has reached the retirement age. Tā 'dàule gàu'lǎude 'swèishu le.

(Find, get at) jǎujau. /There was no way of reaching him. 'Méiyou 'fádz 'jǎujau tā.

Out of reach *or* **beyond one's reach.** /Put the candy out of his reach. is expressed as Put the candy so he can't reach it. Bǎ 'táng 'gēde 'jyàu tā gòubu'jáu. /Such patience is out of my reach. is expressed as I don't have great patience. 'Wǒ méi nèmma 'dàde nàisyīn'fár. or as I can't be so patient. 'Wó kě 'méi nèmma nàifár. /Such food is beyond the reach of poor people. is expressed as Poor people can't buy such food. 'Jèijǔng 'dūngsyi 'chyúngrén 'chr̄bu'chǐ.

READ. kàn; (read aloud or study) nyàn. /Please read the instructions. Chǐng 'kàn jèige 'shwōmíngshū. /Have you read your mail yet? Nǐ 'kànle nǐde 'syìn le ma? /I have read somewhere that this is false. Wǒ yě bù'jr̄dau shr̄ dzài 'nǎr °nyàngwo (°'kàngwo) shwō jèi shr̄ 'jyǎde. /Please read it to me. Chǐng nǐ géi wǒ 'nyànnyan. *or* Chǐng nǐ 'nyàn géi wǒ 'tīngting. /He read the timetable out loud to us. Tā bǎ shr̄jyān'byǎu 'nyàn géi wǒmen 'tīng.

(Predict) 'twēitsè, 'yùtsè. /He tries to read the future. Tā syǎng 'fádz °'twēitsè (°'yùtsè) 'jyānglàide 'shr̄.

READY. (Prepared) hǎule, 'yùbèi'hǎule, 'jwǔnbèi'hǎule; (of food) dé. /When will dinner be ready? 'Fàn shémma 'shr̄hou °'dé (°'yùbèi'hǎule, °'hǎu)? /The coffee is ready. 'Jyāfēi jǔ'déle. /Is everything ready? Yíchyè dōu 'jwǔnbèi'hǎule ma? *or* 'Yùbèi'hǎule ma?

Be ready to *or* **for** (can) 'kéyǐ, néng. /Is the manuscript ready to be printed? 'Gǎudz 'kéyǐ fù'yìnle ma? /Everything is ready for shipment. 'Shémma dōu 'kéyǐ 'lìshr̄ yùn'dzǒu. /I am ready to go anywhere I am sent. Bù'gwǎn 'pài wǒ dàu 'nǎr, 'wǒ dōu néng 'chyù. /Are you ready to forgive him? Nǐ syàn'dzài 'néng 'ráushù tā ma? or expressed as Are you planning to forgive him? Ní 'dǎswàn 'ráushù 'tā ma?

Get ready (in general) 'yùbèi; (take exactly the right precautions in advance) 'jwǔnbèi; **get ready to go out** 'dǎbàn. *See also* **PREPARE.** /I can get ready to go in five minutes. Wǔfēn jūng de 'gūngfu wǒ jyòu kéyǐ 'yùbèi hǎu le 'dzǒu le. /After we decided to go, it took her an hour to get ready. Wǒmen shwō'hǎule yàu 'dzǒu le, tā jyòu chyù 'dǎbàn, °'yǐ dǎbàn (°'yí yùng, °'yí chyù) yùngle yíge jūng'tóu. /For some time the men have been getting ready to go overseas. Bīng wèi 'hǎiwàiywàn'jēng 'jwǔnbèile 'yǒusyē shr̄hou le. /Ready, get set, go! Jàn'hǎu, yù'bèi, 'pǎu!

Ready (at hand) shǒubyār. /I don't have much ready cash. Wó shǒu'byār 'méiyou 'dàije shémma chyán.

REAL. jēn, jēnjèngde; (actually) shr̄jìshang. /Is this real silk or imitation? Jèi shr̄ 'jēnsz̄ 'hái shr̄ rén'dzàusz̄? /This looks like the real thing. 'Jèige gēn 'jēnde yí'yàng. /What was his real reason? Tāde 'jēnde 'lǐyóu shr̄ 'shémma? or expressed

855

<u>as</u> What was his motive at the bottom? Dàu'dǐ tāde 'dùngjī shr̄ 'shémma? / That never happens in real life. Jēn'jèngde 'rénshēng 'jywé búhwèi yǒu 'nèi shr̄. *or* Shŕ'jìshang 'búhwèi yǒu 'nèi shr̄. / It was a real pleasure to meet him. Wǒ 'jēn gāu'syìng °¹'pèngjyànle (°¹'kànjyànle) tā. / Do you know the real facts? <u>is expressed as</u> Do you know the truth of the matter? Nǐ 'jŕdāu jèijyán 'shr̄de jēn'syàng ma?

REALIZE. (Understand) míngbai; (catch on) mwō chīngchule; (see into) chyáuchulai, kànchulai; (know) 'jŕdau, 'syàudé; (expect) syǎngdàu. / I didn't realize that you were interested in it. Wǒ méisyǎng'dàu nǐ dwèiyú jèige hén yǒu 'syìngchyù. *or* Wǒ bù-jŕ'dàu ní 'syǐhwan jèige. / Do you realize what this means? Nǐ °¹'míngbai (°mwō 'chīngchu, °¹'chyáuchūlái, °¹'kànchulái) jèi shr̄ 'dzěmma hwéi 'shèr ma? / It took me a long time to realize what he was trying to say. Wǒ 'fèile hǎu'dàde 'shŕhou tsái °¹'míngbài (°mwō 'chīngchule) tā syǎng'shwō de shr̄ 'shémma. / I realize that this is an important job. Wǒ °¹'jŕdau (°¹'syàudé) jèi shr̄ yíjyàn hén 'jùngyàude 'shèr.

(Achieve) bàndàu; (come true; of a dream) ywán. / He has never realized his desire to own a house. Tā yàu 'jŕ yíswǒ 'fángdz kěshr yìjŕ 'méibàndàu. / I'm afraid that's a dream that will never be realized. Wǒ pà nèige 'mèng yúng'ywán yě 'ywánbùlyǎu. *or* Wǒ pà nèi shèr yúngywán yě bàn bu'dàu.

Realize a profit (make money) jwànchyán. / He realized a big profit on the transaction. Tā dzwò nèibí 'mǎimai jwànle bù'shǎude 'chyán.

REALLY. chíshŕ, jēn, jēnshr̄. / I really wanted to stay home. Wǒ 'jēnshr yàu dzài 'jyā 'dāije laije. / Will the train really start on time? Hwǒchē 'jēn jwǔnshŕ 'kāi ma? / She is really younger than she looks. Chí'shŕ tāde 'swèishu 'méiyou tāde 'yàngdz nèmma 'lǎu. <u>or expressed as</u> She looks older than she is. Tāde 'yàngdz 'kànje bǐ tā rén 'lǎu. / Do you really mean that? Nǐ 'jēn shr̄ nèige 'yìsz ma? <u>or expressed as</u> Are you speaking on the level? Nǐ shr̄ shwō jēn'géde ne ma? / Really? 'Jénde ma? / Well, really! Jēn'géde le!

REASON. (A cause) 'ywángù, 'ywányīn, 'dàulǐ, 'lǐyóu; **the reason why** wèi'shémma. *See also* **WHY.** / What were your reasons for leaving there? Nǐ 'líkāi nèr shr̄ 'shémma °¹'ywángù (°¹'ywányīn, °etc.). / He had a good reason for wanting to leave. Tā yàu 'dzǒu 'yǒu tāde °¹'dàulǐ (°¹'lǐyóu, °etc.). / I can't figure out the reason why he did it. Wǒ jēn 'dzwómwobùchūlái tā wèi'shémma 'nèmmaje. <u>or expressed as</u> I can't figure out what his reasons were for doing it. Wǒ jēn syǎngbùchūlái tā dzwò nèijyàn 'shr̄ shr̄ shémma °¹'dàulǐ (°¹'lǐyóu, °etc.). / We have reason to believe that it was murder. <u>is expressed as</u> We think it was murder and have some evidence. Wǒmen 'rènwéi jèi shr̄ móu'shā shr̄ yǒu syǎngdāngde 'gēnjyù de. / I have reason to believe that we will never see him again. <u>is expressed as</u> There are some things that make me think we won't see him again. Yǒu hǎusyē °¹'shr̄ching (°¹'dìfangr) jyàu wǒ 'jywéde wǒmen dzài jyànbù'jáu tā le.

(Intelligence) 'lǐsyìng. / Some insects almost seem to have reason. Yǒude kwūn-'chúng 'hǎusyàng yě 'yǒu dyǎr 'lǐsyìng 'shr̄de. *or* Yǒude 'chúngdz hǎusyàng yé 'dung dyǎr shémma shr̄de.

Bring someone to reason bǎ . . . gěi shwō 'míngbai gwòlái, bǎ . . . gěi °chywàn 'míngbai (°¹'chywàngwolái, °chywàn 'míngbaigwolái). / He was stubborn, but we brought him to reason. Tā chǐ'chū hén 'gùjŕ láije, 'kěshr wǒmen bǎ tā gěi °shwō-'míngbaigwòláile (°chywàn'míngbaile, °etc.).

It stands to reason dāngrán. / It stands to reason that he wouldn't have done that. Nèige 'dāngrán 'búshr tā 'gànde.

Listen to reason (be reasonable) jyánglǐ. / Please listen to reason. Jyáng dyǎr 'lǐ, hǎu bù'hǎu? *or* Byé bùjyáng'lǐ. / He wouldn't listen to reason. Tā mán-bùjyáng'lǐ. <u>or expressed as</u> He didn't listen to good advice. Tā bùtīng hǎu 'hwà.

Lose one's reason (go crazy) yàufēng le。

Within reason. /He'll pay anything within reason to get it. is expressed as However much it's worth he can pay it. Jř 'dwōshau chyán tā 'dōu néng 'gěi. or as If it's worth it, he'll pay any amount of money. Jř yàushr 'jŕ, tā 'dwōshau 'chyán dōu 'ywànyi 'hwā.

To reason (think logically; use one's head) yùng nǎudz; (think) syǎng; (think it over) syángsyǎng, 'sžswo 'sžswǒ; (figure out) dzwómwo. /That child can't reason. Jèi 'háidz 'búhwèi yùng 'nǎudz. /He reasoned that she would have gone home first. Tā 'syǎng tā yésyu 'syān hwéijyāle. /Let's try to reason it out. Dzámen 'džsyǐ °'dzwómwo 'dzwómwo (°'syángsyǎng, °'sžswǒ 'sžswǒ) shŕ džĕmma hwéi 'shèr.

(Argue, persuade, advise) chywàn; (talk to . . .) gēn . . . 'shwō; (explain to . . .) gēn . . . 'jyǎng. /We reasoned with her until she changed her mind. Wǒmen °'chywàn tā (°gēn tā 'shwō, °gēn tā 'jyǎng) yǐ'jŕ dàu bǎ tāde 'syīn gěi shwō'hwó le.

RECEIPT. (Act of receiving) is expressed as **receive** jyē. /Upon receipt of the telegram, he immediately took the train. Tā yǐ 'jyējau jèi dyàn'bàu, lì'kè jyòu shàngle hwǒ'chē le.

(Paper acknowledging receipt) 'shōujyù, shōutyáur. /Please sign this receipt. 'Chíng nǐ dzài °'shōujyùshang (°shōu'tyáurshang) chyān ge 'míng. /Be sure to get a receipt when you deliver the package. Bǎ jèige 'baur sùng'dàule de 'shŕhou, byé 'wàngle yàu °shōu'tyáur (°'shōujyù).

(Money received) 'shōurù, jìnkwǎn, 'jìnsyàng. /Our receipts will just pay our expenses. 'Wǒmende °'shōurù (°jìn'kwǎn, °'jìnsyàng) jyàng 'gòu 'kāisyàu.

To receipt. /Please receipt this bill. is expressed as Please mark the bill paid. 'Chíng nǐ bǎ jèijāng jàng'tyáur °jù yíjù (°syéshàng) 'fùle. or as Please strike off this bill. 'Chíng nǐ bǎ jèijāng 'tyáur jù'syāu le.

RECEIVE. (Get, acquire) jyē, shōu; (obtain) dé. /Please wait until you receive the letter. 'Chíng ní 'děngje 'jyējau nèifēng 'syìn dzài 'shwō. /We just received the news. Wǒmen gāng 'jyējau jèige 'syāusyi. /That soldier has not received his orders. Jèige 'bīng hái méi'jyēdàu tāde 'mìnglìng ne. /Payment was received. Chyán yǐjing 'shōule. /He didn't receive any compensation for the work. Tā 'dzwòchū nèijyàn 'hwór lái, yì'dyǎr 'bàuchou yě méi'déjáu.

(Experience; especially, suffering) shòu. /He received a wound in the war. Tā dǎ'jàng de 'shŕhou shòu'shāngle. /He's received a lot of criticism. Tā 'shòule bùshàude 'pīpíng.

(Welcome) hwānyíng, 'jāudài. /He was on hand to receive the guests. Tā dzàichǎng °hwānyíng (°'jāudài) 'kèrén.

Be received. /How was your suggestion received? is expressed as How did everybody consider your idea? Džjyā'hwōr 'rènwéi nǐde jyàn'yì džĕmma'yàng? /His speech was well received by the audience. is expressed as Everybody liked to listen to his speech. Tāde yán'jyǎng dà'jyā dōu hěn 'ài tīng. /He was well received in the community. is expressed as Everyone welcomed him very happily. Dà 'jyā jāu'dàide tā °bú'tswò (°hén 'hǎu).

RECENT. syīnjìn. /The television is a comparatively recent invention. Dyànshŕ 'bǐjyàu shŕ yíge syīn'jìn fā'míng de 'dūngsyi. /Is this a recent issue? Jèi shŕ syīn'jìn 'chūde ma?

RECENTLY. jìnlai; (very recently) dzwèijìn; (a few days ago) 'tóujityān; **how recently** (when) 'dwōhwěr. /Have you seen him recently? Nǐ 'jìnlai 'kànjàn tā méiyou? /He has recently been promoted. Tā dzwèi'jìn 'shēngle. /Only recently I met him on the street. Wǒ 'tóujityān hǎi dzài 'jyēshang 'kànjyàn tā láije. /How recently were you there? 'Nǐ shr̀ 'dwōhwěr 'dzài nèr láije?

RECOGNIZE. rèn; (know) 'jr̄dàu. /I recognize him by his hat. Yīnwei tāde 'màudz wǒ bǎ tā 'rènchulaile. /I didn't recognize her in that hat. Tā 'dàishang nèi 'màudz wǒ 'jén bú'rènde tā le. /We recognized the place from your description. Wǒmen 'ànje ní swǒ 'shwō de 'rènchu nèige 'dìfang lái le. /No one recognized his genius while he was alive. Tā 'hwóje de 'shr̀hou méi 'rén 'jr̄dàu tāde 'tyāntsái.

Recognize a speaker 'ràng . . . °fā'yán (°shwō'hwà). /Wait until the chairman recognizes you. 'Děngdàu jǔ'syí 'ràng nǐ °fā'yán, nǐ dzài fā'yán (°shwō 'hwà, nǐ dzài 'shwō).

Recognize a claim rènjàng, 'chéngrèn 'yāuchyóu. /We recognize all claims. Wǒmen 'chywán rèn'jàng. *or* Wǒmen 'chéngrèn swó'yǒude 'yāuchyóu.

Recognize a government 'chéngrèn 'jèngfǔ. /Do they recognize the new government? 'Tāmen 'chéngrèn jèige syīn 'jèngfǔ ma?

RECORD. (Written statement) jìlù; (financial) jàng; **keep records** jìlù; **keep financial records of** bǎ . . . jìdzai 'jàngshang. /Keep a careful record of all expenses. Bǎ 'swóyǒude 'fèiyùng dōu syáng'syìde jìdzai 'jàngshang. /All the records are kept in a filing cabinet. 'Swóyǒude jì'lù dōu dzài jywàndzūng 'gwèidzli bǎu'lyóuje ne.

(Recorded maximum, optimum, etc.) jìlù. /He broke all records for speed. Tāde 'sùdù dǎ'pwò yí'chyède jì'lù. /This heat spell sets a new record. Jèitsżchí-rè dzàule 'syīn jì'lù. /We had a record crop this year. is expressed as Our crop this year is better than all previous ones. Wǒmen 'jīnnyánde 'shōuchéng bǐ 'nèinyán-de dōu 'hǎu. /That's a record for stupidity. is expressed as There isn't anything more stupid than that. 'Dzài yě 'méiyou bǐ 'nèige hǎi 'bènde le.

(Phonograph disk) chàngpyār, chàngpán, hwàsyá'pyāndz. /Do you have many dance records? Nǐde tyàu'wǔde °chàng'pyār (°chang'pán, °hwàsyá'pyāndz) 'dwō budwō?

(Known past; of a particular person) yǐ'chyán dzwǒgwo de 'shr̀. /He has a clean record. Tā yǐ'chyán dzwǒgwo de 'shr̀ méi shémma kě 'pīpíng de. /He has a criminal record. is expressed as He's committed crimes in the past. Tā tséng'jīng fàngwo 'dzwèi. /He had a fine record in college. is expressed as In college his attainments were quite good. Tā dzài 'dàsywé de shr̀hou 'chéngjì hén 'hǎu.

Go on **record** as. /Let me go on record as against this idea. is expressed as Put it down that I'm opposed to this idea. 'Jìje, wǒ jèng'shr̀de 'fǎndwèi 'jèige.

The worst (*or* best, etc.) . . . on **record**. /This is the worst earthquake on record here. is expressed as This earthquake is worse than any we've had here before. 'Jèitsżde dì'jèn yán'jùngde 'chíngsyíng shr̀ 'jèr 'tsúnglái méi'yǒugwode.

To **record** (in writing) jì, jìlù. /Who recorded the proceedings? Hwèi'yìde 'jīnggwò shr̀ 'shéi 'jìde?

(On disks) gwàn pyàndz, gwàn yīn. /What company records for you? Nǐ dzài 'něi yíge gūng'sż 'gwàn 'pyàndz?

(On tape) lù yīn, gwàn lùyindài. /Did you record that song? Ní bǎ nèige gēer lùle yīn le ma?

RECOVER. (Get back) 'jǎujáule, jwēihweilaile, náhweilaile, sometimes other verbs meaning take *or* get plus -hweilaile. /I recovered my watch within a week. Wǒ dzài yíge syīng'chī yǐ'nèi, bá wǒde 'byǎu 'jwēihwéilaile.

(Recuperate) fú'ywán, . . . hǎule, . . . hǎude. /How long did it take you to recover from your operation? Nǐ kāi'dāu yǐ'hòu °'yǎngle dwō 'jyǒu tsái 'hǎu de (°dwō 'jyǒu tsái fú'ywán de)?

Recover oneself hǎule. / He lost his temper for a moment, but soon recovered himself. Tā 'fāle yí'hwěrde 'píchi, kěshr yǐ'hwěr jyòu 'hǎule.

Recover one's self-control jènddìng. / He quickly recovered his self-control. Tā lì'kè jyòu jèn'dìngle.

RED. húng; (red color) 'húngsè, 'húngshǎr, 'húngde 'yánsè. / Red isn't becoming to her. 'Húngde 'yánsè gēn ta bùhé'shr. *or* Tā chwānje 'húngde °bùhǎu'kàn (°bùchèn). / I want to buy a red hat. Wǒ yàu 'mǎi yìdǐng húng 'màudz. / Her face was red with embarrassment. Tā bùhǎu'yìsz, 'lyǎn dōu 'húngle.

REFUSE. (Of a proposal) jyùjywé. / Has she refused him again? Tā 'yòu jyù'jywé tā le ma?

Refuse in other contexts is expressed indirectly. / I offered him a drink, but he refused it. is expressed as I asked him to drink, but he won't. Wǒ 'chǐng tā hē-'jyǒu, kěshr tā bùkěn 'hē. / The manager refused to accept his resignation. is expressed as The manager didn't let him resign. Jǐng'lǐ bù'jwǔn ta tsź'jr. *or as* The manager didn't accept his resignation. Jǐng'lǐ bù'jyēshòu tāde tsź'chéng.

REFUSE. (Discarded stuff) fèiwu, méiyùngde 'dūngsyi. / Throw it away with the rest of the refuse. Bǎ tā gēn chí'tā °fèiwu (°méiyùngde 'dūngsyi) yikwàr 'rēng le ba.

REGARD. (Look at) kàn. / He regarded her face carefully. Tā hěn dž'syì de bǎ tāde 'lyǎn 'kànle yikàn.

Regard someone (*or* something) **as, be regarded as** rènwèi . . . shr. / He's regarded as a great pianist. Yì'bānrén 'rènwéi tā shr hěn 'hǎude gāngchín'jyā. / Her colleagues regard her as an authority on modern Chinese history. Tāde túngshr rènwéi tā shr Jūnggwó jìndàishrde chywánwēi.

Be well regarded. / He's well regarded here. is expressed as People here all think he's not bad. 'Jèrde rén dōu 'jywéde tā bú'tswo. or as He has a very good reputation here. Tā dzài 'jèr hěn yǒu dyǎr 'míngwàng.

Regard (consideration) often expressed verbally as consider kǎulyù, gùlyù, gù. / Show some regard for your parents. Nǐ yé děi gùlyù gùlyù nǐ fùmǔ. or expressed as You ought to think of your parents some. Shāu'wéi yě tì nǐ 'fùmǔ 'syǎng yisyǎng.

In that regard 'jr̀yú 'nèi yidyǎn. / In that regard, I agree with you. Jr̀yú 'nèi yìdyǎn, wǒ 'gēn ni túng'yì.

With regard to, in regard to 'dwèiyú, 'gwānyú, 'jr̀yú. / We'll have to have a little discussion in regard to that last point. 'Dwèiyú dzwèi'hòu nèi yi'dyǎn, wǒmen 'hái déi tǎu'lwùn tǎulwùn. / With regard to your letter of January 1st . . . . 'Gwānyú nǐ 'yíywèyí'hǎude 'syìn . . . .

Send *or* **Give one's regards** chǐngān, wènhǎu, wènān. / Send my regards to your mother. Tì wǒ gěi nínde lǎu 'tàitai °chǐng'ān (°wèn'hǎu, °etc.).

REGRET. hòuhwěi, wǎnsyī. / I've always regretted not having traveled. Wǒ 'cháng-cháng hòu'hwěi méi'chūchyu yóu'lìgwo.

Have regrets is expressed as above. / I have no regrets for what I've done. Wǒ swǒ 'dzwò de shr̀ wǒ 'bìng bùhòu'hwěi.

Send one's regrets. / He said to send his regrets. is expressed as He says he feels sorry. Tā shwō ta hěn bàuchyàn.

REGULAR. (Normal, customary) 'jàulĭde, jèngchángde, pŭtūngde, yŏu'gwēidzéde; or expressed by using 'yīnggāi ought. / This is the regular procedure. 'Jèige shr̀ 'jàulĭde °'shŏusyu (°'chéngsyù). / What's the regular way of writing a business letter. 'Shāngjyède gūng'hán yīnggāi 'dzĕmma syĕ? or Shāngyè gūng'hán °pŭ'tūngde (°jèng-chángde, °'jàulĭde) syĕfar shr̀ dzĕmma yàngr de?

(Orderly) yŏu'jr̀syude. / He lives a very regular life. Tā gwòje yĭjŭng hén yŏu'jr̀syùde 'shēnghwó.

(Of the same pattern) chí, yíyàng. / The hills have a regular outline. Nèisyē 'shān de 'lwúnkwò °dōu yí'yàng (°hĕn 'chí).

(Repeated at regular intervals) is expressed as customarily 'píngcháng, jàulĭ; or as definite, fixed yídìngde. / This happens at regular intervals. Syàng'gé yŏu yí'dìngde shŕjyān. or Gwò yí'dìngde shŕjyān 'jwùn yŏu yítsz̀. / The trains operate on a regular schedule everyday. Hwŏchē mĕityān dōu ànje yí'dìngde shŕjyān 'kāi. / Is there bus service to town? Jèr 'píngcháng yŏu gūnggùngchì'chē dàu chéng'lĭ chyù ma? / He makes a regular thing of it. Tā 'mĕityān jàu'lĭ dzwò 'jèige.

(Real, genuine) is expressed as really jēn. / That storm was a regular flood. Nèijèn bàufēng'yŭ 'jēn chéngle shwĕi'dzāi le.

RELATION. gwānsyi, 'jyāuchíng. / That scene has no relation to the rest of the play. 'Nèi yímù gēn jèi chywánchū 'syì °'háu wú (°méi) 'gwānsyi. / Our relations with the major are excellent. Wŏmen gēn shr̀'jăng de 'jyāuchíng hĕn bú'tswò.

(Relatives; members of the same family) yi'jyā (dze) rén; (not in the same household) bĕnjyā; (by marriage) 'chīnchì. / He is one of my relations. Tā shr̀ wŏde °'chīnchi (°bĕn'jyā). or Tā gen wŏ shr̀ yĭjyā 'rén.

In relation to. / You must judge his work in relation to the circumstances. is expressed as In judging his work, at the same time you must think of the circumstances. Nĭ 'pīping tāde 'gūngdzwò de shŕhou túng'shŕ yĕ 'yīngdāng 'syàngdàu tāde 'hwánjìng. or as You must think of the circumstances and then say how his work is. Nĭ dĕi 'syăng tāde 'hwánjìng 'dzài shwō tā 'dzwòde dzĕmma 'yàng.

Break off relations (of countries) jywéjyāu. / The two countries have broken off relations. 'Jèi lyănggwó jywé'jyāule.

RELATIVE. (Not absolute) syāngdwèide. / Everything in life is relative. Rén'shēngde 'shr̀ching dōushr syāng'dwèide. or 'Hwà dĕi kàn dzài shémma °'dìfang (°'shŕhou) lái'shwō.

Be relative to (depend on) dĕi kàn. / The merits of this proposal are relative to the particular circumstances. Jèige yĭjyàn 'hău buhău yùng dĕi 'kàn dzài shémma 'chíngsyíng jŕ 'syà.

Relatives (kin; members of the same family) yi'jyā(dze) rén; (not in the same household) bĕnjyā; (by marriage) 'chīn chì; **close relatives** jìn chīn. / They're close relatives. Tāmen shr̀ jìn'chīn. / They invited all their friends and relatives to the wedding. Tāmen jyē'hwūn de shŕhou lyán 'chīnchì dài 'péngyou, dōu 'chĭngle.

RELIGION. dzūngjyàu. / She's very tolerant in her attitude toward other religions. Tāde 'tàidu dwèiyu byéde dzūng'jyàu yĕ dōu bùfăn'dwèi. / Some people say Confucianism isn't a religion. 'Yúrén shwō 'Kŭng'jyàu 'búshr dzūng'jyàu.

RELIGIOUS. (Pious) 're̋syĭn. / Quakers are religious people. 'Gwēigéhwèide rén syìn-'jyòu hĕn 're̋syĭn.

REMAIN. (Continue unchanged) 'háishr̀, 'lăushr̀. / These things always remain the same. 'Jèisyē dūngsyi 'lăushr̀ 'jèyàng.

Remain at a place yǐ'jŕ dzài. / He remained at home. Tā yǐ'jŕ dzai 'jyāli.

Remain to be seen or done, etc. hái děi. / That remains to be seen. 'Hái bùnéng 'dǐng ne. / Most of the work still remains to be done. Nèijyàn 'shŕ yǒu yí-'dwōbàr hái děi 'dzwò ne. / Nothing else remains to be done. is expressed as Everything is done. 'Byéde dōu dzwò'wánle.

Remains (of a meal) shēngtsài. / She cleared away the remains of dinner. Tā bǎ shēng'tsài dōu 'nákāile.

(Corpse) shŕshou. / Where did they bury his remains? Tāmen bǎ tāde shŕshou mái 'něr le?

REMARK. (Casual comment) hwà with measure jyù. / That was an unkind remark. 'Nèijyù hwà hén 'swǔn. / Limit your remarks to five minutes. is expressed as Just speak five minutes. 'Syàn ni shwō 'wǔfēn jūng. or as Don't speak for more than five minutes. Byé 'shwōgwò 'wǔfēn jūng.

To **remark on** 'lwùndàu, 'shwōdàu. / He remarked on her appearance. Tā °'lwùndàu (°'shwōdàu) tāde °'shénchì (°'yàngdz).

Remark that shwō. / We've already remarked before that opinions differ on this point. Wǒmen 'dzǎu jyòu shwōgwo dà'jyā dwèiyú 'jèi yìdyǎn 'yìjyàn bù'túng.

REMEMBER. jìde, jìje; (recall) syǎngchilai. / It was in May, as I remember. Wǒ jìde shŕ dzài 'wǔywèli. / Do you remember when he said that? Nǐ 'jìde tā 'shémma shŕhou 'shwōde nèige ma? / Remember to turn out the lights. 'Jìje bǎ dēng gěi 'gwān le. / I can't remember the occasion. Wǒ 'syǎngbuchǐ'lái 'néi yìhwéi 'shŕ.

(Give a gift to) syǎngje, 'làbulyáu. / He always remembers us at Christmas. Tā dzài Shèngdàn'jyé sùng'lǐ de shŕhou 'dzǔng °'syǎngje (°'làbulyáu) wǒmen. / I'll remember you in my will. is expressed as When I write my will I won't forget you. Wó syě yí'jǔ de shŕhou bú'hwèi bá 'nǐ gěi 'wàng le.

Remember someone **to** tì . . . gěi . . . °chǐng'ān (°'wènhòu, °wèn'hǎu). / Remember me to your mother. 'Tì wo gěi nínde lǎu'tàitai °chǐng'ān (°etc.).

REMIND. 'syǎngchilai. / She reminds me of my mother. Kànjyàn 'tā wó 'syǎngchi wǒde 'mǔchin lai. / I'm reminded of an amusing story. Shwō 'jèige jyàu wo 'syǎngchi yíge 'syàuhwar lai.

Remind someone to do something 'tíje . . . yìdyǎr, 'tisyǐng . . . yìshēngr. / Remind me to write him. Nǐ 'tije wǒ dyǎr, 'gěi ta syě yìfēng 'syìn. / If you don't remind me, I'll forget. Nǐ yàu bù'tisyǐng wo yìshēngr, wǒ jyòu syǔ 'wàngle.

REMOVE. (Of stains, ink spots, etc.) bǎ . . . chyù. / This is guaranteed to remove ink spots. Jèige báu'gwǎn néng bǎ mwòshwěi 'dyǎr 'chyù le.

(Of traces, clues, etc.). / They removed every trace of their presence before they left. is expressed as When they went they left no traces. Tāmen 'dzǒude shŕhou, 'yìdyǎr 'hénjì dōu méi'lyóusyà. or as First they restored everything to its original order and then left. Tāmen 'syān bǎ yíchyè dōu hwēifu ywán'jwàng, 'tsái 'dzǒude.

Remove one's hat jāi; (other garments) twō. / Please remove your hats. Chǐng nǐmen bǎ 'màudz 'jāi le.

Remove a growth, an appendix, etc. chyùchulai, lásyalai. / They operated to remove a growth. Tāmen yùng 'shǒu shù bǎ 'lyóudz °'chyùchulaile (°'lásyàlaile).

Remove an official (by higher authority) géjŕ, myǎnjŕ; (by vote) méiyou 'dzài 'sywǎn shàng. / He was removed from office. Tā 'méiyou 'dzài'sywǎn shàng. *or*

Tā bèi gé'jŕle. *or* Tā bèi myǎn'jŕle. / It's about time this official was removed. Jēnshŕ gāi bǎ tā 'gé le.

Remove <u>someone, as from a room</u>, by force tǐchuchyu, rēngchuchyu, hūngchuchyu. / He became boisterous and they had to remove him by force. Tā 'nàude tài 'lìhai le, 'rénjyā jŕ 'háu bǎ ta gěi °'tǐchuchyùle (°'rēngchuchyùle, °'hūngchuchyùle).

Remove <u>objects from some place</u> bàn; (of installations, as a telephone) chāi. / We'll have to remove all these chairs first. Wǒmen déi bǎ jèisye 'yǐdz ban'dzǒu. / I want my telephone removed. Wó syáng bǎ dyànhwà chāidzǒu. / They removed my stove yesterday. Tāmen dzwótyān bǎ wǒde lúdz chāidzǒule.

Remove <u>a population</u> °jyàu (°ràng) . . . bān'dzǒu. / They'll have to remove the people who live in the valley before they can build the dam. Tāmen 'syān děi jyàu dzài shān'gǔli jù de 'rén bān'dzǒule tsái néng syōu 'já.

RENDER. (Cause to be) jyàu, ràng; render <u>someone or something</u> . . . bǎ A nùngde . . . , where A denotes a person or thing; or expressed with resultative compounds. / The (wounds he received in the) accident rendered him completely helpless. Chū'shèrde shŕhou tā shòude 'shāng °jyàu tā (°ràng tā, °bǎ tā nùngde) yì'dyǎr jyèr yě dùng-bu'lyǎu. / This news renders it probable that nothing will happen. <u>is expressed as</u> Having this news probably nothing will happen. Yǒu 'jèige 'syāusyi 'nà jyòu 'dàgài búhwèi chū'shŕle. / The shock rendered him speechless. Jèige 'dǎji °jyàu tā (°bǎ tā nùngde) dōu shwōbuchū 'hwà láile. <u>or expressed as</u> He was shocked to the point of not being able to speak. Tā 'syàde shwōbuchū 'hwà láile.

(Give) gěi, jyāu. / You have rendered invaluable assistance. Ní 'géi wǒmen hěn dà de bāngmáng. <u>or expressed as</u> You've really helped a lot. Nǐ 'jēnshr 'bāngle hěn'dàde'máng. / An account must be rendered monthly. <u>is expressed as</u> Each month an account must be sent in. 'Měi yíge 'ywè, bìděi bǎ 'jàng 'jyāujinchyu. / For services rendered, $10. 'Shòusyùfèi shr 'shŕkwài chyán.

RENT. (Of the person who acquires or of the thing transferred) dzū; (of the person who receives payment) 'dzūgěi. / He had to rent a costume for the party. Tā wèi tsān-'jyā nèige 'hwèi dzūle jyàn 'yīfu. / He rents boats to tourists. Tā yǒu 'chwán 'dzū-gěi 'yóukè. / This car rents for a dollar an hour. Jèilyàng 'chē 'dzū 'yíge jūngtóu 'yíkwài chyán. / I rented a boat yesterday, but haven't paid for it yet. Wǒ dzwótyān 'dzūle yìtyáu 'chwán, °chwánchyán (°chyán, °dzūchyán) hái méi'gěi ne.

Rent (payment) <u>usually expressed with</u> chyán, dzū <u>being used elsewhere in the sentence; sometimes</u> 'dzūchyán; house rent 'fángchyán, fángdzū; X-rent X-chyán. / How much rent do you pay for the house? Nǐde 'fángdz shr 'dwōshau chyán 'dzūde?

REPAIR. syōuli. / Can you repair my shoes in a hurry? Néng bunéng lì'kè bǎ jèishwāng 'syé syōu'hǎu le?

Repairs, repair job, etc. are expressed verbally as above. / The car only needs minor repairs. Jèilyàng 'chē 'jŕ yàu shāu'wēi 'syōuli syōuli. / A complete repair job will take ten days. Yàushr 'wánchywán 'syōuli yísyàr, děi 'shŕtyān.

In bad repair děi 'dà 'syōuli. / The house on the corner is in bad repair. Jǐ-'jyǎur shang nèijyān 'fángdz děi 'dà syōuli yísyà.

REPEAT. Expressed as again dzài (referring to a future action) *or* yòu (referring to a past action), <u>with the specific verb for the thing done a second time; sometimes expressed adverbially as</u> repeatedly fǎnfude . . . . / The play will be repeated next week. Jèichū 'syì 'syalǐbài hái yàu 'dzài yǎn. / He repeated what he had just said. Tā bǎ tā gāngtsái shwō de 'yòu shwōle yíbyàr. / He repeats the same thing over and over again. Tā lǎushr fǎnfude shwō nèijyàn shr.

(Pass on by word of mouth) gàusu 'byéren. /Don't repeat what I've told you. Wǒ 'gàusu nǐ de 'hwà 'búyàu gàusu 'byéren.

Repeat something **after** someone 'gēnje . . . shwō. /Repeat this after me. Nǐ 'gēnje wǒ shwō.

REPLY. (Answer) 'hwéidá, hwéi, 'hwà, 'dáfù; sometimes expressed as say shwō. /He replied that they would be glad to go. Tā hwéi'dá shwō tāmen dōu néng 'lái. /How did you reply to this? Nǐ 'dzěmma °'dáfu de (°hwéidá de)?

A reply 'hwéidá, hwéihwà, 'dáfù. /His reply was quick and direct. Tāde °'hwéidá (°etc.) yòu 'pyàulyàng yòu gān'tswèi.

REPORT. bàugàu. /He reported that everything was in order. Tā bàu'gàu shwō 'shémma dōu nùng'hǎule. /It is reported that you are wasting money. Yǒurén gēn wo shwō nǐ làngfèi 'chyán. /I'll report on this matter tomorrow. Wǒ 'míngtyan bǎ jèijyàn 'shrching 'bàugàu bàugàu. /They reported him to the police. Tāmen bǎ ta gěi bàu'gàu jǐng'chá le.

(Of a reporter or correspondent) is often expressed as write an account syě yídwàn syīnwen. /He reported the fire for his paper. Tā bǎ hwó jǐngde 'chíngsyíng gěi tāde bàu'gwán syěle yídwàn 'syīnwén.

Report for duty bàudàu. /Report for duty Monday morning. Lǐbài'yī 'dzǎushang bàu'dàu.

A report is expressed verbally as in paragraph one. /It was an illuminating report. Nèige bàu'gàude 'nèirúng hěn 'tòuchè. /He gave the report in person. Tā 'chīndz bàu'gàude.

(Sound of a shot) chyāngshēng, 'bēngde yìshēng. /The gun went off with a loud report. Jèige 'chyāng 'bēngde yìshēng 'fàngchuchyule.

Hear a report (rumor) **that** 'tǐngshwō. /I heard a report that you're leaving town. Wǒ 'tǐngshwō nǐ yàu dàu 'byéde dìfang chyù.

REPORTER. (Of news) syīngwénjì'jě.

REPRESENT. (Symbolize). /What does this symbol represent? is expressed as This symbol is of what meaning? Jèige 'jǐhaur shr shémma 'yìsz? or as How do you explain this symbol? Jèige 'jǐhaur dzěmma'jyǎng?

(Portray) shr. /This statue represents Bismarck. Jèige shr'syàng shr Bìsz-'mài.

(Report, make out). /He was represented to me as a first-rate surgeon, but I have reason to doubt it. is expressed as People told me he was a first-rate surgeon . . . . Rén'jyā 'gàusung wo tā shr ge 'hěn 'hǎude 'wàikē 'dàifu; wǒ 'jrdau nèihwà bú'dwèi. or as When people introduced us they told me he was a first-rate surgeon . . . . Rén'jyā 'jyèshau de shrhou shwō tā shr ge 'hěn 'hǎude'wàikē 'dàifu; . . . .

(Exemplify). /He doesn't represent the typical shopkeeper. is expressed as You can't take him as the typical shopkeeper. Tā 'bùnéng 'swànshr 'jēnjèng kāi-'pùdzde. or 'Bùnéng ná 'tā 'dàngdzwò 'jēnjèng kāi'pùdzde. or as The typical shopkeeper isn't the kind he is. 'Jēnjèng kāi'pùdzde 'bùshr 'tā nèiyàngrde.

(Include representatives of) yǒu. /All classes are represented in our membership. Wǒmen 'hwèiywánli 'něi yì'jyéjíde rén dōu 'yǒu.

(Act for; politically) dàibyǎu; (in court) tì . . . chū'tíng. /He has represented us in Congress for years. Tā dzài Gwó'hwèi dāng wǒmende dài'byǎu dāngle 'hǎu-syēnyán le. /He represented China at the Paris Peace Conference in 1919. 'Yī-

'jyǒu'yǐ'jyǒunyán tā dài'byāu 'Jūnggwo dzài 'Bālíhé'hwèi chū'syí. /Who represented the defendant? 'Shéi tǐ bèi'gàu chū'tíngle? /He engaged a young lawyer to represent him in court. Tā 'chǐngle ge nyán'chǐngde lyù'shr̄ lái tǐ ta chū'tíng.

REQUEST. chǐng; (demand) 'yāuchyóu; (pleading) chǐngchyóu; (beg) chyóu. /I'd like to request further (financial) assistance. Wó syǎng 'dzài chǐng syē 'jīntyē. /He requested us to take care of his child. Tā 'chǐng wǒmen 'jàugù tāde 'háidz.

A request chǐngchyóu; (written) chǐngchyóushū; or expressed verbally as above. /Please file a written request. Chǐng 'jyāu yìjāng chǐngchyóu'shū. /I am writing you at the request of a friend. Yǒu yíwèi 'péngyou chyóu wǒ gěi ni syě'syìn.

REQUIRE. (Demand something) yàu. /Do you require a deposit? Nǐ yàu dìngchyán ma? or expressed as Is it necessary to pay a deposit first? 'Shr̄ bushr̄ děi 'syān gěi 'dìngchyán?

(Need) yàu, 'syūyàu. /How much do you require? Nǐ yàu 'dwōshau? /This matter requires consideration. Jèijyàn 'shr̄ching °yàu (°'syūyàu) 'dwō 'kǎulyù kǎulyù.

Require someone to do something jyàu; (less emphatic) yàu; often expressed as have to 'yīnggāi or a similar expression. /They required us to take an examination first. Tāmen jyàu wǒmen 'syān jǐnggwo yíge kǎu'shr̄. /You are required by law to appear in person. Àn fǎ'lyù shwō nǐ yīnggāi 'dzjǐ °chū'myàn (or (if in court) °chū-'tíng).

RESPECT. (Consider worthy of esteem) kàndechǐ, dzwūnjǐng, dzwūnjùng. /I respect your opinion, but I can't always agree with it. Wó hěn dzwūnjùng nǐde 'yìjyàn, kěshr jè 'bìng búshr shwō wó 'láu 'yǐwéi nǐ 'dwèi. /He respects his elders. Tā hěn dzwūn'jǐng tāde 'jǎngbèi. /It's because I respect you. Nà shr wǒ kànde'chí nǐ a.

(Refrain from infringing on) dzwūnjùng, bùchǐfu. /They should respect our rights. Tāmen 'yīnggāi dzwūn'jùng wǒmende 'chywánlǐ. or Tāmen bù'yīnggāi 'chǐfu wǒmen.

Have respect for gùje, pèifu. /Have some respect for other people's opinions. Dzǔng 'yīngdāng 'gùje dyǎr 'byérénde 'yìjyàn. /Everyone he works with has respect for him. Gēn ta dzwò 'shr̄ de rén dōu 'pèifu ta.

In what respect 'dzěmmayàng, dzěmma kàn, tsúng 'něi yǐ'fāngmyàn. /In what respect is this true? 'Dzěmmayàng (shwō) jèige 'tsái shr̄ 'jēnde ne? or 'Jèige děi dzěmma 'kàn tsái shr̄ 'jēnde ne? or Tsúng 'něi yǐ'fāngmyàn kéyǐ shwō 'jèige shr̄ 'jēnde?

In many respects yǒu 'hǎusyē 'dìfang. /In many respects I agree with you. Yóu 'hǎusyē 'dìfang wǒ 'jywéde nǐ hěn 'dwèi.

Respecting 'gwānyú. /There was a question respecting his position. Gwānyú tāde 'dìwèi tséng'jǐng 'fāshēnggwò 'wèntí.

RESPONSIBLE. jùngyau, fù'dzérèn. /It is a most responsible position. Nèige 'shr̄-ching děi 'fù hěn 'dàde 'dzérèn. or 'Nèige shr̄ yíge hěn 'jùngyaude 'chāishr̄.

(Trustworthy) kěkàude. /I consider him a thoroughly responsible individual. Wǒ 'rènwéi tā shr yíge 'jywédwèi chéng'shŕkě'kàude rén.

Be responsible for (give rise to). /His strategy was responsible for the victory. is expressed as The victory was due to his strategy. 'Jèitsz̄ dàshēng 'jàng shr̄ 'yóuyu tāde 'jànlywè. or as Only because of his strategy was the victory possible. 'Yīnwei tāde 'jànlywè tsái néng dàshēng 'jàng.

Be responsible for (accountable for). /You are responsible for the books you

RETURN

take out of the library. is expressed as The books you take out of the library are
your responsibility. Nǐ tsúng túshū'gwǎn jyè de 'shū yóu 'nǐ fù'dzé.

   Be responsible to. /He is responsible only to the President. is expressed as
He takes orders only from the President. Tā jř tǐng dzúng'tǔngde 'míngling.

REST. syē, syōusyi. /Rest awhile. 'Syē yìhwěr. *or* 'Syōusyi yi'hwěr. /I hope you
rest well. Wǒ 'syīwang nǐ hǎu'hǎurde 'syēje. /Try to rest your eyes. 'Syēsye
nǐde 'yǎnjing.

   Rest one's head on 'jěndzài. /She rested her head on the pillow. Tā 'jěndzài
'jěntoushang.

   Rest against (lean against) kàuje. /The ladder is resting against the wall. 'Tǐdz
kàuje 'chyáng 'bǎije ne.

   Rest in. /Our hope rests in him. Wǒmen jyòu °kàn (°kàu, °syīwang) 'tā le.

   Rest on (depend on). /This argument rests on rather weak evidence. is expressed
as This evidence isn't very strong. Jèige 'lǐyóu bú'dà hěn 'chūngdzú.

   Rest with. /The power rests with him. Chywán'bing dzài 'tā shǒuli.

   Rest assured that fàngsyīn. /Rest assured that I'll take care of it. Fàng'syīn
ba, 'wǒ yí'dìng bàn.

   Rest (freedom from activity) is expressed verbally as in paragraph one. /A
little rest would do you a lot of good. Nǐ yàu 'syē yìhwěr, jyòu 'hǎude 'dwō le.

   Be at rest *or* **come to rest** 'tíngjùle, 'jànjùle. /Wait till the pointer is at rest.
'Děngje jèige 'jēn 'tíngjùle.

   Put one's mind at rest (jyàu . . .) 'syīnli jyòu 'ānle. /This will put your mind
at rest. 'Jèi yàng nǐ 'syīnli jyòu 'ānle.

   The rest (remainder) chíyú, byé, 'shèngsyàde. /Where is the rest of the gang?
°Chí'yú nèisyē (°'Byéde) rén dōu dzài 'nǎr. /I'll do the rest of the job. °Chí'yúde
(°'Shèngsyàde 'shŕ) 'wǒ dzwò. /I understood a little and guessed the rest. Wǒ 'jŕ-
dau yì'dyǎr, chí'yúde dōushŕ 'tsāide.

RESTAURANT. fàngwǎndz, fàngwǎr, gwǎndz, fànpùr; (selling Western food) 'syīt-
sāngwǎr; (Moslem) 'hwéihweigwǎr.

RESULT. 'jyēgwǒ. /The results were very satisfactory. 'Jyēgwǒ hén 'mǎnyì. /One
result is that we'll have enough to eat. is expressed as Thus we'll have enough to eat.
'Jèyàng yǐ 'lái wǒmen 'chŕ de dūngsyi shŕ 'gòule. /That fire was the result of your
carelessness. is expressed as That fire was because you weren't careful. Nèihwéi
shŕ'hwǒ shŕ yīngwei nǐ bù'syǎusyīn.

   Result from. /A lot of trouble results from gossip. is expressed as Gossiping
causes a lot of trouble. Shwō syán'hwà °dǐng shēng shŕ'fēi le (°dzwèi chū 'lwàndz).

   Result in. /That disagreement resulted in a complete break between them. is
expressed as Because of that disagreement they broke completely. Yīnwei nèitsżde
'yìjyàn bù'hé, tāmen jyòu wán'chywán jywé'lyèle.

RETURN. 'hwéilái, 'hwéichyù. /When did he return? Tā 'shémma shŕhour 'hwéilaide? /He just returned from work. Tā 'gāng dzwòwán 'gūng 'hwéilai.

   Return something hwán. /Will you return it when you're through? Chǐng ni
yùng'wánle de shŕhou jyòu 'hwán le.

   Return to (resume use of) 'yòu yùng. /He returned to his original plan. Tā
'yòu yùng tā 'běnláide 'jìhwà le.

865

Be **returned** (by an election) bèi 'sywǎn hwéi . . . . /He's been returned to Congress again. Tā yòu bèi 'sywǎn hwéidau Gwó'hwèi chyùle.

Return (time of getting back) 'hwéilái de shŕhou; (act of getting back) <u>expressed verbally as in paragraph one</u>. /I'll take the matter up on my return. Wǒ 'hwéilái de shŕhou 'dzài bàn jeijyàn 'shŕ. /His return was eagerly awaited by everyone. 'Měi yíge rén dōu 'pànje tā 'hwéilai.

(Interest) 'lìchyán. /How much of a return did you get on your investment? Nǐ 'tóudz °déle (°jwànle) dwōshau 'lìchyán?

By return mail. /Try to answer these letters by return mail. <u>is expressed as</u> Try to answer these letters quickly. Syǎng'fár bǎ nèisyē 'syìn jyòu 'hwéile. *or* Syǎng'fár 'kwài bǎ nèisyē 'syìn 'hwéile.

Return ticket (for a return journey) hwéipyàu; **return half of a ticket** 'hwéichyù nèiyí'bàrde pyàu. /I didn't use the return half of the ticket. 'Hwéichyù nèiyí'bàrde pyàu wǒ méi'yùng.

Returns (results) 'jyēgwǒ. /Did the election returns come in yet? Sywǎn'jyǔde 'jyēgwó yǒu'syèrle ma?

REWARD. jyǎnglì; **get a reward** shòushǎng, déjyǎng; **give a reward** (for the recovery of something lost or for the capture of fugitives) sywánshǎng. /You deserve a reward for your hard work. Nǐ 'jēnshr láukǔ'gūnggāu, yīnggāi °shòu'shǎng (°dé'jyǎng). /He was rewarded with a promotion. Yīnwei jyǎng'lì ta, gěi ta 'shēngle. /She offered five dollars reward for the return of her dog. Wèile yàu bǎ 'gǒu 'jàuhwéilái tā sywán'shǎng 'wǔkwài chyán. /His efforts were not rewarded during his lifetime. <u>is expressed as</u> He worked a whole lifetime without getting any benefit. Tā 'mángle yí'bèidz méi 'déjau shémma 'hǎuchù. *or as* He worked hard for a lifetime but received no compensation at all. Tā kǔ'gānle yí'bèidz, 'bìng méi'déje shémma 'bàuchóu.

RIBBON. dwàntyáur, sždài; (as of a typewriter) dàidz. /Give me a yard of white ribbon. Gěi wo yìmǎ 'báide dwàn'tyáur. /The medal had a three-color ribbon. Jèige jyǎng'jāng yǒu yíge sān'shǎrde °sž'dài (°dwàn'tyáur). /I need a new ribbon for my typewriter. Wǒde dǎdz'jī yīnggai 'hwàn yíge 'syīnde 'dàidz.

RICE. (Growing in the field) dàu(dz); **rice grain** (dàu) mǐ; (ready to eat) mǐfàn *or* (including also all staple food made from rice or wheat, or even food in general) fàn. /I'd like a catty of rice. Wǒ yàu yìjīn 'mǐ.

RICH. yǒuchyán, kwò. /His father is very rich. Tā fùchin hěn °'kwò (°yǒu'chyán). /He was adopted by a very rich family. Tā shr bèi yíge kwòrén'jyā shōuchyù'yǎngde.

(Abounding) 'fēngfù; (productive) féi, fù, chǎn'lyàng dzwèi 'dwō, hěn dwō. /Spinach is rich in iron. Bwó'tsàilǐtou 'tyějr hěn 'dwō. /This country is rich in natural resources. Jèi ge gwó'jyāde 'tyānrán wù'chán hěn 'fēngfù. /This is very rich wheat land. Jèikwài'dì jùng 'màidz hěn 'féi. /This is one of the richest oilfields in the world. Jèi shr shr'jyèshang yíge °dzwèi 'fùde (°chǎn'lyàng dzwèi 'dwōde) 'yóutyán.

Strike it rich dzǒuyùn. /My brother struck it rich. Wǒde 'gēge jēn dzǒu'yùn.

The rich 'kwòrén. /This law will benefit the rich. Jèityáu fǎ'lyù dwèiyu 'kwòrén yǒu'lì.

RIDE (RODE, RIDDEN) dzwò; (if one sits astride the vehicle or animal) chí. /We rode in a beautiful car. Wǒmen 'dzwò yílyàng hěn 'pyàulyàngde 'chē. /I rode past the railroad station. Wǒ dzwò'gwòle hwǒchē'jàn le. /We rode to the end of the line. Wǒmen 'dzwòdau dzwèi 'hòude yí'jàr. /Do you know how to ride a bike? Nǐ hwèi chí 'dzsyíng'chē ma? /He's ridden horses all his life. Tā chíle yí'bèidzde 'mǎ. /We rode (horseback) a lot last year. Wǒmen 'chyùnyán chángcháng chí 'mǎ.

(Of the vehicle) dzǒu. /This car rides smoothly. Jèilyàng 'chē dzǒude hén 'wěn.

Ride someone (ridicule) gēn . . . dǎu'lwàn, gēn . . . kāi wán'syàu. /Oh, stop riding me! 'Ài, byé gēn wo °dǎu'lwàn le (°kāi wán'syàu)!

A ride. /Can you arrange a ride for me? Nǐ 'néng bùnéng gěi wǒ 'jǎu yíge byànchē. /It's a short bus ride. is expressed as Ride a short spell on the bus and you get there. Dzwò yìsyǎu'dwàrde gūnggùngchì'chē jyòu 'dàule. /We went for a ride in an airplane. is expressed as We rode in an airplane on a short pleasure trip. Wǒmen dzwòje fēi'jī 'gwàngle yìtàng.

RIGHT. (Correct, proper) dwèi. /That's right! 'Dwèile. /This is the right answer. 'Jèige hwéidá shr 'dwèide. /You're absolutely right. Nǐ 'wánchywán 'dwèi. /He's right about everything. Tā shwō de dōu 'dwèile. /Is this the right way? 'Dzèmma dzòu 'dwèi ma? or 'Dzèmma dzwò 'dwèi ma?

(Of a size) dwèi, héshr. /This one is the right size. Jèige dà'syǎu jèng hé-'shr. or 'Jèige hàu'mǎr jèng 'dwèi.

(Of the weather) hǎu, if the weather desired is good weather; if some other type is desired, the appropriate adjective. /We'll leave tomorrow if the weather is right. Míngr tyār 'hǎu wǒmen jyòu 'dzǒu.

(Of one's mind). /You're not in your right mind. Nǐ 'húdùle. or Nǐ 'nǎujīn bu'chīngchu.

(Of something that has two sides, one of which is designed to be seen) jèng. /Make sure that only the right side of the material shows. 'Chyáuje dyǎr jr jyàu nèige dūngsyide 'jèngmyàr chùng 'wàitou.

(Ninety degrees) jèng. /That's bigger than a right angle. 'Nèige bǐ °'jèng-jyǎu (°jrjyǎu) 'dà yìdyǎr.

(Politically) bǎushǒu. /He's always been on the right politically. Tā yí'syàng shr 'sžsyàng bǎushǒu. /This newspaper follows a rightist policy. Jèige bàujr de lwùndyàn hěn bǎushǒu.

(Opposite of left) yòu. /Take the road on the right. Dzǒu 'yòubyar nèityáu 'lù. /I've lost my right shoe. Wó bǎ 'yòujyǎude 'syé 'dyōule.

A right (privilege; legal) chywán; (social) 'lǐyóu; sometimes expressed with the verb kéyǐ can or may. /They denied his right to the property. Tāmen bùchéng-'rèn tāde tsáichǎn'chywán. /You have no right to behave like this. Nǐ méi 'lǐyou 'jèyàng. /I have a right to go if I wish. Rúgwǒ wǒ 'yàu chyù dehwà, wǒ 'kéyǐ chyù. /I have my rights! (in protest against someone's claim or action) Wǒ yóu'lǐ! or Wǒ lǐ'jrchí'jwàng! or (to an officer of the law who is trying to arrest you) meaning I haven't done anything illegal. Wǒ 'bìng °méifàn'fǎ (°bùfàn'fǎ)! or (to someone who is protesting against your participation in something) Wó yǒu'chywán gwò'wèn! or Wó 'gwàndejáu!

(Moral good) hǎu; **right and wrong** háudǎi, shrfēi. /You seem to have no idea of right and wrong. Nǐ hǎu'syàng °bù'jr háu'dǎi (°shr'fēi bù'míng).

Right (correctly) dwèi. /Do it right or not at all. Yàu 'dzwò jyòu dzwò 'dwèi le, 'yàuburán 'yìdyár yě byé 'dzwò.

(Precisely) jyòu. /Ask him; he's right in the room. Tā jyòu dzài jèige 'wūdzli ne; nǐ 'wèn ta. / The book's right there on the shelf. 'Shū jyòu dzài nèige 'jyàdz-shang ne.

(Immediately, or often added simply to give a polite tone to the sentence) jyòu; (if the idea is that of continuing straight ahead) yìjr̀; sometimes not expressed. / I'll be right there. Wǒ jyòu 'lái. / Go right in the house. Yì'jr̀ dzǒujìn 'fángdz chyù, 'hǎu le. / He drove right on. Tā yǐ'jr̀ 'kāigwòchyule. / Go right ahead. (when answering a request for permission to do something) 'Sying. or 'Kéyǐ. / Sit right down. 'Dzwòsyachyu, 'hǎu le. or 'Dzwò ba.

(Completely) yìjr̀, dōu, jèng. / They fought right to the end. Tāmen yì'jr̀ 'dǎdàu 'dǐ. / The porch runs right around the house. Jèidzwò 'fángdz 'sz̀myàn dōu-shr̀ 'lángdz. / The bullet went right through him. Chyāng'dzěr jèng tsúng tā 'shēn-shang 'chwāngwochyu.

Right away 'gánjǐn, lìkè, 'mǎshang, all followed by jyòu. / Let's go right away, or we'll be late. Wǒmen °'gánjǐn (°lì'kè, °etc.) jyòu 'dzǒu ba, 'yàuburán jyòu 'wǎn le.

Right now syàndzài (jèng). / I'm busy right now. Wǒ syàn'dzài jèng 'mángje ne. or Wǒ syàn'dzài méi 'gūngfu.

All right hǎu. / The doctor said you'd be all right in a few days. 'Dàifu shwō nǐ jityān jyòu kéyi 'hǎu le. / Everything will turn out all right. is expressed as The result will certainly be satisfactory. 'Jyēgwǒ yí'dìng °ywán'mǎn (°méi 'wèntí). / All right, I'll do it if you want me to. 'Hǎu, yàushr nǐ 'jyàu wo dzwò wǒ jyòu 'dzwò.

Do right by, do the right thing by dwèi . . . jù. / You didn't do the right thing by him. Nǐ 'dwèi ta bú'jù. or expressed as You owe him an apology. Nǐ 'dwèibuchi 'tā. / Do you think we did right by him? is expressed as Do you think we can face him? Nǐ 'jywéde wǒmen 'dwèidechǐ ta ma?

Serve someone **right.** / It serves him right! Tā jyòu 'chyàn nèmma yàngr! or Hwó'gāi! or 'Běnlái jyòu 'gāi nèmma 'jr̀ ta.

To right something (turn the proper side up) jènggwolai. / Can you right the boat without any help? Nǐ 'yíge rén néng bǎ 'chwán gěi 'jènggwolái ma?

RING (RANG, RUNG). (Sound) syǎng; (if by striking) dǎ, chyāu. / The bell rings every hour. Jèige 'língr 'měiyìdyǎn jūng °'syǎng (°'dǎ) yítsz̀. / The phone rang. Dyàn-'hwà 'syàngle. / Two shots rang out. Yǒu lyǎngshēngr 'chyāng'syǎng.

(Of the ears) syǎng, jyàuhwàn. / His ears were ringing. Tāde 'ěrdwo jr̀ °syǎng (°'jyàuhwàn). / The sound is still ringing in my ears. Nèige shēng'yīn hái dzài wó 'ěrdwo lǐtou 'syǎng ne.

Ring something (cause to sound) èn (if by pressing a button); yáu (if by swing-ing); dǎ (if by striking); etc. / Ring the bell again. 'Dzài èn yísyà 'líng. / Ring the buzzer. Èn nèige 'líng. / Have you rung the bell? Nǐ jàu 'líng le ma?

Ring true. / His offer rings true. Tā shwōde hǎusyàng shr̀ 'jēnsyīnhwà.

Ring with (resound with). / The valley rang with gun fire. is expressed as The whole valley was the sound of guns. Mǎnshān'gú lǐtou dōu shr̀ chyāng'shēng.

Ring (sound of ringing) 'shēngyīn. / That bell has a peculiar ring. Nèige 'líng-rde 'shēngyīn hěn chí'gwài.

(On a finger) jyèjr̀, (shǒu)lyòudz. / She is wearing a ring on her left hand. Tā dzwóshǒu dàije yige °'jyèjr̀ (°'lyoudz).

(Any circular band) chywàr. / Keep your napkin in this ring. Bǎ nǐde tsān'jīn fàngdzai nèige 'chywārli.

(Circular arrangement of) -chywār. / They stood in a ring. Tāmen 'jànle yǐ-chywār. / There's a ring of trees around the house. Ràuje jèige 'fángdz jùngle yǐ-chywār 'shù. / They've built a ring of cement around the spring. Wéije chywán'ywàn tāmen pūle yǐchywār yáng'hwēi.

(Sports arena) lèitái, táidz. / We had seats near the ring. Wǒmende 'dzwòwèi lí nèige °lèi'tái (°'táidz) hěn 'jìn.

(Gang) hwǒr, hwǒdz. / They broke up the spy ring. Tāmen bǎ nèige jyāndyé-wǎng 'pwòle. or Tāmen bǎ jèihwǒr jyān'dyé dǎ'sànle.

Give someone **a ring** gěi . . . dǎ dyàn'hwà. / Give me a ring tomorrow. 'Míngr gěi wo dǎ dyàn'hwà.

Have a false ring. / Her laughter had a false ring. Tā 'syàude 'jyǎlejyǎ'chǐde.

Be ringed by 'sżwéi dōu shř, 'wéije dōu shř. / The valley is ringed by mountains. Jèige shān'gǔ °'sżwéi (°'wéije) dōu shř 'shān.

RISE (ROSE, RISEN). (Move upward) shēngchilai; (steadily, as a balloon) pyāuchilai; (flying, as a bird or plane) fēichilai, fēishangchyu. / The balloon rose slowly. Nèige chì'chyóu màn'mārde °'shēngchilaile (°'pyāuchilaile). / The plane rose and circled the field. Fēi'jī 'fēichilaile, dzài fēijī'chǎngshang 'ràu.

(Of a curtain) kāi. / When will the curtain rise? 'Shémma shŕhou kāi'mù?

(Extend upward) 'fāuchilai, lí 'dì yǒu. / The mountain rises a thousand feet. 'Shān 'gāuchi yìchyān 'shř lai. or 'Shān dǐngr lí'dì yǒu yìchyān 'chř. / The ground rises a little behind the house. Fáng 'hòutoude 'dì 'gāuchi yì'dyǎr lai.

(Expand upward) fāchilai. / The bread has risen. Jèige myàn'bāu 'fāchilaile.

(Of prices) jǎng. / Prices are still rising. 'Wùjyà hái 'jǎng ne. / Sugar has risen to twice its former price. is expressed as The price of sugar has risen to double what it was. Tángde 'jyàchyán 'jǎngle yí'bèi.

(Of a person) 'chǐlái; (get up in the morning) chǐchwáng; (get up from sitting) jànchilai. / The men all rose as we came in. Wǒmen 'jìnchyu de shŕhou rén dōu 'jànchiláile.

(Of the sun) chūlai. / The sun rises earlier at this time of year. 'Měinyán 'jèige shŕhou 'tàiyang 'chūlaide 'dzǎu. / The sun hasn't risen yet. 'Tàiyang hái méi'chūlai ne.

(Of a voice). / Her voice rose to a scream. is expressed as Her voice got bigger and bigger, until she cried out. Tāde 'shēngyīn ywè lái ywè 'dà, 'jyàuchi-laile.

(Of water) jǎng. / The river is rising fast. Hé('shwěi) 'jǎngde kwài'jí le.

Rise to importance dé'yì, 'chéngwei hěn 'jùngyàude rén. / He rose to importance when he was still young. Tā hái dzài nyán'chīng de shŕhou jyòu yǐjīng 'chéngwei hěn 'jùngyaude 'rén le. or Tā dzài shàu'nyán de shŕhou jyòu hěn déyì le.

Rise to fame chéng'míng, chū'míng. / He rose to international fame almost overnight. Tā yì'jyúchéng'míng. or Tā lì'kè chūle 'míng le. or Tā lì'kè 'míng-mǎn'tyānsyà.

Rise to the occasion. / You can depend on her to rise to the occasion. Nǐ fàng-'syīn ba, °tā 'jřdau dzěmma 'bàn (°'shémma shèr tā dōu néng yìngfude'hǎu).

A rise (of ground) pwō. / The house is on a little rise. Nèige 'fángdz shř dzài yíge syàu'pwōrshang.

(Of prices) expressed verbally with jǎng. / There's been a rise in price since last week. Tsúng 'shànglǐbài chǐ, jǎngle 'jyà le.

(Of temperature) expressed verbally with jǎng. / There was a sudden rise in temperature today. Jyěrde wēn'dù 'hūránde 'jǎngle.

Give rise to underline{is expressed as} cause people to do so-and-so °jyàu (°ràng) rén . . . . /The rumor gave rise to a lot of unnecessary worry. Jèige yáu'yán °jyàu (°ràng) rén bái dān'syīnle yì'chǎng.

RIVER. hé; **Yangtsze River** Chángjyāng, Dàjyāng *or* (just the lower part) Yángdžjyāng; **Yellow River** Hwánghé. / That's a good river for fishing. Nèityáu 'hé dǎ'yú hén 'hǎu.

ROAD. lù, dàu; (thoroughfare) mǎlù; (highway) gūnglù; **main road** dàlù; **side road** syǎulù; **branch road** chàlù. / The road is getting steadily worse. meaning as one goes along it. Nèityáu 'lù ywè 'dzǒu ywè 'hwài. or meaning from day to day Nèityáu 'lù yìtyānyì'tyānde ywè lái ywè 'hwài.

Go on the road páu mǎtóu. / When does the show go on the road? °Jèi 'bǎndz (°Jèige syì'bǎndz) 'shémma shŕhou 'chūchyu páu mǎtóu?

Be on the wrong road (fig.) dzǒu syélù. / The boy is the wrong road and has been stealing things. Jèige 'háidz dzǒu syé'lù, lǎu 'tōu rénde 'dūngsyi.

ROAST. kǎu, shāu; **roast duck** °kǎu (°shāu) 'yādz; etc. / This meat tastes best when roasted. Jèijung ròu kǎuje chŕ dzwèi hǎu. (fig.) /I'm roasting in here; how about you? Wǒ jèr rèszle; 'ní dzěmma'yàng?

ROB. chyǎng. /I've been robbed. Wǒ bèi 'chyǎngle. *or* (fig.) Wǒ shàng'dàngle. *or* Wǒ jyàu rén 'ywānle. /They'll rob you of everything you've got. Tāmen yàu bǎ nǐ 'swóyǒude 'dūngsyi dōu 'chyǎng le. *or* (fig.) Tāmen hěn 'chyǎu jú'gàng.

ROCK. shŕtou; (as contrasted with a pebble) yíkwài 'dà shŕtou. /What kind of rock is this? Jè shr shémma shŕtou? /Don't throw that rock! 'Byé rēng nèikwài 'shŕtou! / The ship was wrecked on a rock. 'Chwán 'jwàngdzài yíkwài 'dà shŕtoushang le. / That's no pebble, that's a rock. 'Nèige 'búshr shŕtou'dzěr shŕ yíkwài 'dà shŕtou.

To rock yáu; **rock** a baby **to sleep** yáujáule; **rock** a house (or something big) yáudùngle. /Rock the baby to sleep. Bǎ 'háidz 'yáuje yáuje jyòu yáu'jáule. / The earthquake rocked the whole house. Dì'jèn bǎ jèi jěng'gèrde 'fángdz dōu jènde jŕ-'dùng.

ROD. gwèr, tyáu. /We need new curtain rods. Wǒmen děi hwàn 'syīnde lyándz'gwèr le. / The parts are connected by an iron rod. Jèisyē 'dwàr dōushr yùng yìgěr °tyě-'tyáu (°tyě'gwèr) 'lyánchilaide.

Fishing rod yúgār.

ROLL. (Change location by rotary motion along a surface or cause to move thus; of a ball, wheel, ring, person, etc.) gúlu; (particularly of a roller or ball) gwǔn; (turn around on an axis, either at one location or changing location) jwàn, with which a verb indicating the method of causing such motion can be used, such as 'twēije (by pushing), 'lāje (by pulling), 'tīje (by kicking). /Roll the barrel over here. Bǎ nèige 'túng gěi °'gúlugwolai (°'gúlu dàu 'jèr lai). / Turn the barrel sideways and roll it up the slope. Bǎ 'túng fàng'dǎule 'twēije °'jwàndau (°'gúludau) 'pwōrshangchyu. /Put the barrel on top of the plank and it'll roll down by itself. Bǎ 'túng gēdzai tyàu'bǎn 'gāude nèi'tourshang, 'džjǐ jyòu kěyi °'gwǔnsyachyule (°'gúlusyachyule). /Give the barrel a push and it'll roll over here. Bǎ 'túng 'twēi yísyàr jyòu 'gúlugwolaile. *or* Yì 'twēi jyòu 'gúlugwolaile. / The ball rolled down the hill. 'Chyóur

°'gwŭnsyà (°'gúlusyà) 'shān chyùle. / Thé rìng rolled ten-feet before it toppled over. 'Hwándz °jwànle (°'gwŭnle, °'gúlule) 'shŕchŕ nèmma 'ywán tsái 'dăusyà. / I rolled out of bed last night. Dzwór 'wănshang wŏ tsúng 'chwángshang °'gwŭn dàu (°'gúludàu, °yĭ 'gúlu gúlu dàu, °yĭ 'gwŭn gwŭndàu, °yĭ fān'shēn fāndàu) 'dìsya chyu le. / The waves keep rolling in. 'Làngtóu yíjènyí'jènde °'gwŭnjìnlai (°'jywàngwŏlai).

(Shape a flat thing into a spiral) jywăn; (sleeves or pant legs only) wăn. / We rolled up the rug. Wŏmen bă dì'tăn °'jywănchiláile (°'jywănchéngle yíge 'jywăr). / He rolls his own cigarettes. Tā 'dzòjĭ 'jywăn yān'jywăr. / Roll up your sleeves. Bă 'syòudz °'jywănchilai (°'wănchilai).

(Press something down by rolling something over it) yà; (if with a large roller, making it flat) nyănpíngle; (make thin by rolling something over it; only for dough) găn. / They rolled the field flat with a roller. Tāmen nă nyăndz bă 'chăngdz yà-'píngle. / Roll the dough out thin. 'Myàn găn 'báu yidyăr.

(Move along on wheels) dzŏu. / This car rolls along smoothly. Jèige 'chē 'dzŏude hĕn 'wĕn.

(Of a ship) yáu, băi. / The ship rolled heavily. 'Chwán °'yáude (°'băide) hĕn 'lìhai.

Roll by (of time). / I get more homesick as the months roll by. Wó syăng'jyā 'syàngde 'yíge ywè bĭ 'yíge ywè 'lìhai.

Roll something into a ball (with palms or fingers) 'tswōchéng ge 'chyóur, 'róuchéng 'chyóur; (with fingers only) 'nyănchéng ge 'chyóur; (enlarging it by rolling it along, as a snowball) 'gwŭnchéng ge 'chyóur.

Roll over (of something lying down, so that the parts facing upward and downward are reversed) fānshēn, fāngwolai; **roll over and over** (either in one place or moving along a surface) dágwĕr. / Roll over! (toward the speaker) 'Fāngwŏ 'shēn lai! or (away from the speaker) 'Fāngwŏ 'shēn chyu! / He rolled over on the ground when his coat caught fire. Tā 'yīshang 'jáule, tā jyòu dzài 'dìshang dăle ge 'gwĕr. / The dog rolled over and over on the ground. 'Gŏu dzài 'dìshang jŕ dă'gwĕr.

A roll (list of names) míngdān; **call the roll** dyănmíng. / Have they called the roll yet? Tāmen dyăn'míngle ma?

A roll of jywăr, jywăndz. / He used a whole roll of wallpaper. Tā yùngle jéng-'jywărde húchyáng'jŕ. / He took out a big roll of bills. Tā 'náchu yí'dàjywăndz chyán-'pyàudz lai. / Do you have rolls of toilet paper? Nĭ yŏu °chéng'jywărde (°'jéng'jywărde) shóu'jŕ ma?

ROOF. (Of a house) fángdĭngr; (of a building) lóudĭngr. / The burglar escaped via the roof of the adjacent house. 'Dzéi tsúng 'jyèbyerde fáng'dĭngrshang 'pàule. / The tin roof is only temporary. Jèige 'fángdzde yángtyé 'dĭngr 'búgwò shŕ 'jànshŕde.

Roof of the mouth shàngtáng. / I burned the roof of my mouth. Wŏ 'tàngle wŏde shàng'táng le.

To roof pū; or expressed with the nouns given above. / The cottage is roofed with tiles. Jèige syău'fángdz °shàngtou 'pūde shŕ 'wă (°shŕ 'wá'dyēngr).

ROOM. wūdz, wūr; (in a hotel) fángjyān. / Where can I rent a furnished room? 'Shémma dìfang néng 'dzū yĭjyan dài 'jyājyu de 'wūdz? / It was a big room with plenty of light. Nèijyān 'wūdz yòu 'dà yòu 'lyàng.

(Rent) fángdzū. / What do you charge for room and board? 'Fángdzū gēn 'fànchyán yĭ'chi nĭ yàu 'dwōshau?

(Space or place) dìfang. / There's no room to sit down. 'Jèr méi dìfang 'dzwò. / Is there room for one more? is expressed as Can you still seat one? 'Hái néng

dzwò yíge ma? /I see little room for improvement. Wǒ 'jywéde néng 'gǎi de dìfang 'méi dwōshǎu le. or expressed as As I see it, there isn't much you can improve.
Wǒ 'kàn, 'méi shémma kě'gǎide.

    To room jù. /Shall we room together? Dzámen 'jù yí'kwàr, 'hǎu ma?

ROOT. gēn, gēr. /The roots are very deep. 'Gēn hěn shēn. /He had to have the
root of his tooth extracted. Tāde yá'gēr děi 'báchulai. /You don't have to pull my
hair out by the roots. Nǐ 'yùngbujáu bá wǒde 'tóufa lyán 'gēr 'báchulai.

    Get to the root of kàn . . . dàu'dǐ shr̄ . . . . /Let's get at the root of the matter.
'Kànkàn jèijyàn 'shr̄ dàu'dǐ shr̄ 'dzěmma hwéi 'shr̄.

    Take root jùnghwó. /Has the rosebush taken root yet? Nèikē 'méigwèi jùng-
'hwóle ma? (fig.) /The custom never really took root. Nèige 'fēngsú 'gēnběn méi
'jēn syīngchilai.

    To root something **out** 'gēnbén gěi °'chúle (°'chǎnchú, °'chyùle). /They're
trying to root out malaria from this region. Tāmen syáng bǎ jèige 'dìfangde 'yàudz
'gēnbén gěi °'chúle (°'chǎnchú).

ROPE. shéngdz. /He slid down the rope. Tā shwùnje 'shéngdz 'lyōusyachyule. /Fix
it with this piece of rope. Ná jèityáu 'shéngdz 'jìshàng 'hǎu le. (fig.) /Don't worry;
give him enough rope and he'll hang himself. Nǐ béng 'gwǎn tā le; tā dzáu'wǎn dzǔng-
'hwài 'dzjí rēchū 'shr̄ lai de.

    Know the ropes. /Wait till you know the ropes better. Syān bǎ 'chíngsyíng
nèng 'shóusyile 'dzài shwō.

    To rope off yùng 'shéngdz 'lán. /A large space was roped off in one corner.
Jǐ'jyǎu nèr yùng 'shéngdz 'lánchū yí'dàkwài 'dìfang chyu.

ROSE. méigwèi hwār; rosebush 'méigwèi(shù) with measure kē. /They presented
the actress with a bouquet of roses. Tāmen 'syàngei nèige nyújú'jyáu yìbǎr méigwèi'hwār. /How do you like my rosebushes? Wǒ jèisyēkē 'méigwèi 'hǎu buhǎu?
(fig.) /This trip has been no bed of roses. Jèi yí'tàng kě bù'shūfu.

    (Color) méigwèidž, méi'gwèishǎr. /She's wearing a rose dress. Tā chwān
yíjyàn 'méigwèishǎrde 'yīfu.

ROUGH. (Not smooth-surfaced) tsū; (of water) expressed as big waves làngdà; (of a
road) bùpíng, hwài. /The bark of this tree is very rough. Jèikē 'shù 'pí hěn 'tsū.
/This table is made of rough planks. Jèijāng 'jwōdz shr̄ tsū'bǎndz dzwòde. /The
water's pretty rough today. Jyērge 'làng hěn 'dà. /How well can this truck take
rough ground? Jèilyàng dzàijùng'chē néng dzǒu bù'píngde 'lù ma?

    (Sketchy) dàjr̀de; a rough draft tsáugǎu. /This'll give you a rough idea. 'Jèige
kěyi jyàu ni míngbai ge dà'gài. /Here's a rough draft of my speech. Jèi shr̄ wó
yán'jyàngde tsáu'gǎu.

    (Not gentle) tsūyě. /His rough manner frightened the children. Tā nèmma
tsū'yěde 'yàngdz bá syǎu'háidzmen dōu 'syàjaule.

    (Severe, difficult). /They had a rough time of it. is expressed as They ex-
perienced a lot of difficulties. Tāmen 'jēnggwò hěn dwō 'máfan.

    To rough it. /He didn't enjoy roughing it last summer. is expressed as Last
summer he certainly didn't like that kind of rough existence. 'Chyùnyán 'syàtyan tā
kě bù'syīhwan nèijǔng bù'shūfude 'shēnghwó.

ROUND. ywán. /They have a round table in the living room. Tāmen kè'tīngli yǒu
yìjāng ywán'jwōdz. /The medicine is in the little round bottle. 'Yàu dzài syǎu

ywán'píngdzli ne. / What a nice round mirror! 'Ài! Jèimyàn ywán'jǐngdz jēn 'hǎu. / That ball doesn't look round to me. Wǒ 'jywéde nèige 'chyóur 'búshr̀ 'ywánde.

(Both ways) láihwéi; **round-trip ticket** láihwéi pyàu. / How much for the round trip? Lái'hwéi 'dwōshau chyán?

In **round numbers** dàgàide 'shùmù; or other expressions with dàgài. / I'm speaking in round numbers. Wǒ 'shwōde shr̀ dà'gàide 'shùmù. / It costs a hundred dollars in round numbers. Dà'gài děi yùng yì'bǎikwài chyán.

A **round** (in a contest) chǎng. / He was eliminated in the second round. Dì'èr-chǎng tā jyòu bèi °dǎsyachyule (°shwāsyalaile). / In what round was the boxer knocked out? 'Něiyi chǎng nèige dǎ'chywánde dzōu pāsyale?

A **round** of dàu. / He ordered another round of drinks. Tā 'yòu gěi 'dàjyā jyàule yídàu 'jyǒu.

Be **on one's rounds** sùng plus a word describing what is delivered; **finish one's rounds** sùng'wán. / The newsboy is on his rounds. Jèige sùng'bàu de háidz sùng'bàu ne. / When will the milkman finish his rounds? Jèige sùngnyóu'nǎi de 'shémma shŕhou sùng'wán?

Make the rounds (get around) chwánde kwài; or expressed as everybody knows it 'shwéi dōu 'jŕdaule. / That story sure made the rounds. Jèige 'shr̀ jēn chwánde 'kwài. or Nèijyàn 'shèr 'shwéi dōu jŕdaule.

To **round** a point of obstruction 'ràugwo. / The ship rounded the Cape of Good Hope this morning. Jīntyan 'dzǎushang 'chwán 'ràugwo Hǎuwàng'jyǎu le.

Round a corner gwǎiwār. / As soon as you round the corner you'll see the store. Nǐ yì gwǎi'wār jyòu 'kànjyan nèige 'pùdz le.

Round off an edge (smooth down) nèngywán, mwóywán. / Round off the edges a little. Bǎ 'byār °'nèng'ywán (°mwó'ywán) yìdyǎr.

Round out something (complete) bǎ . . . tsòu'chíle. / I need this to round out my collection. Wǒ yàu 'jèige háu bǎ wǒ 'dzǎn de tsòu'chíle.

Round (around). / Is there enough candy to go round? is expressed as Is the candy enough to be divided? Táng gòubugòu 'fēn? or as Is the candy enough for everybody to eat? 'Táng 'gòu dàjyāhwǒr 'chr̄de ma?

Round and round jwànje'wārde. / The children were dancing round and round. Jèisyē 'háidzmen jwànje'wārde tyàu'lái tyàu'chyù.

Round the edge of 'sz̀wéi. / There's a border round the edge of it. 'Sz̀wéi 'yánle yìtyáu 'byān.

All year round 'jěngnyán, 'wú'dūng'lǐ'syà. / I now live here all year round. Wǒ syàndzài 'jěngnyán 'jù jèr. or Wǒ shr̀ 'wúdūng'lǐ'syàde 'jùdzài jèr le.

ROW. (Line) lyòu, háng. / He pulled up a whole row of carrots. Tā 'bále yìjěng-'lyòude hú'lwóbe. / They stood in a row waiting. Tāmen 'páile °yí'lyòu (°yì'háng) děng.

To **row** yáu, hwá. / You'll have to row too. 'Nǐ yé děi °'yáu (°'hwá). / Who will row this boat? 'Shéi °yáu (°hwá) jèige 'chwán ne? / Row me across the river. Bá wǒ 'yáugwo 'hé 'nèibyar chyu.

RUB. (With repeated grinding motion) mwó; (scraping, polishing, or rubbing something in, or dirt off) tsā; (in rubbing the hands together, occasionally in other situations) tswō; (with a sidewiping motion) tsèng. / My shoe's rubbing. Wǒde 'syé °jŕ 'tsèng (°mwó) 'jyǎu. / The boat rubbed against the pier. 'Chwán 'tsèngje nèige 'mǎtóu. / He rubbed his hands together. Tā 'tswō'shǒu. / Better rub the clothes hard or they won't get clean. Háishŕ bǎ 'yīshang shŕ'jǐn °'tsā yitsź (°'tswō yitswō) yàuburán syǐbu'gānjing. /Rub her back with alcohol. Yùng hwó'jyou tsź tǎde 'bèi. /You forgot to rub out your name. Nǐ 'wàngle bǎ nǐde 'míngdz gěi 'tsā le.

Rub it in (fig.). /I know I'm wrong, so don't rub it in. Wǒ 'jŕdau wǒ 'tswòle, °jyòu byé 'shwō le (°byé méi'wán le).

RUBBER. syàngpí, jyàupí; <u>in some compounds</u> pí. /They used a lot of rubber in these tires. Jèisyē chē'dài yùngle hěn dwō syàng'pí. /Take this piece of rubber hose. 'Ná jèige pí'gwǎr hǎu le.

Rubbers (overshoes) jyàupí syé, syàngpísyé. /I lost one of my rubbers yesterday. Wǒ 'dzwórge dyōule yìjŕ jyàupí 'syé.

RUG. dǐtǎn. /I like oriental rugs. Wó 'syǐhwan 'dūngfāng dì'tǎn. /That's a nine-by-twelve rug. 'Nèi shŕ yíge 'jyóuchŕ 'kwān, shŕ'èrchŕ'chángde dì'tǎn.

RUIN. hwěi, dzāuta. /The frost will ruin the crop. Jèitsżde 'shwāng yàu bǎ 'jwāngjya géi 'hwěi le. /He's ruining his health. Tā 'dzāuta dżjǐde shēndz. /This material is ruined. Jèige tsái'lyàu °'hwěile (°'dzāutale).

Be ruined (financially) pwōchǎn. /He was ruined in the depression. Tā dzài 'nyántóu bù'hǎude shŕhou pwòle 'chǎn le.

Cause the ruin of <u>something</u> jyàu . . . géi hwěile. /He caused the ruin of his family. Tā jyā shŕ jyàu 'tā géi 'hwěide.

Go to rack and ruin, be in ruins hwěile. /The place is going to rack and ruin. Jèige 'dìfang 'hwěile. /Their house is in ruins. Tāmende 'fángdz 'hwěile.

Ruins (destroyed buildings) lwàndwěi; (remnants of ancient buildings) gǔjì. /They were hunting for bodies among the ruins. Tāmen dzài nèi lwàn'dwěi lǐtou jǎu sž'shŕ ne. /Those are very impressive ruins. Nèi shŕ hén kě'gwānde gǔ'jì.

RULE. (Regulation) gwēijyu. /Smoking is against the rules here. Dzài 'jèr chōu'yān shŕ fàn'gwēijyude. <u>or expressed as</u> Smoking is prohibited here. 'Jèr bù'syǔ chōu-'yān.

(Act of ruling) <u>is expressed verbally as</u> 'tǔngjŕ *or* gwǎn control. /This island has been under foreign rule for years. Jèige 'dǎu bèi 'wàigworén gwǎnle hěn 'jyou le.

As a rule 'syànglái. /As a rule I don't drink. Wǒ 'syànglái bùhē'jyou de.

Be the rule (be customary). /That sort of thing is the rule around here. 'Jèr 'syànglái 'jèmmayàng.

To rule 'tǔngjŕ. /The same family has been ruling for generations. Jèi yí-'syìng yǐjing 'tǔngjŕle 'dwōshau dài le. /He's ruled by his emotions. <u>is expressed as</u> He always does things with emotion. Tā lǎushr 'gǎnchíngyùng'shŕ.

Rule <u>something</u> **out** bǎ . . . °búswànle (°búswàn'shùrle). /This doesn't entirely rule out all possibilities. 'Jèiyàng bìng méi bǎ swóyǒude 'kěnéngsyìng dǒu °búswànle (°búswànshùrle). <u>or expressed as</u> This isn't to say that there are no other ways. 'Jèiyàng 'búshr shwō 'méiyou 'byéde fádz le.

RUN (RAN). (Go fast on foot) pǎu. /You'll have to run if you want to catch the train. Nǐ yàu syǎng 'gǎnshàng nèitàng 'chē, ní ké déi 'pǎu le. /I can walk faster than you can run. Wó 'dzǒude bí ní 'pǎude hái 'kwài. /He ran two miles in fourteen minutes and thirty-two seconds. Tā 'pǎu 'èryǐnglǐ yùng shŕ'sżfēn 'sānshrèr'myǎu.

(Sail or move) dzǒu. /The ship was running before the wind. 'Chwán 'dzǒude hěn shwùn'fēng.

(Be in operation) kāi. / The engine's running. 'Jīchi 'kāije ne.

(Function) is expressed with yùng use. / That car hasn't run well since we bought it. Nèige 'chē dźtsúng wŏmen 'mǎilái yǐ'hòu jyòu bùhǎu'yùng.

(Be in process) kāi, yǎn. / The movie had been running for half an hour when we went in. Wŏmen 'jìnchyu de shŕhou dyàn'yǐng °'yǎnle (°'kāile) 'bànge 'jūngtóu le.

(Flow; of colors) twèisè, twèishǎi, dyàu 'yánshar, dyàushŕ, làushǎr. / These colors are guaranteed not to run. Jèisyē 'yánsè 'gwānbǎu bú °'twèi'sè (°'twèi'shǎi, °etc.).

(Go; of something quoted or sung). / The tune runs like this. is expressed as The tune is like this. Jèige 'dyàur syàng 'jèyàng. / How does the first line run? is expressed as How is the first line sung (or read)? Dì'yīháng dzěmma °'chàng (°'nyàn)? or as How is the first line? Dì'yīháng shŕ 'dzěmma láije?

(Be mostly). / These apples run small. is expressed as These apples are mostly small. Jèisyē 'pínggwŏ chàbudwō 'dōu 'syǎu. / What size do these dresses run in? is expressed as What sizes are there of these dresses? Jèisyē 'yīfu dōu-shŕ 'dwō dà 'hǎur de?

(Of stockings) chōusź, tyàusź. / This kind of stocking won't run. Jèijǔng wǎdz bútyàusź.

Run an apparatus or machine yùng. / Can you run a washing machine? Nǐ 'jŕdau dzěmma yùng syǐ'yīshang de 'jīchi ma?

Run a business dzwò, gwǎn. / I don't think he knows how to run the business. Wŏ 'jywéde tā bú'hwèi dzwò 'mǎimai.

Run a race pǎu, sài. / The first race has already been run. Dì'yīchǎng yǐ-jing °'pǎugwole (°'sàigwole).

Run a risk máusyǎn. / He's running a big risk. Tā 'màu hěn 'dàde 'syǎn.

Run an errand chūchāi. / How many errands have you run today? 'Jīntyan nǐ 'chūle 'jǐtsź 'chāi le?

Run the risk of . . . -ing màuje . . . de wēi'syǎn. / If you wear that pin with the broken catch, you'll run the risk of losing it. Nǐ yàushŕ dài nèige dwànle gōur de byé'jēn, nǐ jyou děi màuje dyōu de wēi'syǎn. or is expressed as If you wear that pin with the broken catch, it'll be easily lost. Nǐ byé'jēnde gōur dwànle, dàije hěn 'rúngyi 'dyōu.

Run across an area (on foot) 'pǎudàu . . . °'nèibyarchyu (°'jèibyarlai). / The chicken ran across the road. Syǎu'jyēr 'pǎudàu dàur 'nèibyar chyu le.

Run across an area (by flowing) lyóudàu . . . °'nèibyarchyu (°'jèibyarlai). / There was a trickle of water running across the floor. Yílyŏur 'shwěi tsúng dì'bǎn 'jèibyar 'lyóudàu 'nèibyar chyù le.

Run across someone or something (see by accident) pèngjyan, 'ǒurán 'kànjyan. / When did you last run across him? Nǐ dzwèi'hòu dzài 'shémma shŕhou 'pèngjyan ta de? / I ran across an article about him the other day. Nèityān wŏ 'ǒurán 'kànjyan yí'dwàr 'gwānyu ta de 'wénjang.

Run aground gēchyǎn. / My boat ran aground. Wŏde 'chwán gē'chyǎnle.

Run something **aground** bǎ . . . nùngde gē'chyǎnle. / He ran the boat aground. Tā bǎ'chwán 'nùngde gē'chyǎnle.

Run along (leave) chyù, dzǎu. / Run along now! 'Chyù ba! or Shàng 'byé-chùr 'chyù ba! or 'Dzǒu ba!

Run along a route (on foot) shwùnje . . . pău. / He ran along the path until he reached the lake. Tā shwùnje 'dàur pău, yì'jŕde pǎude nèige 'hú nèr.

Run along a route (extend along) yánje. / The path runs along the edge of the lake for about a quarter of a mile. Nèige 'lù yánje 'hú yǒu 'sżfēnjr'yī 'lǐ.

Run along a line of thought. / Along what lines does his mind run? Tā shŕ dzěmma ge 'syángfar?

Run around (go out for good times) wár. / He's running around too much; he'll never be able to pass his exams. Tā 'wárde tài 'lìhai le, 'kǎushŕ yúng'ywán yě 'jíbulyǎu 'gé.

Run around a corner or obstruction (on foot) shwùnje . . . 'pǎu. / He ran around the north side of the house and then just seemed to disappear. Tā shwùnje nèige 'fángdz 'běibyār 'pǎuchyule, 'yì hwéi'tóu jyòu kànbu 'jyànle.

Run around something (extend so as to encircle) yánje . . . de jōu'wéi, wéije; run halfway around wéije . . . yí'bàr. / The path runs around the lake. Yánje 'húde jōu'wéi dōu yǒu 'dàur. or Nèi 'dàur 'wéije húbyār 'ràu. / The road runs only halfway around the lake. Wéije hú'byārshang jyòu yǒu yí'bàr yǒu'lù.

Run circles around (fig.) bǐje 'yǎn yé bǐ . . . 'chyáng. / He can run circles around anyone at that business. 'Nèijyàn shŕ tā bǐje 'yǎn yé bǐ 'byérén dzwòde 'chyáng.

Run around to a place (on foot) 'pǎudàu, 'jwàndàu. / The thief ran around to the rear of the house and escaped through the back gate. 'Dzéi °'pǎudàu (°'jwàndàu) 'fángdz'hòutou chyù, tsúng 'hòumér 'pǎule.

Run around with (keep company with) gēn . . . 'hwùn. / He's running around with a fast crowd. Tā 'jǐng gēn yìbāng hú'nàude rén 'hwùn.

Run away (leave quickly, with or without the intention of returning) pǎu. / He ran away when he saw me. Tā yí 'kànjyan wo, jyòu 'pǎule. / Don't let him run away. Byé jyàu ta 'pǎule. / My dog ran away. Wǒde 'góu 'pǎule.

Run away from a place (intending to stay away) tsúng . . . pǎu. / He ran away from home when he was eight. Tā 'bāswèi de shŕhour jyòu tsúng 'jyāli 'pǎule.

Run away from (fig.) 'dwǒkāi. / He always runs away from danger. Tā yúng-'ywǎn shŕ 'kànjyan bù'hǎu jyòu 'dwǒkāi.

Run away with someone (elope) gēn . . . pǎu. / She ran away with the chauffeur. Nèige 'nyǔde gēn kāi'chēde 'pǎule.

Run away with something (abscond) bǎ . . . chwān'pǎule. / He ran away with my best suit. Tā bá wǒ dzwèi'hǎude yítàu 'yīfu gěi chwān'pǎule.

Run away with one (of the imagination). / Don't let your imagination run away with you. Byé hú'sżlwàn'syǎngle. or Byé syángrù'fēifēi.

Run by or past someone or something (on foot) tsúng . . . páng'byār 'pǎugwo-chyù. / He ran right by us without seeing us. Tā tsúng wǒmen páng'byār 'pǎugwo-chyu kěshr méi'kànjyan wǒmen. / He ran right by the house without realizing he had reached it. Tā tsúng nèige 'fángdz páng'byār 'pǎugwochyu kěshr méi'jywéchulai tā 'dàule nèr le.

Run by or past something (extend) dzài . . . páng'byār. / The road runs right by my house. Jèityáu 'lù jyòu dzài wǒde 'fángdz páng'byār 'gwò.

Run down (stop going) tíng. / Wind up the clock before it runs down. Bǎ 'jūng gěi 'shàngshang byé děng 'tíngle tsái 'shàng.

Run down a route (to a lower position; on foot) pǎusyà . . . chyù. / They ran down the hill. Tāmen 'pǎusyà 'shān chyù le.

Run down a route (to a lower position; by flowing) lyóusyalai. / The tears ran down her cheecks. Tāde yǎn'lèi jr̀ 'lyóu.

Run down a route (on foot, but not to a lower position) dzài . . . shang pǎu. / He ran down the road as fast as he could go. Tā dzài nèige 'dàurshang pǐn'mìngde wàngchyán 'pǎu.

Run someone **down** (strike down) bǎ . . . chwàng'dǎule. / He was run down by a truck. Yílyàng dǎ'chē bǎ ta gěi chwàng'dǎule.

Run someone **down** (speak ill of) mà, pīping. / Don't run him down that way; he's doing his best. 'Byé nèmma °'mà (°'pīping) ta; tā nèr 'búshr 'hǎuhāurde 'dzwò ne ma?

Be run down (of a thing) hwàile, pwòle, bùsyíngle; **look run down** (of a person) 'shēntǐ syàng 'hwàile de yàngdz. / The house is run down. Jèijyān 'fángdz °'hwàile (°bù'syíngle, °'pwòle). / She looks terribly run down. Tāde 'shēntǐ hǎu 'syàng hěn'hwàide yàngdz.

Run dry gānle. / The well has never run dry. Jèikóu 'jǐng méi'gāngwo.

Run for a destination pǎudàu. / It's started to rain; let's run for that tree. Syà'yùle, dzámen 'pǎudàu nèikē 'shù nèr chyù ba. but / Run for it! Kwài 'dzǒu ba! or Kwài 'pǎu ba!

Run for an office jìng'sywǎn (dzwò). / Do you think he'll run for mayor? Ní syǎng tā yàu jìng'sywǎn dzwò shr̀'jǎng ma? / Who ran for president that year? 'Nèinyán shr̀ 'shéi jìng'sywǎn dzúng'tǔng?

Run from someone. / Her dog always runs from strangers. is expressed as The minute her dog sees strangers he runs. Tāde 'gǒu yí 'kànjyan 'shēngren jyòu 'pǎu.

Run from A to B (of a vehicle on a route) shr̀ tsúng A kāi(dau) B. / This bus runs from Peiping to Tientsin. Jèige chángtúchǐ shr̀ tsúng Běi'píng kāi Tyānjīn de.

Run from A to B (of a route) shr̀ tsúng A tūngdàu B. / This railroad runs from the ocean to the center of Shensi province. Jèityáu tyě'lù shr̀ tsúng hǎi'byārshang tūngdau 'Shǎnsyǐ'shēngde dāng'jyàr.

Run in a family (of a trait). / That trait runs in their family. is expressed as Everyone in their family has a bit of that. Tāmen 'jyāde rén 'dōu yǒu dyǎr 'nàyàngr.

Run over an edge (overflow) is expressed as in the preceding paragraph, edge being omitted. / The milk is running over the edge of the cup. 'Bēidzlide nyóu'nǎi 'mànde dōu 'lyóuchulaile.

Run (all) over something (cover). / There was ivy running all over the wall. is expressed as The surface of the wall was completely covered with ivy. Chyángshang pá'mǎnle páchyáng'hǔ.

Run over someone (with a vehicle) yàshāngle, yàle; (if it results in death) yàszle. / Someone was run over. Yǒu 'rén ràng 'chē gěi 'yàle.

Run over something (review) 'wēnsyí yíbyàn; (in one's mind) 'syǎngsyǎng. / Run over your part before the rehearsal. 'Yùyǎn yì'chyán, bǎ nǐ nèi yí'bùfen 'wēnsyí yíbyàn. / I ran over in my mind all the persons involved. Wǒ bǎ swóyǒu (gēn 'jèishèr) yǒu'gwānsyide rén dōu 'syǎngle yìsyǎng.

Run someone **in** (take to jail). / I'll have to run you in. Wǒ déi bǎ nǐ dàidàu jǐngchá'jyú °'kānchilai (°'yāchilai, °'jywānchilai).

Run into an interior (on foot) pǎudàu . . . li. / He ran into the house. Tā 'pǎudàu nèige 'fángdzli chyu le.

Run into an interior (extend) 'tūngdàu . . . li. / Does this road run into the city? Jèityáu 'lù tūngdau chéng'lǐtou ma?

Run into an obstruction (of a vehicle) kāidau, jwàng. / The car ran into a tree. Jèilyàng 'chē °kāidau 'shùshang chyù le (°jwàng 'shùshang le).

Run into debt chyànjài, lājàng, gāijàng, chyànjàng. / He's running into debt. Tā syàndzài °chyàn'jàile (°lā'jàngle, °etc.).

Run a vehicle **into** an obstruction bǎ . . . kāidàu. / He ran his car into a tree. Tā bǎ 'chē kāidau 'shùshang le.

Run something **into** something (thrust into). / I ran a splinter into my finger. Wǒ shǒu'jr̄toushang 'jāle yíge 'tser.

Run last. / My horse ran last. Wǒde 'mǎ là 'hòutou le.

Run low ywè lái ywè 'shǎu le. / My money is running low. Wǒde 'chyán ywè lái ywè 'shǎu le.

Run off (hurry away) dzǒu. / Don't run off now! I have some other things to say. Syàn'dzài byé 'dzǒu a! Wǒ 'hái yǒu 'byéde shr̄ching gēn nǐ 'shwō ne.

Run off a route (of a vehicle) kāidau . . . 'wàitou. / The car ran off the road. Jèilyàng 'chē kāidau dàur 'wàitou chyù le.

Run off with (elope or abscond) see **Run away with** above.

Run out yùngwánle, yùnggwāngle. / Our supply of sugar has run out. Wǒmende 'táng yùng °'wánle (°'gwāngle).

Run out of an interior tsúng . . . 'pǎuchulai. / He ran out of the house. Tā tsúng 'wūdzli 'pǎuchulaile.

Run out of something (use up) yùngwánle, yùnggwāngle. / We ran out of ammunition. Wǒmende jyūn'hwǒ yùng'wánle.

Run someone **out of** town, a country, etc. bǎ . . . 'chyū'jù chū'jìngle, bǎ . . . tsúng . . . gǎnchūchyu. / They ran him out of town. Tāmen bǎ tā 'chyū'jù chū'jìngle. / The police ran him out of New York. Jǐng'chá bǎ tā tsúng Nyǒu Ywē 'gǎnchū chyule.

Run over (overflow) lyóuchulai, mànchulai; if said of the container, is expressed in Chinese in terms of the contents. / The water's running over. 'Shwěi dōu °'mǎnde 'lyóuchulaile (°'mànchulaile). / The tub is running over. 'Péndzlide 'shwěi dōu °'mǎnde 'lyóuchulaile (°'mànchulaile).

Run over to a place (if on foot) pǎu; (if not specifying means) chyù. / Run over to the store and see if you can get some sugar. Shàng nèige 'pùdzli °chyù (°pǎu) yí-tàng, kànkan 'néng bunéng 'mǎijáu dyàr 'tang.

Run short kwài yùng'wanle. / Our supplies are running short. Wǒmende 'dūng-syi dōu kwài yùng'wánle.

Run short of something kwài yùng'wánle. / I'm running short of cash. Wǒde 'syànchyán kwài yùng'wánle.

Run through (be found in all of). / There's a strange idea running through the whole book. Jèiběn 'shūde 'jyànjyě °tsúng'tóu dàu'wěi (°tsúng'tóu dàu'lyǎur, °dz̀-'shr̄ jr̀'jūng) dōu hěn 'gwài.

Run through a passage (on foot) dzài . . . pǎu. / He ran through the streets as fast as he could go. Tā pīn 'mìngde dzài 'jyēshang kwài 'pǎu.

Run through one's head dzài . . . 'nǎudzli 'jwànyou. / That tune keeps running through my head. Nèige 'dyàudz 'lǎu dzài wǒ 'nǎudzli 'jwànyou.

Run something **through** a machine. / He ran the meat through the meat-grinder. Tā bǎ 'ròu 'gēdau jyāudāu lǐtou 'jyǎuchulaile.

Run something long **through** a narrow passage bǎ . . . 'chwāngwò . . . . / Run the rope through this loop. Bǎ jèige 'shéngdz 'chwāngwò nèige 'chywār chyu.

Run <u>something pointed</u> **through** <u>something</u> (thrust). / He ran a splinter through his finger. Tā shŏu'jŕtoushang 'jāle ge 'tsěr.

Run to <u>a place</u> (on foot) 'pǎudàu; **run to** <u>a person</u> 'pǎudàu . . . nèr. / The child ran to its mother. Jèige 'háidz pǎudau tā 'mǔchin nèr chyù le.

Run to <u>a place</u> tūng(dàu). / All roads run to Rome. 'Tyáutyáu dà'dàu tūng Lwó'mǎ.

Run until <u>a time</u> (extend) yǐ'jŕ dàu. / His term runs until next year. Tāde rèn-'chĭ yǐ'jŕ dàu 'míngnyan.

Run up <u>a route</u> (to a higher position, by foot) 'pǎushàng . . . chyù. / They ran up the hill. Tāmen 'pǎushàng 'shān chyu le.

Run up <u>a route</u> (by foot, but without getting to a higher position) dzài . . . 'pǎu. / He ran up the road as fast as he could go. Tā dzài 'dàurshang pǐn'mìngde pǎu.

Run up <u>a flag</u> shēngchilai, gwàchilai. / They ran up the flag as soon as they reached the top of the hill. Tāmen yí dàu shān'dǐngrshang 'mǎshang jyòu bǎ 'chídz °'shengchilaile (°'gwàchilaile).

Run up <u>a bill</u>. / She ran up a terrific clothing bill. Tā mǎi 'yīfu 'hwāle hěn 'dwōde chyán.

Run wild (of children). / We're just letting them run wild. Wŏmen 'tài yóuje tāmende 'síngr le.

A run (in a stocking). / Don't look now, but there's a run in your stocking. Byé 'dùng; nǐde 'wàdz chōule yìtyau 'sź.

(Of a play). / That play had an amazingly long run. Nèichū 'syì jēn 'chángde 'lìhai.

(A trip) tàng. / The truck goes a hundred miles on each run. Jèige dzǎijùng'chē 'měiyí'tàng dzŏu 'yìbǎi'lǐ. / It's a long run from coast to coast. <u>is expressed as</u> From this coast to that coast is really not short. Tsúng 'jèiàn dàu 'nèiàn kě 'jēn bú-jìn.

Run of luck. / That run of luck pulled him out of debt. Tā 'fāle jèibǐ 'tsái bǎ tāde 'jài dōu 'hwanle.

In the long run dzwèihòu, 'jyānglái. / You're bound to succeed in the long run. °Dzwèi'hòu (°'Jyānglái) yí'dìng shŕ 'nǐ chéng'gūng.

On the run. / He's coming on the run. Tā 'pǎuje láide.

The run-around. / He's giving her the run-around. Tā shŕ 'yŏudyǎr 'shwǎje nèige 'nyǔde 'wár ne.

The usual run (of things or events) píng'chángde. / That's out of the usual run of things. 'Nèige gēn píng'chángde bùyí'yàng.

A runaway pǎule de; **runaway horse** 'jīngle de 'mǎ. / They finally caught the runaways. Tāmen dàu 'lyǎur bǎ 'pǎule de 'dàihwéiláile. / He was killed by a runaway horse. Yìpǐ 'jīngle de 'mǎ bǎ tā gěi chwàng'sžle.

A running sore núng, núngbāu. / He has a running sore on his foot. Tāde 'jyǎu jǎng'núngle. or Tāde jyaushang yŏu yíge núng'bāu.

<u>Other English expressions.</u> / Make a run for it! Kwài 'dzŏu ba! / After that speech he was out of the running. Tā jyǎng'wán 'nèige jyáng'yǎn yǐ'hòu jyòu bù'tsán-jyā jìng'sywǎn le.

RUNG. (On a ladder) hénggwèr. / Is the top rung strong enough? 'Tīdz 'tóushang nèige héng'gwèr gòu 'jyēshr ma?

RUSH. (Do something in a hurry) is expressed with the appropriate verb for the thing done, and some expression for hurrying, such as chyǎngje, kwàikwāide; (go in a hurry) pǎu. / They rushed to the bank. Tāmen 'pǎudàu yín'háng chyùle. / They rushed through their work. Tāmen 'chyǎngje bǎ tāmende 'shr̀ dzwò'wánle. / They rushed the bill through. Tāmen 'chyǎngje 'tūnggwòle nèige yì'àn. / Rush him to the hospital. Kwài'kwāide bǎ ta sùngdau yī'ywàn chyù. / The blood rushed to his face. is expressed as His face became all red. Tā 'lyǎn chywán 'húngle.

A rush (hurry, tumult) is expressed in terms of be pressed or crowded jǐ or be busy máng. / At five o'clock there's always a rush. 'Wǔdyǎnjūngde shŕhou, 'cháng-cháng hén 'jǐ. / What's your rush? Nǐ °'máng (°'jǐ) shémma? / This is the rush season in our business. Syàndzài shr̀ wǒmen jéjǔng 'shēngyì dzwèi 'mángde shŕ-hou. / It was a rush job. Nèishr̀ 'jíshr̀. or Nèige dzwòde tài 'jíle.

(Of water) is expressed verbally as flow lyóu. / You could hear the rush of water. 'Tīngdejyàn 'shwěi 'lyóude hěn 'jíde shēngyin.

(The plant; growing) lútsǎu; (as material) lúgǎr. / That swamp is full of rushes. Nèige 'shwěi'kēng lǐtou jáng'mǎnle °lú'tsǎu (°lú'wěi).

RUST. syòu. / The knives are covered with rust. Jèisyē 'dāudz dōu (jǎng)'syòule.

To rust jǎng syòu. / Oil the parts or they will rust. Bǎ jèisyē 'jǐchi 'shàng-shang 'yóu, shēngde jǎng'syòu.

SACK. mádài, 'kǒudài, dàidz. / I want a sack of potatoes. Wǒ yàu yì'kǒudài tǔ'dòur.

Get the sack bèi 'tsái. / How many in the office got the sack? Jèige gūngshr̀-'fángli yǒu 'dwōshau rén bèi 'tsáile?

Hit the sack shwèijyàu. / You'd better hit the sack right now. Nǐ dzwèi hǎu 'lìkè chyù shwèi'jyàu chyù.

SAD. (Of a person) fāchóu, bù'bāusyìng, bútùngkwai, bùhǎushòu, nánshòu, bùhǎugwò, nángwò, 'chóuméibù'jǎn. / I don't like to see you looking sad. Nǐ 'chóuméibù'jǎnde 'yàngdz jyàu wǒ syīnli °nán'gwò (°etc.).

(Of a thing or situation) 'ràng rén °fā'chóu (°bùgāu'syìng, °etc.). / What happened to him was very sad. Tā 'dzāule 'nèiyàngrde 'shr̀ching jēn ràng rén °nán-'gwò (°etc.).

(Unfortunate or bad) dzāu, hwài. / That's a sad state of affairs. Nèige 'chíng-sying hěn 'dzāu. / The children's toys are in a pretty sad condition. 'Háidzmende wán'yèr dōu 'hwàile.

SAFE. (Reliable, dependable) báusyǎn, 'láukàu, kěkàu, méi 'wéisyǎn, ānchywán. / Is the bridge safe? Jèige 'chyáu °báu'syǎn ma (°etc.)?

(Not likely to suffer harm or danger, out of danger) bú'jr̀yú yǒu 'wéisyǎn, bú-hwèi yǒu 'wéisyǎn. / You're safe now. Nǐ syàn'dzài 'búhwèi yǒu 'wéisyǎn le.

(Not harmed) 'méi shèr, 'anránwú'shr̀. / The children were safe but their father was still trapped in the burning house. Syǎuháidz dàushr °méi'shèrle (°ānrán-wú'shr̀le) kěshr̀ tāmende fùchin hái dzài jáuje 'hwǒ de fángdzli méichūlai ne.

(Probable, reasonable) yóu 'bǎwò. / That's a safe guess. Nèige 'tsāide yóu 'bǎwò.

(Beyond power of causing trouble or harm) búhwèi 'dzài chū 'máfan. / He's safe in jail; he can't hurt anybody else. Tā dzài 'jyānyùli, °'búhwèi 'dzài chū 'máfan le (°'shāngbulyǎu 'rén le).

A safe (box for valuables) báusyǎnsyāng, báusyǎngwèi. / Please put these in the safe. Láu'jyà, bǎ jèisyē 'gēdzai báusyǎn'syāngli.

SAFETY. 'ānchywán. / Safety first. 'Ānchywán dì'yī. / This is for your safety. Jèi shr̀ wèi nǐ 'ānchywán.

Safety belt ānchywán dài.

Safety pin ānchywán byé'jēn.

SAIL. fān, péng. / That boat has pretty sails. Nèige chwánde 'fān hén hǎu'kàn.

Go for a sail dzwò'chwán wárwar. / Let's go for a sail. Dzámen dzwò'chwán 'wárwar chyù ba.

To sail (of a ship) kāi 'chwán, dzǒu. / When do we sail? Wǒmen 'shémma shŕhou kāi 'chwán? / This boat is sailing slowly. Jèige chwán 'dzǒude hěn 'màn.

(Handle a sailboat) shř, kāi, jyà. / Can you sail a boat? Nǐ hwèi shř 'fānchwán ma?

(Of a person; move smoothly) dwānje 'jyàdz dzǒu. / She sailed out of the room. Nèiwèi 'tàitai dwānje 'jyàdz tsúng wūli 'chūlaile.

Sail the seas hánghǎi. / He's been sailing the seas for years. Tā háng'hǎi yóu 'hǎusyē'nyán le.

SAILOR. (Member of a ship's crew) 'shwéishǒu. / How many sailors are on the boat? 'Chwánshang yǒu 'dwōshau 'shwéishǒu?

(Naval personnel) shwěibīng. / She goes out with a sailor in the U. S. Navy. Tā cháng gēn yíge Měigwo shwěi'bīng chūchyu 'wár.

SAKE. **For the sake of** (because of) wèi; (in order to) wèide shr̀. / This is for the sake of security. Jèige °shr̀ wèi (°wèide shr̀) bǎu dyar 'syán. / I saved the money for the sake of seeing you through college. Wǒ tswún jèibǐ 'chyán °wèide shr̀ (°shr wèi) jyàu ni bǎ dà'sywé nyàn'wánle.

For someone's **sake** (because of) wèi, wèide shr̀; (out of respect for) kàn ... de myàndz, kàn .... le. / I did it for your sake. Wǒ shr wèi 'nǐ 'dzwòde. _or_ Wǒ 'dzwòle wèide shr̀ 'nǐ. _or_ Wǒ shr kàn nǐde 'myàndz tsái dzwòde. / Don't say any more for my sake. Kàn °'wǒ le (°wǒde 'myàndz) byé 'shwō le.

For heaven's sake 'jè shr̀ dzěmma 'shwōde; (local Peiping) lǎutyānyé. / For heaven's sake, cut it out! Hài! 'Jè shr̀ dzěmma 'shwōde! 'Swànle ba! _or_ Hēi! Lǎutyān'yé! 'Swànle ba!

SALE. (Selling). / They made a lot of money through the sale of the family heirlooms. is expressed as They sold the family antiques and made a lot of money. 'Tāmen bǎ jyā-'chwánde 'gúdǔng 'màile, déle yí'dàbǐ chyán.

(Selling at a lowered price) jyǎnjyà. / Is this on sale? Jèige jyǎn'jyà ma? / When are you holding a sale? Nǐmen 'shémma shŕhou jyǎn'jyà?

(Amount sold) 'shēngyî, 'măimài. / Our sales doubled this year. Jīnnyán wŏmende 'măimài 'jyāle yí'bèi.

(Demand) 'syāulù, màichuchyu. / There is no sale for automobiles now. Syàn-'dzài chî'chē °méi'syāulù (°'màibuchū'chyù).

SALT. yán, syányán; in compounds yān; **salt mine** yánkwàng; **salt pit** yánjĭng; **salt water** yánshwĕi. / I want some salt for my meat. Wŏ chr̄ de 'ròuli yàu dyăr 'yán.

Take with a grain of salt (be rather doubtful) yóu dyăr 'hwáiyí; (skeptical) yóu dyăr bú'syìn; (mistrusting) yóu dyăr bùsyāng'syìn. / I always take what she says with a grain of salt. Wŏ dwèiyu tāde 'hwà láu yóu dyăr 'hwáiyí.

To salt (season) gē 'yán, jyā 'yán, fàng 'yán. / Did you salt that soup? Nèige 'tāng nĭ gē 'yán le ma?

(Treat with salt) yān. / Is pork that is salted called "salt pork?" Jūròuli fàng 'yán jyou shr °"yān'ròu" (°" syán'ròu") ma? or Jū'ròu yānle yĭhòu jyou shr °"yān-'ròu" (°" syán'ròu") ma? / We ought to salt the meat away. Wŏmen déi bă jèige 'ròu 'yānshang.

Salt away (save) tswún, dzăn. / I understand he salted away a good deal for his old age. Wŏ jr̄dau tā 'tswúnle bùshăude 'chyán wèi yáng'lăude.

SAME. (Be identical) yíyàng, syāngtúng, shr túng'yàng(r)de. / These two are the same. Jèi lyăngge °yí'yàng (°syāng'túng, °shrtúng'yàng(r)de). / Is this chair the same as the others? Jèibá 'yĭdz gēn 'byéde yí'yàng ma? / He's not the same as he was ten years ago. is expressed as He doesn't resemble the way he was ten years ago. Tā bú'syàng 'shr̄nyán yĭ'chyán 'nà yàngr le.

The same something (as that used before) ywán, 'ywánláide; (one and the same) yĭ; (identical with what it always has been) is expressed as still hái; **the same day** dāngtyăr, dăngtyăr, etc., with other expressions of time; **at the same time** túngshr̄. / Take the same road home that you came on. Nĭ tsúng 'ywán dàur hwéi 'jyā ba. / We came here on the same train. Wŏmen shr̄ dzwò 'yítàng chē láide. / Even though it's the same problem he still can't solve it. Jèi swéirán shr̄ yí'yàngde shèr, tā 'hái shr̄ jyějywébù'lyău. / Can I leave and be back the same day? Wŏ kéyi dàng'tyăr dă lái'hwér ma? / She didn't come in at the same time he did. Tā 'búshr̄ gēn ta túng 'shr̄ 'jìnlaide.

The same as someone else has done is expressed with yĕ also. / I got up, and he did the same. Wó 'chĭláile, tā 'yé 'chĭláile.

All the same (all one kind) chywán yíyàng; (makes no difference) méi (shémma) 'gwānsyi. / That's all the same to me. Nèige wŏ kàn 'méi shémma 'gwānsyi.

At the same time (but) kĕshr. / I think she'll go with us; at the same time, I'm not sure of it. Wó 'syăng tā hwèi gēn wŏmen yíkwàr 'chyù, kĕshr wŏ yòu bùgăn 'shwō yídìng.

In the same boat is expressed as have the same sickness and therefore mutual sympathy 'túngbìngsyāng'lyán. / We're in the same boat. Wŏmen shr̄ 'túngbìngsyāng-'lyán.

Just the same, all the same (regardless of argument or opposition) fănjèng, 'wúlwùnrú'hé, bùgwán 'dzĕmmaje, 'búlwùnrú'hé. / We're going just the same. Bùgwăn 'dzĕmmaje, wŏmen yàu 'dzŏu.

Same here is expressed as I agree wŏ túng'yì or as I approve wŏ dzànchéng or as I also... wó yĕ.... / I'm hungry. Same here! Wŏ 'è le. Wó yĕ 'è le.

The same to you bĭ'tszbĭ'tsz̆. / Happy new year! The same to you! Syīn'syī-syīnsyĭ! Bĭ'tsz̆bĭ'tsz̆!

SATISFY. jyě (release); in compounds jyě. / You must drink water to satisfy your thirst. Ní děi hē 'shwěi tsái néng jyé'kě. / This will not satisfy your hunger. Jèige ní chrle, bùjyě'è.

(Fulfill conditions) héhū, 'mǎndzú; (discharge an obligation) táng; (explain clearly) jyěshrchīngchu. / Does that satisfy your requirements? Nèige 'héhu nǐde syū'yàu ma? / Will this payment satisfy his creditors? Jèibǐ 'chyán néng bǎ 'jàijǔ 'tánggwochyu ma? / Does that satisfy you on this question? Nèmma jyěshr héhu nǐde yìsz ma? *or* Nèige bá nǐde 'wèntí 'jyěshr'chīngchule ma?

Be satisfied (of a person, in general) mǎnyì; (with a quantity or degree of expenditure) jrdzú; (convinced) syìn, syàngsyìn; (contented) gwòyìn, shūfu, tùngkwai. / I'm not satisfied with my new room. Wǒ nèijyān 'syìn 'wūdz wo bùmǎn'yì. / Even though the diamond is that expensive, she still isn't satisfied. Nèikwài dzwànshr 'nèmma gwèi, tā 'hái bùjr'dzú. / I'm not satisfied that she's guilty. Wǒ bú'syìn tā yǒu 'dzwèi. / Were you satisfied with your lunch? Ní wǔ'fàn chrde mǎn'yì ma? / Now are you satisfied? (lit. or sarcastically) Syàn'dzài nǐ gwò'yìn le ba! *or* (Sarcastically) is expressed as Look what a good job you've done! 'Chyáu nǐ 'gàn de 'hǎu'shèr!

SATURDAY. Syīngchǐlyòu, Lǐbàilyòu.

SAVE. (Not spend) shěng. / Save your money. Ní 'shéng dyǎr 'chyán ba.

(Spare, avoid the expense of) shěng, 'yùngbujáu, béng, 'búyùng. / You can save yourself the trouble. Ní kéyi 'shěng yìhwéi 'máfan.

(Keep, hold on to) lyóu, gē, tswún. / Could you save this for me? Ní 'kéyi bǎ jèige gěi wo °'lyóulyour ma (°'lyóuchilai ma)? / I'll save this candy for later. Wó bǎ jèige 'táng 'gēchilai lyóuje 'dàihwěr dzài 'chr.

(Reserve) lyóu, jàn. / Is this seat being saved for anybody? Jèige dzwòr shr gěi 'byérén 'jànde ma?

(Rescue) jyòu. / He saved her life. Tā 'jyòule tāde 'mìng le.

(Collect) tswún, dzǎn, sōují. / He saves stamps. Tā 'dzǎn yóu'pyàu.

(Be careful of) lyóu, 'báuyǎng, 'yángyǎng. / Save your voice. 'Lyóuje nǐde 'sǎngdz ba. *or* 'Yángyǎng nǐde 'sǎngdz ba. *but* / You might as well save your breath is expressed as Just speak fewer idle words. Jyàn'jr 'shǎu shwō fèi'hwà ba. or as Don't waste your lips and tongue. Búyàu 'bái fèi chwún'shé le.

Save the day kàu . . . (gěi) °'dǎnggwochyu (°'tánggwochyu). / He certainly saved the day. Wán'chywán kàu 'tā géi 'dǎnggwochyude.

SAW. jyù. / Could I borrow a saw? Jyè wó bǎ 'jyù 'shrshr.

To saw jyù. / He sawed the logs in half. Tā bǎ mùtou dōu 'jyùcheng lyǎng-jyéer.

SAY (SAID). shwō, jyǎng. / What did you say? Ní shwō 'shémma láije? / The paper says it's going to rain tonight. Bàushang 'shwō jyēr 'wǎnshang yàu syà'yǔ. / What have you got to say for yourself? Ní hái yǒu 'shémma kě 'shwō de ma? or expressed as Give your reason. Ní bá nǐde 'lǐyóu 'shwōshwo. / He said he would go. Tā 'shwōle tā 'ywànyi chyù.

Say, let's say, shall we say °jyòu 'swàn (°dà'gài, °swàn) . . . °dzěmma 'yàng (°ba). / I'll give you enough to cover the expenses, shall we say fifty dollars? Wó gěi ni gòu 'kāisyǎude, jyòu 'swàn 'wǔshrkwài chyán, 'dzěmmayàng? / I'll meet you, say in an hour. Wǒmen 'dàihwěr jyàn, dàgài yíge 'jūngtóu yǐ'nèi ba.

Say (exclamation; by the way or oh) hèi, hē, āiyà. /Say! Did you see the way she acted on the stage? Hèi! Nǐ kàngwo tā dzài 'táishang de nèigǔdz 'jyèr le ma? /Say! I almost forgot. 'Hèi! *or* 'Hē! *or* Āiyà! Chà dyǎr 'wàngle. /Say! It is a big one. Āi'yā! Jēn 'dà!

(Showing disagreement, or detection of something disagreeable) éi, á. /Say! What do you mean? 'Éi! Nǐ 'shémma 'yìsz? /Say! Who do you think you are? Á! Nǐ shr̀ láu'jǐ a?

(Calling someone(ēi, hēi, wēi. /Say! Come over here! 'Ēi! Dàu 'jèr lái!

Let's say (for example) is expressed as such as . . . how about it syàng . . . dzěmma 'yàng. /We'll have to buy some fruit, let's say oranges and peaches. Wǒmen děi mái dyár 'gwǒdz, syàng 'jyúdz le, 'táur le, dzěmma 'yàng?

Have one's say shwōshwo. /I insist on having my say. Wǒ yídìng děi 'shwōshwo.

Have the whole say yǒu 'chywán, ná 'shr̀, ná 'chywán, 'shwō shémma 'shr̀ shémma. /He has the whole say around here. Tā dzài 'jèr yǒu 'chywán.

SCALE. (Layer of covering) lín. /The fish had shiny scales. Nèityáu yúde 'lín jēn 'lyàng.

(Weighing machine, a balance) 'tyānpíng; (a Chinese scale) chèng; (a small Chinese scale) děngdz; (a scale that weighs in pounds) bàng, 'bàngchèng. /Put that on the scale. Bǎ nèige 'gēdzai 'chèngshang 'yāuyau.

(Series of tones) yīnjyē. /She practices scales all day. Tā jěng'tyān jìng lyàn yīn'jyē.

(Graded system) děng, 'děngjí. /What is the scale of wages in this factory? Jèige gūng'chángli °gūng'dzde 'děngjí dzěmmayàng (°gūng'dz fēn 'jǐděng)?

(Series of marks at regular intervals for measurement; on a barometer, thermometer, protractor) dùshur; (on a ruler) 'chr̀tswùn; (on a measuring cup, chemical flask, chart, weighing machine) gé, géer; (on a Chinese weighing instrument) 'chèngsīngr. /The scale on this barometer is hard to read. Jèige chìyā'byǎushangde 'dùshur kànbu'chīngchu.

(Proportion) bǐlì, bǐlìchr̀. /This map has a scale of one inch to one hundred miles. Jèige dì'túde bǐlì'chr̀ yìyǐng'tswùn shr̀ yìbǎiyǐng'lǐ. /This ship model is made exactly to scale. Jèi mwó'syíng shr̀ jàuje ywánláide chwán àn yí'dìngde 'bǐlì dzwòde.

(Relative size) gwēimwó. /They've planned the improvements on a large scale. is expressed as They've planned to improve on a large scale. Tāmen 'jìhwàle yàu 'dàgwēi'mwóde gǎi'lyáng.

Turn the scales byàn, jwǎnbyàn, jwǎn'byàn 'jyúshr̀. /That victory turned the scales in our favor. Nèige shèng'jàng dǎle yǐ'hòu, wǒmende 'jyúshr̀ byàn'hǎule.

To scale (remove scales) gwā lín, gwācha lín, kwācha lín. /Please scale the fish. Láu'jyà, bǎ yú'lín gěi 'gwāgwa.

(Come off in scales) dyàupyér. /The paint is scaling off. Nèitséng yóu'chī dyàu'pyér le.

(Climb) pá. /They scaled the cliff with difficulty. Tāmen 'pá nèige 'shān páde hěn chr̀'lì.

Scale down jyǎn. /All their prices have been scaled down. Tāmen bǎ 'swóyǒude 'jyàchyan dōu 'jyǎnle.

SCARCE. shǎu, 'syǐshǎu, chywē, 'chywēshǎu, nán, nánjǎu, 'kwùnnán. / is food scarce? 'Chrde dūngsyi 'chywē ma? / Jobs are scarce right now. Syàn'dzài 'shr̀-ching hěn nán 'jǎu.

SCATTER. (Sprinkle around) sǎ, rēng. / Scatter some food for the pigeons. Gěi 'gēdz 'sá dyǎr 'shŕ.

(Disband) sàn, fēnsàn. / Wait until the crowd scatters. Děng jèichyún 'rén 'sànle je. / Members of my family are scattered all over. Wǒmen 'jyālide rén dōu fēn'sànle, nǎr dōu yǒu.

(Cause to disband) (by force) bǎ . . . °'hūngsàn (°'gǎnsàn); (by scaring) bǎ . . . dōu syà'pǎule; (by order) jyàu . . . dōu °'sànkai (°'fēnkai); or other resultative compounds with sàn or kāi as the second element. / They scattered the herd of cattle. Tāmen bǎ nèichyún 'nyóu gǎn'sànle.

(Strew). / I found everything scattered. (thrown about) 'Shémma dōu rēngde 'nǎr dōu 'shr̀. or (not packed) 'Shémma dōu 'sànje. or (in disorder) Shémma dōu 'lwànchibā'dzàude (rēngje).

SCENE. (View) jǐngjr, fēngjǐng. / That's a beautiful scene. Nèige 'jǐngjr jēn hǎu'kàn.

(Situation) chíngsying. / Let's reconstruct the scene of the crime. Dzámen bǎ 'nèige 'àndzde 'chíngsying dzài 'yánjyouyánjyou.

(Environment) 'hwánjìng. / A change of scene will do him good. 'Hwànhwan 'hwánjìng dwèiyu 'tā 'hén yǒu 'hǎuchù.

(Setting) bùjǐng. / What is the scene of the play? Jèichū 'syìde bù'jǐng shr̀ shémma?

(Part of a play) chǎng. / This is the third scene of the second act. Jèi shr̀ dì-'èrmùde dì'sānchǎng.

Make a scene nàu(hung), nàu syàuhwar, syānàu. / Don't make a scene. Byé dāngje 'rén nàu 'syàuhwar. / I don't wish to make a scene. Wǒ bú'ywànyi nàugei rén 'kàn.

Behind the scenes (in the theater) hòutái; (out of the public view) hòutái, 'bèidìli, 'àndìli. / I met him in the dressing room behind the scenes. Wǒ dzài hòu'tái hwàjwāng'shr̀li 'pèngjyan tā le. / The details were worked out behind the scenes. 'Syángsyìde 'jyémù shr̀ dzài 'bèidìli 'dzwòde.

SCHOOL. (Place of learning) sywésyàu. / That school has a dormitory. Nèige sywé-'syàu yǒu sù'shè.

(Membership of a school) chywánsyàu, sywé'syàulide rén. / The whole school turned out to welcome him back. °Chywán'syàu (°Sywé'syàulide rén) dōu 'hwānyíng tā 'hwéilai.

(Academic division) ywàn, sywéywàn. / He went to the school of law at the university. Tā shàng 'nèige dà'sywé 'fǎsywé'ywàn le.

(Group devoted to a common aim) pài, pàr. / He belongs to a new school of thought. Tāde 'sz̄syǎng shr̀ 'shǔyú syīn'pàide.

(Group of water animals) chyún. / A school of fish is coming down the river. Yìchyún 'yú shwùnje 'hé 'syàlaile.

Get out of school (at the end of a school day) syàsywé, fàngsywé; (graduate) bìyè. / What time does school get out? 'Shémma shŕhou fàng'sywé? / When did you get out of high school? Nǐ shr 'shémma shŕhou jūngsywé bì'yède?

Go to school shàngsywé. / Do you go to school? Nǐ shàng'sywé le ma?

Schoolbook sywésyàu 'yùng de 'shū.

School building syàushè.

School expenses sywé'syàu jīng'fèi.

To school 'syùnlyàn, jyāu(gei). / They schooled us in military drill. Tāmen 'syùnlyàn wǒmen dzwò 'jyūnshř 'dùngdzwò. / My father schooled me in self-discipline. Wǒ 'fùchin 'jyāugei wó dzěmma dž'jǐ gwǎnje dž'jǐ.

SCIENCE. 'kēsywé. / Have you studied any science? Nǐ 'yánjyougwo 'kēsywé ma?

(Skill) 'sywéwèn. / There's a science to cooking. Dzwò'fàn 'jēn shř dyǎr 'sywéwèn.

SCISSORS. jyǎndz, jyǎndāu.

SCOOP. sháur, sháudz. / Where's the sugar scoop? Táng'sháur dzài 'nǎr ne?

To scoop (dig, on a large scale) wā; (dig, on a small scale) wǎ, wǎi, kwǎi. / Scoop out some grain for the pigs. Gěi 'jū 'wǎi dyǎr 'lyángshr. / This machine is for scooping up sand and gravel. Jèige 'jīchi shř wèi wā 'shādz gēn shŕtou'dzěrgùngde. / She scooped out the inside of the melon. Tā ná 'sháur bǎ gwā'rángr dōu 'wāichulaile.

SCORE. (Points in a game) fēn, fēr, jìlù. / What was the score? 'Dwòshau 'fēr le? or Jì'lù shř 'dwōshau?

(Twenty) èrshŕ; scores (a considerable number) háujǐshŕ.

(Musical) pǔ, ywèpǔ, gēerpǔ, pǔdz, 'yīnywède 'pǔdz, chàng'gēerde 'pǔdz. / Can you read a score at sight? Ywè'pǔ nǐ néng yí'syàr 'nyànsyàlai ma? or expressed as Can you recognize a score? Nǐ néng rèn 'pǔdz ma?

On that score dzài 'nèigeshang, wèi nèige. / You may rest easy on that score. Dzài 'nèigeshang nǐ 'kéyi fàng'syīn le.

Pay off (or settle) a score (pay a debt or get even) swànjàng; (pay a debt) hwánjài, hwánchīng; (get even) bàuchóu, bàufu. / He's sure to pay off that score sometime. 'Dzáuwǎn tā děi 'swàn nèibǐ 'jàng.

To score (make points) dé 'fēr, dé 'fēn. / He scored five points for our team. Tā géi wǒmen 'dwèishang 'déle 'wǔfēr.

(Keep a record) jì fēr, jì fēn. / How does one score this? Jèige'fēr dzěmma 'jì?

(Arrange musically). / This selection is scored for piano. Jèi 'pǔdz shř wèi tán gāng'chín yùngde. 'Tyāuchulai de 'yīnywè shř gěi gāng'chín gēn ywè'dwèi 'yùbèide.

SCRAPE. (Rub with something rough) tsēng; (remove, using something sharp or rough) gwā, gwācha, kwācha, kūcha, kācha; (rubbing with something sharp or rough in order to make smooth or clean) 'dǎmwó; (scour, wipe) tsā; (file) tswò; (by rubbing and scratching) hwá, gwǎ; all of the above are used as main verbs with appropriate postverbs, such as syàchyu (off), gānjing (clean), etc. / We can scape off the paint with a knife. Wǒmen kéyi ná 'dāu bǎ nèitséng you'chǐ 'kāchasyàlai. / Scrape your shoes off before you come in. Bá 'jyǎu °tsēng yitsèng (°tsāyitsā) dzài 'jìnlai. / The bushes scraped against the side of the car. Nèisyē syǎu'shùr bǎ jèige 'chēde 'pángbyār géi 'gwāle.

Scrape along (manage with difficulty) tsòuhe, 'jyāngjyòu, fūyan, dwèifu, myǎnchyang. / Ever since he died, the family has just earned enough to scrape along.

Tsúng tā 'sžle yǐ'hòu, tāmen 'jyā yě jyòushr 'jèng dyǎr 'chyán 'tsòuheje gwò 'řdz.

Scrape something together (collect with difficulty) is expressed simply as collect tsòu (for money), the idea of difficulty being omitted or expressed by other means. / My son is trying to scrape together enough money to buy a car. Wǒde 'érdz jèng syǎng'far tsòu 'chyán yàu mǎi yílyàng 'chē.

A scrape (difficulty) kwùnnan; (trouble) lwàndz. / His father got into a rather bad scrape financially. Tāde 'fùchin dzài 'jīngjìshang 'yùjyànle hěn 'dàde 'kwùnnàn. / He was always getting into scrapes at school. Tā dzài sywé'syàuli 'jìng chū 'lwàndz.

SCRATCH. (With the nails or claws, in order to relieve itching) kwǎi; (with the claws) dāu; (with nails or claws, whether to relieve itching or not) jwā, náu. / The kitten scratched my hand. Nèige syǎu 'māu bá wó 'shǒu °'jwāle (°dàule, °náule). / Will you scratch my back? Láu'jyà, géi wǒ °'jwājwa (°'kwǎikwai, °'náunau) hòu'jínyang.

(Rub or mark with something sharp) hwá; (makr slightly with something sharp) gwǎ; (rub with something rough) tsēng. / Try not to scratch the floor when you move the piano. Nwó gāng'chín de shŕhou byé bǎ 'dìbǎn 'hwále.

(Cut slightly) lá. / Will that stone scratch glass? Nèige 'shŕtou néng lá 'bwōli ma?

(Dig) páu, wā; (dig with the nails) kōu. / We watched the chickens scratching for food. Wǒmen 'kànje nèisyē syǎu 'jyēr páu 'chŕde láije.

(Withdraw from a contest; cancel) chyǔsyāu; be scratched géi chyǔsyāu; (not come out to the contest) bùchūchǎng. / Our horse was scratched. Wǒmen nèipǐ 'mǎ °gei chyǔ'syāu le (°méichū'chǎng).

Scratch out hwále chyù. / Scratch out the last line. Bǎ dzwèi'hòu yì'háng 'hwále chyù.

A scratch (line made by scratching) °hwáde (°gwǎde, °tsēngde, °jwǎde, °náude, °kwǎide, °dāude) 'dàudz; (scratch or a scraped place) yèr; (wound made by scratching or otherwise) shāng. / The desk is covered with scratches. Jèige shū'jwō 'myàrshang yóu hǎusyē 'hwáde 'dàudz. / How did you get that scratch on your chin? Nǐ syàba'kéershangde 'dàudz shŕ 'dzěmma láide?

From scratch (from the beginning) tsúng 'tóur lái. / The whole job had to be done over again from scratch. Jèijyàn shŕching hái 'déi jěng'gèrde tsúng 'tóur dzài 'lái yìhwéi.

SCREAM. rǎng, hǎn, jyàu, rāngrang. / She screamed in terror. Tā 'syàde jŕ 'rǎng.

(Laugh shrilly) 'hāhā 'dà 'syàu. / Everybody screamed at his jokes. Tā nèige 'syàuhwàr 'dòude 'měiyíge rén dōu 'hāhā 'dà 'syàu.

A scream is expressed verbally as above. / I thought I heard a scream. Wǒ 'jywéde wǒ 'tīngjyan 'rǎngle yì'shēng.

Be a scream (very funny) jēn dòu'syàur; (laughable) jen kě'syàu (also derogatory). / That movie is a scream. Nèige dyàn'yǐngr jēn dòu'syàur. or (either it's humorous, or it's so bad it's funny) Nèige dyàn'yǐngr jēn kě'syàu.

SCREW. 'lwósž, lwósždīngr. / These screws need tightening. Jèisyē lwósž'dyēngr děi jínjin le.

To screw (turn, as a screw, or fasten with screws) nǐng. / Screw it in tightly. Níng'jǐn le.

(Fasten with screws or in various other ways) ān. / These pipes screw together very easily. Jèisyē 'gwǎndz hěn 'rúngyi ānde yí'kwàr.

SEA. hǎi. / How far are we from the sea? Wǒmen jèr lí 'hǎi yǒu dwō 'ywǎn? / There was a heavy sea the day we went fishing. is expressed as The day we went fishing, the sea wind and waves were very strong. Wǒmen chyù dǎ'yú de 'nèityān hǎishangde fēng'làng hěn 'dà.

Sea level hǎi'myàn; **above sea level** hǎi'bá. / This land is only 200 feet above sea level. Jèikwài 'dì 'gāu chū hǎi'myàn tsái 'eřbáichř. or Jèikwài 'dì hǎi'bá tsái 'eřbáichř.

At sea (on the ocean) dzài 'hǎishang; (in a boat on the ocean) dzài hǎi'chwánshang. / They've been at sea for three weeks. Tāmen dzài 'hǎishang dāile sā syīng-'chī.

At sea (puzzled) míhu, húdu hútu; (can't understand it) mwò'míngchí'myàu; (can't understand what it is) bù'dǔng shř 'dzěmma hwéi 'shř. / Her answers left me completely at sea. Tā 'hwéidá de 'hwà jyǎn'jřde shř ràng wo mwò'míngchí'myàu.

Go to sea háng'hǎi chyù; (be a sailor; if member of ship's crew) dāng 'shwěishǒu chyù; (if member of the navy) dāng shwěi'bēng chyù, dāng hǎi'jyūn chyù.

Put to sea kāi, dzǒu. / When does the ship put to sea? Nèijř 'chwán 'shémma shřhou 'kāi?

Be seasick yùnchwán. / The rolling of the boat made me seasick. Nèige 'chwán 'yáude wǒ yùn'chwán le.

SEARCH. jǎu, sywéme, sywéle. / I've searched everywhere. Wǒ shémma 'dìfangr dōu 'jǎule.

(Hunt for something by turning things over in a box, drawer, etc.) fān. / I've searched for that pen in the drawer for a long time, but I haven't found it. Nèigwán 'bǐ wǒ dzài 'chōutili 'fānle bàn'tyān, yě méifān'jáu.

(Look for something concealed) sōu; (examine) jyǎnchá. / We'll have to search you. Wǒmen děi °'sōusou (°jyǎn'chá) nǐ.

A search. / Is a search necessary? is expressed verbally as Is it necessary to search? Yí'dìng 'jǎu ma?

SEASON. (One of the four seasons) jì. / Fall is my favorite season. 'Chyōutyan shř wǒ 'dzwèi 'syīhwande yí 'jì.

(Period of the year) shřhou, yi'ji; in compounds chī; **holiday season** 'jyàchī; **fishing season** 'yúchī; etc. / This is the best season for tennis. Jè shř dáwàng'chyóu dzwèi 'hǎude shřhou. / The hotel keeper said this was their best season in many years. Lyú'gwǎn jǎng'gwèide shwō jè shř 'dzěmma syē 'nyán lái 'dzwèi hǎude yíji. / I'll try to get home during the holiday season. 'Jyàchīli wó syǎng hwéi 'jyā.

In season (be ripe) shóu, syàlaile; (come to market) shàngshř. / Are strawberries in season yet? Yáng'méi shàng'shř le ma?

Off season bù'hǎude shřhou. / The hotel is having an off season. Syàn'dzài 'jèng shř jèige lyú'gwǎn 'mǎimai bù'hǎude shřhour.

To season (cure, mature; dry in the air) lyàng; (put aside) gē. / Has this wood been seasoned long enough? Jèige mùtou 'lyàngde gòu 'shřhour le ma?

(Flavor; add salt) °gē (°jyā) 'syándàr; (add salt, sauce, or spices) °gē (°jyā) 'dzwólyòur; **heavily seasoned** kǒujùng. / Have you seasoned the beef stew? Dwùnnyóu'ròuli gē 'dzwólyàur le ma? / The food is too heavily seasoned. Dzwòde 'tsài tài kǒu'jùng le.

Be seasoned (old) lǎu; (experienced) yǒugwo 'jīngyànde. / Those men are seasoned soldiers. Jèisyē 'rén dōu shr̄ 'lǎubīng.

SEAT. dzwòr, dzwòwei, wèidz. / You're in my seat. Nǐ 'dzwòdzai 'wǒde 'dzwòrshang le. / I want two seats for the play. Jèichū 'syì wǒ yàu 'lyǎ dzwòr.

(Of a chair) dzwòr. / The seat of the chair needs repairing. Nèibǎ 'yǐdzde 'dzwòr nèr děi 'shōushrshōushr le.

(Of a garment) 'dzwòde dìfangr, hòutou; (somewhat vulgar, of clothes or the body) 'pìhu, 'pìgu. / The seat of my pants is torn. Wǒ 'kùdzde 'hòutou 'pwòle.

(Central location of, source of) ywányīn, ywángu. / Where does the seat of the trouble seem to be? Jèige 'lwàndzde ywán'yīn shr̄ 'shémma?

Seat of government (national) gwódū, shǒudū, jīngchéng; (provincial) shěng- chéng, shěnghwèi; (district) syànchéng.

Have a seat in Congress shr̄ ge Gwo'hwèide yì'ywán.

Take a seat 'dzwòsyà. / Tell him to take a seat. Ràng ta 'dzwòsya.

To seat (have seats for). / This theater seats several hundred people. Jeige syi'yuándz néng dzwò 'háujíbǎi rén.

Seat someone ràng . . . dzwò. / Seat them in order. Ràng tāmen ànje 'tszsyu 'dzwò.

Be seated 'dzwòsyà, dzwò. / May I be seated? Wǒ 'kéyi 'dzwòsya ma?

SECOND. (Following the first) dièr. / Who's the second man in line? Nèi yí'lyòuli dì- 'èrge 'rén shr̄ 'shéi? / My room is on the second floor. Wǒde 'wūdz dzài (dì)'èr- tséng lóu. / The second was better dressed than the first. Dì'èrge 'dǎbànde bǐ 'tóu- yíge 'hǎu.

(Another) is expressed as again . . . once dzài . . . yí'tsź. / May I have a second helping? Wǒ 'kéyi dzài 'tyān yí'tsź ma? / Give him a second chance. 'Dzài 'ywán- lyàng ta yí'tsź.

Second, in the second place dièr, 'dzàijě, 'dzài shwō, chítsź. / In the second place, I don't want to. Dì'èr ne, wǒ bú'yàu nàyàngr.

Second-hand (old) jyòu; **second-hand goods** (handed on goods) 'gwòshǒu 'hwò, jyòu 'hwò. / We bought most of the furniture second-hand. Dàdwò'shùrde'jyājyù wǒ- men dōu shr̄ 'mǎide 'gwòshǒu 'hwò.

A second (one sixtieth of a minute; of time or angular measure) myǎu.

(A moment) yìhwěr, yísyàr. / Wait a second. 'Děng yìhwěr.

Seconds (goods of an inferior grade) 'èrděng 'hwò, 'tsźděng 'hwò. / These stockings are seconds. Jèisyē 'wàdz dōu shr̄ 'èrděng 'hwò.

To second (parliamentary procedure) fùyì; (approve) dzànchéng. / I second the motion. Wǒ fù'yì. or Wǒ dzàn'chéng 'jèige tí'yì.

SECRET. (Not generally known) 'bìmì(de), mì'mì(de). / It was a secret agreement. Nèige shr̄ yíge 'bìmì'syédìng.

(Hidden, not obvious to the eye) àn. / There's a secret lock on the desk. Nèige shū'jwōrshang yǒu yíge àn'swǒ.

Have a secret meaning (of words, gestures, etc.) àn'hánje yǒu 'yìsz, yǒu àn- 'hánjede 'yìsz.

A secret 'mìmì, 'bìmì. / Can he keep a secret? Tā néng shǒu 'mìmì ma?

or expressed as Is he close-mouthed? Tā dzwěi yán ma? / Let me in on the secret. 'Gàusu wǒ 'nèige 'mìmì.

In secret 'ànjūng, 'bìmì, 'mìmì, tōutōurde, bèi'dìli. / They met in secret to discuss their plans. Tāmen 'ànjūng kāi'hwèi 'shānglyang tāmende 'jìhwa.

SECRETARY. (Stenographer) bìshū, mìshū; (clerk) shújì. / He needs two secretaries to answer all his letters. Tā děi yùng 'lyǎngge mì'shū gwǎn tāde syìnjyàn.

(Officer of a club or company) bìshū, mìshū, wéndǔ, 'wénshū, shújì.

(Government official) bùjǎng. / He's the Secretary of Defense. Tā shr̀ Gwófáng-'bù Bù'jǎng.

SECTION. (Piece) kwàr, fèr, bàr, dwàr. / Cut this stick of bamboo into sections. Bǎ nèige jú'gār 'kǎnchéng jǐ'dwàr.

(Of a citrus fruit) bàr. / Cut this orange into sections. Bǎ nèige 'jyúdz 'chyē-chéng 'bàr.

(Of a class) dzǔ. / What section of the class is he in? Tā dzài jèi 'bānli 'nǎ yǐ'dzǔ?

(Of a department) dzǔ, gǔ, kē, bān, bù, chù, tǐng. / This is the legal section of the department. 'Jèi shr jèi 'sžlide 'fǎlyù'kē.

(Of a written composition) jyé, dwàn. / The part I'm referring to is in chapter one, section three. Wǒ jèng 'tí de nèi'bufen shr̀ dzài dì'yījāng dì'sānjyé.

(Region) dài, kwàr, dìfangr. / I was brought up in this section. Wǒ shr dzài jèi'dài jǎng'dàde.

SECURE. (Safe) báusyǎn, kàudejù, kěkàu, wěn, wěndang, twǒdang, wěngù, twǒkàu. / I feel secure in my new job. Wǒ 'jywéde wǒde 'syīn 'jřyè hěn 'wěndang. / I don't think the foundation of the bridge is very secure. Wǒ syǎng nèige 'chyáude 'dzwòr bù hěn báu'syǎn.

(Firmly fastened) jyēshr. / Is this bolt secure? (on a door) Jeige mén'shwān 'jyēshr ma?

Be secure from °báu'syǎn (°kàude'jù, °jywé) bú'jřyu. / Here we're secure from attack. Dzài 'jèr wǒmen 'jywé bú'jřyu shòu 'gūngjī le.

To secure (acquire) néng, nùng, táuhwan, dǐng. / Can you secure a seat on the plane for me? Nǐ néng dzài fēi'jīshang gěi wo 'néng ge 'dzwò ma?

Secure a loan (to guarantee someone else's loan) dān'bǎu yìbǐ 'jàng; (offer a house, etc., as security for a loan) ná . . . ('dǐ)yā yìbǐ 'jàng. / The bank asked my father to secure the loan before they would lend me the money. Yín'háng jyègei wǒ 'chyán yǐ'chyán, ràng wǒ 'fùshin dān'bǎu jèibǐ 'jàng. / How much do you require to secure this loan? Nǐ yàu ràng wo ná jř 'dwōshǎu chyán de 'dūngsyi °lái 'dǐyā jèi-bǐ 'jàng (° dzwò 'dǐyā)?

SEE (SAW, SEEN). (Look at) kàn, chyáu, chǒu. / May I see your pass? Gěi wo 'kàn-kan nǐde tūngsyíng'jèng. / We've just seen a good movie. Wǒmen gāng 'kànle yíge 'hǎu dyàn'yǐngr.

(Find out) kàn. / See what can be done to change it. 'Kànkan nèige néng 'dzěm-ma 'gǎigai. / I've got to see about getting a new clerk. Wǒ děi 'kànkan dzěmma 'jǎu yíge syīn 'shújì lái.

(Call on) kàn, jyàu. / Come to see me tomorrow. Míng lái 'kàn wo. / You'd better see a doctor about that infection. Nèige chwánrǎn'bìng nǐ děi °'kànkan 'dàifu (°jyàu 'dàifu 'kànkan).

(Meet) jyàn. /See you again. Dzài 'jyàn! /I'd like to see more of you. is expressed as I wish we would meet more times. Wǒ 'ywànyi dzámen dwō 'jyàn jihwèi.

(Make sure; pay attention) jùyì; (don't forget) byé wàngle. /Please see that this letter is mailed today. Láu'jyà, jù'yì jèifēng 'syìn 'jyēr děi 'fāchūchyu.

(Understand) dǔng, míngbai; also (know) syáude, jr̄dau. /I see what you mean. Wǒ 'dǔng nǐde 'yìsz le. /You see, we're planning to leave soon. Nǐ 'jr̄dau, wǒmen jyòu 'dàswàn 'dzǒu le. /See? (friendly or unfriendly) 'Míngbai bumíngbai? /I don't intend to do it, see? Wǒ méi'yàu nèmma 'bàn, 'syáude ba? but /I don't see it that way. is expressed as My way of looking at it isn't the same. Wǒde 'kànfa búshr̀ nàyàngr.

(Realize, grasp) kànchulai. /Do you see the point? Nǐ 'kànchū jèi'dyǎn lái le ma?

(Experience, go through) gwò, jīnggwo. /He's seen better times. Tā 'gwògwo (bǐ jèige) hǎu(de) 'rdz. /He's seen some action. is expressed as He has experienced battle. Tā 'dǎgwo 'jàng. /These boats have seen plenty of service. is expressed as These boats have put out a lot of strength. Jèishwàng 'sywēdz kě jen chūle bùshǎude 'lì.

(Escort someone who is leaving) sùng. /Will anyone see me off? Yǒuren 'sùng wo chyù ma? /Let me see you to the door. Wǒ 'sùng ni dàu mén'kǒur.

See someone through (help through) bāng'máng bāngdàu'dǐ. /Did they see him through the trouble? Tāmen 'bāng tāde 'máng bāngdàudǐle ma?

See light or objects through a window, etc. 'jyēje . . . kàn(de'jyàn); can't see through kàn bu'gwòchyu, kàn bu'jyàn 'nèibyar. /Can you see anything through this glass? 'Jyēje jèikwài 'bwōli kànde'jyàn 'nèibyar ma? /This kind of glass lets light through, but you can't see through it. Jèijǔng 'bwōli °tòu'lyàngr (°tòu'gwāng), kěshr 'kànbu'gwòchyu. /This window is so dirty we can't see through it. 'Chwānghu 'dzāngde dōu kànbu'jyàn °'nèibyar le (or if looking in, like a Peeping Tom) °'lǐbyar le, or (if looking out) °'wàibyar le).

See something through (go through with) dzwòwán, wánchéng, nùngwán, néngwán, gànwán. /I intend to see the project through. Wó 'dàswan bǎ jèijyàn 'jìhwa dzwò'wán.

See through something (be aware of something false) kànchulai, kànchwānle. /I can see through his politeness. Tā nèige jyǎ 'kèchi jyèr, wǒ yí 'kàn jyòu 'kànchūláile. /I can see through her. is expressed as I know what kind of person she is. Wǒ 'jr̄dau tā shr̀ 'dzěmma hwéi 'shr̀.

See to (take care of) jàugu. /I'll see to the arrangements. Wǒ lái 'jàugu yíchyède 'bùjr.

I see . . . (when you've just learned something) 'ywánlái; (Peiping) gǎnching. /I see there was a big fire last night. 'Ywánlái dzwór'wǎnshang jáule yìcháng dà 'hwǒ. /Oh! I see! is expressed as Oh! So it's like that. Òu! 'Ywánláirú'tsz̀. or as A thing like that, eh? 'Nèmma hwéi 'shèr a!

Let me see (let me look) gěi wo °'kànkan (°'chyáuchyau, °'chōuchou); (let me think) ràng wo 'syángsyang, or expressed as wait a minute 'děng yìděng.

Let's see (let us look) 'ràng wǒmen °'kànkan (°'chyáuchyau, °'chōuchou).

SEED. 'jǔngdz̀, dzěr; húr or héer correspond in general to the word pit, but may also be used for the seeds of oranges, dates, grapes, or raisins. /These flowers were grown from seed. Jèisyē 'hwār shr̀ nà 'dzěr 'jǔngchūláide. /Spit out the seeds. Bǎ 'húr tùle.

For seed wèi dá'dzĕrde. / The onions were grown for seed. Jùng jèige 'tsūng shř wèi dá'dzĕrde. / The corn in that field will be used for seed. Nèikwài 'dìlide lǎu'yùmǐ shř wèi dá'dzĕrde.

Go to seed dádzĕr, jyēdzĕr; (of a person; be unlucky) dǎuméi. / The hedge has gone to seed. Jèiháng syǎu'shùr dàle 'dzĕr le. / He looks as if he is going to seed. Tā nèige 'yàngdz syàng 'dǎule 'méi le shřde.

To seed (plant) jùng, syàjǔngr, syàdzĕr. / When did you seed the lawn? Jèi-kwài tsǎu'dì nǐ shémma 'shřhou syàde 'jǔngr a?

(Remove seeds) chyùdzĕr, chyùhúr, chyùhéer. / These raisins have been seeded. Jèisyē 'pútau'gār shř °'chyùle 'dzĕr de (°chyùle 'húr de).

(Arrange superior contestants in a tournament) fēnpèi. / The good players have been seeded. Hǎude 'sywánshŏu yǐjǐng fēnpèi hǎule.

SEEK (SOUGHT). (Look for) jǎu. / They sought high and low, but couldn't find him. Tāmen 'gèchùr dōu jǎu'dàule yé jǎubù'jáu ta.

(Try) syǎngfár, jǐnlyèr. / He sought to persuade her to go. Tā syǎng'fár chy-wàn ta 'chyù laije.

(Ask for) chyóu, chǐng. / We came here to seek your help. Wŏmen shàng 'jèr lai 'chyóu ni bāngbang'máng.

Be sought after yŏurénywár (popular). / He's much sought after in local society. Tā dzài tāmen nèige 'dìfangr hén yŏurén'ywár.

SEEM. hǎu'syàng . . . (shřde), syàng . . . (shřde). / The door seems to be locked. 'Mén hǎu'syàng shř 'swŏshangle (shřde).

Seem to someone jywéde, jywéje. / It seems like a good idea to me. Wŏ 'jywé-de 'nèmmaje tǐng 'hǎu. / How does that seem to you? Nǐ 'jywéde 'nèige dzĕmma-'yàng? / It doesn't seem to me that he'll come. Wŏ jywéde tā bù'lái.

SEIZE. jwā, jwājù; **seize an opportunity** °'jwājù (°'bǎwu, °bǎ'wò) 'jǐhwèi. / He seized my hand. Tā 'jwājin wŏde 'shŏu. / You ought to seize this opportunity. Nǐ dĕi 'jwā-ju jèige 'jǐhwei.

(Take possession of; with or without force) jàn, jànjyù; (with force, someone's personal property) 'chyángjàn, 'bàjàn. / You have no legal right to seize my property! Nǐ 'méiyou 'chywánlì 'jàn wŏde 'chǎnyè. / We seized the town after a short battle. 'Dǎle méi 'dwŏjyŏu, wŏmen jyou bǎ 'chéng 'jànle.

SELDOM. hén shǎu, bùcháng. / He is seldom at home. Tā °'hén shǎu (°bù'cháng) dzài 'jyā. / We seldom go to the movies. Wŏmen °'hén shǎu (°bù'cháng) chyù kàn dyàn'yǐng(r).

SELECT. tyāu, sywǎn, jyǎn, tyāusywǎn. / She selected several dresses to try on. Tā 'tyāule jijyàn 'yīfu lai 'shřle yishř.

Be select (picked out for superior quality) sywǎnchulai de, tyāusywǎnchulai de; (picked out for being either bad or good) tyāuchulai de, jyǎnchulai de. / These are select peaches. 'Jèisyē 'táur shř 'sywǎnchulai de.

(Exclusive; of a school, etc.) is expressed as expensive 'gwèidzú. / She went to a select school. Tā 'rùle yíge 'gwèidzúsywé'syàu.

SELF. (Before an adjective) dz̀; **self-confident** dz̀syìn; **self-satisfied** dàmǎn; **self-sufficient** dz̀dzú. In other cases different expressions are used: **be self-centered** is expressed as **think first of oneself** 'syān syǎngdau 'džjǐ or as **put oneself first** bǎ 'džjǐ gēdzai 'tóu le; **be self-supporting** is expressed as **by oneself to support oneself** 'džjǐ 'gūngji 'džjǐ; **be self-conscious** is expressed as **be unnatural** bú'dzrán; **be self-possessed** is expressed as **be calm** 'lěngjìng.

(Before a noun) calls for various modes of expression. /He has no self-control. is expressed as He can't control himself. Tā bùnéng dž'jr. /I hit him in self-defense. is expressed as I hit him to defend myself. Wǒ wèi dž'wèi tsái 'dǎ ta. /Haven't you any self-respect? is expressed as Can't you respect yourself a bit? Nǐ 'bùnéng dž'dzwūn yìdyǎr ma?

One's better self is expressed as **conscience** 'lyángsyīn or hǎu yàngdz (good appearance). /When it came to making an important decision his better self came through. Dàule jywédìng jùngyau wèntí de shŕhou, tāde lyángsyīn °chūsyànle (°fāsyànle). /He showed his better self at the meeting yesterday. Dzwótyan kāihwèi de shŕhou, tā °lyángsyīn (°hǎude yàngdz) chūsyànle.

Myself, ourselves, yourself, yourselves, himself, herself, themselves are expressed by the proper pronoun plus the following: for intensive effect 'džjǐ or 'džgěr; for reflexive effect bǎ 'džjǐ, gěi 'džjǐ, gēn 'džjǐ or tì 'džjǐ, or by 'džjǐ after the verb of the sentence; for reciprocal effect bítsz; in some cases Chinese leaves the intensive, reflexive, or reciprocal idea unexpressed. /She did it herself. 'Nèi shr tā 'džjǐ dzwòde. /She herself said so. Tā 'džjǐ nèmma 'shwōde. /He hurt himself in the leg. Tā bǎ ('džjǐde) 'twěi 'pèngle. /He must consider himself pretty good to say that. Tā 'nèmma shwō yí'dìng 'jywéje 'džjǐ hái bú'hwài ne. but /She came by herself. Tā 'yíge rén láide. /She isn't herself today. is expressed as She isn't usually this way. Tā 'píngcháng bú'jèiyàngr.

SELL (SOLD). mài. /Did you sell your old piano? Ní bǎ nǐde jyòu gāng'chín 'màile ma? /They sell furniture. Tāmen mài 'jyājyu. /Sugar sells for twenty cents a pound. 'Táng mài 'lyǎngmáu chyán yí'bàng.

(Persuade to accept) ràng . . . jyē'shòu, ràng . . . syìn'fú, ràng . . . syìnfu; **be sold** jyēshòu, syìnfú, syìnfu. /If you had been more tactful, you might have sold him the idea. Nǐ yàushr dzài 'dwō hwèi 'dwèifu dyar 'rén, yěsyu jyou néng 'ràng tā 'jyēshòu nèige 'yìjyan le. /After I told him, he was completely sold on it. Wǒ 'gàusung ta yǐ'hòu, ta swàn 'wánchywán °jyē'shòule (°etc.).

Sell out (get rid of by selling) màichuchyule, màiwánle, màigwāngle, màijìngle. /They sold out their whole stock of bicycles. Tāmen bǎ džsyíng'chēde tswún'hwò dōu °'màichuchyule (°etc.).

Sell out (Betray) mài, chūmài. /He sold us out to the enemy. Tā bá 'wǒmen dzài 'dírénnèr gěi 'màile. or Tā bá 'wǒmen chū'màigei 'dírén le.

SEND (SENT). sùng; (mail) jì; (send out) fā; **send** a message dǎ. /We've sent the manuscript off to the printers. Wǒmen yǐ'rán bǎ 'gǎudz gěi yìnshwā'jyú 'sùngchyule. /Have the invitations been sent out yet? Chǐng'tyē yǐ'rán °'sùngchuchyule (°fāchuchyule) ma? /I sent him a telegram yesterday. Dzwótyan wo gěi ta dǎle dyànbàu le. /Have you sent the letters yet? Syìn 'jìle meiyou?

(Cause to go) ràng, jyàu. /Send him in. Ràng ta 'jìnlai.

Send (someone) for °'pài (°'ràng, °'jyàu, °'dǎfa) . . . chyù. /Can we send him for ice cream? Wǒmen °'ràng (°etc.) ta chyù 'mǎi dyǎr bīngji'líng, 'hǎu buhǎu? or Wǒmen 'ràng ta chyù 'yàu dyǎr bīngji'líng. /I'll send for my trunk later. Yǐhòu wǒ dzai pài 'rén chyù.

Send to someone **for** something jàu. /They sent to him for help. Tāmen 'jàu tā bāng'máng.

SENSE

SENSE. (Faculty of sensation) 'gǎnjywé, 'jřjywé; **sense of hearing** 'tīngjywé; **sense of sight** 'shřjywé; **sense of smell** 'syòujywé; **sense of taste** 'wèijywé; **sense of touch** 'gǎnjywé.

(Meaning) yìsz, 'yìyi, 'dàuli. / That doesn't make sense. Nèige 'méi 'shémma 'dàuli. / There's no sense in doing that. Gàn nèige 'méi 'shémma 'yìsz. / In what sense do you mean what you just said? Nǐ gāng'tsái shwōde 'hwà dàu'dǐ shř 'dzěmma ge 'yìsz?

(Good judgment). / He has sense enough to stay out of trouble. is expressed as He is rather sensible, he won't get into trouble. Tā hái °'míngbai (°'chīngchu), bùhwèi 'chū 'máfan.

Common sense 'chángshř, pǔtūng chángshř; **have common sense** dǔngshř, dǔngshěr. / That's just common sense. Nèi 'búgwò shr cháng'shř. / He lacks common sense. Tā 'búdà dǔng'shř.

In a sense (from one point of view) 'yìfāngmyàn, dzài 'yìfāngmyàn °kàn (°shwō). / In a sense, that's true. Dzài 'yìfāngmyàn shwō, nà shř 'jēnde.

Come to one's senses (come out of a faint) syǐnggwolaile; (be sensible at last) míngbaile.

Have a sense of something jywéde, gǎnjywéde, jywéhuje. / I have a sense of danger. Wǒ 'jywéde hěn 'wēisyǎn. / He has a strong sense of responsibility. Tā jywéde tā 'dzérèn hěn 'jùng. but / He has a sense of humor. Tā shř °jř'chyù de rén (°yǒumwòrde rén).

Lose one's sense of direction (be all turned around) jwànle 'syàng le. / He never loses his sense of direction. Tā yúng'ywán yě bújwàn 'syàng.

To sense jywéde, 'gǎnjywéje, jywéhuje. / I sense vaguely what he means. Wǒ hwǎnghu 'jywédechū dyar tā shř 'shémma 'yìsz. / Do you sense something wrong? Nǐ 'jywéde yǒu 'shémma bú'dwèi ma?

SENTENCE. hwà with measure jyù. / I didn't understand that last sentence. Wǒ bù-'míngbai dzwèi'hòu nèijyù 'hwà.

(Decision of a court) pànjywé. / The judge's sentence was unduly severe. Fǎ-'gwān pàn'jywéde tài 'jùng le. or expressed as The judge passed judgment on that case too severely. Fǎ'gwān bǎ nèige 'àndz pànde tài 'jùng le.

Serve a sentence (be in prison) jyānjìn, túsyíng. / He's already served his sentence. Tā jyān'jìnde řdz yǐ'rán 'mǎn le.

To sentence pàn, dìng. / For how long were you sentenced? is expressed as They sentenced you to be in prison for how long? 'Pànle ni 'dwōshau řdz tú'syíng?

SEPARATE. (Divide) fēn, fēnkai, líkai. / Separate the class into five sections. Bǎ jèi'bān 'fēnchéng wú'dzǔ. / We don't want to be separated. Wǒmen bú'ywànyi 'fēnkai. / Separate the yolks from the whites. Bǎ jǐ'dànde 'hwángr gēn chyēngr 'fēnkai. / The child can't be separated from his mother. Háidz líbukāi mùchin.

(Divide by putting something in between) gé, gékai. / This partition separates the two rooms. Jèishàn 'chyáng bǎ jèi'lyǎngjyān 'wūdz 'gékaile.

(Pull apart) lākai. / Separate the two boys who are fighting. Bǎ jèi'lyǎngge dǎ-'jyà de 'háidz 'lākai.

(Stop living with someone) fēnjyū. / When did she separate from him? Tā tsúng 'shémma shŕhou 'gēn ta fēn'jyūle?

Be separate (stand apart from others) fēnjede, fēnkaide; also (single) dānjede or (another) lìngwài. / We want separate rooms. Wǒmen yàu °'fēnkaide (°'dānjyār-

894

de) 'wūdz. / Put that under a separate heading. Bǎ nèige 'gēdzai lǐng'wài yi'syàng lǐtou. / I'd like to make a separate settlement. is expressed as I'd like to make an agreement alone. Wó syǎng 'dāndú 'dìng ge 'hétung.

SEPTEMBER. Jyǒuywè.

SERIOUS. (In one's moral attitude) 'yánsù; (in one's moral attitude and also in the way one works) 'jēngjǐng, 'jēngjingbaběi, (formal) jēngjùngchíshr̄; (in the way one works) rènjēn, yùngsyǐn, gēsyǐn. / He's a very serious young man. Tā shr̄ 'yíge hěn 'jēngjǐngde 'chīngnyán rén. / He's very serious about his work. Tā dzwò 'shr̄ hěn °rèn-'jēn (°yùng'syǐn, °gē'syǐn). / He's not serious enough about his work. is expressed as He doesn't pay much attention to his work. Tā 'dwèiyú tāde 'shr̄ búdà rèn'jēn. or Tā 'dwèiyú tāde'shr̄ búdà jù'yì.

(On the level) shwō jēn'géde. / Are you serious? Nǐ shr shwō jēn'géde ne ma? / I wasn't serious at all. Wǒ nà shr̀ 'nàuje 'wár ne. or expressed as I was just fooling. Wǒ nà shr̀ 'mǎmahū'hū. or as I didn't take it as anything that counts. Wo gēnběn jyou méi ná nèige dàng hwěi shèr.

(Real) jēnde. / Do you suppose this story is serious? Nǐ 'jywéje jei shèr shr̀ 'jēnde ma?

(Earnest in endeavor) jēn hǎu'hāurde. / Did you make a serious attempt to find him? Nǐ jēn hǎu'hāurde jǎu ta láije ma?

(Important) 'jùngyàu, yàujǐn; (extremely important) 'yánjùng. / This is a serious matter. Jèige 'shr̄ching hěn 'yánjùng.

(Grave) 'yánjùng, lìhai; (of sickness) jùng, 'yàujǐn. / He had a serious accident with his car. Tā jwàng 'chē jwàngde hěn 'lìhai. / Is his illness serious, Doctor? Dàifu, tāde 'bìng 'yàujǐn ma?

(Stern) 'jwāngyán; **look serious** is expressed as tighten one's face 'bēngje 'lyǎn. / She looks very serious. Tāde 'yàngdz hěn 'jwāngyán. / He told the joke with a perfectly serious face. Tā 'bēngje 'lyǎn 'shwōde nèige 'syàuhwàr.

SERIOUSLY. (Earnestly) jēn, dídichywèchywede. / He was thinking seriously of becoming a doctor. Tā °'jēn (°dídichywèchywede) dàng yige 'dàifu.

(Not jesting) jēn, jēnde. / Seriously, did you tell him? °Nǐ 'jēn (°Jēnde nǐ) gàusung tā le ma?

Take someone or something **seriously** dàng hwéi shr̀. / They're not taking this matter seriously. Jèijyan 'shèr tāmen náje 'búdàng hwéi 'shèr. or expressed as They're not taking this matter to heart at all. Jèijyan 'shèr tāmen gēnběn °méiwàngsyǐnli 'chyù (°méigēsyǐn, °méiyùngsyǐn). or as They aren't putting in any effort on this thing. Tāmen dwèi jèijyàn shèr búshāng'jìn. / Don't take him seriously. 'Byé ná ta 'dàng nèmma yǐhwèi 'shèr. or expressed as Don't believe him. 'Byé jēn 'syǐn tāde. or as Don't take what he says to heart. Béng bǎ ta 'gēdzai 'syǐnshang.

SERVE. (Bring; food or drinks) shàng, ná, dwān; (bring food) kāi fàn. / Serve the drinks now, please. Shàng 'jyǒu ba.

(Wait on) tsżhou, fúshr̀. / Who serves this table? Shéi 'tsżhou 'jèijāng 'jwōdz?

(Work) dzwò, gàn; (work for an officer) fúwù; (work for a person) tsżhou, fúshr̀. / How long did you serve in that capacity? 'Nèige shr̄ching nǐ 'dzwòle dwō-'jyǒu le? / He served fifteen years in the army. Tā dzài jyūn'dwèishang 'gànle shr̄-'wǔnyán.

(Help). / Is there any way in which I can serve you? is expressed as Is there anything I can do? Yǒu shémma 'shèr jyàu wo 'dzwòde ma?

(Of a prison term) dzwòjyān. / He is serving a prison term. Tā 'dzài nèr dzwòjyān ne.

(Of a ball) fāchyóu. / He served a mean one. Tā jèige 'chyóu 'fāde jēn 'lìhai. / Whose turn is it to serve? Gāi 'shéi fā'chyóu le?

Serve a need. / I think this will serve your needs. Wó syáng ní yǒu 'jèige jyou 'syíng le.

Serve a summons sùng chwánpyàu. / He served a summons on us. Tā géi wǒmen 'sùnglai chwán'pyàu, chwán wǒmen dàu'tíng.

Serve no purpose. / That serves no purpose at all. 'Nèmmaje yìdyǎr 'yùng yě méi'yǒu.

Serve the purpose. / This will serve the purpose. Yùng 'jèi jyou 'syíng. / What purpose does it serve? Nà yǒu shémma 'yùng ne?

Serve as. / What will serve as a substitute? is expressed as What can you use as a substitute? °Ná (°Yùng, °Shǐ) 'shémma lái dài'tì ya?

A serve (act of serving a ball). / Whose serve is it? is expressed verbally as Whose turn is it to serve? Gāi 'shéi fā'chyóu le?

Other expressions in English. / It serves you right! (Nǐ) hwó'gāi!

SERVICE. (Performance of labor). / He gave us good service for more than ten years. (of an employee) is expressed as He worked well for us for more than ten years. Tā géi wǒmen dzwò'shr 'dzwòle shŕji'nyán le dōu hén 'hǎu. or (of a hotel clerk) is expressed as He served us very well for more than ten years. Tā 'tsżhou wǒmen 'shŕji'nyán le 'tsżhoude hén 'hǎu. or (of a garageman) is expressed as He did repair work for us very well for more than ten years. Tā géi wǒmen 'shōushr shŕji'nyán le 'shōushrde hén 'hǎu. etc.

(Supplying of some need). / Does the rent include maid service? is expressed as Does the rent money take care of tidying up the room? Dzèmma syě 'chyán de fáng'dzū, gwǎn 'shōushr wūdz ma? / Do you have bus service here? is expressed as Do you have public buses here? Nǐmen jèr yǒu gūng'gùngchì'chē ma? / I want to complain about the service. is expressed as The serving here is bad, I must complain. Jèr 'tsżhoude bù'syíng wó děi 'shwōshwo.

(Employment). / In whose service are you? is expressed as For whom do you work? Nǐ gēn 'shwéi dzwò 'shr? / Does she have a civil service job? is expressed as Does she work for the government? Tā géi jèng'fǔ dzwò 'shr ma?

(Armed forces) jyūndwèi. / He enlisted in the service. Tā dàu jyūn'dwèishang 'chyùle. / Service men are admitted free. is expressed as For service people there is no expense. 'Jyūnrén myǎn'fèi.

(Meeting for worship) lǐbài (meaning a Protestant service; note that mísā (mass) is the Roman Catholic term); **hold a service** dzwò lǐbài. / The service begins at 10 o'clock. Lǐbài shŕdyǎn jūng kāishr.

Be at one's service. / I'm at your service. is expressed as When you want something, call me. Nín yǒu 'shémma shŕ de 'shŕhou 'jyàu wǒ. or as If you want something, don't be bashful. Ní yǒu 'shémma 'shr, byé 'kèchi.

Be of service yǒu yùng. / Will this book be of service? Jéiběr 'shū dwèi ni yǒu 'yùng ma?

Do a service (help) bāngmáng. / Could you do me a small service? Nǐ 'kéyi 'bāngbang wǒde 'máng ma?

Use the services of yùng. / Can you use the services of a typist? Nǐ néng 'yùng yíge dǎdz̀'ywán ma?

Funeral service kāidyàu.

Marriage service jyéhwūn.

To service (as an automobile; look over) 'yàn yíyàn; (wash) tsāsyǐ; (repair) shōushr, 'syōulǐ; **service station** chìyóujàn. / I'm leaving my car here to be serviced. Wǒ bá wǒde 'chē 'gēde jèr 'shōushr 'shōushr.

SET. (Put, place) fàng, gē. / Set it over there. Bǎ 'nèige fàngdzai 'nèr. / Set this aside for me. Bǎ 'jèige géi wo 'gēdzai yǐ'byār.

(Put right) dwèi, bwō; **set in order** pái(hǎu). / I want to set my watch. Wǒ yàu 'dwèidwei wǒde 'byǎu. / Has the type been set yet? 'Bǎn pái'hǎule ma? / He set the cards in order. Tā bá kǎ'pyàr 'ànje 'tsz̀syu pái'hǎule.

(Fix) dìng. / He set the price at fifty dollars. Tā bǎ jyàr dìngcheng 'wǔshŕ-kwài 'chyán le. / I must set a limit to expenses. Wǒ hwā 'chyán yí'dìng děi 'dìng-chū ge 'shùr lai.

(Become firm) dìng, níng. / The jelly she made has set. Ta dzwòde dùngdz °dìngchilaile (°níngchilaile).

(Assign) jyàu, ràng, pài; (invite) chǐng. / They set him to counting the money. Tāmen 'ràng ta lái shǔ 'chyán.

(Sit on eggs) fūwō, bàuwō, fūdàn; (of hens) fū syǎujyēr; (place on eggs) ràng . . . fū'wō. / The hens are setting. 'Jī fū syǎu'jyēr ne. / We set a dozen hens each spring. 'Měinyán 'chwūntyān wǒmen ràng shŕ'èrge 'jī fū'wō.

(Go down) làu. / The sun sets at six o'clock tonight. Jyēr 'wǎnshang 'lyòudyǎn jūng làu 'tàiyang.

Set a bone jyē. / Can you set a broken bone? Nǐ hwèi jyē'gǔ ma?

Set a jewel syāng. / The pin has diamonds set in gold. Jèige byé'jēr shŕ 'jīn-dz syāng dzwàn'shŕ de.

Set a trap ān, fàng, syà. / We set traps for the animal. Wǒmen °'syàle (°'ān, °'fàng) yíge dǎi yě'shòu de 'jyādz.

Set an alarm bwō, shàng. / Set the alarm for seven o'clock, will you? Bǎ nàu-jūng °'bwōdau (°'shàngdau) 'chīdyǎn jūng, 'hǎu ma?

Set an example 'dzwò ge 'bǎngyàng, 'dzwò ge 'mwófàn. / He's set a good example for us to follow. Tā géi wǒmen 'dzwòle yíge 'hén hǎude 'bǎngyàng ràng wǒ-men 'mwófǎng.

Set one's heart on jēn 'syǎng. / I set my heart on going today. Wǒ 'jēn syǎng 'jīntyān 'chyù.

Set sail kāichwán.

Set about (begin) chǐtóur, kāishr̀; (be going to) jèng 'yàu. / He set about finishing his report. Tā 'jèng yàu bǎ tāde bàu'gàu nùng'wánle.

Set aside 'gēdzai yǐ'byār, gēchilaile. / This fund has been set aside for an emergency. Jèibǐ 'chyán gēdzai yǐ'byār, děng yǒu 'shr̀ de shŕhou yùng.

Set at ease ràng . . . °swéi'byàn (°byé 'jyūni, °byé 'jyūshu). / We tried to set them at ease. Wǒmen syǎng 'fár ràng tāmen byé 'jyūshu.

Set at liberty jyàu . . . dzǒu, bǎ . . . 'fàngle. / You will be set at liberty. Hwèi bá nǐ fàngle de. *or* Hwèi jyàu nǐ dzǒude.

Set down (land, as a plane) bǎ . . . làu; (write down) syě, jì(lu); (ascribe) swàn. / He set the plane down on the new airfield. Tā bǎ feī'jī làudzai 'syīn fēijī'chángli le. / Set down the main arguments. Bǎ nèige byàn'lwùnde yàu'dyán 'syèsyalai. / He made a mess of his job, but set it down to bad luck. Tá bǎ nèige 'shŕching nùng-'dzǎule, jyou swàn 'yùnchi bù'hǎu jyòu 'wánle.

Set forth shwō, jyǎng, jyěshr. / He set forth his position quite clearly. Tā bǎ tāde 'yìjyan 'shwōde hěn 'chīngchu.

Set in (come) lái. / The rainy season set in early this year. Jīnnyán yǔ'jì láide 'dzǎu.

Set in motion kāi. / By pushing a button he set the machine in motion. Tā yí 'èn 'jīgwan jyou bǎ nèige 'jīchi 'kāikaile.

Set off (start to go) chūfā, dzǒu, dùngshēn, chǐshēn; (increase the effect of) chèn; (cause to explode) fàng; (light) dyǎn. / We're setting off on our hike tomorrow morning. Wǒmende túbùlyǔ'syíng 'míngtyān 'dzǎushàng chū'fā. / That belt sets off her dress nicely. Nèityáu pí'dài bǎ tāde 'yīshang chènde gèng hǎu'kàn le. / He set off the firecracker. Tā bǎ 'pàujang dyǎn'jáule.

Set someone **on** (or against) someone else. / They wouldn't have fought, if he hadn't set them on one another. is expressed as If he hadn't gone between them finding fault, they wouldn't have started to fight. Yàu 'bùshr tā 'tsúngjūng 'tyǎubwō, tāmen hái 'dǎbuchǐ'lái ne. / By clever propaganda they set the two countries against each other. is expressed as They used clever propaganda and incited the two countries to mutual distrust. Tāmen yùng yì'júng 'chyǎumyàude 'sywānchwán bǎ 'nèilyǎng 'gwó 'tyǎubwōde bǐ'tsž bù'hé le.

Set on fire dyǎnjáu; be set on fire jáu, jáuhwǒ, chíhwǒ, shāu. / My cigarette set the newspaper on fire. Wǒde yān'jywǎr bǎ bàu'jř dyǎn'jáule.

Set out see Set off above.

Set right, set straight °shwō (°jyǎng, °'jyěshr) °'chīngchu (°'míngbai). / Set me straight on this. Bǎ jèige géi wo 'jyěshr'chīngchule.

Set to music (compose) gěi . . °byǎn (°dzwò, °syě) gē'pǔdz. / Can you set this poem to music? Nǐ néng gěi jèishou 'shr byǎn yíge 'pǔdz ma?

Set up (start) kāishr, tsái, chǐtóur, dùngshǒu. / When did they set up house-keeping? Tāmen 'shémma shŕhou kāi'shř gwàn 'jyālide 'shŕching? but / His father set him up in business. is expressed as His father helped him to open a business. Tā 'fùchin bāng ta 'kāile yíge 'mǎimài.

A set (collection of things that go together but are not identical) tàu; (collection of things that go together and are almost identical) fù; (of books) bù. / Do you have a complete set of these dishes? Jèige 'dyédz ní yóu jěng'tàude ma? / These buttons are a set. Jèisyē 'nyǒudz shŕ yí'fù.

(Group of people) yìhwǒr, yìchyún, syě 'rén. / He doesn't fit in our set. Tā gēn 'wǒmen °jèiyi'hwǒr (°etc.) shwōbu'lái.

(Scenery) bùjǐng. / Who designed the sets for the play? Jèichū 'syìde bù'jǐng shř 'shéi 'jìhwade?

Radio set wúsyàndyàn.

Be set (decided) 'gùjř, sž. / He has very set opinions. Tāde 'yìjyàn hěn 'gù-jř. or Tā 'sžsyīn'yǎr.

(Ready, prepared) yùbeihǎule, jwǔnbeihǎule, nùnghǎule, nènghǎule. / Are you all set to go? Nǐ dōu yùbei'hǎule yàu 'dzǒu le ma?

Set answer. / He has a set answer for everything. Tā hwéidá shémma wènti dou yùng nèijyu 'hwà.

Set expression (facial). / He always has a set expression on his face. Tāde 'lyǎn láu 'bēngde hén 'jǐn.

SETTLE. (Take up residence; live) jù; (stay) dāi. / In what part of the country did you settle? Nǐmen dzài jèi 'gwóli 'nǎyí'bùfen 'jùsyàláile? / It was the English who first settled in that region. 'Yīnggwo rén syān 'láidàu 'jèiyí'dài 'jùsyàláide.

(Arrange comfortable) dzwò (sit); kàu (recline, lean back). / He settled himself in the chair. Tā 'dzjǐ 'kàudzai 'yǐdzshang le.

(Go to the bottom) chéndyěr, chénsyachyu, làusyachyu. / Wait until the tea leaves settle. Děng chá'yè 'làusyàchyu.

(Sink, as into the ground) syànsyachyu. / The wall has settled a little bit. Jèidwǒ 'chyáng 'syànsyàchyule yìdyar.

(Decide) jywédìng, jyějywé, 'pàndwàn. / Can you settle a question for us? Nǐ néng 'géi wǒmen jyě'jywé yíge 'wèntí ma?

(Satisfy; accomplish) bàn. / All legitimate claims will be settled. 'Swóyǒu hé-'fǎde 'yāuchyóu dōu bànde'dàu.

(Quiet) ràng . . . °bú'nàule (°bùnán'shòu le, °'shūfu le, °bù'téng le, °bú'nàudeheng le, °bù'jēteng le). / This medicine will settle your stomach. Jèige 'yàu néng ràng nǐde 'wèili bùnán'shòu le. or expressed as Take this medicine and your stomach will feel better. Nǐ chrle 'jèige 'yàu 'wèili jyòu bú'nàu le.

(Conclude by agreement) jywédìng, 'dìnggwei'hǎule. / They settled the terms of the treaty. Tāmen bǎ 'tyáujyàn dōu 'dìnggwei'hǎule.

Settle down (live regularly) ānjrhàu; (direct one's attention) ānsyīn, tāsyà 'syīnchyu. / Hasn't he settled down yet? Tāde 'shēnghwó hái méiānjr'hǎu ne ma? / The boy couldn't settle down to his homework. Nèige 'háidz 'tābusyà 'syīn chyu dzài 'jyāli dzwò 'gūngke.

Be settled gùdìng, yǒu yí'dìngjr'gwēi. / He seems very settled in his ways. Tāde 'shēng'hwó'syí'gwàn hǎu'syàng dōu °hěn gù'dìng (°yǒu yí'dìngjr'gwēi).

SEVEN. chī; one-seventh 'chīfēnjr'yī; the seventh dìchī.

SEVENTEEN. shrchī; one-seventeenth shr'chīfēnjr'yī; the seventeenth dìshrchī.

SEVENTY. 'chīshr; one-seventieth 'chīshrfēnjryī; the seventieth dìchīshr.

SEVERAL. ji plus a measure; for emphasis hǎuji plus a measure; **several days** jityān; **several years** jinyán. / I want to stay for several days. Wǒ yàu dzài 'jèr 'dāi jityān. / There are several ways of doing this. Dzwò 'jèige yǒu 'hǎujige 'fádz.

SEVERE. lìhai; (for an illness) jùng, chénjùng, dà; (for an accident) 'yánjùngde; **severe illness** 'lìhaide 'bìng; **have a severe pain** 'tíngde 'lìhai; **severe criticism** 'pīpingde hěn 'lìhai; **severe accident** 'lìhaide yìwài 'shrching. / The judge was very severe. Jèige fǎ'gwān hěn 'lìhai.

(Stern) 'jwāngyán. / I've never seen him look so severe. Wǒ tsúnglái yě méi 'kànjyàngwo tā 'dzěmma yàngr 'jwāngyángwo.

(Hard to endure; especially cold) 'lěngde 'lìhai, tèbyé 'lěng. / Is the winter severe? !Dūngtyān lěngde 'lìhai ma?

(Difficult). / This motor will have to undergo a severe test before it is put into service. is expressed as This motor must be tested carefully before it is used.

899

Jèige fàdùng'jĭ méi'yùng yĭ'chyán déi °hăuhāurde (°'yángéde, °'dzsyìde, °'syáusyău-syĭn'syĭnde) 'sh̀ryàn yísyàr.

(Strict). / Don't be so severe with the child. is expressed as Don't treat the child too harshly. Byé bă 'háidz gwănde tài °'yán le (°'lĭhai le).

(Plain) jyăndan. / That dress has very severe lines. Nèige 'yĭfude 'yàndz hén 'jyăndan. or Nèige 'yĭfude yàngdz jŕgulūng'tūng.

SEW. féng; (specifically of a seam) lyáu; (hem) swŏ; (piece) lyán; (stitch something, as the sole of a Chinese shoe, to make it strong) nà; (sew the upper part of a shoe to the sole) shàng; **do sewing** (use a needle and thread) dzwò 'hwó, dzwò 'jēnsyàn (-hwó), (make clothes) dzwò 'yīshang. / She sews for a living. Tā 'jŕje dzwò 'jēn-syàn'hwó wéi'shēng. / Sew up the seam. Bă 'jèidàu 'fēngr gĕi °'féngshang (°'lyáu-shang).

Sew on a button, etc. dĭng. / Please sew on the buttons. Láu'jyà bă 'jèijige 'nyŏudz gĕi 'dĭngshang.

Sew on a machine yùng 'jīchi dzwò 'hwó.

Sewing machine féngrènjĭ.

SEX. syìngbyé (used only on written documents or when citing them); otherwise, when asking about one's sex, one says male or female (for humans) 'nánde 'nyŭde, (for animals) 'gūngde 'mŭde. / Give your name, age, and sex. Bá nĭde syìng'míng, 'nyán-líng, syìng'byé, dōu 'syĕshang. / What sex is the puppy? Syáu 'gŏur sh̀r 'gūngde háishr 'mŭde?

Sex appeal is expressed as be physically attractive syìnggan. / The new secre-tary has a lot of sex appeal. Jèige syĭn 'shūji hén 'syìnggăn.

SHADE. (Place in shadow) yĭnlyángr. / Let's stay in the shade. Dzámen dàu yĭn'lyángr-li lái ba. / This is a fine shade tree. Jèikē 'shùde shùyĭn'lyángr hén hău.

(Dark part) yĭnyēngr, 'ànde dìfang; **light and shade** yĭn'yáng. / Light and shade are well balanced in that painting. Nèijāng 'hwàr 'yĭn'yáng gwāng syàn 'pèide hĕn 'yún.

(Of color) 'shēnchyăn. / What about this shade (of color)? 'Jèige yánsède shēn-chyăn dzĕmma'yàng? but / Have you any thread to match this shade of blue? is ex-pressed as Have you any kind of thread to match this blue color? Ní yŏu shémma yàngrde syàn pèi 'jèijŭng 'lánshăr ma?

(Minor distinction). / Your translation doesn't get quite the right shade of mean-ing. is expressed as Your translation hasn't grasped the exact meaning. Nĭde 'fānyi 'méiyou 'jwāju nèige jēn'jèngde 'yìsz. or as You translated the meaning not quite right. Ní 'fànde nèige 'yìsz bù 'sh̀rfēn 'chyàdang.

(A blind) 'chwāng(hu)lyár. / Pull down the shades. Bă 'chwānghulyár 'lāsyàlai.

(A slight bit) (yĭ)dyăr. / This hat is a shade more expensive than I thought. Jèige 'màudzde 'jyàchyan bí wó 'syăngde shāu'wēi 'gwèi yĭdyăr. / It's a shade too big. Nèige tài 'dà dyăr le.

To shade (screen) jēju. / Shade your eyes from the glare. Jēju dyár 'yănjīng shēngde hwáng'yăn. or expressed as Cut off the light to keep it from shining in your eyes. 'Dăngje dyár nèige lyàng'gwāng shēngde hwáng'yăn.

(Darken) túshēn, hwàshēn, mwŏshēn, myáu shēn. / Shade this part a little more. Bă 'jèibùfen dzài tú'shēn dyăr.

(Change color gradually) jyàn'jyānde byàn 'yánshar, yĭ'dyăr yĭ'dyărde byàn 'yánshar. / The stage lights shaded from yellow to blue. Wǔ'táide dēng'gwāng tsúng hwáng'yánshar °jyàn'jyānde (°yǐ'dyàryidyàrde) 'byàncheng 'lányánshar le.

SHADOW. (Of a person or thing) yǐngdz, yǐngr. / The trees cast a long shadow in the afternoon. 'Syàbàntyàr shù'yǐngr hěn 'cháng. / He clings to him like his shadow. is expressed as He follows him, form and shadow not apart. Tā 'syíngyǐngbù'líde 'jwēije tā. *but* / He's just a shadow of his former self. is expressed as He's thin, not the way he used to be. Tā 'shòude °'bùshr nà'yàngr le (°gǎile 'yàngr le).

(A little bit) yìdyǎr, háu . . ., 'sǎháu . . . . / There is not a shadow of doubt about the truth of the story. Jèi shèr yí'dìng shr 'jēnde, °yìdyǎr (°'sǎháu) méiyóu kě'yíde.

To **shadow** (watch secretly) 'àn'dì 'jyānshr; (follow secretly) àn'dì 'gēnje. / I hired someone to shadow him. Wǒ 'gùle yíge 'rén àn'dì 'gēnje tā.

SHAKE (SHOOK, SHAKEN). yáu, a general term, meaning to shake in almost any way, but particularly sideways; thus ring a bell by shaking it yáulíng; shake one's head no yáutóu; shake one's head yes dyàntóu; (swing sideways or back and forth) 'yáuhwàng, hwàng, hwàngyou. / He took the boy by the shoulders and shook him. Tā 'jwāju nèi 'háidzde jyān'bǎngr 'yáuhwang tā. / He shook his head yes. Tā 'dyànle dyàn tóur. / He shook his head no. Ta yáule yáu tóur. / He denied it with a shake of his head. is expressed as He didn't answer with words, he just shook his head no. Tā méi'hwéidá shemma 'hwà, 'jyòu 'yáule yáu 'tóur. / Shake the bottle well before using the medicine. Jèi 'yàu méi'yùng yǐ'chyán 'syān déi bǎ píngdz 'yáuyau.

(Hold from the tip and shake up and down, to get out dust, etc.) dǒu, dǒulou. / Shake the dust out of these clothes. Bǎ 'jèisyē 'yīshangshàngde 'tǔ 'dǒulou 'dǒulou.

(Bump up and down, on horseback or in a car) dyān, dyānde. / The road is so bumpy, it feels as if the car would shake apart. 'Jèige dàur tài bù'píng, chē hǎu'syàng dōu kwài 'dyān sǎnle.

(Move) dùnghan. / Our whole house shook during the earthquake. Dì'jèn de 'shríhour wǒmen jēng'gèrde 'fángdz dōu jr 'dùnghan.

(Quiver) fādǒu, chàn, dwōswo, chànwei, dǎchàn, dǒu; (shiver and have one's teeth chatter) dǎjàn, jàn. / He was shaking with cold. Tā 'lěngde jr fā'dǒu. / Her voice shook. Tāde 'shēngyīn jr 'chànwei. / He can't stop his hand from shaking. Tāde 'shóu °jrbú'jùde (°jr) 'dwōswo.

Shake hands 'lāshǒu, 'wòshǒu. / We didn't get a chance to shake hands with the hostess. Wǒmen méi 'dé(dàu) 'jīhwèi gēn 'nyújǔrén 'lāla shǒu.

Shake off (fall off) dyàu, dyàule, 'dyàusyàchyu. / The mud will shake off your shoes easily when it dries. Syéshangde 'ní yì'gān hěn 'róngyide jyòu 'dyàule.

Shake off (get rid of) is expressed indirectly; shake off bad temper is expressed as press down bad temper bǎ 'chì 'yāsyàchyu; shake off responsibilities is expressed as unload responsibilities 'syèle 'dzérèn le; etc. / He shook off his depression and went visiting. is expressed as He took up good spirits, and went out to see people. Tā 'dáchǐ 'jīngshen lái, 'chūchyù kàn 'rén chyule.

Shake up (startle; give a shock to someone) bǎ . . . syà yí'tyàu *or* (cause someone to receive a shock) °jyàu (°shr) . . . shòu yǐ'jīng. / He was really shaken up by the accident. Jèitsz chūshr 'jēn bǎ ta syà yí dà 'tyàu.

SHALL. (In asking someone to express his opinion as to what you should do). / Shall I wait? Wó 'děngje ma? / Let's have dinner now, shall we? Dzámen syàndzài chr 'fàn, 'hǎu buhǎu? / Shall I close the window? Wǒ gwānshang 'chwānghu ba?

SHAPE. (Form) yàngr, yàngdz. / Isn't the shape of that mountain odd! Jèige 'shānde 'yàngdz dwō 'gwài a!

(Condition) 'chíngsyíng, 'jwàngkwàng. / The business is in bad shape. Jèige 'mǎimàide 'chíngsying búda 'hǎu. *but* / I'm in bad shape. is expressed as Lately I haven't felt too good. Wǒ 'jìnlái búda 'hǎu. / What shape is it in? Nèige dzémma-'yàng?

Be in shape (arranged in good order) shōushr, jěngli; (local Peiping) shŕdou, gwēijou, gwēijr. / Is the house in shape for visitors? Fángdz °shōushr (°etc.) 'kéyi ràng 'ren 'jìnlaile ma?

Get something **into shape** bǎ . . . 'nùngchū ge 'yàngr lai. / Get your plans into shape before we discuss them. Dzài wǒmen 'shānglyang yǐ'chyán syān bǎ nǐde 'jì-hwà 'nùngchū ge 'yàngr lai.

Take shape 'you dyǎr °'gwēimwo (°'yàngr) le. / His plan for the dam is taking shape. Tā dzwò 'shwěijá de 'jìhwà 'yóu dyǎr 'gwēimwo le.

To shape something (model with the hands) sù. / He shaped the clay into the image of a human head. Tā yùng 'ní 'sùchéng yíge rén'tóu.

Shape up (take a certain form) 'nùngchéng . . . yàngr. / How are things shaping up? 'Shŕching 'nùngchéng 'shémma yàngr le? *or* 'Shŕching dzémma'yàng?

SHARE. (Part) fèr, bùfen. / You'll have to do your share. Ní děi dzwò 'nǐ nèi'fèr. / Pay your share of the bill. Ní géi 'nǐ nèi'fèr. / We divided the money in equal shares. Wǒmen bǎ 'chyán píngjyūn fēncheng jǐ'fèr.

(Part ownership of a company) gǔdz, gǔr, gǔfèn, gúběn. / How many shares do you hold in that company? Nèige gūng'sžli ní yǒu 'dwōshau 'gǔdz?

To share (divide and use) fēn. / Let's share the cake. Dzámen bǎ jèige 'dàn-gāu fēnle ba.

(Use in common) hé yùng, hé plus a suitable verb. / We three share a bicycle. Wǒmen 'sānge rén 'hé yùng 'yílyàng dżsyíng'chē. / They share a room. is expressed as They live together in one room. Tāmen 'lyǎ hé 'jù 'yìjyān 'wūdz. / May I share your table? is expressed as May I sit here? Wǒ kéyi 'dzwò jèr ma?

(Have in common) dōu yǒu, dōu plus a suitable verb. / We share the same bad habit of always being late. Wǒmen 'lyǎ 'dōu yǒu wǎn'dàude 'máubìng. / They shared the secret. is expressed as They both knew the secret. Tāmen dōu 'jŕdau jèige mì-'mi le.

SHAVE. (Remove hair) gwā, tì. / He shaved the back of my neck for me. Tā géi wǒ 'gwāle 'bwódz hòutou.

(Remove facial hair) gwā lyǎn, gwā húdz, tì húdz. / I have to shave before dressing for the evening. Jyēr 'wǎnshang hwàn 'yīshang yǐ'chyán wó děi 'gwāgwa 'lyǎn.

(Remove thin slices; with any instrument, by scraping) gwā; (with a plane) bàu; (with a knife or axe, etc.) syāu. / Use a plane to shave the edge of the door. Ná 'bàudz bǎ jèige ménde 'byārshang °'gwāgwa (°'bàubau). / If you shave the soap, it will melt faster. Nǐ 'yàushr bǎ yídz 'syāucheng 'pyàr jyou hwàde 'kwài le.

A shave is expressed verbally as in the first two paragraphs. / I went to the barber for a haircut and a shave. Wǒ shàng lǐfa'gwǎn chyù lǐle lǐ 'fà, gwāle gwā °'lyǎn (°'hudz).

SHE (HER, HERS). tā; *or* tā is often lengthened to tā 'nèige rén *or* tā nèige 'nyǔrén; or sometimes one just says that person nèige 'rén; her tā; hers, her tā, 'tāde.

/Who is she? 'Tā shr̀ 'shéi? /If anyone can do it, she can. (Yàushr) 'rén néng 'dzwò de shr̀, 'tā jwūn néng 'dzwò. /I've seen her once. Wǒ 'kànjyangwo tā yí-'tsz̀. /Oh, HER! Òu, 'tā a! /Give this to her. Bǎ jèige gěi 'tā. /This is her hat. Jèi shr 'tāde màudz. /This is hers. Jèige shr 'tāde. Compare HE.

(Used to specify sex) nyǔren, nyǔde (for human beings); mǔde (for animals). /It's a SHE. Shr̀ ge 'nyǔren. *or* Shr̀ ge 'nyǔde. *or* (of an animal) Shr̀ ge mǔde.

Herself. *See* SELF.

SHEEP. yáng, myányáng. /How many head of sheep have you? Ní yǒu 'dwōshautóu 'yáng a?

Black sheep (fig.) méi'chūsyide °'háidz (°rén). /He is the black sheep of the family. Tā shr̀ tāmen 'jyāli méi'chūsyide 'háidz.

SHEET. (Of paper) jāng, pyār. /I want a hundred sheets of paper. Wǒ yàu yi'bǎijāng 'jř.

(Of cardboard, metal, and other stiff things) pyàr. /This machine cuts the aluminum into thin sheets. Jèige 'jīchi bá 'lyǔ 'chyēcheng báu'pyàr.

(On a bed) (chwáng) dāndz; bèidāndz, bèilǐdz, bèilyěr (upper sheet or a sheet sewed to the under side of a quilt, to keep it clean); rùdāndz (under sheet or a sheet sewed to the mattress to keep it clean). /Put clean sheets on the bed. Bǎ 'chwáng 'pūshang 'gānjing 'dāndz. /The sheets are changed every Saturday. 'Měige Lǐbài-lyòu hwàn yí'tsz̀ chwáng'dāndz.

SHELL. (Hard outer covering) kér, chyàur, pyér. /The shells on these walnuts are very thick. Jèisyē 'hétoude 'kér hěn 'hòu.

(Of a turtle) (wángba) kér, (wángba) gàr.

(Of an egg) dànkér, dànpyér, dànchyàur; (of a chicken egg) jīdànkér; (of a duck egg) 'yādàn'kér; etc.

(Framework, of a building) 'chyūchyàur, jyàdz. /After the fire, just the shell of the house was left. Jèige fángdz shāule yǐ'hòu 'jyou shèng yíge 'chyūchyàur le.

(Projectile) dẕdàn, jàdàn, pàudàn. /A shell nearly hit him. Yíge dẕ'dàn chà-'dyǎr méi 'dǎjáu ta.

Sea shell bèngkér, gélibèngdz.

To shell (remove shells, in general) bāupyér, chyùpyér; (for nuts only) chyù-kér. /Are the peas all shelled? Wān'dòu dōu bāu'pyér le ma?

(Bombard) °ná (°yùng) 'pàu °hūng (°gūng, °dǎ). /We shelled the enemy positions for hours. Wǒmen yùng 'pàu gūngle díren 'háujige jūng'tóu.

SHELTER. (Place to stay) ān'shēnde dìfangr, ān'shēnjr'chù, 'jùde 'dìfangr. /We had to find shelter for the night. 'Wǎnshang wǒmen déi 'jǎu ge °'jùde 'dìfangr (°etc.).

(A shack) wōpeng. /We built a crude shelter out of branches. Wǒmen yùng shù'jěr dāle ge 'wōpeng.

Air raid shelter fángkūngdùng.

Fall-out shelter ywándz'chén fángkūngdùng.

To shelter jàugu, jāuhu. /Who'll shelter the refugees? 'Shwéi 'jàugu 'jèisyē tau'nànde ya?

SHINE (SHONE). (Be visible). /Is the sun shining? is expressed as Is the sun out or not? Yǒu 'fàiyang méiyou? or as Is the sun hot or not? 'Tàiyang 'dú budú? / The moon is shining very brightly. is expressed as The moon is very bright. 'Ywèlyàng hěn 'lyàng.

(Give light, of the heavenly bodies or any light) jàu; (dazzle) hwǎng. / The moonlight is shining on the lake. 'Ywègwāng 'jàudzai 'hushang. / That car's head-lights are shining in my eyes. Nèilyàng 'chēde chē'dēng °'jàu (°'hwáng) wǒde 'yǎn.

(Cause to give light) bǎ . . . jàu. / Shine the light over here. Bǎ 'lyàngr wàng 'jèr 'jàujau.

(Polish) tsā. / I want my shoes shined. Wǒ yàu 'tsātsa 'syé.

(Be outstanding) chūsè, lòulyǎn, chūfēngtou. / He really shone in his math class. Tā dzài 'shùsywé'bānshang jěn lòu'lyǎn.

A shine. / Please give me a shine. is expressed as Please shine my shoes. Ching ní bá wǒde 'syé gěi tsā'lyàngle.

Rain or shine (wind and rain no obstacle) 'fēngyǔwú'dzǔ. / We'll come, rain or shine. Wǒmen yí'dìng 'lái, 'fēngyǔwú'dzǔ. or expressed as Whether it's cloudy or fair, we'll certainly come. Bùgwǎn 'yīntyān 'chíngtyān, wǒmen yí'dìng lái.

Have a shine (be shiny) lyàng, fālyàng, shǎngwǎng. / That brass platter has quite a shine on it. Nèige túng'párshang °hěn 'lyàng (°jǐ fā'lyàng, °jǐ shǎn'gwāng). / Look at the shine on that car! Nǐ chyáu nèi 'chē dwō 'lyàng!

SHIP. chwán. / Who is in charge of this ship? Shéi 'gwǎn jèijǐ 'chwán?

(Plane) fēijǐ. / He was piloting a big four-motored ship. Tā 'kāide shǐ 'sżge fādùng'jǐde fēi'jǐ.

To ship (send) sùng; (mail) jì; (send by freight) yùn; (dispatch, as troops) pài-chyǎn. / I want to ship this. Wǒ yàu bǎ 'jèige jì'dzǒu. / Has the case been shipped yet? Nèijǐ 'syāngdz yùn'dzǒule ma? / The government shipped troops to the city to maintain order. 'Jèngfǔ pài'chyǎn rwògān bù'dwèi dàu 'chéngli chyu 'wéichǐ 'jǐ-syù.

Ship out dzwò 'chwán dzǒu. / Has the sailor we met last night shipped out yet? Dzámen dzwór 'wǎnshang 'kànjyàn de nèige shwéi'shǒu 'yǐjing dzwò'chwán 'dzǒule ma?

Be shipped (of soldiers). / They expect to be shipped any day now. is expressed as At any time they will break camp. Tāmen jyòu yàu kāi'bá le.

SHIRT. chènshān, hànshān; **undershirt** chènyī.

Special expressions in English. / Keep your shirt on! is expressed as Don't get excited; take it easy. Byé jāu'jí; màn'márde. / He lost his shirt gambling. is expressed as He gambled and lost everything, even his pants. Tā dǔchyán 'dǔde bǎ 'kùdz dōu 'shūle. / He'd give you the shirt off his back. is expressed as He's capable of giving you anything. Tā 'nénggou bǎ 'shémma dōu 'gěi ni. or as He's extremely generous. Tā 'dàfang'jíle.

SHOE. syé; **cloth shoes** 'bùsyé; **leather shoes** 'písyé; **sports shoes** 'yùndungsyé; etc.

Be in one's shoes. / Put yourself in his shoes. is expressed as If you were he, what would you think? 'Nǐ yàushr 'tā, ní dzěmma'syǎng? or as If you were he, what would you do? 'Nǐ yàushr 'tā, ní dzěmma 'bàn? or as If you were in his position, what would you do? 'Nǐ yàushr 'chùdzai 'tāde 'dìwèi ní 'dzěmma 'bàn? / I'd hate to be in his shoes. Wó ké bu'ywànyì 'chùdzai 'tāde 'dìwei.

Horseshoes májǎng.

To shoe a horse dǐngjǎng, dǐng májǎng. /Who's going to shoe the horses? 'Shéi dǐng má'jǎng a?

SHOOT (SHOT). dǎchyāng; **shoot at** something °kāi (°fàng, °ná, °yùng) chyāng dǎ. /How well can you shoot? is politely expressed as You shoot well, don't you? Ní dǎ 'chyāng yí'dìng 'dǎde 'hǎu ba. or as Do you shoot well? Ní dǎ 'chyāng dǎde 'hǎu ma? /What are they shooting at? Tāmen 'yùng 'chyāng) dǎ 'shémma ne? /He shot me in the arm. Tā ná 'chyāng 'dǎdau wǒ 'gēbeshang le.

(Use; of a gun) yùng. /What kind of bullet does this gun shoot? Jèigǎn 'chyāng yùng 'shémma dz'dàn?

(Move very quickly; run) pǎu, chūng; (run, with a puff of dust) yílyou 'yārde 'pǎu; (run, with a swish) 'sōude yí'syàdz 'pǎu. /A squirrel shot across the road. Yíge 'sūngshǔr dzài 'lùshang 'héngje 'pǎugwòchyule. /A car shot past us. Yílyàng 'chē tsúng wǒmen 'pangbyar 'sōude yí'syàdz jyou 'pǎugwochyule. /On the very last lap of the race our horse shot ahead. Nèi'chǎng sài'mǎ dàule mwò'lyǎur 'wǒmen nèipǐ 'mǎ 'sōude yí'syàdz jyòu 'pǎude 'tóuli chyùle. but /Sharp pains are shooting up and down my leg. is expressed as In my leg, coming up and going down, time after time it pains very severely. Wǒ 'twèishang 'shànglàisyà'chyù yí'jènyí'jènde 'téngde hěn 'lìhai.

Shoot a goal gūngjìn yíge 'chyóur chyu. /Just at the last moment he managed to shoot a goal. Dzwèi'hòu yìfēn'jūng tā hái gūngjìnle yíge 'chyóur chyu.

Shoot an arrow shè'jyàn.

Shoot pictures jàusyàng. /We're planning to shoot a few pictures this morning. Wǒmen 'dǎswan jyēr 'dzǎuchen chyù 'jàu jijǎng 'syàng.

Shoot questions 'wènle yíjèn 'wèntí. /He shot questions at us. Tā 'wènle wǒmen yíjèn 'wèntí.

Shoot out (as flames) 'pūchūlaile. /I opened the furnace door and the flames shot out. Wǒ 'yì kāi lú'mér, hwǒ'myáu 'pūde yí'syàdz jyòu 'chūláile.

Shoot up (grow very fast) jǎng; (Peiping slang for a child growing fast) tswān. /How fast that child has shot up in the last year! 'Nèi háidz 'chyùnyán yì'nyán jǎngle dwō 'gāu a! /Prices have shot up since the war started. Kāi'jàng yǐ'hòu wù'jyà dōu 'jǎngle.

A shoot (new growth) nènyár, syīnyár, syīnjēr, syīntyáu, jyàndz. /The new shoots are coming up. Syīn'yár 'chūlaile.

Bamboo shoots (jú)swǔn.

SHOP. pùdz; in compounds, with preceding elements specifying the kind of thing sold or done, pù, dyàn, jwāng, háng, gwǎn, gàng, chwǎngdz, táng, lóu, jāi, swǒ, jyú, jyū, jyā, shè; **bookshop** shūpù; **barber shop** lǐfàdyàn; **bicycle shop** dzìsyíngchēháng; **butcher shop** (non-Mohammedan, therefore selling pork) jūrougàng, (Mohammedan, selling no pork and concentrating on lamb) yángròuchwǎngdz, etc. /I'm looking for a tobacco shop. Wǒ jèng 'jǎu yānjywǎr'pù ne. /You'll have to take these to a shoe repair shop. Nǐ déi bǎ jèisyē 'syé nádàu 'syōuli'syéde 'pùdzli chyù. /Let's walk down the street and look in the shop windows. Dzámen wàng 'nèibyar 'dzǒudzǒu 'kànkan 'pùdzde 'chwānghu.

(Factory) gūngchǎng. /He's on the night shift at the shop. Tā dzài nèige gūng-'chǎngli dǐng 'yèbān.

Shut up shop shōutār. /It's late; let's shut up shop and go home. Tyān bù'dzǎu le, dzámen shōu'tār hwéi'jyā ba.

Talk shop. /He's always talking shop. is expressed as He never says even

905

three sentences without mentioning his own profession. Tā 'sānjyùhwà bù'lí hěn'háng.

To shop mǎi dūngsyi; shop around 'kàn yikàn. /Where are the best places to shop? 'Shémma dìfang mǎi 'dūngsyi dzwèi 'hǎu a? /I want to shop around a little before I decide. Wó děi 'syān 'kàn lyǎngjyǎer dzai 'mǎi.

SHORE. àn. /How far is it from here to the other shore? Jèr lí dwèi 'àn yǒu dwō 'ywǎn? /Let's pull the boat farther up on shore. 'Dzámen dzài bǎ 'chwán dwō wàng 'ànshang 'lāla.

(Seashore) hǎibyārshang, hǎibīn, hǎiàn. /I want to go to the shore for a vacation. Wǒ yàu dàu hǎi'byārshang chyù 'syōusyisyōusyi.

Be on shore leave syōujyà. /I'm on shore leave. Wǒ 'jèngdzài syōu'jyà.

SHORT. (Not long dwǎn; short story dwǎn'pyān 'syǎushwōr; short wave dwǎnbwō. /I want my hair cut short. Wǒ yàu bǎ 'tóufa jyáu 'dwán dyar. /The days are short now. Tyān 'dwǎn le. /This coat is too short. Jèijyàn shàng'shēr tài 'dwǎn le. but /It's a short distance from here to the lake. is expressed as From here to the lake it's very near. Tsúng 'jèr dàu 'hú nèr °hěn 'jìn (°bù'ywǎn). /We took a short walk in the afternoon. is expressed as In the afternoon we walked a little. 'Syàwǔ wǒmen 'dzǒule °yìdyǎr (°'jìbù) 'lù. or as In the afternoon we walked around a little. 'Syàwǔ 'wǒmen 'sànle sàn 'bù.

(Not tall; low) ǎi. /She is a very short girl. Tā jèige nyǔ'háidz 'gèr tài 'ǎi.

(Not enough) búgòu; (less) shǎu. /That clerk shortchanged me. Nèige 'hwǒji 'jáugéi wǒde 'chyán bú'gòu. or Nèige 'hwǒji shǎu 'jáugéi wǒ 'chyán le.

(Rude; expressed mildly) tsū; (more emphatic) yě; (bad mannered) méi 'gwēijyu. /He was very short with us. Tā gēn wǒmen tài méi 'gwēijyu le.

(Abruptly; immediately) mǎshàng, lìkè, lìshŕkè, dēngshŕ, dāngshŕ, lìshŕ. /He stopped short when he saw us. Tā 'kànjyan wǒmen mǎ'shàng jyòu 'jànjule. /She pulled the horse up short. is expressed as She reined the horse in firmly. Tā bǎ 'mǎ 'lēi'jùle.

Be short of, run short of (lack) dwǎn, 'dwǎn dyar, chywē, 'chywē, dyǎr, 'chywēfǎ, chyàn, chyàn dyar; run short (be insufficient) búgòu, chà. /I'm a little short of money. Wó 'dwǎn dyar 'chyán. /Our supplies were running short. is expressed as Our supplies were becoming not enough. Wǒmende 'dūngsyi yàu búgòu le. /We ran short of paper. is expressed as Our paper was not enough. Wǒmende 'jŕ hái 'chà dyar.

Cut short swōdwǎnle, tí'chyán 'jyésù, ràng . . . 'shǎu. /Her mother's illness cut their vacation short. is expressed as Her mother being sick made them take fewer days' vacation. Tā 'mǔchin yí'bìng ràng tāmen 'shǎu 'wárle jityān.

Fall short (not reach) méi . . . dàu. /The factory fell short of its goal. Jèige gūng'chǎng méi'dzwòdàu ywán'láide 'jìhwa. /The picture fell short of our expectations. Jèige dyàn'yǐngr méi'syàngdàu nèmma chà'jìn.

Make short work of. /We made short work of that argument. is expressed as We stopped up their mouths in an instant. Wǒmen yí'syàr jyòu gěi tāmen 'dìnghwēichyule. /He made short work of the job. is expressed as He had the job done in an instant. Tā yí'syàr jyòu bǎ nèige 'shŕching 'dzwòle.

In short, make a long story short (as a whole) dzǔngjŕ, dzǔngéryánjŕ; (simply, in a word) gàntswèi; (speak simply) 'gàntswèi 'shwō ba; (cut it and speak briefly) 'jyǎndwànjyé 'shwō. /I have neither the time nor the inclination; in short, I refuse. Wǒ shŕ 'jì méi 'gūngfu 'yòu méi 'syìngchyù, gàn'tswèi, wǒ bú'gàn.

Just short of 'chà dyǎr, 'chàbudwō, 'chà yichàr, 'jīhū, jījīhū, kwài. /He came just short of missing the train. Tā 'chà dyǎr jyou méi'gǎnshang 'chē. / They stopped just short of the railroad tracks. is expressed as They almost went on the railroad tracks. Tāmen 'chà dyǎr 'dzǒudau hwǒchē'dàushang. / It's just short of ten o'clock. 'Kwài dàu 'shŕdyǎn jūng le. or 'Chà yi'dyǎr jyou yàu dàu 'shŕdyǎn jūng le.

Nothing short of (absolutely; certainly) jyǎnjŕde; (just) jyòushr; (only) 'jŕ yǒu, chú'fēi . . . bū, fēi(děi) . . . °tsái (°bu). / His action is nothing short of criminal. Tā dzwò de 'shèr jyǎn'jŕde shŕ fàn'fǎ. / Nothing short of a miracle will do any good. 'Fēiděi 'shénsyān tsái 'syíng ne.

Short memory 'jìsying bù'hǎu, 'jìsying tài 'hwài or (when you can't remember someone you've met before) expressed as stupid eyes yǎnjwō.

Short temper 'píchi °bù'hǎu (°tài 'hwài, °tài 'dzāu).

Shorthand sùsyě, sùjì.

A short (short circuit) is expressed verbally as **short circuit** dyànlù bù'tūng, byēle, hwàile, shāuhwàile. / Check the radio and see where the short is. 'Kànkan jèige wúsyàn'dyàn nǎr 'byēle.

Shorts dwǎn kùdz; **undershorts** syǎu kùdz. / Don't you think she looks nice in shorts? Nǐ shwō tā chwān dwǎn 'kùdz dwō hǎu'kàn ne?

SHOT. (Discharge of a gun) 'chyāngsyǎng. / Did you hear a shot? Nǐ 'tīngjyan yìshēng 'chyāngsyǎng ma? or expressed as Did you hear someone shoot? Nǐ 'tīngjyan fàng-'chyāng le ma?

(Aim). / Good shot! Hǎu 'chyāng! or expressed as Shot very accurately! Dǎde jēn 'jwǔn! / That was a bad shot. is expressed as The gun was shot poorly. Nèi 'chyāng dǎde bù'hǎu.

(Marksman) chyāngshǒu. / He's a good shot. is expressed as He's an expert rifleman. Tā shŕ yige 'shénchyāng'shǒu. or as He shoots a gun very well. Tā dǎ 'chyāng 'dǎde hén 'hǎu.

(Lead pellets) chyāngdzěr, shādz. / He loaded the gun with bird shot. Tā 'chyāngli jwāngde shŕ dá 'nyǎurde 'shādz.

(Photograph) syàngpyār. / I took some beautiful shots of the mountains. Wó gěi nèidzwò 'shān jàule jǐjāng hén 'pyàulyang de syàng'pyār. or expressed as I shot several beautiful mountain views. Wǒ 'jàule jǐjāng tíng hǎu'kànde 'shānjǐng.

(Injection) jùshè; **get a shot** shŕ'syíng jù'shè, (colloquial) dǎ 'jēn. / Have you had your typhoid shots? Nǐ dǎle shāng'hán'jēn le ma? (fig.) / His visit was like a shot in the arm to the office. Tā jèi yi'lái gěi wǒmen 'gūngshr'fángrli 'dǎle yì 'mǎ-'fēi'jēn.

(Drink) is expressed as a mouthful kǒu. / I need a shot of whisky. Wó děi °'hē (°lái) yìkǒu wēishr'jì.

A shot in the dark is expressed with try it once °'mēng (°'jwàng, °'pèng) yí-syàr. / It's just a shot in the dark. Nà 'bùgwò 'jyòu shr 'mēng yísyàr.

A long shot (term from horse racing) lěng'mén; (gambling terms referring to a bet on just one number) 'gūdìng, dú'mér. / He likes to play long shots, and once in a while he makes a lot of money. Tā 'syǐhwan yā lěng'mén, 'kèshr 'yǒu shŕhou tā yě néng yíng bùshǎu 'chyán. but / I'm going to try to get a plane reservation for this afternoon; it's a long shot, but maybe I can get one. is expressed as I'm going to go to get a plane reservation for this afternoon; I'm only making a try, but maybe I can get it. Jyèr 'syàwǔ wǒ yàu chyù 'dìng yige fēijǐ'pyàu, bùgwò shŕ °'pèngpeng (°'jwàngjwang) 'shŕshr méi'jwér wǒ jyòu syū 'dìngjau.

907

Take a shot at (with a gun) dǎ . . . yì'chyāng; (with any weapon) dǎ yí'syàdz.
/He took a shot at the sniper. Tā chùngje nèige 'fúbīng 'dàle yí'syàdz. /Let me
take a shot at it. Wǒ lái 'dǎ tā yì'chyāng. or expressed as Let me try. Ràng wo
'shr̀ yisyà.

SHOULD. (Ought to) yīnggāi, yīngdāng. /I should go. Wǒ yīng'dāng 'dzǒule. /I
thought I should go. is expressed as I did think I ought to go. Wǒ 'dàushr̀ 'syǎng-
gwò wǒ 'yīngdāng 'chyù láije. /They should be here by this time. 'Jèige shŕhou
'tāmen yīnggai 'dàu jèr le.

(Were to; in a conditional clause). /If it should rain, do you still want to go? is
expressed as If it rains, will you still want to go? 'Rwòshr̀ syà'yǔ, nǐ 'hái yàu 'chyù
ma?

SHOULDER. (Part of the human body) jyānbǎngr, bǎngdz. /My shoulder hurts. Wǒ jyān'bǎngr 'téng. /Put your head on my shoulder. Bá nǐde 'nǎudai 'jěndau wǒ jyān-
'bǎngrshang.

(Part of a garment) 'yīshangde jyān'bǎngr. /I don't want the shoulders padded.
Wǒ 'yīshang jyān'bǎngr nèr 'búyùng 'dyànchilai.

(Animal's upper foreleg) jǒudz. /The butcher has several (whole) shoulders
hanging in his shop. Nèige jūrou'gàngli 'gwàje hǎuji'gè 'jǒudz.

(Side of a road) lùbyār, dàubyār. /Keep on the pavement, the shoulder's soft.
Byé chūle lù'myàr, lù'byārshang tài 'rwǎn.

Give someone the cold shoulder (be cold to someone) gēn . . . lěng ('lěngdàn).
/What did you give him the cold shoulder for? Nǐ 'wèishémma gēn ta nèmma 'lěngdàn ne?

To shoulder (take or carry on one's shoulders or upper back; as a pack or person) káng; (carry a pole, weighted at each end, on one shoulder) dān, tyāu. /He was
shouldering the pack. Tā 'kángje nèibāu 'dūngsyi láije. /We shouldered our guns
and set out. Wǒmen 'kángje 'chyāng jyòu chū'fāle.

(Push, as with the shoulder) jǐ. /We shouldered our way through the mob.
'Wǒmen tsúng rén'chyúnli 'jǐchūláile.

Shoulder the responsibility fùdzé, °fù (° 'dānfù) 'dzérèn. /We had to shoulder
all the responsibility. Wǒmen děi fù 'wánchywán 'dzérèn.

Shoulder the blame. /Who'll shoulder the blame for this? is expressed as If
there's a mistake, who will take the responsibility? Yàushr 'chūle 'tswǒr shéi fù-
'dzé ya?

SHOW (SHOWN). (Point out) jř. /He showed me where he lived. Tā 'jřgei wǒ tā dzài
'nǎr 'jù. /Can you show me the place on a map? Nǐ 'kéyi dzài dǐ'túshang 'jřgei wo
nèige 'dìfangr ma?

(Go with and point out) dài . . . ('kàn), lǐng . . . 'kàn. /Could you show me the
way? Láu'jyà 'dài wo 'chyù. /Will you show me the room? Láu'jyà 'dài wo kànkan 'wūdz. /I'd like to show you around. is expressed as I'd like to take you everywhere to look. Wó syǎng 'lǐng nǐ 'gèchùr 'kànkan. but /Show the man in. is expressed as Tell the man to come in. Bǎ 'nèige rén chǐng 'jìnlai. /Show him out,
please. Láu'jyà sùng ta 'chūchyu.

(Let someone see) °ná (°dzwò, °etc.) gěi . . . °'kàn (°'chyáu). /Please show
me some red ties. Láu'jyà ná dyǎr 'húngyánshǎrde lǐng'dài gěi wo 'kànkan. /Show
me how to do it. 'Dzwò gěi wo 'kànkan.

(Instruct) gàusu. /Show me how to do it. meaning Tell me how to do it. 'Gàusu wo 'dzĕmma 'dzwò. / Could you show me the way? <u>is expressed as</u> Please tell me how to go. Láu'jyà 'gàusu wo dzĕmma 'dzŏu.

(Be seen) lòu. / Does my slip show? Wŏde chèn'chyún 'lòu bulòu? / Put those letters under the book where they won't show. <u>is expressed as</u> Put those letters under the book; then they can't be seen. Bă nèisyē 'syìn gēdzai nèige shū'dǐsya búyàu jyàu rén 'kànjyan. / I think my arm is hurt, but it doesn't show. <u>is expressed as</u> I think my arm is wounded, but you can't see it. Wŏ 'jywéde wŏde 'gēbe shòu'shāngle, 'kĕshr kànbuchū'lái.

(Let be seen) bă . . . lòuchulai; **show one's face** lòumyàr; **show one's teeth** dẓ yá, tsẓ yá. / That remark of his shows his mean disposition. Tā nèijijyù 'hwà bă tāde hwài 'píchi dōu 'lòuchulaile. / The dog showed his teeth. Nèige 'gŏu °tsẓje (°dẓje) 'yá. / He won't dare show his face here again. Tā bù'găn lòu'myàr le.

(Display). / She doesn't show any consideration for others. <u>is expressed as</u> She doesn't think of other people. Tā bùgĕi 'byé rén 'syăngsyang. / Try not to show any partiality. <u>is expressed as</u> Don't put your heart on one side. Byé pyānsyīn'yăr. / His work showed great concentration. <u>is expressed as</u> From his work you can see he expended concentration. Tsúng tāde 'gūngdzwòli kàndechū'lái tā shr hĕn fèile yìfān 'sẓwŏ. / Do you think he shows any improvement, Doctor? <u>is expressed as</u> Do you think he's getting better, Doctor? Nín °'jywéje (°kàn) tā jyàn 'hău ma? / His work shows signs of improvement. <u>is expressed as</u> His works looks as though it's improving. Tāde 'gūngdzwò kàn 'yàngr hĕn 'yŏu 'jìnbù.

(Indicate). / The thermometer shows a temperature of 85° in this room. <u>is expressed as</u> In this room the thermometer reads 85°. Jèi 'wūli hánshú'byău shr bā-shr'wŭdù. / This gauge shows that the car needs oil. <u>is expressed as</u> From the gauge you can see you must add oil to the car. Tsúng jèige yóu'byăushang 'kéyi 'kànchūlai jèige 'chē dĕi jyā 'yóu.

(Prove) 'jèngmíng. / They weren't able to show why they couldn't go. Tāmen bù'néng 'jyĕshr 'wèi shémma tāmen méi'néng 'chyù. / I won't believe it unless it's shown to me. Chú'fēi gĕi wo 'jèngmíng yí'syàr, yàubùrán wŏ bú'syìn.

(Present, in a theater) yăn, 'byáuyăn. / What are they showing at the theater? Syì'ywándzli yăn 'shémma ne? / They're showing one of the new foreign films. Tā-men nèr 'yăn yíge syīnde 'wàigwo dyàn'yĭngr.

(Present, in a store) băi. / The shops are showing some crazy hats this season. Jèisyē 'pùdz jèi'jyèrli 'băile syē syì'chígu'gwàide 'màudz.

Show off (be vain) syănbei, lòu yìshŏu, chūfengtou; **show** something **off** ná . . . °'lòu (°'syănbei). / Don't you think he shows off a good deal? Nǐ bùjywéde tā °tǐng ài 'syănbei ma (°hĕn ài chū'fēngtou ma)? / She was showing off her jewels. Tā ná tāde 'shŏushr gēn 'dàjyā 'syănbeile yísyàdz.

Show up (appear, of a person) lòumyàr; (contrast) chèn, syăn. / We waited and waited, but he never showed up. Wŏmen 'dĕngle yòu dĕng kĕshr tā shr'jŭng méi-lòu'myàr. / The design shows up well against the dark background. Dyèrde 'yánshar 'àn 'chènde jèige 'hwāyàngr hĕn hău'kàn.

Show up (expose). / I entend to show up your dishonesty. <u>is expressed as</u> I in-tend to take off your mask. Wó 'dăswàn bá nǐde jyămyàn'jyù gĕi 'jāisyalai. <u>or as</u> I want to uncover the truth about you. Wŏde 'yìsz shr yàu 'jyē nǐde 'dǐ. <u>or as I</u> want to disclose the truth. Wŏde 'yìsz shr yàu 'gĕi nǐ 'syèsye 'dǐ. <u>or as</u> I want to shake out the truth. Wŏde 'yìsz shr yàu bá nǐde 'dǐ géi 'dòulou'dòulou.

A show (play) syì, hwàjyù; (movie) dyànyĭngr; (stage show, dancing) tyàuwŭ; (musical comedy or opera) gējyù; (vaudeville) dzáshwăr; (leg show, burlesque) dà-twēisyì. / Did you go to the show last night? Nǐ dzwó'wănshang chyù kàn 'shì chyule ma?

Make a show of (pretend) jyǎ, jwāng, jyǎjwāng. / She makes a show of courtesy. Tā shr̀ jyǎ 'kèchi. / He makes a show of working hard. Tā jwāngde hǎu'syàng tǐng yùng'gūng shrde.

Make a show of <u>oneself</u> (act up) syànyǎn; (lose face) dyōulyǎn, dyōurén, chū-chǒu; (make people laugh) nǎu syàuhwar. / He made an awful show of himself at that party. Dzài nèige yàn'hwèili tā 'nàule ge 'syàuhwàr.

Take a show of hands (raise hands) jyúshǒu. / We voted by a show of hands. Wǒ-men jyú'shǒu byàu'jywé.

Dog show sàigǒuhwèi, góujúng bǐsài.

SHOWER. (Short rain) yíjèn bàu'yǔ, yíjèn, dà'yǔ; **shower of hail** yíjèn 'báudz. / Wait until the shower is over. 'Děng jèijèn bàu'yǔ 'gwòchyù.

(Spraying apparatus) pēndz, pēntóur. / The shower isn't working. Jèige 'pēndz 'hwài le.

(Spray) dwēi, dzwēi. / The wind blew a shower of leaves against the house. 'Fēng bǎ nèi'yí'dzwēi shù'yèdz chùngje nèige 'fángdz 'gwāgwochyule. / We were caught in a shower of sparks from the burning building. Tsúng nèige jáu'hwǒ de 'fáng-dz nèr láile yì'dwēi hwǒ'syīngr fēidàu wǒmen 'shēnshang le.

Take a shower chūngdzǎu, syǐ pēndz, syǐ 'pēntóur; **take a cold shower** 'chūng ge 'léngshwéi 'dzǎu, ná 'lyángshwéi 'chūngchung. / You can take a shower here after the game. Wár'wánle nǐ 'kéyi dzài 'jèr chūng ge 'dzǎu.

To shower *see* **Take a shower** <u>above</u>. / I would like to shower and shave before we leave. Wǒmen dzǒu yi'chyán wǒ yàu chūng ge 'dzǎu gwāgwa 'lyǎn.

(Bestow liberally). / Their friends showered them with presents. Tāmende 'péngyou sùnggei tāmen 'hǎusye 'lǐwù. / We were showered with good wishes when we left for our trip. Wǒmen chǐ'shēn de shŕhou, tāmen gēn wǒmen shwōle 'hǎusyē yílùpíng'ān yíleide 'hwà.

SHUT. gwān(shang). / Shut the door and sit down. Bá mén 'gwānshang 'dzwò yíhwèr. / They shut the dog in the house. Tāmen bá 'gōu 'gwāndzài 'wūli le. / Is it shut tight? Gwān'jǐnle ma?

Shut down (stop) gwān, tíng; (rest) syē; (stop work) tínggūng, syēyè; (close the doors) gwān'mér; (fail) dǎu. / How long will this factory be shut down? Jèige gūng'chǎng tíng 'dwōshǎu 'shŕhou?

Shut off gwān, nǐng; (break a connection) myèle. / Shut off the motor. Bǎ fā-dùng'jǐ 'gwānshang. / Shut off the ignition. Bǎ chē 'gwān le ba. / Shut off the water; it makes too much noise. <u>is expressed as</u> Shut off the water valve; the noise is too great. Bá shwěi'mén 'gwānshang, shēngr tài 'dà. *but* / The water is shut off in the winter to keep the pipes from freezing. <u>is expressed as</u> In the winter the water is stopped to save the pipes from bursting. 'Dūngtyān jyòu bá 'shwěi 'tíng le, 'shěngde bá 'gwǎndz dùng'hwài le.

Shut out buràng . . . 'jìnchuu, bǎ . . . 'gwāndzài 'wàitou; **be shut out** jìnbúchyù, gwāndàu 'wàitou. / Don't forget your key, or you'll be shut out of the house. Byé wàng le 'yàushr bù'rán jìnbu'chyù 'wūdz le. / He went home, but his wife shut him out. Tā hwéi'jyāle, 'kěshr tā 'tàitai °buràng ta 'jìnchyu (°bǎ tā 'gwāndzài 'wài-tou le).

Shut up (close, lock) swǒ, gwān. / When they went to the country, they shut up their house. Tāmen syà'syàng de shŕhou bǎ 'fángdz 'swǒchilaile.

Shut up (put in jail) bǎ . . . °'gwān (°'jywān). / Shut him up for the night. Bǎ tā 'gwān yí'yè.

Shut up (keep indoors) gwāndzài 'wūdzli. / Her work kept her shut up for hours. Tāde 'gūngdzwò bǎ ta gwāndzài wūdzli bàn'tyān. / He shut himself up to study for exams. Tā bǎ dz'gěr 'gwāndzài 'wūrli 'yùbei kǎu'shr̀.

Shut up (don't talk) byé 'shwō le; byé hú'shwō le, byé syā'shwō le (don't talk nonsense); (more emphatic) byé °hú'shwō (°syā'shwō) bá'dàu le.

Be shut is expressed verbally as in the first paragraph. / Something is going on behind those shut doors. Nàr gwānje 'mén jwún yǒu shémma 'shèr ne.

SICK. bìng; (indisposed, out of sorts) nánshòu, bùshūfu, bùshūtan, bùhéshr̀. / I'm geeling a little sick. Wǒ 'jywéde yóu dyǎr bù'shūfu. / The child has a sick look about him. 'Nèi háidz 'kànje syàng yǒu'bìngde 'yàngdz. / He's sick in bed with pneumonia. is expressed as He got pneumonia and is lying in bed. Tā déle fèi'yán 'tǎngdzài 'chwángshang le.

(Nauseated) ěsyin; (about to vomit) yàu 'tù. / I'm going to be sick. Wó 'ěsyin. or Wǒ yàu 'tù.

Be sick of something (not feel like) lǎnde; (be bored, disgusted) nì, 'nìfán; (be disgusted) tǎuyàn; (not want to) búwànyi; (not be pleased at) bùgāusyìng. / I'm sick of working. Wǒ lǎnde dzwò'shr̀. or Wǒ dzwò'shr̀ dzwò'nìle. / We're sick and tired of these complaints. Jèiyàngr 'bàuywàn de 'hwà wǒmen tīng'nìle.

Make one sick ràng . . . °'nìdeheng (°'nìfán, °tǎu'yàn); (be stupid) méiyìsz; (be dull, no fun) wúlyáu. / That sort of thing makes me sick. Nèijǔng 'shr̀ching ràng wo jywéje tǎu'yàn.

The sick (sick people) bìngrén. / This hospital takes very good care of the sick. Jèige yī'ywàn dwèi bìng'rén 'jàugùde hén 'hǎu.

SIDE. (One of the surfaces of an object) byār, myàr; (end) tóu; front side 'jèngmyàr, 'chyánbyār, 'chyánmyàr; back side, rear side 'hòubyār, 'hòumyàr, 'hòutóu, (if the object has only two sides, like a mirror, also 'fǎnmyàr, 'bèimyàr); left side 'dzwǒmyàr, 'dzwǒbyār; right side 'yòumyàr, 'yòubyār; top side 'shàngmyàr, 'shàngbyār, 'shàngtou °nèimyàr (°nèibyār); bottom side 'dǐmyàr, 'syàmyàr, 'syàtóu, 'syàbyār, 'dǐsyà °nèimyàr (°nèibyār). / A cube has six sides. Yíge fāng'kwàr yǒu lyòu 'myàr. / The top side of the silver box is scratched. Yín'héer'shàngmyàr 'hwále syē 'dàudz. / The south side of the house needs painting. Fángdz 'nánbyārde 'chyáng dèi 'shwāshwā le. / The right side of the material is much brighter than the wrong side. (only myàr can be used). Jèige 'lyàudzde 'jèngmyàr bí 'fǎnmyàr lyàngde 'dwō.

(Surface, not top or bottom) byār, 'pángbyār, 'pángmyàr, 'tsèmyàr. / The label is on the side of the box. 'Fēngtyáu dzài 'syàdzde 'tsèmyàr ne. / The picture is taken from the side. Jèijāng syàng'pyār shr̀ tsúng 'tsèmyàr 'jàude. / There's a big garden at the side of the house. Fángdz páng'byār yǒu yíge 'dàhwā'ywàr. but / The lamp has been knocked over on its side. is expressed as The lamp has been hit and is lying down. Bǎ 'dēng pèng'tǎngsyale. / The wrecked car is lying on its side. is expressed as The wrecked car is lying down. Nèige pwò'chē 'tǎngsyale.

(Edge, line bounding a figure) byān, byār. / The land is in the shape of a triangle, with each side 300 feet long. Nèikwài 'dì shr̀ ge sān'jyǎursýng, měi'byàr shr̀ 'sānbáichr̀ 'cháng.

(Part) byār, myàr; east side (of a city) 'dūng chéng, etc. for other directions. / When she talks, you can hear everything she says on the other side of the room. Tā shwō'hwà de shrhou dzài wūdz nèibyār dōu tīngde'jyàn. / His store is on the east side. Tāde 'pùdz dzài 'dūngchéng.

(Bank) byār, àn; (riverbank) héyàr. / They crossed to the other side of the river. Tāmen 'gwò'hé dàu °'nèibyār (°'dwèiàn) chyùle. / There are some trees along the side of the river. Hé'yàrshang 'yǒu syēge 'shù.

911

(Slope) pwōr. / They ran down the side of the hill. Tāmen 'pǎusya shān'pwōr láile.

(Part of the body) byār. / His left side is paralyzed. Tā 'dzwǒbyār 'bànshēn bù'swéi. / He's wounded more seriously on the left side. Tā 'shēnshang 'dzwǒbyār shòude shāng 'jùng. / She told the child to stay close at her side while they crossed the street. Gwò'jyē de 'shŕhour tā 'gàusu nèi háidz jǐn 'gēndzài tā páng'byār. *but* / He's paralyzed on one side. is expressed as Half of his body is paralyzed. Tā 'bànshēn bù'swéi. / He stood with his hands at his side. is expressed as He stood with his hands dangling. Tā 'dǎleje shǒu 'jànje.

(Part of an animal's carcass) shàn. / We bought a whole side of bacon. Wǒmen 'mǎile yíge 'jěngshànde 'làròu.

(Partisan group) byār, tóur; (point of view) fāngmyàn. / Whose side are you on? Nǐ shr nǎi'tóurde? / He fought for the other side in the last war. 'Shànghwéi dǎ'jàng tā dzài 'nèibyār.

(Aspect) fāngmyàn. / Look at every side of the matter. Bǎ jèijyàn 'shŕchingde 'gèfāng'myàn 'dōu 'kànkan. / We discussed the problem from all sides. Wǒmen bǎ nèige 'wèntí tsúng 'gèfāng'myàn 'tǎulwùnle 'tǎulwùn.

(Not front or center) páng, pángbyàrde. / Please use the side door. Chíng dzǒu 'pángmér. / She's on the side porch. Tā dzài páng'byàrde 'lángdzshang ne.

(Not the main; not important) bú'jùngyàu, bú'yàujǐn; (little) syǎu; (rather irrelevant) wú'gwānjǐn'yàu, bù'gwān'tùngyǎng, méi'dàgwānsyi. / I think you're bringing up only side issues. Wǒ 'jywéde ní jr 'tíchǐle 'syēge bú'jùngyaude 'wèntí.

On the side shāudaìje, dàije shǒur, fùdài. / He makes some money working on the side. Ta shāudàije dzwò dyǎr byéde shr jèngle dyǎr chyán. / Besides the salary, you can pick up quite a little on the side. Dzài jèng'syīn yǐ'wài, nǐ hái néng dàije 'shǒur 'ná bù'shǎude chyán. / The store sells mostly clothes, but they carry some household goods on the side. Jèige 'pùdz 'dàbùfèn shr mài'bù, °dài'shǒur (°dàije, °dàije 'shǒur, °fù'dài) hái 'mài dyǎr ṙyùng'pǐn.

Side by side bìngje; (shoulder to shoulder) bìngje jyār, bìngjyān; (together) dzài yíkwàr. / We skated side by side. Wǒmen bìngje 'jyārde lyǒu'bīng.

Choose sides tyāubyār. / Let's choose sides and start playing. Dzámen tyāu-'byār kāi'shŕ 'lái ba.

Take sides syàngje . . . , hùje . . . . / It's difficult to take sides on this question. Jèige 'wèntí hěn nán °'syàngje (°'hùje) nèibyār. / Everybody took sides for or against him. Tāmen búshr fǎn'dwèi tāde, jyòushr 'syàngje tāde.

Sideline dàije, fùdài, dàishǒur; (extra) lìngwài, géwài, yǐwài. / We carry sports equipment as a sideline. Wǒmen fù'dài hái 'mài dyǎr 'tǐyù yùng'pǐn.

Sidelines. / He watched the fistfight from the sidelines. Tā °dzài 'pángbyār (°'dzài yì'byār) 'kànje rénjya dǎ'jyà.

To side jàndzài . . . yì'byār. / She always sides with us in any argument. Yǒu jēnglwùn de 'shŕhour tā 'cháng shr gēn 'wǒmen 'jàndzài yì'byār. / His wife always sides with him. is expressed as His wife always helps him speak. Tāde 'tàitai lǎu jàndzai tā (nèi)yì'byār.

Sidetrack (change the subject) dǎchà, bǎ 'hwàtóur 'chàkāi, chàgwochyu. / He tried to sidetrack me, but I refused to change the subject. Tā 'syàngyàu gēn wo dǎ-chà 'kěshr wǒ háishr bǎ nèige shwō'wánle. / I'm sorry I'm late; I got sidetracked. is expressed as Excuse me; I had some business and am late. Dwèibù'chǐ, wó yǒu dyǎr'shr lái 'wánle.

Sideways (toward one side) wàng 'pángbyār; (toward either side) dzwǒyòu. / The car skidded sideways on the ice. Chē dzài 'bīngshang dzǒuje jr̄ wàng pángbyār hwá. / The elevator was so crowded that I couldn't move backward or foreward or sideways. Jèige dyàn'tī tài 'jǐ le, wǒ chyán'hòu dzwǒ'yòu dōu 'dùngbulyǎu.

SIDEWALK. byāndàu, rénsyíngdàu, 'dzǒudàu.

SIGHT. (Vision). / I have poor sight. is expressed as My eyes aren't very good. Wǒ 'yǎnjīng búdà 'hǎu. or as I can't see things very well. Wǒ kàn 'dūngsyi búdà 'syíng.

(Glance, act of seeing) yǎn. / At first sight I didn't recognize you. Wǒ 'tóuyì-'yǎn méi'rènchū nǐ lái. also expressed as When I first looked at you, I didn't realize it was you. Gāng yí 'kànjyàn nǐ de shŕhou wǒ méi kànchū'lái shŕ nǐ. / They fell in love at first sight. is expressed as They fell in love at the first meeting. Tāmen shŕ yíjyànjūng'chíng.

A sight. / The children were a sight when they came in out of the snow. is expressed as When the children came in out of the snow, you should have seen the way they looked. Nèisyē 'háidz tsúng sywě'dìli 'hwéilái de 'shŕhou nǐ 'chyáu tāmen nà-'yàngr. / It was a terrible sight. is expressed as It was really hard to look at. Nèige 'jēn nán'kàn. or as It wasn't pretty. Nèige bùhǎu'kàn.

Catch sight of 'kànjyàn, 'kànjyàn yǐ'yǎn. / I caught sight of you on the railroad platform. Wǒ dzài hwǒchē'jànshang 'kànjyàn 'nǐ le.

In sight. / The end is now in sight. (lit., as a road) is expressed as Now the end can be seen. Syàn'dzài 'kànjyàn 'tóur le. (fig., as of work) is expressed as We know it's almost done now. Wǒmen 'jŕdàu 'syàndzài kwài 'wán le.

Know by sight. / I know him only by sight. is expressed as I only know who he is when I see him. Wǒ 'kànjyan ta, jŕdau tā shŕ 'shéi, jyòushr le.

Lose sight of (not be able to see) kànbújyàn; (be unable to locate) jǎubujáu; (lose) dyōule. / I lost sight of him in the crowd. Tā dzài 'nèichyún 'rénli wǒ kànbu'jyàn tā le.

On sight yí 'kànjyàn, yí 'jyànjáu. / They had orders to shoot him on sight. Tā-men jyēdàu 'mìnglìng le yí 'kànjyàn tā jyòu bǎ ta 'dásž.

Out of sight. / The ship moved slowly out of sight. Nèige chwán màn'mārde dzǒude kànbu'jyàn le.

Camera sight is expressed as adjusting-focus thing dwèigwāngde or as lens for focusing dwèigwāngjìng, fāngwāngjìng.

Gun sight byáuchǐr.

Go sightseeing (look everywhere) gwàng, gèchù 'kànkan; (make a tour) 'yóulǎn, 'yóulì; (look around) gwāngwàng. / We spent the whole day sightseeing. Wǒmen 'gwàng-le yìjeng'tyān.

Sights (places to be seen) kě'kànde dìfang. / Did you see the sights at the fair? 'Jíshang kě'kànde dìfang nǐ dōu 'kànle ma?

To sight (begin to see) 'kànjyàn. / When will we sight land? Shémma 'shŕhou kéyi 'kànjyàn lùdì a?

(Look through a gun or camera sight) myáu, jàu, 'bǐhwā. / Sight carefully before you shoot the deer. Dǎ nèige 'lù yǐ'chyán déi hǎu'hāurde 'myáumyáu jwǔn.

SIGN. (Of wood or metal, or the bulletin board on which signs are posted) páidz; (of paper) jŕpáidz; (public notice, bulletin) 'gàushr; (marker) 'fúhàur, 'jìhàur; (political sign, or a slogan) byāuyǔ; (a wooden tablet with characters carved on it, over a store to show the name of that store; or presented to a benefactor, with words of thanks carved on it, to be hung outside his house) byàn; (a wooden or paper figure hung outside a store, something like a barber's pole or pawnshop's three balls) hwāngdz; (similar, but also containing characters) 'jāupái. / Can't you see the "No Smoking" sign? Mwòfēi nǐ kànbu'jyàn nèige "Jǐn'jřsyǐ'yàn" de 'páidz ma?

(Gesture) jāuhu; (with the hands only) jāu shǒu. / The waiter gave us a sign to follow him. Nèige 'hwǒjì dǎ ge 'jāuhu ràng wǒmen 'gēnje ta.

(Indication) 'byàushř; (appearance) yàngr; (symptom) 'syànsyàng; (omen) jēngjàu, yùjàur, 'syānjàur; (good omen) jíjàu; (bad omen) 'syūngjàu. / That's a good sign. 'Nèige shř °'yíge 'jíjàur (°hǎu 'syànsyàng). / All signs point toward a cold winter. Kàn jèi'yàngr, 'jǐnnyande) 'dūngtyan yí'dìng hwèi hén 'lěng. / Have you seen any sign of affection between them? Nǐ 'kànchulai tāmen bǐ'tsz you shémma 'byàushř le ma?

(Trace) yǐngr, 'dzūngjì. / There are signs of a wolf. Yǒu lángde 'dzūngjì. *but* / Have you seen any sign of my friend? Nǐ 'kànjyàn wǒ 'péngyou lòu'myàrle ma? or expressed as Have you seen my friend? Nǐ 'kànjyan wǒ 'péngyou le ma?

(Symbol) 'fúhàur; (mark on paper, etc.) hàur. / He got the plus and minus signs mixed up. Tā bǎ 'jèng'fù'hàur dōu nùng'lwànle.

To sign one's name (formal) chyāndz̀; (informal, or in signing in or out) chyānmíng; (of illiterates, with a cross) hwàyǎ. / I forgot to sign the letter. Wǒ 'wàngle dzài jèifēng 'syìnshang chyān'dz̀le. / Sign your name here, please. Chǐng ni dzài 'jèr chyān'míng.

Sign something **away** *or* **over** lǐ 'dz̀jyù bǎ . . . 'jyāugei. / He signed away all his property to the bank. Tā gěi yín'háng lìle ge 'dz̀jyù bǎ 'swóyǒude 'tsáichǎn dōu 'jyāugěi tāmen le. / He signed over control of the business to his son. Tā 'lìle ge 'dzèr bá 'mǎimai 'jyāugei tā 'érdz le.

Sign off. / Radio stations here sign off early in the evening. Dzài 'jèr de wúsyàn'dyàn'tái 'wǎnshang hén 'dzǎude jyòu °tíng'bwōle (°tíng'jř 'bwōsùng le).

Sign on (hire) gù; (take on) shōu; sometimes expressed with look for jǎu; (polite, meaning request the services of) chǐng. / The ship in the harbor is still signing on men. 'Mǎtóulide nèige 'chwán hái 'dzài nèr gù 'rén dāng shwéi'shǒu ne.

Sign on with (agree to work for) dìng hétúng, lǐ hétung. / Will he sign on with us? Tā hwèi 'gēn wǒmen dìng hé'túng ma?

Sign up dìng hé'túng. / He signed up for three years. Tā 'dìngle 'sānnyánde 'hétúng.

Sign someone **up** gen . . . °dìng'hǎu (°shwō'hǎu). / We signed him up for piece work. Tā gēn wǒmen °dìng'hǎule (°shwō'hǎule) dzwò lwùn'jyàn gěichyán de gūng'dzwò.

SIGNAL. (Sign or mark) hàu, jìhaur; (given by an instrument) 'syìnhàu; **air raid signal** jǐngbàu. / A pistol shot will be the signal to start. Fàng yí'chyāng jyòushř kai'syřde 'jìhaur. / A green light is the signal to go ahead. Lyù'dēng shř ràng nǐ 'dzǒude yìjung 'jìhaur. / We sent out an S O S signal. Wǒmen 'fāchūchyù yíge gàu'jí 'syìnhàu.

To signal (use instruments, or an established code) fā'syìnhàu; (make gestures to attract someone's attention) jāuhu, dǎ jāuhu; (sound an air raid signal) °fàng (°fā) jǐngbàu. / The policeman signaled for the cars to stop. 'Jǐngchá 'jāuhu nèisye 'chē 'tíngsyàlái.

SILENCE. (Quiet) jìng, 'ānjìng; (no sound) méishēngr; (no sound or movement) méi'dùngjìngr; or expressed with the literary phrase from the crow and sparrow no sound yāchywèwú'shēng. / I like the silence of the woods. Jèige shù'líndzli °hĕn jìng (°hĕn 'ānjìng, °yāchywèwú'shēngde) wó hén 'syĭhwàn. / The silence in the room was embarrassing. is expressed as No one in the room was talking and it made things a little stiff. Jèi wūdzli méi rén shwō'hwà, yóu dyăr 'jyàng. / His silence about the price surprised us. is expressed as He didn't mention the price, and we thought it was very queer. Tā méi'tí 'jyàchyan, wŏmen 'jywéde hĕn chí'gwài. / Silence! is expressed as A little quiet, please! 'Ānjìng dyăr! or as Don't talk! Byé shwō'hwà le. or as Don't make any noise! Byé 'nàu le! or Byé 'chău! or as Don't let out a sound. Byé chū'shēngr!

In silence yì'shēngrbù'yányude, bù'yánbù'yŭde, 'ānān'jìngjìngde. / He went about his work in silence. Tā yì'shēngrbù'yányude dzài nèr dzwò'shr̀.

To silence °ràng . . . (°bă . . . nùng) 'ānjìngsyàlai. / He silenced the audience and went on speaking. Tā bă 'tīngjùng nùng 'ānjìngsyàlai 'jìsyù 'shwōsyàchyu.

Silence objections 'dŭhwéichyù, 'dìnghwéichyù; (stop . . . from answering) bă . . . 'wènjùle; (make . . . stop talking) ràng . . . méi 'hwà shwō le. / We finally silenced their objections. Dàu'lyăur wŏmen bă 'tāmen 'dŭhwéichyùle.

SILENT. jìng, 'ānjìng, 'jìngchyau'chyāude, méi shēngr, 'yāchywè'wú'shēng; (of a person) bùshwō'hwà (not speak); **be silent about** bùtí (not mention). / The room was silent when we came in. Wŏmen 'jìnlai de shŕhour jèige 'wūdzli 'ānjìng le. / Why are you so silent? Nĭ 'wèishémma bùshwō'hwà ya? / She's too silent to be good company. Tā 'tài búai shwō'hwà, gēn tā dzài yì'chĭ méi shémma'dà 'yìsz. / They were silent about their plans. Tāmen méi'tí tāmende 'jìhwa.

Silent partner (non-participating stockholder) bùgwăn'shŕde gŭ'dūng.

SILK. sz̄; (raw silk) shēngsz̄; (silk material) sz̄jŕpĭn; (satin) dwàndz; (thin silk material) chóudz; (silk crepe) yángjòu; (silk velvet) (sz̄)rúng. / How much is silk by the yard? Chóudz 'dwōshau chyán yì'mă? / I'd like to buy some silk dresses. Wó syăng măi jĭjyàn 'dwàndzde 'yīshang. / I need some silk stockings. Wó syăng 'yàu jishwàng sz̄'wàdz.

(Silk thread) sz̄syàn; (floss) rúngsyàn. / Buy me a spool of silk. Géi wó 'măi yìjóur sz̄'syàn. / My aunt wants some embroidery silk. Wó 'gūgu yàu dyăr syòu-'hwār de sz̄'syàn.

SILVER. yín; **sterling** or **pure silver** 'chwúnyín. / Is this sterling silver? 'Jèige shŕ chwún'yínde ma? / She's wearing a silver ring. Tā 'dàije yíge 'yínjyèjer.

(Utensils of silver) 'yíngchĭ, 'yín dūngsyi. / She received a beautiful set of silver for a wedding present. Tā shōule yìfèr jyéhwūn 'lĭwù, shŕ yitàu hĕn 'pyàu-lyangde 'yínchĭ. / A burglar stole all the silver. Dzéi bă swóyŏude 'yínchĭ dōu 'tōule chyu le.

(Coins) máuchyár. / Give me some silver for these bills. 'Jèijijāng 'pyàudz 'hwàngéi wó dyăr máu'chyár.

Plate with silver 'dùyín; **cover with silver leaf** bāu'yín. / The pin is just lead plated with silver. Jèige byé'jer shŕ 'chyànde 'dùle yìtséng 'yín. or Jèige byé-'jer shŕ 'dùyínde. / Is the teapot sterling silver or just silver plated? Jèige chá'hú shŕ 'chwúnyínde háishr 'dùyínde?

SIMPLE. (Plain) 'jyăndān. / She wars simple clothes. Tā chwānde 'yīshang hén 'jyăn-dān. / He likes the simple life. Tā 'syĭhwàn 'jyăndānde 'shēnghwó. / They're so poor they can only buy the simplest food. Tāmen jēn 'chyúng jyòu néng chŕ 'dzwèi 'jyăndānde chŕde.

(Easy) 'jyăndān, 'rúngyì. / That's simple. Nèige hén 'jyăndān. / That's a simple matter. Nèige 'shr̀ching hén 'jyǎndān. /The work here is fairly simple. Jèr-de 'gūngdzwò 'jyǎndān'jíle.

(Stupid) bèn, shǎ, chr̀dwùn. /I may seem simple, but I don't understand it. Yé-syǔ shr̀ wǒ 'bèn, 'kěshr jèige wǒ bù'míngbai. /She's attractive, but rather simple. Tā hén 'tǎu rén 'syǐhwān 'kěshr yóu dyǎr 'bèn.

(Single) yí . . . . /He had a simple fracture of the arm. is expressed as His arm had the bone broken in one place. Tāde 'gēbeshang yǒu 'yíge 'dìfangr 'gútou 'shéle. /This test tube contains the simple element. Jèige shr̀'gwǎrli 'chéngje 'jyòu-shr̀ 'yíyàngr ywán'sù. /Even a child could start this machine by a simple twist of the wrist. 'Jyòushr̀ yíge syǎu'háidz yě néng yì tái 'shǒu jyòu bǎ jèige 'jīchi 'kāikai. or as Even a child can operate this machine; it's just as easy as turning over the palm of one's hand. 'Jyòushr̀ syǎu'háidz kāi jèige 'jīchi, yě shr̀ 'yìrúfán'jǎng.

(Bare). /These are the simple facts. Jèi 'dōu shr míng'bǎije de 'shr̀. /It's the simple truth. is expressed as It's certainly that way. Nèige jyǎn'jŕde 'jyòushr̀ 'nèmmaje.

SINCE. (Of something still going on) °tsúng (°dz̀'tsúng, °dǎ) . . . °chǐ (°yǐ'lái) . . . yǐ-lái; (of something finished) tsúng (dz̀'tsúng, dǎ) . . . yǐ'hòu, . . . yǐ'hòu. /I haven't had any fun since I got here. Tsúng wǒ 'láile yǐ'hòu méi'jywéde yǒu shémma 'yìsz. /Has anything exciting happened since I saw you last? Tsúng wǒ 'shànghwéi 'kàn-jyan ní yǐ'hòu 'chūle shémma tè'byéde 'shr̀ching le ma? /He hasn't been here since Monday. Tā tsúng syīngchi'yī 'láile yǐ'hòu jyòu méishàng jèr 'lái. /Since when have you worn glasses? Nǐ tsúng shémma 'shŕhour 'chǐ 'dàide yǎn'jyèngr? /He broke his leg and has had it in a cast ever since. is expressed as Since he broke his leg, it's been wrapped up in a cast. Tāde 'twěi shwāi'shéle yǐ'hòu, jyòu yì'jŕ yùng shr̀gāu'múdz 'bāuje. /We quarreled, and I haven't seen her since. Wǒmen dǎ-jyà yǐ'hòu, wǒ hái méi kànjyan tā ne.

(Because) jìrán, jìshr, jì, yīnwei. /Since they couldn't be with us, we had to change our plans. Tāmen jì'rán bù'néng 'tsānjyā, wǒmen déi gǎi'byàn 'jìhwà. /Since you don't believe me, look for yourself. Nǐ jì'rán bú'syìn, nǐ dz̀'jǐ 'kàn chyù ba. /Since you're so smart, you do it. Nǐ 'jì nèmma 'nénggan, 'nǐ dzwò.

SINCERE. 'chéngshr̀, chéngkěn; (have a sincere heart) yǒu 'chéngyì; (have a sincere mind and heart) chéng'syīnchéngyì; (be real) jēnde; (come from a sincere heart) 'chū-yú °'chéngyì (°'jŕchéng). /He's sincere. Tā hěn °'chéngshr̀ (°'chéngkěn). /That letter sounds quite sincere. Nèifēng 'syìn 'kànje hén yǒu 'chéngyì. /I don't believe he's sincere in his promises. Wǒ bú'syìn tā shr̀ 'jēnsyīnde 'dāyingle. or Tā swǒ 'dāying de hwà wǒ bú'syìn shr̀ 'chūyú'chéngyìde.

SING (SANG, SUNG). (Of people) chàng; (of birds) jyàu, shàu. /I can't sing very well. Wǒ 'chàngde bùhén 'hǎu. /Try singing the baby to sleep. is expressed as Sing a song to the baby and lull it to sleep. Gěi háidz chàng ge 'chāngr 'hūng tā shwèi-'jyàu ba. /The birds have been singing all morning. Nyǎur 'jyàule yì'dzāuchen. fig. /Bullets were singing all around us. is expressed as Bullets around us sounded with a swish. Dz̀'dàn 'jyòu dzài wǒmen sz̀jōu'wéi °'sōusoude (°'róurōurde) syǎng.

SINGLE. (One) yí. /I haven't a single thing to eat. Wǒ yì'kǒu 'dūngsyi dōu méide 'chr̄. /He knocked him down with a single blow. Tā 'yísyàdz jyòu bǎ tā dǎ'dǎule. /There isn't a single example of that on record. Gwò'chyù tsúng'lái yě méiyǒu yíge 'jèyàngr-de 'lìdz.

(For one person) dān, 'dānrérde. /I want a single room, if possible. Yàushr̀ bànde'dàu a, wǒ 'yàu yìjyān 'dānrérde 'wūdz. /These sheets are for a single bed. Jèsyē 'dāndz shr̀ wèi 'dānrénchwáng 'yùngde.

(Unmarried) 'méijyé'hwūn; (of a bachelor) dăgwāng'gwèr, gwāng'găr. / Are you married or single? Nǐ jyé'hwūnle méiyou? *or* Nǐ jyé'hwūnle háishr̀ dăgwāng-'gwèr ge?

Single file 'dānháng. / Stand in single file for tickets. Măi'pyàude 'jànchéng 'dānháng.

Single-handed yíge rén, dz̆gěr. / He shot ten of the enemy single-handed. Tā 'yíge rén 'dǎszle 'shŕge 'dírén. / She organized the tea single-handed. Kāi nèige cháhwèi shr̀ tā °'yíge 'rén (°dz̆'gěr) 'bànde.

Singles (tennis) dān. / Let's play singles. Wǒmen lái dān'dǎde ba.

To single out. / They singled him out for special mention. is expressed as They mentioned him alone specially. Tāmen bǎ tā dān'dúde tèbyé 'tíle 'tí.

SIR. 'syānshēng; Chinese usually address a superior by his title, such as jǔsyí (chair-man), shr̀jǎng (mayor); etc.; 'lǎuyé (old-fashioned way of addressing an official); dà-yé (old-fashioned way of addressing the son of a 'lǎuyé). / Sir, could you tell me where Mr. Chang's office is? 'Syānshēng, nǐ néng gàusung wǒ Jāng syānshengde gūngshr̀'fángr dzài 'nǎr? / Yes, sir. Shr̀, °jǔsyí (°shr̀jǎng, °etc.). *or* Shr̀, 'nínne. *but* / No, sir. has no simple translation but requires a statement which is negative or which clarifies the reasons for a negative answer, as Is this yours? No, sir. Jèige shr̀ nǐde ma? Búshr̀ wǒde.

SISTER. (Kinship term) **older sister** jyějye; **younger sister** mèimei; **sisters** jyěmèi, dz̆-mèi. / They are two sisters. 'Tāmen shr̀ lyǎng °'dz̆mèi (°jyěmèi). (polite term) **your older sister** lǐngjyě; **your younger sister** lǐngmèi; **my older sister** jyājyě; **my younger sister** shèmèi.

(Catholic nun) gūnǎinai; (woman who leads a monastic life) syōunyǔ, syōudàude. / There are two sisters having lunch in the restaurant. Yǒu lyǎ °gū'nǎinai (°syōu-nyǔ) dzài jèige fàn'gwárli chr̄ wǔ'fàn ne.

Sister ship jyěmèi °'hàu (°'jyàn), dz̆mèi °hǎu (°'jyàn). / This is the sister ship of the one launched last year. Jèige shr̀ 'chyùnyán syà'shwěi de nèige 'chwánde dz̆-mèi'jyàn.

SIT (SAT). dzwò. / They were sitting when we came in. Wǒmen 'jìnlái de 'shŕhour 'tāmen nèr 'dzwòje ne. / Where are we sitting tonight? Wǒmen jyēr 'wǎnshang 'dzwò-dzai 'nǎr? / She made arrangements to sit for her portrait. Tā 'yùbei 'hǎule 'dzwòdzai nèr ràng rén gěi tā hwà'syàng. / You won't finish today if you just sit there. Nǐ 'yàushr̀ jyòu 'dzwò nèr bú'dùng, 'jyēr nǐ dzwòbù'wánle.

(Have been placed) fàng, gē, bǎi. / That vase has been sitting on the shelf for years. Nèige 'píngdz dzài nèige 'jyàdzshang 'fàngle háujǐ'nyán le.

(Perch) làu. / The pigeons were sitting on the windowsill. Gēdz làude 'chwāng-hu'társhang le.

(Be in session). / The court is sitting. Fǎ'ywàn kāi'tíng le.

Baby-sit kān háidz. / I can't find anyone to baby-sit. Wǒ jǎubu'jáu rén tì wǒ kān 'háidz.

Sit down 'dzwòsyà; sometimes merely dzwò. / He sat down suddenly. Tā 'hū-rán jyòu 'dzwòsyàle. / Sit down over here, won't you? Dzwòdzai 'jèr, 'hǎu ma?

Sit in on something is expressed as listen on the side páng tǐng. / He sat in on all the conferences that day. Nèityān swǒ'yǒude 'hwèi tā dōu °páng 'tǐngle (*or* (attended) °'dàule).

Sit on someone (fig.) gěi . . . 'dǐngdz pèng. / He's very boastful; he just needs to be sat on a little. Tā tài dé'yǐ le, déi 'gěi ta dyǎr 'dǐngdz 'pèng.

SIX

Sit out. /Let's sit this dance out. is expressed as This time let's not dance, let's sit. Jèi'chǎng dzámen 'béng tyàu le, 'dzwòdzwòr ba. /I couldn't sit out that play. is expressed as I couldn't finish looking at the play. Nèichū 'syî wǒ 'kànbusyà-'chyùle.

Sit up (move to an upright position) dzwòchilai; (stay sitting) dzwò. /He sat up suddenly. Tā 'hūrán 'dzwòchǐláile. /The baby has been able to sit up since he was five months old. is expressed as At five months the baby sat up. Jèi háidz 'wǔge 'ywè jyòu 'dzwòchǐláile. or as At five months the baby knew how to sit. Jèi háidz 'wǔge 'ywè jyòu hwèi 'dzwòje le. /We sat up all night talking. Wǒmen 'dzwòdàu nèr 'tánle yí'yède 'tyār. *but* /That will make him sit up and take notice. Nèmmaje jyòu jyàu ta 'bùnéng bù'gwǎn le.

SIX. lyòu; one-**sixth** 'lyòufēnjr̄'yī; the **sixth** dìlyòu.

SIXTEEN. shŕlyòu; one-**sixteenth** shŕ'lyòufēnjr̄'yī; the **sixteenth** dìshŕlyòu.

SIXTY. 'lyòushŕ; one-**sixtieth** 'lyòushŕfēnjr̄'yī; the **sixtieth** dì'lyòushŕ.

SIZE. (Number) hàu, hàur. /I wear size ten stockings. Wǒ chwān 'shŕhàurde 'wàdz. /What size is this shoe? Jèige 'syé shr̀ 'dwōdà 'hàur? /These gloves are a size too small. Jèisyé shǒu'tàur 'syǎu yí'hàur.

(Relative bigness) dàsyǎu; (bigness of body) gèr; (length) chángdwǎn; (thickness) 'hòubáu; (width) kwānjǎi; (height) gāuai. /Try this for size. Shr̀shr jèige dà'syǎu dzěmma'yàng. /You're pretty strong for your size. Ná nǐ jèige 'gèr lái 'shwō, nǐ shr̀ gòu 'jwàngde.

What is the size of . . . (. . . is how big) . . . yǒu dwō'dà, (long) . . . yǒu dwō-'cháng, (high) . . . yǒu dwō 'gāu, (wide) . . . yǒu dwō 'kwān, (thick) . . . yǒu dwō 'hòu. /What size is the house? Jèiswǒ 'fángdz yǒu dwō'dà?

Size up. /He sized up the situation at a glance. is expressed as At one glance he saw the situation clearly. Tā 'yìyǎn jyòu bǎ nèige 'chíngsying kàn'chíngchule.

Good-sized dà. /He's a good-sized man. Tā jèige rén 'gèr hěn 'dà.

Outsized chūhàude. /He wears outsized shoes. Tā 'chwān de 'syé 'dōu shr̀ 'chùle 'hàude.

Undersized (not up to standard) syǎu; (of number) búgòudà. /Their horse is rather undersized. Tāmende 'mǎ búgòudà.

SKIN. (Of a person) ròupyér, pífu. /She has very white skin. Tāde ròu'pyér hěn 'bái.

(Of fruits or vegetables; also the bark of a tree) pí'pyér. /The best part of a potato is near the skin. Shānyau'dàn dzwèi 'hǎude 'dìfangr shr̀ 'kàuje 'pyérde nèi'dǎr.

(Of animals; hide) pí, pídz. /These shoes are made of alligator skin. Jèi'syé shr̀ è'yúpíde.

By the skin of one's teeth chà 'dyǎr méi. /I made the train by the skin of my teeth. Wǒ chà 'dyǎr jyòu 'méigǎnshàng 'chē.

Skin and bones. /That child is just skin and bones. is expressed as That child just has skin covering his bones. Nèi háidz jyǎn'jŕde shr̀ pígāu'gǔ.

Skin deep. /The cut is only skin deep. is expressed as Only the skin is cut. Jyòu lá'pwòle dyǎr 'pyér. /Her beauty is only skin deep. is expressed as Just her expression is beautiful. Tā 'jyòushr̀ wài'byáu hǎu'kàn.

Thick-skinned. /The elephant is a thick-skinned animal. Syàngde 'pí hěn 'hòu. /He's so thick-skinned you can't offend him. is expressed as The skin of his face is really thick, you have no way to hurt his feelings. Tāde lyǎn'pí jēn 'hòu, nǐ méi-'fár bǎ ta dzěmma'yàng.

Thin-skinned. /I'm very thin-skinned. Wǒde ròu'pyér hěn 'báu. /She's too thin-skinned; she can't even take a joke. is expressed as The skin on her face is too thin; if you make a joke with her, she can't take it. Tā lyǎn'pyér tài 'báu, 'gēn ta 'kāi ge wan'syàu tā jyòu gwàbú'jùle.

To skin bāpí, bāupí. /The hunter was skinning the deer. Dǎ'lyède jèng 'bā lù'pí ne.

Skin out of. /She skinned out of her clothes. Tā bǎ 'yīshang °'twōsyàláile (°'bāsyàlaile). /He barely skinned out of that mess. Tā jǐhu méinéng twō'shēn. or expressed as He just escaped that situation. Tā swàn shr̀ bǎ nèige 'shr̀ching bǎi-twōle.

SKIRT. (Part of a dress from the waist down) syà bǎi; (woman's garment hanging from the waist) chyúndz. /I don't look good in skirts and blouses. Wǒ chwān 'chyúndz gēn chèn'shān bùhǎu'kàn. /The skirt of that dress is too tight. Jèijyàn 'yīshangde 'syà-'bǎi tài 'shòu.

To skirt jwàngwochyu, ràugwochyu. /Can I skirt the business district? Wǒ 'kéyi 'ràugwochyu bùdzǒu 'rènau dìfang ma?

SKY. tyān; tyǎr (also means weather). /How does the sky look today? Jyēr 'tyǎr kàn-je 'dzěmmayàng? /The sky is cloudy. Yīn'tyānle.

Out of a clear sky is expressed as suddenly hū'rán('jyān), chōubù'lěngdz, 'lěng-gu'dīngde ('měnggū'dīngde). /Out of a clear sky he quit his job. Tā 'hūrán jyòu tsź-'jr̀le.

To the skies. /He praised her to the skies. Tā bǎ nèige 'nyǔde 'pěngdàu 'tyān-shang chyùle.

SLEEP (SLEPT). shwèi, shwèijyàu. /Did you sleep well? Nǐ (shwèi'jyàu) shwèi'hǎule ma? /I've never slept in this room before. Wó yǐ'chyán méidzài 'jèi wū 'shwèigwò 'jyàu. /I want some place to sleep. Wǒ yàu'jǎu ge 'dìfangr 'shwèishwèi 'jyàu.

(Have space for people to sleep) shwèidesyà, jùdesyà, kéyi shwèi, kéyi jù. /This hotel can sleep 500 people in an emergency. Jèige lyú'gwǎn yǒu 'shr̀ de shr̀-hou jùde'sya 'wúbǎi rén.

Sleep . . . away shwèigwochyu. /He slept the afternoon away. Tā bǎ yí'syàwǔ dōu 'shwèigwochyule.

Sleep . . . off. /He slept off his tiredness. Tā 'shwèile yí'jyàu, jyéle 'fá le.

Get to sleep, go to sleep shwèijáu. /I couldn't get to sleep for hours. Wǒ shwèile 'háujǐge 'jūngtóu yě méishwèi'jáu.

Sleep (act of sleeping) is expressed verbally as in the first paragraph. /I must get some sleep. Wó děi shwèi hwěr 'jyàu. /Did you have a good sleep? Nǐ shwèi-'hàule ma?

SLIGHT. dyǎr, yìdyǎr. /I have a slight cold. Wó 'yǒu dyǎr shāng'fēng. /There is a slight difference. Yóu dyǎr 'bùyí'yàng. /There's not the slightest excuse for being late. Lái'wǎnle, yìdyár 'lí yě méi'yǒu. or expressed as Having come late, what can you say for yourself? Lái'wǎnle hái yǒu shémma kě 'shwōde?

(Slender, fragile; either short or thin) syǎu; (slender) myáutyau; (thin) shòu. /She has a rather slight figure. Tāde 'gèr syàng'dāngde 'syǎu.

To slight (belittle, or snub) kànbùchǐ. /I didn't mean to slight you. Wǒ méiyou kànbù'chǐ nǐ de 'yìsz.

A slight. / She resented the slight. is expressed as Someone slighted her, and she didn't like it. 'Rénjyā kànbùchǐ tā, tā hěn bú'tùngkwài.

SLIP. (Slide) hwá, lyōu, 'chǔlyou; (come loose, of something that should be held tight) 'tūlu. / She slipped and fell. Tā yǐ 'hwá 'tāngsyale. / Don't slip on the ice. Byé dzài 'bīngshang 'chǔlyou'tǎngsya. / See that the knife doesn't slip. Lyóu'shén byé ràng 'dāudz 'hwáde 'shǒushang. / The letter slipped off the table into the wastebasket. Nèifēng 'syìn tsúng 'jwōrshang 'lyǒude dzjǐr'lóurli le. / The canoe slipped down the bank into the water. Nèige syǎu'chwár tsúng 'ānshang 'chǔlyoude 'héli chyù le. but / The vase slipped out of my hands. Nèige 'píngdz tsúng wǒ 'shǒushang °'tūlu ('hwá, °'lyōu, °'chǔlyōu) 'syachyule. / Tie the knot tight, so it won't slip. Bǎ kòur jǐ'jǐn le, byé 'tūlu lou.

(Push with a sliding motion, or stealthily; put something in a small opening) sāi, sēi; (hand something quickly and unobtrusively) tōu'tōurde °'rù (°'chù); (pull something out with a sliding motion or stealthily) chēnchulai, chōuchulai. / He slipped the notebook into his pocket. Tā bǎ nèige rìjǐ'běr 'sāide tā 'dōurli le. / He slipped me a five dollar bill. Tā tōu'tōurde °'rù (°'sāi) géi wo 'wǔkwài 'chyánde 'pyàudz. / He slipped the letter of of its envelope. Tā bǎ nèifēng 'syìn tsúng syìn'fēngrli 'chēnchulaile.

(Move stealthily, or unobserved) (tōu'tōurde) °'dzwān (°'lyōu). / He slipped into the house. Tā tōu'tōurde 'dzwānde nèige 'fángdzli chyù le. / One by one the soldiers slipped past the guard. Nèisyē 'bīng yǐ'gèryí'gèrde tōu'tōurde tsúng wèi-'bīng nèr 'lyōugwochyule. / I'm going to slip out of the room for a minute. Wǒ yàu 'lyōuchū yìhwěr chyù. / This party is dull; let's slip away. Jèige 'hwèi méi'yìsz, 'dzámen 'lyōu le ba.

(Make a casual mistake) tswò, chūtswòr; (forget something) 'wàng dyǎr shémma. / I guess I slipped up somewhere. Wǒ 'jywéde wó nǎr 'tswò le. or Wǒ 'jywéde wǒ 'wàngle dyǎr 'shémma.

(Escape) tswògwochyu. / Don't let the chance slip, if you can help it. Nǐ 'yàushr yóu 'bànfǎ, byé ràng 'jīhwei 'tswògwochyu. or expressed as If you have the means, don't lose this opportunity. Nǐ 'yàushr yóu 'bànfǎ, byé bǎ 'jīhwèi 'dyōu lou.

(Say thoughtlessly) (wúsyīn'jūng) 'shwōchulai. / He let the name slip before he thought. Tā wúsyīn'jūng bǎ nèige 'míngdz 'shwōchulaile.

Slip one's mind. / The matter slipped my mind completely. is expressed as I forgot the whole thing. Nèijyàn 'shr wó jěng'gèr 'wàngle.

Slip into clothes bǎ . . . 'chwānshang; slip into a seat dzài . . . shang 'dzwò.

Slip something into sāi, sēi, jǐ. / We can slip that announcement into the paper somewhere. Wǒmen 'kéyi bǎ nèidwàn 'shēngmíng 'jǐde 'bàushang swéi'byàn 'shémma 'dìfangr.

Slip out of clothes bǎ . . . twōsyalai; slip out of a seat tsúng . . . 'chǐlái.

Slip something over on mēng, dzwàn, ywān, pyàn. / Are you trying to slip something over on me? Nǐ shr yàu 'pyàn wǒ ma?

A slip (woman's undergarment) chènchyún. / Your slip is showing. Nǐde chèn-chyún 'lòuchulaile.

(Casual mistake) tswòr; make a slip chū tswòr. / Did I make a slip? Wǒ chū-'tswòr le ma?

(Case, cover) tàu, tàur. / Please wash the pillow slips. Láu'jyà, bá 'jēn-toutàur 'syǐsyi.

(Small piece) tyáur. / Put a slip of paper in the book to keep your place. Bǎ 'shūli 'jyā yíge jr'tyáur 'dzwò ge 'jìhaur.

(Cutting from a plant, for planting or grafting) jēr, jr̄dz, tyáu. / The rose bush grew from a slip. Nèikē 'méigwèi shr̀ ná 'yíge 'jēr 'chāchulaide.

Slip of the tongue °tūlū (°dzóu) 'dzwěi. / I didn't mean to say that; it was a slip of the tongue. Wǒ méi'dǎswàn nèmma shwō, wǒ shr̀ °'shwō'tūlū (°'shwo'dzǒule) 'dzwěi le.

SLOPE. (An incline) 'pwōdù. / The hill has a 30 degree slope. Jèige shān'pwō yǒu 'sān-shŕ'dù.

(Inclined surface) pwō, pwōr; (slope of a hill) shānpwō, shānpwōr. / My house is on a slope. Wǒde 'fángdz shr̀ dzài 'yíge 'pwōrshang. / They raced down the slope. Tāmen tsúng shān'pwōrshang 'pǎusyalaile.

To slope (down) syésyachyu, pwōsyachyu, lyōusyachyu; (up) syéshangchyu, pwōshangchyu. / The land slopes gradually down to the river. Nèige 'dǐ wàng 'hé nèibyār 'syésyachyule.

(Of shoulders only) lyōu. / His shoulders slope. is expressed as He has shoulders that slide down. Tā 'lyōujyān'bǎngr.

SLOW. màn. / Is it a slow train? Nèi shr̀ ge 'mànchē ma? / My watch is an hour slow. Wǒde 'byǎu 'màn yíge jūng'tóu.

(Of a person's thinking or general movements) 'chŕdwùn. / He's very slow moving. Tā 'dùngdzwò hěn 'chŕdwùn. / He was slow in getting the joke. Tā 'sz̄-syǎng 'chŕdwùn nèige 'syàuhwàr tā bàn'tyān tsái 'míngbai.

Be slow to anger 'búdà 'rúngyì. / She's slow to anger. Tā 'búdà 'rúngyì shēng-'chì.

A slow class (stupid) yì'bān 'bèn 'sywésheng.

A slow fire 'wénhwǒ, 'syáuhwǒr, 'mànhwǒ. / Cook the soup over a slow fire. Yùng 'wénhwǒ 'dzwò jèige 'tāng.

To slow down or **slow up.** / Slow down! 'Màn dyǎr! or Mànsyalai a! / He slows down the work a lot. is expressed as He delays the work. Tā bǎ jèige 'shŕ-ching gěi nàude mànsyalaile.

SLOWLY. màn. / Don't walk so slowly. Byé 'dzǒu 'dzèmma 'màn ne. / Speak slowly. 'Màn dyǎr shwō. / The cars are moving very slowly because the roads are icy. Chē dzǒude hěn 'màn, yīnwèi lù tài 'hwá。

SMALL. syǎu; (very small) yìdyǎr(dà), yì'dyōudyǎr, yìdyōudyòur, búdàdyǎr, (especially of a person, a tiny tot) syǎubùdyǎr. / The room is rather small. 'Wūdz yǒu dyár 'syǎu. / It is a very small room. Jèige 'wūdz shr̀ ge syǎubù'dyǎr. / They began in a small way and soon had a large business. Tāmen chǐ'tóur 'mǎimài 'dzwǒde hén 'syǎu, méi 'dwōshǎu 'r̀dz jyòu dzwò'dàle. / She was wearing a small pin. Tā 'dàide nèige byé'jēr °yì'dyǎrdà (°'búdà'dyǎr, °yì'dyōudyǎr, °yìdyōu'dyòur).

(Small pieces) swèi, swèikwàr. / Chop it up small. Chyē'swèile. or 'Chyē-chéng swèi'kwàr. / Please gather some small pieces of wood. Láu'jyà, 'jyán dyǎr 'swèi 'pǐchái lai.

(Mean) syàlyóu. / That was an awfully small thing to do. 'Nèige shr̀ yí'jyàn hěn 'syàlyóude 'shr̀ching. but / He made me feel pretty small. is expressed as He made me feel ashamed. Tā 'ràng wo 'jywéde hěn °'tsánkwèi (°'bùhǎu'yìsz).

A small matter 'syǎushr̀; or expressed as be unimportant bú'yàujǐn, méigwānsyi, wúswŏwèi. /Where we stay is a small matter. Wŏmen jùdzai 'nǎr °shr̀ jyàn 'syaushr̀ (°dōu bú'yàujǐn). *but* /That's no small matter. 'Nèige hěn 'yàujǐn. *or* 'Nèige hén yŏu'gwānsyi.

Small change 'língchyán. /I haven't any small change. Wŏ méi'yŏu 'língchyán.

Small letters (lower case letters) syǎu dzmŭ, syǎusyě dzmŭ. /Print it all in small letters. Chywán 'yùng 'syǎusyě dz̀'mŭ 'yìn.

Small talk yìngchouhwà. /He's good at small talk, but he's lost in a serious conversation. Tā 'hěn hwèi 'shwō 'yìngchou'hwà, 'kěshr yì'tán jèng'jǐngde jyòu bùsyíng le.

SMELL. wén. /Do you smell smoke? Nǐ 'wénjyàn 'yānwèr le ma? /Smell this bottle and tell me what you think is in it. Wén °yìwén (°yí'syàr, °yǐ'bídz) jèi píngdzli de 'dūngsyi rán'hòu 'gàusu wŏ shr̀ 'shémma.

Smell a rat. /As soon as she mentioned it, I smelled a rat. is expressed as Once I heard her speak, I was a little suspicious. Wŏ yì 'tīngjyàn tā 'shwō, wŏ 'jyòu °'yóu dyǎr yí'syīn (*or* meaning doubtful °'jywéde kě'yǐ).

Smell bad bùhǎuwén, nánwén; (stink) chòu. /It smells bad. 'Nèige bùhǎu'wén. /The garbage smells to high heaven. is expressed as The bad smell of the garbage is great. Nèisyē 'lājǐde 'chòuwèr 'dà le.

Smell good hǎuwén, bùnánwén; (be fragrant) syāng. /That perfume smells good. Nèige 'syāngshwěrde 'wèr hén hǎu'wén.

A smell wèr, 'wèidàu. /What is that smell? 'Nèige shr̀ 'shémma 'wèr a? /Do you like the smell of garlic? Ní 'syǐhwān 'swànwèr ma? /I don't like the smell. Wŏ bù'syǐhwān wén nèi 'wèr.

Sense of smell (technical term) 'syòujywé; usually expressed as nose bídz. /A dog has a very keen sense of smell. Gŏude 'bídz hěn 'líng.

SMILE. lè, syàu. /I like the way she smiles. Wó 'syǐhwān tā 'syàu de nèige 'yàngr.

A smile (smiling appearance) syàu de yàngdz; (cheerful appearance) syàurúngr. /He always has a smile on his face. Tā 'lyǎnshang lǎu 'dàije syàu'rúngr. /You have a pretty smile. Nǐ 'syàu de 'yàngdz hén hǎu'kàn. or expressed as You smile very prettily. Nǐ 'syàude hén hǎu'kàn.

SMOKE. (Fumes) yān. /Open the windows; there's too much smoke in here. Bǎ chwānghu 'kāikai, jè lǐbyar yān tài 'chùng. /Do you see any smoke? Nǐ 'kànjyàn nǎr màu'yānle ma?

(Act of smoking a cigarette) yān (jywǎr) (cigarette). /I'm dying for a smoke. Wŏ 'jèn syǎng lái gēr 'yān chōu.

Go up in smoke (burn up) shāugwāngle, shāuwánle; (fig., be destroyed) wánle. /The house went up in smoke. Nèige 'fángdz dōu shāu'gwāngle. /All our plans went up in smoke. Wŏmen swóyŏude 'jìhwà dōu wánle. or expressed as All our plans dissolved into ashes. Wŏmen swóyŏude 'jìhwà dōu hwàwei hwèi'chénle.

Smoke screen yānmù. /The planes laid down a heavy smoke screen. Nèisyē fēi'jī 'fàngle yì'tséng hěn 'núngde yān'mù.

To smoke (give off smoke) màuyān. /That stove smokes too much. Nèige 'lúdz màu'yān màude tài 'lìhai.

(Preserve by smoke) syūn. /The fishermen here smoke most of their fish. Jèrde dà'yúde bǎ yì'dwōbàn 'yú dōu 'syūnle.

(Stain by smoke) syūnhēile; (spoil by smoke) syūnhwàile. /The chimney of

SO

this lamp is all smoked up. Dēng'jàur dōu ràng 'yān gěi syūn'hēile. /We can't eat that; it's all smoked up. Nèige wōmen 'bùnéng 'chr̄le, dōu ràng 'yān gěi syūn'hwàile.

(Of cigarettes, cigars, etc.) chōuyān, syīyān, chr̄yān. /Do you smoke? Nǐ chōu'yān ma? or Chōu'yān bù'chōu? /I smoke cigars. Wǒ 'chōu sywějyā'yān.

Smoke out syūnchulai. /We'll have to smoke out the animals. Wōmen 'déi bǎ 'nèisyē yě'shòu 'syūnchulai.

SMOOTH. (Level and not rough) píng; (not rough, but not necessarily level; of land, roads, etc.) bù'kēngkengwā'wāde; (extremely smooth and also shiny) 'gwānghwá, gwānglyou; (smooth and also slippery) hwá, hwályou. /Is the road smooth? Dàur 'píng ma? /The sea was very smooth. Hǎi'shwéi hěn °píng (°'píngwěn). /The tires are worn smooth. Pí'dài dōu °mwó'píngle (°mwó'gwāngle). /The cloth has a smooth surface. Jèige 'bù'myàrshang hěn °'gwānghwa (°'gwānglyou, °hwá, °'hwályou). /He got a smooth shave. Tā ba 'lyǎn 'gwāde tǐng °'gwāng (°'gwānglyou).

(Not lumpy) yún, bù'gēlegē'dāde, méigēda. /I hope the paste is smooth. Wǒ 'syīwàng jèige 'jyàngdz dǎde héi 'yún. or Wǒ 'syīwàng jèige 'jyàngdz bú'nèmma 'gēlegē'dāde.

(Calm, steady) wěn. /We had a very smooth ride. Wōmen jèi'tàngchē 'dzǒude hěn 'wěn.

(Suave) 'ywánhwá. /He's a smooth salesman. 'Tā jèige màihwò'ywán hěn 'ywánhwá.

SNAKE. shé, chángchung. /Are there any poisonous snakes around? Jèi yí'dài yǒu dú'shé ma?

SNOW. sywě. /The snow was so thick we couldn't see in front of us. 'Sywě syàde 'tài dà le, dwèi'myàr dōu 'kànbújyàn 'dūngsyi le. /How deep is the snow? 'Sywé yǒu 'dwō shēn? /This is the first snow this winter. Jèi shr̄ lǐ'dūng yǐlái 'tóuyìcháng 'sywě.

Snowdrift sywědwēi.

Snowfall. /We'll have a heavy snowfall tonight. is expressed as A lot of snow will fall tonight. Jyèr 'wǎnshang yàu 'syà yí'chǎng dà'sywě.

Snowstorm fēngsywě, gwāfēng syàsywě. /Snowstorms make traveling difficult. Dzài gwā'fēng syà'sywě de 'tyārli lyǔ'syíng jēn bù'róngyi.

To snow syàsywě. /It snowed a lot last winter. 'Chyùnyán 'dūngtyān 'syàle bù'shǎude 'sywě. /It's snowing! Syà'sywě le.

Be snowed in. /They were snowed in for a whole week. is expressed as A great deal of snow fell, and for a week they couldn't get out of the house. Sywě'syàde 'dàde tāmen yǒu 'yíge lǐ'bài méi'néng tsúng jyāli 'chūlái.

Be snowed under (fig.). /We are snowed under with bills. is expressed as Our bills are heaped up as high as a mountain. Wǒmende jàng'dār 'dwēide yǒu 'shān nèmma 'gāu.

SO. (In this way) jèmma, dzèmma, nèmma, jèmmaje, nèmmaje, 'jèiyàngr, 'nèiyàngr, 'jèmmayàngr, 'dzèmmayàngr, 'nèmmayàngr. /Do it just so. Jyou jèmma 'dzwò. /He's all right now, and I hope he'll remain so. Tā syàn'dzài hǎu le, jyou syīwàng tā néng lǎu jèi'yàngr. /So they say. 'Tāmen dzèmma shwō. /Why are you so gloomy? Nǐ gàn'má 'dzèmma bùgāu'syìng a? /If so, I'll have to go. 'Yàushr̄ 'nàyàngr, wó déi 'dzǒule. /I told you so. Wǒ 'gàusugwo nǐ shr̄ 'dzèmma hwéi 'shr̄. or Wǒ 'dzèmma 'gàusugwo nǐ. /That's not so! 'Búshr̄ 'nèmma hwéi 'shèr!

923

/It certainly is so. 'Dāngrán shr 'nèmma hwéi 'shèr. *but* /So? *or* Is that so? meaning either I don't believe you. *or* Oh! I didn't know that. Ā? *or* 'Jēnde ma? *or* 'Shr ma? *or* Shr 'nèmma je? *or* Shr 'nèmma yàngr ma?

(Also) yě. /I want to go. So do I. Wǒ yàu 'dzǒu le. 'Wó yě yàu dzǒu. /If I can do it, so can you. 'Wǒ yàushr néng 'dzwò, 'ní yě néng 'dzwò. /They're very nice, and so are their children. 'Tāmen rén hěn 'hǎu, tāmende 'háidz 'yé hén 'hǎu.

(Indicating agreement) dwèi le. /He left you a letter. So he did. Tā géi ni 'lyóusyà yìfēng 'syìn. 'Dwèi le. /The door's open. So I see. 'Mén kāile. 'Dwèi le. Wǒ 'chyáujyanle.

(Very; very much) hěn, jēn, tài, 'shrfēn, . . . 'jíle, . . . 'lìhai, . . . de hěn. /You're so clever. Nǐ 'jēn 'tsūngming. /I'm so glad. Nèmmaje hǎu'jíle. /I'd better not go out, my head aches so. Wǒ 'tóuténgde 'lìhai, 'díng hǎu 'byé 'chūchyu le.

(Therefore) 'swóyǐ, yīntsž, 'swóyǐyīn'tsž. /I'm not feeling well so I think I'd better not go. Wǒ jywéde yóu 'dyǎr bù'shūfu, 'swóyi wó 'syǎng 'háishr bù'chūchyu 'hǎu. /They left early and so I missed them. Tāmen 'dzǒude 'dzáu dyǎr, 'swóyi wǒ méi'jyànjau tāmen.

(Well; then) nèmma, shr; so . . . finally °'hǎuma (°'hē) . . . 'kě . . . . /So you think that's a good idea, huh? Nèmma nǐ 'jywéde 'neige hái bú'tswò, á? /So you don't believe me? 'Nǐ shr bù'syǎngsyìn 'wǒ a? /So you don't like it here! Nǐ shr bù'syǐhwān 'jèr a! /So they lived happily ever after. 'Nèmma 'tāmen jyou 'kwàikwàihwó'hwóde gwò'rdz le. /So the work's too hard for you! Ā? Nǐ jywéje 'shèr tài 'máfan le! *or* Óu! nǐ syán shèr tài 'nán le! /So you've finally made up your mind! 'Hē, nǐ 'kě jywé'dìngle! /So you've finally come home! 'Hǎuma, dàu'lyǎur ní 'kě 'hwéilaile!

And so forth, and so on 'déngděng, shémmade. /He had all the symptoms; fever, headache, nervousness, and so on. Tā gè'jǔngde bìng 'syàng shémma fā'shāu, 'tóuténg, 'shénjīnggwò'mǐn 'déngděng 'dōu yǒu.

Or so dà'gài . . . shémmade. /Can you spare a pound or so of sugar? Nǐ 'kéyi 'fēngéi wó dyǎr 'táng ma? Dà'gài yíbàng shémmade.

So as to 'wèideshr . . . (hǎu), . . . 'hǎu, 'nèmma . . . °'kéyi (°'hǎu, °néng). /I did some of the work so as to make things easier for her. Wó bǎ 'neige 'shrching 'dzwòle dyǎr 'wèideshr ràng tā 'dzwòje hǎu 'rúngyì dyǎr.

So far (up to now) yìjrde, 'jrdàu syàndzài wéijr, yísyàng. /So far I'm bored. Yì'jrde wǒ 'jywéde hěn wú'lyáu. /So far, so good. 'Jrdàu syàndzài hái hǎu.

So far as I know (according to what I know) jyù 'wó swǒ 'jrdàude; (I think) wǒ 'jywéde. /So far as I know, he still lives there. Jyù 'wǒ 'jrdàu tā 'hái dzài nèr 'jù。

So long (goodbye) is expressed as see you again dzàijyàn or as see you later hwéitóu jyàn, dāi hwèr jyàn, yǐhwěr jyàn.

So much 'nèmma dwō, etc. /He has so much money he doesn't know what to do with it. Tā yǒu 'nèmma dwō chyán dōu bùjrdàu dzěmma 'bàn le. *but* /I wish she wouldn't cry so much. Wǒ 'syīwang tā 'byé 'dzěmma lǎu 'kū. /Thanks ever so much. 'Dwō syè, 'dwōsyè. *or* Tài 'syèsyè le. /So much for that (that's done); what'll we do next? Nèige °'wán le (°'hǎu le, °'dé le), wǒmen gāi 'dzwò shémma le?

So-so 'méishémma, wúswǒwèi. /How are you feeling? Oh, so-so. Nǐ 'jywéde 'dzěmmayàng? Wúswǒ'wèi.

So that (in order that) *see* **So as to** above; (with the result that) 'swóyǐ, nùngde. /He made it sound good, so that I'd help him. Tā gùyìde 'shwōde hǎu'tīng, hǎu 'ràng wo 'bāngje tā. /It rained very hard, so that the streets were flooded. Yǔ 'syàde hěn 'dà, 'swóyǐ 'jyēshang 'shwěi dōu 'màn le.

So . . . that °tài (°jèmma, °dzèmma, °nèmma, °'jèiyàngrde, °'nèiyàngrde, °jèmma'yàngrde, °dzèmmayàngrde, °nèmma'yàngrde) . . . 'swóyǐ ('jyǎn'jŕde). /He ran so fast he was all out of breath. Tā 'pǎude nèmma 'kwài, swóyí jyǎn'jŕde 'chwǎn-búgwò 'chyèr lái le. /I'm so tired I can hardly keep my eyes open. Wǒ tài 'lèi le, 'swóyǐ jyǎn'jŕde jēngbù'kāi 'yǎn le.

Other English expressions. /So what? The Chinese expressions, like the English, are not very polite. The usual equivalents are 'Nèmma yòu 'dzěmmaje ne? or 'Nèmma yòu 'dzěmma'yàng ne? or 'Nèmma 'dzěmma le? or expressed as What's there to be afraid of? Nà 'pà shémmade?

SOAP. yídz, féidzàu; to describe the form in which the soap is made, use the measures kwài cake, tyáur long bar, bāu or syāng box. /I want a bar of soap. Wǒ yàu yí-tyáur 'yídz. /Do you want a cake of soap, or soap flakes, or powder? Nǐ shŕ 'yàu yí'kwài yídz, shŕ 'yàu yídz'pyàr, 'háishŕ yàu yídz'fěn?

To soap (use soap) shŕ yídz, yùng yídz; (apply soap) dǎ yídz, shàng yídz. /Soap it thoroughly and then rinse it in hot water. Syān bǎ 'yídz dǎ'mǎnlou, rán'hòu dzài dzài 'rèshwéi lǐtou 'tóutou.

SOCIETY. (Social community) 'shèhwèi. /Civic laws are for the good of society. 'Mín-fǎ shŕ wèi 'shèhwèi 'gūngyì tsái 'yǒude. /If boys form into dangerous gangs like that, our whole society is threatened. 'Yàushr 'háidzmen 'dzěmma'yàngrde yí'chyún-yí'chyúnde syā'nàu, wǒmen jěng'gèerde 'shèhwèi dōu shòu 'wēisyé.

(Fashionable group of people) 'gāuděng shèhwèi, 'shànglyóu shèhwèi, 'shàng-děng shè'hwèi. /She's very prominent in local society. Tā dzài 'nèige 'dìfangrde 'shàngděng shè'hwèili hěn chū'fēngtóu.

(Organization) hwèi, 'dzǔjŕ. /He didn't want to join our society. Tā bú'ywàn-yì 'jyàrù wǒmende 'hwèi.

(Companionship). /I enjoy his society very much. is expressed as I like to be with him very much. Wó hěn 'ywànyì gēn ta °dzài yí'kwàr (°lai wǎng).

SOCK. (Short stocking) 'dwǎnwàdz, wàtàur. /I want three pairs of socks. Wǒ yàu sān-'shwāng 'dwǎnwàdz.

(Act of hitting with the fist) dzwěiba. /Give him a sock on the jaw. 'Gěi tā yíge 'dzwěiba.

To sock (hit with the fist) °dǎ (°chwéi, °dzòu, °gěi) yísyàdz. /If you do that again, I'll sock you. Nǐ 'yàushr 'dzài nàyàngr wǒ fēi 'dzòu nǐ bù'syíng.

SOFT. (Not hard) rwǎn. /This pillow is too soft for my taste. 'Jèige 'Jěntou wǒ 'jěn-je tài 'rwǎn. /Is the ground soft? Dì 'rwǎn bù'rwǎn? /The heat makes the pave-ment soft and sticky. Tyār 'rè, mǎ'lù nèngde yòu 'rwǎn yòu 'nyán. /Glass is softer than diamond. 'Bwōli bǐ jīngāng'dzwǎr 'rwǎn. /That material isn't soft enough for a dress. Nèige 'lyàudz yàu 'dzwò 'yīshang búgòu 'rwǎn. /Soft wood will burn quickly. 'Mùtou 'rwǎnde 'jáude 'kwài. or expressed as Wood with a loose fibre burns quickly. 'Sūng 'mùtou 'jáude 'kwài.

(Not bright; gentle, not harsh) róu, róuhe, rwò; (dim) àn. /A soft light would be better. 'Róu dyàrde dēng'gwāng yé'syú 'háu dyǎr.

(Not loud) syǎu. /Make the radio softer. is expressed as Make the sound of the radio smaller. Bǎ wúsyàn'dyànde 'shēngr nùng 'syǎu dyǎr. /She sang in a soft voice. Tā 'syǎu shēngr 'chàng láije.

(Gentle, tender-hearted) syīnrwăn. /You are too soft to be an executive. Nǐ syīn tài 'rwăn, bùnéng 'dzwò gwānrénde 'shèr.

(Flabby physically) rwăn, 'rwănrwò. /I'll get soft if I don't get any exercise. Wŏ yàushr bú'yùndung a, shēnti jyou °'rwăn le (°bù'syíng le). or expressed as If I don't exercise, my physique will be ruined. Wŏ yàushr bú'yùndung a, shēndz'gŭr jyou 'hwài le. /I hate soft men. Wŏ bù'syīhwān yíge 'rén tài 'rwănrwò. or expressed as I don't like a man whose body isn't strong. Shēnti bù'jyēshrde 'rén wŏ bù'syīhwān. or, meaning a weak person, as I hate indecisive people. Wó tău'yàn méi jwŭn'júyì de 'rén.

Soft-hearted syīnrwăn.

SOIL. dì, 'tyándì, 'hàndì; (wet soil for growing rice) 'shwĕidì. /What will grow in this soil? Jèi 'dìli néng 'jùng 'shémma? /This is good rich soil. Jèige 'dì hĕn 'féi.

Soiled dzāng, 'āngdzāng. /Don't let it get soiled. 'Byé bă nèige 'nùng'dzāng lou. /We'll send the soiled clothes to the laundry tomorrow. Wŏmen míngrge bă 'dzāng 'yīshang 'sùngdau syĭyīshang'fángr chyu.

SOLDIER. (Man in uniform, enlisted man or officer) 'jyūnrén; (informal term for enlisted man) bīng; (enlisted man, rather uncomplimentary term) dàbīng; (colloquial term for enlisted man) láudzŭng; (uncomplimentary term for any soldier, enlisted man or officer) chyŏubā. /This captain is a fine soldier. 'Jèige lyán'jăng 'shr yíge hău 'jyūnrén. /Are there any soldiers quartered here? Yŏu 'bīng dzài 'jèr jù'jiá ma? /Is this club for soldiers or officers? 'Jèige jyùlè'bù shr wei 'bīng yùbeide 'háishr 'wèi gwān'jăng yùbeide?

SOLE. (Bottom of a shoe) syédyĕr, chywánjăngr; half sole syéjăngr, chyánjăngr, jăngr. /The soles of these shoes are worn out. Jèi(ji)shwāng 'syéde syé'dyer dōu 'pwò le. /I need new soles on these shoes. Wŏ jèi 'syé dĕi hwàn 'jăngr le.

(Bottom of the foot) jyáujăngr. /I have a pain in the sole of my foot. Wŏ jyáujăngr yóu dyăr 'téng.

Sole (only) wéiyīde, dújyā, jínyŏude; (just) jyòu. /Are we the sole customers? Wŏmen shr jèr wéi'yīde 'jùgu ma? /He is the sole agent for this soda here. Tā shr gèijŭng chǐ'shwĕr 'jèr de dújyā 'dàilǐ. /He reads books for the sole purpose of obtaining knowledge. Tā 'nyàn shū 'jyòu 'wéideshr dé 'jrshr.

To sole hwàn jăngr. /My shoes need to be soled. Wŏde 'syé dĕi hwàn 'jăngr le.

SOLID. (Firm, strong) jyēshr, tsźshr, jyāngù; (local Peiping) bàng. /The construction of the building seems solid enough. Jèidzwò 'lóu gàide chyáu 'yàngr gòu 'jyēshrde. /This chair doesn't feel very solid to me. Wŏ 'jywéde 'jèibă 'yǐdz búda 'jyēshr. /His body is very solid. Tā 'shēndz hĕn °'bàng (°'jyēshr). /The lake is frozen solid. 'Hú 'dùng 'jyēshr le. /Is the ice solid? Bīng 'tsźshr ma?

(Not hollow) sžgadár, sž(ga)tángr; (real throughout) shrde, shrjáur. /Is the beam solid or hollow? Fáng'lyáng shr sžga'dárde 'háishr 'kūngde?

(Whole; of units of time) jĕng, jĕngjēngr; (full) dzú, dzúdzūrde. /He talked to me for a solid hour. Tā gēn wo 'tanle jĕng'jēngde yíge jūng'tóu.

(Real). /This is solid comfort. is expressed as This is really comfort. Jèi 'jēn shr 'shūfu. /You'll get solid pleasure out of this pipe. is expressed as You'll certainly be completely satisfied with this pipe. Jèige yān'dŏu nǐ yí'dìng néng 'shrfēn 'mănyì.

(The same throughout; pure) chwún; (also of colors; local Peiping) yìmǎr; **solid gold** chwúnjīn; **solid mahogany** chwún'húngmù, <u>or expressed as</u> entirely (made of) mahogany chywán shŕ 'húngmù(dzwò)de. /I want a solid blue material. Wǒ 'yàu yí-'kwài °yìmǎr 'lande (°chwún'lánde) 'lyàudz.

(Dependable) kěkàu, kàudejù; (creditable) yǒu'syìnyùng. /You seem to be a solid sort of person. Wǒ kàn nǐ shŕ ge hěn 'kàudejùde 'rén. /This is a solid concern. 'Jèi shŕ 'yíge hén yǒu'syìnyùngde 'pùdz.

A solid 'yìngdūngsyi; (of food) yìngshŕ. /The doctor told him not to eat solids for a few days. 'Dàifu jyàu tā 'jèijityān syān 'byé chŕ yìng'shŕ.

SOME. (A little) dyǎr, yìdyǎr, sye, yìsyē. /Take some meat. 'Lái dyǎr 'ròu. /Give me some more water. Géi wǒ 'dzài lái dyǎr 'shwěi. /I want some of that material. Wǒ 'yàu yì'dyǎr nèige 'lyàudz. /He objected some, but we persuaded him. Tā 'yóu dyǎr fǎn'dwèi, 'kěshŕ women 'bǎ tā shwō'fúle.

(A few) jǐ, hǎuji <u>plus a measure</u>; dyǎr, yìdyǎr, sye, yìsyē. /Could I have some towels? Néng 'gěi wǒ jǐtyau 'shǒujīn ma? /Take some of these books. 'Jèi-syē 'shū 'ná jiber chyu ba.

(A fair quantity of) dyǎr, yìdyǎr, sye, yìsyē, syāngdāngde. /He's a man of some reputation. Tā 'jèige rén 'yóu dyǎr 'míngwàng. /I've been working for some time. Wǒ dzwò'shŕ 'dzwòle you sye 'rdz le. /The garden is some distance from the house. Nèige hwā'ywár lí 'jèige fángdz 'yóu dyǎr dàur.

(Unspecified) yíge (shémma), ge (shémma), shémma. /We've been trying to find some way out of our difficulties. Wǒmen yàu 'syǎng ge shémma 'fádz dǎ'pwò nèige 'kwùnnàn láije. /Some friend of hers gave it to her. 'Tāde yíge 'péngyou 'sùnggěi tāde.

(Certain unspecified ones) yǒu, yǒude. /Some fellows didn't like this movie. Yǒude 'rén bù'syǐhwān 'jèige dyàn'yǐngr. /Some types are better suited for printing this (than this is). Wèi yìn 'jèige 'yǒude dz'tǐ bǐ 'jèige 'hǎu. /Some of these cups are broken. Jèisyē chá'bēi yǒude 'shwāile. /Some of you may disagree with me. Nǐmen jŕ'jūng 'yésyú yǒu 'rén gēn wǒde 'yìjyàn bù'túng.

(At least one, with emphasis) yí(ge) *or* yí <u>plus another measure</u>. /There must be SOME way of finding out! Yí'dìng 'yóu ge 'fádz 'cháchūlái! /No doubt SOME people think so! Yí'dìng 'yǒu rén 'dzěmma 'syǎng!

(Unusually good or bad) hǎu yi <u>plus a measure</u> hǎuma, 'hǎujyāhwo, jēn kéyǐ; (of a person) jēn 'syíng; <u>all of these mean, as in English,</u> it's terrific, <u>either good or bad.</u> /That's some house they live in! Tāmen 'jùde 'hǎu yìswor 'fángdz. *or* Tāmen 'jùde nèiswor 'fángdz 'jēn ké'yǐ. /She's some gal! Hǎu yíge nyǔ'háidz. *or* 'Tā jèige nyǔ'háidz °'hǎuma ('hǎujyāhwo, °jēn ké'yǐ, °jēn 'syíng). /This has been some job! Jèige 'shŕching kě jēn ké'yǐ.

(About) yǒu, dàgài yǒu. /I played with the baby some twenty or thirty minutes. Wǒ gēn 'nèi háidz 'wárle yǒu 'èrsānshŕfēn 'jūng.

Some . . . or other (it doesn't make any difference which) búlwùn něi(ge); (I don't know which) 'jŕbúdìng něi. /Try to get some typist or other to do the job. Syāng-'fár bú'lwun 'jáu něige dǎdz'ywán lái 'dzwò jèige 'shŕ. /It's in some book or other on that shelf. Nèige shr 'dzài shū'jyàdzshang 'jŕbúdìng 'néiběr 'shūli.

Some day *see* SOMETIME.

Some place *see* SOMEWHERE.

SOMEBODY. (An unspecified person) yǒurén; **somebody** (or other) 'yěbú'shr)shéi, 'yěbú(shŕ) 'shémma 'rén. / Somebody phoned you while you were out. Nĭ 'chūchyū de 'shŕhòur 'yŏurén 'gĕi ni 'dădyàn'hwà láije.

(A person of some importance) rénwu, 'dàrénwù. / He's really somebody in that town. Dzài 'nèige 'chéngli tā 'jēn shŕ ge 'rénwu.

SOMEHOW. bùgwăn dzĕmmaje, búlwùn dzĕmmaje; somehow (or other) 'yĕbùdzĕmma, 'yĕbúshŕ 'dzĕmma hwéi 'shèr. / Somehow, I never did meet him. 'Yĕbúshŕ 'dzĕmma hwéi'shèr, wŏ méi'pèngjyàngwo tā. / Somehow or other, that idea seems foolish to me. Yĕbù'dzĕmma wŏ 'jywéde nèige jú'yĭ hĕn 'bèn.

SOMETHING. (A little) dyăr, . . . dyăr, 'dwōshău . . . dyăr. / There is something left of the old temper. 'Lău'píchi hái 'yŏu dyăr. / He knows something about medicine. Tā 'dwōshău 'jŕdau dyăr 'yĭsywé. / That's something like it. Ēi! Jè hái 'syàng dyăr °'hwà (°'yàngr). but / I saw something of him yesterday. is expressed as I saw him for a while yesterday. Wŏ 'dzwóerge 'kànjyan tā yĭ'hwĕr.

(An unspecified thing) shémma. / If you want something, ring the bell. Nĭ 'yàu-shr 'yàu shémma dehwà, èn 'lingr jyòu syíngle. / Wouldn't you like a little something to eat? Nĭ bú'yàu dyăr shémma 'chŕ ma? but / Is something the matter? 'Dzĕmma le? or Shémma 'shŕ?

(A certain thing) dyăr, syē. / There is something peculiar here. Jèr 'yŏu dyăr 'gwài. / There is something else I want. Wŏ hái 'yàu dyăr 'byéde.

(Some significance). / There's something in what you say. is expressed as What you say is rather reasonable. Nĭ 'shwōde 'syāngdāng yŏu'lĭ.

Something or other dyăr 'shémma 'dūngsyi, dyăr 'shémma 'shŕching; yĕbú-shŕ 'shémma ('dzĕmma). / Something or other reminded me of home. 'Yĕbúshŕ 'shémma jyàu wŏ syángchĭ 'jyā lái le. / I'm sure I've forgotten something or other. is expressed as I've certainly forgotten some business. Wŏ yí'dìng 'wàngle dyăr 'shémma °'shŕching (°'dūngsyi).

Be something of swànyige, 'swàn shŕ ge. / He's something of a pianist. Tā 'kéyi swàn yige gāngchín'jyā.

SOMETIME. (In the future) jyānglái; (some day in the future) (jyānglái) nĕityān; (some time in the future) (jyānglái) shémma shŕhou; (one of these days) yŏu nèmma yì-'tyān. / I want to go to Europe sometime. Wŏ 'dàswàn jyāng'lái 'shàng tàng 'Oujou. / Can I have a date with you sometime this week? Jèige 'syīnchi nĕi'tyān wŏmen 'chūchyù 'wárwar, 'hău ma? / I'd like to read it sometime or other. Wŏ 'syáng nĕi-'tyān 'kànkan 'nèige.

(In the past) 'yĕbúshŕ 'shémma shŕhou. / The accident happened sometime last night. Dzwór 'wănshang 'yĕbúshŕ 'shémma shŕhou 'chūde shèr.

SOMETIMES. 'yŏu(de) shŕhou. / I get mixed up sometimes. Wŏ 'yŏu shŕhour jyòu 'nùng'húdule. / Do you ever see her? Sometimes. Nĭ yŏu shŕhou 'kànjyàn tā ma? Yŏu 'shŕhou 'kànjyàn.

SOMEWHAT. 'yŏu dyăr, yìdyăr, syē yìsyē. / This differs somewhat from the usual type. is expressed as This and the usual thing are somewhat not the same. 'Jèige gēn pu'tūngde 'yŏu dyăr 'búdà yí'yàng. / That is somewhat more expensive. Nèige gèng 'gwèi yĭ'dyăr.

SOMEWHERE. năr, shémma dìfangr, yíge dìfangr; somewhere (or other) yĕbúshŕ °'năr (°'shémma 'dìfangr), 'jrbúding °'năr (°'shémma 'dìfangr). / I'm sure I've seen her somewhere before. Wŏ yí'dìng yĭ'chyán dzài 'năr 'kànjyàngwo tā. / She comes from somewhere down south. Tā yĕbú'shŕ tsúng nán'fāng 'shémma 'dìfang 'láide. / I want to go somewhere in the country for my vacation. is expressed as I want to go to a place out of town for my vacation. Wǒ yàu dàu chéng'wài yíge 'dìfang chyù syē'jyà. / That book must be somewhere or other on this shelf. Nèiběr 'shū yí'dìng dzài jèige shū'jyàdzshang 'jr̄búdìng 'nǎr. *but* / That letter must be somewhere in this desk. is expressed as That letter is certainly in this desk. Nèifēng 'syìn yí-'dǐng shr̀ dzài jèi 'jwōdzli ne.

SON. érdz; (baby) syǎuhár; (child) háidz; (modest way of referring to one's own son) syáuchywǎn; (polite way of referring to someone else's son) lìnglǎng, 'gūngdž, shàuye; (never address a younger person as son érdz; it is very insulting). / This is my son. 'Jèi shr̀ 'wǒde syǎu'hár. / How old is your son now? Lìng'láng jīnnyan dwō 'dàle? / All of you bring your sons and daughters. Nǐmen dà'jyā dou bǎ 'syáujye 'dàilai.

SONG. (In general) gēer; (melody) gēchyǔ, chyǔr; (folksong) gēyáu; (children's song) túngyáu; (hillbilly song) shāngēer; (anything sung) chàngr; (short musical composition) syáuchyǔr, syǎudyàur.

(Of birds) is expressed as sound 'shēngyīn. / Can you recognize the songs of different birds? Nǐ 'tīngdechūlái gè'jǔng 'nyǎur jyàu de 'shēngyin ma?

For a song (cheap) pyányi, jyàn. / Here you can pick up things like that for a song. Dzài 'jèr mǎi 'dūngsyi 'pyányi'jíle.

SOON. (In a short while) jyòu, bùjyòu, 'méidwǒjyǒu, yìhwěr, búdàhwěr, méidwǒdà-'hwěr, yì'hwěrde 'gūngfu, bú'dàde 'gūngfu. / I'll be back soon. Wǒ yì'hwěr jyòu 'hwéilái. / He came soon after I left. Wǒ 'dzǒule yǐ'hòu 'méidwǒdà'hwěr tā jyòu 'láile. / The war was soon over. 'Jànshr̀ bù'jyòu jyòu 'gwòchyule.

(Quickly) kwài. / The sooner the better. Ywè kwài ywè 'hǎu. / I won't be back till five at the soonest. Wǒ dzwèi 'kwài yé 'děi 'wúdyǎn 'tsái néng 'hwéilái ne. / Why do you have to leave so soon? Nǐ 'wèishémma yí'dìng yàu 'dzèmma kwài 'dzǒu a?

(Willingly) is expressed as be willing ywànyi, chíngywàn, nìngywàn. / I'd just as soon not go. Wǒ chíng'ywàn bú'chyù. / He said he'd stay home as soon as not. Tā shwō tā 'ywànyì dzài 'jyāli 'dāije. / He'd sooner die than give in. Tā nìng'ywàn 'sž yě 'bùfú'shū.

As soon as (of time) shémma 'shŕhou yǐ . . . jyòu, (gāng) yǐ . . . jyòu. / Let me know as soon as you get here. Nǐ yí'dàu jèr, jyòu 'tūngjr̄ wǒ yìshēngr. / I told you as soon as I knew myself. Wǒ yǐ 'jr̄dàu jyòu 'gàusu nǐ le. / As soon as you feel any pain, take a dose of this. 'Shémma shŕhou yǐ jywéje 'téng, jyòu hē yíjì jèige 'yàu.

No sooner . . . than is expressed as not yet is . . . finished then . . . hái méi . . . 'wán ne jyòu; or as just . . . then . . . gāng . . . jyòu. / No sooner said than done. Yíjyù 'hwà hái méishwō'wán ne jyòu 'déle. / He had no sooner mentioned her name than she came in. Tā gāng yǐ 'shwō tā 'míngdz, tā jyòu 'jìnláile.

Sooner or later 'dzáuwǎn; or expressed as there'll come a day jwǔn yǒu yì-'tyān. / I'll have to see him sooner or later. Wǒ 'dzáuwǎn děi 'jyàn tā. / Sooner or later you'll have to make up your mind. 'Dzáuwǎn ní 'děi jywé'dìng a.

SORE. téng, tùng. / My throat is sore. Wo 'sǎngdz 'téng. / This bruise is sore to the touch. Jèikwài 'shāng yí 'pèng jyòu 'téng. / Look out for my sore toe. is expressed as My toe hurts. Be careful. Wǒ 'nèige jyǎu'jr̄tou 'téng. Lyóu dyǎr 'shén. or as Be careful of my hurt toe. Lyóu'shén wǒde 'hwài jyǎu'jr̄tou.

(Angry) shēngchì. / Don't get sore; I didn't mean anything. Byé shēng'chì, wǒ búshr̀ gù'yìde.

A sore (cut, wound, bruise; some injury received from external causes) shāng;

(boil, pimple) pàu; (swelling) jǔng. / There is a sore on my foot. Wǒ 'jyǎushang yǒu yíkwài 'shāng. / This sore is pretty well healed up now. Jèikwài 'shāng syàn'dzài 'yǐjing jáng'hǎule.

SORROW. Expressed as **be sorrowful** nángwò, shāngsyīn; or as great unhappiness 'fánnǎu. / He's caused his family a great deal of sorrow. Tā 'jēn jyàu tā 'jyālide 'rén nán'gwò. / She's sick with sorrow. Tā shāng'syīn 'jíle. / That is the only real sorrow he's ever had. Nà shr̀ tā shēng'píng wéi'yí jēn jèngde 'fánnǎu.

SORRY. (Repentant) hòuhwěi. / I'm sorry I did it. Wǒ 'hòuhwěi 'dzwòle nèijyàn shr̀. / I'm not sorry I did it. is expressed as I did it and am not a bit repentant. Wǒ 'gànle nèi'dàngdz shr̀ yìdyár ye buhou'hwěi. or Wǒ dzwòle nèi shr̀ bìnbú hòuhwěi.

(Apologetic) bàuchyàn, dwèibuchǐ, dwèibújù; (be embarrassed) yǒu 'dyǎr bùhǎu'yìsz, yǒu 'dyǎr nánwéi'chíng. / Did I bump you? I'm sorry. Wǒ 'pèngle 'nín le ma? Dwèibù'chǐ a. / I'm sorry to be late. Wǒ lái'wǎnle °hěn dwèibu'chǐ (°jēn yǒu 'dyǎr bùhǎu'yìsz).

(Poor, bad) dzāu. / She did a sorry job of cleaning this room. Jèige 'fángdz tā 'dásǎude 'tài dzāu le.

(Pathetic) lángbèibù'kānde. / He's a sorry looking person. Nèige 'rén 'kànje 'jēn shr̀ yǒu dyǎr lángbèibù'kānde 'shénchi.

Be (or Feel) **sorry for** someone jywéje . . . kě'lyán; I feel sorry for . . . . . . 'jēn kě'lyán. / He feels sorry for you. Tā jywéje ní kě'lyán. / I felt sorry for him and didn't press for payment. Wǒ jywéje tā hén kě'lyánde, jyòu 'méiwèn ta yàu nèibǐ 'chyán. / I feel sorry for you. Nǐ 'jēn kě'lyán. / I felt sorry for you; what a fool I was! Wǒ 'ywánlái hái jywéje ní kě'lyán ne; wǒ dzěmma nèmma 'shǎ ya!

SORT. jǔng, lèi, yàngr. See also **KIND.** / What sort of a man is he? Tā shr̀ 'dzěmma yì'jǔng 'rén? or Tā shr̀ 'shémma 'yàngrde 'rén? / We don't allow that sort of thing. Wǒmen jèr bù'syú yǒu 'nèiyàngrde 'shr̀ching. / They have all sorts of books. Tāmen yǒu °'gèjǔngde (°'gèlèide, °'gèshr̀ 'gèyàngrde) 'shū. / He's not a bad sort. is expressed as He's OK. Tā 'rén °bú'hwài (°hái'hǎu).

A sort of nèmma yijǔng. / It's a sort of gift some people have. Yǒusyē 'rén yǒu nèmma yì'jǔng 'tyānfen. / You can't help feeling a sort of admiration for a man like that. Nǐ dwèiyú 'nàyàngrde 'rén déi yǒu nèmma yì'jǔng 'pèifude syīn'lǐ.

Sort of dyǎr. / I'm sort of glad things happened the way they did. 'Shr̀ching 'chéngle 'jèyàngr wó yǒu dyǎr gāu'syìng. / I'd sort of like to go. Wǒ yǒu 'dyǎr syǎng 'chyù. / She's sort of interesting. Tā 'yǒu dyǎr 'yìsz.

Out of sorts (either sick or just nervous and irritable) bùshūfu. / I'm feeling a little out of sorts today. 'Jyēr wǒ 'jywéde 'yǒu dyǎr bù'shūfu.

To sort fēn, fēnlèi, fēnkai; (of people only), fēndzǔ, fēnbār. / I must sort these. Wó déi bǎ 'jè'syē 'fēnfen. / Have these been sorted? Jèisyēge 'fēngwò 'lèi ma? / We sorted the students according to their ability. Wǒmen bǎ 'sywéshēng ànje tāmende 'nénglì °'fēnkaile (°fēn'dzǔ).

SOUND. (Noise) 'shēngyīn, shēngr, syǎng. / I thought I heard a funny sound. Wǒ 'jywéhuje wǒ 'tīngjyànle yì'shēng hěn 'chígwàide 'shēngyīn. / I don't like the sound of the motor. is expressed as The sound of the motor has something wrong. Jèige 'jīchide 'shēngyīn 'yǒu dyǎr bú'dwèi. / What was that sound? 'Nèi shr̀ 'shémma 'syǎng?

(Body of water) hǎijyá, hǎisyá. / Let's go for a sail on the sound. 'Dzámen dàu 'nèige hǎi'jyáli hwáhwá 'chwán chyù.

Be **within sound of** (be able to hear) tīngdejyàn. / She didn't know we were within sound of her voice. Tā bùjr'dàu wŏmen tīngde'jyàn tā shwō'hwà.

Be **soundproof** (be able to cut off sound) néng gé yīn, jyàu 'shēngyīn gwòbu'lái. / The telephone booth has soundproof walls. Jèige dyàn'hwà'gédzde 'chyáng néng gé 'yīn.

To **sound** tīngje. / That shout sounded very close. Nèige 'rǎng de 'shēngyīn 'tīngje 'lí jèr hěn 'jìn. / Your voice sounds funny over the telephone. Nǐde 'shēngyīn 'jyēje dyàn'hwà 'tīngje tǐng tè'byé. / That sounds like thunder. Nèige 'tīngje syàng dǎ'léi shr̀de. / It sounds impossible. is expressed as It sounds as though it can't be done. Nèige 'tīngje syàng bùkě'néng. / How does that sound to you? Nèige nǐ 'tīngje 'dzěmma'yàng? or expressed as What do you think about it? Nèige nǐ 'jywéhuje 'dzěmma'yàng? / What you say about him makes him sound very nice. Nǐ dzěmma yì shwō 'bǎ ta 'shwōde tīng hǎu shr̀de. / He sounds very sincere, but he isn't. is expressed as His words sound sincere; but he's not at all that way. Tāde 'hwà 'tīngje hěn 'chéngkěn, 'kěshr 'shr̀dzài bìng'búshr̀ nèmma hwéi'shr̀.

(Signal by sound). / The bugle sounded retreat. is expressed as The bugle blew retreat. 'Nèige 'chwēi de shr̀ chè'twèi'hàu. / The police sounded an alarm. is expressed as The police department sent out a signal. Jǐngchá'jyú 'fàngle ge 'syìn'hàu. or as The policemen blew their whistles. Jǐng'chá chwēi 'shàur le.

(Measure depth) 'tsèlyáng 'shēndù, 'lyánglyang dwó 'shēn, 'tsèlyang 'tsèlyang dwó 'shēn. / They sounded the lake before they allowed people to swim there. Tāmen syān 'lyánglyang nèige 'hú yŏu dwō 'shēn ránhòu tsái syǔ 'rén chyù yóu'yŭng ne. / They sounded the harbor. Tāmen bǎ 'jèige gǎng'wǎnde 'shēndù 'tsèlyángle 'tsèlyang.

Sound out (question) 'tàntīng. / He sounded me out on the subject. Nèijyàn 'shr̀ tā 'tàntīng wŏde 'kŏuchì láije.

Be **sound** (strong, in good condition) jyēshr; or often simply hǎu. / The floor is old but sound. Jèige dì'bǎn jyǒu le 'kěshr 'jyēshr. / He's still in sound health. Tā 'shēntǐ hái hěn °'hǎu (°'jyēshr). / His mind is still sound. Tāde 'jīngshen hái hěn 'hǎu.

(Reliable) kàudejù; (steady) wěn, 'wěndāng. / Are you sure the business is sound? Nǐ 'shwō nèige 'mǎimai 'wěn ma?

(Reasonable) yóulǐ. / She gave him sound advice. Tā 'chywàn tā 'chywànde hěn yóulǐ. / That's a sound argument. Nèige 'bwóde tīng youlǐ.

(Valid; having a basis) yŏu'gēnjyùde; (legal) héfǎde; (real) jēnjèngde; (reliable) kàudejùde; (really true) 'chyānjēnwàn'chywède. / Can you prove that you have a sound claim to the property? is expressed as You say the property is yours; have you any real proof? Nǐ shwō 'chǎnyè shr̀ 'nǐde, ní yŏu shémma 'chyānjēnwàn'chywède 'jèngjyu ma?

Sound sleep. / I had a sound sleep last night. Dzwóer 'wǎnshang wŏ 'shwèide tīng °'syāng (°'hǎu, °'wěn, °'sź).

Safe and sound méi shr̀. / Did you get home safe and sound? Hwéi'jyā yí'lù méi 'shr̀ ma?

SOUP. tāng. / Give me a bowl of chicken soup, please. Gěi wo lái 'wǎn 'jī tāng.

SOUR. (Acid to taste, or fermented, spoiled) swān; **sour pickles** swāntsài; **sweet and sour spareribs** táng'tsù páigu, 'tyánswān 'páigu. / This fruit is sour. Jèige 'gwǒdz hěn 'swān. / The milk is sour. 'Nyóunǎi 'swān le.

(Disagreeable). / She's a sour old maid. is expressed as That old maid's disposition is very bad. 'Tā jèige lǎu'gūnyang 'píchi jēn 'hwài. / Look at the old sour-puss. is expressed as Look at him with his face so stern and crabby. 'Chyáu ta 'nèmma °běngje (°bǎnje) 'lyǎn.

(Damp). / The cellar smells sour. is expressed as The cellar has a damp smell. Jèige dì'yĭndzli yŏu yìgǔ 'cháuchi wèr.

Sour grapes. / That's nothing but a case of sour grapes with him. is expressed as It must be because he's jealous. (envious) Tā 'nèmmaje 'búgwò shř yīnwei °yǎr-ˈrè 'jyòu shřle (or eating vinegar; more commonly said of women) °chř'tsù 'jyou shřle, or (covetous) °kànje 'byé rén yǎn'húng jyòu shřle).

To sour (become sour) byàn swān. / I'm letting the milk sour. Wŏ 'ràng nèige nyóu'nǎi byàn 'swān lou.

SOURCE. (Point of origin) ywán, 'láiywán. / Where is the source of this river? is ex-pressed as The water source of this river is where? Jèityáu 'héde shwěi'ywán dzài 'nǎr? or as Where does this river start? Jèityáu 'hé tsúng 'nǎr 'fāywán? / What is your source of supplies? Nǐ 'dūngsyi dōu shr dá 'nǎr nùnglái? / What is your source of information? Nǐ jèige 'syāusyi tsúng 'nǎr délai de? but / He's a good source of information. is expressed as He is always ready with information. Tāde 'syāusyi hěn 'língtung.

(Cause) 'ywányīn, gēnyuán, gēn, 'yīnsù. / Have you found the source of the trouble? 'Hwò shř de 'ywányīn dzài 'nǎr ní 'jāuchūláile ma? or more naturally ex-pressed as Did you find out where the source of the trouble is? Hwò'gēn dzài 'nǎr ní 'jāuchūlaile ma? / His success has been a source of great pride to all of us. is ex-pressed as His success gave us no little pride. Tā jèiyìchéng'gūng géi wŏmen dzēng-'gwāng bù'shǎu.

(Literary material) 'tsáilyàu. / This book is based on several published sources. is expressed as This book is based on several kinds of published material. Jèibèr 'shū shř 'gēnjyù háujíjǔng chūbǎngwò de 'tsáilyàu syéde.

SOUTH (SOUTHERN). nán; southeast dūngnán; southwest syīnán; Southern Hemisphere Nánbànchyóu; South Pole Nán'jí. / There's a south wind tonight. Jyēr 'wǎnshang gwā 'nánfēng. / I'd prefer a room facing south. Wŏ 'ywànyi yàu yǐjyān cháu 'nán de 'wūdz.

(Indicating a part or area) nánbù, nánbyǎr, nánfāng. / We traveled through the south of France. Wŏmen lyŭ'syíng 'jīnggwò 'Fàgwode °nánbù (°etc.). / Down south they take things easier. °'Nánbyar (°etc.) dzwò'shř 'búnèmma 'mángmangdau'dàude.

(Indicating an area beyond a border) nánbyar; (to the) south of . . . dzài . . . (de) 'nánbyar. / It's just south of the river. (Nèi) jyòu dzài hé(de) 'nánbyar yĭdyǎr.

SPACE. (Extension) 'kūngjyān. / We cannot conceive of things outside space and time. Wŏmen syǎng 'shémma shřching yě 'chūbùlyǎu 'shřjyān 'kūngjyānde 'chywār. / How fast is that star moving through space? Nèige 'syīngsying dzài 'kūngjyān 'dzŏude yŏu dwō 'kwài?

(Part marked off in some way) dì (land); 'kùngdì, 'kùngdyèr (vacant land); gwò-dàur (passage); kùngr (emptiness). / Is this space big enough to build a house on? Jèikwài 'dì gòu 'gài swòr 'fángde ma? / There's a wide space between the two build-ings. Lyǎ lóu 'jūngjyàr yŏu yí'dàpyàn 'kùngdyèr. / There's a narrow space between our building and the next. Wŏmen 'lóu gēn tāmen 'lóude dāng'jyàr yŏu yí'lyáu syāu gwò'dàur. / How much space do you want between the two desks? Nǐ shwō lyǎ 'jwōdz jūng'jyar lyóu dwódà 'kùngr?

(Extent of time) gūngfu. / He did the work in the space of a day. Tā 'nèijyàn 'shř 'dzwòle yŏu yì'tyānde 'gūngfu. / You ought to have that finished in a short space of time. Nǐ yí'dìng yì'hwěrde 'gūngfu jyòu 'kěyi dzwò'wán.

(Room) dìfangr. / That piano takes up too much space in his room. Tā 'fáng-dzli nèige gāng'chín 'tài jàn 'dìfangr. / Is there any space for my luggage? Yǒu 'dìfangr 'gē wǒde 'syíngli ma? / Write small to save space. Syé 'syáu dyǎr 'shéng dyǎr 'dìfangr.

Stare into space falèng. / He just sat there staring out into space. Tā 'jyòu shř 'dzwòdzai nèr fā'lèng.

To space lyóu(kùngr). / The posts are spaced a foot apart. Nèisyē 'jùdz °jr̄-'jyān (°dāng'jūng) dōu lyóule yìchř̌de 'kùngr.

SPARE. (Free one from something) expressed with a number of verbs in the negative. / Spare me the details. 'Yùngbujáu 'syáng syang syĭ'syĭde gēn wo 'shwō. / He was spared that ordeal. Tā méi'shòujáu nèige 'dzwèi. or as He escaped that ordeal. Nèige 'dzwèi tā swàn 'táukaile.

(Refrain from using) shěng. / I've spared no expense in building the house. Wǒ gài nèige fángdz méishěng chyán. / If you phone him you can spare yourself (the trouble of) going there. Yàushr ni gěi ta 'dǎ ge dyàn'hwà, nǐ jyou bubì dž'jǐ chyù le.

(Keep from destroying). / Kill me but spare my children. Shā wǒ kéyi, kěshr byé shā wǒde haidz. / He alone was spared. Jyòushr tā 'yíge ren méisž. but / His life was spared. Ráule tā yí'mìng.

(Lend) jyè; (give) yún(gei), gěi. / I can spare you some money. Wǒ 'kéyi 'jyè ni dyǎr 'chyán. / Can you spare a cigarette? Nǐ yǒu 'fùyude yān'jywǎr 'yúngei wo yì'gēr ma? / Mister, can you spare a dime? 'Syānsheng, géi wǒ yìmáu 'chyán ba. / Can you spare a minute? Nín néng 'yúnchu yìfen 'jūng lái ma? or expressed as May I trouble you a minute? Wó 'dájyǎu nín yí'syàr, syíng ma?

Spare (extra) fùyu; **spare room** kùng fángdz; **spare time** 'fùyu shŕ'jyān, (syán) gūngfu; **spare tire** bèidài. / I haven't got much spare cash. Wǒ 'méiyou shémma 'fùyu syàn'chyán. / Do you have any spare parts for your radio? Nǐ jèige wúsyàn-dyàn yǒu 'fùyú líng'jyàr ma? / I'll do it in my spare time. Wó yǒu 'gūngfu de shŕ-hou 'dzwò nèige. / I haven't a spare minute. Wǒ 'yìdyǎr syán'gūngfu dōu 'méiyou. / I got to the station with five minutes to spare. is expressed as I got to the station with still five minutes of spare time. Wǒ dàule chē'jàn hái yǒu 'wǔfen jūngde 'fùyu shŕ'jyān.

(Frugal) jyǎndan, shěng. / They've been living on a very spare diet consisting mostly of rice and cabbage. Tāmen chŕ 'fàn 'chŕde jēn 'jyǎndan, jyòu shr 'fàn gēn bái'tsài.

SPEAK (SPOKE, SPOKEN). (Talk) shwō, shwōhwà, jyǎng, jyǎnghwà; (converse) tán (hwà); (discuss) 'tánlwùn, yìlwùn. / Do I speak clearly enough? Wǒ 'shwōde gòu 'chīngchude ma? / Did you speak to me? Nǐ shř gēn wǒ 'shwō ne ma? / He speaks with a slight stammer. Tā shwō'hwà 'yóu dyǎr 'jyēba. / We were just speaking of you. Wǒmen jèr 'jèng shwō 'nǐ ne. / Do you speak English? Nǐ shwō 'Yīngwén ma? / Since that argument they haven't spoken. Tāmen tsúng 'nèihwéi bàndzwéi yǐ-'hòu jyou bí'tsž méishwō'hwà.

(Make a speech) jyǎng, jyǎnghwà, yánjyǎng, jyángyǎn, yǎnshwō. / Who is speaking tonight? Jyèr 'wǎnshang 'shéi jyǎng'yǎn a? / You'll have to speak to the boy about that. Nǐ déi bǎ 'nèijyàn shř gěi nèige 'háidz 'jyǎngjyǎng.

Speak one's mind shwō . . . 'yìjyàn.

Speak for (represent) °tì (°wèi, °dài'byǎu) . . . shwō; (make a bid for) see RESERVE, SELL, etc. / I'm speaking for my friend. Wǒ shř 'tì wǒ 'péngyou 'shwō ya. / We've already spoken for him for our team. is expressed as We've already

933

SPECIAL

asked him to play on our team. Wǒmen 'yǐjīng 'ywēhǎule 'tā lái rù 'wǒmen jèi'dwèi le. / Next Saturday is already spoken for. is expressed as Next Saturday there won't be any time. 'Syà 'syīngchī'lyòu méi 'kùngr le. / Those tickets are already spoken for. is expressed as Those tickets have been reserved. Nèisyējāng 'pyàu 'yǐjǐng yǒu 'rén 'dǐngle.

Speak of see MENTION; nothing to speak of 'méishémma. / Are you hurt? It's nothing to speak of. 'Pèngjaule ma? Méishémma.

Speak up. / Speak up! I can't hear you. 'Dà dyǎr shēngr 'shwō. Wǒ 'tīngbú-'jyàn.

Generally speaking dà'gàide shwō. / Generally speaking, he is home every evening. Dà'gàide shwō, tā 'měityān 'wǎnshang dōu dzài'jyā.

On speaking terms. / We're not on speaking terms. meaning We don't know each other. Wǒmen 'lyǎ méishwōgwò 'hwà. or meaning We aren't friends any longer. Wǒmen 'lyǎ bùshwō'hwà le.

SPECIAL. tèbyé, tèshū. / She bought her gown for a special occasion. Tā shr̀ 'wèi yíjyàn tè'byé 'shr̀ching mǎide nèijyàn yīfer. / I have a special reason. Wǒ 'yǒu yíge tè'byéde 'lǐyóu. / Does this book go in any special place? Jèiběr 'shū děi 'gēdzai shémma tè'byéde 'dìfangr ma? / He's had special training in his field. 'Tā dzài nèi'ménli shǒugwò tè'shūde 'syùnlyàn.

A special train (a train chartered for a particular person or group) 'jwānchē; (an extra train to take care of an unusually large number of passengers) jyāchē. / Is there a special train for the weekend? Jōu'mwò yǒu °jyā'chē (°'jwānchē) ma?

Special delivery píngkwài; or, when the service also includes registering of the mail, 'kwàisyìn. / Send the letter special delivery. Jèifēng 'syìn fā píng'kwài.

SPEECH. Expressed verbally as speak shwōhwà, jyǎnghwà. / Sometimes gestures are more expressive than speech. 'Byǎushr̀ 'yìjyàn yǒude 'shr̀hour 'tàidu bǐ shwō de 'hwà hái chwán'shén. / He has the speech of an educated person. Tīng tā shwō'hwà yì'tīng jyòu 'shr̀ 'shǒugwò 'jyàuyu de 'rén. / He has an impediment in his speech. Tā shwō'hwà 'yóu dyǎr 'jyējyebā'bàde. / You can often tell where a person comes from by his speech. 'Tīng yíge 'rén shwō'hwà jyòu 'wángwǎng 'jr̄dau tā shr̀ 'nǎrde 'rén. or expressed as Often when you hear a person's accent, you know where he's from. Nǐ 'chángchang 'tīng yíge rénde 'kǒuyīn jyòu 'jr̄dau tā shr̀ 'nǎrde 'rén.

(Address) jyángyǎn, yánjyǎng, yǎnshwō. / That was a very good speech. 'Nèige yán'jyǎng 'jyǎngde hén 'hǎu.

Make a speech jyángyǎn, yánjyǎng.

SPEED. 'sùdù, 'súdù, kwàimàn. / The train is moving at a very slow speed. Hwǒ'chē syàn'dzài sù'dù hěn 'màn. / Speed limit 30 miles per hour. °Sù'dù (°'Súdù, °kwài-màn) měisyǎu'shr̀ bùnéng 'chāugwò 'sānshŕlǐ. but / Let's put on a little speed. is expressed as Let's hurry. Dzámen 'kwài dyǎr ba. or as Let's step on the gas. Dzámen jyā dyǎr 'yóu ba. / We're moving at a good speed now. is expressed as We're going fast enough now. Wǒmen syàn'dzài 'dzǒude gòu 'kwàide le. / Full speed ahead! is expressed as Add horsepower and go ahead! Jyā 'dzúlou 'mǎlì wàngchyán 'dzǒu! / We are going at top speed. is expressed as We've added enough horsepower. Wǒmen jyā'dzúle 'mǎlì le. / The greatest speed is needed for this job. is expressed as This job needs to be done fast. 'Jèijyàn shr̀ 'bìděi kwài'kwārde 'dzwò.

(Gear ratio) já, páidǎng. / This car has four speeds. Jèilyàng 'chē yǒu 'sz-dàu °já (°páidǎng).

934

To speed (go fast) pău. /We were speeding along the highway when we saw the accident. Wŏmen 'shwùnje dà'dàu 'pău de 'shŕhour 'kànjyàn nèr chūle 'shŕ le.

(Drive too fast). /We were arrested for speeding. Wŏmen kāi'che kāide tài 'kwài le, jyòu bèi'pŭle.

Speed up. /Speed up the work. is expressed as Tighten the work. 'Jyājĭn 'gūngdzwò. or as You must hurry on that work. Jèige 'hwóer déi 'găn yìgan. or as Hurry in doing that. 'Kwàije dyăr 'dzwò. /Can't you speed things up a little? is expressed as Can't you hurry? Nĭ bùnéng °'kwài (°'gănje) dyăr ma?

SPELL. pĭn, pĭndż. /He doesn't know how to spell yet. Tā hái bú'hwèi pĭn ne. /How do you spell that? Dzĕmma 'pĭn nèige 'dż? /It's spelled the same, but pronounced differently. 'Pĭnfăr yí'yàng, búgwò'nyànfăr bù'túng.

(Relieve) tì. /I'll spell you for a while. Wŏ 'tì nĭ yìhwĕr.

A spell (period of time) jèn, jèndz. /This hot spell won't last long. Jèijèndz 'rèjyèr 'chángbùlyău. /He works for short spells now and then. Tā dzwò 'shèr nèmma yí'jèndz yí'jèndzde. or expressed as Every once in a while he does a few days' work. Tā 'youshŕhou dzwò jĭtyān shèr. or as Now and then he works a little. Tā ŏu'ĕr 'dzwò dyăr shèr. /He had a coughing spell. Tā 'késòule °yí'jèn (°yì'hwèr). /Do you have fainting spells? is expressed as Do you sometimes faint? Ní 'youshŕ-hour 'yūngwòchyu ma?

(Magical charm) syé, 'syéwányèr, syémér, jòu, fú, 'syéjyàu. /We don't believe in spells and charms. Wŏmen búsyìn 'fú la 'jòu le de. or expressed as We don't believe in witchcraft. Wŏmen búsyìn 'syé. (fig.) /Have you come under his spell, too? is expressed as Have you let him charm you, too? Nĭ shŕ 'yĕ jyàu 'tā gĕi 'míjùle ma?

SPEND (SPENT). (Use up, pay out) hwā, yùng; (waste) fèi, 'syāuhàu. /Have you spent your whole salary already? Ní 'yĭjĭng bă 'syīnshwĕi dōu 'hwāle ma? /The enemy spent most of its supplies in that one attack. Dírén yìdwò'bànde gùng'yĭng dōu dzài nèitsż jìn'gūng de 'shŕhou 'syāuhàule. /My money's all spent. Wŏde 'chyán dōu 'hwāle.

(Pay out money) hwā 'chyán, chū 'chyán; spend a lot chū ('dà) °'jyàr (°'jyà-chyan); not to spend much 'bùchū ('dà) °'jyàr (°'jyàchyan). /I'm willing to spend a lot for a piano. Wŏ 'ywànyi 'hwā yí'dàbĭ 'chyán 'măi yíjyà gāng'chín.

(Of time) yùng, fèi, hwā (expend for a purpose); gwò, dāi (pass, stay). /We spent several hours at the museum. Wŏmen dzài bwówu'ywàn dāile 'háujĭge 'jūngtóu. /We spent several hours looking for a suitable gift. Wŏmen °'yùngle (°'fèile, °hwāle) háujĭge jūng'tóude 'gūngfu jău yíjyàn hé'shŕde 'lĭwu. /I want to spend the night here. Wŏ yàu 'dzài jèr °gwò'yè (°'dāi yíyè).

SPENT. (Exhausted) lèijíle, jīn'pílì'jìn. /After the race, the runner was completely spent. Sài'wánle yĭ'hòu, sài'pău de 'rén jyăn'jŕ shŕ jīn'pílì'jìn.

SPIRIT. (Mind, soul) syīn. /The spirit is willing, but the flesh is weak. Syīnyou'yú ér'lìbù'dzú. but /I'll be with you in spirit. is expressed as I'll always be thinking of you. Wŏ yí'dìng lău 'dyànjìje 'nĭ.

(Disposition) 'jĭngshen. /We were told of the defiant spirit of the conquered people. Wŏmen 'tīngshwō dă'bàile de rénde 'jĭngshén hái hĕn chyánghàn. /These tales reveal the spirit of the country. Jèisyē 'gùshr byāusyàn gwójyāde 'jĭngshen. /Well, it's the spirit of the times. 'Nèi shŕ jèige shŕ'dàide 'jĭngshen. or expressed as It's the modern trend. 'Nèi shŕ jèige shŕ'dàide 'cháulyóu.

935

(Feeling, emotion) 'chíngsyù. / A spirit of revolt was evident among the men. Dzài nèichyún rénli hěn 'míngsyànde yǒu yìjǔng 'pànbyànde 'chíngsyù.

(Attitude) 'tàidù. / You don't go about it in the right spirit. Nǐde 'tàidù bú'dwèi. / That's the right spirit! Nèige 'tàidù jyòu jyòu 'dwèi le! or expressed as That's the way! 'Jyòu shr nà 'yàngr! / He tries to judge according to the spirit of the law. is expressed as He tries to judge according to the true meaning of the law. Tā jìn-lyèr ànje 'fǎlyùde jēn'yì lái 'pàndwàn.

(Liveliness) jīngshen (of people or horses); hwānshr (of animals; be lively); hwópwo (of animals and children). / That kid has a lot of spirit. Nèige syǎu'hár tǐng 'jīngshen. / You have a horse with a lot of spirit there. 'Nǐ nèr nèipí 'mǎ hěn yǒu 'jīngshen. / They played the music with spirit. Tāmen dzòu 'ywè 'dzòude hěn yǒu 'jīngshen. / That pup has a lot of spirit. Nèige syǎu'gǒur tǐng 'hwānshr.

(Supernatural being) 'jīnglingr; (ghost) gwěi; (god) shén. / The natives say there's a spirit in this tree. 'Tǔrén shwō jèikē 'shù °nàu 'gwěi (°shr kē'shénshù).

Spirits 'syīnchíng, jīngshen. / I hope you're in good spirits. Wǒ 'syīwàng nǐ syàn'dzài 'syīnchíng bú'tswò. or expressed as I hope you're happy. Wǒ 'syīwàng nǐ syàn'dzài hěn gāu'syìng. / I'm in low spirits. Wǒ 'syīnsyù bù'jyā.

(Concentrated chemical element) jīng; spirits of ammonia 'yǎmwóní'yǎ'jīng.

(Liquor) lyèjyǒu.

SPIT. (Release from the mouth, not vehemently) tùtán; (spit with gusto) tswèi; (vomit) tù. / No spitting. Yán'jìntù'tán. or Jìn'jrtù'tán. / Don't spit on the floor. Byé wàng 'dìshang °tù'tán (°tswèi 'tùmèi). / He spit blood. Tā tù'syě le. / If it tastes bad, spit it out. Yàushr bùhǎu'chr, °'tswèichūlái (°'tùchūlái).

A spit (skewer) tyěchǎdz, gwèr. / We can roast the chicken on a spit. Wǒmen 'kéyi ná °yìgēn 'gwèr (°tyě'chǎdz) 'chāshang jèijr 'jī 'shāushau.

SPLENDID. (Very good) 'dzwèi hǎu, 'tài hǎu, 'jēn hǎu, hǎujíle. / I think what you have done is splendid. Wǒ jywéde nǐ 'dzwòde 'tài hǎu le. / This is splendid weather for swimming. Jèijǔng 'tyānchi fù'shwěi dzwèi 'hǎu. / Splendid! Myǎu'jíle.

(Elaborate) jyāngjyou. / Their house is a little too splendid for my taste. Wǒ 'jywéde tāmende 'fángdz 'tài 'jyāngjyou.

SPOIL. (Ruin) bǎ . . . °gěi (°nùng) °'hwèile (°'hwàile, °'jyǎuhwole, °jyǎule). / The dinner is already spoiled. Jèidwùn 'fàn yǐ'rán nùng 'hwàile. / The bad weather spoiled our vacation. Hwài'tyār bá wǒmende 'jyà géi °'hwèile (°'jyǎuhwole). / Don't spoil my plans by telling the others what I'm going to do. Byé 'gàusu 'byérén wǒ yàu 'gàn shémma, hwéi'tóu bá wǒde 'jìhwà gěi nùng 'hwèile.

(Go bad) hwài, làn. / These apples are beginning to spoil. 'Jèisyē 'pínggwo yǐjing 'làn le. / Food spoils quickly in hot weather. 'Rètyān de 'shŕhou 'dūngsyi 'dzwèi rúngyi 'hwài.

(Overindulge) bǎ . . . °gwàn'hwàile (°dzùng'hwàile, °'fàngdzùng'hwàile). / The little boy is being spoiled by his grandmother. Syǎu'hár jyàu tā dzú'mú gěi gwàn-'hwàile. / He's a spoiled child. Tā jèige 'háidz gwàn'hwàile. / Don't spoil him. Byé 'bǎ tā gwàn'hwàilou.

Spoils 'hǎuchù, dzāng. / They got their share of the spoils, you can be sure. Tāmen yí'dìng fēnjau °'hǎuchù (°'dzāng le).

SPOKE. (Of a wheel) tyáu, chētyáu. / Do you have another bicycle spoke to replace this one? Nǐ 'hái yǒu méiyǒu 'byéde chē'tyáu gěi jèi dzsyíng'chē 'hwàn yi'gēr? / This wheel has a broken spoke. Jèige 'lwúndz 'shéle yìgēr 'tyáu.

SPOON. chŕr, chŕdz, tyáugēng, sháur, gēngchŕ, sháudz. /Do you still feed her with a spoon? Nǐ 'háishr yùng 'chŕdz 'wèi ta ma?

Spoon up wǎichulai, kwàichulai, yǎuchulai. /See if you can spoon up the soup that's left in the kettle. Nǐ 'shr̄shr̄ 'néng bùnéng bǎ 'gwōli 'shèngsyà de nèidyǎr 'tāng 'wǎichulai.

SPORT. (Exercise, physical games) 'yùndung; **sports page** tǐyùlán, yùndunglán. /Do you like sports? Ní 'syǐhwān 'yùndung ma? /Swimming is my favorite sport. Yóu-'yǔng shr̀ wǒ 'dzwèi 'syǐhwan de 'yùndung. /I always read the sports page first. Wǒ yúng'ywǎn shr̀ 'syān kàn 'tǐyùlán. *but* /This is fine sport. is expressed as This is really interesting. Jèi 'jēn yǒu'yìsz.

(Of a person). /She's a poor sport. 'Tā rén hén 'syǎuchi. /He's a good sport, 'Tā rén hén °'dàchi (°'dàfāng).

To sport something new lòu, syànbei. /Aren't you sporting a new tie today? Nǐ jyēr °'lòulou (°syǎnbei) syīn lǐng'dài ya? or expressed as Isn't the tie you're wearing today new? Nǐ 'jīntyán dǎ de lǐng'dài shr̄ bushr̄ 'syīnde ya?

SPOT. (Small mark) dyǎr, dyǎndz; (dirty mark, stain) dzāngdyǎr, dzāngr. /She had on a white dress with red spots. Tā chwānle yíjyàn 'báide dài húng'dyàrde 'yīshang. /Can you get these spots out of my pants? Nǐ néng bá wǒ 'kùdzshangde 'jèijǐkwài 'dzāngr 'chyù le ma?

(Place) dìfangr; (point) dyǎn. /Show me the exact spot you mean. Bá ní swǒ-'shwō de nèiyǐ'dyǎn 'jr̄chūlái. or Bá ní swǒ'shwō de nèige 'dìfang 'jr̄géi wǒ 'kàn-kan.

(Moment) yì'hwěr. /That was a bright spot in an otherwise dull day. is expressed as Of the whole day only that moment was rather interesting. Nèiyíjěng'tyār hǎi 'jyoushr̄ 'nèiyìhwěr 'bǐjyǎu 'yóudyǎr 'yìsz.

On the spot (right there) dzài nèr, dzài nèige 'dìfangr. /I was right on the spot when it happened. Chū'shèr de shr̄hou wǒ 'jèng 'dzài nèr.

On the spot (immediately) lìkè, lìshŕ, dāngshŕ. /They hired him on the spot. Tāmen dāng'shŕ jyòu 'bǎ tā 'gùle.

Be put on the spot dzwòlà, wéinán. /That really put me on the spot. Nèi jyǎn-'jr̄ shr̄ 'jyàu 'wǒ dzwò'là.

To spot *see* **RECOGNIZE**. /I spotted you in the crowd as soon as I saw your hat. is expressed as I saw your hat in the crowd and immediately knew it was you. Dzài 'rénchyúnli wǒ yí'kànjyàn nǐde 'màudz mǎ'shàng jyòu 'jr̄dau shr̄ 'nǐ.

(Stain) nùnghwā. /Will water spot this material? 'Shwěi néng bǎ jèijyàn 'lyàudz nùng 'hwā le ma?

SPREAD. (Lay out) 'dǎkāi, 'tānkāi, 'pūkāi. /Spread the rug out and let me look at it. Bǎ dìtǎn 'tānkāi jyàu wǒ 'chyáuchyau. /He spread the papers out on the table. Tā bá 'jr̄ 'dǎkāi 'pūdzai 'jwōdzshang le.

(Open) 'dǎkāi, 'fēnkāi. /The eagle spread its wings and flew away. Nèige 'yīng 'dǎkāi chr̄'bàngr jyou 'fēile. /Spread your fingers apart. Bá 'nǐde shǒu'jr̄-tou 'fēnkāi.

(Extend) jǎn; (occupy) 'jànchū. /The factory spreads over two acres. Nèige gūng'chǎng 'jànle yǒu 'lyángmǔ dì. /The farm spreads out for miles. Jèikwài 'dì 'jànchūle yóu 'háusyēlǐ 'dì chyù.

(Distribute; throw with the motion of sowing seed, a powdered fertilizer, etc.) să; (spread a thick substance like tar with a shovel or other instrument) tān, tān'píng-lou; (smear butter, etc.; the same motion as tān, only on a much smaller scale) mwŏ. / Spread the fertilizer evenly. (if it is powder) Bă 'féilyàu să'yúnlou. or (if it is manure or a thick substance) Bă 'féilyàu tān'yúnlou. / Spread the honey on the bread. Myàn'bāushang 'mwó dyăr 'fēng'mì. (fig.) / He repaid me in small amounts, spread over several years. is expressed as He divided the money and repaid me a little at a time for several years. Tā 'fēnkai jǐ'nyán yǐ'dyăr yǐ'dyărde băchyán 'hwángei wŏ de.

(Expand) nàuchilai, chwán; (of fire only) yánshāu; (of fire or disease) 'mànyán; (of ideas or of disease) lyóusyíng. / The rumor spread rapidly. 'Yáuyan chwánde hěn 'kwài. / The fire spread rapidly once it got started. 'Hwŏ yǐ 'jáuchǐlái mànyánde tǐng 'kwài. / These ideas are spreading everywhere. Jèisyē 'sžsyăng 'dàuchù lyóu-'syíng. / They tried to stop the disease from spreading. Tāmen syăng bújyàu jèi-bìng 'nàuchilai.

SPRING (SPRANG, SPRUNG). (Jump) bèng, tyàu; (of animals) pū. / He sprang to his feet. Tā yí 'tyàu jyòu 'jànchǐlaile. / The cat sprang at the mouse. Nèige 'māu 'pū nèige 'hàudz.

(Become bent) chyàuchilai; (hump up in the middle) gŭchilai. / The car door has sprung again. Nèige chē'mér yòu 'chyàuchǐláile.

(Pry open by force) 'chyàukāi (by using an instrument); 'nǐngkāi (by twisting with the hands or pliers). / See if we can spring this lock. 'Kànkan wŏmen bă jèige swŏ 'chyàukai 'syíng bùsyíng. / When the police arrived, they found that the lock had been sprung. Jǐng'chá 'dàule de shŕhour jyòu fā'syàn 'swŏ shŕ 'nǐngkāide.

Spring something on someone hū'ránde . . . , lěnggu'dǐngde . . . , chōuhu'lěngdz . . . . / The teacher sprang that test on us without warning. 'Syānsheng hū'ránde 'kăule wŏmen yí'syàr. / What did you spring that question on me for? Nǐ chōuhou-'lěngdz 'wèn wŏ 'nèmma ge 'wèntí gàn 'shémma?

Spring up is expressed as appear, grow, be built, etc. / Mushrooms sprang up all along the lake. 'Mwógu dzài hú'byārshang 'jángchǐláile. / Towns sprang up almost overnight. 'Hū'ránjyan 'jèr yíge 'chéng 'nàr yíge 'jènde jyòu dōu 'gàichǐláile.

Spring (elastic metal device) hwáng, bēnghwáng, lāhwáng, tánhwáng. / The spring seems to be broken. 'Hwáng hău'syàng 'shéle shŕde. / This bed has good springs. Jèige 'chwángde 'hwáng hén 'hău.

(Water source) chywán, 'chwányăn; **spring water** chywánshwěi. / We filled our cups at the spring. Wŏmen dzài 'chwányăn nèr bă 'bēidz 'gwànmănle 'shwěi le. / This mountain has three springs. Jèige 'shān yŏu 'sānge °'chywán (°'chywányan). / Let's have a drink of nice cool spring water. Dzámen 'hē dyăr yòu'lyángyòu'tyánde chywán'shwěi ba.

(Season) chwūntyan, 'chwūnjì. / We won't be leaving town before spring. 'Chwūntyan yǐ'chyán wŏmen 'búhwèi 'líkai jèr. / This is beautiful spring weather. Jēn shr 'chwūngwāngmíng'mèi.

SQUARE. (Equilateral rectangle) (sž)fāngkwàr. / They cut the cake into small squares. Tāmen 'bă 'nèige 'dyānsyin 'chyēchéng 'syău sžfāng'kwàr.

(Carpenter's tool, T square) dǐngdžchŕ.

(Open space in town) kùngchăngr, gwángchăng.

Square (honest, fair) 'gūngdàu, 'chéngshŕde; (literary) 'fāngjèng. / He's a pretty square fellow. Tā shŕ ge 'chéngshŕde 'rén. / Do you think they gave him a square deal? is expressed as Do you think they were fair? Nǐ 'jywéhuje 'tāmen 'gūngdàu ma? / Play square! 'Gūngdàu dyar!

(Square-shaped) ('sż)fāng. / I want a square box. Wǒ 'yàu yíge 'fāng syádz.

(Square unit of measurement) fāng; . . . square . . . jyàn'fāng. / How many square feet does the building cover? Jèidzwo 'lóude 'dìjǐ yǒu 'dwōshau fāng'chǐ? / Our back yard is twenty feet square. Wǒmen hòu'ywàr shr̀ èrshr'chǐ jyàn'fāng. or expressed as Our back yard is twenty by twenty feet. Wǒmen hòu'ywàrde cháng'kwān dōu shr̀ 'èrshr'chǐ. / This scarf is two feet square. Jèige wéi'bwóer shr̀ 'èrchǐ jyàn'fāng.

(Exactly) jèng, jěng, jènghǎu. / The arrow hit the target square in the middle. Jèi yí'jyàn 'jèng shède ba dāng'jyàr. / Hit him square between the eyes. Yí'syàr 'jèng dàde lyǎ 'yǎn dāng'jyàr. / Hit the nail square on the head. Bǎ 'dīngdz dǐng-'jènglou.

To **square**. / I'll square things with you later. Dzámen yǐ'hòu dzài swàn'jàng ba. / My accounts never square at the end of the month. is expressed as My accounts are never cleared up at the end of the month. Wǒde 'jàng 'nǎige ywè'dǐ yě 'méinùng-'chīng.

STAB. jā, tsż, nǎng. / The dead man had been stabbed twice with a dagger. Nèige 'sż-ren shr̀ ràng 'rén ná 'dāudz 'jāle lyǎngsyàdz. / Don't stab yourself with those scissors! Byé ràng 'jyǎndz 'jājau!

Make a stab at (as with a knife) is expressed as above. / He made a stab at him with a knife. Tā ná 'dāudz chùng tā °'bǐhwole (°'jāle) yísyàr.

Make a stab at (try) shr̀. / I'm not sure I can solve this problem, but I'll make a stab at it. Wǒ bùgǎn shwō wǒ néng bǎ jèige 'wèntí 'jyějywéle, 'kěshr wó děi 'shr̀ yísyàdz.

STABLE. (Steady) wěn, 'wěndìng. / She's a pretty stable person. Tā 'jèige rén hén 'wěn. / They haven't had a stable government for centuries. Jíbǎi'nyán le tāmen yě méiyou yíge 'wěndìngde 'jèngfǔ. / The situation on the stock market is pretty stable. Jyāuyì'swǒ 'jyāuyì de 'chíngsying hén 'wěndìng.

A stable mǎpéng, mǎhàu, mǎjywàn. / I can smell the stables. Wǒ 'wénjyan mǎ'jywàn wèr le.

To stable. / The horses will be stabled for the night. 'Wǎnshang déi bǎ 'mǎ shwāndzai mǎ'jywàn lǐtou.

STAIRS. (Leading to a door, outside a building) táijyēr; (leading from one floor to another) lóutī. / Take the stairs to your right. Dzǒu 'yòubyār nèige tái'jyēr.

STAMP. (Step on with the foot) tsǎi; **stamp one's foot** dwò jyǎu. / Stamp on that cigar-ette butt. Bǎ nèige yānjywǎr'tóur 'tsǎile. / Teach that child not to stamp his foot. 'Gàusu nèige 'háidz byé dwò'jyǎu.

(Imprint or impress with a mark) dǎchwōr, gài(tú)jāng; gàiyìn (print). / Please stamp this "Handle with Care." Láu'jyà bǎ jèige "Syǎusyīnchīng'fāng" de 'chwō-dz gei 'dǎshang. / He stamps his name on all his books. Tā bǎ tā 'swóyoude 'shū dōu 'dǎshang tāde 'míngdz le.

(Put on a postage stamp) tyē yóupyàu. / Have you stamped your letter? Nǐde 'syìn nǐ 'tyē you'pyàu le ma? / Give me twenty envelopes stamped, please. Láu'jyà gěi wǒ 'èrshrge °tyē (°dài) yóu'pyàu de syìn'fēngr.

A stamp (instrument that stamps or the mark left by it) chwōdz, 'tújāng, yìn. / Please buy me a rubber stamp. Láu'jyà, géi wǒ 'mǎi yíge syàngpí 'chwōdz lai.

/ Everything that goes out of the office must have his stamp. Tsúng jèr 'náchuchyu de dūngsyi 'dōu déi yǒu tāde 'tújāng.

(Postage) yóupyàu. / I want twenty cents' worth of stamps. Wǒ yàu 'lyǎngmáu chyánde yóu'pyàu. / Give me an air-mail stamp. Géi wǒ yìjāng háng'kūngyóu'pyàu.

Tax stamp yìn'hwā(shwèi'pyàu).

STAND (STOOD). (Rise to one's feet) jànchilai, lìchilai. / The audience stood when they saw the conductor come in. 'Tīngjùng 'kànjyàn jǐ'hwēi 'jìnlai dōu 'jànchilaile.

(Be upright) jàn, lì. / Stand still a minute, will you? Hǎu'hǎurde 'jàn yìhwér 'hǎu ma? / I'm tired of standing here waiting. Wǒ 'jàndzai jèr děng'lèile. / Stand where you were. 'Jàndau nǐ ywán'láide 'dìfangr. / The ladder is standing in the corner. 'Tīdz dzài nèi 'jyǎurshang 'lìje ne.

(Attain a height). / He stands six feet two in his stocking feet. is expressed as Standing and not wearing shoes, he's six feet two. Tā bùchwān 'syé jànje shr 'lyòu-chr̄'èr.

(Set upright) bǎ . . . °lì (°shù). / He stood the box on end. Tā 'bǎ nèige 'syāngdz 'shùchilaile. / Stand your umbrella over there. Bá nǐde 'sǎn 'lìdau nèr.

(Remain). / The old clock has stood on that shelf for years. is expressed as That old clock has been placed on that shelf a good many years. Nèige 'jyòu jūng dzài nèige 'jyàdzshang 'gēle háujǐ'nyán le. / Let the milk stand overnight. is expressed as Put the milk there overnight. Bǎ nyóu'nǎi dzài nèr 'gē yí'yè. / What I said the other day still stands. is expressed as What I said the other day is still effective. Wǒ 'nèityān swǒ'shwō de 'hwà hái yǒu 'syàu. / That statement is wrong, but let it stand. is expressed as That statement is wrong; however, let it be that way. Nèige 'hwà bú'dwèi, déle, jyòu 'nèmmaje ba.

(Endure) shòu, rěn, 'rěnshòu (of people only); jīndejù (of people or things). / I can't stand your friend. Nǐ nèi 'pengyou wǒ 'shòubù'lyǎu. / Will you stop that noise? I can't stand it. Láu'jyà byé 'chǎule, wǒ 'shòubù'lyǎule. / This cloth won't stand much washing. Jèige 'bù jīnbu'jù 'jǐndz 'syǐ. / Can the car stand the punishment it will get on the trip? Jèige 'chē 'dzǒu jèi'tàng jǐnde'jù ma?

(Be). / In this opinion I do not stand alone. is expressed as I am not the only person who expresses this idea. Jèi hwà 'bùshr gwāng wǒ 'yíge rén dzèmma 'shwō. / He stands in danger of losing his job. is expressed as His job may not be secure. Tā nèi 'shr̀ching pà bǎubu'jù. / How much for it as it stands? is expressed as How much do you want for that as it is, not changed? Nèige jyòu 'nàyàngr bú'dùng, yàu 'dwōshau 'chyán? / As things stand now, I'll have to leave. is expressed as With things going as they are now, I'll have to leave. Syàn'dzài 'shr̀ching chéngle 'jèyàngr le wó déi 'dzǒu le. / I stand corrected. Wǒ 'jyēshòu jyōu'jèng.

Stand a chance (have a chance) yǒu 'jīhwèi; (get a chance) 'déjau 'jīhwei. / I'm afraid you don't stand a chance of getting a job here. Wó kǔng'pà nǐ dzài 'jèr 'méiyou 'jīhwèi 'jǎujáu 'shr̀ching. / He entered the contest, but he didn't stand a chance of winning. Tā jyā'rù bǐ'sài láije, kěshr méi'déjau 'jīhwei 'yíng. / He stands a chance of being promoted. Tā yǒu 'shēngshangchyu de 'jīhwei. / He stands a chance of being fired. is expressed as It may happen that he will be fired. Tā pèng'chyǎule jyòu 'syǔ bèi 'tsái.

Stand trial chr̄ gwānsz.

Stand aside 'dwǒkāi. / Stand aside a minute. 'Dwǒkāi yì'hwěr.

Stand back wàng'hòu °'jànjan (°'twèitwei). / Stand back and give her air. Wàng-'hòu 'jànjan, byé 'chǐhuje ta.

Stand by (be near but not participate in something) 'jàndzai yì'byār; yì'byār 'jànje; or expressed as remain aloof with one's hands in one's sleeves syòu'shǒupáng-'gwān. /He stood by, doing nothing while the men fought. Nèisyē 'rén dǎ'jyà de 'shr̄hou tā 'dzài nèr syòu'shǒupáng'gwān.

Stand by (help) bāngmáng. /You know that I'll always stand by you in case of trouble. Nǐ 'jr̄dàu nǐ yǒu shémma 'shr̄ de 'shr̄hou wó 'yǔngwǎn bāng'máng.

Stand by (wait) děng. /Stand by for the latest news bulletin. is expressed as Wait here to listen to the latest news. 'Déngděng tīng dzwèi 'hòude syīn'wén.

Stand by one's word. /You can count on him to stand by his word. is expressed as You can rest easy, that man always means what he says. Nǐ fàng'syīn ba, tā nèige 'rén syàng'lái shr̄ shwō 'hwà swàn 'hwà.

Stand clear of something 'dwǒkāi . . . , lí . . . 'ywán dyǎr. /Stand clear of the sparks. 'Dwǒkāi hwǒ'syīngr 'dyǎr. or Lí hwǒ'syīngr 'ywán dyǎr.

Stand fast jànje bú'dùng. /The others ran away but she stood fast. Byé rén dōu pǎule, 'kěshr̄ tā hái 'jànje méi'dùng.

Stand for (uphold) 'dzànchéng. /That candidate stands for free trade. 'Nèige hòusywǎn'rén dzàn'chéng dz̀'yóu màu'yì.

Stand for (represent) dàibyǎu. /In their code each number stands for a letter. 'Tāmen nèige dyàn'mǎr 'měiyíge shùmu'dzèr dài'byǎu 'yíge dz̀'mǔ.

Stand in with gēn . . . 'dzǒude hěn 'jìn(hu). /Does he stand in with the boss? Tā gēn 'tóur 'dzǒude hěn 'jìn(hu) ma?

Stand out (be noticeable) syányǎn. /Her clothes make her stand out in a crowd. Tāde 'yīshang dzài 'dàtínggwǎng'jùng jr'jyān hěn syán'yǎn.

Stand out of the way see **Stand aside** above. /Stand out of the way. 'Dwǒ kāi 'dàur.

Stand to (surely) jwǔn; (probably) dàgài, yìdwōbàr; it **stands to reason that** ànlǐ. /Now that the race has started, our horse stands to win. Syàn'dzài jèichǎng sài'mǎ yǐjing kāi'shr̄le, 'wǒmen nèi pǐ'mǎ yìdwò'bàr 'yíng. /It stands to reason that she wouldn't do that. An'lǐ tā bú'hwèi 'nèmma 'bàn.

Stand someone **up** (fail to meet). /She stood me up. is expressed as She let me wait in vain. Tā 'ràng wǒ dzài 'nèr 'bái děngle. or as She cheated me; she said she'd come and she didn't. Tā °'pyànle (°'shwànle) wǒ le, 'shwō lái bù'lái.

Stand up to. /Why don't you stand up to your father once in a while? is expressed as Why don't you sometimes discuss the reason with your father? Nǐ wèi-'shémma bù 'yǒushŕhour yě gēn nǐ 'fùchin 'jyǎngjyang 'lǐ. or as Why do you always listen to your father? Nǐ gàn'má 'lǎu tīng nǐ 'fùchinde?

A stand (position) lìchǎng. /You'll have to take a stand either for or against the idea. is expressed as Regarding that idea, whether you approve or oppose it, you must have a stand. Nǐ 'dwèiyú jèige 'yìjyàn shr̄ 'dzànchéng shr̄ fǎndwèi °déi yǒu yíge lì'chǎng (°děi 'jàn yì'byǎr).

(Small table) jwōdz; (place for a small business) tāndz, tār. /The telephone stand is in the hall. Dyànhwà 'jwōr dzài dà'tīngli ne. /There's a newsstand at the corner. Gwai'jyǎur nèr yǒu ge bàu'tār.

Make a stand fángshǒu. /The enemy decided to make a stand outside the city limits. 'Dírén jywé'dìng dzài jèige 'chéngde jyāu'wài fáng'shǒu.

STANDARD. (Norm) 'byāujwǔn. /You can't judge him by ordinary standards. Nǐ bù-néng ná píng'chángde 'byāujwǔn lái 'pàndwàn 'tā. /Who sets the standard of work here? Jèr shr̄ 'shéi 'dìngde 'gūngdzwò 'byāujwǔn na? /The schools have reached a very high standard. Sywé'syàude 'chéngdù dōu hěn 'gāu le. / His work is not up to standard today. 'Jīntyān tāde 'gūngdzwò bùjí'gé. / This leather is below standard. Jèige 'pídz 'chéngshar dī.

Standard of living 'shēnghwó 'byāujwǔn.

Gold standard jīnběnwèi.

Silver standard yínběnwèi.

Standard (established) píngcháng, pǔtūng. / This is the standard size. Jèige dūngsyide dàsyǎn shr hé 'byāujwǎn de.

STAR. (Heavenly body) syīng(sying). / The sky is full of stars tonight. Jyèr 'wǎnshang 'tyānshangde 'syīngsying dōu 'mǎnle. *or* Jyēr 'wǎnshang shr 'mǎntyān 'syīng. / Her dress has white stars on a dark background. Tāde 'yīshang 'dyèr shr 'ànde 'shàngtou yǒu bái 'syīngsying.

(In entertainment or sports) míngsyīng. / There are three stars in that picture. 'Nèijāng dyànyěngr 'pyāndzli yǒu 'sānge míng'syīng.

Star (outstanding) déyìde. / This is my star pupil. 'Jèige shr wǒ déyì de 'sywé-sheng.

To star (mark with a star) hwà 'syīngsying 'jìhàur. / Omit the starred passages. Bǎ hwà 'syīngsying 'jìhàur de nèijǐ'dwàr chyǔ'syāu.

(Play the leading role) dāng 'jújyǎur. / She's starred in every picture she's been in. Tā 'yǎnde měiyíge 'pyāndz dōu shr tā dāng 'jújyǎur.

START. (Begin) kāishr, kāitóur, chǐ tóur; <u>also a verb plus</u> chǐlái. / Has the performance started yet? Byáu'yǎn yǐ'rán kāi'shrle ma? / When will we start taking lessons? Wǒmen 'shémma shŕhou °kāi'shr shàng'kè (°kāi'kè)? / It's starting to rain. 'Syàchí 'yǔ lái le. / The joke started us laughing. <u>is expressed as</u> The joke made us start laughing. Nèige 'syàuhwar jyàu wǒmen 'syàuchǐlaile.

(Set out) chūfā, dzǒu, chyù, dùngshēn, chǐshēn. / When do we start for the country? Wǒmen dàu 'syāngsyà chyu shémma 'shŕhour chǐ'shēn?

(Set going; of a motor) bǎ . . . kāikai; (of a fire) lúng, shēng; (of a rumor or an idea) dzàu; **start a precedent** syān 'chíshr; **start a riot** chíshr. / Start the engine. Bǎ 'jīchi 'kāikai. / Who started the fire? 'Shéi lúngde 'hwǒ? / What started the fire? <u>is expressed as</u> How did the fire start? Hwǒ 'dzěmma 'jáuchǐláide? / Who started this rumor? Shéi 'dzàude jèige 'yáuyán? / I'll start the ball rolling. <u>is expressed as</u> I'll fire the first shot. Wǒ lái 'fàng dìyí'pàu.

A start (beginning) tóur, <u>or expressed verbally</u>; **from start to finish** tsúng'tóur dàu'lyǎur. / This thing has been wrong from the start. Jèi jyàn shr yì kāi'tóur jyòu 'tswò le. / We got an early start. (of work) Wǒmen chǐ'tóur chǐde 'dzǎu. *or* (of a trip) Wǒmen chǐ'shēn chǐde 'dzǎu. / It's important to make a good start. Chǐ'tóur 'chǐde 'hǎu shr tǐng 'yàujǐnde. / He got his start in a small office. Tā °chū'chǐ (°chǐ'chū, °chǐ'tóur) dzài yíge syǎu 'jīgwǎnli dzwò 'shr.

(A lead). / We gave him a start of eight yards. <u>is expressed as</u> We let him have eight yards. Wǒmen sài'pǎu 'ràng tā bā'mǎ.

(Shock). / You gave me quite a start. Nǐ 'syàle wǒ yídà'tyàu. <u>or expressed verbally as</u> She started with surprise. Tā 'syàle yí'tyàu.

STATE. (Situation) chíngsyíng. / I'm in a bad state. Wǒde 'chíngsyíng hwài'tòu le. / Anything is better than the present state of things. 'Dzěmmaje dōu 'bǐ mù'chyánde 'chíngsyíng 'chyáng.

STEADY

(Nation) 'gwójyā; **State Department** Gwówùywàn. / The railroads are owned by the state. Tyě'lù shŕ 'gwójyā 'bànde. / All the states of Europe sent delegates to the convention. Nèige hwèi'yǐ Ōujōu swó'yóude gwó'jyā dōu pàile dài'byǎu le.

(Unit of a nation) shěng (province, used of the Chinese provinces); jōu (one of the states of the United States).

To state shwō. / State your business. Bá 'nǐde 'shŕching 'shwōshwo. / The facts are as stated. Yǐjing shwōgwode 'dōu shŕ 'shŕchíng.

STATEMENT. (Report) bàugàu; (bill) jàngdār; (public bulletin) tūnggàu; (notice sent to an individual) tūngjŕ. / The bank will send you a statement every four months. Yín-'háng měi'sžge ywè gěi ni 'sùng yítsž tūng'jŕ. / Has the store sent a statement of my account? Nèige 'pùdz gěi wo 'sùng jàng'dār láile ma?

(Utterance) hwà. / Have you any statement to make? Nǐ yǒu 'shwō shémma 'hwà yòu 'shwō ma? / Is that statement true? Nèijyù 'hwà kě'kàu ma?

STATION. (Stop) jàn; **train station** chējàn, hwǒchējàn; **bus station** gūng'gùngchìchē-'jàn. / Get off at the next station. 'Syàyíjàn syà 'chē. / Where's the train station? Hwǒchē'jàn dzài 'nǎr? / I'll meet you at the bus station. Gūng'gùngchìchē'jàn 'jyàn.

(Broadcasting unit) dyàntái, wúsyàndyàn'tái. / What stations can you get on your radio? Nǐde wúsyàn'dyàn néng 'shōujau náijǐge dyàn'táide? / This is station Wàn'syáng. **is expressed as** This is Wàn'syáng broadcasting station. Wàn'syáng gwǎng'bwō dyàn'tái.

(Place for research)-chǎng (field); -swǒ (office or building); -chyū (zone). / There's an agricultural experiment station near here. Jèr fù'jìn yǒu yíge 'núngyè shŕyàn'chǎng.

Fire station syāufǎngdwèi.

Police station jǐngchá fēn'jyú, pàichūswǒ, fēnjùswǒ.

To station (assign) pài; (be assigned; one person) jùjá; (be assigned; a group of people) jùtwún, jùfáng. / He's stationed abroad. Tā shŕ 'pài dzài gwó'wài. / The police stationed a man at the door. Pàile yíge jǐng'chá dzài mén'kǒur jàn'gǎng. / Where is your division stationed? Nǐ nèi 'shŕ dzài nǎr jù'fáng?

STAY. (Remain) dāi. / I intend to stay for a week. Wó 'dǎswàn 'dāi yìshīng'chī. / Stay a while. 'Dāi yìhwěr. / Don't stay up late. Byé 'dāi tài 'wǎn le. / They stayed out all night. Tāmen dzài 'wàitou 'dāile yìjěng'yè.

(Live) jù. / Where are you staying? Nǐ 'jùdzài 'nǎr? / I'm staying with friends. Wǒ 'jùdzài 'péngyou jyā.

Stay plus an adjective is expressed by an appropriate stative verb or verbs. / When I fix a thing, it stays fixed. Wǒ 'shōushr 'dūngsyi, 'méi ge 'hwài. / See how long you can stay clean. (to a child) 'Dàu 'chyáuchyau nǐ néng 'gānjing 'dwō-shǎu shŕhou. / He stayed mad for several hours. Tā yí 'chì 'chìle háujǐge jūng-'tóu.

Stay away from . . . lí . . . 'ywǎndyǎr. / Stay away from that place. Lí nèige 'dìfang 'ywándyǎr.

A stay (sojourn) is expressed verbally as live jù. / We had a very pleasant stay at their house. Wǒmen dzài tāmen 'jyā jùde hěn 'tùngkwài.

STEADY. (Firm, not shaky) wěndang, wěn. / This needs a steady hand. Dzwò 'jèige 'shǒu déi 'wěn. / Is the ladder steady enough? 'Tīdz lì'wěndangle ma? / Steady now! 'Wěnje dyǎr! *but* / She has a steady disposition. Tāde 'píchì hén 'hǎu.

943

(Regular) yún (even); cháng (always). /We didn't go fast, but kept up a good steady pace. Wŏmen 'dzŏude bú'kwài, kěshr 'jyăubù dzŏude hěn 'yún. /He's made steady progress. Tā jìn'bùde hěn 'yún. /I'm a steady customer here. Wŏ shr̀ 'jèrde 'chángjŭgu. /He has a steady job now. Syàn'dzài tā 'jăujaule yíge 'chángshr̀.

To steady is expressed as **make steady**. /Steady the ladder so I won't fall. Bă 'tīdz nùng'wěnlou, wŏ byé 'dyàusyalai.

Other expressions in English. /They're going steady. Tāmen lyă 'chéngle. *or* (local Peiping) Tāmen lyă 'paushangle. or expressed as They're always together. Tāmen 'lyă 'lău dzài yí'kwàr.

STEAL (STOLE, STOLEN). (Take dishonestly) tōu. /He'd steal candy from a baby. Jyŏushr syău'hárde 'táng tā yě hwèi 'tōude. /He stole my book. Tā 'tōule wŏde 'shū le. /My car has been stolen. Wŏde 'chē jyàu 'rén gěi tōu'dzŏule. /They stole a large amount from the family treasury. 'Tāmen tsúng jàng'fángrli 'tōule yí'dàbĭ 'chyán. /They stole that hit song from an old folk song. Nèige 'gēer shr̀ tsúng 'jyòu gēerli 'tōuchūláide.

(Go stealthily) tōutōurde, 'tōutoumwō'mwōde plus a verb of motion. /They stole away through the woods. Tāmen tōu'tōurde dă shù'líndz 'păule. /The children stole into the room on tiptoe. 'Háidzmen chyànje 'jyăur 'tōutoumwō'mwōde dàu 'wūli 'chyù le.

Steal the show. /The new actress stole the show. Nèichū 'syì gěi nèige syīn nyŭ'syìdz 'chàngle. or expressed as The new actress suppressed all the other people in the play. Nèichū 'syì nèige 'syīn kwūnjywé bă byérén 'dōu gěi 'yāsyàchyùle.

Stolen goods dzānghwò, dzāng.

STEAM. (Vapor, gas; especially as a source of power) chì; (vapor) jēngchì; (hot vapor) rèchì; **steam heat** nwănchì, chìlúdz; **steam radiator** chì gwăndz, nwănchì gwăndz, nwănchì lúdz; **steam engine** chìjī; **steam roller** chìnyăndz; **steamship** chìchwán. /Melt the glue with steam. Bă nèi 'jyāu gēde rè'chìli 'hwàhwa. /Does it run by steam or electricity? Nèige 'kāichilai shr̀ yùng 'chì háishr̀ yùng 'dyàn a. /Is there steam heat in their house? 'Tāmende 'fángdzli yóu 'nwănchì ma?

Get up steam (of a machine) shàngjyèr; (or people) shàngjyèr, chĭjìn, jyājĭn. /The machine is getting up steam. 'Jīchi yĭjing shàng'jyèrle. /We'll have to get up steam and finish this in a hurry. Wŏmen děi °shàng dyăr 'jyèr (°'chí dyăr 'jĭn, °jyā dyar 'jĭn), 'kwài dyár bă 'jèi nùng'wánle.

To steam (give off steam) màuchì, fàngchì, màu rèchì. /The water's steaming. Shwěi 'màu rè'chyèr le. /Your car is steaming. Nĭde 'chē jr̀ màu'chì.

(Cook by steaming) jēng. /Steam the rice half an hour. Bă 'fàng 'jēng 'bàn-dyăn jūng.

(Move by steam) kāi. /He watched the ship steam out of the harbor. Tā 'kànje nèityáu 'chwán 'kāichu 'găng chyule.

Steam open syūsyu. /He steamed open the letter. Tā 'bă nèifēng 'syìn gēde 'kāishwěishang 'syūsyu jyou 'dăkāile.

Get (*or* Be) **steamed up** (be covered with steam) hāchì; (get excited) chĭjìn, 'syīngfèn. /The windows are steamed up. 'Chwānghushang 'dōu shr̀ hā'chì. /The mirror's getting steamed up. 'Jìngdzshang nùngle hău'syē hā'chì. /He got all steamed up about the idea. Tā dwèiyu nèige 'yìjyàn hén °chĭ'jìn (°'syīngfèn).

STEEL. gāng, gāng tyě. /The bridge is all steel. Jèige 'chyáu 'chywán shr̀ 'gāng dzwòde. /The bullet bounded off his steel helmet. Dž'dàn tsúng tā gāng'kwēishang

944

'bḕngsyàchyùle. / He worked for a while in a steel mill. Tā dzài gāng tyĕgūng'chǎngli 'dzwòle yíjèndz 'shr̀.

STEEP. (Of a slope) dǒu. / That slope is steeper than it looks. Nèige 'pwōr shr̀'jì bǐ 'kànje 'dǒu.

(Of a price) gwèi, gāu. / That's a pretty steep price for that house. Nèiswǒ 'fángdzde 'jyàr kĕ 'jēn gòu 'gwèide.

To steep mēn, pàu. / Let the tea steep a little longer. 'Chá dwō °'mēn (°pàu) yìhwěr.

STEP. (Movement of the foot) bù; (more formal, used especially of dancing and marching) bùdz. / He took one step forward. Tā wàng 'chyán 'màile yí'bù. / I don't know the steps of that dance. Wǒ 'búhwèi 'nèijǔng tyàu'wǔ de 'bùdz.

(Person's way of walking) dzǒu'dàur de yàngr (appearance); jyăubùshēngr (sound). / I thought I heard steps. Wǒ 'jywéje wǒ 'tīngjyàn jyăubù'shēngr le. / I know who it is; I can recognize his step. (if by watching him walk) Wǒ kàn dzǒu'dàur de yàngr jyòu 'jr̄dau shr̀ 'shéi. _or_ (if by listening to him walk) Wǒ 'tīng jyăubù- 'shēngr jyòu 'jr̄dau shr̀ 'shéi.

(Unit of action) bù, 'bùdzòu. / This is only the first step in the process. 'Jèige 'búgwò shr̀ dì'yíbù 'shǒusyù. / This is a great step forward. 'Jèige shr̀ yíge hĕn 'dàde jìn'bù.

(On a stairway) yídèngr °tái'jyēr (°lóu'tī); **steps** táijyēr _or_ (a flight of stairs leading from one floor to another) lóutī. / I stopped and sat on the top step. Wǒ 'jànjùle, dzwòdzài dzwèi 'gāude nèidèng lóu'tīshang le. / He ran up the steps to the porch. Tā 'pǎushang tái'jyēr dàu 'lángdzshang chyù le.

Step by step 'yíbùyí'bùde, 'yìdyăryì'dyărde. / We built up our business step by step. Wǒmende 'shr̀yè shr̀ 'yìdyăryì'dyărde 'dzwòchǐláide.

In (_or_ **Out**) **of step** 'jyăubù, bùdz. / Keep in step with me. Bá 'jyăubù'gēn wo 'dzǒuyí'yàngle. / He's out of step. Tā 'jyăubù bú'dwèi. / He's out of step with the times. Tā lwò'wǔle.

Take steps syăngfár. / I'll have to take steps to stop the gossip. Wó déi syăng- 'fár 'byé ràng tāmen shwō syán'hwà le. / If things don't improve, we'll have to take steps. Yàushr 'shr̀ching hái 'méiyou jìn'bù, wǒmen déi syăng'fár 'bànban.

Watch one's step. / Watch your step! is expressed as Be careful! Lyóu'shén! or as Be careful of your footing! 'Lyóushén jyáu 'dǐsyà! or as Pay attention! Jù- 'yì!

To step (go) dzǒu; in some combinations expressed as stand jàn. / I stepped in a puddle. Wó 'dzǒu dàu shwěi'kēngrli le. / Step lively now! 'Kwài dzǒu. / Step aside. Wàng páng'byār 'jànjan. / Step back a little. Wàng hòu °'jàn dyǎr (°'twèi-twei).

(Put the foot down on) tsǎi. / Don't step on the flowers. Byé 'tsǎilou 'hwār.

(Reach out with the foot) mài; **step over** something 'màigwò; **step up on** something 'màishàng, **step down from** something 'màisyà. / Step over the fence. 'Màigwò nèige 'líba chyù. / He just stepped off the train. Tā 'gāng 'màisyà 'chē lái.

Step in (for a visit). / I just stepped in for a moment. is expressed as I just came to see you a moment; then I must go. Wǒ 'jyòushr lái 'kànkan 'nǐmen yì- 'hwěr déi 'dzǒu.

Step in (intervene) 'chūlai °'lyáu (°'tyáuting, °'shwōhe). / He stepped in to stop the fight. Tā 'chūlai 'gěi tāmen 'shwōhe'shwōhe 'búràng tāmen 'dǎ le.

Step up (move forward) wàng 'chyán dzǒu; (increase) dzēngjyā. / Step right up for your tickets. Wàng 'chyán dzǒu ná 'pyàu chyù. / Try to step up production. Jīn-lyàngr dzēngjyā shēng'chǎn.

STICK (STUCK). (Thrust into) chā; (hook through something) byé; (slip, tuck in) sāi. / Stick this pin in your lapel. Bǎ jèige byé'jēn 'byédzai ní 'lǐngdzshang. / She stuck a flower in her hair. Tā dzài 'toufashang 'chāle yìdwǒ 'hwār. / Someone stuck a knife in the wall. Yǒu 'rén dzài 'chyángshang 'chāle yìbǎ 'dāu. / He stuck the paper in his pocket. Tā bá 'jǐr 'sāi dzai tā 'dǒurli le. but / Don't stick your nose into other people's business. is expressed as Don't mind other people's affairs. Byé gwǎn 'byérénde syán 'shr̀.

(Prick) jā. / That pin is sticking me. Nèige 'jēn 'jāle wǒ le. / He stuck her with a pin. Tā ná 'jēn 'jā ta láije.

(Fasten with glue) bǎ . . . jān; (for thin things like paper) bǎ . . . tyē. / Stick the stamp on the envelope. Bǎ yóu'pyàu 'tyēdzai syìn'fēngrshang. / Stick these pictures in your album. Bǎ jèisyē syàng'pyār 'tyēdzai nǐde syàngpyār'bērshang. / Stick it together with glue. Ná 'jyāu 'jānshang.

(Adhere) jān; (for thin things like paper) tyē. / The paper sticks to my fingers. Jèige 'jǐr jān'shǒu. / There's a piece of gum stuck on my shoe. Yíkwài 'kǒusyāng-'táng 'jāndzai wǒ 'syéshang le. / This label won't stick. Jèige 'fēngtyáu tyēbú'shàng le. / I tried to tear off the label but it stuck. Wǒ 'dǎswàn bǎ nèige 'fēngtyáu 'jyē-syàlai 'kěshr 'jānjùle.

(Be immovable, blocked in some way) chyáshangle, 'chyájùle, or indirect expressions. / This drawer sticks. Jèige 'chōuti 'chyáshangle. or expressed as This drawer can't be pulled open. Jèige 'chōuti °lābu'kāi le (°lābu'dùng le). or as This drawer can't be moved by pushing. Jèige 'chōuti twēibu'dùng le. / Our car is stuck in the mud. is expressed as Our car is sunk in the mud. Wǒmen 'chē °'syàndzai (°'sywàndzai) 'nílí le.

(Place) gē, fàng. / They stuck a "For Rent" sign in the window. Tāmen dzài 'chwānghu ner 'fàngle yìjāng "Tsž'fángjāu'dzū" de 'tyáur. / Stick it over there. 'Syān gēdzài 'nèibyār ba.

(Not change) bùgǎi; also other expressions for working, talking, etc. / Stick to the subject. is expressed as Don't get off the subject. Byé lí 'tí. / Stick to the original. 'Byé gǎi ywán'láide 'yàngr. / He stuck to his story. Tā yì'jr̀de bùgǎi 'dzwèi. / Pick a good brand and then stick to it. Jǎu yíge 'hǎude jyou byé 'gǎi le.

(Remain). / His name stuck in my mind. is expressed as His name made me remember it. Tāde 'míngdz ràng wǒ 'jìdzai 'syīnli le.

Stick it out rěn, rěnnài. / Try to stick it out a little longer. Syǎng'fár dwō 'rěn yì'hwěr. / He stuck it out to the bitter end. Nèige 'shr̀ching tā rěn'nàije dzwò-'wánle.

Stick something out (or up) chū; (especially of an arm, leg, etc.) shēn, jr̀; stick out or stick up (visibly) lòu, lòuchúlai. / He stuck his feet out into the aisle. Tā bá 'jyǎu 'shēndau dzǒu'dàushang le. / Your shirt-tail is sticking out. Nǐ chèn-shān 'hòutou jr̀chulaile. / Watch out for that pipe sticking up over there. Lyóu'shén 'nèibyār 'jr̀chulai de nèige 'gwǎndz.

Stick up for (be partial to) syàng; (help) bāng. / He always sticks up for you. Tā 'lǎu shr̀ 'syàngje nǐ.

Be stuck (of a person). / He's stuck on that problem. is expressed as He really has no rules to go by on that problem. Nèige 'wèntí tā 'jyǎnjr̀ shr̀ méi'jé. / The train broke down and we were stuck there for hours. is expressed as The train broke down and we were stranded there for hours. Hwǒ'chē 'hwài le wǒmen dzài nèr 'dwǔnle háujǐge jūng'tou.

A **stick** (walking stick) shǒujàng, gwǎigwèr, gwǎijàng; (trimmed branch, smooth stick or stake) gwùndz, gwèr; (twig, branch) shùjér. / He knocked on the door with his stick. Tā 'yùng tāde shǒu'jàng chyāu 'mén láije. / I hit him with a stick. Wǒ ná 'gwùndz 'dǎ tā láije. / Pick up the sticks in the yard. Bǎ 'ywàndzlide shù'jér 'jyánchǐlai.

A **stick of** is expressed with various measures including tyáu and gēr; a **stick of** gum yí'kwài kǒusyāng'táng.

STICKY. nyán. / My fingers are sticky from the honey. Wǒ shǒu'jŕtou nùngshang 'mì le, hěn 'nyán.

(Hot and humid) nyán, 'mēnrè. / What a sticky day! Hǎu 'nyánde tyār! or Tyār 'mēnrè!

STIFF. (Hard to bend) yǐng. / How stiff shall I starch your collars? Nǐde 'lǐngdz yàu 'jyāng 'dwó yǐng a? / Use a stiff brush. Yùng yìbǎ 'yǐng 'shwādz. / The book is bound in stiff paper. Nèiběr 'shū dǐngle ge 'yǐng pyér.

(Lame, not supple) swān; **have a stiff neck** 'làule 'jěn le. / I'm stiff from that exercise yesterday. Dzwóer wǒ 'bèngde hwún'shēn fā'swān.

(Thick, viscous) chóu; (too thick to whip) chóude 'dǎ bú'dùngle. / Beat it until it's stiff. Bǎ nèige 'dǎde 'chóude dǎbú'dùng lou. but / Beat the egg whites until stiff. is expressed as Beat up the egg whites. Bǎ jīdàn'chīngr 'dáchǐlai.

(Formal) jyāng, bǎn, běngje. / Don't be so stiff. Byé 'nèmma 'běngje.

Special expressions in English. / Is it a stiff examination? is expressed as Is the examination difficult? Nèige 'kǎude 'nán ma? / He charges stiff fees. is expressed as The prices he wants are too high. Tā 'yàu de 'jyàr tài °'dà (°'gāu, °'dwō). / A good stiff breeze sprang up. Yíjèn syāu lyáng'fēngr 'gwāde tíng 'hǎu. / Please pour me a stiff drink. is expressed as Please give me a strong drink. Láu-jyà géi wǒ 'dàu yìbēi 'chùng dyárde 'jyǒu.

STILL. (Motionless) jù, wēn; or expressed as not move búdùng. / Hold still a minute. Byé 'dùng. / Keep your feet still. Ní 'jyǎu byé 'dùng. / Stand still. 'Jànje byé 'dùng. or Jàn'jù lou. or Jàn'wēn lou. / She sat perfectly still. Tā 'dzwò nèr yì-'dyǎr dōu bú'dùng.

(Quiet) 'ānjìng. / Be still. 'Anjìng dyǎr. or expressed as Don't make noise. Byé 'chǎu. or as Don't speak. Byé 'yányu le. / The whole house was still. Jěng-'gèrde 'fángdzli hěn 'ānjìng. or expressed as Throughout the house there wasn't a sound. Jěng'gèrde 'fángdzli yìdyǎr 'shēngr dōu méi'yǒu. / Keep still about this. is expressed as Don't mention this. Jeige byé gēn rén tí. or as Don't say anything about this. 'Jèige byé 'shwōchuchyu. or as Don't talk about this. 'Dwèiyú 'jèige byé 'yányu tsái 'hǎu.

(Calm and quiet; of water) 'píngjìng. / The lake is still today. 'Jyēr húli hěn 'píngjìng. but / The air is very still. is expressed as There's not a bit of wind. Yìdyǎr 'fēng dōu méi'yǒu. or as There is no wind and it is very silent. Yǒu méi 'fēng yòu 'ānjìng.

(As yet, now as before) hái, hwán, 'réngjyǒu. / I am still waiting to hear from him. Wǒ 'hái dzài 'děngje 'tīng tāde 'syāusyi ne. / He's still the same. Tā 'hái shŕ nà 'yàngr. / He built it while his wife was still alive. Tā 'gài 'nèige de 'shŕ-hour tā 'tàitai hái 'hwóje ne. / Eat it while it's still hot. Chènje hái 'rèje ne, 'chŕ ba. or 'Chŕ ba, chèn 'rèr.

(Even) (hái . . .) dzài; with comparatives using gèng, also (hái . . .) gèng.

/He asked for still more books. Tā 'hái yàu dzài 'dwō jáu dyǎr 'shū. /I want to go still further up the mountain. Nèige 'shān wǒ yàu 'dzài shàng 'gāu dyǎr. *or* Nèige 'shān wǒ yàu 'gèng shàng 'gāu dyǎr.

Even so ... still jyòushr 'jèyàng ... hái; although ... still 'swéirán ... kěshr ... hái. /Even so I still think you did the right thing. Jyòushr 'jèyàng, wǒ 'hái yǐwéi nǐ dzwò'dwèile. /Although I don't like him, still I have to admit he's clever. 'Swéirán wǒ bù'syǐhwan ta, kěshr wǒ 'hái shwō tā 'tsūngming.

STOCK. (Supply; stored goods) tswúnhwò; (goods) dǐhwò, hwò. /I'll look through my stock and see if I have it. Wǒ yàu 'kànkan wǒde tswún'hwòli yǒu nèige méiyǒu. *but* /I want to lay in a stock of soap. is expressed as I want to store a supply of soap. Wǒ yàu 'tswún yìpǐ 'yídz.

(Subscribed capital) gǔpyàu. /I have several shares of their stock. Wó yǒu jí'gǔr tāmende gǔ'pyàn.

(Livestock) shēngkou. /He keeps all kinds of stock on his farm. Tā dzài tāde 'dìli yǎngle 'gèshr'gèyàngrde 'shēngkou.

(Breed) jǔngr. /Are these animals of healthy stock? 'Jèisyē 'shēngkoude 'jungr 'hǎu ma?

In stock. /What do you have in stock? is expressed as What goods do you have stored? Nǐ 'tswúnde yǒu 'shémma 'hwò?

Out of stock. /That size glove is out of stock. is expressed as That size glove is not among the goods. Nèi'hàurde shǒu'tàur °méi'hwòle (or meaning sold out °mài-'wánle).

Put stock in. /I don't put much stock in that reporter's stories. is expressed as I don't believe much of that reporter's news. Wǒ búdà 'syìn nèige syīnwénjì'jěde 'syāusyi.

Take stock. /Next week we're taking stock. is expressed as Next week we're going to check the whole stock. Syàsyīng'chī wǒmen yàu 'chīngching hwò'dǐdz le. /Why don't you stop and take stock of the situation? is expressed as Why don't you stop and investigate the situation? Nǐ wèi'shémma bùtíngsyàlai °'dyàucha jèige 'chíngsying ne? or as ... inspect the situation? ... °'kǎuchá jèige 'chíngsying ne? or as ... study the situation? ... °'yánjyou jèige 'chíngsying ne?

Stock market jyāuyìswǒ; **play the stock market** dzwò dáu'bǎ de 'shēngyì or expressed as buy and sell on margin mǎi'kūng mài'kūngr.

To stock tswún. /Are you stocked up for the winter? 'Jīnnyán 'dūngtyande 'hwò nǐ 'tswúnle ma? /The hotel is well stocked with linen. Jèige lyú'gwǎn 'tswúnle bù'shǎude chwáng'dāndz. /We don't stock that brand. Wǒmen bù'tswún nèijǔng 'páidzde.

STOCKING. (Either short or long stockings) wàdz; (long stockings) 'chángtūngr'wàdz, gāu'yàur'wàdz. /I want three pairs of stockings, size nine and a half. Wǒ yàu 'sān-shwāng 'jyǒuhwàur'bànde 'chángtūngr'wàdz.

In one's stocking feet (without shoes) 'gwāngje wà'dyěr. /He walks around the house in his stocking feet. Tā 'gwāngje wà'dyěr dzài 'fángdzli dzǒulái dzǒu'chyù.

STOMACH. wèi; (abdomen) dùdz; (upper and front part of the body) syīnkǒu. /Rich foods don't set well on my stomach. 'Yóunìde 'dūngsyi wǒ 'chrle °'dùdzli bùhǎu-'shòu (°wèili bùhǎu'gwò). /I have a pain in my stomach. (if in the lower part) Wǒ 'dùdz 'téng. *or* Wǒ °'wèi (°'wèichì) 'téng. *or* (if in the upper part) Wǒ syīn'kǒu 'téng. /Hit him in the stomach. 'Dǎde tā syīn'kǒushang le.

Empty stomach kùngdùr, kūngje wèi. / Don't exercise on an empty stomach. Kùngje 'dùr de 'shŕhour byé 'yùndùng.

To stomach. / I can't stomach such rich food. Wǒ bùnéng 'chŕ dzèmma 'yóunìde 'dūngsyi. / He couldn't stomach the insult. Nèijùngde 'wūrǔ tā shòubù'lyǎu. / I can't stomach going to that party. Wǒ °méi 'wèikou (°bù'syǎng) 'shàng nèige 'yànhwei chyù.

STONE. shŕtou; (pebble) shŕtoudzěr. / The house is built entirely of stone. Jèige 'fángdz jěng'gèrde shŕ 'shŕtou 'gàide. / The stones of the wall are cool. 'Chyángshangde 'shŕtou lyángbu'jyērde. / It's hard walking on these stones. Dzài jèisyē 'shŕtoushang hěn bùhǎu 'dzǒu. / Who threw that stone? Nèige shŕtou'dzěr shŕ 'shéi 'rēngde? / Can you lift that stone? Nǐ néng 'jyúchǐ nèikwài 'shŕtou lái ma? / The kitchen has a stone floor. Chú'fángde dì'bǎn shŕ 'shŕtoude. / We decided to put three stone benches in the garden. Wǒmen jywé'dìng dzài hwā'ywárli gē 'sānge 'shrtou 'dèngdz.

(Grave stone, monument) shŕbēi, jìnyànbēi. / We had a beautiful stone put on his grave. Wǒmen dzài tāde 'fénshang 'lìle yíkwài hén hǎu'kànde shŕ'bēi.

(Gem) bǎushŕ, shŕtour. / Have you any precious stones to declare? Ní yǒu 'shémma bǎu'shŕ děi bǎu'shwèi ma?

(Pit) húr, héer. / I was eating cherries and throwing the stones out the window. Wǒ chŕje 'yīngtau bǎ 'húr jyòu 'rēngde chwānghu 'wàitou chyùle.

A stone's throw. / He lives just a stone's throw from us. is expressed as He lives the distance of an arrow from us. Tā 'jùde dìfangr lí 'wǒmen jèr yě 'jyòushŕ yí'jyàn ywǎn.

Stone-broke. / I am stone-broke. is expressed as I haven't a single cent. Wǒ 'chyúngde yífen chyán yě 'méiyǒule.

Stone-deaf jěng'gèrde 'lúngle.

Stone-blind jěng'gèrde syā le.

STOP. (Bring to a halt) °ràng (°bǎ) . . . °jànju (°tíng); (stop a vehicle) 'dǎjù; (stop someone or something from doing something by putting up a barrier, or by using persuasion) lán, dǎng, 'lánjùle, 'dǎngjùle. / We were stopped by the police. Syún'jǐng °ràng 'wǒmen 'jànjùle (°bǎ wǒmen 'lánjùle). / Stop the car at the next crossing. Bǎ chē tíng dzài 'syà yíge 'shŕdz̀lù'kǒur bǎ. / He was trying to go out, but I stopped him. Tā syǎng 'chūchyù wǒ 'bǎ ta °'lánjùle (°'dǎngjùle). or expressed as He wanted to go out but I wouldn't let him go. Tā syǎng 'chūchyù kěshŕ wǒ méi'jyàu ta 'chūchyù. / If anyone tries to stop you, let me know. 'Yàushr yǒu 'ren 'lan ni a, gàusu wo.

(Halt) tíng, jànju; (of vehicles especially, and sometimes of people walking or working) 'dǎjù. / He stopped short and turned around. Tā nèmma yī 'tíng jyòu 'jwāngwochyùle. / This car will stop on a dime. is expressed as The brakes on this car are very good; it stops in an instant. Jèige 'chē 'já hěn 'líng, yí'syàr jyòu 'jànju. or as The brakes on this car are very good; you say stop and it stops. Jèige 'chē 'já hěn 'líng, 'shwō dǎjù jyòu néng 'dǎjù. / When do we stop for lunch? (if you're either working or driving) Wǒmen 'shémma shŕhour 'dǎjù hǎu chŕ 'fàn chyù? / The passers-by stopped to look. Nèige gwò'lù de 'rén 'jànjule 'kànle yikàn. / My watch just stopped. Wó 'byǎu 'gāng 'tíngle. or expressed as My watch has stopped going. Wó 'byǎu gāng bù'dzǒule.

(Prevent) lán (see first paragraph above), bùràng; (stop pain, bleeding, etc.) jŕ. / Can't you stop him from talking that way? Ní 'kéyi 'lánlan tā byé 'ràng ta nèmma 'shwō ma? / You can't stop me from thinking about it. Nǐ 'méifar bùràng wo 'syǎng nèige 'shŕching. or Wo 'syǎng nèige 'shŕ nǔ lánbù'lyǎu. / This medicine ought to stop the pain. Jèige 'yàu yí'dìng jŕ'téng. / Stop her from hitting him. Bǎ nèige 'nyǔde 'lánjù, byé ràng tā 'dǎ ta.

(Cease) bù . . . le; (when asking someone to stop something) byé (don't). /I've stopped worrying about it. 'Nèijyàn 'shř wó yě bùjāu'jíle. /I stopped having headaches. Wǒ 'dzài méi tóu'ténggwo. /When do you stop work? Nǐ 'shémma shŕhour jyòu búdzwò 'shŕle? /Has it stopped raining? Yǔ bú'syàle ma? /He stopped in the middle of a sentence. Tā 'shwōle 'bànjyù hwà jyòu bù'shwōle. /Stop reading a minute. Syān 'byé nyàn ne. *or* 'Děngdengr 'dzài nyàn. *but* /Stop it! 'Déle ba!

(Stay) jù. /We stopped at a farmhouse overnight. Wǒmen dzài yíge 'núngrén jyāli 'jùle yíyè.

Stop off 'tíng °yitíng (°yihwěr, °yisyàr), 'jàn °yijàn (°yihwěr, °yisyàr). /Let's stop off at the beach. Dzámen dzài hǎi'byārshang 'tíng yísyàr.

Stop over is expressed as stay a couple of days 'jù lyǎngtyān.

Stop up dǔ, tyán. /This hole should be stopped up. Jèige 'kūlung déi 'dǔshang. *or* Jèi 'kēngr dèi 'tyánshang. /My nose is stopped up. Wǒde 'bídz 'dǔjùle.

A stop (stopping place) jàn. /Get off the bus at the next stop. 'Syàyíjàn syà 'chē.

(Act of stopping) is expressed verbally as in the second paragraph. /We made several stops before we got here. Wǒmen 'dàu jèr lái dzài 'dàurshang 'jànjule hǎujǐ'tsż.

Bring to a stop (of a vehicle) bǎ . . . 'dǎjù. /He brought the train to a full stop. Tā bǎ 'chē 'dǎjùle.

STORE. (Shop) dyàn, pùdz, yángháng (*see* **SHOP**). /I know a store where you can buy that. Wǒ 'jřdàu yǒu yíge 'pùdz nǐ néng 'mǎijau 'nèige. /Run down to the grocery store for me. Tì wo 'pǎu yítàng yóuyán'dyàn.

(Storage) usually expressed verbally as tswún. /We have a big store of supplies right now. Syàn'dzài wǒmen 'tswúnle bù'shǎude 'dūngsyi. /We've canned some vegetables to have in store for the winter. Wǒmen bǎ 'tsài 'jwāngle dyǎr 'gwàntou 'tswúnchilai wèi 'dūngtyan chř.

In store for (in the future). /I wonder what's in store for us? is expressed as I don't know what the future will be like for us. Wǒ bùjř'dàu wǒmen 'jyānglái dzěmma 'yàng.

To store (lay away) tswún, shōu, fàng, gē (put). /Where shall I store the potatoes? Wó bǎ jèisyē tǔ'dòur °tswún (°shōu, °fàng, °ge) 'nǎr?

STORM. bàufēngyǔ, dà'fēngdà'yǔ; (snowstorm) bàufēngsywě, dà'fēngdà'sywě. /Do you remember that storm we had last summer? Nǐ hái 'jìde 'chyùnyán wǒmen 'gǎnshàng de nèichǎng bàufēng'yǔ ma? /There was a foot of snow after the storm yesterday. Dzwóer nèi'chǎng dà'fēngdà'sywe yǐ'hòu 'sywé yǒu 'yìchř 'shēn.

Take by storm. /We took the enemy by storm. is expressed as We gave the enemy a blow when he wasn't watching. Wǒmen dzài 'dírén méilyóu'shén de shŕ-hour gěi ta 'láile yísyàdz.

To storm (attack) 'gūngjī. /We stormed the enemy positions. Wǒmen 'gūngjī 'dírénde 'jènde.

STORY. (Narrative) shŕching. /Do you know the story of his life? Nǐ 'jřdau tā nèiyí-'bèidzde 'shŕching ma? /The whole story is in the paper. Nèijyàn 'shŕching jěng-'gèrde jīng'gwò dōu shàngle 'bàu le.

(Short tale) dwǎnpyān syǎushwōr. /She wrote a story for the school magazine. Tā gěi sywé'syàude 'kānwù 'syěle yìpyān dwǎnpyān syǎu'shwōr.

(Joke) syàuhwar. /Know any new stories? 'Jr̄dàu shémma syĭn 'syàuhwàr ma?

(Account) hwà, shwō de hwà, shwōde. / Their stories don't agree. Tāmende 'hwà bùyí'yàng. / That's my story, and I'll stick to it. 'Nà shr̄ wǒ 'shwōde, wǒ yúng'ywǎn nèmma 'shwō. /It's a plausible story. Nèige 'hwà hěn hé'lǐ. / The story goes that he really doesn't know her. is expressed as They say that he really doesn't know her. Tāmen shwō tā 'shr̄dzài 'bìng bù'rènshr nèige 'nyǔde. / So the story goes. is expressed as So they say. 'Tāmen dzèmma 'shwōde. / It'll be another story tomorrow. is expressed as Tomorrow it'll be another way. 'Míngrge jyòu 'lǐngyíge 'yàngrle.

(Floor) lóu with measure tséng. / She lives on the second story. Tā 'jùdzài 'èrtséng'lóu. /It's a four-story building. 'Nèige shr̄ yíge 'sz̀tsénglóude lóu'fáng.

STOVE. lúdz, dzàu. / Put the beans on the stove. Bǎ 'dòur gēde 'lúdzshang. / We bought a new electric stove. Wǒmen 'mǎile yíge 'syĭn dyàn'lúdz.

STRAIGHT. jr̄, jr̄lyou; (in a straight course) yìjr̄. / We need a good straight stick. Wǒmen yàu yí'gēr 'jr̄ gwèr. / Draw a straight line through it. 'Hwà yìtyáu 'jr̄ syàn 'jĭnggwò nèige. / The road is straight for five miles on this side of the bridge. is expressed as On this side of the bridge the road is straight as a pen for five miles. Chyáu 'jèibyār yǒu 'wúlǐ cháng 'bǐjr̄de dà'dàu. / Hold your arm out straight. Bǎ nǐde 'gēbei shēn'jr̄lou. / Look straight down. 'Jr̄je wàngsyà 'kàn. / Stand up straight. Jàn'jr̄lou. /Go straight ahead. Yǐ'jr̄ dzǒu. /Go straight across the square. °'Jr̄je (°Yǐ'jr̄de) wàngchyán 'dzǒu, 'chwāngwò nèige 'chǎngdz chyù. / He walked straight into the telephone pole. Tā yǐ'jr̄de 'dzǒude dyànsyàn'gǎndzshàng le.

(Directly) yǐjr̄de, jr̄jyēde. /Go straight home. Yǐ'jr̄de hwéi'jyā a. / Come straight over after the show. Kànwán 'syì jr̄'jyēde shàng 'jèr lái a.

(Properly) jèng (at right angles to something; 'jèngdàng, dwèi (right, correct). /Is my hat on straight? Wǒde 'màudz dài'jèngle ma? / He can't think straight, much less talk straight. Tā 'syǎngde bú'jèngdang, shwō de 'hwà 'gèng bú'jèngdang.

(Honest) 'chéngshr̄, 'chéngkěn. / He's always been straight with me. Tā 'dwèi wo 'lǎu shr̄ 'nèmma 'chéngkěn.

(Undiluted). / He drank his whiskey straight. is expressed as He drank his whiskey with nothing added to it. Tā 'hē wēishr̄'jì jyou shémma yě méi'chān.

(At a stretch without a break) yísyàr, yìjr̄de, yíchyèr, yíkǒu chyèr. / We worked for fifteen hours straight. Wǒmen yì'jr̄de 'dzwòle shr̄'wǔge jūng'tóu.

A straight face. /I told it with a straight face. Wǒ 'běngje 'lyǎn shwōde.

Get something **straight** nùng °chĭngchu (°míngbai), kàn míngbai, and similar resultative compounds. / Try to get the story straight. Bǎ 'jèige 'shr̄ching kàn-'míngbailou. /Be sure to get your facts straight before you put them into the report. Bǎ 'jēn'syàng nùng °'chĭngchule (°'míngbaile) dzài syě bàu'gàu.

STRANGE. (Unfamiliar) shēng. /It's good to see you among all these strange faces. Dzài jèisyē 'shēngrén lǐtou 'kànjyàn nǐ jēn bú'tswò. /All this is strange to me. Wǒ 'jywéde 'jèige dōu hěn 'shēng.

(Peculiar) gwài, 'chígwài; tèbyé (special, unusual). / There is something strange about this house. Jèige 'fángdz yǒu dyàr tè'byé. / That's a strange thing to say. 'Nèmma shwō 'hwà hěn'chígwài. / He's a strange character. 'Tā nèige rén jēn 'gwài. /It's strange, but true. Nèige hěn tè'byé, 'kěshr bù'jyǎ. /It feels strange to be doing this kind of work. Dzwò 'jèijǔng 'shr̄ching jywéde hěn 'gwài. / Strange to say, I didn't notice it. 'Shwōchǐlai tǐng 'gwài, wǒ méijù'yì.

STRANGER. (Unknown person) 'shēngrén. / I had dinner with a total stranger. Wǒ gēn yíge 'shēngrén dzai yíkwàr chār 'fàn laije.

    Be a stranger to someone or someplace bùshú, búrènshr. / He is a complete stranger to me. Wǒ gēn tā bù'shú. *or* Bú'rènshr tā. / I am a stranger to this place myself. 'Jèr wó yě bù'shú. *or* Jèiyidài 'dìfang wó yě bú'rènshr (lù).

    Be a stranger to something busyígwàn. / He is a stranger to this kind of life. Jèijǔng shēnghwo tā bu'syigwàn.

STREET. jyē, dàjyē, mǎlù, lù; (small street or alley) hútùngr; (lane) syàng. / Be careful when you cross the street. Gwò 'jyē de 'shŕhour lyóu dyǎr 'shén. / What street do I get off at? Wǒ dzài 'nèityáu jyē 'syàlai? / I live at 47 East Chang-an Street. Wǒ 'jùdzài 'Dūngcháng-ān'jyē 'sżshŕ'chíhòu. / The children shouldn't play in the street. 'Háidzmen yí'dìng 'bùnéng dzài 'jyēshang wár. / I ran into him on the street the other day. Wǒ nèityān dzài 'jyēshang 'pèngjyàn 'tā le.

    Dead-end street sżhútùngr.

STRENGTH. lìlyang, jìn, jyèr, jìntóur. / I haven't that much strength. Wǒ 'méiyou nèmma 'dàde 'lìlyang. / I haven't the strength to climb that mountain. Wǒ méi 'jyèr pá 'shān le. / Steel has more strength than almost any other metal. 'Gāng chàbù-'dwō bǐ 'shémma 'jīnshǔ dōu yǒu 'jìn. / I'm afraid this medicine has lost its strength. Wó kǔng'pà jèige 'yàu méi 'lìlyang le.

    (Strong point in a person's character) 'chángchù. / His strength lies in his patience. Tāde 'changchu 'jyòu shŕ néng 'rěn. *but* / He has great strength of character. is expressed as His character is very straight. Tāde rén'géer hen 'jèng.

    (Military strength) jàndoulì, lìlyang. / We haven't tried to judge the strength of the enemy. Wǒmen 'bìng méi'gūjì 'dírénde 'jàndòu'lì.

    On the strength of píng (according to). / We hired those five men on the strength of your recommendation. Wǒmen 'yùng nèiwǔge 'rén shŕ píng 'nǐ 'jyèshàude.

STRETCH. (Stretch out) 'lākāi, dǎkāi, 'chēnkāi; (stretch tight) lājǐnle, bēngjǐnle. / He stretched the clothesline between the trees. Tā bǎ lyàng 'yīshang de 'shéngdz lākai shwāndau 'shùshang le.

    (Extend) jàn, 'jànchūchyu (occupy); 'tūngchū (pass through); 'chūchyù (go). / The wheat fields stretch out for miles. Nèipyàn 'màidz'dì 'jànle yǒu 'háujǐlǐ 'dì. / How far does this road stretch? Jèityáu 'lù °'tūngchū (°'chūchyù) yǒu 'dwōywǎn a?

    (Extend a part of the body) shēn. / It feels good to stretch my legs after that long ride. Pǎule dzèmma 'ywǎn yítàng yǐ'hòu 'shēnshen 'twěi jywéje tǐng 'shūfu. / Can you get that off the shelf if you stretch for it? Nǐ shēnchǐ 'gēbe lái néng bǎ 'nèige tsúng 'jyàdzshang 'gòusyàlai ma? / Stop yawning and stretching. Byé dǎ 'hāchi yě byé shēn 'lǎnyāu. (shēn 'lǎnyāu means lit. to stretch one's lazy waist; thus to stretch the upper part of your body the way you do when you yawn.) *but* / He stretched out on the couch. is expressed as He lay out straight on the couch. Tā 'jŕjrlyóu'lyóur dzài 'chwángshang 'tǎngje.

    (Become larger) dà, sūng. / Will this sweater stretch when I wash it? Jèige máu'yī syà'shwéi yǐ'hòu 'sūng busūng?

    (Become larger when pulled) lādechulai, chēndechulai. / This elastic won't stretch worth two cents. Jèige sūngjǐn'dàr yìdyǎr dōu 'lābùchū'lái.

    (Make larger by pulling) lādà, chēndà. / I stretched the sweater. Wó bǎ nèijyàn máu'yī 'chēndàle.

    (Make larger by putting something inside) chēngdà; (shoes only) pái, sywàn.

/ Can you stretch my shoes a little? Nǐ néng bǎ wǒ jèi shwāng 'syé 'chēngdà yìdyǎr ma?

(Exaggerate) yéngwòchíshr̄. / I think he's stretching the facts a little. Wǒ 'jywéde tā bǎ neige 'shr̄ching 'shwōde yóu dyǎr yéngwòchíshr̄. / Let's stretch a point and let him go. is expressed as Let's loosen a little and let him go. Dzámen °fàng-'sūng (°fàng'kwān) dyǎr, 'ràng ta 'dzǒu ba.

Stretch (length or distance) dwàn, dwàr. / The next stretch of road is not bad. 'Syàbyar nèidwàn 'lù bú'hwài. / There's a long stretch of beach at the edge of the town. Jèige chéng'byārshang yóu tǐng'chángde yídwàr hǎi'tān.

(Elasticity). / Does that rubber band have much stretch? is expressed verbally as Can that rubber band be stretched? Nèige syànpí'chywǎr hái 'lādechū'lái ma?

At a stretch. / He worked about two hours at a stretch. Tā yìkǒu 'chyèr dzwòle lyǎ jūng'tóu.

STRIKE (STRUCK). (Hit) dǎ, dzòu (local Peiping); (hit with a hammer or other instrument) dzáu; (collide) jwàng. *See* **HIT**. / She struck him in the face. Tā dǎle nèige 'nánde yíge 'dzwēiba. / He struck at the dog with a stick. Tā ná shǒu'jàng 'dǎle neige 'gǒu yísyàdz. / He struck the rock sharply with a hammer. Tā ná 'chwéidz shrjìn 'dzáule nèige 'shr̄tóu yísyàdz. / We struck back at the enemy. Wǒmen yísyàdz jyòu bǎ 'dírén gěi 'dǎhwéichyùle. / The ship struck a rock. Chwán 'jwàngdzài 'shr̄toushangle. *but* / That tree's been struck by lightning. is expressed as That tree has been split by thunder. Nèige 'shù ràng léi 'pīle. / The stone struck bottom. is expressed as The stone got to the bottom. Nèige 'shr̄tou dàu'dyěrle. / Wait till the light strikes it. is expressed as Wait until the light illuminates it. 'Děngje ná 'dēng 'jàudau nèr dzài 'shwō.

(Of a clock) dǎ. / Did the clock strike? Jūng 'dǎgwòle ma? / It just struck seven. Gāng 'dǎgwò chī'dyǎn.

(Stop work) bàgūng. / What are they striking for? 'Tāmen wèishémma bà-'gūng? / They promised not to strike during the conference. Tāmen 'dāying dzài 'shānglyang de shr̄hour búbà'gūng.

(Seem to someone) jywéde. / How does that suggestion strike you? Nèige 'yìsz nǐ jywéde dzěmma'yàng? / The situation struck me funny. Nèige 'chíngsying wǒ 'jywéde hén kě'syàu.

(Make a sudden impression on) 'jywéde, syǎngdàu. / That idea really struck my fancy. Nèige 'yìjyàn wǒ 'jywéde jēn 'hǎu. / That idea just struck me. Wǒ gāng-'tsái 'hūrán syǎngdàu de nèmmage 'fár.

(Come upon) 'pèngjyàn (meet); jǎujau (find); fāsyàn (discover); **strike luck** is expressed as go to good luck dzǒu yùn; **strike a gold mine** (either a real mine or a wonderful source of income) is expressed as dig a gold mine 'wājau jīn'kwàng; **strike it rich** fātsái. / Has anyone ever struck oil around here? Yǒu 'rén dzài fù'jìn fā-syàn yóu'kwàng le ma? / You're the first man I've struck who thinks so. Wǒ 'pèngjyàn de 'rén lǐtou yǒu 'jèijǔng 'szsyǎngde 'nǐ shr̄ 'tóuyíge.

Strike a bargain °chéng (°dzwò) yíhàur 'mǎimai. / We finally struck a bargain. Wǒmen dàu'lyǎur °chéngle (°dzwòle) yíhàur 'mǎimai.

Strike a match 'hwá yìgēn yáng'hwǒ.

Strike sparks (by collision) °'jwàngchū (°pèngchu) hwǒ'syīngr lái; (by striking) °'tsēngchū (°'dǎchū) hwǒ'syīngr lái.

Strike off (*or* out) chyǔsyāu (delete); (draw a line through) 'lále chyù, 'hwále chyù. / Strike his name off the list. Bǎ tāde 'míngdz tsúng míng'dārshang 'hwále chyù. / Strike out the last paragraph. Bǎ mwòyí'dwàr chyǔsyāu.

953

Strike up. / The two of them struck up a friendship very quickly. is expressed as The two of them were familiar after a little while. Tāmen 'lyǎ yi'hwěr jyòu 'shóule. / The band struck up the national anthem. Ywè'dwèi dzòuchǐ gwó'gēer lái le.

A strike is expressed verbally as stop work bàgūng. / How long did the miners' strike last? Kwàng'gūng bà'gūng bàle 'dwōjyǒu?

STRING (STRUNG). (Thread or fine string) syàn, syàr; (thick string, rope) shéngr, 'shéngdz. / Could you tie this up with string? Nǐ 'néng ná 'shéngdz bǎ 'jèige 'shwān-shang ma? fig. / There are no strings attached to the offer. is expressed as This affair has no other details. Jèijyàn 'shr̄ching 'méi shémma lǐng'wàide 'jr̄jyé.

(Of a musical instrument or sports racket) syán; (of a piano) yīn (tone). / Do you have violin strings? Ní yǒu syǎutí'chínde 'syán ma? / My racket needs new strings. Wǒde chyóur'pāidz děi hwàn 'syán le. / One of the piano strings is out of tune. Gāng'chínshang yǒu yíge 'yīn bù'jwūnle.

A string of (series of things on a string) chwàn; (a line, column) chwàn, lyóu. / She's wearing a beautiful string of pearls. Tā dàide nèichwàn 'jēnjū 'jēn hǎu'kàn. (In the case of a necklace the measure may also be gwà something that is hung.) / There's a long string of busses waiting to be filled. Yǒu yídà'lyóu kǎ'chē 'děngje shàng 'rén ne.

Pull strings twō rénching (get other people to do things for you). / I never was too good at pulling strings. Wǒ tsúng'lái yě bú'hwèi twō rén'chíng.

To string (stretch; see STRETCH) lā; ān (fix, put). / They strung the electric wire from pole to pole. Tāmen bǎ dyàn'syàn shwùnje 'dyànsyàn'gāndz yì'dwàryi-'dwàrde 'ānshàngle.

(Thread) chwān. / Where can I have my amber beads strung? Shémma 'dìfangr néng bǎ wǒde 'hǔpwo nyàn'jūr gěi 'chwānshang?

(String beans) jái. / Please help me string the beans. Láu'jyà 'bāngje wǒ jái-jai 'dòur.

String (someone) along (trick) shwǎ; (cheat) ywān, pyàn, dzwàn. / Are you stringing me along? Nǐ shr̄ 'shwǎ wo ne ma? / She's been stringing him along for months. Nèige 'nyǔde ná ta 'shwǎje wár 'shwǎle 'háujǐge 'ywè.

Be strung out is expressed as stand in a line jànle °yì'háng (°yì'pái, °yí'lyòu). / The policemen were strung out along the sidewalk. Jǐng'chá 'shwùnje byàn'dàu jàn-le °yì'háng (°yì'pái, °yí'lyòu).

STRONG. (Powerful) yǒulìlyang, yǒujìn, 'lìlyang dà, jyèr dà, chyáng; bàng (colloqui-al); in special combinations other expressions are used as a strong wind 'yìngfēng or fēng hěn chùng. / He has strong hands. Tāde 'shǒu hěn yǒu'jìn. / Are you strong enough to swim that far? Ní yǒu 'nèmma dàde 'lìlyang fù 'nèmma 'ywǎn ma? / The current is pretty strong. is expressed as The water flows very fast. Shwěi 'lyóude hěn 'jí. / I'm not very strong yet (after an illness). is expressed as My body is still soft. Wǒ 'shēndz hai shr̄ 'rwàn. / They are a strong nation. Tāmen shr̄ ge 'chyáng-gwó. / He believes in a strong navy. is expressed as He maintains that one ought to have a large and strong navy. Tā 'jùjāng yīng'gāi yíge chyáng'dàde hǎi'jyūn.

(Firm, solid) jyēshr. / Do you have a good strong rope? Ní yǒu 'jyēshrde 'shéngdz ma? / Is this ladder strong? Jèige 'tīdz 'jyēshr ma? / Is this ladder strong enough to hold me? is expressed as Can this ladder hold me? Jèige 'tīdz 'jǐnde'jù wǒ ma?

(Concentrated) chùng, lìhai. / This drink is too strong. Jèige 'jyǒu tài 'chùng. / She likes strong perfume. Tā 'syǐhwàn wèr 'chùngde syāng'shwěr.

(Numerically large). / This political party isn't very strong yet. is expressed as The influence of this party isn't very great. 'Jèidăngde 'shŕlì hái 'búswăn 'dà. or as There aren't many members of this party. 'Jèidăngde 'dăngywán hái bù'dwō. (In Chinese one must distinguish the two meanings, since a large party is not necessarily a strong one.)

(Intense). / He showed a strong desire to see it. is expressed as He showed that he wanted very much to see it. Kàn tā nèi 'yàngdz 'hĕn syăng yàu 'kànkan nèige. / I have strong feelings on that subject. is expressed as My emotions on that subject are very deep. Nèige 'wèntí wŏ 'gánsyăng hĕn 'shēn. / It made a strong impression on me. is expressed as It gave me a very deep impression. 'Nèige 'gĕi wŏ yíge hĕn 'shēnde 'yìnsyàng.

Be strong-minded (have made up one's mind what one wants) yŏu'júyì. / He's a very strong-minded person. Tā shŕ ge hén yŏu'júyìde rén.

STUDENT. sywésheng. / He's a student at the university. Tā shŕ nèige dà'sywélide 'sywésheng. *but* / She's a serious student of the subject. is expressed as She does research in that field very seriously. 'Tā dzài nèiyì'mérli hĕn rèn'jēnde 'yánjyou.

STUDY. kàn (look at, read); nyàn (read, sometimes read aloud); dú (read); yánjyou (do research); sywé (learn, be a student). / I've studied the situation carefully. Wó bă nèige 'chíngsying dzsyìde 'yánjyoule yánjyou. / We studied the map before we started. Wŏmen chū'fā yí'chyán bă dì'tú 'yánjyoule yí'syàr. / I've studied all the literature on the subject. Wó bă 'gwānyú nèige 'tímude shū gēn 'wénjāng dōu °'kàn-le (°'nyànle, °'dúle). / He's busy studying. is expressed as He's reading books. Tā jèng 'mángje nyàn 'shū ne. / I'm studying medicine at the university. Wŏ dzài dà'sywé lĭtou sywé 'yīsywé. / He studied under some famous men. Tā 'gēnje jige 'míngrén °'sywéde °'yánjyoude (°'nyànde, °'dúde).

A study (problem studied) mér (course); yánjyou (research problem). / Geometry in his principal study. Tā 'yánjyoude 'jŭyàude yì'mér jyòushŕ jĭ'hé. / He is doing very well in his studies. is expressed as He studies all his books very well. Tā 'shū dōu 'nyànde bú'tswò. / This battle would make a good study for a historian. Jèiyí-'jàng hĕn 'jŕde ràng yánjyou lì'shŕde 'yánjyou yísyàr.

(Written results of research) wénjāng (article); dūngsyi (thing); băugàu (report). / He has published several studies in that field. Gwānyu nèi'mér tā fā'byăugwo jipyăn °'wénjāng (°'dūngsyi, °bău'gàu).

(Private library or reading room) shūfáng. / I'll be in the study if you want me. Nĭ 'hwéitóu yàu 'jáu wŏ de'hwà wŏ dzài shū'fáng.

Make a study of yánjyou. / I'll have to make a study of that situation. Wó dĕi 'yánjyouyánjyou nèige 'chíngsying.

STUFF. dūngsyi. / Put some of that stuff on your hand. Bă nèige 'dūngsyi dzài ní 'shŏushang mwó dyăr. / What's that stuff you're eating? Nĭ dzài chŕ 'shémma dūng-syi? / Give me a drink of that stuff, whatever it is. Bùgwăn nèige 'shŕ shémma, 'gĕi wŏ hē dyăr. / Get your stuff out of my room. Bá 'nĭde dūngsyi tsúng 'wŏ wūli 'náchūchyu. / I don't like the stuff he's been writing lately. Tā 'jìnlái 'syéde nèisyē 'dūngsyi wŏ bù'syĭhwan. / Throw that old stuff away. Bă 'nèige 'jyòu dūngsyi 'rēng-lóu ba. *but* / That book is great stuff! is expressed as That book's not bad. Nèibĕr 'shū bú'tswò. / None of that stuff! Byé 'nèmmaje! / No rough stuff allowed. Bù-'syŭ yĕ'mán.

To stuff jwāng (pack); sāi, sēi (cram, squeeze into something); tyán (fill); yē (tuck in, slip in); dŭ (plug up). / She keeps her handbag stuffed full of junk. Tāde pí-'bāuli jwāng'mănle lwànchibā'dzaude dūngsyi. / Stuff your ears with cotton. Bá nĭ 'ĕrdwo ná 'myánhwa °'dŭshang (°'sāishang, °'tyánshang). / Stuff it down that hole.

Bǎ 'nèige 'sāide nèige 'kūlungli. /I stuffed the paper under the cushion. Wó bǎ nèijāng 'jř 'yēde 'dyàndz 'dǐsya le. /He stuffed his things into a suitcase. Tā bǎ tāde 'dūngsyi dōu °'tyánde (°'sāide) 'syāngdzli le. /Did you stuff the peppers? Ní bǎ chín'jyāu 'jwāngshang 'syàr le ma?

(Put filling into something) sywàn. /Since these shoes are too big for him, he stuffed some cotton in them. Jèishwāng 'syé tài 'dà tā sywànle yìdyǎr 'myánhwa.

Stuff oneself is expressed in terms of eating a lot. /Don't stuff yourself. Byé chř tài 'dwō lou. /I can't eat any more; I'm stuffed. Wǒ tài 'bǎu le, 'chřbúsyà'chyù le.

Be stuffed up. /My head is all stuffed up from my cold. is expressed as I have a cold and my head is pushing outwards. Wǒ jāu'lyáng le, 'nǎudai fā'jàng.

STYLE. (Fashion) yàngdz, 'yàngshř, 'shřyàng(r); *also* shřmáur, shřsyíng (be fashionable) *or* mwódēng (be modern, up-to-date). /It's the latest style. 'Nèige shř dzwèi-'syínde 'yàngdz. /Is this dress in style? 'Jèijyàn 'yīfu shř'syíng ma? /I don't like the style of that dress. Wǒ bù'syǐhwan nèijyàn 'yīfude 'yàngdz. /Her clothes haven't any style. 'Tāde 'yīshang bùmwó'dēng. /She has a lot of style. Tā hěn shř'máur.

(Manner of expression) 'bǐfǎ, 'syéfǎr (way of writing); 'hwàfǎr (way of painting); (an artist's personal style) 'tǐtsái, dzwòfēng. /I don't like that author's style. Wǒ bù'syǐhwan nèige dzwò'jyāde dzwo'fēng. /He writes in the style of the last century. Tā syě 'dūngsyi yùng 'shàngyíshř'jìde 'syéfǎr. /His work is in the style of the modern French painters. Tāde 'hwàfǎr shř fǎng 'jìndài 'Fàgwopài.

SUBJECT. tímu (topic); mén, mér (field). /Are you familiar with this subject? Jèige 'tímu nǐ 'shúsyi ma? *or* Nǐ 'dwèiyú 'jèiyìmér 'shúsyi ma? /Don't change the subject. Byé 'gǎi 'tímu a. /What was the subject of his lecture? Tāde jyáng'yǎn shř 'shémma 'tímu? /What subject did you study in school last year? 'Chyùnyán nǐ dzài sywé'syàuli nyàn nǎi'mén?

(National) 'shǔmín, rén. /He's a British subject. Tā shř 'Yīnggwode 'shǔmín. *or* Yīnggworén.

Be subject to (liable) děi dzwūnshǒu, děi gēnjyù, yídìng hwèi (yàu); (can *or* may) kěnéng . . . , kéyǐ . . . ; (easy to get) cháng . . . , róngyi . . . . /Everyone on board was subject to international law. 'Měiyíge rén dzài 'chwánshang dóu děi dzwūn-'shǒu 'gwojigūng'fǎ. /All my actions are subject to his approval. Wǒde yíchyè syíng-'dùng dōu děi gēn'jyù tāde syú'kě. /These rates are subject to change without notice. Búbì 'tūngjř jyàmù jyòu kéyǐ 'byàndùng. /Due to the snowstorm, all trains are subject to delay. Yīnwèi jèichǎng dàfēng'sywé swóyǒude hwǒchē dōu kěnéng wù'dyǎn. /Japan is subject to earthquakes. Rběn °cháng (°róngyi) yǒu dì'jèn. /He is often subject to fits of anger. Tā °hěn róngyi (°cháng) shēng'chì.

SUCCEED. chéng; chénggūng (be successful). /Don't worry if you don't succeed right away. Mǎ'shàng 'yàushř °bù'chéng (°bùnéng chéng'gūng) béng jāu'jí. /The plan didn't succeed equally well in all cases. Jèige 'fǎr dzài 'gèjǔng 'dìfangr yǒude 'chéng yǒude búdà 'chéng.

(Follow, take the place of) jyē (lit. receive). /Who succeeded him in office? Shéi 'jyē tāde 'shřching le? /If he dies, who will succeed him as emperor? 'Yàu-shr tā 'sžlou shéi 'jyēje dzwò 'hwángshang?

Succeed in doing something is expressed with a verb of action followed by hǎule, chéngle, jáule, chǐláile, *or* wánle (see Chinese-English section for each); **succeed in finding** 'jāujáule; **succeed in writing** 'syěwánle, chéngle, 'syěhǎule, 'syěchǐláile; **succeed in doing** 'dzwòchéngle, 'dzwòhǎule, 'dzwòdàule, 'dzwòchǐláile, 'dzwòwánle. /Did you succeed in getting him on the phone? Ní dǎ dyàn'hwà 'jǎu ta 'jǎujaule ma?

SUCCESS. <u>Expressed verbally as</u> chénggūng (complete a task successfully); dzwòchéng, bàuchéng (accomplish work). / He's had a good deal of success in handling such cases. 'Jèiyàngrde shŕching tā bàn'chéngle hău'syéhwéi le. / Congratulations on your success. Nǐ chéng'gūngle, děi géi nǐ dàu'syǐ a. / His play was an instant success. Tā nèichū 'syǐ yǐ'yàn 'mǎshang jyou chéng'gūngle. / Did he make a success of his business? Tāde 'mǎimai °dzwò'chéngle ma (°chéng'gūngle ma)?

(Achievement) chéngjyòu. / He's had several successes in this line. Dzài 'jèi-hángli tā 'yóu dyǎr 'chengjyòu.

See also **SUCCEED.**

SUCH. jèmma, jèyàngr, 'jèmmayàngr, nèmma, nèyàngr, 'nèmmayàngr, 'dzèmma-yàngr; (thus) rútsž; (of one kind) yǐleide. / All such statements are exaggerated. 'Fánshŕ 'jèiyàngrde 'hwà 'dōu shŕ 'yángwòchí'shŕ. *or* Jèiyí'lèide 'hwà dōu dyǎr 'shwōde gwò'hwǒr. / We can't examine every such complaint. 'Jèiyàngrde 'shŕ wǒ-men 'méifár gè 'gèr dōu 'chá. / She never says such things. Tā 'tsúnglái bùshwō 'jèiyàngrde 'hwà. / I never heard of such a thing happening. Wǒ 'méitīng'shwōgwò 'jèiyàngrde shŕching. / Such is life. Rén'shēng jyou shŕ jèmma yi'hwéi 'shŕ. *or* Rú'tsž rén'shēng. / It must have been some such place where I saw him. Wǒ yí'dìng shŕ dzài syàng 'jèmma yàngrde yíge 'dìfangr 'kànjyàngwo tā. / There's no such person here. Jèr 'méiyou 'dzèmma ge 'rén. / I've seldom seen such beauty. Wó hěn 'shǎu kànjyan 'dzèmma hǎu'kànde. / Nobody wanted to work for him, he was such a slave-driver. Tā dài rén nèmma 'hěn, 'méiyou rén 'ywànyi gēn tā dzwò 'shŕ. / I've never tasted such food. Wǒ tsúng'lái yě méi'chŕgwo 'jèyàngrde 'chŕde. / Don't be in such a hurry. Byé dzèmma 'máng a. / He's just such a man as I imagined he would be. Tā 'jèngshŕ wǒ 'syǐnli 'syǎng de 'nèmma yíge 'rén. / He said it in such a way that I couldn't help laughing. Tā 'nèmma yǐ 'shwō ràng wǒ bù'néng bú'syàu.

As such. / They have no hotels, as such, in this region. <u>is expressed as</u> In this region there are no hotel-like hotels. Jèiyí'dài méi syàng'yàngrde lyú'gwǎn. / He's acting chairman, and as such should be respected. <u>is expressed as</u> He's already chairman, and everyone should respect him. Tā jǐ'rán shŕ jǔ'syǐ; dàjyā'hwǒr jyou yīngdāng 'dzwūnjìng tā.

Such as syàng. / Conduct such as this is inexcusable. Syàng 'jèiyàngrde 'syǐng-wei shŕ 'bùnéng 'ywánlyàngde. / It's too cold here for some fruit trees, such as the peach. Jèr 'tyānchi dwèiyú jíjúng 'gwǒdz tài 'lěng, syàng 'táur shémmade.

SUDDEN. méisyǎngdàu syǎngbúdàu (unexpected); <u>or expressed as</u> suddenly *see* **SUDDENLY**, <u>or as</u> at once yísyàdz, 'pāde yísyàdz. / This is so sudden! 'Jèige jēn méisyǎng'dàu. / He died a sudden death. Tā 'hūrán jyòu 'sžle. / Our army made a sudden attack. Wǒmende jyūn'dwèi chǒubu'lěngdz jìn'gūngle yí'syàdz.

All of a sudden *see* **SUDDENLY**. / All of a sudden it began to pour. 'Hūrán tyān syàchi dà'yǔ laile.

SUDDENLY. hūrán, chǒubulěngdz, měnggudǐngde, lěnggudǐngde. / He suddenly turned on us in anger. Tā 'hūrán jyòu gēn wǒmen fā'pǐchi. / Suddenly I remembered that I had to mail a letter. Wǒ °hūrán (°etc.) syángchǐlái děi 'fā yìfēng 'syìn.

SUFFER. shòukǔ (go through hardship); shòudzwèi (go through an ordeal); nánshòu, nángwò (not be feeling well); bùshūfu (be ill, uncomfortable, unhappy); bùhǎushòu, bùhǎugwò (be ill); bú'tùngkwài (feel restrained, unhappy, resentful). / Did you suffer much after your operation? Dùng'shoushù yǐ'hòu nǐ shòu shémma 'dzwèi 'méiyou? / She's suffering from an infected tooth. Tā nàu 'yá ne, tǐng shòu'dzwèide. *but* / Are you suffering any pain? Nǐ 'jywéje 'téng ma?

(Be injured) (nùng) hwàile, (núng)hwèile; shòu swǔnshr (sustain damage; physical or financial); chŕkwēi (get the worst of it). / The buildings along the river

957

suffered severely from the flood. Yánje 'hé de nèisyē 'lóu fā'shwĕi de shŕhour 'dōu gĕi nùng'hwĕile. /Your reputation will suffer if you do it. Nĭ 'yàushr nèmma 'bàn, nĭde 'míngyù jyòu 'hwĕile. /The school didn't suffer much from the fire yesterday. Dzwóerge jáu'hwŏ sywé'syàu méishòu shémma 'swŭnshŕ. /You'll certainly suffer if you insist on doing it that way. Nĭ 'yàushr nèmma 'dzwò yí'dìng chŕ'kwēi. /Our army has suffered heavy losses. Wŏmende jyūn'dwèi shòule hĕn dàde 'swŭnshr.

SUGAR. táng; (rock candy) 'bīngtáng; (powdered sugar) 'báitáng, èr'gùngtáng; (granulated sugar) 'shātáng; (lump sugar) 'fāngtáng; (light brown sugar) 'cháubáitáng; (dark brown sugar) 'hēitáng, 'húngtáng. /Please pass the sugar. Láu'jyà, bā 'táng 'dìgéi wŏ.

To sugar jyātáng, fàngtáng, gētáng. /She's sugaring the cupcakes. Tā wàng nèige 'dyănsyīnshang °jyā'táng ne (°gē'táng ne, °fàng'táng ne).

SUGGEST. shwō (say); tíyì (propose). /Do you have anyone to suggest for the job? Jèige 'shŕching nĭ shwō yùng 'shéi lái 'dzwò? /What do you suggest we do tonight? Nĭ shwō 'jyér 'wănshang wŏmen gàn 'shémma? /I suggest that we ask him to come too. 'Wŏ shwō dzámen 'chĭng tā yí'kwàr lái. /Are you suggesting that I'm wrong? Nĭ shŕ 'shwō wŏ 'tswòle ma?

(Bring to mind) ràng . . . 'syángchĭlai (remind you of something you'd forgotten); 'kànje syàng (look like); 'mwōje syàng (feel like); 'tīngje syàng (sound like); 'chángje syàng (taste like); 'wénje syàng (smell like). /Does this suggest anything to you? Jèige 'ràng nĭ 'syángchĭ dyăr 'shémma lái ma? or Do you think this is like something? 'Jèige nĭ 'jywéje syàng 'shémma? /The shape of the cloud suggests a horse to me. is expressed as I think the shape of that cloud is like a horse. Jèikwài 'yúntsaide 'yàngdz wŏ 'jywéje syàng yìpí 'mă.

SUIT. (Clothes) yīshang, yīfu; with measure tàu or shēn. /This suit doesn't fit him very well. Jèitàu 'yīshang tā 'chwānje bŭdà hé'shŕ. /How do you like her new suit? Ní 'syĭhwan tāde nèishēn 'syīn 'yīfu ma?

(Legal) àndz. /Who is the lawyer handling the suit? 'Năige lyù'shŕ gwăn jèige 'àndz?

(In cards) mén. /Diamonds were his strongest suit. Fāng'kwàr shŕ tā 'shŏuli dzwèi 'bàngde yì'mén.

Follow suit. /I'm out of hearts; I can't follow suit. is expressed as I haven't any hearts; I haven't any way to follow. Wŏ méi húng'táur le, wŏ méi 'fár 'gēnje 'chū. or as I haven't any hearts; I have to fill in one. Wŏ méi húng'táur le, wó dĕi 'dyàn yì'jāng. /If he's going home early, I think I'll follow suit. is expressed as If he's going home early, I think I ought to, too. Tā yàushr 'dzău hwéi 'jyā a, wó 'syăng wŏ yé dĕi nèmma 'bàn.

To suit (satisfy) jywéje °hău (°hé'shŕ); jyàu . . . măn'yì (be satisfied); or jyàu . . . syĭhwan (be pleased, like something). /Does the program suit you? 'Jyémù jèiyàngr ní °'syĭhwan (°'măn'yì) ma? /This gift ought to suit him. Wó syăng jèijyàn 'lĭwu hwèi jyàu tā 'syĭhwande. or Jèijyàn 'lĭwu 'wó syăng tā hwèi măn'yì. /Our prices will suit everybody. Wŏmen dĭng de 'jyàer 'jwŭn jyàu dàjyā'hwŏ dōu măn'yì.

(Be suitable) héshŕ; dwèi (fit, match); syàngfú, 'fúhé (coincide). /This color doesn't suit you. Jèige 'yánsher nĭ 'chwānje bùhé'shŕ. or expressed as This color isn't becoming for you to wear. Jèige 'yánshăr nĭ 'chwānje bùshŕ'yàngr. /A three-room apartment suits our family nicely. Yìswŏ 'sānjyān 'wŭdzde 'fángdz wèi wŏmen 'jyā hĕn hé'shŕ. /This insurance policy will suit your purpose very well. Jèijŭng báu'syăn dwèi 'ní tĭng hé'shŕ.

SUM. (Amount, figure) shùr, shùmu; (total gained by adding numbers) dzŭngshù(r); **a**

sum of money yìbǐ chyán; **a large sum of money** yí'dàbǐ 'chyán; **a small sum of money** hén 'syàude yìbǐ 'chyán. / The sum of all these numbers is 1,000. Jèsyē 'shùmu 'jyāchilai de dzǔng'shùr 'děngyú yí'chyán. / I want to deposit a large sum of money to my account. Wǒ yàu 'dzài wǒ °hùtóushang (°jédzshang) 'twsún yí'dàbǐ 'chyán. / Can you pay me a small sum in advance? Nǐ syān 'fùgéi wǒ °yíge 'syǎushùr (°yì-dyǎr, °yìdyǎr 'chyán) 'syíng bù'syíng? / It's a small sum. Jèige 'shùmu hén 'syǎu. *or* Jèibǐ 'chyán hén 'syǎu.

To sum up 'dzǔngéryán'jr̄ (in a word, or in a nutshell); gwēi'nàchilai (conclude). / To sum up, he's not good at all. 'Dzǔngéryán'jr̄, tā yì'dyǎr dōu bù'hǎu. / He summed up the situation in a few words. Tā yùng jǐ'jyùhwà jyòu bǎ nèige 'chíngsying gwēi'nàchilaile.

SUMMER. 'syàtyān. / Does it rain much here during the summer? Jèr 'syàtyān 'yù-shwei 'dwō ma? / She invited us to her summer cottage. Tā chíng wǒmen dàu tā 'syàtyān bì'shǔ de dìfangr chyù. / I need some summer clothes. Wǒ 'dwan dyǎr 'syàtyānde 'yīfu.

SUN. tàiyang; (local Peiping) lǎuyéer; (sunlight) yánggwāng; **in the sun** 'tàiyang dìli *or* yáng'gwāng 'dǐsya (under the sun). / The sun just went down. 'Tàiyang 'gāng syàchyu. / I couldn't see you because the sun was in my eyes. 'Tàiyang hwáng wǒ-'yǎnjing láije, méi'kànjyan ni. / The sun is pretty hot today. is expressed as The sun today is really severe. Jyèr 'tàiyang jēn 'dú. / Stay out of the afternoon sun. 'Syàwǔ byé dzài 'tàiyang 'dìli dāije. / I've been out in the sun all day. Wǒ dzài wàitou 'tàiyang 'dìli dāile yìjěng'tyān.

Get sunburned jyàu 'tàiyang °'shàile (be overexposed to the sun) (°shàihúngle (get tanned or red), °shàitwǒ'píle (get so burned that the skin peels), °shàihēile (be sunburned)); **have a sunstroke** *or* **be overcome by the sun** jyàu 'tàiyang °shài'yūn-gwòchule (°shài 'hwūngwòchyule, °shàibìngle, °shài'míhule), jùngshǔ, shòushǔ.

SUNDAY. Syīngchǐtyān, Lǐbàityān, Syīngchǐr̀, Lǐbàir̀, Syīngchǐ, Lǐbài.

SUPPER. wǎn fàn. / Supper is ready. Wǎn'fàn 'déle. / We eat supper about six o'clock. Wǒmen dàgài 'lyòudyǎn jūng chr̄ wǎn'fàn.

SUPPLY. (Available amount). / The supply of medicine can't begin to meet the demand. is expressed as The medicine isn't enough to supply the demand. 'Yàu gūngbú'shàng 'màide. or as The medicine that has been stored up isn't enough to supply the demand. 'Tswún de 'yàu gūngbú'shàng 'màide. or as All the medicine available can't meet the demand. 'Yàu shr̀ 'gùngbuyíng'chyóu.

A supply of yìpī (load or shipment of); **a large supply of** bùshǎude . . . ; **a small supply of** méi dwōshǎu . . . , (my) **supply of** (wǒ) jèrde . . . . / We need a fresh supply of tennis balls. Wǒmen děi 'yàu yìpī 'syīn wǎng'chyóu. / I need another supply of carbon paper. is expressed as I need some more carbon paper. Wǒ 'hái děi 'yàu dyǎr fùsyé'jr̀. / I carried a good supply of reading matter with me. Wǒ dàile bù'shǎude 'shū gēn dzá'jr̀ shémmade. / We have just a small supply of these on hand. 'Jèige wǒmen 'shǒuli °'mái dwō'shǎu (°'jyòu yǒu yì'dyǎr). / How large a supply of towels do you have? Nǐ 'tswúnle yǒu 'dwōshǎutyáu 'shǒujin? / My supply of paper is running low. Wǒ jèrde 'jr̀ kwài yùng'wánle.

Supplies dūngsyi, 'jíyǎng (military supplies). / We are running out of supplies. Wǒmende °'dūngsyi (°'jíyǎng) dōu kwài yùng'wánle. / I'm going to town for groceries and other supplies. Wǒ yàu dàu chénglǐ mái dyǎr 'tsài gēn líng'swéide 'dūngsyi.

To supply gūng (supply a demand, or supply money); jyè (lend); sùng, gěi (give); chū (give out, produce). / The store has enough shoes on hand to supply any normal demand. Jèige 'pùdzli tswún de 'syé jàu píng'chángde yàngr 'mài, 'dzěmmaje yě gūngde'shàng. / I'll supply the money for you. Wǒ 'gūng ni 'chyán yùng. / I'll supply the money for your schooling. Wǒ 'gūng ni shàng'sywé. / You supply the money and I'll do the work. 'Nǐ chū 'chyán, 'wo chū 'lì. / That company supplies us with ice. Nèige gūng'sz̄ géi wǒmen sùng'bīng. / I'll supply anything else you need. Nǐ 'hái yàu 'shémma wo dōu kéyi 'géi ni.

SUPPORT. (Hold up) fú (keep something standing erect with hand); jr̄je (support something from underneath by poles); dǐng (carry on one's head; also used of poles); chān (support a person by taking his arm lightly); jyà (support a person or thing by lifting it up forcibly); *see also* **CARRY**; **be able to support** jīndejù. / Support the ladder to keep it from falling. 'Fúje nèige 'tīdz dyār byé 'ràng ta 'dǎulou. / The board was supported by the two benches. Nèikwài 'bǎndz chywán 'jàngje nèilyǎngtyáu 'dèngdz 'jyàje ne. / The house is supported on piles. Jèige 'fángdz dōu 'jàngje nèijigēr 'jùdz °'jr̄je ne (°'dǐngje ne). / He put his arm under hers to support her. Tā (bá shǒu 'gēdau nèi nyǔde gēbei'jóur nèr) 'chānje tā. / That bridge isn't strong enough to support so much weight. Nèige 'chyáu búgòu 'jyēshr jīnbu'jù nèmma 'jùng.

(Uphold) bāng (help); gèng jèng'míng . . . dwèi (give further proof); 'dzànchéng (approve); 'jèngmíng (prove). / I'll support your claims. Wǒ 'bāngje nǐ 'shwǒ. / That supports my argument. Nèmma yǐ'lai 'gèng jèng'ming wǒshwode 'dwèi le. / Does this paper support his policies? Jèige 'bàu 'dzànchéng tāde 'bànfǎ ma? / I've said before that I support this idea. Wó yǐ'chyán 'shwōgwo wǒ 'dzànchéng nèige 'bànfǎ. / Can you offer any evidence to support this statement? Nǐ 'neng náchū shr̀-'shŕ lái 'jèngmíng nèige 'hwà ma?

(Provide maintenance for) yǎnghwo (support anyone); yǎngjyā (support one's own wife or family). / Are you supporting a family? Nǐ déi yǎng'jyā ma?

Supporting role pèi jyǎur.

A support (prop); jùdz (pole); chyáng (wall). / The supports under the porch don't look very strong to me. Nèige 'lángdzde 'jùdz wǒ kàn bú'dà 'jyēshr.

(Act of supporting). / Several relatives depend on him for their support. is expressed verbally as He has several relatives who depend on him to support them. Tā yǒu hóujǐge 'chīnchi dōu 'jàngje tā 'yǎnghwoje. *but* / I'm the main support of my family. is expressed as My family depends mostly on me. Wǒ 'jyā gwò'rdz dwōbàr 'jàngje 'wǒ.

SUPPOSE. (Think) syǎng, 'yǐwéi, jywéde. / I suppose so. Wó syǎng 'shr̀ nàyàngr. / He's all right, I suppose. Wǒ 'jywéde tā bú'tswò. / Do you suppose that this is true? Nǐ 'yǐwéi nèi shr̀ 'jēnde ma? / He is generally supposed to be a rich man. Dà'hwǒr dōu 'yǐwéi tā hěn 'kwò. / It's supposed to be true. Dàjyā'hwǒr dōu 'yǐwéi shr̀ nèmma hwéi 'shr̀.

(Assume true) jyǎ'shè. / Suppose he turns up, what then? Jyǎ'shè tā 'láile, dzěmma 'bàn? / Let's suppose, for the sake of argument, that I'm right. Jyǎshè wǒ shwōde 'dwèi.

(How about) °jyǎ'shè (°'yàushr, °rúg'wǒ) . . . 'dzěmmayàng; (why not . . .) wèishémma bù . . . . / Suppose we go to the show tonight instead of tomorrow. Wǒmen wèi'shémma bù 'jyērge kàn dyàn'yǐngr chyù, 'myérge béng chyù le. / Suppose you wait till tomorrow. Nǐ 'yàushr děng dàu 'myérge 'dzěmmayàng ne? *or* Nǐ 'wèishémma bùděngde 'myérge ne? or expressed as Wait until tomorrow, OK? Nǐ děng dàu 'myérge dzài 'shwō, 'syíng bùsyíng?

Be supposed to yīngdāng, yīnggāi. / I was supposed to go with him. Běn'lái yǐng'dāng shr̀ 'wǒ gēn ta chyù. / You're supposed to do it yourself. Nǐ yīnggāi 'dzjǐ 'dzwò. / It's supposed to rain today. is expressed as Someone said it would rain today. Jyù 'shwō jyēr yàu syà 'yǔ.

960

SURE. (Be certain of something) 'jwǔn jř̄dau (know for certain); gǎn shwō (dare to say). / Are you sure of that? 'Nèige ní 'jwǔn jř̄dau ma? *or* 'Nèige ní gǎn 'shwō ma? *or* expressed as Is that true? Nèige shř̄ 'jēnde ma? / What are you going to do? I'm not sure. Ní 'syǎng gàn 'shémma ya? Wǒ 'hái méi 'jwěr ne (lit. I'm not certain yet). *or* Wǒ bùgǎn 'shwō. *or* Wǒ hái bùjř̄'dàu ne (lit. I don't know yet). / I'm sure of one thing; he dislikes us. Yǒu 'yíyàngr shř̄ wó gǎn 'shwōde, 'jyòushř̄ tā bù'syǐ̄hwan wǒmen.

(Be dependable) kàude jù; jwūn chéng, jwūn syíng (certainly be accomplished); yǒu 'bǎwù (be safe); 'wànwúyi'shř̄ (never miss). / This method is slow but sure. 'Jèige 'fádz 'màn, kěshr jwūn 'syíng. / That investment is a sure thing. Náchū 'chyán lai dzwò 'nèige mǎimai hěn kàude'jù. / Our final victory is absolutely sure. Wǒmende dzwèi'hòu shèng'lì shř̄ 'jywédwèi yóu 'bǎwù.

Be sure and (*or* to) when ordering someone °'yí'dìng (°'bìdìng) (děi). / Be sure and wear your coat. Yí'dìng děi 'chwānshang dyǎr dǎ'yī. / Be sure to lock the door before you go to bed. Shwèijyàu yǐ'chyán yí'dìng yàu swōshang 'mén.

Be sure to (be certain to) yídìng, jwǔn. / He is sure to be back by nine o'clock. Tā 'jyǒudyǎn jūng yí'dìng kéyi 'hwéilai. / Whatever he does is sure to be interesting. Tā 'nùngchū 'shémma lai dōu yí'dìng yóu'yìsz. / I'm sure to forget it if you don't remind me. Ní 'yàushr bù'tí wǒ yìshēngr wǒ yí'dìng jyòu 'wàngle.

Feel sure that jywéde . . . yídìng. / I feel sure that you will be all right. Wǒ 'jywéde ní yí'dìng 'kéyi. / I feel sure of success. Wǒ 'jywéde yí'dìng kéyi 'chéng.

Make sure *see* the first two paragraphs above. When the English means see to it that, there are many Chinese expressions, depending on the method of making sure. The following sentences illustrate various ways of expressing the idea. / Make sure you're on time. Syǎng 'fǎr yí'dìng àn 'shŕhou lái. / I'll make sure we never see him again. Wǒ yí'dìng syǎng 'fǎr ràng wǒmen tsúng'tsz 'dzài yě bú'jyàn tā le. / Make sure there isn't a single mistake. 'Chywèshř̄ dwèi'hǎule, 'yíge tswòr dōu bùnéng 'yǒu. / Make sure the thing works before you buy it. Mǎi yi'chyán děi shř̄-'hǎule.

As sure as fate bí 'syěsya hái 'jwūn (more certain than if it were written down); méi 'wèntí (there's no question about it); méitswòr (there's no mistake about it). / As sure as fate he'll be there. Tā 'jwūn 'dzài nèr yí'dìng méi'tswòr.

Sure (certainly) jēn. / I'd sure like to see them, but I won't have time. Wǒ jēn 'ywànyi 'kànkan tāmen, kěshr wǒ méi 'gūngfu. / You said it would rain, and sure enough it did. Ní shwō 'tyān yàu syà 'yǔ, jyòu jēn 'syàle. *but* / Sure! (OK! Of course!) Hǎu! *or* Ai! *or* Dāng'rán! *or* Yí'dìng!

SURPRISE. (Startle) syà yítyàu, chŕ yìjīng; **be surprised** 'jywéje tè'byé, chígwài (think it's odd), méisyǎngdàu (not have expected it). / Are you surprised that I came? Wǒ 'láile ní 'jywéde hěn 'gwài ma? / He surprised us by doing such a good job. Nèijyàn 'shř̄ tā 'dzwòde 'nèmma hǎu °jēn 'syà wǒmen yí'tyàu (°wǒmen 'jēn shř̄ méisyǎng'dàu, °jēn jyàu wǒmen jywéje chí'gwài). / I'm surprised at you. Ní kě 'jēn ràng wǒ méisyǎng'dàu.

A surprise. / I got the surprise of my life when I saw him. is expressed verbally as I was very surprised when I saw him. Wǒ yí 'kànjyàn tā 'syà wǒ yídà'tyàu. or as To see him was the most unexpected thing in my life. Wǒ néng dzài nèr 'kànjyàn 'tā jēn shř̄ yí'bèidz méisyǎng'dàu de 'shèr. / I've got a surprise for you in this package. is expressed as You can't guess what's in this package. Ní yí'dìng °syǎngbú'dàu (°tsāibù'jáu) jèi 'bāuli shř̄ 'shémma. / That was a surprise. is expressed as Nobody would have thought of it. 'Nèige jēn ràng rén syǎngbú'dàu. / They paid us a surprise visit. Méisyǎng'dàu 'tāmen lái 'kàn wǒmen láile. *but*

961

/Imagine my surprise! is expressed as You can think how surprised and bewildered I was! Nǐ 'syángsyang wǒ nèige chǐ'gwài ba!

To one's surprise méisyǎng'dàu. /I later learned, to my surprise, that he was right. Wǒ 'hòulai 'tīngshwō méisyǎng'dàu tā 'dwèi le.

SWEET. (To the taste) tyán. /Is the lemonade sweet enough? Nèige níngméng'shwèi gòu 'tyánde le ma? /Do you have any sweet pickles? Ní yǒu shémma tyán pàu'tsài ma?

(Not soured). /Is the milk still sweet? is expressed as Hasn't the milk gotten sour? Nyóu'nǎi hái méi'swān ne ma?

(To the smell) syāng; 'syāngtyán (smelling so good that it would probably taste good too). /These flowers smell too sweet. Jèi'syē 'hwār tài 'syāng le. /What's that sweet smell? Nèige nèmma 'syāngtyánsyāng'tyánde shr̀ 'shémma?

(Nice, pleasant) hǎu. /How sweet of you! Nǐ jēn 'hǎu. /She has a very sweet disposition. Tāde 'píchi jēn 'hǎu. /Her voice is very sweet. Tāde 'sǎngdz hén 'hǎu.

SWEETEN. °jyā (°gē, °fàng) táng (add sugar). /We haven't sweetened the cocoa yet. 'Kōukou lǐtou wǒmen hái méijyā 'táng.

SWELL (SWOLLEN). jǔng (enlarge because of infection); jàng (become bigger because of a change in temperature, dampness, etc.; warp). /My foot is beginning to swell up. Wǒde 'jyǎu 'júngchǐláile. /Your ankle looks swollen. Nǐde jyǎu'wàndz 'kànje syàng 'jǔngle shr̀de. /The hot water has made my hand swell. Rè'shwěi bá wǒ 'shǒu gěi pàu'jàngle. /The wood has swelled and the door won't open. 'Mùtou 'jàngle, 'mén kāibu'kāile.

(Increase) dzēngjyā. /Their numbers are swelling fast. Tāmende 'rénshur dzēng'jyāde hěn kwài.

Be swell (very good) hǎujíle, gāujíle, bàngjíle; °hěn (°jēn, °tǐng, °tài) °'hǎu (°'gāu, °'bàng). /Swell! Hǎu'jíle! /That's a swell idea. Nèige 'yìsz tíng 'hǎu. /She's a swell person. Tā nèige 'rén hǎu'jíle.

SWIFT. kwài; (of current) jí. /Is the current swift? 'Shwěi 'lyóude 'jí ma? /He kept up a swift pace. Tā 'dzǒude hěn 'kwài. /The end was so swift that it took everyone by surprise. Nèige 'wánde tài 'kwài le, 'shéi dōu méisyǎng'dàu.

SWIM (SWAM, SWUM). fúshwěi, yóuyǔng, yóushwěi. /Do you know how to swim? Nǐ hwèi yóu'yǔng? /Let's go swimming this afternoon. Jyēr 'syàwǔ 'dzámen fù'shwěi chyù ba. /We'll have to swim the river. Wǒmen děi 'fùgwò jèityáu 'hé chyù. *but* /The blow made my head swim. is expressed as The blow made my head dizzy and my eyes see stars. Nèiyí'syàdz 'dǎde wǒ 'tóuyunyǎn'hwā.

A swim is expressed verbally as above. /We had a good swim. Wǒmen fù'shwěi 'wárde tíng 'hǎu. /I'm going out for a swim. Wǒ yàu chyù 'fùfu 'shwěi.

SYSTEM. 'syìtǔng (organic or organized whole); in compounds also syì; 'jr̀dù (method or policy; of political or social organizations); in compounds also jr̀. /Our railway system isn't very good yet. Wǒmende 'tyělù 'syìtǔng hái 'búswàn 'hǎu. /He's reading about the solar system. Tā jèng 'yánjyou 'tàiyang'syì ne. /We're proud of our school system. Wǒmen 'jywéde wǒmende sywé'syàu 'jr̀dù hái bú'tswò. /We use the metric system here. 'Wǒmen jèr 'yùng 'mǐdá'jr̀.

(Plan, method) fádz, 'fāngfǎ, 'bànfǎ. /What is your system for getting things done? Nǐ yùng 'shémma 'fádz 'dzwòchulaide? /Do you understand the system well enough? 'Nèige fádz nǐ 'shóu bushóu?

TAKE

(Physical tract) is expressed as blood syě or as body shēndz. / He isn't rid of all the poison in his system yet. Tā syēlide 'dú hái méichú'jìng.

TABLE. (Furniture) jwō(dz). / Push the table against the wall. Bǎ 'jwōdz 'twēide kàuje 'chyáng.

(Array of data) byǎu; **timetable** shŕjyānbyǎu; **table of contents** 'mùlù, mùlù-byǎu. / The figures are given in the table on page twenty. Yàujǎude 'shùr dzài dì-'èrshryède 'byǎushang. / He's looking it up in the table of contents. Tā jèng dzài 'mùlù nèr 'jǎu ne. or Tā 'jèngdzai chá 'mùlù ne.

Set the table bǎijwō. / She set the table very attractively. Tā bǎi'jwō 'bǎide hén hǎu'kàn. (fig.) / They set a good table. Tāmen 'yùbèi de 'tsàihén °'hǎu (°'fēng-fù).

Turn the tables on °jŕ (°gěi) . . . 'lái yísyàdz. / Let's turn the tables on him; we can't always be doing what he says. Dzámen déi syǎng 'fár 'jŕje ta le, 'bùnéng 'jìng tīng 'tāde. / Let's turn the tables on him; we can't always let him get the best of us. Dzámen yé gěi 'tā lái yísyàdz ba; byé 'jìng jyàu 'tā jàn 'pyányi.

To table yāchilai, gēdzai yǐ'byār. / They tabled the motion. Tāmen bǎ yì'àn °'yāchilaile (°gēdzai yǐ'byār le).

TAIL. (of animals) yǐba. / The puppy had a clipped tail. Syáu'gǒurde 'yǐba shŕ 'dwòle de.

Tail end (of something that is taking time) mwòmwolyǎur, kwài 'wán le de shŕ-hou; (of something that extends in space) jǐn'hòutou nèi'dwàr, jǐn'hòutou nèi'jyéer. / We arrived at the tail end of the first act. Wǒmen dzài 'tóuyímùde mwòmwo'lyǎur 'dàude. or Wǒmen dzài dì'yímù syǐ kwài 'wánle de shŕhou 'dàude. / The tail end of the train was blocking the road. Hwǒ'chē jǐn'hòutou nèi'jyéer 'jèng bǎ 'lù 'dǎng-shang.

Tail light hòudēng. / I'm having the tail light on my car fixed. Wǒ jèng 'shōu-shr wǒ 'chēshangde hòu'dēng.

Tails (side of coin) mèr. / Heads or tails? Yàu 'dzèr yàu 'mèr.

To tail, tail behind gēnje (lái or chyù on occasion). / We'll tail right behind your car. Wǒmen jǐn 'gēnje nǐde 'chē.

Other English expressions. / His lecture was so confusing we couldn't make head or tail of it. Tāde yán'jyǎng 'lwànchibā'dzǎude, wǒmen jyǎn'jŕ bùjŕ'dàu tā 'shwōde shŕ 'shémma.

TAILOR. tsáifeng. / Where can I find a good tailor? 'Nár yóu hǎu 'tsáifeng?

Tailor (shop) tsáifengpù, syǐfúdyàn. / Take this suit to the tailor to be fixed. Bǎ jèitàu 'yǐfu nádàu tsáifeng'pù chyù 'gǎi yísyàr.

To tailor is expressed by dzwò make. / This skirt is well tailored. Jèige 'chyúndz dzwòde hén 'hǎu. / How long will it take to tailor this coat? Jèijyàn shàng-'yǐ 'děi dzwò 'dwōshau shŕhou?

TAKE (TOOK, TAKEN). (Want or accept) yàu; (choose) tyāu; (buy) mǎi; (rent) dzū. / Will you take a check for the bill? Jŕpyàu nǐ 'yàu buyàu? / Which room will you take? Nǐ yàu 'nèijyān 'wūdz? or Nǐ syǎng tyāu 'něijyān 'wūdz? / I'll take the room with a bath. Wǒ yàu dài syǐdzǎu'fáng de nèijyān wūdz. / I think I'll take the blue hat. Wó syǎng mǎi nèidǐng 'lánshǎrde 'màudz. / Let's take a house in the country for the summer. Dzámen 'syàtyar dzài chéng 'wàitou dzū swǒr 'fáng jù.

963

(Grasp and carry) bān, dĭlou, and various other terms depending on the method of carrying; *see* **CARRY, BRING.** / Here, boy, take my bags! 'Cháfang, bān 'syíngli! *or* 'Cháfang, 'dĭlou 'syángdz!

(Call for and carry away for some purpose) lái . . . chyúdzŏu. / Did the man take my laundry yet? Nèige 'rén lái bá wŏde 'dzāng 'yīfu chyú'dzŏule méiyou?

(Appropriate without permission) jĭ, dǎ, yùng, nádzŏu, chāudzŏu, dàidzŏu. / I wish you wouldn't keep taking my ties! Wŏ 'syīwang nĭ byé 'lǎu °'jĭ (°'dǎ) wŏde lĭng-'dài, 'syíng busyíng? / Who took my book? 'Shéi bá wŏde 'shū °ná'dzŏule (°chāu-'dzoule)? / Don't take my hat! Byé 'chāu wŏde 'màudz! *or* Byé bá wŏde 'màudz dài'dzŏu! / Who took the papers out of my drawer? 'Shéi bá wŏ 'chōutilide wén'jyàn ná'dzŏule? / Has anything been taken from your room? is expressed as Is your room short anything? Nĭ 'wūdzli 'dwǎnle shémma 'dūngsyi méiyou?

(Consider, bring into the picture) ná. / Take that man over there, for example. Jyòu ná 'nèr nèige 'rén dzwò ge 'bĭfang.

(Use) yùng, or expressed with a specific verb appropriate to the particular thing used. / Will you let me take your car? Wŏ 'kéyi yùng nĭde 'chē ma? / I take cream with my coffee. is expressed as When I drink coffee I put cream in it. Wŏ hē kā'fēi gē nǎi'yóu.

(Go by a means of transportation) kāi if one operates the vehicle oneself, otherwise dzwò. / I'm glad you took your car. Syìng'kwēi nĭ bǎ 'chē 'kāilaile. / We're taking the train tomorrow. Wŏmen 'míngtyan dzwò hwŏ'chē dzŏu.

(Capture) gūngsyalai, 'dǎsyàlái, dédau shŏu. / Our troops took the town in two hours. Wŏmende 'jyūndwèi 'lyǎngge jūngtóu de gūngfu jyòu bǎ 'chéng °'gūng-syàláile (°'dǎsyàláile, °dedau 'shŏule).

(Win) yíng. / Who do you think will take the tennis match? Nĭ shwō wǎngchyóur bĭ'sài 'shei hwèi 'yíng?

(Require personnel) yŏu . . . tsái; (require additional personnel) hái dĕi tyān . . . tsái. / It will take two more men to move this safe. Nwó jèige báusyǎn'syāng °'dzài yóu (°hái dĕi tyān) 'lyǎngge rén tsái 'syíng.

(Require time) yùng, dĕi yùng, fèi, dĕi fèi. / How long does the trip take? Yí'chyù yùng 'dwōshau shŕhou? / It took a long time for me to come here. Wŏ shàng 'jèr lai yùngle hǎu'syē 'shŕhou. / How long will it take to press my clothes? Bá wŏ 'yīfu 'tàng yitàng dĕi fèi 'dwōshau shŕhou?

Take a bath syidzǎu. / I'd like to take a bath now. Wó syǎng syàn'dzài syí-'dzǎu.

Take a beating 'āi yídwùn 'dzòu. / He certainly took a whale of a beating. Tā dzú'dzúrde 'āile dwùn 'dzòu. or fig. expressed as He's really lost badly. Tā 'shūde jēn 'tsǎn.

Take a chance on someone shŕshr. / Let's take a chance on him. Dzámen jyòu 'shŕshr ta ba.

Take a nap 'syē yihwěr, 'shwèi yìsyǎu'jyàu, 'mīfeng yìhwěr, dǎge dwěr. / We always take a nap after dinner. Wŏmen chŕ wǎn'fàn yǐ'hòu 'lǎu 'syēyihwěr.

Take a seat dzwò. / Take a seat, please. Chĭng'dzwò (chĭng'dzwò). / Is this seat taken? 'Jèr yŏu rén 'dzwò ma? or expressed as Does this seat have anyone? Jèige 'wèidz yŏu 'rén le ma?

Take a walk 'lyōudalyōuda, dzóudzou, sànsan bù. / Would you like to take a walk? Nĭ syǎng sànsan 'bù ma?

Take advantage of (make good use of) chènje; (use something or someone for one's own benefit) jàn pyányi, chǐfu。 /We should take advantage of the good weather and go on a picnic. Wǒmen yīngdāng chènje 'tyānchi 'hǎu, chyù yě'tsān chyu. /He took advantage of my inexperience. Tā lìyùng wǒ méi 'jīngyàn °jàn wǒde 'pyányi (°'chǐfu wǒ). *but* /Thanks, I'll take advantage of your offer. 'Syèsye, wó yǐ'hòu yí'dìng lái °'máfan nín (°gēn nin chǐng'jyàu, °chǐng nín bāng'máng). *or* 'Syèsye, wó yǐ'hòu yí'dìng jàu'bàn.

Take advice tīnghwà. /Take my advice. Tīng wǒde 'hwà.

Take someone's arm chān. /Let me take your arm. Ràng wo 'chānje ni 'dzǒu.

Take care of a matter bàn. /I took care of that matter. Nèijyàn 'shèr wó 'yǐjing 'bànle.

Take care of a person jàugu. /Please take care of the children. Láujya, 'jàugu dyar syǎu'hár. *but* /Take care of yourself! Dwō'bwō bǎu'jùng! *or* 'Syǎusyīn dyǎr! *or* Dwō 'lyóu dyǎr 'shén! *or* Hǎu'hāurde!

Take charge of a house or family kānjyā. /Who's taking charge of the house while you're away? Nǐ chū'mér de shŕhou 'shéi gěi ni kān'jyā?

Take charge of matters bàn, gwān.

Take hold of jyōu, jwā, dzwàn, ná, tái. *See* **GRASP, HOLD.** /Take hold of this rope and help us pull the boat in. °'Jyōujùle (°'Jwājùle, °'Dzwànjùle, °'Nájùle) jèigēr 'shéngdz hǎu bāngje wǒmen bǎ 'chwán 'lājìnlai. /Will you take the other end of the desk and help me move it? Nǐ 'táije jwōdz 'nèi tóur 'bāngje wǒ 'nwó yinwó, hǎu ma?

Take it easy. /We ought to take it easy in this weather. Syàng 'jèyàngde 'tyār dzámen 'yīngdāng °màn'mār lái (°'dzǒuje 'chyáu, °'yōuje'jyèrde dzwò, °'hàu yǐhwěr). /Take it easy! 'Màndyār lái! *or* Lyóu'shén! *or* Byé jāu'jí!

Take it (that) . . . jyù . . . kàn. /I take it you're in trouble. Jyù wǒ 'kàn, nǐ dà'gài yòu °rě'shŕ (°yǒu 'máfan) le.

Take medicine fú yàu; (if in solid form) chŕ yàu; (if in liquid form) hē yàu. /Have you taken your medicine this morning? Nǐ jyēr 'dzǎuchen chŕ 'yàule ma?

Take offense 'dzàiyì. dzàihu, shēngchì, and other expressions meaning get angry, etc. /You shouldn't take offense at what was said. Gāngtsái nèijyù 'hwà nǐ 'yùngbujáu 'dzàiyì.

Take pictures (*or* photographs) jàusyàng. /Are you allowed to take pictures here? 'Jèr syǔ jàu'syàng ma?

Take place most events which in English are said to take place are expressed by verbs in Chinese, thus chūshŕ an accident takes place, chūbìn a funeral takes place, and so on, therefore, see the other English words involved; *also see* **HAPPEN.**

Take someone's **temperature** shŕbyǎu. /Did the doctor take your temperature this morning? 'Dàifu jyēr 'dzǎuchen gěi ni shŕ'byǎule ma?

Take the blame (for). /I won't take the blame for his mistake. 'Tāde tswòr 'píng shémma 'wǒ rèn? *or* 'Wǒ wèi shémma gěi 'tā dzwò tìsź'gwěi? *or* 'Wǒ tsái bútì 'tā rèn'tswòr ne. /He took all the blame himself. Tā 'yíge rén bēi hēigwō.

Take the trouble to (in making a polite request) láujyà. /Will you take the trouble to look at this for me? Láu'jyà tǐ wo 'kàn yísyàr. *but* /Should I take the trouble to go out there this afternoon? Wǒ jyēr syàwǔ 'yùngdejáu wǎng nèr 'pǎu yítàng ma?

Take one's time. /Let's take our time about getting there. Dzámen màn'mārde wǎng nèr 'chyù, hǎu le. /Can I take my time? Wǒ màn'mārde dzwò, 'syíng ma?

Take something **hard.** / Don't take it so hard. Hé'bǐ wǎng 'syīnli chyù. *or* Hé'bǐ nèmma 'dzàihu. *or* Byé syǎngbu'kāi. *or* Yùngbu'jáu dzwān nyóu 'jǐjyau.

Take sick, be taken sick bìng, débìng, shēngbìng. / When did he take sick? Tā 'shémma shŕhou 'bìngde? / I heard she was taken sick in the theater. Wǒ tīng-'shwō tā dzài syì'ywándzli jyòu 'bìngle.

Take after (resemble) syàng. / Who do you take after, your father or your mother? Nǐ shŕ 'jǎngde syàng nǐ 'fùchin háishr syàng ní 'mǔchin?

Take something **away** is expressed by the various words listed under **CARRY** plus dzǒu *or* chyù. / Have the trunks been taken away yet? 'Syāngdz yǐjing ná'dzǒule ma?

Take something **back** is expressed by the various words listed under **CARRY** plus hwéi. / I won't need your book, so why don't you take it back? Wǒ yùngbu'jáu nǐde 'shū le, nǐ 'náhweichyu déle.

Take something **down** (actual motion) is expressed by words listed under **CARRY, GRASP** *or* **BRING** plus syà(lai). / Take the picture down from the wall. Bǎ nèijāng 'hwàr tsúng 'chyángshang 'jāisyalai.

Take notes or minutes (down) jì, jìsyalai. / Who's taking down the minutes? 'Shéi jì 'jìlu ne? / Will you take this down, please. Chǐng ni bǎ 'jèige 'jìsyalai. / He's taking notes at the conference. Tā jèng dzài hwèi'yìshang jì bǐ'jì ne.

Take someone **down a peg** jyàu . . . syàbu'lái 'tái. / She certainly took him down a peg. Tā kě 'jēn 'jyàu ta syàbu'lái 'tái.

Take someone **for** someone 'yǐwéi . . . shŕ . . . ; or expressed as see wrongly kàntswòle *or* recognize wrongly rèntswòle. / Sorry, I took you for someone else. Dwèibu'jù, wó yǐwéi nǐ shŕ 'lìng yíge rén ne. *or* Dwèibu'jù, wǒ rèn'tswòle 'rén le.

Take for granted. / Don't take so many things for granted. Byé 'tài 'dàyi le. *or* Byé dyǎurlàng'dǎngde. *or* 'Byé jywéde 'shémma dōu tǐng 'rúngyi shŕde. *or* Byé 'yǐwéi méi 'wèntí le shŕde.

Take in (see or look at) kàn, chyáu. / Let's take in a movie this afternoon. Dzámen jyēr 'syàwǔ kàn dyán'yǐngr chyù ba. / We haven't enough time to take in all the sights. Wǒmen méi 'gūngfu bǎ 'swóyǒude 'chywán kàn'dàule.

Take in money jèng, jǐn, jwàn, shōurù. / How much do you take in in a month? Nǐ 'yíge ywè jèng 'dwōshǎu chyán?

Take in people, guests shōu, jù, 'jāudài, yǒu. / Even in the winter this hotel takes in a lot of people. Jyòushr 'dūngtyan de shŕhou jèige lyú'gwǎn yě 'jāudài bù-'shǎude 'kèrén.

Take someone **in** (deceive) bǎ . . . géi 'hǔjù, bǎ . . . gěi 'mēngjù. / He certainly took us in with his stories. Tā 'shwōde jēn bá wǒmen gěi 'mēngjùle.

Take clothes **in** (make smaller) shōujǐn, myānjǐn, chyājǐn. / Will you take this dress in at the waist? Nǐ néng bǎ jèijyàn 'yīfude yāu'shēn shōu'jǐn yìdyǎr ma?

Take a baby **in** one's **arms** bàu. / Will you take the baby in your arms? Nǐ 'bàu yibàu 'háidz, hǎu ma?

Take off (of a plane) chǐfēi, kāi. / When does the plane take off? Fēi'jǐ 'shém-ma shŕhou chǐ'fēi?

Take off clothing; jāi for hats, ties, scarfs, etc.; kwān for a topcoat; twō for shoes, coats, trousers, etc. / Take off your hat. Jāile 'màudz.

Take on (get emotional) syǎngbukāi, 'chóuméi bù'jǎn, 'dzgěr gēn dz̀'gěr gwòbu'chyù. /Don't take on so! Byé syǎngbu'kāi!

Take on <u>personnel</u> (hire) tyān, shōu, gù; jyā (if personnel is additional). /I hear the factory is taking on some new men. Wǒ 'tīngshwō gūng'chǎng gù syīn'rén le.

Take on <u>a job</u> kāishř dzwò, dé, lǎn. /We took on a new job yesterday. Wǒmen 'dzwórge kāishř dzwò 'syīnde 'gūngdzwò. *or* Wǒmen 'dzwórge 'lǎnle yíge 'syīnde 'chāishř.

Take <u>someone</u> on (challenge). /I'll have to take you on for some tennis. Wó děi gēn ni 'sàisai wǎng'chyóur.

Take <u>something</u> out of <u>a place</u> ná, jwā, <u>and other words meaning</u> **GRASP**, **CARRY**, etc. <u>plus</u> chū. /Take the fruit out of the bag. Bǎ 'swéigwǒ tsúng 'kwāngrli 'náchulai.

Take <u>dirt</u> out of <u>something</u> chyùdyàu, nùngsyachyu. /Can you take the spot out of these pants? Nǐ néng bǎ jèityáu 'kùdzshangde 'dzāng °'nùngsyachyu (°chyù'dyàule) ma?

Take <u>it</u> out on <u>someone</u> ná . . . sāchi, ná . . . chūchi, jǎusyun, gēn . . . gwòbu-'chyù. /Well, you don't have to take it out on me! Nǐ yùngbu'jáu ná 'wǒ sā'chi!

Take to <u>someone</u>. /They take to him like their own child. Tāmen'ài ta gēn ài 'dzjǐde 'háidz shřde.

Take to <u>a place</u> (run away to) 'táudàu, 'pǎudàu. /When we approached, the enemy took to the woods. Děngdàu wǒmen 'kwài 'dàule nèr de shřhou, 'dírén táudau shù'líndzli chyù le.

Take <u>something or someone</u> to <u>a place</u> is expressed by the various words listed under **GRASP, CARRY, BRING, SEND** plus dàu, shàng, *or* hwéi. /Who's taking her to the station? 'Shéi sùng ta shàng chē'jàn na? /Please take me home now. Chǐng ni lǐ'shř sùng wǒ hwéi 'jyā ba. /When were you taken to the hospital? Tāmen 'shémma shřhou bǎ ni sùngjìn yī'ywàn de? /Take this letter to the post office. Bǎ jèifēng 'syìn sùngdau yóujèng'jyú chyù. /May I take you to dinner? Wǒ chǐng nǐ chyù chř'fàn, 'hǎu buhǎu?

Take <u>something or someone</u> to <u>a place</u> (of a route or a vehicle). /The train will take you there in three hours. is expressed as If you go by train you can get there in three hours. Nǐ dzwò hwǒ'chē sā'jūngtou yǐ'nèi jyòu kéyi 'dàu nèr. /Where will that road take us? is expressed as That road goes where? Jèityáu 'dàur °tūngdàu (°chyù, °shàng) 'nǎr?

Take up (begin working on) kāishř sywé, chíshř sywé, kāishř nyàn, chíshř nyàn. /I think I'll take up some language this year. Wó syǎng 'jīnnyán chíshř 'sywé dyǎr wàigwo'hwà.

Take <u>something</u> up with <u>someone</u> gēn . . . shānglyang, jǎu . . . , gēn . . . dǎudau, gēn . . . swānjǎng, wèn. /You'll have to take that matter up with someone else. 'Nèijyàn shèr nǐ 'dzwèihǎu chyù gēn 'byérén 'shānglyang.

Take <u>something</u> up (shorten at the bottom) gǎidwǎn. /Take up the gown a little. Bǎ dà-'gwàr gái'dwǎn yìdyǎr.

Take <u>someone</u> up on <u>something</u> gàn, gēn . . . lái, chřjyàng. /He offered me a bet, but I didn't take him up on it. Tā yàu gēn wo dá'dǔ láije, °wǒ méi'gàn (°wǒ méi gēn ta 'lái, °wǒ bùchř'jyàng).

Take up with <u>someone</u> gēn . . . 'wǎnglái, gēn . . . dǎ 'jyāudài. /I wouldn't take up with those people if I were you. 'Wǒ yàushr 'nǐ dehwà, 'jywé bù gēn 'nèibāng rén 'wǎnglái.

The take (amount taken in) is expressed verbally. /What was the take this week at the theater? Syǐ'ywándz 'jèi yíge lǐbài yí'gùng jìnle 'dwōshau chyán?

TALK. shwō, shwō hwà. /Who's he talking to? Tā gēn 'shéi shwō 'hwà? /Let's see, what were we just talking about? Dzámen gāng shwō 'shémma láije? /Don't you think she talks too much? Nǐ 'shr̀ bushr̀ jywéde tā °shwō 'hwà tài 'dwō (°'tài hàu shwō 'hwà, °shwō 'hwà 'tài bù'syǎusyin)? /Why don't you talk sense for a change? Nǐ shwō yìdyár yǒu'yìszde 'syíng busyíng? /Please talk slower. Chǐng 'màn yidyǎr 'shwō.

Talk too much (be garrulous) ài dwō dzwěi, pǐnchi, 'pǐndzwěigwā'shéde; (gossip) ài chwán syán'hwà, ài chwán shé.

Talk loudly (loudly and angrily) rāngrang, chǎu, chěje 'sǎngdz 'hǎn.

Talk something over (discuss) tántan; (figure) 'dǎswandǎswan; (consult) 'shānglyangshānglyang; (instead of getting mad) yǒu 'hwà hǎu'hāur shwō. /We'll have to talk over our plans for tomorrow. Dzámen děi 'tán yìtán gwānyu 'míngtyande 'jì-hwà. or Déi 'dǎswàndǎswan 'myérge 'gàn shémma. /Let's talk this over. Dzámen 'shānglyangshānglyang jèige. or Dzámen yǒu 'hwà hǎu'hāur shwō.

Talk someone into something. /He talked me into coming along. is expressed as My coming is because he persuaded me. Wǒ 'lái shr̀ 'tā chywànde. or as My coming was under his influence. Wǒ 'lái shr̀ shòu 'tāde 'yíngsyang.

Talk back to dǐng . . . yíjyù, gēn . . . táigàng, gēn . . . jyánglǐ, gēn . . . bàn-dzwěi, gēn . . . jēnglwùn, gēn . . . fēnbyàn, gēn . . . fèi 'tùmei, gēn . . . dèngyǎn, bwó, dǐng, gēn . . . yìbān 'jyànshr. /For once he dared to talk back to her. Jēi-hwéi tā kě 'jēn 'dǐngle ta yi'jyù. /I wouldn't talk back to them, if I were you. Wǒ yàushr 'nǐ dehwà, jyòu bù'gēn tāmen jēng'lwùn. /There's no use talking back to them. 'Yùngbujáu 'bwó tāmen.

A talk yánjyǎng, yǎnshwō. /His talk was long and dull. Tāde yán'jyǎng shwōde yòu 'cháng yòu méi'wèr.

(Gossip, empty talk). /Oh, that's just talk! 'Nà búgwò shr̀ °'shwōshwo ér'yǐ (°dàu'tú chwán'shwō, °yǒu'rén nèmma 'shwō ér'yǐ)!

(Malicious gossip) 'syánhwà. /Her actions have caused a lot of talk. Tāde 'syíngwéi 'jāule hěn 'dwō de 'syánhwà.

The talk of the town is expressed as the whole town stormed mǎn'chéng fēng'yǔ. /That affair became the talk of the town. Nèijyàn 'shèr 'nàude mǎn'chéng fēng'yǔ.

TALL. gāu. /How tall are you? Nǐ yǒu dwō 'gāu? /Have you ever seen such a tall building? Nǐ 'jyàngwo jèmma 'gāude 'lóu ma?

Tall order. /That's a pretty tall order, but I'll try to do it. Nǐ jyàu wo 'bàn de jèijyàn 'shèr °bú'dà rúngyi 'bàn (°'yésyu bù'syíng), kěshr wó 'dzǔng hwèi syǎng-fár 'shr̀shr̀ de.

Tall story. /He's really telling tall stories. Tā 'shwōde jēn 'rènau. or Tā yángwò chǐ'shr̀.

TASK. shr̀, 'gūngdzwò, 'léijwèi.

Take someone to task mà, 'mánywàn, swǔn. /Lots of people are taking him to task because of that incident. Hǎu'syē rén wèi 'nèijyàn shèr jr̀ 'mà ta.

TASTE. (To the tongue) wèr; or expressed verbally with cháng (taste). /The five tastes are: sweet, sour, bitter, hot, and salty. Wǔwèi shr̀: 'swān, 'là, 'kǔ, 'tyán, 'syán. /This meat has a strange taste. Jèikwài 'ròude 'wèr hěn 'tèbyé. or Jèi-kwài 'ròu yǒu 'wèr le. /I don't like the taste of this milk. Wǒ bù'syǐhwan jèige nyóu'nǎide 'wèr. /Give me a taste of that soup. °Wǒ lái (°Ràng wo) 'cháng dyǎr nèige 'tāng.

(Preference). /Suit your own taste. Swéi 'nǐ. *or* Ní 'syǐhwan dzěmma 'yàng jyòu dzěmma 'yàng ba.

(Ability to choose). /She has good taste in clothes. Tā hěn 'hwèi chwān 'yǐfu. *or* Tā 'yǐfu chwānde hén 'yǎ.

Poor taste. /That remark was in very poor taste. Shwō 'nèijǔng hwà hěn 'súchi.

To taste cháng; or expressed with the noun wèr, *see* above. /Just taste this coffee! 'Cháng yicháng jèijǔng kā'fēi! /I can't taste a thing with this cold. Wǒ shāng'fēngle, °'shémma wèr dōu 'chángbuchu'lái (°chr 'shémma dōu méi'wèr). /This soup tastes too much of garlic. Jèige 'tāng chángje 'swànwèr tài °'dà (°'chùng, °'núng). /This wine tastes bitter. Jèige 'jyóu wèr fā'kǔ.

(Eat a little) chǐ. /She hasn't tasted anything since yesterday. Tā tsúng 'dzwór chǐ, 'shémma dōu méi'chr.

TAX. shwèi. /How much is the tax on these cigarettes? Yān'jywǎr shàng 'dwōshau shwèi?

Pay taxes, get taxes in jyāushwèi, nàshwèi, bǎ 'shwèichyán 'jyāujinchyu. /I hope I can get my taxes in on time this year. Wǒ 'syīwang wǒ 'jīnnyán néng bǎ 'shwèichyán ànje 'shŕhou 'jyāujinchyu.

To tax shàngshwèi, jēngshwèi, chōushwèi, shōushwèi. /I think they're taxing us too much on our property. Wǒ 'jywéde tāmen dzài dzámende 'chǎnyèshang chōushwèi chōude tài 'dwō le.

(Tiring). /Reading this small print is very taxing on the eyes. Kàn jèmma 'dyǎrde syǎu'dzěr kě 'jēn °fèi'yǎn (°'lèi'yǎn, °shāng'yǎn). /This heat is taxing my strength. Tyār 'rède wǒ dōu kwài 'tān le.

TEA. (Ready to drink) chá; (leaves) cháyè. /I'll take tea, please. 'Syèsye, wǒ hē 'chá (hǎu le). /I'll have a catty of tea, please. Chǐng ni gěi wo yìjīn cháyè.

Have tea hē chá, chr chá. /Let's have tea. °Hē (°Chr) dyǎr 'chá ba.

Have someone over for tea chǐng . . . gwòlái °hē chá (°chr chá, °chr 'chá-dyǎn). /Let's have them over for tea Sunday afternoon. Dzámen lǐbài'tyān 'syàwǔ chǐng tāmen gwòlai chr 'chádyǎn, hǎu buhǎu?

TEACH (TAUGHT). jyāu, 'jyāugěi, jyāuhwéi; less formal 'jyǎng yijyǎng, 'jŕdyǎn, gàusung. /Will you teach me your language? Ní 'jyāu wo shwō nǐde 'hwà, hǎu ma? /Would you teach me something about the customs of your country? Ní 'ywànyi 'jyǎng yijyǎng nǐmen 'gwóli de 'fēngsú ma? /You'll have to teach me how to use this machine. Ní děi °'gàusung (°'jŕdyǎn, °'jyāugei) wo dzěmma 'yùng jèige 'jīchi. /Who taught you how to drive a car? 'Shéi jyāu'hwèile ni kāi 'chē de? /Is music taught here? 'Jèr jyāu yīn'ywè ma? /Is that the way you've been taught to handle tools? 'Shéi jyāugei ni 'nèmma shr 'jyāhwo de?

TEACHER. jyàuywán, jyāushŭde; in addressing a teacher directly usually syānsheng.

TEAM. (Athletic) dwèi plus the game specified; thus **basketball team** lánchyóudwèi, **baseball team** bàngchyóudwèi, etc.

(People working together) °jige rén (°dà(jya)hwǒr, °lyǎngge rén) °yíkwàr (°héchilai) .... /They make a very good team for that work. Tāmen °jige rén (etc.) °yíkwàr (°héchilai) dzwò nèijyan 'shr, jēng 'hǎu.

Team up with is expressed as breathe through the same nose gēn . . . yíge 'bídz chū 'chyèr. /We'll go places if we team up with them. Dzámen yàushr néng gēn tāmen 'yíge bídz chū 'chyèr, 'nà kě jyòu jēn 'lyǎubude le.

TEAR (TORE, TORN). (Something flat and flexible, like paper or cloth) chě (if with one motion); sż (if into many small scraps); either of these plus an appropriate postverb such as kāi open or apart, pwò into shreds or tatters, etc. /Be careful not to tear your clothes. 'Syàusyīn byé bǎ 'yīfu 'chě le. /I hope you tore up my last letter. Wǒ 'syīwàng nǐ bá wǒ 'shàngyīfēng 'syìn 'sż le. /Who tore this package open? 'Shéi bǎ jèige 'bāur 'chěkai le? /I tore my pants. Wó bǎ 'kùdz 'chě le. /Who tore the label off the bottle? 'Shéi bǎ 'píngrshangde jr̄'tyáu gěi 'sżsyachyu le? /I see a page has been torn out of this book. Jèiběr 'shū jyàurén gěi 'chěle yì'pyār chyu.

(If by catching on something) gwāpwòle. /My shirt got torn at the elbow. Wǒ chèn'shārde gēbe'jǒur nèr gwǎ'pwòle.

Tear down a building, **tear up** (wreck) things chāi. /They plan to tear down that dirty old hotel next month. Tāmen yùbei 'syàyíge ywè bǎ nèige yòu'pwò yòu'lǎude lyúgwǎn 'chāi le.

A tear is expressed verbally as above, thus chě'pwòle de dìfang torn place, etc., or by kǒudz hole. /Can this tear be repaired in a hurry? Chě'pwòle de jèi-'kwài néng lì'shŕ 'bùshang ma? or Nǐ néng bǎ jèige 'kǒudz gán'jǐn jyòu 'bùshang ma?

TEAR. (Teardrop) yǎnlèi; often expressed with the verb kū cry. /She breaks out into tears at a moment's notice. Tā shwō 'kū jyòu 'kū. or expressed as Her tears are like tap water. Tā yǎn'lèi gēn dzlái'shwěr shŕde. /Tears won't do you any good. Nǐ 'kū yě méi'yùng.

TELEGRAM. dyànbàu; **send a telegram** °dǎ (°fā) dyànbàu; **transmit a telegram** fā dyàn-bàu; **receive a telegram** °jyē (°shōu) dyànbàu. /Are there any telegrams for me? Yǒu wǒde dyàn'bàu ma? /Can I send a telegram here? Nǐmen 'jèr °dǎ (°'fā) dyàn-'bàu ma? /I want to send a telegram to . . . . (person) Wǒ yàu 'dǎ yíge dyàn'bàu gěi . . . . or (place) Wǒ yàu 'dǎ yíge dyàn'bàu dàu . . . . or Wǒ yàu wàng . . . dǎ dyàn-'bàu. /I received three telegrams last night. Dzwótyan wǎnshang wǒ °'jyēle (°'shōu-le) sānfēng dyàn'bàu.

TELEGRAPH. (Send a telegram) dǎ dyànbàu; (transmit a telegram) fā dyànbàu. /Tele-graph us when you get there. 'Dàu nèr de shŕhou géi wǒmen dǎ ge dyàn'bàu. /I'm going to telegraph my folks for some money. Wǒ yàu gěi 'jyāli dǎ dyàn'bàu hǎu yàu dyǎr 'chyán.

By telegraph yùng dyànbàu. /Shall we send the news by telegraph? Jèige 'syàu-syi wǒmen 'shŕ bushŕ yàu yùng dyàn'bàu fāchū?

Telegraph office dyànbàujyú.

TELEPHONE. dyànhwà. /Do you have a telephone? Nǐ nèr yǒu dyàn'hwà ma? or, if asking someone more conversationally whether his house or office is so equipped, Nǐ 'ān dyàn'hwà le ma? /Can I use your telephone, please? 'Jyè nínde dyàn'hwà 'shŕ-shr, syíng ma?

To telephone dǎ dyànhwà. /Did anyone telephone me? Yǒu wǒde dyàn'hwà ma? or Yǒu 'rén gěi wo dǎ dyàn'hwà láije ma? /Where can I telephone you this evening? Jyēr 'wǎnshang wǒ wàng 'nár gěi ni dǎ dyàn'hwà?

TELEVISION. dyànshŕ.

TELL (TOLD). (Give someone information about something) gàusung, gàusu, gěi . . . 'jyǎng yísyàr, gēn . . . tí. / Tell him your name. 'Gàusung ta nǐ 'jyàu shémma. / Can you tell me how to get to the station? Chǐng ni 'gàusung wo dàu hwǒchē'jàn dzěmma chyù. / Tell me all about it. 'Tùngtùngkwār'kwārde 'gàusung wo. *or* Tsúng-'tóurdàu'lyǎur gěi wo 'jyǎng yísyàr. / Did they tell you anything about their plans for this evening? Tāmen gēn ni 'tíle méití jyēr 'wǎnshang tāmen shř 'yùbei 'gàn shémma? *but* / I told you so! Wó 'dzǎu jyòu gēn ni 'shwōgwo! *or* Nǐ bù'tǐng °hǎurén (°lǎurén) 'yán!

(Order someone to do something) jyàu. / Tell them not to make so much noise. Jyàu tamen byé 'rǎng. / Tell the driver to wait for us. Jyàu nèige kāi'chēde 'ďengje dzámen. / I was told to wait here. Tāmen jyàu wo dzài 'jèr ďeng.

(Know) 'jřdàu. / You never can tell what he's going to do next. Nǐ 'tsúnglái jyòu méi'fár 'jřdàu tā yàu 'gàn shémma.

Tell me *or* **tell us** as an introductory remark to an informal question, is often simply omitted. / Tell me, what are you doing tonight? Nǐ jyēr 'wǎnshang 'gàn shémma?

Tell the difference between fēnchulai, shwōchulai, chyáuchulai. / I can't tell the difference between these two materials. Wǒ °'fēnbuchulái (°'shwōbuchulái, °'chyáubuchulái) jèilyángjǔng 'tsailyàur yǒu shémma bǐyí'yàng. / Even if you'd seen them up close, you couldn't have told them apart. Nǐ jyoushr jàndzai tāmen gēn'chyǎr yě 'fēnbuchulái tamen. / How do you tell one from another? is expressed as What's your method of distinguishing? Nǐ dzěmma 'fēnfǎr?

Tell the truth shwō shř'hwà. / Are you telling the truth? Nǐ shř shwō shř'hwà ne ma?

Tell someone **off** mà . . . yídwùn, jyàusyun . . . yídwùn, shwō . . . yídwùn. / I'm going to tell him off one of these days. Nèityān wǒ fēiděi hǎu'hǎurde 'mà ta yídwùn.

Be able to tell time rènshr jūng. / Can your little boy tell time? Nǐde syǎu'hár rènshr 'jūng le ma?

Don't tell me. / Don't tell me I'm too late! (because I know it perfectly well already) Wó 'wǎn le, 'yùngbujáu 'nǐ shwō! *or* Wǒ 'jřdau wó 'wǎn le, 'nǐ jyòu byé 'shwō le! *or* Nǐ kě byé 'shwō wǒ 'láide tài 'wǎn le! *or* (that can't be) Mwò'fēi wǒ 'jēn 'wǎnle ma?

TEMPERATURE. (Of a person) 'rèdù, 'tǐwēn; (of a person or the weather) 'wēndù. / What's the temperature today? Jīntyande 'wēndù shř dwōshau? *or* 'Jyēr dwōshau 'dù? / She's had a high temperature for three days now. 'Jèisāntyān tāde 'rèdù hěn 'gāu.

Run a temperature fāshāu; **run a high temperature** fā 'dàshāu.

Take one's temperature shřbyǎu, shř 'rèdù, shř 'tǐwēn, shř 'wēndù. / You'd better have the nurse take your temperature. Nǐ ràng kānhù °'shřshr nǐde 'rèdù ba (°gěi ni 'shřshr 'byǎu ba).

TEN. shř; **the tenth** dìshř; **one tenth** shřfēnjr'yī.

TERM. (In office) rèn. / Do you think he deserves another term in office? Nǐ 'jywéde tā °gòu 'dīge (°pèi) °'dzài dzwò yí'rèn (°lyán'rèn) ma?

(In school) sywéchī, jì. / When does the new term at school begin? Sywésyàu 'syà °yìsywé'chī (°yí'jì) 'shémma shřhou kāishř?

(Technical name) is expressed verbally as be called jyàu. / Do you know the term for this part of the machine? Nǐ 'jřdàu jīchide 'jèiyíbùfen jyàu 'shémma?

Terms (conditions) 'tyáujyàn. / What are your terms on this automobile? Ní chū'mài jèilyàng 'chē dōu yōu 'shémma 'tyáujyàn? / I think my terms are pretty fair. Wǒ 'jywéde wǒde 'tyáujyàn hén hé'lǐ.

Be on good terms with. / I've been on very good terms with that man up until lately. Wǒ 'jř dàu dzwèi'jìn gēn 'nèige rén °'wéichřje hén hǎude 'gwānsyì (°'hwùn-de tíng 'hǎu) láije.

Bring someone to terms gēn . . . héjyě. / Can we bring him to terms, or will we have to go to court? Dzámen 'shř bushř néng gēn ta hé'jyě, háishr dèi gēn ta dǎ 'gwānsz?

Not be on speaking terms lyán shwō 'hwà dōu bù'shwō le. / We're not even on speaking terms now. Wǒmen 'syàndzài lyán shwō 'hwà dōu bù'shwō le.

Speak of someone in flattering terms fèngcheng, pěng. / People are always speaking of him in flattering terms. Dà'jyā lǎu ài 'fèngcheng ta.

Be termed. / He is what might be termed a wealthy man. Tā dà'gài kéyi °'swàn-shř (°'shwō shř) yíge 'kwòrén.

TERRIBLE. 'lìhài, dà, added to intensify the unpleasant nature of something already made clear by other words. / Wasn't that a terrible storm last night? Dzwór 'yèli nèijèn bàufēng'yǔ 'shř bushř gòu °'lìhaide (°'dàde)? / I've got a terrible cold. Wǒ jāu'lyáng jāude hěn 'lìhai. but / We had a terrible time at their party. is expressed as We didn't find their party at all interesting. Wǒmen dzài tāmen nèr 'wárde yì-dyár yě méi 'yìsz. / Gee! That's terrible! 'Āiya! 'Nà kě bù'hǎu.

TEST. (Chemically or medically) yàn, hwàyàn. / I think we'd better test this water before we drink it. Wǒ syǎng 'díng háu wǒmen 'syān bá 'shwěi °'yànyàn (°'hwàyàn-hwàyàn) dzài 'hē.

(Physically, mechanically) jyǎnyàn, jyǎnchá; (very general) shř. / Take the machine back to the shop and have it tested. Bǎ 'jīchì náhwéi 'chǎngli chyù °'shř yishř (°jyǎn'yànjyǎnyàn, °jyǎn'chájyǎnchá).

(Examine a person) kǎu. / She tests us once a month. Tā yíge 'ywè 'kǎu wǒ-men yì'hwéi.

Test (examination) kǎushř; or expressed verbally with kǎu as above. / I have to take a test tomorrow. Wǒ míngtyan děi tsānjyā yige kǎu'shř. / You'll have to take a test before you can get your driver's license. Ní děi 'kǎu yísyàr 'tsái néng nájau kāichē'jřjáu.

(Trial). / His music will stand the test of time. is expressed as His music certainly isn't capable of being popular for a short while and then being done for. Tāde yǐn'ywè jywé búhwèi húng yí'jèr jyòu 'wán le.

THAN. bǐ. / Have you something better than this? Ní yóu bǐ jèige 'háu dyǎr de ma? / Can't you work any faster than that? Ní bùnéng dzwòde bǐ 'nèige dzài 'kwài dyǎr ma? / He's a foot taller than you. 'Tā bǐ 'nǐ 'gāu yìchř. but / I'd rather stay home than go to that dull play. is expressed as I much prefer staying home and also don't want to go to that dull play. Wǒ chíng'ywàn dzài 'jyāli 'dāije, yě bù'syǎng chyù kàn nèijǔng wēn 'syì.

Other than . . . , something else than . . . (except) chúle . . . (yǐ'wài). / We have no dictionary other than an out-dated one. Wǒmen jer 'chúle běr 'lǎudzdyán yǐ'wài méiyóu dz'dyǎn le. / Can't you think of something else than going to the movies? Nán-daushwō 'chúle kàndyàn'yǐngr ní jyòu syǎngbuchū byéde 'shèr lái 'gàn ma?

THANK. syè. / He thanked me profusely before he left. Tā gēn wǒ 'syèle yòu syè tsái 'dzŏude. *or* Tā 'chyānsyèwànsyède 'dzŏu de. / They wrote him a letter thanking him. Tāmen gĕi tā syĕle yìfēng syìn 'syèsye tā.

(Blame). / I have only myself to thank for this mess. 'Shr̀ching dàu 'jèijŭng dìbù chywán 'ywàn wŏ dz̀'jĭ buhău.

Polite expressions in which **thanks** *or* **thank you** are used. / Thanks. *or* Thank you. 'Syèsye. *or* Dwō'syè (dwō'syè). *or* Fèi'syìn ('fèi'syìn). *or* (for something not yet done such as a future favor) Láu'jya láu'jyà. / Many thanks. Dwō'syè (dwōsyè). *or* Tài fèi'syìn le. *or* 'Jēn shr fèi'syìn le. / Thanks for the idea. Jèige 'yìsz hĕn 'hău, dwō'syè. / Thanks for coming. 'Máfan ní 'pǎule yítàng. *or* Láu'bù, láu'bù. / Thanks for the flowers. Jēn fèi'syìn le, hái sùng 'hwār lai. / No, thanks. (for a thing offered) (cordial) Dwō'syè, (wŏ) búyàu. *or* (abrupt) Bú'yàu. *or* (for more of something) (Dwō'syè,) búyàule. *or* 'Gòu le gòu le. *or* (for a service, as offered by a host) Dwō'syè, búyùng fèi'syìn le. *or* Tài 'kèchi le, bùgǎn'dāng. *or* (to a servant) 'Búyùng le. *or* (for further service offered) Búyùng dzài fèi'syìn le. *but* / No, thanks! (sarcastically) Hǎu ma, 'nà kĕ bù'syíng! *or* Wó kĕ bú'gàn!

Thanks to someone 'kwēile yŏu . . . bāng'máng, syìngkwēi yŏu . . . bāng'máng. / Thanks to him, I was able to get my trunks all right. Kwēile yŏu 'tā bāng'máng, wŏ tsái bá wŏde 'syāngdz nádau 'shŏu. *but* (sarcastically) / Thanks to you, I didn't get my furlough. 'Dòushr 'nĭde °déjèng (°'gūnglau), jyàu wo méigàusya 'jyà lai.

Thank-you note syètyĕ.

THAT (THOSE). (Someone or something indicated or understood by context) nèi, nèige, nèi plus some specific measure, or is not expressed; nèi alone occurs only in the first part of the sentence, never after a verb. / That's what I want. Wŏ yàu de shr̀ 'nèige. / What does that mean? 'Nèi shr̀ shémma 'yìsz? / How about THAT? 'Nèige dzĕmma 'yàng? / That's the book I've been looking for. Nèi 'jèngshr̀ wó syǎng 'yàu de nèibĕr 'shū. / I don't see why you have to do that before dinner. Wŏ jyou bù'míngbai nĭ 'wèi shémma chr̄ fàn yǐ'chyándĕi 'dzwò 'nèige. / Give me some of those. meaning Give me some of that kind of thing. Gĕi wo dyăr 'nèige. *but* / How ABOUT that? Dzĕmma 'yàng? / How do you know THAT? 'Nèige ní dzĕmma 'jr̄daude? / How do you KNOW that? Ní 'dzĕmma néng 'jr̄dàu ne? / What was that you said a minute ago? Nĭ gāng'tsái shwō de shr 'shémma?

(Of or pertaining to someone or something indicated or understood by context) nèi plus a measure. / Who are those people you were talking to? Nĭ gāng gēn 'tā-men shwō 'hwàr de nèisyē 'rén dōu shr̀ 'shéi? / Those children are making too much noise! Nèisyē 'háidz tài 'chău le! / Just look at that magnificent view, will you! Nĭ 'chyáuchyau nèipyàn 'jĭngjr̀!

(To such a degree) nèmma. / I didn't know the dress was that expensive. Wŏ bùjr̄'dàu jèijyàn 'yīfu yŏu 'nèmma gwèi. / Is it THAT far to your house? Dàu nĭ 'jyā yŏu 'nèmma ywǎn ma? / I don't want that much milk. Wŏ bú'yàu nèmma 'dwō de nyóu'nǎi.

As a relative pronoun, **that** is expressed with de. / Show me the best box of candy that you have. Gĕi wo 'chyáuchyau nĭmen dzwèi 'hǎude nèihéer 'táng. / When was the last time that I saw you? Wŏ 'shàngyítsz̀ shr̀ 'shémma shŕhou 'kànjyàn nĭ de? / Have you read the book that everybody's talking about? Nĭ 'kàngwo dà-'jyāhwŏr jŕ 'shwō de nèibĕr 'shū le ma? / Who's the man that just came in? Gāng 'jìnlaide nèige rén shr̀ 'shéi? / Can we find anybody that knows this town? Dzámen néng 'jǎuje 'shóusyi dì'myàr de 'nèmma yíge rén ma? / Let's meet at the same place that we met last night. Dzámen dzài dzwór 'wănshang jyàn'myàr de nèige 'dìfang jyàn, hǎu le.

As a conjunction, **that** is not expressed in Chinese. / We always knew that he couldn't be trusted. Wŏmen yí'syàng jyou 'jr̄dàu 'tā nèige rén bùkĕ'kàu.

That way nèmma. / I just can't see it that way. Wǒ jyòu shr bùnéng nèmma 'kàn.

So that hǎu. / Let's finish this story so that we can start on something else tomorrow. Dzámen bǎ 'jèidwàr 'gùshr syě'wánle ba, 'myérge hǎu syě 'byéde.

See also THIS.

THE. For showing degrees of definiteness English has the choice between **the,** this, that or no special expression; Chinese has only this jèi plus a measure, that nèi plus a measure, or no special expression. Cases which in English take **the** require in Chinese jèi, nèi, or is often not expressed. / I've been trying to find the hotel all day. Wó 'jǎu °nèige (°jèige) lyú'gwǎn 'jǎule yì'tyān le. / Do you know the person who runs the store? Ní 'rènshr kāi °jèige (°nèige) 'pùdz de rén ma? / Haven't you ever heard the president speak? Ní 'tsúnglái méi'tīngjyangwo dzúng'tǔng yán'jyǎng ma? / The sky is cloudy today. Jyēr yīn'tyān.

When stressed for emphasis on exclusiveness is expressed in Chinese with jèng *just, exactly, precisely.* / He's THE man for the job. Tā 'jèng shr dzwò nèijyàn 'shr de rén.

The . . . the . . . ywè . . . ywè . . . . / The sooner we get paid, the better. Ywè 'dzáu gěi women 'chyán ywè 'hǎu. / The cooler it is, the better I can work. Wǒ shr ywè 'lyángkwai 'dzwòde ywè 'hǎu. *or* 'Tyār ywè 'lyángkwai, wǒ 'dzwòde ywè 'hǎu.

THEATER. (Drama) syì; (place for presenting dramas) syìywán(dz); (place for presenting movies) dyànyǐngrywàn; **attend the theater** kànsyì, tīngsyì; **theater tickets** syìpyàu. / Do you like the theater? Ní 'syǐhwan °kàn (°tīng) 'syì ma? / Do you like this theater? Ní 'syǐhwan jèige syì'ywándz ma? / When does the theater open? Syì'ywándz 'shémma shŕhou 'kāi? / Do you have the theater tickets? Syì'pyàu ní 'náje ne ma?

THEIR, THEIRS. *See* THEY.

THEM. *See* THEY.

THEN. (At that time) 'nèige shŕhou. / I ought to know by then. 'Nèige shŕhou wǒ dà-'gài jyòu kéyi 'jŕdàu le.

(Afterward, next) yǐhòu, 'hòulái. / What do I do then? Yǐ'hòu wǒ 'yòu gāi 'dzěmma yàng ne? / Then what happened? 'Hòulái ne? *or* Yǐ'hòu dzěmma 'yàng le? *or* 'Hòulái 'yòu dzěmma le?

(Also, in addition) hái. / Then there's the trunk; we must have it taken down to the basement. Hái yǒu nèige 'syāngdz; dzámen dzúng děi nádau dì'yǐndzli chyù.

(In that case) nèmma (je). / Then we can forget all about it. 'Nèmma(je) jyòu swànle.

(In the light of what you have said) 'jèmma shwō. / Then you didn't expect me today? 'Jèmma shwō ní méi'syǎngdàu wǒ 'jyèrge hwèi 'lái?

Well then hǎule. / Well then, let's eat. 'Hǎule; dzámen jyòu 'chŕ ba.

Now and then 'yǒu(de)shŕhou, ǒuér. / We go to the movies now and then. Wǒmen 'yǒushŕhou chyù kàn dyàn'yǐngr. / Oh, we see them every now and then. Wǒmen ǒu'ér 'kànjyàn tamen yítsž.

Then and there jyòu, dāng'shŕ jyòu, lì'kè jyòu. / I knew then and there that it was the house to buy. Wǒ lì'kè jyòu kàn'jùngle 'nèiswǒr fángdz le.

THERE. (That place) nàr, nèr, nàli, nèige dìfang. / I've never been there. Wǒ méi-

'dàugwo nèr. / I was through there yesterday, and the roads are still closed. Wǒ 'dzwór 'tsúng nèr 'gwò de shŕhou 'lù hái méi'tŭng ne. / Can you get there by car? Dzwò'chē chyu dàude'lyǎu nèr ma? / How did you get over there? Ní 'dzěmma chyude 'nèr?

(In that respect, concerning that point) nèi, 'nèige dìfang; (with reference to something which has just been said) 'jèige dìfang. / You're wrong there! 'Nèi ní kě bú'dwèi! or 'Jèige dìfang ní kě 'tswò le!

(Exclamation) ài (of consolation); hǐ kàn (of surprise or anger). / There, I wouldn't worry so much. 'Ài, 'wǒ yàushr 'nǐ 'jywé bú nèmma fā'chóu. / There, now you've done it! Nǐ 'kàn, nǐ 'jè búshr 'dzwòchulaile ma? but / There you are! meaning Take a look. Nǐ 'kàn! or meaning It works! 'Syíngle! or meaning It's finished! or It's ready! 'Déle!

Here and there jǐchùr, jige 'dìgang, 'yǒude dìfang. / Here and there in his book he's got some good ideas. Tā nèiběr 'shū yóu jǐ'chùr 'syéde hái swan bú'tswò.

Not all there yǒu yìdyǎr °bàn'fēngr (°shǎ). / Don't be surprised at the way he acts; he's not all there. Nǐ kàn tā 'nèige jyèr byé 'jywéje chí'gwài; tā yóu dyǎr 'shǎ.

There is, there are, there were, there was, with unstressed there and the subject following, yǒu. / There are few good hotels in town. 'Chéngli méiyou jige hǎu lyǔ'gwǎn. / Are there any vacancies? Yǒu kŭng'fáng ma?

THEREFORE. 'swóyǐ; see also SO. / A equals B and B equals C; therefore, A equals C. Yīnwèi 'ēi děngyu 'bǐ, 'bǐ děngyu 'syǐ, 'swóyǐ 'ēi děngyu 'syǐ.

THEY (THEM, THEIR, THEIRS). (Referring to some definite group of people) tāmen; (referring to people in general) rén; (referring to things) jèisyē, nèisyē, dōu, chywán, etc., are sometimes used though often not expressed; them tāmen; their or theirs tāmende (de is often dropped before nouns). / Put them on the table. Dōu gēdzài 'jwōdzshang. / Can they stay with us over the weekend? Tāmen 'néng gēn wǒmen gwò yíge jōu'mwò ma? / Are they the people you told me about? 'Tāmen jyòushr nǐ gēn wo 'tígwo de 'nèisyē rén ma? / Do you know their address? Nǐ 'jŕdau tāmende jù-'jŕ ma? / Are you a friend of theirs? Nǐ 'rènshr tāmen ma? or Nǐ shr tāmende 'pengyou ma? / Well, you know what they say. 'Ài, 'rén búshr cháng 'shwō ma? / They say he's very good. Yǒu rén 'shwō tā hén 'hǎu.

(Referring to persons unknown). / They give concerts here in the summer. 'Syà-tyārde shŕhou dzài 'jèr yǎn'dzòu. / When do they open the dining room? Fàn'tǐng 'shémma shŕhou 'kāi?

Themselves see SELF.

THICK. (In dimension) hòu. / I need a piece of wood about three inches thick. Wǒ yàu yíkwài 'sāntswùn hòu de 'mùtou. / I want a thick steak. Wǒ yàu yíkwài hòu'hǒurde ròu'pái. / Is the ice thick enough for skating? Jèrde 'bīng dùngde 'hòude néng 'lyōu le ma?

(In consistency) chóu, núng. / I don't like such thick soup. Wǒ bù'syǐhwan jèmma °'chóude (°'nungde) 'tāng.

(In distribution or density) yòu 'dwō yòu 'shēn. / The weeds are too thick for walking here. Jèrde 'tsǎu yòu 'dwō yòu 'shēn, bùnéng 'dzǒu.

(Of fog) dà. / The fog is getting thick. 'Wù ywè 'lái ywè 'dà.

(Of an accent) lìhai, jùng. / He has a very thick accent. Tāde 'kǒuyīn hěn °'lì-hai (°'jùng).

Thick and fast. /It's raining thick and fast. 'Yǔ 'syàde gòu °'dàde (°'lìhaide).

Through thick and thin yǒu 'hwànnàn de shŕhou. /He stuck by us through thick and thin. Wǒmen yǒu 'hwànnàn de shŕhou, tā 'jēn gòu 'péngyou.

Be thick-headed bèn. /He's really thick-headed. Tā jēn 'bèn a. /Can't I get this through your thick head? is expressed as Are you so thick-headed, I have no way of speaking to you? Ní 'dzèmma jèmma 'bèn a, wǒ méi'fár gēn ni 'shwō le.

THIEF. dzéi, syǎutǒur, syáuli, tōudǔngsyide. /Have they found the thief yet? Tāmen °'jǎujau (°'dēijau, °'jwājau) nèige tōu'dǔngsyide le ma?

THIN. (In dimension) báu. /This book is thin enough to slip into your pocket. Jèibĕr 'shū 'báude kéyi fàngdzai 'dōur lǐtou. /The walls of my room are too thin to keep out the noise. Wǒ 'wūrlide 'chyáng tài 'báu, pángbyár shémma °'shēngyīn dōu tīngde'jyàn (°'shēngr yě gébu'jù). /Cut the bread thin. Bǎ myàn'bāu chyē'báu yì-dyǎr.

(Distribution or density) syī, shǎu. /The grass is rather thin this year. Jīn-nyánde 'tsáu tǐng 'syī. /My hair is getting thin. Wǒ 'tóufa ywè 'lái ywè °'shǎu (°syī).

(Lacking fatty tissue) shòu. /You're too think; you ought to eat more. Nǐ tài 'shòu; yīngdang dwō 'chř dyǎr. /I was shocked to see how thin he'd gotten. Wǒ 'chyáujyàn tā 'shòuchéng 'nàyàngr le syàle yí'tyàu.

(Of consistency) syī. /This soup is too thin. Jèige 'tāng tài 'syī le.

(Of a sound or the voice) syǎu. /His voice was so thin we could hardly hear him. Tā 'shēngyīn 'syǎude wǒmen jyàn'jŕ tīngbu'jyàn ta.

(Inadequate) bù chūngdzú, bu dzĕmma 'yàng. /That's a pretty thin excuse. Jèige lǐ'yóu °'bù chūng'dzú (°'bù dzĕmma 'yàng).

To thin out (of a crowd) dzǒujìngle, dzǒuwánle, dzǒusànle. /Let's wait until the crowd thins out. Dzámen 'dĕng rén °dzǒu'jìngle (°'dzǒu'wánle, °dzǒu'sànle) 'dzài shwō ba.

(Of plants) báchu jige chyu. /We'll have to thin out these carrots. Jèisyē hú-'lwóbe jùngde tài 'mìle, dzámen dĕi 'báchu jigĕr chyu.

THING. (Indefinite material objects) dǔngsyi; if context defines what type of thing is meant the Chinese may have a more specific word. /What are those things you're carrying? Nǐ 'náde nèisyē shŕ 'shémma dǔngsyi? /I've got to go now; did you see where I put my things? Wó déi 'dzǒu le; nǐ 'kànjyàn wó bá wǒde 'dǔngsyi gēdzai 'nǎr le ma? /Have you packed all your things yet? Nǐde °'dǔngsyi (°'syíngli) dōu jwāng'hǎule ma?

(Indefinite non-material entities) shŕ, shèr. /There've been some funny things going on in that house. Tāmen 'jyā 'jìnlái jìngshr lí'chígǔ'gwàide shèr. /That job's the very thing I want. Nèijyàn 'chāishŕ 'jèngshŕ wǒ syǎng 'dzwòde.

A thing or two. /He certainly knows a thing or two about business. Yàu shwò dzwò 'mǎimai 'tā kě 'jēn yóu lyǎngsyàdz.

Not a thing (intensifying the negative) 'shémma yě bu-, 'shémma yě méi-, yǐ'dyǎr... yě °bu- (°méi-). /I can't see a thing from my seat. Wǒ dzwòdzai 'jèr 'shémma yě chyáubu'jyàn. /We haven't done a thing all week. Wǒmen yíge lǐ'bài 'shémma yě méi'gàn. /I can't think of a thing. Wǒ 'yìdyǎr 'júyì yě méiyǒu. /There's not a thing wrong with me. Wǒ shémma 'máubìng yě méiyǒu.

Of all things jēn chígwài, 'jēn shr méi'yǐngrde 'shŕ. /Well, of all things, what are you doing here? 'Jēn shr méi'yǐngrde 'shŕ, nǐ dzài 'jèr gàn 'má ne?

Poor thing (person). /When her parents died, the poor thing didn't know what to do. Tā 'fùmǔ 'gwòchyu yǐ'hòu, nèige kělyán'chúng bù'jŕdàu 'dzěmmaje 'hǎu le. / You poor thing! Nǐ 'tài ke'lyán le! or Nǐ 'jèi kělyán 'jyèrde!

See things (have hallucinations) 'húlihu'dūde, dzoushér, 'húszlwàn'syǎng, syǎng-'rù'fēifēi. /I think you've been seeing things ever since that accident. Wǒ 'jywéde nǐ 'dztsúng nèitsz chū'shèr yǐ'hòu 'cháng yǒude 'shŕhou 'húlihú'dūde.

Thing as it is used in many other English sentences has no equivalent in Chinese. Some typical examples are given below. /We've heard a lot of nice things about you. Wǒmen 'tīngjyàn bù'shǎu rén °shwō ní 'hǎu (°'kwā ni). /How are things? Dzěmma 'yàng? / Things are pretty tough these days. 'Jèi nyán'tóur gòu 'shòude. /Let's sit down and talk things over. Dzámen 'dzwòsya hǎu'hǎurde 'tántan. /She says she's in love, and I think it's the real thing. Tā shwō tā 'àishangle yíge 'rén, 'wó syǎng 'jèihwéi °shŕ 'jēnde (°dàgài 'chéngle). /They've certainly made a good thing of that shop. Tāmen nèige 'pùdz 'mǎimài dzwòde kě 'jēn bú'tswò.

THINK (THOUGHT). (Use one's brains well) yùng nǎudz. /He's never really learned how to think. Tā 'tsúnglái jyòu bùjŕ'dàu 'dzěmma yùng 'nǎudz.

Think (that or so or not) syǎng, 'syǎngdàu, 'yǐwéi, jywéde, syǎngsyìn, kàn. /I think so. Wó syǎng 'shŕ. or Wó syǎng 'shŕ nèiyàngr. /I thought so. Wó 'syǎng jyòushr 'nèiyàngr. or Gēn wó 'syǎng de yí'yàngr. /I didn't think you'd come. Wǒ méisyǎng'dàu nǐ hwèi 'lái. or Wó 'syáng nǐ bù'láile ne. or Wó 'yǐwéi nǐ bù'láile ne. /I think you're all wrong on that. Wǒ °'jywéde (°syǎng'syìn) nǐ wán'chywán bú-'dwèi. or Wǒ jywéde nǐ 'shwōde 'háuwúdàu'lǐ. /I think I'll go now. Wǒ 'kàn wǒ syàndzài 'dzǒu ba. /I thought you weren't coming along. Wó 'yǐwéi nǐ 'bùgēn wǒmen yíkwàr 'chyù ne.

Think about syǎng. /Why don't you think about it for a while before you make up your mind? Nǐ 'wèi shémma bù'syǎn 'syángsyǎng 'dzài dǎ 'júyì? /What're you thinking about? Ní syǎng 'shémma ne?

Think of (remember, recall) syǎngchilai. /I can't think of his address. Wǒ 'syǎng buchǐ'lái tā jù 'nǎr. /Can you think of that man's name? Ní 'syǎngdechǐ'lái nèige rén de 'míngdz ma?

What do (or does) . . . think of kàn, 'jywéde, shwō. /What do you think of going to the movies tonight? Dzámen jyēr 'wǎnshang chyù kàn ge dyàn'yǐngr, nǐ shwō dzěmma 'yàng? /What do you think of that guy? Nǐ °'kàn (°'jywéde, °'shwō), nèige °'rén (°'jyāhwo, °'syǎudz) dzěmma'yàng?

Think better of. /You're taking a big chance, and I'd think better of it if I were you. Ní yóu dyǎr tài màu'syǎn le, 'wǒ yàushr 'ní wǒ yí'dìng hǎu'hǎurde 'syáng-syǎng. /We think better of him since we've learned the facts. Wǒmen yì 'míngbai shŕ 'dzěmma hwéi 'shŕ yǐ'hòu, dwèi ta 'yìnsyàng hǎu 'dwō le.

Think out loud dzyándzyǔ. /He likes to think out loud. Tā lǎurshr dzyándz'yǔde.

Think something over 'syǎng(yi)syǎng, 'kǎulyù. /I'll have to think it over. Wó děi (dwō) °'syángsyǎng (°'kǎulyukǎulyu).

Think twice. /I'd think twice about that if I were you. Wǒ yàushr 'nǐ, wǒ yí-'dìng, dzài'sānde 'syángsyǎng.

Think something up (fictitious) dzōuchulai, byānchulai; (worthwhile) syǎngchulai, dzwómwochulai. /Who thought this up? 'Jèige shŕ 'shéi °'syǎngchulaide (°'dzōuchu-laide)? /You'd better think up a good excuse for being late. Nǐ lái 'wǎnle, chèn-'dzǎur °'dzōuchu (°'dzwómwochu, °'syǎngchu, °'byānchu) ge 'lǐyóu lai.

Be well thought of. /He's well thought of, don't you think? Nǐ 'shŕ bushŕ 'jywéde dàjyā'hwǒr dōu syǎng'dāngde 'dàijyan ta.

Other English expressions. / Think nothing of it? 'Nǎr de 'hwà! or Méi 'gwānsyi! or Syǎu 'yìsz! or (in response to an apology) Byé 'kèchi!

THIRD. The third dìsān; one third 'sānfēnjr'yǐ.

THIRSTY. kě. / I'm very thirsty. Wǒ ké'jíle. / This salty food makes me thirsty. Chr̄ jèige 'syánde dūngsyi jyàu wo kóu 'kě.

THIRTEEN. shŕsān; the thirteenth dìshŕsān; one-thirteenth shŕ'sānfēnjr'yǐ.

THIRTY. 'sānshŕ; the thirtieth dì'sānshŕ; one-thirtieth 'sānshrfēnjr'yǐ.

THIS (THESE). (Someone or something present, near or just mentioned) jèi, jèige, jèi plus some specific measure; jèi alone occurs only in the first part of the sentence, never after a verb. / What's this? 'Jèi shr̄ shémma? / This is too much for me! Wǒ 'jēn shōubu'lyǎu 'jèige! / Is this yours? Jèi shr 'nǐde ma? / I'd like a pound of these and half a pound of those. Wó 'syǎng lái yíbàng 'jèige bànbàng 'nèige.

(That which is present, near or just referred to) jèi plus a measure. / Do you know this man? Nǐ 'rènde jèige 'rén ma? / What are we going to do this weekend? Dzámen jèige jōu'mwò gàn 'má? / I like this room. Wó 'syǐhwan jèijyān 'wūdz. / Have you met all these people? Jèisyē'wèi nǐ dōu 'jyàngwole ma? / Are these bags yours? Jèisyē kǒu'dài shr 'nǐde ma? / These shoes are too small. Jèishwāng 'syé tài 'syǎu.

(To this degree) jèmma. / I can't eat this much food. Wǒ chr̄bu'lyǎu 'jèmma dwō de dūngsyi. / As long as we've come this far, we might as well go on. Wǒmen jì'rán 'yǐjīng dzǒule jèmma 'ywǎn le, háishr 'jyéje dzǒu ba.

This with certain periods of time requires special terms: **this week** bénlǐbài, běnsyīngchī, 'jèige lǐ'bài, jèige syīng'chī; **this Tuesday** meaning Tuesday of this week 'Bénlǐbài'èr, 'Běnsyīngchī'èr, jèige Lǐbài'èr, jèige Syīngchi'èr; **this month** běnywè, 'jèige ywè; **this year** 'jīnnyán.

This minute lìshŕ, 'mǎshàng, mǎshàng, gánjǐn, gwāigwārde. / Come here this minute! meaning don't argue about it any more Gwāi'gwārde gěi wo 'gwòlai!

After this tsúng'jīnyǐ'hòu. / After this I'll be sure to get to the office on time. Tsúng'jīnyǐ'hòu wǒ yí'dìng 'jwǔnshŕshàng'bàn.

See also **THAT.**

THOROUGH. chèdǐ, rènjēn, jèngjǐng, syìsyīn, bù'mámahu'hūde. / I'll make a thorough investigation. Wǒ yí'dìng chè'dǐde 'chá yísyàr. / That fellow is very thorough in everything he does. Nèige 'rén bù'gwǎn dzwò 'shémma dōu hěn °rèn'jēn (°chè'dǐ, °etc.).

THOUGH. (But) 'búgwò, kěshr, dànshr. / I'll attend, though I may be late. Wǒ yí'dìng 'chyù, °búgwò (°kěshr, °dànshr) 'yěsyu déi 'wǎn yìdyǎr 'dàu. / I think it was his fault, though naturally I'm willing to give him another chance. Wó 'syǎude nèige shr̄ tāde 'tswòr, dànshr wúlwùnrú'hé wo 'ywànyi 'dzài gěi ta yíge 'jīhwèi.

(Even) **though** °'swéirán (°jyòushr) . . . °háishr (°'yě). / I didn't catch my train, though I ran all the way. Wǒ 'swéirán yí'lùr 'jǐnje 'pǎu, °háishr (°yě) méi'gǎnshàng 'chē. / We invited him to our house, even though we don't like him. Wǒmen 'swéirán bù'syǐhwan ta, yé bǎ ta chǐng dàu 'jyāli chyùle. / Though I may miss my train I mean to see you before I go. Wǒ jyòushr bǎ 'chē 'dānwùle, yé děi dzài méi'dzóu yǐ'chyán 'jyànjyan ni.

Look as though 'chyáuje ('kànje) hǎu 'syàng. / It looks as though it may rain. 'Chyáuje hǎu 'syàng yàu syà 'yǔ.

Seem as though hǎu syàng, 'fǎngfú. /It seems as though I know him. Wó °hǎu 'syàng (°'fǎngfú) 'rénshr ta shr̀de.

THOUGHT. 'gāujyàn, 'jyànjyě, 'yìjyàn; or is often expressed verbally as think syǎng. /Have you any thoughts on the subject? Gwānyu jèige 'wèntí, ní yǒu shémma °'gāujyàn (°'jyànjyě, °'yìjyàn)? /A penny for your thoughts. Ní syǎng 'shémma ne? or Ní fā shémma 'lèng? /We'll have to give some thought to this matter. Jèijyàn 'shèr dzámen déi hǎu'hǎurde °'syǎngsyǎng (°'yánjyouyánjyou, °'kǎulyùkǎulyù). /Can't you show a little thought for others? Ní 'nándàu jyòu 'bùnéng tǐ 'byérén 'syǎngsyǎng ma? or Mwò'fēi ní jyòu bùjr̀dàu 'gùje dyǎr 'byérén ma?

THOUSAND. chyān; **the thousandth** dìyìchyān; **one thousandth** 'chyānfēnjr'yī; **ten thousand** wàn; **the ten thousandth** dìyíwàn; **one ten-thousandth** 'wànfēnjr'yī.

THREE. sān; sā (equals sān plus ge).

THROAT. sǎngdz. /I have a sore throat. Wó 'sǎngdz téng. or Wǒ nàu 'sǎngdz ne. out /Every time I see this town, I get a lump in my throat. is expressed as . . . , in my heart, it's hard to bear. Wǒ yí 'kànjyàn jèige chéng, 'syīnli jyòu °nán'shòu (°nán'gwò, °'dúde hěn).

Other English expressions. /Don't jump down my throat! Ní 'yùngbujáu gēn wo °'rǎng (°fā 'píchi)! /He'd cut your throat for a dollar. Jānle 'chyán, tā 'shémma dōu dzwòdechūlái. /I tried to apologize, but the words stuck in my throat. Wó 'běnlái syǎng dàu'chyàn láije, kěshr 'hwà 'méinéng 'shwōchulai.

THROUGH. (Of motion) if attention is centered on a point reached after passing through something, tsúng or dǎ; if attention is centered on the place passed through itself, gwò as postverb with any suitable verb of motion; if one is concerned with the possibility of obstructed passage, tūng be passable; if specifically passing through a door on one's way in, jìn mér. /Who's the lady coming through the door? 'Jèng jìn'mér de nèiwèi 'fúrén shr̀ 'shéi? /The car went through the city gate. Chǐ'chē 'chwāngwò chéngmén chyù le. /Can you get through this street? Jèityáu 'jyē °dzǒudegwò'chyù (°'tūng) ma? /Which door did he come in through? Tā °tsúng (°dǎ) 'nèige mér 'jìnlaide?

(With lines of sight, routes, etc., where motion is not present but only theoretically possible) is expressed as above. /He looked out through the window. Tā tsúng 'chwānghu wàng wài 'kàn. but /Can you see it through this fog? is expressed as In this fog can you see? Dzài 'wùli ní kànde'jyàn ma? /I can't see anything through this window pane. is expressed as With this window pane obstructing (the view) I can't see anything. Wǒ °'jyēje jèikwài 'bwōli (°'géje jèikwài 'bwōli, °yǒu jèikwài 'bwōli 'dǎngje) 'shémma dōu kànbu'jyàn.

(By reason of) 'yīnwèi. /Through his negligence the work will have to be held up two weeks. Yīnwei tā nèmma yì 'lǎhu jèijyàn 'gūngdzwò děi 'dānwù 'lyalǐ'bài. /He got where he is through lots of hard work. Tā 'jr̀ swóyi néng yǒu 'jīntyān shr̀ 'yīnwèi tā tsúng'chyán kěn 'gàn.

(Finished) wán as a postverb or alone. /I think I can get through with this book tonight. Wó syǎng wǒ jyēr 'wǎnshang kéyi bǎ jèiběr 'shū kàn'wán le. /Are you through so soon? Ní jèmma 'kwài jyòu 'wánle? /I'll be through work at five o'clock. Wǒ 'wúdyǎnjūng wán'shèr.

See through someone kàntòule. /Everybody can see through that guy. 'Shéi dōu néng bǎ ta kàn'tòu le.

Through and through chèdǐ, dàujyā. /He knows his business through and through. Tā dwèiyu tā běn'háng 'jēn shr̀ 'jr̀dàude °hěn chè'dǐ (°dàu'jyā le).

Through train tūngchē, jŕdáhwǒ'chē, jŕdákwài'chē.

Through street is expressed verbally. / Is this a through street? is expressed as Can you get through on this street? Jèityáu 'jyē °dzǒudegwò'chyù (°'tūng) ma? or as This street isn't a blind alley, is it? Jèityáu 'jyē 'búshr szhú'tùngr ba?

Through ticket lyánpyàu.

THROUGHOUT. (Indicating time) tsúngtóurdàu'lǎur. / He didn't speak a word throughout the whole meeting. Tā dzài hwèi'yìli tsúngtóurdàu'lǎur 'yíjyù hwà yě méi'shwō.

(Indicating space) chywán, chywántǐ, chywánbù. / The house has been painted throughout. Jèige fángdz yǐjìng chywánbù chīgwòle. / This hotel is famous throughout the world. Jèige lyú'gwǎn °shr 'míngbyànchywán'chyóu (°shr'jyè yǒu'míng).

See also **ALL, WHOLE.**

THROW (THREW, THROWN). (Cast, toss, hurl) rēng, rěng, pyě. / Let's see how far you can throw this rock. 'Kànkàn nǐ néng bǎ jèikwài 'shŕtou °rēng (°rěng, °pyě) dwō 'ywǎn.

(Of a horse) shwāisyalai. / Be careful your horse doesn't throw you. Lyóu'shén byé jyàu 'mǎ bá ni gěi 'shwāisyalai.

Throw a switch (if closing the circuit) kāi, kāikai; (if opening the circuit) gwān, gwānshang. / You'll have to throw that switch to get the machine started. Ní děi 'syān bǎ dyàn'mén 'kāikai, 'jīchì tsái néng 'dùng.

Throw a light in a direction wàng . . . jàu. / Throw that light this way, please. Bǎ nèige 'dēng wàng 'jèibyar 'jàu.

Throw a glance at °dèng (°chyáu, °kàn) . . . yìyǎn. / She threw a glance at us when we came into the room. Wǒmen jìn'wūr de shŕhou tā °'dèngle (°'chyáule, °'kànle) wǒmen yì'yǎn.

Throw oneself at someone gēn . . . °byàu (°nèmma 'chīnrè). / Oh, stop throwing yourself at him! 'Ài, byé 'jìng gēn ta 'byàu le! *or* 'Ài, byé gēn ta nèmma 'chīnrè!

Throw something **away** rēng, rěng, dàu. / Throw the rest of my dinner away. Bá wǒ chŕ'shèngsya de °'rēngle (°'rěngle, °'dàule) ba.

Throw in (add, usually casually) 'dwō lái, 'dzài gěi. / Throw in an extra loaf of bread. 'Dwō lái yíge myàn'bāu.

Throw something **in** (to) (pack carelessly) 'sēidàu, 'dwēidàu. / Throw my things into a bag; I have to catch my train. Bá wǒde 'dūngsyi °'sēidàu (°'dwēidàu) jèige 'bāurli; wó děi 'gán hwǒ'chē.

Throw off an infection bǎ . . . jŕ'hǎule, bǎ . . . chyùle. / I haven't been able to throw off this cold all winter. Wǒ shāng'fēng shàngle yì'dūngtyar le, yě méinéng bǎ bìng °jŕ'hǎule (°'chyùle).

Throw on an outer garment pēishang. / I'll just throw a coat on and go down to the store. Wǒ 'pēishang jyàn dà'yī chyù 'pùdz yítàng.

Throw someone **out** hūngchuchyu, gǎnchuchyu. / We'd better pay our rent soon, or they'll throw us out. Dzámen gán'jǐn bǎ 'fángchyán 'gěile ba, 'yàuburán fáng'dūng jyòu yàu bǎ dzámen °'hūngchuchyu (°'gǎnchuchyu) le. *but* / I've been thrown out of better places than this! is expressed as You don't think I care about this, do you! 'Jè swàn 'shémma! / Do you think they'll throw my application out? is expressed as Do you think they'll give me the brushoff? Nǐ kàn tāmen hwèi 'bǎ wo 'shwāsyalai ma?

TIE

Throw over plans jyǎu, gǎibyàn. /His illness made us throw over our plans for the summer. Tā yí 'bìng bǎ wǒmen 'syàtyar de 'jìhwà géi 'jyǎu le. *or* Wǒmen yīnwei tā 'bìngle jrháu gǎi'byàn wǒmen shǔ'jyàde 'jìhwà.

Throw someone over shwā, shwǎi, rēng, rěng, gēn ... chwēile. /I hear she's throwing him over. Wǒ 'tīngshwō tā yàu bǎ ta géi °'shwā le (°'shwǎi le, °'rēng le, °'rěng le). *or* Wǒ 'tīngshwō tā yàu gēn ta 'chwēi le.

Throw up (vomit) tù. /I throw up every time I ride on a train. Wǒ yí dzwò hwǒ'chē jyòu 'tù.

Throw something up to someone 'twēigěi. /That's the second time you've thrown it up to me! Ní 'dzěmma bǎ nèige 'yòu 'twēigei wǒ le!

Be thrown into disorder nùnglwànle, nùngde 'lwànchibā'dzǎu. /Everything was thrown into disorder. 'Dūngsyi chywan °nùng'lwànle (°'nùngde 'lwànchibā'dzǎu le).

A throw yísyàr 'rēngde. /That was some throw! 'Nèisyàr 'rēngde jēn °'bú-'tswò °'ywǎn, °'kéyi)!

THUMB. dàmejř, dàmjř, dàmegē, dàmgē. /I burned my thumb with a match. Wǒ jyàu yáng'hwǒr bǎ dàme'jř 'shāu le.

THUNDER. dǎléi. /It's beginning to thunder. Dǎ'léi le.

(Make a loud noise) is expressed with devices of intensification. /You shouldn't let him thunder at you like that. Ní biyīng'dāng ràng ta 'nèmma yǒuje 'syìngrde gēn ni 'rǎng. /The train thundered over the bridge. Hwǒ'chē tsúng 'chyáushang 'jīdùng-gūng'dūngde 'gwòchyule.

Thunder (the sound) is expressed verbally as above. /Don't be afraid of thunder. Byé 'pà dǎ'léi. /Did you hear all that thunder last night? Ní dzwór 'wǎnshang 'tīng-jyan dǎ'léi le ma?

(Loud noise). /The speaker couldn't be heard above the thunder of applause. is expressed as Everybody clapped so loudly the speaker could not be heard. Dà'jyā-hwǒr pāi'shǒu 'pāide tài 'syǎng le, yánjyǎngde 'shwōde shr̀ 'shémma dōu tīngbu-'jyàn le.

THURSDAY. Syīngchīsz̀, Lǐbàisz̀.

TICKET. pyàu with particular purpose specified; thus ticket for a play syìpyàu; movie ticket dyànyǐngrpyàu; boat ticket chwánpyàu; plane ticket fēijīpyàu; train ticket hwǒ-chēpyàu; bus ticket (or for any public vehicular conveyance) chēpyàu; round-trip ticket láihwéipyàu; season ticket jìpyàu; commuter's ticket (railway, etc.) chángchī-pyàu; (ticket to be taken at a door or gate as one enters) ménpyàu. /Have you got your tickets yet? Ní 'yàujau 'pyàu le ma? *or* Ní 'mǎijau mén'pyàu le ma? *or* Ní dǎ 'pyàu le ma? /I want a round-trip ticket for Peiping. Wǒ yàu yìjāng shàng Běi-'píng de láihwéi'pyàu.

(List of candidates) 'hòusywǎnrén míng'dār. /Are there any women candidates on the ticket? 'Hòusywǎnrén míng'dārshang yǒu 'nyǔde ma?

TIE. (Bind, fasten) jì; (wrap string around) kwǔn; (secure something movable to something fixed by fastening each to one end of a string or rope) shwān; (tie a person to something by wrapping rope around both, or tie a person's wrists or ankles together, or bandage a person) bǎng; (fasten the ends of two strings or ropes together) jyē; (secure packages or baggage) dǎ; where English has tie up Chinese may add shàng *or* chǐlái to any of the above. /I have to tie my shoelace tighter. Wǒ déi bǎ syé-

981

'dàr jǐ'jǐn yìdyǎr. / Please tie this up for me. Láu'jyà bǎ 'jèige gěi wo °'jǐshang (°'kwùnshang, °etc.). / Let's tie the boat up and have our lunch. Dzámen bǎ 'chwán 'shwānshang hǎu chr̄ 'fàn.

(Equal a score or record) píng (during a particular game or competition); gǎn-shang (match a record previously established). / I don't think we can tie the score now. Wǒ 'jywéde syàndzài píngbu'lyǎu le. / Can you tie that record? Nǐ néng 'gǎn-shang nèige jìlù ma?

Be tied up or **down** (occupied, delayed) yǒu shr̀, kwùn, dwūn. / Are you tied up this evening? Nǐ jyèr 'wǎnshang yǒu 'shr̀ ma? / I'm afraid we'll be tied down in the city all weekend. Kǔng'pà jèige jōu'mwò dzámen yàu °'kwùndzài (°'dwūndzài) chéng 'lǐtou.

A tie (neckwear) lǐngdài; **bow tie** lǐnghwār, lǐngjyēr; **tie a tie** 'dǎ(shang) lǐng-'dài, 'jǐ(shang) lǐng'dài. / Is my tie straight? Wǒde lǐng'dài 'jèng bujèng? / Won't you straighten my tie for me, please? Láu'jyà, bá wó lǐng'dài gěi nùng'jèng le.

(In a railroad roadbed) jěnmù.

(In music) lyánhàur, lyánfú.

TIGHT. jǐn; (motionless) jù; (too small) syǎu; (airtight) yán; (solidly) tsz̀shr; or ex-pressed verbally as gū (bind) or chyā (pinch). / Shut your eyes tight. Bá 'yǎn bì-'jǐn le. / I have to tie my shoelace tighter. Wǒ déi bǎ syé'dàr jǐ'jǐn yìdyǎr. / Pull the rope tight. Bǎ 'shéngdz lā'jǐn le. / This is a tight fit. (general) 'Jèige 'jǐn yì-dyǎr. (of clothes) 'Jèige gūje 'shēndz. or Jèige shr̀ chyā'yàude 'yīfu. / This suit is too tight for me. Jèishr̀r 'yīfu wǒ 'chwānje °'syǎu (°tài 'jǐn, °'gūdeheng). / Hold tight onto the rail or you'll fall. °'Fújùle lán'gār (°'Jyōujùle 'fúshòur), bùrán nǐ jyòu syǔ 'dyàusyachyu. / Shut the lid tight on the glass jar. Bǎ bwōli'píngdzshangde 'gàr °níng'jǐn le (°'yán le, °'tsz̀shrle). / Sit tight; it'll only take a minute. Dzwò-'jùle, yì'hwěr jyòu 'wán.

(Drunk) dzwèi. / Boy, was I tight last night after the party! Hǎu'jyāhwo, dzwór 'wǎnshang nèige 'yìngchou 'wánle yǐ'hòu wó 'kě jēn 'dzwèile!

(With money). / He's pretty tight with his money. Tā dzài yùng'chyánshang hén 'syǎuchì. or expressed as He's a tightwad. Tā shr̀ ge chyán'hěndz. or as He's tight-fisted. Tāde 'shǒu hén 'jǐn.

Be in a tight spot 'yùjyàn 'kwùnnan, dǎuméi, chū máfan. / I've been in tight spots before. Wó yǐ'chyán yě °'yùjyàngwo 'kwùnnan (°dǎugwo 'méi, °chūgwo 'má-fan).

Seal tight dǔ or sāi (cork up, seal up) plus the postverb shàng (up) or sž (dead) or jù (motionless). / Is this water pipe sealed tight? Jèige shwéi'gwǎndz 'jēnggèr °'dǔshàngle (°'sāishàngle) ma? or Jèige shwěi'gwǎndz °dú'sžle ma (°'dǔjùle ma, °'sāi'sžle ma, °'sāijùle ma)?

Sew a deal **up tight** °jwǔn (°jēn) 'lāshàng. / He's got the deal sewed up tight. Nèidàngdz 'mǎimai tā jwǔn 'lāshangle.

TILL. (Up to a time) dàu; tsái (then and not before) in the other part of the sentence; or both. / Let's work till ten tonight. Dzámen jyēr 'wǎnshang yǐ'jr̄ 'dzwòdau 'shr̀-dyǎn ba. / Wait till I come back. 'Dèngdau wǒ 'hwéilai 'dzài shwō. / We can't be-gin till he's finished. 'Fēidéi 'dèng tā 'wánle wǒmen 'tsái néng kāi'shr̄. / I won't be able to see you till next week. Wǒ 'búdàu 'syàyíge lǐ'bài bùnéng 'jyàn ni. or Wǒ 'déi dàu 'syàyíge lǐ'bài tsái néng 'jyàn ni.

To till (plow, plant, etc.) jùng, páu, gēng, jǐng. / That soil hasn't been tilled for at least five years. Nèikwài 'dì yóu 'wǔnyán méi °'jùng le (°'páu le, °etc.).

A till (small drawer for money) is expressed as drawer 'chōutĭ. / How much change is there in the till? 'Chōutĭli yŏu 'dwōshau 'língchyán?

TIME. (Most general term) shŕhou. / It's time to leave. Dàu gāi'dzŏude shŕhou le. / Where were you at that time? 'Nèige shŕhou nĭ dzài 'năr ne? / At times I work twenty-four hours at a stretch. 'Yŏu(de) shŕhou wŏ yí'syàr dzwò èrshr'sżge jūng-'tóu. / It'll probably be some time before I can come here again. Wŏ 'dàgai dĕi 'gwò syē shŕhou tsái néng 'lái jèr. / What was the time in the last race? 'Shàngtsż sài-'pău °yùngle (°de 'jìlù shŕ) 'dwōshau shŕhou?

(Hour of day) dyăn(jūng). / What time? 'Jídyăn(jūng)? or 'Jĭshŕ? / What time do we eat? Dzámen 'jĭshŕ chŕ 'fàn? / What time is it? 'Jídyăn le?

(Day) r̀, tyān. / Let's make it some other time. Dzámen °găi 'r̀ (°găi 'tyān) 'dzài shwō ba.

(Era, age) shŕdài, shŕhou. / I'd like to know more about those times. Wó hén 'syăng 'dwō jŕdau yìdyăr °nèi yíge shŕ'dàide 'shŕ (°'nèisyē shŕhoude 'shŕ). / That was before my time. is expressed as That was at my before. 'Nà shŕ dzài 'wó yĭ-'chyán.

(Occasion) tsż, syà(r), tàng, hwéi. / We'll try to do a little better next time. Wŏmen 'syàyítsż syăng 'fár dzwò 'hăuyìdyăr. / This is the last time I'll ever come here. 'Jèi shŕ wŏ dzwèi'hòu yítsż lái 'jèr le. or expressed as I won't come here again. Wŏ 'dzài yě bùlái 'jèr le.

(The future) 'jyānglái. / Time will tell whether he can do the job. 'Jŕhău 'jyāng-lái 'kàn le.

(Time consumed) 'jūngdyăr. / We'll have to make up our time on Sunday. Wŏ-men dĕi dzài lĭbài'tyān bă 'jūngdyăr 'bŭshàng.

(Pay for time during which work is done) is expressed as money chyán. / You can get your time at the pay window now. Nĭ kéyi dàu lĭng 'syīnshwĕi de 'chwāng-kŏur nèr ná 'chyán chyù le.

(Rhythm) pāidz. / That couple isn't keeping time to the music. Nèiyí'dwèr °'tyàude bùhé 'pāidz (°bú'ànje 'pāidz tyàu).

A long time háu jyŏu. / It's been a long time since I've seen you. Háu 'jyŏu méi'jyàn ni le.

At the same time (concessive) búgwò . . . yě, kěshr . . . yě, dànshr . . . yě. / You're right, but at the same time, something can be said for him too. Nĭ shwōde yóu'lĭ, 'búgwò ní yě bùnéng 'shwō tā wán'chywán bú'dwèi.

Do time, serve time dzwòjyàn.

For the time being 'mùchyán, syàndzài.

From time to time cháng, yŏu 'kùngr (de shŕhou), óuěr, shŕcháng. / I'll drop around from time to time. Wŏ yĭ'hòu °cháng (°yŏu'kùngr jyŏu) 'lái.

Have a . . . time. / Have a good time! Hăo'hăur wár a! / Did you have a nice time last night? Dzwór 'wănshang wárde 'hău ma? / I had a tough time with that exam. Wŏ nèitsż 'kăushŕ syăng'dāng fèi'jìn.

Have time gūngfu, kùngr, syánkùngr. / I haven't had a moment's time to myself. Wŏ 'yídyăr syán'kùngr yě méi'yŏu. / I wonder if we'll have time to see them before they go. Bùjŕdàu dzámen 'shrbushŕ néng yŏu 'kùngr dzài tāmen méidzóu yĭ'chyán 'kànkan tāmen. / We've got no time for such nonsense. Wŏmen méi 'gūngfu nàuje'wár.

In good time, in due time dàu shŕhou, àn shŕhou, kwài, yĭ'hwěr jyòu. / I'll pay you back in good time. Wǒ dàu 'shŕhour jwǔn 'hwán gei ni. /Don't worry; I'll be there in good time. Byé fā'chóu; wó °'jwǔn àn 'shŕhou (°'kwài, °yǐ'hwěr jyòu) 'dàu nèr le.

    In no time (at all) lìkè, lìshŕ, mǎshàng, syàndzài, shwō hwà, all followed by jyòu. /We can finish the job in no time at all. Wǒmen °lǐ'kè (°lǐ'shŕ, °'mǎshàng, °etc.) jyòu néng bǎ nèijyàn 'shèr dzwò'wán le.

    In time (sooner or later) dzáuwǎn. /I'm sure we'll get finished in time. Wǒ syàng'syìn wǒmen dzáu'wǎn jwǔn néng dzwò'wán le.

    In time (soon enough) dàule shŕhou. /I'm sure we'll get it finished in time. Dàule 'shŕhou yí'dìng kéyi dzwò'wán le. /Do you think we'll be in time to catch the train? is expressed as Do you think we can hurry sufficiently to make the train? Ní syǎng dzámen 'nénggòu 'gǎnshàng hwǒ'chē ma?

    In time with the music gēnje yīn'ywè. /He drummed on the table in time with the music. Tā 'gēnje yīn'ywè dzài 'jwōdzshang chyāuchu 'dyǎr lai.

    On time (on schedule) àn 'jūngdyǎr. /Is the express on time? Kwài'chē àn 'jūngdyǎr dàu ma?

    On time (in easy payments) fēnchī. /Do you want to pay cash for this radio, or will you take it on time? Ní mǎi jèige wúsyàn'dyàn shŕ gěi 'syànchyán, háishr 'dǎswàn fēn'chī fù 'kwǎn?

    Time after time, time and again, time and time again 'dwōshau hwéi, 'dwōshau tsż, lyǔ'tsż, 'sānfānwǔ'tsż, bùjr'dàu yǒu 'dwōshau 'hwéi le. /Time after time, I've told you not to shout at me that way. Wǒ 'gàusung ni 'dwōshau 'tsż le nǐ 'byé nèmma 'dàshēng 'hǎn wo. /I've passed that store time and again without realizing you were the owner. Wǒ 'lùgwò nèige 'pùdz bùjŕdàu yǒu 'dwōshau hwéi le, kěshr 'tsúnglái méi fā'syàn 'nǐ shŕ 'dūngjya.

    Work against time pīnje'mìngde 'gǎn.

    Times (conditions) ŕdz; be behind the times lwòwǔ, lwòhòu, gwòshŕ. /Times have been tough lately, haven't they? Jìnlái 'ŕdz búdà 'hǎu(gwò), 'dwèi budwèi? /His ideas are way behind the times. Tāde sżsyǎng tài °lwò'wǔ (°etc.) le.

    Times (in the name of a newspaper) shŕbàu.

    Times (multiplied by) chéng. /Two times two equals four. 'Èr chéng 'èr děngyu 'sż.

    To time (keep track of time used) jìshŕ, jìje shŕhou, kànje byǎu. /From now on we'll have to time our work. Tsúng'jīnyǐ'hòu dzámen dzwò 'shèr děi °jìje dyǎr 'shŕhou le (°kànje 'byǎu 'dzwò).

    (Allot amounts of time) swàn shŕjyān, swàn shŕhou, àn shŕhou. /I didn't get to that point because I timed my speech poorly. Wǒ shŕ'jyān méiswàn'hǎu, swóyi méinéng bǎ 'nèi dyǎn 'shwōchulai. /The show is timed to end by eleven. Yàushr àn 'shŕhou dehwà shŕ'yīdyǎn sàn'syì.

    (Do at the most suitable moment). /She timed that entrance beautifully. is expressed as Her entrance was just the time. Tā 'jìnlaide 'jèng shŕ 'shŕhou. /That speech wasn't very well timed, was it? is expressed as The giving of that speech wasn't the time. 'Nèige yán'jyǎng 'shwōde bùshŕ 'shŕhou.

TIN. syí, syǐ. /That candy dish is made of pure tin. Nèige 'tángdyér shŕ yùng chwún 'syí dzwòde.

    Tin can see CAN.

TIRE. (Be or get fatigued) lèi, fá, kwùn. /I tire very easily in this hot weather. Syàng jèmma 'rède tyār wǒ yǐ 'lái jyòu °'lèi (°'fá) le. / I'm afraid that trip will tire me out too much. Wó kǔng'pà 'chūchyù 'nèmma yítàng yí'dìng hwèi bǎ wo °lèi'hwài (°'lèije) le. / I'm too tired to go on. Wǒ 'lèide bùnéng °'jyēje (°'dzài) wàng'syà dzwò le. / Are you tired? Nǐ 'lèile ma? / I'm tired and I want to go to sleep. Wǒ yòu 'fá yòu 'kwùn, syǎng chyù shwèi'jyàu le.

(Be bored). / I'm tired of this place. Wǒ dzài 'jèr dāi'nǐle.

Be tiring (boring) wúlyáu, wúwèi, méiwèr, jyàu rén chǐ'nǐ, jyàurén méi'jìn. / His talks are always very tiring. Tā shwō 'hwà 'lǎushr °hěn wú'lyáu (°gān'dzàuwú-'wèi). *or* Tāde 'hwà 'tīngje °hěn méi'wèr (°jyàu rén chǐ'nǐ).

A tire chē dài, pí dài, gūlu, lwún dài. / One of my tires blew out coming down here. Wó wǎng jèr 'lái de shŕhou yǒu yíge chē'dài fàng'pàu le. / I need some air in these tires. Jèijǐtyáu chē'dài déi dǎ'chì le. / Check my tires. 'Yànyàn wǒde chē-'dài. *or* °'Kànkàn (°'Chyáuchyáu) chē'dài 'shŕ bushr déi dǎ'chì le. / I need a whole new set of tires. Wǒ chē'dài dōu děi 'hwàn le.

TITLE. (Name of a thing) míngdz, míngr; or a compound ending in míng *or* míngr; **title of a movie** pyānmíng; **title of a book** shūmíng; etc. / I wish I could remember the title of that movie. Wǒ bú'jìde nèige dyàn'yǐngrde °'míngdz le (°pyān'míngle).

(Official term for a person holding some position) míngyì, míngsyán, tóusyán, gwānsyán. / What's your exact title in this office? Nǐ dzài 'jèr jēn'jèngde °míngyì (°'míng'syán, °etc.) shr 'shémma?

(Championship) 'tóuyìmíng, gwàn'jyūn, jǐn'byāu. / Who do you think will win the tennis title this year? Ní syǎng 'jīnnyan 'wǎngchyóu bǐ'sài 'shéi néng dé °'tóu-yìmíng (°gwàn'jyūn, °jǐn'byāu)?

(Legal right to property). / Do you have title to this property? is expressed as Is this property yours? Jèige 'chǎnyè shr 'nǐde ma?

TO. (Marking place or position reached) dzài *or* dàu as a postverb with a verb of motion; often a Chinese verb of motion contains within itself the to idea and no separate word is necessary, thus go to shàng. / We drove to the city yesterday. Dzwótyān wǒmen 'kāi chìchē dàu 'chéngli chyù le. / Nail this announcement to the door. Bǎ jèige tūngjr 'dìngdzài 'ménshang.

(Toward, in the direction of) wǎng, wàng, syàng. / Take the first turn to your right. Jyàn 'wār jyòu wàng 'yòu gwǎi.

(In stating distances rather than motion) lí. *See also* **FROM.** / How far is it to town? Li 'chéng yǒu dwō 'ywǎn?

(Time before an hour). / It's ten minutes to four. is expressed as Lacks ten minutes (not to) four o'clock. Chà 'shŕfēn (búdàu) 'sżdyan. or as (It's) four o'clock short ten minutes. 'Sżdyan chyàn 'shŕfēn. or as It's three-fifty. 'Sāndyán 'wùshr-fēn.

(With reference to, concerning, as regards) dwèi, dwèiyu, gwānyu. / You're very kind to me. Nǐ dwèi(yu) 'wǒ tài 'hǎu le. / What do you say to this? Nǐ °'dwèi-yu (°'gwānyu) 'jèige yǒu shémma 'shwō de?

(Marking resultant state) de; chéng as a postverb with a verb of action, followed by a nominal expression of the resultant state; or simply a postverb with proper meaning. / The dog chewed the pillow to pieces. 'Góu bá 'jěntou jyáu'làn le. or 'Jěntou ràng 'gòu °'jyáuchéng (°'jyáude) syǐ'làn.

(Marking a personal recipient or someone consulted with) gěi, gēn. / Give this to him when he comes in. Tā 'jìnlái de shŕhou bǎ jèige 'gěi ta. / Explain that to me. Bǎ nèige gěi wo 'jyǎng yijyǎng. / Let me put it to you this way. Wo 'jèm-ma yàngr gēn ni shwō ba.

(As compared with) bǐ, dwèi. / We won six to two. 'Lyòu °bǐ (°dwèi) 'èr, wǒmen 'yíngle.

(Shut) shàng as a postverb. / Please pull the door to. Chǐng ni bǎ 'mén 'dài-shang.

To and fro 'láiláichyù'chyùde. / Students were walking to and fro in the park. 'Sywéshengmen dzài gūng'ywánli 'láiláichyùchyùde 'dzǒu.

Other uses of to are bound up with specific other words, as come to, fall to, true to life, etc., thus see the other word.

TOBACCO. yānyè(dz), yāntsǎu.

TODAY. jīntyan, jyēr(ge). / What do you have on the menu today? Nǐmen °'jīntyan (°'jyēr) yǒu shémma 'tsài? / Is today payday? °'Jīntyan (°'Jyēr) shr fā'syīn de rdz ma?

(Modern times) dāngchyán, mùchyán, jīnr, syànjīn, syàndzài. / Today's main problem is doing away with war. °Dāng'chyán (°Mù'chyán, °etc.) de 'jùyàu 'wèntí shr chyǔ'syāu jàn'jēng.

TOE. jyǎujŕtou, jyáujŕtou. / My toes are frozen. Wó bá jyǎu'jŕtou 'dùngle.

(Of a sock or stocking) wàdzjyār. / There's a hole in the toe. Wàdz'jyārshang yǒu yíge 'kūlung.

(Of a shoe) syétóur, (upper part) syélyǎr; (of a boot) sywētóur, sywēlyǎr.

TOGETHER. dzài yíkwàr, dzài yìchǐ, with dzài as a coverb or as a postverb. / They work together very well. Tāmen dzài yí'kwàr dzwò 'shr hěn °hé'shǒur (°hédelái). / Try to put these newspapers together in the right order. Bǎ jèisyē bàu'jŕ ànje 'rdz °'mǎdzài (°'lwòdzài, °'fàngdzài) yí'kwàr. / Let's call them together for a meeting. Bǎ tāmen 'jāujîdzài yì'chǐ kāi yítsz 'hwèi.

(With one will, cooperatively) yìtúng, yìchǐ, túngsyīn. / Let's all push together. Dà'jyā °yì'túng (°yì'chǐ) 'gàn.

Where together might be replaced in English by up, Chinese may use chǐlai as a postverb. / Please add these figures together. Láu'jyà bǎ jèisyē 'shùmù 'jyāchilai.

Together with (including also) lyán. / The price of this ticket together with tax is fifty-two dollars. Jèijāng 'pyàu lyán 'shwèi shr 'wǔshr'èrkwài chyán.

Get together (for fun, talk, etc.) 'jyù yijyù, 'hwèi yihwèi, 'wár yiwár, jyàn-jyan myàr, each with an appropriate plural pronoun or noun expression. / Do you suppose we can get together some evening? Ní syǎng dzámen 'nǎyìtyān 'wǎnshang kéyi °'jyù yijyù ma (°'hwèiyihwèi ma, °etc.)?

TOILET. tsèswǒ, máufáng, byànswǒ; (bathroom) syílyǎnfáng, yùshr; (washroom, as in a restaurant) syíshǒujyān.

TOMORROW. míngtyan, myéngr(ge), myér(ge). / Is tomorrow Wednesday? 'Myéngr-ge shr Syīngchī'sān ma? / I'll see you tomorrow morning. Wǒ myéngr 'dzǎuchen 'jyàn ni. / See you tomorrow! Myéngr 'jyàn! / I'll be back tomorrow. Wǒ 'míng-tyan 'hwéilai.

(Times to come) míngr, 'wèilái, 'jyānglái; the world of tomorrow 'wèiláishr-'jyè.

TONGUE. shétou. /Watch out you don't burn your tongue on this hot soup. Lyóu'shén byé jyàu jèige rè 'tāng bá nǐ 'shétou 'tàngjau.

(Food) shétou, kǒutyáu; often with source specified, as **beef tongue** nyóushétou, nyóukǒutyáu. /I'd like a plate of sliced tongue. Wǒ yàu yì'pár kǒutyáu'pyàr.

(Language) hwà; in compounds yǔ or wén. /What's your native tongue? Nǐ shwō 'nǎrde hwà? or (more formal) Nǐde 'běngwó'yǔ shr̀ 'něiyíge?

On the tip of one's tongue is expressed as on the edge of one's mouth dzài 'dzwěibyǎrshang. /Just a minute; I have his name on the tip of my tongue. Byé 'máng; tā 'míngdz jyòu dzài wó 'dzwěibyǎrshang.

Other English expressions. /Hold your tongue! Jǐ'dzwěi! or Byé 'shwō le! or 'Dé le, 'syíng le!

TONIGHT. wǎnshang, jyēr wǎnshang, jīntyan wǎnshang. /See you tonight! 'Wǎnshang 'jyàn! /What shall we do tonight? Dzámen jyēr 'wǎnshang gàn 'shémma? /Have you seen tonight's paper? Nǐ 'kànle jyēr 'wǎnshangde 'bàu le ma? or expressed as Have you seen today's evening paper? Nǐ 'kànle jyērde wǎn'bàu le ma?

TOO. (Also) yě. /May I come too? Wó 'yě lái, 'syíng ma? /I'd like a half pound of those too. Wó 'yě yàu bànbàng 'nèiyàngrde.

(Excessively). /It's too hot. Tài 'rè le. or Tài 'tàng le. /Am I too late? Wǒ tài 'wǎn le ma? /I think you're asking too much for this hat. Jèidǐng 'màudz nǐ yàu 'jyàr yàude tài °'dà le (°'dwō le). /You're going too far! Nǐ 'tài gwò'hwǒr le! or Ní yě 'tài bùjyǎng 'myàndz le!

All too tài plus an expression such as jēn really. /Our stay here was all too short. Wǒmen dzài 'jèr 'dāide shŕhou °'jēnshŕ (°gēn'běn, °jyǎn'jŕ) tài 'dwǎn le.

Other English expressions. /Too bad! 'Jēn dzāu'gāu! or 'Jēn chà'jìn! or 'Jèshŕ dzěmma 'shwōde! or (Hwó) 'gāi! or 'Jēn kě 'syí!

TOOL. jyāhwo. /Could I borrow your tools? Gěi wo nǐde 'jyāhwo 'yùng yiyùng kéyi ma? /Be careful of those tools. Yùng nèisyē 'jyāhwo de shŕhou 'syàusyīn dyǎr.

(Person used by powerful interests) kwéilěi, shòu 'lìyùng. /The mayor is only a tool of the party. Shŕ'jǎng yě bú'gwò °shŕ 'dǎngde kwéi'lěi (°shòu 'dǎngde lìyùng).

To tool (leather, designs, etc.) is expressed with various verbs, particularly dzwò make, kè carve, tàng (using heat, as to apply gold leaf), etc. /He's been tooling leather for years. Tā dzwò 'píhwo dwō'nyán le.

TOOTH. yá. /This tooth hurts. 'Jèige yá 'téng. /I think I need to have this tooth filled. Wó syǎng wó déi bǎ jèige 'yá 'bǔshang. /This tooth needs to be pulled. Jèige 'yá děi 'bá.

(Of a saw or gear wheel) chŕ, chěr. /This saw has a broken tooth. Jèige 'jyùshang de 'chěr 'bēnle yíge.

TOP. dǐng(r) usually followed by nouns to form compounds; **top of one's head** toudǐng(r); **top of a roof** or **roof top** fangdǐng(r); **top of a car** chēdǐng(r), or (if flexible) chēpéng(r); **top of a mountain** or **mountain top** shāndǐng(r), shāndyān, shāntóu, or meaning peak shānfēng. /How high is the top of that mountain? °Shāndǐngr (°etc.) yǒu dwō 'gāu? /Are you going to put down the top of the car? Nǐ yàu bǎ chē'péngr 'lyàusyalai ma?

(Toy) 'twólwó, nyǎnnyanjwàr. /The boy got a top for his birthday. Syǎu'hár 'shēngr 'déle yíge 'twólwó.

At the top of one's voice pīnje 'míngde, chěje 'sǎngdz, chěje 'bwódz. / You don't have to shout at the top of your voice! Nǐ 'yùngbujáu pīnje 'míngde 'hǎn.

Come out on top dé dìyī, yíng, shèng chénggūng. / I'm glad you came out on top. Nǐ dé dì'yī wó hén gāu'syíng.

From top to bottom lyánshàngdài'syà, tsúngshàng dàu'syà. / We searched the house from top to bottom. Wǒmen lóushànglóu'syà dōu jǎu'byànle.

On (the) top of dzài . . . - °shang (°'shàngbyan, °shàngbyar, °shàngmyan, °shàngmyar, °shàngtou, °shàngtour). / I'm sure my wallet was on top of the chest. Wó 'gǎn shwō wǒde chyán'bāur shr̀ dzài wútúng'gwèishang laije.

Sleep like a top. / I slept like a top all last night. Wǒ dzwór 'wǎnshang shwèide tǐng 'syāng.

Top man (person in charge) tóur, yǒudzge, dzwèi 'nénggàn de rén.

Be tops. / You're tops with me. Dzài 'wǒ kàn nǐ 'jēn °ké'yǐ (°shr̀ dǐ'yī le). or Wó kě 'jēn fú ni fúdau 'jyā le.

To top a score. / He topped my score by at least ten points. Tā chí'mǎ bí wǒ 'dwō shr̀'fēr. or Tā jr̀ 'shǎu 'yíngle wǒ shr̀'fēr.

Top a story gǎngwochyu. / Can you top that one? Nǐ néng 'gǎngwò 'nèige chyù ma?

Top something off. / We'll top the dinner off with some wine. Dzámen chr̄ 'fàn 'mwòmwolyáur děi 'hē dyŕ 'jyǒu.

TOTAL. dzǔngshù(r). / Will you figure out the total for me? Nǐ néng bá dzǔng'shùr gěi wo 'swànchulai ma?

Total (whole). / What is the total amount of the bill? is expressed as The bill altogether is how much? 'Jàng yí'gùngdzǔng shr̀ 'dwōshau? / This car is a total loss. is expressed as This car is completely ruined. Jèilyàng 'chē °wán'chywán (°jěng-'gèer) 'hwěi le.

To total (add up to) is expressed as have yǒu. / His income totals two thousand dollars a year. Tā 'yīnyánde shōu'rù yǒu 'lyǎngchyānkwài chyán.

Total up 'jyāchilai. / Let's total up expenses for the month. Dzámen bǎ jèige 'ywède 'kāisyau 'jyāchilai 'kàn yikàn.

TOUCH. (Make physical contact) mwō, mwōswo, māsa (stroke lightly, with a finger or hand); dyǎn, dyǎnda (touch at lightly with a finger of pointed object); pèng, pèngjau (touch against accidentally; may refer to a force ranging from very light to a heavy collision); āi, āijau (be touching very lightly or move very close to); tsēng, tsēngjau (rub or scrape against); dùng, dùngshóu (move or disturb); jānjau (be in contact with, especially water or something sticky); 'dāladàu, 'dāladzài (hang down so as to reach); 'tūludàu, 'tūludzài (hang down and reach when the thing hanging down is in motion, as a dress touching the floor as a woman walks along); dǐng, dǐngjau (with the head). / Don't touch that; it breaks easily. Byé °'dùng (°'mwō, °'mwōswo, °'māsa, °dùng-'shóu, °'chù, °'chùda, °'dyǎnda, °'āi, °'pèng, °'tsēng); rúngyi 'hwài. / You may look at it but don't touch (it). Syǔ 'kàn, bùsyú 'mwō. or 'Kàn shr̀ kěyi 'kàn, kě byé °'dùng (°dùng'shóu, °etc.). / Please don't touch those books. Byé 'dùng nèisyē 'shū. / These pants are much too long; they almost touch the ground. Nèityáu 'kùdz 'chángde 'jyǎnjr̀ yàu °'dāladàu (°'tūlu) 'dìshàng le. or Nèityáu 'kǔdz 'chángde 'jyǎn-jr̀ yàu °'jānjau (°'tsēngjau) 'dì le. / His head nearly touched the ceiling. Tā 'nǎudài 'kwài yàu °'dǐngjau (°'tsēngjau, °'āijau) tyānhwā'bǎn le.

(Concern). / I admit it's a pretty bad situation, but it doesn't touch us directly. is expressed as . . . but it has nothing to do with us. Wǒ 'chéngrèn 'chíngsying shr̀ bú'dà hǎu, kěshr gēn 'wǒmen méi shémma 'gwānsyi. _or as_ . . . but it doesn't obstruct our work. . . . kěshr 'àibujáu dzámende 'shr̀.

Touch at _or_ **on** a port dzài . . . tíng, dzài . . . kàuàn. / What ports did your boat touch at during your trip? Nǐ dzwòde nèityáu 'chwán dōu dzài 'nǎr °'tíng (°kàu-'àn) láije?

Touch off (give rise to) yǐnchilai. / Her remarks touched off a violent argument. Tāde 'hwà 'yǐnchi yìchǎng dà 'chǎudz lai.

Touch (on) (mention) 'tí(dàu), 'tán(dàu), 'lwùn(dàu), 'shwō(dàu). / What subjects did he touch on in the lecture? Tā yán'jyǎng de shŕhou dōu °'tí dàu °'tándàu, °'lwùndàu, °'shwōdàu) 'shémma le? / I wouldn't touch on any of his family problems if I were you. 'Wǒ yàushr 'nǐ a, 'jywé bù °'shwō (°'lwùn, °'tí, °'tán) tā 'jyāli de 'shèr.

Touch up a photograph bǎ . . . syōubǎn; **touch up** (take care of minor repairs and decorations) jyǎnjyan syīn. / My apartment needs touching up. Wǒ 'jùde dìfang děi jyǎnjyan 'syīn le.

A touch (act of touching) is expressed verbally as in paragraph one above. / One touch and it will break. Yí °'dùng (°'mwō, °'mwōswo, °etc.) jyou °'hwài (°'pwò, °'swèi, °'sǎn). / I felt a gentle touch on my shoulder. Wǒ 'jywéde yǒu rén chīng-'chyēngrde °'tǔnge (°'chùle, °'mwōle, °'dyǎnle, °'pèngle, °'àile, °'tsèngle) wǒ jyān'bǎngr yísyàr.

(Contact through communication). / Keep in touch with me. Cháng 'gwānjàu wo dyǎr. _or_ 'Jyēcháng bú'dwànde gēn wo 'jyējye 'tóu. _or_ 'Cháng gěi wo lái ge °'hwàr (°syèr). / I've been out of touch with things here for several months now. Jèrde 'shèr wó yǒu 'háujǐge 'ywè °méi'tīngjyan shémma le (°méi'gwān le). / Have you lost touch with your friends back home? Nǐ gēn lǎu'jyāde 'péngyou dōu ° mái shémma lái'wǎng le ma (°bùtūng 'syīn le ma)?

A touch of dyǎr, syàr. / There was a touch of humor in his speech. Tāde yán-jyǎng yǒu dyǎr 'yōumwò. _or_ Tāde yánjyǎng 'yǒu nèmma yìdyǎr °'yōumwò (°yàu 'yǐnrén'syàude yìsz). / This soup needs a touch of salt. Jèige 'tānglǐ děi °'sá (°'jyā) dyǎr 'yán. / This chair needs a few more touches of paint. Jèibǎ 'yǐdz hái děi °'yóu (°'chī) lyǎngsyàr. _or_ Jèibǎ 'yǐdz yóu 'jǐchù dìfang hái děi 'yóuyou.

Touch and go sywánhuje; (of living conditions) jyòuhuje, 'jyāngjyòuje. / It's been touch and go for a long time. 'Shèr nèmma 'sywánhuje yóu 'hǎusyē r̀dz le. / Things were touch and go for a long time. 'Hǎusyē r̀dz le nèmma °'jyòuhuje (°'jyāngjyòuje) gwòde.

Feels . . . to the touch mwōje . . . . / That cloth feels nice to the touch. Nèi-kwài 'lyàudz 'mwōje tíng °'rwǎnhwo (°'hwályou).

Be touching (evocative of emotion) 'dùngrén, jyàu rén shòu 'gǎndùng. / How touching! 'Jēn shr̀ jyàu rén róu'má! _or_ (sarcastically) 'Dwō róu'má! / It was a touching scene. (of a play or movie) 'Nèidwàr hěn °'dùngrén (°jyàu rén shòu 'gǎn-dùng). _or_ (of a happening) Nèige 'chíngsying hěn °'dùngrén (°jyàu rén shòu 'gǎn-dùng).

Be (a little) touched yóu dyǎr fēng, 'fēngfengdyan'dyǎnde, yóu shénjīng'bìng. / Don't mind him; he's a little touched. Béng 'lǐ ta; tā °yóu dyǎr 'fēng (°yǒu shén-jīng'bìng, °'fēngfengdyandyǎnde).

Be touchy. / He's touchy about his baldness. is expressed as He doesn't like people to mention that he's bald. Tā °'gèying (°'nìwei) rén shwō tā °'tū (°shr̀ 'tūdz, °'tútóu). / Touchy, isn't he? is expressed as He really gets mad whether you disturb him or not. Tā 'jēn shr̀ 'dùngbudùngr jyòu 'nǎu.

TOWARD(S). (Direction) syàng, wàng, wǎng. / Let's go towards town. Dzámen wàng 'chéngli dzǒu ba. / He's coming toward us now. Tā 'jèng wàng wǒmen 'jèr lái ne.

(Approaching, in specifying a time) dǐng, dàgài. / I'll be there towards late afternoon. Wǒ °dǐng (°dà'gài) 'hòubànshǎngr 'dàu nèr.

(Concerning) dwèi, dwèiyu, gwānyu. / I feel very sympathetic towards him. Wǒ dwèi tā hěn 'byǎu túng'chíng.

TOWEL. 'shǒujīn, hànjīn; **bath towel** dzǎujīn, syídzǎumáujīn, syídzǎubù, tsādzǎubù; **turkish towel** máujīn; **face towel** syǐlyǎn'shǒujīn.

TOWN. chéng (particularly one which has a wall); dìfang (refers to any size); where town means a relatively smaller community, one can say small city syǎuchéng. / How far is the next town? Lí 'syàyíge 'chéng yǒu dwō 'ywǎn? / I won't be coming into town this weekend. Wǒ jèige jōu'mwò bújìn'chéng. / I'd rather live in a town than a village; but a city is still better. Wǒ 'jywéde jùdzài 'syǎuchéngli bǐ 'tswūndzli 'hǎu, 'dàchéngli gèng 'hǎu.

(People of a town) chénglide rén; **the whole town** (everyone in town) 'chywán-chéngde rén. / The whole town's talking about them. 'Chywánchéngde rén dōu dzài 'tánlwùn tāmen.

TRACK. (Of a railroad) hwǒchē dàu, chēgwěi, tyégwěi; (of a streetcar) dyànchē dàu. / Watch out for trains when you cross the tracks. Gwò hwǒchē'dàu de shŕhou lyóu-'shén hwǒ'chē.

(Trail left by walking) jyǎuyèr. / Let's follow his tracks to see where he went. Dzámen gēnje tā jyǎu'yèr dzǒu, kàn tā chyù 'nǎr le.

(Horse racing course) páumáchǎng. / If we want to see the first race, we've got to be at the track at one-thirty. Dzámen yàushr syǎng kàn 'tóuyichǎng sài'mǎ dehwà, ké 'děi 'yìdyǎn'bàn yǐ'chyán dàu páumá'chǎng.

(Running sports) jìngsài; **track and field** tyánjìngsài. / When he was at college, he went out for track. Tā dzài 'dàsywé de shŕhou, tsān'jyā gwò 'jìngsài.

Be off the track bùtyētí, lítí tài 'ywǎn. / What you say is true, but it's off the track. Nǐ 'shwō de dàushr 'dwèi, kěshr °bùtyē'tí (°lítí tài 'ywǎn).

Be on the right track dzǒudwèi, yǒumér, mwōje mér. / You're on the right track. Ní dzǒu'dwèile. or Nǐ jēn yǒu'mér. or 'Syíng, nǐ swàn °yǒu'mér le (°mwō-je 'mér le).

Keep track of. / I hope you don't expect me to keep track of all the details. Ní kě 'byé jrje 'wǒ lái 'gwǎn nèisyē 'língchibā'swèide 'shr.

Lose track of. / I'm afraid I've completely lost track of him. is expressed as Where he's gone to I just don't know. Tā rú'jīn dzài 'nǎr, wó kě 'jēn shr bùjr'dàu. or as I haven't even a little news of him. Gwānyu 'tāde syāusyi wǒ shr 'yìdyár yě méiyou.

Make tracks for gán'jín °dzǒu (°hwéi), kāi'twěi jyòu 'pǎu, sā'yǎdz jyòu 'pǎu. / It's getting rather late, so we'd better make tracks for home. 'Tyān bù'dzǎu le; dzámen gán'jín hwéi 'jyā ba.

To track down a fugitive sōusyún, sōubù. / The police are trying to track down the escaped convict. Jǐng'chá jèng dzài °sōu'syún (°sōu'bù) nèige 'táufàn.

Track down a story 'dyàuchá. / Could you track down that story for me? Nǐ néng tì wo 'dyàuchádyàuchá nèijyàn 'shr ma?

TRADE. (The carrying on of business) 'shēngyì, mǎimai. / Do you have much trade in the summer? 'Syàtyar °'shēngyî (°'mǎimai) °'dwō (°'máng) ma? /Is there any trade across the border? 'Jèr 'yǒu méiyou chūrù'kǒude mǎimai?

(Occupation). /What's your trade? <u>is expressed as</u> What work do you do? Nǐ-'dzwò 'shémma shr̀? <u>or as</u> What line of work are you in? Nín shr̀ dzài 'nèiyìháng? /Why, I'm a butcher by trade, but right now I'm working in a factory. <u>is expressed as</u> My original occupation is butcher, ... Wó 'běnháng shr̀ túdzǎi'yè, kěshr syàn-dzài shr̀ dzài gūng'chǎngli dzwò 'shr̀.

(Customers) 'jǔgù. /I think my product will appeal to your trade. Wó syáng wǒ jèr chū de 'hwò yí'dìng hwèi jyàu nǐde 'jǔgù 'syǐhwan.

To trade jyāu'hwàn. /Let's trade. Dzámen jyāu'hwàn ba.

Trade <u>one thing in for</u> <u>another</u> ná ... tyēhwàn .... /I want to trade this car in for a new one. Wó syǎng ná 'jèilyàng chē tyē'hwàn yílyàng 'syǐnde.

Trade <u>something off</u> (get rid of) dǎuchu 'shǒu chyù, twēichuchyu, màichuchyu. /We've got to trade off some of this old merchandise. Dzámen 'dzúng déi syǎng'fár bǎ jèisyē 'jyòu hwò °dǎuchu 'shǒu chyù (°'twēichuchyu, °'màichuchyu).

Trade on jr̀je ... chr̄'rén, jr̀je ... °jǎu (°jàn) 'pyányi. /She's been trading on her looks for years. Tā jèmmasyē'nyán le jyòushr jr̀je 'múyàngr jàn 'pyányi.

TRAIN. (Railroad) hwǒchē, chē. /When does the train leave? Hwǒ'chē 'shémma shr̀-hou 'kāi? /The train is late. Hwǒ'chē wù'dyǎnle. /I have to catch an early train. Wǒ déi 'gǎn yítàng 'dzǎuchē. /I'll see you to the train. Wǒ 'sùng ni shàng 'chē.

(Column of vehicles) lyòu, dàlyòu; **a train of trucks** yídà'lyòude kǎ'chē.

To train (as for athletic events) lyàn, 'syùnlyàn. /I hope you've been training for our tennis match next week. Dzámen 'syàlǐbài sài wǎng'chyóur, wǒ 'syǐwang nǐ jèisyē 'r̀ dz 'lyànle.

Be trained in (have studied and learned) nyàngwo. /Have you been trained in law? Nǐ 'nyàngwo 'fǎlyù ma?

TRANSLATE. fān, 'fānyì. /How do you translate this? 'Jèige ní dzěmma 'fān(yì)? /Where can I find someone to translate this letter? Dàu 'nǎr chyù 'jǎu ge rén bǎ jèifēng 'syìn gěi wo 'fān(yi)chulai? /That's a difficult expression to translate. 'Jèi-jǔng 'shwōfa hěn nán 'fān(yi). <u>or expressed as</u> That expression is hard to say in Chinese (French, German, etc.). Jèijǔng 'shwōfa hěn 'nán yùng 'Jūngwén shwō. /Please translate this letter into Chinese for me. Chíng ní bǎ jèifeng 'syìn géi wǒ fān(yi)cheng 'Jūngwén.

TRAVEL. 'yóulì, lyǔsyíng. /Where are you planning to travel for your spring vacation? Nǐ chwūn'jyà 'dǎswàn dàu 'nǎr chyù lyǔ'syíng?

(Go some place by car, train, etc.) dzwò; (if one is operating the vehicle one-self) kāi; (if one sits astride, as on horseback or a bicycle) chí. /Which is the best way to travel? Dzwò 'shémma dzwèi 'hǎu?

(Move fast) °dzǒude (°fēide, °etc.) dwō'kwài. /Boy, is this plan traveling! Hǎu'jyāhwo, jèige fēi'jī 'fēide dwō'kwài a!

Travel (movement of traffic). /Travel on this road is always light. <u>is expressed as</u> This road isn't crowded. Jèityáu 'lù(shang) bù'jǐ.

TRAVELER. lyǔkè.

TREAT. (Medically) jr̀. /Has the doctor been treating you long? 'Dàifu gěi ni 'jr̀le 'yǒu syē 'shŕhou le ma?

(Pay for someone else) is usually expressed with chǐng invite; sometimes with gěi give. / How about treating me for a change? 'Yě gāi 'chǐngching 'wǒ le. / I'm treating this time. 'Jèihwéi shr̄ wó chǐng.

(Deal with) yánjyou, jyǎng, gwānyu, 'tǎulwùn. / Can you recommend a book that treats current social problems? Nǐ néng 'jyèshau yìběr °'yánjyou (°jyǎng, °etc.) shè'hwèi'wèntí de 'shū ma?

Treat someone in a specified way dài, dwèifu. / You're not treating me fairly. Nǐ 'dài wo bù'gūngdàu. / How would you treat him in a case like this? Syàng 'jèi-yàngr nǐ 'dzěmma 'dwèifu ta? / How's the world been treating you? is expressed as How've you been these days? 'Jìnlái rú'hé? or 'Jìnlái dzěmma 'yàng?

Treat something as 'yǐwéi, rènwei. / You shouldn't treat that as a laughing matter. Nǐ bù'yīngdang °'yǐwei (°'rènwei) 'nèijyàn shr̀ kě'syàu.

A treat (pleasure) is expressed as be interesting yǒuyìsz, láijìn or as be satisfying gwòyǐn. / It will be a treat to hear the concert. Chyù tǐng nèige yīnywè'hwèi yí'dìng hén °'yǒu'yìsz (°'lái'jìn, °gwò'yǐn).

(Act of paying for someone else) is expressed verbally as in paragraph two. / I insist, dinner's my treat. Bù'sying, 'jèidwùn fàn yí'dìng děi °'ràng 'wó chǐng (°'ràng 'wó gěi). or expressed as This dinner certainly should be regarded as mine. Bù'sying, 'jèidwùn fàn yí'dìng děi swàn 'wǒde.

TREE. shù. / I just missed hitting a tree while driving over here. Wǒ kāi 'chē wàng 'jèr lái de shŕhou chà'dyǎr méiwàng 'shùshang.

Be up a tree. / That problem really has me up a tree. Nèige 'wèntí 'jēn jyàu wo °dzwò'là (°méi'lùr, °mei'jé, °wéi'nán).

TRIAL. (A test) is expressed verbally with shr̄ try. / Why don't you give this automobile a trial? Nǐ 'wèi shémma bù'shr̀shr jèilyàng 'chē? / We'll hire you for a week's trial. Wǒmen 'syān ràng ni dzwò yíge lǐ'bài °'shr̀shr (°shr̀'gūng, °shr̀'shǒur).

(A period of emotional hardship) is expressed with nánshòu be hard to bear. / It must have been a great trial to lose your father. Lìng'dzwūn chyù'shr̀ nǐ yí'dìng hěn nán'shòu.

(In court) is expressed with gwòtíng, kāishěn be tried. / Our case comes up for trial next Monday. Dzámende 'àndz 'syàlǐbài'yī °gwò'tíng (°kāi'shěn).

TRICK. (Knack) méndau, chyàumér, 'jywéjāur. / There's a trick to making a good cake. 'Dyǎnsyin yàu syǎng dzwò'hǎule děi 'jŕdàu nèige °'méndau (°chyàu'mér). Bá 'dyǎnsyīn dzwò'hǎule, yǒu ge 'jywéjāur.

(Mischief). / She's full of tricks, isn't she? Tā °syīn'yǎr jēn 'dwō (°hěn 'hwá-tóu, °jú'yì tǐng 'dwō, °sǒu jú'yì hěn 'dwō), 'shr̀ bushr̀?

(Mannerism). / She's got a trick of frowning when she's thinking. Tā yì 'syǎng shémma jyòu 'jòu méi'tóu.

(In cards) yúfù pái, yílwòr pái. / Who took that last trick? 'Shàngyífù 'pái shr̀ 'shéi 'náde? / All we need is two more tricks now. Dzámen 'dzài ná lyǎnglwòr 'pái jyòu 'gòu le.

(Legerdemain) wányèr, syìfǎr. / He knows some pretty good tricks with cards. Tā 'hěn hwèi jí'shǒur ná jŕ'pái °'wár de wán'yèr (°'byàn de syì'fǎr).

(Treacherous act). / That's a mean trick to play on me. 'Nèiyì'shǒur géi wo 'láide kě 'jēn bú'shàn. or Nèige wán'syàu gēn wo 'kāide kě 'jēn bù'syàu.

(Attempts to disrupt or escape). / Don't try any tricks! Byé °'tōutoumwō-

'mwŏrde (°'gwĕigweiswèi'swèide) °shwă'hwā'jāur (°shwă hwā'hwó, °shwă 'gwĕi, °shř'hwài, °chū 'sōujúyì, °shwă hwá'tóu)!

Turn the trick (accomplish the end in view) líng, syíng, chéng. /Your idea will turn the trick. 'Syíng, nĭ nèi yí'syàdz jwun °'líng (°'syíng, °'chéng).

To trick someone pyàn, dzwàn, mēng, ywān, shwā, kĕng. /Just my luck, tricked again! Jēn dău'méi, 'yòu jyàu rén gĕi °'pyàn le (°dzwàn le, °etc.)! /I had confidence in him, but he tricked me and didn't do as we had agreed he would. Wŏ 'dàushr tĭng 'syìnrèn ta láije, kĕshr tā 'pyàn wo, 'búanje wŏmende 'yìsz 'dzwò.

Trick someone into doing something. /Are you trying to trick me into saying that? Nĭ shr syăng 'tàu wŏde 'hwà ma? or Nĭ shr 'byànje 'fāngrde ràng wo 'shwōchulai a?

TRIP. (Journey) (yítàng)lyŭsyíng, (yítàng)dzŏude; (for pleasure) (yítàng) chūchyu wárde. /How was your trip? Nĭ 'jèitàng °lyŭ'syíng (°chūchyu 'wárde, °'dzŏude) dzĕmma 'yàng? /How long a trip is it? Jèiyí'tàng yŏu dwō 'ywăn?

To trip bàn yìge 'gēndou, bàndàule. /He tripped and fell. Tā 'bànle yìge 'gēndou, bàn'dăule.

Trip someone bàn . . . yìge 'gēndou. /If you don't pull your legs out of the aisle, you're liable to trip someone. Nĭ yàushr bùbá 'twĕi tsúng dzŏu'dàushang 'swō hweilai, hwéi'tóu yí'syàdz 'bàn rén yì 'gēndou.

Trip someone up (fig.) dăulwàn. /If somebody hadn't tripped us up somewhere, we would have finished on time, wouldn't we? Yàushr 'méi rén gēn 'dzámen dău- 'lwàn dehwà, dzámen bújyòu kéyi àn 'shŕhou dzwò'wánle ma?

TROUBLE. (Disturbance) lwàndz; or expressed in proper context as affair shŕ. /The police are trying to break up that trouble down the street. Syún'jĭng 'jèng syáng bă jyē nèitóurde °nèige 'lwàndz (°nèidàngdz 'shř) 'lyăule.

(State of being troubled). /What's the trouble? 'Dzĕmmale? or Shémma 'shèr?

(Inconvenience, exertion) máfan; also other special expressions when used in polite statements or requests. /We've really put him to a lot of trouble. Wŏmen shŕ- 'dzài gĕi tā jăule hĕn dwō 'máfan. /Don't put yourself to any trouble. Hè'bì dz- 'jí jău 'máfan? /Thanks for your trouble. Jēn shŕ 'máfan nín le. or expressed as I have made you tired. Jyàu nín shòu 'lèi. /(It was) no trouble at all! Nărde 'hwà! /Would it be any trouble for you to work tonight? Jyēr 'wănshang 'máfan nĭ dwō 'dzwò hwèr, syíng ma?

Be in trouble. /I'm in trouble. Wŏ chū 'shèr le. or (less emphatic) Wŏ chūle 'máfan le. or (experiencing bad luck) Wó dăule 'méi le. or (because of one's wrongdoings or mistakes) Wó 'tŭngle 'lóudz le. or Wó rĕ 'hwò le.

Look (or Ask) **for trouble** jău °'chár (°'máfan). /Are you asking for trouble? Nĭ shr 'méi chár jău 'chár háishr 'dzĕmmaje? or Nĭ shr yàu jău 'máfan? or Ní jău'dzòu a?

To trouble (afflict physically) ràng . . . bù'shūfu (make uncomfortable). /My arm has been troubling me ever since my accident. Tsúng wŏ chūle 'shř yĭ'hòu wŏde 'gēbe yì'jŕde ràng wo bù'shūfu.

(Put to inconvenience) máfan; or, in polite statements or request, other expressions which achieve a polite tone. /I hope I haven't troubled you. Búhwèi 'máfan nín ba. /May I trouble you for a match? is expressed as I beg a match from you. Gēn nín syín gèr yáng'hwŏ. /Sorry to trouble you. is expressed as It is too bad that I have made you tired. 'Jèshr dzĕmma 'shwōde, jyàu nín shòu 'lèi.

TRUCK. (Vehicle) kǎchē, dàchìchē, dzàijùngchìchē, yùnhwòchì'chē; when the context or situation indicates what type of vehicle is involved, one simply says chē. / Where can I park my truck? Wǒ néng bǎ 'chē tíngdzai 'nǎr?

(Garden produce) is expressed with tsài (vegetables). / The farmer sold all his truck in half a day. 'Jwāngjyarén bàn'tyārde 'gūngfu jyòu bǎ tāde 'tsài mài'gwāngle.

To truck (transport) yùng °kǎchē (°dàchìchē, °etc.) yùn; if the context is clear, one simply says yùn. / It took us two days to truck this furniture across town. Wǒmen fèile 'lyǎngtyānde 'gūngfu tsái bǎ 'jyājyù 'yùndau chéng 'nèibyar chyu.

TRUE. (Factual) jēn; (genuine) jēnjèng; (accurate) jēn *or* jèng in compounds. / Is that story true? 'Nèidwàr 'shèr shr̀ 'jēnde ma? / That picture is a true likeness of you. Nèijāng syàng'pyàr jēn 'syàng nǐ. / He's a true scientist. Tā shr̀ yíge jēn-'jèngde kēsywé'jyā. / You'll find him a true friend. Nǐ yí'dìng hwèi fā'syàn tā 'nèige rén shr̀ ge jēnjèngde 'péngyou. or expressed as You'll certainly find him sufficiently a friend. Nǐ yí'dìng hwèi fā'syàn tā 'nèige rén hěn gòu 'péngyou. / Where's true north from here? °Jēn'běi (°Jèng'běi) dzài 'nǎr?

Be true to one's word shwō 'hwà °'swàn hwà (°jyòu 'swàn). / He's always true to his word. Tā 'syànglái shr̀ shwō 'hwà °'swàn hwà (°jyòu 'swàn).

Is it true that is expressed with 'shr̀. / Is it true that you got a new car? Nǐ 'shr̀ mǎile lyàng syīn 'chē ma?

TRUNK. (Of a tree) shù(gàn), shù(bèn). / Nail the notice on the trunk of that tree. Bǎ °'páidz (°bù'gàu) dīngdau nèige 'shùshang.

(For clothes, etc.) (dà)syāngdz, dàsyāng. / I want to send my trunk through on my ticket. Wó syǎng bǎ 'syāngdz dǎ syíngli'pyàu dài'dzǒu.

(Part of the body) shēndz.

Trunk line (railroad or highway) jènglù, dàlù; (railroad only) gànsyàn.

Trunks (short outside trouser-like garment) kùchǎr, dwǎnkùdz. / These trunks are too tight. Jèityáu kù'chǎr tài 'shòu.

TRUST. kàu (rely on); syìn (believe what someone says); 'syìnrèn (trust in someone's ability or character, also translated as put trust in). / Don't you trust me? Nǐ bú-'syìnrèn wǒ ma? / I guess we've got to trust his story. Wǒ kàn, dzámen jr̀'hǎu 'syìn tade. / I'm looking for a servant that I can trust. Wǒ jèngdzài 'jǎu yíge chéng-'shŕkě'kàude 'yùngrén. / I don't trust this driver. Wǒ 'jywéhuje jèige kāi'chēde kàubu'jù. *but* / You shouldn't trust your memory so much. is expressed as Don't expect your memory to be so good. Nǐ byé 'yǐwéi nǐde 'jìsyìng 'hǎu.

(Have hope) 'syīwàng, or omitted. / I trust you'll be able to come to dinner. Wǒ 'syīwàng nín lái gēn wǒmen chr̄ wǎn'fàn. / I trust you slept well. Nǐ shwèi'hǎu le ba!

(Allow one to act without fear). / Can you trust me until payday? is expressed as Wait till payday and I'll pay you back, OK? Déng wǒ gwān'syǎng de shŕhour dzài 'hwán ni, 'syíng ma?

Trust something to someone 'jyāugěi. / They trusted the money to his care. Tāmen bǎ 'chyán jyāugei 'tā gwǎn le.

Hold in trust (legal). / His father's estate was held in trust for him by his uncle until he was twenty-one. is expressed as His uncle took care of his father's property for him until he was twenty-one, before it was given to him. Tāde 'shūshu tì ta 'gwǎnje tā 'fùchin de chǎn'yè, yì'jŕ dàu tā èrshŕ'yīswèi, tsái 'jyāugei ta.

Put trust in 'syìnrèn. / I'm putting my trust in you. Wǒ 'syìnrèn ni.

Of great trust 'dzérèn hěn 'dà. / He holds a position of great trust. Tāde 'shèr 'dzérèn hěn 'dà.

TRUTH. (Words which state facts) shŕhwà. / That's the truth. Nà shŕ shŕ'hwà. / Are you telling me the truth? Nǐ shŕ gēn wo shwō shŕ'hwà ne ma?

(Element of accuracy) jēngéde. / Do you think there's any truth in that story? Nǐ 'jywéde tā shwō de 'hwà yǒu dyǎr jēn'géde ma?

TRY. (Of a key, a pen, etc.) shŕ. / Did you try the key? 'Yàushr nǐ 'shŕle ma? / Here, try my pen. Ei, 'shŕshr 'wǒde gāng'bǐ.

(Of food) is expressed with dzwò cook or with cháng taste. / I think I'll try some soup. Wǒ syǎng wǒ lái dyǎr 'tāng °'shŕshr (°'chángchang). / I've never tried this dish before. Wǒ 'tsúnglái °méi'dzwǒgwo (°méi'chánggwo) jèijǔng 'tsài.

(Of a case in court; of the judge) shěn. / Who's going to try your case? 'Shéi lái 'shén nǐ jèige 'àndz a?

Try one's patience ràng . . . °jāují °búnài'fán). / Sometimes you try my patience. Yǒu'shŕhou nǐ 'jēn ràng wo °jāu'jí (°búnài'fán).

Try clothes on shŕshr, °'chwānshang (°'dàishang, or other words for wear, depending on what type of clothing is involved) . . . 'shŕshr. / First I'd like to try that suit on. Wǒ 'syān 'chwānshang nèijyàn 'yīshang 'shŕshr. or Wǒ syàn 'shŕshr nèi-jyàn 'yīshang dzài 'shwō.

Try out for a part in a play, radio, football game, etc., is expressed in terms of going to see the proper person and taking a try 'shŕshr kàn 'syíngbusyíng.

Try to (or and) do something syǎngfár; (after the trial) shŕ; often omitted. / Let's try and get there on time. Dzámen syǎng'fár ànje 'shŕhou 'dàu nèr. / Try to do better next time. 'Syàyìhwéi syǎng'fár) dzwò 'háu dyǎr. / We'll try to finish today for sure. Wǒmen syǎng 'fádz jyèr yí'dìng dzwò'wán le. / I tried to follow your instructions. Wǒ ànje nǐ 'gàusung wo de 'fádz 'shŕ láije.

Have (or Make or Take) a try (at) shŕ. / He made several tries, but failed each time. Tā 'shŕle háují'hwéi, 'měihwéi dōu bù'syíng. / Let's take another try at solving the problem. Dzámen 'dzài 'shŕ yìhwéi ba.

Be trying tǎuyàn, gòu °chyáude (°shòude). / That noise outside is very trying, especially when you want to work. Wàitoude nèige 'shēngyin tíng tǎu'yàn, nǐ 'ywè yàu dzwò 'shŕ nèr ywè 'syǎng. / This has been a trying day. 'Jèiyìtyān jēn gòu °'chyáude (°'shòude).

TUESDAY. Syīngchīèr, Lǐbàièr.

TURN. jwàn; (of a person; change position of the body) °jwàngwò (°jwǎngwò) °'shèr (°lyǎr) (lái, chyù); (of the wind) jwàn. / The wheels won't even turn in this mud. 'Gūlu dzài 'nílí lyán 'jwàn dōu bú'jwàn. / He turned and beckoned to us to follow him. Tā °jwàngwo 'shèr lai (°etc.) gēn wǒmen dǎ ge 'jāuhu ràng wǒmen 'gēnje ta. / Looks like the wind is turning. Chyáu 'jèige yìsz jwàn'fēng le. / Try to turn the knob. 'Jwànjwàn nèige 'báshou 'shŕshr.

(Twist) wǎi, nyǒu. / She turned her ankle on the edge of the sidewalk. Tā dzài mǎlyù'yár nèr bá jyǎu'wàndz °'wǎile (°'nyǒule) yísyàr.

Turn an age gwò. / She just turned twenty-one. Tā 'gāng gwò ershryi'swèi.

Turn a corner gwǎiwār. / He just turned the corner. Tā gāng gwǎigwò 'wār chyu.

Turn <u>someone's</u> **head.** / He's one person who won't let praise turn his head. Tā 'nèi rén dzěmma bājye, yě bùgǎi 'júyì.

Turn <u>someone's</u> **stomach.** / I'm afraid this food will turn my stomach. Kǔng'pà wǒ yǐ chr̄ jèijǔng 'tsài, 'syīnli jyòu děi 'nàudeheng.

Turn the tables on gěi . . . 'lái yísyàdz. / Let's turn the tables on them for a change and see how they like it. Wǒmen 'yé gěi 'tāmen 'lái yísyàdz, kànkan 'tāmen dzěmma 'yàng.

Turn the tide against yāsyachyu; **turn the tide for** or **in favor** táichilai; **be turned** (of the tide) byànle, jwǎngwolaile. / The city vote turned the tide against our candidate. Chéng 'lǐtou 'tóude 'pyàu bá wǒmende hòusywǎn'rén gěi 'yāsyachule. / But once he spoke in favor of my proposal the tide was turned. 'Tā yǐ shwō tā 'dzàncheng 'wǒde yìsz, nèige 'syíngshr̄ jyòu °'byànle (°'jwǎngwǒláile).

Turn <u>plus an adjective is expressed with</u> byàn become <u>followed by a stative verb or by a stative verb plus</u> le. / She turned pale when she heard the news. Tā yǐ 'tīngjyàn nèige 'syāusyì 'lyǎnshang lì'shr̄ °byànle 'shǎr le (°byàn'báile). / Don't leave the milk on the table, or it'll turn sour. Byé bǎ nyóu'nǎi 'lyàudzài 'jwōdzshang, 'yàuburán jyòu 'swān le.

Turn around (of a person) °jwàngwò (°jwǎngwò) °'lyǎr (°shěr) (lái or chyù). / He turned around and looked at us. Tā jwàngwò 'lyǎr lai 'kàn wǒmen.

Turn <u>something</u> **around** (physically) 'jwàngwò (lái or chyù). / Let's turn the table around. Bǎ 'jwōdz 'jwàngwolai.

Turn <u>something said</u> **around** (misinterpret) jyěshr tswò. / You're turning my words around. Ní bǎ wǒde 'hwà jyěshr 'tswò le.

Turn back wàng 'hwéi dzǒu. / Let's turn back. Dzámen wàng 'hwéi dzǒu ba.

Turn <u>someone</u> **back** ràng . . . 'hwéichyù. / Turn them back; the road's blocked up ahead. Ràng tāmen 'hwéichyu ba, 'chyánbyar 'dàur bù'tūng.

Turn down <u>a road, etc.</u> wàng . . . gwǎi(wār). / Turn down this road. Wàng 'jèibyar gwǎi'wār.

Turn <u>something</u> **down** (fold it back) syānkai. / Turn down the blanket. Bǎ 'bèiwo 'syānkai.

Turn <u>something</u> **down** (reject) 'jyùjywé; <u>or expressed as</u> not accept bùjyēshòu. / My application for a job was turned down for some reason. Wǒ móu'shr de chǐngchyóu'shū 'yīnwèi dyǎr 'ywángu °bèi 'jyùjywéle (°tāmen méijyē'shòu).

Turn in (go to bed) shwèi, shwèijyàu. / We ought to turn in early tonight. Dzámen jyēr 'wǎnshang yīngdāng °'dzǎu shwèi'jyàu (°'dzáudyǎr 'shwèi).

Turn in <u>a driveway, road, etc.</u> 'jìnchyù. / Turn in at the next drive. 'Syàyíge 'kǒur nèr 'jìnchyu. / Turn in at the next gate. 'Syàyíge mén'kǒur nèr 'jìnchyù.

Turn <u>something</u> **in** hwán. / You'll have to turn in your equipment before we can release you. Ní děi bǎ 'dūngsyi 'hwán le, wǒmen tsái néng tàng ní dsǒu.

Turn into (become) 'byànchéng. / She's turned into an old gossip. Tā 'byànchéng ge 'swèidzwěidz lǎu'tàitai le. / The discussion turned into a brawl. <u>is expressed as</u> As they discussed and discussed, they started fighting. 'Shānglyangshānglyangje 'dǎchiláile.

Turn <u>something</u> **into** <u>something else</u> bǎ . . . 'hwànchéng. / Of course, you can always turn your bonds into cash. 'Dāngrán ní 'shémma shr̄hour dōu néng bǎ gūng'jài 'hwànchéng 'syànchyán.

Turn <u>something</u> **off** 'gwānshàng. / Turn off the light, it hurts my eyes. Dēng tài hwángyǎn le bǎ tā gwánshàng ba. /I wonder if I forgot to turn off the gas. Wǒ 'shr bushr 'wàngle bǎ °chǐ'mén (°méi'chi) 'gwānshangle.

Turn on <u>something</u> (depend on for validity) kàn. /The whole argument turns on that point. 'Swóyǒude 'jēnglwùn dōu kàn 'nèiyìdyán dzěmma 'yàng le.

Turn on <u>someone</u> (cease to agree with or be pleasant to) 'hūrán gēn . . . gwòbu-'chyù, 'jyūrán gēn . . . dǎu'lwàn. /Why are you turning on me so? Nǐ gàn'má 'hūrán gēn wo jèmma gwòbu'chyù? /I didn't expect you'd turn on me too. Méi'syǎngdàu 'nǐ 'jyūrán 'yě hwèi gēn wo dǎu'lwàn.

Turn on one's heel nyǒutóur. /She turned on her heel and left. Tā nyǒu'tóur jyòu 'dzǒule.

Turn <u>something</u> **on** kāikai. /You'd better turn the shower on while the water's still hot. Nǐ chèn'dzǎur chènje 'shwěi hái 'rè bǎ 'pēndz 'kāikai. /Turn on the lights. Bǎ dēng 'kāikai.

Turn out (get up) 'chǐ(lái). /What time do you turn out every morning? Ní 'měi- tyān 'dzǎuchen 'shémma shŕhou 'chǐ?

Turn out (assemble) dàuchǎng, chūsyí, chyù, lái. /How many turned out? Yǒu 'dwōshau rén °dàu'chǎngle (°chū'syíle, °'chyùle, °'láile)? /A large crowd turned out for the meeting. <u>is expressed as</u> The people who came to the meeting were quite numerous. Dàu'hwèide rén hěn 'dwō.

Turn out <u>in a certain way</u>. /How did the party turn out? Nèige 'hwèi dzěmma 'yàng le? /This turned out very well. <u>is expressed as</u> This result is quite good. 'Jèige jyē'gwǒ hén 'hǎu.

Turn <u>someone</u> **out** (expel) hūngchulai, hūngchuchyu. /I've been turned out. Wǒ jyàu rén gěi 'hūngchulaile. /When I mentioned politics, he nearly turned me out of the house. Wǒ yì tí °'gwóshr (°jèngjr̀), tā 'chàdyǎr bǎ wo 'hūngchuchyu.

Turn <u>something</u> **out** (extinguish) 'gwānshàng, nùngmyèle. /Turn out the lights. Bǎ 'dēng °'gwānshàng (°nùng'myè le).

Turn <u>something</u> **out** (produce) chū. /That factory turns out a great many guns in one year. Nèige gūng'chǎng yì'nyán chū hěn 'dwōde chyáng'pàu. /He turns out his books wholesale. Tā chū 'shū chūde yòu 'dwō yòu 'kwài.

Turn over fāngwochyu. /Watch out! We almost turned over that time. Lyóu-'shén! 'Nèihwéi 'chàdyǎr (méi) 'fāngwochyù.

Turn over a new leaf 'gǎigwòdz̀'syīn. /Do you think he's sincere when he says he's going to turn over a new leaf? Tā shwō tā yàu 'gǎigwòdz̀'syīn, nǐ 'jywéde tā 'jēn shr̀ 'yàu nàyàngr ma?

Turn <u>something</u> **over** jēgwolai, fāngwolai. /Turn that box over. Bǎ 'syāngdz °'jēgwolai (°'fāngwolai).

Turn <u>something</u> **over in one's mind** *or* **head** 'syǎng yisyǎng, dzài °'syīnli (°'nǎudz) °'jwànjwàn (°'pánswanpánswan). /Turn it over in your mind first, before you give me your answer. Nǐ 'syān dzài 'syīnli 'jwànjwan dzài 'gàusùng wo. /I've been turning this over in my head for months, but I still can't make up my mind. 'Jèi- jyàn shèr dzài wó 'nǎudzli 'jwànle yóu 'háu jǐge 'ywè le, kěshr wǒ 'háishr nábu- dìng 'júyì.

Turn <u>something</u> **over to** <u>someone</u> 'jyāugěi. /He turned over his business to his son. Tā bǎ 'mǎimai 'jyāugei tā 'érdz le.

Turn to <u>a page</u> 'fāndàu. /You'll find those figures if you turn to page fifty. Nǐ 'fāndàu dì'wǔshr̀'yè jyòu kéyi 'kànjyàn nèisyē 'shùr le.

Turn to <u>someone</u> (for help) chyóu, jǎu. /You can always turn to him for help.

TWELVE

Ní 'dzŭng kéyi °chyóu (°jău) 'tā bāngbang 'máng. / I have no one to turn to. Wŏ 'méi rén kĕ 'chyóu.

Turn up (arise) hwèi yŏu. / Come around next week; maybe some news will have turned up by then. Nǐ 'syàlǐbài 'lái yítàng, dàu 'nèige shŕhou hwòjĕ hwèi yóu dyăr 'syāusyi shémma de.

Turn up (appear unexpectedly; of a person). / He's always turning up when you don't want him. 'Năr bú'yàu ta, tā shàng năr 'chyù.

Turn up a driveway, etc. gwăiwār. / Blow your horn when you turn up the driveway. Gwăi'wār de shŕhou 'ēnèn 'lăba.

Turn something **up** (increase) kāidà dyăr. / You'll have to turn the heat up here if you don't want to freeze. Nǐ yàushr bù'dăswàn āi'dùng dehwà, dzúng déi bă jèrde chǐ'lúdz kāi'dà dyăr. / Turn the radio up, will you? Láu'jyà, bă wúsyàn'dyàn kāi 'dà dyăr!

Turn something **up** (fold back) jywánchilai, myánchilai, wánchilai. / I'll have to turn this cuff up. Wó déi bă jèige syòu'kŏur °'jywánchi (°'myánchi, °etc.) dyăr lai.

A turn bār; **take one's turn** gāi bār; **wait one's turn** dĕngje gāi bār. / You can take your turn now. 'Kéyi gāi nǐde 'bār le. / You'll have to wait your turn. Ní déi 'dĕngje gāi nǐde 'bār nǐ dzài 'chyù.

(A change of direction) is expressed verbally. / Make a left turn at the next corner. is expressed as Turn to the left at the corner. Dàu 'chyántou gwái'jyăur nèr wàng 'dzwó gwăi.

(A change in condition). / He was very ill last week, but he's taken a turn for the better. is expressed as He was very ill last week, but later on he soon got better. Tā 'shànglǐbài bìngde tǐng 'lìhai, kĕshr 'hòulai jyòu jyàn 'hău le.

(Place where direction is changed) °gwăi'wār (°jwăn'wār) de dìfangr; or is expressed verbally. / He took the turn at high speed. Tā gwăi'wār gwăide fēi 'kwài. or 'Jwăn'wār de shŕhour hái 'kāide hĕn 'kwài.

In turn āije 'bārde. / They were given their pay in turn. Tāmen 'yígèryí'gèr āije 'bārde dōu 'lǐngdàu 'chyán le.

Out of turn. / You're talking out of turn. meaning You're talking now when it isn't proper for you to. 'Hái bùgāi 'nǐ shwō 'hwà ne, nǐ jyòu 'shwōle. or meaning You're saying improper things. Nǐ 'chèdàu 'năr chyù le.

Take turns lwúnbār, hwàn, 'dăuhwàn, lwúnlyóu. / Let's take turns at the wheel. Dzámen °lwúnje 'bār (°hwànje, °dău'hwànje, °lwún'lyóuje) 'kāi ba.

Other expressions in English. / Let's take a turn around the park. Dzámen dàu gūng'ywánli °'dzŏudzou (°'jwănjwàn, °'lyòulyòu, °'lyōudalyōuda, °sànsan 'bù). / I've heard that story before, but you gave it a new turn. Nèi'dwàr wŏ 'tīngshwōgwo, 'búgwò 'nǐ shwōde shr 'lìng yíyàngr. / He failed at every turn. Tā °'dzŭng (°'dzĕm-maje yĕ) shr bù'syíng. / You gave me quite a turn. Nǐ 'syàle wo yí'tyàu.

TWELVE. shŕèr; **the twelfth** dìshŕèr; **one-twelfth** shŕ'èrfēnjŕ'yī.

TWENTY. 'èrshŕ; **the twentieth** dì'èrshŕ; **one-twentieth** 'èrshŕfēnjŕ'yī.

TWICE. (Two times) 'lyăngtsż. / I've been here twice already. Wó 'yǐjing láigwo jèr 'lyăngtsż le. but / You'd better think it over twice before you come to any decision. is expressed as You'd better think it over again (or carefully) before you come to any decision. 'Dzwēihău °'dzài (°'dzsyì, °hău'hăurde) syăng yisyăng, rán'hòu dă 'júyì.

Twice as . . . . yíbèi. / That's twice as much as I want. Nèige bí wǒ 'yàude 'dwō yíbèi.

TWO. èr (as an independent numeral in counting; an element in compound numerals; the only form before the measure for ounce lyǎng; with many measures of distance, time, and weight, and before the numbers ten shŕ, hundred bǎi, thousand chyān, and ten thousand wàn); lyǎng (alternates with èr before many measures of distance, time and weight, and before the numerals bǎi hundred, chyān thousand, and wàn ten thousand); lyǎ (equals lyǎng plus the measure ge); **twenty-two** èrshr'èr; **two hundred twenty-two** 'èrbǎi èrshr'èr, 'lyángbǎi èrshr'èr. / Can you lend me two dollars? Nǐ néng jyègei wǒ 'lyǎngkwài chyán ma? / I'd say two or three days. Wǒ kàn yě jyòu shr 'lyǎngsāntyānde 'yàngdz. / Let's go by twos. Dzámen 'lyǎrénlyǎ'rénde dzǒu.

Put two and two together. / I put two and two together and figured he must be sick. Wǒ 'gūmeje tā yídìng 'bìng le.

TYPE. (Kind) jǔng (especially of inherent type); yàng, yàngr, jǔngyàngr (especially as distinguished by appearance, shape, form, etc.); lèi (a class, all the members of which have some common characteristic); pài (a group that people identify by some characteristic); lù (of people characterized by a way of life or habits). *See also* **KIND**. / What type of shoes do you wear? Nǐ chwān 'shémma yàngrde 'syé? / I don't like that type of girl. Wǒ bù'syǐhwan °nèijǔngde 'nyǔrén (*or* (of physical type) °nèiyàngrde 'nyǔrén, *or* (with a well-known characteristic, as the bobby-socks type) °nèipàide 'nyǔrén, *or* (of a certain way of life) °nèilùde 'nyǔrén, °nèilèide 'nyǔrén, *or* (assuming a bad type) °nèijǔng 'jyèrde 'nyǔrén, °nèijǔng 'shénchǐde 'nyǔrén, °nèijǔng 'désyìngde nyǔrén). / I can't tell what type he is. Wǒ 'kànbuchūlái tā shŕ °'nèilùde rén (°'dzěmma yàng de rén).

(Printing) dzèr. *See also* **PRINT**. / The type is too small. Dzèr tài 'syǎu.

To type (engage in the activity of typing) dǎdz̀; (make a copy by typing) 'dǎchūlai. / Do you know how to type? Nǐ hwèi dǎ'dz̀ ma? / Will you type these letters for me, please? Láu'jyà bǎ jèisyē 'syìn géi wó 'dǎchulai.

UGLY. (To the eye) bùhǎukàn, nánkàn, chǒu, chwǔn. / The picture looks ugly to me. Nèijāng 'hwàr 'wǒ jywéde bùhǎu'kàn.

(Of a disposition) bùhǎu, dzāu. / That dog has an ugly disposition. Nèityáu 'gǒu 'syìngching bù'hǎu. / I was in an ugly mood when I got up this morning. Wǒ jyèr 'dzǎushang 'chǐlai de shrhou °'píchi hěn 'dzàu (°'syìnching bù'hǎu).

UMBRELLA. yángsǎn, yǔsǎn; (made of oil paper or oilcloth) yóusǎn; including also parasol sǎn. / It looks like rain; you'd better take an umbrella. Jèi 'tyār syàng yàu syà'yǔ, nǐ dàije dyár 'sǎn ba (°yú'sǎn ba, °etc.).

UNDER. °dzài (°tsung, °dàu) . . . °'syàbyar (°'dǐsya). / Slip the letter under the door. Bǎ jèifēng 'syìn tsúng mén 'syàbyar °'sāijìnchyù (°'tǔngjìnchyù). / Can this boat go under the bridge? Jèige 'chwán néng bunéng tsúng chyáu 'syàbyar 'dzǒu ne?

(By the provisions of) 'gēnjyù, ànje. / Under the new law such actions can be punished by a heavy fine. °'Gēnjyù (°'Anje) 'syīn fǎ'lyù, jèijǔng 'syíngwéi yīnggai shòu yán'jùngde chǔ'fá.

Under side of anything . . . dǐsya, . . . dyěr. / The under side of the boat needs painting. °Chwánde 'dǐsya (°Chwán'dyěr) děi °shàng yóu'chǐ le (°'yóuyou le).

Under the circumstances jìrán shŕ 'jèyàngr ne. / Under the circumstances I'll accept your apology. Jìrán shŕ 'jèyàngr ne, wǒ 'ywánlyàng nǐ.

Under water dzài 'shwéi dǐsya or expressed as in the water dzài 'shwéi lǐtou;

dive under water jā měngdz. /I like to swim under water. Wǒ 'ywànyi dzài 'shwéi °lǐtou (°dǐsya) yóu'yùng.

    Be under discussion dzài 'tǎulwùnjūng. /The matter is under discussion. Jèijyàn 'shr̀ching jèng dzài 'tǎulwùnjūng. <u>or expressed as</u> They're just now discussing the matter. 'Jèng 'tǎulwùn jèijyàn 'shr̀ ne.

    Be under oath chǐgwo shr̀. /You're under oath to tell the truth. Nǐ chǐgwo 'shr̀, děi shwō shr̀'hwà.

    Be under . . . control <u>or</u> **under the control of** gwēi . . . gwǎn, yóu . . , gwǎnli. /The factory is under military control. Nèige gūng'chǎng shr̀ °gwēi jyūn'dwèi 'gwǎn (°yóu jyūn'dwèi 'gwǎnli). <u>but</u> /Is everything under control? 'Méi shémma 'shr̀ ba? <u>or</u> Yí'chyè dōu °rú'yì (°shwìn 'syìn) ma? <u>or</u> 'Shémma dōu 'ānpai'hǎule ma?

    Be snowed under. /He was snowed under in the election. Nèitsz̀ sywán'jyǔ jyǎn'jŕde méi shémma rén 'sywǎn tā.

    Go under (use) yùng. /He goes under an assumed name. Tā yùng yíge 'jyǎ míngdz.

    Plow <u>something</u> **under** chúchyu. /The weeds have been plowed under. Yě'tsǎu dōu 'chúchyule.

UNDERNEATH. (On the under side of) . . . dǐsya. /The garage is underneath the house. Chē'fáng dzài 'wūdz dǐsya.

    (The under side) dǐsya, syàbyar. /These pipes will have to be fixed from underneath. Jèisyē 'gwǎndz děi tsúng 'syàbyar 'syōuli. /Is there an opening underneath? °'Dǐsya (°'Syàbyar) yóu 'kǒur ma? /The box is wooden on top and iron underneath. Jèige 'syāngdz 'shàngtou shr̀ 'mùtoude, 'syàbyar shr̀ 'tyěde.

UNDERSTAND (UNDERSTOOD). (Get the meaning of) dǔng, míngbai. /I don't understand what you mean. Wǒ °bù'dǔng (°bù'míngbai) nǐde 'yìsz. /He said he didn't understand the instructions. Tā shwō tā bù'míngbai nèige shwō'míng. <u>or</u> Tā shwō nèibén shwōmíng'shū tā dōu kànbu'dǔng.

    (Be thoroughly acquainted with) rènshr. /It takes a long time to understand these people. Rènshr 'jèiyàngde rén děi yàu hěn chángde shŕ'jyān.

    (Be of the impression that) jywéje, 'yǐwéi. /He understood that you would meet him. Tā °'jywéje (°'yǐwéi) nǐ néng chyù jyàn ta.

    (Have heard that) 'tīngshwō. /I understand you're going away. Wǒ 'tīngshwō nǐ yàu 'dzǒu.

UNION. (A uniting) <u>expressed verbally with</u> unite lyánhé. /A strong political party was formed by the union of several small groups. Nèige yǒu'lìlyangde jèng'dǎng shr̀ tsúng jǐge 'syáu dzǔ lyán'héchilaide.

    Labor union gūnghwèi.

UNITE. (Form a union) lyán'héchilai, hé'bǐngchilai, 'jyēchilai; (cause to form a union) bǎ . . . tǔngyī. /The outbreak of war united the nation. 'Jànshr̀ de bàu'fā bǎ gwó-'jyā tǔng'yīle. <u>or</u> Chywán'gwó yīnwei kàng'jàn ér 'twánjyēchǐláile. /The two clubs decided to unite. Nèilyǎngge 'hwèi 'jywédìng hé'bǐngchilai. /The country is united behind the president. Jèige gwó'jyā dzài dzúng'tǔng lǐng'dàujŕ'syà tǔng'yīle.

UNIVERSAL. <u>Expressed with</u> chywánshr̀jyè the whole world; 'nánnyúlǎu'shàu everybody etc. /That movie has a universal appeal. Nèige dyàn'yǐngr 'shémma rén 'kànje dōu hwèi 'syǐhwan. /We believe that there is a universal desire for peace. Wǒmen 'syāngsyìn chywánshr̀'jyè dōu 'syīwàng hé'píng.

UNIVERSITY. 'dàsywé. / He was graduated from the university at the age of twenty-two. Tā èrshr'èr swèi dzài nèige 'dàsywé bìde 'yè. / The conference will be held at the university. Nèige 'hwèi yàu dzài 'dàsywéli 'kāi.

UNLESS. chúfēi; or expressed as if not °rwòshr (°yàushr) . . . bu. / We'll go on our trip tomorrow unless it rains. Chú'fēi shr syà'yǔ, 'bùrán 'míngtyān wǒmen yí'dìng chyù lyǔ'syíng. or Rwòshr 'míngtyān búsyà'yǔ, wǒmen yí'dìng chyù lyǔ'syíng.

UNTIL. dàu, búdàu . . . bù. / It rained until four o'clock. 'Yǔ yì'jr syàdau 'szdyǎn jūng (tsái 'jù). / He didn't stop work until past midnight. Tā yì'jrméi'tíngde dzwò- dau 'hòubànyè. / He won't give his answer until next week. Búdàu 'syàsyīngchī tā búhwèi 'dáfu. / He waited until everyone had left the train. Tā 'děngdau 'měi yíge rén dōu syàle 'chē.

Not until is sometimes expressed as dzài . . . yǐ'chyán . . . bu. / We won't leave until you're ready. Dzài nǐ 'yùbèi'hǎule yǐ'chyán wǒmen bù'líkai jèr.

Wait until děng, 'děngdàu. / May I wait until he comes back? Wǒ 'děng tā 'hwéilai, 'hǎu buháu?

UP. 1. Be up (referring to anything that may be happening). / What's up? Chūle shém- ma 'shr le? or 'Dzěmma le? or Shémma 'shr? or 'Dzěmma hwéi 'shr? / I knew something was up when I heard the alarm. Wǒ 'tīngjyan nèige jǐng'líng jyòu 'jrdau shr 'chūle shémma 'shr le.

Be up (of a window) kāije (if it opens upward); gwānje (if it opens downward). / Is the window up? meaning Is the window open? Nèige 'chwānghu 'kāije ne ma? or meaning Is the window closed? Nèige 'chwānghu 'gwānje ne ma?

Be up (of a person, meaning out of bed in the morning) 'chǐláile. / He wasn't up yet when we called on him. Wǒmen 'dàu tā nèr de shŕhou tā hái méi'chǐlai ne.

Be up against it (in financial straits) chyán hěn jǐn, jyǔng. / That family has really been up against it lately. Nèijyār 'rén 'jìnlai 'chyán hén 'jǐn. or Tāmen 'jyā 'jìnlai hén 'jyǔng.

Be up and about (after illness) syàdìle. / He was sick last week, but now he's up and about. Tā 'shàngsyīngchī 'bìngle, syàndzài yǐjing syà'dìle.

Be up to someone yóu, swéi. / It's up to you to decide where we'll go. is ex- pressed as Where we go is for you to decide. Wǒmen shàng 'nǎr chyù, yóu 'nǐ lái jywé'dìng. or as Where shall we go? We'll do what you say. Shàng 'nǎr Wǒmen tīng 'nǐ de.

Be up to something. / What're you up to now? Nǐ syàndzài °gàn (°dzwò) 'shém- ma ne? or meaning What trouble are you making now? Nǐ syàndzài °yòu dǎu shém- ma 'lwàn ne (°byē shémma 'hwài ne, °chū shémma sōu'júyi ne?

Up and coming yǒu 'syīwang. / The new mayor is an up and coming politician. Jèige 'syīn shŕ'jǎng dzài 'jèngjyè hén yǒu 'syīwang.

2. Specific combinations of up with a verb are to be found generally under the appropriate verb entry. The following selections are only illustrative. Up in such combinations is often equivalent to the Chinese postverbs 'chǐlái, shàng, chūlai, kāi, mǎn, wán, gwāng or dàu; in other cases a single Chinese verb is equivalent to the English combination of a verb and up.

Examples with 'chǐlái. / She looked up from her book when she heard the phone. Tā kàn 'shū de shŕhou 'tīngjyan dyàn'hwà syǎng jyòu 'táichi 'tóu lai le. / How fast can he add up a column of figures? Tā bǎ yìháng 'shùr 'jyāchilái dzwèi 'kwài yùng 'dwōshau shŕhou?

Example with shàng. /Did you lock up the house before we left? Wŏmen 'dzŏu de shŕhou, ní 'swŏshang 'mén le ma?

Examples with shàng as a verb. /He went up the ladder to pick some apples. Tā shàng(dau) 'tīdz(shang) (chyù) 'jāi dyăr 'píngwŏ. /He lives on the fifth floor, and we have to walk up. Tā 'jùdzai 'wŭséng lóu; wŏmen déi 'dzŏuje 'shàngchyù. /We live up on a hill. is expressed as We live at a hill's topside. Wŏmen jùdzai 'shānshang.

Example with 'chūlái. /Who brought up this problem? Shéi 'tíchulaide jèige 'wèntí?

Example with a choice of kāi, shàng, or 'chĭlái with different main verbs. /Put the umbrella up; it's raining. Syà'yŭ le; bá 'săn °'dăkai (°'jŕshang, °'jŕchilai) ba.

Examples with up giving the idea of completion, using wán, dàu, or gwāng as verbs or postverbs. /Your time is up. Nĭde shŕ'jyān °'dàule (°'wánle). /We used up all our money to get here. Wŏmen dàu 'jèr lai bá 'swóyŏude 'chyan dōu °yùng-'wánle (°yùng'gwāngle). /My car burned up last week. Shànglĭbài wŏde chē shāu-'gwāngle.

Example with up meaning full măn. /Fill this pail up with water. Bă jèige 'tŭngli jwāng'mănle 'shwĕi.

Examples in which a single Chinese verb covers an English expression of a verb plus up. /Don't forget to call me up tonight. Jyēr 'wănshang byé 'wàngle gĕi wo dă dyàn'hwà. /They were coming up the street to meet us. is expressed as They walked along on the street to meet us. Tāmen dzài 'jyēshang 'dzŏugwŏlai 'jáu wŏ-men. /Prices have gone up a lot in the last year. 'Chyùnyan wùjyà 'jăngde hĕn 'dwō. /The temperature went up to ninety. Wēndù 'jăngdàu 'jyŏushr dù le. /Please hang your hat up in the hall. 'Màudz kéyi 'gwàdzai dà'tīngli. /Hurry up, you're wasting too much time. 'Kwài dyăr, nĭ 'tài dānwù 'gūngfu le. /We invited our friends up for dinner. Wŏmen 'chíng wŏmende 'péngyou chŕ 'fàn. /It's time to make up your mind. Gāi jywé'dìng le. or Gāi dă 'júyî le. /He ran up against a lot of trouble before he was elected. Tā dzài 'bèi'sywán yĭ'chyán yùjyan hĕn 'dwō de 'kwùnnan. /The post sticks up out of the water. is expressed as The post in the water sticks out a section. Nèigèr 'jùdz dzài 'shwĕilitou 'lòuchu yī'jyér lai. /We'll take that plan up at the next meeting. 'Syàtsż hwèi wŏmen yàu 'tăulwùn nèige 'jìhwa. /He walked up the aisle to his seat. is expressed as He walked through the aisle to his seat. Tā tsúng gwò'dàur 'dzŏudau tāde 'dzwòr nèr chyù le. /I don't think he did us justice when he wrote up the story. Wŏ 'jywéde tā 'syĕde nèige 'gùshr bá wŏmen 'syĕde bùgūng'píng.

3. To up prices jyā, jăng. /He's upped his prices since we were here last. Tsúng wŏmen 'shàngtsż láile yĭ'hòu, tā °jăng'jyàrle (°jyā'jyàrle).

Up production 'dzēngjyā. /They're upping production by leaps and bounds. Tā-men 'jèng dzài 'dàlyàng dzēngjyā shēng'chăn.

Up and do something 'măshang jyòu. /I told him what you said, and he up and hit me. Wó bá nĭde 'hwà 'gàusu tā le, tā 'măshang jyòu 'gĕile wŏ yí'syàdz.

UPPER. shàng. /I'd just as soon take the upper berth. Wó kéyi shwèi 'shàngpù. /The fire started on one of the upper floors of this hotel. 'Hwŏ shŕ tsúng jèige lyú'gwăn lóu'shàng chĭde.

URGE. (Ask earnestly) chywàn. /We urged him to take a vacation. Wŏmen 'chywàn tā 'syōusyisyōusyi.

Urge a horse (on or forward) jyàu; or, if by a specific action, expressed by a verb describing the action, such as whipping dă, kicking tī, pulling lā, etc. /He urged his horse forward. Tā jyàu 'mǎ wàng 'chyán dzǒu. *or* Tā dǎje 'mǎ wàng-'chyán dzǒu.

 An urge. /He felt a great urge to go back home. is expressed as He felt that he absolutely had to go back home. Tā 'jywéde 'fēiděi hwéi'jyā bù'kě.

US. *See* WE.

USE. (Utilization, handling, function) is usually expressed verbally as use yùng; be of use gàn . . . yùng, yǒuyùng. /Are you sure you know the proper use of this machine? Nǐ shr 'jēn jrdàu dzěmma'yùng jèige 'jīchi ma? /He's lost the use of his right arm. Tāde 'yòugēbe bùnéng 'yùng le. /What possible use can there be for this gadget? Jèige syàu 'dūngsyi gàn shémma 'yùng a?

 Have no use for someone. /I have no use for that sort of person. meaning There's no vacancy for such a person here. 'Nèiyàngde rén wǒ 'jèr yùngbu'jáu. or meaning I can't stand to have such a person around. 'Nèijǔng rén wǒ °'jàubude (or meaning can't stand contact with such a person, °'rèbude, or meaning can't stand being close to such a person °'jìnbude).

 Be in use yùngje; or a specific verb depending on the object. /You'll have to wait a minute; the telephone's in use now. Nǐ 'děng yihwěr ba; dyàn'hwà syàndzài °'yùngje ne (°yǒu'rén 'dǎje ne). /This type of machine has only been in use for a few years. is expressed as This machine came out only a few years ago. 'Jèiyàngde 'jīchi tsái 'chūle jǐ'nyán.

 Be no use doing so-and-so méiyùng, méi shémma yùng. /There's no use hurrying; we've already missed the train. Wǒmen fǎn'jèng gǎnbu'shàng 'chē le, 'máng yě °méi'yùng (°méi shémma 'yùng).

 What's the use yǒu shémma 'yùng. /What's the use of arguing? Tái'gàng (°Bàn'dzwěi) yǒu shémma 'yùng?

 To use yùng; or a specific verb depending on the thing used. /May I use your telephone? 'Yùngyung nínde dyàn'hwà syíng ma? or expressed as May I borrow your telephone and use it? Jyè nín dyàn'hwà 'shrshǐ, 'hǎu ma? /He's using the telephone right now. Tā jèng dzài dǎ dyàn hwà ne. /She uses too much perfume. Tā 'yùngde syāngshwěi tài 'dwō. /Would you like to use my bike? Nǐ yàu chí wǒde dzsyīng'chē ma?

 Use something **up** yùnggwāngle, yùngwánle; (of money) hwāgwāngle, hwāwánle. /I've used up all my money. Wǒ bǎ 'chyán dōu °hwā'gwāngle (°hwā'wánle, °yùng-'gwāngle, °yùng'wánle).

 Used to (past customary action) expressed with the verb plus a time phrase, such as formerly tsúngchyán, dāngchū, yǐchyán, *or* at earlier times yǐ'chyánde shŕhou. /I used to eat there every day. Wǒ °yǐ'chyán (-de shŕhou) (°dāng'chū) tyān'tyār dzài nèr 'chŕ. /I used to like him very much. Wǒ tsúng'chyán hén 'syǐhwan tā.

 Be used to. /I'm not used to doing it this way. 'Jèmmaje wǒ 'jywéje yóu dyǎr °bú'gwàn (°bù'shóu).

USEFUL. yǒuyùngde. /He gave me some useful information. Tā 'gàusung wǒ syēge yǒu'yùngde °'shŕching (°syāusyi, °'hwà).

USUAL. 'ywánláide, 'píngcháng. /Let's go home the usual way. Wǒmen hái dzǒu °'ywánláide (°'píngcháng dzǒude) nèige 'dàur hwéi'jyā ba. /I had lunch at the usual place. Wǒ 'hái dzài 'ywánlái nèige 'dìfang chŕ 'fan. or expressed as I still eat at that place. Wǒ 'háishr dzài nèige 'dìfang chŕ de 'fàn.

VACATION

VACATION. Expressed verbally as **have** or **take a vacation** fàngjyà, syōujyà. /When's your vacation? Nǐ 'shémma shŕhou °fàng'jyà (°syōu'jyà)? /I'm going to the mountains for my vacation this summer. Jīnnyan 'syàtyan wǒ yàu dàu 'shānshang chyu syōu-'jyà. or Jīnnyan syōu'jyà wǒ yàu dàu 'shānshang chyù.

VALLEY. shāngǔ, shāngōur. /There's a deep valley between the mountains. Shān 'jūngjyàr yǒu yíge hěn 'shēnde °shān'gǔ (°shān'gōur). /The land in river valley is very fertile. is expressed as The land along the river is very fertile. Yánje 'hé de dì hěn 'féi.

VALUABLE. yǒu'jyàjŕde. /They gave us valuable information. Tāmen 'gàusungle wǒ-men dyár yǒu'jyàjŕde 'syāusyi. /How valuable are these things? is expressed as How about the value of these things? Jèige 'dūngsyi 'jyàjŕ dzěmma 'yàng?

    Valuables jŕ'chyánde dūngsyi; (jewelry) syǐrwǎn, húnghwò. /You'd better put your valuables in the safe. Nǐ 'dǐng hǎu bǎ syǐ'rwǎn de dūngsyi gēdzai báusyǎn'gwèi-li.

VALUE. jyàjr; often expressed as be worth money jŕchyán or as be worth it jŕ. /What value do you put on this land? 'Nǐ kàn, jèikwài 'dì jŕ 'dwōer chyán? or 'Nǐ kàn, jèikwài 'dì de 'jyàjŕ dzěmma 'yàng? /Do you think you got good value for your money? Nǐ jywéde nǐ 'hwā de 'chyán 'jŕ ma?

    (Worth; monetary or non-monetary) jyàjr; (only non-monetary) yùng. /This book has no value at all. Jèiběr 'shū yìdyǎr °'jyàjr (°'yùng) yě 'méiyǒu.

    (Given in another monetary system) is expressed with exchanges for so-much money hé . . . chyán. /What's the value of an American dollar in this country? Dzài 'jèr 'yíkwài měi'jīn hé 'dwōer chyán?

    To value an opinion 'jùngshr, 'jywéje hén 'hǎu. /I value his opinion very highly. (generally) Wǒ hěn 'jùngshr tāde 'yìjyàn. or (of a specific opinion) Tā 'nèige 'yì-jyàn wǒ 'jywéje hén 'hǎu.

    Value something at such-and-such an amount °'gūjì (°'swànjiswànji, °'swàn-swàn) . . . jŕ . . . 'chyán. /What do you value your property at? Nǐ 'gūjì nǐde 'tsái-chǎn jŕ 'dwōer chyán?

VARIOUS. hǎusyē, hǎujǐge, syē, syēge, 'gèjǔngbù'túngde, 'gèshŕge'yàngrde, 'hǎusyē-jǔngbù'túngde, jǐ, gèfāng'myànde. /Various friends of mine have said they liked him. °Wǒde gèfāng'myànde 'péngyou (°Wǒ yóu hǎu'syē péngyou) 'dōu shwō hén 'syǐhwan tā. /He suggested various places they could go. Tā shwō yóu °'hǎusyē (°háujǐge, °syē, °'syēge) 'dìfangr tāmen néng 'chyù. /Various books have been written on that subject. Gwānyu jèige 'tímù yǒu °'gèjǔngbù'túngde (°'gèshŕge'yàngrde, °hǎu'syē-jǔngbù'túngde) 'shū.

VEGETABLES. (Type of food) tsài, chǐng tsài, shūtsài. /What kind of vegetables do you grow in your garden? Nǐ 'ywándzli jùng shémma °'tsài (°chǐng'tsài, °shū'tsài)?

    (Member of the vegetable kingdom; plant) 'jŕwù.

VERY. hěn, tǐng, tài, twēi, jēn; (local Peiping) bèr; (after the word modified) jíle, -de'hěn, -deheng, -dehwang, -de'lìhài, -de'lyǎubudé; modifiers put after the word modified are stronger than those put before. /He's a very easy person to get along with. Tā 'jèige rén °hěn 'rúngyi syāng'chù (°hén hǎu shwō'hwàr). or Tā 'píchi hén 'hǎu. /I was very pleased to get his letter. Wǒ 'shōudàu tāde 'syìn hěn 'gāu-syìng. /He spoke very fast. Tā shwōde kwàide'hěn. /I'm very tired. Wǒ 'lèide-heng.

    (Exact, precise) is expressed with jyòushr, jèngshr just precisely or lyán even

1004

including. / The very day I arrived, war was declared. Jyòu shr wǒ 'dàu de nèityān, jyòu sywān'jànle. / He's the very man you want. 'Tā °jyòushr (°jèngshr) nǐ 'yàu de nèige rén. / The very thought of leaving is unpleasant to me. Líkai nèijyàn 'shr wǒ lyán 'syǎng dōu bú'ywànyi syǎng.

Not very bùhěn, bútài, bùdzěmma, búnèmma, búdà. / The bank isn't very far from here. Tsúng 'jèr dàu nèige yín'háng °bú'tài (°bùhén) 'ywǎn.

VICTORY. shèng, shènglì; win a victory déshèng, dédau shèng'lì. / The battle ended in a complete victory for our side. Jèitsz dzwò'jàn 'jyēgwǒ wǒmen wán'chywán shèng-'lì.

VIEW. (Scene) jǐngjr, jǐngjèr; (of a landscape) fēngjǐng. / You get a beautiful view from this window. Tsúng jèige 'chwānghu 'kànchuchyu, jǐng'jèr hén 'hǎu.

(Attitude, opinion) 'yìjyàn, jyànjyě, yìsz, 'kànfǎ. / What are your views on the subject? Dwèiyu jèijyàn 'shr nǐde 'yìjyàn dzěmma 'yàng?

Be in full view of. / He was in full view of the crowd. is expressed as The whole crowd could see him. Nèi yìchyún 'rén dōu kànde 'jyàn tā.

Be on view (of a performance or movie) yǎn, shàngyǎn, kāiyǎn. / The picture will be on view the end of the month. Nèige dyànyǐngr 'pyāndz ywè'dí 'yǎn.

In view of ànje . . . lái 'kàn. / In view of present conditions, all shipping will probably be stopped. 'Ànje syàndzài 'syíngshr lái 'kàn, 'swóyǒude shāng'chwán 'dàgài dōu yòu 'tíng le.

With a view to doing so and so 'dǎswàn. / I'm saving money with a view to buying a home of my own some day. Wó dzǎn 'chyán shr 'dǎswàn 'jyānglái wèi wǒ 'dzjí mái swǒr 'fángdz.

To view 'rènwéi, 'yǐwéi, kànje, jywé. / Most people viewed that possibility with alarm. Dà'dwōshùrde 'rén dōu 'rènwéi nèige shrching kě'pà. / The sergeant viewed the recruits with disgust. Nèige jūng'shr kànje nèichyún syīn'bīng 'syǐnli bùgāu'syǐng.

VILLAGE. tswūndz, tswēr. / This is a small village of about five hundred people. Jè shr yíge syǎu 'tswēr, 'dàgài yóu 'wúbǎi rén. / The village post office is half a mile from here. Jèige 'tswūndzlide yóujèng'jyú lí 'jèr yǒu 'bànlǐ dì.

(People of a village) 'tswūndzli de 'rén. / The whole village gathered to hear the speech. 'Tswūndzli 'swóyǒude rén dōu lái tīng nèige yán'jyǎng.

VINE. wàr; grapevines pútaushù. / What kind of grapes do you get from these vines? Jèige pútau'shùshàng jyē shémma 'pútau?

VIOLENT. měnglyè, 'lìhài, dà, syúng. / There was a violent explosion in the factory yesterday. 'Dzwótyān gūng'cháng lǐtou °fāshēngle yítsz měng'lyè bàu'jà (°'jàde hěn 'lìhai. / I've never seen such a violent wind. Wǒ 'tsúnglái méi'kànjyangwo jèmma °'dàde (°'lìhàide) fēng. / She had a violent headache and called the doctor. Tā 'tóuténgde hěn 'lìhai, jyǎu 'dàifu lái 'kàn yi kàn. / We had a violent argument. Wǒmen tái'gàng táide hěn °'lìhai (°'syúng).

Violent death. / He met with a violent death. Tā shr héng'szde. or expressed as He didn't get to die peacefully. Tā méi'dé °shàn'jūng (°háu'sz).

VISIT. °lái (°chyù) kàn, °lái (°chyù) jyàn; (if very formal) bàifǎng. / We planned to visit them during our summer vacation. Wǒmen dǎ'swànje dzài shǔ'jyà de shŕhou chyù 'kàn tāmen.

A visit is expressed verbally as above. /We had a pleasant visit. Wǒmen 'jyàn-jaule hěn gāu'syìng. /While we're here, I'd like to pay a visit to some friends. Wǒmen 'dzài jèr de shŕhou wó syǎng chyù kàn jǐge 'péngyou.

(To or by a doctor) is expressed by saying the doctor examines kàn. /The doctor charges five dollars for a visit. Jèige 'dàifu kàn yí'tsż yàu 'wǔkwài chyán.

VOICE. (In speaking) 'shēngyīn. /Her voice grates on my ears. Tāde 'shēngyīn °cháu (°'jā) 'ěrdwo.

(In singing) sǎngyīn; or expressed as throat sǎngdz. /He has a good voice for singing popular music. Tāde °'sǎngdz (°sǎng'yīn) chàng lyóusyíng'gēer hén 'hǎu.

(Right to express oneself) fāyánchywán. /Does he have any voice in the discussion? Jèige tǎu'lwùn tā yǒu fāyán'chywán ma?

Lose one's voice sǎngdz yǎle. /She had a bad cold and lost her voice. Tā jāu-'lyáng jāude hěn 'lìhai, 'sǎngdz dōu 'yǎle.

To voice fābyǎu. /Everyone was asked to voice an opinion. Tāmen °chíng (°ràng) 'měiyíge rén fā'byǎu dyǎr 'yìjyàn.

VOLUME. (Book) shū with measure běn or tsè; sometimes běn or tsè alone; běndz, tsèdz. /How many volumes do you have in your library? Nǐde túshū'gwǎnli yǒu 'dwō-shauběr 'shū?

(Space occupied) rúnglyàng. /What's the volume of the cold storage room? Jèige lěngtsáng'shŕde rúng'lyàng dwō'dà?

(Of sound). /Turn up the volume on the radio, please. is expressed as Please turn the radio up bigger. Láu'jyà, bǎ wúsyàn'dyàn kāi 'dà dyǎr.

VOTE. pyàu; (act of voting) byǎujywé. /He was elected by 2,000 votes. Tā dwō 'lyǎngchyǎn'pyàu dāngsywǎnle. /He'll have to win the labor vote in order to be elected. Tā děi 'déjáu 'gūngréndе 'pyàu, tsái sywǎndе'shàng. /The vote proved that the majority of the people were opposed to the law. Jèige byǎu'jywé jèng'míng dà'dwō-shùde 'rénmín fǎn'dwèi jèige 'fǎlyù.

To vote a sum of money is expressed as decide to appropriate yǐ'jywé 'náchulai. /The board voted five hundred dollars for relief. Jèige 'hwèi yǐ'jywé náchu 'wúbǎi-kwài 'chyán lai wèi 'jyòujì yùng.

Vote for sywǎn. /We're voting for a new governor next month. Wǒmen 'syà-ywè sywǎn yíge 'syīn shéng'jǎng.

Be voted down méi'tūnggwò, fǒujywéle. /The proposal was voted down. Jèige °'jyànyì (°'tíyì) °méi'tūnggwò (°fǒu'jywéle).

WAGE. 'gūngchyán. /Your wages will be seventy-five dollars a week starting tomorrow. Nǐde 'gūngchyán shŕ 'chī shŕ'wǔkwài chyán yìsyīng'chī; 'míngtyan kāishŕ lái 'dzwò. /What's the wage scale here? is expressed as How's the treatment (financial or otherwise) here? Jèrde 'dàiyù dzěmma'yàng?

To wage war tsúng'shŕ jàn'jēng, jìn'syíng jàn'jēng, dǎjàng. /That country isn't capable of waging a long war. Nèige gwó'jyā méiyou 'nénglì °tsúng'shŕ (°jìn-'syíng) cháng'chī jàn'jēng. or Nèige gwó'jyā jìnbu'jù 'láu dǎ'jàng.

WAIST. (Of the body) yāu. /She has a very slim waist. Tāde 'yāu jēn 'syì.

(Of a garment) yāu, yāushen. /This suit is too loose in the waist. Jèijyàn 'yīfu 'yāushen tài 'féi.

WAIT. děng; hòu (more polite). / I'll wait for you until five o'clock. Wǒ °'déng (°hòu) nǐ dàu 'wǔdyǎn jūng. / I'm sorry to keep you waiting so long. Dwèibu'jù, ràng nín °děng le (°hòule) 'bàntyān. / We can let that job wait till tomorrow. 'Nèijyàn shr̀ women kéyi děng 'míngtyan dzài 'dzwò. / My parents waited up for me last night. Dzwór 'wǎnshang wǒde fù'mú 'děngje wo laije.

(Postpone) wàng 'hòu nwó. / We've waited dinner an hour for you. Wèi déng 'nǐ women bǎ chr̄'fàn de shr̀'jyān wàng 'hòu 'nwóle 'yìdyǎn jūng.

Wait on (attend to) tsz̀hou, fúshr. / After his leg was broken he had to have someone wait on him. Tsúng tā 'twěi 'hwàile yǐ'hòu, 'láu déi yǒu 'rén °'fúshr (°'tsz̀hou) ta. / Where's the girl who's waiting on this table? Tsz̀hou jèige 'jwōdz de nyǔ'háidz dzài 'nǎr ne?

(Act of waiting). / There will be an hour's wait before the train gets in. is expressed as We have to wait an hour before the train can get in. Wǒmen déi 'děng yíge jūng'tóu 'chē tsái néng 'lái.

Lie in wait for byēje. / They were lying in wait for us. Tāmen 'byēje wǒmen láije.

WAKE (WOKE). (Rouse from sleep) syǐng. / The child woke with a start. Háidz 'hūrán syǐngle. / I woke up early this morning. Jyēr 'dzǎuchen wó 'syǐngde 'dzǎu dyǎr. / Wake up! 'Syǐng yisyǐng! *or* 'Syǐngsyingr!

Wake someone **up** (by calling) jyàusyǐngle, jyàu; (by pushing) twēisyǐngle; (by disturbing) chǎusyǐngle; etc., with a main verb specifying the means used. / Please wake me up at seven o'clock. Láu'jyà. 'Chīdyǎn jūng 'jyàu wo. / Wake me up before you go. Nǐ 'dzǒu yǐ'chyán jyàu'sying wo. / The alarm clock woke me up. Nàu'jūng bá wǒ chǎu'syǐngle. / The children woke me up. Háidzmen bá wǒ °'jyàusyǐngle (°'twēisyǐngle, °'kūsyǐngle).

Wake up to the fact that míngbaile, jr̄daule. / He finally woke up to the fact that the man was his enemy. Tā 'hòulai 'jr̄daule, nèige 'rén shr̀ tāde 'dírén.

A wake (of a ship) shwěilyòu. / Our boat was caught in the wake of the steamer. Wǒmende 'chwán dzǒudau nèige 'lwúnchwánde shwěi'lyòuli chyùle.

WALK. dzǒu. / Do you think we can walk it in an hour? Nǐ syáng wǒmen 'dzǒu 'yìdyǎn jūng dàude'lyǎu ma? / It takes him twenty minutes to walk home from the office. Tā tsúng gūngshr̀'fáng hwéi 'jyā yàu dzǒu 'èrshrfēn jūng.

(Cause to walk) lyòu; **walk a dog** lyòugou. / Walk the horses a while so they won't get overheated. Bá 'mǎ 'lyòu yilyòu, hau °'syāusyau (°'làulau) 'hàn.

A walk (path) dàur, lù, dzǒudàur. / They planted flowers on both sides of the walk. Tāmen dzài 'dàurde 'lyǎngbyār jùngshang 'hwār le.

(Gait) dzǒu'dàurde 'yàngdz. / You can always tell him by his walk. Nèige dzǒu-dàurde 'yàndz nǐ yí 'kàn jyou 'jr̄dau shr̀ 'tā.

(Act of walking). / It's a long walk from here to the station. is expressed as One must walk quite a while from here to the station. Tsúng 'jèr dàu chē'jàn 'chyé děi 'dzǒu hwěr ne.

Take a walk, go for a walk 'dzǒu yidzǒu, sànsan bù, 'lyòudalyòuda, 'lyòuda-lyòuda. / Let's go for a walk in the park. Dzámen dàu gūng'ywán chyù sànsan bù.

In all walks of life. / He has friends in all walks of life. Tāde 'péngyou gàn 'shémmade dōu 'yǒu.

WALL. chyáng; (if it makes an enclosure) wéichyáng. / Hang the picture on this wall. Bǎ 'hwàr gwàdzai jèige 'chyángshang. / He built a high wall around his garden. Tā bǎ tāde hwā'ywándz 'chǐshang 'gāude wéi'chyáng le. (fig.) / Not even her best friends could break down the wall she built around herself. is expressed as Not even her best friends could get close to her. Jyòushr tāde 'dzwèihǎude 'péngyou yě 'bùnéng gēn ta dzěmma 'chīnjin.

Backs to the wall. / We have our backs to the wall. is expressed as We're really where there's no way out. Wǒmen shŕ'dzài shŕ dzǒu'tóuwú'lù.

To wall something up chǐ'chyáng bǎ . . . °'dǔshangle (°'lánshangle, °dǎngshangle). / They've walled up the entrance to the cave. Tāmen chǐle yídzwò 'chyáng bǎ nèige dùngmén'kǒu °'dǔshangle (°'lánshàngle, ° 'dǎngshangle).

WANT. yàu, syǎng; want someone to do something (when asking that person for the favor) syǎng twǒ, dǎswǎn chyóu, dǎswǎn chǐng. / I want to go swimming. Wǒ yàu fù'shwěi chyu. / I want you to do me a favor. Wó syǎng 'twǒ ni bàn jyàn 'shŕ. or Wó 'dǎswan °'chyóu (°'chǐng) ni 'bāng syàr 'máng. / He was wanted by the police for murder. Yīnwei yíjyàn rénmìng 'àndz, syún'jǐng 'jǎu ta láije. / I want some more tea. Wǒ 'hái yàu dyǎr 'chá.

Want something of (or with) someone. / What do you want with him? Ní 'jǎu ta 'gàn shémma? or Ní 'gēn ta yǒu 'shémma shèr?

A want of. / There's a great want of affection in that home. is expressed as The people in that family don't have much love for each other. Nèi yì'jyār rén bí-'tsz 'méi shémma 'gǎnchíng. / That pole is rotting for want of paint. is expressed as That pole, always having no paint, is rotting. Nèigēr 'gāndz lǎu méi'yóu dōu 'làn le.

Live in want. / After the war many families were living in want. 'Jàng dǎ'wán-le yǐ'hòu, yóu 'hǎusyē rén'jyār 'shémma dōu 'chywē.

Wants syǎngyàu de. / My wants are very simple. Wó syǎng'yàu de hén 'jyǎn-dān.

WAR. jàn, jànjēng; World War Shŕ'jyèdà'jàn. / After a long war the country finally gained its independence. Jīnggwò yí'tsz hěn 'chángjyǒude jàn'jēng nèige 'gwó tsái 'swànshŕ dú'lì le. / When did the First World War start? Dì'yítsz Shŕ'jyèdà'jàn shŕ 'shémma shŕhou 'chǐde?

Warship jyūnjyàn; warplane jyūnyùngjī; similarly, other compounds which have war in English often have jyūn armed forces in Chinese. / How many warplanes were produced this year? 'Jīnnyan jyūnyùng'jī yí'gùng chūle 'dwōshau jyà? / An unidentified warship sank our ship. Yítyáu 'gwójìbù'míngde jyūn'jyàn bá wǒmende 'chwán dǎ'chén le.

Be at war dǎjàng. / That country has been at war for five years. Nèi yì'gwó dǎ'jàng yǐjing 'dǎle 'wǔnyán le.

Make war on 'chīnfàn, dǎ, syàng . . . 'tyǎusyìn. / They had no excuse for making war on us. Tāmen méiyou 'líyóu lái °'chīnfàn wǒmen (°'dá wǒmen, °syàng wǒ-men 'tyǎusyìn).

Warring nations jyāujàngwó. / The warring nations finally came to an agreement. Jyāujàn'gwó 'jyēgwǒ swànshr 'chénglìle yíge syédìng.

WARM. nwǎnhwo; (of the sun) dú; (hot, used sometimes where English has warm) rè. / It gets very warm here in the afternoon. 'Syàwǔ jèr hén 'nwǎnhwo. / Isn't the sun warm today? 'Jyèrde 'tàiyang 'dú budú? / We were uncomfortably warm at the theater. Wǒmen dzài syì'ywándzli de shŕhou jēn 'rède nán'shòu. / Put some warm clothes on before you go outside. 'Chwānshang dyǎr 'nwǎnhwo yīshang dzài chūchyu.

(Affectionate) chīnrè. / She closed her letter with warm greetings to the family.

Tā dzài 'syìn hòutou 'jyāshangle yǐ'bǐ, hěn chīn'rè de 'wèn tāmen yī'jyādz 'hǎu.

(Of color) is expressed by specifying them individually. / She looks best in warm colors. is expressed as She looks best wearing bright colors like red and yellow. Tā chwān 'húngde a, 'hwángde a, 'nàyàngr 'pyàulyang de 'yīfu hǎu'kàn.

To warm oneself 'nwǎnhwonwǎnhwo; (by a fire) kǎukau hwǒ. / Come in and warm yourself by the fire. 'Jìnlai, °'káukau 'hwǒ (°'nwǎnhwonwǎnhwo).

Warm someone's **heart** gěi . . . hěn 'dàde 'ānwei. / His kind words warmed our hearts. Tāde 'hwà gěi wǒmen hěn 'dàde 'ānwei.

Warm up rè, nùngrè. / We'll have supper as soon as the soup is warmed up. 'Tāng yí 'rè wǒmen jyou chr̄ 'fàn.

Warm up (before a game) lyànsyí. / The players are warming up before the game. Bǐsài yíchyán nèisyē dwèi'ywán dzài nèr lyàn'syí ne.

Warm up to someone gēn . . . °shóu le (°'chīnjìn le, °hǎu le). / He was shy at first, but soon warmed up to us. Tā 'gēn wǒmen chǐ'syān yóu dyǎr °'shēng (°'weiweiswō'swōde), 'méi dwōshau shŕhou jyou °'shóu le (°etc.).

Be getting warm (in guessing) chàbudwō le. / That isn't the right answer, but you're getting warm. Nǐ 'dáde bú'dwèi, kěshr chàbu'dwō le.

WARN. jǐnggàu. / I've been warned that this road is dangerous. 'Rénjyā jǐng'gàu wo shwō jèige 'lù wéi'syǎn. / I warn you! Wó jǐng'gàu nǐ!

WASH. syǐ; **wash one's hands** or **wash up** syǐ'shǒu. / Who's going to wash the dishes? 'Shéi syǐ 'dyédz a? / These shirts needs to be washed. Jèisyē chèn'shān gāi 'syǐ le. Wash your hands before dinner. Chr̄ 'fàn yǐchyán syísyi 'shǒu. / Can this material be washed? Jèige 'lyàudz néng 'syǐ ma? / I always wash on Monday. Wǒ 'yúngywǎn shŕ Syīngchī'yī syǐ 'dūngsyi. / Let's wash up before dinner. Dzámen chr̄ 'fàn yǐ'chyán syísyi 'shǒu.

Wash one's hands of something búgàn le, syíshǒu bugàn le. / I washed my hands of it. Wǒ bú'gàn le. or Wǒ syíshǒu bu'gàn le.

Wash against (of waves) dǎ. / Listen to the waves washing against the side of the boat. Tīng 'làngtou 'dǎ nèige 'chwánbyār ba.

Wash something **away** chūngdzòule. / Last spring the flood washed away the dam. Jīnnyan 'chwūntyan fā'shwei bǎ 'já gěi chūng'dzòule.

Wash something **up** chūngdau . . . shang. / A lot of shells were washed up on the beach. Hǎusyē gélǐ'bàngdz 'chūngdau hǎi'byārshang laile.

Be all washed up shŕ'bàile. / Our vacation plans are all washed up. Wǒmen syóujyà de 'jìhwa₂ wán'chywán shŕ'bàile.

Wash (clothing) gāi 'syǐ de 'yīfu (before being washed); 'syǐ de 'yīfu (after being washed). / The wash hasn't come back from the laundry yet. Syǐ de 'yīfu hái méi tsúng syǐyǐ'dyàn 'náhweilai ne.

WASTE. fèi; **waste money** bái hwāchyán. / He wastes a lot of time talking. Tā 'hěn dwō de 'shŕhour dōu 'fèidzai shwō syán'hwà shang le.

Waste away shòu, dyàubàng. / During his illness he wasted away until he weighed only a hundred pounds. Tā 'bìng de shŕhou °'shòudàu (°dyàu'bàng dàu) jyou shēng yìbǎi 'bàng le.

(Action of wasting). / This seems like a waste of money. is expressed as This seems to waste money. 'Jèmma yàngr hǎu'syàng shr 'bái hwā'chyán. / That process involves too much waste. is expressed as This process wastes too much. 'Nèijǔng 'dzwòfar tài 'fèi.

1009

Go to waste 'dz̄autà, 'hwāngfèi. / The property went to waste because it wasn't taken care of. Nèidyǎr 'chányè méi hǎu'hǎurde 'gwǎn, dōu °'dz̄autàle (°'hwāngfèile).

Lay waste jàhwěile, dǎhwàile, hūngpíngle. / The army laid waste the entire area. Jyūn'dwèi bǎ jèi yí'dài dōu °jà'hwěile (°etc.).

Wastepaper lànjř,, fèijř. / Put the wastepaper in the basket. Bǎ làn'jř rēng-dzai dzjř'lóuli.

Wasteland hwāngdì. / The plains beyond the mountains are all wasteland. 'Shān 'nèibyarde píng'dì dōu shr hwāng'dì.

WATCH. (Keep looking at) chyáu. / We watched the planes landing at the airport. Wǒ-men chyáu fēi'jī 'lwòdzai fēijī'chǎngshang. / I wasn't watching when we passed that sign. Dzámen 'lùgwo nèige 'pár de shŕhou wǒ méi wàng 'nèibyar 'chyáu. / Watch your step! 'Chyáuje dyǎr 'dàur (dzóu)!

(Keep an eye on and guard) kān. / Watch my car for me, will you please? Láu-'jyà 'chǐng ni gěi wo 'kānje dyǎr 'chē.

Watch out (be careful) lyóushén, 'syǎusyīn. / Watch out when you handle that box of dynamite. Nǐ 'dùng nèisyāngdz jà'yàu de shŕhou °lyóu'shén (°'syǎusyīn dyǎr).

Watch out for (take care of) jàuying. / Don't worry; he's watching out for his own interests. Béng fā'chóu; tā hwèi 'jàuying 'dzji de.

Watch out for someone (guard against) 'dīfáng. / Watch out for him; he's a slippery customer. 'Dīfángje ta dyǎr; tā yóu dyǎr 'hwátóuhwá'nǎude.

Watch over shǒu. / The dog watched over the child all night. 'Góu 'shǒuje syǎu-'hár shǒule yí'yè.

Be on watch, stand watch jàngǎng. / The guards are on watch four hours and rest eight. Wèi'bīngmen shr jàn 'sżge jūngtóu de 'gǎng, 'ránhòu syē 'bāge jūngtóu. / Every sailor on this ship has to stand an eight-hour watch. Jèi chwánshang 'swó-yǒude 'shwéishǒu 'dōu děi 'jàn 'bāge jūngtóu de 'gǎng.

Be on the watch for 'fángbèi, 'jǐngbèi. / The police were warned to be on the watch for trouble. Yǒurén 'mǐbàu jǐng'chá °'fángbèi (°'jǐngbèi) chū'shèr.

A watch (timepiece) byǎu. / What time is it by your watch? Nǐde 'byǎu jí'dyǎn le? / This is a watch repair shop. 'Jèi shr ge 'syōuli jūng'byǎude 'pùdz.

WATER. shwěi. / Please give me a glass of water. Láu'jyà, gěi wo yìbēi 'shwěi. / The water's too cold for swimming today. Jīntyande 'shwěi yóu'yūng tài 'lyáng. / Our house is near the water. Wǒmende 'fángdz °dzài 'shwěibyārshang (°kǎu'shwěi). / Do you like water sports? Ní 'syīhwan 'shwěishang 'yùndùng ma?

By water (of travel) dzwòchwán, dzóu shwěilù. / At this time of the year the only way you can get there is by water. Yīnyán lǐtou de 'jèige shŕhou, ní 'jř néng °dzwò 'chwán chyu (°dzóu shwěi'lù).

Hold water (fig.) yǒujìn. / That argument doesn't hold water. Nèige 'hwà shwōde méi'jìn.

To water (dilute) dwèishwěi. / He was put in jail for watering the milk. Tā wàng nyóu'nǎili dwèi'shwěi, swóyi syà'yùle.

(Of eyes) lyóu yǎnlèi; (of mouth) lyóu kóushwěi. / The smoke from the fire made my eyes water. Jèige 'lúdzli de 'yān syūnde wo jŕ lyóu yǎn'lèi. / That cake makes my mouth water. Nèikwài 'dyánsyīn ràng wo lyóu kóu'shwěi.

Water animals yìng; plants and gardens jyāu. / Don't forget to water the horses before we go. Wǒmen dzài 'dzóu yǐ'chyán byé 'wàngle yìn 'mǎ.

Water <u>plants or gardens</u> jyāu. /When did you last water the flowers? Nǐ 'shém-ma shŕhou jyāude 'hwār?

WAVE. (In water) làng, 'làngtou. /During storms, the waves are sometimes twenty feet high here. Dà'fēng dà'yǔ de shŕhou jèrde 'làng yǒude shŕhou yǒu 'èrshrchŕ gāu.

(In the hair) 'tóufashangde 'wār. /She was afraid that the rain would spoil her wave. Tā kǔngpà 'yú bǎ tā 'tóufashangde 'wār nùng'méile.

To wave 'pyāuyáng, 'pyāudàng, 'pyāuwǔ, 'fēiwǔ. /They watched the flags waving in the breeze. Tāmen kànje nèisyē 'chídz dzài 'fēngli 'pyāuyáng.

(With the hand) jāushǒu. /We waved our hands to attract his attention. Wǒmen syàng ta jāu'shǒu, yǐn ta jù'yì. /He waves to the car to stop at the corner. Tā syàng nèige 'chē jāu'shǒu, ràng ta dzài nèige jyē'jyǎur nèr 'jànje.

WAY. (Route, path) dàu(r), lù, 'dàulù. /Is this the right way to town? Jèityáu 'dàur shr dàu chéng 'lǐtou chyùde ma? or Shàng chéng 'lǐtou chyù dzǒu 'jèityáu lù 'dwèi ma? /We passed a new restaurant on our way home. Hwéi'jyā de shŕhou wǒmen dzài 'dàurshang 'lùgwò yíjyār 'syīn fàn'gwǎndz. (fig.) /They let him go his own way. Tāmen °yóu (°swéi) tā 'chyù le. or Tāmen bù'gwǎn ta le.

(Distance) <u>is expressed with</u> ywǎn be far. /These students are a long way from home. Jèisyē 'sywésheng lí 'jyā hén 'ywǎn. /The village is still quite a way off. Nèige 'tswǔndz hái 'ywǎnje ne.

(Manner) yàng, yàngr; <u>way of acting</u> 'tàidù, chù'shŕde 'fāngfa. /I don't like the way he acts. Wǒ bù'syǐhwan tā °'nàyangr (°nèige 'tàidù, °chù'shŕde 'fāngfa).

(Means, method) fāngfa, fádz. /He still hasn't found a way of making a living. Tā 'hái méi'jǎujau yíge móu'shēngde 'fāngfa ne. /Can you find a way to get him here? Nǐ yǒu 'fádz ràng ta shàng 'jèr lái ma? /We discussed ways and means of putting the plan into operation. Wǒmen tǎu' wùn shŕ'syíng nèige 'jìhwa de °'fāngfa (°'fádz).

Across the way dwèimér, dwèigwòr, dwèimyàr. /His house is just across the way from ours. Tāde 'fángdz jyòu dzài 'wǒmen dwèi'mér.

Be in a bad way yóu dyǎr °bù'shūfu (°bùhǎu'shòu, °bùhǎu'gwò, °bùhé'shr). /He was in a bad way after the party last night. Dzwór 'wǎnshang yàn'hwèi 'wánle yǐhòu tā yóu dyǎr °bù'shūfu (°etc.).

Be in the way àile shr le. /They said we'd just be in the way if we tried to help. Tāmen shwō wǒmen 'bāngbulyǎu 'máng, dàu àile 'shr le.

By the way èi. /By the way, are you coming with us tonight? 'Èi! Wǒ 'shwō, nǐ jyèr 'wǎnshang 'lái bulái a?

By way of (route) tsúng, dǎ. /We'll come back by way of the mountains. Wǒmen yàu dǎ 'shānlù hwéilai. /He went by way of Peiping and came back by way of Tientsin. Tā 'chyù shr tsúng Běi'píng chyùde, 'hwéilai shr tsúng 'Tyānjin hwéilaide.

By way of joking 'búgwò shr °nàuje 'wár (°kāi wán'syàu). /He said it only by way of joking. Tā 'shwō nèige 'búgwò shr °nàuje 'wár (°etc.).

Get under way chūfā. /The ship will get under way at noon. Jèijr 'chwán 'jūngwǔ chū'fā.

Go out of one's way to jìnlì, jìnlyàngr, shŕ'jìn 'fāngfa, byànjrbā'fāngrde. /We went out of our way to make him feel at home. Wǒmen °jǐn'lì (°jǐn'lyàngr, °etc.) ràng ta byé 'gǎnjywé 'jyūsu.

Give way (of a dam or other object) hwài; (of a military force) twèi; **give way to one's emotions** dùng 'gǎnchíng. /When the dam gave way the river flooded the town. Hé'bà 'hwàile, 'shwéi bǎ 'chéng 'yānle. /When our fresh troops arrived, the enemy was forced to give way. Wǒmende 'shēnglì'jyūn yí 'dàu jyòu °bǎ 'dírén géi dǎ'twèile (°jyàu 'dírne wàng 'hòu 'twèi).

Have a way with dwèi . . . yǒu °bànfǎ (°lyángshǒur, °lyǎngsyàdz). /He has a way with women. Tā dwèi 'nyǔrén yǒu lyǎng'syàdz. or expressed as He knows how to please women. Tā hěn hwèi táu 'nyǔrénde hwān syīn.

Have one's way. /She thought it was bad for the child to have his own way all the time. Tā rènwéi lǎu 'yóuje háidzde 'syìngr dwài háidz mēi hǎuchu.

In a way dzài 'yìfāngmyan shwō. /In a way we're lucky to be here. Dzài 'yìfāngmyan shwō, wǒmen dàu 'jèr shr hěn 'syìngyùn.

In some ways 'yǒude dìfangr. /In some ways this plan is better than the other one. Jèige 'jìhwà 'yǒude dìfangr bǐ nèige 'chyáng.

In the way of shémma yàngr. /What've you got in the way of portable radios? Nǐ 'jèr yǒu shémma yàngr de shǒu'tíshr wúsyàn'dyàn?

Make way, get out of the way (lit.) bǎ 'dàur °'ràngkai (°'dwǒkai). /Get that truck out of the way, will you? Bǎ nèige kǎ'chē 'nwónwo °'ràngkai (°'dwǒkai) 'dàur, 'hǎu buhǎu? /Traffic was forced to make way for the fire engines. Jyòuhwǒ'chē láile, 'byéde chē dōu bǎ 'dàur 'ràngkaile. (fig.) /They gave him the money to get him out of the way. is expressed as They gave him the money so he wouldn't make trouble. Tāmen géi ta nèige 'chyán jyòu 'wèideshr ràng ta bùdǎu'lwàn.

Out of the way. /I finally got that work out of the way. is expressed as I finally got that back work done. Wǒ jūngyú bǎ 'shèngsyade jèidyǎr 'shèr dzwò'wánle. /He lives in an out-of-the-way part of the city. is expressed as The place where he lives is too obscure. Tā 'jùde dìfang tài 'bèi.

Pay one's way géi dz'jǐ de 'chyán. /I always pay my own way when I go out with him. Wǒ gēn 'tā yí'kwàr 'chūchyu de shrhour 'dzǔngshr wó géi wǒ dz'jǐ de 'chyán.

Right of way. /We gave the other car the right of way. is expressed as We let the other car go by first. Wǒmen ràng 'nèilyàng chē 'syān gwòchyu.

See one's way clear to jyǎn'jŕde néng. /I can't see my way clear to take a vacation this month. 'Běnywè wó jyǎn'jŕde bùnéng syōu'jyà.

This way 'jèmmayàngr, jèmma; **that way** 'nèmmayàngr, nèmma. /Do it this way. 'Jèmma(yàngr) 'dzwò. or 'Dzèmmaje. or 'Jèmmayàngr.

Work one's way through. /He's working his way through school. Tā dz'jǐ gūng dz'jǐ nyàn 'shū.

Way off in the distance láuywǎnde. /I see them way off in the distance. Wǒ láu'ywǎnde 'kànjyan tāmen.

WE (US, OUR, OURS). wǒmen; (informal, and definitely including the person or persons spoken to) dzámen; **us** wǒmen, dzámen; **our** or **ours** wǒmen(de), dzámen(de) (de is sometimes dropped before nouns), or, in certain formal contexts, bèn as **our company** bénháng, **our country** bēngwó, etc. /We expect to be home this afternoon. Wǒmen 'syàng jyērge 'syàwǔ dzài 'jyā. /My friend has invited both of us to the concert tonight. Wǒde 'péngyou jyēr 'wǎnshang chíng wǒmen 'lyǎ chyù tīng yīn'ywè. /Let's go together. Dzámen yi'túng 'chyù ba. /These are ours. 'Jèisyē shr °'wǒmende (°'dzámende).

WEAR

Ourselves. *See* SELF.

WEAK. (Not solid, frail) bùjyēshr. / This bridge is too weak to support heavy traffic. Jèige 'chyáu tài bù'jyēshr, jīnbu'jù tài 'dwōde chē dzài 'shàngtou 'dzŏu. / The cloth will tear at this weak place. Jèige 'bù dzài jèige bù'jyēshrde dìfang hwèi 'pwò.

(Lacking strength) rwǎn, rwò, rwǎnrwò, róu rwò. / He felt very weak after the operation. Tā dùng shŏu'shù yǐ'hòu jywéde hén rwò. / The country has a weak government. Jèige gwó'jyāde 'jèngfu hén rwǎn'rwò.

(Low in alcoholic content) méi lìlyang, búchùng. / This drink is too weak. Jèige'jyŏu °méi 'lìlyang (°bú'chùng).

(Inadequate) bùsyíng, méi lìlyang. / That's a weak argument. Nèige 'hwà méi-'jìn. / Mathematics is his weakest subject. 'Shùsywé shr̀ tā dzwèi bù'syíngde yì-mér 'gūngkè.

WEALTH. tsáichǎn. / He inherited most of his wealth. Tāde tsái'chǎn dà'bùfen shr̀ °chéng'shòu (°chíngshòu) láide.

WEAR (WORE, WORN). (For most clothes) chwān; (for hats, gloves, decorations) dài; (for something tied, as neckties, belts) jì, dǎ; (for an outer covering, as a cape) pēi; (for suspenders) bēi; (for ornamental pins) chā. / What are you going to wear to dinner tonight? Ní dǎswàn 'jyēr wǎnshang chwān 'shémma chyu chr̄ fàn? / A good coat will wear longer than a cheap one. Yíjyàn 'hǎu yīshang bǐ 'tsżde °jīn 'chwān (°'chwānde r̀dz 'dwō, °'chwānde chángywan). / This dress was worn by my mother at her wedding. Jèijyàn 'yīshang shr̀ wŏ 'mǔchin jyē'hwūn de shr̄hou 'chwānde. / He wears his shoes out very fast. Tā chwān 'syé chwānde jēn 'fèi. or expressed as His shoes are spoiled very fast. Tā 'syé °'hwàide (°'pwòde) jēn 'kwài.

Wear a hole in something is expressed with tsā *or* mwó scrape and other such specific verbs. / The constant erasing wore a hole in the paper. 'Lǎu dzài nèr 'tsā, bǎ jr̆ (nèr) dōu 'tsāle yíge 'kūlung. / The cuffs on my trousers are wearing out. Wǒ kù'jyǎur nèr °mwó'máule byār le (°mwó'yàngle, °mwómá'hwār le, °mwó'hwàile, °mwó'tūlule, °mwó le).

Wear something or someone down mwó; wear smooth mwópíngle, mwógwāngle; wear out mwóhwàile. / We finally wore him down and he did what we asked. 'Jyēgwō wǒmen 'mwóde ta 'ràng ta gàn 'shémma tā jyòu 'gàn shémma. / They finally wore down his resistance. Tāmen dàu'lyáur bǎ ta 'mwóde hwéi'syīnjwǎn'yìle. / The record is so worn down we can hardly hear it. Jèijāng chàng'pyār °mwó'píngle (°mwó'gwāngle, °mwó'hwàile), wǒmen dōu 'tīngbujyàn 'shēngr le.

Wear off 'gwòchyù. / The effect of the drug will wear off in a few hours. Jèige 'yàude 'lìlyàng jǐge jūng'tóu jyòu 'gwòchyule.

Be completely worn out, be worn to a frazzle (of a person) lèijíle, (pí)fájíle, 'jīnpílì'jìn, 'yìdyǎr 'jyēr dōu 'méiyoule. / He came home from the factory completely worn out. Tā tsúng gūngchǎng 'hwéilai yǐ'hòu °lèi'jíle (°etc.).

Tired and worn lèi, 'syīnkǔ, fá, 'pífá. / Her face is tired and worn. Tā 'lyǎn-shang 'dàije hěn 'lèide yàngdz. / He looked tired and worn on Monday morning. Syīngchī'yī 'dzǎuchen tā 'kànje syàng hěn °'lèide (°'syīnkude, °etc.) yàngdz.

Wear (use). / This coat was meant for evening wear. is expressed as This coat is for wearing in the evening. Jèijyàn wài'tàur shr̀ 'wǎnshang 'chwānde. / There's still a lot of wear left in these ties. is expressed as These ties can still be worn awhile. Jèisyētyáu lǐng'dài hái néng 'dǎ sye r̀dz.

(Impairment due to use) is expressed verbally with nwó scrape, kěn bite into

1013

and other appropriate verbs. / The tires got a lot of wear and tear from the rough roads. Jèi jǐtyáu che'dài dzài nèige hwài'dàurshang °'mwóde (°'kénde) hěn 'lìhai.

Men's wear 'nánrén chwānde 'yīfu. / Does this store sell men's wear? Jèige 'pùdz mài 'nánrén chwānde 'yīfu ma?

WEATHER. tyānchi, tyār, 'chìhòu. / We've had a lot of rainy weather lately. is ex-pressed as Recently the weather is always raining. 'Jìnlai °'tyānchi (°'tyār) jǐng syà'yǔ.

Be under the weather is expressed with any of a number of terms meaning not be comfortable, not be well yet, etc. / He caught a bad cold yesterday and he's still pretty much under the weather. 'Dzwórge tā jāu'lyáng jáude tǐng 'lìhai, syàn'dzài 'hái °bù'shūfu ne (°bùhé'shr̀ ne, °bùhǎu'gwò ne, °bùhǎu'shòu ne, °nán'gwò ne, °nán-'shòu ne, ° méi'hǎu ne).

To weather a storm 'jīnggwò. / This old ship has weathered a good many storms. Jèityáu jyòu 'chwán 'jīnggwole bù'shǎude fēng'làng.

Be weathered (or weatherbeaten) 'fēngchwēiyú'dǎde. / The gravestone was old and weathered. Jèikwài shr̀'bēi 'nyándzer 'dwòle, 'fēngchwēiyú'dǎde dōu bù'chǐng-chule.

WEDNESDAY. Syīngchīsān, Lǐbàisān.

WEEK. lǐbài, syīngchī; **this week** jèige lǐbài, jèige syīngchī, bénlǐbài, bénsyīngchī; **last week** shànglǐbài, shàngsyīngchī; **next week** syàlǐbài, syàsyīngchī. / It'll be a week before I see you again. Hái děi gwò °'yíge syīng'chī (°'yìsyīng'chī) wǒ 'tsái néng 'dzài kànjyan nǐ ne. / I'm going to start a new job next week. 'Syàsyīngchī (°'Syàlǐbài) wǒ yàu 'kāishr̀ dzwò yíge 'syīn shr̀ching le. / This factory is on a five-day week. Jèige gūng'chǎng 'yíge lǐ'bài dzwò 'wǔtyān 'gūng.

WEIGH. chēng, yàu. / Please weigh this package for me. Láu'jyà, gěi wo °'yàuyàu (°chēngcheng) jèibāu 'dūngsyi. / She asked the storekeeper to weigh out ten pounds of sugar. Tā chǐng nèige jǎng'gwèide gěi ta °'yàule (°chēngle) 'shr̀bàng 'táng.

Weigh so much yǒu . . . jùng. / This piece of meat weighs four pounds. Jèikwài 'ròu yǒu 'sz̀bàng 'jùng.

Weigh oneself, **get weighed** gwòbàng. / I was weighed the other day at the doc-tor's. Nèityān wǒ dzài 'dàifu nèr 'gwòle gwò 'bàng.

Weigh anchor chǐmáu. / What time did the ship weigh anchor? Jèige 'chwán 'shémma shr̀hou chǐ'máu.

Weigh one's words kǎulyù. / He weighed his words carefully before answering. Tā hwéi'dá yǐ'chyán, kǎu'lyùde hěn dž'syì.

Weigh on. / The responsibility of his job doesn't weigh on him very much. is expressed as He certainly doesn't consider his job very difficult. Tā dwèi nèige 'gūngdzwò 'bìng bù'jywéde wéi'nán.

Weigh something **down** yā. / The canoe is weighed down with supplies. Nèige syǎu 'chwár jyàu 'dūngsyi 'yāde chr̀'shwéi hěn 'shēn.

WEIGHT. 'jùnglyàng. / The weight of the bridge is supported by cables. Jèige 'chyáu de 'jùnglyàng dōu jàngje jèisyē tyě'shéngdz 'dyàuje ne. / The weight of that trunk is two hundred pounds. Nèige dà 'syāngdz de 'jùnglyang yǒu 'èrbǎibàng. (fig.) / This isn't a matter of great weight. 'Jèijyàn shr̀ bú'dà °'jùngyàu (°'yàujǐn).

(Piece of metal used on a balance) fámar; (anything heavy) jùng dūngsyi, chén dūngsyi. / Another two-pound weight should make the scale balance. Dzài 'gēshang lyǎngbàng de 'fámar 'tyānpíng jyou 'píng le. / Put a weight on those papers to keep them from blowing away. Ná yangr 'jùng dūngsyi bá 'jř 'yāshang myǎnde jyàn fēng chwēi pǎu le. *but* (fig.) / You've just lifted a weight off my mind. Nǐ 'jè tsái swàn 'chyùle wǒ yíchwáng 'syīnshr. / Don't attach too much weight to what he says. Tāde 'hwà bú'bì tài °dzài'yì (°wàng 'syīnli chyù, °syǎng'syìn). *or* Tāde 'hwà bú'dà 'jùngyàu.

Gain weight °jáng (°jyā) °tǐjùng (°jǎngbàng); lose weight jyán tǐjùng, dyàubàng, chǐngle. / I've gained a lot of weight since I've been here. Wǒ dàu jèr yǐ'hòu, tǐ'jùng °'jàngle (°'jyāle) bù'shǎu.

Lose weight jyán tǐjùng, dyàubàng, chǐngle. / I've lost of lot of weight since I've been here. Wǒ 'dàujèr yǐ'hòu °'chǐngle (°tǐ'jùng 'jyánle) hěn 'dwō.

To weight jyā 'fènlyang. / Make them balance by weighting this side. 'Jèibyār dzài 'jyā dyǎr 'fènlyang, jyou 'píng le.

WELCOME. (Characterizing something one is glad to hear or have) hǎu. / That's the most welcome news I've heard in months. 'Nèige shř wǒ jèijige 'ywè tīngjyànde dzwèi 'hǎude 'syāusyi.

(In answer to thanks offered, or otherwise indicating concession freely given) is expressed as don't act like a guest byé kèchi *or* búkèchi, or as it's nothing 'méi shémma. / You're welcome. Byé 'kèchi. *or* Bú'kèchi. *or* Méi shémma. / You're welcome to use my car. Nín 'dwōdzen yàu yùng 'chē de shřhou chǐng byé 'kèchi.

Welcome (act of welcoming). / They gave us a warm welcome when we came back. is expressed as When we returned they welcomed us warmly. Wǒmen 'hwéilai de shřhour, tāmen hěn 'rèlyède 'hwānyíng wǒmen láije.

To welcome someone 'hwānyíng. / Welcome to Tientsin! 'Hwānyíng hwānying dàu Tyānjin lái! / They welcomed us to the club. Tāmen 'hwānyíng wǒmen jyā'rù nèige 'hwèi. *but* / Welcome home again! 'Hwéiláile! Hǎu'jíle!

WELL. (In a good way) hǎu, myàu, gāu, bútswò, búhwài, búlài. / They do their work very well. Tāmen dzwò 'shř dzwòde hén 'hǎu. / He's doing very well in his business. Tā 'shēngyì dzwòde hěn bú'tswò. / This job is well done. Jèige shř 'dzwòde hen 'hǎu.

(Not ill) hǎu. / Is your father feeling well these days? Jèisyē 'řdz nín lǎutài-'yé 'hǎu a? / He doesn't look like a well man to me. Tāde °'chìsè (°'yàngr, °'shén-chi, °'yàngdz) wǒ kànje búdà 'hǎu.

(Exclamation) á, hē (of surprise). / Well! I wouldn't have thought THAT of her! 'Hē! Wǒ méisyǎng'dàu tā hwèi 'nàyàngr! / Well what do you know! 'Á, 'jyūránrú'tsž! *or* 'Á, shř 'nèmmaje a!

(Of concession, or just a filler while thinking of what to say) is not expressed directly. / Well, OK then. 'Hǎu, jyou nèmma 'bàn ba. *or* 'Hǎu, jyou 'nèmmaje ba. (In these the hǎu means OK, and does not translate the well, which is implied only by the wording of the whole sentence.)

Well done (in cooking) lǎu lǎudyǎrde. / Do you want your steak well done? Nǐde ròu'pái yàu °'lǎude (°'láudyǎrde) ma?

Well over an amount . . . dwō. / The play attracted well over a thousand people. Jèichū 'syì jyàule yǒu yì'chyān dwō 'dzwòr.

As well, as well as (in addition, in addition to) yòu . . . yòu . . . , yě . . . yě . . . . / She sings, and she plays the piano as well. Tā °yòu (°yě) chàng'gēer °yòu (°yě) tán gāng'chín. / She bought a hat as well as a new dress. Tā mǎile yìshěr syīn 'yī-fu, yòu mǎile yìdǐng 'màudz.

Be just as well that. / It's just as well that you got here when you did. is expressed as Good, you got here just at the right time. Hén 'hǎu, nǐ 'dàude 'jěng shr 'shŕhour. *or* Nǐ 'láide jèng 'hǎu.

Be well off (yóu) lya chyár, (yóu) jige chyán, (yóu) dyar chyán, (yóu) dyǎr 'tsáichǎn. / He is pretty well off. Tā hén 'yóu lya 'chyár. / He left his wife well off. Tā 'sžle yǐ'hòu, gěi tā 'taitai 'lyóusyàle dyǎr 'tsáichǎn.

Can (could, may, might) very well plus a verb yésyǔ, kěnéng, dàgài, shwō buding. / He couldn't very well win the election. Jèitsz shwán'jyù tā °bùkě'néng 'sywǎnshang (°yé'syú sywǎnbu'shàng, °shwōbu'dìng hwei lwò'sywǎn). / She might very well change her mind. Tā hén kěnéng byàn'gwà. *but* / He couldn't very well go by train because he couldn't get a reservation. Tā yīnwei méi'dìngjáu 'dzwòr, swóyi méi 'fár dzwò hwò'chē dzǒu.

Leave well enough alone. / I advise you to leave well enough alone. Wǒ 'chywàn ni byé 'dùng ta le; hwéi'tóu 'lúngdz gěi jr 'yǎba le.

Might as well °gān'tswèi (°burú, °swósying) (dzai *or* yě) . . . swànle. / You might as well go back. Nǐ °gān'tswèi (°burú) 'hwéichyu swànle.

Think well of. / Do you think well of him? Nǐ 'jywéde tā 'dzwòde 'hǎu ma?

A well (for water) jǐng; **salt well** yánjǐng. / How deep a well did you have to dig to get water here? Jèrde 'jǐng děi 'wā 'dwō shēn tsái néng jyàn 'shwěi ne?

To well up (of liquid) mǎn; (of feelings) gōuchilai. / The water is welling up where the pipe is broken. 'Gwǎndz 'hwàile de nèige 'dìfangr 'shwěi dōu 'mǎn le. / That was the last straw; all his feelings on the matter welled up and he said what he'd been wanting to say for so long. 'Nèmma yi lái, bǎ tāde 'syīnshr 'gōuchilaile, tā bǎ yàu shwō de 'hwà 'pīlepā'lǎde dōu 'shwōchulaile.

WEST (WESTERN) syī; **west end** syītóur; **southwest** syīnán; **northwest** syīběi. / There's a strong west wind blowing up. Syīfēng gwāchilaile. / The road goes west. Jèige lù shr wàng syī chyùde. / Go west at the next turn. Jyàn 'wār wàng syī 'gwǎi. / Their house faces west. Tamende fángdz cháu syī.

(Indicating a part or area) syībù, syībyār, syīfāng. / In the west the mountains are higher than they are here. °Syībùde (°etc.) shān bǐ jèrde gāu. / They live in the west part of the province. Tāmen jùdzai jèishěngde °syībù (°etc.).

(Indicating an area beyond a border) syībyar; (to the) **west of** . . . dzai . . . (de) syībyar. / The little island is three miles west of the big one. Nèige 'syáu dǎu dzai 'dà dǎu(de) 'syībyar 'sānlǐ dì. / He lives west of the river. Tā jùdzai 'hé(de) 'syībyar.

WET. shr, cháu; (not dry) bùgān. / Keep a wet dressing on your arm. Nǐ dzài 'gēbeshang 'wéi yíkwài 'shŕbù.

Get wet nùngshŕle, shŕle. / You'll get wet! Nǐ hwéi'tóu nùng'shŕle!

To wet something nùngshŕle, pwōshŕle, etc., the main verb indicating the method used. / They wet the street to keep the dust down. Tāmen bǎ 'jyē pwō'shŕle, bá 'tǔ 'yāsyachyu.

Wet one's pants nyàu kùdz. / The baby wet her pants. Nèige 'háidz nyàule 'kùdz le.

WHAT. shémma; (which) nǎ(yi) *or* něi(yi) plus a measure; (whatever) shémma . . . shémma . . . . / What do you want for supper? Nǐ wǎn'fàn yàu chī 'shémma? / What did you say? Nǐ gāng shwō 'shémma laije? / I don't know what I want. Wǒ bujř'dàu wǒ 'yàu shémma. / What's left? 'Shèngsya shémma le? / What? 'Shémma? / What else? 'Hái (yǒu) shémma? /What's missing? Chà shémma 'dūngsyi? *or* Dyōule 'shémma le? /Do you know what train we're supposed to take? Nǐ 'jřdau wǒmen gāi dzwò 'něiyitàng 'chē ma? /He always says what he thinks. Tā yúng'ywán 'syǎng shémma jyou shwō shémma. /We know what ships were in the harbor. Wǒmen 'jř-dau dzài gáng'kǒu dōu yǒu shémma 'chwán. *but* /What I said was right. Wǒ shwōde hěn 'dwèi.

What (exclamation) shémma, dzěmma, á. /What! Isn't he here yet? 'Shém-ma! Tā 'hai méilái ne!

What a . . . . /What a beautiful flower! Jèige 'hwār 'jēn hǎu'kàn! /What a time I had getting home! Wǒ hwéi 'jyā de shŕhour, 'jèiyitàng a!

What about dzěmmayàng. /What about your appointment? Nǐde ywē'hwèr dzěm-ma'yàng?

What if yàushr . . . °dzěmma'yàng (°dzěmma 'bàn). /What if the train's late? 'Chē yàushr wù'dyǎnle °dzěmma'yàng (°dzěmma 'bàn)?

What kind of shémmayàngrde. /What kind of a house are you looking for? Nǐ jǎu shémma'yàngrde 'fángdz?

What of it yǒu shémma 'gwānsyi ne, yǒu néng dzěmma 'yàng ne. /He didn't get here on time, but what of it? Tā méiànje shŕhou 'dàu, °yǒu shémma 'gwānsyi ne (yǒu néng dzěmma 'yàng ne)?

I'll tell you what dzěmmaje ba. /I'll tell you what; let's go to the movies to-night. 'Dzěmmaje ba; wǒmen jyēr 'wǎnshang kàn dyàn'yǐngr chyù ba.

WHATEVER. (wúlwùn *or* búlwùn *or* bùgwǎn) . . . shémma . . . dōu, shémma . . . shém-ma . . . ; no . . . whatever yì'dyǎr . . . °yě (°dōu) plus a negative expression. /Do whatever you like; I don't car. Nǐ (wúlwùn *or* búlwùn *or* bugwǎn) yàu gàn 'shémma dou 'syíng; wǒ bu'dzàihu. *or* Nǐ 'yàu gàn shémma jyou 'gàn shémma; wǒ bu'dzàihu. /Whatever you do, be sure to tell me about it. Nǐ (wú'lwùn) gàn 'shémma dou yí-'dìng děi 'gàusu wo. /He has no money whatever. Tā yì'dyǎr chyán yě méi'yǒu. /She lost whatever respect she had for him. is expressed as Now she doesn't respect him at all. Tā syàndzài yì'dyǎr dōu chyáubu'chǐ ta le.

WHEAT. màidz. /Do you raise wheat on your farm? Nǐde 'dìli jùng 'màidz ma? /How is the wheat crop this year? Jǐnnyán 'màidz 'shōucheng dzěmma 'yàng?

WHEEL. gūlu, lwúndz, lwúnr; waterwheel shwěichēer. /The front wheels of the car need to be tightened. 'Chēde °chyán'lwúnr (°chyántoude gūlu) děi 'jínjin le. /The waterwheel produces all the power we use on this farm. Jěnggèr núng'chǎng dōu yùng jèi shwěi'chēer fā de 'dyàn.

To wheel something is expressed by a verb indicating the specific method of causing the motion, such as push twēi, plus another verb of motion. /They were wheeling the baby carriage through the park. Tām dzài gūng'ywánli 'twēije yáu'chēer 'lyōuda laije.

Wheel around jwàngwo 'shēn lai. /He wheeled around and looked daggers at me. Tā jwàngwo 'shēn lai hěn'hěrde 'dèngle wo yì'yǎn.

WHEN. 'shémma shŕhou(r) 'jǐshŕ, dwōdzen; (what day) jyēr, 'něiyityān; (what hour) 'jídyǎn jūng. /When can I see you again? Wó °'jǐshŕ (°'dwōdzen, °etc.) néng dzài 'jyànjau ni? /Tell me when to expect you. 'Gàusung wo nǐ (dà'gài) 'shémma shŕ-hou °lái (°'dàu).

(Introducing an expression which specifies the time at which something else occurs) . . . de shŕhou(r). /When the work is done, you can go. Nǐ bǎ 'shèr dzwò-

'wánle de shŕhour, nǐ jyou kéyi 'dzǒu le. /I wasn't home when he called. Tā 'lái de shŕhou wǒ méidzài 'jyā. /I feel very uncomfortable when it's hot. Tyār 'rè de shŕhour wó dzǔng 'jywéde bù'shūfu.

There are times when . . . , there are days when . . . 'yǒude shŕhou. /There are times when I prefer to be alone. 'Yǒude shŕhou wǒ 'ywànyî 'yíge rén 'dāije. /There are days when he's very depressed, and days when he's on top of the world. Tā 'yǒude shŕhou fā'chóu, 'yǒude shŕhou 'gāusyîngde lyǎubu'dé.

(Although) chíshŕ. /He gave the boy some money when he should have known better. Tā gěile nèige syǎu nán'hár dyǎr 'chyán, chí'shŕ tā yīngdāng 'jrdau bùgāi nèmma 'dzwò.

WHENEVER. (wúlwùn) shémma shŕhou . . . , . . . dōu . . . ; shémma shŕhou . . . °shémma shŕhou (°swéibyàn) . . . ; yǐ . . . de shŕhou . . . . /Whenever you ask him, he says no. Ni 'wúlwùn shémma shŕhou 'wèn ta, tā dōu shwō bu'syíng. /Come to see us whenever you have time. Shémma 'shŕhou yǒu 'gūngfu °shémma shŕhou 'lái (°swéi'byàn lái). /Whenever he visits us I feel funny. Tā yǐ lái 'kàn wǒmen de shŕ-hou, wó 'dzǔng jywéde yóu dyǎr chí'gwài.

(Showing surprise) 'nǎr láide. /Whenever did you find time to do all this? Ní 'nǎr láide nèmma syē'shŕhou dzwòle jèmma syē 'shèr?

WHERE. (At or in what place) nǎr, shémma dìfang. /Where's the nearest hotel. Lí jèr dzwèi 'jìn de lyú'gwǎn dzài °'nǎr (°shémma 'dìfang)? /Can you tell me where you live? Nǐ dzài 'nǎr jù? or (very polite) Nín 'fùshang shémma 'dìfang?

(To what place) °dàu (°shàng) °nǎr (°shémma dìfang). /Where're you going? Nǐ °dàu (°shàng) 'nǎr chyù?

(From what place) tsúng °nǎr (°shémma dìfang). /Where did you get those flowers? Nèisye hwār nǐ shr tsúng 'nǎr ná lai de?

(At or in or to which) is expressed with de. /The house where I used to live is on this street. Wó yǐ'chyán 'jùgwo de nèiswǒr 'fángdz jyou dzài 'jèityáu jyēshang. /The restaurant where we wanted to go was closed. Wǒmen yàu 'chyù de nèige fàn-'gwǎndz 'gwānle.

As a conjunction is expressed with dìfang place. /The nurses will be sent where they are needed most. Yàu bǎ jèisye 'kānhu pàidau dzwèi 'syūyàu tamen de 'dìfang chyù. /We found him just where he said he would be. Wǒmen jyou dzài tā 'shwō de nèige dìfang bǎ ta 'jǎujau le.

Whereabouts 'syàlwò. /His whereabouts is a mystery. Tāde syàlwò bù'míng.

WHEREVER. nǎr . . . nǎr . . . , shémma dìfang . . . shémma dìfang . . . . /I'll go wherever you go. Nǐ shàng 'nǎr, wó yě shàng 'nǎr.

WHETHER. Expressed by stating alternatives, sometimes with háishr between them. /I don't know whether they will come. Wǒ bùjr'dàu tāmen 'lái bùlái. /Do you know whether this story is true or not? Nǐ 'jrdàu jèige 'gùshr shr 'jēnde háishr 'jyǎde? /We can't tell whether it'll rain or snow, but it looks like it's going to do something. Wǒmen bùgǎn 'shwō shr yàu syà 'yǔ háishr syà 'sywě, fǎn'jèng kàn 'yàngr shr yàu nàu'tyār.

WHICH. nǎ(yi) or něi(yi) plus a measure; referring to people is also expressed as who shwéi or shéi. /Which of the men will be better for the job? Dzwò nèige 'gūngdzwò 'něiyíge rén 'hǎu? /Which is the one you picked out? 'Nèige shr 'nǐ 'tyāuchulai de? /He didn't know which to take. Tā bùjr'dàu ná 'nèige ('hǎu). /Which book do you want? Nǐ yàu ná 'něiběn shū? /When you look at the twins, it's hard to tell which is which. Nǐ 'kànjyan nèidwèi 'shwàngshengr de shŕhou, hěn nán 'fēnchulai °'nĕige shŕ 'nèige (°'shéi shŕ 'shéi).

As a relative pronoun is expressed with de. /Please return the book which you borrowed. Chíng ni bǎ nǐ jyè de 'shū 'hwánle ba. /The double rooms which are on the second floor are all taken. 'Èrtséng 'lóushangde 'shwāngrén'fángjyān dōu jù'mǎn le.

WHILE. (During the time that) . . . de shŕhou. /I want to arrive while it's still light. Wǒ syǎng chènje 'tyān hái 'lyàngje de shŕhou 'dàu nèr. /I met him while traveling. Wǒ shŕ lyǔ'syíng de shŕhòur 'pèngjyan tāde.

(And yet, but, though) is often omitted. /Some of the students are serious, while others are not. 'Yǒude sywésheng hěn yùng'gūng, chí'yúde bùdzěmma'yàng.

Wait a (little) while 'děng yìhwěr, shāu 'hòu yihòu. /You'll have to wait a little while before you can see him. Nǐ děi shāu 'hòu yihòu tsái néng 'jyàn ta.

Be worth one's while héswàn, shàngswàn, jŕde. /It's not worth your while to do this. Nǐ dzwò jèige °buhé'swàn (°bushàng'swàn, °bu'jŕde, °fànbu'shàng).

To while away the time. /How can we while away the time until dinner? is expressed as We still have to wait a bit for dinner; shall we do a bit of something? Lí chŕ 'fàn hái déi 'hwěr ne, dzámen 'gàn dyar 'shémma ne?

WHITE. bái; (white color) bái 'yánshar. /She was dressed in white. Tā 'chwān de shŕ 'báide. /Would it be all right to wear white shoes? Chwān 'báisyé 'syíng ma? /I want the walls painted white and the ceiling blue. 'Chyáng wǒ yàu 'báide, dǐng'péng yàu 'lánde. /She went white when she heard the news. Tā 'tīngjyan nèige 'syāusyi 'lyǎn dōu 'bái le. /She's able to walk again, but she still looks awfully white. Tā néng syà'dǐ le, kěshr 'lyǎnshang 'háishr shà'bái. /This white will glare in the sun. is expressed as This white color . . . . Jèige bái 'yánshar dzài 'tàiyangdyèrli hwáng'yǎn.

White Christmas is expressed in terms of snowing syàsywě. /Do you think we'll have a white Christmas? Nǐ syǎng jīnnyán shēngdàn'jyé hwèi syà'sywě ma?

The white (part of an egg) dànbái, jīdànchīngr. /To make this cake you'll need the whites of four eggs. Dzwò jèige 'gāu nǐ děi yùng 'szge °jīdànde dàn'bái (°jī-dàn'chīngr).

(Of an eye) báiyǎnjūr, báiyǎnchyóur. /The whites of her eyes are bloodshot. Tāde báiyǎn'jūrli yǒu syě'sèr.

WHO (WHOM, WHOSE). shéi, shwéi; whom shéi, shwéi; whose sheide, shwéide. /Who told you? Shŕ 'shéi 'gàusu nǐde? /Who's that person? 'Nèige rén shŕ 'shéi? /Do you know who was responsible for this? Nǐ 'jŕdau 'shéi °fù jèige 'dzérèn ma (°gwǎn 'jèige ma)? /Whose watch is this? Jèige 'byǎu shŕ 'shéide? /Whose is this? 'Jèige shŕ 'shéide? /I'd like to know whose car this is. Wǒ syǎng 'jŕdau jèige 'chē shŕ 'shéide. /Whom do you wish to see? Nǐ syǎng jàu 'shéi?

Who's who shéi shŕ 'dzěmma hwéi 'shŕ. /Can you tell me who's who at the university? Nǐ 'jŕ dau jèige 'dàsywélide rén 'shéi shŕ 'dzěmma hwéi 'shŕ ma?

As relative pronouns are expressed with de. /The man who just came in is the owner of the store. 'Gāng 'jìnlai de nèige rén shŕ jèige 'pùdzlide láu'bǎn. /She is the girl whom I would like most to marry. 'Tā jyòushr wǒ syǎng 'chǔ de nèiwei syáujye. /I would prefer students whose marks are good. Wǒ bíjyàu syǐhwān gūng-kē 'hǎude sywésheng.

In expressions where the who clause is a parenthetical comment, the information

1019

which follows **who** is in Chinese given as a coordinate expression. / My two children, who are now on vacation, will be back next week. is expressed as My two children are now on vacation; next week they're coming back. Wǒde nèi 'lyàngge 'háidz fàng-'jyàle, 'syàsyīngchī jyou 'hwéilaile.

WHOLE. chywán, yìjěng, jěnggèrjěng. / The whole office was dismissed at noon. Chywán gūngshr̀'fáng de rén 'jūngwǔ jyou kéyi 'dzǒu le. / Look at the thing as a whole. 'Yīngdang 'gèfāngmyàn chywán syàng'dàule. / He sat through the whole play. Tā 'dzwòdzai nèr 'kànle yìjěngchū 'syì. / I intend to stay a whole week. Wǒ 'dǎswàn 'jù ('jěng) yíge lǐ'bài. / I worked a whole day. Wǒ dzwòle yǐ'jěngtyānde 'shr̀.

　　(Not in parts) is expressed as not broken, etc. / Did the pitcher break when you dropped it, or is it still whole? 'Gwàndz shwāi'swèile méiyou?

　　A whole . . . of yídà plus a measure. / He caught a whole string of fish. Tā 'dyàule yí'dàchwàr 'yú. / He told a whole pack of lies. Tā 'sāle yí'dàpyān 'hwǎng.

　　A whole lot of hǎusyē. / I ate a whole lot of candy. Wǒ 'chr̄le hǎusyē 'táng.

　　On the whole dàjr̀shang. / On the whole I agree with you. Wǒ dà'jr̀shang gēn ni túng'yì.

WHOLLY. wánchywán, jyǎnjr̀. / The decision is wholly up to you. Dzwèi'hòu yíjyù 'hwà, wán'chywán dzài 'nǐ le. / This is wholly out of the question. 'Jèi jyǎnjr̀ shr̀ bànbu'dàude.

WHY. 'wèi shémma; (how come) dzěmma. / Why's the train so crowded this morning? Jèige 'chē jyēr 'dzǎuchen °'wèi shémma (°dzěmma) dzěmma 'jǐ a? / Why isn't this work finished yet. 'Jèige gūngdzwo °dzěmma (°wèi shémma) hái méidzwò'wán ne? / I can't imagine any reason why he should refuse to come. Wó 'syǎngbuchu'lái 'wèi shémma tā bú'ywànyi lái. / Do you really plan to go tomorrow? Why not? Nǐ 'míngtyan 'jēn chyù ma? 'Wèi shémma bùchyù ne?

　　Why not (making a suggestion) . . . 'hǎu buhǎu, . . . 'syíng busyíng, etc. / Why not come along? 'Nǐ yě 'lái, 'hǎu buhǎu?

　　Whys and wherefores is expressed with 'wèi shémma, dzěmma why. / They tried to find out the whys and wherefores of his absence. Tāmen 'syǎng 'cháchulai °'wèi shémma (°'dzěmma) tā méi'dàu.

WIDE. kwān. / Is this road wide enough for two-way traffic? Jèityáu 'lù 'lyǎnglyàng chē 'bìngje dzǒu gòu 'kwānde ma? / The window is three feet wide and six feet high. Jèige 'chwānghu yǒu 'sānchr̄ kwān, 'lyòuchr̄ 'gāu.

　　(Of great range) gwǎng, dwō. / This newspaper has a wide circulation. Jèige bàu'jr̀ fā'syíngde hén 'gwǎng.

　　(Far from the mark) ywǎn. / Your last shot was wide of the target. Nǐ dzwèi-'hòu nèiyísyàdz dǎde lí'mùbyāu tài 'ywǎn le. / The bullet went wide of its mark. Jèige dz'dàn dǎde lí mù'byāu tài 'ywǎnle.

　　Wide open (lawless) wú'fǎwú'tyān. / This is a wide open town. Jèige 'chéng wú'fǎwú'tyān.

　　Leave oneself **wide open.** / You left yourself wide open. (for past, present, or future trouble) Nǐ 'dzjǐ yìdyár bǎu'jàng yě méi'yǒu. or (for results already finished) Nà shr̀ 'lài nǐ dz'jǐ bù'syǎusyīn.

　　With wide open eyes dēngje 'yǎnjing. / The baby looked at the kitten with wide open eyes. Nèige syǎu'hár dēngje 'yǎnjing 'kàn nèige syǎu'māur.

　　Make something **wide** nùngdà. / Make the hole wide. Bá 'kǒur nùng'dà.

WILL

Open wide kāidà. /Open the window a bit wider. Bǎ 'chwānghu kāi'dà dyǎr.

WIFE. tàitai; 'àirén (limited to Mainland China). /Where's your wife? Nǐ 'tàitai dzài 'nǎr ne? /Are their wives permitted to see them? Syǔ tāmende 'tàitai 'kàn tāmen ma?

WILD. Expressed differently in various combinations: wild animal yěshòu; wild country hwāngdì, hwāngyě, kwàngyě (hwāng'jyāu), mànhwangyě'dì; wild idea gwài 'júyì; wild storm bàufēngyǔ. /Is there any danger of wild animals in the woods? Jǐn shù'líndzli chyù 'shr bushr hwèi yǒu 'yùjyan yě'shòu de 'wéisyǎn? /A hundred years ago this was all wild country. Yì'bǎinyán yǐ'chyán jèr shr yípyàn hwāng'dì. /I hate to waste time on such a wild idea. Wǒ bú'ywànyi dzài nèmma ge gwài 'júyìshang fèi 'gūngfu. /The ship was wrecked during a wild storm at sea. 'Chwán dzài 'hǎishang jyàu yí-jèn bàufēng'yǔ gěi gwā'hwàile.

Go wild (with joy, excitement, etc.) . . . de 'lyǎubudé, . . . de gēn 'fēngle shrde. /The crowd went wild when the news came out. 'Syāusyi 'chwánchulai yǐ'hòu rén °'syǐhwande 'lyǎubudé (°'lède gēn 'fēngle shrde).

Have a wild time wárde kě 'jēn ké'yǐde, wárde kě 'jēn gòu 'chyáude. /We had a wild time at the party last night. Wǒmen dzwór 'wǎnshang chyù nèige 'hwèi 'wárde kě 'jēn °ké'yǐde (°gòu 'chyáude).

Make a wild shot (at tennis, etc.) 'húdǎ, 'syādǎ. /He'd play a good game of tennis if he didn't make so many wild shots. Tāde wǎng'chyóur yàushr °bù'húdǎ (°bu-'syādǎ) 'kéyi dǎde tǐng bu'tswò.

Run wild (of cattle) bùjywānje, mǎnchùr pǎu. /During the winter the cattle were allowed to run wild. 'Dūngtyār 'nyóu bù'jywānje, mǎn'chùr 'pǎu.

WILL. (Indicating future time) hwèi, yàu; (if in an order) děi; often not separately expressed. /They'll be surprised to see you here. Tāmen dzài jèr 'chyáujyàn ni yí-dìng hwèi 'jywéde hěn chí'gwài. /The order read: You will proceed at once to the next town. 'Mìnglìng shwō: Nǐ lì'kè jyòu děi dàu 'syàyíge 'chéng chyù. /I'll meet you at the corner at three o'clock. Wǒ 'sāndyǎn dzài gwǎi'jyàur nèr 'jyàn ni. /Won't you come in for a minute? 'Jìnlai 'dāi hwěr, dzěmma'yàng? /I won't be but a minute. Wǒ 'yùngbulyǎu 'yìfēnjūng. /Will you reserve a room for me for tomorrow? Nǐ 'míngtyan gěi wo 'lyóu jyān 'wūdz, 'syíng busyíng?

(Denoting habitual behavior) néng. /He'll go for days without smoking a cigarette; then in two days sometimes he'll smoke half a carton. Tā néng 'hǎusyē rdz lyán 'yìgēr yān yě bù'chōu; kěshr tā 'yě néng dzài 'lyǎngtyānli chōu 'wǔbāu 'yān.

(Denoting capacity or ability) kéyi, néng. /This theater will hold a thousand people. Jèige syì'hwándz kéyi dzwò yì'chyān rén. /This machine won't work. Jèige 'jīchi bùnéng 'yùngle. or expressed as This machine is broken. Jèige 'jīchi 'hwàile.

Will something to yí'jūshang syěje . . . °jywāngei (°lyóugei) . . . . /He willed all his property to the city. Tā yí'jūshang 'syěje bǎ tā 'swǒyǒude 'tsáichǎn dōu 'jywāngei dì'myàrshang le. /He willed three hundred dollars to his friend. Tā yí-'jūshang 'syěje lyóugei tā 'péngyou sānbaikwai 'chyán.

As he wills. /We'll have to do as he wills. is expressed as We'll have to do as he says. Wǒmen dzúng děi jàu tā 'shwō de 'bàn. or as We'll have to do according to his ideas. Wǒmen dzúng děi ànje tāde 'yìsz dzwò. or as We'll have to listen to him. Dzámen 'jr hǎu tǐng 'tāde.

A will (document) yíjǔ. /He died without leaving a will. Tā chyù'shr de shr-hou méi'lyóusyà yí'jǔ.

Against one's will. /He went to school against his will. is expressed as He

1021

didn't want to go to school, but he went anyway. Tā 'jŕ bù'syǎng shàng'sywé chyù, kěshr 'háishr 'chyùle.

At will swéibyàn. / The prisoners are free to have visitors at will. 'Chyoufàn kéyi swéi'byàn gēn lái 'kàn tāmen de rén jyàn'myàr.

Have a will of one's own yŏujúyi, 'píchi gòu 'nìngde. / My wife has a will of her own. Wŏ tàitai 'syīnli hén yŏu'júyi. / That child certainly has a will of his own. Nèige 'háidz °hén yŏu'júyi (°'píchi jēn gòu 'nìngde).

With a will 'bàuje jywé'syīnde. / The men set to work with a will. Nèisyē 'rén bàuje jywé'syīnde chyù 'dzwòle.

WIN (WON). / Which team do you think will win? Ní syǎng 'nǎ yídwèi 'yíng? / I'm going to win this game if it's the last thing I do. Wŏ jyòushr 'dzěmma je (°'sżle) yé děi yàu bǎ jèichǎng 'yíng le.

(Attain) dé. / He won first prize in the contest. Nèitsž bǐ'sài 'tā déde tóu-'jyǎng. / His story won everyone's sympathy. is expressed as Whoever heard his story was sympathetic. 'Shéi tīngjyan tāde nèidwàr 'gùshr dōu túng'chíng.

Win someone **over** gǎigwolai, chywàngwolai. / We finally won him over to our way of thinking. Tāde 'sžsyǎng dàu'lyǎur ràng women gěi °'gǎigwolai le (°'chywàngwolaile).

WIND. fēng; **be windy** gwāfēng. / There was a violent wind during the storm last night. Dzwór 'wǎnshangde °bàufēng'yǔ (°dà 'fēng dà 'yǔ) kě (gwāde) jēn 'dà. / A stiff wind made it difficult for the boat to reach port. Nèijèn 'fēng jēn 'yìng, 'chwán dōu 'gwāde bù'rúngyi kāijin 'gǎng chyù le. / He flew the plane into the wind. Tā 'dǐngje 'fēngr 'kāi nèige fēi'jī.

(Breathing, need to breathe) hūsyī; or expressed verbally with breathe chwǎn. / His wind is bad because he smokes too much. Tā chōu 'yān chōude tài 'dwō, swóyi °cháng ài 'chwǎn (°hū'syī bù 'hǎu).

(Empty talk) 'fèihwà. / There was nothing but wind in what he said. Tā 'shwō de 'chywán shŕ 'fèihwà.

Against the wind dǐng fēngr, chyáng fēngr.

In the wind. / There's a rumor in the wind that we may get the afternoon off. Yŏu yíge 'yáuyan shwō dzámen jyēr 'syàwǔ yésyǔ fàng'jyà.

Get wind of 'tīngjyànle dyǎr 'fēngr, 'jŕdaule dyǎr, 'tīngshwōle dyǎr. / I got wind of their plans yesterday. Wŏ 'dzwórge °'jŕdàule dyǎr (°'tīngshwōle dyǎr) tāmende 'jìhwà. or Tāmende 'jìhwa wŏ 'dzwórge 'tīngjyànle dyǎr 'fēngr.

Knock the wind out of dǎde . . . 'chūbulái 'chyèr le. / It knocked the wind out of him. Nèiyí'syàdz 'dǎde ta °'chūbulái 'chyèr le (°'dàusyī yìkŏu 'chì).

Take the wind out of someone's **sails.** / It certainly took the wind out of his sails when he lost his job. Tā shŕ'yěle yǐ'hòu jēn 'shòule dyǎr 'dǎjī.

With the wind shùn fēngr.

To wind chwǎn. / That run upstairs winded me. Wó 'pǎule shàngle lóu, 'pǎude wǒ jŕ 'chwǎn.

Get winded chwǎn. / He's not a good swimmer because he gets winded too easily. Tā yóu'yǔng yóude bù'syíng, 'yóu búdà'hwěr jyou 'chwǎn le.

WIND (WOUND). (Of a spring) shàng. / I forgot to wind my watch. Wŏ 'wàngle shàng 'byǎu le. or Wǒde 'byǎu wàngle shàng 'syán le. / Did you wind up the clock before you came upstairs? Nǐ shàng lóu yǐ'chyán °shàng 'jūng le ma (°bǎ 'jūng 'shàngshang-le ma?

(Follow a curving course) ràu, gwǎi. / The cows were winding their way home through the pasture. 'Nyóu °ràuje (°gwǎije) ('wār) 'dzǒu tsúng tsǎu'dǐ nèr 'chwān-gwochyu hǎu hwéi 'jyā. / The road winds through the old part of town. Nèityáu 'dàur °'gwǎide (°'ràude) 'lǎuchéngli chyùle.

(Twist around something) chán, ràu. / Wind the string into a ball. Bǎ 'shéngdz 'ràuchen ge 'chyóur. / Wind the wire up on this spool. Bǎ 'syàn ràudau syàn'jóur-shang. / They wound the bandage tightly around his arm. Tāmen bǎ bēng'dài dzài tā 'gēbeshang °chánde (°'ràude) tíng 'jǐn. / The snake wound itself around a tree. 'Shé °'ràudau (°'chándau, °'pándau) 'shùshangle.

Wind up business 'lyàulǐ, bànwán, 'jénglǐ, jyéshu. / He had two weeks to wind up his affairs before entering the army. Tā jǐn jyūn'dwèi yǐ'chyán, yóu 'lyàngge syǐng'chǐde 'shŕjyān °'lyàulǐ (°bàn'wán, °etc.) tā 'dzjǐde 'shŕching.

Wind up a speech (finish) is expressed as quickly finish jèng yàu wán, jèng dzwò 'jyéshu. / He was just winding up his speech when we got there. Wǒmen 'jìn-chyù de shŕhou, tāde yán'jyǎng jèng yàu 'wán.

WINDOW. chwānghu. / Which one of you kids broke the window? Nǐmen 'něige háidz bǎ 'chwānghu dǎ'pwòle? / These windows need washing. Jèisyē 'chwānghu děi 'tsā-syǐtsāsyǐ le.

WING. (Of a bird or plane) bǎngdz, chŕbǎngr. / The pigeon broke its wing when it hit the window. 'Gēdz jwàngdzai 'chwānghushang bǎ °'bǎngdz (°chŕ'bǎngr) jwàng'hwàile. / The new airplanes have a tremendous wing spread. Syīn fēi'jǐde 'bǎngdz dà'jíle. / One wing of the plane was sheared completely off when it hit the ground. Fēi'jǐ jyàng'lwò de shŕhou yíge 'bǎngdz pèngde 'dìshang le jěng'gèerde 'shésyalaile.

(Of a house) syāngfáng. / We're planning to build a new wing on the house. Wǒ-men jèng 'dǎswanje bǎ jèige 'fángdz 'jyēchu ge syāng'fáng lai.

(Of the stage) is expressed as in the curtains dzài tái'lyár lǐtou. / He stood in the wings waiting for his cue. Tā 'jàndzai tái'lyár lǐtou 'děngje shàng 'chǎng ne.

On the wing (lit.) is expressed as while flying fēije. / He was trying to shoot ducks on the wing. Tā syǎng yàu dzài nèisyē 'yādz 'fēije de shŕhou kāi 'chyāng lái dǎ. (fig.) / He's such a busy person, you'll have to catch him on the wing. Tā shŕ ge 'mángrén, ní děi 'jwēi a gǎnde tsái jǎude'jáu ta.

Take someone under one's wing jàugu. / She took the newcomer under her wing. Tā hěn 'jàugu něige syīn'láide rén.

WINTER. dūng(tyan). / We usually have a mild winter here. Jèr píng'cháng 'dūngtyan bù'lěng. / It's getting cold enough to wear a winter coat. Jèi tyār 'lěngde děi chwān 'dūngdà'yī le.

(Period of cold weather) 'lěngde shŕhou. / We're in for a spell of winter. 'Dàu-le 'lěngde shŕhou le.

To winter gwò dūngtyan. / Where did you winter last year? Nǐ 'chyùnyan dzài 'nǎr gwòde 'dūngtyan?

WIRE. (Electric) dyànsyàn; (iron or sometimes other metal, whatever the use) tyěsz. / The telephone wires were blown down by the storm. Nèige bàufēng'yǔ bǎ dyàn'syàn gwā'shéle. / We put up wire screens to keep out the flies. Wǒmen 'ānshàng °'tyěsz-'shā (°'tyěshā'chwāng) 'dángdang 'tsāngying.

(A telegram) dyànbàu; send a message by wire dǎ dyànbàu. / Send him a wire to tell him we're coming. Gěi ta dǎ ge dyàn'bàu gàusung ta wǒmen jyou yàu 'lái le. /You'll have to send this message to him by wire. Jèijyàn 'shŕching ní déi gěi ta dǎ ge dyàn'bàu.

To wire (furnish with wires) ān dyànsyàn. /Is the house wired for electricity? Jèige 'fángdz 'ānle dyàn'syàn le ma? or expressed as Does this house have electricity? Jèige 'fángdz yǒu dyàn'dēng ma?

(Telegraph) dǎ dyànbàu. /He wired me to meet him at the train. Tā géi wo dǎle yíge dyàn'bàu ràng wo dàu chē'jàn chyu 'jyē ta. /I'll wire if I can. Yàu 'néng dǎ dyàn'bàu, wǒ géi ni 'dǎ yíge.

WISE. tsūngming. /His decision to remain is very wise. Tā jywé'dìng bù'dzǒu shŕ hěn tsūngmingde. /He's a pretty wise fellow. Tā jèige 'rén hěn 'tsūngming.

Get wise to something míngbai. /He never got wise to their little scheme. Tā yì'jr méi'míngbai tāmende bǎ'syì.

Make someone **wise** gàusu(ng). /Don't you think we ought to make him wise to it? Nǐ syǎng bù'yīnggāi 'gàusung ta ma?

WISH. (Want, want to) syīwang, ywànyi, 'syǎng. /I wish I could stay here longer. Wǒ dàushr °'syīwang (°'ywànyi) néng dzài 'jèr 'dwō dāi syē shŕhòu. /What do you wish for most? Nǐ dzwèi °'syīwang (°syǎng) yàu 'shémma?

(In giving an order) chǐng. /I wish you would finish by twelve o'clock. Chǐng ni shŕ'èrdyǎn jūng dzwò'wán.

(In leave-takings and greetings). /We wished him luck. Wǒmen 'jù ta jū'shŕrú'yì. /We sent him our best wishes for luck in his new job. Wǒmen jù ta syīn'shŕyè yì'fānfēng'shwùn. /Best wishes on your birthday! Géi nǐ bài'shòu! /I've come to wish you good-by. (to the one staying) Wǒ lái gēn nín tsź'syíng. or (to the one leaving) Wǒ lái gěi nín sùng'syíng.

Wish something (off) **on** jyāugei, twēigei. /Who wished this job on me? 'Shéi bǎ jèige 'shŕ 'twēigei 'wǒ le? /Let's wish this off on someone else. Dzámen bǎ jèijyàn 'shŕ °'jyāugei (°'twēigei) 'byérén ba.

A wish syīwang; or often expressed verbally. /Her wish for a trip abroad came true. Tā yàu dàu gwó'wài chyù de 'syīwàng shŕ'syànle. or Tā 'dzǎu jyou °syǎng yàu (°'syīwang) chū'gwó, jēn 'chéngle. /She expressed a wish to spend the summer at the beach. is expressed as She said she wished to spend the summer at the beach. Tā shwō tā °yàu (°'syīwang, °syǎng, °'pànwàng néng) dàu hǎi'byārshang chyù gwò'syà.

WITH. (Accompaniment and closely allied meanings) gēn, hé, túng. /I plan to have lunch with him today. Wǒ 'dǎswàn gēn ta 'jīntyān yí'kwàr chr wǔ'fàn. /Why did you break up with him? Nǐ 'wèi shémma gēn ta jywé'jyāu le? /Rent is rising with the cost of living. Fáng'dzū gēnje 'shēnghwó 'fèiyùng yí'kwàr wàng 'shàng 'jǎng. /Your ideas don't agree with mine. Nǐde 'yìjyan gēn 'wǒde °bùyí'jr. (°bùyí'yàng, °bùsyāng'hé, °bùsyāng'túng). /I beg to differ with you. Wǒ gēn nínde 'jyànjyě bùyí'yàng.

(Having) dài, yǒu. /I want a room with bath. Wǒ yàu yìjyan dài dzǎu'fáng de 'wūdz. /Your friend talks with an accent. Nǐde 'péngyou shwō 'hwà °dài (°yǒu) 'kǒuyīn. /He took a gun with him for protection. Tā dàije yìgǎn 'chyāng 'fángbeifángbei.

(Using as an instrument) ná, yùng, shǐ. /He chopped down the tree with an ax. Tā °ná (°etc.) yìbǎ 'fǔdz bǎ 'shù kǎn'dàu le.

(Including) lyán, jyāshang, dāshang. / The price of cigarettes is twenty cents, with tax. Yān'jywǎrde 'jyàchyán °lyán (°'jyāshang, °'dāshang) 'shwèi shř 'lyǎng-máu chyán.

(Among) dzài . . . li. / The candidate is more popular with the farmers than with business men. Jèige hòusywǎn'rén dzài 'núngrénli bǐ dzài 'shāngrénli 'húng.

(For the sake of) wèi. / He's done some valuable work with the people in rural cummunities. Tā dzài 'syāngsyà wèi 'rénmín dzwòle dyǎr yǒu 'yíchu de 'shřching.

(Because of) yīnwei. / With the hot weather the beaches will be crowded. Yīn-wei tyār 'rè hǎi'byārshang yídìng hén 'jǐ. / I went home with a cold. Yīnwei wǒ 'jàule dyǎr 'lyáng jyou hwéi 'jyā le. / The price of radios went up with the increasing demand. Wúsyàn'dyàndе 'jyàr 'jǎngle, shř 'yīnwei 'mǎide rén 'dwōle.

(Despite) 'swéirán. / With all the work he's done on it, the book still isn't finished. Tā 'swéiránshř bǎ 'gūngfu 'dōu gēshangle, kěshr nèibér 'shū hái méisyě'wán.

With each other bǐtsž. / The two countries were at war with each other for many years. Jèilyǎng'gwó bǐ'tsž dǎ 'jàng dǎle háuji 'nyán le.

With someone's permission 'déjáu . . . de syǔ'kě, . . . tungyìde. / I made all my plans with the commanding officer's permission. Wǒ yi'chyède 'jìhwà dōu °'dé-jáu jǔ'gwǎn 'jǎnggwānde syǔ'kě le (°shř jǎng'gwān túng'yì de).

Be pleased with syǐhwan, jywéde . . . °hǎu'kàn (°etc.). / Are you pleased with the view from your windows? Ní 'syǐhwan nǐ 'chwānghu 'wàitoude 'jǐngjr ma? *or* Nǐ 'jywéde nǐ 'chwānghu 'wàitoude 'jǐngjr hǎu'kàn ma?

Leave . . . with tswúndzai, lyóugei 'jyāugei. / Leave your keys with the hotel clerk. is expressed as Leave your keys at the hotel desk. Bǎ nǐde 'yàushr 'tswún-dzai lyú'gwǎnde 'gwèishang.

Other English expressions. / The house was built with cheap labor. is expressed as The labor that built that house was cheap. Jèige 'fángdz 'gàide 'gūngcheng bù-'syíng. / Do you want something to drink with your meal? is expressed as In addition to what you eat would you also like something to drink? 'Chřde yǐ'wài nín 'hái yàu dyǎr shémma 'hēde ma? / With him, it's all a matter of money. is expressed as As he sees things, it's all a matter of money. Dzài 'tā kàn, nà 'wánchywán shř 'chyán-de gwānsyi.

WITHIN. dzài . . . °lǐtou (°jřnèi, °yǐnèi). / I'll be back within a few hours. Wó jǐge jūngtóu yǐ'nèi jyou 'hwéilai. / Speeding is forbidden within the city limits. Dzài chéng 'lǐtou bù'jwǔn kāide tài 'kwài le.

Other English expressions. / Try to keep within the speed limit. is expressed as Don't drive too fast. Byé bǎ 'chē 'kāide tài 'kwài le. / The letters came within a few days of each other. is expressed as In between the time of the arrival of the two letters not many days were skipped. Lyǎngfēng 'syìn dàu de shřhou jūng'jyàr méigé jityán. / Please stay within calling distance. 'Tīngje dyǎr, byé dzóu'ywǎnle. or expressed as Don't go far away, OK? Byé shàng 'ywǎnchù chyù, 'hǎu ba? *or* Byé dzóu 'ywǎnle, 'hǎu ba? / Are we within walking distance of the beach? is expressed as Can we walk from here to the beach? Tsúng 'jèr dàu hǎi'byārshang 'lyóudaje chyù 'syíng ma? / He doesn't live within his income. Tā búlyàn'rùwéi'chū. *or* Tā 'hwāde dzúng bǐ 'jèngde 'dwō.

WITHOUT. méi, méiyou. / We had to do without a car during the summer. Yí'syàtyan wǒmen méiyou 'chē, jyou nèmma 'dwèifuje 'gwòde. / It's very inconvenient to do this without a car. Dzwò 'jèige 'méi(you) 'chē 'jēn bù'fāngbyan. / She passed without seeing us. Tā 'lùgwò méi'chyáujyan wǒmen. or Tā 'dzǒugwochyu de shřhou méi'kànjyan wǒmen. / He walked right in without any fear. Tā yǐ'jř 'dzǒujìnchyule, 'yìdyár yĕ méihài'pà. / Can I get into the hàll without a ticket? Wǒ méi 'pyàu néng jìn lóu 'lǐtou chyù ma? / Can this be done without being detected? is expressed as Can this be done and not let anyone see it? Yàushr 'nèmmaje, nénggou 'bújyàu rén 'kànchulai ma? or Jèige bújyàu rén 'jřdàu bànde'dàu ma?

Without delay 'gánjǐn, mǎshang. / I want this work finished without delay. Jèijyàn 'shr̀ dĕi °'gánjǐn (°'mǎshang) géi wo bàn'wánle.

It goes without saying hái yùng 'shwō ma, 'yùngbujáu 'shwō le. / It goes without saying that this is an imitation. 'Hái yùng 'shwō ma? or 'Yùngbujáu 'shwō le! Jèi shr̀ ge 'jyǎde.

WOMAN. 'nyǔrén; in compounds nyǔ-. / Who's that pretty woman? Nèige hǎu'kànde 'nyǔrén shr̀ 'shéi? / Do you want a woman doctor? Nǐ yàu 'jǎu yíge 'nyǔdàifu ma? Doesn't he like women? or Is he a woman hater? Tā bù'syǐhwan 'nyǔrén ma? / There are more women than men in this office. Jèige gūngshr̀'fángli 'nyǔde bǐ 'nánde 'dwō.

WONDER. (Feel doubt and curiosity) nàmèr, bumíngbai, budǔng, bujřdàu, jywéde hen chígwài. / I wondered why he didn't apologize. Wǒ °'jywéde hěn 'chígwài (°etc.) tā 'dzěmma búdàu'chyàn ne. / I wonder why he doesn't call me up. Wǒ °nà'mèr (°etc.) tā 'wèishémma bùgéi wo dǎ dyàn'hwà. / I was just wondering what you were doing. Wǒ jèng jèr °nà'mèr (°syǎng) nǐ nèr gàn 'shémma ne.

Not wonder if is expressed in terms of most probably 'dwōbàn or for sure jwǔn. / I shouldn't wonder if he's had car trouble. Tā °'dwōbàn (°'jwǔn) shr̀ 'chē chūle 'máubing le.

A wonder (a person) chū'lèibá'tswèide 'rénwù, lyǎubudé de 'rénwù; (in an uncomplimentary sense) gwàiwu. / She can cook, dance, speak nineteen languages, look pretty without any make-up, please a saint or a sinner—she's really a wonder. Tā hwèi dzwò'fàn, hwèi tyàu'wǔ, hwèi shwō shr̀'jyóujǔng yǔ'yán, 'búyùng dzěmma 'dǎban jyou tǐng 'pyàulyang, hái néng jyàn shémma 'rén shwō shémma 'hwà—tā 'jēn shr̀ ge °chū'lèibá'tswèide (°'lyǎubudé de) 'rénwù.

It's a wonder that nándé. / It's a wonder that you got here at all. Nǐ dàu'lyǎur hwéidau jèr láile, jēn nán'dé.

No wonder nángwài, gwàibude. / No wonder it's cold in here; the window is open. °Nángwài (°'Gwàibude) dzěmma 'lěng a, 'gǎnching nèige 'chwānghu 'kāije ne.

With wonder jywéde chígwài, nàmèr. / Tāmen 'kànje nèige fēi'jī, °jwéde hen chí'gwài (°jř nà'mèr).

Work (or **Do**) **wonders with** (or **for**) . . . dwèi . . . you syǎngbu'dàude °hǎuchu (°syàuyan, °etc.). / The new treatment has worked wonders with the child. Jèige 'syīn jřfar dwèi jř syǎu'hár yǒu syǎngbu'dàude 'syàuyan. or Nèige 'syīn'jřfar jř syǎu'hár jēn yǒu 'chísyàu. / A new hat will do wonders for her morale. Yídǐng 'syīn 'màudz dwèi tade 'jīngshen you syǎngbu'dàude 'hǎuchu. or Yídǐng 'syīn 'màudz néng ràng ta 'tèbyé gāu'syìng.

WONDERFUL. tèbyé hǎu, bàng hǎujíle. / We found a wonderful place to spend the summer. Wǒmen 'jǎujáule yíge 'tèbyé 'hǎude dìfang chyù gwò'syà. / He has a wonderful stamp collection. Tā sōu'jíle yítàu 'tèbyé 'hǎude yóu'pyàu. / It's wonderful. Jēn 'bàng. or Hǎu'jíle.

WOOD. mùtou; firewood pǐchái. / This kind of wood makes a very hot fire. 'Jèijǔng mùtou 'shāuchilai hén 'nwànhwo. / How much wood will you need to build the porch? Gài jèige 'lángdz děi yùng 'dwōshau mùtou? / Pile the wood up neatly behind the house. Bǎ jèisyē 'mùtou dzài 'fángdz hòutou dwèi'jěngchile. / Build a wood fire in the stove. is expressed as Burn some firewood in the stove. Dzài 'lúdzli 'shāu dyǎr pǐ'chái.

Woods (forest) shùlíndz.

WOOL. yángmáu, máu; (of a light, fluffy kind) 'máurúng; **wool thread** 'máusyàn; **wool cloth** or **material** yáng'máu 'lyàudz, 'máuní. / Is this suit made of pure wool? Jèi-tàu 'yīshangde 'lyàudz shr̀ 'chwún(yáng)máude ma? / The store is having a sale on wool blankets. Jèi pùdzde °yáng'máu (°'máusyàn, °'máurúng, °'máu) 'tăndz jèng jyăn'jyà ne.

WORD. dz̀, dzèr. / How do you write that word? Nèige 'dz̀ dzĕmma 'syĕ? / How do you spell that word? Nèige 'dz̀ dzĕmma 'pīn? / You're only allowed fifty words in the message. °'Syìnli (°Dyàn'bàuli) yí'gùng jr̄ syú syé 'wǔshrge 'dz̀. / I remember the tune, but I forgot the words. 'Dyàudz wǒ 'jìde, °'dz̀ (°'dzèr) kĕ dōu 'wànglе. / Not a single word is to be changed. 'Yíge dzèr yĕ bùnéng 'găi.

(Meaning prase or short fragment of speech) yíjyù hwà; sometimes yíge dzèr. / There's not a word of truth in what he says. Tā 'shwō de yíjyù shr̄'hwà yĕ méi-'yǒu. or Tā 'shwō de yíge 'dzèr yĕ bùnéng 'syìn. / He said a few words to the police before he left. Tā gēn jĭng'chá °shwōle jijyù 'hwà (°'dàudaule jijyù) tsái 'dzǒude. / I didn't say a word. Wǒ 'yíjyù hwà yĕ °méi'shwō (°méi'tí). or expressed as I didn't make a sound. Wǒ 'yìshēngr yĕ mei'yányu. / May I have a word with you? Wǒ yǒu jyù 'hwà yàu gēn ni °'títi (°'shwōshwo, °'jyăngjyang, °'shāng-lyangshānglyang, °'tántan).

(Meaning message or speech) hwà, hwàr. / Did he leave any word? Tā 'lyóu-(sya) 'hwàr le ma? / He left word that you're to call him. Tā 'lyóule ge 'hwàr, chǐng nín gĕi ta dă dyàn'hwà, dădau 'dūng jyú 'sān'yǐ'lyòu'jyòu. / You should have left word with their maid. Nǐ gāi gēn tāmen lău'măr lyóu ge 'hwàr. / I'll take your word for it then. Wǒ 'syìn nǐde 'hwà, jyou shr̀ le. / Don't take my word for it; I'm not sure about it myself. °'Wǒde hwà (°'Wǒ shwō de) 'bújyànde jyou 'dwèi; wǒ dz̀'jí yĕ 'búshr̀ 'jwǔn jr̄dau shr̀ 'dzĕmma hwéi 'shr̀.

(Message other than oral; letter) syìn, syèr; (orders) 'mìnglìng. / Have you had any word from your son lately? 'Jìnlai lìng'láng °yǒu 'syìn lái ma (°syĕ 'syìn láile ma)? / The word was given that we would attack at dawn. Yǒu 'mìnglìng shwō yìchǐng 'dzăur jìn'gūng. or °Mìngling 'syàlaile (°'Yǐjing 'fēngdau 'mìnglìng), shwō shr̀ yìchǐng'dzăur jìn'gūng.

Beyond words. / She's beautiful beyond words. Tā shr °'syíngrungbuchu'láide (°'shwōbuchu'láide) 'mĕi. or Tā hău'kànde méi 'fádz 'syíngrúng.

Eat one's words búswànle, búswànhwà, búrènjàng. / He ate his words. Tā búrèn'jàng le. or Tā shwō 'hwà búswàn'hwà.

Give one's word dāying, shwō; (very serious) chǐshr̀. / He gave his word that he would finish the job. Tā °'dāyingle (°'shwōle, °'shwō de shr̀) yí'dìng bă jèi shèr bàn'wánle. / I give you my word (of honor) that this is absolutely true. 'Jèi shr̀ 'chyānjēnwàn'chywède; wó găn gēn ni chǐ'shr̀.

Hard words. / When she spoke, she used hard words. (meaning harsh) Tā 'shwōle sye nán'tīngde hwà. or (meaning difficult to understand) Tā shwō de 'hwà nán'dǔng.

In a word jyăndwànjye'shwō, 'yíjyù 'hwà, 'jrjyēlyău'dàngde shwō ba. / In a word, no! 'Jyăndwànjyé'shwō, (jyoushr) bù'syíng! or 'Yíjyù 'hwà, bù'syíng! or 'Jrjyēlyău'dàngde shwō ba, bù'syíng!

In so many words yĕ 'méishwō 'fēihwà, yì'jrde jyòu, 'yìdyăr méirau'wārde, 'tùngtungkwār'kwàrde. / I told him in so many words what I thought of him. Wǒ yì-dyăr méirau'wārde °'màle (°'shwōle) ta yí'dwùn. or Wó °yĕ 'méishwō 'fēihwà (°yǐ'jrde jyòu °etc.) 'màle ta yí'dwùn.

Have the last word. /She always has to have the last word in an argument. Tā gēn rén °'byàn (°'jēnglwùn), 'fēi °shwō'yíngle (°bǎ rén 'shwōde méi 'hwà le) bù-'jř.

Put in a good word. /Will you put in a good word for me with the old man? (not very serious) Láu'jyà dzài lǎu'tóur nèr géi wo °'shwō jyù hǎu'hwà ba (°'chwēisyu-chwēisyu ba). or (pleading) Chyóuni dzài lǎu'tóur nèr géi wo 'shwō jyù hǎu'hwà ba.

To word tswòtsź, syě, shwō. /How do you want to word this telegram? Jèi-fēng dyàn'bàu dzěmma °'tswò'tsź ne (°'syě ne)? /I think it'd be better if you worded it this way. Wǒ 'jywéje háishr 'dzěmmaje °syě (°shwō, °tswò'tsź) 'hǎu dyǎr.

WORK. (Of physical labor) dzwò gūng; (general or of brain work) dzwò shř, dzwò shèr, bàn gūng; (of a carpenter, barber, or tailor, especially of a woman tailor) dzwò hwó(r); work at hard labor dzwò kǔlì, dzwò 'lìchi hwór, mài lìchi, dzwò 'lèi hwór. /They work forty hours a week at the mill. Tāmen dzài gūng'chángli yìsyīng-'chī dzwò 'sźshrdyǎn'jūng de 'gūng. /He goes out and works all day and comes back at night dead tired. Tā yì'jěngtyār 'chūchyu °bàn 'gūng (°dzwò 'gūng, °dzwò 'shèr), 'yèli hwéi 'jyā de shřhou 'lèide yàu'mìng. /He works every other day. Tā 'gé yìtyān dzwò yìtyān °'gūng (°'shèr). /I'm not working this summer. 'Jīnnyán 'syà-tyan wǒ búdzwò 'shř.

(Be usable, not be out of order) syíng, búhwài, dzǒu, chéng, yǒuyùng, kéyi, gwǎnshř, bàndetūng, 'syíngdechūchyù. /The elevator isn't working. Dyàn'tī °bù-'syíng le (°'hwài le, °bù'dzǒu le). /Do you think that plan might work? Nǐ syǎng nèige 'jìhwà °'syíng ma (°'chéng ma, °yǒu'yùng ma, °'kéyi ma, °bànde'tūng ma, °'syíngdechū'chyù ma)? /How do you think this idea might work out? Nǐ 'jywéde jèige 'bànfa °'syíng ma (°'syíng busyíng)?

Work a typewriter or other apparatus yùng. /Do you know how to work a type-writer? Nǐ hwéi yùng dǎdz'jī ma?

Work a region (as a salesman) dzài . . . mài. /The other salesman has worked this region pretty thoroughly. 'Nèiyíge twēisyàu'ywán yǐjing dzài 'jèiyídài 'dìfang 'màide hěn 'dwō le.

Work someone yùng. /He works his employees very hard. Tā yùng 'rén yùngde hén °kǔ (°'kè).

Work oneself. /She's working herself to death. Tā °dzwò 'shř dzwòde (°'tsǎu-láude, °'tsǎulau 'shèr) tài 'dwō, kwài bǎ tā dz'jǐ 'lèiszle.

Work oneself into a mood. /He worked himself into an angry mood. Tā dž'gěr ywè °'syǎng (°'dzwómen, °'dzāmen) ywè shēng'chì.

Work something into place, loose, etc. nwó, twēi, bān. /They finally worked the box into place. Tāmen dàu'lyǎur bǎ nèige 'syāngdz °'nwódau (°'twēidau, °'bān-dau) nèr chyù le.

Work hard at something yùng gūngfu, syà gūngfu. /He really worked hard at your portrait. Tā dzài 'nǐ nèijāng 'syàngshang jēn °'yùngle (°'syàle) dyǎr 'gūngfu.

Work loose sūng. /A screw worked loose. Yǒu yíge 'lwódz sūngle.

Work something into a context yǐndau, jyādau. /Can you work this quotation into your speech? Nǐ néng bǎ nèijyù 'hwà °'yǐndau (°'jyādau) nǐde jyáng'yǎnli ma?

Work on a book syě. /He's working on a new book. Tā 'jèngdzai syě yìběr syīn 'shu.

Work on someone (try to persuade) syǎng'fár (gēn . . . shwō) ràng. /We're working on him to give us the day off. Wǒmen jèng syǎng'fár (gēn ta shwō) ràng ta 'fàng wǒmen yìtyān 'jyà.

Work on <u>something</u> (repair) syŏuli, shŕdou, shōushr, nùng. / The mechanic's at work on your car now. Syàn'dzài nèige jĭchi'jyàng jèng °'syŏuli (°etc.) nĭde 'chē ne.

Work out <u>a plan</u> dzwò. / The captain is working out a plan of attack. Lyán'jăng jèngdzai dzwò jĭn'gūngde 'jìhwà.

Work out a solution jyĕjywé, 'nùngchu ge 'jyĕgwŏ lai. / It took us a long time to work out a solution to the problem. Wŏmen yùngle hĕn 'dwō de 'shŕjyān tsái bă nèige 'wèntí °'jyĕ'jywé le (°'nùngchu ge 'jyĕgwŏ lai).

Work over <u>someone</u> jyòu; (local Peiping) jywēba. / The lifeguard worked over him for an hour before he could revive him. Jyòuhù'ywán °'jywēbale (°jyòule) ta yŏu yíge jūng'tóu, tā tsái 'hwăngwolai.

Work <u>something</u> over (rework). / He worked his paper over half a dozen times before he was satisfied with it. Tāde 'jywàndz dzwòle yŏu 'lyòuchĭ'hwéi tā tsái jywé-je 'syíng le.

Work up an appetite. / I've worked up an awful appetite. Wŏ 'lèile yíjèn, 'ède 'lìhai. / All that exercise made me work up an appetite. Nèijèn 'yùndùng 'nùngde wŏ è'jíle.

Work one's way through a crowd. / We worked our way through the crowd. Wŏ-men hău 'rúngyi tsái tsúng nèichywún 'rénli 'jĭgwolai.

Work one's way through college dz̀'jĭ gūng dz̀'jĭ shàng dà'sywé.

Work <u>something</u> with one's hands yùng 'shŏu nùng; <u>or other verbs indicating specific action, such as</u> chwāi (knead) *or* róu (roll or shape). / Work the dough thoroughly with your hands. Bă 'myàn yùng 'shŏu °nùng'hăule (°chwāi'hăule, °róu-'hăule).

Work (physical labor) gūng, 'gūngdzwò; (general, but especially brain work) shŕ, shèr. / What kind of work do you do? Nĭ syàndzài 'dzwòde shŕ 'shémma °shŕ (°'shŕching)? / He's doing government work. Tā dzài 'jèngfŭjĭ'gwān dzwò 'shŕ.

Work of art. / That's a work of art. (as a simple statement of fact) 'Nàshŕ yíjyàn 'yìshù'pĭn. *or* (as an aesthetic comment, the expression depending on the type of art involved) 'Nèige °'dzwòde (or, of writing or calligraphy, °'syĕde, or, of painting, °'hwàde, or, of carving, °'kède, or, of architecture or handiwork, °'dzàu-de) 'jēn °'mĕi (°hău'kàn, °yŏu'gūngfu).

A nice piece of work. / That bridge is a nice piece of work. Nèige 'chyáu °de 'gūngcheng (°'dzàude, °'syŏude) jēn 'hău.

Be out of work. / He's been out of work since the factory closed. Tsúng nèige gūng'chăng gwān 'mén yĭ'hòu, tā jyou méi °'shŕ le (°dzwò 'shŕ).

Do light work 'chīngsung hwór, dzwò 'chīngsheng hwór.

Take a lot of work fèile hen dwō 'shŕ. / It took a lot of work to convince him that we were right. Hĕn °fèile dyăr 'shŕ (°'fèile dyăr 'jōujé, °'máfanle yí'jèndz) tsái ràng tāmen 'chéngrèn wŏmen 'dwèi le.

WORLD. (The earth) 'shŕjyè; (everything below heaven) 'tyānsyà; (on earth) dìshang; (among men) 'rénjyān; (the mortal world) 'rénshŕ; (mankind) 'rénlèi; **the whole world** 'chywánshŕjyè, (the whole globe) chywánchyóu, (all mankind) 'shŕjyèshang 'swŏyŏude 'rén, 'rénlèi; **world power** 'chyánggwó, dàchyánggwó; <u>sometimes not ex-pressed in phrases such as</u> **nothing in the world, no one in the world, everyone in the world; World War I** Dì'yítsz̀ 'Shŕjyèdà'jàn; **World War II** Dì'èrtsz̀ 'Shŕjyèdà'jàn. / He's traveled all over the world. Chywánshŕ'jyè tā °'năr dōu 'dàugwo (°dōu dzŏu-'byàn le). *or* Tā 'jōuyóugwo °chywánshŕ'jye (°chywán 'chyóu). / He compiled a chronological chart of world history. Tā byānle yìbĕr 'shŕjyè 'lìshŕ 'dàshŕnyán-

'byǎu. /He's writing a history of the world. Tā jèngdzai syě yìběn 'shřjyè lǐ'shř. /He's been around the world three times. Tā wéije chywán'chyóu dzǒugwō 'sāndzàur. *or* Tā 'sāntsź 'jyōuyóu shř'jyè. /He planned to conquer the world. Tā syǎng 'jēng-fú °'chywán shř'jyè (°tyān'syà). /He's known throughout the world. 'Chywánshřjyè 'dōu jřdàu tā jèige rén. *or* Tā shř 'míngjèn chywán'chyóu. /You can't find another like him in the whole wide world. Syàng 'tā jèiyàngrde rén 'dzǒubyàn 'tyānsyà yě 'jǎubujáu dì'èrge. *or* (with a bad connotation) Tā shř ge 'rénjyānshǎu'yǒu 'dìshangwú-'shwāngde 'bǎubei. /There's not another pearl like this in the whole world. 'Jèige 'jūdz chywánshř'jyè °méiyǒu dì'èrge (°méiyóu bǐde'shàng de, °shř 'dúyí'fèr). /He's a world champion. Tā shř 'tyānsyàwú'dí. /He's the world champion. (in boxing) Tā shř 'shřjyè 'chywánwáng. *or* (in some aspect of track) Tā shř 'shřjyègwàn'jyūn. /The whole world will benefit by this new discovery. 'Jèijǔng 'fāmíng yú °'chywán-shř'jyè (°'shřjyèshang swóyǒude 'rén, °'rénlèi) 'dōu yǒu 'hǎuchù. /All the countries in the world are represented here in New York. Dzài Nyóu'ywē jer 'shřjyè 'gègwóde rén 'dōu yǒu. /He predicted that the end of the world would come in the year 2001 A. D. Tā 'yùyán shwō dzài 'èrchyānlíng'yīnyán shř 'shřjyè mwò'r. /Nothing in the world can compare with this. ('Shřjyèshang) 'dzài yě méiyǒu °'jèmmayàngrde le (*or* (only if it is good) °'jèmma hǎu de le, *or* (only if it is bad) °'jèmma 'bùhǎude le). *or* ('Shřjyèshang) 'shémma yé 'bǐbushàng 'jèige. /No one in the world can do it. (Shřjyèshang) 'shéi yě gànbu'lyǎu. /No one else in the world can do it but you. (Shřjyèshang) chúle 'nǐ 'dzài yě méiyǒu °néng dzwò 'jèige de 'rén le (°'byérén néng dzwò 'jèige de le). /He thinks he's always right and the world is always wrong. Tā jywéje 'shéi dōu bú'dwèi, 'jř yǒu tā dž'gěr 'dwèi. /There's nothing in the world I'd like better. 'Dzài yě méiyóu bǐ 'jèige jyàu wó °'syǐhwān (°ywànyi 'gàn) de le. /You have nothing in the world to worry about. Nǐ yì'dyár yě yùngbujáu °wéi-'nán (°tsǎu'syīn). /What part of the world does this fruit come from? Jèisyē 'shwéi-gwǒ shř °'shémma dìfang 'chūde (°'nǎr láide)?

(Creation of fancy). /He built up a queer sort of world about himself. Tā 'syǐng-ching °'gǔgwài (°'gwàipì). *or* (of insanity) Tā 'fēngfengdyān'dyānde. *or* Tā shř ge 'mwójeng. /He lives in a little world of his own. Tā hěn 'gūpì. *or* Tā 'dzwò-jǐnggwān'tyān. *or* Tā 'gūlòugwǎ'wén. *or* Tā gēn rén 'méi shémma 'láiwǎng.

Do one a world of good. /It'll do him a world of good to get away from home. Tā yàushr 'líkāi jyā °dwèiyu tā °'shřdzài yǒu shwōbu'jǐnde (°'tíng yóu) 'hǎuchù.

In the world after questions words is expressed with 'jèi shř, 'nà shř, 'jèi swàn, 'nà swàn after the subject. /What in the world does he mean? Tā nà shř 'shwōde 'shémma a? *or* Tā 'shwōde nà swàn shř 'shémma 'yìsz a? /When in the world did you move out? Nǐ nà swàn 'shémma shřhòu bān'dzǒu de? /Why in the world do you do this? Nǐ jèi swàn tú 'shémma 'syùde? /Where in the world have you been? Nǐ 'nà shř dàu 'nǎr chyu láije? /Where in the world did you find such a queer thing? Nǐ 'jèi shř tsúng 'nǎr °'sywémwolái (°'nénglái) de 'dzèmma gwàide ge 'dūngsyi?

Not for the world, not for all the world, not for anything in the world jywé bu-kěn. /I wouldn't hurt him for all the world. Wǒ 'jywé bu'kěn jyàu tā °'chř'kǔde (°shòu'dzwèide, °'syīnli nán'shòude).

On top of the world. /He's feeling on top of the world because of his new promotion. Tā 'syīnjìn °shēng'gwān le (°'wèijr 'shēngle), swóyi 'měide 'lyǎubudé.

Think the world of. /My father thinks the world of you. is expressed as My father likes you very much. Wǒ 'fùchin 'shřfen 'syǐhwan nǐ. (*See also* **VERY, LIKE, RESPECT,** etc.)

The world to come. /He worried himself to death thinking about the world to come. Tā 'jǐng chóu sž'hòu dzěmma'yàng, gěi 'chóuszle.

The animal world 'swóyǒude 'dùngwù. /He studied all about the animal world. 'Swóyǒude 'dùngwù tā 'dōu yánjyougwo.

The New World is expressed as the New Continent Syīndàlù. /"The New World" means North and South America. Syīndà'lù shr̀ jř̌je 'Nán'béi'měijōu shwōde.

The scholastic world 'sywéshù'jyè. /He's well known in the scholastic world. Tā dzài 'sywéshùjyè 'tǐng yǒu 'míngchi.

The Western world 'Syīfāng (gègwó). /The whole Western world was shocked. 'Syīfāng 'gègwó chywán dōu dà'jīng.

WORRY. (Fret) jāují, 'gùlyù. /They worry a lot about their children. Tāmen wèi tāmende 'háidz hěn jāu'jí. /What are you worrying about? Nǐ jāu shémma 'jí? /We were worried when you didn't get here on time. Nǐ méian 'shŕhou lái, ràng wǒmen 'jāule yíjèn jí. /You worry too much. Nǐ 'gùlyùde tài gwò'fèn le.

Worry (anxiety) 'wèntí, fánshèr; or expressed verbally as above. /You have too many worries. Nǐde °'wèntí (°'fánshèr) tài 'dwō le. /Most of his worries are about money. Tā °jāu'jí (°'gùlyù) de dwō'bàr dōu shr̀ 'chyán.

WORSE. bǐ . . . (hái) °hwài (°bùhǎu); (more violent) bǐ . . . (hái) 'lìhai; **get worse** or **worse and worse** ywè 'lái ywè 'hwài. /The patient felt worse this morning than he did last night. Jèige 'bìngrén jyēr 'dzǎuchen bǐ dzwór 'wǎnshang hái bù'hǎu. /The road got worse as we went along. Wǒmen 'dzǒu de nèige 'lù ywè 'lái ywè 'hwài le. /Her condition got worse and worse. Tāde 'chíngsying ywè 'lái ywè 'hwài. /It's snowing worse than ever. 'Sywě 'syàde bí yǐ'chyán gèng 'lìhai le.

Not any (or None) the worse. /They don't seem any the worse for having been caught in the storm. is expressed as They were caught in the storm for a spell, but it's of no consequence. Tāmen ràng nèige dà'fēngdà'yǔ 'lwúnle yíjèn, 'bìng méi dzěmma'yàng.

WORST. dzwèi hwài, dzwèi lìhai, dzwèi followed by some other appropriate stative verb meaning bad or serious. /That was the worst accident in the city's history. 'Nèihwèi chū de 'shr̀, shr̀ jèige 'chéng yóu'shŕyǐ'lái dzwèi 'lìhai de yítsz̀. /But wait; I haven't told you the worst! 'Hái yǒu ne; dzwèi dzǎugāude nèi'dyár wǒ hái méi'gàusu ni ne. /The worst of it is that they aren't insured. Dzwèi dzǎu'gāude shr̀ tāmen méibáu'syǎn. /He felt worst about leaving his children. Tā yǐwei 'dzwèi nánshòude shr̀ jyòushr líkai tāde háidz.

At (the) worst nùngbù'hǎu dehwà. /At worst, the storm may last a week. Nùng-bù'hǎu dehwà, jèige bàufēng'yǔ jyòusyǔ néng 'gàn yíge syīng'chī.

If worst comes to worst jyòu swàn 'hwàidau °'jyā (°'tóur, °'jídyǎn, °bù'kěkāi-'jyāu). /If worst comes to worst, we can always sell our property. Jyòu swàn 'hwài dau'jyā, wǒmen 'hái néng byàn'mài wǒmende chǎn'yè ne.

Think (or Believe) the worst of syǎng . . . de 'hwàichù. /He always thinks the worst of everybody. Tā 'láu syǎng 'rénjyàde 'hwàichù.

WORTH. (Of a commodity) jŕ. /That horse is worth five hundred dollars. Nèipǐ 'mǎ jŕ 'wúbǎi kwài chyán. /Will the result be worth all this trouble? 'Jŕde jèmma 'má-fan ma?

(Of a person) chèn. /He's worth a cool million. Tā 'chèn yìbǎi'wàn.

Worth (value) jyàjr. /It is showy but without real worth. Nèige hěn hǎu'kàn kěshr méiyǒu jēn 'jyàjr.

So much money's worth of something de. /Give me a dollar's worth of sugar. Géi wo lái yíkwài 'chyánde 'táng.

Get one's money's worth gòuběr le. /We certainly got our money's worth out of our car. Wǒmen jèilyàng 'chē kě 'jēn gòu'běr le.

Other English expressions. / He was never aware of his secretary's real worth. Tā tsúng'lái jyou méi' jywéchulai tāde 'shūjî shr̀ 'dwōma nán'déde. / He hung on to the property for all he was worth. Tā ná'jùle nèidyǎr 'chǎnyè, shwō 'shémma yě bùfàng'shǒu.

WORTHY. yǒuyìyi(de). / This money will go for a worthy cause. Jèibǐ 'chyán shr̀ wèi yíge yǒu'yìyìde 'mùdi yùngde. / He leads a worthy life. Tāde 'shēnghwo yǒu'yìyi.

Worthy charities °'jèngdāngde (°'jēn bàn'shr̀ de, °yú 'dìfangshang 'jēn yǒu-'hǎuchude) 'tsź̀shàn'shr̀ye.

Be worthy of jŕde; (of a person) pèi. / This plan isn't worthy of further consideration. Jèige 'bànfa °bù'jŕde (°'jŕbude) dzài 'kǎulyù le. / I don't feel I'm worthy of all that praise. Wǒ 'jywéde wǒ bú'pèi ràng 'rénjyā nèmma 'kwājyǎng.

WOULD. yàu, hwèi, néng; or not expressed. / They hoped their wishes would come true. Tāmen pànwàngje tāmende 'syīwang (néng) shr̀'syàn. / I thought that would happen. Wǒ jywéje nèige 'shèr yàu °'lái le (°fā'shēngle). / He said he'd go if I would. Tā shwōle 'wǒ yàu ywànyi 'chyù 'tā yě 'chyù. / She just wouldn't be comforted. Dzěmma 'ānwei ta, tā yě bù'tīng.

(In expressing what might be expected) ywànyi, or a resultative compound in the potential form. / He wouldn't take the job for any amount of money. Gěi ta 'dwōshau chyán tā 'yě bú'ywànyi dzwò nèige 'shr̀. / Do you think this bridge would carry a two-ton truck? Nǐ syǎng jèige 'chyáu 'jĭndejù 'lyǎngdwūnde kǎ'chē ma?

(Past habitual action) is expressed adverbially as 'chángcháng often, lǎu(shr) always or tsúnglái customarily in the past. / He would study for hours without stopping. Tā 'lǎushr yí'chyèr nyàn jidyǎn 'jūngde 'shū, 'yìhwer yě bù'syē.

Would like to syǎng, (syǎng) yàu. / He'd like to have us consider him a friend. Tā 'syǎng gēn wǒmen lěi'wǎng. / What would you like to drink? Nǐ yàu 'hē 'shémma?

Would you please is expressed as a declarative request by chǐng nín. / Would you please give me a cup of tea? Chǐng nín gěi wo yiwǎn 'chá °ba (°hǎu buhǎu)?

WOUND. shāng, but the use of this word alone as a verb is limited; more commonly expressed by resultative compounds with such words as nùng make become, shōu receive, or as dǎ hit, etc. describing the action, as first elements and shāng be wounded as the second element. / How many were wounded? Shāngle 'jǐge rén? / She was wounded herself. Tā bǎ ta dž'jǐ nùng'shāngle. / He was wounded by a gunshot. Tā ràng chyāng'dzér dǎ'shāngle. / Several men were wounded in the explosion. Nèitsz bàu'jà yǒu 'háujige rén shòu'shāng le.

Be (or Feel) wounded (emotionally) shāngsyīn. / She was wounded by his indifference. Nèige 'nánde dwèiyu ta nèmma 'lěngdàn, ràng ta hěn shāng'syīn.

A wound shāng; mortal wound (lit. or fig.) jr̀mìngshāng. / It'll be a couple of months before the wound in his leg will heal. Tā 'twěishangde nèikwài 'shāng hái déi 'lyǎywè tsái néng 'hǎu ne. / To others it was nothing; to him it was a mortal wound. Dzài 'byéren shēngshang bu'swàn shemma, dwèi 'tā, nà shr̀ ge jr̀mìng-'shāng.

WRITE (WROTE, WRITTEN). syě, syě dž. / The children are learning how to read and write. 'Háidzmen jèng sywé nyàn 'shū syě 'dž ne. / He promised to write (a letter) once a week while he was away. Tā 'dāying wo tā 'dzǒule yǐ'hòu yíge syīng'chī 'syě yìfēng 'syìn lai. / Have you written your family a letter yet? Nǐ yǐjing gěi nǐ 'jyāli syě 'syìn le ma? / He wrote an account of the fire for the local paper. Tā bǎ nèige hwó'jǐng gěi běn'dìde bàu'jŕ 'syěle yídwàr 'syāusyi。 / This pen doesn't write well. Jèigwán 'bǐ bùháu °'syě (°'shr̀, °'yùng).

(When filling in a form of some kind) syĕ, tyán. /Write your name in the space at the bottom of the page. Bá nĭde 'míngdz °syĕdzai (°tyándzai) jèi'yè dĭsya de 'kùngr nèr.

(As a career) syĕdzwò. /When she got through college, she planned to write for a career. Tā 'dăswàn nyàn'wán dà'sywé yĭ'hòu jyou ná syĕ'dzwò dàng tāde 'shr̀yè le.

Write a book syĕ shū, dzwò shū. /He wrote a book about his experiences in the army. Tā bă tā dzài jyūn'dwèi de 'jīngyàn °'syĕle (°'dzwòle) yìbĕr 'shū. /Who wrote that book you're reading? Nĭ 'nyàn de nèibĕr 'shū shr̀ 'shéi °'syĕde (°'dzwò-de)?

Write a check or receipt kāi, kāichulai. /Please write out that check for me before I go. Láu'jyà, dzài wó 'dzŏu yĭ'chyán, bă nèige jr̆'pyàu géi wo 'kāichulai, 'hău ba? /He hadn't written out a receipt yet. Shōu'tyáur tā hái méi'kāichulai ne.

Write something down syĕsyalai, jĭsyalai. /Write down that telephone number before you forget it. Bă nèige 'dyànhwà hàu'măr °'syĕsyalai (°'jĭsyalia), byé hwéi-'tóu 'wàng le.

Write something in syĕshang, tyánjinchyu. /My candidate wasn't on the ballot, so I had to write in his name. Wŏ yàu 'sywăn de nèige 'rén 'pyàushang méi'yŏu, swóyi wŏ déi bă tāde 'míngdz °'tyánjinchyu (°'syĕshang).

Write something off gōu. /When the company failed, we had to write off its debts. Nèige 'măimai 'gwānle de shr̀hour, wŏmen bù'débù bă tāde 'jàng (géi) 'gōule.

Be written on (or over) (fig.) kàndechulai. /Honesty is written on his face. Tsúng ta 'lyăn shang jyou kàndechu'lái ta hĕn 'chéngshr̀.

WRONG. tswò. /Did I say the wrong thing? Wŏ shwō'tswòle ma? /I got lost because I took the wrong road. Wó dzŏu'dyŏule, yīnwei wó dzŏu'tswòle 'dàur le. /These figures are wrong. Jèisyē 'shùr 'tswòle. /Was I wrong to wait so long? Wó 'dĕngle dzĕmma 'jyŏu, dĕng'tswòle ma?

Be (or Go) wrong with (mechanically) °yŏu (°chū) 'máubing. /Something is wrong with the telephone. Dyàn'hwà yóu dyăr 'máubing. /Something went wrong with the plane, so the pilot decided to land. Fēi'jī chūle dyăr 'máubing, swóyi nèige fēijī'shr̀ jyòu jywé'dìng làusyalaile.

Be in the wrong tswò. /He admitted he was in the wrong, and paid the fine. Tā chéng'rèn tā 'tswòle, bìngchyĕ 'jyāule fá'jīn le.

To wrong ywānwang. /You wronged me. Nĭ 'ywānwang wŏ le.

Be wronged shòuchyū, shòu wĕichyu, ywān. /They feel that they've been wronged. Tāmen 'jywéde tāmen shòule °'chyū le (°'wĕichyu le). or Tāmen 'jywé-de tamen hĕn 'ywān.

YARD. (Measure of length) mă. /How much is this material a yard? Jèige 'lyàudz 'dwōshau chyán yì'mă?

(Ground around a house) in China such open space is normally enclosed by the house, and is called a court or courtyard ywàndz; sometimes called empty land kūng-dì. /Does this place have a yard for the children to play in? Jèige 'dìfang 'yŏu méi-you yíkwài kūng'dì kéyi ràng hăidzmen 'wárwar?

Lumber yard mùchăngdz.

Railroad yards hwŏchētíngchē'chăng; (specifically for repair) syōuchēchăng.

YEAR. (Of time) nyán; **this year** 'jīnnyán; **last year** 'chyùnyán; **next year** 'míngnyán (sometimes gwònyan); **leap year** rwùnnyán. /What was the year of your birth? Nǐ shř 'něinyán 'shēngde? /I hope to come back next year. Wǒ 'syīwang 'míngnyán hwéilai. /I haven't done this for years. Wǒ 'yóu °jinyán (°'háujinyán, °hǎu'syēnyán) méi 'gàn jèige le. /It will take years to finish this work. Bǎ jèige 'shř̌ching dzwò-'wánle, hái děi 'háujinyán. /This year is a leap year. 'Jīnnyan 'rwùnnyán.

(Of age) swèi. /He's thirty years old. Tā 'sānshrswèi.

Year in and year out 'háujinyán, yǐnyányǐ'nyánde 'háujinyán. /He's been at this job year in and year out. Tā dzwò nèige 'shř̌ching yǐnyányǐ'nyánde 'háujinyán le.

Show one's years jyànlǎu. /She's beginning to show her years. Tā jyàn'lǎu le.

School year sywényán. /How long is the school year here? 'Jèr yǐ'sywényán yǒu dwō'cháng?

Yearbook nyánjyàn.

YELLOW. hwáng, 'hwángsè, 'hwángshǎr, hwángyánsher. /Fill in the background with yellow. Bǎ 'dyèr túchéng 'hwángde. /She's wearing a bright yellow dress. Tā chwānle yíjyàn 'érwángde 'yīshang.

Have a yellow streak dǎrsyǎu. /He seems to have a yellow streak. Tā hǎu-'syàng tyān'shēngde dǎr 'syǎu.

To yellow byànhwáng. /Her wedding dress has yellowed with age. Tāde jyē-'hwūn lǐ'fú 'nyántóur 'dwōle dōu byàn 'hwáng le.

Yellow (part of an egg) jīdànhwángr, dànhwángr. /Separate the yellow from the white. Bǎ jīdànde 'hwángr gēn 'chǐngr 'fēnkai. *or* Bǎ jīdàn'hwángr gēn jīdàn-'chǐngr 'fēnkai.

YES. The affirmative answer to a question is given by repeating the verb of the question in the affirmative (simple) form; this may be reinforced with it is so dwèile *or* shř̌. /Yes, I'll be glad to go. 'Shř̌, wǒ 'ywànyi chyù. /Were you born here? Yes. Nǐ shř̌ 'jèr 'shēngde ma? Shř̌. *or* Dwèile.

To yes. /I'm disgusted with the way he always yesses his boss. Wó tǎu'yàn tā nàyàngr lǎu gēn tāde 'tóur shwō 'shř̌. or expressed as I'm disgusted with the way he always agrees with what his boss says. Wǒ tǎu'yàn ta 'nàyangr lǎushř̌ 'tóur shwō shémma 'shř̌ shémma.

YESTERDAY. dzwótyan, dzwór, dzwórge; **day before yesterday** chyántyan, chyár, chyárge. /I just arrived yesterday. Wǒ 'dzwór tsái 'dàu.

YET. (Up to now, thus far) dàu syàn'dzài (wéi'jř̌) . . . hái . . . . /This is the largest diamond found yet. Dàu syàn'dzài (wéi'jř̌), yǐjing fā'syàn de dzwàn'shř̌, háishr 'jèige dzwèi 'dà.

(Still, even now) hái, réngrán, réngjyòu; dzáuwǎn (sooner or later). /We may be successful yet. Wǒmen °hái (°réngrán, °réngjyòu) ké'néng chéng'gūng. /I'll get him yet. Wǒ dzǎu'wǎn yàu 'gěi ta yisyàdz.

(Further, in addition) yòu, dzài, gèng. /He hopes to work for yet another year. Tā 'syīwàng 'dzài dzwò yi nyán.

(Nevertheless) ránér, 'dàushř̌, 'kěshř̌. /He is old yet active. Tā nyánji hěn 'dà le, °rán'ér (°'dàushř̌) hěn 'hwópwo. /I have come as a friend, yet you treat me as a stranger. Wǒ yǐ 'péngyǒude dìwèi 'dài nǐ, °kěshr (°rán'ér) nǐ 'ná wǒ dàng 'wàiren.

And yet kěshr. / And yet you promised to help me! Nǐ kěshr 'dāyinggwo wǒ 'bāng wo 'máng a!

Not yet hái °bu- (°méi-). / He hasn't come in yet. Tā hái méi'lái ne. / He's not dead yet. Tā hái méi'sž ne.

Not just yet jànshr °bu- (°byé), syān °bu- (°byé). / It won't happen just yet. Jàn'shr búhwèi fā'shěng. / Don't go just yet. Syān byé 'dzǒu ne.

YOU (YOUR, YOURS). (One person) nǐ, (polite) nín; (several people) nǐmen, often omitted and understood from context; your or yours nǐde, nínde (one person), nǐmende (several people) (de is sometimes dropped before nouns). / What do you want? (Nǐ) yàu 'shémma? or (Nǐmen) yàu 'shémma? / This is for you. 'Jèige shr gěi °'nǐ de (°'nǐmen de). / I'll help you one after another. Wǒ 'yígeryí'gèrde 'bāngje nǐmen. / All you people with tickets, this way! Nǐmen 'gèwèi yǒu 'pyàu de, 'jèr lái! / Is this your seat? Jèige shr °'nǐde (°nínde) 'dzwòr ma? / All of you hold on to your tickets! Nǐmen 'gèwèi dōu bǎ 'pyàu 'lyóuje! / This hat is yours. 'Jèige màudz shr °'nǐde (°'nínde). / Yours is prettier than hers. 'Nǐde bǐ 'tāde hǎu'kàn.

(Meaning some indefinite person) is usually not expressed; sometimes rén, occasionally nǐ. / To get there, you take a bus and then the ferry. Shàng nèr 'chyù, syān dzwò gūnggùngchì'chē, rán'hòu dzài dzwò lwún'dù. / It makes you sick to hear about it. 'Tīng nèige ràngrén 'nìdeheng.

Yourself, yourselves see SELF.

YOUNG. nyánchīng, syǎu. / I never worked very hard in my younger days. Wǒ nyán-'chīngde (°'syǎude) shŕhou 'méidzěmme tài nǔ'lì. / I'm not as young as I used to be. Wǒ 'búshr yǐ'chyán nèmma nyán'chīng le. / You're very young for your age. Nǐ 'kànje hěn °syǎu (°nyán'chīng).

(Immature animals) dzǎidz, dzǎr; syǎu followed by the word for the adult animal. / The cat fought to protect her young. Nèige mǔ'māu wèi 'hùje °'dzǎidz (°syǎu-'māu) dǎ'jyà.

(Not far advanced) dzǎu. / The night is still young. is expressed as The day is still early. 'Tyān hái 'dzǎu ne. or as It's still early. Hái 'dzǎuje ne.

YOUR, YOURS. See YOU.

YOUTH. (A young person) 'chīngnyán(rén), nyánchīngrén, nyánchīngde. / He has all the enthusiasm of a youth. Tā chūng'mǎnle chīng'nyánde 'rèchíng. / He is but a youth. Tā bú'gwò shr ge 'chīngnyánrén.

(Time of being young) 'chīngnyánde shŕhou. / His father tried to convince him that youth is the best time of life. Tā 'fùchin gěi ta 'jyǎng, ràng ta 'míngbai 'chīng-nyánde shŕhou shr rén'shēng dzwèi 'hǎude shŕhour.

ZERO. (The written figure) líng, língdž; (if written with the arabic numeral instead of with the Chinese character) chywār. / You should have three zeros in the answer. Nǐ nèige 'dáshùr děi yǒu 'sānge °'líng (°'chywār) tsái 'dwèi ne.

(Point on a scale) língdù; **above zero** língshàng, or unexpressed; **below zero** língsyà. / The thermometer reads five above zero. Nèige hánshǔ'byǎu shr °'wǔdù (°'líng'shàng 'wǔdù). / Does the temperature ever get below zero here? 'Jèr wēn'dù 'dàugwo líng'syà ma?

Visibility zero. / The pilot reported visibility zero. is expressed as The pilot reported that nothing could be seen. Nèige jyàshr'ywán bàu'gàn shwō 'shémma yě kànbu'jyàn.

Weights and Measures

I. English System

    A. Linear Measure

English		Chinese	Metric	Intra-system
inch	吋	tswùn	2.54 cm.	———
foot	呎	chř	0.35 m.	12 inches
yard	碼	mǎ	0.915 m.	3 feet
rod	桿	gǎn	5.04 m.	5.5 yards
mile	哩	lǐ	1.609 km.	1760 yards

    B. Square Measure

In order to convert linear measure to square measure, follow the appropriate mathematical procedures, and prefix the term 平方 píngfāng (or simply 方 fāng) to the corresponding Chinese linear measure term. For instance, one 吋 tswùn (one inch or 2.54 cm.) would become one 平方吋 píngfāngtswùn (or 方吋 fāngtswùn), equivalent to one square inch or 6.45 sq. cm. In addition to those terms which may readily be converted from linear to square measure, there is the following term of area measure which has no linear correspondent and does not take any prefix in Chinese:

English		Chinese	Metric	Intra-system
acre	畝	mǔ	40.469 ares	160 sq. rods

    C. Cubic Measure

In order to convert linear measure to cubic measure, follow the appropriate mathematical procedures, and prefix the term 立方 lìfāng to the corresponding Chinese linear measure term. For instance, one 吋 tswùn (one inch or 2.54 cm.) would become one 立方吋 lìfāngtswùn (one cubic inch or 16.39 cu. cm.)

    D. Capacity

Chinese terms for English measures of capacity are merely transliterations of English terms (for instance, English "pint" = Chinese 品脫 pǐntwō), and the English system of capacity measure is not commonly used in Chinese areas. For these reasons, it would seem of little value to show equivalencies of this type here. The reader is advised to study the capacity measure tables under the Chinese and Metric systems (see below) to learn the measures of this type commonly used by the Chinese.

    E. Weight

English		Chinese	Metric	Intra-system
grain	喱	lí	0.065 gm.	———
dram	特拉姆	tèlāmǔ	1.778 gm.	27.34 grains
ounce	唡	lyǎng	28.4 gm.	16 drams
pound	磅	bàng	453.59 gm.	16 ounces

Weights and Measures

English		Chinese	Metric	Intra-system
stone	呫	shŕ	6.35 kg.	14 pounds
hundredweight	担	dǎn	45.36 kg.	100 pounds
ton	嗊	dwùn	907.18 kg.	2000 pounds

II. Chinese System

A. Linear Measure

Chinese		English	Metric	Intra-system
分	fēn	0.131 in.	3.3 mm.	———
寸	tswun	0.109 ft.	3.3 cm.	10 分 fēn
尺	chŕ	1.094 ft.	3.3 dm.	10 寸 tswùn
丈	jàng	10.94 ft.	3.3 m.	10 尺 chŕ
里	lǐ	0.33 mi.	0.5 km.	150 丈 jàng

B. Square Measure

In order to convert linear measure to square measure, follow the appropriate mathematical procedures, and prefix the term 平方 píngfāng (or simply 方 fāng) to the corresponding Chinese linear measure term. For instance, one 寸 tswùn (0.109 ft. or 3.3 cm.) would become one 平方寸 píngfāngtswùn (or 方寸 fāngtswùn), equivalent to 0.012 sq. ft. or 10.89 sq. cm. In addition to those terms which may readily be converted from linear to square measure, there are the following terms of area measure which have no linear correspondents and do not take any prefix in Chinese:

Chinese		English	Metric	Intra-system
毫	háu	.73 sq. yd.	.614 sq. m.	———
厘	lǐ	7.34 sq. yd.	6.1 sq. m.	10 毫 háu
分	fēn	74.43 sq. yd.	.6144 are	10 厘 lǐ
畝	mǔ	.1647 acre	6.144 ares	10 分 fēn
頃	chǐng	16.47 acres	6.14 hectares	100 畝 mǔ

C. Cubic Measure

In order to convert linear measure to cubic measure, follow the appropriate mathematical procedures, and prefix the term 立方 lìfāng to the corresponding Chinese linear measure term. For instance, one 寸 tswùn (0.109 ft. or 3.3 cm.) would become one 立方寸 lìfāngtswùn (.001 cu. ft. or 35.937 cu. cm.).

D. Capacity

Chinese		English	Metric	Intra-system
撮	tswò	.002 pint	1 ml.	———
勺	sháo	.02 pint	1 cl.	10 撮 tswò
合	hé	.182 pint	1 dl.	10 勺 sháo
升	shēng	.908 quart	1 l.	10 合 hé
斗	dǒu	1.14 pecks	1 dkl.	10 升 shēng
石	shŕ	2.85 bushels	1 hl.	10 斗 dǒu

E. Weight

Chinese		English	Metric	Intra-system
分	fēn	.011 oz.	3.125 dg.	———
錢	chyán	.11 oz.	3.125 g.	10 分 fēn
兩	lyǎng	1.1 oz.	31.25 g.	10 錢 chyán
斤	jīn	1.102 lb.	.5 kg.	16 兩 lyǎng
担	dǎn	110.23 lb.	5 myg.	100 斤 jīn

III. Metric System

A. Linear Measure

Metric		Chinese	English	Intra-system
millimeter	公厘	gūnglí	.039 in.	———
centimeter	公分	gūngfēn	.394 in.	10 mm.
decimeter	公寸	gūngtswùn	3.937 in.	10 cm.
meter	公尺	gūngchř	3.281 ft.	10 dm.
decameter	公丈	gūngjàng	32.81 ft.	10 m.
hectometer	公引	gūngyǐn	328.1 ft.	10 dkm.
kilometer	公里	gūnglǐ	.6214 mi.	10 hm.

B. Square Measure

In order to convert linear measure to square measure, follow the appropriate mathematical procedures, and prefix the term 平方 píngfāng (or simply 方 fāng) to the corresponding Chinese linear measure term. For instance, one 公寸 gūngtswùn (3.937 in. or one decimeter) would become one 平方公寸 píngfānggūngtswùn (or 方公寸 fānggūngtswùn), equivalent to one square decimeter or 15.52 square inches. In addition to those terms which may readily be converted from linear to square measure, there are the following terms of area measure which have no linear correspondent and do not take the prefixes 平方 píngfāng or 方 fāng in Chinese:

Metric		Chinese	English	Intra-system
centiare	公釐	gūnglí	1550 sq. in.	———
are	公畝	gūngmǔ	19.6 sq. yd.	100 centiares
hectare	公頃	gūngchǐng	2.471 acres	100 ares

C. Cubic Measure

In order to convert linear measure to cubic measure, follow the appropriate mathematical procedures, and prefix the term 立方 lìfāng to the corresponding Chinese linear measure term. For instance, one 公寸 gūngtswùn (3.937 in. or one decimeter) would become one 立方公寸 lìfānggūngtswùn (one cubic decimeter or 61.24 cubic inches).

D. Capacity

Metric		Chinese	English	Intra-system
milliliter	公撮	gūngtswò	.27 fl. dram	———

Weights and Measures

Metric		Chinese	English	Intra-system
centiliter	公勺	gūngsháo	.338 fl. oz.	10 ml.
deciliter	公合	gūnghé	6.103 cu. in.	10 cl.
liter	公升	gūngshēng	.908 qt.	10 dl.
decaliter	公斗	gūngdǒu	.284 bu.	10 l.
hectoliter	公石	gūngdàn	2.838 bu.	10 dkl.
kiloliter	公秉	gūngbǐng	35.32 cu. ft.	10 hl.

E. Weight

Metric		Chinese	English	Intra-system
milligram	公絲	gūngsz̄	.015 grain	———
centigram	公毫	gūngháu	.154 grain	10 mg.
decigram	公厘	gūnglí	1.54 grains	10 cg.
gram	公克	gūngkè	15.43 grains	10 dg.
decagram	公錢	gūngchyán	.353 oz.	10 g.
hectogram	公兩	gūnglyǎng	3.527 oz.	10 dkg.
kilogram	公斤	gūngjǐn	2.205 lb.	10 hg.
myriagram	公衡	gūnghéng	22.046 lb.	10 kg.
quintal	公担	gūngdǎn	220.46 lb.	10 myg.
millier	公噸	gūngdwùn	2204.6 lb.	10 q.

Radical Chart

emphasizing the fifty most common forms

1	28 厶	29 又	46 山	66 欠 支	91 片	92 牙	110 矛	111 矢	130 月 肉	154 貝 貝	170 阝 阜	192 邑	193 高
1 一	2 ㄧ	**3**			93 牛 牛		112 石		132 自	133 至	155 赤	156 走	171 隶	172 隹	194 鬼	**11**
3 、	4 丿	30 口	47 巛 川	48 工	49 己	68 斗	69 斤	94 方	70 旡 先	113 ネ 示	114 内	134 臼	135 舌	157	173 隶	195 魚
5 乙	6 亅	口	50	71		136 舛	137 舟	158 身	160 辛	174 青	175 非	196 鳥
2	31 口	巾	51 干	52 幺	72 日	115 禾	138 艮	139 色		
7 二	8 亠		53 士	73 曰	74 月	96 王	116 穴	117 立	140 艸 艹	159	**9**	197 鹵	198 鹿
9 亻 人	32 土 土	广	75 木	玉	**6**	141 虍	143 血	161 車	176 面	177 革	199 麥	200 麻 麻
10 儿	11 入	33 士	34 夂	54 又	55 廾	95 玄 玄	97 瓜	118 竹 竹	142 辰	162 辵 辶 辶	178 韋	179 韭	**12**
12 八	13 冂	35 夊 夊	36 夕	56 弋	57 弓	76 欠	98 瓦	99 甘	144 行	146 西 襾	163 邑 阝	180 音	182 風	201 黃 黃	202 黍
14 冖	15 冫	37	58 彐 彑	59 彡	77 止	78 歹	100 生	101 用	145 衣	164 酉	165 采	181 頁	203 黑	204 黹
16 几	17 凵	大	女	60 彳	79 殳	80 毋	102 田	120 糸 糸	121	166	**8**	183 飛	185 首	205 黽	206 鼎
18 刂 刀	38		4	81 比	82 毛	103	105	缶	**7**	里	184 食 食	207 鼓	208 鼠
19 力	39 子	61 忄	85	104	83 氏	84 气	足	疋	疒	122 冈 网	123 羊	147 見	148 角	167	186 香	**10**	209 鼻	210 齊
20 勹	21 匕	40 宀	62 戈	63 户 戸	86 氵 水	106 白	107 皮	124 羽 羽	125 老 耂	149 言 言	金 金	187	**15**	211 齒
22 匚	23 匚	41 寸	42 小	64 才	火 灬	108 皿	126 而	127 耒	150 谷	151 豆	168 長 镸	**16**
24 十	25 卜	43 尢 尤 允	65 支	67 文	89 爻	90 爿	目 四	128 耳	129 聿	152 豕	153 豸	169 門	188 骨	189 高	212 龍	213 龜
26 卩	27 厂 巴	44 尸	45 屮			131 臣				190 髟	191 鬥	**17**	214 龠

Character Index

The number before the decimal point is the radical number;
the number after the decimal point is the number of strokes.

1	一			**4**	)			**8**	亠
1.0	一	yī		4.2	么	ma		8.4	交	jyāu
1.1	丁	dīng		4.2	久	jyǒu		8.6	京	jīng
1.1	七	chī		4.3	之	jr̄		8.6	享	syǎng
1.2	上	shàng		4.4	乍	jà		8.7	亮	lyàng
1.2	万	wàn		4.4	乏	fá		8.7	变	byàn
1.2	丈	jàng		4.5	乒	pīng		**9**	人 亻
1.2	下	syà		4.7	乖	gwāi		9.0	人	rén
1.2	卫	wèi		4.9	乘	chéng		9.1	亿	yì
1.2	三	sān		**5**	乙			9.2	仆	pú
1.2	与	yǔ		5.1	九	jyǒu		9.2	仍	réng
1.3	丑	chǒu		5.2	飞	fēi		9.2	仇	chóu
1.3	不	bù		5.2	乞	chǐ		9.2	什	shén, shŕ
1.4	世	shr̀		5.2	也	yě		9.2	仓	tsāng
1.4	业	yè		5.7	乳	rǔ		9.2	从	tsúng
1.5	丟	dyōu		5.10	乾	gān		9.2	今	jīn
1.6	两	lyǎng		5.11	乾	gān		9.2	仅	jǐn
1.6	严	yán		5.12	亂	lwàn		9.2	介	jyè
1.7	並	bìng		**6**	]			9.3	仁	sā
1.8	並	bìng		6.1	了	le, lyǎu		9.3	仔	dž, dzǎi
2	|			6.7	事	shr̀		9.3	代	dài
2.2	个	ge, gè		**7**	二			9.3	付	fù
2.3	书	shū		7.0	二	èr		9.3	仟	chyān
2.3	中	jūng, jùng		7.1	亏	kwēi		9.3	仪	yí
2.3	丰	fēng		7.2	云	yún		9.3	他	tā
2.6	串	chwàn		7.2	井	jǐng		9.3	仝	túng
2.8	举	jyǔ		7.2	互	hù		9.3	仗	jàng
2.8	临	lín		7.2	开	kāi		9.3	以	yǐ
3	丶			7.2	五	wǔ		9.3	令	líng, lǐng, lìng
3.2	义	yì		7.3	专	jwān		9.4	任	rén, rèn
3.2	丸	wán		7.3	曲	jī		9.4	企	chǐ
3.3	为	wéi, wèi		7.5	些	syē		9.4	伞	sǎn
3.4	主	jǔ		7.5	况	kwàng		9.4	伕	fū
3.8	為	wéi, wèi						9.4	份	fèn
								9.4	仿	fǎng

9.4	伤	shāng
9.4	优	yōu
9.4	仰	yǎng
9.4	休	syōu
9.4	会	hwěi, hwèi, kwài
9.4	伙	hwǒ
9.4	众	jùng
9.4	价	jyà
9.4	件	jyàn
9.5	你	nǐ
9.5	伴	bàn
9.5	佈	bù
9.5	伯	bwó
9.5	低	dǐ
9.5	但	dàn
9.5	佛	fwó
9.5	来	lái
9.5	作	dzwō, dzwó, dzwò
9.5	位	wèi
9.5	伺	tsż
9.5	体	tǐ
9.5	体	tǐ
9.5	伸	shēn
9.5	似	shr̀, sż
9.5	估	gū
9.5	何	hé
9.5	佔	jàn
9.5	住	jù
9.5	伶	líng
9.6	佩	pèi
9.6	侨	chyáu
9.6	依	yī
9.6	使	shǐ
9.6	供	gūng, gùng
9.6	侄	jŕ
9.6	來	lái
9.6	例	lì
9.7	便	byàn, pyán
9.7	侵	chīn
9.7	侮	wǔ
9.7	保	bǎu
9.7	伏	fú

9.7	俘	fú
9.7	俏	chyàu
9.7	信	syìn
9.7	係	syî
9.7	俗	sú
9.8	們	men
9.8	倍	bèi
9.8	倒	dǎu, dàu
9.8	個	ge, gè
9.8	倣	fǎng
9.8	倘	tǎng
9.8	修	syōu
9.8	倉	tsāng
9.8	候	hòu
9.8	值	jŕ
9.8	俱	jyù
9.8	倆	lyǎ, lyǎng
9.8	借	jyè
9.9	健	jyàn
9.9	偏	pyān
9.9	偶	ǒu
9.9	偺	dzá, dzán
9.9	做	dzwò
9.9	偉	wěi
9.9	停	tíng
9.9	偷	tōu
9.9	假	jyǎ, jyà
9.10	傲	syàu
9.10	傘	sǎn
9.10	傍	bàng, páng
9.11	催	tswēi
9.11	僅	jǐn
9.11	債	jài
9.11	傷	shāng
9.11	傳	chwán
9.11	傾	chǐng
9.11	傻	shǎ
9.12	僱	gù
9.12	像	syàng
9.12	僑	chyáu
9.12	僕	pú
9.13	儀	yí
9.13	億	yì

9.13	儉	jyǎn
9.13	價	jyà
9.13	儍	shǎ
9.13	儆	jǐng
9.13	僵	jyāng
9.14	儘	jǐn
9.15	優	yōu
9.20	儻	tǎng

10		儿
10.2	允	yǔn
10.2	元	ywán
10.3	兄	syūng
10.4	充	chūng
10.4	兇	syūng
10.4	光	gwāng, gwǎng
10.4	先	syān
10.5	兔	tù
10.5	兌	dwèi
10.5	克	kè
10.5	免	myǎn
10.6	兒	er, eŕ, r
10.6	冤	tù
10.8	党	dǎng
10.10	兜	dōu

11		入
11.0	入	rǔ, rù
11.2	内	nèi
11.4	全	chywán
11.6	雨	lyǎng

12		八 八
12.0	八	bā, bá
12.2	公	gūng
12.2	六	lyòu
12.4	共	gùng
12.4	興	syīng, syìng
12.5	兵	bīng
12.6	單	dān
12.6	典	dyǎn
12.6	其	chí

13		冂
13.3	冊	tsè
13.4	再	dzài

25	**卜**	
25.3	占	jān, jàn
25.3	卡	chyǎ, kǎ

26	**卩 巳**	
26.4	印	yìn
26.4	危	wēi
26.5	即	jí
26.6	卸	syè
26.6	卷	jywǎn, jywàn
26.7	卽	jí
26.7	卩	jí

27	**厂**	
27.0	厂	chǎng
27.2	厅	tīng
27.2	历	lì
27.3	厉	lì
27.4	压	yā, yà
27.7	厚	hòu
27.7	厘	lí
27.8	原	ywán
27.9	厢	syāng
27.9	厠	tsè
27.10	厨	chú
27.12	厰	chǎng
27.13	屬	lì

28	**厶**	
28.3	去	chyù
28.5	县	syàn
28.6	叁	sān
28.6	参	shēn, tsān
28.9	參	shēn, tsān

29	**又**	
29.0	又	yòu
29.1	叉	chā, chá, chǎ
29.2	双	shwāng, shwàng
29.2	反	fǎn
29.2	友	yǒu
29.3	及	jí
29.4	发	fā
29.6	取	chyǔ
29.6	叔	shū
29.6	受	shòu

29.11	叠	dyé

30	**口**	
30.0	口	kǒu
30.2	句	jyù
30.2	另	lìng
30.2	可	kě
30.2	叫	jyàu
30.2	司	sz̄
30.2	只	jř, jǐ
30.2	号	háu, hàu
30.2	古	gǔ
30.2	台	tái
30.2	右	yòu
30.2	史	shř
30.2	叶	syé, yè
30.2	叮	dīng
30.2	叼	dyāu
30.3	向	syàng
30.3	吉	jí
30.3	后	hòu
30.3	吓	syà
30.3	吐	tǔ, tù
30.3	吃	chř
30.3	合	gě, hé
30.3	各	gè
30.3	吊	dyàu
30.3	名	míng
30.3	同	túng
30.4	君	jyūn
30.4	吝	lìn
30.4	叫	jyàu
30.4	含	hán, hén
30.4	吞	twūn
30.4	呀	ya
30.4	听	tīng
30.4	吸	syī
30.4	吹	chwēi
30.4	吩	fēn
30.4	否	fǒu
30.4	告	gàu
30.4	吨	dwūn
30.4	启	chǐ
30.4	呈	chéng

30.4	吵	chǎu
30.4	呐	na, ne
30.4	吧	ba
30.5	周	jōu
30.5	咖	kā
30.5	呼	hū
30.5	和	hàn, hé, hè, hwo, hwò
30.5	咕	gū
30.5	味	wèi
30.5	咚	dūng
30.5	命	mìng
30.5	呸	pēi
30.5	呢	ne, ní
30.6	咧	lyē, lyě
30.6	虽	swéi
30.6	咸	syán
30.6	哄	hūng, hǔng
30.6	咳	hài, ké
30.6	哈	hā, hǎ
30.6	哑	yǎ
30.6	咽	yān, yàn, yè
30.6	咬	yǎu
30.6	响	syǎng
30.6	哇	wa, wā
30.6	哆	dwō
30.6	咱	dzá, dzán
30.6	品	pǐn
30.6	哎	āi, ái, ǎi, ài, ēi, ěi
30.7	哭	kū
30.7	哩	lǐ
30.7	哲	jé
30.7	哼	heng, hēng
30.7	员	ywán
30.7	哨	shàu
30.7	哦	é, óu, òu
30.7	哥	gē
30.7	唖	yǎ
30.7	哪	na, nǎ, něi
30.7	唉	āi, ái, ǎi, ài, ēi, ěi
30.8	問	wèn
30.8	啦	la, lā
30.8	啃	kěn

30.8	兽	shòu
30.8	商	shāng
30.8	啞	yǎ
30.8	唷	yōu
30.8	售	shòu
30.8	唯	wéi
30.8	啚	tú
30.8	啐	tswèi
30.8	唾	twò
30.8	啟	chǐ
30.8	啓	chǐ
30.8	啤	pí
30.8	唸	nyàn
30.8	啥	shá
30.8	啊	a, ā, á, ǎ, à
30.9	喇	lá
30.9	哀	āi, ái, ǎi, ài, ēi, ei
30.9	喀	kā
30.9	喉	hóu
30.9	喝	hē, hè
30.9	喊	hǎn
30.9	喂	wèi
30.9	喜	syǐ
30.9	善	shàn
30.9	喫	chī
30.9	喘	chwǎn
30.9	單	dān
30.9	喈	dzá, dzán
30.10	嗎	ma, mǎ
30.10	嗨	hāi
30.10	嗓	sǎng
30.11	嘔	ou, ǒu
30.11	嘗	cháng
30.11	嘟	dū
30.11	嘍	lou, lóu
30.12	嘱	jǔ
30.12	嘩	hwā
30.12	嘿	hēi
30.12	噎	yē
30.12	噌	tsēng
30.12	嘴	dzwěi
30.12	嗳	āi, ái, ǎi, ài, ēi, ei
30.13	噴	pēn, pèn
30.13	噢	àu
30.13	噸	dwūn, dwùn
30.14	嚇	syà
30.14	嚄	hwò
30.15	嚮	syàng
30.16	嚥	yàn
30.16	嚮	syàng
30.16	嚮	syàng
30.17	嚷	rāng, rǎng
30.17	嚴	yán
30.18	嚼	jyáu
30.19	囉	lwō, lwó
30.21	囑	jǔ

31	囗	
31.2	四	sz̀
31.3	囙	yǐn
31.3	回	hwéi
31.3	囘	hwéi
31.3	団	twán
31.4	园	ywán
31.4	囬	hwéi
31.4	困	kwùn
31.5	囯	gwó
31.5	固	gù
31.5	图	tú
31.8	國	gwó
31.8	圈	chywān, jywān, jywàn
31.9	圍	wéi
31.10	園	ywán
31.10	圓	ywán
31.11	團	twán
31.11	圖	tú

32	土 圡	
32.0	土	tǔ
32.3	尘	chén
32.3	在	dzài
32.3	地	de, dì
32.4	坐	dzwò
32.4	坏	hwài
32.4	均	jyūn

32.4	坎	kǎn
32.4	坑	kēng
32.4	块	kwài
32.4	坚	jyān
32.5	坡	pwō
32.5	坿	fù
32.5	坦	tǎn
32.5	拉	lā
32.6	垫	dyàn
32.7	城	chéng
32.7	埋	mái, mán
32.8	培	péi
32.8	埽	sǎu, sàu
32.8	堆	dwēi
32.8	堵	dǔ
32.8	基	jī
32.8	執	jŕ
32.8	堅	jyān
32.8	堂	táng
32.9	場	cháng, chǎng
32.9	堡	bǎu, pǔ
32.9	報	bàu
32.9	堤	dī, tí
32.10	填	tyán
32.10	塑	sù
32.10	塗	tú
32.10	塔	tǎ
32.10	塌	tā
32.10	塊	kwài
32.10	塞	sāi, sài, sēi
32.11	境	jìng
32.11	墙	chyáng
32.11	墊	dyàn
32.11	場	cháng, chǎng
32.11	塵	chén
32.12	墜	jwèi
32.12	墨	mwò
32.12	墳	fén
32.12	增	dzēng
32.13	墻	chyáng
32.13	壁	bì
32.14	壓	yā, yà
32.16	壞	hwài

33	**士**	
33.0	士	shř
33.3	壮	jwàng
33.4	壳	ké
33.4	壯	jwàng
33.4	声	shēng
33.9	壺	hú
33.9	壹	yǐ
33.11	壽	shòu

35	**夂 夊**	
35.2	处	chǔ, chù
35.7	夏	syà
35.6	复	fù

36	**夕**	
36.2	外	wài
36.3	多	dwō, dwó
36.5	夜	yè
36.8	夠	gòu
36.8	够	gòu
36.8	梦	mèng
36.11	夢	mèng
36.11	影	hwǒ

37	**大**	
37.0	大	dà, dài
37.1	天	tyān
37.1	夫	fū
37.1	太	tài
37.2	头	tóu
37.2	失	shř
37.3	买	mǎi
37.3	夺	dwó
37.3	关	gwān
37.3	夹	jyā, jyá
37.3	夸	kwā
37.4	夾	jyā, jyá
37.5	奇	chí
37.5	卖	mài
37.5	奉	fèng
37.5	奋	fèn
37.6	奔	bēn, bèn
37.6	奏	dzòu
37.6	奖	jyǎng

37.6	类	lài
37.7	套	tàu
37.8	奢	shē
37.11	奬	jyǎng
37.11	奪	dwó
37.13	奮	fèn

38	**女**	
38.0	女	nyǔ
38.2	奶	nǎi
38.2	奴	nú
38.3	如	rú
38.3	妇	fù
38.3	她	tā
38.3	妄	wàng
38.3	好	hǎu, hàu
38.3	奸	jyān
38.4	妨	fáng
38.4	妥	twǒ
38.5	妹	mèi
38.5	妻	chī
38.5	始	shř
38.5	姓	syìng
38.5	委	wěi
38.5	姑	gū
38.5	妯	jóu
38.5	姊	jyě
38.5	姐	jyě
38.6	姿	dz
38.6	姨	yí
38.6	娃	wá
38.6	威	wēi
38.6	姪	jŕ
38.6	姦	jyān
38.6	姜	jyāng
38.6	娄	lou, lóu
38.7	娘	nyáng
38.7	娱	yú
38.8	婆	pwó
38.8	婦	fù
38.8	娶	chyǔ
38.8	婚	hwūn
38.9	嫂	sǎu
38.9	婿	syù

38.10	媳	syí
38.10	嫉	jí
38.10	嫁	jyà
38.10	媽	mā
38.11	嫩	nèn, nwùn
38.14	嬭	nǎi
38.14	嬤	mā
38.15	嬸	shěn
38.16	嬾	lǎn
38.17	孃	nyáng

39	**子**	
39.0	子	dz, dž
39.1	孔	kǔng
39.3	孙	swūn
39.3	字	dž
39.3	存	tswún
39.5	学	sywé
39.5	季	jì
39.5	孤	gū
39.6	孩	hái
39.7	孫	swūn
39.13	學	sywé

40	**宀**	
40.2	宁	níng, nǐng
40.2	它	tā
40.3	安	ān
40.3	守	shǒu
40.3	宅	jái
40.4	完	wán
40.5	宝	bǎu
40.5	定	dìng
40.5	宗	dzūng
40.5	实	shŕ
40.5	审	shěn
40.5	官	gwān
40.6	宣	sywān
40.6	室	shř, shŕ
40.6	客	kè
40.7	容	rúng
40.7	宰	dzǎi
40.7	害	hài
40.7	家	jyā
40.8	密	mì

40.8	宿	sù, syǒu		44.4	屁	pì		
40.8	寃	ywān		44.4	尿	nyàu		
40.8	寄	jì		44.4	尾	wěi, yǐ		
40.9	寍	níng, nìng		44.4	局	jyú		
40.9	富	fù		44.5	居	jyū		
40.9	寔	shŕ		44.5	屈	chyū		
40.9	寒	hán		44.6	屋	wū		
40.10	寕	níng, nìng		44.6	屎	shř		
40.10	寜	níng, nìng		44.7	展	jǎn		
40.11	寧	níng, nìng		44.8	屠	tú		
40.11	實	shŕ		44.9	屬	shǔ		
40.12	審	shěn		44.9	屢	lyǔ		
40.12	寫	syě		44.11	屢	lyǔ		
40.12	寬	kwān		44.12	屑	tséng		
40.16	寶	bǎu		44.12	履	lyǔ		
40.17	寶	bǎu		44.18	屬	shǔ		

41 寸

41.0	寸	tswùn
41.2	对	dwèi
41.3	寻	syún, sywé
41.3	导	dǎu
41.4	寿	shòu
41.6	封	fēng
41.6	将	jyǎng, jyàng
41.8	將	jyǎng, jyàng
41.8	專	jwān
41.9	尊	dzwūn
41.9	尋	syún, sywé
41.11	對	dwèi
41.13	導	dǎu

42 小

42.0	小	syǎu
42.1	少	shǎu, shàu
42.3	尖	jyān
42.5	尚	shàng
42.6	嘗	cháng

43 尢 兀 允

43.1	尤	yóu
43.9	就	jyòu

44 尸

44.1	尺	chŕ, chř
44.3	盡	jǐn, jìn

46 山

46.0	山	shān
46.4	岔	chà
46.4	岁	swèi
46.5	岸	àn
46.5	岳	ywè
46.7	島	dǎu
46.8	崩	bēng
46.8	崇	chúng
46.9	憲	dzǎi
46.10	歲	swèi
46.14	嶽	ywè

47 川 巛

47.3	州	jōu
47.4	巡	syún

48 工

48.0	工	gūng
48.2	左	dzwǒ
48.2	巧	chyǎu
48.3	巩	gǔng
48.7	差	chā, chà, chāi

49 己

49.0	已	yǐ
49.1	巴	bā
49.6	巷	syàng

50 巾

50.2	布	bù
50.2	市	shř
50.3	帆	fān
50.3	帆	fān
50.3	师	shř
50.4	希	syī
50.4	帛	jř
50.5	帖	tyē, tyě, tyè
50.5	帘	lyán
50.6	帝	dì
50.6	带	dài
50.7	帮	bāng
50.7	席	syí
50.7	师	shř
50.8	常	cháng
50.8	帶	dài
50.8	帳	jàng
50.9	帽	màu
50.9	幇	bāng
50.11	幕	mù
50.13	幨	lyán
50.14	幫	bāng

51 干

51.0	干	gān, gàn
51.2	平	píng
51.3	年	nyán
51.5	并	bìng
51.5	幸	syìng
51.10	幹	gàn

52 幺

52.0	乡	syāng
52.1	幻	hwàn
52.2	幼	yòu
52.9	幾	jī, jǐ

53 广

53.0	广	gwǎng
53.3	庄	jwāng
53.3	庆	chìng
53.4	床	chwáng
53.4	应	yīng, yìng
53.5	府	fǔ

53.5	庙	myàu
53.5	底	de, dǐ
53.5	店	dyàn
53.6	度	dù
53.7	座	dzwò
53.8	康	kāng
53.9	廂	syāng
53.9	廁	tsè
53.9	廊	láng
53.10	廓	láng
53.12	廣	gwǎng
53.12	廠	chǎng
53.12	廚	chú
53.12	廢	fèi
53.12	廟	myàu
53.22	廳	tǐng

54 又

54.3	巡	syún
54.5	延	yán
54.6	建	jyàn
54.6	廻	hwéi

55 廾

55.4	弄	nèng, nùng

56 弋

56.2	式	èr
56.3	式	sān
56.3	式	shř

57 弓

57.0	弓	gūng
57.1	弔	dyàu
57.1	引	yǐn
57.4	弟	dì
57.5	弧	hú
57.5	弦	syán
57.6	弯	wān
57.7	弱	rwò
57.8	張	jāng
57.8	強	chyáng, chyǎng, jyàng
57.9	强	chyáng, chyǎng, jyàng
57.10	彀	gòu
57.12	彆	byè

57.12	彈	dàn, tán
57.13	彊	chyáng, chyǎng, jyàng
57.19	彎	wān

58 彐 彑 彑

58.2	归	gwēi
58.3	当	dāng, dǎng, dàng

59 彡

59.4	形	syíng
59.8	彫	dyāu
59.12	影	yǐng

60 彳

60.4	彻	chè
60.5	征	jēng
60.5	彼	bǐ
60.5	往	wǎng, wàng
60.6	很	hěn
60.6	後	hòu
60.6	待	dāi, dài
60.7	徒	tú
60.8	得	de, dé, děi
60.8	從	tsúng
60.9	復	fù
60.9	徧	byàn
60.10	微	wēi
60.12	徹	chè
60.12	徵	jēng
60.14	徽	hwēi

61 心 忄 小

61.0	心	syīn
61.1	必	bì
61.3	志	jř
61.3	忍	rěn
61.3	忌	jì
61.3	忙	máng
61.3	忘	wáng, wàng
61.4	忠	jūng
61.4	态	tài
61.4	忽	hū
61.4	快	kwài
61.4	忧	yōu
61.4	念	nyàn

61.5	急	jí
61.5	怪	gwài
61.5	怕	pà
61.5	性	syìng
61.5	思	sz̄
61.5	怎	dzěn
61.5	总	dzǔng
61.5	怨	ywàn
61.6	恨	hèn
61.6	恰	chyà
61.6	恐	kǔng
61.6	恋	lyàn
61.6	恭	gūng
61.6	恢	hwēi
61.6	恶	ě, è, wù
61.6	恼	nǎu
61.7	悚	súng
61.7	患	hwàn
61.7	您	nín
61.7	悟	wù
61.7	悠	yōu
61.8	悶	mēn, mèn
61.8	惨	tsǎn
61.8	惟	wéi
61.8	惡	ě, è, wù
61.8	惦	dyàn
61.8	悲	bēi
61.8	情	chíng
61.9	愣	lèng
61.9	想	syǎng
61.9	慈	tsź
61.9	意	yì
61.9	愚	yū
61.9	愉	yú
61.9	爱	ài
61.9	愁	chóu
61.9	恼	nǎu
61.9	惹	rě
61.9	感	gǎn
61.10	慌	hwāng
61.10	態	tài
61.10	愿	ywàn
61.11	慶	chìng

61.11	慢	màn	64.3	扠	chā	64.5	抬	tái
61.11	慚	tsán	64.3	扛	káng	64.5	拥	yūng
61.11	慭	tsán	64.3	扫	sāu, sàu	64.5	拖	twō
61.11	慘	tsǎn	64.3	执	jí	64.6	拼	pīn
61.11	慣	gwàn	64.3	托	twō	64.6	拿	ná
61.11	憂	yōu	64.3	扣	kòu	64.6	按	àn, èn
61.12	憋	byē	64.4	批	pī	64.6	拳	chywán
61.12	憑	píng	64.4	抛	páu	64.6	挎	kwà
61.13	懈	syè	64.4	扭	nyǒu	64.6	拽	jwāi, jwài
61.13	應	yīng, yìng	64.4	报	bàu	64.6	指	jǐ, jǐr, jír
61.14	懦	nwò	64.4	抄	chāu	64.6	拱	gǔng
61.15	懲	chěng	64.4	扯	chě	64.6	挂	gwà
61.16	懷	hwái	64.4	承	chéng	64.6	拴	shwān
61.16	懶	lǎn	64.4	抖	dǒu	64.6	拾	shŕ
61.19	戀	lyàn	64.4	扶	fú	64.6	挺	tǐng
62	**戈**		64.4	抗	kàng	64.6	挑	tyāu, tyǎu
62.2	成	chéng	64.4	抓	jwā	64.6	挖	wā
62.2	戏	syì	64.4	技	jì	64.7	捉	dzwó, jwō
62.3	戒	jyè	64.4	折	jē, jé, jě, shé	64.7	挟	jyā
62.3	我	wǒ	64.4	护	hù	64.7	捅	tǔng
62.4	或	hwò	64.4	投	tóu	64.7	捐	jywān
62.5	战	jàn	64.5	披	pī	64.7	捆	kwǔn
62.9	戤	děng	64.5	拍	pāi	64.7	捞	lāu
62.10	截	jyé	64.5	拏	ná	64.7	挪	nwó
62.11	戲	syì	64.5	抹	mwǒ, mwò	64.7	挨	āi, ái
62.12	戰	jàn	64.5	拔	bá	64.7	捌	bā, bá
62.13	戲	syì	64.5	把	bǎ, bà, bǎi	64.7	挲	bāi
62.13	戴	dài	64.5	拜	bài	64.7	捕	bǔ
62.14	戳	chwō	64.5	拌	bàn	64.7	捂	wǔ
63	**戶 户**		64.5	抱	bàu	64.8	扫	sǎu, sàu
63.0	戶	hù	64.5	拆	chāi	64.8	捧	pěng
63.4	房	fáng	64.5	抻	chēn	64.8	排	pái, pǎi
63.4	所	swǒ	64.5	抽	chōu	64.8	捱	āi, ái
63.5	扁	byǎn	64.5	抵	dǐ	64.8	掰	bāi
63.6	扇	shān, shàn	64.5	担	dān, dàn	64.8	捵	chēn
64	**手 扌**		64.5	押	yā	64.8	掉	dyàu
64.0	手	shǒu	64.5	拦	lán	64.8	掐	chyā
64.0	才	tsái	64.5	拉	lā	64.8	捶	chwéi
64.1	扎	dzā, jā, já, jà	64.5	拒	jyù	64.8	掩	yǎn
64.2	扔	rēng	64.5	拘	jyū	64.8	接	jyē
64.2	扑	pū	64.5	找	jǎu	64.8	控	kùng
64.2	打	dá, dǎ	64.5	招	jāu	64.8	掘	jywé
			64.5	拐	gwǎi	64.8	捲	jywǎn

64.8	据	jyù	64.11	摺	jé, jě	64.19	攢	dzǎn
64.8	挤	jǐ	64.11	摳	kōu	64.19	攤	tān
64.8	撑	jēng, jèng	64.11	摟	lōu, lǒu	64.20	攫	dzwàn
64.8	掌	jǎng	64.11	摩	mā, mwó	64.20	攬	jyáu
64.8	掛	gwà	64.11	摞	lwò	64.21	攬	lǎn
64.8	捨	shě	64.11	攙	chān			
64.8	探	tàn	64.11	摸	mwō	**65**	**支**	
64.8	掏	tāu	64.12	撇	pyē, pyě	65.0	支	jī
64.8	採	tsǎi	64.12	撒	sā, sǎ	**66**	**攵 攴**	
64.8	推	twēi	64.12	撕	sž	66.2	收	shōu
64.9	揉	róu	64.12	撅	jywē	66.3	攻	gūng
64.9	揰	pèng	64.12	撈	lāu	66.3	改	gǎi
64.9	揑	nyē	64.12	撞	chwàng, jwàng	66.4	放	fàng
64.9	描	myáu	64.12	撰	dzwàn	66.5	故	gù
64.9	揹	bēi	64.12	撣	dǎn	66.5	政	jèng
64.9	插	chā	64.12	撑	dèn	66.6	敵	dí
64.9	提	dǐ, tí	64.12	撤	dwūn	66.6	效	syàu
64.9	揙	dzwàn	64.12	撤	chè	66.7	敗	bài
64.9	攙	chān	64.12	播	bwō	66.7	敏	mǐn
64.9	揍	dzòu	64.12	撥	bwō	66.7	教	jyāu, jyàu
64.9	揭	jyē	64.12	撓	náu	66.7	救	jyòu
64.9	揪	jyōu	64.12	撲	pū	66.8	敞	chǎng
64.9	換	hwàn	64.13	擁	yūng	66.8	散	sǎn, sàn
64.9	搜	sōu	64.13	操	tsāu	66.8	敢	gǎn
64.9	握	wò	64.13	擊	jī	66.9	數	shǔ, shù
64.10	搧	shān	64.13	舉	jyǔ	66.9	敬	jǐng
64.10	擘	bāi	64.13	據	jyù	66.10	敲	chyāu
64.10	擺	bǎi	64.13	撐	gǎn	66.11	敵	dí
64.10	搬	bān	64.13	擋	dǎng	66.11	數	shǔ, shù
64.10	搭	dā	64.13	擔	dān, dàn	66.12	整	jěng
64.10	搗	dǎu	64.14	擣	dǎu	**67**	**文**	
64.10	搞	gǎu	64.14	擰	níng, nǐng, nìng	67.0	文	wén
64.10	搶	chyāng, chyǎng	64.14	擦	tsā	67.2	斉	chí
64.10	搥	chwéi	64.14	擡	tái	**68**	**斗**	
64.10	搋	chwāi	64.14	擤	syǐng	68.0	斗	dǒu, dòu
64.10	搗	wǔ	64.14	擠	jǐ	68.7	斛	hú
64.10	搖	yáu	64.14	擱	gē	**69**	**斤**	
64.10	損	swǔn	64.15	擺	bǎi	69.0	斤	jīn
64.10	攤	tān	64.15	攀	pān	69.4	斧	fǔ
64.10	搯	tāu	64.15	擴	kwò	69.7	斷	dwàn
64.10	搓	tswō	64.16	攏	lǔng	69.8	斯	sž
64.11	摔	shwāi, shwǎi	64.17	攔	lán	69.9	新	syīn
64.11	摘	jāi, jé	64.17	攪	chān			

69.14	斷	dwàn	72.9	暈	yūn, yùn	75.3	村	tswūn	
	70	**方**	72.9	暗	àn	75.3	条	tyáu	
70.0	方	fāng	72.10	暢	chàng	75.3	杓	sháu	
70.4	於	yú	72.11	暴	bàu	75.3	李	lǐ	
70.5	施	shr̄	72.12	曆	lì	75.4	板	bǎn	
70.6	旂	chí	72.12	曉	syǎu	75.4	杯	bēi	
70.6	旁	páng	72.15	曠	kwàng	75.4	枣	dzǎu	
70.6	旅	lyǔ	72.19	曬	shài	75.4	東	dūng	
70.7	族	dzú		**73**	**曰**	75.4	枪	chyāng	
70.10	旗	chí	73.1	电	dyàn	75.4	松	sūng	
	71	**旡 无**	73.1	曰	jyòu	75.4	果	gwǒ	
71.0	无	wú	73.2	曲	chyū, chyǔ	75.4	枕	jěn	
71.5	旣	jì	73.3	更	gēng, gèng, jǐng	75.4	极	jí	
71.7	旤	jì	73.6	書	shū	75.4	枝	jr̄	
71.7	旣	jì	73.8	曾	dzēng, tséng	75.5	柏	bǎi	
	72	**日**	73.8	最	dzwèi	75.5	标	byāu	
72.0	日	r̀	73.9	會	hwěi, hwèi, kwài	75.5	查	chá, jā	
72.2	早	dzǎu		**74**	**月**	75.5	柴	chái	
72.3	旱	hàn	74.0	月	ywè	75.5	柒	chī	
72.4	旺	wàng	74.2	有	yǒu	75.5	亲	chīn, chìng	
72.4	明	míng	74.4	朋	péng	75.5	柔	róu	
72.4	昇	shēng	74.4	服	fú, fù	75.5	某	mǒu	
72.4	昏	hwūn	74.7	望	wàng	75.5	染	rǎn	
72.5	昨	dzwó	74.8	期	chī	75.5	柏	tái	
72.5	春	chwūn	74.8	朝	cháu, jāu	75.5	树	shù	
72.5	显	syǎn		**75**	**木**	75.5	柿	shr̀	
72.5	星	syīng	75.0	木	mù	75.5	枴	gwǎi	
72.5	是	shr̀	75.1	本	běn	75.5	柜	gwèi	
72.6	晌	shǎng	75.1	末	mwò	75.5	柱	jù	
72.6	晒	shài	75.1	未	wèi	75.5	架	jyà	
72.6	時	shr̀	75.2	杀	shā	75.5	栏	lán	
72.6	晃	hwǎng, hwàng	75.2	东	dūng	75.5	柳	lyǒu	
72.7	晚	wǎn	75.2	杂	dzá	75.6	桑	sāng	
72.8	晴	chíng	75.2	权	chywán	75.6	栢	bǎi	
72.8	普	pǔ	75.2	机	jī	75.6	案	àn	
72.8	替	tì	75.2	乐	lè, ywè	75.6	栽	dzāi	
72.8	暑	shǔ	75.3	呆	āi, dāi	75.6	挡	dǎng, dàng	
72.8	晾	lyàng	75.3	杠	gàng	75.6	根	gēn	
72.8	景	jǐng	75.3	杆	gān, gǎn	75.6	格	gé	
72.8	暖	nwǎn	75.3	材	tsái	75.6	桥	chyáu	
72.9	暁	syǎu	75.3	杏	syìng	75.6	桃	táu	
72.9	暂	jàn				75.6	样	yàng	
						75.6	桂	gwèi	

86.5	炸	já, jà
86.5	烂	làn
86.5	炼	lyàn
86.6	热	rè
86.6	烟	yān
86.6	烘	hūng
86.6	烤	kǎu
86.6	烙	làu
86.6	烈	lyè
86.6	烏	wū
86.7	烹	pēng
86.8	然	rán
86.8	煮	jǔ
86.8	無	wú
86.8	焦	jyāu
86.9	煤	méi
86.9	照	jàu
86.9	煖	nwǎn
86.9	煩	fán
86.9	煙	yān
86.9	煎	jyān
86.9	煉	lyàn
86.10	熬	āu, áu
86.10	煽	shān
86.10	熄	syí
86.10	熊	syúng
86.11	熱	rè
86.11	燜	mèn
86.11	熨	yùn
86.11	熟	shóu, shú
86.12	燒	shāu
86.12	燕	yān, yàn
86.12	燙	tàng
86.12	燈	dēng
86.12	燉	dwùn
86.13	營	yíng
86.15	爆	bāu, bàu, pàu
86.16	爐	lú
86.17	爛	làn

87		爪 爫
87.4	爬	pá
87.4	爭	jēng

87.6	愛	ài
87.8	爲	wéi, wèi
87.13	爵	jywé
87.14	爵	jywé

88		父
88.0	父	fù
88.2	爺	yé
88.4	爸	bà
88.6	爹	dyē
88.9	爺	yé

89		爻
89.7	爽	shwǎng

90		爿
90.4	牀	chwáng
90.13	牆	chyáng

91		片
91.0	片	pyān, pyàn
91.0	爿	pyān, pyàn
91.4	版	bǎn
91.8	牌	pái
91.11	牎	chwāng

92		牙
92.0	牙	yá

93		牛 牜
93.0	牛	nyóu
93.3	牠	tā
93.3	牡	mǔ
93.4	物	wù
93.4	牧	mù
93.5	牴	dǐ
93.5	牽	chyān
93.5	牲	shēng
93.6	特	tè
93.6	犧	syǐ
93.7	犎	chyān
93.7	犁	lí
93.8	犂	lí
93.8	犄	jǐ
93.16	犧	syǐ

94		犬 犭
94.2	犯	fàn
94.4	犹	yóu
94.4	狂	kwáng
94.5	狐	hú
94.5	狗	gǒu
94.6	狡	jyǎu
94.6	狠	hěn
94.7	狹	syá
94.7	狼	láng
94.8	猪	jū
94.8	猆	hwò
94.8	猛	měng
94.8	猜	tsāi
94.9	猴	hóu
94.9	猶	yóu
94.9	獻	syàn
94.9	猫	māu
94.10	獅	shr
94.10	獸	dāi
94.11	獄	yù
94.13	獨	dú
94.14	獲	hwò
94.15	獸	shòu
94.16	獻	syàn

95		玄 玄
95.0	玄	sywán

96		玉 王
96.0	玉	yù
96.3	玖	jyǒu
96.4	環	hwán
96.4	玫	méi
96.4	玩	wán
96.5	玻	bwō
96.6	班	bān
96.6	珠	jū
96.7	球	chyóu
96.7	理	lí
96.7	現	syàn
96.8	斑	bān
96.8	琴	chín
96.13	環	hwán

97 瓜			
97.0	瓜	gwā	

98 瓦		
98.0	瓦	wǎ, wà
98.6	瓷	tsź
98.6	瓶	píng
98.11	甄	jwǎn

99 甘		
99.0	甘	gān
99.4	甚	shén, shèn
99.5	甜	tyán

100 生		
100.0	生	shēng
100.6	產	chǎn
100.6	産	chǎn
100.7	甥	shēng

101 用		
101.0	用	yùng
101.1	甩	shwǎi
101.4	甫	béng

102 田		
102.0	田	tyán
102.1	由	yóu
102.1	申	shēn
102.2	男	nán
102.2	甸	mǔ
102.3	画	hwà
102.4	界	jyè
102.5	留	lyóu
102.5	畝	mǔ
102.5	畜	chù, syù
102.6	畢	bì
102.6	略	lywè
102.7	番	fān
102.7	畫	hwà
102.8	當	dāng, dǎng, dàng
102.17	疊	dyé

103 疋		
103.0	疋	pǐ, pǐ
103.7	疏	shū
103.9	疑	yí

104 疒		
104.3	疙	gē
104.3	疕	nywè
104.4	疤	bā
104.4	疮	chwāng
104.5	疹	jěn
104.5	疼	téng
104.5	病	bìng
104.5	疲	pí
104.5	疱	bāu
104.6	痒	yǎng
104.6	痕	hén
104.7	痛	tùng
104.7	痢	lì
104.8	痰	tán
104.8	麻	má
104.9	瘦	shòu
104.9	瘋	fēng
104.9	瘟	wēn
104.10	瘤	lyóu
104.10	瘡	chwāng
104.10	瘧	nywè
104.10	瘢	bān
104.11	癎	chywé
104.15	癢	yǎng

105 癶		
105.7	登	dēng
105.7	發	fā

106 白		
106.0	白	bái
106.1	百	bǎi
106.3	的	de, dí, dì
106.4	皇	hwáng

107 皮		
107.0	皮	pí
107.5	皰	bāu
107.10	皺	jòu

108 皿		
108.4	盂	bēi
108.4	盆	pén
108.5	盐	yán
108.5	盌	wǎn
108.5	益	yì
108.5	監	jyān
108.6	盒	hé
108.6	盛	chéng, shèng
108.6	盤	pán
108.6	蓋	gài
108.8	鹽	yán
108.8	盞	jǎn
108.9	盡	jìn
108.9	監	jyān
108.10	盤	pán
108.19	鹽	yán

109 目 罒			
109.0	目	mù	
109.2	盯	dǐng	
109.3	盲	máng	
109.3	直	jŕ	
109.3	具	jyù	
109.4	盼	pàn	
109.4	眉	méi	
109.4	相	syāng, syàng	
109.4	省	shěng	
109.4	看	kān, kàn	
109.5	眨	jǎ	
109.5	真	jēn	
109.5	眞	jēn	
109.6	眼	yǎn	
109.7	着	jāu, jáu, je, jwó	
109.7	睏	kwùn	
109.8	督	dū	
109.8	睡	shwèi	
109.8	睛	jēng	
109.9	瞄	myáu	
109.10	瞎	syā	
109.10	瞌	kē	
109.12	瞪	dèng	
109.12	瞧	chyáu	
109.12	瞭	lyǎu, lyàu	

110 矛		
110.0	矛	máu

111 矢		
111.3	知	jŕ

118.7	節	jyé	119.11	糟	dzāu	120.8	綳	bēng
118.7	筷	kwài	119.12	糧	lyáng	120.8	絣	bēng
118.8	算	swàn	119.12	糨	jyàng	120.8	帛糸	myán
118.8	筘	chyán				120.8	綿	myán

118.8	箇	ge, gè	120.8	綫	syàn
118.8	管	gwǎn	120.8	繩	shéng
118.8	箍	gū	120.8	維	wéi
118.9	節	jyé	120.8	網	wǎng
118.9	節	jyé	120.9	練	lyàn
118.9	篇	pyān	120.9	編	byān
118.9	箱	syāng	120.9	緞	dwàn
118.9	範	fàn	120.9	線	syàn
118.9	箭	jyàn	120.9	緣	ywán
118.10	篦	bǐ	120.9	緩	hwǎn
118.10	篩	shāi	120.10	縣	syàn
118.11	簍	lǒu	120.10	纏	chán
118.11	篱	lí	120.11	繁	fán
118.12	簡	jyǎn	120.11	縷	lyǔ
118.13	簾	lyán	120.11	繃	bēng
118.13	簽	chyān	120.11	總	dzǔng
118.13	簿	bù	120.11	縱	dzùng
118.13	簸	bwǒ, bwò, pwǒ	120.11	縫	féng, fèng
118.14	籃	lán	120.11	縮	swō
118.14	籌	chóu	120.12	織	jř
118.15	籐	téng	120.12	繙	fān
118.16	籠	lúng	120.12	繐	swèi
118.19	籬	lí	120.12	繞	ràu

120.13	繩	shéng
120.13	繫	jì, syì
120.13	繮	jyāng
120.13	繳	jyāu
120.13	繭	jyǎn
120.14	繼	jì
120.15	纏	chán
120.17	纜	tsái

122.6	罣	gwà
122.8	罪	dzwèi
122.8	署	shǔ
122.9	罰	fá
122.10	罷	ba, bà
122.10	罵	mà
122.10	罰	fá
122.14	羅	lwó

123 羊

123.0	羊	yáng
123.3	美	měi
123.4	羞	syōu
123.4	養	yǎng
123.7	群	chyún
123.7	義	yì
123.7	羣	chyún

124 羽 羽

124.4	翅	chr̀
124.5	習	syí
124.9	翦	jyǎn
124.12	翻	fān

125 老 耂

125.0	老	lǎu
125.2	考	kǎu

126 而

126.0	而	ér
126.3	耐	nài
126.3	耍	shwǎ
126.3	耑	dwān, jwān

127 耒

127.4	耙	bà, pá
127.4	耗	hàu
127.4	耕	gēng, jīng
127.7	耡	chú

128 耳

128.0	耳	ěr
128.3	耶	yē
128.5	職	jŕ
128.5	聊	lyáu
128.6	聯	lyán
128.7	聞	wén
128.7	聖	shèng
128.8	聚	jyù
128.9	聰	tsūng
128.11	聰	tsūng
128.11	聯	lyán
128.11	聲	shēng
128.12	職	jŕ
128.16	聾	lúng
128.16	聽	tīng

130 月 肉

130.0	肉	ròu
130.2	肌	jī
130.3	肚	dǔ, dù
130.3	肛	gāng
130.3	肝	gān
130.4	肮	āng
130.4	肺	fèi
130.4	肥	féi
130.4	股	gǔ
130.4	肿	jǔng
130.4	育	yù
130.4	肩	jyān
130.4	肯	kěn
130.5	脉	mài, mwò
130.5	胖	pàng
130.5	背	bēi, bèi
130.5	胃	wèi
130.5	胜	shèng
130.5	膽	dǎn
130.5	胡	hú
130.6	脈	mài, mwò
130.6	腦	nǎu
130.6	臟	dzāng
130.6	胰	yí
130.6	胭	yān
130.6	胸	syūng
130.6	能	néng
130.6	胶	jyāu
130.6	脊	jí, jǐ
130.7	脖	bwó
130.7	脫	twō
130.7	脚	jyǎu, jywé
130.8	脾	pí
130.8	腌	yān
130.8	腔	chyāng
130.8	腐	fǔ
130.8	腊	là
130.9	腦	nǎu
130.9	腮	sāi
130.9	腸	cháng
130.9	腰	yāu
130.9	腥	syīng
130.9	脚	jyǎu, jywé
130.9	腫	jǔng
130.10	腿	twěi
130.11	膠	jyāu
130.11	膝	syī
130.12	膳	shàn
130.12	膩	nì
130.13	臌	gǔ
130.13	臉	lyǎn
130.13	膽	dǎn
130.13	臊	sāu, sàu
130.13	膿	néng, núng
130.15	臘	là
130.16	臙	yān

131 臣

131.2	臥	wò
131.11	臨	lín

132 自

132.0	自	dz̀
132.4	臭	chòu

133 至

133.0	至	jr̀
133.4	致	jr̀
133.8	臺	tái

134 臼

134.7	舅	jyòu
134.7	與	yǔ
134.9	興	syīng, syìng
134.11	舉	jyǔ
134.12	舊	jyòu

135 舌

135.0	舌	shé
135.1	乱	lwàn

143 血

143.0	血	syě, sywě, sywè
143.6	衇	mài, mwò
143.6	衆	jùng

144 行

144.0	行	háng, syíng
144.6	街	jyē
144.9	衝	chūng, chùng
144.9	衛	wèi
144.10	衞	wèi

145 衣 衤 衣

145.0	衣	yī
145.2	补	bǔ
145.3	衬	chèn
145.3	衫	shān
145.3	表	byǎu
145.4	袤	shwāi
145.5	被	bèi
145.5	袜	wà
145.5	袖	syòu
145.6	袴	kù
145.6	袷	jyá
145.6	裁	tsái
145.6	裂	lyè
145.6	装	jwāng
145.7	補	bǔ
145.7	裙	chyún
145.7	裡	lǐ
145.7	裏	lǐ
145.7	裝	jwāng
145.7	袷	jyá
145.8	褂	gwà
145.8	裹	gwǒ
145.8	製	jr̀
145.9	複	fù
145.9	褐	hè
145.10	褥	rù
145.10	褲	kù
145.10	褫	lē
145.11	褶	jě
145.12	襍	dzá
145.15	襪	wà

145.16	襯	chèn

146 西 覀

146.0	西	syī
146.3	要	yāu, yàu
146.12	覆	fù
146.13	覈	hé

147 見

147.0	見	jyàn
147.0	见	jyàn
147.2	观	gwān, gwàn
147.4	規	gwēi
147.5	覚	jyàu, jywé
147.5	視	shr̀
147.9	親	chīn, chìng
147.13	覺	jyàu, jywé
147.18	觀	gwān, gwàn

148 角

148.0	角	jyǎu
148.2	觔	jīn
148.5	觝	dǐ
148.6	解	jyě, jyè, syè
148.6	解	jyě, jyè, syè

149 言 訁

149.0	言	yán
149.2	訒	rèn
149.2	訂	dìng
149.2	計	jì
149.3	訕	ràng
149.3	訓	syùn
149.3	討	tǎu
149.3	託	twō
149.3	記	jì
149.4	設	shè
149.4	許	syǔ
149.4	訪	fǎng
149.4	講	jyǎng
149.5	評	píng
149.5	詞	tsź
149.5	註	jù
149.5	証	jèng
149.5	診	jěn, jen
149.5	詐	jà

149.6	誠	chéng
149.6	詩	shr̄
149.6	試	shr̀
149.6	該	gāi
149.6	詳	syáng
149.6	誇	kwā
149.6	詼	hwēi
149.6	話	hwà
149.7	認	rèn
149.7	説	shwō
149.7	誤	wù
149.7	語	yǔ
149.7	誌	jr̀
149.8	請	chǐng
149.8	調	dyàu, tyáu
149.8	誰	shéi, shwéi
149.8	談	tán
149.8	諒	lyàng
149.8	論	lìn, lwún, lwùn
149.8	課	kè
149.8	諸	jū
149.9	謀	móu
149.10	謎	mèi, mí
149.10	謡	yáu
149.10	謙	chyān
149.10	謝	syè
149.10	講	jyǎng
149.10	謊	hwǎng
149.11	謹	jǐn
149.12	證	jèng
149.12	識	shŕ, shr̀
149.13	議	yì
149.13	警	jǐng
149.13	譬	pì
149.13	譜	pǔ
149.14	護	hù
149.15	讀	dòu, dú
149.16	變	byàn
149.16	讎	chóu
149.17	讓	ràng
149.19	讚	dzàn

150 谷

150.0	谷	gǔ

167.7	銹	syòu
167.7	鋤	chú
167.8	錶	byǎu
167.8	錯	tswò
167.8	錫	syí
167.8	鋼	gāng
167.8	錘	chwéi
167.8	錢	chyán
167.8	鋸	jyū, jyù
167.8	錦	jǐn
167.8	錐	jwēi
167.9	錨	máu
167.9	鍍	dù
167.9	鍊	lyàn
167.9	鍋	gwō
167.9	鍼	jēn
167.9	鍾	jūng
167.10	鎖	swǒ
167.10	鎬	gǎu
167.10	鎚	chwéi
167.10	鎗	chyāng
167.10	鎮	jèn
167.11	鏡	jìng
167.11	鏈	lyàn
167.11	鏽	syòu
167.11	鏟	chǎn
167.12	鐘	jūng
167.13	鏽	syòu
167.13	鐲	jwó
167.13	鐵	tyě
167.13	鐮	lyán
167.13	鐮	lyán
167.14	鑄	jù
167.15	鑛	kwàng
167.16	鑪	lú
167.17	鑰	yàu
167.17	鑲	syāng
167.19	鑼	lwó
167.19	鑽	dzwān, dzwǎn, dzwàn
167.20	鑿	dzáu

168　長　镸

168.0	長	cháng, jǎng

168.0	長	cháng, jǎng

169　門

169.0	門	mén
169.0	门	mén
169.2	閃	shǎn
169.3	閉	bì
169.4	閏	rwùn
169.4	閒	syán
169.4	閑	syán
169.4	間	jyān, jyàn
169.4	開	kāi
169.5	鬧	nàu
169.5	閘	jā
169.6	閔	gwān
169.6	閨	gwēi
169.9	闊	kwò
169.10	闖	chwǎng
169.10	闢	gwān
169.10	關	gwān
169.10	闔	hé

170　阜　阝

170.2	队	dwèi
170.4	陰	yǐn
170.4	陽	yáng
170.4	防	fáng
170.4	阶	jyē
170.5	阿	ā, à
170.5	附	fù
170.5	阻	dzǔ
170.5	陆	lù, lyòu
170.6	陈	chén
170.6	限	syàn
170.6	降	jyàng, syáng
170.7	院	ywàn
170.7	陞	shēng
170.7	陡	dǒu
170.7	除	chú
170.7	陣	jèn
170.8	陳	chén
170.8	陪	péi
170.8	陰	yǐn
170.8	陷	syàn

170.8	陸	lù, lyòu
170.9	隊	dwèi
170.9	隱	yǐn
170.9	陰	yǐn
170.9	陽	yáng
170.9	隄	dǐ, tí
170.9	階	jyē
170.9	隆	lúng
170.10	隨	swéi
170.10	隔	gé, jyē, jyé, jyè
170.12	隣	lín
170.12	隧	swéi
170.13	隨	swéi
170.13	險	syǎn
170.14	隱	yǐn

172　隹

172.2	难	nán, nàn
172.2	隻	jī
172.4	雄	syúng
172.4	雁	yàn
172.4	雇	gù
172.4	集	jí
172.4	雅	yǎ
172.8	雕	dyāu
172.9	雖	swéi
172.10	雜	dzá
172.10	雞	jī
172.10	雙	shwāng, shwàng
172.11	離	lí
172.11	難	nán, nàn

173　雨　⻗

173.0	雨	yǔ
173.3	雪	sywě
173.4	雲	yún
173.5	雹	báu
173.5	電	dyàn
173.5	零	líng
173.5	雷	léi
173.6	霧	wù
173.6	需	syū
173.8	霍	hwò
173.9	霜	shwāng

173.11	霧	wù	181.4	頓	dwūn, dwùn		186	香
173.13	露	lòu, lù	181.4	頑	wán	186.0	香	syāng
173.13	霸	bà	181.4	預	yù		187	馬
173.16	靈	líng	181.5	領	lǐng	187.0	馬	mǎ
	174	青	181.7	頭	tóu	187.0	马	mǎ
174.0	青	chīng	181.8	顆	kē	187.3	馱	twó
174.8	靜	jìng	181.9	顋	sāi	187.4	駁	bwó
	175	非	181.9	題	tí	187.5	駐	jù
175.0	非	fēi	181.9	顏	yán	187.5	駕	jyà
175.7	靠	kàu	181.10	顛	dyān	187.6	罵	mà
	176	面	181.10	類	lèi	187.6	駿	bwó
176.0	面	myàn	181.10	願	ywàn	187.6	駱	lwò
176.0	面	myàn	181.12	顧	gù	187.8	騎	chí
	177	革	181.14	顯	syǎn	187.8	騐	yàn
177.0	革	gé		182	風	187.9	騙	pyàn
177.4	靴	sywē	182.0	風	fēng	187.10	騰	tēng, téng
177.4	靶	bǎ	182.0	风	fēng	187.11	騾	lwó
177.6	鞍	ān	182.6	颳	gwā	187.12	驕	jyāu
177.6	鞋	syé	182.8	飀	jyù	187.13	驚	jīng
177.6	鞏	gǔng	182.11	飄	pyāu	187.13	驗	yàn
177.8	鞠	jyū	182.11	飆	pyāu	187.16	驢	lyú
177.9	鞦	chyōu		183	飛		188	骨
177.9	鞭	byān	183.0	飛	fēi	188.0	骨	gū, gú, gǔ
177.12	韃	sywé		184	食 食	188.4	骯	āng
177.13	韁	jyāng	184.0	食	shŕ	188.10	髒	bǎng
	179	韭	184.4	飲	yǐn, yìn	188.13	體	tǐ
179.0	韭	jyǒu	184.4	飯	fàn	188.13	髖	dzāng
179.4	韮	jyǒu	184.5	飽	bǎu		189	高
	180	音	184.6	餅	bǐng	189.0	高	gāu
180.0	音	yīn	184.6	餃	jyǎu		190	髟
180.12	響	syǎng	184.6	養	yǎng	190.4	髮	fǎng
180.13	響	syǎng	184.7	餐	tsān	190.8	鬆	sūng
180.13	響	syǎng	184.7	餓	è	190.9	鬍	hú
	181	頁 頁	184.8	餒	wěi		191	鬥
181.0	頁	yè	184.9	餵	wèi	191.0	鬥	dòu
181.0	頁	yè	184.9	餬	hú	191.4	鬧	dòu
181.2	頃	chǐng	184.9	餿	sōu	191.5	鬧	nàu
181.2	頂	dǐng	184.9	饅	mán	191.6	鬨	hùng
181.3	順	shwùn	184.11	饒	ráu	191.10	鬪	dòu
181.3	項	syàng	184.12	饍	shàn	191.14	鬬	dòu
181.4	頇	gù		185	首		194	鬼
			185.0	首	shǒu	194.0	鬼	gwěi

195 魚		
195.0	魚	yú
195.6	鮮	syān, syǎn
195.7	鯉	lǐ
195.9	鰐	è
195.7	鯽	jì
195.9	鯽	jì
195.9	鯽	jì
195.12	鱗	lín
195.16	鱷	è

196 鳥		
196.0	鳥	nyǎu
196.0	鸟	nyǎu
196.2	鸡	jī
196.4	鴈	yàn
196.5	鴨	yā
196.6	鴿	gē
196.7	鵝	é
196.8	鵰	dyāu
196.10	鷄	jī

197 鹵		
197.9	鹹	syán
197.13	鹼	jyán

198 鹿		
198.0	鹿	lù
198.22	麤	tsū

199 麥		
199.0	麥	mài
199.0	麦	mài
199.4	麵	myàn
199.9	麵	myàn

200 麻 麻		
200.0	麻	má
200.3	麼	ma

201 黃 黄		
201.0	黃	hwáng
201.0	黄	hwáng

202 黍		
202.5	黏	nyán

203 黑		
203.0	黑	hēi
203.5	點	dyǎn
203.5	點黨	dyǎn
203.8	黨	dǎng

207 鼓		
207.0	鼓	gǔ
207.5	鼕	dūng

209 鼻		
209.0	鼻	bí

210 齊		
210.0	齊	chí

211 齒		
211.5	齣	chū

212 龍		
212.0	龍	lúng
212.0	龙	lúng

214 龠		
214.5	龢	hé

Comparative Tables of Romanization
Wade-Giles to Pinyin and Yale Systems

WG	P	Y	WG	P	Y
A	a	a	chien	jian	jyan
ai	ai	ai	ch'ien	qian	chyan
an	an	an	chih	zhi	jr
ang	ang	ang	ch'ih	chi	chr
ao	ao	au	chin	jin	jin
			ch'in	qin	chin
CHA	zha	ja	ching	jing	jing
ch'a	cha	cha	ch'ing	qing	ching
chai	zhai	jai	chiu	jiu	jyou
ch'ai	chai	chai	ch'iu	qiu	chyou
chan	zhan	jan	chiung	jiong	jyung
ch'an	chan	chan	ch'iung	qiong	chyung
chang	zhang	jang	cho	zhuo	jwo
ch'ang	chang	chang	ch'o	chuo	chwo
chao	zhao	jau	chou	zhou	jou
ch'ao	chao	chau	ch'ou	chou	chou
che	zhe	je	chu	zhu	ju
ch'e	che	che	ch'u	chu	chu
chei	zhei	jei	chua	zhua	jwa
chen	zhen	jen	ch'ua	chua	chwa
ch'en	chen	chen	chuai	zhuai	jwai
cheng	zheng	jeng	ch'uai	chuai	chwai
ch'eng	cheng	cheng	chuan	zhuan	jwan
chi	ji	ji	ch'uan	chuan	chwan
ch'i	qi	chi	chuang	zhuang	jwang
chia	jia	jya	ch'uang	chuang	chwang
ch'ia	qia	chya	chui	zhui	jwei
chiang	jiang	jyang	ch'ui	chui	chwei
ch'iang	qiang	chyang	chun	zhun	jwun
ch'iao	qiao	chyau	ch'un	chun	chwun
chieh	jie	jye	chung	zhong	jung
ch'ieh	qie	chye			

Comparative Tables of Romanization

WG	P	Y	WG	P	Y
KA	ga	ga	k'ung	kong	kung
k'a	ka	ka	kuo	guo	gwo
kai	gai	gai	k'uo	kuo	kwo
k'ai	kai	kai	LA	la	la
kan	gan	gan	lai	lai	lai
k'an	kan	kan	lan	lan	lan
kang	gang	gang	lang	lang	lang
k'ang	kang	kang	lao	lao	lau
kao	gao	gau	le	le	le
k'ao	kao	kau	lei	lei	lei
ke, ko	ge	ge	leng	leng	leng
k'e, k'o	ke	ke	li	li	li
kei	gei	gei	lia	lia	lya
ken	gen	gen	liang	liang	lyang
k'en	ken	ken	liao	liao	lyau
keng	geng	geng	lieh	lie	lye
k'eng	keng	keng	lien	lian	lyan
ko, ke	ge	ge	lin	lin	lin
k'o, k'e	ke	ke	ling	ling	ling
kou	gou	gou	liu	liu	lyou
k'ou	kou	kou	lo	luo	lwo
ku	gu	gu	lou	lou	lou
k'u	ku	ku	lu	lu	lu
kua	gua	gwa	luan	luan	lwan
k'ua	kua	kwa	lun, lün	lun	lwun
kuai	guai	gwai	lung	long	lung
k'uai	kuai	kwai	lü	lü	lyu
kuan	guan	gwan	lüan	lüan	lywan
k'uan	kuan	kwan	lüeh	lüe	lywe
kuang	guang	gwang	MA	ma	ma
k'uang	kuang	kwang	mai	mai	mai
kuei	gui	gwei	man	man	man
k'uei	kui	kwei	mang	mang	mang
kun	gun	gwun	mao	mao	mau
k'un	kun	kwun	mei	mei	mei
kung	gong	gung			

WG	P	Y	WG	P	Y
ch'ung	chong	chung	hsiao	xiao	syau
chü	ju	jyu	hsieh	xie	sye
ch'ü	qu	chyu	hsien	xian	syan
chüan	juan	jywan	hsin	xin	syin
ch'üan	quan	chywan	hsing	xing	sying
chüeh	jue	jywe	hsiu	xiu	syou
ch'üeh	que	chywe	hsiung	xiong	syung
chün	jun	jyun	hsü	xu	syu
ch'ün	qun	chyun	hsüan	xuan	sywan
E,O	e	e	hsüeh	xue	sywe
en	en	en	hsün	xun	syun
eng	eng	eng	hu	hu	hu
erh	er	er	hua	hua	hwa
			huai	huai	hwai
FA	fa	fa	huan	huan	hwan
fan	fan	fan	huang	huang	hwang
fang	fang	fang	hui	hui	hwei
fei	fei	fei	hun	hun	hwun
fen	fen	fen	hung	hong	hung
feng	feng	feng	huo	huo	hwo
fo	fo	fwo			
fou	fou	fou	**I, YI**	yi	yi
fu	fu	fu	**JAN**	ran	ran
			jang	rang	rang
HA	ha	ha	jao	rao	rau
hai	hai	hai	je	re	re
han	han	han	jen	ren	ren
hang	hang	hang	jeng	reng	reng
hao	hao	hau	jih	ri	r
hei	hei	hei	jo	ruo	rwo
hen	hen	hen	jou	rou	rou
heng	heng	heng	ju	ru	ru
ho	he	he	juan	ruan	rwan
hou	hou	hou	jui	rui	rwei
hsi	xi	syi	jun	run	rwun
hsia	xia	sya	jung	rong	rung
hsiang	xiang	syang			

Comparative Tables of Romanization

WG	P	Y	WG	P	Y
men	men	men	ou	ou	ou
meng	meng	meng	PA	ba	ba
mi	mi	mi	p'a	pa	pa
miao	miao	myau	pai	bai	bai
mieh	mie	mye	p'ai	pai	pai
mien	mian	myan	pan	ban	ban
min	min	min	p'an	pan	pan
ming	ming	ming	pang	bang	bang
miu	miu	myou	p'ang	pang	pang
mo	mo	mwo	pao	bao	bau
mou	mou	mou	p'ao	pao	pau
mu	mu	mu	pei	bei	bei
NA	na	na	p'ei	pei	pei
nai	nai	nai	pen	ben	ben
nan	nan	nan	p'en	pen	pen
nang	nang	nang	peng	beng	beng
nao	nao	nau	p'eng	peng	peng
nei	nei	nei	pi	bi	bi
nen	nen	nen	p'i	pi	pi
neng	neng	neng	piao	biao	byau
ni	ni	ni	p'iao	piao	pyau
niang	niang	nyang	pieh	bie	bye
niao	niao	nyau	p'ieh	pie	pye
nieh	nie	nye	pien	bian	byan
nien	nian	nyan	p'ien	pian	pyan
nin	nin	nin	pin	bin	bin
ning	ning	ning	p'in	pin	pin
niu	niu	nyou	ping	bing	bing
no	no	nwo	p'ing	ping	ping
nou	nou	nou	po	bo	bwo
nu	nu	nu	p'o	po	pwo
nuan	nuan	nwan	pou	bou	bou
nun	nun	nwun	p'ou	pou	pou
nung	nong	nung	pu	bu	bu
nü	nü	nyu	p'u	pu	pu
nüeh	nüe	nywe			
O, E	e	e	SA	sa	sa

Comparative Tables of Romanization

WG	P	Y	WG	P	Y
sai	sai	sai	t'a	ta	ta
san	san	san	tai	dai	dai
sang	sang	sang	t'ai	tai	tai
sao	sao	sau	tan	dan	dan
se	se	se	t'an	tan	tan
sen	sen	sen	tang	dang	dang
seng	seng	seng	t'ang	tang	tang
sha	sha	sha	tao	dao	dau
shai	shai	shai	t'ao	tau	tao
shan	shan	shan	te	de	de
shang	shang	shang	t'e	te	te
shao	shao	shau	tei	dei	dei
she	she	she	teng	deng	deng
shei	shei	shei	t'eng	teng	teng
shen	shen	shen	ti	di	di
sheng	sheng	sheng	t'i	ti	ti
shih	shi	shr	tiao	diao	dyau
shou	shou	shou	t'iao	tiao	tyau
shu	shu	shu	tieh	die	dye
shua	shua	shwa	t'ieh	tie	tye
shuai	shuai	shwai	tien	dian	dyan
shuan	shuan	shwan	t'ien	tian	tyan
shuang	shuang	shwang	ting	ding	ding
shui	shui	shwei	t'ing	ting	ting
shun	shun	shwun	tiu	diu	dyou
shuo	shuo	shwo	to	duo	dwo
so	suo	swo	t'o	tuo	two
sou	sou	sou	tou	dou	dou
ssu, szu	si	sz	t'ou	tou	tou
su	su	su	tsa	za	dza
suan	suan	swan	ts'a	ca	tsa
sui	sui	swei	tsai	zai	dzai
sun	sun	swun	ts'ai	cai	tsai
sung	song	sung	tsan	zan	dzan
szu, ssu	si	sz	ts'an	can	tsan
TA	da	da	tsang	zang	dzang

Comparative Tables of Romanization

WG	P	Y	WG	P	Y
ts'ang	cang	tsang	t'un	tun	twun
tsao	zao	dzau	tung	dong	dung
ts'ao	cao	tau	t'ung	tong	tung
tse	ze	dze	tzu	zi	dz
ts'e	ce	tse	tz'u	ci	tsz
tsei	zei	dzei	WA	wa	wa
tsen	zen	dzen	wai	wai	wai
ts'en	cen	tsen	wan	wan	wan
tseng	zeng	dzeng	wang	wang	wang
ts'eng	ceng	tseng	wei	wei	wei
tso	zuo	dzwo	wen	wen	wen
ts'o	cuo	tswo	weng	weng	weng
tsou	zou	dzou	wo	wo	wo
ts'ou	cou	tsou	wu	wu	wu
tsu	zu	dzu	YA	ya	ya
ts'u	cu	tsu	yai	yai	yai
tsuan	zuan	dzwan	yang	yang	yang
ts'uan	cuan	tswan	yao	yao	yau
tsui	zui	dzwei	yeh	ye	ye
ts'ui	cui	tswei	yen	yan	yan
tsun	zun	dzwun	yi, i	yi	yi
ts'un	cun	tswun	yin	yin	yin
tsung	zong	dzung	ying	ying	ying
ts'ung	cong	tsung	yu	you	you
tu	du	du	yung	yong	yung
t'u	tu	tu	yü	yu	yu
tuan	duan	dwan	yüan	yuan	ywan
t'uan	tuan	twan	yüeh	yue	ywe
tui	dui	dwei	yün	yun	yun
t'ui	tui	twei			
tun	dun	dwun			